ASPLOS XXI

Twenty-First International Conference on Architectural Support for Programming Languages and Operating Systems

April 2–6, 2016
Atlanta, Georgia, USA

Sponsored by:

ACM SIGARCH
ACM SIGOPS
ACM SIGPLAN

Association for Computing Machinery

In co-operation with: ACM SIGBED

With Support from: Apple, Huawei, Microsoft Research, ARM, Baidu, Facebook, Google, Intel, NetApp, Oracle Labs, Akamai, Hewlett Packard Enterprise, IBM Research, Nokia, Qualcomm, VMWare, & IEEE Computer Society

Association for
Computing Machinery

Advancing Computing as a Science & Profession

The Association for Computing Machinery
2 Penn Plaza, Suite 701
New York, New York 10121-0701

ISBN: 978-1-4503-4091-5 **ACM Order No:** 415165

Additional copies may be ordered prepaid from:

ACM Order Department
PO Box 30777
New York, NY 10087-0777, USA

Phone: 1-800-342-6626 (USA and Canada)
+1-212-626-0500 (Global)
Fax: +1-212-944-1318
E-mail: acmhelp@acm.org
Hours of Operation: 8:30 am – 4:30 pm ET

Printed in the USA .

ASPLOS 2016 General Chair's Message

Welcome to Atlanta and Georgia Tech for the 21st meeting of the ASPLOS conference! We hope you enjoy your time here and sample the many attractions our city and campus have to offer.

No conference is a success without a strong technical program. Congratulations are due to the Program Chair Yuanyuan Zhou and the Program Committee members for an outstanding job of selecting papers from a high quality submission field. Their diligence in this very difficult task is reflected in an exciting program and represents a deep commitment to the ASPLOS community. We all owe a debt of gratitude to them. The steering committee, in particular its co-chairs, Rajeev Balasubramonian and Al Davis, and its past chair, Vivek Sarkar, worked hard to keep ASPLOS on track. Our thanks are also due to them!

Increasingly important for a successful conference are the pre-conference organizational activities. Tushar Krishna was responsible for engaging the Workshop Chairs and organizing an excellent sequence of workshop and tutorial programs over the weekend prior to the conference. Special thanks are due to the workshop organizers for their hard work in developing their individual programs. Also again this year we have VEE co-located with us. Thanks in particular to VEE General Chair Vishakha Gupta for working with us and being part of "our team." Web presence is also critical to the success of a conference. Gennady Pekhimenko reflected the diligence of the organizing committee in development and maintenance of the conference website. For a conference this size, registration is a large enterprise. Our registration chair, Sriseshan Srikanth, was tireless in setting up and operating the registration activities. Finances are also complex for a conference of this scale. Many thanks are due to Hadi Esmaeilzadeh and Annabel Satin who managed the finances with the level of detail and importance necessary for flawless operation. Thanks also to Changhee Jung, who did a great job in publicizing the conference and in enabling a smooth publications process in the presence of strict deadlines. Ding Yuan did a great job organizing a poster session with 53 posters, as did Emmet Witchel in organizing the debate.

Our local arrangements chair, Catherine Linder Conte, was recruited to manage the operational logistics before and during a conference that her husband volunteered to run (yet again). Catherine also set up and managed the excursion to the Georgia Aquarium – an event that the attendees will enjoy and we hope will remember for a long time. We did have one luxury in organizing ASPLOS: we had strong support from ACM. Our thanks to SIGARCH chair Sarita Adve, SIGOPS chair Robbert van Renesse, and SIGPLAN chair Michael Hicks. We are grateful to the ACM for their professional logistical and operational support. Special thanks to Ashley Cozzi of the ACM who worked closely with us, whose keen eye guided our planning and approval processes, and whose patience with our enquires and schedules kept our budget and contracts on track. We also had the good fortune of working with a great staff at the Georgia Tech Hotel who made the hosting process simple.

New this year, we welcome IEEE Computer Society as a Technical Co-Sponsor of ASPLOS. IEEE is important to many of our careers and it's great to have them on board. Thanks to the ASPLOS steering committee for allowing the co-sponsorship. Also, SIGBED continues its in-cooperation-with support for the conference thanks to its chair Insup Lee. We owe a debt of gratitude to our sponsorship chair, Dan Tsafrir, who served double-duty as the WACI chair. Dan organized a truly impressive cadre of sponsors. It's too long a list for here, but is listed elsewhere in these proceedings. Without the financial generosity of our sponsors, the conference could not have been possible in its current form. Their support reflects the high regard our sponsors place on the conference and the importance of ASPLOS attendees to the broader community. Much of that support helped bring students to ASPLOS, and Asit Mishra did an exemplary job for us.

As you enjoy the conference, if you meet any of the organizers please take a moment to thank them for their volunteer efforts. The success of the conference reflects their commitment and tireless efforts (any deficiencies, however, are solely my doing!).

Please enjoy ASPLOS 2016 in Midtown, Atlanta, Georgia!

Tom Conte, *ASPLOS 2016 General Chair, Georgia Institute of Technology*

ASPLOS 2016 Program Chair's Message

It is my pleasure and privilege to serve as program chair for ASPLOS 2016 - the Twentieth International Conference on Architectural Support for Programming Languages and Operating Systems. This year's conference has set new records in terms of the number of submissions, and reinforces ASPLOS's tradition of encouraging work on innovative multidisciplinary research spanning computer architecture and hardware, programming languages and compilers, operating systems and networking, and applications.

The 2016 conference saw a record, 232 submissions with a total of 986 (unique 877) paper authors from 240 institutions spread across at least 21 countries and spanning 5 continents: a clear indication that our community is growing, and that ASPLOS is the premier venue of choice for disseminating high quality interdisciplinary work.

There was a wide diversity in topics, ranging from DNA computer storage to human computer interaction, with the most popular being heterogeneous architecture and accelerators, security, reliability and debugging, and memory management. 55 papers self-identified as relating to architecture, 55 to parallelism, 59 to operating systems, 40 to programming models and languages, and 20 to compiler optimizations.

Some Notes on the Review Process: All reviewing and discussion, including that at the PC meeting, was double blind. As in past ASPLOS conferences, I used a 2-phase review process, with each paper receiving 3 reviews in round 1, and a minimum of an additional 2 reviews in round 2. In order to improve the quality of review assignment, in conjunction with the paper title and abstract (with sometimes a need to skim the paper directly), I used a combination of topic and interest match with reviewers, and suggestions for reviewers from both the authors and the round 1 reviewers (during the round 2 assignment).

I continued to monitor reviews for papers through both rounds 1 and 2 as they came in for quality, substance, and tone, to correct any expertise mismatch, and to find experts in the multiple areas each paper might span, including experts outside of the program and external review committees, a step that is essential for a conference with the breadth that ASPLOS covers. Reviewer feedback in this process was extremely helpful.

In keeping with ASPLOS'15 and other conferences, not all papers were moved to round 2. In particular, papers with no round 1 reviews advocating acceptance, and with clear consensus (based both on substantive review content and comment exchange) among the reviewers that the paper did not rise above the acceptance bar for the conference, did not move to round 2. Approximately 35.27% of the papers fell in this category. Each of these decisions involved the active participation of all the reviewers.

After the rebuttal phase, each paper was assigned a discussion lead. The discussion lead's job was to carefully read all reviews, the rebuttal, and prior online comments (several papers had extensive online discussions after both rounds 1 and 2), and then initiate a discussion with the goal of reaching a conclusion on whether papers were to be accepted, rejected, or discussed at the PC meeting. The goal of the discussion lead (and my monitoring) was to ensure that every reviewer participated in the discussion after reading the other reviews and the rebuttal. During this process, if new reviewers were considered required based on the rebuttal content, they were sought.

The program committee meeting was held at the Chicago O'Hare Hilton on November 7th, 2014. All but four PC members were in attendance, due to medical emergencies or health issues. PC members had access to the reviews for all papers for which they had no declared conflict. Paper authors were not revealed during the PC meeting, and since the discussion continued to be blind, PC papers were not singled out for separate discussion. PC members were asked to leave the room for papers for which they were declared as a conflict (which included any papers they were authors on) prior to revealing the paper title and number being discussed.

During the PC meeting, all papers categorized as a preliminary accept (15) were discussed first. The PC also had a chance during and prior to the PC meeting to bring up papers for discussion that were classified as tentatively rejected (i.e., all papers were open for discussion at the PC meeting). The majority of the time during the PC meeting was spent on the papers categorized as needing discussion. The result of the extensive reviewing, online discussion, and PC meeting is now in your hands for your reading pleasure, with 53 accepted papers, 16 of which were shepherded. In addition to the decision process, for every paper where the authors chose to provide a rebuttal, the discussion lead, in collaboration with the other reviewers, provided the authors with a summary outlining the main criteria leading to the decision outcome for the paper (whether or not the rebuttal answered reviewer questions or addressed concerns or shortcomings expressed in the reviews), along with feedback for improvement.

The Program: In addition to the 53 accepted papers, the conference includes two invited keynote speeches. Richard Stanley Williams, a senior fellow at HP, will talk about memristors and sensible machines. Kathryn McKinley from Microsoft Research will give a talk on how to program uncertain things. We will maintain the tradition of past ASPLOS conferences in convening a Wild and Crazy Ideas (WACI) session, organized by Dan Tsafrir, and a debate session organized by Emmett Witchel. Each of which has a group of inspiring speakers line up to provoke thoughts and discussion among the audience and the whole community. Lightning sessions, each morning, managed by Ding Yuan, will provide a quick introduction to the key ideas that will be presented in the talks that day. The authors also have one more chance in the poster session to present their work and get feedback.

Acknowledgements: A big thank you to my 42 program committee members and 79 external review committee members for their hard work and for gracefully handling the extra review load from the unanticipated large increase in the number of papers (up to 17 papers were reviewed by each PC member, and up to 7 papers reviewed by each ERC member, for a total of 1,011 reviews). Thanks also to the 17 outside reviewers who provided additional expert opinions. Kathryn McKinley handled my conflicts, assigning reviewers to these papers and monitoring both online and PC meeting discussion, and Dan Tsafrir handled papers that have conflicts with me and Kathryn. Thanks to Eddie Kohler, HotCRP's author, for hosting the HotCRP and the quick follow up to my questions and on fixes for my occasional bug reports; HotCRP and its coloring and tracking features were extremely useful through the review process. My students Tianyin Xu and Ryan Peng Huang were a tremendous help in managing HotCRP, running statistics, and assisting in the PC meeting, including taking notes and coordinating with PCs who remotely dialed in.

I follow in the footsteps of past PC chairs, with my deepest appreciation to Sarita Adve and Sandhya Dwarkadas for establishing a solid review process and coaching me through the entire conference organization. They have shared with me many tips as well as documents and scripts that they used for ASPLOS(es). The steering committee provided valuable guidance on interpreting and setting policies. The organizing committee and the general chair, Tom Conte, deserve special thanks for taking care of all the logistics and allowing me to focus on the technical program, and for bringing us together for the conference at such a spectacular venue. The publication chair, Changhee Jung, and the web chair, Gennady Pekhimenko, have always provided me timely help in handling the final paper versions and posting things online, respectively. And also special thanks to the local arrangement chair, Catherine Conte, who has been working hard with the hotel and outing place to accommodate the program.

Last, but not least, thanks to the 877 authors of the submitted papers for sending their work in to ASPLOS. I hope you enjoy reading the papers in these proceedings and continue to submit your interdisciplinary work to ASPLOS. The conference provides a unique opportunity for stimulating interaction with experts across a diverse range of sub-disciplines and I look forward to seeing many of you at the conference.

Yuanyuan (YY) Zhou

ASPLOS 2016 Program Chair
University of California, San Diego

Table of Contents

ASPLOS 2016 Conference Organization xii

ASPLOS 2016 Sponsors & Supporters xvi

Keynote Address I
Session Chair: Yuanyuan Zhou *(University of California, San Diego)*

- **Programming Uncertain <T>hings** 1
  Kathryn S. McKinley *(Microsoft Research, Redmond)*

Session 1A: Multicore
Session Chair: David Wentzlaff *(Princeton University)*

- **WiSync: An Architecture for Fast Synchronization through On-Chip Wireless Communication** 3
  Sergi Abadal *(University of Illinois at Urbana-Champaign & Universitat Politecnica de Catalunya)*, Albert Cabellos-Aparicio, Eduard Alarcón *(Universitat Politecnica de Catalunya)*, Josep Torrellas *(University of Illinois at Urbana-Champaign)*
- **ReBudget: Trading Off Efficiency vs. Fairness in Market-Based Multicore Resource Allocation via Runtime Budget Reassignment** 19
  Xiaodong Wang, José F. Martínez *(Cornell University)*
- **Dirigent: Enforcing QoS for Latency-Critical Tasks on Shared Multicore Systems** 33
  Haishan Zhu, Mattan Erez *(The University of Texas at Austin)*

Session 1B: I/O
Session Chair: Shan Lu *(University of Chicago)*

- **Paravirtual Remote I/O** 49
  Yossi Kuperman, Eyal Moscovici *(Technion – Israel institute of Technology & IBM Research-Haifa)*, Joel Nider, Razya Ladelsky *(IBM Research-Haifa)*, Abel Gordon *(IBM Research-Haifa & Stratoscale)*, Dan Tsafrir *(Technion – Israel institute of Technology)*
- **High Performance Packet Processing with FlexNIC** 67
  Antoine Kaufmann *(University of Washington)*, Simon Peter *(The University of Texas as Austin)*, Naveen Kr. Sharma, Thomas Anderson, Arvind Krishnamurthy *(University of Washington)*
- **Specifying and Checking File System Crash-Consistency Models** 83
  James Bornholt, Antoine Kaufmann, Jialin Li, Arvind Krishnamurthy, Emina Torlak, Xi Wang *(University of Washington)*

Session 2A: Memory Management
Session Chair: Ricardo Bianchini *(Rutgers University & Microsoft)*

- **Prudent Memory Reclamation in Procrastination-Based Synchronization** 99
  Aravinda Prasad *(Indian Institute of Science & IBM Linux Technology Center)*, K. Gopinath *(Indian Institute of Science)*
- **Whirlpool: Improving Dynamic Cache Management with Static Data Classification** 113
  Anurag Mukkara, Nathan Beckmann, Daniel Sanchez *(Massachusetts Institute of Technology)*
- **TPC: Target-Driven Parallelism Combining Prediction and Correction to Reduce Tail Latency in Interactive Services** 129
  Myeongjae Jeon, Yuxiong He *(Microsoft Research)*, Hwanju Kim *(University of Cambridge)*, Sameh Elnikety *(Microsoft Research)*, Scott Rixner, Alan L. Cox *(Rice University)*

Session 2B: Reliability and Debugging I

Session Chair: Gilles Muller *(INRIA)*

- **How to Build Static Checking Systems Using Orders of Magnitude Less Code** 143
  Fraser Brown, Andres Nötzli, Dawson Engler *(Stanford University)*
- **TxRace: Efficient Data Race Detection Using Commodity Hardware Transactional Memory** 159
  Tong Zhang, Dongyoon Lee, Changhee Jung *(Virginia Tech)*
- **CoGENT: Verifying High-Assurance File System Implementations** 175
  Sidney Amani, Alex Hixon, Zilin Chen, Christine Rizkallah, Peter Chubb, Liam O'Connor, Joel Beeren, Yutaka Nagashima, Japheth Lim, Thomas Sewell, Joseph Tuong, Gabriele Keller, Toby Murray, Gerwin Klein, Gernot Heiser *(Data61 & UNSW)*

Session 3A: Heterogeneous Architectures and Accelerators I

Session Chair: Calin Cascaval *(Qualcomm)*

- **M3: A Hardware/Operating-System Co-Design to Tame Heterogeneous Manycores** 189
  Nils Asmussen, Marcus Völp, Benedikt Nöthen, Hermann Härtig, Gerhard Fettweis *(Technische Universität Dresden)*
- **Sidewinder: An Energy Efficient and Developer Friendly Heterogeneous Architecture for Continuous Mobile Sensing** 205
  Daniyal Liaqat, Silviu Jingoi, Eyal de Lara, Ashvin Goel, Wilson To, Kevin Lee, Italo De Moraes Garcia *(University of Toronto)*, Manuel Saldana *(Huawei)*
- **OpenPiton: An Open Source Manycore Research Framework** 217
  Jonathan Balkind, Michael McKeown, Yaosheng Fu, Tri Nguyen, Yanqi Zhou, Alexey Lavrov, Mohammad Shahrad, Adi Fuchs *(Princeton University)*, Samuel Payne *(NVIDIA Corporation)*, Xiaohua Liang, Matthew Matl, David Wentzlaff *(Princeton University)*
- **COATCheck: Verifying Memory Ordering at the Hardware-OS Interface** 233
  Daniel Lustig *(Princeton University)*, Geet Sethi *(Rutgers University)*, Margaret Martonosi *(Princeton University)*, Abhishek Bhattacharjee *(Rutgers University)*

Session 3B: Security I

Session Chair: Gernot Heiser *(NICTA & UNSW)*

- **True IOMMU Protection From DMA Attacks: When Copy is Faster than Zero Copy** 249
  Alex Markuze, Adam Morrison, Dan Tsafrir *(Technion – Israel Institute of Technology)*
- **Silent Shredder: Zero-Cost Shredding for Secure Non-Volatile Main Memory Controllers** 263
  Amro Awad *(North Carolina State University)*, Pratyusa Manadhata, Stuart Haber *(Hewlett Packard Lab)*, Yan Solihin *(North Carolina State University)*, William Horne *(Hewlett Packard Lab)*
- **Sego: Pervasive Trusted Metadata for Efficiently Verified Untrusted System Services** 277
  Youngjin Kwon *(The University of Texas at Austin)*, Alan M. Dunn *(Google)*, Michael Z. Lee *(Facebook)*, Owen S. Hofmann *(Google)*, Yuanzhong Xu, Emmett Witchel *(The University of Texas at Austin)*

Wild and Crazy Ideas

Session Chair: Dan Tsafrir *(Technion – Israel Institute of Technology)*

- **Synopsis of the ASPLOS '16 Wild and Crazy Ideas (WACI) Invited-Speakers Session** 291
  Dan Tsafrir *(Technion – Israel Institute of Technology)*

Keynote Address II

Session Chair: Tom Conte *(Georgia Tech)*

- **Brain Inspired Computing** 295
  R. Stanley Williams *(Hewlett Packard Labs)*

Session 4A: Code Generation and Synthesis

Session Chair: Xipeng Shen *(North Carolina State University)*

- **Scaling up Superoptimization** 297
  Phitchaya Mangpo Phothilimthana *(University of California, Berkeley)*, Aditya Thakur *(Google Inc.)*, Rastislav Bodik *(University of Washington)*, Dinakar Dhurjati *(Qualcomm Research)*
- **Lifting Assembly to Intermediate Representation: A Novel Approach Leveraging Compilers** 311
  Niranjan Hasabnis *(Intel)*, R. Sekar *(Stony Brook University)*
- **Architecture-Adaptive Code Variant Tuning** 325
  Saurav Muralidharan, Amit Roy, Mary Hall *(University of Utah)*, Michael Garland *(NVIDIA Corporation)*, Piyush Rai *(IIT Kanpur)*

Session 4B: Energy and Thermal Management

Session Chair: Rajeev Balasubramonian *(University of Utah & HP Labs)*

- **Maximizing Performance Under a Power Cap: A Comparison of Hardware, Software, and Hybrid Techniques** 545
  Huazhe Zhang, Henry Hoffmann *(University of Chicago)*
- **The Computational Sprinting Game** 561
  Songchun Fan, Seyed Majid Zahedi, Benjamin C. Lee *(Duke University)*
- **An Energy-interference-free Hardware-Software Debugger for Intermittent Energy-harvesting Systems** 577
  Alexei Colin, Graham Harvey *(Disney Research, Pittsburgh & Carnegie Mellon University)*, Brandon Lucia *(Carnegie Mellon University)*, Alanson P. Sample *(Disney Research, Pittsburgh)*

Session 5A: Emerging Memory Technologies

Session Chair: Joseph Tucek *(HP Labs)*

- **NVWAL: Exploiting NVRAM in Write-Ahead Logging** 385
  Wook-Hee Kim, Jinwoong Kim, Woongki Baek, Beomseok Nam *(UNIST)*, Youjip Won *(Hanyang University)*
- **High-Performance Transactions for Persistent Memories** 399
  Aasheesh Kolli *(University of Michigan)*, Steven Pelley *(Snowflake Computing)*, Ali Saidi *(ARM)*, Peter M. Chen, Thomas F. Wenisch *(University of Michigan)*
- **High-Density Image Storage Using Approximate Memory Cells** 413
  Qing Guo *(NVIDIA Corporation)*, Karin Strauss *(Microsoft Research & University of Washington)*, Luis Ceze *(University of Washington & Microsoft Research)*, Henrique S. Malvar *(Microsoft Research)*
- **Failure-Atomic Persistent Memory Updates via JUSTDO Logging** 427
  Joseph Izraelevitz *(University of Rochester & Hewett Packard Labs)*, Terence Kelly *(Hewlett Packard Labs)*, Aasheesh Kolli *(University of Michigan & Hewett Packard Labs)*

Session 5B: Cloud Computing

Session Chair: Lingjia Tang *(University of Michigan)*

- **Interference Management for Distributed Parallel Applications in Consolidated Clusters** 443
  Jaeung Han, Seungheun Jeon *(Korea Advanced Institute of Science and Technology)*, Young-ri Choi *(UNIST)*, Jaehyuk Huh *(Korea Advanced Institute of Science and Technology)*
- **Taurus: A Holistic Language Runtime System for Coordinating Distributed Managed-Language Applications** 457
  Martin Maas, Krste Asanović *(University of California, Berkeley)*, Tim Harris *(Oracle Labs, Cambridge)*, John Kubiatowicz *(University of California, Berkeley)*
- **HCloud: Resource-Efficient Provisioning in Shared Cloud Systems** 473
  Christina Delimitrou *(Stanford University & Cornell University)*, Christos Kozyrakis *(Stanford University & EPFL)*

- **CloudSeer: Workflow Monitoring of Cloud Infrastructures via Interleaved Logs** 489
  Xiao Yu *(North Carolina State University)*, Pallavi Joshi, Jianwu Xu *(NEC Laboratories America)*, Guoliang Jin *(North Carolina State University)*, Hui Zhang, Guofei Jiang *(NEC Laboratories America)*

Session 6A: Reliability and Debugging II
Session Chair: Sam H. Noh *(UNIST)*

- **LDX: Causality Inference by Lightweight Dual Execution** 503
  Yonghwi Kwon, Dohyeong Kim *(Purdue University)*, William N. Sumner *(Simon Fraser University)*, Kyungtae Kim, Brendan Saltaformaggio, Xiangyu Zhang, Dongyan Xu *(Purdue University)*
- **TaxDC: A Taxonomy of Non-Deterministic Concurrency Bugs in Datacenter Distributed Systems** 517
  Tanakorn Leesatapornwongsa *(University of Chicago)*, Jeffrey F. Lukman *(Surya University)*, Shan Lu, Haryadi S. Gunawi *(University of Chicago)*
- **RID: Finding Reference Count Bugs with Inconsistent Path Pair Checking** 531
  Junjie Mao, Yu Chen, Qixue Xiao, Yuanchun Shi *(Tsinghua University)*

Session 6B: OS Optimizations
Session Chair: Emmett Witchel *(University of Texas, Austin)*

- **Scalable Kernel TCP Design and Implementation for Short-Lived Connections** 339
  Xiaofeng Lin *(Sina Corporation & ZHIHU Corporation)*, Yu Chen *(Tsinghua University)*, Xiaodong Li *(Sina Corporation)*, Junjie Mao, Jiaquan He, Wei Xu, Yuanchun Shi *(Tsinghua University)*
- **SpaceJMP: Programming with Multiple Virtual Address Spaces** 353
  Izzat El Hajj *(University of Illinois at Urbana-Champaign & Hewett Packard Labs)*, Alexander Merritt *(Georgia Institute of Technology & Hewett Packard Labs)*, Gerd Zellweger *(ETH Zürich & Hewett Packard Labs)*, Dejan Milojicic *(Hewlett Packard Labs)*, Reto Achermann *(ETH Zürich)*, Paolo Faraboschi *(Hewlett Packard Labs)*, Wen-mei Hwu *(University of Illinois at Urbana-Champaign)*, Timothy Roscoe *(ETH Zürich)*, Karsten Schwan *(Georgia Institute of Technology)*
- ***memif:* Towards Programming Heterogeneous Memory Asynchronously** 369
  Felix Xiaozhu Lin *(Purdue University)*, Xu Liu *(College of William & Mary)*

Debate
Session Chair: Emmett Witchel *(University of Texas, Austin)*

- **Programmer Productivity in a World of Mushy Interfaces: Challenges of the Post-ISA Reality** 591
  Emmett Witchel *(The University of Texas at Austin)*

Session 7A: Non-traditional Computer Systems
Session Chair: Dean Tullsen *(University of California, San Diego)*

- **RAPID Programming of Pattern-Recognition Processors** 593
  Kevin Angstadt, Westley Weimer, Kevin Skadron *(University of Virginia)*
- **Proactive Control of Approximate Programs** 607
  Xin Sui, Andrew Lenharth, Donald S. Fussell, Keshav Pingali *(The University of Texas at Austin)*
- **AxGames: Towards Crowdsourcing Quality Target Determination in Approximate Computing** 623
  Jongse Park, Emmanuel Amaro, Divya Mahajan, Bradley Thwaites, Hadi Esmaeilzadeh *(Georgia Institute of Technology)*
- **A DNA-Based Archival Storage System** 637
  James Bornholt, Randolph Lopez *(University of Washington)*, Douglas M. Carmean *(Microsoft Research)*, Luis Ceze, Georg Seelig *(University of Washington)*, Karin Strauss *(Microsoft Research)*

Session 7B: Heterogeneous Architectures and Accelerators II

Session Chair: Josep Torrellas *(University of Illinois at Urbana-Champaign)*

- **Generating Configurable Hardware from Parallel Patterns** 651
  Raghu Prabhakar, David Koeplinger, Kevin J. Brown *(Stanford University)*,
  HyoukJoong Lee *(Stanford University & Google)*, Christopher De Sa *(Stanford University)*,
  Christos Kozyrakis *(Stanford University & EPFL)*, Kunle Olukotun *(Stanford University)*
- **DySel: Lightweight Dynamic Selection for Kernel-based Data-parallel Programming Model** 667
  Li-Wen Chang, Hee-Seok Kim, Wen-mei W. Hwu *(University of Illinois)*
- **Baymax: QoS Awareness and Increased Utilization for Non-Preemptive Accelerators in Warehouse Scale Computers** 681
  Quan Chen *(Shanghai Jiao Tong University & University of Michigan)*,
  Hailong Yang *(Beihang University & University of Michigan)*, Jason Mars, Lingjia Tang *(University of Michigan)*
- **Analyzing Behavior Specialized Acceleration** 697
  Tony Nowatzki, Karthikeyan Sankaralingam *(University of Wisconsin - Madison)*

Session 8A: Security II

Session Chair: Karin Strauss *(Microsoft Research & University of Washington)*

- **PIFT: Predictive Information-Flow Tracking** 713
  Man-Ki Yoon *(University of Illinois at Urbana-Champaign)*,
  Negin Salajegheh, Yin Chen, Mihai Christodorescu *(Qualcomm Research)*
- **HIPStR – Heterogeneous-ISA Program State Relocation** 727
  Ashish Venkat, Sriskanda Shamasunder, Hovav Shacham,
  Dean M. Tullsen *(University of California, San Diego)*
- **ANVIL: Software-Based Protection Against Next-Generation Rowhammer Attacks** 743
  Zelalem Birhanu Aweke, Salessawi Ferede Yitbarek *(University of Michigan)*,
  Rui Qiao *(Stony Brook University)*, Reetuparna Das, Matthew Hicks *(University of Michigan)*,
  Yossi Oren *(Ben-Gurion University of the Negev)*, Todd Austin *(University of Michigan)*

Session 8B: Transactional Memory

Session Chair: Wenguang Chen *(Tsinghua University)*

- **ProteusTm: Abstraction Meets Performance in Transactional Memory** 757
  Diego Didona, Nuno Diegues *(Universidade de Lisboa)*, Anne-Marie Kermarrec *(INRIA)*,
  Rachid Guerraoui *(EPFL)*, Ricardo Neves, Paolo Romano *(Universidade de Lisboa)*
- **CSR: Core Surprise Removal in Commodity Operating Systems** 773
  Noam Shalev, Eran Harpaz , Hagar Porat, Idit Keidar *(Technion)*, Yaron Weinsberg *(IBM Research, Israel)*
- **CASPAR: Breaking Serialization in Lock-Free Multicore Synchronization** 789
  Tanmay Gangwani *(University of Illinois at Urbana-Champaign)*,
  Adam Morrison *(Technion – Israel Institute of Technology)*,
  Josep Torrellas *(University of Illinois at Urbana-Champaign)*

Author Index 805

ASPLOS 2016 Conference Organization

General Chair: Tom Conte *(Georgia Tech, USA)*

Program Chair: Yuanyuan Zhou *(University of California, San Diego, USA)*

Finance Chair: Hadi Esmaeilzadeh *(Georgia Tech, USA)*

Publicity / Publications Chair: Changhee Jung *(Virginia Tech, USA)*

Local Arrangements Chair: Catherine Linder Conte

Workshop / Tutorial Chair: Tushar Krishna *(Georgia Tech, USA)*

Sponsorship Chair: Dan Tsafrir *(Technion - Israel Institute of Technology, Israel)*

Student Travel Chair: Asit Mishra *(Intel Labs, USA)*

Web Chair: Gennady Pekhimenko *(Carnegie Mellon University, USA)*

Poster Session Chair: Ding Yuan (*University of Toronto, Canada*)

WACI Session Chair: Dan Tsafrir (*Technion - Israel Institute of Technology, Israel*)

Debate Session Chair: Emmett Witchel (*University of Texas, Austin, USA*)

Registration Chair: Sriseshan Srikanth (*Georgia Tech, USA*)

Steering Committee:
Sarita Adve *(University of Illinois at Urbana-Champaign, USA)*
Rajeev Balasubramonian *(University of Utah / HP Labs, USA)*
Al Davis *(University of Utah, USA)*
Sandhya Dwarkadas *(University of Rochester, USA)*
Kemal Ebcioglu *(Global Supercomputing, USA)*
Shan Lu *(University of Chicago, USA)*
Ozcan Ozturk *(Bilkent University, Turkey)*
Peter Thiemann *(University of Freiburg, Germany)*
David Wood *(University of Wisconsin, Madison, USA)*

Program Committee:
Sarita Adve *(University of Illinois, Urbana-Champaign, USA)*
Marcos K. Aguilera *(VMware Research Group, USA)*
Jade Alglave *(University College London, UK)*
Mona Attariyan *(Google, USA)*
Rajeev Balasubramonian *(University of Utah / HP-Labs, USA)*
Yungang Bao *(ICT Chinese Academy of Sciences, China)*
Luiz André Barroso *(Google, USA)*
Ricardo Bianchini *(Rutgers University / Microsoft, USA)*
Angelos Bilas *(FORTH / University of Crete, Greece)*

Program Committee (continued): Steve Blackburn *(Australian National University, Australia)*
Calin Cascaval *(Qualcomm, USA)*
Wenguang Chen *(Tsinghua University, China)*
Albert Cohen *(INRIA, France)*
Joe Devietti *(University of Pennsylvania, USA)*
Chen Ding *(University of Rochester, USA)*
Jason Flinn *(University of Michigan, USA)*
Maria Garzaran *(Intel / University of Illinois, Urbana-Champaign, USA)*
Roxana Geambasu *(Columbia University, USA)*
Gernot Heiser *(NICTA / UNSW, Australia)*
Christopher Hughes *(Intel, USA)*
Hillery Hunter *(IBM Research, USA)*
Sanjeev Kumar *(Facebook, USA)*
Kathryn McKinley *(Microsoft Research, USA)*
Gilles Muller *(INRIA, France)*
Madanlal Musuvathi *(Microsoft Research, USA)*
Onur Mutlu *(Carnegie Mellon University, USA)*
Satish Narayanasamy *(University of Michigan, USA)*
Sam H. Noh *(UNIST, Korea)*
Santosh Pande *(Georgia Tech, USA)*
Shankar Pasupathy *(NetApp, USA)*
Koushik Sen *(University of California, Berkeley, USA)*
Xipeng Shen *(North Carolina State University, USA)*
Liuba Shrira *(Brandeis University, USA)*
Karin Strauss *(Microsoft Research / University of Washington, USA)*
Lingjia Tang *(University of Michigan, USA)*
Michael Taylor *(University of California, San Diego, USA)*
Dan Tsafrir *(Technion - Israel Institute of Technology, Israel)*
Joe Tucek *(HP Labs, USA)*
David Wentzlaff *(Princeton University, USA)*
Emmett Witchel *(University of Texas, Austin, USA)*
David Wood *(University of Wisconsin, Madison, USA)*
Ding Yuan *(University of Toronto, Canada)*

External Review Committee: Vikram Adve *(University of Illinois, Urbana-Champaign, USA)*
Gheorghe Almasi *(IBM, USA)*
Sorav Bansal *(IIT Delhi, India)*
Abhishek Bhattacharjee *(Rutgers University, USA)*
Eric Bodden *(Fraunhofer SIT / TU Darmstadt, Germany)*
Michael Bond *(Ohio State University, USA)*
Pradip Bose *(IBM, USA)*
Edouard Bugnion *(EPFL, Switzerland)*
Trey Cain *(Qualcomm, USA)*
Mainak Chaudhuri *(IIT Kanpur, India)*
Lieven Eeckhout *(Ghent University, Belgium)*

External Review Committee (continued):

Steve Reinhardt *(AMD, USA)*
Martin Schulz *(LLNL, USA)*
Marc Shapiro *(Sorbonne University UPMC-LIP6 & INRIA, France)*
Kai Shen *(University of Rochester, USA)*
Tianwei Sheng *(Whova, USA)*
Arrvindh Shriraman *(SFU, Canada)*
Keith Smith *(NetApp, USA)*
Dawn Song *(University of California, Berkeley, USA)*
Niranjan K Soundararajan *(Intel, USA)*
Michael Spear *(Lehigh University, USA)*
Chris Stewart *(Ohio State University, USA)*
Edward Suh *(Cornell University, USA)*
Michael Swift *(University of Wisconsin, Madison, USA)*
Zachary Tatlock *(University of Washington, USA)*
Mohit Tiwari *(University of Texas, Austin, USA)*
Josep Torrellas *(University of Illinois, Urbana-Champaign, USA)*
Martin Vechev *(ETH, Switzerland)*
Carl Waldspurger *(Independent Consultant, USA)*
Cheng Wang *(Google, USA)*
Peng Wu *(Huawei, USA)*
Weiwei Xiong *(Whova, USA)*
Antonia Zhai *(University of Minnesota, USA)*
Wei Zhang *(IBM, USA)*
Xiao Zhang *(Google, USA)*

Additional reviewers:

Doug Burger
Chris Dwyer
Hadi Esmaeilzadeh
Wenhao Jia
Sorin Lerner
Wyatt Lloyd
Xiaosong Ma
Milo Martin
Filip Pizlo
Leonid Ryzhyk
Hovav Shacham
Daniel J. Sorin
Guangyu Sun
Jakub Szefer
Yuan Xie
Junfeng Yang
Zhengya Zhang

ASPLOS 2016 Sponsors & Supporters

Sponsors

ACM SIGARCH | ACM sigops | ACM SIGPLAN

Platinum Supporters

National Science Foundation
WHERE DISCOVERIES BEGIN

Gold Supporters

Apple Inc. | HUAWEI | Microsoft Research

Silver Supporters

ARM | Baidu 百度 | facebook

Google | intel | NetApp

Oracle Labs

Bronze Supporters

Akamai | Hewlett Packard Enterprise | IBM Research

NOKIA Bell Labs | QUALCOMM | vmware

Technical Co-Sponsor

IEEE computer society

In-Cooperation with

acm SIGBED

Programming Uncertain <T>hings (Keynote)

Kathryn S. McKinley
Microsoft Research, Redmond, WA, USA
mckinley@microsoft.com

Abstract

Innovation flourishes with good abstractions. For instance, codification of the IEEE Floating Point standard in 1985 was critical to the subsequent success of scientific computing. Programming languages currently lack appropriate abstractions for uncertain data. Applications already use estimates from sensors, machine learning, big data, humans, and approximate algorithms, but most programming languages do not help developers address correctness, programmability, and optimization problems due to estimates.

To address these problems, we propose a new programming abstraction called Uncertain<T> embedded into languages, such as C#, C++, Java, Python, and JavaScript. Applications use familiar discrete operations for estimates with Uncertain<T>. Overloaded conditional operators specify hypothesis tests and applications use them to control false positives and negatives. A simple compositional operator expresses domain knowledge. We carefully restrict expressiveness such that we can build a runtime that implements correct statistical reasoning at conditionals. Our system relieves developers of the need to implement or deeply understand statistics. We demonstrate substantial programmability, correctness, and efficiency benefits of this programming model for GPS sensor navigation, approximate computing, machine learning, and xBox.

We encourage the community to develop and use abstractions for estimates.

Categories and Subject Descriptors D.3.3 [*Programming Languages*]: Language Constructs and Features

General Terms Languages, Verification, Measurement

Keywords Programming with estimates, Probabilistic programming, Bayesian logic, Lazy evaluation

ASPLOS '16 April 02-06, 2016, Atlanta, GA, USA

DOI: http://dx.doi.org/10.1145/2872362.2872416

Resources

We welcome you to use and contribute to the open source C# implementation of *Uncertain*⟨*T*⟩ (`https://github.com/klipto/Uncertainty`) (Mytkowicz et al. 2015). We have published several papers on the Uncertain<T> programming language (Bornholt et al. 2014, 2015; Sampson et al. 2014), plan more, and have a web page for the latest news (Mytkowicz and McKinley 2016).

Biography

Kathryn S. McKinley is a Principal Research at Microsoft. Her research interests span programming languages, compilers, runtime systems, architecture, performance, and energy. She and her collaborators have produced several widely used tools: the DaCapo Java Benchmarks (30,000+ downloads), TRIPS Compiler, Hoard memory manager, MMTk memory management toolkit, and Immix garbage collector. Her awards include the ACM SIGPLAN Programming Languages Software Award; ACM SIGPLAN Distinguished Service Award; and best & test of time paper awards from ASPLOS, OOPSLA, ICS, SIGMETRICS, IEEE Top Picks, SIGPLAN Research Highlights, and CACM Research Highlights. She was program chair for ASPLOS, PACT, PLDI, ISMM, and CGO and currently a CRA and CRA-W Board member. Dr. McKinley was honored to testify to the House Science Committee (Feb. 14, 2013). She is honored to be among the IEEE and ACM Fellows and to have graduated 22 PhD students. She and her husband have three sons.

Acknowledgements

I particularly thank Todd Mytkowicz, and our collaborators James Bornholt, Na Meng, Diman Tootaghaj, and Adrian Sampson for their contributions.

References

J. Bornholt, T. Mytkowicz, and K. S. McKinley. Uncertain<T>: A first-order type for uncertain data. In *International Conference on Architectural Support for Programming Languages and Operating Systems (ASPLOS)*, 2014.

J. Bornholt, N. Meng, T. Mytkowicz, and K. S. McKinley. Programming the internet of Uncertain <T>hings. In *Sensors to Cloud Architectures Workshop (SCAW)*, pages 1–7, 2015.

T. Mytkowicz and K. S. McKinley. The Uncertain<T> programming language, 2016. URL http://research.microsoft.com/en-us/projects/uncertainty/default.aspx.

T. Mytkowicz, J. Bornholt, A. Sampson, D. Tootaghaj, and K. S. McKinley. Uncertain<T>, 2015. URL https://github.com/klipto/Uncertainty.

A. Sampson, P. Panchekha, T. Mytkowicz, K. S. McKinley, D. Grossman, and L. Ceze. Expressing and verifying probabilistic assertions. In *ACM Conference on Programming Language Design and Implementation (PLDI)*, 2014.

WiSync: An Architecture for Fast Synchronization through On-Chip Wireless Communication *

Sergi Abadal,[†‡] Albert Cabellos-Aparicio,[‡] Eduard Alarcón,[‡] and Josep Torrellas[†]

[†]Univ. of Illinois, Urbana-Champaign, IL, USA
http://iacoma.cs.uiuc.edu

[‡]Univ. Politècnica de Catalunya, Barcelona, Spain
abadal@ac.upc.edu

Abstract

In shared-memory multiprocessing, fine-grain synchronization is challenging because it requires frequent communication. As technology scaling delivers larger manycore chips, such pattern is expected to remain costly to support.

In this paper, we propose to address this challenge by using on-chip wireless communication. Each core has a transceiver and an antenna to communicate with all the other cores. This environment supports very low latency global communication. Our architecture, called *WiSync*, uses a per-core *Broadcast Memory* (BM). When a core writes to its BM, all the other 100+ BMs get updated in less than 10 processor cycles. We also use a second wireless channel with cheaper transfers to execute barriers efficiently. WiSync supports multiprogramming, virtual memory, and context switching. Our evaluation with simulations of 128-threaded kernels and 64-threaded applications shows that WiSync speeds-up synchronization substantially. Compared to using advanced conventional synchronization, WiSync attains an average speedup of nearly one order of magnitude for the kernels, and 1.12 for PARSEC and SPLASH-2.

Keywords on-chip wireless communication; synchronization

1. Introduction

In shared-memory programming, there are several common idioms that require frequent synchronization between potentially far-off processors. One is mutual exclusion to popular locations, which involves repeatedly writing and reading locks and/or other variables. Another is frequently-accessed global barriers, which involve reading and writing counts and flags. Other patterns include repeated broadcasts, reductions, and producer-consumer communications which, in addition to the data communicated, often need flags to coordinate writes and reads.

Computer architectures have traditionally struggled to support these patterns efficiently. Some machines have provided advanced hardware support, such as a barrier network in Cray T3D [12], synchronization registers in Cray T3E [38], a collectives network in Blue Gene/L [15], and fetch-and-Φ operations in the SGI Origin [25]. Also, there are many research proposals for advanced hardware support for synchronization (e.g., [5, 7, 26, 37, 40, 53]). As technology scaling delivers larger manycore chips, these patterns are expected to remain costly to support within the chip.

On-chip wireless technology provides a promising approach to address this challenge [1, 3, 13]. Suppose that each core is augmented with a transceiver (i.e., a transmitter plus a receiver) and an antenna. The transmitter modulates and radiates Radio Frequency (RF) signals through the antenna. The signals propagate throughout the chip and are received by all the receiver antennas tuned to the same frequency.

This environment provides two key supports for the idioms outlined above. First, since all antennas are listening, it naturally supports broadcast. Consequently, global communication is easily supported. Second, the latency of point-to-point communication is at least one order of magnitude lower than in current on-chip networks (i.e., around 5 processor cycles), and not dependent on the distance between source and destination.

There are existing prototypes of on-chip antennas and transceivers using conservative implementations [14, 49, 51, 52]. For example, Yu et al. [51] used standard 65 nm CMOS technology to build an antenna and transceiver that provided a bandwidth of 16 Gbit/s (enough for our purposes, as we will see) with an area of 0.23 mm^2 and a power consumption of 31.2 mW. This design is conservative — a result of the current lack of real uses for this technology beyond sensor networks. However, extrapolating this design using scaling projections [11] backed up by recent implementation trends [2, 19], it seems reasonable to use 22 nm CMOS technology to build a similar transceiver and antenna with an area of 0.1 mm^2 at 16 mW, providing the same 16 Gbit/s or perhaps higher.

In this paper, we present a novel architecture that leverages wireless communication in a large manycore to perform fast synchronization. We call it *WiSync*. The key component of WiSync is a per-core *Broadcast Memory (BM)*. Thanks to

*This work was supported in part by NSF under grants CCF-1012759, CNS-1116237, and CCF-1536795; by the Catalan Government under grant 2014SGR-1427; and by the Spanish State Ministry of Economy and Competitiveness under grant aid PCIN-2015-012.

ASPLOS '16, April 02–06, 2016, Atlanta, GA, USA.
© 2016 ACM. ISBN 978-1-4503-4091-5/16/04... $15.00.
DOI: http://dx.doi.org/10.1145/2872362.2872396.

the wireless communication, when a core writes to its BM, all the other 100+ BMs get updated in less than 10 processor cycles. WiSync uses two wireless channels: one for data transfer, and a cheaper one that transfers only tones to execute barriers very efficiently. We also present an example ISA. The resulting manycore supports multiprogramming, virtual memory, and context switching.

We evaluate WiSync with simulations of 128-threaded kernels and 64-threaded applications. The results show that WiSync speeds-up synchronization substantially. Compared to using advanced conventional synchronization, WiSync delivers an average speedup of nearly one order of magnitude for the kernels, and 1.12 for PARSEC and SPLASH-2.

2. Background

Recent advances in CMOS RF technology [18, 24, 28, 29, 36, 39] have enabled the development of antennas and transceivers that can operate in chip-scale settings. A transceiver is mainly characterized by the frequency band at which it transmits. The width of the frequency band determines the bandwidth provided by the transceiver. Specifically, using simple signal modulation, it can be shown that a given frequency band in GHz results in the same number of Gigabits per second (Gb/s) in bandwidth provided [8]. Common frequency bands for state-of-the-art on-chip wireless networks are 16-20 GHz wide, with a center at around 60 GHz. Hence, the bandwidth of the transceiver is 16-20 Gb/s.

The design of a transceiver involves tradeoffs between area, power consumption, bandwidth, and design complexity. Generally, for a given frequency point, widening the frequency band increases the area and power overheads linearly, up to a certain limit. Beyond that limit, increasing the frequency band implies using more complex and power-hungry RF components which cause a large leap in area and power. In all cases, circuit-level and system-level optimizations can help to reduce area and power without impacting upon the bandwidth.

On the other hand, operating at a higher frequency point (e.g., 90 GHz) reduces the area (since the lateral size of the passive RF components is roughly inversely proportional to the frequency), and generally makes it easier to support wider frequency bands. However, the technology at 100 GHz and higher frequencies is still exploratory.

Currently, there are implementations of on-chip antennas and transceivers working at frequency bands around 60 GHz and 90 GHz [14, 49, 51, 52]. As indicated before, the implementations are conservative because there is a lack of real uses for this technology beyond sensor networks. Yu et al. [51] used 65 nm CMOS technology to build an antenna and transceiver that provided a bandwidth of 16 Gb/s with an area of 0.23 mm^2 and a power of 31.2 mW. At this technology, a zig-zag antenna working at 60 GHz takes an area of approximately 0.02 mm^2 [14].

Using these numbers and scaling projections [11] backed up by recent implementation trends [2, 19], we envision that one could build an antenna and transceiver at 22-nm technology with an area of 0.1 mm^2 at 16 mW, providing the same 16 Gb/s. To reach these figures, we consider a sublinear area scaling, more conservative than the linear trend used in related RF interconnect works [11, 33], as well as a power reduction commensurate with the 1.67x scaling trend predicted in [11]. Alternatively, one can double the bandwidth to 32 Gb/s, with the reduced area but with little gain in power consumption over the 65 nm numbers.

Note that, in the chip, the antenna and transceiver are kept powered-on even if they are not communicating. This is done to reduce start-up/wind-down overhead. Hence, they consume about the same power while transmitting as while not transmitting.

Future Trends. Currently, both industrial and academic researchers are pushing the state-of-the-art toward miniaturization and higher frequencies [18, 19, 20, 28, 35, 48]. Abadal et al. [2] take a wide variety of transceiver designs and extrapolate area and power trends. The trends point toward increasing frequency and reducing area and power. They predict that using CMOS (beyond 22 nm), SiGe BiCMOS, or Graphene technologies at 300 GHz frequencies, one could support bandwidths of 64 Gb/s with an area in the order of 0.01 mm^2. Others [11, 24] make similar predictions, pushing the bandwidth to 100 Gb/s. Overall, we expect that, if the case for on-chip wireless communication in general-purpose computing is made, progress towards these aims will be sped-up.

Other Technologies. There are two emerging technologies that can also offer on-chip broadcast capabilities: transmission lines (TLs) [4, 5, 10, 33, 34, 41, 43] and nanophotonics [6, 21, 23, 42, 46, 47]. While these technologies are more energy-efficient and provide more bandwidth than wireless communication, they are more complicated and less scalable than wireless communication. Indeed, these technologies complicate the floorplan, as they require laying out an extra network. In terms of scalability, TLs are challenged by signal reflection, while nanophotonics by laser power requirements. We discuss them further in Section 8.

3. Overview of WiSync

3.1 Main Idea

Fine-grain synchronization has traditionally been challenging to support efficiently because it involves frequent communication between potentially far-off processors. On-chip wireless technology can address this bottleneck. If each core in a large manycore uses an antenna and a transceiver to send and receive wireless signals, we have two key properties.

First, since all antennas are listening, we naturally have broadcast (or multicast) of writes. Second, the latency of point-to-point communication is at least one order of magnitude lower than in current on-chip networks, and not dependent on the distance between source and destination. Specifically, consider broadcasting a 64-bit datum. Adding up a special address and other bits, the message may be about 80 bits. With current technology, the wireless transfer can be done in five 1-ns cycles; with future technology, it may be doable in 2 ns. Adding to this, wireless technology does not complicate the chip layout because no additional wires are needed. Moreover, both area and power are scalable with CMOS technology.

A limitation of on-chip wireless communication is that, if we use a single data transfer channel to minimize cost, only one core can send data at a time. When the network is busy, a core has to wait; if it is free and the core attempts to send data, there may still be a collision with another core. In this case, the cycle(s) are lost and both cores have to retry. Wireless communication also introduces issues related to reliability and security — e.g., an external entity may disrupt the communication unintentionally or on purpose. In this paper, we do not consider these issues.

WiSync abstracts the wireless capability in the form of a per-core *Broadcast Memory (BM)* that is used by variables declared of type *broadcast* in the program. All BMs are connected to the wireless network, and they all contain the exact same, *replicated* variables. When a core writes to a location in its BM, all the other BMs get automatically updated. There is a total order of writes to BMs across all cores.

Figure 1 shows this idea. Variables *x* and *y* are replicated in all the BMs. Three concurrent writes by different processors can result in different interleavings, but no update is lost and all processors observe the same write interleaving. The jagged line means that the non-local BMs are physically far.

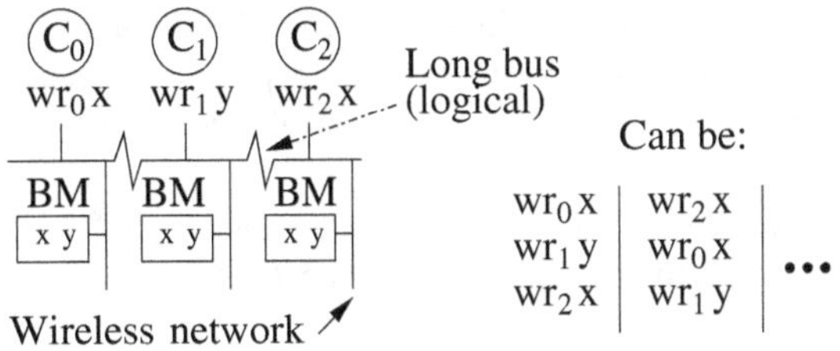

Figure 1: How wireless writes appear in WiSync.

The operating system manages the BM resource with virtual memory, while the program addresses the BM transparently. As a result, WiSync supports multiprogramming — it is likely that a large manycore will be shared by multiple applications — context switching, process migration, and memory access protection.

3.2 WiSync Architecture

Figure 2 shows the WiSync architecture. Each node in the manycore contains: a core with its L1 and L2 caches, a transceiver, two antennas, the BM, and two special bits. The second antenna is for a special, inexpensive *Tone* channel that we discuss later, and adds a very small area and power overhead. The transceiver has three modules: physical layer (PHY), Medium Access Control (MAC), and the Tone Controller. The PHY module interfaces with the antennas by serializing and modulating the data to transmit, detecting the transmission collisions, and demodulating and deserializing the received data. The MAC module determines when a write should be transmitted through the wireless network, and manages the collisions.

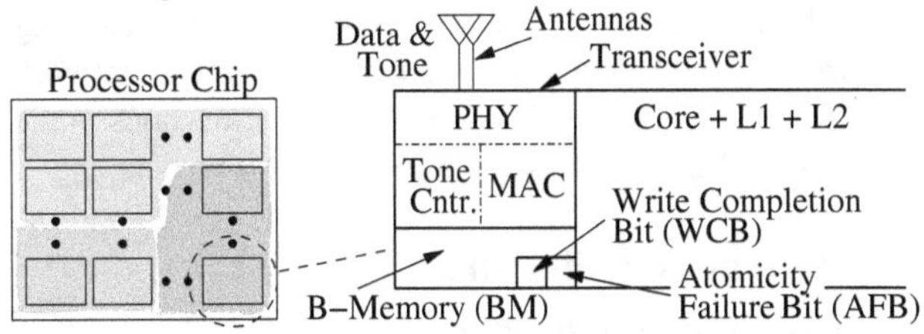

Figure 2: WiSync architecture. The different colors represent different programs running on the chip.

To understand the second antenna and the tone controller, note that, to keep the energy and area footprint of the wireless hardware low, WiSync transfers data in a single frequency band. However, we will see that it is beneficial to add an additional channel that only supports sending a tone. The tone controller manages it.

The BM stores the variables that are communicated through the wireless network. These variables are declared as *broadcast variables* in the program, and are kept replicated in all the BMs. They are uncacheable in the core's L1-L2 cache hierarchy. The core accesses its BM with plain loads and stores, using a range of virtual addresses that are translated in the TLB, but that bypass the L1 and L2 caches. The regular variables use the caches, which are kept coherent with an ordinary cache coherence protocol.

A plain load instruction can read from an address in the local BM into a register. A plain store instruction can store the value of a register into an address in the local BM and (thanks to the wireless network) in *all the BMs*. The write may collide in the wireless network, in which case no BM (including the local one) is updated. The MAC module keeps retrying the wireless transmission until it succeeds, at which point the local BM is also updated.

To reduce overhead, WiSync has *Bulk* load and store instructions. They take a register *R* and a BM address *BM_addr*. A Bulk load loads from four consecutive locations in the local BM starting at *BM_addr* into four registers starting at *R*. A Bulk store stores the four registers to four consecutive locations starting at *BM_addr* in the local and the remote BMs.

WiSync supports atomic read-modify-write (RMW) instructions to the BM, such as Test&Set, Fetch&Inc, Fetch& Add, and Compare-and-Swap (CAS). A RMW instruction involves reading a local BM location, bringing the data to the pipeline, updating the data in the pipeline, and then writing the result to the local BM and (using the wireless network) to all the BMs. To succeed, the instruction must guarantee atomicity from the time it reads from the BM until all the BMs are updated, possibly after several collisions and retries. To provide correct operation, the BM controller has two bits called Write Completion Bit (WCB) and Atomicity Failure Bit (AFB) (Figure 2).

Loads, stores, and RMW instructions can operate on different-sized data, although we will focus on 64-bit operations here.

As shown in Figure 2, multiple programs can be running concurrently and trying to use the BM and wireless network at the same time. Conventional access-bit permissions in the TLB ensure that programs access only their own data.

4. WiSync Architecture

4.1 Organization of the Wireless Transfer

A wireless system can be set up to use a single channel or multiple channels at different frequency ranges. Supporting multiple channels enables parallel wireless communication that can be exploited both within a program and across programs. However, it adds complication. Since we want to keep our system simple and the transceiver small, we choose to use a single channel.

We time-slot the channel in 1-ns slots — equal to the clock period of our 1GHz cores. Typically, we want to use the wireless network for single writes, such as a write to a reduction variable or to a lock. Hence, a transfer involves: a 64-bit datum, its address (11 bits, as we will see), a *Bulk* bit (to denote whether this is the first datum of a Bulk transfer), and a *Tone* bit (to denote whether this is for the tone channel, as we will see). The total size of a transfer is 77 bits.

As discussed in Section 2, current transceivers can transmit at 16-32 Gb/s [51], although in the next few years, this number may go up [24]. Hence, we use 4 cycles to transfer the 77 bits, which gives a required wireless bandwidth of 77b/4ns≈19Gb/s. This is a conservative value [51].

To keep the transceiver simple, WiSync takes 5 cycles for the actual transmission. The second cycle is used for the transceiver to listen if there was a collision in the first cycle. If there was a collision, the transfer is aborted, and the channel is free in the third cycle. Otherwise, the next three cycles send the rest of the message with guaranteed no collision. In this way, the penalty of a collision is 2 cycles instead of 5 cycles. A transmitter-receiver switch capable of working at these speeds has been demonstrated [45].

As per Section 2, a 19 Gb/s bandwidth requires a transmission frequency band of 19 GHz. We choose the central frequency to be 60 GHz, which can be supported with a small transceiver [2]. As shown in Figure 3, we call the resulting channel the Data channel. A transceiver and antenna for a similar frequency range have been built, and shown to consume 31.2 mW [51]. It is widely expected that technology advances will reduce this power.

To help message processing, every wireless message carries the Bulk bit in its first cycle. In ordinary accesses, the bit is zero; in Bulk accesses, it is set. When a transceiver observes the first cycle of a message, it knows the length of the message: if the Bulk bit is zero, the message will take 5 cycles; otherwise it will take 15 cycles.

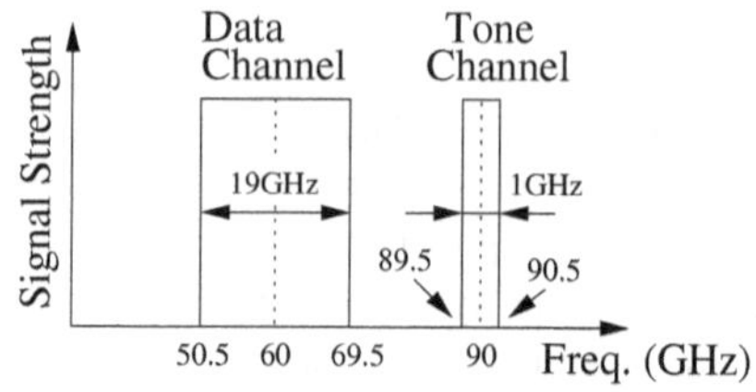

Figure 3: Transmission channels in WiSync.

The reason why a Bulk message only takes 15 cycles rather than 4×5=20 cycles is because we optimize it. Specifically, the second, third, and fourth word of a Bulk message do not need the collision check that occurs in the second cycle of an ordinary message. In addition, they do not need to carry an address, Bulk bit or Tone bit. Hence, given the network bandwidth that we use, these three words transfer their 3×64=192 bits in 10 cycles. The complete Bulk message then takes 5+10=15 cycles to transfer.

When the wireless network is busy, a transceiver ready to send a message waits to send it until the cycle when the network is next expected to be free. This is 15 or 5 cycles after the last message started (depending on whether or not that message was a Bulk one), or after the second cycle if a collision is detected.

In a collision, the MAC module in each of the colliding nodes stops the transmission, discards the messed-up information, and prevents the store from updating the local BM. It then retries the transmission. To maximize the use of the network, the MAC module uses a retry algorithm that temporarily reduces its assertiveness when there is contention. WiSync uses the well-known exponential backoff algorithm [27, 31, 32], which progressively increases the waiting period on a collision.

To reduce contention for the Data channel, WiSync provides an additional channel called the *Tone channel* that offloads the common barrier synchronization pattern. We apply the proposal of Oh et al. [33] for transmission lines, to wireless networks. In the Tone channel, nodes send a tone rather than data.

Specifically, the first core that reaches the barrier sends a message through the Data channel with the Tone bit set. On receiving the message, all the other nodes respond with a continuous tone in the Tone channel, creating repeated collisions. Then, as soon as a core reaches the barrier, its transceiver stops sending the tone. Hence, when the tone finally disappears, all cores have arrived at the barrier.

The Tone channel is also slotted in 1 ns slots. Each message is 1 bit, for a resulting transmission rate of 1 Gb/s. This means that the frequency band of the Tone channel is only 1 GHz. With such a short band, the power needed to support it (i.e., the transceiver extensions and a second antenna) is very small. With the same conservative assumptions we have been using, we estimate it adds 2 mW.

We place this channel at 90 GHz (Figure 3), far from the Data channel to avoid interference. At these high frequencies, signal attenuation is higher, but this is no problem because the Tone channel only transfers a tone rather than data.

4.2 B-Memory Operation and Interface

The BM in a node contains space for all the allocated variables that are declared as *broadcast* type in the programs currently running on the chip. Such variables are replicated in all the BMs and their values are kept consistent at all times. To use the BM efficiently, each BM entry is 64 bits rather than a line. Moreover, for protection, each entry is tagged with the PID of the program or process that allocated it.

When a program allocates a broadcast variable, the variable is allocated in all the BMs, and is tagged with the correct PID. When a core reads or writes a BM entry, the PID is checked in hardware to ensure the action is legal (Section 4.4 describes the address translation). When a variable is deallocated, it is removed from all the BMs.

The optimal size of the BM in each node is likely to be small, e.g., four 4-KB pages. The reason is two-fold. First, large memories require many address bits to be included in each wireless message. With 16KB, we already need 11 bits. Secondly, programs would not usually declare many broadcast variables. If the BM runs out of space for a variable, we envision transparently allocating the variable in a page of regular memory, and access it through the wired network.

4.2.1 Interface to Basic BM Instructions

Loads access the local BM and always succeed. For stores and RMW instructions, WiSync has the *Write Completion Bit (WCB)* and the *Atomicity Failure Bit (AFB)* (Figure 2). These bits are set/reset in hardware and accessible to the software through a register.

The WCB is associated with a store or RMW instruction. It is set when the update operation completes — both the global broadcast and the local BM update. In certain situations, the OS or the user code may benefit from this information. The AFB is associated with a RMW instruction. It is set if its atomicity fails — in which case the instruction completes without the BM write.

When a core executes a store instruction, the transceiver first attempts to broadcast the update to all the remote BMs. If there is a network collision, the transceiver keeps retrying until it succeeds. After it succeeds, the local BM is updated, the WCB gets set, and the pipeline receives the acknowledgment that the store is performed. No subsequent store from the local core can proceed to the global broadcast until the current one has performed all the steps above. Subsequent loads from the local core may or may not be allowed to read any BM address while the current write is in progress, depending on the memory consistency model desired. If loads are allowed to, we have a TSO memory model; if they are not allowed to read any BM address beyond the one being written, we have a sequential consistency model.

When a core executes a RMW instruction, the hardware reads the datum from the local BM into the pipeline, updates the datum in the pipeline, and then tries to write the datum to the BM. As usual, the write involves performing the global broadcast first and, when it succeeds, updating the local BM. It is possible that, after the read from the local BM and before the write manages to get to the wireless network, a remote node updates the variable in the local BM. This is detected in hardware by comparing the addresses of incoming stores to those of pending RMW accesses. In this case, the atomicity of the instruction has failed. As soon as this occurs, the AFB bit gets set. Later, when the write is attempted, it fails — i.e., the RMW instruction neither broadcasts its value nor it updates the local BM. At that time, the WCB gets set because the RMW operation has terminated.

Consequently, a RMW instruction needs to be followed by a software check of the AFB bit. The instruction has executed atomically and, therefore, performed the write, only if AFB=0. If, instead, AFB=1, the write never occurred, and the RMW instruction has to be re-executed. Note that this discussion assumes that the hardware does not allow a load following the RMW instruction to read the AFB register until after the RMW instruction has finished. An exception between the RMW instruction and the AFB check before the wireless transfer has succeeded automatically sets AFB and aborts the wireless transfer. AFB is saved and restored on context switch.

4.2.2 Interface to Tone Channel Instructions

A core has special BM load and store instructions that enable the use of the Tone channel for a particular BM address. They are *tone_ld R, BM_addr* and *tone_st R, BM_addr*.

Recall that we use the Tone channel to implement a barrier: each core needs to tell all the others when it has arrived at the barrier. *Tone_ld* and *tone_st* provide a very efficient implementation. Specifically, when a core reaches the barrier, it performs a *tone_st* operation on the BM location. Note that this is not an ordinary update of the location. Then, the core keeps reading the BM location using *tone_ld*. The load will return a special code when all the participating cores have performed the *tone_st*. In the meantime, the core may choose to do other work, while periodically polling with *tone_ld*.

The implementation of these instructions relies on the tone controller as follows. On a *tone_st*, the hardware does not update the BM location. Instead, the tone controller checks whether it is currently issuing a tone for this address in the Tone channel. If so, the local core is not the first core to arrive at the barrier, and the controller stops issuing the tone; otherwise, the local core is the first one to arrive, and the controller sends a message in the Data channel with the address of the BM location and the Tone bit *set*. The content of the 64-bit data field is immaterial.

The tone controller in any node also performs two actions based on incoming events. First, when it receives a message in the Data channel with the Tone bit set, if the local core

```
retry: fetch&inc R, BM_addr
       if (AFB) {
         jmp retry
       }
       else {
         /* success */
       }
```

(a)

```
retry: ld R_old, BM_addr
       . . . .
       if (!CAS(BM_addr, R_old, R_new)) {
         jmp retry  /* comparison already failed */
       }
       else {
         if (AFB) {
           jmp retry  /* atomicity failure */
         }
         else {
           /* success */
         }
       }
```

(b)

```
for ( ) {
  /* work */
  barrier: local sense = !local_sense
           tone_st (addr)
           spin until (tone_ld(addr)==local_sense)
}
```

(c)

```
Broadcast Writer                    Broadcast Readers
for ( ) {                           for ( ) {
  local_sense = !local_sense          local_sense = !local_sense
  write data                          spin until (release==local_sense)
  count = N                           read data
  release = local_sense               fetch&add (count,-1)
  spin until (count==0)             }
}
```

(d)

Figure 4: Examples of code used for synchronization.

participates in the barrier, it starts issuing a continuous tone in the Tone channel. This will cause repeated collisions with other nodes, which is precisely what we want. We will see in Section 4.4 how barrier participation is detected.

The second action of the tone controller occurs as soon as it detects that the Tone channel has fallen silent. At this point, all the cores have reached the barrier. Then, the controller toggles the value of the local BM location. Such location can only take the values zero or non-zero.

This is a sense-reversing barrier [16]. When a core spinning with *tone_ld* on that address observes that the value has changed, it knows that the barrier has ended. Later, we show how to support multiple concurrent tone barriers.

4.3 Supporting Synchronization Operations

We now outline how WiSync supports some of the popular synchronization operations.

4.3.1 Basic Read-Modify-Write Primitives

Figure 4(a) shows the pseudo-code of the algorithm used to execute a basic RMW operation. The example uses fetch&increment. After the core executes the RMW instruction, it checks the AFB register bit. If it is set, the instruction has been aborted and it has to be retried. Otherwise, the operation performed successfully. Similar pseudo-code is used for test&set and fetch&add.

Figure 4(b) shows pseudo-code for CAS. The code assumes that a CAS returns zero if the content of the BM location is different from the CAS' second argument; otherwise, it returns non-zero. Even if it returns non-zero, however, the CAS may not have executed atomically (and failed to perform the wireless broadcast). Hence, the code checks the AFB register. If it is set, the CAS needs to be retried.

4.3.2 Barriers Using the Data Channel

There are two types of barriers: AND-barriers and OR-barriers. The former are the conventional ones, where a processor arriving at a barrier waits until all other processors have also arrived. For them, we use the popular sense-reversing barrier algorithm [16] with fetch&increment. To save BM space, a single 64-bit BM entry could contain the *Count* variable in one 32-bit word and the *Release* flag in the other word.

OR-barriers (also called Eurekas) are triggered as soon as one of the participating processors detects a certain condition, e.g., overflow of a variable, the solution of a parallel search, or an exception. We implement them as a boolean variable in a BM location. All processors periodically read it; when one detects the condition, it changes the variable. We use a sense-reversing implementation to allow barrier reuse.

4.3.3 Tone Barriers

AND-barriers are supported more efficiently with the Tone channel. As per Section 4.2.2, each core executes the pseudo-code algorithm of Figure 4(c). It implements a sense-reversing barrier with minimal communication. On arrival, the first core sends a message through the Data channel, while later cores simply remove their tone from the Tone channel. Then, all cores spin in their local BM location. When the Tone channel falls silent, the controller toggles the location in all the BMs, which releases all cores. This is a scalable implementation.

4.3.4 Producer-Consumer Operation

To support the single producer, single consumer pattern, we use a BM address for the data and a BM address for a flag. The producer writes the data to the data address, sets the flag, and then spins on the flag until it is cleared. The consumer spins on the flag until it is set, reads the data, and then clears the flag. The process repeats. Often, producer and consumer will use bulk stores and bulk loads, respectively. These instructions trigger reads and uninterruptible writes of multiple BM addresses at a time.

4.3.5 Reduction and Multicast/Broadcast

The BM supports reductions very efficiently. For instance, when all the cores need to add to a single variable, they can use *fetch&add R, BM_addr*. To support different types of reductions, one can include other *fetch&Φ* instructions and, for scientific computations, floating-point versions of them. Very tight reduction loops are supported efficiently.

Multicast/broadcast is the single producer, multiple consumers pattern, and is also supported very efficiently. The producer writes to a BM address and all consumers read from it. To provide ordering between the writer and the readers, we can use an extension of the full-empty flag discussed above. Specifically, we use two additional BM addresses (or store two variables in different halves of the same BM address). One variable is a count, and the other a toggling flag, effectively implementing a sense-reversing barrier.

The pseudo-code is Figure 4(d). The producer writes the data, sets the count to N (the number of readers), toggles the flag, and then spins on the count until it is zero. Each reader spins on the flag until it toggles, reads the data, and then decrements the flag with *fetch&add*. The process repeats.

4.4 BM Entry Allocation and Protection

To access the BM, WiSync uses TLB-based address translation, so that programs do not have to manage memory and can benefit from access protection. However, traditional page-level assignment is suboptimal, as the BM is small and cannot afford the memory wastage due to page-level fragmentation when multiple programs use the BM. Indeed, if each program allocated a single broadcast variable but was assigned a full page, the BM would soon run out of space.

To address this problem, WiSync uses page-level TLB translation but lets different programs use different chunks of the same physical BM page — tagging each chunk with the PID of the program that owns it. Different programs have virtual pages mapped to the same physical BM page, but each program only uses its own, non-overlapping chunks of the physical page.

The smaller the chunk size is, the better the page can be utilized, and there is less fragmentation. However, there is more bookkeeping and tag overhead. In this paper, we do not examine these tradeoffs. Rather, we reckon that using BM effectively is important and, hence, use 64-bit chunks.

When a core allocates an entry in the local and remote BMs, the entry is tagged in hardware with the program's PID. When a core accesses the BM, the address is first translated. Then, at the target BM location, the program's PID is compared to the PID tag (Figure 5). A mismatch is a protection violation.

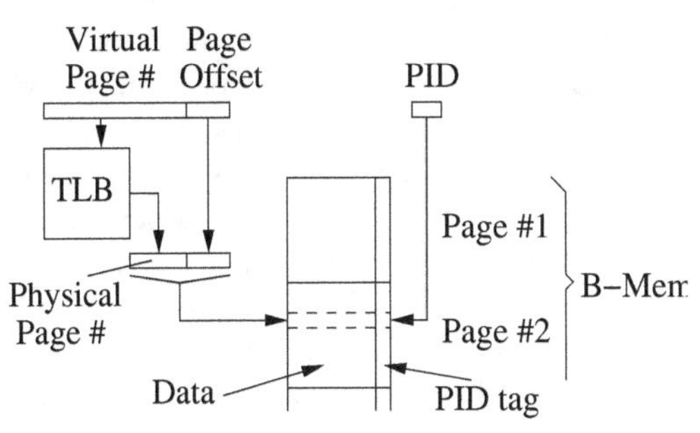

Figure 5: Broadcast memory address translation.

To allocate an entry in the BM, the core uses a special allocation instruction. The instruction broadcasts a message in the wireless network that contains the address (11 bits), PID (e.g., 8 bits), and a few miscellaneous bits. On reception, each node in the chip allocates an entry at the same address in its local BM and tags it with the PID. When this operation succeeds, the local BM allocates and tags an entry at the same address. While it appears inefficient that a variable takes space in all the BMs (even in the BMs of cores that do not run the relevant program), we do it for simplicity.

The allocation of a variable that uses the Tone Channel proceeds similarly. However, in addition, the OS in the receiving nodes records whether or not this variable is locally *armed*. Armed means that there is (or will be) a thread running on the local core that will participate in the tone barrier protocol for the variable. Later, when the node receives a message initiating a tone barrier for a variable, if the variable is locally armed, the tone controller will participate by starting a tone.

This discussion illustrates a restriction in the usage of tone barriers. Unlike in conventional barriers, when a tone barrier is allocated, the runtime needs to know which cores will participate. This is because most of the tone barrier operation is in hardware. If core participation cannot be determined until later on in the program, a tone barrier cannot be used; instead, a Data channel barrier should be used.

5. Implementation Issues

5.1 Sharing the Tone Channel

At any given time, there may be multiple tone barriers (each corresponding to a different BM address) that want to use the Tone channel. WiSync responds by time-multiplexing the Tone channel. Specifically, the Tone channel is slotted with 1-ns slots, and the slots are assigned round-robin to the currently-active tone barriers. A tone barrier is *Active* from the time the first core arrives until the last participating one arrives. Figure 6(a) shows how the slots in the Tone channel are assigned when there are 1, 2, or 3 active tone barriers.

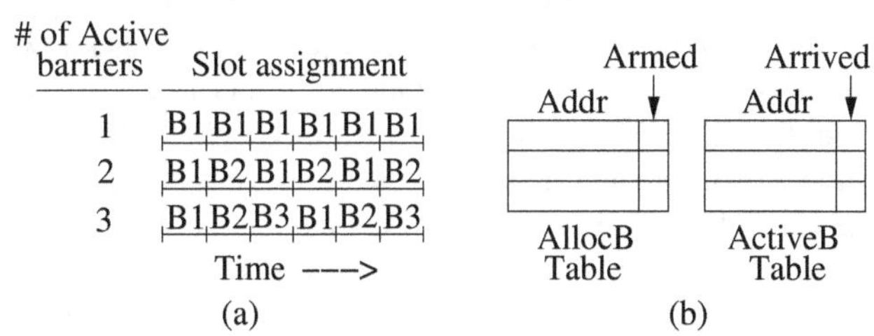

Figure 6: Sharing the Tone channel among several barriers.

To share the Tone channel, the tone controller in each node keeps two tables (Figure 6(b)): one with the *allocated* tone barriers (*AllocB*) and one with the *active* tone barriers (*ActiveB*). These tables contain the same addresses and in the same order in all the nodes of the chip. Such chip-wide consistency is required for correct assignment of slots to barriers. It is easy to support thanks to the wireless broadcast capabilities.

In AllocB, each entry has the BM address of a tone barrier variable plus the local *Armed* bit. When a tone barrier variable is allocated by a program (Section 4.4), an entry is created in the AllocB of all the nodes in the chip. It is also at this point that the OS in each node sets the *Armed* bit to either 1 or 0, as discussed in Section 4.4. Finally, when the tone barrier variable is deallocated (possibly at program termination), its entry is removed from the AllocB of all nodes. At that time, all the entries lower in the table are shifted up.

In ActiveB, each entry has the BM address of the tone barrier variable plus an *Arrived* bit, which indicates whether the local core has arrived at the barrier. The order of the entries in this table determines the round-robin assignment of Tone channel slots to the different active tone barriers.

For a given tone barrier *B*, when the first core arrives at the barrier, the entry for *B* in AllocB is copied to the lowest position in ActiveB. This is done in all the cores. Specifically, if the first-arriving core is the local one, the usual message is sent through the Data channel, the copy is made, and then the *Arrived* bit in the copied entry is set. Instead, if the first-arriving core was a remote one, when the message that it placed in the Data channel is received, the copy is made. Then, if the local *Armed* bit was clear, the *Arrived* bit in the copied entry is set, and no tone is issued in the Tone channel. Effectively, this node refuses to participate in the barrier. On the other hand, if the local *Armed* bit was set, the *Arrived* bit in the copied entry is left clear, and the hardware starts issuing the tone in the Tone channel — but only during the assigned slots. Later, when the local processor arrives, the *Arrived* bit gets set and the local tone terminates.

At any slot assigned to this active barrier, the local tone controller uses the following algorithm. If the *Arrived* bit is zero, issue the tone. Otherwise, listen for the tone; if there is no tone, all cores have arrived. Hence, remove *B*'s entry from ActiveB and shift all the lower entries up.

AllocB and ActiveB are identical across all nodes except for the *Armed* and *Arrived* bits. As a result, all cores know the assignment of slots to individual barriers at all times. Note that the copying of an entry from AllocB to ActiveB starts as soon as the first cycle of the message transfer in the Data channel. The latency of the copy is hidden by the subsequent cycles of the message transmission.

We size AllocB and ActiveB equally, and return an error if an allocation overflows AllocB. In a multiprogramming environment, the OS has to prevent a process from starving out all other processes by using up all the AllocB entries; this can be done by limiting the per-process use of AllocB.

5.2 Context Switching and Thread Migration

The Data channel in WiSync is designed to operate correctly under context switching, thread migration, and multiple threads sharing a core. Consider first a running thread that gets preempted. Even while the thread is preempted, updates from other cores to broadcast variables will reach the local BM and update it. When the thread is rescheduled again, it will see the correct BM state.

A thread can also migrate to another core and resume execution there seamlessly. This is because the state of the BMs is identical in all the nodes. The non-BM state is not relevant to our discussion, as we assume that the cache coherence keeps it coherent. Finally, multiple threads can share a core, and update the same or different BM variables.

The situation is different for programs that use the Tone channel. The reason is that this channel is hardware-managed. In this case, threads can still be preempted, but cannot migrate or share the core with another thread that also uses the same Tone barrier. Indeed, when a tone barrier is allocated, the OS arms or disarms the local AllocB entry, depending on whether a local thread will participate. Migrating a thread would require somehow migrating this state, which is costly. Also, two threads on the same core trying to use the same tone barrier would result in incorrect operation.

5.3 Adaptively Dealing with Contention

Our collision resolution algorithm uses exponential backoff. On a collision, the transmitters back-off for a random number of cycles, whose range increases exponentially with the number of retries. In our design, the range is between 0 and 2^i-1 cycles, where i is a number incremented at every collision and decremented at every successful transmission.

It is possible to use more advanced policies with adaptivity based on the observed contention — a concept analogous to Reactive Synchronization [27]. Adaptive algorithms are not generally used in conventional non-broadcast wireless networks because it is hard to get consensus on the decisions. However, in our scenario, they would be easy to support because all nodes have all the information at all times. In our work, we have not explored such techniques.

6. Evaluation Environment

We use cycle-level execution-driven simulations to model a manycore with 16–256 cores, either with or without WiSync support. The default core count is 64. We use the Multi2sim simulator [44]. Table 1 shows the general parameters of the architecture and, in its lower part, those related to WiSync.

We compare four manycore configurations, as shown in Table 2. *Baseline* is a plain manycore with no wireless hardware. For synchronization, it uses CAS and a sense-reversing centralized barrier. *Baseline+* enhances *Baseline* hardware with: (1) virtual tree-based broadcast in the on-chip network with flit replication at the router crossbars [22], (2) MCS locks [31], and (3) Tournament barriers [31]. *WiSyncNoT* is *WiSync* without the Tone barrier support.

We run two sets of synchronization-intensive kernels and a set of applications (Table 3). The first set of kernels con-

General Parameters	
Architecture	22nm manycore with 16–256 cores (default: 64)
Core	Out of order, 2-issue wide, 1GHz, x86 ISA
ROB; ld/st queue	64 entries; 20 entries
L1 cache	Private 32KB WB, 2-way, 2-cycle RT, 64B lines
L2 cache	Shared with per-core 512KB WB banks
L2 bank	8-way, 6-cycle RT (local), 64B lines
Cache coherence	MOESI directory based
On-chip network	2D-mesh, 4 cycles/hop, 128-bit links
Off-chip memory	Connected to 4 mem controllers, 110-cycle RT
WiSync Parameters	
Per-core BM	16KB, 2-cycle RT, 64-bit wide entry
Tone channel	1Gb/s; 1-cycle transfer latency
Data Tran. channel	19Gb/s; 5-cyc transfer lat; collision detec. cyc 2
Collision handling	Exponential backoff
Transceiv+2Anten	Area: 0.12mm^2; power: 18mW

Table 1: Architecture modeled. RT means round trip.

Config.	BM?	Broadcast HW	Locks	Barriers
Baseline	No	No	CAS	Centralized
Baseline+	No	Virtual Tree	MCS	Tournament
WiSyncNoT	Yes	Wireless	Wireless	Wireless (Data only)
WiSync	Yes	Wireless	Wireless	Wireless (Data+Tone)

Table 2: Architecture configurations compared.

sists of four loops that execute barriers. They include a tight loop that we wrote (*TightLoop*) and Livermore loops 2, 3, and 6 [30]. In TightLoop, each thread adds-up the contents of a 50-element array into a local variable and then synchronizes in a barrier. The process repeats in a loop. For the Livermore loops, we focus on only these three because, as Sampson et al. [37] argue, they are the representative ones with regard to synchronization. We parallelize them and align their data as these authors do.

Barrier Kernels	TightLoop, Livermore loops 2, 3, 6
CAS Kernels	FIFO, LIFO, ADD
Application Suites	SPLASH-2, PARSEC

Table 3: Kernels and applications executed.

The second set of kernels consists of three kernels that execute CAS operations on lock-free data structures. In the ADD kernel, there is a shared queue to which, through a CAS, threads attempt to insert nodes taken from their private memory pools. A given number of instructions are executed between successive node insertions. In the FIFO and LIFO kernels, threads both enqueue and dequeue nodes from the shared queue or stack, respectively. Similarly, a given number of instructions are executed between accesses.

The applications are the entire SPLASH-2 [50] and PARSEC [9] suites. We use the standard input set sizes in SPLASH-2 and *simsmall* in PARSEC. *Dedup* and *fluidanimate* declare arrays of locks larger than the 16KB BM used here. In these cases, we allocate the first 16KB in the BM and the rest in plain memory. Finally, we modified the OpenMP libraries in order to evaluate *freqmine*.

7. Evaluation

7.1 Area and Power Comparison

Table 4 compares the estimated area and power consumption of the transceiver plus the two antennas to two popular 22 nm cores, namely the high performance Xeon Haswell and the energy-efficient Atom Silvermont. The TDP (Thermal Design Power) of an 18-core Haswell chip at 2.1 GHz is 135 W [17]. Correcting for frequency, we roughly estimate a per-core 5 W TDP. The TDP of an 8-core Silvermont chip (Avaton) at 1.7 GHz is 12 W [17]. At 1 GHz, we estimate a per-core 1 W TDP. Area numbers are from the literature.

To estimate the area and power of the transceiver plus the two antennas, we use the 22 nm 60 GHz figures outlined in Section 2. Specifically, a transceiver and one antenna consume 0.1 mm^2 and 16 mW. We then augment the transceiver with circuitry to support the tone channel, and add a second antenna at 90 GHz for the tone channel. Scaling from the 65 nm figures in [14, 49] to 22 nm, we estimate that this additional capability costs 0.04 mm^2 and 2 mW. Hence, the total cost of the transceiver plus the two antennas is 0.14 mm^2 and 18 mW (Table 4).

	Xeon Haswell Core	Atom Silvermont Core	T+2A	(T+2A) /Xeon (%)	(T+2A) /Atom (%)
Area	21.1mm^2	2.5mm^2	0.14mm^2	0.7	5.6
TDP	≈5W	≈1W	18mW	0.4	1.8

Table 4: Comparing two popular cores to the transceiver plus two antennas (T+2A), all at 22 nm.

Overall, we see that the transceiver and two antennas have a small footprint. They account for 0.7% of the area and 0.4% of the power of a Haswell core, and 5.6% of the area and 1.8% of the power of an Atom core.

7.2 Barrier Synchronization Evaluation

We first evaluate the performance of the different barrier configurations using TightLoop, which represents a very demanding environment. Figure 7 shows the number of cycles that each iteration of the loop takes on the different architecture configurations as we change the number of cores from 16 to 256. Note that the Y-axis in this plot and most of the others is *logarithmic*.

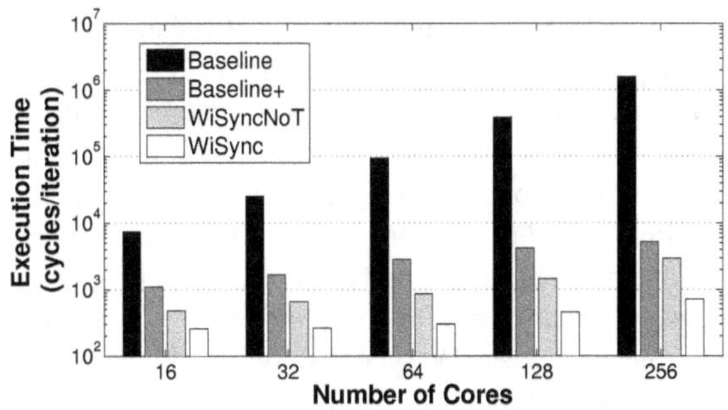

Figure 7: Execution time of TightLoop on different architecture configurations. Note that the Y-axis is *logarithmic*.

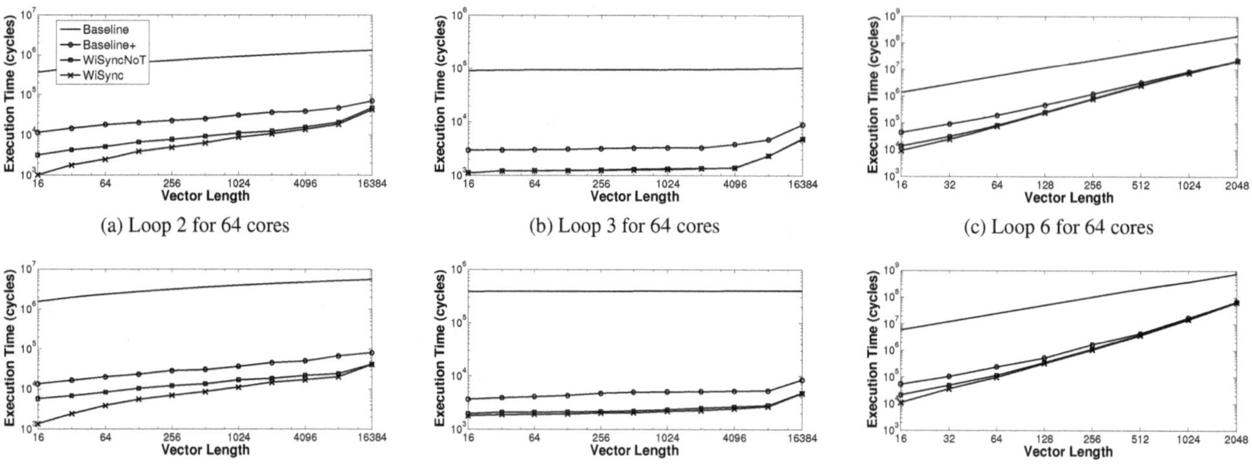

(a) Loop 2 for 64 cores (b) Loop 3 for 64 cores (c) Loop 6 for 64 cores

(d) Loop 2 for 128 cores (e) Loop 3 for 128 cores (f) Loop 6 for 128 cores

Figure 8: Execution time of Livermore loops on different architecture configurations for several vector sizes and core counts.

The figure shows a large difference between the configurations, especially for high core counts. As we increase the core count, the execution time of WiSync remains low, thanks to the Tone channel. WiSync's execution time is about one order of magnitude lower than Baseline+ (which uses a Tournament barrier). It is two to three orders of magnitude lower than Baseline.

WiSyncNoT takes 2–6x longer than WiSync to execute because of collisions in the Data channel. Hence, the Tone channel is useful for barrier-intensive codes. Still, WiSyncNoT's execution time is 2x–4x lower than Baseline+.

Figure 8 shows the execution time of Livermore loops 2, 3, and 6 on the different architecture configurations as we change the vector length. The top and bottom plots correspond to 64-core and 128-core executions, respectively.

Starting with the three upper plots, we see that WiSyncNoT and WiSync are several times faster than Baseline+, and two orders of magnitude faster than Baseline. The gains are highest with small vector lengths, where the overhead of the barrier relative to the computation is most significant. As the vector lengths increase, the computation time becomes higher, and the barrier time (including any collisions) becomes relatively less important. As a result, Baseline+ tends to get closer to WiSyncNoT and WiSync. This is especially the case for Loop 6, which has a large loop body.

We see that WiSync is significantly faster than WiSyncNoT in Loop 2 for modest problem sizes. The reason is similar to that in TightLoop: a burst of arrivals causes collisions in the Data channel in WiSyncNoT which, due to the modest duration of the loop, have a significant impact on latency. WiSync eliminates the collisions by using the Tone channel.

If we examine the lower plots, we see a wider gap between Baseline and the rest of configurations for 128 cores. The difference between WiSync, WiSyncNoT, and Baseline+ follows similar trends as for 64 cores.

Overall, we conclude that, while WiSync's Data channel does well across the board, the Tone channel is even better for some workloads.

7.3 CAS Synchronization Evaluation

We now consider kernels with CAS operations and compare executions using the wireless network and using conventional systems. Since these kernels involve lock-free structures and do not use barriers, the results are independent of the lock and barrier implementation. Consequently, we simply compare WiSync (where CASes use the BM) to Baseline (where CASes use the cache hierarchy).

Figure 9 shows the throughput of the FIFO, LIFO, and ADD CAS kernels on the two architecture configurations as we change the number of instructions that a given processor executes between consecutive CASes. This is shown in the X-axes as critical section size, and small numbers are to the right. The plots show the number of successful CASes per 1,000 cycles. The top and bottom plots correspond to 64-core and 128-core executions, respectively.

The figures show that WiSync is able to attain a much higher CAS throughput than a conventional architecture. For 64 cores, there is little or no difference between the architectures when the number of instructions between CASes is 8-16K or larger. However, the difference increases as the critical section becomes smaller and contention rises. By the time we have about 2K instructions, WiSync delivers a CAS throughput that is about one order of magnitude higher than Baseline. With 128 cores, at about 4K instructions in the critical section, WiSync delivers a one order of magnitude higher CAS throughput than Baseline.

7.4 Full Application Evaluation

We now consider the entire PARSEC and SPLASH-2 application suites running with 64 cores. Figure 10 shows the speedup of Baseline+, WiSyncNoT, and WiSync over the Baseline architecture for all the applications. The two right-

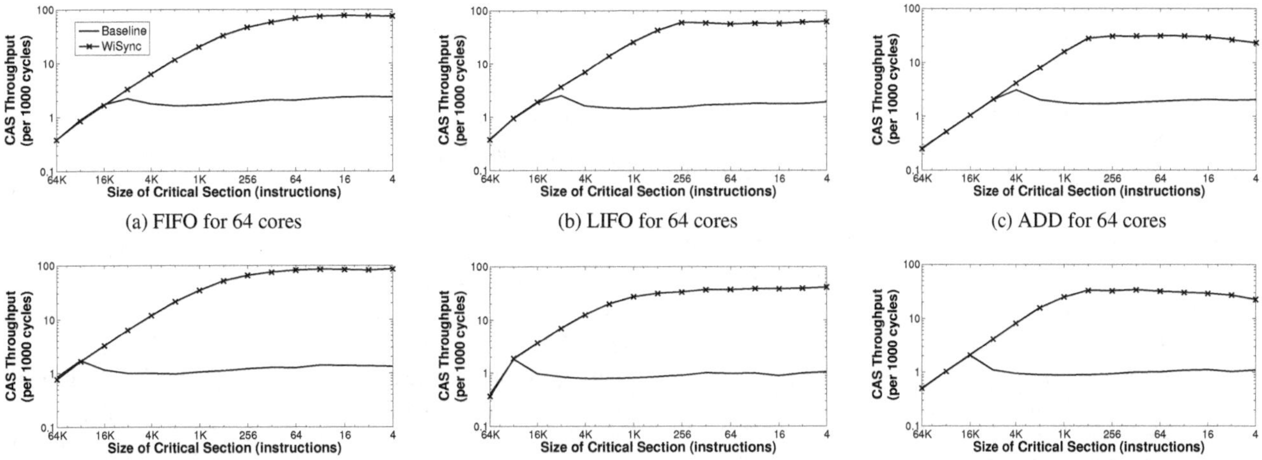

(a) FIFO for 64 cores (b) LIFO for 64 cores (c) ADD for 64 cores

(d) FIFO for 128 cores (e) LIFO for 128 cores (f) ADD for 128 cores

Figure 9: CAS throughput of three kernels on different architecture configurations for several critical section sizes and core counts. In the charts, higher is better.

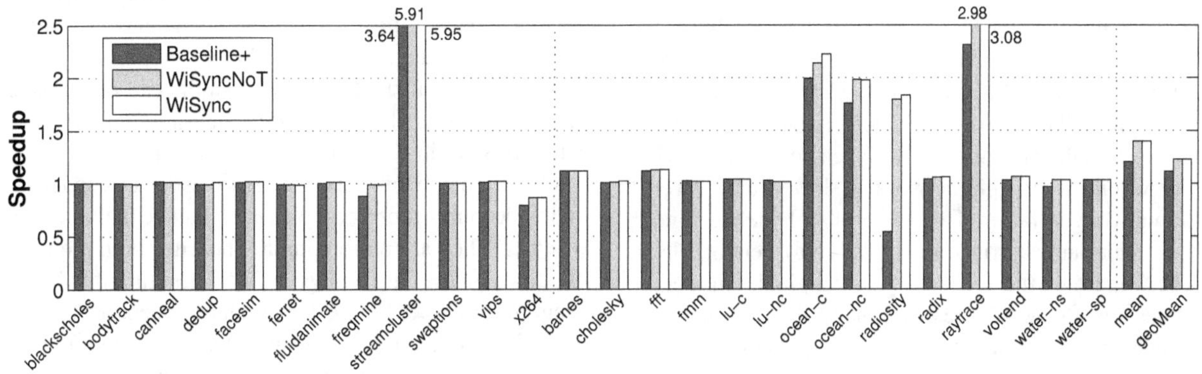

Figure 10: Speedup of different architecture configurations over Baseline running PARSEC and SPLASH-2 for 64 cores.

most set of bars show the arithmetic and the geometric mean, respectively.

Based on the geometric mean, WiSync delivers an average speedup of 1.23 over Baseline. Moreover, compared to the more advanced Baseline+ design that uses MCS locks and Tournament barriers, WiSync delivers an average speedup of 1.12. These are significant improvements. We also see that WiSyncNoT performs on average about the same as WiSync. This is because the wireless Data channel is not very utilized in these applications.

WiSync speeds-up about nine applications. The others have too little synchronization for WiSync to make a difference. WiSync shows its best gains in applications that frequently use barriers, such as *streamcluster* (speedup close to 6) and *ocean*. In addition, significant speedups are also attained in a few lock-intensive applications such as *raytrace* (speedup close to 3) and *radiosity*. Many applications do not use fine-grain synchronization and, therefore, the improvements of WiSync make little difference.

Baseline+ shows low speedups in some applications. This is due to the overhead of its more sophisticated synchronization implementations.

In *dedup* and *fluidanimate*, the locks did not fit in the BM, and we transparently allocated a fraction of the locks in plain memory. However, simulations with an infinitely large BM did not yield any further speedup.

To understand these results better, Table 5 shows the percentage of the cycles in which WiSyncNoT and WiSync use the Data channel. We show data for the most demanding applications and the geometric mean *of all* the applications. From these numbers, we see that, on average, WiSyncNoT and WiSync use the Data channel for 0.2% and 0.1% of the time, respectively. Both utilizations are very low. WiSync's utilization is lower because barrier synchronization uses the Tone channel. In addition, there is little contention. It can be shown that, on average, the latency of a Data channel transfer in WiSyncNoT and WiSync is 9.8 and 5.6 cycles, respectively. Overall, for WiSync to deliver larger speedups, we need applications that use the wireless network more.

7.5 Sensitivity Study

To study the impact of the memory and network latencies on these speedups, we perform a sensitivity study with the configuration variants shown in Table 6. *Default* is the con-

	Str	Rad	W/ns	Flu	Ray	Oc/c	Oc/nc	GM
WT	3.0	2.1	2.0	1.8	1.6	0.8	0.7	0.2
W	0.0	2.1	2.0	1.8	1.6	0.3	0.2	0.1

Table 5: Utilization of the Data channel in WiSyncNoT (*WT*) and WiSync (*W*) in % of the total cycles for the most demanding applications. *GM* is the geometric mean *of all* the applications.

figuration we have used so far. *SlowNet* and *FastNet* increase and decrease, respectively, the network hop latency by two cycles. *SlowNet+L2* additionally makes the L2 cache slower. Finally, *SlowBMEM* makes the BM two cycles slower.

Configuration	L2 RT (Cycles)	BM RT (Cycles)	Net. Hop Lat. (Cycles)
Default	6	2	4
SlowNet	6	2	6
SlowNet+L2	12	2	6
FastNet	6	2	2
SlowBMEM	6	4	4

Table 6: Memory and network configuration variants.

Figure 11 shows the geometric mean speedups of Baseline+, WiSyncNoT, and WiSync over Baseline for the different configurations. The results correspond to 64-core executions. We see that the speedups of WiSync and WiSyncNoT are higher when the on-chip network is slower, and lower when the network is faster. This is because Baseline (and Baseline+) locks and barriers are sensitive to network latency. The impact of the L2 latency is marginal, since all architectures are affected noticeably. Finally, the BM latency barely affects the performance of WiSync and WiSyncNoT, at least for the range considered.

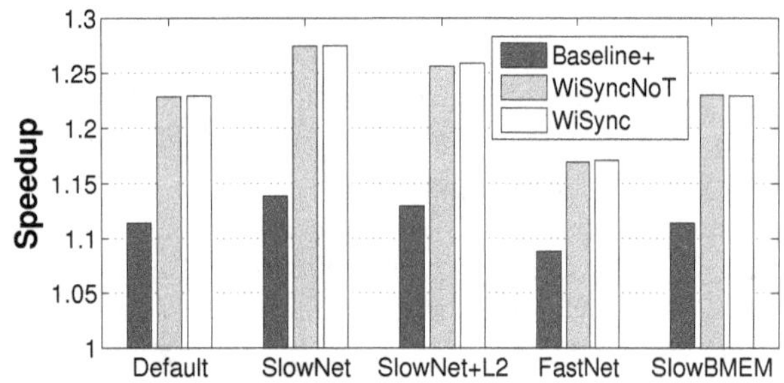

Figure 11: Impact of different memory and network variants on the speedups over Baseline for 64 cores.

8. Related Work

Special hardware support for synchronization. Advanced hardware for synchronization is an active research area (e.g. [5, 7, 12, 15, 25, 26, 37, 38, 40, 53]). Many designs use some form of synchronization in memory or directory, such as the Cray T3E E-registers [38], the SGI Origin fetch-and-Φ operations [25], the buffer of full-empty bit flags in memory banks [53], and the MiSAR on-chip synchronization accelerator [26] to name a few. However, very few designs have ever provided broadcast capabilities, as WiSync does. Perhaps the closest support is Blue Gene/L's network for collectives, broadcast, and reduction [15]. Many designs have optimized barriers, which also include a broadcast step. Some examples are the barrier network in Cray T3D [12], cache coherence protocol optimizations [37], special interconnect hardware for barriers [7], and wired-NOR logic [40].

Transmission Lines (TLs). TLs can provide on-chip broadcast [4, 5, 10, 33, 34, 41, 43]. As a result, they have been used for synchronization. For example, our Tone barrier is inspired in the TLSync TL barrier [33], which also uses tones. Abellan et al. [4, 5] implement locks and barriers using TLs, as they broadcast signals over these TLs. Other designs use TLs for a variety of broadcast networks [10, 34, 43].

Nanophotonics. The transmission of optical signals through nanophotonic waveguides can provide broadcast [21, 23, 46, 47]. Nanophotonics has been proposed for a variety of network architectures [6, 42]. Some proposals use it for on-chip broadcast [21, 23, 46]. Vantrease et al. [47] design a novel form of cache coherence using optical waveguides.

Compared to wireless networks, TLs and nanophotonics are more energy efficient and provide higher bandwidth density. Both advantages are due to the fact that energy is guided rather than radiated. Higher bandwidths can be attained by including several channels within the same link, or by replicating links as in conventional on-chip networks.

On the other hand, network design using TLs and nanophotonics becomes more complex and less scalable than with wireless. They are more complex because both require laying down on the chip a physical infrastructure that interconnects the nodes. TLs are less scalable because they suffer from signal reflections as we connect more nodes to the TL. This requires using amplifying stages between TL segments. Nanophotonics are less scalable due to their laser power needs. Light is modulated by the transmitter and then guided to all the receivers, which extract a fraction of the light each. This causes losses, and requires a high laser power for large destinations sets.

9. Conclusion

This paper proposed to address the challenge of supporting frequent communication due to fine-grain synchronization using on-chip wireless communication. Our architecture, called WiSync, uses a per-core Broadcast Memory (BM). When a core writes to its BM, all the other 100+ BMs get updated in less than 10 processor cycles. In addition to the Data channel for data communication, WiSync proposes the cheap Tone channel, to execute barriers very efficiently. With WiSync, a manycore supports multiprogramming, virtual memory, context switching and, except if the Tone channel is used, process migration. Our evaluation with simulations of 128-threaded kernels and 64-threaded applications showed that WiSync speeds-up synchronization substantially. Compared to using advanced conventional synchronization, WiSync achieved an average speedup of nearly one order of magnitude for the kernels, and 1.12 for the PARSEC and SPLASH-2 applications.

References

[1] S. Abadal, E. Alarcón, M. C. Lemme, M. Nemirovsky, and A. Cabellos-Aparicio. Graphene-enabled Wireless Communication for Massive Multicore Architectures. *IEEE Communications Magazine*, 51(11):137–143, 2013.

[2] S. Abadal, M. Iannazzo, M. Nemirovsky, A. Cabellos-Aparicio, and E. Alarcón. On the Area and Energy Scalability of Wireless Network-on-Chip: A Model-based Benchmarked Design Space Exploration. *IEEE/ACM Transactions on Networking*, 23(5):1, 2015.

[3] S. Abadal, B. Sheinman, O. Katz, O. Markish, D. Elad, Y. Fournier, D. Roca, M. Hanzich, G. Houzeaux, M. Nemirovsky, E. Alarcón, and A. Cabellos-Aparicio. Broadcast-Enabled Massive Multicore Architectures: A Wireless RF Approach. *IEEE MICRO*, 35(5):52–61, 2015.

[4] J. L. Abellán, J. Fernández, and M. E. Acacio. GLocks: Efficient Support for Highly-contended Locks in Many-core CMPs. In *Proceedings of the IEEE International Parallel and Distributed Processing Symposium*, pages 893–905, May 2011.

[5] J. L. Abellán, J. Fernández, and M. E. Acacio. Efficient Hardware Barrier Synchronization in Many-Core CMPs. *IEEE Transactions on Parallel and Distributed Systems*, 23(8): 1453–1466, 2012.

[6] C. Batten, A. Joshi, V. Stojanovic, and K. Asanovic. Designing Chip-Level Nanophotonic Interconnection Networks. *IEEE Journal on Emerging and Selected Topics in Circuits and Systems*, 2(2):137–153, 2012.

[7] C. Beckmann and C. Polychronopoulos. Fast Barrier Synchronization Hardware. *Proceedings of Supercomputing*, November 1990.

[8] S. Benedetto and E. Biglieri. *Principles of Digital Transmission with Wireless Applications.* Springer Science and Business Media, 1999.

[9] C. Bienia, S. Kumar, J. Singh, and K. Li. The PARSEC Benchmark Suite: Characterization and Architectural Implications. In *Proceedings of the 17th International Conference on Parallel Architectures and Compilation Techniques*, pages 72–81, October 2008.

[10] A. Carpenter, J. Hu, O. Kocabas, M. Huang, and H. Wu. Enhancing Effective Throughput for Transmission Line-based Bus. In *Proceedings of the 39th Annual International Symposium on Computer Architecture*, pages 165–176, June 2012.

[11] M. F. Chang, J. Cong, A. Kaplan, M. Naik, G. Reinman, E. Socher, and S.-W. Tam. CMP Network-on-Chip Overlaid With Multi-Band RF-Interconnect. In *Proceedings of the 14th International Symposium on High Performance Computer Architecture*, pages 191–202, February 2008.

[12] Cray Research Inc. CRAY T3D System Architecture Overview, 1993.

[13] S. Deb, A. Ganguly, P. P. Pande, B. Belzer, and D. Heo. Wireless NoC as Interconnection Backbone for Multicore Chips: Promises and Challenges. *IEEE Journal on Emerging and Selected Topics in Circuits and Systems*, 2(2):228–239, 2012.

[14] S. Deb, K. Chang, X. Yu, S. Sah, M. Cosic, P. P. Pande, B. Belzer, and D. Heo. Design of an Energy Efficient CMOS Compatible NoC Architecture with Millimeter-Wave Wireless Interconnects. *IEEE Transactions on Computers*, 62(12): 2382–2396, 2013.

[15] A. Gara, M. A. Blumrich, D. Chen, G. L.-T. Chiu, P. Coteus, M. E. Giampapa, R. A. Haring, P. Heidelberger, D. Hoenicke, G. V. Kopcsay, T. A. Liebsch, M. Ohmacht, B. D. Steinmacher-Burow, T. Takken, and P. Vranas. Overview of the Blue Gene/L System Architecture. In *IBM Journal of Research and Development*, March/May 2005.

[16] J. L. Hennessy and D. A. Patterson. *Computer Architecture: A Quantitative Approach, Fifth Edition.* Morgan Kaufmann, 2012.

[17] Intel Corporation. Intel Products. ark.intel.com, 2015.

[18] C. H. Jan, M. Agostinelli, H. Deshpande, M. a. El-Tanani, W. Hafez, U. Jalan, L. Janbay, M. Kang, H. Lakdawala, J. Lin, Y. L. Lu, S. Mudanai, J. Park, A. Rahman, J. Rizk, W. K. Shin, K. Soumyanath, H. Tashiro, C. Tsai, P. VanDerVoorn, J. Y. Yeh, and P. Bai. RF CMOS Technology Scaling in High-k/Metal Gate Era for RF SoC (System-on-Chip) Applications. In *Proceedings of the IEEE International Electron Devices Meeting*, pages 604–607, December 2010.

[19] S. Kaya, S. Laha, A. Kodi, D. Ditomaso, D. Matolak, and W. Rayess. On Ultra-short Wireless Interconnects for NoCs and SoCs: Bridging the THz Gap. In *Proceedings of the IEEE 56th International Midwest Symposium on Circuits and Systems*, pages 804–808, August 2013.

[20] B. Khamaisi, S. Jameson, and E. Socher. A 210–227 GHz Transmitter With Integrated On-Chip Antenna in 90 nm CMOS Technology. *IEEE Transactions on Terahertz Science and Technology*, 3(2):141–150, 2013.

[21] N. Kirman, M. Kirman, R. Dokania, J. F. Martinez, A. B. Apsel, M. A. Watkins, and D. H. Albonesi. Leveraging Optical Technology in Future Bus-based Chip Multiprocessors. In *Proceedings of the 39th Annual IEEE/ACM International Symposium on Microarchitecture*, pages 492–503, December 2006.

[22] T. Krishna, L. Peh, B. Beckmann, and S. K. Reinhardt. Towards the Ideal On-chip Fabric for 1-to-many and Many-to-1 Communication. In *Proceedings of the 44th Annual International Symposium on Microarchitecture*, pages 71–82, December 2011.

[23] G. Kurian, J. Miller, J. Psota, J. Eastep, J. Liu, J. Michel, L. Kimerling, and A. Agarwal. ATAC: A 1000-Core Cache-Coherent Processor with On-Chip Optical Network. In *Proceedings of the 19th international conference on Parallel Architectures and Compilation Techniques*, pages 477–488, September 2010.

[24] S. Laha, S. Kaya, D. W. Matolak, W. Rayess, D. DiTomaso, and A. Kodi. A New Frontier in Ultralow Power Wireless Links: Network-on-Chip and Chip-to-Chip Interconnects. *IEEE Transactions on Computer-Aided Design of Integrated Circuits and Systems*, 34(2):186–198, 2015.

[25] J. Laudon and D. Lenoski. The SGI Origin: A ccNUMA Highly Scalable Server. In *International Symposium on Computer Architecture (ISCA)*, June 1997.

[26] C.-K. Liang and Milos Prvulovic. MiSAR: Minimalistic Synchronization Accelerator with Resource Overflow Management. In *Proceedings of the 42nd Annual International Symposium on Computer Architecture*, pages 414–426, June 2015.

[27] B.-H. Lim and A. Agarwal. Reactive Synchronization Algorithms for Multiprocessors. In *Proceedings of the International Conference on Architectural Support for Programming Languages and Operating Systems*, November 1994.

[28] O. Markish, B. Sheinman, O. Katz., D. Corcos, and D. Elad. On-chip mmWave Antennas and Transceivers. In *Proceedings of the 9th IEEE/ACM International Symposium on Networks on Chip*, September 2015.

[29] D. Matolak, A. Kodi, S. Kaya, D. DiTomaso, S. Laha, and W. Rayess. Wireless Networks-on-Chips: Architecture, Wireless Channel, and Devices. *IEEE Wireless Communications*, 19(5), 2012.

[30] F. H. McMahon. The Livermore Fortran Kernels: A Computer Test Of The Numerical Performance Range. Technical report, Lawrence Livermore National Laboratory, 1986.

[31] J. M. Mellor-Crummey and M. L. Scott. Algorithms for Scalable Synchronization on Shared-memory Multiprocessors. *ACM Transactions on Computer Systems*, 9(1):21–65, 1991.

[32] R. M. Metcalfe and D. R. Boggs. Ethernet: Distributed Packet Switching for Local Computer Networks. *Communications of the ACM*, 19(7):395–404, 1976.

[33] J. Oh, A. Zajic, and M. Prvulovic. TLSync: Support for Multiple Fast Barriers Using On-chip Transmission Lines. In *Proceedings of the 38th Annual International Symposium on Computer Architecture*, pages 105–115, June 2011.

[34] J. Oh, A. Zajic, and M. Prvulovic. Traffic Steering Between a Low-latency Unswitched TL Ring and a High-throughput Switched On-chip Interconnect. In *Proceedings of the 22nd International conference on Parallel Architectures and Compilation Techniques*, pages 309–318, September 2013.

[35] J.-D. Park, S. Kang, S. Thyagarajan, E. Alon, and A. Niknejad. A 260 GHz Fully Integrated CMOS Transceiver for Wireless Chip-to-chip Communication. In *Proceedings of the IEEE Symposium on VLSI Circuits*, pages 48–49, June 2012.

[36] T. S. Rappaport, J. N. Murdock, and F. Gutierrez. State of the Art in 60-GHz Integrated Circuits and Systems for Wireless Communications. *Proceedings of the IEEE*, 99(8): 1390–1436, 2011.

[37] J. Sampson, R. González, J. F. Collard, N. P. Jouppi, M. Schlansker, and B. Calder. Exploiting Fine-grained Data Parallelism with Chip Multiprocessors and Fast Barriers. In *Proceedings of the 39th Annual IEEE/ACM International Symposium on Microarchitecture*, pages 235–246, December 2006.

[38] S. Scott. Synchronization and Communication in the T3E Multiprocessor. In *International Conference on Architectural Support for Programming Languages and Operating Systems (ASPLOS)*, October 1996.

[39] E. Seok, D. Shim, C. Mao, R. Han, S. Sankaran, C. Cao, W. Knap, and K. K. O. Progress and Challenges towards Terahertz CMOS Integrated Circuits. *IEEE Journal of Solid-State Circuits*, 45(8):1554–1564, 2010.

[40] S. Shang and K. Hwang. Distributed Hardwired Barrier Synchronization for Scalable Multiprocessor Clusters. *IEEE Transactions on Parallel and Distributed Systems*, 6(6):591–605, 1995.

[41] E. Socher and M.-C. F. Chang. Can RF Help CMOS Processors? *IEEE Communications Magazine*, 45(8):104–111, 2007.

[42] C. Sun, M. T. Wade, Y. Lee, J. S. Orcutt, L. Alloatti, M. S. Georgas, A. S. Waterman, J. M. Shainline, R. R. Avizienis, S. Lin, B. R. Moss, R. Kumar, F. Pavanello, A. H. Atabaki, H. M. Cook, A. J. Ou, J. C. Leu, Y.-H. Chen, K. Asanović, R. J. Ram, M. A. Popović, and V. M. Stojanović. Single-chip Microprocessor that Communicates Directly Using Light. *Nature*, 528(7583):534–538, 2015.

[43] G. Sun, S.-H. Weng, C.-K. Cheng, B. Lin, and L. Zeng. An On-chip Global Broadcast Network Design with Equalized Transmission Lines in the 1024-core Era. In *Proceedings of the International Workshop on System Level Interconnect Prediction*, pages 11–18, June 2012.

[44] R. Ubal, P. Mistry, D. Schaa, H. Ave, and D. Kaeli. Multi2Sim: A Simulation Framework for CPU-GPU Computing. In *Proceedings of the 21st International Conference on Parallel Architectures and Compilation Techniques*, pages 335–344, September 2012.

[45] M. Uzunkol and G. M. Rebeiz. A Low-Loss 50-70 GHz SPDT Switch in 90 nm CMOS. *IEEE Journal of Solid-State Circuits*, 45(10):2003–2007, 2010.

[46] D. Vantrease, R. Schreiber, M. Monchiero, M. McLaren, N. Jouppi, M. Fiorentino, A. Davis, N. Binkert, R. Beausoleil, and J. Ahn. Corona: System Implications of Emerging Nanophotonic Technology. In *Proceedings of the 35th International Symposium on Computer Architecture*, June 2008.

[47] D. Vantrease, M. H. Lipasti, and N. Binkert. Atomic Coherence: Leveraging Nanophotonics to Build Race-free Cache Coherence Protocols. In *Proceedings of the 17th International Symposium on High Performance Computer Architecture*, pages 132–143, February 2011.

[48] Z. Wang, P. Y. Chiang, P. Nazari, C. C. Wang, Z. Chen, and P. Heydari. A CMOS 210-GHz Fundamental Transceiver with OOK Modulation. *IEEE Journal of Solid-State Circuits*, 49 (3):564–580, 2014.

[49] N. Weissman and E. Socher. 9mW 6Gbps Bi-directional 85–90GHz Transceiver in 65nm CMOS. In *Proceedings of the 9th European Microwave Integrated Circuits Conference*, pages 25–28, October 2014.

[50] S. Woo, M. Ohara, E. Torrie, J. Singh, and A. Gupta. The SPLASH-2 Programs: Characterization and Methodological Considerations. *ACM SIGARCH Computer Architecture News*, 23(2):24–36, 1995.

[51] X. Yu, J. Baylon, P. Wettin, D. Heo, P. Pande, and S. Mirabbasi. Architecture and Design of Multi-Channel Millimeter-Wave Wireless Network-on-Chip. *IEEE Design & Test*, 31(6): 19–28, 2014.

[52] X. Yu, H. Rashtian, and S. Mirabbasi. An 18.7-Gb/s 60-GHz OOK Demodulator in 65-nm CMOS for Wireless Network-on-Chip. *IEEE Transactions on Circuits And Systems -I: Regular Papers*, 62(3):799–806, 2015.

[53] W. Zhu, V. C. Sreedhar, Z. Hu, and G. R. Gao. Synchronization State Buffer: Supporting Efficient Fine-grain Synchronization on Many-core Architectures. In *Proceedings of the 34th Annual International Symposium on Computer Architecture*, pages 35–45, June 2007.

ReBudget: Trading Off Efficiency vs. Fairness in Market-Based Multicore Resource Allocation via Runtime Budget Reassignment

Xiaodong Wang José F. Martínez

Computer Systems Laboratory
Cornell University
Ithaca, NY 14853 USA
http://m3.csl.cornell.edu

Abstract

Efficiently allocating shared resources in computer systems is critical to optimizing execution. Recently, a number of market-based solutions have been proposed to attack this problem. Some of them provide provable theoretical bounds to efficiency and/or fairness losses under market equilibrium. However, they are limited to markets with potentially important constraints, such as enforcing equal budget for all players, or curve-fitting players' utility into a specific function type. Moreover, they do not generally provide an intuitive "knob" to control efficiency vs. fairness.

In this paper, we introduce two new metrics, Market Utility Range (MUR) and Market Budget Range (MBR), through which we provide for the first time theoretical bounds on efficiency and fairness of market equilibria under *arbitrary* budget assignments. We leverage this result and propose *ReBudget*, an iterative budget re-assignment algorithm that can be used to control efficiency vs. fairness at run-time. We apply our algorithm to a multi-resource allocation problem in multicore chips. Our evaluation using detailed execution-driven simulations shows that our budget re-assignment technique is intuitive, effective, and efficient.

Keywords Multicore architectures; Market equilibria; Scalable resource allocation; Efficiency; Fairness.

1. Introduction

Devising scalable chip-multiprocessor (CMP) designs is an important goal for the upcoming manycore generation. A key challenge to scalability is the fact that these cores will share hardware resources, be it on-chip cache, pin bandwidth, the chip's power budget, etc. Prior work has shown that freely contending for shared resources can penalize system performance [4, 12, 15]. Thus, allocating resources efficiently among cores is key.

Unfortunately, single-resource, and more generally uncoordinated resource allocation, can be significantly suboptimal, due to its inability to model the interactions among resources [4]. A few solutions have been proposed to coordinate resource allocation across multiple resources, and their performance estimation methods range from trial runs [1, 15, 22], to artificial neural networks [4], and to analytical models [12–14]. Unfortunately, these all rely on centralized mechanisms (e.g., global hill-climbing) to optimize system throughput, essentially exploring the global search space sequentially, which may be prohibitively expensive, particularly in large-scale systems.

More recently, a number of market-based approaches have been introduced. Chase et al. propose a static market [11], where the players reveal to the resource supplier the amount of money each is willing to pay as a function of allocated service units, and the central market then allocates the available computing resources so that monetary profit is maximized. Still, because the maximization process is done by the supplier centrally, it is unclear whether it could deal with a large-scale system efficiently.

In the context of distributed computing clusters, Lai et al. propose a market-based solution to resource allocation that allows players to adjust their bids dynamically in response to the others bids to that resource [23]. Resource allocation is done in a largely distributed manner, which enables the system to scale better than centralized approaches. Recently, in our XChange work [37], we also propose one such dynamic market in the context of CMPs, and similarly show that XChange is scalable due to its largely distributed nature: Instead of making the resource allocation decision globally, each core in the CMP is actively optimizing its resource assignment largely independently of each other, and partic-

ASPLOS '16, April 2–6, 2016, Atlanta, Georgia, USA..

http://dx.doi.org/10.1145/2872362.2872382

ipants demands are reconciled through a relatively simple pricing strategy.

XChange also shows that it can achieve a good balance between system efficiency and fairness. The study is purely empirical, however, and thus it does not provide any guarantees on the loss of efficiency and fairness. It is well-known, for example, that market mechanisms in equilibrium can sometimes be highly inefficient—this is known as *Tragedy of Commons* [18]. Therefore, a number of research efforts have focused on quantifying the efficiency loss compared to the optimal resource allocation, known as the *Price of Anarchy (PoA)*. For example, Zhang studies a market where all players have the same amount of money (budget) to purchase resources, and he finds that the overall system efficiency in such a market can be low ($1/\sqrt{N}$ of the maximum feasible utility, where N is the number of market players), but fairness is high (0.828-approximate envy-free, a measure of fairness) [40]. This is consistent with our empirical observations in the XChange work [37].

Recently, Zahedi and Lee propose a resource allocation mechanism named *elasticities proportional* (EP) for CMPs [39], which does provide game-theoretic guarantees such as Pareto efficiency, envy-freeness, etc. However, such guarantees rely on the assumption that an application's utility can be accurately curve-fitted to a Cobb-Douglas function, where the coefficients are used as the "elasticities" of resources. Our XChange work shows that EP can in fact perform worse than expected when such curve-fitting is not well suited to the applications. In addition, although EP is proven to be Pareto-efficient, its efficiency loss compared to global optimality is not quantified.

To improve system efficiency while sacrificing some fairness, our XChange work discusses a *wealth redistribution* technique, which varies the players' budget based on an estimation of their potential for performance gain. However, XChange's wealth redistribution is an on/off technique, providing no "knob" to control the efficiency vs. fairness trade-off. It is also not backed up by a theoretical result that would provide bounds for this trade-off. To the best of our knowledge, there is no theoretic study that is able to quantify the loss of *both* efficiency and fairness under an arbitrary budget assignment.

Contributions

The contributions of this paper are as follows:

— We introduce a new *Market Utility Range (MUR)* metric, which helps us establish a theoretical bound for efficiency loss of a market equilibrium under a constrained budget. Specifically, we show that, if MUR ≥ 0.5, then PoA $\geq (1 - \frac{1}{4\text{MUR}}) \geq 0.5$ (i.e., the efficiency is guaranteed to be at least 50% of the optimal allocation); and that if MUR < 0.5, then PoA $\geq$ MUR.

— We introduce a new *Market Budget Range (MBR)* metric, which helps us evaluate the fairness of a market equilibrium under a constrained budget. We show that any market equilibrium is $(2\sqrt{1+\text{MBR}} - 2)$-approximate envy-free.

— We propose *ReBudget*, a budget re-assignment technique that is able to systematically control efficiency and fairness in an adjustable manner. We evaluate ReBudget on top of XChange, using a detailed simulation of a multicore architecture running a variety of applications. Our results show that ReBudget is efficient and effective. In particular, it can achieve 95% of the maximum feasible efficiency. Furthermore, when combined with the analysis using MUR and MBR metrics, it can provide worst-case fairness guarantees.

2. Market Framework

This paper adopts the general market-based resource allocation framework proposed in our XChange work [37]. In this section, we describe our efficiency and fairness models in the context of that framework.

Assume a market consisting of N players and M resources. Each player i has a utility function $U_i(\mathbf{r_i})$ when it is allocated $\mathbf{r_i} = (r_{i1}, r_{i2}, \ldots, r_{iM})$ resources. We assume that a player's utility functions is concave, nondecreasing, and continuous. Note that this may not always hold in the CMP context (e.g., the utility of the allocated cache space [2, 37]). We describe how we address this issue later in Section 4.

Every player i is allowed to bid b_{ij} for resource j, and the sum of its bids cannot exceed its budget B_i (i.e., the total amount of money it is allowed to spend): $\sum_j b_{ij} \leq B_i$. The market reconciles those bids by adopting a *proportional* allocation scheme, which is widely used [23, 40] and considered fair. The market first collects bids from all the players, and then determines the price of each resource j as follows:

$$p_j = \frac{\sum_{i=1}^{N} b_{ij}}{C_j} \tag{1}$$

where C_j represents the total amount of resource j. As a result, player i gets r_{ij} units of resource j proportionally to its bid: $r_{ij} = \frac{b_{ij}}{p_j}$.

The essence of this type of market-based approach is that it is a largely distributed mechanism: the players independently traverse their local search space to find the bids that maximize their own utilities, bringing the market toward a resource allocation that is Pareto-optimal [25]. In order to find such optimal bids, each player needs to solve an optimization problem, which can be modeled as follows: Given the price p_j of resource j announced by the market, player i is able to compute the sum of other players' bids to that resource: $y_{ij} = \sum_{i' \neq i} b_{i'j} = p_j \times C_j - b_{ij}$. By making the simplification that other players do not change their bids and therefore y_{ij} are constants, player i is able to make a prediction on the amount of resource r_{ij} it can get if it changes its bids from b_{ij} to b'_{ij}:

$$r_{ij} = \frac{b'_{ij}}{b'_{ij} + y_{ij}} C_j \tag{2}$$

Combining this equation with player i's utility function $U_i(\mathbf{r_i})$, the player can obtain its utility function vs. its bids: $U_i(\mathbf{b_i}) = U_i(\frac{b_{ij}}{b_{ij}+y_{ij}} C_j)$. Then the optimization problem a player needs to solve is:

$$\begin{aligned} \text{maximize} \quad & U_i(\mathbf{b}_i) \\ \text{subject to} \quad & \sum_j b_{ij} \leq B_i \end{aligned} \tag{3}$$

Using the Lagrangian multiplier method, we conclude that if such optimal bids exist, there exists a player-specific constant $\lambda_i > 0$ such that, for any resource j:

$$\frac{\partial U_i}{\partial b_{ij}} \begin{cases} = \lambda_i & \text{if} \quad b_{ij} > 0 \\ < \lambda_i & \text{if} \quad b_{ij} = 0 \end{cases} \tag{4}$$

Intuitively, we define λ_{ij} to be the rate of utility change (marginal utility) if player i changes its bid on resource j by one unit: $\lambda_{ij} = \frac{\partial U_i}{\partial b_{ij}}$. From Equation 4, if player i submits non-zero bids on different resources j, the λ_{ij} for all those resources are the same, and equal to λ_i in Equation 4. For resources with zero bids, their λ_{ij} is necessarily smaller than λ_i. Otherwise, it contradicts the condition that the bids maximize the player's utility.

Let's use an illustrative example. Assume player i bids on two resources, with $\lambda_{i1} = 1$ and $\lambda_{i2} = 2$. If the player moves one unit of bid from resource 1 to 2, its utility can be increased by 1 unit (-1 from resource 1 and +2 from resource 2). As a result, the current bids are not optimal, and the player can keep improving its utility by adjusting its bids until λ_{ij} are equal, or the bids on one of the resources drop to zero, beyond which no further profitable movement is possible.

2.1 Market Equilibrium

Market equilibrium is a state where all the players have no incentive to change their bids to improve utilities, and the resource prices remain stable. It is a desirable state because it is proven to be Pareto-optimal (i.e., no other resource allocation can make any one individual better off without making at least one individual worse off [25]). In order to find a market equilibrium, we adopt an iterative bidding–pricing process, similar to the one used in our recent XChange work [37]. Such a process can be divided into two steps: (1) the market broadcasts the current resource prices to all the players, and (2) the players adjust their bids to maximize their own utilities. These two steps are repeated iteratively until the market converges—i.e., for any player, its utility changes negligibly between two iterations. (In our implementation we detect this globally by monitoring prices instead, and assume convergence when they fluctuate within 1%.)

Zhang [40] has shown that a market equilibrium always exists in a *strongly competitive market*, where for any resource j, there always exists at least two players placing non-zero bids.

Lemma 1. *An equilibrium always exists for a strongly competitive market. The market equilibrium may not be unique.*

2.2 Efficiency

Given the existence of a market equilibrium, its system efficiency, also known as social welfare, is an important metric.

Definition 1. *The efficiency of a system is defined as the sum of players' utilities: Efficiency* $= \sum_i U_i(\mathbf{r}_i)$.

Nissan et al. [25] show that the efficiency of a market equilibrium can be low. Papadimitriou introduces the concept of *Price of Anarchy* (PoA) [26], which is the lower bound of the efficiency of a market equilibrium compared with that of the optimal allocation. Mathematically, let $\mathbf{r}_i^*$ denote a feasible resource allocation which maximizes the system efficiency, Ω be the set of resource allocation in market equilibrium (recall that a market equilibrium may not be unique), and $\mathbf{r}^n \in \Omega$ be a market equilibrium outcome. Let us also define optimal efficiency OPT $= \sum_i U_i(\mathbf{r}_i^*)$, and efficiency in market equilibrium Nash$(\mathbf{r^n}) = \sum_i U_i(\mathbf{r}_i^n)$, the Price of Anarchy is then defined as:

Definition 2. *PoA* $= \min_{\mathbf{r^n} \in \Omega} \frac{Nash(\mathbf{r^n})}{OPT}$

Note that PoA is a lower bound, which means that the efficiency of any market equilibrium $\mathbf{r^n}$ is guaranteed to be greater than PoA $\times$ OPT.

Zhang [40] studies PoA in a market with a proportionally balanced budget, where a player is given a budget in proportion to its maximum utility, i.e., the utility when it owns all resources. Zhang then shows:

Lemma 2. *The equilibrium in a market with a proportionally balanced budget has a Price of Anarchy PoA* $= \Theta(\frac{1}{\sqrt{N}})$.

Recall that N is the number of players; thus, Lemma 2 tells us that PoA will worsen with the number of players, and thus it can be prohibitively low in a large market.

2.3 Fairness

Envy-freeness (EF) is widely used to evaluate fairness of a resource allocation in real life [5, 35], and it's recently introduced by Zahedi and Lee in the context of resource allocation in CMPs [39]. It is a metric to evaluate how much a player desires others' resources compared to what it owns.

Definition 3. *Envy-freeness (EF) of an allocation* $\mathbf{r} = (\mathbf{r}_1, \ldots \mathbf{r}_N)$ *is EF*$(\mathbf{r}) = \min_{i,j} \frac{U_i(\mathbf{r}_i)}{U_i(\mathbf{r}_j)}$.

By definition, a resource allocation is envy-free when $EF \geq 1$—i.e., players prefer their own resources to those of others (at worst, they like them equally). Although a market equilibrium is provably envy-free under some form of utility constraints [39], in general it is not. And although it might seem that a market equilibrium would be generally fair as long as every player is endowed with the same budget, Zhang shows that this is not guaranteed [40]. As a result, Zhang defines c-approximate envy-free ($c \leq 1$) as follows:

Definition 4. *A market is c-approximate envy-free, if the envy-freeness of any market equilibrium is larger than c, i.e., for any player i,* $U_i(\mathbf{r}_i) \geq c \cdot \max_j U_i(\mathbf{r}_j)$.

It is straightforward that the equilibrium is more *"fair"* if c is closer to 1 (players envy others less). Zhang then proves [40]:

Lemma 3. *If each player in the market has the same budget, market equilibrium is at least 0.828-approximate envy-free. The bound is tight in the worst case.*

Note that the bounds of efficiency and fairness proven by Zhang [40] may not apply at the same time. Recall that Lemma 2 requires a proportionally balanced budget assignment (i.e., a player's budget is proportional to its maximum achievable utility), while Lemma 3 assumes every player has an equal budget. However, note that in the multicore resource allocation problem that we study, the utility function is in fact a value normalized to the maximum utility (discussed in Section 4.1.1). As a result, the maximum utility is 1 for all the players, and therefore these two markets are equivalent within the scope of this paper.

Thus, by combining Lemma 2 and Lemma 3 in our context, we find although a market with equal budget for all players has a good fairness guarantee, its efficiency can be low ($1/\sqrt{N}$ of optimal allocation in the worst case). In the following sections, we study how budget assignment across players affects the theoretical bound of efficiency and fairness, and how to utilize such theory to design a budget re-assignment scheme to trade off efficiency and fairness systematically.

3. Theoretical Results

In this section, we introduce two new metrics that will serve our goal: *Market Utility Range (MUR)* and *Market Budget Range (MBR)*. By measuring MUR and MBR in the market equilibrium, we can quantitatively understand the bound of loss in efficiency and fairness. In addition, MUR and MBR can be used as a guidance to adjust the budgets across players so that we can control the trade-off between efficiency and fairness more effectively.

3.1 Efficiency

According to Equation 4, in a market with a budget constraint, if player i bids optimally to maximize its utility, its marginal utility of bids $\frac{\partial U_i}{\partial b_{ij}}$ is a player-specific value λ_i, identical for all resources j with non-zero bids. Our intuition is that, the larger the λ_i *variation* across players, the higher "potential" there is to increase system efficiency by budget re-assignment, and therefore the lower PoA efficiency guarantee the current market has.

Consider the following examples: Assume a budget-constrained market with two players (A and B), such that $\lambda_A = 1$ and $\lambda_B = 3$ in equilibrium. It is intuitive that if the market moves 1 unit of budget from A to B, the market's overall efficiency in equilibrium (which is the sum of A's and B's utilities) is likely to increase (e.g., by 2 units, -1 from A and +3 from B). Consider, instead, that $\lambda_A = 1$ and $\lambda_B = 2$. In that case, the same budget re-assignment also points toward a market efficiency increase, but the improvement may be lower than in the first case. Finally, consider that λ_A and λ_B are equal. In that case, the intuitive expectation is that a budget re-assignment will not have an effect in overall market efficiency.

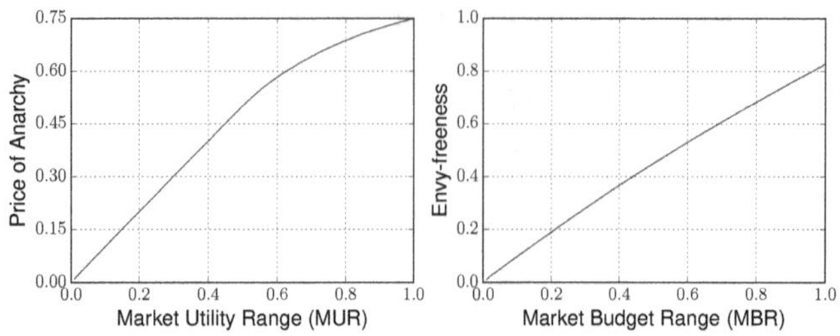

Figure 1: Relationship between Price of Anarchy and Market Utility Range (left), and Envy-freeness and Market Budget Range (right), based on Theorem 1 and Theorem 2, respectively.

Consequently, let's define *Market Utility Range (MUR)* as follows:

Definition 5. *Maximum Utility Range is the maximum variation of marginal utility* λ_i *across the market players,* $MUR = \frac{\min_i \lambda_i}{\max_i \lambda_i}$

By using such definition, we can prove that:

Theorem 1. *If MUR* ≥ 0.5*, the Price of Anarchy of the market equilibrium PoA* $\geq (1-\frac{1}{4MUR}) \geq 0.5$*, i.e., the overall market efficiency is guaranteed to be at least 50% of optimal allocation; If MUR* < 0.5*, PoA* $\geq$ *MUR.*

(The detailed proof can be found later in Section A.1.)

Not only does MUR provide a lower bound of overall market efficiency, it can also be used to guide budget re-assignment to help improve the overall market efficiency. As shown in the examples above, by moving a portion of budget from a player i with lower λ_i to another player i' with higher $\lambda_{i'}$, MUR moves toward 1.[1] As a result, the PoA guarantee increases, and the actual market efficiency hopefully increases accordingly.

3.2 Envy-freeness

A likely side effect of assigning different budgets to different players is that it may impact fairness negatively. It is straightforward that the player with the highest budget is able to purchase more resources than others, and therefore it is likely to be "envied" by others. Hence, we hypothesize that a valuable indicator of envy (or envy-freeness) of a market in equilibrium is the variation of the budget across players:

[1] It is provable that player i's marginal utility of bids λ_i decreases monotonically with a larger budget.

Definition 6. *Market Budget Range is the maximum variation in budget across players,* $MBR = \frac{\min_i B_i}{\max_i B_i}$.

Note that MBR is defined as the minimum budget divided by the maximum budget, so that larger budget variation means lower MBR value. Based on this definition, we can prove the following:

Theorem 2. *A market equilibrium with budget range MBR is* $(2\sqrt{1+MBR}-2)$*-approximate envy-free.*

(A short proof sketch can be found in Section A.2.)

The key insight here is that, by combining Theorem 1 and Theorem 2, we can attempt to adjust the trade-off between efficiency and fairness: As Figure 1 shows, the more aggressively we re-assign the budget to make MUR closer to 1, the higher system efficiency we may achieve. However, it creates a larger variation in players' budgets, which in turn may hurt fairness. Note that such budget re-assignments do not *guarantee* an actual improvement in either the efficiency or the envy-freeness. Nevertheless, our expectation is that, by tightening the efficiency/envy-freeness bounds according to our MUR and MBR theorems, the resulting allocation at equilibrium will tend to move in the desired direction. Therefore, we envision that an algorithm, by using MUR and MBR together, can try to fine-tune a market's trade-off between efficiency and fairness. We show one such algorithm ReBudget in Section 4.2.

4. ReBudget Framework

In this section, we first describe the basic framework for market-based resource allocation. We then describe ReBudget, a practical heuristic based on the theoretical results in Section 3 to assign budgets across players, so that an adjustable trade-off between system efficiency and fairness can be accomplished.

4.1 Market-based Approach

Our basic market-based resource allocation framework, described in Section 2, is a dynamic proportional market. In this framework, the goal is to find a market equilibrium using an iterative bidding–pricing procedure, after which resources are allocated proportionally to bids. This mechanism is detailed in Section 2.1.

Shared cache space and on-chip power are two of the most frequently targeted resources in the literature [6, 9, 24, 27, 34, 38], and our evaluation of ReBudget will focus on these two resources. Our mechanism, however, is a general framework: As long as the resource's utility function can be accurately modeled, and such utility function is non-decreasing, continuous, and concave (or can be made concave), the results of this paper can be applied. (Note that prior studies show that the utility of cache is often non-continuous—e.g., if partitioned by cache ways—and non-concave [2, 37], which is not consistent with our theoretical assumptions. We describe how to address such issue later in Section 4.1.1.)

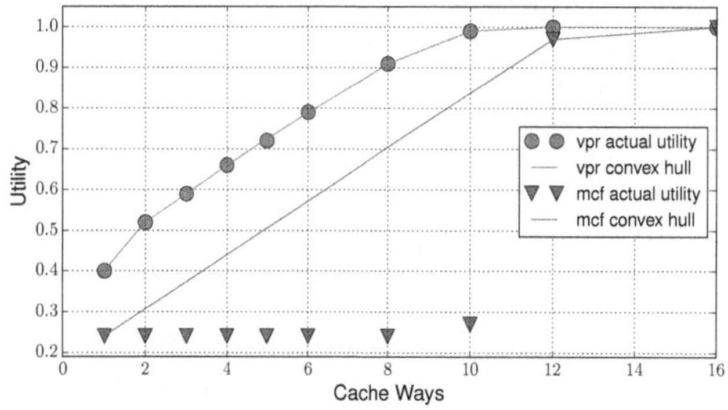

Figure 2: Normalized utility under different cache allocation, running at the highest possible frequency. The x-axis is the number of cache ways enabled. Section 5 describes the setup.

At any point in time, we guarantee that each core will be given a minimum amount resources: one cache region (128 kB), and the power to run at minimum frequency (800 MHz in our setup, Section 5) for free. The remaining cache capacity and power budget are allocated using market-based mechanism. This is to guarantee that each application is able to at least run regardless of its purchasing power.

We now address the two major challenges in designing the market: how to model the players' utility, and how the players bid to maximize their utility.

4.1.1 Utility Function

In the multicore resource allocation problem that we study, we define an application's utility to be its IPC, normalized to the IPC when it's running alone (and thus owns all the resources): $U_i(\mathbf{r_i}) = \text{IPC}(\mathbf{r}_i)/\text{IPC}_{\text{alone}}$. Thus, the possible values of U_i are between 0 and 1. To figure out the performance–resource relationship of the utility function, we adopt the monitoring technique of our recent XChange work [37]: We divide the total execution time of an application into compute and memory phases. The length of the memory phase under different cache allocations is estimated using UMON shadow tags [27] and a critical path predictor [24]. The length of the compute phase and the corresponding power consumption is estimated using the power model developed by Isci et al. [9]. The sum of both phases is an estimation of the execution time given a particular cache-power allocation. Note that this is all modeled dynamically online; no prior off-line profiling is needed whatsoever [37].

Recall that in Section 2, in order to apply the theoretical results, the utility function of a player is required to be concave, continuous, and non-decreasing in shape. However, in computer architecture, this is not always true. On the one hand, power is known to be concave [9, 24], and fine-grained enough to regard it as continuous. For example, Intel's RAPL technique allows setting the CPU power at a granularity of 0.125W [20]. On the other hand, it is well-known that cache capacity is a non-concave, and non-continuous resource [2, 27].

Figure 2 shows the cache utilities of two representative applications, *mcf* and *vpr*. The markers are the utilities (normalized IPC) of each application when it is given different cache ways (no change in power budget). From the figure, we can make two observations:

First, such a utility function is not continuous, as it is partitioned by cache ways which are relatively coarse-grained. To make it continuous, we adopt *Futility Scaling* by Wang and Chen [36], a feedback control mechanism that can precisely keep the partition size close to a target at the granularity of cache lines. We empirically set the allocation granularity to 128 kB, and we call this a *cache region*.

Second, cache utility may not be concave. Although *vpr* shows a concave utility function, *mcf* clearly is not: its normalized utility is flat at 0.2 for 1 to 10 cache ways, and suddenly increases to 1.0 once it secures 12 ways (1.5MB). This is because *mcf*'s working set size is 1.5 MB, and 12 cache ways or more will satisfy its need by reducing the L2 cache miss rate to be almost zero. To address this issue, we apply *Talus*, a technique to convexify cache behavior [2]. Talus works roughly as follows: First, based on an application's actual cache utility, its "convex hull" is derived, which is the convex set of the cache utility. The cache allocation points on the hull are called "point of interest" (*PoI*), which are the desired allocations. Next, to make cache utility continuous on the convex hull, Talus divides the cache partition of a core into two "shadow" partitions. Given an arbitrary cache partition target, Talus first finds its two neighboring *PoIs*, and then adjusts the size of the shadow partitions accordingly. The access stream is also divided correspondingly into the two shadow partitions. More details can be found in Talus [2]. As shown in Figure 2, Talus effectively convexifies the cache behavior to a convex hull, which satisfies the requirement of being concave and non-decreasing.

4.1.2 Bidding Strategy

Now that we have constructed a utility function for each player, according to the market's bidding–pricing procedure (Section 2), the next problem is how each player finds its optimal bids to maximize its utility. Because both cache and power utilities are concave, heuristics such as hill climbing are appropriate in finding optimal solutions [2]. Therefore, we adopt a simple hill-climbing technique as follows:

1. Each player i splits its budget B_i into equal bids b_{ij} across all resources. In addition, S, which is the amount by which a player will shift its budget across resources, is set to be half of the bid.
2. Each player i computes the marginal utility λ_{ij} of all resources j. According to the optimality condition in Equation 4, if a player's bids are such that they maximize the player's utility, then the marginal utilities of all resources which receive non-zero bids are necessarily identical—in other words, the player has no incentive to re-allocate its budget across resources. Otherwise, if λ_{ij} varies for different resources under the current bids, the player will move an amount S of money from a resource k with lower λ_{ik} to another one k' with higher $\lambda_{ik'}$, and such a move will tend to equalize the marginal utility of these two resources (recall that the player's utility function is concave, which means that marginal utility λ_{ij} decreases as bid b_{ij} increases).
3. S is halved, and the process is repeated, until one of the following two conditions is met: *(a)* Either λ_{ij} of the resources stays the same (within 5% difference); or *(b)* S is smaller than 1% of the total budget. Because S decreases exponentially with every step, and λ_{ij} is monotonic, such an algorithm will quickly reach an optimal bids to the resources.

4.2 Budget Re-assignment Algorithm

The mechanism discussed so far applies to individual players in the context of a general budget-constrained market-based mechanism. In this section, we describe ReBudget, a heuristic that works on top of the above mechanism. ReBudget assigns different budgets to players in an adjustable manner, so that a trade-off between system efficiency and fairness can be made.

As is discussed Section 3, MUR and MBR are good metrics to indicate multicore efficiency and fairness. Using MUR, we can identify the lower bound of system efficiency, as shown in Theorem 1. Moreover, due to the concavity of utility, player i's λ_i increases if its budget B_i is reduced. As a result, by reducing the budget of a player with low λ_i, system MUR, which is the maximum variation of marginal utility λ_i across the market players, will move closer to 1, potentially yielding a higher efficiency. On the other hand, however, by creating a larger budget variation across players, MBR will decrease (recall from Section 3.2 that larger budget variation will decrease MBR), therefore opening the door for the level of fairness (i.e., envy-freeness) to decrease as well.

In ReBudget, we attempt to maximize efficiency while guaranteeing a certain level of fairness. The system administrator can set a lowest acceptable envy-freeness level, and using Theorem 2, the minimum MBR can be computed. Then, the budgets of the players are re-assigned based on their λ_i value under market equilibrium: those with lower λ_i will get a reduction in budget. We define a player to be "low λ_i" if its λ_i is smaller than 50% of the maximum λ_i—recall that, in Theorem 1, we find that when MUR is smaller than 0.5, the PoA guarantee starts to decrease linearly. However, at any point in time, the budget variation across players has to be maintained higher than the set MBR value.

We design an iterative method with exponential back-off:

(1) MBR is computed based on the lowest acceptable fairness level set by the administrator. To start the bidding process for the market, each player is assigned an equal budget B. The amount of budget re-assignment, named *step*, is initialized to be $(1-\text{MBR})\cdot\frac{B}{2}$. (2) Players then use their budget to conduct the algorithm we described in Section 4.1.2 to reach a market equilibrium. (3) λ_i of each player is collected. If a player i's λ_i value is lower than 50% of the maximum λ_i in the market, its budget is reduced by one *step*. (4) *step* is halved, and the algorithm returns to (2) to find a market equilibrium again. When *step* is smaller than 1% of each player's initial budget, or when no player's budget is decreased, the resulting market equilibrium is the final outcome.

This algorithm has two advantages: (1) The highest possible budget of any player is B, and the lowest possible budget is $\text{MBR}\cdot B$ (if the player gets a budget decrease in all iterations). Therefore, the maximum variation of players' budget will stay within MBR, and the fairness level set by the designer is guaranteed. (2) The exponentially decreasing *step* ensures that the process is fast, so that the market is still efficient and scalable to deal with large-scale systems.

The above exponential back-off greedy algorithm is a show case of how MUR and MBR can be used to guide budget re-assignment to optimize the system. As we will show in Section 6, such an algorithm is in fact fast and efficient in practice.

4.3 Implementation

We now discuss the hardware and software implementation of ReBudget. On the hardware side, ReBudget requires:

1. Hardware monitors to model an application's utility–resource relationship. As is discussed in Section 4.1.1, we adopt the same monitoring hardware as we do in XChange. As a result, the overhead is 3.7 kB per core [37], and the total overhead of the monitors is less than 1% of the total cache.
2. Extra states per partition and per cache line for partitioning the cache. We adopt Futility Scaling to partition the L2 cache. and it incurs around 1.5% storage overhead of the total cache [36].

On the software side, in order to handle the changing resource demands due to context switches and application phase changes, our budget re-assignment algorithm described in Section 4.2 is triggered every 1 ms to re-allocate resources. Similar to XChange, such an algorithm can be piggybacked to the Linux kernel's APIC timer interrupt, with a low runtime overhead [37].

5. Experimental Methodology

5.1 Architectural Model

We evaluate ReBudget using SESC [28], a highly detailed execution-driven simulator, which we modified in-house to suit our experimental setup. We model 4-way out-of-order cores; Table 1 shows the most important parameters of the CMP. We also faithfully model Micron's DDR3-1600 DRAM timing [19].

Table 1: System configuration.

Chip-Multiprocessor System Configuration	
Number of Cores	8 / 64
Power Budget	80 W / 640 W[a]
Shared L2 Cache Capacity	4 MB / 32 MB
Shared L2 Cache Associativity	16 / 32 ways
Memory Controller	2 / 16 channels
Core Configuration	
Frequency	0.8 GHz - 4.0 GHz
Voltage	0.8 V - 1.2 V
Fetch/Issue/Commit Width	4 / 4 / 4
Int/FP/Ld/St/Br Units	2 / 2 / 2 / 2 / 2
Int/FP Multipliers	1 / 1
Int/FP Issue Queue Size	32 / 32 entries
ROB (Reorder Buffer) Entries	128
Int/FP Registers	160 / 160
Ld/St Queue Entries	32 / 32
Max. Unresolved Branches	24
Branch Misprediction Penalty	9 cycles min.
Branch Predictor	Alpha 21264 (tournament)
RAS Entries	32
BTB Size	512 entries, direct-mapped
iL1/dL1 Size	32 kB
iL1/dL1 Block Size	32 B / 32 B
iL1/dL1 Round-Trip Latency	2 / 3 cycles (uncontended)
iL1/dL1 Ports	1 / 2
iL1/dL1 MSHR Entries	16 / 16
iL1/dL1 Associativity	direct-mapped / 4-way
Memory Disambiguation	Perfect

[a] We anticipate multicore chips with different number of cores will not be fabricated under the same technology, and thus expect the power consumption per core to decrease with the technology. For simplicity, in our evaluation, we use a chip TDP of 10 W per core and a 65-nm power model.

We use Wattch [7] and Cacti [30] to model the dynamic power consumption of the processors and memory system. We adopt Intel's power management approach for Sandy Bridge [29] to approximate the static power consumption as a fraction of the dynamic power that is exponentially dependent on the system temperature [10]. The run-time temperature of the chip multiprocessor is estimated using Hotspot [31] integrated with SESC.

Our multicore chip is able to regulate two shared on-chip resources: power budget and shared last-level cache. The power budget is regulated via per-core DVFS, similar to Intel's RAPL technique [20]. Each core can run at a frequency between 800 MHz and 4 GHz, as long as the total power consumption remains within $p\times 10$ W, where p is the number of processor cores. The last-level (L2) cache is partitioned using Futility Scaling by Wang and Chen [36], at the granularity of 128 kB (one cache region). The total L2 cache capacity is $p\times 512$ kB. Due to the overhead of UMON shadow tags [27], we limit its stack distance to be 16, i.e., the shadow tags can estimate the miss rate for the cache with capacities from 128 kB to 2 MB. We empirically observe that very few of our applications benefit from cache regions larger than 2 MB, and even if they do, such a large cache region is usually not affordable given the limited budget of each player. With a dynamic sampling rate of 32, the shadow tags take up 3.6 kB per core, which is less than 1% of the L2 cache size.

We guarantee that each core will have at least one cache region, and sufficient power budget to allow it to run at the minimum frequency (800 MHz). The remaining resources will be entirely distributed (i.e., no leftovers) based on a market-based resource allocation decision.

Workload Construction

We use a mix of 24 applications from SPEC2000 [32] and SPEC2006 [33] to evaluate our proposal. Each application is cross-compiled to MIPS ISA with -O2 optimization using gcc 4.6.1. For all simulations, we use Simpoints [8] to pick the most representative 200-million dynamic instruction block of each application.

Our evaluation is based on multiprogrammed workloads because we anticipate to allocate resources at the granularity of cores. For multithreading workloads, we can still allocate the resources at thread granularity if each thread is running on a different core.[2] Another choice is to allocate resources at the granularity of applications. All the threads of one application may share the same resources, which is a reasonable assumption, because the demand of the threads tend to be similar across threads of a parallel application in many programming models.

To construct our multiprogrammed workloads, we classify the 24 applications into four classes based on profiling: *Cache-sensitive* (C), *Power-sensitive* (P), *Both-sensitive* (B), and *None* (N). Then, we create six categories of multiprogrammed workloads: *CPBN*, *CCPP*, *CPBB*, *BBNN*, *BBPN*, and *BBCN*. For each category, we randomly generate 40 workloads for 8- and 64-core configurations. The random generation works as follows: for an 8-core (64-core) configuration, 2 (16) applications are randomly selected from each application class (e.g., *CPBN* means 2 (16) applications in each of *C*, *P*, *B*, and *N*, whereas *CCPP* will have 4 (32) applications in *C* and 4 (32) in *P*).

Performance Metrics

A key issue in resource allocation is the figure of merit. As is discussed in Section 4.1, we define an application's utility to be its IPC normalized by the IPC when it's running alone: $U_i(\mathbf{r_i}) = \text{IPC}(\mathbf{r}_i)/\text{IPC}_{\text{alone}}$. The system efficiency can therefore be computed as:

$$\text{Efficiency} = \sum_{i=1}^{N} U_i = \sum_{i=1}^{N} \frac{\text{IPC}_i(\text{r}_i)}{\text{IPC}_i^{\text{alone}}} \quad (5)$$

We realize that this is exactly *weighted speedup*, a common metric to measure system throughput, and has been widely accepted by the community. Therefore, our *Price of Anarchy* study becomes meaningful in computer architecture: it guarantees the lower bound of throughput in market equilibrium.

A system could achieve high throughput (i.e., weighted speedup) by starving one or two applications while benefiting all the others; however, system fairness would suffer as a result, providing a bad experience to some users. Therefore, we evaluate fairness using *envy-freeness* shown in Definition 3, which is a widely used metric in economy, and has recently been introduced by Zahedi and Lee to evaluate fairness in multicore chips [39].

6. Evaluation

We evaluate our proposal in two phases. In the first phase, we analytically study the effectiveness of ReBudget by assuming that the applications' utility functions can be perfectly modeled and convexified. For this phase only, we extensively profile each application using our simulation infrastructure. (Recall that ReBudget does not require off-line profiling; our second phase models utility functions at run-time using hardware monitors, as described in Section 4.1.1.)

We sample 90 cache+power configuration points, with $\{$1-6, 8, 10, 12, 16$\}$ cache regions (10 possible allocations) and $\{$0.8,1.2,1.6,…, 4.0$\}$ GHz (9 possible allocations). For each point, we collect average IPC and power consumption.[3] Then, we derive the convex hull of cache and power, and assume that their utilities are perfectly concave and continuous. Finally, we analytically evaluate the system efficiency and fairness by applying ReBudget and other competing mechanisms to all 240 bundles.

In the second phase, we evaluate ReBudget in a simulated CMP environment (SESC). The application's utility is monitored at run-time, using the technique described in Section 4.1.1. We apply *Talus* [2] and *Futility Scaling* [36] to make cache behavior concave and continuous. Because of practical simulation time constraints, we randomly select one application bundle per category, and run it using detailed simulations. We use these results to validate our first phase evaluation.

We conduct all the experiments on 8- and 64-core CMP configurations, and find that the results are similar. Therefore, we omit the results for the 8-core configuration, and focus on the large-scale 64-core configuration.

[2] Skewing resources within threads in a multi-threaded application (e.g., to alleviate synchronization imbalance) is beyond our scope, can be incorporated orthogonally to our approach, and has been studied elsewhere [3, 16].

[3] Without loss of generality, our evaluation assumes that allocating more than 16 cache regions (2 MB) does not yield any significant additional utility to any application. This is reasonable for the input sets of the applications studied, and it allows us to complete profiling in a reasonable time.

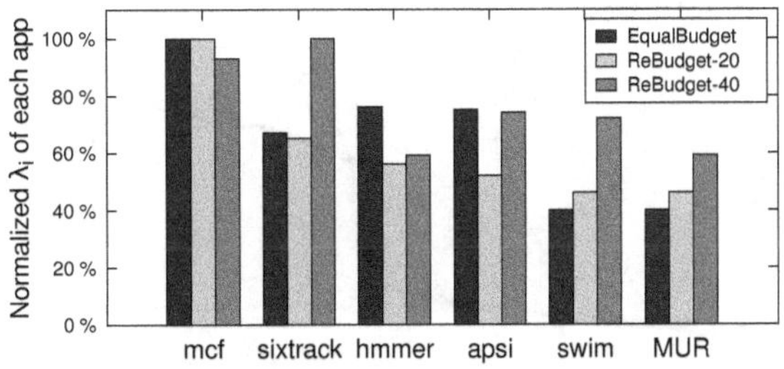

Figure 3: Marginal utility λ_i of each application in a sample *BBPC* bundle. The multiple copies of the same application in the bundle behave essentially the same way, so only one of each is shown. λ_i is normalized to the maximum λ_i in the bundle. MUR metric is also shown.

The allocation mechanisms evaluated are as follows: *EqualShare*, where resources are equally partitioned among all processor cores. Two XChange mechanisms [37]:[4] *EqualBudget*, where resources are partitioned using a market-based procedure assuming equal budgets for all players; and *Balanced*, where each player receives a budget proportional to the utility difference between its maximum (2 MB L2 cache and 4.0 GHz frequency) and minimum (128 kB and 800 MHz) possible allocations, normalized to the former. *ReBudget-step*, where resources are allocated using our ReBudget mechanism such that, at the end of the first iteration (where all players run with equal budget), each player is assigned either its original budget or *step* less. (Recall that *step* is halved in each subsequent iteration.) The initial budget is set to be 100 for all players. Finally, *MaxEfficiency*, which is the resource allocation maximizing system efficiency, is obtained by running an infeasible very fine-grained hill-climbing search (recall that all utilities are concave).

6.1 Efficiency

For the first phase evaluation, Figure 4 reports the efficiency and envy-freeness for EqualShare, MaxEfficiency, as well as XChange's EqualBudget and Balanced, and ReBudget with different aggressiveness (i.e., *step*) based on run-time feedback. The bundles are ordered by the efficiency of EqualShare. We observe that the efficiency of EqualShare compared to MaxEfficiency suddenly increases for the last 40 bundles. Most of these bundles fall into the category of BBPN. EqualShare works well for BBPN workloads because 75% of the apps in the bundle are power sensitive, and equally distributing the power in EqualShare works reasonable well. In addition, although the efficiency can be improved by giving more cache to "B" apps, they are not as cache-sensitive as "C" apps. Therefore, EqualShare in cache performs better for BBPN bundles than others such as CPBN.

[4] Note we convexify applications' utility, which is an improvement over the original XChange.

6.1.1 EqualBudget vs. EqualShare

We first compare the efficiency between EqualBudget market-based mechanism with EqualShare allocation. Figure 4a shows that in a 64-core configuration, 37% of the workloads in EqualBudget are able to achieve 95% of the social welfare of the MaxEfficiency, and over 90% bundles are within 90%. This proves that the market-based mechanism is robust, efficient, and scalable in this setup.

However, there are still 10% of the applications below 90% of the welfare in optimal allocation. We observe that over half of these workloads fall in the category of *BBPC*, where the number of applications favoring both resources (50%) is much higher than the number of applications favoring power (25%) or cache (25%) only. This is reminiscent of the well-known *Tragedy of Commons* [18]. MaxEfficiency strongly favors the apps which prefer only one resource, and the "B" apps, which need both resources, are sacrificed for the sake of higher system efficiency. The EqualBudget mechanism allows all the applications to fairly contend with each other, even though the price is an efficiency that is not as good as MaxEfficiency's.

We look closely at an 8-core experiment using a BBPC bundle that contains four "B" apps (*apsi* and *swim*, 2 copies each), two "C" apps (2 copies of *mcf*), and two "P" apps (*hmmer* and *sixtrack*). The overall efficiency of such bundle with EqualBudget is 90% of MaxEfficiency, and we find its MUR $= 0.40$. Figure 3 shows λ_i value of each app at market equilibrium. We can find that with EqualBudget, "B" app *swim* has the lowest λ_i value, indicating that it is over-budgeted and not use its money efficiently; on the other hand, "C" app *mcf* has the highest λ_i value, showing that a budget increase can lead to a high utility gain.

6.1.2 XChange-Balanced

XChange's Balanced budget assignment is an intuitive way to distribute budget among players to improve efficiency [37]. However, Figure 4a shows that it does not outperform EqualBudget in efficiency too much, but in fact it loses in fairness, as shown in Figure 4b. The reasons are: (1) With the exception of "N"-type apps, which are not sensitive to any resources, the performance difference between minimum and maximum utility of most apps are similar, especially when we give out minimum resources for each player for free. Therefore, the budget assignment is not very different from EqualShare. (2) Blindly setting the player's budget B_i proportionally to his "potential," while ignoring the shape of utility and MUR metric, is ineffective.

6.1.3 ReBudget

We evaluate the our ReBudget mechanism proposed in Section 4.2. We test different aggressiveness, by setting the amount of budget decrease at each iteration (i.e., *step*) to be 20 and 40. Figure 4a clearly shows that by re-assigning the budget more aggressively, efficiency will improve for all

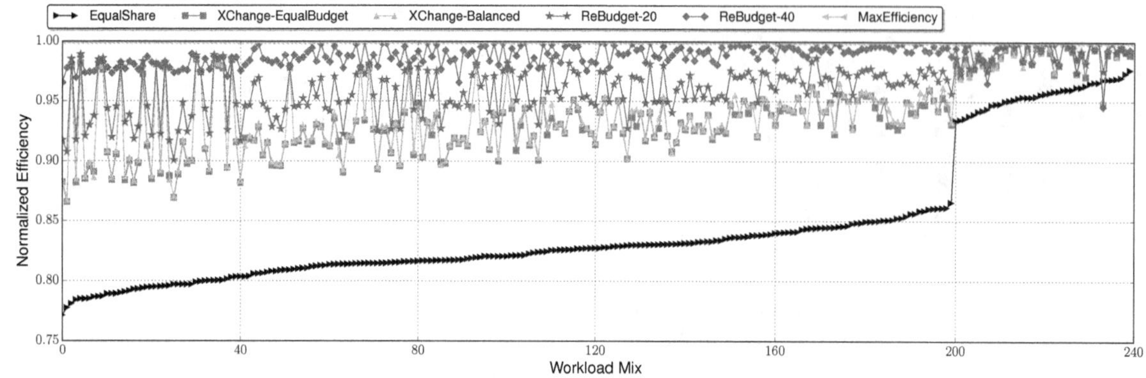

(a) 64-core Efficiency. Higher is better.

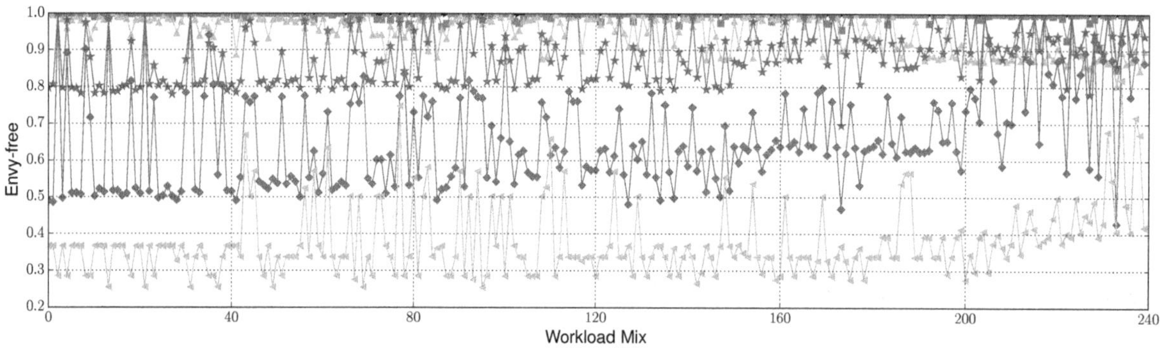

(b) 64-core Envy-freeness. Higher is better.

Figure 4: Comparison of system efficiency (weighted speedup) and envy-freeness among the proposed mechanisms in a 64-core configuration. System efficiency results are normalized to MaxEfficiency. Workloads are ordered by the efficiency of EqualShare.

bundles. Also, for all the 240 bundles, ReBudget-40 achieves 95% of system efficiency of MaxEfficiency.

We look closely at the same 8-core bundle we study in Section 6.1.1. For ReBudget-20, Figure 3 shows that *swim*, whose λ_i at 0.40 is the lowest under EqualBudget, has its value increased to 0.46, because its budget drops from 100 (every player's initial budget) to 61.25 units (minimum budget under ReBudget-20). On the other hand, *mcf*, which has the highest λ_i, has its budget unchanged (100). The budget of other apps are lowered to around 80, because their λ_i values are significantly lower than *mcf*. Note that λ_i of *apsi* and *hmmer* decrease, even though their budgets are reduced. This is because the budget cut of *swim* makes the prices of resources drop significantly. As a result, although *apsi* and *hmmer*'s budgets are reduced, they can actually afford more resources, and their λ_i decreases. Overall, the MUR of ReBudget-20 increases to 46%, compared to 40% in EqualBudget. Correspondingly, the efficiency of ReBudget-20 increases to 96% of MaxEfficiency.

In ReBudget-40, *swim*, whose λ_i is still the lowest in ReBudget-20, get a further budget cut to 20. As a result, its λ_i value increases from 0.46 to 0.72, as shown in Figure 3. *mcf* in this case is no longer the highest in λ_i value: *sixtrack*'s budget is decreased to 30 and it starts to request for more money. Therefore, MUR of the system is increased to 0.59, and the efficiency is now 99% of MaxEfficiency.

6.2 Fairness

We use envy-freeness as the metric to evaluate the fairness, as is discussed in Section 2.3. We first look at the fairness comparison between EqualBudget and MaxEfficiency. As expected, Figure 4b shows that EqualBudget is almost envy-free, where in the worst case, it is still 0.93-approximate envy-free. On the contrary, MaxEfficiency is unfair, which is typically 0.35-approximate envy-free.

Regarding the XChange-Balanced mechanism, the envy-freeness of most workloads stays at 0.9, where in the worst-case it is 0.86-approximate envy-free. It is not as good as EqualBudget, and considering its trivial efficiency gain, and no control over the aggressiveness in making trade-off between efficiency and fairness, we consider such a mechanism to be ineffective.

On the other hand, the envy-freeness of ReBudget has a direct relationship with its aggressiveness. Figure 4b shows that the typical envy-freeness of ReBudget-20 and ReBudget-40 are 0.8 and 0.5, respectively, and none of the

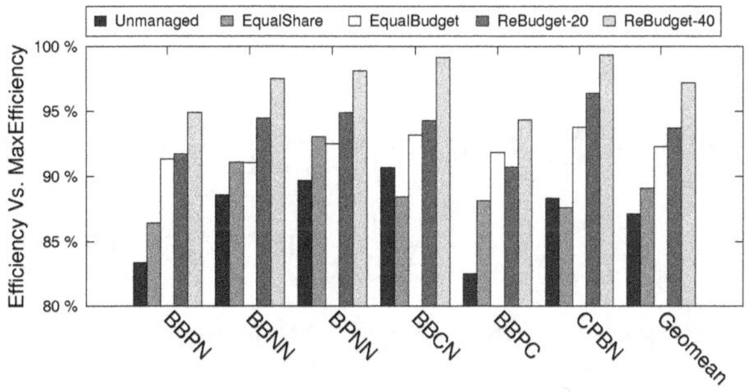

(a) 64-core Efficiency in SESC. Higher is better.

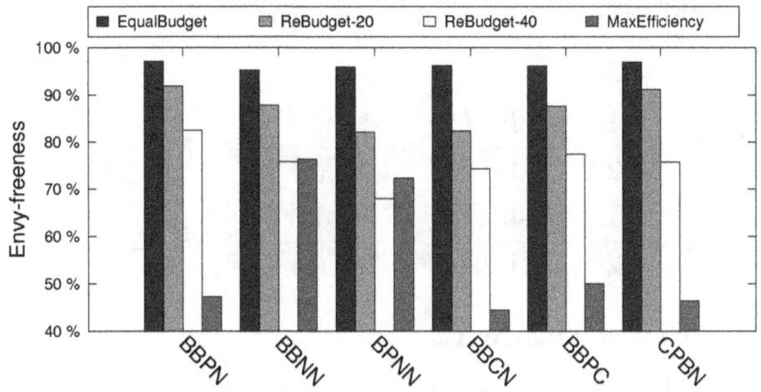

(b) 64-core Envy-freeness in SESC. Higher is better.

Figure 5: Comparison of system efficiency (weighted speedup) and envy-freeness among the proposed mechanisms in a simulated 64-core configuration. System efficiency results are normalized to MaxEfficiency.

bundles violates the theoretic guarantee provided by Theorem 2 (0.53 and 0.19). We notice that there is a gap between the theory and reality. This is because what Theorem 2 states is a theoretic lower bound, which should stand in all cases. Such bound is tight, and it is not hard to construct a market to reach it[5]. Although it does not happen on the applications we use, it could happen in the real life. In addition, we show the envy-freeness of ReBudget-20 is consistently higher than ReBudget-40 for all bundles. Therefore, besides the theoretic guarantee, MBR can be used as an accurate indicator of system fairness.

Combined with the findings in Section 6.1, we can conclude that the more aggressive budgets are adjusted, the higher efficiency, and correspondingly the lower fairness it is achieved. This is appealing, because system designers and administrators can use the *step* as a "knob" to trade off one for the other.

6.3 Simulation Results

Besides the above analytical results, we implement ReBudget in architectural simulator SESC. Figure 5 shows the system efficiency and envy-freeness of the competing mechanisms. Such results are consistent to our analytical evaluation above: ReBudget improves system efficiency over EqualBudget by sacrificing fairness, and the more aggressive budget is re-assigned, the more efficiency improvement it is achieved. On the other hand, EqualBudget achieves the highest in envy-freeness, and MaxEfficiency, which targets at maximizing system efficiency, is the worst in fairness. ReBudget successfully maintains its rank between these two extremes, and aggressiveness gradually hurts system performance as expected.

6.4 Convergence

A very important aspect of the market-based mechanism is how fast our algorithm is in finding the equilibrium allocation. To the best of our knowledge, there is no theoretic lower bound on the convergence time. However, in reality, we find that EqualBudget and XChange-Balanced converge within 3 iterations for 95% of the bundles. ReBudget mechanism spends a few more iterations, because it needs to re-converge after budget adjustment. However, the exponential back-off in budget change guarantees that the ReBudget process converges fast. These findings are in line with prior studies (e.g., Feldman et al. find the convergence time for a dynamic market is ≤ 5 iterations [17]). We also adopt a fail-safe mechanism for the very rare cases that market cannot converge: we simply terminate the equilibrium finding algorithm after 30 iterations.

7. Conclusion

In this paper, we have introduce two new metrics, *Market Utility Range (MUR)* and *Market Budget Range (MBR)*, which help us establish a theoretical bound for the loss of efficiency and fairness of a market equilibrium under a constrained budget, respectively. We have proposed *ReBudget*, a budget re-assignment technique that is able to systematically control efficiency and fairness in an adjustable manner. We evaluate ReBudget on top of our earlier XChange proposal for market-based resource management in CMPs, using a detailed simulation of a multicore architecture running a variety of applications. Our results show that ReBudget is efficient and effective. In particular, when combined with the proposed MUR and MBR metrics, ReBudget is effective at maximizing efficiency under worst-case fairness constraints.

A. Proofs

A.1 Proof of Theorem 1

Johari and Tsitsiklis [21] study the PoA for a market where the players are not constrained by a budget, and the players are maximizing their actual payoff: i.e., its utility minus its resource costs:

$$\text{maximize } U_i(\mathbf{b}_i) - \sum_j b_{ij} \tag{6}$$

We introduce *market utility range* metric $\text{MUR} = \frac{\min_i\{\lambda_i\}}{\max_i\{\lambda_i\}}$ into their proof, so that such proof can be generalized to

[5] Zhang shows an example in EqualBudget case [40].

a market with budget constraint. In a market equilibrium allocation $\mathbf{r}^n$ where player i bids $\mathbf{b}_i^n$, there exists $\lambda_i > 0$ for this player, such that for any resources j:

$$\begin{aligned}\frac{\partial U_i(\mathbf{r}_i^n)}{\partial b_{ij}} &= \frac{\partial U_i(\mathbf{r}_i^n)}{\partial r_{ij}}\frac{\partial r_{ij}}{\partial b_{ij}} \\ &= \frac{\partial U_i(\mathbf{r}_i^n)}{\partial r_{ij}}\frac{1}{p_j^n}(1-\frac{r_{ij}^n}{C_j})\begin{cases} = \lambda_i & \text{if} \quad b_{ij} > 0 \\ < \lambda_i & \text{if} \quad b_{ij} = 0\end{cases}\end{aligned} \tag{7}$$

Let $V_i(\mathbf{r}_i) = \sum_j \frac{\partial U_i(\mathbf{r}_i^n)}{\partial r_{ij}}(r_{ij} - r_{ij}^n) + U_i(\mathbf{r}_i^n)$. We find $\mathbf{r}^n$ for U_i is also the equilibrium allocation for V_i:

$$\frac{\partial V_i(\mathbf{r}_i^n)}{\partial b_{ij}} = \frac{\partial V_i(\mathbf{r}_i^n)}{\partial r_{ij}}\frac{\partial r_{ij}}{\partial b_{ij}} = \frac{\partial U_i(\mathbf{r}_i^n)}{\partial r_{ij}}\frac{\partial r_{ij}}{\partial b_{ij}}.$$

Define Nash(U) to be the system efficiency in market equilibrium, where players have utility function U_i. Because the market equilibrium allocation for U_i is also the equilibrium allocation for V_i, Nash(U) = Nash(V). Also define OPT(U) to be the maximum feasible efficiency of the market. Due to the concavity of the utility function U_i, we have $V_i \geq U_i$ for any resource allocation $\mathbf{r}_i$. Therefore, OPT$(V) \geq$ OPT(U), and:

$$\text{Nash}(U)/\text{OPT}(U) \geq \text{Nash}(V)/\text{OPT}(V)$$

Define $\alpha_{ij} = \frac{\partial U_i(\mathbf{r}_i^n)}{\partial r_{ij}}$, $\beta_i = U_i(\mathbf{r}_i^n) - \sum_j \alpha_{ij} r_{ij}^n$, and $V_i(\mathbf{r}_i) = \sum_j \alpha_{ij} r_{ij} + \beta_i$. Let $W_i(\mathbf{r}_i) = \sum_j \alpha_{ij} r_{ij}$, $B = \sum_i \beta_i$. Then we have:

$$\frac{\text{Nash}(U)}{\text{OPT}(U)} \geq \frac{\text{Nash}(V)}{\text{OPT}(V)} \geq \frac{\text{Nash}(V) - B}{\text{OPT}(V) - B} = \frac{\text{Nash}(W)}{\text{OPT}(W)} \tag{8}$$

Next, we show the *Price of Anarchy* assuming players have utility W_i. The social welfare $W = \sum_i W_i(\mathbf{r}_i) = \sum_i \sum_j \alpha_{ij} r_{ij} = \sum_j \sum_i \alpha_{ij} r_{ij}$. It is easy to find that the optimal social welfare is achieved if for resource j, all C_j is given to the player i that has maximum α_{ij}:

$$\text{OPT}(W) = \sum_j C_j \max_i\{\alpha_{ij}\}$$

For market equilibrium allocation r^n, we have Nash$(W) = \sum_j \sum_i \alpha_{ij} r_{ij}^n$. Define Nash$_j = \sum_i \alpha_{ij} r_{ij}^n$. From Equation 7, each player has $\alpha_{ij}\frac{1}{p_j^n}(1 - \frac{r_{ij}^n}{C_j}) = \lambda_i$ for any resource j if he submits a non-zero bid to it. Therefore, $\alpha_{ij} \geq p_j^n \lambda_i$. Without loss of generality, we define $\alpha_{1j} = \max_i\{\alpha_{ij}\}$. Then we have:

$$\begin{aligned}\text{Nash}_j &= \alpha_{1j} r_{1j}^n + \sum_{i\neq 1} \alpha_{ij} r_{ij}^n \geq \alpha_{1j} r_{1j}^n + \sum_{i \neq 1} p_j^n \lambda_i r_{ij}^n \\ &\geq \alpha_{1j} r_{1j}^n + p_j^n \min_i\{\lambda_i\}(C_j - r_{1j}^n) \\ &\geq \alpha_{1j} r_{1j}^n + \alpha_{1j}\frac{\min_i\{\lambda_i\}}{\lambda_1}(C_j - r_{1j}^n)(1 - \frac{r_{1j}^n}{C_j}) \\ &\geq \alpha_{1j} r_{1j}^n + \alpha_{1j}\frac{\min_i\{\lambda_i\}}{\max_i\{\lambda_i\}}(C_j - r_{1j}^n)(1 - \frac{r_{1j}^n}{C_j}) \\ &= \alpha_{1j}[\frac{\text{MUR}}{C_j}(r_{1j}^n - (1 - \frac{1}{2\text{MUR}}))^2 + C_j(1 - \frac{1}{4\text{MUR}})]\end{aligned}$$

Therefore, if MUR $\geq \frac{1}{2}$, Nash$_j \geq \alpha_{1j} C_j (1 - \frac{1}{4\text{MUR}})$, and:

$$\begin{aligned}\text{Nash}(W) = \sum_j \text{Nash}_j &\geq (1 - \frac{1}{4\text{MUR}})\sum_j \max_i\{\alpha_{ij}\}C_j \\ &= (1 - \frac{1}{4\text{MUR}})\text{OPT}(W) \geq \frac{1}{2}\text{OPT}(W)\end{aligned}$$

If MUR $< \frac{1}{2}$, Nash$_j > \alpha_{1j} C_j \cdot$ MUR, then:

$$\text{Nash}(W) > \text{MUR} \cdot \text{OPT}(W)$$

Combined with Equation 8, we have:

$$\begin{aligned}\text{MUR} \geq \frac{1}{2}: \frac{\text{Nash}(U)}{\text{OPT}(U)} \geq \frac{\text{Nash}(W)}{\text{OPT}(W)} \geq (1 - \frac{1}{4\text{MUR}}) \\ \text{MUR} < \frac{1}{2}: \frac{\text{Nash}(U)}{\text{OPT}(U)} \geq \frac{\text{Nash}(W)}{\text{OPT}(W)} \geq \text{MUR}\end{aligned}$$

A.2 Proof of Theorem 2

We introduce *market budget range* metric MBR $= \frac{B_i}{\max_j\{B_j\}}$ into Zhang's proof of envy-freeness with equal budget [40], so that our results apply to a market with an arbitrary budget assignment for players. The idea for proving a market is c-approximate envy-free is to prove that at market equilibrium, for any feasible bid vector $\mathbf{z}$ with $0 \leq z_j \leq y_{ij}^n$, and it is always the case that $\sum_j z_j = \max_i\{B_i\}$, $U_i(\mathbf{r}_i^n) \geq c \cdot U_i(\frac{z_j}{b_{ij}^n + y_{ij}^n})$.

To prove this, we define the player i's budget range: MBR$_i = \frac{B_i}{\max_j\{B_j\}}$. Similar to Zhang [40], we construct a matrix $\{\hat{b}_{jk}\}$ for $0 \leq j, k \leq M$, where M is the number of resources. Such matrix satisfies the following conditions:

$$\hat{b}_{jj} = \min_j\{b_{ij}, z_j \cdot \text{MBR}_i\},$$

$$\sum_k \hat{b}_{jk} = b_{ij},$$

$$\sum_j \hat{b}_{jk} = z_k \cdot \text{MBR}_i$$

The rest of the proof follows Zhang [40], combined with the fact that MBR$_i = \frac{B_i}{\max_j\{B_j\}} \geq \frac{\min_j B_j}{\max_k B_k} =$ MBR.

Finally, we get that for any player i,

$$\begin{aligned}U_i(\mathbf{x}_i^n) &\geq (2\sqrt{1 + \text{MBR}_i} - 2) \cdot U_i(\mathbf{z}) \\ &\geq (2\sqrt{1 + \text{MBR}} - 2) \cdot U_i(\mathbf{z})\end{aligned}$$

Acknowledgments

We are grateful to Éva Tardos for her feedback during various stages of this project. We thank also the anonymous reviewers for their thoughtful feedback, which helped improve the paper. This work was supported in part by AFOSR Award FA9550-15-1-0311, and a gift from Qualcomm.

References

[1] M. Becchi and P. Crowley. Dynamic thread assignment on heterogeneous multiprocessor architectures. In *Intl. Conf. on Computing Frontiers (FC)*, 2006.

[2] N. Beckmann and D. Sanchez. Talus: A simple way to remove cliffs in cache performance. In *Intl. Symp. on High Performance Computer Architecture (HPCA)*, 2015.

[3] A. Bhattacharjee and M. Martonosi. Thread criticality predictors for dynamic performance, power, and resource management in chip multiprocessors. In *Intl. Symp. on Computer Architecture (ISCA)*, 2009.

[4] R. Bitirgen, E. Ipek, and J. F. Martínez. Coordinated management of multiple interacting resources in chip multiprocessors: A machine learning approach. In *Intl. Symp. on Microarchitecture (MICRO)*, 2008.

[5] S. J. Brams and A. D. Taylor. *Fair Division: From cake-cutting to dispute resolution.* Cambridge University Press, 1996.

[6] J. Brock, C. Ye, C. Ding, Y. Li, X. Wang, and Y. Luo. Optimal cache partition-sharing. In *Intl. Conf. on Parallel Processing (ICPP)*, 2015.

[7] D. Brooks, V. Tiwari, and M. Martonosi. Wattch: a framework for architectural-level power analysis and optimizations. In *Intl. Symp. on Computer Architecture (ISCA)*, 2000.

[8] B. Calder, T. Sherwood, E. Perelman, and G. Hamerley. Simpoint. http://www.cs.ucsd.edu/ calder/simpoint/, 2003.

[9] A. B. Canturk Isci, C.-Y. Cher, P. Bose, and M. Martonosi. An analysis of efficient multi-core global power management policies: Maximizing performance for a given power budget. In *Intl. Symp. on Microarchitecture (MICRO)*, 2006.

[10] P. Chaparro, J. González, and A. González. Thermal-effective clustered microarchitectures. In *Workshop on Temperature-Aware Computer Systems*, 2004.

[11] J. S. Chase, D. C. Anderson, P. N. Thakar, A. M. Vahdat, and R. P. Doyle. Managing energy and server resources in hosting centers. In *ACM Symp. on Operating Systems Principles (SOSP)*, 2001.

[12] J. Chen and L. K. John. Predictive coordination of multiple on-chip resources for chip multiprocessors. In *Intl. Conf. on Supercomputing (ICS)*, 2011.

[13] J. Chen, L. K. John, and D. Kaseridis. Modeling program resource demand using inherent program characteristics. In *Intl. Conf. on Measurement and Modeling of Computer Systems (Sigmetrics)*, 2011.

[14] J. Chen, A. Nair, and L. John. Predictive heterogeneity-aware application scheduling for chip multiprocessors. *IEEE Trans. on Computers*, 63, 2012.

[15] S. Choi and D. Yeung. Learning-based SMT processor resource distribution via hill-climbing. In *Intl. Symp. on Computer Architecture (ISCA)*, 2006.

[16] E. Ebrahimi, R. Miftakhutdinov, C. Fallin, C. J. Lee, J. A. Joao, O. Mutlu, and Y. N. Patt. Parallel application memory scheduling. In *Intl. Symp. on Microarchitecture (MICRO)*, 2011.

[17] M. Feldman, K. Lai, and L. Zhang. A price-anticipating resource allocation mechanism for distributed shared clusters. In *Intl. Conf. on Electronic Commerce (EC)*, 2005.

[18] G. Hardin. The tragedy of the commons. *Science*, 162(3859): 1243–1248, 1968.

[19] M. T. Inc. 2Gb DDR3 SDRAM component data sheet: MT41J256M8. http://www.micron.com/parts/dram/ddr3-sdram/mt41j256m8da-125, July 2012.

[20] Intel Corporation. Intel 64 and IA-32 Architectures Software Developer's Manuals. http://www.intel.com/content/www/us/en/processors/architectures-software-developer-manuals.html, 2014.

[21] R. Johari and J. N. Tsitsiklis. Efficiency loss in a network resource allocation game. *Mathematics of Operations Research*, 29(3):407–435, 2004.

[22] R. Kumar, K. I. Farkas, N. P. Jouppi, P. Ranganathan, and D. M. Tullsen. Single-isa heterogeneous multi-core architectures: The potential for processor power reduction. In *Intl. Symp. on Microarchitecture (MICRO)*, 2003.

[23] K. Lai, L. Rasmusson, E. Adar, L. Zhang, and B. A. Huberman. Tycoon: An implementation of a distributed, market-based resource allocation system. *Multiagent and Grid Systems*, 1, 2005.

[24] R. Miftakhutdinov, E. Ebrahimi, and Y. N. Patt. Predicting performance impact of dvfs for realistic memory systems. In *Intl. Symp. on Microarchitecture (MICRO)*, 2012.

[25] N. Nisan, T. Roughgarden, E. Tardos, and V. V. Vazirani. *Algorithmic game theory*. Cambridge University Press, 2007.

[26] C. Papadimitriou. Algorithms, games, and the Internet. In *Intl. Symp. on Theory of computing*, 2001.

[27] M. K. Qureshi and Y. N. Patt. Utility-based cache partitioning: A low-overhead, high-performance, runtime mechanism to partition shared caches. In *Intl. Symp. on Microarchitecture (MICRO)*, 2006.

[28] J. Renau, B. Fraguela, J. Tuck, W. Liu, M. Prvulovic, L. Ceze, S. Sarangi, P. Sack, K. Strauss, and P. Montesinos. SESC simulator, January 2005. http://sesc.sourceforge.net.

[29] E. Rotem, A. Naveh, D. Rajwan, A. Ananthakrishnan, and E. Weissmann. Power-management architecture of the intel microarchitecture code-named sandy bridge. *IEEE Micro*, 32 (2):0020–27, 2012.

[30] P. Shivakumar and N. P. Jouppi. CACTI 3.0: an integrated cache timing, power, and area model. Technical report, HP Western Research Labs, 2001.

[31] K. Skadron, M. R. Stan, K. Sankaranarayanan, W. Huang, S. Velusamy, and D. Tarjan. Temperature-aware microarchitecture: Modeling and implementation. *ACM Trans. on Architecture and Code Optimization (TACO)*, 1(1):94–125, 2004.

[32] Standard Performance Evaluation Corporation. SPEC CPU2000. http://www.spec.org/cpu2000/, 2000.

[33] Standard Performance Evaluation Corporation. SPEC CPU2006. http://www.spec.org/cpu2006/, 2006.

[34] G. E. Suh, S. Devadas, and L. Rudolph. A new memory monitoring scheme for memory-aware scheduling and partitioning.

In *Intl. Symp. on High Performance Computer Architecture (HPCA)*, 2002.

[35] H. R. Varian. Equity, envy, and efficiency. *Journal of economic theory*, 9(1):63–91, 1974.

[36] R. Wang and L. Chen. Futility scaling: High-associativity cache partitioning. In *Intl. Symp. on Microarchitecture (MICRO)*, 2014.

[37] X. Wang and J. F. Martínez. XChange: A market-based approach to scalable dynamic multi-resource allocation in multicore architectures. In *Intl. Symp. on High Performance Computer Architecture (HPCA)*, 2015.

[38] Y. Xie and G. H. Loh. PIPP: promotion/insertion pseudo-partitioning of multi-core shared caches. In *Intl. Symp. on Computer Architecture (ISCA)*, 2009.

[39] S. M. Zahedi and B. C. Lee. Ref: Resource elasticity fairness with sharing incentives for multiprocessors. In *Intl. Conf. on Architectural Support for Programming Languages and Operating Systems (ASPLOS)*, 2014.

[40] L. Zhang. The efficiency and fairness of a fixed budget resource allocation game. In *Automata, Languages and Programming*, pages 485–496. Springer, 2005.

Dirigent: Enforcing QoS for Latency-Critical Tasks on Shared Multicore Systems

Haishan Zhu
The University of Texas at Austin
haishanz@utexas.edu

Mattan Erez
The University of Texas at Austin
mattan.erez@utexas.edu

Abstract

Latency-critical applications suffer from both average performance degradation and reduced completion time predictability when collocated with batch tasks. Such variation forces the system to overprovision resources to ensure Quality of Service (QoS) for latency-critical tasks, degrading overall system throughput. We explore the causes of this variation and exploit the opportunities of mitigating variation directly to simultaneously improve both QoS and utilization. We develop, implement, and evaluate Dirigent, a lightweight performance-management runtime system that accurately controls the QoS of latency-critical applications at fine time scales, leveraging existing architecture mechanisms. We evaluate Dirigent on a real machine and show that it is significantly more effective than configurations representative of prior schemes.

Categories and Subject Descriptors C.0 [*Computer Systems Organization*]: Hardware/software interfaces

Keywords QoS; Colocation; Latency Distribution; Latency Tail; Run-Time Prediction; DVFS; Cache Partitioning

1. Introduction

There is an growing interest in cloud computing as it can significantly reduce the cost of computation and storage. However, while consolidating the workloads of many clients reduces average cost, the datacenters that house these cloud services require tremendous up-front investment; for example, Facebook recently invested $1 billion on its new datacenter [57]. A major challenge datacenters face today is that this large investment is often underutilized because current individual nodes cannot always meet the processing requirements of customers unless they are not fully utilized [2, 11]. Studies on large data centers have reported average utilization to be between 10% and 50% [2, 11, 41, 62].

The main reason for this underutilization is that many user-facing applications have strict latency requirements such that collocating them with other throughput-oriented batch applications is challenging. The contention from background batch jobs increases the average latency, worst-case execution time (WCET), and the fraction of tasks that exceed the requirements of user-facing latency-critical jobs. However, without "backfilling" nodes with batch jobs, it is practically impossible to fully load them.

Although the problem of meeting latency goals while improving system utilization has been addressed in previous work (e.g., [9, 12, 14, 15, 19, 26–30, 32, 36, 39, 42, 43, 45, 49–51, 58, 60–63]), intensive resource contention also leads to large variation in the execution time of latency-critical tasks even when their average and percentile performance matches the *quality of service* (QoS) goals. In this paper we focus on this little-explored variation problem. We show how variation significantly reduces efficiency. We then propose and evaluate techniques to reduce variation and take advantage of the resulting predictable task completion times.

An interesting characteristic of many user-facing workloads is that there is limited utility in completing tasks faster than the critical latency goal [2, 11, 35]. This is true both for very low-latency tasks, such as those from search, content caching, and delivery workloads [13, 42, 62], and for the somewhat longer latency associated with tasks of live video processing, online stream data analysis, and recognition tasks [6, 17, 38]. In this work, we focus on the latter kind of workloads. Speficailly, we study workloads that are offloaded to the cloud and that are characterized by being both computationally intensive and latency sensitive. Because very fast execution is not beneficial but latency targets are very strict, performance variation leads to poor system utilization—resources are reserved and allocated such that most tasks can finish on time, but are wasted for those tasks that finish quickly. Importantly, the variation in completion time has both slowly- and rapidly-varying components such that managing resources at coarse time scales is not enough to fully utilize a system.

ASPLOS '16 April 2–6, 2016, Atlanta, Georgia, USA.
Copyright © 2016 ACM 978-1-4503-4091-5/16/04…$15.00
DOI: http://dx.doi.org/10.1145/2872362.2872394

To address the challenges and opportunities of rapid variation, we study applications with execution-time constraints, which we call *foreground* (FG) applications by measuring their performance when running with different batch-oriented *background* (BG) applications on a real machine. We focus on variation caused by contention in the memory system because it is the most commonly shared resource and because other resource conflicts (e.g., I/O) can be handled at a coarser granularity by task schedulers [12, 13]. We show that FG applications suffer from significant performance variance when running under contention. We design and implement *Dirigent*, a lightweight resource management runtime that directly reduces the variation of FG jobs at very fine timescales to simultaneously meet their latency targets and provide more resources to BG jobs. Dirigent is based on a novel technique for dynamically predicting the task-to-task completion time within the execution of an FG task and adapting frequency and cache partitioning. This fine time scale management is fundamentally different from prior approaches and is enabled by the lightweight runtime and completion-time predictor.

Our work on Dirigent makes the following contributions:

- We expose the problem of performance variation for latency-critical (foreground) tasks when running under contention. Such variation prevents schedulers and resource managers from maximizing utilization.
- We develop a very lightweight technique for accurately predicting the execution time of foreground tasks at very fine time scales and with very high accuracy; we evaluate this predictor on a real system.
- We further develop the Dirigent lightweight runtime controller that exploits the new trade-off space between reducing the execution time variation of foreground tasks and the throughput of background tasks. Dirigent coordinates all contending processes with the knowledge of expected completion times and deadlines. Dirigent is thus able to improve background-task performance by enabling foreground tasks to yield resources when they are expected to finish faster than their required latency.
- We evaluate Dirigent on a real machine using a range of benchmarks. Results show Dirigent significantly reduces the performance variation of foreground applications while minimizing the background-task throughput degradation when compared to allowing the background jobs to freely contend for resources. On average, Dirigent can achieve 85% reduction in the standard deviation of execution time for foreground applications at the cost of just 9% background task performance loss; this translates into 30% better background throughput than schemes that operate at coarse time scales while also achieving higher completion success rates for the foreground latency-critical tasks.

The rest of this paper is organized as follows. Section 2 provides background on applications of interest and the challenges related to performance variation. Section 3 explains how reducing variation in foreground applications benefits system operation, and discusses the underlying architectural and system mechanisms to control resource use. Section 4 describes the design and implementation of Dirigent. Section 5 presents evaluation results. Section 6 reviews prior QoS management techniques related to Dirigent. Finally, Section 7 concludes the paper and discusses future work.

2. Background

In this section we briefly summarize background most pertinent to Driginent, including a description of our target workloads, and the goals of performance and QoS management techniques in the context of the workloads.

2.1 Target Workloads and Metrics

Based on prior publications, we classify cloud workloads into three categories [2, 6, 8, 17, 35, 38]. The first includes tasks that are not user-facing, for which throughput is the primary concern, and that can be freely scheduled in the background when resources are available. The second class includes short latency-critical user-facing tasks, such as responding to web search requests and content caching. This class of workloads is characterized by short deadlines in the order of tens of milliseconds. The third is an emerging class of workloads that correspond to offloading of work from user devices to the cloud. Examples include online video processing, online stream data analysis, and recognition tasks. Such tasks are user facing and latency critical, yet are also computationally intensive and have relatively long execution times. These tasks can take hundreds of milliseconds or more to finish and therefore can benefit from being offloaded to the cloud [6, 17, 38].

Both the second and third classes are typically user-generated tasks, of which those arising from sophisticated data and sensor processing applications often belong to the third class. Both classes pose challenges for efficient cloud resource usage. In particular, their performance is expressed both in terms of throughput (number of tasks processed per unit time) and in terms of strict latency constraints where only a small fraction of tasks can violate the constraints without severe penalties. Two common and useful measures corresponding to these performance goals are *average execution time* for throughput and *95-percentile execution time* (or other percentile goals) for latency constraints. Note that in evaluating Dirigent in this paper, we use workloads comprised of tasks from the first and the third categories.

2.2 Challenges

The strict performance goals of user-facing tasks can lead to poor system utilization, where nodes do not operate near their peak processing capability. There are two primary reasons for that. First, FG tasks on their own cannot be used to fully utilize a node because it is often undesirable to collocate FG tasks because of aspects relating to how data is sharded across cloud servers and sizes of application states [2, 11, 42]. Second, "backfilling" BG tasks to better utilize nodes is also not always possible because of the detrimental impact this has on FG performance.

The problem with collocating BG and FG tasks is the performance degradation because the contention between FG and BG tasks for limited processor resources frequently violates FG performance goals. In some collocation scenarios, compromised average latency can be easily identified. The bigger challenge is variations in performance that lead to latency violations. Variations in FG completion times happen when long-running BG tasks vary in their characteristics (phases) or when new tasks are scheduled for collocation, altering the interference and contention impact [30, 37, 62].

Prior work that addresses the challenge of collocation has focused on managing interference at relatively coarse granularity by scheduling only tasks that do not interfere much onto the same node [45, 60], by statically throttling BG tasks such that sufficient resources are given to collocated FG tasks [62], by slowly and dynamically adjusting BG task throttling to respond to diurnal load variation [42], or by changing scheduling policies within the OS or across the cloud server to ensure QoS [12, 13, 30, 37, 51, 52, 63].

In contrast to these prior works, Dirigent focuses on very fine time scale to directly minimize task-to-task variation in FG task completion times, which allows Dirigent to free up significantly more resources that can be used by BG tasks without compromising either the throughput or latency targets of the FG tasks. We explain these benefits as well as the mechanisms Dirigent relies on in the next section.

3. Dirigent Principles

In this section we discuss how focusing on reducing the variation in FG task execution benefits system operation and mechanisms to manage variation.

3.1 Benefits of Minimizing Variation

An important insight that Dirigent leverages is that minimizing variation can simultaneously meet the performance targets of latency-critical tasks and improve system utilization. Large variations in the completion time of FG tasks cause inefficiencies in the shared system because they lead to over-provisioned resources for FG tasks and system under-utilization for latency targets to be met. To understand these inefficiencies, consider an FG task that can meet its throughput and latency targets when running alone, but suffers from large variation in execution time when under contention.

Figure 1 shows an example of the execution time probability density function of such a program, where the blue curve represents standalone execution, the red curve shows the behavior under contention, and an ideal curve is shown in green. In standalone execution, FG tasks often complete significantly ahead of the deadline and the throughput achieved (average execution time) is higher than required. As a result hardware is not fully utilized because there is large performance headroom in most FG executions that could be used for other tasks (shown as the highlighted region). However, when a BG task is introduced, too many deadlines are missed despite the average throughput target being maintained.

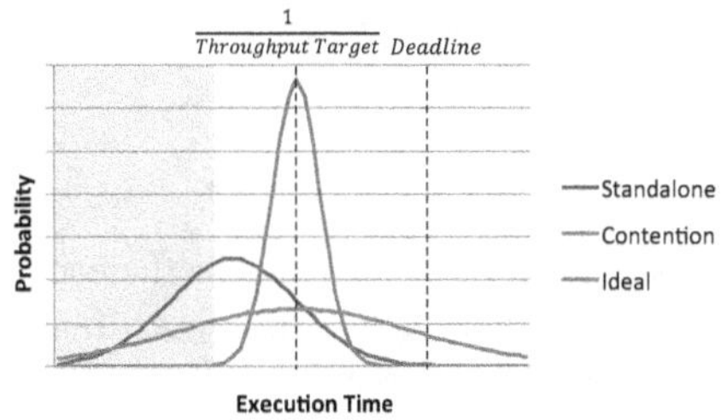

Figure 1: Example FG completion time probability density functions when run alone, under contention, and in an ideal scenario; the shaded region points to underutilized resources when run alone.

Previous work focused on keeping core occupancy high while meeting latency goals [42, 45, 62]. However, by explicitly addressing task-to-task variation at fine time scales within a single task, the ideal (green curve) can be achieved. In this ideal case, both throughput and latency targets are met precisely and core and frequency resources are maximally utilized. Dirigent achieves this ideal curve through unique fine time scale monitoring and control mechanisms.

Furthermore, high variation reduces resource utilization because of task scheduling policies designed for meeting FG task latency constraints. Consider a common reservation-based scheduling policy that ensures on-time completion of FG tasks by reserving sufficient resources to guarantee a 95% latency target [1]. Figure 2 shows how this scheduler operates on two different sets of tasks: tasks of type A, which have high execution time variance, and type B which have low variance. With high variance, the scheduler reserves too much time for the first task (shown in green) because allocation is forced to expand due to the long tail of execution time probability distribution curve, leading to poor system utilization. This does not happen with the low-variance tasks. Significant prior work on scheduling has shown that scheduling tasks with deadlines can be done more aggressively and with higher system resource utilization when variance is low [56].

Dirigent controls fine-grained scheduling and frequency to maximize utilization while meeting QoS goals. In this way overall utility per unit energy is maximized. This is in contrast to a line of prior work that reduces the impact of variation by rapidly adjusting processor clock frequency [5, 21, 31, 40, 41, 59]. Matching frequency to FG compute needs reduces processor energy consumption, but falls short of maximizing efficiency because the processor itself consumes just 25% – 35% of total system power [16, 41, 46].

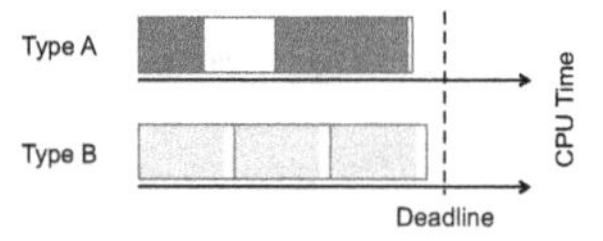

Figure 2: Reservation-based scheduler efficiency with two different task types: type A with high execution time variance and type B with low variance.

3.2 Contention Control Mechanisms

As we explain in Section 4, Dirigent relies on existing mechanisms to manage interference and provide good QoS for the FG jobs. Dirigent uses per-core DVFS and cache partitioning, which we summarize below. We also discuss additional hardware mechanisms that have recently been proposed.

Per-Core dynamic voltage and frequency scaling (DVFS) is a common mechanism for controlling performance and improving processor energy efficiency [23, 33, 47]. Per-core frequency management enables performance adjustments at fine time scales [21, 54], and it can also be used as a throttling mechanism to manage contention and resource usage [19, 22].

Cache partitioning is another well-studied mechanism that provides performance isolation of processes that are collocated and that is used to limit variation and contention [7, 9, 24, 32, 39, 53, 55]. Prior work established the effectiveness of cache partitioning as a QoS mechanism and it has recently been implemented in commercial processors. However, because of the large capacity of the last level cache, changes to cache partitions take significant time to have an impact on execution, an effect termed *cache inertia* [32]. Thus, cache partitioning is effective at relatively long time scales.

While we do not currently use these mechanisms in Dirigent as they are not yet available in commercial processors, there is also a large body of work on QoS mechanisms for managing memory bandwidth and latency resources. Yun et al. studied the performance benefits of memory bandwidth reservation for latency-sensitive applications [61]. Mutlu et al. show different levels of QoS goals and performance benefits that can be achieved by making memory scheduling QoS aware [34, 48–50]. Usui et al. presented QoS aware memory scheduler that handles different priority levels in heterogeneous systems [58]. In other related work, Ebrahimi et al. proposed source throttling, which is a hardware-based mechanism controls the rate at which cores generate requests to shared memory system [14]. Jeong et al. studied the row-buffer locality interference in multicore processors [29]. Zhou et al. proposed an architecture that allows fine-grain micro-architecture resource partitioning among threads [65]. Ma et al. designed a mechanism to control queueing delay of requests in different architecture structures [44]. While other contention sources exist in warehouse scale datacenters, there is a large body of related work that show how intelligent task schedulers can identify and avoid such resource conflicts [12, 13, 30, 36, 37].

4. Dirigent Design and Implementation

Dirigent is composed of three main components: profiler, predictor, and controller. The profiler examines and records the execution of an FG applications offline and in isolation. The profiling information is then used online to predict the expected execution time of the FG application. The controller then partitions resources and throttles tasks to minimize the execution time variation of FG tasks while providing as much resources as possible to BG tasks, thus achieving the goal of simultaneously meeting latency-critical requirements and allowing high processor utilization. The rest of this section discusses in detail the design and initial implementation of Dirigent. Again, we point out that Dirigent is unique in the fine time scales on which it operates.

We implement Dirigent in C++ and evaluate it using a 6-core Intel Xeon E5 2618L-v3 processor, which supports per-core frequency settings and cache partitioning [24].

4.1 Offline Execution Profiler

Dirigent profiles the execution of an FG application when running alone offline. The profiler records progress information that is then used to make accurate online predictions of completion time under contention while a task is still executing. The Dirigent profiler periodically samples the execution progress of the FG task being profiled by measuring and recording a series of (*time*, *progress*) pairs when the FG is running alone without any contention (see Figure 3a). The FG program in the example of Figure 3a has 3 profiled segments and takes $3\Delta T$ time units to execute, where ΔT is the sampling period. We measure *progress* by counting the number of retired instructions using the processor's model-specific performance counter monitors [25], but more abstract metrics can also be used. Note that progress can significantly differ between segments even though the sampling frequency is constant. This is because progress depends on the instruction mix, data access pattern, data set size, and other factors.

Dirigent requires minimal profiling. In our current implementation, the profiler requires no extra hardware as both execution time and instruction count are readily available in most architectures today. Dirigent uses performance counters and `sleep` method for periodic sampling with negligible impact on the running application. Although performance overhead is not a great concern in offline profiling, this low overhead ensures the accuracy of these measurements. Furthermore, note that while our current implementation of Dirigent relies on offline profiling, it is possible to perform online profiling instead, which requires the system to run the FG task a few times while all other tasks are paused to record a stable profiling record.

4.2 Execution Time Predictor

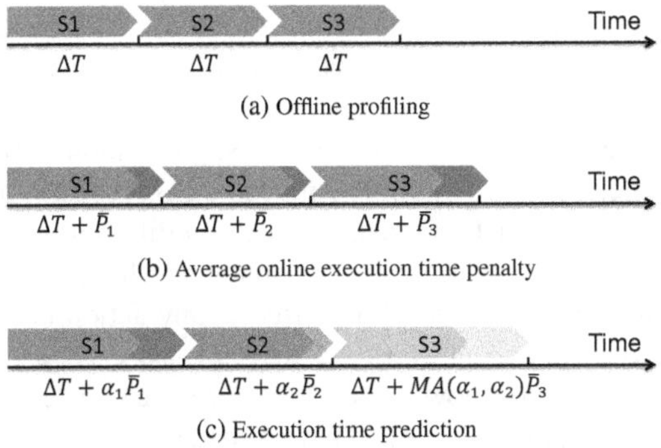

(a) Offline profiling

(b) Average online execution time penalty

(c) Execution time prediction

Figure 3: Execution time predictor example.

To predict FG completion time and control resources, Dirigent periodically samples progress during contended online execution. Dirigent predicts FG completion time by tracking actual progress, comparing this progress to the profiled data, and computing a *time penalty* experienced by the FG process, which is then projected forward to completion as explained below. We pin the Dirigent runtime thread to a core that runs a BG task and again use the `sleep` method to periodically interrupt the BG task and execute the Dirigent runtime task.

The time penalty of a specific segment is computed assuming a fixed rate of progress within each segment. The penalty is the difference between the expected time to make the amount of progress within the profiled segment at the rate of progress experienced in the online segment vs. the profiled time for this segment. This is summarized in Equation 1 where P_i is the penalty for the ith segment and ΔT_i is the duration of that segment. Note that ΔT_i can be slightly different than ΔT in the real implementation because of factors such as errors in timers. We account for that difference in Dirigent to ensure the accuracy of the prediction. Also, we introduce the symbol α_i shown in Equation 1 as shorthand for the ratio of measured vs. expected progress rates for the ith segment.

$$P_i = \frac{Profiled\_progress_i}{Measured\_progress_i} \Delta T_i - \Delta T_i = (\alpha_i - 1)\, \Delta T_i \tag{1}$$

Frequent samples increase the execution time prediction accuracy and the opportunities for performance management, but each prediction and control segment has overhead. We measured this overhead using a subset of our workload mixes. Results show the runtime overhead is minimal and each Dirigent invocation requires on average less than $100\mu s$ (including predictor and throttler). We therefore chose a sampling period $\Delta T = 5ms$ to balance the overhead and effectiveness of online prediction and control. This sampling period provides 100 or more segments in all the FG applications we test with only negligible runtime overhead.

To increase prediction accuracy, Dirigent maintains an exponential moving average (with weight 0.2) of the penalty within each segment across multiple executions of the FG task, which we denote $\overline{P_i} = 0.2P_i + 0.8\overline{P_i}$. Figure 3b shows the average penalty in blue. Note that just like progress, the average penalty can differ significantly across segments. The moving average smooths occasional outlier executions. At a given point in time during a single FG task's execution, Dirigent's predictor uses the penalties observed so far for each segment, the total elapsed time from the start of the process, and the average penalties of the segments yet to execute to compute the expected execution time of the task. The formula is shown in Equation 2, where k is the segment corresponding to current time T, N are the total number of segments in the profiled execution, and $MA\left(\{\alpha_i\}_{i=1}^{k}\right)$ denotes an exponential moving average over the rate factors measured so far in the current execution. This moving average is used as the expected penalty scaling factor for the remainder of the current execution.

$$T_{est,k} = T + \sum_{i=k+1}^{N} \left(MA\left(\{\alpha_i\}_{i=1}^{k}\right) \overline{P_i} + \Delta T_i \right) \tag{2}$$

Figure 3c illustrates how the prediction calculation of Equation 2 is performed. When the example program finishes executing the second segment, the penalty scaling factor α_2 is much smaller than the factor α_1 of the first segment. This difference arises from factors such as OS noise, phase changes of the BG applications, and context switches. The moving average across executions and of executions within the segment smooths out the difference of the scaling, which is then used as the predictive factor for the remaining segment.

In our experiments with Dirigent, we arbitrarily chose a weight of 0.2 for the exponential moving averages and a 5ms sampling interval. As we show in Section 5.2, the predictor is highly accurate with these parameters and is able to predict the expected execution time to within 2%, typically, across multiple applications and different levels of contention. We tested the sensitivity of Dirigent to weight factors in the range of $0.1 - 0.3$ and conclude that Dirigent is robust. We also evaluate Dirigent's sensitivity to sampling periods. We conclude that even 40 samples per execution of the FG task tested provide for accurate completion-time predictions. However, the low performance overhead ($< 100\mu s$ per invocation) enables high sampling frequency for accurate prediction and tight QoS control for FG tasks that widely differ in execution time.

4.3 Performance Controller

Dirigent monitors the performance of FG applications online and uses the predictor to determine whether these applications are progressing faster or slower than necessary to meet their latency goals. Recall that Dirigent does not strive to minimize the execution time of FG tasks, but rather to minimize their execution time variation while meeting their latency targets. As a result, resources for the FG tasks are not over-provisioned. If a FG task is expected to complete before its target time, it is deprioritized and BG tasks can achieve higher throughput. On the other hand, if a FG task is lagging, Dirigent prioritizes resources toward that FG task and away from BG tasks.

In our current implementation of Dirigent, we allocate resource by controlling the frequency at which each core operates, by partitioning the last-level cache (LLC), and by pausing BG tasks when necessary. We chose these mechanisms from the possible ones described in Section 3.2 because they are both effective and available in current systems. We use frequency and task-pausing to control FG progress at fine time scales and cache partitioning at a coarser ones; with large caches, *cache inertia* means significant time passes before the impact of adjusting partitions takes effect [32].

Fine time scale control: The goal of the fine time scale controller is to quickly respond to changes in contention and FG task progress to ensure deadlines are met and minimize performance variance. The controller observes the execution time predictions and decides whether FG tasks can yield resources or whether BG tasks must be throttled and to what extent. A simplified version of the fine time scale controller policy for a single FG task is designed as follows.

At each decision point, the controller determines if the FG task is ahead or behind. If ahead, the controller will check the following three options in order. First, if any background jobs are paused, the control decision is to continue them. Second, if no tasks are paused but some are throttled, the decision is to speed up any throttled BG processes by one speed grade (using existing per-core DVFS mechanisms). Third, if all BG tasks are already running at their maximum frequency, the decision is to throttle the FG task frequency. Similarly, if the FG task is behind schedule, the decision is to speed up to maximum frequency. If it is already at maximum frequency, the decision is to immediately throttle the frequency of the BG tasks. If the BG tasks are already at the minimum frequency, the most intrusive active BG is paused; we define intrusiveness as the number of LLC load misses a task generates, which we obtain from existing performance counters. The throttler controls each core using the `CPUFreq Governor` of Linux [4].

While the Dirigent runtime is very lightweight, the impact of control decisions is not instantaneous. We therefore only make control decisions every some small number of prediction segments (5 in our experiments, arbitrarily). Furthermore, we only take control actions if the expected FG execution time is more than 2% ahead the target deadline and only pause BG tasks if the FG task is expected to complete more than 10% behind its deadline. We chose 2% because it corresponds to the typical error of the predictor and is thus a good safety margin that prevents prematurely slowing down or interfering with a FG task. We chose a larger threshold for pausing because its overhead is greater (again, the value of 10% was arbitrarily chosen within a reasonable value range; sensitivity studies reveal that Dirigent is not sensitive to this choice).

The decision making process is slightly more complicated when there are multiple collocated FG processes along with BG tasks. Each FG task may exhibit different levels of performance degradation even when the interference level is the same for all of them. Furthermore, any action taken on BG tasks will impact all collocated FG tasks. As a result, when all FG tasks show the same performance tendency, we use the same policy described before for a single FG process. Otherwise, BG tasks are throttled based on the performance of the slowest concurrent FG task, and any other FG tasks that are expected to finish sooner than the deadline are throttled down individually.

Coarse time scale control: Dirigent uses cache partitioning for coarse-grain control over the expected execution time of FG tasks, specifically the Cache Allocation Technology recently introduced by Intel [24], which can be used to specify which cache ways may be used by each processor. Because of cache inertia the system's response time to partition changes is fairly slow when compared to the typical short durations of FG tasks. We therefore use statistics collected over multiple executions of a FG task to guide adjustments to cache partitioning. Specifically, our current implementation of Dirigent tracks three measures: (1) the correlation between a FG tasks' execution time and the LLC misses it generates (over multiple executions); (2) a history of the absolute number of LLC misses over executions; and (3) a history of the Dirigent decisions states over time. In our current implementation, we use the history of 10 last executions to compute the measures above. We construct three heuristics to determine whether FG tasks benefit from greater isolation and more dedicated cache ways or whether BG tasks are allowed to utilize a greater portion of the LLC.

First, if there is strong correlation between the execution time of FG tasks and their LLC misses, it indicates that growing the FG partition is likely to improve FG performance. Therefore, if correlation is strong *and* FG tasks have recently missed deadlines, we increase isolation and add one LLC way to the FG partition (removing it from the list of ways utilized by BG tasks). We somewhat arbitrarily chose a correlation coefficient of 0.75 as the threshold determining strong correlation.

Second, Dirigent observes the LLC hit-rate history and if growing the FG partition does not lower FG tasks LLC misses, Dirigent shrinks the foreground partition. This heuristic coupled with the coarse time scale and averaging performed prevents the FG partitions from continuously growing due to anomalous executions.

It is also possible for the correlation between misses and performance to not be strong yet for partitioning to still help:

Table 1: FG and BG Benchmarks

Type	Name	Description
FG	bodytrack	Body tracking of a person
	ferret	Content similarity search
	fluidanimate	Fluid dynamic for animation
	raytrace	Real-time raytracing
	streamcluster	Online clustering of an input stream
Single BG	bwaves	Simulation of blast waves in 3D
	PCA	Principal Component Analysis
	RS	Range Search
Rotate BG	namd	Biomolecular system simulation
	soplex	Linear program solver
	libquantum	Simulation of quantum computer
	lbm	Simulation of fluids with free surfaces

when FG performance is bottlenecked by high memory latency caused by contention from BG tasks. Because Dirigent's fine time scale controller throttles BG tasks when they heavily contend for resources, correlation would not detect the need for stricter partitioning of FG and BG tasks. Therefore, our *third heuristic* grows the FG partition when the controller history indicates that BG tasks are heavily throttled and their utilization of core resources is low. The second heuristic then differentiates between scenarios where BG tasks should be throttled from those where partitioning is more beneficial by shrinking the FG partition back if hit-rate does not improve. We show the effectiveness of our method in Section 5.3.

5. Evaluation

We evaluate Dirigent on a real machine with a range of workloads representative of a wide range of FG and BG behaviors. We first introduce the evaluation infrastructure and workloads. We then discuss a set of experiments that demonstrate the accuracy of Dirigent's completion-time predictor, the effectiveness of the coarse time scale partitioning heuristic, Dirigent's performance benefits compared to a baseline configuration and configurations that roughly correspond to prior work, and the new tradeoff between BG task throughput and FG deadline target that Dirigent enables.

5.1 Workloads and Evaluation Infrastructure

System: We evaluate Dirigent on a 6-core Intel Xeon E6-2618L v3 server processor. The nominal per-core maximum frequency is 2GHz and 9 frequency steps are available for throttling (1.2 – 2.0GHz, though Dirigent uses just 5 equi-spaced frequencies). Turbo Boost is enabled in all experiments. The processor has a 15MB L3 LLC and supports Intel's Cache Allocation Technology, which enables us to partition the cache between FG and BG tasks to provide additional isolation. The system is configured with 4 2133MHz DDR4 channels and has a total of 16GiB. We run a Linux 3.13.0 kernel at runlevel S, which provides an environment with little OS interference and good facilities for implementing both the Dirigent predictor and controller, with an efficient `sleep` implementation and the built-in `CPUFreq Governer`, respectively. We pin all tasks to individual cores and Dirigent is pinned to a core that is shared with a BG task. We set the BG processes to have higher process niceness than the Dirigent runtime and FG processes to have the lowest niceness. We use the configuration above with no explicit resource management as the *baseline configuration*.

Workloads: Table 1 lists the benchmarks we use in the evaluation. We select the subset of PARSEC applications that represent latency-sensitive applications as FG tasks [3]. We chose PARSEC as it is designed to represent emerging and user-facing workloads of the type that are being offloaded to cloud systems. We use a single run of each benchmark with sim-medium inputs as a single FG task. As shown in Figure 4, these tasks span a range of completion times (0.5 – 1.6s) and LLC miss rates. The figure shows the behavior of the FG benchmarks both when running alone and under contention. For this figure, we use 1 FG for all FG tasks and 5 BG cores all running *bwaves*, which falls in the middle of contention range. The FG workloads are all fairly compute-intensive, making them good offload candidates. While they are compute-intensive, they still offer a range of sensitivity to interference from BG tasks both because of LLC and memory access contention. This can be seen by the different correlation levels between LLC miss rate increase and execution time degradation between the different benchmarks. To ensure accurate measurements of these tasks, execution time is measured inside the FG processes using PARSEC's Region of Interests (ROI) interface.

We use two kinds of BG workloads to represent different interference types: BG phase changes and context switches. We use three standalone BG workloads that exhibit strong phase change behavior: the scientific simulation *bwaves* from SPEC 2006 [18] and the machine learning applications Principal Component Analysis (*PCA*) and Range Search (*RS*) from MLPack [10]. All other benchmarks we examined did not provide strong phase behavior, at least with respect to impact on interference, and we omit them from the evaluation—such workloads do not pose significant challenges to the Dirigent predictor.

To mimic varying interference caused by context switches, we select four applications from SPEC 2006 that exhibit a range of memory intensiveness [18], though we arbitrarily chose between all benchmarks that exhibit similar intensity. We then form two-benchmark workloads and randomly switch between the two paired benchmarks each time a FG task completes. The pairs we use are (*lbm+namd*), (*lib+namd*), (*lbm+soplex*), and (*lib+soplex*). We refer these BG workloads as Rotate BG workloads. Figure 5 summarizes the different behaviors of the BG workloads while using a single core running *ferret* as a representative FG workload. The blue bars show the total number of L3 load misses per thousand FG instructions generated by all 6 cores.

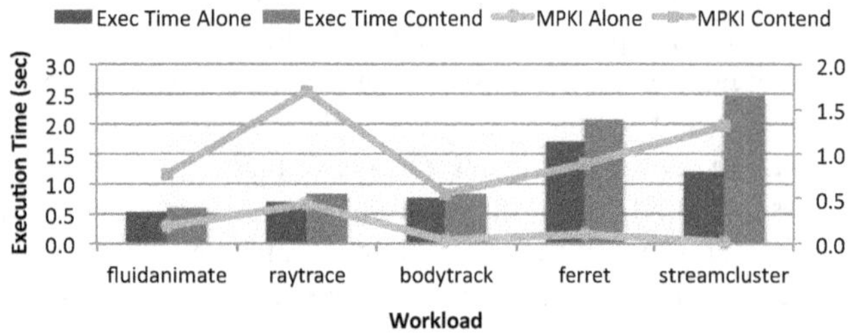

Figure 4: Overview of FG Workloads.

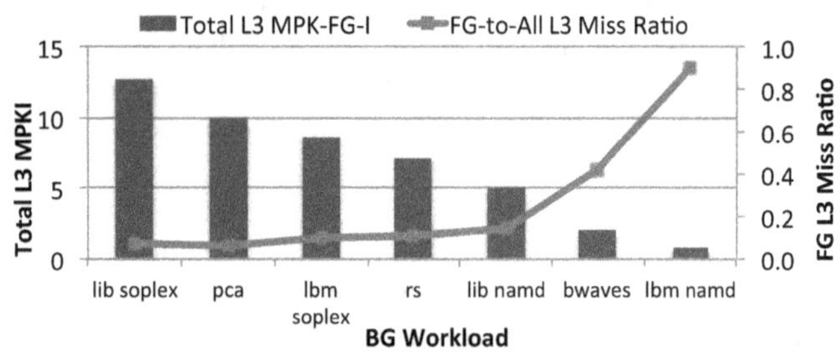

Figure 5: Overview of BG Workloads.

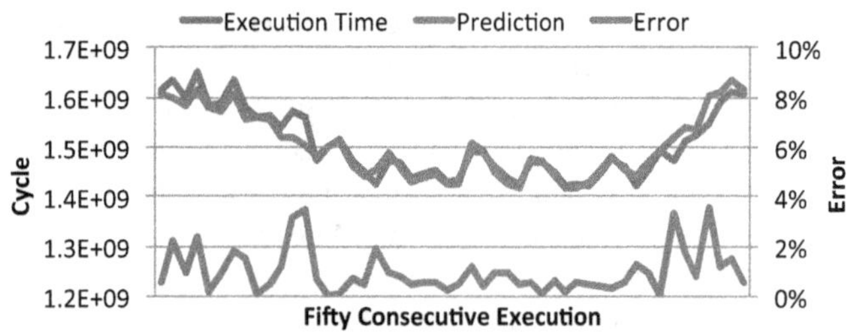

Figure 6: Prediction Trace for *Raytrace* with *RS*.

The red curve shows the fraction of misses generated by FG tasks, which can be interpreted as the ratio between FG task and total memory bandwidth consumption. As can be seen, the BG workloads cover a wide spectrum of behaviors and contention pressure. Similar trends are observed when mixing these BG tasks with other FG workloads.

5.2 Predictor Accuracy

Since the throttling actions of Dirigent are guided by the execution time predictor, it is important to validate its accuracy. Figure 6 shows the execution time, prediction results, and prediction error for 50 consecutive executions of *raytrace* and *RS* workload in the baseline configuration (no explicit resource management). The results shown correspond to a completion-time prediction that is made about half-way through a FG task's execution. Predicted completion closely tracks the actual completion time. Figure 7 shows the average predictor accuracy and the completion time standard deviation normalized to the mean of each workload for all

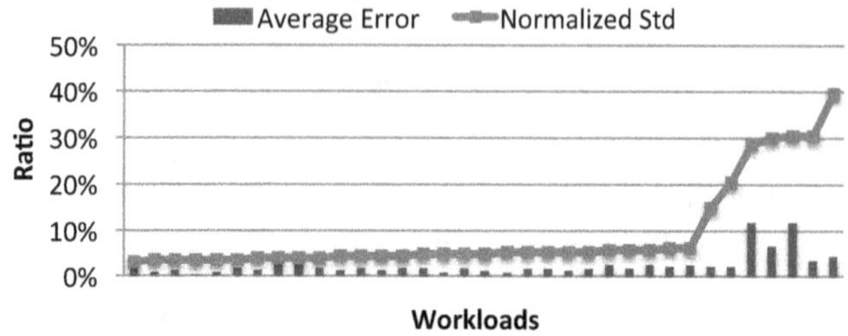

Figure 7: Prediction Accuracy for all FG-BG mixes.

35 workload combinations we use (combinations of one of the 5 FG benchmarks with each of the 7 BG workloads). Average error (ϵ) is computed as shown in Equation 3 at the midpoint of each task over 100 consecutive task executions. The predictor is highly accurate across all these workload combinations with an overall average error of just 2.4%. As expected, higher execution time variation poses greater challenges and predictions tend to be less accurate in such cases; the 5 points with average error of $> 4\%$ all use streamcluster as the FG, with each of the BG we included in the workload. Among those, *RS* gives the highest error rate (12.5%) and the mix between *libquantum* and *namd* gives the lowest error rate (4.4%). Note that the standard deviation of execution time in these cases is significantly larger than predictor errors.

$$\epsilon = \frac{1}{N}\sum_{i=1}^{N}\frac{|predict_i - measure_i|}{measure_i} \tag{3}$$

5.3 Coarse Time Scale QoS Control

To verify the effectiveness of the heuristics used in the coarse time scale QoS controller in Dirigent, we conducted an exhaustive search on cache partitions for 5 arbitrarily chosen workload mixes and show one of the results, for *streamcluster* as the FG task and *PCA* as the BG task in Figure 8. We chose this combination to present because it is one of the few workloads in which FG tasks require a larger partition and therefore stresses the heuristic. As the partition dedicated to the FG tasks grows, the performance of the FG task improves. The knee of the curve representing this exhaustive search is at 5 ways. Dirigent's coarse time scale controller converges to this same partition after just 32 FG task executions (5 coarse time scale controller invocations).

5.4 Dirigent Performance

We use five configurations to evaluate the effectiveness and benefits of Dirigent. In the *Baseline* configuration all cores run at the highest frequency and freely contend for resources. *StaticFreq* sets the FG cores to run at the highest allowed frequencies (2GHz) and BG cores to run at the slowest speed (1.2GHz), giving more resources to FG tasks. *StaticBoth* sets the best static cache partitioning (corresponding

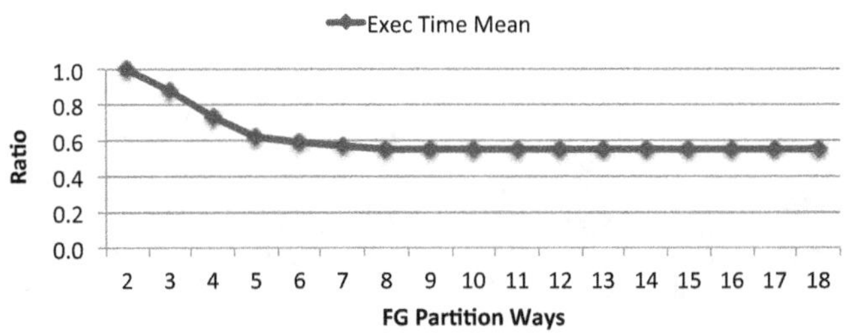

Figure 8: Exhaustive Search on Partition Size.

to Dirigent's heuristic, which we verified is near-optimal) as well as the best frequency for the BG cores. *DirigentFreq* uses Dirigent's fine time scale control only and does not use cache partitioning. *Dirigent* is the full Dirigent implementation that combines coarse time scale cache partitioning with fine time scale frequency control. Note that we omit the coarse time scale-only configuration of Dirigent because it performs just slightly worse than StaticBoth because both use the same partition. Our understanding is that the *StaticBoth* configuration is very similar to the behavior of Heracles [42] in our scenario because the execution time of FG tasks in our experiments are much shorter than polling intervals and controller's optimization convergence time in [42]; our workloads also do not exercise the network.

To quantify the benefits of reduced variation in FG task execution time, we define the deadline for each FG task to be $\mu_{Baseline}+0.3\sigma_{Baseline}$, where $\mu_{Baseline}$ and $\sigma_{Baseline}$ are the average and standard deviation of FG completion time in the *Baseline* configuration; PARSEC does not define latency goals even though the applications do represent potential user-facing tasks. We set the deadline for each benchmark to be slightly larger than the uncontended run time of a task but still far smaller than when contention is unmanaged. In this way Dirigent has the FG run time slack to allow BG jobs to run. The tradeoff between deadline tightness and system throughput is demonstrated later in Section 5.5. For FG tasks, we focus on the *FG success ratio*, which is computed as the fraction of FG task executions that complete within the deadline defined above. For BG tasks, we report *BG performance*, which is the total number of instructions executed during the experiment (across all cores) normalized to *Baseline*. We normalize BG throughput to *Baseline* because running with no constraints results in the highest BG throughput.

Single FG process: Figure 9a and Figure 9b report the performance of both FG and BG tasks in all the workload mixes with one FG process and five BG processes, respectively. The results are summarized in Figure 10 with arithmetic mean of FG success rate and harmonic mean of relative BG throughput.

We make three key observations about these results. First, while BG performance is high with *Basline*, the FG success rate is very poor, averaging just under 60%. Second, while the (semi-)static mechanisms significantly improve FG completion rate (to nearly 100% in the case of *StaticBoth*, BG performance is severely degraded. On average, BG throughput is reduced to $\sim$ 60% that of *Baseline*. Not shown in the graphs is that the FG throughput is improved by 7.5% on average with *StaticFreq*; this is because more BG tasks are throttled more than with the other configurations. Third, the importance of fine time scale control is clearly demonstrated by both *DirigentFreq* and *Dirigent*. Even without cache partitioning, *DirigentFreq* is able to meet the 95% completion target for all but a few workloads and is able to consistently deliver better BG performance than the static schemes (85% of *Baseline* on average). Finally, *Dirigent*, which combines both fine and coarse time scale control, is able to consistently match or exceed both the FG success rate (> 99% on average and 97% in worst success) and BG throughput of all other managed schemes simultaneously; the BG throughput of *Dirigent* comes very close to the throughput of unconstrained execution, averaging 92% and never dropping below 75% of *Baseline*.

We further look at the execution of one of the workload mixes, a *ferret* FG task collocated with five *RS* BG tasks. Figure 11 shows the execution time probability density function curves for the five configurations. Results show that the curves for *Baseline* and *StaticFreq* stretch wide horizontally. Comparing to the *StaticBoth*, the *DirigentFreq* is able to significantly reduce execution time variation by moving the two peaks in *StaticBoth*'s curve closer. *Dirigent* is able to further reshape the curve and merge the two peaks together, achieving even more predictable performance and better BG job throughput. Figure 12 demonstrates the distribution of frequencies that *DirigenttFreq* and *Dirigent* use for cores running BG tasks, and show that partitioning the cache significantly reduces the performance contention on FG performance, allowing BG process to run safely at much higher frequency on average. Overall, *Dirigent* can achieve 85% reduction in the standard deviation of execution time of FG tasks at the cost of only 9% of BG performance loss across all the workload mixes we tested. *DirigentFreq* captures part of the benefits in reducing performance variation, achieving 70% reduction in standard deviation of execution time, but suffers from higher BG performance loss at 15%.

Concurrent FG Processes: Figure 9c uses the same metrics but with workload mixes that have multiple FG processes. These detailed per-workload results are summarized in Figure 13. Due to the large number of possible combinations, it is impractical to exhaustively experiment with all of them. We therefore select five combinations that cover a low to high performance variation range in *Baseline* and measure the performance of these mixes using a varying number of concurrent FG tasks. The workloads in Figure 9c are sorted in ascending order of number of concurrent FG processes

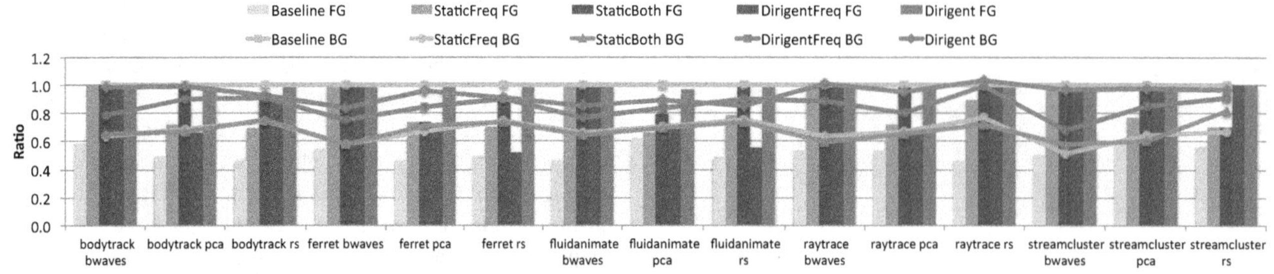

(a) Single BG Workload Mixes

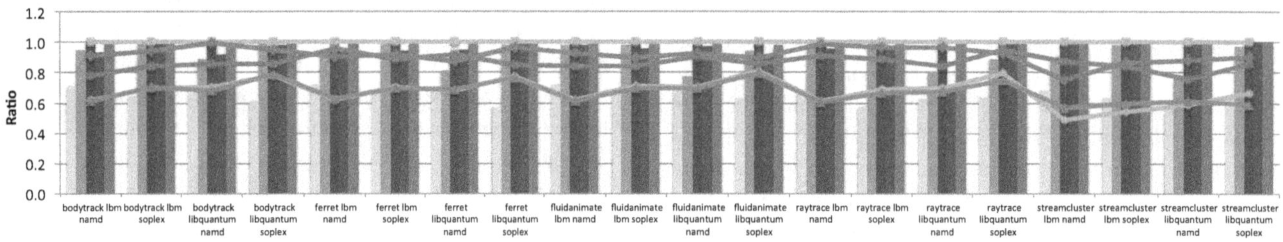

(b) Rotate BG Workload Mixes

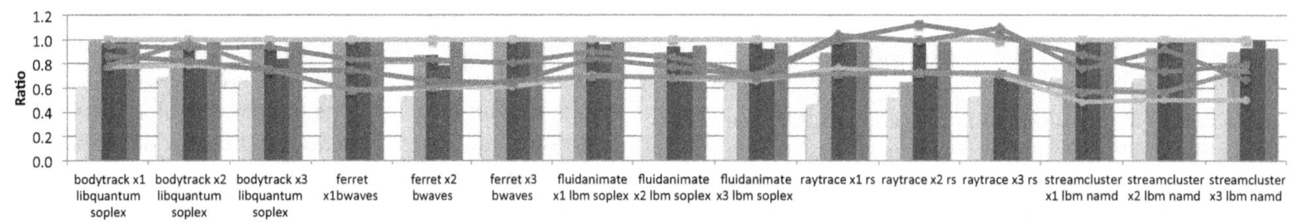

(c) Multiple FGs Workload Mixes

Figure 9: Comparison of FG and BG Performance.

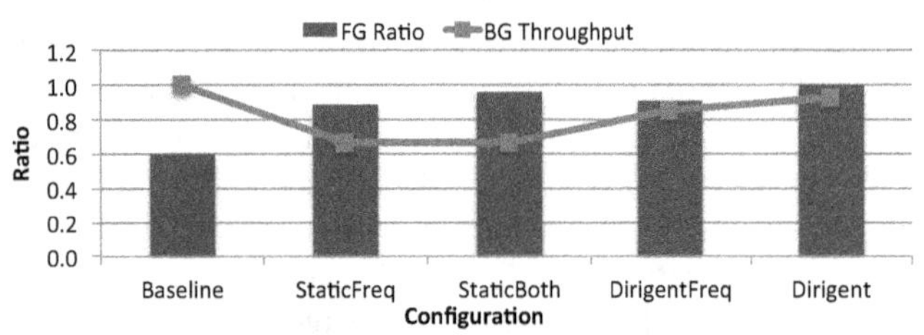

Figure 10: Summary of All Single FG Workload Mixes.

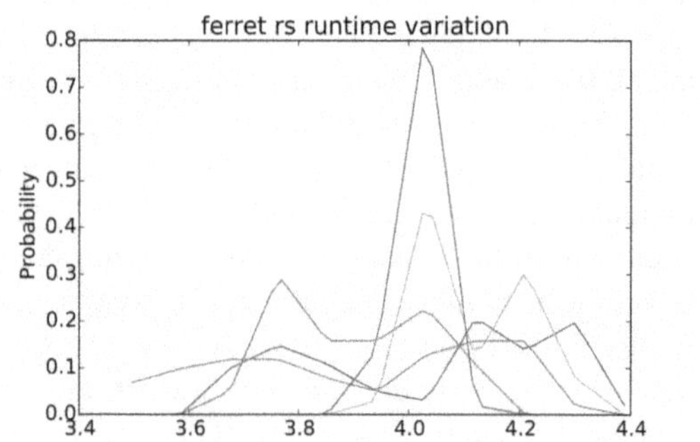

Figure 11: Execution Time Probability Density Function Curve.

within each pair; the total number of FG and BG processes is always 6 (the number of cores).

Overall, the results show similar trends and observations to those exhibited by single-FG process workloads. We discuss two additional insights. First, each FG task may experience different levels of contention due to different FG-BG phase interleavings. This forces the fine-grain controller to use conservative BG performance settings to try and allow even the slowest FG task to complete on target. As seen in Figure 9c, within each FG-BG workload mix with *DirigentFreq*, the general trend is that BG throughput decreases with each additional FG task. This problem is alleviated by the introduction of cache partitioning, as it effectively isolates most of the performance interference between FG and BG tasks. Second, since all FG tasks share the same partition, increasing the number of FG tasks also increases their performance variation. This is shown in Figure 14, where standard

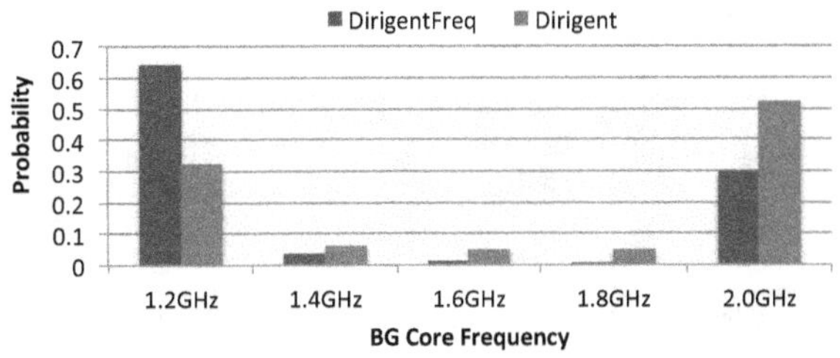

Figure 12: BG Core Frequency Distribution.

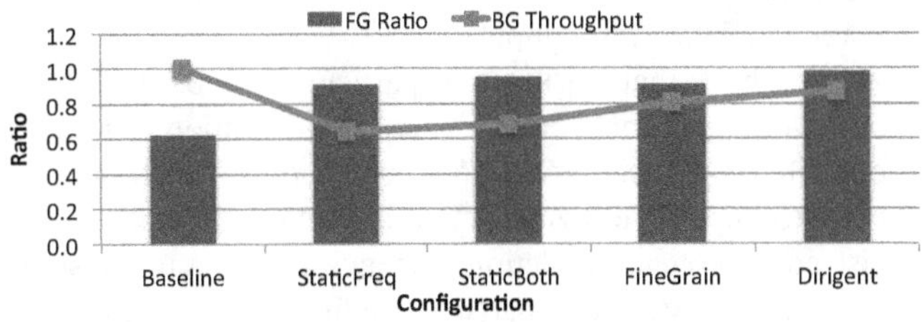

Figure 13: Summary of All Multiple FG Workload Mixes.

deviation for each configuration is normalized to the value in the baseline. While the results show increased variance with more FG processes within each workload mix, *Dirigent* is still able to effectively reduce the performance variation with low BG task performance overhead.

5.5 FG Throughput and BG Performance Tradeoffs

So far we evaluated Dirigent with a fixed FG target execution time that reflects the baseline FG throughput. We now show the tradeoff that Dirigent enables between FG task throughput and BG task performance with precise QoS control. Figure 15 shows one arbitrarily chosen workload: a single *raytrace* FG process and 5 BG *bwaves* processes. We gradually increase the target completion time from the average completion time in standalone execution until it is larger than the average *Baseline* execution time. The blue bars show the average execution time normalized to the standalone execution time, the red bars show the standard deviation at each target normalized to that of *Baseline*, and the green curves show the BG task throughput normalized to *Baseline*.

Dirigent is able to accurately control the execution time across the entire range of target deadlines; the only exception is when the target is set at the standalone execution time because there is no opportunity for collocation without violating QoS. When the deadline is set higher, Dirigent exploits opportunities when FG tasks are running faster than necessary and converts them into BG performance. Importantly, Dirigent effectively enables the tradeoff between FG throughput and BG performance at high system utilization by reducing the variance of FG task execution time. Note that we do not plot the success rates because Dirigent consistently achieves them at the desired $> 99\%$ rate.

6. Related Work

Online QoS Management: Mars et al. proposed an interference characterization methodology and QoS management schemes that target data center applications [45, 60]. Heracles is a performance management runtime that uses multiple control modules leveraging software and hardware mechanisms to enforce QoS for latency sensitive tasks that are collocated with batch jobs [42]. Zhang et al. proposed to identify interference using cycle-per-instruction data, and the results can be used to enforce QoS by static and manual throttling [62]. The above work is most closely related to Dirgient, however, these mechanisms use only coarse time scale statistics and performance variation is not discussed or addressed. As a result the system lacks the ability to adjust contention at fine time granularity, which we demonstrate is crucial to maximizing utilization.

Other related work studies fine-granularity QoS with a focus on saving the energy of executing only FG tasks. PEGASUS improves the energy efficiency of datacenters by dynamically adjusting the power limit of processors [41]. Adrenaline categorizes queries for target applications and only speeds up ones that are likely to fail QoS goals [21]. TimeTrader and Rubik exploit request queueing latency variation and apply any available slack from queueing delay to FG computation to reduce energy consumption [31, 59]. Suh et al. propose to use various execution time prediction mechanisms to guide frequency scaling to save energy [5, 40]. In contrast, Dirigent converts variation in the run time of FG tasks into improved system throughput.

To the best of our knowledge, Dirigent is the first to trade off the performance of latency-critical jobs that finish sooner than required with higher system throughput for BG tasks. A related mechanism proposed by Min et al. tackles fine time granularity QoS problems for GPUs in heterogeneous platforms [28]. However, the progress heuristics used for the GPU were not general and the mechanism proposed is limited to managing main memory bandwidth contention between the CPU and GPU.

Interference Analysis: Interference is a well studied problem and many models and heuristics have been proposed. A good example is the sophisticated model for predicting multicore interference proposed by Zhao et al. [64]. However, this and other prior models do not address deadline-oriented applications because the prediction is made on coarse time scales. Further, these analysis techniques require complex computation that are not suitable for a dynamic lightweight runtime such as Dirigent [62, 64]. Application Heartbeats is a general progress report framework [20], our profiler uses similar concept but on a millisecond scale.

QoS-Aware Scheduling: In addition to the QoS control mechanisms discussed in Section 3.2, task scheduling across multiple nodes in a cloud server or cluster can also be used to manage contention and performance. Kambadur et al. proposed a sample-based interference prediction methodology

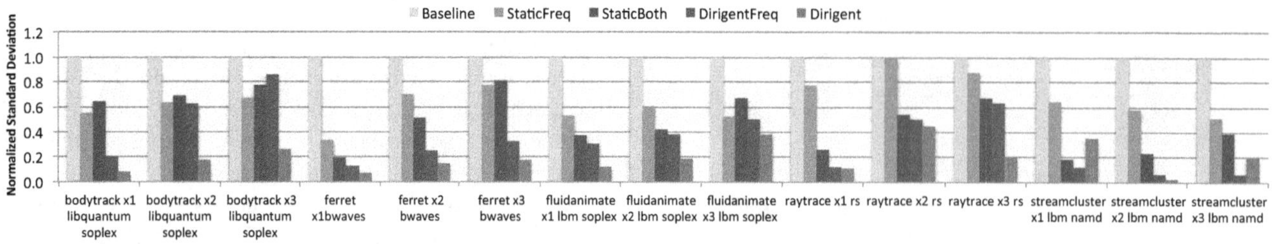

Figure 14: Normalized Standard Variation of Multiple FG Workload Mixes.

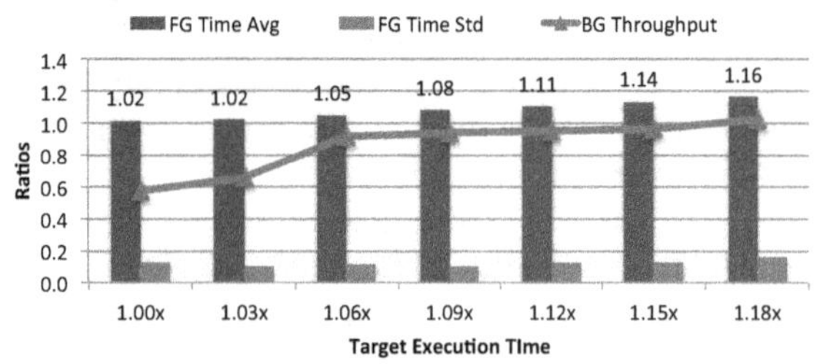

Figure 15: Tradeoff Between FG throughput and BG performance

for identifying application pairs whose collocation should be avoided [30]. SMiTe predicts the SMT-level interference by profiling interference and sensitivity on each kind of shared resources to guide cluster scheduler [63]. Lee et al. designed and implemented a scheduler in the virtual machine hypervisor for soft realtime applications [36]. Leverich et al. analyzed the source of QoS degradations of latency-critical workloads, and devised a new scheduler to handle these issues [37]. Paragon and Quasar are two task schedulers that classify applications and schedule them into data centers by performing resource allocation and assignment to minimizing interference [12, 13]. Q-Clouds and DeepDive are two QoS-aware scheduler that handle contentions and interference in virtual environment [51, 52]. These works are orthogonal to Dirigent and Dirigent can be integrated with these schemes to manage performance on each node.

7. Conclusion

In this work, we expose the problem of performance variation for latency-critical tasks when collocated with batch jobs and the associated challenges and opportunities. We explain how such variation leads to low hardware utilization and resource over-provisioning. Our main insight is that minimizing task-to-task variation offers significant opportunities for improving system utilization without compromising QoS goals. We present the design, implementation, and evaluation of the Dirigent lightweight contention management runtime to exploit these opportunities. Dirigent is effective because it can accurately predict the completion time of a running task at very fine time scales. It can thus control resources during a task's execution to meet deadlines and maximize batch throughput.

We show that Dirigent is particularly well suited for cloud-oriented applications where it is common to run just one latency-critical process per node and use batch-oriented tasks to improve utilization. In this case Dirigent exerts precise control over completion time and resources to boost utilization by $\sim 30\%$ compared to configurations that are similar to previously proposed schemes while providing higher QoS for the latency-critical tasks. We further show that even with multiple concurrent latency-critical tasks, Dirigent is still effective, much more so than alternative techniques, and always achieves very high deadline success rates ($> 98\%$).

We opted to implement Dirigent using existing hardware mechanisms and evaluate it on a real machine. Even without new hardware techniques, Dirigent has low runtime overhead ($< 100\mu s$ per invocation) and we are able to demonstrate the effectiveness and benefits of our techniques. However, for tasks with very tight latency constraints ($\lesssim$ 10ms) additional hardware support may be required. One limitation of the current Dirigent implementation is its dependency on profiling. In this paper we assumed offline profiling but because of the short profiling duration it can be performed online, though it will require pausing all BG tasks while profiling. In future work, we plan to improve the Dirigent prediction and control algorithms to allow concurrent profiling by adding interference offsets into the baseline execution time. A second limitation is that in this first effort with Dirigent, we limited our evaluation to performance variation caused by external interference. Accurate predictions of execution times in the presence of strong input dependence may require interfaces that extend Application Heartbeats [20] or program slicing [40]. Finally, we intend to evaluate Dirigent for parallel applications, where precise control over completion time reduces the overheads associated with synchronization and load imbalance.

Acknowledgment

We thank Huawei, which partially funded this research, the anonymous reviewers who provided valuable feedback and suggestions, and members of the Intel developers forum community who helped answer questions about use of processor features.

References

[1] Alia Atlas and Azer Bestavros. Statistical rate monotonic scheduling. In *Real-Time Systems Symposium, 1998. Proceedings., The 19th IEEE*. IEEE, 1998.

[2] Luiz Andres Barroso and Urs Hoelzle. *The Datacenter as a Computer: An Introduction to the Design of Warehouse-Scale Machines*. Morgan Claypool, 2009.

[3] Christian Bienia. *Benchmarking Modern Multiprocessors*. PhD thesis, Princeton University, January 2011.

[4] Dominik Brodowski and Nico Golde. CPU Frequency and Voltage Scaling Code in the Linux kernel.

[5] Tao Chen, Alexander Rucker, and G Edward Suh. Execution time prediction for energy-efficient hardware accelerators. In *Proceedings of the 48th International Symposium on Microarchitecture*. ACM, 2015.

[6] Yixin Chen and Li Tu. Density-based clustering for real-time stream data. In *Proceedings of the 13th ACM SIGKDD international conference on Knowledge discovery and data mining*. ACM, 2007.

[7] Derek Chiou, Prabhat Jain, Srinivas Devadas, and Larry Rudolph. Dynamic cache partitioning via columnization. In *Proceedings of Design Automation Conference*. Citeseer, 2000.

[8] Jason Clemons, Haishan Zhu, Silvio Savarese, and Todd Austin. Mevbench: A mobile computer vision benchmarking suite. In *Workload Characterization (IISWC), 2011 IEEE International Symposium on*. IEEE, 2011.

[9] Henry Cook, Miquel Moreto, Sarah Bird, Khanh Dao, David A Patterson, and Krste Asanovic. A hardware evaluation of cache partitioning to improve utilization and energy-efficiency while preserving responsiveness. In *ACM SIGARCH Computer Architecture News*. ACM, 2013.

[10] Ryan R. Curtin, James R. Cline, Neil P. Slagle, William B. March, P. Ram, Nishant A. Mehta, and Alexander G. Gray. MLPACK: A scalable C++ machine learning library. *Journal of Machine Learning Research*, 2013.

[11] Jeffrey Dean and Luiz André Barroso. The tail at scale. *Communications of the ACM*, 2013.

[12] Christina Delimitrou and Christos Kozyrakis. Paragon: Qos-aware scheduling for heterogeneous datacenters. *ACM SIGARCH Computer Architecture News*, 2013.

[13] Christina Delimitrou and Christos Kozyrakis. Quasar: Resource-efficient and qos-aware cluster management. *ACM SIGPLAN Notices*, 2014.

[14] Eiman Ebrahimi, Chang Joo Lee, Onur Mutlu, and Yale N Patt. Fairness via source throttling: a configurable and high-performance fairness substrate for multi-core memory systems. In *ACM Sigplan Notices*. ACM, 2010.

[15] Eiman Ebrahimi, Chang Joo Lee, Onur Mutlu, and Yale N Patt. Prefetch-aware shared resource management for multi-core systems. *ACM SIGARCH Computer Architecture News*, 2011.

[16] Xiaobo Fan, Wolf-Dietrich Weber, and Luiz Andre Barroso. Power provisioning for a warehouse-sized computer. In *ACM SIGARCH Computer Architecture News*. ACM, 2007.

[17] Johann Hauswald, Michael A Laurenzano, Yunqi Zhang, Cheng Li, Austin Rovinski, Arjun Khurana, Ronald G Dreslinski, Trevor Mudge, Vinicius Petrucci, Lingjia Tang, et al. Sirius: An open end-to-end voice and vision personal assistant and its implications for future warehouse scale computers. In *Proceedings of the Twentieth International Conference on Architectural Support for Programming Languages and Operating Systems*. ACM, 2015.

[18] John L. Henning. Spec cpu2006 benchmark descriptions. *SIGARCH Comput. Archit. News*, 2006.

[19] Andrew Herdrich, Ramesh Illikkal, Ravi Iyer, Don Newell, Vineet Chadha, and Jaideep Moses. Rate-based qos techniques for cache/memory in cmp platforms. In *Proceedings of the 23rd international conference on Supercomputing*. ACM, 2009.

[20] Henry Hoffmann, Jonathan Eastep, Marco D Santambrogio, Jason E Miller, and Anant Agarwal. Application heartbeats: a generic interface for specifying program performance and goals in autonomous computing environments. In *Proceedings of the 7th international conference on Autonomic computing*. ACM, 2010.

[21] Chang-Hong Hsu, Yunqi Zhang, Michael Laurenzano, David Meisner, Thomas Wenisch, Jason Mars, Lingjia Tang, Ronald G Dreslinski, et al. Adrenaline: Pinpointing and reining in tail queries with quick voltage boosting. In *High Performance Computer Architecture (HPCA), 2015 IEEE 21st International Symposium on*. IEEE, 2015.

[22] Ramesh Illikkal, Vineet Chadha, Andrew Herdrich, Ravi Iyer, and Donald Newell. PIRATE: QoS and performance management in CMP architectures. *ACM SIGMETRICS Performance Evaluation Review*, 2010.

[23] Intel. Intel Product Information.

[24] Intel. Cache Monitoring Technology and Cache Allocation Technology.

[25] Intel. Intel 64 and IA-32 Architectures Software Developer Manuals.

[26] Ravi Iyer. Cqos: a framework for enabling qos in shared caches of cmp platforms. In *Proceedings of the 18th annual international conference on Supercomputing*. ACM, 2004.

[27] Ravi Iyer, Li Zhao, Fei Guo, Ramesh Illikkal, Srihari Makineni, Don Newell, Yan Solihin, Lisa Hsu, and Steve Reinhardt. Qos policies and architecture for cache/memory in cmp platforms. *ACM SIGMETRICS Performance Evaluation Review*, 2007.

[28] Min Kyu Jeong, Mattan Erez, Chander Sudanthi, and Nigel Paver. A qos-aware memory controller for dynamically balancing gpu and cpu bandwidth use in an mpsoc. In *Proceedings of the 49th Annual Design Automation Conference*. ACM, 2012.

[29] Min Kyu Jeong, Doe Hyun Yoon, Dam Sunwoo, Mike Sullivan, Ikhwan Lee, and Mattan Erez. Balancing dram locality and parallelism in shared memory cmp systems. In *High Performance Computer Architecture (HPCA), 2012 IEEE 18th International Symposium on*. IEEE, 2012.

[30] Melanie Kambadur, Tipp Moseley, Rick Hank, and Martha A. Kim. Measuring interference between live datacenter applica-

tions. In *Proceedings of the International Conference on High Performance Computing, Networking, Storage and Analysis*, SC '12, 2012.

[31] Harshad Kasture, Davide B Bartolini Nathan Beckmann, and Daniel Sanchez. Rubik: Fast analytical power management for latency-critical systems. In *Proceedings of the 48th International Symposium on Microarchitecture*. ACM, 2015.

[32] Harshad Kasture and Daniel Sanchez. Ubik: efficient cache sharing with strict qos for latency-critical workloads. *ACM SIGARCH Computer Architecture News*, 2014.

[33] Wonyoung Kim, Meeta S Gupta, Gu-Yeon Wei, and David Brooks. System level analysis of fast, per-core dvfs using on-chip switching regulators. In *High Performance Computer Architecture, 2008. HPCA 2008. IEEE 14th International Symposium on*. IEEE, 2008.

[34] Yoongu Kim, Dongsu Han, Onur Mutlu, and Mor Harchol-Balter. Atlas: A scalable and high-performance scheduling algorithm for multiple memory controllers. In *High Performance Computer Architecture (HPCA), 2010 IEEE 16th International Symposium on*. IEEE, 2010.

[35] Karthik Kumar, Jibang Liu, Yung-Hsiang Lu, and Bharat Bhargava. A survey of computation offloading for mobile systems. *Mobile Networks and Applications*, 2013.

[36] Min Lee, AS Krishnakumar, Parameshwaran Krishnan, Navjot Singh, and Shalini Yajnik. Supporting soft real-time tasks in the xen hypervisor. In *ACM Sigplan Notices*. ACM, 2010.

[37] Jacob Leverich and Christos Kozyrakis. Reconciling high server utilization and sub-millisecond quality-of-service. In *Proceedings of the Ninth European Conference on Computer Systems*, EuroSys '14, 2014.

[38] Chit-Kwan Lin and H. T. Kung. Mobile app acceleration via fine-grain offloading to the cloud. In *6th USENIX Workshop on Hot Topics in Cloud Computing (HotCloud 14)*. USENIX Association, 2014.

[39] Fang Liu, Xiaowei Jiang, and Yan Solihin. Understanding how off-chip memory bandwidth partitioning in chip multiprocessors affects system performance. In *High Performance Computer Architecture (HPCA), 2010 IEEE 16th International Symposium on*. IEEE, 2010.

[40] Daniel Lo, Taejoon Song, and G Edward Suh. Prediction-guided performance-energy trade-off for interactive applications. In *Proceedings of the 48th International Symposium on Microarchitecture*. ACM, 2015.

[41] David Lo, Liqun Cheng, Rama Govindaraju, Luiz André Barroso, and Christos Kozyrakis. Towards energy proportionality for large-scale latency-critical workloads. In *Proceeding of the 41st annual international symposium on Computer architecture*. IEEE Press, 2014.

[42] David Lo, Liqun Cheng, Rama Govindaraju, Parthasarathy Ranganathan, and Christos Kozyrakis. Heracles: improving resource efficiency at scale. In *Proceedings of the 42nd Annual International Symposium on Computer Architecture*. ACM, 2015.

[43] Ying Lu, Tarek Abdelzaher, Chenyang Lu, and Gang Tao. An adaptive control framework for qos guarantees and its application to differentiated caching. In *Quality of Service, 2002. Tenth IEEE International Workshop on*. IEEE, 2002.

[44] Jiuyue Ma, Xiufeng Sui, Ninghui Sun, Yupeng Li, Zihao Yu, Bowen Huang, Tianni Xu, Zhicheng Yao, Yun Chen, Haibin Wang, et al. Supporting differentiated services in computers via programmable architecture for resourcing-on-demand (pard). In *Proceedings of the Twentieth International Conference on Architectural Support for Programming Languages and Operating Systems*. ACM, 2015.

[45] Jason Mars, Lingjia Tang, Robert Hundt, Kevin Skadron, and Mary Lou Soffa. Bubble-up: Increasing utilization in modern warehouse scale computers via sensible co-locations. In *Proceedings of the 44th annual IEEE/ACM International Symposium on Microarchitecture*. ACM, 2011.

[46] David Meisner, Brian T. Gold, and Thomas F. Wenisch. Powernap: Eliminating server idle power. In *Proceedings of the 14th International Conference on Architectural Support for Programming Languages and Operating Systems*, ASPLOS XIV. ACM, 2009.

[47] Rustam Miftakhutdinov, Eiman Ebrahimi, and Yale N Patt. Predicting performance impact of dvfs for realistic memory systems. In *Proceedings of the 2012 45th Annual IEEE/ACM International Symposium on Microarchitecture*. IEEE Computer Society, 2012.

[48] Sai Prashanth Muralidhara, Lavanya Subramanian, Onur Mutlu, Mahmut Kandemir, and Thomas Moscibroda. Reducing memory interference in multicore systems via application-aware memory channel partitioning. In *Proceedings of the 44th Annual IEEE/ACM International Symposium on Microarchitecture*. ACM, 2011.

[49] Onur Mutlu and Thomas Moscibroda. Stall-time fair memory access scheduling for chip multiprocessors. In *Proceedings of the 40th Annual IEEE/ACM International Symposium on Microarchitecture*. IEEE Computer Society, 2007.

[50] Onur Mutlu and Thomas Moscibroda. Parallelism-aware batch scheduling: Enhancing both performance and fairness of shared dram systems. In *ACM SIGARCH Computer Architecture News*. IEEE Computer Society, 2008.

[51] Ripal Nathuji, Aman Kansal, and Alireza Ghaffarkhah. Q-clouds: managing performance interference effects for qos-aware clouds. In *Proceedings of the 5th European conference on Computer systems*. ACM, 2010.

[52] Dejan Novakovic, Nedeljko Vasic, Stanko Novakovic, Dejan Kostic, and Ricardo Bianchini. Deepdive: Transparently identifying and managing performance interference in virtualized environments. Technical Report 183449, EPFL, 2013.

[53] Moinuddin K Qureshi and Yale N Patt. Utility-based cache partitioning: A low-overhead, high-performance, runtime mechanism to partition shared caches. In *Proceedings of the 39th Annual IEEE/ACM International Symposium on Microarchitecture*. IEEE Computer Society, 2006.

[54] Arun Raghavan, Yixin Luo, Anuj Chandawalla, Marios Papaefthymiou, Kevin P Pipe, Thomas F Wenisch, and Milo MK Martin. Computational sprinting. In *High Performance Computer Architecture (HPCA), 2012 IEEE 18th International Symposium on*. IEEE, 2012.

[55] Daniel Sanchez and Christos Kozyrakis. Vantage: scalable and efficient fine-grain cache partitioning. In *ACM SIGARCH Computer Architecture News*. ACM, 2011.

[56] Lui Sha, Tarek Abdelzaher, Karl-Erik Årzén, Anton Cervin, Theodore Baker, Alan Burns, Giorgio Buttazzo, Marco Caccamo, John Lehoczky, and Aloysius K Mok. Real time scheduling theory: A historical perspective. *Real-time systems*, 2004.

[57] Techspot. Facebook to build a $1 billion wind-powered data center in Fort Worth.

[58] Hiroyuki Usui, Lavanya Subramanian, Kevin Chang, and Onur Mutlu. Squash: Simple qos-aware high-performance memory scheduler for heterogeneous systems with hardware accelerators. *arXiv preprint arXiv:1505.07502*, 2015.

[59] Balajee Vamanan, Hamza Bin Sohail, Jahangir Hasan, and TN Vijaykumar. Timetrader: Exploiting latency tail to save datacenter energy for online search. In *Proceedings of the 48th International Symposium on Microarchitecture*. ACM, 2015.

[60] Hailong Yang, Alex Breslow, Jason Mars, and Lingjia Tang. Bubble-flux: Precise online qos management for increased utilization in warehouse scale computers. In *ACM SIGARCH Computer Architecture News*. ACM, 2013.

[61] Heechul Yun, Gang Yao, Rodolfo Pellizzoni, Marco Caccamo, and Lui Sha. Memguard: Memory bandwidth reservation system for efficient performance isolation in multi-core platforms. In *Real-Time and Embedded Technology and Applications Symposium (RTAS), 2013 IEEE 19th*. IEEE, 2013.

[62] Xiao Zhang, Eric Tune, Robert Hagmann, Rohit Jnagal, Vrigo Gokhale, and John Wilkes. Cpi2: Cpu performance isolation for shared compute clusters. In *Proceedings of the 8th ACM European Conference on Computer Systems*, EuroSys '13, New York, NY, USA, 2013. ACM.

[63] Yunqi Zhang, Michael A. Laurenzano, Jason Mars, and Lingjia Tang. Smite: Precise qos prediction on real-system smt processors to improve utilization in warehouse scale computers. In *Proceedings of the 47th Annual IEEE/ACM International Symposium on Microarchitecture*, MICRO-47, 2014.

[64] Jiacheng Zhao, Huimin Cui, Jingling Xue, Xiaobing Feng, Youliang Yan, and Wensen Yang. An empirical model for predicting cross-core performance interference on multicore processors. In *Proceedings of the 22Nd International Conference on Parallel Architectures and Compilation Techniques*, PACT '13, 2013.

[65] Yanqi Zhou and David Wentzlaff. The sharing architecture: sub-core configurability for iaas clouds. In *ACM SIGARCH Computer Architecture News*. ACM, 2014.

Paravirtual Remote I/O

Yossi Kuperman
Technion – Israel institute of Technology & IBM Research—Haifa
skyossi@cs.technion.ac.il

Eyal Moscovici
Technion – Israel institute of Technology & IBM Research—Haifa
emos@cs.technion.ac.il

Joel Nider
IBM Research—Haifa
joeln@il.ibm.com

Razya Ladelsky
IBM Research—Haifa
razya@il.ibm.com

Abel Gordon
IBM Research—Haifa & Stratoscale
abel.gordon@gmail.com

Dan Tsafrir
Technion – Israel institute of Technology
dan@cs.technion.ac.il

Abstract

The traditional "trap and emulate" I/O paravirtualization model conveniently allows for I/O interposition, yet it inherently incurs costly guest-host context switches. The newer "sidecore" model eliminates this overhead by dedicating host (side)cores to poll the relevant guest memory regions and react accordingly without context switching. But the dedication of sidecores on each host might be wasteful when I/O activity is low, or it might not provide enough computational power when I/O activity is high. We propose to alleviate this problem at rack scale by consolidating the dedicated sidecores spread across several hosts onto one server. The hypervisor is then effectively split into two parts: the local hypervisor that hosts the VMs, and the remote hypervisor that processes their paravirtual I/O. We call this model vRIO—paraVirtual Remote I/O. We find that by increasing the latency somewhat, it provides comparable throughput with fewer sidecores and superior throughput with the same number of sidecores as compared to the state of the art. vRIO additionally constitutes a new, cost-effective way to consolidate I/O devices (on the remote hypervisor) while supporting efficient programmable I/O interposition.

1. Introduction

Interposition I/O virtualization decouples logical from physical I/O through an indirection layer. The host exposes a virtual I/O device to its guest virtual machines (VMs). It then intercepts ("traps") VM requests directed at the virtual device, and it fulfills ("emulates") them using the physical hardware. This trap-and-emulate approach [28,54] allows the host to *interpose* on the I/O activity of its guests.

The benefits of I/O interposition are substantial [69]: improving utilization of the physical devices via time and space multiplexing; enabling live migration and suspend/resume using the indirection layer to decouple and recouple VMs from/to the physical device; enabling seamless switching between different I/O channels, which allows for device aggregation, load balancing, and failure masking; and supporting such features as monitoring, software-defined networking (SDN), file-based images, replication, deduplication, snapshots, and security related functionalities such as record-replay, encryption, firewalls, and intrusion detection.

SRIOV The virtual I/O indirection layer hinders performance, mainly due to the overhead generated by *exits* [1], namely, the guest-host context switches upon I/O operations, which are being trapped and emulated. This overhead has motivated hardware vendors to develop the Single Root I/O Virtualization (SRIOV) technology [34,52], whereby a physical I/O device can self-virtualize, supporting multiple virtual instances of itself that can be individually assigned to VMs. SRIOV thus bypasses the host, which is largely removed from the critical data path. The result is significantly better performance for I/O intensive workloads [41,44,46,56,72,76]. There is a serious drawback, however, to using SRIOV, as it eliminates the indirection layer and thus only provides multiplexing out of the benefits of virtual I/O listed above. Notably, SRIOV negates live migration, memory overcommitment, metering, and other such features that rely on interposition and that are crucial for VM environments.

Paravirtualization Consequently, real-world applications of virtualization today, including most enterprise data centers and cloud computing sites, seldom use SRIOV. Instead, they realize virtual I/O through *paravirtualization* [11,58,66,70],

ASPLOS '16, April 2–6, 2016, Atlanta, GA, USA..

ACM 978-1-4503-4091-5/16/04. . . $15.00.
http://dx.doi.org/10.1145/2872362.2872378

exemplified by VMware VMXNET3 [67], KVM virtio [58], and Xen PV [11]. Paravirtual I/O boosts the performance of the virtualization indirection layer while retaining all the aforementioned benefits of interposable virtual I/O. Paravirtualization achieves this goal by requiring guests to install a host-specific device driver that is purely software based. The latter is not modeled after any real device. Rather, it is optimized to minimize the overheads associated with guest-host communication and context switching.

Sidecores While offering an improvement, paravirtualization still hampers performance due to the exits it induces [13, 22, 40, 44, 57, 74]. Recent studies show that the *sidecore* approach is effective in combating this problem [4, 13, 31, 39, 43, 45]. The host's cores are divided to (1) sidecores dedicated to processing virtual I/O, and to (2) *VMcores* for running the VMs that generate the I/O. Each VM writes its I/O requests to memory shared with the host as is usual for the paravirtual I/O model. Unusual, however, is that VM does not trigger an exit. Instead, the host sidecore polls the relevant memory region and processes the request on arrival. The benefit of this approach is twofold: more cycles to the VMs (whose OSes are asynchronous in nature and do not block-wait for I/O) and less cache pollution, yielding a substantial performance improvement. For example, the Elvis system—which implements paravirtual block and net devices on sidecores—is up to 3x more performant than baseline paravirtualization and is oftentimes on par with SRIOV [31].

The sidecore virtual I/O model has an inherent drawback. A sidecore must continuously poll the relevant memory regions of its associated VMs. Therefore, 100% of the sidecore's cycles are consumed, even when the I/O load generated by these VMs is light. In this case, polling wastes valuable CPU cycles that could have otherwise been used to support other, more productive activity. Conversely, it is also possible that the load generated by the corresponding VMs exceeds the processing capabilities of their designated sidecores, and thus the sidecores might become a bottleneck in the system.

Sidecore Consolidation The most notable benefit of virtualization is, arguably, resource consolidation, enabling multiple OSes to multiplex the physical hardware. Experience shows that multiple virtual servers can be adequately serviced by much fewer physical servers. We contend that the same reasoning holds for sidecores, and that applying it will alleviate the problem of having too few or too many per-server sidecores, making this newer I/O model more cost effective.

Departing from the traditional trap-and-emulate virtualization model, the sidecore paradigm already decouples the host's I/O processing from the VM's core, executing it on a different (side)core. In the context of rack scale computing, we propose to take this paradigm a step further and migrate sidecores to a different server. We call this I/O model Paravirtual **R**emote **I/O** (vRIO). In vRIO, hosts are either *VMhosts* or *IOhosts*, consisting of either VMcores or sidecores. VMhosts do not process (and are unaware of) the paravirtual I/O of their VMs. Consolidating the sidecores in IOhosts allows us to achieve superior performance using the same number of CPUs, or comparable performance using fewer CPUs. In exchange for reducing the CPU number, vRIO requires additional networking infrastructure in the rack; we show how this tradeoff yields a cheaper system.

Device Consolidation Supporting the cost-effectiveness of the net/CPU tradeoff is the fact that vRIO introduces a new type of device consolidation for VMs. Splitting the hypervisor into local and remote components makes the remote devices at the IOhost efficiently accessible to local VMs via the paravirtual I/O interface. Note that this feature is complementary to existing device consolidation approaches, such as storage area networks (SANs). The reason: if the VM is configured to use a SAN directly (not as a virtual device), then we lose interposition entirely. Otherwise, the SAN is exposed to the VM as a traditional paravirtual device and so the associated overheads of traditional paravirtualization come into play yet again.

Hypervisor Independence The vRIO model bypasses the local hypervisor, so the vRIO driver is independent of the local hypervisor, thus providing several additional advantages. It is possible, for example, to implement a layer-2 virtual LAN that seamlessly works for virtualized OSes across different processor architectures and hypervisor types. This feature is valuable, as there are nowadays fewer (guest) OSes in widespread use than hypervisors. vRIO also supports bare metal (non-virtual) OSes that install its driver, e.g., they too can be easily incorporated in the aforementioned LAN.

Notably, system-wide services and policies can be implemented for all hypervisor types in one location. Moreover, the IOhost hardware can be specialized for I/O processing.

Minimizing Latency To enjoy the benefits of vRIO, we must make the penalty of adding one hop to the I/O path tolerable. To this end, somewhat surprisingly, we utilize SRIOV. Whereas SRIOV negates interposition in existing I/O models, vRIO is able to use it in a compatible manner. Specifically, the vRIO paravirtual driver installed in the VM generates the same I/O as in traditional paravirtualization. But instead of handing the I/O to the local hypervisor via shared memory, the vRIO driver communicates it to the IOhost through an SRIOV channel. Additionally, vRIO entirely eliminates the overhead of interrupt processing from the virtualization layer by: (1) coupling the SRIOV channel with exitless interrupts [5, 29] at the VMhost; and by (2) polling the Network Interface Controllers (NICs) at the IOhost in accordance to the sidecore paradigm.

Preview of Results vRIO trades off CPUs for NICs and latency for improved resource utilization. We describe supposed vRIO setups that are 8–38% cheaper than the alternative, and we manage to bound vRIO's latency to be at most 1.18x longer than state-of-the-art sidecore paravirtualization for network I/O. The latency is up to 2.20x longer if, in addition to sidecores, we also migrate local block devices to reside in the remote IOhost. The benefit is achieving, e.g., 1.82x the throughput using the same number of sidecores, or 0.92x the throughput using half the number of sidecores.

2. Existing Virtual I/O Models

The vRIO model builds on and extends existing I/O virtualization models. Next, we briefly survey them, highlighting some additional aspects beyond those already mentioned above.

The most naive implementation of virtual I/O devices is *emulation*, whereby the hypervisor implements an interface identical to that of an existing, widely supported hardware device. (For NICs, this is Intel's e1000.) The hypervisor delivers the required functionality by trapping and emulating [28, 54]. Emulation is convenient, because it is hypervisor-agnostic and leaves VMs unaware of being virtualized.

Baseline The cost of emulation is degraded performance, as the physical device was not designed with virtualization in mind, inducing costly exits upon each interaction between the VM and its emulated device. Consequently, installations overwhelmingly prefer *paravirtualization*, which is similar to emulation except that the emulated device does not correspond to any existing hardware but instead is designed to minimize VM-device interactions. Despite being similar in essence across different hypervisors, paravirtual device drivers are hypervisor-specific, because vendors opted to use different interfaces. Thus, VMs must install the appropriate paravirtual device drivers to reap the benefit. In the paper, we use KVM virtio [58] as the state-of-practice representative of paravirtualization. We denote it as the *baseline* configuration.

Optimum Although more performant than naive emulation, paravirtualization still traps upon every I/O request and thus fails to deliver bare metal (non-virtual) performance [41, 46, 56, 72, 76]. The PCI-SIG has thus standardized the SRIOV extension of PCIe [34, 52], which allows physical I/O devices to *self-virtualize* and support multiple virtual instances of themselves such that each instance can be assigned to a different VM. SRIOV outperforms paravirtualization, as I/O requests generated by guests do not trap. But it does not provide bare metal performance, because device interrupts are still handled by the host [5, 14, 22, 29, 31, 40, 44, 72]. The *exitless interrupts* approach (denoted *Eli*) overcomes this barrier, devising a virtual I/O model in which guests directly receive the interrupts of their SRIOV instances without host involvement [5, 29]. SRIOV+Eli provides bare metal performance for VMs. We thus denote it as the *optimum* configuration.

Despite the hype, using SRIOV is problematic, because it negates many of the key benefits of virtualization that rest on interposition. For example, it conflicts with memory overcommitment and host swapping [6], as DMAs do not tolerate page faults, forcing the host to either pin the entire image of the VM to memory [12, 53], or to become aware of all its DMA target buffers via explicit guest-host interaction [4, 15, 41, 62, 71]. SRIOV likewise conflicts with live migration [38, 51, 64, 77], because the source host cannot decouple the device while it is working, and because the target host might not have this particular device. Other problems include the host not being able to meter, account for, suspend, resume, log, isolate, and manipulate the I/O activity [30]. All the features that interposable I/O provides are missing.

Elvis The *sidecore* approach is an interposable I/O model that provides all the benefits of—but is more performant than—traditional paravirtualization. The approach dedicates cores to poll relevant memory regions, observe changes that reflect I/O requests, and process these requests without inducing the overhead of trapping. The sidecore paradigm has been applied to various tasks such as IOMMU virtualization [4], storage virtualization [13], TCP/IP processing [33], and GPU processing [63]. The *Elvis* system applies this paradigm to our baseline KVM virtio setup [31]. It utilizes Eli to deliver exitless interrupts (in the form of IPIs) from host (side)cores to guest cores. Elvis was shown to be superior to the baseline, oftentimes approaching the optimum. The Elvis source code is publicly available [23]; we use it as a representative of the state-of-the-art of interposable virtual I/O.

The number of sidecores utilized by Elvis is static, so their computational power might be too low or to high, thereby wasting valuable cycles or hindering performance. Conceivably, we could dynamically (de)allocate sidecores in response to the changing load [49]. But this approach is limited for two reasons. First, because sidecores are discrete—it is impossible to allocate a fraction of a sidecore even if only a fraction is required. Namely, if only p of the sidecore's cycles are needed, then $1-p$ are wasted. The second, more significant limitation of dynamic sidecore allocation is that it is irrelevant when the aggregated need for VM and I/O processing exceeds the capacity of the individual physical server, for example, because of load imbalance. In such cases, we might consider to resort to live migration so as to hand some of the work to another server. But live migration is a costly, coarse-grained activity that noticeably disrupts service, with reduced response times and downtimes that might reach seconds to tens of seconds [7, 17, 36, 47, 59, 68, 73]; this limitation may explain why Amazon's AWS does not support live migration as some anecdotal evidence suggests [55]. vRIO, in contrast, is better suited to accommodate workload imbalance. (In addition to its other benefits, like I/O device consolidation with efficient programmable interposition.)

3. Cost Effectiveness of vRIO

Using vRIO involves hardware tradeoffs; in this section, we assess the associated cost.

Price Trends The vRIO infrastructure allows the number of processors and other devices local to the server to be reduced (by consolidating them in the IOhost), at the cost of increasing

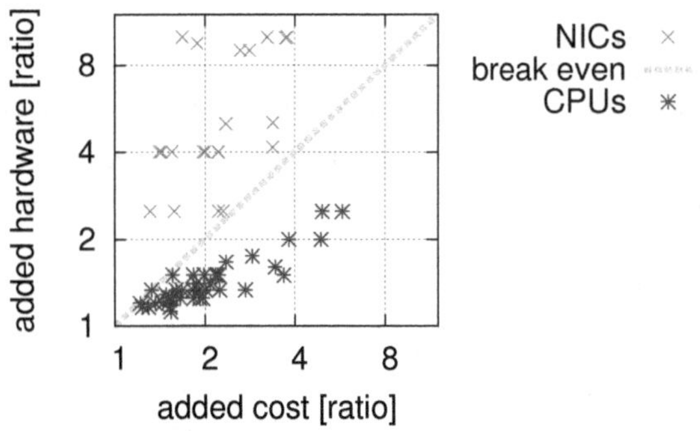

Figure 1. *Within the server, CPU upgrades are costlier than NIC upgrades. CPU data is based on Intel's pricing list [35]. NIC data is based on multiple web sources.*

the number of NICs in that server. Figure 1 shows current trends in NIC and CPU costs that suggest that this tradeoff may be advantageous. The CPU data points in the figure are computed based on the latest pricing list of Intel processors as of this writing [35]. Each data point corresponds to an "adjacent" pair of Xeon CPUs, such that CPUs c_1 and c_2 are adjacent if: (1) the number of cores of c_1 is smaller than that of c_2; (2) the series, version, speed (GHz), and feature size (nm) of the two are identical; and (3) the cache size (MB), power (W), and QPI speed (GT/s) of c_1 are proportionally smaller than or equal to that of c_2. For example, the following two CPUs are adjacent:

c_1: \$3,059 **12**-core 2.3GHz E7-8850 v2 24MB 105W 7.2GT/s QPI 22nm
c_2: \$4,616 **15**-core 2.3GHz E7-8870 v2 30MB 130W 8.0GT/s QPI 22nm

The (x,y) data points in Figure 1 reflect the relative cost of upgrading from c_1 to c_2 and the resulting relative number of added cores: $x = \frac{\$4,616}{\$3,059} \approx 1.51$ and $y = \frac{15\text{cores}}{12\text{cores}} = 1.25$.

The NIC data points in Figure 1 are equivalently computed based on "adjacent" NIC pairs from Chelsio, Dell, Emulex, HotLava, Intel, Mellanox, and SolarFlare. NICs n_1 and n_2 are adjacent if: (1) the throughout of n_1 is smaller than that of n_2; (2) their vendor, product series, port number, form factor, connector type, and offload capabilities are the same; and (3) the power and PCIe generation and lanes of n_1 are proportionally smaller than or equal to that of n_2. For example, the following two Mellanox NICs are adjacent:

n_1: \$560 2x**10**GbE ConnectX-3 MCX312B-XCCT SFP+ PCIe3 x8
n_2: \$1121 2x**40**GbE ConnectX-3 MCX314A-BCCT QSFP PCIe3 x8

The corresponding (x,y) data points in Figure 1 likewise reflect the relative upgrade cost and the consequent added bandwidth. In our example, $x = \frac{\$1121}{\$560} \approx 2$ and $y = \frac{80\text{Gbps}}{20\text{Gbps}} = 4$.

Clearly, all CPU data points in Figure 1 are below the main diagonal, whereas NIC data points are above, indicating that augmenting a server's compute hardware involves a premium absent from augmenting its NICs. A similar observation was made regarding the rapidly declining per-port price of network switches and switch modules [16, 75].[1]

One reason underlying the price trends observed in Figure 1 might perhaps be that the server-class processor market is largely dominated by Intel, whereas NICs are manufactured and sold by multiple competing vendors. A second reason could the objective difficulty involved in designing a general purpose computational processor as opposed to a domain-specific one. Regardless of the reason, the observed trends suggest that utilizing CPUs more efficiently (and thus having to purchase less of them) with the help of some additional networking infrastructure could be cost beneficial.

Cost Benefit of vRIO CPU Consolidation We next exemplify the cost tradeoffs made possible with vRIO. Networking infrastructure involves more than just NICs, so the way to check whether vRIO is cost effective is to assess the price of incorporating it in a real rack setup. We use Dell's website, which associates prices with server components, allowing us to configure them online [21] and to compare prices of equivalent Elvis and vRIO systems. We only apply changes to individual servers, possibly rewiring them to an IOhost instead of the switch, as indicated. We constrain the discussion to a single Dell server model for simplicity, although it is likely cheaper to specialize the IOhost. Our comparison applies to racks with 10GbE or 40GbE switches/cabling. We assume 10GbE, as it is more widely deployed [19]. All setups mentioned in this section can be purchased from Dell as specified. We account for the price of *all* the hardware we use, notably networking hardware.

VMhosts can be connected to their IOhost directly or via a switch. Next, we consider the former alternative, which is cheaper, because it allows us to utilize the existing switch and cabling without hampering performance—vRIO supports the same volume of network traffic as its competitors. In §4.6, we consider the drawbacks of this approach and the alternative of connecting VMhosts to IOhosts through a switch.

Consider three Dell PowerEdge R930 Elvis servers, each equipped with two 10Gbps dual-port NICs and four 18-core CPUs, such that 1/3 of the cores serve as sidecores (we demonstrate the use of such a ratio at the end of §5). We calculate the compute-to-network rate based on a study that measured the per-core network throughput granted by 4 cloud providers (Amazon, Google, Rackspace, and Softlayer) and found it to be between 113–380 Mbps when cores concurrently engage in networking [50]. For our R930, this finding translates to at most $4(\text{CPUs}) \times 18(\text{cores}) \times 380\text{Mbps} = 26.72\text{Gbps}$ per server, which is why it is enough to connect to the switch only 3 out of the 4 per-server 10Gbps ports, as shown in Figure 2a.

We contend (and show below) that vRIO allows for efficient sidecore consolidation, thereby providing all the benefits

[1] The observation regarding the declining cost of networking infrastructure is applicable within the rack, as its size is fixed. It may not be applicable to networking infrastructure between racks in growing data centers that house more and more racks [30]. The scope of this work is rack scale.

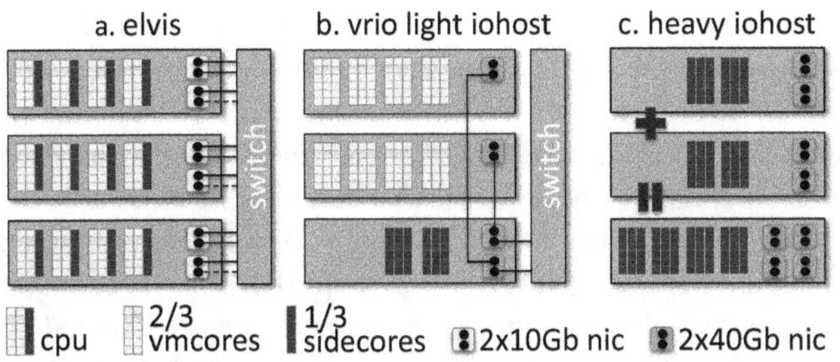

Figure 2. *Elvis sidecores (a) consolidated by vRIO (b), allow an IOhost with only 2 CPUs. Two such "light" IOhosts can be merged into a single "heavy" IOhost (c). If the switch supports 10GbE only, IOhosts are connected to it with 1x40 to 4x10 GbE cables.*

component	*price*	*elvis*	*vmhost*	*light iohost*	*heavy iohost*
base	$6,407	1	1	1	1
18 core CPU	$8,006	4	4	2	4
8GB DRAM	$172		2	8	8
16GB DRAM	$273	18	26		
10Gbps NIC DP	$560	2			
40Gbps NIC DP	$1,121		1	2	4
total server price		$44.5K	$47.0K	$26.0K	$44.2K
total Gbps		40.00	80.00	160.00	320.00
required Gbps		26.72	40.08	160.31	320.63

Table 1. *Dell R930 per-server price, components, and throughput. The CPU is an 18-core 2.5GHz Intel Xeon E7-8890 v3. The NICs pertain to the dual port (DP) Mellanox adapters mentioned earlier; their price includes cable. In the VMhost, we use 2x8GB instead of one 16GB DIMM, as the DIMM number must be even.*

setup	*elvis servers*	*vrio servers*	*elvis price*	*vrio price*	*diff.*
R930 x 3	3	2+1	$133.4K	$120.0K	-10%
R930 x 6	6	4+1	$266.9K	$232.3K	-13%

Table 2. *Overall price of the Elvis and vRIO setups. The $k+j$ notation specifies the number of VMhosts (k) and IOhosts (j).*

regularly associated with virtualization. Specifically, when assuming that the workload is such that most VMs do not typically utilize *all* their resources *all* the time, we contend that vRIO is capable of delivering comparable performance with, e.g., half the number of sidecores (depending on the workload). Alternatively, vRIO is capable of boosting the performance with the same number of sidecores. In this section, we focus on the former case of halving the number. The corresponding vRIO setup is depicted in Figure 2b; halving allows us to use a "lighter" server as the IOhost with half the CPUs, while leaving the overall number of VMcores identical in both the Elvis and vRIO setups across the three servers.

Assigning the VMs that previously ran on the IOhost to the two VMhosts means that each of them should now handle $1\frac{1}{2}$x the VMs. They have exactly that many additional (VM)cores thanks to the sidecore reconfiguration. But they also need a proportionally higher bandwidth: 26.72Gbps $\times\ 1\frac{1}{2}$ = 40.08Gbps per VMhost. The IOhost needs even more: it should handle twice the aggregated throughput of the VMhosts, as every packet transmitted or received by a VMhost must also be (i) received and (ii) retransmitted by the IOhost. The IOhost must therefore handle 2×2(VMhosts) $\times$ 40.08Gbps = 160.31Gbps. We support these bandwidths by installing one and two 40Gbps dual-port NICs in the VMhosts and IOhost, which provide 80 Gbps and 160 Gbps, respectively.

Notably, the use of 40Gbps NICs between VMhosts and IOhosts is agnostic to whether the switch supports 10GbE or 40GbE. And IOhost ports are connected to the switch using either 40GbE-to-4x10GbE cables (assuming a 10GbE switch) or 40GbE cables (assuming a 40GbE switch); in both cases the number of cables connecting the IOhost to the switch is smaller than the corresponding number in the Elvis setup.

Like bandwidth, the memory of the VMhost is $1\frac{1}{2}$x bigger. We use a rate of 4GB per core, so each Elvis server is equipped with 72 (cores) x 4GB = 288 GB, and each VMhost is equipped with 432 GB. Conversely, the IOhost memory requirements are minimal, because its sole purpose is handling the network activity that flows through it. We equip it with 64GB (minimum for R930), which is more than enough.

If we take *two* Elvis 3 x R930 setups and transform them to vRIO, we can merge their two "light" IOhosts into a single "heavy" IOhost as depicted in Figure 2c, thereby utilizing five servers instead of six for increased savings. The throughput and prices of individual R930 server types are specified in Table 1. We list the cost and relative difference between the setups we configured in Table 2, which indicates that the vRIO setups are 10% and 13% cheaper.

Cost Benefit of vRIO Device Consolidation A vRIO setup can use the IOhost to further consolidate other devices, in addition to sidecores—SSDs, for example. Such consolidation is *inherently* orthogonal and complementary to other systems that offer storage consolidation, such as SANs, as: (1) if VMs are allowed to use a SAN directly—not through a paravirtual device—then the host forgoes the ability to perform programmable general-purpose interposition; and (2) if the SAN *is* made available to VMs as a traditional paravirtual device, then the associated excessive overheads take effect. vRIO's goal is to alleviate these overheads and allow for performant programmable interposition. Consequently, it makes sense to expose SANs via vRIO in setups that require interposition.

Returning to our example, the R930 can hold up to eight 3.2TB or 6.4TB FusionIO SX300 PCIeSSDs (that cost $12,706 and $24,063). If we want to improve the performance of an Elvis setup with such drives, we have to install at least one per server, whereas vRIO allows us to consolidate. As with CPUs, consolidation does not necessarily mean we want to reduce the overall number of drives to get a cheaper setup. We can instead use the same number of drives but make all of them efficiently available to all the servers, thereby in-

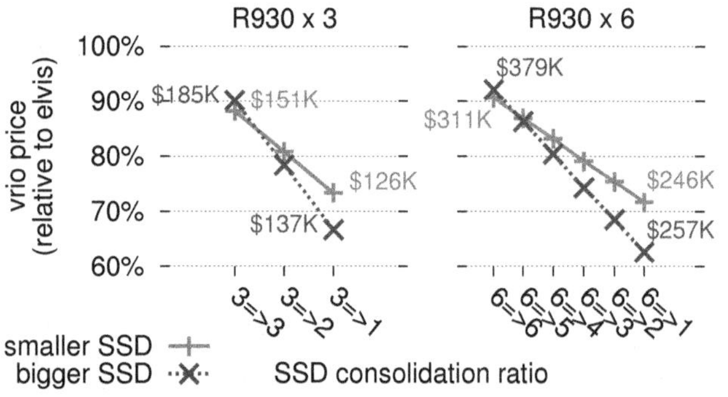

Figure 3. *Price of vRIO relative to Elvis for different drive consolidation ratios (using 3.2TB/6.4TB FusionIO PCIeSSDs).*

creasing the amount of SSD-residing data accessible to each server and boosting overall performance. The SX300 drives deliver up to 2.7GB/sec bandwidth (21.6 Gbps) [60], so consolidating three or six drives requires us to add one or two 2x40Gbps NICs. (The R930 supports up to ten such NICs, so we can add them.)

Let $e \Rightarrow v$ denote the SSD *consolidation ratio*, namely, the number of drives installed in an Elvis setup (e) and in its competing vRIO setup (v). Figure 3 shows the price of the vRIO setups relative to the corresponding Elvis setups, for different consolidation ratios of the aforementioned drives. The cost reduction is between 8%–38%.

4. Design and Implementation

When designing vRIO, our goal is to support sidecore consolidation while trading off as little latency as possible so as to deliver comparable throughput with fewer resources (or better throughput with similar resources) as compared to the state of the art. To this end, we borrow from and extend the three virtual I/O models described in §2.

4.1 Architecture

The vRIO model consists of several components that work together to offload I/O processing from a set of *VMhosts* to their *IOhost*, which houses the VMhosts' sidecores. Usually, VMhosts run guest VMs, but they may also host bare metal OSes as will be discussed later on. We thus use the term *IOclients* to collectively denote the software entities that run on the VMhosts. All I/O processing takes place on the IOhost, on behalf of the IOclients. This transfer of responsibility frees the VMhosts to dedicate more cores to their non-I/O tasks.

vRIO is implemented as a set of drivers in the IOclients and kernel modules in the IOhost. Similarly to the baseline virtio I/O model, vRIO supports both network and block devices. The virtio protocol dictates that guests and host communicate by placing the I/O requests and responses in a shared memory ring buffer (Figure 4a). Elvis follows this protocol, but instead of taking exits on the core of the guest VM, it polls the ring from a different (side)core and allows the VM to continue to compute without interference (Figure 4b). vRIO preserves this architecture but introduces one major change, substituting the shared memory ring with a communications channel (Figure 4c). The latter is exclusively dedicated to encoded I/O traffic that flows between the IOclients and their *I/O hypervisor*—the software that controls the IOhost.

vRIO's dedicated channel is commodity 10Gbps Ethernet, though other interconnects like PCIe [65] or RDMA could be used and would likely provide better performance. Guided by our goal to minimize the latency induced by vRIO, we connect each IOclient to the IOhost through its own SRIOV+Eli instance. Using SRIOV in this manner does not negate interposition, as the I/O hypervisor is free to manipulate the I/O of its clients as it pleases. The only support that vRIO requires from local hypervisors is to assign guests with SRIOV channels. Henceforth, local hypervisors remain uninvolved and unaware of the I/O performed by their guests.

IOclient The IOclient has two driver layers. The first consists of *front-ends*, which expose paravirtual block and net devices to guests, as do virtio and Elvis. The second consists of the *transport* driver, exclusive to vRIO. It is coupled with the aforementioned SRIOV instance and is used to generically support both block and net device types, communicating with the I/O hypervisor as needed. When performing an I/O request, the IOclient hands it to the relevant front-end driver, which in turn hands it to the transport driver. At this point, the request needs to be associated with metadata information, such as the front-end device identifier, type of request, and request size. We directly reuse the virtio protocol—which supplies this information—for this purpose.

The transport driver is responsible for segmenting requests sent to the I/O hypervisor according to the Ethernet protocol. Likewise, it reassembles and decapsulates responses arriving from the I/O hypervisor, before calling the handler functions of the corresponding paravirtual front-end, which notifies the IOclient that a response has arrived.

In virtio and Elvis, the administrator determines the number and type of front-ends assigned to each VM through the local hypervisor. In vRIO, device creation is done via the I/O hypervisor. The transport driver therefore has a secondary role: receiving commands from the I/O hypervisor to create and destroy paravirtual devices in the IOclient.

I/O Hypervisor In the interposable models (virtio, Elvis, vRIO), each front-end device is coupled with an (IO)host back-end, which provides the expected functionality. This emulation layer is where interposition activity takes place, allowing the (IO)host to run services such as block or packet level encryption, SDN, deep packet inspection, intrusion detection, anti-virus, deduplication, and compression.

The vRIO I/O hypervisor consists of a set of *workers*, each running on a different (side)core. Workers service I/O requests from IOclients or from external parties that communicate with them. Requests arrive through IOhost NICs and are directly intercepted by the workers, without going through the TCP/IP stack. A worker that becomes

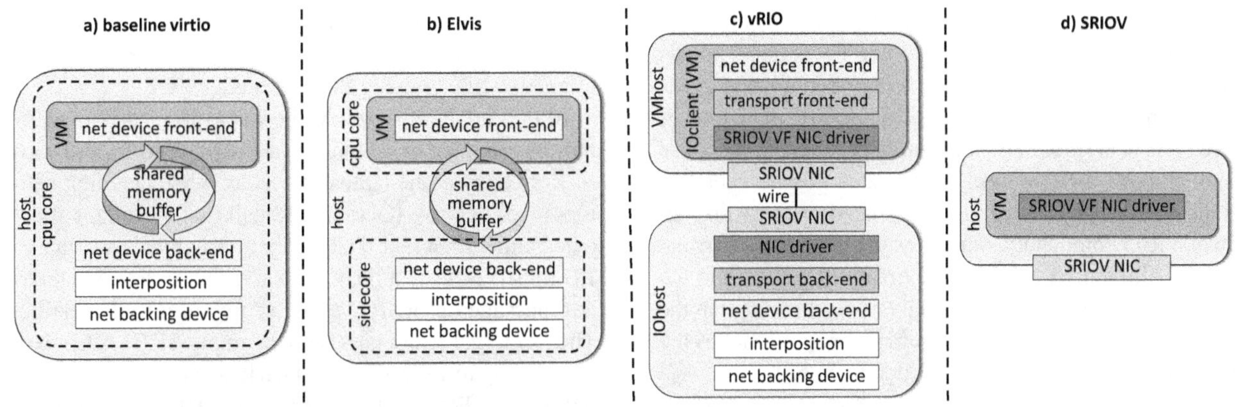

Figure 4. *Side-by-side comparison of the components used for implementing a virtual network device across the four virtual I/O models. The baseline virtio, Elvis, and vRIO are interposable; SRIOV is not. vRIO replaces the shared memory buffers with networking communications. Virtual block devices are not shown but are implemented similarly.*

I/O model	*sync exits*	*guest intrpts*	*intrpt injection*	*host intrpts*	*IOhost intrpts*	*sum*
optimum	0	2	0	0	-	2
vrio	0	2	0	0	0	2
elvis	0	2	0	2	-	4
vrio w/o poll	0	2	0	0	4	6
baseline	3	2	2	2	-	9

Table 3. *Qualitative comparison between the overheads of the different virtual I/O models induced upon a single request-response.*

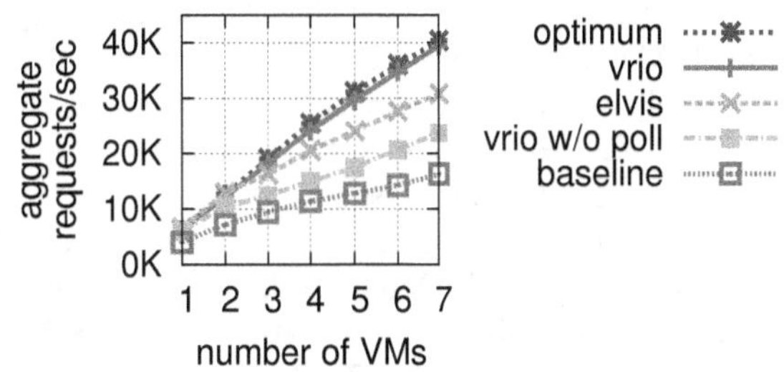

Figure 5. *Turning polling off in vRIO and enabling interrupts substantially degrade the performance of ApacheBench. The performance perfectly correlates with the "sum" column in Table 3.*

idle takes a batch of packets off a relevant NIC receive ring, splits it into sub-batches, and divides the sub-batches between the workers. In a sub-batch, packets are processed in order. For each virtual device *D*, so long as there exists a still-unprocessed packet of *D* designated for processing on the sidecore of worker *W*, then any subsequent requests of *D* will be steered to *W* as well. This policy preserves the order of the original requests and rids network stacks from the need to handle out-of-order packets.

4.2 Interrupts and Exits

Interrupts degrade the performance of virtual setups [5, 29]. But sidecores poll by design, and vRIO carefully uses this property to minimize the overhead. In fact, vRIO completely eliminates the overhead of *virtual* interrupts, partially counteracting the added latency incurred by the extra hop. In this respect, vRIO is superior to Elvis, as will be described next.

Table 3 schematically compares the number of exits and interrupts induced by the virtual I/O models when receiving one network request from an external client and sending back a response. The table contains two vRIO versions—with and without polling at the IOhost. As the comparison is qualitative, we ignore such issues as batching and interrupt coalescing.

Let us go over the table from left to right. Under virtio, a VM induces three synchronous exits: one when sending the response, and two when writing to the end-of-interrupt (EOI) LAPIC register of the virtual hardware after handling the interrupts that notify the VM that (1) a request has arrived and that (2) the response has been sent. The latter interrupts account for the "2" that appears throughout the "guest interrupts" column, as they asynchronously occur in all the I/O models.

Elvis and vRIO do not induce synchronous exits when the virtual NIC is accessed due to their sidecores, whose role is to avoid such exits. Likewise, the optimum avoids these exits as SRIOV provides direct access to the virtual NIC. And none of the models but virtio trigger exits upon EOI because of their use of Eli (which exposes the EOI register directly to the guest by configuring the relevant MSR bitmap to not cause an exit when the guest writes to the EOI register). Similarly, because Eli delivers interrupts of the virtual NIC directly to the VM, all models but virtio avoid the penalty of interrupt injection (4th column in Table 3).

The two virtual device interrupts ("guest interrupts" column) could be the result of two physical interrupts triggered by the backing device, which are handled by the host. The is the case in the baseline and, as it happens, in Elvis ("host interrupts" column). Namely, Elvis's sidecores poll the guest/host shared memory associated with the virtual device (Figure 4b), but they interact with the physical device in the standard interrupt-driven way. In contrast, the optimum and vRIO use SRIOV at the local host and thus do not induce this overhead.

The "IOhost interrupts" column applies to vRIO only. No-poll vRIO treats physical interrupts like Elvis does, letting them drive the IOhost net activity. The number of interrupts is then twice that of Elvis, as every packet reaching the IOhost is received and sent, yielding 4 interrupts per request-response in total. Polling vRIO entirely eliminates this overhead; it polls the NIC, analogously to Elvis's shared memory polling.

Thus, vRIO completely eliminates the overhead of virtual interrupts, allowing it to often outperform Elvis despite the extra hop. Figure 5 supports this analysis by showing that the throughput of ApacheBench is inversely proportional to the "sum" in Table 3 (see experimental details in §5).

4.3 Segmentation and Reassembly

Using Ethernet for VMhost/IOhost communication means that we must segment I/O requests and responses when packet sizes are larger than the maximum transmission unit (MTU), and we must reassemble them at the other end. Of the interposable virtual I/O models, only vRIO suffers from segmentation and reassembly overhead, because shared memory—used by Elvis and the baseline for guest/host communication—does not require segmentation or reassembly.

We optimize the corresponding code paths to reduce this overhead. We configure vRIO to use Ethernet jumbo frames for VMhost/IOhost communication (consisting of 8100 bytes instead of 1500). And we use the TCP segmentation offload (TSO) extension supported by most modern NICs. vRIO works at the raw Ethernet level, but it is nevertheless able to leverage TSO by adding fake TCP/IP headers [20]. This optimization is applicable for chunk sizes as big as 64KB (the maximum buffer size allowed for TCP/IP) and is thus highly effective. Network stacks do not produce packet sizes bigger than 64KB, so the vRIO transport driver only needs to segment block I/O traffic. Reassembly is still done directly by the vRIO software.

4.4 Zero Copying

vRIO copies as little data as possible to minimize CPU consumption and cache pollution. In the IOclient, zero copying is implemented differently for the two front-ends. For the net device, the optimization is straightforward, as the front-end hands a socket buffer (SKB) to the transport driver (T) that already includes all virtio metadata. Then, T adds the aforementioned fake TCP header to the SKB, using existing SKB memory designated for this purpose. It decrements the SKB head pointer to indicate this addition and sends the SKB to the IOhost as explained in §4.3. Receiving is similar: T increments the head pointer and hands the SKB to the front-end.

When the block front-end hands data to T to be *written*, it uses a block I/O buffer, not an SKB. T therefore allocates its own SKB, but it assigns to it pointers of the said block I/O buffer, avoiding a copy. The data is sent, arrives at the IOhost, and is DMAed by the NIC to an IOhost memory buffer. The worker that handles the request reuses this buffer when initiating the corresponding write operation. However, writes to a block device must be aligned to sector size, so the worker uses for zero copy inner portions of the buffer that are aligned, while copying the buffer edges.

When an IOhost *reads*, the data must be copied to the buffers provided by its block system, preventing zero copying.

Zero copy at the IOhost is trickier when handling network messages sent by IOclients. Recall that T utilizes the TSO extension with a fake TCP header to segment messages. The I/O hypervisor must therefore carefully reassemble the original message before it is able to forward it to its destination. The I/O hypervisor starts with an empty SKB. A Linux SKB can map up to 17 fragments, such that each must be contained within a 4KB page. For this reason, vRIO chooses a jumbo frame size of MTU=8100 bytes (rather than the maximal jumbo frame size, which is 9000 bytes). This MTU ensures that each TSO fragment (along with its headers) can be stored in two 4KB pages. At the same time, the maximal size of a single TCP/IP message is 64KB. Thus, the maximal number of per-message TSO fragments is 9, such that 8 of these 9 consist of two 4KB pages and the 9th fragment is smaller than one 4KB page ($64KB - 8100 \times 8 = 736$ bytes). It follows that all the fragments of the original message can be stored in 17 pages as required, ensuring that the I/O hypervisor is able to reassemble the message in a zero copy manner.

4.5 Error Handling

Ethernet is unreliable. Using it as the dedicated communication channel therefore means that vRIO might experience packet loss. For virtual networking I/O, this does not pose a problem, because TCP connections are reliable and retransmit when necessary, and UDP connections might experience loss anyhow. This reasoning does not hold for virtual block I/O, and so vRIO must implement a retransmission mechanism for its block device traffic in order to provide a reliable media.

Block devices may process different requests simultaneously. It is the responsibility of the guest OS disk scheduler (not its driver) to reorder requests, making sure that each *individual* block has only one outstanding request associated with it, while all subsequent requests for that block are pending [10]. Accordingly, vRIO retransmits block requests that it considers lost without worrying that new requests for the same blocks will arrive from the IOclient.

To support retransmission of block requests, vRIO associates a timeout and a unique identifier with each request (or retransmission). The initial timeout is 10ms, and it is doubled upon each subsequent expiration. When a timeout expires, the request is presumed lost and is retransmitted. After the number of unsuccessful retransmissions exceeds some threshold, vRIO concludes that the request cannot be served and raises a device error. vRIO ignores "stale" responses for requests whose unique identifier differs from the current identifier.

We validated the correctness of this mechanism by artificially dropping I/O requests arriving at the IOhost. Furthermore, in our initial experiments, we encountered loss and retransmission of requests "in the wild". vRIO correctly recovered, but the recovery activity affected performance somewhat. Increasing the vRIO receive ring buffers (Rx) from 512 to 4096 packets in the communication channel NIC at the IOhost eliminated this problem.

4.6 Features and Limitations

Device Consolidation Conveniently, efficient sidecore consolidation implicitly allows for efficient I/O device consolidation, for increased utilization. If IOclients are adequately served by fewer devices, consolidation implies comparable or better performance at a lower or the same cost. This benefit is accentuated by expensive devices such as PCIe SSDs. Rack architects can decide to share devices among IOclients instead of limiting their use to individual physical servers. Recall that this type of consolidation is orthogonal, for example, to SANs or NASs: if a SAN/NAS is used directly by IOclients, then there is no interposition, and if it is exposed as a virtual device, then vRIO's advantages come into play.

Friendliness to Heterogeneity Replacing shared memory with network channels as a means of guest-host communication implies that there are no dependencies between the local and remote hypervisors. A handy side-effect of this feature is that the I/O hypervisor is agnostic to the type of the local hypervisor (and its processor architecture), allowing centralized deployment of services and policies that apply to all.

In fact, vRIO does not require a local hypervisor at all. It provides the same services to bare-metal OSes that install its drivers. Bare-metal clouds can thus provide software-based functionality such as firewalls and anti-virus, without "stealing" CPU cycles from the bare-metal machines. (Any software running on the I/O hypervisor cannot be disabled by the IOclient.)

Live Migration The IOhost's transport interface (T) and its net front-end interface (F) are associated with different MAC addresses. T's address is exclusively used for communicating with the IOhost and is unknown to the outside world; any party that wishes to communicate with the IOclient does so via F's address. The T interface can be implemented using an SRIOV instance (T_{sriov}) as described above. But any other NIC will do, notably traditional virtio (T_{virtio}). This architecture facilitates VM live migration between VMhosts that share an IOhost. It allows F to dynamically switch between channeling traffic via T_{sriov} and T_{virtio}. Once T_{virtio} is used, migration can commence as usual. Then, F in the target host switches back to T_{sriov}. Our vRIO implementation correctly runs using T_{virtio}, T_{sriov}, and any other NIC. But we did not implement the dynamic switch.

Migrating a VM away from its IOhost to an arbitrary server (S) is similarly possible, regardless of whether S supports vRIO. First, F notifies the IOhost to stop encapsulating its incoming traffic with vRIO headers. Then, instead of channeling its outgoing traffic (with headers) to the remote IOhost via T_{sriov}, F switches to channel the traffic (without headers) via shared memory to its local hypervisor. This works since the underlying traffic is traditional virtio in both cases. Once F uses traditional virtio, migration can take place as usual. However, if S is a non-vRIO host, it must locally provide the same services previously provided by the IOhost.

Paravirtual block devices (D) migrate as usual: if D is an interface to distributed storage, then this storage will be available in S; otherwise, D's content should be copied to S.

Fault Tolerance vRIO setups as in Figure 2 make the system less fault tolerant. If the IOhost fails, VMhosts cease to be reachable. Reachability in the face of failure can be ensured by connecting VMhosts to their IOhost through the rack switch and configuring the switch to channel IOclient traffic (F addresses) to the appropriate IOhost; this setting requires a costlier switch that can handle the added bandwidth, but it allows for a typical rack arrangement. Alternatively, reachability can be obtained by connecting VMhosts to a secondary fallback IOhost, which requires additional cables and matching ports that would increase price and complexity.

Recall that the IOclient corresponds to F's MAC address. Thus, assuming reachability, the network can recover from an IOhost failure by falling back on regular virtio. Virtual block device activity can similarly recover if D is backed by distributed storage; otherwise, if the storage resides exclusively on the IOhost, losing it is akin to losing a local drive.

Energy An inherent downside of the sidecore approach is that polling consumes energy. In principle, this cost can be reduced [4] by trading off some latency and utilizing the CPU's monitor/mwait capability, which enables the core to enter a low-power state until a monitored cache range is modified [8]. This optimization is outside the scope of this work.

5. Evaluation

Methodology We do not have the resources to conduct an evaluation with setups as described in §3. Instead, we focus on the individual (side)core and compare the performance it delivers in the different I/O models. Our testbed system consists of up to 7 servers: two VMhosts, one IOhost, and four load generators. The VMhosts are IBM System x3550 M4 machines, each with: two 8-core Intel 2.2GHz Xeon E5-2660 CPUs; 56GB memory; and an Intel x520 dual port 10Gbps SRIOV NIC, allowing 20Gbps per VMhost. The IOhost is an IBM System x3650 M4 with: two 8-core Intel 2.7GHz Xeon E5-2680 CPUs; 128GB memory (we made sure the IOhost only uses a small fraction of it); and two NICs identical to that of the VMhosts, supporting 40Gbps. The load generators are IBM System x3550 M2 machines, each with: two 4-core 2.93GHz Intel Xeon 5500 CPUs; 12GB memory; and an Emulex OneConnect dual port 10Gbps NIC. VMhost hypervisors are KVM/QEMU, hosting VMs configured with one VCPU and 1GB of memory each, backed by 2MB pages. All machines run Linux 3.9: guests, hosts, and bare metal. We turn off hyperthreading and all power

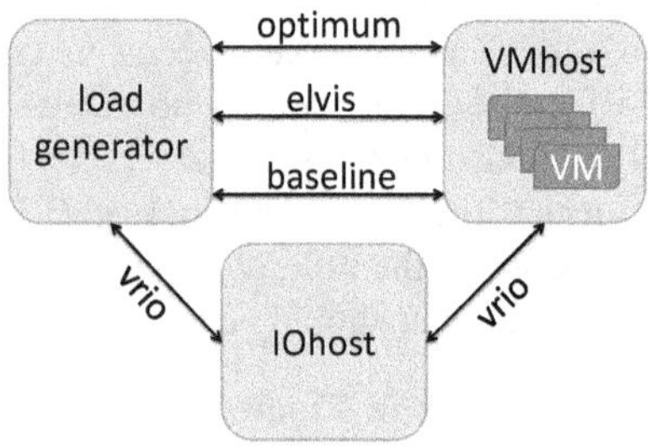

Figure 6. *Simplest experimental setup.*

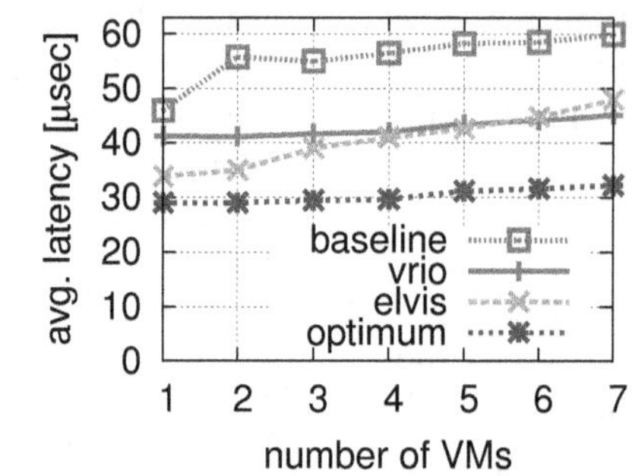

Figure 7. *Netperf RR latency.*

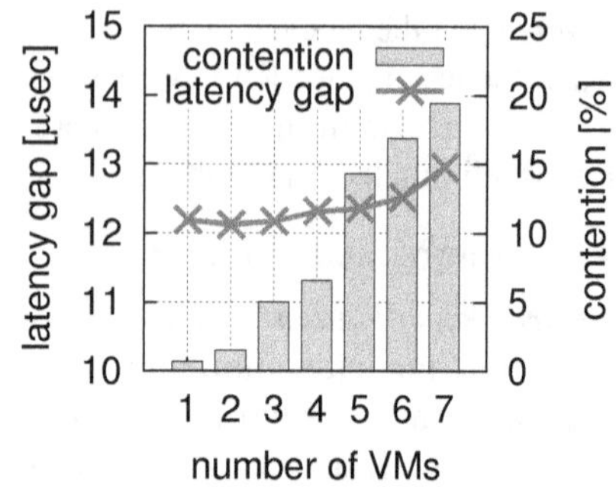

Figure 8. *Netperf RR/vRIO contention.*

optimizations—sleep states (Cstates) and dynamic voltage and frequency scaling (DVFS)—to avoid reporting artifacts caused by nondeterministic events.

Although IOhost specialization is an inherent vRIO advantage, our IOhost is different from the VMhosts because we did not have enough identical machines available. Note, however, that we only use a small fraction of the IOhost in our experiments and carefully equalize the number of cores available to each competing setup, as explained in detail below.

We evaluate vRIO against the I/O models we have considered thus far (§2)—the KVM/virtio baseline as the state of practice [58], Elvis as the state of the art [31], and SRIOV+Eli as the non-interposable optimum [5, 29]. We use the benchmarks: (**1**) Netperf UDP RR (request-response), a standard tool to measure network latency [37], repeatedly sending one byte and waiting for a byte response; (**2**) Netperf TCP stream, a tool to measure the maximal throughput sent over one TCP connection—we use a 64B packet size to stress the I/O models, as bigger sizes quickly saturate the network links and hide the differences; (**3**) Apache [24, 25], an HTTP web server driven by ApacheBench [9]; (**4**) Memcached [26], an in-memory key-value storage server driven by Memslap [3]; and (**5**) Filebench, a filesystem and storage benchmark that generates both micro and macro workloads (as specified later) [48].

We execute each experiment 5 times and present averages. The standard deviation for all the Elvis, vRIO, and optimum models is less than 2% of the average, and it is less the 5% for all the baseline experiments, which are less stable due to nondeterministic scheduling of vhost threads.

Latency The most troubling aspect of vRIO is the impact of adding a hop to the I/O path. We evaluate this impact in the *least* favorable conditions for vRIO—when no interposition is involved. With interposition, the relative weight of vRIO overheads is reduced. For example, if interposition takes 100μs per-packet and vRIO adds 10μs, then performance drops by less than 10% regardless of the I/O model we compare against. We initially use our simplest experimental setup, depicted in Figure 6. For all I/O models but vRIO the setup consists of one VMhost directly communicating with one generator. With vRIO, the two communicate indirectly via the IOhost. Only one 8-core CPU is used on the VMhost.

Using Netperf RR, we measure the latency of the I/O models as a function of N—the number of VMs in the VMhost that run the benchmark. For each given N, we constrain the number of active cores to be $N+1$ for Elvis, vRIO, and the baseline: for Elvis, the extra core is in the VMhost serving as a sidecore; the baseline is similar, but Linux uses the core to run I/O threads and VCPUs as it pleases; and for vRIO, the extra (side)core resides on the IOhost. In the optimum SRIOV/Eli setup, we use only N cores, as an extra core would stand idle with only N VMs, seeing it has no host I/O threads or interrupts to process. (Later, we conduct another experiment where we equalize the number of cores for the optimum setup.)

The results, shown in Figure 7, indicate that the optimum enjoys close to perfect scalability, with 30–32μs latency on average per request-response; vRIO exhibits a similar slope, yet its latency is about 12μs higher—-this is the cost of the added hop. A closer examination of the difference between the latencies of vRIO and the optimum reveals that it slowly increases with N from about 12μs to 13μs, as depicted in Figure 8 (left y-axis). The small increase is due to "contention" over the remote sidecore of vRIO, as exemplified by Figure 8 (right y-axis), which shows the fraction of packets that had to wait at the IOhost before being processed.

The real competitor of vRIO, however, is Elvis, as both support interposition whereas the optimum does not. Initially ($N=1$), the latency of vRIO is 8μs longer than Elvis's. This gap pertains to the 1.18x increased latency we report in the introduction, and it is the highest performance degradation induced by vRIO that we observed for network workloads. As the number of VMs increases, the gap shrinks until vRIO becomes faster than Elvis at $N=6$ due to the manner by which vRIO reduces interrupts activity (§4.2).

The tail latency is shown in Table 4. The results are mixed, with Elvis and vRIO fairing better at different percentiles: Elvis has lower 99.9% and 99.99% latency, but vRIO has a lower 99.999% and maximal latency.

Throughput The Netperf stream throughput is shown in Figure 9. Elvis and the optimum achieve similar performance, and vRIO is 5–8% lower. The degradation is due to the added processing time incurred by the vRIO driver, quantified in

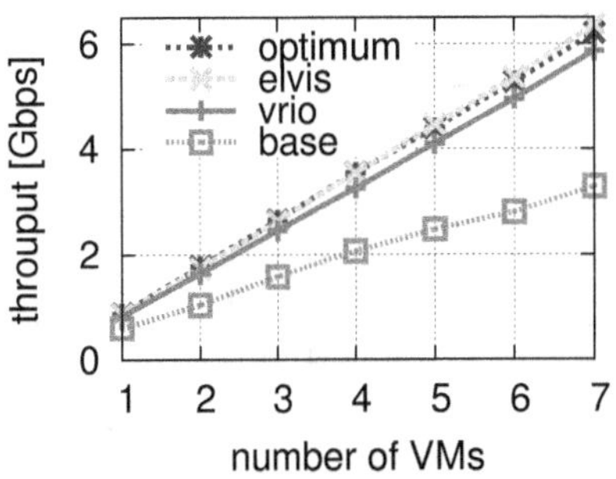

Figure 9. *Netperf stream throughput of vRIO is 5–8% smaller than the optimum.*

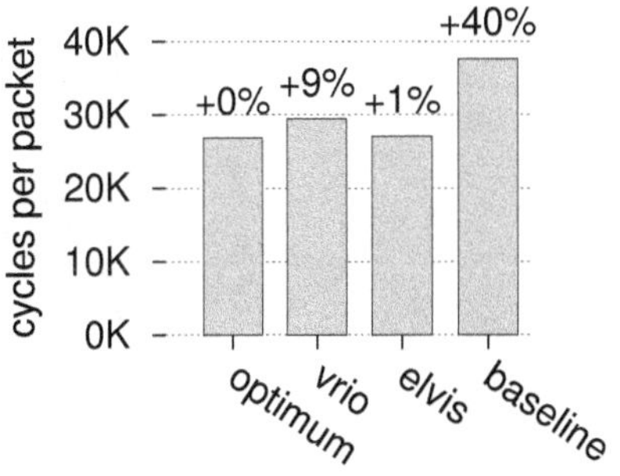

Figure 10. *Netperf stream's per-packet processing time with one VM (N=1).*

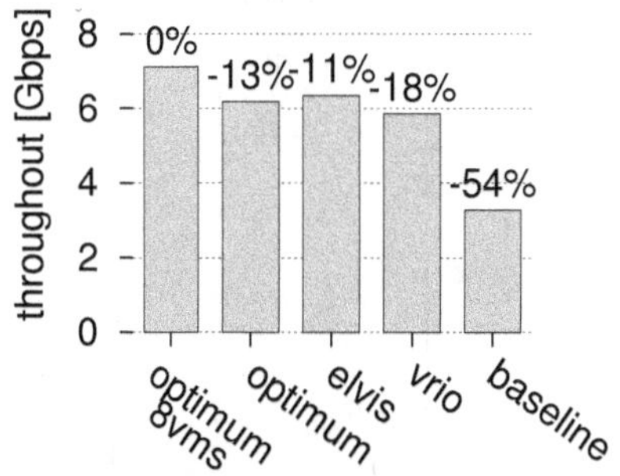

Figure 11. *Optimum with N+1=8 cores ("8vms") shows the cost of interposition.*

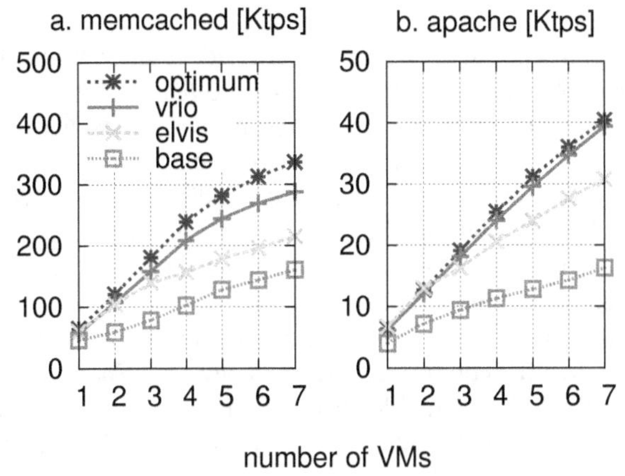

Figure 12. *Benchmarks performance (kilo transactions/second).*

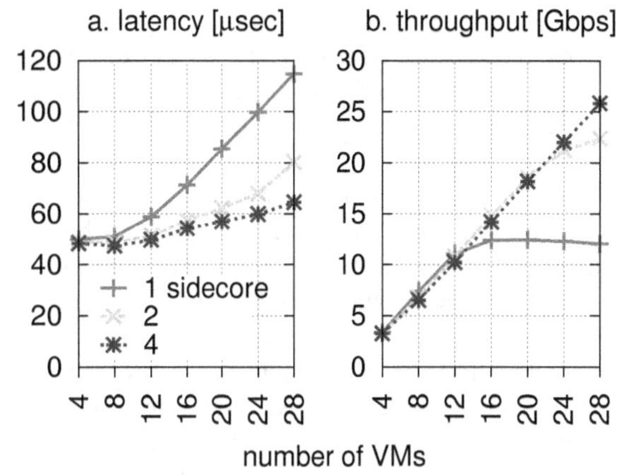

Figure 13. *vRIO's IOhost scalability—latency and throughput.*

percentile	*optimum*	*elvis*	*vrio*
99.9%	35	53	60
99.99%	42	71	156
99.999%	214	466	258
100%	227	480	274

Table 4. *Tail latency in microseconds for one VM.*

Figure 10. Since vRIO spends 9% more cycles on processing each packet, its throughput is lower.

The number of VMs in our experiments so far was fixed (N), so the optimum used one less core. Next, we equalize the number of cores by comparing the $N = 7$ throughput results (Figure 9) to that of the optimum setup utilizing 8 cores to run $N = 8$ VMs. Figure 11 shows the outcome. As expected, this setup yields superior throughput, highlighting the price paid for having the ability to interpose on the I/O of the VMs.

Macrobenchmarks Figure 12 displays the performance of Memcached and Apache. The results—showing that vRIO approaches the optimum whereas Elvis falls behind—coincide with that of the latency experiment for higher N values (Figure 7). As noted in §4.2, when load is high, Elvis is inferior to vRIO, because it needs to handle additional physical interrupts, whereas vRIO polls the device and thus avoids the associated overheads. Notably, the cost of interrupts is substantial despite the fact that both the hardware (NIC) and software (OS) employ interrupt coalescing [5, 29].

IOhost Scalability When consolidating the I/O processing of several VMhosts onto one IOhost, scalability is a concern. We assess vRIO's scalability by serving *all* the machines at our disposal (see beginning of §5) with one IOhost. We configure the two 16-core VMhosts to simulate four 8-core VMhosts: each physical VMhost has two 8-core CPUs and two 10Gbps ports, so we partition it to two logical VMhosts such that each CPU is exclusively associated with a single port.

In this experiment, we systematically increase the load by adding one VM to each of the four logical VMhosts. In the first run there are 4 VMs (one per VMhost), in the second there are 8, and in the final run there are 28 (seven VMs per VMhost). Each VMhost is connected to its own load generator, yielding a setup where the IOhost collectively serves eight multicore machines divided to four VMhost/load-generator pairs.

Figure 13a shows the results of this experiment with Netperf RR and an IOhost that utilizes 1, 2, and 4 sidecores. More sidecores reduce the observed latency. Yet, even with 4 sidecores, the latency increases. This degradation, however,

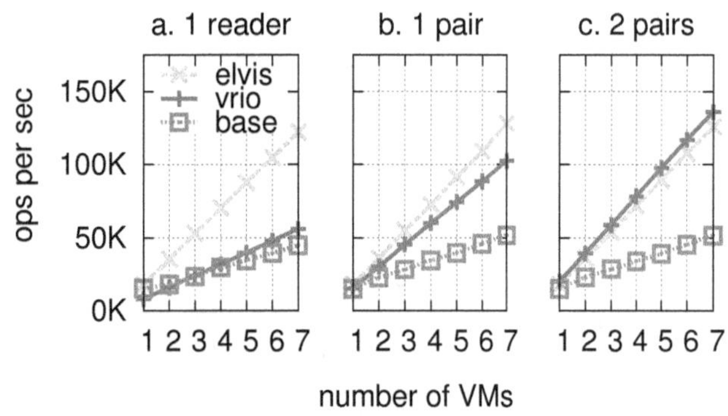

Figure 14. *The vRIO Filebench/ramdisk results improve with increased concurrency until, counterintuitively, it outperforms Elvis.*

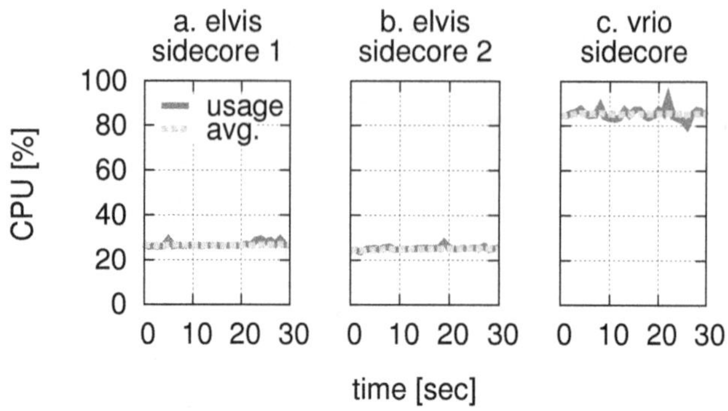

Figure 15. *The CPU utilization and running average indicate that vRIO makes better use of its sidecore cycles as compared to Elvis.*

turned out to be due to NUMA effects on the load generators. Each generator has two 4-core CPUs with a single PCIe bus that is directly connected to CPU 0. Initially, this CPU generates the load. Since we designate one core for interrupt handling only, $N = 16$ is the first run that uses a core from CPU 1, causing the drop in performance. Beyond that, every additional core being used on CPU 1 further increases the average DRAM latency and hence the overall performance.

We repeat the experiment using Netperf stream (Figure 13b) and find that throughput scales linearly while sidecores are not saturated, and that a sidecore gets saturated when servicing about 13 VMs, processing around 13Gbps. Indeed, the curves are converged for N=4,8,12 (and then for N=16,20,24). We conclude that handling VMs from different VMhosts on the same sidecore does not affect performance; only the *number* of VMs is significant, regardless of where the VMs are hosted.

Making a Local Device Remote Suppose we want to accelerate VM storage performance using fast I/O block devices, but we are unwilling to purchase a device for each physical server, or we want all servers to enjoy the devices of the other servers. Further suppose that the devices must be interposable (unlike, say, SAN), so they cannot be used directly by the VMs. With vRIO, these goals can be easily achieved by placing the device(s) at the IOhost rather than locally. We next evaluate the performance implications.

We simulate the device using ramdisk, exposing 1GB to each VM. We use three instances of Filebench: (1) a reader, (2) a reader and a writer ("pair"), and (3) two readers and two writers ("2 pairs"), such that the readers and writers perform 4KB random I/O within their VM. To avoid benchmarking the guests' filesystem cache, we open the virtual block device with O_DIRECT, so all I/O requests pass the guest-host boundary. We do not benchmark the optimum setup, because there is no such thing as an SRIOV ramdisk.

Figure 14 depicts the results. The reader effectively measures latency (inverse of throughput). It shows that vRIO scales somewhat better than the baseline but worse than Elvis. This result refers to the 2.2x latency reported in the introduction. vRIO improves with one pair, and, counterintuitively, outperforms Elvis with two pairs. The reason is the number of involuntary context switches in Elvis guests, which is two orders of magnitude higher as compared to vRIO. The relatively low latency of the local ramdisk combined with the relatively high number of CPU cycles required to process each request results in threads contending over the CPU, degrading throughput.

We utilized a ramdisk to approximate the overhead incurred by vRIO on future, faster I/O devices. When applied to SATA SSDs available to us, the reader's baseline and vRIO throughput become 75%–95% and 83%–95% relative to Elvis.

Improving Utilization Resources consolidation is suitable when VMs make partial use of them. In our context, it means that their I/O is semi-intensive and so they do not require all the computational power of their sidecores. Our next experiment consists of two VMhosts, each running five VMs, utilizing 5+1 cores (N=5). All VMs run Filebench's Webserver I/O personality, modeling a block device workload generated by a typical webserver. The workload includes 30K files of variable sizes with a mean size of 28KB. Each webserver has 4 threads performing open, read, and close operations while updating a log file. We empty the hypervisor page caches before each run. We evaluate three setups: (1) Elvis with two sidecores, one per VMhost; (2) vRIO with a single "consolidated" sidecore at the IOhost serving both VMhosts; and (3) the baseline serving the five VMs with six cores (N+1) on each VMhost. All VMs have a 1GB ramdisk block device, but in vRIO it is remote rather than local.

Figures 15a–b show the CPU used by the Elvis sidecores. Both are underutilized, spending together about 150% CPU on useless polling. Figure 15c shows that the consolidated vRIO sidecore is more effective. Figure 16a shows the resulting throughput. We see that vRIO is significantly better than the baseline but is 8% below Elvis. This outcome constitutes a typical consolidation tradeoff in virtual environments: sacrificing some performance (-8%) to get significant savings in physical resources (halving the sidecore number).

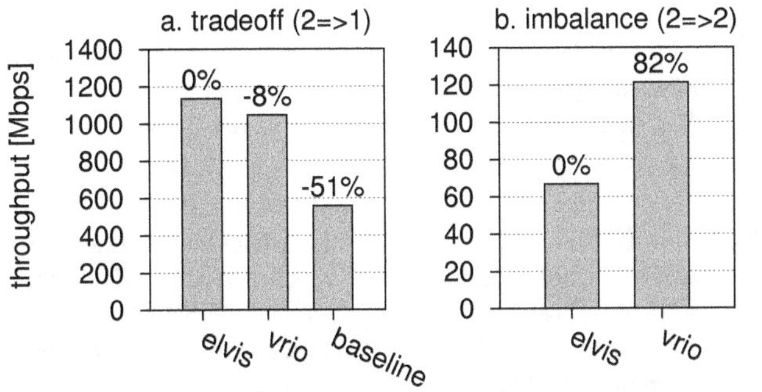

Figure 16. *With sidecore consolidation, we can use fewer or the same resources and get comparable (a) or better (b) performance.*

Load Imbalance Resource consolidation is most suitable to handle load imbalance. Suppose our budget consists of two sidecores, and we need to decide where to place them. In vRIO, we consolidate them at the IOhost, whereas in Elvis we allocate one per VMhost. Suppose that only one VMhost currently requires service (the Webserver personality of Filebench) while the other is idle or engaged in activity that requires little I/O. To increase the imbalance, the Webserver makes use of I/O interposition for seamless encryption. We use AES-256 as the encryption algorithm and invoke it through standard Linux APIs. In vRIO, two sidecores can process the VMhost's I/O and encryption, whereas in Elvis the VMhost can only make use of its one local sidecore. Figure 16b shows the outcome: vRIO provides an 82% improvement over Elvis with the same sidecore budget. This performance boost is an inherent benefit of vRIO.

Heterogeneity Finally, we demonstrate that vRIO enables hypervisor agnostic I/O interposition. We run Netperf stream within a Linux IOclient that is: (1) a VM hosted on VMware ESXi 5; (2) a VM hosted on KVM; and (3) a bare metal OS. All setups attain line rate and have comparable CPU utilization in both sidecore and VMcore. We perform another test involving an IBMPOWER 710 with a 1Gbps Intel 82571EB NIC to show that vRIO is also hardware platform agnostic. We install the vRIO driver on the host OS, making it a bare-metal client that involves no virtualization. We run the same test on an x86 guest after installing a 1Gbps NIC in it so as to have comparable setups. Here too both servers attain line rate and have comparable CPU usage (under 10%). We conclude that it is possible to seamlessly run vRIO services on the IOhost for multiple hardware platforms and hypervisor types.

6. Related Work

The sidecore approach is a parallelization technique to accelerate the execution of virtual machines by polling relevant memory regions via host cores external to the VMs. Rather than taking exits on the cores that run the VMs, the host sidecores continuously observe the requests of VMs and service them accordingly, thereby (1) eliminating the direct and indirect overheads of exits, and (2) offloading the corresponding work to sidecores, freeing VM cores to process other activities. In essence, the sidecore approach offloads work from guest cores to host cores while replacing the costly trap-and-emulate guest/host communication mechanism with simple, much faster load/store operations directed at the coherent memory caches.

The sidecore approach was first introduced in 2007 by Kumar et al. [27, 39]. They used it to accelerate network interrupts and page table management processing of paravirtual guests. In 2009, Liu and Abali reintroduced the same concept, calling it virtualization polling engine (VPE) and using it to additionally accelerate the receive and transmit network I/O paths [45]. In 2012, Ben-Yehuda et al. implemented a block device on a sidecore [13]. In 2013, Har'el et al. proposed Elvis [31]—used in this paper—combining the sidecore paradigm with exitless interrupts [5, 29] and making it applicable to any virtio device (block, as well as net) such that it linearly scales with the number of cores (VMs).

All of the aforementioned sidecore work was done using paravirtualization, whereby the guest VM code is changed to explicitly cooperate with a host that runs on sidecore, rather than on the same core with regular trap-and-emulate exits. Conversely, Amit et al. exposed a virtual IOMMU ("vIOMMU") to unmodified VMs, and they were able to substantially improve performance by running the vIOMMU code on a sidecore, keeping the VMs unaware of the fact they are not using the physical IOMMU [4].

Landau et al. proposed a hardware extension ("SplitX") that allows the hypervisor and its unmodified guests to run on disjoint sets of cores, such that *every* exit occurring on a VM core is delivered to, and is serviced by, a host sidecore [40].

The insight underlying vRIO is that, logically, the functionality of sidecores is very similar to that of I/O devices, and therefore it could be advantageous to consolidate them. Thus, different than all the above studies, vRIO takes the sidecore approach a step further by migrating sidecores to another server, reaping the benefits of consolidation as outlined above. In this respect, vRIO is reminiscent of supercomputer architectures that distinguish between I/O nodes and compute nodes [2,18,32,42,61]. But such architectures—if used to run VMs—either hinder programmable interposition or induce the overheads of traditional interposable virtual I/O.

7. Conclusions

Given that sidecores are an effective way to optimize for virtual I/O, we show that it makes sense—in terms of price and performance—to consolidate them remotely across the network rather than to spread them across the rack.

Acknowledgments

We thanks the anonymous reviewers for their feedback. This research was funded in part by the Israeli Ministry of Science and Technology (grant #3-9779) and the European Union's Seventh Programme (grant agreement No. FP7-609828).

References

[1] Keith Adams and Ole Agesen. A comparison of software and hardware techniques for x86 virtualization. In *ACM International Conference on Architectural Support for Programming Languages and Operating Systems (ASPLOS)*, pages 2–13, 2006. http://dx.doi.org/10.1145/1168857.1168860.

[2] N.R. Adiga, G. Almasi, G.S. Almasi, Y. Aridor, R. Barik, and many others. An overview of the BlueGene/L supercomputer. In *ACM/IEEE Supercomputing (SC)*, pages 1–22, 2002. http://dx.doi.org/10.1109/SC.2002.10017.

[3] Brian Aker. Memslap - load testing and benchmarking a server. http://docs.libmemcached.org/bin/memslap.html. libmemcached 1.1.0 documentation. Accessed: Jan 2015.

[4] Nadav Amit, Muli Ben-Yehuda, Dan Tsafrir, and Assaf Schuster. vIOMMU: efficient IOMMU emulation. In *USENIX Annual Technical Conference (ATC)*, pages 73–86, 2011. http://www.usenix.org/events/atc11/tech/final_files/Amit.pdf.

[5] Nadav Amit, Abel Gordon, Nadav Har'El, Muli Ben-Yehuda, Alex Landau, Assaf Schuster, and Dan Tsafrir. Bare-metal performance for virtual machines with exitless interrupts. *Communications of the ACM (CACM)*, 59(1):108–116, Jan 2016. http://dx.doi.org/10.1145/2845648.

[6] Nadav Amit, Dan Tsafrir, and Assaf Schuster. VSwapper: A memory swapper for virtualized environments. In *ACM International Conference on Architectural Support for Programming Languages and Operating Systems (ASPLOS)*, pages 349–366, 2014. http://dx.doi.org/10.1145/2541940.2541969.

[7] M.R. Anala, M. Kashyap, and G. Shobha. Application performance analysis during live migration of virtual machines. In *IEEE International Advance Computing Conference (IACC)*, pages 366–372, 2013. http://dx.doi.org/10.1109/IAdCC.2013.6514252.

[8] N. Anastopoulos and N. Koziris. Facilitating efficient synchronization of asymmetric threads on hyper-threaded processors. In *IEEE International Parallel and Distributed Processing Symposium (IPDPS)*, pages 1–8, 2008. http://dx.doi.org/10.1109/IPDPS.2008.4536358.

[9] Apachebench. http://en.wikipedia.org/wiki/ApacheBench. Accessed: Jan 2015.

[10] Remzi H. Arpaci-Dusseau and Andrea C. Arpaci-Dusseau. *Operating Systems: Three Easy Pieces*, chapter 37. Arpaci-Dusseau Books, LLC, 0.90 edition, 2015. http://pages.cs.wisc.edu/~remzi/OSTEP/file-disks.pdf.

[11] Paul Barham, Boris Dragovic, Keir Fraser, Steven Hand, Tim Harris, Alex Ho, Rolf Neugebauer, Ian Pratt, and Andrew Warfield. Xen and the art of virtualization. In *ACM Symposium on Operating Systems Principles (SOSP)*, pages 164–177, 2003. http://dx.doi.org/10.1145/945445.945462.

[12] Adam Belay, George Prekas, Ana Klimovic, Samuel Grossman, Christos Kozyrakis, and Edouard Bugnion. IX: A protected dataplane operating system for high throughput and low latency. In *USENIX Symposium on Operating System Design and Implementation (OSDI)*, pages 49–65, 2014. https://www.usenix.org/system/files/conference/osdi14/osdi14-paper-belay.pdf.

[13] Muli Ben-Yehuda, Eran Borovik, Michael Factor, Eran Rom, Avishay Traeger, and Ben-Ami Yassour. Adding advanced storage controller functionality via low-overhead virtualization. In *USENIX Conference on File and Storage Technologies (FAST)*, pages 187–194, 2012. https://www.usenix.org/legacy/events/fast12/tech/full_papers/Ben-Yehuda2-2-12.pdf.

[14] Muli Ben-Yehuda, Michael D. Day, Zvi Dubitzky, Michael Factor, Nadav Har'El, Abel Gordon, Anthony Liguori, Orit Wasserman, and Ben-Ami Yassour. The Turtles project: Design and implementation of nested virtualization. In *USENIX Symposium on Operating System Design and Implementation (OSDI)*, pages 423–436, 2010. http://www.usenix.org/events/osdi10/tech/full_papers/Ben-Yehuda.pdf.

[15] Muli Ben-Yehuda, Jimi Xenidis, Michal Ostrowski, Karl Rister, Alexis Bruemmer, and Leendert van Doorn. The price of safety: Evaluating IOMMU performance. In *Ottawa Linux Symposium (OLS)*, pages 9–20, 2007. https://www.kernel.org/doc/mirror/ols2007v1.pdf#page=9.

[16] Jason Blosil, David Fair, and David Fair. 10GbE – key trends, drivers and predictions. SNIA presentation: http://www.snia.org/sites/default/files/SNIA_ESF_10GbE_Webcast_Final_Slides.pdf, July 2012. (Accessed: Aug 2015).

[17] Vojtech Cima. An analysis of the performance of block live migration in openstack. URL http://tinyurl.com/live-migration-openstack, 2014. Accessed: Jan 2016.

[18] Peter F. Corbett and Dror G. Feitelson. The vesta parallel file system. *ACM Transactions on Computer Systems (TOCS)*, 14(3):225–264, Aug 1996. http://dx.doi.org/10.1145/233557.233558.

[19] Crehan Research. Another year of robust growth and record shipments for branded data center switches. http://www.crehanresearch.com/wp-content/uploads/2015/03/CREHAN-2014-Data-Center-Switching-CR.pdf, Mar 2015. (Accessed: Aug 2015).

[20] B. Davie and J. Gross. A stateless transport tunneling protocol for network virtualization (STT). http://tools.ietf.org/id/draft-davie-stt-04.txt, Sep 2013. Network Working Group; Internet-Draft; draft-davie-stt-04. Accessed: Jan 2016.

[21] Dell Inc. Dell PowerEdge R930 4-socket rack server. http://www.dell.com/us/business/p/poweredge-r930/pd, Jul 2015. Prices as of 31 July, 2015.

[22] Yaozu Dong, Xiaowei Yang, Xiaoyong Li, Jianhui Li, Kun Tian, and Haibing Guan. High performance network virtualization with SR-IOV. In *IEEE International Symposium on High-Performance Computer Architecture (HPCA)*, pages 1–10, 2010. http://dx.doi.org/10.1109/HPCA.2010.5416637.

[23] Virtual I/O acceleration—the Elvis source code. https://github.com/abelg/virtual_io_acceleration, 2013. (Accessed: Mar 2015).

[24] The Apache HTTP server project. http://httpd.apache.org. Accessed: Jan 2015.

[25] Roy T. Fielding and Gail Kaiser. The Apache HTTP server project. *IEEE Internet Computing*, 1(4):88–90, Jul 1997. http://dx.doi.org/10.1109/4236.612229.

[26] Brad Fitzpatrick. Distributed caching with memcached. *Linux Journal*, 2004(124):5, Aug 2004. http://dl.acm.org/citation.cfm?id=1012889.1012894.

[27] Ada Gavrilovska, Sanjay Kumar, Himanshu Raj, Karsten Schwan, Vishakha Gupta, Ripal Nathuji, Radhika Niranjan, Adit Ranadive, and Purav Saraiya. High-performance hypervisor architectures: Virtualization in HPC systems. In *Workshop on System-level Virtualization for HPC (HPCVirt)*, 2007. http://www.csm.ornl.gov/srt/hpcvirt07/papers/paper10.pdf.

[28] Robert P Goldberg. Survey of virtual machine research. *IEEE Computer*, 7(6):34–45, 1974. http://dx.doi.org/10.1109/MC.1974.6323581.

[29] Abel Gordon, Nadav Amit, Nadav Har'El, Muli Ben-Yehuda, Alex Landau, Assaf Schuster, and Dan Tsafrir. ELI: Bare-metal performance for I/O virtualization. In *ACM International Conference on Architectural Support for Programming Languages and Operating Systems (ASPLOS)*, pages 411–422, 2012. http://dx.doi.org/10.1145/2150976.2151020.

[30] James Hamilton. AWS innovation at scale. https://www.youtube.com/watch?t=113&v=JIQETrFC_SQ, Nov 2014. (Accessed: Aug 2015).

[31] Nadav Har'El, Abel Gordon, Alex Landau, Muli Ben-Yehuda, Avishay Traeger, and Razya Ladelsky. Efficient and scalable paravirtual I/O system. In *USENIX Annual Technical Conference (ATC)*, pages 231–242, 2013. https://www.usenix.org/conference/atc13/technical-sessions/presentation/har%E2%80%99el.

[32] R.A. Haring, M. Ohmacht, T.W. Fox, M.K. Gschwind, D.L. Satterfield, and many others. The IBM Blue Gene/Q compute chip. *IEEE Micro*, 32(2):48–60, March 2012. http://dx.doi.org/10.1109/MM.2011.108.

[33] Tomas Hruby, Herbert Bos, and Andrew S. Tanenbaum. When slower is faster: On heterogeneous multicores for reliable systems. In *USENIX Annual Technical Conference (ATC)*, pages 255–266, 2013. https://www.usenix.org/conference/atc13/technical-sessions/presentation/hruby.

[34] Intel. PCI-SIG SR-IOV primer: An introduction to SR-IOV technology. http://www.intel.com/content/www/us/en/pci-express/pci-sig-sr-iov-primer-sr-iov-technology-paper.html, Jan 2011.

[35] Intel Corporation. Intel processor pricing effective June 07, 2015. http://tinyurl.com/intel-cpu-prices-2015-07, June 2015. (Accessed: Aug 2015, via http://www.intel.com/go/processor_pricing).

[36] Hai Jin, Li Deng, Song Wu, Xuanhua Shi, and Xiaodong Pan. Live virtual machine migration with adaptive, memory compression. In *IEEE International Conference on Cluster Computing (CLUSTER)*, pages 1–10, 2009. http://dx.doi.org/10.1109/CLUSTR.2009.5289170.

[37] Rick A. Jones. A network performance benchmark (Revision 2.0). Technical report, Hewlett Packard, 1995. http://www.netperf.org/netperf/training/Netperf.html. Accessed: Jan 2015.

[38] Asim Kadav and Michael M. Swift. Live migration of direct-access devices. In *USENIX Workshop on I/O Virtualization (WIOV)*, pages 95–104, 2008. http://usenix.org/events/wiov08/tech/full_papers/kadav/kadav.pdf.

[39] Sanjay Kumar, Himanshu Raj, Karsten Schwan, and Ivan Ganev. Re-architecting VMMs for multicore systems: The *sidecore* approach. In *Workshop on Interaction between Operating Systems and Computer Architecture (WIOSCA)*, 2007. http://www.ideal.ece.ufl.edu/workshops/wiosca07/Paper3.pdf.

[40] Alex Landau, Muli Ben-Yehuda, and Abel Gordon. SplitX: Split guest/hypervisor execution on multi-core. In *USENIX Workshop on I/O Virtualization (WIOV)*, 2011. http://www.usenix.org/events/wiov11/tech/final_files/Landau.pdf.

[41] Joshua LeVasseur, Volkmar Uhlig, Jan Stoess, and Stefan Götz. Unmodified device driver reuse and improved system dependability via virtual machines. In *USENIX Symposium on Operating System Design and Implementation (OSDI)*, pages 17–30, 2004. https://www.usenix.org/legacy/publications/library/proceedings/osdi04/tech/full_papers/levasseur/levasseur.pdf.

[42] Jianwei Li, Wei-Keng Liao, A. Choudhary, R. Ross, R. Thakur, W. Gropp, R. Latham, A. Siegel, B. Gallagher, and M. Zingale. Parallel netCDF: A high-performance scientific I/O interface. In *ACM/IEEE Supercomputing (SC)*, page No. 39, 2003. http://dx.doi.org/10.1109/SC.2003.10053.

[43] Guangdeng Liao, Danhua Guo, Laxmi Bhuyan, and Steve R King. Software techniques to improve virtualized I/O performance on multi-core systems. In *ACM/IEEE Symposium on Architectures for Networking and Communications Systems (ANCS)*, pages 161–170, 2008. http://dx.doi.org/10.1145/1477942.1477971.

[44] Jiuxing Liu. Evaluating standard-based self-virtualizing devices: A performance study on 10 GbE NICs with SR-IOV support. In *IEEE International Parallel and Distributed Processing Symposium (IPDPS)*, pages 1–12, 2010. http://dx.doi.org/10.1109/IPDPS.2010.5470365.

[45] Jiuxing Liu and Bulen Abali. Virtualization polling engine (VPE): Using dedicated CPU cores to accelerate I/O virtualization. In *ACM International Conference on Supercomputing (ICS)*, pages 225–23, 2009. http://dx.doi.org/10.1145/1542275.1542309.

[46] Jiuxing Liu, Wei Huang, Bulent Abali, and Dhabaleswar K. Panda. High performance VMM-bypass I/O in virtual machines. In *USENIX Annual Technical Conference (ATC)*,

pages 29–42, 2006. http://usenix.org/legacy/event/usenix06/tech/liu.html.

[47] Dražen Lučanin, Foued Jrad, Ivona Brandic, and Achim Streit. Energy-aware cloud management through progressive SLA specification. In *International Conference on Economics of Grids, Clouds, Systems, and Services (GEOCON)*, pages 83–98. Springer, 2014. http://dx.doi.org/10.1007/978-3-319-14609-6_6.

[48] J. Mauro, S. Shepler, and V. Tarasov. Filebench. http://sourceforge.net/projects/filebench/. Accessed: Oct, 2012.

[49] Eyal Moscovici, Yossi Kuperman, Joel Nider, Razya Ladelsky, Abel Gordon, and Dan Tsafrir. Dynamic sidecore allocation. In preparation.

[50] David Mytton. Network performance at AWS, Google, Rackspace and Softlayer. https://blog.serverdensity.com/network-performance-aws-google-rackspace-softlayer, Apr 2014. (Accessed: Aug 2015).

[51] Zhenhao Pan, Yaozu Dong, Yu Chen, Lei Zhang, and Zhijiao Zhang. CompSC: Live migration with pass-through devices. In *ACM International Conference on Virtual Execution Environments (VEE)*, pages 109–120, 2012. http://dx.doi.org/10.1145/2151024.2151040.

[52] PCI-SIG. Single root I/O virtualization and sharing 1.1 specification. http://www.pcisig.com/specifications/iov/single_root/, Jan 2010.

[53] Simon Peter, Jialin Li, Irene Zhang, Dan R. K. Ports, Doug Woos, Arvind Krishnamurthy, Thomas Anderson, and Timothy Roscoe. Arrakis: The operating system is the control plane. In *USENIX Symposium on Operating System Design and Implementation (OSDI)*, pages 1–16, 2014. https://www.usenix.org/system/files/conference/osdi14/osdi14-paper-peter_simon.pdf.

[54] Gerald J. Popek and Robert P. Goldberg. Formal requirements for virtualizable third generation architectures. *Communications of the ACM (CACM)*, 17(7):412–421, Jul 1974. http://dx.doi.org/10.1145/361011.361073.

[55] Jesse Proudman. Live migration is a perk, not a panacea. URL https://www.blueboxcloud.com/insight/blog-article/live-migration-is-a-perk-not-a-panacea, Oct 2014.

[56] Himanshu Raj and Karsten Schwan. High performance and scalable I/O virtualization via self-virtualized devices. In *IEEE International Symposium on High Performance Distributed Computing (HPDC)*, pages 179–188, 2007. http://dx.doi.org/10.1145/1272366.1272390.

[57] Kaushik Kumar Ram, Alan L. Cox, Mehul Chadha, and Scott Rixner. Hyper-Switch: A scalable software virtual switching architecture. In *USENIX Annual Technical Conference (ATC)*, pages 13–24, 2013. https://www.usenix.org/conference/atc13/technical-sessions/presentation/ram.

[58] Rusty Russell. virtio: towards a de-facto standard for virtual I/O devices. *ACM Operating System Review (OSR)*, 42(5):95–103, 2008. http://dx.doi.org/10.1145/1400097.1400108.

[59] Felix Salfner, Peter Tröger, and Andreas Polze. Downtime analysis of virtual machine live migration. In *International Conference on Dependability (DEPEND)*, pages 100–105, 2011. http://tinyurl.com/DEPEND11-vm-downtime.

[60] SanDisk Corp. Fusion ioMemory SX300 spec. http://www.fusionio.com/load/-media-/302x3j/docsLibrary/SX300_DS_Final_v3.pdf, 2014. (Accessed: Aug 2015).

[61] K.E. Seamons, Y. Chen, P. Jones, J. Jozwiak, and M. Winslett. Server-directed collective I/O in Panda. In *ACM/IEEE Supercomputing (SC)*, page No. 57, 1995. http://dx.doi.org/10.1145/224170.224371.

[62] Arvind Seshadri, Mark Luk, Ning Qu, and Adrian Perrig. SecVisor: A tiny hypervisor to provide lifetime kernel code integrity for commodity OSes. In *ACM Symposium on Operating Systems Principles (SOSP)*, pages 335–350, 2007. http://dx.doi.org/10.1145/1294261.1294294.

[63] Mark Silberstein, Bryan Ford, Idit Keidar, and Emmett Witchel. GPUfs: Integrating a file system with GPUs. In *ACM International Conference on Architectural Support for Programming Languages and Operating Systems (ASPLOS)*, pages 485–498, 2003. http://dx.doi.org/10.1145/2451116.2451169.

[64] R. Takano, H. Nakada, T. Hirofuchi, Y. Tanaka, and T. Kudoh. Cooperative VM migration for a virtualized HPC cluster with VMM-bypass I/O devices. In *IEEE International Conference on E-Science (e-Science)*, pages 1–8, 2012. http://dx.doi.org/10.1109/eScience.2012.6404487.

[65] Cheng-Chun Tu, Chao-tang Lee, and Tzi-cker Chiueh. Secure I/O device sharing among virtual machines on multiple hosts. In *ACM International Symposium on Computer Architecture (ISCA)*, pages 108–119, 2013. http://dx.doi.org/10.1145/2485922.2485932.

[66] VMware, Inc. VMware ESX server 2 - architecture and performance implications. Technical Report ESX-ENG-Q305-122, VMware, 2005. https://www.vmware.com/pdf/esx2_performance_implications.pdf.

[67] VMware, Inc. Performance evaluation of VMXNET3 virtual network device. http://www.vmware.com/pdf/vsp_4_vmxnet3_perf.pdf, 2009.

[68] William Voorsluys, James Broberg, Srikumar Venugopal, and Rajkumar Buyya. Cost of virtual machine live migration in clouds: A performance evaluation. In *International Conference on Cloud Computing*, pages 254–265. Springer-Verlag, 2009. http://dx.doi.org/10.1007/978-3-642-10665-1_23.

[69] Carl Waldspurger and Mendel Rosenblum. I/O virtualization. *Communications of the ACM (CACM)*, 55(1):66–73, Jan 2012. http://dx.doi.org/10.1145/2063176.2063194.

[70] Andrew Whitaker, Marianne Shaw, and Steven D. Gribble. Denali: Lightweight virtual machines for distributed and

networked applications. Technical Report 02-02-01, University of Washington, 2002. http://www.cs.washington.edu/tr/2002/02/UW-CSE-02-02-01.pdf.

[71] Paul Willmann, Scott Rixner, and Alan L. Cox. Protection strategies for direct access to virtualized I/O devices. In *USENIX Annual Technical Conference (ATC)*, pages 15–28, 2008. https://www.usenix.org/legacy/event/usenix08/tech/full_papers/willmann/willmann.pdf.

[72] Paul Willmann, Jeffrey Shafer, David Carr, Aravind Menon, Scott Rixner, Alan L. Cox, and Willy Zwaenepoel. Concurrent direct network access for virtual machine monitors. In *IEEE International Symposium on High-Performance Computer Architecture (HPCA)*, pages 306–317, 2007. http://dx.doi.org/10.1109/HPCA.2007.346208.

[73] Timothy Wood, Prashant Shenoy, Arun Venkataramani, and Mazin Yousif. Black-box and gray-box strategies for virtual machine migration. In *USENIX Symposium on Networked Systems Design and Implementation (NSDI)*, pages 17–17, 2007. http://usenix.org/event/nsdi07/tech/full_papers/wood/wood.pdf.

[74] Cong Xu, Sahan Gamage, Hui Lu, Ramana Kompella, and Dongyan Xu. vTurbo: Accelerating virtual machine I/O processing using designated turbo-sliced core. In *USENIX Annual Technical Conference (ATC)*, pages 243–254, 2013. https://www.usenix.org/conference/atc13/technical-sessions/presentation/xu.

[75] Frank Yang. 10GBASE-T economics. http://www.commscope.com/Blog/10gbase-t-economics/, 2012. (Accessed: Aug 2015).

[76] Ben-Ami Yassour, Muli Ben-Yehuda, and Orit Wasserman. Direct device assignment for untrusted fully-virtualized virtual machines. Technical Report H-0263, IBM Research, 2008. http://tinyurl.com/IBM-TR-H-0263.

[77] Edwin Zhai, Gregory D. Cummings, and Yaozu Dong. Live migration with pass-through device for Linux VM. In *Ottawa Linux Symposium (OLS)*, pages 261–268, 2008. https://www.kernel.org/doc/ols/2008/ols2008v2-pages-261-267.pdf.

High Performance Packet Processing with FlexNIC

Antoine Kaufmann[1] Simon Peter[2] Naveen Kr. Sharma[1]
Thomas Anderson[1] Arvind Krishnamurthy[1]

[1]University of Washington [2]The University of Texas at Austin

{antoinek,naveenks,tom,arvind}@cs.washington.edu simon@cs.utexas.edu

Abstract

The recent surge of network I/O performance has put enormous pressure on memory and software I/O processing subsystems. We argue that the primary reason for high memory and processing overheads is the inefficient use of these resources by current commodity network interface cards (NICs).

We propose FlexNIC, a flexible network DMA interface that can be used by operating systems and applications alike to reduce packet processing overheads. FlexNIC allows services to install packet processing rules into the NIC, which then executes simple operations on packets while exchanging them with host memory. Thus, our proposal moves some of the packet processing traditionally done in software to the NIC, where it can be done flexibly and at high speed.

We quantify the potential benefits of FlexNIC by emulating the proposed FlexNIC functionality with existing hardware or in software. We show that significant gains in application performance are possible, in terms of both latency and throughput, for several widely used applications, including a key-value store, a stream processing system, and an intrusion detection system.

Keywords Network Interface Card; DMA; Flexible Network Processing; Match-and-Action Processing

1. Introduction

Data center network bandwidth is growing steadily: 10 Gbps Ethernet is widespread, 25 and 40 Gbps are gaining traction, while 100 Gbps is nearly available [47]. This trend is straining the server computation and memory capabilities; I/O processing is likely to limit future server performance. For example, last-level cache access latency in Intel Sandy Bridge processors is 15 ns [34] and has not improved in newer processors. A 40 Gbps interface can receive a cache-line sized (64B) packet close to every 12 ns. At that speed, OS kernel bypass [5; 39] is a necessity but not enough by itself. Even a single last-level cache access in the packet data handling path can prevent software from keeping up with arriving network traffic.

We claim that the primary reason for high memory and processing overheads is the inefficient use of these resources by current commodity network interface cards (NICs). NICs communicate with software by accessing data in server memory, either in DRAM or via a designated last-level cache (e.g., via DDIO [21], DCA [20], or TPH [38]). Packet descriptor queues instruct the NIC as to where in server memory it should place the next packet and from where to read the next arriving packet for transmission. Except for simple header splitting, no further modifications to packets are made and only basic distinctions are made among packet types. For example, it is possible to choose a virtual queue based on the TCP connection, but not, say, on the application key in a memcache lookup.

This design introduces overhead in several ways. For example, even if software is only interested in a portion of each packet, the current interface requires NICs to transfer packets in their entirety to host memory. No interface exists to steer packets to the right location in the memory hierarchy based on application-level information, causing extraneous cache traffic when a packet is not in the right cache or at the right level. Finally, network processing code often does repetitive work, such as to check packet headers, even when it is clear what to do in the common case.

The current approach to network I/O acceleration is to put fixed-function offload features into NICs [46]. While useful, these offloads bypass application and OS concerns and can thus only perform low-level functions, such as checksum processing and packet segmentation for commonly used, standard protocols (e.g., UDP and TCP). Higher-level offloads can constrain the system in other ways. For example, remote direct memory access (RDMA) [42], is difficult to adapt to many-to-one client-server communication models [32; 13], resulting in diminished benefits [25]. On some

ASPLOS '16 April 2–6, 2016, Atlanta, Georgia, USA.
ACM 978-1-4503-4091-5/16/04.
DOI: http://dx.doi.org/10.1145/2872362.2872367

high-speed NICs, the need to pin physical memory resources prevents common server consolidation techniques, such as memory overcommit.

To address these shortcomings, we propose FlexNIC, a flexible DMA programming interface for network I/O. FlexNIC allows applications and OSes to install packet processing rules into the NIC, which instruct it to execute simple operations on packets while exchanging them with host memory. These rules allow applications and the OS to exert fine-grained control over how data is exchanged with the host, including where to put each portion of it. The FlexNIC programming model can improve packet processing performance while reducing memory system pressure at fast network speeds.

The idea is not far-fetched. Inexpensive top-of-rack OpenFlow switches support rule-based processing applied to every packet and are currently being enhanced to allow programmable transformations on packet fields [9]. Fully programmable NICs that can support packet processing also exist [35; 51; 10] and higher-level abstractions to program them are being proposed [22]. We build upon these ideas to provide a flexible, high-speed network I/O programming interface for server systems.

The value of our work is in helping guide next generation NIC hardware design. Is a more or less expressive programming model better? At one extreme, we can offload the entire application onto a network processor, but development costs will be higher. At the other extreme, fixed-function offloads, such as Intel Flow Director, that match on only a small number of packet fields and cannot modify packets in flight are less expressive than FlexNIC, but forego some performance benefits, as we will show later.

This paper presents the FlexNIC programming model, which is expressive and yet allows for packet processing at line rates, and quantifies the potential performance benefits of flexible NIC packet steering and processing for a set of typical server applications. When compared to a high-performance user-level network stack, our prototype implementation achieves 2.3× better throughput for a real-time analytics platform modeled after Apache Storm, 60% better throughput for an intrusion detection system, and 60% better latency for a key-value store. Further, FlexNIC is versatile. Beyond the evaluated use cases, it is useful for high performance resource virtualization and isolation, fast failover, and can provide high-level consistency for RDMA operations. We discuss these further use cases in §6.

We make four specific contributions:

- We present the FlexNIC programming model that allows flexible I/O processing by exposing a match-and-action programming interface to applications and OSes (§2).
- We implement a prototype of FlexNIC via a combination of existing NIC hardware features and software emulation using dedicated processor cores on commodity multi-core computers and I/O device hardware (§2.4).
- We use our prototype to quantify the potential benefits of flexible network I/O for several widely used networked applications, including a key-value store, data stream processing, and intrusion detection (§3–5).
- We present a number of building blocks that are useful to software developers wishing to use FlexNIC beyond the use cases evaluated in this paper (§2.3).

Our paper is less concerned with a concrete hardware implementation of the FlexNIC model. While we provide a sketch of a potential implementation, we assume that the model can be implemented in an inexpensive way at high line-rates. Our assumption rests on the fact that OpenFlow switches have demonstrated this capability with minimum-sized packets at aggregate per-chip rates of over a half terabit per second [47].

2. FlexNIC Design and Implementation

A number of design goals guide the development of FlexNIC:

- **Flexibility.** We need a hardware programming model flexible enough to serve the offload requirements of network applications that change at software development timescales.
- **Line rate packet processing.** At the same time the model may not slow down network I/O by allowing arbitrary processing. We need to be able to support the line rates of tomorrow's network interfaces (at least 100 Gb/s).
- **Inexpensive hardware integration.** The required additional hardware has to be economical, such that it fits the pricing model of commodity NICs.
- **Minimal application modification.** While we assume that applications are designed for scalability and high-performance, we do not assume that large modifications to existing software are required to make use of FlexNIC.
- **OS Integration.** The design needs to support the protection and isolation guarantees provided at the OS, while allowing applications to install their own offloading primitives in a fast and flexible manner.

To provide the needed flexibility at fast line rates, we apply the reconfigurable match table (RMT) model recently proposed for flexible switching chips [8] to the NIC DMA interface. The RMT model processes packets through a sequence of match plus action (M+A) stages.

We make no assumptions about how the RMT model is implemented on the NIC. Firmware, FPGA, custom silicon, and network processor based approaches are all equally feasible, but incur different costs. However, we note that a typical commodity switch uses merchant silicon to support sixteen 40 Gbps links at a cost of about $10K per switch in volume, including the switching capacity, deep packet buffers, protocol handling, and a match plus action (M+A) table for route control. In fact, it is generally believed that converting to the more flexible RMT model will *reduce* costs in the next generation of switches by reducing the need for specialized protocol processing [8]. As a result, we believe that adding line-rate FlexNIC support is both feasible and likely less expensive than adding full network processor or FPGA support.

In this section, we provide a design of FlexNIC, present a set of reusable building blocks implemented on FlexNIC, and describe how we emulate the proposed FlexNIC functionality with existing hardware or in software.

2.1 Motivating Example

To motivate FlexNIC and its design, we consider the performance bottlenecks for the popular Memcached key-value store [2] and how they could be alleviated with NIC support. Memcached is typically used to accelerate common web requests and provides a simple *get* and *put* interface to an associative array indexed by application-level keys. In these scenarios, service latency and throughput are of utmost importance.

Memory-efficient scaling. To scale request throughput, today's NICs offer receive-side scaling (RSS), an offload feature that distributes incoming packets to descriptor queues based on the client connection. Individual CPU cores are then assigned to each queue to scale performance with the number of cores. Additional mechanisms, such as Intel's FlowDirector [23], allow OSes to directly steer and migrate individual connections to specific queues. Linux does so based on the last local send operation of the connection, assuming the same core will send on the connection again.

Both approaches suffer from a number of performance drawbacks: (1) Hot items are likely to be accessed by multiple clients, reducing cache effectiveness by replicating these items in multiple CPU caches. (2) When a hot item is modified, it causes synchronization overhead and global cache invalidations. (3) Item access is not correlated with client connections, so connection-based steering is not going to help.

FlexNIC allows us to tailor these approaches to Memcached. Instead of assigning clients to server cores, we can *partition* the key space [30] and use a separate key space request queue per core. We can install rules that steer client requests to appropriate queues, based on a hash of the requested key in the packet. The hash can be computed by FlexNIC using the existing RSS hashing functionality. This approach maximizes cache utilization and minimizes cache coherence traffic. For skewed or hot items, we can use the NIC to balance the client load in a manner that suits both the application and the hardware (e.g., by dynamically repartitioning or by routing hot requests to two cores that share the same cache and hence benefit from low latency sharing).

Streamlined request processing. Even if most client requests arrive well-formed at the server and are of a common type—say, GET requests—network stacks and Memcached have to inspect each packet to determine where the client

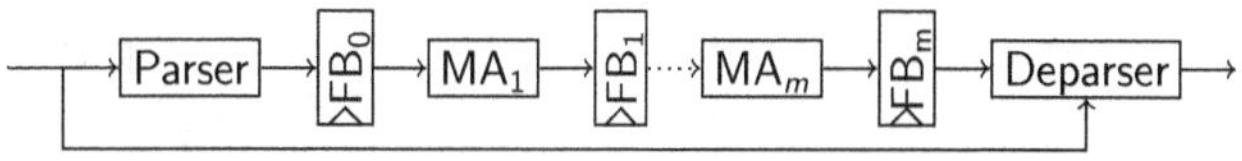

Figure 1. RMT switch pipeline.

payload starts, to parse the client command, and to extract the request ID. This incurs extra memory and processing overhead as the NIC has to transfer the headers to the host just so that software can check and then discard them. Measurements using the Arrakis OS [39] showed that, assuming kernel bypass, network stack and application-level packet processing take half of the total server processing time for Memcached.

With FlexNIC, we can check and discard Memcached headers directly on the NIC before any transfer takes place and eliminate the server processing latency. To do so, we install a rule that identifies GET requests and transfers only the client ID and requested key to a dedicated fast-path request queue for GET requests. If the packet is not well-formed, the NIC can detect this and instead transfer it in the traditional way to a slow-path queue for software processing. Further, to support various client hardware architectures, Memcached has to convert certain packet fields from network to host byte order. We can instruct the NIC to carry out these simple transformations for us, before transferring the packets into host memory.

2.2 FlexNIC Model

We now briefly describe the RMT model used in switches and then discuss how to adapt it to support application-specific optimizations of the type described above. We provide hardware implementation details where they impact the programming model.

RMT in switches. RMT switches can be programmed with a set of rules that match on various parts of the packet, and then apply data-driven modifications to it, all operating at line rate for the switched packets. This is implemented using two packet processing pipelines that are connected by a set of queues allowing for packets to be replicated and then modified separately. Such a pipeline is shown in Figure 1. A packet enters the pipeline through the parser, which identifies all relevant packet fields as described by the software-defined parse graph. It extracts the specified fields into a field buffer (FB_0) to be used in later processing stages. The relevant fields pass through the pipeline of M+A stages ($MA_1..MA_m$) and further field buffers ($FB_1..FB_m$). In a typical design, $m = 32$. An M+A stage matches on field buffer contents using a match table (of implementation-defined size), looking up a corresponding action, which is then applied as we forward to the next field buffer. Independent actions can be executed in parallel within one M+A stage. The deparser combines the modified fields with the original packet data received from the parser to get the final packet. To be able to operate at high line rates, multiple

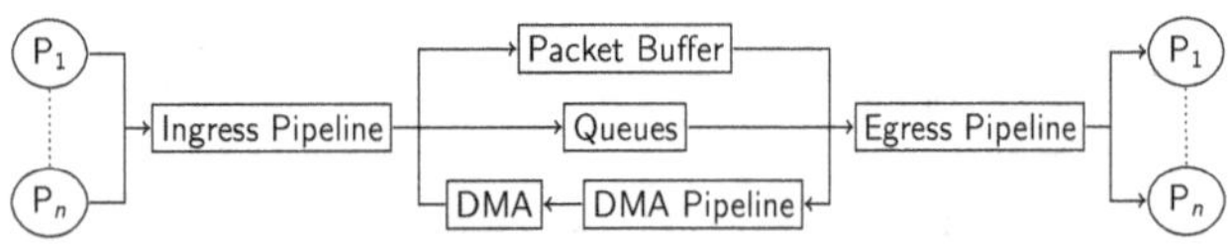

Figure 2. RMT-enhanced NIC DMA architecture.

parser instances can be used. In addition to exact matches, RMT tables can also be configured to perform prefix, range, and wildcard matches. Finally, a limited amount of switch-internal SRAM can maintain state across packets and may be used while processing.

Applying RMT to NICs. To gain the largest benefit from our approach, we enhance commodity NIC DMA capabilities by integrating three RMT pipelines with the DMA engine, as shown in Figure 2. This allows FlexNIC to process incoming and outgoing packets independently, as well as send new packets directly from the NIC in response to host DMA interactions.

Similar to the switch model, incoming packets from any of the NIC's Ethernet ports ($P_1..P_n$) first traverse the ingress pipeline where they may be modified according to M+A rules. Packet fields can be added, stripped, or modified, potentially leaving a much smaller packet to be transferred to the host. Modified packets are stored in a NIC-internal packet buffer and pointers to the corresponding buffer positions are added to a number of NIC-internal holding queues depending on the final destination. In addition to host memory, hardware implementations may choose to offer $P_1..P_n$ as final destinations, allowing response packets to be forwarded back out on the network without host interaction. From each holding queue, packets are dequeued and (depending on the final destination) processed separately in the *DMA pipeline* or the *egress pipeline*. Both can again apply modifications.

If host memory is the final destination, the DMA pipeline issues requests to the DMA controller for transferring data between host memory and packet buffer. DMA parameters are passed to the DMA engine by adding a special DMA header to packets in the DMA pipeline, as shown in Table 1.

This design is easily extended to include support for CPU cache steering [20; 38] and atomic operations [37] if supported by the PCIe chipset. We can use this design to exchange packets with host memory or to carry out more complex memory exchanges. Packet checksums are calculated on the final result using the existing checksum offload capabilities.

Control flow. In general, actions execute in parallel, but FlexNIC also allows us to define dependencies among actions up to a hardware-defined limit. Compilers are responsible for rejecting code with too many dependencies for a particular hardware implementation. Dependencies are simply defined as "executes-before" relationships and may be chained. When mapping a rule set to a hardware pipeline,

Field	Description
`offset`	Byte offset in the packet
`length`	Number of bytes to transfer
`direction`	From/To memory
`memBase`	Start address in memory
`cache`	Cache level to send data to
`core`	Core Id, if data should go to cache
`atomicOp`	PCIe atomic operation [37]

Table 1. Header format for DMA requests.

dependencies constrain which physical pipeline stages can be used for executing individual actions.

Such control flow dependencies are useful to restrict application-level access to packet filtering under kernel bypass [39; 5]. The OS inserts early ingress rules that assign incoming packets to a subset of the installed application rules by tagging packets with an identifier. Rule subsets are associated with applications by requiring them to match on the identifier. If such rules are inserted appropriately by the OS, then applications only receive packet flows deemed accessible by them (e.g., by matching on a specific MAC or IP address first).

Constraints. To make packet processing at high line-rates feasible, the RMT model is explicitly not freely programmable and several restrictions are imposed upon the user. For example, processing primitives are limited. Multiplication, division and floating point operations are typically not feasible. Hashing primitives, however, are available; this exposes the hardware that NICs use today for flow steering. Control flow mechanisms, such as loops and pointers, are also unavailable, and entries inside M+A tables cannot be updated on the data path. This precludes complex computations from being used on the data path. We expect the amount of stateful NIC memory to be constrained; in particular, our experimental results assume no per-flow state.

Programming language. The programming interface to FlexNIC is inspired by the P4 language [9] proposed for configuring programmable switches. Parsers, deparsers, packet headers, and M+A rules can be defined in much the same way, but we also allow handling NIC-internal SRAM in M+A stages, with additional actions for accessing this memory. Integration of the DMA controller, the other major change from RMT switches, does not require language extensions, but we add action verbs to simplify programming.

Example. Figure 3 shows the pseudo-code of a FlexNIC program that implements memory efficient scaling as described in the motivating example of Section 2.1. This program makes use of all the required elements of our model. To execute this program, the FlexNIC parser extracts the referenced packet fields out of incoming packets and passes them to the M+A stages in the ingress pipeline. RMT tables in the ingress pipeline then determine whether the fields match the **IF** declarations in the program. The hash in line 4, which

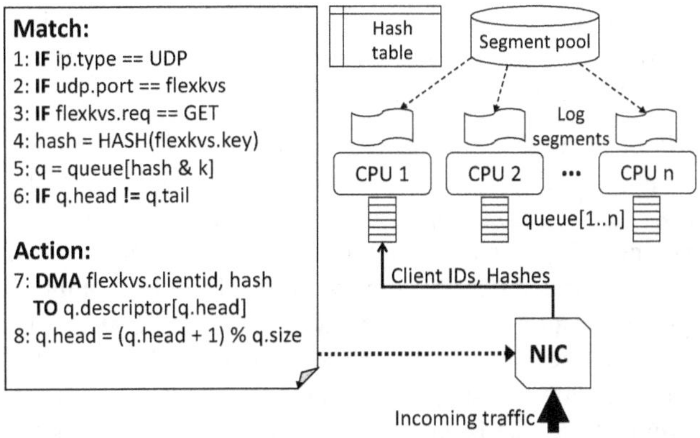

Figure 3. FlexNIC receive fast-path for FlexKVS: A rule matches GET requests for a particular key range and writes only the key hash together with a client identifier to a host descriptor queue. The queue tail is updated by FlexKVS via a register write.

is needed to determine the destination queue, is computed for every incoming packet after parsing (for example, using the CRC mechanism used for checksums) and discarded if not needed later. Line 5 uses a match table to map ranges of hashes to queues of the cores responsible for those keys. `q.head` and `q.tail` in line 6 are maintained in the NIC-internal SRAM and are compared in the ingress pipeline. The action part is inserted into the DMA pipeline. The DMA pipeline generates packet headers to instruct the DMA engine to transfer the specified packet and metadata fields out of the pipeline buffers to the host memory address of the next queue entry. Finally, line 8 updates `q.head` in the NIC-internal SRAM in any pipeline stage of the DMA pipeline. A description of how the FlexKVS application integrates with the FlexNIC pipeline is deferred to Section 3.

2.3 Building Blocks

During the use case exploration of FlexNIC, a number of building blocks have crystallized, which we believe are broadly applicable beyond the use cases presented in this paper. These building blocks provide easy, configurable access to a particular functionality that FlexNIC is useful for. We present them in this section and will refer back to them in later sections.

Multiplexing: Multiplexing has proven valuable to accelerate the performance of our applications. On the receive path, the NIC has to be able to identify incoming packets based on arbitrary header fields, drop unneeded headers, and place packets into software-defined queues. On the send path, the NIC has to read packets from various application-defined packet queues, prepend the correct headers, and send them along a fixed number of connections. This building block is implemented using only ingress/egress M+A rules.

Flow and congestion control: Today's high-speed NICs either assume the application is trusted to implement congestion control, or, as in RDMA, enforce a specific model in hardware. Many protocols can be directly encoded in an RMT model with simple packet handling and minimal per-flow state. For example, for flow control, a standard pattern we use is to configure FlexNIC to automatically generate receiver-side acks using ingress M+A rules, in tandem with delivering the payload to a receive queue for application processing. If the application falls behind, the receive queue will fill, the ack is not generated, and the sender will stall.

For congestion control, enforcement needs to be in the kernel while packet processing is at user level. Many data centers configure their switches to mark an explicit congestion notification (ECN) bit in each packet to indicate imminent congestion. We configure FlexNIC to pull the ECN bits out before the packet stream reaches the application; we forward these to the host operating system on the sender to allow it to adjust its rate limits without needing to trust the application.

Other protocols, such as TCP, seem to be stateful and require complex per-packet logic; although we believe it possible to use FlexNIC to efficiently transmit and receive TCP packets, we leave that discussion for future work.

Hashing: Hashing is essential to the scalable operation of NICs today, and hashes can be just as useful when handling packets inside application software. However, they often need to be re-computed there, adding overhead. This overhead can be easily eliminated by relaying the hardware-computed hash to software. In FlexNIC, we allow flexible hashing on arbitrary packet fields and relay the hash in a software-defined packet header via ingress or DMA rules.

Filtering: In addition to multiplexing, filtering can eliminate software overheads that would otherwise be required to handle error cases, even if very few illegal packets arrive in practice. In FlexNIC, we can insert ingress M+A rules that drop unwanted packets or divert them to a separate descriptor queue for software processing.

2.4 Testbed Implementation

To quantify the benefits of FlexNIC, we leverage a combination of hardware and software techniques that we implement within a test cluster. Whenever possible, we re-use existing hardware functionality to achieve FlexNIC functionality. When this is impossible, we emulate the missing functionality in software on a number of dedicated processor cores. This limits the performance of the emulation to slower link speeds than would be possible with a hardware implementation of FlexNIC and thus favors the baseline in our comparison. We describe the hardware and software emulation in this section, starting with the baseline hardware used within our cluster.

Testbed cluster. Our evaluation cluster contains six machines consisting of 6-core Intel Xeon E5-2430 (Sandy Bridge) systems at 2.2 GHz with 18MB total cache space. Unless otherwise mentioned, hyperthreading is enabled, yielding 12 hyperthreads per machine. All systems have an

Intel X520 (82599-based) dual-port 10Gb Ethernet adapter with both ports connected to the same 10Gb Dell PowerConnect 8024F Ethernet switch. We run Ubuntu Linux 14.04.

Hardware features re-used. We make use of the X520's receive-side scaling (RSS) capabilities to carry out fast, customizable steering and hashing in hardware. RSS in commodity NICs operates on a small number of fixed packet header fields, such as IP and TCP/UDP source and destination addresses/ports, and are thus not customizable. We attain limited customization capability by configuring RSS to operate on IPv6 addresses, which yields the largest contiguous packet area to operate upon—32 bytes—and then moving the relevant data into these fields. This is sufficient for our experiments, as MAC addresses and port numbers are enough for routing within our simple network. RSS computes a 32-bit hash on the 32 byte field, which it also writes to the receive descriptor for software to read. It then uses the hash as an index into a 128-entry redirection table that determines the destination queue for an incoming packet.

Software implementation. We implement other needed functionality in a software NIC extension that we call Soft-FlexNIC. Soft-FlexNIC implements flexible demultiplexing, congestion control, and a customizable DMA interface to the host. To do this, Soft-FlexNIC uses dedicated host cores (2 send and 2 receive cores were sufficient to handle 10Gb/s) and a shared memory interface to system software that mimics the hardware interface. For performance, Soft-FlexNIC makes use of batching, pipelining, and lock-free queueing. Batching and pipelining work as described in [19]. Lock-free queueing is used to allow scalable access to the emulated host descriptor queue from multiple Soft-FlexNIC threads by atomically reserving queue positions via a compare and swap operation. We try to ensure that our emulation adequately approximates DMA interface overheads and NIC M+A parallelism, but our approach may be optimistic in modelling PCI round trips, as these cannot be emulated easily using CPU cache coherence interactions.

Baseline. In order to provide an adequate comparison, we also run all software on top of the high-performance Extaris user-level network stack [39] and make this our baseline. Extaris runs minimal code to handle packets and is a zero-copy and scalable network stack. This eliminates the overheads inherent in a kernel-level network stack and allows us to focus on the improvements that are due to FlexNIC.

3. Case Study: Key-Value Store

We now describe the design of a key-value store, FlexKVS, that is compatible with Memcached [2], but whose performance is optimized using the functionality provided by FlexNIC. To achieve performance close to the hardware limit, we needed to streamline the store's internal design, as we hit several scalability bottlenecks with Memcached. The authors of MICA [30] had similar problems, but unlike MICA, we assume no changes to the protocol or client software. We discuss the design principles in optimizing FlexKVS before outlining its individual components.

Minimize cache coherence traffic. FlexKVS achieves memory-efficient scaling by partitioning the handling of the key-space across multiple cores and using FlexNIC to steer incoming requests to the appropriate queue serving a given core. Key-based steering improves cache locality, minimizes synchronization, and improves cache utilization, by handling individual keys on designated cores without sharing in the common case. To support dynamic changes to the key assignment for load balancing, FlexKVS's data structures are locked; in between re-balancing (the common case), each lock will be cached exclusive to the core.

Specialized critical path. We further optimize FlexKVS by offloading request processing work to FlexNIC and specializing the various components on the critical path. FlexNIC checks headers, extracts the request payload, and performs network to host byte order tranformations. With these offloads, the FlexKVS main loop for receiving a request from the network, processing it and then sending a response consists of fewer than 3,000 x86 instructions including error handling. FlexKVS also makes full use of the zero-copy capabilities of Extaris. Only one copy is performed when storing items upon a SET request.

Figure 3 depicts the overall design, including a set of simplified FlexNIC rules to steer GET requests for a range of keys to a specific core.

3.1 FlexKVS Components

We now discuss the major components of FlexKVS: the hash table and the item allocator.

Hash table. FlexKVS uses a block chain hash table [30]. To avoid false sharing, each table entry has the size of a full cache line, which leaves room for a spin-lock, multiple item pointers (five on x86-64), and the corresponding hashes. Including the hashes on the table entries avoids dereferencing pointers and touching cache lines for non-matching items. If more items hash to an entry than there are available pointers the additional items are chained in a new entry via the last pointer. We use a power of two for the number of buckets in the table. This allows us to use the lowest k bits of the hash to choose a bucket, which is easy to implement in FlexNIC. k is chosen based on the demultiplexing queue table size loaded into the NIC (up to 128 entries in our prototype).

Item allocation. The item allocator in FlexKVS uses a log [44] for allocation as opposed to a slab allocator used in Memcached. This provides constant-time allocation and minimal cache access, improving overall request processing time. To minimize synchronization, the log is divided into fixed-size segments. Each core has exactly one active segment that is used for satisfying allocation requests. A centralized segment pool is used to manage inactive segments, from which new segments are allocated when the active segment is full. Synchronization for pool access is required, but is infrequent enough to not cause noticeable overhead.

Item deletion. To handle item deletions, each log segment includes a counter of the number of bytes that have been freed in the segment. When an item's reference count drops to zero, the item becomes inactive and the corresponding segment header is looked up and the counter incremented. A background thread periodically scans segment headers for candidate segments to compact.When compacting, active items in the candidate segment are re-inserted into a new segment and inactive items deleted. After compaction, the segment is added to the free segment pool.

3.2 FlexNIC Implementation

The FlexNIC implementation consists of key-based steering and a custom DMA interface. We describe both.

Key-based steering. To implement key-based steering, we utilize the hashing and demultiplexing building blocks on the key field in the FlexKVS request packet, as shown in Figure 3. When enqueuing the packet to the appropriate receive queue based on the hash of the key, the NIC writes the hash into a special packet header for software to read. This hash value is used by FlexKVS for the hash table lookup.

Custom DMA interface. FlexNIC can also perform the item log append on SET requests, thereby enabling full zero-copy operation for both directions, and removal of packet parsing for SET requests in FlexKVS. To do so, FlexKVS registers a small number (four in our prototype) of log segments per core via a special message enqueued on a descriptor queue. These log segments are then filled by the NIC as it processes SET requests. When a segment fills up, FlexNIC enqueues a message to notify FlexKVS to register more segments.

FlexNIC still enqueues a message for each incoming request to the corresponding core, so remaining software processing can be done. For GET requests, this entails a hash table lookup. For SET requests, the hash table needs to be updated to point to the newly appended item.

Adapting FlexKVS to the custom DMA interface required adding 200 lines for interfacing with FlexNIC, adding 50 lines to the item allocator for managing NIC log segments, and modifications to request processing reducing the original 500 lines to 150.

3.3 Performance Evaluation

We evaluate different levels of integration between FlexKVS and the NIC. The baseline runs on the Extaris network stack using UDP and RSS, similar to the Memcached configuration in Arrakis [39]. A more integrated version uses FlexNIC to perform the hash calculation and steer requests based on their key, and the third version adds the FlexNIC custom

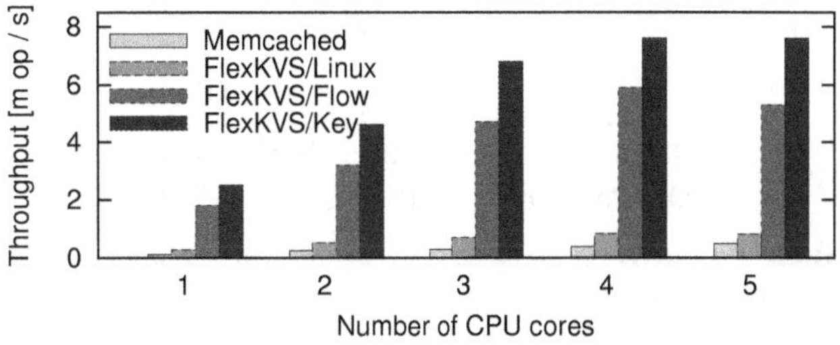

Figure 4. FlexKVS throughput scalability with flow-based and key-based steering. Results for Memcached and FlexKVS on Linux are also provided.

DMA interface. FlexKVS performance is reduced by hyperthreading and so we disable it for these experiments, leaving 6 cores per machine.

Key-based Steering. We compare FlexKVS throughput with flow-based steering against key-based steering using FlexNIC. We use three machines for this experiment, one server for running FlexKVS and two client machines to generate load. One NIC port of each client machine is used, and the server is connected with both ports using link aggregation, yielding a 20 Gb/s link. The workload consists of 100,000 key-value pairs of 32 byte keys and 64 byte values, with a skewed access distribution (zipf, $s = 0.9$). The workload contains 90% GET requests and 10% SET requests. Throughput was measured over 2 minutes after 1 minute of warm-up.

Figure 4 shows the average attained throughput for key- and flow-based steering over an increasing number of server cores. In the case of one core, the performance improvement in key-based steering is due to the computation of the hash function on the NIC. As the number of cores increases, lock contention and cache coherence traffic cause increasing overhead for flow-based steering. Key-based steering avoids these scalability bottlenecks and offers 30-45% better throughput. Note that the throughput for 4+ cores with key-based steering is limited by PCIe bus bandwidth, as the workload is issuing a large number of small bus transactions. We thus stop the experiment after 5 cores. Modifying the NIC driver to use batching increases throughput to 13 million operations per second.

Specialized DMA interface. The second experiment measures the server-side request processing latency. Three different configurations are compared: flow-based steering, key-based steering, and key-based steering with the specialized DMA interface described above. We measure time spent from the point an incoming packet is seen by the network stack to the point the corresponding response is inserted into the NIC descriptor queue.

Table 2 shows the median and 90th percentile of the number of cycles per request measured over 100 million requests. Key-based steering reduces the number of CPU cycles by 38% over the baseline, matching the throughput results pre-

	Steering		
	Flow	Key	DMA
Median	1110	690	440
90th Percentile	1400	1070	680

Table 2. FlexKVS request processing time rounded to 10 cycles.

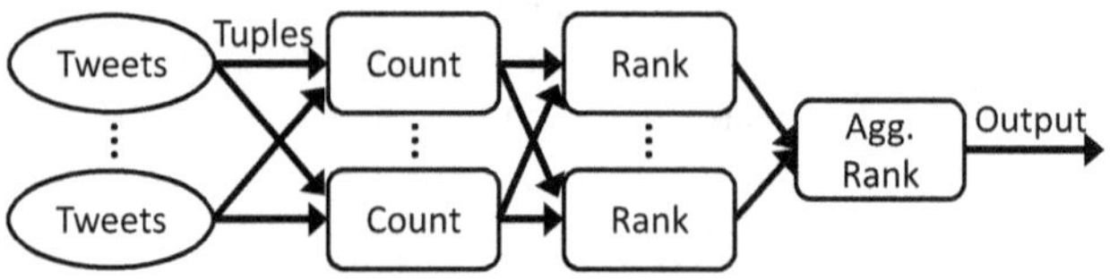

Figure 5. Top-n Twitter users topology.

sented above. The custom DMA interface reduces this number by another 36%, leading to a cumulative reduction of 60%. These performance benefits can be attributed to three factors: 1) with FlexNIC limited protocol processing needs to be performed on packets, 2) receive buffer management is not required, and 3) log-appends for SET requests are executed by FlexNIC.

We conclude that flexible hashing and demultiplexing combined with the FlexNIC DMA engine yield considerable performance improvements in terms of latency and throughput for key-value stores. FlexNIC can efficiently carry out packet processing, buffer management, and log data structure management without additional work on server CPUs.

4. Case Study: Real-time Analytics

Real-time analytics platforms are useful tools to gain instantaneous, dynamic insight into vast datasets that change frequently. To be considered "real-time", the system must be able to produce answers within a short timespan (typically within a minute) and process millions of dataset changes per second. To do so, analytics platforms utilize data stream processing techniques: A set of *worker nodes* run continuously on a cluster of machines; data *tuples* containing updates stream through them according to a dataflow processing graph, known as a *topology*. Tuples are emitted and consumed worker-to-worker in the topology. Each worker can process and aggregate incoming tuples before emitting new tuples. Workers that emit tuples derived from an original data source are known as *spouts*.

In the example shown in Figure 5, consider processing a live feed of tweets to determine the current set of top-n tweeting users. First, tweets are injected as tuples into a set of counting workers to extract and then count the user name field within each tuple. The rest of the tuple is discarded. Counters are implemented with a sliding window. Periodically (every minute in our case), counters emit a tuple for each active user name with its count. Ranking workers

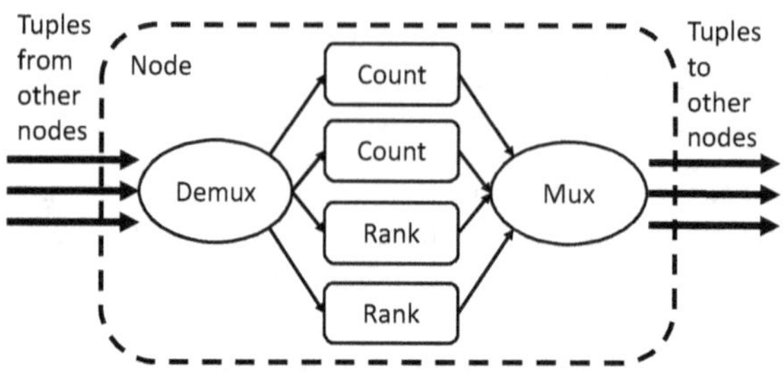

Figure 6. Storm worker design. 2 counters and 2 rankers run concurrently in this node. (De-)mux threads route incoming/outgoing tuples among network connections and workers.

sort incoming tuples by count. They emit the top-n counted users to a single aggregating ranker, producing the final output rank to the user.

As shown in Figure 5, the system scales by replicating the counting and ranking workers and spreading incoming tuples over the replicas. This allows workers to process the data set in parallel. Tuples are flow controlled when sent among workers to minimize loss. Many implementations utilize the TCP protocol for this purpose.

We have implemented a real-time analytics platform FlexStorm, following the design of Apache Storm [49]. Storm and its successor Heron [28] are deployed at large-scale at Twitter. For high performance, we implement Storm's "at most once" tuple processing mode. In this mode, tuples are allowed to be dropped under overload, eliminating the need to track tuples through the topology. For efficiency, Storm and Heron make use of multicore machines and deploy multiple workers per machine. We replicate this behavior.

FlexStorm uses DCCP [27] for flow control. DCCP supports various congestion control mechanisms, but, unlike TCP, is a packet-oriented protocol. This simplifies implementation in FlexNIC. We use TCP's flow-control mechanism within DCCP, similar to the proposal in [17], but using TCP's cumulative acknowledgements instead of acknowledgement vectors and no congestion control of acknowledgements.

As topologies are often densely interconnected, both systems reduce the number of required network connections from per-worker to per-machine connections. On each machine, a demultiplexer thread is introduced that receives all incoming tuples and forwards them to the correct executor for processing. Similarly, outgoing tuples are first relayed to a multiplexer thread that batches tuples before sending them onto their destination connections for better performance. Figure 6 shows this setup, which we replicate in FlexStorm.

4.1 FlexNIC Implementation

As we will see later, software demultiplexing has high overhead and quickly becomes a bottleneck. We can use FlexNIC to mitigate this overhead by demultiplexing tuples

```
Match:                            Action:
IF ip.type == DCCP                SWAP(dccp.srcport, dccp.dstport)
IF dccp.dstport == FlexStorm      dccp.type = DCCP_ACK
                                  dccp.ack = dccp.seq
                                  dccp.checksum = CHECKSUM(dccp)
                                  IP_REPLY
```

Figure 7. Acknowledging incoming FlexStorm tuples in FlexNIC.

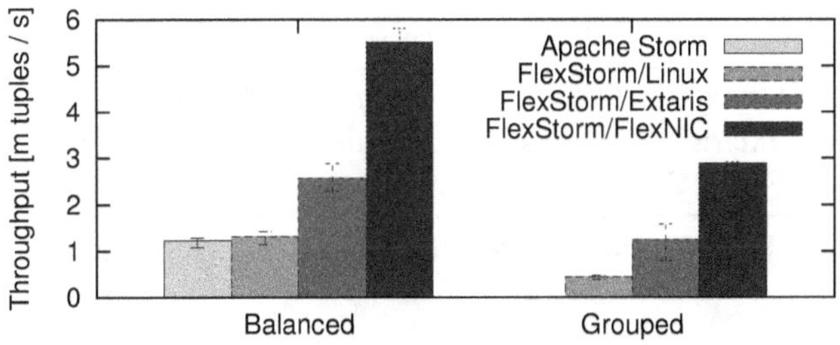

Figure 8. Average top-n tweeter throughput on various Storm configurations. Error bars show min/max over 20 runs.

in the NIC. Demultiplexing works in the same way as for FlexKVS, but does not require hashing. We strip incoming packets of their headers and deliver contained tuples to the appropriate worker's tuple queue via a lookup table that assigns destination worker identifiers to queues. However, our task is complicated by the fact that we have to enforce flow control.

To implement flow-control at the receiver in FlexNIC, we acknowledge every incoming tuple immediately and explicitly, by crafting an appropriate acknowledgement using the incoming tuple as a template. Figure 7 shows the required M+A pseudocode. To craft the acknowledgement, we swap source and destination port numbers, set the packet type appropriately, copy the incoming sequence number into the acknowledgement field, and compute the DCCP checksum. Finally, we send the reply IP packet, which does all the appropriate modifications to form an IP response, such as swapping Ethernet and IP source and destination addresses and computing the IP checksum.

To make use of FlexNIC we need to adapt FlexStorm to read from our custom queue format, which we optimize to minimize PCIe round-trips by marking whether a queue position is taken with a special field in each tuple's header. To do so, we replace FlexStorm's per-worker tuple queue implementation with one that supports this format, requiring a change of 100 lines of code to replace 4 functions and their data structures.

4.2 Evaluation

We evaluate the performance of Storm and various FlexStorm configurations on the top-n user topology. Our input workload is a stream of 476 million Twitter tweets collected between June–Dec 2009 [29]. Figure 8 and Table 3 show average achievable throughput and latency at peak load on this workload. Throughput is measured in tuples processed per second over a runtime of 20 seconds. Latency is also measured per tuple and is broken down into time spent in processing, and in input and output queues, as measured at user-level, within FlexStorm. For comparison, data center network packet delay is typically on the order of tens to hundreds of microseconds.

We first compare the performance of FlexStorm to that of Apache Storm running on Linux. We tune Apache Storm for high performance: we use "at most once" processing, disable all logging and debugging, and configure the optimum amount of worker threads (equal to the number of hyperthreads minus two multiplexing threads). We deploy both systems in an identical fashion on 3 machines of our evaluation cluster. In this configuration Apache Storm decides to run 4 replicas each of spouts, counters and intermediate rankers. Storm distributes replicas evenly over the existing hyperthreads and we follow this distribution in FlexStorm (Balanced configuration). By spreading the workload evenly over all machines, the amount of tuples that need to be processed at each machine is reduced, relieving the demultiplexing thread somewhat. To show the maximum attainable benefit with FlexNIC, we also run FlexStorm configurations where all counting workers are executing on the same machine (Grouped configuration). The counting workers have to sustain the highest amount of tuples and thus exert the highest load on the system.

Without FlexNIC, the performance of Storm and FlexStorm are roughly equivalent. There is a slight improvement in FlexStorm due to its simplicity. Both systems are limited by Linux kernel network stack performance. Even though per-tuple processing time in FlexStorm is short, tuples spend several milliseconds in queues after reception and before emission. Queueing before emission is due to batching in the multiplexing thread, which is configured to batch up to 10 milliseconds of tuples before emission in FlexStorm (Apache Storm uses up to 500 milliseconds). Input queueing is minimal in FlexStorm as it is past the bottleneck of the Linux kernel and thus packets are queued at a lower rate than they are removed from the queue. FlexStorm performance is degraded to 34% when grouping all counting workers, as all tuples now go through a single bottleneck kernel network stack, as opposed to three.

Running all FlexStorm nodes on the Extaris network stack yields a 2× (Balanced) throughput improvement. Input queuing delay has increased as tuples are queued at a higher rate. The increase is offset by a decrease in output queueing delay, as packets can be sent faster due to the high-performance network stack. Overall, tuple processing latency has decreased 16% versus Linux. The grouped configuration attains a speedup of 2.84× versus the equivalent Linux configuration. The bottleneck in both cases is the demultiplexer thread.

Running all FlexStorm nodes on FlexNIC yields a 2.14× (Balanced) performance improvement versus the Extaris

	Input	Processing	Output	**Total**
Linux	6.68 μs	0.6 μs	12 ms	**12 ms**
Extaris	4 ms	0.8 μs	6 ms	**10 ms**
FlexNIC	–	0.8 μs	6 ms	**6 ms**

Table 3. Average FlexStorm tuple processing time.

version. Using FlexNIC has eliminated the input queue and latency has decreased by 40% versus Extaris. The grouped configuration attains a speedup of 2.31×. We are now limited by the line-rate of our Ethernet network card.

We conclude that moving application-level packet demultiplexing functionality into the NIC yields performance benefits, while reducing the amount of time that tuples are held in queues. This provides the opportunity for tighter real-time processing guarantees under higher workloads using the same equipment. The additional requirement for receive-side flow control does not pose an implementation problem to FlexNIC. Finally, demultiplexing in the NIC is more efficient. It eliminates the need for additional demultiplexing threads, which can grow large under high line-rates.

We can use these results to predict what would happen at higher line-rates. The performance difference of roughly 2× between FlexNIC and a fast software implementation shows that we would require at least 2 fully utilized hyperthreads to perform demultiplexing for FlexStorm at a line-rate of 10Gb/s. As line-rate increases, this number increases proportionally, taking away threads that could otherwise be used to perform more analytics.

5. Case Study: Intrusion Detection

In this section we discuss how we leverage flexible packet steering to improve the throughput achieved by the Snort intrusion detection system [43]. Snort detects malicious activity, such as buffer overflow attacks, malware, and injection attacks, by scanning for suspicious patterns in individual packet flows.

Snort only uses a single thread for processing packets, but is commonly scaled up to multiple cores by running multiple Snort processes that receive packets from separate NIC hardware queues via RSS [19]. However, since many Snort patterns match only on subsets of the port space (for example, only on source or only on destination ports), we end up using these patterns on many cores, as RSS spreads connections by a 4-tuple of IP addresses and port numbers. Snort's working data structures generally grow to 10s of megabytes for production rule sets, leading to high cache pressure. Furthermore, the Toeplitz hash commonly used for RSS is not symmetric for the source and destination fields, meaning the two directions of a single flow can end up in different queues, which can be problematic for some stateful analyses where incoming and outgoing traffic is examined.

	Hashing			FlexNIC		
	Min	Avg	Max	Min	Avg	Max
Kpps	103.0	103.7	104.7	166.4	167.3	167.9
Mbps	435.9	439.8	444.6	710.4	715.6	718.6
Accesses	546.0	553.3	559.3	237.0	241.4	251.0
Misses	26.7	26.7	26.7	19.0	19.2	19.2

Table 4. Snort throughput and L3 cache behavior over 10 runs.

5.1 FlexNIC Implementation

Our approach to improve Snort's performance is similar to FlexKVS. We improve Snort's cache utilization by steering packets to cores based on expected pattern access, so as to avoid replicating the same state across caches. Internally, Snort groups rules into port groups and each group is then compiled to a deterministic finite automaton that implements pattern matching for the rules in the group. When processing a packet, Snort first determines the relevant port groups and then executes all associated automatons.

We instrument Snort to record each distinct set of port groups matched by each packet (which we call *flow groups*) and aggregate the number of packets that match this set and the total time spent processing these packets. In our experience, this approach results in 30-100 flow groups. We use these aggregates to generate a partition of flow groups to Snort processes, balancing the load of different flow groups using a simple greedy allocation algorithm that starts assigning the heaviest flow groups first.

This partitioning can then be used in FlexNIC to steer packets to individual Snort instances by creating a mapping table that maps packets to cores, similar to the approach in FlexStorm. We also remedy the issue with the Toeplitz hash by instructing FlexNIC to order 4-tuple fields arithmetically by increasing value before calculating the hash, which eliminates the assymetry.

5.2 Evaluation

We evaluate the FlexNIC-based packet steering by comparing it to basic hash-based steering. For our experiment, we use a 24GB pcap trace of the ICTF 2010 competition [1] that is replayed at 1Gbps. To obtain the flow group partition we use a prefix of 1/50th of the trace, and then use the rest to evaluate performance. For this experiment, we run 4 Snort instances on 4 cores on one socket of a two-socket 12-core Intel Xeon L5640 (Westmere) system at 2.2 GHz with 14MB total cache space. The other socket is used to replay the trace via Soft-FlexNIC implementing either configuration.

Table 4 shows the throughput and L3 cache behavior for hashing and our improved FlexNIC steering. Throughput, both in terms of packets and bytes processed, increases by roughly 60%, meaning more of the packets on the network are received and processed without being dropped. This improvement is due to the improved cache locality: the number of cache accesses to the L3 cache per packet is reduced by 56% because they hit in the L2 or L1 cache, and the number of misses in the L3 cache per packet is also reduced by roughly 28%. These performance improvements were achieved without modifying Snort.

We conclude that flexible demultiplexing can improve application performance and cache utilization even without requiring application modification. Application memory access patterns can be analyzed separately from applications and appropriate rules inserted into FlexNIC by the system administrator.

6. Other Applications

So far we discussed our approach in the context of single applications and provided case studies that quantify the application-level improvements made possible by FlexNIC. In this section, we identify additional use cases with some preliminary analysis on how FlexNIC can be of assistance in these scenarios. First, we discuss how to enhance and optimize OS support for virtualization (§6.1). Then, we present a number of additional use cases that focus on the use of flexible I/O to improve memory system performance (§6.2).

6.1 Virtualization Support

FlexNIC's functionality can aid virtualization in a number of different ways. We discuss below how FlexNIC can optimize the performance of a virtual switch, how it can provide better resource isolation guarantees, and how it can assist in transparent handling of resource exhaustion and failure scenarios.

Virtual Switch. Open vSwitch (OvS) [40] is an open source virtual switch designed for networking in virtualized data center environments. OvS forwards packets among physical and virtual NIC ports, potentially modifying packets on the way. It exposes standard management interfaces and allows advanced forwarding functions to be programmed via OpenFlow [31] M+A rules, a more limited precursor to P4 [9]. OvS is commonly used in data centers today. It supports various advanced switching features, including GRE tunneling.

To realize high performance packet forwarding without implementing all of OpenFlow in the OS kernel, OvS partitions its workflow into two components: a system userspace daemon and a simple kernel datapath module. The datapath module is able to process and forward packets according to simple 5-tuple and wildcard matches. If this is not enough to classify a flow, the packet is deferred to the userspace daemon, which implements the full matching capabilities of OpenFlow. After processing, the daemon relays its forwarding decision, potentially along with a concise 5-tuple match for future use, back to the datapath module.

To show the overhead involved in typical OvS operation, we conduct an experiment, sending a stream of packets from 4 source machines to 8 VMs executing on a single server

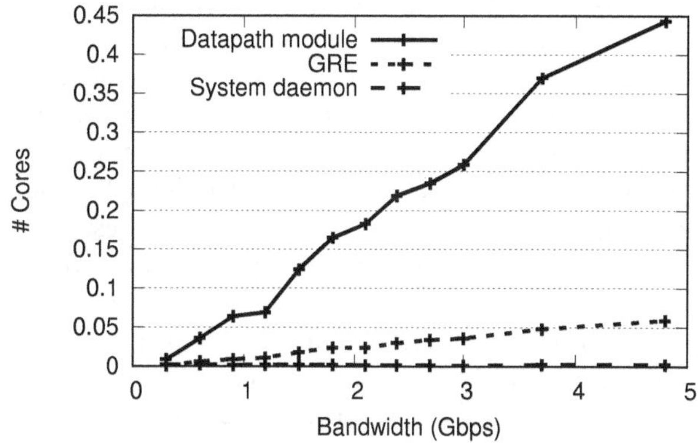

Figure 9. CPU utilization of OvS while tunneling.

machine that executes OvS to forward incoming packets to the appropriate VM. The traffic from the source machines is GRE tunneled and the tunnel is terminated at the server, so OvS decapsulates packets while forwarding. We repeat the experiment as we increase the offered traffic at the clients.

Figure 9 shows the CPU overheads involved in this simple experiment, broken down into system daemon, datapath module, and GRE decapsulation overhead. We can see that the CPU overhead of the datapath module increases linearly with increasing traffic, as it has to carry out more matching and decapsulation activity. On average, the datapath module increases CPU utilization by 10% for each Gb of traffic offered. We can extrapolate these results to understand what would happen at higher line rates: We would require 1 full CPU core at 10 Gb/s, up to 4 CPU cores devoted to OvS handling on a 40 Gb/s link and up to 10 CPU cores on a 100 Gb/s link. The overhead for GRE decapsulation increases linearly, too, but at a slower pace: roughly 1% per offered Gb. The overhead of the system daemon stays flat, which is expected, as it is used only for more complex functionality.

To remove these overheads, we can implement the functionality of the kernel datapath module within FlexNIC. To do so, we simply offload the 5-tuple and wildcard match rules. If actions are as simple as GRE tunnel decapsulation, we can implement them in FlexNIC, too, by removing the relevant packet headers after matching, and gain even more savings. More complex actions might need to be relayed back to kernel-space, saving only the overhead of OvS processing.

We conclude that today's data center environments require flexible packet handling at the edge, which in turn requires CPU resources. While the amount of consumed CPU resource is tenable at 10 Gb/s, it can quickly become prohibitive as line rates increase. FlexNIC allows offloading a large fraction of these overheads, freeing up valuable CPU resources to run application workloads.

Resource isolation. The ability to isolate and prioritize network flows is important in a range of load conditions [3]. A server receiving more requests than it can handle could decide to only accept specific request types, for example based on a priority specified in the request header. On servers that are not fully saturated, careful scheduling can reduce the average latency, for example by prioritizing cheap requests over expensive requests in a certain ratio and thereby reducing the overall tail latency. Achieving isolation implies minimizing the required resources that need to be invested before a priority can be assigned or a request can be dropped [14; 33]. As network bandwidth increases, the cost of classifying requests in software can quickly become prohibitive. FlexNIC can prioritize requests in hardware, and enqueue requests in different software queues based on priorities, or even reject requests, possibly after notifying the client.

Resource virtualization. Cloud services can be consolidated on a single server using resource virtualization. This allows the sharing of common hardware resources using techniques such as memory overcommit to save cost. However, traditional DMA operations require the corresponding host memory to be present, which is achieved by pinning the memory in the OS. With multi-queue NICs, kernel-bypass [39; 5], and RDMA, the amount of memory pinned permanently can be very large (cf. FaRM [13]), preventing effective server consolidation. Even without pinning, accesses to non-present pages are generally rare, so all that is required is a way to gracefully handle faults when they occur. Using FlexNIC, the OS can insert a rule that matches on DMA accesses to non-present regions and redirects them to a slow-path that implements these accesses in software. In this way these faults are handled in a manner fully transparent to applications.

Fast failover. User-level services can fail. In that case a hot standby or replica can be an excellent fail-over point if we can fail-over quickly. Using FlexNIC, an OS detecting a failed user-level application can insert a rule to redirect traffic to a replica, even if it resides on another server. Redirection can be implemented by a simple rule that matches the application's packets and then forwards incoming packets by rewriting the headers and enqueuing them to be sent out through the egress pipeline. No application-level modifications are necessary for this approach and redirection can occur with minimal overhead.

6.2 Flexible Memory Steering

FlexNIC's flexible packet processing provides additional opportunities for enhancing communication abstractions as well as optimizing memory system performance. We describe some of these use cases below.

Consistent RDMA. RDMA provides low latency access to remote memory. However, it does not support consistency of concurrently accessed data structures. This vastly complicates the design of applications sharing memory via RDMA (e.g., self-verifying data structures in Pilaf [32]). FlexNIC can be used to enhance RDMA with simple application-level consistency properties. For example, when concurrently writing to a hashtable, FlexNIC could check whether the target memory already contains an entry by atomically [37] testing and setting a designated memory location and, if so, either defer management of the operation to the CPU or fail it.

Cache flow control. A common problem when streaming data to caches (found in DDIO-based systems) is that the limited amount of available host cache memory can easily overflow with incoming network packets if software is not quick enough to process them. In this case, the cache spills older packets to DRAM causing cache thrashing and performance collapse when software pulls them back in the cache to process them. To prevent this, we can implement a simple credit-based flow control scheme: The NIC can increment an internal counter for each packet written to a host cache. If the counter is above a threshold, the NIC instead writes to DRAM. Software acknowledges finished packets by sending an application-defined packet via the NIC that decrements the counter. This ensures that packets stay in cache for as long as needed to keep performance stable.

GPU networking. General purpose computation capabilities on modern GPUs are increasingly being exploited to accelerate network applications [18; 24; 48; 26]. So far all these approaches require CPU involvement on the critical path for GPU-network communication. GPUnet [26] exploits P2P DMA to write packet payloads directly into GPU memory from the NIC, but the CPU is still required to forward packet notifications to/from the GPU using an in-memory ring buffer. Further, GPUnet relies on RDMA for offloading protocol processing to minimize inefficient sequential processing on the GPU. With FlexNIC, notifications about received packets can be written directly to the ring buffer because arbitrary memory writes can be crafted, thereby removing the CPU from the critical path for receiving packets. In addition FlexNIC's offload capabilities can enable the use of conventional protocols such as UDP, by offloading header verification to hardware.

7. Related Work

NIC-Software co-design. Previous attempts to improve the NIC processing performance used new software interfaces to reduce the number of required PCIe transitions [16] and to enable kernel-bypass [41; 50; 15]. Remote direct memory access (RDMA) goes a step further, entirely bypassing the remote CPU for this specific use-case. Scale-out NUMA [36] extends the RDMA approach by integrating a remote memory access controller with the processor cache hierarchy that automatically translates certain CPU memory accesses into remote memory operations. Portals [4] is similar to RDMA, but adds a set of offloadable memory and packet send operations triggered upon matching packet arrival. A machine model has been specified to allow offload of various communication protocols using these operations [12]. Our approach builds upon these ideas by providing a NIC programming model that can leverage these features in an application-defined way to support efficient data delivery to the CPU, rather than complete offload to the NIC.

High-performance software design. High-performance key-value store implementations, such as HERD [25], Pilaf [32], and MICA [30], use NIC hardware features, such as RDMA, to gain performance. They require client modifications to be able to make use of these features. For example, they require clients to issue RDMA reads (Pilaf) or writes (HERD) to bypass network stacks, or for clients to compute hashes (Pilaf, MICA). FaRM [13] generalizes this approach to other distributed systems. In contrast, FlexNIC requires modifications only in the server's NIC.

Furthermore, FlexNIC allows logic to be implemented at the server side, reducing the risk of client-side attacks and allowing the use of server-sided state without long round-trip delays. For example, FlexKVS can locally change the runtime key partitioning among cores without informing the client—something that would otherwise be impractical with tens of thousands of clients.

MICA [30] can be run either in exclusive read exclusive write (EREW) or concurrent read exclusive write (CREW) mode. EREW eliminates any cache coherence traffic between cores, while CREW allows reads to popular keys to be handled by multiple cores at the cost of cache coherence traffic for writes and reduced cache utilization because the corresponding cache lines can be in multiple cores' private caches. FlexKVS can decide which mode to use for each individual key on the server side based on the keys' access patterns, allowing EREW to be used for the majority of keys and CREW to be enabled for very read heavy keys.

Programmable network hardware. In the wake of the software-defined networking trend, a rich set of customizable switch data planes have been proposed [9; 31]. For example, the P4 programming language proposal [9] allows users rich switching control based on arbitrary packet fields, independent of underlying switch hardware. We adapt this idea to provide similar functionality for the NIC-host interface. SoftNIC [19] is an attempt to customize NIC functionality by using dedicated CPU cores running software extensions in the data path. We extend upon this approach in Soft-FlexNIC.

On the host, various programmable NIC architectures have been developed. Fully programmable network processors are commercially available [35; 10], as are FPGA-based solutions [51]. Previous research on offloading functionality to these NICs has focused primarily on entire applications, such as key-value storage [7; 11] and map-reduce functionality [45]. In contrast, FlexNIC allows for the flexible offload of performance-relevant packet processing functionality, while allowing the programmer the flexibility to keep the rest of the application code on the CPU, improving programmer productivity and shortening software development cycles.

Direct cache access. Data Direct I/O (DDIO) [21] attaches PCIe directly to an L3 cache. DDIO is software-transparent and as such does not easily support the integration with higher levels of the cache hierarchy. Prior to DDIO, direct cache access (DCA) [20] supported cache prefetching via PCIe hints sent by devices and is now a PCI standard [38]. With FlexNIC support, DCA tags could be re-used by systems to fetch packets from L3 to L1 caches. While not yet supported by commodity servers, tighter cache integration has been shown to be beneficial in systems that integrate NICs with CPUs [6].

8. Conclusion

As multicore servers scale, the boundaries between NIC and switch are blurring: NICs need to route packets to appropriate cores, but also transform and filter them to reduce software processing and memory subsystem overheads. FlexNIC provides this functionality by extending the NIC DMA interface. Performance evaluation for a number of applications shows throughput improvements of up to 2.3× when packets are demultiplexed based on application-level information, and up to 60% reduction in request processing time if the DMA interface is specialized for the application on a commodity 10 Gb/s network. These results increase proportionally to the network line-rate.

FlexNIC also integrates nicely with current software-defined networking trends. Core network switches can tag packets with actions that can be executed by FlexNIC. For example, this allows us to exert fine-grained server control, such as load balancing to individual server cores, at a programmable core network switch when this is more efficient.

Acknowledgments

This work was supported by NetApp, Google, and the National Science Foundation (CNS-0963754, CNS-1518702). We would like to thank the anonymous reviewers and our shepherd, Steve Reinhardt, for their comments and feedback. We also thank Taesoo Kim, Luis Ceze, Jacob Nelson, Timothy Roscoe, and John Ousterhout for their input on early drafts of this paper. Jialin Li and Naveen Kr. Sharma collaborated on a class project providing the basis for FlexNIC.

References

[1] `http://ictf.cs.ucsb.edu/ictfdata/2010/dumps/`.

[2] `http://memcached.org/`.

[3] G. Banga, P. Druschel, and J. C. Mogul. Resource containers: A new facility for resource management in server systems. In *3rd USENIX Symposium on Operating Systems Design and Implementation*, OSDI, 1999.

[4] B. W. Barrett, R. Brightwell, S. Hemmert, K. Pedretti, K. Wheeler, K. Underwood, R. Riesen, A. B. Maccabee, and T. Hudson. *The Portals 4.0.1 Network Programming Interface*. Sandia National Laboratories, sand2013-3181 edition, Apr. 2013.

[5] A. Belay, G. Prekas, A. Klimovic, S. Grossman, C. Kozyrakis, and E. Bugnion. IX: A protected dataplane operating system for high throughput and low latency. In *11th USENIX Symposium on Operating Systems Design and Implementation*, OSDI, 2014.

[6] N. L. Binkert, A. G. Saidi, and S. K. Reinhardt. Integrated network interfaces for high-bandwidth TCP/IP. In *12th International Conference on Architectural Support for Programming Languages and Operating Systems*, ASPLOS, 2006.

[7] M. Blott, K. Karras, L. Liu, K. A. Vissers, J. Bär, and Z. István. Achieving 10Gbps line-rate key-value stores with FPGAs. In *5th USENIX Workshop on Hot Topics in Cloud Computing*, HotCloud, 2013.

[8] P. Bosshart, G. Gibb, H.-S. Kim, G. Varghese, N. McKeown, M. Izzard, F. Mujica, and M. Horowitz. Forwarding metamorphosis: Fast programmable match-action processing in hardware for SDN. In *ACM Conference on SIGCOMM*, 2013.

[9] P. Bosshart, D. Daly, G. Gibb, M. Izzard, N. McKeown, J. Rexford, C. Schlesinger, D. Talayco, A. Vahdat, G. Varghese, and D. Walker. P4: Programming protocol-independent packet processors. *SIGCOMM Computer Communication Review*, 44(3):87–95, July 2014.

[10] Cavium Corporation. OCTEON II CN68XX multi-core MIPS64 processors. `http://www.cavium.com/pdfFiles/CN68XX_PB_Rev1.pdf`.

[11] S. R. Chalamalasetti, K. Lim, M. Wright, A. AuYoung, P. Ranganathan, and M. Margala. An FPGA Memcached appliance. In *21st ACM/SIGDA International Symposium on Field Programmable Gate Arrays*, FPGA, 2013.

[12] S. Di Girolamo, P. Jolivet, K. Underwood, and T. Hoefler. Exploiting offload enabled network interfaces. In *23rd IEEE Symposium on High Performance Interconnects*, HOTI, 2015.

[13] A. Dragojević, D. Narayanan, O. Hodson, and M. Castro. FaRM: Fast remote memory. In *11th USENIX Symposium on Networked Systems Design and Implementation*, NSDI, 2014.

[14] P. Druschel and G. Banga. Lazy receiver processing (LRP): A network subsystem architecture for server systems. In *2nd USENIX Symposium on Operating Systems Design and Implementation*, OSDI, 1996.

[15] P. Druschel, L. Peterson, and B. Davie. Experiences with a high-speed network adaptor: A software perspective. In *ACM Conference on SIGCOMM*, 1994.

[16] M. Flajslik and M. Rosenblum. Network interface design for low latency request-response protocols. In *2013 USENIX Annual Technical Conference*, ATC, 2013.

[17] S. Floyd and E. Kohler. Profile for datagram congestion control protocol (DCCP) congestion control ID 2: TCP-like congestion control. RFC 4341, Mar. 2006.

[18] S. Han, K. Jang, K. Park, and S. Moon. PacketShader: A GPU-accelerated software router. In *ACM Conference on SIGCOMM*, 2010.

[19] S. Han, K. Jang, A. Panda, S. Palkar, D. Han, and S. Ratnasamy. SoftNIC: A software NIC to augment hardware. Technical Report UCB/EECS-2015-155, EECS Department, University of California, Berkeley, May 2015. `http://www.eecs.berkeley.edu/Pubs/TechRpts/2015/EECS-2015-155.html`.

[20] R. Huggahalli, R. Iyer, and S. Tetrick. Direct cache access for high bandwidth network I/O. In *32nd Annual International Symposium on Computer Architecture*, ISCA, 2005.

[21] Intel Corporation. Intel data direct I/O technology (Intel DDIO): A primer, Feb. 2012. Revision 1.0. `http://www.intel.com/content/dam/www/public/us/en/documents/technology-briefs/data-direct-i-o-technology-brief.pdf`.

[22] Intel Corporation. Flow APIs for hardware offloads. Open vSwitch Fall Confernce Talk, Nov. 2014. `http://openvswitch.org/support/ovscon2014/18/1430-hardware-based-packet-processing.pdf`.

[23] Intel Corporation. Intel 82599 10 GbE controller datasheet, Oct. 2015. Revision 3.2. `http://www.intel.com/content/dam/www/public/us/en/documents/datasheets/82599-10-gbe-controller-datasheet.pdf`.

[24] K. Jang, S. Han, S. Han, S. Moon, and K. Park. SSLShader: Cheap SSL acceleration with commodity processors. In *8th USENIX Symposium on Networked Systems Design and Implementation*, NSDI, 2011.

[25] A. Kalia, M. Kaminsky, and D. G. Andersen. Using RDMA efficiently for key-value services. In *ACM Conference on SIGCOMM*, 2014.

[26] S. Kim, S. Huh, X. Zhang, Y. Hu, A. Wated, E. Witchel, and M. Silberstein. GPUnet: Networking abstractions for GPU programs. In *11th USENIX Symposium on Operating Systems Design and Implementation*, OSDI, 2014.

[27] E. Kohler, M. Handley, and S. Floyd. Datagram congestion control protocol (DCCP). RFC 4340, Mar. 2006.

[28] S. Kulkarni, N. Bhagat, M. Fu, V. Kedigehalli, C. Kellogg, S. Mittal, J. M. Patel, K. Ramasamy, and S. Taneja. Twitter Heron: Stream processing at scale. In *2015 ACM SIGMOD International Conference on Management of Data*, SIGMOD, 2015.

[29] J. Leskovec and A. Krevl. SNAP Datasets: Stanford large network dataset collection, June 2014. `http://snap.stanford.edu/data`.

[30] H. Lim, D. Han, D. G. Andersen, and M. Kaminsky. MICA: A holistic approach to fast in-memory key-value storage. In *11th USENIX Symposium on Networked Systems Design and Implementation*, NSDI, 2014.

[31] N. McKeown, T. Anderson, H. Balakrishnan, G. Parulkar, L. Peterson, J. Rexford, S. Shenker, and J. Turner. Openflow: Enabling innovation in campus networks. *SIGCOMM Computer Communication Review*, 38(2):69–74, Mar. 2008.

[32] C. Mitchell, Y. Geng, and J. Li. Using one-sided RDMA reads to build a fast, CPU-efficient key-value store. In *2013 USENIX Annual Technical Conference*, ATC, 2013.

[33] J. C. Mogul and K. K. Ramakrishnan. Eliminating receive livelock in an interrupt-driven kernel. *ACM Transactions on Computer Systems*, 15(3):217–252, Aug. 1997.

[34] D. Molka, D. Hackenberg, and R. Schöne. Main memory and cache performance of Intel Sandy Bridge and AMD Bulldozer. In *2014 Workshop on Memory Systems Performance and Correctness*, MSPC, 2014.

[35] Netronome. NFP-6xxx flow processor. `https://netronome.com/product/nfp-6xxx/`.

[36] S. Novakovic, A. Daglis, E. Bugnion, B. Falsafi, and B. Grot. Scale-out NUMA. In *19th International Conference on Architectural Support for Programming Languages and Operating Systems*, ASPLOS, 2014.

[37] PCI-SIG. Atomic operations. PCI-SIG Engineering Change Notice, Jan. 2008. `https://www.pcisig.com/specifications/pciexpress/specifications/ECN_Atomic_Ops_080417.pdf`.

[38] PCI-SIG. TLP processing hints. PCI-SIG Engineering Change Notice, Sept. 2008. `https://www.pcisig.com/specifications/pciexpress/specifications/ECN_TPH_11Sept08.pdf`.

[39] S. Peter, J. Li, I. Zhang, D. R. K. Ports, D. Woos, A. Krishnamurthy, T. Anderson, and T. Roscoe. Arrakis: The operating system is the control plane. In *11th USENIX Symposium on Operating Systems Design and Implementation*, OSDI, 2014.

[40] B. Pfaff, J. Pettit, T. Koponen, E. Jackson, A. Zhou, J. Rajahalme, J. Gross, A. Wang, J. Stringer, P. Shelar, K. Amidon, and M. Casado. The design and implementation of Open vSwitch. In *12th USENIX Symposium on Networked Systems Design and Implementation*, NSDI, 2015.

[41] I. Pratt and K. Fraser. Arsenic: A user-accessible Gigabit Ethernet interface. In *20th IEEE International Conference on Computer Communications*, INFOCOM, 2001.

[42] RDMA Consortium. Architectural specifications for RDMA over TCP/IP. `http://www.rdmaconsortium.org/`.

[43] M. Roesch. Snort - lightweight intrusion detection for networks. In *13th USENIX Conference on System Administration*, LISA, 1999.

[44] M. Rosenblum and J. K. Ousterhout. The design and implementation of a log-structured file system. *ACM Transactions on Computer Systems*, 10(1):26–52, Feb. 1992.

[45] Y. Shan, B. Wang, J. Yan, Y. Wang, N. Xu, and H. Yang. FPMR: MapReduce framework on FPGA. In *18th ACM/SIGDA International Symposium on Field Programmable Gate Arrays*, FPGA, 2010.

[46] P. Shinde, A. Kaufmann, T. Roscoe, and S. Kaestle. We need to talk about NICs. In *14th Workshop on Hot Topics in Operating Systems*, HOTOS, 2013.

[47] A. Singh, J. Ong, A. Agarwal, G. Anderson, A. Armistead, R. Bannon, S. Boving, G. Desai, B. Felderman, P. Germano, A. Kanagala, J. Provost, J. Simmons, E. Tanda, J. Wanderer, U. Hölzle, S. Stuart, and A. Vahdat. Jupiter rising: A decade of Clos topologies and centralized control in Googles datacenter network. In *ACM Conference on SIGCOMM*, 2015.

[48] W. Sun and R. Ricci. Fast and flexible: Parallel packet processing with GPUs and Click. In *9th ACM/IEEE Symposium on Architectures for Networking and Communications Systems*, ANCS, 2013.

[49] A. Toshniwal, S. Taneja, A. Shukla, K. Ramasamy, J. M. Patel, S. Kulkarni, J. Jackson, K. Gade, M. Fu, J. Donham, N. Bhagat, S. Mittal, and D. Ryaboy. Storm@Twitter. In *2014 ACM SIGMOD International Conference on Management of Data*, SIGMOD, 2014.

[50] T. von Eicken, A. Basu, V. Buch, and W. Vogels. U-Net: a user-level network interface for parallel and distributed computing. In *15th ACM Symposium on Operating Systems Principles*, SOSP, 1995.

[51] N. Zilberman, Y. Audzevich, G. Covington, and A. Moore. NetFPGA SUME: Toward 100 Gbps as research commodity. *IEEE Micro*, 34(5):32–41, Sept. 2014.

Specifying and Checking File System Crash-Consistency Models

James Bornholt Antoine Kaufmann Jialin Li Arvind Krishnamurthy Emina Torlak Xi Wang
University of Washington
{bornholt,antoinek,lijl,arvind,emina,xi}@cs.washington.edu

Abstract

Applications depend on persistent storage to recover state after system crashes. But the POSIX file system interfaces do not define the possible outcomes of a crash. As a result, it is difficult for application writers to correctly understand the ordering of and dependencies between file system operations, which can lead to corrupt application state and, in the worst case, catastrophic data loss.

This paper presents *crash-consistency models*, analogous to memory consistency models, which describe the behavior of a file system across crashes. Crash-consistency models include both litmus tests, which demonstrate allowed and forbidden behaviors, and axiomatic and operational specifications. We present a formal framework for developing crash-consistency models, and a toolkit, called FERRITE, for validating those models against real file system implementations. We develop a crash-consistency model for `ext4`, and use FERRITE to demonstrate unintuitive crash behaviors of the `ext4` implementation. To demonstrate the utility of crash-consistency models to application writers, we use our models to prototype proof-of-concept verification and synthesis tools, as well as new library interfaces for crash-safe applications.

Categories and Subject Descriptors D.4.3 [*Operating Systems*]: File Systems Management; D.2.4 [*Software Engineering*]: Software/Program Verification

Keywords Crash consistency; file systems; verification

1. Introduction

Many applications interact with file systems and use them as persistent storage that will be preserved in the face of hardware or software crashes. To achieve the integrity properties they desire, these applications must use file system interfaces correctly. Failure to do so can lead to corrupted application state and catastrophic data loss [83]. Recent studies by Pillai et al. [62] and Zheng et al. [92] show that even mature applications contain serious persistence bugs, making incorrect assumptions about the behavior of the file system interface.

```
/* "file" has old data */
fd = open("file.tmp", ...);
write(fd, new, size);
close(fd);
rename("file.tmp", "file");
```

(a)

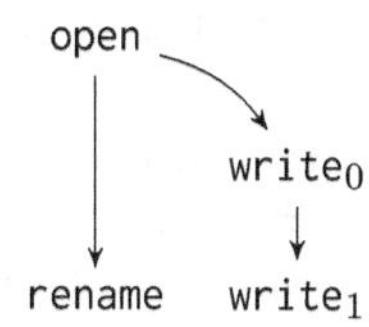

(b)

file's on-disk state	possible executions seen on disk
new	open, $\texttt{write}_0$, $\texttt{write}_1$, rename, ...
	open, $\texttt{write}_0$, rename, $\texttt{write}_1$, ...
	open, rename, $\texttt{write}_0$, $\texttt{write}_1$, ...
old	open, crash
	open, $\texttt{write}_0$, crash
	open, $\texttt{write}_0$, $\texttt{write}_1$, crash
empty	open, rename, crash
partial new	open, $\texttt{write}_0$, rename, crash
	open, rename, $\texttt{write}_0$, crash

(c)

Figure 1. A common replace-via-rename pattern (a) caused the "`ext4` data loss" incident of 2009 [84]. Only the ordering edges in (b) are enforced by the `ext4` file system, which may split the single `write` into smaller actions $\texttt{write}_n$. Unexpected on-disk states (c) arise if the system crashes during execution.

To illustrate the challenges in writing crash-safe applications, consider the 2009 "`ext4` data loss" incident, where multiple users reported that "pretty much any file written to by any application" became empty after a system crash [19, 84]. The root cause was the pattern in Figure 1(a), intended to atomically update "`file`" using a temporary file. Due to modern file system optimizations, the effects of the program do not necessarily reach disk in the order they are executed—only the orderings in Figure 1(b) are enforced. These ordering relaxations are usually invisible to applications and provide significant performance gains. But if the machine crashes during out-of-order execution, the relaxations can become visible. In this case, the `rename` can reach the disk before the

ASPLOS '16 April 2–6, 2016, Atlanta, Georgia, USA
Copyright © 2016 ACM 978-1-4503-4091-5/16/04. . . $15.00
DOI: http://dx.doi.org/10.1145/2872362.2872406

writes. If the machine crashes before the writes persist, users can see empty or partial files, and lose the old file completely, as Figure 1(c) shows. One possible fix is to add an fsync(fd) before close to ensure atomicity: applications will see either the old or the new data.

Who is to blame for such a bug? On one hand, application writers argue that file systems are "broken" [56] and are too aggressive about buffering and reordering file operations. On the other hand, file system developers argue that this behavior is allowed by POSIX and, as with relaxed memory orderings, is necessary for performance [41]. This trade-off between consistency and performance has long been a point of contention in file system design [26].

The key challenge for application writers is to understand the precise behavior of file systems across system crashes. The POSIX standard is largely silent on the guarantees file system interfaces should provide in the event of crashes (see §2.1). In practice, application writers make assumptions about the crash guarantees provided by file systems, and base their applications on these assumptions (e.g., file system-specific optimizations adopted by GNOME [45] and SQLite [77]). Being too optimistic about crash guarantees has led to serious data losses [10, 46, 62, 92]. But being too conservative leads to expensive and unnecessary synchronization, costing energy, performance, and hardware lifespan [55]. It is thus critical to describe crash guarantees of file systems in an unambiguous and accessible manner.

We propose to describe the behavior of file systems across crashes as *crash-consistency models*, analogous to the memory consistency models [1, 75] used to describe relaxed memory orderings. For example, the application in Figure 1 assumes *sequential crash-consistency*—after a crash, the system appears as if it committed the system calls in order. The ext4 file system, however, implements a weaker model, which allows rename to be reordered across a write.

Crash consistency models, as with memory consistency models, take two forms:

- *Litmus tests*: small programs that demonstrate allowed or forbidden behaviors of file systems across crashes; and
- *Formal specifications*: axiomatic and operational descriptions of crash-consistency behavior using logic and (non-deterministic) state machines, respectively.

These forms of specification serve different purposes, and neither can supplant the other. Formal specifications provide complete descriptions of (dis)allowed crash behaviors and, as such, provide a basis for automated reasoning about crash guarantees of applications. Litmus tests, on the other hand, provide a precise and intuitive description that is well suited for communicating to application developers, as well as for validating formal models against file system implementations.

We have developed FERRITE, a toolkit for executing litmus tests against formal specifications of crash-consistency models (to ensure that the specifications agree with the tests) and against real file systems (to validate our models). FERRITE exhaustively explores all possible crash behaviors of a given litmus test, both by explicit enumeration and SMT-based model checking. The enumerator (built on QEMU [7]) executes tests against actual file system implementations, while the symbolic model checker (built in Rosette [80]) executes tests against formal specifications. We have used FERRITE both to confirm known crash-safety problems and to uncover new problems in existing work. Unlike FiSC [88] and eXplode [89], which use model checking to discover file system bugs, FERRITE focuses on distilling the crash guarantees provided by a file system interface.

We show the utility of crash-consistency models with two proof-of-concept tools for application writers:

- A verifier that proves that a program provides intended crash guarantees (such as atomicity and durability) with respect to an operational crash-consistency model;
- A synthesizer that inserts a minimal set of fsync invocations into a program to make it satisfy intended guarantees with respect to an axiomatic crash-consistency model; and,

Crash-consistency models also suggest new OS extensions to better support writing crash-safe applications. Our experience with designing and using these tools shows that crash-consistency models offer a pragmatic formal basis for reasoning about crash safety, much as memory consistency models do for reasoning about the correctness of parallel programs.

In summary, the main contributions of this paper are: (1) litmus tests and formal specifications for precisely describing file system crash-consistency models, (2) a toolkit called FERRITE for running litmus tests against formal specifications and file system implementations, and (3) example applications of crash-consistency models.

The rest of this paper is organized as follows. §2 gives background on POSIX file systems. §3 introduces litmus tests and their results using FERRITE. §4 presents formal specifications. §5 describes how FERRITE works. §6 demonstrates applications of crash-consistency models. §7 relates to previous work. §8 concludes.

2. Background

This section provides background on POSIX file systems and on out-of-order writes to disk in real-world implementations.

2.1 The POSIX file system interface

The POSIX standard [30] defines a set of system calls for file system access [67]. Applications allocate a file descriptor for a file or directory using open, to further perform file operations (e.g., write and read) or directory operations (e.g., link, unlink, mkdir, and their *at variants [79]). They may explicitly flush data to disk using sync or fsync, and deallocate a file descriptor using close. A call to close frees in-memory data structures but need not flush data to disk [43].

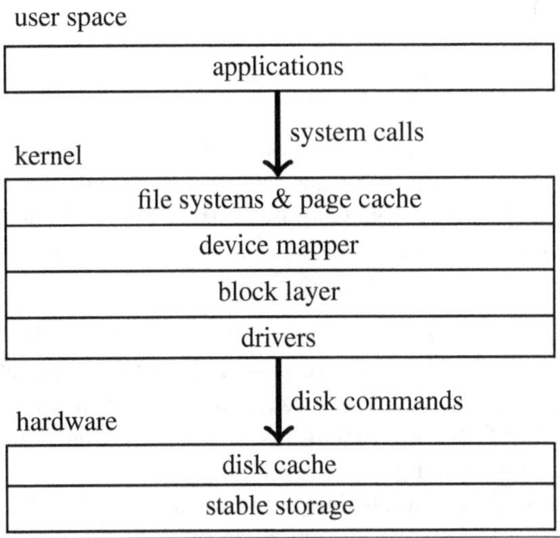

Figure 2. Linux I/O path example: from applications to disk.

As the effects of file and directory operations may be cached in memory, the `fsync` system call is key to providing data integrity in the face of crashes. POSIX defines the rationale for `fsync` [58]:

> The `fsync()` function is intended to force a physical write of data from the buffer cache, and to assure that after a system crash or other failure that all data up to the time of the `fsync()` call is recorded on the disk.

But POSIX is largely silent on crash guarantees of calls other than `fsync`. For example, the standard requires `rename` to be atomic, in the sense that when there is no crash, reading from the destination path can return only the old or new file content, not an intermediate state. But POSIX does not specify what should happen when a crash occurs [6]. As shown in Figure 1, file systems can exhibit unexpected crash behaviors for system calls such as `rename`.

2.2 Out-of-order writes

File systems implement a variety of mechanisms to provide data integrity in the face of crashes. Early file systems relied on check-and-repair tools such as `fsck` [51] to fix inconsistent state on disk after a crash. Modern file systems adopt techniques such as write-ahead logging (or journaling) [27, 28, 54], log-structured file systems [69], copy-on-write (or shadowing) [11, 17, 29, 44, 68], and soft updates [25, 50], among many others [15, 16, 24, 57, 59, 85]. But the modern operating system's I/O stack complicates reasoning about file system guarantees, as it often consists of multiple layers, each with its own caching and reordering policies [72].

As an example, Figure 2 shows a typical data path taken by applications when storing data to disk on Linux. First, applications invoke system calls such as `write` to transfer data from user space into the kernel. A file system may simply copy the data to the page cache and return to user space; pushing data further down the stack will happen later, when the kernel decides to flush the data or applications explicitly invoke system calls like `fsync`. Lower-level layers perform their own optimizations by caching and batching writes. For example, the device mapper may cache data using a faster, secondary disk (e.g., `bcache` and `dm-cache`), while the block layer may sort and merge writes, as well as device drivers and disk controllers [32].

Due to these optimizations, the I/O stack generally persists data to disk out of program order. Ordinarily, the intermediate states are invisible to applications, which retrieve data from the cached, up-to-date version, and so behave as if the system calls were executed sequentially (as required by POSIX). But if the system crashes, the intermediate states can be exposed. Our goal in this paper is to precisely describe the guarantees provided by file systems in the face of crashes, without the need to understand details of the I/O stack or file system implementation.

2.3 Assumptions

Unless otherwise specified, we assume that file systems are POSIX-compliant, running in their default configuration mode, on a single disk, and accessed by a single-threaded application. We focus on what applications should expect from file systems upon a clean reboot after a fail-stop crash. We do not consider disk corruption caused by buggy kernels, broken hardware, or malicious users.

3. Litmus tests

In memory consistency models, a litmus test is a small program and an outcome that communicates the reordering behavior of the memory system to application writers [4, 31]. We adopt litmus tests to document the crash behavior of file systems. A file system litmus test shows a guarantee the application writer might expect to hold—for example, that a later write being persisted implies an earlier write is also persisted. Developers can precisely document the behavior of their file system by listing whether certain litmus tests hold or not. Litmus tests are also useful for cross-validating formal specifications against real implementations.

This section illustrates file system crash-consistency behaviors using litmus tests. Our FERRITE toolkit can execute these litmus tests against a variety of file systems. We show several examples in which a litmus test clarifies ambiguous documentation or corrects misconceptions in prior research.

3.1 Specifying litmus tests

In FERRITE, a litmus test consists of three parts: initial setup, main body, and final checking. It can include POSIX file system calls and control flow constructs (e.g., dealing with errors if a call fails). For presentation purposes, we omit error handling in this section, assuming that all system calls succeed.

Below is a simple example of a litmus test:

```
initial:
  f ← creat("f", 0600)
main:
  write(f, "data")
  fsync(f)
  mark("done")
  close(f)
exists?:
  marked("done") ∧ content("f") ≠ "data"
```

The initial setup is optional. It starts with "initial:" and contains statements to create an initial file system state for the main body. It ends with an implicit sync (i.e., whole-system flush). If the initial setup is omitted, the main body of the test runs against an empty file system.

The main body starts with "main:" and runs after the initial setup. The program may crash at any point in the main body. A special pseudo-function mark labels externally visible events (e.g., printing messages on screen or responding to users); the label can be any unique string. We show next how to use marks to describe durability properties.

The final part is a list of predicates to be tested. A predicate in the list holds if there exists a (possibly crashing) execution of the program whose final state satisfies the predicate. The helper function content($name$) returns the file content for the given file name, or ∅ if the file does not exist; marked($label$) returns true iff the program crashes after the given label.

In the above example, the initial state consists of an empty file f. The main body of the test appends "data" to the file, calls fsync, and closes the file. In the final part, the predicate checks whether there exists an execution in which the file does not contain "data" after the "done" point.

In the rest of this section, we use litmus tests to show file system behavior that may be unintuitive to application writers. The predicates in the final section are *surprising* outcomes: a "sequential" file system that performs no reordering will disallow all these surprising behaviors (i.e., none of the tests' predicates will hold).

3.2 Litmus tests for file operations

We use FERRITE to develop existing litmus tests for two types of file writes: append and overwrite. Append writes are generally more complicated, involving multiple steps (e.g., updating inode, data block, and bitmap [5]) and delayed allocation [78]. Moreover, the on-disk state depends on how the file system orders updates to metadata (e.g., file size) and new data. The following litmus tests elucidate the intended behavior of appends and overwrites.

Prefix-append (PA). The prefix-append (PA) litmus test checks whether, in the event of a crash, a file always contains a prefix of the data that has been appended to it:

```
initial:
  N ← 2500
  as, bs ← "a" * N, "b" * N
  f ← creat("file", 0600)
  write(f, as)
main:
  write(f, bs)
exists?:
  content("file") ⋢ as + bs
```

This property, also referred as "safe append" [61, 77], ensures that no out-of-thin-air or garbage data can appear in a file. Many applications (e.g., Chrome [10]) assume prefix append. But popular file systems, such as ext4 in default configuration, do *not* guarantee this property, as we show in §3.5.

Ordered-file-overwrites. Most file systems reorder file writes, which can lead to surprising results for application writers who assume that these writes happen in program order. The following two litmus tests express this common but unsound assumption.

The **ordered-same-file-overwrites** test checks whether overwrites to the same file are ordered:

```
initial:
  N ← 40 * 1024
  f ← creat("f", 0600)
  write(f, "0" * N)
main:
  pwrite(f, "1", N - 1) # overwrite at offset N - 1
  pwrite(f, "1", 0)     # overwrite at offset 0
exists?:
  content("f")[0] = "1" ∧ content("f")[N - 1] = "0"
```

The **ordered-two-file-overwrites** test checks whether overwrites to different files are ordered:

```
initial:
  f ← creat("f", 0600)
  g ← creat("g", 0600)
  write(f, "0")
  write(g, "0")
main:
  pwrite(f, "1", 0) # overwrite f at offset 0
  pwrite(g, "1", 0) # overwrite g at offset 0
exists?:
  content("f") = "0" ∧ content("g") = "1"
```

3.3 Litmus tests for directory operations

Litmus tests for directory operations check whether operations to the same directory or to two different directories can be reordered. The tests are similar to those for file overwrites and so we omit them. There is a debate about whether POSIX prescribes different guarantees for directory operations as opposed to file operations [6].

3.4 Litmus tests for file-directory operations

The interplay between file and directory operations is subtle and can have surprising consequences. We develop three litmus tests to demonstrate such behavior. The first test checks whether updates to a file and to its parent directory can be reordered. The next two tests check two widely assumed *atomicity properties* of rename, which are referred to as "safe rename" in the literature. We show (§3.5) that "safe rename" properties are not guaranteed by most file systems, despite widespread beliefs otherwise [46, 61, 62].

file system	kernel	PA	ARVR	ACVR
journaling				
ext4	Linux	●	●	●
xfs	Linux	○	●	●
log-structured				
f2fs [39]	Linux	●	●	●
nilfs2	Linux	○	●	●
copy-on-write				
btrfs [68]	Linux	○	○	●
soft updates (SU+J)				
ufs2 [50]	FreeBSD	●	●	●

Figure 3. Characterizing file system implementations with litmus tests using FERRITE:

○: FERRITE found no execution satisfying any of the test's predicates.

●: FERRITE found an execution which allows unintuitive behavior and may surprise application writers.

Implied-directory-fsync. This test checks whether an `fsync`-ed update to a file can be reordered with the creation of that file (i.e., an update to its parent directory):

```
main:
  f ← creat("file", 0600)
  write(f, data)
  fsync(f)
  mark("written")
exists?:
  marked("written") ∧ content("file") = ∅
```

Atomic-replace-via-rename (ARVR). The ARVR test checks whether replacing file contents via `rename` is atomic across crashes (i.e., the file contains either old or new data):

```
initial:
  g ← creat("file", 0600)
  write(g, old)
main:
  f ← creat("file.tmp", 0600)
  write(f, new)
  rename("file.tmp", "file")
exists?:
  content("file") ≠ old ∧ content("file") ≠ new
```

Atomic-create-via-rename (ACVR). The ACVR test is a variation of the ARVR test in which the destination file name does not exist initially. The test checks whether the destination file is either absent or present in its entirety:

```
main:
  f ← creat("file.tmp", 0600)
  write(f, data)
  rename("file.tmp", "file")
exists?:
  content("file") ≠ ∅ ∧ content("file") ≠ data
```

3.5 Characterizing file systems with litmus tests

We applied FERRITE to check the litmus tests presented in this section against commonly used file systems on Linux 4.1 and FreeBSD 10.2, all in default configuration mode (§5 will detail how FERRITE works). Our evaluation covers file systems using a wide range of crash recovery techniques. As explained earlier, most file systems reorder file overwrites and some even reorder directory operations; this is consistent with previous reports and we omit the corresponding results.

We highlight three tests—PA, ARVR, and ACVR—for which FERRITE's results differ from common belief and previous studies. The results are shown in Figure 3. Unlike ambiguous documentation, these litmus tests show precisely which unexpected behaviors are allowed by each file system.

Prefix-append (PA) is not guaranteed by several file systems, including `ext4`, Samsung's new file system `f2fs`, and FreeBSD's default `ufs2`. This is particularly surprising for `ext4`'s default `data=ordered` mode. According to this mode's documentation [42],

> [`ext4`] logically groups metadata information related to data changes with the data blocks into a single unit called a transaction. When it's time to write the new metadata out to disk, the associated data blocks are written first.

Many application writers and researchers interpreted this to mean that metadata updates (e.g., file size) would always reach disk after file data, and thus the prefix-append property should hold [10, 55, 62].

However, we observed files with out-of-thin-air trailing nulls (i.e., binary zeros): a crash after appending 2500 "a"s and then 2500 "b"s resulted in a file of 4096 bytes, with 2500 "a"s and 1596 nulls. We further observed that `ext4` updated the file size to 4096 without writing the file data block (i.e., 2500 "a"s and 1596 "b"s) first, which it did not consider as an "associated data block." When ChromeOS developers observed similar behavior, the `ext4` developers explained that it is "working as intended" [10]. Failing to anticipate this behavior causes application crashes (upon recovery) or even corrupted data.

Atomic replace-via-rename (ARVR) is not guaranteed by most file systems, including `ext4`. After the "`ext4` data loss" incident [84], the `ext4` developers changed the behavior of the file system to accommodate applications that use the replace-via-rename pattern but do not call `fsync` before `rename` (see Figure 1). The new behavior is described in the `ext4` documentation [42]:

> [T]he data blocks of the new file are forced to disk before the `rename()` operation is committed. This provides roughly the same level of guarantees as `ext3`, and avoids the "zero-length" problem that can happen when a system crashes before the delayed allocation blocks are forced to disk.

The documentation seems to imply that it is safe to omit `fsync` in replace-via-rename, as understood by many application writers and researchers [41, 46, 62]. For example, GNOME and dpkg removed these calls to `fsync` on `ext4` to improve performance, causing some users to lose data.

Applying FERRITE to the ARVR litmus test shows this optimization to be unsound on `ext4`. Recent `ext4` *does* have a special workaround to reduce the chance of replace-via-rename producing zero-length files by forcing out the new data blocks upon `rename`. However, `rename` does *not* wait for this flush to complete, and therefore provides no atomicity guarantee—it is possible to end up with only partial new content after a crash. Of the file systems we tested, `btrfs` is the only one that provides the replace-via-rename atomicity guarantee [13].

Atomic create-via-rename (ACVR) offers atomicity guarantees different to those of atomic replace-via-rename (ARVR) on some file systems. For example, `btrfs` guarantees ARVR, but not ACVR. For this reason, the term "safe rename" [62] can cause confusion for application writers.

Our results show that litmus tests provide a precise and intuitive way of communicating crash-consistency behavior. In contrast, documentation for file systems is often ambiguous, and so the intent of file system developers can be easily misinterpreted by application writers.

4. Formal specifications

Litmus tests are an effective medium for communicating file system crash behavior to application writers. But tests alone are insufficient for constructing automated reasoning tools, which improve application reliability and programmer productivity. This section presents a formal framework for specifying file system crash-consistency models, analogous to memory consistency models. In §6, we use formal crash-consistency models expressed in this framework to develop automated verification and synthesis tools.

A crash-consistency model defines the permissible states of a file system after a crash. We develop two styles of specification: *axiomatic* and *operational*. Axiomatic models describe valid crash behaviors declaratively, using a set of axioms and ordering relations, while operational models are abstract machines that simulate relevant aspects of file system behavior (such as crashes, caching, etc.). We show both kinds of models for two example file systems: `seqfs`, an ideal file system with strong crash consistency guarantees (analogous to sequential consistency [38]), and `ext4`, a real file system with weak consistency guarantees (analogous to a weak memory model).

4.1 Axiomatic specifications

An axiomatic crash-consistency model consists of a set of rules, or axioms, that specify whether a given *execution* of a program is allowed. We first define programs and their executions (Definitions 1–3), and then define crash-consistency models (Definitions 4–7).

Program Executions. Programs update the state of an underlying *file system* (Definition 1). As is common in axiomatic specifications of memory models, we describe executions of programs in terms of the *events* (Definition 2) that they generate, such as writing a block to a file or renaming a file. These events are atomic, so we model high-level operating system procedures as emitting sequences of atomic events (e.g., a system call to write $k \times n$ bytes generates a sequence of n atomic write events that write k bytes each). We distinguish between two kinds of events: *update events* modify the state of the underlying file system, while *synchronization events* constrain the order in which events may be generated when executing a program. A sequence of events is called a *trace* (Definition 3), and a crash-consistency model decides whether a given trace is permissible for a program.

Definition 1 (File Systems). A *file system* σ is a tuple $\langle \sigma_{meta}, \sigma_{data} \rangle$, where σ_{meta} is a map from *object identifiers* (i.e., names) to natural numbers (analogous to inode numbers), and σ_{data} is a map from natural numbers (inode numbers) to *file system objects* (analogous to inodes). Object identifiers i are drawn from a countably infinite set of symbols $\mathbb{I} = \mathbb{F} \cup \mathbb{D}$, consisting of disjoint sets of file identifiers $\mathbb{F}$ and directory identifiers $\mathbb{D}$. We write f and d to denote file and directory identifiers, respectively, and we write $\sigma(i)$ to denote the object $\sigma_{data}(\sigma_{meta}(i))$. A file object $\sigma(f)$ is a tuple $\langle b, m \rangle$, where b is a finite string of bits, and m is a finite key-value map of file metadata. A directory object $\sigma(d)$ is a map from object identifiers to natural numbers. We write $\sigma(i) = \bot$ when the object $\sigma(i)$ has not been created; that is, $\sigma_{meta}(i) = \bot$.

Definition 2 (Events). A *file system event* represents an atomic access to the file system σ. There are two kinds of events: *update events* and *synchronization events*. Update events atomically modify the file and directory objects in σ. Synchronization events synchronize accesses to (parts of) σ.

Update events include writes to file (meta)data and updates to directory maps:

- *write*(f, a, d) updates the address a of the file f to contain the data d (i.e., $b[a] = d$ for $\sigma(f) = \langle b, m \rangle$ after the update).
- *setattr*(f, k, v) updates the metadata attribute k of the file f to contain the value v (i.e., $m[k] = v$ for $\sigma(f) = \langle b, m \rangle$ after the update).
- *extend*(f, a, d, s) sets the "size" attribute of f to s, and writes the data d to the address a (i.e., $m[\text{"size"}] = s$ and $b[a] = d$ for $\sigma(f) = \langle b, m \rangle$ after the update). *extend* is used to implement file append operations.
- *link*(i_1, i_2) updates i_2's binding to reflect that of i_1 (i.e., $\sigma_{meta}(i_2) = \sigma_{meta}(i_1)$ and $\sigma_{meta}(i_1)$ is unchanged after the update).
- *unlink*(i) removes the binding for i (i.e., $\sigma_{meta}(i) = \bot$ after the update).

- *rename*(i_1, i_2) links i_2 to i_1 and unlinks i_1 when $i_1 \neq i_2$; otherwise nothing changes.

Synchronization events include write barriers, as well as externally observable non-file-system events (such as sending a message over the network) and events for the beginning and end of a transaction:

- *fsync*(i) synchronizes accesses to the file or directory i.
- *sync*$()$ synchronizes accesses to all files and directories in the file system.
- *mark*(l) marks an externally observable event identified by the unique label l.
- *begin*$()$ begins a new transaction.
- *commit*$()$ ends the current transaction.

Definition 3 (Traces)**.** A *trace* t_P is a sequence of file system events generated during the execution of a program P. We write $\leq_{t_P}$ to denote the total order on events induced by the trace t_P: $e_1 \leq_{t_P} e_2$ iff e_1 occurs before e_2 in the trace t_P. Each program P has a *canonical trace*, τ_P, which is free of crashes and generates events in the order specified by the syntax of P. A trace t_P is *valid* iff it satisfies the following conditions:

- t_P is a permutation of τ_P.
- t_P respects the synchronization semantics of τ_P. That is, $e_i \leq_{t_P} e_j$ when $e_i \leq_{\tau_P} e_j$ and any of the following hold:
  - e_i is an *fsync*, *sync*, *mark*, *begin*, or *commit* event;
  - e_j is a *sync*, *begin*, or *commit* event;
  - e_j is an *fsync* event on i and e_i is an update event on i.
- t_P respects the update semantics of τ_P. That is, applying the update events in the order specified by t_P to a file system σ leaves σ in the same state as applying the update events in the order specified by τ_P.

A *crash* trace, c_P, is a prefix of a valid trace t_P that respects transactional semantics: c_P contains the same number of *begin* and *commit* events. Both the empty trace and t_P itself are crash traces of t_P. We omit the subscript P from the notation when the program P is irrelevant or clear in context.

Example 1. To illustrate our model of file systems, events, and traces, consider the following litmus test:

```
initial:
  f ← creat("f", 0600)
  g ← creat("g", 0600)
  write(f, "0")
  write(g, "0")
main:
  pwrite(f, "1", 0)
  pwrite(g, "1", 0)
  fsync(g)
exists?:
  content("f") = "0" ∧ content("g") = "1"
```

Suppose that we execute this test on an empty file system σ (i.e., $\sigma(i) = \bot$ for all identifiers i). The initial setup updates the abstract state of σ to include the bindings $\sigma(\mathsf{f}) = \langle b, m\rangle$ and $\sigma(\mathsf{g}) = \langle b, m\rangle$, where b = "0" and m = {permissions $\mapsto$ "0600", ...}. Assuming that the `pwrite` operations generate one *write* event each, the canonical trace for the litmus test is $\tau = [e_0, e_1, e_2]$, where $e_0 = \mathit{write}(\mathsf{f}, 0, \text{"1"})$, $e_1 = \mathit{write}(\mathsf{g}, 0, \text{"1"})$, and $e_2 = \mathit{fsync}(\mathsf{g})$. The valid traces, besides τ, are $t_1 = [e_1, e_0, e_2]$ and $t_2 = [e_1, e_2, e_0]$. None of the other permutations of τ are valid traces because they violate barrier semantics. Any prefix of τ, t_1, or t_2 forms a crash trace—intuitively, a crash trace represents the crash of a valid execution at a particular point.

Crash-Consistency Models. A crash-consistency model (Definition 4) determines which valid program traces are permissible, and therefore, what file system states may be observed after a crash. The strongest consistency model is *Sequential Crash-Consistency* (SCC) (Definition 5), which permits no re-ordering of events in the canonical trace. That is, an execution of a program P may only emit the canonical trace τ_P. As a result, the crash behavior of an application running under SCC is easy to reason about, and it can be connected directly to program text. SCC can be thought of as the analogue of sequential consistency for memory models.

Real file systems, however, implement *weaker* models (Definition 6), which permit additional valid traces. In particular, we say that a crash consistency model M_1 is weaker than a model M_2 iff M_1 permits a superset of the valid traces permitted by M_2 for every program. The model provided by the `ext4` file system, for example, is weaker than SCC, permitting re-orderings of updates to different files (among other relaxations). Definition 7 gives an axiomatic specification of `ext4` in our framework, obtained by reading the documentation and empirically observing its behavior on litmus tests using FERRITE. As we show in §6, such a specification clarifies the contract between the application and the underlying file system, and enables automatic synthesis of a minimal set of barriers that ensure atomicity and durability after a crash.

Definition 4 (Crash-Consistency Model)**.** A crash-consistency model M relates an arbitrary valid trace of a program P to its canonical trace. We say that M *permits* t_P iff $M(t_P, \tau_P)$ evaluates to true.

Definition 5 (Sequential Crash-Consistency (SCC))**.** A valid trace t_P of a program P is *sequentially crash-consistent* iff $t_P = \tau_P$. That is, $\mathsf{SCC}(t_P, \tau_P) \triangleq t_P = \tau_P$.

Example 2. Consider the litmus test from Example 1. For this test, SCC permits only the canonical trace $\tau = [e_0, e_1, e_2]$. No crash trace (i.e., prefix) of τ results in the specified final state $\mathsf{content}(f) = \text{"0"} \land \mathsf{content}(g) = \text{"1"}$, and so the SCC model does not allow the surprising behavior of this test.

Example 3. FSCQ [14] is a file system that is verified to be crash-safe: a machine-checkable proof in Coq shows that FSCQ will always recover correctly after a crash. FSCQ wraps each POSIX system call into a transaction committed to a write-ahead log, and so each system call is both atomic and persistent. In our formalization, the canonical trace τ_P for a program P running on FSCQ includes a *begin* event before the sequence of events generated by each system call, and a *commit* event after those events. For example, a `write` system call on FSCQ may produce the canonical trace $\tau_P = [begin, write_0, \dots, write_n, commit]$ (with one $write_i$ per block). This canonical trace yields only two valid crash traces: the empty trace and τ_P itself.

Definition 6 (Weaker Crash-Consistency Model)**.** A crash-consistency model M_1 is *weaker* than the model M_2 iff $M_2(t_P, \tau_P) \implies M_1(t_P, \tau_P)$ for every valid trace t_P and its corresponding canonical trace τ_P.

Definition 7 (`ext4` Crash-Consistency)**.** Let t_P be a valid trace and τ_P the corresponding canonical trace. We say that t_P is `ext4` *crash-consistent* iff $e_i \leq_{t_P} e_j$ for all events e_i, e_j such that $e_i \leq_{\tau_P} e_j$ and at least one of the following conditions holds:

1. e_i and e_j are metadata updates to the same file: $e_i = setattr(f, k_i, v_i)$ and $e_j = setattr(f, k_j, v_j)$.
2. e_i and e_j are writes to the same block in the same file: $e_i = write(f, a_i, d_i)$, $e_j = write(f, a_j, d_j)$, and $sameBlock(a_i, a_j)$, where *sameBlock* is an implementation-specific predicate.
3. e_i and e_j are updates to the same directory: $args(e_i) \cap args(e_j) \neq \emptyset$, where $args(link(i_1, i_2)) = \{i_1, i_2\}$, $args(unlink(i_1)) = \{i_1\}$, and $args(rename(i_1, i_2)) = \{i_1, i_2\}$.
4. e_i is a write and e_j is an extend to the same file: $e_i = write(f, a_i, d_i)$ and $e_j = extend(f, a_j, d_j, s)$.

Example 4. Consider again the litmus test from Example 1. The `ext4` crash-consistency model permits every valid trace (i.e., τ, t_1, and t_2) of the program. Crash traces (i.e., prefixes) of two of these traces (t_1 and t_2) satisfy the predicate `content`$(f) =$ "0" $\wedge$ `content`$(g) =$ "1", and so unlike SCC, `ext4` allows the surprising behavior of this test. The programmer can ensure that the test exhibits only the SCC behaviors on `ext4` by inserting an `fsync(f)` barrier after the write to `f`.

Note that a crash-consistency model does not include an explicit model of hardware disk behavior. Instead, the reorderings and caching behaviors of hardware disks are implicit in the allowed reorderings and in the semantics of update and synchronization events. In §5, we describe how FERRITE simulates the intermediate states of the hardware disk after a crash, and so a crash-consistency model developed with FERRITE implicitly captures hardware behavior.

4.2 Operational specifications

An operational crash-consistency model takes the form of a non-deterministic state machine M, which uses idealized components—maps and tuples—to abstract the implementation details of real file systems. We model the persistent (on-disk) and volatile (in-core) state of a file system σ with a tuple $\langle \sigma_{inCore}, \sigma_{onDisk} \rangle$, where σ_{inCore} and σ_{onDisk} are themselves tuples of the form $\langle \sigma_{meta}, \sigma_{data} \rangle$, as defined previously (Definition 1). Events update the volatile state of the files they interact with, occurring in the order specified by the syntax of a program P. The state machine M non-deterministically chooses to persist (some of) these updates to disk, or to crash.

$$\frac{\sigma' = \textsc{Flush}(\textsc{Apply}(P[p], \sigma))}{\langle \sigma, p \rangle \rightarrow \langle \sigma', p+1 \rangle}\ \textsc{StepSeq}$$

$$\frac{}{\langle \sigma, p \rangle \rightarrow \langle \sigma, \bot \rangle}\ \textsc{Crash}$$

Figure 4. An operational model for SCC (Definition 5).

$$\frac{\sigma' = \textsc{Apply}(P[p], \sigma)}{\langle \sigma, p \rangle \rightarrow \langle \sigma', p+1 \rangle}\ \textsc{Step} \qquad \frac{}{\langle \sigma, p \rangle \rightarrow \langle \sigma, \bot \rangle}\ \textsc{Crash}$$

$$\frac{\sigma' = \textsc{PartialFlush}(\sigma)}{\langle \sigma, p \rangle \rightarrow \langle \sigma', p \rangle}\ \textsc{NonDet}$$

Figure 5. A sample of the `ext4` operational model.

Figure 4 shows an example operational specification of sequential crash-consistency. We model the machine state as a pair $\langle \sigma, p \rangle$, where $\sigma = \langle \sigma_{inCore}, \sigma_{onDisk} \rangle$ is the current state of the file system, and p the program counter (an index into the program P). The APPLY function executes the semantics of an event as given in Definition 2. The FLUSH function flushes the volatile state of all files to disk. The STEPSEQ rule says that the volatile state is flushed to disk at every step. In other words, $\sigma_{inCore} = \sigma_{onDisk}$ at any point during execution. The non-deterministic rule CRASH can halt the program at any point (denoted by setting the program counter to $\bot$). It is easy to see that a machine executing these two rules can only produce the canonical trace (or its prefix) of any program P.

Figure 5 shows the key rules for an operational specification of `ext4`. The `ext4` model permits more non-determinism than the sequential model: the NONDET rule may transition without performing the next event in the program. The PARTIALFLUSH function non-deterministically flushes none, some, or all of each file in the file system. For space reasons, we omit a full description of the rules for `ext4`, but in §6.2, we describe a Dafny-based verifier for application-level properties that uses this operational crash-consistency model.

5. Making specifications executable

This section describes FERRITE, a suite of automated tools for reasoning about crash-consistency models. FERRITE consists of two tools—an explicit enumerator and a bounded model checker—which exhaustively explore all possible crash behaviors of a litmus test (§3). The enumerator executes litmus tests against actual file system implementations to determine the set of all possible crash behaviors. The model checker executes litmus tests symbolically against an axiomatic specification (§4.1). Together, these tools enable

disk commands	description
write($blockID$, $data$)	write data to a given block
flush()	flush disk cache to stable storage
trim($blockID$)	wipe a given block
mark($label$)	label externally observable event

Figure 6. Disk commands supported by FERRITE's virtual disk; `mark` is a pseudo-command that corresponds to the pseudo-function of the same name in litmus tests (see §3.1).

file system developers to create high fidelity specifications of crash behavior: the model checker ensures that the formalizations (dis)allow representative behaviors encoded in litmus tests, and the enumerator ensures that the litmus tests are indeed representative of the behavior of the actual file system implementations.

5.1 Executing tests against file system implementations

The possible reordering behaviors of a file system are often subtle even to their developers. Prior experience with memory models has demonstrated the utility of tools such as DIY [3] that execute litmus tests against real hardware to observe possible outcomes. To help specification writers understand the behaviors allowed by a file system, FERRITE includes an explicit enumerator that executes all possible crash traces of a litmus test against an actual file system implementation.

The enumerator takes as input a litmus test P and a target file system, and reports all possible outcomes of P on that file system, including potential crashes. The system calls made by P pass through several layers of the I/O stack (Figure 2), each of which is free to reorder or buffer them according to its own rules. Eventually, the operating system produces *disk commands*, shown in Figure 6, which are sent to the hardware storage device. The storage device is then free to reorder and buffer those events according to its own rules. The state of persistent storage after a crash therefore depends on both the trace of disk commands and the behavior of the storage device.

To generate all possible crash states of the test P, FERRITE needs to observe two sets of traces: (1) all possible sequences of disk commands sent to the hardware, and (2) all possible reorderings of those commands made by the hardware. FERRITE determines the possible sequences of disk commands by executing P many times, as is common for testing memory models [3, 4]. But producing hardware reorderings is trickier, since it also requires producing all intermediate states of the persistent storage in order to simulate crashes. In particular, interposing on the hardware to inspect intermediate states or produce a crash at a certain point would be expensive and imprecise. Instead, FERRITE abstracts the behavior of storage hardware with a *disk model*, producing only the command reorderings that satisfy a chosen disk model.

A disk model captures the allowed behaviors of the disk hardware. FERRITE implements a default disk model that resembles a disk with a large volatile cache and arbitrary schedules. Specifically, it allows two disk operations o_i and o_j to be reordered unless one of the following is true:

- either o_i or o_j is a `flush`;
- o_i and o_j are changes to the same block;
- o_i is a `mark` command.

Capturing hardware behavior in a disk model allows FERRITE to easily simulate a crash at any point during P's execution, and observe the resulting intermediate state. This guarantees that all possible crash states are observed.

The enumerator executes litmus tests by intercepting system calls and forwarding them to an underlying guest OS running in QEMU [7]. The guest OS has an attached virtual disk provided by FERRITE. The target file system, running in the guest OS, issues disk commands to this virtual disk, which are forwarded to FERRITE to be recorded in a trace. Once execution of P is complete, the enumerator produces all possible reorderings of the trace according to the chosen disk model, and for each trace, produces all possible prefixes. Each prefix produces a disk image file that corresponds to a possible disk state after a crash. The enumerator finally mounts the disk image as a loopback device in the guest OS to recover the state of the files written by P. Optionally, the enumerator can then verify the predicates in the final section of the litmus test (§3.1) against the possible states. We have applied enumeration to run litmus tests against file systems on Linux and FreeBSD, with results presented in §3.5 earlier.

Limitations. The result of the enumerator is dependent on a particular implementation of the file system and the rest of the I/O stack. It is useful to show that certain system calls *can* be reordered by the file system (assuming QEMU and the I/O stack are correct). It cannot prove that two system calls must always be ordered even if it never sees a counter-example in the output; we cross-validated with documentation and with file system developers for those cases.

5.2 Executing tests against specifications

Axiomatic specifications of crash consistency are useful only to the extent that they faithfully capture the behavior of file system implementations. Prior experience with memory models [82] has shown that it is easy to accidentally write a specification that is under-constrained (allowing behaviors that should be forbidden) or over-constrained (forbidding behaviors that should be allowed). To help file system developers avoid these pitfalls when specifying crash-consistency models, FERRITE includes a model checker that symbolically executes a litmus test against a specification, ensuring that the specification (dis)allows the behaviors encoded in the test.

The model checker takes as input a litmus test P (§3) and an axiomatic specification of a crash-consistency model M (§4), and checks whether the predicates specified in the `exists?` section of the test are satisfied by any execution of the body. Conceptually, the model checker works by generating all crash traces of P that are permitted by M

```
; SCC permits no reorderings
(define (SCC-reorder? e1 e2) #f)

; ext4 forbids the reorderings in Definition 7
(define (ext4-reorder? e1 e2)
  (and
    (not (metadata-same-ino-deps? e1 e2))            ; (1)
    (not (same-file-block-deps? e1 e2 BLOCK_SIZE))   ; (2)
    (not (dir-same-ino-deps? e1 e2))                 ; (3)
    (not (file-write-extend-deps? e1 e2))))          ; (4)
```

Figure 7. Rosette specifications of the reordering rules for the SCC (Definition 5) and ext4 (Definition 7) models.

(Definition 4), and checking each predicate against that set. In particular, the checker produces the set of crash traces $T = \{c_P \mid c_P \text{ is a crash trace of } t_P \text{ and } M(t_P, \tau_P)\}$, where τ_P is the canonical trace of P. Then, it checks whether any predicate in P is satisfied by some trace in T. If so, the crash-consistency model M allows some surprising behavior. This outcome can be cross-checked against the actual file system implementation using FERRITE to confirm the model is not too weak.

We implemented the model checker in Rosette [80], a programming language that extends Racket [23] with features for program synthesis and verification, based on an underlying SAT or SMT solver [21, 81]. The specification writer uses Rosette to encode the axiomatic specification of the crash-consistency model M, and the model checker provides a simple DSL for expressing the litmus test P. The specification M is written simply as a procedure that takes as input two events from the canonical trace, $e_1 \leq_{\tau_P} e_2$, and returns true iff M allows these two events to be reordered. Figure 7 shows the specifications for the SCC and ext4 models, both of which are direct translations of Definitions 5 and 7, respectively, into Rosette's syntax. Given these inputs, the model checker uses Rosette to symbolically execute P against M, relying on the SMT solver to implicitly check P's exists? predicates against the traces permitted by M, as described above.

We applied the model checker to validate the SCC and ext4 specifications against our litmus tests (§3). The SCC specification, by construction, does not permit any of the surprising results in the tests, and our model checker confirmed this to be the case. The ext4 specification, on the other hand, is expected to allow some of the litmus tests, since the actual ext4 implementation does as well (§3.5). The model checker confirms that the specification behaves like the implementation on all tests. All of the checks complete within a few seconds. In general, implementing a SAT/SMT-based tool that scales to our litmus tests—which manipulate files with thousands of bytes—would require hand-crafted encodings and significant time investment (as with the specialized encodings [48, 82, 90] for checking litmus tests against memory models). However, Rosette's aggressive partial evaluation allows our model checker to scale to these litmus tests without manual intervention.

6. Experience with specifications

In this section we demonstrate that formal specifications are useful for building tools that can aid application writers. We also discuss how applications can benefit from support from the operating system and hardware.

6.1 Synthesis

Rather than require application writers to manually ensure crash safety of their programs, formal crash-consistency specifications allow us to *synthesize* sufficient barriers for an implementation so that it satisfies the desired crash-safety properties. In particular, the application writer develops the program P assuming sequential crash-consistency. The synthesizer then transforms P, by inserting a minimal set of barriers, so that the resulting program P' behaves just like P under a given weaker crash-consistency model, such as ext4.

We built a proof-of-concept synthesizer on top of the FERRITE model checker described in §5.2. The synthesizer uses Rosette's implementation [80] of counterexample-guided inductive synthesis (CEGIS) [73, 74] to generate candidate programs P' and verify that they preserve P's guarantees on every permitted trace. The synthesizer generates candidate programs P' by inserting new fsync invocations into P. Moreover, the synthesizer automatically *optimizes* the insertion of barriers, such that the program P' contains the minimal number of additional fsync invocations necessary to guarantee the desired safety properties.

To illustrate, consider the atomic-replace-via-rename (ARVR) litmus test in §3.4. This program guarantees atomicity under SCC. But recall from Figure 3 that it does not do so on ext4: after a crash, it is possible for "file" to contain neither the old nor the new file contents. To guarantee atomicity, we must insert additional synchronization. A naive solution would be to insert an fsync after each call in this program, but this is unnecessarily conservative and potentially inhibits performance. Our synthesizer instead chooses to insert an fsync(f) after the write operation. This single fsync is sufficient to guarantee atomicity for this program on ext4. The synthesizer automatically generates and verifies this program in under 30 seconds, with similar performance on all the other litmus tests in §3. While our synthesizer is a proof-of-concept, common optimizations (e.g., Fender [37]) would allow it to scale to larger programs.

6.2 Verification

To demonstrate the use of operational crash-consistency models (§4.2), we developed a verification framework in Dafny [40] based on our operational model of ext4, and we applied it to prove crash safety of several small programs. Dafny proofs in our framework are unbounded, unlike those produced by the FERRITE model checker. In particular, given a procedure that takes as input a file, Dafny proves its crash-safety with respect to all possible file sizes. FERRITE, in contrast, expects a bound on the file size, as provided in our litmus tests.

Our framework models the file system with Dafny's built-in strings and maps: files are strings, and directories are maps. Each system call is simply a procedure with associated pre- and post-conditions. We express non-determinism using Dafny's havoc statements. For example, the CRASH rule in Figure 5 can be modeled as "`if (*) crash();`," where the havoc statement `*` means that the given branch is taken non-deterministically. We similarly use havoc statements to implement non-deterministic flushes (the NONDET rule in Figure 5) and to represent garbage data. Because Dafny closely resembles a conventional imperative language, applications can be implemented in Dafny against our abstract interface, and extracted to implementations against real file system interfaces.

We verified crash safety of several small programs using our Dafny framework. For example, we verified the unbounded version of the ARVR litmus test used in synthesis above. Our framework's use of Dafny's language features made proof automation highly effective: it required only 6 annotations to verify ARVR.

6.3 OS support

Recent research in memory consistency models [1] designs programming abstractions that hide the details of memory reordering where possible (using concurrency libraries), but exposing them when necessary for peak performance (such as through C11 atomics). In addition to providing a basis for synthesis and verification tools, crash-consistency models also suggest a similar design for programming abstractions that offer crash-consistency guarantees. This section discusses two such interfaces. The first is a simple interface to expose the key characteristics of a file system's crash-consistency behavior to the application, akin to C11 atomics. The second is a radical design that provides applications with sequential crash-consistency (SCC) guarantees. We prototyped both designs using our litmus tests and Dafny verification framework.

Exposing file system characteristics. File system developers often hesitate to promise strong crash-consistency guarantees. Instead, many applications try to exploit the characteristics of specific file systems and implement per-file-system optimizations. Consider the following code snippet from GNOME [45], which skips an `fsync` call for replace-via-rename if the file system magic number is a known constant:

```
struct statfs buf;
fstatfs(fd, &buf);
if (buf.f_type == BTRFS_SUPER_MAGIC || buf.f_type == ...)
      // ... skip fsync(fd) ...
```

This practice is risky because the file system's behavior may depend on specific versions or mount options, which applications can easily overlook. One solution is to provide interfaces for applications to query the possible behaviors of the current file system. For example, a flag could expose whether the file system guarantees atomic replace-via-rename (§3):

```
if (buf.f_charcs & FC_ATOMIC_REPLACE_VIA_RENAME) ...
```

Applications can then make their optimizations and expectations explicit, making them more portable and easier to reason about. We implemented a prototype on Linux by exposing such information through the reserved bits of `statfs`. §7 discusses other proposed high-level interfaces (e.g., file system transactions and barriers).

End-to-end I/O stack. Reasoning about crash consistency is made difficult by the complexity of the I/O stack, as shown in §2.2. An alternative approach, embraced by exokernel designs [22, 34], is to reduce or eliminate the kernel from the I/O path. While these designs focus on improving end-to-end performance, we believe that they can also offer better reliability and more explicit crash-consistency guarantees.

As a demonstration, we implemented a prototype I/O stack by porting the persistent log and a `megaraid` driver from the Arrakis operating system [60] to Linux. It has a small code base—200 LOC for the log and 4,000 LOC for the driver—and completely bypasses the existing file system I/O stack. The persistent log provides strong crash-consistency guarantees: log entries reach disk in same order as they are appended, and applications will see only complete log entries after the system crashes. We derived a formal proof of the properties of the persistent log implementation using Dafny (with 25 annotations). To measure performance, we modified LevelDB 1.18 to use the log and measured the time to append 100,000 `Put(key, val)` entries to the log; the backend was an LSI Logic MegaRAID SAS-3 3108 RAID controller. The time reduced from 14.4 s on `ext4` to 4 s when using the log. We believe that this is a promising direction to build end-to-end storage systems with well-defined crash behavior.

7. Related work

Our work is motivated by past research that finds crash-safety bugs in both applications and file systems, that explores better programming abstractions for crash safety, and that provides formal models of file systems.

Bugs in storage systems. Storage systems need to tolerate system crashes and are difficult to get right [47, 64]. Techniques such as model checking [88, 89] and static analysis [70] have been proven to be effective in finding bugs in applications and file systems. FERRITE differs from these tools in two ways. First, it does not focus on finding bugs in file systems. Rather, §3.5 shows incorrect or imprecise crash models used in previous work (i.e., bugs in their models). Second, Ferrite presents the first formalization of file system crash-consistency models; these models can be used with automated reasoning tools, as we showed through synthesis and verification in §6. The models in previous work are not formal models and cannot be used this way.

FERRITE was inspired by recent work from Pillai et al. [62] and Zheng et al. [92] on crash-safety bugs. Their work showed that even applications carefully designed and engineered to tolerate crashes may be vulnerable to data losses, and that it remains challenging to develop crash-safe applications on top of POSIX file systems.

A major challenge for both application writers and file system developers is that the POSIX file interface under-specifies crash behaviors, leading to conflicting interpretations. Our crash-consistency models address this challenge by providing litmus tests and formal specifications for precisely describing crash behavior. Precise, formal models clarify misinterpretations and provide a basis for automated reasoning tools.

Formal specification and verification of file systems. Several projects have explored formally specifying and verifying file systems. Bevier et al. specified the Synergy file system in Z [9] and verified its implementation in ACL2 [8]. Kang and Jackson used Alloy [35] to model a file system for flash-based storage devices, with a focus on flash-specific features such as wear leveling. Wenzel used Isabelle/HOL [86] to formalize common Unix file system abstractions and reason about their security properties. The Commuter tool [18] formalizes the commutativity of the POSIX interface and studies its scalability implications. SibylFS [66] is a recent effort in formalizing POSIX and testing implementation conformance. To our knowledge, we propose the first formal framework for describing crash-consistency behaviors of POSIX file systems. On the other hand, our framework focuses on crash consistency, and we do not model POSIX details such as permissions and symbolic links.

Another line of work is applying formal verification to implementing a POSIX-like file system [33]. On-going work includes BilbyFs [36], FSCQ [14], and Schellhorn et al.'s verified flash file system [71]. It would be interesting to apply our framework to analyzing the crash-consistency guarantees of these file systems once they are complete and available.

File system interfaces. One limitation of POSIX is that applications have to resort to expensive `fsync` calls to express ordering requirements even when they do not need durability. Kernel developers have proposed to extend Linux with an `fbarrier` system call [20] to improve performance for such applications. Other extensions to better support ordering include Featherstitch [24], OptFS [16], and xsyncfs [57].

A number of proposals offer transactional semantics for file system operations [52, 59, 63, 65, 76, 85, 87]. Emerging storage devices provide new hardware primitives, such as Fusion-io's multi-block atomic writes and new SCSI commands (ATOMIC WRITE and draft SCATTERED WRITE), that could be used to simplify file system implementations and provide stronger crash-consistency guarantees [32, 53].

Memory consistency models. Development and analysis of memory consistency models is an active area of research, and our approach draws on the general themes and ideas from this work. A memory model determines the semantics of reads in a multi-threaded shared-memory system; in particular, it specifies which writes to a memory location a given read may observe. Memory models are described through a combination of litmus tests (e.g., [3, 4]), axiomatic specifications (e.g., [2, 82, 90]), and operational specifications (e.g., [12, 91]). Litmus tests have the advantage of being easy to understand; operational models offer a direct basis for building simulation tools; and axiomatic models are best suited for formal reasoning and concise descriptions of complex systems (e.g., [49]). Many tools have been developed to check that these forms of specification agree with each other (e.g., [48, 82, 90]), as well as with the behavior exhibited by hardware (e.g., [4]).

Compared to memory models, crash-consistency models have simpler ordering constraints: all possible program behaviors can be described in terms of reorderings of a canonical trace. Memory models, in contrast, generally involve constraints over many ordering relations [2] and even many speculative executions [49]. On the other hand, crash-consistency models involve richer data structures, such as files and directories, and the notion of crashes.

8. Conclusion

The guarantees that file systems should provide in the face of crashes are under-specified by the POSIX standard, leaving application writers to guess how to achieve data integrity and improve performance. This paper showed that crash-consistency models, in the form of litmus tests and formal specifications, effectively describe the contract between the file system and the application. We presented FERRITE, a toolkit for constructing crash-consistency models by exploring the possible crash behaviors of a file system. While developing models for common file systems, we identified and clarified several widely misunderstood guarantees in the literature.

Crash-consistency models enable tools for writing crash-safe applications. We demonstrated proof-of-concept synthesis and verification tools, and discussed opportunities for improved programming interfaces that build on these models. We hope that both file system developers and application writers can benefit from precise specifications of crash behavior. All of FERRITE's source code is publicly available at: `http://sandcat.cs.washington.edu/ferrite`.

Acknowledgments

We thank Zach Tatlock, our shepherd Joseph Tucek, and the anonymous reviewers for feedback on earlier versions of this paper. This work was supported in part by NSF under grant #1064497, by DARPA under contract FA8750-16-2-0032, and by a gift from the VMware University Research Fund.

References

[1] S. V. Adve and H.-J. Boehm. Memory models: A case for rethinking parallel languages and hardware. *Communications of the ACM*, 53(8):90–101, Aug. 2010.

[2] J. Alglave. A formal hierarchy of weak memory models. *Formal Methods in System Design*, 41(2):178–210, Oct. 2012.

[3] J. Alglave, L. Maranget, S. Sarkar, and P. Sewell. Fences in weak memory models. In *Proceedings of the 22nd International Conference on Computer Aided Verification (CAV)*, pages 258–272, Edinburgh, UK, July 2010.

[4] J. Alglave, L. Maranget, S. Sarkar, and P. Sewell. Litmus: Running tests against hardware. In *Proceedings of the 17th International Conference on Tools and Algorithms for the Construction and Analysis of Systems*, pages 41–44, Saarbrücken, Germany, Mar.–Apr. 2011.

[5] R. H. Arpaci-Dusseau and A. C. Arpaci-Dusseau. *Operating Systems: Three Easy Pieces*. Arpaci-Dusseau Books, 0.90 edition, Mar. 2015.

[6] Austin Group. 0000672: Necessary step(s) to synchronize filename operations on disk, 2013. `http://austingroupbugs.net/view.php?id=672`.

[7] F. Bellard. QEMU, a fast and portable dynamic translator. In *Proceedings of the 2005 USENIX Annual Technical Conference*, pages 41–46, Anaheim, CA, Apr. 2005.

[8] W. R. Bevier and R. M. Cohen. An executable model of the synergy file system. Technical Report 121, Computational Logic, Inc., Oct. 1996.

[9] W. R. Bevier, R. M. Cohen, and J. Turner. A specification for the synergy file system. Technical Report 120, Computational Logic, Inc., Sept. 1995.

[10] N. Boichat. Issue 502898: ext4: Filesystem corruption on panic, June 2015. `https://code.google.com/p/chromium/issues/detail?id=502898`.

[11] J. Bonwick. ZFS: The last word in filesystems, Oct. 2005. `https://blogs.oracle.com/bonwick/entry/zfs_the_last_word_in`.

[12] G. Boudol and G. Petri. Relaxed memory models: An operational approach. In *Proceedings of the 36th ACM Symposium on Principles of Programming Languages (POPL)*, pages 392–403, Savannah, GA, Jan. 2009.

[13] Btrfs. What are the crash guarantees of overwrite-by-rename? `https://btrfs.wiki.kernel.org/index.php/FAQ`.

[14] H. Chen, D. Ziegler, T. Chajed, A. Chlipala, M. F. Kaashoek, and N. Zeldovich. Using Crash Hoare Logic for certifying the FSCQ file system. In *Proceedings of the 25th ACM Symposium on Operating Systems Principles (SOSP)*, Monterey, CA, Oct. 2015.

[15] V. Chidambaram, T. Sharma, A. C. Arpaci-Dusseau, and R. H. Arpaci-Dusseau. Consistency without ordering. In *Proceedings of the 10th USENIX Conference on File and Storage Technologies (FAST)*, pages 101–116, San Jose, CA, Feb. 2012.

[16] V. Chidambaram, T. S. Pillai, A. C. Arpaci-Dusseau, and R. H. Arpaci-Dusseau. Optimistic crash consistency. In *Proceedings of the 24th ACM Symposium on Operating Systems Principles (SOSP)*, pages 228–243, Farmington, PA, Nov. 2013.

[17] H. Chu. MDB: A memory-mapped database and backend for OpenLDAP. In *Proceedings of the 3rd International Conference on LDAP*, Heidelberg, Germany, Oct. 2011.

[18] A. T. Clements, M. F. Kaashoek, N. Zeldovich, R. T. Morris, and E. Kohler. The scalable commutativity rule: Designing scalable software for multicore processors. In *Proceedings of the 24th ACM Symposium on Operating Systems Principles (SOSP)*, pages 1–17, Farmington, PA, Nov. 2013.

[19] J. Corbet. ext4 and data loss, Mar. 2009. `http://lwn.net/Articles/322823/`.

[20] J. Corbet. That massive filesystem thread, Mar. 2009. `https://lwn.net/Articles/326471/`.

[21] L. de Moura and N. Bjørner. Z3: An efficient SMT solver. In *Proceedings of the 14th International Conference on Tools and Algorithms for the Construction and Analysis of Systems*, pages 337–340, Budapest, Hungary, Mar.–Apr. 2008.

[22] D. R. Engler, M. F. Kaashoek, and J. W. O'Toole. Exokernel: An operating system architecture for application-level resource management. In *Proceedings of the 15th ACM Symposium on Operating Systems Principles (SOSP)*, pages 251–266, Copper Mountain, CO, Dec. 1995.

[23] M. Flatt and PLT. Reference: Racket. Technical Report PLT-TR-2010-1, PLT Design Inc., 2010. `http://racket-lang.org/`.

[24] C. Frost, M. Mammarella, E. Kohler, A. de los Reyes, S. Hovsepian, A. Matsuoka, and L. Zhang. Generalized file system dependencies. In *Proceedings of the 21st ACM Symposium on Operating Systems Principles (SOSP)*, pages 307–320, Stevenson, WA, Oct. 2007.

[25] G. R. Ganger and Y. N. Patt. Metadata update performance in file systems. In *Proceedings of the 1st Symposium on Operating Systems Design and Implementation (OSDI)*, pages 49–60, Monterey, CA, Nov. 1994.

[26] D. Giampaolo. *Practical File System Design with the BE File System*. Morgan Kaufmann Publishers, 1999.

[27] J. Gray. Notes on data base operating systems. In *Operating Systems, An Advanced Course*, pages 393–481. Springer-Verlag, 1977.

[28] R. Hagmann. Reimplementing the cedar file system using logging and group commit. In *Proceedings of the 11th ACM Symposium on Operating Systems Principles (SOSP)*, pages 155–162, Austin, TX, Nov. 1987.

[29] D. Hitz, J. Lau, and M. Malcolm. File system design for an NFS file server appliance. In *Proceedings of the Winter 1994 USENIX Technical Conference*, San Francisco, CA, Jan. 1994.

[30] IEEE and The Open Group. The open group base specifications issue 7, 2013.

[31] Intel Corporation. *Intel 64 and IA-32 Architectures Software Developer's Manual*, 2015. rev. 57.

[32] W. K. Josephson, L. A. Bongo, D. Flynn, and K. Li. DFS: A file system for virtualized flash storage. In *Proceedings of the 8th USENIX Conference on File and Storage Technologies (FAST)*, pages 1–15, San Jose, CA, Feb. 2010.

[33] R. Joshi and G. J. Holzmann. A mini challenge: Build a verifiable filesystem. *Formal Aspects of Computing*, 19(2): 269–272, June 2007.

[34] M. F. Kaashoek, D. R. Engler, G. R. Ganger, H. M. Briceño, R. Hunt, D. Mazières, T. Pinckney, R. Grimm, J. Jannotti, and K. Mackenzie. Application performance and flexibility on exokernel systems. In *Proceedings of the 16th ACM Symposium on Operating Systems Principles (SOSP)*, pages 52–65, Saint-Malo, France, Oct. 1997.

[35] E. Kang and D. Jackson. Formal modeling and analysis of a Flash filesystem in Alloy. In *Proceedings of the 1st Int'l Conference of Abstract State Machines, B and Z*, pages 294–308, London, UK, Sept. 2008.

[36] G. Keller, T. Murray, S. Amani, L. O'Connor, Z. Chen, L. Ryzhyk, G. Klein, and G. Heiser. File systems deserve verification too. In *Proceedings of the 7th Workshop on Programming Languages and Operating Systems*, Farmington, PA, Nov. 2013.

[37] M. Kuperstein, M. Vechev, and E. Yahav. Automatic inference of memory fences. In *Proceedings of 10th International Conference on Formal Methods in Computer-Aided Design*, pages 111–120, Lugano, Switzerland, Oct. 2010.

[38] L. Lamport. How to make a multiprocessor computer that correctly executes multiprocess programs. *IEEE Transactions on Computers*, 26(9):690–691, Sept. 1979.

[39] C. Lee, D. Sim, J.-Y. Hwang, and S. Cho. F2FS: A new file system for flash storage. In *Proceedings of the 13th USENIX Conference on File and Storage Technologies (FAST)*, pages 273–286, Santa Clara, CA, Feb. 2015.

[40] K. R. M. Leino. Dafny: An automatic program verifier for functional correctness. In *Proceedings of the 16th International Conference on Logic for Programming, Artificial Intelligence and Reasoning (LPAR)*, pages 348–370, Dakar, Senegal, Apr.–May 2010.

[41] Linux kernel. Bug 15910 - zero-length files and performance degradation, 2010. `https://bugzilla.kernel.org/show_bug.cgi?id=15910`.

[42] Linux kernel. Ext4 filesystem, 2015. `https://www.kernel.org/doc/Documentation/filesystems/ext4.txt`.

[43] Linux man-pages. `close` - close a file descriptor, 2013. `http://man7.org/linux/man-pages/man2/close.2.html`.

[44] R. A. Lorie. Physical integrity in a large segmented database. *ACM Transactions on Database Systems*, 2(1):91–104, Mar. 1977.

[45] R. Lortie. more on dconf performance, btrfs and fsync, Dec. 2010. `https://blogs.gnome.org/desrt/2010/12/19/more-on-dconf-performance-btrfs-and-fsync/`.

[46] R. Lortie. ext4 file replace guarantees, June 2013. `http://www.spinics.net/lists/linux-ext4/msg38774.html`.

[47] L. Lu, A. C. Arpaci-Dusseau, R. H. Arpaci-Dusseau, and S. Lu. A study of Linux file system evolution. In *Proceedings of the 11th USENIX Conference on File and Storage Technologies (FAST)*, pages 31–44, San Jose, CA, Feb. 2013.

[48] S. Mador-Haim, R. Alur, and M. M. K. Martin. Generating litmus tests for contrasting memory consistency models. In *Proceedings of the 22nd International Conference on Computer Aided Verification (CAV)*, pages 273–287, Edinburgh, UK, July 2010.

[49] J. Manson, W. Pugh, and S. V. Adve. The Java memory model. In *Proceedings of the 32nd ACM Symposium on Principles of Programming Languages (POPL)*, pages 378–391, Long Beach, CA, Jan. 2005.

[50] M. K. McKusick. Journaled soft-updates. In *BSDCan*, Ottawa, Canada, May 2010.

[51] M. K. McKusick and T. J. Kowalski. Fsck: The UNIX file system check program. UNIX System Manager's Manual (SMM), Oct. 1996.

[52] Microsoft. Alternatives to using Transactional NTFS, 2015. `https://msdn.microsoft.com/en-us/library/windows/desktop/bb968806(v=vs.85).aspx`.

[53] C. Min, W.-H. Kang, T. Kim, S.-W. Lee, and Y. I. Eom. Lightweight application-level crash consistency on transactional flash storage. In *Proceedings of the 2015 USENIX Annual Technical Conference*, pages 221–234, Santa Clara, CA, July 2015.

[54] C. Mohan, D. Haderle, B. Lindsay, H. Pirahesh, and P. Schwarz. ARIES: A transaction recovery method supporting fine-granularity locking and partial rollbacks using write-ahead logging. *ACM Transactions on Database Systems*, 17(1):94–162, Mar. 1992.

[55] Mozilla. Bug 421482 - Firefox 3 uses `fsync` excessively, 2008–2015. `https://bugzilla.mozilla.org/show_bug.cgi?id=421482`.

[56] S. Neumann. Re: fsync in glib/gio, Mar. 2009. `https://mail.gnome.org/archives/gtk-devel-list/2009-March/msg00098.html`.

[57] E. B. Nightingale, K. Veeraraghavan, P. M. Chen, and J. Flinn. Rethink the sync. In *Proceedings of the 7th Symposium on Operating Systems Design and Implementation (OSDI)*, pages 1–14, Seattle, WA, Nov. 2006.

[58] Open Group. fsync - synchronise changes to a file. The Single UNIX Specification, Version 2, 1997. `http://pubs.opengroup.org/onlinepubs/7908799/xsh/fsync.html`.

[59] S. Park, T. Kelly, and K. Shen. Failure-atomic `msync()`: A simple and efficient mechanism for preserving the integrity of durable data. In *Proceedings of the ACM EuroSys Conference*, pages 225–238, Prague, Czech Republic, Apr. 2013.

[60] S. Peter, J. Li, I. Zhang, D. R. K. Ports, D. Woos, A. Krishnamurthy, T. Anderson, and T. Roscoe. Arrakis: The operating system is the control plane. In *Proceedings of the 11th Symposium on Operating Systems Design and Implementation (OSDI)*, pages 1–16, Broomfield, CO, Oct. 2014.

[61] T. S. Pillai, V. Chidambaram, J.-Y. Hwang, A. C. Arpaci-Dusseau, and R. H. Arpaci-Dusseau. Towards efficient, portable application-level consistency. In *Proceedings of the 9th Workshop on Hot Topics in Dependable Systems*, Farmington, PA, Nov. 2013.

[62] T. S. Pillai, V. Chidambaram, R. Alagappan, S. Al-Kiswany, A. C. Arpaci-Dusseau, and R. H. Arpaci-Dusseau. All file systems are not created equal: On the complexity of crafting crash-consistent applications. In *Proceedings of the 11th*

Symposium on Operating Systems Design and Implementation (OSDI), pages 433–448, Broomfield, CO, Oct. 2014.

[63] D. E. Porter, O. S. Hofmann, C. J. Rossbach, A. Benn, and E. Witchel. Operating systems transactions. In *Proceedings of the 22nd ACM Symposium on Operating Systems Principles (SOSP)*, pages 161–176, Big Sky, MT, Oct. 2009.

[64] V. Prabhakaran, A. C. Arpaci-Dusseau, and R. H. Arpaci-Dusseau. Model-based failure analysis of journaling file systems. In *Proceedings of the 35th Annual IEEE/IFIP International Conference on Dependable Systems and Networks (DSN)*, pages 802–811, Yokohama, Japan, June–July 2005.

[65] V. Prabhakaran, T. L. Rodeheffer, and L. Zhou. Transactional flash. In *Proceedings of the 8th Symposium on Operating Systems Design and Implementation (OSDI)*, pages 147–160, San Diego, CA, Dec. 2008.

[66] T. Ridge, D. Sheets, T. Tuerk, A. Giugliano, A. Madhavapeddy, and P. Sewell. SibylFS: formal specification and oracle-based testing for POSIX and real-world file systems. In *Proceedings of the 25th ACM Symposium on Operating Systems Principles (SOSP)*, Monterey, CA, Oct. 2015.

[67] D. M. Ritchie and K. Thompson. The UNIX time-sharing system. *Communications of the ACM*, 17(7):365–375, July 1974.

[68] O. Rodeh, J. Bacik, and C. Mason. BTRFS: The Linux B-tree filesystem. *ACM Transactions on Storage*, 9(3), Aug. 2013.

[69] M. Rosenblum and J. Ousterhout. The design and implementation of a log-structured file system. In *Proceedings of the 13th ACM Symposium on Operating Systems Principles (SOSP)*, pages 1–15, Pacific Grove, CA, Oct. 1991.

[70] C. Rubio-González, H. S. Gunawi, B. Liblit, R. H. Arpaci-Dusseau, and A. C. Arpaci-Dusseau. Error propagation analysis for file systems. In *Proceedings of the 2009 ACM SIGPLAN Conference on Programming Language Design and Implementation (PLDI)*, pages 270–280, Dublin, Ireland, June 2009.

[71] G. Schellhorn, G. Ernst, J. Pfähler, D. Haneberg, and W. Reif. Development of a verified flash file system. In *Proceedings of the 4th International ABZ Conference*, pages 9–24, Toulouse, France, June 2014.

[72] K. Shen, S. Park, and M. Zhu. Journaling of journal is (almost) free. In *Proceedings of the 12th USENIX Conference on File and Storage Technologies (FAST)*, pages 287–293, Santa Clara, CA, Feb. 2014.

[73] A. Solar-Lezama. *Program synthesis by sketching*. PhD thesis, University of California, Berkeley, 2008.

[74] A. Solar-Lezama, L. Tancau, R. Bodik, V. Saraswat, and S. Seshia. Combinatorial sketching for finite programs. In *Proceedings of the 12th International Conference on Architectural Support for Programming Languages and Operating Systems (ASPLOS)*, pages 404–415, San Jose, CA, Oct. 2006.

[75] D. J. Sorin, M. D. Hill, and D. A. Wood. *A Primer on Memory Consistency and Cache Coherence*. Morgan & Claypool, 2011.

[76] R. P. Spillane, S. Gaikwad, M. Chinni, E. Zadok, and C. P. Wright. Enabling transactional file access via lightweight kernel extensions. In *Proceedings of the 7th USENIX Conference on File and Storage Technologies (FAST)*, pages 29–42, San Francisco, CA, Feb. 2009.

[77] SQLite. Atomic commit in SQLite, 2013. `https://www.sqlite.org/atomiccommit.html`.

[78] A. Sweeney, D. Doucette, W. Hu, C. Anderson, M. Nishimoto, and G. Peck. Scalability in the XFS file system. In *Proceedings of the 1996 USENIX Annual Technical Conference*, San Diego, CA, Jan. 1996.

[79] The Open Group. Technical standard: Extended API set part 2, Oct. 2006.

[80] E. Torlak and R. Bodik. A lightweight symbolic virtual machine for solver-aided host languages. In *Proceedings of the 2014 ACM SIGPLAN Conference on Programming Language Design and Implementation (PLDI)*, pages 530–541, Edinburgh, UK, June 2014.

[81] E. Torlak and D. Jackson. Kodkod: A relational model finder. In *Proceedings of the 13th International Conference on Tools and Algorithms for the Construction and Analysis of Systems*, pages 632–647, Braga, Portugal, Mar.–Apr. 2007.

[82] E. Torlak, M. Vaziri, and J. Dolby. MemSAT: Checking axiomatic specifications of memory models. In *Proceedings of the 2010 ACM SIGPLAN Conference on Programming Language Design and Implementation (PLDI)*, pages 341–350, Toronto, Canada, June 2010.

[83] L. Tung. Bitcoin developers offer $10,000 virtual bounty to fix mystery Mac bug, Nov. 2013. `http://goo.gl/Ssbj8T`.

[84] Ubuntu. Bug #317781: Ext4 data loss, Jan. 2009. `https://bugs.launchpad.net/ubuntu/+source/linux/+bug/317781`.

[85] R. Verma, A. A. Mendez, S. Park, S. Mannarswamy, T. Kelly, and C. B. M. III. Failure-atomic updates of application data in a Linux file system. In *Proceedings of the 13th USENIX Conference on File and Storage Technologies (FAST)*, pages 203–211, Santa Clara, CA, Feb. 2015.

[86] M. Wenzel. Some aspects of Unix file-system security, Aug. 2014. `http://isabelle.in.tum.de/library/HOL/HOL-Unix/Unix.html`.

[87] C. P. Wright, R. Spillane, G. Sivathanu, and E. Zadok. Extending ACID semantics to the file system. *ACM Transactions on Storage*, 3(2):1–42, June 2007.

[88] J. Yang, P. Twohey, D. Engler, and M. Musuvathi. Using model checking to find serious file system errors. In *Proceedings of the 6th Symposium on Operating Systems Design and Implementation (OSDI)*, pages 273–287, San Francisco, CA, Dec. 2004.

[89] J. Yang, P. Twohey, D. Engler, and M. Musuvathi. EXPLODE: A lightweight, general system for finding serious storage system errors. In *Proceedings of the 7th Symposium on Operating Systems Design and Implementation (OSDI)*, pages 131–146, Seattle, WA, Nov. 2006.

[90] Y. Yang, G. Gopalakrishnan, G. Lindstrom, and K. Slind. Nemos: a framework for axiomatic and executable specifications of memory consistency models. In *IPDPS*, 2004.

[91] Y. Yang, G. Gopalakrishnan, and G. Lindstrom. UMM: An operational memory model specification framework with inte-

grated model checking capability. *Concurrency and Computation: Practice & Experience*, 17:465–487, Apr. 2005.

[92] M. Zheng, J. Tucek, D. Huang, F. Qin, M. Lillibridge, E. S. Yang, B. W. Zhao, and S. Singh. Torturing databases for fun and profit. In *Proceedings of the 11th Symposium on Operating Systems Design and Implementation (OSDI)*, pages 449–464, Broomfield, CO, Oct. 2014.

Prudent Memory Reclamation in Procrastination-Based Synchronization

Aravinda Prasad
Indian Institute of Science, Bangalore &
IBM Linux Technology Center
aravinda@csa.iisc.ernet.in

K Gopinath
Indian Institute of Science, Bangalore
gopi@csa.iisc.ernet.in

Abstract

Procrastination is the fundamental technique used in synchronization mechanisms such as Read-Copy-Update (RCU) where writers, in order to synchronize with readers, defer the freeing of an object until there are no readers referring to the object. The synchronization mechanism determines when the deferred object is safe to reclaim and when it is actually reclaimed. Hence, such memory reclamations are completely oblivious of the memory allocator state. This induces poor memory allocator performance, for instance, when the reclamations are ill-timed. Furthermore, deferred objects provide hints about the future that inform memory regions that are about to be freed. Although useful, hints are not exploited as deferred objects are not *"visible"* to memory allocators.

We introduce Prudence, a dynamic memory allocator, that is tightly integrated with the synchronization mechanism to ensure visibility of deferred objects to the memory allocator. Such an integration enables Prudence to (i) identify the safe time to reclaim deferred objects' memory, (ii) have an inclusive view of the allocated, free and about-to-be-freed objects, and (iii) exploit optimizations based on the hints about the future during important state transitions. Our evaluation in the Linux kernel shows that Prudence integrated with RCU performs 3.9× to 28× better in micro-benchmarks compared to SLUB, a recent memory allocator in the Linux kernel. It also improves the overall performance perceptibly (4%-18%) for a mix of widely used synthetic and application benchmarks. Further, it performs better (up to 98%) in terms of object hits in caches, object cache churns, slab churns, peak memory usage and total fragmentation, when compared with the SLUB allocator.

ASPLOS '16, April 02–06, 2016, Atlanta, GA, USA

DOI: http://dx.doi.org/10.1145/2872362.2872405

Categories and Subject Descriptors D.4.7 [*Operating Systems*]: Organization and Design; D.1.3 [*Programming Techniques*]: Concurrent Programming—Parallel programming; D.4.2 [*Operating Systems*]: Storage Management—Allocation/deallocation strategies

General Terms Design, Synchronization, Performance

Keywords Read-Copy-Update (RCU), Memory Reclamation, Dynamic Memory Allocator

1. Introduction

The evolution of multicore systems has increased the need for highly scalable synchronization mechanisms. Traditional lock-based synchronization techniques such as reader-writer locks do not scale for large multicore systems [4, 44]. This has led to the exploration of non-traditional synchronization mechanisms such as Read-Copy-Update (RCU) [31, 34, 37], where synchronization is achieved via procrastination [32]. Although synchronization via procrastination was first proposed in the 1980s [27], there is an increased interest in such techniques in the recent past [1, 9, 23, 29, 30, 43] as they achieve near-linear scalability even at high core counts.

Synchronization via procrastination has been applied to various data structures such as lists, trees [1, 9, 23], hash tables [32, 39, 41, 42], and used in number of operating systems including DYNIX/PTX [37], Linux [2], Tornado [16], K42 [5]. RCU is widely used in the Linux kernel [33] with several subsystems using the RCU synchronization primitive to achieve better scalability [36, 38].

In order to update an object, writers in synchronization via procrastination, create a new version of the object and defer the freeing of the old object versions until there are no readers referring to the old version. As a consequence, multiple versions of the object exist at the same time resulting in readers accessing stale data. Such staleness, however, is acceptable in many situations [32]. This is a radical departure from traditional synchronization mechanisms where writers update objects in place.

From the memory allocator's stance, synchronization via procrastination generates high stress on the memory allocator. This is because of frequent allocation and freeing of objects as each update operation allocates a new object and defers the freeing of the old version of the object. Furthermore, the synchronization mechanism determines when the old version of the object is safe to reclaim and when it is actually reclaimed. Normally such memory reclamations are batched and either offloaded to worker threads or processed in the background to avoid interference with the application [21, 35, 40, 43]. This induces unconventional allocation and freeing patterns on the underlying memory allocators; object allocation is spread over an interval of time, whereas freeing occurs in bursts. Existing memory allocators are not designed to handle such allocation patterns.

Additionally, procrastination-based synchronization mechanisms throttle the amount of memory reclamations performed at a time depending on the backlog of the deferred objects. However, such throttling is completely oblivious of the memory allocator state. Ill-timed throttling by the synchronization mechanism can adversely affect the performance of memory allocators and further cause out-of-memory situations when the update rates are high.

Apart from its impact on the memory allocator's performance, the deferred freeing of objects has an inherent property that interests memory allocators from the perspective of providing hints about the future. Intuitively such insight into the memory regions that are about to be freed are valuable to memory allocators. However, existing memory allocators cannot take advantage of hints about the future as deferred objects are not *visible* to memory allocators.

It is important to note that in conventional synchronization mechanisms (such as reader-writer locks), readers and writers have mutual exclusion. Thus, writers neither copy and update an object nor wait for the readers to free the old version of the object. Instead, objects are updated in place. Hence, such synchronization mechanisms neither provide hints about the future nor exhibit such pathological effect on memory allocators. In addition, they are not impacted by the performance of memory allocators as writers do not allocate a new object and free the old version of the object.

We introduce Prudence, a dynamic memory allocator based on slab allocator [8] principles, but that tightly integrates with procrastination-based synchronization mechanism to gain visibility into the deferred objects. In memory allocator parlance, we are integrating a specific mutator (synchronization via procrastination) with the underlying memory allocator to gain visibility to the lifetime information of the objects. This enables the memory allocator to efficiently handle the objects that are deferred for freeing. Such an integration enables Prudence to wait until the completion of readers referring to the old version of the object before reclaiming the associated memory. Furthermore, integration with the synchronization mechanism enables Prudence to have an inclusive view of the allocated, free and about-to-be-freed objects equipping Prudence to properly time the reclamation of deferred objects. Additionally, Prudence exploits optimizations based on hints about the future during important state transitions.

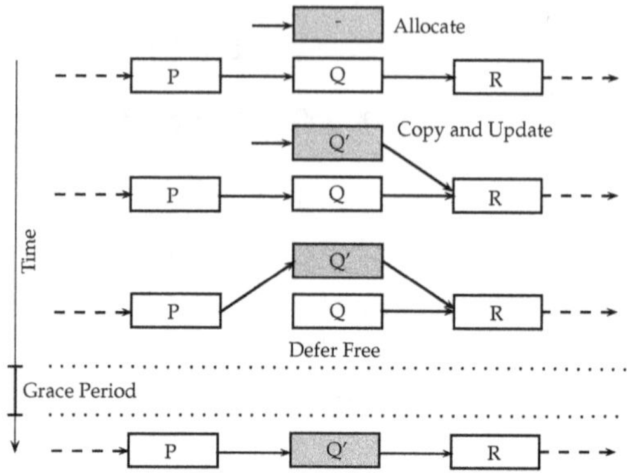

Figure 1. Procrastination-based synchronization technique applied to linked list update operation

Prudence provides a simple *turnkey* replacement for existing subsystems to defer the freeing of an object. Hence, any increased complexity of such an enhancement is limited to memory allocators and does not extend to subsystems using synchronization via procrastination.

We evaluate our idea with the RCU synchronization mechanism in the Linux kernel along with a slab-based memory allocator. Our evaluation of Prudence integrated with RCU shows 3.9× to 28× performance improvement for micro-benchmarks compared to the SLUB allocator. Prudence improves the overall performance of widely used synthetic (Postmark, Netperf) and application (Apache, PostgreSQL) benchmarks. Further, it performs better (up to 98%) in terms of object hits in caches, object cache churns, slab churns, peak memory usage and total fragmentation when compared with the SLUB allocator.

To the best of our knowledge, Prudence is the first memory allocator designed to handle reclamation of deferred objects in the memory allocator by tightly integrating with the synchronization mechanism. In addition, it exploits optimizations based on hints about the future.

We briefly introduce procrastination-based synchronization mechanism and the slab memory allocator (§2) followed by the impact on memory allocators due to processing deferred objects in a synchronization setting (§3). The design of Prudence memory allocator is then covered in §4 with evaluation of Prudence in the Linux kernel in §5.

2. Background

2.1 Synchronization via Procrastination

In this section, we explain synchronization via procrastination using the example of a linked list update operation. Readers in synchronization via procrastination traverse the list concurrently with writers without explicitly synchronizing with the writers. Hence the wait-free readers scale lin-

```
writer(...) {
  ...
  old_object = list_update(...);
  rcu_register_callback(cb_func, old_object);
  ...
}

/* Invoked after a grace period by RCU */
cb_func(void *old_object) {
  free(old_object);
}
```

Listing 1. The RCU defer free API

early with near-zero overhead. However, writers are responsible for guaranteeing consistent view of data structures to readers.

A writer updating object Q (Figure 1), instead of updating it in place, allocates a new object, copies the contents of Q to the new object and performs the update on the new object. The writer inserts the updated object Q′ and removes the old object Q from the list. Once object Q is removed from the list, no new readers can gain reference to it. But there could be pre-existing readers referring to it. Hence, the writer defers the freeing of object Q until the completion of the pre-existing readers. As readers traversing the list are wait-free and hence make progress, the number of readers referring to object Q eventually becomes zero.

The synchronization mechanism keeps track of the deferred objects in the system and waits for the completion of pre-existing readers before reclaiming the deferred objects' memory. Different techniques are available to identify the completion of pre-existing readers [22]. One such technique employed by RCU in the Linux kernel restricts readers from (i) holding reference to an object outside the read-side critical section and (ii) relinquishing the CPU inside a read-side critical section. Hence, a context switch on a CPU implies the completion of all prior read-side critical sections on that CPU i.e., there are no readers holding reference to deferred objects on that CPU. Therefore, a context switch on all the CPUs after an update operation implies that there are no readers in the entire system holding reference to the object deferred during the corresponding update operation [31, 34]. Hence, a deferred object has to wait for a context switch on all the CPUs to ensure the completion of pre-existing readers. Such a wait time after which a deferred object is eligible for freeing is called a grace period. RCU invokes memory reclamation routine for the deferred objects which have waited for a grace period.

RCU can wait for the completion of pre-existing readers for several deferred objects without explicitly tracking each and every deferred object. This is because a context switch on all the CPUs after a set of deferred frees ensures the completion of the pre-existing readers for these deferred objects.

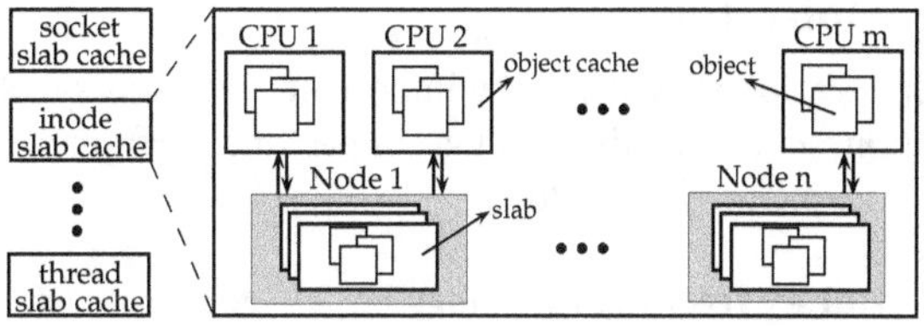

Figure 2. Structure of a slab allocator

2.2 Defer freeing an object

The code snippet in Listing 1 shows the API provided by RCU for writers to asynchronously defer the freeing of an object. A writer after updating an object registers a callback function with RCU to defer free the old version of the object. RCU invokes the callback function `cb_func`, which performs the actual freeing, once the deferred object is safe for freeing, i.e., after the completion of the grace period.

2.3 Slab Allocator

A slab allocator [8] is a dynamic memory allocator that efficiently manages allocation requests for objects of the same type and size. The slab allocator consists of caches (referred as slab caches) of commonly used objects. For example, slab allocators in OS kernels have different slab caches for commonly used objects such as inodes, threads.

Each individual slab cache constitutes a per-CPU object cache and a per-NUMA node list of slabs as depicted in Figure 2. The per-CPU object cache (hereafter referred as object cache) is a cache of free objects. The per-NUMA node list (hereafter referred as node list) contains the list of slabs belonging to the same NUMA domain. A slab is one or more contiguous pages of memory, split-up into equal sized objects.

Object caches are filled by moving the required number of objects from slabs in the node list. A slab is marked fully allocated, partially allocated or free depending on the number of objects available in the slab. The slab is considered fully allocated or full when all of its objects are moved to object caches.

The slab allocator attempts to serve an allocation request by looking for a free object in the current CPU's object cache. An allocation request successfully served from the object cache involves minimal work and is efficient; such an allocation is referred as cache hit. An allocation request that cannot be served from the object cache requires refilling of the object cache from the current node's list of slabs. If all the slabs in the node list are full, the slab cache is grown by allocating one or more slabs from the page allocator.

Similarly, upon free, the slab allocator puts the object into the current CPU's object cache. In case the object cache overflows, the objects are flushed into the respective slabs in the node list. If the number of free slabs crosses the threshold, the slab cache is shrunk by returning the pages associated with the free slabs to the page allocator.

3. Motivation

In this section we discuss the important aspects of synchronization via procrastination that impact the performance of dynamic memory allocators.

3.1 Bursty freeing of memory

Real-world applications perform thousands of update operations during a single grace period interval [40]. Each update operation defers the freeing of one or more objects. For example, tree re-balancing results in multiple deferred objects [9]. Hence, there can be thousands of deferred objects awaiting the completion of the grace period. The synchronization mechanism initiates the memory reclamation of eligible deferred objects after the completion of the grace period. As a result, freeing of objects occurs in bursts.

Bursty freeing of objects causes object cache overflow resulting in object cache flushing. Moreover, object cache flushing can happen in parallel on all CPUs as deferred objects are processed in parallel on all CPUs [40]. Parallel flushing of object caches on all CPUs causes contention on the node list lock. In addition, it increases the number of free slabs in the node list resulting in slab cache shrinking when the number of free slabs exceeds the threshold.

The worst case occurs when the synchronization mechanism schedules memory reclamation of deferred objects soon after refilling the object cache. Freeing deferred objects during reclamation causes object cache overflow. This results in object cache flush, which wastes resources and time spent by memory allocator in refilling the object cache.

Prudence acts with caution by considering the number of deferred objects waiting for reclamation when performing object cache refill/flush.

3.2 Extended object lifetimes

Lifetime of an object (including that of a deferred object) is the time interval between the allocation of an object and freeing of that object back to the memory allocator. Although deferred objects are safe for freeing soon after the completion of the grace period, they are in fact freed only when processed by the synchronization mechanism.

The synchronization mechanism incurs delays in processing the deferred objects and hence the memory associated with the deferred objects may not be reclaimed immediately after the completion of the grace period. For example, as RCU has to explicitly process individual deferred objects by invoking the registered callback functions, the processing of deferred objects towards the end of the queue is delayed. Additionally, processing of deferred objects is further delayed due to external factors such as triggering of interrupts and preemption.

Furthermore, to avoid latency spikes and jitters due to processing of deferred objects, the number of deferred objects processed at a given time is throttled by the synchronization mechanism [21, 35, 40]. Throttling limits the number of deferred objects processed at a time, further delaying the memory reclamation of safe deferred objects.

All these factors result in extended object lifetimes. Existing memory allocators are not aware of safe deferred objects. Hence, they cannot reuse/reallocate these deferred objects until the objects are processed by the synchronization mechanism.

3.3 High object cache and slab churn rate

Bursty freeing of memory and extended object lifetimes, together amplify the performance impact on dynamic memory allocators. Extended object lifetimes result in object cache refill and slab cache grow operations, because memory allocator cannot reuse safe deferred objects until processed by the synchronization mechanism. Bursty freeing of memory, however, results in object cache flush and slab cache shrink. Together they result in high object cache and slab churn rates.

Additionally, throttling the number of deferred objects processed at a given time is completely oblivious of the memory allocator state. Ill-timed throttling induces poor memory allocator performance. For instance, the synchronization mechanism may (i) limit the number of deferred objects processed when the object cache is empty causing object cache refill (ii) process more deferred objects when the object cache is full leading to object cache flushing. Hence, throttling may cause unnecessary object cache refill/flush operations.

Object cache refill/flush and slab cache grow/shrink operations are expensive and impact the performance of memory allocators. Our evaluation in the Linux kernel reveals that the object allocation cost, compared to cache hit, is $4\times$ expensive if it involves object cache refill and $14\times$ expensive if it involves slab cache grow operation. Hence, unnecessary object cache and slab churns are better avoided.

Increasing the size of object cache does not help in avoiding high object churns, instead it causes even higher churn rate. An allocation request that cannot be served from the object cache due to non-availability of objects results in more objects getting refilled in the object cache. If such object cache refill is followed by bursty freeing of objects, the object cache can overflow resulting with more number of objects flushed from object cache. Normally half of the object cache is flushed during the overflow. Moreover, increasing the size of object cache does not eliminate extended object lifetimes. We believe such issues are better handled by having deferred objects visible to the memory allocator.

3.4 Denial-of-service attacks

Extended object lifetimes can be exploited to create denial-of-service attacks by generating a load on the system that triggers high rate of deferred frees. Due to extended object lifetimes, the number of deferred objects waiting for reclamation increases steadily and ultimately exhausts the entire memory in the system. Such DoS attacks have been reported

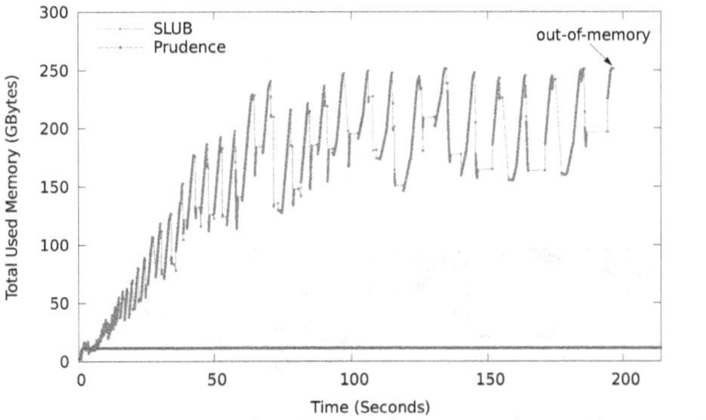

Figure 3. Impact of RCU on the SLUB allocator in the Linux kernel can be seen. Variations in the total used memory incurred by Prudence (up to a few hundred MB) is not noticeable in the graph.

for RCU implementation in the Linux kernel where a malicious user performs file open-close operations in a tight loop to generate high rate of deferred objects [35].

Prudence eliminates extended object lifetimes by having deferred objects visible to the memory allocator. Prudence can reallocate deferred objects immediately after they are eligible for freeing without waiting for processing by an entity external to the memory allocator.

3.5 Evaluating the impact of RCU in the Linux kernel

We evaluate the impact of RCU on the SLUB allocator [10] in the Linux kernel. The test machine is an Intel Xeon E5-4640 processor with 4 CPU sockets, 8 cores per socket for a total of 32 CPUs; with two-way hyper-threading enabled the total number of logical CPUs available is 64. The test machine has 252 GB of physical memory running Linux kernel 3.17.0.

We stress the RCU subsystem by running a workload that continuously performs linked list update operation on all the CPUs. Each CPU updates a different list and hence does not contend for list lock. Every update operation results in the allocation of a new object followed by defer freeing of the old version of the object. We use 512 bytes as object size and sample the total used memory in the system every 10 ms. The result is plotted in Figure 3.

The total used memory in the system increases during the update operation as several object allocation requests result in slab cache growth leading to allocation of pages from the page allocator. This is followed by a steep drop in the total used memory due to bursty free of objects triggered after the completion of grace periods. Free burst increases the number of free slabs resulting in slab cache shrinking leading to returning of pages to the page allocator.

Heavy slab churns are clearly evident from Figure 3 with spikes of slab cache grow and shrink operations. However, Figure 3 does not reveal heavy object churns. This is because flushing/refilling of object cache does not affect the total used memory in the system unless they result in slab cache grow/shrink.

Even though the rate at which the objects, both allocated and deferred free are the same, the total used memory in the system gradually increases and ultimately the system hits out-of-memory (OOM) at the 196th second. Increase in the total used memory is due to extended object lifetimes as RCU is unable to keep up the rate of processing the deferred objects resulting in many objects waiting for reclamation. Existing RCU implementation in the Linux kernel expedites the processing of deferred objects when the system is under memory pressure. This can be observed at around 70 seconds when RCU attempts to process more deferred objects as the memory pressure increases. Despite this, RCU fails to keep up with the rate at which objects are deferred for freeing resulting in OOM.

Ideally, the total used memory should remain the same as the rate at which objects, both allocated and deferred free are the same. Prudence achieves near-ideal performance which is explained in §5.5.

3.6 Hints about the future

We look at the deferred frees from the perspective of providing hints about the memory regions that are about to be freed. Such hints enable dynamic memory allocators to know the future free operations in advance. Moreover, the hints are precise and bound to happen, unlike predictions. Intuitively any hint about the future is valuable. We believe that the hints about the future can be exploited to enhance the performance of dynamic memory allocators.

Prudence demonstrates that optimizations based on hints are viable by exploiting the hints during important state transitions.

4. The Prudence Dynamic Memory Allocator

Prudence is a slab-based [8] dynamic memory allocator integrated with procrastination-based synchronization mechanism. The basic design principle of Prudence is to have deferred objects visible and processed in the memory allocator.

In order to equip memory allocators with the capability to observe and reclaim deferred objects, the memory allocator should (i) provide an interface to other subsystems to defer the freeing of an object, (ii) be capable of identifying the safe time to reclaim the deferred objects' memory.

To incorporate requirement (i) Prudence exports a new API to defer the freeing of an object. The code snippet in Listing 2 shows how to asynchronously defer free an object using Prudence. The new API is a simple *turnkey* replacement for the existing API provided by synchronization mechanisms. With the new API, subsystems can request Prudence to reclaim the deferred objects instead of registering a callback function with the synchronization mechanism. In addition, Prudence allows subsystems to issue regular allocation and free operations along with the deferred free.

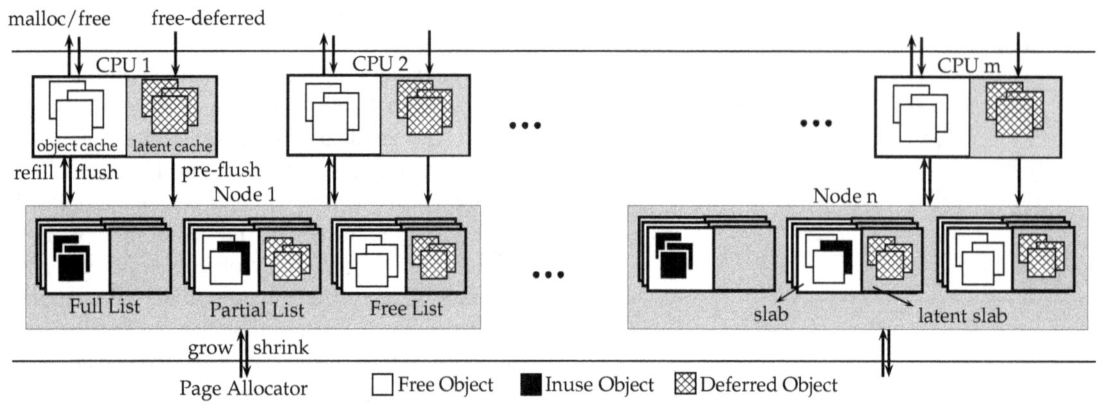

Figure 4. An individual slab cache in Prudence memory allocator

```
writer(...) {
  ...
  old_object = list_update(...);
  free_deferred(old_object);
  ...
}
```

Listing 2. Defer freeing an object in Prudence

For requirement (ii) we tightly integrate the synchronization mechanism with the memory allocator. Procrastination-based synchronization mechanisms employ different memory reclamation schemes to identify the completion of pre-existing readers referring to a deferred object. Generally, to identify the grace period, these schemes maintain the state of the object (active or deferred free) along with the state of the readers. We modify the synchronization mechanism to provide information on the grace period state to the memory allocator and further integrate such information with the deferred objects. Prudence identifies the safe time to reclaim a deferred object depending on whether the grace period is ongoing or completed. However, the synchronization mechanism is still responsible for computing the grace period.

4.1 Latent Cache and Latent Slab

Prudence introduces latent caches and latent slabs to efficiently handle deferred objects and to effectively exploit hints about the future. Both latent caches and latent slabs hold deferred objects that are not yet eligible for reuse/reclamation. A latent cache is defined for every object cache and holds deferred objects at object cache level. Similarly, a latent slab is defined for every slab and holds deferred objects belonging to that slab as shown in Figure 4. Objects in latent caches and latent slabs remain hidden until the completion of the grace period. After the completion of the grace period, objects in the latent cache are merged with the object cache and objects in the latent slab are merged with the slab.

Prudence enforces a limit on the size of a latent cache. The limit is set to the size of the object cache. Once the limit is reached, subsequent objects deferred for freeing are placed into the latent slab. The rationale for setting such a limit is a proactive measure to avoid object cache overflow when the safe deferred objects in latent cache are merged with the object cache. The limit is not applicable to a latent slab as it holds only the deferred objects that belong to the slab. Hence the size of the latent slab cannot exceed the size of the slab.

Latent cache/latent slab completely eliminates the extended object lifetimes because there is no delay incurred in reclaiming the deferred objects. The deferred objects are tracked and processed in the memory allocator and are considered for reallocation immediately after the completion of the grace period. They need not wait for processing from an entity external to the memory allocator.

4.2 Exploiting hints about the future

Information on the objects that are about to be freed is available to Prudence from latent caches/slabs. Prudence uses this information during cache refill and flush operations to avoid performance impact. In addition, Prudence employs optimizations that take advantage of hints about the future to improve memory allocator attributes. This section describes the optimizations employed by Prudence along with the pseudo-code (presented in Algorithm 1) for important functions.

Object cache refill: In cases when an allocation request cannot be served from an object cache, Prudence checks for deferred objects in the latent cache that have waited for a grace period. Eligible deferred objects, if any, are merged into the object cache and the allocation request is served from the object cache (lines 8-11). Object cache refill is required only when there are no eligible deferred objects in latent cache (line 12).

Prudence considers the number of deferred objects in the latent cache while performing an object cache refill. The object cache is partially refilled if there are deferred objects waiting for the completion of the grace period in the latent cache. For example, if the object cache size is o and there are

Algorithm 1 Prudence

```
1: function MALLOC(size)
2:     slab_cache ← GET_SLAB_CACHE(size)
3:     obj_cache ← slab_cache[current.cpu].obj_cache
4:     object ← GET_OBJECT(obj_cache)
5:     if object then                                  ▷ Cache Hit
6:         return object
7:     latent_cache ← slab_cache[current.cpu].latent_cache
8:     MERGE_CACHES(obj_cache, latent_cache)
9:     object ← GET_OBJECT(obj_cache)                  ▷ Retry
10:    if object then
11:        return object
12:    return REFILL_OBJECT_CACHE(obj_cache)

13: function REFILL_OBJECT_CACHE(obj_cache)
14:    objs_to_refill ← obj_cache.size − latent_cache.count
15:    LOCK(current.node)
16:    while objs_to_refill > 0 do
17:        if NOT_LIST_EMPTY(node.partial_list) then
18:            Pick a slab S from node.partial_list such that
19:                the total fragmentation is minimized
20:        else if NOT_LIST_EMPTY(node.free_list) then
21:            Pick the first slab S from node.free_list
22:        else break
23:        REFILL(obj_cache, S, objs_to_refill)
24:        objs_to_refill ← objs_to_refill − S.free_objs
25:    UNLOCK(current.node)
26:    object ← GET_OBJECT(obj_cache)                  ▷ Retry again
27:    if object then       ▷ Successful partial/complete refill
28:        return object
29:    if GROW(slab_cache) then                        ▷ Add more slabs
30:        return GET_OBJECT(obj_cache)
31:    if deferred objects waiting for grace period then
32:        Wait for a grace period and retry allocation
33:    else return 0                                   ▷ Trigger out of memory

34: function FREE_DEFERRED(object)
35:    object.gp_state ← GET_GRACE_PERIOD_STATE()
36:    slab_cache ← GET_SLAB_CACHE(object.size)
37:    obj_cache ← slab_cache[current.cpu].obj_cache
38:    latent_cache ← slab_cache[current.cpu].latent_cache
39:    if latent_cache.count < threshold then          ▷ Fast Path
40:        PUT_OBJECT(object, latent_cache)
41:        if ((obj_cache.count + latent_cache.count)
42:            > obj_cache.size) then
43:            SCHEDULE_IDLE_PREFLUSH(latent_cache)
44:        return
45:    FLUSH(obj_cache)
46:    MERGE_CACHES(obj_cache, latent_cache)
47:    if latent_cache.count < threshold then          ▷ Retry
48:        PUT_OBJECT(object, latent_cache)
49:    else                            ▷ Put object into latent slab
50:        PUT_OBJECT(object, object.latent_slab)
51:        PRE_MOVE_SLAB(object.slab)

52: function PRE_MOVE_SLAB(slab)
53:    LOCK(current.node)
54:    if IS_ON_NODE_FULL_LIST(slab) then
55:        MOVE_TO_NODE_PARTIAL_LIST(slab)
56:    else if slab.allocated = slab.deferred then
57:        MOVE_TO_NODE_FREE_LIST(slab)
58:    UNLOCK(current.node)
59:    if free_slabs > free_limit then SHRINK(slab_cache)

60: function MERGE_CACHES(obj_cache, latent_cache)
61:    for obj in latent_cache do
62:        if GRACE_PERIOD_COMPLET(obj.gp_state) then
63:            MOVE_TO_OBJ_CACHE(obj) ▷ Safe for reuse
64:        if obj_cache.count = obj_cache.size then
65:            break
```

d deferred objects in the latent cache, then $o - d$ objects are refilled (line 14). This avoids overflowing the object cache later when d deferred objects are merged into the object cache.

Latent cache pre-flush: Prudence initiates latent cache pre-flush if it foresees an object cache flush after a grace period. Such cases arise when the number of objects in object cache and latent cache together exceed the size of the object cache (lines 41-43). Pre-flushing moves deferred objects in the latent cache to the respective latent slabs.

Prudence schedules pre-flushing during CPU idle time (inspired by [17]). Utilizing CPU idle time eliminates the interference of pre-flushing with object allocation, free and deferred free calls. However, pre-flushing is not performed if idle cycles are unavailable. In such cases, flushing is performed at the time of merging the latent cache with their object cache (line 45).

The number of deferred objects moved from the latent cache to the latent slabs during pre-flush operation is decided based on (i) the number of objects in object cache and latent cache and (ii) object allocation, free and deferred free rate during recent few grace period intervals. The deferred objects in the latent cache are aggressively pre-flushed when the latent cache is almost full and the allocation rate is lower than the free/deferred free rate. Prudence takes a less aggressive approach by intermittently sleeping or yielding the CPU when the allocation rate is higher than the free/deferred free rate, because higher object allocation rate empties the object cache faster. Pre-flushing is terminated when the number of objects in object cache and latent cache together falls below the size of the object cache.

In cases where a grace period is completed during the process of pre-flushing, the eligible/safe deferred objects in the latent cache are merged into the object cache and the pre-flushing is continued. This is beneficial as it avoids the merging of deferred objects from latent cache to object cache during an allocation request.

The pre-flushing of different latent caches is likely to spread over an interval of time. Hence, pre-flushing reduces the lock contention on the node list. In current memory allocators, due to bursty freeing of objects, flushing happens in parallel on all CPUs soon after the completion of grace periods causing high contention on the node list lock.

Object cache flush: As already mentioned, Prudence attempts to avoid flushing the object cache by partially refilling the object cache during object cache refill. Further, it pre-flushes the latent cache if it foresees an object cache flush after a grace period. However, object cache flushing cannot be eliminated. For instance, flushing is required when a series of free operations overflows the object cache.

In Prudence, the number of objects flushed during an object cache flush depends on the number of deferred objects in the latent cache (similar to object cache refill technique). More objects are flushed if there are more deferred objects in the latent cache.

Slab pre-movement: Similar to other slab-based allocators [10, 18], Prudence groups the slabs that are full, partially full and free as shown in Figure 4. Prudence performs pre-movement of a slab between full, partial and free lists if it foresees such a movement in the future (lines 54-57). For example, pre-movement of a full slab from the full list to the partial list is performed when an object associated with the full slab is deferred for freeing. Pre-movement avoids contention on the node list lock as movement of slabs is spread over an interval of time. Whereas, in the case of existing memory allocators, slab movement is triggered in parallel on all CPUs after the completion of a grace period due to the bursty freeing of objects causing high contention on the node list lock.

Reduces total fragmentation: Slab-based allocators consume more memory than requested due to unused objects in the object caches and slabs. Total fragmentation f_t measures the excess memory consumed by the allocator and is defined as the ratio of the allocated and the requested memory [6, 8]:

$$f_t = \frac{allocated}{requested} = \frac{slabs\_allocated \times slab\_size}{objects\_requested \times object\_size}$$

Prudence reduces total fragmentation by considering deferred objects in the latent slab at the time of selecting a slab for object cache refill (lines 17-21). We explain the slab selection optimization with the help of an example.

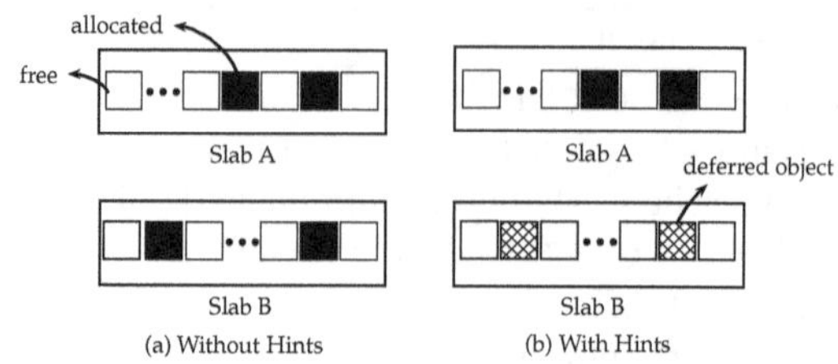

Figure 5. Prudence considers hints on deferred objects during slab selection for object cache refill to reduce total fragmentation [6, 8] and hence selects slab A.

Consider two slabs A and B belonging to a slab cache with two allocated objects in both the slabs as shown in Figure 5(a). It is possible to have slabs in such a state after a couple of allocation and free cycles. We consider this scenario to demonstrate how Prudence chooses a better slab to reduce the total fragmentation when information on deferred objects is available.

For existing memory allocators, with information on the allocated/free objects in a slab, there is no advantage of selecting slab A over slab B or vice versa to refill the object cache. Hence, let us assume slab B is selected for object cache refill.

Now consider this scenario when information on deferred objects is available to the memory allocator as shown in Figure 5(b). Let the slabs A and B be in the same state as before. However, let us assume that the two allocated objects in slab B are deferred for freeing. The memory regions corresponding to these deferred objects will be free after the grace period. With that hint, there is an advantage of selecting slab A over slab B to refill the object cache, because, it is known that the entire slab B will be free after the completion of the grace period. Hence, the pages associated with slab B can be returned to the page allocator if slab A is chosen. This reduces total fragmentation as the number of requested objects remains the same in both the cases, however, the number of allocated slabs will be reduced by one in Prudence.

Furthermore, Prudence does not select a slab for object cache refill when most of the allocated objects in that slab are deferred for freeing (unless it needs to grow the slab cache). This is based on the hope that a few remaining allocated objects will be freed/deferred for freeing in the future. If that happens, the pages associated with the slab can be returned to the page allocator.

Handling memory pressure: Dynamic memory allocators invoke out-of-memory (OOM) handlers to reclaim memory when the system is running low on memory. OOM handlers are disruptive and kill processes to reclaim the memory.

Prudence delays the triggering of OOM handlers if there are several deferred objects waiting for the completion of the grace period (line 31). This can avoid killing of processes to reclaim the memory as the deferred objects can be reallocated after the grace period.

4.3 Reuse of existing optimizations

Slab allocators have been used for decades in many operating systems, libraries and utilities and are highly optimized for performance based on empirical studies and mathematical models. Prudence reuses such optimizations employed in the existing memory allocators. For example, our implementation of Prudence in the Linux kernel reuses the existing heuristics employed by SLUB allocator to decide the size of the object cache, the size of a slab, the threshold after which the slab shrinking should be considered. Other factors influencing the performance such as the slab coloring scheme to improve the hardware cache utilization are also reused.

5. Evaluation

We implement Prudence in the Linux kernel by tightly integrating with the RCU subsystem. Two new APIs `kfree_deferred()` and `kmem_cache_free_deferred()`[1] are exported by Prudence to enable other kernel subsystems to defer free an object. Kernel subsystems that use RCU are modified to use the new APIs, while the rest of the kernel subsystems continue to use SLUB as the memory allocator.

Prudence, analogous to RCU, does not need to explicitly track each and every deferred object in latent cache or latent slab. All these deferred objects are eligible for reuse/reallocation after the completion of the grace period.

5.1 Experiment setup

The test machine is as detailed in §3.5. A mix of micro, synthetic (Postmark, Netperf) and application benchmarks (Apache, PostgreSQL) have been selected to measure the performance of Prudence.

We compare our results with the SLUB allocator in the Linux kernel. The SLUB allocator is the recent allocator in the Linux kernel based on the slab allocation principle [8] and is the default allocator in the Linux kernel. The SLUB implementation in the Linux kernel has better object management techniques, less metadata footprint and lower total fragmentation compared to the earlier SLAB allocator in the Linux kernel [28]. SLUB also performs better on large multicore systems compared to the SLAB allocator [28].

5.2 Micro Benchmark

We execute `kmalloc()/kfree_deferred()` operations in a tight loop, for different object sizes, on all CPUs and measure the total number of allocation/deferred free operations executed per second. A total of 5 million pairs of allocation and deferred free operations are executed per CPU per object size. The benchmark is run thrice and we report the average value across three runs along with the standard deviation.

[1] `kmem_cache_free_deferred()` requires slab cache identifier as an additional argument [8, 18]

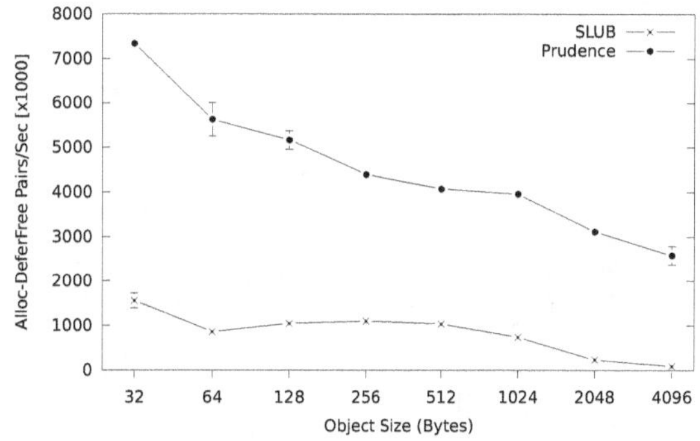

Figure 6. `kmalloc()/kfree_deferred()` pairs of operations executed per second for different allocation size requests

Prudence performs 3.9× to 28.6× better than SLUB on the number of `kmalloc()/kfree_deferred()` pairs executed per second as shown in Figure 6. The improvement is due to eliminating extended object lifetimes and avoiding unnecessary object cache and slab churns. The improvement is higher for larger objects, with the highest improvement of 28.6× achieved for 4096 bytes object size. Larger objects are normally optimized for memory efficiency, hence have fewer objects in object cache and smaller slabs. Fewer objects in object cache result in more frequent object cache refill/flush and smaller slabs result in frequent slab churns. Hence, avoiding unnecessary object cache refill/flush and slab churns results in better performance for larger objects.

5.3 Synthetic and application benchmark details

Postmark-1.51: Postmark [26] simulates the behavior of a mail server by executing file read, append, create and delete operations stressing the underlying filesystem. We execute 64 instances of Postmark on an ext4 filesystem. Each instance operates on a pool of 500 files and 100 directories.

Netperf-2.6.0: The Netperf [25] benchmark measures the performance of network. We execute TCP Connect/Request /Response (TCP_CRR) test on localhost.

Apache-2.4.6: We use ApacheBench (`ab`) [14] part of Apache HTTP server [15] to benchmark the Apache server. The benchmark measures the number of requests the Apache server handles per second. We execute `ab` on localhost with 128 parallel instances.

PostgreSQL-9.2.7: We benchmark PostgreSQL [20] using `pgbench` [19]. The `pgbench` tool, part of PostgreSQL, performs a sequence of SQL operations in multiple concurrent database sessions generating stress similar to TPC-B. We run `pgbench` with 64 threads and 128 clients on localhost.

All the benchmarks execute a fixed number of transactions/jobs on a fresh boot. The number of transactions/jobs is chosen such that each run executes for 5-10 mins. We repeat the run three times and present the average of three runs

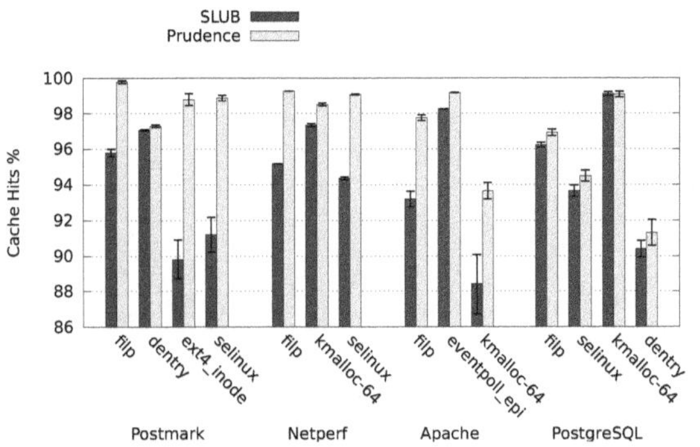

Figure 7. Improvement in the percentage of allocation requests served from the object cache

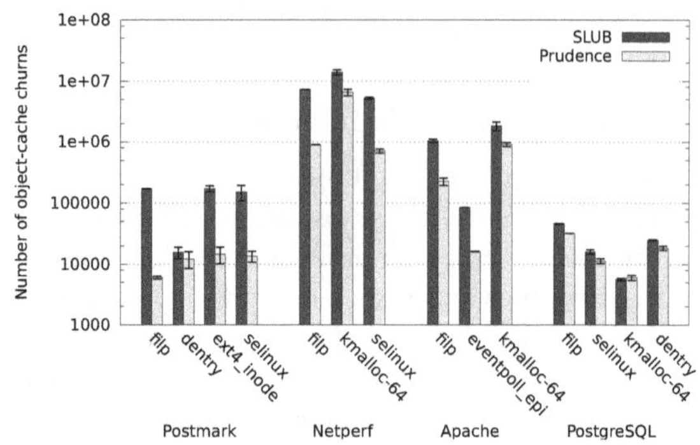

Figure 8. Number of object cache churns incurred by different slab caches

along with the standard deviation. Fixed number of transactions/jobs executed for every benchmark enables a fair comparison of absolute numbers of the memory allocator attributes.

We use the same names for the slab cache as used in the Linux kernel here. The `filp` slab cache holds objects for file descriptor table, `eventpoll_epi` holds objects related to Linux specific poll() system call [12], `dentry` holds directory entry objects, `ext4_inode` holds inodes of ext4 filesystem and `selinux` holds Security Enhanced Linux (SELinux) related objects. We use `kmalloc-64` to represent kmalloc slab cache of size 64 bytes.

We report the performance of the slab caches which have performed more than a million allocation and deferred free operations per run. Each benchmark stresses different slab caches depending on the type of operation/transaction performed. For example, the `ext4_inode` slab cache is stressed a lot while running the Postmark benchmark, however, it has fewer than a few hundred allocations and deferred free requests when running Netperf.

5.4 Results

In this section we report the performance of Prudence.

Object cache hits: Prudence performs better in terms of cache hits for all the slab caches as shown in Figure 7. Improvement in cache hits is due to better management of deferred objects through latent cache. The latent cache ensures immediate availability of deferred objects in the object cache for subsequent allocation requests after the completion of a grace period. This results in serving more requests from the object cache, improving cache hits. In the SLUB allocator, deferred objects are not immediately available for allocation after the completion of a grace period and hence it frequently runs out of objects in object cache requiring to refill the object cache.

Furthermore, when object cache overflows, Prudence flushes only the required number of objects by considering the number of deferred objects in the latent cache. This avoids unnecessary flushing of more objects from the object cache increasing cache hits.

Object cache churns: Prudence reduces the number of object cache churns (pairs of object cache refill/flush operations) by 25.97% to 96.47% compared to the SLUB allocator (except for PostgreSQL `kmalloc-64` which increased by 6%) as shown in Figure 8. Improvement in churn rate is due to avoiding unnecessary refill and flush operations caused by bursty freeing of objects together with extended object lifetimes. If Prudence foresees an object cache flush due to bursty freeing, then subsequent deferred objects are moved to latent slabs. Extended object lifetimes is completely eliminated using latent caches reducing unnecessary object cache refills. Furthermore, improvement in churn rate is due to avoiding unnecessary object cache flushes by performing partial refill of object cache. In addition, more objects are flushed during object cache overflow by considering deferred objects in the latent cache.

Increase in object cache churn rate in the case of PostgreSQL `kmalloc-64` is due to PostgreSQL triggering several free operations outside the context of deferred frees on the `kmalloc-64` slab cache. These free operations interfere with the decisions taken by Prudence resulting in more object cache churns.

Slab churns: Figure 9 shows the number of slab churns (pairs of slab grow/shrink operations) performed by Prudence and SLUB during benchmark execution. Prudence reduces the number of slab churns by 21% to 98.3% except for Postmark `dentry`. Although the slab churn rate for `dentry` is reduced by 3.1%, the reduction is not as high as compared to other slab caches. The number of slab churns for Netperf `filp` is reduced drastically from 364K in SLUB to 6K in Prudence.

Improvement in slab churn rate is due to avoiding unnecessary slab grow/shrink operations caused by bursty freeing of objects together with extended object lifetimes. Further, reduction in the number of object cache churns also reduces the number of slab churns.

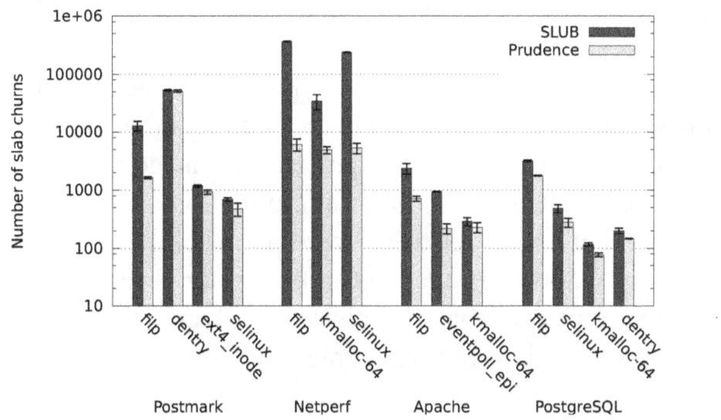

Figure 9. Number of slab churns incurred by different slab caches

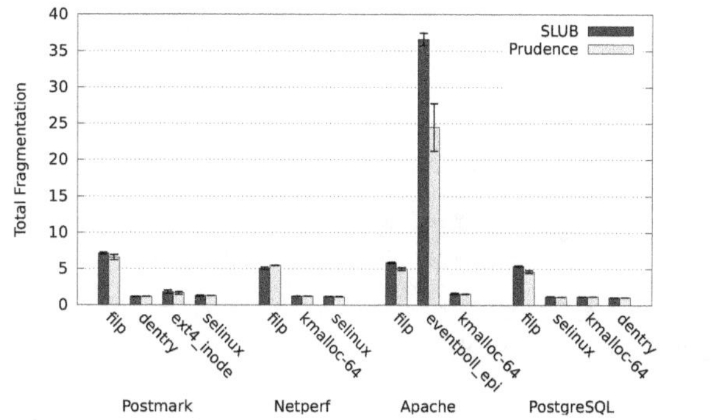

Figure 11. Total Fragmentation [6, 8] measured after the completion of each run for different slab caches

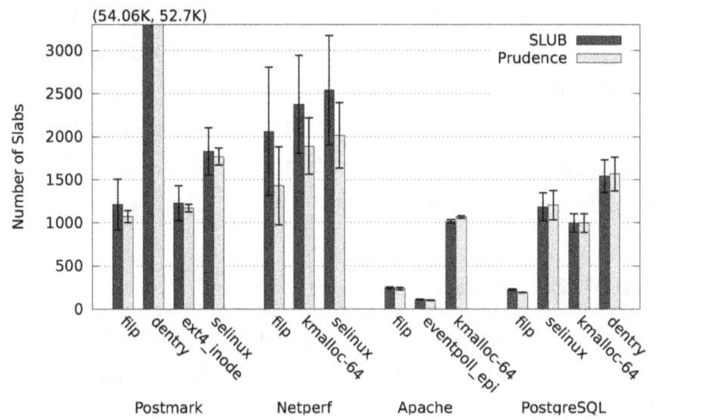

Figure 10. Peak slab usage for different slab caches

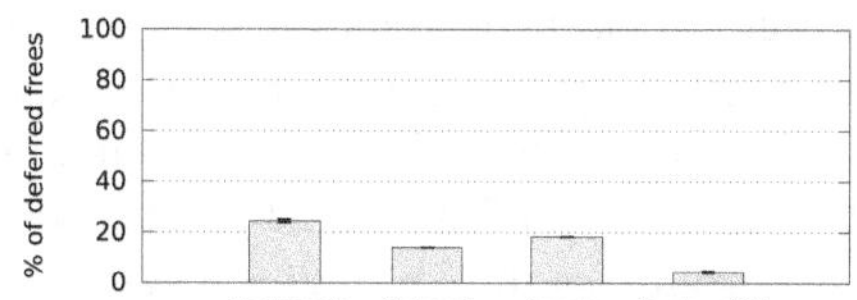

Figure 12. Percentage of deferred frees out of total memory free operations

Peak slab usage: Figure 10 shows the peak number of slabs allocated by Prudence and SLUB. Peak slab usage also indicates the maximum memory consumed by respective slab caches during the execution of the benchmark. Prudence reduces the peak slab usage by 2.5% to 30.6% for most of the slab caches and performs equally well (±2% change) for others compared to SLUB (except for Apache `kmalloc-64` which increased by 5%). Reduction in the peak slab consumption is due to eliminating extended object lifetimes. In Prudence, deferred objects are immediately available for reuse/reallocation after the completion of grace period which avoids unnecessary slab grow operations.

The intensity of slab churns is clearly evident from the peak slab usage. For example, in the case of Netperf `filp`, the peak number of slabs allocated is 2060, however, a total of 364K slab churns are incurred in SLUB. In Prudence, the peak slab usage for Netperf `filp` is reduced to 1429 and the number of slab churns incurred is only 6K.

Total fragmentation: We measure the total fragmentation after the completion of each run (as followed in [8]). Prudence reduces fragmentation for many slab caches (7% to 33% reduction) and performs equally well (±2% change) for the other slab caches compared to the SLUB allocator as shown in Figure 11. However, the total fragmentation is increased by 8.7% for the Netperf `filp` slab cache.

The SLUB allocator selects the first slab in the node partial list to refill the object cache. Prudence, as mentioned already, selects a slab considering the number of deferred objects in the latent slab. The number of slabs in the node partial list can be high and traversing the entire list to select a slab increases refill latency. Hence, Prudence traverses the first 10 slabs in the node partial list reducing the opportunity to improve total fragmentation. This is a trade-off between improving total fragmentation and reducing latency.

Throughput: Overall performance improvement depends on how much an application exercises the memory allocator [6–8, 13]. Prudence is designed to optimize deferred frees and hence the number of frees occurring in the context of RCU deferred frees indicates the opportunity for optimization. Figure 12 shows the percentage of deferred frees out of the total free operations triggered by each benchmark. The percentage of deferred frees varies from 4.4% for PostgreSQL to 24.4% for Postmark.

Figure 13 shows the average throughput improvement by Prudence compared to the SLUB allocator. Postmark achieves the highest performance improvement of 18%. Objects in different slab caches such as `filp`, `ext4_inode` are deferred for freeing during file deletions and are allocated during file creation. The improvement in throughput is due to better handling of deferred objects during file creation and deletion. Netperf and Apache respectively trigger 14% and

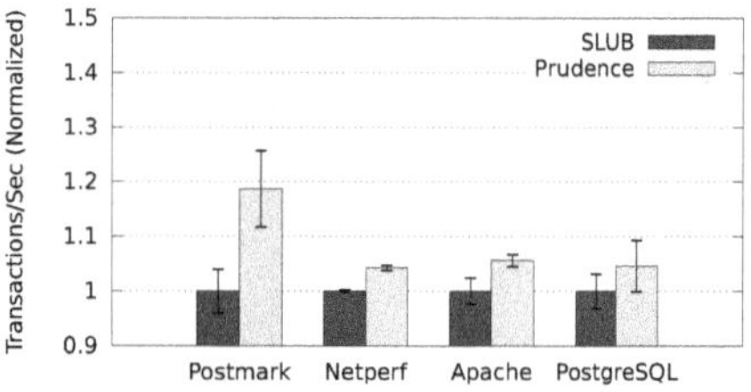

Figure 13. Improvement in overall performance of Prudence compared to SLUB

18% of deferred frees over total free operations and achieve 4.2% and 5.6% improvement in performance. In both the benchmarks, objects are deferred for freeing during connection tear town. Additionally, in case of Apache, objects are deferred for freeing during the removal of the target file descriptor from epoll [12] instance. PostgreSQL achieves 4.6% improvement in performance. However, the variation in the throughput is high for both SLUB and Prudence.

In all the benchmarks the SELinux subsystem allocates and defer frees `selinux` objects during creation and deletion of various resources such as files and sockets.

5.5 Endurance

We discuss the impact of RCU on Prudence for the experiment mentioned in §3.5. It is evident from Figure 3 that Prudence does not suffer from high slab churns or extended object lifetimes.

The total memory used in Prudence increases initially because the initial set of objects deferred for freeing are available for reallocation only after waiting for a grace period. However, Prudence hits equilibrium once the rate at which deferred objects are eligible for reallocation reaches the rate at which objects are allocated. Hence, the total used memory after the initial increase remains almost the same. Prudence still incurs slab churns, however they are fewer in number. These slab churns are not noticeable in Figure 3 because of small variations in the total used memory. Furthermore, Prudence is not susceptible to denial-of-service attacks as it eliminates extended object lifetimes.

6. Related Work

Previous work attempts to optimize memory reclamation in the synchronization mechanism only. The RCU implementation in the Linux kernel employs such optimizations which include offloading the reclamation of deferred frees to kernel threads [11] and throttling the number of objects reclaimed based on the backlog [40]. TRASH [39] also employs throttling to reclaim deferred objects based on backlog. Masstree [30] and CITRUS [1] mention that a technique similar to RCU is employed for memory reclamation. However, further details on memory reclamation are not provided. Silo [43] performs memory reclamation either in the main thread or in a background task. However, none of these mechanisms exploit the hints provided by deferred objects on the future free operations.

A completely orthogonal work predicts the object lifetimes to enable optimization in the memory allocator [3, 24]. However, predictions are not precise and can go wrong. With Prudence, hints provide precise information on the memory regions that are about to be freed and such frees are guaranteed to happen. Prudence can be further optimized based on predictions of object lifetimes for objects that are freed outside of the deferred free context.

7. Conclusion

We introduce Prudence, a dynamic memory allocator designed to handle memory reclamation of deferred objects by tightly integrating it with procrastination-based synchronization mechanism. Prudence avoids poor memory allocator performance induced by synchronization mechanisms by properly timing the memory reclamations. It also employs novel optimizations exploiting hints about the future and further demonstrates that such optimizations improve the performance of memory allocators.

Acknowledgments

We would like to thank our shepherd Emmett Witchel, the anonymous reviewers, Paul McKenney, Sorav Bansal, Murali Krishna Ramanathan and Vinayaka Pandit for their constructive comments which helped to improve this paper. Many thanks to Akshatha Deshpande, Sunita Rao, Ananth Narayan, Arpith K Sharma, Ashish Panwar and Madhuri Prasad.

References

[1] Maya Arbel and Hagit Attiya. Concurrent updates with rcu: Search tree as an example. In *Proceedings of the 2014 ACM Symposium on Principles of Distributed Computing*, PODC '14, pages 196–205, New York, NY, USA, 2014. ACM.

[2] Andrea Arcangeli, Mingming Cao, Paul E McKenney, and Dipankar Sarma. Using Read-Copy-Update Techniques for System V IPC in the Linux 2.5 Kernel. In *USENIX Annual Technical Conference, FREENIX Track*, pages 297–309, 2003.

[3] David A Barrett and Benjamin G Zorn. Using lifetime predictors to improve memory allocation performance. In *ACM SIGPLAN Notices*, volume 28, pages 187–196. ACM, 1993.

[4] Andrew Baumann, Paul Barham, Pierre-Evariste Dagand, Tim Harris, Rebecca Isaacs, Simon Peter, Timothy Roscoe, Adrian Schüpbach, and Akhilesh Singhania. The Multikernel: A New OS Architecture for Scalable Multicore Systems. In *Proceedings of the ACM SIGOPS 22nd Symposium on*

Operating Systems Principles, SOSP '09, pages 29–44, New York, NY, USA, 2009. ACM.

[5] Andrew Baumann, Jeremy Kerr, Jonathan Appavoo, Dilma Da Silva, Orran Krieger, and Robert W Wisniewski. Module hot-swapping for dynamic update and reconfiguration in K42. In *6th Linux. Conf. Au*, 2005.

[6] Emery D Berger, Kathryn S McKinley, Robert D Blumofe, and Paul R Wilson. Hoard: A scalable memory allocator for multithreaded applications. *ACM Sigplan Notices*, 35(11):117–128, 2000.

[7] Emery D Berger, Benjamin G Zorn, and Kathryn S McKinley. Oopsla 2002: reconsidering custom memory allocation. *ACM SIGPLAN Notices*, 48(4S):46–57, 2013.

[8] Jeff Bonwick. The Slab Allocator: An Object-Caching Kernel Memory Allocator. In *USENIX summer*, volume 16. Boston, MA, USA, 1994.

[9] Austin T. Clements, M. Frans Kaashoek, and Nickolai Zeldovich. Scalable address spaces using rcu balanced trees. In *Proceedings of the Seventeenth International Conference on Architectural Support for Programming Languages and Operating Systems*, ASPLOS XVII, pages 199–210, New York, NY, USA, 2012. ACM.

[10] Jonathan Corbet. The SLUB allocator. `http://lwn.net/Articles/229984/`, 2007.

[11] Jonathan Corbet. Relocating rcu callbacks. `http://lwn.net/Articles/522262/`, 2012.

[12] Jonathan Corbet. Epoll evolving. `https://lwn.net/Articles/633422/`, 2015.

[13] Jason Evans. A scalable concurrent malloc (3) implementation for freebsd. In *Proc. of the BSDCan Conference, Ottawa, Canada*, 2006.

[14] The Apache Software Foundation. Apache HTTP server benchmarking tool. `https://httpd.apache.org/docs/2.2/programs/ab.html`, 2015.

[15] The Apache Software Foundation. Apache HTTP Server Project. `http://httpd.apache.org/`, 2015.

[16] Benjamin Gamsa, Orran Krieger, Jonathan Appavoo, and Michael Stumm. Tornado: Maximizing locality and concurrency in a shared memory multiprocessor operating system. In *OSDI*, volume 99, pages 87–100, 1999.

[17] Richard Golding, Peter Bosch, John Wilkes, USENIX Association, et al. Idleness is not sloth. In *USENIX*, pages 201–212, 1995.

[18] Mel Gorman. *Understanding the Linux virtual memory manager*. Prentice Hall, 2004.

[19] The PostgreSQL Global Development Group. pgbench. `http://www.postgresql.org/docs/devel/static/pgbench.html`, 2015.

[20] The PostgreSQL Global Development Group. PostgreSQL. `http://www.postgresql.org/`, 2015.

[21] Dinakar Guniguntala, Paul E McKenney, Josh Triplett, and Jonathan Walpole. The read-copy-update mechanism for supporting real-time applications on shared-memory multiprocessor systems with Linux. *IBM Systems Journal*, 47(2):221–236, 2008.

[22] Thomas E Hart, Paul E McKenney, Angela Demke Brown, and Jonathan Walpole. Performance of memory reclamation for lockless synchronization. *Journal of Parallel and Distributed Computing*, 67(12):1270–1285, 2007.

[23] Philip W Howard and Jonathan Walpole. Relativistic red-black trees. *Concurrency and Computation: Practice and Experience*, 2013.

[24] Hajime Inoue, Darko Stefanović, and Stephanie Forrest. On the prediction of java object lifetimes. *Computers, IEEE Transactions on*, 55(7):880–892, 2006.

[25] Rick Jones. NetPerf. `http://www.netperf.org/`, 2012.

[26] Jeffrey Katcher. Postmark: A new file system benchmark. Technical report, Technical Report TR3022, Network Appliance, 1997. www. netapp. com/tech_library/3022. html, 1997.

[27] H. T. Kung and Philip L. Lehman. Concurrent manipulation of binary search trees. *ACM Trans. Database Syst.*, 5(3):354–382, September 1980.

[28] Christoph Lameter. SLUB: The unqueued slab allocator. `http://lwn.net/Articles/229096/`, 2007.

[29] Ran Liu, Heng Zhang, and Haibo Chen. Scalable read-mostly synchronization using passive reader-writer locks. In *2014 USENIX Annual Technical Conference (USENIX ATC 14)*, pages 219–230, Philadelphia, PA, June 2014. USENIX Association.

[30] Yandong Mao, Eddie Kohler, and Robert Tappan Morris. Cache craftiness for fast multicore key-value storage. In *Proceedings of the 7th ACM European conference on Computer Systems*, pages 183–196. ACM, 2012.

[31] Paul E McKenney. *Exploiting Deferred Destructions: An Analysis of Read-Copy-Update Techniques in Operating System kernels*. PhD thesis, Oregon Health & Science University, 2004.

[32] Paul E McKenney. Structured deferral: synchronization via procrastination. *Communications of the ACM*, 56(7):40–49, 2013.

[33] Paul E McKenney. RCU Linux usage. `www.rdrop.com/users/paulmck/RCU/linuxusage.html`, 2014.

[34] Paul E McKenney, Jonathan Appavoo, Andi Kleen, Orran Krieger, Rusty Russell, Dipankar Sarma, and Maneesh Soni. Read-copy update. In *AUUG Conference Proceedings*, page 175. AUUG, Inc., 2001.

[35] Paul E McKenney, Dipankar Sarma, Ingo Molnar, and Suparna Bhattacharya. Extending RCU for realtime and embedded workloads. In *Ottawa Linux Symposium, pages v2*, pages 123–138, 2006.

[36] Paul E McKenney, Dipankar Sarma, and Maneesh Soni. Scaling dcache with RCU. *Linux Journal*, 2004(117):3, 2004.

[37] Paul E McKenney and John D Slingwine. Read-copy update: Using execution history to solve concurrency problems. In *Parallel and Distributed Computing and Systems*, pages 509–518, 1998.

[38] James Morris. Have You Driven an SELinux Lately? In *Linux Symposium Proceedings*, 2008.

[39] Robert Olsson and Stefan Nilsson. Trash a dynamic lc-trie and hash data structure. In *High Performance Switching and Routing, 2007. HPSR'07. Workshop on*, pages 1–6. IEEE, 2007.

[40] Dipankar Sarma and Paul E McKenney. Making RCU safe for deep sub-millisecond response realtime applications. In *Proceedings of the 2004 USENIX Annual Technical Conference (FREENIX Track)*, pages 182–191, 2004.

[41] Josh Triplett, Paul E McKenney, and Jonathan Walpole. Scalable concurrent hash tables via relativistic programming. *ACM SIGOPS Operating Systems Review*, 44(3):102–109, 2010.

[42] Josh Triplett, Paul E McKenney, and Jonathan Walpole. Resizable, Scalable, Concurrent Hash Tables via Relativistic Programming. In *USENIX Annual Technical Conference*, page 11, 2011.

[43] Stephen Tu, Wenting Zheng, Eddie Kohler, Barbara Liskov, and Samuel Madden. Speedy transactions in multicore in-memory databases. In *Proceedings of the Twenty-Fourth ACM Symposium on Operating Systems Principles*, pages 18–32. ACM, 2013.

[44] David Wentzlaff and Anant Agarwal. Factored operating systems (fos): the case for a scalable operating system for multicores. *SIGOPS Oper. Syst. Rev.*, 43:76–85, April 2009.

Whirlpool: Improving Dynamic Cache Management with Static Data Classification

Anurag Mukkara Nathan Beckmann Daniel Sanchez

Computer Science and Artificial Intelligence Laboratory
Massachusetts Institute of Technology
{anuragm, beckmann, sanchez}@csail.mit.edu

Abstract

Cache hierarchies are increasingly non-uniform and difficult to manage. Several techniques, such as scratchpads or reuse hints, use static information about how programs access data to manage the memory hierarchy. Static techniques are effective on regular programs, but because they set fixed policies, they are vulnerable to changes in program behavior or available cache space. Instead, most systems rely on dynamic caching policies that adapt to observed program behavior. Unfortunately, dynamic policies spend significant resources trying to learn how programs use memory, and yet they often perform worse than a static policy.

We present Whirlpool, a novel approach that combines static information with dynamic policies to reap the benefits of each. Whirlpool statically classifies data into *pools* based on how the program uses memory. Whirlpool then uses dynamic policies to tune the cache to each pool. Hence, rather than setting policies statically, Whirlpool uses static analysis to guide dynamic policies. We present both an API that lets programmers specify pools manually and a profiling tool that discovers pools automatically in unmodified binaries.

We evaluate Whirlpool on a state-of-the-art NUCA cache. Whirlpool significantly outperforms prior approaches: on sequential programs, Whirlpool improves performance by up to 38% and reduces data movement energy by up to 53%; on parallel programs, Whirlpool improves performance by up to 67% and reduces data movement energy by up to 2.6×.

CCS Concepts

• Computer systems organization → Multicore architectures.

Keywords Non-uniform cache access (NUCA), Data movement, Static analysis, Cache modeling.

ASPLOS '16, April 2–6, 2016, Atlanta, Georgia, USA.

ACM 978-1-4503-4091-5/16/04... $15.00.
http://dx.doi.org/10.1145/2872362.2872363

1. Introduction

Future systems will be limited by data movement, which is orders of magnitude more expensive than basic compute operations. For example, at 28 nm a 64-bit floating-point multiply-add consumes 20 pJ, while sending 256 bits across the chip costs 300 pJ, an on-chip access to a 1 MB cache costs about 1 nJ, and an off-chip DRAM access costs 20-50 nJ—1000× more energy than the multiply-add [21, 36, 59]. The trend towards lean, specialized cores means that, for efficiency reasons, caches are increasingly distributed across the chip and have non-uniform access latencies (NUCA [37]).

While distributed caches are more efficient, they are also harder to manage. Their non-uniform latency and energy means that *data placement* is critical to limit data movement. But data placement is hard: applications need to fit their most intensely-used data in nearby banks, while competing with each other for scarce capacity. Data placement is a spatial scheduling problem that, to solve well, requires accurate information about how programs use memory.

Unfortunately, all the relevant information is not generally available: static analysis or profiling can reveal program semantics (i.e., how a program uses memory), but not its dynamic or input-dependent behavior; and dynamic policies have difficulty efficiently recovering program semantics. To see this in more detail, consider the extremes of static vs. dynamic design. At one extreme, scratchpad-based systems expose the distributed memories to software, relying on static analysis to place data. Scratchpads work well on regular access patterns, but cope poorly with irregular, input-dependent, or rapidly changing patterns and varying resources in shared systems [38, 41]. At the other extreme, cache-based systems expose a flat address space that programs access through undifferentiated loads and stores, relying on hardware-managed caches to transparently retain the right data. Most memory systems are cache-based, but recovering program semantics from this limited interface is difficult and expensive. For example, classic dynamic NUCA schemes migrate data towards the requester in response to each access, which increases data movement and requires expensive lookups [7, 9, 28]. As memory systems become more complex, ignoring program semantics becomes increasingly inefficient.

Prior work exploits static information in cache-based systems through prefetch [34], bypass [48], and cache priority [27] hints. Hints let software override dynamic policies and control the cache, reaping the benefits of static information when it is accurate. However, hints suffer from the same problems as scratchpads: with uncertain or dynamic behavior, hints are often inaccurate and hurt performance [41, 47].

The key idea of this paper is to combine static information with dynamic policies to reap the benefits of each. Rather than using static information to set fixed policies, we instead use it to inform dynamic policies. The insight is that, while uncertainty makes it hard to statically predict how data will be used, it is often easy to accurately group data with similar usage patterns. This approach lets dynamic policies make better decisions at lower overhead.

We demonstrate this idea through Whirlpool, a *classification-based* approach to improve data placement in multicores. In Whirlpool, programs divide their data into a small number of memory *pools*, e.g. one for each major data structure. We find that for most programs, a few pools (three or four) suffice. Hardware then monitors each pool dynamically and adapts the memory system to keep the most valuable data near where it is used. Unlike hints, pools do not encode static policies; rather, they make it easy for hardware to find the right policies dynamically. Whirlpool thus combines static program semantics with dynamic policies, and robustly adapts to changes in program behavior or available resources (Sec. 2).

Whirlpool has both software and hardware components (Sec. 3). In software, Whirlpool provides a memory allocator that groups semantically similar data and tags each page with a pool id. In hardware, Whirlpool extends prior NUCA techniques [9, 11] to monitor each pool and control its placement. Whirlpool needs only a few pools, so it adds small overheads. We first evaluate Whirlpool by manually applying it to several SPEC CPU2006 and PBBS benchmarks. We show that Whirlpool achieves significant performance gains, of up to 38%, when managing a large NUCA cache, and reduces data movement energy by up to 53%. Through case studies, we also show that Whirlpool improves the performance of parallel applications on a 16-core chip by up to 67% and reduces data movement energy by up to 2.6×.

We then use the insights gained from manually porting applications to design *WhirlTool*, a profiling tool that automatically discovers pools in unmodified binaries (Sec. 4). We evaluate WhirlTool on a comprehensive set of benchmarks and program mixes, and find that it works as well or better than our careful manual classification.

In summary, Whirlpool gives a promising way to combine static program semantics and dynamic policies to reduce data movement.

2. Motivation and Background

In this section, we motivate Whirlpool's hybrid, static-dynamic design and discuss related work.

2.1 How static classification reduces data movement

Consider the multicore shown in Fig. 1. This chip has a NUCA cache of twenty-five 512 KB banks shared by four surrounding cores, similar to the Oracle SPARC M7 [3] (see Appendix A for detailed methodology). We consider the benchmark `dt` (Delaunay triangulation) from the PBBS suite [60], running in the leftmost core. Our goal is to use this distributed cache capacity as efficiently as possible by placing `dt`'s most intensely used data near where `dt` is running.

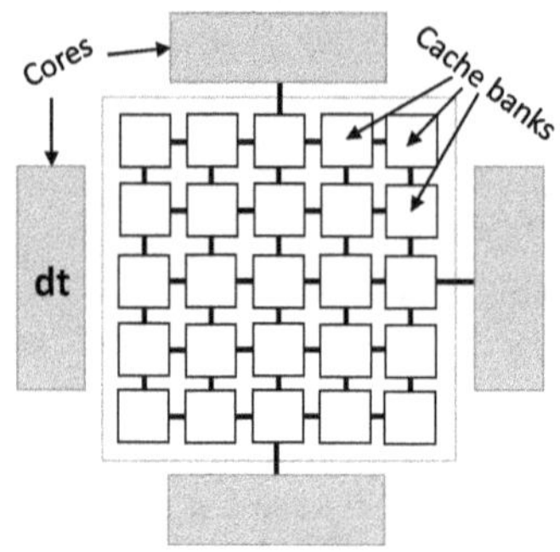

Figure 1: Multicore chip with a distributed last-level cache.

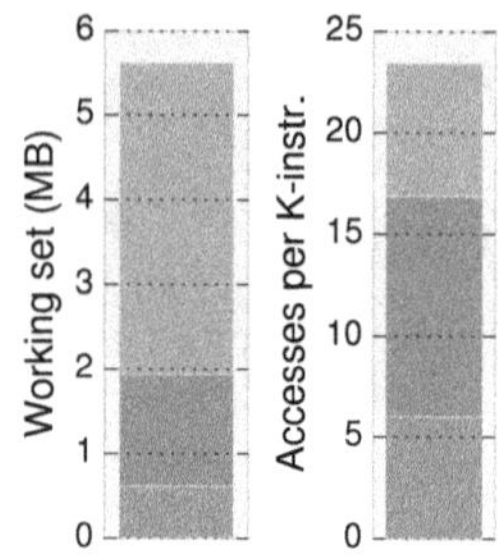

Figure 2: Breakdown of `dt`'s working set and access pattern.

Fig. 2 shows how `dt` accesses memory. It has a 6 MB working set that easily fits in the cache. It accesses three data structures: points, vertices, and triangles, which take 0.5 MB, 1.5 MB, and 4 MB, respectively. Accesses are split roughly evenly across the three data structures, so their access *intensity* (i.e., accesses per MB) varies: points are accessed most intensely, followed by vertices and triangles.

How should we place `dt`'s data to reduce data movement? Many commercial processors adopt a static NUCA (S-NUCA) design that hashes addresses evenly across banks [37, 53]. Fig. 3 shows how S-NUCA places `dt`'s data. This figure shows all 25 cache banks, with colors indicating where data is placed. Because S-NUCA spreads `dt`'s 6 MB working set across 12.5 MB of cache, banks are left half-empty.

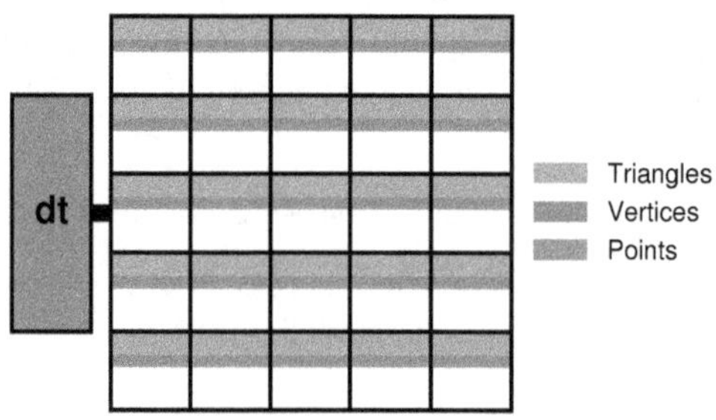

Figure 3: S-NUCA places `dt`'s data unnecessarily far away.

Since capacity is available in closer banks, we can reduce data movement by concentrating `dt`'s data closer to where `dt` is running. Fig. 4 shows how Jigsaw [9, 11], the NUCA scheme that Whirlpool builds on, places `dt`'s data. Jigsaw tightly packs `dt`'s working set near the left of the chip, but it cannot distinguish between the different data structures because it is blind to program semantics.

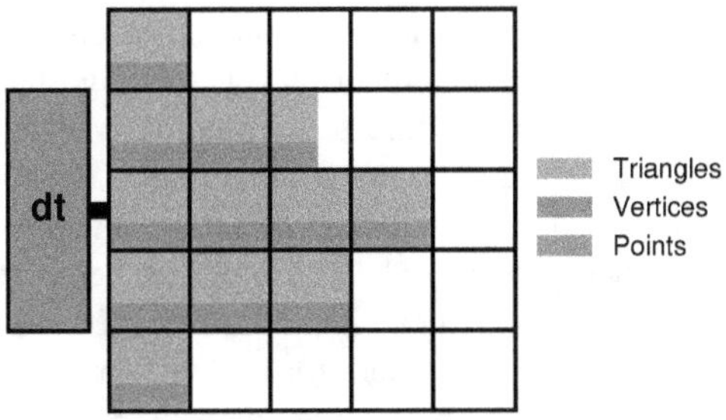

Figure 4: Jigsaw places `dt`'s data closer, but does not distinguish between types of data.

We can reduce data movement further by placing the most intensely accessed data even closer to where `dt` is running. Fig. 5 shows how Whirlpool places `dt`'s data. Whirlpool classifies data into pools statically, but dynamically monitors each pool to decide data placement. In this case, because points is most intensely accessed, it is placed in the closest cache banks. Likewise, vertices is placed in three next-closest banks, and triangles in the closest remaining banks.

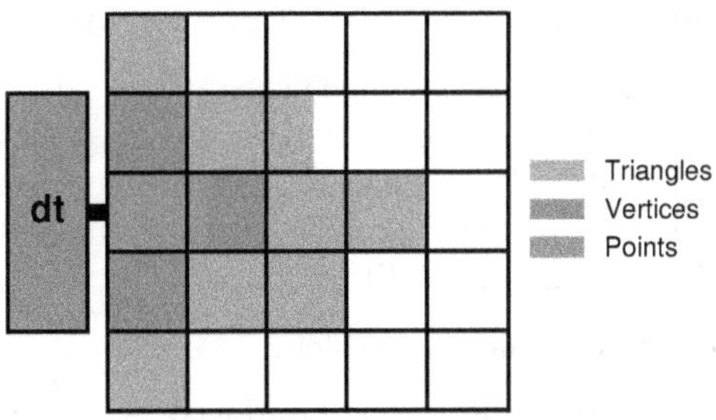

Figure 5: Whirlpool statically classifies `dt`'s data into pools, and dynamically places intensely-accessed pools nearby.

Whirlpool improves `dt`'s performance by 19% over S-NUCA and by 15% over Jigsaw, and reduces data movement energy (cache and memory dynamic energy) by 42% over S-NUCA and by 27% over Jigsaw.

This example shows how static, program-level data classification can help dynamic policies reduce data movement. By identifying key data structures statically, Whirlpool can place data without wasting resources in learning how data is used. By contrast, many prior schemes that achieve a similar data placement do so by migrating data on demand [18, 43, 68]. The extra data movement from migrations can exceed the energy savings of smart data placement (see Sec. 2.3). Hence, static classification is crucial to Whirlpool's benefits.

2.2 How dynamic policies reduce data movement

Whirlpool leverages static data classification from either the programmer or an automatic profile-guided tool. Whirlpool also monitors each pool at run-time and uses this dynamic information to reconfigure the cache. By decoupling classification and policy, Whirlpool robustly adapts to changes in application behavior and system configuration. By contrast, other techniques that involve application-level or code changes, such as software prefetching [47], reuse/non-temporal hints [12, 14, 27, 48, 63], or loop tiling [20, 39, 64], directly encode a fixed policy in the program and cannot adapt to changing application or system behavior.

To see why adapting dynamically is important, consider `lbm` from SPEC CPU2006. On each timestep, `lbm` operates on two grids, source and destination, with markedly different access patterns: source is accessed more often and enjoys good reuse, while destination sees little reuse. At the end of each timestep, `lbm` swaps the source and destination pointers, resulting in an alternating access pattern to both memory pools, shown in Fig. 6. Whirlpool continuously monitors both pools and adopts different policies on even and odd phases, caching source data near `lbm` and bypassing accesses to the destination grid. As a result Whirlpool outperforms Jigsaw by 4.8%, and reduces data movement energy by 12%. By contrast, each pool looks the same on average, so the best static placement yields no improvement over Jigsaw.

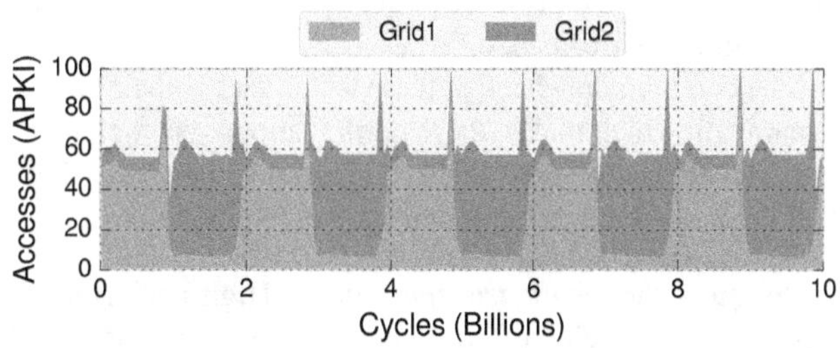

Figure 6: `lbm` has two pools that, though indistinguishable on average, have markedly different access patterns in alternating program phases.

This example shows that while static *classification* into pools may suffice, dynamic *policies* are needed to reduce `lbm`'s data movement. Moreover, program phase changes are not the only source of unpredictability. The appropriate caching policy depends on many factors that are hard to capture statically: irregular reference patterns, different program inputs, cache contention in shared systems, etc. Sec. 3 explores how Whirlpool's dynamic policies adapt to these sources of dynamic variability.

2.3 Related work

Whirlpool builds upon many prior memory management techniques. Broadly, these techniques fall into two categories, based on whether they consider modifying the program to improve memory system behavior. Table 1 summarizes the pros and cons of each technique.

Techniques that require program changes: Architectures with software-managed scratchpad memories provide the highest efficiency and degree of control, letting programmers

Scheme	Static information	Dynamic policy	Spatial placement	Single-lookup	Easy to use
Scratchpads	✓	✗	✓	✓	✗
Code hints	✓	✗	✗	✓	✓
Cache replacement	✗	✓	✗	✓	✓
Private D-NUCA	✗	✓	✓	✗	✓
Shared D-NUCA	✗	✓	✓	✓	✓
Whirlpool	✓	✓	✓	✓	✓

Table 1: Desirable properties achieved by prior memory system management techniques.

or compilers manage data placement and movement. But scratchpads are hard to use. Even with advanced compilers, only highly regular programs can use them well [41]. Scratchpads also do not support dynamic adaptation.

For these reasons, most memory systems use cache hierarchies instead. Caches are transparent by default, but programs can include various types of access hints such as software prefetch instructions and non-temporal hints to bypass the cache hierarchy [12, 14, 27, 48, 63]. However, these techniques embed specific static policies in the program, which may degrade performance.

The common drawback of these techniques is their lack of dynamism, which makes these optimizations risky: changes in workload behavior or system configuration may make these optimizations ineffective or detrimental to performance.

Techniques that work transparently: High-performance replacement policies often dynamically classify data and treat lines of each class differently. For example, RRIP [33] classifies lines as reused and non-reused; IbRDP [50] classifies them by the PC of their last memory access; and SHiP [65] classifies lines by PC or memory address.

Similarly, Whirlpool's classification could also improve replacement decisions. We explored a Whirlpool-based replacement policy that extends DRRIP [33] to adapt insertion priority across pools (similar to TA-DRRIP [32, 33] and CAMP [49]). However, we found that the benefits from static classification within a monolithic cache were marginal: cache replacement is a simpler problem than data placement, and dynamic replacement policies like DRRIP and SHiP perform well at relatively low overhead. We therefore focus on the harder problem of NUCA data placement.

Dynamic NUCAs (D-NUCAs) try to reduce data movement by placing data near where it is used. These schemes can be broadly classified into two categories based on whether they start from a private or shared cache organization.

Private-baseline D-NUCAs treat the cache as a fine-grained hierarchy, accessing the closest banks first, then checking farther-away banks on a miss [6, 37, 68]. Upon a hit, these D-NUCAs move data closer to the accessing core, displacing other data further away, similar to how high-performance replacement policies promote lines upon reuse. Hence, over time, private-baseline D-NUCAs gradually place frequently-used data nearby.

However, private-baseline D-NUCAs suffer from two problems. First, migrating data in response to each access increases overall data movement and wastes significant energy [7]. Second, since addresses do not have a known location, they also require complex lookup mechanisms (e.g., multi-level lookups, broadcasts, or directories) that add area, latency, and energy [6, 51, 68]. For example, schemes that use global directory lookups beyond the local cache bank would not reduce `dt`'s data movement for vertices or triangles—the majority of its data accesses. As a result, prior work has consistently shown that it is far more efficient to avoid moving data among banks in response to accesses [7, 9, 22, 28, 51].

Shared-baseline D-NUCAs [4, 9, 19, 28] leverage the virtual memory system to control data placement. A page's location is tracked in software and infrequently updated in response to program behavior. Unlike private-baseline D-NUCAs, shared-baseline D-NUCAs can locate data in a single lookup and thereby avoid excessive data migration. However, they respond more slowly to changes in program behavior and must also place data at a page granularity.

We compare against schemes from each class: IdealSPD, an idealized private-baseline D-NUCA, and Awasthi et al. [4], a representative shared-baseline D-NUCA (see Appendix A).

Whirlpool achieves the advantages of the above techniques while minimizing their drawbacks. It leverages static, program-level data classification to achieve a good data placement without frequently migrating data, and it adapts to unpredictable run-time variability.

2.4 Jigsaw: Our baseline system

Whirlpool builds on Jigsaw, a partitioned, shared-baseline D-NUCA. We now briefly describe Jigsaw's main features; please see prior work for details [8, 9, 11].

Virtual caches: Jigsaw builds *virtual caches* (VCs) by combining partitions of physical cache banks, as shown in Fig. 7a (colors represent VCs). Pages are mapped to a specific VC through the TLB. Jigsaw uses three kinds of VCs: each thread has a thread-private VC; all threads in the process share a process VC; and all threads in the system share a global VC. Pages start as private to the thread that allocates them, and are upgraded lazily: an access from another thread upgrades the page to the process VC, and an access from another process upgrades the page to the global VC.

To support Whirlpool, we extend Jigsaw to allow applications to define additional VCs and map pages to them.

Single-lookup accesses: Jigsaw stores the placement of each VC in a small structure called the *virtual cache translation buffer* (VTB). In Jigsaw, each core requires just 3 VTB entries (for its thread-private, process, and global VCs). Each VTB entry is essentially a configurable hash function that maps an address to its *unique location*—in Jigsaw, data does *not* migrate in response to accesses. Jigsaw thus provides

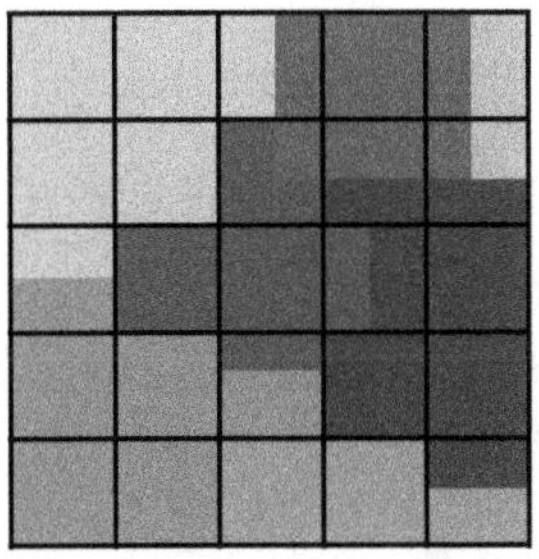

(a) Jigsaw groups bank partitions into virtual caches (VCs).

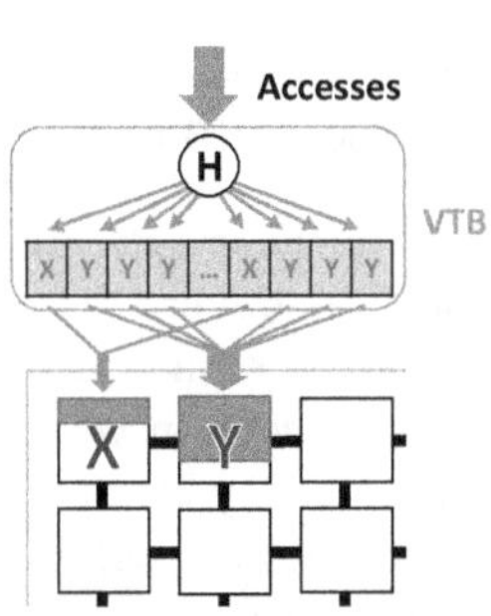

(b) The VTB controls data placement across banks.

Figure 7: Overview of Jigsaw, our baseline NUCA system.

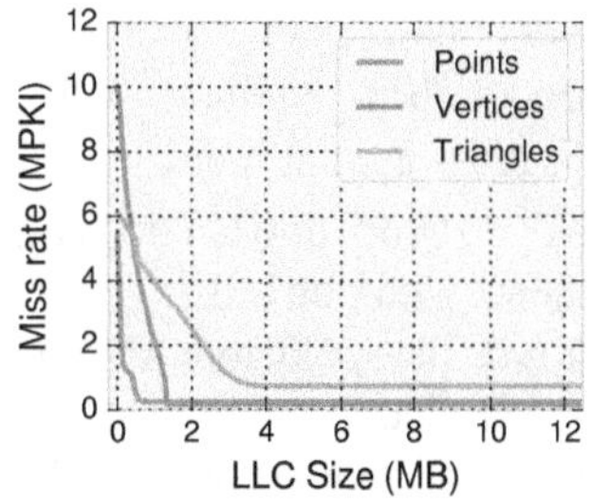

(a) Miss rate curves.

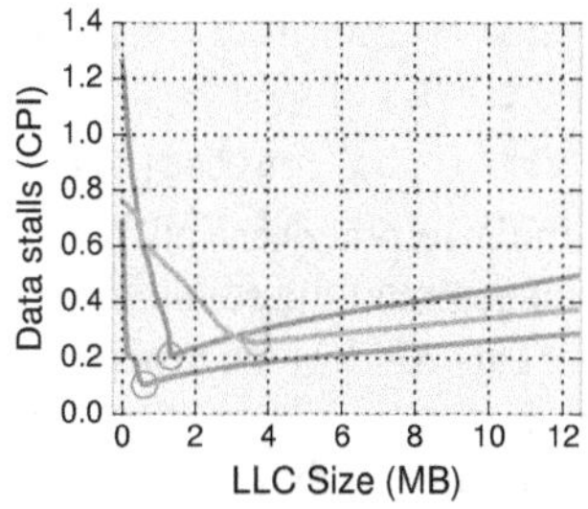

(b) Memory latency curves.

Figure 8: `dt`'s memory performance vs. VC size: (a) Last-level cache misses. (b) Cycles per instruction stalled on data.

single-lookup accesses. The VTB controls data placement by dividing the access stream across banks, as shown in Fig. 7b.

Reconfigurations: A lightweight OS runtime periodically (every 25 ms in our implementation) reconfigures the cache, sizing and placing VCs to minimize data movement. It does so using a simple model of memory access time that accounts for both cache misses and cache access latency. To account for cache misses, Jigsaw monitors *miss rate curves*, i.e. miss rate vs. VC size [11, 52]. To account for cache access latency, Jigsaw uses the average latency to the closest cache banks needed for a given VC size. From these components, the total latency of a VC is simply the sum of VC access latency (access rate $\times$ network and bank latency) and memory latency (miss rate $\times$ miss penalty).[1]

The runtime builds the total latency curves for each VC and uses them to partition cache capacity. Traditional cache partitioning schemes try to minimize cache misses and partition using miss rate curves [52, 55]. By using latency curves instead of miss rate curves [11], Jigsaw will not use cache banks when their reduction in miss rate does not offset their added network latency. For example, `dt` fits in half the cache banks, so the remaining banks are not used (Fig. 4).

Whirlpool chooses VC sizes identically to Jigsaw, with the only difference being that each memory pool gets its own VC. Fig. 8a shows the miss rate curves for `dt`, and Fig. 8b shows the latency curves and the sizes chosen for each VC: in this case, the full working set fits on cache, so Jigsaw chooses the sizes that minimize each VC's total latency.

After sizing VCs, the reconfiguration algorithm places them in cache banks. We use Jigsaw's trading placement algorithm [11], which initially places data using a simple, greedy heuristic, and then trades capacity between VCs to reduce data movement. The key idea is *access intensity*: lines that are accessed more frequently pay a larger penalty for poor placement, and should therefore be placed closer to cores that access them. Intensity is given as access rate per capacity, i.e. a VC's access rate divided by its size (APKI per MB). For example, the pools in `dt` are accessed at a similar rate, but since `points` is one-eighth the size of `triangles`, its access intensity is $8\times$ larger. Intensity essentially says how many accesses are affected by placing a chunk of capacity of fixed size, and it lets us compute if trading capacity between two VCs reduces data movement.

Jigsaw outperforms state-of-the-art D-NUCAs and adds small overheads [9, 11]. In hardware, Jigsaw adds less than 0.6% area overhead over LLC banks; in software, Jigsaw consumes less than 0.4% of system cycles. Whirlpool extends Jigsaw to support static classification of data into pools by building VCs for each pool. We make small modifications to Jigsaw to exploit opportunities presented by static classification, but do not modify its core hardware mechanisms or software reconfiguration runtime.

3. Whirlpool with Manual Classification

We now present the design of Whirlpool and explore how it reduces data movement by combining static, program-level classification with dynamic caching policies.

Whirlpool classifies data used by an application into different regions, which we call memory pools. Memory pools let Whirlpool manage data that has similar access patterns as a single entity. It is also the granularity at which Whirlpool gathers information to drive dynamic policies.

In this section, we present an interface that lets an application programmer create memory pools and tag data used by the application to different pools. We then explore how Whirlpool improves placement through case studies. In Sec. 4, we present a profiling framework that automatically classifies data into memory pools.

3.1 Application programming interface

In our implementation, a pool is an independent region of heap-allocated memory. Our memory allocator ensures that pages belong to exactly one pool (or none) at a time, so that we can use the virtual memory system to classify data into pools, as in Jigsaw.

The programmer creates a new memory pool by calling:

```
pool_t pool_create();
```

[1] This simple model ignores memory-level parallelism, but we find it works well. Alternatively, we could model energy; this would penalize misses more and change tradeoffs somewhat.

which returns an id for the newly created pool. To allocate `size` bytes of memory from the pool, the programmer calls:

```
void* pool_malloc(size_t size, pool_t pool_id);
```

Similarly, other variants like `pool_calloc`, `pool_realloc`, etc. augment the standard arguments with `pool_id`.

This API lets the programmer tune the application's cache performance by providing high-level hints at memory allocation time. At first, it might seem to be a tedious task for the programmer to reason about the access patterns and cache locality of different data. However, we find it often suffices to identify a few prominent data regions and allocate them to different pools. Thus, only a few lines of code need to be modified to port applications manually to Whirlpool.

Table 2 shows the applications we have manually ported, their key data structures, and the lines of code changed. Overall, Whirlpool improves performance on these applications by 7.3% over Jigsaw and reduces data movement energy by 12%. Detailed results are presented in Sec. 4.

Application	Pools	Data structures	LOC
Breadth-first search	4	Vertices, edges, frontier, visited	16
Delaunay triangulation	3	Points, vertices, triangles	11
Maximal matching	3	Vertices, edges, result	13
Delaunay refinement	3	Vertices, triangles, misc	8
Maximal independent set	3	Vertices, edges, flags	13
Spanning forest	3	Union-find parents, output tree, input edges	13
Minimal spanning forest	3	Union-find parents, output tree, input edges	11
Convex hull	2	Points, hull array	10
401.bzip2	4	arr1, arr2, ftab, tt	43
470.lbm	2	Source and destination grids	21
429.mcf	2	Nodes and arcs	14
436.cactusADM	2	Pugh variables, staggered-leapfrog grid data	53

Table 2: Pools found manually in various applications, plus lines of code (LOC) modified while porting to Whirlpool.

3.2 Modifications to baseline system

System calls to manage VCs: We expose VCs to user-level programs with a few additional system calls: `sys_vc_alloc` allocates a user-level VC, returning its unique id; `sys_vc_free` deallocates an existing VC; and `sys_vc_tag` tags a range of pages with a user-level VC. We also modify `sys_mmap` to optionally tag new pages with a specific VC. These system calls perform the adequate checks to ensure safety (e.g., allowing each process to map pages only to its own user-level VCs).

Our allocator uses this low-level interface to map each pool to a different VC and tag pages from each pool with the right VC id. Our implementation is built on top of Doug Lea's malloc [40], but other allocators could be used instead.

Support for more VCs per core: The baseline Jigsaw system supports 3 VTB entries per core for thread-private, process, and global VCs. To support user-level VCs, we add extra VTB entries and utility monitors (specifically, GMONs [11]). As we will see, supporting up to 4 pools is enough for most programs. In the 4-core system, Whirlpool adds 6 KB in VTB entries and 24 KB of monitors, or 0.3% of cache area.

Bypassing VCs: Programs often have data structures that get negligible reuse in the cache, and it is more efficient for them to bypass the cache entirely [62]. Bypassing is particularly beneficial in Whirlpool, since its static classification helps accurately identify data that should be bypassed.

We therefore extend Jigsaw to support bypassing VCs. We add a bypass bit to each VTB entry. Bypassed VCs have no LLC space allocated, and their L2 misses go directly to main memory. Bypassing is allowed only if the VC is accessed by a single thread. Coherence is maintained by invalidating the VC in the LLC when it enters bypassing mode (extending Jigsaw's existing reconfiguration mechanism [11]), and by invalidating the VC in the L2 when it exits bypassing mode. Finally, Jigsaw's software runtime decides whether to bypass a VC by modifying the inputs to its existing partitioning algorithm. Specifically, it excludes cache access latency in its access latency model if the VC is allocated no space. With this trivial change, the partitioning algorithm will only allocate space to a VC when bypassing hurts performance (see below).

We evaluate both Jigsaw and Whirlpool with this optimization, but since Jigsaw does not separate data that gets reuse from data that does not, we find that VC bypassing is more useful in Whirlpool.

Other Jigsaw components are unmodified. In particular, the OS remains in charge of reconfiguring the cache, and the reconfiguration algorithm stays the same. Additional VCs add 0.2% of system cycles to reconfigurations.

3.3 Whirlpool case studies

We now present several case studies that show how Whirlpool adapts to various sources of variability.

Whirlpool benefits from bypassing: Whirlpool decides whether to bypass VCs by modifying the latency curve. Fig. 9 shows how this is done for the PBBS benchmark `mis` (maximal independent set). Whirlpool changes Jigsaw's memory latency model to model bypassing for VCs accessed by a single thread. Specifically, the total latency curve at a VC size of zero excludes the cache access latency. This is the only change needed, as the partitioning algorithm will then only allocate space if doing so reduces data movement vs. bypassing.

`mis` has two pools, vertices and edges. Vertices cache well, but edges do not. Whirlpool gives the full cache to vertices and bypasses edges. This is only possible because of Whirlpool's static classification, which quickly identifies edges so they can be bypassed. Jigsaw does not separate accesses to vertices and edges, so it cannot allocate capacity specifically to vertices and it must always check the cache to maintain coherence.

Fig. 10 analyzes `mis`'s performance, data movement energy, and LLC accesses. We compare Whirlpool against S-

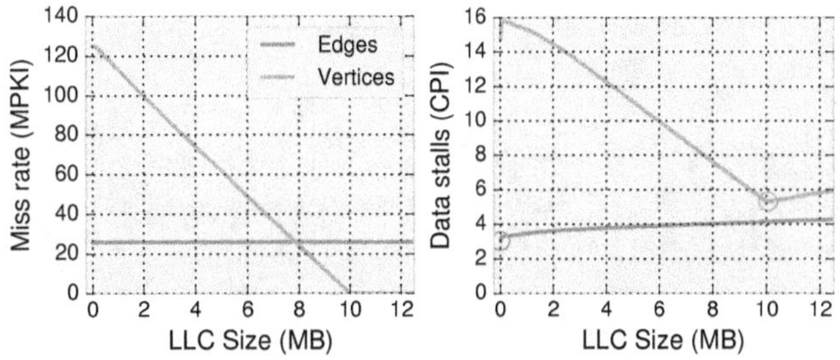

(a) Miss rate curves. (b) Memory latency curves.

Figure 9: mis's memory performance vs. VC size. Vertices cache well, but edges are streaming. Whirlpool bypasses edges and gives the cache to vertices.

NUCA caches with LRU and DRRIP replacement; IdealSPD, an idealized private-baseline D-NUCA policy that is an upper-bound over several prior D-NUCAs; the shared-baseline, page-migration D-NUCA proposed by Awasthi et al. [4]; and Jigsaw, extended to support bypassing (see Appendix A).

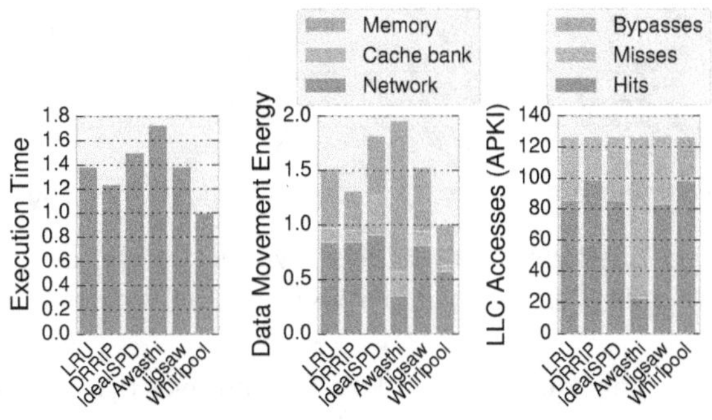

Figure 10: Breakdown of mis's performance, energy, and accesses for different caching schemes.

Whirlpool reduces data movement because its static classification lets it adopt the right policy for each pool. Whirlpool gives enough space to fit vertices, achieving a similar hit rate to DRRIP and thus reducing memory energy. It also immediately bypasses accesses to edges, *without first checking a cache bank*. This reduces network and cache bank energy significantly over the other policies. In contrast, IdealSPD checks multiple banks (nearby banks first, then remote banks), and thus consumes the most energy. Meanwhile, Awasthi gets stuck at a small capacity allocation, incurring more misses than the other schemes. (Although Awasthi performs poorly on mis and several other benchmarks, it outperforms S-NUCA and saves energy on average; see Sec. 4.) Whirlpool improves mis's performance by 38% over Jigsaw and reduces data movement energy by 53%.

Whirlpool adapts to application phases: Unlike prior techniques that leverage static information through fixed policies, Whirlpool uses dynamic policies that can adapt to time-varying program behavior. Fig. 6 showed one example for the SPEC CPU2006 benchmark lbm; Fig. 11 shows another for the PBBS benchmark refine (Delaunay refinement).

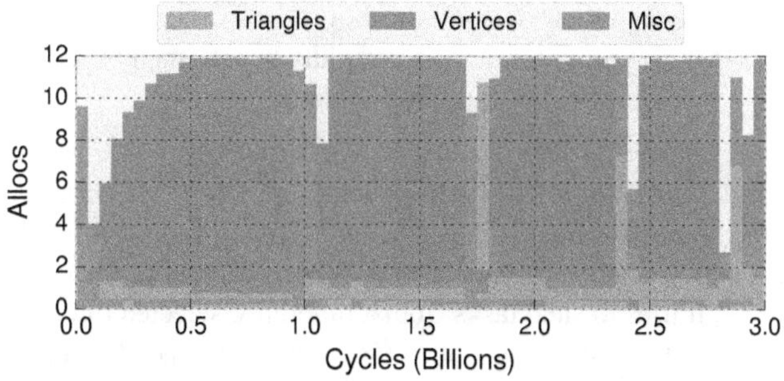

(a) Cache allocations sorted vertically by distance.

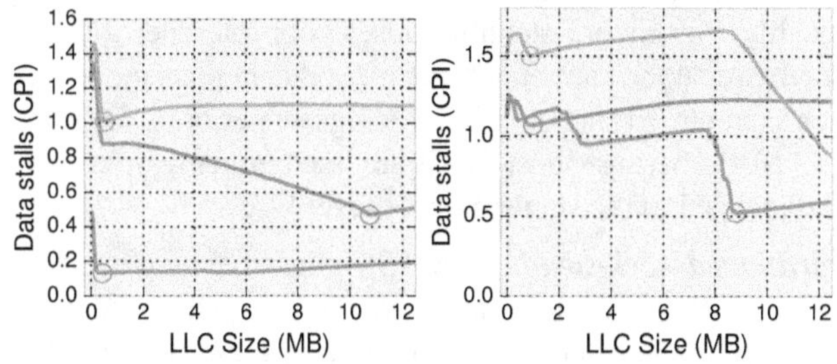

(b) Latency curves at $\frac{1}{2}$ B cycles. (c) Latency curves at 1 B cycles.

Figure 11: refine has irregular phase changes. Whirlpool dynamically adapts its allocations and placement to retain the data structures that have reuse.

refine accesses two main data structures, triangles and vertices, as well as other miscellaneous data in the misc pool. For most of refine's execution, its working set fits easily on chip (Fig. 11b). However, at irregular intervals, its behavior changes for roughly 100 M cycles: vertices becomes streaming, triangles starts fitting on cache, and misc's working set increases substantially (Fig. 11c).

Whirlpool adapts to this unpredictable behavior, changing its allocations and placement to retain the data structures that cache best. Fig. 11a shows how Whirlpool allocates and places cache space for refine. Time is shown in cycles along the x-axis, and allocations are indicated by color along the y-axis. Additionally, allocations are sorted by distance from the core along the y-axis from bottom to top.

For most of refine's execution, triangles and misc are given small allocations placed near the core, and vertices is given most of the remaining cache space. This placement minimizes data movement because it fits vertices in the cache, and accesses to triangles and misc *miss quickly*. In refine, bypassing triangles and misc is not advantageous (see Fig. 11b), but placing them nearby helps by reducing network traffic.

During phase changes, this pattern inverts: vertices is streaming and is given a small allocation placed near the core, and the remaining cache space is given to either triangles or misc (depending on whether triangles fits).

3.4 Whirlpool with parallel applications

In addition to reducing data movement in sequential applications, Whirlpool benefits parallel applications by running tasks close to their data. Whirlpool makes small changes to task-parallel runtimes, letting it rapidly benefit many applications with minimal programmer burden.

Conventional work-stealing: Work-stealing [13] is the most widely-used scheduling technique for task-parallel programs. Each thread has a queue of ready tasks, to which it enqueues and dequeues work. When a thread runs out of work, it tries to steal tasks from a randomly-selected thread's queue. Work-stealing makes task enqueues and dequeues cheap and achieves good load balance, but, over time, each core ends up accessing data used by many tasks, hurting locality. Since work-stealing causes poor reference locality, D-NUCAs alone cannot achieve a good data placement [11]. For example, as shown in Fig. 13, Jigsaw performs the same as S-NUCA because most data is accessed from multiple cores and mapped to the single process-level VC.

Partitioned work-stealing (PaWS): Inspired by prior work on locality-aware placement and stealing [11, 16, 67], we develop simple extensions to improve reference locality. We leverage that, in many applications, the data accessed by each task is known when the task is created. PaWS partitions program data evenly among cores, and enqueues tasks to the core that has its input data instead of the thread's local queue, as shown in Fig. 12. PaWS also preferentially steals tasks from neighboring cores instead of at random.

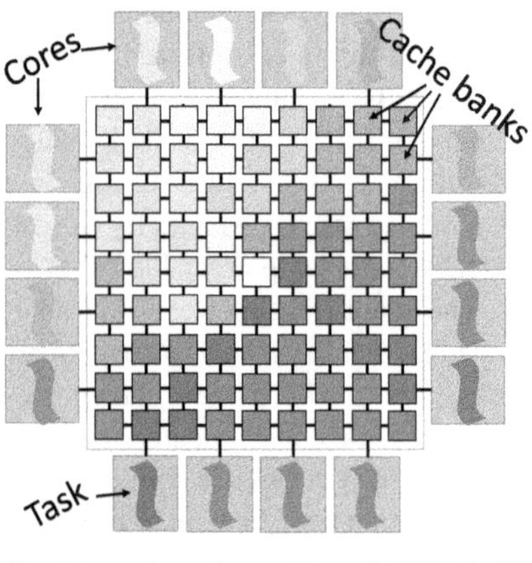

Figure 12: Partitioned work-stealing (PaWS) in Whirlpool on a 16-core system. In PaWS, each core works on a partition of the input and preferentially steals tasks from nearby cores. Colors indicate affinity between tasks and data.

We evaluate PaWS on six memory-intensive applications from several benchmark suites: `mergesort` [57], `delaunay` [60], `fft` [26], `pagerank` [58], `connectedComponents` [5], and `triangleCounting` [5]. The first three use regular data structures that are trivial to evenly partition across cores. The last three are irregular graph algorithms, for which different partitionings can have a large impact on performance. We use METIS [35] to evenly partition their input graphs while minimizing the number of edges across partitions.

Fig. 13 shows that PaWS improves performance moderately over Jigsaw when running on a 16-core system (up to 19% on `pagerank`). Jigsaw + PaWS improves performance because locality improves in the private caches and more data remains in the thread-private VC for longer. However, over time, work-stealing still causes a large fraction of the data to be accessed from multiple cores, leading to poor data placement in Jigsaw (and other schemes, e.g. R-NUCA [28]).

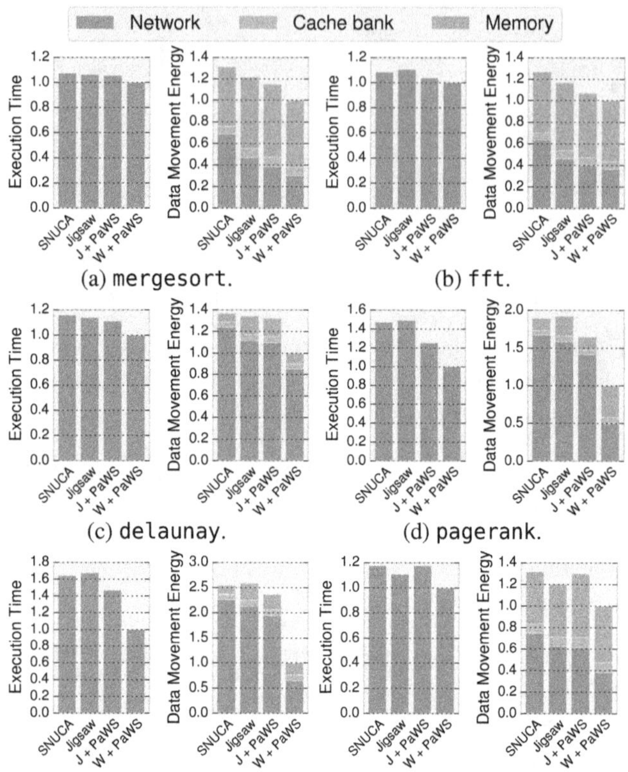

Figure 13: Performance of S-NUCA, Jigsaw, Jigsaw with PaWS, and Whirlpool with PaWS on parallel applications.

Whirlpool with PaWS: Whirlpool makes it easy for PaWS to benefit from improved spatial placement in shared caches. We simply map data from each partition to a separate pool. Although load imbalance causes data to be accessed by multiple cores, each pool's VC is still placed close to the cores that use it. As shown in Fig. 13, this results in much higher gains over Jigsaw: from 6.5% higher performance and 22% lower data movement energy on `mergesort`, to 67% higher performance and 2.6× lower data movement energy on `connectedComponents`.

In summary, Whirlpool with PaWS dramatically improves the performance and efficiency of parallel programs. Moreover, it requires only small changes to existing schedulers, and retains a familiar and productive programming model.

4. WhirlTool: Automated Data Classification

While specifying pools manually gives full control to the programmer, modifying program code is not always practical. We now use the insights from Sec. 3 to design Whirl-

Tool, a profile-guided tool that automatically classifies data into pools. WhirlTool works on unmodified binaries, often matches and sometimes outperforms our manual classification, and introduces small overheads. WhirlTool is publicly available at `http://people.csail.mit.edu/sanchez`.

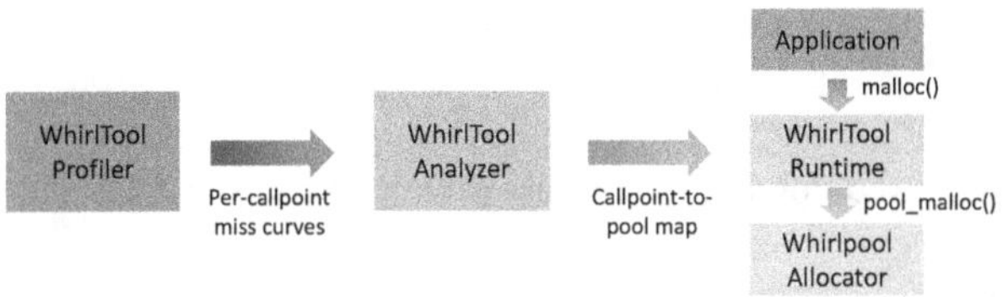

Figure 14: WhirlTool overview.

WhirlTool consists of three main components, shown in Fig. 14. First, the *WhirlTool profiler* tracks a program's memory allocations and profiles their access patterns. Specifically, we sample their stack distance distributions at regular intervals. Second, the *WhirlTool analyzer* clusters allocations into pools using the profiled stack distributions. Third, the *WhirlTool runtime* replaces the default memory allocator and transparently maps each allocation to its assigned pool. Profiling and analysis are performed once (e.g., during compilation).

4.1 WhirlTool profiler

To limit profiling information, Whirlpool identifies memory allocations by their *callpoint*, and profiles all allocations from the same callpoint as a single entity. This heuristic is motivated by our experience in manually porting applications, where we observed that semantically different data tend to be allocated from different points. Specifically, we produce each callpoint id by walking the stack and hashing the last two return PCs.

WhirlTool profiles applications to gather the miss rate curve of each callpoint [24, 61], then uses a distance metric based on miss rate curves to cluster callpoints into a small number of pools (discussed below). The profiler periodically records miss rate curves for all callpoints, which is important to distinguish allocations that are similar on average but whose behavior varies over time (e.g., `lbm` in Sec. 2.2).

We implement the profiler as a Pintool [44], though we note that profiling could be done in Jigsaw hardware directly. We sample miss rate curves every 50 M instructions. This produces 200 KB–1.25 MB of data on our benchmarks. We train WhirlTool with short runs (e.g., using SPEC CPU2006 train input sets) by default. As we show in Sec. 4.4, WhirlTool is quite robust to input set changes.

4.2 WhirlTool analyzer

The *WhirlTool analyzer* progressively clusters callpoints into a small number of pools. Clustering uses a distance metric between pools that reflects *how many additional misses are incurred by clustering them.*

Distance metric: WhirlTool computes the distance between two pools by using their miss rate curves. First, WhirlTool estimates the *combined miss rate curve*, i.e., the curve that would result if both pools were grouped. We have developed a simple method to compute this curve, presented in Appendix B. Second, WhirlTool computes the *partitioned miss rate curve*, i.e., the curve that results from partitioning capacity between both pools. This results in fewer misses than the combined curve, since partitioning favors the pool that uses the cache best.

In principle, we could find the optimal partitioning between both pools at every size, but in practice doing so is computationally expensive [9, 52]. Instead, we compute the convex hulls of each input miss rate curve (a linear-time operation [45]), and then partition the full capacity in a single pass using convex optimization (i.e., hill climbing). This performance could be practically realized by using partitioning within each VC to achieve convex performance [10].

On a single interval, we define the distance between two pools as the area between their combined and partitioned curves. Fig. 15 shows an example. We combine a cache-friendly pool (`m1`) with two other pools (`m2` and `m3`) in the left and right figures. In the left figure, both `m1` and `m2` cache well, so there is little penalty from combining them. This is reflected in the small difference between their combined and partitioned miss rate curves. However, in the right figure, `m3` does not cache well, and it thus interferes more with `m1`. Combining these pools is a bad idea, since doing so will add many unnecessary misses to `m1`. This is reflected in the larger difference between their combined and partitioned miss rate curves.

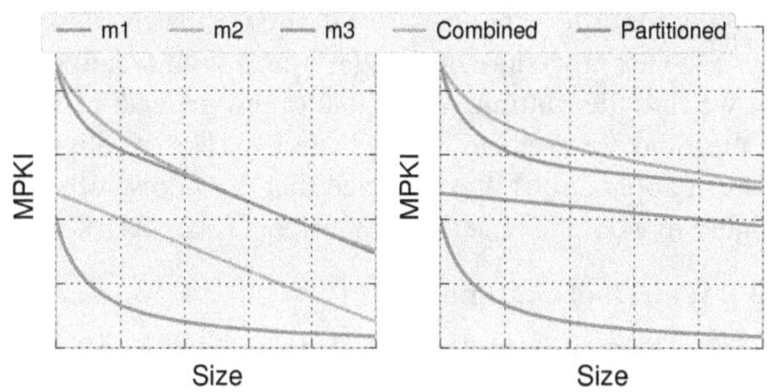

Figure 15: WhirlTool measures the distance between two pools as the additional misses incurred by combining the pools vs. partitioning them separately.

Finally, the distance between two pools is the sum of distances of their per-interval curves. This way, pools accessed in non-overlapping intervals have a small distance, even though they may have very distinct access patterns when active. This benefits programs that use different data over distinct phases, as they can use a small number of pools without degradation.

Agglomerative clustering: WhirlTool uses a simple algorithm to cluster callpoints into pools. It first places each callpoint in a separate pool, and computes the pairwise distances

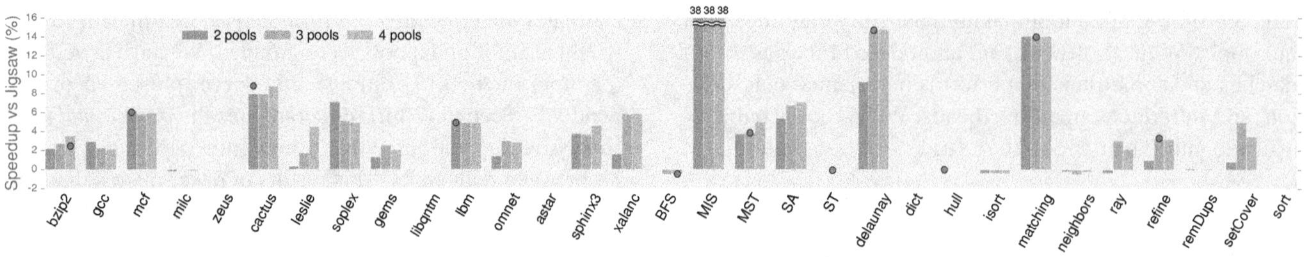

Figure 16: Speedup of WhirlTool over Jigsaw with 2, 3, and 4 pools. A red dot shows the performance achieved by manual classification for the applications we ported by hand (Table 2).

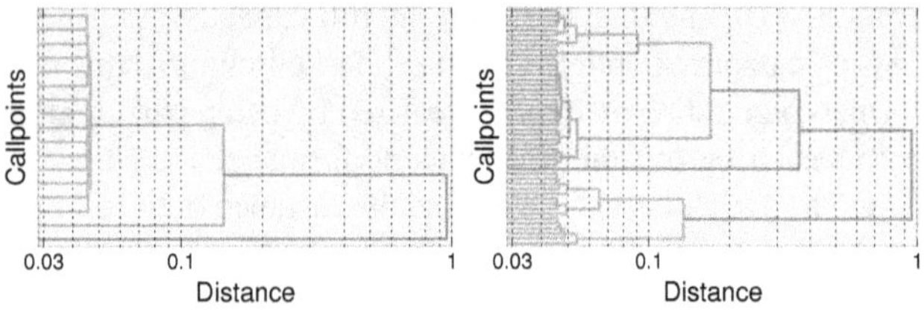

(a) dt. (b) omnetpp.

Figure 17: Hierarchical clustering with WhirlTool. Each graph shows the distance (x-axis) among callpoints and clusters (y-axis). Colors indicate how WhirlTool clusters callpoints into 3 pools.

between all pools. Then it proceeds iteratively. Each iteration merges the two closest pools, and computes the distance of the resulting pool to all the remaining pools. The result is a hierarchical clustering that gives the callpoint-to-pool mapping for different numbers of desired pools, as shown in Fig. 17. This procedure takes $O(n^2)$ time with n callpoints, but we find the runtime acceptable (a few seconds) for the applications we evaluate, which have 10s-100s of callpoints. In most applications, we observed that 2-4 pools suffice to capture most of the benefits of Whirlpool (Sec. 4.4).

4.3 WhirlTool runtime

WhirlTool's runtime replaces the system's memory allocator. On each allocation call, the tool finds the callpoint id and calls the Whirlpool allocator with the corresponding pool. Allocations from an unprofiled callpoint use the thread-private pool. This instrumentation incurs small overheads, at most 0.01% over all our benchmarks (some of which have frequent allocations).

4.4 WhirlTool analysis

Sensitivity to the number of pools: Fig. 16 shows how WhirlTool's performance changes with the number of pools. Each group of bars show the performance of a specific application over Jigsaw. Each bar in the group shows performance for a given number of pools, from 2 to 4. We include SPEC CPU2006 and single-threaded PBBS applications running with their largest input sets. WhirlTool uses profiling data from the train input sets for SPEC CPU2006 and the small input sets for PBBS applications. For manually-ported applications (Sec. 3), a dot shows the number of pools used by manual classification (x-axis) and the performance it achieves (y-axis). As we can see, performance improves by 5-15% for several applications, and `mis` is 38% faster.

In general, moving from 2 to 3 pools improves performance somewhat on a few applications, while 4 pools shows negligible improvements. Some applications (e.g., `gcc`, `soplex`) show a slight decrease in performance with more pools. This happens because these applications have significant variability, and partitioning their data more finely makes phase changes somewhat worse. Given these results, we consider 3 pools to be the right tradeoff, and use 3 pools in subsequent results.

WhirlTool vs. manual classification: Fig. 16 also shows that WhirlTool matches the performance of manual classification for most applications, and outperforms it in some cases (e.g., `bzip2`). Only `cactus` performs slightly worse with automatic classification.

Sensitivity to training data: WhirlTool's performance is robust across input sets on most applications. To quantify this, we compare WhirlTool's performance when using the default training input sets (train/small) for profiling vs. the full input sets used in our experiments (ref/large). WhirlTool's performance is only significantly different in 4 out of the 31 applications, shown in Fig. 18. In these applications, the training inputs result in lower performance than when using the full inputs, e.g. by 5.5% for `leslie` and by 6.7% for `omnet`. This happens because the training inputs exhibit different access patterns than the full inputs. However, over all benchmarks WhirlTool is robust to different inputs, yielding just 0.4% lower performance on training inputs.

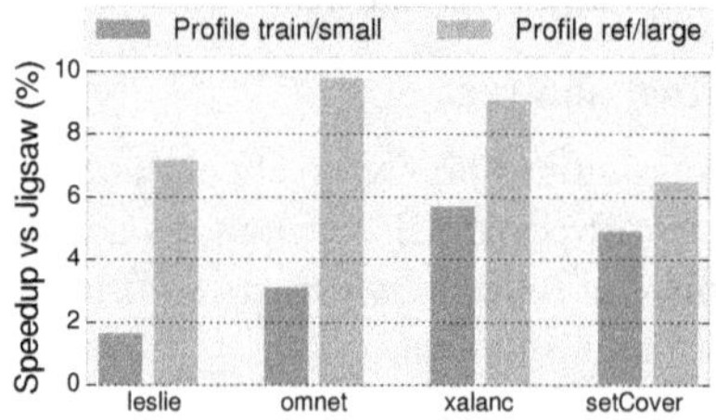

Figure 18: WhirlTool's sensitivity to training inputs.

4.5 WhirlTool evaluation

Fig. 19 and Fig. 20 give two examples of how WhirlTool achieves similar benefits to manual classification.

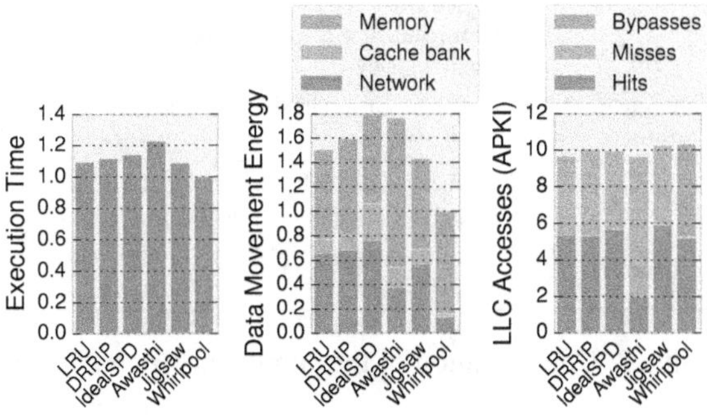

Figure 19: Breakdown of `cactus`'s performance, energy, and accesses for different caching schemes.

`cactus` has two memory regions, only one of which gets good reuse. WhirlTool correctly identifies these pools, letting Whirlpool cache the former near the core and bypass the latter (Fig. 19). Meanwhile, Jigsaw cannot distinguish between pools and must use more cache banks to retain the working set. As a result, Whirlpool significantly reduces network traffic over Jigsaw, and reduces overall data movement energy by 42%. Reducing network traffic also reduces network latency, and Whirlpool improves performance over Jigsaw by 8.6%.

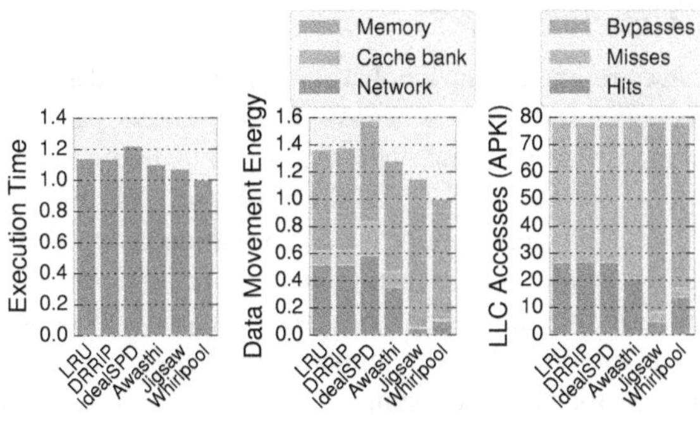

Figure 20: Breakdown of `SA`'s performance, energy, and accesses for different caching schemes.

`SA` offers an interesting contrast. Rather than using fewer banks to reduce network latency over Jigsaw, Whirlpool uses more banks to reduce cache misses (Fig. 20). WhirlTool identifies the pools in `SA` that cache well, and Whirlpool can thus retain more of the working set and reduce main memory accesses. But in order to do so, it uses more banks—which can be seen in the higher network energy. Overall, this is a good tradeoff, and Whirlpool reduces data movement energy by 15% over Jigsaw while improving performance by 7.3%.

Single-threaded applications: We now extend these case studies across many benchmarks. Fig. 21 compares Whirlpool's overall performance and data movement energy with S-NUCA, IdealSPD, Awasthi et al., and Jigsaw over the 31 memory-intensive applications from SPEC CPU2006 and PBBS.

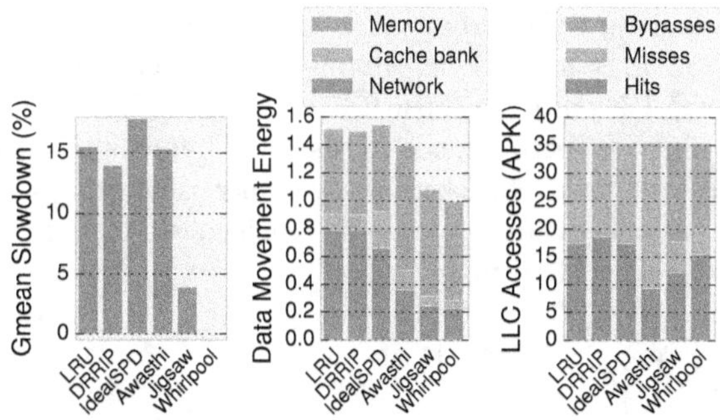

Figure 21: Breakdown of overall performance, energy, and accesses for different caching schemes across all single-threaded benchmarks.

Individual applications see large improvements, e.g., up to 53% lower data movement energy and 38% speedup in `mis`. However, average gains are more muted: Whirlpool reduces data movement energy over Jigsaw by 8.0%, and improves performance by 3.9%. As currently coded, many applications do not expose their memory access heterogeneity across different address regions. With more careful coding, WhirlTool may be able to extract more heterogeneity and improve performance further. As shown in Fig. 21, Whirlpool achieves this by *(a)* placing data closer, which reduces network energy and latency, *(b)* caching data that is more likely to hit, and *(c)* bypassing more selectively than Jigsaw. By contrast, S-NUCA with LRU incurs 51% more data movement energy than Whirlpool and 15% worse performance; S-NUCA with DRRIP incurs 50% more data movement energy and 14% worse performance; IdealSPD incurs 54% more data movement energy and 18% worse performance; and Awasthi incurs 40% more data movement energy and 15% worse performance. However, while S-NUCA variants are generally slower, IdealSPD has a more bimodal behavior: it performs close to Jigsaw on benchmarks that fit within its private region (e.g., `bzip2`), but performs the worst of all schemes on benchmarks that do not fit due to unnecessary multi-level lookups that slow down misses and add data movement energy. Similarly, Awasthi performs much better than S-NUCA on benchmarks with small working sets, but performs poorly on benchmarks that need more than four cache banks (Awasthi's initial allocation). As a result, Awasthi significantly reduces network latency and energy but incurs more misses than S-NUCA.

Fig. 21 also shows that, while Whirlpool and Jigsaw both benefit from bypassing, Whirlpool benefits more because it can distinguish and bypass pools with no reuse. Without bypassing, Jigsaw is 0.2% slower, while Whirlpool is 1.2% slower.

Multi-programmed mixes: We run 20 mixes of randomly-chosen, memory-intensive SPEC CPU2006 applications, at both 4 and 16 cores. Fig. 22 shows the distribution of weighted speedups in both cases. Each line shows the weighted speedup of a single scheme over the Jigsaw baseline, sorted along workload mixes (x-axis) by improvement (inverse CDF). Whirlpool outperforms Jigsaw by up to 13% at 4 cores (5.1% gmean), by up to 6.4% at 16 cores (3.0% gmean), and improves performance consistently. Improvements are larger with fewer cores because, with more applications, Jigsaw has many choices to improve cache performance even with a single VC per application.

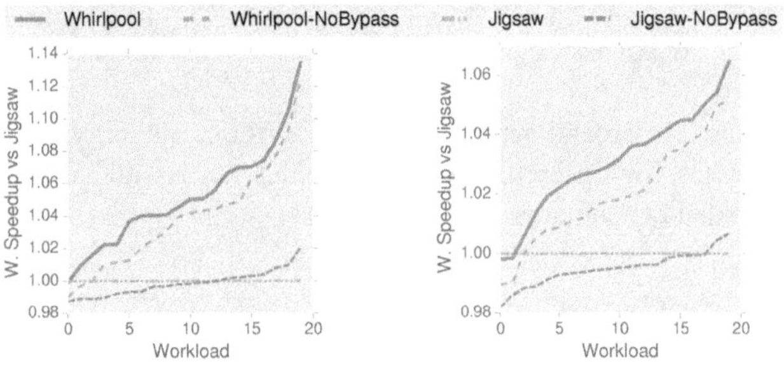

(a) 4 cores. (b) 16 cores.

Figure 22: Weighted speedup of Whirlpool over Jigsaw for 4- and 16-core systems.

Other schemes perform considerably worse. On 4- and 16-core mixes, Whirlpool outperforms S-NUCA by 32%/62% respectively, DRRIP by 25%/52%, IdealSPD by 30%/50%, and Awasthi by 18%/25%. This is because Jigsaw gathers detailed information about each VC over all possible allocations, allowing it to carefully optimize data placement at each reconfiguration.

5. Additional Related Work

Awasthi et al. [4] propose a D-NUCA scheme that uses page coloring to periodically migrate a few most heavily accessed pages to nearby banks. The scheme uses simple hardware extensions and an OS runtime, similar to Whirlpool. Because Awasthi manages individual pages, it doesn't require tagging pools. But per-page monitoring also limits the information Awasthi can gather, and it therefore places pages incrementally using a simple heuristic that can get stuck in local optima (see Fig. 9). In contrast, Whirlpool monitors pools in detail, models end-to-end latency, and performs full reconfigurations, achieving lower AMAT.

SLIP [22] is an insertion policy for single-core NUCAs that seeks to minimize data movement energy. SLIP samples per-page reuse distance distributions, stores them in main memory, and uses an energy optimization unit to decide where to insert lines from different pages. Unlike Jigsaw and Whirlpool, SLIP does not extend to chips with multiple, distributed cores. SLIP also incurs significant storage and logic overheads to decide how far away to insert cache lines at runtime, as it performs very fine-grained (per-page) classification. Instead, Whirlpool relies on distinguishing among the few main classes of data in the program, which makes online adaptation inexpensive.

Cores	4/16 cores, x86-64 ISA, Nehalem-like OOO, 2 GHz [56]
L1 caches	32 KB, 8-way set-associative, split D/I, 4-cycle latency
L2 caches	128 KB private per-core, 8-way set-associative, inclusive, 6-cycle latency
L3 cache	512 KB per bank, 4-way 52-candidate zcache [54], 9 cycle bank latency
Coherence protocol	MESI, 64 B lines, in-cache directory, no silent drops; sequential consistency
NUCA NoC	5×5/9×9 mesh, 128-bit flits and links, X-Y routing, 3-cycle pipelined routers, 2-cycle links
Memory	1/4 MCUs, 1 channel/MCU, 120 cycles zero-load latency, 12.8 GB/s per channel

Table 3: Configuration of the simulated 16-core CMP.

Recent work has studied page placement for systems with heterogeneous and non-uniform main memory (NUMA) [1, 23, 69]. NUMA techniques also have different goals and constraints than NUCA: main memory is larger and has significantly lower bandwidth, so these designs primarily seek to balance bandwidth over network distance and capacity, and reconfigurations are much more infrequent. Agarwal et al. [2] propose an API that lets programmers give hints on whether allocated memory should be placed in bandwidth- or capacity-optimized memory. Unlike this work, Whirlpool includes a fully-automatic variant and places data dynamically.

6. Conclusions

We have presented Whirlpool, a classification-based approach to manage distributed caches. Whirlpool statically classifies data into different pools, which allows dynamic policies to tune the cache to each pool. Unlike prior work, Whirlpool conveys semantic, application-level information about memory usage without fixing the caching policy. We have presented a simple API that allows programmers to classify data, and a profiling tool that works in unmodified binaries and achieves similar performance to manual classification. By leveraging this rich information, Whirlpool significantly outperforms prior work.

A. Experimental Methodology

We perform microarchitectural, execution-driven simulation using zsim [56]. We simulate systems with 4 and 16 OOO cores with parameters in Table 3. The 4-core system has a NUCA cache with 5×5 with 512 KB banks (3.1 MB/core), as shown in Fig. 1. The 16-core system has 9×9 banks (2.5 MB/core), as shown in Fig. 12. We compute data movement (uncore) energy using McPAT 1.1 [42] at 22 nm for caches and NoC, and Micron DDR3L datasheets [46] for main memory. Additionally, we evaluated systems with stream prefetchers: Whirlpool's performance relative to other schemes is unchanged. We do not include prefetchers because they add undesirable data movement energy, especially in mixes.

We compare Whirlpool with D-NUCA and S-NUCA configurations. Jigsaw and Whirlpool both use latency-aware capacity allocation and trading data placement [11]. For private-baseline D-NUCAs, we model an idealized shared-private D-NUCA scheme, IdealSPD, which we grant additional capacity. In IdealSPD, each core has a private 1.5 MB L3 that replicates the 3 closest NUCA banks, followed by a fully-provisioned directory and an exclusive, S-NUCA L4. L4 banks act as a victim cache and are accessed in parallel with the directory to minimize latency. IdealSPD upper-bounds D-NUCA schemes that partition the LLC between private and shared regions, as private (L3) regions do not reduce the capacity of the shared (L4) region. Herrero et al. [30] show that this idealized scheme *always* outperforms several state-of-the-art private-baseline D-NUCA schemes that include shared-private partitioning, selective replication, and adaptive spilling (DCC [29], ASR [6], and ECC [30]), often significantly (up to 30%). For shared-baseline D-NUCAs, we compare against Awasthi et al. [4], discussed in Sec. 5. We have implemented Awasthi as proposed, sweeping implementation parameters α_A, α_B to find the values that perform best. Other shared-baseline D-NUCAs use placement heuristics that compare unfavorably to Awasthi and Whirlpool; e.g., R-NUCA [28] achieves 6.8%/7.2% lower performance than Awasthi on 4-/16-core mixes of SPEC CPU2006.

We use SPEC CPU2006 and PBBS [60] apps. In single-program experiments, SPEC apps are executed for 10 B instructions after fast-forwarding 20 B instructions, and PBBS apps are fast-forwarded to the start of their region of interest, and run for the full region. We consider the applications with >5 L2 MPKI: 15 from SPEC CPU2006 (`bzip2`, `gcc`, `mcf`, `milc`, `zeusmp`, `cactusADM`, `leslie3d`, `soplex`, `GemsFDTD`, `libquantum`, `lbm`, `astar`, `omnetpp`, `sphinx3`, and `xalancbmk`) and 16 from PBBS (all but `nbody`).

We also simulate mixes of single-threaded SPEC CPU2006 apps, using a fixed-work methodology similar to prior work [9, 31, 33]: we run random mixes with 1 B instructions per app after fast-forwarding for 20 B instructions. All apps are kept running until all finish 1 B instructions, and we only consider the first 1 B instructions of each app.

B. Modeling Combined Miss Rate Curves

As discussed in Sec. 4, WhirlTool's distance metric needs to estimate the combined miss rate curve of several callpoints. Several prior models predict shared cache interference [15, 17, 25, 66], but these are somewhat complex and computationally expensive. We instead develop a simpler model that lets WhirlTool rapidly estimate the effect of combining pools.

We model the combined miss rate curve using the *flow* of lines through the cache. For simplicity, consider LRU replacement. The idea behind flow is that lines enter the cache at MRU, and are pushed towards LRU by other lines entering the cache, until they are eventually evicted. Flow is the rate that lines are being pushed towards LRU. However, flow is not constant—hits promote lines rather than evicting them, so flow decreases as lines hit (see Fig. 23). Hence, *the flow at a given point in the miss rate curve is equal to the miss rate at that size.*

Flow is useful because it gives a simple way to combine miss rate curves: when two pools are merged, accesses from either pool push lines from both pools towards LRU. In other words, flow is additive. But the rate at which lines are pushed depends on both their fraction of flow—infrequently-accessed pools have little effect on the combined miss rate curve—and how far they have already been pushed. Listing 1 gives pseudocode for the model.

```
def combineMissCurves(m1, m2):
    s1, s2 = 0, 0
    for s = 0 to N:
        m[s] = m1[s1] + m2[s2]
        s1 += m1[s1] / m[s]
        s2 += m2[s2] / m[s]
    return m
```

Listing 1: Simple model for combining miss rate curves.

One way to think about this model is that it has a single "write head" at `s` and two "read heads" at `s1` and `s2`. At each step, it writes `m` by reading the input miss rate curves at `m1` and `m2`, then moves the read heads through their input curves according to their relative flows. Fig. 23a shows an example.

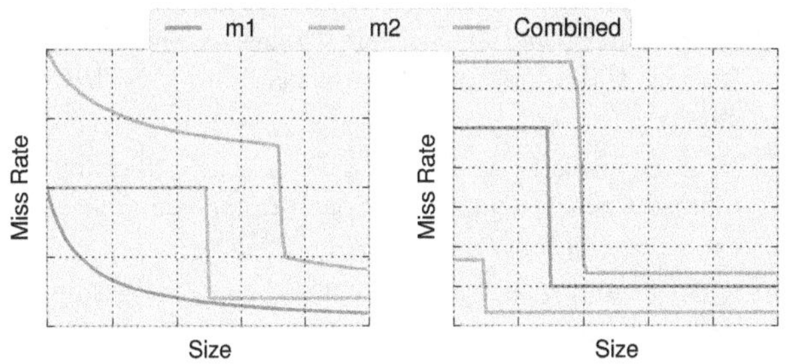

(a) Combining m1 and m2. (b) Combining similar pools.

Figure 23: WhirlTool's simple model to combine miss rate curves.

This model has several desirable properties. It is commutative and associative, so the order in which pools are combined does not matter. It will correctly recombine similar access patterns into a similar result, so the model is insensitive to arbitrary divisions of single pool into subpools (see Fig. 23b). It also produces small changes when adding a pool that is accessed infrequently.

Acknowledgments

We thank Harshad Kasture, Suvinay Subramanian, Po-An Tsai, Xiaosong Ma, and the anonymous reviewers for their helpful feedback. This work was supported in part by NSF grants CCF-1318384 and CAREER-1452994, and by a Samsung GRO award.

References

[1] N. Agarwal, D. Nellans, M. O'Connor, S. W. Keckler, and T. F. Wenisch, "Unlocking bandwidth for GPUs in CC-NUMA systems," in *Proc. HPCA-21*, 2015.

[2] N. Agarwal, D. Nellans, M. Stephenson, M. O'Connor, and S. W. Keckler, "Page Placement Strategies for GPUs within Heterogeneous Memory Systems," in *Proc. ASPLOS-XX*, 2015.

[3] K. Aingaran, D. Smentek, T. Wicki, S. Jairath, G. Konstadinidis, S. Leung *et al.*, "M7: Oracle's Next-Generation Sparc Processor," *IEEE Micro*, no. 2, 2015.

[4] M. Awasthi, K. Sudan, R. Balasubramonian, and J. Carter, "Dynamic hardware-assisted software-controlled page placement to manage capacity allocation and sharing within large caches," in *Proc. HPCA-15*, 2009.

[5] S. Beamer, K. Asanović, and D. Patterson, "The GAP benchmark suite," *arXiv:1508.03619 [cs.DC]*, 2015.

[6] B. M. Beckmann, M. R. Marty, and D. A. Wood, "ASR: Adaptive selective replication for CMP caches," in *Proc. MICRO-39*, 2006.

[7] B. M. Beckmann and D. A. Wood, "Managing wire delay in large chip-multiprocessor caches," in *Proc. MICRO-37*, 2004.

[8] N. Beckmann, "Design and analysis of spatially-partitioned shared caches," Ph.D. dissertation, Massachusetts Institute of Technology, 2015.

[9] N. Beckmann and D. Sanchez, "Jigsaw: Scalable software-defined caches," in *Proc. PACT-22*, 2013.

[10] N. Beckmann and D. Sanchez, "Talus: A Simple Way to Remove Cliffs in Cache Performance," in *Proc. HPCA-21*, 2015.

[11] N. Beckmann, P.-A. Tsai, and D. Sanchez, "Scaling Distributed Cache Hierarchies through Computation and Data Co-Scheduling," in *Proc. HPCA-21*, 2015.

[12] K. Beyls and E. D'Hollander, "Generating cache hints for improved program efficiency," *J. Syst. Architect.*, vol. 51, no. 4, 2005.

[13] R. D. Blumofe and C. E. Leiserson, "Scheduling multithreaded computations by work stealing," *J. ACM*, vol. 46, no. 5, 1999.

[14] J. Brock, X. Gu, B. Bao, and C. Ding, "Pacman: Program-assisted cache management," in *Proc. ISMM*, 2013.

[15] D. Chandra, F. Guo, S. Kim, and Y. Solihin, "Predicting inter-thread cache contention on a chip multi-processor architecture," in *Proc. HPCA-11*, 2005.

[16] Q. Chen, M. Guo, and H. Guan, "LAWS: locality-aware work-stealing for multi-socket multi-core architectures," in *Proc. ICS*, 2014.

[17] X. E. Chen and T. M. Aamodt, "A first-order fine-grained multithreaded throughput model," in *Proc. HPCA-15*, 2009.

[18] Z. Chishti, M. D. Powell, and T. Vijaykumar, "Optimizing replication, communication, and capacity allocation in CMPs," in *Proc. ISCA-32*, 2005.

[19] S. Cho and L. Jin, "Managing distributed, shared L2 caches through OS-level page allocation," in *Proc. MICRO-39*, 2006.

[20] S. Coleman and K. S. McKinley, "Tile size selection using cache organization and data layout," in *Proc. PLDI*, 1995.

[21] W. J. Dally, "GPU Computing: To Exascale and Beyond," in *Supercomputing '10, Plenary Talk*, 2010.

[22] S. Das, T. M. Aamodt, and W. J. Dally, "SLIP: reducing wire energy in the memory hierarchy," in *Proc. ISCA-42*, 2015.

[23] M. Dashti, A. Fedorova, J. Funston, F. Gaud, R. Lachaize, B. Lepers *et al.*, "Traffic management: a holistic approach to memory placement on NUMA systems," in *Proc. ASPLOS-XVIII*, 2013.

[24] C. Ding and Y. Zhong, "Predicting whole-program locality through reuse distance analysis," in *Proc. PLDI*, 2003.

[25] D. Eklov, D. Black-Schaffer, and E. Hagersten, "StatCC: a statistical cache contention model," in *Proc. PACT-19*, 2010.

[26] M. Frigo, C. E. Leiserson, and K. H. Randall, "The Implementation of the Cilk-5 Multithreaded Language," in *Proc. PLDI*, 1998.

[27] X. Gu, T. Bai, Y. Gao, C. Zhang, R. Archambault, and C. Ding, "P-OPT: Program-directed optimal cache management," in *Proc. LCPC-21*, 2008.

[28] N. Hardavellas, M. Ferdman, B. Falsafi, and A. Ailamaki, "Reactive NUCA: near-optimal block placement and replication in distributed caches," in *Proc. ISCA-36*, 2009.

[29] E. Herrero, J. González, and R. Canal, "Distributed cooperative caching," in *Proc. PACT-17*, 2008.

[30] E. Herrero, J. González, and R. Canal, "Elastic cooperative caching: an autonomous dynamically adaptive memory hierarchy for chip multiprocessors," in *Proc. ISCA-37*, 2010.

[31] A. Hilton, N. Eswaran, and A. Roth, "FIESTA: A sample-balanced multi-program workload methodology," *Proc. MoBS*, 2009.

[32] A. Jaleel, W. Hasenplaugh, M. Qureshi, J. Sebot, S. Steely Jr, and J. Emer, "Adaptive insertion policies for managing shared caches," in *Proc. PACT-17*, 2008.

[33] A. Jaleel, K. B. Theobald, S. C. Steely Jr, and J. Emer, "High performance cache replacement using re-reference interval prediction (RRIP)," in *Proc. ISCA-37*, 2010.

[34] N. P. Jouppi, "Improving direct-mapped cache performance by the addition of a small fully-associative cache and prefetch buffers," in *Proc. ISCA-17*, 1990.

[35] G. Karypis and V. Kumar, "A fast and high quality multilevel scheme for partitioning irregular graphs," *SIAM J. Sci. Comput.*, vol. 20, no. 1, 1998.

[36] S. W. Keckler, W. J. Dally, B. Khailany, M. Garland, and D. Glasco, "GPUs and the future of parallel computing," *IEEE Micro*, no. 5, 2011.

[37] C. Kim, D. Burger, and S. W. Keckler, "An adaptive, non-uniform cache structure for wire-delay dominated on-chip caches," in *Proc. ASPLOS-X*, 2002.

[38] R. Komuravelli, M. D. Sinclair, M. Kotsifakou, P. Srivastava, S. V. Adve, and V. S. Adve, "Stash: Have your scratchpad and cache it too," in *Proc. ISCA-42*, 2015.

[39] M. D. Lam, E. E. Rothberg, and M. E. Wolf, "The cache performance and optimizations of blocked algorithms," in *Proc. ASPLOS-IV*, 1991.

[40] D. Lea, "A memory allocator," http://gee.cs.oswego.edu/dl/html/malloc.html, 2000.

[41] J. Leverich, H. Arakida, A. Solomatnikov, A. Firoozshahian, M. Horowitz, and C. Kozyrakis, "Comparing memory systems for chip multiprocessors," in *Proc. ISCA-34*, 2007.

[42] S. Li, J. H. Ahn, R. D. Strong, J. B. Brockman, D. M. Tullsen, and N. P. Jouppi, "McPAT: an integrated power, area, and timing modeling framework for multicore and manycore architectures," in *Proc. MICRO-42*, 2009.

[43] J. Lira, C. Molina, and A. González, "LRU-PEA: A smart replacement policy for non-uniform cache architectures on chip multiprocessors," in *Proc. ICCD*, 2009.

[44] C.-K. Luk, R. Cohn, R. Muth, H. Patil, A. Klauser, G. Lowney *et al.*, "Pin: building customized program analysis tools with dynamic instrumentation," in *Proc. PLDI*, 2005.

[45] A. A. Melkman, "On-line construction of the convex hull of a simple polyline," *Information Processing Letters*, vol. 25, no. 1, 1987.

[46] Micron, "1.35V DDR3L power calculator (4Gb x16 chips)," 2013.

[47] T. C. Mowry, M. S. Lam, and A. Gupta, "Design and evaluation of a compiler algorithm for prefetching," in *Proc. ASPLOS-V*, 1992.

[48] S. Palanca, V. Pentkovski, S. Tsai, and S. Maiyuran, "Method and apparatus for implementing non-temporal stores," 2001, US Patent 6,205,520.

[49] G. Pekhimenko, T. Huberty, R. Cai, O. Mutlu, P. B. Gibbons, M. Kozuch *et al.*, "Exploiting compressed block size as an indicator of future reuse," in *Proc. HPCA-21*, 2015.

[50] P. Petoumenos, G. Keramidas, and S. Kaxiras, "Instruction-based reuse-distance prediction for effective cache management," in *Proc. SAMOS*, 2009.

[51] M. K. Qureshi, "Adaptive spill-receive for robust high-performance caching in CMPs," in *Proc. HPCA-15*, 2009.

[52] M. K. Qureshi and Y. N. Patt, "Utility-based cache partitioning: A low-overhead, high-performance, runtime mechanism to partition shared caches," in *Proc. MICRO-39*, 2006.

[53] S. Rusu, H. Muljono, D. Ayers, S. Tam, W. Chen, A. Martin *et al.*, "Ivytown: A 22nm 15-core enterprise Xeon® processor family," in *Proc. ISSCC*, 2014.

[54] D. Sanchez and C. Kozyrakis, "The ZCache: Decoupling ways and associativity," in *Proc. MICRO-43*, 2010.

[55] D. Sanchez and C. Kozyrakis, "Vantage: Scalable and efficient fine-grain cache partitioning," in *Proc. ISCA-38*, 2011.

[56] D. Sanchez and C. Kozyrakis, "ZSim: fast and accurate microarchitectural simulation of thousand-core systems," in *Proc. ISCA-40*, 2013.

[57] D. Sanchez, R. M. Yoo, and C. Kozyrakis, "Flexible architectural support for fine-grain scheduling," in *Proc. ASPLOS-XV*, 2010.

[58] N. Satish, N. Sundaram, M. M. A. Patwary, J. Seo, J. Park, M. A. Hassaan *et al.*, "Navigating the maze of graph analytics frameworks using massive graph datasets," in *Proc. SIGMOD*, 2014.

[59] J. Shalf, S. Dosanjh, and J. Morrison, "Exascale computing technology challenges," in *Proc. High Performance Computing for Computational Science (VECPAR)*, 2010.

[60] J. Shun, G. E. Blelloch, J. T. Fineman, P. B. Gibbons, A. Kyrola, H. V. Simhadri *et al.*, "Brief announcement: the problem based benchmark suite," in *Proc. SPAA*, 2012.

[61] D. K. Tam, R. Azimi, L. B. Soares, and M. Stumm, "RapidMRC: approximating L2 miss rate curves on commodity systems for online optimizations," in *Proc. ASPLOS-XIV*, 2009.

[62] G. Tyson, M. Farrens, J. Matthews, and A. R. Pleszkun, "A modified approach to data cache management," in *Proc. MICRO-28*, 1995.

[63] Z. Wang, K. McKinley, A. L. Rosenberg, and C. C. Weems, "Using the compiler to improve cache replacement decisions," in *Proc. PACT-11*, 2002.

[64] M. E. Wolf and M. S. Lam, "A data locality optimizing algorithm," in *Proc. PLDI*, 1991.

[65] C.-J. Wu, A. Jaleel, W. Hasenplaugh, M. Martonosi, S. C. Steely Jr, and J. Emer, "SHiP: signature-based hit predictor for high performance caching," in *Proc. MICRO-44*, 2011.

[66] X. Xiang, B. Bao, C. Ding, and Y. Gao, "Linear-time modeling of program working set in shared cache," in *Proc. PACT-20*, 2011.

[67] R. M. Yoo, C. J. Hughes, C. Kim, Y.-K. Chen, and C. Kozyrakis, "Locality-aware task management for unstructured parallelism: A quantitative limit study," in *Proc. SPAA*, 2013.

[68] M. Zhang and K. Asanovic, "Victim replication: Maximizing capacity while hiding wire delay in tiled chip multiprocessors," in *Proc. ISCA-32*, 2005.

[69] S. Zhuravlev, S. Blagodurov, and A. Fedorova, "Addressing shared resource contention in multicore processors via scheduling," in *Proc. ASPLOS-XV*, 2010.

TPC: Target-Driven Parallelism Combining Prediction and Correction to Reduce Tail Latency in Interactive Services

Myeongjae Jeon†, Yuxiong He†, Hwanju Kim*[1], Sameh Elnikety†, Scott Rixner‡, Alan L. Cox‡

†Microsoft Research
Redmond, WA, USA

*University of Cambridge
Cambridge, UK

‡Rice University
Houston, TX, USA

Abstract

In interactive services such as web search, recommendations, games and finance, reducing the tail latency is crucial to provide fast response to every user. Using web search as a driving example, we systematically characterize interactive workload to identify the opportunities and challenges for reducing tail latency. We find that the workload consists of mainly short requests that do not benefit from parallelism, and a few long requests which significantly impact the tail but exhibit high parallelism speedup. This motivates estimating request execution time, using a predictor, to identify long requests and to parallelize them. Prediction, however, is not perfect; a long request mispredicted as short is likely to contribute to the server tail latency, setting a ceiling on the achievable tail latency.

We propose TPC, an approach that combines prediction information judiciously with dynamic correction for inaccurate prediction. Dynamic correction increases parallelism to accelerate a long request that is mispredicted as short. TPC carefully selects the appropriate target latencies based on system load and parallelism efficiency to reduce tail latency.

We implement TPC and several prior approaches to compare them experimentally on a single search server and on a cluster of 40 search servers. The experimental results show that TPC reduces the 99th- and 99.9th-percentile latency by up to 40% compared with the best prior work. Moreover, we evaluate TPC on a finance server, demonstrating its effectiveness on reducing tail latency of interactive services beyond web search.

[1] Currently with EMC

ASPLOS '16 April 2–6, 2016, Atlanta, Georgia, USA.

DOI: http://dx.doi.org/10.1145/http://dx.doi.org/10.1145/2872362.2872370

Categories and Subject Descriptors D.4.1 [*Operating Systems*]: Process Management—Threads

General Terms Algorithm, Design, Performance

Keywords Interactive Service, Tail Latency, Parallelism, Thread Scheduling, Machine Learning, Web Search

1. Introduction

Interactive online services such as web search, financial trading, and online games provide consistently fast responses to every user request, which translates to requirements on the tail for request response times [9, 19]. Reducing response latency is important because it generates extra revenues: The saved latency can be used for adding extra capabilities and new features. It can also be used for cost savings as the system capacity increases: Under the same latency SLA and input workload, fewer servers are deployed when servers employ the latency reduction techniques to support the higher load. This paper presents an approach to reduce the tail latency of interactive services, where we use web search as a driving example.

For large-scale commercial search engines, the web index is typically partitioned among many servers, and therefore a user request (or query) is processed on several servers [3, 8, 20]. The slowest server determines the request latency. On a single server, it is important to reduce the tail latency rather than the average. We illustrate this point with a simple example of a cluster containing 40 search servers. Here, the request response is aggregated from the 40 servers, and to obtain a 99th-percentile latency of X time units, each server must achieve a substantially stricter tail latency [9, 19], specifically $\sqrt[40]{99/100} \times 100 = 99.98$ th-percentile latency of X.

We characterize the server workload to investigate how to reduce tail latency. The study shows that computation time dominates disk and network IO as well as queueing latencies. CPU is the bottleneck resource, making parallel processing on a multi-core server a promising approach. Moreover, data center environments collect extensive telemetry data, including system load, query logs, and workload information, which can be exploited to provide better performance.

However, workload characterization reveals important challenges. Queries exhibit large latency variability, where the service demand of long queries is orders of magnitude higher than the median. Moreover, not all queries benefit equally from parallelization: Parallelization has a non-negligible overhead, particularly for short queries. This motivates estimating request execution time, using a predictor, to identify which queries are long. Prediction, however, is not perfect; a long request mispredicted as short is likely to contribute to the server tail latency. In effect, prediction inaccuracy sets a ceiling on the achievable tail latency reduction.

Prior work on using parallel processing to reduce query latency falls into two categories according to whether prediction information is used. (1) Techniques in the first category ignore per-query prediction information completely. For example, recent work [20, 33] determines the parallelism degree before running the query according to system load without differentiating short and long queries, resulting in substantial overhead as short requests are parallelized. Another approach [15] increases the parallelism degree during query execution, but misses the opportunity to parallelize long queries early, leading to longer completion time and impacting the tail latency. (2) Recent work in the second category relies primarily on per-query prediction information [21]. The parallelism degree can be decided according to the predicted query execution time. The latency reduction is, however, limited because the mispredicted long queries impact the tail substantially.

To overcome the limitations of the prior work, we propose a novel approach that exploits prediction information judiciously with dynamic correction for inaccurate prediction. Dynamic correction ramps up the degree of parallelism to accelerate long queries mispredicted as short. Ramping up parallelism must be done carefully: If it is invoked too early, it wastes resources that could have been used to reduce the tail latency. If it is invoked too late, the request completes late directly impacting the tail latency.

Our main contribution is TPC, standing for Target-driven parallelism combining Prediction and Correction, which is an algorithm to reduce the very high tail latency. TPC exploits several factors jointly, including per-query prediction information, instantaneous system load information, statistical workload information (*i.e.*, average parallelism speedup). It has three key insights:

First, TPC determines a common *target* completion time to determine how aggressively to parallelize requests and when to invoke dynamic correction. The target is used for two purposes: (1) to allocate the least amount of resources so that majority of requests complete before the target, and (2) to determine which requests take longer than expected, e.g., due to under-estimating their service demands. The requests taking longer than the target are likely to impact the tail. If additional resources are available, they are allocated to accelerate those requests. The target value depends on the current system load and overall parallelism efficiency of requests.

Second, TPC applies *predictive parallelism*: it predicts the execution time of each request to compute its degree of parallelism. More precisely, TPC selects the smallest parallelism degree so that the request meets its target completion time while accounting for the request parallelism efficiency. As a result, short requests complete within the target using sequential execution and long requests are parallelized to meet the target using minimum resources.

Third, TPC introduces *dynamic correction* to handle mispredictions — long requests that are mispredicted as short and execute sequentially or with a low parallelism degree. TPC increases parallelism for requests that exceed the target completion time while considering the available spare resources, reducing latency for the very high-percentile.

To assess the benefits of TPC, we implement it in the context of Microsoft Bing search engine and evaluate it experimentally using a production workload. The empirical results show that TPC consistently outperforms the prior work [20, 21, 33]. TPC effectively reduces the very high-percentile latency. The server 99.9th-percentile latency is reduced by up to 40% compared with the best prior work. Moreover, as each server completes requests by meeting the computed target resulting in lower latency variance and lower tail latency, at the cluster level tail latency is reduced. Our results show that the 99th-percentile tail latency of a 40-server cluster is reduced by 66% compared with sequential and 29% compared with the best prior work.

Furthermore, we generalize the TPC approach to a wider class of CPU-intensive interactive services exhibiting the properties of highly-variant request demand, parallelizable request execution and predictable sequential execution time. As an example, we implement TPC on a finance server and show its effectiveness on reducing tail latency.

We structure the paper around our contributions: First, we conduct a comprehensive workload characterization that shows the opportunities and challenges of using parallelization to reduce request tail latency (Section 2). Second, we develop a new policy, TPC, that applies prediction information judiciously with dynamic correction under inaccurate prediction (Section 3). Third, we implement and evaluate TPC experimentally in a commercial search engine. We find that TPC consistently outperforms the prior work (Section 4). Finally, we implement and evaluate TPC on a finance server, demonstrating its effectiveness beyond web search (Section 5).

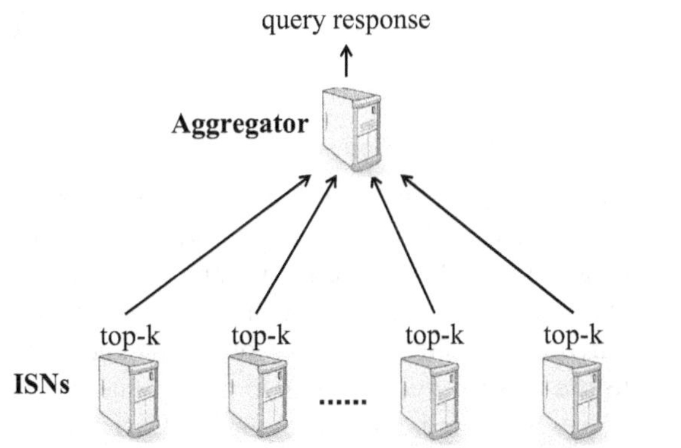

Figure 1. Index serving system architecture.

2. Workload Characterization

The index serving system in a search engine retrieves documents relevant to user queries, generating an interactive workload that we characterize carefully to motivate TPC design.

2.1 System Overview

System architecture. Figure 1 illustrates the *partition-aggregate* architecture of an index serving system. It consists of an aggregator (also known as a broker) and search servers called index serving nodes (ISNs). The index contains information about web documents, is document-sharded [3] and distributed among the ISNs. When a user sends a query and the query response is not cached, the aggregator propagates the query to all ISNs hosting the web index. Each ISN searches its fragment of the web index to return the top-k most relevant results to the aggregator. The aggregator receives the results from the ISNs, and merges them to compute the response to the user query. The aggregator waits for all of its ISNs to respond so it will not miss any search results. ISNs are the workhorse of the index serving system. They constitute over 90% of the total hardware resources and account for the majority of the query processing time. This architecture is similar to others discussed in prior work [3, 8, 20].

Query processing. The ISN manages a number of worker threads that can process several queries concurrently on multiple cores. Newly arrived queries first join the waiting queue of the ISN. When a worker thread is idle, it dequeues a query from the waiting queue and starts to process it. The worker thread searches its web index fragment to produce a list of documents matching the keywords in the query. As there are a fixed number of worker threads, some queries may experience a delay in the waiting queue. Thus, a query's response time consists of both its queueing delay and execution time.

2.2 Computationally Bound Workload

Several factors make web search a computationally bound workload. First, the inverted indices are sharded across a large number of ISNs, each of which has 10s of GBs of DRAM for caching its part of these indices. This caching substantially reduces the amount of disk I/O performed by the ISNs [20]. For example, under production workloads, the average amount of disk I/O by each ISN is only 0.3 KB/s. Consequently, the CPU spends little or no time blocked on disk I/O. Second, a search engine is an interactive application. Therefore, it is not operated at extremely high loads to avoid queueing delay and quality degradation [20]. Our measurements show that even under a relatively high CPU utilization of 73%, the average queueing delay at the ISN is 0.35 ms. Third, the time for network I/O is a small fraction of the overall query latency. The average time for network I/O per query is only 2.13 ms, while the computation by the CPU represents the largest fraction, with a service demand of 13.47 ms on average or up to more than 200 ms. We have observed this small impact of the non-computation parts regardless of the query length. Therefore, query latency reduction is best achieved by speeding up the computation.

Queries running concurrently exhibit little interference or memory contention. [20] reports that a query suffers less than a 5% slowdown while running together with other queries at 50% CPU utilization, as compared to running alone. We have observed similar behavior under our workloads. In summary, we have a computationally bound workload with little interference among queries. So, we believe that *query parallelization has a good chance of reducing latency.*

2.3 Latency Variability

Server requests have varying computational demands. Most queries are short, with more than 85% taking below 15 ms. A few queries are, however, very long, taking up to 200 ms. In particular, the average service demand is 13.47 ms, while the 99th-percentile service demand is 200 ms, which is 15 times the average. The gap between the median and the 99th-percentile is even larger at 56 times. We observe that this variability is fairly consistent across a few hundred ISNs in the index serving cluster.

Many factors affect query execution time, and we discuss two typical factors responsible for long execution. First, long queries tend to have more documents to match and score, which consumes more processor cycles. Second, long queries involve the intersection of inverted indices for a larger number of keywords. It is known that the average latency of queries with ten keywords can be approximately an order of magnitude greater than that of queries with only two keywords [36].

The distributed query processing further increases latency variability. In a partition-aggregate cluster where a search query runs in parallel and its results are aggregated over a large number of ISNs (in Figure 1), speeding up the long queries at each ISN is necessary to reduce the cluster tail latency, which directly affects end-to-end response time. Our experimental evaluation on a Bing search cluster (in Section 4.5) also shows that reducing tail latency of the clus-

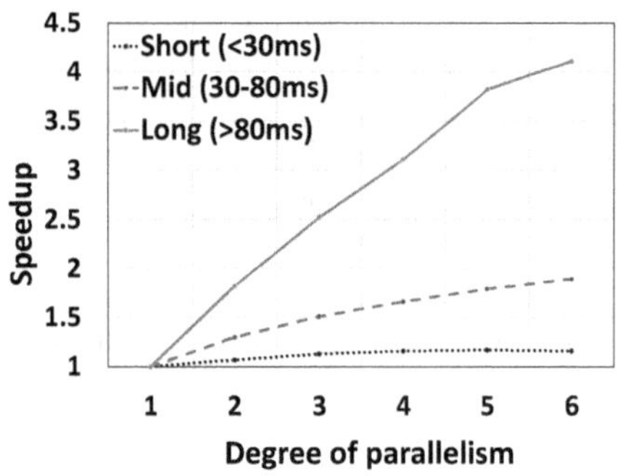

Figure 2. Average speedup for processing queries in parallel grouped by their execution time.

ter requires reducing a much higher percentile at each ISN. Thus, each server should be optimized for both moderate (*e.g.*, 95th- to 99th-percentile) and even high (*e.g.*, higher than 99th-percentile) tail latency. We conclude that *to deliver low-latency responses to users, it is crucial to speed up long queries at each ISN.*

2.4 Query Parallelization Efficiency

Multiple threads can process a single query to exploit the modern multi-core processors. We adopt a state-of-the-art query parallelization approach from prior work [20], where the index data is partitioned into small tasks, forming a task pool, and the query threads retrieve tasks from the pool and process them. A query can be assigned a number of threads upon the start of query execution [20], and later on the scheduler can add additional threads to a query during its execution [15]. As observed in many applications [1, 11, 23, 33, 38], parallelization incurs overhead due to various factors, such as task creation, synchronization and speculated execution [15, 20]. The parallelization efficiency varies among queries for two reasons, which impact on short queries: (1) Some steps are not parallelized, *e.g.*, query parsing and rescoring of the top results. (2) Load imbalance among tasks adversely affects parallelism speedup [12].

We study query parallelization efficiency empirically using a production index and query log. We classify the queries into three classes based on execution time and show the speedup with different parallelism degrees in Figure 2. The long queries that run more than 80 ms achieve more than 4 times speedup on 6 threads, reducing their mean execution time from 168 ms to 41 ms. In contrast, using 6 threads, the short queries that complete in under 30 ms achieve only 1.16 times speedup. In addition, medium queries that run between 30 and 80 ms have modest speedup, around 2 times with parallelism degree 6. The parallelization efficiency thus depends on the query service demand, as has been observed in other search workloads [12]. We conclude that *parallelization is more effective for long queries than short queries.*

2.5 Impact of Prediction Accuracy

Prior work uses machine learning techniques to predict (sequential) execution time of a query before running it to identify long queries [21, 26]. We adopt a predictor [21] that uses both term and query features such as IDF (inverted document frequency) and the number of augmented keywords, and uses a boosted-tree regressor to predict query execution time. Regressor accuracy is commonly measured using L1 error, representing the difference of the predicted and actual query execution time. The L1 error of our predictor is 14 ms using production indices and query logs. To illustrate the impact of prediction accuracy on tail latency, we present a more intuitive view from a classifier's perspective as we show in the experimental evaluation: The predictor identifies long queries, classifying each query as either long or short. Classifier accuracy is measured using precision (the fraction of detections which are truly long queries) and recall (the fraction of truly long queries which are detected).

High recall is essential; We should identify the majority of long queries and subsequently process them faster to reduce their response time. A misprediction due to imperfect recall means that a long query is processed as a short query and therefore is likely to increase tail latency. In contrast, misprediction due to imperfect precision is directly related to how many short queries are mispredicted as long, resulting in higher overhead: Resources are wasted to parallelize short queries with no benefit for reducing tail latency.

Across the 40 ISNs, the average recall is 0.86 and precision is 0.91 for identifying queries running longer than a latency threshold of 80 ms. Since the workload has 4% of long queries ($>$ 80 ms) and the predictor correctly identifies 86% of them, the remaining long queries, which are 0.56% of all queries, are misidentified as short. These mispredicted long queries will not affect the 99th-percentile tail latency (as they are less than 1%) but they significantly affect the higher tail such as 99.9th-percentile (as they constitute more than 0.1% of all queries). Prediction alone cannot effectively reduce any tail latency beyond the 99.44th-percentile.

2.6 Implications for Tail Latency

This workload characterization shows both opportunities and challenges for reducing tail latency. On one hand, parallelization can effectively reduce query execution time particularly for long queries. On the other hand, queries exhibit different parallelization efficiency, and impact the tail differently according to their service demands. Execution time prediction identifies the majority of long queries (accelerating them to reduce tail latency) and identifies the majority of short queries (avoiding their parallelism overhead). However, it is not sufficient to reduce latency in very high percentiles because of the mispredicted long queries.

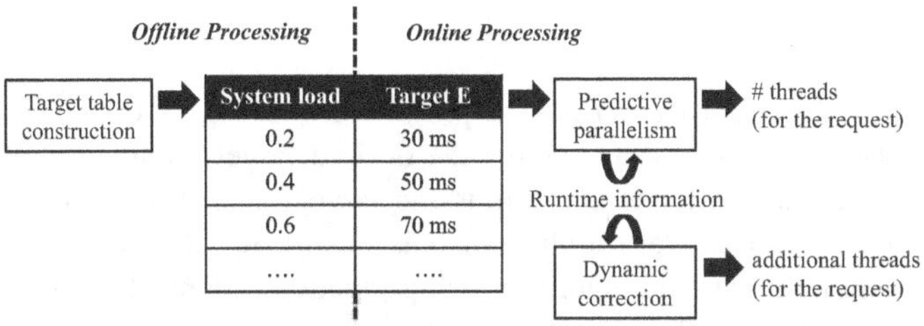

Figure 3. Online/Offline processing workflow in TPC.

3. TPC Algorithm

We propose TPC — Target-driven parallelism combining Prediction and Correction — which exploits the benefits of prediction and uses dynamic parallelism to handle the issues of mispredicted long queries. Ramping up parallelism on mispredicted queries can further reduce tail latencies beyond using prediction alone. However, the challenge is to determine "when" to start ramping up the parallelism dynamically. If we do this too early, we end up wasting resources of parallelizing queries that will not impact the tail; if we do it too late, we end up increasing latency. TPC carefully selects the appropriate *target* latencies based on system load to leverage prediction and dynamic correction to reduce tail latency.

TPC computes a target completion time E for all requests based on current system load. Resources are allocated to a request such that it completes within the target E. Short requests can complete within E using sequential execution, but long requests must be parallelized.

If the predicted sequential execution time is longer than E, parallelism is carefully used to shorten the request completion time to be within E using the minimum resources. Providing extra resources to complete a request earlier than E is not beneficial to reducing the tail, and it takes resources that could have been used by other requests to meet E.

Since prediction is not 100% accurate, long requests mispredicted as short would affect the tail. We develop a dynamic correction mechanism, to ramp up request parallelism and use available idle cores to speed up the requests that have not completed as expected, mitigating the tail.

Figure 3 presents an overview of TPC. As scheduling decisions must be made quickly, we split the scheduling algorithm into two parts: online and offline. The *offline* component constructs a table, called the *target table*, that maps the system load to target completion time E. We develop an efficient algorithm using gradient descent method to search for the appropriate targets. During *online* processing, TPC utilizes the target E from the table according to the current system load, and it determines the parallelism degree of requests through two steps: predictive parallelism and dynamic correction. *Predictive parallelism* decides the parallelism degree before executing the request. It exploits the predicted request execution time and request parallelism efficiency to meet E by using minimum resources. When a request does not complete by the target time E, TPC employs *dynamic correction*, increasing its parallelism at runtime to complete it faster. We next focus on the online component of TPC: predictive parallelism and dynamic correction.

3.1 Predictive Parallelism

We use the predicted request execution time to parallelize the long requests, reducing tail, and execute the short requests sequentially, saving resources.

Inputs. Predictive parallelism takes three inputs to decide request parallelism degree: *(1) Target completion time.* TPC reads the current system load to retrieve the target completion time E from the target table. *(2) Predicted request execution time.* To identify long requests, TPC uses a predictor from prior work [21] to estimate request execution time L before running a request. *(3) Parallelization efficiency.* The degree of parallelism should depend on the parallelization efficiency. To illustrate, consider the case of perfect parallelization efficiency, in which the response time decreases linearly with increased parallelism. Here, we should use as many cores as possible. In contrast, if parallelization efficiency is too low, response time does not decrease with increased parallelism, making sequential execution the best option. Realistic requests fit between these extremes, and better efficiency allows a higher degree of parallelism.

We use a speedup profile to model request parallelization efficiency. The speedup profile maps request parallelism degree to its speedup. We denote it by $\{S_i | i = 1, 2, ...P\}$, where S_i is the request speedup with parallelism degree i and P is the maximum degree. In practice, request speedup is hard to predict accurately. However, since long requests exhibit better speedup than short ones, we classify requests into groups based on their sequential execution time and measure the average speedup in each group, *e.g.*, as shown in Figure 2. Given a request, we use its predicted sequential execution time to determine its group and retrieve the speedup profile.

Algorithm. Upon request arrival, TPC retrieves the target completion time E based on system load, predicts the execution time L of the request, and identifies its speedup profile $\{S_i\}$. With a speedup S_i, the request execution time using parallelism degree i is estimated as $T_i = L/S_i$. *TPC finds the smallest parallelism degree d to meet E*, i.e., $d = \arg\min_{1 \le i \le P}\{T_i | T_i \le \text{E}\}$. Putting extra resources to complete a request much earlier than E is not beneficial to reducing the tail, as it consumes resources that could have been used by other requests to meet their target completion time.

3.2 Dynamic Correction

If a request has not completed within the target E, TPC increases the request's parallelism degree dynamically at runtime to complete the request quickly.

Motivation. In Section 2.5, we demonstrate that using prediction alone cannot reduce latency beyond 99.44th-percentile due to the limited predictor accuracy: There are

0.56% of requests are long but misidentified as short requests. For reducing even higher percentile latency, *e.g.*, 99.9th or higher, dynamic correction is needed to recover prediction errors.

Technique. When a request has not finished its execution by the target E, TPC dynamically increases the request's parallelism degree at runtime to complete the request quickly. In particular, TPC increases the request parallelism degree up to using all the available resources or reaching the maximum parallelism degree of the request. The available resources can be measured in several ways, including number of idle cores (or hardware contexts with SMT), and the number of idle worker threads. In the experiments, TPC uses the number of idle worker threads. Dynamic correction accelerates long requests mispredicted as short, and therefore reduces the very high percentile tail latency that predictive parallelism cannot optimize effectively.

Synergy between Predictive Parallelism and Dynamic Correction. When request execution time is predictable, dynamic correction may not be as efficient as predictive parallelism. First, prediction allows us to parallelize those really long requests at the very beginning of query execution with high parallelism while dynamic correction would defer the decision and prolong their execution time. Moreover, when we identify a request as long, we can parallelize the request early using smaller parallelism degree to meet its target E, whereas dynamic correction parallelizes the request late using a higher parallelism degree. Since the parallelism efficiency decreases with increasing parallelism degree, predictive parallelism completes the request while using fewer resources.

Therefore, TPC uses predictive parallelism to parallelize the majority of long requests effectively using fewer resources, and it applies dynamic correction to only mispredicted long requests when necessary. The two techniques are synergistic in reducing the tail latency.

3.3 Computing the Target Table

Instantaneous load on a server varies over time [29], impacting the availability of idle resources. This motivates the need for adaptation to exploit the currently available idle resources. TPC defines target table to map the current load value to its corresponding target completion time. When load increases, TPC chooses a larger target because the system has fewer spare sources. It parallelizes requests less aggressively and uses spare resources for really long requests only. This section describes a systematic way to construct the target table, which searches the desired targets across loads using gradient descent method. Our algorithm is applicable to a variety of system load metrics, such as request arrival rate, number of active threads, and processor utilization.

We formally represent the target table Φ as a list of (load, target) pairs with m entries, *i.e.*, $\Phi = [(d_0, e_0), ..., (d_i, e_i), ..., (d_{m-1}, e_{m-1})]$. Here (d_i, e_i) denotes a (load, target) pair and the loads are sorted in ascending order, *i.e.*, $d_{i-1} < d_i$. For a given instantaneous load d, TPC chooses a target value $E = e_i$ such that $d_{i-1} < d \leq d_i$.

Algorithm 1 describes the procedure — BUILDTARGETTABLE — that searches for the desired target completion times across loads and builds the target table. Instead of using exhaustive search, which is costly, we develop an efficient heuristic algorithm using greedy gradient descent method. The algorithm takes two inputs: an initial target table and the search step size. For example, when using the number of active threads as load metric, the initial table consists of load values $\{d_i\}$ ranging from $0, 1, 2, ..., \hat{d}, \infty$. Here $\hat{d}$ is the maximum number of active threads observed under the production setting. The entry ∞ maps to any load $d > \hat{d}$. Moreover, we initialize the targets $\{e_i\}$ in the table to a set of small values, *e.g.*, the latency of an unloaded system where every single request is parallelized using all cores, which gives the smallest target we may ever achieve.

BUILDTARGETTABLE searches for the desired target values iteratively using gradient descent method. Starting from the initial table, we increase the target value of each load entry one by one with step size δ (Line 7) and measure the latency impact of a set of new tables experimentally using MEASURETAIL (Line 8). MEASURETAIL is an experimental procedure that takes a target table as input, runs a predefined experiment to cover all production load ranges, and returns a weighted sum of their tail latencies across the load ranges. Among all the new tables $\{tmpTable_i\}$, we identify the one $tmpTable_{i^*}$ that gives the smallest tail latency (Line 10). If this latency is smaller than that of the current table, we update the target table to $tmpTable_{i^*}$ and continue the search (Line 12). Otherwise, if the current table has smaller latency, we stop the search and return the current table as our final target table (Line 15).

The complexity of BUILDTARGETTABLE is measured using the number of times MEASURETAIL is invoked. It is upper bounded by mE_{max}/δ, where E_{max} denotes the maximum latency target. In an interactive system like web search, the value of E_{max} is within a few hundred milliseconds. The step size δ presents a tradeoff between search time and search quality. We use 1ms in our experiments because it is the smallest unit for tail latency measurements. The result of E_{max}/δ bounds the number of iterations we take to complete the search in the while loop (Line 5). Comparing with exhaustive search incurring cost of $(E_{max}/\delta)^m$, our search algorithm is much more efficient. We demonstrate its effectiveness empirically in Section 4.

There are a few remarks related to target table construction. (1) Section 4.6 compares several system load metrics and shows the number of active threads of long queries is a good metric, which we use as default. (2) The target table can be computed periodically as system parameters change. (3) At web search clusters, the workloads are fairly evenly partitioned and well balanced across ISNs. Our experimen-

Algorithm 1 Algorithm for Target Table Construction

```
procedure BuildTargetTable(initial target table Φ0, step size δ)
    Φ = Φ0                                  ▷ initialize target table Φ
    m = |Φ|                                 ▷ get the number of entries of Φ
    curLatency = MeasureTail(Φ)
    while true do
        for i = 0; i < m; i++ do
            tmpTable_i = [(Φ.d_0, Φ.e_0), ..., (Φ.d_i, Φ.e_i + δ), ..., (Φ.d_{m-1}, Φ.e_{m-1})]
            newLatency_i = MeasureTail(tmpTable_i)
        end for
        i* = argmin_{0≤i<m}(newLatency_i)
        if newLatency_{i*} < curLatency then
            Φ = tmpTable_{i*}               ▷ update the table
            curLatency = newLatency_{i*}
        else
            return Φ;                       ▷ found the final target table
        end if
    end while
end procedure
```

tal results on a cluster of 40 ISNs show that these ISNs have the same target table.

Summary. TPC reduces server tail latency using three insights. (1) It coordinates request completion time using a common target, which is used to identify long requests that are likely to impact the tail, and thus accelerates them through parallelization. (2) It applies predictive parallelism to parallelize the majority of long requests from the beginning of request execution using minimum resources, and to execute short requests sequentially. (3) It exploits dynamic correction to speed up long requests mispredicted as short, further reducing the tail.

4. Experimental Evaluation

We implement TPC along with competing techniques in the index serving nodes (ISNs) of Microsoft Bing, and conduct evaluation using production workload. We show that TPC consistently outperforms prior work across loads in reducing tail latency. In a nutshell, TPC reduces both the 99th-percentile and 99.9th-percentile latency in the ISN by up to 40% compared to the best performing policy (Figure 4 and 5). Moreover, TPC reduces the 99th-percentile latency in a cluster of 40 ISNs by 29% from the best prior work (Figure 8(a)). The saved latency improves user experiences on multiple folds, including providing faster response, enabling extra capabilities such as better ranking, or using a larger web index size.

4.1 Experimental Setup and Methodology

Machine setup and workload. Each ISN machine has two 2.27GHz 6-core Intel Xeon processors with hyperthreading enabled for a total of 24 concurrent hardware threads. The ISN manages a 160 GB web index partition on SSD and uses 17 GB of memory to cache recently accessed web index data. The number of worker threads is set to 28 as a worker thread may occasionally block for disk or network I/O. The Windows OS scheduler dynamically schedules worker threads on the available cores.

We conduct experiments both on a single ISN and across a cluster of 40 ISNs. We employ a client that plays queries from a trace of 100K user queries using a Poisson process in an open loop. We vary the load by changing the query arrival rate, *i.e.*, queries per second (QPS). The cluster setup includes an aggregator as illustrated in Figure 1, and Section 4.5 discusses the cluster experiments. All other experiments are conducted using the single-ISN setup.

Algorithm	Information use		
	Predicted exec. time	System load	Para. efficiency
TPC	✓	✓	✓
AP	✗	✓	✓
Pred	✓	✗	✗
WQ-Linear	✗	✓	✗

Table 1. Information used in parallelism policies.

Policies for comparison. We compare TPC to the following parallelization strategies from prior work. Table 1 compares the information used in choosing the parallelism degree for a query.

- **AP**. Adaptive Parallelism (AP) approach [20] takes into account the average parallelism speedup of all queries and the waiting queue length. The algorithm chooses the parallelism degree for a query such that the total response time of all queries in the system is minimized.
- **Pred**. Pred [21] predicts query execution time using machine learning to parallelize long queries using a *fixed* parallelism degree. All other queries are executed sequentially.
- **WQ-Linear**. Work Queue Linear (WQ-Linear) [33] considers only system load, which is the number of queries waiting in the queue. Queries are parallelized with a degree inversely proportional to the system load.
- **Sequential**. Baseline system with sequential execution.

TPC and Pred use a state-of-art predictor [21], which is memory efficient and achieves high accuracy as explained in Section 2.5. As queries executed across ISNs share common characteristics and features, we build the predictor from one selected ISN and distribute it to all ISNs. Therefore, the cost of building the predictor is constant and not affected by the size of cluster.

We limit the maximum parallelism degree to six in TPC and AP. TPC measures system load using the number of active threads running long queries, and it uses the number of idle worker threads as the available resources for dynamic correction. To model parallelism efficiency, queries are classified into three groups, short (<30 ms), mid (30–80 ms), and long (>80 ms) as depicted in Figure 2. We discuss other groupings and load metrics in the sensitivity study in Section 4.6.

Performance metrics. We use the *99th-percentile* (P99) and *99.9th-percentile* (P99.9) of query response time as the tail latency metrics. Query response time of the ISN or the cluster is measured from the time it receives the query to the time it responds to the client. We do not report response quality (*i.e.*, relevance scores) because parallelism decisions do not affect the response quality [20].

4.2 Comparison to Competing Techniques

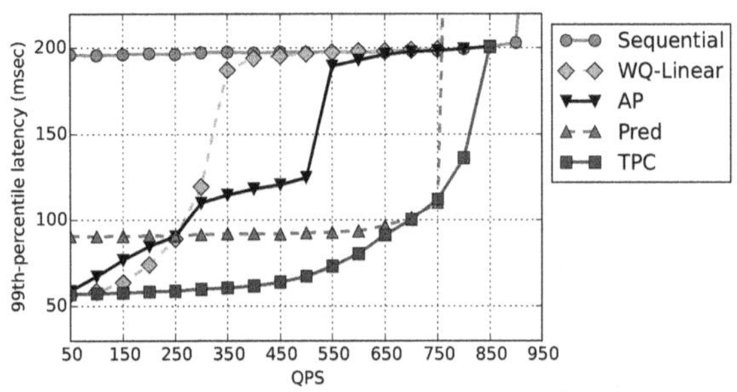

Figure 4. 99th-percentile latency for parallelism policies.

We compare TPC with AP, Pred and WQ-Linear to show the importance of using both query and system load information in TPC. Figure 4 presents P99 latencies of the policies. We vary the load over a wide range from 50 to 900 QPS over the x-axis. For Pred, queries predicted to execute longer than 80 ms run with 3-way parallelism following the reported guidelines [21].

Exploiting predicted query execution time. Figure 4 shows that using per-query information, both TPC and Pred significantly reduce tail latency even at moderate and heavy load. For example, in the range of 500–700 QPS, TPC and Pred achieve approximately 100 ms at P99, while all other approaches have 200 ms or higher P99 latency. TPC and Pred achieve such low tail latencies by parallelizing long queries only; avoiding parallelizing short queries gives more resources to long queries. In contrast, WQ-Linear and AP have high tail latencies since they do not differentiate long and short queries that have different parallelization efficiency and different impact on tail latency. Thus, as load increases, they reduce the parallelism degree for all queries, but short queries may still get parallelized unnecessarily, wasting resources, and long queries are not sufficiently parallelized.

Table 2 shows the query parallelism degree distribution for TPC and AP at low (150 QPS) and high (600 QPS) load. Due to high prediction accuracy, TPC is able to parallelize long queries with high degrees in both loads. At 150 QPS, 98.1% of long queries exploit the maximum degree 6. While

QPS	Policy	Group	1T	2T	3T	4T	5T	6T
150	TPC	Short	93.7	0.8	0.5	0.5	0.3	4.2
		Long	0	0	0.4	0.5	1.0	98.1
	AP	Short	0	1.5	30.5	43.9	15.1	9.0
		Long	0	1.5	29.8	44.9	14.4	9.4
	Pred	Short	98.1	0	1.9	0	0	0
		Long	18.6	0	81.4	0	0	0
600	TPC	Short	96.8	0.6	0.4	0.3	0.2	1.7
		Long	0.3	2.5	5.5	8.4	10.3	73.0
	AP	Short	57.0	42.1	0.9	0	0	0
		Long	55.5	43.3	1.2	0	0	0
	Pred	Short	98.1	0	1.9	0	0	0
		Long	18.6	0	81.4	0	0	0

Table 2. Parallelism degree distribution by percentages.

the ratio decreases to 73% at high load, up to 91.7% of long queries are parallelized with fairly high degrees (>3). Moreover, short queries are rarely parallelized. In contrast, AP gives short and long queries the same parallelism. Thus, long queries receive fewer parallelism degree and less resources compared with TPC. The situation gets worse at higher load: At 600 QPS, 98.8% of long queries are executed with 1 or 2 threads.

Exploiting system load. TPC and Pred have similar tail latency under heavy load, but TPC reduces tail latency from 100 ms of Pred to 60 ms under low to moderate load. The reason is that Pred does not adapt to varying system load and it always parallelizes long queries using the same parallelism degree. In comparison, TPC has more flexibility; it decides which queries to parallelize and by how much according to system load.

We use Table 2 to compare TPC to Pred in detail. At 150 QPS, TPC selects a higher degree for long queries than Pred. Interestingly, even those long queries that are mispredicted as medium or short are often given high degree if idle cores are available. Moreover, unlike Pred, TPC can select any degree among the possible options for better performance. For example, at 600 QPS, although TPC still prefers high parallelism degree for long queries, it exploits all parallel degrees to execute long queries, adapting to transient overload or underload. This adaptation allows TPC to perform better than Pred, which uses fixed parallelism for long queries.

In summary, these results show that it is essential to use both predicted query execution time and adapting to system load to reduce tail latency.

4.3 Using Predictive Parallelism Alone

We discuss if predictive parallelism alone is adequate. Figure 5 compares TPC with the prior policies with respect to a higher-percentile latency, *i.e.*, P99.9. Optimizing for the higher tail at each ISN is important because to reduce tail latency at the aggregator, we need to reduce a much higher percentile at each ISN (further details in Section 4.5). Figure 5 shows that TPC provides the lowest P99.9 latency, outperforming all other policies. Under moderate and high

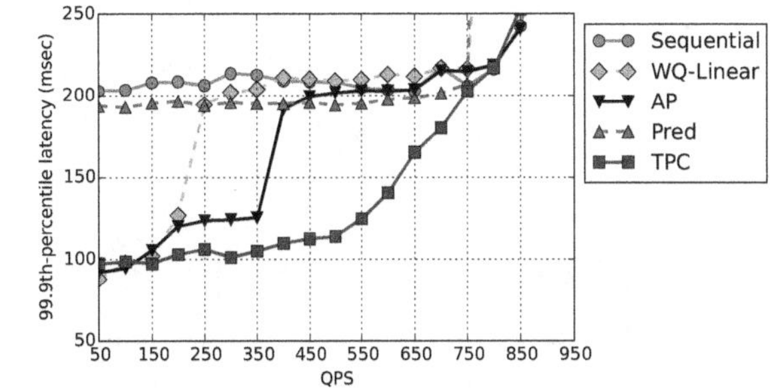

Figure 5. 99.9th-percentile latency for parallelism policies.

load (>400 QPS), TPC reduces the P99.9 latency by up to 40% compared with the best results from prior work. More specifically, the relative latency gap from AP and WQ-linear to TPC is similar to that for the P99 latency (Figure 4). Pred, however, performs poorly at P99.9, almost as high as Sequential, for all the loads, although Pred performs reasonably well for P99 latency.

The primary reason for a big difference on the performance of Pred with respect to the P99 and P99.9 latency is the limited accuracy of the predictor. As discussed in Section 2.5, assuming a tail latency target of 80 ms, which is set for Pred, some long queries are misidentified as short, and they constitute 0.56% of total queries. These queries do not affect P99 (as they are less than 1%) but P99.9 (as they are more than 0.1%). This is why Pred, which uses prediction only, performs poorly for the higher percentile latency. In contrast, TPC uses dynamic correction to recover from prediction errors, effectively reducing the higher tail latency.

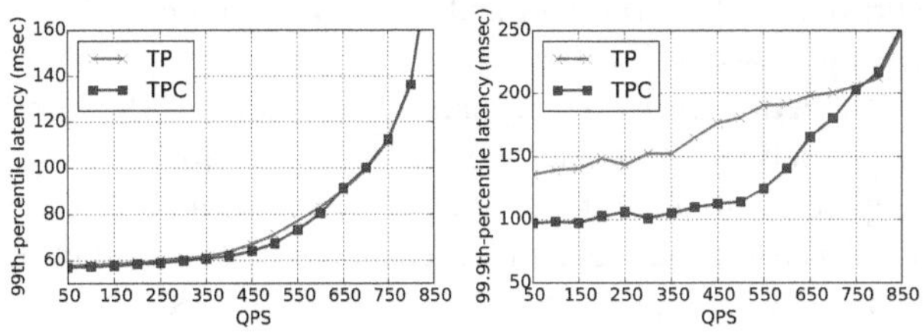

(a) 99th-percentile latency

(b) 99.9th-percentile latency

Figure 6. Tail latency for TP and TPC.

To measure the contribution of dynamic correction at TPC, we compare it with TP, which is the same as TPC but does not employ dynamic correction. Figure 6(a) and 6(b) show the P99 and P99.9 latency, respectively, TPC and TP. As expected, for P99 latency, they perform almost the same since prediction is accurate enough to reduce P99 range. However, TPC is better in P99.9 latency. As Figure 6(b) shows, dynamic correction reduces P99.9 by 40–65 ms more than TP. The analysis on the query parallelism degree distribution shows that adding dynamic correction increases the percentage of the long queries parallelized with high degrees (> 3) from 95% to 99.5% at 150 QPS and from 79.2% to 91.7% at 600 QPS.

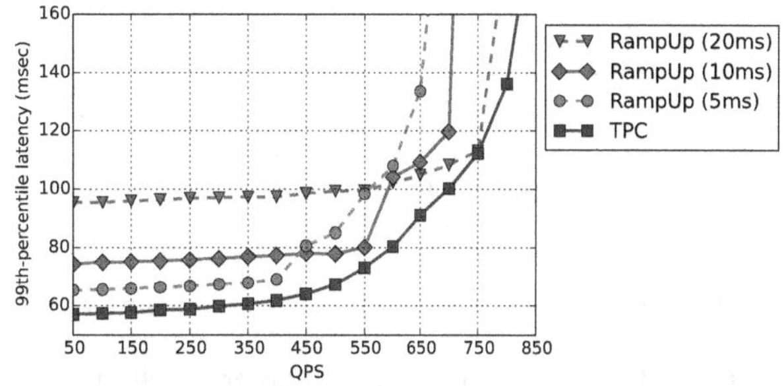

Figure 7. 99th-percentile latency of TPC and RampUp.

4.4 Using Dynamic Correction Alone

This section compares TPC with the policies that employ dynamic correction without prediction, in order to study how dynamic correction alone performs. We introduce policies that increase the query parallelism degree dynamically during its execution, which we call RampUp. RampUp starts a query with sequential execution. Then, if the query does not complete in a predefined time interval, it increases the query parallelism degree by 1 until the query either completes or reaches its maximum parallelism degree (which is set to six). Using RampUp, short queries complete sequentially, while long queries get higher parallelism and more resources. It achieves the goal of parallelizing long queries without knowing query execution time. We use different thread ramp-up intervals (5, 10, and 20 ms) to evaluate RampUp. For example, an interval of 5 ms means that we add a thread to the query at each 5 ms of execution up to 6 threads per query. The smaller the interval is, the higher the parallelism degree the query receives.

Figure 7 compares TPC with RampUp for P99 and shows that TPC achieves lower latency than RampUp for a large range of loads. TPC outperforms RampUp because it accurately predicts query execution time, making parallelism decision early before executing a long query, whereas RampUp intrinsically has delay in increasing parallelism, resulting in higher latency. To reduce the delay, RampUp has to add up parallelism quickly (*e.g.*, at every 5 ms interval). It effectively reduces tail latency at light load, but this comes with high parallelism overhead at high load.

Even when the RampUp policy takes load into account, *i.e.*, using the best RampUp interval at any given load, the latency is still higher than TPC. The reason is that as long as the RampUp interval is not 0 (which is the case except very light load), it cannot parallelize the long queries from the very beginning and it takes longer to complete those queries than TPC. Compared to using RampUp with wide range of intervals, TPC outperforms the best RampUp strategy at every arrival rate across a large load range. For extremely lightly (or heavily) loaded systems, both RampUp and TPC execute queries with maximum parallelism (or sequentially).

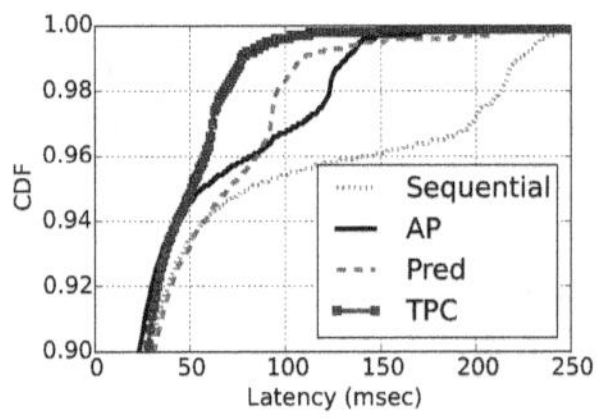

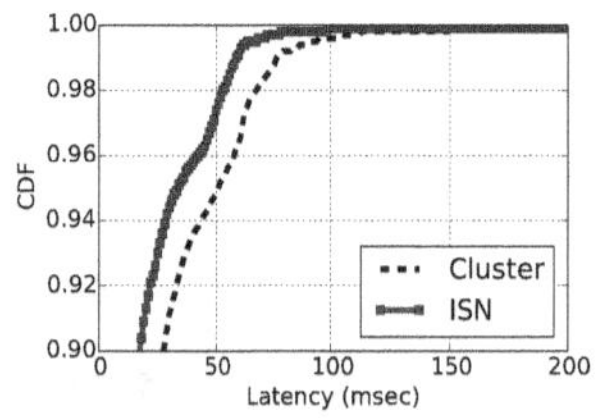

(a) Aggregator latency (b) ISN v.s. aggregator for TPC

Figure 8. CDF of latency for a cluster of 40 ISNs at 300 QPS (zoomed to high cumulative fractions).

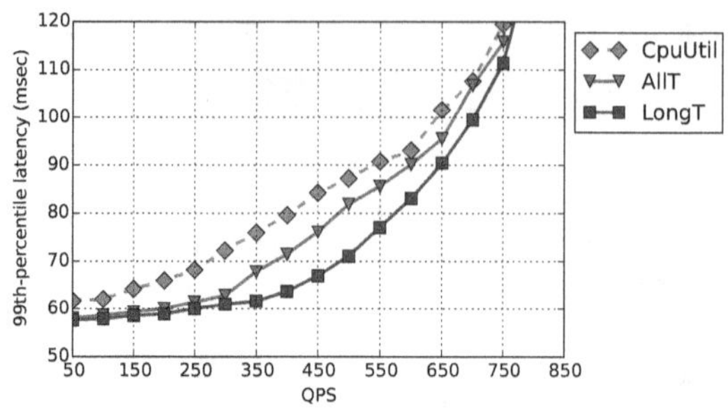

Figure 9. 99th-percentile latency of TPC for load metrics.

Both Section 4.3 and 4.4 show that using either predictive parallelism or dynamic parallelism alone is not sufficient. TPC integrates them to effectively lower tail latency.

4.5 Tail Latency in Cluster of ISN machines

This section discusses how TPC improves query responsiveness in a cluster of 40 ISNs. We compare four strategies (Sequential, AP, Pred, and TPC) and measure response times at an aggregator. For each query, the aggregator waits for all ISNs to collect and merge the results. The aggregator latency is thus decided by the slowest response from the ISNs. Latency at the aggregator includes network, I/O, and queueing delay as well as query processing at the ISNs.

Figure 8(a) shows the cumulative distribution of query response times from the aggregator at 300 QPS, where Y-axis depicts high cumulative probability fractions to focus on slowest query responses. The results show that TPC outperforms all other policies consistently over a wide range of tail latency targets, from P95 onwards, leading to much fewer slow responses at the aggregator. In particular, TPC has less than 0.4% of queries taking longer than 100 ms, whereas AP and Pred have 3.3% and 1.7%. Therefore TPC is the only policy that is able to lower P99 aggregator latency below 100 ms — P99 latency of AP, Pred, and TPC are 132.2, 108.9, and 77.7 ms, respectively. TPC reduces P99 aggregator latency by 29% compared with the best performing approach from prior work.

Next, Figure 8(b) compares cumulative distributions for the latency of TPC at the aggregator and an individual ISN. As the figure shows, in order to reduce tail latency at the aggregator, we need to reduce latency of higher tail at the ISN. For example, the latency of 77.7 ms, which we observe in P99 at the aggregator, appears at the P99.8 at the ISN. This indicates that taming P99 aggregator latency requires reducing P99.8 ISN latency, which is higher tail.

4.6 Sensitivity Study

System load metric. Figure 9 compares various metrics for identifying instantaneous system load. We show the results of our baseline (using the number of active long threads (LongT)), and two alternatives (using CPU utilization (CpuUtil) and the total number of active threads (AllT)). The server retrieves CpuUtil by sending a query to Windows performance counters periodically, for which we use Performance Data Helper (PDH) APIs [30]. The intervals are set to 25 ms in our system considering a tradeoff between more accurate information and lower overhead.

Because CpuUtil is a moving average heavily weighted from the past, Figure 9 shows that it performs worse than other two metrics in capturing instantaneous system load. The performance of CpuUtil becomes worse with increased load, as more queries are aggregated in a sampling interval. For example, under 100 QPS, the utilization for 3 past queries may be aggregated. However, under 500 QPS, that for 13 past queries may be aggregated, more likely misrepresenting the instantaneous load.

In contrast, accounting for the number of active threads is a good proxy to measure instantaneous system load. In particular, LongT is the best because threads running long queries are more likely to stay longer in the system, affecting the resource availability of the newly scheduled query, while short queries are transient and could have completed right after the new queries start.

Prediction accuracy. Dynamic correction in TPC recovers prediction errors and helps cover the performance gap compared with a perfect predictor. We mimic a perfect predictor by using the sequential execution time collected in advance for each input query. We compare TPC using its current predictor with using the perfect predictor, and the results show that they perform rather similarly. More specifically, at P99, the performance difference between using the current predictor and the perfect predictor is only 4.0% on average across all loads. For much higher percentiles, dynamic correction helps to recover from prediction errors and reduce the performance gap. For example, their performance difference in P99.9 is 7.8% on average across the loads. This is a significant improvement over TP (*i.e.*, TPC without dynamic correction): TP has 44.1% higher latency than using the perfect predictor. These results show that dynamic correction effectively compensates prediction error, making TPC more resilient to inaccurate predictors.

The number of parallelism efficiency groups. With more groups, predictive parallelism can potentially apply more accurate speedup efficiency information given query execution time. For example, by grouping queries into long, mid, and short separately, we obtain more latency reduction than treating all queries indifferently. However, when we increase from 3 groups to 6 groups (we obtain 6 groups by evenly dividing each of the 3 groups into 2 subgroups), no further improvement exists — the most improvement we observe across loads is 0.65%. This is because the speedup profiles of queries among neighboring groups have become similar when we divide the groups even further. It supports why our algorithms use parallelism efficiency profiles of 3 groups.

5. Applicability Beyond Web Search

This section summarizes the properties of the interactive workloads where TPC can effectively reduce tail latency. We show that another application — a finance server — satisfies these properties, and TPC reduces its P99 by 52% compared with sequential execution and by 20% compared to the best prior work.

TPC preferred workload properties. (1) CPU processing dominates the latency, (2) Request service demands exhibit high variability, (3) Requests are parallelizable and the parallelism degree can vary at runtime, and (4) Per-request execution time can be estimated before running the request.

Discussion. Several interactive services are often computationally intensive [14, 27, 34]. Increasing the degree of parallelism is supported by several threading frameworks and runtimes, such as Cilk Plus [5], TBB [7], and TPL [25]. If the request service demand is constant, tail latency becomes lower and there is little opportunity to differentiate processing among requests. On the other hand, the higher the variability, the higher the tail latency, leading to bigger benefits from TPC. Request service demand can be known or estimated in several settings [17, 41].

5.1 Evaluation Using a Finance Server

Banks and fund management companies evaluate thousands of financial derivatives everyday, submitting requests that value derivatives and use the results to make immediate trading decisions. Finance servers are interactive and reducing their tail latency is crucial because slower responses are lost investment opportunities. We use Intel TBB runtime to parallelize request execution and evaluate TPC on finance servers.

Workload. We implement an option pricing server that uses Monte Carlo methods for complex path-dependent Asian options. Request processing is CPU-bound, has a regular structure, and consists of iterations. Request sequential execution time can be estimated accurately (as a function of the structure size and number of iterations). To parallelize a request, we fork a number of tasks at each iteration matching the parallelism degree and join them after the computation.

Experimental setup. For evaluation, input requests contain 10% long requests, for which the service demand is 9 times that of a short request, and requests are issued following a Poisson distribution. We vary the load by controlling the mean inter-arrival rate of requests, *i.e.*, requests per second (RPS). We compare TPC to two parallelization policies, AP and Pred, and to Sequential for reference. In both TPC and AP, the maximum degree of parallelism is four. Pred does not adjust to the load, and we use its best setting with parallelism degree two for long requests.

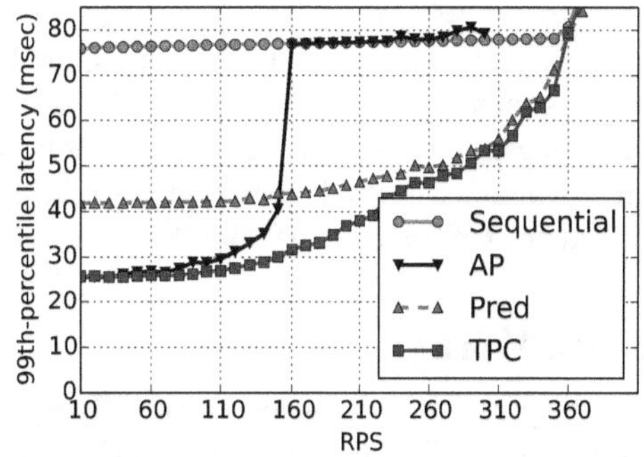

Figure 10. 99th-percentile latency for finance server.

Experimental results. TPC consistently outperforms the three other policies over a wide range of loads as depicted in Figure 10, which shows P99 latency. At light and moderate load, TPC reduces the tail latency over Pred by up to 40% because TPC exploits system load and uses the available resources more aggressively in speeding up long requests. At high load, TPC reduces the tail latency over AP by up to 50% because TPC exploits per-request predicted execution time to parallelize long requests only.

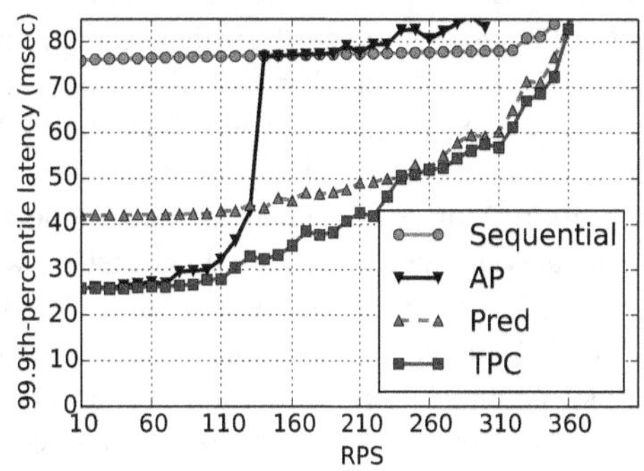

Figure 11. 99.9th-percentile latency for finance server.

Figure 11 depicts P99.9 latency, which has a similar trend as P99. While web search requires dynamic correction to reduce P99.9 to recover from prediction errors, the finance server never calls dynamic correction because the estimated stencil computation time is accurate. At 200 RPS, with TPC, there are on average 3.5 concurrent requests in the system competing for server resources. At this load, TPC runs short requests sequentially and long requests with degree four resulting in short tail latency (P99=37 ms, P99.9=41 ms). In contrast, AP (which does not exploit the request service demand) runs all requests with average degree 3.9, resulting in high tail latency (P99=77 ms, P99.9=79 ms) as extra CPU resources are needed to parallelize short requests. Pred (which does not use system load to adapt the parallelism degree) runs short requests sequentially but executes long request with degree two rather than a higher degree, contributing to higher tail latency (P99=46 ms, P99.9=48 ms).

6. Related Work

Section 4 compares TPC with several recent algorithms that decide request parallelism degree on interactive server systems, and we do not repeat them here. Prior work shows how to adapt parallel program execution to runtime variability and hardware characteristics [4, 16, 24, 28, 31] either to improve performance of a single program or to reduce average latency on a multiprogrammed environment where job characteristics are unknown a priori. This work addresses a different problem, and we focus on interactive server systems such as web search.

Search query parallelization. Frachtenberg [12] proposes a heuristic to predict which queries to parallelize based on runtime information. Query first runs sequentially for a subset of the index partition, and the ratio of hits to documents is determined. If the ratio is above a threshold, the query is assumed to have good parallelization speedup and is then parallelized; otherwise, the query runs sequentially. Haque *et al.* propose few-to-many incremental parallelism, which dynamically increases parallelism to reduce tail latency [15]. This approach is similar to using load-aware RampUp but without prediction. Compared with TPC, long queries under the above two approaches do not get the resources to speed up their execution at the earliest possible time. It thus has a similar limitation with RampUp policy in Section 4, and we show that TPC provides lower tail latencies by combining prediction with dynamic correction. Moreover, their work uses the total number of instantaneous queries as their load metric, which is coarse-grained. We propose a more general table construction method that allows various (coarse- and fine-grained) load metrics, enabling additional latency savings (Figure 9). Tatikonda *et al.* propose a fine-grained intra-query parallelism approach [36], which has some similarities to how we parallelize a query. However, this paper does not discuss how to decide the parallelism degree, which is the focus of this work.

Predicting query execution time for search engine. Macdonald *et al.* [26] propose a framework to predict execution time of web search queries under early termination. Jeon *et al.* [21] improve upon the prior query predictor [26] by incorporating more features, query rewriting, and boosted-tree regressor, resulting in better accuracy. Our work uses the predictor proposed in [21] to predict query execution time.

Other techniques for reducing response times in interactive services. In web search, graphics processors (GPU) [10], SIMD instructions [35], and core frequency scaling [18] have been used to accelerate the processing of a query. In particular, core frequency scaling offers a complementary acceleration mechanism to reduce tail latency [18]. Parallelism can achieve additional speedup beyond a single core, and this potential speedup comes with a key challenge: competition among concurrent queries for cores, which we address in this work.

There are studies on reducing the response time for web search queries across different system components, for example, optimizing caching [2, 13] and prefetching [22] to mitigate I/O costs and improving network protocols between ISNs and aggregators [37, 40]. Moreover, response quality can be traded off to reduce response time, especially under heavy load or other exceptional situations in which the servers could not process queries fast enough [6]. For the case where other sources of variability, such as interference from other workloads and hardware variability, contribute to tail latency, Dean *et al.* [9] propose to submit multiple copies of a query to different replicas, and cancel the slower query. These studies are complementary to our work.

Today's data analytics clusters have been optimized to offer timely responses for parallel jobs [32, 39]. Compared to web search, their framework is fundamentally different: Schedulers are often decentralized and pick a set of machines to serve a scheduled job. They reduce latency by sampling the machine status and improving the assignment of jobs to machines.

7. Conclusions

Interactive services are designed to reduce the tail latency of user requests. We introduce TPC, a new algorithm that determines request parallelism degree by combining predictive parallelism and dynamic correction. We evaluate TPC experimentally on both web search and finance servers. The results show that it significantly reduces the tail latency compared with prior work.

Acknowledgments

We thank anonymous reviewers for their valuable comments and suggestions. We also thank Chenyu Yan, Fang Liu, Jun Zhao, and Junhua Wang from Microsoft Bing for their collaboration and support during this work.

References

[1] M.-C. Albutiu, A. Kemper, and T. Neumann. Massively parallel sort-merge joins in main memory multi-core database systems. *VLDB*, 5(10):1064–1075, June 2012.

[2] R. Baeza-Yates, A. Gionis, F. Junqueira, V. Murdock, V. Plachouras, and F. Silvestri. The impact of caching on search engines. In *SIGIR*, 2007.

[3] L. A. Barroso, J. Dean, and U. Hölzle. Web search for a planet: The google cluster architecture. *IEEE Micro*, 23(2):22–28, Mar. 2003.

[4] F. Blagojevic, D. S. Nikolopoulos, A. Stamatakis, C. D. Antonopoulos, and M. Curtis-Maury. Runtime scheduling of dynamic parallelism on accelerator-based multi-core systems. *Parallel Comput.*, 33(10-11):700–719, Nov. 2007.

[5] R. D. Blumofe, C. F. Joerg, B. C. Kuszmaul, C. E. Leiserson, K. H. Randall, and Y. Zhou. Cilk: An efficient multithreaded runtime system. In *PPOPP*, 1995.

[6] B. B. Cambazoglu, F. P. Junqueira, V. Plachouras, S. Banachowski, B. Cui, S. Lim, and B. Bridge. A refreshing perspective of search engine caching. In *WWW*, 2010.

[7] G. Contreras and M. Martonosi. Characterizing and improving the performance of intel threading building blocks. In *IISWC*, 2008.

[8] J. Dean. Challenges in building large-scale information retrieval systems: invited talk. In *WSDM*, 2009.

[9] J. Dean and L. A. Barroso. The tail at scale. *Commun. ACM*, 56(2):74–80, Feb. 2013.

[10] S. Ding, J. He, H. Yan, and T. Suel. Using graphics processors for high performance ir query processing. In *WWW*, 2009.

[11] S. Eyerman and L. Eeckhout. The benefit of smt in the multi-core era: Flexibility towards degrees of thread-level parallelism. In *ASPLOS*, 2014.

[12] E. Frachtenberg. Reducing query latencies in web search using fine-grained parallelism. In *WWW*, 2009.

[13] Q. Gan and T. Suel. Improved techniques for result caching in web search engines. In *WWW*, 2009.

[14] R. Guida. Parallelizing a computationally intensive financial r application with zircon technology. In *The R User Conference*, 2010.

[15] M. E. Haque, Y. H. Eom, Y. He, S. Elnikety, R. Bianchini, and K. S. McKinley. Few-to-many: Incremental parallelism for reducing tail latency in interactive services. In *ASPLOS*, 2015.

[16] Y. He, W.-J. Hsu, and C. E. Leiserson. Provably efficient online nonclairvoyant adaptive scheduling. *IEEE Trans. Parallel Distrib. Syst.*, 19(9):1263–1279, Sept. 2008.

[17] Y. He, S. Elnikety, and H. Sun. Tians scheduling: Using partial processing in best-effort applications. In *ICDCS*, 2011.

[18] C.-H. Hsu, Y. Zhang, M. A. Laurenzano, D. Meisner, T. Wenisch, J. Mars, L. Tang, and R. G. Dreslinski. Adrenaline: Pinpointing and reining in tail queries with quick voltage boosting. In *HPCA*, 2015.

[19] V. Jalaparti, P. Bodik, S. Kandula, I. Menache, M. Rybalkin, and C. Yan. Speeding up distributed request-response workflows. In *SIGCOMM '13*, 2013.

[20] M. Jeon, Y. He, S. Elnikety, A. L. Cox, and S. Rixner. Adaptive parallelism for web search. In *EuroSys '13*, 2013.

[21] M. Jeon, S. Kim, S.-W. Hwang, Y. He, S. Elnikety, A. L. Cox, and S. Rixner. Predictive parallelization: Taming tail latencies in web search. In *SIGIR*, 2014.

[22] S. Jonassen, B. B. Cambazoglu, and F. Silvestri. Prefetching query results and its impact on search engines. In *SIGIR*, 2012.

[23] J. Kwon, K.-W. Kim, S. Paik, J. Lee, and C.-G. Lee. Multi-core scheduling of parallel real-time tasks with multiple parallelization options. In *RTAS*, 2015.

[24] J. Lee, H. Wu, M. Ravichandran, and N. Clark. Thread tailor: dynamically weaving threads together for efficient, adaptive parallel applications. In *ISCA*, 2010.

[25] D. Leijen, W. Schulte, and S. Burckhardt. The design of a task parallel library. In *OOPSLA*, 2009.

[26] C. Macdonald, N. Tonellotto, and I. Ounis. Learning to predict response times for online query scheduling. In *SIGIR*, 2012.

[27] J. Mars, L. Tang, R. Hundt, K. Skadron, and M. L. Soffa. Bubble-up: increasing utilization in modern warehouse scale computers via sensible co-locations. In *MICRO*, 2011.

[28] C. McCann, R. Vaswani, and J. Zahorjan. A dynamic processor allocation policy for multiprogrammed shared-memory multiprocessors. *ACM Trans. Comput. Syst.*, 11(2):146–178, May 1993.

[29] D. Meisner, C. M. Sadler, L. A. Barroso, W.-D. Weber, and T. F. Wenisch. Power management of online data-intensive services. In *ISCA*, 2011.

[30] MSDN. Using the pdh functions to consume counter data. `http://msdn.microsoft.com/en-us/library/windows/desktop/aa373214(v=vs.85).aspx`.

[31] S. C. Muller, G. Alonso, A. Amara, and A. Csillaghy. Pydron: Semi-automatic parallelization for multi-core and the cloud. In *OSDI*, 2014.

[32] K. Ousterhout, P. Wendell, M. Zaharia, and I. Stoica. Sparrow: Distributed, low latency scheduling. In *SOSP*, 2013.

[33] A. Raman, H. Kim, T. Oh, J. W. Lee, and D. I. August. Parallelism orchestration using dope: the degree of parallelism executive. In *PLDI*, 2011.

[34] S. Ren, Y. He, S. Elnikety, and K. S. McKinley. Exploiting processor heterogeneity in interactive services. In *ICAC*, 2013.

[35] B. Schlegel, T. Willhalm, and W. Lehner. Fast sorted-set intersection using simd instructions. In *ADMS*, 2011.

[36] S. Tatikonda, B. B. Cambazoglu, and F. P. Junqueira. Posting list intersection on multicore architectures. In *SIGIR*, 2011.

[37] B. Vamanan, J. Hasan, and T. Vijaykumar. Deadline-aware datacenter tcp (d2tcp). In *SIGCOMM*, 2012.

[38] K. Veeraraghavan, D. Lee, B. Wester, J. Ouyang, P. M. Chen, J. Flinn, and S. Narayanasamy. Doubleplay: Parallelizing sequential logging and replay. In *ASPLOS*, 2011.

[39] S. Venkataraman, A. Panda, G. Ananthanarayanan, M. J. Franklin, and I. Stoica. The power of choice in data-aware cluster scheduling. In *OSDI*, 2014.

[40] C. Wilson, H. Ballani, T. Karagiannis, and A. Rowtron. Better never than late: meeting deadlines in datacenter networks. In *SIGCOMM*, 2011.

[41] Y. Zhu and V. J. Reddi. High-performance and energy-efficient mobile web browsing on big/little systems. In *HPCA*, 2013.

How to Build Static Checking Systems Using Orders of Magnitude Less Code

Fraser Brown Andres Nötzli Dawson Engler

Stanford University

{mlfbrown,noetzli,engler}@stanford.edu

Abstract

Modern static bug finding tools are complex. They typically consist of hundreds of thousands of lines of code, and most of them are wedded to one language (or even one compiler). This complexity makes the systems hard to understand, hard to debug, and hard to retarget to new languages, thereby dramatically limiting their scope.

This paper reduces the complexity of the checking system by addressing a fundamental assumption, the assumption that checkers must depend on a full-blown language specification and compiler front end. Instead, our program checkers are based on drastically incomplete language grammars ("micro-grammars") that describe only portions of a language relevant to a checker. As a result, our implementation is tiny—roughly 2500 lines of code, about two orders of magnitude smaller than a typical system. We hope that this dramatic increase in simplicity will allow developers to use more checkers on more systems in more languages.

We implement our approach in µchex, a language-agnostic framework for writing static bug checkers. We use it to build micro-grammar based checkers for six languages (C, the C preprocessor, C++, Java, JavaScript, and Dart) and find over 700 errors in real-world projects.

Categories and Subject Descriptors F.3.2 [*Semantics of Programming Languages*]: Program analysis; D.3.4 [*Processors*]: Parsing

Keywords Micro-grammars; Parsing; Bug Finding; Static Analysis

1. Introduction

Research on bug finding has exploded in the past couple decades. While researchers have explored many approaches, the dominant, near-universal trend has been towards increasing complexity. The unsound dataflow analysis of early tools has given way to SAT solvers, theorem provers, and full-blown symbolic execution. While these new systems find interesting bugs, they also miss bugs due to their complexity. The more complex a tool is: the worse it scales; the harder it is to debug and understand; and the more assumptions it makes, limiting the programs it can check.

Our own work has followed this standard path, going from static analysis to symbolic execution. The complaints above are drawn both from our own difficulties dealing with the day-to-day cost of increasing complexity and from commiserations with other researchers. As a personal data point, the inherent difficulty in reasoning about symbolic execution—where each judgment is typically the result of thousands of previous low-level, feedback-directed decisions—meant that we once spent about six months uneasily trying to replicate *our own* results with *our own* tool with only mixed success [18]. As another, we have even struggled with the simpler approach of static analysis. During development, a commercial tool from our group switched the order in which it traversed the true and false branches of an `if` statement, leading to a disturbing change in the set of bugs the tool found (and missed). "Fixing" the problem was deemed too difficult, and the developers just rolled back the change, forfeiting the new bugs that it had found [6].

This paper is our reaction to these (and other) bitter experiences, and to the metastizing complexity throughout the field. We have taken the simplest bug finding approach—static analysis—and further reduced its complexity by about two orders of magnitude. This reduction is mostly due to one technical innovation, a new approach to parsing based on dramatically incomplete *micro-grammars*. Instead of depending on a full-blown language specification and compiler front end, our checkers are deliberately based on micro-grammars, partial grammars designed to extract checker-specific features that later passes analyze for bugs. Our checkers are often less than forty lines of code, and the parsers that they run on are less than 200. Checking an entirely new language—building its checker and associated

ASPLOS '16 April 2–6, 2016, Atlanta, Georgia, USA.
Copyright © 2016 ACM 978-1-4503-4091-5/16/04. . . $15.00
DOI: http://dx.doi.org/10.1145/2872362.2872364

parser—might take merely a couple hours. We have written such checkers for C, C preprocessor, C++, Java, JavaScript, and Dart code. Furthermore, because our system uses micro-grammars instead of parsing and defining an entire language, it is tiny itself—roughly 2500 lines of code. It is not hard to understand a system that you can print on a dozen sheets of paper. As a result, it is not hard to customize, extend, rewrite, or reimplement that system. We hope that this stark simplification will allow more people to build and use static bug finders.

The main intellectual contribution of this paper is the concept of micro-grammars, along with techniques to define them in a principled way. Our main experimental results:

1. The approach works: as Table 1 shows, it is general and robust enough to find over 700 bugs in widely-used systems written in six different languages.
2. Despite ignoring most of the language, our checkers are not limited to checking simple syntactic properties. We reimplement two flow-sensitive checkers (§ 4) originally built using a traditional checking system, and show that despite being orders of magnitude simpler, they find a similar number of true bugs.
3. Micro-grammar checkers are not weak, and can help debug more sophisticated tools. When we check the same property as a state-of-the-art commercial tool and compare our results on the same code base, we find a roughly comparable number of bugs; we also find 190 bugs that the commercial tool misses. As a result, we think that our approach may be used as a safety net for more complex tools.
4. We repeatedly show (§ 5.1) that adopting an existing checker in our system to a new, previously unchecked language is a matter of writing a few lines of code (even when going from C++ to JavaScript!). Furthermore, writing a new checker from scratch is often in the tens of lines (§ 5.2). This ease is in contrast to traditional static checking systems, which, because of their detailed dependency on exact language semantics, might take months or years to retarget to a new language.
5. Micro-grammars allow us to run the exactly same checker and parser combination, unaltered, on many different languages (§ 6).

Checker	System	Bugs	False
Blocking while Locking	Linux (C)	124	0
Null Pointer	Linux (C)	233	12
	OpenJDK (Java)	42	3
	LLVM (C++)	10	1
	Firefox (C)	63	3
	Firefox (C++)	61	33
	Firefox (Java)	3	2
	Firefox (JavaScript)	25	6
	Node.js (JavaScript)	7	1
	All	444	61
Redundant Nested Macro Conditions	Linux (C macro)	7	0
	Firefox (C macro)	16	0
	All	23	0
Equals wo/ Hashcode	OpenJDK (Java)	73	2
	Dart SDK (Dart)	13	0
	All	93	2
Non-Observable Collection	Dart SDK (Dart)	2	0
Redundant Branches	Linux (C)	34	6
	OpenJDK (Java)	5 (8*)	1
	LLVM (C++)	2	0
	Firefox (C)	3	3
	Firefox (C++)	4	2
	All	48 (8*)	12
Redundant Conditions	Linux (C)	6	0
	OpenJDK (Java)	3	0
	Firefox (C++)	6	0
	LLVM (C++)	1	0
	All	16	0
Suspicious Loop Conditions	Linux (C)	5	2
	OpenJDK (Java)	2	0
	Firefox (C)	1	0
	Firefox (C++)	1	32‡
	LLVM (C++)	0	5
	Node.js (JavaScript)	2	0
	All	11	39
Total		761 (8*)	116
Spurious Null Check†	Dart SDK (Dart)	3	0
Incorrect Length Check†	Dart SDK (Dart)	152	0

* Generated code † Style and performance checkers
‡ Repeated patterns in related files

Table 1. Errors in all systems. We check Linux 4.4-rc7, Firefox 39.0, OpenJDK 8 b132, Node.js 0.12.7, LLVM 3.6.2 and Dart SDK 1.13.2 (including Core Libraries).

2. Overview

Traditional checking systems use front ends designed to parse a complete language grammar. These parsers reject any input that does not lead to a legal parse based on the full language specification. In contrast, our system is built on incomplete micro-grammars that intentionally ignore the vast majority of the input language.

Micro-grammar parsing differs from traditional parsing for bug finding in two ways:

1. A traditional parser returns an error (and perhaps tries to recover) when it fails to parse a program. In contrast, when a micro-grammar parser hits non-matching input, it simply slides forward by one token and tries again. This "sliding window" approach (similar to common regular expression matching) matches all constructs described by the micro-grammar and skips past those that the micro-grammar does not match. Ultimately, it consumes the entire input.

Component	Traditional	Using micro-grammars
Language	Full language grammar	Micro-grammar
Error handling	Exit or report	Advance one token, retry
Output	Complete representation	Incomplete representation

Table 2. Comparing our system to a traditional system.

2. Within a grammar rule, developers can perform fine-grained input skipping by using `wildcard` non-terminals—non-terminals that lazily match any input up to a suffix.

For example, we can write a micro-grammar that matches `if` statements but does not care about the details of expressions: "`S` → `if ( wildcard )`." When applied to a file with five `if` statements, the parser returns five parse trees. While a traditional parser creates a tree with (roughly) one node for every token, our parser returns a tree where lists of tokens match to each `wildcard` node. For example, parsing "`if (x == y)`" with the `if` statement micro-grammar would result in a normal `if` node and a `wildcard` node containing "`["x", "==", "y"]`". Table 2 summarizes these differences between our system and a traditional canonical one.

Implementation We implement the micro-grammar approach in μchex, a language-agnostic framework for writing static bug checkers. Like a traditional system, μchex breaks its input stream into tokens, feeds these lexed tokens to a parser, and runs a checker on the parser's output. In our system, though, checker developers can easily define their own lexers, parsers, and checkers, a process that sometimes takes less than a day (or even a couple hours). This shows one of the surprising benefits of ignoring most of a language; often, parts of languages overlap enough that they can share almost the same micro-grammar (§ 5 and § 6). Concretely, this means we can combine pieces of existing parsers and checkers to form new ones, even for syntactically different languages.

We now walk through how to check a new language from scratch. First, developers specify a lexer by supplying a list of keywords, operators, and a set of regular expressions for identifiers, literals, and comments. We use the Haskell Parsec library to make lexing easy; a typical specification is around ten lines of code [32].

Developers then build parsers recursively by defining a parser for each non-terminal and composing these parsers together to accept a micro-grammar. Adding a new non-terminal to a grammar equates to combining its parser with an existing one. For example, to create a parser for C's control flow, we first write parsers for `if` statements, `while` loops, `for` loops, etc. Each of these small parsers is around six lines of code, and we glue them together into a 156 line C control flow parser (Section 4.1.2 shows a concrete example of this process). The small parsers can be reused in other parsers; for example, our Dart control flow parser

Grammar	Parsec
`S → F B`	`s = f >> b`
`F → foo`	`f = rsrvd "foo"`
`B → bar | baz`	`b = rsrvd "bar" <|> rsrvd "baz"`

Figure 1. The context-free grammar and its Parsec equivalent on the right.

(§ 5.2.2) shares many parsers (and 75 lines of code) with the C version. For convenience, μchex ships with a library of combinable parsers.

The parsing step, like the lexing step, is built on top of the Haskell Parsec library. This compact (3475 LOC) parser combinator library supports infinite-lookahead parsers for $LL(k)$ grammars. It fits well with our approach because it makes combining parsers for different non-terminals easy. For example, Figure 1 shows how each non-terminal of a grammar can correspond to a single Parsec parser, and how those Parsec parsers can be combined.

Finally, users build checkers using μchex's framework, which provides a set of built-in functions for common checking operations. Though μchex supports generic checking, we have tuned it especially for "belief-style" checkers [20]. Beliefs are facts implied by code. For example, "`x/y`" implies a belief that `y` is non-zero and an unlock "`unlock(l)`" implies a belief that `l` is locked. In general, if we assume that a programmer does not intend to crash their program, then a given program statement implies that they believe the statement's preconditions hold. Therefore, contradicting beliefs signify errors.

In our system, the user implements a checking function that produces beliefs and then uses those beliefs to find bugs. μchex automatically applies the checking function to tree nodes and propagates the beliefs that it produces through the tree. It supports forward or backward flow-sensitive analyses as well as custom propagation methods. Users control how beliefs propagate through join points, and μchex provides libraries for computing domination and post-domination.

To repeat: while we present belief-style checkers in this paper, and support them in our framework, the micro-grammar approach is not limited to this type of checking. Furthermore, while we chose to implement the system in Haskell, our approach is not limited to this language; in fact, we wrote our initial system in Python. Both versions are comparable in size and our core result—the dramatic reduction in the size of the checking system—is caused by micro-grammars, not by a specific implementation.

3. Micro-grammars

We discuss practical aspects of micro-grammars in Section 3.1 and define them more formally in Section 3.2.

3.1 Parsing with micro-grammars

Below, we discuss how we implement the two distinctive features of our approach: the wildcard non-terminals that we use to selectively ignore parts of a language and the "sliding window" strategy that advances by one token when it fails to parse.

Wildcards The simplest wildcard rule that µchex implements is `SkipTo`, which skips tokens until it reaches a suffix `P`. We construct a `SkipTo` parser with semantics corresponding to the following grammar:

```
AnyToken   → token, token ∈ language
SkipTo(P)  → P | AnyToken SkipTo(P)
```

`AnyToken` matches any token in the input, and `SkipTo` matches the suffix `P` or `AnyToken` followed by `P`. The following micro-grammar uses `SkipTo` to accept any substring that contains one "a" followed by zero or more tokens and ending in "cd":

```
SkipB → a SkipTo(cd)
```

Given the input string "abcd", the `SkipB` production would accept, and its wildcard non-terminal would match "b". Given the input string "abc", however, the `SkipB` production would not match, since "abc" does not fully contain `SkipB`'s suffix ("cd").

Wildcard matching is lazy (as opposed to greedy), meaning that wildcards match the fewest number of tokens possible. Otherwise, any wildcard would necessarily consume the entire input. All wildcard rules (such as `SkipTo`) are parameterized by a suffix that defines the end of the wildcard matching. In our implementation, to decide whether a rule containing a wildcard applies, the parser does a lookahead and checks whether the rule suffix appears in the input. If not, that particular rule does not match. Tokens consumed by wildcard non-terminals are stored in special wildcard nodes in the parser output.

Sliding window approach When a µchex parser does not match, it slides forward by one token and retries; in other words, it always consumes the entire input, and matches input to productions whenever those productions accept. Without this mechanism, the parser might get stuck. For example, without "sliding window," `SkipB` fails to parse "XabcdXabcd", since the first token of the input is not "a". With it, parsing "XabcdXabcd" with `SkipB` returns two identical parse trees (and accepts the entire input string).

Our approach semantically corresponds to adding the following rule to a micro-grammar with the top symbol `P`:

```
P' → SkipTo(P) P' | ϵ
```

Commit points The "sliding window" approach allows micro-grammars to ignore irrelevant parts of the input language. Clearly, though, badly-written micro-grammars may ignore too much, thereby skipping input that is relevant to the checker. For example, early in the project, we defined a `try` parser (incorrectly) so that its wildcard non-terminal could never find its suffix. As a result, we marched through the input, ignoring `try`s and sliding forward one token until `eof`. We solved this problem with *commit points*, warnings that sound when parsers consume too much. Users create commit points by specifying *commit tokens*, tokens that must lead to a successful match of the rule in which they appear. After users create a commit point, the parser yells each time it "slides forward" after consuming the commit token (e.g. `try`).

Compositional parsers µchex implements a feature called *compositional parsers* that allows users combine parsers by applying one parser to the output of another. It is usually easier to write a grammar for two different constructs separately and later compose these grammars (as opposed to intermixing them into a single micro-grammar). For example, writing a grammar for `if` conditions and the expressions that they contain is far harder than writing a single grammar for `if` conditions and a single grammar for expressions. µchex takes advantage of this by allowing users to run parsers on the `wildcard` node output of other parsers. Applying parsers to `wildcard` nodes replaces those nodes with subtrees, but has no effect on the other, non-`wildcard` nodes. We walk through an example of compositional parsers in Section 4.1.1.

3.2 Defining micro-grammars

Micro-grammars capture portions of the input that interest the checker, such as `for` loops or `try` blocks. Checkers depend on these input snippets being parsed correctly; otherwise, the checkers might be wrong, since they are operating on a mis-parse. To avoid this problem, we intuitively want the micro-grammar's parse tree to look like a less detailed version of the original grammar's parse tree—a version with the same structure where some subtrees are replaced by `wildcard` nodes. We formalize this intuitive definition below. Later, we give an example of a micro-grammar that violates the definition and discuss how it confounds the checker.

Suppose we are interested in writing a checker for a certain construct (an `if` statement or `for` loop, for example) that appears in a language G, where $G = (N, \Sigma, R, S)$, with N its set of non-terminals, Σ its terminals, R its productions, and S a start symbol [29]. Also, suppose that the grammar is structured in such a way that there is a non-terminal $C \in N$ that that models our construct of interest. We say that $G' = (N', \Sigma, R', S')$ is a micro-grammar of G iff the following two conditions are met:

1. The language $L(G)$ accepted by G is a subset of the language $L(G')$ accepted by G'
2. Let `MATCH` be a function that takes a non-terminal P and some input X in $L(G)$, and returns the set of all substrings of X that are matched by P. We require that there is a non-terminal $C' \in N'$ so that $\texttt{MATCH}(C, X) \subseteq \texttt{MATCH}(C', X)$ for all $X \in L(G)$.

We need the first element of the definition because, without it, our parsers would get stuck on any input that did not match any rule. This would cause them to potentially miss check-able constructs later in the source code.

The second condition describes the fact that we want our micro-grammars to have the same overall structure as the original grammar, but with some subtrees replaced by `wildcard` nodes. To make `MATCH` concrete, consider a grammar G for a C-like language and its non-terminal `ifStmt` that matches `if` statements:

```
IfStmt → if '(' Expr ')' '{' Body '}'
```

If G accepts the following code snippet `Sentence`:

```
int x = 4, y = 5;
if(x == y) { return x; }
x++;
if(x < y) { if (x < 0) { return 0; } return y; }
```

Then `MATCH(IfStmt, Sentence)` is a list of three substrings:

```
[ "if(x == y) { return x; }",
  "if(x < y) { if (x < 0) { return 0; } return y; }",
  "if (x < 0) { return 0; }" ]
```

In the following paragraph, we walk through an example of an incorrect micro-grammar and its effect on the checker.

Incorrect micro-grammars We want to write a micro-grammar to check `if` conditions in a language defined by the following grammar:

```
S    → if Cond Expr ';'
Cond → '(' Expr ')'
Expr → '(' Expr ')' | Expr '+' Expr | IntLiteral
```

This grammar describes `if` statements that check integer expressions. Based on this full grammar, we might be tempted to create the following micro-grammar:

```
S'    → if Cond' SkipTo(';')
Cond' → '(' SkipTo(')')
```

The problem with this micro-grammar is that the rule for `Cond'` matches the first closing parenthesis that it encounters. For example, for the input "`if ((a + b) * c) ;`", `Cond'` matches "`((a + b)`", while the original non-terminal, `Cond`, matches the entire condition: "`((a + b) * c)`". As a result, our checker will check an `if` statement that does not actually exist in the source code ("`a + b`"), potentially yielding a false positive. Furthermore, it might miss a true bug in the condition that it mis-parsed ("`((a + b) * c)`"). This problem arises because `Cond'` violates the second condition of the micro-grammar definition.

The correct micro-grammar for extracting conditions is:

```
S'      → if Cond' SkipTo(';')
Cond'   → '(' Balance
Balance → SkipTo(')' | Cond' Balance)
```

In contrast to the previous attempts, this micro-grammar balances parentheses to make sure that the non-terminal of interest (`Cond'`) matches the same substrings as the original non-terminal (`Cond`). Now, our checker only checks `if` statements as they appear in the source code.

4. How do micro-grammar based checkers compare to traditional ones?

Because our checkers only understand a fraction of the checked language, an obvious concern is that they either cannot implement more complex analyses or fail to find a compelling number of bugs. We address those concerns by:

1. Showing that µchex is not limited to detecting simple syntactic patterns by implementing two flow-sensitive checkers from our previous work [19, 20]. These checkers detect 420 errors in Linux and Firefox, two systems that have been extensively checked for over a decade.
2. Comparing one of these checkers' results to those of an advanced, widely used commercial system. Both systems find 43 of the same bugs; SystemX finds an additional 73 bugs we miss, but we find 190 bugs it misses.

These results, presented in the next two sections, demonstrate that micro-grammars are effective and useful despite their simplicity.

4.1 Reimplemented checkers

We implement a null pointer dereference checker (§ 4.1.1) and a deadlock checker (§ 4.1.2).

4.1.1 Null Pointer checker

Our Null Pointer checker uses belief analysis to detect potential null pointer dereferences. It flags when a dereferenced pointer "`*p`" (which implies a belief that p is non-null) is post-dominated by a check against `NULL` (which implies a belief that p could be null). While these checks are occasionally harmless, they often signify null pointer dereferences or even security vulnerabilities [13]. The following bug shows a common pattern that this checker finds—a dereference hoisted above a null check. It was copy-pasted eleven times in the same file:

```
    /* arch/ia64/sn/pci/pcibr/pcibr_reg.c */
199 union br_ptr __iomem *ptr = (union br_ptr __iomem *)
      ↪ pcibus_info->pbi_buscommon.bs_base;
200
201 if (pcibus_info) ...
```

The pointer `pcibus_info` is dereferenced (implying a belief that it is non-null) in line 199 and checked against null in line 201. To detect errors like this one, the checker does a forward analysis of each function's parse tree. It keeps track of pointers that are dereferenced and flags an error whenever a previously dereferenced pointer is checked.

Implementation The checker uses two parsers, one for control flow, the other for expressions.

The control flow parser is composed of several small parsers for different control flow constructs such as functions, `if` statements, `for` loops, etc. In total it is 156 lines of code. We reuse this parser repeatedly for other checkers in this paper (even checkers that operate on other languages in Section 6). It implements a micro-grammar with non-terminals for each control flow construct and semantics corresponding to:

```
S           → Function
Function    → Ident ('(') FnArgs SkipTo('{') Body '}'
FnArgs      → SkipTo(',' FnArgs | ')')
```

```
Body        → '{' Statements '}' | Statement
Statements  → Statement Statements | ε
Statement   → IfStmt | WhileStmt Body | ... | Line
IfStmt      → if Balanced('(', ')') Body [Else]
Else        → else Body
... // more constructs
Line        → SkipTo(';')
```

In addition to parsing control flow it also parses straight-line statements such as "int x = y;" using the Line non-terminal. The parsers that correspond to each of these non-terminals are only three to nine lines of code. For example, the following parser code corresponds to the IfStmt non-terminal in the micro-grammar above:

```
ifParser = do
  position <- pRsrvd "if"
  cond <- balancedP
  thBr <- bodyParser
  elseBr <- elseParser
  return $ IfThenElse position cond thBr elseBr
```

The ifParser is composed of other parsers: balancedP for balanced parentheses and their content, bodyParser for the true branch body, and elseBr for the false branch body. This parser returns an IfThenElse tree node.

A second 29-line parser extracts the structure of C expressions. We run this (compositional) parser *after* running the control flow parser (§ 3.2), using it to parse tokens that have matched to wildcard nodes. For example, before using the expression parser, the content of an if condition node might be:

```
wildcard: ["a", "==", "foo", "(", ")"]
```

After using the expression parser, its content would be:

```
binOp "==" ("a") (call "foo" [])
```

The end result of applying both parsers to the source code—first the control flow parser, next the expression parser—is a parse tree for C control flow and basic expressions.

The Null Pointer checker then operates on this tree, performing a forward, flow-sensitive traversal over each function's parse to compute a set of all pointers dereferenced (and therefore believe to be "not null") on *all* incoming paths. Each time the checker encounters a null pointer check "p == NULL" it looks up p in the "not null" set and emits an error if p is present.

The checker computes the "not null" set by recursively traversing the parse tree, and, at each node, pattern matching against patterns for dereferences and assignments. If a pointer is dereferenced, it is added to the "not null" set; if it is reassigned, it is removed from that set. For example, encountering a tree for the code phrase "x = p->q," our checker would add p to the "not null" set and remove x from the set.

The analysis splits at fork points (if statements, switch statements, etc) and, when these paths rejoin, the analysis adds new dereferences that occur on all paths and removes dereferences that were killed on at least one path.

Results We find 233 true bugs and twelve false positives in Linux, for a false positive rate of 5%; the original checker from [20] detected 102 bugs and 4 false positives (4% false positive rate). Our false positives arose mostly from correlations between the nullness of the dereferenced pointer and other variables and for_each macros. The checker also finds 63 bugs and 3 false positives in Firefox.

4.1.2 Deadlock checker

This checker flags instances where a potentially blocking function is called while interrupts are disabled, a spinlock is held, or a mutex is held. The first two cases can cause deadlock; the third is at least a performance bug. The following security bug in Linux is representative of the major errors that this checker finds:

```
    /* arch/frv/kernel/traps.c */
169 spin_lock_irq(&atomic_op_lock);
170 if (__get_user(z, p) == 0) {
171   if (__put_user(y, p) == 0)
172     goto done2;
173 goto error2;
174 }
175 spin_unlock_irq(&atomic_op_lock);
```

At line 169, the programmer locks atomic_op_lock and then immediately calls "__get_user()" and, perhaps, "__put_user()", which read and write memory from user space; these routines sleep if the user memory that they access is paged out. Because users can control residency, they can trigger this bug for a denial-of-service attack.

This checker is a twist on a deadlock checker from our prior work [19]. The original checker entered a no-block state when it detected a lock acquisition or interrupt disable operation. It flagged any blocking calls that it encountered in this no-block state. In hindsight, this checker missed errors when Linux's labyrinthine control flow and aggressive use of function pointers caused it to miss paths from acquisitions (or disables) to blocking operations.

We implement a twist on this checker as a safety net against its false negatives. Since our checker and the original check the same property in different ways, they will each find bugs that the other misses. As opposed to identifying blocking calls after locking or disabling calls, we flag variations on the following code pattern:

```
block();
unlock(l);
```

Here, "unlock(l)" implies the programmer believes l is locked on the current path, including the place where the block call was made.

Implementation Like the Null Pointer checker, the Deadlock checker does a forward analysis of parses for C control flow and expressions. Its main computed data structure is a set of beliefs about whether the program can block. When it encounters a blocking call, it adds a can-block belief to the set, and when it sees an unlocking call (or enabling call), it adds a cannot-block belief to the set. It clears the belief set when it encounters a lock or disabling call. The checker flags an error whenever the belief set contains both a can-block belief and a cannot-block belief.

Type	SystemX Bugs	SystemX False	Shared Bugs	Shared False	µchex Bugs	µchex False
Intra-procedural	7	2	43	1	190	11
Inter-procedural	≤ 55	≥ 3	n/a		n/a	
Aliasing	≤ 11	≥ 0	n/a		n/a	
Total	≤ 73	≥ 5	43	1	190	11

Table 3. Comparison of bugs by type between SystemX and µchex for Linux 4.4-rc7. µchex currently does not support inter-procedural and aliasing analyses but manages to find more intra-procedural bugs. Most of the SystemX reports are not examined, thus we report the known numbers as bounds.

Results This checker finds 124 bugs in the Linux 4.4-rc7 source code and no false positives. The checker finds such a clean set of errors because it conservatively flags instances where a blocking call is made on *all* paths coming into an unlocking call, though blocking calls on *any* path are actually wrong. Compared to the results of the original implementation [19], we find a similar amount of bugs (124 instead of 123) on a newer version of the kernel, which is encouraging.

4.2 Comparison with commercial system

Micro-grammar based checkers are able to find bugs—but how do they compare to state-of-the-art static analysis tools? This section presents a case study comparing our Null Pointer checker's reports against the reports generated by a similar (but more advanced) checker implemented in a widely-used commercial tool, subsequently referred to as SystemX.[1] The company behind the tool has been developing static checkers for more than a decade, with a team that currently numbers in the low hundreds. SystemX detects bugs using an inter-procedural analysis with alias tracking and some amount of path sensitivity, while µchex does a simple intra-procedural analysis. Even though µchex is far simpler, it finds 44 out of 122 of SystemX's reports. Furthermore, and surprisingly, µchex also manages to find 190 bugs that SystemX does not. Table 3 summarizes these results.

Of course, the two tools' results are not entirely comparable. SystemX has been analyzing the kernel for over five years, and many of its most important reports have already been fixed, leaving only a residue of the total detected bugs behind. Still, we believe that our results, a direct comparison of SystemX and µchex on the same code base, show that micro-grammars are a useful approach for two reasons: 1) their results are similar to those of a more advanced system and 2) they can actually be used to improve that system. False negatives are a perennial problem for unsound checking tools. Front end based tool builders might debug their checkers by writing smaller, equivalent checkers in µchex (in thirty lines of code), or even constructing a corresponding micro-grammar based system themselves.

As a counter against potential bias in our results, we did not configure or run SystemX ourselves. The company configured their analysis for Linux, while a Linux maintainer who regularly checks the kernel with SystemX configured and built the analyzed kernel (version 4.4-rc7). He configured the checker to run with as many `CONFIG_` options enabled as viable (roughly 6900) while disabling as few as necessary (roughly 100), and built the kernel for the x86-64 architecture. We merely accessed the reports afterwards. We compared every report issued by SystemX against those found by µchex (rather than only a subset) to avoid selection bias.

Results Table 3 summarizes the result of our comparison: the Shared column describes categories and counts of bugs that both tools found, while the SystemX and µchex columns detail the distinct bugs that each tool found. In total, SystemX generated 122 bug reports (false and true), while µchex generated 245. The table tells a two-sided story: we find bugs that SystemX misses, but we also miss bugs that SystemX finds. In the next paragraphs, we first explore the reasons for our false negatives, and then discuss the mechanisms behind our true positives.

SystemX uses two analysis strategies that we do not, inter-procedural analysis and alias tracking, which account for 66 bugs; these bugs are undetectable without these two analysis strategies, and since µchex does not use them, it misses these errors. Based on our past experiences building checking tools, we believe simple inter-procedural analysis can be readily added to µchex. µchex could also implement trivial alias tracking, but non-trivial alias tracking is challenging without a full understanding of the checked language.

SystemX's inter-procedural analysis accounts for two types of µchex false negatives: bugs where the dereference appears in one function and the check in another (53 out of 55 cases) and bugs where µchex conservatively assumes that a function might reassign a pointer (two cases). The following code snippet from Linux illustrates the second type of false negative:

```
    /* drivers/staging/rts5208/rtsx.c */
446 if (chip->srb->sc_data_direction == ...)
    ...
469 else {
470     scsi_show_command(chip);
471     rtsx_invoke_transport(chip->srb, chip);
472 }
    ...
478 if (!chip->srb) ;
```

Even though "`chip->srb`" is dereferenced in line 446 and checked in line 478, µchex conservatively assumes that `scsi_show_command` could change the value of "`chip->srb`" (since `chip` is passed to `scsi_show_command`), so both the dereference and the null check may be correct. SystemX, on

[1] For confidentiality we omit the system name.

the other hand, analyzes the content of `scsi_show_command`, and flags an error on line 478 since the function does not alter "`chip->srb`."

µchex misses seven bugs that are detectable without additional analysis strategies. Three false negatives result from minor differences in how µchex and SystemX propagate beliefs through loops and `goto`s. Such differences are expected when comparing the results of different tools and could likely be resolved by replicating SystemX's propagation strategy (if it were public). The last four false negatives are due to our false positive suppression strategy of removing all "not null" beliefs when encountering C preprocessor directives. Without this suppression strategy, we find a less clean set of errors, but detect four more SystemX bugs.

While µchex misses a couple of bugs, it also finds 190 bugs that SystemX does not. The following error is an example:

```
    /* fs/fscache/object.c */
228 new_state = state->work(object, event);
241 if (state->work) {
242   if (unlikely(state->work == ((void *)2UL))) {
243     _leave(" [dead]");
244     return;
245   }
246   goto restart_masked;
247 }
```

In line 228, function pointer "`state->work`" is dereferenced. In line 241, it is checked against null (with no intervening assignments). Strangely, in the next line, it is also checked for equality against the integer literal `2UL`. It is unclear why SystemX misses this error—we believe the error is simple enough that its developers would certainly want to know about their mistake.

Some of the false negatives in SystemX are caused by the fact that it only analyzes x86-64 builds: µchex finds 18 bugs in `arch` (in `arch/alpha`, `arch/cris`, `arch/a64`, and `arch/x86`), while the commercial tool finds only two, both in `arch/x86`. In general, µchex is not limited to checking a specific build configuration; it examines every function in every file of the source code. The Linux SystemX scan maintainer tries to approximate this by configuring the build with `CONFIG_COMPILE_TEST`, so SystemX at least checks non-x86 drivers. Otherwise, their true bug rate would be lower.

5. How hard is it to check a new language?

Because micro-grammars ignore most of the checked language, they allows us to check entirely new languages in a few lines of code, instead of the tens (or hundreds) of thousands of lines that a traditional approach requires. This section demonstrates how micro-grammars make it easy to:

1. Retarget existing checkers to a new language. In Section 5.1 we take the C Null Pointer checker from Section 4.1.1 and its associated parsers and modify them to find errors in C++, Java, and JavaScript. Table 4 summarizes the changes necessary to check these three different languages (and to find 211 bugs).
2. Create new checkers for new languages. In Section 5.2 we build: 1) a checker for the C preprocessor (CPP) that finds 23 bugs and 2) four checkers for Dart that find 15 bugs and 152 performance errors.

Language	Checking function (LOC)	Parser (LOC)
Base (C)	78	156
C++	+11	+16
Java	+1	+1
JavaScript	+2	+15

Table 4. Lines of code shared between the different versions of the Null Pointer checker (checking function and its parser). Line counts indicate changes from the language above to add support for a specific language. While line counts are a somewhat imprecise proxy for the amount of work required, the low counts are encouraging.

5.1 Adapting an existing checker to a new language

Bugs in one language often appear in others. Unfortunately, the structure of traditional checking tools makes it hard to retarget checkers to new languages. Creating a front end from scratch can take months or years. Even adapting a prebuilt front end is not easy, since front ends are complicated, and so is integrating one with a checking tool. As one data point, it took us years to add Java checking to our C static tool, both in an academic and later in an industry setting.

This section demonstrates that retargeting micro-grammar checkers can be nearly trivial by measuring how much effort it takes to port Section 4's Null Pointer checker from C to C++, Java, and JavaScript. For each language, our goal is to implement a useful checker, one that finds true bugs and few false positives, using the smallest number of modifications (akin to a minimum viable product). We discuss the adaptions and results for each target language and conclude with a brief discussion of the case study.

C++ Adapting the C Null Pointer checker to check C++ requires 27 lines of code, and the adapted checker finds 71 bugs. Without these adaptions, the original tool finds 50 of the same bugs (and 9 of the same false positives) on Firefox, but flags over one hundred additional false reports. To suppress these, we implement support for `try` statements and templated identifiers within the micro-grammar. Finally, we adjust the checker to conservatively reset all "not null" beliefs when it encounters a function call that looks like it might be in the same class as the current code. Methods like these ("`foo()`" as opposed to "`bar.foo()`") can change the state of any member variable of the class; in other words, they might change the value of a pointer between the dereference and the check, invalidating our error report.

In contrast to C, C++ supports classes with operator overloading, which presents both a problem and an opportunity for µchex. We can end up with false positives if a class overloads the dereference (`->`) and logical negation (`!`) operators, since we do not know what beliefs the overloaded operators imply. On the other hand, developers have expectations about operator's behavior, and completely violating these assumptions is bad style. For example, "`!`" and "`->`" are overloaded for implementing smart pointers, pointers that ease memory management but follow traditional dereference and negation rules. µchex finds null smart pointer dereferences for free, while a traditional system would require quite a bit of modification to support checking them. We find a number of bugs involving Firefox's custom smart pointers (such as `nsRefPtr` and `nsComPtr`).

In total, the checker finds 61 bugs in Firefox and 33 false positives. Out of the false positives, 24 are caused by callbacks that change a member in the calling class. For example, "`mActor->StartDestroy()`" indirectly destroys `mActor`, which makes the subsequent null check valid. In LLVM, the checker finds 10 bugs and a single false positive. The checker finds the following bug in LLVM:

```
/* lib/Transforms/InstCombine/InstCombineAddSub.cpp */
456 Value *Opnd0_0 = I0->getOperand(0);
457 Value *Opnd0_1 = I0->getOperand(1);
458 Value *Opnd1_0 = I1->getOperand(0);
459 Value *Opnd1_1 = I1->getOperand(1);
    ...
488 FastMathFlags Flags;
489 Flags.setUnsafeAlgebra();
490 if (I0) Flags &= I->getFastMathFlags();
491 if (I1) Flags &= I->getFastMathFlags();
```

The code checks `I0` and `I1` on lines 490 and 491 even though they are dereferenced on lines 456–459. In addition, the conditions do not match the dereferences in their bodies ("`I->getFastMathFlags();`").

Java The analogue of a null pointer dereference in Java is a `NullPointerException` when performing operations on `null` object. Adapting the already-adapted C++ Null Pointer checker to check Java requires 2 lines of code; the only real change is representing the dereference operator as "`.`" instead of "`->`."

The Java Null Pointer checker finds the following issue in OpenJDK:

```
/* jdk/src/share/classes/com/sun/crypto/provider/
    CipherCore.java */
int outputCapacity = output.length - outputOffset;
int minOutSize = (decrypting?
    (estOutSize - blockSize):estOutSize);
if ((output == null) ...) ...
```

Calling "`output.length`" implies that `output` cannot be `null`, whereas the check "`output == null`" implies a belief that `output` *can* be null. Therefore, we flag an error.

JavaScript Adapting the Java checker to JavaScript requires 17 lines of code that extend its micro-grammar with support for nested functions. Without this adaption, the JavaScript checker mis-parses functions to the point that the checker is unable to operate. To suppress false positives, we change the checker to only consider the left-hand sides of binary logical operator expressions as null checks. For example, in "`a || b`," we consider only `a` to have been checked. We do this because, in JavaScript, "`expr1 || expr2`" returns `expr1` if it evaluates to true and `expr2` otherwise (instead of returning a boolean value). This operator is commonly used to express that `expr2` is a fallback, meaning that there is value to including `expr2` even if it is guaranteed never to evaluate to false.

The JavaScript checker finds 25 bugs in Firefox and 7 in Node.js with 6 and one false positive, respectively. The following example shows a dereference just before a check in Firefox:

```
/* browser/devtools/styleinspector/computed-view.js */
this.sheet = rule.parentStyleSheet;

if (!rule || !this.sheet) ...
```

Discussion Our case study shows that it is possible to adapt a checker to new languages by slightly changing the checker and its micro-grammar. While these adapted checkers can be tuned further to find even more bugs, it is surprising that so few changes yield such useful results, especially compared to the amount of work that it would take to migrate a traditional checking system to a new language.

5.2 Writing a checker for a new language from scratch

We now demonstrate how easy it is to write a new checker from scratch for a new language by doing so for both Dart (§ 5.2.2) and CPP code (§ 5.2.1). These languages are very different: Dart is a new scripting language developed by Google, and CPP is an old, primitive language with many pitfalls. Nevertheless, the micro-grammar approach makes implementing checkers for both of these languages possible with very little code overhead.

5.2.1 C preprocessor (CPP)

When developers use the C preprocessor to conditionally compile code in big source files, the directives become distant and nested, making it challenging to keep track of all the active definitions ("if-def hell"). Our checker extracts all CPP conditional checks and flags logical contradictions. The following Linux example shows a representative error:

```
/* sound/pci/au88x0/au88x0_core.c */
#ifndef CHIP_AU8810
...
#ifdef CHIP_AU8810
    temp = (temp & 0xfeffffff) | ((f & 1) << 0x18);
    temp = (temp & 0xfdffffff) | ((f & 1) << 0x19);
#endif
...
#ifdef CHIP_AU8810
    temp =
      ((f & 1) << 0x18) | (temp & 0xfcffffef) |
      ↪  FIFO_BITS;
#endif
...
#endif
```

Lines 878–1035 are guarded by a check that verifies that `CHIP_AU8810` is not defined. Nested within this guarded piece of code, there are two pieces of code that are guarded by checks that verify that `CHIP_AU8810` *is* defined, rendering the code within them useless. The checker finds 16 bugs in Firefox and 7 bugs in Linux with no false positives. We implement 40 lines of checker and parser to achieve these results.

We extract preprocessor directives and traverse their parse to determine whether conditions have been redundantly checked. The checker produces beliefs about whether a variable is `defined` or `undefined` and flags tautological and (often more important) contradictory checks. When the checking function encounters a check such as "`#ifdef foo`", it generates a belief `checked` for `foo`. Directives like "`#define foo`" or "`#undef foo`" remove that belief because they change `foo`. The checker conservatively resets all beliefs when encountering an "`#include`" directive, because the included file could define or undefine anything. In contrast to the previous belief-style checkers, this checker propagates beliefs path-sensitively: µchex propagates the belief that `foo` has been checked through the branches of an "`#ifdef`" but not beyond the corresponding "`#endif`".

5.2.2 Dart

The CPP language is old and relatively simple; this section shows that it is similarly easy to write a parser and checker for features of a new, much more sophisticated language. We check Dart, an optionally-typed language that compiles to JavaScript and has been used in production since 2013.

We did not conceive of the checkers in this section ourselves; in fact, none of us authors has ever written a line of Dart. Instead, we solicited a list of common errors from active Dart developers and created a checker for each one, validating its errors with experts. Clearly, even though these checkers are small and easy to build, they still find real-world errors that matter to developers.

Three of the checkers in the next paragraphs operate on the output of the same 207 line Dart control flow parser (where 75 lines are reused from the C version). One checker runs on an independent 7 line parser. We describe their implementations and the bugs that they find in the following.

Equals without hashcode This checker flags overridden Dart "==" methods that lack a corresponding `hashCode` methods. In Dart (as in Java), classes inherit an "==" (`equals`) method from the root of the of the class hierarchy. This default method only checks whether two objects are the same instance—whether they are the same exact object. Programmers can override the default "==" method with a custom implementation. Dart expects users to override the `hashCode` method when overriding "==," because equal objects should hash to the same value. Missing `hashCode` implementations may cause wrong behavior: for example, many elements that are equal according to the overridden method might end up in a different bucket in a `HashMap` because their `hashCodes` differ.

Our 28-line checking function runs on a control flow parse and does a backwards analysis of each Dart class. When it encounters a "==" method, it adds a `needs_hashCode` belief to the belief set. When it sees a `hashCode` method, it removes this belief. Finally, if it reaches the beginning of a class and the `needs_hashCode` belief remains, the checker flags an error. Below is a Dart class where the "==" function is overridden without also overriding `hashCode`:

```
/* sdk/pkg/analysis_server/lib/
   src/services/index/indexable_file.dart */
class IndexableFile implements IndexableObject {
...
@override
bool operator ==(Object object) =>
  object is IndexableFile && object.path == path;
}
```

The checker finds 13 instances of overriden "==" methods without `hashCode` and no false positives. We confirmed these errors with Dart developers. Seven of the errors that this tool found on a previous version of the analyzed code have been fixed (though independent of our reports). Our Java version of the checker finds 73 bugs and 2 false positives in OpenJDK.

Non-observable @Observable collections When writing Dart Polymer elements—Dart web elements that rely on the Polymer package—developers may use the "`@Observable`" annotation. Placed before data structures, this annotation enables a two-way binding between DOM nodes and object models. If programmers add the annotation to collections without making their contents observable (using the `toObservable` function or an `Observable` version of the collection), changes to that collection's elements in the DOM are not reflected in the data model for the collection.

The checker (26 lines of code) traverses the parsed Dart control flow, seeking annotation nodes. If it detects that a new collection object has been annotated, it verifies that that collection's value has been converted `toObservable` (or that the collection's name contains `Observable`, making it an observable collection).

We find two instances of this error in Dart code (out of twenty-two observable annotations in the code that we check):

```
/* sdk/runtime/observatory/lib/
   src/elements/flag_list.dart */
@observable List<ServiceMap> modifiedFlags =
  new List<ServiceMap>();
@observable List<ServiceMap> unmodifiedFlags =
  new List<ServiceMap>();
```

Style: spurious null check Though not an error, null checks in overridden "==" functions are not necessary, since Dart handles this case automatically. To find this style issue, we parse Dart control flow and implement a checker (9 lines of code) that finds "==" functions containing a null check. For each null check, the checker produces a warning.

Performance: incorrect length check In Dart, lists and list-backed data structures implement the `isEmpty` function, which runs in constant time. Despite this, many people check lists' "`.length`" against 0, a check that runs in linear time. This check usually results in a small performance hit but adds up when repeated. The checker consists of a separate parser (7 lines of code) and a checking function that flags everything the parser returns. It finds 152 instances of the issue in Dart code.

Discussion These results show that the micro-grammar approach is not limited to detecting low-level bugs in old languages—it can be just as readily applied to new, modern programming languages. Optimistically, our results suggest that micro-grammars could speed the adoption of new languages by enabling developers to easily write checkers for them. In fact, micro-grammars are a good fit for budding languages because they are robust to evolving language grammars. As languages mature, developers can adjust their checkers with very little overhead.

Finally, we were happily surprised by the fact that micro-grammars allowed us to find bugs not only in systems we do not understand, but also in *languages* we do not understand.

6. Does the same checker run on different languages' source code?

One of our most unexpected results is that the same checker and parser combination can find bugs in many different languages. The intuition behind this fact is that if languages share a common heritage, some portion of their grammars may be similar, even though they may otherwise differ significantly. Micro-grammars can capture the overlapping portion while ignoring the rest of the grammar.

This section explores this unexpected result by running the same checker, unaltered, charcter-for-character, on C, C++, Java, and JavaScript code. We detect programming logic errors in the form of tautological branching decisions. Such redundant or impossible operations often hint at high-level conceptual errors [20, 47, 49]. With the exception of a few stylized (and often commented) cases, programmers write code to perform useful work; if they perform an action, it is because they believe it serves a purpose. To detect these errors, we implement the following checkers:

Redundant Branches finds `if` statements with redundant branches: "`if (x) { a(); } else { a(); }`"

Redundant Conditions finds `if` statements with repeated conditions:
"`if (x) { a(); } else if (x) { b(); }`"

Suspicious Loop Condition finds `for` loop headers where the condition contradicts the increment:
"`for (i = 0; i < len; i--) ...`"

While these errors are thought of as simple, they can be some of the most difficult to diagnose [6], because they often cause code to silently compute an incorrect result.

6.1 Redundant Branches

The Redundant Branches checker flags instances where both true and false branches of an `if` statement perform syntactically identical actions. With some exceptions, checking a condition implies that the programmer must handle different cases as a result of that condition. Performing identical actions in both cases is suspicious.

The following error in LLVM (changed in version 3.7.0) is a good example:

```
/* lib/Target/X86/AsmParser/X86AsmParser.cpp */
if (isParsingIntelSyntax()) {
  Operands.push_back(X86Operand::CreateReg(
    X86::DX, NameLoc, NameLoc));
  Operands.push_back(DefaultMemDIOperand(
    NameLoc));
} else {
  Operands.push_back(X86Operand::CreateReg(
    X86::DX, NameLoc, NameLoc));
  Operands.push_back(DefaultMemDIOperand(
    NameLoc));
}
```

Here, the LLVM assembler's parsing code checks if the input assembly uses Intel syntax, which it must handle differently (versus AT&T syntax). Unfortunately, both branches contain identical code, thereby leading to (potentially silent) mis-parses. Our checker, despite not understanding C++ and certainly not understanding what this program does, easily detects this bug.

The checker uses the C control flow parser. It examines each `if` node in the parse tree and if both branches are syntactically equal, it flags an error. The checker filters out `if` statements with empty consequent blocks (the surprisingly common "`if (x) ;`"). It also filters out errors that appear in chained `if` statements, because repeated branches often indicate multiple cases without a commitment to different actions in every case. This extra false positive filtration can be easily disabled.

The checker finds 48 true bugs and 12 false positives running unaltered on C, C++, Java, and JavaScript code. We find 8 additional instances in generated code in OpenJDK. Our true bugs often seem to result from copy-paste errors. Our false positives, on the other hand, mostly consist of instances where programmers use duplicate logic to document that different cases lead to the same actions. Programmers also occasionally insert these kinds of statements for future use. In practice, identical branch blocks are suspicious enough that they are commonly accompanied by a comment.

6.2 Redundant Conditions

This checker flags sequences of nested `if` statements where more than one `if` statement contains the same condition. The most straightforward errors that this checker finds mirror those in Section 6.1, where it appears that the programmer copied code but performed an incomplete rewrite. For example, the checker finds the following error in OpenJDK:

```
    /* nashorn/src/jdk/nashorn/internal/codegen/types/
       BooleanType.java */
131 } else if (to.isLong()) {
132   convert(method, OBJECT);
133   invokeStatic(method, JSType.TO_UINT32);
134 } else if (to.isLong()) {
135   convert(method, OBJECT);
136   invokeStatic(method, JSType.TO_LONG);
137 } else if ...
```

The condition "`to.isLong()`" is checked on lines 131 and 134. The code in the body of the first check, however, appears to handle `UInt32`s (instead of `Long`s). This has two ramifications: 1) `Long`s are handled as `UInt32`s and 2) `UInt32`s are not handled at all.

Like the Redundant Branches checker, this checker runs on parsed C control flow structures. For each `if` node in the program graph, it gathers all the chained `if` nodes attached to it. It flags an error if any of the conditions are not unique. It filters out duplicate cases with side-effects ("`if (x++)`").

This checker finds 16 errors in C, C++, Java, and JavaScript. The checker could potentially yield many false positives because it only does rudimentary filtering of conditions with side-effects. In practice, the filter is good enough to avoid all false positives on the systems that we check.

6.3 Suspicious Loop Condition

All four languages—C, C++, Java and JavaScript—have `for` loops, which they define similarly as containing four parts: the initialization, the condition, the afterthought, and the body. Often, developers use `for` loops to traverse a range of numbers. In this case, the condition defines either the lower or the upper bound of the range and the afterthought defines the direction of the traversal. Our Suspicious Loop Conditions checker identifies pairings of loop conditions and afterthoughts that are suspicious because the direction of change in the afterthought moves the value away from the condition. The following code is an error in OpenJDK:

```
/* jdk/test/java/io/pathNames/GeneralWin32.java */
for (char d = 'C'; d <= 'Z'; d--) {
  File df = new File(d + ":\\");
  if (df.exists()) return d;
}
```

Windows uses alphabetical identifiers for volumes. Instead of traversing these identifiers from "`C:`" to "`Z:`" in order to find an active drive, the `for` loop explores the range below "`C:`", which consists of illegal identifiers. Because of the narrow range of `char`, the loop will wrap around and terminate, silently skipping most of the intended lookups.

This checker uses the `for` loop header parser (which is also used in the C control flow parser):

```
S → for '(' SkipTo(';') SkipTo(';') SkipTo(')')
```

The checking function extracts variables that are compared with an expression (e.g. "`x < expr`") and the nature of that comparison (e.g. "<"). From the afterthought, it extracts variables that are incremented or decremented. Then, it checks that comparisons on a variable are consistent with the operation on that variable in the afterthought.

We run the unmodified checker on C, C++, Java and JavaScript code. The checker detects 11 true bugs and 39 false positives. With the exception of one of the false positives, the variable in question is an unsigned integer, so under- and overflow are defined behaviors, and the behavior may be intentional (though somewhat questionable).

7. Related Work

To the best of our knowledge, the concept of micro-grammars is new, as is the thorough, deliberate use of language incompleteness to simplify program checkers. Our empirical result that checkers can ignore the bulk of a programming language and yet be effective is viewed as "surprising" (to pick the most diplomatic word) by nearly everyone in the programming language community we have discussed it with.

Simplicity The systems community has a long tradition of arguing for and acting on simplicity. This ranges from broad principles such as KISS (and others compiled in [31]) and some forms of the end-to-end argument for moving functionality out of layers [43]. Some examples of artifacts that aimed to be more simple in useful ways than their predecessors are the RISC computer [38] and Unix [42] as a reaction to Multics [12] (and then Plan9 as a reaction to Unix complexity [40]). One way to view this paper is that we have extended the reasoning that systems should be simple to also apply to the tools that check them. In this context, many of the arguments for ease of modification, understanding, speed, and correctness made in prior work also hold.

Incompleteness Our sliding window approach for micro-grammars is similar to traditional parsers that perform error recovery [2, 26]. When a malformed input triggers a parse error in such parsers, the parser skips ahead until it finds a successful match. While our approach skips ahead and retries in a similar fashion when no rule applies, we additionally use bounded skipping within rules using wildcard non-terminals. Often error recovery in traditional parsers works well (perhaps because languages have somewhat evolved to enable it), which gives encouragement to our approach.

In the context of program checkers, the closest parallel to incomplete grammars is that some unsound static tools skip portions of code (functions, files, and directories) that they cannot parse (some tools can also skip paths in code they understand to make progress [30]). Of these tools, the closest analogue we know to our approach is the use of pre-compilation filters that remove code constructs (such as compiler-specific assembly statements) that the tool cannot parse [6]. We believe that skipping code is a common practice but often not reported because of negative connotations. While these prior approaches skip code, they combine the risks of incomplete parsing with the complexity of traditional approaches: rather than leveraging their incompleteness for simplicity, they use full-blown, complex front ends with the added challenge that they silently discard code, often in ways that are hard to reason about. In comparison, micro-grammars give orders of magnitude reduction in tool complexity, while also making the line between parsed and skipped code both explicit and more precise.

The use of incomplete grammars to parse programs can be viewed as similar to natural language processing (NLP) [9], where a key problem is to parse corpora (e.g., newspaper articles) using woefully incomplete grammars and do something useful with the result. The fact that the NLP field has obtained many interesting results using incomplete grammars perhaps makes it less of a surprise that micro-grammars can work for the more regular programming languages. NLP often benefits from the fact that many of the statements one cares about are *upward entailing* [21], i.e. missing information does not invalidate them: "Bob is 18" is true whether or not we miss that he is also African. A similar dynamic occurs with code checkers, which often only need a small set of program constructs to detect violations of their properties. For example, a lock checker may only need lock acquisition and release and control flow, but can ignore other statements in the program since they cannot invalidate the facts implied by these operations.

Finally, our deliberate strategy of skipping over code that the micro-grammar cannot parse has some similarities in spirit to failure oblivious computing [41], which discards the result of computations that caused errors (such as memory corruption or division by zero) in order to make progress.

Program Checking Using micro-grammars makes µchex and its checkers dramatically simpler than past systems for effective static bug finding. While line counts are not public, even early tools appear to be orders of magnitude more complex, including PREfix [30], ESP [16], ESC [22, 33], the leak detection analysis of Xie et al. [48], and Wagner's security work [45, 46].

A key reason for the complexity in the past work is that from the very beginning, the standard approach to source code analysis has been to build tools on top of sophisticated language front ends. Examples for such front ends for C include `gcc`, EDG [25], `clang` [1], and CIL [34]. These front ends are complex. For example, the most widely-used commercial front end, EDG, consists of almost one million lines of code. As a consequence of using traditional front ends, even bug-finding tools known for their simplicity such as the PREfast system [3] (which performs only intra-procedural analysis and makes heavy use of annotations) are forced to be significantly larger than a micro-grammar approach. In addition, those tools can be limited by the capabilities of their front end: Despite years of effort `clang` still has issues compiling parts of the Linux kernel [10].

At the opposite end of the spectrum, there are many different approaches to dynamic bug finding. The simplest are concrete dynamic tools such as Purify [27] and Valgrind [36] taint analysis, including TaintCheck [37] and Dytan [11]. These side-step the need for a programming language specification, but instead need an analogous understanding of machine code, which empirically appears at least as difficult.

More recently, researchers have pushed dynamic analysis further by using symbolic execution [7], such as klee [8], DART [24], Woodpecker [15], DiSE [39], and CUTE [44]. Because these approaches execute code paths while reasoning about many (potentially all) possible values, they can check properties we cannot. Overall, these approaches are significantly more complex than traditional static analysis, which in turn is significantly more complex and heavier weight than our approach. As a result, while they can find some errors we cannot (the converse applies as well), they generally apply to significantly less code—one way to see this is to compare the hundreds of bugs we find to the typically order of magnitude fewer found in these other papers.

Ambitious researchers have combined static and dynamic analysis in various ways, such as CCured [35], SLAM [4, 5], Bandera [14], and FeaVer [28]. We view these approaches as somewhat orthogonal to ours, and hope that using micro-grammars could help reduce complexity in such systems.

Others have taken a language-based approach to prevent bugs, such as Vault [17] and Foster et al. [23]. Switching languages requires significant work on the part of the programmer. We view our work as relatively independent of language-based approaches, but hope that the ease of writing micro-grammar checkers for new languages might somewhat mitigate the stress of adopting them.

8. Conclusion

We challenge the long-standing assumption that static bug finding tools must be based on a complete language front end. In this paper, we find bugs despite the fact—and at times *because* of the fact—that our checkers are built on micro-grammars, incomplete fragments of a language. Because our system does not require a complete language specification, it allows developers to check new languages easily. Furthermore, the partial parses on which our checkers operate surprisingly often match constructs that appear identically in multiple languages; as a result, a checker and parser written for one language can run un- or slightly-altered on many others. Finally, since our design reduces the complexity of program checking by orders of magnitude, we hope it it will increase the number of developers writing checkers and checking systems—and the number of dangerous bugs detected.

Acknowledgments

We thank Ben Holtz, Dave Jones, Adam Bender, Keith Schwarz, and David Terei for their expertise; David Dill, Stephen Cooper, and the anonymous reviewers for their feedback; and Mary Jane Swenson for her endless assistance. This research is supported by DARPA Subcontract No. 1190029-276707.

References

[1] clang: a C language family frontend for LLVM. `http://clang.llvm.org/`.

[2] Alfred V Aho, Ravi Sethi, and Jeffrey D Ullman. *Compilers: Principles, Techniques, and Tools*. 1986.

[3] Thomas Ball, Byron Cook, Vladimir Levin, and Sriram K. Rajamani. Slam and static driver verifier: Technology transfer of formal methods inside microsoft. In *IFM.*, 2004.

[4] Thomas Ball and Sriram K Rajamani. Bebop: A symbolic model checker for boolean programs. In *Proceedings of the Seventh International SPIN Workshop on Model Checking of Software*, 2000.

[5] Thomas Ball and Sriram K. Rajamani. Automatically validating temporal safety properties of interfaces. In *Proceedings of the Eighth International SPIN Workshop on Model Checking of Software*, 2001.

[6] Al Bessey, Ken Block, Ben Chelf, Andy Chou, Bryan Fulton, Seth Hallem, Charles Henri-Gros, Asya Kamsky, Scott McPeak, and Dawson Engler. A few billion lines of code later: Using static analysis to find bugs in the real world. *Commun. ACM*, 53(2), 2010.

[7] Robert S. Boyer, Bernard Elspas, and Karl N. Levitt. Select – a formal system for testing and debugging programs by symbolic execution. *ACM SIGPLAN Notices*, 10(6), 1975.

[8] Cristian Cadar, Daniel Dunbar, and Dawson Engler. KLEE: Unassisted and automatic generation of high-coverage tests for complex systems programs. In *Proceedings of Symp. on Operating Systems Design and Implementation*, 2008.

[9] Erik Cambria and Bebo White. Jumping NLP curves: A review of natural language processing research. In *IEEE Computational Intelligence Magazine*, 2014.

[10] clang. Bug 4068 - compiling the linux kernel with clang. `https://llvm.org/bugs/show_bug.cgi?id=4068`, 2009.

[11] James Clause, Wanchun Li, and Alessandro Orso. Dytan: a generic dynamic taint analysis framework. In *Proceedings of International Symp. on Software Testing and Analysis*, 2007.

[12] Fernando J Corbató, Jerome H Saltzer, and Chris T Clingen. Multics: the first seven years. *Proceedings AFIPS 1972 SJCC*, 40, 1972.

[13] Jonathan Corbet. Fun with null pointers, part 1. `http://lwn.net/Articles/342330/`, 2009.

[14] James C. Corbett, Matthew B. Dwyer, John Hatcliff, Shawn Laubach, Corina S. Păsăreanu, Robby, and Hongjun Zheng. Bandera: Extracting finite-state models from Java source code. In *Proceedings of the 22nd International Conference on Software Engineering*, 2000.

[15] Heming Cui, Gang Hu, Jingyue Wu, and Junfeng Yang. Verifying systems rules using rule-directed symbolic execution. In *Proceedings of International Conference on Architectural Support for Programming Languages and Operating Systems*, 2013.

[16] Manuvir Das, Sorin Lerner, and Mark Seigle. Esp: path-sensitive program verification in polynomial time. In *Proceedings of the ACM SIGPLAN 2002 Conference on Programming Language Design and Implementation*, 2002.

[17] Robert DeLine and Manuel Fähndrich. Enforcing high-level protocols in low-level software. In *Proceedings of the ACM SIGPLAN 2001 Conference on Programming Language Design and Implementation*, 2001.

[18] Dawson Engler. Making finite verification of raw c code easier than writing a test case. Invited talk, International Conference on Runtime Verification, 2011.

[19] Dawson Engler, Benjamin Chelf, Andy Chou, and Seth Hallem. Checking system rules using system-specific, programmer-written compiler extensions. In *Proceedings of Operating Systems Design and Implementation*, 2000.

[20] Dawson Engler, David Yu Chen, Seth Hallem, Andy Chou, and Benjamin Chelf. Bugs as deviant behavior: A general approach to inferring errors in systems code. In *Proceedings of the 18th ACM Symposium on Operating Systems Principles*, 2001.

[21] Kai Von Fintel. NPI-licensing, strawson-entailment, and context-dependency. In *Journal of Semantics*, 1999.

[22] Cormac Flanagan, K Rustan M Leino, Mark Lillibridge, Greg Nelson, James B Saxe, and Raymie Stata. Extended static checking for Java. In *Proceedings of the ACM SIGPLAN 2002 Conference on Programming Language Design and Implementation*, 2002.

[23] Jeffrey S Foster, Manuel Fähndrich, and Alexander Aiken. A theory of type qualifiers. In *Proceedings of the SIGPLAN '99 Conference on Programming Language Design and Implementation*, 1999.

[24] Patrice Godefroid, Nils Klarlund, and Koushik Sen. DART: Directed automated random testing. In *Proceedings of the ACM SIGPLAN 2005 Conference on Programming Language Design and Implementation*, 2005.

[25] Edison Design Group. EDG C++ compiler front-end. `http://www.edg.com`.

[26] Dick Grune and Ceriel J.H. Jacobs. *Parsing Techniques: A Practical Guide (2nd ed)*. 2008.

[27] Reed Hastings and Bob Joyce. Purify: Fast detection of memory leaks and access errors. In *Proceedings of the USENIX Winter Technical Conference*, 1992.

[28] Gerard J Holzmann and Margaret H Smith. Software model checking: Extracting verification models from source code. In *Invited Paper. Proceedings PSTV/FORTE99*, 1999.

[29] John E. Hopcroft, Rajeev Motwani, and Jeffery Ullman. *Introduction to Automata Theory, Languages, and Computation, Third Edition*. Pearson Education, Inc, 2007.

[30] Intrinsa. A technical introduction to PREfix/Enterprise. Technical report, Intrinsa Corporation, 1998.

[31] Butler W. Lampson. Hints for computer system design. In *Proceedings of the Eighth ACM Symposium on Operating Systems Principles*, 1983.

[32] Daan Leijen and Erik Meijer. Parsec: Direct style monadic parser combinators for the real world. 2002.

[33] K Rustan M Leino, Greg Nelson, and James B Saxe. ESC/Java user's manual. Technical note 2000-002, Compaq Systems Research Center, 2001.

[34] George C. Necula, Scott McPeak, S.P. Rahul, and Westley Weimer. Cil: Intermediate language and tools for analysis and transformation of c programs. In *Proceedings of Conference on Compiler Construction*, 2002.

[35] George C. Necula, Scott McPeak, and Westley Weimer. Ccured: type-safe retrofitting of legacy code. In *Proceedings of Symp. on Principles of Programming Languages*, 2002.

[36] Nicholas Nethercote and Julian Seward. Valgrind: a framework for heavyweight dynamic binary instrumentation. In *Proceedings of the ACM SIGPLAN 2007 Conference on Programming Language Design and Implementation*, 2007.

[37] James Newsome and Dawn Song. Dynamic taint analysis for automatic detection, analysis, and signature generation of exploits on commodity software. In *Proceedings of Network and Distributed Systems Security Symp.*, 2005.

[38] David A. Patterson. Reduced instruction set computers. *Communications of the ACM*, 21(1), 1985.

[39] Suzette Person, Guowei Yang, Neha Rungta, and Sarfraz Khurshid. Directed incremental symbolic execution. In *Proceedings of ACM SIGPLAN Conf. on Programming Language Design and Implementation*, 2011.

[40] Rob Pike, Dave Presotto, Ken Thompson, and Howard Trickey. Plan 9 from bell labs. In *Proceedings of the Summer 1990 UKUUG Conference*, 1990.

[41] Martin Rinard, Cristian Cadar, Daniel Dumitran, Daniel M. Roy, Tudor Leu, and Jr. William S. Beebee. Enhancing server availability and security through failure-oblivious computing. In *Proceedings of the 6th conference on Symposium on Operating Systems Design & Implementation*, 2004.

[42] D.M. Ritchie, K. Thompson, Dennis M Ritchie, and Ken Thompson. The UNIX time-sharing system. *Communications of the ACM*, 17(7), 1974.

[43] Jerome H Saltzer, David P Reed, and David D Clark. End-to-end arguments in system design. *ACM Transactions on Computer Systems*, 2(4), 1984.

[44] Koushik Sen, Darko Marinov, and Gul Agha. CUTE: A concolic unit testing engine for C. In *Proceedings of the 13th ACM SIGSOFT International Symposium on Foundations of Software Engineering*, 2005.

[45] David Wagner and Drew Dean. Intrusion detection via static analysis. In *Proceedings of the 2001 IEEE Symposium on Security and Privacy*, 2001.

[46] David Wagner, Jeffrey S. Foster, Eric A. Brewer, and Alexander Aiken. A first step towards automated detection of buffer overrun vulnerabilities. In *Network and Distributed System Security Symposium*, 2000.

[47] Xi Wang, Nickolai Zeldovich, M. Frans Kaashoek, and Armando Solar-Lezama. Towards optimization-safe systems: Analyzing the impact of undefined behavior. In *Proceedings of the Twenty-Fourth ACM Symposium on Operating Systems Principles*, 2013.

[48] Yichen Xie and Alex Aiken. Context- and path-sensitive memory leak detection. In *Proceedings of the International Symp. on Foundations of Software Engineering (FSE)*, 2005.

[49] Yichen Xie and Dawson Engler. Using redundancies to find errors. *Proceedings of the 10th ACM SIGSOFT International Symposium on Foundations of Software Engineering*, 27(6), 2002.

TxRace: Efficient Data Race Detection Using Commodity Hardware Transactional Memory

Tong Zhang Dongyoon Lee Changhee Jung

Virginia Tech

{ztong, dongyoon, chjung}@vt.edu

Abstract

Detecting data races is important for debugging shared-memory multithreaded programs, but the high runtime overhead prevents the wide use of dynamic data race detectors. This paper presents TxRace, a new software data race detector that leverages commodity hardware transactional memory (HTM) to speed up data race detection. TxRace instruments a multithreaded program to transform synchronization-free regions into transactions, and exploits the conflict detection mechanism of HTM for lightweight data race detection at runtime. However, the limitations of the current best-effort commodity HTMs expose several challenges in using them for data race detection: (1) lack of ability to pinpoint racy instructions, (2) false positives caused by cache line granularity of conflict detection, and (3) transactional aborts for non-conflict reasons (e.g., capacity or unknown). To overcome these challenges, TxRace performs lightweight HTM-based data race detection at first, and occasionally switches to slow yet precise data race detection only for the small fraction of execution intervals in which potential races are reported by HTM. According to the experimental results, TxRace reduces the average runtime overhead of dynamic data race detection from 11.68x to 4.65x with only a small number of false negatives.

Categories and Subject Descriptors D.1.3 [*Programming Techniques*]: Concurrent Programming; D.2.5 [*Software Engineering*]: Testing and Debugging

Keywords data race; concurrency bug detection; hardware transactional memory; dynamic program analysis

1. Introduction

Data races are an important class of concurrency errors in shared-memory multithreaded programs. A data race occurs when two threads access the same memory location, at least one of the two accesses is a write, and their relative order is not explicitly enforced by synchronization primitives such as locks [8, 49, 56].

Data races often lie at the root of other concurrency bugs such as unintended sharing, atomicity violation, and order violation [46]. There are many real-world examples showing the severity of data races, including the northeastern blackout [64], mismatched Nasdaq Facebook share prices [57], and security vulnerabilities [73]. Moreover, data races make it difficult to reason about the possible behaviors of programs. The C/C++11 standards [8, 33, 34] give no semantics to programs with data races, and the data race semantics for Java programs [49] is considered to be too complex [69].

To address this problem, a variety of dynamic data race detectors [19, 21, 32, 58, 65, 75] have been proposed to help programmers write more reliable multithreaded programs. However, such dynamic tools often add too much runtime overhead. For example, FastTrack, a state-of-the-art happens-before based detector, incurs a 8.5x slowdown for Java programs [21] and a 57x slowdown for C/C++ programs [18]. For different set of benchmarks, Intel's Inspector XE incurs a 200x slowdown [62], and Google's ThreadSanitizer incurs a 30x slowdown [65]. Such high overhead hinders the widespread use of dynamic data race detectors in practice, despite their good detection precision.

This paper presents TxRace, a new software data race detector that leverages commodity Hardware Transactional Memory (HTM) to speed up dynamic data race detection. Transactional Memory (TM) [28] was proposed to simplify concurrent programming as a new programming paradigm, and hardware support for transactional memory has recently become available in commodity processors such as Intel's Haswell processor [29, 31]. TxRace exploits the observation that the conflict detection mechanism of HTM can be repurposed for lightweight data race detection in conventional multithreaded programs not originally developed for TM.

However, naively leveraging HTM does not automatically guarantee efficient data race detection. Rather, the limitations of the current commodity HTMs expose three challenges in using them for data race detection: (1) As the

ASPLOS '16 April 02-06, 2016, Atlanta, GA, USA.

DOI: http://dx.doi.org/10.1145/2872362.2872384

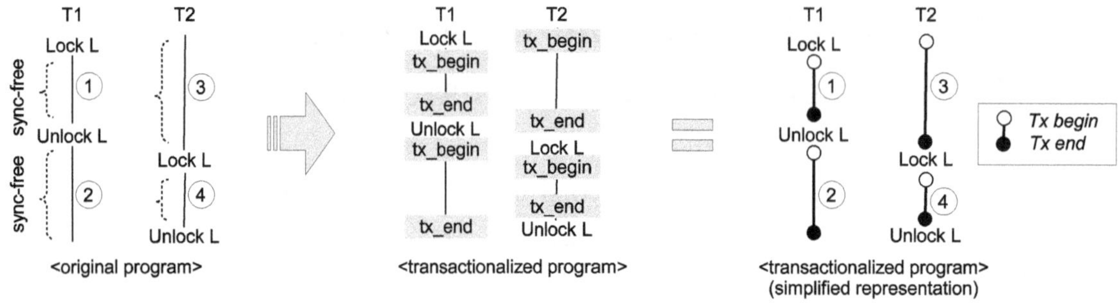

Figure 1: Transactionalization. TxRace statically instruments synchronization-free regions into transactions and leverages HTM for lightweight data race detection at runtime.

HTMs are designed to transparently guarantee atomicity and isolation between concurrent transactions, they do not provide a way to pinpoint racy instructions or conflicting addresses; (2) Since data conflicts are detected at the cache line granularity, false alarms could be reported due to the false sharing; and (3) Due to the best-effort nature of existing commodity HTMs, transactions may abort for reasons other than data conflicts, including exceeding the hardware capacity, interrupts and exceptions.

To overcome these challenges, TxRace first instruments a multithreaded program to transform all code regions between synchronizations (including critical sections) into transactions (Figure 1). At runtime, TxRace then performs a two-phase data race detection comprising fast and slow paths. During the initial fast path, TxRace detects potential data races using the low-overhead data conflict detection mechanism of HTM. In this stage, the detected races are only potential races, as the conflict might be due to false sharing in the cache line. When a data conflict is detected, the current HTMs do not identify the instruction that caused the transaction to abort, the conflicting address, or the other conflicting transaction. TxRace addresses this problem by artificially aborting all the (in-flight) concurrent transactions, rolling back them to the state before the data conflict occurred, and then performing software-based *sound*[1] (no false negative) and *complete* (no false positive) data race detection [21, 32, 65] for the concurrent code regions. This work refers to the rollback and subsequent re-execution with software-based data race detection as the slow path, which enables TxRace not only to pinpoint racy instructions but also to filter out any false positives. TxRace also relies on the slow path to cover the code regions, which cannot be monitored by transactions due to the limitations of existing commodity HTMs. This conservative approach reduces the chance of missing data races at the cost of runtime overhead, and TxRace includes an optimization technique to avoid repeated capacity aborts.

[1] In this paper, a dynamic analysis is *sound* if it does not incur false negatives; and *complete* if it does not report false positives, for the analyzed execution as in [16, 21, 22, 72]. Some [6, 9, 19] refer to a dynamic analysis to be *precise* (instead of *complete*) when there is no false positive, and others [18, 66] swap the definitions of soundness and completeness.

The experimental results show that using Intel's Restricted Transactional Memory (RTM) and Google's ThreadSanitizer (TSan) for the fast and slow paths respectively, TxRace achieves runtime overhead reduction of dynamic data race detection from 11.68x (TSan) to 4.65x (TxRace) on average. Using an HTM-based detector during the fast path may lead to missing data races if they do not overlap in concurrent transactions (and for other reasons). Nevertheless, TxRace incurs only a few false negatives (high recall of 0.95) for tested applications.

This paper makes the following contributions:

- To the best of our knowledge, TxRace is the first software scheme that demonstrates how commodity hardware transactional memory can be used to build a lightweight dynamic data race detector.
- TxRace proposes novel solutions to address the challenge in designing HTM-based data race detector. They enable TxRace to pinpoint racy instructions, remove false data race warnings caused by false sharing, and handle non-conflict transactional aborts efficiently.
- The paper presents experimental results showing cost effectiveness of TxRace compared to a state-of-the-art happens-before based data race detector and its random sampling based approach.

2. Background and Challenges

This section briefly introduces hardware transactional memory systems and discusses the challenges in using them in data race detection.

2.1 Hardware Transactional Memory

Transactional Memory (TM) [28] provides programmers with transparent support to execute a group of memory operations in a user-defined transaction in an atomic (all or nothing) and isolated (the partial state of a transaction is hidden from others) manner. Hardware support for transactional memory has been implemented in IBM's Blue Gene/Q supercomputers [26] and System z mainframes [35]; Sun's (canceled) Rock processor [17]; Azul's Vega processor [14]. Recently, HTM has become available in commodity pro-

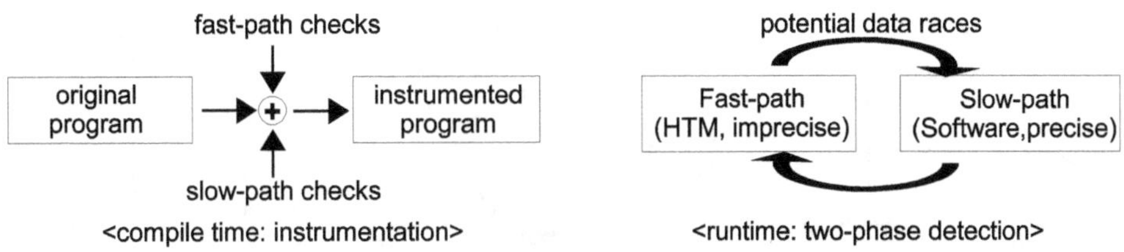

Figure 2: TxRace Overview

cessors used in desktops such as Intel's Haswell processor [29, 31].

TxRace leverages Intel's Transactional Synchronization Extensions (TSX) introduced in the Haswell processors. Intel TSX includes Hardware Lock Elision (HLE) and Restricted Transactional Memory (RTM) supports, where the latter enables general-purpose transactional memory. Intel RTM provides a new set of instructions comprising *xbegin*, *xend*, *xabort*, and *xtest* to help programmers initiate, complete, abort a transaction, and check its status, respectively. Intel RTM uses the first level (L1) data cache to track transactional states, and leverages the cache coherence protocol to detect transactional conflicts [23, 74]. Intel RTM supports *strong isolation*, which guarantees transactional semantics between transactions and non-transactional code [51]. For conflict management, Intel RTM uses a simple *requester-wins* policy in which on a conflicting request, the requester always succeeds and the conflicting transactions abort [7].

2.2 Challenges in Using HTM for Race Detection

At first glance, it might be expected that HTMs can trivially provide lightweight data race detection. However, the commercial HTMs, including Intel RTM, share limitations that hinder their adoption for data race detection.

First, though HTMs can detect the presence of data conflicts and abort, HTMs including Intel RTM do not provide programmers with the problematic instructions that caused the transaction to abort, or with the affected memory addresses. Moreover, the concurrent transactions to which the competing instructions belong may have been successfully committed according to TM semantics. This implies that programmers cannot reason about the pairs of memory accesses involved in the data race.

Second, HTMs detect data conflict by leveraging a cache coherence mechanism. Conflicts are therefore discovered at the cache-line granularity (64-bytes in the Intel Haswell processor). This may produce false warnings in data race detection due to non-conflicting operations on variables that share a cache line. By comparison, traditional dynamic data race detectors identify data races at the word (or byte) granularity, significantly reducing the likelihood of false positives.

Third, HTMs have bounded resources, and irrevocable I/O operations are not supported. Intel RTM does not support arbitrarily long transactions, simply aborting any transactions exceeding the capacity of the hardware buffer for transactional states [27, 61]. Moreover, changing privilege level always forces a transaction abort. The implication is that a transaction should not include any system call.

Finally, a transaction in best-effort (non-ideal) commodity HTMs including Intel RTM may be aborted for an unknown reason (neither due to data conflict nor due to capacity overflow). Intel's reference manuals [29, 31] illustrate some causes of unknown aborts, such as operating system context switches for interrupt or exception handling. However, neither the exact abort reason nor the problematic instruction is provided to programmers, which makes it hard to work around such a transaction abort.

3. Overview of TxRace

TxRace is a lightweight software dynamic data race detector that leverages hardware transactional memory support in modern commodity processors. The key insight is that TxRace can detect potential data races with a very low runtime overhead by initially relying on the conflict detection mechanism of HTM. The detected races are potential because the data conflict between transactions might be caused by false sharing in the same cache line. When transactions commit without data conflicts, TxRace incurs only the small runtime overhead of the transactional execution. In this sense, this HTM-based check is called *fast path* in which TxRace first takes to quickly identify potential data races. To address the aforementioned challenges of HTM-based detectors, on a data conflict, TxRace artificially aborts all concurrent (in-flight) transactions, rolls them back to the state before the data conflict occurs, and performs software-based sound and complete data race detection in an on-demand manner. Such re-execution with software-based detection is called *slow path*, which allows TxRace not only to pinpoint racy instructions but also to filter out false positives caused by false sharing.

Figure 2 shows an overview of TxRace. It consists of a compile-time instrumentation and a two-phase data race detection at runtime. TxRace inserts fast path transactional codes (e.g., *xbegin*, *xend*) and slow path sound and complete data race detection codes (e.g.,FastTrack [21], ThreadSanitizer [65]) into the original program at compile-time. Then, TxRace makes use of the two-phase data race detection at runtime. This allows TxRace to selectively perform sound and complete (but slow) data race detection for only a small fraction of the whole execution, leading to significant run-

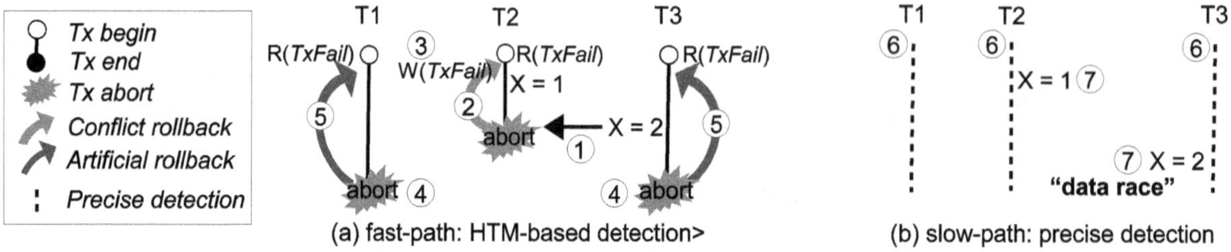

Figure 3: TxRace Runtime Example

time overhead reduction compared to a traditional dynamic data race detection.

As illustrated in Figure 1, TxRace transforms program regions between synchronizations (*synchronization-free regions*) into transactions. Then, TxRace performs HTM-based race detection between program regions that overlap in parallel at runtime. For example, for an execution where program regions ① and ③ overlap, TxRace checks potential data races between those two regions. Similarly, program regions between ② and ③; or between ② and ④ are checked when they run concurrently. On the other hand, the original synchronization lock *L* prevents the program regions ① and ④ (and corresponding transactions) from being overlapped at runtime. Therefore, the HTM will never observe conflicting memory accesses in critical sections protected by the same lock. In the following figures, a white circle corresponds to the beginning of a transaction, a black circle to its end.

After compile-time instrumentation, TxRace detects data races at runtime using the fast and slow paths as follows. Figure 3 shows an example with three threads, T1, T2, and T3, each performing one transaction. Suppose the shared variable *X* is not protected by the common lock, so that the transactions of T2 and T3 may run concurrently. During the fast path, each transaction begins by first reading a shared global flag named *TxFail* (as a part of instrumented code together with *xbegin*). Then, TxRace relies on HTM to detect data conflicts. Suppose a transaction in T3 causes another transaction in T2 to abort by accessing the shared variable *X* (step ①). Intel RTM employs a *requester-wins* conflict resolution strategy in which on a conflicting request, the requester always succeeds and the conflicting transactions abort [7]. Thus, the concurrent transactions of T1 (no conflict) and T3 (winner) may proceed further. To pinpoint the precise data race condition, TxRace immediately aborts the in-flight transactions by making the aborted transaction in T2 update *TxFail* (step ③) right after its rollback. Intel RTM supports *strong isolation* that guarantees transactional semantics between transactions and non-transactional code [51]. Together with the requester-wins policy, the strong isolation property in Intel RTM cause a transaction to abort if there is a conflicting access from a non-transaction code. Therefore, the update to *TxFail* causes all the concurrent transactions to abort artificially (step ④) as they have read *TxFail* at the beginning of the transaction. When all the concurrent transactions are rolled back (step ⑤), they resume execution on the slow path in which HTM is no longer used (step ⑥), but software-based sound and complete data race detection is performed (step ⑦) instead. When the slow path finishes for the program regions where potential data races are detected, TxRace switches back to the fast path in which HTM is used for the next program regions.

4. Fast Path HTM-based Race Detection

This section first describes how TxRace instruments original programs to detect potential data races as well as how it handles different types of transactional aborts, and then discuss optimization techniques used for reducing performance overhead.

4.1 Transactionalization

To exploit HTM for potential data race detection, TxRace transforms a code region between synchronization operations (including a critical section) into a transaction as illustrated in Figure 1. To be specific, at compile-time, TxRace inserts transaction begin instructions (*xbegin*) at thread entry points and after synchronization operations; and transaction end instructions (*xend*) at thread exit points and before synchronization operations. System calls require special consideration due to HTM limitations. Intel RTM, for example, aborts a transaction if a change in privilege level takes place. Consequently, TxRace ends the current transaction prior to each system call and begins a new transaction immediately after the system call in order to guarantee forward progress.

Furthermore, TxRace instruments each transaction to read the shared flag *TxFail* immediately after *xbegin*. As discussed in Section 3, Intel RTM uses the *requester-wins* policy that allows the requester to succeed on a conflicting request and aborts the conflicting transactions [7]; and supports *strong isolation* that guarantees transactional semantics between transactions and non-transactional code [51]. These two properties cause an in-flight transaction to abort on a conflicting access from non-transaction code. As TxRace makes transactions read *TxFail* when they start, when a data conflict is detected, the aborted transaction can artificially abort other in-flight transactions by writing to the flag *TxFail*. For example in Figure 3, when the aborted transaction in T2 writes to *TxFail*, the concurrent in-flight transactions

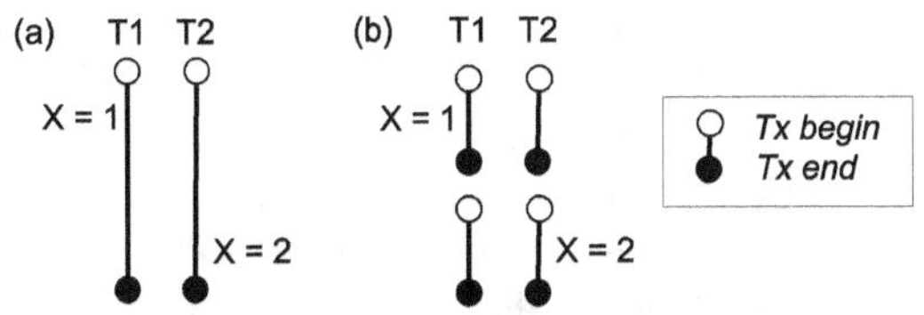

Figure 4: (a) Race detected with long transactions (b) Race missed with short transactions

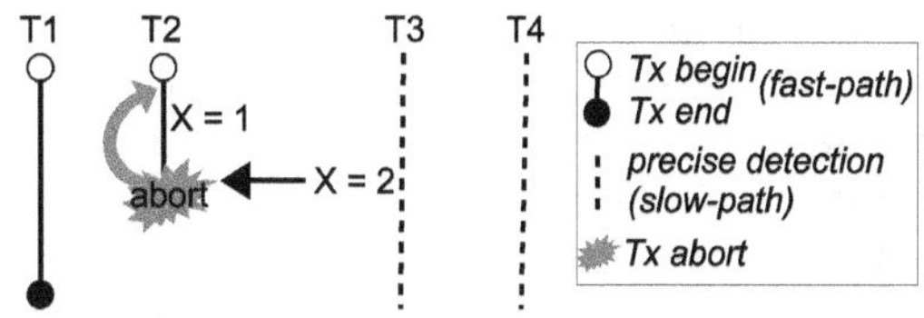

Figure 5: Detecting data races between fast and slow paths using the strong isolation property of HTM

in T1 and T3 which have read *TxFail* get aborted. Similar techniques have been used to abort in-flight transactions in hybrid TM systems [11, 15, 44] or to enable transactional lock elision [2].

HTMs can only detect those data races that result in conflicts between concurrent transactions. This suggests that maximizing the size of the transactions inserted at compile-time will minimize the likelihood of false negatives. It would be ideal to transform each synchronization-free region into a single transaction. However, as mentioned above, TxRace cuts transactions across systems calls inevitably. A performance optimization called *loop-cut* discussed further in Section 4.3 may also lead to cut a transaction originally formed for a synchronization-free region.

Figure 4 (a) and (b) show that the length of transactions can affect the detection of data races. Both (a) and (b) show unsynchronized and potentially-concurrent writes to the shared variable *X* from threads T1 and T2: a race condition. In (a), each thread executes a single lengthy transaction. The long transaction length increases the likelihood that the two transactions will overlap, and in this case the data race on *X* is detected. In (b), each thread executes two transactions, and the data race on *X* is more likely to be missed (a false negative) as a result. As shown in (b), suppose the first transaction in T1 includes *X=1* and successfully commits prior to the beginning of the second transaction in T2, which includes *X=2*. However, if the two transactions do not overlap, then neither will abort. For this reason, similar to other overlap-based data race detectors [5, 12, 18, 20], TxRace may miss data races if they happen far apart in time. Though perfect soundness is thus out of reach, the experimental results in Section 8 show that TxRace trades only a few false negatives (recall of 0.95) for excellent performance.

4.2 Handling Transactional Aborts

The best-effort Intel RTM does not guarantee that a transaction will eventually commit and make progress. In addition to data conflicts, there are many architectural and micro-architectural conditions that may cause a transaction to abort. When a transaction is aborted, Intel RTM rolls back the transaction to the point where it begins and reports the abort type(s) in the register. TxRace handles transaction aborts according to the abort reason as follows, while juggling the competing goals of reducing false negatives, decreasing overhead, and offering a forward progress guarantee.

Conflict. A transaction aborted due to a data conflict indicates a potential data race. To conduct precise data race detection, TxRace updates the shared flag (named *TxFail*) that every transaction begins by reading, forcing all the concurrent (in-flight) transactions to abort and roll back (Figure 3). TxRace then performs slow path software-based sound and complete data race detection among the code regions that overlapped with the aborted code region. Once a potential data race is detected by the fast path, the software-based slow-path detector will winnow out the false positives and to find data races if one exists.

Retry. A transaction aborted with "retry" status might succeed if retried. If this flag is set in conjunction with the conflict flag described above, TxRace treats the case as a conflict and follows the slow path. Otherwise, TxRace retries the transaction.

Capacity. When a transaction is aborted due to overflow, TxRace makes only the thread that observed the capacity abort fall back to slow path. Unlike the case for data conflicts, TxRace does not artificially abort the other concurrent transactions (by not updating the shared flag *TxFail*) since there is no indication of a potential data race with concurrent transactions. Using concurrent slow and fast path executions minimizes performance overhead while still giving TxRace high detection coverage (fewer false negatives) and the guarantee of forward progress. Figure 5 demonstrates how TxRace can detect data races when both fast and slow paths run at the same time. Here, threads T1 and T2 are on the fast path, while threads T3 and T4 are on the slow path due to capacity aborts. In this case, data races between threads T1 and T2 can be detected using HTM-based fast-path detection, and data races between thread T3 and T4 can be detected using precise slow-path detection. The interesting case is a race condition between fast path and slow path threads. If T2 is on the fast path and T3 is on the slow path as shown in the example, the strong isolation property of Intel RTM ensures that the transaction in T2 will be aborted in the event that T3 makes the conflicting access to the variable *X* that T2 has accessed. In this case, TxRace handles the conflict abort as described above. Because T3 is already in the slow path, the precise data race condition can be identified once TxRace puts T2 in the slow path.

Unknown. A transaction may abort with an unknown (unspecified) reason. As TxRace enforces that a transaction does not include a system call (Section 4.1), this is most likely due to unexpected operating system context switches to handle interrupts, exceptions, etc. To guarantee forward progress while achieving high detection coverage (fewer false negatives), TxRace treats this case the same as the capacity abort.

Debug/Nested. The debug bit is set when a transaction aborts upon encountering a debug breakpoint, while the nested bit is set when a transaction was aborted during a nested transaction. Neither of these conditions may happen as a result of the TxRace transactionalization process; no debug breakpoints are used, and TxRace does not introduce nested transactions. TxRace simply ignores this case.

4.3 Optimization

To reduce performance overhead at runtime, TxRace applies several optimizations in the fast path. First, TxRace checks if the program is in the single-threaded mode or not (e.g., in the very beginning of program execution before spawning child threads). If so, there should be no races, thus TxRace simply does not use HTM to monitor the program execution to avoid unnecessary cost of transactions. If a function is profiled to be invoked in both single-threaded and multi-threaded modes, then at compile-time TxRace clones the function and instruments only the version that is called in multithreaded mode.

Second, Txrace reuses the same static analysis algorithm that Google TSan uses to avoid unnecessary data race checks. If a memory operation is statically proven to be data race free, then TSan does not instrument it. TxRace also does not insert transaction codes for those code regions that are not instrumented by Google TSan to hook memory accesses for data race detection.

Third, for regions containing a small number of memory operations, the overhead associated with HTMs exceeds the cost of the software-based slow path. If a code region contains fewer than K memory operations, TxRace favors the slow path. In our experiment we chose $K = 5$.

Finally, TxRace leverages our so-called *loop-cut* optimization for transactions that includes loops with a large number of iterations; these loops are a frequent cause of capacity aborts. By default, TxRace falls back to the slow path when a transaction experience a capacity abort to obtain better detection capability for those code regions at the cost of some performance overhead. To reduce this overhead, the loop-cut optimization aims to end the long transaction before prior to a capacity abort. TxRace first profiles an application with representative input to identify the candidate loops for the loop-cut optimization. In this study, TxRace leverages the Last Branch Recorder (LBR), a branch tracing facility in Intel processors [30], which allows TxRace to identify the last branch taken before a transaction aborts. Then, TxRace inserts the following loop-cut logic to the end of the candidate loop body.

The high level idea is for TxRace to keep track of the number of loop iteration (called *loop-cut-threshold*). When the transaction experiences a capacity abort in the loop, TxRace takes the slow path at first (default behavior), but when the same loop is executed next time, TxRace uses this loop-cut-threshold to cut the current transaction early in the middle of loop iterations, placing the rest of the iterations into another transaction to avoid capacity aborts. As discussed above, short transactions cut by loop-cut optimization may lead to false negatives.

HTM semantics make this implementation slightly tricky. Note that as the loop is a part of transaction, it is not possible to use a counter incremented per loop iteration to obtain the precise loop-cut-threshold value; updates to the counter will not survive a transaction abort. TxRace addresses this problem by setting a small initial estimate loop-cut-threshold (two in our experiment) and by incrementing and decrementing the estimate when the transaction commits/aborts, respectively (outside the transaction). This approach enables TxRace to estimate the last largest loop-cut-threshold allowing the transaction to commit. This work calls this scheme, which dynamically learns the loop-cut-threshold at runtime, *TxRace-DynLoopcut*.

As another scheme, *TxRace-ProfLoopcut* profiles an application with representative input to figure out the initial loop-cut-threshold value beforehand. This approach allows TxRace to avoid even the very first capacity abort. Similar to *TxRace-DynLoopcut*, *TxRace-ProfLoopcut* handles misprofiling by adjusting the threshold when the transaction commits or aborts accordingly. Section 8.2 evaluates the effectiveness of the two loop-cut optimization schemes.

5. Slow Path Software-based Race Detection

For software-based data race detection during the slow path, TxRace uses Google's ThreadSanitizer (TSan) [62, 65], an open-source state-of-practice data race detector. Similar to the well-known sound and complete FastTrack algorithm [21], TSan keeps track of the happens-before order for each memory location using a shadow memory. Then, TSan detects data races when accesses to shared locations are not ordered. This process requires instrumenting (1) synchronization operations to track the happens-before order; and (2) memory operations to look up shadow memory and compare their happens-before order. By design, TSan is complete (no false positive). However, to bound memory overhead, TSan maintains N (default 4) shadow cells per 8 application bytes, and replaces one random shadow cell when all shadow cells are filled. This may affect soundness (no false negative) of data race detection. Thus, this work configured TSan to have enough number of shadow cells to be sound as well.

The potential interplay of fast and slow path threads necessitates additional overhead during the fast path. A naive fast path could rely solely on HTM to detect potential data

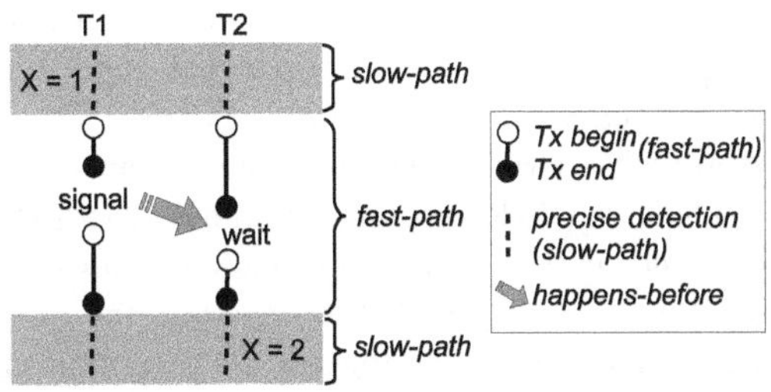

Figure 6: Tracking the happens-before order of synchronizations on the fast path eliminates false warnings on the slow path

races, obviating the need to track the happens-before order imposed by synchronization operations. However, threads may alternate between fast and slow paths for precise data race detection. When TSan finishes in the slow path, TxRace resumes the use of the fast path to monitor the next regions, achieving better performance. This design requires TxRace to keep track of the happens-before order of synchronization operations even during the fast path to remove false warnings during slow path. Figure 6 describes this feature in more detail. Suppose that threads T1 and T2 have executed the slow path, fast path, and slow path in turn for some reason other than conflicting accesses to *X*, and that there was a happens-before order between *signal* and *wait* that appeared during the fast path. If TxRace does not track this happens-before order during the fast path, the slow path data race detector would report a data race between *X=1* and *X=2*, which is a false warning. The performance overhead breakdown in Section 8.2 shows that tracking synchronization operations is not that expensive during the fast path.

6. False Negatives

TxRace is complete (no false positive) but unsound (some false negative). There are four main reasons why TxRace could miss data races. First, fast-path HTMs do not detect data conflicts between transactions that do not overlap in time, as discussed in Section 4.1. This is different from sound (happens-before based) data race detectors such as FastTrack or Google's TSan, which identify races by tracking the happens-before order of synchronization operations. In this sense, TxRace resembles overlap-based data race detectors [5, 12, 18, 20].

Second, when a transaction is aborted due to data conflict and TxRace writes the shared flag *TxFail* to abort others, there is no guarantee that some of the already-running transactions will not commit before they see the write. In this case, even though TxRace triggers the slow path, the race will not occur again and thus cannot be detected.

Third, race detection between the fast and slow paths (Figure 5) only works in one direction. If the slow path thread makes a shared memory access *before* the fast path thread makes a conflicting access, then the HTM's strong isolation guarantee does not apply. As a result, when the opposite of the situation in Figure 5 happen, TxRace will not trigger the slow path, and the race will not be detected.

Finally, TxRace by nature shares the limitations of the underlying HTM system. As of now, Intel Haswell processor does not support more concurrent transactions than the total number of hardware threads available. This implies that the number of threads that can be monitored by HTM during fast path is limited.

During evaluation, the thread count was restricted to be smaller than the hardware thread counts, ruling out the forth reason. All of the observed false negatives were due to non-overlapping transactions.

7. Implementation

TxRace instrumentation framework is implemented in the LLVM compiler framework [39]. As a very first process, we translate application source codes into LLVM IR (Intermediate Representation) and perform instrumentation as a custom transformation pass. During this process, we do not include external libraries such as standard *libc*, *libc++*, *libm*, etc., assuming that such libraries are thread safe, and users are interested in detecting data races in application codes. External libraries may be included into our scope when their LLVM IR is provided. It is worthwhile to note that we included all the internal libraries that are provided with core application codes such as *gsl*, *libjpeg*, *glib*, *libxml2*, etc. in PARSEC benchmark suite [3] into our analysis.

Instrumentation for fast path needs to intercept synchronization operations and the program points before/after system calls so that transaction begin/end codes can be inserted. For example, a new transactional region starts after a new thread starts or after each system call. As we do not include standard C/C++ libraries into our scope, we instrument system calls at the library call boundary; i.e., before and after calls to library functions that may invoke system calls such as synchronization (e.g., *PThread* library); standard I/O (e.g., *read*, *write*); and dynamic memory management library (e.g., *malloc*, *free*). For the third party libraries whose source codes are not available, dynamic binary instrumentation tools [10, 48, 55] can be used to profile the program with representative input and to identify a list of external library functions invoking system calls. Misprofiling would result in unknown aborts caused by undetected system calls. TxRace falls back to slow path in case of unknown aborts (by default), thus misprofiling only adds runtime overhead, and does not harm detection coverage.

For slow path, we use off-the-shelf Google's ThreadSanitizer (TSan) [62, 65], an open-source state-of-practice happens-before based data race detector. For each memory location and synchronization variable, TSan keeps track of happens-before order information into shadow memory. TSan supports compile-time instrumentation for data race detection using Clang frontend [68] and LLVM passes [39]. For simplicity, we instrument fast/slow path codes together into the original program. For example, the same memory access hook is instrumented for both fast/slow paths. Depending on the fast or slow path, the hook performs TSan data race detection for slow path or it does nothing for fast path. For better performance, it would be ideal to clone the codes and have separate fast/slow path codes to remove the redundancy similar to [38, 67]. We leave this optimization as a future work.

The implementation of TxRace can be downloaded from https://github.com/lzto/TxRace

8. Evaluation

Our evaluation answers the following questions:

- What is the overhead of TxRace data race detection? Is it efficient?
- Does TxRace effectively detect data races? How many false negatives are there?
- Is TxRace cost-effective compared to other approaches? Is it better than a sampling-based approach, or a full happens-before based detector?

8.1 Methodology

We ran experiments on a 3.6GHz quad-core Intel Core^{TM}i7-4790 processor, with 16GB of RAM, running Gentoo Linux (kernel 4.0.4). Intel's Restricted Transactional Memory (RTM) is used for HTM-based fast path data race detection. Intel Haswell processor supports the same number of concurrent transactions as the hardware threads available, which is four (eight with hyperthreading) in our case. On the other hand, Google's ThreadSanitizer (TSan) is used for software-based slow path data race detection.

TxRace was evaluated using 1) PARSEC benchmark suite [3] that is designed to be representative of next-generation shared-memory programs including emerging workloads; and 2) Apache web server [1]. We used *simlarge* input for all the 13 application in PARSEC, and tested Apache using ab (ApacheBench) by sending 300,000 requests from 20 concurrent clients over a local network. Performance was reported in terms of overhead with respect to the original execution time without data race detection. We compare our system (named *TxRace* in the result) with off-the-shelf Google's ThreadSanitizer (named *TSan*). All results are the mean of five trials with four worker threads (except the scalability analysis).

8.2 Performance Overhead

Table 1 shows the TxRace execution statistic, the number of detected data races, and overall performance results. The first column provides the application name. The next four columns show transaction statistics during HTM-based fast path data race detection: the number of total committed transactions, the number of data conflict aborts, the number of capacity (overflow) aborts, and the number of unknown (unspecified) aborts. The next two columns give the number of races detected by TSan and TxRace. The applications in which TxRace cannot detect all the races reported by TSan are marked with asterisk. The next three columns show the original, TSan, and TxRace execution times. The first is the execution time of the original application (with no transactions, memory hooks, etc.); the second is the execution time when TSan is used; the third is the execution time of our system TxRace. The last two columns show TSan's and TxRace's overhead with respect to the original execution.

Examining the results, we see that TxRace's overhead is generally low. On average, TxRace reduces runtime overhead of dynamic data race detection from 11.68x to 4.65x (geometric means), showing 60% reduction ratio. For some applications such as *vips* and *streamcluster*, TxRace achieved more than 10 times speedup over TSan.

Figure 7 shows a breakdown of the overhead normalized to the original execution time (baseline) for all benchmarks. The black portion in each bar (xbegin/xend) represents the pure fast path overhead in which transactions are executed, but no slow path is taken even when they get aborted (simply run untransactionalized code). For most applications, this overhead is pretty low (the geometric mean of 17%), except *swaptions* and *streamcluster*. Upon further investigation, we found out that these two applications have tight loops that have system calls in the loop body. In this case, TxRace ends and begins new transactions around the system calls. This results in tight short transactions whose management cost now becomes dominant. The next overhead comes from handling aborts due to data conflicts (157%), which includes running slow path software-based data race detection. This low-overhead result shows the benefits of using HTM-based potential data race detection beforehand, which allows TxRace to selectively perform the software-based dynamic data race detection only for small fraction of execution intervals. Finally, the remaining performance overhead comes from handling capacity and unknown aborts (126% and 66%, respectively). To achieve small false negatives, TxRace takes the conservative approach of using slow path software-based detector to monitor program regions that fast path HTM cannot cover. We envision that if there is an ideal HTM such that a transaction aborts only if there is a data conflict and do not have capacity/unknown aborts, then the runtime overhead of TxRace would be improved significantly as TxRace only falls back to slow path when necessary (only when a data conflict occurs).

Figure 8 shows the scalability of TxRace. We varied the number of worker threads from 2, 4 to 8, and measured the runtime overhead normalized to the original execution time with 2, 4, and 8 worker threads, respectively. For comparison of two and four thread cases, some applications such as *swaptions* and *streamcluster* show lower runtime overhead for four thread cases, but most of the remaining applications show small differences in normalized runtime over-

application	committed transactions	conflict aborts	capacity aborts	unknown aborts	TSan races	TxRace races	original time(ms)	TSan time(ms)	TxRace time(ms)	TSan overhead	TxRace overhead
blackscholes	131105	2	0	7	0	0	253	467	460	1.85x	1.82x
fluidanimate	17778944	696789	10321	36614	1	1	539	8217	3724	15.23x	6.9x
swaptions	160640076	2599	557497	54317	0	0	868	5875	3446	6.77x	3.97x
freqmine	84	0	3	26	0	0	3973	55611	4569	14x	1.15x
vips	707547	16793	23403	14985	112	79(*)	953	1139087	60320	1195x	63.28x
raytrace	143	12	0	14	2	2	4546	23130	12203	5.09x	2.68x
ferret	208052	379	2413	4263	1	1	1060	11390	5852	10.74x	5.52x
x264	36808	245	423	5358	64	64	595	3837	3332	6.45x	5.6x
bodytrack	9950991	36004	47050	2004723	8	6(*)	503	6429	4479	12.78x	8.9x
facesim	12827334	1611	3372	38563	9	8(*)	2439	89242	28027	36.59x	11.49x
streamcluster	756908	170805	230	832	4	4	1430	39042	4253	25.9x	2.97x
dedup	2185219	106618	13889	40177	0	0	2748	13292	11513	4.84x	4.19x
canneal	3200570	25187	2896	106419	1	1	3499	15367	10375	4.39x	2.97x
apache	310781	227	446	9793	0	0	6916	21089	13600	3.05x	1.97x
geo.mean										11.68x	4.65x

Table 1: TxRace Execution Statistics and Performance.

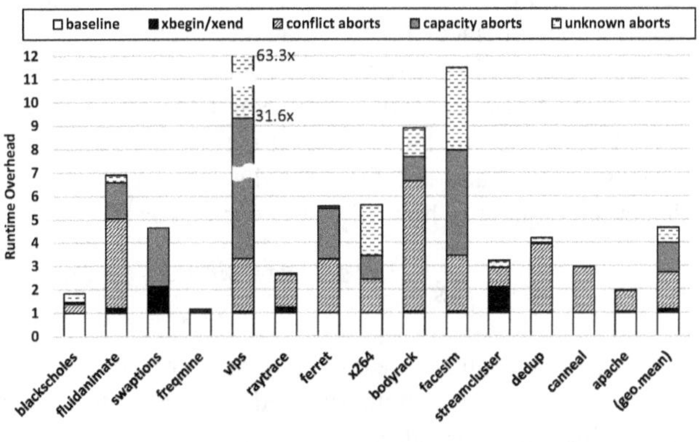

Figure 7: Breakdown of runtime overhead.

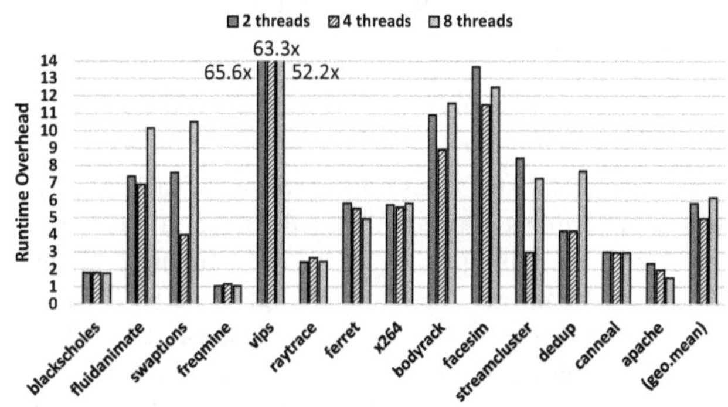

Figure 8: Scalability of TxRace

head. Upon further investigation, we found out that the number of capacity aborts (geometric mean of 644 vs. 474) and unknown aborts (geometric mean of 8377 vs. 4651) decreases from two to four thread cases. The reduction in capacity aborts makes sense as many applications in PARSEC benchmark take advantage of data parallelism, and thus each worker thread is likely to have smaller dataset with more worker threads. On the other hand, the number of conflict aborts (geometric mean of 244 vs. 1242) increases from two to four thread cases (likely due to increased concurrency). After all, the mixture of the increase and the decrease in transactional aborts causes different applications to show variation in performance overhead.

Another interesting result of this experiment is the high overhead incurred for some applications with eight threads (e.g., *fluidanimate*, *swaptions*, *streamcluster*, and *dedup*). Examining the results, we found that the number of unknown aborts increases significantly for eight thread case (geometric mean of 42251, which is 5x and 9x more than two and four thread cases, respectively). As Intel Haswell processor does not provide additional information regarding unknown aborts, further investigation was not possible, but we suspect that eight concurrent transactions enabled by hyperthreading might lead to increased unkonwn aborts.

Finally, we evaluate the effectiveness of the loop-cut optimization discussed in the Section 4.3. Figure 9 presents the normalized runtime overhead of TSan and three different types of TxRace. They differ from each other based on how they handle a transaction that includes a loop with a large number of iterations, causing capacity aborts frequently. *TxRace-NoOpt* stands for the basic scheme without optimization that TxRace simply falls back to slow path every time when a transaction gets aborted for the capacity reason. *TxRace-DynLoopcut* represents the optimized scheme that for a transaction including a loop, TxRace dynamically learns the loop iteration count (called *loop-cut-threshold*) that do not cause a capacity abort at runtime. When the transaction gets aborted, TxRace falls back to the slow path at first. However, when the same loop is executed next time, TxRace uses the loop-cut-threshold to terminate the transaction early in the middle of loop iterations and starts a new transaction to avoid capacity aborts. *TxRace-ProfLoopcut* is similar to the above dynamic scheme, but it profiles the program with representative input to collect the initial loop-cut-threshold, and avoids even the very first capacity aborts. Fig-

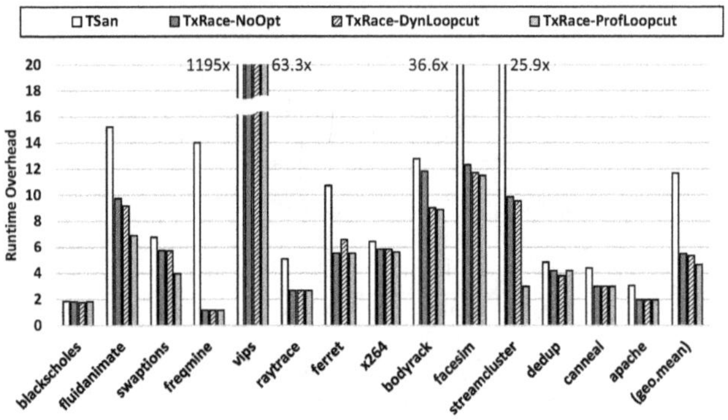

Figure 9: Effectiveness of loop-cut optimization

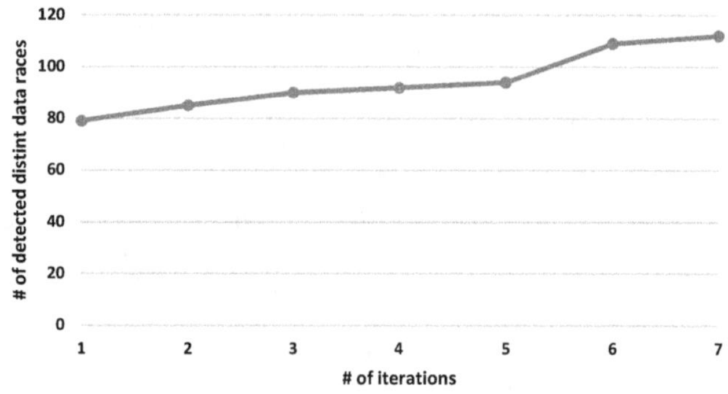

Figure 10: The number of detected distinct data races across multiple runs for *vips*

ure 9 shows the benefits of leveraging the loop-cut optimization. In all cases, TxRace is more efficient than TSan. On average, *TxRace-ProfLoopcut* shows the best result (4.65x) in terms of performance overhead, and *TxRace-DynLoopcut* which does not require profiling the threshold also performs better than TSan (5.34x).

8.3 False Negatives

In this section, we study false negatives of TxRace. HTMs detect data conflicts between transactions that are concurrently overlapped in time. As a result, similar to other overlap-based data race detectors [5, 12, 18, 20], TxRace may miss data races if they happen far apart in time. The sixth and seventh columns of Table 1 represent the average number of data races reported by happens-before based TSan and our overlap based TxRace. Here, each race is in a form of racy instruction pair, and we count the number of static instances.

There are three applications (*vips*, *bodytrack*, and *facesim*) that TxRace detects less data races than TSan. It turns out that the missed three cases of *bodytrack* and *facesim* are due to the common *initialization* idiom, in which a data structure is allocated within a thread and initialized without any synchronization while the structure is still local to the thread, and then it becomes accessible to other threads, by adding it to a global data structure. For example in *facesim*, a structure is initialized when a thread pool is created at the beginning of program execution, then it becomes shared at a later time. TxRace missed such races because conflicting accesses do not overlap.

On the other hand, for *vips*, though the number of data race found for each test run remains about the same (average of 79), we observed that TxRace actually finds different sets of data races across different runs. This makes sense because TxRace's nature of the overlap-based detection makes it sensitive to underlying OS scheduler. Figure 10 shows that when we accumulate the distinct data races detected, TxRace can find all the data races (112) found by TSan after seven runs. Note that for *vips*, TxRace (63.3x) is order of magnitude faster than TSan (1195x).

8.4 Cost-Effectiveness of Data Race Detection

TxRace is complete (no false positive) but unsound (some false negative). In essence, TxRace aims to be a cost-effective solution that exploits a critical tradeoff of soundness for performance. To quantitatively evaluate how cost-effective TxRace is, we rely on a popular economic analysis term called *cost-effectiveness ratio* where the denominator is the effectiveness and the numerator is the cost. The original ratio is inverted and redefined for the context of data race detection to quantify how cost-effective it is as follows:

$$CostEffectiveness = \frac{Race\_Detection\_Effectiveness}{Race\_Detection\_Cost}$$

As a metric to evaluate the data race detection effectiveness, we use *recall* that is commonly used to measure the quality of classifiers in information retrieval and bug detection communities [4, 36, 43, 71]. Intuitively, high recall leads to less false negatives (undetected data races). In the context of data race detection, *recall* is defined as follows:

$$recall = \frac{|Reported\_Data\_Races \cap Real\_Data\_Races|}{|Real\_Data\_Races|}$$

For comparison to TSan, $Real\_Data\_Races$ is defined as the data races reported by TSan. To calculate the cost effectiveness (CE), we use TxRace's runtime overhead normalized to TSan's. Table 2 summarizes how much more cost-effective TxRace is compared to TSan for each benchmark application (here TSan's CE is 1). TxRace turns out to be 2.38x (geometric mean) more cost-effective than TSan across the benchmark applications. This is mainly because in TxRace, only small portion of memory accesses are investigated for software-based data race detection (slow path). On the other hand, the majority of memory accesses are dealt with by transactional execution (fast path) at a very low runtime cost.

To justify such a high cost-effectiveness of TxRace, we also compare TxRace with TSan with sampling. Sampling memory operations is an intuitive way to reduce runtime overhead of dynamic data race detection. However, it also comes with false negative issues because some data races

application	overhead	recall	cost-effectiveness
blackscholes	0.99	1	1.02
fluidanimate	0.45	1	2.21
swaptions	0.59	1	1.7
freqmine	0.08	1	12.17
vips	0.05	0.71	13.32
raytrace	0.53	1	1.9
ferret	0.51	1	1.95
x264	0.87	1	1.15
bodytrack	0.7	0.75	1.08
facesim	0.31	0.89	2.83
streamcluster	0.11	1	8.71
dedup	0.87	1	1.15
canneal	0.68	1	1.48
apache	0.65	1	1.55
geo.mean	0.38	0.95	2.38

Table 2: Cost-Effectiveness of TxRace vs. TSan

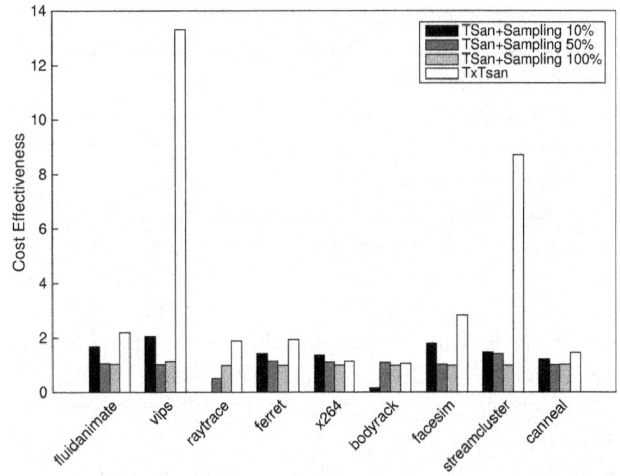

Figure 11: Cost-Effectiveness of TxRace vs. Sampling

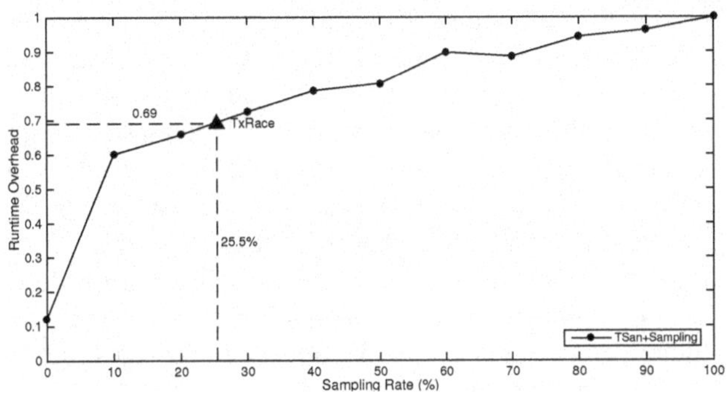

Figure 12: Runtime overhead for *bodytrack*

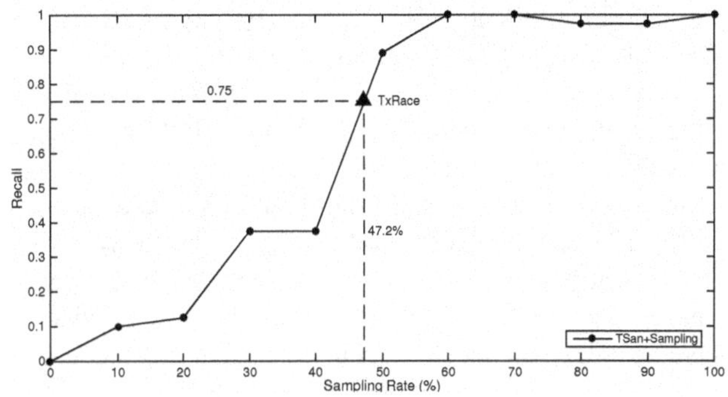

Figure 13: Recall for *bodytrack*

might be missed at a low sampling rate. To study if TxRace is more cost-effective than sampling, we vary the sampling rate and measure the resulting runtime overhead and the recall of TSan for every benchmark. As a represetative application, we present the result of *bodytrack* in detail. Figure 12 shows the runtime overhead normalized to 100% sampling (full coverage), and Figure 13 shows the recall at different sampling rates while treating 100% as an oracle. As expected, both the runtime overhead and recall increase as the sampling rate increases. On the other hand, the normalized runtime overhead and the recall of TxRace are 0.69 and 0.75, respectively. This implies that TxRace adds an overhead equivalent to sampling about 25.5% of memory operations, but its recall is equivalent to 47.2% sampling, which shows its cost effectiveness.

Lastly, Figure 11 presents the cost-effectiveness of TxRace compared to TSan with sampling across nine applications in which TxRace/TSan detect at least one data race. For some applications such as *fluidanimate*, *vips*, and *facesim*, 10% sampling turns out to be more efficient than 50% or 100% sampling cases. It turns out that the data race in such applications manifest often at runtime, thus they get detected even at the low sampling frequency. In other words, the number of dynamic instances of the data race is quite high even though the number of static instance (unique race condition) is small (e.g., one for *fluidanimate*), thus reaching the recall of almost 1 (no false negative) at the low frequency. After all, for almost all applications execpt *x264*, TxRace outperforms TSan with sampling in terms of the cost-effectiveness.

9. Related Work

This section discusses closely related work comparing TxRace with existing data race detection techniques. To the best of our knowledge, TxRace is the first approach to leverage a commodity HTM for speeding up data race detection.

Eraser [63] introduced lockset-based approach, which infers data race through violation of locking discipline. As lockset-based algorithms do not consider non-mutex synchronization operations such as conditional variables, they are incomplete (generate false positives) compared to the approach that tracks happens-before order of synchronization operations using vector clocks. FastTrack [21] is known to be the most optimized algorithm in this category, which reduced runtime overhead significantly compared to prior works such as MultiRace [58]. Google's ThreadSanitizer, which TxRace used for its slow path, also tracks happens-before order similar to FastTrack. However, high runtime overhead is still a major concern.

Several strategies have been explored to reduce the overhead of dynamic data race detection. LiteRace [50] and Pacer [9] use sampling; RaceMob [37] crowdsources (distributes) runtime checks across different users; Wester et al. [70] parallelizes data race detection; Lee et al. [40, 41] uses offline symbolic analysis; and Goldilocks [19], Choi et al. [13], and Chimera [42] leverage static analysis to remove checks for statically proven race-free memory operations. Matar et al. [52] exploit Intel TSX (same as ours) to speed up data race detection, but they leveraged HTM simply to replace locks that are used to provide atomicity in metadata updates/checks, which is different from TxRace. We believe that TxRace can use these techniques to further reduce the runtime cost of the slow path.

Greathouse et al. [24] presents a demand-driven race detector. They use hardware performance counters in modern processors to monitor cache events indicating data sharing to turn on race detection. Due to limitation in current hardware, they could identify W→R data sharing events only, and though all are presumably possible, not all cache sharing causes data races. On the other hand, TxRace uses data conflict detection mechanism in HTM to identify potential data races and to trigger on-demand race detection.

The recent advances in overlap-based data race detectors [5, 12, 18, 20] have shown their cost-effectiveness and practical benefits by trading soundness for better performance. DataCollider [20] and Kivati [12] use hardware code/data breakpoint mechanism in processors to detect data races. They set a data breakpoint to trap conflicting accesses by other threads. This is similar to conflict detection mechanism in HTM, which detects concurrent conflicting accesses. After setting up the breakpoint, they insert a short amount of time delay to the thread to increase detection probability. The detection window in HTM spans the whole length of a transaction, so the detection probability is likely to be higher than the breakpoint based approach at the cost of false positive. Moreover, the small number of breakpoints (four for x86 hardware) limits its coverage. As another overlap-based detector, IFRit [18] exploits compiler analysis to form interference-free regions where data races can be detected when they overlap. The scope of IFRit may be longer than TxRace's transactional region in some cases, but it could be very short (e.g., basic block) in other cases since each region may start after the variable is defined in the SSA form. For performance reasons, IFRit gives up data race detection for those short-scope regions, which TxRace may cover.

Data race detection also has been the subject of intense research by hardware community. In general, hardware-assisted data-race detectors store metadata (e.g., locksets, vector-clocks) in the cache, piggyback them on coherence protocol messages, and compare them to detect data races.

HARD [76] is a hardware-based implementation of the lockset algorithm, whereas ReEnact [60] and CORD [59] implement happens-before based algorithm in hardware. RADISH [16] proposes hardware-software co-design to enable always-on sound and complete data race detections in which hardware performs the vast majority of race checks and software backs up hardware resource limitations. Conflict Exceptions [47] extends a standard coherence protocol and caches to detect data conflicts between synchronization-free regions, as TxRace does. SigRace [54] employs custom hardware address signature where the memory addresses accessed by a processor are hash-encoded and accumulated, and uses it do detect the outcome of potential data races rather than the race itself. Then SigRace relies on checkpointing/rollback to identify actual racing instructions. Similarly, TxRace uses the same insight to use lightweight check first, then do expensive one later only if necessary.

Perhaps RaceTM [25] is the most closely related to our work, as it also proposes to use hardware transactional memory in detecting data races. However, their approach is hardware-only solution that requires additional hardware extension to conventional HTMs like LogTM [53]. For example, RaceTM requires two additional bits (debug read/write bits) for every cache line. They added support to provide the conflict address and responsible racy instructions as well.

Finally, even if TxIntro [45] is not a data race detector, it combines hardware performance counters (such as HITM, cache miss, and PEBS) with Intel's TSX to infer the conflicting data linear address. We envision that TxRace can leverage such supports to design more efficient slow path if the future generation of commodity processor provides such information to the users.

10. Conclusion

The spread of shared-memory multiprocessor architectures has spurred development of multithreaded programs. However, such programs are subject to concurrency bugs including data races. Unfortunately, traditional dynamic data race detectors are too slow to use in many cases. This paper describes TxRace, a new software dynamic data race detector that exploits commodity hardware transactional memory support to enable dynamic data race detection with a low runtime overhead. Leveraging existing HTM support allows TxRace to use a precise but expensive dynamic data race detector only for a small fraction of the whole execution in an on-demand manner, leading to performance improvement. The experiment results show that TxRace achieves runtime overhead reduction of dynamic data race detection by 60% on average with only a few false negatives (high recall of 0.95).

Acknowledgments

We thank Jaeheon Yi, Jungwoo Ha, and Richard M. Yoo for helpful discussion and their feedback; James Davis for his careful proofreading; and the anonymous reviewers for insightful comments. The work is supported in part by an award from Google.

References

[1] The apache http server. http://httpd.apache.org.

[2] Y. Afek, A. Levy, and A. Morrison. Software-improved hardware lock elision. In *Proceedings of the 2014 ACM Symposium on Principles of Distributed Computing*, PODC '14, pages 212–221, 2014. ISBN 978-1-4503-2944-6.

[3] C. Bienia, S. Kumar, J. P. Singh, and K. Li. The PARSEC Benchmark Suite: Characterization and Architectural Implications. In *Proc. of the 17th PACT*, Oct. 2008.

[4] C. Bishop et al. *Pattern recognition and machine learning*. Springer New York:, 2006.

[5] S. Biswas, M. Zhang, M. D. Bond, and B. Lucia. Efficient, software-only data race exceptions. In *Proceedings of the 2015 ACM SIGPLAN International Conference on Object-Oriented Programming, Systems, Languages, and Applications*, OOPSLA '15, 2015.

[6] S. Biswas, M. Zhang, M. D. Bond, and B. Lucia. Valor: Efficient, software-only region conflict exceptions. In *Proceedings of the 2015 ACM SIGPLAN International Conference on Object-Oriented Programming, Systems, Languages, and Applications*, OOPSLA 2015, pages 241–259, 2015. ISBN 978-1-4503-3689-5.

[7] J. Bobba, K. E. Moore, H. Volos, L. Yen, M. D. Hill, M. M. Swift, and D. A. Wood. Performance pathologies in hardware transactional memory. In *Proceedings of the 34th Annual International Symposium on Computer Architecture*, ISCA '07, pages 81–91, 2007. ISBN 978-1-59593-706-3.

[8] H.-J. Boehm and S. V. Adve. Foundations of the c++ concurrency memory model. In *Proceedings of the 2008 ACM SIGPLAN Conference on Programming Language Design and Implementation*, PLDI '08, pages 68–78, 2008.

[9] M. D. Bond, K. E. Coons, and K. S. McKinley. Pacer: Proportional detection of data races. In *Proceedings of the 2010 ACM SIGPLAN Conference on Programming Language Design and Implementation*, PLDI '10, pages 255–268, 2010. ISBN 978-1-4503-0019-3.

[10] D. Bruening, T. Garnett, and S. Amarasinghe. An infrastructure for adaptive dynamic optimization. In *Proceedings of the International Symposium on Code Generation and Optimization: Feedback-directed and Runtime Optimization*, CGO '03, pages 265–275, 2003. ISBN 0-7695-1913-X.

[11] I. Calciu, J. Gottschlich, T. Shpeisman, G. Pokam, and M. Herlihy. Invyswell: A hybrid transactional memory for haswell's restricted transactional memory. In *Proceedings of the 23rd International Conference on Parallel Architectures and Compilation*, PACT '14, pages 187–200, 2014.

[12] L. Chew and D. Lie. Kivati: Fast detection and prevention of atomicity violations. In *Proceedings of the 5th European Conference on Computer Systems*, EuroSys '10, pages 307–320, 2010. ISBN 978-1-60558-577-2.

[13] J.-D. Choi, K. Lee, A. Loginov, R. O'Callahan, V. Sarkar, and M. Sridharan. Efficient and precise datarace detection for multithreaded object-oriented programs. In *Proceedings of the ACM SIGPLAN 2002 Conference on Programming Language Design and Implementation*, PLDI '02, pages 258–269, 2002. ISBN 1-58113-463-0.

[14] C. Click. Azuls experiences with hardware transactional memory. In *In HP Labs - Bay Area Workshop on Transactional Memory*, 2009.

[15] L. Dalessandro, F. Carouge, S. White, Y. Lev, M. Moir, M. L. Scott, and M. F. Spear. Hybrid norec: A case study in the effectiveness of best effort hardware transactional memory. In *Proceedings of the Sixteenth International Conference on Architectural Support for Programming Languages and Operating Systems*, ASPLOS XVI, pages 39–52, 2011. ISBN 978-1-4503-0266-1.

[16] J. Devietti, B. P. Wood, K. Strauss, L. Ceze, D. Grossman, and S. Qadeer. Radish: Always-on sound and complete ra detection in software and hardware. In *Proceedings of the 39th Annual International Symposium on Computer Architecture*, ISCA '12, pages 201–212, 2012. ISBN 978-1-4503-1642-2.

[17] D. Dice, Y. Lev, M. Moir, and D. Nussbaum. Early experience with a commercial hardware transactional memory implementation. In *Proceedings of the 14th International Conference on Architectural Support for Programming Languages and Operating Systems*, ASPLOS XIV, pages 157–168, 2009. ISBN 978-1-60558-406-5.

[18] L. Effinger-Dean, B. Lucia, L. Ceze, D. Grossman, and H.-J. Boehm. Ifrit: Interference-free regions for dynamic data-race detection. In *Proceedings of the ACM International Conference on Object Oriented Programming Systems Languages and Applications*, OOPSLA '12, pages 467–484, 2012. ISBN 978-1-4503-1561-6.

[19] T. Elmas, S. Qadeer, and S. Tasiran. Goldilocks: A race and transaction-aware java runtime. In *Proceedings of the 2007 ACM SIGPLAN Conference on Programming Language Design and Implementation*, PLDI '07, pages 245–255, 2007. ISBN 978-1-59593-633-2.

[20] J. Erickson, M. Musuvathi, S. Burckhardt, and K. Olynyk. Effective data-race detection for the kernel. In *In Proceedings of the 9th USENIX conference on Operating systems design and implementation*, OSDI '10, 2010.

[21] C. Flanagan and S. N. Freund. Fasttrack: Efficient and precise dynamic race detection. In *Proceedings of the 2009 ACM SIGPLAN Conference on Programming Language Design and Implementation*, PLDI '09, pages 121–133, 2009. ISBN 978-1-60558-392-1.

[22] C. Flanagan, S. N. Freund, and J. Yi. Velodrome: A sound and complete dynamic atomicity checker for multithreaded programs. In *Proceedings of the 29th ACM SIGPLAN Conference on Programming Language Design and Implementation*, PLDI '08, pages 293–303, 2008. ISBN 978-1-59593-860-2.

[23] B. Goel, R. Titos-Gil, A. Negi, S. A. McKee, and P. Stenstrom. Performance and energy analysis of the restricted transactional memory implementation on haswell. In *Proceedings of the 2014 IEEE 28th International Parallel and Distributed Processing Symposium*, IPDPS '14, pages 615–624, Washington, DC, USA, 2014. ISBN 978-1-4799-3800-1.

[24] J. L. Greathouse, Z. Ma, M. I. Frank, R. Peri, and T. Austin. Demand-driven software race detection using hardware performance counters. In *Proceedings of the 38th Annual International Symposium on Computer Architecture*, ISCA '11, pages 165–176, 2011. ISBN 978-1-4503-0472-6.

[25] S. Gupta, F. Sultan, S. Cadambi, F. Ivancic, and M. Roetteler. Racetm: Detecting data races using transactional memory. In *Proceedings of the Twentieth Annual Symposium on Parallelism in Algorithms and Architectures*, SPAA '08, pages 104–106, 2008. ISBN 978-1-59593-973-9.

[26] R. Haring, M. Ohmacht, T. Fox, M. Gschwind, D. Satterfield, K. Sugavanam, P. Coteus, P. Heidelberger, M. Blumrich, R. Wisniewski, a. gara, G. Chiu, P. Boyle, N. Chist, and C. Kim. The ibm blue gene/q compute chip. *IEEE Micro*, 32 (2):48–60, Mar. 2012. ISSN 0272-1732.

[27] W. Hasenplaugh, A. Nguyen, and N. Shavit. Quantifying the capacity limitations of hardware transactional memory. In *WTTM '15: 7th Workshop on the Theory of Transactional Memory*, July 2015.

[28] M. Herlihy and J. E. B. Moss. Transactional memory: Architectural support for lock-free data structures. In *Proceedings of the 20th Annual International Symposium on Computer Architecture*, ISCA '93, pages 289–300, 1993. ISBN 0-8186-3810-9.

[29] Intel. Intel architecture instruction set extensions programming reference. chapter 8: Intel transactional synchronization extensions, 2012. https://software.intel.com/sites/default/files/m/9/2/3/41604.

[30] Intel. Intel 64 and ia-32 architectures software developers manual, 2013. http://download.intel.com/products/processor/manual/325462.pdf.

[31] Intel. Intel 64 and ia-32 architectures optimization reference manual. chapter 12: Intel tsx recommendations, 2014. http://www.intel.com/content/dam/www/public/us/en/documents/manuals/64-ia-32-architectures-optimization-manual.pdf.

[32] Intel. Intel inspector xe, 2015. http://software.intel.com/en-us/intel-inspector-xe.

[33] International Organization for Standardization. ISO/IEC 14882:2011: Information technology – Programming languages – C++, 2011.

[34] International Organization for Standardization. ISO/IEC 9899:2011: Information technology – Programming languages – C, 2011.

[35] C. Jacobi, T. Slegel, and D. Greiner. Transactional memory architecture and implementation for ibm system z. In *Proceedings of the 2012 45th Annual IEEE/ACM International Symposium on Microarchitecture*, MICRO-45, pages 25–36, 2012. ISBN 978-0-7695-4924-8.

[36] C. Jung, S. Lee, E. Raman, and S. Pande. Automated memory leak detection for production use. In *Proceedings of the 36th International Conference on Software Engineering*, 2014.

[37] B. Kasikci, C. Zamfir, and G. Candea. Racemob: Crowdsourced data race detection. In *Proceedings of the Twenty-Fourth ACM Symposium on Operating Systems Principles*, SOSP '13, pages 406–422, 2013. ISBN 978-1-4503-2388-8.

[38] K. Kelsey, T. Bai, C. Ding, and C. Zhang. Fast track: A software system for speculative program optimization. In *Proceedings of the 7th Annual IEEE/ACM International Symposium on Code Generation and Optimization*, CGO '09, pages 157–168, 2009. ISBN 978-0-7695-3576-0.

[39] C. Lattner and V. Adve. Llvm: A compilation framework for lifelong program analysis & transformation. In *Proceedings of the International Symposium on Code Generation and Optimization: Feedback-directed and Runtime Optimization*, CGO '04, pages 75–, 2004. ISBN 0-7695-2102-9.

[40] D. Lee, M. Said, S. Narayanasamy, Z. Yang, and C. Pereira. Offline symbolic analysis for multi-processor execution replay. In *Proceedings of the 42Nd Annual IEEE/ACM International Symposium on Microarchitecture*, MICRO 42, pages 564–575, 2009. ISBN 978-1-60558-798-1.

[41] D. Lee, M. Said, S. Narayanasamy, and Z. Yang. Offline symbolic analysis to infer total store order. In *Proceedings of the 2011 IEEE 17th International Symposium on High Performance Computer Architecture*, HPCA '11, pages 357–358, 2011. ISBN 978-1-4244-9432-3.

[42] D. Lee, P. M. Chen, J. Flinn, and S. Narayanasamy. Chimera: Hybrid program analysis for determinism. In *Proceedings of the 33rd ACM SIGPLAN Conference on Programming Language Design and Implementation*, PLDI '12, pages 463–474, 2012. ISBN 978-1-4503-1205-9.

[43] S. Lee, C. Jung, and S. Pande. Detecting memory leaks through introspective dynamic behavior modelling using machine learning. In *Proceedings of the 36th International Conference on Software Engineering*, 2014.

[44] Y. Lev, M. Moir, and D. Nussbaum. PhTM: Phased transactional memory. In *TRANSACT '07: 2nd Workshop on Transactional Computing*, aug 2007.

[45] Y. Liu, Y. Xia, H. Guan, B. Zang, and H. Chen. Concurrent and consistent virtual machine introspection with hardware transactional memory. In *Proceedings of the 2014 IEEE 20th International Symposium on High Performance Computer Architecture*, HPCA '14, 2014.

[46] S. Lu, S. Park, E. Seo, and Y. Zhou. Learning from mistakes: A comprehensive study on real world concurrency bug characteristics. In *Proceedings of the 13th International Conference on Architectural Support for Programming Languages and Operating Systems*, ASPLOS XIII, pages 329–339, 2008. ISBN 978-1-59593-958-6.

[47] B. Lucia, L. Ceze, K. Strauss, S. Qadeer, and H.-J. Boehm. Conflict exceptions: Simplifying concurrent language semantics with precise hardware exceptions for data-races. In *Proceedings of the 37th Annual International Symposium on Computer Architecture*, ISCA '10, pages 210–221, 2010. ISBN 978-1-4503-0053-7.

[48] C.-K. Luk, R. Cohn, R. Muth, H. Patil, A. Klauser, G. Lowney, S. Wallace, V. J. Reddi, and K. Hazelwood. Pin: Building customized program analysis tools with dynamic instrumentation. In *Proceedings of the 2005 ACM SIGPLAN Conference on Programming Language Design and Implementation*, PLDI '05, pages 190–200, 2005. ISBN 1-59593-056-6.

[49] J. Manson, W. Pugh, and S. V. Adve. The java memory model. In *Proceedings of the 32Nd ACM SIGPLAN-SIGACT Symposium on Principles of Programming Languages*, POPL '05, pages 378–391, 2005. ISBN 1-58113-830-X.

[50] D. Marino, M. Musuvathi, and S. Narayanasamy. Literace: Effective sampling for lightweight data-race detection. In *Pro-*

ceedings of the 2009 ACM SIGPLAN Conference on Programming Language Design and Implementation, PLDI '09, pages 134–143, 2009. ISBN 978-1-60558-392-1.

[51] M. Martin, C. Blundell, and E. Lewis. Subtleties of transactional memory atomicity semantics. *IEEE Comput. Archit. Lett.*, 5(2):17–17, July 2006. ISSN 1556-6056.

[52] H. S. Matar, I. Kuru, S. Tasiran, and R. Dementiev. Accelerating precise race detection using commercially available hardware transactional memory support. In *5th Workshop on Determinism and Correctness in Parallel Programming*, WoDet '14, 2014.

[53] K. E. Moore, J. Bobba, M. J. Moravan, M. D. Hill, and D. A. Wood. LogTM: Log-based transactional memory. In *Proceedings of the 2006 IEEE 12th International Symposium on High Performance Computer Architecture*, pages 254–265, Feb. 2006.

[54] A. Muzahid, D. Suárez, S. Qi, and J. Torrellas. Sigrace: Signature-based data race detection. In *Proceedings of the 36th Annual International Symposium on Computer Architecture*, ISCA '09, pages 337–348, 2009.

[55] N. Nethercote and J. Seward. Valgrind: A framework for heavyweight dynamic binary instrumentation. In *Proceedings of the 2007 ACM SIGPLAN Conference on Programming Language Design and Implementation*, PLDI '07, pages 89–100, 2007. ISBN 978-1-59593-633-2.

[56] R. H. B. Netzer and B. P. Miller. What are race conditions?: Some issues and formalizations. *ACM Lett. Program. Lang. Syst.*, 1(1):74–88, Mar. 1992. ISSN 1057-4514.

[57] PCWorld. Nasdaq's facebook glitch came from race conditions, May 2012. http://www.pcworld.com/article/255911/nasdaqs_facebook_glitch_came_from_race_conditions.html.

[58] E. Pozniansky and A. Schuster. Multirace: Efficient on-the-fly data race detection in multithreaded c++ programs: Research articles. *Concurr. Comput. : Pract. Exper.*, 19(3):327–340, Mar. 2007. ISSN 1532-0626.

[59] M. Prvulovic. Cord: Cost-effective (and nearly overhead-free) order-recording and data race detection. In *Proceedings of the 2006 IEEE 12th International Symposium on High Performance Computer Architecture*, HPCA '06, 2006.

[60] M. Prvulovic and J. Torrellas. Reenact: Using thread-level speculation mechanisms to debug data races in multithreaded codes. In *Proceedings of the 30th Annual International Symposium on Computer Architecture*, ISCA '03, pages 110–121, 2003. ISBN 0-7695-1945-8.

[61] C. G. Ritson and F. R. Barnes. An evaluation of intel's restricted transactional memory for cpas, 2013.

[62] P. Sack, B. E. Bliss, Z. Ma, P. Petersen, and J. Torrellas. Accurate and efficient filtering for the intel thread checker race detector. In *Proceedings of the 1st Workshop on Architectural and System Support for Improving Software Dependability*, ASID '06, pages 34–41, 2006. ISBN 1-59593-576-2.

[63] S. Savage, M. Burrows, G. Nelson, P. Sobalvarro, and T. Anderson. Eraser: A dynamic data race detector for multithreaded programs. *ACM Trans. Comput. Syst.*, 15(4):391–411, Nov. 1997. ISSN 0734-2071.

[64] SecurityFocus. Software bug contributed to blackout, Feb. 2004. http://www.securityfocus.com/news/8016.

[65] K. Serebryany and T. Iskhodzhanov. Threadsanitizer: Data race detection in practice. In *Proceedings of the Workshop on Binary Instrumentation and Applications*, WBIA '09, pages 62–71, 2009. ISBN 978-1-60558-793-6.

[66] Y. Smaragdakis, J. Evans, C. Sadowski, J. Yi, and C. Flanagan. Sound predictive race detection in polynomial time. In *Proceedings of the 39th Annual ACM SIGPLAN-SIGACT Symposium on Principles of Programming Languages*, POPL '12, pages 387–400, 2012. ISBN 978-1-4503-1083-3.

[67] M. Susskraut, T. Knauth, S. Weigert, U. Schiffel, M. Meinhold, and C. Fetzer. Prospect: A compiler framework for speculative parallelization. In *Proceedings of the 8th Annual IEEE/ACM International Symposium on Code Generation and Optimization*, CGO '10, pages 131–140, 2010.

[68] T. C. Team. Clang 3.8 threadsanitizer, 2015. http://clang.llvm.org/docs/ThreadSanitizer.html.

[69] J. Ševčík and D. Aspinall. On validity of program transformations in the java memory model. In *Proceedings of the 22Nd European Conference on Object-Oriented Programming*, ECOOP '08, pages 27–51, 2008. ISBN 978-3-540-70591-8.

[70] B. Wester, D. Devecsery, P. M. Chen, J. Flinn, and S. Narayanasamy. Parallelizing data race detection. In *Proceedings of the Eighteenth International Conference on Architectural Support for Programming Languages and Operating Systems*, ASPLOS '13, pages 27–38, 2013. ISBN 978-1-4503-1870-9.

[71] R. Wilcox. *Introduction to Robust Estimation and Hypothesis Testing*. Elsevier Science & Technology, 2012. ISBN 9780123869838.

[72] Y. Xie, M. Naik, B. Hackett, and A. Aiken. Soundness and its role in bug detection systems. In *In Proceedings of the Workshop on the Evaluation of Software Defect Detection Tools*, 2005.

[73] J. Yang, A. Cui, S. Stolfo, and S. Sethumadhavan. Concurrency attacks. In *The 4th USENIX Workshop on Hot Topics in Parallelism*, Berkeley, CA, 2012. USENIX. URL `https://www.usenix.org/conference/hotpar12/concurrency-attacks`.

[74] R. M. Yoo, C. J. Hughes, K. Lai, and R. Rajwar. Performance evaluation of intel® transactional synchronization extensions for high-performance computing. In *Proceedings of the International Conference on High Performance Computing, Networking, Storage and Analysis*, SC '13, pages 19:1–19:11, 2013. ISBN 978-1-4503-2378-9.

[75] Y. Yu, T. Rodeheffer, and W. Chen. Racetrack: Efficient detection of data race conditions via adaptive tracking. In *Proceedings of the Twentieth ACM Symposium on Operating Systems Principles*, SOSP '05, pages 221–234, 2005. ISBN 1-59593-079-5.

[76] P. Zhou, R. Teodorescu, and Y. Zhou. Hard: Hardware-assisted lockset-based race detection. In *Proceedings of the 2007 IEEE 13th International Symposium on High Performance Computer Architecture*, HPCA '07, pages 121–132, 2007. ISBN 1-4244-0804-0.

COGENT: Verifying High-Assurance File System Implementations

Sidney Amani, Alex Hixon, Zilin Chen, Christine Rizkallah, Peter Chubb,
Liam O'Connor, Joel Beeren, Yutaka Nagashima, Japheth Lim, Thomas Sewell, Joseph Tuong,
Gabriele Keller, Toby Murray, Gerwin Klein, Gernot Heiser

Data61 (formerly NICTA) and UNSW, Australia
first.last@data61.csiro.au

Abstract

We present an approach to writing and formally verifying high-assurance file-system code in a restricted language called COGENT, supported by a certifying compiler that produces C code, high-level specification of COGENT, and translation correctness proofs. The language is strongly typed and guarantees absence of a number of common file system implementation errors. We show how verification effort is drastically reduced for proving higher-level properties of the file system implementation by reasoning about the generated formal specification rather than its low-level C code. We use the framework to write two Linux file systems, and compare their performance with their native C implementations.

Categories and Subject Descriptors D.4.5 [*Operating Systems*]: Reliability—Verification; D.2.4 [*Software Engineering*]: Software / Program Verification—Formal methods; D.3.2 [*Programming Languages*]: Language Classification—Applicative (functional) languages

Keywords file systems; verification; domain-specific languages; co-generation; Isabelle/HOL

1. Introduction

Operating systems (OS) code is critical for the dependability and security of computer systems. In monolithic systems, most OS services are part of the kernel and are included in the trusted computing base (TCB) of any application. While microkernels can help reduce the TCB [10, 17, 29, 47], in practice we need more, because most applications depend on the correct operation of a significant number of OS services.

ASPLOS '16, April 02 – 06, 2016, Atlanta, GA, USA.

ACM 978-1-4503-4091-5/16/04...$15.00.
http://dx.doi.org/10.1145/10.1145/2872362.2872404

File systems, which constitute the largest fraction of code in Linux after device drivers, have among the highest defect density of Linux kernel code [38]. Furthermore, new file systems are frequently added for new media types or for new performance and reliability trade-offs. The lack of support for correctly writing new file systems is a standard bottleneck.

Formal verification in the style of seL4 [26] or Ironclad [15] is the only approach to fully solve this problem. While formal verification for file systems has seen a surge in activity in recent years [9, 11, 18], it has however not yet reached that same level of detail and assurance. In the most advanced and deepest of these verifications, Chen et al. [8] formally shows crash-resilience of the FSCQ file system implemented in the Coq prover [6]. Even this verification still relies on generating Haskell code from the Coq implementation, and executing that generated code with a full Haskell run-time at user level. This proof crosses an important barrier for formal verification: it removes human intervention from the link between the code that runs and the model that is verified. However, the trusted code base is still huge: the run-time is larger than the file system, the code generation step from Coq is unverified, and the semantics of the target language (Haskell) is complex and informal. While certainly an impressive result, for high-assurance systems on potentially resource-constrained devices, this is not yet good enough.

As motivated in [23], we design a new language called COGENT to bridge the gap between verifiable formal model and low-level code. In separate work [36], we define the formal semantics of COGENT, describe the COGENT compiler in detail which generates C code and an Isabelle/HOL specification, and show how the seven main stages of automatic compiler-produced proof work that connect the C and the Isabelle/HOL specification. In this paper, we show how to reason about COGENT programs, how COGENT is used to implement two Linux file systems, and we analyse how COGENT reduces the effort of reasoning about a low-level C implementation in order to more productively reason about high-level functional specifications — similar in style to Chen et al's verification. To this end, we verified two high-level functional correctness properties of one of the two Linux file systems. These are properties that would form key building blocks in, for instance, a proof of crash resilience.

COGENT goes further than just bridging the gap from model to code. It also provides tools for file system programmers *without any formal verification expertise* to *provably* avoid common errors: The language is type safe, i.e. the type system is strictly enforced. The compiler and type system in turn enforces basics like memory safety, but also the absence of any undefined behaviour on the C level, null pointer dereferences, buffer overflows, memory leaks, and pointer mismanagement in error handling. Mismanagement of pointers in error-handling code is a wide-spread problem in Linux file systems specifically [41], and Saha et al. [42] shows that file systems have among the highest density of error-handling code in Linux. In the verification of seL4, a significant fraction of the overall effort went into proving absence of such errors [25] – COGENT's *linear type system* [49] provides this for free and assists the programmer with memory allocation handling. Memory safety and memory leaks are problems with file systems, but also more generally in systems code [43]. The infamous Heartbleed bug for instance, was a buffer overflow [16], the recent "goto-fail" defect in Apple's SSL/TLS implementation was an error-handling problem obscured by `goto`s in an `if`-cascade [37], and the recent memory leak in Android Lollipop also was part of error-handling code [30]. All of these problems are prevented on the language level by COGENT, and are enforced by its certifying compiler. Few other languages come with type-system guarantees that address problems like memory leaks without significant overhead or large language run-times (e.g. Rust), and none come with a formal semantics and a machine-checked proof of their guarantees.

COGENT compiles to straight C code that can be compiled by gcc or CompCert [27, 28]. The generated C code also falls into the fragment understood by Sewell et al.'s gcc translation validation tool [46], providing a pathway to extend the verification all the way to binary level if needed. We designed COGENT with the code patterns and common errors in Linux file systems in mind. As detailed in separate work [36], its semantics is sequential (allowing asynchronous I/O, but not full concurrency), restricted to total functions, and contains no built-in loops or recursion. This simplifies reasoning, both for the compiler and on top of the language. Iterators, external abstract functions, and types that rely on sharing, are implemented in a formally modelled foreign function interface, supported by a custom template-style C extension. In our file system implementation, a small library of abstract data types (ADTs) and iterators is sufficient, and the foreign-function interface is powerful enough to provide interoperability with an existing red-black tree implementation in C.

In summary, we make the following contributions:

1. We demonstrate the use of COGENT for implementing actual file systems (Section 3).
2. We present proofs of high-level correctness properties of a file system implemented in COGENT and discuss how COGENT facilitates such proofs (Section 4).
3. We discuss the effort involved in implementing file systems with verified properties in COGENT (Section 5).
4. We evaluate the COGENT-implemented file systems against their native C counterparts (Section 5).

2. Overview of Our Approach

2.1 COGENT

COGENT is tailored to writing systems code, with a specific focus on file systems. It is intentionally more restrictive than general-purpose functional languages, to enable the use of efficient and powerful reasoning techniques on its high-level semantics, to avoid the need for an elaborate language run-time, and to enable the COGENT compiler to output an automatic proof that the C code it generates correctly implements the behaviour of the COGENT program [36]. In this paper, we further demonstrate how to prove functional correctness of the COGENT program.

COGENT manages to avoid a garbage collector, unlike most existing high-level languages such as Java, Haskell, and OCaml, by implementing a *linear type system* [49], which ensures that each linearly typed object is used exactly once. The type system not only provides memory safety, but also makes memory leaks compile-time errors. Traditional pure functional languages, such as Haskell, that disallow side effects, favour frequent copies of dynamically allocated data structures and make it hard to reason about the performance of the generated code. COGENT's linear type system increases performance by allowing the compiled code to modify data structures in-place. The type system supports parametric polymorphism. While doing so might not be an obvious choice for a language geared towards systems programming, it is particularly important in the context of COGENT, which relies on external ADTs to implement data structures that cannot be implemented with linear types.

COGENT also supports higher-order functions. In contrast to general-purpose functional languages, however, all functions in COGENT have to be defined on the top-level. This restriction is necessary to avoid the run-time overhead and heap allocations necessary to implement closures otherwise.

As an example, Figure 1 depicts a snippet of COGENT from our ext2 implementation, specifically the `ext2_inode_get()` function. This function looks up an inode on disk, given its inode number `inum`. Lines 3–4 declare the type of this function. It takes 3 arguments: an `ExState`, which is a reference to an ADT embodying the outside environment of the file system; an `FsState`, a reference to a COGENT structure that holds the file system state, and a `U32`, an unsigned 32-bit integer that in this case is the

```
1 type RR c a b = (c, <Success a | Error b>)
2
3 ext2_inode_get : (ExState, FsState, U32) ->
4       RR (ExState, FsState) (VfsInode) (U32)
5 ext2_inode_get (ex, state, inum) =
6     let ((ex, state), res) =
7       ext2_inode_get_buf (ex, state, inum)
8     in res
9     | Success (buf_blk, offset) ->
10        -- read the inode, from the offset
11        let ((ex, state), res) =
12          deserialise_Inode (ex, state,
13                             buf_blk, offset,
14                             inum)
15          !buf_blk
16        in res
17        | Success inode ->
18            let ex =
19              osbuffer_destroy (ex, buf_blk)
20            in ((ex, state), Success inode)
21        | Error () ->
22            let ex =
23              osbuffer_destroy (ex, buf_blk)
24            in ((ex, state), Error eIO)
25    | Error (err) -> ((ex, state), Error err)
26
27 osbuffer_destroy:(ExState, OsBuffer)->ExState
```

Figure 1. Looking up an inode Ext2, in COGENT.

number of the inode to be looked up. It returns a result of type RR (defined on line 1), which is a pair. Its first component c is mandatory data that must always be returned, while the second component is a *tagged union* value which signals whether the function succeeded (Success a) or not (Error b), where a and b are result values for the respective cases. ext2_inode_get() (line 4) always returns both the ExState and FsState; when successful it also returns a VfsInode reference to the looked-up inode; otherwise it instead returns also a U32 error code.

ext2_inode_get() first calls (line 6–7) the COGENT function ext2_inode_get_buf(), which, after more calculation, internally calls an ADT function to read the corresponding block from disk. We match (lines 8, 9, 25) on the result res to make a case distinction: for Success (line 9), the result contains a reference buf_blk to a buffer, plus the offset offset of the inode in that buffer. We use these to deserialise the inode from the buffer into a VfsInode structure.

In this situation, linear types are unnecessarily restrictive. Passing the linear value buf_blk to deserialise_Inode() in line 12 would consume it, so deserialise_Inode() would have to return it as an additional result for it to be used again later on in the program. This is overly complicated, given that deserialise_Inode() never modifies the buffer. The "!" operator (in "!buf_blk", line 15) allows us temporarily to escape the use-once restriction of the linear type system: it indicates that within the right-hand side of = here, buf_blk is used read-only and can therefore be referenced multiple times without consuming it. The type system prevents deserialise_Inode() from modifying the buffer that is holding the inode being deserialised. Moreover, it ensures that no references to buffer or parts of it can be returned, as this would result in aliasing.

For the Error case (line 25), the result includes an error code that is simply propagated to the caller along with the return values that were mandatory. The Success/Error case distinction is repeated following the attempt to deserialise the inode from the buffer. In either case, the buffer must be released, by calling the ADT function osbuffer_destroy(), whose type signature (line 27) suggests it consumes the buffer.

Note that in this function, COGENT's linear type system would flag an error if the buffer buf_blk was never released. ext2_inode_get() will only type-check if all of the Error cases are handled. Also observe that the mandatory ExState and FsState values are threaded through the function. The ExState value encompasses all external state, and so includes for instance Linux's buffer cache. Because COGENT is a pure functional language, it makes side effects explicit. This means this ExState is passed to osbuffer_destroy() explicitly, which then returns a new ExState reference that encompasses the external state of the world after the buffer has been released. This does not mean that large structures are copied at run-time. In practice, COGENT's linear type system allows the ExState update in osbuffer_destroy() to be performed in-place. The same is true for the other functions that each consume and return an ExState or FsState.

It is obvious from Figure 1 that COGENT's current surface syntax for error handling is unnecessarily verbose. The textual overhead for the regular error handling pattern can easily be reduced by additional syntactic sugar in a future language iteration without touching the verification infrastructure – we merely focused on verification first.

2.2 COGENT File Systems

We implement two file systems in COGENT, to drive the development of the language and as case studies for automatic proof generation. The first is an almost feature-complete revision 1 ext2 implementation: it passes the Posix File System Test Suite [35], except for the ACL and symlink tests (as we have not implemented those features). Its performance is comparable to Linux's native ext2 implementation. For contrast, the second is a new flash file system called BilbyFs [23] whose design strikes a balance between the simplicity of JFFS2 and the performance of UBIFS, the two most popular Linux flash file systems.

The COGENT implementations of ext2 and BilbyFs share a common library of ADTs that includes fixed-length arrays for words and structures, simple iterators for implementing for-loops, and COGENT stubs for accessing a range of Linux APIs such as the buffer cache and its native red-black tree implementation, plus iterators for each ADT. The in-

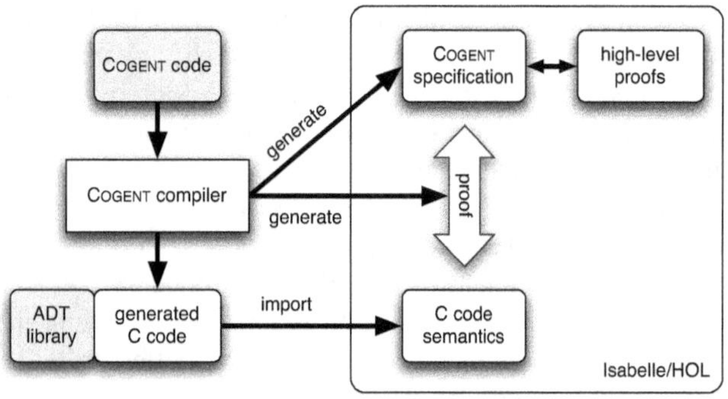

Figure 2. Code/Proof Co-Generation Process.

terfaces exposed by these ADTs are carefully designed to ensure compatibility with COGENT's linear type system.

For full functional correctness, these ADTs need to be verified separately. We have done so for a smaller instance (the `WordArray` ADT) to validate the cross-language semantics, but have not verified for instance the red-black tree implementation, although it is certainly feasible to do so. For example, a verification of a red-black tree implementation (although in a higher-order logic and thus not usable in our framework) is part of the Isabelle/HOL [34] standard library.

The ext2 implementation showcases COGENT's ability to enable the re-engineering of existing file systems, and thus its potential to provide an incremental upgrade path to increase the reliability of existing systems code. BilbyFs, on the other hand, provides a glimpse of how to design and engineer new file systems that are not only performant, but amenable to being verified as correct against a high-level specification of file system correctness. To this end, BilbyFs pursues aggressive modular decomposition, whereas the structure of the ext2 implementation mirrors that of its native Linux counterpart. Section 3 presents the two file systems in more detail.

2.3 Automatic Code/Proof Co-Generation

Details of the code/proof co-generation form the topic of separate work [36]. We provide a brief summary below.

Figure 2 shows the code and proof generation process: the COGENT compiler generates C code, which is then compiled by some C compiler, linking against the ADT library, to produce binary files. Besides the C code, the COGENT compiler also generates a formal specification in Isabelle/HOL that precisely encodes the semantics of the source COGENT program, and a refinement proof that this semantics is correctly implemented by the C code. The specification can be used to prove higher-level properties about the COGENT program.

The generated C code can be compiled by standard compilers such as gcc, and also CompCert. We assign the generated C language subset a semantics, which is from Norrish's *C Parser* [50], originally developed for the seL4 verification. Since Norrish's C Parser also supplies the C semantics for Sewell et al.'s gcc translation validation tool [46], we can in future extend the compiler-generated proofs for the C code to the binary level.

The refinement proofs state that every behaviour exhibited by the C code can also be exhibited by the COGENT code and, furthermore, that the C code is always well-defined, including that e.g. the generated C code never dereferences a null pointer, and never causes signed overflow. It also implies that the generated C code is type-safe and memory-safe, meaning the code will never try to dereference an invalid pointer, or try to dereference two aliasing pointers of incompatible types. In conjunction with the COGENT typing proofs, generated by the COGENT compiler for the input program, we get additional guarantees that the generated code handles all error cases, is free of memory leaks, and never *double-free*s a pointer.

These proofs do *not* guarantee, for instance, that the implementation always behaves as a proper file system — e.g. that data written to disk will always be able to be read back. Providing that kind of additional guarantee requires proving the COGENT code functionally correct against a high-level specification of file system functionality.

In later sections, we show how to reason on top of the COGENT formal specification in Isabelle/HOL, leveraging COGENT's purely functional semantics. Reasoning here is simpler than reasoning on C code directly because the COGENT semantics is represented as pure functions in the logic, making it possible to reason equationally about it via Isabelle's powerful rewriting engine. We return to this point in Section 4.

If desired, one could further formalise different logics on top of our generated COGENT specification to further simplify reasoning about different domain-specific properties. For example, a Crash Hoare Logic [8] to simplify reasoning about crash safety.

3. File Systems in COGENT

As mentioned in Section 2, we have implemented two file systems in COGENT: an ext2 implementation, and a new raw flash file system called BilbyFs. Both file system implementations sit below Linux's virtual file system switch (VFS) module, using C stub code to provide the top-level entry points expected by the VFS. These C stubs call directly into the top-level COGENT functions that implement each file system, using locking to prevent two COGENT functions from executing concurrently (because our current verification technology does not support concurrency).

An ADT provides a common interface to the VFS within COGENT, while each file system uses a separate ADT for interfacing with the physical storage medium, as these differ between the two. Both ADTs capture all relevant properties of the underlying media, and should be fully re-usable for other file systems targeting the same media.

3.1 ext2

ext2 is a well-known file system for block devices. While on large block devices it has long been supplanted by journaling file systems, which provide better reliability guarantees in the event of a crash, it remains popular for smaller block devices like SD cards and USB flash memory.

The COGENT ext2 implementation follows ext2fs of Linux 3.14.12; essentially we transliterated the Linux implementation into COGENT. This approach tests COGENT's ability to let systems programmers (re)implement their code, and in the process gain (proof-) guaranteed type- and memory-safety, as well as absence of undefined behaviour, missing error cases and memory leaks (as discussed in Section 1).

In its current state, our ext2 implementation has a number of limitations compared to Linux ext2fs. Each of these is straightforward to remove, except the lock that forces the code to run without concurrency. It emulates an early version (revision 1) of ext2, with 1k blocks and 128byte inodes. It also does not yet support read-ahead or direct-IO, and uses a simpler block allocation algorithm than Linux, so the order of blocks on disk is different, leading to different seek times, and different on-disk fragmentation. The implementation also currently elides extended attributes, quotas, reserved blocks and symlinks; however, none of these features are exercised by the benchmarks presented in Section 5.

3.2 BilbyFs

BilbyFs is meant to serve as a case study in how to design new file systems that are fully verifiable, meaning that not only is their generated C code proved to always implement their COGENT semantics, but that their COGENT semantics can also be verified to satisfy high-level correctness properties, such as full functional correctness against an abstract specification of file system correctness.

Unlike ext2, BilbyFs is not a block device file system. Instead it is a file system for raw flash devices, like those on embedded devices. BilbyFs' design draws inspiration from the two most popular raw flash file systems, JFFS2, which was merged into Linux in 2001; and the newer UBIFS, which was merged in 2008. BilbyFs' design balances the simplicity of JFFS2 with the run-time performance properties of UBIFS. Like each of these file systems, BilbyFs is a log-structured file system. Like JFFS2 and UBIFS, it provides crash-tolerance by structuring flash updates in atomic transactions, and discarding incomplete transactions when re-mounting following a crash.

Like UBIFS, BilbyFs writes data to the flash asynchronously, allowing otherwise small writes to be batched into large transactions to improve metadata packing and throughput [19]. Like JFFS2, however, BilbyFs eschews storing the flash *index*, which records the on-flash location of each file system object, on the flash. Instead it maintains the index in memory. This means that the index must be re-

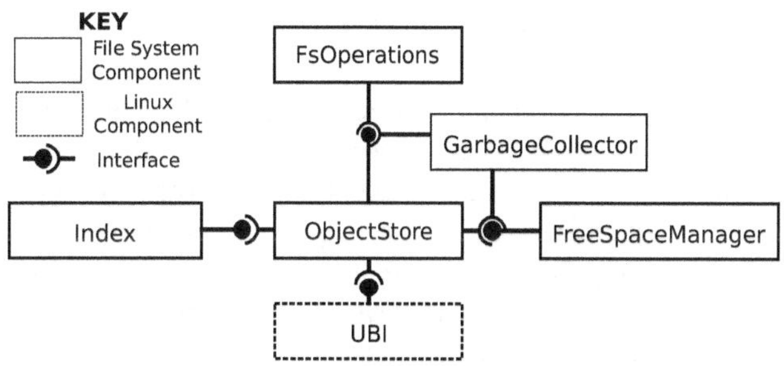

Figure 3. The modular design of BilbyFs.

constructed at mount time, and limits the maximum medium size that can be supported.

As mentioned, BilbyFs' design is rooted in aggressive modular decomposition, to reduce the cost of completing a manual proof of full functional correctness of its COGENT code, building on top of the automatic correctness proofs generated by the COGENT compiler. Recent research [32] provides evidence suggesting that the effort required for manual verification scales quadratically with the size of the statement to be proved. This indicates that increasing modularity will reduce the overall verification effort.

BilbyFs' modular design is depicted in Figure 3. At the bottom level, BilbyFs interfaces with Linux's UBI component via a COGENT ADT. It uses UBI to read and write the flash, allowing UBI to handle wear levelling and manage logical erase blocks as it does for UBIFS. The in-memory Index component, one level up, implemented in COGENT, tracks the on-flash address of each file system object. The ObjectStore uses this Index to provide an abstract interface for reading and writing generic objects on flash. To do so it also makes use of the FreeSpaceManager, which in turn is used by the GarbageCollector to free erase blocks no longer in use. Finally, the FsOperations component implements the top-level file system operations and objects, like inodes directory entries and data blocks. This decomposition ensures that the key file system logic is confined to the FsOperations component, while the physical representation of objects on flash is handled by the ObjectStore.

3.3 Reusable Abstract Data Types

As mentioned, the two file systems share a common ADT library (7 ADTs in total). It includes the `WordArray` type mentioned in Section 2, for arrays of primitive words; a separate polymorphic `Array` type for (linear) heap values; common utility functions like iterators for implementing `for`-loops with early exit and accumulators, and (inline) functions for manipulating machine words; a heapsort implementation; and polymorphic linked lists. It also includes stubs for accessing existing kernel APIs, including the buffer cache (e.g. `osbuffer_destroy()` from Figure 1), the page cache, a native red-black tree implementation, checksum functions, time and date functions, and the VFS.

Some care is needed when designing ADTs that respect and enforce the constraints of COGENT's linear type system. For example, the function for accessing an element of the general polymorphic `Array` type must make sure that the element cannot be accessed a second time, inadvertently giving two writable references to a single value, which violates the constraints of the linear type system. This is why we have a separate `WordArray` type for strings of (non-linear) machine words. When accessing array-elements read-only, no such removal is needed: the type system guarantees that the aliasing is safe in such cases.

While designing and implementing ADTs thus requires some skill, it should be a relatively rare activity because ADTs are freely reusable. Given that our current ADT library is shared between the two relatively different file systems, we expect that it should be completely reusable for other file system implementations as well.

4. Formal Verification

Recall from Section 2.3 that the COGENT compiler generates C code as well as a high-level Isabelle/HOL specification from the input COGENT program. In this section, we describe how this high-level specification facilitates further, formal reasoning at much reduced effort compared to traditional functional correctness verification as typified by e.g. seL4 [26]. To this end, we describe two BilbyFs high-level functional correctness properties that we proved.

4.1 Top-Level Correctness Specification

These proofs show that the `sync()` and `iget()` operations of BilbyFs are *functionally correct*, meaning that they behave correctly in accordance with a *top-level*, abstract specification for these operations. This abstract specification is written directly in Isabelle's higher-order logic. It is short enough that a human can audit it to ensure that it accurately captures the intended behaviour of these operations. A complete description of our top-level specifications is available in separate work [3]. The top-level specifications for `sync()` and `iget()` are depicted in Figure 4. The total line count of both specifications including all their dependencies is 239 lines of Isabelle/HOL.

`sync()` and `iget()` each implement the corresponding functions expected of the Linux VFS layer. The `sync()` operation synchronises the current in-memory state of the file system to physical storage. The in-memory state may differ from the physical state because, as mentioned in Section 3.2, BilbyFs buffers pending writes in memory to improve metadata packing and throughput. The top-level *abstract file system* (AFS) specification for `sync()`, afs_sync, operates over the abstract file system state *afs*, which tracks the state of the physical storage medium (med), the pending in-memory medium updates (updates), and whether the file-system is currently read-only (is_readonly). The specification says that `sync()` first checks whether the file system is read-only, in which case an appropriate Error code is returned with the file system state unchanged (lines 2 and 3). Otherwise, it applies the in-memory updates to the physical medium.

Its specification is sufficiently nondeterministic to capture the behaviour of a correct file system under the situation when the in-memory updates are only partially applied, perhaps because of a flash device failure part-way through. For this reason, the specification allows any number of updates n (line 5) to succeed, between 0 and the total number of updates currently in-memory (i.e. length (updates *afs*)). It then (lines 8 and 9) applies the first n updates *toapply* to the physical medium med *afs* of file system state *afs*, and remembers the updates that remain to be applied *rem*. If all updates were applied, it returns Successfully, yielding the new file system state (lines 10 and 11). Otherwise (lines 12 to 14), it returns an appropriate error code, selected nondeterministically because the specification abstracts away from the precise reason *why* the failure might have occurred. In case of an I/O error (eIO), the file system is also put into read-only mode.

The `iget()` operation looks-up inodes on the physical medium. It takes a inode number *inum* and a VFS inode structure *vnode*. It first (line 2) checks whether an inode with the given inode number exists in the file system. To do so it must consult both the in-memory and on-medium state, computing via the expression updated_afs *afs* what the file system state *would be* if it were synchronised to the medium. If the inode number is not present (lines 11 and 12) an appropriate error code is returned. Otherwise, the `iget()` specification reads the inode with that number from the medium (line 4) and then returns appropriately based on whether the inode read succeeded (lines 6 and 7) or produced an error (lines 8 an 9). In the case of Success, the inode must be converted to a VFS inode structure for inter-operating with the Linux VFS. Observe that the `iget()` specification does not return an updated *afs* structure: thus its type signature automatically captures that it can never modify the abstract file system state.

Note that the `iget()` specification intentionally elides interaction with the Linux inode cache. These are managed by a trivial amount of C code that sits between the Linux VFS layer and the BilbyFs implementation as produced by the COGENT compiler. Incorporating them into the COGENT implementation of BilbyFs (and thus into e.g., the `iget()` specification) would add little value, as these caches would be just large unverified ADTs and opaque to COGENT and the verification.

4.2 Functional Correctness Proof

We prove the correctness of the BilbyFs `sync()` and `iget()` operations, against their top-level specifications of Figure 4. The proof follows the modular decomposition of the BilbyFs implementation from Figure 3 (see Section 3.2). For both

```
afs_sync afs ≡
 if is_readonly afs then
  return (afs, Error eRoFs)
 else do
  n ← select{0..length (updates afs)};
  let updates = updates afs;
    (toapply, rem) = (take n updates, drop n updates);
    afs = (afs⦇med := apply_updates toapply (med afs),
                 updates := rem⦈);
  in if rem = [] then
    return (afs, Success ())
  else do
    e ← select {eIO, eNoMem, eNoSpc, eOverflow};
    return (afs⦇is_readonly := (e = eIO)⦈, Error e)
  od
 od
```

```
afs_iget afs inum vnode ≡
 (if inum ∈ dom (updated_afs afs) then
  do
   r ← read_afs_inode afs inum;
   case r of
    Success inode ⇒
      return (inode2vnode inode, Success ())
   | Error e ⇒
      return (vnode, Error e)
  od
 else
  return (vnode, Error eNoEnt))
```

Figure 4. Top-level specifications for `sync()` and `iget()`, against which their BilbyFs COGENT implementations are verified.

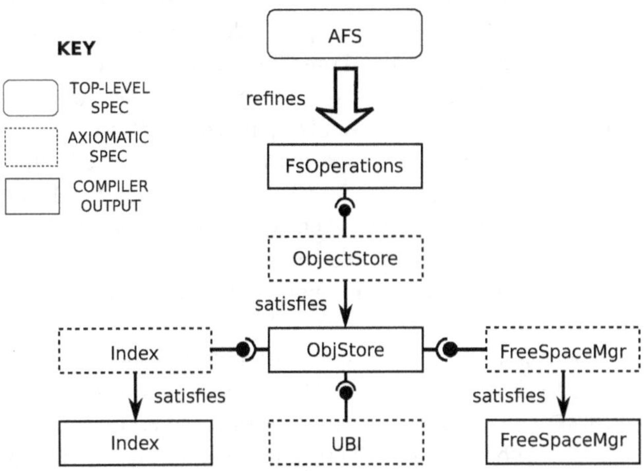

Figure 5. Modular functional correctness proof of BilbyFs.

operations, we prove the full component chain up to the UBI component.

Figure 5 depicts the structure of this proof. At the top, we prove that the code for the VFS-facing component of BilbyFs, called FsOperations, correctly *refines* its high-level specification as given in the abstract file system specification (AFS) of Figure 4. To complete this proof we formally define how to map the abstract file system state (*afs* of Figure 4) to the concrete file system state as implemented in COGENT. For instance, the abstract in-memory list of updates (updates *afs* of Figure 4) corresponds to an in-memory buffer where pending medium-writes are stored. The mapping from the former to the latter requires parsing the physical buffer contents (a list of bytes). In addition, the physical medium state (med *afs*) corresponds to the state of the UBI component of BilbyFs, which provides the interface to the flash storage. Similar to the in-memory buffer, mapping the state of the UBI component to its abstract representation in the AFS requires logically mimicking the file system `mount` operation, to parse the entire physical medium. In this sense, our proofs deal directly with the raw bytes stored in-memory and on-flash by the file system.

The FsOperations proof relies on formal assumptions about the ObjectStore. Those assumptions form an *axiomatic* specification of the ObjectStore, which serves as a compact representation of its correctness that abstracts away from its implementation details.

For `sync()`, the proof proceeds by establishing that the ObjectStore implementation indeed satisfies these axioms. This proof in turn makes use of axiomatic specifications for the components on which the ObjectStore relies, the Index and FreeSpaceManager, whose COGENT implementations we also prove satisfy their axioms. The proof bottoms out at the UBI component which, being entirely abstract, is captured by an axiomatic specification only. The validity of the entire functional correctness proof then rests on the validity of the assumptions encoded in the UBI specification. We return to these assumptions later in Section 4.4.

4.3 Ease of Proof

While they establish a similar property, these proofs are far simpler than e.g. the comparable functional correctness proofs of seL4 [26]. Just as with seL4, the functional correctness proof here relies on establishing global invariants of the abstract specification and its implementation. For BilbyFs, the invariants include e.g. the absence of link cycles, dangling links and the correctness of link counts, as well as the consistency of information that is duplicated in the file system for efficiency.

Importantly, unlike with seL4, none of the invariants have to include that in-memory objects do not overlap, or that object-pointers are correctly aligned and do point to valid objects. All of these details are handled automatically by

COGENT's type system and are justified by the C code correctness proofs generated by the COGENT compiler.

Even better, when proving that the file system correctly maintains its invariants, we get to reason over pure, functional specifications of the COGENT code. Because they are pure functions, these specifications do not deal with mutable state (as e.g., the seL4 ones do). Thus when proving that they satisfy their invariants, or refine the top-level AFS, we need not resort to cumbersome machinery like separation logic [40]: each function can be reasoned about by simply unfolding its definition, and the presence of separation between objects x and y follows trivially from x and y being separate variables.

Functional programmers have long recognised, and advocated for, the benefits afforded by reasoning over pure functions. COGENT puts these benefits directly into the hands of verification engineers without the need for a large, untrusted run-time system.

4.4 Assumptions and Invariants

As mentioned above, the BilbyFs proofs rest on the assumptions made about the Linux UBI component, as encoded in its axiomatic specification. At present, these assumptions are a little more restrictive than could be expected of a flash memory in practice. In particular, the axiom for the ubi_write function, which takes a buffer and writes it to the flash, states that either the entire write succeeds, or it fails leaving the flash unchanged. In practice, this write may be spread across multiple flash pages, each of which may succeed or fail and for which failure may leave the flash page only partially-written, or even corrupted [48]. With additional work, these assumptions can be made fully realistic.

The proofs assume that the file system invariant holds before invoking `sync()` and `iget()`, and we prove that these operations maintain it. The invariant talks about the contents of erase-blocks and wbuf, the in-memory buffer that stores pending updates. It asserts that the contents of erase-blocks and wbuf must form a valid log, i.e., data can be parsed as a sequence of valid transactions. After parsing, the logical representation of a transaction is a list of file system objects such as inode, directory entry and data blocks. The invariant also says that each transaction has a unique transaction number that indicates the order in which transactions must be applied when mounting the file system.

5. Evaluation

We evaluate COGENT from two perspectives: its ease-of-use as a systems language and verification target, and how well file systems implemented in COGENT perform.

5.1 Experience with COGENT

5.1.1 COGENT as a systems implementation language

In order to shed light on COGENT's usability as a systems programming language, we briefly describe the experience of developing our ext2 and BilbyFs implementations. In both cases, we started from a C implementation. In the case of ext2, this was Linux's ext2fs implementation; for BilbyFs it was our own implementation of the file system that was used to prototype its modular design. The two file systems were written by separate developers, but in the case of BilbyFs the same developer wrote both its C and COGENT implementations. Both developers were already familiar with functional programming, the ext2 developer is an undergraduate student.

Naturally, the COGENT language evolved in the process – at the time of the initial implementations, the language had linear types but no polymorphism and limited support for loops. The developers jointly wrote the shared ADT library, and the ext2 developer spent considerable time assisting with COGENT toolchain design and development. Unfortunately, this makes it infeasible to give accurate effort estimates for how long each file system would have taken to write had the language and toolchain been stable, as they are now.

Having to adopt COGENT's functional style was not a major barrier for either developer; indeed one reported that COGENT's use of nested `let`-expressions for sequencing and error handling aided his understanding of the potential control paths of his code. While both had to get used to the linear type system, both reported that this happened quite quickly and that the linear type system generally did not impose much of a burden when writing ordinary COGENT code. Both developers noted the usefulness of COGENT's linear types for tracking memory allocation and catching memory leaks.

Where linear types did cause friction was mostly when having to design the shared ADT interfaces to respect the constraints of the type system, as mentioned earlier in Section 3.3. Another place where linear types caused friction was when implementing the `rename()` operation in COGENT. `rename()` takes two directory arguments, the source and target directory of the file to be renamed. In case of renaming a file without changing its directory, these two arguments are identical. As COGENT does not allow such aliasing, we need two versions of this operation, leading to about 150 lines of essentially replicated code.

Both developers reported that the strong type system provided by COGENT decreased the time they usually would have spent debugging, which is to be expected. Logic bugs, which cannot be captured by the static semantics, can remain in COGENT code and are harder to debug because of lack of tool support. The developers, however, found comparatively few bugs in the COGENT code; the vast majority of bugs were in the C wrapper code or, to a lesser degree, in the C ADT implementations. Both developers reported that they felt that the COGENT support for a template-style C extension increased productivity in writing ADT implementations. Another reported benefit of COGENT's pluggable

ADTs was the ability to switch-in different ADT implementations to aid debugging.

System	native C	COGENT	generated C
ext2	4,077	2,789	12,066
BilbyFs	4,021	4,643	18,182

Table 1. Implementation source lines of code, native vs. COGENT, measured with sloccount. Generated line counts include ADTs.

Table 1 shows the source code sizes of the two systems. For the native ext2 system (i.e. the Linux code) we exclude code that implements features our COGENT implementation does not currently support. We can see that for the ext2 system, the COGENT implementation is about 2/3 the size of C. BilbyFs' COGENT implementation is larger than ext2's relative to their respective native C implementations. This is because BilbyFs makes much heavier use of the various ADTs from the common ADT library, some of which present fairly verbose client interfaces in their current implementation.

The current COGENT language can be viewed as a core language: we intentionally kept it minimal, without much syntactic sugar or support for common usage patterns. Rather than speculating about the optimal set of language shortcuts, we implemented the two case studies in the core language. This was obviously a source of frustration for both developers, but it gave us a better understanding of which additions are actually worthwhile. For example, code sequences as depicted in Figure 1, where the error handling code simply frees all the memory allocated in the sequence so far before returning an error value, are common. The programmer should not have to write such boilerplate code, especially because the type system provides sufficient information for the compiler to identify the objects that have to be destroyed before returning. Language support for this and other common patterns can be added fairly easily: as the compiler will just desugar these patterns into core language constructs, they do not affect the verification or code generation at all, and are orthogonal to the issues discussed here.

The blowout in size of the generated C code in Table 1 is mostly a result of normalisation steps applied by the COGENT compiler. Most of this is easily optimised away by the C compiler. However, we found that gcc's optimiser does an unsatisfactory job of optimising operations on large structs, resulting in unnecessary copy operations left in the code. This could be addressed by producing more optimised COGENT output for such cases.

It is also quite difficult to analyse performance of COGENT code, as links between assembly output and COGENT source code tend to be convoluted.

5.1.2 COGENT as a verification target

COGENT was carefully designed to provide a usable verification target for higher-level reasoning on top of its functional semantics. Specifically, we took care to ensure its semantics could be directly encoded as a pure, side-effect-free function in Isabelle's higher-order logic.

Recall from Section 2.3 that the COGENT compiler proves refinement, which means that reasoning about the generated specification is sound with respect to the generated C code, in that any property proved of the former is guaranteed to hold for the latter.

The linear type system is critical here, as we can only give COGENT a purely functional semantics because the linear types limit aliasing. Pure functions are naturally easy to reason about, especially by exploiting powerful yet sound automated tools like Isabelle's rewriting engine.

Compared to the seL4 project [26], the proofs generated by the COGENT compiler roughly correspond to the second refinement step from the intermediate executable specification to C code (except that the COGENT code is higher-level). Klein at al. [26] reports that one third of the total seL4 verification effort went into that step (not counting re-usable libraries and frameworks), so we can confidently predict that our co-generation automates at least a third of the overall effort of producing a completely verified file system. The savings are likely to be higher, as COGENT already proves a number of properties like correct pointer typing that in seL4 needed complex invariants established in the first refinement step, from abstract to executable specification [25].

The verification found six defects in the already tested and benchmarked BilbyFs implementation. Three of these occurred in serialisation functions, and three in the `sync()` implementation itself. Serialisation and de-serialisation are mechanical and tedious to write, which makes them prime candidates for further language and proof generation support.

The effort for verifying the complete file system component chain for the functions `sync()` and `iget()` in BilbyFs was roughly 9.25 person months, and produced roughly 13,000 lines of proof for the 1,350 lines of COGENT code. 4.5 person months, $\approx$4,000 lines of proof, of these were spent on serialisation/de-serialisation functions ($\approx$850 lines of COGENT code), which, as mentioned, could be further automated. An additional $\approx$1,500 of the $\approx$13,000 lines of proof are libraries. The `sync()`-specific proof size is just about 5,700 lines and took 3.75 person months for $\approx$300 lines of COGENT code. The `iget()` proofs took 1 person month for $\approx$1,800 lines of proof and $\approx$200 lines of COGENT code.

This compares favourably with traditional C-level verification as for instance in seL4, which spent 12 person years with 200k lines of proof for 8,700 source lines of C code. Roughly 1.65 person months per 100 C source lines in seL4 are reduced to $\approx$0.69 person months per 100 COGENT source lines in COGENT.

5.2 COGENT performance

The evaluation platform for the ext2 file system is a four-core i7-6700 running at 3.1 GHz, with a Samsung HD501JL 7200RPM 500G SATA disk, running Linux kernel 4.3.0-

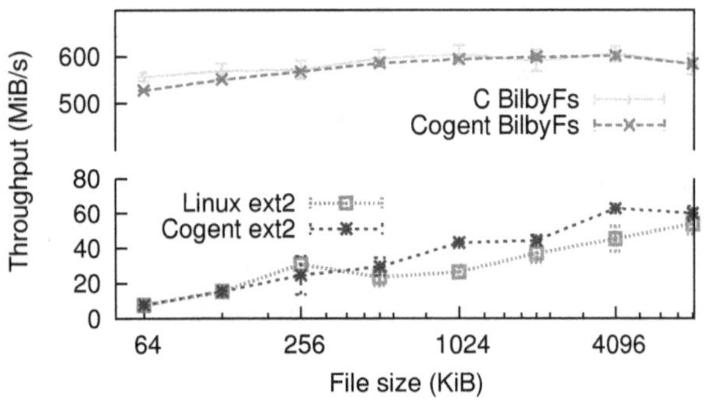

Figure 6. IOZone throughput for random 4 KiB writes.

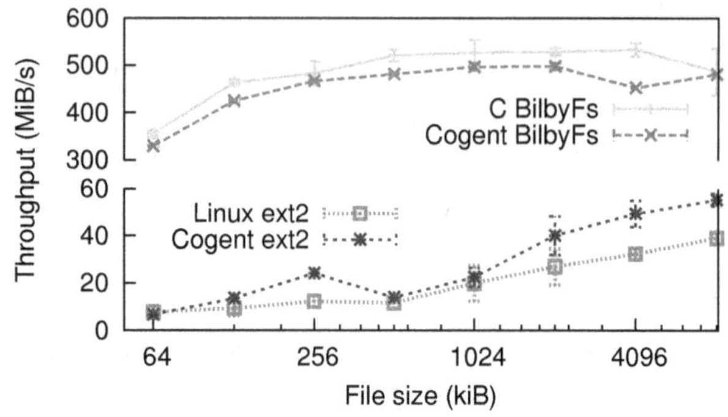

Figure 7. IOZone throughput for sequential 4 KiB writes.

1 from the Debian 8.0 distribution. To reduce run-to-run variability, we disable all but one core. For the BilbyFs evaluations we use a Mirabox with 1 GiB of NAND flash, a Marvell Armada 370 single-core 1.2 GHz ARMv7 processor and 1 GiB of DDR3 memory, running Linux kernel 3.17 from the Debian 6a distribution.

5.2.1 I/O microbenchmarks

We use the IOZone file system microbenchmarks [20] to evaluate basic performance. We use the default settings for an automated run, but include the cost of 'flush' at the end of each write for ext2.

Figure 6 shows performance on random writes. For BilbyFs, we do not include the cost of 'flush' at the end of each write since it completely hides the overhead of the COGENT implementation. BilbyFs shows a 5% throughput degradation in the worst case (64KiB files) for the COGENT version. The CPU load is around 20% compared to 15% on the C version. This is mostly the effect of redundant memory copy operations in the generated C code when passing structs on the stack.

On the other hand COGENT ext2 shows a modest improvement in throughput. CPU usage for COGENT and native Linux are the same at around 10%. We used `blktrace` to investigate; it appears that the COGENT implementation is slightly slower, which means that disk I/O operations hit the disk more often, instead of being merged in the I/O queue. We speculate that the on-disk firmware does a better job of scheduling disk writes than the Linux CFQ I/O scheduler.

Figure 7 shows sequential write performance. Again, COGENT outperforms Linux native for ext2, with very similar CPU load (around 10%). Indirect blocks have to be allocated at 512 KiB and a double-indirect block at 1024 KiB, causing the dips at these points. Again, tracing the I/O patterns show more, and more frequent, disk I/Os for the COGENT implementation. BilbyFs shows a throughput degradation of about 10% with CPU usage of 20% compared to the 15% of the C version. This degradation is explained by the same reasons presented for Figure 6.

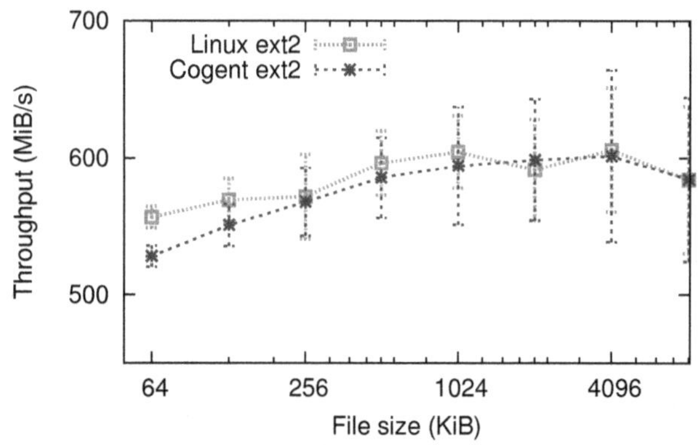

Figure 8. Random write performance on RAM disk.

In order to identify overheads resulting from the use of COGENT, without disk artifacts perturbing the results, we re-run the ext2fs benchmarks on a RAM disk, created as follows:

```
modprobe rd rd_size=1048576
dd if=/dev/zero of=/dev/ram0 bs=1M
mkfs -t ext2 -O none -r 0 -I 128 -b 1024 \
  /dev/ram0
```

Figure 8 shows that without physical I/O, COGENT is slightly slower than native Linux, as expected. This confirms that the performance differences observed in the IO benchmarks are indeed the result of disk artifacts. The ($\pm 8\%$) error bars (showing standard deviation on ten runs) are because of CPU contention with other system activity; they are larger for COGENT because its slightly longer running time gives more opportunity for such contention.

5.2.2 File-system macro benchmarks

For a macro benchmark that exposes present limitations of COGENT, we run *postmark* [22], a benchmark that emulates a busy mail server by creating and deleting many small files. For ext2 tests, we configure the benchmark to start with 50,000 files of size 10,000 bytes each, and run on a RAM disk, so that I/O latency will not mask COGENT overheads. BilbyFs results are on a RAM disk that emulates the MTD

System	Total time sec	creation files/sec	read rate kB/sec
C ext2	10	5025	248
COGENT ext2	21	2393	118
C BilbyFs	6	33375	431
COGENT BilbyFs	10	20025	259

Table 2. Postmark run summary, CPU usage is 100% in all cases.

interface, this time on the same i7 machine that we use for the ext2 tests. BilbyFs' file creation times are much faster than ext2's, so we increased the initial number of files to 200,000.

Table 2 shows the results, each of the values is the mode of ten runs. Typically five or six of the ten runs have essentially the same performance, the rest is worse as benchmarking overlaps with unavoidable system activity. We can see significant degradation of the COGENT implementations, a factor around two for ext2 on the RAM disk, and 1.5 times for BilbyFs.

Profiling COGENT ext2 performance shows that most of the time is spent in converting from in-buffer directory entries to COGENT's internal data type. A better implementation of the directory handling code could reduce this problem.

BilbyFs' bottleneck is in a function that summarises information about newly created files for the log. The same function shows as a bottleneck in both C and COGENT versions, but in the COGENT version it takes about three times as long.

The underlying reason for these results is that the COGENT compiler is at present overly reliant on the C compiler's optimiser. In particular, it passes many structs on the stack, which result in much extra copying, which the C compiler fails to optimise away. Further work is needed to generate code that is more in line with the C compiler's optimisation capabilities.

6. Related Work

Functional verification of file systems belongs to systems verification in general. Klein [24] gives an overview of the early work in this area. The more recent achievements are the comprehensive verification of the seL4 microkernel [25, 26], the verification stack of the Verisoft project [1, 2], the increase of verification productivity in CertiKOS [12, 13], and the full end-to-end application verification in Ironclad [15], which builds on a modified verified Verve kernel [51].

We share the vision for end-to-end systems verification with Ironclad, with verified file systems as a major component, but we are not ready to sacrifice performance as they do. Although our case studies interface with Linux for meaningful evaluation, COGENT is designed to integrate with the verification stack of the seL4 kernel, which will allow a verified COGENT file system to run in protected isolation from legacy applications for a truly minimal TCB.

Verified File Systems Early Z specifications of file systems are those by Morgan and Sufrin [33] for UNIX, and Bevier et al [7] for a custom file system. Arkoudas et al [5] verify two key operations on the block-level of a file system, but the result remains partial and the authors even argue that system components such as file systems will probably always remain beyond the reach of full correctness proofs.

Joshi and Holzman [21] proposed a file system verification challenge, which our work fits into. The aim of this paper was not to provide a full file system verification, but rather to show that high-level file system properties are possible to prove down to the low-level implementation at the same proof productivity as reasoning about higher-level specifications. There is plenty of previous work that shows proofs about such high-level specifications. Our work closes the gap to code. For instance, Hesselink and Lali [18] manage to prove a file refinement stack that goes down to a formal model, but assumes an infinite storage device and other simplifications, and does not end in code. The Event B refinement proof by Damchoom et al [9] similarly does not end in code. In theory, Event B can generate code from low-level models, but neither of these verifications are close enough to achieve usable file system implementations, let alone high performance.

The most realistic high-level Flash file system verification work to date is conducted using the KIV tool [39] and goes from the Flash device layer up to a Linux VFS implementation [11, 44, 45]. The verification work is still in progress and the current code generation from low-level models targets Scala running on a Java Virtual Machine, which implies run-time overheads and dependency on a large language runtime. It may be fruitful to investigate a COGENT backend for this work.

Maric and Sprenger [31] investigate the issue of crash tolerance in file systems, and previously Andronick [4] formally analysed similar issues for tearing in smart cards with persistent storage. COGENT does not provide any special handling for crash tolerance, but the generated specifications are detailed enough to facilitate reasoning about it. Chen et al [8] take cash tolerance to the level of a complete file system in a proof that includes functional correctness of an implementation in Coq. This Coq implementation is roughly on the same level as the Isabelle/HOL specifications generated out of COGENT. Their work is a strong argument that COGENT is hitting the right level of abstraction.

Another stream of work in the literature focuses on more automatic techniques such as model checking and static analysis [14, 41, 52]. While in theory these techniques could be used to provide similar guarantees as COGENT, this has not yet been achieved in practice. Instead of providing guarantees, such analyses are more useful as tools for efficiently finding defects in existing implementations. They also do not provide a path to further higher-level reasoning.

7. Conclusions

We have presented an approach to prove the functional correctness of low-level file system code. We build on COGENT, a certifying compiler that produces C code, Isabelle/HOL specifications, and translation correctness proofs, and we prove properties about the generated specifications in Isabelle/HOL. Composed with the compiler correctness proof, we obtain proofs about the C code.

We find that COGENT not only allows non-experts in formal verification to write provably-safe, fully realistic file system code, it is also the key step to lowering the effort and complexity for the full mechanical verification of file systems against high-level formal specifications.

Our evaluation shows that on a real disk our present file system implementations in COGENT have almost identical throughput with their C counterparts, with slightly more CPU usage. Furthermore, we find that this degradation can, in many cases, be avoided by improving the COGENT compiler output, such that it is less dependent on the optimiser of the underlying C compiler.

COGENT is a sequential language. Although it allows asynchronous disk access, obvious future work is full concurrency. While not a trivial transition, we believe the linear type system of COGENT will help: it lets the compiler keep track of memory locations and side effects. Moreover, the high-level functional semantics can already be executed fully concurrently — sequentialisation happens through the explicit states that the programmer can see and pass through the program in COGENT, making interaction points explicit. Given additional suitable synchronisation primitives, if those states become more fine-grained, more concurrency becomes available.

Acknowledgements

We would like to thank Andrew Baumann and Leonid Ryzhyk for insightful feedback on earlier drafts of this paper.

NICTA is funded by the Australian Government through the Department of Communications and the Australian Research Council through the ICT Centre of Excellence Program.

This material is based on research sponsored by Air Force Research Laboratory and the Defense Advanced Research Projects Agency (DARPA) under agreement number FA8750-12-9-0179. The U.S. Government is authorised to reproduce and distribute reprints for Governmental purposes notwithstanding any copyright notation thereon. The views and conclusions contained herein are those of the authors and should not be interpreted as necessarily representing the official policies or endorsements, either expressed or implied, of Air Force Research Laboratory, the Defense Advanced Research Projects Agency or the U.S. Government.

References

[1] ALKASSAR, E., HILLEBRAND, M., LEINENBACH, D., SCHIRMER, N., STAROSTIN, A., AND TSYBAN, A. Balancing the load — leveraging a semantics stack for systems verification. *Journal of Automated Reasoning: Special Issue on Operating System Verification 42, Numbers 2–4* (2009), 389–454.

[2] ALKASSAR, E., PAUL, W., STAROSTIN, A., AND TSYBAN, A. Pervasive verification of an OS microkernel: Inline assembly, memory consumption, concurrent devices. In *Proceedings of Verified Software: Theories, Tools and Experiments 2010* (Edinburgh, UK, Aug. 2010), vol. 6217 of *Lecture Notes in Computer Science*, pp. 71–85.

[3] AMANI, S., AND MURRAY, T. Specifying a realistic file system. In *Workshop on Models for Formal Analysis of Real Systems* (Suva, Fiji, Nov. 2015), pp. 1–9.

[4] ANDRONICK, J. Formally Proved Anti-tearing Properties of Embedded C Code. In *Proceedings of Second International Symposium on Leveraging Applications of Formal Methods, Verification and Validation* (Paphos, Cyprus, Nov. 2006), pp. 129–136. Invited Speaker.

[5] ARKOUDAS, K., ZEE, K., KUNCAK, V., AND RINARD, M. C. Verifying a file system implementation. In *Proceedings of the 6th International Conference on Formal Engineering Methods* (Seattle, WA, USA, Nov. 2004), vol. 3308 of *Lecture Notes in Computer Science*, pp. 373–390.

[6] BERTOT, Y., AND CASTÉRAN, P. *Interactive Theorem Proving and Program Development. Coq'Art: The Calculus of Inductive Constructions.* Texts in Theoretical Computer Science. An EATCS Series. 2004.

[7] BEVIER, W., COHEN, R., AND TURNER, J. A specification for the Synergy file system. Tech. Rep. Technical Report 120, Computational Logic Inc., Austin, Texas, USA, Sept. 1995.

[8] CHEN, H., ZIEGLER, D., CHAJED, T., CHLIPALA, A., KAASHOEK, M. F., AND ZELDOVICH, N. Using Crash Hoare logic for certifying the FSCQ file system. In *Proceedings of the 25rd ACM Symposium on Operating Systems Principles* (Monterey, CA, Oct. 2015), pp. 18–37.

[9] DAMCHOOM, K., BUTLER, M., AND ABRIAL, J.-R. Modelling and proof of a tree-structured file system in Event-B and Rodin. In *Proceedings of the 10th International Conference on Formal Engineering Methods* (Kitakyushu-City, Japan, Oct. 2008), vol. 5256 of *Lecture Notes in Computer Science*, pp. 25–44.

[10] ELPHINSTONE, K., AND HEISER, G. From L3 to seL4 – what have we learnt in 20 years of L4 microkernels? In *ACM Symposium on Operating Systems Principles* (Farmington, PA, USA, Nov. 2013), pp. 133–150.

[11] ERNST, G., SCHELLHORN, G., HANEBERG, D., PFÄHLER, J., AND REIF, W. Verification of a virtual filesystem switch. In *Proceedings of Verified Software: Theories, Tools and Experiments 2013* (Menlo Park, CA, USA, May 2013), vol. 8164 of *Lecture Notes in Computer Science*, pp. 242–261.

[12] GU, L., VAYNBERG, A., FORD, B., SHAO, Z., AND COSTANZO, D. CertiKOS: A certified kernel for secure cloud

computing. In *Proceedings of the 2nd Asia-Pacific Workshop on Systems (APSys)* (2011).

[13] Gu, R., Koenig, J., Ramananandro, T., Shao, Z., Wu, X. N., Weng, S., Zhang, H., and Guo, Y. Deep specifications and certified abstraction layers. In *Proceedings of the 42nd ACM SIGPLAN-SIGACT Symposium on Principles of Programming Languages* (2015), pp. 595–608.

[14] Gunawi, H. S., Rubio-González, C., Arpaci-Dusseau, A. C., Arpaci-Dussea, R. H., and Liblit, B. EIO: error handling is occasionally correct. In *Proceedings of the 6th USENIX Conference on File and Storage Technologies* (Feb. 2008), pp. 207–222.

[15] Hawblitzel, C., Howell, J., Lorch, J. R., Narayan, A., Parno, B., Zhang, D., and Zill, B. Ironclad apps: End-to-end security via automated full-system verification. In *USENIX Symposium on Operating Systems Design and Implementation* (Broomfield, CO, US, Oct. 2014), pp. 165–181.

[16] The Heartbleed bug. http://heartbleed.com, https://www.openssl.org/news/secadv_20140407.txt, Apr. 2014. Accessed March 2015.

[17] Herder, J. N., Bos, H., Gras, B., Homburg, P., and Tanenbaum, A. S. MINIX 3: A highly reliable, self-repairing operating system. *ACM Operating Systems Review 40*, 3 (July 2006), 80–89.

[18] Hesselink, W. H., and Lali, M. I. Formalizing a hierarchical file system. In *Proceedings of the 14th BCS-FACS Refinement Workshop* (Eindhoven, The Netherlands, Nov. 2009), vol. 259 of *Electronic Notes in Theoretical Computer Science*, pp. 67–85.

[19] Hunter, A. A brief introduction to the design of UBIFS, 03 2008.

[20] IOzone filesystem benchmark. http://www.iozone.org/.

[21] Joshi, R., and Holzmann, G. J. A mini challenge: build a verifiable filesystem. *Formal Aspects of Computing 19*, 2 (2007), 269–272.

[22] Katcher, J. PostMark: A new file system benchmark. Tech. Rep. TR-3022, NetApp, October 1997.

[23] Keller, G., Murray, T., Amani, S., O'Connor-Davis, L., Chen, Z., Ryzhyk, L., Klein, G., and Heiser, G. File systems deserve verification too! In *Workshop on Programming Languages and Operating Systems (PLOS)* (Farmington, Pennsylvania, USA, Nov. 2013), pp. 1–7.

[24] Klein, G. Operating system verification — an overview. *Sādhanā 34*, 1 (Feb. 2009), 27–69.

[25] Klein, G., Andronick, J., Elphinstone, K., Murray, T., Sewell, T., Kolanski, R., and Heiser, G. Comprehensive formal verification of an OS microkernel. *ACM Transactions on Computer Systems 32*, 1 (Feb. 2014), 2:1–2:70.

[26] Klein, G., Elphinstone, K., Heiser, G., Andronick, J., et al. seL4: Formal verification of an OS kernel. In *ACM Symposium on Operating Systems Principles* (Big Sky, MT, US, Oct. 2009), pp. 207–220.

[27] Leroy, X. Formal certification of a compiler back-end, or: Programming a compiler with a proof assistant. In *Proceedings of the 33rd ACM SIGPLAN-SIGACT Symposium on Principles of Programming Languages* (Charleston, SC, USA, 2006), pp. 42–54.

[28] Leroy, X. Formal verification of a realistic compiler. *Communications of the ACM 52*, 7 (2009), 107–115.

[29] Liedtke, J. Improving IPC by kernel design. In *Proceedings of the 14th ACM Symposium on Operating Systems Principles* (Asheville, NC, US, Dec. 1993), pp. 175–188.

[30] Memory leak in Android Lollipop's rendering engine. https://code.google.com/p/android/issues/detail?id=79729#c177, Dec. 2014. Accessed March 2015.

[31] Maric, O., and Sprenger, C. Verification of a transactional memory manager under hardware failures and restarts. In *Proceedings of the 19th International Symposium on Formal Methods (FM)* (May 2014), vol. 8442 of *Lecture Notes in Computer Science*, pp. 449–464.

[32] Matichuk, D., Murray, T., Andronick, J., Jeffery, R., Klein, G., and Staples, M. Empirical study towards a leading indicator for cost of formal software verification. In *International Conference on Software Engineering* (Firenze, Italy, Feb. 2015), p. 11.

[33] Morgan, C., and Sufrin, B. Specification of the UNIX filing system. *IEEE Transactions on Software Engineering 10*, 2 (1984), 128–142.

[34] Nipkow, T., Paulson, L., and Wenzel, M. *Isabelle/HOL — A Proof Assistant for Higher-Order Logic*, vol. 2283 of *Lecture Notes in Computer Science*. 2002.

[35] POSIX filesystem test project. http://sourceforge.net/p/ntfs-3g/pjd-fstest/ci/master/tree/. Retrieved Jan., 2016.

[36] O'Connor, L., Rizkallah, C., Chen, Z., Amani, S., Lim, J., Nagashima, Y., Sewell, T., Hixon, A., Keller, G., Murray, T., and Klein, G. COGENT: Certified compilation for a functional systems language. *CoRR abs/1601.05520* (2016).

[37] Apple's SSL/TLS bug. https://www.imperialviolet.org/2014/02/22/applebug.html, Feb. 2014. Accessed March 2015.

[38] Palix, N., Thomas, G., Saha, S., Calvès, C., Lawall, J., and Muller, G. Faults in Linux: ten years later. In *Proceedings of the 16th International Conference on Architectural Support for Programming Languages and Operating Systems* (Newport Beach, CA, US, 2011), pp. 305–318.

[39] Reif, W., Schellhorn, G., Stenzel, K., and Balser, M. Structured specifications and interactive proofs with KIV. In *Automated Deduction – A Basis for Applications*, vol. 9 of *Applied Logic Series*. 1998, pp. 13–39.

[40] Reynolds, J. C. Separation logic: A logic for mutable data structures. In *Proceedings of the 17th Annual IEEE Symposium on Logic in Computer Science* (Copenhagen, Denmark, July 2002).

[41] Rubio-González, C., and Liblit, B. Defective error/pointer interactions in the Linux kernel. In *Proceedings of the 20th International Symposium on Software Testing and Analysis* (Toronto, ON, Canada, July 2011), pp. 111–121.

[42] SAHA, S., LAWALL, J., AND MULLER, G. An approach to improving the structure of error-handling code in the Linux kernel. In *Conference on Language, Compiler and Tool Support for Embedded Systems (LCTES)* (Chicago, IL, USA, Apr. 2011), pp. 41–50.

[43] SAHA, S., LOZI, J.-P., THOMAS, G., LAWALL, J. L., AND MULLER, G. Hector: Detecting resource-release omission faults in error-handling code for systems software. In *Dependable Systems and Networks (DSN), 2013 43rd Annual IEEE/IFIP International Conference on* (2013), IEEE, pp. 1–12.

[44] SCHELLHORN, G., ERNST, G., PFÄHLER, J., HANEBERG, D., AND REIF, W. Development of a verified Flash file system. In *Proceedings of the 4th International Conference on Abstract State Machines, Alloy, B, TLA, VDM, and Z* (Toulouse, France, June 2014), vol. 8477 of *Lecture Notes in Computer Science*, pp. 9–24.

[45] SCHIERL, A., SCHELLHORN, G., HANEBERG, D., AND REIF, W. Abstract specification of the UBIFS file system for flash memory. In *Proceedings of the Second World Congress on Formal Methods (FM)* (Nov. 2009), vol. 5850 of *Lecture Notes in Computer Science*, pp. 190–206.

[46] SEWELL, T., MYREEN, M., AND KLEIN, G. Translation validation for a verified OS kernel. In *ACM SIGPLAN Conference on Programming Language Design and Implementation* (Seattle, Washington, USA, June 2013), pp. 471–481.

[47] SINGARAVELU, L., PU, C., HÄRTIG, H., AND HELMUTH, C. Reducing TCB complexity for security-sensitive applications: Three case studies. In *Proceedings of the 1st EuroSys Conference* (Leuven, BE, Apr. 2006), pp. 161–174.

[48] TSENG, H.-W., GRUPP, L., AND SWANSON, S. Understanding the impact of power loss on flash memory. In *Proceedings of the 48th Design Automation Conference* (2011), ACM, pp. 35–40.

[49] WADLER, P. Linear types can change the world! In *Programming Concepts and Methods* (1990).

[50] WINWOOD, S., KLEIN, G., SEWELL, T., ANDRONICK, J., COCK, D., AND NORRISH, M. Mind the gap: A verification framework for low-level C. In *International Conference on Theorem Proving in Higher Order Logics* (Munich, Germany, Aug. 2009), pp. 500–515.

[51] YANG, J., AND HAWBLITZEL, C. Safe to the last instruction: automated verification of a type-safe operating system. In *Proceedings of the 2010 ACM SIGPLAN Conference on Programming Language Design and Implementation* (Toronto, Ont, CA, June 2010), pp. 99–110.

[52] YANG, J., SAR, C., AND ENGLER, D. EXPLODE: a lightweight, general system for finding serious storage system errors. In *USENIX Symposium on Operating Systems Design and Implementation* (Nov. 2006), pp. 131–146.

M3: A Hardware/Operating-System Co-Design to Tame Heterogeneous Manycores

Nils Asmussen[†] Marcus Völp[†*] Benedikt Nöthen[‡] Hermann Härtig[†] Gerhard Fettweis[‡]

Operating-Systems Chair[†] and Vodafone Chair Mobile Communications Systems[‡]
Technische Universität Dresden
Nöthnitzer Straße 46, 01187 Dresden, Germany
{nils.asmussen,marcus.voelp,benedikt.noethen,hermann.haertig,gerhard.fettweis}@tu-dresden.de

Abstract

In the last decade, the number of available cores increased and heterogeneity grew. In this work, we ask the question whether the design of the current operating systems (OSes) is still appropriate if these trends continue and lead to abundantly available but heterogeneous cores, or whether it forces a fundamental rethinking of how systems are designed. We argue that:

1. hiding heterogeneity behind a common hardware interface unifies, to a large extent, the control and coordination of cores and accelerators in the OS,
2. isolating at the network-on-chip rather than with processor features (like privileged mode, memory management unit, ...), allows running untrusted code on arbitrary cores, and
3. providing OS services via protocols over the network-on-chip, instead of via system calls, makes them accessible to arbitrary types of cores as well.

In summary, this turns accelerators into first-class citizens and enables a single and convenient programming environment for all cores without the need to trust any application.

In this paper, we introduce network-on-chip-level isolation, present the design of our microkernel-based OS, M^3, and the common hardware interface, and evaluate the performance of our prototype in comparison to Linux. A bit surprising, without using accelerators, M^3 outperforms Linux in some application-level benchmarks by more than a factor of five.

* New affiliation: SnT-CritiX, University of Luxembourg

ASPLOS '16 April 2–6, 2016, Atlanta, Georgia, USA.

DOI: http://dx.doi.org/10.1145/2872362.2872371

Categories and Subject Descriptors C.1.3 [*Other Architecture Styles*]: Heterogeneous (hybrid) systems; D.4.7 [*Organization and Design*]: Distributed systems; D.4.6 [*Security and Protection*]: Access controls

Keywords Heterogeneous architectures; Accelerators; On-chip networks; Operating systems; Capabilities

1. Introduction

In recent years, computer architecture followed two major trends: increased parallelism and heterogeneity. We expect that future systems will continue to follow these trends and confront us with even more heterogeneous cores.

1.1 Heterogeneity

Today, workloads in many application areas run on computer systems, which combine general-purpose CPUs and special-purpose accelerators to achieve the required performance and energy efficiency. For example, in addition to CPU/GPU combinations, which have become mainstream in many daily life devices, we find accelerators to assist in cryptography [21], multimedia [47], object caching [28], signal processing [5, 37], the processing of massive multidimensional data-sets [46] and machine learning [30], to mention just a few.

In their respective domains, special-purpose solutions show large performance and energy advantages over general-purpose solutions. For example, Lim et al. have presented an FPGA-based accelerator for memcached [28] that shows a 16 times performance-per-watt improvement over an Atom CPU. Liu et al. demonstrated that an machine learning accelerator [30] can achieve 20% better performance than a GPU-based solution, while requiring 128 times less energy.

Increased leakage currents and limited heat dissipation capabilities already make it impossible to operate all parts of a chip at full frequency over extended periods of time. To mitigate these effects, which lead to dark silicon, computer architects already proposed mixtures of largely heterogeneous processing elements to accelerate frequently recurring patterns in general-purpose workloads [43], and also to integrate special-purpose accelerators [18] for specific application domains.

In summary, we expect hardware platforms to continue to increase in heterogeneity. Unfortunately, current operating-systems (OSes) rely on specific hardware features such as a privileged mode, exceptions, and a memory management unit (MMU). Furthermore, the OS design requires a kernel, available on every core that should be a *first-class citizen*, i.e., which has access to OS services and can run untrusted code. Of course, special-purpose cores could be equipped with all the hardware features required by current OSes to make them first-class. However, this leads either to large porting efforts for the OS kernel because it needs to run on various different cores. Or it forces hardware vendors to produce cores that are equal at the architectural level, which limits the benefits of accelerators since their advantages stem also from their architectural differences to general-purpose cores.

1.2 Second-class vs. First-class Citizens

Accelerators are currently treated as devices, i.e., *second-class citizens*. Although this model is suitable for timers, network cards or storage devices, we consider it less appropriate for accelerators that execute software or for reconfigurable circuits like FPGAs, which are becoming increasingly common. At first, as more and more accelerators execute increasingly complex software, their need for OS services like filesystems, network stacks or inter-process communication mechanisms increases. Second, applications might want to offload parts of their computation onto accelerators and of course, do not want to switch to a completely different and limited programming environment. We therefore believe that it is crucial to remove the barrier between general-purpose cores and accelerators and treat both as first-class citizens.

1.3 Abundantly Available Cores

Although the increase of single-thread performance has mostly stopped due to the break-down of Dennard scaling [12], Moore's law still leads to about twice as many integrated transistors every 18 months, which are used to integrate more cores on a chip as a response to the stop of Dennard scaling. Today, there are already research projects with hundreds [3] to even one thousand [24] cores on a chip and we believe that chips with that many cores will become commercially available in the future. These large number of cores, while probably not all usable at all times due to power and heat constraints, offer new opportunities and trade offs. For example, having enough cores allows the OS to place each application on its own core. By cleverly balancing the load and powering off unused cores, the OS can make sure that it stays within the power budget. This approach is beneficial because it avoids both the direct and the indirect costs of context switches. That is, applications no longer share hardware resources like registers, caches, and translation lookaside buffers (TLBs).

1.4 Contributions

Our goals are therefore to, at first, integrate arbitrary cores as first-class citizens into the system, and second, leverage the fact that cores are abundantly available. To achieve that, we integrate cores and memories into a packet-switched network-on-chip (NoC) and equip each core with a *data transfer unit* (DTU) as the common hardware component. The DTU, offering message passing and memory access, is thereby the only means for the core to communicate with other cores or memories. Thus, controlling the DTU allows us to control the core and therefore also the software running on the core. OS services like filesystems and network stacks are provided based on a core-neutral communication protocol between DTUs. Our contributions are as follows:

1. We introduce data transfer units and the concept of NoC-level isolation, which enables uniform control and coordination of heterogeneous cores.
2. We evaluate new OS design opportunities and trade-offs that become possible through NoC-level isolation and abundantly available cores.
3. We describe the design of our OS prototype, M^3, where we combine the above findings into a microkernel-based system. As a proof of concept, we implemented a filesystem and pipes. M^3 is available as open source at `https://github.com/TUD-OS/M3`.
4. Finally, we evaluate the performance of our prototype to show the feasibility of the OS design. By trading system utilization for supporting heterogeneous cores and by accelerating data transfers via the DTU, M^3 outperforms Linux as a representative of a traditional OS by more than a factor of five in some application-level benchmarks.

The rest of the paper is organized as follows: After relating this paper to previous work in Section 2, we introduce our approach to tame heterogeneous manycores based on NoC-level isolation and DTUs in Section 3. In Section 4, we detail our hardware/OS co-design of the DTU and the OS prototype M^3. Finally, we evaluate our prototype in Section 5, conclude in Section 6, and sketch directions for future work in Section 7.

2. Related Work

As this paper is about a hardware/operating-system co-design, the related work can be split into similar hardware components and similar OS designs.

2.1 Hardware-Level Isolation and Message Passing

At first, memory management units (MMUs) and memory protection units (MPUs) are related to the DTU described in this paper. They are typically tightly integrated with the core architecture and used for memory translation and/or protection, controlled by the OS kernel. More recently, IOMMUs have been introduced to add translation and protection to I/O

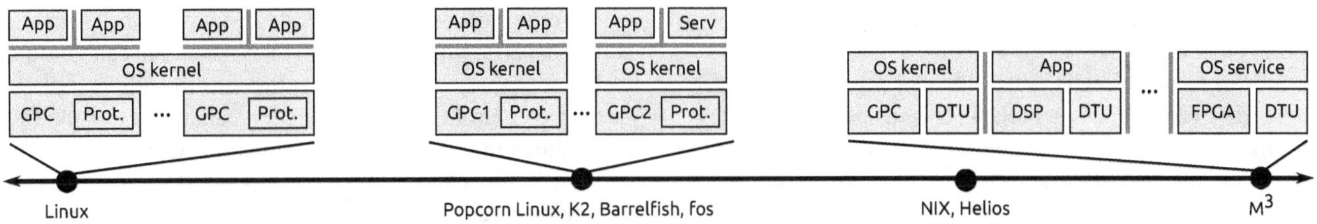

Figure 1. Design space for heterogeneity, enforcing isolation (red lines) and providing OS services.

devices. Furthermore, hardware components have been proposed to connect heterogeneous cores over a NoC in a secure way [16, 36]. However, all of them are dealing with memory accesses only. Instead, the purpose of the DTU is to abstract from the heterogeneity of the cores and provide the features that are required to make all cores first-class citizens. In particular, this includes the ability to perform secure and efficient message passing between cores.

Besides approaches for memory accesses, various work [4, 20, 25, 31, 34] has been done on (user-level) message passing architectures. For example, Alpert et al. describe protected message passing in userland on the Shrimp multicomputer [4]. Protection is thereby based on virtual memory support in the core. Similarly, the MAGIC component in the FLASH multiprocessor [20, 25], is designed as a core that executes software to allow the implementation of a variety of protocols like cache coherency. It does also require cooperation with an OS kernel. In summary, all approaches rely on core-specific features like virtual memory and/or an OS kernel on the sending/receiving core for special cases. Since our goal is to integrate arbitrary cores into the system and simple accelerators in particular, the DTU has to be core-agnostic and needs to handle all operations without involving an OS kernel on the same core.

2.2 Operating Systems

When exploring related OS work and comparing it with our design, we find different approaches to heterogeneity, isolation, and providing OS services. As depicted in Figure 1, traditional OSes like Linux are built to execute a shared kernel on homogeneous cores. Isolation between the OS kernel and applications and between applications is thereby implemented via processor features like a privileged mode, exceptions, and MMUs (denoted by *Prot.* for protection features in the figure) that we find in general-purpose cores (GPC). OS services are offered via system calls that perform a mode switch from user mode into privileged mode.

To let Linux support heterogeneous cores, approaches like Popcorn Linux [7] and K2 [29] have been suggested, which run multiple Linux instances on potentially heterogeneous cores. Since they are still based on Linux running on general-purpose cores, isolation and OS services are realized in the traditional way. Like with standard Linux, accelerators are treated as devices.

Moving further to the right, we find the multi-kernel design with Barrelfish [8] as one implementation. Barrelfish aims to support many heterogeneous cores as well and designs the OS as a distributed system to improve scalability. Similarly, fos [44] targets manycores and thus introduces the concept of *service fleets* that are spread among the whole chip. Both Barrelfish and fos use message passing to access OS services that may run on a different core. However, the design of Barrelfish and fos is based on the traditional way of isolation and executing a kernel on every core, required for message passing and resource access in case of fos and for memory isolation and capability management in Barrelfish.

NIX [6], based on Plan 9 [35], relaxes the requirement on executing a kernel on every core by introducing application cores. In contrast to still existing time sharing cores, application cores do not execute a kernel to prevent *OS noise*, i.e., interference with the application caused by the OS through e.g., interrupt handling. Application cores can still access OS services by communicating via message passing with a time sharing core. Although NIX supports cores that are not able to execute a kernel, the communication in NIX is based on shared memory and isolation requires MMUs on all cores. In contrast to NIX, our approach does not rely on this.

Helios [33], a derivative from Singularity [14], reduces the requirements one step further by using software isolation instead of address space protection. Thereby, neither an MMU nor a privileged mode is required. However, Helios still executes a *satellite kernel* on every core and requires a timer device, an interrupt controller, exceptions, and a quite large amount of memory (at least 32 MiB).

In this paper, we evaluate the rightmost point in this spectrum (see Figure 1) by removing all requirements on processor features. We achieve that by abstracting the heterogeneity of the cores via a common hardware component per core, called DTU, which contains all the features that are required for an OS to treat the attached core as a first-class citizen. This allows us to hide any kind of processor, including very simple ones, behind a DTU. For example, a general-purpose core, a digital signal processor (DSP), an application-specific integrated circuit (ASIC), an FPGA, etc. Based on the DTU, we isolate at the NoC-level by remotely controlling the communication capabilities of DTUs and offer OS services via core-neutral communication protocols. In this paper, we use the term *processing element* (PE) to denote the combination of core, local memory (scratchpad or cache) and DTU.

Similar to M^3, GPUfs [40], GPUnet [22] and PTask [39] strive to make GPUs first-class citizens. However, they specifically target GPUs, while we aim to find a general solution to integrate arbitrary PEs as first-class citizens.

3. Taming Heterogeneous Manycores

To address the problem of heterogeneous PEs, we move the kernel to dedicated PEs and thereby let the applications run on bare-metal, as shown in Figure 1. That is, no applications are running on the *kernel PEs*, while no kernel is running on the *application PEs*. Similar to previous works [6, 10, 41], system calls are not handled on the same core by performing a mode switch, but by sending a message over the DTU to the corresponding kernel PE. However, the main motivation in the mentioned works is the improvement of performance, while ours is the support of heterogeneous cores.

Despite the differences between the kernel in M^3 and a traditional kernel, they share their main responsibility: making the final decision of whether an operation is allowed or not. Typically, a traditional kernel, in contrast to applications, is running in the privileged processor mode. With M^3, privilege is not defined by the processor mode, but by the DTU. Similarly to the processor mode, all DTUs are privileged at boot, i.e., any communication is allowed. During boot, the DTUs of the application PEs are downgraded by the kernel to become unprivileged. Due to the similarities to traditional kernels, we also use the term *kernel* for the entity that exercises the mentioned responsibility and the term *kernel PE* for naming the entire PE on which this entity runs.

3.1 Data Transfer Unit

In our approach, a DTU is a small hardware component that is present in each PE and thereby serves two purposes:

1. It is the only interface for the PE to PE-external resources like other PEs or memories.
2. It abstracts from the heterogeneity of the PEs to allow a uniform control of different PEs.

For our OS design, the DTU needs to support both message passing and remote memory access. Message passing is essential for the PE-neutral protocols used to provide filesystems, network stacks, access to devices and so on, while memory access is required to use PE-external memories.

The DTU should be attached to the core as a device with memory mapped registers. In this way, the DTU can be core-agnostic and existing instruction set architectures can be reused without any change.

3.2 NoC-level Isolation

Since we assume that all PEs are potentially different, the processor features used for isolation in classical OSes are different in every PE or are not even available. Therefore, we enforce isolation at the NoC-level instead of within one core. That is, applications run on bare-metal and can thus use their core in any way they like. Instead, to isolate applications, we control the communication capabilities of the PE, i.e., control the exchange of information with other PEs or memories. Since the DTU is the only interface to other PEs or memories, controlling the DTU suffices to control the application on that PE. This is done by a kernel, running on a different PE. In this way, a kernel isolates the applications at the NoC-level by remotely controlling their DTUs.

3.3 Abundantly Available Cores

Although we expect that future platforms will have many cores, we do not assume that, at any point in time, cores outnumber the threads of execution in the system. Instead, we plan to support the multiplexing of a core[1] among a group of threads that can run on that same core, but to not context-switch periodically, but only if required. With this, we optimize for the common case with abundantly available cores: two interacting applications are running on separate cores at the same time and can thus directly communicate with each other. That is, communication does not mean to transition the execution from the sender to the receiver, but both are running in parallel and are putting their cores in a low power state when waiting. For a communication that involves longer wait times, we plan to inform the kernel about a potentially reusable core, which can then perform a context switch to another thread of execution, if necessary. In this case, the kernel needs to switch back to the old thread before the interrupted communication can be completed. We leave the details of context switching (and migration, because it requires the same mechanism) as future work.

3.4 Discussion

This approach has several advantages:

1. Applications do not share resources like registers, caches or TLBs with kernels and, in the common case, not with other applications as well. Therefore, when performing system calls, registers do not need to be saved or restored and, when the call is finished, cache or TLB misses do not happen because no entries have been evicted.
2. As no kernel is running on application PEs, supporting arbitrary PEs becomes much easier. First, the kernel PEs could be homogeneous. Second, only the application needs to be compiled for the targeted PE(s) and, if desired, be prepared for hardware features it wants to make use of. Thus, new application PEs can be added without requiring any change to a kernel.
3. Furthermore, as no application is running on the kernel PEs, a kernel does not need to run in privileged mode, support context switching or use paging to isolate itself

[1] This will be restricted to the subset of the cores that support it, i.e., some accelerators might be excluded.

from the application. Instead, the only hardware feature that a kernel needs to support is the DTU to communicate with the applications and control them from the outside.

4. OS kernels and services do not necessarily benefit from the same hardware features (instruction extensions, number of functional units, memory architecture etc.) as the application. Giving them different PEs allows to accelerate both in the best possible way.

The disadvantage of this design is the decrease in system utilization, because a PE is idling (for a certain time) if the application on that PE is waiting for an incoming message or the completion of a memory transfer. However, it is expected that the power consumption and heat generation will be the limiting factors in the future. That is, even if an OS could fully utilize all PEs at all times, physical limits will prevent it from doing so. Furthermore, abundantly available cores will allow the OS in most cases to not reuse the core for a different application immediately, since enough free cores are available. For this reason we believe that this can be relaxed in favor of supporting heterogeneous cores (which are controlled remotely) and an increase in performance, because the state of the application (e.g., in the cache and TLB) is kept during most communications.

Note that, despite the separation in kernel PEs and application PEs, it does not mean that they require different cores. In fact, the kernel of our prototype implementation does not need any specific processor feature and can thus run on any core, where a DTU is attached and for which a C++ compiler is available. But of course our approach *allows* to specialize a kernel PE by e.g., adding specific instructions to the core to accelerate certain operations, if desired.

4. Design and Implementation

To evaluate the feasibility of the described approach, we built a prototype for both the DTU and the OS. The DTU was thereby co-designed with the OS to reflect the requirements of the OS in the feature-set of the DTU. In particular, our goal is to treat all PEs as first-class citizens whether or not they support OS kernels. For example, the core might have no privileged mode or memory protection to protect a kernel. Another reason is that the core can be an FPGA that should only host the circuit to accelerate a specific computation.

4.1 Prototype Platform

To investigate how an OS could look like if PEs do not support an OS kernel, we chose to use the Tomahawk platform [5], which is a multiprocessor system-on-a-chip (MPSoC) for mobile communication applications. Tomahawk consists of multiple PEs, connected over a network-on-chip and one DRAM module. The PEs are Xtensa RISC cores that do not have a privileged mode and also no MMU. Furthermore, they employ a scratchpad memory (SPM) instead of caches as the only directly addressable memory. SPM is often used for accelerators, because in contrast to caches, they can be tailored to the accelerators needs by adding multiple independent SRAM banks to perform multiple accesses in parallel [11].

M^3 supports two versions of Tomahawk: The first is a silicon chip, which employs 8 PEs, each having a SPM of 32 KiB for code and 32 KiB for data and a predecessor of the here described DTU, that does only support data exchange, but no message passing with the features described in Section 4.4. The second is cycle-accurate simulator of Tomahawk, based on the Cadence Xtensa SystemC framework [9], that we modified to include the DTU described in this paper. It supports an arbitrary number of PEs, each having a SPM of 64 KiB for code and 64 KiB for data. Although this version of Tomahawk is currently only available as a simulator, it has already been sent to the chip manufacturer and will thus also be available as a silicon chip next year. M^3 runs on both Tomahawk versions, but we describe and evaluate the simulator-based version because it supports more PEs and employs the described DTU (on the current hardware, some features need to be emulated in software).

4.2 Limitations

Our prototype platform has currently two major limitations:

1. Instead of a cache, a core employs only a small SPM, limiting the size of code and data and thus the complexity of applications that can run on it (without manually managing it like a cache).
2. Virtual memory is not supported, but a core accesses the SPM and external memory with physical addresses. The SPM can be accessed directly with load/store instructions, whereas the external DRAM (or other PE's SPMs) requires an explicit transfer into the SPM over the DTU first, leading to a distributed memory architecture.

However, to us, this was not a limitation, but a feature: simple accelerators, which we strive to support in particular, typically lack these features. Starting with a platform that consists of simple accelerator-like cores only, allowed us to explore how to design the system in a way that these cores are supported as first-class citizens. In future work, we will address these limitations to optionally support caches and virtual memory, as described in Section 7.

4.3 Overview and Terminology

Before diving into the details, this section briefly sketches the general concepts of isolation, communication, and remote memory access, and introduces the terminology used in this paper. At the hardware side, as shown in Figure 2, the DTU consists of a number of *endpoints* (EPs). Each endpoint can be configured to be a *send endpoint*, a *receive endpoint*, or a *memory endpoint*. The configuration registers (`buffer`, `target`, `credits`, and `label`) are only writable by kernel PEs, while the `data` register is writable by the application PE as well. Initially, all registers are writable at all PEs and the kernels downgrade the permissions at the application PEs during boot[2]. To let applications communicate, a kernel establishes communication *channels* by remotely configuring endpoints. Afterwards, no kernel PE is involved, but the sender and receiver communicate directly (as indicated by the thick arrow in Figure 2).

At the software side, the kernels provide *Virtual Processing Elements* (VPEs) as an abstraction for PEs. Applications consist of at least one VPE, whereas each VPE is assigned to exactly one PE at any point in time. The kernels use *capabilities* [13] to manage the permissions of the VPEs by maintaining a capability table per VPE. In Figure 2, the receiver uses a *receive gate* object, which is associated with the *receive capability* and bound to a receive endpoint. Analogously, the sender uses a *send gate* associated with the *send capability* and bound to a send endpoint. For memory access, the concept is analogous, but the *target* register at the send endpoint specifies a region of memory instead of a receive endpoint.

this case. As the memory transfer occurs without involving an OS kernel and without involving software on the passive side (where the data is read from or written to), it is a form of RDMA.

An endpoint is therefore a hardware representation of a capability, similar to CHERI [45]. In contrast to CHERI, we did not extend the instruction set architecture, but the DTU acts as a device attached to the core.

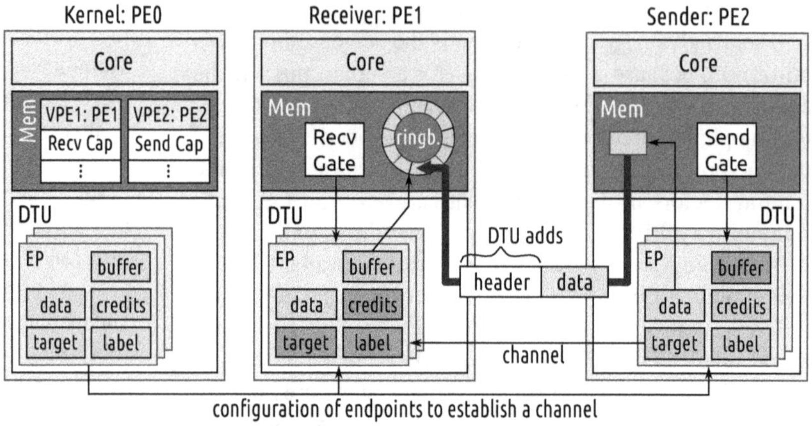

Figure 2. Communication between two PEs via the DTUs, set up by a kernel. The receiver has a receive endpoint configured for receiving messages and the sender has a send endpoint for sending messages to the receive endpoint.

4.4 Data Transfer Unit

For our prototype, we built a DTU and integrated one instance in each PE of the Tomahawk platform.

4.4.1 Endpoints

To support both memory access and message-based communication we provide endpoints to establish communication channels. Each DTU contains a set of endpoints, which can be configured for different operations.

With a send endpoint, a message can be sent by specifying the address and size of the data to send via the `data` register. This requires that the `target` register has been configured to point to the receive endpoint and that the registers `credits` and `label` have been set accordingly (the following sections provide more detail on them). The `buffer` register is not used for send endpoints.

For receive endpoints, the `buffer` register specifies the location and size of the ringbuffer, which can only be done by a kernel PE (see Section 4.4.4). Received messages are placed into the ringbuffer by the DTU without involving any software. If permitted by the sender, a reply can be send via the `data` register. The other registers are unused.

For memory endpoints, the `target` register specifies the remote memory region and the permissions (read or write). When reading, the `data` register denotes the location the read data should be transferred to, while when writing, it denotes the data to write. `Label` and `credits` are not used in this case.

[2] If desired, a kernel can also upgrade the permissions of an application PE again to turn it into a kernel PE, but this is not done in our prototype.

In the current implementation, the software polls a DTU register to wait for received messages or completed memory transfers. In future work, we will put the core into a low-power state and the DTU will wake it up for these events.

4.4.2 Messages

Messages consist of a header and a payload. The header is automatically prepended to the payload by the DTU and contains a label, the length of the message, and information for a potential reply (see Section 4.4.4). A label, originally introduced by KeyKOS [19] as *numeric tag*, is a value that is chosen by the receiver when the channel is created and unforgeable by the sender to securely identify the sender. Typically, the receiver sets it to the address of the object that corresponds to the sender, so that no additional lookup in a hash table or a similar data structure is necessary to find the object needed for the requested operation.

We believe that device interrupts should be sent as messages as well to integrate them with the existing concepts. This would allow to wait for them as for any other message, interpose them, sent them to any PE, independent of the core, etc. However, we have not yet implemented this idea, because of the lack of devices in the prototype platform.

4.4.3 Ringbuffer

Ringbuffers at the receive endpoints allow receivers to simultaneously accept messages from multiple senders. Ringbuffers are allocated in the local memory of the PE and organized in fixed-size slots. The size of the slots, which corresponds to the maximum message size, is configurable per endpoint. Upon the reception of a message, the DTU writes the received message at the current write position in the ringbuffer and moves the write position forward. The software in turn advances the buffer's current read position to indicate that a message has been processed. To manage the ringbuffer space, we use a credit system, similar to the one in Intel QuickPath [2]. That is, the receiver hands out credits to its senders and thereby limits the number of messages per sender. If a sender has no credits left, message sending is denied by the DTU until the credits have been refilled by either the receiver (typically when replying) or an OS kernel. For most scenarios, the receiver should not hand out more credits than buffer space is available, because messages are dropped if no space is left.

4.4.4 Replies

A channel is unidirectional in the sense that only the sender can start a communication. But since a reply is an important and also performance-critical operation, the DTU supports direct replies on received messages without requiring a dedicated channel back to the sender.

To enable replies, the sender specifies any of its endpoints as receive endpoint for the reply and transmit this information to the receiver. We decided to store the reply information in the message header, i.e., in the receiver's ringbuffer. To reply, the receiver selects the message to reply to and the DTU accesses the message header to extract the destination. Naturally, storing this security-critical information at a software accessible location requires additional protection. Therefore, if replies should be enabled for a ringbuffer, an OS kernel ensures these ringbuffers are placed in read-only memory and do not overlap before configuring a receive endpoint.

4.5 Operating System

In parallel to the just described DTU, we have built an operating-system prototype called M^3, which is short for **m**icrokernel-based syste**m** for heterogeneous **m**anycores (or L4 [27] $\pm$ 1), and follows the design introduced in Section 3. M^3 consists of a kernel, running on a dedicated PE[3], OS services and the library *libm3*.

4.5.1 Microkernel Approach

We chose to build the OS as a microkernel-based system. That is, the kernel provides only the necessary mechanisms to let applications implement the actual functionality of the OS. In particular, filesystems, network stacks and drivers are therefore implemented as applications; hence we use the term *application* to refer to both user applications and OS services in this paper.

Besides the well known security and reliability advantages of microkernels, the DTU and our approach of having dedicated application and kernel PEs eliminates the most important criticism of microkernels: Since message passing is performed directly between applications via DTUs, without kernel involvement or context or address-space switches, it is very fast. As reported in Section 5, it is even faster than a Linux system call on Xtensa and ARM.

[3] In the future, multiple instances of the kernel will be supported.

4.5.2 Library

The library libm3 provides abstractions for communicating with the kernel or OS services, accessing files, using the DTU etc. and contains only little architecture-specific code. Currently, only the PE initialization is architecture-specific, which makes libm3 easily portable to architectures other than Xtensa. Due to the small SPMs in our prototype, which we believe is a common limitation of accelerators and other PEs without kernel support, libm3 provides lightweight abstractions rather than a POSIX-compliant environment. This choice also results in performance improvements, as demonstrated in the evaluation.

4.5.3 Capabilities

Inspired by L4 microkernels [23, 26, 42], M^3 uses capabilities to manage the permissions of applications. A capability is thereby a pair consisting of a kernel object and permissions for this object. The kernel maintains a table of capabilities per VPE, similar to the file descriptor table in UNIX systems.

M^3 provides two operations to *exchange* capabilities between VPEs (*delegate* and *obtain*) and one operation to undo the exchange (*revoke*):

1. *Delegate*: Grant another VPE access to a capability.
2. *Obtain*: Request access to a capability from another VPE.
3. *Revoke*: Undo all grants of a capability recursively.

Naturally, VPEs can only delegate and revoke capabilities they possess themselves. To revoke a capability recursively, i.e., including all grants, the kernel maintains a tree that records all delegation/obtain operations, similar to the *mapping database* found in some L4 microkernels [23, 26, 42].

In L4 microkernels, a capability exchange is performed via inter-process communication (IPC). In particular, a single message allows to exchange both information and capabilities. In contrast, in M^3, IPC does not involve the kernel and is instead performed directly between applications. However, to exchange capabilities, the kernel needs to be involved as it manages all capabilities. For that reason, M^3 offers two options to exchange capabilities, which are both realized as system calls to the kernel: first, one can exchange capabilities with another VPE, provided that the requesting VPE has a capability for the other. Second, applications can exchange capabilities with services. The second additionally involves communication with the service to negotiate details and allow the service to deny the capability exchange. The required communication channel between kernel and service is created at service registration. In the current prototype, send and receive capabilities are virtualizable, i.e., they can be interposed by a proxy to e.g., monitor the communication, but memory capabilities are not. This is due to the lack of virtual memory support in our prototype platform.

4.5.4 Gates

A *gate* is the software abstraction used for communication and memory access over the DTU. M^3 provides three different kinds of gates:

- *receive gates* to receive messages,
- *send gates* to send messages to receive gates and
- *memory gates* to access remote memory.

As receive gates can receive messages at any point in time, they can only be moved to different endpoints or PEs after invalidating all connected send gates and ensuring that no transfer is in progress. In contrast, send gates and memory gates are easily movable. Hence, the kernel only allows to delegate/obtain send and memory capabilities, but not receive capabilities.

The kernel is responsible for managing the memories in the system. That is, it decides which application can use which parts of which memories. Our current prototype contains only one DRAM module and all PEs have SPMs instead of caches. Therefore, code, static data, heap, and stack are placed in the SPM, owned by the application currently running on that PE. Applications can however request a region of the DRAM via a system call to obtain a memory gate, which provides access to the region via explicit data transfers over the DTU.

To actually send messages or access memory, receiving a send or memory gate is not sufficient. A kernel needs to configure an endpoint at the application PE first, which is requested via a system call, because only a kernel has the permissions to configure endpoints. This indirection allows a kernel to defer the reply to the system call until the receiver is ready to receive messages. Furthermore, since the DTU provides only a limited number of endpoints (8 in our prototype platform) and applications might need more send gates or memory gates[4] than endpoints are available, multiplexing is used to share the endpoints among these gates. This is done by libm3, which checks before the usage of a gate whether the endpoint is appropriately configured. If not, the corresponding system call is performed.

4.5.5 Virtual PEs

Applications consist of multiple Virtual PEs, whereas each VPE is bound to a specific PE at any point in time. Although our current prototype does not yet support it, we plan to allow the migration of VPEs and also time-sharing of PEs among multiple VPEs. As far as the kernel is concerned, each VPE represents a single activity, i.e., does not use parallelism. Instead, new VPEs can be created to make use of more than one PE. However, an application is of course free to implement user-level thread-switching on a single PE or, if a PE supports it, use a timer interrupt and a small interrupt routine to switch between threads preemptively.

VPEs are created via a system call to the kernel, which instructs the kernel to select a suitable and unused PE. Thereby, the application can request a specific type of PE – for example a specific accelerator. If found, the kernel creates a VPE kernel object and a VPE capability for the VPE that requested it. Furthermore, the requesting VPE receives a memory gate for the memory that the VPE can access. In the current prototype, the memory gate refers to the local memory of the PE. If caches are available, it will be some PE-external memory and the kernel will configure the cache/DTU to access it.

The memory gate is used by libm3 to perform application loading as it provides complete control of the PE. libm3 supports two operations: First, applications can clone themselves onto this PE, similar to a `fork` in UNIX. Second, they can load an executable from the filesystem (see Section 4.5.8) onto the PE, similar to `exec`. The former is intended only for homogeneous PEs, the latter for both homogeneous and heterogeneous PEs.

When using the clone operation, libm3 transfers the code, static data, the used portion of the heap and the stack to the corresponding locations of the memory denoted by the memory gate. Since each PE has its own local memory, this does neither require virtual memory nor position independent code: the regions are simply copied to the same addresses in the other PE.

In the current C++ implementation of libm3, the clone operation can be used to execute C++ lambdas on other PEs, as the following example shows:

```
int a = 4, b = 5;
VPE vpe("test");
vpe.run([a,&b]() {
    auto &s = Serial::get();
    s << "Sum: " << (a + b) << "\n";
    return 0;
});
int result = vpe.wait();
```

At first, the VPE is created via a system call, selecting a PE of the same type as the requesting PE in this case. Second, all state is copied to the other PE and the given function is called. Arguments can be passed to the lambda by capturing them – either by value or by reference. However, since our prototype platform does not support to access PE-external memories with load/store instructions, values of the caller cannot be directly manipulated. Instead, this has to be done explicitly by using message passing or memory gates. This can be achieved by exchanging capabilities with the VPE before and/or after running the lambda. Note that

[4] Multiplexing is currently unsupported for receive gates, because they are more difficult to move, as described before.

the execution of the lambda happens asynchronously. The method `wait` can be called to wait until the lambda has finished execution and to receive an exit code. In case the lambda does not return after some time, the owner of the VPE capability could revoke it to let the kernel reset the associated PE, thereby making it available again for others.

4.5.6 Message Passing

We chose to make message passing asynchronous on the lowest level. That is, after a message is sent, which is done by programming the memory-mapped registers of the DTU accordingly, the application is free to perform other work until the reply has been received (if any is expected). This is because the kernel is executing on a different PE and not involved if two applications communicate. Since an asynchronous model is often more difficult, most abstractions of libm3 combine the send operation with waiting for the reply, making it synchronous again.

To simplify the message-based communication, libm3 provides easy-to-use C++ abstractions for marshalling and unmarshalling. Inspired by previous L4 marshalling frameworks [15], it overloads the C++ shift operators to marshal an object into the message or unmarshal it again.

4.5.7 Pipes

Based on the so far described basic primitives, libm3 offers a pipe concept, similar to a pipe in UNIX. On M^3, a pipe is a unidirectional data channel between exactly one writer and exactly one reader. The data is thereby transferred over a software-managed ringbuffer in the DRAM, to which both reader and writer have access. Although the SPM and the ringbuffer provided by the DTU could be used, we decided in favor for the DRAM, because the SPM might be too small, if an application needs several pipes to other applications. By using the DRAM, large ringbuffers can be used to maximize the parallelism of readers and writers.

To manage access to the ringbuffer, messages are used to synchronize reader and writer. That is, after writing new data to the ringbuffer, the writer notifies the reader with a message, which in turn will read the data from the ringbuffer, after it received the message. In this way, the state of the ringbuffer is exchanged with messages, while the ringbuffer in DRAM contains only the data that is transmitted through the pipe. It is important to note that, after setting up the pipe, the kernel is not involved in the communication. That is, the actual pipe-based communication happens directly between the PE of the reader and PE of the writer.

4.5.8 Filesystem

As a filesystem is an essential and performance-critical component of an OS, we have designed and implemented a filesystem, called *m3fs*, as a proof of concept for a service provided by an application in M^3. m3fs is currently an in-memory filesystem, because our prototype platform lacks persistent storage. However, the organization of the data has been chosen to be suitable for persistent storage as well, so that we can support it later.

For opening files, closing files, meta-data operations like `mkdir`, `link` etc., the service is contacted to perform these operations. The actual data transfers are done without involving m3fs, because the applications directly read or write to the memory, where the file is stored[5]. The application needs to ask m3fs for the locations of the file fragments that it wants to access first. m3fs will then delegate memory capabilities for the requested fragments in memory to the application. The concept is therefore somewhat similar to GoogleFS [17], where meta-data is separated from data storage as well.

The filesystem is organized like classical UNIX filesystems, consisting of a superblock, an inode and block bitmap, an inode table and directories with pointers to the inodes. The data of an inode is stored in a tree of tables containing extents. As in other modern filesystems [32, 38], an extent is a pair of a starting block number and a number of blocks. The reason for this organization is that the applications get access to the data in form of memory capabilities, representing contiguous pieces of memory. To maximize the performance and scalability, these pieces of memory should be as large as possible to reduce the number of times m3fs has to be contacted. Storing the contiguous pieces in the form of extents avoids the need to first scan through a list of block numbers to determine the contiguous pieces.

To relieve the application programmers from obtaining memory capabilities from m3fs, determining at which offset of that memory the application needs to access etc., libm3 offers POSIX-like abstractions (`open`, `read`, `write`, `seek`, `close`, ...) to the application. That is, the application uses a local buffer for reading and writing, and libm3 will translate that into memory reads or writes at the appropriate location and will, if necessary, request further memory capabilities.

In this way, we optimize the data transfers for performance and scalability, because we believe that they are more performance-critical than meta-operations. For example, because a file consists of a list of extents, each potentially having a different length, seeking gets more expensive. However, most seek operations can be done in libm3 by seeking within the already obtained memory capabilities (extents).

A further consequence of this design is that, even if m3fs is storing the data in random access memory, like in our prototype, the fragmentation of files (of how many extents they consist) is important. The reason is, that the more extents a file has, the more often the application needs to communicate with m3fs to request further memory capabilities. Additionally, the seeking performance suffers with an increasing number of extents. For that reason, write operations extend files by a large number of blocks at once to minimize the

[5] In the current prototype, files are already in DRAM. If persistent storage was involved, m3fs would first load the file into DRAM, i.e., into the buffer cache.

fragmentation and the close operation truncates it to the actually used space. As the evaluation in Section 5.7 shows, as long as the extents are sufficiently large, the performance degradation with multiple extents is minimal.

To support multiple filesystems, libm3 offers a virtual filesystem (VFS) that allows to mount filesystems at specific paths. Besides m3fs, it provides a pipe filesystem to integrate pipes into the VFS, making it transparent for applications whether they access a pipe or a file in m3fs.

5. Evaluation

Our evaluation strives to answer the following questions:

- How fast are system calls via DTU?
- How fast are file operations with m3fs?
- What is the performance impact of file fragmentation?
- How fast are OS-intensive applications?
- How far does M^3 scale with a single service/kernel?
- What performance can be achieved by accelerators?

5.1 Methodology

To answer these questions, we compare our prototype to Linux in as many benchmarks as possible. We used two general approaches: first, we conducted micro-benchmarks to compare the performance of system calls and filesystem operations. Second, to prevent large porting efforts, we obtained traces from applications on Linux to compare both OSes in more realistic settings. Due to prohibitively long simulation times, we could not use standard benchmarks, but were required to use short running applications.

For both M^3 and Linux we used cycle-accurate simulators, whose computation performances are equivalent. M^3 was running on the Tomahawk platform, which can be started with an arbitrary number of PEs, each containing 64 KiB of SPM for instructions and 64 KiB for data with no caches and no MMU. Linux 3.18 was running on the simulator provided by Cadence with an Xtensa core, which contains an instruction and data cache, each with a capacity of 64 KiB, and an MMU. Furthermore, we configured the cost for a cache miss on Linux to be equivalent to the transfer time for loading a cache line (32 Bytes) via the DTU. That is, loading data from DRAM takes the same time in both setups. Due to the larger variation of the results on Linux, we discarded the results of the first two runs of all benchmarks to ensure that the caches are warm. For results still subject to a standard deviation of more than 1%, we show error bars in the figures.

Unfortunately, Linux does not provide support for multiple PEs in the simulator. To achieve a fair comparison, we made sure that, if comparing to Linux, M^3 did not take advantage of multiple PEs, i.e., at no point in time multiple PEs were doing useful work in parallel. This is because a second PE was only involved if the first PE sent a message to the second, in which case the first one waited until the second one replied, so that the execution merely transitioned from PE to PE.

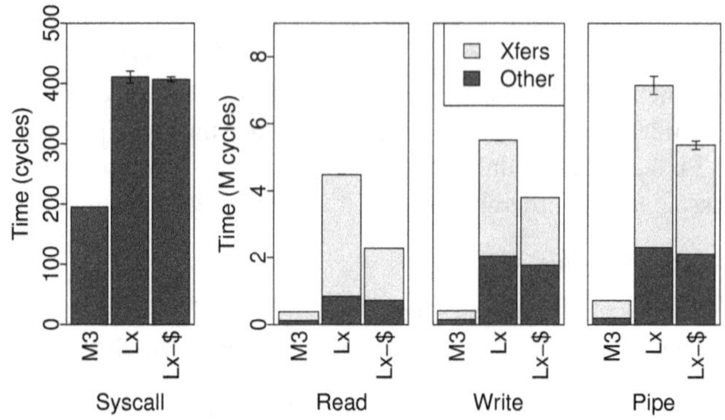

Figure 3. Comparison of system calls and file operations. Lx-$ shows the time on Linux without cache misses.

5.2 Linux on Xtensa vs. Linux on ARM

To ensure that our results are not specific to Xtensa, because e.g., Linux could be less optimized for Xtensa than for other architectures, we did also run some of the benchmarks on an ARM Cortex-A15. Apart from data transfers being slower on Xtensa, because the core does not have a cache line prefetcher (see Section 5.4 for more details), which prevents Xtensa to saturate the memory bandwidth, we saw comparable results. For example, a Linux system call requires 320 cycles on ARM and 410 cycles on Xtensa, creating a 2 MiB large file has 2.4 million cycles overhead on ARM and 2.2 million cycles on Xtensa, and copying a 2 MiB file has 3.2 million cycles overhead on both architectures.

5.3 System Calls

System calls on M^3 are done by sending a message via the DTU to the kernel PE and waiting for the reply of the kernel, while classical system calls switch from user mode into privileged mode on the same PE. To compare their performance, we performed a *null system call* on both M^3 and Linux, i.e., the system call function has an empty body. As can be seen in the left part of Figure 3, a system call on M^3 via DTU takes about 200 cycles, while it takes about 410 cycles on Linux. On M^3, the actual message transfers take about 30 cycles and the other 170 cycles are required for marshalling the messages, programming the DTU registers, unmarshalling the messages and figuring out the system call function to call. On Linux, most of the time is spent with saving and restoring the machine state, because the user application and the kernel share these hardware resources. Note that on Linux, we have removed outliers caused by interrupts from the results since they would have had large effects on the standard deviation in this case due to the short time for a single system call.

5.4 Filesystem and Pipe

Next, we conducted micro-benchmarks to evaluate m3fs and pipes. Since m3fs is an in-memory filesystem, we compared it to Linux's tmpfs. For all our benchmarks, we transferred 2 MiB of data, using a buffer size of 4 KiB, because 4 KiB is the sweet spot on Linux (M^3 benefits from larger buffer sizes until all available space in the SPM is used for the buffer). On M^3, the file was not fragmented (see Section 5.5 for the influence of fragmentation) and m3fs used a block size of 1 KiB. On Linux, tmpfs used a block size 4 KiB. We performed the following benchmarks:

1. *Read*: read a file, discarding the data,
2. *Write*: write precomputed data into a new file, and
3. *Pipe*: transfer data between two processes/VPEs.

On Linux, all three benchmarks used `read/write` system calls to perform the transfer. We also compared copying a file using `mmap` on Linux, but do not show it here, because of Linux's bad performance due to cache thrashing between the page fault handling of the kernel and the `memcpy` of the application. On M^3, the time for copying is the sum of the times for reading and writing the file.

To understand the differences between M^3 and Linux, we have broken down the results into the time for the data transfer ("Xfers") using the DTU or `memcpy` in the kernel, and the remaining time ("Other"). As Figure 3 shows, a large portion of the difference is made up by data transfers. This is because the data transfer on M^3 is performed by the DTU, which transfers 8 Byte per cycle without involving the core (similar to DMA). In contrast to that, Linux is copying the data via `memcpy`. Unfortunately, Xtensa does not have a cache line prefetcher, which could detect the data access pattern of `memcpy` and thus prefetch the next cache lines in the background. Therefore, `memcpy` cannot saturate the memory bandwidth on Xtensa. We believe that, with a cache line prefetcher and load/store instructions that operate on more bytes at once, the transfer time could reach the theoretical limit of 8 Byte per cycle, like with the DTU.

Apart from the differences for the data transfers, Figure 3 shows that M^3 incurs much less OS overhead. This is because on Linux, a system call is done for every 4 KiB block, doing in part the same work over and over again. On M^3, after the locations of the file fragments in the DRAM have been obtained, only libm3 is involved, which only needs to determine where to read or write. For example, `read` on Linux requires ~380 cycles for entering/leaving the kernel, ~400 cycles for retrieving the file pointer, doing security checks and executing function prologs/epilogs and ~550 cycles for page cache related operations (`get`, `put`, etc.). M^3 on the other hand needs ~70 cycles to get to the read function and ~90 cycles to determine the location for reading.

Another difference is that Linux is overwriting each block with zeros before handing it out to a writing application, while m3fs can instruct the DTU to zero blocks in the background, i.e., in parallel to handling requests. In the benchmarks, we assume that enough zero blocks are available, which will be the case in realistic scenarios since there will always be time where m3fs is idling.

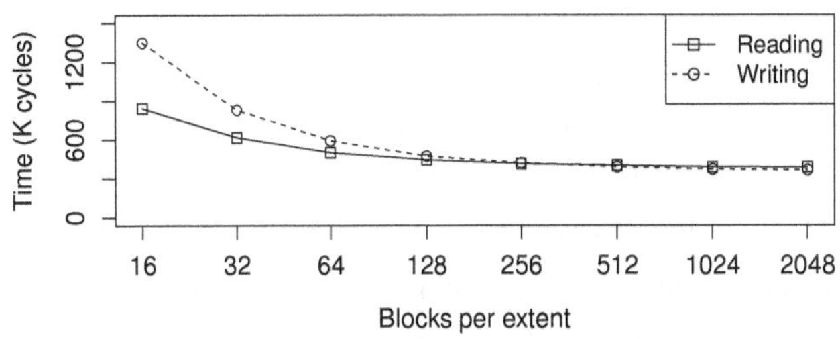

Figure 4. Read/write time, depending on file fragmentation

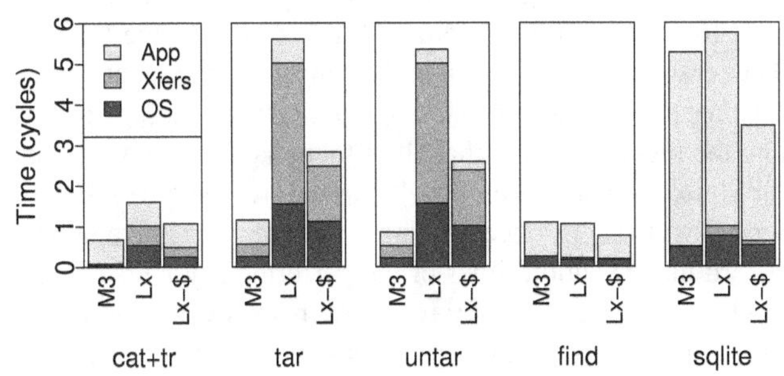

Figure 5. Comparison with application-level benchmarks. Lx-$ shows the time on Linux without cache misses.

5.5 Impact of File Fragmentation

As mentioned, the performance of reading and writing files with m3fs depends on file fragmentation, i.e., the number of extents the file consists of. To quantify this, we ran the read-/write benchmarks with varying numbers of extents per file, as shown in Figure 4. That is, for reading, the 2 MiB large file was prepared to have 16 to 2048 blocks per extent. And for writing we let the application allocate the corresponding number of blocks at once. As the results show, the sweet spot is 256 blocks, so that we chose to allocate that number of blocks at once when appending to a file. This leads to a good write performance and will probably also limit the file fragmentation, so that the read performance is good as well.

5.6 Application-level Benchmarks

To compare M^3 to Linux in more realistic settings, we performed application-level benchmarks. Since the computation performance of the cores is identical for both M^3 and Linux, we chose mostly applications that make extensive use of the OS. For a more compute-heavy application, we used sqlite. We ran the following five benchmarks:

1. *cat+tr*: creates a child process/VPE and lets it write a 64 KiB large file into a pipe, while the parent reads from

that pipe, replaces all occurrences of "a" with "b" and writes the result into a new file

2. *tar*: creates a tar archive with files between 60 and 500 KiB and 1.2 MiB in total
3. *untar*: unpacks the same tar archive
4. *find*: searches for files within a directory tree of 40 items
5. *sqlite*: creates a table, inserts 8 entries and selects them

As the first benchmark is simple to implement, we did that ourselves, using the same code for M^3 and Linux, except for programming against libm3 in case of the former. The reasons for including it in the benchmarks are that it uses all presented concepts of M^3 (application loading, pipes, and the filesystem) and that all of them have their equivalent on Linux. The other four benchmarks were first run on Linux with BusyBox [1], once running it with `strace` and again to record the execution times of the performed syscalls (to exclude the overhead of `strace`). The results were combined into a data structure that specifies which syscall to execute including its arguments. For all unsupported syscalls[6] and for the computation time, wait commands were inserted into the data structure. On M^3, we ran a program that replays the syscalls from the data structure using the corresponding API on M^3 or waits as long as specified. That is, we assume that computation and the unsupported syscalls require the same time on both systems.

The results are shown in Figure 5, which we have broken down into the time for the application (computation and on M^3 unsupported system calls), data transfers and the OS overhead to explain the differences between M^3 and Linux. Note however, that the results are in favor of Linux because on Linux, only the system call itself (e.g., `open`) is added to the OS overhead, while the time spent in a library call (e.g., `fopen`) is added to the application time. On M^3, the entire library call is added to OS overhead.

In case of *cat+tr*, M^3 is about twice as fast, which stems from `VPE::run` being faster than `fork`, less overhead for accessing files/pipes and the avoidance of context switches. Note that, as mentioned, although both the reader and writer are running time-multiplexed on one core on Linux, M^3 does not take advantage of the two cores involved. That is, like Linux with multiple cores, M^3 could achieve better performance by letting reader and writer work in parallel.

For *tar* and *untar*, M^3 requires only 20% and 16%, respectively, of the time Linux takes. This is caused on the one hand by faster data transfers and on the other hand by less OS overhead for `read` and `write`, as already described in Section 5.4. However, Linux does not suffer from many system calls in this case, because both benchmarks use `sendfile` to transfer the data.

[6] In these benchmarks, we ignored `access`, `ioctl`, `getuid`, `geteuid`, `getpid`, `getrlimit`, `setrlimit`, `rt_sigaction`, `rt_sigprocmask`, `brk`, `fcntl`, `fchown`, `chown`, `chmod` and `chdir`.

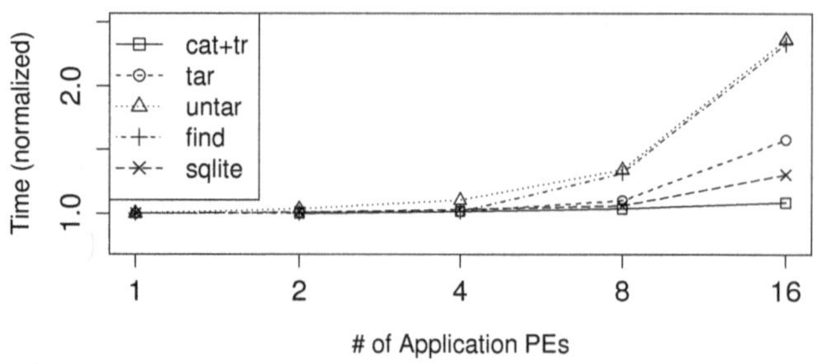

Figure 6. Scalability of the OS design, showing the average time per benchmark instance, normalized to the time with only one benchmark instance (flatter is better).

Find shows a different picture as Linux is slightly faster than M^3. This is because *find* consists mostly of `stat` calls, which work similarly on both systems. On Linux, a traditional syscall is done, which searches for the inode denoted by the given path, whereas M^3 does the same by calling m3fs, using message passing. Furthermore, `stat` is well optimized on Linux, so that M^3 is actually a bit slower.

Finally, *sqlite* is only slightly faster on M^3, because computation makes up the majority of the execution time.

5.7 Scalability

Another interesting point of this OS design is of course the scalability. Before using multiple instances of services or the kernel, we wanted to evaluate how far it scales using a single instance. That is, how many PEs a single instance can handle without significantly decreasing the performance. To evaluate that, we ran the application-level benchmarks again, with varying number of benchmark instances[7] in parallel. That is, we run one instance of the same problem on each core, so that equal time per instance means perfect scalability. Thereby, we replaced the reading/writing from/to the DRAM with a spinning loop of the same time to evaluate only the scalability of the software, i.e., we assume that the NoC (in terms of memory transfers; messages are still sent) and the DRAM scale perfectly.

As the results in Figure 6 indicate, all benchmarks scale very well with up to 4 instances, while degrading a bit with 8 instances. Using 16 instances, the performance of *find* and *untar* decreases significantly, while *tar* and *sqlite* are still acceptable and *cat+tr* show nearly no degradation. Thus, we believe that a single service/kernel instance can handle at least 8 PEs. Of course, *cat+tr* scales almost perfectly because after the setup phase, only the reader and writer communicate with each other. The *sqlite* benchmark spends the majority of the time with computation, so that it scales very well. For *tar* and *untar*, most of the time, files are read and written, which scales almost perfectly, too. Occasionally in *tar* and *untar* and quite often in *find*, m3fs is called, which queue up with an increasing number of benchmark instances.

[7] Since *cat+tr* requires two PEs per benchmark instance, there are no results for 1 Application PE.

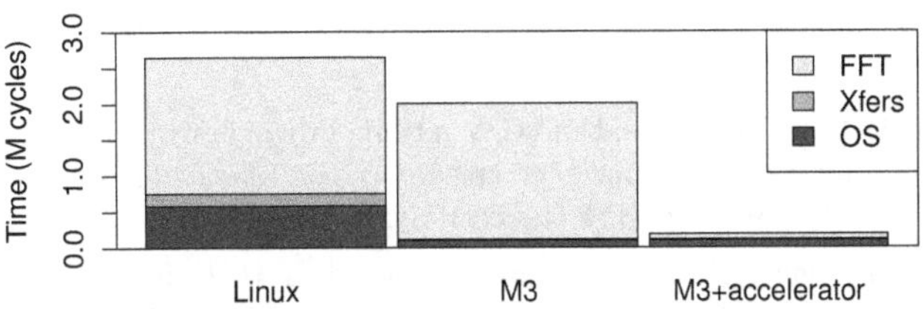

Figure 7. Performance benefits of an FFT accelerator core.

5.8 Accelerator

So far, the benchmarks used standard Xtensa cores. To show the feasibility of integrating an accelerator and to demonstrate the performance advantages, we added a core with instruction extensions for a fast fourier transformation (FFT) to our prototype platform. In mobile communication, FFTs are typically used within a filter chain, where e.g., data is received over the mobile network, transformed using the FFT, and passed forward to the next element in the chain. Thus, we built a similar scenario that lets an application (the *parent*) create a VPE, assigned to the FFT core. Afterwards, it executes the FFT application (the *child*) on that VPE and creates a pipe between itself and the child. The parent is generating random numbers, 32 KiB of data in total, and writes them into the pipe, while the child reads from that pipe, performs the FFT and writes the result into a file (it could be another pipe as well).

To show the performance benefits, we ran this benchmark first on Linux using a software FFT, second, on M^3 using only standard Xtensa cores with the same software FFT, and third, on M^3 using the FFT accelerator. It is worth noting that the code for the parent is identical for the software version and the accelerator version. It merely receives a different path to the executable to run on the VPE. The results in Figure 7 show at first, that the accelerator has a huge performance benefit over the software version (about a factor of 30). Second, `exec`, the pipe communication and the write to the file on Linux has much more overhead than their equivalent on M^3, especially compared to the FFT time when using the accelerator. This shows that the fast abstractions of M^3 lower the bar for using accelerators.

6. Conclusion

In this paper, we presented a new point in the design space for operating systems (OSes) by co-designing the OS with the hardware to support arbitrary cores as first-class citizens. That is, we support isolation on all cores to run untrusted code and provide access to OS services on all cores. This is achieved by abstracting from the heterogeneity of the cores by introducing a common hardware component, called data transfer unit (DTU), next to each core that supports remote memory access and message passing. By leveraging the fact that it is expected that future platforms will contain a large number of cores, we introduce kernel cores, where only the kernel is running and application cores, which are owned by one application at a given time. Cores and thus applications are thereby isolated at the network-on-chip-level via remotely controlling their DTUs, because a DTU is the only component that has access to core-external resources.

We demonstrated the feasibility of this design by implementing the DTU and the OS for a prototype platform, whose cores do not have support for an OS kernel and where we could integrate accelerators. We showed how basic OS abstractions like application loading, pipes, and filesystems can be built and that they work across heterogeneous cores. In our evaluation, we illustrated how this design can outperform Linux in some application-level benchmarks by more than a factor of five without exploiting accelerators.

7. Future Work

As we have laid the foundation for supporting arbitrary PEs as first-class citizens by starting with the challenging part of building an OS for PEs without kernel support in this work, we will extend this to more feature-rich PEs in future work. In particular:

- We plan to add caches to the PEs or replace the SPM with caches. The cache will use the DTU to load/store cache lines from/into DRAM. In this way, the DTU remains the only component with access to PE-external resources and it thus suffices to control the DTU.
- Furthermore, we want to support virtual memory to enable copy-on-write, demand paging, etc. This can be done by by managing the page tables remotely, similarly to managing the DTU endpoints remotely.
- Finally, we plan to support POSIX-compliant applications. So far, our prototype platform prevented us from directly running existing and complex applications due to the small SPM and the distributed memory architecture. As soon as caches and virtual memory are supported, we will add a POSIX emulation layer, similar to the already existing emulation layer for the filesystem API, that was used to replay system call traces.

As already mentioned in the paper, we currently do not support multiple instances of services or the kernel, because we wanted to explore first how far a single instance can scale. In the future, we will design synchronization protocols to allow multiple instances.

8. Acknowledgments

We would like to thank our shepherd, Gernot Heiser, the anonymous reviewers, Björn Brandenburg, Jeronimo Castrillon, Pramod Bhatotia, and Michael Roitzsch for their helpful suggestions. This work is in part funded through the German Research Council DFG through the Cluster of Excellence Center for Advancing Electronics Dresden (cfaed).

References

[1] BusyBox. `http://www.busybox.net/`. last checked: 01/19/2015.

[2] An introduction to the Intel® QuickPath interconnect. `http://www.intel.de/content/dam/doc/white-paper/quick-path-interconnect-introduction-paper.pdf`. last checked: 01/19/2015.

[3] J. Ahn, M. Fiorentino, R. G. Beausoleil, N. Binkert, A. Davis, D. Fattal, N. P. Jouppi, M. McLaren, C. M. Santori, R. S. Schreiber, S. M. Spillane, D. Vantrease, and Q. Xu. Devices and architectures for photonic chip-scale integration. *Applied Physics A*, 95(4):989–997, 2009.

[4] R. Alpert, C. Dubnicki, E.W. Felten, and K. Li. Design and implementation of NX message passing using Shrimp virtual memory mapped communication. In *Proceedings of the 1996 International Conference on Parallel Processing*, volume 1, pages 111–119, Aug 1996.

[5] Oliver Arnold, Emil Matus, Benedikt Noethen, Markus Winter, Torsten Limberg, and Gerhard Fettweis. Tomahawk: Parallelism and heterogeneity in communications signal processing MPSoCs. *ACM Transactions on Embedded Computing Systems*, 13(3s):107:1–107:24, March 2014.

[6] F.J. Ballesteros, N. Evans, C. Forsyth, G. Guardiola, J. McKie, R. Minnich, and E. Soriano-Salvador. NIX: A case for a manycore system for cloud computing. *Bell Labs Technical Journal*, 17(2):41–54, 2012.

[7] Antonio Barbalace, Marina Sadini, Saif Ansary, Christopher Jelesnianski, Akshay Ravichandran, Cagil Kendir, Alastair Murray, and Binoy Ravindran. Popcorn: Bridging the programmability gap in heterogeneous-ISA platforms. In *Proceedings of the Tenth European Conference on Computer Systems (EuroSys '15)*, pages 29:1–29:16, New York, NY, USA, 2015. ACM.

[8] Andrew Baumann, Paul Barham, Pierre-Evariste Dagand, Tim Harris, Rebecca Isaacs, Simon Peter, Timothy Roscoe, Adrian Schüpbach, and Akhilesh Singhania. The multikernel: A new OS architecture for scalable multicore systems. In *Proceedings of the ACM SIGOPS 22nd Symposium on Operating Systems Principles (SOSP '09)*, pages 29–44, New York, NY, USA, 2009. ACM.

[9] Cadence. Xtensa customizable processor. `http://ip.cadence.com`. last checked: 01/19/2015.

[10] Koushik Chakraborty, Philip M. Wells, and Gurindar S. Sohi. Computation spreading: Employing hardware migration to specialize CMP cores on-the-fly. In *Proceedings of the 12th International Conference on Architectural Support for Programming Languages and Operating Systems (ASPLOS XII)*, pages 283–292, New York, NY, USA, 2006. ACM.

[11] Emilio G. Cota, Paolo Mantovani, Giuseppe Di Guglielmo, and Luca P. Carloni. An analysis of accelerator coupling in heterogeneous architectures. In *Proceedings of the 52nd Annual Design Automation Conference (DAC '15)*, pages 202:1–202:6, New York, NY, USA, 2015. ACM.

[12] R.H. Dennard, V.L. Rideout, E. Bassous, and A.R. LeBlanc. Design of ion-implanted MOSFET's with very small physical dimensions. *Solid-State Circuits, IEEE Journal of*, 9(5):256–268, Oct 1974.

[13] Jack B. Dennis and Earl C. Van Horn. Programming semantics for multiprogrammed computations. *Communications of the ACM*, 9(3):143–155, March 1966.

[14] Manuel Fähndrich, Mark Aiken, Chris Hawblitzel, Orion Hodson, Galen Hunt, James R. Larus, and Steven Levi. Language support for fast and reliable message-based communication in Singularity OS. In *Proceedings of the 1st ACM SIGOPS/EuroSys European Conference on Computer Systems*, pages 177–190, New York, NY, USA, 2006. ACM.

[15] Norman Feske. A case study on the cost and benefit of dynamic RPC marshalling for low-level system components. *ACM SIGOPS Operating Systems Review*, 41(4):40–48, July 2007.

[16] L. Fiorin, G. Palermo, S. Lukovic, V. Catalano, and C. Silvano. Secure memory accesses on networks-on-chip. *IEEE Transactions on Computers*, 57(9):1216–1229, Sept 2008.

[17] Sanjay Ghemawat, Howard Gobioff, and Shun-Tak Leung. The Google file system. In *Proceedings of the Nineteenth ACM Symposium on Operating Systems Principles (SOSP '03)*, pages 29–43, New York, NY, USA, 2003. ACM.

[18] N. Hardavellas, M. Ferdman, B. Falsafi, and A. Ailamaki. Toward dark silicon in servers. *IEEE Micro*, 31(4):6–15, July 2011.

[19] Norman Hardy. KeyKOS architecture. *ACM SIGOPS Operating Systems Review*, 19(4):8–25, October 1985.

[20] John Heinlein, Kourosh Gharachorloo, Scott Dresser, and Anoop Gupta. Integration of message passing and shared memory in the Stanford FLASH multiprocessor. In *Proceedings of the Sixth International Conference on Architectural Support for Programming Languages and Operating Systems*, pages 38–50, New York, NY, USA, 1994. ACM.

[21] K.U. Jarvinen and J.O. Skytta. High-speed elliptic curve cryptography accelerator for koblitz curves. In *16th International Symposium on Field-Programmable Custom Computing Machines (FCCM '08)*, pages 109–118, April 2008.

[22] Sangman Kim, Seonggu Huh, Yige Hu, Xinya Zhang, Amir Wated, Emmett Witchel, and Mark Silberstein. GPUnet: Networking abstractions for GPU programs. In *Proceedings of the International Conference on Operating Systems Design and Implementation*, pages 6–8, 2014.

[23] Gerwin Klein, Kevin Elphinstone, Gernot Heiser, June Andronick, David Cock, Philip Derrin, Dhammika Elkaduwe, Kai Engelhardt, Rafal Kolanski, Michael Norrish, Thomas Sewell, Harvey Tuch, and Simon Winwood. seL4: Formal verification of an OS kernel. In *Proceedings of the ACM SIGOPS 22nd Symposium on Operating Systems Principles*, pages 207–220, New York, NY, USA, 2009. ACM.

[24] George Kurian, Jason E. Miller, James Psota, Jonathan Eastep, Jifeng Liu, Jurgen Michel, Lionel C. Kimerling, and Anant Agarwal. ATAC: A 1000-core cache-coherent processor with on-chip optical network. In *Proceedings of the 19th International Conference on Parallel Architectures and Compilation Techniques (PACT '10)*, pages 477–488, New York, NY, USA, 2010. ACM.

[25] J. Kuskin, D. Ofelt, M. Heinrich, J. Heinlein, R. Simoni, K. Gharachorloo, J. Chapin, D. Nakahira, J. Baxter, M. Horowitz, A. Gupta, M. Rosenblum, and J. Hennessy. The Stanford FLASH multiprocessor. In *Proceedings of the 21st Annual International Symposium on Computer Architecture*, pages 302–313, Apr 1994.

[26] Adam Lackorzynski and Alexander Warg. Taming subsystems: Capabilities as universal resource access control in L4. In *Proceedings of the Second Workshop on Isolation and Integration in Embedded Systems (IIES '09)*, pages 25–30, New York, NY, USA, 2009. ACM.

[27] J. Liedtke. On micro-kernel construction. In *Proceedings of the Fifteenth ACM Symposium on Operating Systems Principles (SOSP '95)*, pages 237–250, New York, NY, USA, 1995. ACM.

[28] Kevin Lim, David Meisner, Ali G. Saidi, Parthasarathy Ranganathan, and Thomas F. Wenisch. Thin servers with smart pipes: Designing SoC accelerators for memcached. In *Proceedings of the 40th Annual International Symposium on Computer Architecture (ISCA '13)*, pages 36–47, New York, NY, USA, 2013. ACM.

[29] Felix Xiaozhu Lin, Zhen Wang, and Lin Zhong. K2: A mobile operating system for heterogeneous coherence domains. In *Proceedings of the 19th International Conference on Architectural Support for Programming Languages and Operating Systems (ASPLOS '14)*, pages 285–300, New York, NY, USA, 2014. ACM.

[30] Daofu Liu, Tianshi Chen, Shaoli Liu, Jinhong Zhou, Shengyuan Zhou, Olivier Teman, Xiaobing Feng, Xuehai Zhou, and Yunji Chen. PuDianNao: A polyvalent machine learning accelerator. In *Proceedings of the Twentieth International Conference on Architectural Support for Programming Languages and Operating Systems*, pages 369–381. ACM, 2015.

[31] K. Mackenzie, J. Kubiatowicz, M. Frank, W. Lee, W. Lee, A. Agarwal, and M.F. Kaashoek. Exploiting two-case delivery for fast protected messaging. In *Fourth International Symposium on High-Performance Computer Architecture*, pages 231–242, Feb 1998.

[32] Avantika Mathur, Mingming Cao, Suparna Bhattacharya, Andreas Dilger, Alex Tomas, and Laurent Vivier. The new ext4 filesystem: current status and future plans. In *Proceedings of the Linux Symposium*, volume 2, pages 21–33, 2007.

[33] Edmund B. Nightingale, Orion Hodson, Ross McIlroy, Chris Hawblitzel, and Galen Hunt. Helios: Heterogeneous multiprocessing with satellite kernels. In *Proceedings of the ACM SIGOPS 22nd Symposium on Operating Systems Principles (SOSP '09)*, pages 221–234, New York, NY, USA, 2009. ACM.

[34] Mike Parker, Al Davis, and Wilson Hsieh. Message-passing for the 21st century: Integrating user-level networks with SMT. In *Proceedings of the 5th Workshop on Multithreaded Execution, Architecture and Compilation*, 2001.

[35] Rob Pike, Dave Presotto, Ken Thompson, Howard Trickey, et al. Plan 9 from Bell Labs. In *Proceedings of the Summer 1990 UKUUG Conference*, pages 1–9. London, UK, 1990.

[36] J. Porquet, A. Greiner, and C. Schwarz. NoC-MPU: A secure architecture for flexible co-hosting on shared memory MPSoCs. In *Design, Automation Test in Europe Conference Exhibition (DATE), 2011*, pages 1–4, March 2011.

[37] Wajahat Qadeer, Rehan Hameed, Ofer Shacham, Preethi Venkatesan, Christos Kozyrakis, and Mark Horowitz. Convolution engine: Balancing efficiency and flexibility in specialized computing. *Communications of the ACM*, 58(4):85–93, March 2015.

[38] Ohad Rodeh, Josef Bacik, and Chris Mason. BTRFS: The Linux B-tree filesystem. *ACM Transactions on Storage (TOS)*, 9(3):9:1–9:32, August 2013.

[39] Christopher J. Rossbach, Jon Currey, Mark Silberstein, Baishakhi Ray, and Emmett Witchel. PTask: Operating system abstractions to manage GPUs as compute devices. In *Proceedings of the Twenty-Third ACM Symposium on Operating Systems Principles (SOSP '11)*, pages 233–248, New York, NY, USA, 2011. ACM.

[40] Mark Silberstein, Bryan Ford, Idit Keidar, and Emmett Witchel. GPUfs: Integrating a file system with GPUs. In *Proceedings of the Eighteenth International Conference on Architectural Support for Programming Languages and Operating Systems (ASPLOS '13)*, pages 485–498, New York, NY, USA, 2013. ACM.

[41] Livio Soares and Michael Stumm. FlexSC: Flexible system call scheduling with exception-less system calls. In *Proceedings of the 9th USENIX Conference on Operating Systems Design and Implementation (OSDI '10)*, pages 1–8, Berkeley, CA, USA, 2010. USENIX Association.

[42] Udo Steinberg and Bernhard Kauer. NOVA: A microhypervisor-based secure virtualization architecture. In *Proceedings of the 5th European Conference on Computer Systems (EuroSys '10)*, pages 209–222, New York, NY, USA, 2010. ACM.

[43] M.B. Taylor. A landscape of the new dark silicon design regime. *IEEE Micro*, 33(5):8–19, Sept 2013.

[44] David Wentzlaff and Anant Agarwal. Factored operating systems (fos): The case for a scalable operating system for multicores. *ACM SIGOPS Operating Systems Review*, 43(2):76–85, April 2009.

[45] Jonathan Woodruff, Robert N.M. Watson, David Chisnall, Simon W. Moore, Jonathan Anderson, Brooks Davis, Ben Laurie, Peter G. Neumann, Robert Norton, and Michael Roe. The CHERI capability model: Revisiting RISC in an age of risk. In *Proceeding of the 41st Annual International Symposium on Computer Architecuture (ISCA '14)*, pages 457–468, Piscataway, NJ, USA, 2014. IEEE Press.

[46] Lisa Wu, Raymond J. Barker, Martha A. Kim, and Kenneth A. Ross. Navigating big data with high-throughput, energy-efficient data partitioning. In *Proceedings of the 40th Annual International Symposium on Computer Architecture (ISCA '13)*, pages 249–260, New York, NY, USA, 2013. ACM.

[47] Wei Yu and Yun He. A high performance CABAC decoding architecture. *IEEE Transactions on Consumer Electronics*, 51(4):1352–1359, Nov 2005.

Sidewinder: An Energy Efficient and Developer Friendly Heterogeneous Architecture for Continuous Mobile Sensing

Daniyal Liaqat
University of Toronto
dliaqat@cs.toronto.edu

Silviu Jingoi
University of Toronto
silviu@cs.toronto.edu

Eyal de Lara
University of Toronto
delara@cs.toronto.edu

Ashvin Goel
University of Toronto
ashvin@eecg.toronto.edu

Wilson To
University of Toronto
wilson.to@mail.utoronto.ca

Kevin Lee
University of Toronto
kevinalexander.lee@mail.utoronto.ca

Italo De Moraes Garcia
University of Toronto
italo.demoraesgarcia@mail.utoronto.ca

Manuel Saldana
Huawei
manuel.saldana@huawei.com

Abstract

Applications that perform continuous sensing on mobile phones have the potential to revolutionize everyday life. Examples range from medical and health monitoring applications, such as pedometers and fall detectors, to participatory sensing applications, such as noise pollution, traffic and seismic activity monitoring. Unfortunately, current mobile devices are a poor match for continuous sensing applications as they require the device to remain awake for extended periods of time, resulting in poor battery life. This paper presents Sidewinder, a new approach towards offloading sensor data processing to a low-power processor and waking up the main processor when events of interest occur. This approach differs from other heterogeneous architectures in that developers are presented with a programming interface that lets them construct application specific wake-up conditions by linking together and parameterizing predefined sensor data processing algorithms. Our experiments indicate performance that is comparable to approaches that provide fully programmable offloading, but do so with a much simpler programming interface that facilitates deployment and portability.

Categories and Subject Descriptors C.1.3 [*Processor Architectures*]: Heterogeneous (hybrid) systems

Keywords Mobile Computing, Continuous Sensing, Energy Efficiency, Heterogeneous Architecture

1. Introduction

Modern smartphones are fitted with a wide assortment of sensors. A typical smartphone, such as the LG Nexus 5, contains an accelerometer, barometer, compass, gyroscope, proximity sensor, ambient light sensor, hall effect sensor, geo-spatial positioning sensors (GPS, GLONASS, Beidou), a microphone and two cameras. Despite having such a rich array of sensors, most of them go unused most of the time. The way smartphones are typically used is that the user will open an application such as a game, news or social media application, interact for a few minutes and then put their device to sleep. Taking advantage of this usage pattern, mobile processors have been heavily optimized to rely on a low-power sleep state when not in use in order to improve battery life.

While this approach has fared well with how devices are currently used, it falls short in the face of emerging continuous sensing applications, examples of which range from context-aware applications [11, 16], such as medical applications that improve our well-being [15, 26, 32] to applications that use participatory sensing to get a better understanding of the physical world, such as noise pollution monitoring [21, 22], traffic prediction [17] or earthquake early warning [23]. While the processing demands of these applications are modest most of the time, they require continuous collection of sensor data, which prevents the processor from entering its' low-power sleep state, resulting in poor battery life and ultimately, a slow emergence of continuous sensing applications.

It is generally accepted that the solution to this problem lies in a heterogeneous architecture where one or more low-power, peripheral processors (known as a sensor hub) collect and process sensor data while the main processor is in its sleep state. When the low-power sensor hub detects an event of interest, it wakes up the main processor, allowing for further processing of sensor data. The programming model for this heterogeneous architectures remains, however, an open research question. On one end of the spectrum, researchers have proposed a **fully programmable model** [19, 27, 31] that allows application developers to write arbitrary code that runs on the low-power processor. While this would provide potentially great flexibility and power savings, there are many drawbacks. Application developers would not only have to be familiar with programming the low-power processor, they would have to account for hardware differences between devices. It is also unclear how this model would support different applications that

ASPLOS '16, April 02-06, 2016, Atlanta, GA, USA

DOI: http://dx.doi.org/10.1145/2872362.2872398

are running concurrently. On the other end is **predefined activity**, an approach where hardware manufacturers provide a low-power processor which is hardwired to detect a few specific events. Both Apple and Android provide frameworks for detecting predefined activities such as significant motion and steps [2, 3]. Another example is the Motorola Moto X smartphone [7, 10] that has a dedicated Natural Language Processor which is used to wake up the device when the user says a certain phrase such as "OK Google Now". Such frameworks are very easy to use from a developer's point of view and provide significant energy savings, but they are very limited because they only allow detection of events that have been pre-programmed into the device by the manufacturer.

This paper presents *Sidewinder*, a new approach for continuous mobile sensing that splits the work of energy-efficient event detection between the platform and the application developer. With Sidewinder, the platform implements common sensor data processing algorithms (e.g., windowing, noise reduction, feature extraction, admission control) that execute on a low-power sensor hub, and application developers construct custom wake-up conditions by linking together and parameterizing these sensor data processing algorithms. The custom wake-up conditions execute on the low-power sensor hub and, when events of interest are detected, the main processor is woken up and the rest of the application code is invoked.

While heterogeneous architectures have been used previously, the innovation in Sidewinder is the collaborative approach where the platform provides sensor processing algorithms and developers parameterize and chain these algorithms together to create wake-up conditions. Processing algorithms are written natively for the low-power sensor hub so application developers do not need to worry about writing code for the underlying heterogeneous architecture.

To evaluate the benefits of Sidewinder, we developed applications that use accelerometer readings or audio data to detect several events of interest. Additionally, we built a prototype implementation that extends a Nexus 4 phone with a low-power sensor hub. To enable us to conduct controlled and repeatable experiments, we mounted our prototype on a robot. Simulations conducted on accelerometer and audio traces collected in various environments show that Sidewinder can reduce the average energy required to run continuous sensing applications by up to 96% compared to keeping the phone awake at all times, while matching the detection recall and precision of the always on approach. Moreover, for most of our usage scenarios, Sidewinder achieves over 90% of the power savings achieved by a "perfect" wake-up mechanism, indicating that an implementation that supports custom code offloading will achieve only marginal additional improvements.

The rest of this paper is organized as follows. Section 2 describes the Design of Sidewinder and 3 describes how we implemented the design. Sections 4 and 5 present our evaluation method and results. Finally, Sections 6 and 7 describe our work in the context of related work and conclude the paper.

2. Design

Continuous mobile sensing approaches have to address two main constraints: maximizing detection accuracy and minimizing energy consumption. Users expect high precision and recall and user experience is adversely affected when the application misses or over-reports events of interest. Achieving both high recall and precision requires highly specialized algorithms tuned to the event of interest. Specifically, our experience suggests that getting the last few percentage points in precision and recall is difficult and requires complex algorithms and fine parameter tuning. Additionally, these complex algorithms typically run on a fully featured processor, which is detrimental to battery life since a large portion of energy savings comes from keeping the main processor in a sleep state.

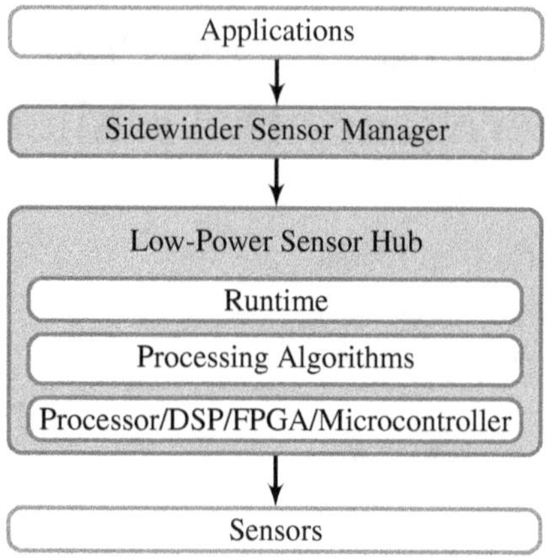

Figure 1: Proposed system architecture. The sensor manager is part of the OS, and the Sensor Hub and Sensors are hardware provided by the manufacturer

We achieve our two main goals (energy efficiency and high precision/recall) by using a multi-stage pipeline of algorithms to create a more complex classifier. Earlier stages are used to achieve the majority of available energy savings and later stages can then optimize for high detection precision and recall. For example, a voice recognition algorithm may have three stages, the first stage determines if microphone data contains sound, the second stage determines if the sound is human speech and the third stage converts the speech to text. The first two stages are relatively simple and can be run on a less powerful, more energy efficient processor. They have high recall but may have low precision (i.e. they will let through a high proportion of events that contain speech, but not all events passed through will contain speech). Since the first two stages are run on a low-power processor and reduce the amount of time the main processor has to be awake, this will result in an overall saving of energy.

Based on this observation, Sidewinder encourages continuous mobile sensing applications to be structured as pipelines of processing algorithms of increasing complexity: simple yet high recall, moderate precision algorithms that run continuously on a low-power sensor hub, providing energy efficient wake-up mechanisms for higher complexity algorithms that run on the main CPU and provide both high recall and high precision.

To facilitate the creation of wake-up conditions capable of running on a low-power sensor hub, Sidewinder provides a set of commonly used sensor data processing algorithms that are ready to run on the sensor hub. These algorithms can be parameterized and chained together to create wake-up conditions.

We conjecture: 1) that it is possible to implement custom wake-up conditions for a wide range of applications by configuring a small set of common processing algorithms; and 2) that this approach will achieve comparable energy savings to an alternative implementation that supports full programmability.

2.1 Sidewinder

Sidewinder is a new approach for continuous mobile sensing that divides the responsibility of energy-efficient event detection between the manufacturer and the application developer. The manufacturer provides a low-power sensor hub and implements common sensor data processing algorithms that execute on the sensor hub. Applications construct custom wake-up conditions for events of interest in their application code. These wake-up conditions are then pushed to and executed continuously on the low-power sensor hub and, when events of interest are detected, the main processor is woken up and the application code is notified.

Figure 1 shows the architecture of a system that uses Sidewinder. Applications interact with a sensor manager to define a custom wake-up condition. The manager contains an API for parameterizing and chaining algorithms that are available on the low-power sensor hub. Developers can use this API to create their wake-up conditions. The low-power sensor hub contains commonly used algorithms for windowing, filtering, transformations, feature extraction and admission control. Once configured by the developer, the wake-up condition is converted into an intermediate language by the sensor manager and pushed to a runtime or interpreter on the low-power sensor hub. When running on the sensor hub, the custom wake-up condition wakes the main CPU if an event of interest occurs.

We next describe the components of Sidewinder based on whether their implementation is the responsibility of the device manufacturer, the operating system, or the application developer.

2.1.1 The Manufacturer

The manufacturer is responsible for providing the hardware and software of the low-power sensor hub. The hardware could be a network of one or more processors, Digital Signal Processors (DSP), FPGAs or microcontrollers. For example, there could be one larger processor to handle all sensors and algorithms or a DSP for the microphone and an FPGA for each of the other sensors. The manufacturer also needs to provide a runtime to manage this hardware and an implementation of common sensor data processing algorithms. The runtime needs to be able to receive wake-up condition configurations from applications, configure the hardware and algorithms, execute the resulting wake-up condition and notify applications when an event of interest occurs.

The runtime could use an interpreter approach where it executes each algorithm, a compiler approach where it generates an executable or it could reconfigure FPGAs according to the requirements of the wake-up condition and the hardware available. In the case of FPGAs the algorithms will most likely be pre-compiled and the runtime would need to reconfigure according to the specific configuration.

The runtime provides a decoupling layer between the mobile platform (Android, iOS, etc.) and the hardware since the runtime is responsible for managing the hardware. And since the manufacturer will be providing both the runtime and hardware, any architecture for the low-power sensor hub can be used.

2.1.2 The Application Developer

The application developer creates custom wake-up conditions for their event(s) of interest. One important aspect of Sidewinder is that common sensor data processing algorithms are provided to the developer by the platform. This means for example, if the developer needs to use an FFT, they do not need to implement it themselves or find a library. Instead, they would use the system API to create a wake-up condition that uses an FFT. The API allows developers to parametrize the FFT and if needed, chain it with other algorithms together to create more advanced wake-up conditions. They can then use the API to push their wake-up condition to the low-power sensor hub.

Because wake-up conditions are defined by configuring generic algorithms designed to support a large set of applications, as opposed to writing custom code specific to any application, their performance may be suboptimal by design. To ensure that user experience is not adversely affected when the application misses events of interest, application developers should create conservative wake-up conditions that provide for high recall at the expense of lower precision. This approach will ensure that no events of interest are overlooked, but will result in some unnecessary wake-ups, i.e., false positives. Therefore, to ensure that the application does not adversely affect user experience by over reporting, additional filtering needs to be executed on the main processor on a wake-up event to eliminate any false positives. In Section 5, we show that while the moderate precision of wake-up conditions does result in additional energy use, the approach is nevertheless able to achieve 90% of the power savings achieved by an "ideal" wake-up mechanism.

2.1.3 The Operating System

The operating system needs to provide the API (part of the Sensor Manager in Figure 1) that allows developers to create wake-up conditions and push/receive data to/from the low-power sensor hub. A wake-up condition is pushed to the sensor hub in the form of an intermediate code to decouple the platform from the hub. The operating system will also need to provide a driver to allow communication with the hardware. Depending on the mobile platform (Android, iOS, Windows 10 Mobile), it is likely that the manufacturer will provide the driver.

2.2 Advantages

Sidewinder has many benefits:

Lower programming complexity. Programming complexity is decreased because application developers can use the predefined processing algorithms, rather than implementing their own. The intermediate language makes Sidewinder language independent so that developers can write their classifier in the same language as their application.

Better optimization. The hardware and software of the low-power processor is implemented by the manufacturer, allowing for much greater optimization by experts.

Better security. Providing access to these algorithms via an API has significant security advantages over the fully programmable offloading approach because application developers cannot execute arbitrary code on the low-power processor.

Improved portability. Programmers do not have to be aware of the specifics of the underlying hardware, nor create a version for every type of platform. Manufacturers are free to use any type of hardware they want (processor, DSP, FPGA or networks of processors/DSPs/FPGAs) as long as it can interpret and execute the intermediate language.

3. Implementation

In this section we outline our implementation of the components mentioned in the design section. We also describe the applications we developed to evaluate Sidewinder. We implemented Sidewinder on the Android platform. It is important to note that there are many different valid implementations of our design, ours is just an example of a valid implementation.

3.1 Sensor Manager

The Sidewinder sensor manager is based off the Android sensor manager [8]. It contains information about the available sensors and processing algorithms and gives developers access to them via the API.

3.2 API

The API allows developers to create wake-up conditions. It contains four major components:

- $ProcessingPipeline$. This represents the entire wake-up condition from the input sensors to the final output. The pipeline consists of one or more processing branches.
- $ProcessingBranch$. Branches represent the flow of data from either a sensor to an algorithm or between two algorithms. At

```java
public class SignificantMotion implements SensorEventListener {

    public void createClassifier() {
        ProcessingPipeline significantMotion = new ProcessingPipeline();

        ProcessingBranch[] branches = new ProcessingBranch[3];
        branches[0] = new ProcessingBranch(SidewinderSensorManager.ACCELEROMETER_X);
        branches[1] = new ProcessingBranch(SidewinderSensorManager.ACCELEROMETER_Y);
        branches[2] = new ProcessingBranch(SidewinderSensorManager.ACCELEROMETER_Z);

        branches[0].add(new MovingAverage(10));
        branches[1].add(new MovingAverage(10));
        branches[2].add(new MovingAverage(10));

        Algorithm vm = new VectorMagnitude();
        Algorithm ac = new MinThreshold(15);

        significantMotion.add(branches);
        significantMotion.add(vm);
        significantMotion.add(ac);

        SidewinderSensorManager sManager = (SidewinderSensorManager) getSystemService(
                SENSOR_SERVICE);
        sManager.push(significantMotion, this);
    }

    @Override
    public void OnSensorEvent(SensorData data) {
        // Do something with data
    }
}
```

(a) Java representation

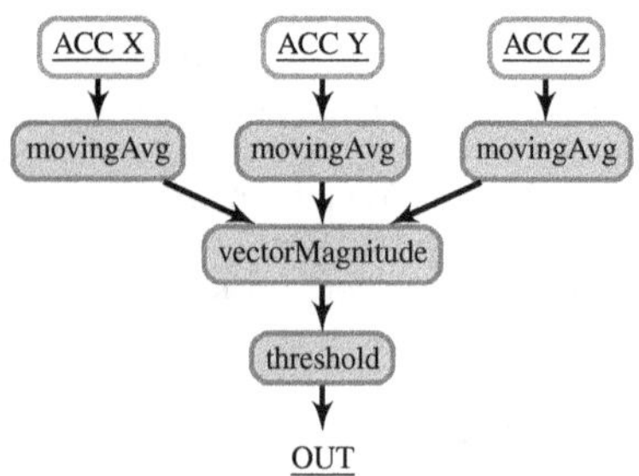

(b) Conceptual representation

```
ACC_X -> movingAvg(id=1, params={10});
ACC_Y -> movingAvg(id=2, params={10});
ACC_Z -> movingAvg(id=3, params={10});
1,2,3 -> vectorMagnitude(id=4);
4 -> minThreshold(id=5, params={15});
5 -> OUT;
```

(c) Intermediate representation

Figure 2: Various representations of a Significant motion pipeline

the start of the classifier pipeline, there may be any number of branches, each receiving data from any of the available sensor channels. At the end of the pipeline, there must be only one branch remaining. This means that if the pipeline contains multiple branches, aggregation algorithms need to be used to reduce the number of branches until a single branch is left.

- *Algorithm.* An algorithm is some operation that accepts one or more branches and produces one branch. For example, a moving average or admission control (threshold) algorithm accepts one branch and produces one branch. A vector magnitude algorithm accepts one or more branches and produces one. At the API level, these algorithms are simply stubs that represent the algorithm implantations at the low-power processor level.
- *SensorEventListener.* This is the Android SensorEventListener. It is a callback method that is registered with the sensor manager that will be called when the custom wake-up condition is satisfied.

An example of a significant motion wake-up condition is given in Figure 2a. A conceptual diagram of the condition is given in Figure 2b. First a ProcessingPipeline object is created. Next, three branches, one for each axis of the accelerometer are created and each branch is given one axis as its source. Then, three MovingAverage algorithms are created, each with window size of 10, and one MovingAverage is added to each of the branches. A VectorMagnitude object and MinThreshold object are also created. The order in which these algorithms and branches are added to the ProcessingPipeline specify how they are chained together. Since the MinThreshold is the last algorithm in the pipeline, if it produces any result, the callback method will be invoked. Now that the pipeline is configured, it, along with a SensorEventListener, is pushed to the SidewinderSensorManager.

3.3 Intermediate language

The intermediate language allows decoupling between the sensor manager and the low-power processor implementation. Upon receiving a wake-up condition configuration, the sensor manager generates its associated intermediate code. The intermediate code for the significant motion wake-up condition is shown in Figure 2c. Having the intermediate code allows developers to write their conditions in the same language as their application. In the intermediate code, each algorithm has a unique ID (generated by the sensor manager). In the example, the moving average algorithms are given IDs from 1, 2 and 3. Then the vector magnitude is setup to receive data from algorithms 1, 2 and 3 and the result of the vector magnitude is given to the admission control algorithm. Finally, the admission control algorithm is fed to OUT. A value being sent to OUT indicates that an event of interest has occurred and the main processor should be woken up.

3.4 Hardware

Our prototype is built around a Google Nexus 4 phone running Android 4.2.2. Since the Nexus 4 does not have an easily programmable sensor hub built in, we implemented our low-power sensor hub using a Texas Instruments (TI) MSP430 or LM4F120 microcontroller attached to an accelerometer sensor and a microphone. We chose to focus our efforts on these sensors because in our experience they are the most commonly used.

The Nexus 4 and microcontroller communicate over the UART [9] port made available by the Nexus 4 debugging interface via the audio interface jack. The serial connection provides sufficient bandwidth to support low bit-rate sensors, such as the accelerometer, a microphone or GPS. However, extending the prototype to work with higher bit-rate sensors like the camera would require a higher bandwidth data bus, such as I^2C [6].

3.5 Runtime

The main responsibility of the Sidewinder runtime is to execute the intermediate language. In this regard, the implementation of the runtime is very flexible. Our implementation of the runtime resembles a simple interpreter (written in C). It contains implementations of algorithms and a list of all available algorithms. Upon receiving a new configuration, the runtime allocates memory for each algorithm in the configuration. The interpreter then waits for sensor data to be available and feeds the data into the appropriate algorithm. If the algorithm produces a result, it sets a flag. The interpreter checks the flag and if necessary sends the result to the next algorithm. The flag is required because some algorithms may not always produce a result. A moving average with a window size of N will not produce a result until it has received N data points and a threshold will only produce a result when the threshold is met. The final algorithm feeds into OUT, indicating that the main processor should be woken up.

3.6 Processing Algorithms

Our algorithms are written in C and packaged with the runtime. Each algorithm operates on its own instance of a data structure. The data structure is created by the runtime and stores the algorithm ID, type, size, data, whether a result is available and the result. It can also contain any other data needed by the algorithm. Each time the algorithm needs to be run, the interpreter invokes the algorithm and passes it its data structure. The algorithm operates on the data available in the structure and, if required, stores the result in the structure and sets the hasResult flag. We implemented the following algorithms:

- **Windowing** Partitioning sensor data into rectangular or Hamming windows.
- **Transform**
  - Fast Fourier Transform (FFT) from time-domain to frequency-domain
  - Inverse Fast Fourier Transform (IFFT) from frequency-domain to time-domain.
- **Data Filtering**
  - Noise-reduction algorithms such as a moving average and exponential moving average.
  - FFT-based low-pass filtering.
  - FFT-based high-pass filtering.
- **Feature Extraction**
  - Magnitude of acceleration vector computation.
  - Zero Crossing Rate computation.
  - A set of statistical functions.
  - Determination of magnitude of dominant frequency.
- **Admission Control** Configurable high or low thresholds.

3.7 Applications

We developed six applications to run on the mobile device and, for each of the applications, we constructed a wake-up condition using the algorithms presented in Section 3.6.

3.7.1 Accelerometer Applications

We decided to use a robotic dog to conduct controlled and repeatable experiments. We developed three applications that detect activities that an AIBO ERA 210 robot can perform: walking, posture transitions, and headbutts. We chose these actions because they have similar acceleration signatures to human activities. It should be noted that, although classifiers to detect these activities will be similar (i.e. similar sensors used, similar algorithms and order of algorithms), each classifier requires its algorithms be parametrized specifically to the activity. This reinforces that a small set of algorithms can be used for numerous classifiers based on how they are chained and parameterized.

A walking robot has a similar acceleration signature as a human, though at a lower intensity. The headbutts are meant to represent very infrequent human actions such as falling. We found that robot stance transitions between the normal and sitting postures are very similar in their acceleration signature to humans sitting down and standing up. In Section 5 we show that the energy saving measured in our experiments with the robot approximate closely the results of experiments conducted on limited traces collected from human subjects.

Steps Counts how many steps the robot takes when it walks. The algorithm is based on the human step detection algorithm proposed by Ryan Libby [18]. The application takes in raw accelerometer readings and applies a low-pass filter on the x-axis acceleration. It then searches for local maxima in the filtered x-axis acceleration. Local maxima between $2.5\,m/s^2$ and $4.5\,m/s^2$ are detected as steps.

Transitions Detects transitions between sitting and standing. The application monitors changes in acceleration due to gravity on the y and z axes to determine the orientation of the device. If the z-axis (up-down relative to the dog) acceleration is between $9m/s^2$ and $11m/s^2$, and the acceleration on the y-axis (front-back relative to the dog) is between $-1m/s^2$ and $1m/s^2$, the device is in a horizontal position and the robot is assumed to be in a standing posture. Similarly, if the z-axis acceleration is

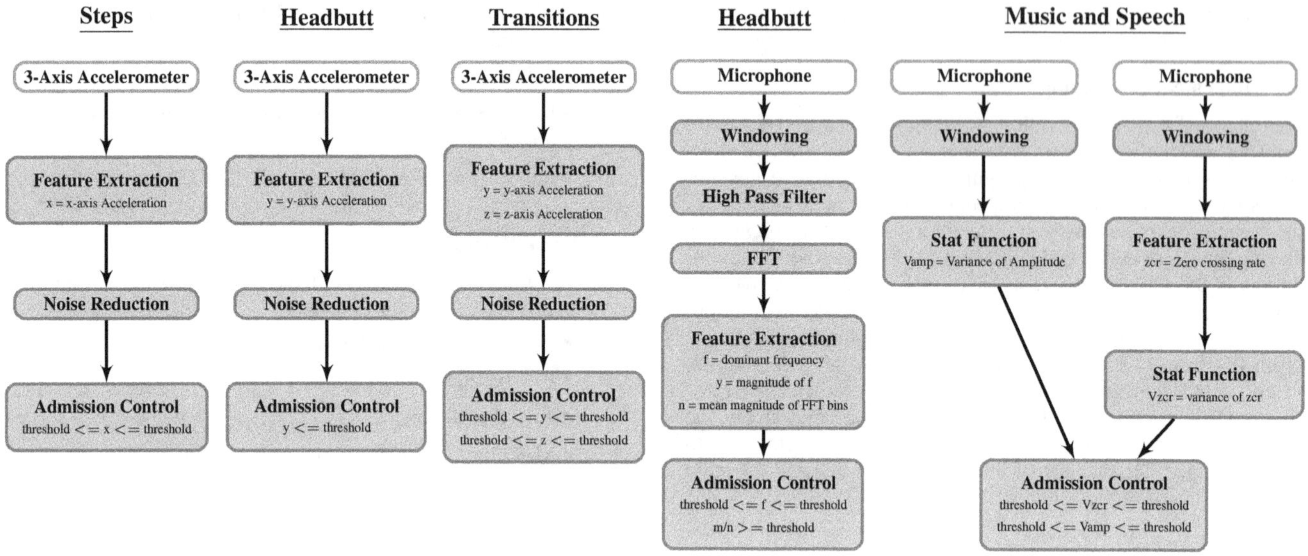

Figure 3: Wake-up conditions pipelines for each of the applications.

between $7.5m/s^2$ and $9.5m/s^2$, and the acceleration on the y-axis is between $3.5m/s^2$ and $5.5m/s^2$, the device is in an angled position and the robot is assumed to be in a sitting posture. The application detects transitions by looking for posture changes.

Headbutts Detects a sudden forward head movement. The application monitors the y-axis acceleration and searches for local minima between $-3.75\ m/s^2$ and $-6.75\ m/s^2$.

3.7.2 Audio Applications

We developed the following three microphone based applications.

Siren Detector Detects sirens originating from emergency vehicles. The application applies a 750 Hz high-pass filter in order to remove a significant potion of sounds that aren't sirens. The data in each window is transformed to the frequency domain using a FFT in order to extract the magnitude of the dominant frequency and the mean magnitude of all frequency bins. The ratio of the magnitude of the dominant frequency and the mean frequency is used to determine if the window contains pitched sounds. Pitched sounds between 850 Hz and 1800 Hz that last longer 650 ms are classified as sirens.

Music Journal Creates a list of all the songs heard during the day using the web services provided by Echoprint.me [4]. Audio data is partitioned into windows and passed to two branches for feature extraction. The first branch computes the variance of the amplitude over the entire window. The second branch further partitions the data into smaller windows and computes the zero crossing rate (the rate at which the signal changes from positive to negative or vice versa) for each sub-window. It then calculates the variance in zero crossing rate across the set the sub-windows. Finally, an admission control step uses thresholds (different for music and speech detection) on the extracted features to determine if an event of interest has occurred. Data is then passed to the Echoprint.me web service to identify the song.

Phrase Detection Similar to Music Journal, except different parameters are used in the wake-up condition and Google Speech API was used for speech-to-text translation.

We created a wake-up condition for each of these six applications using the processing algorithms described in section 3.6. Figure 3 shows the conceptual pipeline representation for each condition we constructed. Each one ends with an admission control step with configurable thresholds. The wake-up condition is satisfied when the relevant data or extracted features meet the admission control threshold.

3.8 Discussion

This section describes important questions that will need to be answered by hardware vendors to implement Sidewinder.

Identifying processing algorithms. Defining the appropriate set of common algorithms that should be included in the API and executed on the low-power processor for each sensor is a key challenge. First, there is a trade-off between algorithm generality and accuracy. Simple generic algorithms can support a large set of applications, albeit no specific application is likely to experience optimal performance. Conversely, a highly specialized algorithm may provide optimal performance but is only applicable to a limited set of applications. Second, there is also a trade-off between algorithm complexity and power savings. More complex algorithms can reduce energy consumption by preventing unnecessary wake-ups due to increased accuracy. On the other hand, more complex algorithms have higher computational demands, which require a larger and hungrier peripheral processor.

While determining the complete set of algorithms to be included as part of the runtime is beyond the scope of this paper, we anticipate that it will include algorithms for windowing, data filtering, feature extraction, admission control and transformations. Ideally, this set of algorithms should be standardized by the platform (ex. Android or iOS).

Access to sensor data. A related question is determining what data the sensor hub should pass to the application following a wake-up. Some applications may be interested in the raw sensor data, while others may want to use the filtered data or extracted features. Ideally, an API would allow developers to specify what data their application should receive when an event of interest occurs. Our current implementation passes a buffer of raw sensor data to the application.

Sizing. When creating the sensor node of the prototype implementation we evaluated two microcontrollers having different power consumption levels. We noticed that the lower power microcontroller was not able to run some algorithms (such as Fast Fourier Transforms) in real-time. Determining the optimal number, type and size of processors to include in the sensor hub is an open research question. Each sensor (or small group of related sensors) may be supported by its own dedicated low-power processor. Alternatively, a larger processor could be used to serve the entire sensor hub. Identifying a sweet spot between the maximum number of concurrent algorithm executions, energy budget, cost and physical size of the sensor node is an open challenge and is a decision the hardware manufacturer will have to make.

Sensor fusion. Fusing inputs from multiple sensors is a common technique used for improving the accuracy of sensing applications. Whether low power sensor hubs should include support for sensor fusion, however, is not clear. On the one hand, such support could increase energy efficiency by reducing the occurrence of unnecessary wake-ups. On the other, sensor fusion tends to be application specific and the added complexity may negate any energy benefits. The current implementation allows sensor fusion at the main processor level. Once a wake-up condition triggers and passes raw data to the application, the application has the ability to run sensor fusion algorithms on the data.

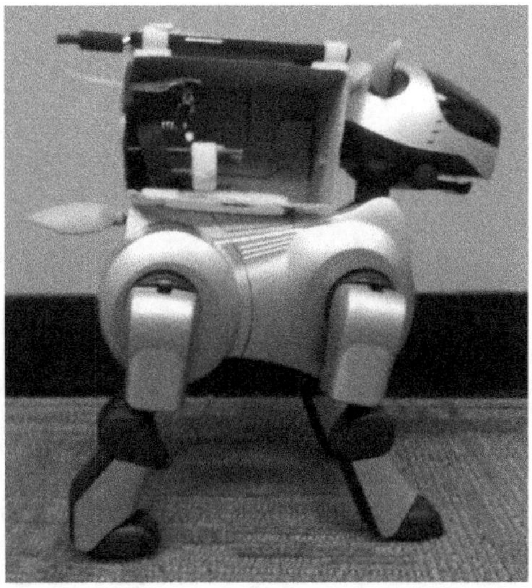

Figure 4: Aibo robotic dog used for data collection

4. Evaluation

Our evaluation is based on a trace-driven simulation. We measured power usage for our hardware to create a power model and collected accelerometer and audio traces. This data was fed into our simulator which modeled the behavior and power consumption of our devices under various configurations and applications.

We power profiled the Google Nexus 4 in order to create a model to estimate power consumption based on the outputs from the simulator. The results of the power profile are summarized in Table 1. During all the measurements, the devices' screen, WiFi and GPS were turned off. While the device is sleeping, its power usage is very low, consuming only 9.7 mW. While awake, the power consumption is significantly higher, averaging 323 mW. During our power measurements we noticed that additional energy is consumed during transitions between the asleep and awake states. Each transition takes about 1 second. During a wake-up transition, the average power consumption goes up to 384 mW, while during an awake-to-asleep transition the average power consumption is 341 mW.

We implemented the low-power processor on two different microcontrollers. One was a Texas Instruments (TI) MSP430 and the other a TI LM4F120. The MSP430 has the advantage of requiring very little power, consuming only 3.6 mW while awake. However, it has limited memory and cannot perform complex analysis of sensor data in real-time. In our tests, it was unable to run the FFT-based low-pass filter in real-time. The TI LM4F120 is powered by a Cortex-M4 processor. It can batch a higher number of accelerometer readings and can run all our filters in real time. However, this microcontroller has an energy footprint an order of magnitude greater than the MSP430, consuming an average of 49.4 mW while awake.

4.1 Trace Collection

Audio traces We collected three half-hour audio traces in different environments: an office, a coffee shop and outdoors. We used audio mixing software to add audio events of interest to the collected traces. The audio events of interest include music (5% of each trace), speech (5% of each trace), and sirens (2% of each trace). The events of interest were randomly selected from a library of audio files.

Human accelerometer traces We collected six hours of accelerometer traces from three different individuals while they perform routine daily activities: morning commute using public transit, working in a retail store, and working in an office. Between 20% and 37% of each trace is spent walking.

Robotic accelerometer traces We collected synthetic traces by having a robot perform multiple runs with a prototype smartphone attached to its back. For each run, the robot logged the start and end of each action, which we use as the ground truth for our experiments. The smartphone ran an application that kept the device always awake and continuously recorded accelerometer readings for all three axes.

To enable us to conduct controlled and repeatable experiments, we mounted the prototype smartphone on the back of an AIBO ERA 210 robot dog (see Figure 4). Because the robot's actions can be scripted, this setup provides an efficient and reliable way to determine ground truth. In contrast, labeling data collected from human subjects with ground truth is error prone and labor intensive.

In each run, the robot performed five different actions: standing idle, walking, sit-to-stand transitions, stand-to-sit transitions, and headbutts. We created runs with three different levels of activity. Runs in groups 1, 2 and 3 spent 90%, 50% and 10% of the time standing idle, respectively. The reminder of the time was allocated as follows: 73% for walking, 24% for transitions between sitting and standing, and 3% for headbutts. This setup allows us to experiment with detecting actions that are common, somewhat frequent, and rare. In total, the robot executed 18 different runs: 9 for group 1, 6 for group 2 and 3 for group 3. We generated more runs for groups 1 and 2 because of the lower activity levels compared to group 3. To eliminate bias, the list of actions was generated randomly for each run, based on the expected probabilities of each action.

While our robotic testbed allows us to run live experiments, we chose instead to use trace-based simulation for several reasons. First, it took the robot close to an hour to complete a single experiment. Secondly, a thorough exploration of the configuration space of the various sensing approaches we consider would have required months of continuous live experiments. Moreover, taking fine grain power consumption measurements while the robot is in motion is not trivial.

4.2 Configurations

We used the simulator to evaluate the recall and precision of our applications under the following configurations.

- **Duty Cycling** The applications wake-up at fixed time intervals to collect sensor data for 4 seconds and run the event detection

State	Average Power Consumption (mW)	Average Duration
Awake, running sensor-driven application	323	N/A
Asleep	9.7	N/A
Asleep-to-Awake Transition	384	1 second
Awake-to-Asleep Transition	341	1 second

Table 1: Google Nexus 4 power profile.

algorithms. If an action is detected, the phone is kept awake for another 4 seconds, otherwise it goes to sleep for N seconds. N is referred to as the sleep interval. For our experiments, we use a sleep interval of 2, 5, 10, 20 and 30 seconds. As the sleep interval increases, more power is saved but recall suffers.

- **Batching** Similar to Duty Cycling, except when the phone is asleep sensor data is cached. When the device wakes, a batch of data from the sleep cycle is given to the application. We use the same sleep interval for Batching Cycling as we did for Duty Cycling.
- **Predefined Activity** This configuration simulates the Android's built-in significant motion detector. We constructed simple classifiers to wake up the device and invoke the callback method in the application when significant activity is detected (significant acceleration or sound).
- **Sidewinder based Classifier** For each of the applications, we constructed wake-up conditions to invoke the application when events of interests are detected.
- **Oracle** A hypothetical ideal implementation that only wakes up when the event of interest occurs. Such a wake-up condition would achieve perfect detection precision and recall, with the lowest possible power consumption. The difference between the power consumption of this method and the Sidewinder configuration provides an upper bound on the potential additional benefits of custom code offloading.

4.3 Metrics

For each sensing approach and trace, the simulator calculated the amount of sleep and awake time, the total number of wake-up events, and the recall and precision of the application. Using this data and the energy model derived from measurements of our prototype, we estimate the average power consumption. For the *Duty Cycling* experiments, the power model accounts only for the energy consumption of the Nexus 4. For *Batching* and *Predefined Activity*, the model also includes the cost of a low-power TI MSP430 microcontroller. Finally, experiments configured to use *Sidewinder* include the cost of the TI MSP430, with the exception being the siren detector which required the more powerful TI LM4F120 to run FFT in real time.

5. Results

In this section we present the results of simulations conducted on the accelerometer and audio traces described in Section 4.1. We answer the following questions:

1. How much power can be saved with more energy efficient sensing approaches?
2. How close to optimal is Sidewinder?
3. How does Sidewinder compare to Predefined Activities?
4. How well do Duty Cycling and Batching perform?

Wake-up Mechanism	Sirens	Music	Phrase
Oracle	16.8	27.2	14.7
Predefined Activity	51.9	51.9	51.9
Sidewinder	63.1*	32.3	35.6

* Includes the more powerful TI LM4F120

Table 2: Average power consumption for the audio applications. Values measured in milliwatts.

5. How representative are the accelerometer experiments on the AIBO of expected performance with humans?

Figure 5 presents the power usage, relative to Oracle, of replaying the synthetic accelerometer traces under the various sensing configurations. For each application[1], the graph presents additional power consumption over Oracle, measured in percent. Results are averages across runs of the same group. In order to make it easier to compare across approaches, we calibrated all approaches so that they all achieve 100% recall. Duty Cycling is the one approach that cannot achieve 100% recall with any reasonable sleep interval. Figure 6 shows the recall for Duty Cycling at 90% idle. All sensing approaches achieved similar average precision (Headbutts: 89%, Transitions: 91%, Walking: 93%).

Table 2 shows the average results from running the the simulations on the collected audio traces. We omitted the results for Duty Cycling and Batching because they are similar to the results from the simulations on accelerometer traces.

5.1 How Much Power can be Saved?

The Oracle in our work is a hypothetical ideal which is in a sleep state most of the time and only wakes up when events of interest occur. It has perfect recall, precision and the best possible power usage. Always Awake, on the other hand, never sleeps and therefore, and has the worst possible power usage. The difference in power usage between these two approaches represents the power that could be saved by better sensing approaches. Always Awake consumed on average 323mW of power. In our most demanding scenario, step detection with 10% idle, the Oracle consumed on average 266mW. For the least demanding, step detection with 10% idle, the Oracle consumed on average 16.4mW. This means, depending on the scenario, *there is potential to reduce power consumption by 17.7% to 94.9%.*

5.2 How Close to Optimal is Sidewinder?

By comparing the performance of the Sidewinder approach to Oracle we observe that the Sidewinder approach achieves between 92.7% and 95.7% of the of the possible power savings [2] for our

[1] Results for Batching are shown with a 10s sleep interval as the other results were similar to Duty Cycling

[2] $(AllwaysAwake - Sidewinder)/(AllwaysAwake - Oracle)$

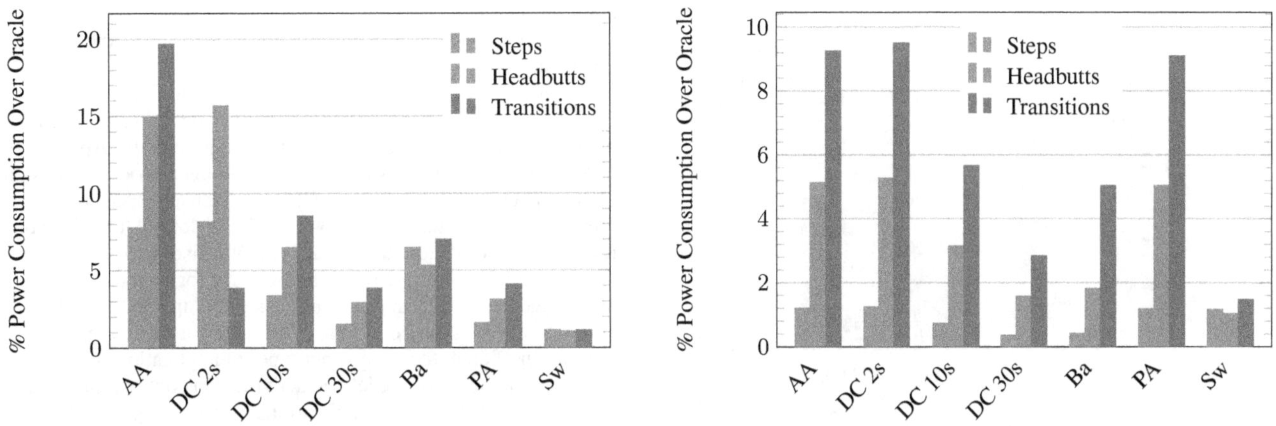

(a) 90% Idle

(b) 10% Idle

Figure 5: Power usage of Always Awake (AA), Duty Cycling (DC) with various sleep intervals, Batching (Ba) with 10s sleep interval, Predefined Activity (PA) and Sidewinder (Sw) relative to Oracle for synthetic accelerometer traces

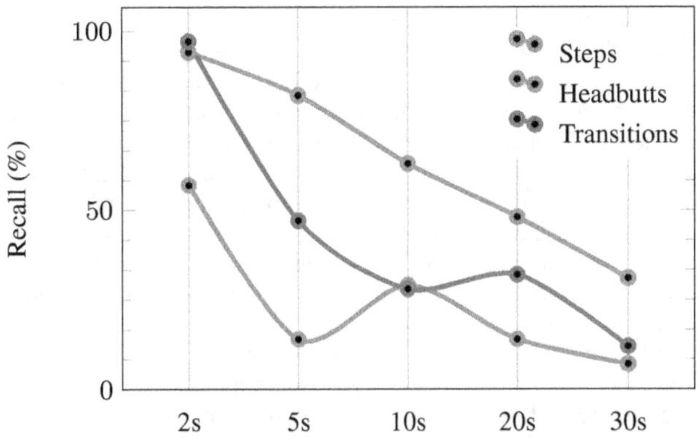

Figure 6: Recall for Duty Cycling on synthetic accelerometer traces with 90% idle

accelerometer-based applications. Audio applications performed similarly with saving between 85% and 98%.

The suboptimal nature of wake-up conditions is illustrated by the phrase detection application. Whereas, the Oracle only wakes up when the phrase of interest occurs (<1% of each trace), our wake-up condition powers up the device every time it detects a speech segment (approximately 5% of each trace). However, even with this limitation, Sidewinder achieves 93% of the possible energy saving for this application.

We conclude *it is possible to build a wide range of classifiers based on a set of generic processing algorithms, and that the resulting classifier achieves the large majority of available power savings. Moreover any additional power saving that custom code may achieve are likely to be very limited.*

5.3 Sidewinder vs. Predefined Activity

To make the comparison to Predefined Activity as fair as possible, we explored the parameter space to determine the best thresholds for *significant acceleration* and *sound intensity*[3]. We chose values that minimize power consumption, while maintaining 100% detection recall. Thus the parameters used in this scenario are over-fitted to our test data and represent a best case scenario that skews the results in favor of Predefined Activity.

As expected, the power consumption resulting from the use of significant activity detectors (significant sound, significant motion) are proportional to the amount of activity in the trace and the popularity of the event of interest.

In the accelerometer experiments, Predefined Activity has similar power consumption to Sidewinder for *steps*, which is a common event, but consumes 4.7 and 6.1 times more power to detect *headbuttss* and *transitions*, which are less frequent events. In the experiments performed on the audio traces, Predefined Activity consumed 18% less power for *sirens* than Sidewinder, but 45% and 60% more power for *music journal* and *phrase detection*, respectively. Due to the higher complexity of the wake-up condition used for siren detection, the power consumption model had to account for the powerful TI LM4F120 microcontroller instead of the MSP430, which consumes an additional 40 mW.

We conclude that a *a small number of predefined activities are unlikely to support efficiently a wide range of applications. This is particularly the case for applications interested in infrequent events.*

5.4 Sidewinder vs. Duty Cycling and Batching

Duty Cycling performs poorly. Short sleep intervals actually result in an increase in power consumption (339 mW compared to an average of 323 mW for Always Awake) due to frequent transitioning between awake and asleep states. Longer sleep intervals are more effective at saving energy, but they do so by sacrificing recall. For example, a sleep interval of 10 seconds reduces the Headbutts and Transitions recall bellow 30%.

Batching achieves perfect recall, but requires long batching intervals to achieve large energy savings. Therefore, this approach is not appropriate for applications with timeliness constrains. For example, the user of a gesture recognition application [20, 29] would not be satisfied if the application detects the performed gesture after a delay of more than a couple of seconds. We anticipate that in practice realistic batching intervals are in the order of a few seconds, depending on the sensor data acquisition rate and the size of the data buffer. Additionally, the device often wakes up to find out that no events occurred in the current batch.

[3] Two predefined activites supported by our hardware

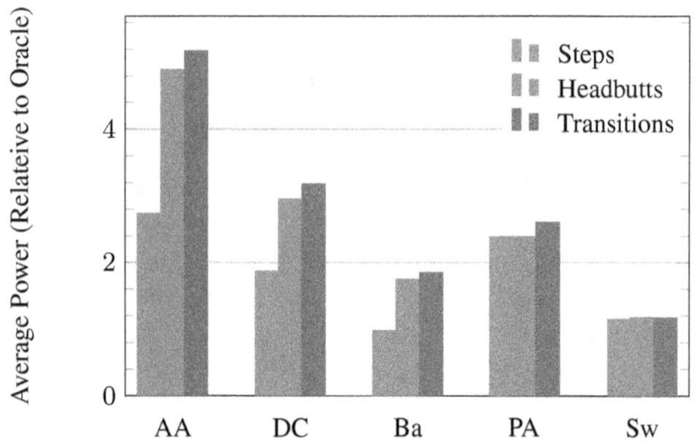

Figure 7: Power usage of Always Awake (AA), Duty Cycling (DC), Batching (Ba), Predefined Activity (PA) and Sidewinder (Sw) relative to Oracle for human traces

In most cases *Duty Cycling and Batching consumed 2.4 to 7.5 times more power than Sidewinder. To achieve significant power saving, Duty Cycling and Batching have to either sacrifice recall or timeliness.*

5.5 Human Traces

Figure 7 shows the results from running the step detector application on traces collected from three human subjects. Since these traces are not annotated with ground truth, we use the steps detected by an *Always Awake* configuration as the baseline for determining recall. For Duty Cycling and Batching we show only a sleep interval of 10 seconds. All approaches except Duty Cycling (82%) had 100% recall.

The results from these experiments show benefits very similar to the synthetic experiments for runs with low and medium levels of activity. The Sidewinder approach achieves at least 91% of the available power saving in each of the traces.

Additionally, we note that the generic wake-up condition performs poorly. We attribute the relatively high power consumption to the fact the human subjects were performing a wide range of activities. While most of the activities were not events of interest, they resulted in unnecessary wake-ups.

6. Related Work

The idea of waking up a device when an event of interest occurs has been around since the inception of mobile phones. The phone's radio transceiver wakes up the device when an incoming call or a text message is received [5]. Wake on Wireless [30] extended this idea by augmenting a PDA with a low-power radio that would send a wake-up message when an incoming call is received. Similarly, Wake on WLAN [24] allows remote wake-up of wireless networking equipment.

Turducken [31] generalizes the "wake on event of interest" approach to several types of applications and to multiple components operating at increasingly small power-levels. Little Rock [27] applies Turducken's multi-tiered architecture to sensing on mobile devices. Reflex [19] complements the idea proposed by Turducken by providing a shared memory abstraction to be used by the different processors. Little Rock and Reflex expose application developers to the heterogeneous architecture. In contrast, Sidewinder hides the heterogeneous nature of the system from the application developer. Creating an application that makes use of Sidewinder does not require the developer to write low-level code for the low-power sensor hub. Instead, developers create custom wake-up conditions by configuring pipelines of commonly used algorithms. This approach increase portability, while achieving the majority of the potential power savings.

Smartphone manufacturers have started to incorporate low-power processors into their architectures, but have only implemented limited APIs that provide fixed functionality. Apple's M7 and M8 motion co-processors are used to collect, process, and store sensor data even while the main CPU is asleep and applications can retrieve historical motion data via the CoreMotion API [3]. Some recent Android devices allow batching of sensor readings [1], and the Motorola Moto X provides recognition for a small number of predefined activities that can be used as wake-up conditions [7, 10]. While these wake-up conditions work well for some applications, they are inefficient for many other types of applications that are not interested in the set of predefined activities. In contrast, Sidewinder supports a wide variety of applications by providing developers an easy mechanism to create custom wake-up conditions.

Most of the previously noted works focused on system architecture modification in order to lower the cost of sensing. Alternative approaches have also been explored. Ace [25] is a middleware that supports continuous context-aware applications while mitigating sensing cost for acquisition of context attributes (such as AtHome and IsDriving). It achieves power savings when multiple applications request strongly correlated context attributes. Additionally, it can reduce power consumption when a "cheaper" sensor exists, which can determine the value of a different context attribute that has a strong correlation with the requested context attribute (e.g. use the accelerometer to check if the user is jogging instead of using the GPS to determine if the user is at work). A middleware such as Ace is a great example of a library that can run on top of Sidewinder and achieve additional power savings. Sensor fusion has also been an active focus of related research. Data from multiple sensors can be used to increase context-awareness in mobile devices [12, 14].

While our focus was on power-efficient acquisition of sensor data, next generation mobile perception applications face related problems regarding partitioning of application code. MAUI [13] enables fine-grained energy-aware offload of mobile application code to remote servers. Similarly, Odessa [28] uses code-offloading to address the issue of processing sensor data on resource constrained mobile devices.

7. Conclusion

In this paper we proposed *Sidewinder*, a new approach for continuous mobile sensing. In this approach, the platform implements common sensor data processing algorithms that execute on a low-power processor, and application developers construct wake-up conditions for events of interest by selecting among the set of predefined common processing algorithms and tuning their parameters. We presented an extensive evaluation showing the benefits of using Sidewinder as wake-up mechanisms for the multiple accelerometer and audio-based applications.

Our immediate future work includes developing an FPGA-based prototype, performing a thorough exploration of what algorithms should be included as part of the platform and analyzing their power and computational requirements. We would also like to explore supporting multiple concurrent applications while still maintaining predictable performance. When receiving multiple wake-up conditions, the sensor manager can attempt to improve performance by combining the pipelines that use common algorithms.

Another interesting extension includes adding "smartness" to the low-power sensor hub. Application developers may face challenges in selecting the optimal algorithms and configuration parameters for their wake-up conditions. But given feedback from the more complex algorithms running on the application level, self-learning mechanisms may be able to tune the paramers used on the wake-up conditions. It is easy to imagine an application notifying the sensor hub about wake-ups when events of interest were not actually detected (i.e. false positives). However, it will be more difficult to automatically identify events of interest missed by the wake-up condition running on the low-power node (i.e. false negatives).

References

[1] Android 4.4 sdk. http://developer.android.com/about/versions/android-4.4.html, .

[2] Android motion sensors. http://developer.android.com/guide/topics/sensors/sensors_motion.html, .

[3] Core motion framework reference. https://developer.apple.com/library/ios/documentation/coremotion/reference/coremotion_reference/index.html.

[4] Echoprint - open source music identification. http://echoprint.me/.

[5] Qualcomm - 3g/4g connectivity (gobi). https://developer.qualcomm.com/mobile-development/maximize-hardware/3g4g-connectivity-gobi.

[6] I2c. URL https://en.wikipedia.org/w/index.php?title=I%C2%B2C&oldid=670659499. Page Version ID: 670659499.

[7] Moto x. http://www.motorola.com/motox.

[8] SensorManager | android developers. URL https://developer.android.com/reference/android/hardware/SensorManager.html.

[9] Universal asynchronous receiver/transmitter. URL https://en.wikipedia.org/w/index.php?title=Universal_asynchronous_receiver/transmitter&oldid=673411359. Page Version ID: 673411359.

[10] X8 mobile computing system. http://www.motorola.com/us/X8-Mobile-Computing-System/x8-mobile-computing-system.html.

[11] M. Baldauf, S. Dustdar, and F. Rosenberg. A survey on context-aware systems. *International Journal of Ad Hoc and Ubiquitous Computing*, 2(4):263–277, 2007.

[12] G. Biegel and V. Cahill. A framework for developing mobile, context-aware applications. In *Pervasive Computing and Communications, 2004. PerCom 2004. Proceedings of the Second IEEE Annual Conference on*, pages 361–365. IEEE, 2004.

[13] E. Cuervo, A. Balasubramanian, D.-k. Cho, A. Wolman, S. Saroiu, R. Chandra, and P. Bahl. Maui: making smartphones last longer with code offload. In *Proceedings of the 8th international conference on Mobile systems, applications, and services*, pages 49–62. ACM, 2010.

[14] H. W. Gellersen, A. Schmidt, and M. Beigl. Multi-sensor context-awareness in mobile devices and smart artifacts. *Mobile Networks and Applications*, 7(5):341–351, 2002.

[15] K. Hameed. The application of mobile computing and technology to health care services. *Telematics and Informatics*, 20(2):99–106, 2003.

[16] J.-y. Hong, E.-h. Suh, and S.-J. Kim. Context-aware systems: A literature review and classification. *Expert Systems with Applications*, 36(4):8509–8522, 2009.

[17] B. Hull, V. Bychkovsky, Y. Zhang, K. Chen, M. Goraczko, A. Miu, E. Shih, H. Balakrishnan, and S. Madden. Cartel: a distributed mobile sensor computing system. In *Proceedings of the 4th international conference on Embedded networked sensor systems*, pages 125–138. ACM, 2006.

[18] R. Libby. A simple method for reliable footstep detection in embedded sensor platforms, 2009.

[19] X. Lin, Z. Wang, R. LiKamWa, and L. Zhong. Reflex: Using low-power processors in smartphones without knowing them. *Proc. Conf. Architectural Support for Programming Languages and Operating Systems (ASPLOS)*, March 2012.

[20] J. Liu, L. Zhong, J. Wickramasuriya, and V. Vasudevan. uwave: Accelerometer-based personalized gesture recognition and its applications. *Pervasive and Mobile Computing*, 5(6):657–675, 2009.

[21] N. Maisonneuve, M. Stevens, M. E. Niessen, P. Hanappe, and L. Steels. Citizen noise pollution monitoring. In *Proceedings of the 10th Annual International Conference on Digital Government Research: Social Networks: Making Connections between Citizens, Data and Government*, pages 96–103. Digital Government Society of North America, 2009.

[22] N. Maisonneuve, M. Stevens, M. E. Niessen, and L. Steels. Noisetube: Measuring and mapping noise pollution with mobile phones. In *Information Technologies in Environmental Engineering*, pages 215–228. Springer, 2009.

[23] S. E. Minson, B. A. Brooks, C. L. Glennie, J. R. Murray, J. O. Langbein, S. E. Owen, T. H. Heaton, R. A. Iannucci, and D. L. Hauser. Crowdsourced earthquake early warning. 1(3): e1500036–e1500036. ISSN 2375-2548. doi: 10.1126/sciadv.1500036. URL http://advances.sciencemag.org/cgi/doi/10.1126/sciadv.1500036.

[24] N. Mishra, K. Chebrolu, B. Raman, and A. Pathak. Wake-on-wlan. In *Proceedings of the 15th international conference on World Wide Web*, pages 761–769. ACM, 2006.

[25] S. Nath. Ace: exploiting correlation for energy-efficient and continuous context sensing. In *Proc. of the 10th Conference on Mobile Systems, Applications, and Services (MobiSys)*, pages 29–42. ACM, 2012.

[26] D. Preuveneers and Y. Berbers. Mobile phones assisting with health self-care: a diabetes case study. In *Proceedings of the 10th international conference on Human computer interaction with mobile devices and services*, pages 177–186. ACM, 2008.

[27] B. Priyantha, D. Lymberopoulos, and J. Liu. Littlerock: Enabling energy-efficient continuous sensing on mobile phones. *Pervasive Computing, IEEE*, 10(2):12–15, 2011.

[28] M.-R. Ra, A. Sheth, L. Mummert, P. Pillai, D. Wetherall, and R. Govindan. Odessa: enabling interactive perception applications on mobile devices. In *Proceedings of the 9th international conference on Mobile systems, applications, and services*, pages 43–56. ACM, 2011.

[29] T. Schlömer, B. Poppinga, N. Henze, and S. Boll. Gesture recognition with a wii controller. In *Proceedings of the 2nd international conference on Tangible and embedded interaction*, pages 11–14. ACM, 2008.

[30] E. Shih, P. Bahl, and M. J. Sinclair. Wake on wireless: an event driven energy saving strategy for battery operated devices. In *Proc. of the 8th Conference on Mobile Computing and Networking(MobiCom)*, pages 160–171. ACM, 2002.

[31] J. Sorber, N. Banerjee, M. D. Corner, and S. Rollins. Turducken: Hierarchical power management for mobile devices. In *Proc. of the 3rd Conference on Mobile Systems, Applications, and Services (MobiSyS)*, Seattle, WA, June 2005.

[32] C. C. Tsai, G. Lee, F. Raab, G. J. Norman, T. Sohn, W. G. Griswold, and K. Patrick. Usability and feasibility of pmeb: a mobile phone application for monitoring real time caloric balance. *Mobile networks and applications*, 12(2-3):173–184, 2007.

OpenPiton: An Open Source Manycore Research Framework

Jonathan Balkind Michael McKeown Yaosheng Fu Tri Nguyen
Yanqi Zhou Alexey Lavrov Mohammad Shahrad Adi Fuchs
Samuel Payne * Xiaohua Liang Matthew Matl David Wentzlaff

Princeton University

{jbalkind,mmckeown,yfu,trin,yanqiz,alavrov,mshahrad,adif}@princeton.edu,
spayne@nvidia.com, {xiaohua,mmatl,wentzlaf}@princeton.edu

Abstract

Industry is building larger, more complex, manycore processors on the back of strong institutional knowledge, but academic projects face difficulties in replicating that scale. To alleviate these difficulties and to develop and share knowledge, the community needs open architecture frameworks for simulation, synthesis, and software exploration which support extensibility, scalability, and configurability, alongside an established base of verification tools and supported software. In this paper we present OpenPiton, an open source framework for building scalable architecture research prototypes from 1 core to 500 million cores. OpenPiton is the world's first open source, general-purpose, multithreaded manycore processor and framework. OpenPiton leverages the industry hardened OpenSPARC T1 core with modifications and builds upon it with a scratch-built, scalable uncore creating a flexible, modern manycore design. In addition, OpenPiton provides synthesis and backend scripts for ASIC and FPGA to enable other researchers to bring their designs to implementation. OpenPiton provides a complete verification infrastructure of over 8000 tests, is supported by mature software tools, runs full-stack multiuser Debian Linux, and is written in industry standard Verilog. Multiple implementations of OpenPiton have been created including a taped-out 25-core implementation in IBM's 32nm process and multiple Xilinx FPGA prototypes.

1. Introduction

Multicore and manycore processors have been growing in size and popularity fueled by the growth in single-chip transistor count and the need for higher performance. This trend has been widespread across the industry with manycore processors being fabricated by numerous vendors [49, 70, 82, 84, 86]. Academia has also heavily studied multicore and manycore [28, 47, 87], though often through the use of software simulation [14, 21, 31, 50, 59, 81] and modeling [43, 72] tools. While software tools are convenient to work with and provide great flexibility, they do not provide the high performance, characterization fidelity (power, area, and frequency), and ability to perform research at-scale that taking a manycore design to RTL, FPGA, or silicon implementation can provide.

A major barrier limiting manycore research is the lack of an easy to use, highly scalable, open source, manycore processor design. In order to maximize benefit, such a design and framework would have robust software tools, be easily configurable, provide a mature tool ecosystem with OS support, be written in an industry standard HDL, be easily synthesizable to FPGA and ASIC, and provide a large test suite. Building and supporting such an infrastructure is a major undertaking which has prevented such prior designs. Our

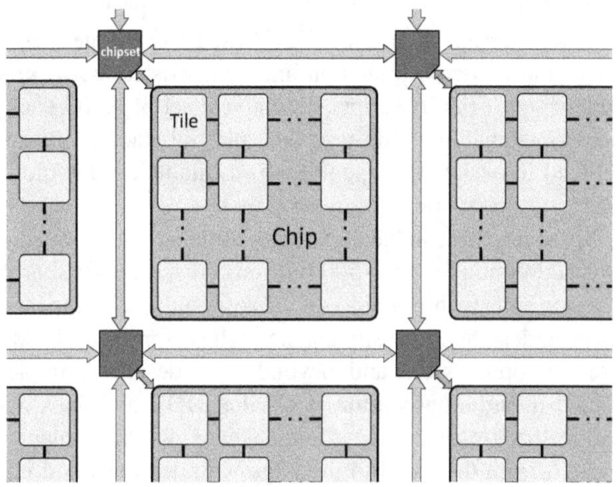

Figure 1: OpenPiton Architecture. Multiple manycore chips are connected together with chipset logic and networks to build large scalable manycore systems. OpenPiton's cache coherence protocol extends off chip.

* Now at Nvidia

ASPLOS '16, April 02 - 06, 2016, Atlanta, GA, USA

DOI: http://dx.doi.org/10.1145/2872362.2872414

framework, OpenPiton, attacks this challenge and provides all of these features and more.

OpenPiton is the world's first open source, general-purpose, multithreaded manycore processor. The OpenPiton platform shown in Figure 1 is a modern, tiled, manycore design consisting of a 64-bit architecture using the mature SPARC v9 ISA with a distributed, directory-based, cache coherence protocol (shared distributed L2) implemented across three physical, 2D mesh Networks-on-Chip (NoCs). OpenPiton contains a pipelined dual-precision FPU per core and supports native multithreading to hide memory latency. OpenPiton builds upon the industry hardened OpenSPARC T1 [6, 58, 78] core, but sports a completely scratch-built uncore (caches, cache-coherence protocol, NoCs, scalable interrupt controller, NoC-based I/O bridges, etc), a new and modern simulation and synthesis framework, a modern set of FPGA scripts, a complete set of ASIC back-end scripts enabling chip tape-out, and full-stack multiuser Debian Linux support. OpenPiton is available for download at `http://www.openpiton.org`.

OpenPiton is scalable and portable; the architecture supports addressing for up to 500-million cores, supports shared memory both within a chip and across multiple chips, and has been designed to easily enable high performance 1000+ core microprocessors and beyond. The design is implemented in **industry standard Verilog HDL** and does not require the use of any new languages. OpenPiton enables research from the small to the large with demonstrated implementations from a single lite-core, PicoPiton, on a Xilinx Artix 7 operating at 29.5MHz up to Piton, our 25-core custom ASIC implementation of OpenPiton, taped-out at 1GHz in 32nm silicon.

OpenPiton has been designed as a platform to enable at-scale manycore research. An explicit design goal of OpenPiton is that it should be easy to use by other researchers. To support this, OpenPiton provides a high degree of integration and configurability. Unlike many other designs where the pieces are provided, but it is up to the user to compose them together, OpenPiton is designed with all of the components integrated into the same easy to use build infrastructure providing **push-button scalability.** Computer architecture researchers can easily deploy OpenPiton's source code, add in modifications and explore their novel research ideas in the setting of a fully working system. Over 8000 targeted, high-coverage test cases are provided to enable researchers to innovate with a safety net that ensures functionality is maintained. OpenPiton's open source nature also makes it easy to release modifications and reproduce previous work for comparison or reuse.

Beyond being a platform designed by computer architects for use by computer architects, OpenPiton enables researchers in other fields including OS, security, compilers, runtime tools, systems, and even CAD tool design to conduct research at-scale. In order to enable such a wide range

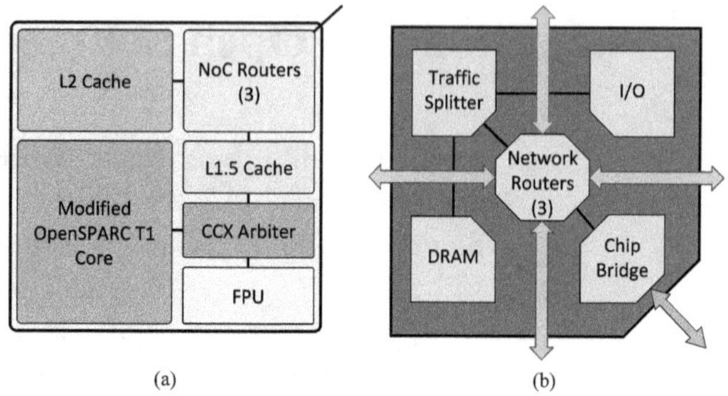

Figure 2: Architecture of (a) a tile and (b) chipset.

of applications, OpenPiton is configurable and extensible. The number of cores, attached I/O, size of caches, number of TLB entries, presence of an FPU, number of threads, and network topology are all configurable from a single configuration file. OpenPiton is easy to extend; the presence of a well documented core, a well documented coherence protocol, and an easy to interface NoC make adding research features easy. Research extensions to OpenPiton that have already been built include several novel memory system explorations, an Oblivious RAM controller, and a new in-core thread scheduler. The validated and mature ISA and software ecosystem support OS and compiler research. The release of OpenPiton's ASIC synthesis, FPGA synthesis, and back-end (Place and Route) scripts make it easy for others to port to new process technologies or FPGAs. In particular, this enables CAD researchers who need large netlists to evaluate their algorithms at-scale.

The following are our key contributions:

- Creation and release of the world's first open source, general-purpose, multithreaded manycore processor.
- Detailed description of the OpenPiton architecture including a novel coherent memory system that seamlessly integrates on-chip and off-chip networks.
- Presentation of multiple use-cases of configurability and extensibility of the OpenPiton Architecture.
- Comparison of FPGA and ASIC implementations of OpenPiton
- Characterization of backend synthesis runtimes.
- Characterization of the test coverage of the OpenPiton test suite.
- Qualitative comparison against prior open source processors.

2. Architecture

OpenPiton is a tiled-manycore architecture, as shown in Figure 1. It is designed to be scalable, both intra-chip and inter-chip.

Intra-chip, tiles are connected via three networks on-chip (NoCs) in a 2D mesh topology. The scalable tiled architecture and mesh topology allow for the number of tiles within an OpenPiton chip to be configurable. In the default configuration, the NoC router address space supports scaling up to 256 tiles in each dimension within a single OpenPiton chip (64K cores/chip).

Inter-chip, an off-chip interface, known as the chip bridge, connects the tile array (through the tile in the upper-left) to off-chip logic (chipset). The chipset may be implemented on an FPGA, ASIC, or integrated on an OpenPiton chip. The chip bridge extends the three NoCs off-chip, multiplexing them over a single link.

The extension of NoCs off-chip allows the seamless connection of multiple OpenPiton chips to create a larger system, as illustrated in Figure 1. The cache-coherence protocol extends off-chip as well, enabling shared-memory across multiple chips. A core in one chip may be cache coherent with cores in another chip. This enables the study of even larger shared-memory manycore systems.

2.1 Tile

The architecture of a tile is shown in Figure 2a. A tile consists of a modified OpenSPARC T1 [58] core, an L1.5 cache, an L2 cache, a floating-point unit (FPU), a CCX arbiter, and three NoC routers.

The L2 and L1.5 caches connect directly to all three NoC routers and all messages entering and leaving the tile traverse these interfaces. The CPU Cache-Crossbar (CCX) is the crossbar interface used in the OpenSPARC T1 to connect the cores, L2 cache, FPU, I/O, etc. [6]. The L1.5 is responsible for transducing between CCX and the NoC router protocol. The CCX arbiter de-multiplexes memory and floating-point requests from the core to the L1.5 cache and FPU, respectively, and arbitrates responses back to the core.

2.2 Core

OpenPiton uses the OpenSPARC T1 [58] core with minimal modifications. This core was chosen because of its industry-hardened design, multi-threaded capability, simplicity, and modest silicon area requirements. Equally important, the OpenSPARC framework has a stable code base, implements a mature ISA with compiler and OS support, and comes with a large test suite.

In the taped out OpenPiton core, the default configuration for OpenPiton, the number of threads is reduced from four to two. This was primarily done to reduce the area requirement of the core and to reduce the pressure on the memory system. By default, the stream processing unit (SPU), essentially a cryptographic functional unit, is also removed from the core to save area. Instructions intending to utilize the SPU will trigger a trap and are emulated in software. The default TLB size is 16 entries to reduce area (which reflects the reduction in the number of threads), but it can be increased to 64 or decreased down to 8 entries.

Additional configuration registers were added to enable extensibility within the core. They are implemented as memory-mapped registers in an alternate address space (one way to implement CPU control registers in SPARC). These configuration registers can be useful for adding additional functionality to the core which can be configured from software, e.g. enabling/disabling functionality, configuring different modes of operation, etc.

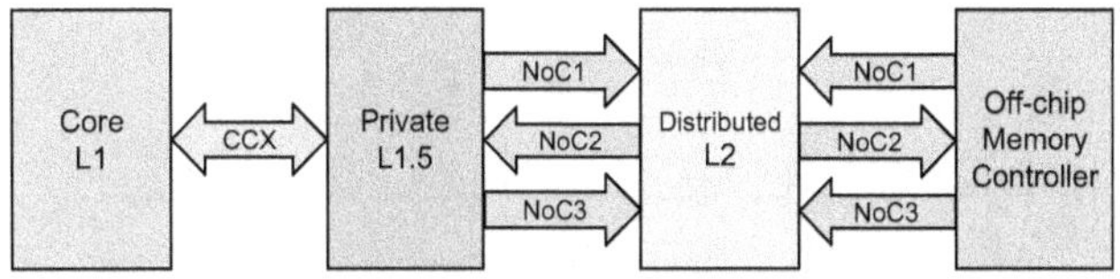

Figure 3: OpenPiton's memory hierarchy datapath.

Many of the modifications to the OpenSPARC T1 core, like the ones above, have been made in a configurable way. Thus, it is possible to configure the core to the original OpenSPARC T1 specifications or a set of parameters different from the original OpenSPARC T1 as is the default OpenPiton core. More details on configurability are discussed in Section 3.1.

2.3 Cache Hierarchy

OpenPiton's cache hierarchy is composed of three cache levels, with private L1 and L1.5 caches and a distributed, shared L2 cache. Each tile in OpenPiton contains an instance of the L1 cache, L1.5 cache, and L2 cache. The data path through the cache hierarchy is shown in Figure 3.

2.3.1 L1 Cache

The L1 cache is reused, with minimal modifications, from the OpenSPARC T1 design. It is tightly integrated to the OpenSPARC T1 pipeline, and composed of two separate caches: the L1 data cache and L1 instruction cache. The L1 data cache is an 8KB write-through cache; it is 4-way set-associative and the line size is 16-bytes. The 16KB L1 instruction cache is similarly 4-way set associative but with a 32-byte line size. Both L1 caches' sizes can be configured, as detailed in Section 3.1.2.

There are two issues with the original OpenSPARC T1 L1 cache design which made it suboptimal for use in a scalable multicore and hence required changes in OpenPiton. First, write-through caches require extremely high write-bandwidth to the next cache level, which is likely to overwhelm and congest NoCs in manycore processors with distributed caches. This necessitates a local write-back cache. Second, the cache communication interface needs to be compliant with OpenPiton's cache coherence protocol, i.e., tracking MESI cache line states, honoring remote invalidations, and communicating through OpenPiton's NoCs instead of the OpenSPARC T1's crossbar. Rather than modifying the existing RTL for the L1s, we introduced an extra cache level (L1.5) to tackle both issues.

2.3.2 L1.5 Data Cache

The L1.5 serves as both the glue logic, transducing the OpenSPARC T1's crossbar protocol to OpenPiton's NoC

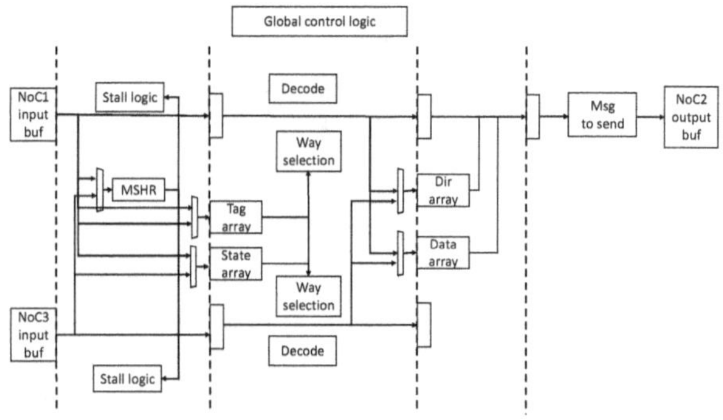

Figure 4: The architecture of the L2 cache.

coherence packet formats, and a write-back layer, caching stores from the write-through L1 data cache. It is an 8KB 4-way set associative write-back cache (the same size as the L1 data cache by default) with configurable associativity and size. The line size is the same as the L1 data cache at 16-bytes.

The L1.5 communicates requests and responses to and from the core through CCX. The CCX bus is preserved as the primary interface to the OpenSPARC T1. The L1.5 CCX interface could relatively easily be replaced with other interfaces like AMBA or AXI to accommodate different cores. When a memory request results in a miss, the L1.5 translates and forwards request to the L2 through the network-on-chip (NoC) channels. Generally, the L1.5 issues requests on NoC1, receives data on NoC2, and writes back modified cache lines on NoC3, as shown in Figure 3.

While the L1.5 was named as such during the development of the Piton ASIC prototype, in traditional computer architecture contexts it would be appropriate to call it the "private L2" and to call the next level cache the "shared/distributed L3". The L1.5 is inclusive of the L1 data cache; each can be independently sized with independent eviction policies. As a space- and performance-conscious optimization, the L1.5 does not cache instructions–these cache lines are bypassed directly between the L1 instruction cache and the L2. It is possible to modify the L1.5 to also cache instructions.

2.3.3 L2 Cache

The L2 cache is a distributed write-back cache shared by all tiles. The default cache configuration is 64KB per tile and 4-way set associativity, but both the cache size and associativity are configurable. The cache line size is 64 bytes, larger than caches lower in the hierarchy. The integrated directory cache has 64 bits per entry, so it can precisely keep track of up to 64 sharers by default.

The L2 cache is inclusive of the private caches (L1 and L1.5). Cache line way mapping between the L1.5 and the L2 is independent and is entirely subject to the replacement policy of each cache. In fact, since the L2 is distributed, cache lines consecutively mapped in the L1.5 are likely to be strewn across multiple L2 tiles (L2 tile referring to a portion of the distributed L2 cache in a single tile). By default, OpenPiton maps cache lines using constant strides with the lower address bits across all L2 tiles, but Coherence Domain Restriction (CDR) [30], an experimental research feature integrated into OpenPiton, can be used to interleave cache lines belonging to a single application or page across a software-specified set of L2 tiles.

As shown in Figure 4, the L2 cache is designed with dual parallel pipelines. The first pipeline (top) receives cache miss request packets from lower in the cache hierarchy on NoC1 and sends memory request packets to off-chip DRAM and cache fill response packets to lower in the cache hierarchy on NoC2. The second pipeline (bottom) receives memory response packets from off-chip DRAM and modified cache line writeback packets from lower in the cache hierarchy on NoC3. The first L2 pipeline contains 4 stages and the second pipeline contains only 3 stages since it does not transmit output packets. The interaction between the L2 and the three NoCs is also depicted in Figure 3.

2.4 Cache Coherence and Memory Consistency Model

The memory subsystem maintains cache coherence with a directory-based MESI coherence protocol. It adheres to the TSO memory consistency model used by the OpenSPARC T1. Coherent messages between L1.5 caches and L2 caches communicate through three NoCs, carefully designed to ensure deadlock-free operation.

The L2 is the point of coherence for all memory requests, except for non-cacheable loads and stores which directly bypass the L2 cache. All other memory operations (including atomic operations such as compare-and-swap) are ordered and the L2 strictly follows this order when servicing requests.

The L2 also keeps the instruction and data caches coherent. Per the OpenSPARC T1's original design, coherence between the two L1 caches is maintained at the L2. When a line is present in a core's L1 instruction cache and is loaded as data, the L2 will send invalidations to the relevant instruction caches before servicing the load.

High-level features of the coherence protocol include:

- 4-step message communication
- Silent eviction in Exclusive and Shared states
- No acknowledgments for dirty write-backs
- Three 64-bit physical NoCs with point-to-point ordering
- Co-location of L2 cache and coherence directory

2.5 Interconnect

There are two major interconnection types used in OpenPiton, the NoCs and the chip bridge.

2.5.1 Network On-chip (NoC)

There are three NoCs in an OpenPiton chip. The NoCs connect tiles in a 2D mesh topology. The main purpose of the NoCs is to provide communication between the tiles for cache coherence, I/O and memory traffic, and inter-core interrupts. They also route traffic destined for off-chip to the chip bridge. The NoCs maintain point-to-point ordering between a single source and destination, a feature often leveraged to maintain TSO consistency. In a multi-chip configuration, OpenPiton uses similar configurable NoC routers to route traffic between chips.

The three NoCs are physical networks (no virtual channels) and each consists of two 64-bit uni-directional links, one in each direction. The links use credit-based flow control. Packets are routed using dimension-ordered wormhole routing to ensure a deadlock-free network. The packet format preserves 29 bits of core addressability, making it scalable up to 500 million cores.

To ensure deadlock-free operation, the L1.5 cache, L2 cache, and memory controller give different priorities to different NoC channels; NoC3 has the highest priority, next is NoC2, and NoC1 has the lowest priority. Thus, NoC3 will never be blocked. In addition, all hardware components are designed such that consuming a high priority packet is never dependent on lower priority traffic. While the cache coherence protocol is designed to be logically deadlock free, it also depends on the physical layer and routing to also be deadlock free.

Classes of coherence operations are mapped to NoCs based on the following rules, as depicted in Figure 3:

- NoC1 messages are initiated by requests from the private cache (L1.5) to the shared cache (L2).
- NoC2 messages are initiated by the shared cache (L2) to the private cache (L1.5) or memory controller.
- NoC3 messages are responses from the private cache (L1.5) or memory controller to the shared cache (L2).

2.5.2 Chip Bridge

The chip bridge connects the tile array to the chipset, through the upper-left tile, as shown in Figure 1. All memory and I/O requests are directed through this interface to be served by the chipset. Its main purpose is to transparently multiplex the three physical NoCs over a single, narrower link in pin-limited chip implementations.

The chip bridge contains asynchronous buffers to bridge between I/O and core clock domains. It implements three virtual off-chip channels over a single off-chip physical channel, providing the necessary buffering and arbitration logic. The off-chip channel contains two 32-bit unidirectional links, one in each direction, and uses credit-based flow control. At 350MHz, Piton's target I/O frequency, the chip bridge provides a total bandwidth of 2.8GB/s.

2.6 Chipset

The chipset, shown in Figure 2b, houses the I/O, DRAM controllers, chip bridge, traffic splitter, and inter-chip network routers. The chip bridge brings traffic from the attached chip into the chipset and de-multiplexes it back into the three physical NoCs. The traffic is passed to the inter-chip network routers, which routes it to the traffic splitter if it is destined for this chipset. The traffic splitter multiplexes requests to the DRAM controller or I/O devices, based on the address of the request, to be serviced. If the traffic is not destined for this chipset, it is routed to another chipset according to the inter-chip routing protocol. Traffic destined for the attached chip is directed back through similar paths to the chip bridge.

2.6.1 Inter-chip Routing

The inter-chip network router is configurable in terms of router degree, routing algorithm, buffer size, etc. This enables flexible exploration of different router configurations and network topologies. Currently, we have implemented and verified crossbar, 2D mesh, 3D mesh, and butterfly networks. Customized topologies can be explored by re-configuring the network routers.

We have proven that our network routing protocols can safely extend and be further routed (under some constraints) off chip while maintaining their deadlock-free nature.

2.7 Floating-point Unit

We utilize the FPU from OpenSPARC T1 [58]. In OpenPiton, there is a one-to-one relationship between cores and FPUs, in contrast to the OpenSPARC T1, which shares one FPU among eight cores [6]. This was primarily done to boost floating-point performance and to avoid the complexities of having shared FPUs among a variable number of tiles. The CCX arbiter always prioritizes the L1.5 over the FPU in arbitration over the shared CCX interface into the core.

3. Platform Features

This section discusses the flagship features of OpenPiton that make it a compelling platform for doing manycore research.

3.1 Configurability

OpenPiton was designed to be a configurable platform, making it useful for many applications. Table 1 shows OpenPiton's configurability options, highlighting the large design space that it offers.

3.1.1 PyHP for Verilog

In order to provide low effort configurability of our Verilog RTL, we make use of a Python pre-processor, the Python Hypertext Processor (PyHP) [63]. PyHP was originally designed for Python dynamic webpage generation and is akin to PHP. We have adapted it for use with Verilog code. Parameters can be passed into PyHP and arbitrary Python code

Component	Configurability Options
Cores (per chip)	Up to 65,536
Cores (per system)	Up to 500 million
Threads per Core	1/2/4
TLBs	8/16/32/64 entries
L1 I-Cache	16/32KB
L1 D-Cache	8/16KB
Floating-Point Unit	Present/Absent
Stream-Processing Unit	Present/Absent
L1.5 Cache	Number of Sets, Ways
L2 Cache	Number of Sets, Ways
Intra-chip Topologies	2D Mesh, Crossbar
Inter-chip Topologies	2D Mesh, 3D Mesh, Crossbar, Butterfly Network
Bootloading	SD Card, UART

Table 1: Supported OpenPiton Configuration Options

can be used to generate testbenches or modules. PyHP enables extensive configurability beyond what is possible with Verilog generate statements alone. The motivation for using PyHP came from the inability to view the intermediate code after pre-processing Verilog generate statements, which made debugging difficult.

3.1.2 Core Configurability

As mentioned previously, the cores at the heart of OpenPiton are two-way threaded by default with an FPU per tile. OpenPiton preserves the OpenSPARC T1's ability to modify TLB sizes, thread counts, and the presence or absence of the FPU and SPU. As shown in Table 1, OpenPiton offers the option to select from 1 to 4 hardware threads, vary the TLB between 8 and 64 entries (in powers of two), and choose whether or not to include an FPU, an SPU, or both in each tile. Additionally, the L1 data and instruction caches can be doubled in size. Future support will include configuration of the L1 caches' associativity.

3.1.3 Cache Configurability

Leveraging PyHP, OpenPiton provides parameterizable generic flop-based memories for simulation in addition to the infrastructure for using custom or proprietary SRAMs. This enables the configurability of cache parameters. The associativity and size of the L1.5 and L2 caches are configurable, though the line size remains static. OpenPiton also includes scripts which automate the generation of correctly sized RAMs necessary for FPGA implementations, providing a push-button approach to FPGA implementation.

3.1.4 Manycore Scalability

PyHP also enables the creation of scalable meshes of cores, drastically reducing the code size and complexity in some areas adopted from the original OpenSPARC T1. OpenPiton automatically generates all core instances and wires for connecting them from a single template instance. This reduces code complexity, improves readability, saves time when modifying the design, and makes the creation of large meshes straightforward. The creation of large two-dimensional mesh interconnects of up to 256x256 tiles is reduced to a single instantiation. The mesh can be any rectangular configuration and the dimensions do not need to be powers of two. This was a necessary feature for our 5x5 (25-core) tape-out.

3.1.5 NoC Topology Configurability

Two-dimensional mesh is not the only possible NoC connection topology for OpenPiton. The coherence protocol only requires that messages are delivered in-order from one point to another point. Since there are no inter-node ordering requirements, the NoC can easily be swapped out for a crossbar, higher dimension router, or higher radix design. Currently, OpenPiton can be configured with a crossbar, which has been tested with four and eight cores with no test regressions. Other NoC research prototypes can easily be integrated and their performance, energy, and other characteristics can be determined through RTL or gate-level simulation, or by FPGA emulation.

3.1.6 Multi-chip Scalability

Similar to the on-chip mesh, PyHP enables the generation of a network of chips starting with the instantiation of a single chip. OpenPiton provides an address space for up to 8192 chips, with 65,536 cores per chip. In conjunction with the scalable cache coherence mechanism built into OpenPiton, half-billion core systems can be built. This configurability enables the building of large systems to test ideas at scale.

3.1.7 Case Study: PicoPiton

To demonstrate the elasticity of OpenPiton's design space, we created a minimized configuration called PicoPiton, which fits on a Digilent Nexys 4 DDR board. Currently, this board costs only $160 (US) for academic purchase, making it an ideal solution for low-cost academic prototyping with OpenPiton. The small area of this board required size reductions for many structures. The final version of PicoPiton is single threaded with no FPU, SPU, or chip bridge, 8 TLB entries and a 32KB L2 cache. PicoPiton is able to reach a clock frequency of 29.5MHz and is shown in Figure 5 executing "Hello, world!" over a serial connection.

3.2 Extensibility

One of the most prominent design goals for OpenPiton was to create a framework which could easily be extended. This enables rapid prototyping of research ideas backed by infrastructure for validation, characterization, and implementation. This section discusses some of the ways in which OpenPiton is extensible and presents case studies demonstrating how OpenPiton has already been used in research.

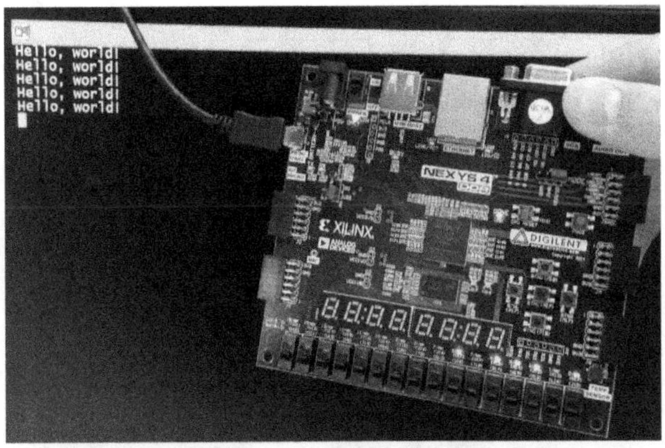

Figure 5: PicoPiton printing Hello World to UART.

3.2.1 Core Replacement

Given their importance [28, 41], support for heterogeneous systems architectures in OpenPiton is compelling. Future plans for OpenPiton include building a heterogeneous mesh of cores and accelerators connected to OpenPiton's NoC and memory system. Integrating an OpenSPARC T2 core would be straightforward as it uses a similar CCX crossbar interface. With the removal of the CCX arbiter, the L1.5 could likely communicate with any other TSO-compliant core. If the core's L1 cache were a write-back cache, a simple transducer could potentially replace the L1.5 cache entirely.

3.2.2 Accelerators

Accelerators can be easily connected to the NoC thereby enabling integration into the cache coherence protocol. As OpenPiton's coherence protocol is open source and documented, this provides a unique opportunity for accelerator researchers. Accelerators which participate in the coherence protocol can work cooperatively and in parallel with other accelerators or general purpose cores, utilizing OpenPiton's modern NoC based architecture and cache-coherence protocol. OpenPiton enables this type of research at scale, only possible previously through high-level simulation.

3.2.3 AXI-Lite Bridge

OpenPiton includes an AXI4-Lite bridge that provides connectivity to a wide range of I/O devices by interfacing memory mapped I/O operations from the NoCs to AXI-Lite. Given OpenPiton prototypes make use of Xilinx FPGAs, Xilinx-provided intellectual property (IP) cores compatible with AXI and AXI-Lite interfaces can be seamlessly integrated with OpenPiton. The Xilinx UART IP core, which uses the AXI-Lite interface, has been successfully integrated into the OpenPiton FPGA prototypes through memory mapped I/O. By using a standard interface like AXI, many I/O devices can be interfaced with OpenPiton and existing drivers can be reused.

3.2.4 Case Studies

Several case studies demonstrate how the OpenPiton platform has thus far been used to enable research.

Execution Drafting Execution Drafting [46] (ExecD) is an energy saving microarchitectural technique for multithreaded processors which leverages duplicate computation. ExecD is a more ad-hoc case study, as it required modification to the OpenSPARC T1 core. Therefore, it was not as simple as plugging a standalone module into the OpenPiton system. Instead the core microarchitecture needed to be understood and the implementation tightly integrated with the core. However, the integration of ExecD into OpenPiton revealed several implementation details that had been abstracted away in simulation, such as tricky divergence conditions in the thread synchronization mechanisms. This reiterates the importance of taking designs to implementation in an infrastructure like OpenPiton.

ExecD takes over the thread selection decision from the OpenSPARC T1 thread selection policy and instruments the front-end to achieve energy savings. ExecD is a good example of the addition of configuration registers in OpenPiton. It utilizes some of the configuration register address space to set whether ExecD is enabled, which thread synchronization method is used, etc.

Coherence Domain Restriction Coherence Domain Restriction [30] (CDR) is a novel cache coherence framework designed to enable large scale shared memory with low storage and energy overhead. CDR restricts cache coherence of an application or page to a subset of cores, rather than keeping global coherence over potentially millions of cores. In order to implement it in OpenPiton, the TLB is extended with extra fields and both the L1.5 and L2 cache are modified to fit CDR into the existing cache coherence protocol. CDR is specifically designed for large scale shared memory systems such as OpenPiton. In fact, OpenPiton's million-core scalability is not feasible without CDR because of increasing directory storage overhead.

Oblivious RAM Oblivious RAM (ORAM)[29, 32, 75] is a memory controller designed to eliminate memory side channels. An ORAM controller was integrated into the 25-core Piton ASIC, providing the opportunity for secure access to off-chip DRAM. The controller was directly connected to OpenPiton's NoC, making the integration straightforward. It only required a handful of files to wrap an existing ORAM implementation.

3.3 Platform Stability

One of the benefits of OpenPiton is its stability, maturity, and active support. Much of this is inherited from using the OpenSPARC T1 core, which has a stable code base and has been studied for years allowing the code to be reviewed and bugs fixed by many people. In addition, it implements a mature, commercial ISA, SPARC V9. This means that there is existing full tool chain support for OpenPiton, including Debian Linux OS support, a compiler, and an assembler. SPARC is an actively supported platform, with a number of supported OSs and Oracle recently releasing Linux for SPARC in late 2015[1]. Porting the OpenSPARC T1 hypervisor required changes to fewer than 10 instructions, and a newer Debian Linux distribution was modified with readily available, open source, OpenSPARC T1-specific patches written as part of Lockbox[15, 20].

Another feature inherited from using the OpenSPARC T1 core is the large test suite. This includes tests for not only the core, but the memory system, I/O, cache coherence protocol, etc. When making research modifications to OpenPiton, this allows the researcher to rely on an established test-suite to ensure that their modifications did not introduce any regressions. In addition, the OpenPiton documentation details how to add new tests to validate modifications and extend the existing test suite.

OpenPiton provides additional stability on top of what is inherited from OpenSPARC T1. The tool flow was updated to modern tools and ported to modern Xilinx FPGAs. OpenPiton is also used extensively for research internally. This means there is active support for OpenPiton and the code is constantly being improved and optimized. In addition, the open sourcing of OpenPiton will strengthen its stability as a community is built around it.

3.4 Validation

OpenPiton features more than 8000 directed assembly tests for testing not only core functionality, but that of the extensions like ExecD (Section 3.2.4). Validation is done through a mix of assembly tests, randomized assembly test generators, and tests written in C. Scripts are provided that run large regressions in parallel with the SLURM job scheduler and automatically produce pass/fail reports, coverage reports, and even run chip synthesis to verify that synthesis-safe Verilog has been used.

3.4.1 Randomized Testing

The OpenPiton test suite contains a number of randomized assembly test generators written in Perl, known as "PAL" files. These tests have a number of parameters and can be seeded to generate as many test instances as are desired. 2100 of the core OpenPiton tests make use of these PAL test generators, handling behaviors covering memory, branches, ALU, FPU, thread scheduling, and more.

3.4.2 C Tests

While the OpenPiton validation methodology focuses primarily on directed and randomized assembly tests, the infrastructure also supports the use of tests written in C. We have written a small stable of C tests akin to microbenchmarks which can perform any standard C functions (including console I/O but excluding file I/O) and link against static libraries.

[1] Linux for SPARC is hosted at `https://oss.oracle.com/projects/linux-sparc/`

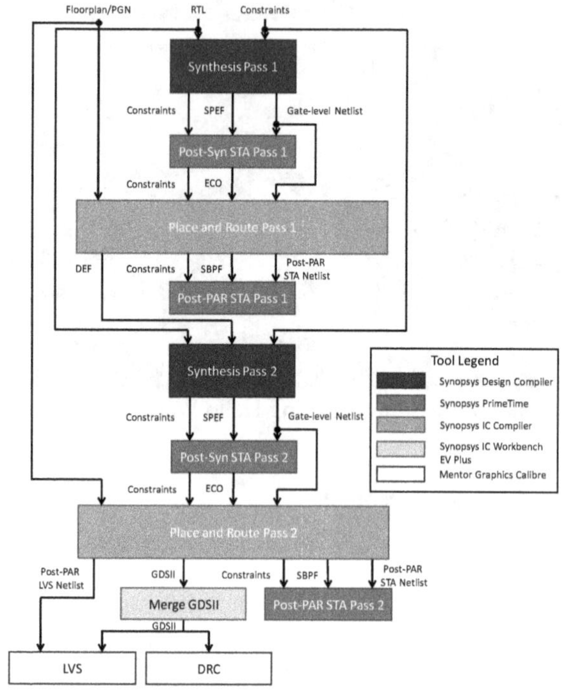

Figure 6: Synthesis and back-end tool flow.

3.4.3 Coverage Reports

In order to gain an understanding of how effective the testing regime is at a given time and to best focus testing efforts, coverage reports are automatically generated alongside the results of a regression. These reports include coverage breakdowns per module and per module instantiation and include line, toggle, condition, branch and finite state machine coverage.

3.5 Synthesis and Back-end Support

OpenPiton provides scripts to aid in synthesis and back-end for generating realistic area results or for taping-out new designs based on OpenPiton. The scripts are identical to the ones used to tape-out the Piton ASIC prototype, however references to the specific technology used have been removed due to proprietary foundry IP concerns and the scripts have been made process agnostic. Directions are included with OpenPiton which describe how to port to a new foundry kit. This allows the user to download OpenPiton, link to the necessary process development kit files, and run the full tool flow to tape-out a specific instance of OpenPiton. In this sense, OpenPiton is portable across process technologies and provides a complete ecosystem to implement, test, prototype, and tape-out research.

The tool flow provided with OpenPiton is shown in Figure 6 and is mainly a Synopsys tool flow. The figure shows a two-pass flow, however the number of passes is configurable. Increasing the number of passes improves the quality of results, but with diminishing returns. The Verilog RTL along with design constraints are first passed to Synopsys Design Compiler, which synthesizes a gate-level netlist from the behavioral RTL. The resulting netlist, along with the constraints, are passed to Synopsys PrimeTime to perform post-synthesis static timing analysis (STA). This analyzes the gate-level netlist against the constraints specified and reports the results. If the constraints are not met, Synopsys PrimeTime may output an engineering change order (ECO) file, which suggests modifications to the netlist to meet the constraints.

The gate-level netlist, constraints, ECO file, and physical floorplan (specified by the user) are passed to Synopsys IC Compiler to perform placement and routing (PAR). However, before PAR, the ECO modifications are applied to the gate-level netlist to give Synopsys IC Compiler a better chance of meeting the constraints. After PAR is complete, the post-PAR netlist is again passed to Synopsys PrimeTime, along with the constraints, to perform STA and check the design against the constraints. Although not shown in the figure, Synopsys PrimeTime may output an ECO file again, which can be fed back into Synopsys IC compiler, along with the post-PAR netlist and physical layout library to apply the ECO. We have found the ECOs from PrimeTime to be very useful in meeting timing.

The output of this flow is a fully placed and routed design in GDSII format. If it meets the constraints, design rule checking (DRC) and layout versus schematic checking (LVS) are performed. However, it is likely the constraints may not be met after the first pass. In this case, results can be improved by performing the same flow up to this point a second time, while passing physical information from the output of the first IC Compiler pass and the ECO from the output of PrimeTime. Any number of passes through this flow is possible, but we saw diminishing returns after two passes. If constraints are still not met, it may be the case that the constraints and/or floorplan must be modified.

After a GDSII of the design that meets the constraints is obtained, it must be merged with the GDSII of any third-party IP to generate the final GDSII. This is done with the Synopsys IC Workbench EV Plus tool. After the final merged GDSII is generated, it is passed to Mentor Graphics Calibre for LVS and DRC checking. DRC requires the GDSII and the DRC deck from the process development kit. LVS only requires the GDSII and the post-PAR gate-level netlist.

A final consideration for synthesis and back-end flow is what to use for the input RTL. If one were to give the full OpenPiton RTL as input to synthesis, the flow would take an unreasonable amount of time and may not even complete successfully. For this reason, the design is generally broken down into hierarchical blocks. The leaf blocks are run through the flow first, and imported as black-boxes in

Figure 7: Two Virtex 6 (ML605) boards connected by the chip bridge.

Board	Frequency (1 Core)	Cores
Xilinx VC707 (Virtex-7)	67MHz	4
Digilent Genesys 2 (Kintex-7)	60MHz	2
Digilent Nexys 4 DDR (Artix-7)	29MHz	1
Xilinx ML605 (Virtex-6)	18MHz	2

Table 2: FPGA Boards Currently Supported by OpenPiton

the flow for modules higher in the hierarchy. This is done until the top-level chip is reached. Since the hierarchy may depend on process technology, design modifications, etc. the OpenPiton synthesis and back-end scripts make it easy to modify and define new module hierarchies.

3.5.1 Gate-level Simulation

Gate-level simulation provides more accurate results than behavioral simulation because it is based on post-synthesis netlists and can account for delays through standard cells. OpenPiton extends the gate-level simulation framework from the OpenSPARC T1 and is capable of simulating the entire chip or any sub-modules. Since timing information is available from the standard cells, gate-level simulation is able to check for potential timing violations in the design. The gate-level simulation results can also be compared against the behavioral simulation outputs for functional verification or fed into PrimeTime PX to estimate power consumption. Gate-level power estimation is valuable, as it provides more accurate power estimates than tools that rely on modeling in software simulations.

3.6 Prototyping

This section discusses the prototype implementations of specific OpenPiton instances, which validate it as a viable, modern, and competitive platform.

Figure 8: OpenPiton running on a Xilinx VC707 board executing Tetris on full-stack multiuser Debian Linux

3.6.1 FPGA Prototypes

OpenPiton has been successfully ported to the Virtex-6 (ML605 Evaluation Board), Artix-7 (Digilent Nexys 4 DDR), Kintex-7 (Digilent Genesys 2) and Virtex-7 (VC707 Evaluation Board) Xilinx FPGA platforms, as shown in Table 2, to prototype the design and provide improved test throughput. These prototypes validate the full spectrum of OpenPiton's configurability, from the PicoPiton Artix-7 design at the low-end intended for very small prototypes, to the Virtex-7, which is large enough to fit four OpenPiton cores.

The Virtex and Kintex designs have the same features as the ASIC prototype, validating the feasibility of that particular design (multicore functionality, etc.), and can even include the chip bridge to connect multiple FPGAs via a FPGA Mezzanine Card (FMC) link, as shown in Figure 7. All of the FPGA prototypes feature the NoC to DDR transducer, located on an external FPGA for Piton.

After verifying the functionality of the NoC to AXI-Lite bridge in simulation, it took just a few hours to integrate a serial port and run the first I/O-based "Hello, world!" test on PicoPiton as shown in Figure 5. We expect users of the OpenPiton FPGA prototypes to achieve a similarly quick turnaround from initial Verilog implementation to getting results at speeds far surpassing behavioral simulation.

OpenPiton on the Virtex and Kintex boards can load baremetal programs over a serial port and can boot full stack multiuser Debian Linux from an SD or MicroSD card, depicted in Figure 8 running Tetris. Booting Debian on the VC707 board running at 67MHz takes about 12 minutes, compared to 45 minutes for the original OpenSPARC T1, which relied on a tethered MicroBlaze for its memory and I/O requests. This improvement combined with the move to Xilinx's Vivado Suite for FPGA synthesis and implementation drastically increased productivity when testing operating system or hardware modifications.

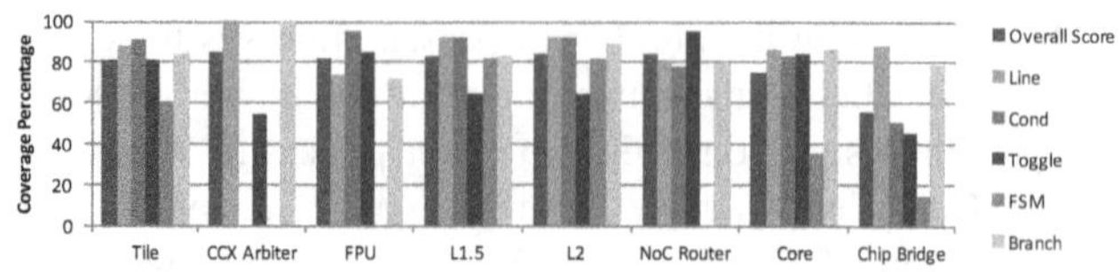

Figure 9: Test suite coverage results by module (default OpenPiton configuration).

3.6.2 ASIC Prototype

The Piton ASIC prototype was taped out in March 2015 on IBM's 32nm SOI process with a target clock frequency of 1GHz. It features 25 tiles in a 5x5 mesh on a 6mm x 6mm ($36mm^2$) die. Each tile is two-way threaded including ExecD and CDR, while ORAM was included at the chip level. The ASIC provides validation of OpenPiton as a research platform and shows that ideas can be taken from inception to silicon with OpenPiton.

4. Results

This section provides experimental results from OpenPiton simulation and prototyping.

4.1 Simulation

Verilog simulation in OpenPiton utilizes Synopsys VCS, though there are plans to expand to other Verilog simulators in the future. OpenPiton Verilog simulation runs at 4.85 kilo-instructions per second (KIPS) per tile with Synopsys VCS on a 2.4GHz Intel Westmere Xeon E7-4870 processor. While simulation speed varies with tile count, test stimuli, etc., this value is obtained from averaging across the OpenPiton test suite, which includes various numbers of cores and instruction mixes, and is normalized to a single tile. While the simulation speed may seem slow compared to many architectural simulators, it is a very detailed RTL simulation. In addition, the ability to synthesize OpenPiton to an FPGA makes up for this shortcoming.

Another important metric of OpenPiton is the design coverage resulting from executing the full test suite. This provides an idea of how well the test suite exercises the design. In addition, running coverage after making modifications can give insight into how well the modifications are tested. Figure 9 shows the different types of coverage (line, condition, toggle, FSM, branch) resulting from running the full OpenPiton test suite for all major architectural blocks.

Each architectural block includes the coverage of all blocks beneath it in the module hierarchy. For example, the tile coverage results include the weighted average of coverage results from the CCX arbiter, FPU, L1.5, L2, NoC router, and OpenSPARC T1 core. The missing bars in the figure are not due to zero coverage, but due to the coverage tool's inability to identify that type of coverage for that particular

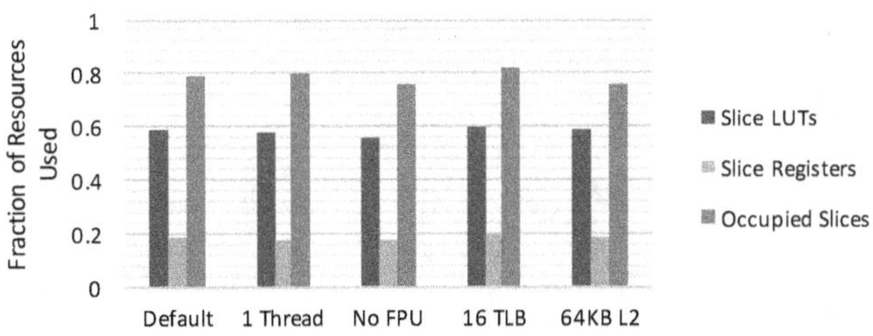

Figure 10: Virtex 6 area comparison for different configurations.

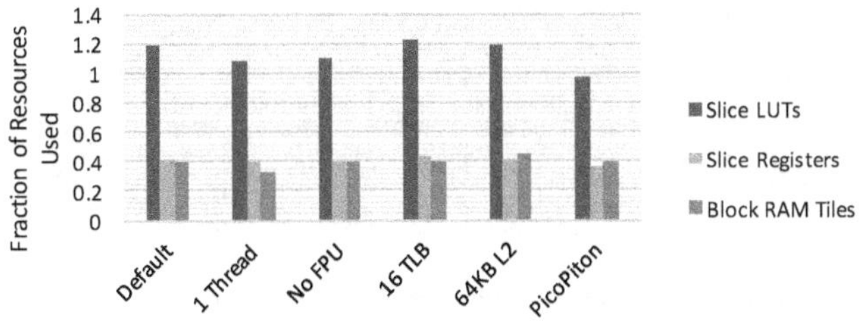

Figure 11: Artix 7 area comparison for different configurations.

design. For example, the CCX arbiter does not have a bar for condition coverage, as there are no complex conditional statements in that design. The interconnections also see low coverage as some paths are not thoroughly used (e.g. the chip bridge sees little NOC1 traffic and NOC2/NOC3 traffic is largely unidirectional when cross-chip sharing is minimal). Overall, the coverage is good, which demonstrates that the OpenPiton test suite does a good job of exercising the OpenPiton design.

4.2 Prototyping

Our FPGA prototyping efforts have so far resulted in prototypes for four different Xilinx boards: Virtex 6 (ML605), Artix 7 (Nexys 4 DDR), Kintex 7 (Genesys 2), and Virtex 7 (VC707). These prototypes are capable of achieving clock frequencies of 18MHz, 29.5MHz, 60MHz, and 67MHz respectively, as summarized in Table 2.

The default configuration discussed here has two threads, 8 entry TLBs, 8KB L1D, 16KB L1I, 8KB L1.5, 32KB L2, and the FPU included. The area breakdowns for the default configuration on each board are listed in Table 3. Note that the default configuration is too large for the Artix 7 and had to be pared down to fit. Figures 10 and 11 show the resource utilization for different configuration options on the Virtex 6 (post-place and route) and Artix 7 (post-synthesis) FPGAs, as a proportion of the available resources on each FPGA. These figures indicate the rough cost of modifying a particular configuration value, but have some counter-intuitive results. For example, increasing the L2 to 64KB on the Virtex 6 causes Xilinx ISE to better map the design to included BRAM, thus decreasing the amount of area used.

	Slice LUTs	Slice Regs	Occupied Slices
Virtex 6 240T	88,682	56,141	29,691
(Available)	150,720	301,440	37,680
	Slice LUTs	Slice Regs	Block RAM Tiles
Artix 7 100T	75,253	52,993	53
(Available)	63,400	126,800	135
	Slice LUTs	Slice Regs	Block RAM Tiles
Kintex 7 325T	68,976	50403	54
(Available)	203,800	407,600	445
	Slice LUTs	Slice Regs	Block RAM Tiles
Virtex 7 485T	68,303	51,084	23
(Available)	303,600	607,200	1,030

Table 3: Default resource utilization vs available resources for each FPGA.

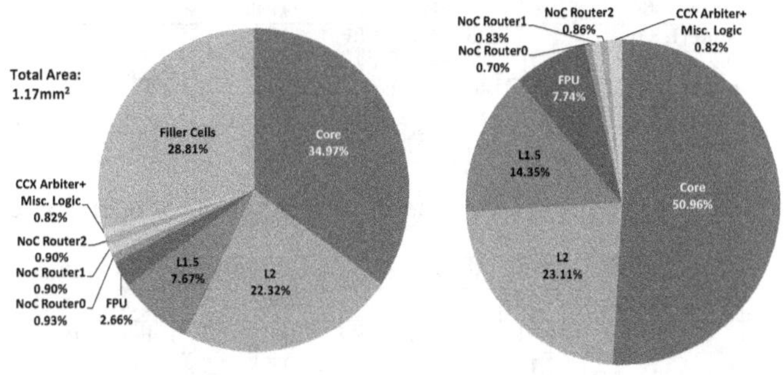

(a) ASIC Piton (b) FPGA PicoPiton

Figure 12: Tile area breakdown.

Submodule	SYN	PAR	STA	ECO	DRC	LVS	Total
NoC Router	0.32	2.35	0.02	N/A	0.04	0.04	2.80
L1.5	0.40	15.45	0.05	3.55	0.24	0.12	34.18
Core	1.16	36.82	0.19	3.51	1.09	0.32	78.04
Tile	1.11	22.95	0.12	2.69	2.10	0.49	55.89
Chip	4.20	79.19	0.67	11.36	9.04	0.93	104.91

Table 5: Time durations (in hours) of selected synthesis and back-end stages for selected submodules. If any stage executes more than once (STA or for multi-pass flow), the maximum duration is shown.

The area breakdown of a default single tile on Artix 7 is shown in Figure 12b. This breakdown is based on Xilinx Vivado "cells", rather than LUT or BRAM utilization.

4.3 ASIC Prototype

The Piton ASIC prototype was taped-out on the IBM 32nm SOI process with a target clock frequency of 1GHz. The area breakdown of a single tile is shown in Figure 12a. The total tile area is 1.17mm^2 with about 30% of the area taken up by filler cells. Space was overprovisioned by about 30% (70% utilization) in floorplanning stages to give PAR a better chance of meeting the constraints. This space was filled with filler cells after the design was successfully PARed.

Measuring with a 2.4GHz Intel Westmere machine, the synthesis and back-end scripts take 78 hours (3.25 days), 56 hours (2.3 days), and 104 hours (4.3 days) to run the full tool flow for the core, the tile, and the whole chip with

Processor	Architecture	Performance	FPU	OS	MMU	HW Multithreaded	Multicore/ Manycore/GPU	Prototype Core Count	NoC	HDL	Back-end Scripts	License	Last Update
pAVR [57]	8b AVR	Low	✗	✗	✗	✗	No	-	✗	VHDL	✗	GPL v2	Mar 2009
openMSP430 [36, 55]	16bMSP430	Low	✗	✗	✗	✗	No	-	✗	Verilog	✗	BSD	Jul 2015
CPU86 [34]	16b x86	Low	✗	✓	✗	✗	No	-	✗	VHDL	✗	GPL	Jun 2014
Zet [4]	16b x86	Low	✗	✓	✗	✗	No	-	✗	Verilog	✗	GPL v3	Nov 2013
LatticeMico32 [71]	32b LatticeMico32	Low	✗	✓	✗	✗	No	-	✗	Verilog	✗	GPL	Oct 2015
ZPU [5]	32b MIPS	Low	✗	✓	✗	✗	No	-	✗	VHDL	✗	FreeBSD & GPL	Apr 2015
SecretBlaze [11]	32b MicroBlaze	Low	✗	✗	✗	✗	No	-	✗	VHDL	✗	GPL v3	Dec 2012
AltOr32 [53]	32b ORBIS	Low	✗	✓	✗	✗	No	-	✗	Verilog	✗	LGPL v3	Feb 2015
aeMB [8, 51, 73]	32b MicroBlaze	Medium	✗	✓	✗	✓	No	-	✗	Verilog	✗	LGPL v3	Feb 2012
Amber [54]	32b ARM v2a	Medium	✗	✓	✗	✗	No	-	✗	Verilog	✗	LGPL	Nov 2015
OpenRISC [56, 79]	32b/64b ORBIS	Medium	✓	✓	✓	✗	No	-	✗	Verilog	✗	LGPL	Dec 2012
MIPS32 r1 [3]	32b MIPS32 r1	Medium	✗	✓	✗	✓	No	-	✗	Verilog	✗	LGPL v3	Jul 2015
LEON 3 [24, 65]	32b SPARC V8	Medium	✓($)	✓	✓	✗	SMP/AMP	-	✗	VHDL	✗	GPL	May 2015
OpenScale [18]	32b MicroBlaze	Medium	✗	✓	✗	✗	Manycore	FPGA/6	✓	VHDL	✗	GPL v3	Jan 2012
XUM [2, 47]	32b MIPS32 r2	High	✗	✓	✗	✓	Manycore	FPGA/8	✓	Verilog	✗	LGPL v3	Jul 2015
MIAOW GPGPU [9]	AMD Southern Islands	High	✓	✗	✗	✓	GPU	FPGA/1	✓	Verilog	✗	BSD 3-Clause & GPL v2	Jan 2016
Simply RISC S1 [68]	64b SPARC V9	High	✓	✓	✓	✗	No	-	✗	Verilog	✗	GPL v2	Dec 2008
BERI [1, 83]	64b MIPS/CHERI	High	✓	✓	✓	✓(BERI2)	Multicore	FPGA/4	✗	Bluespec	✗	BERI HW-SW	Jun 2015
OpenSPARC T1/T2 [6, 7]	64b SPARC V9	High	✓	✓	✓	✓	Multicore	ASIC/8	✗	Verilog	✗	GPL v2	2008
RISC-V Rocket [42, 67]	64b scalar RISC-V	High	✓	✓	✓	✗	Manycore	ASIC/2	✓	Chisel	✗	BSD 3-Clause	Jan 2016
RISC-V Boom [22, 66]	64b scalar RISC-V	High	✓	✓	✓	✗	Manycore	FPGA/?	✓	Chisel	✗	BSD 3-Clause	Jan 2016
OpenPiton	64b SPARC V9	High	✓	✓	✓	✓	Manycore	ASIC/25	✓	Verilog	✓	BSD 3-Clause & GPL v2	Jan 2016

Table 4: Taxonomy of differences of open source processors (table data last checked in January 2016).

Submodule	SYN	PAR	STA	ECO	DRC	LVS	Peak
NoC Router	5.38	3.55	0.57	N/A	1.40	1.33	5.38
L1.5	19.91	5.97	1.43	5.00	1.73	1.46	19.91
Core	27.19	7.99	1.96	15.05	2.54	4.03	27.19
Tile	28.04	7.71	1.90	13.62	2.48	8.84	28.04
Chip	8.37	64.54	1.34	64.65	8.54	>41	64.65

Table 6: Peak memory usage (in GByte) of selected synthesis and back-end stages for selected submodules. If any stage executes more than once (STA or for multi-pass flow), the maximum peak usage is shown.

25 tiles respectively. These runtimes are obtained by adding up the run times of all synthesis and back-end stages, from synthesis first pass to DRC and LVS passes. Table 5 details runtimes of individual synthesis and back-end stages for select submodules of the Piton ASIC prototype. For stages in the flow that execute more than once, such as STA or when using a multi-pass flow, the maximum duration for that stage is shown.

Resource requirements for synthesis and back-end scripts, particularly main memory usage, are not excessive. Table 6 (max value is taken for stages that execute more than once) shows that the most memory intensive step of the synthesis and back-end flow requires just over 64GB for the top-level 25-tile chip, making it possible for a high-end desktop at the time of this publication to successfully run through OpenPiton's synthesis and back-end flow.

5. Enabled Applications

Open source platforms such as OpenPiton are designed for flexibility and extensibility, and thus can be easily modified. Researchers leveraging such platforms need not re-implement others' work, which is advantageous for those who lack adequate resources to build infrastructure from scratch. These platforms' independence from a specific target implementation technology also prevents them from going obsolete [80]. In this section, we outline potential applications of the OpenPiton platform in different research domains.

5.1 Architecture

OpenPiton is great tool for computer architecture research and prototyping. In addition to supporting traditional microarchitecture research, OpenPiton offers research opportunities in memory subsystems thanks to its scratch-built uncore. Researchers may also explore manycore scalability, NoCs, and NoC-attached accelerators and I/O.

OpenPiton lowers the barrier to implementing ideas in RTL, while providing accurate estimations of a design's area, power and frequency. The extensive test suite complements the physical implementation by providing behavioral and/or gate-level simulated, and FPGA-emulated validation.

5.2 Operating Systems

While OS researchers have studied how best to add OS support for manycore systems [12, 16, 17, 85], the scarcity of high core-count systems is a barrier to innovation in this space. OpenPiton can enable such research because it can scale to large fabrics while providing support for modern Debian Linux running on an FPGA at tens of MHz.

5.3 Security

Open source processors are widely used by researchers in the security community. While some researchers simulate using open source processors to verify their ideas [13, 77], others build proof-of-concept implementations on FPGA [23, 38, 39, 69, 78]. OpenPiton's substantial test suite, support for an OS and hypervisor, and unique manycore infrastructure, make it a suitable test environment for the security community to further examine novel ideas.

5.4 Compilers

OpenPiton's scalability can assist compiler researchers in understanding how their solutions scale on real hardware. It enables the investigation of future programming models for parallel architectures [62, 64], or how to add automatic parallelization constructs into current languages [19]. The use of the SPARC ISA makes compiler research convenient due to pre-existing compiler support (e.g., GCC).

5.5 Reliability Analysis

Transient and permanent faults can be injected into the RTL of a target design to simulate the effects of faults on system functionality. Consequently, metrics such as architectural vulnerability factor (AVF), failures in time (FIT), and mean time to failure (MTTF) can be estimated. Many studies [25, 26, 48, 60, 61, 89] have used open source processors to perform fault injection. They have also been used in thermal and power management reliability modeling [33, 35] as well as wearout fault modeling studies [74].

With advances in the scalability of reliability analysis tools, researchers can now evaluate the reliability of larger circuits. Moreover, efficient fault simulation schemes have been developed to explore the reliability of multicore and manycore processors [33, 40]. OpenPiton enables researchers to study how different solutions, across the entire design hierarchy, affect the reliability of a manycore. It also facilitates researchers to perform manycore-oriented reliability studies, such as the reliability of NoC architectures [27] and cache coherence protocols.

5.6 Education

Educators have shown the value of using FPGAs in teaching microprocessor architecture [52, 76]. Downloaded from `http://www.openpiton.org`, the OpenPiton platform comes push-button packaged to run on FPGA, including the widely used and subsidized ($160 Academic, currently) Digilent Nexys 4 DDR Artix-7 FPGA Board. In addition, because OpenPiton ships with synthesis and back-end scripts, students learning digital circuits can easily leverage its ASIC flow, in a similar approach to [44], on a real modern manycore processor.

6. Related Work

This section qualitatively compares OpenPiton to other open source platforms available for research implementation and prototyping. Table 4 highlights the main differences between these platforms and OpenPiton.

Most of the open source platforms have rudimentary OS support, frequently only for embedded real time operating systems (RTOS) like eCos [45] by ZPU [5]. Few have memory management units (MMU) needed for full operating system support. In addition, many projects who do support system calls/OSs/memory mapped I/O often require a tethered host core to proxy through. In contrast, leveraging the OpenSPARC T1 core, OpenPiton is a standalone system that has robust OS and hypervisor support.

Most designs in Table 4 are soft-IPs, synthesizable to FPGAs for rapid prototyping, but have not been demonstrated in ASIC. In contrast, OpenPiton supports both FPGA and ASIC usage paradigms. Additional low-end available processors, not shown in Table 4 are mentioned in two surveys [10, 37]. Moreover, technology limitations [88] and the end of Dennard scaling [28] have resulted in a paradigm shift to multi/manycore and heterogeneity [41] and created demand for a truly open source manycore design. Though some designs have limited multicore scalability (i.e. OpenSPARC T1&T2 [6, 7]), OpenPiton is specifically engineered for scalable core count and chip count.

Some recent academic projects [1, 42, 67, 83] are centered around high-level synthesis (HLS) tools, citing the use of past HDL's as archaic and error-prone. In contrast, OpenPiton does not try to innovate in this space. We deliberately use Verilog to leverage industrial-grade design/verification/synthesis flow to significantly reduce design time. Moreover, universal familiarity with Verilog makes OpenPiton easier to access and understand.

While the RISC-V platform provides a crossbar for multicore implementations [67], OpenScale [18], XUM [47], and OpenPiton benefit from scalable mesh networks.

Last, to the best of our knowledge, OpenPiton is the only platform that includes the ASIC back-end (place-and-route) scripts, assisting users with porting the design to other process technologies. Furthermore, the industrial-grade CPU core design together with robust software ecosystem will prove useful to future research projects.

7. Conclusion

The OpenPiton processor design and framework enables researchers to conduct manycore research at-scale and bring novel ideas to implementation using a mature tool chain, a mature ISA, and a complete test suite. OpenPiton can scale from small designs to large designs as proven with implementations in ASIC silicon as well as in many prototyped FPGA boards. OpenPiton is configurable and extensible and comes with a complete verification infrastructure. We are optimistic that OpenPiton will serve as an important tool for scalable manycore processor research and enable more researchers to bring their designs to implementation.

Acknowledgements

This work was partially supported by the NSF under Grants No. CCF-1217553, CCF-1453112, and CCF-1438980, AFOSR under Grant No. FA9550-14-1-0148, and DARPA under Grants No. N66001-14-1-4040 and HR0011-13-2-0005. Any opinions, findings, and conclusions or recommendations expressed in this material are those of the authors and do not necessarily reflect the views of our sponsors.

References

[1] Beri processor 'arcina' release 1. https://github.com/CTSRD-CHERI/beri. Accessed Jan. 2016.

[2] eXtensible Utah Multicore (xum). https://github.com/grantae/mips32r1_xum. Accessed Jan. 2016.

[3] Mips32 release 1. https://github.com/grantae/mips32r1_core. Accessed Jan. 2016.

[4] Zet processor. http://zet.aluzina.org/index.php/Zet_processor. Accessed Jan. 2016.

[5] Zylin cpu. https://github.com/zylin/zpu. Accessed Jan. 2016.

[6] *OpenSPARC T1 Microarchitecture Specification*. Santa Clara, CA, 2006.

[7] *OpenSPARC T2 Core Microarchitecture Specification*. Santa Clara, CA, 2007.

[8] Aeste Works. Aemb multi-threaded 32-bit embedded core family. https://github.com/aeste/aemb. Accessed Jan. 2016.

[9] R. Balasubramanian, V. Gangadhar, Z. Guo, C.-H. Ho, C. Joseph, J. Menon, M. P. Drumond, R. Paul, S. Prasad, P. Valathol, and K. Sankaralingam. Enabling gpgpu low-level hardware explorations with miaow: An open-source rtl implementation of a gpgpu. *ACM Trans. Archit. Code Optim.*, 12(2), June 2015.

[10] R. R. Balwaik, S. R. Nayak, and A. Jeyakumar. Open-source 32-bit risc soft-core processors. *IOSR Journal od VLSI and Signal Processing*, 2(4):43–46, 2013.

[11] L. Barthe, L. Cargnini, P. Benoit, and L. Torres. The secretblaze: A configurable and cost-effective open-source soft-core processor. In *Parallel and Distributed Processing Workshops and Phd Forum (IPDPSW), 2011 IEEE International Symposium on*, pages 310–313, May 2011.

[12] A. Baumann, P. Barham, P.-E. Dagand, T. Harris, R. Isaacs, S. Peter, T. Roscoe, A. Schüpbach, and A. Singhania. The multikernel: A new os architecture for scalable multicore systems. In *Proceedings of the ACM SIGOPS 22Nd Symposium on Operating Systems Principles*, SOSP '09, pages 29–44, New York, NY, USA, 2009. ACM.

[13] M. Bilzor, T. Huffmire, C. Irvine, and T. Levin. Evaluating security requirements in a general-purpose processor by combining assertion checkers with code coverage. In *Hardware-Oriented Security and Trust (HOST), 2012 IEEE International Symposium on*, pages 49–54, June 2012.

[14] N. Binkert, B. Beckmann, G. Black, S. K. Reinhardt, A. Saidi, A. Basu, J. Hestness, D. R. Hower, T. Krishna, S. Sardashti, R. Sen, K. Sewell, M. Shoaib, N. Vaish, M. D. Hill, and D. A. Wood. The gem5 simulator. *SIGARCH Computer Architecture News*, 39(2):1–7, Aug. 2011.

[15] D. Bittman, D. Capelis, and D. Long. Introducing seaos. In *Information Science and Applications (ICISA), 2014 International Conference on*, pages 1–3, May 2014.

[16] S. Boyd-Wickizer, H. Chen, R. Chen, Y. Mao, F. Kaashoek, R. Morris, A. Pesterev, L. Stein, M. Wu, Y. Dai, Y. Zhang, and Z. Zhang. Corey: An operating system for many cores. In *Proceedings of the 8th USENIX Conference on Operating Systems Design and Implementation*, OSDI'08, pages 43–57, Berkeley, CA, USA, 2008. USENIX Association.

[17] S. Boyd-Wickizer, A. T. Clements, Y. Mao, A. Pesterev, M. F. Kaashoek, R. Morris, and N. Zeldovich. An analysis of linux scalability to many cores. In *Proceedings of the 9th USENIX Conference on Operating Systems Design and Implementation*, OSDI'10, pages 1–8, Berkeley, CA, USA, 2010. USENIX Association.

[18] R. Busseuil, L. Barthe, G. Almeida, L. Ost, F. Bruguier, G. Sassatelli, P. Benoit, M. Robert, and L. Torres. Open-scale: A scalable, open-source noc-based mpsoc for design space exploration. In *Reconfigurable Computing and FPGAs (ReConFig), 2011 Int. Conference on*, pages 357–362, Nov 2011.

[19] S. Campanoni, T. Jones, G. Holloway, V. J. Reddi, G.-Y. Wei, and D. Brooks. Helix: Automatic parallelization of irregular programs for chip multiprocessing. In *Proceedings of the Tenth International Symposium on Code Generation and Optimization*, CGO '12, pages 84–93, New York, NY, USA, 2012. ACM.

[20] D. J. Capelis. Lockbox: Helping computers keep your secrets. Technical Report UCSC-WASP-15-02, University of California, Santa Cruz, Nov. 2015.

[21] T. E. Carlson, W. Heirman, and L. Eeckhout. Sniper: exploring the level of abstraction for scalable and accurate parallel multi-core simulation. In *Proceedings of 2011 International Conference for High Performance Computing, Networking, Storage and Analysis*, SC '11, pages 52:1–52:12, New York, NY, USA, 2011. ACM.

[22] C. Celio, D. A. Patterson, and K. Asanović. The berkeley out-of-order machine (boom): An industry-competitive, synthesizable, parameterized risc-v processor. Technical Report UCB/EECS-2015-167, EECS Department, University of California, Berkeley, Jun 2015.

[23] D. Champagne and R. Lee. Scalable architectural support for trusted software. In *High Performance Computer Architecture (HPCA), IEEE 16th Int. Symposium on*, pages 1–12, Jan 2010.

[24] Cobham Gaisler AB. Grlib ip core users manual. May 2015.

[25] A. da Silva and S. Sanchez. Leon3 vip: A virtual platform with fault injection capabilities. In *Digital System Design: Architectures, Methods and Tools (DSD), 2010 13th Euromicro Conference on*, pages 813–816, Sept 2010.

[26] M. Ebrahimi, L. Chen, H. Asadi, and M. Tahoori. Class: Combined logic and architectural soft error sensitivity analysis. In *Design Automation Conference (ASP-DAC), 2013 18th Asia and South Pacific*, pages 601–607, Jan 2013.

[27] M. Ebrahimi, M. Daneshtalab, and J. Plosila. High performance fault-tolerant routing algorithm for noc-based many-core systems. In *Parallel, Distributed and Network-Based Processing (PDP), 2013 21st Euromicro International Conference on*, pages 462–469, Feb 2013.

[28] H. Esmaeilzadeh, E. Blem, R. St. Amant, K. Sankaralingam, and D. Burger. Dark silicon and the end of multicore scaling. In *Proceedings of the 38th Annual International Symposium on Computer Architecture*, ISCA '11, pages 365–376, New York, NY, USA, 2011. ACM.

[29] C. W. Fletcher, L. Ren, A. Kwon, M. van Dijk, and S. Devadas. Freecursive oram: [nearly] free recursion and integrity verification for position-based oblivious ram. In *Proceedings of the Twentieth Int. Conference on Architectural Support for Programming Languages and Operating Systems*, ASPLOS '15, pages 103–116, New York, NY, USA, 2015. ACM.

[30] Y. Fu, T. M. Nguyen, and D. Wentzlaff. Coherence domain restriction on large scale systems. In *Proceedings of the 48th International Symposium on Microarchitecture*, MICRO-48, pages 686–698, New York, NY, USA, 2015. ACM.

[31] Y. Fu and D. Wentzlaff. Prime: A parallel and distributed simulator for thousand-core chips. In *Performance Analysis of Systems and Software (ISPASS), 2014 IEEE International Symposium on*, pages 116–125, March 2014.

[32] O. Goldreich and R. Ostrovsky. Software protection and simulation on oblivious rams. *J. ACM*, 43(3):431–473, May 1996.

[33] M.-Y. Hsieh. A scalable simulation framework for evaluating thermal management techniques and the lifetime reliability of multithreaded multicore systems. In *Int. Green Computing Conference and Workshops*, pages 1–6, July 2011.

[34] HT-Lab. Cpu86: 8088 fpga ip core. `http://ht-lab.com/freecores/cpu8086/cpu86.html`. Accessed Jan. 2016.

[35] H. Hua, C. Mineo, K. Schoenfliess, A. Sule, S. Melamed, R. Jenkal, and W. Davis. Exploring compromises among timing, power and temperature in three-dimensional integrated circuits. In *Design Automation Conference, 2006 43rd ACM/IEEE*, pages 997–1002, 2006.

[36] T. Instruments. Msp430x1xx family users guide, 2006.

[37] R. Jia, C. Lin, Z. Guo, R. Chen, F. Wang, T. Gao, and H. Yang. A survey of open source processors for fpgas. In *Field Programmable Logic and Applications (FPL), 2014 24th International Conference on*, pages 1–6, Sept 2014.

[38] O. Khalid, C. Rolfes, and A. Ibing. On implementing trusted boot for embedded systems. In *Hardware-Oriented Security and Trust, IEEE Int. Symposium on*, pages 75–80, June 2013.

[39] S. T. King, J. Tucek, A. Cozzie, C. Grier, W. Jiang, and Y. Zhou. Designing and implementing malicious hardware. *LEET*, 8:1–8, 2008.

[40] M. Kochte, M. Schaal, H. Wunderlich, and C. Zoellin. Efficient fault simulation on many-core processors. In *ACM/IEEE Design Automation Conference*, pages 380–385, June 2010.

[41] R. Kumar, K. Farkas, N. P. Jouppi, P. Ranganathan, and D. M. Tullsen. Single-isa heterogeneous multi-core architectures: The potential for processor power reduction. In *Microarchitecture, 2003. MICRO-36. Proceedings. 36th Annual IEEE/ACM Int. Symposium on*, pages 81–92. IEEE, 2003.

[42] Y. Lee, A. Waterman, R. Avizienis, H. Cook, C. Sun, V. Stojanovic, and K. Asanović. A 45nm 1.3ghz 16.7 double-precision gflops/w risc-v processor with vector accelerators. In *European Solid State Circuits Conference (ESSCIRC), ESSCIRC 2014 - 40th*, pages 199–202, Sept 2014.

[43] S. Li, J. H. Ahn, R. Strong, J. Brockman, D. Tullsen, and N. Jouppi. Mcpat: An integrated power, area, and timing modeling framework for multicore and manycore architectures. In *Microarchitecture, 2009. MICRO-42. 42nd Annual IEEE/ACM Int. Symposium on*, pages 469–480, Dec 2009.

[44] J. Lu and B. Taskin. From rtl to gdsii: An asic design course development using synopsys® university program. In *Microelectronic Systems Education (MSE), 2011 IEEE International Conference on*, pages 72–75, June 2011.

[45] A. J. Massa. *Embedded software development with eCos*. Prentice Hall Professional, 2003.

[46] M. McKeown, J. Balkind, and D. Wentzlaff. Execution drafting: Energy efficiency through computation deduplication. In *Microarchitecture (MICRO), 2014 47th Annual IEEE/ACM International Symposium on*, pages 432–444, Dec 2014.

[47] B. L. Meakin. Multicore system design with xum: The extensible utah multicore project. Master's thesis, The University of Utah, 2010.

[48] N. Mehdizadeh, M. Shokrolah-Shirazi, and S. Miremadi. Analyzing fault effects in the 32-bit openrisc 1200 microprocessor. In *Availability, Reliability and Security. ARES 08. Third International Conference on*, pages 648–652, March 2008.

[49] B. Miller, D. Brasili, T. Kiszely, R. Kuhn, R. Mehrotra, M. Salvi, M. Kulkarni, A. Varadharajan, S.-H. Yin, W. Lin, A. Hughes, B. Stysiack, V. Kandadi, I. Pragaspathi, D. Hartman, D. Carlson, V. Yalala, T. Xanthopoulos, S. Meninger, E. Crain, M. Spaeth, A. Aina, S. Balasubramanian, J. Vulih, P. Tiwary, D. Lin, R. Kessler, B. Fishbein, and A. Jain. A 32-core risc microprocessor with network accelerators, power management and testability features. In *IEEE Int. Solid-State Circuits Conf. Digest of Tech. Papers*, pages 58–60, Feb 2012.

[50] J. Miller, H. Kasture, G. Kurian, C. Gruenwald, N. Beckmann, C. Celio, J. Eastep, and A. Agarwal. Graphite: a distributed parallel simulator for multicores. In *IEEE 16th Int. Symp. on High Performance Computer Architecture*, pages 1–12, 2010.

[51] S. T. S. Ngiap. Aemb 32-bit microprocessor core datasheet, November 2007.

[52] J. Olivares, J. Palomares, J. Soto, and J. Gámez. Teaching microprocessors design using fpgas. In *Education Engineering (EDUCON), 2010 IEEE*, pages 1189–1193, April 2010.

[53] OpenCores. Altor32 - alternative lightweight openrisc cpu. `http://opencores.org/project,altor32`. Accessed Jan. 2016.

[54] OpenCores. Amber arm-compatible core. `http://opencores.org/project,amber`. Accessed Jan. 2016.

[55] OpenCores. Openmsp430. `http://opencores.org/project,openmsp430`. Accessed Jan. 2016.

[56] OpenCores. Or1200 openrisc processor. `http://opencores.org/or1k/OR1200_OpenRISC_Processor`. Accessed Jan. 2016.

[57] OpenCores. pAVR. `http://opencores.org/project,pavr`. Accessed Jan. 2016.

[58] Oracle. OpenSPARC T1. `http://www.oracle.com/technetwork/systems/opensparc/opensparc-t1-page-1444609.html`.

[59] P. M. Ortego and P. Sack. Sesc: Superescalar simulator. In *17th Euro micro conf. on real time systems*, pages 1–4, 2004.

[60] I. Parulkar, A. Wood, J. C. Hoe, B. Falsafi, S. V. Adve, J. Torrellas, and S. Mitra. Opensparc: An open platform for hardware reliability experimentation. In *Fourth Workshop on Silicon Errors in Logic-System Effects (SELSE)*. Citeseer, 2008.

[61] A. Pellegrini, R. Smolinski, L. Chen, X. Fu, S. Hari, J. Jiang, S. Adve, T. Austin, and V. Bertacco. Crashtest'ing swat: Accurate, gate-level evaluation of symptom-based resiliency solutions. In *Design, Automation Test in Europe Conference Exhibition (DATE), 2012*, pages 1106–1109, March 2012.

[62] C. D. Polychronopoulos. *Parallel programming and compilers*, volume 59. Springer Science & Business Media, 2012.

[63] PyHP. PyHP Official Home Page. `http://pyhp.sourceforge.net`.

[64] A. Raman, A. Zaks, J. W. Lee, and D. I. August. Parcae: A system for flexible parallel execution. In *Proc. of the ACM SIGPLAN Conf. on Programming Language Design and Implementation*, pages 133–144, New York, NY, USA, 2012.

[65] Aeroflex Gaisler AB. Sparc v8 32-bit processor leon3/leon3-ft companioncore data sheet, March 2010.

[66] UC Berkeley Architecture Research. The berkeley out-of-order risc-v processor. `https://github.com/ucb-bar/riscv-boom`. Accessed Jan. 2016.

[67] UC Berkeley Architecture Research. Rocket core. `https://github.com/ucb-bar/rocket`. Accessed Jan. 2016.

[68] S. RISC. Simply risc s1 core. `http://www.srisc.com/?s1`. Accessed Jan. 2016.

[69] P. Schaumont and I. Verbauwhede. Thumbpod puts security under your thumb. *Xilinx® Xcell J*, 2003.

[70] L. Seiler, D. Carmean, E. Sprangle, T. Forsyth, M. Abrash, P. Dubey, S. Junkins, A. Lake, J. Sugerman, R. Cavin, R. Espasa, E. Grochowski, T. Juan, and P. Hanrahan. Larrabee: A many-core x86 architecture for visual computing. *ACM Trans. Graph.*, 27(3):18:1–18:15, Aug. 2008.

[71] L. Semiconductor. Latticemico32 open, free 32-bit soft processor. `http://www.latticesemi.com/en/Products/DesignSoftwareAndIP/IntellectualProperty/IPCore/IPCores02/LatticeMico32.aspx`. Accessed Jan. 2016.

[72] Y. S. Shao, B. Reagen, G.-Y. Wei, and D. Brooks. Aladdin: A pre-rtl, power-performance accelerator simulator enabling large design space exploration of customized architectures. In *The 41st Annual Int. Symposium on Computer Architecture*, pages 97–108, Piscataway, NJ, USA, 2014. IEEE Press.

[73] S. Shengfeng, Z. Dexue, and Y. Guoping. Soc verification platform based on aemb softcore processor [j]. *Microcontrollers & Embedded Systems*, 4:016, 2010.

[74] J. C. Smolens, B. T. Gold, J. C. Hoe, B. Falsafi, and K. Mai. Detecting emerging wearout faults. In *Proc. of Workshop on SELSE*, 2007.

[75] E. Stefanov, M. van Dijk, E. Shi, C. Fletcher, L. Ren, X. Yu, and S. Devadas. Path oram: An extremely simple oblivious ram protocol. In *Proceedings of the 2013 ACM SIGSAC Conference on Computer and Communications Security*, CCS '13, pages 299–310, New York, NY, USA, 2013. ACM.

[76] A. Strelzoff. Teaching computer architecture with fpga soft processors. In *ASEE Southeast Section Conference*, 2007.

[77] J. Szefer and R. Lee. Architectural support for hypervisor-secure virtualization. In *Proceedings of the Seventeenth International Conference on Architectural Support for Programming Languages and Operating Systems*, ASPLOS XVII, pages 437–450, New York, NY, USA, 2012. ACM.

[78] J. Szefer, W. Zhang, Y.-Y. Chen, D. Champagne, K. Chan, W. Li, R. Cheung, and R. Lee. Rapid single-chip secure processor prototyping on the opensparc fpga platform. In *Rapid System Prototyping (RSP), 2011 22nd IEEE International Symposium on*, pages 38–44, May 2011.

[79] J. Tandon. The openrisc processor: open hardware and linux. *Linux Journal*, 2011(212):6, 2011.

[80] J. Tong, I. Anderson, and M. Khalid. Soft-core processors for embedded systems. In *Microelectronics, 2006. ICM '06. International Conference on*, pages 170–173, Dec 2006.

[81] R. Ubal, B. Jang, P. Mistry, D. Schaa, and D. Kaeli. Multi2sim: A simulation framework for cpu-gpu computing. In *Proceedings of the 21st International Conference on Parallel Architectures and Compilation Techniques*, PACT '12, pages 335–344, New York, NY, USA, 2012. ACM.

[82] S. R. Vangal, J. Howard, G. Ruhl, S. Dighe, H. Wilson, J. Tschanz, D. Finan, A. Singh, T. Jacob, S. Jain, et al. An 80-tile sub-100-w teraflops processor in 65-nm cmos. *Solid-State Circuits, IEEE Journal of*, 43(1):29–41, 2008.

[83] R. N. M. Watson, J. Woodruff, D. Chisnall, B. Davis, W. Koszek, A. T. Markettos, S. W. Moore, S. J. Murdoch, P. G. Neumann, R. Norton, and M. Roe. Bluespec Extensible RISC Implementation: BERI Hardware reference. Technical Report UCAM-CL-TR-868, University of Cambridge, Computer Laboratory, Apr. 2015.

[84] D. Wentzlaff, P. Griffin, H. Hoffmann, L. Bao, B. Edwards, C. Ramey, M. Mattina, C.-C. Miao, J. F. Brown III, and A. Agarwal. On-chip interconnection architecture of the Tile Processor. *IEEE Micro*, 27(5):15–31, Sept. 2007.

[85] D. Wentzlaff, C. Gruenwald, III, N. Beckmann, K. Modzelewski, A. Belay, L. Youseff, J. Miller, and A. Agarwal. An operating system for multicore and clouds: Mechanisms and implementation. In *Proceedings of the 1st ACM Symposium on Cloud Computing*, SoCC '10, pages 3–14, New York, NY, USA, 2010. ACM.

[86] D. Wentzlaff, C. J. Jackson, P. Griffin, and A. Agarwal. Configurable fine-grain protection for multicore processor virtualization. In *Proceedings of the Annual Int. Symp. on Computer Architecture*, pages 464–475, Washington, DC, USA, 2012.

[87] D. H. Woo and H.-H. S. Lee. Extending amdahl's law for energy-efficient computing in the many-core era. *Computer*, (12):24–31, 2008.

[88] D. Yeh, L.-S. Peh, S. Borkar, J. Darringer, A. Agarwal, and W.-M. Hwu. Thousand-core chips [roundtable]. *Design Test of Computers, IEEE*, 25(3):272–278, May 2008.

[89] M. Zandrahimi, H. Zarandi, and A. Rohani. An analysis of fault effects and propagations in zpu: The world's smallest 32 bit cpu. In *Quality Electronic Design (ASQED), 2010 2nd Asia Symp. on*, pages 308–313, Aug 2010.

COATCheck: Verifying Memory Ordering at the Hardware-OS Interface

Daniel Lustig *
Princeton University
dlustig@nvidia.com †

Geet Sethi *
Rutgers University
geet.sethi@rutgers.edu

Margaret Martonosi
Princeton University
mrm@princeton.edu

Abhishek Bhattacharjee
Rutgers University
abhib@cs.rutgers.edu

Abstract

Modern computer systems include numerous compute elements, from CPUs to GPUs to accelerators. Harnessing their full potential requires well-defined, properly-implemented memory consistency models (MCMs), and low-level system functionality such as virtual memory and address translation (AT). Unfortunately, it is difficult to specify and implement hardware-OS interactions correctly; in the past, many hardware and OS specification mismatches have resulted in implementation bugs in commercial processors.

In an effort to resolve this verification gap, this paper makes the following contributions. First, we present COATCheck[1], an address translation-aware framework for specifying and statically verifying memory ordering enforcement at the microarchitecture and operating system levels. We develop a domain-specific language for specifying ordering enforcement, for including ordering-related OS events and hardware micro-operations, and for programmatically enumerating happens-before graphs. Using a fast and automated static constraint solver, COATCheck can efficiently analyze interesting and important memory ordering scenarios for modern, high-performance, out-of-order processors. Second, we show that previous work on Virtual Address Memory Consistency (VAMC) does not capture every translation-related ordering scenario of interest, and that some such cases even fall outside the traditional scope of consistency. We therefore introduce the term *transistency model* to describe the superset of consistency which captures all translation-aware sets of ordering rules.

* The first two authors contributed equally to this paper.

† The work was performed while this author was at Princeton University.

[1] Consistency Ordering and Address Translation Checker

ASPLOS '16 April 2–6, 2016, Atlanta, Georgia, USA.

DOI: http://dx.doi.org/10.1145/2872362.2872399

1. Introduction

Computer systems are becoming increasingly complex, with multiple processing elements (e.g., multicore CPUs, GPUs, and other accelerators) running multiple layers of system software (user code, libraries, operating systems, hypervisors, etc.). These heterogeneous systems frequently enable inter-element communication by presenting the user with an abstraction of shared virtual memory, even when the underlying hardware may contain discrete physical memory blocks [11, 42]. Harnessing these systems' full potential requires careful coordination between the hardware and the OS to ensure that the memory consistency model(s) (MCMs) and address translation (AT) mechanisms are properly-implemented. Unfortunately, the ability to rigorously verify these subsystems and their interactions with each other remains a vexing problem.

Recent years have seen increased attention being paid to the need for well-defined memory models and analysis techniques at each layer of the hardware-software stack. Many architectures and programming languages have recently developed formal consistency model specifications [10, 13, 30] and tools to help analyze them [3, 40]. However, most (but not all [38, 39]) of these models ignore the implications of virtual-to-physical address translation, such as synonyms and page permission updates, on memory ordering. Furthermore, these tools cannot verify the underlying implementations of these models, leaving a verification gap within which bugs often arise.

A key challenge is that microarchitectural events (i.e., those which are not architecturally visible) and OS behavior can affect memory ordering in ways for which standard (i.e., non-translation-aware) memory consistency analysis can be fundamentally insufficient [38, 39]. Proper implementation of a memory model requires correctness to be maintained through library calls, through system calls, and through the varying and/or unpredictable behavior of the microarchitecture. Events within each of these layers interact with and affect the state of memory, and, crucially, *events within these low-level layers may behave differently from the "normal" accesses described by the formal memory model.* For example, on the x86-64 architecture, which implements the relatively strong total store ordering (TSO) memory model [32], events such as page table accesses may be inherently racy: page table walks are automatically issued by hardware, can happen at any time, and are often not ordered with respect to most fences [16, 20].

No existing notion of memory consistency captures the strictest possible translation-aware set of orderings. As we show in this paper, even data-race-free programs [1], sequentially consistent machines [23], and systems obeying sequential consistency for virtual address memory consistency (SC-for-VAMC) [38, 39] can nevertheless be prone to (perhaps surprising) ordering bugs. These bugs relate to the checking of metadata which is not directly associated with the virtual *or* the physical address being accessed; this places it outside the scope of memory consistency, including VAMC. We therefore use the term *memory transistency model* to refer to any set of memory ordering rules which explicitly takes virtual-to-physical address translation issues into account, even through the extra layers of indirection needed above.

To aid in the analysis of transistency models and their implementations, this work develops techniques and tools—collectively called COATCheck—for verifying memory ordering enforcement in the context of virtual-to-physical address translation. COATCheck extends existing tools and techniques [26, 29] to allow users to reason about system calls, interrupts, microcode, and so on. The goal of COATCheck is to improve the ability to specify and verify system behaviors at an already bug-prone interface [38, 39] whose complexity is worsening with heterogeneous parallelism. Our contributions are as follows.

First, we demonstrate a comprehensive yet tractable methodology for specifying and statically verifying memory ordering enforcement at the hardware-OS interface. We develop a Domain-Specific Language (DSL) called μspec within which each component in a system (e.g., each pipeline stage, each cache, each TLB) can independently specify its own contribution to memory ordering using the languages of first-order logic and μhb graphs [26, 27, 29]. μspec extends the constraint-based approach of previous work [29] to support modeling of TLB occupancy, page table walk microcode, activities that emit memory references despite not being part of the user-level instruction stream, system calls for memory allocation (e.g., `malloc/mmap`), and interrupts (e.g., inter-processor interrupts to maintain TLB coherence). The μspec approach allows components to be swapped in and out without affecting others, thereby providing a more modular approach to memory ordering verification.

Second, we develop a fast and general-purpose constraint solver which automates the analysis of μspec specifications, thereby allowing interactive exploration of memory ordering scenarios more complex than previous tools have handled. We demonstrate the use of COATCheck (the methodology and the tool) on several case studies that highlight interesting challenges at the hardware-OS boundary: a sophisticated model of an Intel Sandy Bridge-like processor running Linux, as well as classes of translation-related bugs recently identified by processor vendors. The full toolset (the DSL, models, litmus tests, and analysis tool) is open-source and publicly available.[2]

Finally, we use COATCheck to identify cases in which transistency goes beyond the traditional scope of consistency. We demonstrate cases where even sequentially consistent (or, following recent work, SC for VAMC [38, 39]) code may be buggy due to improper handling of page table entry status bits for virtual address synonyms. Overall, our work offers formal, yet practical tools for memory ordering checking, and it broadens the very scope of memory consistency.

Initially: `[x]=0, [y]=0`	
Thread 0	**Thread 1**
`St [x] ← 1`	`St [y] ← 2`
`Ld [y] → r1`	`Ld [x] → r2`
Proposed outcome: `r1=2, r2=1`	

(a) Litmus test code

Initially: `[x]=0, [y]=0`	
Thread 0	**Thread 1**
`St PA1←1`	
	`St PA2←2`
	`Ld PA1→r2`
`Ld PA2→r1`	
Outcome `r1=2, r2=1` permitted	

(b) A possible execution showing how the proposed outcome is observable, *if* `x` and `y` point to different physical addresses.

Initially: `[x]=0, [y]=0`	
Thread 0	**Thread 1**
`St PA1←1`	
	`St PA1←2`
	`Ld PA1→r2`
`Ld PA1→r1`	
Outcome `r1=2,r2=1` forbidden	

(c) The execution is forbidden if `x` and `y` point to to the same physical address. (Only one possible interleaving is shown.)

Figure 1: The litmus test outcome is permitted if TSO is considered to apply only to virtual addresses or if `x` and `y` are not synonyms, and forbidden otherwise.

2. Overview

2.1 Background and Motivation

As motivation, consider the litmus test[3] in Figure 1a. As written, `x` and `y` appear to be distinct addresses. Under that assumption, Figure 1b shows that even a strong MCM such as sequential consistency (SC) [23] considers the proposed final values to be observable, because an event interleaving exists to achieve that value outcome. If instead, as in Figure 1c, `x` and `y` are actually synonyms (i.e., both map to the same physical address), the test is forbidden by SC, because

[2] `http://github.com/daniellustig/coatcheck`.

[3] Litmus tests are small programs testing some aspect of a MCM. Each proposes a particular outcome (i.e., the value returned by each load) and then specifies/tests whether that outcome is permitted or forbidden by the MCM's rules.

if the addresses are the same, no interleaving of the threads produces the proposed outcome. While simple, this example highlights how memory ordering verification is fundamentally incomplete unless it explicitly accounts for address translation when determining expected behaviors and verifying correctness.

Relationship to Past Work: The bulk of prior MCM work has focused on the high-level programming language and hardware layers [2, 10, 13, 30, 32, 40]. However, abstractions effective at these levels (e.g., SC-for-DRF [1], TSO [43]) are often ineffective at the hardware level, as high-performance data structures and low-level hardware operations are often inherently weakly ordered and racy. For example, although x86 processors implement the Total Store Ordering (TSO) MCM, *page table walks are TSO-ordered with respect to neither normal memory accesses nor* `mfence` *instructions (which enforce orderings between all normal loads and stores)* [16, 20]. Likewise, many parallel data structures bypass software memory models in favor of higher-performance (but less portable) assembly implementations that interface more directly with the non-SC hardware memory model [10, 24, 25, 31].

Romanescu et al. were the first to distinguish between MCMs meant for virtual addresses (VAMC) and those for physical addresses (PAMC) [38, 39]. They considered hardware to be responsible for enforcing the latter, and a combination of hardware and OS for the former. Accordingly, traditional hardware models such as TSO would fall under PAMC, while synonyms, page mapping changes, and side effects (i.e., page status bits) would be added to form VAMC. COATCheck provides a rigorous means of specifying and verifying the interaction between the two models. This paper also goes beyond the VAMC-PAMC distinction to identify cases in which ordering bugs can be found even when both VAMC and PAMC are made sequentially consistent.

PipeCheck and CCICheck verify memory ordering enforcement through the use of microarchitecture-level happens-before (μhb) graphs [26, 27, 29]. PipeCheck performs MCM verification by enumerating a complete family of μhb graphs for any given litmus test. CCICheck extends PipeCheck to handle coherence-consistency interface issues. COATCheck extends both of these by providing a fully-general DSL for specifying ordering enforcement, and by demonstrating how PAMC, VAMC, and transistency in general can be analyzed using μhb graphs.

2.2 The COATCheck Approach

Figure 2 shows layers at which memory ordering issues might be considered. Our work enables the building and verification of detailed models for hardware-OS memory ordering implications, particularly focusing on layers 3, 4, and 5 in Figure 2. This allows us to analyze memory ordering in an execution stream that includes library and kernel code, as well as microcode-level events such as the hardware page table walks executed on behalf of the program at TLB misses. Previously, incomplete specifications, incorrect implementations, or poor coordination between the layers could (and did [5, 6, 18, 21]) cause bugs. These include forbidden multithreaded outcomes becoming observable, legal data disappearing due to incorrect updates of page table entry dirty bits, processors experiencing deadlock/livelock, and any number of other undesirable outcomes.

1. At the highest level: Programmer-written source code is transformed into compiler-generated low-level code.
2. After dynamic linking with libraries: Compiler-generated user-level code with user-level OS support (e.g., syscalls).
3. After addition of OS kernel work (e.g., system call handlers, interrupts): User and kernel level code.
4. After the addition of microcode: Microcode and post-ISA user and kernel code.
5. After mapping onto a given microarchitecture: Micro-ops (or low-level instructions) traversing pipeline structures.

Figure 2: In a typical system layering, our approach supports memory order verification for Levels 3, 4, and 5. OS code Insertion (Section 3.3) creates Kernel-Level Litmus Tests that lie at Layer 3. The further insertion of ghost instructions (Section 3.4) creates ELTs that lie at Layer 4. Finally, with designer input via μspec, the constraint solver and graph enumeration explore microarchitecturally-aware event orderings at Layer 5.

COATCheck overcomes these problems by building *modular* models of memory ordering enforcement at the hardware-OS interface. In particular, each component (a pipeline stage, a page table walker, an OS mechanism, etc.) can specify its own independent contribution to memory ordering enforcement. Prior to verification, the independent contributions of the components which form the system under test are merged into a single overall specification. The COATCheck tool then uses this combined specification to generate families of μhb graphs to statically verify the overall correctness of the system.

Figure 3 shows the overall COATCheck toolflow. First, traditional (i.e., address translation-unaware) litmus tests are converted into *enhanced litmus tests* which include all (micro) code relevant to memory ordering. Second, the enhanced litmus test is analyzed according to the rules of the μspec specification of the orderings enforced at various parts of the system. This produces a set of constraints describing the conditions under which the outcome proposed by the litmus test would be observable. Third, the constraints are analyzed by the COATCheck constraint solver tool to determine whether any observable execution (in the form of a μhb graph) can be found. We analyze each step in detail in the sections that follow.

After describing the overall flow, Section 6 gives the concrete example of how a system consisting of Intel Sandy Bridge-like hardware, a Linux-like OS, and interesting litmus tests as software can be modeled and analyzed using COATCheck. This is followed with an analysis of the perfor-

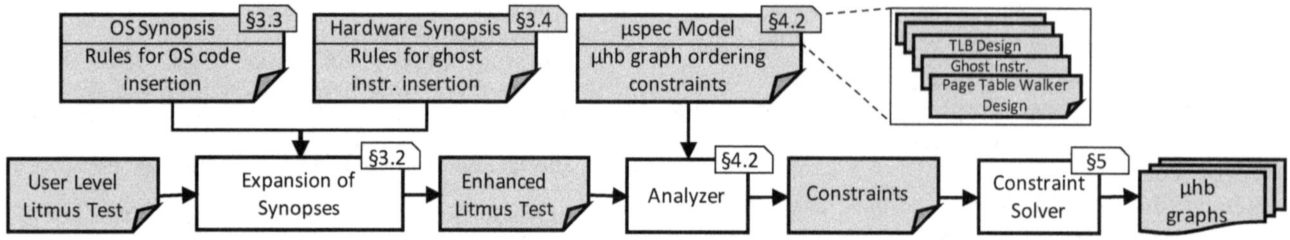

Figure 3: COATCheck flow diagram. Section numbers are listed in the top-right of the appropriate boxes.

mance of the COATCheck constraint solver, using the above system as a case study.

3. Beyond Traditional Litmus Tests

Litmus tests have become a standard tool in memory model analysis. This section describes how we derive *Enhanced Litmus Tests* (ELTs) which account for address translation operations, page table walks, remappings, memory-accessing microcode, and other operations relevant to memory ordering and other system-level operations that execute concurrently with, and on behalf of, user-level code.

3.1 Enhanced Litmus Tests: An Overview

ELTs use three key constructs in moving beyond traditional, user-level litmus tests. First, ELTs describe virtual and physical addresses as distinct and simultaneous entities. In the same way that traditional litmus tests propose an outcome consisting of a set of values returned by the loads in the program, ELTs likewise propose as part of the outcome the physical addresses used by each access. In this way, the analysis of later sections can directly test whether a proposed set of address translation outcomes is legal.

Second, ELTs incorporate relevant chunks of OS activity, such as map/remap functions (MRFs) or inter-processor interrupts (IPIs) as used in software TLB coherence [37, 46]. They similarly include events such as the sending of IPIs, register reads/writes which cause the enabling/disabling of interrupts, and so on.

Third, ELTs include "ghost instructions" which model lower-than-ISA operations (e.g., page table walks) executed by the hardware on behalf of user-level or system-level code, even if these instructions are not fetched, decoded or issued as part of the normal ISA-level instruction stream. The combined power of address tracking, ghost instructions and OS module insertions gives ELTs sufficient expressive power to test all aspects of memory ordering enforcement as it relates to address translation.

Figure 4 presents an example flow from user-level litmus test to ELT. Our example shows the *store buffering* (`sb`) litmus test, which will be further discussed in Section 7. The stated test outcome is forbidden under sequential consistency (because it does not represent any simple interleaving of the four user-level instructions), but as its name implies, it is observable under models such as TSO which allow store buffering/store→load reordering to be visible. We form a more system-oriented example by inserting an extra system call to `mprotect` at the beginning of thread 0 in Figure 4a.

3.2 Litmus Test Expansion Synopses

As Figure 4 shows, each ELT comes about as the result of a sequence of modification passes. We systematize this transformation in the form of *litmus test expansion synopses*, or simply *synopses* for short. Each synopsis is a "recipe" for expanding each instruction in an input litmus test into one or more instructions in an output litmus test. As described below, there is some flexibility in what the recipes look like: the original instruction may or may not be maintained, and instruction expansions may insert new code into other threads as well. Furthermore, each expanded instruction may be inserted either before or after the original instruction. In this way, synopses serve as succinct representations of behaviors that we hope might one day become more rigorously and precisely formalized.

3.3 From User-Level to Kernel-Aware Litmus tests

Incorporating system calls and kernel-level code into a user-level litmus test requires multiple changes. First, in the invoking thread (e.g., Thread 0 in Figure 4a), we must be able to substitute the system call with a module of memory reference operations that correctly encapsulate the system call behavior relevant to memory ordering verification. Figure 4b continues the example of Figure 4a by expanding the system call into a set of four instructions on the invoking Thread 0. The expanded regions are shaded in blue.

It is worth noting that this expansion can affect multiple threads at once. Because one of the instructions expanded in Thread 0 triggers an inter-processor interrupt (IPI), we also add a three instruction interrupt handler to all of the other threads (in this case, Thread 1a). Notably, since the relative timing of Thread 0 and Thread 1a has not yet been established, it is also impossible (at this point) to determine the relative ordering of Threads 1a and 1b. For example, while it is clear that the interrupt handler must happen sometime after the interrupt is originally triggered, there is little other synchronization between the threads. Any such orderings will be filled in later by the μspec specification of IPI behavior in the microarchitecture in question.

Initially: [x]=0, [y]=0	
Core 0/Thread 0	**Core 1/Thread 1a**
syscall mprotect [x], r/w	
St [x] ← 1	St [y] ← 1
Ld [y] → 0	Ld [x] ← 0
Outcome: Permitted	

(a) Original user-level test.

Initially: [x]=0, [y]=0, VA x → PA a (R/O, acc, !dirty), VA y → PA b (R/W, acc, dirty), VA z → PTE for VA x (R/W, acc, dirty)		
Core 0	**Core 1**	
User Thread 0	**User Thread 1a**	**Int. Hndlr. Thread 1b**
St [z/PTE(x)] ← R/W	St [y/b] ← 1	invlpg [x]
invlpg [x]	Ld [x/a] → 0	Send ACK
Send IPI		iret
Wait for Acks		
St [x/a] ← 1		
Ld [y/b] → 0		
Outcome: Permitted		

(b) User+Kernel litmus test. On core 1, threads 1a and 1b will be interleaved in some fashion, but the interleaving cannot be statically determined. The "R/W" store value is shorthand to indicate that the entire PTE is written, but with the R/W bit set.

Initially: [x]=0, [y]=0, VA x → PA a (R/O, acc, !dirty), VA y → PA b (R/W, acc, dirty), VA z → PTE for VA x (R/W, acc, dirty) VA w → PTE for VA y (R/W, acc, dirty)		
Core 0	**Core 1**	
User Thread 0	**User Thread 1a**	**Int. Hndlr. Thread 1b**
St [z/PTE(x)] ← R/W	St [y/b] ← 1	IPI Recv
invlpg [x]	Ld PML4E(x)	save state
Send IPI	Ld PDPTE(x)	disable ints
Wait for IPI Acks	Ld PDE(x)	invlpg [x]
Ld PML4E(x)	Ld PTE(x)	Send Ack
Ld PDPTE(x)	Ld [x/a] → 0	iret
Ld PDE(x)		
Ld PTE(x)→clean		
LdAtomic PTE(x)→clean		
StAtomic PTE(x)←dirty		
St [x/a] ← 1		
Ld [y/b] → 0		
Outcome: Permitted		

(c) Microarchitecture-level litmus test (ELT). However, page table accesses for [y], accessed bit updates, etc., are not even expanded in this example; the real situation would potentially grow even larger.

Figure 4: To represent the memory accesses taking place at the microarchitecture level, we expand user-level litmus tests into *enhanced litmus tests*.

OS Synopses: On the invoking core, an *OS synopsis* specifies a mapping from each system call into a simple pre-defined sequence of microops capturing the effects of that system call on address translation and consistency. When the system call contains an inter-processor interrupt (IPI), the OS synopsis also instantiates pre-defined interrupt handler threads on those cores, again using a sequence of statically-determined instructions. Each interrupt handler may be arbitrarily interleaved with the other thread(s) assigned to that core, subject to μspec constraints (Section 4.2).

We do not curently model the complexities of OS decision making or data structures; our OS synopses currently include only memory accesses which update the paging structures and any synchronization used to enforced orderings with respect to these updates. However, these synopses could be made more sophisticated as needed; we believe that attempting to formalize the relationship between these OS synopses and the full OS code would make for interesting follow-up work.

3.4 Memory-Accessing Microcode: Ghost Instructions

During V-P translation, there are many microcode operations which are *not* fetched as ISA-level instructions (either user or kernel) but which still play a key role in enforcing consistency. These microcode operations are used to support hardware page table walks, TLB refills, accessed/dirty bit updates, and so on. We refer to these operations as *ghost instructions*, as they are present but not visible to the user or to the OS kernel.

The presence and behavior of ghost instructions depends heavily both on the architecture and on the microarchitecture in question. At an architecture level, operations such as page table walks may be specified as being enforced entirely by hardware, entirely by software, or anywhere in between. COATCheck is flexible enough to cover any point on this spectrum. We break this problem into two parts: the specification of the instructions (and ghost instructions) which are emitted to cause ordering to be enforced (this section), and the specification of the orderings enforced between these instructions at different points in their executions (Section 4.2).

Figure 4c depicts an ELT derived from Figure 4b. Darker red-shaded regions are microcode operations that have been expanded at this phase; lighter blue regions remain those expanded in the previous step. For this test scenario, thread 0's access to [x] requires a page table walk, because the TLB entry for that virtual address would have been invalidated by the invlpg instruction. Also, since the initial condition states that the page containing [x] is clean, hardware would also mark the page as dirty prior to the write (specified to occur on x86 using a LOCKed atomic operation [20]). Other accesses may also take TLB misses and trigger page table walks themselves, although (for space reasons) the figure does not show all of them. Finally, the ELT includes hardware operations for receiving the interrupt, saving state, and disabling nested interrupts via the microcode preamble to thread 1b. In this example, hardware is responsible for saving state, but software is responsible for restoring it. This again highlights the degree of collective responsibility between hardware and OS for ensuring ordering correctness.

Microarchitecture Synopses: As with the OS synopses, our *microarchitecture synopses* currently consist of rela-

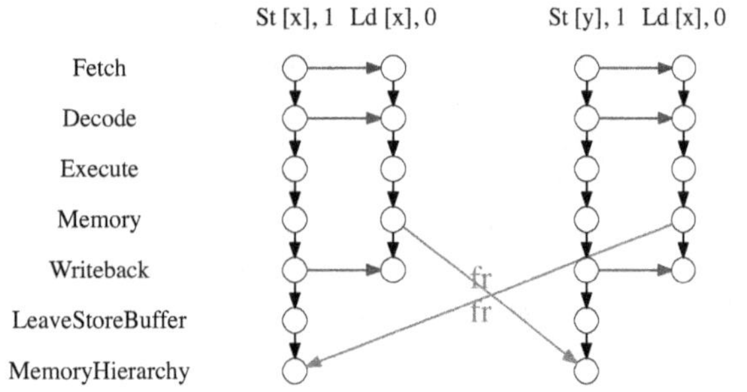

Figure 5: μhb graph for the test of Fig. 4a, without the syscall.

tively straightforward pre-defined expansions which insert page table walk ghost instructions next to each normal instruction. Unlikely as it may be, for completeness we perform this expansion for every instruction, as each instruction may cause a TLB miss and hence trigger a page table walk, and every instruction may update the associated page status bits. Likewise, the expansions of loads in our current synopses include ghost instructions corresponding to accessing both clean and dirty pages, as both possibilities must be considered. The comprehensive enumeration performed by the μspec models may choose to use all ghost instructions, or it may choose to ignore optional possibilities which are not needed (e.g., PT walks not needed during TLB hits) or impossible (e.g., a page being clean and dirty simultaneously).

As with the OS synopses, we envision microarchitecture synopses becoming more sophisticated as needed. Further, we envision that the notion of such synopses will ultimately become part of future microarchitectural specifications too.

4. μspec: A μhb Graph-Centric Ordering Specification Language

4.1 Background: μhb Graphs

Microarchitecture-level happens-before (μhb) graphs capture consistency model enforcement at the implementation level [26, 27]. Figure 5 gives an example. Nodes in a μhb graph represent events corresponding to a particular instruction (column) at a particular physical location (row). For example, a node may represent a particular instruction passing through a particular pipeline stage. Edges represent happens-before orderings guaranteed by some property of the microarchitecture: an instruction flowing through a pipeline, a FIFO-ordered structure, the passage of a message, and so on.

All edges in a μhb graph are equivalent, regardless of their label. This allows the transitive closure of two μhb graphs to itself always be a legal μhb graph, and it implies that *any* cycle in a μhb graph indicates that the execution is infeasible. This places μhb graphs in contrast to some other existing approaches in which only specific subsets of a happens-before graph are analyzed for cycles [3].

```
Axiom "ReadsFrom":
forall microops "r", IsRead r =>
  exists microop "w", IsWrite w /\
  SamePhysicalAddress w r /\ SameData w r /\
  EdgeExists ((w, AccessMemory), (r, AccessMemory), "rf").
```

Figure 6: μspec syntax example.

4.2 μspec: A DSL for Specifying μhb Graph Orderings

μspec is a domain specific language in which hardware or software component designers express the ordering relationships enforced by that component. Through the μspec specification, designers provide a set of μhb graph-focused *axioms* which must all be satisfied for a given test to be considered observable [29]. This axiomatic approach is widely used in memory model analysis [2, 3, 28, 32], but μspec extends this down to a lower level of abstraction.

μspec axioms are first order logic (i.e., AND, OR, NOT, EXISTS, FORALL) statements built on top of instruction- and μhb graph-related predicates. The instruction-related predicates are used to constrain an axiom to a relevant subset of instructions. For example, an axiom that states a property relating two reads to the same physical address would use the two predicates `IsRead` and `SamePhysicalAddress`.

The core μspec axiom is the predicate `EdgeExists` (or, in plural form, `EdgesExist`). This predicate takes three arguments: a source μhb node, a destination μhb node, and a label. The nodes are in turn formed of two components: an instruction, and a microarchitectural location or event. These correspond to the column and row of the node in the μhb graph, respectively. The edge label is purely cosmetic, as all edges in a μhb graph are equivalent (Section 4.1).

Figure 6 gives an example of the μspec syntax. The `ReadsFrom` axiom asserts that for every read `r`, there must be some corresponding write `w` to the same *physical* address. Further, this write must match the value returned by the read. When such a read is found, the axiom specifies that an edge labeled "rf" should be added to the μhb graph between the two μhb nodes (w, AccessMemory) and (r, AccessMemory). If there is more than one candidate for w which satisfies `SamePhysicalAddress` and `SameData`, then each possibility (and sub-cases derived thereof) will be considered independently by the constraint solver (Section 5).

Each axiom in a μspec model specification represents an independent and ideally localized property of one particular mechanism. Component models are formed by conjoining (i.e., logically ANDing) the axioms within a model. Likewise, system models are built by conjoining the models of the components forming the system. The overall system specification therefore consists of a first order logic formula whose satisfiability determines whether a proposed execution is feasible on the system being analyzed.

The approach of separating out individual axioms makes μspec models highly modular: axioms can be added or removed as necessary without affecting any of the other axioms or components. In other words, this approach allows microarchitecture-specific axioms to be easily swapped out for another set while OS- and architecture-level are kept unchanged, to give just one example. While μspec cannot (yet) automate the extraction of a specification from Verilog or HDLs, it does greatly reduce the effort required to express ordering requirements and expectations, and we hope to elaborate on this aspect in future work.

5. Constraint Solver and Software Implementation

As described in Section 4.2, the μspec specification of a system produces a first-order logic formula whose satisfiability corresponds to the feasibility of a particular execution. The COATCheck constraint solver accepts this formula and some litmus test as inputs, and it searches to find any execution of that test which satisfies all of the constraints of the model. If one can be found, then the proposed outcome is observable. If not, then the proposed outcome is forbidden. In PipeCheck, which introduced μhb graphs, the graphs were generated using naive exhaustive enumeration [26, 27]. However, the PipeCheck approach does not scale to the sizes and numbers of graphs needed to handle ELTs.

5.1 Constraint Solver Algorithm

The preliminary step in the solving process is to eliminate the quantifiers in the formula. Doing so produces a quantifier-free propositional logic formula that is more directly amenable to being solved. Since the domain of each quantifier is concrete in the context of some particular litmus test, the quantifiers are removed by simply converting each `forall` into a conjuction (AND) over its domain (i.e., cores, threads, or instructions). Likewise, each `exists` is converted into a disjunction (OR).

The solver algorithm itself resembles and is inspired by the Davis-Putnam-Logemann-Loveland (DPLL) algorithm widely used in SAT solvers [14]. We apply it to μhb graphs, making our solver resemble a primitive but effective SMT solver for the theory of acyclic directed graphs. At a high level, the solver uses a backtracking approach: given a starting point, it generates a list of subcases of "either-or" edge additions, and it then recursively descends into each subcase, abandoning those which cannot satisfy the given conditions and stopping when it reaches a leaf node (i.e., an acyclic graph). Although we could have used an off-the-shelf SAT or SMT solver, our custom solver provided significantly better debugging ability and status visualization (e.g., of partially-completed μhb graphs and decision trees) than would have been possible with a black-box solver. We found this empirically to be very useful during our work.

5.2 Software Toolchain

We implemented the COATCheck methodology into the complete working toolflow shown in Figure 3. In normal operation, the tool takes as input a user-level litmus test, HW/OS synopses (Section 3.1), and μspec models (Section 4.2). For low-level debugging, the tool also allows the direct input of a manually-written ELT (bypassing the synopses). The ELT and component μspec models feed into the model analyzer, which applies the axioms of the models to the ELT to generate a tree of μhb graph constraints. The constraints are then passed to the constraint solver to determine if the outcome is feasible.

Our core analysis infrastructure is written in Coq to allow for formal verification [44]. However, we have not yet completed any formal proofs of correctness; this remains an open problem, and in any case, the specifications of expected behavior often simply do not yet exist. We therefore leave this to future work, and we instead extract the Coq code to OCaml to build COATCheck as a standalone tool.

Because we aim for backwards compatibility with existing MCM analysis frameworks, we interface our tool with `herd` and the `litmus` format [3]. This allows us to draw from a large existing body of litmus tests. Although these tests do not distinguish virtual and physical addresses, they serve as valuable sanity checks for the basic correctness of a pipeline model. Furthermore, hardware models from previous work [26, 27, 38, 39] can be easily adapted into μspec and our OS models, and hence into COATCheck as well.

6. Detailed Processor+OS Model Case Study

This section presents an in-depth case study of how hardware and software designers might use COATCheck and μspec to model a high-performance out-of-order processor and OS, respectively. The resulting μspec model is the one used for Section 7's litmus test case studies, and Section 8 performance results.

6.1 Basic Overview

Our case study model has three main parts, two of which are provided by the hardware designer and one of which is provided by someone familiar with the OS. The first component is a μspec model which describes a given processor microarchitecture. This model provides a set of μspec axioms representing the ordering constraints enforced by the hardware. In this case study, this hardware component is inspired by the Intel Sandy Bridge microarchitecture, and was developed in detail using public documentation [19, 20], information gleaned from patents [16], and some educated guesses used to fill in gaps. Many of the low-level details remain proprietary, so it cannot be an exact match, but the paper nevertheless refers to this as our *SandyBridge* model. Table 1 gives an overall enumeration of the μspec axioms in this model.

The second component is a SandyBridge hardware synopsis (Section 3.4) which specifies how litmus tests might be expanded by hardware when executed on SandyBridge. These expansions pertain to hardware page table walks or other hardware-initiated events (i.e., ghost instructions) in-

Axiom	Description
Reads	Path (Pipeline stage sequence) and μhb orderings for read instructions
Writes	Path/orderings for write instructions
mfence	Path/orderings for `mfence`
invlpg	Path/orderings for `invlpg`
iret	Path for `iret` instruction
RMW	Atomicity of LOCKed RMW operations
FetchPO	Program Order enforced at Fetch
DispatchPPO	Fetch order maintained at Dispatch
CommitPPO	Dispatch order maintained at Commit
StBufPPO	Commit order maintained at Store Buffer
Write Serialization	Per-physical address total order on all writes reaching `AccessCache`
SLR	Speculative Load Reordering
IPIInsertions	IPI handlers embedded within user thread
IPIOrdering	Enumeration of all nestings of IPI handlers
IPIReceive	Paths for OS code modeling receiving of IPI
IPIRecvAtomicity	OS code modeling receving of IPI is atomic
IPIAcks	IPI handlers must complete before issuing thread allowed to proceed
TLBEntries	Paths for PT walks and TLB entry μhb nodes
TLBEntriesNoDups	No concurrent duplicate TLB entries

Table 1: Axioms for SandyBridge model. Some axioms include macros which expand to address other orderings not listed.

serted within the litmus test. The third component is the Linux OS synopsis (Section 3.3) that specifies code sequences for system calls and for interrupt handlers. Our Linux synopsis is derived from careful inspection of the Linux source code (and, for the architecture-specific portions, the 64-bit x86 version). Note that there is no μspec model for the Linux component; this is because the software specifies the instructions to be executed (i.e., the column headings in a μhb graph), while the hardware actually executes the instructions (i.e., the nodes and edges in the graph).

In general, the μspec model and hardware synopsis rely on hardware knowledge, and the OS synopsis relies on OS knowledge, but the three components compose together; no single designer must be fluent across all components. In the text that follows, we discuss several important-to-model aspects of hardware-OS behavior. For each, we describe how the μspec model, the hardware synopsis and the OS synopsis work together to reflect the appropriate hardware-OS behavior.

6.2 Memory Dependency Prediction and Disambiguation

The first type of functionality we consider is a sophisticated, high-performance store buffer (SB) forwarding mechanism. We focus on capturing the key role address translation plays in the store buffer. If the implementation operated using only virtual addresses, for example, then it would be unable to detect virtual address synonyms, leading to problems such as the one in Figure 7. Placing the TLB on the critical path would avoid this problem; however, this would

x and y are synonyms
Thread 0
`St [x/PA1] ← 1`
`St [y/PA1] ← 2`
`Ld [x/PA1] → r1`
Proposed outcome: `r1=1`

Figure 7: Store buffer forwarding implementations must be able to detect synonyms to ensure that each load receives its value from the latest store to the same physical address

come with a performance cost. This realistic example reveals the perhaps-surprising complexity involved in the seemingly straightforward process of store buffer forwarding. We start by describing the mechanism, and we then describe its implementation in μspec. Hardware or OS synopses are not used in modeling this feature, so they are not discussed.

Mechanism: High-performance forwarding in our SandyBridge model consists of memory dependency prediction and memory disambiguation [19]. The prediction stage anticipates dynamic same-physical address dependencies between stores and loads to try to preemptively prevent consistency violations that might arise. The disambiguation stage later ensures that all predictions were correct. This pairing ensures that synonyms can be detected while keeping the TLB off of the forwarding critical path.

The mechanism we model works as follows. All stores write their virtual address and data into the SB in parallel with accessing the TLB. The physical address is later written into the SB as well, once the TLB provides it. Loads, in parallel with accessing the TLB, write their lower 12 bits ("index bits") into a CAM-based load buffer that holds all loads that have not yet committed. Due to the minimum 4KB page size, these lower 12 bits will always be identical between virtual and physical addresses.

Initially, each load compares its index bits against the index bits of all older stores present in the store buffer. If no index match is found among the filled-in entries, then clearly no match exists. If an older entry is allocated but not filled in (because its address was not yet generated), it is predicted to cause no dependencies. If an index match is found, the load will then compare high-order bits. If the load's virtual tag matches the virtual tag of the store, the store will forward its value to the load[4]. If not, the load compares its physical tag against the store's physical tag, stalling if either instruction's TLB access has not yet returned a translation. If the physical tags match, the store will forward its data to the load. Otherwise, the load will have determined that no dependency exists between the load and that particular store.

In addition to the above, our model must also reflect disambiguation, in which stores determine whether their speculations were legal. Before each store commits, it checks the load buffer to see if any younger loads matching the same

[4] Homonyms are handled on Linux/x86 by flushing non-global TLB entries on each context switch.

```
DefineMacro "StoreBufferForwardPTag":
exists microop "w", (
    SameCore w i /\ IsAnyWrite w /\ ProgramOrder w i /\
    SameIndex w i /\ ~(SameVirtualTag w i) /\
    SamePhysicalTag w i /\ SameData w i /\ EdgesExist [
      ((w, SB-VTag/Index/Data), (i, LB-SB-IndexCompare),
          "SBEntryIndexPresent");
      ((w, SB-PTag), (i, LB-SB-PTagCompare),
          "SBEntryPTagPresent");
      ((i, SB-LB-DataForward), (w, (0, MemoryHierarchy)),
          "BeforeSBEntryLeaves");
      ((i, LB-SB-IndexCompare), (i, LB-SB-VTagCompare),
          "path");
      ((i, LB-SB-VTagCompare), (i, LB-SB-PTagCompare),
          "path");
      ((i, LB-PTag), (i, LB-SB-PTagCompare), "path");
      ((i, LB-SB-PTagCompare), (i, SB-LB-DataForward),
          "path");
      ((i, SB-LB-DataForward), (i, WriteBack), "path")] /\
    ExpandMacro STBNoOtherMatchesBetweenSrcAndRead).
```

Figure 8: μspec Macro describing instance of SB-Forwarding

physical address have speculatively executed before it. If so, it squashes and replays them.

μspec Axioms: Based on that store buffer mechanism, Figure 8 shows a μspec model snippet of one piece of the prediction and disambiguation mechanism; other pieces are analogous but omitted for space reasons. The figure shows a μspec snippet for the sub-case in which a load has an index match, virtual tag miss, and physical tag match with a previous store.

The first part of the code, '`exists microop "w"`', will only evaluate to true if there is at least one microop that satisfies the enclosed statements. The middle part enforces orderings via two types of μhb edges: some ensuring that the write `w` is still in the store buffer when the load `i` searches for it, and some describing the path `i` itself takes through the forwarding mechanism. Finally, it expands a macro (not pictured due to space reasons) checking that the store is in fact the youngest matching store in the store buffer. The model accomplishes this by ensuring that for all stores in between, either the virtual and physical tags do not match or the indexes of the middle stores are not present (because they have not yet executed).

Other possibilities exist for memory disambiguation. An advantage of μspec is that the axioms representing the approach we describe above can be easily replaced by those representing other solutions (e.g., load reexecution [15]).

6.3 Memory Mapping/Remapping Functions, System Calls, and Interrupts

A second component of our *Linux+SandyBridge* model reflects the functionality of system calls and interrupts as they relate to memory mapping/remapping functions. This section describes mechanisms for how these work, particularly noting which parts are implemented in hardware and OS. The model also serves as an example of how key hardware-

```
DefineMacro "EmbeddedIn" t1 t2:
forall microops "i1", OnCore c i1 => OnThread t1 i1 => (
  forall microops "i2", OnCore c i2 => OnThread t2 i2 => (
    AddEdge ((i1, Commit), (i2, Fetch), "EmbeddedIn") \/
    AddEdge ((i2, Commit), (i1, Fetch), "EmbeddedIn"))).

Axiom "IPIOrdering":
forall threads "t1", forall threads "t2",
~(IsMainThread t1) => ~(IsMainThread t2) =>
~(SameThread t1 t2) =>
  ExpandMacro EmbeddedIn t1 t2 \/
  ExpandMacro EmbeddedIn t2 t1.
```

Figure 9: Enumerating thread interleavings using μspec. The user specifies only the constraint that there exists some embedding; the solver later enumerates the possibilities.

OS functionality is reflected in our SandyBridge μspec model and the hardware and OS synopses.

Mechanism: Although x86 TLB lookups and page table walks are performed by the hardware, x86 TLB coherence is OS-managed. To support this, x86 provides the privileged `invlpg` instruction, as well as the support for cores to communicate via inter-processor interrupts (IPIs). `invlpg` is a privileged instruction which serializes the instruction stream and invalidates the TLB entry containing the mapping corresponding to the specified virtual address. As a serializing instruction, `invlpg` causes all previous instructions to commit and drains all pending writes in the store buffer to memory before fetching the following instruction. `invlpg` also ensures that the next access to the virtual page invalidated will be a TLB miss, thus forcing the latest version of the corresponding page table entry to be brought into the TLB.

Linux Synopsis: Our Linux synopsis expands the system call `mprotect` into code snippets which 1) update the PTE appropriately, 2) invalidate the now-stale TLB entry on the current core, and 3) send TLB shootdowns to other cores via IPIs and interrupt handlers. The interrupt handler performs its own `invlpg` operation before sending an acknowledgment to the sender and returning from the interrupt.

SandyBridge Synopsis: The SandyBridge synopsis reflects ghost instructions added to reflect hardware-initiated memory references. In this case, the hardware synopsis first adds a ghost instruction representing the reception of the interrupt. This allows the μspec model to draw μhb edges reflecting that operation. Second, it adds a ghost instruction representing a write to the `FLAGS` register bit that determines whether interrupts are enabled, as on x86, after receiving an interrupt, subsequent interrupts are disabled until re-enabled by the handler or the OS. Interrupt re-enabling is handled by the OS code expanding to sequences containing either `iret` or `cli` instructions; both implicitly model writes to the `FLAGS` register as well.

μspec Axioms: Figure 9 shows how the orderings between these events are specified within our `SandyBridge` μspec model. This snippet shows a macro `EmbeddedIn` and an axiom `IPIOrdering` that makes use of it. The user simply specifies the set of possibilities, and the solver (Section 5) automatically and efficiently enumerates all ways the axiom can be satisfied. A separate macro (not shown) adds pipeline- and store buffer-draining μhb edges representing the fact that interrupts are precise [19].

6.4 Page Table Walks

Mechanism: On the x86 architecture, the page table walker is built into the hardware [20]. This means that page table walk loads are not issued by the user or by the OS; instead, they are contained entirely within hardware and are invisible to the user.

SandyBridge Synopsis: Every potential page table walk is instantiated by the microarchitecture synopsis as a set of ghost instruction loads of the page table entry. (The TLB is modeled as described in Section 6.6.)

μspec Axioms: Our model handles these ghost loads as follows. First, it does not draw Fetch, Dispatch, etc. nodes in the paths (i.e., columns) for these special loads, as they do not pass through the pipeline. Second, the axiom never uses predicates such as `SameVirtualTag` with them, since page table walks are done using only physical addresses. Third, since the loads are not TSO-ordered, they do not search the load buffer as in Section 6.2. Lastly, it adds exceptions to, e.g., the `mfence` axioms to omit μhb edges touching these instructions. The model does ensure, however, that page table walks are ordered with respect to `invlpg` [16].

6.5 Status Bit Updates

Mechanism: When a page table accessed or dirty bit needs to be updated due to a memory access, our SandyBridge pipeline waits until the triggering instruction reaches the head of the reorder buffer. At that point, the processor injects microcode implementing the update into the buffer. It also must ensure that the update is ordered against younger instructions to prevent later loads from reading the now-stale state of the PTE from before the update.

SandyBridge Synopsis: For each store, the hardware synopsis instantiates dirty bit updates as ghost instructions performing a LOCKed RMW operation on the bits in memory. These instructions are inserted just before the triggering instruction. At a low level, we represent the read and the write of the RMW as separate microops, and atomicity is guaranteed by the μspec axioms described below.

μspec Axioms: The ghost instructions in a status bit update do traverse the Dispatch, Issue, and Commit stages, unlike the ghost page table walks, as the status bit updates do propagate through most of the pipeline and affect architectural state. They are not fetched, however. The orderings enforced for these ghost instructions are modeled in μspec by adding μhb edges to enforce that 1) all previous accesses must have committed, reflecting the condition that the triggering instruction be at the head of the ROB, and 2) each update has LOCK semantics (i.e., `mfence` semantics plus atomicity).

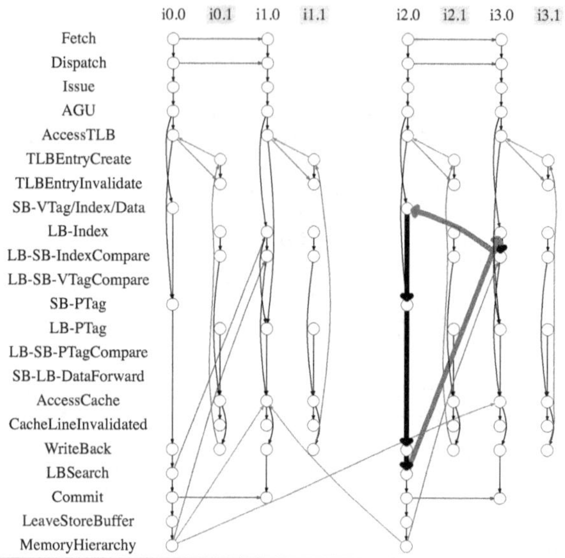

Initially: `[x]=0, [y]=0,` `VA x → PA a (R/W, acc, dirty),` `VA y → PA a (R/W, acc, dirty),`			
Core 0		**Core 1**	
`(i0.0)`	`St [x/a] ← 1`	`(i2.0)`	`St [y/a] ← 2`
`(i0.1)`	`Ld PTE(x)`	`(i2.1)`	`Ld PTE(y)`
`(i1.0)`	`Ld [y/a]→ r1`	`(i3.0)`	`Ld [x/a] → r2`
`(i1.1)`	`Ld PTE(y)`	`(i3.1)`	`Ld PTE(x)`
Outcome: Forbidden; r1 = 2, r2 = 1			

Figure 10: Litmus test `n5`. Cycle shown with thicker edges.

6.6 Modeling TLB Occupancy

μspec Axioms: To model TLB occupancy in μhb graphs, we add two special new nodes to the paths of page table walk and status bit update ghost instructions. For page table walks and status bit updates, after the last memory access of the walk completes, the insertion of the entry into the TLB corresponds to a *TLB entry creation* event. Some time later, there is a *TLB entry invalidation* event that takes place for the same entry. Note that this invalidation, in general, occurs long after the page table walk has completed. This approach, which resembles the value-in-cache-line (ViCL) mechanism developed previously [29], tracks the ordering of TLB state changes and applies equally well to microarchitectural variants such as allowing in-place updating of TLB status bits.

We then add a constraint stating that each instruction must read from a TLB entry which exists and which contains matching data (translation and status). More precisely, for a given instruction i accessing virtual address v and physical address p, this means that there must exist a ghost instruction g such that the data returned (for walks) or written (for updates) by g is a PTE mapping the tag of v to the tag of p. The relevant model axiom also checks for status and permission bits in the same way. Once the entry is found,

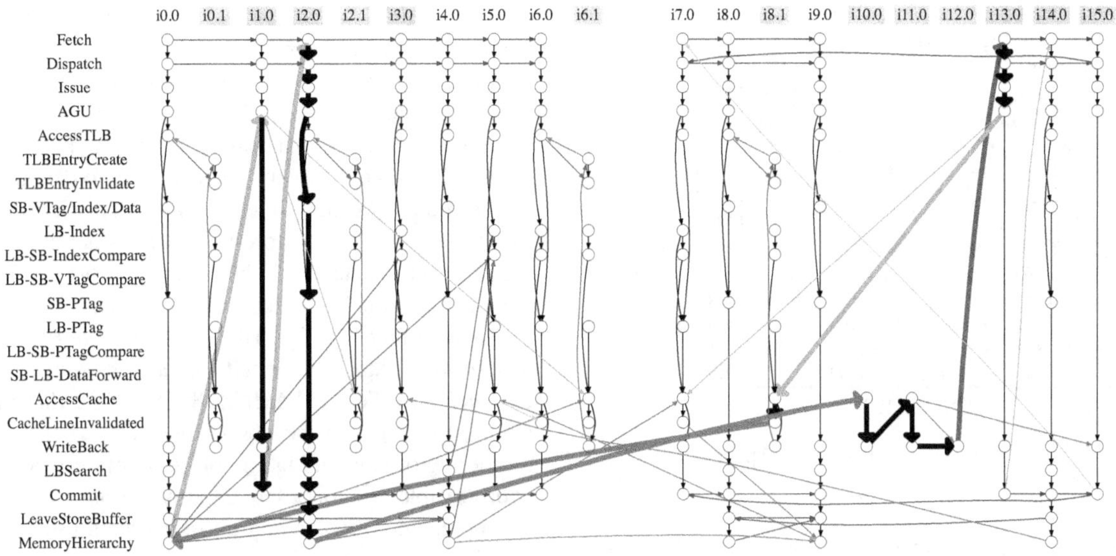

Figure 11: Cyclic graph illustrating one possible ordering for litmus test `ipi8` [38, 39]. Because the graph is cyclic (highlighted with thicker edges), this outcome is not observable in this case. In this case, the cycle was found before the PTEs for y were even enumerated. For this test, all executions lead to cyclic graphs, and hence the outcome is not observable, as expected.

the axiom adds two μhb edges representing that 1) the TLB entry must be created before the instruction can access it, and 2) the TLB entry must be accessed before it is invalidated.

Note that each page table walk may be but need not be associated with a particular instruction. A TLB prefetch could trigger a page table walk at any point in an execution, and so there may be "floating" walks. The TLB occupancy model operates in exactly the same way in both cases.

7. Case Study Litmus Tests

In this section, we study three interesting test cases in the context of the system modeled in Section 6.

7.1 Dependence Checks and Store Buffer Forwarding

As described in Section 2, `n5_synonym` tests whether the store buffer forwarding mechanism takes physical addresses into account. If either core's store buffer does not realize that the two accesses from that core are synonyms, either load may be allowed to bypass the store before it, leading to an illegal outcome. Figure 10 shows one of the μhb graphs by which COATCheck verifies that such an (erroneous) outcome is impossible on our SandyBridge model[5].

The particular execution of Figure 10 shows the scenario in which the processor speculates that the store and load access different addresses and hence (under TSO rules) may be reordered. As in previous litmus tests, the red shading denotes hardware microcode operations (PT walks) executed on behalf of the user-level code. The columns of the μhb graph are annotated with instruction labels (user-level or microcode) corresponding to those in the litmus test.

When the load (i3.0) executes, it finds that the store buffer contains no previous entries with the same index (because in this scenario, the store (i2.0) has not yet issued). This leads to a happens-before edge (shown in thick blue in the figure) between the `LB-SB-IndexCompare` stage of (i3.0) and the `SB-VTag/Index/Data` stage of (i2.0). However, when the store (i2.0) does eventually execute, the condition under which it would not squash the speculatively-executed load is if the load buffer has no entries matching the same index. This could occur only if the load had not yet entered the load buffer. This situation would cause there to be a happens-before edge (also shown in thick blue) from the `LBSearch` stage of the (i2.0) store back to the `LB-Index` stage of the load (i3.0), thereby completing a happens-before cycle indicating that the scenario cannot occur in practice.

7.2 Page Remappings and TLB Shootdowns

Figure 11 shows the μhb graph for the Figure 12 scenario involving address remappings and TLB shootdowns. This scenario is derived from previous work [38, 39]; however, we fill in some underspecified page mappings and initial conditions and adapt it to x86-TSO. The original test also considered two outcomes, one of which was observable and the other of which was forbidden. Here, we split this into two tests; we treat the permitted variant as a separate test and a sanity check that the legal outcome remains observable.

At a high level, thread 0 changes the mapping for x (i0.0), triggers a TLB shootdown (i2.0), and sends a message to thread 1 (i4.0). Thread 1 receives the message (i7.0) and writes to x (i8.0), whose mapping was just modified. Cor-

[5] In reality, the solver would have stopped searching as soon as it detected a cycle, and it may not have filled in any still-incomplete portions of the graph. However, the complete graph is drawn here for clarity

Initially: [x]=0, VA x → PA a (R/W, acc, dirty), (other mappings omitted for space reasons)			
Core 0		**Core 1**	
Thread 0		**Thread 1a**	
(i0.0)	St [z/PTE(x)] ← (VA x → PA b)	(i7.0)	Ld [y/c] → 2
		(i8.0)	St [x/a] ← 3
(i0.1)	Ld PTE(z)	(i8.1)	Ld PTE(x) → TLB
(i1.0)	invlpg [x]	(i9.0)	St [y/c] ← 4
(i2.0)	St [w/APIC] ← mrf	**Thread 1b**	
(i2.1)	Ld PTE(w)→ TLB	(i10.0)	Ld [w/APIC] → mrf
(i3.0)	Ld [v/d] → ack	(i11.0)	Ld EFLAGS → (IF)
(i4.0)	St [y/c] ← 2	(i12.0)	St EFLAGS ← (!IF)
(i5.0)	Ld [y/c] ← 4	(i13.0)	invlpg
(i6.0)	Ld [x/b] ← 1	(i14.0)	St [v/d] ← ack
(i6.1)	Ld PTE(x)→ TLB	(i15.0)	iret
Outcome: Forbidden			

Figure 12: Code for litmus test ipi8

rectness dictates that this write use the new rather than the old mapping; however, this particular test has the load using the *old, stale* translation in an effort to have COATCheck verify that such a situation is unobservable. Thread 1 (i9.0) sends a message back to thread 0 (via i5.0), which checks (i6.0) that the value at x (according to the new mapping) was not overwritten by the thread 1 store (i8.0) (as it used the old mapping). These orderings (plus the remaining low-level details) cause COATCheck to find μhb cycles in all cases.

This graph combines many COATCheck features: IPIs and their handlers, microcode which does not pass through the entire pipeline, orderings enforced (or not) by fences on different types of orderings, and so on. The scale and complexity of these analyses emphasizes the need for tools like COATCheck to automate the enumeration of such graphs and identify the cycle (thicker highlighted lines) to demonstrate non-observable outcomes.

7.3 OS Responsibility for Synonym Tracking

A third case study discusses maintaining coherence among the status bits in a synonym set. Our SandyBridge hardware does *not* guarantee that dirty bit update ghost instructions will also update all synonym pages [20]; the OS is responsible for identifying and updating dirty bits for any synonym PT entries. This can lead to a scenario in which data may be lost if this coordination is not implemented correctly.

Suppose x and y are synonyms mapped to PA a whose PTEs are both marked as clean. When a store is done to x, hardware will mark its PTE as dirty. Suppose the OS intends to swap out the physical page holding PA a and hence needs to check if the page is dirty. If it does so by only checking the PTE for y (and *not* checking the PTE for its synonym x), then a naive OS may incorrectly think the physical page is clean. We have implemented the model for this scenario (μhb graph not shown due to space reasons) and while the analysis accounts for all known happens-before orderings, an acyclic μhb graph can be found, indicating the event may be observable.

Fixing this case requires that at page eviction time, a less-naive OS such as Linux checks whether PTEs for *all* members of a synonym set are marked clean. The ELT would therefore contain an extra load of PTE(x) and a proposed outcome indicating that this load returned a clean PTE. COATCheck would then detect a violation of the SandyBridge Reads axiom, which requires that each load return the value of the latest store to that physical address (since the dirty bit update would be ordered before the load), and conclude that the bad outcome is no longer observable.

This example highlights the fact that *memory transistency models are broader in scope than memory consistency models, including SC-for-VAMC* [38, 39]. Note that in the example, the bug may be observable even when there is no reordering of any kind taking place. In other words, the bug is observable even on a sequentially consistent system. Furthermore, since the two non-ghost instructions access different virtual and physical addresses, and the status bit updates target a different PTE than the non-ghost load uses, the necessary ordering requirement (i.e., to check the state of the synonym pages) is also outside the scope of VAMC. Hence, there may be a translation-related memory ordering bug even on a SC-for-VAMC system. COATCheck is the first MCM analysis framework which can capture and reason about this additional level of indirection, and it can do so regardless of which layer of Figure 2 is used to solve it.

8. Automated Verification Software

8.1 Test Characteristics

We have performance tested COATCheck on a wide-ranging set of 118 litmus tests. We include a number of tests from Intel and AMD manuals and other prior work to sanity check that our SandyBridge model (Section 6) behaves as expected [7, 17, 32, 45].

Another category of litmus tests are modifications of the "standard" tests above to directly test address translation and OS interface issues. We either derived these from previous work [38, 39] or custom wrote them to test new functionality or scenarios. In some cases these originate as user-level codes and follow the full transformation path shown in Figure 3. In a few cases, we wrote the tests directly as ELTs to expediently achieve the desired test scenario. In general, these litmus tests lead to larger graphs, because they employ more of the ghost instructions and system call modules that lead to test size growth en route to an ELT.

Lastly, we also include the case studies of Section 7, plus numerous variants thereof. In all, this gives us a wide-ranging suite of tests on which we perform our analysis.

8.2 Performance Results

Figure 13 shows the full runtimes for our COATCheck implementation. Performance measurements were taken on a server with a 3.2GHz Intel Xeon E5-2667 v3 CPU. The runtimes shown in this graph are for the path from ELT

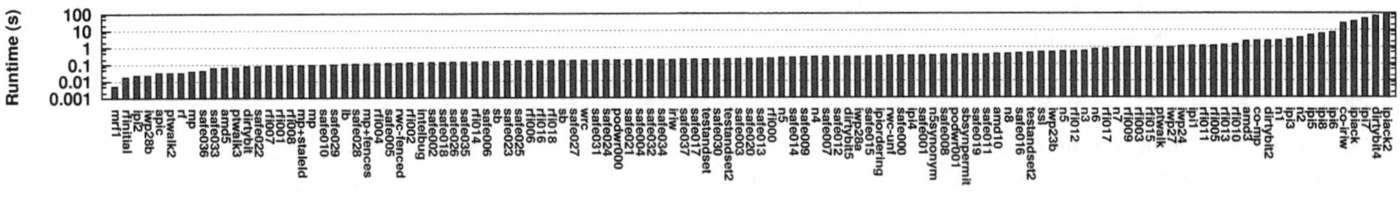

Figure 13: Execution times for full litmus test suite, sorted from smallest to largest run time.

through the constraint solver of Section 5. Recall that a cyclic μhb graph means that the event cannot be observed, and an acyclic μhb graph means that it is possible to observe. Therefore, when performing cycle checks, the cycle-checker can stop its analysis *for a given graph* as soon as a single cycle has been found in it. Likewise, when performing cycle checks for a litmus test intended to be forbidden, one can stop the checking *for the whole litmus test* as soon as a single acyclic graph has been found; one acyclic graph indicates an outcome intended to be forbidden might be observable.

Figure 13 shows the runtimes of the tests, sorted in increasing order. All 118 tests complete in less than 100 seconds, and many are even faster. All tests taking more than 30 seconds were created for this paper to test address translation, IPIs, TLB behavior, and so on. Although these μhb graphs are the largest for which such enumerate-and-check approaches have been used—they often an order of magnitude larger than those from the original PipeCheck work—our runtimes are similar to or less than those of PipeCheck. This shows that even though μspec is more general than previous work on μhb graphs [26, 27], the COATCheck constraint solver algorithm and its implementation are orders of magnitude more efficient. This allows COATCheck to be suitable even for interactive verification, thereby dramatically improving ease of use and debugging in practice.

9. Related Work

Computer architects and verification experts have long studied MCMs and in recent years researchers have made significant progress in formalizing MCM specifications and analysis [3, 13, 23, 28, 30, 32, 40]. These efforts have clearly demonstrated that 1) there is a need for rigor when analyzing memory models, 2) both informal and formal hardware and software models are highly prone to bugs [4, 36], and 3) it can take years to develop models which are sound with respect to hardware, sound with respect to the intention of the designers, and usable by programmers [8–10].

While these contributions have shed light on how to correctly design high-performance shared memory systems, they do not distinguish virtual and physical addresses and do not adequately cover hardware-OS interactions. As such, researchers have only recently focused on the relationship between MCMs and address translation [38, 39]. While our efforts are partly inspired by their observations, their virtual address memory models do not as comprehensively span system layers as ours do. For example, the more abstract VAMC [38, 39] does not reason about the interactions of OS activities like system calls and interrupts, microarchitectural activities like microcode injection, and low-level details like hardware page table walks. Instead, COATCheck formalizes a methodology to understand their interactions, and to verify that their relationship with MCMs actually meets specifications. In fact, these low-level details are essential, not just to design correct systems in the face of increasing system complexity (e.g., with heterogeneous systems and unified address spaces [34, 35]), but also to ensure that various recent TLB proposals on optimizations like prefetching [12, 41], coalescing [33], range TLBs [22], and TLB shootdowns [37, 46] operate correctly.

10. Conclusions

Memory consistency models have long been difficult to define, implement, and analyze. The need to properly handle hardware-OS interface issues such as address translation only adds new complexity. This paper provides methods and a full, efficient toolflow for automatically specifying and verifying memory ordering at the hardware-OS interface. Through many detailed case studies, our work also pushes beyond existing definitions of "consistency" to the more general notion of "transistency", because the ordering requirements in some of our tests cannot be expressed by consistency models alone. The COATCheck toolset facilitates further exploration of hardware-OS memory ordering issues, both in support of system verification itself, and also in the context of forward-looking definitions and explorations of consistency and transistency.

Acknowledgments

We thank Guilherme Cox, Yatin Manerkar, Caroline Trippel, Jan Vesely, and the anonymous reviewers for their helpful feedback. This work was supported in part by C-FAR (under the grant HR0011-13-3-0002), one of the six SRC STARnet Centers, sponsored by MARCO and DARPA, and in part by the National Science Foundation (under grants CCF-1117147 and CCF-1253700).

References

[1] S. V. Adve and M. D. Hill. Weak ordering—a new definition. *17th International Symposium on Computer Architecture (ISCA)*, 1990.

[2] J. Alglave. A formal hierarchy of weak memory models. *Formal Methods in System Design (FMSD)*, 41(2):178–210, 2012.

[3] J. Alglave, L. Maranget, and M. Tautschnig. Herding cats: Modelling, simulation, testing, and data-mining for weak memory. *ACM Transactions on Programming Languages and Systems (TOPLAS)*, 36(2):7:1–7:74, July 2014.

[4] J. Alglave, M. Batty, A. F. Donaldson, G. Gopalakrishnan, J. Ketema, D. Poetzl, T. Sorensen, and J. Wickerson. GPU concurrency: Weak behaviours and programming assumptions. *20th International Conference on Architectural Support for Programming Languages and Operating Systems (ASPLOS)*, 2015.

[5] AMD. Revision guide for AMD Athlon 64 and AMD Opteron processors. Publication number 25759. Revision: 3.79. 2009. URL `http://support.amd.com/TechDocs/25759.pdf`.

[6] AMD. Revision guide for AMD family 10h processors. publication number 41322. revision: 3.92. 2012.

[7] AMD. AMD64 architecture programmer's manual. `http://developer.amd.com/resources/documentation-articles/developer-guides-manuals/`, 2013.

[8] D. Aspinall and J. Sevcik. Java memory model examples: Good, bad and ugly. *1st International Workshop on Verification and Analysis of Multi-threaded Java-like Programs (VAMP)*, 2007.

[9] M. Batty, S. Owens, S. Sarkar, P. Sewell, and T. Weber. Mathematizing C++ concurrency. In *38th Symposium on Principles of Programming Languages (POPL)*, 2011.

[10] M. Batty, K. Memarian, S. Owens, S. Sarkar, and P. Sewell. Clarifying and compiling C/C++ concurrency: From C++11 to POWER. In *39th Symposium on Principles of Programming Languages (POPL)*, 2012.

[11] Benedict R. Gaster. HSA memory model. *Hot Chips Tutorial*, 2013. URL `http://hsafoundation.com/hot-chips-2013-hsa-foundation-presented-deeper-detail-hsa-hsail/`.

[12] A. Bhattacharjee and M. Martonosi. Inter-core cooperative TLB for chip multiprocessors. In *15th International Symposioum on Architectural Support for Programming Languages and Operating Systems (ASPLOS)*, 2010.

[13] H.-J. Boehm and S. V. Adve. Foundations of the C++ concurrency memory model. In *29th Conference on Programming Language Design and Implementation (PLDI)*, 2008.

[14] M. Davis, G. Logemann, and D. Loveland. A machine program for theorem-proving. *Communications of the ACM*, 5 (7), 1962.

[15] K. Gharachorloo, A. Gupta, and J. Hennessy. Two techniques to enhance the performance of memory consistency models. *International Conference on Parallel Processing (ICPP)*, 1991.

[16] A. Glew, G. Hinton, and H. Akkary. Method and apparatus for performing page table walks in a microprocessor capable of processing speculative instructions, Oct. 21 1997. URL `https://www.google.com/patents/US5680565`. US Patent 5,680,565.

[17] Intel. Intel 64 architecture memory ordering white paper. 2007. SKU 318147-001.

[18] Intel. Intel Core Duo processor and Intel Core Solo processor on 65 nm process specification update. Document number 309222. Revision number 20., 2009.

[19] Intel. Intel 64 and IA-32 architectures optimization reference manual, 2013.

[20] Intel. Intel 64 and IA-32 architectures software developer's manual, 2013.

[21] Intel. Intel Xeon processor E5 product family specification update. Reference number 326510-018., 2015.

[22] V. Karakostas, J. Gandhi, F. Ayar, A. Cristal, M. D. Hill, K. S. McKinley, M. Nemirovsky, M. M. Swift, and O. Ünsal. Redundant memory mappings for fast access to large memories. In *42nd International Symposium on Computer Architecture (ISCA)*, 2015.

[23] L. Lamport. How to make a multiprocessor computer that correctly executes multiprocess programs. *IEEE Transactions on Computing*, 28(9), 1979.

[24] N. M. Lê, A. Guatto, A. Cohen, and A. Pop. Correct and efficient bounded FIFO queues. *25th Symposium on Computer Architecture and High-Performance Computing (SBAC-PAD)*, 2013.

[25] N. M. Lê, A. Pop, A. Cohen, and F. Zappa Nardelli. Correct and efficient work-stealing for weak memory models. *18th Symposium on Principles and Practice of Parallel Programming (PPoPP)*, 2013.

[26] D. Lustig, M. Pellauer, and M. Martonosi. PipeCheck: Specifying and verifying microarchitectural enforcement of memory consistency models. *47th International Symposium on Microarchitecture (MICRO)*, 2014.

[27] D. Lustig, M. Pellauer, and M. Martonosi. Verifying correct microarchitectural enforcement of memory consistency models. *IEEE Micro Top Picks of 2014*, 35(3):72–82, May 2015.

[28] S. Mador-Haim, L. Maranget, S. Sarkar, K. Memarian, J. Alglave, S. Owens, R. Alur, M. M. K. Martin, P. Sewell, and D. Williams. An axiomatic memory model for POWER multiprocessors. In *24th International Conference on Computer Aided Verification (CAV)*, 2012.

[29] Y. A. Manerkar, D. Lustig, M. Pellauer, and M. Martonosi. CCICheck: Using μhb graphs to verify the coherence-consistency interface. *48th International Symposium on Microarchitecture (MICRO)*, 2015.

[30] J. Manson, W. Pugh, and S. V. Adve. The Java memory model. In *32nd Symposium on Principles of Programming Languages (POPL)*, 2005.

[31] P. E. McKenney, T. Riegel, J. Preshing, H. Boehm, C. Nelson, and O. Giroux. Towards implementation and use of `memory_order_consume`. *ISO SC22 WG21 N4321*, November 2014.

[32] S. Owens, S. Sarkar, and P. Sewell. A better x86 memory model: x86-TSO. In *22nd International Conference on Theorem Proving in Higher Order Logics (TPHOLs)*, 2009.

[33] B. Pham, V. Vaidyanathan, A. Jaleel, and A. Bhattacharjee. CoLT: Coalesced large-reach TLBs. In *45th International Symposium on Microarchitecture (MICRO)*, 2012.

[34] B. Pichai, L. Hsu, and A. Bhattacharjee. Architectural support for address translation on GPUs. In *19th International Conference on Architectural Support for Programming Languages and Operating Systems (ASPLOS)*, 2014.

[35] J. Power, M. Hill, and D. Wood. Supporting x86-64 address translation for 100s of GPU lanes. In *20th International Symposium on High Performance Computer Architecture (HPCA)*, 2014.

[36] W. Pugh. The Java memory model is fatally flawed. *Concurrency - Practice and Experience*, 12(6):445–455, 2000.

[37] B. Romanescu, A. Lebeck, D. Sorin, and A. Bracy. UNified instruction/translation/data (UNITD) coherence: One protocol to rule them all. In *16th International Symposium on High Performance Computer Architecture (HPCA)*, 2010.

[38] B. F. Romanescu, A. R. Lebeck, and D. J. Sorin. Specifying and dynamically verifying address translation-aware memory consistency. In *15th International Conference on Architectural Support for Programming Languages and Operating Systems (ASPLOS)*, 2010.

[39] B. F. Romanescu, A. R. Lebeck, and D. J. Sorin. Address translation aware memory consistency. *IEEE Micro*, 31(1), Jan 2011.

[40] S. Sarkar, P. Sewell, J. Alglave, L. Maranget, and D. Williams. Understanding POWER multiprocessors. In *32nd Conference on Programming Language Design and Implementation (PLDI)*, 2011.

[41] A. Saulsbury, F. Dahlgren, and P. Stenstrom. Recency-based TLB preloading. In *27th International Symposium on Computer Architecture (ISCA)*, 2000.

[42] T. C. Schroeder. Peer-to-peer & unified virtual addressing. *NVIDIA GPU Technology Conference*, 2011.

[43] P. Sewell, S. Sarkar, S. Owens, F. Zappa Nardelli, and M. O. Myreen. x86-TSO: a rigorous and usable programmer's model for x86 multiprocessors. *Communications of the ACM*, 53(7), 2010.

[44] The Coq development team. *The Coq proof assistant reference manual, version 8.0*. LogiCal Project, 2004. URL `http://coq.inria.fr`.

[45] The diy development team. *A don't (diy) tutorial, version 5.01*, 2012. `http://diy.inria.fr/doc/index.html`.

[46] C. Villavieja, V. Karakostas, L. Vilanova, Y. Etsion, A. Ramirez, A. Mendelson, N. Navarro, A. Cristal, and O. Unsal. DiDi: Mitigating the performance impact of TLB shootdowns using a shared TLB directory. In *20th International Conference on Parallel Architectures and Compilation Techniques (PACT)*, 2011.

True IOMMU Protection from DMA Attacks: When Copy is Faster than Zero Copy

Alex Markuze Adam Morrison Dan Tsafrir

Computer Science Department
Technion—Israel Institute of Technology

Abstract

Malicious I/O devices might compromise the OS using DMAs. The OS therefore utilizes the IOMMU to map and unmap every target buffer right before and after its DMA is processed, thereby restricting DMAs to their designated locations. This usage model, however, is not truly secure for two reasons: (1) it provides protection at page granularity only, whereas DMA buffers can reside on the same page as other data; and (2) it delays DMA buffer unmaps due to performance considerations, creating a vulnerability window in which devices can access in-use memory.

We propose that OSes utilize the IOMMU differently, in a manner that eliminates these two flaws. Our new usage model restricts device access to a set of shadow DMA buffers that are never unmapped, and it copies DMAed data to/from these buffers, thus providing sub-page protection while eliminating the aforementioned vulnerability window. Our key insight is that the cost of interacting with, and synchronizing access to the slow IOMMU hardware—required for zero-copy protection against devices—make *copying preferable to zero-copying*.

We implement our model in Linux and evaluate it with standard networking benchmarks utilizing a 40 Gb/s NIC. We demonstrate that despite being more secure than the safest preexisting usage model, our approach provides up to 5× higher throughput. Additionally, whereas it is inherently less scalable than an IOMMU-less (unprotected) system, our approach incurs only 0%–25% performance degradation in comparison.

Categories and Subject Descriptors D.1.3 [*Operating Systems*]: Security and Protection

ASPLOS '16, April 2–6, 2016, Atlanta, Georgia, USA..

ACM 978-1-4503-4091-5/16/04…$15.00.
http://dx.doi.org/10.1145/2872362.2872379

Keywords IOMMU; DMA attacks

1. Introduction

Computer systems face the threat of a *DMA attack* [8, 45] in which a hardware device compromises the host system using direct memory access (DMA) operations to arbitrary physical memory locations. An attacker can mount a DMA attack by (1) remotely taking over a device, e.g., by exploiting a network interface card (NIC) firmware vulnerability [20, 21], or (2) physically introducing a malicious device, e.g., by intercepting hardware shipments [3] or plugging in a malicious iPod [8, 11, 12, 19]. The attacking device can then use DMAs to gain access to the host OS [8, 11, 12, 19, 20], install a backdoor [3, 16, 47], steal sensitive data [11, 12, 17, 19, 45], or crash the system [33, 46]. An errant device [33] or buggy driver [9, 18, 23, 49] might also inadvertently mount a DMA attack.

OSes leverage hardware I/O memory management units (IOMMUs) [5, 7, 25, 30] to implement *intra-OS protection* [50] and prevent arbitrary DMAs. The IOMMU treats the address in a DMA as an I/O virtual address (IOVA) [36] and maps it to a physical address using OS-provided mappings, blocking the DMA if no mapping exists. OSes use transient IOMMU mappings that restrict device DMAs only to valid DMA targets [6, 14, 26, 39]. The OS maps a DMA buffer when a driver requests a DMA. The device now "owns" the buffer and OS code may not access it. When the device notifies the OS that the DMA has completed, the OS destroys the mapping—preventing further device access—and OS code may access the buffer again. Systems that isolate drivers as untrusted out-of-kernel components [15, 23, 35, 43] apply the same technique to protect data in the trusted kernel.

In practice, unfortunately, implementations of the above intra-OS protection design *do not fully protect from DMA attacks*. They suffer from two problems: lack of *sub-page protection* and providing only *deferred* protection.

No sub-page protection IOMMU protection works at the granularity of pages [5, 7, 25, 30]. Mapped data—e.g., network packets—is usually allocated with standard kernel

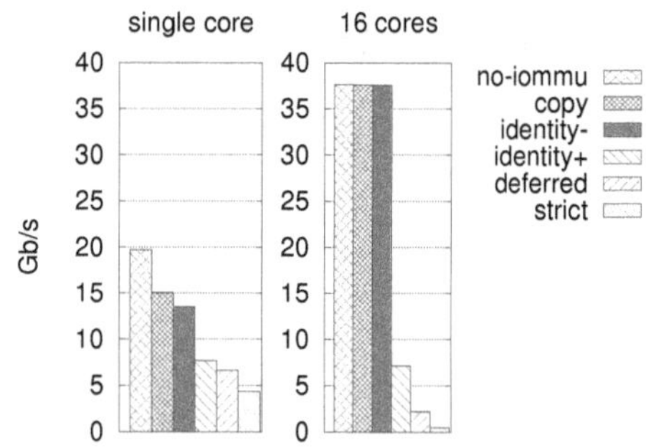

Figure 1: *IOMMU-based OS protection cost: Linux TCP throughput (1500 B packets) over 40 Gb/s ethernet, measured with single/multiple netperf instances. (copy is our intra-OS protection; identity± is recent work [42] tackling another Linux bottleneck.)*

`malloc`, which can satisfy multiple allocations from the same page [13]. Thus, sensitive data that should not be accessible to the device may get co-located on a page IOMMU-mapped for a device.

Deferred protection Unmapping an IOVA requires invalidating the IOTLB, a TLB that caches IOMMU mappings. IOTLB invalidation is expensive, e.g., requiring ≈ 2000 cycles on an Intel Sandy Bridge machine [37]. Worse, IOTLB interaction is serialized with a lock, which becomes a bottleneck for concurrent IOTLB invalidations [42]. As a result, OSes by default implement *deferred* protection, in which IOTLB invalidations are batched to amortize their cost, instead of *strict* protection that invalidates on each unmap. Figure 1 depicts the issue for Linux, our case study here, and followup work [42] that attempted to address it; other OSes make similar trade-offs [42].

Deferred protection weakens security by creating a window in which a device can access unmapped IOVAs that have since been reused. While exploiting this window is not in the scope of this paper, we remark that it is not theoretical—we have been able to crash Linux using it.

True DMA attack protection We propose an alternative intra-OS protection design addressing the two flaws above. We use the IOMMU to restrict device access to a set of permanently-mapped *shadow DMA buffers* and *copy* DMAed data to/from these buffers, thereby achieving byte-granularity protection while never needing to invalidate the IOTLB. Our key insight is that *copying is typically cheaper than invalidating the IOTLB*, for two reasons. First, in many I/O workloads DMA buffers are simply small enough that copying them costs less than an IOTLB invalidation—e.g., 1500-byte ethernet packets. Second, in multicore workloads, the IOTLB-related lock contention under strict protection significantly increases invalidation costs and makes even larger copies, such as 64 KB, profitable.

Still, copying huge DMA buffers costs more than an IOTLB invalidation. Huge buffers, however, occur in workloads such as GPU usage, whose DMA frequency is low enough that the standard zero-copy strict protection does not incur much overhead. (Basically, most time is spent on data transfer/processing.) In these cases, we copy only the sub-page head/tail of the buffer (if any), and map/unmap the rest.

iommu protection model		*sub-page protect*	*no vulnerability window*	*single core perf.*	*multi core perf.*
strict	Linux	✗	✓	✗	✗
	FAST'15 [38]	✗	✓	✓	✗
	ATC'15 [42]	✗	✓	✓	✗
defer	Linux	✗	✗	✓✗	✗
	FAST'15 [38]	✗	✗	✓	✗
	ATC'15 [42]	✗	✗	✓	✓
copy (shadow buffers)		✓	✓	✓	✓

Table 1: *Our contribution relative to the state of the art.*

Performance We focus on 40 Gb/s networking, as it represents demanding I/O workloads that trigger millions of DMAs per second. We evaluate our design in Linux using standard networking benchmarks. Our protection scheme achieves comparable throughput to state-of-the-art deferred protection [42]—which is less secure—and provides throughput $5\times$ higher relative to strict protection—which is still less secure—while reducing CPU consumption by up to $2.5\times$.

The maximal I/O throughput that our protection scheme can scale to is inherently less than the throughput achievable in a native execution without an IOMMU, due to the CPU and memory traffic overhead incurred by copying. (For example, if the native execution requires 100% CPU to sustain the I/O throughput, our scheme's overhead would lead to reduced throughput.) We show, however, that on modern hardware our scheme *scales to the demanding 40 Gb/s rates*: it incurs only 0–25% throughput degradation and less than 20% increased CPU use.

Contributions To summarize, we make three contributions: (1) observing that copying DMA buffers is preferable to IOTLB invalidation; (2) providing a truly secure, fast, and scalable intra-OS protection scheme with strict sub-page safety; and (3) implementing the new scheme in Linux and evaluating it with networking workloads at 40 Gb/s. Table 1 highlights the differences between our newly proposed scheme and the state-of-the-art (further deails provided below).

2. Background: IOMMU-Based OS Protection

IOMMUs prevent DMAs not authorized by the OS from accessing main memory (see § 2.1). IOMMUs can provide inter- and intra-OS protection [48, 50]. Inter-OS protection is used by hypervisors to prevent a guest OS from directing DMAs at the memory of another guest OS or of the hypervisor. This form of protection uses static IOMMU mappings that reflect a guest's physical-to-host address mappings [50].

It thus does not frequently change IOMMU mappings and is not our focus. We focus on *intra-OS* protection, in which the OS protects itself from attacks by devices (§ 2.2).

2.1 IOMMU Operation

We describe the IOMMU operation in the Intel x86 architecture [30]; other architectures are similar [5, 7, 25]. The IOMMU treats the target address of a DMA as an *I/O virtual address* (IOVA) [36] and attempts to translate it to a physical address. Translations are done based on per-device *IOVA mappings* that the OS creates, which also include the type of access allowed to the mapped IOVA—read, write or both. The DMA is then routed to the physical address to which its IOVA maps; if no valid mapping exists, the DMA is blocked and the OS is notified. IOVA mappings are at page granularity; they are maintained in a per-device page table (similar to a standard MMU page table).

The IOMMU has an IOTLB that caches IOVA mappings. The OS must therefore *invalidate* any IOTLB entries associated with an IOVA mapping after modifying or destroying the mapping. The IOMMU supports both *global* invalidations, which invalidate every cached mappings, and invalidations of specific IOVA pages (i.e., at page granularity). The OS invalidates the IOTLB by posting an invalidation command to the IOMMU's *invalidation queue*, a cyclic buffer in memory from which the IOMMU reads and asynchronously processes IOMMU commands. The OS can arrange to be notified when the invalidation completes. It does this by posting an *invalidation notification* instructing the IOMMU to update a memory location after invalidating the IOTLB, which allows the OS to busy wait on this location.

2.2 Intra-OS Protection via the DMA API

OSes base IOMMU-based intra-OS protection on a *DMA API* [6, 14, 26, 39] that a driver must use to authorize an expected DMA. The basic idea is that, before programming a device to issue a DMA to some buffer, the driver invokes a `dma_map` call to map the buffer in the IOMMU. Once the DMA completes, the driver invokes a `dma_unmap` call to destroy the mapping.[1] We describe the Linux DMA API [14, 36, 40] in detail; other OSes are similar [6, 26, 39].

• `dma_map`: This operation receives a buffer's address and size, as well as desired device access rights (read, write or both). It allocates a sufficiently large IOVA interval I from the device's IOVA space, creates a mapping from I to the buffer in the device's IOMMU page table, and returns I's starting IOVA. From this point, the device can access the buffer and so the OS/driver are not allowed to modify the buffer and should not expect to read valid data from it.

• `dma_unmap`: This operation receives an IOVA that maps to a DMA buffer. It unmaps the buffer in the IOMMU by looking up the IOVA interval I containing the IOVA and then removing the mappings of I from the device's IOMMU page table. I is deallocated, so that future `dma_map` calls can reuse it. From this point, the driver/OS can access the buffer again, and the device should not attempt to access any IOVA in I.

• `dma_alloc_coherent` of shared buffers: DMA buffers through which a driver posts commands and receives responses, such as DMA descriptor rings and "mailbox" data structures, need to be accessed simultaneously by both driver and device. The `dma_alloc_coherent` operation facilitates this—it allocates memory for such use and maps it in the IOMMU. The driver/OS can access this memory but must do so defensively, since the device can also access it. `dma_alloc_coherent` allocates memory in pages, and so the pages of a buffer it allocates are never shared with any other allocation. Buffers allocated with `dma_alloc_coherent` are freed using `dma_free_coherent`, at which point they are unmapped as in `dma_unmap`.

2.2.1 Strict vs. Deferred Protection

To prevent a device from accessing an unmapped buffer, `dma_unmap` must invalidate the IOTLB after removing an IOVA mapping from the IOMMU page table. IOTLB invalidation is an expensive operation for two reasons: First, the hardware is slow—invalidation can take ≈ 2000 cycles to complete [37]. Second, the IOMMU invalidation queue is protected by a lock, which becomes a bottleneck for concurrent IOTLB invalidations [42].

As a result, *strict* protection—in which an `dma_unmap` invalidates the IOTLB—adds prohibitive overheads for high-throughput I/O workloads such as 10–40 Gb/s networking (§ 6). These workloads generate millions of DMAs per second, and often run on multiple cores because the desired throughput cannot be achieved by a single core [34].

To avoid these overheads, OSes by default trade off security for performance and use *deferred* protection, in which the IOTLB is invalidated asynchronously *after* the `dma_unmap` returns. In Linux, for example, `dma_unmap` batches IOTLB invalidations by adding the unmapped IOVAs to a global list. The IOTLB is then invalidated after batching 250 invalidations or every 10 milliseconds, whichever occurs first. The unmapped IOVAs are also deallocated at this time, so that they can be reused later. Other OSes make similar compromises [42].

Unfortunately, this approach still imposes unacceptable overheads on multi-core workloads, because the global list of pending invalidations is itself lock-protected and becomes a bottleneck [42]. To address this, IOTLB invalidations must be batched locally on each core instead of globally [42]. This, however, increases the vulnerability window in which a device can access unmapped IOVAs [42].

3. Assumptions & Attacker Model

Assumptions Our focus is protecting the OS from *unauthorized* DMAs to targets not mapped with the DMA API (see § 2.2). Attacks carried out with authorized DMAs—

[1] The API also has map/unmap operations for non-consecutive scatter/gatter lists, which work analogously.

e.g., a malicious disk tampering with file contents—are out of scope. Peer-to-peer attacks mounted by a device against another device [53] are also out of scope, as peer-to-peer traffic does not go through the IOMMU. [2] We do not consider interrupt-based attacks [51], which are prevented with low overhead using the IOMMU's interrupt remapping feature [53].

We assume that the IOMMU is secure and trustworthy. We also assume that it correctly identifies the device issuing a DMA (i.e., DMAs cannot be spoofed)—this holds on PCIe-only systems and systems that do not have multiple devices behind PCI or PCI-to-PCIe bridges [44, 53]. Finally, we assume that the IOMMU prevents DMAs from compromising the OS during boot—this is true on platforms with a secure boot process, e.g., Intel's TXT feature [1, 28].

Attacker model The attacker controls a set of DMA-capable hardware devices but cannot otherwise access the OS. [3] We thus assume that device drivers are trusted—in particular, to correctly use the DMA API—which is the case in the commodity OSes we focus on. Note, however, that our shadow buffers design can be implemented in systems that isolate drivers as untrusted components [15, 23, 35, 43], in which case this assumption is not needed.

4. Current Intra-OS Protection Weaknesses

The current Intra-OS protection deployed by commodity OSes does not fully protect from DMA attacks, due to two weaknesses: lack of *sub-page protection* and providing only *deferred* protection by default.

No sub-page protection Because IOMMU protection works at page-level granularity (§ 2.1), it cannot protect memory at the byte-level granularity specified by the DMA API. Thus, a device can access any data co-located on a page in which a DMA buffer begins or ends. DMA buffers are typically allocated with standard kernel `malloc` calls, which co-locate multiple allocations on the same page [13]. This makes it possible for data that should not be accessible to the device to reside on a page that gets mapped in the IOMMU.

We argue that addressing this weakness by fixing the relevant `malloc` callers to allocate DMA buffers in quantities of pages will be hard and problematic. First, one would have to reason about every `malloc()` call and determine if a subset of the buffer could end up being used for DMA, because DMA buffer allocations can occur outside of drivers (e.g., in the socket or and storage layers). This requires significant effort, is error-prone, and adds maintenance overhead. In contrast, having the DMA API provide byte-level protection is simpler and automatically benefits the entire kernel. Moreover, allocating DMA-able buffers in page quantities would impose significant memory overhead, proportional to the allocated data. In contrast, the memory overhead of shadow buffers is proportional only to the DMAs *in flight*.

Deferred protection Due to performance reasons, OSes by default implement deferred protection, which performs IOTLB invalidations asynchronously instead of invalidating the IOTLB on each `dma_unmap` (§ 2.2.1). A DMA buffer may thus remain accessible to the device after a `dma_unmap` of the buffer returns. Several attacks can be carried out in this window of vulnerability. For example, after an incoming packet passes firewall inspection, a malicious NIC can modify the packet into a malicious one [15]. Moreover, an unmapped buffer may get reused by the OS, exposing the device to arbitrary sensitive data.

Such attacks appear feasible. We have observed that overwriting an unmapped DMA buffer within 10 μs of its `dma_unmap`[4] can cause a Linux kernel crash—and with deferred protection, buffers can remain mapped for up to 10 milliseconds. This indicates it may be practical to compromise the OS through such an attack vector. While we leave exploiting deferred protection to future work, we contend that OSes require strict protection for true security.

5. Intra-OS Protection via DMA Shadowing

Here we describe our secure intra-OS protection design, which provides strict protection at sub-page (byte-level) granularity and requires no changes to the DMA API. The basic idea is simple: we restrict a device's DMAs to a set of *shadow DMA buffers* that are permanently mapped in the IOMMU, and copy data to (or from) these buffers from (or to) the OS-allocated DMA buffers. Our design thus obviates the need for unmappings and IOTLB invalidations, but adds the additional cost of copying. However, the insight driving our design is that because of the slow IOMMU hardware and the synchronization required to interact with it, copying is typically preferable to an IOTLB invalidation (as shown in § 6).

Realizing the DMA shadowing idea poses several challenges that we discuss in detail below: The design must carefully manage NUMA locality and synchronization issues to minimize overheads (§ 5.3), and it must handle DMA buffers whose size is such that copying would impose prohibitive overheads (§ 5.5).

5.1 Design Goals

Apart from secure intra-OS protection, DMA shadowing sets to achieve the following goals:

• **Transparency:** Implementing DMA shadowing must not require changes to the DMA API, allowing the design to be easily integrated into existing OSes. We discuss this when

[2] Peer-to-peer attacks can be prevented using PCIe Access Control Services (ACS) [41, § 6.13], as explained by Zhou et al. [53].

[3] For example, the attacker cannot exploit a kernel vulnerability from userspace to reconfigure the IOMMU or authorize DMAs to arbitrary targets.

[4] The overwrite was caused by a bug in our copy-based intra-OS protection mechanism (§ 5), whose effect—a DMA buffer being overwritten after being unmapped—is similar to a DMA attack.

`iova_t acquire_shadow(`*buf*, *size*, *rights*`)`	Acquires a shadow buffer and associates it with the OS buffer *buf*. The acquired shadow buffer is of at least *size* bytes, and device access to it is restricted as specified in *rights* (read/write/both). Returns the IOVA of the shadow buffer. The pool guarantees that if a page of the shadow buffer holds another shadow buffer, then both shadow buffers have the same access rights.
`void* find_shadow(`*iova*`)`	Looks up the shadow buffer whose IOVA is *iova* and returns the OS buffer associated with it.
`void release_shadow(`*shbuf*`)`	Releases the shadow buffer *shbuf* back to the pool, disassociating it from its OS buffer.

Table 2: *API of shadow DMA buffer pool (§ 5.3).*

presenting the design in § 5.2. We do, however, extend the API to allow optional optimizations (§ 5.4).

• **Scalability:** The design must minimize synchronization, particularly coarse-grained locks, so that it does not impose bottlenecks on multi-core I/O workloads (see § 2.2.1). We address this in § 5.3.

• **Generality:** While our focus is on the high-throughput I/O workloads that are most sensitive to DMA API performance, our design must support all workloads—providing intra-OS protection only from *some* devices will not offer full protection from DMA attacks. This boils down to supporting huge DMA buffers efficiently, which we discuss in § 5.5.

5.2 DMA Shadowing Implementation of the DMA API

We implement the DMA API as a layer on top of a *shadow buffer pool* that is associated with each device. This pool manages buffers that are permanently mapped in the IOMMU and accessible only to the associated device. The shadow buffer pool interface is shown in Table 2; its implementation is described in § 5.3.

The DMA API operations acquire a shadow buffer from the pool, copy data to (or from) the OS buffer from (or to) the shadow buffer, and finally release the shadow buffer, as follows:

• `dma_map` acquires a shadow buffer of the appropriate size and access rights from the pool. The shadow buffer will be associated with the mapped OS buffer until the shadow buffer is released back to the pool. If the `dma_map` is for data meant to be read by the device, the `dma_map` now copies the OS buffer into the shadow buffer. Finally, it returns the shadow buffer's IOVA.

• `dma_unmap` finds the shadow buffer associated with the OS buffer, based on its IOVA argument. If the `dma_unmap` is for a buffer meant to be written to by the device, `dma_unmap` now copies the contents of the shadow buffer into the OS buffer. (The `dma_unmap` arguments include the size and access rights of the buffer, so this is easy to do.) It then releases the shadow buffer and returns.

The scatter/gather (SG) operations are implemented analogously, with each SG element copied to/from its own shadow buffer.

• For `dma_alloc_coherent` and `dma_free_coherent`, we use the standard DMA API implementation with strict protection. These are infrequent operations (typically invoked at driver initialization and destruction) that are not performance critical. Furthermore, the standard implementation already provides byte-level protection by guaranteeing that `dma_alloc_coherent` memory is allocated in page quantities.

Security DMA shadowing maintains the security semantics of the DMA API, even though the device can always access all the shadow buffers: The implementation reads from an OS buffer at `dma_map` time and writes at `dma_unmap` time, and the pool guarantees that every IOMMU-mapped page holds only shadow buffers with the same access rights. Thus, bytes a device reads can only come from data previously copied from an OS buffer mapped for read or read/write access. Similarly, bytes a device writes are either overwritten by some later copy and never observed by the OS, or are copied out on `dma_unmap`, implying that the target OS buffer was mapped for write access.

DMA shadowing allows a device compromised at some point in time to read data from buffers used at earlier points in time. This does not constitute a security violation, since our attacker model (§ 3) assumes that a device is *always* controlled by the attacker, which implies that the OS *never* places sensitive data in a shadow buffer.

5.3 Shadow Buffer Pool

Each device is associated with a unique shadow buffer pool. The shadow buffer pool is essentially a fast and scalable multi-threaded segregated free list memory allocator [31] that provides the DMA API with shadow DMA buffers (Table 2). It carefully manages NUMA locality and uses lightweight fine-grained synchronization, enabling multiple pool (and hence DMA API) operations to run concurrently. The pool assigns shadow buffers with IOVAs that encode information about the shadow buffer and its free list. It leverages this information to implement `find_shadow` in $O(1)$ time.

Pool design A pool maintains a unique set of free lists from which shadow buffers are acquired. Each list holds free shadow buffers of a particular size *and device access rights.*

That is, for each shadow buffer size class, the pool maintains three free lists—read, write or both. Acquisitions of shadow buffers whose size exceeds the maximum free list size class are described in § 5.5.

Each core maintains its own set of free lists, to allow fast concurrent free list operations (we describe how this is implemented later on). Both shadow buffers and free list metadata are allocated from the core's NUMA domain.

Shadow buffers are *sticky*, in the sense that a shadow buffer acquired from some free list always returns to the same list upon release, even if it is released by a different core. This prevents shadow buffers allocated on one NUMA domain from being acquired later on another NUMA domain, where they would be more expensive to access. In addition, keeping a shadow buffer in the same free list means that its IOMMU mapping never changes. Otherwise, we would have to modify the mapping and invalidate the IOTLB when a shadow buffer moves between free lists with incompatible access rights.

Shadow buffer metadata Each NUMA domain maintains an array of shadow buffer metadata structures for each size-class. (Using an array allows looking up a metadata structure based on its index, which is encoded in the IOVA, as explained later on.) The metadata of *free* shadow buffers—those not currently acquired by the DMA API—doubles as nodes in a singly linked list from which shadow buffers are acquired/released (Figure 2). When a shadow buffer is acquired, its metadata is updated to point to the OS buffer being shadowed. This allows finding the OS buffer when the DMA API needs it (i.e., the `find_shadow` operation). The metadata is not mapped in the IOMMU and is not accessible to the device.

Free list synchronization The free list supports concurrent acquires and releases of shadow buffers with minimal synchronization and cross-core cache coherence traffic. Shadow buffers are acquired from the free list only by the core that owns the list. However, they may be released back to the free list by other cores.

To support these operations efficiently, the free list maintains pointers to the head and tail of the list on distinct cache lines (Figure 2). Shadow buffers are acquired from the head and released to the tail. Acquires are lockless, with the owner core simply removing the head node from the list. Shadow buffer releases are done under a lock that is co-located on the tail pointer's cache line. The released shadow buffer's metadata node is appended to the linked list. If the list was previously empty, the head pointer is updated as well. This is safe to do because when an acquire operation finds the list empty, it allocates a new shadow buffer and returns it, relying on a later release to add the shadow buffer to the free list.

In addition, to avoid false sharing, the free list contains a second read-only pointer to the shadow buffer metadata array, which resides on a separate cache line and from which non-owner cores read.

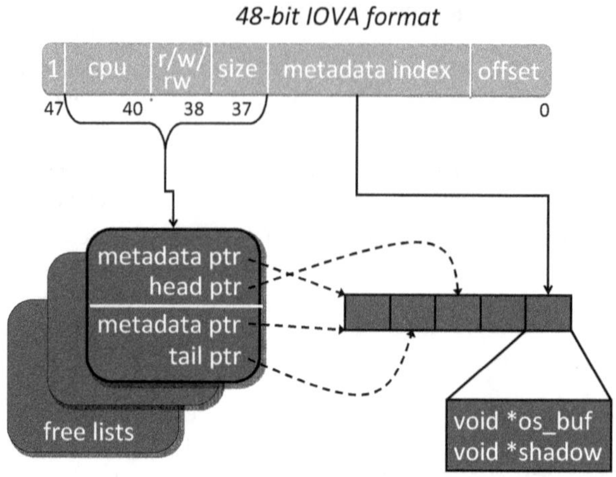

Figure 2: *Shadow buffer IOVA and free list structures. Bits 37–46 of a shadow buffer's IOVA encode its free list, and bits 0–36 encode its metadata structure. For free shadow buffers, the* `os_buf` *metadata field points to the next node in the free list.*

Shadow buffer allocation Free lists are initially empty. A shadow buffer is allocated when a core tries to acquire a shadow buffer from an empty free list. The core then:

- allocates a new shadow buffer from its NUMA domain,
- stores its address in the next unused metadata node in the domain's metadata array,[5]
- obtains an IOVA for the buffer by encoding the list and metadata node (as described below),
- maps the IOVA to the new shadow buffer in the device's IOMMU page table, and returns.

To provide byte-level protection, the pool guarantees that if several shadow buffers are co-located on the same page, the device has the same access rights to all of them. It achieves this by allocating memory for shadow buffers in page (4 KB) quantities. For small shadow buffers, the pool breaks up allocated pages into multiple shadow buffers. One of these shadow buffers is then returned as usual, and the rest are placed in a private cache to satisfy future allocations. (We do not want to insert them into the free list, to avoid having to synchronize with shadow buffer releases.)

IOVA encodings A shadow buffer's IOVA uniquely identifies its metadata structure. The IOVA encodes the shadow buffer's free list—identified by the owner core id, size class, and access rights—and the index of the metadata structure in the metadata array of the owner core's NUMA domain.

x86 IOVAs are presently 48 bits wide [30]. We reserve the MSB to signify that the IOVA encodes shadow buffer metadata. The remainder bits can be divided in numerous ways. Figure 2 shows the encoding used in our prototype

[5] This next-unused index is lock-protected. Shadow buffer allocation is an infrequent operation, so this lock does not pose a contention problem.

implementation, which supports shadow buffers of two size-classes, 4 KB and 64 KB: 7 bits for core id, 2 bits for access rights (read/write/both), 1 bit for size class, and 37 bits to encode the metadata structure index. Notice that for a size class C, the least significant $\lceil \log_2 C \rceil$ bits are not used in the index encoding, as they are used for addressing within the shadow buffer. Thus, when decoding an IOVA we first identify the appropriate size class and then extract the metadata index. We remark that one can have more size classes by using less bits for the index and/or core id fields.

The half of the IOVA space with MSB clear serves as a fallback, in case a NUMA domain exhausts a shadow buffer metadata array. In such a case, we allocate the metadata using kernel `malloc` and the IOVA with an external scalable IOVA allocator [42]. The IOVA-to-metadata mapping in these fallback cases is maintained in an external hash table.

Memory consumption Shadow DMA buffer use corresponds to *in flight* DMAs. Because shadow buffers are not used for huge DMA operations (§ 5.5), typical shadow buffer memory consumption should be modest—for example, we observe < 256 MB consumed by shadow buffers in our experiments (§ 6). Moreover, the OS can impose a limit on the memory allocated to shadow buffers and/or free unused shadow buffers under memory pressure. (When a shadow buffer is freed, it must be unmapped from the IOMMU, including an IOTLB invalidation. This should not adversely affect performance as long as memory pressure-related freeing does not happen frequently.)

5.4 Copying Optimizations

The main overhead of DMA shadowing is in the copying to/from the OS buffers—the shadow pool operations are fast and scalable. We have explored several options for optimizing copying:

Copying hints: DMA buffers often end up not full—for example, a networking driver maps MTU-sized buffers for incoming packets, but the arriving packets can be much smaller. To avoid copying useless data, we let drivers register an optional *copying hint*, which is a function that is given a DMA buffer as input and returns the amount of data that should be copied. For example, our prototype implementation uses a copying hint that returns the length of the IP packet in the buffer. It is the driver writer's responsibility to ensure that the copying hint is fast and secure, since its input is untrusted.

Smart `memcpy`***:*** We have attempted to use optimized `memcpy` implementations that use SIMD instructions and/or streaming (non-temporal) stores [29]. However, we have found that on our machines, these do not provide an overall benefit over the standard `memcpy` implementation based on the x86 `REP MOVSB/STOSB` instruction. We suspect the reason is that this instruction is optimized in our processors, which have an enhanced `REP MOVSB/STOSB` (ERMS) feature.

5.5 Handling Huge DMA Buffers

Copying is not *always* preferable to an IOTLB invalidation—copying a large enough buffer can greatly exceed invalidation cost, even after factoring in the lock contention involved. We observe, however, that huge DMA buffers have infrequent DMA map/unmaps. This is because the rate of IO operations decreases, as more time is spent on transferring the data to/from the device and processing it afterwards. For example, while a 40 Gb/s NIC can DMA incoming 1500-byte packets at a rate of 1.7 M packets/sec, Intel's solid-state drive (SSD)—whose DMA buffers are at least 4 KB—provides up to 850 K IOPS for reads and up to 150 K IOPS for writes [27]. When DMA map/unmap rate is low, the overhead of IOMMU unmapping becomes insignificant, which makes it possible to reuse the standard zero-copy DMA mapping technique.

To maintain byte-level protection, we propose using a hybrid approach that copies only the sub-page head/tail of the OS DMA buffer, and maps the remainder in the IOMMU. One can use an external scalable IOVA allocator [42] to obtain a range of IOVAs for mapping the head/tail shadows with the remainder between them. On `dma_unmap`, this mapping is destroyed, including invalidating the IOTLB.

6. Evaluation

We implement DMA shadowing in Linux 3.19. Our implementation consists of ≈ 1000 LOC. We focus our evaluation on 40 Gb/s networking, as it represents demanding I/O workloads that trigger millions of DMAs per second. Our evaluation seeks to answer the following questions:

- How does the overhead imposed by copying DMA buffers compare to the overhead of existing IOMMU-based protection?
- What is the performance effect of DMA shadowing on I/O intensive workloads?

To this end, our DMA shadowing implementation focuses on the copying-related parts of the design. Moreover, we enable DMA shadowing only for the device being tested. We thus do not implement fallbacks to standard IOVA allocation and handling of huge DMA buffers, both of which do not occur in our benchmarks.

Evaluated systems We compare DMA shadowing (denoted *copy*) to Linux 3.19 with the IOMMU disabled (*no iommu*), i.e., with no DMA attack protection. We also compare to a Linux 3.19 variant that uses identity mappings for IOVAs [42], with both strict (*identity+*) and deferred (*identity-*) protection. We use this variant instead of the baseline Linux because it significantly outperforms Linux under both modes, as it resolves a Linux bottleneck in IOVA assignment during `dma_map` [42].

Experimental setup Our setup consists of two Dell PowerEdge R430 machines. Each machine has dual 2.40 GHz Intel Xeon E5-2630 v3 (Haswell) CPUs, each with 8 cores,

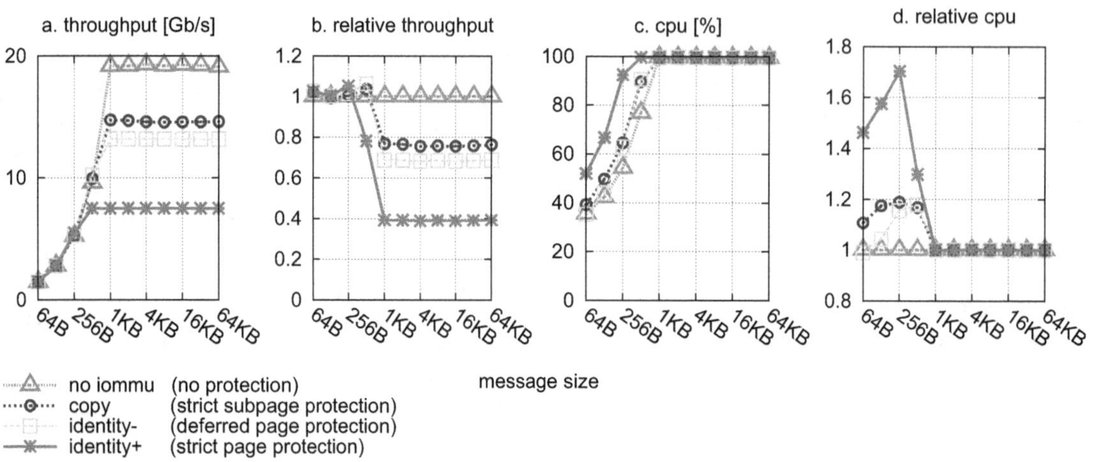

Figure 3: *Single-core TCP receive (RX) throughput and CPU utilization (netperf TCP STREAM)*

for a total of 16 cores (hyperthreading is disabled). Each machine has two 16 GB 1867 MHz DDR4 DIMMs (one per socket), for a total of 32 GB of memory. One machine runs the evaluated kernel and the other serves as the traffic generator. The traffic generator runs with its IOMMU disabled. The machines are connected back-to-back with 40 Gb/s NICs: an Intel Fortville LX710 on the evaluated machine and a Mellanox ConnectX3 on the traffic generator. The machines are configured for maximum performance, with dynamic control of the clock rate (Turbo Boost) disabled.

Methodology We configure the NIC drivers to use one receive ring per core, to avoid measurement noise from uneven load balancing between the cores. We configure even interrupt distribution between the cores for the same reason. We run measurements on idle systems. Each benchmark runs for 60 seconds, to amortize any sporadic noise. We report averages of 10 runs.

Benchmarks We evaluate TCP/IP throughput and latency using netperf [32], a standard network benchmarking tool. We evaluate both receive (RX) and transmit (TX) throughput, by performing separate experiments in which the evaluation machine is a netperf receiver/transmitter. (We further detail each experiment below, as we present it.) We additionally study an application workload using memcached [22], a popular high-performance key-value store used by web applications for object caching. We run a memcached instance per core, to avoid lock contention in multi-threaded memcached, and measure aggregated throughput under a memslap [4] workload. We use the default memslap configuration of 64-byte keys, 1 KB values, and 90%/10% GET/SET operations.

Single-core TCP throughput We measure the throughput obtained in netperf's TCP STREAM test, varying its *message size*—the amount of data that the sending machine repeatedly writes to the TCP socket. We first evaluate single-core throughput: Figure 3 shows throughput and CPU utilization in the RX test, in which the evaluation system is the receiver. For small message sizes (up to 512 B), the evaluated systems are not the bottleneck—as evidenced by the CPU utilization—and they all obtain the same throughput.[6] Thus, overheads translate into different CPU utilization: *copy* has CPU overhead of $1.1\times$–$1.2\times$ compared to *no iommu*, and *identity+* has CPU overhead of $1.3\times$–$1.7\times$. With larger messages, the bottleneck shifts to the receiver and overheads translate into throughput. Interestingly, *copy* is the best performer after *no iommu*—outperforming *identity-* by 10% despite providing stronger protection, and obtaining $0.76\times$ the throughput of *no iommu*. The overhead of strict protection in *identity+* is much larger, and *copy* obtains $2\times$ its throughput.

To understand the source of these overheads, Figure 5a breaks down the average packet processing time. IOMMU-related map/unmap overhead dominates both zero-copy schemes. IOMMU page table management costs both *identity-* and *identity+* 0.17 μs, and *identity+* additionally spends 0.61 μs on IOTLB invalidation. In contrast, *copy* spends 0.02 μs on shadow buffer management and 0.11 μs on copying from the shadow buffer (`memcpy`)—that is, *copying a 1500 B ethernet packet is* $5.5\times$ *faster than invalidating the IOTLB*.

Figure 4 shows transmit (TX) throughput[7] and CPU utilization. For messages sizes < 512 B, *copy* performs comparably to *identity+* and *identity-*, while providing better security. Unlike the RX case, however, with larger messages *copy* obtains the worst throughput—10% to 20% worse than the other designs. In addition, *copy* is the only design that

[6] The limiting factor is the sender's system call execution rate.

[7] Notice that peak *no iommu* TX throughput differs from peak RX throughput. The reason is that the RX test measures true *single-core* RX throughput—running netperf and handling interrupts on the same core—whereas in the TX test the receiver does not limit networking in this way. We do this to guarantee that the receiver is not the bottleneck in the TX test.

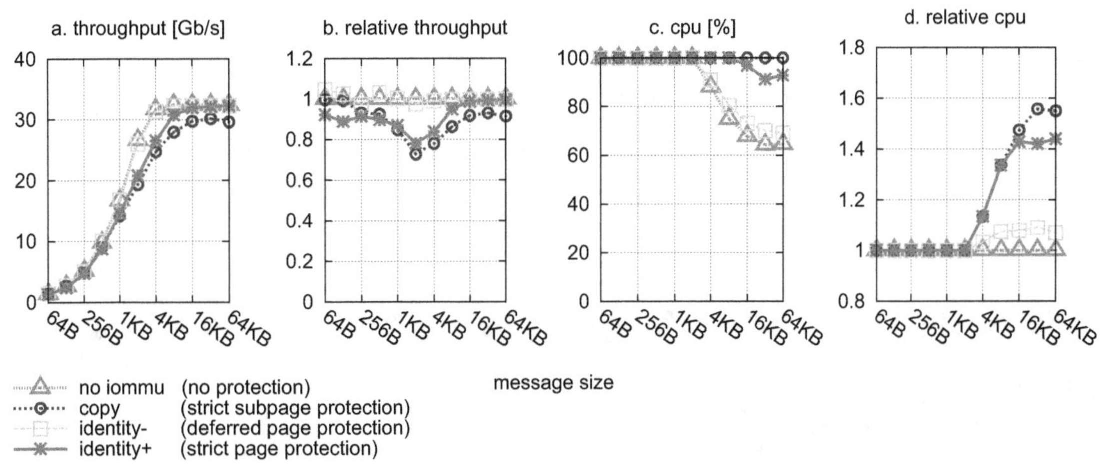

Figure 4: *Single-core TCP transmit (TX) throughput and CPU utilization (netperf TCP STREAM)*

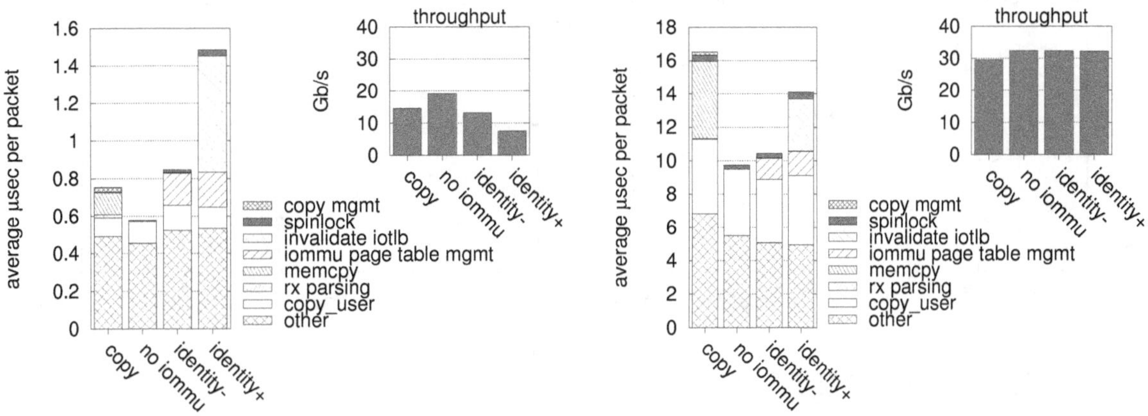

a. Receive (RX)

b. Transmit (TX)

Figure 5: *Average packet processing time breakdown in single-core TCP throughput tests (64 KB message size).*

keeps the CPU 100% busy with 64 KB messages, a 1.4× CPU overhead over *no iommu*. The reason for *copy*'s behavior is the TCP segmentation offload (TSO) feature of the evaluated machine's NIC. With TSO, the driver can pass the NIC a packet of up 64 KB, and the NIC breaks it internally and transmits MTU-sized packets on the wire. Consequently, *copy* needs to copy 64 KB DMA buffers, as opposed to the RX case, in which the buffers are bounded by the 1500 B MTU. Figure 5b depicts the effect of this larger copy operation. First, the `memcpy` time for *copy* increases to 4.65 μs. (This is 40× that of the RX case.) Second, *copy* spends $\approx 2\,\mu$s on "other" tasks. We attribute this increase to cache pollution: A 64 KB buffer copy evicts all data from the core's 32 KB L1 cache, replacing it with data that the core will not later use (as opposed to the RX case). Interestingly, IOMMU-related overhead of *identity+* is 4.58 μs, roughly the same as the `memcpy` time in *copy*. It is the cache pollution that tips the scale slightly in favor of *identity+*.

Multi-core TCP throughput As a single core cannot sustain the 40 Gb/s wire throughput even without an IOMMU, we explore multi-core TCP throughput. We run 16 netperf client/server instances (one per core) on each machine. We report aggregated TCP throughput and CPU utilization, for RX in Figure 6 and for TX in Figure 7. (Here CPU utilization is over all cores, i.e., eight 100% busy cores translate to a 50% utilization.)

We observe a striking difference between *identity+* and the other designs. For RX, *identity+* obtains 5× worse throughput than the other designs (which obtain comparable throughput among each other) across all message sizes. For TX, *identity+* is 5× worse for small message sizes, but closes the gap as message size increases. Moreover, *identity+* is the only design that always has 100% CPU utilization, both for RX and TX. The reason for this is a dramatic increase in overhead compared to the single-core case. The average packet processing time breakdown in Figure 8 depicts this: First, IOTLB invalidation time in *identity+* in-

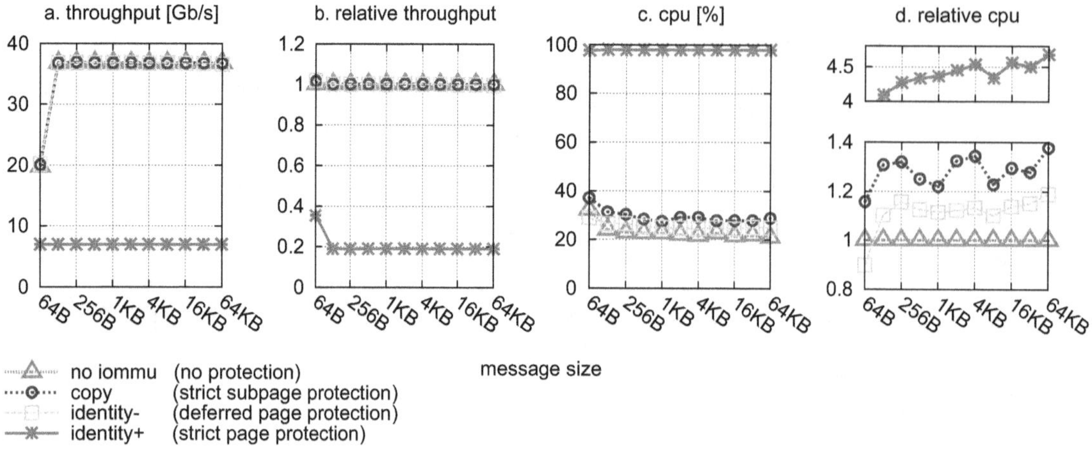

Figure 6: *16-core TCP receive (RX) throughput and CPU utilization (netperf TCP STREAM).*

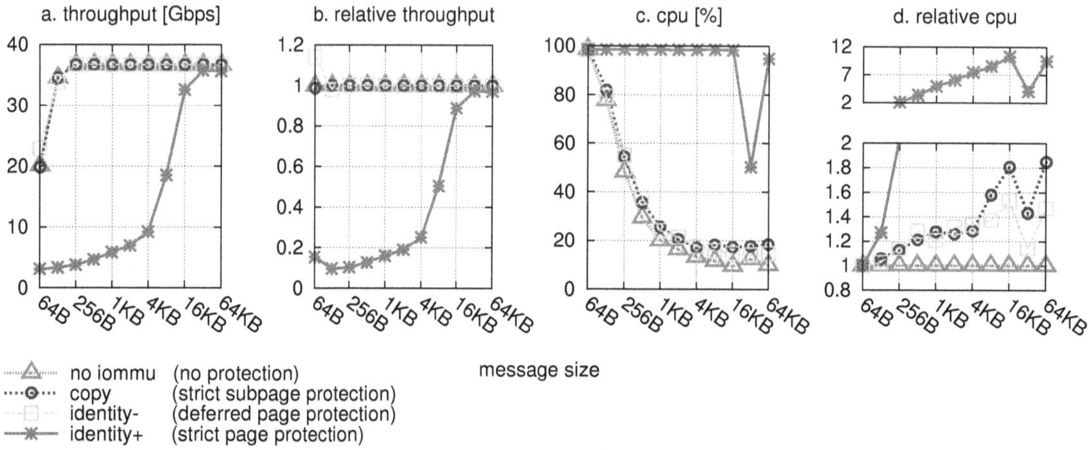

Figure 7: *16-core TCP transmit (TX) throughput and CPU utilization (netperf TCP STREAM).*

creases to 2.7 μs (however, it remains unchanged for TX). More significantly, *identity+* now suffers from contention on the IOTLB lock (§ 2.2.1). In RX, which requires more MTU-sized packets/second to sustain line rate, this contention is more severe—$\approx$ 70 μs per packet—than in TX, where TSO causes packet rate to decrease as message size increases. This is why on TX, *identity+* eventually manages to drive 40 Gb/s, whereas for RX its throughput remains constant. In short, Figure 8b shows that IOTLB invalidation lock overhead *is even more expensive* than the 64 KB buffer `memcpy` done by *copy* in TX, including the resulting cache pollution.

The *copy* design achieves comparable throughput to *no iommu*, with up to 60% CPU overhead, for both RX and TX. While *identity-* also achieves this throughput, with lower CPU overheads of up to 20%, it trades off strict OS protection in order to do so.

TCP latency We measure TCP latency with a single-core netperf request/response benchmark. This benchmark measures the latency of sending a TCP message of a certain size (which we vary) and receiving a response of the same size. Figure 9 shows the resulting latency and CPU utilization. In this benchmark, per-byte costs are not the dominating factor: observe that although the message size increases by 1024$\times$ from 64 B to 64 KB, the latency only increases by $\approx 4\times$. Indeed, the protection-related overheads in the *copy* and the *identity* designs do not make a noticeable impact on the overall latency, and all designs obtain comparable latency to *no iommu*. The overheads are more observable through the CPU utilization, which is broken down (for 64 KB messages) in Figure 10. We find that *identity+* spends almost half its time on IOMMU-related tasks, whereas the *copy* overheads of shadow buffer management and copying constitute 20% of its time, and less than 10% of the overall CPU time.

memcached Our memcached benchmark consists of multiple memslap instances generating load on 16 memcached instances running on the evaluation machine. The results, depicted in Figure **??**, exhibit a similar trend to the multi-core TCP throughput benchmark. Except for *identity+*, all designs obtain comparable memcached transactional throughput, which is 6.6$\times$ that of the throughput *identity+* ob-

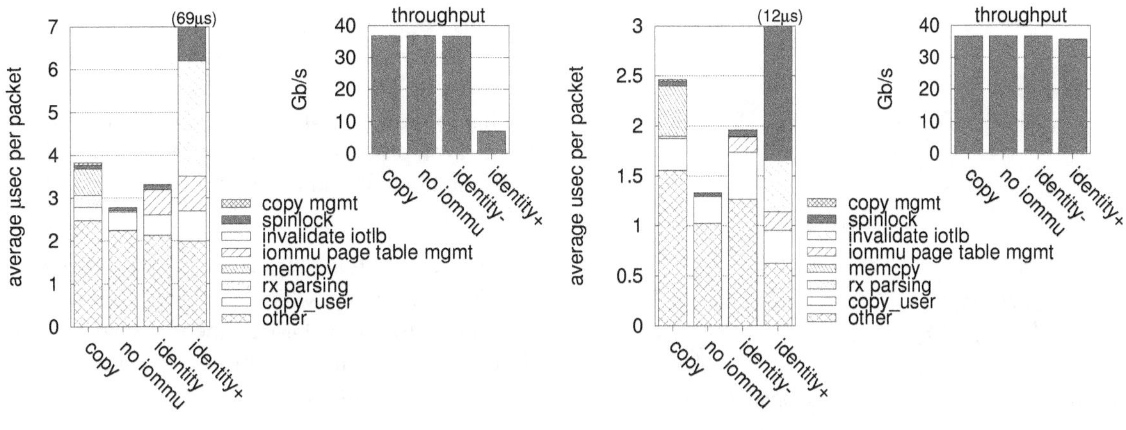

a. Receive (RX)

b. Transmit (TX)

Figure 8: *Average packet processing time breakdown in 16-core TCP throughput tests (64 KB message size).*

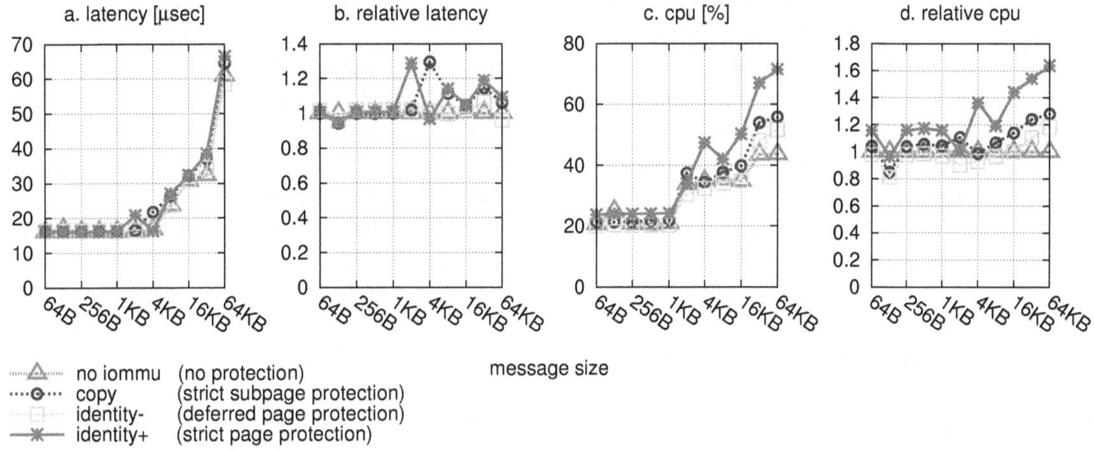

Figure 9: *TCP latency (single-core netperf TCP request/response).*

tains. We thus see that for a realistic demanding workload, *copy* provides full DMA attack protection at essentially the same throughput and CPU utilization (< 2% overhead) as *no iommu*.

Memory consumption Our prototype implementation of *copy* supports shadow buffers of two size classes, 4 KB and 64 KB. Although a size class of C bytes can have at most $2^{37-\lceil \log_2 C \rceil}$ shadow buffers (§ 5.3), we use a more practical bound of 16 K buffers. Thus, in the worst case, *copy* could consume about 2.1 GB (4 KB × 16 K = 64 MB plus 64 KB × 16 K = 1 GB, for each of the two NUMA domains).

In practice, however, we expect memory consumption to be dramatically less. This is because shadow DMA buffer allocations correspond to *in flight* DMAs. To test this, we measured shadow DMA buffer memory consumption during our benchmarks. We observe 64 MB of shadow buffers being allocated to shadow TX buffers, and 96 MB to shadow RX buffers—i.e., ≈ 13× less than the worst case bound.

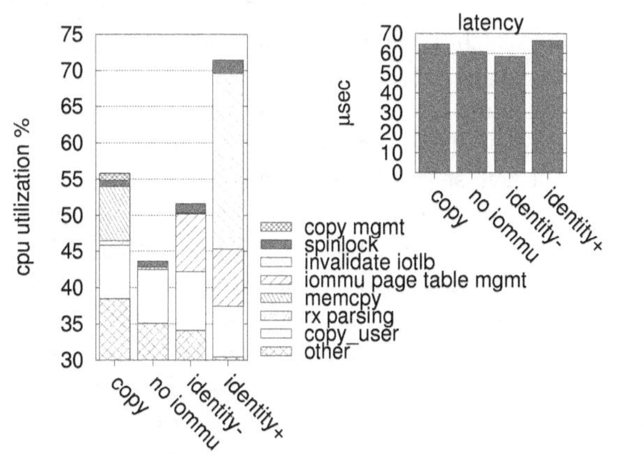

Figure 10: *Single-core TCP request/response CPU utilization breakdown (64 KB message size).*

Summary Our results show that *copy* provides full protection from DMA attacks with comparable or better per-

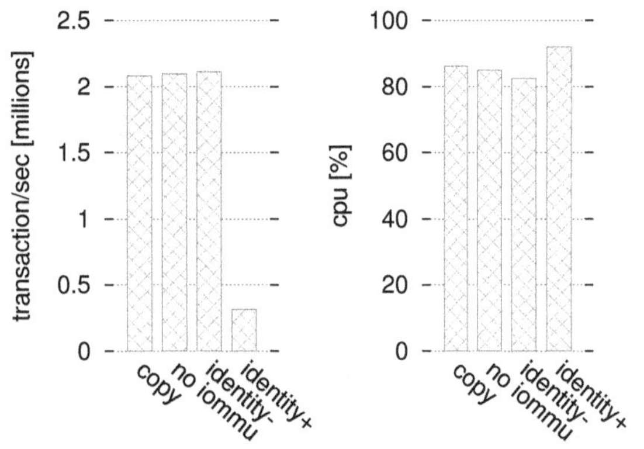

Figure 11: *memcached: aggregated throughput (16 instances).*

formance than the existing, less secure designs. Compared to *identity+*, which does not provide byte-level protection, *copy* provides comparable (< 10% less) or far better throughput (2×–5×), comparable latency, and better or comparable CPU utilization. Compared to *identity-*, which lacks byte-level protection and may allow devices to access unmapped memory, *copy* obtains comparable throughput and latency with 1×–1.4× CPU overhead. Finally, *copy* obtains 0.76×–1× the throughput of *no iommu*, which is defenseless against DMA attacks, with a 20% increase in CPU utilization (which translates to an overhead of 1.8×).

7. Related work

IOMMU-based OS protection Willmann et al. [50] describe five IOMMU-based protection strategies, each of which lacks one or more of the properties provided by our design—strict intra-OS protection (§ 2.2.1) at byte granularity with efficiency and scalability that support high-throughput I/O such as 10–40 Gb/s networking. EiovaR [38] provides strict protection but at page granularity, and it shares the scalability bottlenecks of Linux. Peleg et al. [42] describe scalable protection schemes, but these require deferred protection for high-throughput and are at page granularity. In SUD [15], usermode drivers communicate with the OS through shared IOMMU-mapped buffers, which act similarly to our shadow buffers. While SUD also protects from malicious drivers, it does not appear compatible with high-throughput I/O requirements. Even for 1 Gb/s networking, SUD incurs up to 2× CPU overhead due to context switches, and must use batching—hurting latency—to obtain acceptable throughput [15]. Arrakis [43] provides direct application-level access to devices for efficient I/O. To protect themselves from DMA attacks, Arrakis applications must thus use a DMA API-like scheme, making our shadow buffers relevant there.

Copying-based protection Linux supports an SWIOTLB mode [2] in which the DMA API is implemented by copying DMA buffers to/from dedicated *bounce buffers*. This mode makes no use of the hardware IOMMU and thus provides no protection from DMA attacks. Instead, its goal is to allow systems without an IOMMU to work with devices, such as 32-bit devices, that cannot address the entire physical address space. Horovitz et al. describe a protection scheme similar to shadow DMA buffers [24] in the context of a software cryptoprocessor. However, they do not discuss implementation details and do not provide a performance evaluation.

Hardware solutions Basu et al. [10] propose a hardware IOMMU design in which mappings self-destruct after a threshold of time or DMAs, thereby obviating the need to destroy the mapping in software. However, this hardware is not currently available.

8. Conclusion

Due to lack of byte-granularity protection and trading off security to obtain acceptable performance when using IOMMUs, OSes remain vulnerable to DMA attacks. We propose a new way of using IOMMUs, which fully defends against DMA attacks. Our new usage model restricts device access to a set of shadow DMA buffers that are never unmapped, and copies DMAed data to/from these buffers. It thus provides sub-page byte-granularity protection while closing the current vulnerability window in which devices can access in-use memory. Our key insight is that the gains of zero-copy for IOMMU protection are negated by the cost of interacting with the slow IOMMU hardware and the synchronization it entails, making copying preferable to zero-copying in many cases.

We show that, despite being more secure than the safest preexisting usage model, our DMA shadowing approach provides up to 5× higher throughput. Moreover, while DMA shadowing cannot indefinitely scale with I/O throughput due to the overhead of copying, we show that it *does scale* to 40 Gb/s rates and incurs only 0%–25% throughput degradation as compared to when the IOMMU is disabled.

With malicious devices being used in the wild [3, 52], defending against DMA attacks becomes an increasingly pressing problem. DMA shadowing provides full protection from DMA attacks at reasonable overheads, and we hope to see it deployed in practice.

Acknowledgments

This research was funded in part by the Israeli Ministry of Science and Technology grant #3-9779, by the Israel Science Foundation (grants 1227/10 and 1749/14), by Yad HaNadiv foundation, and by Mellanox, which additionally graciously donated NICs.

References

[1] Intel TXT Overview. `https://www.kernel.org/doc/Documentation/intel_txt.txt`. Linux kernel documentation.

[2] Dma issues, part 2. https://lwn.net/Articles/91870/. (Accessed: January 2016).

[3] Inside TAO: Documents Reveal Top NSA Hacking Unit. *Der Spiegel*, Dec 2013. http://www.spiegel.de/international/world/the-nsa-uses-powerful-toolbox-in-effort-to-spy-on-global-networks-a-940969.html. (Accessed: January 2016).

[4] B. Aker. Memslap - load testing and benchmarking a server. http://docs.libmemcached.org/bin/memslap.html. libmemcached 1.1.0 documentation.

[5] AMD Inc. AMD IOMMU architectural specification, rev 2.00. http://developer.amd.com/wordpress/media/2012/10/488821.pdf, Mar 2011.

[6] Apple Inc. Thunderbolt device driver programming guide: Debugging VT-d I/O MMU virtualization. https://developer.apple.com/library/mac/documentation/HardwareDrivers/Conceptual/ThunderboltDevGuide/DebuggingThunderboltDrivers/DebuggingThunderboltDrivers.html, 2013. (Accessed: January 2016).

[7] ARM Holdings. ARM system memory management unit architecture specification — SMMU architecture version 2.0. http://infocenter.arm.com/help/topic/com.arm.doc.ihi0062c/IHI0062C_system_mmu_architecture_specification.pdf, 2013.

[8] D. Aumaitre and C. Devine. Subverting Windows 7 x64 Kernel with DMA attacks. In *Hack In The Box Security Conference (HITB)*, 2010. http://esec-lab.sogeti.com/static/publications/10-hitbamsterdam-dmaattacks.pdf. (Accessed: January 2016).

[9] T. Ball, E. Bounimova, B. Cook, V. Levin, J. Lichtenberg, C. McGarvey, B. Ondrusek, S. K. Rajamani, and A. Ustuner. Thorough static analysis of device drivers. In *ACM EuroSys*, pages 73–85, 2006.

[10] A. Basu, M. D. Hill, and M. M. Swift. I/O memory management unit providing self invalidated mapping. https://www.google.com/patents/US20150067296, 2015. US Patent App. 14/012,261.

[11] M. Becher, M. Dornseif, and C. N. Klein. FireWire: all your memory are belong to us. In *CanSecWest Applied Security Conference*, 2005.

[12] A. Boileau. Hit by a Bus: Physical Access Attacks with Firewire. In *Ruxcon*, 2006. http://www.security-assessment.com/files/presentations/ab_firewire_rux2k6-final.pdf. (Accessed: January 2016).

[13] J. Bonwick. The Slab allocator: An object-caching kernel memory allocator. In *USENIX Summer Annual Technical Conference*, pages 87–98, 1994.

[14] J. E. Bottomley. Dynamic DMA mapping using the generic device. https://www.kernel.org/doc/Documentation/DMA-API.txt. Linux kernel documentation.

[15] S. Boyd-Wickizer and N. Zeldovich. Tolerating Malicious Device Drivers in Linux. In *USENIX Annual Technical Conference (ATC)*, pages 117–130, 2010.

[16] J. Brossard. Hardware bakdooring is pratical. In *Black Hat*, 2012. http://www.toucan-system.com/research/blackhat2012_brossard_hardware_backdooring.pdf. (Accessed: January 2016).

[17] B. D. Carrier and J. Grand. A hardware-based memory acquisition procedure for digital investigations. *Digital Investigation*, 1(1):50–60, Feb 2014.

[18] A. Chou, J. Yang, B. Chelf, S. Hallem, and D. Engler. An empirical study of operating systems errors. In *ACM Symposium on Operating Systems Principles (SOSP)*, pages 73–88, 2001.

[19] M. Dornseif. 0wned by an iPod. In *PacSec*, 2004. https://pacsec.jp/psj04/psj04-dornseif-e.ppt. (Accessed: January 2016).

[20] L. Duflot, Y.-A. Perez, G. Valadon, and O. Levillain. Can you still trust your network card? Technical report, French Network and Information Security Agency (FNISA), Mar 2010. http://www.ssi.gouv.fr/uploads/IMG/pdf/csw-trustnetworkcard.pdf. (Accessed: January 2016).

[21] L. Duflot, Y.-A. Perez, and B. Morin. What if You Can't Trust Your Network Card? In *Conference on Recent Advances in Intrusion Detection*, pages 378–397, 2011.

[22] B. Fitzpatrick. Distributed caching with memcached. *Linux Journal*, 2004(124), Aug 2004.

[23] J. N. Herder, H. Bos, B. Gras, P. Homburg, and A. S. Tanenbaum. Failure resilience for device drivers. In *IEEE/IFIP Annual International Conference on Dependable Systems and Networks (DSN)*, pages 41–50, 2007.

[24] O. Horovitz, S. Rihan, S. A. Weis, and C. A. Waldspurger. Secure support for I/O in software cryptoprocessor. https://patents.google.com/patent/US20150269091A1, 2015. US Patent App. 14/663,217.

[25] IBM Corporation. PowerLinux servers — 64-bit DMA concepts. http://pic.dhe.ibm.com/infocenter/lnxinfo/v3r0m0/topic/liabm/liabmconcepts.htm. (Accessed: January 2016).

[26] IBM Corporation. AIX kernel extensions and device support programming concepts. http://public.dhe.ibm.com/systems/power/docs/aix/71/kernextc_pdf.pdf, 2013. (Accssed: July 2015).

[27] Intel Corporation. Intel SSD Data Center Family Product Brief. http://www.intel.com/content/www/us/en/solid-state-drives/data-center-family.html.

[28] Intel Corporation. Intel Trusted Execution Technology. http://www.intel.com/content/dam/www/public/us/en/documents/white-papers/trusted-execution-technology-security-paper.pdf, 2012.

[29] Intel Corporation. Intel 64 and IA-32 Architectures Software Developers Manual, Volume 3: System Programming Guide. http://download.intel.com/products/processor/manual/325384.pdf, 2013.

[30] Intel Corporation. Intel Virtualization Technology for Directed I/O, Architecture Specification - Architecture Speci-

fication - Rev. 2.3. http://www.intel.com/content/dam/www/public/us/en/documents/product-specifications/vt-directed-io-spec.pdf, Oct 2014.

[31] M. S. Johnstone and P. R. Wilson. The memory fragmentation problem: Solved? In *ACM International Symposium on Memory Management (ISMM)*, pages 26–36, 1998.

[32] R. A. Jones. A network performance benchmark (revision 2.0). Technical report, Hewlett Packard, 1995. http://www.netperf.org/netperf/training/Netperf.html.

[33] A. Kadav, M. J. Renzelmann, and M. M. Swift. Tolerating hardware device failures in software. In *ACM Symposium on Operating Systems Principles (SOSP)*, pages 59–72, 2009.

[34] B. H. Leitao. Tuning 10Gb network cards on Linux. In *Ottawa Linux Symposium (OLS)*, pages 169–189, 2009.

[35] J. LeVasseur, V. Uhlig, J. Stoess, and S. Götz. Unmodified device driver reuse and improved system dependability via virtual machines. In *USENIX Symposium on Operating System Design and Implementation (OSDI)*, pages 17–30, 2004.

[36] Linux. Documentation/intel-iommu.txt, Linux 3.18 documentation file. https://www.kernel.org/doc/Documentation/Intel-IOMMU.txt. (Accessed: January 2016).

[37] M. Malka, N. Amit, M. Ben-Yehuda, and D. Tsafrir. rIOMMU: Efficient IOMMU for I/O devices that employ ring buffers. In *ACM International Conference on Architectural Support for Programming Languages and Operating Systems (ASPLOS)*, pages 355–368, 2015.

[38] M. Malka, N. Amit, and D. Tsafrir. Efficient Intra-Operating System Protection Against Harmful DMAs. In *USENIX Conference on File and Storage Technologies (FAST)*, pages 29–44, 2015.

[39] V. Mamtani. DMA directions and Windows. http://download.microsoft.com/download/a/f/d/afdfd50d-6eb9-425e-84e1-b4085a80e34e/sys-t304_wh07.pptx, 2007. (Accessed: January 2016).

[40] D. S. Miller, R. Henderson, and J. Jelinek. Dynamic DMA mapping guide. https://www.kernel.org/doc/Documentation/DMA-API-HOWTO.txt. Linux kernel documentation.

[41] PCI-SIG. PCI Express 2.0 Base Specification Revision 0.9. https://www.pcisig.com/specifications/iov/ats, Sep 2006.

[42] O. Peleg, A. Morrison, B. Serebrin, and D. Tsafrir. Utilizing the IOMMU Scalably. In *USENIX Annual Technical Conference (ATC)*, pages 549–562, 2015.

[43] S. Peter, J. Li, I. Zhang, D. R. K. Ports, D. Woos, A. Krishnamurthy, T. Anderson, and T. Roscoe. Arrakis: The Operating System is the Control Plane. In *USENIX Symposium on Operating System Design and Implementation (OSDI)*, pages 1–16, 2014.

[44] F. L. Sang, Éric Lacombe, V. Nicomette, and Y. Deswarte. Exploiting an I/OMMU vulnerability . In *International Conference on Malicious and Unwanted Software (MALWARE)*, pages 7–14, 2010.

[45] P. Stewin and I. Bystrov. Understanding DMA Malware. In *Conference on Detection of Intrusions and Malware & Vulnerability Assessment (DIMVA)*, pages 21–41, 2012.

[46] M. Swift, B. Bershad, and H. Levy. Improving the reliability of commodity operating systems. *ACM Transactions on Computer Systems (TOCS)*, 23(1):77–110, Feb 2005.

[47] A. Triulzi. I 0wn the NIC, now I want a shell! In *PacSec*, 2008. http://www.alchemistowl.org/arrigo/Papers/Arrigo-Triulzi-PACSEC08-Project-Maux-II.pdf. (Accessed: January 2016).

[48] C. Waldspurger and M. Rosenblum. I/O virtualization. *Communications of the ACM (CACM)*, 55(1):66–73, Jan 2012.

[49] D. Williams, P. Reynolds, K. Walsh, E. G. Sirer, and F. B. Schneider. Device driver safety through a reference validation mechanism. In *USENIX Symposium on Operating System Design and Implementation (OSDI)*, pages 241–254, 2008.

[50] P. Willmann, S. Rixner, and A. L. Cox. Protection strategies for direct access to virtualized I/O devices. In *USENIX Annual Technical Conference (ATC)*, pages 15–28, 2008.

[51] R. Wojtczuk and J. Rutkowska. Following the White Rabbit: Software attacks against Intel VT-d technology. http://invisiblethingslab.com/resources/2011/SoftwareAttacksonIntelVT-d.pdf, Apr 2011.

[52] K. Zetter. How the NSA's Firmware Hacking Works and Why It's So Unsettling. *Wired*, Feb 2015. http://www.wired.com/2015/02/nsa-firmware-hacking/. (Accessed: July 2015).

[53] Z. Zhou, V. D. Gligor, J. Newsome, and J. M. McCune. Building Verifiable Trusted Path on Commodity x86 Computers. In *IEEE Symposium on Security and Privacy (S&P)*, pages 616–630, 2012.

Silent Shredder: Zero-Cost Shredding for Secure Non-Volatile Main Memory Controllers

Amro Awad
North Carolina State University
ajawad@ncsu.edu

Pratyusa Manadhata
Hewlett Packard Labs
pratyusa.k.manadhata@hpe.com

Stuart Haber
Hewlett Packard Labs
stuart.haber@hpe.com

Yan Solihin
North Carolina State University
solihin@ncsu.edu

William Horne
Hewlett Packard Labs
william.horne@hpe.com

Abstract

As non-volatile memory (NVM) technologies are expected to replace DRAM in the near future, new challenges have emerged. For example, NVMs have slow and power-consuming writes, and limited write endurance. In addition, NVMs have a data remanence vulnerability, i.e., they retain data for a long time after being powered off. NVM encryption alleviates the vulnerability, but exacerbates the limited endurance by increasing the number of writes to memory.

We observe that, in current systems, a large percentage of main memory writes result from data shredding in operating systems, a process of zeroing out physical pages before mapping them to new processes, in order to protect previous processes' data. In this paper, we propose *Silent Shredder*, which repurposes *initialization vectors* used in standard counter mode encryption to completely eliminate the data shredding writes. Silent Shredder also speeds up reading shredded cache lines, and hence reduces power consumption and improves overall performance. To evaluate our design, we run three PowerGraph applications and 26 multi-programmed workloads from the SPEC 2006 suite, on a gem5-based full system simulator. Silent Shredder eliminates an average of 48.6% of the writes in the initialization and graph construction phases. It speeds up main memory reads by 3.3 times, and improves the number of instructions per cycle (IPC) by 6.4% on average. Finally, we discuss several use cases, including virtual machines' data isolation and user-level large data initialization, where Silent Shredder can be used effectively at no extra cost.

Keywords Encryption; Hardware Security; Phase-Change Memory; Data Protection

1. Introduction

With the arrival of the era of big data and in-memory analytics, there is increasing pressure to deploy large main memories. The traditional use of DRAM as main memory technology is increasingly becoming less attractive, for several reasons. The need to refresh volatile DRAM cells incurs large power consumption, which limits the amount of DRAM we can deploy in the same package. Second, scaling down DRAM cell size becomes difficult as the charge in DRAM cell capacitor needs to be kept constant to meet the retention time requirements [27]. Considering these DRAM limitations, computer system designers are rightfully considering emerging Non-Volatile Memories (NVMs) as replacements for DRAM. NVMs are non-volatile and require no refresh power; some of them have a read latency comparable to DRAM, while at the same time they may scale better than DRAM [6, 8, 41].

Currently, there are still serious challenges in using NVMs as the main memory. Writing to NVM cells is often slow, requires large power consumption, and has limited write endurance, e.g., 10-100 million writes in Phase Change Memory [6, 8, 30, 41, 45]. Another serious challenge is the data remanence vulnerability, where NVMs retain data for NVMs a long time after a system is powered off whereas DRAM loses data quickly. Obtaining an NVM chip and scanning it can reveal data in memory. Memory encryption has been proposed to ward off data remanence attacks [16, 43]. While effective in dealing with the vulnerability, memory encryption worsens the write endurance problem. A good encryption scheme must have the *diffusion* property; the change in one bit in original data should

ASPLOS '16, April 2–6, 2016, Atlanta, Georgia, USA..

http://dx.doi.org/10.1145/2872362.2872377

change many bits in the encrypted data [36]. However, as pointed out by Young et al. [43], techniques to reduce the number of writes in NVMs, such as Data Comparison Write (DCW) and Flip-N-Write (FNW), lose effectiveness due to diffusion because these techniques are inspired by the observation that few bits will have their values changed after successive cache line writes.

Therefore, with memory encryption, reducing the number of writes is of paramount importance. The goal of this paper is to find opportunities to reduce the number of writes to an encrypted NVM used as main memory. Specifically, we focus on the problem of ***data shredding***, which is one of the most frequent operating system (OS) operations [14]. Data shredding is the strategy to initialize to zero each physical memory page before mapping it to a process [13, 32, 35]. The OS performs shredding to avoid inter-process data leak, where a process accidentally or intentionally reads the old data of another process. Also, hypervisors perform shredding to avoid inter-virtual machine (VM) data leak in virtualized systems. Our experiments show that data shredding can contribute to a large portion of the overall number of main memory writes, significantly costing processor cycles and memory bandwidth. Furthermore, up to 40% of the page fault time can be spent in page zeroing [38].

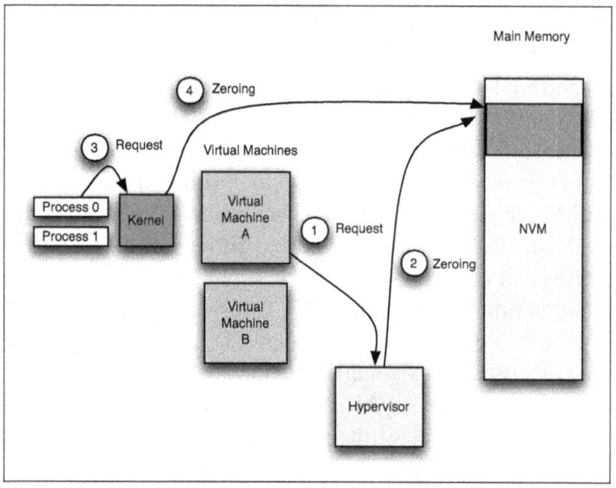

Figure 1. Example of duplicate data sherdding.

The frequency of shredding will further increase where there are many running processes or many virtual machines sharing a system, which is becoming increasingly more common in servers, due to virtualization and server consolidation. Data shredding can also occur multiple times for a single memory page. For example, as shown in Figure 1, hypervisors manage memory allocations across virtual machines in virtualized systems. As shown in Step 1, a VM requests host physical memory pages. However, the hypervisor needs to zero out the data to prevent inter-VM data leak [7, 9], as shown in Step 2. Furthermore, when a process requests memory pages, the Kernel/OS inside the VM zeroes out physical pages before mapping them to a new process to prevent inter-process data leak, as shown in Steps 3 and 4, respectively. The impact of data shredding necessitates that we rethink how data shredding should be implemented.

Virtual machines and local nodes' kernels may prefer to request memory allocations with large granularity, for several reasons. The hypervisor or resource manager does not need to go through a large number of extra page table walks beyond the page table walks that occur at the virtual machine or local node level, hence reducing the cost of address translation misses. Another reason is to reduce the intervention between virtual machines or local nodes and resource managers, hence a better scalability. Accordingly, for instance, assume a system with hundreds of terabytes of memory and a large number of nodes, memory allocations can be in order of gigabytes or terabytes. Zeroing out such large amount of memory would be very slow. Furthermore, there is a chance that the virtual machine or the local node never writes the whole space, but shredding the whole assigned physical space is still required.

Previous work targeted speeding up zeroing pages in the context of DRAM main memory [21, 34, 42]. However, since writes to DRAM are cheap, these studies proposed speeding up the zeroing operation, but not eliminating it. For example, Jiang et al. [21] suggest offloading the zeroing to a DMA engine, while Sehsadri et al. [34] shift the zeroing to within the DRAM. However, in both studies, the writes to the main memory still occur, and hence these methods are not suitable for use in NVM-based main memory.

In this paper, we present a secure NVMM controller, *Silent Shredder*, that *completely* eliminates writes to NVM due to data shredding. Silent Shredder eliminates shredding-related writes to NVM-based main memory by exploiting *initialization vectors (IVs)* used in symmetric encryption. We prevent data leakage and eliminate shredding-related writes at the same time with minimal cost. One key insight for avoiding shredding-related writes is that to protect data privacy of a process, it is sufficient for the OS to make a data page unintelligible when the page is allocated to another process. By making the page unintelligible rather than zeroing it, the old data of a process is protected from being read by another process. The second insight is that when data in a newly allocated page is read, for software compatibility, the controller should skip the actual reading from NVM and instead should supply a zero-filled block to the cache. Silent Shredder achieves these goals by repurposing the IVs: it manipulates IVs to render data pages unintelligible and to encode the shredded state of a page. Note that Silent Shredder works with all modes of symmetric encryption that use IVs, including the counter mode used in recent secure NVM proposals. By avoiding shredding-related writes to NVM and the subsequent reads from NVM, Silent Shredder improves NVM's write endurance, increases read performance, and reduces power consumption. All these are achieved using low-cost modifications to a standard counter-mode encrypted memory system.

To evaluate our design, we use gem5, a detailed full-system simulator, to run 3 graph analytics applications from the PowerGraph framework and 26 multi-programmed workloads from the SPEC 2006 benchmark suite. Silent Shredder eliminates about *half* (48.6%, on average) of the writes in the initialization and graph construction phases. Furthermore, it speeds up the memory reads by an average of 3.3 times and improves the instructions per cycle (IPC) by an average of 6.4%.

The rest of the paper is organized as follows. We briefly describe NVM technologies, data shredding, and encrypted NVMs in Section 2. In Section 3, we present a motivational example. In Section 4, we introduce several design options for eliminating data shredding and discuss their advantages and disadvantages. Later, we motivate our choice of Silent Shredder as the preferred design and then show that our design can be implemented at zero cost when using secure NVMM controllers. We introduce our evaluation methodology in Section 5 and present evaluation results and a parameter sensitivity study in Section 6. In Section 7, we discuss several use cases, security concerns, and remediation for Silent Shredder. We discuss related work in Section 8 and conclude with a summary in Section 9.

2. Background

In this section, we briefly describe emerging NVM technologies, memory encryption, and data shredding in OSes.

2.1 Non-Volatile Memories (NVMs)

Phase-Change Memory (PCM), Spin-Transfer Torque (STT-RAM) and Memristor are among emerging non-volatile memory technologies, some of which are considered as candidates for replacing DRAM for use as the main memory. Their read latencies and densities are either competitive or comparable with DRAM, and they may scale better than DRAM. However, NVMs suffer from slow and power consuming writes, and generally have limited write endurance, e.g., 10-100 million writes with Phase Change Memory [30]).

When used as main memory, NVMs may provide *persistent memory*, where regular store instructions can be used to make persistent changes to data structures in order to keep them safe from crashes or failures. Persistent memory enables *persistent memory allocations* [11, 23, 24, 39], and may allow future systems to fuse storage and main memory [1, 4, 26]. When an application or a VM requests and uses a persistent page, the OS should guarantee that its page mapping information is kept persistent, so the process or the VM can remap the page across machine reboots [24, 39]. There has been research on explicit software programming frameworks for exploiting persistent memory, e.g., ATLAS [15].

However, NVMM suffers from a serious security vulnerability: it retains data long after a system is powered off. Obtaining physical access to NVMM (through theft, repair, or improper disposal) allows attackers to read the plaintext of data [16, 43]. Accordingly, NVMM should be paired with at least some form of memory encryption.

2.2 Memory Encryption

There are two general approaches for encrypting NVMM. One approach assumes the processor is not modified, and the NVMM controller encrypts the main memory content transparently to the processor [16]. To minimize performance overheads, cold data, i.e, infrequently used data, stays encrypted, but hot data is proactively decrypted and stored in plaintext in memory. Another approach assumes that the processor can be modified and the processor chip is the secure base. Any data sent off chip in the main memory is encrypted. There are many example systems using the latter approach, including some recent studies [31, 40, 43].

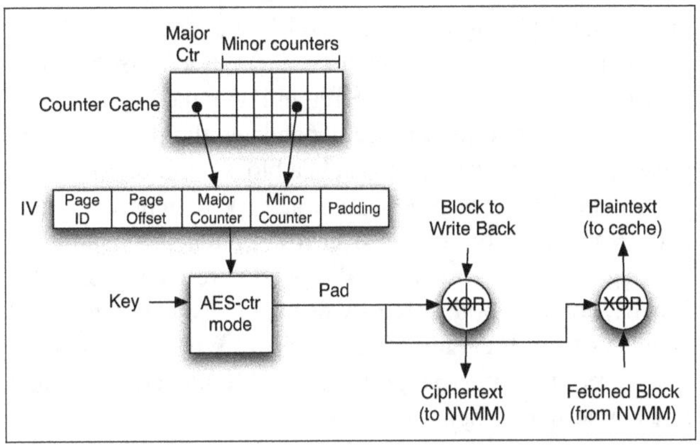

Figure 2. State of the art counter mode encryption. AES is shown for encryption/decryption but other cryptographic algorithms are possible.

There are several encryption modes that can be used to encrypt the main memory. One mode is *direct encryption* (also known as electronic code book or ECB mode), where an encryption algorithm such as AES is used to encrypt each cache block as it is written back to memory and decrypt the block when it enters the processor chip again. Direct encryption reduces system performance by adding decryption latency to the last level cache (LLC) miss latency. Another mode is *counter mode* encryption, where the encryption algorithm is applied to an *initialization vector* (IV) to generate a one-time pad. This is illustrated in Figure 2. Data is then encrypted and decrypted via a simple bitwise XOR with the pad. With counter mode, decryption latency is overlapped with LLC miss latency, and only the XOR latency is added to the critical path of LLC miss. In state-of-the-art design, the IV of a counter mode encryption consists of a unique ID of a page (similar to a page address, but is unique across the main memory and swap space in the disk), page offset (to distinguish blocks in a page), a per-block *minor* counter (to distinguish different versions of the data value of a block over time), and a per-page *major* counter (to avoid overflow in counter values).

For the rest of the paper, we assume counter mode processor-side encryption, similar to earlier papers [31, 40, 43], because counter mode is more secure: Encryption in ECB mode, without the use of counters or IVs is vulnerable to several attacks based on the fact that identical blocks of plaintext will encrypt to identical blocks of ciphertext, wherever they occur in memory; vulnerabilities include dictionary and replay attacks. Memory-side encryption, e.g. with secure DIMMs, is vulnerable to bus snooping attacks. In addition, processor-side encryption makes it easier to interface with the OS, use per-user and per-application keys, and expose key management to users and applications (where appropriate).

Counters are kept in the main memory, but are also cached on chip with one major counter of a page co-located in a block together with all minor counters of a page. For example, in [40], a 4KB page has a 64-bit major counter that is co-located with 64 7-bit minor counters in a 64-byte block. Any parts of the IV are not secret and only the key is secret. The security of counter mode depends on the pad not being reused, hence at every write back, a block's minor counter is incremented prior to producing a new IV to generate a new pad. When a minor counter overflows, the major counter of the page is incremented and the page is re-encrypted [40]. Finally, counter mode integrity needs to be ensured to avoid attackers from breaking the encryption. While counters are not secret, they must be protected by Merkle Tree to detect any tampering to their values [31].

2.3 Data Shredding

Avoiding data leak between processes requires clearing, e.g., zeroing, a memory page of a process before allocating it to another process. The cost of data shredding is high. For example, a recent study showed that up to 40% of the page fault time is spent in page zeroing [38]. Different operating systems adopt different zeroing strategies. For example, in FreeBSD, the free pages are zeroed out early and kept in a memory pool ready for allocation. Once a process needs a new page to be allocated, a new virtual page is mapped to one of the zeroed physical pages [2]. In Linux, the kernel guarantees that a newly allocated virtual page is initially mapped to a special physical page called the *Zero Page*. The Zero Page is shared by all new allocated pages. The actual allocation of a physical page happens when the process writes to the page for the first write, using a mechanism referred to as copy-on-write (COW). During COW, a physical page (from another process) is zeroed out and the virtual page is remapped to it [13]. Similar mechanisms are deployed by hypervisors to avoid data leak between virtual machines [7].

The zeroing step itself can be implemented with different mechanisms [18]. One mechanism relies on using temporal store instructions, e.g., `movq` in the x86 instruction set, which brings each block into the cache before writing zero to it. The use of temporal store can cause cache pollution, where useful blocks are evicted and cause subsequent cache misses. The impact of cache pollution increases when dealing with large pages, such as 2MB and 1GB size pages. In addition, the mechanism works well if all cache blocks of the page are used shortly after zeroing; however, often this is not the case. Also, without additional mechanisms, zeroing blocks of the page in the cache is not secure as it does not persist the modifications to the NVMM right away. Hence, upon system failures, the zeroing may be lost, and data leak may occur.

Another zeroing mechanism is using non-temporal store instructions, such as `movntq` in x86. Such store instructions bypass the entire cache hierarchy and write directly to the main memory; any blocks that are currently cached are invalidated. Non-temporal stores avoid cache pollution, but they also come with a risk of invalidating soon-to-be accessed or initialized blocks. Some overheads remain unchanged, e.g, the number of store instructions used, and latency and power from using memory bus bandwidth.

There have been proposals to improve zeroing performance. Some studies have proposed offloading the zeroing step to the DRAM controller or the DMA engine, so that the CPU time is not wasted in zeroing pages and cache pollution is avoided [18, 21, 34]. Such techniques are effective in DRAM main memory, but with NVMM, the zeroing still results in high performance overheads due to high power consumption and latency of writes in NVMs, and reduced write endurance. Since our paper targets memory controllers for NVMM, we consider techniques that zero out pages in main memory and bypass the caches entirely, but with a significant reduction in the actual zeroing operations.

3. Motivation

We start with an example to study the impact of kernel shredding on system performance. Assume a simple code that allocates and initializes $SIZE$ bytes of memory, as shown in the code snippet in Figure 3. As explained earlier

```
// Allocating SIZE bytes
char * ALLOC= (char *) malloc(SIZE);
// Setting all allocated memory to 0
// Point 0
memset(ALLOC,0,SIZE);
// Point 1
memset(ALLOC,0,SIZE);
// Point 2
```

Figure 3. A code sample for initializing allocated memory.

in Section 2, the Linux kernel allocates and zeroes out a physical page right after the first write. Accordingly, the first store instruction in the first `memset` causes a page fault, the page fault handler then allocates a new physical page and zeroes it out, and finally maps it to the application process. As the application's `memset` resumes after the page fault, if the region is the size of a page, page zeroing is redundantly repeated. Overall, the first memset incurs the following delay: kernel page allocation, kernel zeroing, and program zeroing. In contrast, the second memset only has the program zeroing delay. Since program zeroing follows a similar mechanism as kernel zeroing, the second `memset`'s delay is a good proxy of kernel zeroing latency. `memset` is more optimized than the kernel zeroing process- it uses non-temporal stores when the size of the memory to be initialized is bigger than the LLC, and hence avoids cache pollution. Hence it takes less time than kernel zeroing and in our experiments, `memset`'s time is a conservative proxy for kernel zeroing time. Figure 4 shows the time spent to execute the first vs. the second `memset`.

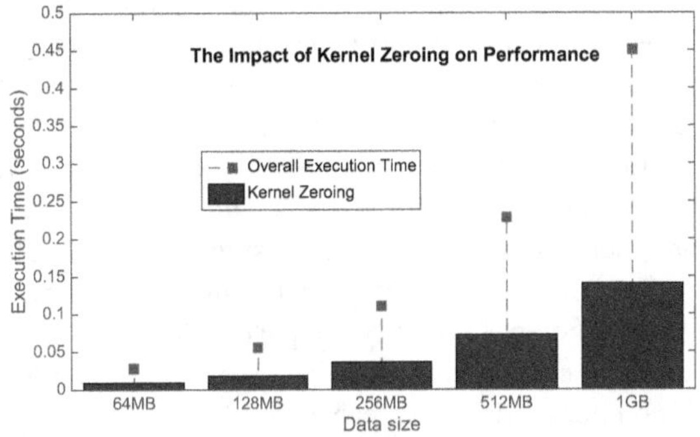

Figure 4. The impact of kernel zeroing on performance.

The overall execution time is the time taken by the first memset (which includes page zeroing, page faults, and program zeroing), and the height of the blue bars is the time taken by the second memset (which only incurs program zeroing). We observe that on average, roughly 32% of the first `memset` time is spent in kernel zeroing. Our observation is consistent with previous studies that showed that up to 40% of the page fault time is spent in kernel zeroing [38]. Note that writing latency for NVMs is multiple times slower than that of DRAM, and hence the page zeroing is expected to become dominant and to contribute for most of the page fault time.

Now let us examine real applications. Figure 5 shows the number of writes to the main memory for several graph analytics applications from the PowerGraph suite [20]. The number of writes was collected using performance counters. A system call was added to collect the number of times the kernel calls the `clear_page` function. For all real system experiments, we use Linux kernel 3.16.2 on a 12-core Intel Xeon E5-2620 CPU machine with 16GB main memory. The data sets we use are publicly released data sets from Netflix and Twitter [10, 44].

For each application, the first bar represents the number of writes when using temporal kernel zeroing (zero-

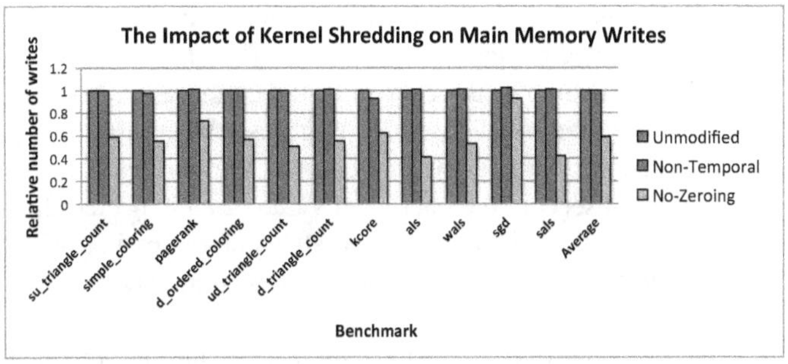

Figure 5. Impact of zeroing on the overall number of writes to the memory.

ing in caches). The second bar represents the number of writes when using non-temporal kernel zeroing (bypassing the cache hierarchy). Finally, the third column shows the number of writes to the main memory when zeroing is avoided in the main memory. We obtained the third bar by counting the number of writes caused by kernel zeroing in the non-temporal case and deducting it from the overall number of writes. We observe that in big data applications, such as graph analytics, a large percentage of the overall number of writes to the main memory is caused by kernel zeroing. The main reason behind this is that many data analytics applications exhibit a write-once read-many times behavior, where the graph is rarely modified after the graph construction phase.

In summary, we found that kernel zeroing can contribute very significantly to the execution time and the number of main memory writes, regardless of whether temporal or non-temporal writes are used. While such overheads are costly with DRAM main memory, they are multiple times more costly with NVMM due to the slow and power consuming nature of writes, and the reduction in NVMs' lifetime until write endurance limit is reached.

4. Silent Shredder Design

In this section, we explore several design alternatives for data shredding and motivate the design choices in Silent Shredder.

4.1 Attack Model

Silent Shredder is designed to protect against attacks carried out by attackers who have physical access to the computers. The attackers can scan a computer's bus or main memory, tamper with main memory content, or play man in the middle between the computer's processor and the main memory. This attack model is the same as the models assumed in prior memory encryption studies [31, 40, 43]. Such attacks are possible due to several reasons such as lax physical security guarding server rooms in cloud computing facilities, improper disposal of computers at the end of their service, and malicious administrators or repairmen. Attackers may insert a bus snooper or a memory scanner to read out data communicated off the processor chip. They may also insert devices to overwrite the content of the main memory, or act as a man in the middle by returning false data requested by the processor chip. They may conduct known-plaintext attacks by observing the encrypted value of an expected data item, or employ dictionary-based attacks by guessing original values according to encrypted values' frequency.

We leave out side-channel attacks because they are beyond the scope of this paper and there are many side-channel protection mechanisms in the literature that can be added to Silent Shredder as needed.

Silent Shredder requires the OS to communicate page zeroing to hardware. This requires minimal modifications to the OS's page fault handler; however, it requires the OS to be trusted, as an untrusted OS can maliciously avoid page zeroing in order to cause data leak between processes. If the OS is not trusted, then processes must run in secure enclaves. Although beyond the scope of this paper, we believe that Silent Shredder can be adapted relatively easily to work with secure enclaves. For example, the hardware can notify Silent Shredder directly when a page from an enclave is going to be deallocated. Further discussion about several security concerns when using counter-mode encryption and their remediations can be found in Section 7.1.

4.2 Skipping the Zeroing Writes

The main goal of shredding data is to prevent data leakage between processes or VMs when a page is reused. One key observation we make is that page zeroing is only one way to prevent data leakage. Writing any unintelligible or random content into the page before the page is reused achieves the same goal, as the process which gets the page will not be able to read any meaningful data from the page. In traditional (non-encrypted) memory, however, there is no advantage to writing a random pattern to a page compared to writing zeros to the page. In fact, writing zeros to a page is more efficient as various instruction sets may provide a special instruction to zero an entire cache block (e.g., `dcbz` in PowerPC).

However, in encrypted memory, the nature of cryptographic encryption can be exploited to initialize a reused page with a random pattern *for free*. For example, consider a page of data encrypted with the key K_1. Before the page is reused, if we change the key to a different one, K_2, then subsequent decryption of the page will result in unintelligible data. The nature of encryption ensures that the new decrypted data is not correlated with the initial data, nor is it any easier to break encryption when attackers read data decrypted with a different key. Most importantly, the entire initialization writes to the reused page are completely eliminated, resulting in significant performance improvement, power savings, and write endurance improvement.

The above technique can be achieved by giving every process a unique key, instead of the entire system using one key. However, giving each process a unique encryption key seriously complicates key management. First, the architecture and the OS need to ensure that no key is reused and all keys are securely stored. Second, it complicates data sharing among processes: shared pages need to be encrypted/decrypted using a common key that is known to all sharing processes. Third, from a practical perspective, the memory controller has no easy way to identify the process that owns the physical address of the memory read/write request; hence it is unable to decrypt the data without the correct key. Addressing this requires the process ID or the process-specific key to be passed along with every memory request.

These challenges make the deployment of such a design costly. Thus, in Silent Shredder, we assume that processes share a single cryptographic key. In order to provide a way to initialize a reused page with a random pattern without using process-specific keys, we exploit the feature of counter-mode encryption where the initialization vector (IV) is what is encrypted to generate a pad. Essentially, if a block is encrypted with an IV, IV_1, but decrypted with a different IV, IV_2, then even when the two IVs differ by just one bit, the decrypted data is unintelligible. This is because $Data \neq D_K(IV_2) \oplus \big(E_K(IV_1) \oplus Data\big)$ where E_K and D_K are encryption and decryption using the key K. Therefore, to initialize a reused page with unintelligible random data, it is sufficient to modify the page's IVs. Note that this is true of any encryption mode that uses IVs, though we focus on counter mode in this paper.

The next logical question is which parts of the IV should be modified. The page ID and the page offset components in an IV should not be modified as they ensure spatial uniqueness of the IV of a block. This leaves us with the per-page major counter and the per-block minor counter. We now discuss several possible approaches with different trade offs. One option is to increment all the minor counters in a page. This changes the IVs of all blocks in a page and avoids actual page zeroing. However, this option has drawbacks. One drawback is that since minor counters are typically small, e.g., 7 bits are recommended [40], incrementing minor counters induces a high probability of minor counter overflow, which causes expensive page re-encryption. Essentially, a block in a page can only be written back from the LLC to the NVMM $2^7 = 128$ times before the page needs to be re-encrypted. Page re-encryption involves reading all blocks of a page from memory into the cache, incrementing the page's major counter, resetting all minor counters of the page, and writing back all blocks of the page from the cache to the NVMM. Page re-encryption is an expensive operation in DRAM main memory and is significantly more expensive in NVMM. Hence it should be avoided whenever possible.

To avoid increasing the frequency of page re-encryption, we can pursue a second option, where we increment the major counter and leave all minor counters unchanged. Since the major counter of a page is used to encrypt or decrypt all blocks in the page, incrementing the major counter is sufficient to initialize a reused page to a random pattern. Accordingly, we do not increase the frequency of page re-encryption since minor counters are unchanged.

A major drawback with both of these techniques is that they assume that the OS or applications are not implemented with the expectation that a newly-allocated page will have zero values. However, our observation is that this assumption is not valid in modern systems. For example, in Linux, we find that the `libc` system library's runtime load (`rtld`) code contains an error-checking assertion that verifies that pointer variables in a newly-allocated page have the value of zero (`NULL`). Hence the two techniques give rise to software compatibility challenges.

However, we can pursue another approach when such assertion removal is not possible or not desirable. In this situation, we would still like to avoid zeroing writes but allow Silent Shredder to return a zero value when reading any cache block from a newly allocated page. This requires a third option as follows. When a reused page is initialized, the major counter of the page is incremented, and simultaneously all the minor counters are reset to zero. We reserve the value zero in a block's minor counter to indicate that when the block is read, zeros are returned to the processor instead of a random pattern. The zero minor counter is not used during regular page re-encryption; for example, when a minor counter overflows, the minor counter will be reset to 1 instead of zero. Upon an LLC miss, the minor counter value for the block is checked. If it is zero, then the cache block is not fetched from memory. Instead, a zero-filled block is allocated in the cache, and returned to the `ld` or `st` instruction that accesses the block. This approach has the side benefit of reducing page re-encryption frequency as it lengthens the time until page re-encryption. For the rest of the paper, we use the third option to accomplish page shredding, where the major counter is incremented and minor counters are reset.

Note that without the Silent Shredder mechanism, shredding a memory page in conventional NVMM will cause every minor counter on a page to be incremented, *in addition to* writing zeros to the main memory. Thus, Silent Shredder does not increase the number of writes to counters, but it completely avoids page zeroing writes.

4.3 Silent Shredder's Design

We now discuss Silent Shredder's overall design. Figure 6 illustrates the high-level mechanism. First, when the OS wants to shred a page, p, the OS uses a mechanism to give a hint to the hardware, e.g., by writing p's physical address to a memory-mapped register in the Memory Controller (MC). This is shown in the figure as Step 1. The MC then sends an invalidation request to the cache and coherence controller of remote caches and also the local cache (Step 2). The coherence controller sends out invalidation requests to any blocks in the page that may be shared in the caches of other cores. In addition, the block containing p's counters is also invalidated from other cores' counter caches. This step is necessary for keeping the caches coherent, even though the blocks will not be actually written. When a remote core has a cache miss, it will be forced to reload updated counters for the page and the missing block in the page.

After the invalidation, the counters can be changed (Step 3) by incrementing the major counter of the page p and resetting all the minor counters to zero. Finally, the counter cache controller acknowledges (Step 4) the completion of updating counters, and the MC signals the completion to the processor. At this time, the zeroing is completed without any blocks in the page ever written to the NVMM.

Note that steps 2, 3, 4 and 5 are correctness requirements for any kind of bulk zeroing that bypasses the cache hierarchy, e.g., non-temporal zeroing and DMA engine support. Most modern integrated memory controllers have the ability to invalidate and flush cache lines; DMA region writes should invalidate any stale data in the cache hierarchy [3, 34]. Furthermore, a simple serializing event, e.g., `sfence`, can be implemented to ensure that all invalidations have been posted and that the counter values have been updated. For example, in Linux, non-temporal zeroing stores are followed by `sfence` to guarantee that all writes have been propagated to main memory. A similar approach can be adopted in Silent Shredder, e.g., following shredding the command with `sfence` or `pcommit`, where the memory controller guarantees that serializing events such as `sfence` or `pcommit` will not be marked completed until all invalidations are posted and all counters are updated.

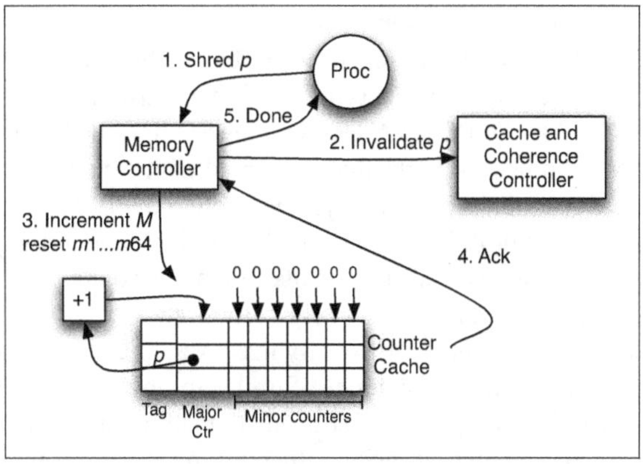

Figure 6. Silent Shredder's shredding mechanism.

Figure 7 shows how a LLC miss is serviced. Suppose the LLC misses on a block, x. The block address of the miss is passed to the counter cache (Step 1), resulting in the minor counter being read out. The minor counter for the block x is then compared to zero. If the minor counter value is not zero, then a request to fetch the block x is passed on to the memory controller (Step 3a), which then obtains x from the NVMM, decrypts it, and returns it to the LLC (Step 4). On the other hand, if the value of the minor counter is zero, then a zero-filled block is returned to the LLC.

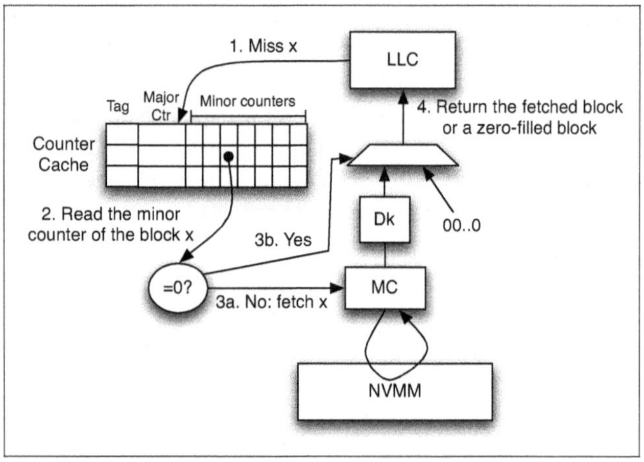

Figure 7. Silent Shredder's mechanism for servicing an LLC miss.

Overall, Silent Shredder's mechanism achieves the following savings compared to traditional page zeroing mechanisms:

1. During page shredding, none of the cache blocks of the page are written.
2. When any of the 64 blocks in a shredded page is read for the first time, the NVMM is not accessed, and instead a zero-filled block is installed in the cache.

Both of these savings improve performance, both during and after shredding. Furthermore, the first item reduces power consumption and improves write endurance of NVMM due to skipping writes.

Silent Shredder's Extensibility: Silent Shredder can be implemented with any encryption mode that uses IVs: CBC, PCBC, CFB, OFB, and CTR. Such encryption modes have the well-known property that encrypted data cannot be decrypted without both the encryption key and the IV that were used to encrypt it. In our scheme, Silent Shredder zeros out the minor counter and increments the major counter in the IV, thereby changing the IV originally used for encryption, making the encrypted data totally irrecoverable.

Counter Cache Persistency: Similar to any scheme that relies on IVs, Silent Shredder needs to maintain the counter cache's persistency by using either a battery-backed write-back counter cache, or a write-through counter cache. For the rest of the paper, we assume a battery-backed write-back counter cache. However, even in case of write-through counter cache, the overhead for counter cache is minimal per page zeroing (64B block per 4096B page write).

Data Recovery: In our case, recovering data in case of disasters is the same as with secure DIMMs. For security reasons, encryption keys need to be stored outside the DIMM or stored securely in the DIMM, e.g. encrypted with a master recovery key. Similar mechanisms to recover keys apply to both cases. In addition, the IVs must be backed up to NVMM. Once the keys and the IVs are obtained, the data can be recovered. In addition, redundancy and key sharing can be used for recovery.

5. Evaluation Methodology

We use a modified version of Linux kernel 3.4.91 in our experiments. Specifically, we replace the `clear_page` function used to clear new physical pages with our shredding mechanism. We use a memory-mapped I/O register for writing the physical address of the page to be shredded. We use the default page size of 4KB. Shredding any page larger than 4KB, such as 2MB and 1GB, can be done by sending a shred command for each 4KB of the large page. In Linux, the function for clearing large pages, `clear_huge_page`, already calls the `clear_page` function for each 4KB. Therefore, no more modifications are needed. We run our modified Linux kernel on gem5, a full system cycle-accurate simulator [12]. We extended gem5's memory controller to include a counter cache and a memory-mapped I/O register. We run 26 SPEC CPU2006 benchmarks with the reference input [5]. We also run 3 benchmarks from PowerGraph benchmark suite: page rank, simple coloring and kcore [20]. All benchmarks were compiled with default settings and optimizations.

Our goal is to study the potential benefits for Silent Shredder under environments with high level of data shredding as a proof of concept. Data shredding is a performance bottleneck during graph construction and initialization phases. Hence we checkpoint the PowerGraph benchmarks at the beginning of the graph construction phase, and the SPEC benchmarks at the beginning of the initialization phase. In the baseline configuration without Silent Shredder, we assume that when receiving a shred command, shredded cache blocks are invalidated and written back (if dirty) to the main memory. In other words, the baseline shredding uses non-temporal stores. Such an assumption guarantees that similar number of instructions are executed when comparing Silent Shredder with the baseline; similar kernel binary and checkpoints are used. For fair comparison, we assume that for both the baseline and Silent Shredder, invalidation of all cache blocks is sent right after receiving the shredding command.

We warm up the system caches for 1 billion cache accesses and then run the applications until at least one core has executed 500 million instructions (a total of approximately 4 billion instructions for an 8-core system). For SPEC benchmarks, we run an instance of the benchmark on each core.

The system configuration used in our simulations is shown in Table 1. Similar to the expected trend of modern cache hierarchies, our system has a 4-level cache hierarchy [37]. L4 and L3 caches are shared among all cores, while L1 and L2 caches are private for each core. We also assume a battery-backed writeback counter cache.

Each valid cache block in the counter cache maps to a single physical page in the main memory. Each block contains 7-bit minor counters, one for each cache block in

Table 1. Configurations of the baseline system.

Processor	
CPU	8 cores x86-64 processor, 2GHz clock
L1 Cache	2 cycles, 64KB size, 8-way, LRU, 64B block size
L2 Cache	8 cycles, 512KB size, 8-way, LRU, 64B block size
L3 Cache	25 cycles, 8MB size, 8-way, LRU, 64B block size
L4 Cache	35 cycles, 64MB size, 8-way, LRU, 64B block size
Coherency Protocol	MESI
Main Memory	
Capacity	16 GB
# Channels	2 channels
Channel bandwidth	12.8 GB/s
Read Latency	75 ns
Write Latency	150 ns
Counter Cache	10 cycles, 4MB size, 8-way, 64B block size
Operating System	
OS	Gentoo
Kernel Version	3.4.91

that page, and a 64-bit major counter for that page. In Section 6.4, we discuss the reason behind our choice of the capacity of the counter cache to be 4MB. The latency of the counter cache was obtained using the CACTI 6.0 tool [25].

6. Evaluation

In this section, we evaluate the potential benefits that come from our design. We start by showing the reduction of the number of main memory writes as a result of using Silent Shredder. Later, we show how our design also reduces read traffic and improves performance as additional benefits.

6.1 Write Reduction

The main goal of Silent Shredder is to reduce the number of writes occurring as a result of the kernel zeroing process for shredding previous data. We find that an average of 48.6% of the main memory writes in the initialization phase could be eliminated. Figure 8 shows the percentage of writes to the main memory that we could save by using Silent Shredder.

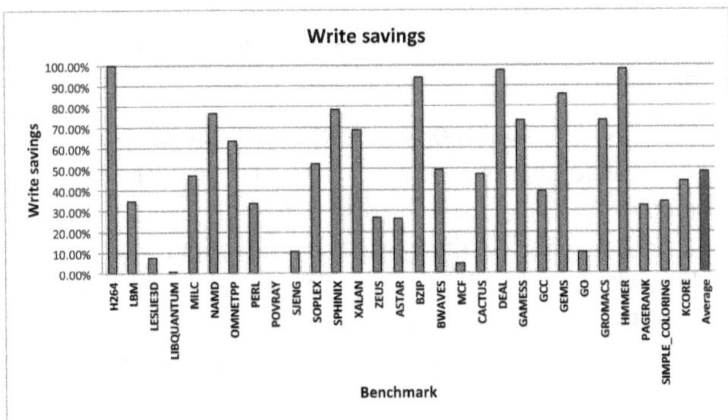

Figure 8. Savings on writes to the main memory.

From Figure 8, we observe that kernel zeroing contributes to large percentage of main memory writes for some applications. A few applications, e.g., H264, DealII and Hmmer, have a very small ratios of main memory writes to instructions. Accordingly, we find that for such applications the majority of main memory writes result from the kernel zeroing operation. Note that since we simulate the full system, the kernel zeroing can be a result of the application initialization code itself, loading system libraries, writing metadata or any other system activities. Since our work targets shredding from the kernel perspective, we count all kernel shredding writes, regardless of the semantics of the program.

Eliminating a significant number of writes is very important; it reduces the memory traffic, increases performance by eliminating slow and power consuming NVMM writes, and increases the lifetime of the NVMM. Our evaluation focuses on the start up or graph initialization phase which is important because the graphs get rarely modified after initialization, hence significant percentage of the main memory writes occur at this phase. The startup phase is not the only scenario where Silent Shredder is effective. In a system that is highly loaded, data shredding will occur frequently because the high load from multiple workloads are placing a high pressure on the physical memory. For example, most data center servers today are not very good in terms of energy proportionality (idle power is approximately 50% of peak power), and therefore peak energy efficiency is achieved when the data centers are highly loaded resulting in very high processor utilization rates [19]. A highly loaded system will suffer from a high rate of page faults, and page fault latency is critical in this situation.

6.2 Read Traffic Reduction

Another important advantage of using Silent Shredder is the ability to recognize shredded cache blocks from their minor counter values. Once a read to a shredded block is detected, a zero-filled block will be returned to the cache hierarchy without the need to read the invalid data from the main memory. We find a surprisingly large percentage of the initialization read traffic can be eliminated.

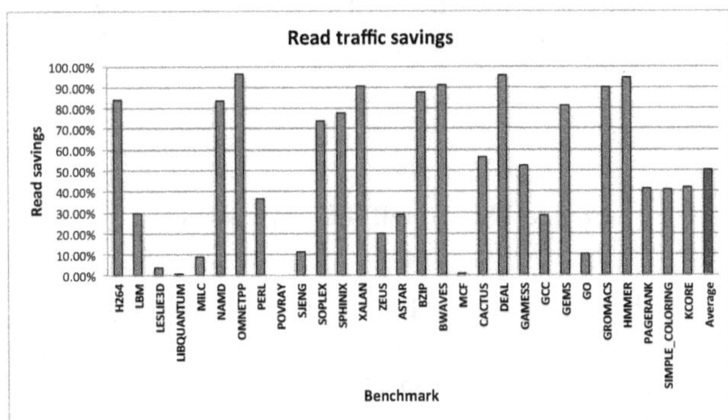

Figure 9. Percentage of the saved main memory read traffic.

As shown in Figure 9, an average of 50.3% of the read traffic during the initialization phase is due to reading shredded pages. Reducing the read traffic is crucial for systems that run memory-intensive benchmarks with limited memory bus bandwidth. Identifying that a block is shredded happens quickly: any shredded block read request can be completed once its minor counter value is read. Figure 10 shows the speed up ratio of the average memory read latency for each benchmark. On average, Silent Shredder achieves an average memory read speed up ratio of $3.3\times$ across the benchmarks.

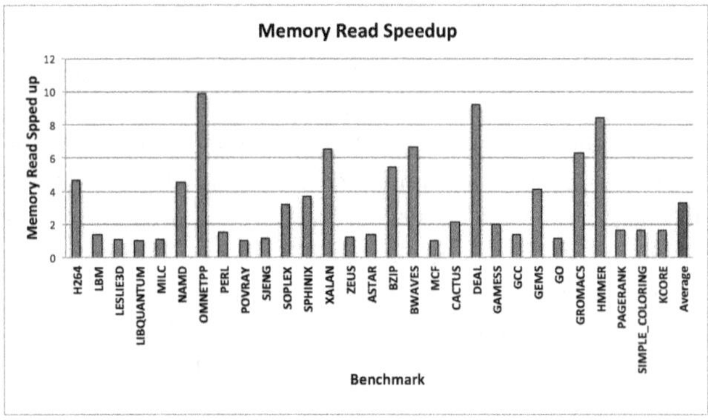

Figure 10. The speed up of the main memory reads.

6.3 Overall Performance Improvement

As mentioned earlier, in addition to eliminating shredding writes, Silent Shredder also speeds up reading shredded cache lines. These two improvements together improve the IPC. Figure 11 shows the relative IPC when using Silent Shredder (higher is better), normalized to the baseline.

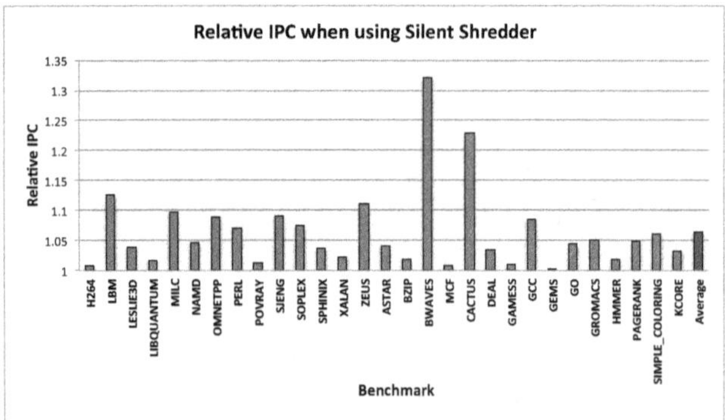

Figure 11. Overall IPC improvement.

We observe an average IPC improvement of 6.4% among all benchmarks, with a maximum of 32.1% for `Bwaves`. The overall IPC improvement depends on the fraction of instructions that access either main memory or shredded cache blocks.

6.4 Counter Cache Size

The IV cache should be fast enough so that encryption, specifically OTP generation, starts as soon as possible. Accordingly, the IV cache needs to be as small as possible while achieving a high hit rate.

From Figure 12, we observe that increasing the cache size beyond 4MB has little impact on reducing the cache miss rate. However, increasing the cache size brings significant reduction in the cache miss rate until reaching a capacity of 4MB. Accordingly, we believe that a size of 4MB is the smallest cache size that achieves a reasonable cache miss rate.

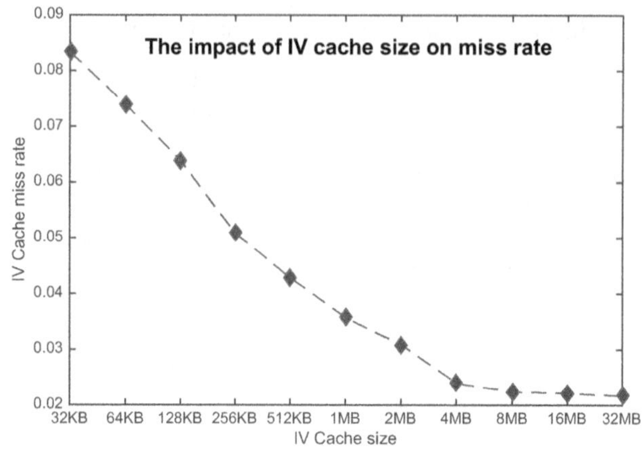

Figure 12. The impact of cache size on miss rate.

7. Discussion

In this section, we start by discussing several security concerns when using Silent Shredder and counter-mode encryption in general, and describe possible remediations. We then discuss different use cases and applications that can benefit from Silent Shredder at no extra cost.

7.1 Security Concerns

Several security concerns can arise when using counter-mode encryption in general. Other concerns arise when relying on hardware to achieve operating system privileged tasks. In this section, we discuss the concerns and their remediations.

- ***Tampering with Memory and Encryption Counter Values***: Since data is already encrypted, tampering with the memory values can cause unpredictable behavior. However, tampering with or replaying the counter values can be a security risk. While out of the scope of this paper, to avoid such risk, techniques such as Bonsai Merkle Trees can be used for authenticating the counter values with low overhead (about 2%) [31, 40]. The only information that could be leaked to an adversary is whether a page is shredded or not; a minor counter of 0 will indicate shredding, however, such information is useless. If we want to hide such information, the only modification needed is to encrypt the IV counters when writing to the main memory.
- ***Losing Counter Cache Values in Case of Power Loss***: In counter-mode encryption, the counter cache must be backed up to NVMM whenever there is a crash or power

loss. Hence the counter cache must be battery-backed and guaranteed to be persistent. In addition, the kernel should have a mechanism to verify the integrity of the stored counter values. If the integrity has been violated, then the kernel should report an error and stop execution of the system. Further error handling mechanisms are needed to recover from this error, which are beyond the scope of this paper.

Another way for achieving persistence of the counter cache would be a write-through implementation, i.e., any update to the counter cache is also updated in NVMM. In the latter case, non-temporal stores or DMA engine zeroing write zeros to NVMM *in addition to* the counter cache block. However, in Silent Shredder only the counter cache block is written to NVMM.

- ***Using the Shred Command from User Space***: As explained earlier, the Shred command hints the memory controller with a physical page address to shred. Allowing user-space applications to issue shred commands can be a security risk. Accordingly, we implement the shred command so that it can be executed only by the kernel (kernel-mode) and only when the kernel allocates a new physical page to a process. Any attempt to write the memory-mapped I/O register of the memory controller from a user-space process will cause an exception.

7.2 Other Use Cases for Silent Shredder

While our main goal in this paper is data shredding, Silent Shredder can be used in other areas.

- ***Virtual Machine Isolation in Virtualized Environments***: In VMs, zeroing out pages is used heavily to shred any physical page before allocating to a VM [7]. This zeroing happens in addition to the kernel shredding occurring inside the VM to protect applications' data. VMs typically request large pools of pages and prefer large pages due to the reduced translation overhead; large pages skip one or more levels of translation and hence speed up the page table walk process [29]. Furthermore, large allocations can reduce the number of hypervisor interruptions. Silent Shredder can speed up the VM requests by completely avoiding zeroing out pages. In case of highly-shared systems, the hypervisor continuously reclaims physical memory pages from VMs in a process called memory ballooning, in order to be able to satisfy requests from VMs with higher memory demand [7]. Accordingly, data shredding will be very frequent and hence Silent Shredder can be of substantial use.
- ***Initializing Large Blocks of Memory***: Some applications tend to zero out large amount of allocated memory, e.g., a sparse matrix, as part of the initialization phase. Such initialization can benefit from the hardware support provided by Silent Shredder. Applications would invoke a system call to provide the kernel with the starting virtual address and the number of pages to be zeroed out. The system call would be translated by the kernel shred command with the corresponding physical address.
- ***Zero Initialization in Managed Programming Languages***: In managed languages, such as Java and C#, the language specifications require initializing new objects with zeros. Similarly, unmanaged native languages, such as C++, have started using zero initialization to improve memory safety [28]. Silent Shredding can be used to zero initialize allocated memory pages with low overhead. It only requires a system call to the kernel, providing it with the virtual address of the page(s) desired for zero initialization. The kernel will simply submit a shred command with the physical address of each page to be zero initialized.

8. Related Work

In this section, we discuss prior work related to our work. Since our work is interdisciplinary and has intersections with different research problems, we summarize previous work by the problems they addressed.

Data Shredding: Data shredding is the process of erasing data previously written by a process to prevent interprocess data leak. Chow et al. [18] discuss the importance of shredding data during page deallocation and investigate both temporal and non-temporal ways to zero out pages for shredding purposes. Currently, modern operating systems deploy shredding by zeroing out pages [2, 13, 32, 35]. Our work achieves the shredding process at zero-cost by eliminating the need to write to the main memory.

Improving Initialization Performance: Jiang et al. [21] suggest offloading the zeroing process to a dedicated DMA engine close to the memory controller. Their design reduces both cache pollution and wasted processor time. Seshadri et al. [34] observe that significant memory bus bandwidth could be wasted by initialization. Accordingly, they suggest the zeroing operation to occur within DRAM by dedicating a zero row inside each DRAM subarray. Their design, RowClone, efficiently reduces the fraction of bus bandwidth used for initialization. However, in both the previously mentioned work, writes to the memory cells still occur. Lewis et al. [22] propose reducing the memory access required to fetch uninitialized blocks on a store miss by using a specialized cache to keep track of uninitialized regions of memory. While their work and Silent Shredder have similar advantages, our design's main goal is to efficiently protect applications' data. Speeding up applications and reducing memory traffic are additional advantages of the way we shred data. Yang et al. [42] study the performance implications when using temporal versus non-temporal stores for zeroing data. Sartor et al. [33] propose new ISA instructions to speed up zeroing in managed languages. Their solution, however, requires that the kernel zeros out processes' new physical pages in main

Table 2. Comparison between Silent Shredder and other initialization techniques.

Mechanism	Features					
	No Cache Pollution	Low Processor Time	Fast to Read/Write	No Memory Writes	Persistent	No Memory Bus Writes
Non-temporal stores	✓	✗	✗	✗	✓	✗
Temporal stores	✗	✗	✓	✗(indirectly)	✗	✗(indirectly)
DMA bulk zeroing engine	✓	✓	✗	✗	✓	✗
RowClone (DRAM-specific)	✓	✓	✗	✗	✓	✓
Silent Shredder	✓	✓	✓	✓	✓	✓

memory; hence Silent Shredder can be of great importance when using such a scheme. Table 2 presents a brief summary of the features of the most related initialization techniques. Note that for both temporal and non-temporal stores, the processor needs to execute a large `for` loop of `movq/movntq` instructions to zero out the whole page. In the case of temporal stores, it can also pollute caches and indirectly increase the main memory writes, as shown in Section 3. Furthermore, Silent Shredder enables fast read/write operations for the initialized blocks; shredded lines can be quickly recognized from their IV values. Silent Shredder also achieves persistent shredding, because the IV values must be backed up in case of power failure, otherwise, recovering the data will be impossible.

Secure Non-Volatile Memory Controllers: Chhabra and Solihin [16] propose encrypting cache lines when writing to the main memory. Their design aims to efficiently avoid revealing data when NVMM chips get stolen. However, their implementation does not protect from bus-snoop, dictionary-based and replay attacks. Later, Young et al. [43] propose a design that uses counter-mode based encryption that eliminates bus-snoop attacks, replay attacks, dictionary-based attacks, and physical NVM access attacks. Their design, DEUCE, uses AES counter mode for encrypting cache lines before writing back to the main memory. Our secure NVMM controller is based on a design similar to the one in DEUCE. Accordingly, it prevents all the previously mentioned attacks.

Write-aware Non-Volatile Memory Controllers: Writes to NVM-based main memory are expensive in terms of latency, energy requirements, and lifetime reduction. Accordingly, many previous work have targeted reducing the actual number of writes to NVM-based main memory [30, 45]. Qureshi et al. [30] propose to dynamically change the bound of the main memory using start and gap registers to uniformly distribute writes across memory cells. Later, Zhou et al. [45] suggest using differential writes, i.e., first read the previous data, compare it with the new data, and then only write the cells whose values have changed. Cho and Lee [17] propose Flip-N-Write technique, their technique suggests that memory words can be written in a flipped manner to reduce the number of bits having their value changed and hence reducing the number of actual writes. In the context of secure NVMM controllers, Young et al. [43] observe that techniques such as Flip-N-Write and differential writes are inefficient in presence of encryption. They propose to reduce the number of writes by avoiding re-encrypting the unmodified partitions of a cache line. Our work is orthogonal and can be easily integrated with their design, DEUCE. DEUCE targets reducing the need for changing cells' values when a cache line write is certain to occur. However, Silent Shredder eliminates the cache line writes completely when shredding new pages.

9. Conclusion

NVM technologies are serious contenders for replacing DRAM as main memory in the near future. However, they face two key challenges for widespread adoption: limited write endurance and data remanence vulnerability. NVM encryption alleviates the data remanence vulnerability, but exacerbates the endurance challenge by increasing the number of main memory writes. In this paper, we propose an approach to reduce the number of writes to encrypted NVM by completely eliminating the writes occurring due to OS data shredding. Our approach, Silent Shredder, manipulates counter mode encryption IV values to render memory pages unintelligible and hence obviates the writing of zeros to memory pages. For software compatibility, we encode IV values in a manner so that Silent Shredder quickly identifies shredded blocks from their IV values and then returns a zero block instead of returning unintelligible data stored in shredded pages. As a byproduct, this process also speeds up reading shredded cache lines. Hence Silent Shredder reduces the number of writes and speeds up reading in encrypted NVM, and hence reduces power consumption and improves overall system performance. We believe that encryption will be commonly used in NVMM for data protection; hence our Silent Shredder approach can contribute significantly to NVMM adoption by increasing NVMM lifetime and improving overall system performance.

Acknowledgments

A large portion of this work was done when Amro Awad was an intern at HP Labs and in collaboration with his Ph.D. advisor Yan Solihin. We would like to thank the anonymous reviewers for their generous feedback.

References

[1] Intel 3D XPoint. URL `http://newsroom.intel.com/docs/DOC-6713`.

[2] FreeBSD. URL `http://www.freebsd.org/doc/en_US.ISO8859-1/articles/vm-design/prefault-optimizations.html`.

[3] Intel. Intel 64 and IA-32 Architectures Software Developer's Manual, Volume 3a, Chapter 11, Page 12. April 2012.

[4] The Machine: A new kind of computer. URL `http://www.hpl.hp.com/research/systems-research/themachine/`.

[5] SPEC, SPEC CPU2000 and CPU2006, http://www.spec.org/.

[6] Huai, yiming, et al. "observation of spin-transfer switching in deep submicron-sized and low-resistance magnetic tunnel junctions." Applied Physics Letters 84.16: 3118-3120, 2004.

[7] *Understanding Memory Resource Management in VMware vSphere® 5.0.*

[8] Exploring high-performance and energy proportional interface for phase change memory systems. *the proceedings of the IEEE 20th International Symposium on High Performance Computer Architecture (HPCA-20), 2013*, 0:210–221, 2013. ISSN 1530-0897. .

[9] R. H. Arpaci-Dusseau and A. C. Arpaci-Dusseau. *Operating Systems: Three Easy Pieces.* Arpaci-Dusseau Books, 0.80 edition, May 2014.

[10] J. Bennett and S. L. and. The Netflix Prize. In *In KDD Cup and Workshop in conjunction with KDD*, 2007.

[11] K. Bhandari, D. R. Chakrabarti, and H.-J. Boehm. Implications of CPU caching on byte-addressable non-volatile memory programming. Technical report, 2012.

[12] N. Binkert, B. Beckmann, G. Black, S. K. Reinhardt, A. Saidi, A. Basu, J. Hestness, D. R. Hower, T. Krishna, S. Sardashti, R. Sen, K. Sewell, M. Shoaib, N. Vaish, M. D. Hill, and D. A. Wood. The gem5 simulator. *SIGARCH Comput. Archit. News*, 39(2):1–7, Aug. 2011. ISSN 0163-5964. . URL `http://doi.acm.org/10.1145/2024716.2024718`.

[13] D. Bovet and M. Cesati. *Understanding The Linux Kernel.* Oreilly & Associates Inc, 2005. ISBN 0596005652.

[14] M. Calhoun, S. Rixner, and A. L. Cox. Optimizing kernel block memory operations. In *IEEE 4th Workshop on Memory Performance Issues, Feb. 2006.*

[15] D. R. Chakrabarti, H.-J. Boehm, and K. Bhandari. Atlas: Leveraging locks for non-volatile memory consistency. In *the proceedings of the 2014 ACM International Conference on Object Oriented Programming Systems Languages & Applications*, pages 433–452. ACM, 2014.

[16] S. Chhabra and Y. Solihin. i-NVMM: A Secure Non-volatile Main Memory System with Incremental Encryption. In *"the proceedings of the 38th Annual International Symposium on Computer Architecture (ISCA-38), 2011*, ISCA '11, pages 177–188, New York, NY, USA, 2011. ACM. ISBN 978-1-4503-0472-6. . URL `http://doi.acm.org/10.1145/2000064.2000086`.

[17] S. Cho and H. Lee. Flip-n-write: A simple deterministic technique to improve pram write performance, energy and endurance. In *the proceedings of the 42nd Annual IEEE/ACM International Symposium on Microarchitecture, 2009. MICRO-42*, pages 347–357, Dec 2009.

[18] J. Chow, B. Pfaff, T. Garfinkel, and M. Rosenblum. Shredding your garbage: Reducing data lifetime through secure deallocation. In *the proceedings of the 14th Conference on USENIX Security Symposium (SSYM-14), 2005*, SSYM'05, pages 22–22, Berkeley, CA, USA, 2005. USENIX Association. URL `http://dl.acm.org/citation.cfm?id=1251398.1251420`.

[19] X. Fan, W.-D. Weber, and L. A. Barroso. Power provisioning for a warehouse-sized computer. In *the proceedings of the 34th Annual International Symposium on Computer Architecture (ISCA), 2007*, ISCA '07, pages 13–23, New York, NY, USA, 2007. ACM. ISBN 978-1-59593-706-3. . URL `http://doi.acm.org/10.1145/1250662.1250665`.

[20] J. E. Gonzalez, Y. Low, H. Gu, D. Bickson, and C. Guestrin. Powergraph: Distributed graph-parallel computation on natural graphs. In *the proceedings of the 10th USENIX Conference on Operating Systems Design and Implementation (OSDI-10), 2012*, OSDI'12, pages 17–30, Berkeley, CA, USA, 2012. USENIX Association. ISBN 978-1-931971-96-6. URL `http://dl.acm.org/citation.cfm?id=2387880.2387883`.

[21] X. Jiang, Y. Solihin, L. Zhao, and R. Iyer. Architecture support for improving bulk memory copying and initialization performance. In *the proceedings of the 2009 18th International Conference on Parallel Architectures and Compilation Techniques (PACT-18), 2009*, PACT '09, pages 169–180, Washington, DC, USA, 2009. IEEE Computer Society. ISBN 978-0-7695-3771-9. . URL `http://dx.doi.org/10.1109/PACT.2009.31`.

[22] J. Lewis, B. Black, and M. Lipasti. Avoiding initialization misses to the heap. In *the proceedings of the 29th Annual International Symposium on Computer Architecture (ISCA-29), 2002*, pages 183–194, 2002. .

[23] R.-S. Liu, D.-Y. Shen, C.-L. Yang, S.-C. Yu, and C.-Y. M. Wang. NVM Duet: Unified working memory and persistent store architecture. In *ACM SIGPLAN Notices*, volume 49, pages 455–470. ACM, 2014.

[24] I. Moraru, D. G. Andersen, M. Kaminsky, N. Binkert, N. Tolia, R. Munz, and P. Ranganathan. Persistent, protected and cached: Building blocks for main memory data stores. *Technical Report CMU-PDL-11-114*, 2012.

[25] N. Muralimanohar and R. Balasubramonian. Cacti 6.0: A Tool to Model Large Caches.

[26] O. Mutlu and L. Subramanian. Research Problems and Opportunities in Memory Systems. *Invited Article in Supercomputing Frontiers and Innovations (SUPERFRI), 2015.*, pages 32–34.

[27] P. J. Nair, D.-H. Kim, and M. K. Qureshi. Archshield: Architectural framework for assisting dram scaling by tolerating high error rates. In *the proceedings of the 40th Annual International Symposium on Computer Architecture (ISCA-40), 2013*, ISCA '13, pages 72–83, New York, NY, USA, 2013. ACM. ISBN 978-1-4503-2079-5. . URL `http://doi.acm.org/10.1145/2485922.2485929`.

[28] G. Novark, E. D. Berger, and B. G. Zorn. Exterminator: Automatically correcting memory errors with high probability. In *the proceedings of the ACM SIGPLAN Conference on Programming Language Design and Implementation (PLDI), 2007*. Press, 2007.

[29] B. Pham, A. Bhattacharjee, Y. Eckert, and G. Loh. Increasing tlb reach by exploiting clustering in page translations. In *the proceedings of the IEEE 20th International Symposium on High Performance Computer Architecture (HPCA), 2014*, pages 558–567, Feb 2014. .

[30] M. Qureshi, J. Karidis, M. Franceschini, V. Srinivasan, L. Lastras, and B. Abali. Enhancing lifetime and security of PCM-based Main Memory with Start-Gap Wear Leveling. In *the proceedings of the 42nd Annual IEEE/ACM International Symposium on Microarchitecture (MICRO-42), 2009*, pages 14–23, Dec 2009.

[31] B. Rogers, S. Chhabra, M. Prvulovic, and Y. Solihin. Using address independent seed encryption and bonsai merkle trees to make secure processors os- and performance-friendly. In *the proceedings of the 40th Annual IEEE/ACM International Symposium on Microarchitecture (MICRO-40), 2007*, MICRO 40, pages 183–196, Washington, DC, USA, 2007. IEEE Computer Society. ISBN 0-7695-3047-8. . URL `http://dx.doi.org/10.1109/MICRO.2007.44`.

[32] M. Russinovich and D. A. Solomon. *Windows Internals: Including Windows Server 2008 and Windows Vista, Fifth Edition*. Microsoft Press, 5th edition, 2009. ISBN 0735625301, 9780735625303.

[33] J. B. Sartor, W. Heirman, S. M. Blackburn, L. Eeckhout, and K. S. McKinley. Cooperative cache scrubbing. In *the proceedings of the 23rd International Conference on Parallel Architectures and Compilation (PACT-23), 2014*, pages 15–26. ACM, 2014.

[34] V. Seshadri, Y. Kim, C. Fallin, D. Lee, R. Ausavarungnirun, G. Pekhimenko, Y. Luo, O. Mutlu, P. B. Gibbons, M. A. Kozuch, and T. C. Mowry. Rowclone: Fast and energy-efficient in-dram bulk data copy and initialization. In *the proceedings of the 46th Annual IEEE/ACM International Symposium on Microarchitecture (MICRO-46), 2013*, MICRO-46, pages 185–197, New York, NY, USA, 2013. ACM. ISBN 978-1-4503-2638-4. . URL `http://doi.acm.org/10.1145/2540708.2540725`.

[35] A. Singh. *Mac OS X Internals*. Addison-Wesley Professional, 2006. ISBN 0321278542.

[36] W. Stallings. *Cryptography and Network Security (6th ed.)*. 2014.

[37] J. Stuecheli. Power8. In *Hot Chips. Vol. 25. 2013.*, 2013.

[38] S. Valat, M. Pérache, and W. Jalby. Introducing kernel-level page reuse for high performance computing. In *the proceedings of the ACM SIGPLAN Workshop on Memory Systems Performance and Correctness*, page 3. ACM, 2013.

[39] H. Volos, A. J. Tack, and M. M. Swift. Mnemosyne: Lightweight persistent memory. *ACM SIGPLAN Notices*, 46 (3):91–104, 2011.

[40] C. Yan, B. Rogers, D. Englender, D. Solihin, and M. Prvulovic. Improving cost, performance, and security of memory encryption and authentication. In *the proceedings of the 33rd International Symposium on Computer Architecture (ISCA-33), 2006*, pages 179–190, 2006. .

[41] J. J. Yang, D. B. Strukov, and D. R. Stewart. Memristive devices for computing. *Nature nanotechnology*, 8(1):13–24, 2013.

[42] X. Yang, S. M. Blackburn, D. Frampton, J. B. Sartor, and K. S. McKinley. Why nothing matters: The impact of zeroing. In *the proceedings of the 2011 ACM International Conference on Object Oriented Programming Systems Languages and Applications (OOPSLA), 2011*, OOPSLA '11, pages 307–324, New York, NY, USA, 2011. ACM. ISBN 978-1-4503-0940-0. . URL `http://doi.acm.org/10.1145/2048066.2048092`.

[43] V. Young, P. J. Nair, and M. K. Qureshi. DEUCE: Write-Efficient Encryption for Non-Volatile Memories. In *the proceedings of the 20th International Conference on Architectural Support for Programming Languages and Operating Systems (ASPLOS-20), 2015*, ASPLOS '15, pages 33–44, New York, NY, USA, 2015. ACM. ISBN 978-1-4503-2835-7. . URL `http://doi.acm.org/10.1145/2694344.2694387`.

[44] R. Zafarani and H. Liu. Social computing data repository at ASU, 2009. URL `http://socialcomputing.asu.edu`.

[45] P. Zhou, B. Zhao, J. Yang, and Y. Zhang. A durable and energy efficient main memory using phase change memory technology. In *the proceedings of the 36th Annual International Symposium on Computer Architecture (ISCA-36), 2009*, ISCA '09, pages 14–23, New York, NY, USA, 2009. ACM. ISBN 978-1-60558-526-0. . URL `http://doi.acm.org/10.1145/1555754.1555759`.

Sego: Pervasive Trusted Metadata for Efficiently Verified Untrusted System Services

Youngjin Kwon[1] Alan M. Dunn[2*] Michael Z. Lee[3*]
Owen S. Hofmann[2*] Yuanzhong Xu[1] Emmett Witchel[1]

[1]The University of Texas at Austin [2]Google [3]Facebook

{yjkwon, yxu, witchel}@cs.utexas.edu {amdunn, osh}@google.com mzlee@fb.com

Abstract

Sego is a hypervisor-based system that gives strong privacy and integrity guarantees to trusted applications, even when the guest operating system is compromised or hostile. Sego verifies operating system services, like the file system, instead of replacing them. By associating trusted metadata with user data across all system devices, Sego verifies system services more efficiently than previous systems, especially services that depend on data contents. We extensively evaluate Sego's performance on real workloads and implement a kernel fault injector to validate Sego's file system-agnostic crash consistency and recovery protocol.

General Terms Security, Verification

Keywords Application protection, Virtualization-based security, Paraverification, Crash consistency

1. Introduction

A seemingly endless parade of privileged software compromises (e.g., OS-level zero-day exploits commanding half-million dollar ransoms as revealed by the Hacking Team emails [39]) and a desire to migrate sensitive computations to the cloud have energized research into removing trust from privileged software like the host operating system or hypervisor.

Once privileged software is untrusted, there are two approaches to system services: replace or verify (in this paper by verify we mean check at runtime that the behavior matches a specification). Many systems (e.g., Haven [11] and MiniBox [25]) force an application to link into its address space much of its own trustworthy software, e.g., to protect persistent storage. Haven includes an entire library operating system. Finer-grained systems like Overshadow [14], Appsec [30], parts of Virtual Ghost [16, 17], and Inktag [23] verify system services at runtime, for example, using the guest file system, but checking that the guest OS is operating correctly (e.g., by verifying the cryptographic hash value of a secure file).

The advantage of replacement is that the application has complete control over its software trusted computing base (TCB). The disadvantage is that complex libraries, including library operating systems, have large attack surfaces that are likely vulnerable to the types of runtime compromise that plague existing complex libraries and operating systems. Systems that do not trust privileged software, but verify its behavior at runtime, incur time and computational expense to encrypt and hash data as it passes through the trust boundaries of the system. For example, SGX-enabled processors encrypt and decrypt data as it passes from the processor cache (trusted) to RAM (untrusted). Inktag and Overshadow encrypt and hash data as it passes from trusted RAM (protected by the hypervisor) to untrusted RAM (protected by the untrusted guest OS).

Exacerbating the performance and complexity problems of these systems is guest OS services that examine the contents of memory pages actively used by user-level code. For example, kernel memory sharing (KSM) reduces physical memory use by looking for pages with identical contents (as often occurs when running multiple virtual machines). Memory compaction copies memory to physically contiguous regions to enable those regions to be mapped efficiently with a single TLB entry (e.g., a 2MB page for Intel's x86 architecture). Whenever an untrusted guest OS touches a memory page of a secure process in Inktag and Overshadow, it triggers a hypervisor page fault and the hypervisor must encrypt and hash the page's data.

Finally, file system recovery is difficult to do efficiently when the OS is not trusted. Many file system operations that appear atomic (e.g., creating a file) consist of a sequence of updates to persistent storage. Journaling file systems make

* This work is done when the authors were graduate students of The University of Texas at Austin

ASPLOS '16, April 2–6, 2016, Atlanta, Georgia, USA..

http://dx.doi.org/10.1145/http://dx.doi.org/10.1145/2872362.2872372

file system operations efficient to perform and recover, but at the cost of complex data structures that introduce more intermediate states. The hypervisor has two problems managing persistent metadata: it cannot trust the OS's existing file system metadata and it generates new intermediate states during secure file operations (e.g., the secure process must first tell the hypervisor it wants to create a file before it tells the OS). Crashes that occur during the new state transitions must be cleaned up properly by the hypervisor. Fast recovery of persistent data for guest OS crashes is important because the guest can be malicious and crashing is a malicious behavior that can erase or make unavailable persistent data for secure processes and harms availability if it requires costly recovery.

This paper introduces Sego, a system that efficiently verifies system services at runtime; Sego makes protected, trusted metadata pervasive across all system devices, eliminating the trust boundary that necessitates encryption and hashing. In the Sego model, data stays in plain text, but it is protected by trusted components that have access to the trusted metadata. For example, Sego protects RAM using the extended page tables and secure page metadata, which is managed by the trusted hypervisor. Persistent storage is protected by persistent metadata that is accessed only by the trusted virtual block device.

Sego is faster than InkTag or Overshadow for workloads where the untrusted OS touches secure memory, because those systems must lock pages touched by the OS, and encrypt and hash their contents. Sego is 13%–15% faster for IO-bound workloads, up to 2× faster for memory-intensive workloads with KSM active, and up to 19% faster when memory compaction is active. For the file system, Sego efficiently recovers files purposefully or mistakenly deleted by the guest OS. Previous systems, e.g., InkTag and Haven, provide secure file recovery after a guest OS crash; however, they require a full disk scan to find and recover all pieces of secure files. Sego's recovery time is proportional to the size of the recovered data, not the size of the storage device. For example, Sego is 11× faster than Inktag recovering a 100MB secure file from a 24GB virtual disk, even if the virtual disk is completely cached in host memory.

The cost of pervasive metadata is a modified interface. In Sego, the untrusted OS manipulates pages by reference, making a hypercall so the hypervisor will perform the operation after verifying that the OS's request is legal (e.g., the OS is not trying to overwrite one trusted application with another's data). Sego changes the interface for untrusted software to make verification of memory page operations more efficient (designing interfaces that are efficient to verify is called paraverification [23]).

Our Sego prototype is implemented as part of the KVM hypervisor, and the QEMU hardware emulator. While Sego's model of pervasive metadata is amenable to pushing the TCB into hardware, our goal was to build a prototype that executes on currently available hardware. Therefore, Sego modifies the hypervisor (protecting the CPU), uses nested paging (to protect RAM), and modifies the hypervisor's virtualized block device (to protect the file system). We modify the guest Linux operating system to conform to Sego's security model. It no longer manipulates memory directly, but uses hypercalls to initialize, copy, and test pages. We extensively evaluate Sego's performance on various real workloads, implement a kernel fault injector to validate Sego's crash consistency and recovery protocol, and demonstrate improved performance.

The contributions of this paper are the following.

1. Develop a model for secure computing where trusted metadata and untrusted data remain coupled, across all devices on which they reside (§3).
2. Design an efficient, secure data recovery protocol for applications that rely on a journaling file system provided by an untrustworthy operating system (§4).
3. Prototype and evaluate a trusted hypervisor that efficiently verifies untrusted system services that depend on data contents (§5, §6).

2. Overview and Background

This section explains the parts of Sego[1] that derive from other untrusted privileged code systems (keeping the paper self-contained). Because it is implemented in the hypervisor, Sego's lineage traces back to InkTag [23] and Overshadow [14], but much of Sego's assumptions are shared with other designs such as Haven [11], SP^3 [37], SecPod [35], and Virtual Ghost [17], though we emphasize the portions that are most relevant to Sego's novel contributions.

2.1 Threat model

Sego completely removes trust of the guest operating system. Therefore, Sego assumes the guest OS can (try to) read or modify any area of a user application's memory, and intercept or manipulate data en route to an IO device. It can modify control flow when a user application returns from a system call or interrupt. An attacker can intentionally crash the OS at any point to subvert an application. For example, when a user application updates its security settings (stored in a file), the attacker can crash the OS before the changes are made persistent and pretend as if the updates were persisted. The OS can try to revert file contents. For example, when a user application deletes a file and writes a new version of the file with the same name, the attacker can modify OS file metadata to point to the old version of file, rolling back the file's state.

The benefit of removing trust from the operating system is that it prevents the operating system from being a shared vulnerability across the entire system. Currently, if an OS is dynamically compromised using a vulnerability in one application, then all applications on the platform are untrustworthy. Systems like Sego allow trusted applications to continue

[1] Sego is from super-ego. It restrains the untrusted OS, ensuring well-adjusted behavior, regardless of purity of intent.

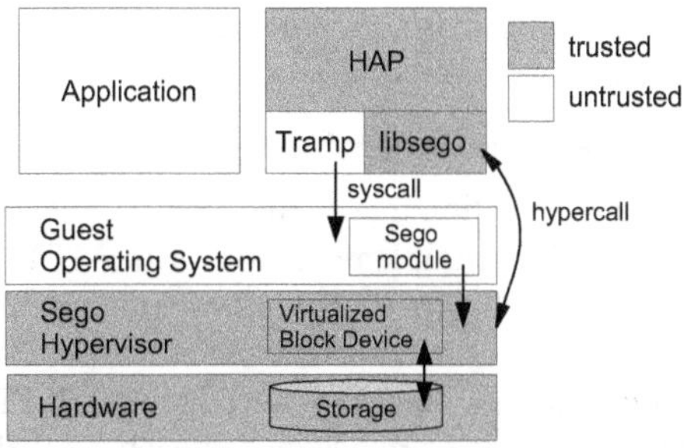

Figure 1: Sego design overview. In Sego, high-assurance processes (HAPs) make hypercalls to the virtual machine hypervisor to verify the runtime behavior of the operating system. The hypervisor and the virtualized block device are trusted. The section labeled Tramp is untrusted trampoline code and data used by the HAP to make system calls.

to function with a compromised and even overly hostile operating system.

To protect the application from OS, Sego relies on a trusted hypervisor and assumes hardware faithfully executes hypervisor code. Like most work in untrusted OSes, Sego does not prevent application bugs or application collusion with the OS. Applications can establish trusted channels through the untrusted operating system just as they can across a network, with Sego providing trusted identifiers. However, once an application trusts another application, Sego provides no protection.

Sego (and related systems) do not guarantee OS availability. A compromised OS can simply shut down or refuse to schedule processes. While such activity would be disruptive, it is also easily detected.

2.2 Sego security guarantees

Figure 1 shows an overview of the Sego architecture. Sego's trusted application code executes in a **high-assurance process, or HAP**. After booting the OS, the Sego hypervisor can start a HAP in such a way that the HAP can verify its own initial code and data, bootstrapping trustworthy execution in a way similar to a trusted program module (TPM) or software guard extensions (SGX). The details are identical to Inktag [23]. Once running, the Sego hypervisor ensures that a HAP's process context (registers) and trusted address space are isolated from the operating system. Context switches are handled by the hypervisor which hides information about the HAP's program counter and register contents from the guest OS. The Sego hypervisor uses hardware nested page tables to ensure privacy and integrity for the HAP's address space including code and allocated memory. The Sego hypervisor provides full address space privacy and integrity for the HAP's data and control flow. While we explain the high-level ideas, details are available from previous systems [14, 23]. Sego views the HAP's address space as a set of secure 4KB pages (called `S-pages`) that contain the HAP's code and data. Sego protects S-pages using nested paging (a set of page tables accessible to the hypervisor and not to the guest operating system). If the guest OS accesses S-page data, the nested page table hardware faults and transfers control to the Sego hypervisor, which considers the OS action malicious and denies the operation (possibly terminating the OS).

Rather than extensively tracking guest OS state, the Sego hypervisor uses paraverification, where the hypervisor protects important guest data structures (like the page tables) and the guest clearly communicates its actions and intent to the hypervisor. We assume the Sego hypervisor can start as part of a trusted booting process [3], though the details are out of scope for this work. In order to operate on S-page data, a guest OS must make a hypercall and the hypervisor will perform the action after verifying that the OS action comports with the HAP's intent, as expressed to the hypervisor via a set of hypercalls. While the Sego hypervisor contains new hypercalls to verify guest OS operations, these functions are generally simple and only minimally increase the hypervisor attack surface. Section 3 provides more detail.

Sego supports secure persistent file storage (called `S-files`). HAPs allocate S-pages to load S-files into memory so that the OS cannot read or modify contents of S-files. To protect S-files resident in persistent storage, the Sego hypervisor maintains some per-file and per-file-data-block metadata and uses it to verify accesses to secure files (§ 5.1).

The Sego hypervisor refers to each object that it guarantees privacy and integrity by an identifier known as an **OID**. For example, OIDs name secure files and anonymous memory regions. They are 64-bits long in the prototype.

Sego does not manage network I/O, however applications can safely communicate over the network via mechanisms such as transport layer security (TLS [18]), that enable secure communication over an untrusted channel.

2.3 libsego

HAPs must express their intent to the hypervisor, so the hypervisor can verify OS activity. For example, if the HAP wants to read data from a file, it must inform the hypervisor of its intent and then perform the system calls to open and read the data. Forcing the HAP programmer to make many additional hypercalls would be burdensome, but fortunately it is unnecessary because system calls always require the same hypercalls to precede them.

HAPs link a small library (less than 5,000 lines) called `libsego` to get Sego services without having to change their code. libsego mostly handles system calls and can be viewed as a small modification to the C runtime library. For example, when a HAP tries to access an S-file, it transparently invokes recovery operations (§4) if needed.

Each HAP also contains a small amount of *untrusted trampoline* code that interacts with the operating system. The Sego hypervisor switches control between secure HAP code and the untrusted trampoline, and all system calls are issued from the trampoline, protecting HAP control flow. All system call arguments are copied into trampoline memory, and results are copied out by the HAP.

For example, when a HAP calls `open`, code in libsego translates the path name into an identifier (OID) and then makes a hypercall to allow the hypervisor to check permissions. If the hypervisor approves the open, the libsego code calls the operating system by copying arguments into the trampoline, then transferring control to it via the hypervisor. When the system call returns, libsego verifies the results. For example, if the hypervisor approved the open, but the operating system claimed that no such file exists, libsego must take action to reconcile the discrepancy, if possible (see Section 4). libsego verifies system call parameters and the return value to prevent Iago attacks (§ 5.5).

3. Secure pages

Sego provides a uniform view of protected and trusted metadata with its associated data across all system devices (libsego, hypervisor, and virtualized block device): secure metadata and the data to which it refers are always logically coupled, no matter where the data resides. Previous systems that eliminate trust in privileged software provide an abstraction for secure data, but they all require complex management of secure data as it transitions between being protected by the system's TCB and residing in untrusted storage.

Sego (and many similar systems) manage secure data in fixed-sized units we call secure pages (S-pages). S-page data and metadata can reside in a processor's cache, in RAM, or in persistent storage. An S-page in Sego is a block of data with secure metadata specifying the persistent object (OID) and offset, uniquely representing the memory. Sego maintains the same secure metadata for S-pages across all system devices pervasively.

To contrast Sego S-pages with previous systems, SGX [24] only considers on-chip cache secure storage, so SGX-secured data is encrypted and MACed (message-authentication code) by hardware when it resides in RAM (or on persistent storage). The InkTag hypervisor also encrypts and MACs secure data as it moves to untrusted storage.

The Sego model assumes S-page metadata is bound to its data across all devices. This binding can be provided directly by the hardware, or emulated with some combination of hardware and trusted software. In our prototype, Sego is implemented in a hypervisor, and it protects S-pages in RAM using hardware memory protection (nested page tables) to ensure the untrusted guest OS cannot access them. The Sego hypervisor reads and writes S-page metadata to storage devices, emulating device support. Our Sego prototype does not encrypt or MAC data in order to protect it; it uses alternate techniques, such as nested paging and trusting the hypervisor's handling of block I/O.

Sego will terminate any untrusted privileged software that directly manipulates S-page data. Therefore, untrusted privileged software must be rewritten to access S-pages by reference. Fortunately, privileged software's access to S-page data is generally limited and stylized (e.g., it mostly needs to copy the data, and occasionally needs more complex operations like checking if two pages have equal contents). As we quantify in Section 6, modifying Linux to operate on user pages by reference is non-invasive. Sego modifies 1,572 lines of guest kernel code.

3.1 Pervasive metadata for S-page

An S-page abstraction that spans all system devices simplifies the model and implementation of the TCB, making security easier to achieve. It also allows efficient, protected S-page access for untrusted privileged software. For example, Sego requires less metadata per page than InkTag. InkTag requires 64 bytes of metadata for each 4KB disk sector[2], while Sego requires only 20 bytes[3]. Much of InkTag's overhead is for maintaining cryptographic hashes and initialization vectors for persistent data. While InkTag uses nested paging, Sego simplifies its use. In Sego, an S-page always resides in a trusted nested page table, while InkTag must move S-pages between trusted and untrusted nested page tables. Sego's approach is simpler because it knows when S-files are being read from IO devices and where the S-files are being placed in memory, so it can allocate the proper type of memory page (§ 3.3). InkTag does not trust IO devices, so it first reads encrypted S-file blocks into an untrusted page table and decrypts and moves them to a trusted page table when the HAP accesses the S-file data. Therefore, Sego's memory page management code is more than $10\times$ smaller than InkTag's (which is less than a thousand lines of code).

3.2 Pages in Sego

Sego views persistent and in-memory storage as objects that contain a sequence of 4KB blocks. Each block can be in one of three states:

Untrusted. An untrusted block may be freely used by untrusted software, privileged and unprivileged. Sego does not maintain metadata for untrusted blocks. All other blocks are **trusted**.

Reserved. A reserved block is protected by Sego and cannot be accessed directly by untrusted privileged software, but it contains incomplete metadata. Reserved blocks are used during non-atomic transitions, like when a memory frame is allocated to receive protected data from disk.

S-page. An S-page is protected by Sego and cannot be directly accessed by untrusted privileged software. Sego maintains the OID and the offset of each S-page. It sometimes tracks additional metadata, for example it adds a sequence number to anonymous memory S-pages.

Table 1 describes the interface the untrusted operating system uses to create and manipulate S-pages. The untrusted operating system uses its data structures (e.g., a `struct page` in Linux) to distinguish the states of physical frames. For example, if it needs a new empty page for a HAP, rather than initialize the page itself, it invokes the `OPAGE` hypercall, which zeroes the page, and protects it from the OS.

[2] OID and offset: 16B, hash: 16B, previous hash: 16B, IV: 16B.

[3] OID and offset: 16B, version number: 4B.

Hypercall	Description
`RESV(fr)`	Reserve a physical frame (fr), e.g., in preparation for a disk read. untrusted→reserved
`POPL(fr)`	Populate a reserved physical frame (fr) as S-page, e.g., in completion of a disk read. reserved→S-page
`SET_PT(fr)`	Guest OS requests Sego hypervisor to map and verify an S-page. S-page previously `POPL`ed, `0PAGE`ed or `COW`ed. S-page →verified S-page
`0PAGE(fr)`	Zero-initialize a new frame (fr). The Sego hypervisor protects the page and fills it with zeros. untrusted→S-page
`COW(dst, src)`	The Sego hypervisor copies the S-page data and meta-data, thereby marking *dst* a copy of *src*. S-page →two S-pages
`FREE(fr)`	Release an S-page. If the S-page contains sensitive data (i.e., is not already a zero page), it is zeroed by the Sego hypervisor. S-page →untrusted

Table 1: Sego interface for the untrusted operating system to request services from the hypervisor to manage physical memory frames. The description of the call concludes with the state change induced on the frame.

3.3 Reading and writing the buffer cache

Untrusted disk blocks can be read into untrusted memory frames, but the Sego **virtualized block device** will refuse to read untrusted data into trusted physical memory. The virtualized block device is code that executes in the hypervisor that implements the block device interface used by the OS. It is a necessary part of any hypervisor that exposes a physical or virtual block device to a guest. The untrusted OS must first reserve a frame before passing the frame to the virtualized block device as the destination of a read. When the virtualized block device receives a request for an S-page disk block, it ensures that the destination frame is reserved, then reads the S-page data into the frame and the S-page metadata from storage into hypervisor memory. Once the reserved frame is filled with data and its associated metadata is in place, the reserved frame becomes an S-page. Sego maintains S-page metadata in trusted storage as described in Section 5.1.

3.4 OS-generated S-pages

In addition to regular files, applications (including HAPs) have memory pages that do not come from a file on disk, but are instead generated by the operating system. For example, `malloc` will call `mmap` to generate anonymous memory to hold dynamically allocated data. When an application calls `fork()`, it expects its anonymous memory to become copy-on-write: if, after the fork, either the parent or child attempts to write to anonymous memory, the operating system creates a private copy of the page for that process. Maintaining copy-on-write semantics and verifying its correctness for these anonymous regions is challenging for Sego.

The Sego hypervisor tracks each HAP's anonymous memory regions as S-pages, analogous to the handling of files. Each anonymous memory S-page has an OID that refers to the owning HAP, and an offset that specifies the location of the page in the HAP's virtual address space. When the parent process calls `fork()`, the Sego hypervisor clones all anonymous S-page metadata into the new process (via the `COW` hypercall). Although the hypervisor clones S-page metadata, the data segments for cloned S-pages may be shared, as long as the data remains read-only. Copy-on-write faults are processed by the guest OS and validated by the hypervisor.

To track S-pages generated by copying or zero-initialization, Sego relies on an S-tag to represent the contents of the page. An S-tag is a vector with several fields updated by the Sego hypervisor that tracks the state of the S-page as it is copied and modified.

The S-tag for the S-page has four fields:

$$\langle \textit{OID, offset, sequence number, dirty bit} \rangle$$

The S-tag is updated as follows: every time the S-page becomes writable, the S-page's OID and offset are copied into the corresponding fields in the S-tag. The sequence number is incremented, and the dirty bit set to indicate that the page may have been written. If the S-page becomes read-only, the dirty bit is cleared. When the untrusted OS tries to map the copy-on-write pages (using the `SET_PT` hypercall), Sego looks up the corresponding S-tag by OID and offset and verifies the mapping.

3.5 Discussion

There are advantages and disadvantages to the Sego model for secure data. Security-conscious users want their cloud data encrypted while "at rest." In the Sego model secure data is stored in plaintext. Sego's security model would be strengthened by hardware enforcement of trusted metadata, which would protect persistent data from malicious administrators, if not physical attacks. A security-conscious user can always use encryption and MACing with Sego, though at some performance cost.

An important question is whether hardware support for encryption and hashing will erase Sego's performance gains over an approach like InkTag. Currently, IO bandwidth is growing faster than encryption/hashing performance, keeping encryption/hashing a bottleneck for InkTag- and Overshadow-like approaches. CPU vendors are improving the performance of cryptographic operations. For AES-GCM (128 bit) the Intel Xeon E5 processor achieves 1GB/s throughput per core [6] and a blog reports up to 1.5GB/s on an Intel i7 4570HQ [7]. Sego shows a 13%–15% speedup over InkTag for an IO-bound workload using a single SSD, which has 250MB/s of write bandwidth (§6.4). Assuming the faster AES speed, Sego's performance win is reduced to 8%. However, recent SSDs can sustain 520MB/s IO bandwidth (e.g., Samsung 850 SSD Pro [9]) which would bring Sego's win back up to 34%. We obtained the 850 and measured Sego's sequential read performance as 37% faster than Inktag's.

Sego's elimination of encryption and hashing is important as the bandwidth of high-end IO devices are increasing faster than processor speeds (e.g., PureStorage announced 5GB/s–9GB/s of IO bandwidth in the FlashArray//m product [8]).

Device bandwidth can also be increased using RAID striping. Figures for how memory bandwidth differs between system and enclave memory for SGX are not yet available.

3.6 Future work

We hope Sego is attractive to device manufacturers because it gives device manufacturers a path to integrate trusted metadata into their devices and improve performance. Hardware support for trusted metadata would close the security gap of data not being encrypted at rest because even at rest, data is protected by hardware.

Another advantage of hardware support is that emulating secure devices can be expensive. The situation is similar to device support for virtualization [28]. As software virtualization gained popularity, device manufacturers directly supported virtualization, improving performance. If Intel's SGX [24] forms the basis for a new generation of trusted software, Intel and other device manufacturers might embrace the Sego model of pervasive trusted metadata because then they could support it in hardware, limiting the TCB and improving performance. For example, the Sego's virtualized block device could be implemented in an intelligent SSD [19]. Ultimately, technology trends and marketplace demands will determine the fate of trusted computing.

4. Secure files

A Sego block storage device is an array of 4 kB blocks, each of which can be untrusted, reserved, or a persisted S-page. Blocks by default are untrusted, but they are reserved by the virtualized block device when identified as the eventual location of in-memory S-page data and become persisted S-pages when data is committed. Users access secure data on disk via S-files, which are just like normal files, but privacy and integrity is guaranteed by the virtualized block device and hypervisor (the Sego TCB). In addition to per-block trusted metadata, Sego maintains the following per-file metadata: OID, file length, and access control information. Per-file metadata is persisted and managed by the hypervisor, in storage that appears as a file in the host system (though the file cannot be read or written by the guest operating system or any guest applications).

Sego provides fast recovery of secure persistent storage for guest OS crashes. One contribution of InkTag was to ensure the integrity of persistent storage in the presence of guest OS and hypervisor crashes. While InkTag's mechanism has been adopted by other untrusted OS projects [11], recovery for crashes (secure `fsck`) requires a complete scan of any attached disks. Sego must be able to recover from hypervisor crashes, but recovery continues to require a full disk scan, just as it does in InkTag. Sego focuses on the more common case of guest OS crashes.

Recovery of persistent data should be fast. The guest OS can be malicious and crashing is a malicious behavior harms availability if it requires costly recovery.

Fast recovery is difficult. The Sego hypervisor cannot trust the indexing structures of the guest OS (e.g., the journal) and must not harm I/O scheduling with many additional sync operations or reordering barriers. Sego's pervasive metadata model allows `libsego`, the Sego hypervisor and the virtualized block device to work cooperatively by sharing uniform view of metadata, detecting any inconsistency between S-file and S-file metadata and recover the S-file.

4.1 Sego's S-file model

To facilitate fast recovery and to preserve the security guarantees of S-files, the model for S-files is somewhat limited relative to normal files:

- **No sparsity.** S-files are not sparse; they must contain on-device disk blocks for all file data.
- **No shrinking.** S-files may be `ftruncate`d only to zero length, or a length larger than the file's current length. If a file's length is extended via `ftruncate`, it is filled with zeroes to preserve the "No sparsity" property.
- **sync required.** A HAP cannot be sure that a file change is resident on secondary storage until it returns from a sync operation (e.g., `sync`, `fsync`, `fdatasync`). POSIX programs must also sync to be sure file updates are committed to storage, but the Sego hypervisor does more aggressive caching than most file systems.

Sego's recovery guarantee for secure files is that any data present on a storage device or in a device queue at the time of a guest OS crash is recoverable after the crash. Sego further provides privacy, integrity and prevention of rollback attacks for S-files. Recovery is initiated by HAPs (optionally, transparently) when they first access an S-file after a guest crash.

The Sego hypervisor and the virtualized block device collaborate to verify access to S-files, and to efficiently recover them. Sego storage maintains the invariant that each block of a secure file is stored at **a unique location**. For example, there can be only one block whose per-block metadata identifies it as OID X, offset 0. If there is more than one block corresponding to an offset of a secure file, then the OS can direct writes to only one of those blocks and direct reads to the other block, thereby achieving a **roll back attack**. The unique location allows the virtualized block device to locate an S-file's S-pages without scanning all of persistent storage, making recovery efficient.

The Sego hypervisor must track S-file length because it cannot rely on the OS. For instance, consider a S-file persisted up to length Y, and the OS records length $Y - x$ due to a legitimate journal rollback or a malicious action. If the Sego hypervisor believes the $Y - x$ is correct and allows a HAP to write data to that offset, the S-file will have multiple data blocks for the same offset.

Challenge of journaling file systems. Modern file systems like ext4, NTFS and XFS [33] support journaling for crash consistency, but these guest OS mechanisms only create challenges for Sego recovery: Sego cannot trust OS journals,

Recovery target	Inconsistency	Detected
S-file (RSF)	Sego creates an S-file but OS does not	When HAP opens the S-file
S-file length (RSL)	S-file length is different from persistent storage	When guest OS boots
Committed block (RCB)	Sego loses persistent data from an S-file	When HAP opens a S-file
Reserved block (RRB)	S-file data block corrupted (not correctly committed)	When Sego hypervisor runs secure fsck

Table 2: Recovery actions for S-files in Sego.

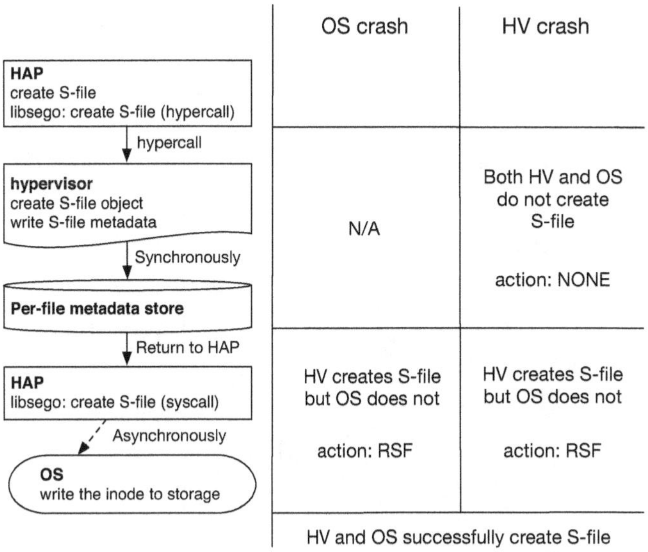

Figure 2: Windows of vulnerability while creating an S-file.

and must not harm a well-behaved OS performing proper recovery from a journal. The default behavior of journaling file systems, when a HAP writes a block of data, is for the OS to write a modified `inode` into its journal and to asynchronously write the data. When the data write reaches persistent storage, the Sego hypervisor increases the length of the S-file. A crash at this point would cause a (well-behaved) OS to believe the data block had not made it safely to persistent storage (because the modified inode has only been written to the journal, not to its on-storage location), and the file's length would remain unchanged. In recovery, the OS would disregard the uncommitted journal transaction, causing the OS and hypervisor to believe the S-file has different lengths (with the hypervisor believing the file is longer). To resolve this type of inconsistency, Sego introduces a novel recovery mechanism.

4.2 Recovery from OS crashes

Table 2 shows Sego recovery actions for different types of S-file inconsistencies between the hypervisor and OS. For simplicity, we discuss each cases individually, but it is possible that a single file needs multiple different recovery actions.

To prevent data loss, Sego must accurately track S-file existence (see §5.1 for hypervisor on-storage data structures). S-file creation is not atomic, so there is a window of vulnerability between when the Sego hypervisor believes an S-file exists and the OS believes the corresponding S-file exists. `libsego` checks on open for such inconsistencies and recovers by recreating the missing S-file in the OS file system (case RSF).

Figure 2 shows the timeline of events on the left, and the consequences of an OS or hypervisor (HV) crash on the right. A HAP creates an S-file, causing libsego to make a hypercall. The hypervisor creates the S-file and before it writes the metadata, if the hypervisor were to crash, both it and the OS would agree that the S-file does not yet exist. Once the hypervisor syncs its per-file metadata, then on a OS crash it would believe the file exists, while the OS would not. This is the most common disagreement between the hypervisor and the OS in our experiments (§6). Once the OS has (asynchronously) written the new inode to its location on storage, the hypervisor and OS would again agree on the state of the file system were either to crash. The OS region is marked N/A during hypervisor execution, because the OS cannot crash while it is not executing.

For writes, `libsego` extends the length of an S-file before writing data. If the OS crashes after the S-file length is extended, but before the OS persists the new S-page, Sego must recover the correct length of the written data (case RSL). The virtualized block device tracks the length of the S-file, shares the S-file state with the Sego hypervisor, and persists the metadata even when the guest crashes. The Sego hypervisor can determine the true (persisted) length of the S-file by examining the shared state from the virtualized block device without exhaustively searching storage. Figure 3 illustrates this complex case, specifying the possible disagreements between OS and hypervisor and the actions necessary to reconcile state after a crash.

The most challenging recovery case is recovering committed data blocks (case RCB). RCB arises when the guest OS rolls back an uncommitted journal transaction and the OS's notion of the length of the S-file is shorter than what the hypervisor's metadata says. When a HAP opens an S-file, `libsego` compares the OS length and the hypervisor length, and if the OS length is shorter, `libsego` initiates data recovery. A HAP indicates target S-pages in memory to hold recovered data with a recovery hypercall, and the hypervisor and the virtualized block device find and return the missing data. Importantly, this does not require searching through all persistent blocks. RCB can ignore all non-secure data block because the trusted block bitmap (§5.2) allows the hypervisor to distinguish trusted from untrusted blocks. `libsego` then makes system calls to write the recovered data into the S-file to allow the OS to come to agreement with the hypervisor on the contents of the S-file. Note that the guest OS is isolated from all recovery actions, and cannot access any recovery information.

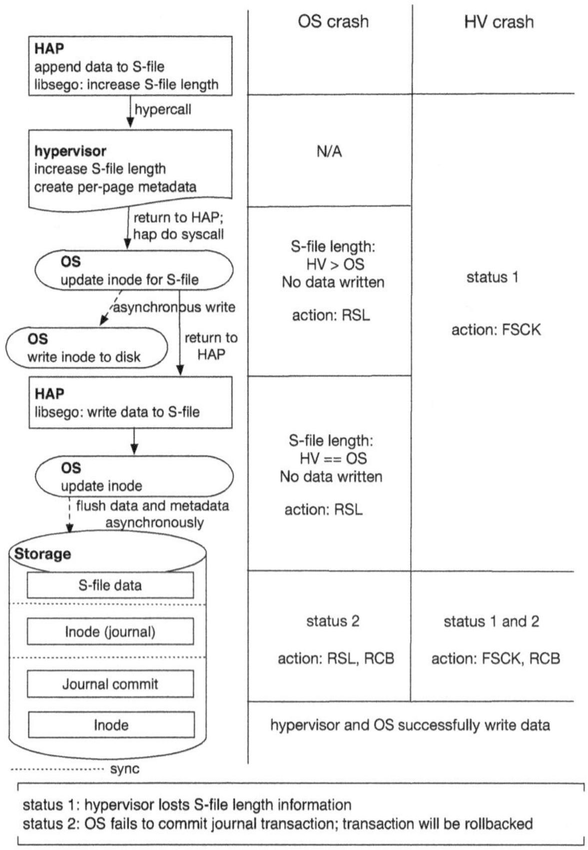

Figure 3: Appending data to S-file. Guest OS uses journaling file system (Ext3 ordered mode in this figure). The dotted line "sync" implies the successive two blocks are stored in order, guaranteeing that the first is persisted before the second.

Hypervisor crashes will not lose secure file data, but recovering from a hypervisor crash requires a complete disk scan (InkTag's secure `fsck`). RRB recovery can only occur during a secure `fsck`. We leave optimizations for hypervisor crash recovery as future work.

4.3 Secure deletion: preventing file rollback attack

Deleting S-files creates a challenge for maintaining unique block locations, because the data and metadata for a single S-file can be scattered across a storage device. Consider a user who deletes a file, and then creates a file with new contents but the same name. The delete must somehow invalidate all blocks on the storage device before it can safely return, yet synchronously updating the metadata for every block in a file will be slow, especially for disks.

Sego provides a fast delete operation by adding a version number which is incremented on delete (as other file systems have done, e.g., LFS [31]). Sego defines the **effective OID** for a file as $hash(OID|verion)$. The hypervisor increments the version number when the HAP deletes a secure file by calling `ftruncate(0)` or `unlink`. The hypervisor and the virtualized block device maintain a mapping from original OID to effective OID. For crash consistency, the mapping

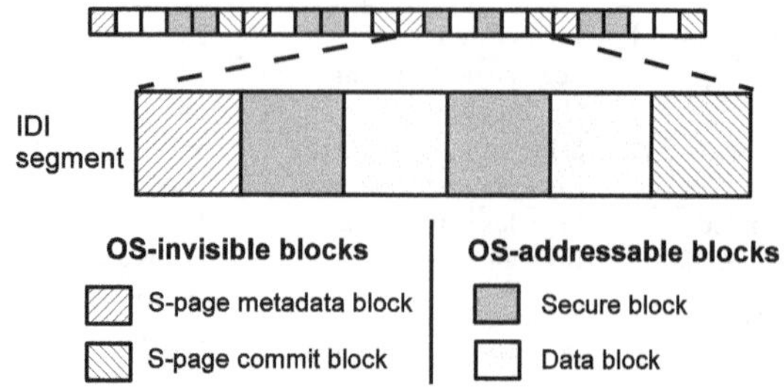

Figure 4: Sego storage layout. The untrusted OS reads and writes OS-addressable blocks, which are arranged in segments on the backing store and interleaved with OS-invisible blocks, that store S-page metadata.

information is synchronously persisted to per-file metadata store. The hypervisor stores the effective OID in per-block metadata, so the virtualized block device can separate active blocks and deleted block for secure files. Effective OIDs allow for fast, secure deletion of S-files.

5. Implementation

This section describes our prototype implementation of Sego for efficient, pervasive metadata and crash recovery.

5.1 Storage layout

The Sego hypervisor views persistent storage as a sequence of 4KB blocks. The Sego's virtualized block device executes on behalf of the hypervisor and helps track S-page and S-file metadata.

Figure 4 illustrates the persistent storage layout of *OS-addressable* blocks, which contain untrusted data or S-page data and may be read directly (for untrusted data) or indirectly (for S-pages) by the guest OS. The storage image also contains *OS-invisible* blocks, which contain metadata for S-pages. OS-addressable blocks are arranged in *segments* on the storage device, with OS-invisible blocks interleaved at a fixed ratio. The Sego hypervisor presents the OS-addressable blocks to the untrusted guest as a contiguous virtual block device. Sego interleaves its metadata, defining a virtual storage image format that we call interleaved data image or **IDI**.

For each segment of OS-addressable blocks, metadata for S-pages contained within those blocks is stored in two OS-invisible blocks. The *leading* invisible block stores S-page metadata such as OID and offset, and the *trailing* invisible block stores a commit block, that atomically indicates the completion of an update to both S-page metadata and data.

5.2 Implementing pervasive metadata

The Sego hypervisor (running as part of the Linux `kvm` module), its virtualized block device (running as part of the userspace `qemu` process), and the guest kernel share information about the state of physical frames in memory and on disk.

Trusted block bitmap The untrusted guest kernel and the virtualized block device share a bitmap of the trusted blocks, indicating which blocks contain S-file data (the trusted block bitmap). Before submitting a disk request, the guest kernel (specifically, the `VirtIO` driver) checks the bitmap, and invokes a hypercall for a secure disk operation if the blocks contains S-file data.

Sharing S-page metadata with the virtualized block device The Sego hypervisor and the virtualized block device share a map of physical memory to exchange S-page metadata. The map is indexed by the guest physical address of an S-page and contains S-page metadata for each entry. When the virtualized block device receives a write request with data in guest physical memory and a virtual disk address as a destination, it checks the shared map to see whether the request comes from an S-page, updates the secure block bitmap if necessary, and writes the S-page metadata, along with the data to virtual disk. When the virtualized block device receives a read request, it verifies the block's status by looking it up in shared memory: the destination physical frame must be marked as an S-page if the block is trusted or marked as untrusted if the block is untrusted. If the destination physical frame is an S-page, the virtualized block device populates the S-page metadata in the shared map by reading the S-page metadata block. The size of S-page metadata is 30 bytes[4] for each 4KB S-page, which is at most 0.7% of total memory size.

5.3 Recovering S-files

To aid secure recovery, the virtualized block device and the Sego hypervisor share a memory region. Once `qemu` boots, it allocates a fixed amount of memory and sends the address to the hypervisor via `ioctl` interface.

When `libsego` requests `RCB` recovery (see Table 2 in §4.2) to the hypervisor, the hypervisor maps the shared memory, signals the virtualized block device to fetch recovery data and send the recovery data to `libsego`. Most importantly, the Sego hypervisor never trusts any information from OS and the OS cannot access or modify the shared memory during the `RCB` recovery.

The first 4K page of the shared memory contains information for recovery such as OID and range of offset. Once the virtualized block device gets signal for a recovery request, it searches corresponding blocks for the S-file with the block bitmap information (without full scan of disk such as what InkTag does) and copies found data to the shared memory for recovery.

Sego restores S-page and S-file metadata consistency following a hypervisor crash (not guest OS crash) via an `fsck`-like process that reads the entire disk. Blocks having both associated S-page metadata and a valid commit block are considered secure blocks. If a block has S-page metadata, but no commit block, then it is considered reserved. Because the hypervisor cannot be sure whether or not private data has been written to the OS-addressable block, the virtualized block device can only zero the block on disk to recover the reserved block. (`RRB` recovery)

[4] OID: 8B, offset: 8B, version number: 4B, sector number: 8B, state variable: 2B.

5.4 Optimizing storage access

The InkTag storage layout is designed for crash consistency. When the OS writes a block for a secure file, the write is transformed into three writes. First, S-page metadata is written to the leading metadata block, which is invisible to guest OS. Then, the data is written to the OS-addressable block. Last, the commit block is written to indicate the completion of the previous two writes. To reduce seeks on disk, the InkTag's virtualized block device[5] writes metadata, data and commit block sequentially within each segment. The host (hypervisor) I/O scheduler can merge and reorder I/O request from the InkTag's virtualized block device so InkTag must `sync` after each write to guarantee that the three writes are persisted in order.

Sego batches writes to a single segment, writing leading metadata, all data blocks, and then the commit block in order. This process eliminates a sync for every data block written to a segment, beside the first. Segments are 64KB in our prototype.

5.5 Preventing Iago attacks

Sego prevents known Iago attacks [12]. It prevents attacks on `mmap` as InkTag does, using a user-provided token returned by the OS from `mmap`, which allows the user to verify that newly memory mapped regions do not overlap old ones. Sego saves and restores the `fs` and `gs` registers on context switches, because the `gcc` toolchain uses them for thread-local storage and other purposes.

Sego only supports unnamed POSIX semaphores, which reside in the processes' address space, disabling the OS from modifying their values. Sego uses uClibc for HAPs and the resume path in `sem_wait` checks whether the thread is being woken up by another thread/process doing a `sem_post`. This check ensures that a waiting process will not proceed when the OS wakes it up for any reason except a corresponding `sem_post`.

6. Evaluation

In this section, we evaluate the performance and crash recovery of the Sego system. For IO benchmarks we use a 3.4GHz quad-core Intel i7-3770, with a 500GB HDD and a 256GB SSD and for the server benchmarks we use a 2.8GHz quad-core Intel i7-860 with a 160GB HDD and a 256GB SSD. Sego is originally implemented at Linux 2.6.36 and QEMU 0.12.5[6] and ported to Linux 3.19.3 and QEMU 2.3.2. Our test system uses Ubuntu 14.04.4. Our guest VMs use a single virtual CPU, 2GB memory and a 12GB disk image. For the InkTag experiments, we turn off MAC functionality to

[5] This is the similar component to Sego's virtualized block device and used for InkTag's storage layout

[6] The server benchmark, crash test and IO benchmarks are done using the older code base.

Service	Application	Non-HAP	InkTag	Sego
KSM	429.mcf	521	1095 (110%)	548 (5%)
	471.omnetpp	319	478 (49%)	333 (4%)
	470.lbm	218	351 (61%)	230 (5%)
	Graph analysis	200	278 (39%)	202 (1%)
Comp.	Memory read	237	298.6 (25%)	251.4 (6%)

Table 3: Execution time with KSM (in second) and memory compaction (in millisecond). Application slowdown is normalized by Non-HAP.

Domain	Masked	Short	Recovery			Total
			RSF	RSL	RCB	
File system	51	9	40	2	1	103
Kernel	85	7	10	0	1	103

Table 4: Random fault injection experiments, with faults injected to file system code and into the entire kernel. Either the benchmark ran correctly (faults Masked), the OS and Sego hypervisor both observed the same amount of data in affected files (Short), or Sego recovered a secure file, secure length, and possibly secure data (RSF, RSL, and RCB).

Domain	Recovery			Success	Total
	RSF	RSL	RCB		
File system	29	7	0	150	150
Kernel	26	0	0	150	150

Table 5: Random fault injection experiment for git

emulate GCM [20] (or upcoming hardware support for SHA hashing [5]). Sego modifies 1,572 lines of Linux kernel code for guest OS and 5,411 lines of KVM hypervisor code. InkTag modifies 962 lines of guest kernel code and 4,068 lines of hypervisor code.

6.1 Performance comparison with modern OS services

This section compares the efficiency of Sego and InkTag when a HAP runs with modern kernel services: kernel samepage merging (KSM) and memory compaction. Table 3 shows application slowdown when the applications execute with KSM and/or compaction enabled. To quantify the overhead from KSM, we run three memory-intensive benchmarks from SPEC CPU 2006[7] and a graph analysis application [2]. KSM uses its default configuration, where a dedicated kernel thread scans 100 pages on every invocation and sleeps 20 milliseconds between invocations. The KSM thread constantly scans and test secure memory, causing severe performance interference (up to 2×) by InkTag's cryptographic operations. To analyze compaction overhead and thereafter memory access delay, we use synthetic microbenchmark: this benchmark maps 500MB of secure memory, requests compaction and read the memory after compaction finishes. Our investigate reveals 64MB secure memory is moved by compaction (InkTag hypervisor encrypts the pages). When HAP reads the pages, InkTag decrypts the pages, which causes 19% slowdown of memory read performance.

6.2 Crash Consistency

We evaluate Sego's crash consistency via directed and randomized fault injection. We analyze file system code to determine four windows of vulnerability for different types of data loss and use System Tap [21] to inject faults at the beginning, middle and end points of each window (directed crash test). These experiments stress worst case behaviors that would be difficult to generate with user-level workloads. For example, when extending a file, Linux often merges the length and data updates into a single inode write, but we test a crash between these updates. Sego recovers from all faults in the directed crash tests for the `ext3`, `ext4`, `vFAT`, and `btrfs` filesystems.

We further validate that Sego can withstand and recover from faults by randomly injecting faults into a guest (that has an `ext3` file system). We use a kernel fault injection model [13, 34, 38], updating a copy of the injection framework from Swift et. al. [34] for modern kernels. We use two fault distributions, one for the whole kernel and one that targets file system code. These distributions are based on recent real-world fault studies [15, 26, 29, 38]. Our results are in Table 4. Our software fault injection framework is available online.[8]

A fault injection trial starts with the execution of four HAPs concurrently writing 20MB S-files, while 20 randomly selected faults are injected. Then four more HAPs are created to write additional 20MB S-files, all data is synced to storage and the system reboots. After the reboot, all of the S-files are read by the HAPs.

Table 4 shows the results of injecting random kernel and file system faults. Sego can detect and recover from every case where the OS and Sego hypervisor disagree on the state of the affected S-files. In our experiment, the RCB recovery happens when the guest OS believes the S-file does not exist (though the S-file actually exists and data are persisted). Thus, the recovery procedure is combined with two recovery mechanisms: re-creating the S-file (RSF) and recovering blocks of the S-file (RCB).

We do the fault injection evalution to version control system, git. We make git (v1.2.3) run as HAP and configure the git to store all meta-information and object files as secure files. The evaluation starts with initializing repository, adding 20MB file and commiting the file, followed by sync. Git can persist meta-information (index, header for initial commit) and objects for current snapshot. Faults are injected with the same configuration used in table 4. 30MB file is added and commited to the repository and system shuts down. After reboot, we run git's consistency checking tool (`git fsck`). If git successfully finishes the consistency check, we count it as success. Table 5 shows the result. Sego recovers every trial enough for git to successfully run `git fsck`.

[7] We choose these three benchmarks because they have enough memory accesses to show a difference between InkTag and Sego.

[8] `https://github.com/ut-osa/fault-injection`

Recovery time for a secure file in Sego.

File Size	4KB	1MB	10MB	50MB	100MB
Disk	0.02	0.03	0.36	1.63	3.49
SSD	0.01	0.02	0.16	0.78	1.51

Recovery time for InkTag.

	Fully cached	Half cached	Not cached
SSD	17	41	65

Table 6: Recovery time (seconds). A 24GB virtual disk is stored on an SSD and the host caches different amounts of the virtual disk during recovery.

Server		Linux VM	Sego
Apache	throughput (req/s)	1526	1411 (7.5%)
	latency (ms)	65.5	70.9 (8.2%)
OpenLDAP	insert (ms)	1307.7	1515.7 (15.9%)
	query (ms)	1079.8	1118.2 (3.6%)
	delete (ms)	1269.4	1459.5 (15.0%)
DokuWiki	1 client (s)	7.9	11.1 (40%)
	16 client (s)	11.3	16.9 (49%)

Table 7: Server application performance.

Sego recovery provides an optimized path for recovering secure data that is maliciously erased by the operating system. If the malicious OS executes `rm -rf /`, Sego has trusted metadata distinguishing all secure disk blocks so it preserves their contents and rejects any subsequent OS writes to them. As haps try to access the deleted S-files, Sego recovers their contents by searching just the secure data on the disk, not the entire disk contents. Table 6 shows the amount of time it takes to recover S-files. To measure the recovery time of Sego, we delete (`rm -f`) an S-file and have a HAP reopen the S-file to recover the data. Most of the time is spent in the disk controller (~90%) reading secure data, and the HAP successfully recovers the entire contents of the S-file. The second table shows recovery time of InkTag. InkTag has to scan entire disk to recover the length of S-files and inconsistent blocks since it cannot trust the on-disk metadata of OS. We measure the time by running `fsck -c` (the option that scans for bad blocks) on the virtual disk to estimate InkTag fsck time. Sego's recovery time is 19× faster than InkTag when the entire virtual disk is already in the host buffer cache. Because Sego maintains fine-grained metadata, it does not need to recover the entire disk after a crash, it can recover only missing secure data.

6.3 Server applications

We build several server applications as HAPs, and evaluate their performance. The clients run in a different machine connected over 1Gbps Ethernet.

For the Apache webserver, we use the `ab` benchmarking tool to measure the performance overhead in Sego. The benchmark executes 10,000 requests, at a concurrency level of 100. Table 7 shows the results; throughput and latency overheads are below 9%.

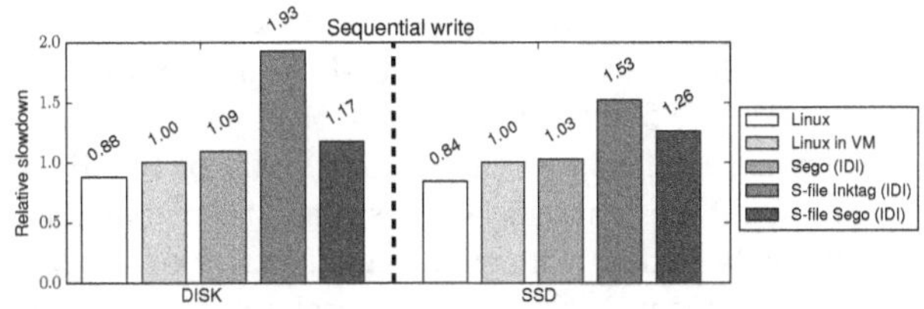

Figure 5: Sequential IO performance of disk and SSD. We normalize I/O throughput by the number of Linux VM; Slowdown of Linux is less than 1.

SSD	Linux in a VM	S-file Sego	
grep-src	0.20	0.22	(10.1%)
Fortune 50	1.80	1.95	(8.3%)

Table 8: GNU grep execution time in seconds. The standard deviation over 20 trials is less than 4% of the mean.

We build the OpenLDAP [4] server as a HAP, using Berkeley DB as the backend and secure all database and log files as S-files. We measure the overhead of inserting, querying, and deleting 200 entries, and the results are shown in Table 7. The overhead is 3.6% for queries, and under 16% for insert and delete. The server calls an `fdatasync` for inserts and deletes, in which the Sego hypervisor synchronizes the per-file metadata for crash consistency.

We run DokuWiki [1] as a HAP in Sego and follow the methodology from the InkTag paper [23]. DokuWiki is a PHP-based wiki that stores wiki data as S-files. We use the same corpus of wiki edits used in the InkTag benchmarks. We run a sequence of operations against DokuWiki via its XML-RPC interface, with a 90% read workload, where each write advances a wiki page to its next version. Sego runs DokuWiki's CGI binary as a HAP. We measure the slowdown for a sequence of 20 operations, averaged across 5 trials. Our results are shown in Table 7.

6.4 IO benchmarks

Figure 5 shows the sequential write performance of Sego on both disk and SSD. The micro-benchmark performs 200MB of sequential write with a 64K request size. The interleaved disk image (labeled IDI) has a segment size of 64KB and a 4KB block each for the metadata and commit blocks.

The write penalty for IDI is reasonably low ($< 10\%$), Sego's S-file write performance is 17% and 26% slower on disk and SSD respectively. We measure between 8 to 10 MB of additional metadata writes when writing a 200 MB S-file on SSDs. Sego outperforms InkTag by 76% and 27% in disk and SSD respectively because Sego reduces the number of `sync` by our I/O optimization and eliminates encryption and MAC for IO data. Our investigation identifies 13%–15% IO performance is improved by removing the cryptographic protection.

To measure IO performance with a real application, we compile GNU grep (v2.18) as a HAP and search for a string (that is not found) in the grep source code and through a directory of the most recent form 10-K filing from the top 50 of the Fortune 500 (termed Fortune 50). The grep source code contains 918 files with an average file size of 10 KB and the Fortune 50 files contains 49 files (one of the companies is not publicly traded) with an average file size of 4.6 MB. Table 8 shows the wall-clock time for each setting. Grepping large and small files on Sego has about a 10% overhead though it is slightly worse when search through many small files. Opening an S-file induces an additional hypercall to check for file recovery, which shows up when working with many small files.

7. Related work

There has been significant work on providing verifiable system services built on untrustworthy operating systems. We summarize the contribution of many systems in a taxonomy to determine what has been done in the state of the art and what work remains.

Table 9 summarizes several recent systems, explains what properties they achieve and how they achieve them. Most abbreviations used in the table are explained in the caption. The table is divided into regions. The first region is about privacy and integrity of physical memory and address space mappings. The next region is about storage. Some systems distinguish storage for user's cryptographic keys; some systems support protected files; some assume applications will use their keys to encrypt and MAC their data. Sego and InkTag have focused on problems that arise with verifying the untrusted file system, while Haven replaces the untrusted file system with a library OS and most other systems assume a simple library for encrypted and MACed files. OS page indicates if a system allows the OS to temporarily swap a protected application's page to persistent storage (which it does to manage a limited amount of physical memory). Then follows access control, with HV acct indicating if the trusted system supports a user account distinct from, but parallel to OS accounts. In the final section, Split app indicates if the system requires an application to do privilege separation to isolate its security-sensitive components (which represents a significant barrier to entry).

Techniques for protecting the privacy and integrity of RAM is the area of widest innovation. RAM protection is the performance-sensitive basis for supporting applications on a hostile operating system, so it is logical that it is the focus of innovation. Most existing systems have not addressed address space privacy, so a hostile operating system can effectively get a page-granularity trace of any application's execution (and an effective attack has been published [36]).

A fundamental distinction is between systems that try to provide a protected file system and those that rely on applications (perhaps augmented with libraries) to protect their own data via encryption. Systems that support an untrusted file system (e.g., Sego and Overshadow) can `mmap` secure files, which provides compatibility with current systems and a variety of services and optimizations. For example, `mmap` is the way Linux loads applications. It provides demand paging for executables and provides a basis for metadata-efficient integrity verification. Supporting a file system allows systems like Overshadow and Sego to support OS paging. Finally, verifiable file system support can include flexible access control.

Many recent systems have avoided providing file system support, relying on cryptography and do-it-yourself application libraries (e.g., virtual ghost and MiniBox). The simplicity of leaving the file system out of the list of system services that need to be verified is appealing. Without file system support, it is straightforward to support simple data storage for a single application (much like the app-centric storage model of iOS). If a user has privacy and integrity for a set of encryption keys, they can use those keys to encrypt and HMAC files. Encryption on files works well for a HAP to protect data that a future instance of the same HAP will access.

All features provided by an untrusted file system can probably be reimplemented by trusted applications, though these features include complex semantics and important performance optimizations. For example, application-directed paging would require new interfaces to allow applications to make swapping decisions. Paging requires the application and hypervisor to dynamically protect the privacy and integrity of memory pages and the integrity of their mapping. Virtual ghost has a design for OS paging, but does not implement it in their prototype, hence the Y/N. As another example of how systems compensate for lack of file system support, TLR relies on special hardware to prevent memory rollback attacks.

It is difficult to provide access control without a file system. Several systems feature user accounts in the hypervisor (though virtual ghost has a VM instead). Such accounts might be sufficient for the hypervisor to maintain per-user encryption keys. However, providing user and group-based access control common in file systems using only cryptography is still an open problem, especially for access revocation [10, 22].

minimizing the code in a HAP is desirable. It uses a shared wimpy kernel service that verifies only low-level I/O with the untrusted OS, not higher level services like file system operations (e.g., demand paging or copy-on-write).

8. Conclusion

Sego guarantees trustworthy services for user applications even when the guest operation system is malicious. We propose pervasive metadata for efficient verification and demonstrate substantial performance improvements for modern system services as well as IO-bound workloads. Sego provides crash consistency and recovery for secure data, which is validated by experiment. We believe Sego contributes a step forward for "secure" cloud computing.

System	RAM privacy	RAM integrity	AS privacy	AS integrity	User keys	FS privacy	FS integrity	FS crash	OS Paging	HV acct	Split app
Sego	EPT	EPT	None	PV & HV	Secure file	HV & Virtualized block device		HV recovery	Yes	No	No
InkTag [23]	EPT & Encrypt	EPT & HMAC	None	PV & HV	Secure file	Encrypt & Namespaces	Per-sector HMAC	Disk scan	Yes	No	No
Overshadow [14]	Shadow page table	HMAC	None	HV	Secure file	Encrypt	File HMAC	None	Yes	No	No
Haven [11]	HW Enclave	HW Enclave & HMAC	None	HW Enclave	LibOS file system	Shield module	Shield module	Disk scan	Yes	NA	No
Virtual Ghost [17]	Compiler & ISA	Compiler	None	ISA	TPM & VM	None	None	None	Y/N	Yes	No
MiniBox [25] TrustVisor [27]	EPT	EPT & vTPM	Pinned text	HV	μTPM & TPM	App	App	None	No	Yes	Yes
TLR [32]	ARM TrustZone memory		ARM TrustZone translation tables		Encrypt & memory HW	None	None	None	No	No	Yes

Table 9: A comparison of techniques that support applications running on untrusted operating systems. AS–address space, FS–file system, HV–hypervisor, EPT–extended page tables, PV–paravirtualization, attrs–attributes, PCR–platform configuration register. NA means the category is not applicable.

Acknowledgement

We thank the anonymous reviewers and Dan Tsafrir for shepherding this paper. This research is supported by NIH R01 LM011028-01 and NSF CNS-1228843.

References

[1] DokuWiki. `https://www.dokuwiki.org/`.

[2] HPC Graph Analysis. `http://www.graphanalysis.org/benchmark/`.

[3] Intel Trusted Execution Technology. `http://www.intel.com/technology/security/`.

[4] OpenLDAP. `http://www.openldap.org/`.

[5] Intel SHA Extensions, 2013. `https://software.intel.com/en-us/articles/intel-sha-extensions`.

[6] AES-GCM Encryption Performance on Intel Xeon E5 v3 Processors, 2015. `https://software.intel.com/en-us/articles/aes-gcm-encryption-performance-on-intel-xeon-e5-v3-processors`.

[7] AES-NI SSL performance, 2015. `https://calomel.org/aesni_ssl_performance.html`.

[8] FlashArray//m Technical Specs, 2015. `http://www.purestorage.com/products/technical-specifications/`.

[9] Samsung V-NAND SSD, 2015. `http://www.samsung.com/global/business/semiconductor/minisite/SSD/global/html/ssd850pro/specifications.html`.

[10] Randy Baden, Adam Bender, Neil Spring, Bobby Bhattacharjee, and Daniel Starin. Persona: an online social network with user-defined privacy. In *SIGCOMM*, 2009.

[11] Andrew Baumann, Marcus Peinado, and Galen Hunt. Shielding applications from an untrusted cloud with haven. In *OSDI*, 2014.

[12] Stephen Checkoway and Hovav Shacham. Iago attacks: Why the system call API is a bad untrusted RPC interface. In *ASPLOS*, March 2013.

[13] Peter M. Chen, Wee Teck Ng, Subhachandra Chandra, Christopher Aycock, and David Rajamani, Gurushankarand Lowell. The rio file cache: Surviving operating system crashes. In *ASPLOS*, pages 74–83, 1996.

[14] Xiaoxin Chen, Tal Garfinkel, E. Christopher Lewis, Pratap Subrahmanyam, Carl A. Waldspurger, Dan Boneh, Jeffery Dwoskin, and Dan R. K. Ports. Overshadow: A virtualization-based approach to retrofitting protection in commodity operating systems. In *ASPLOS*, May 2008.

[15] Andy Chou, Junfeng Yang, Benjamin Chelf, Seth Hallem, and Dawson Engler. An empirical study of operating systems errors. In *SOSP*, pages 73–88, 2001.

[16] John Criswell. *Secure virtual architecture: security for commodity software systems*. PhD thesis, University of Illinois at Urbana-Champaign, 2014.

[17] John Criswell, Nathan Dautenhahn, and Vikram Adve. Virtual Ghost: Protecting Applications from Hostile Operating Systems. In *ASPLOS*, 2014.

[18] Tim Dierks and Eric Rescorla. RFC 5246: The Transport Layer Security (TLS) Protocol: Version 1.2. `http://tools.ietf.org/html/rfc5246`, 2008.

[19] Jaeyoung Do, Yang-Suk Kee, Jignesh M. Patel, Chanik Park, Kwanghyun Park, and David J. DeWitt. Query processing on smart ssds: Opportunities and challenges. In *ACM International Conference on Management of Data (SIGMOD)*, 2013.

[20] Morris Dworkin. NIST Special Publication 800-38D: Recommendation for Block Cipher Modes of Operation: Galois/Counter Mode (GCM) and GMAC. `http://csrc.nist.gov/publications/nistpubs/800-38D/SP-800-38D.pdf`, 2007.

[21] Frank Ch. Eigler. Problem solving with systemtap. In *The Ottawa Linux Symposium*, pages 261–268, 2006.

[22] Ariel J Feldman, Aaron Blankstein, Michael J Freedman, and Edward W Felten. Social Networking with Frientegrity: Privacy and Integrity with an Untrusted Provider. In *USENIX Security*, 2012.

[23] Owen S. Hofmann, Sangman Kim, Alan M. Dunn, Michael Z. Lee, and Emmett Witchel. InkTag: Secure Applications on an Untrusted Operating System. In *ASPLOS*, 2013.

[24] Intel Corporation. *Software Guard Extensions Programming Reference*, 2015. https://software.intel.com/sites/default/files/managed/48/88/329298-002.pdf.

[25] Yanlin Li, Adrian Perrig, Jonathan McCune, James Newsome, Brandon Baker, and Will Drewry. MiniBox: A two-way sandbox for x86 native code. Technical Report CMU-CyLab-14-001, CyLab, Carnegia Mellon University, 2014.

[26] Lanyue Lu, Andrea C Arpaci-Dusseau, Remzi H Arpaci-Dusseau, and Shan Lu. A study of linux file system evolution. In *FAST*, pages 31–44, 2013.

[27] Jonathan M. McCune, Yanlin Li, Ning Qu, Zongwei Zhou, Anupam Datta, Virgil Gligor, and Adrian Perrig. TrustVisor: Efficient TCB reduction and attestation. In *IEEE S&P*, May 2010.

[28] Gil Neiger, Amy Santoni, Felix Leung, Dion Rodgers, and Rich Uhlig. Intel virtualization technology: Hardware support for efficient processor virtualization. In *Intel Technology Journal*, volume 10, 2006.

[29] Nicolas Palix, Gaël Thomas, Suman Saha, Christophe Calvès, Julia Lawall, and Gilles Muller. Faults in linux: Ten years later. In *ASPLOS*, pages 305–318, 2011.

[30] Jianbao Ren, Yong Qi, Yuehua Dai, Xiaoguang Wang, and Yi Shi. Appsec: A safe execution environment for security sensitive applications. In *VEE*, 2015.

[31] Mendel Rosenblum and John K. Ousterhout. The design and implementation of a log-structured file system. *ACM Trans. Comput. Syst.*, 10(1), February 1992.

[32] Nuno Santos, Himanshu Raj, Stefan Saroiu, and Alec Wolman. Using ARM trustzone to build a trusted language runtime for mobile applications. In *ASPLOS*, 2014.

[33] Adam Sweeney, Doug Doucette, Wei Hu, Curtis Anderson, Mike Nishimoto, and Geoff Peck. Scalability in the xfs file system. In *USENIX ATC*, 1996.

[34] Michael M. Swift, Brian N. Bershad, and Henry M. Levy. Improving the reliability of commodity operating systems. In *SOSP*, pages 207–222, 2003.

[35] Xiaoguang Wang, Yue Chen, Zhi Wang, Yong Qi, and Yajin Zhou. Secpod: a framework for virtualization-based security systems. In *USENIX ATC*, 2015.

[36] Yuanzhong Xu, Weidong Cui, and Marcus Peinado. Controlled-channel attacks: Deterministic side channels for untrusted operating systems. In *IEEE S&P*, 2015.

[37] Jisoo Yang and Kang G. Shin. Using hypervisor to provide data secrecy for user applications on a per-page basis. In *VEE*, pages 71–80, 2008.

[38] Takeshi Yoshimura, Hiroshi Yamada, and Kenji Kono. Is linux kernel oops useful or not. In *HotDep*, 2012.

[39] Kim Zetter. Hacking team leak shows how secretive zero-day exploit sales work. *Wired*, 2015.

Synopsis of the ASPLOS '16 Wild and Crazy Ideas (WACI) Invited-Speakers Session

Dan Tsafrir

Technion – Israel Institute of Technology

dan@cs.technion.ac.il

Abstract

The Wild and Crazy Ideas (WACI) session is a longstanding tradition at ASPLOS, soliciting talks that consist of forward-looking, visionary, inspiring, creative, far out or just plain amazing ideas presented in an exciting way.[1]

The first WACI session took place in 1998. Back then, the call for talks included a problem statement, which contended that "papers usually do not get admitted to [such conferences as] ISCA or ASPLOS unless the systems that they describe are mature enough to run [some standard benchmark suites, which] has a chilling effect on the idea generation process—encouraging incremental research" [1]. The 1998 WACI session turned out to be a great success. Its webpage states that "there were 42 submissions [competing over] only eight time slots, [which resulted in] this session [having] a lower acceptance rate than the conference itself" [2].

But the times they are a-changin' [3], and the WACI session no longer enjoys that many submissions (Figure 1), perhaps because nowadays there exist many forums for researchers to describe/discuss their preliminary ideas, including: the "hot topics in" workshops [4–7]; a journal like CAL, dedicated to early results [8]; main conferences soliciting short submissions describing "original or unconventional ideas at a preliminary stage" in addition to regular papers [9]; and the many workshops co-located with main conferences, like ISCA '15, which hosted 13 such workshops [10].

Regardless of the reason for the declining number of submissions, this time we've decided to organize the WACI session differently to ensure its continued high quality. Instead of soliciting talks via an open call and hoping for the best, we proactively invited speakers whom we believe are capable of delivering excellent WACI presentations. That is, this year's WACI session consists exclusively of invited speakers. Filling up the available slots turned out to be fairly easy, as most of the researchers we invited promptly accepted our invitation. The duration of each talk was set to be eight minutes (exactly as in the first WACI session from 1998) plus two minutes for questions.

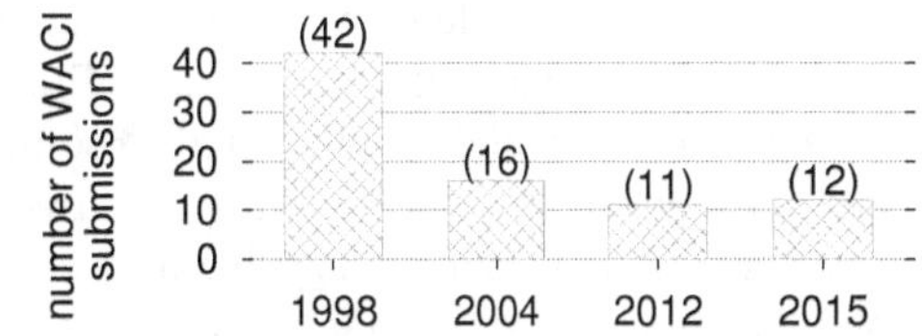

Figure 1. *The number of submissions to the WACI session has declined over the years [2, 11–13]. We contacted WACI session chairs from other years* ($\geq$ 2010) *in an attempt to obtain more data, but they did not maintain it in their records. They typically agreed, however, that the numbers were depressingly low.*

The talks are outlined below. We believe they are interesting and exciting, and we hope the attendees of the session will find them stimulating and insightful.

1. The ASPLOSian Singularity

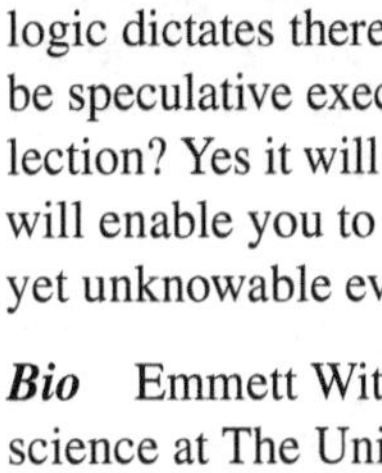

Emmett Witchel, University of Texas at Austin.

Abstract The technological singularity is the inflection point where machine intelligence recursively self-improves, making it inevitable that machines surpass human intelligence with unknowable motivations. Therefore, logic dictates there will be an ASPLOSian singularity. Will it be speculative execution, a file system or require garbage collection? Yes it will! Our delightful and information-dense talk will enable you to understand and profit from this inevitable yet unknowable event.

Bio Emmett Witchel is an associate professor in computer science at The University of Texas at Austin, since receiving his doctorate from MIT in 2004. He and his group are interested in operating systems, security, and architecture.

[1] Amusing elements in the presentations are tolerated ;-) but are in fact optional.

ASPLOS '16, April 2–6, 2016, Atlanta, GA, USA.

ACM 978-1-4503-4091-5/16/04... $15.00.
http://dx.doi.org/10.1145/2872362.2876512

2. The Elephant in the Room Cannot Write Parallel Code

Yoav Etsion, Technion – Israel Institute of Technology.

Abstract Dennard scaling (or end thereof) has stopped the clock and drove us to multicore architecture. Soon afterwards, Dark Silicon and the power wall sent us to develop various hardware accelerators. Today, many in the computer architecture community believe that future computer systems will be parallel, heterogeneous, and littered with hardware accelerators. This view draws attention to the proverbial Elephant in the room: Can humans really program such systems? In my talk, I wish to argue for an idea that is so wild and crazy that only few dare say it out loud: Automatic Code Parallelization.

Bio Yoav Etsion is an Assistant Professor at Technion – Israel Institute of Technology, where he is a member of both Electrical Engineering and Computer Science departments. In addition, he is a founding member of the Technion Computer Engineering research center (TCE). Previous to that, he was a Senior Researcher at the Barcelona Supercomputing Center (BSC-CNS). Prof. Etsion received his PhD from the Hebrew University in 2010, and he is a member of the ACM and IEEE. His research interests include computer architecture, HW/SW interoperability, operating systems, and parallel programming models.

3. Silicon Meets Biotech: Building Better Computers by Incorporating Biological Parts

Luis Ceze, University of Washington.

Abstract Hybrid silicon and biochemical systems are worth serious consideration: time is ripe for computer architects to consider incorporating biomolecules as an integral part of computer design. I'll provide examples of using biology to improve storage, compute and sensing, leading to systems that would be impossible with just silicon or biology alone. Biotechnology has benefited tremendously from progress in silicon technology developed by the computer industry; perhaps now is the time for the computer industry to borrow back from the biotechnology industry.

Bio Luis Ceze is the Torode Family Associate Professor in the Computer Science and Engineering Department at the University of Washington. His research focuses on the intersection between computer architecture, programming languages and biology. He is a recipient of an NSF CAREER Award, a Sloan Research Fellowship, a Microsoft Research Faculty Fellowship and the 2013 IEEE TCCA Young Computer Architect Award. When he is not working, he is fond of either eating or cooking.

4. Wean the Screen: Systems Challenges for Practical, Non-Visual User Interfaces

Don Porter, Stony Brook University.

Abstract Mark Weiser's vision of ubiquitous computing has been an exciting goal for systems researchers. A prevailing approach to making computers more ubiquitous is proliferating display devices. Although proliferating displays is inexpensive and feels futuristic, this approach misses important opportunities for computing to intrude into our lives. Some activities and situations simply preclude monitors, such as taking a shower, driving a car, or jogging. Moreover, many computer users develop repeated stress injuries that limit time at a traditional computer, and a significant fraction of the population is blind or has reduced vision. Finally, technology itself is trending toward small displays, such as thermostats, watches, and some devices may have no onboard display. This talk explores systems challenges that must be solved in order for systems to support practical user interfaces with little-to-no visual component. As an example, consider responding to email while jogging; the user may be able to look at a few images on a phone or watch, but the primary interaction mode would be audio. The user will need to refer to data outside of her email application, such as checking her calendar, updating a document, or adding data to a spreadsheet.

Bio Don Porter is an Assistant Professor of Computer Science at Stony Brook University. Porter's research interests broadly involve developing more efficient and secure computer systems. Porter earned a PhD and MSc from The University of Texas at Austin, and a BA from Hendrix College.

5. Data Untangling Begins at Home

Vishakha Gupta, Intel.

Abstract Imagine all your documents, emails, photos were not digital but print. Now imagine you had to find photos from an event ten years ago. Assuming you still had those pictures, you might be able to pull up a few from an album created at the time. If you like to hoard and are really really organized, you might be able to find them. Even if you are very organized though, you would probably not be able to easily find pictures of all the games your daughter played in when she was a kid. Storage and classification systems are both impediments to these types of tasks. Then came computers and that made things... worse. Storage may have become cheaper and more abundant but that only made the organization and search problem worse. Solutions like Apple's Spotlight try to free the user from the need to organize and classify data but are still very limited in their understanding of what the user really wants to find or look at; not to mention that those needs may change. What if we never had to worry about where any file got saved on our permanent storage? What if all we understood were elements in life like messages, photos, events, tutorials, conversations but had no idea of how they mapped to storage, just how they mapped to our lives. What if size and number were not a problem? What if one search revealed connections we had even forgotten about? What if I said graphs on next generation memories could make all this possible and more?

Bio Vishakha Gupta is a Research Scientist at the best software lab in the industry at a hardware company called Intel. At around the time she joined Intel in 2011, after begrudgingly leaving Georgia Tech, she fell in love with graphs for some reason and now wants to apply them to solve every problem on the planet. If numerous mathematicians can, why can't she? Other than that, she likes working on systems problems, particularly when it comes to dealing with large memories and big data.

6. We Have People for That

Emery Berger, University of Massachusetts Amherst.

Abstract Since 1960, the world population has been growing by 1 billion people roughly every 12 years. I dub this More's Law. Today, there are more than 7 billion people in the world. Also today, almost 4 billion of them are wasting their vast potential staring into their mobile phone screens. These converging trends mean that there are vast unused human computational resources waiting to be tapped. I argue that getting these people to do anything even remotely productive will make the world a better place.

Bio Emery Berger is a Professor in the College of Information and Computer Sciences at the University of Massachusetts Amherst, where he co-directs the PLASMA lab (Programming Languages and Systems at Massachusetts) and is a regular visiting researcher at Microsoft Research. He is the creator of a number of influential software systems including Hoard, a fast and scalable memory manager that accelerates multithreaded applications (used by companies including British Telecom, Cisco, Credit Suisse, Reuters, Royal Bank of Canada, SAP, and Tata, and on which the Mac OS X memory manager is based); DieHard, an error-avoiding memory manager that directly influenced the design of the Windows 7 Fault-Tolerant Heap; and DieHarder, a secure memory manager that was an inspiration for hardening changes made to the Windows 8 heap. He is currently serving / surviving as Program Chair for PLDI 2016, and maintains his blood-caffeine level at roughly 0.94.

7. Making Reconfigurable Fabric Actually Reconfigurable

Chris Rossbach, VMware and University of Texas at Austin.

Abstract A wealth of research and engineering effort has been devoted to enabling an era of FPGA ubiquity through improvements to front-end programmability and through better support for familiar interfaces to resources such as memory. Despite this effort, using FPGAs in a setting where reconfiguration is a common operation remains a surprisingly radical idea. The same is true for related systems-level concerns such as sharing and virtualization. This talk considers the challenges associated with making reconfigurable resources actually reconfigurable and sharable, and sets a technical course for restructuring and improving system software in a way that enables more widespread use of FPGAs.

Bio Chris Rossbach is a Senior Researcher at VMware Research Group, an Assistant Professor at the University of Texas at Austin, and an alumnus of Microsoft Research's Silicon Valley Lab. He received his PhD in computer science from The University of Texas at Austin in 2009. Chris's research focuses on operating system and architectural support for emerging hardware, particularly those that leverage concurrency. He is interested in concurrency in the broadest sense, but has a particular affinity for exploring abstractions that enable systems to take advantage of concurrency to improve performance and mechanisms that simplify the development of parallel programs.

8. Remembrances From Future Spaces: Nano-Computing and the Imitation Game in 2050

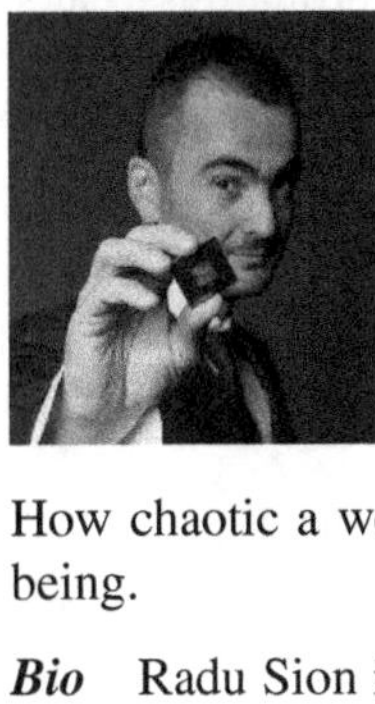

Radu Sion, Stony Brook University.

Abstract We will talk about small things, happiness, and free energy. We explore the year 2050. How to power up your computing using your sweat. Whether the singularity will really happen or stop at passing the Turing test. How chaotic a world in which energy is free may end up being.

Bio Radu Sion is the CEO of Private Machines Inc., and a Professor of Computer Science at Stony Brook (on leave). Radu and his group are interested in systems, cybersec and large scale computing. Radu is currently leading Private Machines Inc., a cyber security startup designing the next generation secure cloud computing technologies.

9. A Captain of Industry Who Is Me Changes The Technology Business Forever

James Mickens, Harvard University.

Abstract It's not clear what hardware designers and OS architects should be doing these days. Moore's Law is dead. File descriptor tables have already been invented. Making computers more power-efficient is supposed to save the earth for future people, but the future people are not here yet, and if they're anything like the current people, we already don't like them. It is well-known that making things go fast is very fun and occasionally useful. We can make software go fast by moving it to hardware. So, I propose that we take the top five applications that a platform executes, and implement them in hardware, leaving only a thin software layer to coordinate the particularly tricky parts. So, uh, let's implement Linux in hardware. We should also implement Firefox in hardware. And Emacs. OK AND VI TOO. You vi people are so needy. Stockholm syndrome will do that to you.

Bio James Mickens is an IEEE Knight of the Republic, an ACM Templar for Non-Open Access, and a Royal Proceeding of Her Majesty's Royal Proceedings. His appreciation for syntactically correct code has led him to be called "a semicolon in human form." His online shopping habits have too many dimensions to be k-means clustered, so he is only shown ads about dinosaurs and ancient siege machines. This does not bother James Mickens, and explains why he spends his summers attacking France with triceratops horns.

Acknowledgments

We warmly thank Apple and Netapp for sponsoring this session, and the speakers for boldly accepting the challenge. The session chair would like to additionally thank YY Zhou, the ASPLOS '16 program chair, for supporting this year's experiment of changing the format of the WACI session.

References

[1] John Kubiatowicz. The ASPLOS '98 wild and crazy ideas session: Call for talks. URL `http://www.cs.berkeley.edu/~kubitron/asplos98/call.html`, 1998. Accessed: January 2016.

[2] John Kubiatowicz. The ASPLOS '98 wild and crazy ideas session. URL `http://www.cs.berkeley.edu/~kubitron/asplos98/index.html`, 1998. Accessed: January 2016.

[3] Bob Dylan. The times they are a-changin'. URL `http://www.bobdylan.com/us/songs/times-they-are-changin`, 1964. Accessed: January 2016.

[4] HotCloud '16: USENIX workshop on hot topics in cloud computing. URL `https://www.usenix.org/conference/hotcloud16`, 2016. Accessed: January 2016.

[5] HotStorage '16: USENIX workshop on hot topics in storage and file systems. URL `https://www.usenix.org/conference/hotstorage16`, 2016. Accessed: January 2016.

[6] HotOS '15: USENIX workshop on hot topics in operating systems. URL `https://www.usenix.org/conference/hotos15`, 2015. Accessed: January 2016.

[7] HotSec '16: USENIX summit on hot topics in security. URL `https://www.usenix.org/conference/hotsec16`, 2016. Accessed: January 2016.

[8] CAL: IEEE Computer Architecture Letters. URL `http://www.computer.org/web/cal/about`. Accessed: January 2016.

[9] Call for papers of ATC '16: USENIX Annual Technical Conference. URL `https://www.usenix.org/conference/atc16/call-for-papers`, 2016. Accessed: January 2016.

[10] Workshops of ISCA '15: ACM/IEEE International Symposium on Computer Architecture. URL `http://www.ece.cmu.edu/calcm/isca2015/workshop_tutorial.php`, 2015. Accessed: January 2016.

[11] Steve Keckler, Steve Blackburn, and Emmett Witchel. The Wild and Crazy Idea Session IV. URL `http://www.cs.utexas.edu/users/skeckler/wild04/`, 2004. Accessed: January 2016.

[12] Alexandra (Sasha) Fedorova. 2012 WACI (provocative ideas) session. Private email correspondence, 2016.

[13] John Criswell. 2015 WACI session. Private email correspondence, 2016.

Brain Inspired Computing

R. Stanley Williams
Hewlett Packard Labs
stan.williams@hpe.com

Abstract

The computer industry is facing a potential existential crisis: how to continue exponential increases in computing performance and efficiency after the end of transistor size scaling at roughly 5 nm feature sizes, which in principle is only two generations or as little as four years away. This challenge has demanded a great deal of attention from a variety of industrial, government and academic experts in various aspects of computing. In particular, the IEEE Rebooting Computing Initiative has held four Summits at which evolutionary and revolutionary approaches for computing ranging from new types of transistors to new architectures have been proposed and examined. In addition, the International Technology Roadmap for Semiconductors (ITRS), which for over two decades coordinated the efforts of the semiconductor industry and its supply chain to keep integrated circuits for processors and memory on the path of exponential increases in transistor count, has changed the emphasis of its efforts toward systems and applications, and is collaborating closely with Rebooting Computing.

The good news to come out of these efforts is that there are many proposals that have the potential to dramatically improve computer energy efficiency. Now the challenge is to begin a comprehensive research effort that can advance these ideas to the point where they can be implemented or rejected. This effort will require contributions from multiple institutions and disciplines, and will almost certainly involve international cooperation and competition as well. These issues have been recognized recently by the US White House Office of Science and Technology Policy, which announced a new Nanotechnology-Inspired Grand Challenge for Future Computing on October 20, 2015.

Of the many proposals for Future Computing, perhaps the most intriguing is to look to the human brain for inspiration on how to improve energy efficiency. A major problem is that there is very little agreement about how brains actually compute, so that the term 'neuromorphic computing' has taken on a wide variety of concepts and interpretations. I acknowledge that I know very little about what brains actually do, but in looking over various ideas that have been proposed I can already see significant opportunities for improving the computers we will have in the near future. Further, I anticipate that as neuroscientists learn more about cortical architecture and neuron function, electrical engineers will be inspired to design specialized devices and circuits that are hyper-optimized to perform particular valuable computations, and that these structures will be integrated onto heterogeneous system-on-chip or system-in-package engines as accelerators and co-processors. The reason why this strategy should succeed now is two-fold: the end of transistor scaling means that general purpose processors will no longer improve faster than special purpose hardware can be designed, and the power dissipation of scaled transistors will likely be so large that it will not be possible to operate all of the circuitry on a chip simultaneously – the 'dark-silicon' problem. The materials and technologies that will provide the new electronic functionalities for these neuromorphic accelerators have already been under development for over a decade and are the basis for the non-volatile memories that promise to change computing from a processor centric to a memory driven architecture. Can this be a path toward exponential improvements by increasing the amount of computation per unit of energy expended? The answer to this question likely involves the types of computation to be performed. I will discuss the speed versus limited precision of an example of a brain-inspired accelerator – an analog dot product engine that multiplies a fixed matrix by a variable vector in a single clock cycle, which is a type of computation in memory useful for a variety of algorithms. I will outline an idealized research program to harvest and utilize discoveries in neuroscience for brain inspired computing.

I will conclude by speculating on the possible relationship between chaotic behaviour of neurons and intuition, i.e. the ability to solve a problem for which there is no pre-existing pathway connecting two apparently unrelated states in a huge mass of data.

Categories and Subject Descriptors B.0 [GENERAL]

General Terms Performance, Design

Keywords neuromorphic computing; cortical architecture; system-on-chip; dark silicon; non-volatile memory; neuromorphic co-processors and accelerators

Bio

R. Stanley Williams is a Senior Fellow at Hewlett Packard Enterprise. He has received recognition for business, scientific and academic achievement, including being named one of the top 10 visionaries in the field of electronics by EETimes, the 2014 IEEE Outstanding Engineering Manager Award, the 2009 EETimes Innovator of the Year ACE Award, the 2007 Glenn T. Seaborg Medal for contributions to Chemistry, the 50th Anniversary Laureate Lecturer on Electrical and Optical Materials for the TMS, the 2004 Herman Bloch Medal for Industrial Research, the inaugural Scientific American 50 Top Technology leaders in 2002, and the 2000 Julius Springer Award for Applied Physics.

ASPLOS '16, April 02-06, 2016, Atlanta, GA, USA
ACM 978-1-4503-4091-5/16/04.
http://dx.doi.org/10.1145/2872362.2872417

Scaling up Superoptimization

Phitchaya Mangpo Phothilimthana
University of California, Berkeley
mangpo@eecs.berkeley.edu

Aditya Thakur
Google Inc.
avt@google.com

Rastislav Bodik
University of Washington
bodik@cs.washington.edu

Dinakar Dhurjati
Qualcomm Research
dinakard@qti.qualcomm.com

Abstract

Developing a code optimizer is challenging, especially for new, idiosyncratic ISAs. Superoptimization can, in principle, discover machine-specific optimizations automatically by searching the space of all instruction sequences. If we can increase the size of code fragments a superoptimizer can optimize, we will be able to discover more optimizations.

We develop LENS, a search algorithm that increases the size of code a superoptimizer can synthesize by rapidly pruning away invalid candidate programs. Pruning is achieved by selectively refining the abstraction under which candidates are considered equivalent, only in the promising part of the candidate space. LENS also uses a bidirectional search strategy to prune the candidate space from both forward and backward directions. These pruning strategies allow LENS to solve twice as many benchmarks as existing enumerative search algorithms, while LENS is about 11-times faster.

Additionally, we increase the effective size of the superoptimized fragments by relaxing the correctness condition using contexts (surrounding code). Finally, we combine LENS with complementary search techniques into a cooperative superoptimizer, which exploits the stochastic search to make random jumps in a large candidate space, and a symbolic (SAT-solver-based) search to synthesize arbitrary constants. While existing superoptimizers consistently solve 9–16 out of 32 benchmarks, the cooperative superoptimizer solves 29 benchmarks. It can synthesize code fragments that are up to 82% faster than code generated by `gcc -O3` from WiBench and MiBench.

Categories and Subject Descriptors D.1.2 [*Automatic Programming*]: Program Transformation; D.3.4 [*Programming Languages*]: Processors-Optimization

Keywords Superoptimization, Program Synthesis, SMT

ASPLOS '16 April 2–6, 2016, Atlanta, Georgia, USA.
Copyright © 2016 ACM 978-1-4503-4091-5/16/04…$15.00
DOI: http://dx.doi.org/10.1145/http://dx.doi.org/10.1145/2872362.2872387

1. Introduction

Code optimization is more important today than ever before. For example, CERN's internal study demonstrated that using a highly optimizing compiler with profile-guided optimizations increased the power efficiency of its data center by 65% [15]. Another study shows that loop optimizations alone improved energy consumption of applications running on battery-operated portable devices by up to 10 times [16]. Code optimizers may also reduce costs of devices by enabling developers to select lower-power computing resources and smaller memory [7].

Developing a code optimizer still remains a challenging problem. The task of implementing a code optimizer is further exacerbated by the development of different instruction set architectures (ISAs) for different types of processors. For example, ARM alone has over 30 variants of ISAs [35], and new architectures are constantly being developed [8, 10, 12, 19, 22, 29, 36]. Even when compiling for widely-used architectures, like x86 or ARM, compilers may miss some optimizations that human experts can recognize. Many of these optimizations are local and very specific to the architectures. Although the expert developers can specify peephole optimizations in the compilers to perform these local rewrites, they may still miss some optimizations, and their rewrite rules may be buggy [17].

Superoptimization, introduced by Massalin [18], is a program optimization technique that *searches* for a correct and optimal program given an optimality criterion, instead of relying on rewrite rules. Thus, a superoptimizer can be used for automatically generating peephole optimization rules for compilers [5, 11] or optimizing small sequences of instructions produced by compilers on the fly [1, 24, 25]. With this technique, we can avoid buggy human-written rewrite rules and potentially discover even more optimizations. Note that superoptimization subsumes instruction selection, instruction scheduling, and local register allocation. A superoptimizer is shown to optimize a complex multiplication kernel and offer 60% speedup over an optimizing compiler [24].

Our aim is to develop a search technique that can synthesize optimal programs more consistently and faster than existing techniques. We experimented with the most common superoptimization search techniques: symbolic (SAT-solver-based) [27, 31], enumerative [5, 6, 9, 11, 18, 32, 34], and stochastic [24, 25] search. A symbolic search could synthesize arbitrary constants, but it was the slowest. An enumerative search synthesized relatively small programs the fastest, but it could only synthesize up to three ARM instructions within an hour. A sliding window decomposition [20] could scale symbolic and enumerative search to larger programs, but it does not guarantee the optimality of the final output programs. A stochastic search could synthesize larger programs compared to symbolic and enumerative search, but it sometimes could not find the optimal program. This is because a stochastic search can get stuck at local minima.

We develop LENS, an enumerative search algorithm that rapidly prunes away invalid candidate programs. It employs a bidirectional search to prune the search space from both forward and backward directions. It also refines the abstraction under which candidates are considered equivalent selectively via an incremental use of test cases. In our experiment, these pruning techniques increase the number of benchmarks the enumerative search can solve from 11 to 20 (out of 22) and offer 11x reduction on the search time on average.

Although LENS performs better than the existing enumerative algorithms, it still cannot synthesize ARM code with more than five instructions or GreenArrays (GA) [12] code with more than 12 instructions. To scale this search algorithm to synthesize larger code, we introduce a context-aware window decomposition. With this decomposition, our enumerative search can synthesize an optimal (or nearly optimal) ARM program of 16 instructions within 10 minutes.

Optimizing code may require creating new constants or transforming the code fragment globally, which cannot be achieved by the enumerative search with the window decomposition. Thus, we compensate these limitations by combining stochastic and symbolic search into our superoptimizer, yielding a cooperative superoptimizer.

Finally, we develop GREENTHUMB, a framework for constructing superoptimizers for different architectures and testing different search techniques. The framework nicely facilitates testing various search techniques against each other and ensuring they work well for various ISAs. We instantiate GREENTHUMB for two very different ISAs—ARM and GA—for the testing purpose.

This paper makes the following contributions:

- the LENS algorithm, a bidirectional enumerative search with selective refinement (Section 3)
- the context-aware window decomposition, which scales a superoptimization technique that can optimize relatively small programs to larger programs (Section 4)
- the cooperative superoptimizer, which exploits strengths of different search techniques (Section 5)
- GREENTHUMB, a framework for constructing superoptimizers that provides efficient back-end search algorithms and can be extended to new ISAs (Section 6)

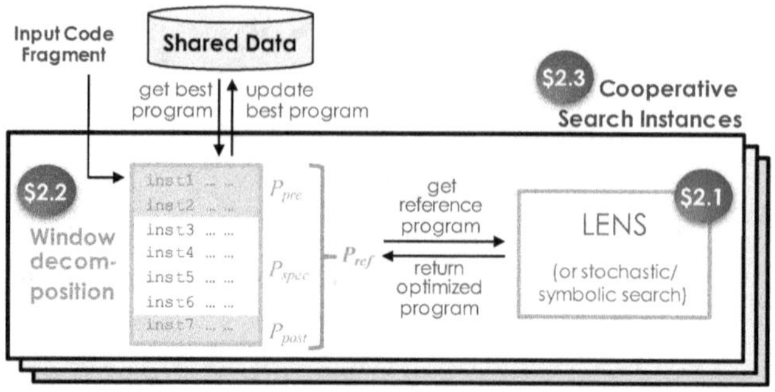

Figure 1. Interaction between the main components in our superoptimizer

2. Overview and Insights

Figure 1 displays the interaction between the LENS algorithm (Section 2.1), the context-aware window decomposition (Section 2.2), and the cooperation of multiple search instances (Section 2.3), which can either employ LENS or different search techniques. The terminology used in this paper is defined as follows.

- A *program* is a sequence of instructions without loops and branches.
- A *reference program* is a program to be optimized.
- A *program state* contains values in the locations of interest such as registers, stacks, and memory.
- A *test input* is a program state that is used for checking correctness (being equivalent to a reference program).
- A *test output* is an expected program state after executing a candidate program on a given test input. A pair of a test input and a test input constitutes a *test case.*
- An *equivalence verification* is a process to verify if a candidate program is equivalent to a reference program on all inputs using a constraint solver.

2.1 Search Technique

A search technique searches for a program that is semantically equivalent to a reference program but faster according to a given performance model. This section provides our insights on how we design our search technique.

2.1.1 Problem Formulation

Let p_{spec} be a program we want to optimize. The set of test inputs $I = (i_1, ..., i_n)$ and test outputs $O = (o_1, ..., o_n)$ can be generated. Each test case (i_k, o_k) is an input-output pair such that $p_{spec}(i_k) = o_k$. We formalize the superoptimization problem as a graph search problem. A node u in the graph represents a vector of n program states. The initial node s represents I, and the goal node t represents O. There is an edge from node u—representing program states $(x_1, ..., x_n)$—to node v—representing program states $(y_1, ..., y_n)$—labeled with an instruction $inst$,

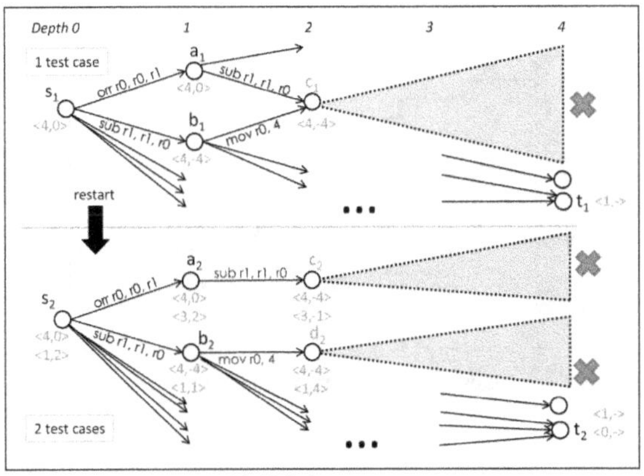

(a) Existing strategy

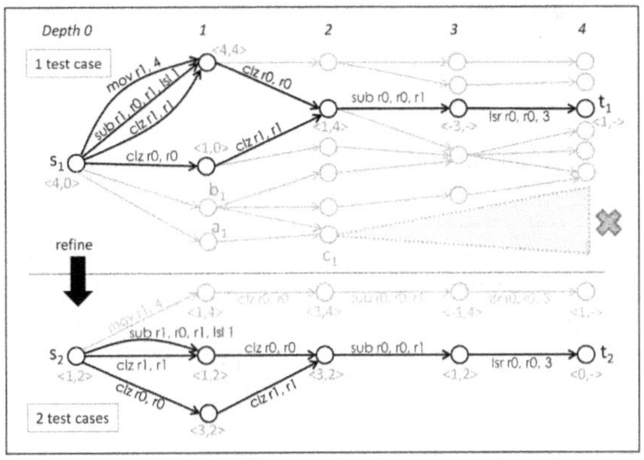

(b) Selective refinement via incremental use of test cases

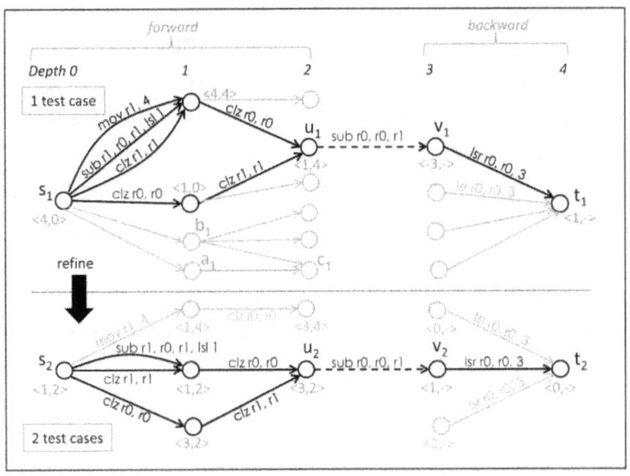

(c) Bidirectional strategy

Figure 2. Search graphs of ARM programs of length 4. In (b) and (c), the highlighted paths are programs that pass the test cases. Assume programs are executed on 4-bit machine.

if $inst(u) = v$, an abbreviation for $\bigwedge_{i=1}^{n} inst(x_i) = y_i$. We use $u \rightsquigarrow v$ to denote a set of all paths from u to v, which represents a set of instruction sequences. A program that passes all n test cases corresponds to a path from s to t. Therefore, the superoptimization problem reduces to searching for a path p from s to t such that $cost(p) < cost(p_{spec})$. We use $q \oplus r$ to denote concatenation of programs q and r.

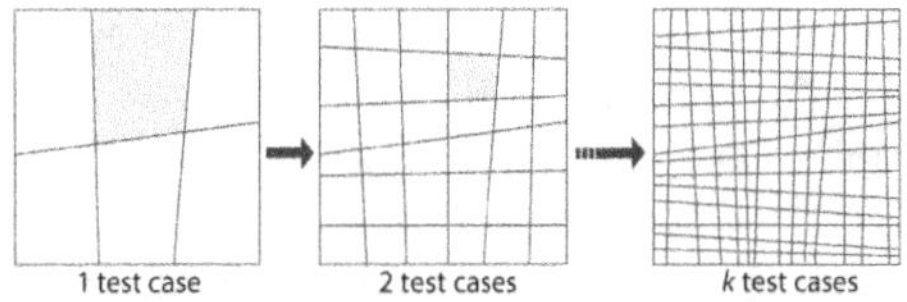

(a) Existing strategy

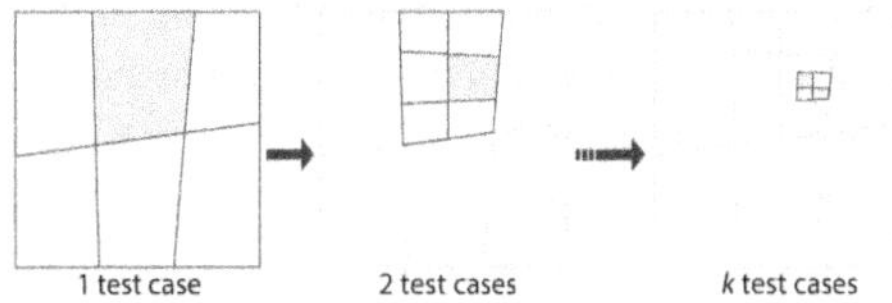

(b) Selective refinement via incremental use of test cases

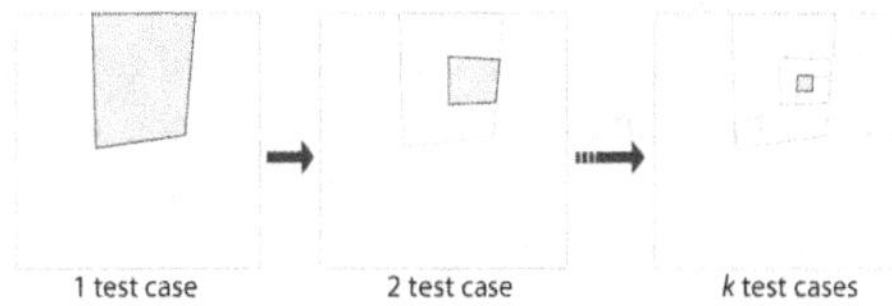

(c) Bidirectional strategy

Figure 3. Division of search space of length d programs. Yellow boxes represent feasible equivalence classes.

2.1.2 Enumerative Search Algorithms

In this section, we illustrate the differences between existing enumerative algorithms and the LENS algorithm. Assume we want to synthesize an ARM program of four instructions using only two registers. A program state is represented by `<r0,r1>`. Figure 2 shows the search graphs constructed by different algorithms, which will be explained in detail.

Existing Algorithms Enumerative algorithms enumerate all possible programs whose cost are less than $cost(p_{spec})$ and search for a program that is equivalent to p_{spec}. The existing successful enumerative program synthesizers [2, 3, 6, 9, 32] apply an *equivalence class* concept, grouping programs into equivalence classes based on their behaviors on a set of test inputs. The search enumerates all possible behaviors, which can be many orders of magnitude fewer than all possible programs. Grouping programs based on a set of test cases is effectively abstracting the search space. The fewer the test cases, the more abstract the equivalence classes are; each equivalence class may contain more programs that are, in fact, not equivalent. Node u in the search graph essentially corresponds to the equivalence class containing programs $s \rightsquigarrow u$, which have the same behavior according to the set of inputs I.

The SIMD synthesizer [6] and the SyGus enumerative solver [3] are enumerative synthesizers that solve similar problems to ours. Both synthesizers use equivalence classes in a similar way to prune the search space. Here, we will explain their pruning strategy using our new formulation. Let p be a program prefix from s to u. The algorithm searches for a program postfix q such that $q(u) = t$. If there is no such q, the search can prune all program prefixes in the same equivalence class as p away. The top part of Figure 2(a) illustrates this idea. $s_1 \rightsquigarrow c_1$ corresponds to programs in the same equivalence class. The algorithm only needs to explore the subgraph rooted at c_1 once to prune away all paths from s_1 to c_1.

We observed two main sources of inefficiency in the existing algorithms. The first source of inefficiency comes from restarts. A restart happens when the search finds a *feasible* program, a program that passes the current set of test cases but is not equivalent to p_{spec}; the abstraction is too coarse. The counterexample generated by a constraint solver is added to the test cases to refine the abstraction, and the search restarts building a new graph from scratch with respect to the updated I and O. Upon restarting, the search *forgets* which programs it has already pruned away, so it revisits them again. Figure 2(a) illustrates that the search revisits its programs from s_1 to c_1 in the new graph. Conceptually, when a new counterexample is found, the algorithm redivides the search space entirely as shown in Figure 3(a). The figure visualizes the space of all programs of size d (four in the example in Figure 2) divided into equivalence classes.

The second source of inefficiency comes from using more test cases than necessary. Consider programs p_1 and p_2 whose behaviors are the same on the first test case but different on the second one. If there is no q such that $(p_1 \oplus q)(I[1]) = O[1]$ with respect to the first test case, the search can also prune away p_2. However, since p_1 and p_2 are not in the same equivalence class because of the second test case, the search does not prune away p_2. Figure 2(a) illustrates that the additional test case splits programs $s_1 \rightsquigarrow c_1$ into two equivalence classes $s_2 \rightsquigarrow c_2$ and $s_2 \rightsquigarrow d_2$, so the search has to traverse the same subgraphs at c_2 and d_2 separately, to find out that both of them cannot reach t_2.

LENS *Algorithm* Our enumerative search does not have the aforementioned inefficiencies. It does not restart the search and uses just enough test cases to prune the search space. More specifically, when a counterexample is found, we build a new search graph according to the next test case only on the programs that pass all previous test cases, as shown in Figure 2(b). The search graph of test case 2 only includes programs that pass test case 1 (the highlighted paths in the search graph of test case 1). Therefore, we never revisit programs from s_1 to c_1. Conceptually, when we find a counterexample, we refine the search by only subdividing the *feasible* equivalence class, as shown in Figure 3(b).

Additionally, we discover that when we search for a program of length d, we can in fact direct the search to a feasible equivalence class without constructing the other equivalence classes of programs of size d, as shown in Figure 3(c). This can be achieved through bidirectional search, which builds the search graph from both s and t, as shown in Figure 2(c).

2.2 Context-aware window decomposition

A context-aware window decomposition scales search techniques that can solve relatively small problems to larger

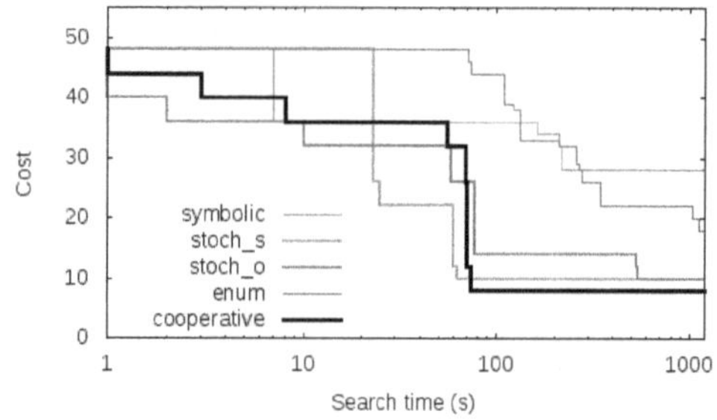

(a) Costs of best programs found over time

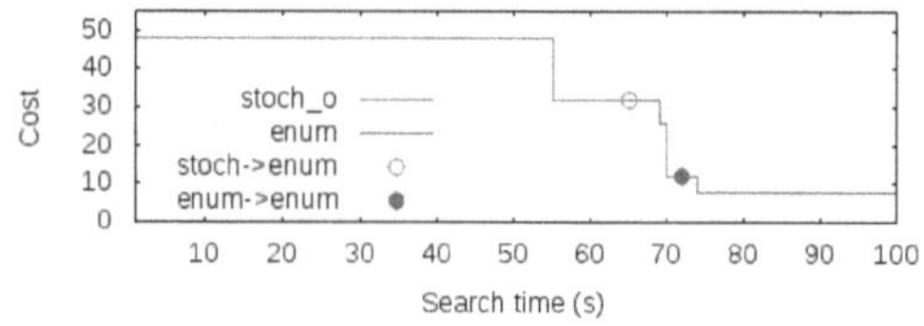

(b) Trace to the best program found by cooperative search. Circles indicate communications between search instances.

Figure 4. Optimizing a sequence of GA instructions from a SHA-256 program. 'stoch_s' is stochastic search that starts from random programs. 'stoch_o' is stochastic search that starts from the correct reference program.

problems without losing much optimality of the final solutions. The key idea is to inform the superoptimizer about the precise precondition and postcondition under which the optimized fragment will be executed. We harvest a precondition and postcondition from a context—code surrounding the code to be optimized—and used them to relax the correctness condition. The decomposition selects a random code fragment p_{spec} in a reference program and optimizes the fragment in the context of the prefix p_{pre} and the postfix p_{post} (as depicted in Figure 1). This process repeats until none of the fragments in the program can be optimized further. Consequently, this decomposition increases the *effective size* of programs that the superoptimizer can synthesize.

2.3 Cooperative search

A cooperative superoptimizer runs multiple search instances of enumerative, stochastic, and symbolic search. The superoptimizer exploits the strengths of all search techniques through communication between search instances, exchanging the best programs they have discovered so far.

To demonstrate the effectiveness of the cooperative superoptimizer, we show how it optimized a GA code fragment from a SHA-256 program. According to Figure 4(a), the cooperative superoptimizer was the only superoptimizer that found the best known code, while being as quick as the stochastic superoptimizer. Although some of the other techniques might seem better at the beginning, the cooperative superoptimizer eventually found the best solution that the other techniques could not; the cooperation costs some overhead but eventually pays off. Note that all supertoptimizers execute the same number of search instances. The detailed descriptions of these five superoptimizers are in Section 7.3.

Figure 4(b) depicts how the cooperative superoptimizer arrived at the best solution. A stochastic instance that started mutating from the correct reference program first found a better solution, so it updated the best program shared between the search instances. An enumerative instance took that newly updated program, applied the context-aware window decomposition, and found two better solutions before another enumerative search instance took the latest best program, applied window decomposition, and found the final best program. Our experiment shows that the cooperative superoptimizer increased the number of benchmarks in which the superoptimizer found best known solutions *consistently* from 23 to 29 (out of 32) over using the enumerative search alone. We define a superoptimizer as *consistent* at solving a benchmark if it found best known solutions in all runs.

3. The LENS Algorithm

In Section 2, we outlined the LENS algorithm's pruning strategies. For the sake of simplification, we assumed that the size of the synthesized program was fixed *a priori*. The complete description provided in this section explains how the algorithm simultaneously grows the program size and refines the search.

3.1 Representation of Search Graphs

Each test case (i_k, o_k) is associated with a forward search graph F_k of program prefixes of length ℓ_F, and a backward search graph B_k of program postfixes of length ℓ_B. The root s_k of F_k is labeled with the input i_k, and the root t_k of B_k is labeled with the output o_k. We store $F_1, ..., F_n$ in the nested map M_F such that $M_F[u_1][u_2]...[u_n]$ returns the set of programs p of length ℓ_F such that $p(i_1) = u_1, p(i_2) = u_2, ..., p(i_n) = u_n$. For example, in the search graphs in Figure 2(c), $M_F[\langle 1,4\rangle][\langle 3,2\rangle]$ maps to three programs: (1) `sub r1, r0, r1, lsl 1; clz r0, r0`, (2) `clz r1, r1; clz r0, r0`, and (3) `clz r0, r0; clz r1, r1`. We use $Progs(M_F)$ to refer to all programs stored inside M_F.

The backward search graphs are stored differently, but to simplify the explanation of our algorithm, let us assume that the backward search graph offers the same interface; there is a map M_B such that $M_B[u_1][u_2] \ldots [u_n]$ returns the set of programs p of length ℓ_B such that $p(u_1) = o_1, p(u_2) = o_2, ..., p(u_n) = o_n$. Our efficient implementation of the backward search graphs is described in Section 3.3.3.

3.2 The Algorithm

Algorithm 1 displays our main algorithm. We first create one test case. Therefore, at the beginning, we start the search from F_1 containing only s_1, and B_1 containing only t_1. Then, the main loop performs two actions—search and expand—in each iteration. The search phase searches for programs of size $\ell_F \ell_B + 1$ that pass all test cases. When the search phase is complete, the expand phase increases the size of programs we will be searching in the next iteration by one. This process repeats until timeout.

Algorithm 1 Main search

```
1:  n ← 1                                          ▷ Number of test cases
2:  ℓ_F ← 0, ℓ_B ← 0
3:  p_spêc ← ReduceBitwidth(p_spec)
4:  cost ← cost(p_spec)
5:  (I, O) ← GenTest(p_spêc)
6:  M_F ← Init(I), M_B ← Goal(O)
7:  while true do
8:      for all inst ∈ Insts do                    ▷ Searching Phase
9:          (M_F, M_B) ← Connect(M_F, M_B, inst, 1)
10:     if Forward?(ℓ_F, ℓ_B) then                 ▷ Expanding Phase
11:         M_F ← ExpandForward(M_F), ℓ_F ← ℓ_F + 1
12:     else
13:         M_B ← ExpandBackward(M_B), ℓ_B ← ℓ_B + 1
```

Algorithm 2 Connect and refine

```
Global variables: I, O, cost, n, p_spec, p_spêc
function CONNECT(M_F, M_B, inst, k)
    if k > n then                                  ▷ Pass all test cases
        for all p ∈ M_F, p' ∈ M_B do               ▷ M_F, M_B are sets of programs
            if cost(p ⊕ inst ⊕ p') < cost then
                Verify(p ⊕ inst ⊕ p')
                                                   ▷ Build search graph on test case k
    if M_F is not a map then                       ▷ M_F is a set of programs
        M_F ← BuildForward(M_F, I[k])
    if M_B is not a map then                       ▷ M_B is a set of programs
        M_B ← BuildBackward(M_B, O[k])

    for all u ∈ keys(M_F) do                       ▷ Search for a connection
        v ← inst(u)
        if v ∈ keys(M_B) then                      ▷ Find a connection, so refine the search
            (M_F[u], M_B[v]) ←
Connect(M_F[u], M_B[v], inst, k + 1)
    return (M_F, M_B)

function VERIFY(p̂)
    if p̂ ≡ p_spêc then                            ▷ Check via a constraint solver
        for all p ∈ IncreaseBitwidth(p̂) do
            if p ≡ p_spec then                     ▷ Found a better program!
                cost ← cost(p)
                yield p
    else
        n ← n + 1
        (I[n], O[n]) ← CounterExample(p_spêc, p̂)
```

The expanding phase (on line 10–13) increases the size of programs by expanding all leaf nodes of either F_1 or B_1. *Forward?* is a heuristic function that decides whether to expand forward or backward. In particular, we expand each leaf node u in F_1 by adding $u \xrightarrow{inst} v$ for all $inst \in Insts$, where $Insts$ is a set of all possible instructions. Similarly, we expand each leaf node v in B_1 backward by adding $u \xrightarrow{inst} v$ for all $inst \in Insts$.

The searching phase (on line 7–9) find programs that pass all n test cases by finding an instruction that can connect leaf nodes in $F_1, ..., F_n$ to leaf nodes in $B_1, ..., B_n$ respectively. The main algorithm calls *Connect* to find such programs. $Connect(M_F, M_B, inst, k)$, shown in Algorithm 2, searches for programs in $Progs(M_F) \oplus inst \oplus Progs(M_B)$ that pass test cases k to n. It maintains the invariant that all programs in $Progs(M_F) \oplus inst \oplus Progs(M_B)$ pass all test cases 1 to $k - 1$. This invariant is the key to refining the search only on a feasible equivalence class.

After F_k and B_k are built, the loop on lines 12–15 searches for a leaf node u in F_k and v in B_k that can be connected by $inst$. $keys(M_F)$ and $keys(M_B)$ on line 12 and 14 are sets of leaf nodes in F_k and B_k. If $inst$ can connect u to v, programs in $Progs(M_F[u]) \oplus inst \oplus Progs(M_B[v])$ pass test case k, so the algorithm refines the search on $Progs(M_F[u]) \oplus inst \oplus Progs(M_B[v])$ with the next test case $k + 1$. For our running example in Figure 2(c), we find an instruction `sub r0, r0, r1` connecting u_1 and v_1 of test case 1, so we refine the search on the highlighted programs $s_1 \rightsquigarrow u_1 \rightarrow v_1 \rightsquigarrow t_1$.

When we recursively call *Connect*, M_F will eventually become a set of programs instead of a nested map, as well as M_B. Lines 7–10 take care of building F_k for programs in M_F and B_k for programs in M_B. F_k and B_k for each k are built once and saved on line 15 to be used later when *Connect* is called with different $inst$s. If there are no more test case left, lines 2–5 verify all programs in $M_F \oplus inst \oplus M_B$ against the reference program. *Verify* function performs equivalence verification. If the two programs are not equivalent, an counterexample is added to I and O on line 25. If they are equivalent, the algorithm yields the candidate program and continues searching for solutions with lower costs until timeout.

3.3 Implementation Details

3.3.1 Challenges of Backward Search

We have identified two main challenges in implementing backward search in a program synthesizer. First, the synthesizer needs to evaluate an instruction backward; it needs an inverse function for every instruction. Second, in the forward direction, an instruction $inst$ is a one-to-one function that map a state u to v. In contrast, in the backward direction, $inst$ is a one-to-many function that map the state v to a set of states, one of which is u.

Fortunately, we can mitigate these challenges by reducing bitwidth, using only four bits to represent a value. First, we can avoid implementing an inverse emulator by constructing an inverse function table for every instruction. We execute every instruction on all possible combinations of 4-bit input arguments' values and memorize them in the inverse table. Second, the small bitwidth also reduces the number of states an instruction can transition to in the backward direction. For example, in 32-bit domain, an inverse instruction *add* transitions from one state to 2^{32} states; in contrast, in 4-bit domain, the same instruction only transitions to 2^4 states.

3.3.2 Reduced Bitwidth

Let bit be the actual bitwidth and $\hat{bit}$ be the reduced bitwidth, which is four in our case. The reduced bitwidth not only enables the backward search but also allows us to initially divide the search space more coarsely, which is desirable because the search graph even for a single test can be very large. For example, an ISA with four 32-bit registers can have $2^{32\times4}$ states and, hence, up to $2^{32\times4}$ nodes in the graph.

Apart from the second-step equivalence verification (line 20 of Algorithm 2), the search algorithm operates in the reduce-bitwidth domain. Therefore, we need both reduced-bitwitdh and precise versions of a program state and an ISA emulator. We implement an emulator that can be parameterized by bitwidth to instantiate both versions. For example, the precise ARM emulator interprets instruction `movt r0, 1` as writing 1 to the top 16 bits of a 32-bit register. The 4-bit ARM emulator should interpret the same instruction as writing 1 to the top 2 bits of a 4-bit register. Implementing a parameterizable program state is simple. We just need to use a specified number of bits to represent each entry in a program state.

Additionally, we must have a way to convert programs between the two domains. In particular, at the beginning, we convert the reference program p_{ref} from the precise domain to the reduced-bitwidth domain (line 3 in Algorithm 1) by replacing constants appearing in the program with their reduced-bitwidth counterparts. We replace a constant c using the following function α:

$$\hat{c} = \alpha(c) = \begin{cases} \hat{bit} & \text{if } shift?(c) \wedge (c = bit) \\ \hat{bit} - 1 & \text{if } shift?(c) \wedge (c = bit - 1) \\ \hat{bit}/2 & \text{if } shift?(c) \wedge (bit/2 \leq c < bit - 1) \\ 1 & \text{if } shift?(c) \wedge (1 < c < bit/2) \\ c \bmod 2^{\hat{bit}} & \text{otherwise} \end{cases}$$

where $shift?(c)$ checks if c is a shift operand. α is designed to preserve semantics of shift operations in a meaningful way. For example, it translates shift by 31 in 32-bit domain to shift by 3 in 4-bit domain. Apart from shift constants, α simply masks in the lowest $\hat{bit}$ bits.

During this conversion, we memorize every replacement of c with $\hat{c}$, so that we can map each reduced-bitwidth constants back to the set of original constants to obtain candidate programs in the precise domain. We construct the replacement map γ by storing $\gamma[\hat{c}] \leftarrow \gamma[\hat{c}] \cup \{c\}$ for every constant c in p_{ref}. Before the precise equivalence verification, the reduced-bitwidth constant $\hat{c}$ is replaced with every constant in the set $\gamma[\hat{c}]$ (line 19 in Algorithm 2) with the expectation that one of them will lead to a correct solution.

We are able to optimize many bitwidth-sensitive programs (e.g. population count and computing higher-order half of multiplication) using this reduced-bitwidth trick.

3.3.3 Data Structure for Backward Search Graph

We could store backward search graphs the same way we store forward search graphs. However, it would require a

Routine	Non-context-aware	Context-aware
Equivalence verification	$p_{spec} \equiv p$	$p_{pre} \oplus p_{spec} \oplus p_{post} \equiv p_{pre} \oplus p \oplus p_{post}$
Input text-cases update	$I = I \cup \{i_{ce}\}$	$I = I \cup \{p_{pre}(i_{ce})\}$
Output text-cases update	$O = O \cup \{p_{spec}(i_{ce})\}$	$O = O \cup \{p_{pre} \oplus p_{spec}(i_{ce})\}$

Table 1. The differences between non-context-aware and context-aware decomposition. p is a candidate program. i_{ce} is the input counterexample returned by the constraint solver if the candidate program is not equivalent to the reference program.

large amount of memory because in the backward direction, an instruction is a one-to-many function; one program postfix can appear in a large number of backward equivalence classes. Instead of using a nested map to store all backward search graphs, we construct n separate maps to store n backward search graphs $B_1, ..., B_n$. We can find a program postfix p such that $p(u_1) = o_1, ..., p(u_n) = o_n$, by looking up $Y[u_1] \cap ... \cap Y[u_n]$. The pseudocode in Algorithm 1 and Algorithm 2 has to be modified slightly to support this data structure.

4. Context-Aware Window Decomposition

We can scale a search technique that can synthesize relatively small programs to optimize larger programs using a decomposition. Let p_{ref} be a large program to be optimized, and L be a window size. We can decompose p_{ref} into $p_{pre} \oplus p_{spec} \oplus p_{post}$ such that $length(p_{spec}) < L$, and optimize p_{spec}, the code inside the window. Peephole optimizations will try to optimized p_{spec} alone, or in the best scenario, with a precondition that is often not precise. The precondition and postcondition relax the correctness condition and provide invariants that may be exploited by the search. Therefore, we believe that optimizing p_{spec} with the most precise precondition and postcondition, essentially in the context of its prefix p_{pre} and postfix p_{post}, can lead to finding a better program. We call this decomposition a *context-aware window decomposition*. In our implementation, we pick a random position of the window and optimize the program. This process repeats until we cannot optimize the program at any window's position anymore.

To support the context-aware decomposition, we need to modify search algorithms slightly. Note that any search technique can be modified to be context-aware. Recall that a search technique looks for a program p such that for each $i \in I, o \in O \,.\, p(i) = o$. To make the search context-aware, we do not need to change this search routine, but only need to adjust the equivalence condition used during equivalence verification and the way test cases are updated as shown in Table 1. Normally, when we find p that passes all test cases, we uses a constraint solver to verify if $p_{spec} \equiv p$. If they are not equivalent, the constraint solver will return an input counterexample i_{ce}, which we use to update the test inputs I and test outputs O as shown in Column 'non-context-aware'. Then, the search continues to find a new candidate program, and so on. To make the search context-aware, we ask the constraint solver if p is equivalent to p_{spec} in the context of p_{pre} and p_{post}, in particular if $p_{pre} \oplus p_{spec} \oplus p_{post} \equiv p_{pre} \oplus p \oplus p_{post}$. If they are not equivalent, the constraint solver will return i_{ce}, which is an input to p_{pre} (not directly to p), so we have to update the test cases differently as shown in Column 'context-aware'.

Concrete Example

Assume we want to optimize the following ARM program:

```
P_pre:  cmp r3, r4
        moveq r1, #0        // mov if r3 = r4
        movne r1, #1        // mov if r3 != r4
P_spec: cmp r2, #31
        movhi r1, #0        // mov if r2 > 31
        andls r1, r1, #1    // and if r2 <= 31
```

The decomposition selects the window as labeled; p_{post} is empty. Without p_{pre}, p_{spec} cannot be improved because no faster code modifies `r1` as p_{spec} does. With p_{pre}, however, the superoptimizer learns that the value of `r1` is either 0 or 1 at the beginning of p_{spec}, so the last instruction `r1 = r1 & 1` does not have any effect. Thus, the superoptimizer can simply remove it. Note that we do not have to explicitly infer this precondition of p_{spec}. It is implicit, captured by running p_{pre} along with p_{spec} during test case evaluations and equivalence verification. We also find that p_{post} helps the superoptimizer discover faster code.

5. Cooperative Superoptimizer

To utilize strengths of different search techniques, we introduce a cooperative superoptimizer that combines all search techniques in a simple fashion. The cooperative superoptimizer launches all search techniques in parallel and may run more than one search instance of each search technique.

5.1 Terminology

This section defines the terminology and symbols of variations of different search techniques used in the rest of the paper. The base search algorithms are symbolic (SM), stochastic (ST), and enumerative (E). There are two modes of search. Synthesize mode (s) is when a search does not use a starting correct program except for equivalence verification. Optimize mode (o) is when a search uses a starting correct program beyond equivalence verification. The table below summarizes the symbols we use.

Symbol	Description
E^s	enumerative on entire code fragment
E^o	enumeratvie with decomposition
SM^s	symbolic on entire code fragment
SM^o	symbolic with decomposition
ST^s	stochastic that starts from a random program
ST^o	stochastic that starts from the input correct program

5.2 Communication between Search Instances

The search instances aid each other by exchanging information about the current best solution equivalent to p_{ref}. When a search instance finds a new best program, it updates the shared best solution p_{best}. The other search instances may obtain p_{best} to aid in their search processes. In particular, different types of search techniques utilize p_{best} as follows:

- E^s and SM^s do not use p_{best}.
- E^o and SM^o apply the context-aware window decomposition on p_{best}.
- ST^s reduce its search space by only exploring programs with up to $length(p_{best})$ instructions.
- ST^o restarts the search from p_{best}. In practice, it is better to allow some divergence among stochastic instances. Therefore, our stochastic instances check p_{best} every 10,000 mutations and restart the search from p_{best} only if $cost(p_{best})$ is much less than the cost of the local best solution; in our implementation, we restart when the difference is more than 5.

5.3 Practical Configuration of Search Instances

We present a configuration for allocating search instances that worked well in our experiment; however, it might not be optimal. Our cooperative superoptimizer executes N search instances with the following distributions: $N/2 - 1$ E^o, one E^s, two ST^s, three ST^o, and the rest for SM^o. We dedicate almost half of the threads for enumerative search because it performs the best in most benchmarks (see Section 7.1). Multiple enumerative instances attempt to optimize different parts of the program at the same time, reducing overall search time to find a final solution. We allocate one thread for E^s because if the size of the final solution is small, E^s will find an optimal solution quickly. A few ST^s instances are allocated because they can perform very well on some benchmarks on which E performs poorly. We also dedicate a few threads for ST^o instances because they often help E^o instances reach the final solution faster. Finally, we allocate the rest of the resources to SM^o, which helps discover optimizations that involve synthesizing arbitrary constants. For search instances that use the window decomposition, we use four sizes of window L, $2L$, $3L$, and $4L$, where L is a constant specific to the ISA.

6. Implementation

We develop GREENTHUMB [21], a framework for building superoptimizers for different ISAs and testing search techniques. We define the semantics of an ISA by implementing an ISA emulator in Rosette [30], which is built on top of Racket. The enumerative and stochastic search uses the emulator to execute a sequence of instructions on concrete program states. Additionally, since the emulator is written in Rosette, we also obtain, for free, (i) the program equivalence verifier, and (ii) the symbolic search for that particular ISA.

We instantiate GREENTHUMB to build superoptimizers for two very different ISAs.

ARM is a RISC architecture that is widely used in many devices. We implement a superoptimizer for ARMv7-A and model the performance cost function based on ARM Cortex-A9 [4]. An ARM program state includes 32-bit registers, memory, and condition flags. The default instruction representation provided by GREENTHUMB, which includes opcode and operands, is extended to support ARM instructions by including a condition code suffix and optional shift. We also extend GREENTHUMB's stochastic search by adding new mutation rules: mutating condition code, and mutating optional shift. The smallest window size L is set to 2. Recall that there are four sizes of window L, $2L$, $3L$, and $4L$.

GreenArrays GA144 is a low-power processor, composed of many small cores [12]. It is a stack-based 18-bit processor. Each core has two registers, two small stacks, and memory. Each core can communicate with its neighbors using read and write instructions. The program state for GA includes registers, stacks, memory, and a communication channel, similar to the one used in the superoptimizer in Chlorophyll [20]. A communication channel is an ordered list of (data, neighbor port, read/write) tuples representing the data that the core receives and sends. For two programs to be equivalent, their communication channels have to be identical. Only one GA instruction, fetch-immediate, has an operand, which is for specifying the immediate constant value, so we extend the stochastic search to mutate an operand only for that opcode. We set the smallest window size L to 7. We model the performance cost based on GA144's instruction timing [12].

Limitations

We do not model memory access latency variations caused by misses at different levels of caches. We assign the same cost to all loads and stores. Therefore, our performance model is imprecise; as a result the superoptimizer may output a program that is actually slower than other candidates it has explored. To work around this problem, the superoptimizer can output the best ten programs instead of only the best one. This way, we can try running all of them on the real machine and select the fastest one empirically.

The second limitation is that the superoptimizer can only optimize code without loops and branches. In order to optimize across multiple basic blocks with loops and branches, we will need to modify the superoptimizer.

7. Experimental Evaluation

Our key result is that we improve on the state of the art in superoptimization, represented by STOKE [24, 25], the stochastic superoptimizer. On large benchmarks, our implementation of STOKE produced ARM programs of length 10–27 and GA programs of length 18–32. Our cooperative superoptimizer optimized the benchmarks faster (12x faster on average) and obtained better solutions (the performance cost of our code is, on average, 18% lower than that of stochastic search).

We implemented all search techniques as well as ARM and GA emulators in our framework using Racket. Since all search techniques are implemented in the same language and using the same emulator, we can compare them fairly. As discussed in Section 7.5, we tried to make a fair comparison between all search techniques.

This section presents detailed evaluation of our algorithms, starting from the new enumerative algorithm, using the following benchmark suites.

ARM Hacker's Delight Benchmarks consist of 16 of the 25 programs identified by [13] drawn from Hacker's Delight [33]. We excluded the first nine programs from our set of benchmarks because they are very small. We used code produced by `gcc -march=armv7-a -O0` as the input programs to the superoptimizers. Their sizes ranged from 16 to 60 instructions. The timeout was set to one hour.

GA Benchmarks consist of frequently-executed basic blocks from MD5, SHA-256, FIR, sine, and cosine functions from the Chlorophyll compiler's benchmarks [20]. We used Chlorophyll without superoptimization to generate these basic blocks. The sizes of the input programs in this benchmark suite ranged from 10 to 56 instructions. The timeout was set to 20 minutes.

7.1 Experiment I: Evaluating the LENS algorithm

Experiment I is designed to evaluate the base search techniques: SM^s, E^s, and ST^s. Recall that superscript ^{s} indicates synthesize mode (no window decomposition). This experiment will help us answer which search technique is a suitable building block for a superoptimizer with window decomposition. For each benchmark, we ran each search technique on a single thread 16 times.

Hypothesis A *Enumerative search is faster and can solve larger benchmarks than the other base search techniques.*

E^s is superior in terms of speed and scalability: it was the fastest search; it solved all except two benchmarks; and it could solve larger benchmarks than other synthesizers. Regarding consistency—which is desirable because it obviates the need for redundant instances, improving the chances of finding optimal solutions—almost all of E^s 16 search instances found optimal solutions in each of its solved benchmarks. Note that there is small amount of randomness in the enumerative search because the initial test cases are generated randomly.

There were a total of 22 benchmarks in which one of the search techniques found optimal solutions in at least one of the 16 runs. Columns SM^s, E^s, and ST^s of Figure 5 summarize the results. Figure 5(a) displays the number of benchmarks *solved* by each search technique, categorized by size. A search technique *solved* a benchmark if it an optimal solution in one of its run. Row 'benchmarks' in Figure 5(b) summarizes the numbers of solved benchmarks. Row 'instances' displays the average numbers of search instances that found optimal solutions per solved benchmark. In terms of search time, we evaluated each search technique against E^s by comparing the best runs of the benchmarks they both solved. Row 'E^s speedup' shows how much faster E^s was on average compared to a particular search technique.

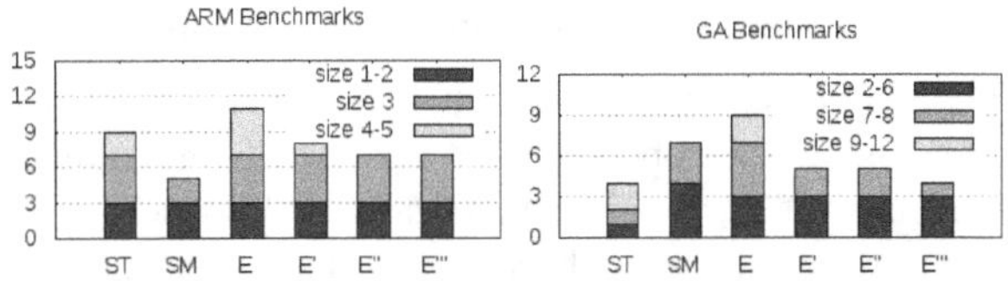

(a) Number of solved benchmarks, categorized by size

Solved	ST^s	SM^s	E^s	$E^{s\prime}$	$E^{s\prime\prime}$	$E^{s\prime\prime\prime}$
Benchmarks	13	12	20	13	12	11
Instances	7.2	13.5	14.9	15.8	15.5	15.9
E^s speedup	14x	52x	1x	2.7x	5.2x	11x

(b) Total number of solved benchmarks, average number of instances per solved benchmark, and search time speedup by E^s

Figure 5. Comparing base search techniques

According to Figure 5(a), E^s could synthesize larger ARM programs than ST^s and SM^s could. For GA, E^s could synthesize larger programs than SM^s could. While E^s and ST^s were comparable at synthesizing large GA programs, ST^s was much worse at synthesizing smaller GA programs. This might be because the cost function of ST^s does not fit well with these GA benchmarks, or the mutations we have are not the best for GA. Interestingly, the largest GA benchmark, which E^s failed to solve, was solved by ST^s. This result suggests that sometimes the cost function can be very effective in guiding the search in some particular problems. Another benchmark that E^s failed to solve can be solved by SM^s. This is because the optimal program contains a constant not included in the pre-defined constant list of E^s and ST^s.

Hypothesis B *The* LENS *algorithm improves on the existing enumerative algorithms.*

With the same experimental setting, we compared multiple versions of enumerative search:

- E^s: LENS with all pruning strategies
- $E^{s\prime}$: E^s without backward search (unidirectional search)
- $E^{s\prime\prime}$: $E^{s\prime}$ without reduced-bitwidth trick
- $E^{s\prime\prime\prime}$: $E^{s\prime\prime}$ without refinement through incremental test cases. $E^{s\prime\prime\prime}$ represents the existing enumerative search but without the stack representation [6].

Columns E^s–$E^{s\prime\prime\prime}$ of Figure 5 summarizes the results. The pruning strategies we introduce not only increase the size of code an enumerative search can solve but also speed up the search; E^s was, on average, 11x faster than $E^{s\prime\prime\prime}$.

7.2 Experiment II: Evaluating window decomposition

Experiment II is designed to test the effectiveness of context-aware window decomposition. We test E^o, which is context-aware, against a modified version of E^o, which is not context-aware, on the 12 benchmarks that E^s cannot synthesize optimal solutions from the previous experiment. Recall that the superscript ^{o} indicates optimize mode (see Section 5.1). On ARM benchmarks, we ran a superoptimizer using 32 E^o search instances on a 16-core hyper-threaded machine. On GA benchmarks, we ran 16 search instances on a 16-core Amazon EC2 machine. For each benchmark, we repeated the experiment three times.

Hypothesis C *The context-aware window decomposition technique enables the enumerative search to find better code than does the non-context-aware window decomposition.*

Considering the best out of the three runs, in six benchmarks, the context-aware decomposition found solutions with 1.3x–3x lower cost than did the non-context-aware decomposition. In the rest, both of them found solutions with the same costs.

7.3 Experiment III: Evaluating cooperative search

Experiment III is designed to evaluate superoptimizers based on different search techniques with context-aware window decomposition. We use the same experimental set up as in Section 7.2. We evaluate the following five versions of superoptimizers, each of which runs N search instances ($N = 32$ for ARM, and $N = 16$ for GA).

Superoptimizer	Search instances used
$\widetilde{ST}^s$	all ST^s instances with no communication
$\widetilde{ST}^o$	all ST^o instances with no communication
$\widetilde{SM}$	one SM^s instance, $N-1$ SM^o instances
$\widetilde{E}$	one E^s instance, $N-1$ E^o instances
$\widetilde{C}$	one E^s, $N/2-1$ E^o, two ST^s, three ST^o, and the rest for SM^o instances

Search instances of each superoptimizer communicate with each other except in $\widetilde{ST}^s$ and $\widetilde{ST}^o$, which represent STOKE implemented in our framework. In $\widetilde{E}$, $\widetilde{SM}$, and $\widetilde{C}$, we add one instance of an enumerative or symbolic search in synthesize mode (E^s or SM^s) because these instances can find an optimal solution should the optimal solution be small.

Hypothesis D *The enumerative superoptimizer can often synthesize best known programs more consistently and faster than the stochastic and symbolic superoptimizers.*

$\widetilde{E}$ was *consistent* on 2.1x, 2.6x, and 1.4x more benchmarks than $\widetilde{ST}^s$, $\widetilde{ST}^o$, and $\widetilde{SM}$. We define a superoptimizer as *consistent* at solving a benchmark if it found programs as optimal as the best known solution in all runs. Consistency is desirable because in practice we want to find the best program in one run not multiple runs. Then, we did a pair-wise comparison of the median search time between $\widetilde{E}$ and each of the other superoptimizers on the benchmarks they both solved consistently. We found that $\widetilde{E}$ was also on average 9x, 4.6x, and 14x faster than $\widetilde{ST}^s$, $\widetilde{ST}^o$, and $\widetilde{SM}$.

Figure 6 shows the performance costs of the best correct programs found in each of three runs; the lower the better. The reported costs of each benchmarks are normalized by the cost of the best known program of that particular benchmark. Table 2 reports the median time to finding the best known solutions for the various superoptimizers. If a superoptimizer did not find a program as optimal as the best known solution on one or more runs on a benchmark, the table excludes that corresponding entry.

Hypothesis E *The cooperative superoptimizer improves on the enumerative superoptimizer by utilizing the strengths of other search techniques.*

We compare $\widetilde{C}$ and $\widetilde{E}$. While $\widetilde{E}$ uses only enumerative search instances, $\widetilde{C}$ uses enumerative as well as symbolic and stochastic search instances. According to the result, $\widetilde{C}$ was consistent at finding best known solutions on 29 out of 32 benchmarks, while $\widetilde{E}$ was consistent on 23 benchmarks. $\widetilde{C}$ and $\widetilde{E}$ were comparable in term of search time; $\widetilde{C}$ was 33% faster, on average. Columns $\widetilde{C}$ of Figure 6 and Table 2 display the costs of the best correct programs found by $\widetilde{C}$ and its median time to find the best known solutions for all benchmarks. Compared to the algorithm used in the state-of-the-art superoptimizer (STOKE), $\widetilde{C}$ was, on average, 12x faster than the best of $\widetilde{ST}^s$ and $\widetilde{ST}^o$. The performance cost of code produced by $\widetilde{C}$ is, on average, 18% lower than that of the best from $\widetilde{ST}^s$ and $\widetilde{ST}^o$.

We also tested $\widetilde{C}'''$—the cooperative superoptimizer with the enumerative search without our pruning strategies—to examine how much the performance of the enumerative instances affect the performance of the cooperative superoptimizer. Columns $\widetilde{C}'''$ of Figure 6 and Table 2 display the costs of the best correct programs found by $\widetilde{C}'''$ and its median time to find the best known solutions. According to the result, $\widetilde{C}'''$ could not consistently solve seven benchmarks that $\widetilde{C}$ could. Hence, we conclude that our pruning strategies in the enumerative search are crucial for obtaining the best performance out of the cooperative superoptimizer.

7.4 Experiment IV: Runtime speedup over `gcc -O3`

Experiment IV is designed to test the effectiveness of the cooperative superoptimizer against an optimizing compiler. We measure the execution time of all benchmarks in this experiment on an actual ARM Cortex-A9.

Hypothesis F *Cooperative superoptimizer can optimize code generated from a non-optimizing compiler and obtain code as fast as generated from an optimizing compiler.*

From the experiment in Section 7.3, $\widetilde{C}$ optimized code generated from `gcc -O0` and produced code as fast as `gcc -O3` code for all ARM benchmarks. In fact, $\widetilde{C}$ found faster code than those generated from `gcc -O3` on five benchmarks. One of them is 17.8x faster. Thus, for the new architectures for which we do not have good optimizing compilers, our superoptimizer can help generating efficient code.

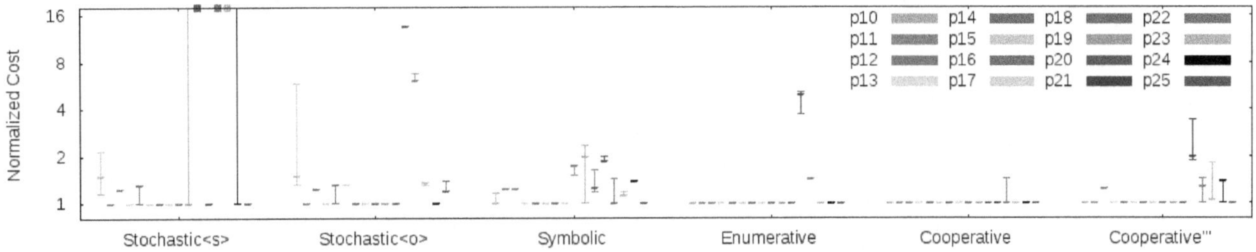

(a) ARM Hacker's Delight Benchmarks

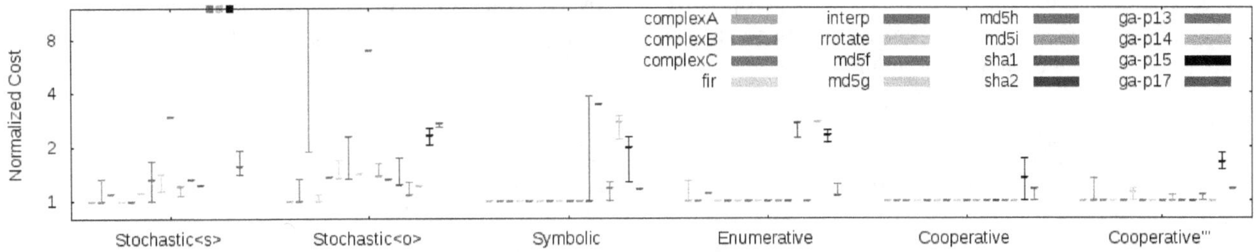

(b) GA Benchmarks

Figure 6. Costs of best programs found by the different superoptimizers (normalized by the cost of the best known program). A **dash** represents the cost of the best program found in one run. A dash may represent more than one run if the best programs found in different runs have the same cost. If one or two runs did not find any correct program that is better than the input program, the vertical line is extended past the chart. If none of the runs found a correct program that is better than the input program, a **rectangle** is placed at the top of of the chart.

(a) ARM Hacker's Delight Benchmarks

Benchmarks	$\widetilde{ST}^s$	$\widetilde{ST}^o$	$\widetilde{SM}$	$\widetilde{E}$	$\widetilde{C}$	$\widetilde{C}'''$
p10	-	-	-	145	**88**	188
p11	244	188	-	**49**	92	1171
p12	-	-	-	**566**	646	-
p13	13	6	85	3	3	**2**
p14	-	-	755	19	11	**9**
p15	837	-	591	26	**8**	**8**
p16	**5**	**5**	83	-	7	6
p17	15	12	82	11	**6**	72
p18	21	38	-	**7**	9	89
p19	-	**21**	-	76	36	49
p20	-	254	-	129	**113**	365
p21	1316	-	-	-	**1139**	-
p22	-	-	-	-	-	-
p23	-	-	-	707	**665**	-
p24	-	1440	-	**73**	151	-
p25	72	-	47	2	2	**1**

(b) GA Benchmarks

Benchmarks	$\widetilde{ST}^s$	$\widetilde{ST}^o$	$\widetilde{SM}$	$\widetilde{E}$	$\widetilde{C}$	$\widetilde{C}'''$
complexA	**45**	258	136	-	72	63
complexB	-	-	186	**43**	52	-
complexC	-	-	**7**	-	21	17
fir	**7**	-	501	153	23	63
interp	119	-	109	12	**7**	22
rrotate	-	-	104	108	**92**	-
md5f	-	-	832	97	71	**34**
md5g	-	-	1078	206	**163**	259
md5h	-	-	44	2	**1**	**1**
md5i	-	-	690	549	**520**	-
sha1	-	-	-	**20**	24	178
sha2	-	-	-	-	**179**	214
ga-p13	-	-	-	**27**	127	-
ga-p14	-	-	-	-	**187**	281
ga-p15	-	-	-	-	-	-
ga-p17	-	-	-	-	-	-

Table 2. Median time in seconds to reach best known programs. "-" indicates that the superoptimizer failed to find a best known program in one or more runs. Bold denotes the fastest superoptimizer to find a best known program in each benchmark.

Hypothesis G *Cooperative superoptimizer can further optimize real-world code generated by an optimizing compiler.*

We compiled *WiBench* [37] (a kernel suite for benchmarking wireless systems) and *MiBench* [14] (an embedded benchmark suite) using `gcc -O3` for ARM. We extracted basic blocks from the compiled assembly and selected 13 basic blocks that contain more than seven instructions and have more data processing than load/store instructions. For six out of 13 code fragments, $\widetilde{C}$ found faster fragments compared to those generated by `gcc -O3`, offering up to 82% speedup.

Table 3 summarizes characteristics of the program fragments found by $\widetilde{C}$ that are faster than those generated by `gcc -O3`. Column 'runtime speedup' reports how much faster the fragments are when running on an actual ARM processor. The last column demonstrates that different base search techniques contribute to finding the best solutions in many benchmarks. For example, in the `wi-txrate5a` benchmark from WiBench's rate matcher kernel, a SM^o instance first optimized the input program, and then a ST^o instance optimized the program found by the SM^o instance and arrived at the best known solution. In `mi-bitshift` from MiBench's

Optimization 1

before (a):
```
cmp    r1, #0
mov    r3, r1, asr #31
add    r2, r1, #7
mov    r3, r3, lsr #29
movge  r2, r1
ldrb   r0, [r0, r2, asr #3]
add    r1, r1, r3
and    r1, r1, #7
sub    r3, r1, r3
asr    r1, r0, r3
and    r0, r0, #1
```

after (b):
```
cmp    r1, #0
mov    r3, r1, asr #31
add    r2, r1, #7
mov    r3, r3, lsr #29
movge  r2, r1
ldrb   r0, [r0, r2, asr #3]
bic    r1, r2, #248
sub    r3, r1, r3
asr    r1, r0, r3
and    r0, r1, #1
```

Optimization 2

before (b):
```
cmp    r1, #0
mov    r3, r1, asr #31
add    r2, r1, #7
mov    r3, r3, lsr #29
movge  r2, r1
ldrb   r0, [r0, r2, asr #3]
bic    r1, r2, #248
sub    r3, r1, r3
asr    r1, r0, r3
and    r0, r1, #1
```

after (c):
```
asr    r3, r1, #2
add    r2, r1, r3, lsr #29
ldrb   r0, [r0, r2, asr #3]
and    r3, r2, #248
sub    r3, r1, r3
asr    r1, r0, r3
and    r0, r1, #1
```

Figure 7. Optimizations that the cooperative superoptimizer discovered when optimizing `mi-bitarray` benchmark. Blue highlights the difference between before and after each optimization. (a) is the original program. (b) is the intermediate program. (c) is the final optimized program.

Program	gcc -O3 length	Output length	Search time (s)	Speed -up	Path to best code
p18	7	4	9	2.11	E^s
p21	6	5	1139	1.81	E^o*, SM^o*, ST^o*
p23	18	16	665	1.48	$ST^o* \rightarrow E^o*$
p24	7	4	151	2.75	$ST^o* \rightarrow E^o* \rightarrow ST^o \rightarrow E^o*$
p25	11	1	2	17.8	E^s
wi-txrate5a	9	8	32	1.31	$SM^o \rightarrow ST^o$
wi-txrate5b	8	7	66	1.29	E^o
mi-bitarray	10	6	612	1.82	$SM^o* \rightarrow E^o*$
mi-bitshift	9	8	5	1.11	E^o
mi-bitcnt	27	19	645	1.33	$E^o \rightarrow ST^o \rightarrow E^o \rightarrow ST^o \rightarrow E^o$
mi-susan	30	21	32	1.26	ST^o

Table 3. Execution time speedup over `gcc -O3` code and search instances involved in finding the solution. In the last column, $X \rightarrow Y$ indicates that Y uses the best code found by X. $*$ indicates exchanging of the best code among search instances of the same search technique.

bit shift benchmark, an E^o instance immediately found the best program by applying the optimization explained in the concrete example in Section 4. In p21 from Hacker's Delight, the path to the best known solution involves passing the latest best programs between many E^o, SM^o, and ST^o instances repeatedly.

To illustrate how the different types of search instances work together in practice, we explain how the cooperative superoptimizer found the best program in the `mi-bitarray` benchmark, getting a specific bit in an array. The superoptimizer found two optimizations (Optimization I and II) displayed in Figure 7. The code in blue is inside a window, and the rest are the context used in the window decomposition. First, a SM^o instance optimized code inside a small window of two instruction to one instruction. The SM^o instance was able to perform this optimization because it can synthesize an arbitrary constant, in this case, 248. After the SM^o instance discovered Optimization I, an E^o instance optimized the code further. Optimization II performed by the E^o instance, in fact, consists of two different optimizations. The first optimization transforms:

```
cmp   r1, #0
add   r2, r1, #7
movge r2, r1        // mov when r1 >= 0 (signed)
```

to:

```
asr r3, r1, #2            // r3 = r1 s>> 2
add r2, r1, r3, lsr #29 // r2 = r1 & (r3 u>> 29)
```

eliminating the `cmp` instruction and the conditional suffix. Note that this transformation is valid in any context. In the second optimization, the superoptimizer learned from the postfix—specifically at the instruction `sub r3, r1, r3`—that only the difference between the values of `r1` and `r3` matters, and the exact values of `r1` and `r3` do not. This particular optimization illustrates that not only precondition but postcondition also helps the superoptimizer discover more optimizations. Notice that the E^o instance used the constant 248, found by SM^o, to synthesize the final code, as the optimized fragment contains 248. Hence, in order to obtain the final code in this benchmark, we need the enumerative search, the symbolic search, and the context-aware window decomposition all together.

7.5 Existing Superoptimizers' Implementations

The original stochastic superoptimizer (STOKE) [24, 25] is for x86. Consequently, we could not use STOKE in our experiments. STOKE can evaluate approximately 10^6 candidates per second by executing programs natively [25] or running emulators on a cluster of machines [24]. Without an ability to run programs natively or an access to run programs on a cluster of machines, one will not be able to achieve this kind of performance. Nevertheless, our stochastic superoptimizer is able to evaluate approximately 20,000 candidates per second and synthesize up to 10 ARM instructions within an hour using emulators on one machine with 32 cores. However, the optimized program with 10 instructions that our stochastic superoptimizer synthesized is not optimal, so it is not reported in the experiment in Section 7.1. Note that the size of our ARM search space is similar to x86 search space explored in the original STOKE without JIT [24]: they both have 400–1,000 different variations of opcodes [26]. Although ARM has much fewer actual opcodes than x86, many variations are created by the combination of opcodes, optional shift, and conditional suffixes.

Similarly, we created $E^{s'''}$ by modifying E^s to implement the algorithm used in the SIMD synthesizer [6] and the SyGus enumerative solver [3]. We note that $E^{s'''}$ does not use the stack-based program representation, used in [6] to remove search space symmetries due to register renaming. We did not use this representation because we observed that some optimal programs cannot be obtained from this representation, unless we introduce new pseudo-instructions for peaking into the stack and dropping values from the stack. Note that this optimization is orthogonal from the search algorithm and can improve our search technique.

8. Related Work

Symbolic search is popular in program synthesis tools such as Sketch [27] and Rosette [31]. This search technique is also used in the Chlorophyll compiler's superoptimizer [20]. Although constraint solvers have many clever pruning strategies (e.g. conflict clauses) and heuristics to make decisions, constraint solvers are not optimized for program synthesis problems. Component-based synthesis [13] introduces an alternative encoding, which significantly improves the performance of a symbolic search; however, even with this encoding, the symbolic solver from SyGus'14 competition still did not perform well [3]. Another pruning strategy using divide-and-conquer to break QFBV formula potentially reduces synthesis time by many orders of magnitude [28], but it is likely synthesizing the same program as given. The refutation-based approach used in the CVC4 solver [23], the winner of SyGus'15 competition, is also not suitable for superoptimization problems because it tends to produce very large solutions with many if-else constructs.

Stochastic search, first used in STOKE [24, 25], randomly mutates a program to another using cost function to determine the acceptance of the mutation. STOKE is the first superoptimizer that is able to synthesize large programs (10–15 x86 instructions) in under an hour. The use of cost function to guide the search is one of the keys to its effectiveness. The weakness of this search is a possibility to get stuck at local minima and, as a result, fail to reach an optimal solution.

Enumerative search is used in many superoptimizers and program synthesizers. Enumerative search can be extremely fast if it is done right, as the winning teams of two synthesis competitions (ICFP'13 [2] and SyGus'14 [3]) employed this technique. This is because an enumerative search is highly customized to solve a particular problem it is designed for. The problem domain knowledge can be encoded into the search as systematic pruning strategies or just as ad-hoc heuristics, such as which branch in the search tree should be explored first. In our experience, building an enumerative search is easy, but building a fast enumerative search is difficult because a fast enumerative algorithm requires many clever pruning strategies to make the search tractable.

We have tried existing pruning strategies including using virtual registers [34] and a stack-base program representation [6] to reduce symmetry, using a canonical form [5], and memorization [2]. However, these pruning strategies alone do not work for our problem domain as well as for [2, 3, 6]. This is because our search space is bigger. For example, the SIMD synthesizer usually considers only a small number of instructions that are predicted from the input non-vectorized programs. However, we cannot restrict the search space in the same way because our goal is to find the optimal code fragment, which may require unexpected instructions. The SyGus and ICFP competitions only include programs that take in one argument and produce one return value. Thus, we have introduced new pruning strategies that make program synthesis problems more tractable.

However, new pruning strategies are still needed if we want to solve synthesis problems with even bigger search space. For example, memorization similar to [2] should accelerate the search even more. However, from our experience, the memorization system requires a decent amount of engineering effort to support quick lookup in a very large database that contains more than billion programs in order to speed up our synthesis process. We did not spend enough effort to implement a very efficient memorization system, so our superoptimizer does not currently utilize this technique.

9. Conclusion

This paper introduced the LENS algorithm, which can optimize larger program fragments compared to existing techniques. To optimize even larger program fragments, we applied a context-aware window decomposition, optimizing a subfragment of the entire code with the precise precondition and postcondition from the surrounding context. Lastly, we improved upon the LENS algorithm by combining symbolic and stochastic search into our system. To make superoptimization even more practical, we can cache superoptimized code to avoid an expensive search when optimizing programs we have seen before.

In summary, we introduced strategies to scale up superoptimization to optimize real-world programs. We hope that our work will enable program developers to use a superoptimizer to further optimize code generated from an optimizing compiler, when performance is critical. Similarly, we also hope to enable a rapid compiler construction for a new ISA by side stepping the laborious development of traditional compiler optimizations by using superoptimization.

Acknowledgments

This work is supported in part by Qualcomm Innovation Fellowship, MSR Fellowship, Grants from NSF (CCF–1139138, CCF–1337415, and ACI–1535191), U.S. Department of Energy, Office of Science, Office of Basic Energy Sciences Energy Frontier Research Centers (FOA–0000619), and DARPA (FA8750–14–C–0011), as well as gifts from Google, Intel, Mozilla, Nokia, and Qualcomm.

References

[1] Souper. `http://github.com/google/souper`. URL `http://github.com/google/souper`.

[2] T. Akiba, K. Imajo, H. Iwami, Y. Iwata, T. Kataoka, N. Takahashi, M. Moskal, and N. Swamy. Calibrating research in program synthesis using 72,000 hours of programmer time. Technical report, MSR, 2013.

[3] R. Alur, R. Bodik, E. Dallal, D. Fisman, P. Garg, G. Juniwal, H. Kress-Gazit, P. Madhusudan, M. M. K. Martin, M. Raghothaman, S. Saha, S. A. Seshia, R. Singh, A. Solar-Lezama, E. Torlak, and A. Udupa. Syntax-guided synthesis. In *SyGus Competition*, 2014.

[4] ARM. *Cortex-A9: Technical Reference Manual*, 2012. URL `http://infocenter.arm.com/help/topic/com.arm.doc.ddi0388i/DDI0388I_cortex_a9_r4p1_trm.pdf`.

[5] S. Bansal and A. Aiken. Automatic generation of peephole superoptimizers. In *ASPLOS*, 2006.

[6] G. Barthe, J. M. Crespo, S. Gulwani, C. Kunz, and M. Marron. From relational verification to simd loop synthesis. In *PPoPP*, 2013.

[7] J. Bungo. The use of compiler optimizations for embedded systems software. *Crossroads*, 15(1):8–15, Sept. 2008.

[8] A. Duller, D. Towner, G. Panesar, A. Gray, and W. Robbins. picoarray technology: the tool's story. In *Design, Automation and Test in Europe*, 2005.

[9] J. Galenson, P. Reames, R. Bodik, B. Hartmann, and K. Sen. Codehint: Dynamic and interactive synthesis of code snippets. In *ICSE*, 2014.

[10] V. Govindaraju, C.-H. Ho, T. Nowatzki, J. Chhugani, N. Satish, K. Sankaralingam, and C. Kim. Dyser: Unifying functionality and parallelism specialization for energy-efficient computing. *Micro, IEEE*, Sept 2012.

[11] T. Granlund and R. Kenner. Eliminating branches using a superoptimizer and the gnu c compiler. In *PLDI*, 1992.

[12] GreenArrays. *Product Brief: GreenArrays GA144*, 2010. URL `http://www.greenarraychips.com/home/documents/greg/PB001-100503-GA144-1-10.pdf`.

[13] S. Gulwani, S. Jha, A. Tiwari, and R. Venkatesan. Synthesis of loop-free programs. In *PLDI*, 2011.

[14] M. R. Guthaus, J. S. Ringenberg, D. Ernst, T. Mudge, R. Brown, and T. Austin. Mibench: a free, commercially representative embedded benchmark suite. In *IEEE International Symposium on Workload Characterization*, 2001.

[15] Intel. Reducing Data Center Energy Consumption. Technical report, 2008.

[16] M. Kandemir, N. Vijaykrishnan, and M. Irwin. Compiler optimizations for low power systems. In *Power Aware Computing*, Series in Computer Science. Springer US, 2002.

[17] N. P. Lopes, D. Menendez, S. Nagarakatte, and J. Regehr. Provably correct peephole optimizations with alive. In *PLDI*, 2015.

[18] H. Massalin. Superoptimizer: a look at the smallest program. In *ASPLOS*, 1987.

[19] P. Merolla, J. Arthur, F. Akopyan, N. Imam, R. Manohar, and D. Modha. A digital neurosynaptic core using embedded crossbar memory with 45pj per spike in 45nm. In *Custom Integrated Circuits Conference (CICC), 2011 IEEE*, 2011.

[20] P. M. Phothilimthana, T. Jelvis, R. Shah, N. Totla, S. Chasins, and R. Bodik. Chlorophyll: Synthesis-aided compiler for low-power spatial architectures. In *PLDI*, 2014.

[21] P. M. Phothilimthana, A. Thakur, R. Bodik, and D. Dhurjati. Greenthumb: Superoptimizer construction framework. In *Proceedings of International Conference on Compiler Construction*, 2016.

[22] W. Qadeer, R. Hameed, O. Shacham, P. Venkatesan, C. Kozyrakis, and M. A. Horowitz. Convolution engine: Balancing efficiency and flexibility in specialized computing. In *ISCA*, 2013.

[23] A. Reynolds, M. Deters, V. Kuncak, C. Tinelli, and C. Barrett. Counterexample-guided quantifier instantiation for synthesis in smt. In *CAV*, 2015.

[24] E. Schkufza, R. Sharma, and A. Aiken. Stochastic superoptimization. In *ASPLOS*, 2013.

[25] E. Schkufza, R. Sharma, and A. Aiken. Stochastic optimization of floating-point programs with tunable precision. In *PLDI*, 2014.

[26] R. Sharma. Personal communication, June 2015.

[27] A. Solar-Lezama, L. Tancau, R. Bodik, S. Seshia, and V. Saraswat. Combinatorial sketching for finite programs. In *ASPLOS*, 2006.

[28] V. Srinivasan and T. Reps. Synthesis of machine code from semantics. In *PLDI*, 2015.

[29] The Linley Group. Processor watch: Getting way out of box. `http://www.linleygroup.com/newsletters/newsletter_detail.php?num=5038`, 2013. Accessed: 2014-11-13.

[30] E. Torlak and R. Bodik. Growing solver-aided languages with Rosette. In *Onward!*, 2013.

[31] E. Torlak and R. Bodik. A lightweight symbolic virtual machine for solver-aided host languages. In *PLDI*, 2014.

[32] A. Udupa, A. Raghavan, J. V. Deshmukh, S. Mador-Haim, M. M. Martin, and R. Alur. Transit: Specifying protocols with concolic snippets. In *PLDI*, 2013.

[33] H. S. Warren. *Hacker's Delight*. Addison-Wesley Longman Publishing Co., Inc., Boston, MA, USA, 2002.

[34] H. S. Warren. A hacker's assistant. Oct. 2008. URL `http://www.hackersdelight.org/aha/aha.pdf`.

[35] Wikipedia. List of arm microarchitectures. `http://en.wikipedia.org/wiki/List_of_ARM_microarchitectures`, 2014. Accessed: 2014-11-13.

[36] C. Zhang. *Dynamically Reconfigurable Architectures for Real-time Baseband Processing*. PhD thesis, Lund University, 2014.

[37] Q. Zheng, Y. Chen, R. Dreslinski, C. Chakrabarti, A. Anastasopoulos, S. Mahlke, and T. Mudge. Wibench: An open source kernel suite for benchmarking wireless systems. In *Workload Characterization (IISWC), 2013 IEEE International Symposium on*, 2013.

Lifting Assembly to Intermediate Representation: A Novel Approach Leveraging Compilers *

Niranjan Hasabnis
Intel †
niranjan.hasabnis@intel.com

R. Sekar
Stony Brook University
sekar@cs.stonybrook.edu

Abstract

Translating low-level machine instructions into higher-level intermediate language (IL) is one of the central steps in many binary analysis and instrumentation systems. Existing systems build such translators manually. As a result, it takes a great deal of effort to support new architectures. Even for widely deployed architectures, full instruction sets may not be modeled, e.g., mature systems such as Valgrind still lack support for AVX, FMA4 and SSE4.1 for x86 processors. To overcome these difficulties, we propose a novel approach that leverages knowledge about instruction set semantics that is already embedded into modern compilers such as GCC. In particular, we present a learning-based approach for automating the translation of assembly instructions to a compiler's architecture-neutral IL. We present an experimental evaluation that demonstrates the ability of our approach to easily support many architectures (x86, ARM and AVR), including their advanced instruction sets. Our implementation is available as open-source software.

1. Introduction

Binary analysis and instrumentation form the basis of many popular systems for program debugging and monitoring (e.g., Valgrind [37], DynamoRio [13] and Pin [36]), processor virtualization (e.g., QEMU [12]), and malware analysis (e.g., BitBlaze [49] and BAP [14]). Numerous techniques and solutions in software security, including taint-tracking [38, 42, 44], control-flow integrity [6, 57], sandboxing untrusted code [23, 32, 54], malware analysis [22, 52, 55], and automated exploit and signature generation [10, 19], rely on binary analysis/instrumentation.

A central challenge faced by all these systems is the accurate modeling of instruction semantics. Errors in the model will invalidate binary analysis results. Worse, they may cause instrumented programs to crash or fail in other ways. The size and complexity of modern instruction sets compounds instruction semantics modeling: the popular x86 architecture supports over 1000 instructions that are documented in a 1500-page manual. Despite its roots in RISC, ARM v7A includes several instruction sets such as Thumb, ThumbEE and Jazelle that cause the instruction set size to balloon to about 1200, and the manual to about 1000 pages.

Existing binary analysis and instrumentation systems rely on manually developed models of instructions. Given the size of modern instruction sets, manual modeling poses a daunting challenge even for a single architecture. Supporting multiple architectures such as PowerPC, x86, ARM, SPARC, and MIPS using this approach can be prohibitive. It is no wonder that even mature systems such as Valgrind[1] support only a limited number of platforms, and moreover, omit instruction subsets such as AVX, FMA4, and SSE4.1 on x86, and ThumbEE and Jazelle on ARM.

In contrast with previous binary analysis and instrumentation works, all of which relied on manual instruction semantics modeling, we present *a novel automated approach* in this paper. Our approach leverages the knowledge of instruction sets that is already encoded in existing compilers such as GCC [40] and LLVM [24]. Specifically, their code generators can translate their (architecture-neutral) intermediate language to assembly code for many different architectures. We present techniques to (a) automatically "extract" this semantics, and (b) to test the accuracy of extracted semantics. Our approach offers several important benefits:

- *Automated instruction semantics modeling.* Our approach can greatly reduce the manual efforts needed in modeling instruction set semantics.
- *Architecture-neutrality.* This feature has long been recognized as important, starting with early works such as EEL [35] and UQBT [17]. However, the focus of these works was on the analysis and instrumentation steps that followed a *manually implemented* step to lift assembly to an intermediate language (IL). Our work addresses the significant challenge left open by these (and other subsequent) works, namely, automating the lifting step.
- *Leveraging well-tested compiler code.* Compilers are among the most extensively tested pieces of software —

* This work was supported in part by grants from NSF (CNS-0831298 and 1319137), AFOSR (FA9550-09-1-0539) and ONR (N00014-15-1-2378).

† This work was completed as a PhD student at Stony Brook University.

ASPLOS '16, April 02–06, 2016, Atlanta, GA, USA.

ACM 978-1-4503-4091-5/16/04...$15.00.
DOI: http://dx.doi.org/10.1145/2872362.2872380

[1] We used Valgrind version 3.7.0 for our testing.

both during development and in the field. As a result, errors in instruction semantics are likely to have been found and fixed. By extracting this "debugged" instruction semantics, our approach reduces the likelihood of errors that are all too common in manually lifted assembly [1, 3–5].

1.1 Approach Overview and Contributions

Problem Formulation. Modern compilers such as GCC rely on an architecture-specific *machine description (MD)* to drive their code generator. However, as discussed in Section 2, these MDs are interpreted using large amounts of architecture-specific C-code. Indeed, many MD rules directly contain C-code! As a result, it is not feasible to extract instruction semantics by directly processing the MDs. We therefore formulate the model extraction problem as a machine-learning problem: given examples of IL to assembly translation produced by a compiler, learn a mapping from assembly to IL.

Algorithm for Learning Assembly to IL Mappings. While there exist a vast array of machine-learning algorithms, most of them are focused on the problem of classification or regression, i.e., given an input, they output a (small) integer or a real-value. The output in our learning problem are more complex, consisting of tree-structured[2] IL snippets. Secondly, machine learning algorithms are designed with the assumption that errors can be tolerated, and indeed, are a necessary component of any solution that generalizes well. In contrast, translation errors are unacceptable in our context. To our knowledge, the only previous works that satisfy these constraints are on finite-state transducers (FSTs). However, these algorithms (e.g., OSTIA [39]) operate on strings, and do not address two major challenges that arise in our problem context: *parameterized translation* and *tree-structured data*. We describe these challenges in Section 3, and develop efficient techniques to overcome them.

Efficient Lifting of Whole Binaries to IL. Our learning algorithm maps (short) *sequences* of assembly instructions into IL. Given a long instruction sequence, there can be multiple ways to lift it to an IL sequence. As a result, a straight-forward lifting algorithm can have an exponential complexity. In Section 4, we show how to exploit dynamic programming to realize a linear-time lifting algorithm.

Correctness of Extracted Mappings. While compilers use the MD rules to translate IL to assembly, we are using them in the reverse direction. This raises a question as to the correctness of the approach. We provide a conceptual justification of correctness in Section 5, followed by a more formal treatment and experimental evaluation in Section 6.4.

Experimental Evaluation. Our evaluation in Section 6 establishes the following:

- *Ability to support complex instruction sets.* Our system can extract the semantics for about 1100 user-level instructions on x86, including advanced instruction sets such as SSE and AVX; and about the same number for ARM, including its Thumb, VFP, and SIMD instructions.
- *Completeness.* We show that our approach can successfully lift about 99.5% of Ubuntu/x86 and 99.8% of Debian/ARM binaries. Most of the missed instructions are various forms of NOPs and other instructions that are never used by GCC. Because of the simplicity of these instructions, it took us only a few hours to manually extend the model to incorporate these instructions.
- *Architecture-neutrality.* It took *just 9 person-hours* to support ARM, and 3 hours to support AVR, a popular microcontroller used in platforms such as Arduino.
- *Performance.* We trained the system using 1.4GB of code generator logs. This training produced a transducer with 4830 states in 10 minutes. We then used this transducer to lift all the binaries from the entire Ubuntu/x86 and Debian/ARM distributions, which total about 100M instructions. This testing took approximately 8 hours.

In a companion paper [41], we describe the application of the semantics derived by our approach. A short summary of this application is discussed in Section 6.5. Comparison with related work is presented in Section 7, followed by concluding remarks in Section 8.

Our system is available as open-source software [27].

2. Background and Problem Formulation

Compiler researchers have long worked to develop architecture-independent code generators [20]. These code generators translate code in an architecture-neutral intermediate language (IL) into assembly code. Their operation is driven by *machine descriptions* (MDs) that describe the instruction set of a target architecture. The core component of an MD is a set of rules, each mapping a snippet of IL into an assembly instruction (or in some cases, a sequence of assembly instructions). This general structure is applicable to modern compilers such as GCC and LLVM, but due to GCC's mature support for numerous architectures, our implementation is based on GCC. An example rule from GCC's x86 MD is shown below:

```
[(set (match_operand:0 "register_operand" "=a")
  (div (match_operand:1 "register_operand" "0" )
    (match_operand:2 "nonimmediate_operand" "qm")))
  (clobber (reg: FLAGS_REG))]
 ⟶ "div %2"
```

This rule consists of an RTL[3] pattern corresponding to the divide instruction. This RTL snippet states that the result of dividing operand 1 by operand 2 is stored in operand 0. At the assembly level, the first two operands are same and implicit, a fact captured by (the cryptic) match constraints "**0**" and "**=a**" in the RTL. The applicability of the pattern is constrained by several other (architecture-specific) con-

[2] We are referring to a parse tree of the IL snippet.

[3] RTL is the name of GCC's IL.

straints as well, including "***register_operand***" and "**qm**." Often, compilers do not need to reason about the exact value of flags after each and every arithmetic or logical instruction. Hence this rule indicates that flags are modified without specifying exactly how[4].

It may seem that MD rules can be used in reverse to translate assembly to IL, but unfortunately, as illustrated by the above example, the rules are not self-contained. Several details, such as the meanings of the constraints and the printing of assembly-level operands (i.e., how %2 is substituted in the above example) are hard-coded into architecture-specific C-functions. Even the output assembly may not be specified for some rules: instead, the right-hand side of the rule may consist of C-code that, when compiled and executed, will return a string representing the output assembly instruction! Reversing these rules will hence require all such C-code to be inverted. Computing inverses of arbitrary C-functions is an intractable problem in general, so we need alternative methods. One possibility is to rely on human experts to study these C-functions and hand-generate the inverses. Unfortunately, we find that the amount of C-code that needs handling is far too much to make this approach attractive. For instance, the x86 MD in GCC consists of 1500 rules (40K lines), *but a far larger 90K lines of C-code.* Moreover, such manual efforts can introduce new bugs, thus negating the primary benefit of MDs, i.e., they have been tested extensively.

To overcome the above problems, we develop a *black-box* approach that *observes* the IL-to-assembly translations actually produced by a compiler, and *learns* a mapping from these observations. Such an approach eliminates the need to understand the semantics of MDs or the associated architecture-specific code. This, in turn, makes the technique easier to apply to a broad range of compilers, including those that rely on even more programmatic MDs than GCC. While coverage is a concern with learning-based approaches, note that in the context of this problem, large amounts of training data can be readily obtained by compiling (a virtually endless supply of) open-source software, and recording the IL-to-assembly mappings.

We formulate the assembly-to-IL lifting problem as one of *learning a parameterized translation* on *trees* representing assembly and IL snippets. We say "parameterized" because the translations involve parameters, which correspond to operands in the assembly and IL. In addition, we operate on parse-trees (rather than strings), as their structure provides additional clues for the learning algorithm, and moreover, the notion of parameters is more easily understood in the context of trees. The following abstract example will help illustrate some of the key requirements of the learning algorithm we will describe in the next section.

[4] Static analysis and instrumentation techniques typically require sound instruction semantics, but can typically cope with incompleteness, e.g., when flags (or in some cases, other operands) are specified as clobbered. This is why the incompleteness of `div` semantics does not pose a problem. For a more detailed discussion, see Section 6.4.1.

Example 1. We use a first-order term notation to represent trees. For instance, $a(e, b(c, d))$ represents a tree with the root symbol a and two children. The first child is the (leaf) symbol e, while the second child is a tree with the root symbol b and two subtrees c and d that are leaves. The following table shows a list of pairs given to the learning algorithm, and a (possible) rule learned from them:

Asm	IL	Rule learned
$a(4,2)$	$s(2, b(2,2,8))$	
$a(1,1)$	$s(1, b(2,1,2))$	$a(x,y) \longrightarrow s(y, b(2,y,\mathbf{f}(x)))$
$a(7,3)$	$s(3, b(2,3,14))$	

Here, $\mathbf{f}$ is a function that multiplies its argument by 2, while x and y are universally quantified variables that represent parameters. This example has been chosen to illustrate several common features we observe in the assembly to IL translation. For instance, parameters may be reordered because IL tends to list its destination operand first, while assembly may list it last. Parameter duplication is also common since assembly typically uses two-operand format for most operations, while IL uses 3-operand format. It is also relatively common for IL to add additional operators such as b — for instance, a constant 10 in assembly may be represented as (`cint` 10) in IL. Finally, constants may be transformed using simple functions such as $\mathbf{f}$, e.g., they may be offset or scaled by a small number. Thus, the learning algorithm needs to be able to recognize such transformations.

Some of the constants in the first two columns correspond to parameters, while others, such as the first child of b, don't. The learning algorithm needs to distinguish between them by observing several examples.

Operating on trees means that we need to first parse assembly code as well as RTL. The latter task is easy because RTL uses an S-expression syntax that is easy to parse, and moreover, it is a one-time effort. Parsing assembly, on the other hand, is an architecture-specific task. To minimize its development effort, we build a "rough" parser, one that recognizes the nesting of operators and operands to build a tree, but is unaware of many other syntactic distinctions, e.g., the differences between addressing modes. As a result, the entire parser code for x86 is less than 100 lines.

3. Learning Algorithm

We begin by enumerating the key requirements for the algorithm for learning translations:

1. *Error-free:* Translation errors cannot be tolerated, because they will undermine the soundness of tools relying on the mapping derived by the approach. At a minimum, our algorithm should avoid errors on the training data; ideally, it will have no errors (except, possibly, missing translations) on test data.

2. *Fully automatic:* This algorithm should not require manual supervision or any form of intervention.

3. *Parameterized translation:* Both assembly and RTL consist of operands that often range over large domains (e.g., 32-bit integers), and may go through transformations such as the addition or multiplication by small constants, big endian to little endian conversions, etc. Our algorithm should be able to learn such common transformations.

4. *Scalable to handle large data sets:* As mentioned before, a large amount of labeled training data is available in the context of this problem, and so we seek an algorithm that is efficient enough to exploit it.

To the best of our knowledge, previous techniques do not satisfy several of these requirements. For instance, machine-learning techniques target applications that can tolerate errors. Often, a conscious trade-off is made that modestly increases the error rate in order to achieve better generalization from training samples. This is particularly true in the context of modern machine translation literature, where the focus is on the very difficult problem of natural language translation.

In the simpler setting of string translations, techniques that focus on minimizing errors have been developed. Specifically, Oncina et al [39] developed an algorithm called OSTIA for learning so-called *onward subsequential transducers*[5] from examples. Being *onward* means that the transducer emits as much of the output as possible at each transducer state, instead of waiting until all of the input is examined. Doing so exposes commonalities among states, enabling more generalization (achieved by merging similar states).

A key property of OSTIA is its guarantee of zero errors on the training data. However, OSTIA does not support the concept of parameters such as those shown in Example 1, or transformations on them. As noted in Example 1, even the identification of parameters is nontrivial. Moreover, OSTIA operates on strings, while our translation algorithm operates on trees. While trees can be flattened into a string representation, this is undesirable for many reasons. First, important structural information, which can provide clues for the learning algorithm, is lost. Second, the kind of parameter reordering shown in Example 1 leads to a situation where almost no output can be emitted until all of the input is read[6]. This leads to degenerate transducers that emit all their output in the very last state, with the output being distinct for every distinct input. In effect, this leads to a degenerate case of learning, namely, *exact recall,* which memorizes input/output pairs observed during training, and can recall the output when a previously seen input is presented again. We will use this exact recall algorithm as a baseline for our comparison, while developing a new algorithm that satisfies all the requirements listed above. Our system, called LISC (Learning Instruction Semantics from Code generator), uses three main steps as discussed below: (1) *training data collection,* (2) *parameterization,* and (3) *transducer construction.*

[5] Transducers are very similar to automata: while automata accept an input language, transducers perform translations, and as such, their transitions not only consume inputs but also emit outputs.

[6] This is because the last parameter of the input produces the first parameter of the output, so the only output that can be produced before consuming all input is the symbol "s".

3.1 Training data collection

We first use GCC to compile many source code packages and collect concrete pairs of assembly and IL-snippets produced by the code generator. Note that this collection occurs at the very last step of code generation: at this point, GCC has completed register allocation, so the RTL refers to hardware registers. This factor simplifies the learning step. A few example pairs are shown below, where the RTL has been abbreviated a bit to improve readability.

Asm	RTL
`sub $8, %eax`	`(set (reg eax) (+ (reg eax) (cint -8)))`
`sub %ebx, %eax`	`(set (reg eax) (- (reg eax) (reg ebx)))`
`sub %eax, 8(%esp)`	`(set (mem (+ (reg esp) (cint 8))) (- (mem (+ (reg esp) (cint 8)))(reg eax)))`

Both the assembly and IL are represented as first-order terms after parsing. For instance, the term pair corresponding to the first row of the table is

$$\langle sub(8, eax), \quad set(reg(eax), +(reg(eax), \ cint(-8)))\rangle$$

Note that a function $\mathbf{g}(n) = -n$ has been applied to the parameter 8, similar to the function $\mathbf{f}(n) = 2n$ used in Example 1. Other features of Example 1, such as parameter reordering and duplication, are also present.

Typically, there is just a single assembly instruction per pair, but there are instances where there is a sequence of them. Our algorithm makes no distinction between these cases, treating the sequence operator as yet another assembly-level operator.

3.2 Parameterization

The goal of parameterization is to (a) identify all parameters from a concrete pair $\langle A, I\rangle$, and (b) determine any functions that are being applied to these parameters. Since we cannot definitively identify a parameter by just looking at one $\langle A, I\rangle$ pair, *we conservatively flag every constant (i.e., a leaf in the term) in assembly as a* ***potential parameter***[7].

We next identify, for each pair $\langle A, I\rangle$, the ways to derive each of the leaf terms in I from the potential parameters identified in A. Our design here is based on our observation that there are only a small number of transformations that are commonly found in assembly to IL mappings:

- *eq:* Identity is the most common transformation.
- $+, -$: Addition or subtraction of a small integer $k > 0$.
- $*, /$: Multiplication or division by a small integer $k > 0$.

[7] Non-leaf subterms represent expressions containing an operator at their root. Since we expect operators to have different semantics (if not syntax) in assembly and IL, we do not consider them as parameters. In contrast, constants such as "8" or "`eax`" can be copied over from assembly to RTL or vice-versa, and hence we consider them as potential parameters.

- $2^k, \log_2$: These occur when a multiplication operation by a power of two is translated into a shift operation.
- *Numeric conversions* such as big-endian to little-endian.
- *Subword extraction,* e.g., extracting a specific byte of a 32-bit value. We have observed this often in the context of SIMD instructions, where multiple 8-bit values from RTL are packed into a single 32-bit assembly operand.

Our parameterization algorithm starts with a small set $\mathbf{f}_1, \ldots, \mathbf{f}_r$ of transformation functions such as those listed above. (We explicitly omit more complex functions, e.g., $kx + l$ or kx^2.) Then, for each leaf l in I and each potential parameter x in A, it checks if $\mathbf{f}_i(x) = l$. If there is no such $\mathbf{f}_i$, l is left as is. Otherwise, l is replaced by a combination of all such transformations, plus l itself. If there is any potential parameter x that is unused in any of these transformations, then it is eliminated from consideration as a parameter. We illustrate this procedure using a few examples below.

In/out pair		After parameterization	
$a(5,b)$	$t(s)$	$a(5,b)$	$t(s)$
$a(2,c)$	$t(6)$	$a(x,c)$	$t(\{6, x*3, x+4\})$
$a(4,c)$	$t(8)$	$a(x,c)$	$t(\{8, x*2, x+4\})$
$d(2,4)$	$u(5,3)$	$d(x,y)$	$u(\{5, x+3, y+1\}, \{3, x+1, y-1\})$
$d(5,6)$	$u(7,6)$	$d(x,y)$	$u(\{7, x+2, y+1\}, \{6, x+1, y\})$

Figure 1. Examples of parameterization

In the first row, the arguments of a are not considered parameters, as they bear no relationship to the leaf s. In the second row, the leaf 2 is identified as a potential parameter. It may either be multiplied by 3, or added to 4 in order to yield the leaf 6 in IL. It is also possible that 6 is a constant that won't be affected by changes to the parameter value 2. While parameterizing, we capture all these three possibilities by using a set notation for the output parameter value, with the semantics that *<u>all</u> of the expressions in the set yield the correct value* for the output parameter.

The fourth and fifth rows involve two parameters instead of one, but as before, we simply replace each leaf in I by a set of expressions. If the learning algorithm, at some point, concludes that the same parameterized rule is implied by two distinct examples, then the two parameterized pairs are merged, provided the following conditions hold:

- they match at every non-leaf position, and
- the intersection of corresponding leaves is nonempty.

The intersection corresponding to rows 4 and 5 will yield the IL-term $u(y+1, x+1)$. (Since the sets consist of just a single expression, we have omitted the braces around them.)

3.3 Transducer construction

Our transducer operates on terms, and is hence a tree-transducer. Such a transducer is similar to a trie or an acyclic DFA. Like a DFA, a transducer operates in time that is linear in the size of its input, and hence it provides fast translation from assembly into IL. At the same time, a tree transducer differs from a DFA in two important ways:

- a transducer's transitions specify not only the input symbols that must match, but also output symbols that are emitted on each transition.
- unlike a string transducer, whose input consumption (and output emission) occurs in a strictly left-to-right manner, a *tree transducer* traverses its input (and emits output) in any order, as long as it visits parent nodes before children.

procedure $MkDucer(S, \mathbf{R})$:
$j = select(\mathbf{R}_A)$; Record j in S
for each b in $\mathbf{R}_A[j]$ **do**
  $\mathbf{R}_b = \{\langle R_A, R_I\rangle \in \mathbf{R} \mid root(R_A[j]) = b\}$
  $T_b = mcp(\mathbf{R}_b)$
  Create new state S_b
  Create a transition from S to S_b annotated with T_b
  $\mathbf{R}'_b = \{residue(R, T_b) \mid R \in \mathbf{R}_b\}$
  if $\mathbf{R}'_b = \emptyset$
    then mark S_b final
  else $MkDucer(S_b, \mathbf{R}'_b)$

Figure 2. Transducer construction algorithm

Our algorithm $MkDucer$ for constructing a transducer is shown in Fig. 2. We begin with an intuitive illustration of this algorithm on the example of Fig. 1, which results in the transducer shown in Fig. 3. The states of the transducer are annotated with a set of $\langle A, I\rangle$ pairs and a position to be examined next in A. The start state S_0 of the transducer is associated with the entire set $\mathbf{R}$ of $\langle A, I\rangle$ pairs from Fig. 1. At S_0, there is only one option for the next position to examine, i.e., the root of A, so we don't show it explicitly.

Inputs in Fig. 1 are of the form $a(x, y)$ or $d(x, y)$, so we create a transitions from S_0 to capture these two cases. The output is of the form $t(z)$ in the first case. In the second case, we obtain an output of $u(y+1, x+1)$ using the merge step described at the end of Section 3.2. We annotate the edges from S_0 with these $\langle in, out\rangle$ pairs.

State S_1 corresponds to the first three rows of Fig. 1. At S_1, we have examined $a(x, y)$, the *maximal common prefix (mcp)* of the three (assembly) terms, and emitted $t(z)$, the mcp of the three IL terms. (A prefix of a term is obtained by omitting some of its subterms.) The subterms omitted in

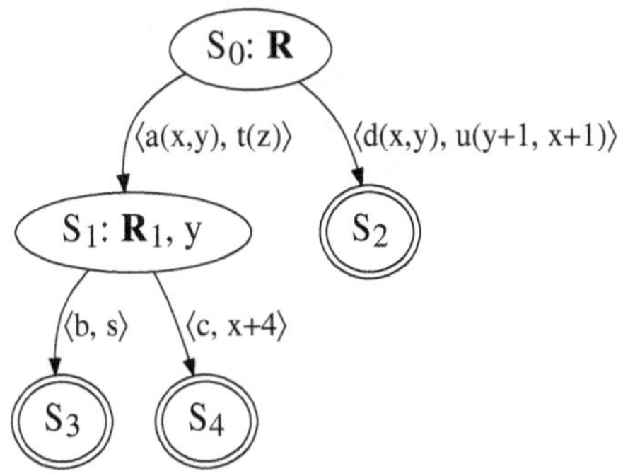

Figure 3. Result of $MkDucer$ (Fig. 2) on Fig. 1

the prefix are called *residues* — they represent the yet-to-be-examined parts of the assembly instruction, and the yet-to-be determined parts of the output. Note that a residue consist of lists of subterms $[t_1, \ldots, t_n]$ that we call as a *fringe*. The state S_1 is annotated with this set $\mathbf{R}_1$ of residues. From the first three rows of Fig. 1, it is easy to see

$$\mathbf{R}_1 = \{\langle [5, b], s\rangle, \langle [2, c], 6\rangle, \langle [4, c], 8\rangle\}$$

We have omitted brackets when a fringe is singleton.

$MkDucer$ uses a helper function *select* to determine the next position to visit from S_1. Suppose that y represents this position. This choice is noted in S_1. Since there are two possible values for y, namely, b and c, two transitions are created out of S_1. On each of these transitions, the output is fully determined, so S_3 and S_4 are marked as final states, and $MkDucer$ terminates.

Now we proceed to a technical description of $MkDucer$. An invocation of $MkDucer(S, \mathbf{R})$ builds a subtree rooted at a state S. A prefix of the input and output terms, as specified by the path from the transducer root to S, has been examined. $\mathbf{R}$ represents the residues of $\langle A, I\rangle$ pairs that are compatible with this prefix. Thus, *each element* of $\mathbf{R}$ is a pair of fringes $\langle R_A, R_I\rangle$, where R_A and R_I are each sequences of subterms of a parameterized pair $\langle A, I\rangle$ that have not been captured in the common prefix.

$MkDucer$ uses a helper *select* to pick the next input position to examine. Since we are interested in selecting from input positions, *select* is a function of $\mathbf{R}_A$, the input components of $\mathbf{R}$. (For simplifying the illustration, this selection was identified using a variable name in Fig. 3, but the algorithm uses an integer index into the fringe array.)

Next, we partition $\mathbf{R}$ on the basis of the symbols occurring at this selected position. The partition corresponding to a symbol b is denoted $\mathbf{R}_b$. The members of $\mathbf{R}_b$ agree on this symbol b, but they may share more. We use the function mcp to identify their *maximal common prefix* T_b. We then create a new state S_b and a transition from S to S_b annotated with T_b.[8] This annotation means that T_b will be examined on this transition, so we compute what is left to be examined in $\mathbf{R}_b$ using the function *residue*. If the residue is empty, then we are done, and we mark S_b as final. Otherwise we make a recursive call to complete the transducer subtree rooted at S_b.

To complete this algorithm, we define mcp and *residue*:

DEFINITION 1 (***Maximal common prefix***). *$mcp(t_1, ..., t_n)$ is the largest term t such that every t_i is an instance of t. It is defined inductively as follows:*

- *If t_1 or t_2 is a variable x, or $root(t_1) \neq root(t_2)$ then $mcp(t_1, t_2) = x$*
- *If t_1 and t_2 represent sets of expressions (from Section 3.2) then if $t_1 \cap t_2 = \phi$ then $mcp(t_1, t_2) = x$, otherwise it is $t_1 \cap t_2$*
- *Otherwise $t_1 = c(t_{11}, \ldots, t_{1r})$ and $t_2 = c(t_{21}, \ldots, t_{2r})$, and $mcp(t_1, t_2) = c(mcp(t_{11}, t_{21}), \ldots, mcp(t_{1r}, t_{2r}))$*

For two fringes $T_1 = [t_{11}, \ldots, t_{1r}]$ and $T_2 = [t_{21}, \ldots, t_{2r}]$, $mcp(T_1, T_2) = [mcp(t_{11}, t_{21}), \ldots, mcp(t_{1r}, t_{2r})]$.

DEFINITION 2 (***Residue***). *If t_1 is an instance of t_2 then $residue(t_1, t_2) = [t_{11}, \ldots, t_{1r}]$ such that t_1 is obtained by substituting the ith variable in t_2 by t_{1i}, for $1 \leq i \leq r$. Otherwise the residue is undefined.*
For two fringes $T_1 = [t_{11}, \ldots, t_{1r}]$ and $T_2 = [t_{21}, \ldots, t_{2r}]$, $residue(T_1, T_2) = [residue(t_{11}, t_{21}), ..., residue(t_{1r}, t_{2r})]$

We illustrate mcp and $residue$ in the following tables:

t_1	t_2	$mcp(t_1, t_2)$
$t(s)$	$u(5, 3)$	x
$\{5, x + 3\}$	$\{5, x + 2\}$	5
$\{5, y + 1\}$	$\{7, y + 1\}$	$y + 1$
$a(5, a(b, c))$	$a(4, a(b, b))$	$a(x, a(b, y))$

t_1	t_2	$residue(t_1, t_2)$
$t(6)$	$t(x)$	6
$a(5, a(b, c))$	$a(x, a(b, y))$	$[5, c]$
$a(b, \{x + 2, y * 3\})$	$a(x', y')$	$[b, \{x + 2, y * 3\}]$

Defining *select*. For the basic version of $MkDucer$, it is easy to define *select*. It chooses only non-parameter positions. Among non-parameter positions, it chooses a position that minimizes the number of immediate children of the current state. If only parameter positions remain, this basic version of the algorithm fails. For the related problem of building matching automata for trees, such a choice has been shown to be optimal [45–47]. Extensions to this basic algorithm are described later in this section.

Building DAG Transducers. Since assembly language grammars typically have a fixed number of operands with very limited depth, cycles are not useful (or even meaningful) in our transducers. However, DAG structure can still be useful, as it can produce considerable space savings.

While conversion to DAG is usually thought of as a bottom-up post-processing optimization, such an approach wastes significant resources: Tree automata can be exponentially larger than DAG automata, so post-processing techniques can perform exponentially worse than direct DAG construction approaches.

Given our choice of passing only residues ("unseen inputs and unemitted outputs") into $MkDucer$, there is a simple and elegant approach for direct DAG construction: before creating a new state S_b corresponding to $\mathbf{R}_b$, simply check if there already exists another state S' with the same residue, and if so, create a transition to the existing state, and avoid the recursive call. Such an approach works correctly because $MkDucer$'s behavior is fully determined by the argument $\mathbf{R}$, and hence two invocations that pass in the same $\mathbf{R}$ will result in identical subautomata.

[8] By the properties of mcp, T_b includes the maximal part of the output that can be determined at this point. Eagerly emitting output in this manner isn't critical for this version of the algorithm but *is* important for an optimization we discuss later.

Improving *select.* Typically, branching on parameter positions can be avoided if the assembly language parser is capable of distinguishing between basic operand types, such as immediates and registers. However, in the interest of simplicity, our parser does not make this distinction, so we needed to generalize *select* further. Secondly, even if a better parser were available, this generalization makes $MkDucer$ more powerful, capable of handling complexities that would trip up the basic version. Thirdly, this generalization can produce space savings by avoiding multi-way branches with numerous branches, instead using two-way branches.

When *select* is unable to find a non-parameter position to branch on, or when the branching factor is too large, it builds if-then-else branches. If the position contains parameters of different types such as integers and strings, then the branch will be on the basis of type. Otherwise, *select* compares with a constant that divides the current set of residues into two equal halves. Values less than this constant will follow the then-branch, while the rest will follow the else-branch.

Extending *select* in this manner requires the mcp and $residue$ operations to be extended so that we can deal with inequalities. Due to space constraints, we omit the details here, but an interested reader can find them in Reference [50], which studies the problem of building matching automata for network packets.

4. Efficient Lifting of Whole Binaries to IL

We next turn our attention to the problem of using the assembly-to-IL mapping learned in the previous section to lift whole binaries to IL. In order to do this, binaries need to be first disassembled. While this is a nontrivial problem itself, recent works (e.g., [56, 57]) have developed robust solutions, at least for our experimental platform. Thus we focus on the next step, namely, lifting (long) sequences of assembly instructions to IL.

Lifting would be straight-forward if the mapping derived in the last section operated on a single assembly instruction at a time. However, there are many instances where the translation operates on multiple instructions at the same time. This arises typically because compilers require some primitives that cannot be realized using a single instruction. For instance, manipulating stack canaries requires multiple assembly instructions that should not be separated for security reasons. Handling such groups is necessary not only because some instructions may occur only in groups[9], but also because it is advantageous to reconstruct the higher-level primitives when lifting up back to IL.

The most obvious approach for lifting in the presence of instruction groups is to use a greedy approach that maximizes the size of each group that can be lifted in one run of the transducer. The greedy strategy is motivated by the observation that larger sequences can reconstruct more of the high-level information. Unfortunately, it can be easily shown that a greedy strategy is not optimal: a greedy choice early on in the assembly sequence may preclude the use of many larger groups later on. Indeed, a greedy strategy is not even guaranteed to find *any* solution at all, unless it uses backtracking. Moreover, such a backtracking approach can have an exponential worst case complexity.

On further reflection, it becomes clear that the exponential blowup occurs due to repeated efforts to solve overlapping subproblems. By recognizing this structure, we develop an efficient algorithm that uses dynamic programming. The subproblems we consider correspond to prefixes of the given sequence $A_1 \cdots A_n$ of assembly instructions. We let C_j denote the minimum cost of lifting the prefix $A_1 \cdots A_j$. To compute this cost, we need to assign a cost GC to each group of assembly instructions that can be lifted by a single pass of the transducer. To express our preference for larger groups, we set $GC(B_1 B_2 \cdots B_r) = -r$ if the transducer can translate $B_1 B_2 \cdots B_r$, otherwise the cost is set to ∞.

The minimum cost C_j is given by the following equation, where k denotes the size of largest group that can be translated by the transducer.

$$C_j = \underset{1 \leq i \leq k}{Min} \; [C_{j-i} + GC(A_{j-i+1} A_{j-i+2} \cdots A_j)]$$

To see why this is correct, note that a minimum cost partitioning (into groups) of $A_1 \cdots A_j$ must have a last group. The size of this group cannot be larger than k, the largest group for which the transducer provides a translation. Moreover, preceding this last group is a partitioning of $A_1 \cdots A_{j-i}$. Clearly, the cost of this group should be C_{j-i} or else we can replace this partitioning with a lower-cost way and hence have a contradiction. This establishes the correctness of the above equation.

To analyze the complexity of computing C_j, note that it can be computed starting with $j = 1$ and going to $j = n$. Thus, we need to perform the "min" operation above n times. Each run of this min operation takes $O(k)$ time. Note that k should be property of the machine description used in the compiler, and should be small. In our experiments on x86, $k \leq 4$. When k is treated a constant, computing C_j takes $O(n)$ time. Thus we have a linear-time algorithm for lifting whole binaries to IL.

As with other dynamic programming algorithms, it is not enough to compute the minimum cost, but we also need to identify the corresponding partitions. But this step is routine, so we don't describe it further.

5. Soundness

Code generators use machine descriptions to perform IL to assembly translations, so a natural question is whether it is sound to use them in reverse. We begin by describing how MDs are developed and used, and how this use supports their use in reverse. A more formal and rigorous treatment is provided in Section 6.4.

[9] In fact, we find that many instructions that operate on the gs register on x86 occur in such multi-instruction bundles.

Machine descriptions are developed by enumerating instructions in the target architecture, and specifying the semantics of those instructions in IL. Thus, the developer view indeed corresponds to an assembly to IL mapping. Secondly, note that the IL-to-assembly mapping performed by a code generator must be sound, or else it will generate incorrect code. Therefore, an assembly instruction must perform all of the actions that are included in IL. This suggests that perhaps the assembly instruction could do more than what was asked for by the IL, e.g., change an additional register. If so, assembly-to-IL translation does not capture these extra actions. However, consider the fact that the IL optimizer performs several optimizations such as removal of redundant computations and reordering of code snippets. These would be unsound if we allowed an IL snippet to be replaced by an assembly instruction that modified CPU state in ways beyond what was stated in IL. Modern compilers such as GCC make use of many such optimizations even on the lowest levels of their IL. Undocumented effects of assembly instructions will invalidate these optimizations, thereby leading to the generation of incorrect code. Since code generators undergo extensive testing (by virtue of compiling vast amounts of code), it is reasonable to expect that such bugs in MDs would long have been found and fixed.

Finally, and most importantly, we have previously formulated the notion of correctness of code generators [26]. Based on this formulation, we have developed an automated testing approach for checking the equivalence of IL semantics and the corresponding assembly instruction. We summarize this formulation, and our experimental results in applying this formulation, in Section 6.4.

6. Evaluation

Our evaluation addresses completeness (Section 6.1), architecture-neutrality (Section 6.2), performance (Section 6.3) and correctness (Section 6.4). Additionally, we evaluate the effectiveness of the extracted model by developing an application using it (Section 6.5). Our implementation platform is Linux, and the architectures we target are x86, ARM and AVR. AVR processors are widely used in embedded systems: they underpin the popular Arduino platform, as well as numerous automotive applications.

All experiments were performed on a quad-core Intel i7 processor running 32-bit Ubuntu-14.04 OS. Compilers and other tools needed for ARM and AVR were obtained using cross-compilers for these architectures.

6.1 Completeness

For completeness experiments, we first build a transducer using the set of concrete pairs observed while compiling a set of programs (P_{train}). We then use this transducer to translate assembly instructions from a set of test binaries (P_{test}). We used `objdump` for disassembly, as it is quite robust on Linux.

P_{train}	% insns lifted		LISC (%)		Missing Mnemonics (absolute)
	Exact Recall	LISC	Missing Mnemonics	Missing Operands	
`openssl-1.0.1f` `+binutils-2.22`	63.72	98.46	1.05	0.49	464
`+ffmpeg-2.3.3`	68.21	98.74	1.03	0.23	377
`+glibc-2.21`	68.74	98.80	1.01	0.19	346
`+ffmpeg-2.3.3`[10]	69.07	98.89	0.88	0.23	303
`+gstreamer-1.4.5`	71.07	99.10	0.79	0.11	221
`+qt-5.4.1`	72.45	99.21	0.69	0.09	161
`+linuxkern-3.19`	73.97	99.49	0.44	0.07	49
`+Manual`	74.04	100.00	0.00	0.00	0

Figure 4. Completeness result for x86

P_{test} consisted of all the unique instructions in all binaries (including kernel modules) on a standard Linux desktop distribution. While the total number of instructions in these binaries approaches a trillion, after eliminating exact duplicates, we arrived at about 40M instructions in P_{test}. Note than neither P_{test} nor P_{train} include instructions executable only in kernel mode, as GCC never generates them.

We provide two types of numbers on completeness: the first, expressed as a percentage, concerns the fraction of the approximately 40M unique instructions in P_{test} that could not be translated by LISC. To interpret these percentages, we compare them with that obtained by the baseline technique of *exact recall* (ER), which is able to translate an instruction in $A \in P_{test}$ only if $A \in P_{train}$. Note that ER is a good baseline because (a) the previously known transducer algorithm OSTIA reduces to ER in our setting, and (b) ER provides the same correctness guarantee as our system, i.e., the system will correctly lift any $A \in P_{train}$.

Our second completeness metric is an absolute number: it counts the fraction of (distinct) instruction mnemonics that are not lifted by LISC. Note that both x86 and ARM support about 1200 distinct mnemonics.

The training data set, which was always a subset of P_{test}, was varied as follows. We started with P_{train} consisting of two binaries `openssl` and `binutils`. We then identified the binary that had the lowest completion rate with this training data, and then added that binary to P_{train}. This step was repeated until maximum possible completeness was obtained. This is not 100% because some instructions are never generated by the compiler used in our experiments. We now discuss these completeness results for each architecture.

6.1.1 Completeness Results for x86

Coverage on P_{test}. The results for x86 are shown in Figure 4. Rows in the figure list the packages that were added to P_{train} in each round. So `+ffmpeg` in the second experiment means that `ffmpeg` was added to the base training data of `openssl` and `binutils` in second iteration. We used `gcc-4.6.4` for 32-bit x86 with commonly used GCC flags (`-O2`, `-msse1`, `-msse4.2`, `-mavx`, `-mi387`, `-mmmx`, etc.) to

[10] `ffmpeg` was recompiled with SSE, i387, AVX enabled one-by-one.

P_{train}	% insns lifted		LISC (%)		Missing Mnemonics (absolute)
	Exact Recall	LISC	Missing Mnemonics	Missing Operands	
Openssl + binutils	34.58	88.21	6.86	4.94	814
+libfftw	44.60	92.77	6.01	2.22	553
+swig	51.43	95.67	3.72	0.61	422
+gcc	62.54	96.26	1.73	2.01	366
+libc	65.41	97.87	1.37	0.76	314
+gs	67.69	98.92	1.02	0.04	276
+slapd	69.54	98.95	0.85	0.2	246
+busybox	71.45	99.61	0.3	0.09	196
+libpoppler	71.90	99.66	0.3	0.04	126
+lib7z	72.10	99.78	0.21	0.01	76
+manual	72.23	100.00	0.00	0.00	0

Figure 5. Completeness result for ARM

capture a more complete set of instructions in the compiled packages. P_{test} consisted of all x86 binaries (including kernel modules) found on Ubuntu-14.04 desktop installation. To the best of our knowledge, Ubuntu uses GCC to produce these binaries. These binaries (9237 of them) were disassembled using `objdump-v2.24`.

After training LISC with a combination of `openssl` and `binutils`, which contain about 0.35M unique instructions, we could lift 98.46% of the 38M unique instructions in all of x86 binaries on Ubuntu-14.04. By adding a few more packages to the training set, coverage was increased to about 99.5%. At this point, the training data included about 3.1M unique instructions. Obtaining 100% coverage requires a small amount of manual effort, since the missing instructions are not used by GCC. This point is further elaborated below.

Coverage of Mnemonics. While counting instructions, we have counted a single mnemonic with different modes (byte vs word) separately. With this way of counting, there are 1187 total mnemonics on x86. (Recall that this number excludes instructions that are only available in the kernel mode.) Of these 1187, 49 mnemonics (4%) appear only in hand-written assembly, and are not generated by GCC. These include instructions such as `nop` and `enter` (inserted by the assembler), some rarely used arithmetic instructions (e.g., `aaa`, and `aad` operations on binary-coded decimals) and instructions to set/clear flag bits (e.g., `cld`), and low-level instructions such as `cpuid`, `invpcid`, and `rdtsc`.

Advanced instruction set extensions such as `sse`, `avx` and `fma` are covered in the semantics extracted by LISC. This contrasts with the fact that many of these extensions are not supported by mature (and popular) tools such as Valgrind.

We manually modeled these missing instructions. Since many of the instructions were simple, this wasn't a hard task, and took us only a few hours of effort.

6.1.2 Completeness Results for ARM

Coverage on P_{test}. For ARM, P_{test} contained all instructions obtained by compiling all binaries (7.3K in total) found on Debian-7.8.0 desktop installation, yielding a total of about 55M unique instructions. We used `gcc-4.7.3` cross-compiler for 32-bit ARM cortex-v7A [8], and used `arm-linux-gnueabi-objdump-v2.24` as the disassembler. The results are summarized in Figure 5. About 99.8% coverage could be obtained on P_{test} after training with about a dozen binary packages.

Coverage of Mnemonics. By our count, there are about 1200 distinct mnemonics supported by ARM v7A, of which 76 (about 6%) were missing in the learned semantic model because they were unused by `gcc-4.7.3`. These can be classified as: a few miscellaneous instructions (such as `dbg` and `dmb`), some low-level instructions (such as `isb`, `mcr2`, `mrs`, and `wfi`), and a few other advanced instructions (such as `vtbl`, `vtbx`, and `vstm`).

The total time taken to implement code changes for supporting ARM, including the time for testing and debugging, was around 9.5 person-hours.

6.1.3 Completeness Results for AVR

We then selected the AVR [9] processor. We trained LISC by using the same base packages for training as the earlier experiments, and used `avr-gcc-v4.8.2` cross-compiler to compile them. We then tested the extracted model on a few coreutils binaries (`ls`, `cp`, `cat`, `echo` and `head`) for AVR.[11] We used `avr-objdump-v2.23.1` disassembler to disassemble these binaries. Unfortunately, we could not get complete `coreutils` package to cross-compile. The extracted model covered 72 of the 76 AVR mnemonics. Our system was able to translate all of the assembly instructions from the input binaries.

Manual modeling was required for just 4 mnemonics (`break`, `nop`, `wdr`, and `sleep`).

6.2 Effort for supporting multiple architectures

Component (language)	Arch-neutral code	x86	ARM	AVR
Log collection (C)	70	-	-	-
Parameterization and transducer construction (OCaml)	2400	-	-	-
Assembly lexer (Ocamllex)	74	10	12	7
Assembly parser (OCamlyacc)	76	75	60	89
Utility code (scripts)	500	50	16	15

Figure 6. Breakdown of LISC implementation effort

Figure 6 shows the breakdown of the number of lines of code that is architecture-specific. Log collection adds a small amount of code to GCC to record ⟨assembly, IL⟩ pairs for learning. (Recall that testing data comes directly from binaries.) This code, as well as the code for learning the transducer, is architecture neutral.

Manual effort needed to support a new architecture is very small. It takes less than 100 lines of OCaml Lex and

[11] These binaries were obtained by using `avr-gcc-v4.8.2` cross-compiler to compile source code of these utilities. We did not attempt to run these binaries, as that is not needed for our experiments.

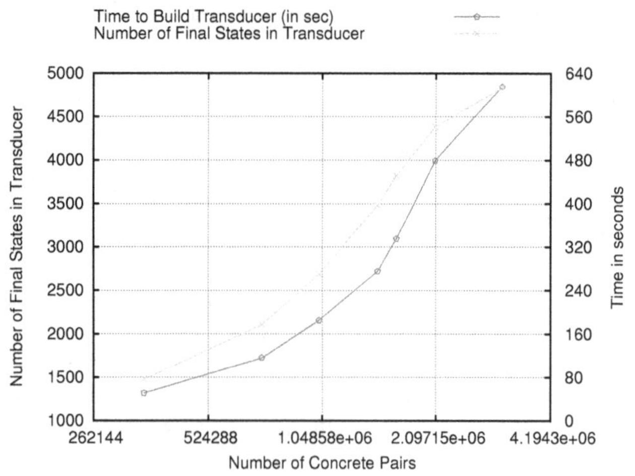

Figure 7. x86 Transducer Details

Yacc code to support each architecture. Note that this code is particularly easy to write since we are not writing full parsers for assembly, but a "rough" parser that can make out the approximate tree structure.

The effort for supporting ARM, including the development of about 100 lines of code, and verifying that all components "work as expected" took about 9.5 person-hours.

The effort required for AVR was about 3.5 person-hours.

6.3 Performance

Figure 7 captures the performance of the learning algorithm. Note that the chart shows both time and size on the Y-axis. The Y-axis is linear, while the X-axis is logarithmic. So, although the transducer time may visually appear to increase super-linearly, the actual increase is close to linear. The time needed by the algorithm is relatively small, about 10 minutes for the largest training data consisting of about 3.5M concrete pairs on x86. We have not optimized space usage yet, but it is reasonable already — about 200MB for the largest transducer we have built.

The performance charts for ARM are qualitatively similar, but the actual transducer construction is almost four times as fast, and space usage is about half as much as the x86 transducer.

Performance for Lifting Entire Binaries. We described a linear-time dynamic programming algorithm for lifting binaries. We have experimentally verified that its runtime increases roughly in proportion to the size of the binary that is lifted. Due to space constraints, we will just summarize its performance below.

Using this algorithm to translate all binaries on Ubuntu and Debian took approximately 8 hours each. The total time includes the disassembly time, which is approximately a fifth of the total time to lift a binary.

6.4 Correctness of translation

We experimentally evaluate correctness in three ways.

- *Semantic equivalence test:* We rely on ArCheck [26] to test the correctness of the mappings derived by our approach.
- *Consistency test:* Note that it is possible for distinct IL-snippets to result in the generation of the same assembly instruction A. In this case, A may be lifted to two distinct IL-snippets, which may seem like an error in lifting. We describe a systematic investigation to analyze them.
- *Loop-back test:* Given a binary with a list $\mathcal{A}$ of assembly instructions, lift it up to IL $\mathcal{I}$ using LISC, and then use GCC to generate code for $\mathcal{I}$ and check that this code matches $\mathcal{A}$.

6.4.1 Semantic equivalence test

Here, we rely on ArCheck [26], which defines two notions of correctness:

- *Soundness:* This notion permits IL to leave some effects of assembly instructions unspecified, e.g., the IL may indicate that certain registers (or memory locations) are *clobbered.* In particular, IL may over-approximate the effects of assembly, but it cannot miss any effects.
- *(Strong) Equivalence:* Here the semantics of IL and assembly must be identical. In other words, the IL precisely captures the effect of assembly.

ArCheck currently supports 140 of the basic x86 instructions. We used it to verify the soundness of the IL produced by LISC for all these instructions. While this does not eliminate the possibility of soundness errors for the remaining instructions, it does validate our approach, and suggests that such errors are unlikely.

The only soundness problem we have observed so far arises in the context of a call instruction. In particular, an IL-level call indicates the number of actual parameters, but this information is unavailable at the assembly level. We can address this problem by lifting a call instruction to indicate no parameters at the IL level.

We also used ArCheck to verify that the IL produced by LISC preserves strong equivalence for 109 of the 140 instructions. For the remaining 31, differences arise due to CPU flags as discussed below.

Impact on Binary Analysis/Instrumentation. Soundness is a requirement for most applications of binary analysis and instrumentation. Without soundness, the lifted IL would be incorrect in some cases, and lead to problems and failures. Equivalence is desirable but not critical for all applications. Indeed, we observe that equivalence failures arise primarily in the context of CPU flags, which are typically left unspecified after most arithmetic and logical instructions. GCC uses only a small subset of these instructions (e.g., the compare instruction) to translate conditionals, and hence specifies flags accurately for this subset.

Binary analyses typically rely on abstraction — what is needed is a sound approximation, which is what we focus on. Instrumentation involves preserving original code, while adding new code to maintain metadata or to enforce policies. For instructions whose IL is not strongly equivalent, a simple liveness analysis of over-approximated fields can be performed. Specifically, a static analysis can be used to determine if subsequent instructions rely on any of state (say, flags) that is over-approximated in the IL; if not, then the approximation cannot have any negative effect. On the other hand, if there is a possible use, then the instrumentation system can be designed to ensure that the exact same instruction is emitted again, thereby preserving the original semantics.

6.4.2 Consistency test

The approach discussed above shows that every pair $\langle I, A\rangle$ produced by the code generator represents a sound translation of assembly code A to IL I. However, this leaves the following question open: if the code generator produces the same assembly code A for two distinct IL snippets I_1 and I_2, which of these should be used as the IL for A? The following possibilities arise:

- If any one of the IL translations preserves strong equivalence, then choose this IL as the preferred translation.
- Otherwise, there exist n sound ILs $I_1, \ldots, I_n$ for an assembly instruction A, but none of them are strongly equivalent to A. Since each of $I_1, \ldots, I_n$ is a sound approximation, their intersection is also a sound approximation of A. Moreover, this intersection is likely to be more complete than any individual I_j, and indeed, may be strongly equivalent.

For the ILs learned by LISC for x86, we made the following observations:

- Of the total 1187 mnemonics in x86, around 24% map to multiple possible ILs.
- Of these 24%, a vast majority of them — specifically, 22% — mapped to at least one IL that was strongly equivalent to the assembly instruction.
- For the remaining 2%, we apply the intersection operation. We found that for most of them, differences arise because the ILs define different subsets of CPU flags. By taking the intersection, we were able to achieve strong equivalence for most of these mnemonics.

Similarly for ARM, we made the following observations:

- Of the nearly 1200 assembly mnemonics, 15% (around 180) had multiple possible ILs.
- A vast majority of these — about 14% — mapped to at least one IL that was semantically-equivalent to the assembly instruction.
- For almost all of the remaining 1%, we applied the intersection operation and obtained semantic equivalence.

6.4.3 Loop-back test

There are factors to be noted in this context. First, note that GCC is unable to regenerate code for instructions such as nop that it never generates on its own. Second, due to the fact that two distinct assembly instructions A_1 and A_2 could be equivalent to the same IL, it is possible that lifting A_1 and regenerating code may result in A_2. We compensate for both factors in our test.

We have successfully performed this test on most of the data in P_{test} but not all. This is because GCC is not designed to accept externally produced RTL and translate it. As a result, our attempts to translate the lifted RTL can fail inexplicably in some cases. Moreover, the fact that GCC may not recognize some of the manually-introduced ILs (about 5% of assembly mnemonics) introduces an additional challenge. Our efforts have been focused on understanding GCC internals to model such instructions in a GCC-friendly way.

Despite these challenges, we have been able to carry out the loop-back tests successfully for several large binaries such as vim, gedit, python interpreter, latex, wireshark, mplayer, and packages from coreutils, binutils, and SPEC. In total, around 67% x86 binaries, 74% ARM binaries and 94% AVR binaries from our test data pass loop-back test. (Note that these numbers refer to entire binaries that passed the test. If we counted the instructions that were successfully regenerated, that number would be much closer to 100%.)

6.5 Application of extracted semantic model

We have applied our model for binary analysis, specifically, for implementing a robust shadow stack [41]. Shadow stack provides strong protection against stack smashing and ROP attacks, but the technique has not been deployed because previous approaches suffered from false positives on complex programs. In particular, complex code ends up using return instructions for purposes other than returning from a function call. A deep and precise static analysis is necessary to identify such uses of return instructions, and instrument them differently from normal returns. We applied the detailed instruction semantic models derived by LISC to perform this static analysis. As a result, we were able demonstrate the absence of false positives on a wide range of large and complex applications.

7. Related work

Binary analysis and instrumentation. Most previous binary analysis/instrumentation systems, including DynamoRio [13], Pin [36], QEMU [12], Valgrind [37], SecondWrite [7], CodeSurfer [11], UQBT [17] and many other systems [16, 21, 31, 33, 48] require a hand-written target instruction specification to drive the translator. We are not aware of other efforts that use compilers to fully automate this effort.

Some previous [15, 29] have developed assembly-to-IR translators by relying on QEMU's support for multiple architectures. Specifically, they have written a backend for

QEMU to translate QEMU's IR to LLVM's IR. BAP [14], on the other hand, directly uses Valgrind's assembly to IR translator. These methods thus inherit any completeness issues from QEMU and Valgrind, which manifest as (a) support for only the most commonly used platforms, and (b) missing support for new and advanced instruction sets.

DisIRer [30] and Dagger [2] are two efforts that leverage compiler infrastructures to lift binaries to an IL. Dagger relies on the LLVM infrastructure, but their approach for lifting is manual. Hence it requires a considerable amount of additional code development, as well as a good understanding of LLVM internals.

DisIRer's goals are similar to ours: using MDs in reverse to lift binaries. However, as discussed earlier, there are many parts of MDs that are not specifications, and the only way to invert them is if we understand the C-code involved, and manually write functions to invert them. This requires a large amount of manual development effort for each architecture, thus negating the main advantage of using compiler MDs.

Language translation and transducers. Modern language translations efforts have been focused on natural languages. However, the complexity of natural languages implies that a certain rate of errors must be accepted. Our goals are thus closer to some of the earlier works, such as OSTIA [39] that emphasize error-free translation of simpler languages. (This relationship has already been discussed earlier in this paper.)

While we have defined tree transducers as automata, many earlier works have defined them using a formalism similar to grammars [43, 53]. Nevertheless, we are not aware of works that fully automate the learning of tree transducers. Language translation works that rely on tree transducers (e.g., [53]) still require humans to specify a (weighted) transducer, with the weights being derived using a learning process [25]. (Their choice of weighted transducers has again been influenced by the complexity of natural languages.)

While our goal has been to learn assembly to IL mappings, Derive [28] goes in the other direction: it learns the machine encoding of assembly instructions. There are some similarities between our work and theirs, e.g, they too want to identify simple transformations such as endian conversions. However, they do not concern themselves many of the problems we address, such as the learning of tree transducers (it is hard to represent machine code encodings as a parse tree), or avoiding strong assumptions about the structure of assembly code, or the interpretation of operands.

Collberg's [18] effort was more ambitious, attempting to learn MDs from a C-compiler. His approach is to construct very simple C-programs that perform operations such as an addition, analyze the instructions produced, and deduce the semantics. The approach was reported to work on common arithmetic operations. However, it is unclear how the approach can be generalized beyond simple arithmetic operations on registers.

Matching Automata and Decision Trees. The problem of efficiently matching terms has been studied extensively in the context of functional and logic programming, as well as automated theorem-proving. Given a set of terms $t_1, ..., t_n$, the problem is one of compiling the terms into an automaton that speeds up the identification of the term t_i that matches a given query term s. As compared to string matching, the key differences are (a) the need to handle variables, and (b) the ability to vary the order of traversing the nodes in the term so as to build more compact and efficient automata. Reference [45] discusses an array of techniques to handle a wide range of queries that arise in automated reasoning systems.

The criteria used for constructing compact matching automata are closely related to those used to construct decision trees in machine learning. While machine learning techniques rely on heuristics such as information gain that aren't guaranteed to construct optimal trees, it has been shown that under certain conditions, an *optimal* matching automaton can be constructed [46, 47]. Reference [51] extended the approach to matching network packets, and in that context, demonstrated major gains in terms of space and runtime over a previous technique [34] that relied on information gain. Many of the concepts used in this paper, such as mcp and $residue$, as well as the implementation of the $select$ function, have been based on that work [50, 51]. The main difference is that the current paper develops algorithms for learning translations on trees, while those previous works were focused on the (simpler) problem of term matching.

8. Conclusion

In this paper, we described an automated black-box approach called LISC for learning assembly-to-IL translators. Our experiments validate the hypothesis that by leveraging the knowledge already encoded in today's compilers, instruction semantics for diverse architectures can be obtained with relative ease. We showed that new architectures can be supported with as little as several hours of effort.

In a companion paper [41], we have demonstrated an application of the semantic model derived in this paper for performing a detailed static analysis on binaries. In our future work, we plan to study several additional applications that require accurate analysis and instrumentation of large binaries. Moreover, to aid other researchers working on similar problems, we have made an open-source version of LISC available for download from our laboratory web site [27].

Our approach can only recover the semantics of instructions generated by the compiler that feeds the ⟨assembly, IL⟩ pairs for our learning algorithm. Manual instruction modeling is required for those missing instructions. However, this factor does not reduce the value of our work: as our evaluation shows, manual effort is limited to about a twentieth of the instruction set. Moreover, these instructions tend to be very simple in nature (e.g., NOPs), so the effort needed is reduced by one to two orders of magnitude over a fully manual approach for modeling instruction semantics.

References

[1] Bad rounding in cvtsi2ss instruction. https://bugs.kde.org/show_bug.cgi?id=319393.

[2] Dagger. http://dagger.repzret.org.

[3] Incorrect decoding of vpbroadcastb,w reg,reg forms. https://bugs.kde.org/show_bug.cgi?id=340725.

[4] insn_basic test might crash because of setting and not clearing DF flag. https://bugs.kde.org/show_bug.cgi?id=326983.

[5] Power lxvw4x instruction uses 4 32 byte loads. https://bugs.kde.org/show_bug.cgi?id=339433.

[6] Martín Abadi, Mihai Budiu, Úlfar Erlingsson, and Jay Ligatti. Control-flow Integrity Principles, Implementations, and Applications. *ACM Trans. Inf. Syst. Secur.*

[7] Kapil Anand, Matthew Smithson, Aparna Kotha, Khaled Elwazeer, and Rajeev Barua. Decompilation to Compiler High IR in a Binary Rewriter. Technical report, Univ of Maryland, 2010.

[8] ARM. ARM Architecture Reference Manual ARMv7A and ARMV7-R edition. http://infocenter.arm.com/help/index.jsp?topic=/com.arm.doc.ddi0406c/index.html, 2014.

[9] Atmel. Atmel AVR 8-bit Instruction Set. www.atmel.com/images/Atmel-0856-AVR-Instruction-Set-Manual.pdf, 2014.

[10] Thanassis Avgerinos, Sang Kil Cha, Brent Lim Tze Hao, and David Brumley. AEG: Automatic Exploit Generation. In *Network and Distributed System Security Symposium*, 2011.

[11] Gogul Balakrishnan, Radu Gruian, Thomas Reps, and Tim Teitelbaum. CodeSurfer/x86 — A Platform for Analyzing X86 Executables. In *Compiler Construction*, 2005.

[12] Fabrice Bellard. QEMU, a Fast and Portable Dynamic Translator. In *Proceedings of the Annual Conference on USENIX Annual Technical Conference*, ATEC '05, 2005.

[13] Derek L. Bruening. *Efficient, Transparent, and Comprehensive Runtime Code Manipulation.* PhD thesis, Cambridge, MA, USA, 2004.

[14] David Brumley, Ivan Jager, Thanassis Avgerinos, and Edward J. Schwartz. BAP: A Binary Analysis Platform. In *Proceedings of the 23rd International Conference on Computer Aided Verification*, CAV'11, 2011.

[15] Vitaly Chipounov and George Candea. Dynamically Translating x86 to LLVM using QEMU. Technical Report EPFL-TR-149975, 2010.

[16] Cristina Cifuentes, Brian Lewis, and David Ung. Walkabout - A Retargetable Dynamic Binary Translation Framework. In *Workshop on Binary Translation*, 2002.

[17] Cristina Cifuentes, Mike Van Emmerik, and Norman Ramsey. The Design of a Resourceable and Retargetable Binary Translator. In *Reverse Engineering, 1999. Proceedings. Sixth Working Conference on*, 1999.

[18] Christian S. Collberg. Reverse Interpretation + Mutation Analysis = Automatic Retargeting. In *Proceedings of the ACM SIGPLAN 1997 Conference on Programming Language Design and Implementation*, PLDI '97, 1997.

[19] Manuel Costa, Jon Crowcroft, Miguel Castro, Antony Rowstron, Lidong Zhou, Lintao Zhang, and Paul Barham. Vigilante: End-to-end Containment of Internet Worm Epidemics. *ACM Trans. Comput. Syst.*, 26(4), December 2008.

[20] Jack W. Davidson and Christopher W. Fraser. Code Selection Through Object Code Optimization. *ACM Trans. Program. Lang. Syst.*, 1984.

[21] Thomas Dullien and Sebastian Porst. REIL: A platform-independent intermediate representation of disassembled code for static code analysis. 2009.

[22] Manuel Egele, Christopher Kruegel, Engin Kirda, Heng Yin, and Dawn Song. Dynamic Spyware Analysis. In *2007 USENIX Annual Technical Conference on Proceedings of the USENIX Annual Technical Conference*, ATC'07, 2007.

[23] Úlfar Erlingsson, Martín Abadi, Michael Vrable, Mihai Budiu, and George C. Necula. XFI: Software Guards for System Address Spaces. In *Proceedings of the 7th Symposium on Operating Systems Design and Implementation*, OSDI '06, 2006.

[24] LLVM Foundation. The LLVM Compiler Infrastructure Project. http://llvm.org.

[25] Jonathan Graehl, Kevin Knight, and Jonathan May. Training Tree Transducers. *Comput. Linguist.*, 2008.

[26] Niranjan Hasabnis, Rui Qiao, and R. Sekar. Checking Correctness of Code Generator Architecture Specifications. In *Proceedings of the 13th Annual IEEE/ACM International Symposium on Code Generation and Optimization*, CGO '15, 2015.

[27] Niranjan Hasabnis and R Sekar. LISC - Learning Instruction Semantics from Code Generator - software release. http://seclab.cs.sunysb.edu/seclab/lisc/.

[28] Wilson C. Hsieh, Dawson R. Engler, and Godmar Back. Reverse-Engineering Instruction Encodings. In *Proceedings of the General Track: 2001 USENIX Annual Technical Conference*, 2001.

[29] Chun-Chen Hsu, Pangfeng Liu, Chien-Min Wang, Jan-Jan Wu, Ding-Yong Hong, Pen-Chung Yew, and Wei-Chung Hsu. LnQ: Building High Performance Dynamic Binary Translators with Existing Compiler Backends. In *Parallel Processing (ICPP)*, 2011.

[30] Yuan-Shin Hwang, Tzong-Yen Lin, and Rong-Guey Chang. DisIRer: Converting a Retargetable Compiler into a Multiplatform Binary Translator. *ACM Trans. Archit. Code Optim.*, 7, December 2010.

[31] Johannes Kinder and Helmut Veith. Jakstab: A Static Analysis Platform for Binaries. In *Proceedings of the 20th International Conference on Computer Aided Verification*, CAV '08, 2008.

[32] Vladimir Kiriansky, Derek Bruening, and Saman P. Amarasinghe. Secure Execution via Program Shepherding. In *USENIX Security Symposium*, 2002.

[33] Julian Kranz, Alexander Sepp, and Axel Simon. GDSL: A Universal Toolkit for Giving Semantics to Machine Language. In *Programming Languages and Systems*, Lecture Notes in Computer Science. 2013.

[34] Christopher Kruegel and Thomas Toth. Using Decision Trees to Improve Signature-Based Intrusion Detection. In *RAID*, 2003.

[35] James R. Larus and Eric Schnarr. EEL: Machine-independent Executable Editing. In *Proceedings of the SIGPLAN 1995 Conference on Programming Language Design and Implementation*, June 1995.

[36] Chi-Keung Luk, Robert Cohn, Robert Muth, Harish Patil, Artur Klauser, Geoff Lowney, Steven Wallace, Vijay Janapa Reddi, and Kim Hazelwood. Pin: Building Customized Program Analysis Tools with Dynamic Instrumentation. In *Proceedings of the 2005 ACM SIGPLAN Conference on Programming Language Design and Implementation*, PLDI '05, 2005.

[37] Nicholas Nethercote and Julian Seward. Valgrind: A Framework for Heavyweight Dynamic Binary Instrumentation. In *Proceedings of the 28th ACM SIGPLAN Conference on Programming Language Design and Implementation*, PLDI '07, 2007.

[38] James Newsome and Dawn Song. Dynamic Taint Analysis for Automatic Detection, Analysis, and Signature Generation of Exploits on Commodity Software. In *Network and Distributed System Security Symposium (NDSS)*, 2005.

[39] J. Oncina, P. García, and E. Vidal. Learning Subsequential Transducers for Pattern Recognition Interpretation Tasks. *IEEE Trans. Pattern Anal. Mach. Intell.*, 1993.

[40] GNU Project. The GNU Compiler Collection. `http://gcc.gnu.org`.

[41] Rui Qiao, Mingwei Zhang, and R. Sekar. A Principled Approach for ROP Defense. In *Proceedings of the 31st Annual Computer Security Applications Conference*, ACSAC 2015, 2015.

[42] Feng Qin, Cheng Wang, Zhenmin Li, Ho-seop Kim, Yuanyuan Zhou, and Youfeng Wu. LIFT: A Low-Overhead Practical Information Flow Tracking System for Detecting Security Attacks. In *Proceedings of the 39th Annual IEEE/ACM International Symposium on Microarchitecture*, MICRO 39, 2006.

[43] William C. Rounds. Mappings and grammars on trees. *Mathematical systems theory*, 4(3), 1970.

[44] Prateek Saxena, R Sekar, and Varun Puranik. Efficient Fine-grained Binary Instrumentation with Applications to Taint-tracking. In *Proceedings of the 6th annual IEEE/ACM international symposium on Code generation and optimization*, CGO '08, 2008.

[45] R. Sekar, I. V. Ramakrishnan, and Andrei Voronkov. Handbook of automated reasoning. chapter Term Indexing, pages 1853–1964. Elsevier Science Publishers B. V., Amsterdam, The Netherlands, The Netherlands, 2001.

[46] R. C. Sekar, R. Ramesh, and I. V. Ramakrishnan. Adaptive Pattern Matching. In *Proceedings of the 19th International Colloquium on Automata, Languages and Programming*, ICALP '92, 1992.

[47] RC Sekar, R Ramesh, and IV Ramakrishnan. Adaptive Pattern Matching. *SIAM Journal on Computing*, 24(6):1207–1234, 1995.

[48] Alexander Sepp, Julian Kranz, and Axel Simon. GDSL: A Generic Decoder Specification Language for Interpreting Machine Language. *Electronic Notes in Theoretical Computer Science*, 2012. Third Workshop on Tools for Automatic Program Analysis (TAPAS' 2012).

[49] Dawn Song, David Brumley, Heng Yin, Juan Caballero, Ivan Jager, Min Gyung Kang, Zhenkai Liang, James Newsome, Pongsin Poosankam, and Prateek Saxena. BitBlaze: A New Approach to Computer Security via Binary Analysis. In *Proceedings of the 4th International Conference on Information Systems Security. Keynote invited paper.*, December 2008.

[50] A. Tongaonkar and R. Sekar. Condition Factorization: A Technique for Building Fast and Compact Packet Matching Automata. *IEEE Transactions on Information Forensics and Security*, 2016.

[51] Alok Tongaonkar, R. Sekar, and Sreenaath Vasudevan. Fast Packet Classification Using Condition Factorization. In *Proceedings of the 7th International Conference on Applied Cryptography and Network Security*, ACNS '09, 2009.

[52] P. Vogt, F. Nentwich, N. Jovanovic, E. Kirda, C. Kruegel, and G. Vigna. Cross-Site Scripting Prevention with Dynamic Data Tainting and Static Analysis. In *In Proceeding of the Network and Distributed System Security Symposium (NDSS)*, 2007.

[53] Kenji Yamada and Kevin Knight. A Syntax-based Statistical Translation Model. In *Proceedings of the 39th Annual Meeting on Association for Computational Linguistics*, ACL'01, 2001.

[54] Bennet Yee, David Sehr, Gregory Dardyk, J. Bradley Chen, Robert Muth, Tavis Ormandy, Shiki Okasaka, Neha Narula, and Nicholas Fullagar. Native Client: A Sandbox for Portable, Untrusted x86 Native Code. In *Security and Privacy, 2009 30th IEEE Symposium on*, 2009.

[55] Heng Yin, Dawn Song, Manuel Egele, Christopher Kruegel, and Engin Kirda. Panorama: Capturing System-wide Information Flow for Malware Detection and Analysis. In *Proceedings of the 14th ACM Conference on Computer and Communications Security*, CCS '07, 2007.

[56] Mingwei Zhang, Rui Qiao, Niranjan Hasabnis, and R. Sekar. A Platform for Secure Static Binary Instrumentation. In *ACM SIGPLAN/SIGOPS International Conference on Virtual Execution Environments (VEE)*, 2014.

[57] Mingwei Zhang and R. Sekar. Control Flow Integrity for COTS Binaries. In *Proceedings of the 22nd USENIX Conference on Security*, SEC'13, 2013.

Architecture-Adaptive Code Variant Tuning

Saurav Muralidharan
University of Utah
sauravm@cs.utah.edu

Amit Roy
University of Utah
aroy@cs.utah.edu

Mary Hall
University of Utah
mhall@cs.utah.edu

Michael Garland
NVIDIA Corporation
mgarland@nvidia.com

Piyush Rai
IIT Kanpur
piyush@cse.iitk.ac.in

Abstract

Code variants represent alternative implementations of a computation, and are common in high-performance libraries and applications to facilitate selecting the most appropriate implementation for a specific execution context (target architecture and input dataset). Automating code variant selection typically relies on machine learning to construct a model during an offline learning phase that can be quickly queried at runtime once the execution context is known. In this paper, we define a new approach called architecture-adaptive code variant tuning, where the variant selection model is learned on a set of source architectures, and then used to predict variants on a new target architecture without having to repeat the training process. We pose this as a multi-task learning problem, where each source architecture corresponds to a task; we use device features in the construction of the variant selection model. This work explores the effectiveness of multi-task learning and the impact of different strategies for device feature selection. We evaluate our approach on a set of benchmarks and a collection of six NVIDIA GPU architectures from three distinct generations. We achieve performance results that are mostly comparable to the previous approach of tuning for a single GPU architecture without having to repeat the learning phase.

Categories and Subject Descriptors C.4 [*Performance of Systems*]: Modeling Techniques; D.2.8 [*Metrics*]: Performance Measures; D.3.4 [*Processors*]: Optimization

Keywords autotuning; cross-architectural tuning; input-adaptive; multi-task learning; device feature selection

ASPLOS '16, April 02-06, 2016, Atlanta, GA, USA

DOI: http://dx.doi.org/10.1145/2872362.2872411

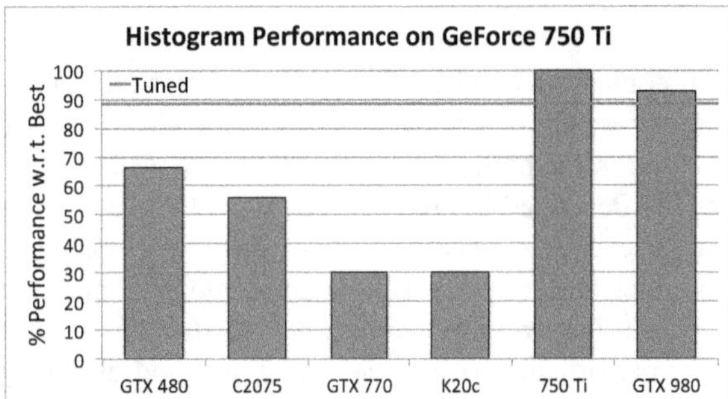

Figure 1: Histogram performance on the GeForce 750 Ti when trained on other architectures. The tuned line shows the performance of our system when trained using data from all architectures other than 750 Ti.

1. Introduction

Modern high-performance computing hardware has grown increasingly complex with the proliferation of deep memory hierarchies, hierarchical parallelism and latency vs. throughput-optimized processor cores. Achieving high performance on such systems thus often requires the use of automatic performance tuning (*autotuning*) software [6, 18, 32, 37, 38]. Autotuners systematically navigate a search space of possible implementations of a computation to find the implementation(s) that best meets a specific optimization criteria, usually performance. *Code variants* in such systems represent alternative implementations of a computation. Each code variant has the same interface, and is functionally equivalent to the other variants but may employ fundamentally different algorithms or implementation strategies.

Prior work on code variant selection and related code optimization systems have successfully employed machine

This research was funded in part by the U.S. Government. The views and conclusions contained in this document are those of the authors and should not be interpreted as representing the official policies, either expressed or implied, of the U.S. Government.

learning to develop an optimization model during an offline training phase [1, 11, 16, 23, 24, 29, 30, 35]. Such a model can be queried to perform variant selection at runtime once properties of the input dataset are available. These systems, however, require the variant selection model(s) to be re-trained every time the software is installed on a new architecture or if the underlying hardware is upgraded. This training process is typically very time-consuming and heavy on system resources; we are required to evaluate each variant v for each input i when collecting the training data. This paper evaluates the following question: *Can we develop a methodology to reuse results of training on two or more source architectures to create a variant selection model for a different target architecture without training on the target architecture?* While the overall approach we present in this paper is general, we simplify the problem by focusing on only NVIDIA GPUs.

As a motivating example, consider the Histogram operation: it counts the number of observations that fall into one of a set of disjoint bins. Consider the six code variants for Histogram in the high-performance GPU CUB library [26], which are described in Figure 3. There are two variants that do not use atomic operations, two that use global memory atomics and two that use shared memory atomics. The best variant is therefore *architecture-sensitive*, based on the relative performance of atomic operations, and also *input-sensitive*, e.g., affected by input size and mean sample distribution.

Figure 1 shows performance for Histogram on the GeForce 750 Ti GPU (Maxwell), when using a variant selection model trained on six different GPU architectures. The x-axis captures results when trained on the corresponding GPU. The y-axis represents percentage performance achieved by the variant selected by a model with respect to the best-performing variant (exhaustive search), averaged across all inputs in a test dataset. From the figure, it is clear that while variant selection models trained and tested on the same architecture perform well (above 95% of exhaustive search), this is not the case when models trained on architecture X are deployed on architecture Y (X $\neq$ Y), with performance dropping to as low as 30% of exhaustive in some cases.

While an architecture-specific model yields high performance, the time-consuming training phase must be repeated for each application and target architecture. In this paper, we instead develop a system that automatically constructs code variant selection model(s) on a target architecture using only training data from a set of source architectures specified by the programmer, together with information that characterizes each architecture. On the target, no variants are executed during the model construction process, since no training data from the target is required. Our system thus enables the construction of performance-portable software that quickly and automatically adapts to both changing inputs and new hardware architectures. In Figure 1, the line labeled 'Tuned' shows performance achieved by our system trained on data from every architecture except the 750 Ti.

We treat the cross-architectural tuning problem as a *multi-task* [8] learning problem, where each separate task denotes an architecture. Features that characterize each architecture (hereafter referred to as *device features*) are collected automatically (a one-time operation) on each architecture. Device features not relevant to the application in question are pruned away. The resulting device features are then used in the multi-task learner to come up with variant selection model(s) for the target architecture.

This paper makes the following contributions: (1) it develops the first automated approach (to our knowledge) to cross-architecture autotuning, which uses multi-task learning to develop a model on a target architecture from training on different source architectures; (2) it summarizes a wealth of empirical data for six computations and six GPU architectures across three distinct generations that captures reasons behind architectural sensitivity to code variant selection; and, (3) it demonstrates that device feature selection is valuable in building a successful code variant selection model on new architectures, discussing the strengths and limitations of the approach.

2. System Overview

The automated system described in this paper extends the Nitro autotuning framework [29]. Nitro provides a library interface that permits expert programmers to express code variants along with meta-information that aids the system in selecting among the set of variants at runtime. Figure 2(a) illustrates the approach in Nitro. A learning algorithm – Support Vector Machine (SVM) classifier by default – constructs a code variant selection model on the target architecture as a result of an offline training phase on the same architecture. For each architecture, training data has the form $\{(\mathbf{x}_1, y_1), \ldots, (\mathbf{x}_N, y_N)\}$, where each $\mathbf{x}_i$ represents an input feature vector and each y_i represents the best variant for that input. When presented with a new, unseen input at runtime, the model predicts the best variant to use.

Figure 2(b) shows how we have extended Nitro to support architecture-adaptive tuning. We can omit the training data collection on the target architecture by using previously-collected training data from one or more source architectures. To capture the signature of the target architecture and its relationship to the source architectures, we rely on *device features*, listed in Table 1. On NVIDIA platforms, these features are obtained in three possible ways: most are discovered instantaneously using the built-in `deviceQuery` program bundled with the CUDA toolkit. `Static` device features are easily-obtained published specifications that augment what is returned by `deviceQuery`. If any other features are needed, then `Custom` features can be added. We observed that there were no features that captured the cost of atomic operations, which vary significantly across GPU generations. Therefore,

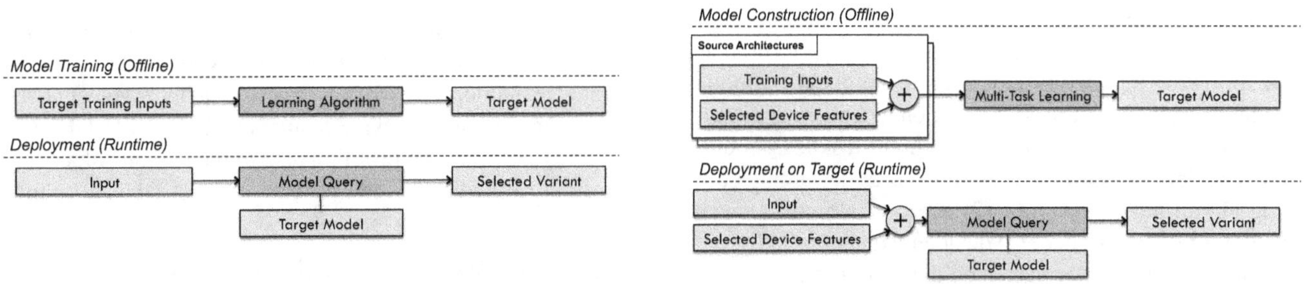

(a) Overview of the original Nitro system.

(b) Architecture-adaptive tuning overview.

Figure 2: Comparison of the original Nitro system with architecture-adaptive tuning. When tuning across architectures, values of the device features selected through DFS are obtained on both the source (during model construction) and target (during deployment). These are then concatenated with feature values of the relevant input data point ('+' operator in the figure).

	Fermi		Kepler		Maxwell	
Feature	**480**	**C2075**	**770**	**K20c**	**750**	**980**
deviceQuery						
`global_mem (GB)`	1.5	5.2	4.0	4.7	2.0	4.0
`cuda_cores`	480	448	1536	2496	640	2048
`clock_rate (MHz)`	1401	1147	1110	706	1268	1216
`mem_clock_rate (MHz)`	1848	1566	3505	2600	2700	3505
`mem_bus_width (bits)`	384	384	256	320	128	256
`l2_cache_size (KB)`	768	768	512	1280	2048	2048
`shared_mem_per_block (KB)`	48	48	48	48	48	48
`copy_engines`	1	2	1	2	1	2
Static						
`peak_gbps`	177.4	144.0	224.0	208.0	86.4	224.0
`peak_gflops_sp`	1345	1030	3213	3520	1389	4612
`peak_gflops_dp`	168	515	134	1170	43	156
Custom						
`shared_atomic (msec)`	0.193	0.238	0.281	0.361	0.011	0.006
`global_atomic (msec)`	0.402	0.488	0.034	0.051	0.063	0.036

Table 1: Values of GPU device features for 6 architectures.

	480		C2075		770		K20c		750		980	
	H	**S**	**H**	**S**	**H**	**S**	**H**	**S**	**H**	**S**	**H**	**S**
480	1	1	0.9	0.8	0.3	-0.4	0.6	0.3	-0.8	-0.6	0.2	-0.4
C2075	0.9	0.8	1	1	0	-0.8	0.5	-0.3	-0.6	0	-0.3	-0.8
770	0.3	-0.4	0	-0.8	1	1	0.9	0.8	-0.8	-0.6	0.3	1
K20c	0.6	0.3	0.5	-0.3	0.9	0.8	1	1	-1	-1	-0.1	0.8
750	-0.8	-0.6	-0.6	0	-0.8	-0.6	-1	-1	1	1	0	-0.6
980	0.2	-0.4	-0.3	-0.8	0.3	1	-0.1	0.8	0	-0.6	1	1

Table 2: Cosine similarity between architectures for Histogram (*H*) and SpMV (*S*). Values closer to +1 indicate similarity, while values closer to -1 indicate dissimilarity.

we added to Nitro two microbenchmarks that measure this; other microbenchmarks could be added to the `Custom` set as needed. Device feature values for the six GPU architectures we consider in this paper are also listed in Table 1.

We pose the problem of architecture-adaptive tuning as a *multi-task learning* (MTL) problem. MTL algorithms learn multiple tasks simultaneously to capture intrinsic relatedness between tasks. In our system, each separate architecture is represented as a task, and inter-task relationships are learned using MTL algorithms. We use *feature concatenation* for MTL, which derives the code variant selection model for the target architecture and is formally described in Section 3.1. In earlier stages of this research, we implemented and explored other MTL algorithms such as weighted kernels and probabilistic SVMs [7], but found that variant selection performance was far more affected by device feature selection than MTL algorithms.

We have discovered that using the full set of 13 device features does not yield the most accurate predictions, and which features are most relevant to code variant selection is application-specific. Therefore, our system performs *device feature selection (DFS)* to pinpoint the small number of device features relevant to the current application.

Each code variant stresses different components of the hardware architecture, such as the DRAM subsystem, floating-point performance, parallelism, machine balance, etc. To demonstrate that device feature selection is application-specific, Table 2 approximates the similarity between architectures for two benchmarks: Histogram and Sparse Matrix-Vector Multiplication (SpMV). Each entry in the table corresponds to the *cosine-similarity* (cosine of the angle between vectors) between device feature vectors of the corresponding architectures. Thus, values closer to +1 indicate similarity, while values closer to -1 indicate dissimilarity. Note that the optimal set of device features for both the benchmarks are different, since Histogram and SpMV variants stress different components of the hardware architecture. Thus, two architectures which are very similar for the SpMV computation may be completely different for Histogram. For example, the entry corresponding to (C2075, 750) shows that for Histogram, the C2075 and 750 are quite dissimilar (a fact confirmed in Figure 1), while the same pair of architectures is relatively similar for the SpMV benchmark.

3. Tuning Process

Our system employs a two-phase device feature selection (DFS) strategy to automatically find the best-performing subset of device features (in terms of final variant selection performance) for each computation. These selected device features may then be used by a multi-task learning algorithm to automatically construct variant selection models. The following subsection describes the process of model training using the feature concatenation technique. The subsections that follow describe how the multi-task learner constructs variant selection models on the target architecture using (1) all device features; (2) device features found by profile DFS (P-DFS); and, (3) device features found by performing cross-validation search on the output of P-DFS.

3.1 Model Construction using MTL

The feature concatenation strategy for multi-task learning appends device features to input features and builds an SVM model based on this new training dataset. More formally, let there be M source architectures and N training inputs. Further, let $\{\mathbf{a}_1, \mathbf{a}_2, ..., \mathbf{a}_M\}$ denote device feature vectors for each of the M source architectures. Then, for a given source architecture s, the corresponding training set is:

$$T_s = \{([\mathbf{x}_1 \circ \mathbf{a}_s], y_{s1}), \ldots, ([\mathbf{x}_N \circ \mathbf{a}_s], y_{sN})\}$$

where $\{\mathbf{x}_1, \ldots, \mathbf{x}_N\}$ is the set of N input feature vectors from the training set, and each y_{si} denotes the label (best variant) for training input i on architecture s; $[\circ]$ denotes vector concatenation. The full training set is then: $T = \bigcup_{s=1}^{M} T_s$, which is used to train an SVM classifier. During testing, the device features of the target architecture are concatenated with the input features before querying the model.

3.2 Utilizing the Full Set of Device Features

A straightforward solution to the architectural tuning problem is to feed the entire device feature set to the multi-task learner when it builds the variant selection model for the target. In this subsection, we describe how this naïve strategy works.

Source Architecture Side On the source architectures, when the user invokes the autotuning system, input features and corresponding variant labels are collected automatically, as in the original Nitro system [29]. This information is also recorded in a repository, to be retrieved when needed by target architectures. The device feature values for the source architecture in question are also collected and recorded in the repository.

Target Architecture Side On the target architecture, the user invokes a function in the autotuner, which automatically (1) retrieves the data collected from the source architectures from the repository; and (2) collects device feature values of the target. Each training input from the source architectures is of the form $\langle I, v\rangle$, where I represents an input feature vector and v represents the label of the best variant for that input. Using this together with device feature values for each source architecture, a variant selection model for the target architecture is constructed as explained in Section 3.1.

3.3 Profile Device Feature Selection (P-DFS)

With a restricted set of source architectures, extraneous device features can confuse the multi-task learner, as demonstrated in Section 6.2. We now describe an improvement over using the full set of device features called profile DFS (P-DFS), which uses the profiling data of the variants of a computation to predict the device features most relevant to that computation.

Application Proxies An application proxy is a small program that takes an *intensity* value ϕ as input, ranging from 0 to 5, and produces a GPU kernel with roughly `ϕ * 20%` instructions of a particular kind. The first column of Table 3 lists the application proxies used by our system. Thus, the `SP-GFLOP` proxy generates kernels with single-precision floating point instructions, the `ATOMIC` proxy generates kernels with atomic add instructions and so on. As a concrete example, when the `SP-GFLOP` proxy is provided an intensity value of 2, the proxy generates a CUDA kernel with roughly 40% single-precision floating point arithmetic instructions. The following code snippet shows the generated kernel code:

```
// 6 loads and stores, 4 floating-point instructions
A[i] = A[i+1]*beta + alpha;
A[i+1] = A[i+2]*beta + alpha;
A[i+2] = A[i+3];
```

Here, `A` is an array of type `float32`, `alpha` and `beta` are scalars (also of type `float32`), and `i` is the array index.

Each proxy P_j, where j ranges from 1 to 5 (total number of proxies) is associated with a set of device features F_j, representing the hardware component(s) that it stresses. The `ATOMIC` proxy, for example, is associated with the `shared_atomic` and `global_atomic` features. The first and last columns in Table 3 list these associations for each proxy.

Application Proxy Profiling For each proxy P_j, the system automatically collects tuples of the form $\langle C_{\phi j}, \phi\rangle$, where $C_{\phi j}$ represents the profiling data of a single run of proxy P_j, and ϕ is the intensity with which it is run. Each proxy has a subset of relevant profiling metrics, which are also listed in Table 3 (column 3). Running a proxy at every intensity from 0 to 5, we obtain a set of $\langle C_{\phi j}, \phi\rangle$ tuples that can be used to train a machine learning model. A model is built for every proxy, which can then be queried with profiling data of code variants.

Source Architecture Side The P-DFS approach requires collecting the following data on at least one source architecture: (1) profiling metrics C_v of each code variant v on each training input; and (2) profiling metrics of application proxies at different intensities $\langle C_{\phi j}, \phi\rangle$. Thus, in addition to invoking the autotuner as described in Section 3.2, the user is required to initiate profiling data collection. This automatically collects all the required profiling data and stores it in the repository.

Target Architecture Side On the target, the construction of variant selection models proceeds as in Section 3.2. How-

Proxy	Description	Profiling Metrics	Device Features
SP-GFLOP	Single precision floating-point	flop_count_sp, inst_fp_32, flop_sp_efficiency	peak_gflops_sp, cuda_cores, clock_rate
DP-GFLOP	Double precision floating-point	flop_count_dp, inst_fp_64, flop_dp_efficiency	peak_gflops_dp, cuda_cores, clock_rate
ATOMIC	Atomic operation latency	atomic_transactions_per_request, atomic_transactions, l2_atomic_transactions, l2_atomic_throughput, atomic_throughput	global_atomic, shared_atomic
MEM-BW	Global memory bandwidth	l1_cache_global_hit_rate, l1_cache_local_hit_rate, gld_transactions, gst_transactions, local_load_transactions, local_store_transactions, gld_transactions_per_request, gst_transactions_per_request, local_load_transactions_per_request, local_store_transactions_per_request, stall_memory_dependency, gld_efficiency, gst_efficiency, l2_l1_read_hit_rate, l2_read_transactions, l2_write_transactions, dram_read_transactions, dram_write_transactions, l2_l1_read_transactions, l2_l1_write_transactions, l2_utilization	peak_gbps, mem_clock_rate, mem_bus_width, l2_cache_size
SH-MEM-BW	Shared memory bandwidth	shared_load_transactions, shared_store_transactions, shared_load_transactions_per_request, shared_store_throughput	shared_mem_per_block

Table 3: GPU application proxies with corresponding profiling metrics and device features.

ever, this time, only device features selected by the P-DFS system are used for training the variant selection model.

Algorithm 1 provides an overview of the P-DFS process. The profiling data for the proxies at various intensities $\langle C_{\phi j}, \phi \rangle$ is first retrieved from the repository. This is then used to construct a set of models, one for each proxy. If we denote the model for proxy P_j as λ_j, then querying λ_j with the profiling metrics of a variant C_v will yield the intensity value corresponding to P_j for the variant. By querying each proxy model using the profiling data of the variants in the computation (also retrieved from the repository), and examining the predicted intensity values, the best proxies can be found. These are recorded for each input and in the final step, a majority voting scheme is used to select a global best set of proxies. The device features associated with the winning proxies (last column of Table 3) is returned as output of the P-DFS system.

Algorithm 1 Profile Device Feature Selection

```
▷ V: Set of variants
▷ I: Set of training inputs
▷ P: Set of application proxies
global_best ← {}
for v ∈ V do
    ▷ For each kernel in variant v
    for k ∈ kernels[v] do
        ▷ For each training input
        for i ∈ I do
            intensity ← {}
            for p ∈ P do
                ▷ Profiling data for kernel k on input i
                t ← profile[k, i]
                ▷ Predict intensity for proxy p on profile
                intensity[p] = intensity-predict(t, p)
            best_proxies[i] = {x : intensity[x]is highest}
        ▷ Add best proxies across inputs to global best
        global_best ∪ = majority-vote(best_proxies)
return global_best
```

3.4 Cross-Validation Device Feature Selection (CV-DFS)

Although device features obtained as a result of P-DFS are relevant to the computation in question, there may still be

Algorithm 2 Cross-Validation Device Feature Selection

1: ▷ *S:* Set of source architectures
2: ▷ *D:* Set of device features from P-DFS
3: global_best ← {}
4: ▷ *For each source architecture*
5: **for** $s \in$ S **do**
6:     best_accuracy ← 0
7:     best_set ← ∅
8:     ▷ *Assign a temporary target*
9:     target ← s
10:     sources ← $S - \{s\}$
11:     $T_s \leftarrow$ {**training-data**(x): $x \in$ sources}
12:     $T_t \leftarrow$ **training-data**(target)
13:     **for** $d \in$ **subsets**[D] **do**
14:         ▷ *Get device feature values of source and target*
15:         $DF_s \leftarrow$ {**df-values**(d, x): $x \in$ sources}
16:         $DF_t \leftarrow$ **df-values**(d, target)
17:         ▷ *Train MTL model using* T_s *and* DF_s
18:         model ← **mtl-train**(T_s, DF_s)
19:         ▷ *Predict and calculate accuracy w.r.t.* T_t
20:         accuracy ← **predict**(model, T_t, DF_t)
21:         **if** accuracy > best_accuracy **then**
22:             best_accuracy ← accuracy
23:             best_set ← d
24:     ▷ *Record best features and their frequencies*
25:     global_best ∪ = best_set
26: ▷ *Return the k most frequently occurring features*
27: **return most-frequent**(global_best, k)

extraneous features that confuse the variant selection model on the target. To obtain an even more pruned and relevant set of device features, we employ a cross-validation DFS (CV-DFS) strategy. An overview of CV-DFS is provided in Algorithm 2.

CV-DFS is performed on the target architecture, and does not require any extra data collection on the source architectures (over P-DFS). The algorithm proceeds by assigning one of the source architectures as a temporary target (Line 9 in Algorithm 2). Then, with the remaining source architectures, every subset of device features (currently restricted to size three) is exhaustively used to build a variant selection model for the temporary target (Line 18, **mtl-train** function) and performance of this model on the temporary target's training data is evaluated (Line 20, the **predict** function). This process is iteratively performed for each source architecture, and the k device features that perform best over all source architectures are chosen. By default, k is set to one (i.e., return the best device feature).

CV-DFS relies on the assumption that device features that yield good prediction performance on source architectures are likely to be good predictors on the target for the same computation. As demonstrated in Section 6, this assumption holds for most applications.

```python
from nitro import *
import glob

histogram = code_variant("histogram", 6)
# Record training data in store
histogram.record = True
histogram.device_id = "gtx_480"
# Create autotuner instance
tuner = autotuner("histogram")
inputs = glob.glob("training/*.jpg")
tuner.set_training_args(inputs)
# Tune for current architecture
tuner.tune([histogram])
```

Listing 1: Histogram tuning example - source architecture.

```python
from nitro import *

histogram = code_variant("histogram", 6)
histogram.profiling_based_dfs = True
histogram.search_based_dfs = True
# Create autotuner instance
tuner = autotuner("histogram")
# Build model from source data
tuner.tune_from_source([histogram])
```

Listing 2: Histogram tuning example - target architecture.

4. Implementation

The Nitro framework [29] provides C++ and Python interfaces for code variant tuning. Variants, input features, and optional constraints are specified using the C++ interface within the application, while a separate Python script is used to customize the tuning process. For the system described in this paper, we extend Nitro's Python tuning interface with additional functions and options.

The function `tune_from_source` automatically builds models for the target architecture using source training data and device feature values. We have implemented a storage system for variant training data using `Redis` [34]. The variant name, together with the device identifier is used to index into the store, where the variant training data, optional profiling data (for both the variants and proxy applications), and device feature values are kept. The `tune_from_source` function automatically retrieves the right data and builds the models. Users have the option of toggling both P-DFS (using the `profiling_based_dfs` knob) and CV-DFS (using the `search_based_dfs` knob). If P-DFS is enabled, then per-input profiling data must also be collected on at least one of the source architectures (using the `profile` function). Listings 1 and 2 provide examples of how this interface is used on the source and target sides, respectively.

5. Benchmarks

Figure 3 lists the benchmarks we use to evaluate our system's effectiveness, including a description of the set of variants, the features used, and number of inputs for training and test datasets. All of these benchmarks are derived from high-performance CUDA libraries that already included code variants. By using existing high-performance libraries, we are able to focus the experiment on the small amount of additional code required to apply our automated system to these benchmarks. The training and test inputs come from standard sources, as described, and the training inputs are not included in the test inputs. Further, we choose training inputs such that all variants are well-represented in the training set for each benchmark.

Histogram Histograms are very commonly used as building blocks in a number of domains, especially image processing. We use the variants implemented in the high-performance CUDA Unbound (CUB) library [26]. We evaluate three variants and two grid-mapping strategies, thus giving rise to six code variants. We use three features. We construct a 256-bin histogram for grayscale images, with pixel values ranging from 0 to 255. For training and testing, we use the images from the INRIA Holidays Dataset [21] (converted to grayscale). Out of the 1491 images in the dataset, 200 are used for training and the rest for testing.

Sparse Matrix-Vector Multiplication (SpMV) SpMV is used in many iterative methods for solving large-scale linear systems. For this experiment, we use the variants provided by the CUSP library [4]. We use 5 features and a training set consisting of 54 matrices from the UFL Sparse Matrix collection [15]. For the 100 matrices in the test set, we selected 10 matrices each from a set of 9 groups in the UFL collection at random (with the exception of the Williams group, which has only 7 matrices in the UFL collection), and generated 13 matrices related to stencils.

Sort We use 3 high-performance GPU sorting algorithms: Merge Sort, Locality-Optimized Segmented Sort, and Radix Sort as variants for this benchmark. The Merge and Locality Sorts are part of the ModernGPU [3] library of GPU primitives, while the Radix Sort implementation is provided in CUB [26].

Sorting is performed on 32 and 64-bit floating point keys. We train a combined model for both data types and report performance achieved on a test set consisting of both types of data. The training set consists of 60 sequences for each data type, thus giving us a total of 120 instances. For testing, we use a total of 600 sequences, 300 for each data type. Further, each of the 300 instances is divided into 3 categories, 100 consisting of uniformly random keys, 100 consisting of reverse sorted keys, and 100 consisting of almost sorted keys. The "almost sorted" category is generated by taking a sorted sequence and randomly swapping 20-25% of the keys. Key lengths are varied from 100K to 20M keys.

Breadth-First Search (BFS) BFS is used as a basis for algorithms that analyze sparse relationships (such as social networks and electronic design automation) represented as graphs. Variants are selected from a set of highly optimized BFS implementations for GPUs described in [28], part of a larger set of GPU primitives provided in the Back40 Library [25]. We consider a set of six variants provided in the library, which are designed for different types of input graphs. We use a set of 5 features. The training set for BFS consists of a set of 20 graphs and the test set consists of all the graphs in the DIMACS10 group in the UFL Sparse Matrix collection. We run 100 randomly-sourced BFS traversals for each graph to evaluate each variant. Further, we use traversed edges per second (TEPS) as the optimization metric.

Linear Solvers and Preconditioners Many large-scale scientific simulations such as computational fluid dynamics (CFD) and structural mechanics [20] involve solving partial differential equations (PDE) systems. Typically, solutions to a PDE involve solving the underlying sparse linear system using software toolkits [2, 31]. One of the challenges in effectively using such toolkits is the selection of an appropriate ⟨linear solver, preconditioner⟩ combination as this selection impacts both the performance and convergence of the computation. For this experiment, we use 6 ⟨linear solver, preconditioner⟩ combinations from the CULA Sparse toolkit [31], which is a GPU library for solving large sparse linear systems. Features used for this benchmark are based on the work by Bhowmick et al. [5]. We use symmetric sparse matrices from [15] to represent sparse linear systems.

Matrix Transposition In-place transposition of square matrices is a well-studied problem. Transposition of a non-square matrix is a much more involved process, requiring $O(mn \log mn)$ work. Catanzaro et al. [10] describe a set of in-place matrix transposition algorithms which perform the operation in $O(mn)$ time. These algorithms are packaged as an open-source library [9]. We use four variants from this library for our experiment: two for general row-to-column and column-to-row transposition, and another two specialized for skinny matrices. We use four features related to the dimensions of the matrix. Matrix dimensions are chosen from a uniform-random distribution with the constraint that the matrix fits in the memory of the GTX 480 GPU (the GPU with lowest memory capacity). The matrices are populated with 64-bit double precision values. 194 such matrices are used for training and 1000 for testing.

6. Results

We run our experiments on six NVIDIA GPUs characterized by the device features in Table 1: (1) GeForce GTX 480, (2) Tesla C2075, (3) GeForce GTX 770, (4) Tesla K20c, (5) GeForce 750 Ti, and (6) GeForce GTX 980. As shown in Table 1, these graphics cards span three GPU architecture families: Fermi, Kepler, and Maxwell. We use CUDA Toolkit version 6.5 for our experiments[1]. The host system is an Intel Core i7-4770 CPU (3.4 Ghz) with 32 GB of RAM. GPU profiling metrics are collected using the `nvprof` tool. Each profiling metric is normalized with respect to the total number of issued instructions in the GPU kernel.

[1] Except for Solvers, which requires CUDA 6.0 (due to CULA).

Benchmark	Variants	Description	Features	Description	(#Training, #Testing) I/Ps
SpMV	CSR, CSR-VEC	Performs SpMV on CSR-formatted matrices. CSR assigns a thread to each row. CSR-Vec assigns a warp to each row.	AvgNZPerRow, RL-SD, MaxDeviation	Features related to row length.	(54, 100)
	DIA, ELL	Perform SpMV on DIA and ELL formatted matrices.	DIA-Fillin, ELL-Fillin	Fillin ratio for DIA and ELL formats.	
Solver	CG-Jacobi, CG-Bjacobi, CG-Fainv	Conjugate gradients method with Jacobi, Blocked Jacobi and Factorized Approximate Inverse preconditioners	NNZ, #Rows	Number of nonzeros and rows.	(26, 100)
	BiCGStab-Jacobi BiCGStab-BJacobi BiCGStab-Fainv	BiConjugate gradients Stabilized method with Jacobi, Blocked Jacobi and Factorized Approximate Inverse preconditioners	Trace DiagAvg, DiagVar, DiagDominance LBw Norm1	Trace of a matrix. Features related to diagonal elements of a matrix. Left bandwidth of a matrix. 1-norm of a matrix.	
BFS	EC-Fused, EC-Iterative	Expand incoming vertex frontier, filter, and produce outgoing vertex frontier. Fused version invokes single kernel that steps through BFS iterations. Iterative version invokes a separate kernel for each BFS iteration.	AvgOutDeg, Deg-SD, MaxDeviation	Features related to graph out-degree.	(20, 138)
	CE-Fused, CE-Iterative	Contract incoming edge frontier, filter, and produce outgoing edge frontier.	#Vertices, #Edges	Number of vertices and edges.	
	2-Phase-Fused 2-Phase-Iterative	Isolates vertex expansion and edge contraction workloads into separate kernels			
Histogram	Sort-ES, Sort-Dynamic	Sort data first, and then do a quick run-length detection. Even-Share (ES) version assigns an even share of inputs to thread blocks, dynamic uses a queue.	N, N/#Bins SubSampleSD	Sequence of length and average length. Standard deviation of sub-sample.	(200, 1291)
	Global-Atomic-ES Global-Atomic-Dynamic	Compute Histogram using global atomic add operations.			
	Shared-Atomic-ES Shared-Atomic-Dynamic	Compute Block-level Histogram using shared memory atomicAdd, and then reduce to final Histogram.			
Sort	Merge Sort	Merge sort from ModernGPU library.	N	Input size.	(120, 600)
	Locality Sort	Locality sort from ModernGPU library.	NBits	32 or 64 bits.	
	Radix Sort	Radix sort from CUB.	#AscSeq	# Ascending sub-sequences.	
Transpose	R2C, C2R	R2C, C2R variants from inplace library	M, N RowMajor	Number of rows, columns. Is in row-major layout.	(194, 1000)
	Skinny R2C Skinny C2R	R2C, C2R specialization for skinny matrices	CoPrime	Are M and N co-prime.	

Figure 3: Variants and features used for each benchmark. The last column lists the sizes of training and testing sets.

6.1 Architecture Sensitivity of Benchmarks

We first ask the question whether architecture differences significantly impact code variant selection. For this purpose, we identify the best variant (found through exhaustive search) for each input in the testing set across all benchmarks and architectures. Figure 4 provides a measurement of the architectural sensitivity of each benchmark. Here, the x-axis is the set of benchmarks, and the y-axis is the percentage of test inputs for which at least one architecture selects a different best variant than the others. In other words, it is the percentage of test inputs for which the exact same variant of the benchmark was not selected across all architectures. Figure 5 is similar, except it depicts architectural sensitivity of benchmarks within GPUs of each generation - namely, Fermi, Kepler, and Maxwell. Figure 5 shows that differences in variant selection are usually less pronounced within the same architectural family, but not always. Further data is shown in Table 4, where each sub-table represents a benchmark and a row represents the distribution of variant selection (via exhaustive search) across all test inputs for a particular architecture. We use these two figures and the table in the remainder of this subsection.

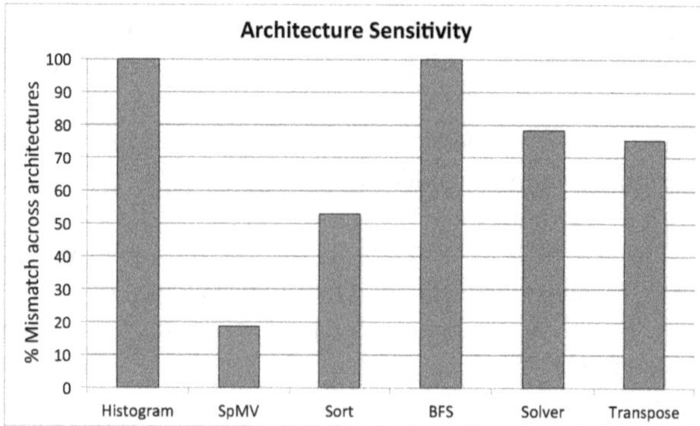

Figure 4: Architecture-sensitivity of each benchmark. The y-axis represents the percentage of test inputs for which at least one architecture selects a different best variant than the others.

From one generation to the next, new architecture features and machine configurations may dramatically affect

	SpMV			
	CSR	CSR-VEC	DIA	ELL
GTX 480	0.00	50.52	19.59	29.90
C2075	0.00	54.64	19.59	25.77
GTX 770	0.00	49.48	19.59	30.93
K20c	3.09	48.45	18.56	29.90
750 Ti	4.12	45.36	20.62	29.90
GTX 980	0.00	56.70	18.56	24.74

	BFS					
	EC-Fused	EC-Iter	CE-Fused	CE-Iter	2P-Fused	2P-Iter
GTX 480	0.00	0.70	90.91	4.90	1.40	2.10
C2075	0.00	0.71	90.00	7.86	1.43	0.00
GTX 770	0.71	59.29	0.71	37.86	0.00	1.43
K20c	24.64	0.00	75.36	0.00	0.00	0.00
750 Ti	13.04	0.00	86.96	0.00	0.00	0.00
GTX 980	4.29	0.00	94.29	0.00	1.43	0.00

	Transpose			
	R2C	C2R	Skinny R2C	Skinny C2R
GTX 480	44.10	55.10	0.00	0.80
C2075	45.50	53.80	0.00	0.70
GTX 770	42.50	56.90	0.00	0.60
K20c	25.10	74.30	0.00	0.60
750 Ti	45.00	54.40	0.00	0.60
GTX 980	32.90	66.40	0.00	0.70

	Solver					
	CG-J	CG-BJ	CG-FAI	BiCGStab-J	BiCGStab-BJ	BiCGStab-FAI
GTX 480	12.90	15.05	6.45	35.48	23.66	6.45
C2075	13.98	12.90	6.45	32.26	30.11	4.30
GTX 770	6.45	10.75	13.98	35.48	23.66	9.68
K20c	11.83	13.98	5.38	36.56	24.73	7.53
750 Ti	18.28	11.83	6.45	34.41	16.13	12.90
GTX 980	12.90	16.13	7.53	37.63	17.20	8.60

	Sort		
	Locality	Merge	Radix
GTX 480	3.50	27.17	69.33
C2075	7.50	47.00	45.50
GTX 770	2.50	26.00	71.50
K20c	1.67	36.00	62.33
750 Ti	33.50	4.50	62.00
GTX 980	39.00	17.17	43.83

	Histogram					
	Sort-ES	Sort Dynamic	GA-ES	GA-Dynamic	SA-ES	SA-Dynamic
GTX 480	0.64	36.30	0.00	0.00	7.13	55.93
C2075	0.00	33.73	0.00	0.00	26.92	39.34
GTX 770	0.08	73.56	4.49	0.40	0.24	21.23
K20c	0.00	85.18	0.08	0.00	4.49	10.26
750 Ti	0.00	0.00	0.00	0.00	97.84	2.16
GTX 980	0.00	0.00	0.00	0.00	0.16	99.84

Table 4: Variant selection histograms across different benchmarks and architectures. Each sub-table represents the distribution of variant selections across test data for a particular benchmark.

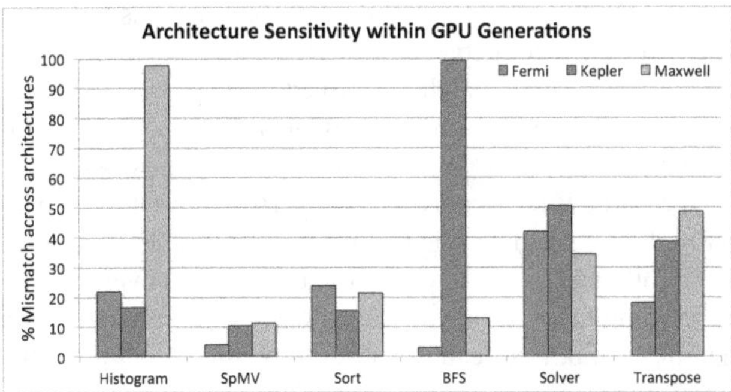

Figure 5: Architecture-sensitivity within GPUs of the same generation.

variant selection (e.g., support for atomic operations). But within a single generation, different selections are usually attributed to differences in (1) raw performance metrics (clock speed, memory bandwidth, floating point performance, etc.); or, (2) parallelism (number of cores). These architecture differences are captured in the device features of Table 1. From Figures 4 and 5 and Table 4, we see that Histogram reflects significant differences both across and within an architecture generation. The Maxwell generation devices (GTX 980 and 750 Ti) use the shared-atomic variants (SA-ES and SA-Dynamic) almost exclusively due to their low latency of shared memory atomics. However, these two devices rarely select the same shared-atomic variant, with the GTX 980 preferring SA-Dynamic and 750 Ti preferring SA-ES for most inputs. The Dynamic variants treat the input as a queue and atomically dequeue work in tiles for processing. Due to the reliance of these variants on atomics, the GTX 980 prefers them compared to the 750 Ti (the GTX 980's performance on atomics is nearly twice that of the 750 Ti, as Table 1 shows). The Kepler and Fermi devices predominantly use the Sort-Dynamic, SA-ES and SA-Dynamic variants, with the Kepler devices (GTX 770 and K20c) preferring the sorting-based variant over the shared-atomic ones. We believe that the slightly lower performance of shared atomics on Kepler when compared to the Fermi devices (GTX 480 and C2075) is the reason for this.

For BFS, most of the differences arise on the GTX 770 architecture. Specifically, the EC-Iterative and CE-Iterative variants are rarely selected by any architecture except the GTX 770. As described in Figure 3, the Iterative variants invoke a separate kernel for each BFS kernel, while the Fused versions use a single kernel to step through BFS iterations. Notice that `l2_cache_size` is a relevant device feature for BFS (Table 5, second column) and the GTX 770 has the lowest L2 cache size of all GPUs (Table 1). Since doing more work in a single kernel invocation typically increases L2 cache usage, we suspect that this is the reason for the GTX 770 preferring the Iterative variants over Fused ones.

Sort and Transpose exhibit architecture sensitivity, but not to the extent shown by Histogram and BFS and mostly across generations. The Maxwell generation of devices prefers to pick Locality sort over Merge sort, when compared to devices from other generations. The lower cost of atomic operations on Maxwell is most likely the reason for

Benchmark	Best Device Features	Proxies predicted by P-DFS	Best Feature by CV-DFS
Histogram	peak_gbps, shared_atomic, mem_bus_width	MEM-BW, ATOMIC	shared_atomic
SpMV	peak_gbps, mem_speed	MEM-BW, SH-MEM-BW	peak_gbps
Sort	global_atomic, l2_cache_size, shared_atomic	MEM-BW, ATOMIC	shared_atomic
BFS	global_atomic, shared_atomic, l2_cache_size, peak_gbps	MEM-BW, ATOMIC, SH-MEM-BW	shared_atomic
Solvers	global_atomic, shared_atomic, l2_cache_size, peak_gbps	MEM-BW, ATOMIC, SH-MEM-BW	shared_atomic
Transpose	global_atomic, shared_atomic, l2_cache_size, peak_gbps	MEM-BW, SH-MEM-BW	peak_gbps

Table 5: Best device features for each benchmark, proxies predicted by P-DFS, and the best features chosen by CV-DFS.

this, as Locality sort uses a dynamic work queue from which tasks are peeled off atomically. For Transpose, the bigger devices from the Kepler and Maxwell generations (the K20c and the GTX 980, respectively), tend to slightly prefer the C2R variant over R2C compared to other cards.

Finally, we notice from Table 4 that for the SpMV and Solver benchmarks, variants tend to be picked uniformly across architectures. We believe the primary reason for this is the fact that SpMV and Solver variants are optimized for various sparsity patterns of the input matrix and not necessarily for architecture-specific features; thus making them predominantly input-dependent. We were able to confirm this for the SpMV variants in the CUSP library by analyzing their source code, but not for the related Solver variants from CULA, which are closed-source.

6.2 Prediction Performance

First we look at how well device feature selection detects the relevant features for each benchmark. Table 5 shows the best subset of device features found by exhaustive search and by cross-validation search for each benchmark in the second and fourth columns, respectively. The third column shows the application proxies predicted by P-DFS for each benchmark. This exhaustive search finds the subset that yields best prediction accuracy on the target's test data. Since cross-validation DFS may predict a different subset of device features for every target, the last column of the table shows the device feature that occurs most frequently among all targets. We notice that P-DFS correctly predicts the proxies relevant to each benchmark. For example, it predicts that atomics are relevant to Histogram and BFS. Also, cross-validation search, guided by proxies found by P-DFS, discovers most of the important device features or nearby ones found via exhaustive search for all benchmarks. Another interesting observation is that although all the benchmarks we consider are predominantly memory bandwidth-bound, some benchmarks such as Histogram and BFS contain variants that rely on the use of global and shared-memory atomics. This reinforces our earlier point that the magnitude of architectural similarity is a function of the device features relevant to a benchmark's variants, and is not the same across all benchmarks.

Now we examine how well the different variant selection models derived from multi-task learning compare in their effectiveness against the original Nitro system (training and testing performed on the target architecture) and exhaustive search. In Figure 6, the benchmarks appear on the x-axis, with each bar representing a different target architecture (the remaining 5 architectures are used as sources). The y-axis shows percentage performance achieved compared to exhaustive search, as defined in the previous subsection. Bars labeled *Full Set* represent performance achieved when multi-task learning uses all device features, while the *P-DFS* and *CV-DFS* bars represent performance achieved by using device features selected by the profile DFS, and profiling followed by cross-validation DFS, respectively. While performing cross-validation DFS, we restrict the maximum size of each device feature subset to 3, since we found that increasing this beyond 3 rarely resulted in performance improvements. Also, we use the default value of 1 for the CV-DFS parameter k (number of most frequently occurring device features) in our evaluation. While we discovered that higher values suited certain benchmarks (for example, Histogram performs 2.5% better on average across all architectures when k is set to 2), we avoid varying k on a per-benchmark basis to remain consistent.

We expected the original Nitro bar would be an upper bound on performance, as it is training on the target architecture. Indeed we see a modest performance loss for Histogram. Performance is comparable for Transpose and Sort for all architectures, and BFS for Fermi and Maxwell generations but not Kepler. The reasons for these deviations in performance were explained in Section 6.1, but effectively they indicate instances where the learning phase did not see similar scenarios. Surprisingly, multi-task learning actually outperforms the original Nitro for the Solver and SpMV benchmarks on some architectures. This is a significant result considering the fact that we performed no training runs on the

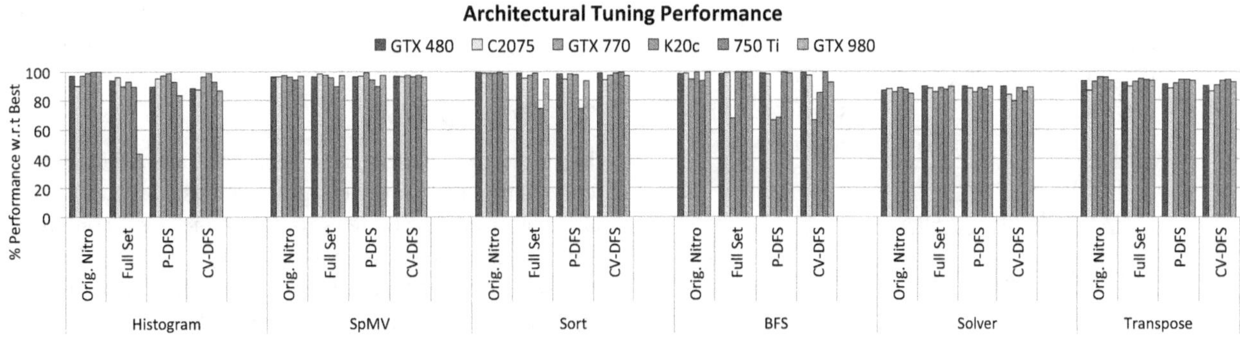

Figure 6: Device feature selection performance.

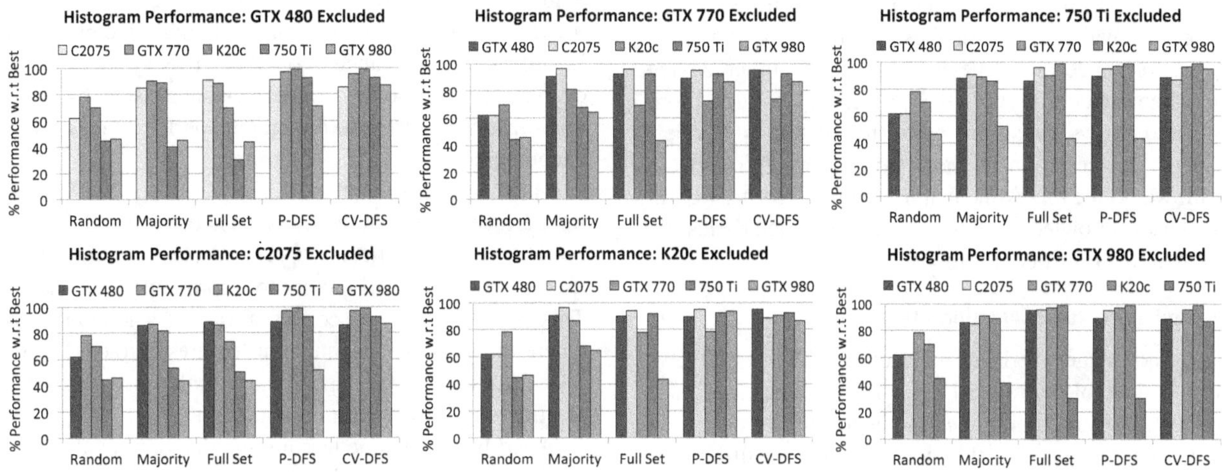

Figure 7: Device feature selection performance for Histogram on a restricted set of architectures.

target. It is an indication that multi-task learning is inferring useful relationships between similar architectures, thus effectively increasing the amount of training data available for model training compared to using only one architecture.

Now consider the differences between the three DFS strategies. Cross-validation yields the best performance for Histogram, SpMV, and Sort on almost all architectures, and is comparable to the other two DFS approaches for Solver and Transpose. The full set is preferable for the K20c version of BFS. The effect of using incorrect device features is more pronounced on a restricted set of source architectures. Space does not permit us to present our system's performance on all source:target combinations for all the benchmarks. However, to demonstrate how sensitive the performance is to the correct feature set, we perform the same experiment as above for Histogram, but iteratively remove one architecture from the total set - resulting in 4 source architectures instead of 5. This seemingly small change has substantial effects on performance.

Figure 7 shows the results for this experiment. Here, each sub-figure shows the performance of MTL with different device feature sets when a specific GPU is excluded from the list of architectures. In this experiment, we also compare against two simpler reference schemes: random selection and majority vote (*Random* and *Majority* in Figure 7, respectively). *Random* simply chooses a valid variant uniformly at random for each test input. It indicates the extent of input sensitivity, as it works well when variants have similar performance across inputs. We report the average of 1000 runs in this case for consistent results. *Majority* chooses the most frequently predicted variant among all source architectures for a given input as the predicted variant for the target. To accomplish this, a variant selection model for each source architecture is built separately using the original Nitro system. Since these two schemes do not make use of any architectural characteristics, their performance (especially on a set of restricted architectures) can be used to indicate and quantify the importance of device feature selection.

For all the source:target combinations, we notice a marked improvement in performance for *P-DFS* and *CV-DFS* over *Full Set*, demonstrating the importance of device feature selection. Further, the performance of *CV-DFS* is at least comparable to *P-DFS*, and often significantly better, especially on Fermi and Maxwell. In comparison, *Random* and

	P-DFS	CV-DFS
Histogram	4.70	100.50
SpMV	3.36	12.42
Sort	4.14	56.61
BFS	3.89	30.27
Solver	4.59	36.80
Transpose	4.26	48.24

Table 6: Device feature selection overhead (time in seconds).

Majority fare relatively poorly. In particular, the tendency of Maxwell devices (750 Ti and GTX 980) to strongly prefer the shared atomic variants over others (Table 4) seems to confuse the majority vote scheme. This is confirmed by the fact that removal of either of these devices improves *Majority* performance on all devices except the other device in the same generation. CV-DFS proves to be much more robust, and shows consistent performance across devices, even when devices from the same generation are removed. Overall, we notice that while majority vote performs well in simple cases, knowledge of architectural characteristics via device features is critical for robust performance.

6.3 Device Feature Selection Overhead

Table 6 shows the overhead incurred by P-DFS and CV-DFS[2] . As the table shows, P-DFS is fastest, since it primarily involves construction of the models for the various proxies, followed by querying the models on the profiling data of the code variants. CV-DFS takes longer, since all subsets of size $<= 3$ must be evaluated by the algorithm. Note that CV-DFS takes less time in comparison to gathering training data from source architectures, as we do not evaluate each $\langle I, v \rangle$ pair.

The CV-DFS strategy has a number of parameters that can be adjusted by the user. The value of these parameters can greatly affect the time taken to execute CV-DFS. Users can adjust the training subset size, feature subset size and the number of source architectures to use for CV. Reducing the values of any of these aforementioned parameters significantly reduces CV-DFS execution time. In our experiments we used the full training set, and feature subset sizes from 1 to 3 on all the source architectures.

6.4 Summary

Overall, multi-task learning produces results comparable to training on the target architecture in most cases, and even better results in a few cases. It falls short when the training data fails to capture a sufficiently similar scenario, and it improves from additional training data available from multiple sources. Finally, we observe that device feature selection improves performance particularly when less training data is available, and that in such cases, CV-DFS produces superior results but introduces more overhead than other approaches.

[2] Since the repository is stored on the local network, we do not include communication overheads.

7. Related Work

Performance counters have been used to predict and guide code tuning and compiler optimizations. Cavazos et al. [11] use performance counters to determine good compiler optimization settings. Machine learning is used to learn relationships between performance counter and optimal code optimization settings. Our framework, on the other hand, uses machine learning to build a relationship between performance counters and best device feature subsets, which are subsequently used in the cross-architectural tuning pipeline. Another system introduced by Parello et al. [30] uses performance counter data to systematically optimize programs by identifying performance anomalies. This system uses a decision tree to iteratively fix performance issues by applying optimization schemes to remedy the performance anomalies encountered.

Machine learning has been extensively used in guiding performance optimizations, as heuristics and exhaustive search are not practical. Supervised classification has been used to predict unroll factors to improve performance [35]. This problem can be seen as a variant selection problem where the selection depends on features extracted from the code itself. Our work specifically looks at variants whose performance depends on input dataset.

Apart from machine learning-guided optimizations, there has been prior work on input adaptivity. Ding et al. [16] address this problem by extending the PetaBricks language [1] to support input sensitivity. The language enables users to define domain-specific features of the input. The PetaBricks autotuner generates a number of implementations of the algorithm (each optimized for a specific input size). These implementations are used as variants that the machine learning algorithm predicts based on the given input features. Our framework focuses on streamlining the process of selecting variants and adapting selection across architectures and hence does not automatically generate variants but rather lets the user define the variants. G-ADAPT [23] is a framework that discovers decisions for GPU code optimizations. This system was subsequently adapted to handle input sensitivity. The G-ADAPT framework achieves this by employing machine learning (Regression Trees) to build a mapping from input to GPU code optimizations. This is achieved by an iterative search for the set of near-optimal optimization parameters for a given input. Both of the above frameworks address the input adaptivity problem but do not support cross-architectural adaptation.

Magni et al. [24] address the tuning of OpenCL code across architectures by applying a *thread-coarsening* transformation to the code. A machine learning technique is employed to predict the optimal coarsening factor for these transformations. Our framework does not apply transformations to the code but rather works with an existing set of variants and does not require training on the target architecture.

A number of systems support the tuning of optimization parameters. Such systems can aid in variant generation and tuning using parameterized templates which specify how to generate new variants based on the actual values of the parameters in the template. Such systems include Active Harmony [36] (integrated with the CHiLL loop transformation framework [12] to generate variants), POET [39], Orio [19], Sequoia [33], the X-Language [17] and [27].

A number of frameworks aid in the development of efficient and portable applications for specific domains. Examples of such systems include ATLAS [38], PhiPAC [6], and OSKI [37] for linear algebra, FFTW [18] and SPIRAL [32] for signal processing, and [13],[14],[22].

In summary, to our knowledge we are the first to adapt code variant selection across architectures without re-training, formulating this as a multi-task learning problem.

8. Conclusions

This paper has presented a novel approach to cross-architecture autotuning, which uses multi-task learning to develop a model on a target architecture from training on different source architectures. On a set of benchmark applications and a collection of six NVIDIA GPUs from three distinct architecture generations, we achieve performance results comparable to the previous approach of tuning for a single architecture without having to repeat the learning phase, demonstrating the promise of multi-task learning for addressing performance portability across architectures. We view this work on variant selection as an initial step towards a more general approach to learning an optimization model on one set of resources and adapting to a different set of resources at runtime. Many questions remain: improving models for outliers, examining very different architectures, and other autotuning problems such as parameter selection. Tuning across different architecture classes such as CPU and GPU is particularly challenging, as higher-level device features (e.g. `gflops/gbps` ratio) and profiling metrics that remain valid across architecture classes must be used. These challenges will become increasingly important to future architectures, as complexity grows and systems become more dynamic.

Acknowledgments

We would like to thank NVIDIA Corporation for generous equipment donations, and members of the NVIDIA research group including Duane Merrill and Albert Sidelnik for valuable discussions. We would also like to thank the reviewers who suggested additional experiments to improve the paper. This research was funded by DARPA contract HR0011-13-3-0001.

References

[1] J. Ansel, C. Chan, Y. L. Wong, M. Olszewski, Q. Zhao, A. Edelman, and S. Amarasinghe. PetaBricks: A language and compiler for algorithmic choice. In *Proceedings of the 2009 ACM SIGPLAN conference on Programming language design and implementation*, PLDI '09, pages 38–49, New York, NY, USA, 2009. ACM.

[2] S. Balay, W. D. Gropp, L. C. McInnes, and B. F. Smith. Efficient management of parallelism in object oriented numerical software libraries. In *Modern Software Tools in Scientific Computing*, pages 163–202. Birkhäuser Press, 1997.

[3] S. Baxter. Modern GPU library. `http://nvlabs.github.io/moderngpu/`.

[4] N. Bell and M. Garland. Implementing sparse matrix-vector multiplication on throughput-oriented processors. In *SC '09: Proc. Conference on High Performance Computing Networking, Storage and Analysis*, Nov. 2009.

[5] S. Bhowmick, B. Toth, and P. Raghavan. Towards low-cost, high-accuracy classifiers for linear solver selection. In *Proceedings of the 9th International Conference on Computational Science: Part I*, ICCS '09, pages 463–472, Berlin, Heidelberg, 2009. Springer-Verlag. ISBN 978-3-642-01969-2.

[6] J. Bilmes, K. Asanovic, C.-W. Chin, and J. Demmel. Optimizing matrix multiply using PHiPAC: A portable, high-performance, ANSI C coding methodology. In *Proceedings of the 11th International Conference on Supercomputing*, ICS '97, pages 340–347, New York, NY, USA, 1997. ACM. ISBN 0-89791-902-5.

[7] E. V. Bonilla, F. V. Agakov, and C. K. I. Williams. Kernel multi-task learning using task-specific features. In *Proceedings of the 11th International Conference on Artificial Intelligence and Statistics (AISTATS)*, 2007.

[8] R. Caruana. Multitask learning. *Mach. Learn.*, 28(1):41–75, July 1997. ISSN 0885-6125.

[9] B. Catanzaro. In-place matrix transposition. `https://github.com/bryancatanzaro/inplace`.

[10] B. Catanzaro, A. Keller, and M. Garland. A decomposition for in-place matrix transposition. In *Proceedings of the 19th ACM SIGPLAN Symposium on Principles and Practice of Parallel Programming*, PPoPP '14, pages 193–206, New York, NY, USA, 2014. ACM.

[11] J. Cavazos, G. Fursin, F. Agakov, E. Bonilla, M. F. P. O'Boyle, and O. Temam. Rapidly selecting good compiler optimizations using performance counters. In *Proceedings of the International Symposium on Code Generation and Optimization*, CGO '07, pages 185–197, Washington, DC, USA, 2007. IEEE Computer Society. ISBN 0-7695-2764-7.

[12] C. Chen. Model-guided empirical optimization for memory hierarchy. In *Ph.D dissertation, University of Southern California*, May 2007.

[13] M. Christen, O. Schenk, and H. Burkhart. PATUS: A code generation and autotuning framework for parallel iterative stencil computations on modern microarchitectures. In *Proceedings of the 2011 IEEE International Parallel & Distributed Processing Symposium*, IPDPS '11, pages 676–687,

Washington, DC, USA, 2011. IEEE Computer Society. ISBN 978-0-7695-4385-7.

[14] K. Datta, S. Kamil, S. Williams, L. Oliker, J. Shalf, and K. Yelick. Optimization and performance modeling of stencil computations on modern microprocessors. *SIAM Rev.*, 51(1): 129–159, Feb. 2009. ISSN 0036-1445.

[15] T. Davis. The University of Florida Sparse Matrix Collection. *ACM Transactions on Mathematical Software*, 38:1:1–1:25, 2011.

[16] Y. Ding, J. Ansel, K. Veeramachaneni, X. Shen, U.-M. O'Reilly, and S. Amarasinghe. Autotuning algorithmic choice for input sensitivity. In *Proceedings of the 36th ACM SIGPLAN Conference on Programming Language Design and Implementation*, PLDI 2015, 2015.

[17] S. Donadio, J. Brodman, T. Roeder, K. Yotov, D. Barthou, A. Cohen, M. J. Garzarán, D. Padua, and K. Pingali. A language for the compact representation of multiple program versions. In *Proceedings of the 18th International Conference on Languages and Compilers for Parallel Computing*, LCPC'05, pages 136–151, Berlin, Heidelberg, 2006. Springer-Verlag.

[18] M. Frigo and S. G. Johnson. The fastest fourier transform in the west. In *Proceedings of the 1998 International Conference on Acoustics, Speech, and Signal Processing, ICASSP '98*, 1997.

[19] A. Hartono, B. Norris, and P. Sadayappan. Annotation-based empirical performance tuning using Orio. In *Proceedings of the 2014 IEEE 28th International Parallel and Distributed Processing Symposium*, IPDPS '09, pages 1–11. IEEE Computer Society, 2009.

[20] M. A. Heroux, P. Raghavan, and H. D. Simon. *Parallel Processing for Scientific Computing (Software, Environments and Tools)*. Society for Industrial and Applied Mathematics, Philadelphia, PA, USA, 2006.

[21] H. Jégou, M. Douze, and C. Schmid. Hamming embedding and weak geometric consistency for large scale image search. In A. Z. David Forsyth, Philip Torr, editor, *European Conference on Computer Vision*, volume I of *LNCS*, pages 304–317. Springer, oct 2008.

[22] S. Kamil, C. Chan, L. Oliker, J. Shalf, and S. Williams. An auto-tuning framework for parallel multicore stencil computations. In *International Parallel and Distributed Processing Symposium (IPDPS)*, 2010.

[23] Y. Liu, E. Z. Zhang, and X. Shen. A cross-input adaptive framework for GPU program optimizations. In *Proceedings of the 2009 IEEE International Symposium on Parallel & Distributed Processing*, IPDPS '09, pages 1–10, Washington, DC, USA, 2009. IEEE Computer Society. ISBN 978-1-4244-3751-1.

[24] A. Magni, C. Dubach, and M. F. P. O'Boyle. A large-scale cross-architecture evaluation of thread-coarsening. In *Proceedings of the International Conference on High Performance Computing, Networking, Storage and Analysis*, SC '13, pages 11:1–11:11, New York, NY, USA, 2013. ACM.

[25] D. Merrill. Back40 Computing, . `http://code.google.com/p/back40computing/`.

[26] D. Merrill. CUDA Unbound (CUB), . `http://nvlabs.github.io/cub/`.

[27] D. Merrill, M. Garland, and A. Grimshaw. Policy-based tuning for performance portability and library co-optimization. In *Proc. Innovative Parallel Computing (InPar 2012)*, May 2012.

[28] D. Merrill, M. Garland, and A. Grimshaw. Scalable GPU graph traversal. In *Proceedings of the 17th ACM SIGPLAN symposium on Principles and Practice of Parallel Programming*, PPoPP '12, pages 117–128, New York, NY, USA, 2012. ACM. ISBN 978-1-4503-1160-1.

[29] S. Muralidharan, M. Shantharam, M. Hall, M. Garland, and B. Catanzaro. Nitro: A framework for adaptive code variant tuning. In *Proceedings of the 2014 IEEE 28th International Parallel and Distributed Processing Symposium*, IPDPS '14, pages 501–512. IEEE Computer Society, 2014.

[30] D. Parello, O. Temam, A. Cohen, and J. Verdun. Towards a systematic, pragmatic and architecture-aware program optimization process for complex processors. In *Proceedings of the ACM/IEEE SC2004 Conference on High Performance Networking and Computing, Pittsburgh, PA, USA*, 2004.

[31] E. Photonics and NVIDIA. CULA | sparse. `http://www.culatools.com/`.

[32] M. Püschel, J. M. F. Moura, J. Johnson, D. Padua, M. Veloso, B. Singer, J. Xiong, F. Franchetti, A. Gacic, Y. Voronenko, K. Chen, R. W. Johnson, and N. Rizzolo. SPIRAL: Code generation for DSP transforms. *Proceedings of the IEEE, special issue on "Program Generation, Optimization, and Adaptation"*, 93(2):232– 275, 2005.

[33] M. Ren, J. Y. Park, M. Houston, A. Aiken, and W. J. Dally. A Tuning Framework for Software-Managed Memory Hierarchies. In *International Conference on Parallel Architectures and Compilation Techniques*, pages 280–291, October 2008.

[34] S. Sanfilippo and P. Noordhuis. Redis. `http://redis.io`.

[35] M. Stephenson and S. Amarasinghe. Predicting unroll factors using supervised classification. In *Proceedings of the International Symposium on Code Generation and Optimization*, CGO '05, pages 123–134, Washington, DC, USA, 2005. IEEE Computer Society.

[36] A. Tiwari, C. Chen, J. Chame, M. Hall, and J. Hollingsworth. A scalable auto-tuning framework for compiler optimization. In *Parallel Distributed Processing, 2009. IPDPS 2009. IEEE International Symposium on*, pages 1–12, May 2009.

[37] R. Vuduc, J. W. Demmel, and K. A. Yelick. OSKI: A Library of Automatically Tuned Sparse Matrix Kernels. *Journal of Physics: Conference Series*, 16(1):521, 2005.

[38] R. C. Whaley, A. Petitet, and J. J. Dongarra. Automated empirical optimization of software and the ATLAS project. *Parallel Computing*, 27(1–2):3 – 35, 2001.

[39] Q. Yi, K. Seymour, H. You, R. Vuduc, and D. Quinlan. POET: Parameterized optimizations for empirical tuning. In *Parallel and Distributed Processing Symposium, 2007. IPDPS 2007. IEEE International*, pages 1–8, 2007.

Scalable Kernel TCP Design and Implementation for Short-Lived Connections

Xiaofeng Lin
Sina Corporation, ZHIHU Corporation
jerrylin.lxf@gmail.com

Yu Chen
Department of Computer Science and Technology, Tsinghua University
yuchen@mail.tsinghua.edu.cn

Xiaodong Li
Sina Corporation
xiaodong2@staff.sina.com.cn

Junjie Mao Jiaquan He Wei Xu Yuanchun Shi
Department of Computer Science and Technology, Tsinghua University
maojj12@mails.tsinghua.edu.cn, objectkuan@gmail.com, weixu@tsinghua.edu.cn, shiyc@tsinghua.edu.cn

Abstract

With the rapid growth of network bandwidth, increases in CPU cores on a single machine, and application API models demanding more short-lived connections, a scalable TCP stack is performance-critical.

Although many clean-state designs have been proposed, production environments still call for a bottom-up parallel TCP stack design that is backward-compatible with existing applications.

We present Fastsocket, a BSD Socket-compatible and scalable kernel socket design, which achieves table-level connection partition in TCP stack and guarantees connection locality for both passive and active connections. Fastsocket architecture is a ground up partition design, from NIC interrupts all the way up to applications, which naturally eliminates various lock contentions in the entire stack. Moreover, Fastsocket maintains the full functionality of the kernel TCP stack and BSD-socket-compatible API, and thus applications need no modifications.

Our evaluations show that Fastsocket achieves a speedup of 20.4x on a 24-core machine under a workload of short-lived connections, outperforming the state-of-the-art Linux kernel TCP implementations. When scaling up to 24 CPU cores, Fastsocket increases the throughput of Nginx and HAProxy by 267% and 621% respectively compared with the base Linux kernel. We also demonstrate that Fastsocket can achieve scalability and preserve BSD socket API at the same time. Fastsocket is already deployed in the production environment of Sina WeiBo, serving 50 million daily active users and billions of requests per day.

Categories and Subject Descriptors D.4.4 [*Operating Systems*]: Communications Management—Network communication

Keywords TCP/IP; multicore system; operating system

1. Introduction

Recent years have witnessed a rapid growth of mobile devices and apps. These new mobile apps generate a large amount of the traffic consisting of short-lived TCP connections [39]. HTTP is a typical source of short-lived TCP connections. For example, in Sina WeiBo, the typical request length of one heavily invoked HTTP interface is around 600 bytes and the corresponding response length is typically about 1200 bytes. Both the request and the response only consume one single IP packet. After the two-packet data transaction is done, the connection is closed, which closely matches the characteristics of short-lived connection. In this situation, the speed of establishment and termination of TCP connections becomes crucial for server performance.

As the number of CPU cores in one machine increases, the scalability of the network stack plays a key role in the performance of the network applications on multi-core platforms. For long-lived connections, the metadata management for new connections is not frequent enough to cause significant contentions. Thus we do not observe scalability issues of the TCP stack in these cases. However, it is challenging to reach the same level of scalability for short-lived connections as that of long-lived connections, since it involves frequent and expensive TCP connection establishment and termination, which result in severe shared resource

ASPLOS '16 April 2–6, 2016, Atlanta, Georgia, USA.
Copyright © 2016 ACM 978-1-4503-4091-5/16/04. . . $15.00
DOI: http://dx.doi.org/10.1145/2872362.2872391

contentions in the TCP Control Block (TCB) and Virtual File System (VFS).

TCB Management The TCP connection establishment and termination operations involve managing the global TCBs which are represented as TCP sockets in the Linux kernel. All these sockets are managed in two global hash tables, known as the *listen table* and the *established table*. Since these two tables are shared system-wide, synchronization are inevitable among the CPU cores.

In addition, the TCB of a connection is accessed and updated in two phases:

1. Incoming packets of the connection are received in the interrupt context through network stack on the CPU core that receives the NIC (Network Interface Controller) interrupt.
2. Further processing of incoming packets payload in user-level application and transmission of the outgoing packets are accomplished on the CPU core running the corresponding application.

It is ideal that for a given connection, both phases are handled entirely on one CPU core, which maximizes CPU cache efficiency. We refer to this property as *connection locality*. Unfortunately, in the current Linux TCP stack, these two phases often run on different CPU cores, which seriously affects scalability.

VFS Abstraction A socket is abstracted by VFS and exposed to user-level applications as a socket *File Descriptor* (FD). As a result, the performance of opening and closing a socket FD in VFS has a direct impact on the efficiency of the TCP connection establishment and termination. However, there are severe synchronization overheads in processing VFS shared states, e.g., `inode` and `dentry`, which results in scalability bottlenecks.

Serious lock contention are observed on an 8-core production server running HAProxy as an HTTP load balancer for WeiBo to distribute client traffic to multiple servers. From profiling data collected by *perf*, we observed that `spin_lock` consumes 9% and 11% of total CPU cycles in TCB management and VFS respectively. Even worse, due to contention inside the network stack processing, there is a clear load imbalance across all CPU cores, though packets are evenly distributed to these CPU cores by NIC.

Production Environment Requirements In production environment, such as data center, the network server/proxy applications have three fundamental requirements:

1. Compatibility of TCP/IP related RFC: Different applications follow different TCP/IP related RFCs. As a result, the TCP/IP implementation in production environment also need to support commonly accepted RFCs as far as possible.
2. Security: TCP may be attacked in a variety of ways(DDoS, Connection hijacking, etc.). These attacks result of a thorough security protection of TCP [13] in OS kernel.
3. Resource Isolation and Sharing: TCP/IP stack needs to support diverse existed NIC hardware resources, and should isolated or share data with other name space or sub-systems (disks, file systems, etc.)

Extensive researches [12, 21, 22, 27, 30, 38] are focused on system support for enabling network-intensive applications to achieve performance close to the limits imposed by the hardware. Some work proposes a brand new I/O abstraction to make the TCP stack scalable [21]. However, applications have to be rewritten with the new API. Recent research projects [12, 22, 30] attempt to solve the TCP stack scalability problem using modified embedded TCP stack lwIP [26] or custom-built user-level TCP stack from the ground up. Though these design can improve the performance of network stack, it does not fully replicate all kernel's advanced networking features (Firewall/Netfilter, TCP veto, IPsec NAT and other vulnerabilities defenses for security, TCP optimizations for wireless net, cgroup/sendfile/splice mechanism for resource isolating or sharing, etc.) which are heavily utilized by our performance-critical applications.

Therefore, currently it remains an open challenge to completely solve the TCP stack scalability problem while keeping backward compatibility and full features to benefit existing network applications in the production environment.

In this paper, we present Fastsocket to address the aforementioned scalability and compatibility problems in a backward compatible, incrementally deployable and maintainable way. This is achieved with three major changes: 1) partition the globally shared data structures, the listen table and established table; 2) correctly steer incoming packets to achieve connection locality for any connection; and 3) provide a fast path for socket in VFS to solve scalability problems in VFS and wrap the aforementioned TCP designs to fully preserve BSD socket API.

In the production environment, with Fastsocket, the contention in TCB management and VFS is eliminated and the effective capacity of HAProxy server is increased by 53.5%. Our experimental evaluations show that in short-lived connection benchmark of web servers and proxy servers handling short-lived connections, Fastsocket outperforms base Linux kernel by 267% and 621% respectively.

This paper makes three key contributions:

1. We introduce a kernel network stack design which achieves table-level partition for TCB management and realizes connection locality for arbitrary connection types. Our partition scheme is complete and naturally solves all potential contentions along the network processing path, including the contentions we do not directly address such as timer lock contention.
2. We demonstrate that BSD socket API does not have to be an obstacle in network stack scalability for commodity hardware configuration. The evaluation using real-world applications and benchmarks shows throughput

with Fastsocket can scale up to 20.4x on a 24-core machine with 10G NIC, using the BSD socket API. The results suggest that there is no scalability reasons to give up the BSD socket API. Moreover, this compatibility ensures that existing network applications do not need modifications to use Fastsocket.

3. We demonstrate that with moderate modifications in kernel, we can build a highly scalable kernel network stack. By integrating into the kernel framework, our design can preserve robustness and all features of kernel network stack, which makes it a practical scheme for production environment deployment. Fastsocket follows this idea and has been massively deployed in the Sina WeiBo production environment.

The rest of this paper is organized as follows. In Section 2, we discuss the challenges in scaling TCP stack while being backward compatible in more detail. We describe the Fastsocket design in Section 3. Section 4 evaluates Fastsocket in the production environment and with several benchmarks as well. Section 5 presents related work and we conclude in Section 6.

2. Challenges

In this section, we focus on the scalability bottlenecks: TCB management and VFS abstraction. We analyze the challenge to completely solve these bottlenecks and parallelize TCP stack while keeping backward compatibility.

2.1 Bottleneck in TCB Management

Management of global TCBs is a major scalability bottleneck for the TCP stack on multi-core platforms. Due to mutual exclusion requirement when operating these global TCBs, locks are widely used, leading to potential lock contentions when multiple CPU cores need to update the TCBs (represented as sockets in Linux) concurrently.

Global Listen Table

While establishing passive connections with concurrent clients requesting the same service port, a global listen socket is used to set up connections on all CPU cores, which is a major scalability bottleneck.

Both Linux `SO_REUSEPORT` [23] and Megapipe [21] address this scalability problem using socket-level partition. For example, in `SO_REUSEPORT`, each application process creates a private copy of the original listen socket and these copies are linked into a single bucket list in the listen table. When handling new connections, kernel traverses the list and randomly selects a listen socket copy from all others in `NET_RX` SoftIRQ . Application processes accept new connections from its own listen socket copy only. As a result, they can remove the global listen socket bottleneck based on this socket-level partition. However, this solution hits another scalability problem. Though in `NET_RX` SoftIRQ kernel can use multiple listen sockets to avoid intensive contention, it has to *traverse* the bucket list to choose a listen socket for any connection request. In this case, the complexity of finding a listen socket is *O(n)*, where *n* is number of CPU core in the server. Therefore, when the number of CPU cores increases, the cost of matching a listen socket becomes serious enough to be a bottleneck. Our benchmarks with `SO_REUSEPORT` show that the function that matches a listen socket, `__inet_lookup_listener()`, consumes only 0.26% CPU cycles on a single core machine, but the overhead soars to an average of 24.2% per-core with 24 CPU cores.

Although Megapipe has a different implementation, it uses the same socket-level partitioning design as `SO_REUSEPORT` and suffers from the same problem.

It may be worth attempting to use a naive table-level partition scheme, in which each CPU core has its own local listen table containing the copied listen socket to avoid searching the bucket list with a *O(n)* complexity. However, this partition breaks the TCP stack. For example, if one process in the application crashes, the operating system will destroy the copied listen socket created by the process. In this case, there is no copied listen socket in the local listen table of that certain CPU core. When a `SYN` packet is delivered to the CPU core, it cannot match any listen socket in the local socket table and the connection request from client would be rejected with a `RST` packet, even if other application processes (on other CPU cores) are available to handle the client connection, which breaks the TCP robustness.

Global Established Table

A new socket is created and added into the established table to represent an established connection for both passive and active connections. Linux currently adopts per-bucket locks to synchronize concurrent modifications to the established table shared by multiple CPU cores. This locking granularity works fine on a 8-core machine serving hundreds of concurrent connections. However, the global design of established table will inevitably lead to considerable lock contentions when both the CPU cores and concurrent connections in a single server grow rapidly. Therefore, lock granularity refinement is just an optimization but not a thorough solution to the scalability problem.

Naive partition of the global established table into per-core local tables does not work, because there is no guarantee that in `NET_RX` SoftIRQ any incoming packet is always processed on the same CPU core that has the corresponding socket in the local established table. As a result, it is possible that the socket is created by one CPU core and inserted into the local table of the CPU core while a subsequent packets of the connection arrives on the other CPU core. In this condition, the packet would be rejected and the TCP connection breaks with this naive partition design.

Through the above analysis, it is still challenging to realize a *full partition of TCB management*, that is when managing any socket, no lock is ever contended and the cost is constant regardless of number of CPU cores.

2.2 Lack of Connection Locality

Incoming and outgoing packets in a single connection can be handled by two different CPU cores, which causes CPU cache bouncing and performance degradation. Therefore, for maximum scalability, it is desirable to achieve *complete connection locality*, i.e., all activities for a given connection are always handled on the same CPU core, including both passive and active connections.

It is worth noting that complete connection locality is not only a performance optimization, but also the key prerequisite to partition the established table, as we discussed in the previous section. If we can ensure a connection is always handled on the same CPU core, we naturally solve the established table partition problem.

The *completeness* is the real challenge, which has not been solved by various optimizations to *improve* connection locality in a best-effort way that only provide a probabilistic guarantee.

For passive connections, Affinity-Accept [29] and Megapipe [21] achieves connection locality by making the application accept new connections on the CPU core where the application is running. Unfortunately, this design does not apply to active connections that are heavily used in proxy and RPC (Remote Procedure Call) applications. This is because active connections are initiated in the applications which has no control over selection of the CPU core the connection will be processed later in NET_RX SoftIRQ .

To improve connection locality, RFS (Receive Flow Deliver) was introduced into Linux [6, 7]. RFS introduces a table to track connections in the system. In the table, RFS records on which CPU core each connection is processed in application and delivers incoming packets according to the table. However, managing the table introduces considerable overhead and complete connection locality cannot be guaranteed due to the table size limit.

Modern NIC provides advanced features such as FDir (Flow Director) [9] to deliver incoming packets intelligently. FDir works in two modes: ATR (Application Target Routing) or Perfect-Filtering. ATR works similarly to RFS but differs in that ATR samples outgoing packet and maintains the connection-CPU-mapping table in the NIC. Since the mapping is based on sampling and the size of hardware table is limited, it is actually a best-effort solution instead of a complete solution. With Perfect-Filtering, users can program NIC to a limited extent to decide which CPU core to deliver an incoming packet to, based on the IP address and TCP port of the packet. However, it is impractical to use Perfect-Filtering to realize active connection locality, as there lacks a general pattern of the IP address and TCP port we can leverage to program the delivery policy to the NIC.

Even if there is a design realizing active connection locality, in order to achieve complete connection locality, the design cannot break the passive connection locality, which makes it even more challenging to implement complete connection locality.

2.3 Additional Overhead for Compatibility

Socket has an abstraction in VFS as a special file type and VFS associates each socket with corresponding `inode` and `dentry` data structures in the same way as other file types. As discussed in [14], when sockets are frequently allocated, VFS spends much effort to manage the globally visible `inodes` and `dentries`, which involves expensive synchronization.

Mainline Linux kernel and research[14] use fine-grained locking mechanism,sloppy counter,lock-free protocol, etc. to improve the efficiency of VFS synchronization. However, we believe it is unnecessary for socket to inherit such overheads, even if they are becoming smaller, as `inode` and `dentry` are actually not being used by socket at all, because of the fundamental differences between networking and a disk file.

Recent researches have proposed two kinds of new designs to address the scalability problem of VFS for socket and TCP stack. For example, a user-level TCP stack [22] and a new IO API design [21]. These new designs avoid synchronization at the cost of advanced TCP stack features and backward compatibility.

The user-level TCP stack, mTCP [22], or modified embedded TCP stack, lwIP [12, 30], used by rescent research works, eliminates VFS overhead and bypasses all the complexity of kernel to achieve high performance. However, the performance gain is not free. First, these TCP stacks implement a light version of TCP stack. Many advanced features such as namespace and firewall, which are very useful in practice, are not implemented. Overtime, these stacks could replicate the kernel functions, but it will be a very complex and expensive development process. Second, the APIs provided by these network stacks are not fully compatible with BSD socket, VFS and RFCs, leading to expensive code changes in applications. Finally, to enable a NIC to work with these TCP stacks, we can no longer share the NIC with the kernel, preventing other "normal" applications from running on the same NIC port. All these limitations make it impractical for us to deploy in production environment.

Megapipe [21], on the other hand, introduces a new I/O API which completely bypasses VFS and maintains the in-kernel advantages that user-level TCP stack does not provide. However, Megapipe is no longer compatible with socket API. To deploy Megapipe, we need to modify all existing applications and tools. Some of the modifications are nontrivial as Megapipe presents a different network programming model. The incompatibility severely limits the real-world applicability of Megapipe.

Our goal is to redesign a kernel-level TCP stack that keeps compatibility to the BSD socket API while achieving

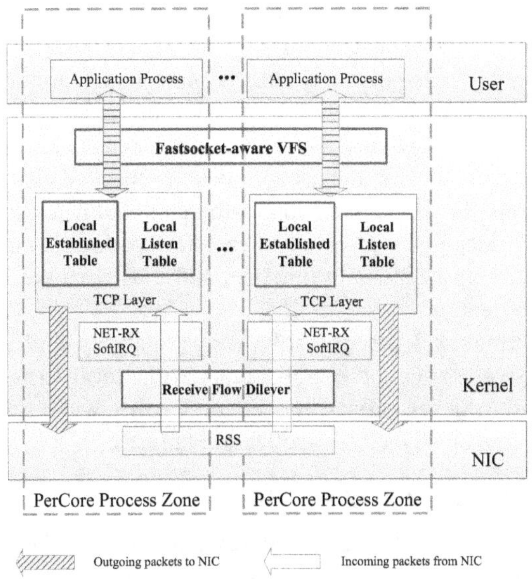

Figure 1: Fastsocket Architecture

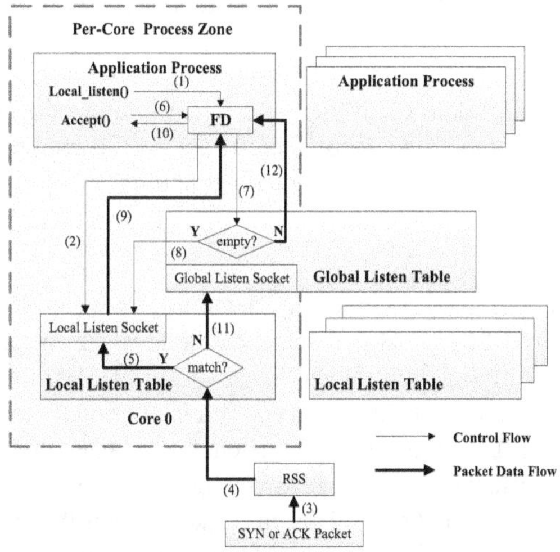

Figure 2: Local Listen Table

high scalability and low overhead, which is the genuine demand for large-scale production environment.

3. Fastsocket Design

3.1 Architecture Overview

Figure 1 presents an architecture overview of Fastsocket. Fastsocket provides three components, the partitioned TCB data structures (the Local Listen Table and the Local Established Table), Receive Flow Deliver (RFD), and Fastsocket-aware VFS, which are highlighted with bold box in Figure 1. The three modules cooperate to provide Per-Core Process Zones in which all activities for a given connection, from NIC interrupts up to application accesses, are executed on a single CPU core with minimum cross-core synchronization.

To build the Per-Core Process Zone, we have made improvements to the shared data structure, the connection-core binding and the VFS abstraction implementation:

1. Fastsocket fully partitions the data structure and management of both global TCB tables. Thus, when `NET_RX` SoftIRQ reaches the TCP layer, Fastsocket uses per-core Local Listen Table and per-core Local Established Table for a full partitioning of TCB management.
2. Before an incoming packet enters the network stack, Fastsocket uses Receive Flow Deliver to steer the packet to a proper CPU core where the corresponding local table is managed and its relating application process is running. This way, Fastsocket achieves maximum connection locality and minimize CPU cache bouncing.
3. The kernel VFS layer is the key to the socket API abstraction and compatibility. Fastsocket-aware VFS bypasses unnecessary and lock-intensive VFS routines and uses socket-special fast path instead to eliminate scalability bottlenecks, while retaining enough states to provide all socket API functionalities.

The remaining of this section describes each of the three Fastsocket component designs in detail.

3.2 Full Partition of TCB Management

In this section, we describe ways to use Local Listen Table and Local Established Table to implement table-level partitions of the listen sockets and established sockets management.

3.2.1 Local Listen Table

We propose Local Listen Table to realize table-level partition for listen sockets while guaranteeing the robustness of the TCP stack. In addition, passive connection locality is also achieved with Local Listen Table.

In the kernel TCP setup stage, Fastsocket allocates a *local listen table* for each CPU core and maintains the original *global listen table* for robustness.

On startup, the first process of a server application typically `listen()`s on a certain TCP port to wait for client requests. The kernel correspondingly creates a listen socket in the global listen table. Then the server forks multiple processes and binds them with different CPU cores. These child processes inherit the listen socket and are ready to accept new connections and process accepted connections in parallel.

With Fastsocket, each process invokes `local_listen()` to inform the kernel that the process wants to handle incoming connections from the CPU core to which it has been bound (1). As Figure 2 shows, for the process bound on CPU core 0, a new listen socket is copied from the original listen socket and inserted into the local listen table of CPU core 0 (2). We refer to the copied listen socket as the *local lis-*

ten socket and the original listen socket as the *global listen socket*.

Steps (3) to (6) and (8) to (10) in Figure 2 illustrates the fast (normal) path of setting up a passive connection using local listen table, and step (7), (11) and (12) illustrate slow (abnormal) path to handle the fault condition.

Fast Path

When a `SYN` packet comes in (3) and it is delivered to CPU core 0 by RSS, the kernel searches the local listen table of CPU core 0 to match a local listen socket (4). Without any failures, the local listen socket which is previously inserted by `local_listen()` will be matched (5). After the three-way handshake is done, a ready connection is placed in the accept queue of the local listen socket. When the process bound on core 0 issues `accept()` for new connections (6), the kernel first checks the accept queue of the global listen socket (7). Under normal operation, the accept queue is always empty. This check is done without locking, as we will explain later in this section. Then the kernel will check the local listen table of core 0 for any ready connection (8). Naturally, the previously ready connection can be found (9) and returned to application process (10).

Therefore, with a table-level partition of Local Listen Table, every operation (except for the lock-free check) is on the local table, which eliminates the synchronization bottleneck during the establishment of a passive connection.

As a by-product, we also achieve passive connection locality as all processing (in application process and the kernel interrupt context) of any passive connection runs on the same CPU core.

Slow Path

Application failures complicate things a bit, as we have described in Section 2.1. Under certain unusual circumstance, it is possible that the copied listen socket in the local listen table of certain CPU core is missing.

In Fastsocket, Figure 2 shows, when a `SYN` packet cannot match a local listen socket in the local listen table, the kernel will set up a new connection with the global listen socket in the global listen table (11). When any application process calls `accept()` (6), the ready connection in the global listen socket will be found since the accept queue of the global listen socket is checked first (7). The kernel can then `accept()` the connection from the global listen socket to the application process, just what the legacy TCP stack does (12).

As we have mentioned before, we need to check the accept queue of the global listen socket first, prior to accepting a new connection from the local listen socket. This is because on a busy server, there are always new connections in the local listen socket. If we check the local listen socket first, we will keeping processing connections in the local listen socket and starve the connection in the global listen socket.

In addition, no locking is needed when checking the global listen socket, since it is done by checking whether the accept queue pointer is `NULL` using a single atomic read operation. If there is a new connection in the accept queue (very rare), we have to lock the global listen socket. When the socket is locked, the accept queue is checked again and we accept the new connection from the global listen socket. Though locking is involved in the slow path, this circumstance rarely happens in practice, and thus does not cause lock contentions.

In summary, Fastsocket solves any scalability bottlenecks in passive connection establishment with Local Listen Table, and achieves passive connection locality while keeping robustness of TCP under application failures.

3.2.2 Local Established Table

We propose Local Established Table to partition the established table for locally accessing established sockets.

Operations of Local Established Table are designed as follows:

- Fastsocket allocates a *local established table* for each CPU core when kernel initializes network stack.
- New established sockets are inserted into the local established tables.
- In `NET_RX` SoftIRQ , the kernel checks the local established table to match an established socket for any incoming packet.

As described in Section 2.1, we need to make sure that for any connection, inserting and matching the established socket are carried out on the same CPU core to make this design work. Fastsocket provides the guarantee we will describe in Section 3.3.

With Local Established Table, established sockets management is fully partitioned across the CPU cores and this design eliminates scalability problems in the established table regardless of the number of CPU cores in a single machine.

At this point, Fastsocket has achieved table-level partition for both listen table and established table and a full partition of TCB management is achieved.

3.3 Complete Connection Locality

As shown in previous section, Local Listen Table design realizes the passive connection locality. In this section, we propose Receive Flow Deliver (RFD) to solve the active connection locality problem described in Setion 2.2 to achieve the complete connection locality.

Build Active Connection Locality

The key insight is that the kernel can encode the current CPU core id into the source port when making an active connection request. To achieve this, we use a hash function $hash(p)$ that maps ports to CPU cores. When the application running on CPU core c attempts to establish an active connection, RFD chooses a port p_{src} so that $c = hash(p_{src})$. Upon receiving a response packet, RFD picks the destination port of the received packet p_{dst} which is the port RFD previously chosen, determines which CPU core should handle the packet by $hash(p_{dst})$, and steers the packet to the selected CPU core, if this is not the CPU core currently handling the packet. In this way, RFD guarantees that each active connection is always processed by the same CPU core, which eliminates the non-local connection problem.

Retain Passive Connection Locality

Passive connections and active connections can exist in one machine simultaneously, and incoming traffic consists of both passive incoming packets and active incoming packets. Before decoding the CPU core id from the destination port of incoming packets, RFD has to distinguish the two incoming packet categories since the hash function is designed for active connections and should only be applied to active incoming packets. Otherwise, RFD would break the passive connection locality from Local Listen Table.

To determine whether an incoming packet is a passive incoming packet or an active incoming packet, RFD applies the following rules in order:

1. If the source port of an incoming packet is in the range of the well-known (less than 1024) ports, it should be an active incoming packet. We assume the kernel never picks a port within the well-known ports as the source port under normal conditions.
2. If the destination port is a well-known port, it is a passive incoming packet for the same reason.
3. (optional) If neither of the previous condition meets, we see whether the packet can match a listen socket. If so, it indicates that it is a passive incoming packet because it is not allowed to start an active connection with a source port that was previously listened. Otherwise, the packet is an active incoming packet.

The classification work could be done within the first two quick checks when the application is serving on well-known ports, which is usually the case. A precise classification, if required, can be guaranteed by applying the third rule directly(the first two rules should be skipped in this case).

Leverage Hardware Features

RFD can work correctly without any hardware NIC features. However, as synchronization is required when RFD needs to steer a packet to a different CPU core, it is beneficial for RFD to take advantage of advanced NIC features such as FDir and offload the steering work to the NIC.

As Section 2.2 describes, there are two modes in FDir: Perfect-Filtering and ATR. When using Perfect-Filtering, RFD may program the hash function into NIC in order to offload the steering work completely to hardware. When using ATR mode, the majority of incoming packets are delivered to the right CPU core thanks to the sampling of NICs and the rest of them are left to RFD to handle. Thus, RFD can be used either with Perfect-Filtering for maximum performance benefits at a cost of extra NIC configuration, or with ATR to enhance connection locality of the system with minimal maintenance efforts, and coexists with other applications requiring the ATR mode.

Our RFD Implementation

To choose a proper hash function, we need to consider the capability of the underlying NIC hardware and the software overhead for extra packet steering work in RFD.

In our implementation of Fastsocket, we use the following hash function:

$hash(p)$ = `p & (ROUND_UP_POWER_OF_2(n) - 1)`

where `ROUND_UP_POWER_OF_2(x)` returns the next power of two of x and n is the number of CPU cores we have.

This function can be easily programmed into the FDir in Perfect-Filtering mode which supports bit-wise operations only.

We can introduce some randomness to improve security by randomly selecting the bits used in the operation. It helps prevent malicious attacks that try to make the server process all connections on the same CPU core. We can also leverage existing efforts on defending such attacks [5, 25] on top of Fastsocket. The defensing work could be left to the dedicated network security devices as well. The security solutions are beyond the scope of this paper.

With Local Listen Table and Receive Flow Deliver, Fastsocket has achieved complete connection locality.

3.4 Fastsocket-aware VFS

In some operating systems, such as Linux, socket is managed by VFS abstraction among other file types. However, sockets are fundamentally different from files on disk [21].

1. **Sockets are not on disk.** Due to the slow speed of disks, `dentry` and `inode` are used as memory caches for the metadata of files on the slow disk. However, sockets exist in memory for their entire lifecycle and cannot benefit from the caching mechanism for which `dentry` and `inode` are designed.
2. **Directory path is never used to identify socket.** Usually, directory path is used to identify the disk files, and internally the kernel maps the directory path to a `dentry` and its corresponding `inode` to find the file. However, sockets are accessed directly through the `private_data` field of file structures. As a result, `dentry` and `inode` are not being used to identify sockets.

Therefore, we can see that `dentry` and `inode` are functionally useless for sockets, but still associated with sockets to be compatible with VFS abstraction. As discussed in 2.3, the useless dentry and inode introduce tremendous synchronization overhead when sockets are allocated frequently.

We propose Fastsocket-aware VFS to tackle the VFS scalability bottleneck for sockets while keeping the Fastsocket compatible with legacy VFS.

Avoid Unnecessary Overhead Fastsocket-aware VFS provides a fast path in the VFS processing for sockets to avoid the unnecessary overhead. Specifically, Fastsocket-aware VFS skips most initialization/destruction work of dentry and inode when creating/destroying a socket, which involves acquiring several locks and managing the dentry and inode in various tables and links.

Keep Compatibility We cannot remove dentry and inode from socket completely, as the remove will break the compatibility with legacy sockets. For example, widely used system tools such as *lsof* and *netstat* will fail, since they access the corresponding socket status through */proc* file system, which relies on dentry and inode (but does not require them to be completely initialized). Fastsocket-aware VFS only keeps the necessary states and functions of dentry and inode to support */proc* file system, which is a small price to pay to achieve compatibility.

In short, Fastsocket-aware VFS internally customizes VFS for sockets to improve scalability while externally keeping VFS compatibility for socket applications and system tools.

4. Evaluation

To evaluate the performance and scalability of Fastsocket, we focus on the following two questions in this section:

1. Does Fastsocket benefit real applications?
2. How does Fastsocket scale, compared to the state-of-the-art Linux TCP kernel stack implementations, especially for short-lived TCP connection handling?

To answer the first question, we evaluate Fastsocket on a 8-core server running HAProxy as HTTP load balancer in a production environment and we observe a 53.5% improvement in the effective capacity by deploying Fastsocket. In addition, we also carry out an experimental evaluation with Nginx and HAProxy, the two most important component in our infrastructure. The results show that their throughputs with Fastsocket outperform the base Linux by 267% and 621% respectively on a 24-core machine.

For the second question, The results show that the throughput with Fastsocket on a 24-core system scales to 20x while Linux 3.13 with SO_REUSEPORT [23] achieves only 12x. In addition, we collect statistics on locking and L3 shared cache missing rate in order to illustrate how and why each individual design benefits the overall performance.

With the excellent scalability performance of Fastsocket from the evaluation result, we demonstrate that BSD socket API is no longer the scalability obstacle for TCP stack.

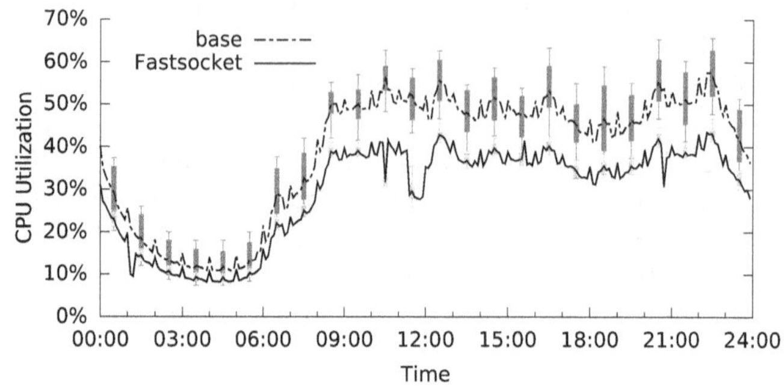

Figure 3: CPU utilization of two 8-core HAProxy servers in the Sina WeiBo production environment. One is with Fastsocket and the other is not. The upper line presents the average CPU utilization of the server without Fastsocket in one day and the lower line is with Fastsocket. We adopt a box plot [37] to visually convey the spread of 8 CPU core utilization for the two servers, which are sampled every hour.

4.1 Experiment Setup

Our testing environment consists of three machines, each of which has two 12-core Intel Xeon E5 2697 v2 processors, 64GB memory and a dual-port Intel 82599 10GE NIC. RSS is enabled on the NICs if FDir is not explicitly configured. The number of NIC queues is configured according to the number of CPU cores involved. We configure NIC interrupt affinity and XPS (Transmit Packet Steering) [8] to assign each RX and TX queue to one CPU core. As the baseline kernel has trouble in fully utilizing CPU resources with a single listen socket, all benchmarks listen on different IP addresses but on the same port 80.

All benchmarks fork multiple processes per server application and pin each process to a different CPU core. We use *connections per second* to measure throughput, as our main concern is the cost associated with connection establishment and termination. Unless otherwise stated, *http_load* [2] is used as the HTTP workload generator.

In order to saturate the benchmark servers with Fastsocket, we have to deploy Fastsocket on the clients and backend servers to increase their throughput to the same level.

4.2 Application Performance

4.2.1 Production Environment Evaluation

We have deployed Fastsocket on production servers running HAProxies in the Sina WeiBo production system. We collected the CPU utilization on two servers handling the same amount of requests (ensured by the load balancer) during the same period of time. Each server has two 4-core CPUs and 1GE NIC (without FDir support). *HTTP Keep-alive*[3] is disabled on HAProxy. One server is Fastsocket-enabled and the other is not. Figure 3 presents the results.

When serving client requests, we need to guarantee some service-level agreement (SLA), such as the 99.9th percentile response latency. In our production environment, we need to keep the CPU utilization under a certain threshold, in our case, 75%, to achieve the SLA. If any CPU core reaches the threshold, the workload handled by that CPU core will suffer a long latency, causing a latency SLA violation, even if other CPU cores are still idle. We describe this situation as the server has reached its *effective capacity*. The effective capacity is determined by the *most utilized* CPU core. Therefore, the load balance among different CPU cores and avoiding a "hot" CPU core is an important performance optimization.

As Figure 3 shows, without Fastsocket, the average CPU utilization is relatively high. Moreover, the variation of CPU utilization is very high among the 8 CPU cores (the error bar shows the max and min CPU utilization on different CPU cores). The underlying reason is using shared resources and lock contentions in the Linux kernel. For example, when multiple CPU cores try to get new connections from the shared accept queue, they need to first acquire the listen socket lock, as described in Section 2.1. The first CPU core will take the connection and there would probably be no connection left for the last CPU core when the core acquires the lock in turn. This can happen each time when kernel informs application that there are new connections ready to be accepted, which makes certain CPU cores have more connections to process and introduces the sustaining load variances among different CPU cores.

In the contrast, with Fastsocket, the average CPU utilization is considerably reduced because of the lower overhead in lock contention. Even better, the utilization of all CPU cores is perfectly balanced since Fastsocket eliminates shared resources and lock contentions in TCP stack.

Take a busy time 18:30 as an example. Without Fastsocket, average CPU utilization is 45.1%, while for the server with Fastsocket, the number is 34.3%, revealing that Fastsocket can improve CPU efficiency by 31.5% in handling the same amount of real traffic. Without Fastsocket, the CPU utilization varies from 31.7% to 57.7%, and with Fastsocket, the utilization of all CPU cores is very close to each other, ranging from 32.7% to 37.6%. We reasonably assume that the CPU consumption of a server is linear with the traffic it is supporting. Thus, the effective capacity and the utilization of the most utilized CPU core are inversely proportional. As a result, Fastsocket has improved effective capacity by

$$\frac{(37.6\%)^{-1} - (57.7\%)^{-1}}{(57.7\%)^{-1}} = 53.5\%$$

In addition, these production servers are relatively old machines that only have 8 CPU cores. The scalability problem only gets worse with the increasing number of CPU cores in the very near future. Fastsocket will become more crucial in the new multi-core machines. Nonetheless, the 53.5% performance boost by Fastsocket is still a big cost-saving in the production environment.

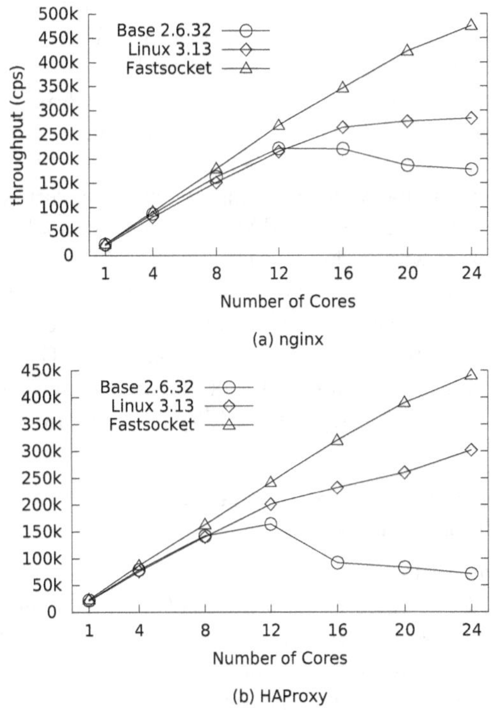

Figure 4: Connections per second throughput of the Nginx and HAProxy tests

4.2.2 Nginx

We perform Nginx benchmark to evaluate Fastsocket with the real-world web server. We disable HTTP Keep-alive on Nginx to allow the emulated clients to establish multiple short-lived connections. *Http_load* fetches a 64 bytes static file from Nginx with a concurrency of 500 multiplied by the number of CPU cores. The file is cached in memory so no disk I/O is involved. As the listen socket contention is eliminated by Fastsocket, we disabled `accept_mutex` in the Fastsocket test.

The throughput of Nginx on 1 to 24 CPU cores are shown in Figure 4(a). Fastsocket with Linux 2.6.32 on 24 CPU cores achieves 475K connections per second, with a speed up of 20.0x. The throughput of Nginx with base 2.6.32 kernel increases non-linearly up to 12 CPU cores and drops dramatically to 178K with 24 CPU cores. The latest 3.13 kernel only achieves the throughput to 283K when using 24 CPU cores. Here we observe that the latest kernel does not completely solve the scalability bottlenecks, preventing it from scaling beyond 12 CPU cores. We will show the reason later in Section 4.2.4.

4.2.3 HAProxy

In addition to Nginx, we present our HAProxy benchmark, to demonstrate the active connection (to the backend servers)

performance. We setup a client running *http_load* with concurrency of 500 multiplied by number of CPU cores and a backend server sending a constant 64-byte page.

Figure 4(b) presents the throughput of HAProxy. Fastsocket outperforms Linux 3.13 by 139K connections per second and base 2.6.32 by 370K when using 24 CPU cores, though the single CPU core throughputs are very close among all the three kernels. HAProxy is a proxy application and different with Nginx in that it makes frequently active connections to backend servers. With Receive Flow Deliver, Fastsocket introduces connection locality for active connections and greatly reduces CPU cache bouncing. This local processing of connections is important since Receive Flow Deliver increases throughput by 15%, as shown in Section 4.2.4.

4.2.4 Analysis on Fastsocket Performance Improvements

Lock Contention

To understand the effect of Fastsocket on reducing lock contentions, we have run the HAProxy benchmark with 24 CPU cores for 60 seconds and used *lockstat* [4] statistics to measure lock contentions. Table 1 presents the hottest locks, their contention counts in the baseline Linux and their contention count changes after enabling Fastsocket.

For the baseline kernel, `dcache_lock` and `inode_lock` in VFS suffer from the most severe contention and Fastsocket-aware VFS eliminates these unnecessary contentions as discussed in Section 3.4.

Socket is shared between interrupt context and process context in the TCP stacks by multiple CPU cores, therefore, a `slock` is used to protect the shared state of socket. Using Local Listen Table and Receive Flow Deliver, we achieve complete connection locality, therefore, each socket is processed only on a single CPU core, which eliminates any socket sharing across CPU cores. Thus we reduce the contentions on `slock` to 0 when enabling Local Listen Table and Receive Flow Deliver.

TCP processing involves other kernel systems, e.g., Epoll and Timer. `Ep.lock` avoids parallel socket status updating on the event ready list of epoll instance. `Base.lock` protects modifications to per-socket timers managing TCP timeouts. They suffer the same `slock` contention problem, since they are in the critical path of TCB processing. When Fastsocket has achieved complete connection locality, these lock contentions are naturally eliminated as Table 1 shows.

`Ehash.lock` is the per-bucket lock protecting the global established table. Contentions on this lock have been completely eliminated by adopting the Local Established Table.

After Fastsocket is deployed, locks (esp. *spinlocks*) consumes no more than 6% CPU cycles and most of the locks can be acquired without contention due to the partitioned data structure in Fastsocket. As a result, lock contention is no longer a performance bottleneck in our TCP stack.

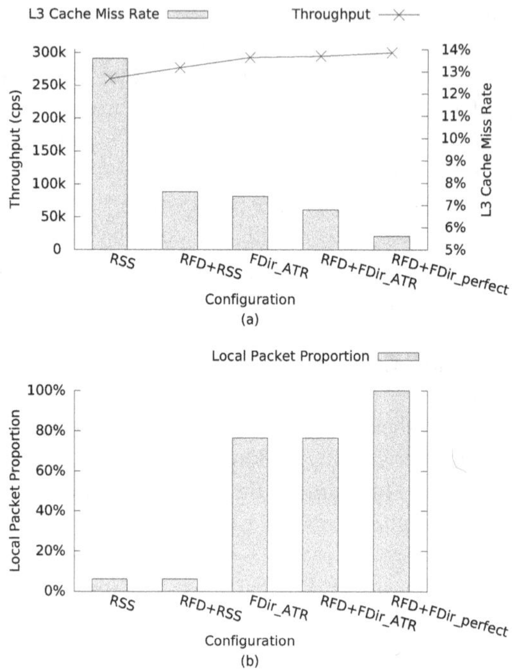

Figure 5: Throughput, L3 cache miss rate and local packet proportion with different NIC packets delivering features enabled

Connection Locality

To evaluate Receive Flow Deliver in more detail, we conduct experiments with RFD enabled or disabled, combined with different NIC packet delivering features including RSS, FDir in ATR mode (FDir_ATR) and FDir in Perfect-Filtering mode (FDir_Perfect). The experiment is carried out on a SandyBridge server with 16 CPU cores as the latest CentOS 6 does not support `ioatdma` [10] on IvyBridge yet, which would affect CPU cache usage patterns in the test. Fastsocket-aware VFS and Local Listen Table are always enabled in these experiments.

We did not perform the experiment of using FDir_Perfect without Receive Flow Deliver, because as discussed in Section 2.2, it will cause correctness problems.

We use throughput and L3 cache miss rate as metrics to illustrate the connection locality effect of RFD combined with different NIC packets delivering features. In addition, for active connections, we count the number of *local packets*, i.e. packets received from NIC and later processed in application on the same CPU core, as well as the total number of packets received. We present the percentage of local packets among all packets received to illustrate the effectiveness in preserving connection locality.

The throughput, L3 cache miss rates are presented in Figure 5(a) and local packet proportion data in Figure 5(b).

When RSS is enabled, the NIC evenly distributes incoming packets to different CPU cores, regardless of where the packets would be processed by applications. As a result, the local packet proportion is 6.2%, showing that the majority

Table 1: Lock Contention Counts (HAProxy benchmark with 24 CPU cores for 60 Seconds)

V = Fastsocket-Aware VFS, L = Local Listen Table, R = Receive Flow Deliver, E = Local Establish Table

lock	Baseline	Δ				Fastsocket
		+V	V +L	VL +R	VLR +E	
dcache_lock	26.4M	-26.4M	-	-	-	0
inode_lock	4.3M	-4.3M	-	-	-	0
slock	422.7K	+451.6K	-852.0K	-22.3K	-	0
ep.lock	1.0M	+906.4K	-1.3M	-649.7K	-	0
base.lock	451.3K	+337.2K	-277.6K	-510.9K	-	8
ehash.lock	868	+754	+466	+499	-2.6K	0

of incoming packets are received and processed on different CPU cores. In this case, the software Receive Flow Deliver forwards these non-local packets to the right CPU core to avoid further overhead from non-local connection problem. This reduces L3 cache miss rate by 6 percentage point and consequently improves throughput by 6.1% (from 261k to 277k).

For FDir_ATR, the local packet proportion rises to 76.5% and Receive Flow Deliver provides another performance improvement of 0.8% compared to FDir_ATR alone. Though the L3 cache miss rate when using FDir_ATR is close to RSS+RFD, FDir_ATR delivers a majority of packets to the right CPU core in NIC hardware and thus reduces software overhead on packet steering. At the same time, Receive Flow Deliver makes FDir_Perfect practical for accurately distributing incoming packets with a 100% local packet proportion, which gives us 1.8% reduction in L3 cache miss rate and 2.4% throughput improvement (from 293k to 300k) compared to only using FDir_ATR.

5. Related Work

Reducing Shared Resource Contentions In [14, 21], `inode` and `dentry` of VFS has been identified as the bottleneck for socket scalability and a more fine-grained lock scheme is proposed to mitigate inter-core shared resource contention. Megapipe [21] proposes a new channel design to bypass VFS completely. However, Megapipe loses compatibility with VFS abstraction. This forces legacy applications to modify their code and causes some system tools to misbehave, such as *netstat* and *lsof*. As described in Section 3.4, we adopt a more moderate design which retains the compatibility and remove locks associated with inode and dentry.

Locks in the listen socket is another hot spot identified by recent researches. Affinity-Accept [29], SO_REUSEPORT [23] and Megapipe [21] solve the single socket problem by cloning a listen socket copy for each CPU core. But these designs are still based on the global listen table. This is a potential scalability bottleneck Fastsocket has solved the problem completely with Local Listen Table.

Achieving Connection Locality Some researchs [34, 36, 38, 40–42] analyze and modify modern OSes, such as OpenSolaris, FreeBSD, Linux, Windows, etc., for high-performance TCP/IP network. In [38], two variations on a partitioned network-stack design for scalability in FreeBSD are described, and compared in evaluation with a conventional locked implementation. One variation protects partitioned data structures with locks that are global, but in practice uncontended. A second associates partitioned data structures whose instances may be accessed only by specific threads, providing synchronisation; Willman describes substantial overhead from context switching. Affinity-Accept [29] and Megapipe [21] achieve acceptable connection locality in the case of passive connection. Fastsocket goes further by realizing complete connection locality on both passive and active connections with Local Listen Table and Receive Flow Deliver.

Batching System Calls and zero-copy Communication FlexSC [32] and Megapipe [21] proposed system call batching to save the cost of context switch. It is possible to implement system call batching in Fastsocket and simulate the BSD socket API in the user library. Since we focus on the scalability problem in TCP stacks in this paper, integrating system call batching is left as future work. Zero-copy reduces data movement overheads and simplifies resource management [28]. POSIX OSes have been modified to support zero-copy through page remap- ping and copy-on-write [15]. Fastsocket can use zero-copy technologies in POSIX OSes [33].

Relaxing System Call Restrictions on Semantics Existing literatures [16, 21] have blamed the *lowest available file descriptor* in POSIX specification for poor scalability and relaxed the rule. However, there are applications implemented based on the rule. For example, the latest HAProxy assumes that file descriptor should never exceed the current connection number based on the file descriptor rule and uses file descriptor as the index of a connection array for connection management [1]. To achieve compatibility, we have not introduced these semantics changes in Fastsocket.

User-level Network Stacks Application-specific extensibility was one of the main motivations behind user-level networking. For example, application-specific customization of the networking stack in a user-level networking system was shown to be beneficial by enabling application-controlled flow control and feedback. There have been several user-level network stacks that try to accelerate the performance [17–20, 22]. However, they lack the full BSD socket API, general and robust implementation of kernel network stack, as described in Section 1. Fastsocket, on the other hand, is built into the Linux kernel and is designed to be compatible with both existing applications and mature network stack components in the kernel. The compatibility achieved by Fastsocket makes it easier to deploy our proposal to production systems.

Library operating systems with hardware virtualization Library operating systems: Exokernels extend the end-to-end principle to resource management by implementing system abstractions via library operating systems linked in with applications [19]. Library operating systems often run as virtual machines. Hardware support for virtualization naturally separates control and execution functions, e.g., to build type-2 hypervisors [35], run virtual appliances [24]. IX [12] and Arrakis [30] uses hardware virtualization to separate the I/O dataplane from the control plane. IX uses a full Linux kernel as the control plane; provides three-way isolation between the control plane, networking stack, and application; and proposes a dataplane architecture that optimizes for both high throughput and low latency. Arrakis uses Barrelfish [11] as the control plane and includes support for IOMMUs and SR-IOV. As far as we know, IX and Arrakis use modified embedded TCP stack lwIP, which missed many advanced features as described in Section 1, which are very useful in practice.

Reserving Cores for Network IsoStack [31] aims to improve network system efficiency with a novel architecture that designates one CPU core to handle all network stack work to remove contentions, while all other CPU cores run applications. However, when adopting IsoStack in 10G and even 40G network, the dedicated single CPU core will be overloaded, especially in the CPU-intensive short-lived connection scenarios. Fastsocket shows that full partition of TCB management is a more efficient and feasible alternative to scale TCP stack.

6. Conclusion

This paper introduces Fastsocket, a new scalable TCP socket which successfully partitions shared socket tables including the listen table and established table. Fastsocket further implements PerCore Process Zone to avoid lock contentions and keep compatibility at the same time.

The key designs are 1) Local Listen Table which partitions the global listen table and guarantees passive connection locality, 2) Local Established Table which partitions the global established table and guarantee full partition on TCB management. 3) Receive Flow Deliver which guarantees active connection locality which coexists with passive connection locality, and 4) Fastsocket-aware VFS which avoids heavy lock contentions on sockets while keeping compatible with existing applications.

Nginx and HAProxy evaluation on Intel 24-core shows Fastsocket improves the performance by 267% and 621% respectively and retains full BSD socket API, which benefits existing socket applications and their developers as well. Moreover, all these modifications are not intrusive to the Linux kernel, which means Fastsocket can gracefully fit into the existing Linux kernel. Because of both high scalability and compatibility, Fastsocket has been deployed in Sina Weibo system to serve requests from all over the world. All Fastsocket source code is publicly available at https://github.com/fastos/fastsocket.

Acknowledgments

This research is carried out by Sina&Tsinghua&Intel's cooperation. We thank Intel, especially Mr. Xu Chen, for their hardware and expertise. And also thank Sixing Xiao for his early research work. This research is supported by Natural Science Foundation of China under Grant No. 61170050, National Science and Technology Major Project of China (2012ZX01039-004),The National High Technology Research and Development Program of China (2015AA011505).

References

[1] Haproxy. `http://haproxy.1wt.eu/`.

[2] http_load - multiprocessing http test client. `http://www.acme.com/software/http_load/`.

[3] Hypertext transfer protocol – http/1.0. `http://tools.ietf.org/html/rfc1945`.

[4] Lock statistics. `https://git.kernel.org/cgit/linux/kernel/git/torvalds/linux.git/tree/Documentation/lockstat.txt`.

[5] Tcp syn flooding attacks and common mitigations. `http://tools.ietf.org/html/rfc4987`.

[6] Rfs hardware acceleration. `http://lwn.net/Articles/406489/`, 2010.

[7] rfs: Receive flow steering. `http://lwn.net/Articles/381955/`, 2010.

[8] xps: Transmit packet steering. `http://lwn.net/Articles/412062/`, 2010.

[9] Intel 82599 10 gigabit ethernet controller datasheet. `http://www.intel.com/content/www/us/en/ethernet-controllers/82599-10-gbe-controller-datasheet.html`, 2014.

[10] Intel i/o acceleration technology: Intel network adapters user guide. `http://web.mit.edu/cron/documentation/dell-server-admin/en/IntelNIC/ioat.htm`, 2014.

[11] A. Baumann, P. Barham, P.-E. Dagand, T. Harris, R. Isaacs, S. Peter, T. Roscoe, A. Schüpbach, and A. Singhania. The multikernel: A new os architecture for scalable multicore systems. In *Proceedings of the ACM SIGOPS 22Nd Symposium on Operating Systems Principles*, SOSP '09, pages 29–44, New York, NY, USA, 2009. ACM.

[12] A. Belay, G. Prekas, A. Klimovic, S. Grossman, C. Kozyrakis, and E. Bugnion. Ix: A protected dataplane operating system for high throughput and low latency. In *Proceedings of the*

11th USENIX Conference on Operating Systems Design and Implementation, OSDI'14, pages 49–65, Berkeley, CA, USA, 2014. USENIX Association.

[13] S. M. Bellovin. A look back at "security problems in the tcp/ip protocol suite". In *Proceedings of the 20th Annual Computer Security Applications Conference*, ACSAC '04, pages 229–249, Washington, DC, USA, 2004. IEEE Computer Society.

[14] S. Boyd-Wickizer, A. T. Clements, Y. Mao, A. Pesterev, M. F. Kaashoek, R. Morris, and N. Zeldovich. An analysis of linux scalability to many cores. In R. H. Arpaci-Dusseau and B. Chen, editors, *OSDI*, pages 1–16. USENIX Association, 2010.

[15] H.-k. J. Chu. Zero-copy tcp in solaris. In *Proceedings of the 1996 Annual Conference on USENIX Annual Technical Conference*, ATEC '96, pages 21–21, Berkeley, CA, USA, 1996. USENIX Association.

[16] A. T. Clements, M. F. Kaashoek, N. Zeldovich, R. T. Morris, and E. Kohler. The scalable commutativity rule: designing scalable software for multicore processors. In M. Kaminsky and M. Dahlin, editors, *SOSP*, pages 1–17. ACM, 2013.

[17] S. Communications. Introduction to openonload: Building application transparency and protocol conformance into application acceleration middleware. `http://www.solarflare.com/content/userfiles/documents/solarflare_openonload_intropaper.pdf`, 2011.

[18] D. Ely, S. Savage, and D. Wetherall. Alpine: A user-level infrastructure for network protocol development. In *USITS*. USENIX, 2001.

[19] G. R. Ganger, D. R. Engler, M. F. Kaashoek, H. M. Briceo, R. Hunt, T. Pinckney, and V. Inc. Fast and flexible application-level networking on exokernel systems. *ACM Transactions on Computer Systems*, 20:49–83, 2000.

[20] H. S. Gunawi, A. C. Arpaci-Dusseau, and R. H. Arpaci-Dusseau. Deploying safe user-level network services with icTCP. In *OSDI*, pages 317–332. USENIX Association, 2004.

[21] S. Han, S. Marshall, B.-G. Chun, and S. Ratnasamy. Megapipe: A new programming interface for scalable network i/o. In *Proceedings of the 10th USENIX Conference on Operating Systems Design and Implementation*, OSDI'12, pages 135–148, Berkeley, CA, USA, 2012. USENIX Association.

[22] E. Jeong, S. Wood, M. Jamshed, H. Jeong, S. Ihm, D. Han, and K. Park. mtcp: a highly scalable user-level tcp stack for multicore systems. In *11th USENIX Symposium on Networked Systems Design and Implementation (NSDI 14)*, pages 489–502, Seattle, WA, Apr. 2014. USENIX Association.

[23] M. Kerrisk. The so_reuseport socket option. `http://lwn.net/Articles/542629/`, 2013.

[24] I. Krsul, A. Ganguly, J. Zhang, J. A. B. Fortes, and R. J. Figueiredo. Vmplants: Providing and managing virtual machine execution environments for grid computing. In *Proceedings of the 2004 ACM/IEEE Conference on Supercomputing*, SC '04, pages 7–, Washington, DC, USA, 2004. IEEE Computer Society.

[25] G. Loukas and G. Öke. Protection against denial of service attacks. *Comput. J.*, 53(7):1020–1037, Sept. 2010.

[26] lwIP community. lwip - a lightweight tcp/ip stack - summary. `http://savannah.nongnu.org/projects/lwip/`, 2012.

[27] E. M. Nahum, D. J. Yates, J. F. Kurose, and D. Towsley. Performance issues in parallelized network protocols. In *Proceedings of the 1st USENIX Conference on Operating Systems Design and Implementation*, OSDI '94, Berkeley, CA, USA, 1994. USENIX Association.

[28] V. S. Pai, P. Druschel, and W. Zwaenepoel. Io-lite: A unified i/o buffering and caching system. *ACM Trans. Comput. Syst.*, 18(1):37–66, Feb. 2000.

[29] A. Pesterev, J. Strauss, N. Zeldovich, and R. T. Morris. Improving network connection locality on multicore systems. In P. Felber, F. Bellosa, and H. Bos, editors, *EuroSys*, pages 337–350. ACM, 2012.

[30] S. Peter, J. Li, I. Zhang, D. R. K. Ports, D. Woos, A. Krishnamurthy, T. Anderson, and T. Roscoe. Arrakis: The operating system is the control plane. In *Proceedings of the 11th USENIX Conference on Operating Systems Design and Implementation*, OSDI'14, pages 1–16, Berkeley, CA, USA, 2014. USENIX Association.

[31] L. Shalev, J. Satran, E. Borovik, and M. Ben-Yehuda. Isostack: Highly efficient network processing on dedicated cores. In *Proceedings of the 2010 USENIX Conference on USENIX Annual Technical Conference*, USENIXATC'10, pages 5–5, Berkeley, CA, USA, 2010. USENIX Association.

[32] L. Soares and M. Stumm. FlexSC: Flexible system call scheduling with exception-less system calls. In R. H. Arpaci-Dusseau and B. Chen, editors, *OSDI*, pages 33–46. USENIX Association, 2010.

[33] T. Suzumura, M. Tatsubori, S. Trent, A. Tozawa, and T. Onodera. Highly scalable web applications with zero-copy data transfer. In *Proceedings of the 18th International Conference on World Wide Web*, WWW '09, pages 921–930, New York, NY, USA, 2009. ACM.

[34] S. Tripathi. Fireenginea new networking architecture for the solaris operating system. `http://www.scn.rain.com/~neighorn/PDF/FireEngine_WP.pdf`, 2004.

[35] R. Uhlig, G. Neiger, D. Rodgers, A. L. Santoni, F. C. M. Martins, A. V. Anderson, S. M. Bennett, A. Kagi, F. H. Leung, and L. Smith. Intel virtualization technology. *Computer*, 38(5):48–56, May 2005.

[36] R. N. M. Watson. Introduction to multithreading and multiprocessing in the freebsd smpng network stack. `http://www.watson.org/~robert/freebsd/netperf/20051027-eurobsdcon2005-netperf.pdf`, 2005.

[37] D. F. Williamson, R. A. Parker, and J. S. Kendrick. The box plot: a simple visual method to interpret data. *Annals of internal medicine*, 110(11):916–921, 1989.

[38] P. Willmann, S. Rixner, and A. L. Cox. An evaluation of network stack parallelization strategies in modern operating systems. In *Proceedings of the Annual Conference on USENIX '06 Annual Technical Conference*, ATEC '06, pages 8–8, Berkeley, CA, USA, 2006. USENIX Association.

[39] S. Woo, E. Jeong, S. Park, J. Lee, S. Ihm, and K. Park. Comparison of caching strategies in modern cellular backhaul

networks. In H.-H. Chu, P. Huang, R. R. Choudhury, and F. Zhao, editors, *MobiSys*, pages 319–332. ACM, 2013.

[40] P. Xie, B. Wu, M. Liu, J. Harris, and C. Scheiman. Profiling the performance of tcp/ip on windows nt. *Computer Performance and Dependability Symposium, International*, 0:133, 2000.

[41] H. youb Kim and S. Rixner. Performance characterization of the freebsd network stack. `http://www.cs.rice.edu/CS/Architecture/docs/kim-tr05.pdf`, 2005.

[42] H. Zou, W. Wu, X.-H. Sun, P. DeMar, and M. Crawford. An evaluation of parallel optimization for opensolaris network stack. In *Local Computer Networks (LCN), 2010 IEEE 35th Conference on*, pages 296–299, Oct 2010.

SpaceJMP: Programming with Multiple Virtual Address Spaces

Izzat El Hajj[3,4,*], Alexander Merritt[2,4,*], Gerd Zellweger[1,4,*], Dejan Milojicic[4], Reto Achermann[1], Paolo Faraboschi[4], Wen-mei Hwu[3], Timothy Roscoe[1], and Karsten Schwan[2]

[1]Department of Computer Science, ETH Zürich [2]Georgia Institute of Technology
[3]University of Illinois at Urbana-Champaign [4]Hewlett Packard Labs

[*]Co-primary authors

Abstract

Memory-centric computing demands careful organization of the virtual address space, but traditional methods for doing so are inflexible and inefficient. If an application wishes to address larger physical memory than virtual address bits allow, if it wishes to maintain pointer-based data structures beyond process lifetimes, or if it wishes to share large amounts of memory across simultaneously executing processes, legacy interfaces for managing the address space are cumbersome and often incur excessive overheads.

We propose a new operating system design that promotes virtual address spaces to first-class citizens, enabling process threads to attach to, detach from, and switch between multiple virtual address spaces. Our work enables data-centric applications to utilize vast physical memory beyond the virtual range, represent persistent pointer-rich data structures without special pointer representations, and share large amounts of memory between processes efficiently.

We describe our prototype implementations in the DragonFly BSD and Barrelfish operating systems. We also present programming semantics and a compiler transformation to detect unsafe pointer usage. We demonstrate the benefits of our work on data-intensive applications such as the GUPS benchmark, the SAMTools genomics workflow, and the Redis key-value store.

1. Introduction

The volume of data processed by applications is increasing dramatically, and the amount of physical memory in machines is growing to meet this demand. However, effectively using this memory poses challenges for programmers. The main challenges tackled in this paper are addressing more physical memory than the size of a virtual space, maintaining pointer-based data structures across process lifetimes, and sharing very large memory objects between processes.

We expect that main memory capacity will soon exceed the virtual address space size supported by CPUs today (typically 256 TiB with 48 virtual address bits). This is made particularly likely with non-volatile memory (NVM) devices – having larger capacity than DRAM – expected to appear in memory systems by 2020. While some vendors have already increased the number of virtual address (VA) bits in their processors, adding VA bits has implications on performance, power, production, and estate cost that make it undesirable for low-end and low-power processors. Adding VA bits also implies longer TLB miss latency, which is already a bottleneck in current systems (up to 50% overhead in scientific apps [55]). Processors supporting virtual address spaces smaller than available physical memory require large data structures to be partitioned across multiple processes or these structures to be mapped in and out of virtual memory.

Representing pointer-based data structures beyond process lifetimes requires data serialization, which incurs a large performance overhead, or the use of special pointer representations, which results in awkward programming techniques. Sharing and storing pointers in their original form across process lifetimes requires guaranteed acquisition of specific VA locations. Providing this guarantee is not always feasible, and when feasible, may necessitate mapping datasets residing at conflicting VA locations in and out of the virtual space.

Sharing data across simultaneously executing processes requires special communication with data-serving processes (e.g., using sockets), impacting programmability and incurring communication channel overheads. Sharing data via traditional shared memory requires tedious communication and synchronization between all client processes for growing the shared region or guaranteeing consistency on writes.

To address all these challenges, we present SpaceJMP, a set of APIs, OS mechanisms, and compiler techniques that constitute a new way to manage memory. SpaceJMP applications create and manage Virtual Address Spaces (VASes) as first-class objects, independent of processes. Decoupling VASes from processes enables a single process to activate multiple VASes, such that threads of that process can switch

ASPLOS '16 April 02 - 06, 2016, Atlanta, GA, USA

ACM 978-1-4503-4091-5/16/04... $15.00
DOI: http://dx.doi.org/10.1145/2872362.2872366

between these VASes in a lightweight manner. It also enables a single VAS to be activated by multiple processes or to exist in the system alone in a self-contained manner.

SpaceJMP solves the problem of insufficient VA bits by allowing a process to place data in multiple address spaces. If a process runs out of virtual memory, it does not need to modify data mappings or create new processes. It simply creates more address spaces and switches between them. SpaceJMP solves the problem of managing pointer-based data structures because SpaceJMP processes can always guarantee the availability of a VA location by creating a new address space. SpaceJMP solves the problem of data sharing by allowing processes to switch into a shared address space. Clients thus need not communicate with a server process or synchronize with each other on shared region management, and synchronization on writes can be lightweight.

SpaceJMP builds on a wealth of historical techniques in memory management and virtualization but occupies a novel "sweet spot" for modern data-centric applications: it maps well to existing hardware while delivering more flexibility and performance for large data-centric applications compared with current OS facilities.

We make the following contributions:

1. We present SpaceJMP (Section 3): the OS facilities provided for processes to each create, structure, compose, and access multiple virtual address spaces, together with the compiler support for detecting unsafe program behavior.
2. We describe and compare (Section 4) implementations of SpaceJMP for the 64-bit x86 architecture in two different OSes: DragonFly BSD and Barrelfish.
3. We empirically show (Section 5) how SpaceJMP improves performance with microbenchmarks and three data-centric applications: the GUPS benchmark, the SAMTools genomics workflow, and the Redis key-value store.

2. Motivation

Our primary motivations are the challenges we have already mentioned: insufficient VA bits, managing pointer-based data structures, and sharing large amounts of memory – discussed in Sections 2.1, 2.2, and 2.3 respectively.

2.1 Insufficient Virtual Address Bits

Non-Volatile Memory (NVM) technologies, besides persistence, promise better scaling and lower power than DRAM, which will enable large-scale, densely packed memory systems with much larger capacity than today's DRAM-based computers. Combined with high-radix optical switches [76], these future memory systems will appear to the processing elements as single, petabyte-scale "load-store domains" [33].

One implication of this trend is that the physical memory accessible from a CPU will exceed the size that VA bits can address. While almost all modern processor architectures support 64-bit addressing, CPU implementations pass fewer

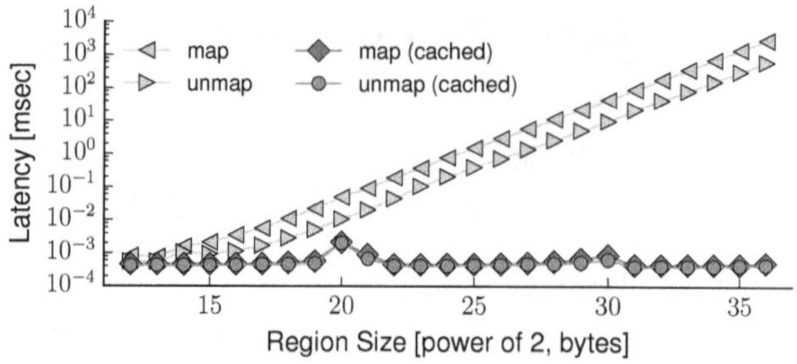

Figure 1: Page table construction (mmap) and removal (munmap) costs in Linux, using 4KiB pages. Does not include page zeroing costs.

bits to the virtual memory translation unit because of power and performance implications. Most CPUs today are limited to 48 virtual address bits (i.e., 256 TiB) and 44-46 physical address bits (16-64 TiB), and we expect a slow growth in these numbers.

The challenge presented is how to support applications that want to address large physical memories without paying the cost of increasing processor address bits across the board. One solution is partitioning physical memory across multiple OS processes which would incur unnecessary inter-process communication overhead and is tedious to program. Another solution is mapping memory partitions in and out of the VAS, which has overheads discussed in Section 2.4.

2.2 Maintaining Pointer-based Data Structures

Maintaining pointer-based data structures beyond process lifetimes without serialization overhead has motivated emerging persistent memory programming models to adopt region-based programming paradigms [15, 21, 78]. While these approaches provide a more natural means for applications to interact with data, they present the challenge of how to represent pointers meaningfully across processes.

One solution is the use of special pointers, but this hinders programmability. Another solution is requiring memory regions to be mapped to fixed virtual addresses by all users. This solution creates degenerate scenarios where memory is mapped in and out when memory regions overlap, the drawbacks of which are discussed in Section 2.4.

2.3 Sharing Large Memory

Collaborative environments where multiple processes share large amounts of data require clean mechanisms for processes to access and manage shared data efficiently and safely. One approach uses a client-server model whereby client processes communicate with key-value stores [24, 63, 67] that manage and serve the data. This approach requires code to be rewritten to use specific interfaces and incurs communication overhead. Another approach is using shared memory regions, but current OS mechanisms for doing so have many limitations discussed in Section 2.4.

2.4 Problems with Legacy Methods

Legacy methods for interacting with memory are based on interfaces exposed over a *file* abstraction. As systems become increasingly memory centric, these interfaces introduce performance bottlenecks that limit scalability [35], and their complexity and usability create challenges for programmers.

Changing memory maps in the critical path of an application has significant performance implications, and scaling to large memories further exacerbates the problem. Using file-based methods such as `mmap` is slow and not scalable [20]. Figure 1 shows that constructing page tables for a 1 GiB region using 4 KiB page takes about 5 ms; for 64 GiB the cost is about 2 seconds. Frequent use of such interfaces quickly becomes an expensive operation, especially when applications must access all pages within a region.

In addition to performance implications, the flexibility of legacy interfaces is also a major concern. Memory-centric computing demands careful organization of the virtual address space, but interfaces such as `mmap` only give limited control. Some systems do not support creation of address regions at specific offsets. In Linux, for example, `mmap` does not safely abort if a request is made to open a region of memory over an existing region; it simply writes over it. Moreover, in current systems, memory sharing is tied to coarse-grained protection bits configured on the backing file, such as user-group, or access control lists (ACL). This requires a translation between different security models which may want to operate at different granularities. That along with linkers that dynamically relocate libraries or OSes that randomize the stack allocation prevents applications from sharing memory effectively.

3. Design

We now describe the design of SpaceJMP and define the terminology used in this paper. SpaceJMP provides two key abstractions: *lockable segments* encapsulate sharing of in-memory data, and *virtual address spaces* represent sets of non-overlapping segments. We also describe semantics for safe programming of segments and address spaces.

3.1 Lockable Segments

In SpaceJMP, all data and code used by the system exist within *segments*. The term has been used to refer to many different concepts over the years; in SpaceJMP, a segment should be thought of as an extension of the model used in Unix to hold code, data, stack, etc.: a segment is a single, contiguous area of virtual memory containing code and data, with a fixed virtual start address and size, together with metadata to describe how to access the content in memory. With every segment we store the backing physical frames, the mapping from its virtual addresses to physical frames and the associated access rights.

For safe access to regions of memory, all SpaceJMP segments can be *lockable*. In order to switch into an address

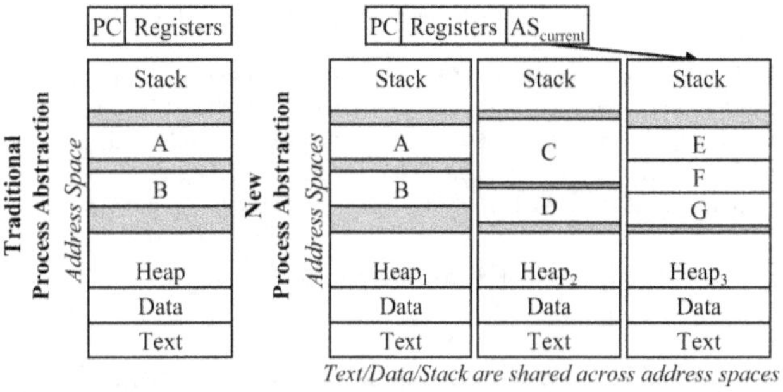

Figure 2: Contrasting SpaceJMP and Unix.

VAS API – for applications.

```
vas_find(name) → vid
vas_detach(vh)
vas_create(name,perms) → vid
vas_clone(vid) → vid
vas_attach(vid) → vh
vas_switch(vh)
vas_ctl(cmd,vid[,arg])
```

Segment API – for library developers.

```
seg_find(name) → sid
seg_attach(vh,sid)
seg_detach(vh,sid)
seg_ctl(sid,cmd[,arg])
seg_attach(vid,sid)
seg_detach(vid,sid)
seg_clone(sid) → sid
seg_alloc(name,base,size,perms) → sid
```

Figure 3: SpaceJMP interface.

space, the OS must acquire a reader/writer lock on each lockable segment in that address space.

Each lock acquisition is tied to the access permissions for its corresponding segment: if the segment is mapped read-only, the lock will be acquired in a shared mode, supporting multiple readers (i.e., multiple reading address spaces) and no writers. Conversely, if the segment is mapped writable, the lock is acquired exclusively, ensuring that only one client at a time is allowed in an address space with that segment mapped.

Lockable segments are the unit of data sharing and protection provided in SpaceJMP. Together with address space switching, they provide a fast and secure way to guarantee safe and concurrent access to memory regions to many independent clients.

3.2 Multiple Virtual Address Spaces

In most contemporary OSes, a process or kernel thread is associated with a single virtual address space (VAS), assigned when the execution context is created. In contrast, SpaceJMP virtual address spaces are first-class OS objects, created and manipulated independently of threads or processes. The contrast between SpaceJMP and traditional Unix-like (or other) OSes is shown in Figure 2. SpaceJMP can emulate regular Unix processes (and does, as we discuss in the next section), but provides a way to rapidly switch sections of mappings to make different sets of segments accessible.

The SpaceJMP API is shown in Figure 3. A process in SpaceJMP can *create*, *delete*, and *enumerate* VASes. A VAS can then be *attached* by one or more processes (via `vas_attach`), and a process can *switch* its context between

```
type *t; vasid_t vid; vhandle_t vh; segid_t sid;

// Example use of segment API.        // Example use of VAS API.
va=0xC0DE; sz=(1UL«35);                vid=vas_find("v0");
vid=vas_create("v0",660);              vh=vas_attach(vid);
sid=seg_alloc("s0",va,sz,660);         vas_switch(vh);
seg_attach(vid, sid);                  t=malloc(...); *t = 42;
```

Figure 4: Example SpaceJMP usage.

different VASes to which it is attached at any point during its execution. A VAS can also continue to exist beyond the lifetime of its creating process (e.g., it may be attached to other processes).

The average user only needs to worry about manipulating VASes. Advanced users and library developers may directly manipulate segments within the VAS. Heap allocators, for instance, must manage the segments that service the allocations (see Section 4). Segments can be *attached* to, or *detached* from a VAS. In practice, some segments (such as global OS mappings, code segments, and thread stacks) are widely shared between VASes attached to the same process. `seg_attach` and `seg_detach` allow installing segments that are process-specific by using the `vid` handle (`vh`) or globally for all processes attached to a VAS using the `vid`.

Rather than reinventing the wheel, our permission model for segments and address spaces use existing security models available in the OS. For example, in DragonFly BSD, we rely on ACLs to restrict access to segments and address spaces for processes or process groups. In Barrelfish, we use the capability system provided by the OS (Section 4.2) to control access. To modify permissions, the user can *clone* a segment or VAS and use the `seg_ctl`, or `vas_ctl`, to change the meta-data of the new object (e.g., permissions) accordingly.

A spawned process will still receive its initial VAS by the OS. The exposed functionality to the user process, however, allows it to construct and use additional VASes. A typical call sequence to create a new VAS is shown in Figure 4.

3.3 Programming Semantics for Safe Execution

Multiple VASes per process is a powerful feature for writing applications in a data-driven world. However, this feature introduces new kinds of unsafe memory access behavior that programmers must carefully avoid. We provide the user with a compiler tool to detect such unsafe behavior.

This section defines semantics for programming with SpaceJMP safely. The *common region* refers to the memory segments that a process maps to all VASes such as the stack, code, and globals. A VAS should not store a pointer that points to another VAS, except in the common region, which is shared by all VASes. Therefore any pointer not in the common region of a VAS is valid only when that VAS is active. Moreover, pointers to the common region should only be stored in the common region because they are not meaningful to other processes that may attach a VAS. This ensures that a VAS remains independent from any process.

The following rules define safe and unsafe behavior:

- If a pointer p is obtained when a VAS v is active via allocation in or loading from the non-common region:
  - Dereferencing p is safe in v and unsafe otherwise
  - Storing to p a pointer q is safe if q points to the non-common region of v and unsafe otherwise
- If a pointer p is obtained via allocation on the stack or is a global or function pointer:
  - Dereferencing and storing to p is always safe
- If a pointer p is loaded from the common region:
  - The safety properties of p must be the same as that of the originally stored pointer

Compiler support for detecting violations of these rules is discussed in Section 4.3.

4. Implementation

We built 64-bit x86 implementations of SpaceJMP for the DragonFly BSD and Barrelfish operating systems, which occupy very different points in the design space for memory management and provide a broad perspective on the implementation trade-offs for SpaceJMP. We first discuss the DragonFly BSD implementation, since it is the most mature and the platform for the majority of results in Section 5.

4.1 DragonFly BSD

DragonFly BSD [27] is a scalable, minimalistic kernel originally derived from FreeBSD4, supporting only the x86-64 architecture. Our SpaceJMP implementation includes modifications to the BSD memory subsystem and an address-space-aware implementation of the user space `malloc` interfaces.

Memory subsystem: DragonFly BSD has a nearly identical memory system to FreeBSD, both of which derive from the memory system in the Mach kernel [65]. The following descriptions therefore also apply to similar systems.

The BSD memory subsystem is based on the concept of *VM objects* [65] which abstract storage (files, swap, raw memory, etc.). Each object contains a set of physical pages that hold the associated content. A SpaceJMP segment is a wrapper around such an object, backed only by physical memory, additionally containing global identifiers (e.g., a name), and protection state. Physical pages are reserved at the time a segment is created, and are not swappable. Furthermore, a segment may contain a set of cached translations to accelerate attachment to an address space. The translations may be globally cached in the kernel if the segment is shared with other processes.

Address spaces in BSD, as in Linux, are represented by two layers: a high-level set of region descriptors (virtual offset, length, permissions), and a single instance of the architecture-specific translation structures used by the CPU. Each region descriptor references a single VM object, to inform the page fault handler where to ask for physical pages. A SpaceJMP segment can therefore be created as a VM object and added directly to an address space, with minimal modifications made to the core OS kernel implementation.

Sharing segments with other processes is straightforward to implement as they can always be attached to an existing address space, provided it does not overlap a previously mapped region. Sharing an address space is slightly more complicated: as mentioned in Section 3, we only share segments that are also visible to other processes. Doing so allows applications to attach their own private segments (such as their code or their stack) into an address space, before they can switch into it. Those segments would typically heavily conflict as every process tends to have a stack and program code at roughly the same location. The underlying address space representation that BSD uses (the `vmspace` object) always represents a particular instance of an address space with concrete segments mapped. Therefore, sharing a `vmspace` instance directly with other processes will not work. Instead, when sharing an address space, the OS shares just the set of memory segments that comprise the VAS. A process then attaches to the VAS, creating a `vmspace`, which it then can switch into.

A slight modification of the process context structure was necessary to hold references to more than one `vmspace` object, along with a pointer to the current address space. Knowing the active address space is required for correct operation of the page fault handler and system calls which modify the address space, such as the segment attach operation.

Inadvertent address collisions may arise between segments, such as those for stack, heap, and code. For example, attaching to a VAS may fail if a (global) segment within it conflicts with the attaching process' (private, fixed-address) code segments. Our current implementation in DragonFly BSD avoids this by ensuring both globally visible and process-private segments are created in disjoint address ranges.

Runtime library: We developed a library to facilitate application development using the SpaceJMP kernel interface, avoiding complexities such as locating boundaries of process code, globals, and stack for use within an address space across switches. The library performs much of the bookkeeping work involved in attaching an address space to a process: private segments holding the process' program text, globals, and thread-specific stacks are attached to the process-local `vmspace` object by using the VAS handle.

Furthermore, the library provides allocation of heap space (`malloc`) within a specific segment while inside an address space. SpaceJMP complicates heap management since programs need to allocate memory from different segments depending on their needs. These segments may not be attached to every address space of the process, and moreover a call to free up memory can only be executed by a process if it is currently in an address space which has the corresponding segment attached.

To manage this complexity, the SpaceJMP allocator is built over Doug Lea's dlmalloc [48], providing the notion of a memory space (mspace). An mspace is an allocator's internal state and may be placed at arbitrary locations. Our library supports distinct mspaces for individual segments, and provides wrapper functions for `malloc` and `free` which supply the correct mspace instance to dlmalloc, depending on the currently active address space and segment.

VAS switching: Attaching to a global VAS creates a new process-private instance of a `vmspace` object, where the process code, stack, global regions are mapped in. A program or runtime initiates a switch via a system call; the kernel identifies the `vmspace` object specified by the call, then simply overwrites `CR3`[1] with the physical address of the page table of the new VAS. Other registers, such as the stack pointer, are not modified. A kernel may also transparently initiate a switch, e.g., after a page fault, or triggered via any other event.

4.2 Barrelfish

Barrelfish [7] is a research operating system structured as a "multikernel", a distributed system of cores communicating solely via asynchronous messages.

In contrast to BSD, Barrelfish prohibits dynamic memory allocation in the kernel. Instead, Barrelfish has user-space memory servers which allocate physical memory to applications. Each memory region is typed using a capability system inspired by seL4 [31]. Retyping of memory is checked by the kernel and performed by system calls. The security model guarantees that a user-space process can allocate memory for its own page tables (and other kernel-level objects) and frames for mapping memory into the virtual address spaces.

The capability system provides fine-grained access control to resources, allowing processes great flexibility in implementing policies, and safely performs security-relevant actions via explicit capability invocations. Therefore, SpaceJMP is implemented almost entirely in user space with no additional logic added to the kernel: all VAS management operation translate into explicit capability invocations.

We use this functionality to explicitly share and modify page tables without kernel participation. In particular, we implemented a SpaceJMP-service to track created VASes in the system, together with attached segments and attaching processes, similar to the kernel extensions employed in BSD. Processes interact with the user-level service via RPCs.

Upon attaching to a VAS, a process obtains a new capability to a root page table to be filled in with mapping information. Switching to the VAS is a capability invocation to replace the thread's root page table with the one of the VAS. This is guaranteed to be a safe operation as the capability system enforces only valid mappings. Initially, all page tables other than the root of a VAS are shared among the attached processes, allowing easy propagation of updated mappings.

[1] *Control register*—indicates currently active page table on an x86 CPU core.

The Barrelfish kernel is therefore unaware of SpaceJMP objects. To enforce their proper reclamation we can rely on the capability revocation mechanism: revoking the process' root page table prohibits the process from switching into the VAS. The result is a pure user space implementation of SpaceJMP, enabling us to enforce custom policies, such as alignment constraints or selecting alternative page sizes.

4.3 Compiler Support

This section describes the implementation of a compiler tool for detecting unsafe behavior according to the semantics presented in Section 3.3. A trivial solution would be to tag all pointers with the ID of the address space they belong to, and insert checks on the tags before any pointer dereference. However, because checking every pointer dereference is too conservative, we present a compiler analysis to prove when dereferences are safe, and a transformation that only inserts checks where safety cannot be proven statically. These are briefly described in this section while detailed algorithms, optimizations, and evaluation are left for future work.

The analysis begins by finding the potentially active VASes at each program point and the VASes each pointer may be valid in. It produces the following sets of information:

- $VAS_{valid}(p)$: For each pointer p, the set of IDs for VASes that p may be valid in. $VAS_{valid}(p)$ may also contain two special values:
    - v_{common}: p may point to the common region
    - v_{unkown}: the ID of the VAS p may point to is unkown statically
- $VAS_{in}(i)$ and $VAS_{out}(i)$: For each relevant program instruction i, the set of IDs for VASes which may be current before and after i executes.

The instructions relevant to the analysis are shown in Figure 5 along with how they impact the analysis information. We provide an additional instruction *vcast* that enables users to cast pointers across VASes to override the safety rules.

After obtaining these two sets of information, the analysis uses them to identify all load or store instruction that may dereference a pointer in the wrong address space. These include any load or store instruction i that dereferences a pointer p such that at least one of the following three conditions hold:

1. $(|VAS_{valid}(p)| > 1) \vee (VAS_{valid}(p) \ni v_{unkown})$ (The VAS that p points to is ambiguous)
2. $|VAS_{in}(i)| > 1$ (The current VAS when i is executed is ambiguous)
3. $VAS_{valid}(p) \neq VAS_{in}(i)$ (The VAS that p points to may not be the same as the current VAS)

For these instructions, the transformation inserts a check before i that checks if the VAS which p points to matches the currently active VAS.

Instruction	**Description**	**Impact on Analysis**
switch v	Switch to VAS v	$VAS_{out}(i) = \{v\}$
x = vcast y v	Cast y to VAS v	$VAS_{valid}(x) = \{v\}$
x = alloca	Stack allocation	$VAS_{valid}(x) = v_{common}$
x = *global*	Global variable	$VAS_{valid}(x) = v_{common}$
x = malloc	Heap allocation	$VAS_{valid}(x) = VAS_{in}(i)$
$x = y$	Copy (arith., casts)	$VAS_{valid}(x) = VAS_{valid}(y)$
x = phi y z ...	Phi instructions	$VAS_{valid}(x) = VAS_{valid}(y) \cup VAS_{valid}(z) \cup ...$
$x = *y$	Loads	$VAS_{valid}(x) = VAS_{in}(i)$ or v_{unkown} if stack dereference
$*x = y$	Stores	No impact
x = foo(y, ...)	Function calls	Update VAS_{valid} of parameters and VAS_{in} at function entry
ret x	Returns	Update VAS_{valid} and VAS_{out} at callsites

Figure 5: SSA Instructions Relevant to Analysis

The analysis information is also used to identify stores that may store pointers to illegal locations. These include any store instruction i of a pointer v to a pointer p such that i does not meet any of the following conditions:

1. $VAS_{valid}(p) = \{v_{common}\}$ (The store is to the common region)
2. $(|VAS_{valid}(p)| = 1) \wedge (VAS_{valid}(p) = VAS_{valid}(v))$ (The stored pointer points within the region it is stored to)

For these instruction, the transformation inserts checks that ensure that either p points to the common region or that p and v both point to the current VAS.

The VASes of pointers used in checking code is obtained by inserting appropriate tracking code where those pointers are defined. VASes of pointers across function boundaries are tracked via a global array. VASes of pointers that escape to the common region are tracked via tagged pointers (using the unused bits of the pointer), though shadow memory may also be used for this purpose.

4.4 Discussion

Current implementations of SpaceJMP are relatively unoptimized, and there are several directions for improvement.

On the compiler analysis side, there are situations where our conservative algorithm will insert unnecessary safety checks which a more involved analysis would elide.

More effective caching of page table structures would be beneficial for performance, but imposes additional constraints on the virtual addresses to be efficient. For example, mapping an 8 KiB segment on the boundaries of a PML4 slot requires 7 page tables[2]. By restricting the virtual addresses of segments, to avoid crossing such high-level page table boundaries, page table structures can be cached more efficiently.

The hardware side is also an interesting source of future work. Modern x86-64 CPUs support tagging of TLB entries

[2] One PML4 table, two tables each of PDPT, PDT, PT.

Name	Memory	Processors	Freq.
M1	92 GiB	2x12c Xeon X5650	2.66 GHz
M2	256 GiB	2x10c Xeon E5-2670v2	2.50 GHz
M3	512 GiB	2x18c Xeon E5-2699v3	2.30 GHz

Table 1: Large-memory platforms used in our study.

with a compact (e.g., 12-bit) *address space identifier* to reduce overheads incurred by a full TLB flush on every address space switch. Our current implementations reserve the tag value zero to always trigger a TLB flush on a context switch. By default, all address spaces use tag value zero. The user has the ability to pass hints to the kernel (`vas_ctl`) to request a tag be assigned to an address space.

The trade-off can be complex: use of many tags can decrease overall TLB coverage (particularly since in SpaceJMP many address spaces share the same translations) and result in lower performance instead of faster context switch time.

Furthermore, this trade-off is hardware-specific. Only a single TLB tag can be current in an x86 MMU, whereas other hardware architectures (such as the "domain bits" in the ARMv7-A architecture [3] or the protection attributes in PA-RISC [81]) offer more flexible specification of translations, which would allow TLB entries to be shared across VAS boundaries. In any case, efficient dynamic use of TLB identifiers is a topic for future work.

5. Evaluation

In this section, we evaluate potential benefits afforded through SpaceJMP using three applications across domains: (i) a single-threaded benchmark derived from the HPCC GUPS [64] code to demonstrate the advantages of fast switching and scalable access to many address spaces; (ii) Redis$_{JMP}$, an enhanced implementation of the data-center object-caching middleware Redis, designed to leverage the multi-address-space programming model and lockable segments to ensure consistency among clients; and (iii) a genomics tool to demonstrate ease of switching with complex, pointer-rich data structures. The applications have not been instrumented with the safety checks described in Section 4.3.

Three hardware platforms support our measurements, code-named *M1*, *M2*, and *M3*, as shown in Table 1. All are dual-socket server systems, varying in total memory capacity, core count, and CPU micro-architecture; symmetric multi-threading and dynamic frequency scaling are disabled. Unless otherwise mentioned, the DragonFly BSD SpaceJMP implementation is used.

5.1 Microbenchmarks

This section explores trade-offs available with our solution for address space manipulation, and further evaluates its performance characteristics as an RPC mechanism (Figure 7). We begin first with an evaluation of VAS modification overheads, followed by a breakdown of context switching costs with and without TLB tagging optimizations.

Operation	DragonFly BSD		Barrelfish	
`CR3` load	130	**224**	130	**224**
system call	357	–	130	–
`vas_switch`	1127	**807**	664	**462**

Table 2: Breakdown of *context switching*. Measurements on *M2* in cycles. Numbers in **bold** are with tags enabled.

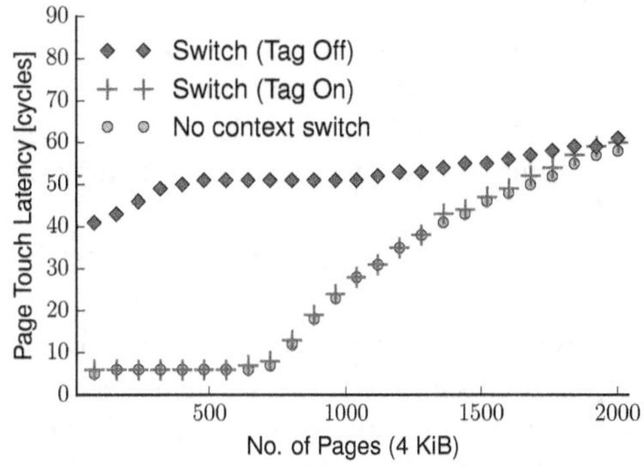

Figure 6: Impact of TLB tagging (*M3*) on a random-access workload. Tagging retains translations, and can lower costs of VAS switching.

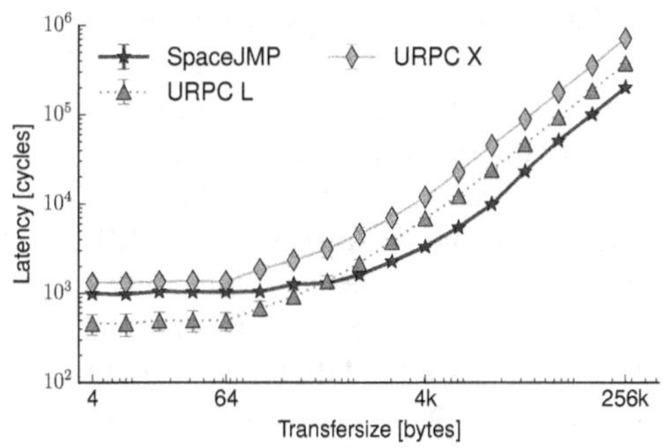

Figure 7: Comparison of URPC and SpaceJMP on Barrelfish (*M2*) as an alternative solution for fast local RPC communication.

Recall from Figure 1 that **page table modification does not scale**, even in optimized, mature OS implementations. The reason is because entire page table subtrees must be created – costs which are directly proportional to the region size and inversely proportional to page size. When restricted to a single per-process address space, changing translations for a range of virtual addresses using `mmap` and `munmap` incurs these costs. Copy-on-write optimizations can ultimately only reduce these costs for large, sparsely-accessed regions, and random-access workloads that stress large areas incur higher page-fault overheads using this technique. With SpaceJMP, these costs are removed from the critical path by switching translations instead of modifying them. We demonstrate this performance impact on the GUPS workload in Section 5.2.

Given the ability to switch into other address spaces at arbitrary instances, a process in SpaceJMP will cause **context switching** to occur at more frequent intervals than is typical, e.g., due to task rescheduling, potentially thousands of times per second. Table 2 breaks down the immediate costs imposed due to an address space switch in our DragonFly BSD implementation; a system call imposes the largest cost. Subsequent costs are incurred as TLB misses trigger the page-walking hardware to fetch new translations.

While immediate costs may only be improved within the micro-architecture, subsequent costs can be improved with **TLB tagging**.

Notice in Table 2 that changing CR3 register becomes more expensive with tagging enabled, as it invokes additional hardware circuitry that must consider extra TLB-resident state upon a write. Naturally, these are hardware-dependent costs. However, the overall performance of switching is improved, due to reduced TLB misses from shared OS entries.

We directly measured the impact of tagging in the TLB using a random page-walking benchmark we wrote. For a given set of pages, it will load one cache line from a randomly chosen page. A write to CR3 is then introduced between each iteration, and the cost in cycles to access the cache line are measured. Lastly, we enable tags, shown in Figure 6. The benefits, however, tail off: with tags, the cost of accessing a cache line reduces to the cost incurred without writes to CR3 as the working set grows. As expected, benefits gained using tags are limited by a combination of TLB capacity (for a given page size), and sophistication of TLB prefetchers. In our experiment, access latencies with larger working sets match that of latencies where the TLB is flushed.

Finally, we compare the **latency of switching address spaces** in SpaceJMP, with issuing a remote procedure call to another core. In this benchmark, an RPC client issues a request to a server process on a different core and waits for the acknowledgment. The exchange consists of two messages, each containing either a 64-bit key or a variable-sized payload. We compare with the same semantics in SpaceJMP by switching into the server's VAS and accessing the data directly by copying it into the process-local address space. Figure 7 shows the comparison between SpaceJMP and different RPC backends.

Our point of comparison is the (highly optimized) Barrelfish low latency RPC, stripped of stub code to expose only the raw low-level mechanism. In the low-latency case, both client and server busy-wait polling different circular buffers of cache-line-sized messages in a manner similar to FastForward [36]. This is the best-case scenario for Barrelfish RPCs – a real-world case would add overhead for marshalling, polling multiple channels, etc. We see a slight difference between intra (URPC L) and inter-socket (URPC X) performance.

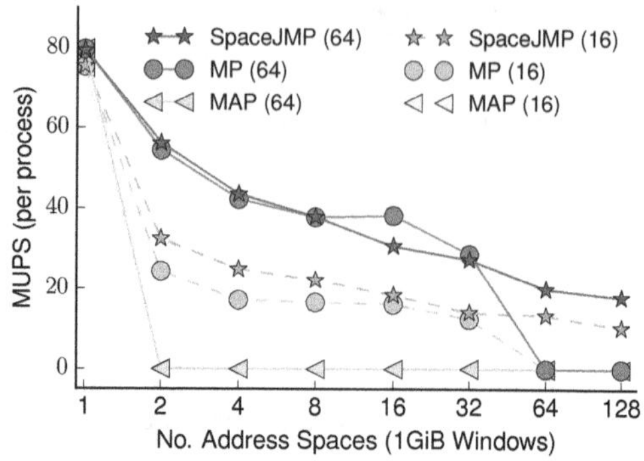

Figure 8: Comparison of three designs to program large memories with GUPS (*M3*). Update set sizes 16 and 64.

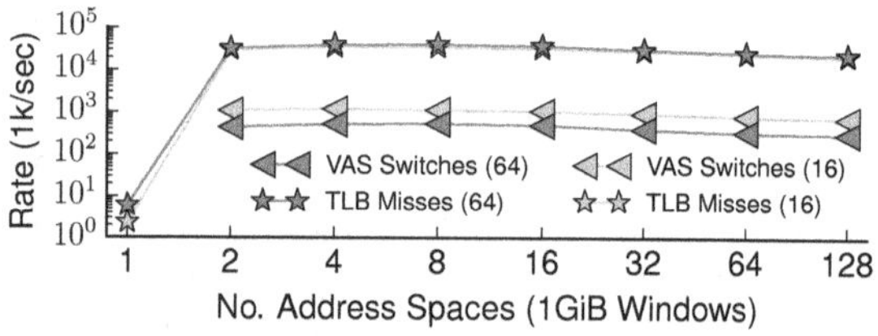

Figure 9: Rate of VAS switching and TLB misses for GUPS executed with SpaceJMP, averaged across 16 iterations. TLB tagging is disabled. A larger window size would produce a greater TLB miss rate using one window.

In all cases, the latency grows once the payload exceeds the buffer size. SpaceJMP is only out-performed by intra-socket URPC for small messages (due to system call and context switch overheads). Between sockets, the interconnect overhead for RPC dominates the cost of switching the VAS. In this case, using TLB tags further reduced latency.

5.2 GUPS: Addressing Large Memory

To deal with the limits of addressability for virtual memory, applications adopt various solutions for accessing larger physical memories. In this section, we use the GUPS benchmark [64] to compare two approaches in use today with a design using SpaceJMP. We ask two key questions: (i) how can applications address large physical memory regions, and (ii) what are the limitations of these approaches?

GUPS is appropriate for this: it measures the ability of a system to scale when applying random updates to a large in-memory array. This array is one large logical table of integers, partitioned into some number of *windows*. GUPS executes a tight loop that, for some number of updates per iteration, computes a random index within a given window for each update and then mutates the value at that index. After each set of updates is applied, a new window is randomly chosen. Figure 8 illustrates the performance comparison between three different approaches, where performance is reported as the rate of million updates applied per second.

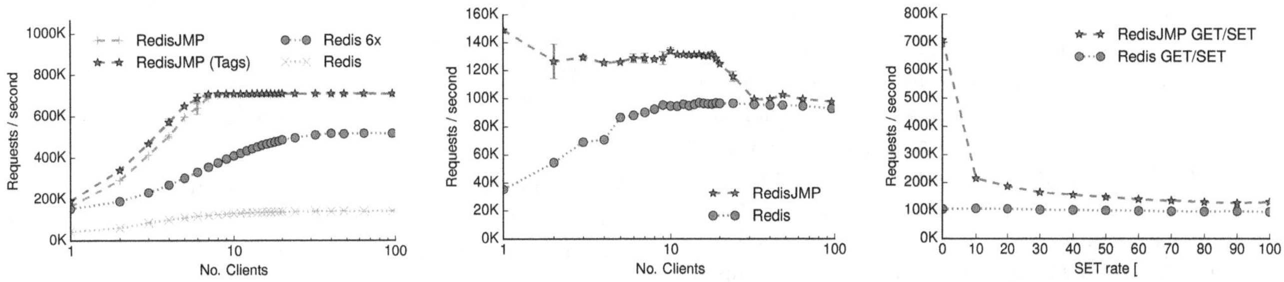

(a) Throughput of GET requests (b) Throughput of SET requests (c) Varying GET and SET requests

Figure 10: Performance comparison of Redis vs. a version of Redis using SpaceJMP

The first approach (MAP) leverages **address space remapping**: a traditional process may logically extend the reachability of its VAS by dynamically remapping portions of it to different regions of physical memory. Our implementation of this design uses the BSD `mmap` and `munmap` system calls (configured to attach to existing pages in the kernel's page cache) opening new windows for writing.

The second traditional approach (MP) uses **multiple processes**: each process is assigned a distinct portion of the physical memory (a window). In our experiment, one process acts as master and the rest as slaves, whereby the master process sends RPC messages using OpenMPI to the slave process holding the appropriate portion of physical memory. It then blocks, waiting for the slave to apply the batch of updates before continuing, simulating a single thread applying updates to a large global table. Each process is pinned to a core.

We compare these techniques with **VAS switching**, modifying GUPS to take advantage of SpaceJMP. Unlike the first technique, we do not modify mappings when changing windows, but instead represent a window as a segment in its own VAS. Pending updates are maintained in a shared heap segment mapped into all attached address spaces. Figure 9 illustrates the rate of VAS switching and TLB misses.

Discussion. For a single window – no remapping, RPC, or switching – all design configurations perform equally well. Changing windows immediately becomes prohibitively expensive for the MAP design, as it requires modification of the address space on the critical path. For the MP and SpaceJMP designs, the amount of CPU cache used grows with each added window, due to cache line fills from updates, as well as the growth in required page translation structures pulled in by the page-walker. The SpaceJMP implementation performs at least as well as the multi-process implementation, despite frequent context switches, with all data and multiple translation tables competing for the same set of CPU caches (for MP, only one translation table resides on each core). At greater than 36 cores on *M3*, the performance of MP drops, due to the busy-wait characteristics the OpenMPI implementation. The same trends are visible across a range of update set sizes (16 and 64 in the figure). Finally, a design leveraging SpaceJMP is more flexible, as a single process can independently address multiple address spaces without message passing.

This experiment shows that SpaceJMP occupies a useful point in the design space between multiple-process and page-remapping techniques – there is tangible benefit from switching between multiple address spaces rapidly on a single thread.

5.3 Redis with Multiple Address Spaces

In this section, we investigate the trade-off in adapting an existing application to use SpaceJMP and the potential benefits over traditional programming models.

We use Redis (v3.0.2) [67], a popular in-memory key-value store. Clients interact with Redis using UNIX domain or TCP/IP sockets by sending commands, such as SET and GET, to store and retrieve data. Our experiments use local clients and UNIX domain sockets for performance.

We compare a basic single-threaded Redis instance with Redis_{JMP}, which exploits SpaceJMP by eliding the use of socket-based communications. Redis_{JMP} avoids a server process entirely, retaining only the server data, and clients access the server data by switching into its address space. Redis_{JMP} is therefore implemented as a client-side library, and the server data is initialized lazily by its first client.

This client creates a new lockable segment for the state, maps it into a newly created address space, switches into this address space, and runs the initialization code to set-up Redis data-structures. We replaced the Redis memory allocator with one based on SpaceJMP, and moved all Redis global variables to a statically-allocated region inside the lockable segment.

Each client creates either one or two address spaces with the lockable segment mapped read-only or read-write, and invokes commands by switching into the newly created address space, executing server code directly. Our Redis_{JMP} implementation currently supports only basic operations for simple data-types. Some Redis features such as publish–subscribe would be more challenging to support, but could be implemented in a dedicated notification service.

Redis$_{JMP}$ uses locked segments to provide parallel read access to Redis state, but two further modifications were needed to the Redis code. First, Redis creates heap objects even on GET (read-only) requests for parsing commands, which would require read-write access to the lockable segment for all commands. We therefore attached a small, per-client scratch heap to each client's server address space. Second, Redis dynamically grows and shrinks its hash-tables asynchronously with respect to queries; we modified it to resize and rehash entries only when a client has an exclusive lock on the address space.

We used the *redis-benchmark* from the Redis distribution to compose the throughput of Redis$_{JMP}$ with the original on a single machine (*M1*). The benchmark simulates multiple clients by opening multiple file descriptors and sending commands while asynchronously polling and waiting for a response before sending the next command. For SpaceJMP we modified *redis-benchmark* to use our API and individual processes as clients that all attach the same server segment.

Fig. 10a and Fig. 10b show the performance of the GET and SET commands (4-byte payload) for a regular Redis server and Redis$_{JMP}$. In case of a single client (one thread), SpaceJMP outperforms a single server instance of Redis by a factor of *4x* for GET and SET requests, by reducing communication overhead.

The maximum read throughput of a single-threaded Redis server is naturally limited by the clock-speed of a single core, whereas Redis$_{JMP}$ allows multiple readers to access the address space concurrently. Therefore, we also compare throughput of a single Redis$_{JMP}$ instance with six independent Redis instances (Redis 6x) paired with six instances of *redis-benchmark* running on the twelve core machine.

Even in this case, at full utilization Redis$_{JMP}$ is still able to serve *36%* more requests than 6 regular Redis instances. We also compare SpaceJMP with and without TLB tagging enabled and notice a slight performance improvement using tags until the synchronization overhead limits scalability. For TLB misses, we measured a rate of 8.9M misses per second with a single client and 3.6M per core per second at full utilization (using 12 clients). With TLB tagging, the miss rate was lower, 2.8M misses per second for a single client and 0.9M per core per second (using 12 clients). The total number of address space switches per second is equals to two times the request rate for any number of clients.

For SET requests we sustain a high request rate until too many clients contend on the segment lock. This is a fundamental SpaceJMP limit, but we anticipate that a more scalable lock design than our current implementation would yield further improvements. Fig. 10c shows maximum system throughput while increasing the percentage of SET requests. The write lock has a large impact on throughput even when 10% of the requests are SETs, but Redis$_{JMP}$ still outperforms traditional file-based communication.

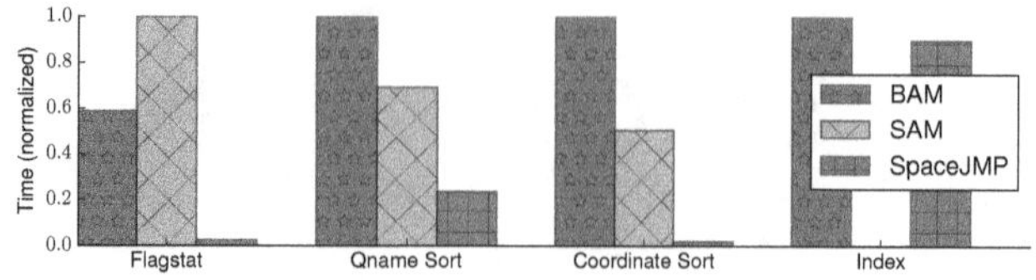

Figure 11: SAMTools vs. an implementation with SpaceJMP. BAM and SAM are alternative in-memory serialization methods; SpaceJMP has no serialization.

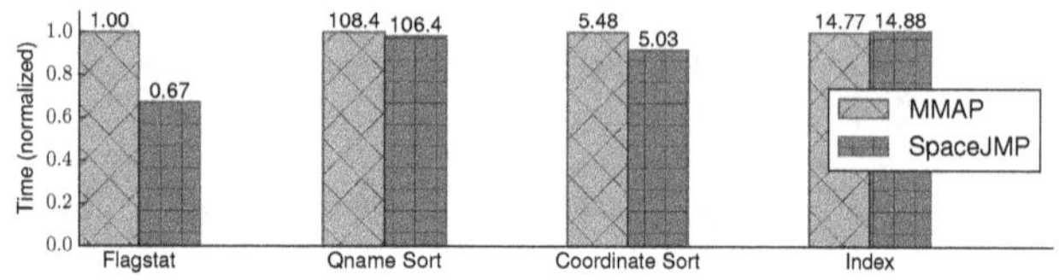

Figure 12: Use of `mmap` vs. SpaceJMP in SAMTools. Absolute runtime in seconds shown above each bar.

In summary, small changes are needed to modify an existing application to use SpaceJMP, but can make a single-threaded implementation both scale better and sustain higher single-thread performance by reducing IPC overhead.

5.4 SAMTools: In-Memory Data Structures

Finally, we show the benefit of using SpaceJMP as a mechanism to keep data structures in memory, avoiding both regular file I/O and memory-mapped files.

SAMTools [50] is a toolset for processing DNA sequence alignment information. It operates on multiple file formats that encode aligned sequences and performs various operations such as sorting, indexing, filtering, and collecting statics and pileup data. Each of these parses file data, performs a computation, and may write output to another file. Much of the CPU time in these operations is spent converting between serialized and in-memory representations of data.

We implement a version of SAMTools that uses SpaceJMP to keep data in its in-memory representation, avoiding frequent data conversions such as serialization of large data structures; such procedures comprise the majority of its execution time. Instead of storing the alignment information in a file according to a schema, we retain the data in a virtual address space and persist it between process executions. Each process operating on the data switches into the address space, performs its operation on the data structure, and keep its results in the address space for the next process to use.

Figure 11 compares the performance of using SpaceJMP to the original SAMTools operations on Sequence Alignment/Map (SAM) and BGZF compressed (BAM) files of sizes 3.1 GiB and 0.9 GiB respectively. It is evident from the graph that keeping data in memory with SpaceJMP results in significant speedup. The SAM and BAM files are stored using an in-memory file-system so the impact of disk access in the original tool is completely factored out. The performance improvement comes mainly from avoiding data conversion between pointer-rich and serialized formats.

We also implement a version of SAMTools that uses memory-mapped files to keep data structures in memory. Processes access data by calling `mmap` on a file. Region-based programming is used to build the data structures within the file. To maximize fairness, we make `mmap` as lightweight as possible by using an in-memory file system for the files, and pass flags to `mmap` to exclude regions from the core file and inform the pager to not gratuitously sync dirty pages back to disk. Moreover, we stop timers before process exit to exclude the implicit cost of unmapping data.

Figure 12 compares the performance of SpaceJMP to its counter-part using memory-mapped files. It is evident that the SpaceJMP has comparable performance. Therefore, the flexibility provided by SpaceJMP over memory-mapped files (i.e., not using special pointers or managing address conflicts) comes at a free cost. Moreover, with caching of translations enabled, it is expected that SpaceJMP's performance will improve further.

It is noteworthy that flagstat shows more significant improvement from SpaceJMP than the other operations in Figure 12. That is because flagstat runs much quicker than the others so the time spent performing a VAS switch or `mmap` takes up a larger fraction of the total time.

6. Related work

SpaceJMP is related to a wide range of work both in OS design and hardware support for memory management.

System software Memory management is one of the oldest areas of computer systems with many different design considerations that have been proposed so far. The most familiar OSes support address spaces for protection and isolation.

Strong isolation limits flexibility to share complex, pointer rich data structures and shared memory objects duplicate page table structures per process. OpenVMS [61] shares page tables for the subtree of a global section. Munroe patented sharing data among multiple virtual address spaces [59].

Threads of a process usually share a single virtual address space. The OS uses locks to ensure thread safety which leads to contention forcing memory management intensive programs to be split up into multiple processes to avoid lock contention [79]. RadixVM [20] maintains a radix tree from virtual addresses to meta data and allows concurrent operations on non-overlapping memory regions. VAS abstractions as first-class citizens provides a more natural expression of sharing and isolation semantics, while extending the use of scalable virtual memory optimizations.

Cyclone [37] has memory regions with varying life times and checks the validity of pointers in the scopes where they are dereferenced. Systems like QuickStore [80] provide shared-memory implementations of object stores, leveraging the virtual memory system to make objects available via their virtual addresses. Quickstore, however, incurs the cost of in-place pointer swizzling for objects whose virtual address ranges overlap, and the cost itself of mapping memory. SpaceJMP elides swizzling by reattaching alternate VASes, and combines VAS-aware pointer tracking for safe execution.

BSD operating system kernels are designed around the concept of virtual memory objects, enabling more efficient memory mappings, similar to UVM [23].

Prior 32-bit editions of Windows had only 2 GiB of virtual address space available for applications but allowed changing this limit to 3 GiB for memory intensive applications [56]. Furthermore, Address Windowing Extensions [57] gave applications means to allocate physical memory above 4 GiB and quickly place it inside reserved windows in the 32-bit address space, allowing applications to continue using regular 32-bit pointers.

Some single-address-space operating systems (SASOSes) (e.g., Opal [17, 18] and IVY [51]) eliminated duplicate page tables. Nevertheless, protection domains need to be enforced by additional hardware (protection lookaside buffers) or page groups [47]. Systems like Mondrix [83] employ isolation by enforcing protection on fixed entry and exit points of cross-domain calls, much like traditional "call gates" or the CAP computers' "enter capabilities" [82]. Such mechanisms complement SpaceJMP by providing protection capabilities at granularities other than a page within a VAS itself.

Also, SASOSes assume large virtual address spaces, but we predict a limit on virtual address bits in the future. More recent work such as SMARTMAP [12] evaluates data-sharing on high-performance machines. Distributed shared memory systems in the past [46] gained little adoption, but have recently acquired renewed interest [60].

Our work is influenced by the design of Mach [65], particularly the concept of a *memory object* mappable by various processes. Such techniques were adopted in the Opal [17] and Nemesis [38] SASOSes to describe memory *segments* characterized by fixed virtual offsets.

Lindstrom [52] expands these notions to shareable *containers* that contain code segments and private memory, leveraging a capability model to enforce protection. Application threads called *loci* enter containers to execute and manipulate data. *loci* motivated our approach to the client–server model.

In the 90s, research focused on exporting functionality to user space, reducing OS complexity, and enabling applications to set memory management policies [32, 38, 66]. Our work is supported by such ideas, as applications are exposed to an interface to compose virtual address spaces, with protection enforced by the OS, as with seL4 [31] and Barrelfish [7].

The idea of multiple address spaces has mainly been applied to achieve protection in a shared environment [17, 73], and to address the mismatch of abstractions provided by the OS interfaces [2, 66]. Some operating systems also provide similar APIs in order to simplify kernel development by executing the kernel directly in user-space [26, 30]. Dune [8] uses virtualization hardware to sandbox threads of a process in their own VAS. Further work has used them to transparently manage costs in NUMA systems [11, 25, 43, 54, 62, 68, 77, 85] or HPC applications [13]. SpaceJMP goes further by promoting a virtual address space to a first-class citizen in the OS, allowing applications to compose logically related memory regions for more efficient sharing.

Anderson *et al.* [1] recognized that increased use of RPC-based communication requires both sender and receiver to be scheduled to transfer data involving a context switch and kernel support (LRPC [9]) or shared memory between cores (URPC [10]). In both cases, data marshalling, cache misses, and buffering lead to overhead [16, 45, 75]. Compared to existing IPC mechanisms like Mach Local RPC [28] or overlays [49] SpaceJMP distinguishes itself by crossing VAS boundaries rather than task or process boundaries.

Ideally, bulk-data transfer between processes avoids copies [19, 41, 70, 72], although there are cases where security precludes this [29, 41].

Collaborative data processing with multiple processes often requires pointer-rich data structures to be serialized into a self-contained format and sent to other processes which induces an overhead in web services but also in single multicore machines [14, 39, 42, 71].

Hardware support Multiple address spaces are also supported by hardware. We have already discussed the trade-offs involved in tagged TLBs, and observed that SpaceJMP would benefit from a more advanced tagging architecture than that found in x86 processors. The HP PA-RISC [53] and Intel Itanium [40, 84] architectures both divide the virtual address space as windows into distinct address regions. The mapping is controlled by region registers holding the VAS identifier.

Our research is further complemented by Direct Segments [6]. SpaceJMP segments are currently backed by the underlying page table structure, but integrating our segments API with Direct Segments would yield further benefits. Alternatively, RMM [44] proposes hardware support that adds a redundant mapping for large ranges of contiguous pages. RMM seems like a good match for SpaceJMP segments, requiring fewer TLB entries than a traditional page-based system. SpaceJMP could be extended straightforwardly to implement RMM's eager allocation strategy. Other work proposes hardware-level optimizations that enable finer granularities than a page [44, 69].

Large pages have been touted as a way to mitigate TLB flushing cost, but such changes require substantial kernel modifications [74] and provide uncertain benefit to large-memory analytics workloads [6], as superpage TLBs can be small. Superpages on NUMA systems may be unfavorable [34].

Bailey *et al.* [5] argue the availability of huge and fast non-volatile, byte addressable memory (NVM) will fundamentally influence OS structure. Persistent storage will be managed by existing virtual memory mechanisms [22, 58] and accessed directly by the CPU. Atlas [15] examines durability when accessing persistent storage by using locks and explicit publishing to persistent memory. The approach in this paper provides a foundation for designing more memory centric operating system architectures.

Compiler-based program analysis for pointer safety introduces runtime checks with associated overhead. These could be made more efficient by labeling pointers with address space information. Some architectures such as ARM's *aarch64* [4] support the notion of "tagged pointers" where some bits (8, in aarch64) in every pointer can be made available to software and not passed to the MMU.

Lockable segments may benefit from hardware transactional memory (HTM) support: encapsulating the address space switch in an HTM-supported transactions can avoid the need of locking (or other synchronization) and improve performance of shared regions.

7. Conclusion

SpaceJMP extends OS memory management with lockable segments and multiple address spaces per process as a way to more efficiently execute data-centric applications which use massive memory and/or pointer-rich data structures.

However, we also claim that SpaceJMP has broader applicability. For example, SpaceJMP can also help in handling the growing complexity of memory. We expect future memory systems will include a combination of several heterogeneous hardware modules with quite different characteristics: a co-packaged volatile performance tier, a persistent capacity tier, different levels of memory-side caching, private memory (for example, only accessible by accelerators), and so on. Applications today use cumbersome techniques such as explicit copying and DMA to operate in these environments. SpaceJMP can be the basis for tying together a complex heterogeneous memory system and provide the application support for efficient programming. Another potential application is sandboxing, using different address spaces to limit access only to trusted code.

Our ongoing work is exploring these possibilities, but we also plan to address other issues such as the persistency of multiple virtual address spaces (for example, across reboots), and apply optimizations on address space creation, such as copy-on-write, snapshotting, and versioning.

So far, our experience has been encouraging, and we hope that SpaceJMP becomes a solid foundation for using memory in next-generation hardware platforms with high demands for data and with very large memories.

8. Acknowledgements

We thank the anonymous reviewers and our shepherd, Galen Hunt, for their many helpful suggestions. We would also like to thank our University colleagues and many Hewlett Packard Labs staff for their valuable insights and feedback.

References

[1] Thomas E. Anderson, Henry M. Levy, Brian N. Bershad, and Edward D. Lazowska. The Interaction of Architecture and Operating System Design. In *Proceedings of the Fourth International Conference on Architectural Support for Programming Languages and Operating Systems*, ASPLOS IV, pages 108–120, Santa Clara, California, USA, 1991.

[2] Andrew W. Appel and Kai Li. Virtual Memory Primitives for User Programs. In *Proceedings of the Fourth International Conference on Architectural Support for Programming Languages and Operating Systems*, ASPLOS IV, pages 96–107, Santa Clara, California, USA, 1991.

[3] ARM Ltd. *ARM Architecture Reference Manual: ARMv7-A and ARMv7-R Edition*, 2014. ARM DDI 0406C.c.

[4] ARM Ltd. ARMv8-A Architecture. Online, 2015. `http://www.arm.com/products/processors/armv8-architecture.php`.

[5] Katelin Bailey, Luis Ceze, Steven D. Gribble, and Henry M. Levy. Operating System Implications of Fast, Cheap, Non-volatile Memory. In *Proceedings of the 13th USENIX Conference on Hot Topics in Operating Systems*, HotOS'13, pages 2–2, Napa, California, 2011.

[6] Arkaprava Basu, Jayneel Gandhi, Jichuan Chang, Mark D. Hill, and Michael M. Swift. Efficient Virtual Memory for Big Memory Servers. In *Proceedings of the 40th Annual International Symposium on Computer Architecture*, ISCA '13, pages 237–248, Tel-Aviv, Israel, 2013.

[7] Andrew Baumann, Paul Barham, Pierre-Evariste Dagand, Tim Harris, Rebecca Isaacs, Simon Peter, Timothy Roscoe, Adrian Schüpbach, and Akhilesh Singhania. The Multikernel: A New OS Architecture for Scalable Multicore Systems. In *Proceedings of the ACM SIGOPS Twenty-Second Symposium on Operating Systems Principles*, SOSP '09, pages 29–44, Big Sky, Montana, USA, 2009.

[8] Adam Belay, Andrea Bittau, Ali Mashtizadeh, David Terei, David Mazières, and Christos Kozyrakis. Dune: Safe User-level Access to Privileged CPU Features. In *Proceedings of the 10th USENIX Conference on Operating Systems Design and Implementation*, OSDI'12, pages 335–348, Hollywood, CA, USA, 2012.

[9] Brian N. Bershad, Thomas E. Anderson, Edward D. Lazowska, and Henry M. Levy. Lightweight Remote Procedure Call. *ACM Trans. Comput. Syst.*, 8(1):37–55, February 1990.

[10] Brian N. Bershad, Thomas E. Anderson, Edward D. Lazowska, and Henry M. Levy. User-level Interprocess Communication for Shared Memory Multiprocessors. *ACM Trans. Comput. Syst.*, 9(2):175–198, May 1991.

[11] William J. Bolosky, Michael L. Scott, Robert P. Fitzgerald, Robert J. Fowler, and Alan L. Cox. NUMA Policies and Their Relation to Memory Architecture. In *Proceedings of the Fourth International Conference on Architectural Support for Programming Languages and Operating Systems*, ASPLOS IV, pages 212–221, Santa Clara, California, USA, 1991.

[12] Ron Brightwell, Kevin Pedretti, and Trammell Hudson. SMARTMAP: Operating System Support for Efficient Data Sharing Among Processes on a Multi-core Processor. In *Proceedings of the 2008 ACM/IEEE Conference on Supercomputing*, SC '08, pages 25:1–25:12, Austin, Texas, 2008.

[13] Javier Bueno, Xavier Martorell, Rosa M. Badia, Eduard Ayguadé, and Jesús Labarta. Implementing OmpSs Support for Regions of Data in Architectures with Multiple Address Spaces. In *Proceedings of the 27th International ACM Conference on International Conference on Supercomputing*, ICS '13, pages 359–368, Eugene, Oregon, USA, 2013.

[14] Bryan Carpenter, Geoffrey Fox, Sung Hoon Ko, and Sang Lim. Object Serialization for Marshalling Data in a Java Interface to MPI. In *Proceedings of the ACM 1999 Conference on Java Grande*, JAVA '99, pages 66–71, San Francisco, California, USA, 1999.

[15] Dhruva R. Chakrabarti, Hans-J. Boehm, and Kumud Bhandari. Atlas: Leveraging Locks for Non-volatile Memory Consistency. In *Proceedings of the 2014 ACM International Conference on Object Oriented Programming Systems Languages & Applications*, OOPSLA '14, pages 433–452, Portland, Oregon, USA, 2014.

[16] Satish Chandra, James R. Larus, and Anne Rogers. Where is Time Spent in Message-passing and Shared-memory Programs? In *Proceedings of the Sixth International Conference on Architectural Support for Programming Languages and Operating Systems*, ASPLOS VI, pages 61–73, San Jose, California, USA, 1994.

[17] Jeff Chase, Miche Baker-Harvey, Hank Levy, and Ed Lazowska. Opal: A Single Address Space System for 64-bit Architectures. *SIGOPS Oper. Syst. Rev.*, 26(2):9–, April 1992.

[18] Jeffrey S. Chase, Henry M. Levy, Miche Baker-harvey, and Edward D. Lazowska. How to Use a 64-Bit Virtual Address Space. Technical report, Department of Computer Science and Engineering, University of Washington, 1992.

[19] Ting-Hsuan Chien, Chia-Jung Chen, and Rong-Guey Chang. An Adaptive Zero-Copy Strategy for Ubiquitous High Performance Computing. In *Proceedings of the 21st European MPI Users' Group Meeting*, EuroMPI/ASIA '14, pages 139:139–139:144, Kyoto, Japan, 2014.

[20] Austin T. Clements, M. Frans Kaashoek, and Nickolai Zeldovich. RadixVM: Scalable Address Spaces for Multithreaded Applications. In *Proceedings of the 8th ACM European Conference on Computer Systems*, EuroSys '13, pages 211–224, Prague, Czech Republic, 2013.

[21] Joel Coburn, Adrian M. Caulfield, Ameen Akel, Laura M. Grupp, Rajesh K. Gupta, Ranjit Jhala, and Steven Swanson. NV-Heaps: Making Persistent Objects Fast and Safe with Next-generation, Non-volatile Memories. In *Proceedings of the Sixteenth International Conference on Architectural Support for Programming Languages and Operating Systems*, ASPLOS XVI, pages 105–118, Newport Beach, California, USA, 2011.

[22] Jeremy Condit, Edmund B. Nightingale, Christopher Frost, Engin Ipek, Benjamin Lee, Doug Burger, and Derrick Coetzee. Better I/O Through Byte-addressable, Persistent Memory. In *Proceedings of the ACM SIGOPS Twenty-Second Symposium on Operating Systems Principles*, SOSP '09, pages 133–146, Big Sky, Montana, USA, 2009.

[23] Charles D. Cranor and Gurudatta M. Parulkar. The UVM Virtual Memory System. In *Proceedings of the 1999 USENIX Annual Conference*, ATEC '99, pages 9–9, Monterey, California, 1999.

[24] Danga Interactive. memcached - a distributed memory object caching system. Online, April 2015. `http://memcached.org/`.

[25] Mohammad Dashti, Alexandra Fedorova, Justin Funston, Fabien Gaud, Renaud Lachaize, Baptiste Lepers, Vivien Quema, and Mark Roth. Traffic Management: A Holistic Approach to Memory Placement on NUMA Systems. In *Proceedings of the Eighteenth International Conference on Architectural Support for Programming Languages and Operating Systems*, ASPLOS '13, pages 381–394, Houston, Texas, USA, 2013.

[26] Jeff Dike. *User Mode Linux*. Upper Saddle River, NJ, USA, 2006.

[27] Matt Dillon. DragonFly BSD Sources. `http://www.dragonflybsd.org/`, June 2015.

[28] Richard Draves. A Revised IPC Interface. In *USENIX MACH Symposium*, pages 101–122. USENIX, 1990.

[29] Peter Druschel and Larry L. Peterson. Fbufs: A High-bandwidth Cross-domain Transfer Facility. In *Proceedings of the Fourteenth ACM Symposium on Operating Systems Principles*, SOSP '93, pages 189–202, Asheville, North Carolina, USA, 1993.

[30] Aggelos Economopoulos. A peek at the DragonFly Virtual Kernel (part 1). `https://lwn.net/Articles/228404/`, March 2007.

[31] Dhammika Elkaduwe, Philip Derrin, and Kevin Elphinstone. Kernel Design for Isolation and Assurance of Physical Memory. In *Proceedings of the 1st Workshop on Isolation and Integration in Embedded Systems*, IIES '08, pages 35–40, Glasgow, Scotland, 2008.

[32] D. R. Engler, M. F. Kaashoek, and J. O'Toole, Jr. Exokernel: An Operating System Architecture for Application-level Resource Management. In *Proceedings of the Fifteenth ACM Symposium on Operating Systems Principles*, SOSP '95, pages 251–266, Copper Mountain, Colorado, USA, 1995.

[33] Paolo Faraboschi, Kimberly Keeton, Tim Marsland, and Dejan Milojicic. Beyond Processor-centric Operating Systems. In *15th Workshop on Hot Topics in Operating Systems*, HotOS XV, Kartause Ittingen, Switzerland, May 2015.

[34] Fabien Gaud, Baptiste Lepers, Jeremie Decouchant, Justin Funston, Alexandra Fedorova, and Vivien Quéma. Large Pages May Be Harmful on NUMA Systems. In *Proceedings of the 2014 USENIX Conference*, USENIX ATC'14, pages 231–242, Philadelphia, PA, 2014.

[35] Simon Gerber, Gerd Zellweger, Reto Achermann, Kornilios Kourtis, Timothy Roscoe, and Dejan Milojicic. Not Your Parents' Physical Address Space. In *15th Workshop on Hot Topics in Operating Systems*, HotOS XV, Kartause Ittingen, Switzerland, May 2015.

[36] John Giacomoni, Tipp Moseley, and Manish Vachharajani. FastForward for Efficient Pipeline Parallelism: A Cache-optimized Concurrent Lock-free Queue. In *Proceedings of the 13th ACM SIGPLAN Symposium on Principles and Practice of Parallel Programming*, PPoPP '08, pages 43–52, Salt Lake City, UT, USA, 2008.

[37] Dan Grossman, Greg Morrisett, Trevor Jim, Michael Hicks, Yanling Wang, and James Cheney. Region-based Memory Management in Cyclone. In *Proceedings of the ACM SIGPLAN 2002 Conference on Programming Language Design and Implementation*, PLDI '02, pages 282–293, Berlin, Germany, 2002.

[38] Steven M. Hand. Self-paging in the Nemesis Operating System. In *Proceedings of the Third Symposium on Operating Systems Design and Implementation*, OSDI '99, pages 73–86, New Orleans, Louisiana, USA, 1999.

[39] Marjan Hericko, Matjaz B. Juric, Ivan Rozman, Simon Beloglavec, and Ales Zivkovic. Object Serialization Analysis and Comparison in Java and .NET. *SIGPLAN Not.*, 38(8):44–54, August 2003.

[40] Intel Corporation. *Intel Itanium Architecture Software Developer's Manual*. Document Number: 245315.

[41] Bär Jeremia and Föllmi Claudio. Bulk Transfer over Shared Memory. Technical report, ETH Zurich, Feburary 2014. `http://www.barrelfish.org/dsl-bulk-shm-report.pdf`.

[42] Matjaz B. Juric, Bostjan Kezmah, Marjan Hericko, Ivan Rozman, and Ivan Vezocnik. Java RMI, RMI Tunneling and Web Services Comparison and Performance Analysis. *SIGPLAN Not.*, 39(5):58–65, May 2004.

[43] Stefan Kaestle, Reto Achermann, Timothy Roscoe, and Tim Harris. Shoal: Smart Aladdress and Replication of Memory For Parallel Programs. In *Proceedings of the 2015 USENIX Annual Technical Conference*, USENIX ATC 15, pages 263–276, Santa Clara, CA, USA, July 2015.

[44] Vasileios Karakostas, Jayneel Gandhi, Furkan Ayar, Adrián Cristal, Mark D. Hill, Kathryn S. McKinley, Mario Nemirovsky, Michael M. Swift, and Osman Ünsal. Redundant Memory Mappings for Fast Access to Large Memories. In *Proceedings of the 42Nd Annual International Symposium on Computer Architecture*, ISCA '15, pages 66–78, Portland, Oregon, 2015.

[45] Vijay Karamcheti and Andrew A. Chien. Software Overhead in Messaging Layers: Where Does the Time Go? In *Proceedings of the Sixth International Conference on Architectural Support for Programming Languages and Operating Systems*, ASPLOS VI, pages 51–60, San Jose, California, USA, 1994.

[46] Pete Keleher, Alan L. Cox, Sandhya Dwarkadas, and Willy Zwaenepoel. TreadMarks: Distributed Shared Memory on Standard Workstations and Operating Systems. In *Proceedings of the USENIX Winter 1994 Technical Conference*, WTEC'94, pages 10–10, San Francisco, California, USA, 1994.

[47] Eric J. Koldinger, Jeffrey S. Chase, and Susan J. Eggers. Architecture Support for Single Address Space Operating Systems. In *Proceedings of the Fifth International Conference on Architectural Support for Programming Languages and Operating Systems*, ASPLOS V, pages 175–186, Boston, Massachusetts, USA, 1992.

[48] Doug Lea. dlmalloc: A Memory Allocator. `http://g.oswego.edu/dl/html/malloc.html`, April 2000.

[49] J.R. Levine. *Linkers and Loaders*. Morgan Kauffman, 2000.

[50] Heng Li, Bob Handsaker, Alec Wysoker, Tim Fennell, Jue Ruan, Nils Homer, Gabor Marth, Goncalo Abecasis, Richard Durbin, and 1000 Genome Project Data Processing Subgroup. The Sequence Alignment/Map format and SAMtools. *Bioinformatics*, 25(16):2078–2079, 2009.

[51] Kai Li. IVY: A Shared Virtual Memory System for Parallel Computing. *ICPP (2)*, 88:94, 1988.

[52] A. Lindstrom, J. Rosenberg, and A. Dearle. The Grand Unified Theory of Address Spaces. In *Proceedings of the Fifth Workshop on Hot Topics in Operating Systems*, HotOS-V, pages 66–71, May 1995.

[53] Michael J. Mahon, Ruby Bei-Loh Lee, Terrence C. Miller, Jerome C. Huck, and William R. Bryg. The Hewlett-Packard Precision Architecture: The Processor. *Hewlett-Packard Journal*, 37(8):16–22, August 1986.

[54] Zoltan Majo and Thomas R. Gross. Memory Management in NUMA Multicore Systems: Trapped Between Cache Contention and Interconnect Overhead. In *Proceedings of the International Symposium on Memory Management*, ISMM '11, pages 11–20, San Jose, California, USA, 2011.

[55] Collin McCurdy, Alan L. Coxa, and Jeffrey Vetter. Investigating the TLB Behavior of High-end Scientific Applications on Commodity Microprocessors. In *Proceedings of the IEEE International Symposium on Performance Analysis of Systems and Software*, ISPASS '08, pages 95–104, 2008.

[56] Microsoft Corp. 4-Gigabyte Tuning: BCDEdit and Boot.ini. `https://msdn.microsoft.com/en-us/library/windows/desktop/bb613473(v=vs.85).aspx`.

[57] Microsoft Corp. Address Windowing Extensions. `https://msdn.microsoft.com/en-us/library/windows/desktop/aa366527(v=vs.85).aspx`.

[58] Iulian Moraru, David G. Andersen, Michael Kaminsky, Niraj Tolia, Parthasarathy Ranganathan, and Nathan Binkert. Consistent, Durable, and Safe Memory Management for Byte-addressable Non Volatile Main Memory. In *Proceedings of the First ACM SIGOPS Conference on Timely Results in Operating Systems*, TRIOS '13, pages 1:1–1:17, Farmington, Pennsylvania, 2013.

[59] Steven Jay Munroe, Scott Alan Plaetzer, and James William Stopyro. Computer System Having Shared Address Space Among Multiple Virtual Address Spaces. Online, January 20 2004. US Patent 6,681,239, `https://www.google.com/patents/US6681239`.

[60] Jacob Nelson, Brandon Holt, Brandon Myers, Preston Briggs, Luis Ceze, Simon Kahan, and Mark Oskin. Latency-Tolerant Software Distributed Shared Memory. In *Proceedings of the 2015 USENIX Annual Technical Conference*, USENIX ATC 15, pages 291–305, Santa Clara, CA, July 2015.

[61] Karen L. Noel and Nitin Y. Karkhanis. OpenVMS Alpha 64-bit Very Large Memory Design. *Digital Tech. J.*, 9(4):33–48, April 1998.

[62] Stanko Novakovic, Alexandros Daglis, Edouard Bugnion, Babak Falsafi, and Boris Grot. Scale-out NUMA. In *Proceedings of the Nineteenth International Conference on Architectural Support for Programming Languages and Operating Systems*, ASPLOS '14, pages 3–18, Salt Lake City, Utah, USA, 2014.

[63] John Ousterhout, Parag Agrawal, David Erickson, Christos Kozyrakis, Jacob Leverich, David Mazières, Subhasish Mitra, Aravind Narayanan, Diego Ongaro, Guru Parulkar, Mendel Rosenblum, Stephen M. Rumble, Eric Stratmann, and Ryan Stutsman. The Case for RAMCloud. *Commun. ACM*, 54(7):121–130, July 2011.

[64] S.J. Plimpton, R. Brightwell, C. Vaughan, K. Underwood, and M. Davis. A Simple Synchronous Distributed-Memory Algorithm for the HPCC RandomAccess Benchmark. In *Proceedings of the 2006 IEEE International Conference on Cluster Computing*, pages 1–7, Sept 2006.

[65] Richard Rashid, Avadis Tevanian, Michael Young, David Golub, Robert Baron, David Black, William Bolosky, and Jonathan Chew. Machine-independent Virtual Memory Management for Paged Uniprocessor and Multiprocessor Architectures. In *Proceedings of the Second International Conference on Architectual Support for Programming Languages and Operating Systems*, ASPLOS II, pages 31–39, Palo Alto, California, USA, 1987.

[66] Barret Rhoden, Kevin Klues, David Zhu, and Eric Brewer. Improving Per-node Efficiency in the Datacenter with New OS Abstractions. In *Proceedings of the 2Nd ACM Symposium on Cloud Computing*, SOCC '11, pages 25:1–25:8, Cascais, Portugal, 2011.

[67] Salvatore Sanfilippo. Redis. `http://redis.io/`, August 2015.

[68] Scott Schneider, Christos D. Antonopoulos, and Dimitrios S. Nikolopoulos. Scalable Locality-conscious Multithreaded Memory Allocation. In *Proceedings of the 5th International Symposium on Memory Management*, ISMM '06, pages 84–94, Ottawa, Ontario, Canada, 2006.

[69] Vivek Seshadri, Gennady Pekhimenko, Olatunji Ruwase, Onur Mutlu, Phillip B. Gibbons, Michael A. Kozuch, Todd C. Mowry, and Trishul Chilimbi. Page Overlays: An Enhanced Virtual Memory Framework to Enable Fine-grained Memory Management. In *Proceedings of the 42nd Annual International Symposium on Computer Architecture*, ISCA '15, pages 79–91, Portland, Oregon, 2015.

[70] Piyush Shivam, Pete Wyckoff, and Dhabaleswar Panda. EMP: Zero-copy OS-bypass NIC-driven Gigabit Ethernet Message Passing. In *Proceedings of the 2001 ACM/IEEE Conference on Supercomputing*, SC '01, pages 57–57, Denver, Colorado, 2001.

[71] Audie Sumaray and S. Kami Makki. A Comparison of Data Serialization Formats for Optimal Efficiency on a Mobile Platform. In *Proceedings of the 6th International Conference on Ubiquitous Information Management and Communication*, ICUIMC '12, pages 48:1–48:6, Kuala Lumpur, Malaysia, 2012.

[72] Brian Paul Swenson and George F. Riley. A New Approach to Zero-Copy Message Passing with Reversible Memory Aladdress in Multi-core Architectures. In *Proceedings of the 2012 ACM/IEEE/SCS 26th Workshop on Principles of Advanced and Distributed Simulation*, PADS '12, pages 44–52, Washington, DC, USA, 2012.

[73] M. Takahashi, K. Kono, and T. Masuda. Efficient Kernel Support of Fine-grained Protection Domains for Mobile Code. In *Proceedings of the 19th IEEE International Conference on Distributed Computing Systems*, ICDCS '99, pages 64–73, Washington, DC, USA, 1999.

[74] Madhusudhan Talluri and Mark D. Hill. Surpassing the TLB Performance of Superpages with Less Operating System Support. In *Proceedings of the Sixth International Conference on Architectural Support for Programming Languages and Operating Systems*, ASPLOS VI, pages 171–182, San Jose, California, USA, 1994.

[75] Chandramohan A. Thekkath, Henry M. Levy, and Edward D. Lazowska. Separating Data and Control Transfer in Distributed Operating Systems. In *Proceedings of the Sixth International Conference on Architectural Support for Programming Languages and Operating Systems*, ASPLOS VI, pages 2–11, San Jose, California, USA, 1994.

[76] Dana Vantrease, Robert Schreiber, Matteo Monchiero, Moray McLaren, Norman P Jouppi, Marco Fiorentino, Al Davis, Nathan Binkert, Raymond G Beausoleil, and Jung Ho Ahn. Corona: System implications of emerging nanophotonic technology. In *ACM SIGARCH Computer Architecture News*, volume 36, pages 153–164. IEEE Computer Society, 2008.

[77] Ben Verghese, Scott Devine, Anoop Gupta, and Mendel Rosenblum. Operating System Support for Improving Data Locality on CC-NUMA Compute Servers. In *Proceedings of the Seventh International Conference on Architectural Support for Programming Languages and Operating Systems*, ASPLOS VII, pages 279–289, Cambridge, Massachusetts, USA, 1996.

[78] Haris Volos, Andres Jaan Tack, and Michael M. Swift. Mnemosyne: Lightweight Persistent Memory. In *Proceedings of the Sixteenth International Conference on Architectural Support for Programming Languages and Operating Systems*, ASPLOS XVI, pages 91–104, Newport Beach, California, USA, 2011.

[79] David Wentzlaff and Anant Agarwal. Factored Operating Systems (Fos): The Case for a Scalable Operating System for Multicores. *SIGOPS Oper. Syst. Rev.*, 43(2):76–85, April 2009.

[80] Seth J. White and David J. DeWitt. Quickstore: A high performance mapped object store. In *Proceedings of the 1994 ACM SIGMOD International Conference on Management of Data*, SIGMOD '94, pages 395–406, New York, NY, USA, 1994. ACM.

[81] John Wilkes and Bart Sears. A comparison of Protection Lookaside Buffers and the PA-RISC Protection Architecture. Technical Report HPL–92–55, Computer Systems Laboratory, Hewlett-Packard Laboratories, Palo Alto, CA, USA, March 1992.

[82] M. V Wilkes. *The Cambridge CAP Computer and Its Operating System (Operating and Programming Systems Series)*. North-Holland Publishing Co., Amsterdam, The Netherlands, The Netherlands, 1979.

[83] Emmett Witchel, Junghwan Rhee, and Krste Asanović. Mondrix: Memory Isolation for Linux Using Mondriaan Memory Protection. In *Proceedings of the Twentieth ACM Symposium on Operating Systems Principles*, SOSP '05, pages 31–44, Brighton, United Kingdom, 2005.

[84] Rumi Zahir, Jonathan Ross, Dale Morris, and Drew Hess. OS and Compiler Considerations in the Design of the IA-64 Architecture. In *Proceedings of the Ninth International Conference on Architectural Support for Programming Languages and Operating Systems*, ASPLOS IX, pages 212–221, Cambridge, Massachusetts, USA, 2000.

[85] Jin Zhou and Brian Demsky. Memory Management for Many-core Processors with Software Configurable Locality Policies. In *Proceedings of the 2012 International Symposium on Memory Management*, ISMM '12, pages 3–14, Beijing, China, 2012.

memif: Towards Programming Heterogeneous Memory Asynchronously

Felix Xiaozhu Lin
Purdue ECE
xzl@purdue.edu

Xu Liu
College of William & Mary
xl10@cs.wm.edu

Abstract

To harness a heterogeneous memory hierarchy, it is advantageous to integrate application knowledge in guiding frequent memory move, i.e., replicating or migrating virtual memory regions. To this end, we present memif, a protected OS service for asynchronous, hardware-accelerated memory move. Compared to the state of the art – page migration in Linux, memif incurs low overhead and low latency; in order to do so, it not only redefines the semantics of kernel interface but also overhauls the underlying mechanisms, including request/completion management, race handling, and DMA engine configuration.

We implement memif in Linux for a server-class system-on-chip that features heterogeneous memories. Compared to the current Linux page migration, memif reduces CPU usage by up to 15% for small pages and by up to 38× for large pages; in continuously serving requests, memif has no need for request batching and reduces latency by up to 63%. By crafting a small runtime atop memif, we improve the throughputs for a set of streaming workloads by up to 33%. Overall, memif has opened the door to software management of heterogeneous memory.

Categories and Subject Descriptors D.4.7 [*OPERATING SYSTEMS*]: Organization and Design

Keywords Operating Systems; Heterogeneous Memory; Data-intensive Computing

1. Introduction

Memory accesses have become a major performance bottleneck in modern data-intensive applications, e.g. big data and high performance computing (HPC) workloads. The reasons are large working sets and cache/prefetcher-unfriendly access patterns. These applications often incur substantial last-level cache misses, suffering from long memory latency [19, 61].

To bridge the speed gap between CPU and memory, modern computers have already employed complex memory hierarchies, including multi-level caches and non-uniform memory access (NUMA) designs. Moreover, emerging architectures are embracing heterogeneous memory, a mixture of fast and slow memory banks that also have significantly different capacities. Fast memories are often built as on-chip SRAM [4], embedded DRAM [23], or die-stacked memory [1, 7]; slow memories are often DRAM or NVRAM.

Unsurprisingly, heterogeneous memory raises new challenges to the hardware-software stack. Most prior work seeks to make memory heterogeneity transparent to applications: this includes hardware mechanisms that manage fast memory as a large cache [40] or part of main memory [54] and OS support that monitors memory access patterns and moves memory data accordingly [45].

Despite the efficacy of the transparent approaches, we believe that they miss a key opportunity: user knowledge. To this end, our driving vision is to empower user, i.e., a synergy among programmer, runtime, and compiler, to explicitly control a heterogeneous memory hierarchy. Towards this vision, we first lay the software foundation by abstracting heterogeneous memories as individual *pseudo* NUMA nodes. The NUMA abstraction for heterogeneous memory, despite its dismissal in prior work [45], enables us to reuse mature OS facilities with great ease. To the best of our knowledge, our work is the first implementation of NUMA abstraction on real heterogeneous memory hardware.

Based on the abstraction, our top design challenge is to support moving *virtual* memory regions – either replicating or migrating them – as requested by applications. Such an OS service is both desirable and feasible: on one hand, impromptu, frequent memory move is proven vital to the use of heterogeneous memory [20, 52], of which faster memories usually have limited capacity and thus have to be used efficiently; on the other hand, modern hardware has already provided good support for memory move, including ample

ASPLOS '16, April 2–6, 2016, Atlanta, Georgia, USA..

ACM 978-1-4503-4091-5/16/04. . . $15.00.
DOI: http://dx.doi.org/10.1145/2872362.2872401

off-chip memory bandwidth [19, 29], cache-coherent DMA engines [58], and a variety of page sizes.

However, moving memory regions *efficiently* is challenging. Without a careful design, the overheads of kernel interface, virtual memory management and byte copy can easily overshadow what applications can benefit from fast memory. As we will show in Section 2, the closest service in commodity OSes, page migration for NUMA [33], is intensive on both CPU and virtual memory. Point solutions, such as exposing DMA engines to userspace or reserving large chunks of physical memory, are unsafe or impractical to generic workloads.

To address this challenge, we present memif, an OS service offering asynchronous, DMA-accelerated memory move. Unlike userspace DMA drivers, memif is protected and compatible with commodity OSes. To make memif's interface low overhead and low latency, we apply two primary ideas: *i)* making user and kernel directly share *lock-free* data structures, including a unique red-blue lock-free queue; *ii)* using kernel threads to fetch memory move requests and post completion notifications without synchronizing with applications. Both ideas are rarely seen in existing kernel subsystems, such as GPU or NIC drivers. Accordingly, we overhaul kernel mechanisms that are known expensive: page lookup, race handling, and DMA engine reconfiguration.

To offer a proof of concept, we design and implement memif on the Texas Instruments KeyStone II, a server-class system-on-chip (SoC) featuring heterogeneous memory [59]. Compared to Linux page migration, memif reduces CPU usage by up to 15% for small pages (4KB) and up to 38× for large pages (2MB); in continuously serving user requests, it does not require request batching and reduces the latency by up to 63%. On top of memif, we showcase a simple runtime for supporting streaming workloads and gain up to 33% throughput by tapping into KeyStone II's heterogeneous memory.

Overall, memif lays the foundation for software to directly manage heterogeneous memory at medium (hundreds of KB) or coarse (multiple MB) granularities. Atop memif, we expect that compilers or runtime will decide *when* and *where* to move memory by leveraging their domain knowledge. Together, the OS, runtime, and compiler will enable efficient exploitation of memory heterogeneity without burdening application programmers.

We have made the following contributions:

- A novel user interface that enables applications to submit memory move requests and receive completion notifications asynchronously, with no batching and little user/kernel synchronization;
- A suite of overhauled kernel mechanisms for detecting races (instead of avoiding them), efficiently looking up pages, and quickly reconfiguring the DMA engine;
- A detailed cost breakdown, evaluation, and application case study of memif on real heterogeneous memory hardware.

The full source code of memif is available at: `http://xsel.rocks/p/memif`

2. Background and Motivation

In this section, we highlight the importance of user-guided memory move, identify the inadequacies of existing support, and present our design considerations.

2.1 A Case for User-guided Memory Move

Memory move, i.e., migration or replication, is a key theme in managing heterogeneous memory [20, 52, 54]: a faster memory often has a much lower capacity and cannot hold the working sets of many data-intensive workloads. For instances, many important HPC applications work on terabytes of data [49]; typical big data applications consume data at high rates, e.g., tens of GB per second, with their relative simple compute [29, 61]. To benefit from heterogeneous memories, one must frequently move data in and out of fast memory based on recent or future memory access.

Underutilized off-chip memory bandwidth Fortunately, the ample main memory bandwidth in modern platforms creates rich opportunities for "background" memory move in parallel to foreground computation. Prior work has discovered that scale-out server workloads often utilize less than 10% of off-chip bandwidth [19]; a recent study [29] shows that offline data analytics has bursty memory demand and often uses less than 15% of bandwidth on average; online data analytics often has less than 50% bandwidth utilization and is described as "good and smooth".

User's knowledge is the key The knowledge of programmer, compiler, and runtime is proven essential to exploiting complex memory hierarchies [31, 38]. Compared to transparent approaches that hide memory move from users, a user-guided approach has three key advantages:

- With a full understanding of program design, users can guide data move for catering to complex memory access patterns.
- Unlike transparent management that often reacts based on recent memory access, users are able to move memory proactively or even speculatively for optimal performance.
- User-guided optimization relieves system software of continuous monitoring of application memory access, a mechanism known to incur non-trivial (>10%) runtime overhead [39].

2.2 Existing OS Support Is Inadequate

Ideally, an OS should empower applications to guide memory move efficiently and with ease. Unfortunately, such a service is missing from today's OS.

Page migration for NUMA As we put heterogeneous memory under the NUMA abstraction, existing OS support for migrating pages across NUMA nodes seems a natural fit. However, the mechanism is far from efficient.

To illustrate the problem, we test page migration built in the Linux kernel on both ARM and x86 platforms. In migrating 1500 4KB pages with one `mbind()` syscall, a server-class ARM SoC (see Section 6 for details) shows a throughput of 0.30 GB/sec. On a 2×8 Xeon E5-4650 NUMA machine, the same test shows a throughput of 0.66 GB/sec; even when we migrate 1 million pages in one syscall, the throughput is only 1.41 GB/Sec. All observed throughputs are below 10% of the corresponding memory bandwidths.

Looking deeper into the Linux kernel, we find migrating a page is CPU-bound: in addition to copying bytes from source to destination, CPU performs page table walk, cache flush, page table update with TLB flush, as well as page allocation and free operations. For each page these operations take around 15 μs (of which only 4 μs is for copying bytes) on our ARM-based test platform. The major inefficiencies are twofold: first, CPU is used in copying bytes; second, the kernel mechanism is tailored for synchronous syscalls and repeats some heavy operations for each page with little reuse. Using huge pages will improve the throughput, however, it does not address the inefficiencies and may introduce new performance problems [21]. We will present more overhead details in Section 6.

Direct access of DMA engine Ad-hoc support for memory move often bypasses the kernel infrastructure for efficiency. Userspace DMA drivers enable applications to directly operate DMA engines with no OS overhead. However, this approach has three flaws. First, unless there exists IOMMU for DMA, an application can abuse the unprotected drivers for accessing almost any data in physical memory. Second, lacking a good way of learning memory move completion, applications often have to periodically poll the DMA engine. Third, assigning a DMA engine to a particular application prevents multiple applications from sharing the engine.

Large carveout memory Another common ad-hoc optimization is to amortize the memory move cost over large chunks of physically contiguous memory. This is often done by reserving the chunks during boot time and later linearly mapping them to application's address space. Although effective for certain uses, e.g., embedded multimedia, this approach leads to memory waste and declines all the benefits of kernel memory management. Even worse, it often necessitates an in-application page allocator [60] for managing the large chunks, which fragments the OS features.

2.3 Design considerations

To address these inadequacies, we aim to design an OS service with the following considerations.

Architectural assumptions Our design depends on one common architectural feature: a DMA engine supporting scatter-gather transfer [15], which can move multiple physical memory regions in a single transfer [23, 58]. We consider two optional features greatly beneficial to performance and software simplicity: cache coherence between CPU and DMA engine, which relieves software of expensive cache maintenance; non-aliasing CPU cache, which allows applications and kernel to coherently share data structures from separate address spaces.

Design requirements & goals Our OS service should meet the following basic requirements: *i) asynchronous*, it offloads byte copy to a DMA engine, freeing CPU for user workloads, *ii) protected*, only the kernel code can access the DMA engine and virtual memory states, and *iii) compatible* with commodity monolithic OS kernels such as Linux. Furthermore, it should achieve two performance goals:

- Low overhead. First, the service interface has to be lightweight. Frequent memory move requests, as discussed in Section 2.1, motivate us to minimize user/kernel crossings that are known to significantly interfere with user workloads [55]. Furthermore, the underlying kernel mechanism should incur minimum cost, as every cycle it spends will diminish the benefit from fast memory. This is challenging: although DMA frees CPU from copying bytes, the asynchronous interface introduces new, non-trivial costs, in addition to the existing overhead of physical and virtual memory management.
- Low latency. It is important not to delay application memory requests, because CPU workloads often do not see massive parallelism and are less likely to have enough work to fill the time gap of long wait. Furthermore, quickly pushing application requests to the DMA engine increases the parallelism between CPU and DMA and thus better utilizes the memory bandwidth.

Design decisions At first glance, our two goals appear incompatible: on one hand, conventional wisdom suggests amortizing overhead by delaying and processing requests in batches; on the other hand, individual requests should be serviced with minimum delay. Towards balancing and meeting the two goals, we make the following decisions:

1. Minimize syscalls: make applications and the kernel communicate mostly through shared data structures.
2. Eliminate user-level request batching: make kernel threads proactively "pull" individual requests from application and "post" notifications back – without user/kernel crossings or synchronization. This departs from prior syscall-

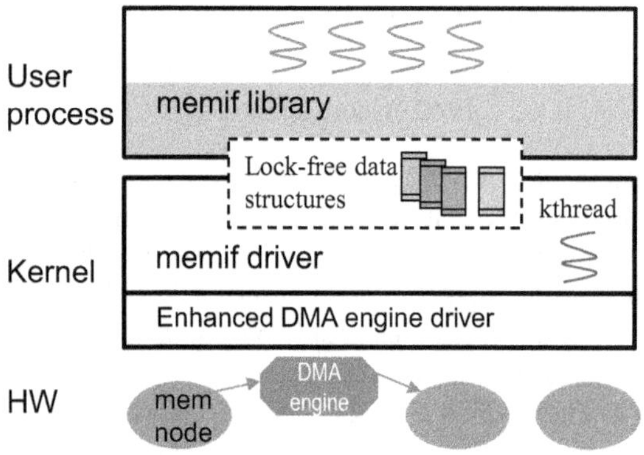

Figure 1. An overview of memif

```
int memfd = MemifOpen("/dev/memif0")
struct mov_req *req;
/* Request to move memory regions */
for (int i = 0; i < 10; i++) {
  req = AllocRequest(memfd);
  /* populate all the fields */
  req->src_base = ...
  ...
  SubmitRequest(req); /* non-blocking */
}

/* Do computation ... */

if (req = RetrieveCompleted()) /* Is any move completed? */
  /* Todo: Consume the memory with compute ... */
  ...
/* No other work, sleep until any move is completed. */
poll(fdset);  /* fdset is a set containing memfd. */
...
MemifClose(memfd);
```

Figure 2. A simple example of using the memif user API

minimizing approaches [24, 53] that make applications "push" batched requests to the kernel.

3. Exploit the asynchrony of the new interface for optimizing the kernel mechanism.

3. memif in a Nutshell

Implemented as a kernel-mode driver accompanied by a small user library (as shown in Figure 1), memif provides an asynchronous, hardware-accelerated service to replicate and migrate virtual memory regions. It supports two types of move:

- *Replication* implements the semantics of `memcpy()`: an application asks for copying data across two virtual memory regions that are already allocated in its address space. Replication incurs low OS cost: memif does not need to manage virtual memory or physical pages, and is indifferent to potential races between CPU and DMA.
- *Migration* provides the same semantics as page migration for NUMA: an application specifies one of its virtual memory regions and one destination memory node; memif replaces the existing backing pages with new pages allocated from the destination memory; it then fills the new pages with data from the old pages. memif also detects and reports any race between CPU and DMA.

The* memif *interface Simply put, the interface allows an application to submit move requests and later receives the completion notifications without blocking. More specifically, the application first opens a memif device file and owns the corresponding memif instance. The application then communicates with the underlying memif driver via a set of shared, lock-free queues: it submits move requests through enqueueing and receives completion notifications through dequeueing. A syscall is only needed when memif's kernel worker thread is idle and thus needs a kick-start; the memif user library, based on its observation of the queue color, will determine the need for such a syscall and make the syscall automatically (§4.4).

Later, if the application becomes idle, it can call `poll()` to sleep while still listening for any notifications from memif, just like a network server waiting for I/O events.

It is worth noting that multiple application threads, in accessing memif concurrently, are unable to cause data races. By design, all operations on data structures of the lock-free interface are atomic. This leaves no room for data race regardless of the application access patterns.

Execution of the* memif *driver The memif driver serves requests one by one and moves memory regions accordingly. In making a "kick-start" syscall, an application thread enters the kernel to execute the memif driver for just one request; it exits the kernel as soon as the resultant DMA transfer starts. Once the request is completed, a memif kernel thread takes charge of serving all the queued requests without userspace involvement. Meanwhile, the application may continue to submit new requests asynchronously – no syscall or locking is needed. Upon the completion of each request, the driver posts a notification by enqueueing the completed request for the application. After all submitted requests (including the new ones submitted asynchronously) are completely drained, the kernel thread goes back to sleep.

4. The Interface Design

In this section we present the exterior and interior of the memif interface. We first describe the user API (§4.1), then dive in the kernel interface design (§4.2 and 4.3), and last describe how the user API is implemented atop the kernel interface (§4.4).

4.1 The User API

We next describe the memif user API from a programmer's perspective. To make the discussion concrete, we also show a simple code example in Figure 2.

```
int MemifOpen(const char *device_name);
int MemifClose(int memfd);
```

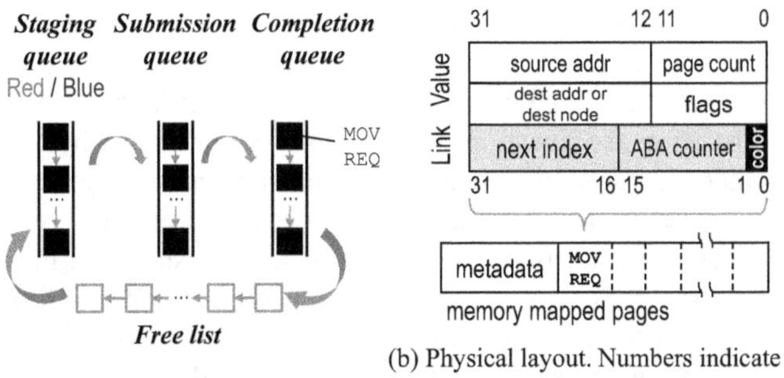

(a) Logic view

(b) Physical layout. Numbers indicate bit offsets. Link is used for queues.

Figure 3. The core of the memif kernel interface: lock-free data structures that are shared between userspace and kernel

Each memif instance exposes a Linux device file. Given a device file name, the above two functions initialize a memif instance and clean it up, respectively.

```
struct mov_req *AllocRequest(int memfd);
void FreeRequest(struct mov_req *req);
```

These two functions allocate and free a `mov_req` structure, respectively. `mov_req` is a hardware-independent representation of a move request, which specifies a virtual memory region consisting of multiple pages in an application's address space. Figure 3(b) shows all fields of a `mov_req`. After a blank `mov_req` is allocated, the programmer is responsible for populating all the fields in `mov_req` with the desired parameters.

```
int SubmitRequest(struct mov_req *req);
```

This function submits a new move request to memif. By calling it, the caller application is oblivious to whether a syscall will be made; instead, the memif library will decide so judiciously. We will discuss the details in Section 4.4. The function is non-blocking; it returns the error code or 0 on success.

```
struct mov_req *RetrieveCompleted(void);
```

This function attempts to retrieve one completion notification from memif. If there is no pending notification, the function returns `NULL` immediately without blocking.

In addition to the non-blocking retrieval, an application can wait for memif notifications while sleeping by calling a POSIX syscall `poll()`, as demonstrated in Figure 2. Supporting `poll()` is useful. First, it allows sleep for saving CPU cycles. Second, `poll()` is generic: through one invocation, applications can blocking wait for memif notifications and other types of I/O events at the same time, such as those of disk and network.

4.2 Kernel Interface

The memif kernel interface, which backs the user API, consists of two components per memif instance:

- One memif device file: just like normal Linux device files, it supports `open()`, `close()`, `mmap()`, and `poll()`. In addition, it supports a new `ioctl` command `MOV_ONE`;
- A set of data structures shared between userspace and kernel: three queues implemented as singly linked lists and one free list. All the shared data structures reside in a set of pinned pages that are first allocated by the memif driver and then mapped into the application's address space. These data structures are lock-free: they can be concurrently accessed by application threads and any kernel contexts without synchronization.

Shared data structures As shown in Figure 3 (b), the internal layout of the memory-mapped area starts with the metadata for the list and queues followed by an array of `mov_req` entries. As shown in Figure 3 (a), the memif initialization procedure chains all the `mov_req` entries in the free list through their `link` fields. Subsequent enqueueing and dequeueing operations update these `link`s and thus logically move `mov_req`s among the following queues:

- *Staging queue* holds the submitted requests that are not yet known to the kernel.
- *Submission queue* holds the requests that are known to the kernel and are currently waiting to be processed.
- *Completion queue* holds the completed requests posted back to the application. In practice, we have implemented the queue as two: one for successful moves and the other for failed ones; we refer to them as one for brevity.

The new `ioctl` command, `MOV_ONE`, only does one thing: entering the kernel, it dequeues a `mov_req` from the *submission* queue and executes the memif driver for the request.

Why lock-free? All the three queues are based on a classic lock-free queue design [47] (the first queue is augmented with a red/blue color as will be discussed later). Lock-free data structures provide a unified, conceptually simple mechanism that allows concurrent access to the memif queues. No single kernel locking mechanism provides this benefit. Synchronization using sleepable locks, e.g., semaphores, prevents the *completion* queue from being accessed by interrupt handlers for notification delivery. Synchronization using non-sleepable spinlocks, on the other hand, exposes kernel to lockup hazards: a misbehaving application failing to release a spinlock will deadlock the kernel.

In theory, any lock-free data structures supporting `set` operations including `add` and `remove` can be used for the memif interface. Having considered other lock-free data structures including singly or doubly linked list [25, 57], we chose lock-free queue for its simplicity and low overhead.

It is worth noting that the use of lock-free data structures is uncommon in user/kernel communication: existing work often makes user and kernel share normal queues (i.e. not lock-free) [24, 53], since user and kernel only access these queues synchronously. With the asynchrony of the memif interface, normal queues no longer work: the integrity of the shared interface data structures must be guaranteed under any user/kernel access pattern.

Why a red-blue queue? We further extend the *staging* queue to be a novel *red-blue* lock-free queue: unlike a vanilla lock-free queue that only guarantees the atomicity of each queue operation, the new design guarantees the atomicity of each queue operation together with the access of a queue-wide flag, i.e. the queue color.

This feature is critical to memif. To minimize latency, threads from both an application and the kernel share not only the *staging* queue but also a key flag, which indicates which thread is responsible for flushing all the queued requests for execution. While moving requests in/out of the queue, all the threads also pass around the responsibility of flushing the queue. To do so, each thread must manipulate both the queue and the flag exclusively; otherwise a race condition will occur. This raises non-trivial challenge: were memif to employ a vanilla lock-free queue and a normal flag, it would require a lock for protecting the two, breaking lock freedom and incurring lockups.

The red-blue queue realizes the feature with a novel idea. It encodes the flag, dubbed "queue color", in each link inside the queue; it atomically propagates the flag as the queue grows. As a result, the flag can be manipulated as part of an atomic queue operation. Lock freedom is retained.

We will sketch the internals of a red-blue lock-free queue in Section 4.3 and show its use in Section 4.4.

Safety Concerns Directly sharing data structures between userspace and kernel naturally raises safety concerns. Fortunately, the memif interface does not jeopardize kernel's integrity. First, the only object references, the link field in `mov_req`, are indices into the array of `mov_req`, which will be validated by the memif driver before use. Second, as discussed above, as applications hold no lock, their use of memif will never lock up the kernel. Last, one memif device is owned by one process. Multiple memif devices maintain separate copies of queues and free lists and are therefore isolated from each other.

However, it is still possible that applications abuse the memif service for excessive data movement. Such problems are not introduced by the memif interface and can be prevented by the driver without safety risks.

4.3 Internals of Red-blue Lock-free Queue

As mentioned in Section 4.2, application or kernel may need exclusive access to both a *staging* queue and its color. To avoid introducing a lock, our key idea is to "entangle" color in the atomic queue operations. We next provide a generic, memif-agnostic description of how this is implemented.

To provide some background, a classic lock-free queue [47] is often implemented as a singly linked list. It uses compare-and-swap (CAS), an atomic CPU instruction, to update the links between its elements. To enqueue or dequeue, a thread checkpoints the link to be modified, prepares a new version of the link on the side, and then tries to "swap in" the new link with a CAS. Guaranteed by hardware, the swap attempt will succeed if and only if the checkpoint is still up-to-date; otherwise, the queue must have just been modified by another concurrent thread, and the whole procedure is retried.

Based on the design, our red-blue lock-free queue encodes one color bit in each element link, as shown in Figure 3 (b). This allows performing a queue operation (i.e., link update) and setting/getting color with a single CAS. Compared to the classic design, the overhead added by coloring is negligible. We next overview the queue interface and its implementation.

```
color_t set_color(queue_t q, color_t new);
```

This function attempts to change one queue's color to `new`, which, as a rule, will only succeed on an empty queue. Inside, the function first checks if the queue is empty, i.e., whether the head's `next` link is `NULL`. If so, it then follows the aforementioned procedure to swap in a `NULL` link encoding the new color. On success, the old color is returned.

```
color_t enqueue(queue_t q, element_t e);
element_t dequeue(queue_t head);
```

A queue's color is maintained and returned as part of the enqueueing and dequeueing functions. The enqueueing function extracts the color from the old tail's `next` link during checkpointing; it then propagates the color to the new tail's `next` link during CAS. On success, it returns the color to the caller. Since the dequeueing function returns the dequeued element, the caller can simply extract the color from the element's `next` link.

From a high-level perspective, our red-blue lock-free queue is a generic design that maintains a queue-wide property (not limited to a binary color value) as part of the atomic queue operations.

4.4 Putting It Together: Implementing the User API

Most memif user functions presented in Section 4.1 are thin wrappers around the kernel interface: opening or closing the device file, getting a `mov_req` from the free list or putting one back, and dequeuing a `mov_req` from the *completion* queue. The only non-trivial one is `SubmitRequest()`, for which simplified pseudo code is listed and explained below.

```
1  SubmitRequest(request) {
2    color = enqueue(staging_queue, request);
3    if (color == BLUE) { /* user should flush */
4  flush:
5      while (request = dequeue(staging_queue))
6        enqueue(submission_queue, request);
7      old_color = set_color(staging_queue, RED);
8      if (old_color == -1) /* queue not empty */
9        goto flush;
10     if (old_color == RED)
11       return;
12     ioctl(MOV_ONE);
13   }
14 }
```

This function first deposits a `mov_req` in the *staging* queue (line 2). As described in Section 4.1, the *staging* queue has a blue or red color indicating who should flush it: blue for the application and red for the kernel. If the color is red, the function does nothing but return, knowing that an active kernel thread will later flush the entire queue including the just enqueued request; if the color is blue, the function flushes all `mov_req`s from the *staging* queue to the *submission* queue (line 4–6). At the end of flushing, the function attempts to change the the queue's color from blue to red (line 7). If the attempt fails because the queue is no longer empty (line 8) – one another application thread may have just submitted new requests – flushing is retried. On success, the function invokes `ioctl()` to issue a `MOV_ONE` command (line 12). After the queue color is changed to red, any subsequent requests will accumulate in the *staging* queue, waiting to be flushed by the kernel thread.

There is no race among concurrent application threads attempting to flush the *staging* queue: only the thread that successfully changes the queue color from blue to red will call `ioctl()`; other threads, in attempting to change the queue color, will see the color is already red and quit (line 10).

5. The memif Driver

As mentioned in Section 3, the memif driver serves `mov_req` requests. To break down the challenges faced by the driver, we list the major operations in fulfilling each `mov_req` in Table 1. For these operations, the table shows baseline designs that are closely modelled after the Linux page migration – except DMA and notification delivery. In this section, we discuss key optimizations applied to individual operations (also summarized in Table 1) and then present a complete execution workflow with the optimized operations.

5.1 Gang Page Lookup

To move a virtual memory region, the memif driver needs to locate all the physical page descriptors. Conceptually, given the virtual address of each page, the driver should walk the page table to locate the page table entry (PTE) that leads to the corresponding physical page descriptor. Since all pages targeted by a request are virtually contiguous, we leverage the fact that most of their PTEs are adjacent. Thus, only for the first page in the region, the driver descends "vertically" from the page table root down to the PTE; for each of the remaining pages, the driver walks "horizontally" to traverse neighboring PTEs without starting over from the root.

5.2 Lightweight Race Detection

In migrating each page, the baseline workflow modifies the user address space twice (in Remap and Release) as summarized in Table 1 and illustrated in Figure 4(a). The implications are two. First, changing PTE and TLB has significant direct cost, e.g., up to a couple of μs based on our measurement; in addition, flushing TLB also has indirect cost [2, 55]. Second, since modifying user address space is a heavy action, any code trying to do so must first obtain a sleepable lock as required by the Linux kernel. This prevents Release from being done in non-sleepable contexts such as interrupt handlers.

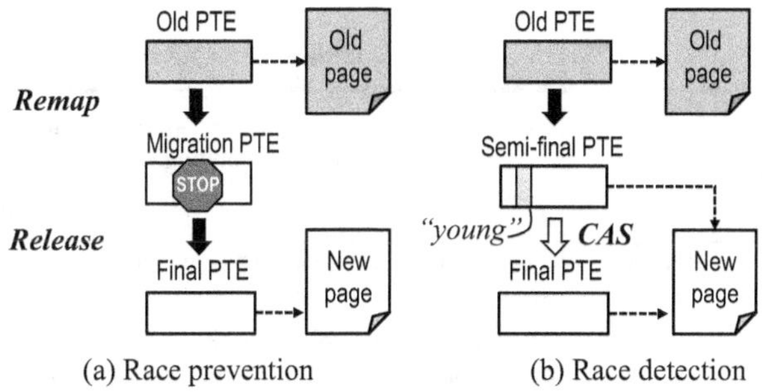

Figure 4. A comparison of (a) race prevention as in Linux page migration for NUMA and (b) race detection in memif

In retrospect, modifying user address space in Remap used to be warranted: the installed migration PTE *prevents* races between CPU and DMA by blocking any user thread attempting to modify pages being migrated. With the legacy synchronous interface, blocking applications is the only way to handle race: applications have no other way to learn migration completion and therefore cannot actively avoid races.

Fortunately, since the memif interface explicitly delivers completion notifications to applications, the memif driver can be relieved of race *prevention* and instead simply performs race *detection*, therefore skipping installing migration PTEs. Based on this rationale, we have built the following mechanism.

Proceed and fail The driver detects races and treats them as program errors, as shown in Figure 4(b). In Remap, the driver installs a semi-final PTE, in which all bits are identical to the final PTE (the one installed by the baseline Release) except that the "young" bit is set. With the Linux design, the young bit will be cleared by the kernel automatically when the page is accessed for the first time or when the page is migrated. When it comes to Release, the memif driver tries to clear the young bit: it uses a CAS instruction to swap in the final PTE in which young bit is cleared as it should be. The CAS will fail if any code has modified the semi-final PTE or any page reference has occurred causing its young bit to be cleared. In such a case, the driver sends a `SEGFAULT` signal to the application. On success, no TLB flush is needed since the semi-final PTE never enters TLB.

Alternative: proceed and recover We have also considered handling races more transparently at the price of higher complexity and overhead: upon a race, memif aborts the migration, restores the original mapping, and gracefully notifies the application of the race. This could be useful in case one application decides to stop waiting for an outstanding memory move and demands immediate memory access.

To implement this feature, the driver provides a custom page fault handler for aborting migration when race is de-

	Baseline Operations	Optimized Operations	Major Costs
1. Prep → *R & M*	For each page: based on the user-provided virtual address, look up the corresponding physical page descriptor.	For the whole request: given the virtual address range, find all physical page descriptors with gang page lookup. **See Section 5.1.**	**++Per-request: ++Page lookup** --Per-page: --Page lookup
2. Remap → *M*	For each page: allocate a new page on the destination memory. Replace the page table entry (PTE) with a special migration PTE, so that any process trying to access the page will be blocked until the migration ends. Flush TLB.	For each page: allocate a new page on the destination memory. Replace the page table entry (PTE) with one pointing to the new page. Set the "young" bit in the PTE. Flush TLB. **See Section 5.2.**	Per-page: Page allocation Replace PTE TLB flush
3. DMA/cfg → *R & M*	For the whole request: assemble a scatter-gather list and pass the list to the DMA engine driver. The DMA engine driver programs the chain of transfer descriptors and triggers the transfer.	For the whole request: assemble a scatter-gather list and pass the list to the DMA engine driver. The DMA engine driver reuses a chain of transfer descriptors and triggers the transfer. **See Section 5.3.**	Per-request: Initialize the list Per-page: **++Reuse descriptor** --Write descriptor
(... DMA transfer ...)			
4. Release → *M*	For each page: replace the migration PTE with the final one pointing to the new page. Flush TLB. Free the old page.	For each page: use a CAS to clear the "young" bit in the PTE and report any race happened during the DMA transfer. **See Section 5.2.** Free the old page.	Per-page: **++CAS** --Replace PTE --TLB flush Page freeing
5. Notify → *R & M*	For the request: enqueue the completed `mov_req` to the *completion* queue and wake up any waiting application threads.		Per-request: Enqueue notif.

Time ***R: operation needed in replication M: operation needed in migration*** -- *Cost in baseline only* ++ ***Cost in optimized only***

Table 1. The major operations of the memif driver in serving one move request

tected. Remap installs a special PTE so that any write to a migrating page will be trapped as a page fault and handled by the custom fault handler. This handler restores the old PTE, drops the outstanding DMA transfer, and enqueues the aborted `mov_req` to notify the application. The CPU's new write that causes the race will thus be preserved.

5.3 Minimal Reconfiguration of DMA Engine

Perhaps a bit surprisingly, the overhead of configuring DMA engine is non-trivial as compared to the saved CPU cycles. A modern DMA engine often offers sophisticated mechanisms to copy data. For instance, the TI EDMA3 engine [58] exposes an array of transfer descriptors. Consisting of 12 parameters, one transfer descriptor commands the engine to copy a chunk of bytes as if the bytes are organized in a three-dimensional array. To implement scatter-gather transfers [15], CPU can chain descriptors by writing to a specific field in each descriptor to indicate the next descriptor that the engine should execute. According to our knowledge, the configurable descriptors and chaining interface are popular in other DMA engines such as Intel's Crystal Beach 3 [28].

To move a memory region which spans multiple pages, the DMA engine driver composes a chain of descriptors. Without assuming IOMMU, DMA requires one descriptor to cover a physically contiguous area. As a result, the driver dedicates each descriptor to one page, the largest physically contiguous memory area that applications are guaranteed to get.

The major overheads of DMA engine configuration are thus two: *i)* calculating the parameters for each descriptor; *ii)* writing to each descriptor which is in unbuffered, uncached I/O memory. It sometimes takes 4-5 μs to configure one descriptor according to our measurement.

To minimize the first overhead, we have done an obvious optimization to cache calculated parameters since each descriptor always copies a page. To minimize the second overhead, we reuse descriptor chains that have been configured for previous transfers. In order to do so, we enhance the DMA engine driver so that it maintains the knowledge of existing descriptor chains. In a simple example, since the enhanced driver knows that "starting from descriptor 42, there exists a chain of 32 descriptors, each configured for a 4KB transfer", it can reuse part of or the whole chain in the next transfer. For each reused descriptor, the driver only needs to overwrite the source and destination fields, reducing the second overhead by 4×.

5.4 Putting It Together: Driver Execution

With the above optimization applied, the refined operations and their costs are shown in Table 1. Thanks to the lock-free data structures (§4.2), these operations are performed in three different kernel contexts to achieve the smallest latency

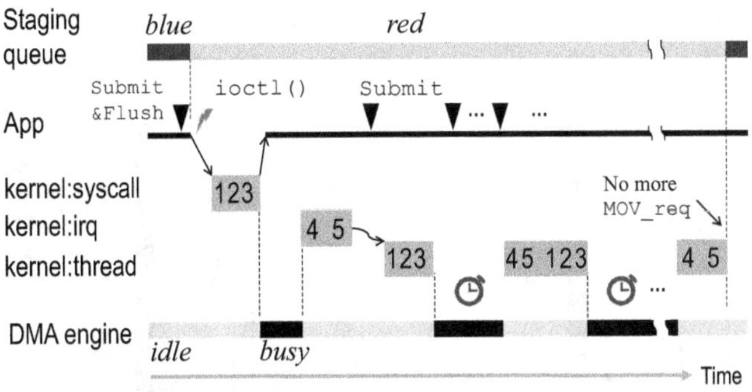

Figure 5. An example execution of memif driver. The numbers are referring to the driver operations summarized in Table 1. Time on x-axis is not drawn to scale.

possible: the caller's process, interrupt handlers, and kernel threads. We next describe the three execution paths in the memif driver. An example execution timeline is shown in Figure 5.

Syscall path As mentioned in Section 4.4, an application invokes `ioctl(MOV_ONE)` to enter the memif driver. Executed in the context of the application process, the driver does operation 1–3 for one queued request. Right after activating the DMA engine, the execution returns to userspace.

Interrupt path When the DMA engine completes data copy for a request, an interrupt is fired. The interrupt handler performs Release (4) and Notif (5) immediately. Note that this is made possible through our lightweight race detection described in Section 5.2; otherwise, modifying address space in Release (4) is forbidden in interrupt handlers as it may lock up the kernel. Last, the interrupt handler wakes up a kernel thread.

Kernel thread path Once woken up, the kernel thread issues all queued requests from the *submission* queue and the *staging* queue. Inspired by network interface drivers [48], the kernel thread switches between the interrupt-driven mode and polling mode depending on the amount of data to move. For small requests (less than 512KB in our implementation) for which completion time is short and predictable, the kernel thread turns off the DMA interrupt and sleeps shortly before performing Release(4) and Notify(5). This is shown in Figure 5. Otherwise, the kernel thread leaves the interrupt on and lets the interrupt handler perform Release and Notify. Finally, when queues are emptied, the kernel thread colors the *staging* queue as blue, indicating that the application is responsible for flushing the queue from now on.

Why use a kernel thread? As schedulable entities, kernel threads are able to acquire sleepable locks such as semaphores, thus capable of time-consuming operations such as Remap(2). More importantly, kernel threads can be executed on cores other than the ones where data-intensive application runs [55], shielding the latter from frequent context switches and CPU exceptions, both known costly.

Table 2. A summary of the test platform, the TI KeyStone II SoC

Hardware	Specs
CPU	4x Cortex-A15, each @ 1.2GHz
Memory	*Fast*: 6 MB on-chip SRAM Measured bandwidth: 24.0 GB/sec *Slow*: 8 GB DDR3 1600MHz Measured bandwidth: 6.2 GB/sec
DMA Engine	TI EDMA3: coherent; 6 transfer controllers; 512 entries for transfer descriptors.

Table 3. A summary of the memif source code

	Library	Driver	DMA	Test	Total
KSLoC	0.8	3.3	0.8	1.7	6.6

6. Prototype & Evaluation

In this section, we describe our test platform and prototype (§6.1), present the evaluation methodology (§6.2) and results (§6.3 – 6.5), and discuss our limitations (§6.7).

6.1 Test Platform & Prototype

We have prototyped memif atop the Texas Instruments KeyStone II SoC [59]. A server-class SoC, KeyStone II powers microservers such as the HP Proliant m800 [26]. As summarized in Table 2, the SoC embraces two types of memory, both cached. An on-chip controller manages two memories and implements coherency between CPU and other bus masters including the DMA engine.

Applying the NUMA abstraction As mentioned in Section 1, we have abstracted the heterogeneous memories as pseudo NUMA nodes. In order to do so, we have ported an existing ARM NUMA patchset [37] to KeyStone II. One challenge is the physical address of SRAM is lower than any DDR bank, luring the kernel to use the capacity-limited SRAM for booting and then crash due to out of memory. To prevent this, we have patched the Linux boot memory allocator so that the SRAM bank only becomes visible after the booting. By that time, all kernel subsystems and the userspace, e.g., the `numactl` utility, can see and use two NUMA nodes: the CPU cores and the DRAM (slow) are on the same node, while the SRAM (fast) is on the other node.

***Implementing* memif** Table 3 summarizes the new implementation source code introduced by our memif prototype. The user library and driver share the implementation of lock-free data structures. Based on Linux 3.10, the memif driver is compiled as a standalone kernel module. Only minor changes are made to the rest of the kernel, e.g., reverse memory mapping, to export a handful of internal functions to the module.

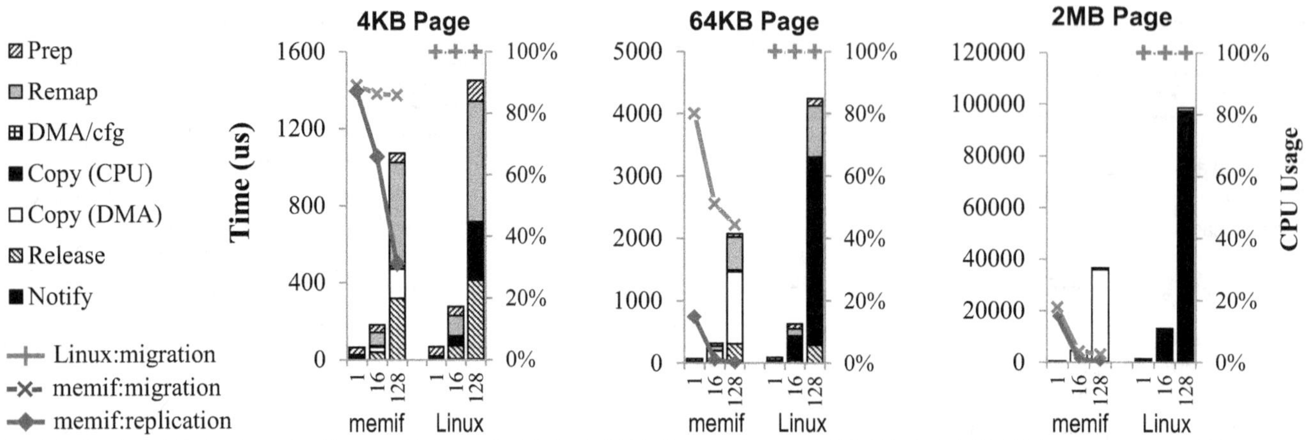

Figure 6. The time breakdown (columns; left y-axis) and CPU usage (lines; right y-axis) in fulfilling a single `mov_req`. Each subfigure is for a different page size as marked on top. Numbers on the x-axis indicate the number of pages in each `mov_req`.

We have applied the DMA enhancement described in Section 5.3 to EDMA3 on KeyStone II. Because EDMA3 is unfortunately not supported by TI's official kernel tree, we have to port a similar driver from TI's DaVinci SoC. In bringing up EDMA3, we have also implemented memory-to-memory transfer for it and added a couple of locks for thread-safety.

6.2 Methodology

We test whether memif has achieved the goals of low cost and low latency as set in Section 2. We benchmark memif replication and migration by moving memory from the slow node to the fast node, and compare memif migration with Linux page migration. In addition to testing the default 4KB page, we further investigate how memif will be impacted by typical large pages. Given that large page support is not yet mature on our ARM-based test platform, we emulate the impact by modifying the kernel so it moves extra bytes while keeping other operations unchanged. By doing so, we have slightly overestimated the cost of page table walk as using large pages often reduces the page table depth by one or two, which, however, is negligible as compared to the total cost.

6.3 Cost Analysis

As has been shown in Figure 6, memif provides memory move service at low cost. Compared to the Linux page migration (labelled as "Linux"), memif *i)* moves the same amount of pages with much lower CPU usage and *ii)* does so in much shorter time for most cases.

By comparing the three subfigures for different page granularities, we can see how memif gains the edge. When small (4KB) pages are in use, the overheads of managing virtual memory and physical pages are the majority. memif manages to offset the overhead with its interface and mechanism optimizations described in Section 4 and 5; memif loses its advantage over Linux only in the extreme case where each request only targets one page. When page size becomes medium (64KB) or large (2MB), byte copy cost starts to dominate and the DMA benefit gradually eclipses every other cost, giving memif a clear win.

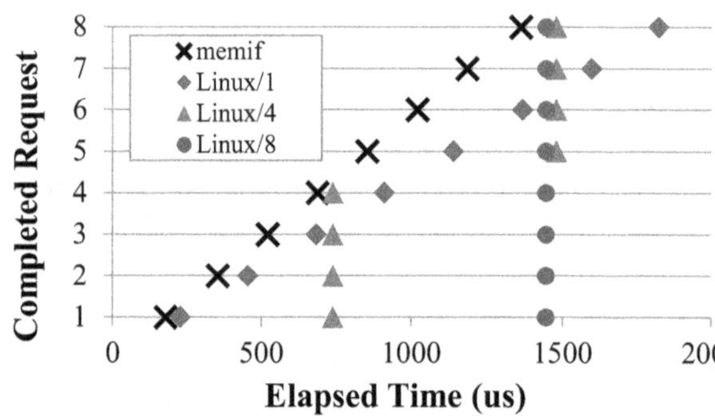

Figure 7. The latency in completing a sequence of eight migration requests, each covering sixteen 4KB pages. Numbers in legend indicate the count of requests batched in each syscall.

It is worth noting that the time breakdown in Figure 6 is not always accurate. Since memif is asynchronous, its operations do not always have counterparts in the Linux page migration code. In such cases, we identify rough equivalences with best effort.

6.4 Request Latency

In continuously serving requests, the asynchronous interface of memif incurs minimum latency at the cost of only one user/kernel crossing. To demonstrate this, we write an application to submit a sequence of eight requests (each targeting 16 pages) to memif; in comparison, we use a second application to perform the same task by using NUMA migration syscalls, and vary the number of requests batched in each syscall from one, to four, and to eight. As shown in Figure 7, the memif-based application receives each notification soon after the corresponding request is completed. Through the course, the application only makes one syscall – `ioctl()`

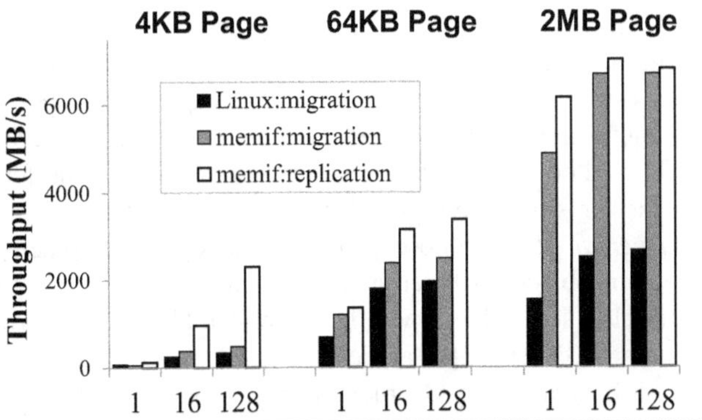

Figure 8. The memory move throughputs across different page granularities. Numbers on x-axis indicate the number of pages in each move request.

Table 4. The throughputs of streaming workloads on top of a mini runtime that uses memif. Numbers are in MB/Sec.

	StreamCluster.pgain	STREAM.triad	STREAM.add
Linux	1440.1	2384.1	2390.1
Memif	1778.4 (+23.5%)	3184.4 (+33.6%)	3186.9 (+33.3%)

for the first request. In contrast, the second application is unable to reduce latency and overhead at the same time: it either has to send each request in a separate syscall to favor latency and suffers from high syscall overhead, or it has to batch multiple requests in one syscall and thus suffers from high latency.

6.5 Throughput

Thanks to its low cost, memif is able to achieve a significantly higher throughput in memory move. We compare an application that streams migration requests to memif with `migspeed`, a Linux NUMA utility released with the standard `numactl` library. As shown in Figure 8, except for the extreme case where each request covers only one 4KB page (the leftmost columns), the memif-based application outperforms `migspeed` by at least 40% (small pages) and up to 3× (large pages). The throughput of memif replication is even higher as compared to the memif migration: the simpler semantics of replication eliminates the need for virtual memory management.

6.6 Case study: A Mini Runtime for Streaming Workloads

To study how memif could be used by real applications, we craft a mini runtime library that uses memif for parallel streaming workloads. The runtime is based on a simple idea: using the fast memory as an array of prefetch buffers and managing outstanding moves just like asynchronous I/O requests. As soon as one application starts, the runtime fills all buffers by replicating data from the slow memory asynchronously. During execution, once a buffer is ready, the runtime invokes the workload's compute function to consume the buffer with all available CPU cores; immediately after any buffer is consumed, the runtime requests to fill the buffer with fresh data again. If all prefetched data are consumed when memory move is still in flight, the runtime invokes compute function to consume data in the slow memory. We implement the runtime with around 400 SLoC.

We have ported three compute kernels from two well-known benchmarks, STREAM [43] and StreamCluster [6]. The throughputs measured on our test platform are shown in Table 4. Our experience suggests that *i)* memif is practical and easy to use and *ii)* a synergy between memif and runtime/compiler offers a promising framework to boost application performance.

6.7 Limitation

Memory move at fine granularity Despite the great efficiency improvement over the state of the art, the cost of memif is still non-trivial when it moves small memory regions – a few to tens of small pages, as has been shown in Figure 6. This is a fundamental limitation rooted in our basic design requirements (§2.3): user/kernel crossings cannot be completely eliminated since virtual memory mappings and DMA engine have to be protected by the kernel; the management of virtual and physical memory cannot be made free due to their software cost. As the granularity of memory region shrinks, all these are emerging as the major cost.

Without an overhaul of the hardware/software stack, user-guided approaches may never be as efficient as transparent, hardware-only approaches for very fine-grained memory move, e.g., at 2 KB [54]. Yet, to data-intensive workloads with large working sets, moving memory at a medium (hundreds of KB) or large (multiple MB) granularity creates a highly valuable balance between efficiency and flexibility.

Platform limitations In testing a variety of data-intensive applications, e.g., wordcount [61] and psearchy [9], we find many of them see little performance gain from memif. Our investigation shows the causes as two limitations of the KeyStone II platform. First, the 6 MB fast memory is not significantly larger than the 1 MB per-core last-level cache. As a result, applications whose working sets fit in the fast memory are also likely cache-friendly. Second, as applications can only use 4 KB pages, memif has to move memory at a relative high cost as discussed above.

We expect the limitations to disappear from emerging platforms as large fast memory and medium/large pages become pervasive. For instance, fast memory is expected to be as large as 1/8 of the main memory [45]. With them, memif will substantially benefit a much wider range of applications.

Implementation limitations As a research prototype, the current memif cannot automatically swap out fast memory; it can only move anonymous pages but not pages backed by files; its support for moving pages shared among processes is primitive. Furthermore, although by design memif is capable of serving multiple concurrent applications, we have not evaluated the feature. Down the road, we plan to coevolve the memif prototype with emerging heterogeneous memory hardware and examine the implementation more thoroughly.

7. Related Work

Heterogeneous Memory Architecture Memory heterogeneity is common. Small on-chip SRAM, often known as scratchpad memory, is widely used in embedded systems for its low power and high predictability [4]. However, ranging from tens of KB [27] to a few hundreds of KB [42], it is too limited for today's data-intensive workloads. Such small capacities often warrant pure user-level memory management via compilers [18, 44, 56] or runtime [3]. Lacking kernel support, these solutions are unsafe in multiprogrammed environments.

GPGPU often embraces a variety of memory types in one memory hierarchy, making proper placement of program data critical to good performance. Unlike memif, most software work on GPU memory [13, 36] focuses on static data placement rather than dynamic data move.

Memory move Memory move is a key facility in managing complex memory hierarchies. Most software approaches move memory without application's awareness. Treating SRAM as the main memory and DRAM as a paging device, RAMPage [41] transparently copies data between the two. Targeting heterogeneous memory, Meswani *et al.* propose a hardware counter that assists OS to track memory hotness and to migrate pages accordingly [45]. Memory move is also widely used for NUMA. To increase threads and data affinity, kMAF [17] monitors memory access by injecting page faults and migrates pages dynamically across NUMA nodes. To alleviate memory traffic congestion, Carrefour [16] dynamically replicates pages among NUMA nodes. Shoal [31] transparently replicates program arrays among NUMA nodes using DMA. In moving memory, most of the prior work relies on Linux page migration which we have shown as inefficient. Unlike any of them, memif exposes memory move as an OS service.

A few studies improve the mechanism of memory move. Goglin *et al.* [22] augment Linux page migration with a lazy option, migrating a page upon its first access on the new memory node. Compared to memif, they defer migration without addressing the major inefficiency. Bock *et al.* [8] propose a new hardware feature for pinning pages in CPU cache so that the pages remain accessible while being migrated. Compared to memif, they do not reduce the OS overhead of migration. Lepers *et al.* [35] speed up Linux page migration by mainly reducing the use of locks. Compared to memif, they freeze applications during migration, and do not exploit DMA for byte copy.

For heterogeneous memory, memif opens the door to a classic approach – codesigning task scheduling and data move, as has been applied to CPU cache [14] and GPU [30].

User's knowledge User's knowledge has been long known important in managing complex memory hierarchies. For CPU cache, software prefetching [11] is a classic technique to hide latency. Targeting heterogeneous memories, memkind [12] is a user-level heap manager that exposes a variety of memory properties to applications. Similarly, TLM malloc [46] allows programmers to allocate buffers on fast or slow memory under the guidance of profiling. Pena *et al.* [50] propose a profiler for optimally placing program objects in heterogeneous memories. NUMA systems also see rich support for compiler [10, 51] or programmer [32, 38, 39] to guide page replication or migration. These programming abstractions and profiling techniques are complementary to memif and can be retrofitted to guide memory move.

Efficient user/kernel interface High-performance kernel subsystems, such as GPU driver and network stack [24, 53], often directly share buffers with userspace. To use their services, applications push batched requests to kernel using syscall, thus removing the need for explicit synchronization. This is reasonable in handling a stable stream of requests, e.g. in packet I/O applications. The kernel thread in memif is inspired by FlexSC [55], in which all syscalls are greedily deferred until the caller process becomes idle and then get executed in dedicated kernel threads. Similar to them, memif minimizes the use of syscalls; unlike them, memif minimizes the latency in serving memory move requests, as has been discussed in Section 2. Thus, memif eliminates user-level batching and enables user and kernel to asynchronously access the shared data structures in the interface.

Event delivery mechanisms in modern OSes, such as `epoll` [5] and `kqueue` [34], hold pending notifications in kernel buffers. Since the buffers are invisible to userspace, applications have to use syscalls to retrieve the notifications. Unlike them, the memif driver delivers notifications to applications asynchronously without requiring any syscall.

8. Conclusions

We present memif, a lightweight OS service for moving memory regions across heterogeneous memories. memif is asynchronous, hardware-accelerated, and safe to use. memif has achieved low latency and low overhead through a lightweight interface built around a set of shared lock-free data structures and a suite of key optimizations for its kernel mechanisms. Through a prototype atop heterogeneous memory hardware, we have demonstrated that memif enables applications to leverage their knowledge in exploiting heterogeneous memories with ease.

Acknowledgments

The authors thank Texas Instruments for donating the Keystone II evaluation modules and the anonymous reviewers for their useful feedback.

References

[1] S. Anthony. Intel unveils 72-core x86 knights landing cpu for exascale supercomputing. ExtremeTech, 2013.

[2] ARM. ARM architecture reference manual: Armv7-a and armv7-r edition, 2014.

[3] J. Balart, M. Gonzalez, X. Martorell, E. Ayguade, Z. Sura, T. Chen, T. Zhang, K. Obrien, and K. Obrien. A novel asynchronous software cache implementation for the cell-be processor. In *Languages and Compilers for Parallel Computing*, pages 125–140. Springer, 2008.

[4] R. Banakar, S. Steinke, B.-S. Lee, M. Balakrishnan, and P. Marwedel. Scratchpad memory: Design alternative for cache on-chip memory in embedded systems. In *Proceedings of the Tenth International Symposium on Hardware/Software Codesign*, pages 73–78, 2002.

[5] G. Banga, J. C. Mogul, and P. Druschel. A scalable and explicit event delivery mechanism for unix. In *Proceedings of the Annual Conference on USENIX Annual Technical Conference*, pages 19–19, 1999.

[6] C. Bienia, S. Kumar, J. P. Singh, and K. Li. The parsec benchmark suite: Characterization and architectural implications. In *Proceedings of the 17th International Conference on Parallel Architectures and Compilation Techniques*, pages 72–81, 2008.

[7] B. Black, M. Annavaram, N. Brekelbaum, J. DeVale, L. Jiang, G. Loh, D. McCauley, P. Morrow, D. Nelson, D. Pantuso, P. Reed, J. Rupley, S. Shankar, J. Shen, and C. Webb. Die stacking (3d) microarchitecture. In *Microarchitecture, 2006. MICRO-39. 39th Annual IEEE/ACM International Symposium on*, pages 469–479, Dec 2006.

[8] S. Bock, B. R. Childers, R. Melhem, and D. Mossé. Concurrent page migration for mobile systems with os-managed hybrid memory. In *Proceedings of the 11th ACM Conference on Computing Frontiers*, pages 31:1–31:10, 2014.

[9] S. Boyd-Wickizer, A. T. Clements, Y. Mao, A. Pesterev, M. F. Kaashoek, R. Morris, and N. Zeldovich. An analysis of linux scalability to many cores. In *Proceedings of the 9th USENIX Conference on Operating Systems Design and Implementation*, pages 1–8, 2010.

[10] F. Broquedis, N. Furmento, B. Goglin, P.-A. Wacrenier, and R. Namyst. ForestGOMP: An efficient OpenMP environment for NUMA architectures. *Intl. Journal of Parallel Programming*, 38(5-6):418–439, 2010.

[11] D. Callahan, K. Kennedy, and A. Porterfield. Software prefetching. *SIGOPS Oper. Syst. Rev.*, 25(Special Issue):40–52, Apr. 1991.

[12] C. Cantalupo, V. Venkatesan, J. R. Hammond, K. Czurylo, and S. Hammond. User extensible heap manager for heterogeneous memory platforms and mixed memory policies. Architecture document, 2015.

[13] G. Chen, B. Wu, D. Li, and X. Shen. Porple: An extensible optimizer for portable data placement on gpu. In *Proceedings of the 47th Annual IEEE/ACM International Symposium on Microarchitecture*, pages 88–100, 2014.

[14] D. Chiou, S. Devadas, J. Jacobs, P. Jain, V. Lee, E. Peserico, P. Portante, L. Rudolph, G. E. Suh, and D. Willenson. Scheduler-based prefetching for multilevel memories. *Lab. Comput. Sci., MIT, Boston, MA, Group Memo*, 444, 2001.

[15] J. Corbet. The chained scatterlist api. `https://lwn.net/Articles/256368/`, 2007.

[16] M. Dashti, A. Fedorova, J. Funston, F. Gaud, R. Lachaize, B. Lepers, V. Quema, and M. Roth. Traffic management: A holistic approach to memory placement on numa systems. In *Proceedings of the Eighteenth International Conference on Architectural Support for Programming Languages and Operating Systems*, pages 381–394, 2013.

[17] M. Diener, E. H. Cruz, P. O. Navaux, A. Busse, and H.-U. Heiß. kmaf: Automatic kernel-level management of thread and data affinity. In *Proceedings of the 23rd International Conference on Parallel Architectures and Compilation*, pages 277–288, 2014.

[18] A. Dominguez, S. Udayakumaran, and R. Barua. Heap data allocation to scratch-pad memory in embedded systems. *Journal of Embedded Computing*, 1(4):521–540, 2005.

[19] M. Ferdman, A. Adileh, O. Kocberber, S. Volos, M. Alisafaee, D. Jevdjic, C. Kaynak, A. D. Popescu, A. Ailamaki, and B. Falsafi. Clearing the clouds: A study of emerging scale-out workloads on modern hardware. In *Proc. ACM Int. Conf. Architectural Support for Programming Languages & Operating Systems (ASPLOS)*, pages 37–48, 2012.

[20] Y. Gao, F. Zhang, and J. Bakos. Sparse matrix-vector multiply on the keystone ii digital signal processor. In *High Performance Extreme Computing Conference (HPEC), 2014 IEEE*, pages 1–6, Sept 2014.

[21] F. Gaud, B. Lepers, J. Decouchant, J. Funston, A. Fedorova, and V. Quéma. Large pages may be harmful on numa systems. In *2014 USENIX Annual Technical Conference (USENIX ATC 14)*, pages 231–242, June 2014.

[22] B. Goglin and N. Furmento. Enabling high-performance memory migration for multithreaded applications on linux. In *Parallel Distributed Processing, 2009. IPDPS 2009. IEEE International Symposium on*, pages 1–9, May 2009.

[23] P. Hammarlund, R. Kumar, R. B. Osborne, R. Rajwar, R. Singhal, R. D'Sa, R. Chappell, S. Kaushik, S. Chennupaty, S. Jourdan, S. Gunther, T. Piazza, and T. Burton. Haswell: The fourth-generation intel core processor. *IEEE Micro*, (2):6–20, 2014.

[24] S. Han, S. Marshall, B.-G. Chun, and S. Ratnasamy. Megapipe: A new programming interface for scalable network i/o. In *Presented as part of the 10th USENIX Symposium on Operating Systems Design and Implementation (OSDI 12)*, pages 135–148, 2012.

[25] T. L. Harris. A pragmatic implementation of non-blocking linked-lists. In *Proceedings of the 15th International Conference on Distributed Computing*, pages 300–314, 2001.

[26] HP. Data sheet: Hp proliant m800 server cartridge, 2014.

[27] Intel. Product brief: Intel ixp425 network processor. `ftp://download.intel.com/design/network/ProdBrf/27905105.pdf`, 2006.

[28] Intel. Intel xeon processor e5-1600/e5-2600/e5-4600 v2 product families, 2014.

[29] T. Jiang, Q. Zhang, R. Hou, L. Chai, S. Mckee, Z. Jia, and N. Sun. Understanding the behavior of in-memory computing workloads. In *Workload Characterization (IISWC), 2014 IEEE International Symposium on*, pages 22–30, Oct 2014.

[30] A. Jog, E. Bolotin, Z. Guz, M. Parker, S. W. Keckler, M. T. Kandemir, and C. R. Das. Application-aware memory system for fair and efficient execution of concurrent gpgpu applications. In *Proceedings of Workshop on General Purpose Processing Using GPUs*, pages 1:1–1:8, 2014.

[31] S. Kaestle, R. Achermann, T. Roscoe, and T. Harris. Shoal: Smart allocation and replication of memory for parallel programs. In *2015 USENIX Annual Technical Conference (USENIX ATC 15)*, pages 263–276, July 2015.

[32] R. Lachaize, B. Lepers, and V. Quéma. Memprof: A memory profiler for numa multicore systems. In *Proc. of the 2012 USENIX Annual Technical Conference (USENIX ATC 12)*, pages 53–64, 2012.

[33] C. Lameter. Local and remote memory: Memory in a linux/numa system. In *Linux Symposium*, 2006.

[34] J. Lemon. Kqueue-a generic and scalable event notification facility. In *USENIX Annual Technical Conference, FREENIX Track*, pages 141–153, 2001.

[35] B. Lepers, V. Quema, and A. Fedorova. Thread and memory placement on numa systems: Asymmetry matters. In *2015 USENIX Annual Technical Conference (USENIX ATC 15)*, pages 277–289, July 2015.

[36] C. Li, Y. Yang, Z. Lin, and H. Zhou. Automatic data placement into gpu on-chip memory resources. In *Code Generation and Optimization (CGO), 2015 IEEE/ACM International Symposium on*, pages 23–33, Feb 2015.

[37] Linaro. Numa support for arm. `https://wiki.linaro.org/LEG/Engineering/Kernel/NUMA`, 2013.

[38] X. Liu and J. Mellor-Crummey. A tool to analyze the performance of multithreaded programs on NUMA architectures. In *Proceedings of the 19th ACM SIGPLAN Symposium on Principles and Practice of Parallel Programming*, pages 259–272, 2014.

[39] X. Liu and J. M. Mellor-Crummey. A data-centric profiler for parallel programs. In *Proc. of the 2013 ACM/IEEE Conference on Supercomputing*, 2013.

[40] G. H. Loh and M. D. Hill. Efficiently enabling conventional block sizes for very large die-stacked dram caches. In *Proceedings of the 44th Annual IEEE/ACM International Symposium on Microarchitecture*, pages 454–464, 2011.

[41] P. Machanick, P. Salverda, and L. Pompe. Hardware-software trade-offs in a direct rambus implementation of the rampage memory hierarchy. In *Proceedings of the Eighth International Conference on Architectural Support for Programming Languages and Operating Systems*, pages 105–114, 1998.

[42] T. Maeurer and D. Shippy. Introduction to the cell multiprocessor. *IBM journal of Research and Development*, 49(4):589–604, 2005.

[43] J. D. McCalpin. Memory bandwidth and machine balance in current high performance computers. *IEEE Computer Society Technical Committee on Computer Architecture (TCCA) Newsletter*, pages 19–25, Dec. 1995.

[44] R. McIlroy, P. Dickman, and J. Sventek. Efficient dynamic heap allocation of scratch-pad memory. In *Proceedings of the 7th International Symposium on Memory Management*, pages 31–40, 2008.

[45] M. Meswani, S. Blagodurov, D. Roberts, J. Slice, M. Ignatowski, and G. Loh. Heterogeneous memory architectures: A hw/sw approach for mixing die-stacked and off-package memories. In *High Performance Computer Architecture (HPCA), 2015 IEEE 21st International Symposium on*, pages 126–136, Feb 2015.

[46] M. Meswani, G. Loh, S. Blagodurov, D. Roberts, J. Slice, and M. Ignatowski. Toward efficient programmer-managed two-level memory hierarchies in exascale computers. In *Hardware-Software Co-Design for High Performance Computing (Co-HPC), 2014*, pages 9–16, Nov 2014.

[47] M. M. Michael and M. L. Scott. Nonblocking algorithms and preemption-safe locking on multiprogrammed shared memory multiprocessors. *J. Parallel Distrib. Comput.*, 51(1):1–26, May 1998.

[48] J. C. Mogul and K. K. Ramakrishnan. Eliminating receive livelock in an interrupt-driven kernel. *ACM Trans. Comput. Syst.*, 15(3):217–252, Aug. 1997.

[49] D. D. Neteworks. Ddn solution brief – accelerate seismic processing. `http://www.ddn.com/pdfs/SeismicProcessing_SolutionBrief.pdf`, 2013.

[50] A. Pena and P. Balaji. Toward the efficient use of multiple explicitly managed memory subsystems. In *Cluster Computing (CLUSTER), 2014 IEEE International Conference on*, pages 123–131, Sept 2014.

[51] G. Piccoli, H. N. Santos, R. E. Rodrigues, C. Pousa, E. Borin, and F. M. Quintão Pereira. Compiler support for selective page migration in numa architectures. In *Proceedings of the 23rd International Conference on Parallel Architectures and Compilation*, pages 369–380, 2014.

[52] L. E. Ramos, E. Gorbatov, and R. Bianchini. Page placement in hybrid memory systems. In *Proceedings of the International Conference on Supercomputing*, pages 85–95, 2011.

[53] L. Rizzo. netmap: A novel framework for fast packet i/o. In *USENIX Annual Technical Conference*, pages 101–112, 2012.

[54] J. Sim, A. Alameldeen, Z. Chishti, C. Wilkerson, and H. Kim. Transparent hardware management of stacked dram as part of memory. In *Microarchitecture (MICRO), 2014 47th Annual IEEE/ACM International Symposium on*, pages 13–24, Dec 2014.

[55] L. Soares and M. Stumm. Flexsc: Flexible system call scheduling with exception-less system calls. In *Proc. USENIX Conf. Operating Systems Design and Implementation (OSDI)*, pages 1–8, 2010.

[56] S. Steinke, L. Wehmeyer, B.-S. Lee, and P. Marwedel. Assigning program and data objects to scratchpad for energy reduction. In *Design, Automation and Test in Europe Conference and Exhibition, 2002. Proceedings*, pages 409–415, 2002.

[57] H. Sundell and P. Tsigas. Lock-free and practical doubly linked list-based deques using single-word compare-and-swap. In *Principles of Distributed Systems*, volume 3544 of

Lecture Notes in Computer Science, pages 240–255. Springer Berlin Heidelberg, 2005.

[58] Texas Instruments. Enhanced dma (edma3) controller. literature no.: Spruel2b, 2009.

[59] Texas Instruments. Multicore DSP+ARM KeyStone II System-on-Chip (SoC), 2013.

[60] Texas Instruments. Cmem overview. `http://processors.wiki.ti.com/index.php/CMEM_Overview`, 2014.

[61] L. Wang, J. Zhan, C. Luo, Y. Zhu, Q. Yang, Y. He, W. Gao, Z. Jia, Y. Shi, S. Zhang, C. Zheng, G. Lu, K. Zhan, X. Li, and B. Qiu. Bigdatabench: A big data benchmark suite from internet services. In *High Performance Computer Architecture (HPCA), 2014 IEEE 20th International Symposium on*, pages 488–499, Feb 2014.

NVWAL: Exploiting NVRAM in Write-Ahead Logging

Wook-Hee Kim, Jinwoong Kim, Woongki Baek, Beomseok Nam, Youjip Won

Ulsan National Institute of Science and Technology (UNIST)
{okie90,jwkim,wbaek,bsnam}@unist.ac.kr

Hanyang University
yjwon@hanyang.ac.kr

Abstract

Emerging byte-addressable non-volatile memory is considered an alternative storage device for database logs that require persistency and high performance. In this work, we develop *NVWAL* (NVRAM Write-Ahead Logging) for SQLite. The proposed NVWAL is designed to exploit byte-addressable NVRAM to maintain the write-ahead log and to guarantee the failure atomicity and the durability of a database transaction. The contribution of NVWAL consists of three elements: (i) byte-granularity differential logging that effectively eliminates the excessive I/O overhead of filesystem-based logging or journaling, (ii) transaction-aware lazy synchronization that reduces cache synchronization overhead by two-thirds, and (iii) user-level heap management of the NVRAM persistent WAL structure, which reduces the overhead of managing persistent objects.

We implemented NVWAL in SQLite and measured the performance on a Nexus 5 smartphone and an NVRAM emulation board - Tuna. Our performance study shows the following: (i) the overhead of enforcing strict ordering of NVRAM writes can be reduced via NVRAM-aware transaction management. (ii) From the application performance point of view, the overhead of guaranteeing failure atomicity is negligible; the cache line flush overhead accounts for only 0.8∼4.6% of transaction execution time. Therefore, application performance is much less sensitive to the NVRAM performance than we expected. Decreasing the NVRAM latency by one-fifth (from 1942 nsec to 437 nsec), SQLite achieves a mere 4% performance gain (from 2517 ins/sec to 2621 ins/sec). (iii) Overall, when the write latency of NVRAM is 2 usec, NVWAL increases SQLite performance by at least 10x compared to that of WAL on flash memory (from 541 ins/sec to 5812 ins/sec).

ASPLOS '16, April 2–6, 2016, Atlanta, Georgia, USA

DOI: http://dx.doi.org/10.1145/2872362.2872392

Categories and Subject Descriptors H.2.7 [*Database Management*]:Logging and recovery

Keywords Write-ahead-logging; Non-volatile memory

1. Introduction

In the era of mobile computing, SQLite [3] is arguably the most widely deployed relational database management system because Android devices extensively use it to persistently manage application data for a wide range of apps such as contact managers, Twitter, and even web browsers. Due to its serverlessness, compactness, and the ability to form an integral part of a program, SQLite has become a core component of the Android software stack.

Despite its popularity, SQLite is far from being satisfactory in terms of efficiently exploiting the underlying hardware resources, mainly because the EXT4 filesystem journals the database journaling operation [17, 21, 23, 33, 38]. Beginning with SQLite 3.7, write-ahead logging (WAL) has become available as an alternative option to rollback journal modes. The WAL recovery scheme is designed in such a way that any update operation to a database page has to first be recorded in a permanent log file. WAL significantly improves the performance of SQLite because WAL needs fewer `fsync()` calls as it modifies a single log file instead of two, i.e., a database file and a rollback journal file [23]. However logging a single database transaction in SQLite WAL mode still entails at least 16 KBytes I/O traffic to underlying storage mainly due to metadata journaling overhead in the EXT4 file system [23].

The recent advances of byte-addressable NVRAM (Non-Volatile RAM) open up a new opportunity to reduce the high latency of NAND flash memory and the I/O overhead of block granularity journaling [10, 14, 35, 37, 41, 43]. As the log file is often much smaller than the database file and is accessed very frequently, high performance NVRAM is considered to be a promising alternative storage device for write-ahead logs. First, NVRAM can be used as a disk replacement; each page in a log file can be flushed to the NVRAM file system with low latency using a legacy block device I/O interface [15, 18, 22]. Alternatively, in order to take advantage of the fine granularity of byte-addressable

NVRAM, each log record in a transaction can be stored in NVRAM as a persistent object [15, 36].

In this work, we take the latter approach and implement write-ahead logging for NVRAM (*NVWAL*) in SQLite. Our implementation of NVWAL allows reordering of memory write operations and minimizes the overhead of the cache line flush via byte-granularity differential logging. In addition, NVWAL reduces the overhead required to manage persistent objects via user-level heap management, while guaranteeing the failure atomicity. NVWAL is not a completely novel logging data structure, but it orchestrates SQLite, the OS persistent heap manager, and NVRAM layers to effectively leverage high performance NVRAM.

Over the past decades, processor design for volatile memory has evolved. Modern processors often do not preserve the ordering of memory write operations unless a memory barrier instruction is explicitly invoked. However, NVRAM must constrain the ordering of write operations to ensure correct recovery from system failures [37]. In order to avoid limiting NVRAM write concurrency and improve write throughput, several memory persistency models are being considered for emerging NVRAM technologies [37]. Assuming one of these NVRAM persistency models, NVRAM heap managers such as NV-Heaps [9] and Heapo [16], and NVRAM file systems such as SCMFS [46], PMFS [11], and BPFS [10] have been proposed. Using these NVRAM file systems or NVRAM heap managers, applications can deal with the ordering issues of NVRAM writes.

Database write-ahead logging does not have to strictly enforce the ordering of memory write operations as long as it guarantees that a commit flag is flushed only after all the dirty records are logged in WAL. Therefore, the proposed NVWAL does not call cache line flush instructions per log entry, but delays calling them in a lazy manner in order to reduce the overhead of the cache line flush by 1/3x.

It has been reported that flushing cached data to NVRAM can be extremely costly, especially when applications frequently call cache flush operations [47]. However, our performance study shows that the cost of data persistence in SQLite is no higher than 4.6% of query execution time, and the cost ratio even decreases when we insert a larger number of records in a transaction. SQLite throughput is governed both by I/O performance and by CPU performance. CPU overhead accounts for a dominant fraction of the transaction processing time. I/O constitutes about 30% of query processing time when SQLite WAL is stored in slow storage [23]. However, when the WAL is stored in fast devices such as NVRAM, the I/O overhead becomes much less significant than when the WAL log is located in the slow block device and when it is maintained through the expensive filesystem interface.

The main contributions of this work are as follows.

- **Byte-granularity differential logging**
  In stock SQLite WAL mode, write-ahead logging stores an entire B-tree page in a log file. In order to reduce the I/O overhead of SQLite logging on NVRAM, our NVWAL writes only the dirty portion of a B-tree page, so as to take advantage of the byte-addressability of NVRAM.
- **Transaction-aware memory persistency guarantee**
  In order to persist memory writes and to prevent incorrect reordering of the memory writes, cache line flush instructions and memory barriers must be called properly. We develop a transaction-aware persistency guarantee via *lazy synchronization*, which guarantees the atomicity and the durability of the database. This transaction-aware memory persistency guarantee enforces the persist order only between a set of log-write operations and the commit operation. It eliminates the unnecessary overhead of enforcing memory write ordering constraints.
- **User-level NVRAM management for WAL**
  The NVWAL structure is designed to minimize the overhead of managing non-volatile memory objects. Allocating and deallocating non-volatile memory blocks using a kernel-level NVRAM heap manager has high overhead due to ensuring consistency in the presence of failures. In order to avoid such overhead, we pre-allocate a large NVRAM block and manage the user-level heap inside the block where we store multiple WAL frames. The user-level NVRAM management helps reduce the number of expensive system calls to the NVRAM heap manager interface.
- **Effect of NVRAM latency on application performance**
  We observe that database transactions are less sensitive to NVRAM latency than expected. This is because the I/O overhead does not account for a large fraction of transaction execution time. In addition, we reduce the overhead of guaranteeing the failure atomicity via NVWAL. Consequently, we make the performance of SQLite more insensitive to NVRAM latency. This result holds a profound implication for NVRAM and CPU manufacturers because they need to invent and improve non-volatile material compounds and architectures to meet the expected application performance [34].

Combining all these elements, NVWAL on NVRAM yields transaction throughput 10x higher than that of WAL on flash memory (541 ins/sec vs. 5812 ins/sec).

The rest of the paper is organized as follows: In section 2, we briefly discuss the background. In section 3, we present our design and implementation of NVWAL on SQLite. In section 4, we discuss how the transaction-aware memory persistency guarantee can enforce minimal ordering of NVRAM write operations while guaranteeing durability and failure atomicity. Section 5 provides the performance results and analysis. In section 6, we discuss other research efforts related to this study. We conclude the paper in section 7.

2. Background: Write-Ahead Logging

In database systems, transactions make modifications to copies of database pages in volatile buffer cache memory and write the dirty pages to persistent storage when the transactions commit. In SQLite write-ahead logging (WAL) mode, the dirty pages are appended to a separate log file and the original pages remain intact in the database file. If a system crashes before a transaction commits or if a transaction aborts, dirty pages written by the aborted transaction can be simply ignored by the WAL recovery process because the original pages are available in the database file.

In WAL mode, the checkpointing process periodically batches the dirty pages in the log to the database file. When all the dirty pages in the log are written and checkpointed to the database file, the log is truncated so that it does not grow infinitely. Checkpointing occurs whenever all database sessions are closed or the number of log entries reaches the predefined limit (1000 pages in SQLite).

Write-ahead logging on block device storage guarantees the *atomicity* and *durability* of transaction commits and the ordering of transaction commits via `fsync()` system calls. In SQLite, a transaction commit mark is stored in the log frame header of the last appended dirty page, and the dirty pages and their checksum bytes are flushed to block device storage all together by `fsync()` system call. The order of transaction commits is guaranteed in SQLite by enforcing the commit marks of transactions, which are appended to the log file in the order of the commits. Because the commit mark and the dirty pages are flushed by the same `fsync()` system call in SQLite, SQLite is subject to the latent system failure issues pointed out by [48]. However, resolution of these problems lies beyond the scope of this paper.

3. NVWAL: Design and Implementation

For the past several decades, memory technologies have evolved rapidly and now non-volatile memory devices such as phase-change RAM (PCRAM) and spin-transfer torque (STT) MRAM promise large capacity, high performance, low power consumption, and unlimited endurance. STT-MRAM is expected to meet the requirements of various computing domains because its performance is expected to be within an order of magnitude of that of DRAM [10, 11, 37].

However, as the price of NVRAM is not likely to be as low as that of flash memory, it is hard to expect that NVRAM will replace flash memory in the near future. On the other hand, it can also be inferred that NVRAM will not replace volatile DRAM without major changes in the software stack: volatility of memory is inevitable in current software and hardware design because system errors will be permanent if everything is non-volatile [6]. Therefore, we design and implement an SQLite write-ahead logging scheme for a system that has NVRAM along with DRAM and block device storage, as illustrated in Figure 1(b).

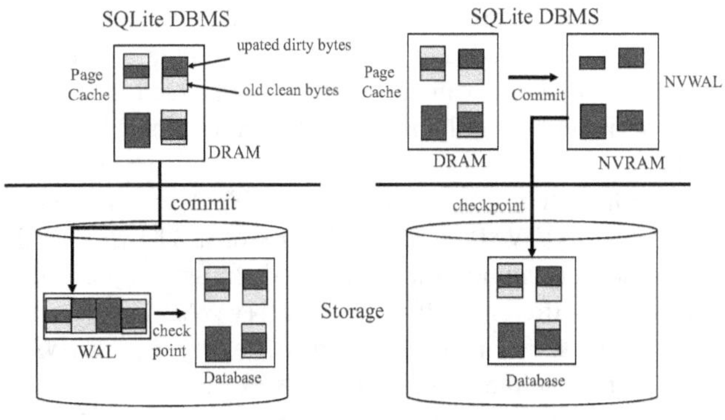

(a) Write-Ahead Logging (b) NVWAL

Figure 1: Write-Ahead Logging in NVRAM

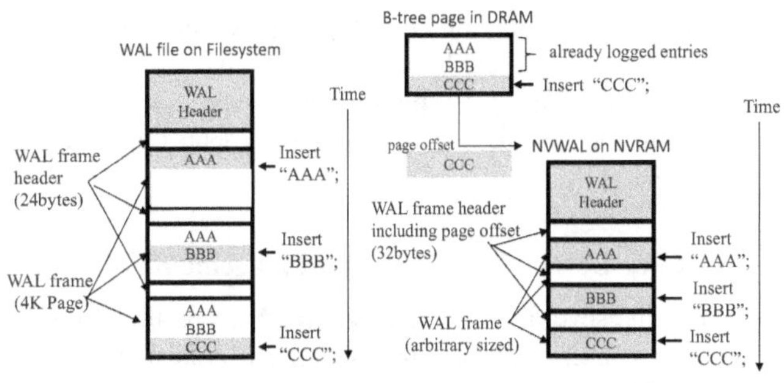

(a) Write-Ahead Logging in SQLite (b) Byte Addressable Differential Logging

Figure 2: Byte Granularity Differential Logging

3.1 Write-Ahead Logging on NVRAM

A fair number of studies have proposed to store the database transaction logs in NVRAM [5, 8, 15, 42, 44]. When a transaction commits, the updated pages are either synchronized to a database file in journaling modes, or appended to a log file in WAL mode. Because transactions in WAL mode do not directly update the database file but buffer the frequent small updates in the write-ahead logs, storing write-ahead logs in high performance NVRAM can replace expensive block I/O traffic with lightweight memory write instructions; such a setup can take advantage of the byte-addressability of NVRAM as well. Figure 1(a) shows how NVRAM can be leveraged to accelerate database transactions.

3.2 Byte Granularity Differential Logging in NVWAL

In SQLite, write-ahead logging is designed to work with block device storage systems. It flushes an entire B-tree page (4 KBytes in normal SQLite configuration) to a WAL log file no matter how small a portion of the page is dirty. The size of the B-tree is aligned with the filesystem block size to avoid read-modify-write and torn-write problems in databases and file systems [31]. In most cases, a single database transaction yields changes in a small fraction of a B-tree page and leaves most of the contents of the B-tree page intact. In NVWAL, we exploit the byte-addressability of NVRAM and employ byte-granularity *differential logging* (also often referred to as *delta encoding*), which has been widely used in various systems including flash memory database systems [4, 13, 26, 28].

As illustrated in Figure 2(b), the NVWAL structure consists of an NVWAL header and pairs of a 32 bytes WAL frame header and arbitrary-sized WAL frames (log entries) created by differential logging. The NVWAL header contains database file metadata as in the legacy SQLite WAL header and a pointer to the available space for the next WAL frame to be stored (*next_frame*). Each WAL frame header consists of a commit flag, a checkpointing id number, a database page number, an in-page offset, a frame size, and checksum bytes for the WAL frame. For each WAL frame, we identify which portion of the B-tree page is dirty and truncate the preceding and trailing clean regions so that only the dirty portions of the B-tree page are flushed to NVRAM, as shown in Figure 2. By minimizing the memory copy, we can avoid the unnecessary overhead of cache line flush instructions.

3.3 User-Level NVRAM Heap Management

There exist several well-designed proposals on how to manage non-volatile memory pages under a persistent namespace and how to map the pages to application processes [9, 35, 41, 43, 46]. BPFS [10] is a transactional file system for NVRAM. NV-Heap [9] and Heapo [16] are heap-based persistent object stores that allow programmers to implement in-memory data structures without difficult reasoning about thread safety, atomicity, or memory access ordering.

For NVWAL, we employed Heapo [1] as our NVRAM heap manager so that (i) SQLite can map NVRAM to its address spaces, (ii) a non-volatile memory page can be identified by a persistent namespace and its address even when system reboots, and (iii) the NVRAM pages can be protected by access permission as in the file system. It should be noted that Heapo does not enforce memory persistency; the applications are responsible for properly adopting a persist barrier, memory barrier, and cache line flush to guarantee the failure atomicity.

System call is expensive. It crosses the protection boundary and the parameters are copied. The system call overhead becomes even more expensive if we rely on a kernel when allocating and deallocating NVRAM pages. Thus, we develop a user-level heap management scheme for NVWAL. This scheme allows us to manage the log at the user level and to minimize the system call interference. Instead of relying on a kernel feature to protect an object against corruption and against the race condition, we implement a simple tri-state flag for each NVRAM block, i.e., *free*, *in-use*, and *pending*.

```
input: WalHeader wh, PagePtr p, bool commit
while p do
    available_space = wh.getAvailableSpace() ;
    dirty_frame = compute_WAL_frame(p) ;
    if available_space < dirty_frame.size then
        /* get an nvram block in pending mode */
        block=nv_pre_malloc(BLOCK_SZ) ;
        ptr = wh.add_new_block(block) ;
        dmb(); /* data memory barrier */
        cache_line_flush(ptr,ptr+sizeof(void*)) ;
        dmb(); /* data memory barrier */
        persist_barrier() ;
        /* mark in-use flag of nvram block */
        nv_malloc_set_used_flag(block) ;
    end
    next_nv_frame = wh.next_frame ;
    /* store a dirty WAL frame in NVRAM */
    memcpy(next_nv_frame, dirty_frame, ..) ;
    nvFramePtrList.add(next_nv_frame) ;
    p=p.next ;
end
f=nvFramePtrList.first() ;
dmb() ; /* data memory barrier */
while f do
    cache_line_flush(f,f+f.header.frame_size) ;
    f=nvFramePtrList.next() ;
end
dmb(); /* data memory barrier */
persist_barrier() ;
if commit==true then
    lastFrame = nvFramePtrList.last() ;
    lastFrame.commitMark |= COMMIT ;
    dmb() ;
    cache_line_flush(lastFrame.commitMark,...);
    dmb() ;
    persist_barrier() ;
end
```

Algorithm 1: `sqliteWriteWalFramesToNVRAM()`

To enable user level heap management, we implemented `nv_pre_malloc()` and `nv_malloc_set_used_flag()` system calls on top of Heapo so that the system could manage the status of the allocated NVRAM blocks. `nv_pre_malloc()` allocates a set of NVRAM pages that occupy a consecutive address space, maps them to a fraction of the virtual address space of a process, and sets the status of the block to *pending*. When NVWAL persistently saves the address of a newly allocated NVRAM block in another NVRAM block as in a linked list, it calls `nv_malloc_set_used_flag()` to change its status from

[1] Heapo is available at https://github.com/ESOS-Lab/HEAPO

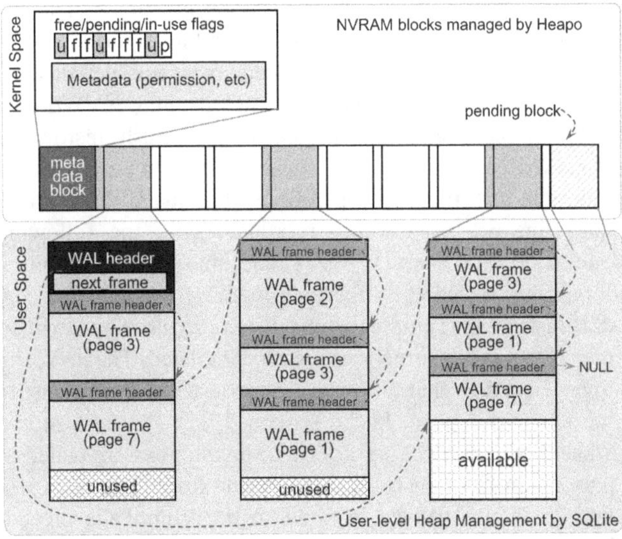

Figure 3: NVRAM Block Management in NVWAL

pending to *in-use*. If the system crashes while an NVRAM block is still in *pending* status, the SQLite NVWAL recovery process can safely deallocate the block.

Algorithm 1 shows how NVWAL allocates and manages NVRAM blocks. Figure 3 illustrates an example of NVWAL block management. The NVWAL heap consists of a metadata block and a set of pages from NVRAM. The metadata block contains the permission and the state of each block: free, pending or in-use.

In the example shown in Figure 3, if a transaction commits a new dirty page p, SQLite searches for page p's WAL frame in the write-ahead log. If page p's WAL frame is not in the log, the entire page p and its WAL frame header are copied to the available space of the last NVRAM block in the linked list if they fit. If the available space in the last NVRAM block is not large enough to hold them, we allocate another NVRAM block from Heapo, add the block to the linked list of NVRAM blocks, set the status of the block to *in-use*, and store the dirty WAL frame and its header in the newly allocated NVRAM block. If page p's WAL frames are found in the log, the differences between the page and the WAL frame are computed to construct a small WAL frame, as described in section 3.2; the small differential log entry is stored as a WAL frame in the NVRAM log. With the pre-allocated large NVRAM block, NVWAL reduces the number of calls to the expensive NVRAM heap manager's `nvmalloc()`. In the experiments we will describe in section 5, each NVRAM block stores 4.9 WAL frames on average when we fix the size of each NVRAM block to 8 KBytes.

4. Transaction-Aware Memory Persistency Guarantee

When NVRAM is used to replace block device storage, the atomicity and the durability of the database transactions

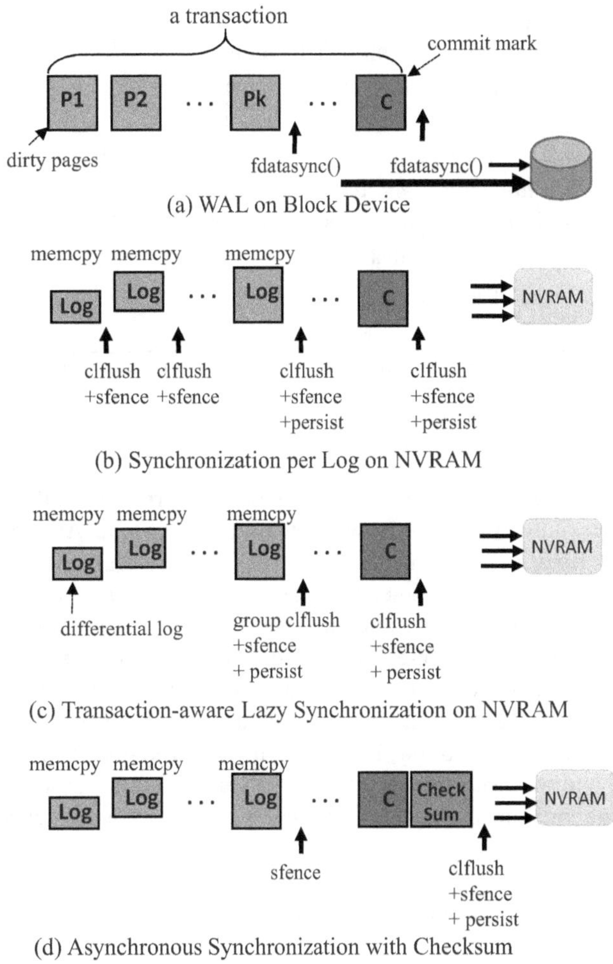

Figure 4: Transaction-Aware Persistency Guarantee

must be ensured in the memory operations. NVWAL requires that we explicitly flush the appropriate cache lines to NVRAM to enforce the ordering constraints. The WAL recovery algorithm is based on the assumption that log entries are stored in the order of database transactions. Unfortunately, memory write operations can be arbitrarily reordered in today's processor designs. Without the hardware support `sfence` or `mfence` alone cannot guarantee the propagating of memory writes to NVRAM because writes can be cached in L1 or L2 caches. In order to guarantee that memory write operations flush data all the way down to NVRAM, cache line flush operations such as `clflush` should accompany `persist barrier` instructions such as Intel's `PCOMMIT`, as shown in Figure 4(b). `Persist barrier` ensures that the cache lines queued in the memory subsystem are persisted in NVRAM. Otherwise, a commit mark can be written to NVRAM before log entries are stored.

In X86 processors, `clflush` instruction invalidates and flushes a cache line from the memory cache hierarchy. In the ARM v7 architecture, there exist two cache flush in-

```
input: u32 start, u32 end
u32 lineLen = getCachelineLen();
/* Align start to cache line boundary*/
start = start & ~(lineLen - 1);
u32 mva = start;
while mva < end do
    /* clean data cache line to PoC by MVA */
    dccmvac(mva) ;
    mva = mva + lineLen ;
end
```

Algorithm 2: cache_line_flush() system call for ARM v7

structions: `dccimvac` and `dccmvac`. The former invalidates the flushed cachelines while the latter does not. Android 4.4 has not implemented the `clflush()` system call. For NVWAL, we implemented a `cache_line_flush()` system call using a `dccmvac` instruction, as shown in Algorithm 2. `cache_line_flush()` calls `dccmvac` instead of `dccimvac` because write-ahead logging in SQLite does not, indeed, need cache invalidation due to its append-only nature. We implemented `cache_line_flush()` as a system call despite the overhead of the kernel mode switch because the `dccmvac` instruction needs to access register 15 in privileged mode.

4.1 Transaction-Aware Memory Persistency Guarantee

We exploit the ordering and persistency constraints in write-ahead logging and develop a transaction-aware memory persistency guarantee scheme. The idea is simple and straightforward. A log-commit operation consists of two phases: (i) logging: writing a sequence of logs to NVRAM and (ii) commit: putting the commit mark to NVRAM to validate the logs. We enforce the ordering and persistency guarantee requirement only between the two phases by calling the expensive `clflush`, `sfence`, and `persist barrier`. The reason behind this is that the ordering of writing WAL frames does not necessarily have to be preserved as long as a transaction's commit mark is written after all the WAL frames are written to NVRAM. It should be noted that (i) SQLite is a serverless DBMS that does not allow multiple write transactions to run concurrently and (ii) a write transaction requires an exclusive lock on the entire database file.

Under a transaction-aware memory persistency guarantee, so that the processors can better utilize caches and memory banks, NVWAL allows processors to flush the WAL frames to NVRAM in any order. That is, NVWAL separates the phase in which the logs are being copied to NVRAM (`memcpy()`) and the phase in which the respective logs are synchronized to NVRAM (`cache_line_flush(p)`). Figure 4(c) schematically illustrates the behavior of the transaction-aware memory persistency guarantee. The details of the implementation can be found in Algorithm 1.

There are a few implementation specific issues that deserve further elaboration. We implemented NVWAL in ARM based platform. The cache line flush instruction in an ARM, `dccmvac`, is non-blocking. In order to ensure that the memory operations that mark the commit flag (line 30–34) are not reordered with the following `cache_line_flush()`, the cache line flush instruction should be preceded by the data memory barrier, `dmb`. The `dmb` instruction completes only when any previous explicit memory access instructions are all completed. The `dmb()` in line 22 ensures that all WAL frames are written at least to the L1 or L2 cache. In the proposed *lazy synchronization*, a batch of non-blocking `dccmvac` instructions are called in line 23–26 in order to flush the cache lines. The `dmb()` in line 27 is also needed in order to block until the preceding `cache_line_flush()` flushes all the WAL frames to NVRAM. `dmb()` in line 32 also ensures that the memory operation that marks the commit flag is not reordered with `cache_line_flush()`.

The commit mark resides at the WAL frame header and is one bit long. As in a prior work [10], we assume that NVRAM devices guarantee atomic writes for 8 bytes. This means that even if a random power failure occurs, capacitors in DIMM guarantee no corruption of 8 bytes. Because the commit mark is just a bit flag, the commit mark can be safely flushed to NVRAM with 8 bytes padding. If atomic writes can be done in the unit of a cache line, as in [35], cache line padding is necessary to prevent `cache_line_flush()` from flushing an unintended memory region.

4.2 Asynchronous Commit

We can further allow processors to utilize caches and memory banks by compromising the consistency using checksum bytes. Under this mechanism, we do not explicitly enforce the barrier between the logging phase and the commit phase. Instead, we compute the checksum of the logs that must precede the commit mark and store the checksum along with the commit mark. Figure 4(d) illustrates NVWAL with asynchronous log-commit; NVWAL asynchronously writes log entries, a commit mark, and checksum bytes without calling the cache line flush instructions.

Suppose a system crashes after it flushes a commit mark and checksum bytes but before all log entries are written to NVRAM. In the recovery phase, the checksum bytes will be found to be inconsistent with the written log entries and this will invalidate the commit mark of the transaction. Thus, the database recovery process can consider that the transaction has been aborted. However there is a chance that the written checksum bytes accidentally match the unwritten log entries. Hence, although the chance is very low, a system crash may corrupt a database file. We consider this asynchronous synchronization NVWAL as a performance comparison target because it minimizes the overhead of enforcing memory constraints.

4.3 Checkpointing and Crash Recovery

In WAL, the committed dirty pages in NVRAM are written back to the original database file in block device storage via periodic checkpointing. In NVWAL, we reconstruct the dirty pages by combining the log entries in the NVWAL log and the respective original database pages. When all the dirty pages are flushed to the database file via `fsync()`, the NVRAM blocks for the write-ahead logs can be safely truncated from the end of the list to the beginning. For each NVRAM block, we first set the tri-state flag of the NVRAM block to *free* and then call Heapo's `nvfree()` system call.

In SQLite WAL mode, the log file contains a complete history of dirty pages committed by transactions. When a system crashes, SQLite can recover the transactions by replaying the logs. The recovery algorithm of NVWAL is not very different from SQLite's stock recovery algorithm except that the dirty pages are reconstructed from byte-addressable WAL frames. However, complications can arise if the system crashes while updating the metadata of the NVRAM blocks.

NVWAL is for a forth-coming architecture, which is not available yet. Without a persist barrier, we are unable to perform a physical power-off test for NVWAL because `clflush` and the emulated persist barrier do not guarantee the failure atomicity. Instead, we resort to discussing the NVRAM recovery algorithm under various failure cases that can occur while a transaction is executing `sqliteWriteWalFramesToNVRAM()`.

- If a system fails while allocating an NVRAM block (line 6 of Algorithm 1), the allocated NVRAM block is marked as *pending*, but SQLite may not have written its reference in another persistent NVRAM block. When the system recovers, the heap manager can reclaim any pending NVRAM blocks to prevent a memory leak.
- If a system crashes after an NVRAM reference was stored in the WAL header but before the block was marked as in-use, the SQLite recovery process will find that the block was freed by the NVRAM heap manager's recovery process and the block's reference can be safely deleted.
- If system crashes while copying a dirty WAL frame to NVRAM using `memcpy()` (line 22 of Algorithm 1), SQLite can easily recover from the failure because the frame's transaction has not written a commit mark, thus the transaction is considered to have been aborted. In database transactions, writing a commit mark is the last operation of the transaction commit process.
- Recovery from checkpointing process' failure is also trivial and not different from legacy checkpointing recovery. Because the write-ahead logs will not be deleted before all the dirty pages are persistently stored in the database file, the SQLite recovery process can simply replay the checkpointing process to recover from the failure.

4.4 NVWAL and Persistency Model

In this section, we briefly discuss NVWAL implementation for strict and relaxed persistency models.

Memory persistency, proposed by Pelley et al [37], is a framework that provides an interface for enforcing the ordering constraints on NVRAM writes. The ordering constraints are referred to as "persists" to distinguish them from regular writes to the volatile memory [37]. Similar to memory consistency, memory persistency is largely classified into two classes – *strict persistency* and *relaxed persistency*.

Strict persistency integrates memory persistency into the memory consistency [37]. Under strict persistency, persist order must match the volatile memory order specified by the memory consistency model. Strict persistency is a simple and intuitive model in the sense that it provides a unified framework to reason about possible volatile memory and persist orders. In addition, it requires no additional persist barriers because the existing memory barriers can be used to specify persist ordering constraints. Strict persistency, however, may significantly limit persist performance because it enforces strict ordering constraints between persist operations.

In contrast, relaxed persistency decouples the memory consistency and persistency models [37]. Under relaxed persistency, persist order may deviate from the volatile memory order specified by the memory consistency model. Relaxed persistency requires persist barriers to enforce the order of persist operations. A representative relaxed persistency model is *epoch persistency* [10, 37]. In epoch persistency, persist barriers are used to divide persist operations into different persist epochs. Persist barriers ensure that all the persists before the barrier occur strictly before any persist after the barrier. Persists in the same epoch, however, are allowed to concurrently execute, potentially improving persist performance. A major disadvantage of relaxed persistency is the increased programming complexity; programmers must correctly annotate their code using the two types of barriers (i.e., memory and persist barriers).

With memory persistency, it is the responsibility of the underlying hardware to enforce the ordering constraints of NVRAM writes specified in the (annotated) code. Therefore, no extra code is required to explicitly flush appropriate cache lines to NVRAM, easing the programmer's burden.

Strict persistency significantly simplifies the NVWAL implementation shown in Algorithm 1 because all the cache-flush operations and persist barriers can be safely removed. However, we conjecture that strict persistency may degrade the performance of NVWAL because it enforces strict (but unnecessary) ordering constraints between persists when writing the log entries to NVRAM.

Relaxed persistency simplifies the NVWAL implementation shown in Algorithm 1 because all the cache-flush oper-

# of insertion per txn	1	2	4	8	16	32
# of cache line flushes	139.49	153.32	181.224	236.52	349.168	574.464

Table 1: Average number of cache line flushes per transaction for the experiments shown in Figure 5

ations can be safely removed. We expect that relaxed persistency, because it can dynamically reorder persist operations when copying the WAL frames from DRAM to NVRAM, will induce a level of performance for NVWAL higher than that possible when using strict persistency. Due to the unavailability of real hardware that can implement strict and relaxed persistency, we leave a performance evaluation of NVWAL under various memory persistency models to our future work.

5. Experiments

We implemented NVWAL in SQLite 3.7.11 and integrated it with an NVRAM heap manager - *Heapo* [16]. We first measure the performance of NVWAL using a *Tuna* NVRAM emulation board [2, 29].

Tuna is an NVRAM emulation board with Xilinx Zynq XC7Z020 ARM-FPGA SoC. The Tuna board consists of an ARM Cortex-A9 processor with L2 caches and FPGA programmable logic that controls the read/write latency of one of the two DRAMs in order to emulate NVRAM. The emulated NVRAM has a separate power switch for non-volatility emulation. The frequency of the emulated NVRAM is 400MHz (DDR3-800) while that of the volatile DRAM is 533MHz (DDR3-1066); the data width of the emulated NVRAM is 64 bits while that of DRAM is 32 bits. The size of the cache line is 32 bytes. The write latency of the emulated NVRAM can be adjusted between 400 nsec and 2000 nsec.

5.1 Overhead of Ordering Constraints

First, we quantify the overhead of enforcing the ordering constraints in SQLite write-ahead logging. In the configuration denoted as *E* (eager synchronization), we make SQLite write-ahead logging call `cache_line_flush()` system call and memory barrier immediately after each `memcpy()` function call per log entry as illustrated in Figure 4(b). In the other configuration, denoted as *L* (lazy synchronization), SQLite calls a batch of `cache_line_flush()` system calls for all the dirty log entries in a transaction right before its commit mark is stored, as illustrated in Figure 4(c).

We run the experiments on a Tuna NVRAM emulation board and set the write latency of the NVRAM to 500 nsec as in [37]. Figure 5 shows the benefits of lazy synchronization. As we insert more records into the database table in a single transaction, more dirty bytes are written to NVRAM and the time spent for memory writes increases. Table 1 shows how many cache lines are flushed per transaction (the number of

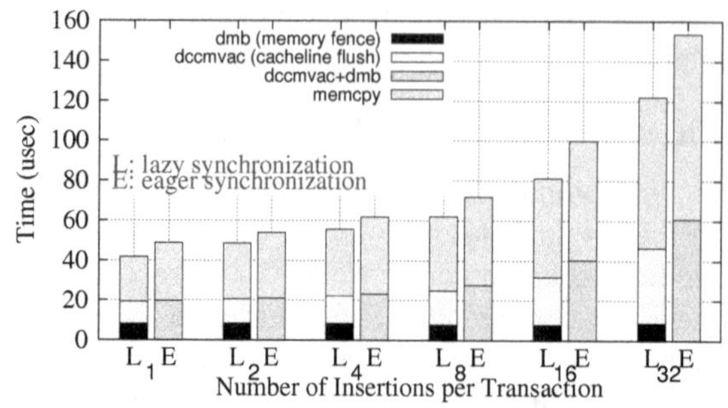

Figure 5: Quantifying the benefit of allowing processors to reorder memory writes

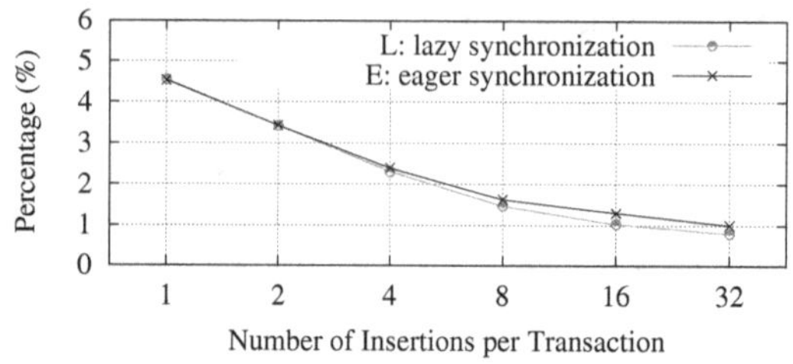

Figure 6: Proportion of ordering constraint overhead to query execution time

called dccmvac instructions) with varying the number of insertions per transaction. When each transaction inserts a single data record, the time spent on `dccmvac`, `dmb`, and kernel mode switching is only 19.3 usec per transaction. Considering that the query execution time is 424 usec, this overhead is just 4.6% of the query execution time as shown in Figure 6. However, when a transaction inserts 32 data records, the query execution time is 5828 usec while the overhead of the write ordering constraints is 46.5 usec (only 0.8 % of the execution time). SQLite throughput is governed more by the computation performance than by the I/O performance, especially when a WAL file is located in fast NVRAM. Hence, improving the I/O performance by reordering the memory writes does not significantly affect the ratio of the ordering constraint overhead to the query execution time, as shown in Figure 6.

In eager synchronization, denoted as *E*, we do not allow reordering of memory writes. But, in lazy synchronization denoted as *L*, we call `memcpy()` for all dirty portions of the WAL frames in a transaction before NVWAL explicitly calls `dccmvac`. Therefore the dirty bytes in the L1 or L2 cache could have been already evicted. I.e., in lazy synchronization, the overhead of `dccmvac` is masked by the overhead of `memcpy()`. As in epoch persistency, the lazy synchronization decouples the volatile memory order from the persist order, which fits quite well with the database transaction concept.

# of operation per txn	1	2	4	8	16	32
Insert	4431.8	4874.2	5767.1	7536.6	11141.1	18350.0
Insert (Diff)	726.8	863.0	1139.7	1684.0	2776.0	4984.0
Delete	4890.6	5685.2	7274.4	10452.9	16842.7	22282.2
Delete (Diff)	1555.2	2236.8	3576.9	5863.0	9412.6	11452.9
Update	4096	4210.6	4440.0	4882.4	5832.7	7733.2
Update (Diff)	647.7	830.3	1186.5	1857.9	3191.5	5529.6

Table 2: Average number of bytes written to NVRAM

The amounts of time spent on `memcpy()` in both schemes are similar in the experiments, as shown in Figure 5. However, in *E*, the `dccmvac` and `dmb` together perform up to *23% slower* than does `dccmvac` in *L* because *E* does not allow the reordering of memory writes. By separating `memcpy()` and `dccmvac`, write-ahead logging can eliminate about 2∼23% of the total overhead of enforcing persistency (19.3 ∼ 46.4 usec vs. 19.7 ∼ 60.7 usec). The overhead of `dmb` in *L* is negligible because `dmb` is called at most only four times in our implementation.

5.2 Differential Logging and I/O

Table 2 shows the I/O volume written to NVRAM with byte granularity differential logging and with legacy block granularity logging. For the insert, update, and delete operations, byte-granularity differential logging eliminates 73∼84%, 29∼85%, and 49∼69% of the unnecessary I/Os to NVRAM, respectively. In SQLite, each B-tree page appends a newly inserted set of data to the end of the used region. Thus, the size of a WAL log entry generated by byte-granularity differential logging is often small. But, for the update and delete operations, because it has to shift some log entries to avoid fragmentation issues, the write-ahead logging may touch a large portion of the B-tree page. Therefore, the insert transaction gets the most performance benefit from byte-granularity logging while the performance benefits for the update and delete transactions are moderate.

5.3 Transaction Throughput and NVRAM Latency

For the experiments shown in Figure 7, we measure the throughput of NVWAL with the SQLite benchmark app Mobibench [1] with varying the latency of NVRAM. Using Mobibench, we submit 1,000 transactions that insert, update, or delete a single 100-byte data record per transaction. In the experiments, we do not include the time for periodic checkpointing that sporadically flushes the logged WAL frames to the slow block device storage. It should be noted that checkpointing affects the performance of only one out of hundreds of transactions; this overhead is not relevant to the write latency of NVRAM.

The write latency of NVRAM is likely to be higher than the write latency of DRAM. For example, phase change memory, because it has access latencies in the hundreds of nanoseconds, is about 2∼5 times slower than DRAM [10, 24]. In the experiments, we vary the write latency of NVRAM from 400 nsec to 1900 nsec. Overall, as the write

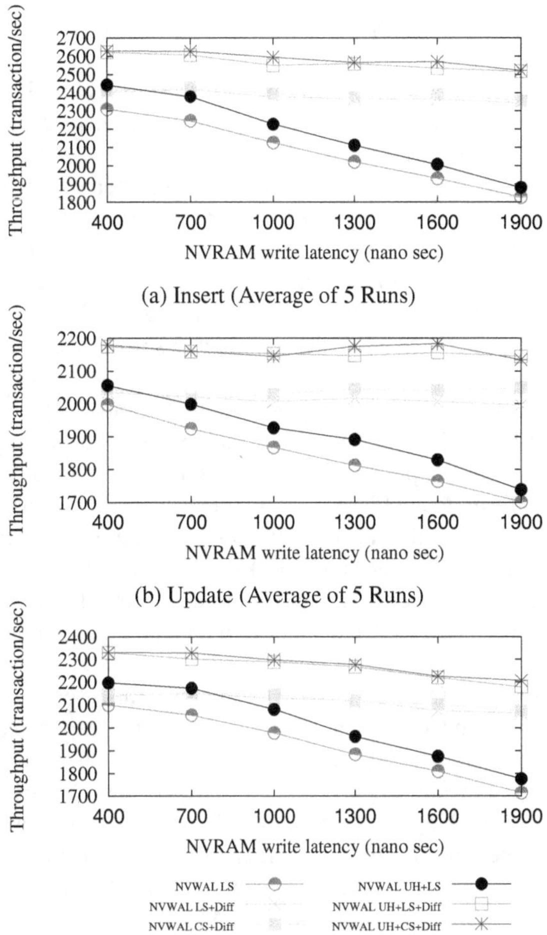

(a) Insert (Average of 5 Runs)

(b) Update (Average of 5 Runs)

(c) Delete (Average of 5 Runs)

Figure 7: Transaction throughput with varying latency of NVRAM (Average of 5 runs on Tuna)

latency increases, the transaction throughput decreases in a linear fashion. However, the latency adjustment affects the throughput of some NVWAL schemes more severely than it does others. Due to the unavailability of persist barrier instruction, we simulate the persist barrier overhead by introducing a 1 usec delay using `nop` instructions. We also assume the PoC is the system main memory - DRAM and NVRAM. In most cases, the PoC is the system main memory and `dccmvac` flushes data to the main memory. However, ARM architecture does not prohibit the implementation of outer caches beyond the PoC. We believe the outer cache should be disabled when NVRAM is used. Otherwise, outer caches should be explicitly flushed before the persist barrier instruction is called.

NVWAL LS denotes the NVWAL scheme with *lazy synchronization*, which calls cache line flush instructions in a lazy manner without hurting the correctness of the database transactions as illustrated in Figure 4(c). *NVWAL LS* does not employ byte-granularity differential logging and user-level heap; it calls Heapo's `nvmalloc()` system call for every dirty WAL frame.

In *NVWAL LS+Diff*, SQLite performs lazy synchronization. Additionally, it adopts *byte-granularity differential logging*. When the B-tree node size is 4 Kbytes, *NVWAL LS* calls 128 cache line flush instructions, one memory barrier instruction, and one persist barrier instruction for each WAL frame. It then calls another cache line flush instruction, memory barrier instruction, and persist barrier instruction for a commit mark. However, in *NVWAL LS+Diff*, the average number of cache line flush instructions per transaction is reduced, and hence *NVWAL LS+Diff* consistently outperforms *NVWAL+LS*, yielding up to 28% higher throughput.

In *NVWAL CS+Diff*, NVWAL asynchronously flushes log entries without explicitly calling cache line flush instructions, as illustrated in Figure 4(d). In this variant of NVWAL, we call the cache line flush instruction and memory barrier only for a commit mark and checksum bytes. In this way, we minimize the overhead of the ordering constraints. However, the performance benefit comes with a potential inconsistency.

In *NVWAL UH+LS*, NVWAL employs the user-level heap, which reduces the number of calls to the expensive NVRAM heap manager's `nvmalloc()` function. In the experiments shown in Figure 7, we call Heapo's `nvmalloc()` and allocate 8Kbytes NVRAM block that can store two WAL frames. By saving the overhead of calling an expensive NVRAM heap manager's function, *NVWAL UH+LS* achieves a 6% performance gain over *NVWAL LS*.

In *NVWAL UH+LS+Diff*, NVWAL employs user-level heap, lazy synchronization, and byte-granularity differential logging. Interestingly, the performance of *NVWAL UH+LS+Diff* is comparable to that of *NVWAL UH+CS+Diff*, which uses an user-level heap, byte granularity differential logging, and checksum bytes. Because *NVWAL UH+CS+Diff* minimizes the number of bytes to be written to NVRAM and also minimizes the overhead of the `cache_line_flush()` system calls and memory barrier, it shows the highest transaction throughput. Considering that *NVWAL UH+CS+Diff* is vulnerable to the inconsistency problem that is inherent in probabilistic checksum bytes, *NVWAL UH+LS+Diff*'s comparable performance makes it a promising write-ahead logging scheme for NVRAM, because it does not compromise the correctness of database transactions.

As the write latency of NVRAM increases, the benefit of using the proposed schemes becomes more significant. When the write latency of NVRAM is set to 1942 nsec, *NVWAL UH+LS+Diff* yields throughput up to 37% higher than that of *NVWAL LS*.

5.4 The Real Numbers: Nexus 5

In the last set of experiments, we examine the performance of NVWAL using a commercially available smartphone - the Nexus 5, which has a 2.26 GHz Snapdragon 800 processor, 2 GB DDR memory and 16 GB SanDisk iNAND eMMC 4.51 SDIN8DE4 formatted with an EXT4 file system. As for the NVRAM emulation on Nexus 5, we assume that a specific address range of DRAM is NVRAM, i.e., that NVRAM is attached to the memory bus. NVRAM write latency is varied by inserting `nop` instructions. The stock SQLite WAL implementation does not use the emulated NVRAM but stores log pages in flash memory instead. We fix the CPU frequency to the maximum 2.26 GHz to reduce the standard deviation of the experiments. The Snapdragon 800 processor's cache line size is 64 bytes. We run Mobibench using SQLite 3.7.11 and Android 4.4 on Nexus 5.

Recent studies [17, 23, 30] have reported that SQLite on flash memory suffers from unexpected I/O volume and that SQLite write-ahead logging unnecessarily doubles the I/O traffic in the current implementation (SQLite 3.7.11). In order to fix these problems and compare the performance of SQLite WAL on flash memory against that on NVWAL in a fair way, we implemented two optimizations that help avoid the unnecessary I/O traffic and that significantly improve the performance of SQLite on flash memory.

For each dirty page, SQLite creates a 24-byte frame header that consists of page number, commit mark, checksum values, etc., and that appends the dirty page to it. Due to the additional 24-byte frame header of the WAL frames, each WAL frame becomes larger than the page size, which causes the WAL frames not to be aligned with the page boundaries. With such misaligned pages, a write operation for a single database page causes at least two pages to be written to the block device storage. In order to resolve the misaligned WAL frame problem, we modified SQLite's B-tree split algorithm so that it splits an overflow page early and the last 24 bytes of all B-tree pages are not used. By doing so, 24 bytes of WAL frame header and WAL frame can be merged and stored in a single page of a WAL file. We implemented the same split algorithm for NVWAL.

Another ad-hoc improvement we made on SQLite WAL is *pre-allocation of WAL log pages* as in WALDIO [30]. For each dirty page, a transaction calls `write()` that appends one or two pages to the end of a log file. As the appended pages increase the size of the WAL log file, the increased file size must be updated in an inode. Because the writes in WAL mode are all sequential and because the size of the log file keeps increasing until checkpointing truncates it, pre-allocating multiple pages once will help the next transactions write log frames without increasing the file size. The only negative aspect of this pre-allocation is that it may waste several disk pages if there is no next transaction. In terms of EXT4 journal overhead, allocating two new pages causes overhead slightly higher than that induced by allocating only one page. However, that overhead is much smaller than the overhead for allocating another page later. The size of the pre-allocated pages can be fixed at a specific number based

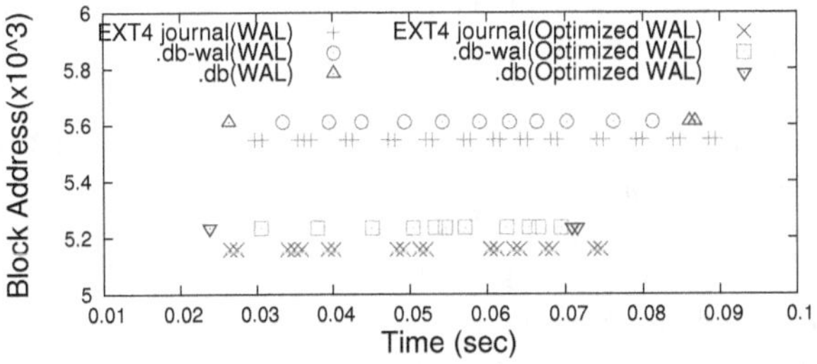

Figure 8: Block Trace of SQLite Insert Transaction with Optimizations

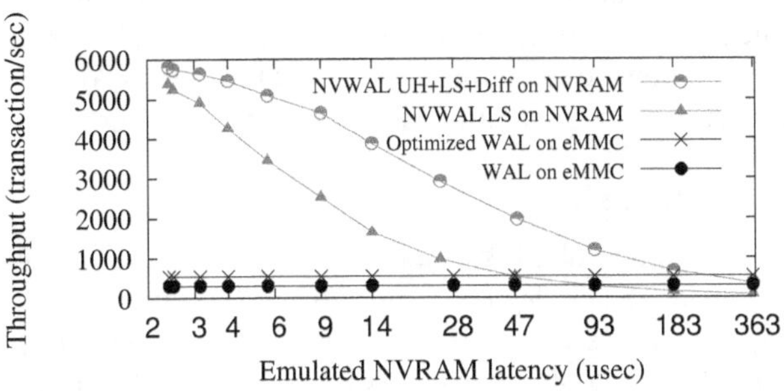

Figure 9: Transaction Throughput of NVWAL on Emulated NVRAM vs. Optimized WAL on eMMC Memory (Average of 5 Runs)

on the database access patterns or the size can be doubled every time the pre-allocated pages fill up.

Figure 8 shows a block I/O trace of 10 transactions in stock SQLite WAL mode and another block I/O trace of 10 transactions in our optimized WAL mode. For a single insert transaction, one block (4KB) is written to the `.db-wal` file but two blocks(16KB, 4KB) are written to the EXT4 journal to update the metadata of the log file in the ordered-mode EXT4 journal. In our optimized WAL mode, SQLite pre-allocates 8 pages when a transaction writes a log frame for the first time, even if the system needs just one page. If another transaction needs to write log frames while there is no available pre-allocated page, we double the number of pages to be pre-allocated each time and SQLite allocates 16 new pages to the log file. Compared to the block trace of the WAL mode, allocating multiple log pages in advance reduces EXT4 journal accesses by 40% (172 KB vs. 284 KB), and the batch execution time in our optimized WAL mode decreases from 90 msec to 74 msec.

In Figure 9, we measure the transaction throughput of NVWAL on Nexus 5. We run 1000 insert transactions with an empty SQLite database table. Each transaction inserts a single 100-byte record into the table. The NVRAM write latency on the Nexus 5 is varied by adding `nop` instructions after each `clflush` instruction, which is also used to emulate the NVRAM write latency in [15]. We set the checkpointing interval to 1000 dirty WAL frames, which is the default setting in SQLite. As for the sporadic checkpointing overhead, we amortize the overhead across 1000 transactions.

Our optimized WAL on flash memory yields 541 transactions/sec while *NVWAL LS* and *NVWAL UH+LS+Diff* on NVRAM (DRAM with 2 usec write latency) exhibit 5393 and 5812 transactions/sec, respectively. As we increase the write latency, the throughput of NVWAL decreases. When the write latency becomes 47 usec, *NVWAL LS* on the emulated NVRAM shows throughput similar to that of WAL on flash memory. When the write latency is set to 230 usec, *NVWAL UH+LS+Diff* also shows performance similar to that of WAL on flash memory. We need to stress that an NVRAM write latency of 230 usec is very conservative.

The experiments on the Nexus 5 are not precisely identical to the experiments on the Tuna board because the former do not include the overhead of checkpoint operation, whereas the latter include the checkpointing overhead. Hence, the experiments on the Nexus 5 stand for the sustained throughput, while the experiments on the Tuna stand for the peak throughput.

6. Related Work

Condit et al. [10] designed a file system *BPFS* and a hardware architecture for persistent, byte-addressable memory. BPFS proposes a new *epoch barrier* instruction that specifies an ordering of groups of persists. BPFS uses short-circuit shadow paging, which provides atomic, fine-grained updates to persistent storage. However, *epoch barrier* instruction requires a modification of the memory hierarchy because it considers cache-bypassing writes, and because cache flushes cause inefficiency.

Fang et al. [12] proposed to write log records directly into storage class memory (SCM), which provides an *epoch barrier* without caching them in volatile DRAM. In their logging scheme, log records stored in SCM are periodically archived to a WAL file in block device storage. Unlike our NVWAL, their logging scheme requires log records to be stored twice - once in NVRAM and once in block device storage before they are applied to the database file.

SCMFS proposed by Wu et al. [46] is another file system designed for non-volatile memory; it uses only `clflush` and `mfence` instructions without any modification to the hardware; however, it is unclear if this design guarantees consistency if the system crashes.

With non-volatile memory, memory write errors from application bugs can cause serious and permanent system corruption. Moraru et al [35] proposed *NVMalloc* - a memory allocator for NVRAM that prevents memory wear-out and increases robustness against erroneous memory writes. *NV-Heaps* [9], Mnemosyne [43], *Heapo* [16], and Atlas [7] are persistent object management systems for NVRAM. These works are complementary to our work as NVWAL can utilize persistent and byte-addressable heap managers or file systems.

In the future, when NVRAM and a good implementation of the transactional memory support such as Mnemosyne [43] become available, it may be possible to eliminate some use cases of SQLite because some application developers use SQLite as a failure atomic persistent storage. However, RDBMS provides the same level of failure atomic persistent storage, with the added benefit of using declarative query language (SQL), pre-implemented relational operators, indexing, and query optimization, to name just a few of them. Hence, we expect that NVWAL and persistent heap will be complementary to each other, rather than in competition.

In Android smartphones, due to the overhead of journaling activity, one of the major performance bottlenecks has been shown to be the storage of the device [17, 21, 27]. Recently, a fair amount of work has been done to leverage the non-volatility of NVRAM to resolve the performance and scalability issues of database logging [5, 8, 12, 15, 19, 20, 22, 25, 32, 39–42, 44, 45]. Kim et al. [23] proposed a version-based B-tree for flash memory. The version-based B-tree (*CDDS*) has also been studied for NVRAM by Venkataraman et al. [41]. CDDS allows atomic updates on NVRAM without requiring logging. *NV-tree* is another B-tree for NVRAM, specifically designed to achieve data consistency on NVRAM while reducing the number of cache line flush operations.

NV-Logging proposed by Huang et al. [15], proposes a per-transaction logging method for OLTP systems using NVRAM; this allows us to avoid the bottleneck of centralized log buffers. Unlike NVWAL, NV-Logging [15] calls `clflush` immediately after every `memcpy()` operation. Huang et al. [15] compared their per-transaction logging against that of an *NV-Disk* [20, 22] - NVRAM accessed via standard file I/O interface; they showed that replacing the disk or flash memory with NVRAM without redesigning the file system cache and I/O interface can cause the system to suffers from high overhead [15]. Our NVWAL is different from NV-Logging in that NV-Logging focuses on scalability issues of processing concurrent queries, while SQLite does not allow concurrent transactions.

The related work most similar to ours is SQLite/PPL, recently proposed by Oh et al. [36]. They proposed a per-page logging scheme for SQLite; this system stores the disk-based WAL frames in PCM memory, which takes no account of byte-addressability, reordering of memory writes, or the overhead of managing a persistent heap.

Lee et al. [25] proposed to merge the buffer cache and the journal for byte-addressable NVRAM by converting the buffer cache blocks to journal logs simply by changing the status of the blocks to a frozen state. The method of *Blurred Persistence*, proposed by Lu et al. [32], blurs the boundary between volatility and persistency by allowing processors to persist uncommitted data in NVRAM and by detecting the uncommitted data later via *execution in log* if necessary. Our work is different from theirs in that NVWAL targets database systems that retain DRAM, not NVRAM, as a volatile buffer cache.

Pelley et al. [37] conducted a memory trace analysis and showed that replacing a disk with NVRAM, which supports a *persist barrier*, can achieve significantly higher throughput than that of disks. To further improve the performance of OLTP, they proposed a *group commit* protocol that persists the committed transactions in batches in order to reduce the number of required barriers. Our method of transaction-aware lazy synchronization is different from their idea of group commit in that they assumed that the ordering of memory writes would be enforced through the *persist barrier*, which does not exist yet, while we evaluated SQLite WAL on real hardware an emulated NVRAM board with ARM v7 instructions and no modifications to the processor design.

7. Conclusions

Emerging non-volatile memory devices are expected to substitute slow block device storage so as to persistently store frequently accessed data. In this work, we design and implement write-ahead-logging on NVRAM (NVWAL) and show that NVWAL can minimize the overhead of managing and synchronizing log entries on NVRAM via i) transaction-aware lazy synchronization, ii) a user-level NVRAM block manager, and iii) byte-granularity differential logging.

Through our extensive performance evaluation, we show that database logging can be optimized to be insensitive to NVRAM latency, and that the overhead of guaranteeing the failure atomicity is almost free. NVWAL with the optimizations exhibits transaction throughput up to 37% higher than that of non-optimized WAL on NVRAM; when NVRAM latency is smaller than 2 usec, NVWAL achieves at least 10x higher than that of legacy WAL on flash memory.

We can draw three lessons from this study. First, employing an NVRAM in database logging is not an option but a necessity. Second, the aggregate overhead of the persist barrier instructions is insignificant from the application's point of view. Third, NVRAM latency is barely propagated to SQLite performance. NVWAL significantly decreases the logging overhead in SQLite and makes the workload further CPU bound. As a result, SQLite performance becomes relatively insensitive to NVRAM latency.

8. Acknowledgments

We would like to thank our shepherd Shankar Pasupathy and the anonymous reviewers for their suggestions on early drafts of this paper. This research was supported by MKE/KEIT (No.10041608, Embedded System Software for New Memory based Smart Devices). The corresponding author of this paper is Beomseok Nam.

References

[1] Mobibench. *https://github.com/ESOS-Lab/Mobibench.*

[2] OpenNVRAM. *http://opennvram.org/.*

[3] Sqlite. *http://www.sqlite.org/.*

[4] S. Agarwal, R. Garg, M. S. Gupta, , and J. E. Moreira. Adaptive incremental checkpointing for massively parallel systems. In *Proceedings of the 18th annual international conference on Supercomputing*, 2004.

[5] J. Arulraj, A. Pavlo, and S. R. Dulloor. Let's talk about storage & recovery methods for non-volatile memory database systems. In *Proceedings of the 2015 ACM SIGMOD International Conference on Management of Data*, pages 707–722. ACM, 2015.

[6] K. Bhandari, D. R. Chakrabarti, and H.-J. Boehm. Implications of cpu caching on byte-addressable non-volatile memory programming. *http://www.hpl.hp.com/techreports/2012/HPL-2012-236.pdf*, 2012.

[7] D. Chakrabarti, H.-J. Boehm, and K. Bhandari. Atlas: Leveraging locks for non-volatile memory consistency. In *Proceeding of the 2014 ACM International Conference on Object Oriented Programming Systems Languages & Applications (OOPSLA)*, pages 433–452, 2014.

[8] A. Chatzistergiou, M. Cintra, and S. D. Viglas. Rewind: Recovery write-ahead system for in-memory non-volatile datastructures. *Proceedings of the VLDB Endowment*, 8(5):497–508, 2015.

[9] J. Coburn, A. M. Caulfield, A. Akel, L. M. Grupp, R. K. Gupta, R. Jhala, and S. Swanson. NV-Heaps: Making persisten objects fast and safe with next-generation, non-volatile memories. In *Proceedings of the 16th International Conference on Architectural Support for Programming Languages and Operating Systems (ASPLOS)*, 2011.

[10] J. Condit, E. B. Nightingale, C. Frost, E. Ipek, B. C. Lee, D. Burger, and D. Coetzee. Better i/o through byte-addressable, persistent memory. In *Proceedings of the 22nd ACM Symposium on Operating Systems Principles (SOSP)*, 2009.

[11] S. R. Dulloor, S. Kumar, A. Keshavamurthy, P. Lantz, D. Reddy, R. Sankaran, and J. Jackson. System software for persistent memory. In *Proceedings of the 9th ACM European Conference on Computer Systems (EuroSys)*, pages 15:1–15:15, 2014.

[12] R. Fang, H.-I. Hsiao, B. He, C. Mohan, and Y. Wang. High performance database logging using storage class memory. In *Proceedings of the 27th International Conference on Data Engineering (ICDE)*, pages 1221–1231, 2011.

[13] R. Gioiosa, J. C. Sancho, S. Jiang, and F. Petrini. Transparent, incremental checkpointing at kernel level: A foundation for fault tolerance for parallel computers. In *Proceedings of the ACM/IEEE SC2005 Conference*, 2005.

[14] G. Graefe. A survey of B-tree logging and recovery techniques. *ACM Transactions on Database Systems*, 37(1), Feb. 2012.

[15] J. Huang, K. Schwan, and M. K. Qureshi. Nvram-aware logging in transaction systems. *Proceedings of the VLDB Endowment*, 8(4), 2014.

[16] T. Hwang, J. Jung, and Y. Won. Heapo: Heap-based persistent object store. *ACM Transactions on Storage (TOS)*, 11(1), 2014.

[17] S. Jeong, K. Lee, S. Lee, S. Son, and Y. Won. I/O stack optimization for smartphones. In *Proceedings of the USENIX Annual Technical Conference (ATC)*, 2013.

[18] J. Jung and Y. Won. nvramdisk: A transactional block devie driver for non-volatile ram. *IEEE Transactions on Computers*, http://dx.doi.org/10.1109/TC.2015.2428708, 2015.

[19] J. Jung, Y. Won, E. Kim, H. Shin, and B. Jeon. Frash: Exploiting storage class memory in hybrid file system for hierarchical storage. *ACM Transactions on Storage (TOS)*, 6(1):3, 2010.

[20] D. Kim, E. Lee, S. Ahn, and H. Bahn. Improving the storage performance of smartphones through journaling in non-volatile memory. *Consumer Electronics, IEEE Transactions on*, 59(3):556–561, 2013.

[21] H. Kim, N. Agrawal, and C. Ungureanu. Revisiting storage for smartphones. In *Proceedings of the 11th USENIX conference on File and Storage Technologies (FAST)*, 2013.

[22] J. Kim, C. Min, and Y. I. Eom. Reducing Excessive Journaling Overhead with Small-Sized NVRAM for Mobile Devices. *IEEE Transactions on Consumer Electronics*, 6(2), June 2014.

[23] W.-H. Kim, B. Nam, D. Park, and Y. Won. Resolving journling of journal anomaly in android i/o: Multi-version b-tree with lazy split. In *Proceedings of the 11th USENIX conference on File and Storage Technologies (FAST)*, 2014.

[24] B. C. Lee, E. Ipek, O. Mutlu, and D. Burger. Architecting phase change memory as a scalable DRAM alternative. In *Proceedings of the 36th International Symposium on Computer Architecture (ISCA)*, 2009.

[25] E. Lee, H. Bahn, and S. H. Noh. Unioning of the buffer cache and journaling layers with non-volatile memory. In *Proceedings of the 11th USENIX conference on File and Storage Technologies (FAST)*, 2013.

[26] J. Lee, K. Kim, and S. Cha. Differential logging: A commutative and associative logging scheme for highly parallel main memory database. In *Proceedings of the 17th International Conference on Data Engineering (ICDE)*, 2001.

[27] K. Lee and Y. Won. Smart layers and dumb result: Io characterization of an android-based smartphone. In *Proceedings of the 12th International Conference on Embedded Software (EMSOFT 2012)*, 2012.

[28] S.-W. Lee and B. Moon. Design of flash-based dbms: An in-page logging approach. In *Proceedings of 2007 ACM SIGMOD International Conference on Management of Data (SIGMOD)*, 2007.

[29] T. Lee, D. Kim, H. Park, and S. Yoo. Fpga-based prototyping systems for emerging memory technologies. In *Proceedings of the 25th IEEE International Symposium on Rapid System Prototyping (RSP)*, 2014.

[30] W. Lee, K. Lee, H. Son, W.-H. Kim, B. Nam, and Y. Won. Waldio: Eliminating the filesystem journaling in resolving the journaling of journal anomaly. In *Proceedings of the 2015 USENIX Anual Technical Conference (ATC)*, 2015.

[31] M. Li and P. P. C. Lee. Toward i/o-efficient protection against silent data corruptions in raid arrays. In *Proceedings of the*

30th International Conference on Massive Storage Systems and Technology (MSST), 2014.

[32] Y. Lu, J. Shu, and L. Sun. Blurred persistence in transactional persistent memory. In *Proceedings of the 31st International Conference on Massive Storage Systems and Technology (MSST)*, 2015.

[33] H. Luo, L. Tian, and H. Jiang. qNVRAM: quasi non-volatile ram for low overhead persistency enforcement in smartphones. In *Proceedings of the 6th USENIX Workshop on Hot Topics in Storage and File Systems (HotStorage)*, 2014.

[34] J. S. Meena, S. M. Sze, U. Chand, and T.-Y. Tseng. Overview of emerging nonvolatile memory technologies. *Nanoscale research letters*, 9(1):1–33, 2014.

[35] I. Moraru, D. G. Andersen, M. Kaminsky, N. Tolia, N. Binkert, and P. Ranganathan. Consistent, durable, and safe memory management for byte-addressable non volatile main memory. In *Proceedings of the ACM Conference on Timely Results in Operating Systems (TRIOS)*, 2013.

[36] G. Oh, S. Kim, S.-W. Lee, and B. Moon. Sqlite optimization with phase change memory for mobile applications. *Proceedings of the VLDB Endowment (PVLDB)*, 8(12):1454–1465, 2015.

[37] S. Pelley, P. M. Chen, and T. F. Wenisch. Memory persistency. In *Proceedings of the 41st International Symposium on Computer Architecture (ISCA)*, pages 265–276, 2014.

[38] K. Shen, S. Park, and M. Zhu. Journaling of journal is (almost) free. In *Proceedings of the 11th USENIX conference on File and Storage Technologies (FAST)*, 2014.

[39] M. Son, S. Lee, K. Kim, S. Yoo, and S. Lee. A small non-volatile write buffer to reduce storage writes in smartphones. In *Proceedings of the 2015 Design, Automation & Test in Europe Conference & Exhibition*, DATE '15, pages 713–718, San Jose, CA, USA, 2015. EDA Consortium. ISBN 978-3-9815370-4-8.

[40] C. A. N. Soules, G. R. Goodson, J. D. Strunk, and G. R. Ganger. Metadata efficiency in versioning file systems. In *Proceedings of the 2nd USENIX conference on File and Storage Technologies (FAST)*, pages 43–58, 2003.

[41] S. Venkataraman, N. Tolia, P. Ranganathan, and R. H. Campbell. Consistent and durable data structures for non-volatile byte-addressable memory. In *9th USENIX conference on File and Storage Technologies (FAST)*, 2011.

[42] S. D. Viglas. Data management in non-volatile memory. In *Proceedings of the 2015 ACM SIGMOD International Conference on Management of Data*, pages 1707–1711. ACM, 2015.

[43] H. Volos, A. J. Tack, and M. M. Swift. Mnemosyne: Lightweight persistent memory. In *16th International Conference on Architectural Support for Programming Languages and Operating Systems (ASPLOS)*, 2011.

[44] T. Wang and R. Johnson. Scalable logging through emerging non-volatile memory. *Proceedings of the VLDB Endowment*, 7(10):865–876, 2014.

[45] Q. Wei, J. Chen, and C. Chen. Accelerating file system metadata access with byte-addressable nonvolatile memory. *ACM Transactions on Storage (TOS)*, 11(3):12, 2015.

[46] X. Wu and A. L. N. Reddy. SCMFS: A file system for storage class memory. In *Proceedings of the ACM/IEEE SC2011 Conference*, 2011.

[47] Y. Zhang and S. Swanson. A study of application performance with non-volatile main memory. In *Proceedings of the 31st International Conference on Massive Stroage Systems (MSST)*, 2015.

[48] M. Zheng, J. Tucek, D. Huang, F. Qin, M. Lillibridge, E. S. Yang, B. W. Zhao, and S. Singh. Torturing databases for fun and profit. In *Proceedings of the 11th USENIX Symposium on Operating Systems Design and Implementation (OSDI 14)*, pages 449–464, Oct. 2014.

High-Performance Transactions for Persistent Memories

Aasheesh Kolli
University of Michigan
akolli@umich.edu

Steven Pelley
Snowflake Computing
steven.pelley@snowflake.net

Ali Saidi
ARM
ali.saidi@arm.com

Peter M. Chen
University of Michigan
pmchen@umich.edu

Thomas F. Wenisch
University of Michigan
twenisch@umich.edu

Abstract

Emerging non-volatile memory (NVRAM) technologies offer the durability of disk with the byte-addressability of DRAM. These devices will allow software to access persistent data structures directly in NVRAM using processor loads and stores, however, ensuring consistency of persistent data across power failures and crashes is difficult. Atomic, durable transactions are a widely used abstraction to enforce such consistency. Implementing transactions on NVRAM requires the ability to constrain the order of NVRAM writes, for example, to ensure that a transaction's log record is complete before it is marked committed. Since NVRAM write latencies are expected to be high, minimizing these ordering constraints is critical for achieving high performance. Recent work has proposed programming interfaces to express NVRAM write ordering constraints to hardware so that NVRAM writes may be coalesced and reordered while preserving necessary constraints. Unfortunately, a straightforward implementation of transactions under these interfaces imposes unnecessary constraints. We show how to remove these dependencies through a variety of techniques, notably, deferring commit until after locks are released. We present a comprehensive analysis contrasting two transaction designs across three NVRAM programming interfaces, demonstrating up to 2.5x speedup.

Categories and Subject Descriptors D.4.2 [*Operating Systems*]: Storage Management—Main memory

Keywords Non-Volatile Memory, Memory Persistency, Recoverability, Transactions

ASPLOS '16 April 2–6, 2016, Atlanta, Georgia, USA.
Copyright © 2016 ACM 978-1-4503-4091-5/16/04... $15.00
DOI: http://dx.doi.org/10.1145/2872362.2872381

1. Introduction

New types of memory technology are emerging that could significantly change how software handles persistent data. These new technologies, such as phase-change memory, spin-transfer torque MRAM, memristors, and the recently announced Intel/Micron 3D XPoint technology [15], are non-volatile like magnetic disk and flash memory, but offer much faster access latencies than existing non-volatile storage technologies (though likely not as fast as DRAM). Future systems will likely attach these non-volatile memories (NVRAM) directly to the memory bus and allow processors to access them at word granularity via load and store instructions [14, 27].

For compatibility, some software will continue to access persistent data in NVRAM through a block-based, file system interface. However, we expect many programs to access persistent data structures directly in NVRAM using processor loads and stores. Doing so eliminates the need to maintain separate on-disk and in-memory copies of persistent data, and eliminates the overhead of traversing the file system each time persistent data is read or written.

Ensuring that persistent data is consistent despite power failures and crashes is difficult, especially when manipulating complex data structures with fine-grained accesses. One way to ease this difficulty is to access persistent data through atomic, durable transactions, which make groups of updates appear as one atomic unit with respect to failure. Transactions also provide mechanisms for controlling concurrency; in this paper, we assume that transactions use locks in volatile memory for concurrency control. Because of the power and convenience of transactions, many prior works propose providing them on top of NVRAM [8, 22, 33, 34]. We focus our analysis on static transactions (transactions for which lock sets are known a priori), as detailed in Section 3.

Implementing transactions on NVRAM requires the ability to order writes to the NVRAM.[1] For example, in write-ahead logging [24], the commit record for a transaction may only be written to NVRAM after all log records for that transaction have been written; otherwise a failure may cause the system to recover to a state in which only some of the updates are present. We call writes to NVRAM *persists*, and we call constraints on the order of NVRAM writes *persist dependencies*.

Whereas specifying and honoring persist dependencies is essential for correctness, *minimizing* persist dependencies is likely to be essential for performance. Future NVRAM technologies are likely to be slower than DRAM [19], and will only be able to keep up with CPU speeds through techniques such as parallelism, batching, and re-ordering [35], all of which are possible only in the absence of ordering constraints. Pelley and co-authors show that minimizing persist dependencies can make as much as a 30× difference in performance [27].

This paper considers how to implement NVRAM transactions in a way that minimizes persist dependencies. We show that a simple transaction system design enforces many unnecessary persist dependencies and that these dependencies greatly slow down common transaction workloads, that most of the unnecessary dependencies arise as a consequence of performing the commit step of the transaction while locks are held, and how to remove these dependencies by deferring this commit until after locks are released.

Deferring commits leads to the new challenge of correctly ordering the deferred commit operations across all outstanding transactions. To ensure transaction serializability, commit order must match the order in which locks were originally acquired during transaction execution. We show how to minimize persist dependencies through a combination of techniques, including distributed logs [32], deferred commit [10, 16], Lamport/vector clocks to serialize transactions [18], a subtle epoch-based mechanism to recycle log storage, and relaxed persistency models [27].

We implement a transaction system for NVRAM that defers commits, and we measure its performance on simulated NVRAM with a range of device speeds. For two transaction-processing workloads, we find that performance improves by up to 50% under relaxed persistency models [27] and by up to 150% under Intel's recent x86 ISA extensions for NVRAM [14].

We first introduce a brief formalism to enable reasoning about persist dependencies (Section 2). We then derive the minimal persist ordering requirements to implement correct transactions under an idealized programming interface that can specify arbitrary ordering constraints to hardware (Section 3). Such a programming interface is unrealistic; we summarize practical interfaces proposed in the literature and in recent extensions to the x86 ISA (Section 4). We then analyze a straightforward transaction implementation, synchronous commit transactions (SCT), demonstrating how it overconstrains persist ordering (Section 5). Instead, we propose deferred commit transactions (DCT), which can achieve minimal ordering constraints under sufficiently expressive interfaces (Section 6). We evaluate our transaction implementations using the TPCC and TATP transaction processing workloads (Section 7) and end with a survey of related work (Section 8).

[1] Ensuring recoverability without transactions also requires the ability to order writes.

2. Ordering constraints

The ability to order writes is critical to all software that uses persistent storage. Constraining the order that writes persist is essential to ensure consistent recovery, and minimizing these constraints is key to enabling high performance.

Formally, we express an ordering relation over memory events *loads* and *stores*, which we collectively refer to as *accesses*. The term *persist* refers to the act of durably writing a store to persistent memory. We assume persists are performed atomically (with respect to failures) at 8-byte granularity. By "thread", we refer to execution contexts—cores or hardware threads. We use the following notation (adopted from [17]):

- L_a^i: A load from thread i to address a
- S_a^i: A store from thread i to address a
- M_a^i: A load or store by thread i to address a

We reason about two ordering relations over memory events, *volatile memory order* and *persist memory order*. Volatile memory order (VMO) is an ordering relation over all memory events (loads and stores) as prescribed by the memory consistency model for multiprocessors [1]. Persist memory order (PMO) deals with the same events but may have different ordering constraints than VMO. [27] uses the term *persistency model* to describe the types of constraints that hardware allows software to express on the persist memory order.

We denote these ordering relations as:

- $A \leq_v B$: A occurs no later than B in VMO
- $A \leq_p B$: A occurs no later than B in PMO

An ordering relation between stores in PMO implies the corresponding persist actions are ordered; that is,
$A \leq_p B \rightarrow B$ may not persist before A.

3. Transactions under Idealized Ordering

It is not easy for software to express persist dependencies. Simply ordering the instructions that store data to NVRAM is not sufficient: writes to memory (including NVRAM) are cached and may not be written from the CPU cache to NVRAM in the same order the corresponding instructions were executed [2].

In this section, we suppose that software has the ability to specify precisely the persist dependences for all writes to NVRAM. While this is unrealistically expressive, it provides a useful baseline upon which to build an idealized transaction system that minimizes persist dependencies. In later sections, we implement transactions built on more realistic interfaces and show how a naive implementation of transactions on these interfaces introduces unnecessary ordering constraints.

The most precise way to specify persist dependencies is as a partial order over all persists. This partial order can be expressed as a directed acyclic graph (DAG), where a node in the graph represents a persist, and an edge exists from node A to node B iff the persist represented by node A must occur no later than the persist represented by node B (note that this condition can be satisfied by performing the two persists atomically). In a system with idealized ordering, the software can express a constraint between any two persists, including persists that occur on separate threads.

We next describe how to build a simple transaction system, given the ability to express general partial orders over all NVRAM writes.

3.1 Transaction design

There are many ways to implement transactions [12], with one basic design choice being which version to log of the data being modified in a transaction: the data before the modification (undo logging [8, 11, 21]), the data after the modification (redo logging [33]), or both (e.g., ARIES [24]). In this paper, we implement transactions with undo logging. We believe this design fits well with storing data directly in NVRAM: both committed and uncommitted data are stored in place, so software can always read the most recent data directly from the in-place data structure (assuming appropriate locks are held). In contrast, if transactions are implemented with a redo log, reads of uncommitted data must be intercepted and redirected to the redo log.

We further implement several common optimizations required to achieve high transaction concurrency. We implement per-thread, distributed logs [32, 33], to avoid the scalability constraints of a centralized log. Our undo log records a copy of data (physical undo records) before it is mutated rather than a "synchronous log-and-update" approach (like PMFS [11]), as the latter requires more persist ordering constraints. We leverage checksum-based log entry validation [28] so that non-atomic writes to a log entry can proceed in parallel, but recovery software can deduce whether a log record was fully written without requiring a separate "valid" bit. This optimization eliminates one persist ordering constraint and is similar to the torn-bit optimization in Mnemosyne [33] and eager commit [22]. We assume concurrency control via arbitrarily fine-grain locking—a transaction must hold all required locks before executing (i.e. static transactions). Requiring a transaction to hold all locks before executing implies that all the data that can possibly be modified by the transaction is known a priori. If such knowledge is not available, a program must execute a read phase to identify all regions it might touch and acquire all locks, and then begin execution (similar to the approach used to implement deterministic transactions [29]).

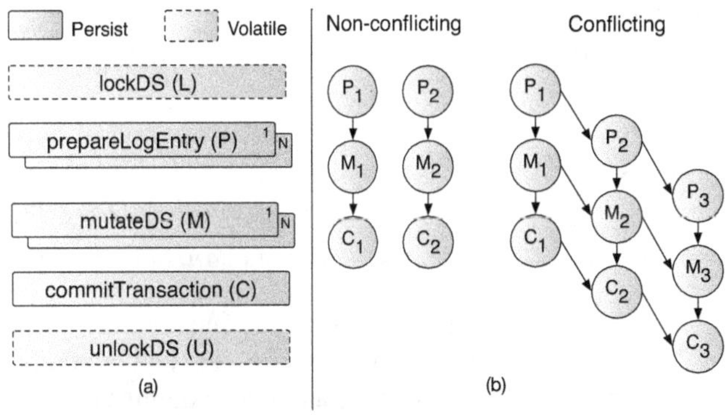

Figure 1. (a) Steps in an undo transaction. (b) Persist dependencies in a transaction sequence.

Figure 1(a) depicts the high-level steps of an undo-logging transaction. Steps outlined in a dotted box modify only volatile memory locations; those outlined in a solid box write to persistent memory. We briefly describe each step:

- **lockDS (L):** Acquire all locks to ensure mutual exclusion of the transaction. Locks are held in volatile memory.
- **prepareLogEntry (P):** Allocate log space and copy the prior state of all data that will be mutated to the log.
- **mutateDS (M):** Modify the data structure in place.
- **commitTransaction (C):** Commit the transaction by marking the undo log entry invalid; the transaction will no longer be undone during recovery.
- **unlockDS (U):** Release all locks acquired by lockDS.

We represent transactions with three persist nodes, corresponding to the three steps that perform durable writes, $prepareLogEntry$ (P), $mutateDS$ (M) and $commitTransaction$ (C).

3.2 Minimal Persist Dependencies

We next analyze the minimal persist dependencies required for correct recovery of an undo-logging transaction. We consider two transactions, T_m and T_n, which acquire lock sets $Locks_m$ and $Locks_n$, respectively. The transactions conflict if their lock sets intersect (i.e., they mutate overlapping data). We require order across conflicting transactions (the order in which they acquire locks); the subscripts indicate this order—in our example, $m < n$. $transactionStep_m$ indicates completion of a particular step in the transaction T_m (and all its associated persists). Recovery correctness requires the following order relationships:

$$prepareLogEntry_m \leq_p mutateDS_m \quad (1)$$

$$mutateDS_m \leq_p commitTransaction_m \quad (2)$$

$$\forall(m,n):$$
$$(unlockDS_m \leq_v lockDS_n) \wedge (Locks_m \cap Locks_n \neq \phi)$$

$$prepareLogEntry_m \leq_p prepareLogEntry_n \quad (3)$$
$$mutateDS_m \leq_p mutateDS_n \quad (4)$$
$$commitTransaction_m \leq_p commitTransaction_n \quad (5)$$

- Within one transaction, the log entry must be complete before data structure mutation (Eq. 1), and mutation must be complete before the transaction commits (Eq. 2). These dependencies ensure that any incomplete transaction can be rolled-back during recovery.
- Between conflicting transactions, preparing the log, mutating data, and commit must be ordered (Eqs. 3, 4, 5). These dependencies ensure that: (1) Mutations from conflicting transactions persist in lock-acquisition order (Eq. 4). (2) During recovery, active log entries from conflicting transactions can be undone in the appropriate order (Eqs. 3, and 5). Note that no dependencies exist between non-conflicting transactions.

3.3 Persist critical path analysis

In later sections, we evaluate alternative transaction implementations by comparing their persist dependency critical path to the ideal persist dependency DAG. Conflicting transactions incur additional dependencies that are absent among non-conflicting transactions. Hence, we characterize the critical path under two extreme scenarios, one where all transactions are non-conflicting, and one where all transactions conflict. Figure 1(b) depicts the ideal DAG for conflicting and non-conflicting transaction sequences. Nodes in this figure correspond to the (concurrent) sets of persist operations performed in each transaction step (we omit steps that modify only volatile state). Edges indicate persist dependency between nodes (more precisely, pairwise persist dependencies between all persists represented by each node).

Under each scenario, we assume x transactions are performed, and t threads concurrently execute those transactions. In the non-conflicting scenario, the x transactions all acquire disjoint locks and modify disjoint data. Therefore, there are no persist order dependencies across threads; the critical path is determined solely by persist ordering constraints that arise on a single thread. In this scenario, the ideal persist critical path length is 3—the intra-transaction ordering constraints—independent of x or t.

In the conflicting scenario, we assume all x transactions mutually conflict (they all require a lock in common). Therefore, the persist critical path follows the total order of these x transactions, as established by the order the locks are acquired. In this case, the persist critical path propagates through the commit node of each transaction, resulting in a critical path length of $x + 2$ persist operations. Again, the critical path is independent of the number of threads t.

While persist critical paths for an ideal DAG are quite short, achieving this ideal is difficult with currently proposed programing interfaces, which we summarize next.

4. Memory persistency models

Section 3 supposes that software is able to specify arbitrary ordering relationships among all persists, for example, in the form of a DAG. With this ability, a transaction implementation can minimize the number of persist dependencies and maximize NVRAM performance.

However, it is impractical to expect hardware to allow software to specify arbitrary persist dependencies, as this would require the hardware to track and honor an arbitrary DAG among persists. Instead, hardware will likely provide persist ordering mechanisms similar to those for ordering memory accesses in shared-memory multiprocessors. Industry has already begun following this course [14].

In currently shipping processor architectures, persist dependencies must be enforced either by using a write-through cache or by explicitly flushing individual cache lines (e.g., using the *clflush* instruction on x86). Moreover, these flush operations must be carefully annotated with fences to prevent hardware and compiler reorderings (details appear in [2]). These mechanisms are quite slow because they give up much of the performance benefits of CPU caches. Because cache flushes are so slow, Intel has recently announced extensions to its x86 ISA to optimize cache line flushing [14]. However, these mechanisms tie the ordering required between writes to NVRAM to the ordering required between a write to NVRAM and subsequent CPU instructions (Chidambaram, et al. describe this as the distinction between ordering and durability [6]).

Researchers have proposed other means to express persist dependencies. Condit and co-authors propose an *epoch barrier*, which ensures writes before the barrier are ordered before writes after the barrier [9]. Pelley and co-authors liken the problem of ordering persists to the problem of ordering memory accesses in a multiprocessor [27]. Just as there is a design space for multiprocessor memory consistency models, Pelley lays out a design space for NVRAM memory *persistency* models. We use *Total Store Order* as the underlying consistency model in this paper. We briefly summarize four persistency models, on which we build our transaction implementations.

4.1 Strict persistency

Under strict persistency, PMO is identical to VMO. So, for any two stores ordered by the consistency model, the corresponding persists are also ordered. Formally,

$$M_a^i \leq_v M_b^j \leftrightarrow M_a^i \leq_p M_b^j \quad (6)$$

Whereas strict persistency is the most intuitive persistency model, it is not the best performing. By ordering persists per VMO, strict persistency enforces orderings typically not required for recovery correctness [27]. Thus, researchers have proposed more relaxed persistency models, in which PMO may have fewer ordering constraints than VMO.

4.2 Epoch persistency

The *epoch persistency model* introduces a new memory event, the "persist barrier" (different from memory consistency barriers). We denote persist barriers issued by thread i as PB^i. Under epoch persistency, any two memory accesses on the same thread that are separated by a persist barrier in VMO are ordered in PMO.

$$M_a^i \leq_v PB^i \leq_v M_b^i \rightarrow M_a^i \leq_p M_b^i \quad (7)$$

Persist barriers separate a thread's execution into ordered epochs (persists within an epoch are concurrent). While persist barriers order persists from one thread, epoch persistency relies on another property, *strong persist atomicity*, to order persists from different threads.

Strong persist atomicity: Memory consistency models often guarantee that stores to the same address by different processors are serialized (this is called *store atomicity*). Pelley argues persistency models should similarly provide *strong persist atomicity* (SPA), to preclude non-intuitive behavior, such as recovering to states unreachable under fault-free execution [27]. SPA requires that conflicting accesses (accesses to the same address, at least one being a store) must persist in the order they executed.

$$\begin{aligned} S_a^i \leq_v M_a^j \rightarrow S_a^i \leq_p M_a^j \\ M_a^i \leq_v S_a^j \rightarrow M_a^i \leq_p S_a^j \end{aligned} \quad (8)$$

4.3 Strand persistency

Strand persistency divides program execution into *strands*. Strands are logically independent segments of execution that happen to execute in the same thread. Strands are separated by the *new strand* (NS) memory event. New strand events from thread i are denoted as NS^i. The new strand event clears all prior PMO constraints from prior instructions, effectively making each strand behave as if it were a separate thread (with respect to persistency). Memory accesses within a strand are ordered using persist barriers (Eq. 7). Under strand persistency, two memory accesses on the same thread separated by a persist barrier are ordered in PMO only if there is no intervening strand barrier. Memory accesses across strands continue to be ordered via SPA (Eq. 8).

$$\begin{aligned} (M_a^i \leq_v PB^i \leq_v M_b^i) \wedge (\nexists NS^i : M_a^i \leq_v NS^i \leq_v M_b^i) \\ \rightarrow M_a^i \leq_p M_b^i \end{aligned} \quad (9)$$

4.4 Eager sync

In addition to the persistency models proposed by Pelley, we also consider *eager sync*, our attempt to formalize the persistency model implied by Intel's recent x86 ISA extensions to optimize NVRAM performance [14]. We briefly describe these new instructions:

- $CLWB$: Requests write back of modified cache line to memory; the cache line may be retained in a clean state.
- $PCOMMIT$: Ensures that stores that have been accepted to memory are persistent.

Using these two instructions, stores on one thread to addresses A and B can be guaranteed to persist in the order $S_A^i \leq_p S_B^i$, using the following pseudo-code:

```
st A; CLWB A; SFENCE; PCOMMIT; SFENCE; st B;
```

We use the term "sync barrier" to refer to the code sequence $SFENCE; PCOMMIT; SFENCE$. A sync barrier issued by thread i will be denoted as SB^i. The first $SFENCE$ orders the $PCOMMIT$ with the earlier stores and $CLWB$s, while the second orders the younger stores with the $PCOMMIT$. A sync barrier differs from a persist barrier under epoch and strand persistency in two ways: (1) The second $SFENCE$ ensures that a younger store will *not* be globally visible until all stores older than the $PCOMMIT$ become persistent. In contrast, a persist barrier does not affect the global visibility of subsequent stores, it only orders the corresponding persists. (2) The $PCOMMIT$ persists only those stores that have been accepted to memory (e.g., using $CLWB$); a persist barrier orders the persists in PMO for all stores that precede the persist barrier in VMO.

Sync barriers affect the visibility of subsequent stores, with two important implications:

- Delaying store visibility until prior stores become persistent will likely add stalls to thread execution, especially because NVRAM persists may take 100s of nanoseconds [19] and a $PCOMMIT$ must persist all stores that have been accepted to memory.
- Since global visibility of a store can be delayed until prior stores have become persistent, the visibility of a store can act as a signal that all earlier stores are persistent. Astonishingly, such stalling of volatile events for persist events, can, in some cases, lead to fewer persist dependencies and better performance than epoch persistency (as we show in Section 6).

5. Synchronous commit transactions (SCT)

Section 3 showed how to implement transactions under an idealized programming model allowing arbitrary persist dependencies. We next examine how to implement transactions using more realistic mechanisms.

We first discuss an intuitive transaction implementation, which we call synchronous commit transactions (SCT). However, as we will show, SCT enforces unnecessary persist dependencies and overconstrains the persist critical path. Below, we describe and analyze SCT under epoch, eager sync, and strand persistency (we omit analysis under strict persistency to save space; all our designs will work under strict persistency).

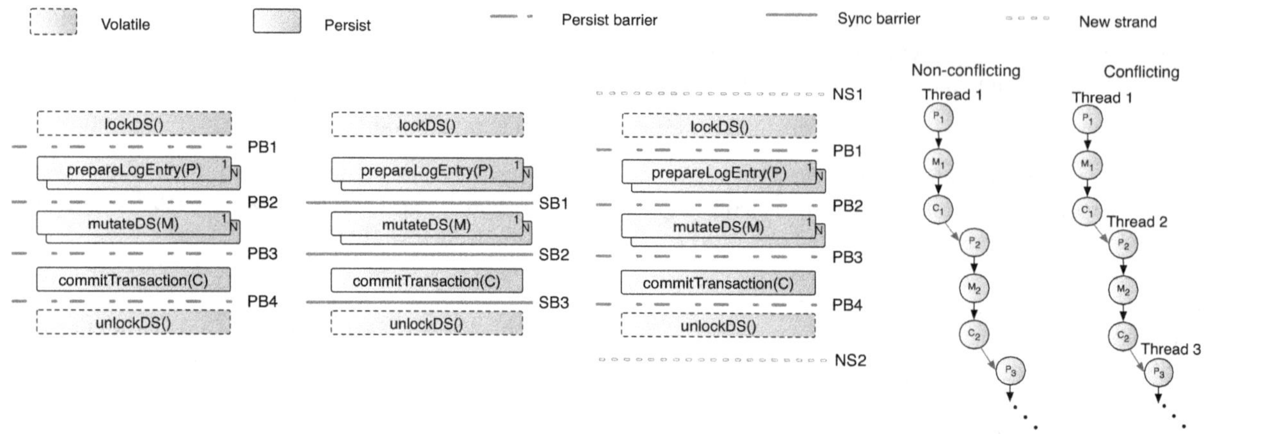

(a) SCT under epoch persistency (b) SCT under eager sync (c) SCT under strand persistency (d) Persist critical path (epoch persistency)

Figure 2. Synchronous-commit transactions under epoch persistency, eager sync and strand persistency. The red arrows in (d) represent the unnecessary dependencies enforced when compared to the minimal dependencies shown in Figure 1b.

5.1 SCT under Epoch Persistency

Epoch persistency enforces intra-thread persist dependencies via persist barriers, and inter-thread dependencies (for conflicting transactions) via persist barriers and SPA (Eq. 8). Figure 2(a) depicts a synchronous-commit transaction annotated with the four persist barriers required for correctness.

Intra-transaction dependencies: $PB2$ and $PB3$ ensure proper intra-transaction ordering of $prepareLogEntry$, $mutateDS$, and $commitTransaction$ (Eqs. 1 and 2).

Inter-transaction dependencies: Conflicting transactions (T_m and T_n) are synchronized through the common locks in their lock sets and hence through $unlockDS_m$ and $lockDS_n$. Since T_m happens in VMO before T_n, from SPA (Eq. 8), we have:

$$unlockDS_m \leq_v lockDS_n \rightarrow unlockDS_m \leq_p lockDS_n$$

The VMO of $prepareLogEntry$, $PB2$ (or $PB3$ or $PB4$), and $unlockDS$ in T_m imply:

$$prepareLogEntry_m \leq_p unlockDS_m$$

The VMO of $lockDS$, $PB1$, and $prepareLogEntry$ in T_n imply:

$$lockDS_n \leq_p prepareLogEntry_n$$

Applying transitivity to the above three equations, we observe that conflicting transactions prepare their log entries in order, satisfying Eq. 3. It is important to note that $PB1$ is critical to ensuring the correct order. Similarly, the VMO of $lockDS$, $PB1$ (or $PB2$), $mutateDS$, $PB3$ (or $PB4$), and $unlockDS$ ensures that conflicting transactions mutate the data structure in order, satisfying Eq. 4. VMO of $lockDS$, $PB1$ (or $PB2$ or $PB3$), $commitTransaction$, $PB4$, and $unlockDS$ ensure that conflicting transactions commit in order, satisfying Eq. 5.

Thus, the four persist barriers in Figure 2(a) are necessary and sufficient to ensure transactional persist ordering requirements. Unfortunately, these four persist barriers create a persist critical path longer than the path that would be possible had the software been able to specify the precise dependencies between all persists (Section 3).

From the VMO of $commitTransaction$, $PB4$, and $unlockDS$ in T_m and Eq. 7, we have:

$$commitTransaction_m \leq_p unlockDS_m$$

Similarly, VMO of $lockDS$, $PB1$, and $prepareLogEntry$ in T_n implies:

$$lockDS_n \leq_p prepareLogEntry_n$$

We have already shown:

$$unlockDS_m \leq_p lockDS_n$$

Applying transitivity to the above three equations, we have:

$$commitTransaction_m \leq_p prepareLogEntry_n$$

So, under epoch persistency, conflicting transactions are serialized. Moreover, transactions on the same thread are always serialized, even if they do not conflict. Figure 2(d) shows the persist critical path under epoch persistency: $3x$ for conflicting transactions and $3(x/t)$ for non-conflicting transactions. Both are longer than the minimal critical path (Figure 1(b)). Whereas SCT under epoch persistency is simple and intuitive, performing all steps of a transaction while holding locks overconstrains the persist dependency graph and lengthens the persist critical path.

5.2 SCT under Eager Sync

Eager sync enforces both intra-thread and inter-thread (for conflicting transactions) persist dependencies via sync barriers. Figure 2(b) depicts a synchronous-commit transaction annotated with the three sync barriers required for correctness. We also assume that all the $CLWB$s required to be issued before the sync barriers are issued along with the stores in the functions $prepareLogEntry$, $mutateDS$ and $commitTransaction$.

Intra-transaction dependencies: $SB1$ and $SB2$ ensure correct intra-transaction ordering of $prepareLogEntry$, $mutateDS$, and $commitTransaction$, satisfying Eqs. 1,2.

Inter-transaction dependencies: We again consider conflicting transactions T_m and T_n. $SB3$ ensures $unlockDS_m$ is not globally visible until $commitTransaction_m$ persists to NVRAM. $prepareLogEntry_n$ cannot be executed until T_n acquires its locks ($lockDS_n$), which happens after $unlockDS_m$ becomes globally visible. By stalling the global visibility of $unlockDS_m$ until $commitTransaction_m$ persists (because of $SB3$), we ensure that:

$$commitTransaction_m \leq_p prepareLogEntry_n$$

It is important to note that a sync barrier between $LockDS$ and $prepareLogEntry$ is not required to achieve the above dependency. The above dependency is the same (over-constraining) dependency incurred under epoch persistency, which serializes all conflicting transactions. $SB3$ also enforces that non-conflicting transactions within the same thread are serialized (as under epoch persistency). SCT under eager sync enforces the same ordering constraints as SCT under epoch persistency, resulting in the same persist critical path (Figure 2(d)).

5.3 SCT under Strand Persistency

Strand persistency makes it possible to remove unnecessary persist dependencies between transactions on the same thread (left graph of Figure 2(d)) by placing the transactions on different *strands*. Our implementation of SCT is shown in Figure 2(c). We start and end every transaction on a new strand ($NS1$, $NS2$ in Figure 2(c)). As a result, each transaction behaves as if on its own logical thread (from the perspective of the persistent memory, from Eq. 9). Such a design removes the dependence between successive non-conflicting transactions on the same thread. Conflicting transactions continue to be ordered due to the dependencies caused by the lock/unlock operations (as under epoch persistency).

It is important to note that in the SCT design for strand persistency (Figure 2(c)), $NS1$ ensures that each transaction starts on a new strand, and $NS2$ ensures that memory events executed after the transaction (but prior to the next transaction), don't end up serializing transactions on the same thread. For example, transaction systems may perform some book-keeping (say, update transaction count) at the end of every transaction. Without $NS2$, such bookkeeping could end up causing conflicts between otherwise non-conflicting transactions.

To achieve high concurrency, our SCT implementation uses per-thread (distributed) logs. In practice, log space is limited, and must ultimately be recycled. As a consequence, transactions that share no locks may nonetheless conflict if they reuse the same log space. We enforce the necessary ordering by adding a lock for the log entry to the transaction's lock sets.

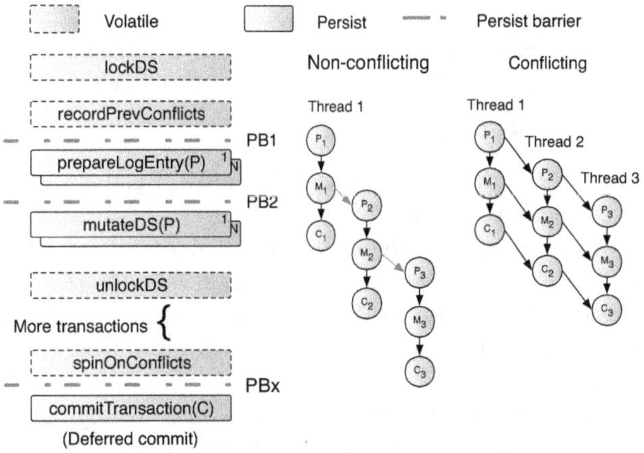

(a) DCT under epoch persistency (b) Persist critical path

Figure 3. Deferred commit transactions under epoch persistency and the resulting persist ordering constraints.

Under ideal implementations of strand persistency, the achievable persist concurrency is limited only by the available log space. In practice, we expect future systems to limit strand concurrency. In a system with t threads and s strands, the maximum concurrency under strand persistency is similar to a system with $s \times t$ threads under epoch persistency. Under strand persistency, the SCT persist critical path for non-conflicting transactions improves to $3(x/st)$ (the persist critical path for conflicting transactions remains $3x$). Whereas strand persistency improves the SCT persist critical path, it remains longer than the theoretical minimum.

6. Deferred commit transactions (DCT)

SCT generates longer critical paths than needed when implemented on realistic persistency models. In this section, we describe deferred commit transactions (DCT), which generate shorter critical paths than SCT.

The key idea in DCT is for a transaction to release locks after mutating the data structure and to defer commit until later. This idea has been explored as a mechanism for managing lock contention for transaction systems with a centralized log [16]. We use this idea to break the persist order dependence between $commitTransaction$ and $prepareLogEntry$ of consecutive conflicting transactions. However, performing the commit after the lock release implies that the persists from $commitTransaction$ are no longer synchronized by the respective locks and could result in conflicting transactions committing out of order. [2] To ensure that conflicting transactions commit in order (Eq. 5) we modify transactions to explicitly track (in volatile memory)

[2] This is not a problem with a centralized log, as they are serialized by the lock for the log.

their predecessor conflicting transactions and commit after all predecessors have committed. Next, we describe DCT implementations under the three persistency models.

6.1 DCT under Epoch Persistency

Figure 3(a) shows the implementation of DCT and the associated "deferred-commit" block.

Intra-transaction dependencies: Persist barrier $PB2$ helps satisfy Eq. 1 by guaranteeing that $prepareLogEntry$ is ordered before $mutateDS$. The commit-after-mutate rule (Eq. 2) is ensured by PBx (a barrier from a subsequent transaction).

Inter-transaction dependencies: For conflicting transactions T_m and T_n, the persist barriers $PB1$ and $PB2$, along with the SPA guarantees of $unlockDS_m$ and $locksDS_n$, ensure that the log entries are prepared in order, satisfying Eq. 3. SPA (Eq. 8) of the conflicting regions of the data structure ensure that Eq. 4 is satisfied. DCTs need to explicitly track prior conflicting transactions to ensure the commit-in-order rule (Eq. 5). We achieve this order by having the transaction $spinOnConflict$ (conflicts are recorded in the log entry) after the lock release and then $commitTransaction$ following a persist barrier PBx. It is important to note that, instead of having a designated barrier to order the commit, we rely on a barrier from a subsequent transaction. As a result, the $commitTransaction$ step may occur concurrently with persists from a subsequent transaction and does not add to the persist critical path. Next, we describe the challenges that arise from deferring commits and the bookkeeping required to address them.

6.1.1 Inferring undo order during recovery

By allowing transaction commits to be deferred, we can arrive at a state where multiple conflicting uncommitted transactions must apply undo log entries at recovery. The recovery protocol must infer the order of these log entries and perform the undo operations in reverse order. As we use distributed logs, deducing this order is non-trivial. Mnemosyne [33] uses a single global atomic counter to assign each new transaction an incrementing global timestamp (log entries can be undone in the decreasing order of timestamps). However, such an approach implies that all transactions conflict (they all update the global counter), and results in an artificially conflated persist critical path. One might consider recording a timestamp in each log entry, but reliably ordering nearly concurrent events via wall-clock timestamps is challenging, especially if execution is distributed over multiple cores/chips.

Since we only need to order log entries for conflicting transactions, we extend all locks to contain logical time stamps (i.e., Lamport clocks [18]). When a transaction acquires a lock, it records and increments the current lock timestamp, ensuring subsequent conflicting transactions will see a higher timestamp. Timestamps are logged in the new $recordPrevConflicts$ function, shown in Figure 3(a). If a transaction acquires multiple locks, all of their timestamps must be recorded. Recovery uses these timestamps to deduce the correct undo order.

6.1.2 Enforcing correct commit order

To ensure correct recovery, conflicting transactions must commit in order. DCT requires an explicit software mechanism to track and enforce this order. We extend each lock with a pointer to the log entry of the last transaction to acquire that lock. When a transaction acquires all of the locks in its lock set, it records the pointers to previous conflicting transactions (one per lock) in volatile memory, shown as $recordPrevConflicts$ in Figure 3(a). Then, it records a pointer to its own log entry in each lock.

At commit, a transaction must verify that preceding conflicting transactions have committed. Using the recorded pointers, it examines each preceding log entry for a commit marker, spinning until all are set ($spinOnConflicts$ in Figure 3(a)). However, if a log entry is recycled, its commit marker is now stale. Along with the commit marker, $recordPrevConflicts$ records a log generation number associated with every log entry. The log generation number is incremented if the log entry is recycled. The combination of the commit marker and the log generation number is used to deduce whether an earlier transaction has committed.

Once all of the conflicting log entries are committed, the transaction may commit ($commitTransaction$ in Figure 3(a)). (Note that, rather than simply spinning, an intelligent transaction manager could instead further defer commit and execute additional transactions on this thread). The spin loop prior to commit orders conflicting transactions in VMO. A persist barrier is required between $spinOnConflicts$ and $commitTransaction$ (PBx) to ensure the conflicting transaction commits are also ordered in PMO.

6.1.3 Persist critical path analysis

Figure 3(b) shows the persist critical path for DCT under epoch persistency. DCT succeeds in matching the critical path length of the ideal dependence DAG for conflicting transactions as derived in Section 3. For transactions on a single thread, it reduces the critical path by allowing commit operations to be batched.

For non-conflicting transactions on the same thread, the $prepareLogEntry$ and $mutateDS$ steps remain (unnecessarily) serialized. The $commitTransaction$ step overlaps with the $prepareLogEntry$ step of the subsequent transaction. Hence, the non-conflicting persist critical path length is $(2(x/t)+1)$. For conflicting transactions, the persist critical path traverses the $commitTransaction$ step of each transaction, and its path length is $x+2$.

6.2 DCT under Eager Sync

The implementation of DCT under the eager sync persistency model is shown in Figure 4(a). While similar to the DCT implementation under epoch persistency, we require

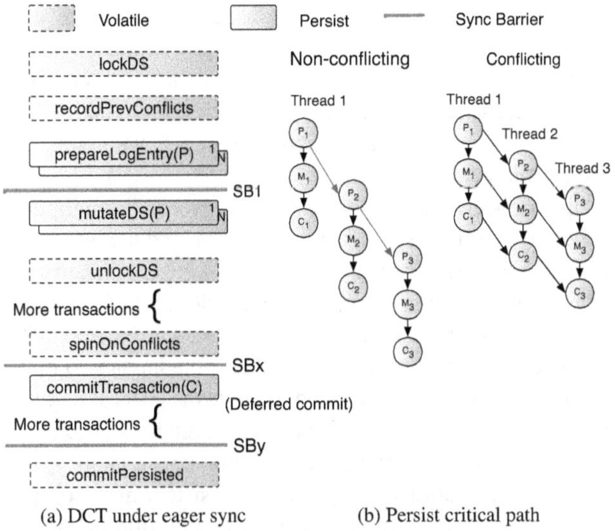

Figure 4. Deferred commit transactions under eager sync and the resulting persist ordering constraints.

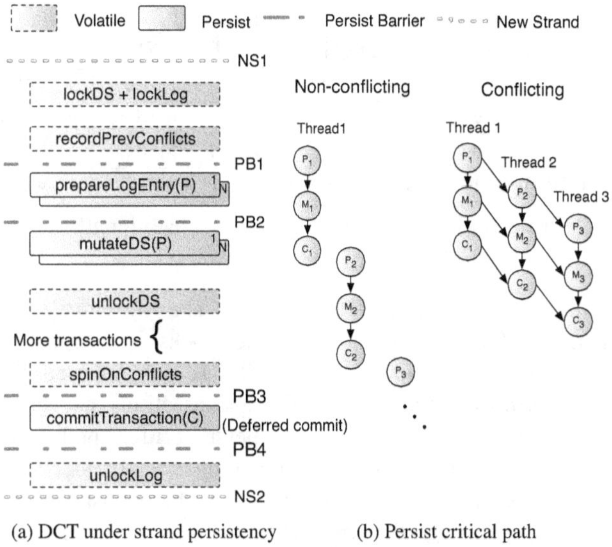

Figure 5. Deferred commit transactions under strand persistency and the resulting persist ordering constraints.

some subtle changes to account for the differences between a persist barrier and a sync barrier detailed in Section 4.2. It is important to note that we require only one sync barrier within the transaction, rather than the two persist barriers required for DCT under epoch persistency.

Intra-transaction dependencies: The sync barrier $SB1$, ensures order between $prepareLogEntry$ and $mutateDS$, satisfying Eq. 1. The sync barrier Sbx (which belongs to a subsequent transaction) ensures that $mutateDS$ and $commitTransaction$ are ordered correctly, satisfying Eq. 2.

Inter-transaction dependencies: We discuss inter-transaction dependencies using two conflicting transactions T_m and T_n. Within T_m, $SB1$, ensures that $unlockDS_m$ doesn't become globally visible until $prepareLogEntry_m$ becomes persistent. In transaction T_n, $prepareLogEntry_n$ cannot be executed before the locks are acquired using $lockDS_n$. However, $lockDS_n$ cannot be completed until $unlockDS_m$ becomes globally visible. Transitively, $SB1$, ensures that log entries are prepared in order, satisfying Eq. 3. Cache coherence ensures that at any given time, only the latest values of any conflicting regions of the data structure persist, satisfying Eq. 4.

Since SPA (Eq. 8) is not provided under eager sync, we cannot use the same coding pattern as used in the epoch persistency DCT implementation to ensure conflicting transactions commit in order. Instead, we have a $commitPersisted$ bit associated with every log entry, which is set after $commitTransaction_m$ is guaranteed to be have persisted (ensured by SBy in Figure 4(a)). We modify the $spinOnConflict$ function to spin on the $commitPersisted$ bits of conflicting transactions, rather than the log entries. Once a transaction observes that the $commitPersisted$ bit of earlier conflicting transactions have been set, it can be committed and be certain that the correct commit order has been followed.

It is important to note that we do not need dedicated sync barriers, SBx and SBy, for every transaction. We instead rely on sync barriers from a subsequent transaction, implying that both $mutateDS$ and $commitTransaction$ are persisted concurrently with later transactions. So, only the persists belonging to $prepareLogEntry$ fall on the persist critical path on a single thread, as depicted in Figure 4(b). For non-conflicting transactions, the persist critical path traverses all the $prepareLogEntry$ steps of each transaction executed on one thread and is $x/t + 2$. For the conflicting case, the persist critical path traverses the $commitTransaction$ step of all the transactions and is $x + 2$. Note that DCT under eager sync incurs a shorter persist critical path than under epoch persistency for non-conflicting transactions, whereas they exhibit the same persist critical path for conflicting transactions.

Discussion: DCT under eager sync and Mnemosyne (asynchronous mode) [33] are similar in that each transaction may add at most one persist epoch delay to the execution critical path. Whereas DCT amortizes the cost of $mutateDS$ and $commitTransaction$ over subsequent transactions on the same thread, Mnemosyne offloads log truncation to a separate helper thread.

6.3 DCT under Strand persistency

Figure 5(a) shows our implementation of DCT under strand persistency. As with the SCT implementation under strand persistency, we expose additional persist concurrency by placing each transaction on a new strand, removing the dependencies between non-conflicting transactions on the same thread. Similar to SCT, we introduce a log entry lock to a transaction's lock set, so that transactions which

	Non-conflicting		Conflicting	
Persistency Model	**SCT**	**DCT**	**SCT**	**DCT**
Epoch	$3x/t$	$2x/t+1$	$3x$	$x+2$
Eager sync	$3x/t$	$x/t+2$	$3x$	$x+2$
Strand	$3x/st$	$3x/st$	$3x$	$x+2$

Notation: x- total transactions, t-threads, s-strands/thread

Table 1. Summary of persist critical path lengths.

conflict on a log entry are serialized. The log entry lock is acquired along with all the other locks in a transaction's lock set. However, the log entry is only released after $commitTransaction$, serializing transactions that share log space. Figure 5(b) shows the persist critical paths for the conflicting and non-conflicting scenarios. In the conflicting case, as under epoch persistency, the persist critical path passes through the $commitTransaction$ step of each transaction, leading to the ideal persist critical path length of $x + 2$ edges. In the non-conflicting case, the persist dependency critical path improves, but may still fall short of the ideal DAG if the number of strands supported in hardware is limited. The persist critical path for non-conflicting transactions goes through transactions which share log space and is $3x/st$ where t is the number of threads and s the number of strands per thread (similar to SCT under strand). With support for at least two strands per thread, DCT under strand persistency outperforms DCT under epoch persistency.

Table 1 summarizes the critical paths for SCT and DCT under various persistency models and workloads.

7. Evaluation

We evaluate transactional systems implementing both SCT and DCT to examine their performance trade-off as a function of persist latency for two transaction processing workloads. In general, we expect DCT to have slower volatile execution performance, due to the bookkeeping overheads required to order commits. However, as persist latency increases, it rapidly becomes the performance bottleneck, and DCT overtakes SCT. As the NVRAM programming interface remains unclear, we also compare the performance achieved under different persistency models for both SCT and DCT. Strict persistency performs much worse than all other persistency models, so we omit it from the discussion.

7.1 Methodology

We implement our transactional systems as a C++ library providing a simple API comprising only three entry points: `beginTransaction()`, `prepareLogEntry()`, and `endTransaction()`. The system manages bookkeeping, log serialization, commit ordering, and inserting the necessary barriers to enforce persist dependencies.

Because memory-bus-attached NVRAM devices are not yet available, we use a region of DRAM as a proxy. We execute our workloads writing persistent data to DRAM to establish their volatile execution performance. We then re-execute the workloads with lightweight pin instrumentation [23] to record all persist operations and barriers. From these traces, we construct the persist critical path (taking into account ordering within and across threads). We assume 8-byte atomic persists.

Under epoch and strand persistency, overall throughput is limited by the slower of volatile execution and the latency to drain all persists. However, in the case of eager sync, overall throughput is limited by volatile execution, which includes the stalls associated with executing the sync barriers. The overhead of a sync barrier only includes the latency to make the stores persistent and does not include the costs associated with issuing and executing the corresponding $CLWB$s.

As the hardware characteristics, raw device latency, and scheduling limitations of a practical persistent memory system are as yet unknown, we vary our assumption for persist performance and report the resulting throughput. Cumulative persist latency is determined by how fast, on average, an epoch of persists can drain subject to queueing, scheduling, device-level concurrency, and coalescing effects. We abstract these effects as a single average latency per persist epoch (i.e., latency per dependency edge in the critical path). As we expect persist throughput to be the performance bottleneck when transactions are short, load on the persistent memory system will be high and queueing delays substantial. Hence, the average persist epoch latency is likely a small integer multiple of the NVRAM device latency, we study the the range of 0-4μs.

We perform experiments on an Intel Xeon E5645 processor (2.4GHz). We analyze throughput for transactions selected from two widely studied transaction processing workloads. We study the *New Order* transaction from TPCC [30], which is its most frequent write transaction. A New Order transaction simulates a customer buying different items from a local warehouse. The transaction is write-intensive and requires atomic updates to several tables. We also study the *Update Location* transaction from TATP [26], a benchmark that models a mobile carrier database. Update Location records the hand-off of a user from one cell tower to another. In contrast to New Order, Update Location transactions are much shorter, updating a small record in a single table. We execute workloads for 10M transactions running on four threads. We assume four strands per thread under strand persistency.

7.2 Performance analysis

Figure 6 contrasts SCT and DCT performance across workloads, persistency models, and average persist epoch latencies depicting throughput (millions of transactions per sec (MTPS)) versus persist epoch latency (micro seconds).

Each performance result with epoch and strand persistency (Figure 6) comprises a flat region, followed by a curve where throughput rapidly falls off. In the flat regions, where average persist epoch latency is low, overall throughput is

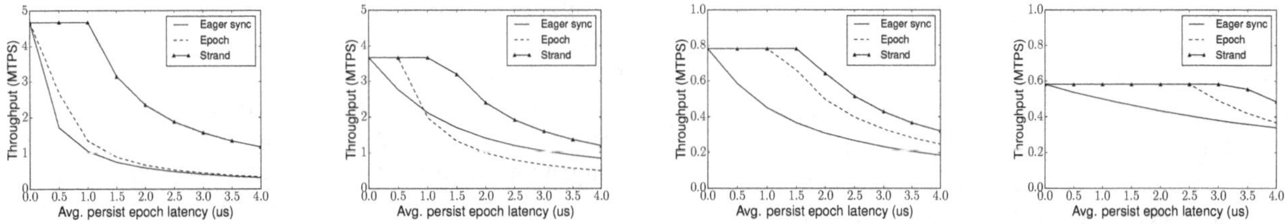

(a) Update Location (SCT) (b) Update Location (DCT) (c) New Order (SCT) (d) New Order (DCT)

Figure 6. SCT and DCT performance for Update Location and New Order under various persistency models.

limited by volatile execution. At the knee, which we call the "break-even" latency, volatile execution and the persist critical path are equal. Higher break-even latency implies tolerance for slower NVRAM technologies. Performance then drops off rapidly as average persist epoch latency increases and asymptotically reaches zero. In contrast, for eager sync, since sync barriers cause stalls in volatile execution, performance begins to drop-off at the first non-zero average persist epoch latency.

Volatile execution performance of SCT exceeds DCT. As expected, the additional bookkeeping required to implement DCT penalizes volatile execution speed—SCT transactions are faster than DCT transactions (if persist epoch latency is neglected) by 20%, 25% for Update Location and New Order respectively.

SCT performance across persistency models: Figures 6(a) and 6(c) show the performance of SCT, for Update Location and New Order, for different persistency models. SCT under eager sync always performs worse than under epoch persistency. This behavior is to be expected as SCT exhibits similar persist critical paths under epoch persistency and eager sync. With similar persist critical paths, the performance under epoch persistency is always better than under eager sync. Under epoch persistency, performance is determined by the slower of volatile execution and time taken to drain the persists. However, in the case of eager sync, the time taken to drain persists (stalls due to sync barriers), slows volatile execution.

Also, as expected, SCT performs better under strand persistency than under epoch persistency, due to a shorter persist critical path. Hence, SCT performs best under strand persistency and the worst under eager sync.

DCT performance across persistency models: The performance trade-offs for DCT are more complex. Figure 6(b) shows that the performance of DCT under epoch persistency is worse than under eager sync above $1\mu s$ persist latency. DCT incurs a longer persist critical path under epoch persistency than under eager sync, especially for workloads where transactions rarely conflict, like Update Location. Hence, beyond the break-even latency, the performance under epoch persistency declines faster than under eager sync.

	Update Location	New order
Epoch persistency	0.5	2
Eager sync	0.5	1
Strand persistency	1.5	2.5

Table 2. The average persist epoch latency (in μs), at which DCT breaks even with SCT.

For New Order (Figure 6(d)), we see that DCT performs better under epoch persistency than under eager sync. This behavior is caused by multiple factors: (1) The break-even latency for epoch persistency is $2.5\mu s$, so epoch persistency performance degrades only for persist latencies above $2.5\mu s$. (2) New Order has more conflicting transactions than Update Location, so the difference in persist critical path between epoch and eager sync is smaller. (3) The crossover point at which eager sync begins outperforming epoch persistency lies beyond $4\mu s$, which is not shown in the graphs. It is not clear that a memory technology that incurs more than $4\mu s$ average persist epoch latency is viable as a main memory.

As expected, DCT under strand persistency performs best for both workloads (Figures 6(b) and 6(d)) as the persist critical path under strand persistency is the shortest.

SCT vs. DCT across persistency models: The performance trade-off (for all persistency models) between SCT and DCT depends upon two competing factors: (1) the better volatile performance of SCT, and (2) the shorter persist critical paths of DCT. As a result, for lower average persist epoch latencies, SCT performs better, but as latency increases, DCT outperforms SCT by up to 50% under epoch and strand persistency and 150% under eager sync.

In Table 2, we summarize the average persist epoch latency, where SCT and DCT provide the same performance, under each persistency model. Table 2 indicates: (1) DCT breaks-even with SCT at higher latencies for New Order than Update Location. New Order is a larger transaction, hiding longer persist delays under volatile execution. (2) Strand persistency exhibits the highest SCT-DCT break-even latencies, as it incurs the smallest difference in persist critical path between DCT and SCT.

8. Related work

The emergence of new persistent memory technologies has spurred research in many areas of computer science, including file systems [4, 9, 11], databases [5, 7, 13, 21, 32], persistent data structures [8, 33], and concurrent programming [3].

Several systems share our goal of providing a transaction interface to persistent memory. NV-Heaps [8] provides a persistent object system with transactional semantics that prevents persistence-related pointer and memory allocation errors. Mnemosyne [33] allows programmers to declare or allocate persistent data and write this data through special instructions or via transactions. Rio Vista [21] provides transactions on top of flat memory regions.

Prior systems have generally not sought to optimize concurrency of writes to persistent memory. For example, Rio Vista assumes persistent memory is fast enough to not require concurrent accesses [21]. NV-Heaps uses epoch barriers to order persistent writes and assumes that memory accesses execute serially [8]. Mnemosyne uses cache-flush operations to order updates to persistent memory [33].

Unlike these systems, our paper focuses on maximizing the concurrency of writes to persistent memory by reducing ordering constraints between persistent memory accesses. We believe that freeing the underlying persistent memory system to reorder, parallelize, and combine writes will be essential to supporting high-performance, transaction-oriented workloads. To our knowledge, our work is the first to explore the implications of various recently proposed persistency models on transaction software.

Recent work by Lu and co-authors shares our goal of reducing ordering constraints among persistent writes [22]. Their system distributes the commit status of a transaction among the data blocks to eliminate an ordering constraint within a transaction (similar to the torn bit in Mnemosyne [33]), and uses hardware support (multi-versioned CPU cache and transaction IDs) to enable conflicting transactions to persist out of order. Their techniques are complementary to the ones we propose for reducing ordering constraints. In addition, their system assumes that flushing is required to guarantee ordering (as in eager sync), whereas we explore other memory persistency models.

Our work builds on prior proposals to allow software to communicate ordering dependencies among writes to persistent memory. In shipping systems, order can be enforced by flushing persistent writes from the CPU cache to memory (e.g., via write-through caches or `clflush` instructions) and then issuing a memory barrier (e.g., `mfence`) [31]. However, flushing data to persistent storage is not necessarily the best way to ensure the order in which data is made durable [6]. To relax ordering requirements, Condit and co-authors propose using *epoch barriers* to ensure an ordering between writes before and after the barrier [9]. Pelley and co-authors expand this into a design space for memory persistency models [27].

Others propose hardware support to increase the apparent speed of persistent memory by adding a nonvolatile CPU cache [34] or by assuming sufficient residual power to complete all pending writes [25]. Reducing persist latency makes it less important to allow concurrent writes to persistent memory. Our work makes the more conservative assumption that data must be written to the main persistent memory to be considered durable. Transactions can also be accelerated via other hardware support for persistent memory, such as editable atomic writes [7].

9. Conclusions

New non-volatile memory technologies make it possible to store persistent data directly in memory. Achieving the full performance benefits of doing so requires minimizing the constraints on the order of writes to NVRAM. In this paper, we show how to design transaction systems that specify and communicate these constraints to hardware in a way that reduces the dependencies between NVRAM writes. Our DCT transaction design reduces the persist critical path and improves performance by up to 50% under epoch and strand persistency and up to 150% under eager sync.

Acknowledgments

We would like to thank the anonymous reviewers for their valuble feedback. This work was supported by the National Science Foundation under the award NSF-CCF-1525372.

References

[1] Sarita V. Adve and Kourosh Gharachorloo. "Shared Memory Consistency Models: A Tutorial." In *IEEE Computer*, Vol. 29 No. 12, December 1996.

[2] Kumud Bhandari, Dhruva R. Chakrabarti, and Hans-J. Boehm. "Implications of CPU Caching on Byte-addressable Non-Volatile Memory Programming." *Technical Report HPL-2012-236, Hewlett-Packard*, 2012.

[3] Dhruva R. Chakrabarti, Hans-J. Boehm, and Kumud Bhandari. "Atlas: Leveraging Locks for Non-volatile Memory Consistency." In *Conference on Object-Oriented Programming, Systems, Languages, and Applications*, 2014.

[4] Peter M. Chen, Wee Teck Ng, Subhachandra Chandra, Christopher M. Aycock, Gurushankar Rajamani, and David E. Lowell. "The Rio File Cache: Surviving Operating System Crashes." In *International Conference on Architectural Support for Programming Languages and Operating Systems*, 1996.

[5] Shimin Chen, Phillip B. Gibbons, and Suman Nath. "Rethinking Database Algorithms for Phase Change Memory." In *Conference on Innovative Data Systems Research*, 2011.

[6] Vijay Chidambaram, Thanumalayan Sankaranarayana Pillai, Andrea C. Arpaci-Dusseau, and Remzi H. Arpaci-Dusseau. "Optimistic Crash Consistency." In *Symposium on Operating Systems Principles*, 2013.

[7] Joel Coburn, Trevor Bunker, Meir Shwarz, Rajesh K. Gupta, and Steven Swanson. "From ARIES to MARS:Transaction

Support for Next-Generation Solid-State Drives." In *Symposium on Operating System Principles*, 2013.

[8] Joel Coburn, Adrian M. Caulfield, Ameen Akel, Laura M. Grupp, Rajesh K. Gupta, Ranjit Jhala, and Steven Swanson. "NV-Heaps: Making Persistent Objects Fast and Safe with Next-Generation, Non-Volatile Memories." In *International Conference on Architectural Support for Programming Languages and Operating Systems*, 2011.

[9] Jeremy Condit, Edmund B. Nightingale, Christopher Frost, Engin Ipek, Benjamin Lee, Doug Burger, and Derrick Coetzee. "Better I/O Through Byte-Addressable, Persistent Memory." In *Symposium on Operating Systems Principles*, 2009.

[10] David J. DeWitt, Randy H. Katz, Frank Olken, Leonard D. Shapiro, Michael R. Stonebraker, and David A. Wood. "Implementation Techniques for Main Memory Database Systems." In *International Conference on Management of Data*, 1984.

[11] Subramanya R. Dulloor, Sanjay Kumar, Anil Keshavamurthy, Philip Lantz, Dheeraj Reddy, Rajesh Sankaran, and Jeff Jackson. "System Software for Persistent Memory." In *European Conference on Computer Systems*, 2014.

[12] Jim Gray and Andreas Reuter. "Transaction Processing: Concepts and Techniques." *Morgan Kaufmann Publishers, Inc.*, 1993.

[13] Jian Huang, Karsten Schwan, and Moinuddin K. Qureshi. "NVRAM-aware Logging in Transaction Systems." In *Proceedings of the VLDB Endowment*, 2014.

[14] Intel. "Intel Architecture Instruction Set Extensions Programming Reference (319433-023)." `https://software.intel.com/sites/default/files/managed/0d/53/319433-023.pdf`, 2014.

[15] Intel and Micron. "Intel and Micron Produce Breakthrough Memory Technology." `http://newsroom.intel.com/community/intel_newsroom/blog/2015/07/28/intel-and-micron-produce-breakthrough-memory-\technology`, 2015.

[16] Ryan Johnson, Ippokratis Pandis, Radu Stoica, Manos Athanassoulis, and Anastasia Ailamaki. "Aether: A Scalable Approach to Logging." In *Proceedings of the VLDB Endowment*, 2010.

[17] Aasheesh Kolli, Steven Pelley, Ali Saidi, Peter M. Chen, and Thomas F. Wenisch. "Persistency Programming 101." In *Non-Volatile Memories Workshop*, 2015.

[18] Leslie Lamport. "Time, Clocks, and the Ordering of Events in a Distributed System." In *Communications of the ACM*, Vol. 21, July 1978.

[19] Benjamin C. Lee, Engin Ipek, Onur Mutlu, and Doug Burger. "Architecting Phase Change Memory as a Scalable Dram Alternative." In *International Symposium on Computer Architecture*, 2009.

[20] Eunji Lee, Hyokyung Bahn, and Sam H. Noh. "Unioning of the Buffer Cache and Journaling Layers with Non-volatile Memory." In *Conference on File and Storage Technologies*, 2013.

[21] David E. Lowell and Peter M. Chen. "Free Transactions with Rio Vista.". In *Symposium on Operating Systems Principles*, 1997.

[22] Y. Lu, J. Shu, L. Sun, and O. Mutlu. "Loose-Ordering Consistency for Persistent Memory." In *International Conference on Computer Design*, 2014.

[23] Chi-Keung Luk, Robert Cohn, Robert Muth, Harish Patil, Artur Klauser, Geoff Lowney, Steven Wallace, Vijay Janapa Reddi, and Kim Hazelwood. "Pin: Building Customized Program Analysis Tools with Dynamic Instrumentation." In *Conference on Programming Language Design and Implementation*, 2005.

[24] C. Mohan, Don Haderle, Bruce Lindsay, Hamid Pirahesh, and Peter Schwarz. "ARIES: A Transaction Recovery Method Supporting Fine-Granularity Locking and Partial Rollbacks Using Write-Ahead Logging." In *ACM Transactions on Database Systems*, Vol. 17 No. 1, 1992.

[25] Dushyanth Narayanan and Orion Hodson. "Whole-System Persistence." In *International Conference on Architectural Support for Programming Languages and Operating Systems*, 2012.

[26] Simo Neuvonen, Antoni Wolski, Markku Manner, and Vilho Raatikka. "Telecom Application Transaction Processing Benchmark." `http://tatpbenchmark.sourceforge.net/`.

[27] Steven Pelley, Peter M. Chen, and Thomas F. Wenisch. "Memory Persistency." In *International Symposium on Computer Architecture*, 2014.

[28] Vijayan Prabhakaran, Lakshmi N. Bairavasundaram, Nitin Agrawal, Haryadi S. Gunawi, Andreas C. Arpaci-Dusseau, and Remzi H. Arpaci-Dusseau. "IRON File Systems." In *Symposium on Operating Systems Principles*, 2005.

[29] Alexander Thomson and Daniel J. Abadi. "The Case for Determinism in Database Systems." In *Proceedings of the VLDB Endowment*, 2010.

[30] Transaction Processing Performance Council (TPC). "TPC Benchmark B." `http://www.tpc.org/tpc_documents_current_versions/pdf/tpc-c_v5-11.pdf`.

[31] Shivaram Venkataraman, Niraj Tolia, Parthasarathy Ranganathan, and Roy H. Campbell. "Consistent and Durable Data Structures for Non-Volatile Byte-Addressable Memory." In *Conference on File and Storage Technologies*, 2011.

[32] Tianzheng Wang and Ryan Johnson. "Scalable Logging through Emerging Non-Volatile Memory." In *Proceedings of the VLDB Endowment*, 2014.

[33] Haris Volos, Andres Jaan Tack, and Michael M. Swift. "Mnemosyne: Lightweight Persistent Memory." In *International Conference on Architectural Support for Programming Languages and Operating Systems*, 2011.

[34] Jishen Zhao, Sheng Li, Doe Hyun Yoon, Yuan Xie, and Norman P. Jouppi. "Kiln: Closing the Performance Gap Between Systems With and Without Persistence Support." In *International Symposium on Microarchitecure*, 2013.

[35] Jishen Zhao, Onur Mutlu, and Yuan Xie. "FIRM: Fair and High-performance Memory Control for Peristent Memory Systems." In *International Symposium on Microarchitecure*, 2014.

High-Density Image Storage Using Approximate Memory Cells *

Qing Guo★ Karin Strauss† ‡ Luis Ceze‡ † Henrique S. Malvar†

★NVIDIA †Microsoft Research ‡University of Washington

Abstract

This paper proposes tailoring image encoding for an approximate storage substrate. We demonstrate that indiscriminately storing encoded images in approximate memory generates unacceptable and uncontrollable quality degradation. The key finding is that errors in the encoded bit streams have non-uniform impact on the decoded image quality. We develop a methodology to determine the relative importance of encoded bits and store them in an approximate storage substrate. The storage cells are optimized to reduce error rate via *biasing* and are tuned to meet the desired reliability requirement via *selective error correction*. In a case study with the progressive transform codec (PTC), a precursor to JPEG XR, the proposed approximate image storage system exhibits a 2.7× increase in density of pixels per silicon volume under bounded error rates, and this achievement is additive to the storage savings of PTC compression.

Categories and Subject Descriptors I.4.2 [*Image Processing and Computer Vision*]: Approximate methods; B.3.4 [*Memory Structures*]: Reliability, Testing, and Fault-Tolerance

Keywords Approximate Storage; Image Encoding; Multi-level Cells

1. Introduction

Images and video consume significant storage space in both consumer devices and in the cloud. The emergence of new applications and new devices with even greater image and video recording capabilities will only reinforce this trend. This will result in pressure on storage system capacity, which is exacerbated by replicas of the data in multiple user devices and the cloud. Luckily, this also relaxes the requirements on the quality of data stored in devices because there is always a high-fidelity copy stored in the cloud. This paper proposes an image encoding algorithm co-designed with a solid-state storage system that supports multiple reliability levels, resulting in high-density image storage. This allows users to have more images stored locally, potentially at a lower quality, all backed up by full-quality images in the cloud.

Solid-state memories with multi-level cell (MLC) capability improve storage density by subdividing the range of values in a cell into a greater number of levels, each of which being representative of a digital state. Creating more levels to store multiple bits in a single cell improves density, but it also increases the cost of storage dramatically because read and write circuits with much higher precision are required to ensure that data can be reliably read and written.

Recently proposed approximate storage techniques [27] relax the costly reliability requirements by allowing occasional errors. Examples of data that can tolerate these errors are samples of signal inputs that are already noisy, such as image sensors – an error in one pixel in a raw image affects quality in a localized manner. However, images are rarely stored in raw format long-term; instead, they are typically encoded in compressed form to save space.

Image compression techniques such as JPEG trade-off image quality against image size via quantization techniques. This quantization step is lossy, yet applied in a deterministic way so that all loss happens at encoding time. In contrast, approximate storage errors are inherently non-deterministic and accrue over time. This paper makes the observation that the latter type of error may create large distortions once the image is decoded because it has not been accounted for at encoding time. Because image encoding schemes typically transform pixels to the frequency domain (where some components matter more than others) and employ entropy encoding (lossless compression), changes in different bits in the compressed file lead to different kinds of distortion in the output image. Hence, to preserve quality in the decoded image, different bits should be subject to different levels of approximation (*i.e.*, exposed to different error rates).

An intuitive solution for reducing the error rates of an unreliable substrate is to treat it as a noisy channel and uniformly apply an error correcting code to it. This approach treats source and channel encoding independently, and is optimal when the conditions for the well-known separation

* This work was done when the author Qing Guo was an intern at Microsoft Research and a student at the University of Rochester.

ASPLOS '16 April 2–6, 2016, Atlanta, Georgia, USA.

DOI: http://dx.doi.org/10.1145/2872362.2872413

theorem apply [8, 9]. Unfortunately, at least one of these conditions does not apply when the source is image data (which in general cannot be modeled as being generated from a source with stationary statistics) or when the channel is MLC storage (where the error probability depends on the value stored and manufacturing variations). In other words, if we apply an error-correcting code (channel coding) uniformly to the entire storage space, we essentially make all cells similarly reliable, which is wasteful when storing parts of the encoded image data that can tolerate higher error rates.

This paper advocates for a cooperative design of image encoding algorithms and approximate storage systems to maximize storage density while minimizing image distortion. The key idea is to determine the relative importance of encoded bits created by the encoding algorithm, and store them into separate regions of approximate storage, each of which tuned to match the error tolerance of the bits it stores. This exploits the case that, when the conditions for the separation theorem do not apply, best compression is achieved by joint source-channel coding [8, 32].

We demonstrate our techniques via a case study of the progressive transform codec (PTC) [17] – a precursor to JPEG XR – and a phase-change memory (PCM) storage substrate. Our results show that the proposed scheme achieves extra quality versus space trade-off that is fundamentally *not* possible with the deterministic quantization in the algorithms of the JPEG family. Compared to plain PTC-encoded images stored in precise PCM cells, our proposed system increases the storage substrate density by over 2.7× with negligible quality degradation in the decoded images.

2. Background

This section presents background on image encoding, multi-level phase-change memory, and approximate storage.

2.1 Image Encoding

Image encoding algorithms use a variety of strategies to reduce the size of a raw image. These algorithms may be lossless or lossy. Often, the lossy algorithms (*e.g.*, JPEG [23]) are capable of achieving better compression rates with tolerable degradation in image quality. Hence, we focus on lossy image encoding. The specific algorithm used in this work is the progressive transform codec (PTC) [16, 17] – a precursor to the state-of-the-art JPEG XR [5]. PTC has been used in several practical applications, such as in game texture storage for Xbox games.

PTC processes the pixels in the image through typical steps including time-to-frequency transformation, quantization, coefficient mapping from a 2D array to 1D, and entropy encoding (shown in Figure 1). These steps are also used by most image codecs, including the popular JPEG [5, 17, 23]. What makes PTC unique is the use of the hierarchical lapped biorthogonal transform (HLBT) instead of the discrete cosine transformation (DCT) or wavelets, a ping-pong style scanning pattern for macroblocks, and an adaptive run-length/Golomb-Rice (RLGR) entropy encoding [17, 18].

PTC image encoding process. Figure 1 shows that PTC encodes an image in six steps: the raw image is partitioned into rectangular blocks (1), each of which is transformed into the frequency domain using the HLBT (2). Next, the HLBT frequency-domain coefficients are quantized, *i.e.*, scaled and rounded to the nearest integers (3). The quantization resolution and hence the number of bits used to represent the coefficients is determined by a target quality, typically measured by peak signal to noise ratio (PSNR). Then, coefficients with similar frequencies are spatially gathered and grouped via a 'clustering' step (4). Next, a reordering step visits the coefficient array in a hierarchical ping-pong manner (5), resulting in a vector with lower frequency coefficients clustered in the beginning and higher frequency coefficients clustered toward the end. Lower frequency coefficients tend to have greater absolute values and to be more important to image quality [15, 17]. Finally, this vector is divided into fixed-size macroblocks (MB), each of which is subsequently encoded using the adaptive RLGR algorithm (6).

The RLGR algorithm encodes all of the coefficients in a macroblock along the vertical direction, *i.e.*, *bit-plane encoding* [29]. The number of bit planes is determined by the maximum absolute value of the coefficients. The encoding process begins at the first bit plane (*e.g.*, bit plane 0 in Figure 1), and progressively encodes column-by-column toward the last bit plane (*e.g.*, bit plane 4). Notably, coefficients toward the beginning of a macroblock are likely to have greater absolute values than those toward the end of a macroblock (thanks to the clustering and the reordering steps), which translates into longer runs of *zeros* in the bit planes and results in a better compression rate. For each individual coefficient, the most important pieces of information are the *sign* and the bit position of the most significant *one* (underlined) that determine the magnitude of the coefficient. The remaining bits on the right hand side of the most significant *one* refine the corresponding coefficient value, and hence are called 'refinement bits'. Prior work observed that the entropy in the refinement bits is so high that there is little to gain in encoding them [16]. As such, refinement bits are simply appended to the coded bitstream of the macroblock.

A bit plane is encoded in one of the following three modes (Figure 1). In the 'no run' mode, the coder reads a single bit and encodes it. In the 'full run' mode, the coder finds m continuous 0s ($m = 2^k$) from the input and uses a single 0 to represent them. If the number of 0s is short for a full run ($m < 2^k$), the coder uses binary compression, $binary(m,k)$, to encode the value of m with k bits, and the coder is in 'partial run' mode. To achieve a good compression rate, the RLGR coder adaptively switches between run modes (controlled by parameter k) based on the inputs it has observed. The RLGR coder outputs 'control bits' and 'run-length' bits. The control bits inform the decoder the mode used in the encoding and

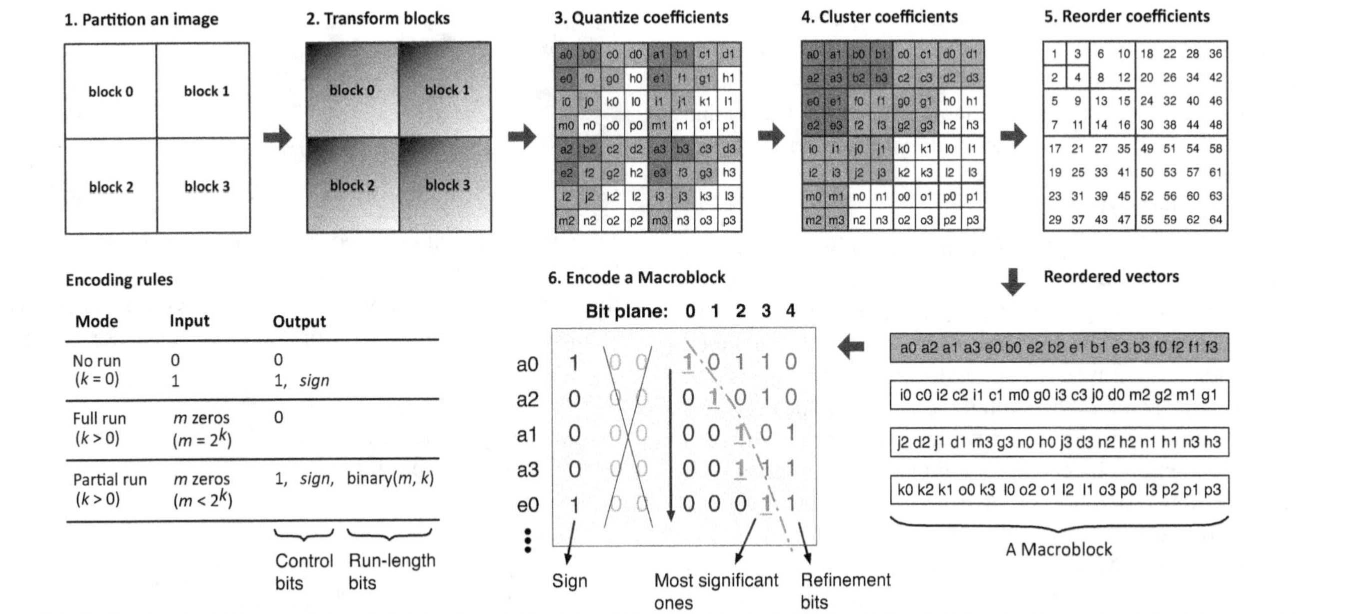

Figure 1. Simplified encoding steps in the PTC image codec.

the sign of the corresponding coefficient, and the run-length bits convey the number of 0s in a partial run. Both control and run-length bits are precision critical; an error in either a control or a run-length bit may affect the decoding of all of the subsequent bits in the bit plane, which results in the distortion of multiple spots in the decoded image.

2.2 Multi-Level Cells

Memory technologies with a large dynamic range (*e.g.*, between the minimum and maximum charges in a NAND Flash, or between the minimum and maximum resistances in emerging resistive memories) allow for dividing the analog range into more than two levels, each of the levels representing a distinct digital value. In contrast to a single-level cell (SLC) that stores binary states, a multi-level cell (MLC) encodes more than two bits into a single memory cell. Figure 2 illustrates a 4-level cell: the analog range is uniformly (in log scale) partitioned into four levels, L_0, L_1, L_2 and L_3, corresponding to binary values of '10', '11', '01', and '00', from lowest to highest resistance. A Gray code is used to minimize the Hamming distance between the codes from adjacent levels.

Phase-change memory (PCM) represents the stored information by the resistance of a chalcogenide material, which ranges from $10^3\Omega$ (in the crystalline state) to $10^{6.5}\Omega$ (in the amorphous state) [21]. An SLC PCM cell can be programmed into one of its two states by driving a write current through the chalcogenide material; the magnitude and the duration of the current pulse determine which resistance level the cell finally settles in. Programming an MLC PCM cell is more challenging because the dynamic range is partitioned into more levels, each mapping to a narrower 'band' than an SLC cell. This requires higher precision write and read circuitry. In practice, MLC PCM often employs a *write-and-verify* approach, which iteratively issues a write pulse and a subsequent checker read. The write process completes when the resistance of the cell is within the boundaries of the target level ($2T$) [3, 21]; alternatively, a write fails when the number of trials exceeds a predefined limit, which creates a write error. We model the final write resistance as a normal distribution around the target resistance of that level, as suggested in prior work [30, 33].

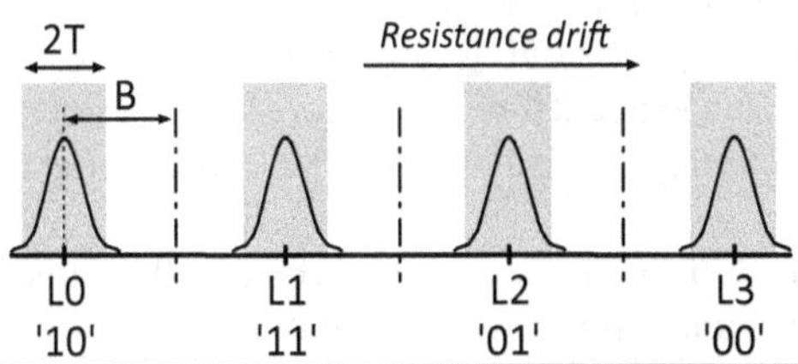

Figure 2. A 4-level cell: The analog (resistance) range (x axis) is in log scale, where levels are uniformly distributed. Write operations set cell resistance according to a normal distribution around the target resistance in the middle of the range.

A critical issue with MLC PCM is resistance drift [12, 13] – an effect of structural relaxation that causes the resistance of a cell to increase over time. Resistance drift is a major source of *retention errors*, in which a cell is written to one of the levels and, by the time it is read, it has shifted to another level (*e.g.*, an L_0 value drifts beyond $L_0 + B$ in Figure 2). The drift effect increases with the target resistance and the elapsed time from the last write. In a 4-level PCM cell like in Figure 2, for instance, level L_2 suffers the most resistance drift and often dominates the combined error rate of the cell. The drift from L_3 does not cause an error. Prior work proposes tri-level cells [30], in which the most drift-prone level (*i.e.*, L_2) is removed from a 4-level cell. Alternative solutions for mitigating retention errors include tackling the time component of the drift, employing error-correcting codes [2, 14, 24, 36], or periodically scrubbing the entire memory [1]. Recently, IBM and Macronix proposed novel circuit techniques that allow reliable reads from 4-level and 8-level PCM cells in the presence of resistance drift [31, 34].

2.3 Approximate Storage

Approximate Storage [27] offers an alternative approach to the costly error control mechanisms. Instead of detecting errors and correcting them, an approximate storage system exposes errors to the application in a controlled manner: programmers are given the option to specify the objects that can tolerate errors. As a result, the precision-critical objects are still protected (yet in a more costly manner) whereas the error-tolerant objects are stored in memory regions with relatively low reliability for the benefits of increased density and performance.

Naive Image Mapping to Approximate Storage. As described previously, the encoded PTC bits have different importance, *i.e.*, errors in them have a different impact on the resulting decoded image. For example, an error in a low frequency coefficient affects the corresponding entire block and may be visible in the decoded image, making the quality degradation unacceptable in many cases.

If all bits of an encoded image are indiscriminately stored in unoptimized and untuned approximate cells, errors, already at a high rate due to the lack of optimization, affect all encoded bits equally. Such naive use of approximate storage for images invariably leads to either density loss due to wasteful overprovisioning of error correction resources to maintain image quality, or lower storage requirements at the risk of polluting precision-critical bits, which affects image quality.

Figure 3 illustrates an example where a 40 dB image (left) is stored in unoptimized 8-level approximate cells and is read, decoded, and reconstructed 28 seconds later (right). Despite improving density by 3×, this degrades image by about 22 dB. Without any cell optimization or error correction, maintaining the image quality (40 dB) at decode time would have required the use of a much higher target quality level (50 dB), which uses a smaller quantization factor at encode time, resulting in almost doubled encoded image size. Alternatively, error correction can be used to protect the image against errors at the cost of additional storage overheads (*e.g.*, about a third extra storage for BCH-16).

3. Effective Approximate Storage for Images

This paper advocates that bits with different importance in output image quality should be treated differently with respect to how they are stored and that cells storing these bits should be optimized and tuned to appropriate error levels. Careful matching of cell error properties with encoded bits via cooperative design of the encoding algorithm with selective error correction storage can significantly improve image quality while getting most of the density benefit that approximate storage offers.

Figure 3. Original encoded image (left, error rate = 10^{-16}, PSNR = 40 dB) and the same image naively stored in unoptimized and untuned approximate cells, with unacceptable quality degradation (right, error rate = 10^{-3}, PSNR = 18 dB).

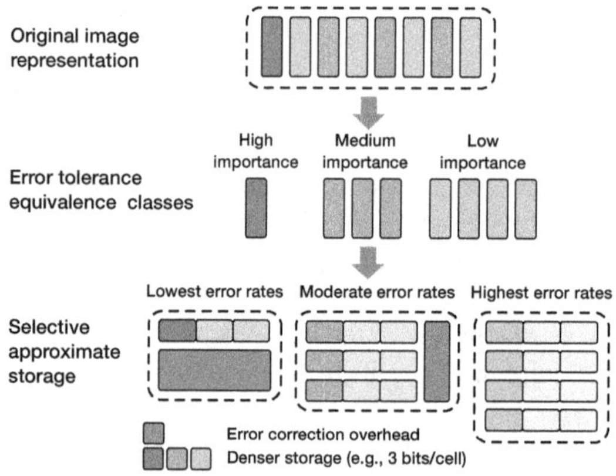

Figure 4. Example mapping of encoded bits into error tolerance classes, which are placed in storage with appropriately designed error rates.

As Figure 4 shows, we start by analyzing the PTC image encoding format (top) and identifying groups of bits with similar error rate requirements to form *error tolerance classes* (middle). Next, we optimize a multi-level PCM cell design for high density (*e.g.*, 3×) at reasonably high error rates (*e.g.*, 10^{-3}). Finally, bits in different error tolerance classes are stored by the modified algorithm into regions of a single optimized storage substrate (bottom), yet protected by appropriate error correction codes with different resulting error rates and storage overheads. The end result is high storage density with little image quality degradation.

This approach is most suitable to smartphones and other mobile devices. They make it very easy to take photos and users want to have all their pictures available to them on these devices. However, given the importance of small form-factor, the amount of solid-state storage available in these devices is limited. Since these devices are commonly backed by the cloud, it is acceptable to allow image quality degradation, as there can always be a full-quality version of the image stored in the cloud.

4. Approximation-Aware Encoding Algorithm

We analyze the PTC algorithm to identify bits in different error tolerance classes and make two observations. First, lower frequency coefficients, often higher in value, are the most important coefficients for image quality. Luckily, PTC (and other image encoding algorithms) already organizes coefficients based on the frequency which they refer to, typically from lower to higher frequency. As a result, lower frequency coefficients will be present in the first few macroblocks and can be easily mapped to memory that offers low error rates. Second, control bits affect output quality more than the run-length bits, and run-length bits affect the output quality significantly more than refinement bits. Consequently, these classes of encoded bits should be stored in memory regions of increasing density and error rates, respectively. Section 8 confirms this intuition, and Section 2.1 explained how PTC generates these types of bits. Back to Figure 4, the red shape represents control and run-length bits for the lowest frequency coefficients, the orange shapes represent control and run-length bits for other coefficients, and the yellow shapes represent refinement bits for all coefficients.

Modifications to PTC. The original PTC algorithm partitions data into macroblocks, which makes it straightforward to direct different macroblocks to different regions of storage. However, for each macroblock, PTC stores control, run-length and refinement bits in the same bitstream. During encoding, refinement bits are already segregated from control and run-length bits and appended at the end of a macroblock. However, the latter two need to be pulled apart into different bitstreams if they are to be stored into memory regions with different error characteristics. The algorithm uses a header – typically stored in the precise memory region – to record the mapping between macroblocks' bitstreams and the regions of memory that store them.

Implementation effort and quality control. We envision these modifications to be implemented by a programmer expert in image encoding who is familiar with the methodology proposed here and the various error correction options provided by the storage hardware, along with their corresponding error rates. The final algorithm is packaged in a library. This cooperative design effort may be undertaken by memory manufacturers, who ship their hardware along with supporting libraries, or by system integrators designing a product that includes digital imaging, where the library is never exposed. Final users of these products are exposed to a single knob that sets the expected quality of the image – this is exactly how users interface with lossy encoding algorithms (such as JPEG) today. This is possible because, from a user's perspective, errors caused by approximate storage are simply one more source of image quality loss.

Application to other encoding algorithms and data types. Although we use PTC as the base encoding algorithm, the same principles can be easily applied to other codecs that employ time-frequency transformation, quantization, and entropy encoding. For example, modern video codecs such as H.264 [39] apply motion estimation to predict the current video frame, and the difference frame between the original and its prediction is encoded with an image codec, which has the a similar structure to JPEG, JPEG XR, or PTC. In essence, the proposed scheme can be applied to other types of data where more important bits coexist with less important bits (*e.g.*, video, audio, and sensor data).

5. Storage Substrate Optimization

Our next goal is to optimize a PCM storage substrate to offer high density while maintaining reasonable error rates. We use a technique called *biasing* [33, 37] that, when used in combination with very low frequency scrubbing, achieves low error rates in a 4-level configuration (2 bits/cell) and reasonably low error rates in an 8-level configuration (3 bits/cell).

5.1 Biased Levels

A multi-level cell maps each of the levels within the analog range (in the case of PCM, the range between the highest and lowest resistances) onto a distinct digital value. Before biasing was proposed, each level in a multi-level PCM cell was assigned the same width in log space (Figure 2). However, such uniform partitioning of the resistance range can lead to unnecessary drift-related errors in dense approximate cells. Biasing addresses this problem by tuning the positions of the resistance levels for minimizing the combined (write and drift) error rate.

A cell suffers two types of errors. A *write error* occurs when the write circuitry is unable to set the cell resistance at the target level before exceeding a maximum number of trials, leaving the cell in an undesired resistance level. Material relaxation causes cell resistances to drift to higher resistance levels, resulting in the second type of errors – *drift errors*. Drift unidirectionally increases the cell resistance and its effect is more significant in higher resistance levels than the lower ones (Section 7). As such, the second highest level in a uniform cell (L_2 in Figure 2) becomes the most drift-prone level and dominates the drift error rate of the cell. The highest level (L_3 in Figure 2) does not suffer from drift errors because it is the highest range of resistances.

We use *biasing* to reposition and resize each resistance level (Figure 5). The drift error rate of the cell can be minimized by equalizing the drift error rate of each individual level (assuming the stored data maps to each level with an even probability). As shown in Figure 5, levels are wider in value ranges where drift is more likely to have an effect, *i.e.*, the higher resistance levels. Biasing is optimized based on a fixed elapsed time since the last write. This assumes that the system will scrub the storage contents and reset resistance levels to the target resistance at this scrubbing interval. It is worth noting that cells will work at different scrubbing

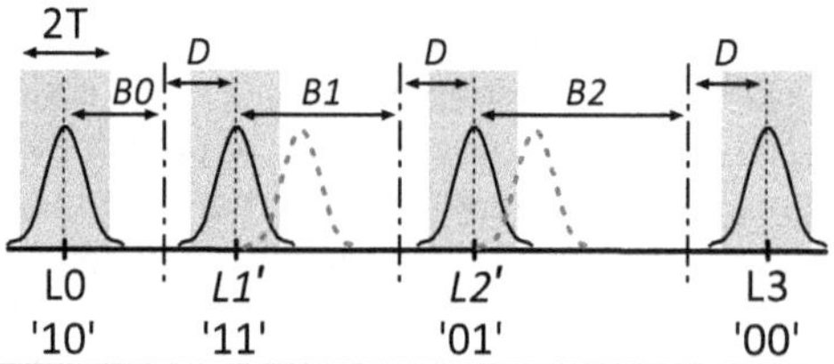

Figure 5. Cell configured with biased levels. The goal is to reduce drift-induced errors by equalizing the error rate of each individual level.

intervals, but they will suffer higher error rates compared to the interval they were optimized for because levels' error rates will not be completely equalized. To understand why this is the case, imagine an optimal biasing configuration for interval t. When this interval is extended to $t + t_\Delta$, resistances are allowed to drift longer distances. Since the drift for higher resistances is stronger than for lower ones, at interval $t + t_\Delta$ a cell optimized for interval t will experience higher error rates in higher levels. As such, to equalize error rates, the optimization needs to compensate by making the higher levels even wider than before, and the lower levels even narrower than before.

In addition, note that target resistances are no longer placed at the center of each level, dividing each level into two bands; the left band is made narrower (D) to leave more room for drift in the right band (B_i). However, as the target resistance is moved to lower values and D is reduced, the write error rate begins to increase because the tail of the write resistance distribution gets closer to the lower end of that level. The sizing of D and B_i is therefore a trade-off between write error rate and drift error rate. Errors are minimized by equalizing the number of errors of each type.

Once the resistance range is partitioned into biased levels, the next step is to map digital values to individual biased levels. Both in general and in our encoded images, *zeros* are the most common ('00' for 4-level cells and '000' for 8-level cells), so the value *zero* should be mapped to the highest level, which is immune to drift. We observe no other value that is more common than others for images, so the values for the remaining levels are assigned by using a simple Gray code.

Cell density. Based on the cell parameters we assume in this work (Section 7), we advocate for two cell configurations: 4- and 8-level cells. Notably, none of the two meet the uncorrectable bit error rate of commercial solid-state storage products today (10^{-16}) in their raw form [4, 20]; however, reasonably low error rates can be achieved via biasing and the industrial standard reliability can be reached with error correction codes. Even optimized with biasing, unfortunately, a 16-level cell suffers prohibitively high error rates (*i.e.*, the write error rate is around 10^{-4}, and the drift error rate is in the order of 10^{-1} after 1 second of writing), which cannot be brought down to a reasonable level by error correction codes that have storage overheads low enough to justify the increase in number of levels.

We use 2-level and 3-level cells as precise baselines since they both exhibit very low error rates. The 2-level cell has a simpler structure and presents a better performance in terms of read and write speed. In contrast, the 3-level cell offers higher density while maintaining a low error rate. However, additional circuits are required to convert the data from the rest of the system to the form that is stored in the 3-level cells. We use 4-level and 8-level cells as approximate memory cells.

5.2 Scrubbing to Reduce the Effect of Drift

After biasing is applied, drift may still be an issue in the long-term. To mitigate excessive drift, scrubbing can be used to rewrite a cell and bring the resistance level back down. Based on our PCM cell model, we expect the scrubbing period to be in the order of 10^7 seconds (3 months) – so infrequent that it is likely to be imperceptible. The average access bandwidth required by scrubbing at this frequency is on the order of 100 bits/second per gigabit of storage – a negligible figure. Also, if data is going to be scrubbed anyway, this may also be a good opportunity to perform wear leveling.

6. Providing Error Rate Diversity

Once cells are optimized, they can finally be tuned to provide different levels of reliability. The storage controller is responsible for offering a variety of error correction codes, each of which presenting a different trade-off between the error correction capability and the storage overhead. The complexity – and hence the area, power, and latency overheads – of the error correction circuits can be reduced by using codes within the same family (*e.g.*, BCH-4 and BCH-16).

Region configuration. The controller is responsible for organizing the storage into regions, each with a different error correction capability. The controller stores a region-to-configuration map in a table resident in the controller, which is backed by a preconfigured precise region of storage that persists during power cycles. System software sends special configuration commands to the controller for region allocation and configuration. Once configured, the controller uses the requested address and the information in the region-to-configuration map to determine which region the request targets and the appropriate error correction capability to use in servicing the request. The number of different regions is small (*e.g.*, 8), so the region-to-configuration map can support variable-size regions and be fully associative.

Hardware/software interface. The code implementing the modified algorithm must be able to allocate storage in different configurations. Assuming a storage system that is directly accessible through the processor address space, each bitstream can simply be allocated via a persistent object interface, and pointed to by the header. If a file system is used, then all storage in a block needs to be in the same configuration. The file system provides calls to specify the memory configuration when opening streams and to concatenate multiple streams to form a single file. If no changes to the file system are possible or desirable, the multi-precision memory may be exposed as an independent volume, providing an 'image store' that maintains and serves the collection of images using approximate storage, where each image can be linked from the main file system. The operating system or the storage controller is responsible for any necessary maintenance tasks, such as wear leveling, refreshing the memory to limit degradation over time, and reconfiguring the storage after power failure.

Storage region sizing. Regions with different error correction capabilities have different storage overheads for metadata. As such, different regions will need different number of cells for storing the same amount of data. The entire storage space may be managed in one of the two ways. Static management simply partitions the storage into multiple regions at manufacturing time. This approach is inflexible in that it does not allow a different proportion of storage to be dedicated to a region. The second approach is to allow dynamic reconfiguration of regions to match application demands. In this case, region resizing causes additional complexity. Assuming the storage device leaves manufacturing with all regions initialized to the strongest available error correction by default, when a region is configured for the first time, it grows in density, and thus in usable size. A simple way to cope with this is to expose this region as two regions, one of the original size before reconfiguration, and a virtual one with the surplus storage. This makes addressing simpler. A region can only be reconfigured to a smaller size if the system can accommodate the contents of the surplus region elsewhere.

7. Experimental Setup

This section describes experimental setup, assumptions, and parameters used for this study.

Encoding algorithm. We implement our algorithm modifications on top of the PTC codec [16–18]. Besides its state-of-the-art performance, we choose PTC because of its relatively simple reference code, which makes it easier to design and implement modifications. In addition, we expect that the results we report here for PTC, in terms of the impact of bit errors on reconstructed image quality, should be similar if we implement the same modifications in other codecs. That is essentially because of the orthogonality of transforms. Developers modifying other codecs can follow a methodology similar to the one presented in this paper to identify and process most important and less important groups of bits separately.

Input images. All quality measurements are based on 24 grayscale raw images at 768×512 pixels resolution in the Kodak PCD image set [6]. These images provide diversity in types of features they include, which make them ideal for benchmarking image encoding algorithms. Color images have a color component in addition to the grayscale component. The color component is encoded in the same manner as the grayscale one and typically produces slightly more refinement bits. Higher resolution images with more pixels would have similar behavior. As such, we choose to use small grayscale images because this makes the algorithm simple to modify and experiments fast to run, yet they still provide a conservative lower bound on the benefits of cooperatively designing the algorithm and hardware.

Cell model. All experiments assume a PCM cell model with resistance range between $10^3\Omega$ and $10^{6.5}\Omega$ [21]. We use the power-law drift model from prior studies [12, 13]:

$$R_d(t) = R_w \cdot \left(\frac{t}{t_w}\right)^{\nu} \tag{1}$$

where R_w is the initial resistance at the time the write operation concludes (t_w), and R_d is the drift resistance after an elapsed time t. The drift exponent ν grows with $\log R_w$. Configurations and parameter settings for 4-level cells and 8-level cells are summarized in Table 1 and Table 2, respectively. Note that, compared to uniform cells, biased cells have target levels ($\log R_T$) and level boundaries ($\log R_B$) moved toward lower resistances by appropriate amounts, resulting in lower drift-induced errors at the cost of increased write errors (as discussed in Section 5.1). The overall drift error rate can be minimized by equalizing the drift error rates for all the levels (except for the first level and the last level). Cells are optimized for a scrubbing interval $t = 10^7$s (about 3 months) after they are written. During scrubbing, their original target resistances are restored.

We use an iterative *write-and-verify* writing mechanism [3, 38]: a *RESET* pulse followed by a series of *SET* pulses are generated to heat the PCM, with a checker read after each write trial until the desired resistance level has been reached. Each pulse has the same width (duration) but different amplitude. Equation 2 describes the in-house model that emulates the writing process:

$$R_w = R_0 + (R_w - R_0) + \sqrt{|\Delta \cdot (R_w - R_0)|} \cdot N(0,1) \tag{2}$$

where R_0 and R_w are the original and the final resistance, respectively, and N is the normal distribution. Δ measures the imprecision of the writing circuitry (in this case, 10%). Another parameter is T (shown in Figure 5). A writing process will succeed when the final resistance falls into the $2T$ range of a level, or abort after a predefined number of trials. This model generates a normal distribution of final write resistance values, with means shown in the $logR_T$ column (Table 1 and Table 2), and a standard variation of $T/3$. We use $T = 0.1$, like prior work [22, 25]. With the selected target write error rate (10^{-6}), our model shows that the maximum number of trials in a biased 4-level cell and a biased 8-level cell are seven and nine, respectively.

We model the read circuitry in Cadence SPECTRE, and conclude that a current-mode sensing mechanism (similar to that used by Bedeschi *et al.* [3]) and an analog-to-digital converter are capable of distinguishing the worst-case resistance difference for all cell configurations.

Level	Data	$\log R_T$		$\log R_B$		$\mu(v)$		$\sigma(v)$	Write BER		Drift BER	
		u	b	u	b	u	b		u	b	u	b
0	10	3.00	3.00	3.58	3.35	0.001	0.001	$0.4\mu(v)$	very low	2.5×10^{-6}	very low	very low
1	11	4.17	3.60	4.75	4.27	0.027	0.012				very low	very low
2	01	5.33	4.52	5.92	6.25	0.073	0.040				0.3656	very low
3	00	6.50	6.50	–	–	0.120	0.120				–	–

Table 1. Uniform (u) and biased (b) 4-level cell parameters. R_T denotes the mean resistance of a level, and R_B denotes the resistance at the upper boundary of the level. v follows normal distribution, with $\mu(v)$ being interpolated from prior work [30, 38].

Level	Data	$\log R_T$		$\log R_B$		$\mu(v)$		$\sigma(v)$	Write BER		Drift BER	
		u	b	u	b	u	b		u	b	u	b
0	100	3.00	3.00	3.25	3.14	0.001	0.001	$0.2\mu(v)$	5.6×10^{-14}	5.6×10^{-6}	very low	very low
1	101	3.50	3.28	3.75	3.44	0.010	0.006				very low	0.0005
2	111	4.00	3.58	4.25	3.75	0.020	0.012				0.0058	0.0040
3	110	4.50	3.90	4.75	4.12	0.040	0.018				0.6774	0.0042
4	010	5.00	4.28	5.25	4.62	0.060	0.031				0.9700	0.0043
5	011	5.50	4.78	5.75	5.33	0.080	0.051				0.9960	0.0044
6	001	6.00	5.47	6.25	6.36	0.100	0.080				0.9991	0.0045
7	000	6.50	6.50	–	–	0.120	0.120				–	–

Table 2. Uniform (u) and biased (b) 8-level cell parameters.

Metrics. We evaluate the proposed scheme through a combination of two metrics: peak signal to noise ratio (PSNR) and memory density. PSNR is commonly used in the image processing community to measure the quality of reconstructed images. It compares the original image – pixel by pixel – against the decoded image that contains errors from lossy compression algorithm (*e.g.*, quantization) and memory subsystem (in this case, uncorrected write errors and drift errors). The higher the PSNR value, the smaller the difference between the original and the reconstructed images. We evaluate the approximate memory system with images from several PSNR targets, *i.e.*, 35 dB, 38 dB, 40 dB, and 42 dB. For most images, 40–42 dB range denotes high image quality, with distortion visually imperceptible; whereas, 38 dB and 35 dB represent moderate and low quality, respectively.

Memory density is defined as the average number of *data* bits stored by a cell. Error-prone memories (*e.g.*, PCM) commonly use error correction codes (ECC) to recover from certain number of errors. The storage overhead of error correction code reduces memory density.

Simulation. We conduct Monte Carlo simulations to model write-induced errors caused by circuit imprecision (Equation 2), in which a disturbance factor Δ is applied to the write target. Read-induced errors are modeled in a similar manner. Process variation is taken into account and is reflected by the parameter v in the cell model (Equation 1, Tables 1 and 2) – the drift effect varies from cell to cell.

Due to the nondeterministic error patterns in the approximate memory system, we run each image in the benchmark through our stochastic model 100 times (errors appear in random locations every time) and report the minimum (rather than the average) PSNR for each image, which gives a conservative estimate of the quality loss.

8. Evaluation

In this section, we demonstrate the benefits of tailoring the PTC image encoding algorithm to a PCM approximate storage substrate. We start by showing the overall quality and space improvement of an optimized design over the baseline. We then show how errors affect different types of encoded bits and the resulting image quality, evaluate the benefit of optimizing the PCM substrate, and illustrate how hardware and software are tuned for best density versus image quality trade-off. We also show results obtained using the proposed algorithm and methodology on a Flash substrate.

8.1 Overall Gains

Figure 6 compares quality versus memory area of a fully optimized design and intermediate alternatives against PTC on SLC PCM. The memory area (x-axis) is measured by the number of memory cells being used, normalized to the image size. The y-axis shows the reconstructed image quality after having been encoded and stored in the approximate memory for a scrubbing interval (10^7s). As high-density memory cells often suffer higher error rates, image quality and memory area are at odds. As such, the further left a curve is, the better the quality versus memory area trade-off it represents.

From right to left, the worst performance comes from the PTC algorithm on SLC PCM (2LC), where the quality and area trade-off is solely controlled by the quantization factor; previously proposed tri-level PCM (3LC) results in a 1.58× (*i.e.*, $log_2 3$) increase in density without any quality loss from the encoded images. However, the circuitry to deal with base transformations adds complexity to the memory system interface. In comparison, the biased 4-level (Bias4LC) cell, which requires no complex base transformation circuitry, results in a higher density (1.85× over 2LC), while still maintaining the same level of image quality. The only cost of biasing is the optimization of cell levels and boundaries at design time.

Finally, we see three biased 8-level cell configurations on the left. Note that all of them use error correction because at this density the quality degrades dramatically if no error correction is used (10 dB range, which is unacceptable). The configurations shown include error correction applied thoroughly and equally to the entire storage (Bias8LC TC), selective error correction applied based on the algorithm's needs (Bias8LC SC), and an idealized correction mechanism that has no storage overhead and corrects all errors (8LC ideal). Despite gaining 2.28× in density over 2LC, the Bias8LC TC uses more correction strength than necessary to maintain high quality. In contrast, by carefully choosing the appropriate ECC scheme for each encoded bits class, Bias8LC SC achieves a density of 2.73× over 2LC (less than 10% lower then the ideal 8-level cell density gain, *i.e.*, 3×), while keeping quality loss at an acceptable level ($\leq$ 1 dB loss).

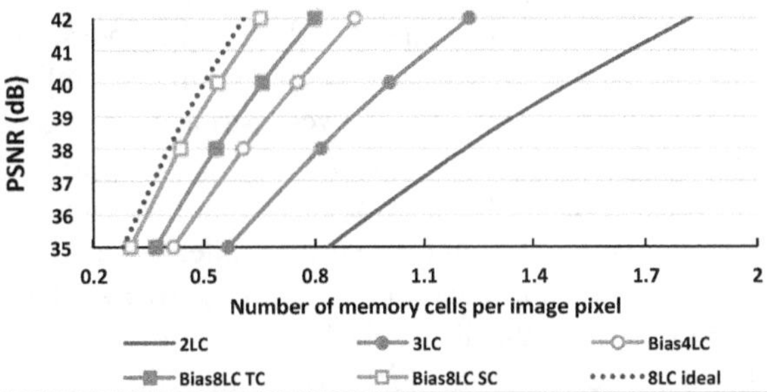

Figure 6. Overall benefits of the fully optimized design. Bias4LC, Bias8LC TC, and Bias8LC SC assume a scrubbing interval of 10^7 seconds.

8.2 Effect of Errors on Encoded Bit Types

We evaluate the impact of different coded bitstreams on the quality of reconstructed images. Our goal is to keep the quality loss within 1 dB of the encoded image. For example, a target quality of 40 dB will allow degradation only down to 39 dB.

We first evaluate the effects of control, run-length, and refinement bits across all the macroblocks. Intuitively, control bits are more precision-critical than run-length bits, then followed by refinement bits (Section 3). Figure 7 corroborates this by applying variable error rates over a subset of bits based on their types and measuring the resulting quality degradation. All images are encoded with a target quality of 40 dB. Each curve is labeled with three letters representing whether the error rate (in the x axis) is applied (A) or not (P) to each of control, run-length, and refinement bit types, respectively.

P-P-P does not suffer any failures and maintains the quality at the target 40 dB. Refinement bits affect image quality the least. As such, P-P-A can tolerate quite high error rates (this curve starts dropping only when BER reaches 10^{-4}). Next, P-A-P and P-A-A (with the introduction of run-length errors) can tolerate failure rates up to 10^{-7} with no or very little image quality degradation. Control bits are the most error-sensitive (A-P-P and A-A-A), also degrading quality quickly as failure rates go above 10^{-7}. This analysis supports the idea of adjusting error correction selectively, maintaining a lower error rate for control and run-length bits (10^{-7}), and a higher error rate (10^{-3}) for refinement bits. Due to the large gap between the error rate requirements for refinement bits and other types of bits, we fix refinement error rates at 10^{-3}, committing 0.2 dB of our 1 dB quality degradation budget.

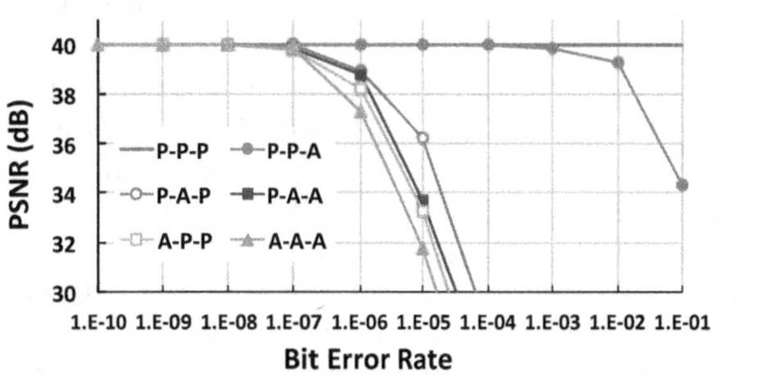

Figure 7. Image quality degradation with approximate bit streams. P denotes precise substrate, A denotes approximate substrate with BERs varying along the x-axis. The first letter represents control bits, the second represents run length bits, and the third represents refinement bits.

Next, we study the effect of different macroblocks on quality. Section 4 states that the first macroblock, which holds the lowest frequency coefficients, plays the most important role on the decoded image quality. Figure 8 verifies this statement by applying strong correction (at an error rate of 10^{-16}) to the first n macroblocks in a coded image with a total of 128 macroblocks, variable error rates for control and run-length bits in the remaining blocks, and the fixed error correction (at an error rate of 10^{-3}) for refinement bits in all blocks.

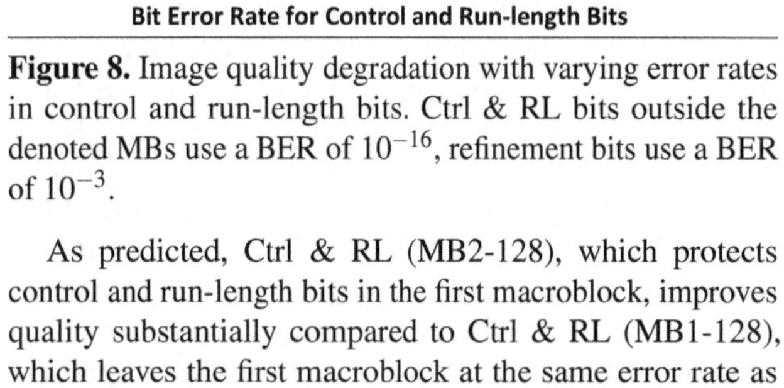

Figure 8. Image quality degradation with varying error rates in control and run-length bits. Ctrl & RL bits outside the denoted MBs use a BER of 10^{-16}, refinement bits use a BER of 10^{-3}.

As predicted, Ctrl & RL (MB2-128), which protects control and run-length bits in the first macroblock, improves quality substantially compared to Ctrl & RL (MB1-128), which leaves the first macroblock at the same error rate as other macroblocks. On the other hand, raising the precision level of additional macroblocks has diminishing returns. These results suggest that protecting the first macroblock's control and run-length bits with a strong error correction to reach industrial standard error rates (10^{-16}), and then protecting the remaining control and run-length bits with an intermediary strength code (10^{-6}) keeps quality well within the 1 dB degradation limit.

8.3 Effect of Substrate Biasing

With target error rates for error tolerance classes in hand, we turn our attention to bringing the PCM substrate up to these standards. We start by making the substrate as good as it can possibly be for an arbitrary scrub rate ($10^7 s$, or approximately 3 months) by optimizing cells via biasing. Figure 9 illustrates the effect of biasing on error rates, for both 4-level and 8-level cells, reporting combined error rates across all levels. Error rates grow over time because of drift effects.

We initially focus on uniform cells (Uniform 4LC and Uniform 8LC). As expected, error rates for 4-level cells are always lower than for 8-level cells because fewer levels allow more room for drift in each level. However, both types of cells start showing excessively high error rates even only an hour after being written. In contrast, Biased 4LC maintains very low drift error rates during the entire range of time (10^{-20} at 10^{10}s). The raw bit error rate (RBER) of the biased 4LC is dominated by write errors. Biased 8LC provides an error rate of about 10^{-3}, which is two orders of magnitude lower than Uniform 8LC at 10^7s. Coincidentally, it also matches the needs of the most error tolerant bits (*i.e.*, the refinement bits). This allows us not to use any error correction at all for these bits, eliminating unnecessary metadata overhead.

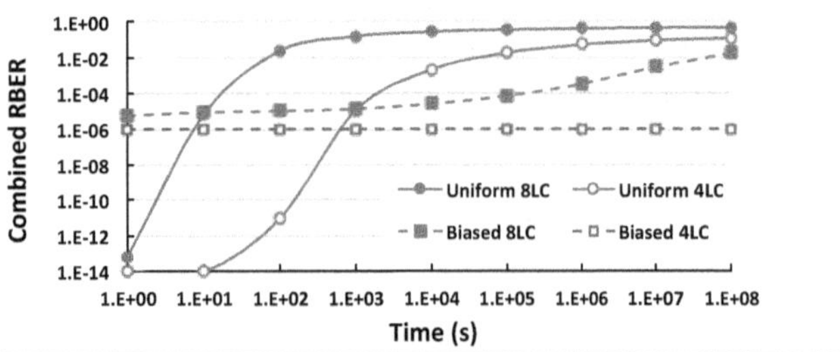

Figure 9. Combined RBERs of uniform and biased PCM cells.

Figure 10 provides insight on which cell configuration offers the best trade-off between overall density, including error correction to maintain the uncorrectable bit error rate (UBER) at the industrial standard rates (10^{-16}) [4, 20], and scrubbing overhead. SLC and 3LC cells have RBERs as low as precise memory, and hence do not require error correction. 3LC provides 1.58× higher density over SLC. The densities of uniform cells (*i.e.*, 4LC, 8LC, and 16LC), although high for short scrubbing intervals (so short that makes them unattractive), fall sharply at longer intervals, since drift-induced errors accrue fast. In contrast, biasing suppresses the growth of drift errors significantly: Bias4LC has a stable 1.86× density gain (the delta between this and the ideal 2× is caused by the ECC that protects against the write errors), and Bias8LC experiences a much smoother density degradation, achieving 2.28× density improvement at 10^7s (*i.e.*, the target scrubbing interval).

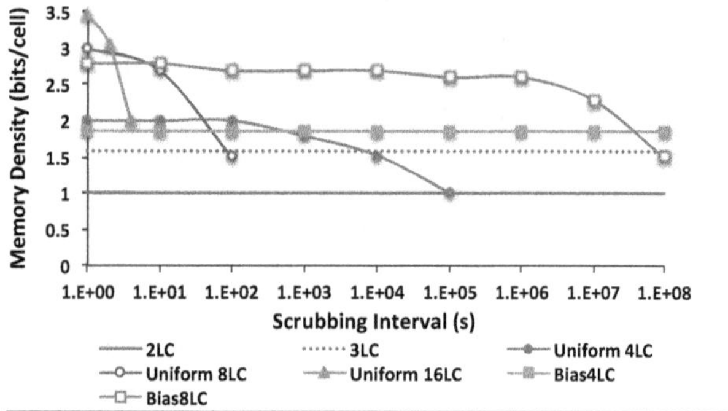

Figure 10. Density comparison (target UBER = 10^{-16}).

8.4 Assigning Error Correction to Encoded Bit Types

Once both the algorithmic error rate requirements are determined and the substrate is optimized for lowest possible error rates, we match the two via error correction. This relies on understanding the trade-offs between storage overhead of the error correction mechanism and its correcting power. Figure 11 presents a variety of error correction mechanisms (with storage overheads), and the correspondence between a variety of RBER values and their resulting UBERs when using each of these mechanisms. The biased 8LC cell already meets the demands of refinement bits, so they don't need any correction. For control and run-length bits in the first macroblock, we need a correction mechanism that accepts a RBER of 10^{-3} and produces a UBER of 10^{-16}. BCH-16 is the code that provides this capability with the lowest storage overhead (31.2%). Luckily, the bits that need such a strong error correction are only a small fraction (2.1%) of all bits. Finally, BCH-6 provides a 10^{-6} UBER at an overhead of 11.7% for the remaining bits that need any correction (81.7%).

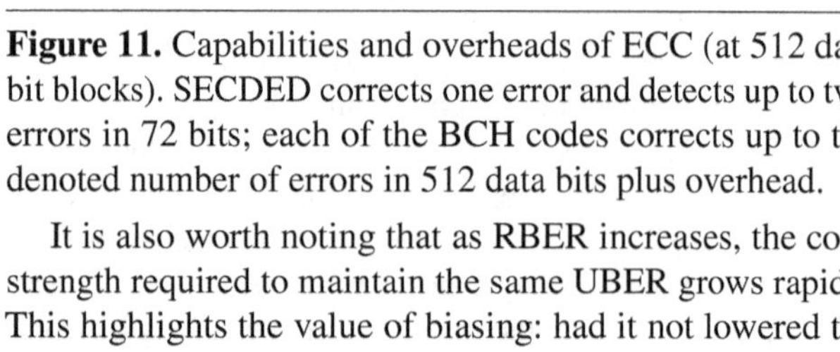

Figure 11. Capabilities and overheads of ECC (at 512 data bit blocks). SECDED corrects one error and detects up to two errors in 72 bits; each of the BCH codes corrects up to the denoted number of errors in 512 data bits plus overhead.

It is also worth noting that as RBER increases, the code strength required to maintain the same UBER grows rapidly. This highlights the value of biasing: had it not lowered the error rate by two orders of magnitude, the 8-level cell design would have offered RBER so high that the overhead of correcting all errors would have made it prohibitive.

8.5 Sensitivity to Scrubbing Period

The scrubbing period chosen for the biasing optimization is long enough to create insignificant overhead and short enough to preserve quality. This section shows what would happen if we used this cell design with other scrubbing intervals. Note that these results do not assume a cell redesign, they only show what would happen if designers decided to use these cells "out-of-spec" for different scrubbing intervals. Thus, if the interval is shorter than the specified, write errors dominate the RBER of the cell; if the interval is longer, drift errors dominate instead.

Figure 12 shows how error correction selection would have changed for different scrubbing intervals (assuming less than 1 dB quality degradation). It compares thorough correction (Bias8LC TC) with selective correction (Bias8LC SC) side-by-side at each interval. As the scrubbing interval increases (towards the right of x-axis), stronger ECC mechanisms must be employed to suppress the growth of drift errors, resulting in higher storage overheads. On the other hand, larger intervals reduce system energy and bandwidth overheads due to data movement and checker bits computation generated by the scrubbing. Although we select 10^7 seconds as the target scrubbing interval for the dense, approximate image storage system, shorter intervals might also be acceptable for other systems if higher density is the top priority.

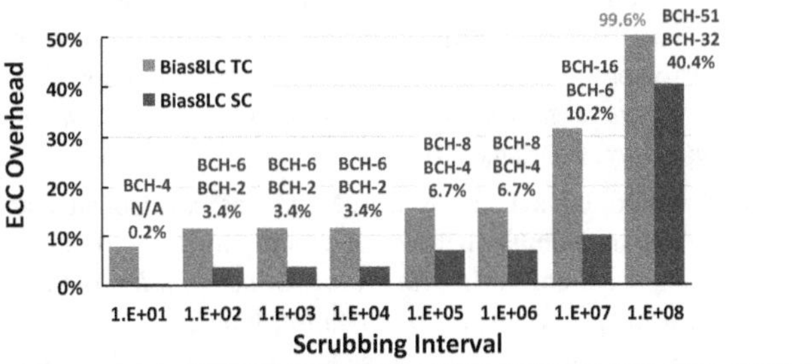

Figure 12. Trade-off between ECC storage overhead and scrubbing interval. Above each set of bars, the code in the first row is applied to all the bits in thorough correction (TC); the selective correction (SC) uses the first-row ECC for the control and run-length bits in MB1, and the second-row ECC for the control and run-length bits in other MBs, and leaves all refinement bits unprotected. The third row shows the total overhead.

The main takeaway from these results, however, is that selectively applying error correction only where needed can significantly reduce the loss in density while bringing the memory to the algorithmically-required error rates, as evidenced by the large difference in each pair of bars. Thanks to the biasing (optimized at the scrubbing interval of 10^7s), only 10.2% storage overhead (brought down from almost 32%) is required. This is what ultimately allows us to reach storage density 2.73× over the 2-level baseline.

8.6 Applicability to Flash

Although the proposed co-design of image encoding algorithm and approximate memory bases the study on multi-level PCM, the framework is readily applicable to other technologies, *e.g.*, Flash. Multi-level Flash (*e.g.*, TLC NAND Flash) is supported by major manufacturers [19, 28]. In such devices, ECCs (BCH and LDPC are common) are applied to a sector of 512 bytes (or greater, 1024 bytes). Figure 13 compares various BCH codes in terms of error correction capability and storage overhead (similar to Figure 11 but at a larger granularity).

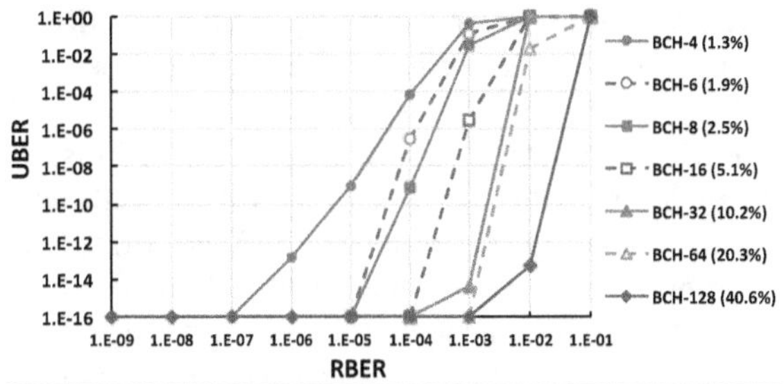

Figure 13. Capabilities and overheads of error correcting codes commonly used with Flash. Each code is able to correct the denoted number of errors in a 512-byte Flash sector and the associated ECC checker bits.

Prior studies report that TLC NAND Flash devices have an initial RBER of 10^{-4}, which increases gradually with the number of program/erase cycles [35]. Combining this knowledge with the methodology presented in this paper, a TLC Flash would use BCH-16 for the cells that store the control and run-length bits in MB1, and BCH-6 for the remaining control and run-length bits, and leave all refinement bits uncorrected. This results in 2.96× higher density than SLC while maintaining a less than 1 dB quality loss. In comparison, thorough correction, which uses BCH-16 uniformly, achieves 2.85× higher density. However, these numbers only apply to a brand new device. As RBER increases along with program/erase cycles, stronger ECCs are gradually required. For instance, RBER reaches 10^{-3} after approximately 3000 program/erase cycles. At this point, the density improvement of selective correction and thorough correction lower to 2.88× and 2.49×, respectively, making selective correction more attractive.

9. Related Work

Sampson *et al.* [27] observed that not all applications need high-precision storage (*i.e.*, storage that has really low error rates) for all kinds of data, and proposed trading-off storage accuracy for other desirable characteristics including density, performance, endurance, and energy efficiency. However, practical and crucial issues such as how to identify data structures that have different levels of error tolerance and how to manage them within a single storage system were not addressed. This paper advances prior work by demonstrating a methodology of quantifying the reliability requirements of different parts of an encoded image and optimizing an approximate storage substrate to meet them. On top of the image quality versus storage space trade-off already enabled by the algorithms in the JPEG family, programmers are offered explicit control over mapping application data onto multiple approximation levels to gain extra space savings.

Seong *et al.* [30, 37] proposed tri-level cell PCM, which was motivated by the fact that the uniform 4-level cell suffered high error rates due to drift. The tri-level cell was architected as a precise memory in prior work (and is used as a baseline in this paper). In this work we exploit practical use of cells with more levels as approximate storage. Cell reliability is significantly improved via *biasing* and the storage density is enhanced via *selective error correction*.

Yoon *et al.* [37] proposed *biasing* to address the drift issue in PCM. We leverage this idea to tune MLC PCM cells and minimize the combined (*i.e.*, write and drift) error rate at a certain scrubbing interval. Xu and Tong [33] proposed an adaptive drift mitigation approach for PCM, which stores a 'timestamp' in a reference cell along with the cells that store the data. When reading the data, the controller uses the timestamp to decide the level boundries of the cells. Sala *et al.* [26] proposed dynamic thresholding for multi-level cells. This mechanism adapts read circuitry parameters according to the elapsed time since the cells were written. Unlike these and other techniques that dynamically tune the read circuits to offset the drift effect, *biasing* settles the optimal positions for levels at manufacturing time, requiring lower area overheads and hence lower costs.

Holcomb and Fu [11] proposed an automated method that maps a data word onto multiple approximate MLCs such that the worst-case error is minimized at the word-level. The scheme is based on uniformly partitioned levels and certain levels that cause high error rates are removed. In contrast, this work uses biased levels that make better use of the resistance range of storage cells. In addition, it leverages relative importance of bits to choose their mapping to different types of approximate storage cells, and observes that a non-uniform distribution of values may lead to higher than expected error rates if the mapping between values and levels in a cell is not favorable.

In multimedia communication systems, Guo *et al.* [10] and Frescura *et al.* [7] explored an unequal error protection approach to protect image and video data against channel errors during transmission. The idea is to choose different coding parameters and redundancy levels based on the parts of the compressed bitstream. Specifically, maximum redundancy is used for headers and lower redundancy for less important parts of the compressed data. While similar in spirit, this technique is different from our work in at least two key aspects. First, we focus on storage systems, which have very different properties compared to wireless channels (*e.g.*, packet drop/loss is the main issue in wireless channels). Second, our proposal adjusts error correction at a much finer granularity, considering component frequency as well as the kind of bitstream (control, run-length, and refinement). This leads to a completely different algorithmic structure. To our knowledge, our proposal is the first to apply selective reliability to image storage.

10. Conclusion

We proposed to cooperatively design image encoding and storage mechanisms for denser approximate storage. The key idea is to identify the relative importance of encoded bits on output image quality and perform error correction accordingly. The result is over 2.7× the density of the image storage with little quality degradation (less than 1 dB). We focused on PTC image encoding and PCM, but our ideas also apply to other storage substrates and other algorithms that use time-frequency transformation followed by quantization and entropy coding (*e.g.*, audio and video).

Acknowledgments

The authors would like to thank Adrian Sampson and Kathryn McKinley for feedback and early discussions on this work and the anonymous reviewers for the useful comments and suggestions.

References

[1] M. Awasthi, M. Shevgoor, K. Sudan, B. Rajendran, R. Balasubramanian, and V. Srinivasan. Efficient scrub mechanisms for error-prone emerging memories. In *Proceedings of the 18th International Symposium on High Performance Computer Architecture*, February 2012.

[2] R. Azevedo, J. Davis, K. Strauss, M. Manasse, P. Gopalan, and S. Yekhanin. Zombie memory: Extending memory lifetime by reviving dead blocks. In *Proceedings of the 40th International Symposium on Computer Architecture*, June 2013.

[3] F. Bedeschi, R. Fackenthal, C. Resta, E. M. Donze, M. Jagasivamani, E. C. Buda, F. Pellizzer, D. W. Chow, A. Cabrini, G. Calvi, R. Faravelli, A. Fantini, G. Torelli, D. Mills, R. Gastaldi, and G. Casagrande. A bipolar-selected phase change memory featuring multi-level cell storage. *IEEE Journal of Solid-State Circuits*, 44(1):217–227, 2009.

[4] Y. Cai, E. F. Haratsch, O. Mutlu, and K. Mai. Error patterns in MLC NAND Flash memory: Measurement, characterization, and analysis. In *Proceedings of the Conference on Design, Automation and Test in Europe*, DATE '12, pages 521–526, San Jose, CA, USA, 2012. EDA Consortium.

[5] F. Dufaux, G. J. Sullivan, and T. Ebrahimi. The JPEG XR image coding standard. *IEEE Signal Processing Magazine*, 26: 195–199, June 2009.

[6] R. Franzen. Kodak Lossless True Color Image Suite: PhotoCD PCD0992, 2002.

[7] F. Frescura, M. Giorni, C. Feci, and S. Cacopardi. JPEG2000 and MJPEG2000 transmission in 802.11 wireless local area networks. *IEEE Transactions on Consumer Electronics*, 49(4): 861–871, Nov 2003.

[8] M. Gastpar and M. Vetterli. Source-channel communication in sensor networks. *Information Processing in Sensor Networks*, pages 162–177, 2003.

[9] M. Gastpar, B. Rimoldi, and M. Vetterli. To code, or not to code: Lossy source-channel communication revisited. *Transactions on Information Theory*, pages 1147–1158, 2003.

[10] Z. Guo, Y. Nishikawa, R. Y. Omaki, T. Onoye, and I. Shirakawa. A low-complexity FEC assignment scheme for motion JPEG2000 over wireless network. *IEEE Trans. on Consum. Electron.*, 52(1):81–86, Feb. 2006.

[11] D. Holcomb and K. Fu. QBF-based synthesis of optimal word-splitting in approximate multi-level storage cells. In *Workshop on Approximate Computing Across the System Stack (WACAS), 2014*, March 2014.

[12] D. Ielmini, A. L. Lacaita, and D. Mantegazza. Recoverty and drift dynamics of resistance and threshold voltages in phase-change memories. *IEEE Transactions on Electron Devices*, 54(2):308–315, February 2007.

[13] D. Ielmini, S. Lavizzari, D. Sharma, and A. L. Lacaita. Physical interpretation, modeling and impact on phase change memory (PCM) reliability of resistance drift due to chalcogenide structural relaxation. In *Proceedings of the International Electron Devices Meeting*, December 2007.

[14] A. N. Jacobvitz, R. Calderbank, and D. J. Sorin. Coset coding to extend the lifetime of memory. In *Proceedings of the 2013 IEEE 19th International Symposium on High Performance Computer Architecture (HPCA)*, pages 222–233, 2013.

[15] H. S. Malvar. *Signal Processing with Lapped Transforms*. Artech House, 1992. http://research.microsoft.com/apps/pubs/default.aspx?id=77707.

[16] H. S. Malvar. Fast progressive wavelet coding. In *Proceedings of the Data Compression Conference*, DCC '99, pages 336–343, Washington, DC, USA, 1999

[17] H. S. Malvar. Fast progressive image coding without wavelets. In *Proceedings of the Data Compression Conference*, pages 243–252, March 2000.

[18] H. S. Malvar. Adaptive Run-Length / Golomb-Rice encoding of quantized generalized gaussian sources with unknown statistics. In *Proceedings of the Data Compression Conference*, DCC '06, pages 23–32, Washington, DC, USA, 2006.

[19] Micron. Micron TLC NAND. http://www.micron.com/products/nand-flash/tlc-nand.

[20] N. Mielke, T. Marquart, N. Wu, J. Kessenich, H. Belgal, E. Schares, F. Trivedi, E. Goodness, and L. R. Nevill. Bit error rate in NAND flash memories. In *IEEE International Reliability Physics Symposium, 2008. IRPS 2008.*, pages 9–19, April 2008.

[21] T. Nirschl, J. B. Philipp, T. D. Happ, G. W. Burr, B. Rajendran, M.-H. Lee, A. Schrott, M. Yang, M. Breitwisch, C.-F. Chen, E. Joseph, M. C. Lamorey, R. Cheek, S.-H. Chen, S. Zaidi, S. Raoux, Y.-C. Chen, Y. Zhu, R. Bergmann, H. L. Lung, and C. Lam. Write strategies for 2 and 4-bit multi-level phase-change memory. In *IEEE International Electron Devices Meeting, 2007. IEDM 2007.*, pages 461–464, 2007.

[22] N. Papandreou, H. Pozidis, A. Pantazi, A. Sebastian, M. Breitwisch, C. Lam, and E. Eleftheriou. Programming algorithms for multilevel phase-change memory. In *2011 IEEE International Symposium on Circuits and Systems (ISCAS)*, pages 329–332, May 2011.

[23] W. B. Pennebaker and J. L. Mitchell. JPEG: Still image data compression standard. Technical report, Springer, 1993.

[24] M. K. Qureshi. Pay-as-you-go: Low-overhead hard-error correction for phase change memories. In *Proceedings of the 44th Annual IEEE/ACM International Symposium on Microarchitecture*, pages 318–328, 2011.

[25] M. K. Qureshi, M. M. Franceschini, L. A. Lastras-Montaño, and J. P. Karidis. Morphable memory system: A robust architecture for exploiting multi-level phase change memories. In *Proceedings of the 37th Annual International Symposium on Computer Architecture*, ISCA '10, pages 153–162, New York, NY, USA, 2010.

[26] F. Sala, R. Gabrys, and L. Dolecek. Dynamic threshold schemes for multi-level non-volatile memories. *IEEE Transactions on Communications*, 61(7):2624–2634, July 2013.

[27] A. Sampson, J. Nelson, K. Strauss, and L. Ceze. Approximate storage. In *Proceedings of the 46th International Conference on Microarchitecture*, December 2013.

[28] Samsung. Samsung SSD Product Story: 3-bit/cell MLC NAND Flash. http://www.samsung.com/global/business/semiconductor/minisite/SSD/global/html/why/MlcNandFlash.html.

[29] J. W. Schwartz and R. C. Barker. Bit-plane encoding: A technique for source encoding. *IEEE Transactions on Aerospace and Electronic Systems*, AES-2(4):385–392, July 1966.

[30] N. H. Seong, S. Yeo, and H.-H. S. Lee. Tri-level-cell phase change memory: Toward an efficient and reliable memory system. In *Proceedings of the 40th International Symposium on Computer Architecture*, June 2013.

[31] M. Stanisavljevic, A. Athmanathan, N. Papandreou, H. Pozidis, and E. Eleftheriou. Phase-change memory: Feasibility of reliable multilevel-cell storage and retention at elevated temperatures. In *Reliability Physics Symposium (IRPS), 2015 IEEE International*, pages 5B.6.1–5B.6.6, April 2015.

[32] S. Vembu, S. Verdú, and Y. Steinberg. The source-channel separation theorem revisited. *IEEE Transactions on Information Theory*, 41:44–45, January 1995.

[33] X. Wei and Z. Tong. A time-aware fault tolerance scheme to improve reliability of multilevel phase-change memory in the presence of significant resistance drift. *IEEE Transactions on Very Large Scale Integration (VLSI) Systems*, 19(8):1357–1367, 2011.

[34] J. Y. Wu, W. S. Khwa, M. H. Lee, H. P. Li, S. C. Lai, T. H. Su, M. L. Wei, T. Y. Wang, M. BrightSky, T. S. Chen, W. C. Chien, S. Kim, R. Cheek, H. Y. Cheng, E. K. Lai, Y. Zhu, H. L. Lung, and C. Lam. Greater than 2-bits/cell mlc storage for ultra high density phase change memory using a novel sensing scheme. In *2015 Symposium on VLSI Technology*, 2015.

[35] E. Yaakobi, L. Grupp, P. Siegel, S. Swanson, and J. Wolf. Characterization and error-correcting codes for tlc flash memories. In *2012 International Conference on Computing,*

Networking and Communications (ICNC), pages 486–491, Jan 2012.

[36] D. H. Yoon, N. Muralimanohar, J. Chang, P. Ranganathan, N. P. Jouppi, and M. Erez. FREE-p: Protecting non-volatile memory against both hard and soft errors. In *Proceedings of the 2011 IEEE 17th International Symposium on High Performance Computer Architecture*, pages 466–477, 2011.

[37] D. H. Yoon, J. Chang, R. S. Schreiber, and N. P. Jouppi. Practical nonvolatile multilevel-cell phase change memory. In *Proceedings of the International Conference on High Performance Computing, Networking, Storage and Analysis (SC'13)*, pages 21:1–21:12, 2013.

[38] W. Zhang and T. Li. Helmet: A resistance drift resilient architecture for multi-level cell phase change memory system. In *IEEE/IFIP 41st International Conference on Dependable Systems Networks (DSN)*, pages 197–208, June 2011.

[39] T. Wiegand, G.J. Sullivan, G. Bjontegaard, and A. Luthra. Overview of the H.264/AVC video coding standard In *IEEE Transactions on Circuits and Systems for Video Technology*, vol. 13, pp. 560–576, July 2003.

Failure-Atomic Persistent Memory Updates via JUSTDO Logging

Joseph Izraelevitz
U. Rochester/Hewlett Packard Labs
jhi1@cs.rochester.edu

Terence Kelly
Hewlett Packard Labs
terence.p.kelly@hpe.com

Aasheesh Kolli
U. Michigan/Hewlett Packard Labs
akolli@umich.edu

Abstract

Persistent memory invites applications to manipulate persistent data via LOAD and STORE instructions. Because failures during updates may destroy transient data (e.g., in CPU registers), preserving data integrity in the presence of failures requires failure-atomic bundles of updates. Prior failure atomicity approaches for persistent memory entail overheads due to logging and CPU cache flushing. Persistent caches can eliminate the need for flushing, but conventional logging remains complex and memory intensive. We present the design and implementation of JUSTDO logging, a new failure atomicity mechanism that greatly reduces the memory footprint of logs, simplifies log management, and enables fast parallel recovery following failure. Crash-injection tests confirm that JUSTDO logging preserves application data integrity and performance evaluations show that it improves throughput 3× or more compared with a state-of-the-art alternative for a spectrum of data-intensive algorithms.

Categories and Subject Descriptors D.4.5 [*Operating Systems*]: Reliability—fault-tolerance

Keywords non-volatile memory, persistent memory, crash-resilience, failure-atomicity, transactions

1. Introduction

Emerging byte-addressable non-volatile memory (NVM) device technologies are widely expected to augment and perhaps eventually supplant conventional DRAM as density scaling limitations constrain the latter [37]. Meanwhile, persistent memory implemented with conventional device technologies (e.g., non-volatile DIMMS based on DRAM, flash storage, and supercapacitors [51]) offers similar attractions: Regardless of how it is implemented, persistent memory invites applications to manipulate persistent application data directly via ordinary LOAD and STORE instructions. By contrast, on today's conventional hardware with volatile byte-addressable memory and non-volatile block-addressed storage, complex multi-layered software stacks—operating systems, file systems, and database management systems—provide indirect and mediated access to persistent data.

Eliminating the memory/storage distinction and the associated layers of intermediary software promises to streamline software and improve performance, but direct in-place manipulation of persistent application data allows a failure during an update to corrupt data. Mechanisms supporting program-defined *failure-atomic sections* (FASEs) address this concern. FASEs can be implemented as transactional memory with additional durability guarantees [14, 52] or by leveraging applications' use of mutual exclusion primitives to infer consistent states of persistent memory and guarantee consistent recovery [9]. These prior systems offer generality and convenience by automatically maintaining UNDO [9, 14] or REDO [52] logs that allow recovery to roll back FASEs that were interrupted by failure. Maintaining such logs inevitably entails space and time overheads; flushing logs from transient CPU caches to persistent memory incurs additional time and memory-bandwidth overheads.

Persistent CPU caches eliminate the need to flush caches to persistent memory and can be implemented in several ways, e.g., by using inherently non-volatile bit-storage devices in caches [61] or by maintaining sufficient standby power to flush caches to persistent memory in case of power failure. The amount of power required to perform such a flush is so small that it may be obtained from a supercapacitor [53] or even from the system power supply [32]. Preserving CPU cache contents in the face of detectable non-corrupting application software failures requires no special hardware: STOREs to file-backed memory mappings persist beyond process crashes [33].

However, even if persistent caches eliminate the cache flushing overheads of FASE mechanisms, the overhead of conventional UNDO or REDO log management remains. A simple example illustrates the magnitude of the problem: Consider a multi-threaded program in which each thread uses a FASE to atomically update the entire contents of a long linked list. Persistent memory transaction systems [14, 52] would serialize the FASEs—in effect, each thread acquires a global lock on the list—and would furthermore

ASPLOS '16 April 2–6, 2016, Atlanta, Georgia, USA
Copyright © 2016 ACM 978-1-4503-4091-5/16/04...$15.00
DOI: http://dx.doi.org/10.1145/2872362.2872410

maintain a log whose size is proportional to the list modifications to support rolling back changes. A mutex-based FASE mechanism for persistent memory [9] avoids serializing FASEs by allowing concurrent updates via hand-over-hand locking but must still maintain per-thread logs, proportional in size to the amount of modified list data.

The key insight behind our approach is that mutex-based critical sections are intended to execute to completion; unlike optimistic transactions, they do not abort due to conflict. While it is possible to implement rollback for lock-based FASEs [9], we might instead simply *resume* FASEs following failure and execute them to completion. This insight suggests a design that employs minimalist logging in the service of FASE resumption rather than rollback.

Our contribution, JUSTDO logging, unlike traditional UNDO and REDO logging, does not discard changes made during FASEs cut short by failure. Instead, our approach resumes execution of each interrupted FASE at its last STORE instruction then executes the FASE to completion. Each thread maintains a small log that records its most recent STORE within a FASE; the log contains the destination address of the STORE, the value to be placed at the destination, and the program counter. FASEs that employ JUSTDO logging access only persistent memory, which ensures that all data necessary for resuming an interrupted FASE will be available during recovery. As in the Atlas system [9], we define a FASE to be an outermost critical section protected by one or more mutexes; the first mutex acquired at the start of a FASE need not be the same as the last mutex released at the end of the FASE (see Figure 1). Auxiliary logs record threads' mutex ownership for recovery.

Our approach has several benefits: By leveraging persistent CPU caches where available, we can eliminate cache flushing overheads. Furthermore the small size of JUSTDO logs can dramatically reduce the space overheads and complexity of log management. By relying on mutexes rather than transactions for multi-threaded isolation, our approach supports high concurrency in scenarios such as the aforementioned list update example. Furthermore we enable fast *parallel* recovery of all FASEs that were interrupted by failure. JUSTDO logging can provide resilience against both power outages and non-corrupting software failures, with one important exception: Because we sacrifice the ability to roll back FASEs that were interrupted by failure, bugs *within* FASEs are not tolerated. Hardware and software technologies for fine-grained intra-process memory protection [12, 54] and for software quality assurance [7, 8, 19, 42, 60] complement our approach respectively by preventing arbitrary corruption and by eliminating bugs in FASEs.

In this paper, we describe the design and implementation of JUSTDO logging and evaluate its correctness and performance. Our results show that JUSTDO logging provides a useful new way to implement persistent memory FASEs with improved performance compared with a state-of-the-art system: On five very different mutex-based concurrent data structures, JUSTDO logging increases operation throughput over 3× compared with crash resilience by the state-of-the-art Atlas FASE mechanism [9].

The remainder of this paper is organized as follows: Section 2 presents key concepts and terminology used in our paper. Section 3 reviews persistent memory technologies and their implications for software. Section 4 presents our assumptions regarding the system on which JUSTDO logging runs and the programming model that our approach supports. Section 5 describes the design of JUSTDO logging, and Section 6 presents the details of our current implementation. Section 7 evaluates the correctness and performance of our approach, and Section 8 concludes with a discussion.

2. Concepts & Terminology

Application data typically must satisfy application-level invariants or other correctness criteria. We say that data are *consistent* if the relevant application-level correctness criteria hold, otherwise the data are *corrupt*. *Failures* are events that may corrupt application data; familiar examples include application process crashes, operating system kernel panics, and abrupt power outages. We say that a failure is *tolerated* if application data consistency either is unaffected by the failure or is restored by post-failure recovery procedures. We distinguish between *corrupting* and *non-corrupting* failures; the former preclude successful recovery by corrupting application data directly or by corrupting data necessary for recovery (e.g., logs). A corrupting failure may be caused, for example, by a STORE through a pointer variable containing an invalid address.

We say that data are *persistent* if they survive tolerated failures intact and are accessible by recovery code, otherwise the data are *transient*. Similarly we say that memory locations, memory address ranges, processor cache lines, and other places where data may reside are persistent or transient depending on whether or not the data they contain will be available to recovery code following any tolerated failure. For example, a *persistent memory region* is a contiguous range of virtual addresses whose contents will survive tolerated failures. Note that persistence does not imply consistency: Failure may render persistent data irreparably corrupt, making recovery impossible.

We reserve the term *non-volatile* for characterizing device technologies that retain data even in the absence of supplied power; examples include memristor, STT-RAM, and PCM. Similarly the term *volatile* characterizes device technologies such as DRAM that require continuously supplied power to retain data. We emphasize that our persistent/transient distinction is orthogonal to volatility. For example, while non-volatile memory (NVM) facilitates the implementation of memory that is persistent with respect to certain kinds of failure, persistent memory also admits alternative implementations that do not involve NVM. Moreover, NVM

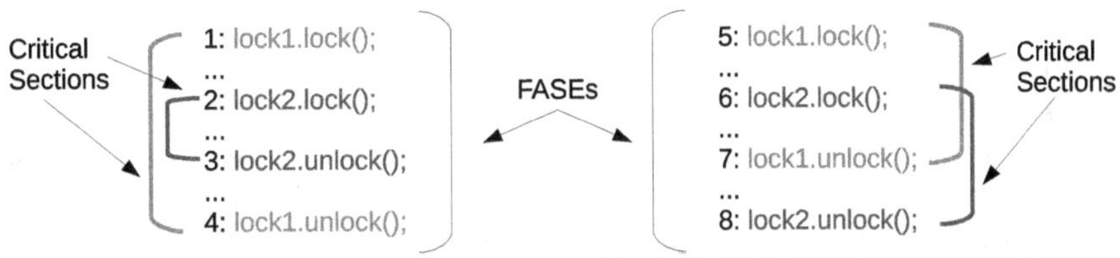

Figure 1. Two examples of lock-delimited FASEs. Left (lines 1–4): Nested. Right (lines 5–8): Hand-over-hand.

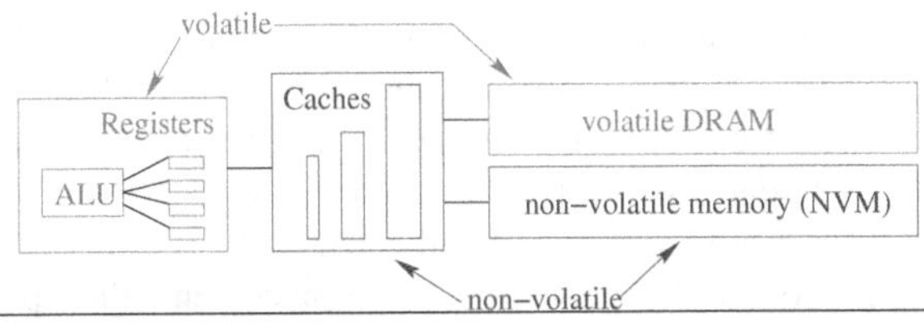

Figure 2. Hybrid architecture incorporating both conventional volatile CPU registers and DRAM in addition to non-volatile CPU caches and NVM.

need not be persistent according to our definition: For example, if thread stacks on a particular computer are reclaimed by the operating system following abnormal process termination, then stack data are not available to recovery code and are therefore transient, even if every byte of memory on the machine is non-volatile.

We distinguish between *partial* and *whole-system* persistence. The latter applies when the entire state of a machine survives tolerated failures, whereas the former describes situations in which some data is persistent and some is transient. Partial persistence results when applications designate only some data as persistent (e.g., a persistent memory region containing long-term application data) and allow the remainder to be transient (e.g., per-thread function call stacks). Partial persistence is a natural match for future *hybrid architectures* that incorporate both volatile and non-volatile components, as depicted in Figure 2.

We conclude this section by using our definitions to briefly define our hardware and software system model, characterize the failures that JUSTDO logging can tolerate, and describe situations where our approach is likely to offer good performance; all of these topics are covered in greater detail in subsequent sections. JUSTDO logging is designed with future hybrid architectures in mind (Figure 2). More specifically, our system model (Section 4) and our design (Section 5) assume that CPU registers are transient but that both CPU caches and (part of) main memory are persistent, and our programming model assumes partial persistence. JUSTDO logging tolerates non-corrupting failures that were not caused by software bugs within a failure-atomic section. We expect JUSTDO logging to achieve good performance if it is inexpensive to impose ordering constraints on modifications to persistent data—as would be the case with persistent caches and/or persistent STORE buffers integrated into the CPU in addition to persistent memory.

3. Related Work

Hardware for Persistence Memory footprints of modern workloads are increasing at a rate higher than Moore's law [56]. With the end of DRAM scaling (the memory technology of choice for decades) on the horizon, much research has focused on incorporating alternative, denser memory technologies into future architectures [22, 23, 40, 56]. Potential DRAM replacement technologies such as phase change memory (PCM) [23], memristor [48] and spin-torque transfer memory (SST-RAM) [3] offer higher densities and are furthermore non-volatile. These non-volatile memory (NVM) device technologies facilitate the implementation of memory that is persistent with respect to power outages. Systems with persistent memory allow persistent data manipulation via processor LOADs and STOREs [37], a stark deviation from traditional disk/flash based durability. The prospect of persistent memory has sparked new research on file systems [10, 15, 18, 24], database systems [11, 13, 20, 27, 53], and persistent programming and data structures [9, 14, 52, 58].

Ensuring recovery requires constraining the order in which STOREs attain persistence. If memory is persistent but CPU caches are not, carefully synchronized cache flushing must be used to ensure that STOREs reach memory in the desired order [5]. Intel has recently announced ISA extensions to optimize cache flushes for systems with persistent memory [41]. Pelley et al. recently introduced memory persistency models that build on memory consistency models [1] to provide guarantees on the order in which STOREs become persistent [37].

The different NVM device technologies offer different read/write/endurance characteristics and are expected to be deployed accordingly in future systems. For example, while PCM and Memristor are mainly considered as candidates for main memory, STT-RAM is expected to be used in caches [61]. Non-volatile caches imply that STOREs become persistent upon leaving the CPU's STORE buffers. Persistent caches can also be implemented by relying on stand-by power [32–34] or employing supercapacitor-backed volatile caches to flush data from caches to persistent memory in the case of a failure [53]. Recent trends show that non-volatile caches are possible in the near future [53].

Software for Persistence Disk-based database systems have traditionally used write-ahead logging to ensure consistent recoverability [31]. Changing workloads, data models, and storage media have inspired numerous refinements and specializations represented by systems such as eNVy [55], Berkeley DB [35], Stasis [44], MARS [13], and Rio Vista [27]. Proper transactional updates to files in file systems can simplify complex and error-prone procedures such as software upgrades. Transactional file updates have been explored in research prototypes [36, 47]; commercial implementations include Microsoft Windows TxF [30] and Hewlett Packard Enterprise AdvFS [50]. Transactional file update is readily implementable atop more general operating systems transactions, which offer additional security advantages and support scenarios including on-the-fly software upgrades [39]. At the opposite end of the spectrum, user-space implementations of persistent heaps supporting failure-atomic updates have been explored in research [59] and incorporated into commercial products [6]. Logging-based mechanisms in general ensure consistency by discarding changes from an update interrupted by failure. In contrast, for idempotent updates, the update cut short by failure can simply be re-executed rather than discarding changes, reducing required logging (similar to [4, 21]).

Persistent memory has inspired research on programming interfaces with durability semantics. Kiln [61] and Lu et al. [28] describe mechanisms that provide atomicity and durability guarantees for systems with persistent caches and persistent memory, however, the programmer remains responsible for ensuring isolation. Whole-system persistence [32], a combined hardware and software technique, gives consistency guarantees for power failures, but does not tolerate software errors. Mnemosyne [52] and NV-Heaps [14] extend transactional memory to provide durability guarantees for ACID transactions on persistent memory. Mnemosyne emphasizes performance; the use of REDO logs, for example, postpones the need to flush data to persistence to a single end-of-transaction batch. NV-heaps, an UNDO log system, emphasizes programmer convenience, providing garbage collection and strong type checking to help avoid pitfalls unique to persistent memory, e.g., pointers to transient data inadvertently stored in persistent memory. Given the ubiquity of lock-based concurrency control, Atlas [9] provides durability guarantees for mutex-based FASEs. Like JUSTDO logging, Atlas guarantees failure atomicity for FASEs defined as outermost critical sections (see Figure 1). Mnemosyne, NV-Heaps, and Atlas can all tolerate abrupt power failures, non-corrupting kernel panics, and non-corrupting process crashes; they do not tolerate corrupting software errors because the latter may corrupt persistent application data directly or may corrupt logs needed for recovery.

The Atlas system, which we compare against in our evaluation (Section 7), illustrates the tradeoffs among convenience, compatibility, generality, and performance that confront any implementation of FASEs. Atlas employs per-thread UNDO logging to ensure the atomicity of FASEs. An UNDO log entry is created for every STORE to persistent memory that is executed by a thread in a program. The log entry must be made persistent before the corresponding STORE can occur. Unlike the isolated transactions of NV-heaps and Mnemosyne, the outermost critical sections that constitute Atlas FASEs may be linked by dependencies: Sometimes an outermost critical section that has completed must nonetheless be rolled back during recovery. Reclaiming UNDO log entries no longer needed for recovery is therefore a non-trivial task in Atlas and is performed in parallel by a separate helper thread. Because dependencies between FASEs must be explicitly tracked, Atlas requires persistent memory updates to be synchronized via locks, which precludes the use of `atomics` (in the sense of C++11) in the current version of Atlas. Atlas emphasizes generality, programmer convenience, and compatibility with conventional lock-based concurrency control; a sophisticated infrastructure is required to support these advantages, and the requisite UNDO logging and log pruning carry performance overheads. Specifically, the size of UNDO logs is proportional to the amount of data modified in the corresponding FASE, and the complexity of tracking dependencies for log reclamation can grow with the number of FASEs.

4. System Model & Programming Model

System Model Figure 2 illustrates our system model. As in prior work [28, 61], we consider a system in which both main memory and processor caches are persistent, i.e., their contents survive tolerated failures intact. We place no restrictions on how persistent memory and persistent caches are implemented. A tolerated failure on such a system causes all processor state to be lost but the contents of the caches and memory survive and are available upon recovery. We assume that power failures and non-corrupting fail-stop software failures have these consequences.

If caches are persistent, a STORE will become persistent once it reaches the coherence layer; release fences force the STORE into persistence. By comparison, on an x86 system with persistent memory but without persistent caches, STOREs can be pushed toward persistence using a `CLFLUSH`. On future Intel systems, new flushing instructions such as `CLFLUSHOPT` and `CLWB` will provide fine-grained control over persistence with lower overhead [16]. Flushing instructions will be used with `SFENCE` and `PCOMMIT` to constrain persistence ordering.

Programming Model JUSTDO logging leverages mutex-based concurrency control to infer FASEs. We assume that failure-atomic modifications to shared data in persistent memory are performed in critical sections delimited by lock acquisitions and releases: A thread that holds one or more locks may temporarily violate application-level consistency invariants, but all such invariants are restored before the thread releases its last lock (Atlas makes the same assumption [9]). Therefore, data in persistent memory are consistent in the quiescent state in which no thread holds any locks, and we accordingly equate outermost critical sections with FASEs: JUSTDO logging guarantees that a quiescent (and thus consistent) state is restored following a failure. At FASE exit, all modifications are guaranteed to be persistent, therefore JUSTDO applications may safely emit output dependent on a FASE—e.g., acknowledging to a remote client that a transaction has completed—immediately after exiting the FASE. Aside from standard lock-mediated data accesses, JUSTDO logging supports unsynchronized read-write (but not write-write) races, which are condoned for C++ `atomics`. Although JUSTDO's approach to failure atomicity is designed for concurrency, it can be adapted to serial code by simply delimiting FASEs as in parallel software.

As in prior approaches [9, 14, 52] our technique allows the programmer to specify explicitly which data is to be preserved across failure by placing it in persistent memory; such control is useful for, e.g., hybrid architectures that incorporate both DRAM and NVM. In such partially persistent systems that expose both persistent and transient memory to applications, JUSTDO logging requires that FASEs access only persistent memory.

Our current implementation of JUSTDO logging is a C++ library with bindings for C and C++. The library requires FASEs to reside in functions that consolidate boilerplate required for recovery and requires that STOREs occur via special JUSTDO library calls. Future compiler support could eliminate nearly all of the verbosity that our current prototype requires and could eliminate opportunities for incorrect usage.

As in prior implementations of persistent memory FASEs, JUSTDO logging maintains logs crucial to recovery in the address space of a running application process. Application software bugs or OS bugs that corrupt the logs or the application's data in persistent memory cannot be tolerated by any of these approaches, but detectable non-corrupting software failures can be tolerated. The main difference between JUSTDO logging and the earlier approaches to persistent memory FASEs is that JUSTDO logging does not tolerate software failures *within* FASEs: Our approach of resuming execution at the point of interruption is inappropriate for such failures, and our approach does not have the ability to roll back a FASE interrupted by failure.

Use Cases Two widespread and important use cases, which we call *library-managed persistence* and *mandatory mediated access*, are well suited to the strengths and limitations of JUSTDO logging and its synergies with complementary technologies for fine-grained fault isolation and software quality assurance techniques.

JUSTDO logging can provide the foundation for high-performance thread-safe libraries that manage persistent data structures on behalf of application logic. In such scenarios, exemplified today by SQLite [45] and similar software, the library assumes responsibility both for orderly concurrent access to shared data in persistent memory and for recovering persistent memory to a consistent state following failures. JUSTDO logging enables expert library developers to write lock-based FASEs in library routines and employ JUSTDO logging to ensure consistent recoverability with low overhead during failure-free operation. A well-designed JUSTDO-based library will consolidate persistent data updates in small FASEs that lend themselves readily to powerful software quality assurance techniques [7, 8, 19]. One advantage of this approach is that JUSTDO logging is employed only in the expert-written library and is not visible to application developers; one limitation of this use case is that FASEs cannot span library calls.

A related use case involves application logic of questionable quality or security that must be constrained to manipulate valuable persistent data only indirectly, via a trusted high-quality intermediary. A widespread example of this pattern is commercial relational database management systems, which mediate application access to database tables while upholding data integrity constraints and preventing arbitrary modifications of the database by buggy, misguided, or malicious application logic. JUSTDO logging provides a new high-performance logging strategy for the intermediary in mandatory mediated access scenarios. OS process boundaries coupled with user permissions can isolate untrusted application code from trusted intermediary software, allowing only the latter direct access to persistent data. However this isolation strategy, widely used today in high-integrity database configurations, requires application logic to communicate with trusted code via heavyweight inter-process communication (IPC) mechanisms. Research on fine-grained intra-process isolation [12], together with JUSTDO logging, suggests a lightweight alternative: Application logic accesses persistent data via a *library* linked into the same address space as the application, precisely as in the library-managed persistence scenario, but with a crucial difference: The intra-process isolation mechanism protects both the data and the trusted library from untrusted application code. Such a strategy eliminates the overhead of IPC between application code and the trusted intermediary without weakening protection.

5. Design

JUSTDO logging implements lock-delimited failure-atomic sections (FASEs) by recording sufficient information during the execution of a FASE such that, if a crash occurs, each FASE can resume at the last STORE it attempted prior to the failure.

The key data structure for our technique is the JUSTDO log, a small per-thread log. This thread-local log contains only a *single active entry* at any one time, and is written before every STORE within a FASE. The single active log entry contains only the *address* to be written, the *new value* to be written there, the *size* of the write, and the *pro-*

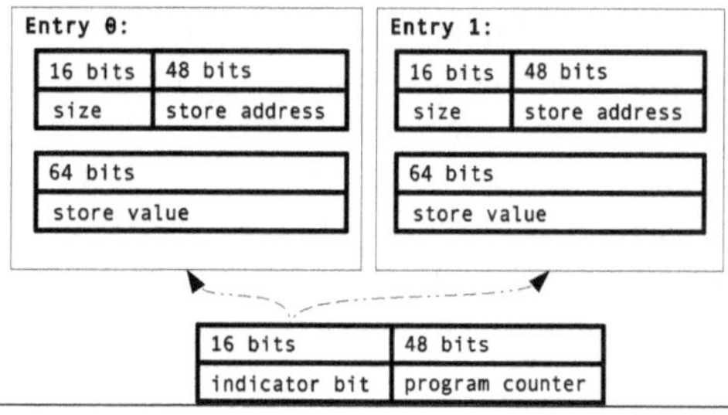

Figure 3. JUSTDO log format.

gram counter. Immediately after the log entry is completed, the corresponding STORE is performed. Conceptually, the JUSTDO log is a "done to here" note; recovery code leverages the idempotence of STOREs to transform at-least-once execution of the most recent STORE before a failure into correct resumption.

To recover using a crashed program's set of per-thread JUSTDO logs, recovery threads re-enter each interrupted FASE at the program counter indicated in the FASE's JUSTDO log, re-acquire the appropriate locks, re-execute the idempotent STORE, and continue execution until the end of each FASE.

Successful recovery requires additional steps when writing a JUSTDO FASE. In particular, we must ensure that the instructions in a FASE do not access data that was stored in transient memory, which will not have survived the failure. We satisfy this requirement by mandating that all LOADs and STOREs within a FASE access only persistent memory. Furthermore, we must ensure that instructions in a FASE do not depend on data held only in volatile CPU registers. We satisfy this requirement by preventing register promotion [26, 43] of memory values within FASEs. Finally, the recovery-time completion of each FASE must respect all mutual exclusion constraints present in the program. We ensure this by recording the locks acquired and released in each FASE in thread-local lock logs.

This section describes the design of the JUSTDO log and our auxiliary data structures. For brevity we largely omit release fences from our discussion. We employ release fences as necessary to constrain the order in which STOREs attain persistence.

5.1 JUSTDO Log

The JUSTDO log is updated for every STORE within a FASE. Our approach transforms every STORE in the original crash-vulnerable FASE to both a log update and then the STORE in the JUSTDO-fortified FASE.

Figure 3 illustrates the format of the entire thread-local JUSTDO log. The log is implemented as a tightly packed struct where each field holds critical recovery information. To ensure atomic updates to the log, it actually holds two entries, although only one is active at a time. In each entry, we store the destination address, size, and new value. The program counter value is shared between the entries, and we use the high order bits of the program counter to indicate which entry is active. On Intel x86, virtual addresses are 48 bits, facilitating this tight packing [16]. Additional bits in the size field and indicator bit are reserved for future use (e.g., flags indicating an atomic store).

To update the log, both the new value and destination address are STOREd (with the size packed into the high order bits of the address pointer) in the inactive entry, followed by a release fence to ensure that the writes have reached the persistent cache. Subsequently, we STORE the new program counter (with the indicator bit set for the recently updated entry).

After the log has been successfully updated, we execute a release fence (again to ensure that the updates are persistent), then complete the persistent STORE by writing the new value to the destination address.

5.2 Persistent-Only Accesses

We require that all memory LOADs and STOREs within FASEs access only persistent data. This requirement extends to thread-local locations that would ordinarily be transient, such as variables on the stack. By mandating that FASEs can access only persistent data we ensure that no updates in a FASE are dependent on state destroyed by failure.

The persistent-only access requirement means that any thread-local memory locations that might be accessed in the FASE (including those normally stored on the stack) must be moved to persistent memory prior to entering the first critical section of a FASE, and, if desired, moved out of persistent memory at the end of a FASE.

While this "persistent-only access" restriction may appear limiting, we find that it is compatible with familiar design patterns. Consider, for example, the ubiquitous "container" pattern as applied to persistent data: (nearly) all of the container metadata maintained by the library code is persistent; similarly, the data stored in a persistent container is also persistent. User code will ensure that its (possibly large) data values are persistent before passing pointers to them into the library; the library can verify that the data are in persistent memory via range checking. It is straightforward to migrate into persistent memory the relatively small amount of transient data passed on the stack between client and library (e.g., the pointer to persistent data). Unlike physical logging-type systems, our technique only requires the data to be written to persistence once, and is consequently insensitive to data size (see Section 7.4). The "small transient state property" is typical of the exported methods of shared persistent data structures and their maintenance operations (e.g., rebalancing).

5.3 Register Promotion in FASEs

Register promotion is a compiler optimization that eliminates redundant LOADs from memory by caching memory locations in CPU registers [26, 43]. Register promotion in FASEs is problematic for JUSTDO logging. Consider a value in persistent memory that within a FASE is LOADed into a register upon which two subsequent STOREs depend. If, due to register promotion, the value is not re-LOADed from persistent memory prior to influencing the second STORE, recovery from a crash immediately after the first STORE is impossible: The crash erases the register containing the value upon which the second STORE depends.

Our current implementation prevents such anomalies by selective use of the C/C++ "`volatile`" keyword. We employ a templated type wrapper within FASEs to ensure that LOADs within FASEs occur via `volatile` pointers and are therefore not elided by compiler optimization. Note that STOREs are not affected by this LOAD-specific mechanism. Manual inspection of the assembly code generated for our FASEs confirms that our current approach prevents problematic register promotions without affecting STOREs.

The penalty of disabling register promotion within FASEs in our current prototype is that FASE execution time is roughly doubled, i.e., crash-resilient JUSTDO-fortified critical sections are twice as slow as crash-vulnerable transient critical sections. Compared to the logging overheads of alternative failure atomicity mechanisms, our overhead is lower (Section 7). In the future, a JUSTDO-aware compiler could more selectively disable register promotion in FASEs, allowing it where it does not preclude recovery, thus improving performance.

5.4 Lock Logs

Recovering from failure by resumption requires that every recovery thread know which locks it holds, and furthermore that no locks are held forever; otherwise safety violations or deadlock can occur. Our design supports arbitrary lock implementations; our current prototype employs standard pthread mutexes.

To preserve lock ownership information across crashes, we require that locks reside in a persistent memory region. Threads maintain two per-thread persistent logs to facilitate proper restoration of lock ownership during recovery: a *lock intention log* and a *lock ownership log*. The purpose of the former is to speed recovery by obviating the need to inspect all locks in persistent memory, whereas the latter is used to reassign locks to recovery threads. The size of a thread's lock ownership and lock intention logs at a particular point in time is proportional to the number of locks held by the thread.

Immediately prior to attempting a lock acquisition, a thread declares its intent by recording the lock address in the lock intention log. Immediately after acquiring the lock, the thread records the acquisition in the lock ownership log using a JUSTDO store. To unlock a mutex, a thread performs the same operations in reverse order: It first uses a JUSTDO store to remove the lock from its lock ownership log, then unlocks the mutex, and finally removes the lock from the lock intention log. This protocol ensures that following a crash the per-thread lock intention logs collectively record all locks that *might* be locked, and the lock ownership logs record which thread has locked each lock that is *certainly* locked.

5.5 Recovery

Recovery begins by using the per-thread lock intention logs to *unlock* all mutexes that might have been locked at the moment of failure. Without lock intention logs, unlocking all mutexes would require inspecting them all or using generational locks in the manner of NV-heaps [14]. The lock intention log enables both arbitrary mutex implementations and fast recovery.

After unlocking all mutexes, recovery spawns one thread per non-empty JUSTDO log; a recovery thread's duty is to execute to completion a corresponding FASE that had been cut short by failure. Each recovery thread inherits a JUSTDO log and the pair of lock logs left behind by its deceased predecessor.

Recovery threads begin by acquiring all locks in their respective lock ownership logs, then waiting at a barrier for all other threads to do likewise. Once all locks have been acquired by all recovery threads, each thread re-executes the STORE instruction contained in its JUSTDO log. Finally, each recovery thread jumps to the program counter value contained in the JUSTDO log and continues execution of the interrupted FASE. Recovery threads track the number of mutexes they hold, and when this count drops to zero the FASE has been completed and the thread exits.

Interestingly, recovery *must* be executed with an interleaving of instructions (either in parallel or by context switching across recovery threads): Some FASEs may be blocked waiting for other FASEs to release mutexes. This interleaving requirement is actually an advantage, because our approach naturally supports parallel recovery. Furthermore, once our recovery threads have re-acquired all of their locks and passed the barrier, access to shared persistent state is properly synchronized by the appropriate mutexes. Consequently, the resurrected application may spawn ordinary (non-recovery) threads that operate, with appropriate synchronization, upon persistent memory *even before our recovery threads have completed the execution of interrupted FASEs.* In other words, the restoration of consistency to persistent memory can proceed in parallel with resumed application execution. Section 7.3 presents recovery time measurements of crashed processes that manipulated large volumes of persistent data via JUSTDO logging.

Reasoning about the barrier employed by recovery makes it easy to show that our approach tolerates failures during recovery. No persistent memory state is altered before our recovery threads reach the barrier, so a crash before this point has no effect and recovery may simply be attempted again. After our recovery threads pass the barrier, they execute FASEs under the protection of JUSTDO logging, precisely as in an ordinary execution of the program.

6. Implementation

Our current JUSTDO logging prototype is a C++ library with bindings for both C++ and C. Annotations for JUSTDO-enabled FASEs are a straightforward, if tedious, transformation of transient (non-crash-resilient) code, somewhat analogous to the annotations employed in software transactional memory systems. We hope that future work, integrating compiler support, can automate nearly all of the chores surrounding annotations while also providing additional type safety guarantees to ensure that the "persistent-only accesses" rule is followed within FASEs. In the meantime, however, JUSTDO integration requires every possible code path and access within a FASE to be identified and annotated at compile time, making JUSTDO integration significantly more complex than other failure atomicity systems. Other systems, such as Atlas, do not need to know all possible FASE code paths at compile time. Compared with prior FASE implementations, our current prototype deliberately trades programmer convenience and generality for performance.

Our library contains three major elements: the `jd_root`, the `jd_obj`, and the JUSTDO routine. The first two are C++ classes and are entry points into our library. The JUSTDO routine consolidates the boilerplate required to execute an application-defined FASE under JUSTDO logging. The remainder of this section illustrates the use of these elements in a detailed example shown in Figures 4, 5, 6, and 7. Our example code failure-atomically transfers money from `acnt1` to `acnt2`; for clarity we omit type casts and the use of the `volatile` keyword. Our example code shows the usage of JUSTDO annotations and how to set up a JUSTDO FASE.

By definition, persistent memory outlives the processes that access it. Therefore JUSTDO logging requires mechanisms to enable newly created processes to locate persistent memory containing data of interest and to make the data accessible to application software. At a high level, we follow the same straightforward approach taken by prior research implementations of FASEs and by emerging industry standards for persistent memory [38, 46]: A file system (or the moral equivalent thereof) maps short, memorable, human-readable strings (names) to long persistent byte sequences, and processes use an `mmap`-like interface to incorporate into their address spaces the persistent data thus located. More specifically, our JUSTDO logging prototype uses the Atlas [9] implementation of persistent memory regions, which supports memory allocation methods `nv_malloc` and `nv_calloc` and contains a header for its root pointer (accessed via `Get/SetRegionRoot` methods), as shown in our example code.

6.1 `jd_root`

The `jd_root` object is the main entry point to the JUSTDO library. This object is placed in a well-known location in the persistent region that is accessible by recovery code via `GetRegionRoot`.

The `jd_root` is a global object and is the factory object for `jd_obj`s, which are thread-local. The `jd_root` maintains a list of the `jd_obj`s that have been allocated to threads.

During recovery, the `jd_root` object is responsible for unlocking all mutexes and coordinating lock re-acquisitions across recovery threads. Finally, it initiates thread-local recovery, in which recovery threads jump back into their respective FASEs.

6.2 `jd_obj`

The `jd_obj` is a thread local object for executing a FASE under JUSTDO logging. It contains both the JUSTDO log structure and its associated lock logs. `jd_obj` exports methods `jd_lock`, `jd_store`, and `jd_unlock`; consequently most lines within a JUSTDO FASE will touch the `jd_obj`.

The `jd_obj` also provides a handle to thread-local persistent memory that is used to persist variables normally on the stack; this handle facilitates compliance with the "persistent-only access" rule of Section 5.2. In an *exception* to the "persistent-only access" rule, each thread maintains a *reference* to its `jd_obj` on the stack. Following a crash, this reference is correctly re-set in each recovery thread. This exception allows a recovery thread to share a reference to its `jd_obj` with its failed predecessor.

6.3 JUSTDO routine

A JUSTDO routine is a function containing a JUSTDO FASE. Such functions have a defined prototype and are annotated to enable recovery. During recovery, the JUSTDO routine's stack frame provides thread-local scratch space that would be inconvenient to obtain otherwise. The annotations are illustrated in our example code at line 10 in `transfer_justdo` of Figure 5.

A JUSTDO routine complies with several annotation requirements. It takes three arguments: a `jd_obj` and two `void` pointers for the arguments and return values. We also require that the first line of the JUSTDO routine be a special macro: `JD_ROUTINE_ON_ENTRY` (line 12).

There are two ways to execute a JUSTDO routine, corresponding to normal (failure-free) execution and recovery. During failure-free operation, invocation of a JUSTDO routine simply executes the function (and FASE) as written.

During recovery, however, the execution of a JUSTDO routine is different. A recovery thread that has acquired mutexes as described in Section 5.5 invokes the JUSTDO routine, passing as an argument a reference to the the `jd_obj` that it inherits from its failed predecessor thread and NULL for the remaining two arguments, `args` and `rets`. The `JD_ROUTINE_ON_ENTRY` macro in the JUSTDO routine determines from the `jd_obj` that it is running in recovery mode and uses the JUSTDO log within the `jd_obj` to cause control to jump to the last STORE within the FASE executed prior to failure. When a recovery thread unlocks its last mutex, it

```
struct Root { int* accounts;
              lock* locks;
              jd_root* jdr; };
Root* rt;
struct Args { int acnt1,acnt2,amount; };
struct Returns { bool success; };
struct Locals { int acnt1, acnt2;
              bool success; };
```

Figure 4. JUSTDO logging example (Globals)

knows that its assigned FASE has completed and therefore it exits.

6.4 Recovery Implementation

Having introduced all library constructs and their design, we can now summarize the entire recovery procedure:

1. The application detects a crash and invokes JUSTDO recovery via `jd_root`.
2. The `jd_root` resets all locks using the lock intention logs.
3. The `jd_root` spawns recovery threads for every active `jd_obj`.
4. Each recovery thread re-acquires locks using its lock ownership logs in its `jd_obj`, then barriers.
5. Following the barrier, the recovery threads invoke interrupted JUSTDO routines with their inherited `jd_obj`.
6. Each recovery thread uses the `JD_ROUTINE_ON_ENTRY` macro to jump to the program counter as indicated by its JUSTDO log.
7. When a recovery thread's lock count reaches zero, it exits.

```
// jd_routine for account transfer
void transfer_justdo(jd_obj* jdo,
 void* args, void* rets){
  JD_ROUTINE_ON_ENTRY(jdo);
  // copy locals off the stack
  jdo->set_locs<Locals>();
  jdo->locs->acnt1 = args->acnt1;
  jdo->locs->acnt2 = args->acnt2;
  jdo->locs->amount = args->amount;
  // begin FASE
  jdo->jd_lock(
   rt->locks[jdo->locs->acnt1]);
  jdo->jd_lock(
   rt->locks[jdo->locs->acnt2]);
  // increment first account
  jdo->jd_store(
   &rt->accounts[jdo->locs->acnt1],
   rt->accounts[jdo->locs->acnt1] +
   jdo->locs->amount);
  // decrement second account
  jdo->jd_store(
   &rt->accounts[jdo->locs->acnt2],
   rt->accounts[jdo->locs->acnt2] -
   jdo->locs->amount);
  // end FASE
  jdo->jd_unlock(
   rt->locks[jdo->locs->acnt1]);
  jdo->jd_unlock(
   rt->locks[jdo->locs->acnt2]);
  // outside FASE, can access transient
  rets->success = true;
}
```

Figure 5. JUSTDO logging example (JUSTDO Routine)

7. Experiments

In the current state of our prototype it is difficult to retrofit JUSTDO logging onto large and complex real-world legacy applications, so our evaluations employ small benchmarks. We implemented five high-throughput concurrent data structures to evaluate the performance and recoverability of JUSTDO logging. Each data structure is implemented in three variants: a *Transient* (crash vulnerable) version, a JUSTDO crash-resilient version, and a version fortified with the Atlas crash-resilience system [9]. The five algorithms are the following:

Queue The two-lock queue implementation of Michael and Scott [29].

Stack A locking variation on the Treiber Stack [49].

Priority Queue A sorted list traversed using hand-over-hand locking. This implementation allows for concurrent accesses within the list, but threads cannot pass one another.

Map A fixed-size hash map that uses the sorted-list priority queue implementation for each bucket, obviating the need for per-bucket locks.

Vector An array-based resizable vector in the style of the contiguous storage solution proposed by Dechev et al. [17]. This algorithm supports lookups and updates during resizing.

The queue and stack are lock-based implementations of algorithms in the `java.util.concurrent` library. The vector's design allows it to exploit atomic STORE instructions, and our transient and JUSTDO versions of the vector take advantage of this feature. Atlas supports only mutex-based synchronization and consequently our Atlas version of the vector uses a reader-writer lock instead, which incurs a non-negligible performance overhead. In all other respects, the

```
int main(){
  int rid =
   LoadPersistentRegion("my_region");
  rt = GetRegionRoot(rid);
  // initialize our root if needed
  if(rt == NULL) {
    rt = nv_malloc(sizeof(Root),rid);
    rt->accounts =
     nv_calloc(sizeof(int),N_ACCTS,rid);
    rt->locks =
     nv_calloc(sizeof(lock),N_ACCTS,rid);
    rt->jdr =
     nv_malloc(sizeof(jd_root),rid);
    new(rt->jdr) justdo_root(jdr);
    SetRegionRoot(rt,rid);
  }
  // otherwise recover if needed
  else{rt->jdr->recover();}
  // get a thread local jd_obj
  jd_obj* jdo = rt->jdr->new_jd_obj();
  // conduct transfer
  Args args;
  args.acnt1 = 3;    // arguments passed
  args.acnt2 = 5;    // into FASE
  args.amount = 50; // via jd_routine
  Returns rets;
  transfer_justdo(jdo,args,rets);
  // delete jd_obj
  rt->jdr->delete_jd_obj(jdo);
}
```

Figure 6. JUSTDO logging example (main)

```
// The equivalent transient routine
bool transfer_transient(int acnt1,
 int acnt2, int amount){
  lock(rt->locks[acnt1]);
  lock(rt->locks[acnt2]);
  accounts[acnt1] += amount;
  accounts[acnt2] -= amount;
  unlock(rt->locks[acnt1]);
  unlock(rt->locks[acnt2]);
  return true;
}
```

Figure 7. JUSTDO logging example (equivalent transient routine)

three versions of each of our five data structures differ only in the implementation—or non-implementation—of crash resilience.

Note that our implementations of these data structures admit parallelism to varying degrees. Our stack, for example, serializes accesses in a very small critical section. At the other extreme, our hash map admits parallel accesses both across and within buckets. We therefore expect low-parallelism data structures to scale poorly with worker thread count whereas high-parallelism data structures should exhibit nearly linear performance scaling.

7.1 Correctness Verification

Conventional hardware suffices for the purposes of verifying the crash-resilience guarantees of JUSTDO logging because both conventional CPU caches and conventional DRAM main memory can be *persistent with respect to process crashes*: Specifically, STOREs to a file-backed memory mapping are required by POSIX to be "kernel persistent," meaning that such STOREs are guaranteed to outlive the process that issued them; neither `msync` nor any other measures are required after a STORE to obtain this guarantee [33].

To test JUSTDO recovery we installed a 128 GB JUSTDO-fortified hash map in a file-backed memory mapping on a server-class machine (described in more detail in Section 7.2). After building the hash table, we used all sixty of the server's hardware threads to perform inserts and removes in equal proportion on random keys in the hash table. Our hash buckets are implemented as sorted linked lists, so corruption (if present) will manifest as dangling pointers within a bucket, resulting in a segmentation fault or assertion failure. At intervals of two seconds, we killed the threads using an external `SIGKILL`. On restarting the process, we performed JUSTDO recovery before continuing execution. This test was conducted for approximately four hours. We constructed similar tests for each of our other four concurrent data structures; these additional tests also injected crashes every two seconds and ran for over twelve hours. No inconsistencies or corruption occurred.

7.2 Performance Evaluation

The goal of our performance evaluation is to estimate the overhead of JUSTDO crash resilience compared with high-performance transient (crash-vulnerable) versions of the same concurrent algorithms. We took care to ensure that the transient versions of our five algorithms exhibit quite good performance; these versions provide reasonable performance baselines. For example, running on newer hardware, our transient hash map achieves per-core throughput approaching published results on the state-of-the-art MICA concurrent hash table [25].

Our results are conservative/pessimistic in the sense that our experiments involve small data-intensive microbenchmarks that magnify the overheads of crash resilience to the greatest possible extent. In real applications, concurrent accesses to shared persistent data structures might *not* be a performance bottleneck, and therefore by Amdahl's law [2] the overheads of any crash resilience mechanism would likely be smaller. This effect is shown in Section 7.4, where the overhead of initializing large data values eliminates the overhead of persistence.

Our tests consist of microbenchmarks with a varying number of worker threads. Tests are run for a fixed time interval using a low overhead hardware timer, and total operations are aggregated at the end. For the duration of microbenchmark execution, each thread repeatedly chooses a random operation to execute on the structure. Unless stated otherwise (see Section 7.4), keys and values are eight-byte integers, are generated in transient memory, and are copied into persistent memory upon entry into a FASE. For our evaluations of queues, stacks, and priority queues, threads choose randomly between `insert` or `remove`; these three data structures were sized such that most accesses were served from the CPU caches. Therefore performance for our stack and queues is limited by synchronization.

Our vector and map evaluations drew inspiration from the standard YCSB benchmark [57]. For vectors and maps, the containers are filled to 80% of the key range, then we perform `overwrite` operations for random keys in the range. The `overwrite` operation replaces the value only if it exists, but otherwise does not modify the data structure. We sized our vectors and maps so that the vast majority of these two structures did *not* fit in the CPU caches; keys for accesses were drawn randomly from a uniform distribution. Most accesses miss in the CPU caches, therefore our vector and map are limited by memory performance.

During each test, threads synchronize only through the tested data structure. To smooth performance curves, pages are prefaulted to prevent soft page faults. For data structures with high memory allocator usage (all except the vector), we implemented a simple thread-local bump pointer block pool to prevent bottlenecking on `malloc` and to minimize the impact of Atlas's custom memory allocator, which tends to underperform at high thread counts. Variables within the data structures are appropriately padded to prevent false sharing. To generate random numbers, threads use thread-local generators to avoid contention.

Software threads for all experiments are pinned to specific hardware threads. Our thread pinning progression fills all cores of a socket first, then fills the corresponding hyperthreads. Once all cores and hyperthreads are filled, we add additional sockets, filling them in the same order. For all machines, we ran every experimental configuration five times and took the average.

Compilation for the transient and JUSTDO data structures was done using gcc 4.8.4 with the `-O3` flag. Atlas structures were compiled using the clang and llvm-based Atlas compiler, again with the `-O3` flag set.

"Persistent Cache" Machines We conducted performance tests on three machines. The first is a single-socket workstation with an Intel Core i7-4770 CPU running at 3.40 GHz. The CPU has four two-way hyperthreaded cores (eight hardware threads). It has a shared 8 MB L3 cache, with per-core private L2 and L1 caches, 256 KB and 32 KB respectively. The workstation runs Ubuntu 12.04.5 LTS.

Our second machine is a server with four Intel Xeon E7-4890 v2 sockets, each of which has 15 cores (60 hardware threads total). The machine has 3 TB of main memory, with 37.5 MB per-socket L3 caches. L2 and L1 caches are private per core, 256 KB and 32 KB respectively. The server and the workstation are used to mimic machines that implement persistent memory using supercapacitor-backed DRAM (e.g., Viking NVDIMMs [51]) and supercapacitor-backed SRAM.

Figures 8 and 9 show aggregate operation throughput as a function of worker thread count for all three versions of our data structures—transient, JUSTDO-fortified, and Atlas-fortified. Our results show that on both the workstation and the server, JUSTDO logging outperforms Atlas for every data structure and nearly all thread counts. JUSTDO performance ranges from three to one hundred times faster than Atlas. JUSTDO logging furthermore achieves between 33% and 75% of the throughput of the transient (crash-vulnerable) versions of each data structure. For data structures that are naturally parallel (vector and hash map), the transient and JUSTDO implementations scale with the number of threads. In contrast, Atlas does not scale well for our vectors and maps. This inefficiency is a product of Atlas's dependency tracking between FASEs, which creates a synchronization bottleneck in the presence of large numbers of locks.

Future NVM-based main memories that employ PCM or resistive RAM are expected to be slower than DRAM, and thus the ratio of memory speed to CPU speed is likely to be lower on such systems. We therefore investigate whether changes to memory speed degrade the performance of JUSTDO logging. Since commodity PCM and resistive RAM chips are not currently available, we investigate the implications of changing memory speed by under-clocking and over-clocking DRAM. For these experiments we use a third machine, a single-socket workstation with a four-core (two-way hyperthreaded) Intel i7-4770K system running at 3.5 GHz with 32 KB, 256 KB private L1 and L2 caches per core and one shared 8 MB L3 cache. We use 32 GBs of G.SKILLs TridentX DDR3 DRAM operating at frequencies of 800, 1333 (default), 2000, and 2400 MHz.

For our tests involving small data structures (queue, stack, and priority queue), the performance impact of changing memory speed was negligible (under 1% change)—which is not surprising because by design these entire data structures fit in the L3 cache. For our tests involving larger data structures deliberately sized to be far larger than our CPU caches and accessed randomly (map and vector), we find that the ratio of transient (crash-vulnerable) throughput to

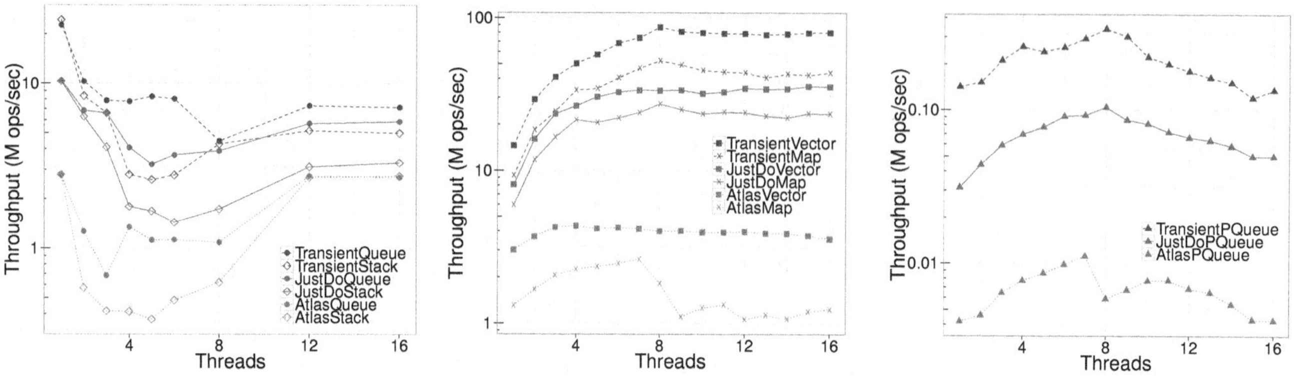

Figure 8. Throughput on workstation (log scale)

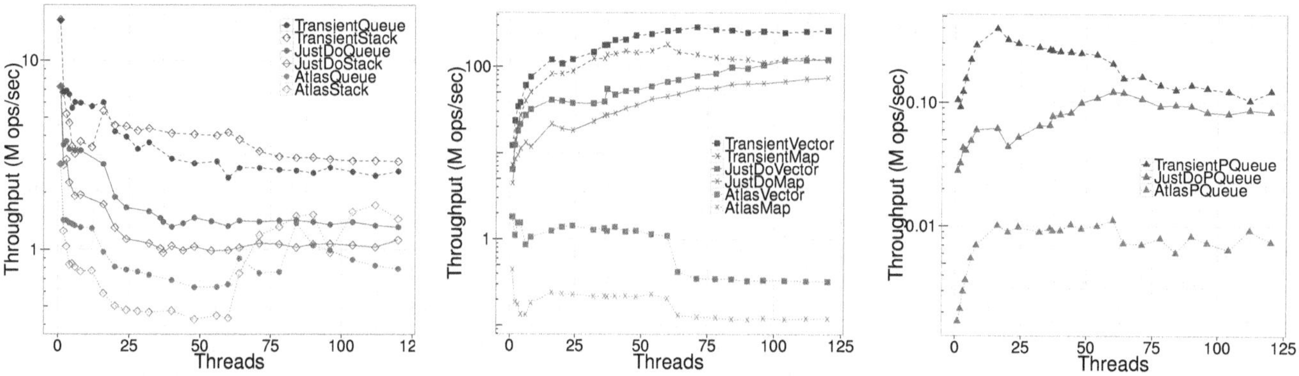

Figure 9. Throughput on server (log scale)

JUSTDO logging throughput remains constant (between 1.93 and 2.00) as memory speed varies over a 3× range. Varying memory speed does not change the overhead of of JUSTDO logging.

"Transient Cache" Machines To investigate how JUSTDO logging will likely perform on machines without persistent caches, but with persistent main memory, we modified our JUSTDO library to use the synchronous CLFLUSH instruction to push STOREs within FASEs toward persistent memory. This x86 instruction invalidates and writes back a cache line, blocking the thread until it completes. While Intel has announced faster flushing mechanisms in future ISAs [41], this instruction is the only method on existing hardware. Our CLFLUSH-ing version uses the CLFLUSH instruction where before it used only a release fence, forcing dirty data back to persistent storage in a consistent order.

We performed CLFLUSH experiments on our i7-4770 workstation and compared with Atlas's "flush-as-you-go" mode, which also makes liberal use of CLFLUSH in the same way (see Figure 10). As expected, JUSTDO logging takes a serious performance hit when it uses CLFLUSH after every STORE in a FASE, since the reduced computational overhead of our technique is overshadowed by the more expensive flushing cost. Furthermore, the advantage of a JUSTDO log that fits in a single cache line is negated because the log is repeatedly invalidated and forced out of the cache. The cache line invalidation causes a massive performance hit. For the JUSTDO map using four worker threads, the L3 cache miss ratio increases from 5.5% to 80% when we switch from release fences to CLFLUSHes. We expect that the new Intel instruction CLWB, which drains the cache line back to memory but does not invalidate it, will significantly improve our performance in this scenario when it becomes available.

In contrast to JUSTDO logging, Atlas's additional sophistication pays off here, since it can buffer writes back to memory and consolidate flushes to the same cache line. Atlas outperforms the JUSTDO variants by 2–3× across our tested parameters on "transient cache" machines.

7.3 Recovery Speed

In our correctness verification test (Section 7.1), which churned sixty threads on a 128 GB hash table, we also recorded recovery time. After recovery process start-up, we spend on average 2000 microseconds to mmap the large hash table back into the virtual address space of the recovery process. Reading the root pointer takes an additional microsecond. To check if recovery is necessary takes 64 microseconds. In our tests, an average of 24 FASEs were interrupted by failure, so 24 threads needed to be recovered. It took

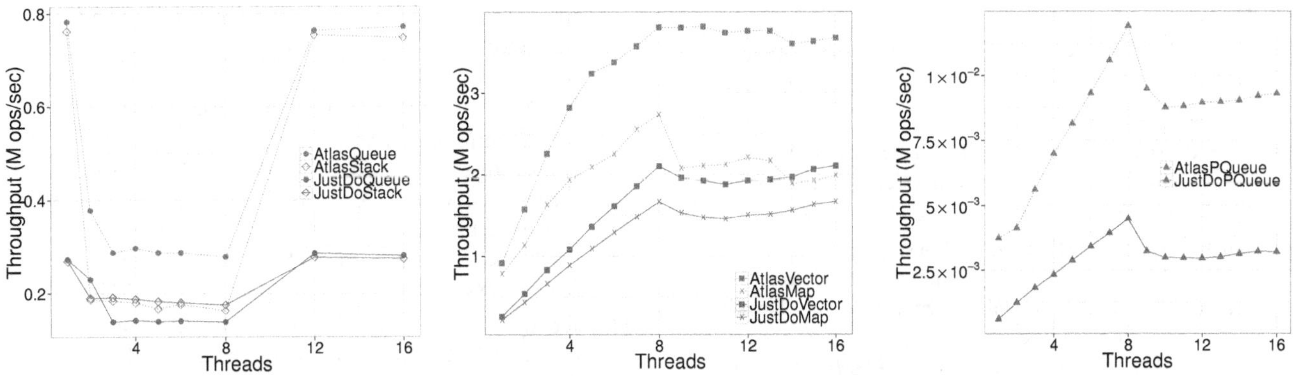

Figure 10. Throughput on workstation using CLFLUSH (linear scale)

on average 2700 microseconds for all recovery threads to launch, complete their FASEs in parallel, and terminate. (To put these numbers in perspective, during failure-free execution a FASE in these tests took on the order of one microsecond.) From start to finish, recovering a 128 GB hash table takes under 5 ms.

7.4 Data Size

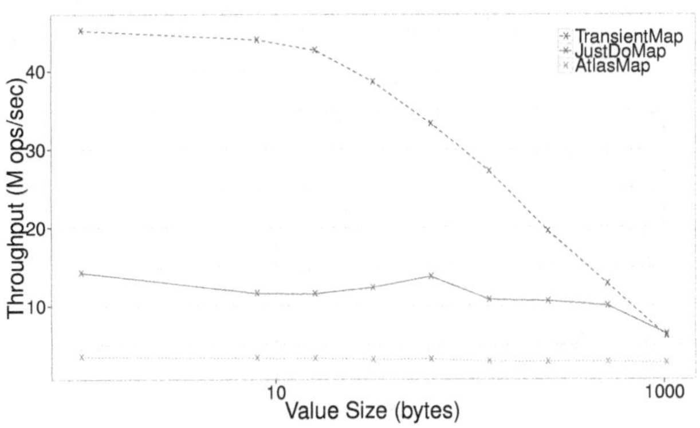

Figure 11. Throughput on server as a function of value size (linear scale)

Figure 11 shows throughput as a function of data size on the various key-value (hash map) implementations. Tests were run on the server machine with eight threads, assume a persistent cache, and vary value sizes from a single byte to one kilobyte. For each operation, values were created and initialized with random contents by the operating thread; the Atlas and JUSTDO variants allocate and initialize data in persistent memory. Allocation and initialization quickly become bottlenecks for the transient implementation. The JUSTDO implementation is less sensitive to data size, since it operates at a slower speed, and value initialization does not begin to affect throughput until around half a kilobyte. At one kilobyte, the allocation and initialization of the data values becomes the bottleneck for both implementations, meaning the overhead for persistence is effectively zero beyond this data size. In contrast to the transient and JUSTDO implementations, the Atlas implementation is nearly unaffected by data size changes: Atlas's bottleneck remains dependency tracking between FASEs.

Note that only Atlas copies the entire data value into a log; in the case of a crash between initialization of a data value and its insertion, Atlas may need to roll back the data's initial values. In contrast, JUSTDO logging relies on the fact that the data value resides in persistent memory. After verifying that the data is indeed persistent, the JUSTDO map inserts a pointer to the data. The "precopy" of JUSTDO copies only the value's pointer off the stack into persistent memory. Consequently, it is affected by data size only as allocation and initialization become a larger part of overall execution. Obviously, the transient version never copies the data value as it is not failure-resilient.

8. Conclusions

We have shown that JUSTDO logging provides a useful new way to implement failure-atomic sections. Compared with persistent memory transaction systems and other existing mechanisms for implementing FASEs, JUSTDO logging greatly simplifies log maintenance, thereby reducing performance overheads significantly. Our crash-injection tests confirm that JUSTDO logging preserves the consistency of application data in the face of sudden failures. Our performance results show that JUSTDO logging effectively leverages persistent caches to improve performance substantially compared with a state-of-the-art FASE implementation.

Acknowledgments

This work was partially supported by the U.S. Department of Energy under Award Number DE-SC-0012199. We thank Dhruva Chakrabarti, Adam Izraelevitz, Harumi Kuno, Mark Lillibridge, Brad Morrey, Faisal Nawab, Michael Scott, Joe Tucek, the ASPLOS reviewers, and our shepherd Mike Swift for suggestions that greatly improved our paper.

References

[1] Sarita V. Adve and Kourosh Gharachorloo. "Shared Memory Consistency Models: A Tutorial." In *IEEE Computer*, Vol. 29 No. 12, December 1996.

[2] Gene M. Amdahl. "Validity of the Single Processor Approach to Achieving Large Scale Computing Capabilities." In *Spring Joint Computer Conference*, 1967.

[3] Dmytro Apalkov, Alexey Khvalkovskiy, Steven Watts, Valdimir Nikitin, Xueti Tang, Daniel Lottis, Kiseok Moon, Xiao Luo, Eugene Chen, Adrian Ong, Alexander Driskill-Smith, and Mohamad Krounbi. "Spin-transfer Torque Magnetic Random Access Memory (STT-MRAM)." In *Journal on Emerging Technologies in Computing Systems (JETC)—Special issue on memory technologies*, 2013.

[4] Brian N. Bershad. "Fast Mutual Exclusion for Uniprocessors." In *International Conference on Architectural Support for Programming Languages and Operating Systems (ASPLOS)*, 1992.

[5] Kumud Bhandari, Dhruva R. Chakrabarti, and Hans-J. Boehm. "Implications of CPU Caching on Byte-addressable Non-Volatile Memory Programming." *Technical report HPL-2012-236, Hewlett-Packard*, 2012.

[6] Aviv Blattner, Ram Dagan, and Terence Kelly. "Generic Crash-Resilient Storage for Indigo and Beyond." *Technical report HPL-2013-75, Hewlett-Packard*, 2013. `http://www.labs.hp.com/techreports/2013/HPL-2013-75.pdf`

[7] Cristian Cadar, Daniel Dunbar, and Dawson Engler. "KLEE: Unassisted and Automatic Generation of High-Coverage Tests for Complex Systems Programs." In *Symposium on Operating Systems Design and Implementation (OSDI)*, 2008.

[8] Cristian Cadar, Vijay Ganesh, Peter M. Pawlowski, David L. Dill, and Dawson R. Engler. "EXE: Automatically Generating Inputs of Death." In *Conference on Computer and Communications Security (CCS)*, 2006.

[9] Dhruva R. Chakrabarti, Hans-J. Boehm, and Kumud Bhandari. "Atlas: Leveraging Locks for Non-Volatile Memory Consistency." In *International Conference on Object Oriented Programming Systems Languages and Applications (OOPSLA)*, 2014.

[10] Peter M. Chen, Wee Teck Ng, Subhachandra Chandra, Christopher Aycock, Gurushankar Rajamani, and David E. Lowell. "The Rio File Cache: Surviving Operating System Crashes." In *International Conference on Architectural Support for Programming Languages and Operating Systems (ASPLOS)*, 1996.

[11] Shimin Chen, Phillip B. Gibbons, and Suman Nath. "Rethinking Database Algorithms for Phase Change Memory." In *Biennial Conference on Innovative Data Systems Research (CIDR)*, 2011.

[12] David Chisnall, Colin Rothwell, Robert N.M. Watson, Jonathan Woodruff, Munraj Vadera, Simon W. Moore, Michael Roe, Brooks Davis, and Peter G. Neumann. "Beyond the PDP-11: Processor support for a memory-safe C abstract machine." In *International Conference on Architectural Support for Programming Languages and Operating Systems (ASPLOS)*. 2015.

[13] Joel Coburn, Trevor Bunker, Meir Schwarz, Rajesh Gupta, and Steven Swanson. "From ARIES to MARS: Transaction Support for Next-Generation, Solid-State Drives." In *Symposium on Operating Systems Principles (SOSP)*, 2013.

[14] Joel Coburn, Adrian M. Caulfield, Ameen Akel, Laura M. Grupp, Rajesh K. Gupta, Ranjit Jhala, and Steven Swanson. "NV-Heaps: Making Persistent Objects Fast and Safe with Next-Generation, Non-volatile Memories." In *International Conference on Architectural Support for Programming Languages and Operating Systems (ASPLOS)*, 2011.

[15] Jeremy Condit, Edmund B. Nightingale, Christopher Frost, Engin Ipek, Benjamin Lee, Doug Burger, and Derrick Coetzee. "Better I/O Through Byte-addressable, Persistent Memory." In *Symposium on Operating Systems Principles (SOSP)*, 2009.

[16] Intel Corporation. "Intel Architecture Instruction Set Extensions Programming Reference." No. 319433-023, October 2014.

[17] Damian Dechev, Peter Pirkelbauer, and Bjarne Stroustrup. "Lock-free Dynamically Resizable Arrays." In *International Conference on Principles of Distributed Systems (OPODIS)*, 2006.

[18] Subramanya R. Dulloor, Sanjay Kumar, Anil Keshavamurthy, Philip Lantz, Dheeraj Reddy, Rajesh Sankaran, and Jeff Jackson. "System Software for Persistent Memory." In *European Conference on Computer Systems (EuroSys)*, 2014.

[19] Patrice Godefroid, Nils Klarlund, and Koushik Sen. "DART: Directed Automated Random Testing." In *Conference on Programming Language Design and Implementation (PLDI)*, 2015.

[20] Jian Huang, Karsten Schwan, and Moinuddin K. Qureshi. "NVRAM-aware Logging in Transaction Systems." In *Proceedings of the VLDB Endowment*, 2014.

[21] Marc de Krujf and Karthikeyan Sankaralingam. "Idempotent Processor Architecture." In *International Symposium on Microarchitecture (MICRO)*, 2011.

[22] Emre Kultursay, Mahmut Kandemir, Anand Sivasubramaniam, and Onur Mutlu. "Evaluating STT-RAM as an Energy-Efficient Main Memory Alternative." In *International Symposium on Performance Analysis of Systems and Software (ISPASS)*, 2013.

[23] Benjamin C. Lee, Engin Ipek, Onur Mutlu, and Doug Burger. "Architecting Phase Change Memory As a Scalable DRAM Alternative." In *International Symposium on Computer Architecture (ISCA)*, 2009.

[24] Eunji Lee, Hyokyung Bahn, and Sam H. Noh. "Unioning of the Buffer Cache and Journaling Layers with Non-volatile Memory." In *Conference on File and Storage Technologies (FAST)*, 2013.

[25] Hyeontaek Lim, Dongsu Han, David G. Andersen, and Michael Kaminsky. "MICA: A Holistic Approach to Fast In-Memory Key-value Storage." In *Conference on Networked Systems Design and Implementation (NSDI)*, 2014.

[26] Raymond Lo, Fred Chow, Robert Kennedy, Shin-Ming Liu, and Peng Tu. "Register Promotion by Sparse Partial Redundancy Elimination of Loads and Stores." In *Conference*

on *Programming Language Design and Implementation (PLDI)*, 1998.

[27] David E. Lowell and Peter M. Chen. "Free transactions with Rio Vista." In *Symposium on Operating Systems Principles (SOSP)*, 1997.

[28] Youyou Lu, Jiwu Shu, Long Sun, and Onur Mutlu. "Loose-Ordering Consistency for Persistent Memory." In *International Conference on Computer Design (ICCD)*, 2014.

[29] Maged M. Michael and Michael L. Scott. "Simple, Fast, and Practical Non-Blocking and Blocking Concurrent Queue Algorithms." In *Symposium on Principles of Distributed Computing (PODC)*, 1996.

[30] Microsoft Developer Network. "Alternative to using Transactional NTFS." `http://msdn.microsoft.com/en-us/library/hh802690.aspx`, Accessed 17 September 2014.

[31] C. Mohan, Don Haderle, Bruce Lindsay, Hamid Pirahesh, and Peter Schwarz. "ARIES: A Transaction Recovery Method Supporting Fine-granularity Locking and Partial Rollbacks Using Write-ahead Logging." In *ACM Transactions on Database Systems*, Vol. 17 No. 1, March 1992.

[32] Dushyanth Narayan and Orion Hodson. "Whole-System Persistence." In *International Conference on Architectural Support for Programming Languages and Operating Systems (ASPLOS)*, 2012.

[33] Faisal Nawab, Dhruva R. Chakrabarti, Terence Kelly, and Charles B. Morrey III. "Procrastination Beats Prevention: Timely Sufficient Persistence for Efficient Crash Resilience." In *International Conference on Extending Database Technology (EDBT)*, 2015. `http://openproceedings.org/2015/conf/edbt/paper-336.pdf`

[34] Faisal Nawab, Dhruva R. Chakrabarti. Terence Kelly, and Charles B. Morrey III "Zero-Overhead NVM Crash Resilience." In *Non-Volatile Memories Workshop (NVMW)*, 2015. `http://nvmw.ucsd.edu/2015/assets/abstracts/41`

[35] Micheal A. Olson, Keith Bostic, and Margo Seltzer. "Berkeley DB." In *USENIX Annual Technical Conference (FREENIX track)*, 1999.

[36] Stan Park, Terence Kelly, and Kai Shen. "Failure-Atomic `msync()`: A Simple and Efficient Mechanism for Preserving the Integrity of Durable Data." In *European Conference on Computer Systems (EuroSys)*, 2013. `http://doi.acm.org/10.1145/2465351.2465374`

[37] Steven Pelley, Peter M. Chen, and Thomas F. Wenisch. "Memory Persistency." In *International Symposium on Computer Architecture (ISCA)*, 2014. `http://dl.acm.org/citation.cfm?id=2665671.2665712`

[38] "Persistent Memory Programming." `http://pmem.io/`, Accessed 12 August 2015.

[39] Donald E. Porter, Owen S. Hofmann, Christopher J. Rossbach, Alexander Benn, and Emmett Witchel. "Operating System Transactions." In *Symposium on Operating Systems Principles (SOSP)*, 2009.

[40] Moinuddin K. Qureshi, Vijayalakshmi Srinivasan, and Jude A. Rivers. "Scalable High Performance Main Memory System Using Phase-change Memory Technology." In *International Symposium on Computer Architecture (ISCA)*, 2009.

[41] Andy Rudoff. "In a World with Persistent Memory." In *Non-Volatile Memories Workshop (NVMW)*, 2015.

[42] Leonid Ryzhyk, Peter Chubb, Ihor Kuz, Etienne Le Sueur, and Gernot Heiser. "Automatic Device Driver Synthesis with Termite." In *Symposium on Operating Systems Principles (SOSP)*, 2009.

[43] A.V.S. Sastry and Roy D.C. Ju. "A New Algorithm for Scalar Register Promotion Based on SSA Form." In *Conference on Programming Language Design and Implementation (PLDI)*, 1998.

[44] Russell Sears and Eric Brewer. "Stasis: Flexible Transactional Storage." In *Symposium on Operating Systems Design and Implementation (SOSP)*, 2006.

[45] SQLite `http://www.sqlite.org/`, Accessed 15 January 2016.

[46] "Storage Networking Industry Association (SNIA) Non-Volatile Memory Programming Model." `http://www.snia.org/tech_activities/standards/curr_standards/npm`, Accessed 10 January 2016.

[47] Richard P. Spillane, Sachin Gaikwad, Manjunath Chinni, Erez Zadok, and Charles P. Wright. "Enabling Transactional File Access via Lightweight Kernel Extensions." In *Conference on File and Storage Technologies (FAST)*, 2009.

[48] Dmitri B. Strukov, Gregory S. Snider, Duncan R. Stewart, and R. Stanley Williams. "The missing memristor found." In *Nature*, Vol. 453 No. 7191, May 2008.

[49] R. Kent Treiber. "Systems Programming: Coping with Parallelism." *Technical Report RJ 5118, IBM Almaden Research Center*, 1986.

[50] Rajat Verma, Anton Ajay Mendez, Stan Park, Sandya Mannarswamy, Terence Kelly, and Charles B. Morrey III. "Failure-Atomic Updates of Application Data in a Linux File System." In *Conference on File and Storage Technologies (FAST)*, 2015. `https://www.usenix.org/system/files/conference/fast15/fast15-paper-verma.pdf`

[51] Viking Technology. "NVDIMM Technology: ArxCis-NV." `http://www.vikingtechnology.com/nvdimm-technology`, Accessed 10 August 2015.

[52] Haris Volos, Andres Jaan Tack, and Micheal M. Swift. "Mnemosyne: Lightweight Persistent Memory." In *International Conference on Architectural Support for Programming Languages and Operating Systems (ASPLOS)*, 2011.

[53] Tianzheng Wang and Ryan Johnson. "Scalable Logging through Emerging Non-Volatile Memory." In *Proceedings of the VLDB Endowment*, 2014.

[54] Jonathan Woodruff, Robert N. M. Watson, David Chisnall, Simon W. Moore, Jonathan Anderson, Brooks Davis, Ben Laurie, Peter G. Neumann, Robert Norton, and Michael Roe. "The CHERI capability model: Revisiting RISC in an age of risk." In *International Symposium on Computer Architecture (ISCA)*, 2014.

[55] Micheal Wu and Willy Zwaenepoel. "eNVy: A Non-Volatile, Main Memory Storage System." In *International Conference*

on Architectural Support for Programming Languages and Operating Systems (ASPLOS), 1994.

[56] Cong Xu, Dimin Niu, Naveen Muralimanohar, Rajeev Balasubramonian, Tao Zhang, Shimeng Yu, and Yuan Xie. "Overcoming the challenges of crossbar resistive memory architectures." In *Symposium on High Performance Computer Architecture (HPCA)*, 2015.

[57] "Yahoo! Cloud Serving Benchmark (YCSB)." `https://github.com/brianfrankcooper/YCSB/wiki`, Accessed 4 August 2015.

[58] Jun Yang, Qingsong Wei, Cheng Chen, Chundong Wang, Khai Leong Yong, and Bingsheng He. "NV-Tree: Reducing Consistency Cost for NVM-based Single Level Systems." In *Conference on File and Storage Technologies (FAST)*, 2015.

[59] Sunghwan Yoo, Charles Killian, Terence Kelly, Hyoun Kyu Cho, and Steven Plite. "Composable Reliability for Asynchronous Systems." In *USENIX Annual Technical Conference (ATC)*, 2012. `https://www.usenix.org/system/files/conference/atc12/atc12-final206-7-20-12.pdf`

[60] Anna Zaks and Rajeev Joshi. "Verifying Multi-threaded C Programs with SPIN." Model Checking Software. Springer Berlin Heidelberg, 2008.

[61] Jishen Zhao, Sheng Li, Doe Hyun Lee, Yuan Xie, and Norman P. Jouppi. "Kiln: Closing the Performance Gap Between Systems With and Without Persistence Support." In *International Symposium on Microarchitecture (MICRO)*, 2013.

Interference Management for Distributed Parallel Applications in Consolidated Clusters

Jaeung Han*, Seungheun Jeon*, Young-ri Choi†, and Jaehyuk Huh*

School of Computing, KAIST*, School of Electrical and Computer Engineering, UNIST†

{juhan,shjeon,jhuh}@calab.kaist.ac.kr, ychoi@unist.ac.kr

Abstract

Consolidating multiple applications on a system can improve the overall resource utilization of data center systems. However, such consolidation can adversely affect the performance of some applications due to interference caused by resource contention. Despite many prior studies on the interference effects in single-node systems, the interference behaviors of distributed parallel applications have not been investigated thoroughly. With distributed applications, a local interference in a node can affect the whole execution of an application spanning many nodes. This paper studies an interference modeling methodology for distributed applications to predict their performance under interference effects in consolidated clusters. This study first characterizes the effects of interference for various distributed applications over different interference settings, and analyzes how diverse interference intensities on multiple nodes affect the overall performance. Based on the characterization, this study proposes a static profiling-based model for interference propagation and heterogeneity behaviors. In addition, this paper presents use case studies of the modeling method, two interference-aware placement techniques for consolidated virtual clusters, which attempt to maximize the overall throughput or to guarantee the quality-of-service.

Categories and Subject Descriptors C.1.4 [*Parallel Architectures*]: Distributed architectures; C.4 [*Performance of Systems*]: Modeling techniques; D.4.1 [*Process Management*]: Scheduling

Keywords Resource contention, consolidated system, cloud computing, distributed parallel application, interference model, placement algorithm

ASPLOS '16, April 2–6, 2016, Atlanta, Georgia, USA.

http://dx.doi.org/10.1145/2872362.2872388

1. Introduction

An increasing number of cores in multi-core processors have been exacerbating contention on shared architectural resources such as shared last-level caches (LLC) and memory bandwidth. Such contention causes performance interference among applications in consolidated systems where different types of applications share a physical machine. With the growing popularity of cloud computing and system virtualization, such a consolidation of divergent applications on the same system has become common. To mitigate the performance interference problem, recent studies have been exploring schemes to reduce performance variation or to support a certain level of performance guarantee, regardless of the behaviors of co-running applications [7, 13, 15, 16, 21].

However, most of the prior work have isolated the effect of interference within a physical system. Their models assume that the interference occurring in a system affects only the applications running on the same system. For example, in the recent studies to control the interference [13, 21], the performance of a critical application running on a single physical system is protected from co-running batch applications. By estimating the resource contention and performance impact by the co-running applications, the studies have prevented batch applications from reducing the performance of the critical application lower than a threshold.

However, in clouds, another important class of applications are distributed parallel applications, which span multiple physical systems (nodes). In such distributed parallel applications, the effect of interference in a physical node affects the final latency of the applications differently, depending on how their parallelism is utilized. For example, in one type of distributed applications, the interference in one of the nodes can propagate to the entire participating systems, if load balancing is not dynamically adjusted. In this case, one slow node can delay the whole execution of the application, since the other nodes cannot proceed to the next stage until the delayed one is completed. A different type of distributed applications can be resilient to such an isolated interference, minimizing the propagating effect. Furthermore, when multiple nodes suffer from different intensities of interference, the final latency of distributed applications may depend on how the different levels of interference manifest themselves in the parallel execution.

For distributed applications in consolidated systems, this paper investigates how interference in a subset of nodes affects the final execution times of the applications, exploring techniques to model the interference effect. Unlike prior studies which have been isolating interference estimation within a physical system boundary [13, 21], to the best of our knowledge, this paper is one of the first studies to investigate the interference effect on distributed systems and to propose a method to estimate the effect. Such interference management is important to guarantee the quality of service of distributed applications, or to improve the overall throughput of consolidated clusters.

The proposed interference-aware performance model covers two different aspects of interference manifestation in distributed systems. First, the *interference propagation* model estimates how interference in a subset of nodes determines the final latency. Second, the *interference heterogeneity* model converts different interference intensities in a subset of nodes to a homogeneous intensity in the same or different numbers of nodes, to simplify the estimation model. Combining the two aspects, the proposed technique can estimate the final performance of a distributed application under different interferences in a subset of nodes with a small number of profiling runs.

Based on the proposed modeling technique, this paper investigates interference-aware placement algorithms for distributed applications as a case study. Using the performance model, two algorithms based on a simulated annealing technique find the best placement of multiple distributed applications on a cluster of physical nodes with two different goals. The first algorithm finds the best placement for maximizing the overall throughput. The second algorithm finds the best placement to support a certain level of performance guarantee for an application while improving the throughput of the other applications. Our experimental results show that the placement algorithms can effectively improve the overall performance with quality-of-service (QoS) support using the proposed interference model.

The main contributions of this paper are as follows. First, this paper investigates how the final performance of a distributed application is determined when a subset of the nodes suffer from various intensities of interference. Second, this paper proposes a method to build an interference-aware performance model for distributed applications. Although it requires profiling runs to characterize the interference propagation behaviors of applications, the method reduces the required profiling runs significantly, compared to a naive design. Third, using the proposed model, this paper explores interference-aware placement algorithms for distributed applications on a cluster of physical nodes. By reflecting the interference propagation behaviors, the placement algorithms improve the overall throughput or support QoS for distributed applications.

Limitations: As the first effort to model the interference in distributed applications, this paper assumes that each distributed application is known a priori, and the interference model of the application is constructed with a small number of separate profiling runs. The model from the separate profiling runs cannot be adjusted dynamically during application execution. In addition, it allows to predict the effects of pairwise interaction in each node. In each node, the model assumes that only up-to two distinct applications share the node resources. A similar approach has been used in the prior work [13]. Mars et al. first used a profile-based model construction for pairwise co-location as the initial mechanism of interference management [13]. Their subsequent work extended the profile-based approach to on-line estimation which supports co-locations of multiple applications [21]. Supporting a dynamic model for more than two distributed applications in each node will be our future work.

The rest of the paper is organized as follows. Section 2 describes a prior technique to quantify and model interference in a single node system. Section 3 investigates two aspects, propagation and heterogeneity of interference in distributed systems. Section 4 proposes a modeling method to minimize required profiling runs, and validates our model. Section 5 proposes two interference-aware placement algorithms, and shows the experimental results. Section 6 presents the validation results with a commercial cloud service. Section 7 presents the related work and Section 8 concludes the paper.

2. Background and Motivation

2.1 Prior Techniques for Quantifying Interference

This section presents a prior technique proposed by Mars et al. to model the effect of interference for pairwise applications running on single-node systems [13]. Among various sources of performance interferences, shared last-level caches (LLC) and memory bandwidth have been dominantly contended resources for compute-intensive applications [13, 16, 21]. If one application evicts cachelines for a co-running application or consumes scarce memory bandwidth excessively, the performance of the co-running application is adversely affected. In this paper, we use the effect of shared cache and memory bandwidth interference as the primary source of performance interference, although the technique can be generalized to different types of interferences such as network and disk I/O bandwidth, as discussed by the prior studies [13, 16, 21].

To model the interference behavior of distributed applications, we employ a technique proposed by a prior study, to model the interference behavior within a physical node boundary. The single-node technique called *Bubble-Up*, measures how the performance of each application is degraded by different intensities of interference. Based on the

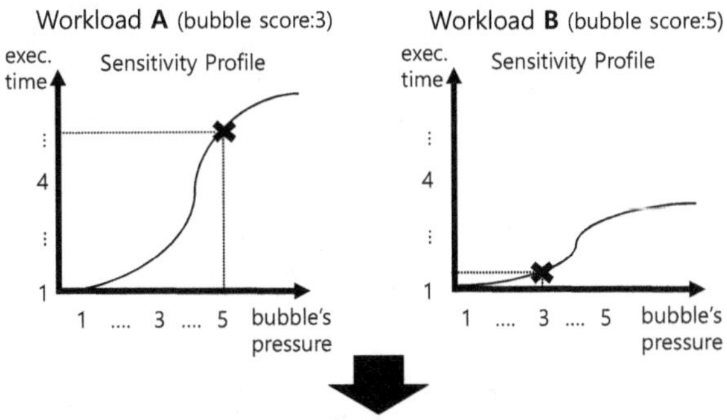

Workload	Estimated exec. time
A	5
B	1.3

Figure 1. Estimating execution times of consolidated workloads with interference sensitivity curves and bubble scores

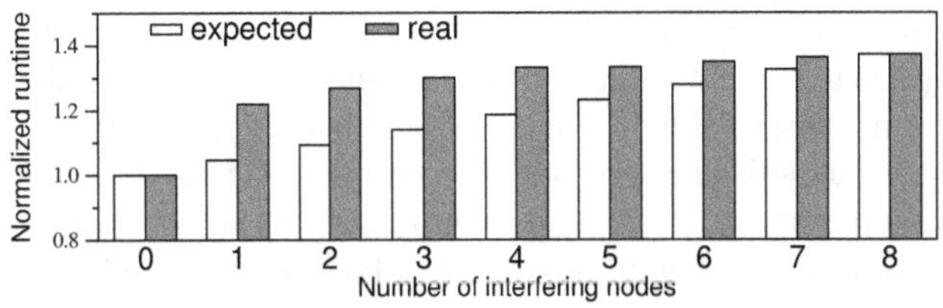

Figure 2. Execution time of 126.lammps over various numbers of nodes executing 462.libquantum

performance changes, the technique generates interference response curves (*sensitivity profile*) for each application with profiling runs [13]. In addition to the per-application interference sensitivity profile, it also measures how much interference the application generates to co-runners, and normalizes the generated interference to a score (*bubble score*). Using the per-application sensitivity profile and the bubble score generated by the application, the interference management system can estimate the performance of any two applications when the two applications are scheduled to the same system. The study divides applications to mission-critical tasks and batch ones, and the batch applications are scheduled only when they do not degrade the performance of mission-critical ones beyond a threshold [13, 21].

A key component of the interference modeling technique is to normalize the interference intensity to a bubble score. To generate interference intensity in a controlled manner, the study designs *bubble*, a small interference-generation program, which exercises the memory subsystem by creating different levels of cache misses and external memory accesses. Using the bubble program, the performance of each application is measured with different pre-defined levels of interference. With profiling runs for each application under different interference levels, the scheme measures how much performance degradation the application exhibits under a given level of interference. In Figure 1, the interference sensitivity profile for each workload models the execution time increase pattern by the pressure increase using the co-running *bubble*.

The same bubble program is also used to measure how much interference an application generates. Based on the performance degradation of the bubble program itself, when it is co-run with a target application, the interference intensity the application causes is converted to a bubble score. In essence, the bubble-based approach provides an interference normalization method, so that the interference effect of every pair of co-running applications does not need to be profiled a priori. For each application, the per-application sensitivity profile and bubble score need to be measured, without knowing what another application will be co-run. When two applications are deployed to a system, their possible performance interference can be estimated by examining the sensitivity profiles and bubble scores of the two applications. Figure 1 shows the procedure to estimate the performance of two co-running applications by combining the sensitivity curves and bubble scores.

The subsequent study by Yang et al. extended the bubble-based interference model to on-line measurement which also supports co-locations of multiple applications in a single node [21]. The interference response and generation models of applications are constructed on the fly by executing profiling runs with bubble occasionally. They optimized the occurrence of profiling runs, by tracking changes of the system behavior.

A different prior approach, *DeepDive* uses an interference model with resource usage statistics for interference management [16]. The interference model estimates possible interference and performance degradation, from the resource usage statistics of co-running applications. When a task is submitted, it runs on an isolated virtual machine (VM) without interference to characterize the behavior of the application for a short period of time, collecting key resource usage statistics such as cache misses or I/O accesses. Once the characterization of the application is completed with the short dynamic profiling run, the task is migrated to an appropriate node, by estimating the possible interference by the new application and the existing applications based on the resource usage statistics. Instead of normalizing interference levels to bubble scores, the approach directly models interference with memory and I/O usage statistics. It also exploits the migration capability of virtualization to avoid separate profiling runs, although the effectiveness of the approach relies on the stability of application behaviors since only a short initial run must be able to represent the whole execution.

2.2 Motivation

In this paper, we use the same approach as the bubble-based interference measurement for each individual node participating the execution of distributed applications. Using an interference generation program similar to *bubble*, we generate several different intensities of interference in each node.

The main contribution of this work is how each individual interference in distributed nodes should be combined to determine the final performance of distributed applications.

As a motivating example, Figure 2 presents how the final runtime of a parallel application is determined by interference in a subset or all of the nodes. For the experiments, 32 dual-core virtual machines are deployed to run the `lammps` application in an 8-node cluster. The detailed configuration is presented in Section 3.1. Along with the parallel application, instances of `libquantum` run in a subset of nodes, as an interfering co-runner. The figure shows the normalized execution times when interference occurs by the co-running `libquantum` applications in 0-8 physical nodes.

To demonstrate the importance of interference modeling of parallel applications, the figure presents an expected performance with a *naive* proportional interference model. With the naive proportional model, the interference in a node affects the final execution time of the application proportionally. For example, if a task in a single node within an n-node cluster is slowed down due to interference, it affects the overall performance by a factor of $1/n$. The first set of bars shows the expected execution times of the application (`lammps`) with the naive model, and the second set of bars shows the real execution times of the same application. The x-axis represents the number of nodes where instances of `libquantum` are running, and thus `lammps` is experiencing interference.

As shown in the figure, the expected execution time with the naive proportional model increases linearly with the number of interfering nodes. However, the real runs exhibit completely different curves. Even when a single node suffers from interference, the execution time is significantly increased. Further increases of interfering nodes delay the execution with much slower rates. Such behavior of `lammps` is due to its parallelism and synchronization pattern. A slowdown in a single node will block the progress of the other nodes.

As shown by the motivation example, the performance of distributed applications cannot be simply estimated by the proportional aggregation of the performance of participating nodes. To address the problem, this paper proposes a modeling method for distributed applications under interference.

3. Modeling Interference

This section presents the interference sensitivity behaviors of distributed applications. First, we analyze the performance degradation when the number of nodes suffering from interference increases. Such *interference propagation* determines the performance of distributed applications, with a given number of nodes under the same interference intensity. Second, we investigate how heterogeneous intensities of interference in multiple nodes are reflected in the final performance of the applications.

Type	Name	Size	Abbrev.
SPEC MPI2007	104.milc	mref	M.milc
	107.leslie3d	mref	M.lesl
	113.GemsFDTD	mref	M.Gems
	126.lammps	mref	M.lmps
	132.zeusmp2	mref	M.zeus
	137.lu	mref	M.lu
NPB	cg	class D	N.cg
	mg	class D	N.mg
HADOOP	Kmeans	75 MB	H.KM
SPARK	PageRank	1M vertices with 12M edges	S.PR
	Collaborative Filtering	30 users on 100 movies	S.CF
	WordCount	4.2GB	S.WC
SPEC CPU2006	403.gcc	ref	C.gcc
	429.mcf	ref	C.mcf
	436.cactusADM	ref	C.cact
	450.soplex	ref	C.sopl
	462.libquantum	ref	C.libq
	483.xalancbmk	ref	C.xbmk

Table 1. Application configuration and data set

3.1 Methodology

For our study, we use a cluster composed of eight physical host nodes connected via a 10 Gigabit Ethernet switch. Each of the hosts is configured with two Intel Xeon Octa-core E5-2650 processors and 64 GB memory. The Xen hypervisor with version 4.3.2 is used, and the guest operating system for virtual machines (VMs) is a para-virtualized Linux of kernel version 3.2.59. For each VM, it is configured to have two virtual CPUs (vCPUs) with 5 GB memory. Since a host has 16 physical cores in total, the total 8 VMs can be placed on each of the hosts. Since we use compute-intensive workloads, the experimental setup does not over-commit the total vCPUs more than the available physical cores.

Table 1 shows application workloads and their input sizes used in our experiments. Four types of parallel workloads, SPECMPI2007, NPB, Hadoop, and Spark are used to investigate the interference model for distributed applications. Applications in SPECCPU2006, which are not parallel workloads, are used as possible batch-oriented co-running workloads in Section 5. For the experiments, each distributed application uses 32 dual-core VMs (i.e. 64 vCPUs in total) running on 8 physical nodes with 16 cores. For each workload, we restricted that four VMs which belong to the same application, are always executed together on a host node in experiments. Therefore, only up-to two applications can be co-located in a node, reducing the complexity of our analysis.

3.2 Interference Propagation

The first aspect of interference modeling for distributed applications is how the effect of interference occurring in a subset of nodes propagates to the execution of the whole ap-

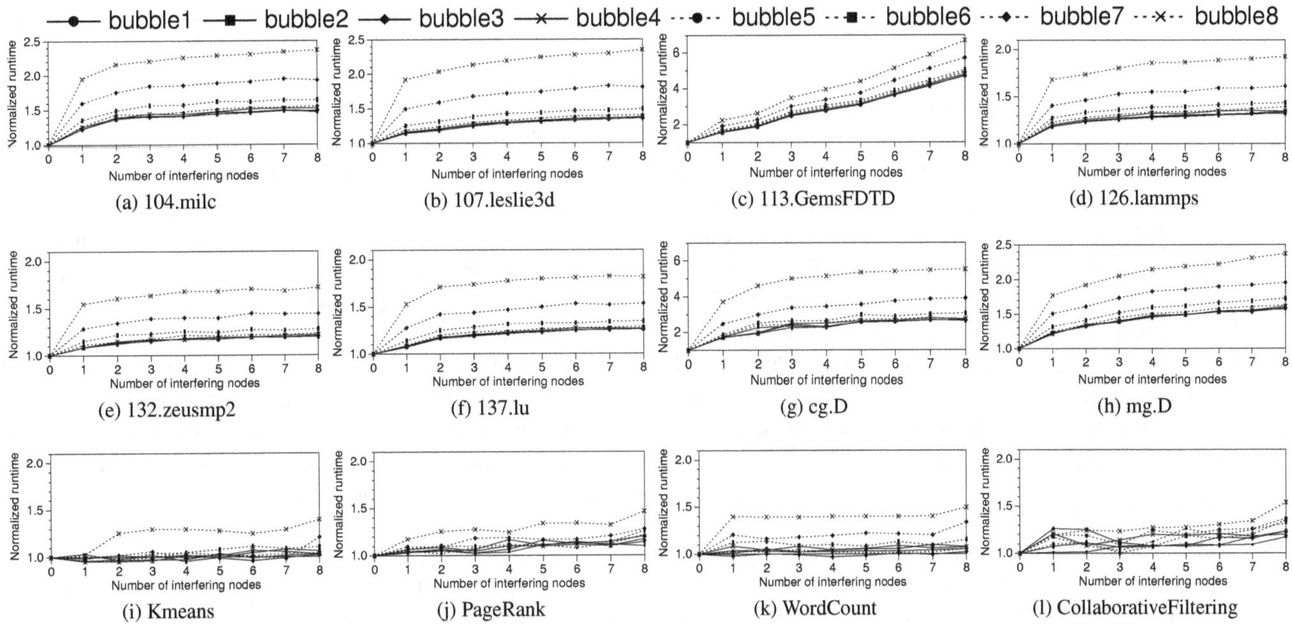

Figure 3. Execution time with varying bubble pressures with from 1 to 8 interfering nodes (normalized to no-interference)

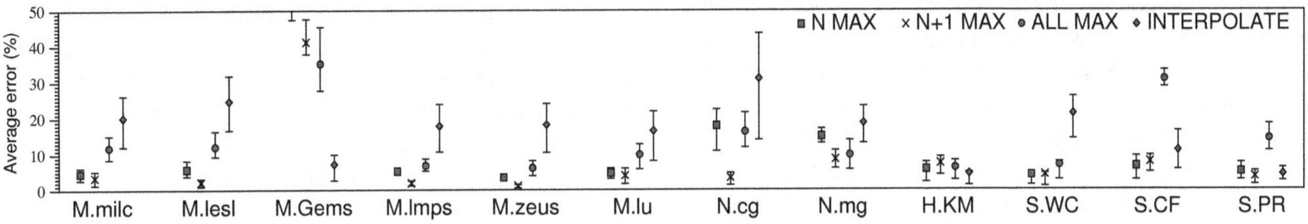

Figure 4. Average error by converting heterogeneous interference to homogeneous one with four policies on 8 hosts

plication spanning multiple nodes. In this section, we first present how the performances of our benchmark applications change when the number of physical nodes with interference (*interfering nodes*) increases. To simplify the analysis, all the interfering nodes suffer from the same interference intensity with the same bubble pressure. Figure 3 presents the normalized execution times when the number of interfering nodes increases from 1 to 8 physical nodes. The x-axis is the number of interfering nodes. Each graph shows 8 curves with different bubble pressures from 1 to 8 generated by a co-running bubble.

As shown in the figure, applications exhibit different interference propagation behaviors. In general, there are roughly three types of applications. In the first type, `high propagation`, the interference in one or two nodes affects the execution times significantly. The majority of applications, including `M.milc`, `M.lesl`, and `M.lmps`, exhibit such behaviors. The high propagation property becomes stronger with higher bubble pressures. In the second type, `proportional propagation`, such as `M.Gems`, the execution times increase proportionally to the number of interfering nodes. The behavior of this type of applications is similar to the collection of single-node applications. As more individual nodes are slowed down, the performance is proportionally degraded. Note that unlike the other MPI-based applications we used, `M.Gems` does not use any allreduce/allgather routines, and has much smaller numbers of barriers, having the low collective operations and showing linear increase patterns. The final type, `low propagation`, such as `H.KM` and `S.PR`, is relatively resilient to the interference, since it has low requirements for LLC capacity and memory bandwidth. Even if a co-running application monopolizes the shared resources, this type of applications is not affected significantly.

Various distributed workloads we examined exhibit different interference propagation behaviors. Furthermore, even in the same propagation type of applications, the performance curves quite differ, since the resilience to local interference varies by application behaviors. Even though application experts may know the general behavior of each application, and even its memory resource demand and usage pattern, it is extremely difficult to estimate the actual performance impact from the interference. Based on the observation, we conclude that per-application interference propagation models are necessary to estimate the performance of each application, when some nodes have performance interference.

However, one critical problem of profiling and modeling the propagation behaviors of distributed applications is the number of profile runs to build the model. For single-node applications used by Mars et al. [13], it is necessary only to run each application with different levels of bubble pressure. For distributed applications running on multiple physical nodes, profiling runs must examine all possible numbers of interfering nodes, increasing the time complexity of the profiling run significantly. A naive method is to run with *N* different interference setups for an *N*-node cluster, and for each setup, different levels of bubble pressure must be examined. In Section 4, we will propose a scheme to reduce the required profiling runs drastically.

3.3 Interference Heterogeneity

The second difficulty of modeling interference for distributed applications is the heterogeneity of interference intensity in multiple interfering nodes. In the previous section, it is assumed that every interfering node suffers from the same level of interference. However, in real consolidated systems, each node may have a different interference level. If profiling runs must examine all possible intensities in different numbers of interfering nodes, the profiling space will become intractable. To resolve the explosion of the profiling space, we propose a method to convert the heterogeneous intensity in interfering nodes, to a homogeneous one. With this mapping, the model only needs to have the performance sensitivity curves with homogeneous intensity, as shown in Figure 3.

The rationale behind the feasibility of conversion process is that in some applications, the worst interference dominates the execution, while the average interference determines the overall interference level in other applications. In this work, we investigate and formulate four different mapping policies. First, `N max` policy considers only the number of interfering nodes under the worst interference intensity. For example, suppose there are four interfering nodes. If two of them suffer from the same high pressure, and the rest of two nodes are under lower pressures, the overall execution time of an application is similar to that of the same application with only two interfering nodes with the same high pressure. The effect of two interfering nodes with lower pressures is ignored. Second, `N+1 max` policy slightly augments `N max` policy. Instead of considering only the top intensity nodes, in this policy, the rest of interfering nodes are merged to an extra interfering node with the same top pressure, instead of ignoring them. For the same example of four interfering nodes, the heterogeneous intensity is mapped to a homogeneous intensity with 3 nodes with the same top pressure. The third policy, `all max`, assumes that the effect of the worst pressure even in a single node propagates directly to all the nodes. Therefore, it is mapped to a homogeneous intensity in which the worst pressure occurs in every node. The final policy, `interpolate`, uses an average intensity from all nodes as a representative interference in all the nodes. Note that in this work, we present a converting methodology to handle the heterogeneous intensity, and our methodology will be able to accommodate the addition of new policies, if any, for applications with entirely different behaviors.

Using the four different policies, we evaluate the behaviors of our workloads. However, examining all possible combinations of intensity levels from 1 to 8 with from 0 to 8 interfering nodes requires a large number of experimental runs which were impossible to test with our limited computing resources. With 8 physical systems, the total number of heterogeneous settings is 12,870. To find the best mapping policy, we use a sample-based approach. We randomly selected 60 heterogeneous interference configurations, and examined which of the four policies matches each application behavior.

Figure 4 presents the detailed error rates with the four different policies for each application. For each policy, an error bar with the minimum and maximum error rates is also presented. As shown in the figure, although not a single policy is the best for all applications, one or two policies for each application have very small error rates. Table 2 shows the best policy for each application with the average error, and standard deviation. As shown in the table, for distributed applications, at least, one of the policies can convert heterogeneous intensity to homogeneous intensity effectively with less than 9% average error and low standard deviation.

To find the best mapping policy, the profiling method must examine a statistically meaningful number of samples. For 12,870 total configurations, the 60 samples have a margin of error of about +/−1.7 on 99% confidence level, assuming the population distribution is normal and the standard deviation of the population follows the sample standard deviation. Due to the relatively low standard deviation as shown in Table 2, the confidence interval is short even on 99% confidence level. With a certain number of sample runs, the best mapping policy of each application can be found. Once the best policy is determined, only homogeneous intensity runs are necessary to build a model for the application.

3.4 Interference Model

To estimate the performance of distributed applications under diverse interferences in a subset of nodes, three modeling parameters must be obtained by profiling runs. First, the profiling process must measure the *bubble score* of each application, which is the interference intensity generated by the application. For MPI-based applications, the master participates in the computation like slaves. Thus, they generate a similar intensity of interference in all participating nodes, since each process exhibits a similar memory system behavior. However, for Hadoop and Spark applications, the master

Workload	Best policy	Avg. error(%)	Std. dev.
M.milc	N+1 MAX	3.50	2.18
M.lesl	N+1 MAX	2.20	1.60
M.Gems	INTERPOLATE	7.34	5.93
M.lmps	N+1 MAX	1.91	0.93
M.zeus	N+1 MAX	1.11	0.82
M.lu	N+1 MAX	4.01	2.35
N.cg	N+1 MAX	3.37	2.26
N.mg	N+1 MAX	8.62	3.16
H.KM	INTERPOLATE	4.55	1.41
S.WC	N MAX	4.15	7.95
S.CF	N MAX	6.60	4.96
S.PR	N+1 MAX	3.69	2.60

Table 2. The best heterogeneity mapping policy

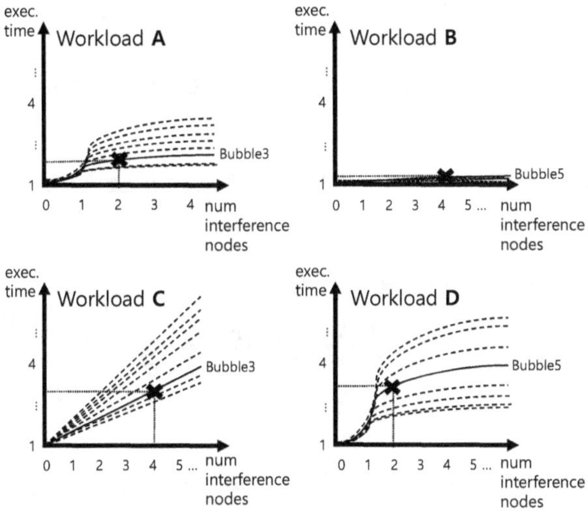

Workload A,B,C,D's placement to 8 nodes

NODE 1	NODE 2	NODE 3	NODE 4	NODE 5	NODE 6	NODE 7	NODE 8
A	B	A	A	B	A	B	C
B	C	C	D	C	D	D	D

Workload	Bubble point	Bubble list	Converted bubble list
A (N+1 max)	5	[3, 2, 1, 1]	[3, 3, 0, 0]
B (ALL max)	3	[5, 2, 2, 1]	[5, 5, 5, 5]
C (INTERPOLATE)	2	[3, 5, 3, 1]	[3, 3, 3, 3]
D (N max)	1	[5, 5, 3, 2]	[5, 5, 0, 0]

Figure 5. Sensitivity profiles, bubble scores, and heterogeneity mapping policies

does not process any task, generating much lower interference. Thus, only among slaves, the interference levels are similar. In this work, we use the average interference intensity generated in all participating nodes as the bubble score of an application. However, further optimization is possible to consider the difference between the master and slaves for Hadoop and Spark applications. Second, to address the interference heterogeneity, the profiling process must find the per-application best mapping policy between heterogeneous and homogeneous interferences. Third, for each bubble pressure, the profiling runs must measure the interference sensitivity curves for increasing numbers of interfering nodes to represent interference propagation property as in Figure 3.

Algorithm 1 Binary-brute algorithm

var T: double[n][$m+1$]; //initially $T[i][j] = null$
    t_0: double;
t_0 := measure(0, 0); //exec. time with no interference
for each i in $0..n-1$ **do**
    $T[i][0] := 1$; //norm. time with no interference
    $T[i][m]$:= measure($i+1, m$)/t_0; //with max nodes at $i+1$
    T := profile_binary_row(T, i, 0, m, t_0);
    T := interpolate_row(T, i);
end for

Figure 5 describes sensitivity curves and heterogeneity mapping policies for four workloads. The top table in the figure shows an example placement where workloads A, B, C, and D are placed in 8 nodes, with two different workloads sharing each node. In the bottom table, the workload column shows the best mapping policy for each workload, and the second column is the bubble scores of workloads. The third pressure list column is the heterogeneous interference actually occurring by the example placement, and the converted pressure list shows the homogeneous intensity converted by the best mapping policy of each application. With the information on the model, the performance of workloads A, B, C, and D can be estimated for the example placement. For example, workload A receives pressures of 3,2,1,1 with the placement. The heterogeneous interference can be converted to 3,3,0,0, since the best mapping policy is `N+1 max` for the workload. Then, using the curves for the pressure value of 3 with two interfering nodes, the performance of A under the interference is estimated.

4. Profiling Method and Model Validation

4.1 Interference Propagation Profiling

To profile the execution times of a distributed application under various interference settings efficiently, we devise two algorithms, *binary-brute* and *binary-optimized*. These algorithms selectively profile the execution times of a distributed application to construct the sensitivity curves with different bubble pressures and with different numbers of homogeneous interfering nodes as in Figure 3.

Each of the algorithms computes a matrix of execution times normalized to those under no interference for a distributed application. In an $n \times (m+1)$ matrix, called T, where n is the total number of bubble pressures, and m is the total number of hosts, $T[i][j]$ is a normalized execution time when the number of interfering nodes with $i+1$ bubble pressure is j.

Algorithm *binary-brute* measures the execution of a target application for each different bubble level, which corresponds to each curve in Figure 3. For each curve, instead of examining all possible numbers of interfering nodes, it measures the execution times with a few selected numbers

Algorithm 2 Binary-optimized algorithm

```
var T: double[n][m + 1]; //initially T[i][j] = null
    t0: double;
t0 := measure(0, 0); //exec. time with no interference
T[0][m] := measure(1, m)/t0; //with max nodes at min bub.
T[n − 1][m] := measure(n, m)/t0; //with max nodes at max bub.
for each i in 0..n − 1 do
    T[i][0] := 1; //norm. time with no interference
end for
T := profile_binary_row(T, n − 1, 0, m, t0);
T := interpolate_row(T, n − 1);
T := profile_binary_col(T, m, 0, n − 1, t0);
T := interpolate_col(T, m);
T := interpolate_all(T);
```

of interfering nodes (using function *measure*). The selection process uses a binary-search algorithm to eliminate unnecessary runs, and thus, if the performance difference with two different numbers of interfering nodes is small enough, then the profiling process does not need to run for the number of interfering nodes between the two setups (in function *profile_binary_row*). Once this profiling process is done, we predict each of unmeasured execution times by interpolating existing execution time values (in function *interpolate_row*).

Algorithm *binary-optimized* further reduces the profiling runs by exploiting the shape of curves is similar, regardless of bubble pressures. It constructs one curve with the highest bubble pressure with the same binary search as *binary-brute*. In addition to the top curve, it similarly measures or predicts the execution time with the maximum number of interfering nodes at different bubble pressures (in functions *profile_binary_col* and *interpolate_col*). By constructing the top curve and measuring the distance between curves among different pressure levels, the other curves with lower bubble pressures can be inferred, assuming their shapes do not change significantly. We can predict an unmeasured $T[i][j]$ by doing a sum by proportion based on the existing execution times (in function *interpolate_all*) as $T[i][j] := 1 + \frac{(T[i][m]-1)*(T[n-1][j]-1)}{T[n-1][m]-1}$.

4.2 Cost Reduction and Accuracy

We compare the performance of these two algorithms with random based algorithms, in terms of profiling cost and accuracy. The random-30% and random-50% algorithms randomly select 30% and 50% of all interference settings, respectively, and predict the execution times of other settings by interpolating the existing execution times. Note that in these algorithms, settings with no interference and with interference in all hosts for each bubble pressure are always selected and measured to construct sensitivity curves effectively.

Table 3 shows the accuracy of each of the four algorithms. The average profiling cost of an algorithm is computed as the average percentage of measured interference settings over all settings. The average error is computed as the average percentage of the difference between an estimated normalized execution time and a measured one for all settings. Figure 6 and Figure 7 present the average error and cost for each of the applications, respectively. In the results, for the binary-brute algorithm, it has the lowest error, but requires the highest cost among all the algorithms. For the binary-optimized algorithm, it shows a moderate error and requires the lowest cost. Considering both of profiling cost and accuracy, the binary-optimized algorithm can be used effectively to construct the sensitivity curves of an application, compared to the binary-brute and random based algorithms.

Prediction Algorithm	Average cost(%)	Average error(%)
binary-optimized	18.45	3.16
binary-brute	59.44	0.56
random-50%	49.23	5.31
random-30%	29.23	13.55

Table 3. Profiling cost and accuracy

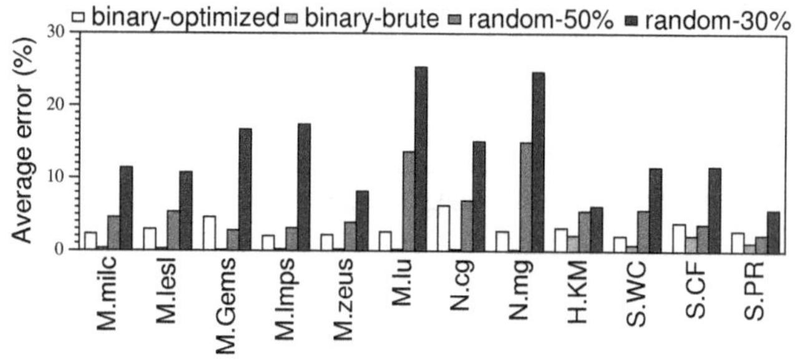

Figure 6. Prediction errors with four profiling techniques

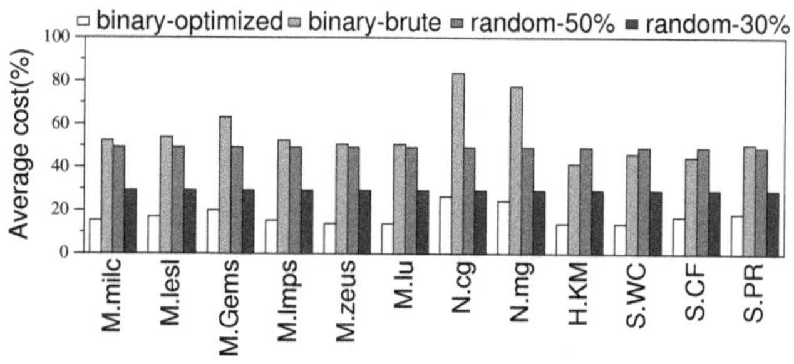

Figure 7. Profiling cost with four profiling techniques

Workload	Bubble	Workload	Bubble	Workload	Bubble
M.milc	4.3	M.lesl	3.9	M.Gems	2.4
M.lmps	1.0	M.zeus	1.4	M.lu	4.6
N.cg	3.9	N.mg	5.0	H.KM	0.2
S.WC	0.3	S.CF	0.5	S.PR	0.7
C.gcc	4.8	C.mcf	5.4	C.cact	3.8
C.sopl	4.9	C.libq	6.6	C.xbmk	4.3

Table 4. Bubble scores for the benchmark applications

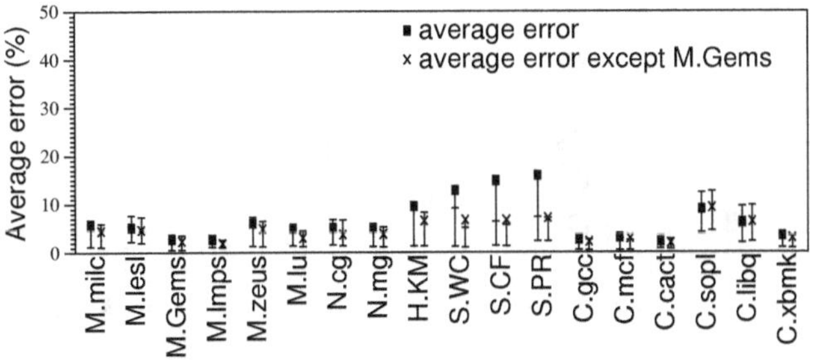

Figure 8. Average validation errors for applications

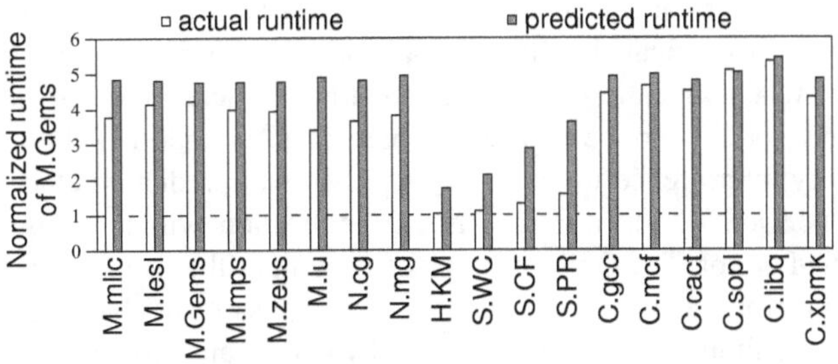

Figure 9. Validation errors with M.Gems

4.3 Model validation

We experimentally validate the interference-aware performance model by running two applications together in a cluster of multiple systems. We use the same system configuration as described in Section 3.1. For each application, the interference propagation model is constructed as in Figure 3, and the best interference heterogeneity mapping policy is also determined as in Table 2. Table 4 shows the measured bubble score for all applications, ranging from 0.2 to 6.6. They generate widely different intensities of interference.

Figure 8 presents the average error including 25% - 75% error bars for each application, when the application is co-running with all the applications (including itself). Most of workloads have less than 10% errors with the majority of them under 5%. The Spark applications have high error rates over 10%, but their average error rates are reduced significantly without the problematic co-runner, `M.Gems`. Figure 9 presents the predicted and actual runtimes of all applications running with `M.Gems`. `M.Gems` is one of the most unpredictable applications among our workloads, since its behavior is relatively unstable, depending on the co-running applications. It uniquely uses latency-sensitive blocked I/Os instead of common asynchronous I/Os. In Xen, when there are some idle CPU resources to dedicatedly execute Dom0 which handles network I/Os, the blocked I/O performance can be boosted. Since `M.Gems` is very sensitive to the availability of CPU for Dom0, our prediction accuracy is low for the Spark and Hadoop applications that have fluctuating CPU loads.

4.4 Limitations

Static Profiling: The first limitation of this study is its model construction method based on static profiling. This study assumes a priori knowledge of each application, and through separate profiling runs, the propagation and heterogeneity behaviors are measured before the application is used in production environments. The profiling is done only once for each application until the application binary or physical system configuration changes, and this study proposed to reduce the number of profiling runs with a binary search method and statistical sampling. Due to the static nature of model construction, the model may not reflect the dynamic changes of behavior accurately. For example, if an application has clear phase changes during its execution, and each phase has a different interference model behavior, the current single static model provides only an average behavior across different phases.

Pairwise Interaction: The second limitation of this study is its pairwise interaction within a node. In each node, only up-to two different applications can be co-located to accurately model their interaction in the current modeling method. A possible solution for extending the model is to design a method to combine bubble pressures from multiple applications to a single score. Although the bubble design varies by resource types, in our bubble design for LLC and memory bandwidth, the dominant factor is LLC miss. In our scoring scheme, each score increase by 1 corresponds to the doubling of LLC misses. For example, when the same two bubble scores, *S*, are combined, the result score will be the sum of *S+1* and extra pressure by collision of the two combined applications. The extra pressure may be dependent on the original score, and this extra pressure estimation requires an additional modeling and validation effort.

Average Bubble Scoring: The proposed technique assumes that all the processes from an application across different nodes generate similar interference intensities, and uses a single average bubble score for the application. In the benchmark applications, the majority of MPI and Hadoop applications use the same program running on many nodes, and thus each process of the same application exhibits very similar LLC miss behaviors. Furthermore, as the balanced data distribution across processes attempts to equalize the amount of data handled by each process, the similarity among processes is very strong in our benchmark applications. One exception was the master node for certain applications, in which the master node performs significantly different tasks from the other worker nodes. A future extension of this study will be to support heterogeneous tasks within an application with potentially different bubble scores.

5. Case Studies

5.1 Placement Algorithm

When the interference propagation model and interference heterogeneity handling policy are profiled for each appli-

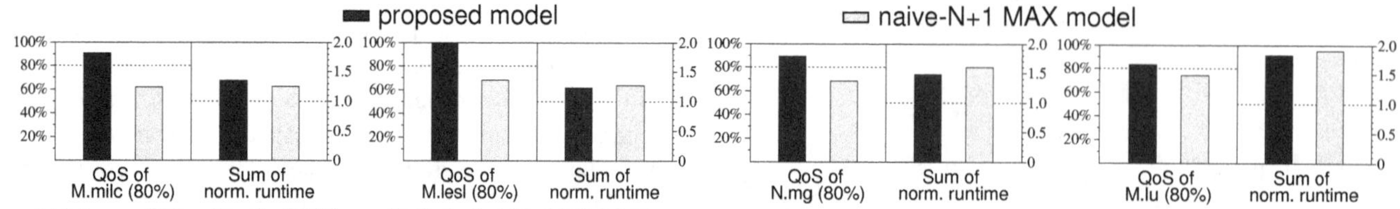

(a) M.zeus+C.libq+*M.mlic*+S.WC (b) C.xbmk+*M.lesl*+H.KM+N.mg (c) C.sopl+*N.mg*+S.CF+N.cg (d) *M.lu*+C.cact+M.lmps+M.Gems

Figure 10. QoS guarantee and runtimes normalized to solo runs

cation, a placement algorithm finds the best placement of applications to satisfy given constraints in a set of cluster nodes. Since the exhaustive search of all possible mappings is impossible, we develop an interference-aware VM placement algorithm based on simulated annealing [9]. A similar placement algorithm based on stochastic hill climbing has been studied for web-service workloads [12]. The placement algorithm attempts to find the global optimal point by locating a good approximation, although it is not guaranteed to find the optimal solution.

The algorithm starts by hypothetically mapping VMs randomly over hosts. To find the best VM placement under interference, it randomly selects two VMs running different workloads and swaps the locations of two VMs, if the new VM placement performs better while it satisfies given QoS constraints. The above process is repeated until the number of iterations reaches a predefined threshold. For each step with a hypothetical placement, the placement algorithm estimates the normalized execution time of each application using the proposed interference model. Note that this algorithm provides a reasonably good way to prove the effectiveness of our model as shown in the results below. However, other techniques rather than simulated annealing can be used, and they can also benefit from the interference model.

In this section, the experiments used the same system configuration described in Section 3.1. However, in these runs, each distributed application is running with 16 VMs, and four applications with total 64 VMs fully share the 8-node cluster with 16 cores per node. Since the current model supports only pairwise co-locations of different applications, our placement algorithms consider a set of 4 VMs running the same application in a host as a unit, instead of an individual VM (even though the algorithms in Sections 5.2 and 5.3 are described based on the unit of an individual VM). In this way, only one or two application workloads will be placed in a host. Since SPECCPU2006 applications are single-threaded applications, if a SPECCPU2006 application is chosen, 32 instances of the same application are running on 16 VMs, with 2 instances per VM, as a VM has two cores.

5.2 QoS-Aware Placement

An important use scenario is to support QoS guarantee for mission-critical distributed applications. When a mission-critical application is running, other less critical applications may or may not be allowed to share physical nodes. Without any interference model, it is impossible to predict whether the QoS of the mission-critical application will be satisfied or not. The QoS-aware placement algorithm is based on the aforementioned interference-aware placement algorithm with simulated annealing. After hypothetically distributing VMs for given workloads randomly over hosts in the system, the algorithm randomly selects two VMs running different workloads, and swaps the locations of the two VMs, if the new placement satisfies the delay constraint for the applications with the QoS requirement. In case that the current placement state already meets the delay constraint, it swaps randomly selected VMs only if the new VM placement still meets the constraint, and has a shorter total execution time. The above process is repeated for predefined iterations. The placement algorithm attempts to reduce the overall execution time while meeting the QoS constraint first.

Figure 10 presents the QoS support status and the sum of normalized runtimes for four application mixes. In the figure, one of the four applications for a mix (in italic) is a target application for QoS. The algorithm finds a placement to support the QoS for the application, and to maximize the overall performance. For the experiment, the QoS constraint is to guarantee 80% of the execution time compared to a solo run where the target application is running without any interference. For comparison, the result also shows a naive model for distributed applications. In the naive model, heterogeneous interference is converted to a homogeneous one with the `N+1 max` policy, which is the static best one, if we select a single policy for all the applications. Once the heterogeneity is eliminated, the overall performance is estimated proportionally by the number of interfering nodes (as the expected performance is estimated in Figure 2).

As shown in the figure, using the proposed model supports the QoS guarantee effectively within 80% of the solo run performance. However, using the naive model can violate the QoS as shown in the gray bar. The right side of the figures shows the sum of normalized runtimes. The execution time of each application is normalized to that in the

Index	Workload combination			
High perf. difference between best and worst (20%∼)				
HW1	N.mg	N.cg	H.KM	M.lmps
HW2	M.zeus	C.libq	H.KM	M.Gems
HW3	C.libq	N.cg	H.KM	S.PR
HM1	M.zeus	S.WC	M.Gems	S.PR
HM2	H.KM	M.Gems	M.lu	C.xbmk
HM3	S.CF	H.KM	M.Gems	M.Gems
Medium perf. difference between best and worst (5∼20%)				
MW	N.mg	H.KM	H.KM	M.lesl
MM	C.cact	C.libq	M.Gems	M.lmps
MB	N.cg	M.milc	C.libq	C.xbmk
Low perf. difference between best and worst (∼5%)				
L	M.lesl	M.zeus	M.zeus	N.mg

Table 5. Selected workload combinations

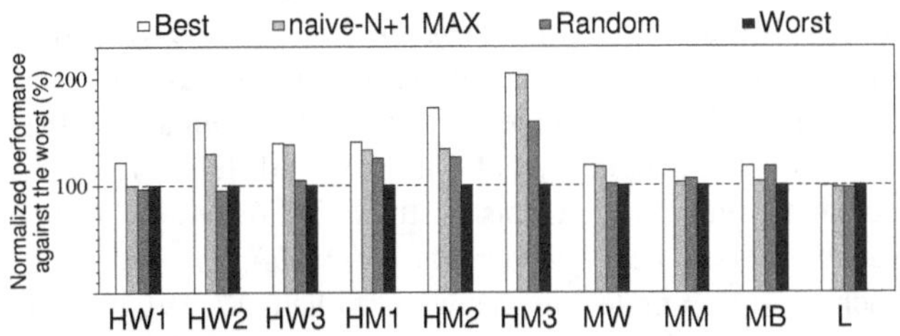

Figure 11. Normalized performance improvement

solo run, and the sum is weighted by the number of VMs used by each application. For example, 16 VMs of a SPEC-CPU2006 application have the same weight as the other distributed applications using the same number of VMs. For the mix (a), the proposed model increases the overall runtime slightly compared to the naive model to support QoS. For the rest of mixes, the overall runtimes are similar to or slightly shorter than those with the naive model.

5.3 Placement for Performance

Using the same placement algorithm as the QoS-aware placement, the second policy finds the placement for the best overall performance without any QoS constraints. For each application in a placement, its performance is defined as the speedup over the execution time of the same application in the worst placement. The overall combined performance from all the applications in a placement is the weighted average of the speedups from the applications, and the weight of each application is proportional to the number of VMs used by the application.

We chose 10 mixes with different behaviors as given in Table 5, to examine the effectiveness of our placement algorithm in real machines with a spectrum of mix characteristics. We ran each mix using three goals, *Best* maximizes the overall performance, *Worst* finds the worst performing placement for comparison, and *Random* shows the average results of five random placements. In addition, we also use the naive model explained in the previous section. In Table 5, the mixes are divided into high, medium, and low by the performance difference between the best and worst placements. The low difference mixes do not suffer from interference since generated interferences by applications are small or co-running applications are not very sensitive to interference. However, we still examine those mixes to show that the placement algorithm does not negatively affect such low difference cases either.

Figure 11 presents the average speedup of four applications for each mix. For the mixes with high difference, the placement algorithm quite effectively finds a good placement with a large performance improvement of up-to 105% for `HM3`. The average improvements with high and medium differences against the worst placement are 56.59% and 16.98%, respectively. For the naive model, the average improvements with high and medium differences are 39.86% and 7.94%, respectively. However, it shows unpredictable performance, which is often better or worse than the random placement. For all mixes, the best placement with our model exhibits the best performance. The result indicates that the proposed placement algorithm using the interference model effectively finds a good placement, and avoids the worst placement.

6. Results on Amazon EC2

To validate our modeling method for larger systems, we ran experiments with the Amazon EC2 service. For our experiments, we use 32 VM instances with *c4.2xlarge* type, which is configured with 8 vCPUs, 15 GiB memory, and high network performance. The interference model proposed in this paper requires to measure interference occurring in physical systems. However, in the public Amazon EC2 cloud, it is impossible to control the placement of VMs or to measure current interference from their co-running VMs. Thus, we co-locate applications within a VM provided by EC2. The experiments use four vCPUs to execute an application workload, while we reserve the remaining four vCPUs to execute bubble programs (or another application workload). The total number of vCPUs for a distributed application is 128.

There are two critical limitations of this EC2-based setup for our study. First, there is unmeasured interference from VMs owned by other users running on the same physical system. Second, the EC2 service may relocate VMs to different physical systems while they are not active. Therefore, it is very difficult to experiment on consistent physical systems with interference fully measured. To mitigate these uncontrollable effects, we selected four workloads which have relatively short execution times, to finish all the experiments before the system status changes. For application workloads, we use `M.milc`, `M.Gems`, `M.zeus` and `M.lu`.

For each of the four applications, the interference model is constructed with the proposed modeling method. Figure 12 shows the normalized execution times when the number of homogeneous interfering VMs (which execute bubble

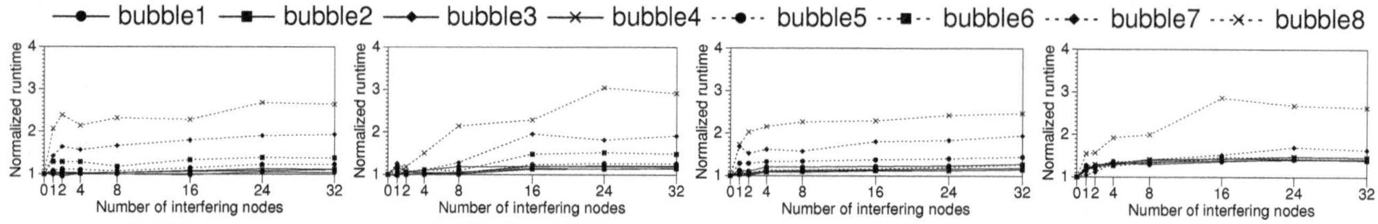

(a) 104.milc (b) 113.GemsFDTD (c) 132.zeusmp2 (d) 137.lu

Figure 12. Execution time with varying bubble pressures and with from 1 to 32 interfering nodes on Amazon EC2

Workload	Best policy	Avg. error(%)	Std. dev.
M.milc	N+1 MAX	12.01	7.27
M.Gems	N+1 MAX	11.49	6.28
M.zeus	ALL MAX	6.40	4.52
M.lu	N MAX	5.28	4.36

Table 6. The best heterogeneity mapping policy on EC2

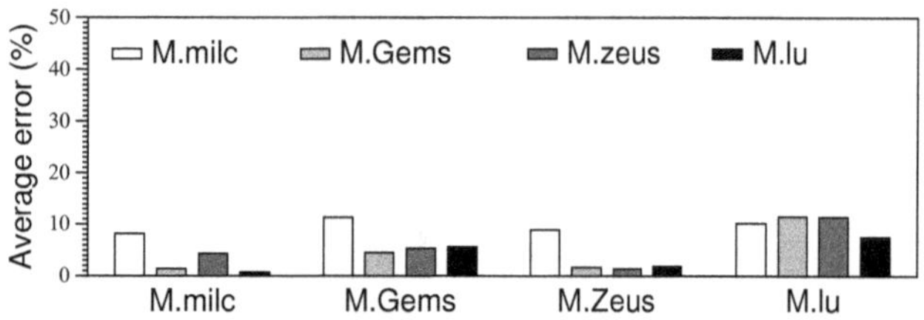

Figure 13. Validation errors for applications on EC2

programs along with the application workload) is 0, 1, 2, 4, 8, 16, 24 or 32. Table 6 shows the best mapping policy for each application with the average error and standard deviation. To find the interference heterogeneity model for each application, we randomly sample 100 heterogeneous interference settings, and measure the execution times on the selected settings. For each of the applications, the average error for the best mapping policy on Amazon EC2 is higher than that on our private cluster. A major reason is because we cannot control the placement of VMs and VMs by other users are likely running with our VMs on Amazon EC2.

Similar to Section 4.3, we run two applications together on 32 VMs to validate our model. Figure 13 shows the average performance estimation error for each application when it is executed together with all the other applications. For the benchmark workloads, the average errors are 3-10%.

The sensitivity curves, best mapping policy, and bubble score for an application are dependent on physical system configurations as well as the application behaviors. Therefore, separate interference-aware performance models need to be constructed for Amazon EC2. However, with the model parameters newly measured from the EC2 system, our model can still predict the performance under interference with modest errors for the larger scale systems.

7. Related Work

There have been earlier efforts on investigating techniques to reduce the effects of shared cache and NUMA. Zhuravlev et al. proposed scheduling algorithms in which threads are grouped and distributed among sockets in a multicore system such that the overall cache miss rate of the system is minimized [24]. A co-scheduling algorithm was proposed to group VMs with complementary resource demands [14]. In each time slice, it schedules tasks with different resource demands, reducing hotspots on the chip. To reduce shared cache impacts between threads (or VMs), low overhead cache partitioning techniques were studied [17, 19]. Nathuji et al. proposed to compensate the negative performance impact due to shared cache by provisioning additional resources for VMs running in a single system [15].

Besides cache contention, NUMA can complicate thread and VM scheduling and impact performance significantly. Blagodurov et al. developed a NUMA-aware scheduling algorithm that migrates the memory of threads to maintain NUMA affinity [3]. The effects of NUMA on shared memory and MPI-based applications have been investigated in virtualized environment [11]. To support NUMA systems, a commercial hypervisor, VMware ESX, provided optimization to migrate the memory of VMs [1], but shared LLC contention was not taken into account on scheduling. To minimize the effects of cache sharing and NUMA affinity for a cloud system, Ahn et al. proposed contention-aware scheduling techniques, which use live VM migration to schedule VMs dynamically for single-threaded workloads [2].

There have been several studies to reduce resource contention and balance load over physical hosts by using VM migrations. Wood at al. proposed techniques to monitor the resource usages of VMs, and initiate VM migrations to mitigate hotspots [20]. In VMware's Distributed Resource Scheduler (DRS) [10], it migrates running VMs for load balancing across physical hosts, based on the resource requirements specified by users. Similarly, VM migration is triggered when CPU utilization of a physical system becomes larger than some threshold for load balancing [6]. A decentralized migration technique was proposed to monitor network affinity between pairs of VMs, and migrate VMs to minimize communication overhead among VMs [18]. Scheduling techniques based on VM migration can be also used for parallel workloads to reduce the latency caused by interference at runtime.

Performance prediction models can be used to schedule VMs efficiently. Zhu et al. proposed a power-aware consolidation algorithm for scientific workflows, which consolidates tasks with dissimilar resource requirements on the same node [23]. An interference-aware scheduling algorithm was studied for data-intensive applications in a virtualized data center, which characterizes the applications based on CPU and I/O resource usages [5]. In a task scheduling algorithm for MapReduce applications, it mitigates the effect of interference using an exponential interference prediction model, while improving data locality [4].

Several techniques to identify interference and predict the effect of interference have been investigated to improve performance of applications or resource utilization [13, 16, 21, 22], and also QoS-aware resource management techniques have been studied [7, 8]. CPI^2 detects interference based on CPI data and possibly throttles applications which affect the performance of other co-running applications badly [22]. Delimitrou and Kozyrakis investigated a QoS-aware scheduler that uses collaborative filtering techniques to classify an incoming workload regarding the effects of heterogeneous resources and interference [7], and developed a QoS-aware cluster management system which allows users to specify performance constraints (such as throughput) of applications, instead of resource reservation, and uses similar classification techniques for resource management [8]. The effects of heterogeneity caused by co-running jobs as well as different machine types have been analyzed for web-service applications in warehouse-scale computers, and a system (called Whare-Map) which maps jobs to heterogeneous machines using stochastic hill climbing technique has been proposed [12].

8. Conclusion

This study investigated how interference in individual nodes affects the overall performance of distributed parallel applications. Extending a prior *Bubble-Up* technique for modeling the interference effect in single-node applications, this work proposed a scheme to model interference propagation across multiple nodes and to address interference heterogeneity. Using the proposed performance model, the paper investigated two interference-aware placement algorithms, one for ensuring the QoS, and the other for maximizing the overall throughput of applications, as case studies. The proposed model can be used for the overall energy reduction to minimize the wasted CPU resources, when interference in some nodes is unavoidable for distributed applications with high interference propagation. A limitation of this study is, as one of the first studies for interference effect on distributed applications, that it relies on the profiling-based model construction for pairwise co-locations of the applications. Extending it to an online mechanism supporting co-location of multiple applications is our future work.

Acknowledgments

This work was supported by the National Research Foundation of Korea (NRF) grant funded by the Korea government (MSIP) (No. 2013R1A2A2A01015514) and by Institute for Information & communications Technology Promotion (IITP) grant funded by the Korea government (MSIP) (No. R0190-15-2012, High Performance Big Data Analytics Platform Performance Acceleration Technologies Development)

References

[1] VMware ESX Server 2 NUMA Support. White paper. .

[2] Jeongseob Ahn, Changdae Kim, Jaeung Han, Young-ri Choi, and Jaehyuk Huh. Dynamic virtual machine scheduling in clouds for architectural shared resources. In *Proceedings of the 4th USENIX Conference on Hot Topics in Cloud Computing (HotCloud)*, 2012.

[3] Sergey Blagodurov, Sergey Zhuravlev, Mohammad Dashti, and Alexandra Fedorova. A case for NUMA-aware contention management on multicore systems. In *Proceedings of the 2011 USENIX Conference on USENIX Annual Technical Conference (ATC)*, 2011.

[4] Xiangping Bu, Jia Rao, and Cheng-zhong Xu. Interference and locality-aware task scheduling for MapReduce applications in virtual clusters. In *Proceedings of the 22nd International Symposium on High-performance Parallel and Distributed Computing (HPDC)*, 2013.

[5] Ron C. Chiang and H. Howie Huang. Tracon: interference-aware scheduling for data-intensive applications in virtualized environments. In *Proceedings of 2011 International Conference for High Performance Computing, Networking, Storage and Analysis (SC)*, 2011.

[6] Hyung Won Choi, Hukeun Kwak, Andrew Sohn, and Kyusik Chung. Autonomous learning for efficient resource utilization of dynamic VM migration. In *Proceedings of the 22nd annual international conference on Supercomputing (ICS)*, 2008.

[7] Christina Delimitrou and Christos Kozyrakis. Paragon: QoS-aware scheduling for heterogeneous datacenters. In *Proceedings of the 18th International Conference on Architectural Support for Programming Languages and Operating Systems (ASPLOS)*, 2013.

[8] Christina Delimitrou and Christos Kozyrakis. Quasar: Resource-efficient and QoS-aware cluster management. In *Proceedings of the 19th International Conference on Architectural Support for Programming Languages and Operating Systems (ASPLOS)*, 2014.

[9] RW Eglese. Simulated annealing: a tool for operational research. *European journal of operational research*, 46(3):271–281, 1990.

[10] Ajay Gulati, Ganesha Shanmuganathan, Anne Holler, and Irfan Ahmad. Cloud-scale resource management: Challenges

and techniques. In *Proceedings of the 3rd USENIX Conference on Hot Topics in Cloud Computing (HotCloud)*, 2011.

[11] Jaeung Han, Jeongseob Ahn, Changdae Kim, Youngjin Kwon, Young-ri Choi, and Jaehyuk Huh. The effect of multi-core on HPC applications in virtualized systems. In *Proceedings of the 5th Workshop on Virtualization in High-Performance Cloud Computing (VHPC)*, 2011.

[12] Jason Mars and Lingjia Tang. Whare-map: Heterogeneity in "homogeneous" warehouse-scale computers. In *Proceedings of the 40th Annual International Symposium on Computer Architecture (ISCA)*, 2013.

[13] Jason Mars, Lingjia Tang, Robert Hundt, Kevin Skadron, and Mary Lou Soffa. Bubble-Up: Increasing utilization in modern warehouse scale computers via sensible co-locations. In *Proceedings of the 44th Annual IEEE/ACM International Symposium on Microarchitecture (MICRO)*, 2011.

[14] Andreas Merkel, Jan Stoess, and Frank Bellosa. Resource-conscious scheduling for energy efficiency on multicore processors. In *Proceedings of the 5th European Conference on Computer Systems (EuroSys)*, 2010.

[15] Ripal Nathuji, Aman Kansal, and Alireza Ghaffarkhah. Q-clouds: managing performance interference effects for qos-aware clouds. In *Proceedings of the 5th European conference on Computer systems (EuroSys)*, 2010.

[16] Dejan Novaković, Nedeljko Vasić, Stanko Novaković, Dejan Kostić, and Ricardo Bianchini. DeepDive: Transparently identifying and managing performance interference in virtualized environments. In *Proceedings of the 2013 USENIX Conference on Annual Technical Conference (ATC)*, 2013.

[17] Moinuddin K. Qureshi and Yale N. Patt. Utility-based cache partitioning: A low-overhead, high-performance, runtime mechanism to partition shared caches. In *Proceedings of the 39th Annual IEEE/ACM International Symposium on Microarchitecture (MICRO)*, 2006.

[18] Jason Sonnek, James Greensky, Robert Reutiman, and Abhishek Chandra. Starling: Minimizing communication overhead in virtualized computing platforms using decentralized affinity-aware migration. In *Proceedings of the 2010 39th International Conference on Parallel Processing (ICPP)*, 2010.

[19] G. Edward Suh, Srinivas Devadas, and Larry Rudolph. A new memory monitoring scheme for memory-aware scheduling and partitioning. In *Proceedings of the 8th International Symposium on High-Performance Computer Architecture (HPCA)*, 2002.

[20] Timothy Wood, Prashant Shenoy, Arun Venkataramani, and Mazin Yousif. Black-box and gray-box strategies for virtual machine migration. In *Proceedings of the 4th USENIX Conference on Networked Systems Design & Implementation (NSDI)*, 2007.

[21] Hailong Yang, Alex Breslow, Jason Mars, and Lingjia Tang. Bubble-flux: Precise online QoS management for increased utilization in warehouse scale computers. In *Proceedings of the 40th Annual International Symposium on Computer Architecture (ISCA)*, 2013.

[22] Xiao Zhang, Eric Tune, Robert Hagmann, Rohit Jnagal, Vrigo Gokhale, and John Wilkes. CPI2: Cpu performance isolation for shared compute clusters. In *Proceedings of the 8th European Conference on Computer Systems (EuroSys)*, 2013.

[23] Qian Zhu, Jiedan Zhu, and Gagan Agrawal. Power-aware consolidation of scientific workflows in virtualized environments. In *Proceedings of the 2010 International Conference for High Performance Computing, Networking, Storage and Analysis (SC)*, 2010.

[24] Sergey Zhuravlev, Sergey Blagodurov, and Alexandra Fedorova. Addressing shared resource contention in multicore processors via scheduling. In *Proceedings of the 15th International Conference on Architectural Support for Programming Languages and Operating Systems (ASPLOS)*, 2010.

Taurus: A Holistic Language Runtime System for Coordinating Distributed Managed-Language Applications

Martin Maas* Krste Asanović* Tim Harris† John Kubiatowicz*

* University of California, Berkeley † Oracle Labs, Cambridge

Abstract

Many distributed workloads in today's data centers are written in managed languages such as Java or Ruby. Examples include big data frameworks such as Hadoop, data stores such as Cassandra or applications such as the SOLR search engine. These workloads typically run across many independent language runtime systems on different nodes.

This setup represents a source of inefficiency, as these language runtime systems are unaware of each other. For example, they may perform Garbage Collection at times that are locally reasonable but not in a distributed setting.

We address these problems by introducing the concept of a *Holistic Runtime System* that makes runtime-level decisions for the entire distributed application rather than locally. We then present Taurus, a Holistic Runtime System prototype. Taurus is a JVM drop-in replacement, requires almost no configuration and can run unmodified off-the-shelf Java applications. Taurus enforces user-defined coordination policies and provides a DSL for writing these policies.

By applying Taurus to Garbage Collection, we demonstrate the potential of such a system and use it to explore coordination strategies for the runtime systems of real-world distributed applications, to improve application performance and address tail-latencies in latency-sensitive workloads.

1. Introduction

A large portion of workloads that are running in cloud data centers are written in managed languages such as C#, Go, Java, JavaScript/node.js, PHP/Hack, Python, Ruby or Scala. According to a recent survey [48], 4 out of the 6 most popular languages are managed languages, and many widely used cloud frameworks – such as Hadoop [66], Cassandra [1] or Spark [68] – are written in these languages.

ASPLOS '16, April 02-06, 2016, Atlanta, GA, USA
ACM 978-1-4503-4091-5/16/04.
http://dx.doi.org/10.1145/2872362.2872386

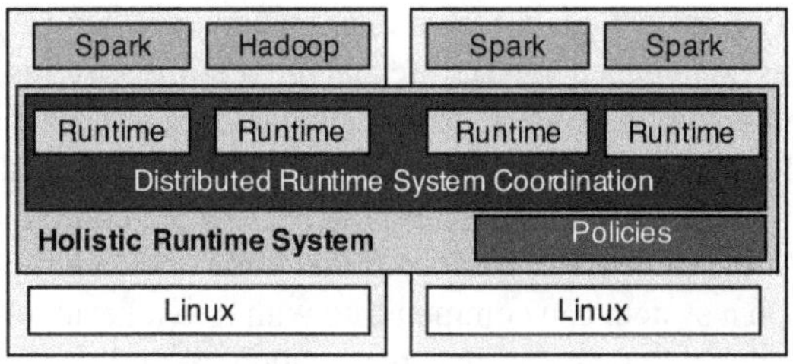

Figure 1: A Holistic Runtime System coordinates individual runtimes across machines based on a policy.

We see this trend continuing: Companies such as Twitter [17] or Facebook [8, 14] are writing most of their code in Scala and PHP/Hack. At the same time, cloud platforms such as Google AppEngine [7] or Microsoft Azure [13] are supporting managed language as explicit targets. Finally, many web startups write their code in languages such as Python, Ruby or JavaScript, as it allows them to iterate quickly.

Unfortunately, managed languages are known to cause performance overheads in some use cases [25, 38], and much work has been done to address these. However, most of this work looks at individual nodes. When running *distributed managed applications* and frameworks such as Hadoop or Spark at a rack or data-center scale, the application spans many processes across multiple nodes, each with its own runtime system. As we show in this paper, this causes problems beyond those encountered within an individual runtime system. Specifically, the language runtime systems on different nodes make completely independent decisions, such as about when to perform GC or how to JIT their code. This causes performance problems for many workloads, including both throughput-oriented and latency-sensitive jobs.

To address these problems, we propose what we call a *Holistic Runtime System* (Figure 1). A Holistic Runtime System is a distributed language runtime system that treats the runtimes underlying a distributed application as a distributed system itself and enables them to make decisions globally rather than individually. As such, it adopts some of the ideas from distributed operating systems [26, 44, 49, 53, 57] and applies them to language runtimes systems. This approach is motivated by today's low-latency data center networks and a trend towards rack-scale machines that enable a tighter integration of nodes in distributed systems. At the same time, data center workloads interact at ever smaller time-scales. These developments make it both feasible and necessary to integrate the runtime systems in a cluster more closely.

One design point would be a monolithic distributed runtime system with a single-system view [45]. However, this approach raises challenges with (1) compatibility with existing applications, (2) predictability by hiding the distinction between local and remote memory, (3) failure isolation, and (4) scalability bottlenecks such as those from distributed GC across a shared heap. We therefore propose an intermediate approach that retains the boundaries between individual runtime systems but enables coordination between them. Applications do not need to be aware that the runtime systems they are running across are part of the same logical entity. This enables running unmodified workloads, where the Holistic Runtime transparently applies policies for GC, compilation, etc. At the same time, workloads that know they are running on such a system can communicate with it to take advantage of its global knowledge and coordination capabilities.

To demonstrate the effectiveness of this approach, we built Taurus, a Holistic Language Runtime System for Java, with a specific focus on GC. Taurus is based on the OpenJDK Hotspot JVM and is a JVM drop-in replacement. It requires no modification of the application: once installed, running a Java application will automatically run it with Taurus, which joins it into the distributed system so that it can partake in global decision-making. Applications can then supply *policies* (written in a special DSL) to instruct Taurus how to coordinate language events (such as GC) between nodes.

We run two real-world workloads with Taurus. By using Taurus to coordinate GC, we show that it can reduce the execution time of a Spark PageRank workload by 21% and eliminate many GC-related stragglers for a Cassandra workload (reducing the 99.99%ile latency from 65.7 ms to 33.8 ms for reads, 40.7 ms to 10.1 ms for updates). At the same time, Taurus adds negligible overhead, scales to at least 180 nodes and is robust against failures (mostly isolating its faults from the applications and runtimes that it manages).

In this paper, we first make the case that the approach we take with the Holistic Runtime System – and Taurus in particular – is promising (Section 2). We then give an overview of the design of a Holistic Runtime System (Section 3), followed by a description of our policy DSL (Section 4) and the specific implementation details of Taurus (Section 5). We then evaluate Taurus on real-world workloads and microbenchmarks (Section 6). Finally, we present related work (Section 7) and draw our conclusions (Section 8).

2. Motivation & Case Studies

In this section, we make the case for using a Holistic Runtime System and why it is time to look at language runtime systems from a distributed systems perspective.

2.1 Opportunities of Managed Languages

The primary reason for using managed languages is arguably an increase in productivity, driven by features such as dynamic typing, class resolution at runtime, reflection and GC. The latter is particularly important: automatic memory management reduces the engineering overhead from managing explicit pointers and eliminates many sources of errors. Further advantages of managed languages include opportunities for dynamic optimization – data center workloads are often running for a long time and can therefore amortize JIT overheads. Many managed runtimes also compact memory during execution; this is important for long-running applications, since they can otherwise experience performance degradation from fragmentation and loss of locality.

2.2 Problems for Distributed Applications

The advantages of managed languages often come at the cost of substantial overheads over native code. These overheads have been well-studied. The most significant challenge is often considered to be GC, with thousands of academic papers in this area. Other overheads include JIT compilation and profiling [25], type resolution [19], as well as overheads from boxed types, indirection and additional safety checks [38]. Many previous works address these challenges for individual runtime systems on a single machine, and tremendous progress has been made. However, when running distributed applications across multiple runtime systems, a largely orthogonal set of problems emerges. We divide these problems into four categories:

Lack of Coordination between Nodes. Runtime systems on different nodes are unaware of each other. This means that they make all decisions independently, e.g., when to perform GC. As we show in the next section, this can have a significant impact on distributed workloads, both batch workloads and interactive jobs. Similar problems have been reported in several real-world deployments [9, 15, 33].

Interference within Nodes. Runtime systems on the same node do not coordinate. While co-scheduling of data center workloads is well-investigated and has been addressed by many projects [27, 30, 35, 43], most of these projects do not look at managed-language-specific issues such as GC interference or instruction cache pollution from multiple copies of the same code. Some distributed Java applications have 100s of instances on the same node – this can make these overheads substantial, and motivated the Multi-tasking Virtual Machine project [41] and JSR-121 [11]. However, MVM never achieved widespread adoption, presumably due to concerns about failure propagation and difficulty of deployment (two issues we are addressing in this work).

Slow Elasticity. Managed language runtimes take a long time to boot and reach their full performance, partly due to warming up the code cache. This introduces overhead when adding processes at a fine granularity, as well as time skew.

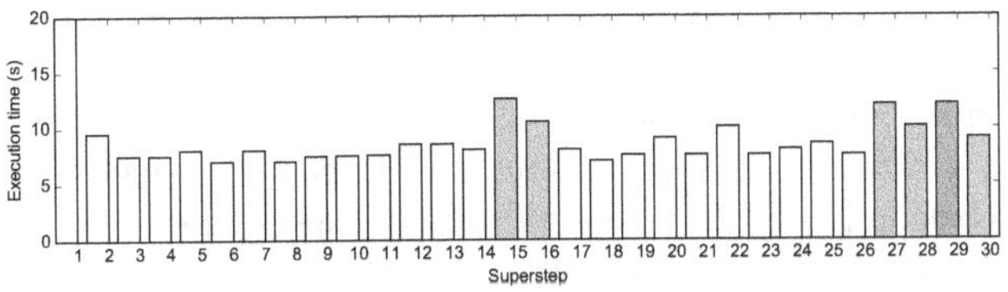

(a) Baseline System (no coordination)

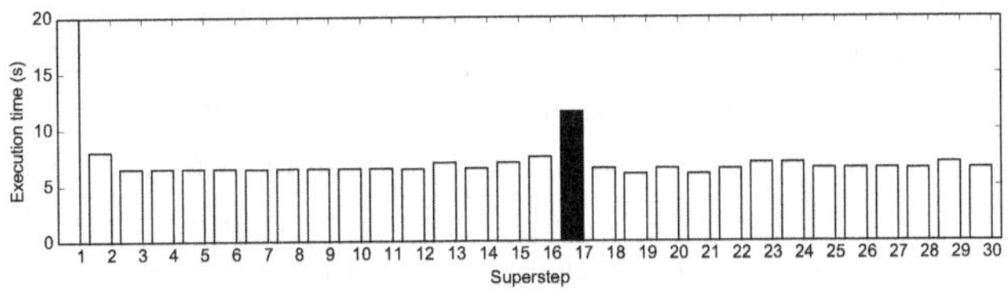

(b) Coordinating GC (Stop-the-Universe)

Figure 2: Relation between GC and the superstep durations of Spark PageRank (shade represents the number of nodes performing GC during a superstep; white = no GC). As soon as one node performs GC, the superstep takes much longer.

Redundancy. Every runtime system has its own JIT. As distributed workloads often run the same executable on every node (or even multiple instances of the same executable), this causes wasteful re-JITing of shared code. Companies such as Microsoft are therefore starting to forego the JIT in favor of statically pre-compiled binaries [3, 10]. However, this loses benefits from profile-directed dynamic optimization (e.g., trace-driven compilation and dynamic inlining).

2.3 Case Studies

We will now show how the first problem materializes in the two main categories of workloads encountered in data centers: throughput-oriented "batch" workloads such as big data computations (where we care about the completion time) and latency-sensitive "interactive" workloads (where we care about the distribution of response times).

2.3.1 Batch Workloads

We illustrate the problems caused by a lack of coordination between runtime systems for batch workloads, using iterative computations in Apache Spark [68] as an example. Spark is a popular Scala framework for distributed computation. It can run a wide range of workloads, including graph computations [34], machine learning, database workloads [67] and stream computations [69].

Many Spark workloads are very memory-intensive. Spark is based on applying operators and transformations to large distributed data sets; as a result, it exercises the heap significantly. Spark, by default, uses the parallel scavenge/serial mark-sweep-compact stop-the-world GC in the Hotspot JVM, which has very high collection performance but frequently incurs short pauses to perform young-generation GC (on the order of 100s of ms) and every once in a while incurs very long pauses (up to multiple seconds) for full GC.

These long pauses cause difficulties during iterative computations. Figure 2 shows an example of a 30-superstep PageRank computation – the example from the original Spark paper [68] – on a 16-node cluster (Section 6.2 describes the setup in detail). During each superstep, Spark launches a number of tasks on each worker node. Once all tasks have completed, the nodes exchange results and can only continue after this exchange has completed. As a result, this step effectively acts as a barrier between supersteps.

In the absence of GC, every superstep takes a similar time (Figure 2a). However, when one node performs a full GC, it pauses for multiple seconds and all other nodes have to wait at the barrier for that node to become available again. While waiting, they cannot do any work themselves. Worse, when they continue, they will at some point incur a GC as well, and become the reason for other nodes to wait.

The root cause of this problem is that the runtime systems make independent decisions about when to perform GC. The memory on the different nodes fills up at a different rate, and therefore their GCs will occur at different times. But what if the system was globally coordinated? In that case, the best decision would be to let all nodes do GC at the same time: since nodes have to wait for a single node in GC, they can use that time efficiently by performing their own GC. We call this policy *Stop-the-Universe*. Figure 2b shows its effect: even on this relatively small workload, it leads to a speedup of 21% (excluding the initial loading of the graph from disk).

We note that this problem is common to all distributed iterative computations with global barriers. This includes many Machine Learning algorithms (e.g., Logistic Regression) and graph workloads (e.g., Shortest Path). The problem is somewhat reminiscent of inter-thread synchronization in parallel workloads and the OS Noise problem in HPC [63]. Both are often solved using gang-scheduling, and *Stop-the-Universe* can be seen as its language-runtime equivalent.

Similar problems have recently been confirmed for Naiad workloads [33]. This indicates that this class of problems applies to a wider range of workloads and runtime systems.

2.3.2 Interactive Workloads

We now demonstrate a different set of problems which is encountered by latency-sensitive workloads. This includes data stores such as Cassandra [1], client applications such as the SOLR search engine [60] or systems-level software such as ZooKeeper [39]. Data center applications are interacting at ever smaller time-scales (such as in algorithmic trading, real-time bidding for ads, or low-latency storage [52]). Further, applications are often composed of hundreds of services [29] and the expected latencies for individual services have decreased to micro-second granularities. In such a scenario, stragglers are a significant problem since a single straggler can cause an entire request to miss its deadline. GC can be a significant contributor to this problem – even minor-GC pauses at the order of milliseconds are problematic when services operate at micro-second granularity.

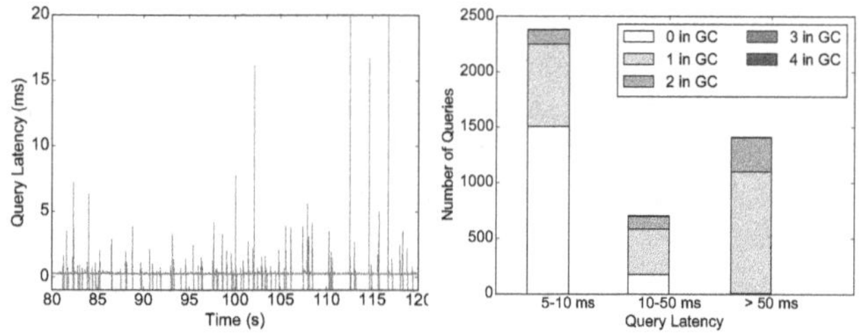

(a) Request latencies over time (b) Stragglers coinciding with GC

Figure 3: Correlation between stragglers in Cassandra read queries and GC. Grey lines in (a) are minor GCs and latencies of (potentially concurrent) request are averaged over 10ms intervals. The average request latency was 277 us.

We use the Cassandra key-value store as an example. Cassandra uses consistent hashing to replicate data across a subset of nodes. Requests can be sent to any node, which then assembles a quorum by contacting the replicas. While Cassandra uses a concurrent collector, it still experiences multi-millisecond pauses for young-generation GC (note that most concurrent collectors still introduce some form of jitter like this). To show the impact of these pauses, we ran a 4-node Cassandra cluster with the YCSB benchmark [28] for 10M queries (details can be found in Section 6.3). While the average latency for reads was 277 us, we occasionally incurred latencies that were over 100× larger. Figure 3a shows that these spikes mostly coincide with GC pauses (grey lines). Figure 3b shows that, in fact, most requests longer than 10 ms coincided with a GC pause, either in the node that received the request or in a node required to assemble a read or write quorum (concurrent work [31] presents related results). Note that these numbers might even understate the impact of GC, due to correlated omission in YCSB [65].

The fundamental problem is, once again, ignoring the language runtime system as part of the distributed system. Runtime systems make their GC decisions independently and collect as soon as their young generation fills up, stalling the application without warning. For example, two replicas holding the same entry can go down for GC at the same time, making it impossible to assemble a quorum. Further, services often have a choice where to send a request – for example, Cassandra requests can be handled by any node. However, when sending a request to a node that starts a GC pause before sending a response, we introduce a straggler.

Many of these problems could be avoided in a globally coordinated system. One approach is to expose the state of all runtime systems to the logic that directs requests to different servers (e.g., the load balancer). This makes it possible to avoid nodes that are close to GC – we call this *Request Steering*. Another strategy is to globally schedule GC such that there is always a sufficient number of replicas of any service available – we call this approach *Staggered GC*. Concurrent work [62] also confirms the efficiency of similar strategies.

2.4 What Does Software Do Today?

Problems such as the ones above have been reported for a wide range of applications and frameworks, including Hadoop [9], SOLR [60] and financial applications [4, 15]. They are often solved by rewriting parts of the application in a native language such as C++ and managing large data structures off-heap [16, 42]. Others use non-idiomatic Java (e.g., large byte arrays), split applications into smaller VMs or control allocation carefully to avoid GC pauses. In fact, the latest versions of Spark and Cassandra both use such techniques (note that our experiments use versions from before these changes). The problem with these approaches is that they lose many advantages of using a managed language in the first place, including safety and productivity.

There is also anecdotal evidence that some distributed applications treat GC as a failure mode like others, and restart the process when a full GC is necessary. The problem with this approach is that it is only viable if GC is rare. As we saw in Section 2.3, major GCs may occur every few minutes.

In the past, some applications also tried to control GC explicitly, using functions such as `System.gc`. This turned out insufficient, since it was difficult for application developers to make good decisions based on the knowledge available. Some runtime systems hence ignore such calls today.

We have also seen a commercial application that steers requests away from nodes paused for GC, similar to our proposed strategy above [15]. Implementation of such strategies is facilitated through language extensions such as C#'s GC Notification API [6] that allow applications to respond to upcoming GC pauses [62]. However, while explicitly designed for this use, we have not seen these APIs being widely used. Our hypothesis is that the mechanism is too low-level; programmers still need to solve distributed systems problems such as multi-node coordination or failures. Making the implementation of such strategies much easier is our key goal.

A final solution to the problem are concurrent garbage collectors such as C4 [61] or G1 [5]. These collectors avoid GC pauses; however, this comes at a performance cost from constantly having to trace and compact the heap, and performing extra book-keeping on every reference access to keep collector and mutator in sync (e.g., resulting in a large number of traps). This means that more memory bandwidth and CPU resources are used for GC to achieve the same GC throughput as a parallel stop-the-world collector. Furthermore, most concurrent GCs still introduce short pauses or jitter – with the very short request latencies required by many services today, this can still be problematic. In fact, we believe that it may be preferable to tolerate rare, predictable stop-the-world pauses over jitter from concurrent GC.

While all these solutions work, they often result in error-prone ad-hoc approaches, reduce productivity, redo a large amount of work, are not portable or yield poor performance. We believe it is time for a general solution to the problem, and propose Holistic Runtime Systems as such a solution.

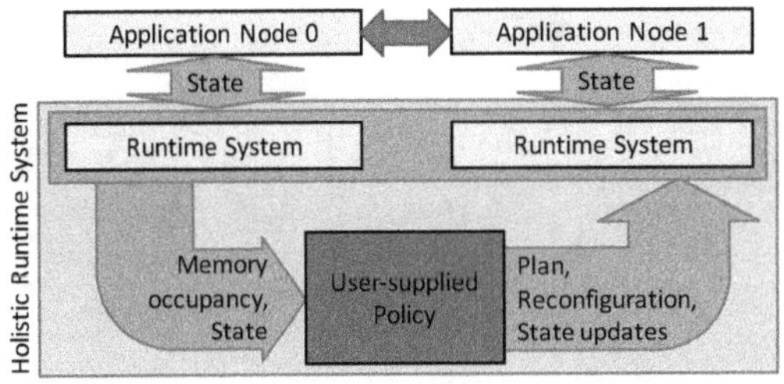

Figure 4: The Holistic Runtime System approach.

3. System Overview

We now give a high-level overview of the Holistic Runtime System approach and our implementation, Taurus. A Holistic Runtime System is a distributed language runtime system that coordinates a set of language runtimes across a cluster. It aims to be a general solution that enables developers to deploy and experiment with strategies to work around the problems from Section 2.3 while abstracting away many sources of errors and increasing productivity.

From the perspective of the application that is running across the runtime systems, nothing changes: the application processes are still isolated, and there is no shared heap. Traditionally, each runtime system would now make decisions independently, based on its settings. For example, the Hotspot JVM allows users to configure the GC, generation sizes, tenure rates, and many others. In a Holistic Runtime, these decisions are made globally for the entire distributed workload, through a configurable *policy* provided by the application. We show how policies are defined in Section 4.

Coordination works by dividing time into epochs of varying length. At the end of each epoch, a *leader* executes the policy. The policy considers the state of all the nodes and produces a *plan* that contains runtime events to be executed during the next epoch, as well as information to be shared between the nodes. This plan is then distributed to the other nodes and executed in a decentralized manner (reminiscent of the approach taken in systems such as Tesselation [27] for decentralized scheduling). At the end of the epoch, all nodes report back to the leader with any state updates, so that the next epoch can begin (Figure 4).

Holistic Runtimes enable a wide range of coordination patterns, while abstracting away the challenges of maintaining the distributed system, failure tolerance, time synchronization and interfacing to the runtime system. In Taurus, our prototype, we use these mechanisms to implement and investigate GC coordination. However, the same mechanisms could be used to coordinate JITs, share profiling data, reduce startup times or co-tune applications on the same node.

3.1 Design Decisions and Goals for Taurus

One of our primary goals for Taurus is compatibility. While it would be possible to design an entirely new system (and potentially language) from the ground up, it would be challenging to bring up workloads for it: many existing workloads require a fully standard-compliant runtime system, and even close approximations (such as Apache Harmony [2]) do not work reliably. We therefore decided to base our work on the OpenJDK Hotspot JVM, which is the reference implementation of Java and runs the vast majority of software.

Another important goal is usability. For Taurus to be useful, its deployment must be substantially easier than reimplementing coordination at the application level. We therefore designed Taurus to be a drop-in replacement; the goal is that the user only has to install a different `java` executable and everything else behaves the exact same way as before. Behind the scenes, this executable calls into Hotspot and brings up Taurus, which then connects the runtime systems.

A final goal is failure isolation. For the system to be adopted, it must also not substantially increase the probability of failure in any part of the system. For this reason, Taurus has fault tolerance built in and can tolerate node-failures by electing leaders and migrating state using a distributed consensus protocol (Section 5.3). This is an important argument for foregoing a model that supports a single-system view (which might reduce failure isolation between nodes).

We are also concerned about failure propagation into the JVM. We therefore avoid direct changes to the Hotspot code base but instead interact with the JVM through its management interface. Hotspot provides a rich interface to install libraries and performance monitors within the JVM, which can communicate to the outside world. Taurus itself is implemented as a co-process for Hotspot – this ensures that most errors in Taurus are staying outside the JVM process barrier, and failures do not bring down the JVM.

3.2 Components of the System

Figure 5 shows the high-level components of Taurus. With Taurus installed, every JVM instance is augmented with a *monitor* process at startup, to form a *Holistic Runtime Instance*. The monitor connects to the JVM's management interface, which allows it to monitor memory occupancy and other internals, and trigger JVM operations (Section 5.1). The monitor also opens a communication channel to the application space of the JVM. This allows the application to exchange information with Taurus (Section 3.4). Using this feature is optional and requires modifying the application.

On startup, the monitor instantiates a *client*, which exposes an RPC interface that other nodes can connect to (Section 5.2). Monitors also connect to a consensus layer that provides us with a set of replicated, consistent storage. This layer is used for features such as leader election or node discovery (Section 5.3). We use an implementation of the Raft consensus protocol [51] – we assume that this layer is available on startup, but it could also be launched automatically.

When launching a Holistic Runtime Instance, the application can select a policy, usually through a new set of special command line flags (we use the `-XX:HVM:flag=value` namespace, which is not used by Hotspot; adding new `-XX` arguments does not break J2SE-compliance).

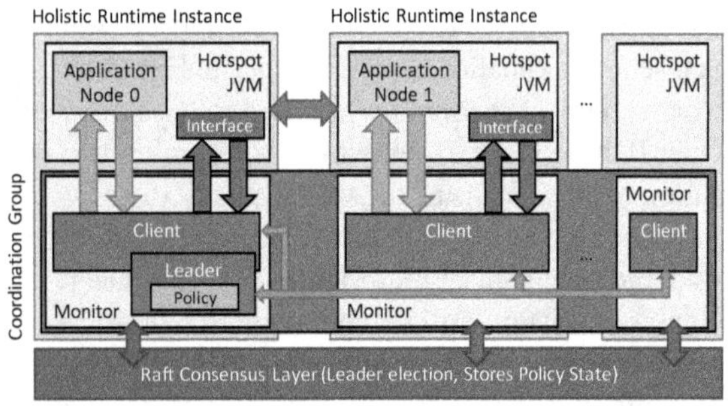

Figure 5: The high-level components of Taurus.

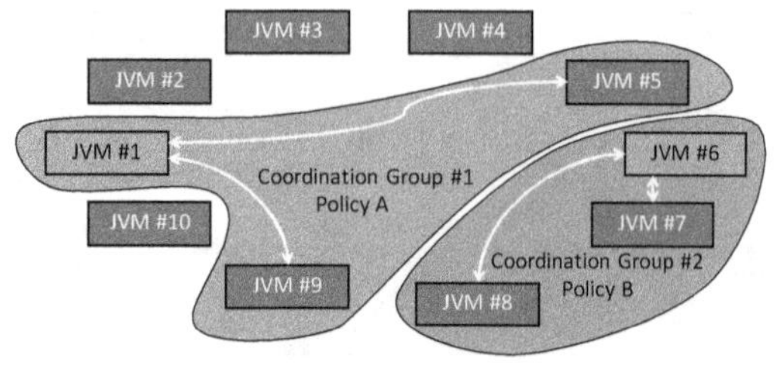

Figure 6: Cluster divided into multiple coordination groups. Orange nodes are the leaders, which execute the policy and distribute the results to the remaining nodes in the group.

3.3 Policy Execution

Policies are the core of Taurus: they describe the strategies for coordinating the different runtime systems. Taurus's policies are written in a high-level DSL we describe in Section 4.

Policy execution in Taurus follows a two-level approach. Using the consensus layer for all coordination in the entire cluster would result in scalability issues, and prevent us from fully exploiting fast rack-level interconnects. Instead, Taurus allows multiple policies to be active within the same cluster and operate on what we call a *coordination group*.

A coordination group is a subset of runtime systems that is subject to a policy at a given time (Figure 6). Every runtime system can be a member of at most one coordination group, and policies can choose to add or remove unclaimed runtimes from their group. Coordination groups operate independently from each other and the consensus layer is only used to handle group membership, leader election and recovery (we assume such changes to be infrequent). This means that a Holistic Runtime System can manage a large set of machines while fine-grained coordination occurs for subsets of nodes, such as those within a rack or an application.

A policy is a pure function that takes as input the state of the coordination group (e.g., memory occupancy of all runtime systems, or user-defined state as described in Section 3.4) and produces a plan that contains runtime events for the next epoch and state updates. It also contains coordination group changes (e.g., runtime systems to add or remove).

Each coordination group has an elected leader; all other nodes are followers. The leader establishes a synchronized time base for the group and is responsible for executing the policy once every epoch. When a runtime system instance is launched with a policy selected, it will try to become the leader for this policy by contacting the consensus layer. If there is no leader yet, the node will become the leader, spawn off a *leader* thread, and start executing the policy. Otherwise, it will become a *follower* and connect to the existing leader.

By using this approach, we address the scalability issues since no global consensus is necessary within the coordination group; the only scalability bottleneck is the leader, which needs to receive one sample from each member of the group per epoch and distribute the plan (in Section 6.4.3, we show that this scales well to at least 180 nodes). Furthermore, failures in the coordination group are "softer" than failures in the global consensus layer. While they may lead to performance degradation, missing a few epochs will not cause a failure of the application running on Taurus – they can be fixed up throughout later epochs (work in cluster scheduling shows that such an *optimistic* approach can work well in a distributed setting [58]). The downside is that since we are not relying on the consensus layer within coordination groups, we need to be able to recover from both leader and follower failures (Section 5.4).

3.4 Communication with the Application

In addition to coordination at the runtime system level, Taurus can optionally communicate with the application itself. This is useful to implement policies such as the *Steering* policy from Section 2.3.2, where the runtime system needs to communicate to the application which nodes to avoid. The abstraction we chose is a shared set of key-value pairs visible to both the runtime system and the application space.

For this purpose, each monitor installs a globally visible class in the application space that provides thread-safe static methods `HVM.getKeyValuePair(k)` and `HVM.setKeyValuePair(k,v)`. To use them in an application, it suffices to add a .jar file to the classpath.

The executing policy receives as part of its input the full set of key-value pairs on all nodes of the coordination group, and can produce (as part of its plan) updates to key-value pairs on any node. This allows policies to implement a wide range of communication patterns with the application.

3.5 Reconfiguration

When launching a new policy, its coordination group only contains one node. The policy can query the list of available *runtimes* in the cluster, and whether they are a member of any other group. They can then select non-claimed nodes to add to their coordination group as part of the plan. These nodes join during the next epoch, and are considered during the next execution of the policy (conflicts are avoided by making policy executions atomic with respect to each other). Node terminations or failures are visible in a similar way: the policy can see a node that has timed out and can remove it from its coordination group (Section 5.4).

```
policy AutoAdd {
  run(Set<Runtime> s = runtimes) {
    foreach(Runtime r : s) {
      if (r.status == UNASSIGNED) {
        plan <- ReconfigureAddMember(r);
      }}}}
```

(a) Policy that automatically adds unassigned runtimes.

```
policy STU {
  extern double cutoff = 10.0;

  run(Set<Member> stu = members,
      Set<Member> collect = members) {
    if (!(stu.filter([Member m : (! m.busy) &&
          m.memory.old > cutoff]).empty())) {
      plan <- MajorGC(collect);
    }}}
```

(b) *Stop-the-Universe* Policy that performs a full GC for all members in `collect` if at least one of `stu` has reached a memory occupancy of `cutoff`.

```
policy Example {
  import STU(cutoff=90.0);
  import AutoAdd();

  run() {
    STU(members.filter([Member m:
        m.runtime.tag == "gc"]), members);
    AutoAdd(runtimes);
    plan <- EpochLength(200.0); //ms
  }}
```

(c) Composing policies: `Example` imports and calls into `STU` (with two dynamic parameters), then `AutoAdd`.

Figure 7: Examples of policies written in our DSL.

4. Policy Description Language

To facilitate the development of policies (and therefore adoption), we designed a DSL for policy descriptions (Figure 7).

Each policy declaration (which gives the policy a unique name) contains a `run` block that describes the policy function and defines policy parameters. This block contains a sequential program that can access any state visible to the system and builds up a plan. However, instead of a fully Turing-complete language, we do not provide general for or while loops but only `foreach` loops over finite sets; this ensures that policies *always terminate*, which prevents the leader getting stuck (a key advantage of using a DSL).

In addition to the primitive types `double`, `int` and `string` and two parameterized collection types `Set` and `Map`, the language provides two composite types to describe runtime systems (two types are required to distinguish between runtime systems that are under the control of the policy and those registered but not under the policy's control):

```
policy PingPong {
  state Map<Member,int> prev = 0;

  run() {
    foreach (Member m : members) {
      int pp = m.kv("pingpong").toInt(0);
      if (prev.get(m) != pp) {
        plan <- SetKV(m, "pingpong", pp+1);
        prev.set(m, pp+1);
      }
    }
    plan <- EpochLength(200.0);
  }}
```

Figure 8: Example policy using key-value pairs and policy state. The policy monitors a key-value pair and increases it when it sees a change; the application does the same.

- `Runtime`: A runtime that is part of the Holistic Runtime but not necessarily the current coordination group. This type is used for group management (e.g., adding/removing). It contains fields such as the runtime's server, command line, tags set at startup, and group membership.
- `Member`: A member of the policy's coordination group. This type is used to actually interact with the runtime system. It contains fields for memory occupancy of the different subspaces, GC statistics, whether the node is unresponsive (`busy`) and KV pairs.

Note that the `Members` are a subset of the `Runtimes`; given a `Member m`, the corresponding `Runtime` can be accessed with `m.runtime`. The sets of all runtimes and all members can be accessed using global keywords `runtimes` and `members`. Note that the `runtimes` set can become large, which is why monitors cache it instead of updating it from the consensus layer every epoch (comparing only a version number to check for updates).

The language allows filtering sets with a predicate. An example can be found in Figure 7b. In this case, a filter predicate is used to determine the set of members with a certain memory occupancy, and check whether it is empty.

We provide a special construct of the form `plan <- Action(...)` to add commands to the policy's plan. A plan is effectively the policy's return value and contains a set of commands to execute on each runtime system. Some commands take parameters, such as a subset of members or runtimes they apply to (e.g., adding a set of runtimes, performing GC on a set of members). By repeatedly using this construct, the policy creates the plan for the next epoch.

A member's key-value pairs are accessed through a `kv` field in `Member`, and updates to them are added to the plan (Figure 8). Key-value pairs are stored as strings and it is often necessary to convert values to or from primitive types such as integers. To prevent error conditions in the case of malformed strings, all such conversions need to be provided a default value that is used in case the conversion fails.

Finally, policies support state that is kept around between epochs using the `state` keyword (Figure 8). Note that all state variables also need a default value that is used in case of errors (e.g., if a key is not found in a Map, or on failure).

4.1 Configurability and Composability

We hypothesize that most workloads will require variations of a small set of basic policies, potentially with some application-specific extensions (Section 6.1). Composability is therefore an important feature in our Policy DSL: it allows us to build a repository of basic policies over time, and combine them into application-specific solutions. To achieve this flexibility, policies need to be configurable and composable.

We allow policies to be included into other policies through an `import` statement. This will include the policy and allows it to be called within the `run` block. Figure 7c shows an example of this. Policies are parametrizable with two types of parameters: dynamic and static parameters. Static parameters are defined at the time of import and do not change at runtime (these are the parameters defined as "extern" outside the run block). Dynamic parameters are given to the policy whenever it is called from within another policy. Figure 7b shows examples for both types of parameters: `cutoff` is static, while `stu` is dynamic. All parameters can have default values.

4.2 Policy Compilation

Our DSL is embedded into C++11, and we reuse many C++ features including numerical and logical operations, if statements and stream operators. A recursive-descent parser written in Python transforms our policy code into C++ code, which is then compiled into a dynamic library. The parser does not split the code down to individual tokens but only into pieces that can be directly transformed into C++ (e.g., the predicate within a filter). We then find and replace any DSL-specific keywords and idioms with their C++ equivalents (considering scopes, strings, etc.). Policies are transformed into classes, foreach loops into iterators and filter predicates into C++11 lambda expressions. We use C++11 move semantics to chain filters without copying data.

5. Implementation

After the high-level design, we will now present implementation details of Taurus. Taurus is entirely written in C++11, to avoid GC-induced pauses in the system itself.

5.1 JVM Interface

The monitor connects to Hotspot through three different interfaces (Figure 9). It queries memory occupancy information through `jstat`, which exposes the JVM's performance counters by writing them to a shared page that can be mapped by a different process (by default, Hotspot updates these counters every 50ms; as we require a finer granularity, we set the interval to 1ms instead). This means that

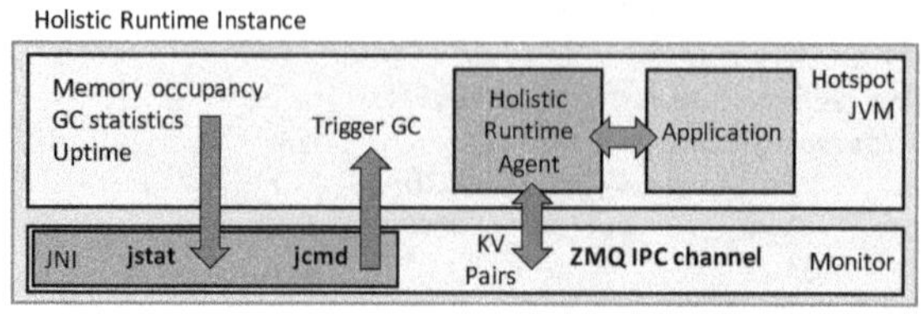

Figure 9: Interface between Hotspot and the monitor.

the monitor can access this data without blocking on the JVM. Commands in the JVM (primarily triggering of Major GC) are performed through the `jcmd` interface, which allows calling into the JVM to trigger activities (it may stall if the JVM is unresponsive, such as in a GC pause). Finally, key-value pairs are exposed to the Java application through a *Java agent* that is installed into the JVM's application space at start-up. This agent connects to the monitor through an IPC mechanism provided by the ZMQ library [37], which is the same library we use for inter-node communication. The agent then updates key-value pairs in the `HVM` class (Section 3.4), which is accessible from the application. The agent is also responsible for triggering minor GCs: since Hotspot does not support this, the agent can force a minor GC by allocating unreachable objects until the young generation is full (using the `MemoryPoolMXBean` interface to determine how much memory it needs to fill).

5.2 Inter-node Communication

Inter-node communication is implemented using a simple RPC protocol. We use ZMQ [37] for communication, since it gives us a higher level of abstraction than regular sockets (e.g., managing concurrency and high-level communication patterns), and supports low-latency communication over Infiniband. Our RPC protocol is using Protocol Buffers [64].

Adding a node is simple: The leader (prompted by its policy) sends a reconfigure request to the node's client, which will then send a request to join the leader's coordination group. The leader then confirms the join request and sends the plan of the currently active epoch to the client, after which the node is part of the group. Leader and client also repeatedly exchange timestamps through a separate connection, to determine the drift between them (no special hardware is needed for this). From then on, all timestamps are expressed relative to the leaders's clock.

5.3 Consensus Layer

We use LogCabin [12, 51], Stanford's Raft implementation, as our consensus layer. We run three LogCabin instances, and runtime systems can connect to any of them. LogCabin provides a small amount of consistent, highly replicated storage. We use this storage to track the set of instances currently registered with Taurus, as well as active policies. The set of instances has a version number; for performance, nodes cache the instances locally and only compare against the version number once per epoch.

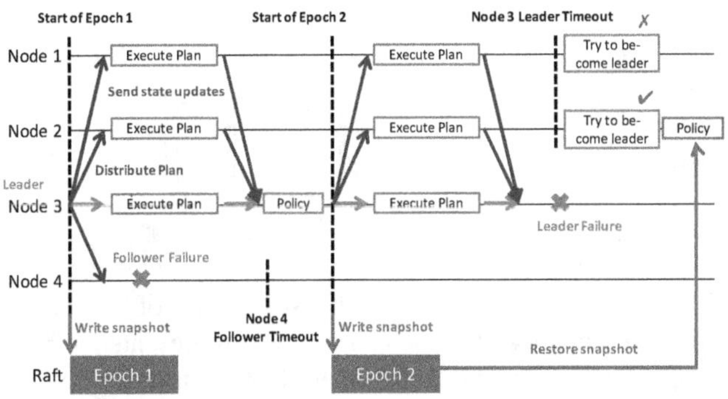

Figure 10: A sample policy execution in Taurus. When a follower fails, the policy sees it as unavailable. When the leader fails, another node becomes leader, restores the policy from the last executed epoch, and continues (marking all other nodes as unavailable for the next epoch, before stabilizing).

When launching a new JVM, its monitor will connect to LogCabin and create an entry for its runtime system instance. This includes information such as its command line options and address/port (the monitor selects a free port automatically on startup). Next, it will try to launch a policy and become the leader for it, if requested through a command line option. When the policy runs, it can detect other instances in the cluster and add them to its coordination group. (To help policies distinguish between multiple distributed applications, it is possible to supply a flag with a unique application ID to all JVMs belonging to one application; the first node with this ID will become the leader and runs the policy, which adds the other nodes.)

5.4 Execution & Failure Handling

Once a leader has brought up the policy, it enters a loop that consists of three stages, visualized in Figure 10:

1. Distribute the current plan to all nodes in the coordination group (at the beginning, the plan is empty).
2. Followers execute the instructions in the plan, then atomically take a sample of their state, and send it to the leader. If they cannot take a sample in time, they will send a response that they are "busy" (which can happen if the JVM is in a GC pause or if there is contention in the system).
3. The leader collects state updates from all followers. Once the epoch has ended, it marks all nodes from which it has not received an update as "unavailable", executes the policy, produces a new plan, and sends it to all nodes (including unavailable ones; failure is discussed below).

The length of the epoch is set by the plan itself and can adapt to the circumstances (e.g., if the workload is exhibiting irregular allocation rates, the policy can decide to decrease the epoch to react more quickly to changes). However, in this case policy authors have to be careful about control loops.

Leader failures are tolerated by storing the policy metadata (including the last plan) to the consensus layer every epoch (i.e., the epoch is made persistent before sending out a plan). All followers have a timeout by which they expect the next plan to arrive. If no plan arrives, they assume that the leader has failed and will attempt to become leader themselves by trying to write the entry of the current epoch. If it has been written before, it means that the original leader is either still alive and the message was delayed, or that some other node has become leader in its place. In that case, the node will continue as a follower. If the node succeeds in writing the policy entry, it becomes the next leader, pulls the policy data from the consensus layer, and starts executing.

This approach moves all the failure handling into the consensus layer, simplifying fault tolerance. At the same time, it puts little load on the consensus layer in the absence of failures (requiring only the leader to access it, once per epoch). This maintains the advantages of the two-level approach.

6. Evaluation

We now demonstrate how Taurus coordinates GC in real-world applications and characterize its coordination performance and overheads through microbenchmarks.

We performed most of our evaluation on a 16-node cluster connected with 40 GbE using Mellanox dual port MCX314A-BCBT cards. Each node has an Intel IvyBridge E5-1680V2 3.0GHz CPU with 8 cores (16 hardware threads) and 64GB RAM. In addition to our workloads, the cluster ran YARN, as well as HDFS and Tachyon file systems. To show generality and scalability of the system, we also run a scalability microbenchmark on a set of 200 `g1-small` instances on Google Compute Engine.

All nodes are running Linux 3.13.0. We run a snapshot of LogCabin from 4/10/15 with the `Segmented` storage module on a RAM disk (as we do not require persistence across machine failures). We use OpenJDK 1.7.0_75, ZeroMQ 4.0.5 and Google Protocol Buffers 2.6.1. Unless noted otherwise, we used the default settings for all applications.

6.1 GC Policies & Applying Taurus to Applications

To make efficient use of Taurus, it is important to apply policies that address the specific GC problems of a given application. Looking at a range of workloads, we discovered that most GC policies we found could be expressed as a combination of three fundamental strategies:

- *Schedule*: Trigger GC at suitable/convenient times.
- *Redirect*: If a task can be handled by multiple nodes, choose a node that is not unavailable due to GC.
- *Hand-off*: If a node has sole responsibility for a task or a piece of data, hand it to another node before GC.

We dub these fundamental strategies *S*, *R* and *H*. Looking at published literature and our own work, we can describe a wide range of policies in terms of these strategies:

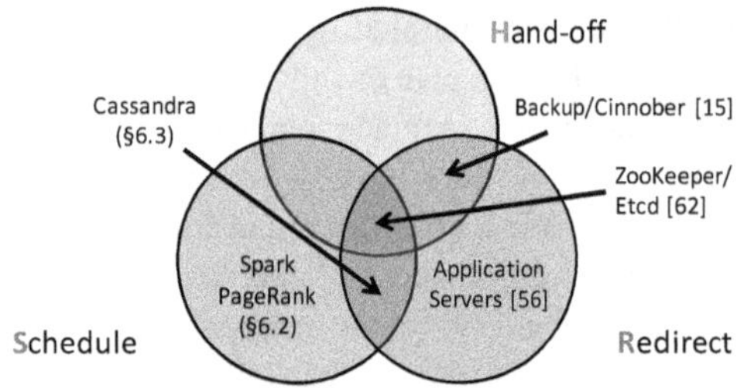

Figure 11: Mapping of GC policies to base strategies.

1. **Stop-the-Universe (S).** Synchronize GCs between all nodes in the distributed system. This strategy is useful for iterative batch workloads (Section 2.3.1).
2. **GC-when-Idle (S).** Trigger GC during a period of idleness. E.g., for in-memory computations, perform GC in the backing data store (e.g., HDFS) during computation.
3. **Steering (R).** In a system where multiple servers can handle requests (e.g., sharded search engines such as SOLR [60], or replicated services), steer requests away from nodes close to GC. Steering can happen within applications (e.g., picking replicas) or at a load-balancer.
4. **Staggering (S).** In a system that requires quorums of replicas for consistency, ensure that only one of the replicas is performing GC at any given time.
5. **Backup (SR).** Have two instances of a component, but use only one of them and trigger GC on the other [15].
6. **Leadership Transfer (H).** When the leader of a system is about to stall for GC, use the system's recovery mechanism to hand off leadership to another replica [62].
7. **Timeout Extension.** Stop connections or leases from timing out during GC pauses (a common problem [18]).

Applications can combine these policies to fit their needs. Figure 11 shows examples: Spark (Section 6.2) benefits from *Stop-the-Universe* (*S*), Cassandra (Section 6.3) uses *Steering* & *Staggering* (*SR*), a Zookeeper-like system [62] has been shown to benefit from a *Steering*, *Staggering* & *Leadership Transfer* (SRH), and replicated application servers [56] have been shown to benefit from *Steering* (*R*) alone.

We note that there is a connection between the fundamental policies and their implementation complexity: *S* oftentimes requires no changes to the application, *R* does require changes but those are minimal if it is possible to modify the replica selection algorithm already available in applications, while *H* can be more work, unless the application already has a hand-off mechanism as part of its failover handling.

Taurus enables and simplifies the implementation of these policies, and we hypothesize that they provide a basic set that can be combined to cover most applications. Using the two examples from Section 2.3, we now show how Taurus can be used to improve these workloads by implementing three of the fundamental policies above.

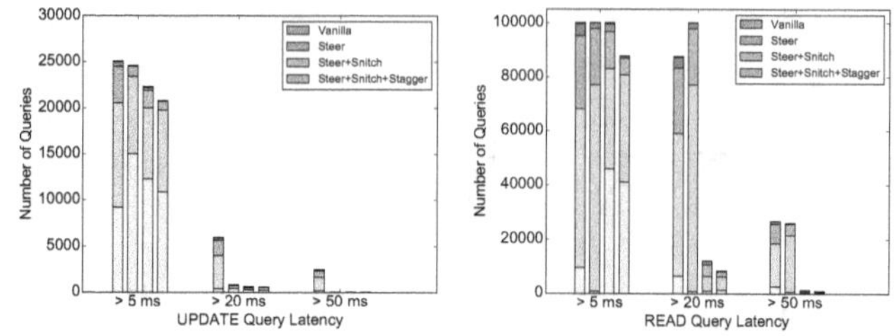

Figure 12: Cumulative latency distributions of the slowest 100K queries (99.9 percentile) of a representative run. Stacked bars represent the number of GCs during a request.

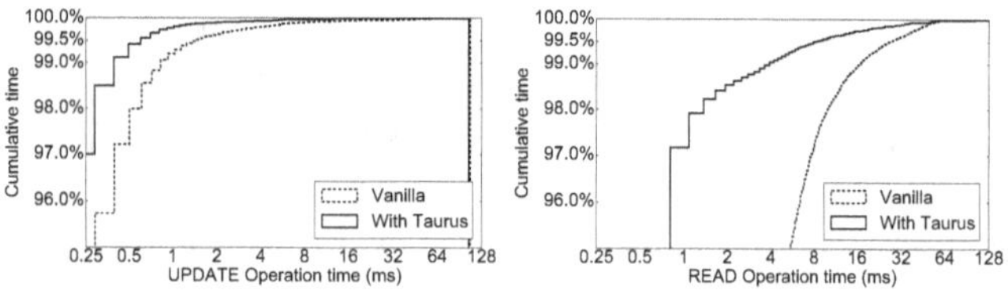

Figure 13: Fraction of total execution time (sum of all query latencies) spent in requests of at least a certain length.

6.2 Case Study: Apache Spark

As an example for a batch workload, we used the Spark PageRank workload from Section 2.3.1. As discussed there, this workload benefits from a Stop-the-Universe (STU) policy, and implementing it in Taurus is simple. In fact, all parts have already appeared in the paper: the improved PageRank workload in Figure 2b is the result of using the STU policy from Figure 7. We used Spark 1.1.1 on 16 nodes with 32GB heaps. No modification to Spark was required, and even this simple policy reduced execution time by 21%.

6.3 Case Study: Apache Cassandra

As an example for an interactive workload, we improve Cassandra tail-latencies (Section 2.3.2). We run a YCSB snapshot from 3/11/15 against Cassandra 1.0.6 with a replication factor of 3 and a cluster size of 8. We run workload A on a keyspace with 10M entries for 100M queries (50s warmup). We chose a 32GB heap with a 4GB young generation.

The average latencies were 173.6 us for updates and 522.8 us for reads, but some requests were over 100× slower: Figure 12 shows the distribution of the slowest 100K queries (>5ms latency), which is the tail from the 99.9 percentile. Our goal was to remove as many of the stragglers (>20ms) as possible. To this end, we applied multiple of the GC coordination policies from Section 6.1:

Request Steering (Steer). Requests in Cassandra can be sent to any node. A main source of stragglers are nodes that stall for GC while processing a request. To avoid this, we expose all nodes that are close to GC to the load balancer (in our case the YCSB client). We implemented a policy that monitors the young-generation occupancy of each node every 10ms epoch and maintains a key-value pair per node. When a node's occupancy reaches 80%, the key-value pair is set to 1. YCSB then checks these key-value pairs before dispatching each request. If the key-value pair is 1, YCSB sends the request to a different node (we hence maintain additional connections to each Cassandra node). This eliminates most update stragglers over 20ms but does not improve reads (Figure 12). This is because updates can be delayed while reads need to contact a quorum of replicas.

Snitch Steering (Snitch). In order to serve a read query, the node executing the query has to assemble a quorum of replicas. This quorum is chosen based on a *Snitch*, a feature in Cassandra that is normally used to describe the data center topology. We modified Cassandra's dynamic snitch to read the key-value pairs and select replicas that are not close to GC. Figure 12 shows this improves reads substantially.

Staggering (Stagger). Additional read stragglers stem from multiple GCs occurring at the same time. To address this, we modified the policy to ensure that only one node is performing GC at any time. Each epoch, we trigger a minor GC on the node with the highest memory occupancy over 80%, if any, and trigger no other GC before it has finished. For our 8-node cluster, this is sufficient. Larger clusters could stagger GC by triggering simultaneous GCs on nodes 3 steps apart in the Cassandra ring (to avoid stalling multiple replicas belonging to the same key).

The overall impact of all coordination techniques is shown in Figure 13. The y axis shows the fraction of total time spent in requests of at least the latency on the x axis (averaged over 10ms intervals). As our coordinated version is well to the left of the original (note the log scale), we eliminate a large fraction of stragglers. On a per-request basis, the 99.99%ile latency improves from 65.7 ms to 33.8 ms for reads (40.7 ms to 10.1 ms for updates) and the 99.999%ile from 128.6 ms to 54.6 ms for reads (67.7 ms to 21.0 ms for updates).

Note that we use an untuned configuration of Cassandra, with a large heap and young generation. In practice, Cassandra deployments are heavily hand-tuned. We argue that with a system such as Taurus, tuning becomes less important.

6.4 Microbenchmarks

We now characterize the coordination performance, scalability and overheads of Taurus using microbenchmarks.

6.4.1 Coordination Granularity

We are first interested in the granularity of coordination that Taurus enables, specifically the minimum sustainable epoch length. We ran Taurus on a Java program that sleeps for one second at a time in an infinite loop, and ran it for different policies and epoch lengths (Figure 14). We report how often clients fail to report back by the end of the epoch; this indicates that the epoch was too short. In all cases, we let the system reach a stable state before performing our measurements. Error bars here and later are the σ of 5 runs.

8-Null and 16-Null are a policy that does nothing and only checks for new runtimes (on 8 and 16 nodes). In both

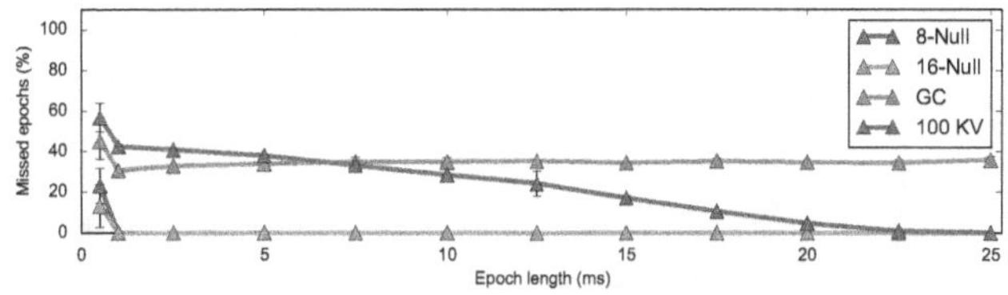

Figure 14: Missed epochs depending on the epoch length.

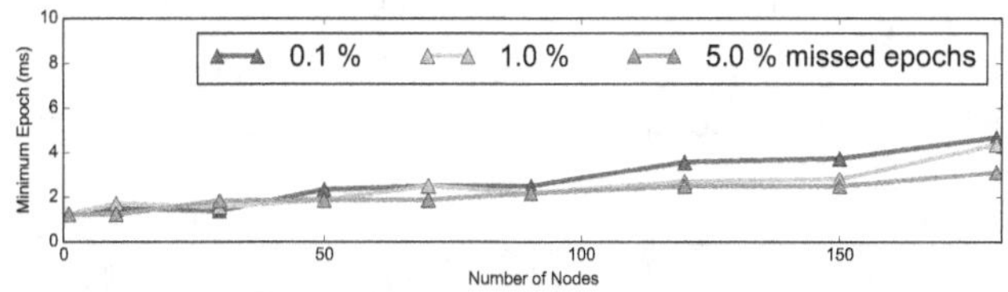

Figure 15: Scaling to 180 Google Compute Engine nodes.

cases, no epochs were missed until going below 2ms, indicating the minimum sustainable epoch length is 1-2ms (for the scale we looked at). Since the minimum jstat sampling rate of the Hotspot JVM is 1ms, this is sufficient.

We also experimented with two other policies: `KV` sets 100 key-value pairs every epoch on each node – this stresses communication and increases the minimum epoch length to 20ms. We also ran a policy that triggers a full GC every 10s (`GC`), on a workload that always allocates data. As expected, this misses a constant fraction of epochs due to GC pauses.

6.4.2 Scalability

To demonstrate that Taurus scales to a large number of nodes in a more realistic data center deployment, we ran the same benchmark on a set of up to 180 Google Compute Engine `g1-small` instances. We performed a run with a policy that constantly measures the number of missed epochs and adjusts their length in a binary search fashion until a target fraction of missed epochs is reached (note that in a large deployment, there are always going to be some missed epochs).

Figure 15 shows that even in such a deployment without Infiniband, Taurus performs well and can achieve epoch times below 10ms. With ping latencies of around 300us (and LogCabin running on a separate set of nodes), we believe these results to be reasonable. As we saw in Section 6.3, a 10ms epoch is sufficient even for fine-grained coordination in latency-sensitive systems. In addition to helping us determine the minimum epoch length, this experiment also shows an example of a policy that automatically adjusts the epoch length (a good strategy to make policies more portable).

6.4.3 Performance Breakdown

We are now interested in how different components of the execution contribute to the epoch length. Figure 16 shows the different contributors. For the leader, we ran a policy that reads out all nodes' GC statistics while varying the coordination group size (with four JVMs per node). For the followers, we chose the KV policy from Section 6.4.1, varying the number of key-value pairs.

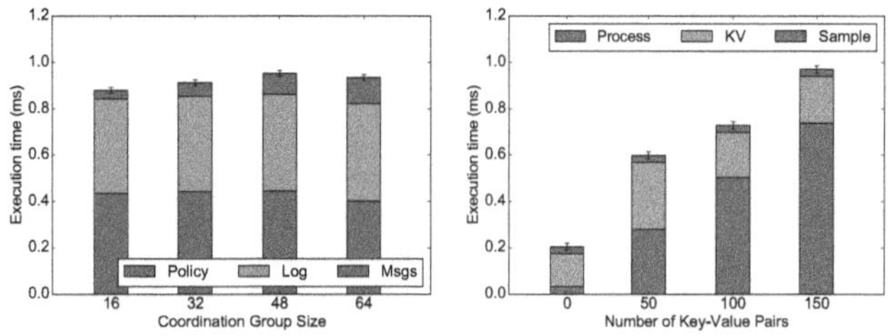

(a) Leader Execution (b) Follower Execution

Figure 16: Impact and scalability of the different components of policy execution, for both the leader and followers.

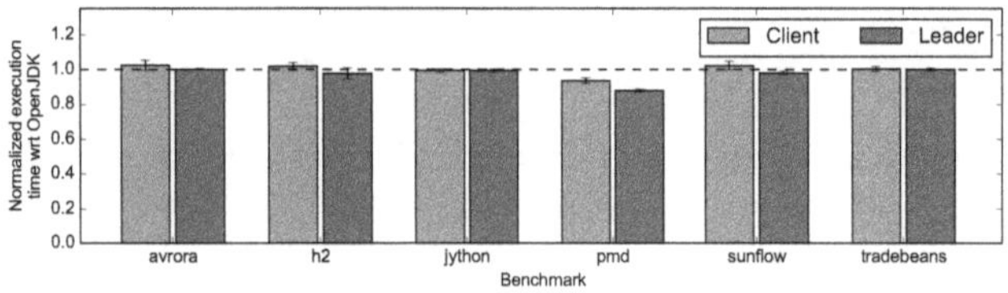

Figure 17: Overhead of running Dacapo with Taurus.

The leader's execution limits the coordination granularity as much as the epoch length. The bottleneck appears to be the access to LogCabin: snapshotting the epoch takes about 400us on average (with a LogCabin instance on the leader's node). The policy takes a similar amount, as it needs to perform one access to the LogCabin cluster as well, in order to check version numbers. Sending out plans is a small fraction, and scales linearly to the coordination group size.

For followers, the execution time is currently dominated by receiving, decoding and applying the instructions of the plan (which grows with the number of key-value pairs). It is likely that a better plan format could reduce these overheads. Neither sampling the JVM nor communicating Key-Value pairs to the JVM appear to be a substantial bottleneck.

6.4.4 Overhead

To determine the overhead of Taurus, we used the Dacapo benchmarks [22] (we chose the subset that worked correctly with OpenJDK 7). We compare the performance degradation both for followers and leaders. Taurus does not introduce substantial overheads, at most 3.0% (Figure 17). Given that JVMs are known to be sensitive to changes in the environment and that we introduce many such changes (e.g., adding an agent, using management interfaces, changing the sampling interval), we believe most of the differences in performance to be noise (e.g., the speed-up for pmd).

7. Related Work

There has been a large amount of work on GC – Jones and Lins [40] provide a comprehensive survey. Recently, there has been renewed interest in GC in the Big Data setting [31, 33, 45, 46, 54]. Proposed solutions range from approaches similar to our request steering [15, 31, 55, 56, 62] to region-based memory management for avoiding GC [33, 50], to specialized collectors [32, 61]. Our approach is different in that we provide a general mechanism to implement many of these approaches, instead of a new approach in itself.

The Holistic Runtime System has similarities to previous work on Distributed JVMs [20, 21, 47, 70, 71]. However, these JVMs are targeted at monolithic applications, not distributed workloads. There are also projects that share some of our goals: Forseti [24] investigates holistic heap sizing. The MVM [41] looked at running multiple applications in the same JVM. A^2-VM [59] cooperatively schedules Java applications across machines, making the JVM and its services resource-aware to enable cluster-wide thread scheduling based on policies (which bear some resemblance to Taurus's policies). Finally, Terracotta [23] deploys Java applications across JVMs through clustering. The last two differ from Taurus in that they provide a platform for writing distributed workloads rather than a transparent support layer.

Taurus also has similarities with work on cluster schedulers [36, 58]. While they schedule and coordinate workloads as well, they do so at a much coarser granularity. However, it is possible that a system such as Taurus could eventually be integrated into the cluster scheduler, to reuse its available information and failover mechanisms.

8. Future Work and Conclusion

We presented the design of a Holistic Runtime System to coordinate distributed applications in data centers. We introduced Taurus, a prototype of such a system that can be used to coordinate GC. Taurus is a JVM drop-in replacement, runs unmodified real-world applications, requires no modifications to the underlying runtime system and provides a simple DSL to implement policies. Our goal is to enable developers to implement their own policies and use Taurus as a research vehicle for exploring coordination strategies.

We believe that Taurus can be used beyond GC. Specifically, it could be used for distributed monitoring and profiling, coordinating code generation and reducing interference between JVMs. It would also be possible to integrate Taurus with other runtime systems than the JVM, to coordinate workloads across different programming languages.

Acknowledgements

We would like to thank Michael Armbrust, Peter Kessler, Kay Ousterhout, Philip Reames, Mario Wolczko, Reynold Xin and the anonymous reviewers for their feedback on this and earlier versions of this work. Thanks are owed to Peter Bailis for pointing out the snitch mechanism in Cassandra, and to Daniel Goodman for coining the term "Stop-the-Universe".

Precursor work was done at Oracle Labs, Cambridge. Research at UC Berkeley was partially funded by DARPA Award Number HR0011-12-2-0016, DOE grant #DE-AC02-05CH11231, the Center for Future Architecture Research, a member of STARnet, a Semiconductor Research Corporation program sponsored by MARCO and DARPA, and ASPIRE Lab industrial sponsors and affiliates Intel, Google, Huawei, LG, NVIDIA, Oracle, and Samsung. Any opinions, findings, conclusions, or recommendations in this paper are solely those of the authors and do not necessarily reflect the position or the policy of the sponsors.

Martin Maas, the first author, is dedicating this paper to his newlywed wife Yucy. "Taurus" is her zodiac sign.

References

[1] "The Apache Cassandra Project." [Online]. Available: http://cassandra.apache.org/

[2] "Apache Harmony." [Online]. Available: http://harmony.apache.org/

[3] "ART vs Dalvik - introducing the new Android runtime in KitKat." [Online]. Available: http://www.infinum.co/the-capsized-eight/articles/art-vs-dalvik-introducing-the-new-android-runtime-in-kit-kat

[4] "Credit Suisse Case Study." [Online]. Available: http://www.azulsystems.com/customers/creditsuisse

[5] "G1: One Garbage Collector To Rule Them All." [Online]. Available: http://www.infoq.com/articles/G1-One-Garbage-Collector-To-Rule-Them-All

[6] "Garbage Collection Notifications." [Online]. Available: https://msdn.microsoft.com/en-us/library/cc713687(v=vs.110).aspx

[7] "Google App Engine: Platform as a Service."

[8] "Hack: a new programming language for HHVM." [Online]. Available: https://code.facebook.com/posts/264544830379293/hack-a-new-programming-language-for-hhvm/

[9] "HDFS Issue 7244: "Reduce Namenode memory using Flyweight pattern"." [Online]. Available: https://issues.apache.org/jira/browse/HDFS-7244

[10] "Inside .NET Native (Channel 9)." [Online]. Available: http://channel9.msdn.com/Shows/Going+Deep/Inside-NET-Native

[11] "JSR-000121 Application Isolation API Specification." [Online]. Available: https://jcp.org/aboutJava/communityprocess/final/jsr121/

[12] "LogCabin (GitHub)." [Online]. Available: http://github.com/logcabin/logcabin

[13] "Microsoft Windows Azure." [Online]. Available: http://www.windowsazure.com/

[14] "On Garbage Collection." [Online]. Available: http://hhvm.com/blog/431/on-garbage-collection

[15] "Predictable Low Latency: "Cinnober on GC pause-free Java applications through orchestrated memory management"," Tech. Rep. [Online]. Available: http://www.cinnober.com/sites/cinnober.com/files/news/Cinnober%20on%20GC%20pause%20free%20Java%20applications.pdf

[16] "Project Tungsten: Bringing Spark Closer to Bare Metal." [Online]. Available: https://databricks.com/blog/2015/04/28/project-tungsten-bringing-spark-closer-to-bare-metal.html

[17] "Twitter Shifting More Code to JVM, Citing Performance and Encapsulation As Primary Drivers." [Online]. Available: http://www.infoq.com/articles/twitter-java-use

[18] "ZooKeeper SessionExpired events," in *Apache HBase Reference Guide.* Apache HBase Team. [Online]. Available: http://hbase.apache.org/book.html

[19] O. Anderson, E. Fortuna, L. Ceze, and S. Eggers, "Checked Load: Architectural Support for JavaScript Type-checking on Mobile Processors," in *Proceedings of the 2011 IEEE 17th International Symposium on High Performance Computer Architecture*, 2011.

[20] J. Andersson, S. Weber, E. Cecchet, C. Jensen, and V. Cahill, "Kaffemik - a Distributed JVM Featuring a Single Address Space Architecture," in *Proceedings of the 2001 Symposium on Java Virtual Machine Research and Technology Symposium*, 2001.

[21] Y. Aridor, M. Factor, and A. Teperman, "cJVM: A single system image of a JVM on a cluster," in *Proceedings of the 1999 International Conference on Parallel Processing*, 1999.

[22] S. M. Blackburn, R. Garner, C. Hoffman, A. M. Khan, K. S. McKinley, R. Bentzur, A. Diwan, D. Feinberg, D. Frampton, S. Z. Guyer, M. Hirzel, A. Hosking, M. Jump, H. Lee, J. E. B. Moss, A. Phansalkar, D. Stefanović, T. VanDrunen, D. von Dincklage, and B. Wiedermann, "The DaCapo Benchmarks: Java Benchmarking Development and Analysis," in *Proceedings of the 21st Annual ACM SIGPLAN Conference on Object-Oriented Programing, Systems, Languages, and Applications*, 2006.

[23] J. Bonér and E. Kuleshov, "Clustering the Java Virtual Machine using Aspect-Oriented Programming," in *Proceedings of the 6th International Conference on Aspect-Oriented Software Development*, 2007.

[24] C. Cameron, J. Singer, and D. Vengerov, "The Judgment of Forseti: Economic Utility for Dynamic Heap Sizing of Multiple Runtimes," in *Proceedings of the 2015 ACM SIGPLAN International Symposium on Memory Management*, 2015.

[25] T. Cao, S. M. Blackburn, T. Gao, and K. S. McKinley, "The Yin and Yang of Power and Performance for Asymmetric Hardware and Managed Software," in *Proceedings of the 39th Annual International Symposium on Computer Architecture*, 2012.

[26] D. Cheriton, "The V Distributed System," *Commun. ACM*, vol. 31, no. 3, pp. 314–333, Mar. 1988.

[27] J. A. Colmenares, G. Eads, S. Hofmeyr, S. Bird, M. Moretó, D. Chou, B. Gluzman, E. Roman, D. B. Bartolini, N. Mor, K. Asanović, and J. D. Kubiatowicz, "Tessellation: Refactoring the OS Around Explicit Resource Containers with Continuous

Adaptation," in *Proceedings of the 50th Annual Design Automation Conference*, 2013.

[28] B. F. Cooper, A. Silberstein, E. Tam, R. Ramakrishnan, and R. Sears, "Benchmarking Cloud Serving Systems with YCSB," in *Proceedings of the 1st ACM Symposium on Cloud Computing*, 2010.

[29] G. DeCandia, D. Hastorun, M. Jampani, G. Kakulapati, A. Lakshman, A. Pilchin, S. Sivasubramanian, P. Vosshall, and W. Vogels, "Dynamo: Amazon's Highly Available Key-value Store," in *Proceedings of Twenty-first ACM SIGOPS Symposium on Operating Systems Principles*, 2007.

[30] C. Delimitrou and C. Kozyrakis, "Quasar: Resource-efficient and QoS-aware Cluster Management," in *Proceedings of the 19th International Conference on Architectural Support for Programming Languages and Operating Systems*, 2014.

[31] H. Fan, A. Ramaraju, M. McKenzie, W. Golab, and B. Wong, "Understanding the Causes of Consistency Anomalies in Apache Cassandra," *Proceedings of the VLDB Endowment*, vol. 8, no. 7, 2015.

[32] L. Gidra, G. Thomas, J. Sopena, M. Shapiro, and N. Nguyen, "NumaGiC: A Garbage Collector for Big Data on Big NUMA Machines," in *Proceedings of the Twentieth International Conference on Architectural Support for Programming Languages and Operating Systems*, 2015.

[33] I. Gog, J. Giceva, M. Schwarzkopf, K. Viswani, D. Vytiniotis, G. Ramalingan, M. Costa, D. Murray, S. Hand, and M. Isard, "Broom: sweeping out Garbage Collection from Big Data systems," in *Proceedings of the 15th USENIX/ACM Workshop on Hot Topics in Operating Systems (HotOS 2015)*, 2015.

[34] J. E. Gonzalez, R. S. Xin, A. Dave, D. Crankshaw, M. J. Franklin, and I. Stoica, "GraphX: Graph Processing in a Distributed Dataflow Framework," in *Proceedings of the 11th USENIX Conference on Operating Systems Design and Implementation*, 2014.

[35] T. Harris, M. Maas, and V. J. Marathe, "Callisto: Co-scheduling Parallel Runtime Systems," in *Proceedings of the Ninth European Conference on Computer Systems*, 2014.

[36] B. Hindman, A. Konwinski, M. Zaharia, A. Ghodsi, A. D. Joseph, R. Katz, S. Shenker, and I. Stoica, "Mesos: a platform for fine-grained resource sharing in the data center," in *Proceedings of the 8th USENIX Conference on Networked Systems Design and Implementation*, 2011.

[37] P. Hintjens, "ZeroMQ: The Guide," Tech. Rep., 2010. [Online]. Available: http://zguide.zeromq.org/page:all

[38] G. C. Hunt and J. R. Larus, "Singularity: Rethinking the Software Stack," *SIGOPS Oper. Syst. Rev.*, vol. 41, no. 2, pp. 37–49, Apr. 2007.

[39] P. Hunt, M. Konar, F. P. Junqueira, and B. Reed, "ZooKeeper: Wait-free Coordination for Internet-scale Systems," in *Proceedings of the 2010 USENIX Annual Technical Conference*, 2010.

[40] R. Jones and R. Lins, *Garbage Collection: Algorithms for Automatic Dynamic Memory Management*. Wiley, Sep. 1996.

[41] M. Jordan, L. Daynès, G. Czajkowski, M. Jarzab, and C. Bryce, "Scaling J2EE Application Servers with the Multi-tasking Virtual Machine," Sun Microsystems, Inc., Mountain View, CA, USA, Tech. Rep., 2004.

[42] M. Kornacker, A. Behm, V. Bittorf, T. Bobrovytsky, C. Ching, A. Choi, J. Erickson, M. Grund, D. Hecht, M. Jacobs, I. Joshi, L. Kuff, D. Kumar, A. Leblang, N. Li, I. Pandis, H. Robinson, D. Rorke, S. Rus, J. Russell, D. Tsirogiannis, S. Wanderman-Milne, and M. Yoder, "Impala: A modern, open-source SQL engine for hadoop," in *Seventh Biennial Conference on Innovative Data Systems Research*, 2015.

[43] M. A. Laurenzano, Y. Zhang, L. Tang, and J. Mars, "Protean Code: Achieving Near-Free Online Code Transformations for Warehouse Scale Computers," in *Proceedings of the 47th Annual IEEE/ACM International Symposium on Microarchitecture*, 2014.

[44] E. D. Lazowska, H. M. Levy, G. T. Almes, M. J. Fischer, R. J. Fowler, and S. C. Vestal, "The Architecture of the Eden System," in *Proceedings of the Eighth ACM Symposium on Operating Systems Principles*, 1981.

[45] M. Maas, K. Asanovic, T. Harris, and J. Kubiatowicz, "The Case for the Holistic Language Runtime System," in *First International Workshop on Rack-scale Computing (WRSC '14)*, 2014.

[46] M. Maas, T. Harris, K. Asanovic, and J. Kubiatowicz, "Trash Day: Coordinating Garbage Collection in Distributed Systems," in *Proceedings of the 15th USENIX/ACM Workshop on Hot Topics in Operating Systems (HotOS 2015)*, 2015.

[47] M. Maas and R. McIlroy, "A JVM for the Barrelfish Operating System," in *2nd Workshop on Systems for Future Multi-core Architectures (SFMA '12)*, 2012.

[48] L. A. Meyerovich and A. S. Rabkin, "Empirical Analysis of Programming Language Adoption," in *Proceedings of the 2013 ACM SIGPLAN International Conference on Object Oriented Programming Systems Languages & Applications*, 2013.

[49] S. Mullender, G. van Rossum, A. Tananbaum, R. van Renesse, and H. van Staveren, "Amoeba: a distributed

operating system for the 1990s," *Computer*, vol. 23, no. 5, pp. 44–53, May 1990.

[50] K. Nguyen, K. Wang, Y. Bu, L. Fang, J. Hu, and G. Xu, "FACADE: A Compiler and Runtime for (Almost) Object-Bounded Big Data Applications," in *Proceedings of the Twentieth International Conference on Architectural Support for Programming Languages and Operating Systems*, 2015.

[51] D. Ongaro and J. Ousterhout, "In Search of an Understandable Consensus Algorithm," in *Proceedings of the 2014 USENIX Annual Technical Conference*, 2014.

[52] J. Ousterhout, P. Agrawal, D. Erickson, C. Kozyrakis, J. Leverich, D. Mazières, S. Mitra, A. Narayanan, G. Parulkar, M. Rosenblum, S. M. Rumble, E. Stratmann, and R. Stutsman, "The Case for RAMClouds: Scalable High-performance Storage Entirely in DRAM," *SIGOPS Oper. Syst. Rev.*, vol. 43, no. 4, pp. 92–105, Jan. 2010.

[53] J. K. Ousterhout, A. R. Cherenson, F. Douglis, M. N. Nelson, and B. B. Welch, "The Sprite Network Operating System," *Computer*, vol. 21, no. 2, pp. 23–36, Feb. 1988.

[54] K. Ousterhout, R. Rasti, S. Ratnasamy, S. Shenker, and B.-G. Chun, "Making Sense of Performance in Data Analytics Frameworks," in *12th USENIX Symposium on Networked Systems Design and Implementation (NSDI 15)*, 2015.

[55] A. Portillo-Dominguez, M. Wang, J. Murphy, and D. Magoni, "Adaptive GC-Aware Load Balancing Strategy for High-Assurance Java Distributed Systems," in *16th International Symposium on High Assurance Systems Engineering (HASE)*, 2015.

[56] A. O. Portillo-Domínguez, M. Wang, D. Magoni, P. Perry, and J. Murphy, "Load balancing of Java applications by forecasting garbage collections," 2014.

[57] M. Schwarzkopf, M. P. Grosvenor, and S. Hand, "New Wine in Old Skins: The Case for Distributed Operating Systems in the Data Center," in *Proceedings of the 4th Asia-Pacific Workshop on Systems*, 2013.

[58] M. Schwarzkopf, A. Konwinski, M. Abd-El-Malek, and J. Wilkes, "Omega: flexible, scalable schedulers for large compute clusters," in *Proceedings of the 8th European Conference on Computer Systems*, 2013.

[59] J. Simão, J. Lemos, and L. Veiga, "A2-VM : A Cooperative Java VM with Support for Resource-Awareness and Cluster-Wide Thread Scheduling," in *On the Move to Meaningful Internet Systems: OTM 2011*, ser. Lecture Notes in Computer Science, 2011.

[60] D. Smiley and D. E. Pugh, *Apache Solr 3 Enterprise Search Server*. Packt Publishing Ltd, 2011.

[61] G. Tene, B. Iyengar, and M. Wolf, "C4: The Continuously Concurrent Compacting Collector," in *Proceedings of the International Symposium on Memory Management*, 2011.

[62] D. Terei and A. Levy, "Blade: A Data Center Garbage Collector," *arXiv:1504.02578 [cs]*, Apr. 2015, arXiv: 1504.02578.

[63] D. Tsafrir, Y. Etsion, D. G. Feitelson, and S. Kirkpatrick, "System Noise, OS Clock Ticks, and Fine-grained Parallel Applications," in *Proceedings of the 19th Annual International Conference on Supercomputing*, 2005.

[64] K. Varda, *Protocol buffers: Google's data interchange format*, 2008.

[65] N. Wakart, "Correcting YCSB's Coordinated Omission problem," Mar. 2015. [Online]. Available: http://psy-lob-saw.blogspot.com/2015/03/fixing-ycsb-coordinated-omission.html

[66] T. White, *Hadoop: The Definitive Guide: The Definitive Guide*. O'Reilly Media, 2009.

[67] R. S. Xin, J. Rosen, M. Zaharia, M. J. Franklin, S. Shenker, and I. Stoica, "Shark: SQL and Rich Analytics at Scale," in *Proceedings of the 2013 ACM SIGMOD International Conference on Management of Data*, 2013.

[68] M. Zaharia, M. Chowdhury, M. J. Franklin, S. Shenker, and I. Stoica, "Spark: Cluster Computing with Working Sets," in *Proceedings of the 2nd USENIX Conference on Hot Topics in Cloud Computing*, 2010.

[69] M. Zaharia, T. Das, H. Li, S. Shenker, and I. Stoica, "Discretized Streams: An Efficient and Fault-tolerant Model for Stream Processing on Large Clusters," in *Proceedings of the 4th USENIX Conference on Hot Topics in Cloud Ccomputing*, 2012.

[70] W. Zhu, C.-L. Wang, and F. Lau, "JESSICA2: a distributed Java Virtual Machine with transparent thread migration support," in *Proceedings of the IEEE International Conference on Cluster Computing*, 2002.

[71] J. N. Zigman and R. Sankaranarayana, "dJVM-A distributed JVM on a Cluster," Australian National University, Tech. Rep., 2002.

HCloud: Resource-Efficient Provisioning in Shared Cloud Systems

Christina Delimitrou
Stanford University & Cornell University
cdel@stanford.edu

Christos Kozyrakis
Stanford University & EPFL
kozyraki@stanford.edu

Abstract

Cloud computing promises flexibility and high performance for users and cost efficiency for operators. To achieve this, cloud providers offer instances of different sizes, both as long-term reservations and short-term, on-demand allocations. Unfortunately, determining the best provisioning strategy is a complex, multi-dimensional problem that depends on the load fluctuation and duration of incoming jobs, and the performance unpredictability and cost of resources.

We first compare the two main provisioning strategies (reserved and on-demand resources) on Google Compute Engine (GCE) using three representative workload scenarios with batch and latency-critical applications. We show that either approach is suboptimal for performance or cost. We then present HCloud, a hybrid provisioning system that uses both reserved and on-demand resources. HCloud determines which jobs should be mapped to reserved versus on-demand resources based on overall load, and resource unpredictability. It also determines the optimal instance size an application needs to satisfy its Quality of Service (QoS) constraints. We demonstrate that hybrid configurations improve performance by 2.1x compared to fully on-demand provisioning, and reduce cost by 46% compared to fully reserved systems. We also show that hybrid strategies are robust to variation in system and job parameters, such as cost and system load.

Categories and Subject Descriptors: Computer systems organization [*Distributed architectures*]: Cloud computing

Keywords: datacenter; provisioning; QoS; latency; resource efficiency; hybrid; cloud computing

ASPLOS '16, April 02 - 06, 2016, Atlanta, GA, USA

ISBN 978-1-4503-4091-5/16/04...$15.00
DOI: `http://dx.doi.org/10.1145/2872362.2872365`

1. Introduction

An increasing amount of computing is now hosted in public clouds, such as Amazon's EC2 [1], Windows Azure [65] and Google Compute Engine [24]. Cloud platforms provide two major advantages for end-users and cloud operators: *flexibility* and *cost efficiency* [7,8,29]. Users can quickly launch jobs without the overhead of setting up a new infrastructure every time. Cloud operators can achieve economies of scale by building large-scale datacenters (DCs) and by sharing their resources between multiple users and workloads.

Users need to provision resources along two dimensions; first they must decide between *reserved* and *on-demand* resources. *Reserved resources* are dedicated for long periods of time (typically 1-3 years [1]) and offer consistent service, but come at a significant upfront cost. In the other extreme are *on-demand resources*, which are progressively obtained as they become necessary. The user pays only for resources used at each point, however, the per hour cost is 2-3x higher compared to reserved resources, and acquiring new instances induces instantiation overheads. Second, users must determine the *amount of resources* (instance size) an application needs. While dedicated machines provide more predictable performance they come at a high cost. On the other hand, smaller instances are prone to external interference, resulting in unpredictable quality of service. In this paper we present a provisioning system that navigates these trade-offs.

Since provisioning must determine the necessary resources, it is important to understand the extent of this unpredictability. Performance varies both across instances of the same type (spatial variability), and within a single instance over time (temporal variability) [6, 23, 32, 34, 38, 42, 50, 51, 53, 56, 64]. Figure 1 shows the variability in performance for a Hadoop job running a recommender system using Mahout [41] on various instance types on Amazon EC2 [1] and on Google Compute Engine (GCE) [24]. Analytics such as Hadoop and Spark [67] are throughput-bound applications, therefore performance here corresponds to the completion time of the job. The instances are ordered from smallest to largest, with respect to the number of virtual CPUs and memory allocations they provide. We show 1 vCPU `micro`, 1-8 vCPU standard (`stX`) and 16 vCPU memory-optimized

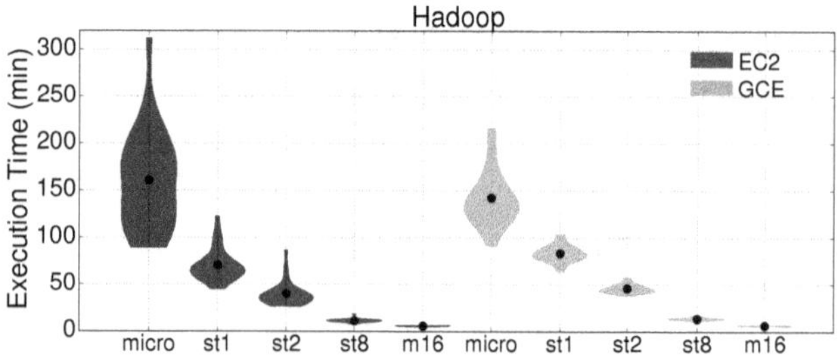

Figure 1: Performance unpredictability on Amazon EC2 and Google Compute Engine for a Hadoop job.

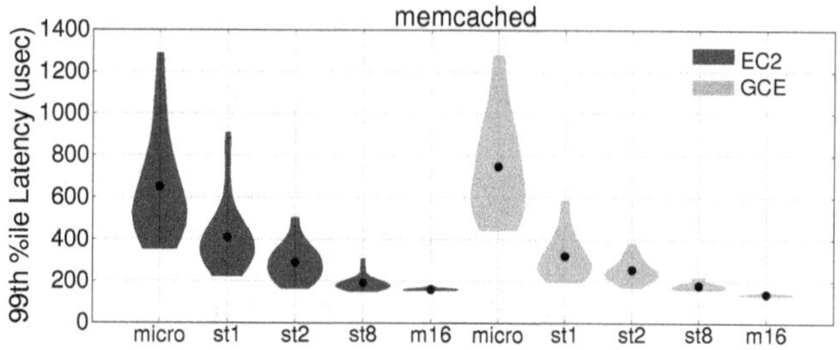

Figure 2: Performance unpredictability on Amazon EC2 and Google Compute Engine for memcached.

Configuration	Cost	Perf. unpredictability	Spin-up	Flexibility	Typical usage
Reserved	High upfront, low per hour	no	no	no	long-term
On-demand	No upfront, high per hour	yes	yes	yes	short-term
Hybrid	Medium upfront, medium per hour	low	some	yes	long-term

Table 1: Comparison of system configurations with respect to: cost, performance unpredictability, overhead and flexibility.

instances (`mX`) [1, 24]. Each graph is the violin plot of completion time of the Hadoop job over 40 instances of the corresponding type. The dot shows the mean performance for each instance type. It becomes clear that especially for instances with less than 8 vCPUs unpredictability is significant, while for the micro instances in EC2 several jobs fail to complete due to the internal EC2 scheduler terminating the VM. For the larger instances (`m16`), performance is more predictable, primarily due to the fact that these instances typically occupy a large fraction of the server, hence they have a much lower probability of suffering from interference from co-scheduled workloads, excluding potential network interference. Between the two cloud providers, EC2 achieves higher average performance than GCE, but exhibits worse tail performance (higher unpredictability).

Figure 2 shows a similar experiment for a latency-critical service (memcached) on the same instance types. Note that the number of memcached clients is scaled by the number of vCPUs of each instance type, to ensure that all instances operate at a similar system load. Unpredictability is even more pronounced now, as memcached needs to satisfy tail latency guarantees [14], as opposed to average performance. The results from above hold, with the smaller instances (less than 8 vCPUs) experiencing significant variability in their tail latency. Performance jitter decreases again for the 8-16 vCPU VMs, especially in the case of the memory-optimized instances (`m16`). Additionally GCE now achieves better average and tail performance compared to EC2.

The goal of this work is to optimize *performance over cost for cloud systems*, similarly to the way work on system design and resource management optimized performance per Watt for small- and large-scale systems [36, 37, 60, 61, 71]. We first explore the implications of the two main provisioning approaches (reserved and on-demand resources), with respect to performance variability and cost efficiency. We perform this analysis on Google Compute Engine (GCE) [24] using three representative workload scenarios with batch and latency-critical applications, and increasing levels of load variability. We assume no a priori knowledge of the applications in each scenario, except for the minimum and maximum aggregate load, which is needed for a comparison with an idealized statically-reserved provisioning strategy. Our study reveals that while reserved resources are superior with respect to performance (2.2x on average over on-demand), they require a long-term commitment, and are therefore suitable for use cases over extended periods of time. Fully on-demand resources, on the other hand, are more cost-efficient for short-term use cases (2.5x on average), but are prone to performance unpredictability, because of instantiation overheads and external interference. We show that to achieve reasonable performance predictability with either strategy, it is crucial to understand the resource preferences and sensitivity to interference of individual applications [21, 43, 54]. Recent work has shown that a combination of lightweight profiling and classification-based analysis can provide accurate estimations of job preferences with respect to the different instance types, the sensitivity to interference in shared resources, and the amount of resources needed to satisfy a job's performance constraints [21].

Next, we design HCloud, a *hybrid provisioning system* that uses both reserved (long-term) and on-demand (short-term) resources. Hybrid provisioning strategies can offer the best of both worlds by leveraging reserved resources for the steady long-term load, and on-demand resources for short-term resource needs. The main challenge with hybrid provisioning is determining how many/what resources to obtain and how to schedule jobs between reserved and on-demand resources. Table 1 shows the differences between the three provisioning strategies with respect to *cost, performance unpredictability, instantiation overheads* and *provisioning flexibility*.

We demonstrate that by quickly determining the resource preferences of new jobs, and accounting for system load and instance characteristics, hybrid provisioning strategies improve both resource efficiency and QoS-awareness. They maximize the usage of the already-provisioned reserved resources, while ensuring that applications that can tolerate some performance unpredictability will not delay the scheduling of interference-sensitive workloads. We also compare the performance, cost and provisioning needs of hybrid systems against fully reserved and fully on-demand strategies over a wide spectrum of workload scenarios. Hybrid strategies achieve within 8% of the performance of fully reserved systems (and 2.1x better than on-demand systems), while improving their cost efficiency by 46%. Reserved resources are utilized at 80% on average in steady-state. Finally, we perform a detailed sensitivity analysis of performance and cost with job parameters, such as duration, and system parameters, such as pricing, and load.

2. Cloud Workloads and Systems

2.1 Workload Scenarios

We examine the three scenarios shown in Figure 3 and summarized in Table 2. Each scenario consists of a mix of batch (Hadoop workloads running over Mahout [41] and Spark jobs) and latency-critical workloads (memcached). This mix corresponds to what most online services consist of today, by servicing user requests and analyzing data in the background. The batch jobs are machine learning and data mining applications, including recommender systems, support vector machines, and matrix factorization. memcached is driven with loads that differ with respect to the read:write request ratio, the size of requests, the inter-arrival time distribution, the client fanout and the dataset size.

The first scenario has minimal load variability (*Static*). In steady-state the aggregate resource requirements are 854 cores. Approximately 55% of cores service batch jobs and the remaining 45% latency-critical services. The difference between maximum and minimum load is 10% and most jobs last several minutes to a few tens of minutes.

Second, we examine a scenario with mild, long-term load variability (*Low Variability*). The steady-state minimum load requires on average 605 cores, while in the middle of the scenario the load increases to 900 cores. The surge is mostly caused by an increase in the load of the latency-critical applications. On average 55% of cores are needed for batch jobs and the remaining 45% for the latency-critical services.

Finally, we examine a scenario with large, short-term load changes (*High Variability*). The minimum load drops at 210 cores, while the maximum load reaches up to 1226 cores for short time periods. Approximately 60% of cores are needed

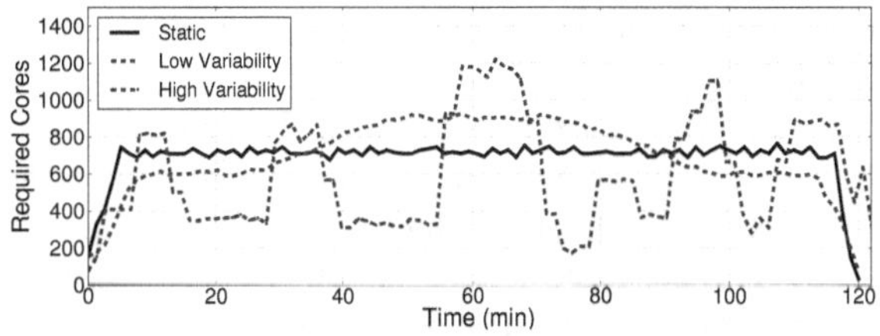

Figure 3: The three workload scenarios.

	Workload Scenarios		
	Static	Low Var	High Var
max:min resources ratio	1.1x	1.5x	6.2x
batch:low-latency – in jobs	4.2x	3.6x	4.1x
– in cores	1.4x	1.4x	1.5x
inter-arrival times (sec)	1.0	1.0	1.0
ideal completion time (hr)	2.1	2.0	2.0

Table 2: Workload scenario characteristics.

for batch jobs and 40% for the latency-critical services. Because of the increased load variability, each individual job is shorter (8.1 min duration on average).

The ideal duration for each scenario, with no scheduling delays or degradation due to interference, is 2 hours.

2.2 Cloud Instances

We use servers on Google Compute Engine (GCE) for all experiments. For provisioning strategies that require smaller instances we start with the largest instances (16 vCPUs) and partition them using Linux containers [5, 13]. The reason for constructing smaller instances as server slices as opposed to directly requesting various instance types is to introduce controlled external interference which corresponds to typical load patterns seen in cloud environments, rather than the random interference patterns present at the specific time we ran each experiment. This ensures *repeatable experiments* and *consistent comparisons* between provisioning strategies.

We model interference by imposing external load that fluctuates $\pm 10\%$ around a 25% utilization [8, 21]. The load is generated by both batch and latency-critical workloads. Section 5.1 includes a sensitivity study to the external load.

We only partition servers at the granularity of existing GCE instances, e.g., 1,2,4,8 and 16 vCPUs. Whenever we refer to the cost of an on-demand instance, we quote the cost of the instance that would be used in the real environment, e.g., a 2 vCPU instance. Similarly, we account for the spin-up overhead of the instance of the desired size, wherever applicable. Finally, all scheduling actions, such as autoscale and VM migration performed by GCE are disabled.

2.3 Cloud Pricing

Google Compute Engine currently only offers on-demand instances. To encourage high instance usage, it provides sustained usage monthly discounts [24]. Although discounts reduce the prices of on-demand instances, they do not approximate the price of long-term reserved resources. The most popular alternative pricing model is the one used by AWS, which includes both long-term resource reservations and short-term on-demand instances. Because this pricing model offers more provisioning flexibility and captures the largest fraction of the cloud market today, we use it to evaluate the different provisioning strategies. Specifically, we approximate the cost of reserved resources on GCE based on the reserved to on-demand price ratio for EC2, adjusted to the prices of GCE. In Section 5.3 we discuss how our results translate to different pricing models, such as the default GCE model and the pricing model used by Windows Azure.

3. Provisioning Strategies

The two main cloud resource offerings are *reserved* and *on-demand* resources. Reserved instances require a high upfront investment, but have 2-3x lower per-hour cost than on-demand resources, offer better availability, and consistent performance. On-demand resources are charged in a pay-as-you-go manner, but incur spin-up overheads and performance unpredictability due to external load. We ignore spot instances for this work, since they do not provide any availability guarantees. Both with reserved and on-demand resources, the user must also determine the size and number of acquired instances.

Ideally, a provisioning strategy achieves three goals: (1) *high workload performance*, (2) *high resource utilization (minimal overprovisioning)*, and (3) *minimal provisioning and scheduling overheads*. We initially study the three leftmost provisioning strategies described in Table 3.

3.1 Statically Reserved Resources (SR)

This strategy statically provisions reserved resources for 1 year, the shortest contract for reserved resources on EC2. Reserved resources are readily available as jobs arrive, eliminating the overhead of spinning up new VMs. Because SR only reserves large instances (16 vCPUs), there is limited interference from external load, except potentially for some network interference. Because of its static nature, SR must provision resources for the peak requirements of each scenario, plus a small amount of overprovisioning. Overprovisioning is needed because all scenarios contain latency-critical jobs that experience tail latency spikes when using nearly-saturated resources [7, 8, 14, 35]. We explain the insight behind the amount of overprovisioning in Section 3.3. Peak requirements can be easily estimated for static scenarios. For scenarios with load variability, static provisioning results in significant resource underutilization.

3.2 Dynamic On-Demand Resources (OdF, OdM)

We now examine two strategies that acquire resources as they become necessary. On-demand Full (OdF) only uses large instances (16 vCPUs), which are less prone to external interference (see Section 1). On-demand Mixed (OdM) acquires instances of any size, including smaller instances with 1-8 vCPUs. While OdM offers more flexibility, it suffers from substantial external interference in the smaller instances. There are ways to improve predictability in on-demand provisioning strategies, e.g., by sampling multiple instances for each required instance and only keeping the well-behaved ones [23]. Although this addresses performance variability across instances, it is still prone to temporal variation within a single instance. Additionally, it is only beneficial for long-running jobs that can afford the overhead of sampling multiple instances. Short jobs, such as real-time analytics (100msec-10sec) cannot tolerate long scheduling delays and must rely on the initial resource assignment.

	SR	OdF	OdM	HF	HM
Reserved resources	Yes	No	No	Yes	Yes
On-demand resources	No	Yes (full servers)	Yes	Yes (full servers)	Yes

Table 3: Resource provisioning strategies.

Moreover, each new instance incurs overheads to spin up the new VMs. This is typically 12-19 seconds for GCE, although the 95th percentile of spin-up overheads is 2 minutes. Smaller instances tend to incur higher overheads. Therefore provisioning strategies must also decide how long to retain resources after a job completes. If a workload scenario has no or little load variability, instances should be retained to amortize spin-up overheads. We determine retention time by drawing from work on processor power management. The challenge there is to determine when to switch to low power modes that enable power savings but incur overheads to revert to an active mode [40, 45, 59]. Given that the job inter-arrival time in our scenarios is 1 second, we set the retention time to 10x the spin-up overhead. [1] Section 5.1 shows a sensitivity analysis to retention time. Only instances that provide predictably high performance are retained past the completion of their jobs.

3.3 The Importance of Resource Preferences

Traditionally, end-users have to specify how many resources each job should use; unfortunately this is known to be error-prone and to lead to resource overprovisioning [8, 11, 21, 39, 54]. Moreover, it offers no insight on the sensitivity of each job to interference from other jobs, external or not, running on the same physical server. This is suboptimal for both statically-reserved and on-demand strategies, which may acquire more/fewer resources than needed. SR may colocate jobs that interfere negatively on the same instance. OdF and OdM may acquire instance types that are prone to higher interference than what certain jobs can tolerate.

[1] The benefit of longer retention time varies across instance sizes due to differences in spin-up overheads.

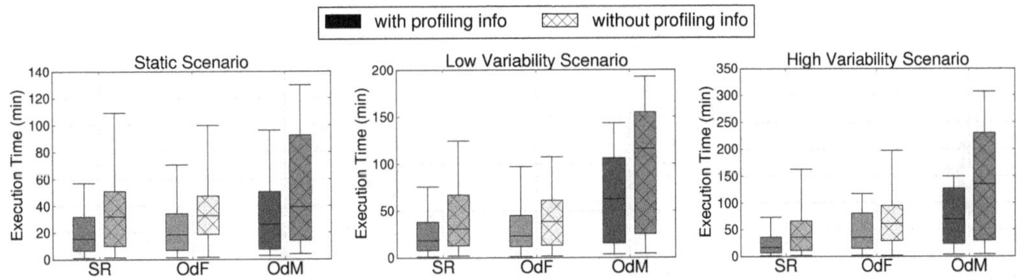

(a) Performance of batch applications for the three scenarios.

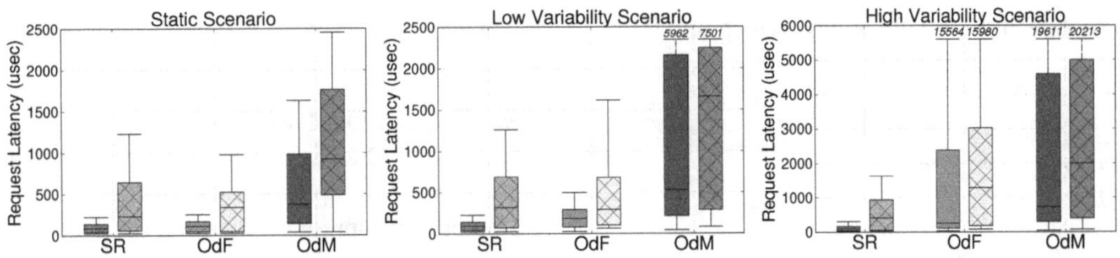

(b) Performance of latency-critical applications for the three scenarios.

Figure 4: Performance of jobs of the three scenarios with the three provisioning strategies. The boundaries of the boxplots depict the 25th and 75th percentiles, the whiskers the 5th and 95th, and the horizontal line in each boxplot shows the mean.

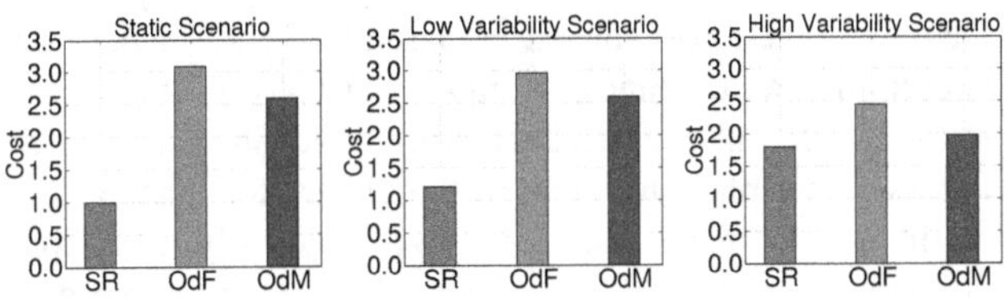

Figure 5: Cost of fully reserved and on-demand systems.

The recently-proposed Quasar cluster manager provides a methodology to quickly determine the resource preferences of new, unknown jobs [21]. When a job is submitted, it is first profiled on two instance types, while injecting interference in two shared resources, e.g., last level cache and network bandwidth. This signal is used by a set of classification techniques which find similarities between the new and previously-scheduled jobs with respect to instance type preferences and sensitivity to interference. A job's sensitivity to interference in resource i is denoted by c_i, where $i \in [1, N]$, and $N = 10$ the number of examined resources [21]. Large c_i values mean that the job puts a lot of pressure in resource i. To capture the fact that certain jobs are more sensitive to specific resources we rearrange vector $C = [c_1, c_2, ..., c_N]$ by order of decreasing magnitude of c_i, $C' = [c_j, c_k, ..., c_n]$. Finally, to obtain a single value for C', we use the order preserving encoding: $Q = c_j \cdot 10^{(2\cdot(N-1))} + c_k \cdot 10^{(2\cdot(N-2))} + ... + c_n$, and normalize Q in $[0, 1]$. Q denotes the resource quality a job needs to satisfy its QoS constraints. High Q denotes a resource-demanding job, while low Q a job that can tolerate some resource interference.

We use Quasar's estimations of resource preferences and interference sensitivity to improve provisioning. For SR, we use these estimations to find the most suitable reserved resources available with respect to size and interference using a simple greedy search [21]. Accounting for resource preferences reduces overprovisioning to 10-15%. For OdF, the estimations are used to select the minimum amount of resources for a job, and to match the resource capabilities of instances to the interference requirements of a job. For OdM, this additionally involves requesting an appropriate instance size and type (standard, compute- or memory-optimized). Note that because smaller instances are prone to external interference, provisioning decisions may have lower accuracy.

Finally, we detect suboptimal application performance and revisit the allocation decisions at runtime [3, 4, 12, 21, 55]. Once a job is scheduled its performance is monitored and compared against its expected QoS. If performance drops below QoS the cluster manager takes action [21]. At a high level, we first try to restore performance through local actions, e.g., increasing the resource allocation on the server where the application already resides, and then through rescheduling. The latter is unlikely in practice.

3.4 Provisioning Strategies Comparison

Performance: We first compare the performance impact of the three provisioning strategies, with and without Quasar's information on job preferences. Figure 4 shows the performance achieved by each of the three strategies for the three workload scenarios. We separate batch (Hadoop, Spark) from latency-critical applications (memcached), since their critical performance metric is different: completion time for

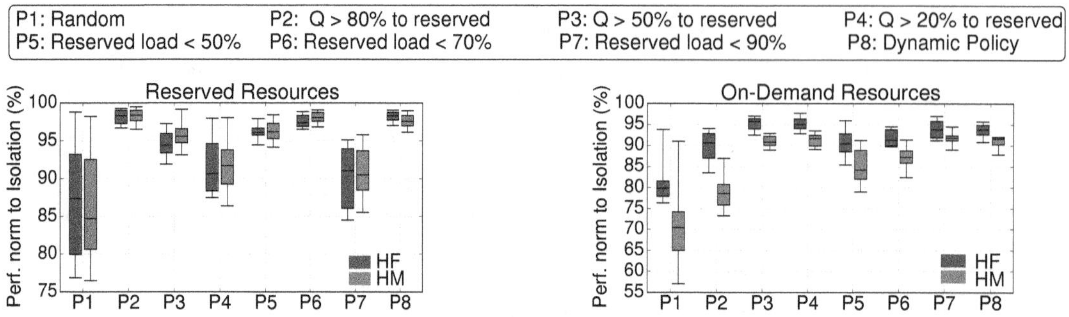

Figure 6: Sensitivity to the policy of mapping jobs to reserved versus on-demand resources for HF and HM.

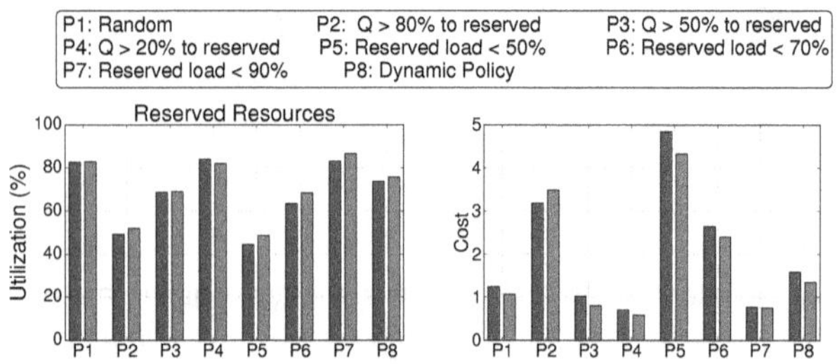

Figure 7: Utilization of reserved resources and cost with different application mapping policies for HF and HM.

the batch jobs and request latency distribution for memcached. The boundaries in each boxplot depict the 25th and 75th percentiles of performance, the whiskers the 5th and 95th percentiles and the horizontal line shows the mean. When Quasar is not used, the resources for each job are sized based on user-defined reservations. For batch jobs (Hadoop and Spark) this translates to using the default framework parameters (e.g., 64KB block size, 1GB heapsize for Hadoop), while for memcached resources are provisioned for peak input load [54]. OdM requests the smallest instance size that satisfies the resource demands of a job. SR allocates resources on the reserved instances with the most available resources (least-loaded).

It is clear from Figure 4 that all three strategies benefit significantly from understanding the jobs' resource preferences and interference sensitivity. Specifically for SR, there is a 2.4x difference in performance on average across scenarios. The differences are even more pronounced for latency-critical jobs, where the performance metric of interest is tail latency. In all following results, we assume that provisioning strategies take job preferences into account, unless otherwise specified.

We now compare the performance achieved by the three provisioning strategies. The static strategy SR achieves the best performance for all three scenarios, both for batch and latency-critical jobs. OdF behaves near-optimally for the static scenario, but worsens for the scenarios where variability is present, primarily due to spin-up overheads to obtain new resources. OdM achieves the worst performance for every scenario (2.2x worse than SR on average), in part because of the spin-up overheads, but primarily because of the performance unpredictability it experiences from external load in the smaller instances. Memcached suffers a 24x and 42x increase in tail latency in the low- and high-variability scenarios, as it is more sensitive to resource interference.

Cost: Figure 5 shows the relative cost of each strategy for the three scenarios. All costs are normalized to the cost of the static scenario with SR. Although strategy SR appears to have the lowest cost for a 2 hour run (2-3x lower per hour charge than on-demand), it requires at least a 1-year commitment with all charges happening in advance. Therefore, unless a user plans to leverage the cluster for long periods of time, on-demand resources are dramatically more cost-efficient. Moreover, SR is not cost effective in the presence of high workload variability, since it results in significant overprovisioning. Between the two on-demand strategies, OdM incurs lower cost, since it uses smaller instances, while OdF only uses the largest instances available. However the cost savings of OdM translate to a significant performance degradation from unpredictability (Figure 4).

4. Hybrid Provisioning Strategies

The previous section showed that neither fully reserved nor fully on-demand strategies are ideal. Hybrid provisioning strategies that combine reserved and on-demand resources have the potential to achieve the best of both worlds. The main challenge now becomes determining which jobs should be scheduled on on-demand versus reserved resources.

4.1 Provisioning Strategies

We design HCloud, a hybrid provisioning system that uses both reserved and on-demand resources, and discuss two strategies HCloud employs. The first strategy (HF) only uses large instances for on-demand resources, to constrain unpredictability. The second strategy (HM), uses a mix of on-demand instance types to reduce cost, including smaller instances that experience interference from external load. The retention time policy for on-demand resources is the same as for the purely on-demand strategies OdF and OdM. The

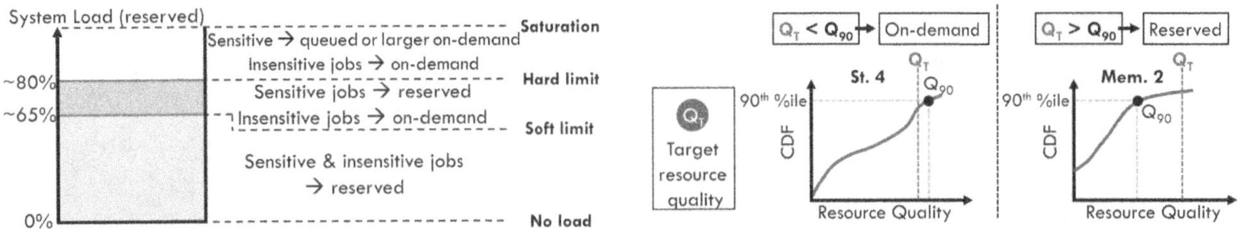

Figure 8: Application mapping scheme between reserved and on-demand instances for HF and HM.

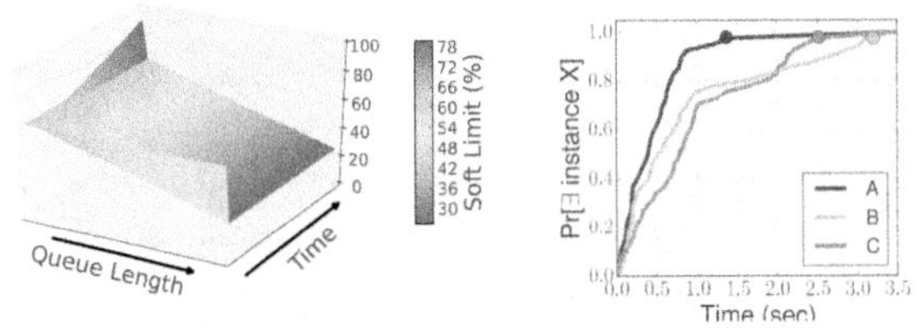

Figure 9: Determining the soft utilization limit (left) and the expected waiting time (right) in HF and HM.

reserved resources are large instances, as with the statically-provisioned strategy. We configure reserved instances to accommodate the minimum steady-state load, e.g., 600 cores for the low variability scenario to avoid overprovisioning. For scenarios with low steady-state load but high load variability the majority of resources are on-demand. Since HF uses large instances for both reserved and on-demand resources, it primarily uses on-demand instances to serve overflow load. In contrast HM can leverage smaller on-demand instances to also accommodate jobs that can tolerate some interference in shared resources.

HCloud addresses two challenges: first, it determines how many resources each incoming job needs to satisfy its QoS, and second, it determines whether a new job should be scheduled on on-demand or reserved resources.

4.2 Application Mapping Policies

We first consider a baseline policy that maps applications between the reserved and on-demand resources randomly using a fair coin. Figure 6 shows the performance of applications mapped to reserved (left) and on-demand resources (right) for the two hybrid strategies in the high variability scenario. Performance is normalized to the performance each job achieves if it runs with unlimited resources in isolation. Figure 7 also shows the utilization of reserved instances and the total cost for the 2 hour scenario normalized to the cost of the static scenario with SR. Because the number of jobs is large, approximately half of them are scheduled on reserved and half on on-demand resources [27]. The random policy hurts performance for jobs mapped to either resource type. In reserved resources, performance degrades as more workloads than the instances can accommodate are assigned to them, and are therefore queued. In on-demand resources, performance degrades for two reasons. First, because on-demand resources introduce instantiation overheads, and, more prominently, because jobs that are sensitive to interference and should have been mapped to reserved resources underperform due to external load.

Ideally, the mapping policy should take into account the sensitivity of jobs to performance unpredictability. The following three policies shown in Figure 6 set a limit to the jobs that should be mapped to reserved resources based on the quality of resources they need. $P2$ assigns jobs that need quality $Q > 80\%$ to the reserved instances to protect them from the variability of on-demand resources. $P3$ and $P4$ set stricter limits, with $P4$ only assigning very tolerant to unpredictability jobs to on-demand resources. As we move from $P2$ to $P4$ the performance of jobs in the on-demand instances improves, as the number of jobs mapped to them decreases. In contrast, the performance of jobs scheduled to reserved resources worsens due to increased demand and queueing delays. In general, performance is worse for HM in on-demand resources, due to the increased performance variability of smaller instances.

It is clear that there needs to be an upper load limit for reserved resources. The next three policies $P5 - P7$ set progressively higher, static limits. For low limits, e.g., 50-70% the performance of jobs on reserved resources is near-optimal. In contrast, jobs assigned to on-demand resources suffer substantial degradations, since job mapping is only determined based on load and not resource preferences. For a utilization limit of 90%, the performance of jobs in reserved resources degrades due to excessive load. Low utilization in reserved resources also increases cost, as additional on-demand instances have to be obtained. Therefore a static utilization limit that does not account for resource preferences of jobs is also suboptimal.

Based on these findings we design a dynamic policy to separate jobs between reserved and on-demand resources. The policy adheres to three principles. First, it utilizes reserved resources before resorting to on-demand resources. Second, applications that can be accommodated by on-demand resources should not delay the scheduling of jobs sensitive to interference. Third, the system must adjust the utilization limits of reserved instances to respond to performance degradations due to excessive queueing.

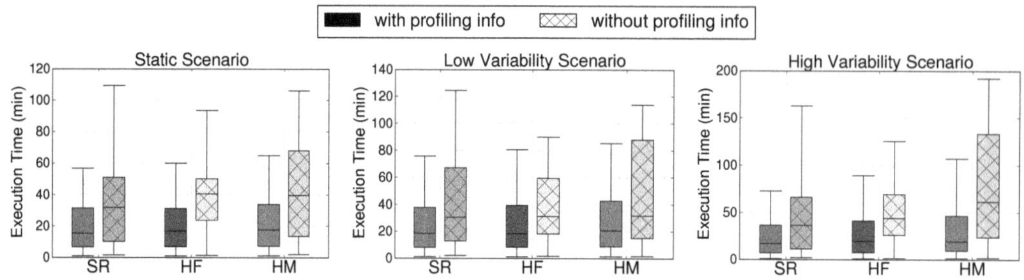

(a) Performance of batch applications for the three scenarios.

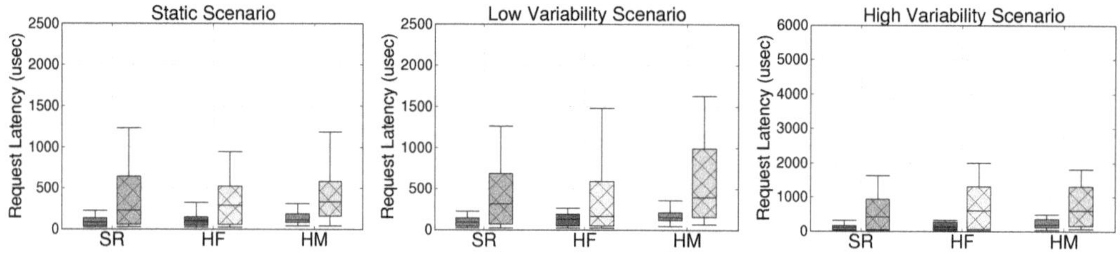

(b) Performance of latency-critical applications for the three scenarios.

Figure 10: Performance of the three scenarios with the statically-reserved and hybrid strategies. The boundaries of the boxplots depict the 25th and 75th percentiles, the whiskers the 5th and 95th percentiles and the horizontal line in each boxplot the mean.

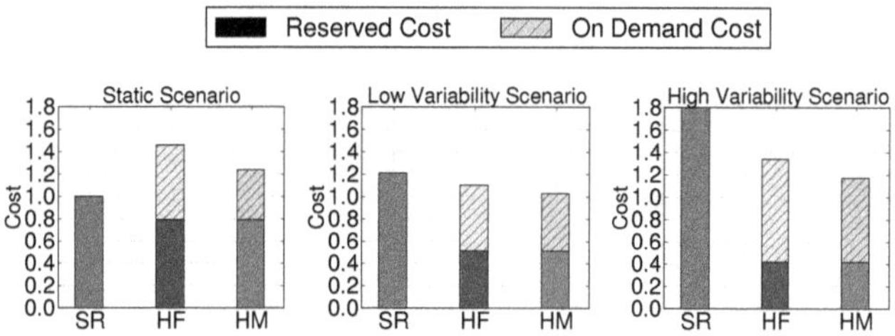

Figure 11: Cost comparison between SR, HF and HM.

Figure 8 explains the dynamic policy. We set two utilization limits for reserved resources. First, a *soft limit* (experimentally set at 60-65% utilization), below which all incoming jobs are allocated reserved resources. Once utilization exceeds this limit, the policy differentiates between jobs that are sensitive to performance unpredictability and insensitive ones. The differentiation is done based on the resource quality Q a job needs to satisfy its QoS constraints and the knowledge on the quality of previously-obtained on-demand instances. Once we determine the instance size a job needs (number of cores, memory and storage), we compare the 90th percentile of quality of that instance type (monitored over time) against the target quality (Q_T) the job needs. If $Q_{90} > Q_T$ the job is scheduled on the on-demand instance, otherwise it is scheduled on the reserved instances. Examining the 90th percentile is sufficient to ensure accurate decisions for the majority of jobs. Tightening this constraint to higher percentiles increases the utilization of reserved resources, and/or the cost from acquiring additional on-demand instances.

Second, we set a *hard limit* for utilization, when jobs need to be queued before reserved resources become available. At this point, any jobs for which on-demand resources are satisfactory are scheduled in on-demand instances and all remaining jobs are locally queued [52]. An exception occurs for jobs whose queueing time would exceed the instantiation overhead of a large on-demand instance (16 vCPUs); these jobs are instead assigned to on-demand instances. Queueing time is estimated using a simple feedback loop based on the rate at which instances of a given type are being released over time. For example, if out of 100 jobs waiting for an instance with 4 vCPUs and 15GB of RAM, 99 were scheduled in less than 1.4 seconds, the system will estimate that there is a 0.99 probability that the queueing time for a job waiting for a 4 vCPU instance will be 1.4 seconds. Figure 9b shows a validation of the estimation of waiting time for three instance types. The lines show the cumulative distribution function (CDF) of the probability that an instance of a given type becomes available. The dots show the estimated queueing time for jobs waiting to be scheduled on instances with 4 (A), 8 (B) and 16 vCPUs (C) in the high variability scenario. In all cases the deviation between estimated and measured queueing time is minimal.

Third, we adjust the soft utilization limit based on the rate at which jobs get queued. If the queued jobs increase sharply, the reserved instances should become more selective in the workloads they accept, i.e., the soft limit should decrease. Similarly, if no jobs get queued for significant periods of time, the soft limit should increase to accept more jobs. We use a simple feedback loop with linear transfer functions to adjust the soft utilization limit of reserved instances as

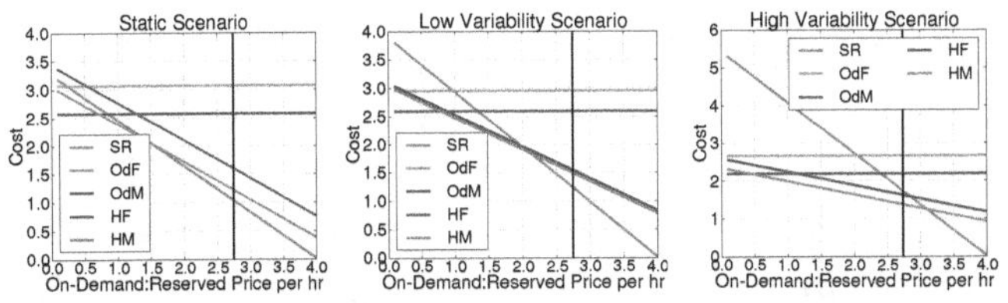

Figure 12: Sensitivity of provisioning cost to on-demand:reserved resource cost.

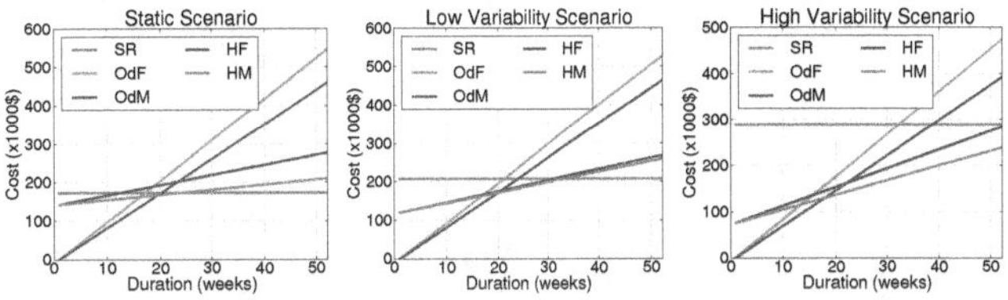

Figure 13: Sensitivity of provisioning cost to workload scenario duration.

a scenario progresses. Figure 9a shows how the soft limit changes with execution time and queue length.

4.3 Provisioning Strategies Comparison

Performance: Figure 10 compares the performance achieved by the static strategy SR and the two hybrid strategies (HF and HM), with and without determining the resource preferences of new jobs. As expected, using the profiling information improves performance significantly for the hybrid strategies, for the additional reason that it is needed to decide which jobs should be scheduled on reserved resources (2.4x improvement on average for HF and 2.77x for HM). When using the profiling information, strategies HF and HM come within 8% of the performance of the statically reserved system (SR), and in most cases outperform strategies OdF and OdM, especially for scenarios with load variability. The main reason is that HF and HM differentiate between jobs that can tolerate the unpredictability of on-demand instances, and jobs that need the predictable performance of a fully controlled environment. Additionally hybrid strategies hide some of the spin-up overhead of on-demand resources by accommodating part of the load in the reserved instances.

Cost: Figure 11 shows the relative cost of strategies SR, HF and HM for the three scenarios. While the static strategy (SR) is more cost-efficient in the static scenario where provisioning is straight-forward, the hybrid strategies incur significantly lower costs for both scenarios with load variability. Therefore, unless load is almost completely static, SR requires high cost, and significant overprovisioning. Additionally, because of the lower per-hour cost of reserved resources in HF and HM, the hybrid strategies have lower per-hour cost than fully on-demand resources as well. For HF and HM, most of the cost per hour comes from on-demand resources, since reserved instances are provisioned for the minimum steady-state load. Finally, between the two hybrid strategies, HM incurs lower cost since it uses smaller instances.

5. HCloud Analysis & Robustness

5.1 Sensitivity to Job & System Parameters

We first evaluate the sensitivity of the previous findings to various system and workload parameters.

Resource cost: The current average cost ratio of on-demand to reserved resources per hour is 2.74. Figure 12 shows how the relative cost of the three scenarios varies when this ratio changes. All costs are normalized to the cost for the static scenario using SR. We change the ratio in $[0.01, 4]$ by scaling the price of reserved resources; beyond that point the cost of SR per hour becomes practically negligible. Initially (0.01), strategies using on-demand resources (OdF, OdM) are significantly more cost-efficient, especially for scenarios with variability. For the static scenario, even when on-demand resources are much cheaper than reserved, SR, HF and HM incur similar charges as the fully on-demand systems. For each scenario, there is a price ratio for which SR becomes the most cost-efficient strategy. As variability increases, this value becomes larger (e.g., for the high variability scenario the ratio must be 3 for SR to be more cost-efficient than HM). Note that SR still requires at least a 1-year commitment, in contrast to on-demand strategies. Finally, the hybrid strategies, HF and HM, achieve the lowest per-hour cost for extended ratio ranges, especially for scenarios with load variability.

Scenario duration: Figure 13 shows the cost of each strategy, as scenario duration increases. Because we compare aggregate costs (instead of per-hour), this figure shows the absolute cost in dollars. For the static scenario, cost-wise, strategy HM is optimal only if duration is $[20 - 25]$ weeks. For durations less than 20 weeks, OdM is the most cost-efficient, while for durations exceeding 25 weeks the statically-reserved system (SR) is optimal. This changes when there is load variability. For the scenario with high variability and durations over 18 weeks, HM is the most cost-efficient strategy, with the significantly overprovisioned reserved system (SR) never being optimal. Note that the charge for SR doubles beyond the 1 year (52 weeks) mark.

Spin-up overhead: Figure 14a shows the 95th percentile of performance for different spin-up overheads in the high variability scenario. The statically-reserved strategy (SR) is not affected by this change. Because in this scenario resources are frequently recycled, increasing the spin-up overheads significantly affects performance. This is more pronounced for strategies using exclusively on-demand resources (OdF, OdM). The additional degradation for OdM comes from the performance unpredictability of smaller instances.

External load: Figure 14b shows the sensitivity of performance to external load (system load due to jobs beyond those

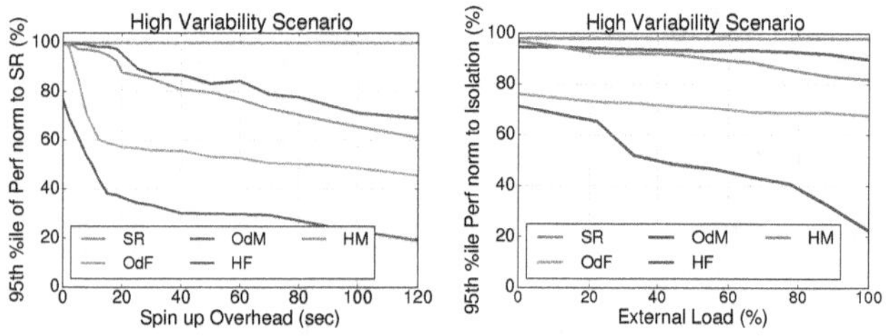

Figure 14: Performance sensitivity to instance spin-up time and external load.

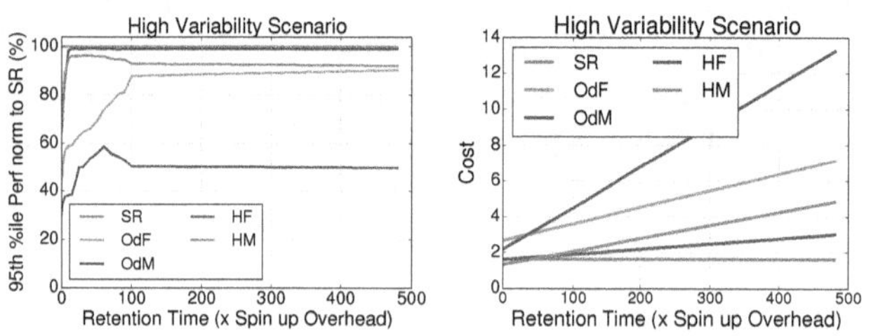

Figure 15: Performance and cost sensitivity to resource retention time.

provisioned with our strategies). SR provisions a reserved system, therefore there is no external load to affect performance. OdF and HF are also tolerant to external load, since they only use large instances, which are less prone to interference. For HM, performance degrades minimally until 50% load, beyond which point the estimations on resource quality become inaccurate. OdM suffers the largest performance degradation since all of its resources are susceptible to external interference.

Retention time: Figure 15 shows the 95th latency percentile and cost for the high variability scenario, as the time for which idle instances are maintained changes. As expected, releasing well-behaved instances immediately hurts performance, since it introduces higher spin-up overheads to acquire new resources. This is especially true here, where load changes frequently. Higher retention time also increases cost for OdF and OdM, while SR remains unchanged; the difference for hybrid strategies is small. An unexpected finding is that excessive resource retention hurts performance slightly for OdM and HM. The primary reason is the temporal variability in the quality of on-demand resources, which degraded by the time new jobs were assigned to them.

Workload characteristics: Figure 16 shows the 95th percentile of performance for the five strategies as the percentage of jobs that are sensitive to interference increases. We modify the high variability scenario used before, such that the number of jobs that cannot tolerate performance unpredictability increases. In the left-most part of the graph, most jobs are batch Hadoop applications, which can tolerate some resource contention; as we move to the right part of the graph

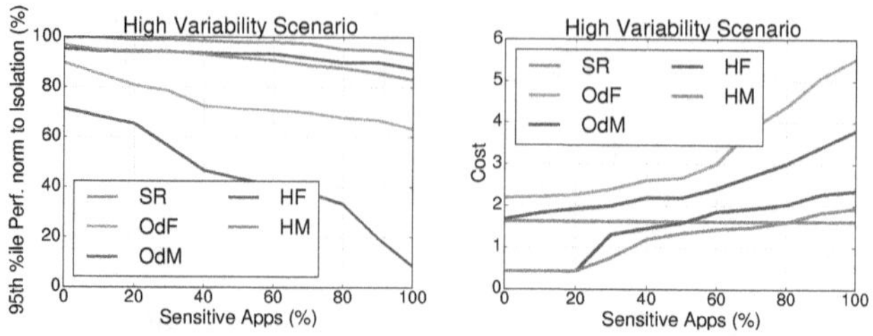

Figure 16: Performance and cost sensitivity to application characteristics.

the majority of jobs are latency-critical memcached applications and real-time Spark jobs.

The statically-provisioned strategy (SR) behaves well even when most applications need resources of high quality, since it is provisioned for peak load, and there is no external load affecting application performance. The two hybrid strategies also behave well, until the fraction of sensitive applications increases beyond 80%, at which point queueing in the reserved resources becomes significant. The purely on-demand strategies are the ones that suffer the most from increasing the fraction of sensitive applications. OdF and especially OdM significantly degrade the performance of scheduled workloads, both due to increased spin-up overheads, and because more applications are now affected by external resource contention.

With respect to cost, increasing the fraction of applications that are sensitive to interference impacts all strategies except for SR. Since HF and HM can use the reserved resources for the sensitive jobs, their cost increases only beyond the 30% mark, at which point more on-demand resources have to be purchased to avoid increased queueing in the reserved resources. The two on-demand strategies experience a significant cost surge, since increasing the fraction of sensitive applications results in a lower degree of co-scheduling and makes acquiring new resources necessary.

5.2 Provisioning Overheads

In the presented strategies, the provisioning overheads include job profiling and classification (Quasar), provisioning decisions, spin-up of new on-demand instances (where applicable), and rescheduling actions. The profiling that generates the input signal for classification takes 5-10 sec, but only needs to happen the first time a job is submitted. Classification itself takes 20msec on average. Decision overheads include the greedy scheduler in the static strategy (SR) and the job mapping policy between reserved and on-demand resources in the hybrid strategies. In all cases decision overheads do not exceed 20msec, three orders of magnitude lower than the spin-up overheads of on-demand instances (10-20sec on average). Finally, job rescheduling due to suboptimal performance is very infrequent for all strategies except OdM, where it induces 6.1% overheads to the execution time of jobs on average.

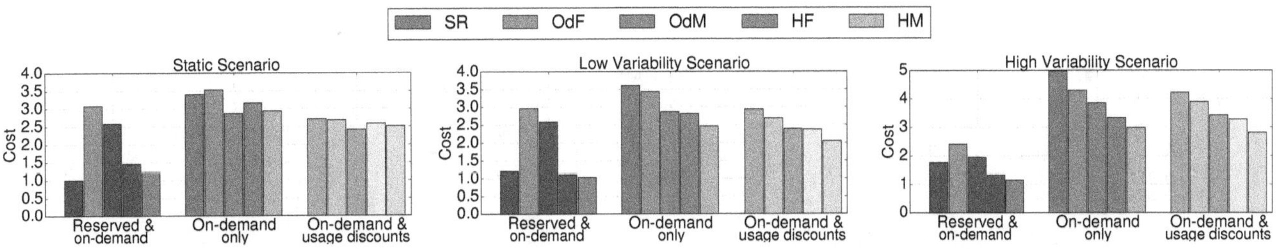

Figure 17: Sensitivity to the cloud pricing model for the three workload scenarios.

5.3 Different Pricing Models

So far we have assumed a pricing model similar to Amazon's AWS. This is a popular approach followed by many smaller cloud providers. Nevertheless, there are alternative approaches. GCE does not offer long-term reservations. Instead it provides *sustained usage monthly discounts* to encourage high utilization of on-demand resources. The higher the usage of a set of instances for a fraction of the month, the lower the per-hour price for the remainder of the month. Microsoft Azure only offers on-demand resources at the moment.

Even without reserved resources, the problem of selecting the appropriate instance size and configuration, and determining how long to retain an instance remains. Figure 17 shows how cost changes for the three workload scenarios, under the Azure (on-demand only) and GCE (on-demand + usage discounts) pricing models, compared to the AWS pricing model (reserved + on-demand). We assume that the resources will be used at least for one month, so that GCE's discounts can take effect. Cost is normalized to the cost of the static scenario under the SR strategy using the *reserved & on-demand* pricing model. Even with the alternative pricing models using the hybrid strategies and accounting for resource preferences of new jobs significantly benefits cost. For example, for the high variability scenario, HM incurs 32% lower cost than OdF with the Windows Azure pricing model; similarly for the GCE model with discounts, HM achieves 30% lower cost than OdF.

GCE decouples the usage from the specific instance used. For example, it does not differentiate between using a single instance of type A for 3 weeks, or 3 instances of type A for 1 week each. This introduces new optimization opportunities to maximize the time a certain instance type is used during a month. We defer such considerations to future work.

5.4 Resource Efficiency

Apart from lowering cost, we must ensure that a provisioning strategy is not wasteful in terms of resources. Figure 18 shows the resource allocation for each strategy throughout the duration of the high variability scenario. SR is provisioned statically for the peak requirements plus a 15% overprovisioning to avoid operating close to saturation, as described in Section 3.1. Because all instances are private (limited external interference) and resources are readily available, SR achieves near-ideal execution time (~2hr). However, due to the high load variability, system utilization is rarely high, resulting in poor resource efficiency. The majority of resources is only used in the interval between 32 and 60 minutes.

Figure 20 shows the CPU utilization of each instance throughout the execution of the high variability scenario for the five provisioning strategies. CPU utilization is sampled every 2 seconds and averaged across the cores of an instance. For the hybrid strategies we separate the reserved (bottom) from the on-demand resources (top). Servers are ranked from most- to least-utilized at each point in time during the execution of the scenario. Figure 19 also shows server resources in the order in which on-demand instances are obtained. For strategies with only reserved resources, the y-axis corresponds to server IDs.

Strategy OdF obtains resources as they become necessary, therefore inducing spin-up overheads frequently due to the constant load change, and resulting in increased execution time (132 min). It also introduces some overprovisioning, as it only requests the largest instances to constrain performance unpredictability. Because instances are released after remaining idle for a while, the average number of active instances is smaller than for SR. OdM does not overprovision allocations noticeably since it uses smaller instances, however, it significantly hurts performance, resulting in the scenario taking 48% more time. Performance degradation is partially the result of variability in the quality of instances, and of the high instance churn, due to their poor performance. 43% of obtained instances were released immediately after use.

The hybrid strategies (HF and HM) provision reserved resources for the minimum, steady-state load and use on-demand resources beyond that. HF needed in total 72 on-demand instances, of which 34 are used on average. HM needs a higher number of on-demand resources, because it uses smaller instances, and because it releases poorly-performing resources. 11% of on-demand instances obtained by HM were released immediately after use. Note that this is significantly lower than for OdM since only jobs that can tolerate performance unpredictability are assigned to on-demand resources. This issue is even less pronounced when

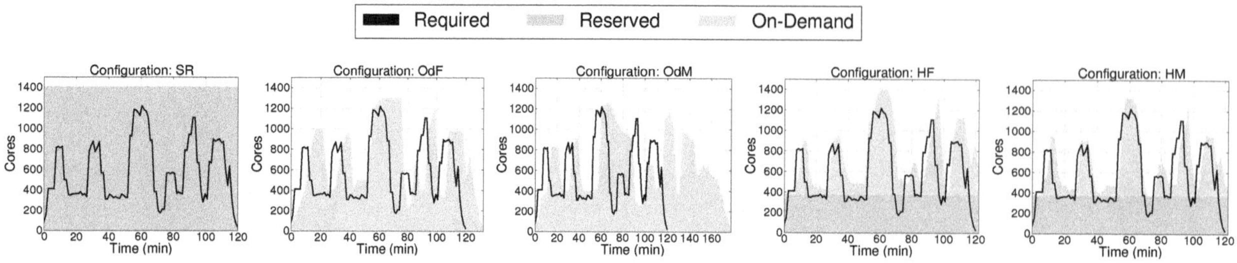

Figure 18: Resource allocation graphs for the five provisioning strategies in the case of the high variability scenario.

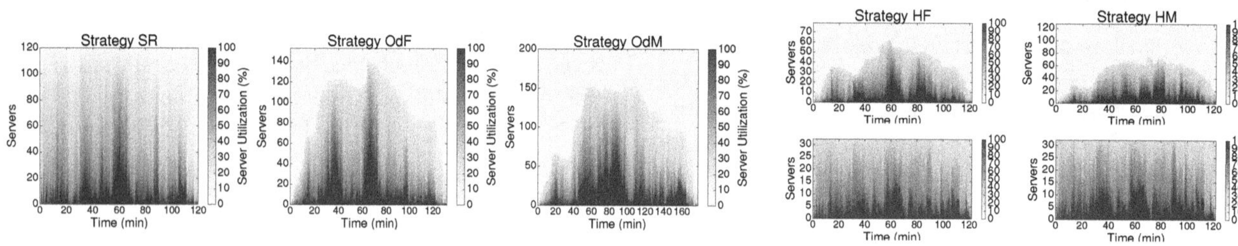

Figure 19: Resource utilization for the high variability scenario across the five provisioning strategies. Servers are ordered from most to least utilized at each point in time during the execution of the scenario.

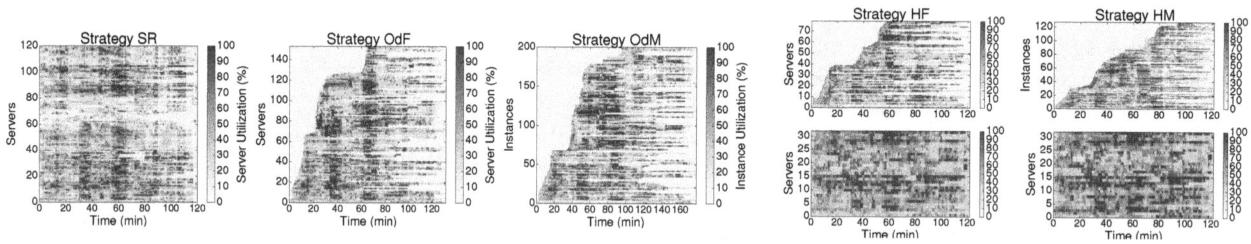

Figure 20: Resource utilization for the high variability scenario across the five provisioning strategies. Instances are ranked in the order in which they are obtained. For HF and HM we separate reserved (bottom) from on-demand (top) resources.

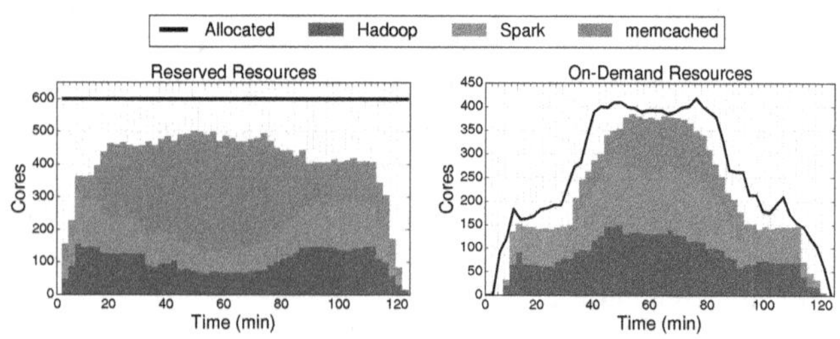

Figure 21: Breakdown of allocation per application type.

all on-demand resources are large instances (HF). Finally, spin-up overheads induce some delay in execution, which amounts to 2.6% over SR.

Figure 21 breaks down the allocation of the low variability scenario by application type, for HM. Initially the reserved resources are used for most jobs, until load reaches the soft utilization limit. Beyond that, the interference-sensitive memcached occupies most of the reserved resources, while batch workloads are mostly scheduled on the on-demand side. When the memcached load exceeds the capabilities of the reserved resources, part of its load is serviced by on-demand resources to avoid long queueing delays, although it is often allocated larger instances to meet its resource quality requirements.

5.5 Additional Provisioning Considerations

Spot instances: Spot instances consist of unallocated resources that cloud providers make available through a bidding interface. Spot instances do not have availability guarantees, and may be terminated at any point if the market price exceeds the bidding price for an instance type. Incorporating spot instances in provisioning for non-critical tasks or jobs with very relaxed performance requirements can further improve cost-efficiency. We will consider how spot instances interact with the current provisioning strategies in future work.

Reducing unpredictability: Resource partitioning (cache, memory or network bandwidth partitioning) can reduce unpredictability in fully on-demand systems. We plan to investigate how resource partitioning complements the current provisioning decisions.

Data management: In our current infrastructure both reserved and on-demand resources reside in the same physical cluster. When reserved resources are deployed as a private facility, provisioning must also consider how to minimize data transfers and replication across the two clusters.

6. Related Work

Cluster management: The prevalence of cloud computing has motivated several new designs for cluster management. Systems like Mesos [30], Torque [62], Tarcil [22], and Omega [57] all address the problem of allocating resources in large, shared clusters. Mesos is a two-level scheduler. It has a central coordinator that makes resource offers to application frameworks, and each framework has an individual scheduler that handles its assigned resources. Omega on the other hand, follows a shared-state approach, where multiple concurrent schedulers can view the whole cluster state, with conflicts being resolved through a transactional mechanism [57]. Tarcil leverages information on the type of resources applications need to employ a sampling-base distributed scheduler that returns high quality resources within a few milliseconds [22]. Dejavu identifies a few workload classes and reuses previous allocations for each class, to minimize reallocation overheads [63]. CloudScale [58], PRESS [26], AGILE [48] and the work by Gmach et al. [25] predict future resource needs online, often without a priori knowledge. Finally, auto-scaling systems, such as Rightscale [55], automatically scale the number of physical or virtual instances used by webserving workloads, to accommodate changes in user load.

A second line of work tries to identify the specific resources that are appropriate for incoming tasks [16, 18–20, 44, 46, 66]. Paragon uses classification to determine the impact of platform heterogeneity and workload interference on an unknown, incoming workload [17, 18]. It then uses this information to achieve high application performance and high cluster utilization. Paragon, assumes that the cluster manager has full control over all resources, which is often not the case in public clouds. Nathuji et al. developed a feedback-based scheme that tunes resource assignments to mitigate memory interference [47]. Yang et al. developed an online scheme that detects memory pressure and finds colocations that avoid interference on latency-sensitive workloads [66]. Similarly, DeepDive detects and manages interference between co-scheduled workloads in a VM environment [49]. Finally, CPI2 [70] throttles low-priority workloads that induce interference to important, latency-critical services. In terms of managing platform heterogeneity, Nathuji et al. [46] and Mars et al. [43] quantified its impact on conventional benchmarks and Google services, and designed schemes to predict the most appropriate servers for a workload.

Hybrid clouds: Hybrid clouds consist of both privately-owned and publicly-rented machines and have gained increased attention over the past few years for several reasons, including cost-efficiency, future growth, as well as security and privacy concerns [2, 10, 31, 33, 69]. Breiter et al. [10] describe a framework that allows service integration in hybrid cloud environments, including actions such as overflowing in on-demand resources during periods of high load. Farahabady et al. [31] present a resource allocation strategy for hybrid clouds that attempts to predict the execution times of incoming jobs and based on these predictions generate Pareto-optimal resource allocations. Finally, Annapureddy et al. [2] and Zhang et al. [69] discuss the security challenges of hybrid environments, and propose ways to leverage the private portion of the infrastructure for privacy-critical computation.

Cloud economics: The resource pricing of cloud providers has been extensively analyzed. Ben-Yehuda et al. [9] contest whether the pricing strategy of spot instances on EC2 is indeed market-driven, and discuss alternative strategies. Deelman et al. [15] present cost-efficient cloud provisioning strategies for specific astronomy applications. Li et al. [38] compare the resource pricing of several cloud providers to assist users provision their applications. Finally, Guevara et al. [28] and Zahed et al. [68] incorporate the economics of heterogeneous resources in market-driven and game-theoretic strategies for resource allocation in shared environments.

7. Conclusions

We have discussed the resource offerings available on cloud providers today and showed their advantages and pitfalls with respect to cost, performance, and instantiation overheads. We then presented HCloud, a hybrid provisioning system that uses both reserved and on-demand resources. HCloud obtains information on the resource preferences of incoming jobs, and determines which jobs should be mapped to on-demand versus reserved resources and how many resources they should each receive. We showed that hybrid strategies can provide the best of both worlds in terms of performance and cost-efficiency; they preserve QoS for the majority of jobs, improve performance by 2.1x compared to fully on-demand resources, and reduce cost by 46% compared to fully reserved resources.

Acknowledgements

The authors sincerely thank Mendel Rosenblum, John Ousterhout, Daniel Sanchez, David Lo, and the anonymous reviewers for their feedback on earlier versions of this manuscript. This work was supported by the Platform Lab and NSF grant CNS-1422088. Christina Delimitrou was supported by a Facebook Graduate Fellowship.

References

[1] Amazon ec2. `http://aws.amazon.com/ec2/`.

[2] K. Annapureddy. Security challenges in hybrid cloud infrastructures. In *Aalto University, T-110.5290 Seminar on Network Security*. 2010.

[3] Autoscale. `https://cwiki.apache.org/cloudstack/autoscaling.html`.

[4] Aws autoscaling. `http://aws.amazon.com/autoscaling/`.

[5] G. Banga, P. Druschel, and J. Mogul. Resource containers: a new facility for resource management in server systems. In *Proceeedings of OSDI*. New Orleans, 1999.

[6] S. K. Barker and P. Shenoy. Empirical evaluation of latency-sensitive application performance in the cloud. In *Proceedings of the First Annual ACM SIGMM Conference on Multimedia Systems (MMsys)*. Scottsdale, AR, 2010.

[7] L. Barroso. Warehouse-scale computing: Entering the teenage decade. *ISCA Keynote, SJ, June 2011*.

[8] L. Barroso and U. Hoelzle. *The Datacenter as a Computer: An Introduction to the Design of Warehouse-Scale Machines*. MC Publishers, 2009.

[9] O. A. Ben-Yehuda, M. Ben-Yehuda, A. Schuster, and D. Tsafrir. Deconstructing amazon ec2 spot instance pricing. In *ACM TEAC, 1(3), September 2013*.

[10] G. Breiter and V. Naik. A framework for controlling and managing hybrid cloud service integration. In *Proceedings of the 2013 IEEE International Conference on Cloud Engineering (IC2E)*. Redwood City, CA, 2013.

[11] M. Carvalho, W. Cirne, F. Brasileiro, and J. Wilkes. Long-term slos for reclaimed cloud computing resources. In *Proceedings of ACM Symposium on Cloud Computing (SOCC)*. Seattle, WA, 2014.

[12] J. Chase, D. Anderson, P. Thakar, A. Vahdat, and R. Doyle. Managing energy and server resources in hosting centers. In *Proceedings of the Symposium on Operating Systems Principles (SOSP)*. Banff, CA, 2001.

[13] Linux containers. `http://lxc.sourceforge.net/`.

[14] J. Dean and L. A. Barroso. The tail at scale. In *Communications of the ACM (CACM), Vol. 56 No. 2, Pages 74-80*.

[15] E. Deelman, G. Singh, M. Livny, B. Berriman, and J. Good. The cost of doing science on the cloud: The montage example. In *Proceedings of Supercomputing (SC)*. Austin, TX, 2008.

[16] C. Delimitrou, N. Bambos, and C. Kozyrakis. QoS-Aware Admission Control in Heterogeneous Datacenters. In *Proceedings of the International Conference of Autonomic Computing (ICAC)*. San Jose, CA, USA, 2013.

[17] C. Delimitrou and C. Kozyrakis. iBench: Quantifying Interference for Datacenter Workloads. In *Proceedings of the IEEE International Symposium on Workload Characterization (IISWC)*. Portland, OR, September 2013.

[18] C. Delimitrou and C. Kozyrakis. Paragon: QoS-Aware Scheduling for Heterogeneous Datacenters. In *Proceedings of the Eighteenth International Conference on Architectural Support for Programming Languages and Operating Systems (ASPLOS)*. Houston, TX, 2013.

[19] C. Delimitrou and C. Kozyrakis. QoS-Aware Scheduling in Heterogeneous Datacenters with Paragon. In *ACM Transactions on Computer Systems (TOCS), Vol. 31 Issue 4*. December 2013.

[20] C. Delimitrou and C. Kozyrakis. Quality-of-Service-Aware Scheduling in Heterogeneous Datacenters with Paragon. In *IEEE Micro Special Issue on Top Picks from the Computer Architecture Conferences*. May/June 2014.

[21] C. Delimitrou and C. Kozyrakis. Quasar: Resource-Efficient and QoS-Aware Cluster Management. In *Proceedings of the Nineteenth International Conference on Architectural Support for Programming Languages and Operating Systems (ASPLOS)*. Salt Lake City, UT, USA, 2014.

[22] C. Delimitrou, D. Sanchez, and C. Kozyrakis. Tarcil: Reconciling Scheduling Speed and Quality in Large Shared Clusters. In *Proceedings of the Sixth ACM Symposium on Cloud Computing (SOCC)*. Kohala Coast, HI, 2015.

[23] B. Farley, A. Juels, V. Varadarajan, T. Ristenpart, K. D. Bowers, and M. M. Swift. More for your money: Exploiting performance heterogeneity in public clouds. In *Proceedings of the ACM Symposium on Cloud Computing (SOCC)*. San Jose, CA, 2012.

[24] Google compute engine. `https://developers.google.com/compute/`.

[25] D. Gmach, J. Rolia, L. Cherkasova, and A. Kemper. Workload analysis and demand prediction of enterprise data center applications. In *Proceedings of the IEEE International Symposium on Workload Characterization (IISWC)*. Boston, MA, 2007.

[26] Z. Gong, X. Gu, and J. Wilkes. Press: Predictive elastic resource scaling for cloud systems. In *Proceedings of the International Conference on Network and Service Management (CNSM)*. Niagara Falls, ON, 2010.

[27] G. R. Grimmett and D. R. Stirzaker. Probability and random processes. 2nd Edition. Clarendon Press, Oxford, 1992.

[28] M. Guevara, B. Lubin, and B. Lee. Navigating heterogeneous processors with market mechanisms. In *Proceedings of the IEEE Symposium on High Performance Computer Architecture (HPCA)*. Shenzhen, China, 2013.

[29] J. Hamilton. Cost of power in large-scale data centers. `http://perspectives.mvdirona.com`.

[30] B. Hindman, A. Konwinski, M. Zaharia, A. Ghodsi, A. Joseph, R. Katz, S. Shenker, and I. Stoica. Mesos: A platform for fine-grained resource sharing in the data center. In *Proceedings of the USENIX Sumposium on Networked Systems Design and Implementation (NSDI)*. Boston, MA, 2011.

[31] M. Hoseinyfarahabady, H. Samani, L. Leslie, Y. C. Lee, and A. Zomaya. Handling uncertainty: Pareto-efficient bot scheduling on hybrid clouds. In *Proceedings of the International Conference for Parallel Processing (ICPP)*. Lyon, France, 2013.

[32] A. Iosup, N. Yigitbasi, and D. Epema. On the performance

variability of production cloud services. In *Proceedings of IEEE/ACM International Symposium on Cluster, Cloud and Grid Computing (CCGRID)*. Newport Beach, CA, 2011.

[33] V. Khadilkar, K. Y. Oktay, B. Hore, M. Kantarcioglu, S. Mehrotra, and B. Thuraisingham. Risk-aware data processing in hybrid clouds. TR-UTDCS-31-11, 2011.

[34] Y. E. Khamra, H. Kim, S. Jha, and M. Parashar. Exploring the performance fluctuations of hpc workloads on clouds. In *Proceeedings of IEEE International Conference on Cloud Computing Technology and Science (CloudCom)*. Indianapolis, IN, 2010.

[35] L. Kleinrock. Queueing systems volume 1: Theory. pp. 101-103, 404.

[36] E. Lau, J. E. Miller, I. Choi, D. Yeung, S. Amarasinghe, and A. Agarwal. Multicore performance optimization using partner cores. In *Proceedings of the USENIX Workshop on Hot Topics in Parallelism (HotPar)*. Berkeley, CA, 2011.

[37] J. Laudon. Performance/watt: the new server focus. In *ACM SIGARCH Computer Architecture News: dasCMP*. Vol. 33 Issue 4, p. 5-13, November 2005.

[38] A. Li, X. Yang, S. Kandula, and M. Zhang. Cloudcmp: Comparing public cloud providers. In *Proceeedings of Internet Measurement Conference (IMC)*. Melbourne, Australia, 2010.

[39] Host server cpu utilization in amazon ec2 cloud. `http://goo.gl/nCfYFX`.

[40] J. Lorch and A. Smith. Reducing processor power consumption by improving processor time management in a single-user operating system. In *Proceeedings of Annual International Conference on Mobile Computing and Networking (Mobicom)*. New York, NY, 1996.

[41] Mahout. `http://mahout.apache.org/`.

[42] D. Mangot. Ec2 variability: The numbers revealed. `http://goo.gl/NAH2lm`.

[43] J. Mars and L. Tang. Whare-map: heterogeneity in "homogeneous" warehouse-scale computers. In *Proceeedings of the International Symposium on Computer Architecture (ISCA)*. Tel-Aviv, Israel, 2013.

[44] J. Mars, L. Tang, R. Hundt, K. Skadron, and M. L. Soffa. Bubble-up: increasing utilization in modern warehouse scale computers via sensible co-locations. In *Proceeedings of the IEEE/ACM International Symposium on Microarchitecture (MICRO)*. Porto Alegre, Brazil, 2011.

[45] S. M. Martin, K. Flautner, T. Mudge, and D. Blaauw. Combined dynamic voltage scaling and adaptive body biasing for lower power microprocessors under dynamic workloads. In *Proceeedings of International Conference On Computer Aided Design (ICCAD)*. 2002.

[46] R. Nathuji, C. Isci, and E. Gorbatov. Exploiting platform heterogeneity for power efficient data centers. In *Proceeedings of the International Conference on Autonomic Computing (ICAC)*. Jacksonville, FL, 2007.

[47] R. Nathuji, A. Kansal, and A. Ghaffarkhah. Q-clouds: Managing performance interference effects for qos-aware clouds. In *Proceeedings of EuroSys France*, 2010.

[48] H. Nguyen, Z. Shen, X. Gu, S. Subbiah, and J. Wilkes. Agile: Elastic distributed resource scaling for infrastructure-as-a-service. In *Proceedings of the International Conference on Autonomic Computing (ICAC)*. 2013.

[49] D. Novakovic, N. Vasic, S. Novakovic, D. Kostic, and R. Bianchini. Deepdive: Transparently identifying and managing performance interference in virtualized environments. In *Proceeedings of the USENIX Annual Technical Conference (ATC)*. San Jose, CA, 2013.

[50] S. Ostermann, A. Iosup, N. Yigitbasi, R. Prodan, T. Fahringer, and D. Epema. A performance analysis of ec2 cloud computing services for scientific computing. In *Lecture Notes on Cloud Computing*. Volume 34, p.115-131, 2010.

[51] Z. Ou, H. Zhuang, J. K. Nurminen, A. Ylä-Jääski, and P. Hui. Exploiting hardware heterogeneity within the same instance type of amazon ec2. In *HotCloud*. 2012.

[52] K. Ousterhout, P. Wendell, M. Zaharia, and I. Stoica. Sparrow: Distributed, low latency scheduling. In *Proceeedings of the Symposium on Operating Systems Principles (SOSP)*. Farminton, PA, 2013.

[53] M. Rehman and M. Sakr. Initial findings for provisioning variation in cloud computing. In *Proceeedings of CloudCom*. Indianapolis, IN, 2010.

[54] C. Reiss, A. Tumanov, G. Ganger, R. Katz, and M. Kozych. Heterogeneity and dynamicity of clouds at scale: Google trace analysis. In *Proceeedings of ACM Symposium on Cloud Computing (SOCC)*. 2012.

[55] Rightscale. `https://aws.amazon.com/solution-providers/isv/rightscale`.

[56] J. Schad, J. Dittrich, and J.-A. Quiané-Ruiz. Runtime measurements in the cloud: Observing, analyzing, and reducing variance. *Proceeedings VLDB Endow.*, 3(1-2):460–471, Sept. 2010.

[57] M. Schwarzkopf, A. Konwinski, M. Abd-El-Malek, and J. Wilkes. Omega: flexible, scalable schedulers for large compute clusters. In *Proceeedings of EuroSys*. 2013.

[58] Z. Shen, S. Subbiah, X. Gu, and J. Wilkes. Cloudscale: elastic resource scaling for multi-tenant cloud systems. In *Proceeedings of ACM Symposium on Cloud Computing (SOCC)*. Cascais, Portugal, 2011.

[59] T. Simunic and S. Boyd. Managing power consumption in networks on chips. In *Proceeedings of Design Automation Conference (DAC)*. Paris, France, 2002.

[60] S. Swanson, A. Putnam, M. Mercaldi, K. Michelson, A. Petersen, A. Schwerin, M. Oskin, and S. J. Eggers. Area-performance trade-offs in tiled dataflow architectures. In *Proceeedings of ACM SIGARCH Computer Architecture News, v.34 n.2, p.314-326, May 2006.*

[61] K. Therdsteerasukdi, G. Byun, J. Cong, F. Chang, and G. Reinman. Utilizing rf-i and intelligent scheduling for better throughput/watt in a mobile gpu memory system. In *Transactions on Architecture and Code Optimization (TACO) 8(4)*. 2012.

[62] Torque resource manager. http://www.adaptivecomputing.com/products/open-source/torque/.

[63] N. Vasić, D. Novaković, S. Miučin, D. Kostić, and R. Bianchini. Dejavu: accelerating resource allocation in virtualized environments. In *Proceedings of the Seventeenth International Conference on Architectural Support for Programming Languages and Operating Systems (ASPLOS)*. 2012.

[64] G. Wang and T. S. E. Ng. The impact of virtualization on network performance of amazon ec2 data center. In *Proceeedings of IEEE International Conference on Computer Communications (INFOCOM)*. San Diego, CA, 2010.

[65] Windows azure. http://www.windowsazure.com/.

[66] H. Yang, A. Breslow, J. Mars, and L. Tang. Bubble-flux: precise online qos management for increased utilization in warehouse scale computers. In *Proceeedings of the International Symposium on Computer Architecture (ISCA)*. 2013.

[67] M. Zaharia, M. Chowdhury, T. Das, A. Dave, J. Ma, M. McCauley, M. Franklin, S. Shenker, and I. Stoica. Spark: Cluster computing with working sets. In *Proceedings of the USENIX Sumposium on Networked Systems Design and Implementation (NSDI)*. San Jose, CA, 2012.

[68] S. M. Zahed and B. C. Lee. Ref: Resource elasticity fairness with sharing incentives for multiprocessors. In *Proceeedings of the Nineteenth International Conference on Architectural Support for Programming Languages and Operating Systems (ASPLOS)*. Salt Lake City, UT, 2014.

[69] J. Y. Zhang, P. Wu, J. Zhu, H. Hu, and F. Bonomi. Privacy-preserved mobile sensing through hybrid cloud trust framework. In *Proceeedings of IEEE International Conference on Cloud Computing (CLOUD)*. 2013.

[70] X. Zhang, E. Tune, R. Hagmann, R. Jnagal, V. Gokhale, and J. Wilkes. Cpi2: Cpu performance isolation for shared compute clusters. In *Proceeedings of EuroSys*. Prague, 2013.

[71] L. Zhao, R. Iyer, J. Moses, R. Illikkal, S. Makineni, and D. Newell. Exploring large-scale cmp architectures using manysim. In *IEEE Micro, vol.27 n.4, July 2007.*

CloudSeer: Workflow Monitoring of Cloud Infrastructures via Interleaved Logs

Xiao Yu
North Carolina State University
xyu10@ncsu.edu

Pallavi Joshi Jianwu Xu
NEC Laboratories America
pallavijoshi84@gmail.com
jianwu@nec-labs.com

Guoliang Jin
North Carolina State University
guoliang_jin@ncsu.edu

Hui Zhang Guofei Jiang
NEC Laboratories America
{huizhang, gfj}@nec-labs.com

Abstract

Cloud infrastructures provide a rich set of management tasks that operate computing, storage, and networking resources in the cloud. Monitoring the executions of these tasks is crucial for cloud providers to promptly find and understand problems that compromise cloud availability. However, such monitoring is challenging because there are multiple distributed service components involved in the executions.

`CloudSeer` enables effective workflow monitoring. It takes a lightweight non-intrusive approach that purely works on interleaved logs widely existing in cloud infrastructures. `CloudSeer` first builds an automaton for the workflow of each management task based on normal executions, and then it checks log messages against a set of automata for workflow divergences in a streaming manner. Divergences found during the checking process indicate potential execution problems, which may or may not be accompanied by error log messages. For each potential problem, `CloudSeer` outputs necessary context information including the affected task automaton and related log messages hinting where the problem occurs to help further diagnosis. Our experiments on OpenStack, a popular open-source cloud infrastructure, show that `CloudSeer`'s efficiency and problem-detection capability are suitable for online monitoring.

Categories and Subject Descriptors D.2.5 [*Software Engineering*]: Testing and Debugging—Debugging aids, Distributed debugging, Monitors; D.4.5 [*Operating Systems*]: Reliability; D.4.8 [*Operating Systems*]: Performance

Keywords Cloud Infrastructures; Distributed Systems; Log Analysis; Workflow Monitoring

ASPLOS '16 April 2–6, 2016, Atlanta, Georgia, USA

DOI: http://dx.doi.org/10.1145/2872362.2872407

1. Introduction

With the fast growth of the global cloud-computing market, many dedicated software infrastructures have emerged to provide convenient access to cloud-based computing, storage, and networking resources. For example, Amazon Elastic Compute Cloud (EC2) [3] and Microsoft Azure [10] are two widely used public cloud infrastructures that enable users to easily create computing platforms in the cloud with multiple servers and configurable resources. In the open-source community, OpenStack [11] has been gaining popularity steadily in recent years [1].

Cloud infrastructures provide access to cloud resources via a series of management tasks, e.g., tasks enabling users to spawn virtual machines (VMs), stop VMs, and delete VMs. To execute a task, cloud infrastructures coordinate multiple internal service processes distributed on different server nodes, each of which takes part in the whole execution (e.g., a scheduler to assign VMs to different nodes and hypervisors on assigned nodes to boot up VMs). The distributed and multi-process nature of task executions introduces extra complexity and non-determinism, which can sometimes result in subtle problems.

From the perspective of cloud providers, monitoring is an important way to help the identification and diagnosis of execution problems that compromise cloud availability. The provider-side administrators expect to know through monitoring if each task execution completes successfully and in time. When execution problems occur, administrators also expect enough information from monitoring that can guide the diagnosis. However, cloud infrastructures usually do not expose enough execution details. De facto practices include checking the outcomes of test requests [8] and monitoring running statuses of service processes and resource usages to detect abnormalities. Unfortunately, test requests may fail to exercise and expose problems in specific problematic execution paths, and resource usages may not reveal problems that do not cause usage irregularities (e.g., expected inter-service messages not sent or received). As a result, revealing internal execution steps across service processes for direct monitoring in the workflow level is challenging.

Monitoring logs is another common practice to find and diagnose problems. For example, Amazon CloudWatch [2] provides a log-streaming interface for real-time log monitoring on VM instances. There are also open-source projects, such as Logstash [9], to support a similar feature for centralizing distributed logs from multiple server nodes to a single location. However, it is tedious and labor-intensive to manually monitor and understand numerous distributed and interleaved log messages by human effort. In a real-world banking system, that some of the authors had experiences with, there were 200 full-time operators dedicated to 24x7 log monitoring with 67 screens for 190 subsystems.

To facilitate monitoring through logs, we present a non-intrusive lightweight approach for *workflow monitoring*. Our prototype for OpenStack, `CloudSeer`, purely works on logs that are readily available in existing cloud infrastructures. `CloudSeer` is backed by the observations that logging is a general practice for complex software systems and logs implicitly carry workflow information. In these logs, not only error messages, but also sequence-based information, can help monitor and discover execution problems. To enable log-based workflow monitoring, `CloudSeer` addresses the following key challenges.

Working with interleaved log sequences. When a cloud infrastructure is executing multiple tasks in parallel, log messages from different executions are usually interleaved in log files. Even in a single execution, asynchronous operations among different services can interleave log messages in different ways. To recover workflow information, it is necessary, but not straightforward, to identify the correspondence between log messages and task executions. Some existing work [18] assumes that messages have unique request and thread identifiers, which can distinguish messages from different task executions. However, such an assumption does not always hold. While working with OpenStack, we found that there could be multiple non-unique identifiers representing different entities (e.g., VMs, physical machines, and networks) in different log messages. Only the combinations of some identifiers may identify sequences of log messages that belong to different task executions.

Working in an online scenario. The sooner a problem is noticed, the quicker can it be fixed and the more can its effects be mitigated. Existing work [21, 24, 29] on detecting problems using data mining and clustering on logs can only operate in an offline manner, since they require task or program executions to finish so that logs are available in their entirety beforehand. Such a design delays problem detection and is more problematic if the executions may not finish at all. In the monitoring scenario, the detection of execution problems should be quick without the need to wait for the tasks to finish.

Detecting problems without explicit error messages. Execution problems can manifest in different forms. Some of them may not be easily noticeable, e.g., performance degradation and silent failures that do not come with explicit error messages. From the logging practices in OpenStack [11], we found that failures were not always accompanied with indicative error messages. A recent study [31] on logging practice also reports that over half of the studied failures were not properly logged. Thus, only looking for error messages might not reveal subtle execution problems.

Providing workflow information. As a monitoring approach, just reporting a failure is not enough for administrators to diagnose the failure and take further actions. The context of a failure, particularly, workflow [14, 23], is useful for guiding administrators to narrow down and isolate possible causes. A monitoring approach should leverage log messages to include such information in failure reports.

`CloudSeer` addresses these challenges by combining an offline modeling stage (Section 3) and an online checking stage (Section 4). In the offline modeling stage, `CloudSeer` builds an automaton for each task via the logs generated by multiple correct executions. The result automaton depicts the task workflow, in which state transitions capture temporal dependencies between log messages. We introduce this automaton to serve two roles. `CloudSeer` uses it as a specification to identify log sequences in the online checking stage. The automaton is also a bookkeeper to keep track of the execution progress or context on-the-fly by maintaining automaton states. The bookkeeping enables the automaton to be used as an informative output that provides context information when `CloudSeer` detects a potential problem.

In the online checking stage, `CloudSeer` works on a log stream that consists of interleaved log messages from distributed services. It uses the pre-built automata to identify individual log sequences out of interleaved ones, and check them for divergences that may indicate execution problems.

We define two divergence criteria for two symptoms of execution problems: (1) error messages and (2) expected log messages not appearing within a time interval. While the first case is straightforward as it represents failures that are properly caught and handled by a system, the second case indicates unhandled silent failures that are not accompanied by error messages (e.g., when a key service stops responding) or performance degradation. In this paper, we do not distinguish between silent failures and performance degradation. Our goal is to show that `CloudSeer` is capable of detecting different kinds of execution problems, rather than directly identifying the root causes of the detected problems.

To ensure efficiency for monitoring via interleaved logs, we design effective heuristics that leverage non-unique message identifiers to group related log messages into growing sequences on-the-fly. Based on the heuristics, `CloudSeer` associates a limited number of automaton instances with each sequence and checks if the sequence followed by a

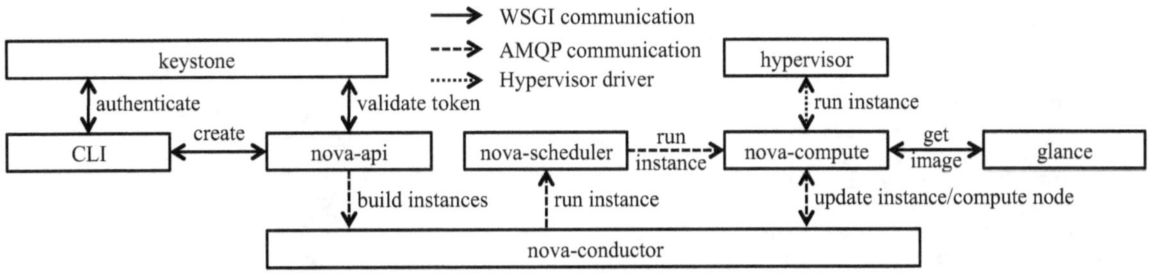

Figure 1. Inter-service interactions when booting a VM

new message still conforms with its associated automaton instances. As a result, CloudSeer is able to avoid the brute-force checking on each message against all automaton instances, thus significantly reducing performance overhead.

During the checking process, CloudSeer marks and reports automaton instances that satisfy the divergence criteria. The reported instances provide workflow information about the task and the step within the task where the problem is occurring. Administrators can then use the provided information to understand and mitigate ongoing problems.

We evaluate CloudSeer by a series of experiments on primitive VM tasks of OpenStack (Section 5). The experiments evaluate how accurate and efficient CloudSeer checks interleaved log sequences and its capability of detecting some injected common problems. The results show that the checking accuracy of CloudSeer is at least 92.08% on interleaved logs, with a satisfactory efficiency (an average of 2.36s/1k-messages in our test bed), making it suitable for the monitoring scenario. The results further show CloudSeer's problem-detection capability with a precision of 83.08% and a recall of 90.00% on the injected problems.

2. Overview

We start with a general description about a representative cloud infrastructure, OpenStack, and a common set of logging characteristics that exist in similar systems. Then, we use examples based on OpenStack to briefly describe how CloudSeer monitors task executions through logs.

2.1 Cloud-Infrastructure Example: OpenStack

OpenStack is an open-source cloud-infrastructure platform. It consists of multiple service components that manage computing, storage, and networking resources in the cloud. For example, the component nova provides a set of tasks to manage VMs. Cloud users can issue task commands, e.g., "nova boot" and "nova stop" from the command-line interface (CLI) to boot up and stop VMs.

The execution of a task involves coordination between multiple service components. Figure 1 depicts how service components interact during the booting of a VM. When a user executes a task with the "nova boot" command, a request is sent to nova-api, which is a web service built using Web Server Gateway Interface (WSGI). The authentication service, keystone, authenticates the incoming request. If authenticated, the scheduling service, nova-scheduler, selects a compute server on which to boot up a new VM. The compute service, nova-compute, running on the compute server, obtains the appropriate VM image from glance, which provides VM images. The VM hypervisor then takes over the request from nova-compute to launch the VM. The proxy service, nova-conductor, records states of VMs in the database and manages remote procedure calls (RPCs) across service boundaries using Advanced Message Queuing Protocol (AMQP).

2.2 Logging Characteristics

We are aware of two logging characteristics that make the log-based workflow monitoring not straightforward. The two characteristics are the manifestation of a set of underlying system behaviors, which are common in similar systems and not specific to OpenStack examples.

First, besides the message interleaving caused by simultaneous task executions, log messages from the same execution might also be interleaved. This is caused by asynchronous operations (e.g., AMQP communications in OpenStack), which create multiple execution paths through different service processes. As a result, log messages from different paths could be interleaved without a fixed ordering, making task workflows more complicated to monitor.

Second, there is often no single and unique identifier associated with log messages related to a task execution. In cloud infrastructures, each service manages its own resources (e.g., users, VMs, and images are managed by different services) and logs them with identifiers based on resource types. Those identifiers may not be propagated across different services during a task execution, because different services do not share the knowledge on different resources. For instance, a hypervisor knows which VM is running, but it has no knowledge about the user whom the VM belongs to. Consequently, different log messages may not share common identifiers.

We use an example in OpenStack to further illustrate the two characteristics. Figure 2 shows simplified log messages for two executions of the "nova boot" task. To ease the explanation, we simplify messages by substituting timestamps with numbers at the beginning of the messages, remov-

```
(1) api accepted IP1
(2) api accepted IP2
(3) api [UUID1] IP1 "POST /UUID2/servers"
(4) api [UUID3] IP2 "POST /UUID4/servers"
(5) scheduler [UUID1] Scheduling instance UUID5.
(6) scheduler [UUID3] Scheduling instance UUID6.
(7) api [UUID3] IP2 "GET /UUID4/servers/UUID6"
(8) compute [UUID1] Starting instance UUID5.
(9) api [UUID1] IP1 "GET /UUID2/servers/UUID5"
(10) compute [UUID3] Starting instance UUID6.
(11) compute Instance UUID5 spawned successfully.
(12) compute Instance UUID6 spawned successfully.
```

Figure 2. Simplified Log Sequences for Booting VMs in OpenStack

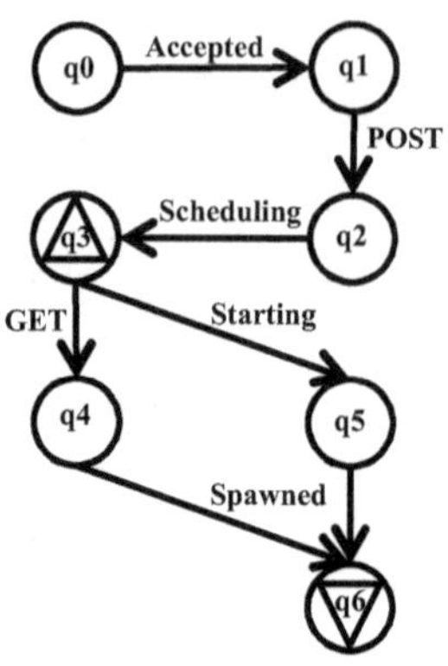

Figure 3. The Automaton for Booting a VM

ing logging levels, replacing identifiers (IPs, URLs, UUIDs, etc.) with simple text (e.g., replace the actual IP address with just *IP1*), and shortening text in the messages (e.g., `api` for `nova-api`). The identifiers in log messages indicate different resources, e.g., the identifiers in square brackets indicate users who initiate the tasks, the identifiers preceded by the text "`Instance`" indicate VMs, and the identifiers in the message bodies may indicate tenants or VMs.

In Figure 2, there are two interleaved log sequences, $1 \rightarrow 3 \rightarrow 5 \rightarrow 8 \rightarrow 9 \rightarrow 11$ and $2 \rightarrow 4 \rightarrow 6 \rightarrow 7 \rightarrow 10 \rightarrow 12$. Messages $8 \rightarrow 9$ in the first sequence and $7 \rightarrow 10$ in the second one show two different orderings for one pair of log messages. This is because the service `nova-scheduler`, which generates messages 5 and 6, uses asynchronous AMQP communications to schedule VM instances *UUID5* and *UUID6* to compute nodes. Such asynchronicity causes `nova-api` (generating messages 7 and 9) and `nova-compute` (generating messages 8 and 10) to execute their parts of the task in parallel, resulting in two possible orderings.

It is also noticeable how diversified the log identifiers are. For instance, messages 1 and 5 from the same sequence do not have any common identifiers. On the other hand, many a time some messages can connect other seemingly disconnected ones. For instance, message 3 shares *IP1* and *UUID1* with messages 1 and 5, respectively. It can effectively establish the relation between messages 1 and 5. This observation suggests that shared identifiers, regardless of how far they are propagated across services, can create a chain that transitively connects messages together. This observation thus enables a heuristic that separates interleaved log sequences.

2.3 Demonstration of CloudSeer

We show the basic idea of `CloudSeer` using the example in Figure 2. We assume that we have already built a task automaton using logs collected from multiple normal executions of booting VMs. Figure 3 shows the automaton for the "`nova boot`" task, and it is simplified accordingly as what we have done for the log sequence in Figure 2. Section 3 describes the modeling step in detail.

The Task Automaton. The automaton in Figure 3 represents the booting-VM workflow by encoding the dependencies among log messages. The automaton takes message templates as inputs. The message templates are log messages without variable parts. Determining the variable parts requires certain domain knowledge. We consider IP addresses, UUIDs, and numbers as the variable parts in log messages.

To model interleaved messages caused by asynchronous operations, we introduce two special types of states in addition to the conventional automaton states: the *fork* states ($q3$ in Figure 3) and the *join* states ($q6$). A *fork* state has multiple outbound transitions for log messages that do not have dependencies with each other but share the same precedent, and each outbound transition transits to a new state from the fork state (e.g., $q4$ and $q5$ are forked from $q3$ after consuming the messages "`GET`" and "`Starting`"). A *join* state has multiple inbound transitions for a log message that must always be followed by some other messages, and all inbound transitions transit to the same join state (e.g., $q4$ and $q5$ join to $q6$ after consuming the message "`Spawned`").

Checking Interleaved Sequences. `CloudSeer` takes one log message at a time. It checks if the message belongs to a growing log sequence and if the growing sequence with the new message still conforms with its corresponding automaton. This checking process continues until a message completes a sequence or satisfies divergence criteria.

To leverage multiple identifiers to determine the association of a message with a developing log sequence, `CloudSeer` uses a data structure, *identifier set*, as the signature of each log sequence. An *identifier set* stores identifiers appearing in all messages of a sequence.

Table 1 shows the process of `CloudSeer` checking log messages. The column "Identifier Set" presents the identifier set after processing the corresponding message shown in the column "Message." Due to space limit, we use the symbol $UUID1/2$ to represent $UUID1$ and $UUID2$ in the column "Identifier Set." The column "Instance Transition" shows the state transitions of automaton instances. The label before each identifier set and state transition indicates the log sequence under checking.

`CloudSeer` considers messages 1 and 2 to be the beginning of two new sequences because their identifier sets do

Message	Identifier Set	Instance Transition
(1) `Accepted`	1: $\{IP1\}$	1: $\{q0\} \rightarrow \{q1\}$
(2) `Accepted`	2: $\{IP2\}$	2: $\{q0\} \rightarrow \{q1\}$
(3) `POST`	1: $\{IP1, UUID1/2\}$	1: $\{q1\} \rightarrow \{q2\}$
(4) `POST`	2: $\{IP2, UUID3/4\}$	2: $\{q1\} \rightarrow \{q2\}$
(5) `Scheduling`	1: $\{IP1, UUID1/2/5\}$	1: $\{q2\} \rightarrow \{q3\}$
(6) `Scheduling`	2: $\{IP2, UUID3/4/6\}$	2: $\{q2\} \rightarrow \{q3\}$
(7) `GET`	2: $\{IP2, UUID3/4/6\}$	2: $\{q3\} \rightarrow \{q3, q4\}$
(8) `Starting`	1: $\{IP1, UUID1/2/5\}$	1: $\{q3\} \rightarrow \{q3, q5\}$
(9) `GET`	1: $\{IP1, UUID1/2/5\}$	1: $\{q3, q5\} \rightarrow \{q4, q5\}$
(10) `Starting`	2: $\{IP2, UUID3/4/6\}$	2: $\{q3, q4\} \rightarrow \{q4, q5\}$
(11) `Spawned`	1: $\{IP1, UUID1/2/5\}$	1: $\{q4, q5\} \rightarrow \{q6\}$
(12) `Spawned`	2: $\{IP2, UUID3/4/6\}$	2: $\{q4, q5\} \rightarrow \{q6\}$

Table 1. Demonstration of Checking Process

not have any common element. Therefore, `CloudSeer` creates a new identifier set and a new automaton instance for each of these two messages.

The identifiers in message 3 have a common element with the identifier set of the first sequence ($\{IP1\}$) only. Therefore, `CloudSeer` associates the message with the sequence "1." It then tests if the message causes the corresponding automaton instance to make a state transition. As the transition happens, `CloudSeer` extends the identifier set of the sequence with the UUIDs in the message. When message 4 arrives, `CloudSeer` associates the message with sequence "2" since the IP address $IP2$ appears in the current identifier set for that sequence. For the rest of the messages, `CloudSeer` repeats this checking process until the two automaton instances accept their log sequences.

Interpreting Results. When an incoming message, or lack thereof, satisfies divergence criteria, `CloudSeer` is able to report the diverged automaton instance indicating a problematic execution. For investigation, the diverged instance provides useful information that includes the ongoing task with its normal workflow, and the execution point where the problem occurs in the form of the current automaton state(s) and all log messages consumed so far.

For example, in Figure 2, if a problem occurs in the compute node assigned to run the VM $UUID5$, the message 8 or 11 may not appear. Such a case is detectable by a "timeout" criterion that specifies a time period in which an automaton instance must consume a message. `CloudSeer` would then report an instance with the states $\{q3, q4\}$ or $\{q4, q5\}$, depending on if the message 8 has appeared. Then, a knowledgeable administrator may quickly narrow down the problem to immediately before booting the VM (if $\{q3, q4\}$, network could be the main cause) or during the booting process (if $\{q4, q5\}$, I/O or hypervisor could be the main cause).

3. Modeling Task-Based Log Sequences

The offline modeling process creates automata from logs generated by correct task executions. `CloudSeer` uses the output automata to check interleaved logs in the online scenario. For each task to model, the modeling process takes *log sequences* from multiple executions of the task. The term log sequence denotes all log messages ordered by their timestamps (or in the order they arrive) from a single execution. Since asynchronous operations among services may cause some messages to be interleaved in different ways, using multiple log sequences of a task helps the modeling process reconstruct *temporal dependencies*, which describe the order relation of log messages to represent the task workflow.

The modeling process consists of three steps: (1) preprocessing log sequences to extract key log messages for the task workflow; (2) mining temporal dependencies in the preprocessed log sequences; and (3) constructing automata from the mined temporal dependencies.

3.1 Preprocessing

The preprocessing step takes log sequences as input. A log sequence LS is a vector of log messages $\langle m_1, m_2, ..., m_n \rangle$. Each log message m_i in LS has two attributes: a template t representing the constant text of m_i, and a value set S_v containing values in the variable parts of m_i. There are different ways to determine the template t and the value set S_v of a log message m, and we consider numbers, IP addresses, and UUIDs as variable parts, where UUID is in the form of a well-formatted string. We use regular expressions to match and extract them to create $m.S_v$, and $m.t$ is naturally the part of m after the extraction.

For a set of log sequences S_{LS} collected from multiple executions of a task, the preprocessing step keeps key log messages in each log sequence of S_{LS} and removes all other messages which are considered less relevant to the task workflow. To determine if a log message m is a key message, this step counts the appearance of $m.t$ in each log sequence of S_{LS}. The message m is a key message if $m.t$ appears the same number of times in every sequence.

The preprocessing provides two benefits. First, it removes irregular log messages from loops, conditional choices, and periodical background tasks. Such messages are irrelevant to the task workflow and would introduce excessive possibilities when `CloudSeer` checks the interleaved log sequences. We consider that keeping only key messages is sufficient and efficient for the monitoring purpose. Second, the result sequences bring out in-sequence message interleaving caused by asynchronous operations. Capturing and modeling such interleaving is important for recovering the task workflow.

3.2 Mining Temporal Dependencies

Given a set of preprocessed log sequences S_{LS}, *temporal dependencies* describe the order relation in which collaborative services generate log messages. We define the following two types of temporal dependencies over log templates $\{t_1, t_2, ..., t_n\}$ shared by sequences in S_{LS}: (1) a strong dependency $t_i \xrightarrow{strong} t_j$ iff t_j is always next to t_i for each of their occurrences in S_{LS}; (2) a weak dependency $t_i \xrightarrow{weak} t_j$ iff t_i always happens before t_j in S_{LS}, but it is not necessarily followed by t_j immediately. Any pair of t_i and t_j

not having the two dependencies is considered to not have any specific order. For example, in Figure 2, the messages "`accepted`" and "`POST`" have a strong dependency, since both the occurrences $1 \rightarrow 3$ and $2 \rightarrow 4$ follow one specific order. On the other hand, the message "`Scheduling`" (5 and 6) always leads "`Starting`" and "`GET`" ($5 \rightarrow 8 \rightarrow 9$ and $6 \rightarrow 7 \rightarrow 10$), but the latter two messages do not follow a specific order. Therefore, the messages "`Starting`" and "`GET`" have weak dependencies with "`Scheduling`." The weak dependencies imply that the execution becomes asynchronous after the message "`Scheduling`" and before "`Starting`" and "`GET`."

To mine temporal dependencies, this step consists of three parts. It first enumerates and collects all pairs of log templates for each sequence in S_{LS}. For example, given a sequence $\langle a, b, c\rangle$, this step enumerates pairs of $(a, b), (a, c), (b, c)$. Then it classifies all collected pairs into strong and weak temporal dependencies based on their definition. Finally, it performs a reduction of transitive relations on the classified temporal dependencies. The transitive relations are the result of enumerating all message pairs. In particular, for any dependencies $a \rightarrow b$ and $b \rightarrow c$ before the reduction, there must be a dependency $a \rightarrow c$. The reduction removes such dependencies as $a \rightarrow c$ to keep the result dependencies minimal.

3.3 Constructing Automata

This step constructs a *task automaton* that encodes the mined temporal dependencies. A task automaton is a septuple $(Q, \Sigma, \Delta, q_0, F, Q_f, Q_j)$ where: (1) Q is a set of states of a task execution; (2) Σ is a set of log message templates; (3) Δ is a transition function $Q \times \Sigma \rightarrow \mathcal{P}(Q)$ based on the temporal dependencies; (4) q_0 is an initial state; (5) F is a set of final states; (6) $Q_f \subset Q$ contains fork states, which lead transitions to multiple other states by messages not dependent on each other but having weak temporal dependencies with the previous message; (7) $Q_j \subset Q$ contains join states, to which multiple states converge on a message having weak temporal dependencies with multiple previous messages.

The construction of a task automaton is as follows. All log templates in the temporal dependencies constitute the input set Σ. Each input in Σ is assigned a state, indicating the state after taking the input. Then, the assigned states with the mined dependency pairs constitute transitions in Δ. To determine the first transition from the initial state q_0, this step looks up an input that does not depend on any others. To determine the final states F, the fork states Q_f, or the join states Q_j, this step looks for the states without any outbound transitions, have multiple outbound transitions, or have multiple inbound transitions in Δ. For each fork state, this step adds a self-loop to the transition function to allow state forking, as shown in the rows 7 and 8 of Table 1. In addition, we limit a fork state to take self-transitions at most the number of its outbound transitions, so that the automaton only processes a finite length of log sequence.

Algorithm 1: Checking Individual Sequences

Input: a log message m; an automaton group G, empty by default
Output: the updated automaton group G after its automaton instances consume the message m
Global: a set of task automata M for different tasks

```
1 G′ ← CopyInstances(G);
2 if G′ is empty then
3 |  G′ ← InitializeInstances(M);
4 G ← {};
5 foreach a in G′ do
6 |  if TryInputMessage(a, m.t) is true then
7 |  |  G ← G ∪ {a};
8 return G;
```

4. Checking Interleaved Log Sequences

In the online checking stage, `CloudSeer` uses task automata from the previous offline modeling stage to check interleaved log sequences. The input and output of this checking stage are as follows. `CloudSeer` takes one log message at a time from a log stream. The input message belongs to one of some interleaved log sequences being generated. Based on the task automata, `CloudSeer` outputs (1) an accepting automaton instance, if the last message completes a correct log sequence; (2) an erroneous automaton instance, if the last message meets problem-detection criteria; or (3) no output, indicating more log messages are expected.

We start from the basic case for individual log sequences assuming tasks are executed one by one. Then we relax this assumption and present the full checking algorithm. Finally, we discuss our problem detection criteria.

Basic case: individual sequences. `CloudSeer` needs to choose a correct automaton from multiple task automata to check incoming log messages belonging to the current log sequence. Since `CloudSeer` takes one log message at a time, it does not know the right choice of automaton for sure until an automaton accepts the last message, completing the current log sequence.

Algorithm 1 shows the checking algorithm for individual sequences. Its main idea is using an *automaton group G* to keep track of all possible automata for the sequence being checked. *G* initially contains instances created from a global set of task automata M (Lines 2 to 3). Each automaton instance a in *G* represents one possible task, and it maintains its own state transitions based on input messages.

For each log message m with the current automaton group G, the algorithm finds the automaton instances that make state transitions with m (Lines 5 to 7, determined by the function *TryInputMessage* that lets an instance decide whether it can consume m), and it passes them to the next invocation by returning the updated G. A final state of any instance in the result *G* indicates the completion of checking a log sequence. On the other hand, an empty *G* indicates that none of the automaton instances can consume m.

Checking interleaved sequences. We extend the checking algorithm shown in Algorithm 1 in two ways. First, the

Algorithm 2: Checking Interleaved Sequences

Input: a log message m
Output: an accepting or erroneous automaton instance, if the message m completes a correct log sequence, or meets an error criterion; no output otherwise
Global: a set of identifier sets $\mathcal{I}$; a set of automaton groups $\mathcal{G}$; a relation set $R : \mathcal{I} \times \mathcal{G}$

1 $S_{id} \leftarrow$`GetIdentifierValues`$(m.S_v)$;
2 $\mathcal{I}_{max} \leftarrow$`ComputeMaxIdentifierSets`$(S_{id}, \mathcal{I})$;
3 $\mathcal{G}_{max} \leftarrow$`GetAutomatonGroups`$(R, \mathcal{I}_{max})$;
4 $\mathcal{G}_{after} \leftarrow \{\}$;
5 **foreach** G *in* $\mathcal{G}_{max}$ **do**
6 $\quad G' \leftarrow$ Apply Algorithm 1 with m and G;
7 $\quad$**if** G' *is not empty* **then**
8 $\quad\quad \mathcal{G}_{after} \leftarrow \mathcal{G}_{after} \cup \{(G, G')\}$;
9 **if** $|\mathcal{G}_{after}| = 1$ **then**
10 $\quad G, G' \leftarrow$`Single`$(\mathcal{G}_{after})$;
11 $\quad ID \leftarrow$`GetAssociatedIdentifierSet`(R, G);
12 $\quad R \leftarrow R \setminus \{(ID, G)\}$;
13 $\quad ID' \leftarrow$`ExpandOrCreateIdentifierSet`$(ID, m.S_v)$;
14 $\quad R \leftarrow R \cup \{(ID', G')\}$;
15 **else if** $|\mathcal{G}_{after}| > 1$ **then**
16 $\quad NID \leftarrow$`CreateIdentifierSet`$(m.S_v)$;
17 $\quad \mathcal{G}' \leftarrow \{\}$;
18 $\quad$**foreach** (G, G') *in* $\mathcal{G}_{after}$ **do**
19 $\quad\quad ID \leftarrow$`GetAssociatedIdentifierSet`(R, G);
20 $\quad\quad NID \leftarrow$`ExpandOrCreateIdentifierSet`$(NID, ID)$;
21 $\quad\quad \mathcal{G}' \leftarrow \mathcal{G}' \cup \{G'\}$;
22 $\quad R \leftarrow R \cup [\{NID\} \times \mathcal{G}']$;
23 **else**
24 $\quad$**Divergence Recovery and Problem Detection**
25 $a, \mathcal{I}, \mathcal{G}, R \leftarrow$`PruneIfAcceptingOrErroneous`$(\mathcal{I}, \mathcal{G}, R, \mathcal{G}_{after})$;
26 **return** a or $None$;

new algorithm keeps multiple automaton groups simultaneously to track interleaved sequences, where each automaton group tracks the log messages from one task execution. Second, to avoid exhaustively trying every incoming message on all automaton groups, the algorithm associates an *identifier set* with each automaton group, which helps determine the proper automaton group to use on-the-fly.

An identifier set is a signature for an automaton group, and it is generated based on the log sequence that has been checked by the automaton group. During the growth of a sequence, its corresponding identifier set incrementally stores identifiers appearing in log messages of the sequence. Identifier sets serve as the key to determine whether an incoming message belongs to a sequence. This is based on an observation that a log message is likely to belong to a sequence with whose identifier set the message shares the greatest number of common identifiers. Since each automaton group is associated with an identifier set, the checking algorithm can find the most likely automaton group(s) to consume an input message without trying all the groups.

Algorithm 2 shows the detail of checking interleaved log sequences. The algorithm first gets the automaton group(s) associated with the identifier set(s) having the greatest number of common identifiers with the incoming message m (Lines 1 to 3). Then the algorithm uses Algorithm 1 with the selected automaton groups to check m (Lines 4 to 8). The checking may result in three cases: (1) only one automaton group left (the branch from Lines 9 to 14); (2) multiple automaton groups taking m (the branch from Lines 15 to 22); or (3) none of the selected automaton groups to take m (the branch from Lines 23 to 24). After handling the three cases, the algorithm looks for and returns any automaton instance that is in the accepting state, or identifies a potential problem. The algorithm also cleans up related identifier sets, automaton groups, and their relations (Lines 25 to 26).

We describe the handling of the three cases below:

Case (1): decisive checking. When there is only one decisive automaton group, which shares the greatest number of common identifiers with the incoming message and can consume the message, the algorithm applies the steps from Lines 10 to 14 to update the associated identifier set and the relation between the set and the group. In particular, Line 13 expands the set ID by including new identifiers in the message m, i.e., $ID \cup m.S_v$. If the set is associated with multiple automaton groups besides the group taking the message m, the algorithm creates a new identifier set from the original one, and it then expands the new set with new identifiers in m, i.e., two sets ID and $ID \cup m.S_v$. Upon the acceptance of an automaton instance, Line 12 removes the old relation between the original automaton group and its associated identifier set, and Line 14 adds the new relation.

Case (2): brute force and heuristics. There can be multiple automaton groups from Lines 4 to 8. These automaton groups all share the same greatest number of identifiers with the incoming message and can consume the message, but they may have different identifier sets. The algorithm cannot decisively determine an automaton group among all the chosen ones, so it has to keep all of them before and after taking a message to explore different possibilities. For example, suppose there are two automaton groups G_1 and G_2 with identifier sets ID_1 and ID_2, both of which share the most identifiers with an incoming message m. G_1 and G_2 make their own state transitions to G_1' and G_2' by taking the message m. The algorithm keeps (ID_1, G_1) and (ID_2, G_2), and it adds $(ID_1 \cup ID_2 \cup m.S_v, G_1')$ and $(ID_1 \cup ID_2 \cup m.S_v, G_2')$ to the relation set R. When the message after m comes in, the extended identifier set $(ID_1 \cup ID_2 \cup m.S_v)$ gives G_1' and G_2' an equal chance to check the message. As a result, the algorithm tracks both possibilities: G_1' and G_2, or G_1 and G_2'. Upon the acceptance of an automaton instance, the algorithm removes all automaton groups, identifier sets, and relations that are related to the other possibilities.

To reduce the number of possible automaton groups to track, we introduce two heuristics to deal with the two causes of having multiple automaton groups. First, if two identifier sets share the same number of identifiers with an incoming message, the function *ComputeMaxIdentifierSets* also computes the numbers of identifiers that are different between these sets and the message, and it selects the set with the least difference. Second, if there are multiple automaton groups associated with the same identifier set, the function *GetAutomatonGroups* randomly selects one group when it finds multiple equivalent groups. Two automaton groups are equivalent if they contain automaton instances of the same kind, and the instances of the same kind are in the same state.

Case (3): divergence recovery. Divergences during the checking on the message m result in an empty set returned from Algorithm 1. Such divergences may not indicate execution problems under the following four causes. We provide a recovering heuristic for each of these causes, and these causes are prioritized in the ascending order based on our knowledge of their recovering cost and side effect: (a) m is not in the Σ of any automaton; (b) m starts a new log sequence, so there is no corresponding automaton group; (c) the chosen identifier set is likely not correct, so the automaton group is unable to take m; and (d) m does not arrive in the order defined by the modeled temporal dependencies.

`CloudSeer` applies the recovering heuristics one by one until it recovers. For the cause (a), the algorithm allows unrecognizable messages to pass through. Such messages are usually not of interest to the checking process. If an error message appears, the error-message criterion described below can capture it. For the cause (b), Algorithm 1 is applied with an empty automaton group to create new automaton instances for tracking a new sequence.

If the first two heuristics cannot resolve the divergence, it is likely that the algorithm has chosen a wrong automaton group (the cause (c)). Such situation can sometimes happen if two interleaved log sequences share some identifiers, e.g., the same user boots two VMs at the same time. The algorithm tries another automaton group that has less common identifiers than the best match to take the message.

The unexpected message reordering may fail all other heuristics (the cause (d)). In this situation, a message B arrives earlier than another message A, which should not happen according to the dependency $A \rightarrow B$ from the modeling stage. There are two possible reasons for such reordering: $A \rightarrow B$ is a false dependency or a message-delivery delay causes A to arrive late. We consider that it is unnecessary to determine the particular reason in `CloudSeer`'s usage scenario, so we treat all such reordering as the result of false dependencies encoded in task automata and remove such dependencies from the automaton instances.

Figure 4 shows an example of the removal step. The graph on the left side shows an automaton with a false temporal dependency $B \rightarrow C$. To remove $B \rightarrow C$ from the automaton and make it accept a new sequence $ACBD$, the algorithm first removes the state transition from $q2$ to $q3$, and it adds two new transitions $q1 \rightarrow q3$ and $q2 \rightarrow q4$ (shown by dashed arrows in the right-side graph of Figure 4). The state $q1$ thus becomes a fork state, and $q4$ becomes a join state. These changes reflect two weakened dependencies $A \rightarrow C$ and $B \rightarrow D$ as the results of removing $B \rightarrow C$.

Problem Detection. We implement two simple criteria in `CloudSeer` to detect common execution problems. The two criteria are based on two common manifestations of execution problems: (1) the presence of error messages, indicating task failures; (2) the absence or delay of messages, indicating task failures or performance degradation.

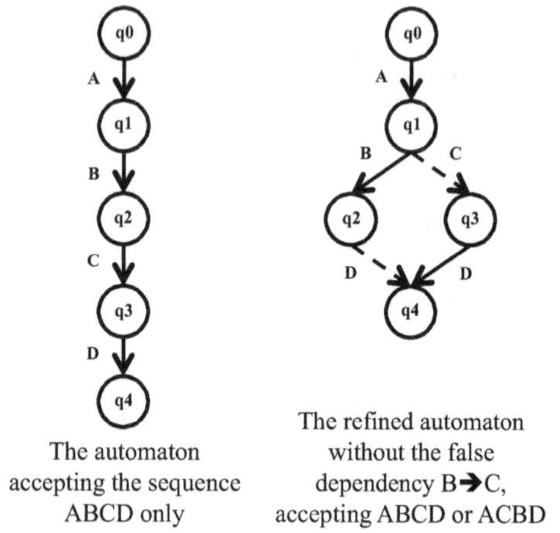

Figure 4. Removing Dependencies

Error-message criterion is in effect when an error message (determined by its logging level) arrives, and the checking algorithm in Algorithm 2 results in a state of divergence, as shown in Line 24. This criterion then applies the functions *ComputeMaxIdentifierSets* and *GetAutomatonGroups* to identify and output the most likely automaton group that may be associated with the error message.

Timeout criterion marks any automaton groups that do not take any messages within a specified time period. The marked automaton groups become the outputs of Algorithm 2. The timeout value may vary in different systems and configurations. Determining such values is not in the scope of this paper, and we leave it for future work.

5. Evaluation

We present a series of systematic experiments conducted on OpenStack to evaluate the following aspects of `CloudSeer`.

Checking Accuracy. The accuracy that `CloudSeer` correctly checks interleaved log sequences is fundamental to `CloudSeer`'s problem detection. We measure the accuracy based on logs collected from correct task executions. `CloudSeer` is supposed to recognize and accept all log sequences in the correct logs. Therefore, any nonacceptance would indicate inaccuracies.

Efficiency. To show `CloudSeer`'s capability of working in the monitoring scenario, we measure the throughput of `CloudSeer` consuming log messages and present how the identifier-based heuristic affects the checking efficiency.

Capability of Problem Detection. With typical execution problems that are injected to certain weak points in the OpenStack system, we show how well `CloudSeer` detects them and provides automaton instances as useful information related to the detected problems.

Task	Description	Msgs	Trans
Boot	Create a new VM.	23	34
Delete	Delete a VM.	9	9
Start	Start a stopped VM.	7	7
Stop	Stop a running VM.	6	6
Pause	Pause a running VM in memory.	7	7
Unpause	Bring back a paused VM.	7	7
Suspend	Suspend a running VM to disk.	6	6
Resume	Bring back a suspended VM.	7	7

Table 2. VM Tasks for Experiments

5.1 Test Bed

We deploy an OpenStack instance in a five-node cluster as the test bed for our experiments. The OpenStack version is *Havana*. In our deployment, there are one controller node, one network node running network-related services, and three compute nodes. We follow the installation guide of OpenStack [5] to deploy this instance.

We set the logging levels for all `nova` service components to *INFO*. Therefore, `nova-api`, `nova-scheduler`, and `nova-compute` generate *INFO*-level messages for VM-related tasks. Such a setting is typical for deployment, and our evaluation suggests that *INFO* level is sufficient to provide workflow information without imposing excessive burdens on servers.

We deploy our prototype of `CloudSeer` alongside Elasticsearch [7], which is a central log database, on the controller node. To centralize logs from OpenStack services, we deploy Logstash [9] on each server node. Logstash parses log messages generated by OpenStack services on each server node and sends the parsed messages to both `CloudSeer` and Elasticsearch on the controller node. While Logstash instances on multiple server nodes create a log stream, Elasticsearch stores all log messages in the stream. We use the log stream and stored log messages in different experiments.

5.2 Workload Generator

To evaluate `CloudSeer` with interleaved log sequences, we implement a workload generator that simulates multiple users submitting OpenStack tasks concurrently through the command-line interface. This generator can create various workloads varying in the number of concurrent users and the number of tasks submitted by each user.

The generator uses eight primitive and typical VM-related tasks to create workloads, and they are listed in Table 2. To obtain the automaton for each task, we keep running the task and applying the modeling algorithm on the output logs, until logs from any subsequent task executions do not change the result automaton. In this way, the result automaton is likely to be concise regarding key log messages and complete regarding relations between messages. The number of runs for modeling each task ranges from 200 to 800, depending on the extent of nondeterminism within task executions. In Table 2, the column "Msgs" shows the number of messages in the log sequence of each execution

Grp.	Data Sets	Users	Single UID?	Total Tasks
1	$1-10$	2	N	1600
2	$11-20$	3	N	2400
3	$21-30$	4	N	3200
4	$31-40$	2	Y	1600
5	$41-50$	3	Y	2400
6	$51-60$	4	Y	3200

Table 3. Experiments for Accuracy and Efficiency

Injection Point	Type	Responsibilities
AMQP-Sender	Net	Request RPCs to services that control VMs, e.g., `nova-scheduler` and `nova-compute`.
AMQP-Receiver	Net	Receive and process RPC requests.
Image-Create	I/O	On each `nova-compute` server node, create a new VM image from an image template.
Image-Delete	I/O	When destroying a VM, delete all related files.
WSGI-Client	Net	Send HTTP-based requests to query image information stored by `glance` services.
WSGI-Server	Net	Process queries of image information.

Table 4. Execution Points for Failure Injection

after preprocessing, and the column "Trans" shows the number of transitions in the corresponding automaton.

For each simulated user, the generator randomly populates tasks by the following regular expression:

$$(Boot\ (StopStart \mid PauseUnpause \mid SuspendResume)*\ Delete)+$$

This expression produces multiple task groups, starting with a "boot" task and ending with a "delete" task. Within each task group, there can be multiple pairs of "stop/start," "pause/unpause," and "suspend/resume" tasks on the same VM. When booting a VM, we use CirrOS [6] as the guest system. To ensure the completion of each submitted task, we set each user to wait 15 seconds between two tasks.

5.3 Experiment Design

We design six groups of experiments (shown in Table 3) to evaluate checking accuracy and efficiency of `CloudSeer`. These experiments test two potential factors that may affect the results of accuracy and efficiency: the number of tasks being executed concurrently, and the diversity of identifiers appearing in logs. We control the first factor by setting various concurrent users in the workload generator (shown in the column "Users"). To control the second factor, we set the generator to simulate users with identical or different user identifier (shown in the column "Single UID?") when submitting tasks. We repeat the experiment of each combination of the two factors for 10 times to produce different combinations of interleaved log sequences (shown in the column "Data Sets"). Each simulated user in an experiment is set to submit 80 tasks, resulting in the total numbers shown in the column "Total Tasks."

The evaluation of checking accuracy and efficiency requires measuring multiple aspects of `CloudSeer`'s checking algorithm in a repeatable way. Therefore, we use the same set of stored log messages to feed `CloudSeer` multiple times to ensure consistent measurements.

To show the capability of problem detection, we randomly inject execution problems to the test bed to mimic

Grp.	Acc. Range	Median	% Interleaved ($\geq 2, 3, 4$)
1	$93.24\% - 100.0\%$	96.83%	48.50%
2	$96.82\% - 100.0\%$	98.09%	$65.00\%, 31.17\%$
3	$95.78\% - 98.72\%$	97.22%	$74.34\%, 48.63\%, 22.84\%$
4	$96.15\% - 97.47\%$	97.47%	49.00%
5	$94.16\% - 99.37\%$	98.07%	$64.67\%, 32.71\%$
6	$92.08\% - 97.87\%$	96.51%	$80.12\%, 55.59\%, 30.06\%$

Table 5. Experiment Results for Accuracy

Grp.	Ave. Msgs	Ave. Time	Ave. 1k	% Decisive
1	2164	3.91s	1.81s	83.13%
2	2990	6.25s	2.09s	80.76%
3	3849	8.98s	2.33s	78.18%
4	2158	4.32s	2.00s	80.12%
5	2989	7.37s	2.47s	75.48%
6	3820	11.57s	3.03s	71.43%

Table 6. Experiment Results for Efficiency

the real-world scenario, and let `CloudSeer` monitor the test bed for the injected problems. We configure the workload generator to use four users to submit tasks concurrently. In addition, we configure the timeout value of task automata to be 10 seconds based on the performance of our test bed.

We choose six execution points to inject execution problems and apply `CloudSeer` to detect them. Table 4 shows these injection points and their major responsibilities for tasks in the scope of our experiments. These injection points are potentially error-prone because of network and I/O, and they reflect general and typical failure patterns that have been well studied [17, 19, 20]. During the experiment, we enable these injection points one at a time and set every enabled injection point with a 25% chance to trigger an execution problem. The problem is chosen randomly by the injection point from: (a) delaying execution by a significant amount of time to simulate a performance problem, (b) aborting the current thread to simulate an unexpected exception, and (c) ignoring a network-based request or returning an incorrect file-system status, to simulate network or I/O specific problems. We use the workload generator to keep running tasks until each injection points triggers 10 execution problems. Then we examine whether the problems reported by `CloudSeer` match with the injected ones.

5.4 Checking Accuracy

Since there are nearly 15,000 log sequences from the experiment, it is impractical to manually determine whether `CloudSeer` accurately checks each of them with the correct automaton instance. Instead, we approximate the checking accuracy using the following formula:

$$Accuracy = 1 - \frac{\#\ of\ Not\text{-}Accepted\ Sequences}{\#\ of\ Interleaved\ Sequences}$$

We only use the number of interleaved log sequences from parallel task executions in the denominator. False temporal dependencies are the only cause of checking inaccuracies in sequential executions, because other checking heuristics are not in effect. As our task modeling is sufficient for sequential executions, we exclude them from the accuracy calculation for a close approximation. Since we cannot precisely control whether and how OpenStack executes parallel task requests, we estimate the number of interleaved sequences caused by parallel executions using the number of automaton instances simultaneously tracked by `CloudSeer`.

We determine the number of not-accepted sequences by counting automaton instances that are not in accepting states. We also compare the number of instances of each task with the number of tasks populated by the workload generator. If they do not match, we manually check related automaton instances to identify accepted instances that may happen to accept messages from multiple sequences, and we count them as not-accepted ones. However, we cannot identify the case where an accepted instance may happen to take messages from multiple sequences of the same kind of task.

Table 5 presents the experiment results. The column "Acc. Range" gives the accuracy ranges showing the worst and the best results in each experiment group, and the column "Median" gives the median values. The column "% Interleaved" shows the average percentages of interleaved sequences in each experiment group. For the groups 1 and 4, the percentages are of interleaved sequences from at least two executions being in parallel (shown by the first percentage in each row). For the groups having more than two users, we also show the percentages of interleaved sequences from at least three and four executions being in parallel (shown by the second and the third percentages in each row).

The results suggest that `CloudSeer` is accurate enough to check most interleaved log sequences. Among six groups of experiments, the worst accuracy is 92.08% in one experiment of the group 6, while two experiments in the groups 1 and 2 result in a perfect accuracy. Based on the data in Table 5, we find no substantial links between the accuracy and the number of paralleled task executions or the diversity of identifiers. On the other hand, there are about 271 sequences that are for sure not accurately checked by `CloudSeer`. They end up not being accepted or being accepted by wrong automaton instances. Such inaccuracies are caused by message-interleaving patterns that invalidate the heuristics on identifier sets and divergence recovery.

5.5 Efficiency

Table 6 presents the results of efficiency by measuring the checking time for each data set listed in Table 3. The column "Ave. Msgs" shows the average number of messages produced by each experiment group. The columns "Ave. Time" and "Ave. 1k" present the average checking time and the average time per 1000 messages in each experiment. The column "% Decisive" presents the percentage of decisive checking led by the identifier-based heuristic, i.e., case (1) in Algorithm 2, among all cases. These results reflect the throughput of the checking algorithm of `CloudSeer` (Algorithm 2), but not the overhead of Logstash delivering logs from each server node to the centralized location.

Injection Point	Tasks	D	A	S	Detected	F/P	F/N
AMQP-Sender	45	3	3	4	9	0	1
AMQP-Receiver	85	3	5	2	10	1	0
Image-Create	256	3	5	2	*10	3	1
Image-Delete	240	1	3	6	8	3	2
WSGI-Client	208	3	3	4	10	3	0
WSGI-Server	87	5	3	2	8	1	**2

*. `CloudSeer` caught an unplanned and unexpected performance problem.
**. One of the injected problems does not reflect on logs.

Table 7. Detection Results

Overall, the results suggest a satisfactory checking efficiency regarding the throughput and reveal two key observations that are related to the achieved efficiency. First, the identifier-based heuristic is effective in improving the overall checking efficiency. The higher the percentage of decisive checking is, the less the checking time is needed. In particular, comparing groups with similar numbers of log messages, e.g., groups 1 and 4, we conclude that the throughput is proportional to the percentage of decisive checking. Second, both the number of parallel executions and the diversity of identifiers can affect the efficiency. The diversity of identifiers directly affects the chance of applying the expensive brute-force and divergence-recovery algorithms, as the throughputs of groups 4, 5, 6 are lower than those of groups 1, 2, 3. Subtly, the number of parallel executions affects the number of candidate identifier sets, which further increases the chance of not having decisive checking in the first place.

5.6 Capability of Problem Detection

Table 7 presents the detection results. The column "Tasks" shows the number of tasks running for each injection point, as we keep running OpenStack tasks until each point triggers 10 problems. The execution problems come randomly from three types: column "D" for delaying execution, column "A" for aborting execution, and column "S" for network or I/O specific problems. The column "Detected" shows the number of true problems detected by `CloudSeer`. The columns "F/P" and "F/N" are false positives and false negatives.

Among all 60 injected problems, 17 of them have related error messages. The other 43 problems do not lead to any error messages. Within these 43 problems, 25 of them are execution failures, and the other 18 are performance problems that are not supposed to generate any error messages.

`CloudSeer` detects 16 problems by the error-message criterion and 38 problems by the timeout criterion. These results show a precision of 83.08% and a recall of 90.00%. To verify true positives and investigate causes of false positives and false negatives, we manually check relevant automaton instances produced by `CloudSeer` and the task-submission logs by the workload generator. We also check the injection history that records injection time and VM information.

We identify two major factors affecting the precision and recall of `CloudSeer` reporting execution failures. The checking accuracy is by nature a major reason, which causes both false positives and false negatives. In Table 7, eight false positives and two false negatives are the results of inaccurate checking. We find that the major cause of such inaccuracies is message ordering missed by task automata due to insufficient modeling.

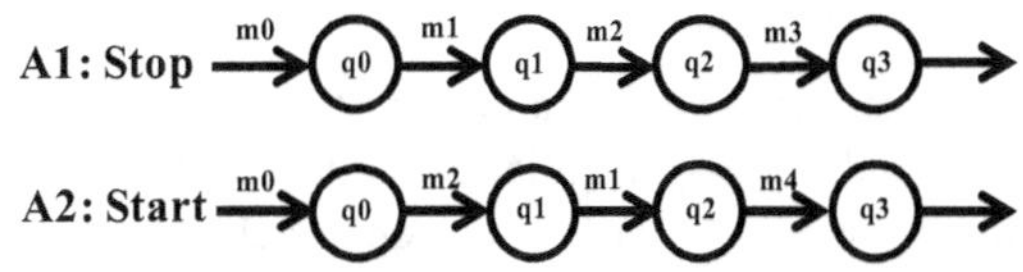

m0, m1, m2, m3	[A1, A2]	m0, m2, m1, m3	[A1, A2]
m1, m2, m3	[A1, A2]	m2, m1, m3	[A1, A2]
m2, m3	[A1]	m1, m3	[A2]
m3	[A1]	m3	[?]

Figure 5. Normal and Reordering Cases

Figure 5 presents a simplified but representative case of message reordering. $A1$ and $A2$ represent automaton excerpts for the tasks "Stop" and "Start." Both automata can consume the messages m_1 and m_2, but in different orders. The concrete messages for m_1 and m_2 are "`Lifecycle event`" from a callback registered with the VM hypervisor and "`Instance destroyed`" from the `nova-compute` service. For a normal log sequence m_0, m_1, m_2, m_3 (bottom left of Figure 5), `CloudSeer` would choose $A1$ as the automaton for the sequence after checking messages followed by m_3. However, $m_1 \rightarrow m_2$ turns out to be a false dependency, where the two messages could be sometimes reordered when the server workload increases (bottom right of Figure 5). Coincidentally, it happens that $A2$ is able to recognize the reordered messages. Therefore, `CloudSeer` would keep $A2$ instead of $A1$ for the sequence without triggering divergence-recovery strategies. Consequently, $A2$ could trigger a timeout because the expected message m_4 never comes, leading to a false positive. Meanwhile, `CloudSeer` may find another automaton instance to consume the unhandled message m_3, leading to a potential false negative if the instance should have triggered a timeout. A straightforward mitigation of such reordering is to involve manual efforts in refining the task automata once false dependencies are identified during the checking process.

In addition, multiple error messages for a single execution problem lead to three false positives and three false negatives. Our error-message criterion assumes that each execution problem would be associated with only one error message. However, we find that occasionally different services may generate error messages at the same time for the same injected problem. In such cases, after associating an error message with an automaton instance, `CloudSeer` stops choosing that instance to check any other messages. Consequently, if identifier values in the extra error messages match with existing identifier sets, `CloudSeer` may find other automaton instances to associate with, which leads to false positives. Any falsely associated automaton instances would lose the capability of detecting problems of their own log sequences, so potentially lead to false negatives.

6. Related Work

In essence, we contribute an approach that monitors interleaved logs and reports potential execution problems in an automated lightweight manner. The approach uses the task automaton as the workflow abstraction to provide context information out of unstructured logs for further problem diagnosis. Based on our main contribution, we differentiate our approach from existing work as follows.

Mining workflow models from logs. Recent work [14, 15, 22, 23, 28] uses logs or traces to create workflow models for software testing, debugging, and the understanding of system behaviors. Notably, CSight [14] creates finite state machines by mining temporal invariants in logs of concurrent systems. Lou *et al.* [23] propose an intuitive automaton model and corresponding mining algorithms for reconstructing concurrent workflows from event traces.

Compared to such work, `CloudSeer` specifically addresses the log-monitoring problem using workflow models. To make workflow models suitable for both monitoring and system-behavior understanding that helps problem diagnosis, we adapt the idea of mining workflow models by tailoring such models to be lightweight specifications (i.e., task automata). With the tailored models, `CloudSeer` can effectively and efficiently check interleaved log sequences for the purpose of monitoring; meanwhile, it can also output monitoring results represented in workflow models that are understandable by administrators. Furthermore, we add on-the-fly refinement to task automata in order to mitigate false dependencies from mining and message-delivery delays in the production environment.

Log analysis for distributed systems. Some log-analysis approaches apply data-mining and machine-learning techniques on logs of distributed systems [16, 18, 21, 24, 25, 29]. Some of these approaches also focus on workflow-based analysis. Fu *et al.* [18] proposes an approach that learns workflow models from unstructured logs and uses the models to detect performance anomalies in new input logs. The Mystery Machine [16] relies on a tremendous amount of log data to infer dependency models for critical-path analysis.

Compared to these approaches, `CloudSeer` addresses the following two key points. First, in the monitoring scenario that `CloudSeer` targets, the log-message set for analysis keeps growing and changing. Such dynamics make these techniques tend to be unstable and inefficient to produce results, because they rely on existing offline logs in which there are sufficient data points representing both normal and abnormal executions. On the other hand, `CloudSeer` separates the analysis into offline and online phases. The offline phase produces task automata as stable models for the ground truth of correct-execution logs. Then the online phase leverages the models to identify partial log sequences and look for potential problems along the growing of logs.

Second, some of the workflow-based approaches require a unique and global identifier for each request. As we discussed in Section 2, although the use of identifiers in logs is ubiquitous, there is usually no single and unique identifier that is propagated across all distributed components. In `CloudSeer`, we lift the requirement of such unique and global identifiers by introducing the identifier-based heuristics. The heuristics work on-the-fly to associate multiple identifiers that should belong to the same log sequence, but are used by different distributed components.

In addition, lprof [32] is a request-flow profiler for distributed systems. It reconstructs request flows from logs and assists the diagnosis of performance anomalies. lprof relies on static analysis on Java bytecode to identify logging information, such as request identifiers for attributing log messages to flows. To the contrary, `CloudSeer` is language-agnostic and complements lprof on systems where static analysis is tedious or difficult to implement.

Log-based failure diagnosis. Insight [26] and SherLog [30] use error logs and other artifacts, such as source code, to infer or reproduce failure paths. These failure-diagnosis techniques work on a single-thread or single-request basis. `CloudSeer` may be beneficial to these techniques when being applied to complex systems, because `CloudSeer` can provide abstracted log sequences including erroneous ones from parallel task executions.

Distributed tracing frameworks. There are frameworks targeting at tracing large-scale distributed systems [4, 12, 13, 27]. These frameworks require instrumentation in specific system components, e.g., network library, to generate traces for further analysis. Compared to these frameworks, `CloudSeer` purely works on logs that are readily available in existing running systems, so it does not require any special instrumentation. Since logging is a common practice in developing large-scale systems, `CloudSeer` is highly usable on existing production systems with general logs.

7. Conclusion

We present `CloudSeer`, a lightweight non-intrusive approach for log-based workflow monitoring in cloud infrastructures. `CloudSeer` effectively and efficiently checks interleaved log sequences for execution problems with or without error log messages. It outputs task-automaton instances representing possible erroneous sequences as hints for further diagnosis. Our experiments on OpenStack show that `CloudSeer`'s checking accuracy is high on interleaved logs, with a satisfactory efficiency for the online monitoring scenario. The experiment with injected execution problems further shows that `CloudSeer` is capable for online execution-problem detection.

Acknowledgments

We would like to thank anonymous reviewers for their thoughtful feedback that helps us improve this paper and Tao Wang for proofreading.

References

[1] 2013 Path to an OpenStack-Powered Cloud Survey Results Highlight Aggressive OpenStack Adoption Plans by Enterprises. http://www.redhat.com/en/about/press-releases/2013-path-to-an-openstack-powered-cloud-survey-results-highlight-aggressive-openstack-adoption-plans-by-enterprises.

[2] Amazon CloudWatch. https://aws.amazon.com/cloudwatch/.

[3] Amazon Elastic Compute Cloud. http://aws.amazon.com/ec2/.

[4] Apache HTrace. http://htrace.incubator.apache.org/.

[5] Architecture. OpenStack Installation Guide, http://docs.openstack.org/havana/install-guide/install/apt/content/ch_overview.html.

[6] CirrOS: A Tiny Cloud Guest. https://launchpad.net/cirros.

[7] Elasticsearch. http://www.elasticsearch.org/overview/elasticsearch/.

[8] Logging and Monitoring. OpenStack Operations Guide, http://docs.openstack.org/openstack-ops/content/logging_monitoring.html.

[9] Logstash. http://www.elasticsearch.org/overview/logstash/.

[10] Microsoft Azure. http://azure.microsoft.com/en-us/.

[11] OpenStack. http://www.openstack.org/.

[12] Zipkin. http://zipkin.io/.

[13] P. Barham, A. Donnelly, R. Isaacs, and R. Mortier. Using Magpie for Request Extraction and Workload Modelling. In *Proceedings of the 6th Conference on Symposium on Opearting Systems Design & Implementation - Volume 6*, OSDI'04, pages 18–18, Berkeley, CA, USA, 2004. USENIX Association.

[14] I. Beschastnikh, Y. Brun, M. D. Ernst, and A. Krishnamurthy. Inferring Models of Concurrent Systems from Logs of Their Behavior with CSight. In *Proceedings of the 36th International Conference on Software Engineering*, ICSE 2014, pages 468–479, New York, NY, USA, 2014. ACM.

[15] I. Beschastnikh, Y. Brun, M. D. Ernst, A. Krishnamurthy, and T. E. Anderson. Mining Temporal Invariants from Partially Ordered Logs. *ACM SIGOPS Operating Systems Review*, 45(3):39–46, Jan. 2012.

[16] M. Chow, D. Meisner, J. Flinn, D. Peek, and T. F. Wenisch. The Mystery Machine: End-to-end Performance Analysis of Large-scale Internet Services. In *Proceedings of the 11th USENIX Conference on Operating Systems Design and Implementation*, OSDI'14, pages 217–231, Berkeley, CA, USA, 2014. USENIX Association.

[17] T. Do, M. Hao, T. Leesatapornwongsa, T. Patana-anake, and H. S. Gunawi. Limplock: Understanding the Impact of Limpware on Scale-Out Cloud Systems. In *Proceedings of the 4th Annual Symposium on Cloud Computing*, SOCC '13, pages 14:1–14:14, New York, NY, USA, 2013. ACM.

[18] Q. Fu, J.-G. Lou, Y. Wang, and J. Li. Execution Anomaly Detection in Distributed Systems through Unstructured Log Analysis. In *Proceedings of the 2009 Ninth IEEE International Conference on Data Mining*, ICDM '09, pages 149–158, Washington, DC, USA, 2009. IEEE Computer Society.

[19] P. Joshi, H. S. Gunawi, and K. Sen. PREFAIL: A Programmable Tool for Multiple-Failure Injection. In *Proceedings of the 2011 ACM International Conference on Object Oriented Programming Systems Languages and Applications*, OOPSLA '11, pages 171–188, New York, NY, USA, 2011. ACM.

[20] X. Ju, L. Soares, K. G. Shin, K. D. Ryu, and D. Da Silva. On Fault Resilience of OpenStack. In *Proceedings of the 4th Annual Symposium on Cloud Computing*, SOCC '13, pages 2:1–2:16, New York, NY, USA, 2013. ACM.

[21] K. Kc and X. Gu. ELT: Efficient Log-based Troubleshooting System for Cloud Computing Infrastructures. In *2011 30th IEEE Symposium on Reliable Distributed Systems (SRDS)*, pages 11–20, Oct 2011.

[22] D. Lo, L. Mariani, and M. Pezzè. Automatic Steering of Behavioral Model Inference. In *Proceedings of the the 7th Joint Meeting of the European Software Engineering Conference and the ACM SIGSOFT Symposium on The Foundations of Software Engineering*, ESEC/FSE '09, pages 345–354, New York, NY, USA, 2009. ACM.

[23] J.-G. Lou, Q. Fu, S. Yang, J. Li, and B. Wu. Mining Program Workflow from Interleaved Traces. In *Proceedings of the 16th ACM SIGKDD International Conference on Knowledge Discovery and Data Mining*, KDD '10, pages 613–622, New York, NY, USA, 2010. ACM.

[24] J.-G. Lou, Q. Fu, S. Yang, Y. Xu, and J. Li. Mining Invariants from Console Logs for System Problem Detection. In *Proceedings of the 2010 USENIX Conference on USENIX Annual Technical Conference*, USENIXATC'10, pages 24–24, Berkeley, CA, USA, 2010. USENIX Association.

[25] K. Nagaraj, C. Killian, and J. Neville. Structured Comparative Analysis of Systems Logs to Diagnose Performance Problems. In *Proceedings of the 9th USENIX Conference on Networked Systems Design and Implementation*, NSDI'12, pages 26–26, Berkeley, CA, USA, 2012. USENIX Association.

[26] H. Nguyen, D. J. Dean, K. Kc, and X. Gu. Insight: In-situ Online Service Failure Path Inference in Production Computing Infrastructures. In *Proceedings of the 2014 USENIX Conference on USENIX Annual Technical Conference*, USENIX ATC'14, pages 269–280, Berkeley, CA, USA, 2014. USENIX Association.

[27] B. H. Sigelman, L. A. Barroso, M. Burrows, P. Stephenson, M. Plakal, D. Beaver, S. Jaspan, and C. Shanbhag. Dapper, a Large-Scale Distributed Systems Tracing Infrastructure. Technical report, Google, Inc., 2010.

[28] N. Walkinshaw and K. Bogdanov. Inferring Finite-State Models with Temporal Constraints. In *Proceedings of the 2008 23rd IEEE/ACM International Conference on Automated Software Engineering*, ASE '08, pages 248–257, Washington, DC, USA, 2008. IEEE Computer Society.

[29] W. Xu, L. Huang, A. Fox, D. Patterson, and M. I. Jordan. Detecting Large-Scale System Problems by Mining Console Logs. In *Proceedings of the ACM SIGOPS 22nd Symposium on Operating Systems Principles*, SOSP '09, pages 117–132, New York, NY, USA, 2009. ACM.

[30] D. Yuan, H. Mai, W. Xiong, L. Tan, Y. Zhou, and S. Pasupathy. SherLog: Error Diagnosis by Connecting Clues from Runtime Logs. In *Proceedings of the Fifteenth Edition of ASPLOS on Architectural Support for Programming Languages and Operating Systems*, ASPLOS XV, pages 143–154, New York, NY, USA, 2010. ACM.

[31] D. Yuan, S. Park, P. Huang, Y. Liu, M. M. Lee, X. Tang, Y. Zhou, and S. Savage. Be Conservative: Enhancing Failure Diagnosis with Proactive Logging. In *Proceedings of the 10th USENIX Conference on Operating Systems Design and Implementation*, OSDI'12, pages 293–306, Berkeley, CA, USA, 2012. USENIX Association.

[32] X. Zhao, Y. Zhang, D. Lion, M. F. Ullah, Y. Luo, D. Yuan, and M. Stumm. lprof: A Non-intrusive Request Flow Profiler for Distributed Systems. In *Proceedings of the 11th USENIX Conference on Operating Systems Design and Implementation*, OSDI'14, pages 629–644, Berkeley, CA, USA, 2014. USENIX Association.

LDX: Causality Inference by Lightweight Dual Execution

Yonghwi Kwon[1] Dohyeong Kim[1] William N. Sumner[2] Kyungtae Kim[1]
Brendan Saltaformaggio[1] Xiangyu Zhang[1] Dongyan Xu[1]

[1]Department of Computer Science, Purdue University, USA
[2]School of Computing Science, Simon Fraser University, Canada
[1]{kwon58,kim1051,kim1798,bsaltafo,xyzhang,dxu}@purdue.edu [2]wsumner@sfu.ca

Abstract

Causality inference, such as dynamic taint anslysis, has many applications (e.g., information leak detection). It determines whether an event *e* is causally dependent on a preceding event *c* during execution. We develop a new causality inference engine LDX. Given an execution, it spawns a slave execution, in which it mutates *c* and observes whether any change is induced at *e*. To preclude non-determinism, LDX couples the executions by sharing syscall outcomes. To handle path differences induced by the perturbation, we develop a novel on-the-fly execution alignment scheme that maintains a counter to reflect the progress of execution. The scheme relies on program analysis and compiler transformation. LDX can effectively detect information leak and security attacks with an average overhead of 6.08% while running the master and the slave concurrently on seperate CPUs, much lower than existing systems that require instruction level monitoring. Furthermore, it has much better accuracy in causality inference.

Keywords Causality Inference, Dual Execution, Dynamic Analysis

1. Introduction

Causality inference during program execution determines whether an event is causally dependent on a preceding event. Such events could be system level events (e.g., input/output syscalls) or individual instruction executions. A version of causality inference, *dynamic tainting*, is widely used to detect *information leak*, namely, sensitive information is undesirably disclosed to untrusted entities, and *runtime attacks*, in which exploit inputs subvert critical execution state such as stack and heap (Qin et al. 2006; Song et al. 2008; Kemerlis et al. 2012; Clause et al. 2007; Bosman et al. 2011).

Most existing causality inference techniques are based on program dependences, especially data dependences. There is data dependence between two events if the former event defines a variable and the later event uses it. These techniques have a few limitations. *First*, they have difficulty in handling control dependence. There is control dependence between a predicate and an instruction if the predicate directly determines whether the instruction executes. The challenge lies in that control dependences sometimes lead to strong causality, but some other times lead to very weak causality that cannot be exploited by attackers and hence should not be considered. Most existing solutions (McCamant and Ernst 2008; Kang et al. 2011; Cox et al. 2014) rely on detecting syntactic patterns of control dependences and hence are incomplete. *Second*, existing techniques are expensive (e.g., a few times slow-down (Kemerlis et al. 2012)), as memory accesses need to be instrumented to detect data dependences. *Third*, the complexity in implementation is high. Dependence tracking logic needs to be defined for each instruction, which is error-prone for complex instruction sets. Instrumenting third party libraries, various languages and their runtimes, is very challenging.

We observe that these limitations root at tracking causality by monitoring program dependencies. We propose to directly infer causality based on its defintion. In (Lewis 1973), *counterfactual causality* was defined as follows. An event *e* is causally dependent on an earlier event *c* if and only if the absence of *c* also leads to the absence of *e*. Program dependence tracking in some sense just approximates counterfactural causality. Our technique works as follows. It perturbs the program state at *c* (the *source*) and then observes whether there is any change at *e* (the *sink*). There are a number of challenges. (1) We need at least two executions to infer causality. Thus, we must prune the differences caused by non-determinism such as different external event orders. (2) Meaningful comparison of states across executions requires execution alignment. Due to perturbation, the event *e* may occur at different locations. Naive approaches such as using program counters hardly work due to path differences (Xin et al. 2008). (3) The second execution is not a simple replay of the first one, as the perturbation may cause path differences and then input/output syscall differences. (4) Ideally, the two executions should proceed in parallel. Otherwise, the execution time is at least doubled.

The core of our technique is a novel runtime engine LDX, which stands for *Lightweight Dual eXecution.* Its execution model is similar to *Dual Execution* (DualEx) (Kim et al. 2015). Given an original execution (the *master*), a new execution (the *slave*) is derived by mutating the source(s). Later, by comparing the output buffer contents of the two executions at the sink(s), we can determine if the sink(s) are causally dependent on the source(s). The master and the slave are coupled and run concurrently. The slave tries to reuse syscall and nondeterministic instruction outcomes (e.g., `rdtsc`) from the master to avoid nondeterminism. To avoid side effects, the slave often ignores output syscalls. Since perturbation may cause path differences and hence syscall differences, an on-the-fly execution alignment scheme is necessary. DualEx has a very expensive alignment scheme based on *Execution Indexing* (Xin et al. 2008). The slow-down reported in (Kim et al. 2015) is three orders of magnitude. In contrast, LDX features a novel lightweight *on-the-fly alignment scheme* that maintains a *counter* that reflects the progress of execution. The counter is computed in such a sophisticated way

ASPLOS '16 April 2–6, 2016, Atlanta, Georgia, USA.
Copyright © 2016 ACM 978-1-4503-4091-5/16/04...$15.00
DOI: http://dx.doi.org/10.1145/2872362.2872395

that an execution with a larger counter value must be ahead of another with a smaller one. The slave blocks if it reaches a syscall earlier than the master. If different paths are taken in the executions, the scheme can detect them and instructs the executions to perform their syscalls independently. It also allows the executions to realign by ensuring that they have the same counter value at the join point of the different paths. *Without such fine-grained alignment, when the slave encounters a syscall different from that in the master, it cannot decide if the master is running behind (so that it can simply wait) or the two are taking different paths so that the syscall will never happen in the master.*

Our contributions are summarized in the following.

- We study the limitations of program dependence based causality and propose counterfactual causality instead.
- We develop a lightweight dual execution engine that enables practical counterfactual causality inference.
- We develop a novel scheme that computes a counter cost-effectively at runtime using simple arithmetic operations. The counter values from multiple executions indicate their relative progress, facilitating runtime alignment. The scheme handles language features such as loops, recursion, and indirect calls.
- Our evaluation shows that LDX outperforms existing program dependence based dynamic tainting systems LIBDFT (Kemerlis et al. 2012) and TAINTGRIND (Khoo 2013). In the effectiveness aspect, LIBDFT and TAINTGRIND can only detect 31.47% and 20% of the true information leak cases and attacks detected by LDX. Also, LDX does not report any false warnings. In the efficiency aspect, the overhead of LDX is 6.08% to the original execution while it requires running the master and the slave concurrently on two separate CPUs. In contrast, the other two cause a few times slowdown although they do not require the additional CPU and memory. Note that the counter scheme allows aligning and continuing executions in the presence of path differences, which makes LDX superior to TIGHTLIP (Yumerefendi et al. 2007), which often terminates when it detects misaligned syscalls.

Limitations. LDX requires access to source code. Specifically, the target application should be compiled with LLVM because our analysis and instrumentation techniques are implemented in a LLVM pass. LDX occupies more resources than a single execution. In the worst case scenario, it may double the resource consumption on memory, processor, and external resources such as files on disk. Our performance evaluations assume that the machine has enough capacity to accomodate such resource duplication. In practice, if the slave and the master executions are coupled most of the time, only the processor and memory consumptions are doubled because the slave can shares most external I/Os with the master. LDX may have false positives. For example, low level data races that are not protected by any locks may induce non-deterministic state differences and eventually lead to undesirable output differences. However, for shared memory accesses protected by locks, LDX ensures the same synchronization order across the master and the slave. Furthermore, heap addresses are non-deterministic across the two runs, if heap pointer values are emitted as part of the output, LDX reports causality even though the two pointers may be semantically equivalent. However, In our experience, pointer values are rarely printed as part of the outputs at sink points.

LDX may also have false negatives. The current implementation may not capture causality through covert channels. For example, information can be disclosed through execution time and file metadata (e.g. last accessed time). We will leave it to our future work. Furthermore, program execution may run into extremal conditions (e.g., running out of disk/memory space), the current implementation of LDX does not handle such conditions.

2. Counterfactual Causality

Counterfactual causality (CC) (Hume 1748; Lewis 1973) is the earliest and the most widely used definition of causality: an event e is causally dependent on an event c if and only if, if c were not to occur, e would not occur. Later, researchers also introduce the notion of causal strength: c is a *strong cause* if and only if it is the necessary and sufficient condition of e (Miller and Johnson-Laird 1976; Kushnir and Gopnik 2005; Cheng 1997). Otherwise, c is a weak cause.

We adapt the definition in the context of program and program execution as follows. *Given an execution, we say a variable y at an execution point j is causally dependent on a variable x at an earlier point i, if and only if mutating x at i will cause change of y at j.* The causality is strong if and only if any change to x must lead to some change of y. We call this causality a *one-to-one mapping*. The causality is weak if multiple x values lead to the same y value. We call it a *many-to-one mapping*. The strength of the causality is determined by how many x values map to the same y.

Most existing causality inference techniques including dynamic tainting are based on tracking program dependences, especially data dependencies. Two events are causally related if there is a dependence path between them during execution. As we discussed in Section 1, these techniques have inherent limitations because *program dependences are merely approximation of CC.* Next, we discuss the relation between CC and dynamic program dependences to motivate our design.

(1) *Most Data Dependences Are Essentially Strong CCs.* Consider Fig. 1 (a). There is a strong CC between s at the source (line 1) and x at the sink (line 4) as any change to s leads to some change at the sink, and there is a data dependence path $4 \rightarrow 3 \rightarrow 1$ between the two. Other data dependences have similar characteristics, which implies that conventional dynamic tainting (based on data dependence) tracks strong CCs. On the other hand, if there is a technique that infers all strong CCs, it must subsume dynamic tainting.

(2) *Control Dependences Induce Both Strong and Weak CCs.* In Fig. 1 (b), assume the true branch is taken and $x = 1$. We can infer that s must be 10; there is strong causality between x and s. This strong CC is induced by the control dependence 14→13, together with data dependences $15 \rightarrow 14$ and $13 \rightarrow 11$. If control dependence is not tracked (like in most existing dynamic tainting techniques), the CC is missed. However in many cases, control dependences only lead to weak CC. In case (c), assume $s = 50$ and hence $x = 1$. There is a dependence path $25 \rightarrow 24 \rightarrow 23 \rightarrow 21$ if control dependence $24 \rightarrow 23$ is tracked. However, the casuality between x at 25 and s at 21 is weak as many values of s lead to the same $x = 1$. Such weak causality is very difficult for the attacker to exploit. For example with $x = 1$, the adversary can hardly infer s's value, even with the knowledge of the program. Moreover in code injection attacks, the attacker can hardly manipulate the sink (e.g. function return address) by changing the source. According to (Bao et al. 2010), if control dependences are not tracked, 80% strong CCs are missed; if all control dependences are tracked, strong CCs are never missed but 45% of the detected causalities are weak. In some large programs, an output event is causally dependent on almost all inputs with 90% of them being weak causalities that cannot be exploited. In summary, control dependences are a poor approximation of strong CCs.

(3) *Tracking both Data and Control Dependences May Still Miss Strong CCs.* Fig. 1 (d) presents such a case. Assume $s = 10$ and hence the else branch is executed. As such, x is not updated. However, the fact that x is not updated (and hence has the value of 0) allows the adversary to infer $s = 10$. It is a strong CC: any change

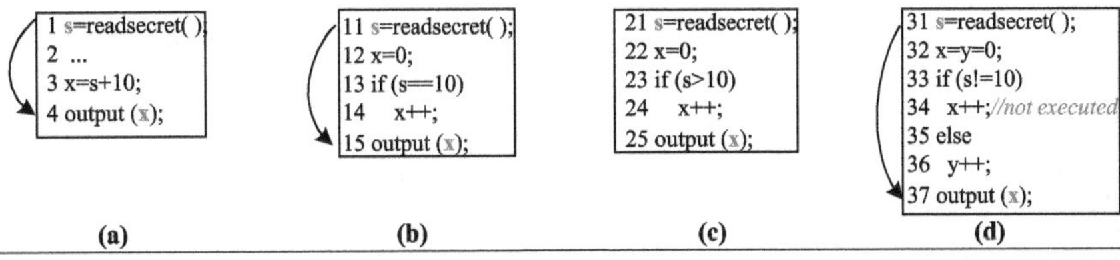

Figure 1. Examples to illustrate the comparison of counterfactual causality and program dependences. Arrows denote strong causalities between x at the sink and s at the source. Case (a) shows strong CC by data dependence; (b) shows strong CC by control dependence; (c) shows control dependence does not imply (strong) CC; (d) strong CC missed by both data and control dependences.

to s makes x have a different value. Unfortunately, such strong CC cannot be detected by tracking program dependences as line 37 is only data dependent on line 32 as the true branch is not executed. More cases are omitted due to the space limitations. They can be found in our technical report (tr).

The above discussion suggests that program dependences are a poor approximation of strong CCs. Hence, we propose LDX, a cost-effective technique that allows us to directly infer strong CCs, strictly following the definition.

3. Overview and Illustrative Example

We use an example to illustrate LDX. Here we are interested in information leak detection. We mutate the secret inputs. If output differences are observed at the sinks, there are strong CCs between the sinks and the secret inputs, and hence leaks.

Specifically, given the master execution, LDX creates a slave and runs the two concurrently in a closely coupled fashion. The master interacts with the environment and records its syscall outcomes. In most cases, the slave does not interact with the environment, but reuses the master's syscall outcomes, to eliminate state differences caused by nondeterministic factors such as external event orders. The slave mutates the sources, which potentially leads to path differences and hence syscall differences. A novel feature of LDX is to tolerate syscall differences in a cost-effective manner. It maintains a counter for each execution that indicates the progress. Execution points (across runs) with the same counter value and the same PC are guaranteed to *align* (in terms of control flow). An execution with a larger counter value is ahead of another with a smaller value. Aligned syscalls can share their outcomes; if the slave encounters a syscall with a counter larger than that in the master, the slave blocks until the master catches up; if the slave encounters an input syscall that does not have an alignment in the master, it will execute the syscall independently. The counter is computed as follows. It is incremented by 1 at each syscall. When two executions take different branches of a predicate –since the branches may have different numbers of syscalls– the values added to the counter may be different. The technique compensates the counter in the branch that has a smaller increment so that the counter must have the same value when the join point of the branches is reached. As such, the executions are re-synchronized.

Cnt	Master	Cnt	Slave	Action
1	1. read();	1	1. read();	M exec, S. copies
2	2. open();	2	2. open();	M exec, S. copies
3	12. open();	3	12. open();	M and S exec
4	13. read();	4	13. read();	M and S exec
		5	17. write();	M waits, S exec
		6	7. read();	M waits, S exec
7	11. send();	7	11. send();	Compare

Figure 3. Syscall traces and the synchronization action sequence by LDX for the example in Fig. 2 with `title` the secret. The shaded entries are aligned.

Example. Consider the program in Fig. 2 (a). It reads information of an employee, computes his/her raise and sends it to a remote site. If the employee is a regular staff, function `SRaise()` is called to compute the raise (line 4). If he/she is a manager, function `MRaise()` is called (line 6). Moreover, the program reads the department information to compute the bonus for the manager. Finally (lines 10 and 11), the name and the raise are reported to a remote site. `SRaise()` opens and reads a contract file that describes the rate of raise. `MRaise()` calls `SRaise()` to compute the basic raise, using a different contract file. Furthermore, it saves all the junior managers with a salary higher than `C1` to a local file.

The control flow graphs (CFGs) and their instrumentation for counter computation (i.e. code along CFG edges) are shown in Fig. 2 (b). The number beside a node denotes the counter value at the node, computed by the instrumentation starting from the function entry. It can be intuitively considered as the maximum number of syscalls encountered along a path from the entry to the node. In `SRaise()`, the counter is incremented twice along edges $Entry \rightarrow 12$ and $12 \rightarrow 13$ before the two syscalls. The total increment is hence 2, as shown beside the exit node. In `MRaise()`, the counter value of line 15 is 2, although the edge is not instrumented. This is because of the increments inside `SRaise()`. The true branch of line 16 has an increment of 1 due to the `write` syscall. To ensure identical counter values at the join point, the false branch (i.e., edge $16 \rightarrow 18$) is compensated with $+1$. As a result, the total increment of `MRaise()` is 3 along any path. Similarly in `main()`, the path $3 \rightarrow 5 \rightarrow 6 \rightarrow 7 \rightarrow 8 \rightarrow 10$ has an increment of 4, due to the three syscalls inside `MRaise()` and the syscall at line 7. As such, we compensate the edges $4 \rightarrow 10$ and $9 \rightarrow 10$ by $+2$ and $+4$, respectively.

Assume `title=STAFF` is the secret. In the slave, it is mutated to `MANAGER`. Also assume `age=JUNIOR`. Fig. 3 shows the syscall sequences of the two executions and the corresponding counter values. The first two entries are the syscalls at lines 1 and 2 in both executions, and they align due to the same counter value. Hence, the slave *copies* the syscall results from the master. The two executions diverge at line 3 and different syscalls are encountered. In particular, the master executes two syscalls inside `SRaise()` and the slave *executes* the two syscalls inside `SRaise()` in a different context, followed by the `write` at line 17 and the `read` at 7. Since these syscalls do not align, both the master and the slave execute them separately. Assume the master finishes its (true) branch first and continues to the `send` syscall at line 11. At this time, the counter is 7 in the master and larger than the slave's. The master blocks until the slave's counter also reaches 7, at which the two syscalls (at line 11) align again. Since the syscall is a sink, LDX compares the outputs and identifies differences. It hence reports a leak. Note that even though there is no direct data flow from `title` to `raise`, the value of `raise` still leaks the secret `title` through control dependences. Many existing techniques cannot detect such causality. □

One may notice in Fig. 3 that the third and the fourth syscalls in both executions have the same counter. In fact, both are syscalls

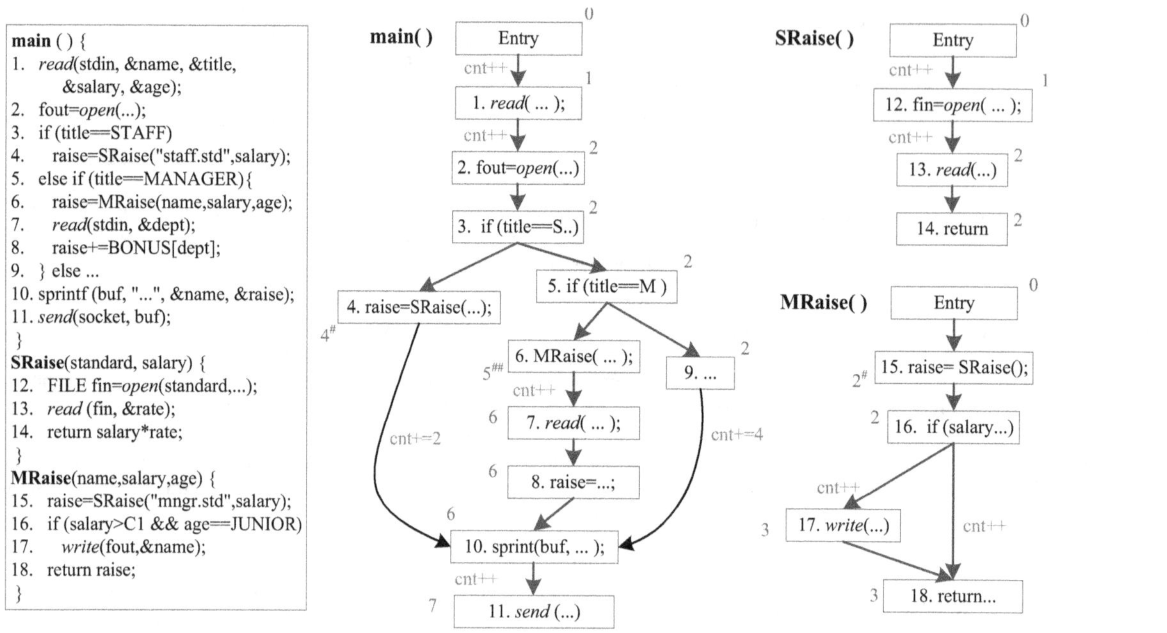

(a) Program (b) Control Flow Graphs and Instrumentation

Figure 2. Illustrative Example. The code along control flow edges represents instrumentation. #cnt+=2 inside **SRaise**(); ##cnt+=3 in **MRaise**().

in `SRaise()`. To recognize syscalls that are different but have the same counter value and the same PC, LDX compares their parameters.

Fixed versus Dynamically Computed Counter values. One may also be curious that why LDX does not assign a fixed counter value to each syscall. This is because a function may be invoked under different contexts such that the counter value computed for a syscall inside the function may vary.

Use of LDX. LDX is fully automated during production runs. It has a predefined configuration of sources (e.g., socket receives) and sinks (e.g., file writes). The user can also choose to annotate the sources and sinks in the code during instrumentation. At runtime, all the specified sources are mutated. If output differences are observed at any sink, LDX considers that there is strong causality between the sink and some source(s) and reports an exception. It does not require running multiple times for individual sources.

4. Basic Design

The basic design consists of two components. The first is for counter computation and the second is for synchronizing the executions and sharing syscall results. For now, we assume programs do not have loops, recursion, or indirect calls. They are discussed in later sections (loops/recursion in Section 5 and indirect calls in Section 6).

4.1 Counter Computation

In LDX, each execution maintains a counter to allow progress comparison across runs. The basic idea of counter computation is to ensure that the current counter value represents the maximum number of syscalls along a path from the beginning of the program to the current execution point. If the program does not have any loops, recursion, or indirect calls, such a number can be uniquely computed. Hence, our instrumentation compensates the paths other than the one that has the maximum number of syscalls, by incrementing the counter, to make sure the counter must have the same value (i.e. the maximum number of syscalls) along any path. Intuitively, when the two executions take different branches of a predicate, the counter computation ensures that they align when the branches join again, because the counter will have the same value regardless of the branch taken.

Algorithm 1 Basic Counter Instrumentation Algorithm.

Input: The CFGs of the m functions of a program P, denoted as $\langle N_1, E_1\rangle$, ..., $\langle N_m, E_m\rangle$
Output: Instrumented CFGs
1: **function** INSTRUMENTPROG
2: **for** $\langle N_i, E_i\rangle$ in reverse topological order of the call graph **do**
3: INSTRUMENTFUNC ($\langle N_i, E_i\rangle$)
4: **end function**
Input: The CFG of a function F, denoted as $\langle N, E\rangle$
Output: The instrumented CFG
5: **function** INSTRUMENTFUNC
6: **for** each node $n \in N$ **do**
7: $cnt[n] \leftarrow 0$
8: **for** node $n \in N$ in topological order **do**
9: $cnt[n] \leftarrow max_{p \to n \in E}(cnt[p])$
10: **if** n is a syscall **then**
11: $cnt[n] \leftarrow cnt[n] + 1$
12: **for** each edge $p \to n \in E$ **do**
13: **if** $cnt[p] \neq cnt[n]$ **then**
14: instrument $p \to n$ with "$cnt+=$"$\cdot cnt[n] - cnt[p]$
15: **if** n is a call to user function F_x **then**
16: $cnt[n] \leftarrow cnt[n] + FCNT[F_x]$
17: $FCNT[F] \leftarrow cnt$[exit node of F]
18: **end function**

The instrumentation procedure is presented in Algorithm 1. It consists of two functions: INSTRUMENTPROG() that instruments the program and INSTRUMENTFUNC() that instruments a function. INSTRUMENTPROG() instruments functions in the reverse topological order. As such, when a function is instrumented, all its callees must have been instrumented. In INSTRUMENTFUNC(), $cnt[n]$ contains the number of maximum syscalls along a path from the function entry to n. In lines 6-7, $cnt[]$ is initialized to 0. Then in the loop from lines 8-16, the algorithm traverses the CFG nodes in the topological order and computes $cnt[]$. In particular, $cnt[n]$ is first set to the maximum of $cnt[p]$ for all its predecessors p (line 9). It is further incremented by one if n is a syscall (lines 10-11). Then for any incoming edge $p \rightarrow n$, the algorithm instruments it with a counter increment of $cnt[n] - cnt[p]$, ensuring the counter value must be $cnt[n]$ along all edges (lines 12-14). After that, if n denotes a function call to F_x, $cnt[n]$ is incremented by the counter of the function $FCNT[F_x]$, which denotes the maximum number of syscalls that can happen inside F_x along any path (line 15-16). Note that this increment does not cause any instrumentation on n because the increment denoted by $FCNT[F_x]$ is realized inside F_x. At the end, $FCNT[F]$ is set to the computed counter value for the exit node. It will be used in counter computation in the callers of F.

Example. In Fig. 2, the algorithm first instruments `SRaise()`. The $cnt[]$ values are showed beside the nodes. Observe that $cnt[12] = 1$ and $cnt[13] = 2$, which lead to the instrumentation on $entry \rightarrow 12$ and $12 \rightarrow 13$. $FCNT[\texttt{SRaise}] = cnt[14] = 2$. `MRaise()` is instrumented next. Due to $FCNT$ [`SRaise`], $cnt[15] = 2$. Note that node 15 is not instrumented. Node 18 has two predecessors and thus $cnt[18] = max(cnt[17], cnt[16]) = 3$, which entails the instrumentation on $16 \rightarrow 18$. At last, function `main()` is instrumented. $cnt[10] = max\ (cnt[8], cnt[4], cnt[9]) = cnt[8] = 6$, causing the instrumentation on $4 \rightarrow 10$ and $9 \rightarrow 10$. □

Algorithm 2 Syscall Wrapper for Master.

Input: Syscall id *sys_id* and parameters *args*.
Output: Syscall return value.
Definition: Q_m the syscall outcome queue maintained by the master; O_s the latest sink syscall by the slave; cnt_m and cnt_s the local counters in master and slave, respectively; $ready_m$ the counter value in master exposed to the slave; similarly, $ready_s$ the counter value in the slave exposed to the master.

```
1: function SYSCALLWRAPPER(sys_id, args)
2:     if sys_id denotes a sink syscall then
3:         while cnt_m > ready_s do
4:             {}
5:         if cnt_m < ready_s ∨ O_s.sys_id ≠ sys_id ∨ O_s.args ≠ args then
6:             report causality
7:     r ← SYSCALL (sys_id, args)
8:     Q_m.enq(⟨cnt_m, sys_id, args, r⟩)
9:     ready_m ← cnt_m
10:    return r
11: end function
```

4.2 Dual Execution Facilitated by Counter Numbers

To support dual execution, LDX intercepts syscalls to perform synchronization and syscall outcome sharing. In the master, when a syscall is encountered, if it is not a sink, LDX executes the syscall and saves the outcome for potential reuse by the slave. Otherwise, it waits for the slave to reach the same sink so that their parameters can be compared. In the slave, upon a syscall, it first checks whether it is ahead of the master. If so, it waits until the master finishes the corresponding syscall so that it can copy the master's result. If the corresponding syscall does not appear in the master (due to path differences), which can be detected by the counter scheme, the slave executes the syscall.

Execution Control in the Master. Algorithm 2 shows the controller of the master. It is implemented as a syscall wrapper. Each syscall in the master must go through the controller. Inside the controller, cnt_m and cnt_s denote the current counter values in the master and the slave, respectively. They are local to their execution and invisible to the other execution. It also uses two shared variables $ready_m$ and $ready_s$ to facilitate synchronization. They are assigned the values of cnt_m and cnt_s when the master and the slave are ready to disclose the effects of the current syscall to the other party.

Lines 2-6 handle a sink syscall. At line 3, the master spins until the slave catches up. Note that the value of $ready_s$ is the same as cnt_s when the state of the slave's syscall denoted by cnt_s becomes visible. There are four possible cases after the master gets out of the spin loop.

(1) $cnt_m < ready_s$. This happens when there is not a syscall denoted by the value of cnt_m in the slave. For example in Fig. 2, assume the master takes the false branch at line 3 and is now at line 7 with $cnt_m = 6$ while the slave takes the true branch and now it just returns from the call to `SRaise()` at line 4 with $cnt_s = ready_s = 4$. Assume we make line 7 a sink. Then the master will wait at line 7. However, the next time $ready_s$ is updated (in the slave) is at line 11, at which $ready_s = 7$, larger than $cnt_m = 6$.

(2) $cnt_m \equiv ready_s$ but the syscall in the slave represented by $ready_s$ is different from the sink syscall in the master. This is due to path differences.

(3) $cnt_m \equiv ready_s$ and both the master and the slave align at the same sink syscall. However, their arguments are different.

(4) The counters, syscalls, and arguments are all identical.

The first three cases denote causality between the source and the sink, suggesting leak or exploit. The last case is benign. In the first two cases, there is causality because the sink (in the master) disappears in the slave with the input perturbation. The three comparisons at line 5 correspond to the first three cases, respectively.

If the current syscall is not a sink, lines 7-8 in the algorithm perform the real syscall and enqueue the syscall and its outcome, which may be reused by the slave. At last (line 9), $ready_m$ is set up-to-date, indicating the syscall outcome for cnt_m is ready (for the slave).

Execution control in the slave is similar. Details can be found in our technical report (tr).

Syscall Handling. LDX's policy of handling syscalls is similar to that in *dual execution* (DualEx) (Kim et al. 2015). For most input/output syscalls, the slave simply reuses the master's syscall outcome if their alignments in the master can be found. Otherwise, it *executes* the syscall. To avoid undesirable interference, the slave may need to construct its own copy of the system state before executing the syscall. For example, before the slave executes a file read, the file needs to be cloned, opened, and then seeked to the right position. Some special syscalls are always executed independently such as process creation. Since the policy is not our contribution, we refer the interested reader to (Kim et al. 2015).

Dual Execution Model Comparison between LDX and DualEx (Kim et al. 2015). Similar to LDX, DualEx also has the master and the slave. However, its synchronization and alignment control is through a third process called the *monitor*. Both the master and the slave simply send their executed instructions to the monitor, which builds a tree-like execution structure representation called *index* and aligns the executions based on their indices. The monitor also determines if a process needs to be blocked, achieving lockstep synchronization. As such, its overhead is very high (i.e., 3 orders of magnitude). In contrast, LDX is much more lightweight. It is based on counter values and uses spinning to achieve synchronization.

5. Handling Loops

The basic design assumes programs without loops. Handling loops is challenging because the number of iterations for a loop is unknown at compile time. The master and the slave may iterate different numbers of times due to the perturbation at sources, leading to different increments to the counters and hence difficulty in alignment. Our solution is to synchronize two corresponding loops at the iteration level. In particular, it aligns the ith iteration of the master with the ith iteration of the slave by synchronizing at the backedges, i.e. the edge from the end of the loop body back to the loop head. It is analogous to having a barrier at the end of each iteration. Along the backedge, LDX also resets the counter to the value before it en-

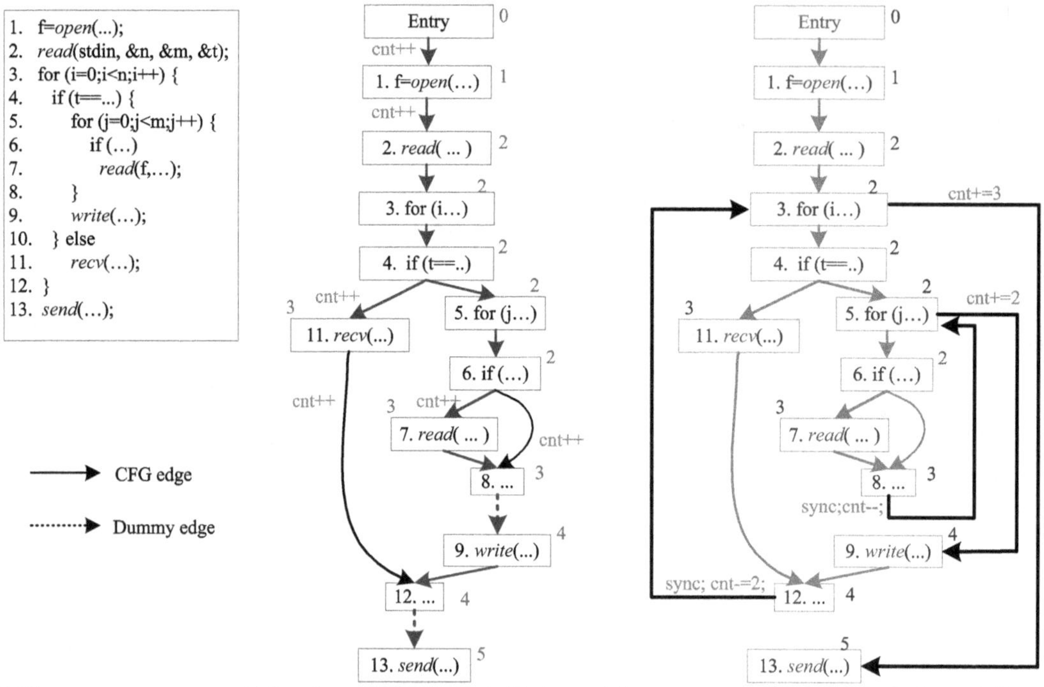

(a) Program **(b) Transformed CFG and Part of Instrumentation** **(c) Loop Edge Instrumentation**

Figure 4. Loop Example.

tered the loop. Doing so, the value of the counter is bounded and does not grow with the number of iterations. If an execution gets out of the loop, its counter is incremented by the maximum number of syscalls along any path inside the loop. As such, a counter value beyond the loop is larger than any counter values within the loop, correctly indicating that the execution beyond the loop is ahead of the one in the loop.

Algorithm 3 Counter Instrumentation with Loops.

Input: The CFG of a function F, denoted as $\langle N, E\rangle$
Output: The instrumented CFG

```
1: function INSTRUMENTFUNCWITHLOOP
2:     for each back edge t → h ∈ E do
3:         Let h → n be the exit edge of the loop
4:         E ← E − {t → h, h → n}    ▷ Remove loop exit and back edges
5:         E ← E ∪ {t → n}                          ▷ Add dummy edge
6:     INSTRUMENTFUNC(⟨N, E⟩)
7:     remove all dummy edges and their instrumentation
8:     restore all the removed edges in the original CFG
9:     for each original back edge e : t → h do
10:        instrument e with "sync(); cnt− ="·cnt[t] − cnt[h]
11:    for each original loop exit edge e : h → n do
12:        instrument e with "cnt+ ="·cnt[n] − cnt[h]
13: end function
```

Algorithm 3 presents the instrumentation algorithm for a function with loops. It transforms the CFG to an acyclic graph by removing loop edges. As such, the $cnt[]$ values in the acyclic graph are statically computable. The computed $cnt[]$ values are then leveraged to construct the instrumentation, including that for the original loop edges. Particularly, the algorithm first removes all the backedges and the loop exit edges (line 2-5). A loop exit edge is from the loop head h to the next statement n beyond the loop. A *dummy edge* is inserted from the end of the loop body t to the next statement n beyond the loop. Our discussion focuses on `for` and `while` loops, `do-while` loops can be similarly handled.

At line 6, the acyclic graph is instrumented through INSTRUMENTFUNC(). After that, the dummy edges and their instrumentation are removed as they do not denote real control flow (line 7). The backedges and loop exit edges are then restored. Lines 9-10 instrument the backedges. For a backedge $t \to h$, the instrumentation first calls a barrier function `sync()`, which is similar to lines 3-4 in Algorithm 2, to synchronize with the backedge of the same iteration in the other execution. It then resets the counter to the value at h such that the counter increment of the next iteration has a fresh start. Lines 11-12 instrument the loop exit edges. For a loop exit $h \to n$, the instrumentation increments the counter by the difference between $cnt[n]$ and $cnt[h]$. Intuitively, it raises the counter to the value of $cnt[n]$.

Example. Fig. 4 (a) shows a loop example. There are two loops: the i loop and the j loop. Their iteration numbers are determined by the inputs from line 2. Figure (b) shows the transformed CFG and part of the instrumentation generated by INSTRUMENTFUNC() in the basic design. Observe that the backedges $8 \to 5$ and $12 \to 3$, the loop exit edges $3 \to 13$ and $5 \to 9$ are removed. Dummy edges $8 \to 9$ and $12 \to 13$ are added. They do not represent real control flow, but allow $cnt[9]$ to be computed as $cnt[8]+1$ and $cnt[13] = cnt[12]+1$. Figure (c) shows the instrumentation for backedges and loop exit edges. Note that the CFG in (c) is the original CFG. The backedge $8 \to 5$ is instrumented with the call to the barrier function and the decrement of the counter by $cnt[8] - cnt[5] = 1$. The loop exit edge $5 \to 9$ is instrumented with the counter increment of $cnt[9] - cnt[5] = 2$, which makes the counter value of node 9 always larger than those within loop j. The instrumentation for loop i is similar.

Fig. 5 shows the dual execution when the loop bounds n and m are the sources. Assume the master executes with $n = 1$ and $m = 2$ and the slave executes with $n = 2$ and $m = 1$. Along the syscall sequences, we also show the loop iterations to facilitate understanding. The first three syscalls (up to inside the first iteration of j) align in the two executions. At Ⓐ, the two executions are

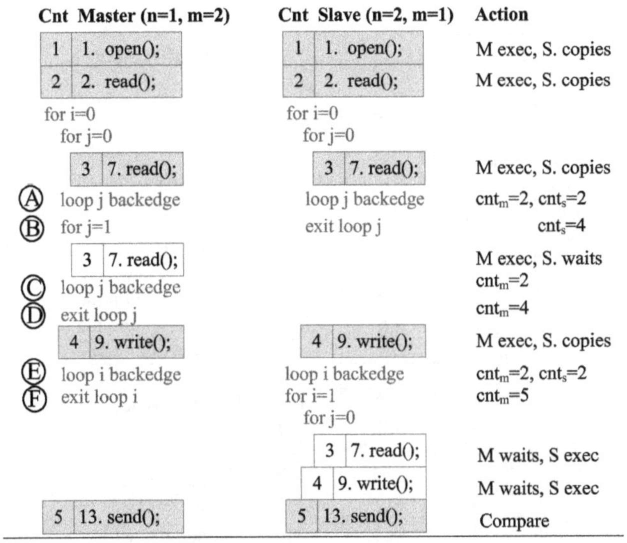

Figure 5. Syscalls and the sequence of synchronizations by LDX for the example in Fig. 4 with `n` and `m` the sources. The shaded entries are aligned. The indentation shows the loop nesting.

synchronized and counters are reset to 2. However at Ⓑ, the slave exits loop j while the master continues to the second iteration of j. As such, the slave's counter becomes 4, which blocks its execution. At Ⓒ, the master finishes the second iteration of j and its counter is reset to 2. At Ⓓ, the master also exits loop j and its counter is incremented to 4, which aligns the two syscalls at line 9. At Ⓔ, the two runs are synchronized at the backedge of loop i and their counters are reset to 2 due to the instrumentation on $12 \rightarrow 3$. At Ⓕ, the master exits the i loop; its counter becomes 5 due to the instrumentation on $3 \rightarrow 13$, which blocks its execution as the master needs the parameters of the `send()` from the slave to infer causality. In contrast, the slave executes the remaining i iteration before it reaches the aligned sink (line 13). □

Recursive functions are handled similarly. Also note that we only need to instrument loops that include syscalls. Hot loops are usually computation intensive and should not have syscalls. Therefore, they are unlikely to be instrumented.

6. Handling Indirect Function Calls

The challenge for handling indirect calls is that the call targets are usually unknown at compile time. As a result, we cannot use the counter values in the callee(s) to compute those in the caller. To handle indirect calls, LDX saves a copy of the current counter to the stack when an indirect call is encountered, and resets the counter to 0 such that the two executions start a fresh alignment from the indirect call site. When the executions return from the indirect call, the counter value is restored. As such, we do not need to know the precise counter increment inside the indirect call to support alignment in the caller. LDX supports components that cannot be instrumented such as third party libraries and dynamic loaded libraries by synchronizing at their interface. `Longjmp` and `setjmp` are ignored during the CFG analysis. They are supported at runtime by saving a copy of the counter stack at the `setjmp` which will be restored upon the `longjmp`. Moreover, an artificial sink is inserted before the `longjmp` so that if one process `longjmps` but the other does not, LDX reports exception. More details can be found in (tr).

7. Handling Concurrency and Library Calls

LDX supports real concurrency, which is completely different from DualExec (Kim et al. 2015). Threads have their own counters. Threads in the master and the slave are paired up. LDX treats pthread library calls as syscalls. The two executions hence synchronize on those calls and share the outcomes of lock acquisitions and releases. Note that sharing synchronization outcomes induces very similar thread schedules in the two executions. However, path differences may lead to synchronization differences which may in turn lead to deadlocks in LDX if not handled properly. We taint locks that have encountered differences and avoid sharing synchronization outcomes for those locks. Moreover, low-level data races that are not protected by any locks may induce non-deterministic state differences, leading to false positives in strong CC inference. In Section 8, our experiment shows that false positives rarely happen (for the programs we consider). Intuitively, non-determinism during computation may not lead to non-determinism at the sinks.

Light-weight Resource Tainting. In our current implementation, a file/directory is considered a resource. Taint metadata is associated with each resource. When an operation for a resource is misaligned, the resource is tainted to indicate state differences so that any future syscalls on the resource cannot be coupled. When a tainted resource is accessed by the other execution, LDX will create a copy of the related resource(s) so that the master and the slave operate on their own copies, without causing interference. For example, if the master creates a directory while the slave does not, the directory is tainted. When the slave tries to access the directory later, it gets into the de-coupled mode. The slave's syscall will be performed on a clone of the parent directory without the created directory. Similarly, if a file is renamed or removed from a directory in one execution but not the other, the file is tainted. Any following acceses to the file lead to de-coupled execution.

Handling Library Calls. Regarding local file outputs, the slave does not perform any outputs to the disk if they are aligned. Instead, it skips the calls or buffer the output values for causality inference if local file outputs are considered sinks. The slave ignores its own signals and receives its signals from the master. Upon a signal, LDX allows the slave to execute the signal handler. Handler invocations are handled similar to indirect calls. Note that the slave may invoke system calls to cause different signals or events such as creating threads or processes different from the master. LDX buffers such different system calls and all the system calls caused by such signals and events for causality inference. The threads and processes unique to either execution run in the de-coupled mode.

Handling UI Library Calls. LDX is intended to be transparent to the user. Hence, it is undesirable to have two (almost identical) user interfaces. Therefore, LDX allows the master to handle all the UI library calls as usual. The slave does not have its own interface. It tries to reuse the UI library call outcomes from the master as much as possible. Misaligned UI library calls, if they are input related, return random values to the slave. Misaligned output UI calls are ignored, or buffered for causality inference if the outputs are considered sinks.

8. Evaluation

LDX is implemented in LLVM 3.4. We evaluate its runtime performance, the capability of handling misaligned syscalls, and the effectiveness of causality inference with two applications: information leak detection and attack detection. Experiments are on a machine with Intel i7-4770 3.4GHz CPU (4 cores), 8GB RAM, and 32-bit LinuxMint 17.

Benchmark Programs. We used 28 programs as shown in Table 1. They include four different subsets: SPECINT2006 (the first 12); the network and system related set for information leak detection (the next 5), the vulnerable program set for attack detection (the next 6), and the concurrency set (the last 5) for evaluation of concurrency control. The detailed introduction of these programs can be found in (tr).

Table 1. Benchmarks and Instrumentation.

Program	LOC	Instrumented instances				Syscalls		Max Cnt.	Dyn. Cnt.		Mutated inputs
		Inst.	Loop	Recur.	FPTR	Sinks	Total		Value	Stack*	
400.perlbench	128K	5540 (1.56%)	10233	634	852	4	62	72K	3392	2.91/7	Input perl source file
401.bzip2	5739	43 (0.24%)	360	0	57	4	10	7	4.5	0/1	Input data file
403.gcc	385K	791 (0.07%)	45702	2928	463	3	31	424	96.1	0.11/5	Input C source file
429.mcf	1579	27 (1.32%)	44	1	0	3	11	8	4.3	0/0	Input data file
445.gobmk	157K	235 (0.22%)	7910	74	47	3	15	37	1.7	1.68/4	Input data file
456.hmmer	20K	1762 (3.59%)	1611	11	13	4	25	281	83.2	0/1	Input file and arguments
458.sjeng	10K	26 (0.13%)	978	10	1	4	12	6	2.7	0.07/1	Input data file
462.libquantum	2611	52 (1.08%)	153	11	0	3	17	8	1	0/0	Input arguments
464.h264ref	36K	102 (0.09%)	1994	38	362	4	20	101	26.4	0.26/2	Configuration file
471.omnetpp	26K	121 (0.09%)	6102	46	838	2	22	20	4.5	2.3/6	Configuration file
473.astar	4285	56 (0.47%)	224	0	1	1	18	51	32.8	0.12/1	Configuration file
483.xalancbmk	266K	116 (0.01%)	28381	312	10265	5	25	5	1.5	1.34/9	Input XML file
Firefox	14M	83 (0.01%)	21	0	9	3	26	71	41.2	0.09/1	nsIURI object accesses
lynx	204K	13157 (6.92%)	6799	109	1179	6	132	15M	578K	0.3/6	Cookie, network packet
nginx	287K	4672 (4.27%)	1541	21	850	6	110	518	17.9	3.8/7	Configuration file
tnftp	152K	2452 (6.31%)	1093	17	210	8	125	5878	2623	0.01/1	Input arguments
sysstat	29K	811 (6.94%)	271	0	1	3	47	365	70.7	0.01/1	Returns of lib. calls
gif2png	16K	246 (7.76%)	62	0	0	7	36	76	18.2	0/0	Input image file
mp3info	9252	205 (8.34%)	91	0	0	3	31	88	6.4	0/0	Input mp3 file
prozilla	13K	1116 (8.19%)	285	0	14	5	67	5680	713	0/0	Network packet
yopsweb	1961	282 (5.93%)	97	0	1	4	44	24	3.7	0/1	Network packet
ngircd	66K	1052 (6.70%)	417	24	1031	4	62	2863	1524	0/1	Network packet
gocr	54K	2801 (5.48%)	2581	4	2	3	24	23K	2182	0/1	Input image file
Apache	208K	640 (0.61%)	2700	23	183	6	126	89	43.7	1.56/4	Input HTML file
pbzip2	4527	735 (6.74%)	226	0	3	4	49	1997	578.83	0/0	Input data file
pigz	5766	996 (5.85%)	434	2	15	6	54	9288	432.82	0.99/1	Input data file
axel	2583	342 (8.24%)	162	1	3	6	35	271	73.66	0/0	Network packet
x264	98K	2071 (1.30%)	2218	1	2295	8	49	881	76.58	15K/18K	Input video file

* It shows avg/max

Instrumentation Details. Table 1 shows the instrumentation details. Columns 3-6 describe the numbers of instrumented instructions (and their percentage), instrumented loops, instrumented recursive functions, and instrumented indirect calls. The next two columns show the number of sinks and syscalls instrumented. For programs that have network connections, we use the outgoing networking syscalls as sinks. For other programs, we treat the local file outputs as sinks. The "max cnt." column shows the maximum counter value in a program. It denotes the largest number of syscalls along some static program path. For `firefox`, we were not able to instrument the whole program as LLVM failed to generate the whole program bitcode (supposedly larger than 600MB). We identified the source files for event processing and the JS engine and only instrumented those. The resulted object files are then linked with the rest.

We have a few observations. (1) We have some large and complex programs such as `lynx`, `403.gcc`, and `apache`. (2) The percentage of instrumented instructions is low (3.44% on average). (3) Some programs (e.g., `403.gcc` and `400.perlbench`) have a large number of recursive functions and indirect calls. LDX handles all of them.

The last column of Table 1 shows the source mutations. For the SPEC and network/system programs, we mutate the data files and the configuration files. For the vulnerable program set, we mutate the inputs from untrusted sources and detect whether differences are observed at function return addresses (for buffer overflow attacks) and at parameters of memory management functions (for integer overflow attacks). We perform off-by-one mutations. In order to avoid invalid mutations, we only mutate data fields, not magic values or structure related values.

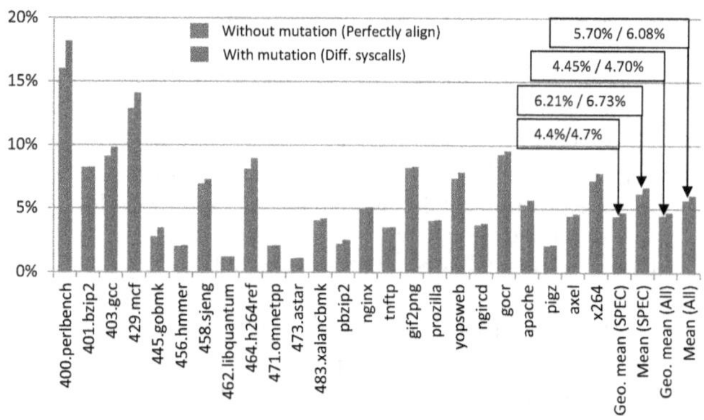

Figure 6. Normalized overhead of LDX.

8.1 Performance

We study the performance of LDX using SPECINT2006 and programs that are not interactive and have non-trivial execution time. For server programs such as `nginx` and `apache`, we run the server and send 10,000 requests, and then measure the throughtput. For web servers such as `apache`, we use `ApacheBench` to provide the requests. `Firefox` and `lynx` are omitted because they are interactive. `Sysstat` and `mp3info` are also excluded as their running time is trivial (¡0.01sec). We use the reference inputs for SPEC. We run each program twice. In the first run, we do not mutate the input so that the master and the slave perfectly align. The overhead is thus for counter maintenance and syscall outcome sharing. In the second run, the master and the slave execute with different inputs. Since they can take different paths and have different syscalls, the overhead includes that for synchronization and realignment. The results are shown in Fig. 6. The baseline is the native execution time for the uninstrumented programs with the original inputs. The geometric means of the overhead are 4.45% and 4.7%, while the arithmetic means are 5.7% and 6.08%. Observe that the overhead of LDX is very low. We have also measured the overhead of LIBDFT (Kemerlis et al. 2012), one of the state-of-the-art dynamic tainting implementations that works by instruction level monitoring. Its slow-down over native executions is roughly 6X on average. LDX is also three orders of magnitude faster than *dual execution* (Kim et al. 2015).

Another observation is that the input differences and hence the syscall differences do not cause much additional overhead. As we will show later, the syscall differences are not trivial. This is because our alignment scheme allows the misaligned syscalls to execute separately and concurrently. The "dyn. cnt." columns in Table 1 show the runtime characteristics of the counter values. Observe that the average counter values are much smaller than the maximum values (column 9). The maximum depth of the stack is also small, meaning that we rarely encounter nesting indirect calls.

Table 2. Dual Execution Effectiveness.

Program	Input 1 / Input 2		# of syscall diffs	
	LDX	TightLip	Input 1	Input 2
lynx	O / X	O / O	1801 (4.13%)	1272 (3.0%)
nginx	O / X	O / O	202 (13.92%)	181 (13.02%)
tnftp	O / X	O / O	2443 (19.19%)	381 (15.74%)
sysstat	O / X	O / O	53 (7.42%)	58 (19.21%)
gcc	O / X	O / O	38161 (24.99%)	3590 (3.11%)
xalancbmk	O / X	O / O	102 (2.60%)	91 (2.32%)
gobmk	O / X	O / O	345 (1.68%)	114 (0.55%)
perlbench	O / X	O / O	17 (7.08%)	11 (4.58%)
bzip2	O / X	O / O	53 (54.63%)	49 (50.51%)
mcf	O / X	O / O	20 (0.01%)	17 (0.01%)
sjeng	O / X	O / O	729 (45.45%)	132 (8.22%)
h264ref	O / X	O / O	141 (31.68%)	12 (2.69%)
hmmer	O / -	O / -	2 (0.03%)	-
libquantum	O / -	O / -	1 (12.5%)	-
omnetpp	O / -	O / -	0	-
astar	O / -	O / -	11 (73.33%)	-

8.2 Effectiveness of Dual Execution

In this experiment, we answer the question why we need to align the master and the slave. The experiment is in the context of detecting information leak. For each program, we construct two input mutations with the following goal: one input mutation leads to sink differences (and hence leakage) and the other does not. Both mutations may trigger syscall differences. We also compare LDX with TIGHTLIP, which does not align executions and often has to terminate at syscall differences, reporting leakage. Table 2 presents the results. Symbol 'O' denotes that leakage is reported and 'X' denotes normal termination without any warning. The last two columns show the syscall differences before the sink difference and their percentage over the total number of dynamic syscalls. We have the following observations. (1) LDX correctly identifies that one input mutation causes leakage while the other one does not (except for the last four cases), whereas TIGHTLIP reports leakage for both input mutations. Note that a lot of syscall differences are not output related. (2) The syscall differences caused by input mutations are not trivial and are sometimes substantial. LDX can properly handle all such differences. (3) For numerical computation oriented programs (i.e., the last four in the table), we were not able to construct the input mutation that does not cause leakage as any input mutation always leads to sink differences.

8.3 Effectiveness of Causality Inference

Comparison with Dynamic Tainting. We first compare LDX with TAINTGRIND (Khoo 2013) and LIBDFT (Kemerlis et al. 2012) [1].

[1] We have tried DECAF (formerly TEMU), but encountered build problems.

Table 3. Comparison with Dynamic Tainting

Program	# of tainted sinks			Total # of sinks
	LDX	TAINTGRIND	LIBDFT	
gcc	3	0	0	146
perlbench	1	0	0	5
bzip2	7	0	0	20
mcf	12	4	3	36
gobmk	68	39	39	84
hmmer	17	4	4	29
sjeng	83	8	6	112
libquantum	4	2	2	7
h264ref	28	3	3	37
omnetpp	24	4	2	52
astar	16	3	3	53
xalancbmk	45	21	0	419
lynx	5	3	1	8
nginx	10	5	0	22
tnftp	5	2	0	32
sysstat	6	3	0	12
gif2png	1	1	1	7
mp3info	1	1	1	8
prozilla	1	1	1	100799
yopsweb	1	1	0	41
ngircd	1	1	1	597
gocr	1	1	1	5
total	340	107	68	-

We compare the number of tainted sinks for all the benchmarks. For the set of programs with vulnerabilities, their sinks include function returns and memory management library calls. The results are shown in Table 3. The three columns in the middle report the number of tainted sinks. The last column shows the total number of sinks encountered during execution.

We have the following observations. (1) The tainted sinks reported by TAINTGRIND and LIBDFT and are only 31.47% and 20% of those reported by LDX. This is because the other two are based on tracking data dependences. As we discussed in Section 2, data dependences are essentially strong causalities. Hence, LDX can detect what the other two detect. In addition, LDX can detect strong causalities induced by control dependences. We have validated that all the sinks reported by LDX have one-to-one mappings with the tainted inputs (i.e., no false positives). (2) The tainted sinks reported by TAINTGRIND are a superset of those reported by LIBDFT. Further inspection shows that LIBDFT does not correctly model taint propagation for some library calls. This indeed illustrates a practical challenge for instruction tracking based causality inference, which is to correctly model taint behavior for the large number of instructions and libraries. The last six rows show the results for the vulnerable program set. Observe that LDX can detect the attacks by correctly inferring the causality between the untrusted inputs and the critical execution points.

Effectiveness for Concurrent Programs. LDX supports real concurrency by sharing the thread schedule as much as possible between the two executions (Section 7). However, low level races may introduce non-deterministic state differences, leading to false positives in causality inference. In this experiment, we collect 5 concurrent programs. For each program, we mutate the input and dual execute it 100 times. We used the standard inputs provided with the programs. As shown in column 3 of Table 4, the number of tainted sinks rarely changes, whereas syscall differences do change (column 2) due to low level races. However, the syscall difference changes are not substantial because LDX was able to enforce the same schedule for most cases. This supports the effectiveness of the concurrency control of LDX (for the programs we consider). The tainted sink changes for `x264` are caused by the execution statistics report (e.g., the bits processed per sec.). Although LDX forces the master and the slave to share the same schedule and the same timestamps, the number of bits processed per unit time is non-deterministic *across tests* and beyond control. The tainted sink changes for `axel` are because the program makes Internet connections in each run, which are non-deterministic.

Table 4. Effectiveness of concurrent programs.

Program	# of syscall diffs (Min/Max/Std. Dev.)	# of tainted sinks (Min/Max/Std. Dev.)
Apache	114 / 123 / 1.66	39 / 39 / 0
pbzip2	288 / 332 / 11.59	8 / 8 / 0
pigz	490 / 546 / 18.50	14/ 14 / 0
axel	1173 / 1252 / 25.39	813 / 834 / 6.5
x264	854 / 1211 / 89.38	350 / 353 / 0.3

Input Mutation. LDX performs off-by-one mutation on sources, which must detect any strong CCs as proved in (tr). However in some rare cases it may also detect weak causalities. We conduct an experiment to study different mutation strategies. We observe that other strategies do not supercede off-by-one. Details can be found in (tr).

8.4 Case Studies

403.gcc. In this study, we use the source code of `nginx` as input. Fig. 7 shows part of input code on the left. We specify the configuration `NGX_HAVE_POLL` as the source. The master has `NGX_HAVE_POLL` defined but the slave does not. As such, the master includes `poll.h` while the slave does not. This corresponds to 7_2, 8_2, and 10_2 (Fig. 7) occurring in the master but not in the slave. Later on, both executions re-align at 216_1 and run in the coupled mode. In fact, 216 and 217 are in an output loop that emits the preprocessed code. Due to the earlier differences, the preprocessed code is different. The differences manifest as parameter differences during executions of 216_i, 217_i in the master and 216_j, 217_j in the slave. The leak is reported. Note that the causality is strong as one can infer from the preprocessed code the value of `NGX_HAVE_POLL`.

Other tools such as LIBDFT and TAINTGRIND are not able to detect the causality as it is induced by control dependences, Fig. 7 shows the relevant `gcc` code on the right. At line 472, `gcc` reads the value of `NGX_HAVE_POLL` and stores it. Later, when the preprocessor reaches the "`#if NGX_HAVE_POLL`" statement inside `do_if()`, it reads the stored value and compares it with 0. The outcome is stored to `skip` at line 1329. Then, the variable is copied to `pfile->state.skipping` (line 1331), which later determines if the code block guarded by the if statement should be skipped or not. Note that although there are data dependences 472 → 1329 and 1329 → 1331, the connection between `pfile->node->value` and `skip` at line 1329 is control dependence, which breaks the taint propagation in LIBDFT and TAINTGRIND.

Firefox. In this case, we detect information leak in a `firefox` extension `ShowIP 1.2rc5` that displays the IP of current page. It sends the current url to a remote server. LDX instruments the event handling component and part of the JS engine in `firefox` to align JS code block executions that correspond to page loading and user event handling. It successfully detects the leak whereas TAINTGRIND and LIBDFT fail because the leak goes through control dependences. Details can be found in (tr).

9. Related Work

Dual Execution. LDX is closely related to dual execution (Kim et al. 2015). The main differences are the following. (1) LDX is very lightweight (6.08% overhead) whereas (Kim et al. 2015) relies on the expensive execution indexing (Xin et al. 2008), causing 3 orders of magnitude slowdown. (2) LDX allows threads to execute concurrently whereas (Kim et al. 2015) does not. (3) The applications are different. The low overhead of LDX makes it a plausible causality inference engine in practice. (4) Their dual execution models are different as explained in Section 4.2. TIGHTLIP (Yumerefendi et al. 2007) also uses the master-and-slave execution model to detect inforamtion leak. It uses a window to tolerate syscall differences. The simple approach can hardly handle nontrivial differences.

Execution Replication and Replay. Execution replication has been widely studied (Birman 1985; Chereque et al. 1992; Tulley and Shrivastava 1990; Black et al. 1998; Castro et al. 2003; Berger and Zorn 2006; Vandiver et al. 2007; Chun et al. 2008; Hosek and Cadar 2015). The premise is similar to n-version programming (Chen and Avizienis 1995), which runs different implementations of the same service specification in parallel. Then, voting is used to produce a common result tolerating occasional faults. There are many security applications (Cox et al. 2006; Bruschi et al. 2007; Lvin et al. 2008; Salamat 2009; McDermott et al. 1997; Yumerefendi et al. 2007) of execution replication by detecting differences among replicas. There are also works in execution replay (Hower and Hill 2008; Montesinos et al. 2009; Narayanasamy et al. 2006; Sorrentino et al. 2010; Park et al. 2009; Veeraraghavan et al. 2012; Chandra et al. 2011; Goel et al. 2005; Kim et al. 2010). In contrast, LDX align different paths during execution. RAIL (Chen et al. 2014) re-runs applications with previous inputs to identify information disclosure after a vulnerability is fixed. To handle state divergence between the original and replay executions, it requires developers to annotate the program. DORA (Viennot et al. 2013) is a replay system that records execution beforehand to replay with a modified version of the application. Instead, LDX runs two executions of an application with input perturbation to infer causality at real-time. LDX focuses on aligning two executions accurately using a counter algorithm, while (Viennot et al. 2013) relies on heuristics to tolerate non-determinism.

Dynamic Taint Tracking. Most dynamic tainting techniques (Song et al. 2008; Kemerlis et al. 2012; Clause et al. 2007; Bosman et al. 2011; Qin et al. 2006; Attariyan and Flinn 2010) work by tracking instruction execution and hence are expensive. They have difficulty handling control dependences (McCamant and Ernst 2008). Some have limited support by detecting patterns (Kang et al. 2011) or handling special dependences (Bao et al. 2010). In particular, (Attariyan and Flinn 2010) identifies and handles a subset of important control dependencies using several heuristics. LDX provides a solution to such problems by detecting strong CC based on the definition of causality instead of program dependencies. Approaches for quantifying information flow (McCamant and Ernst 2008; Heusser and Malacaria 2010; Backes et al. 2009; Mardziel et al. 2014) aim to precisely ascertain figures like the number of sensitive bits of information that an attacker may infer, the number of attack attempts required, or strategies for identifying secrets. Hardware based solutions (Tiwari et al. 2009b,a; Li et al. 2011; Tiwari et al. 2011) have been proposed to speed up or improve accuracy of taint analysis.

Secure Multiple Execution (SME). SME (Devriese and Piessens 2010; Austin and Flanagan 2012; Capizzi et al. 2008) splits an execution into multiple ones for different security levels: the low execution does the public outputs and the high execution does the confidential outputs. SME can enforce the non-interference policy. It blocks or terminates when the two executions diverge, which is intended for non-interference. In comparison, LDX focuses on causality inference and tolerates execution divergence.

Statistical Fault Localization (SFL). Recent approaches in SFL (Bai et al. 2015; Baah et al. 2010; Shu et al. 2013) use causal inference methodology in order to mitigate biases such as confoundings. In particular, suspiciousness scores that guide to locate faults can be distorted by such biases, producing inaccurate results. They run a

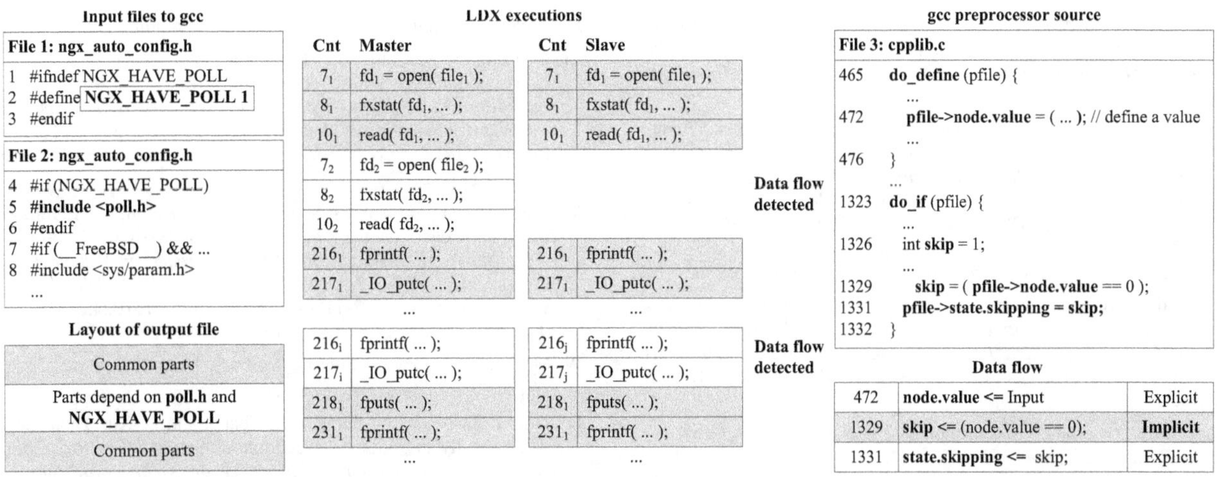

Figure 7. Case study on `403.gcc`. Input files on the left; relevant gcc code on the right; dual execution in the middle.

program over a set of inputs repeatedly to identify the causal effect of a statement on program failures. Such causal effect is then used to improve the performance and accuracy of SFL by reducing confounding bias. Instead, LDX infers causality by running multiple executions concurrently while tolerating execution divergence caused by the input purturbation.

10. Conclusion

We present LDX, a causality inference engine by lightweight dual execution. It features a novel numbering scheme that allows LDX to align executions. LDX can effectively detect information leak and security attacks. It has much better accuracy than existing systems. Its overhead is only 6.08% when executing both the master and the slave concurrently on separate CPUs. This is much lower than systems that work by instruction level tracing although they do not require the additional CPU and memory.

11. ACKNOWLEDGMENTS

We thank the anonymous reviewers for their constructive comments. This research was supported, in part, by DARPA under contract FA8650-15-C-7562, NSF under awards 1409668 and 0845870, ONR under contract N000141410468, and Cisco Systems under an unrestricted gift. Any opinions, findings, and conclusions in this paper are those of the authors only and do not necessarily reflect the views of our sponsors.

References

Lightweight dual-execution engine project website. `https://sites.google.com/site/ldxprj`.

M. Attariyan and J. Flinn. Automating configuration troubleshooting with dynamic information flow analysis. In *Proceedings of the 9th USENIX Conference on Operating Systems Design and Implementation*, OSDI'10, pages 1–11, Berkeley, CA, USA, 2010. USENIX Association. URL `http://dl.acm.org/citation.cfm?id=1924943.1924960`.

T. H. Austin and C. Flanagan. Multiple facets for dynamic information flow. In *POPL*, 2012.

G. K. Baah, A. Podgurski, and M. J. Harrold. Causal inference for statistical fault localization. In *Proceedings of the 19th International Symposium on Software Testing and Analysis*, ISSTA '10, pages 73–84, New York, NY, USA, 2010. ACM. ISBN 978-1-60558-823-0. doi: 10.1145/1831708.1831717. URL `http://doi.acm.org/10.1145/1831708.1831717`.

M. Backes, B. Kopf, and A. Rybalchenko. Automatic discovery and quantification of information leaks. In *Proceedings of the 2009 30th IEEE Symposium on Security and Privacy*, SP '09, pages 141–153, Washington, DC, USA, 2009. IEEE Computer Society. ISBN 978-0-7695-3633-0. doi: 10.1109/SP.2009.18. URL `http://dx.doi.org/10.1109/SP.2009.18`.

Z. Bai, G. Shu, and A. Podgurski. Numfl: Localizing faults in numerical software using a value-based causal model. In *Software Testing, Verification and Validation (ICST), 2015 IEEE 8th International Conference on*, pages 1–10, April 2015. doi: 10.1109/ICST.2015.7102597.

T. Bao, Y. Zheng, Z. Lin, X. Zhang, and D. Xu. Strict control dependence and its effect on dynamic information flow analyses. In *Proceedings of the 19th International Symposium on Software Testing and Analysis*, ISSTA '10, pages 13–24, New York, NY, USA, 2010. ACM. ISBN 978-1-60558-823-0. doi: 10.1145/1831708.1831711. URL `http://doi.acm.org/10.1145/1831708.1831711`.

E. D. Berger and B. G. Zorn. Diehard: Probabilistic memory safety for unsafe languages. In *Proceedings of the 2006 ACM SIGPLAN Conference on Programming Language Design and Implementation*, PLDI '06, pages 158–168, New York, NY, USA, 2006. ACM. ISBN 1-59593-320-4. doi: 10.1145/1133981.1134000. URL `http://doi.acm.org/10.1145/1133981.1134000`.

K. P. Birman. Replication and fault-tolerance in the isis system. *SIGOPS Oper. Syst. Rev.*, 19(5):79–86, Dec. 1985. ISSN 0163-5980. doi: 10.1145/323627.323636. URL `http://doi.acm.org/10.1145/323627.323636`.

D. Black, C. Low, and S. K. Shrivastava. The voltan application programming environment for fail-silent processes. *Distributed Systems Engineering*, 5(2):66–77, 1998.

E. Bosman, A. Slowinska, and H. Bos. Minemu: The world's fastest taint tracker. In *Proceedings of the 14th International Conference on Recent Advances in Intrusion Detection*, RAID'11, pages 1–20, Berlin, Heidelberg, 2011. Springer-Verlag. ISBN 978-3-642-23643-3. doi: 10.1007/978-3-642-23644-0_1. URL `http://dx.doi.org/10.1007/978-3-642-23644-0_1`.

D. Bruschi, L. Cavallaro, and A. Lanzi. Diversified process replic for defeating memory error exploits. *Performance, Computing, and Communications Conference, 2002. 21st IEEE International*, 0:434–441, 2007. ISSN 1097-2641. doi: http://doi.ieeecomputersociety.org/10.1109/PCCC.2007.358924.

R. Capizzi, A. Longo, V. N. Venkatakrishnan, and A. P. Sistla. Preventing information leaks through shadow executions. In *ACSAC*, 2008.

M. Castro, R. Rodrigues, and B. Liskov. Base: Using abstraction to improve fault tolerance. *ACM Trans. Comput. Syst.*, 21(3):236–269, Aug. 2003. ISSN 0734-2071. doi: 10.1145/859716.859718. URL `http://doi.acm.org/10.1145/859716.859718`.

R. Chandra, T. Kim, M. Shah, N. Narula, and N. Zeldovich. Intrusion recovery for database-backed web applications. In *Proceedings of the Twenty-Third ACM Symposium on Operating Systems Principles*, SOSP '11, 2011.

H. Chen, T. Kim, X. Wang, N. Zeldovich, and M. F. Kaashoek. Identifying information disclosure in web applications with retroactive auditing. In *11th USENIX Symposium on Operating Systems Design and Implementation (OSDI 14)*, pages 555–569, Broomfield, CO, Oct. 2014. USENIX Association. ISBN 978-1-931971-16-4. URL https://www.usenix.org/conference/osdi14/technical-sessions/presentation/chen_haogang.

L. Chen and A. Avizienis. N-version programminc: A fault-tolerance approach to rellablllty of software operatlon. In *Fault-Tolerant Computing, 1995, Highlights from Twenty-Five Years., Twenty-Fifth International Symposium on*, pages 113–, Jun 1995. doi: 10.1109/FTCSH.1995.532621.

P. Cheng. From covariation to causation: A causal power theory. *Psychological Review, 104*, pages 367–405, 1997.

M. Chereque, D. Powell, P. Reynier, J.-L. Richier, and J. Voiron. Active replication in delta-4. In *Fault-Tolerant Computing, 1992. FTCS-22. Digest of Papers., Twenty-Second International Symposium on*, pages 28–37, July 1992. doi: 10.1109/FTCS.1992.243618.

B.-G. Chun, P. Maniatis, and S. Shenker. Diverse replication for single-machine byzantine-fault tolerance. In *USENIX 2008 Annual Technical Conference on Annual Technical Conference*, ATC'08, pages 287–292, Berkeley, CA, USA, 2008. USENIX Association. URL http://dl.acm.org/citation.cfm?id=1404014.1404038.

J. Clause, W. Li, and A. Orso. Dytan: A generic dynamic taint analysis framework. In *Proceedings of the 2007 International Symposium on Software Testing and Analysis*, ISSTA '07, pages 196–206, New York, NY, USA, 2007. ACM. ISBN 978-1-59593-734-6. doi: 10.1145/1273463.1273490. URL http://doi.acm.org/10.1145/1273463.1273490.

B. Cox, D. Evans, A. Filipi, J. Rowanhill, W. Hu, J. Davidson, J. Knight, A. Nguyen-Tuong, and J. Hiser. N-variant systems: A secretless framework for security through diversity. In *Proceedings of the 15th Conference on USENIX Security Symposium - Volume 15*, USENIX-SS'06, Berkeley, CA, USA, 2006. USENIX Association. URL http://dl.acm.org/citation.cfm?id=1267336.1267344.

L. P. Cox, P. Gilbert, G. Lawler, V. Pistol, A. Razeen, B. Wu, and S. Cheemalapati. Spandex: Secure password tracking for android. In *23rd USENIX Security Symposium (USENIX Security 14)*, pages 481–494, San Diego, CA, Aug. 2014. USENIX Association. ISBN 978-1-931971-15-7. URL https://www.usenix.org/conference/usenixsecurity14/technical-sessions/presentation/cox.

D. Devriese and F. Piessens. Noninterference through secure multi-execution. In *S&P*, 2010.

A. Goel, K. Po, K. Farhadi, Z. Li, and E. de Lara. The taser intrusion recovery system. In *Proceedings of the twentieth ACM symposium on Operating systems principles*, SOSP '05. ACM, 2005.

J. Heusser and P. Malacaria. Quantifying information leaks in software. In *Proceedings of the 26th Annual Computer Security Applications Conference*, ACSAC '10, pages 261–269, New York, NY, USA, 2010. ACM. ISBN 978-1-4503-0133-6. doi: 10.1145/1920261.1920300. URL http://doi.acm.org/10.1145/1920261.1920300.

P. Hosek and C. Cadar. Varan the unbelievable: An efficient n-version execution framework. In *Proceedings of the Twentieth International Conference on Architectural Support for Programming Languages and Operating Systems*, ASPLOS '15, pages 339–353, New York, NY, USA, 2015. ACM. ISBN 978-1-4503-2835-7. doi: 10.1145/2694344.2694390. URL http://doi.acm.org/10.1145/2694344.2694390.

D. R. Hower and M. D. Hill. Rerun: Exploiting episodes for lightweight memory race recording. In *Proceedings of the 35th Annual International Symposium on Computer Architecture*, ISCA '08, pages 265–276, Washington, DC, USA, 2008. IEEE Computer Society. ISBN 978-0-7695-3174-8. doi: 10.1109/ISCA.2008.26. URL http://dx.doi.org/10.1109/ISCA.2008.26.

D. Hume. An enquiry concerning human understanding. 1748.

M. G. Kang, S. McCamant, P. Poosankam, and D. Ong. DTA++: Dynamic taint analysis with targeted control-flow propagation. In A. Perrig, editor, *NDSS 2011, 18th Annual Network & Distributed System Security Symposium*, Washington, DC, USA, Feb. 2011. Internet Society. URL http://www.isoc.org/isoc/conferences/ndss/11/pdf/5_4.pdf.

V. P. Kemerlis, G. Portokalidis, K. Jee, and A. D. Keromytis. Libdft: Practical dynamic data flow tracking for commodity systems. In *Proceedings of the 8th ACM SIGPLAN/SIGOPS Conference on Virtual Execution Environments*, VEE '12, pages 121–132, New York, NY, USA, 2012. ACM. ISBN 978-1-4503-1176-2. doi: 10.1145/2151024.2151042. URL http://doi.acm.org/10.1145/2151024.2151042.

W. M. Khoo. wmkhoo/taintgrind - github, Nov. 2013. URL https://github.com/wmkhoo/taintgrind/.

D. Kim, Y. Kwon, W. N. Sumner, X. Zhang, and D. Xu. Dual execution for on the fly fine grained execution comparison. In *Proceedings of the Twentieth International Conference on Architectural Support for Programming Languages and Operating Systems*, ASPLOS '15, pages 325–338, New York, NY, USA, 2015. ACM. ISBN 978-1-4503-2835-7. doi: 10.1145/2694344.2694394. URL http://doi.acm.org/10.1145/2694344.2694394.

T. Kim, X. Wang, N. Zeldovich, and M. F. Kaashoek. Intrusion recovery using selective re-execution. In *Proceedings of the 9th USENIX conference on Operating systems design and implementation*, OSDI'10. USENIX Association, 2010.

A. Kushnir and A. Gopnik. Young children infer causal strength from probabilities and interventions. *Psychological Science, 16 (9)*, pages 678–683, 2005.

D. Lewis. Counterfactuals. *Oxford: Blackwell*, 1973.

X. Li, M. Tiwari, J. K. Oberg, V. Kashyap, F. T. Chong, T. Sherwood, and B. Hardekopf. Caisson: A hardware description language for secure information flow. In *Proceedings of the 32Nd ACM SIGPLAN Conference on Programming Language Design and Implementation*, PLDI '11, pages 109–120, New York, NY, USA, 2011. ACM. ISBN 978-1-4503-0663-8. doi: 10.1145/1993498.1993512. URL http://doi.acm.org/10.1145/1993498.1993512.

V. B. Lvin, G. Novark, E. D. Berger, and B. G. Zorn. Archipelago: Trading address space for reliability and security. In *Proceedings of the 13th International Conference on Architectural Support for Programming Languages and Operating Systems*, ASPLOS XIII, pages 115–124, New York, NY, USA, 2008. ACM. ISBN 978-1-59593-958-6. doi: 10.1145/1346281.1346296. URL http://doi.acm.org/10.1145/1346281.1346296.

P. Mardziel, M. S. Alvim, M. Hicks, and M. R. Clarkson. Quantifying information flow for dynamic secrets. In *Proceedings of the 2014 IEEE Symposium on Security and Privacy*, SP '14, pages 540–555, Washington, DC, USA, 2014. IEEE Computer Society. ISBN 978-1-4799-4686-0. doi: 10.1109/SP.2014.41. URL http://dx.doi.org/10.1109/SP.2014.41.

S. McCamant and M. D. Ernst. Quantitative information flow as network flow capacity. In *Proceedings of the 2008 ACM SIGPLAN Conference on Programming Language Design and Implementation*, PLDI '08, pages 193–205, New York, NY, USA, 2008. ACM. ISBN 978-1-59593-860-2. doi: 10.1145/1375581.1375606. URL http://doi.acm.org/10.1145/1375581.1375606.

J. McDermott, R. Gelinas, and S. Ornstein. Doc, wyatt, and virgil: prototyping storage jamming defenses. In *Computer Security Applications Conference, 1997. Proceedings., 13th Annual*, pages 265–273, Dec 1997. doi: 10.1109/CSAC.1997.646199.

G. Miller and P. N. Johnson-Laird. Language and perception. *Cambridge: Cambridge University Press*, 1976.

P. Montesinos, M. Hicks, S. T. King, and J. Torrellas. Capo: A software-hardware interface for practical deterministic multiprocessor replay. In *Proceedings of the 14th International Conference on Architectural Support for Programming Languages and Operating Systems*, ASPLOS XIV, pages 73–84, New York, NY, USA, 2009. ACM. ISBN 978-1-

60558-406-5. doi: 10.1145/1508244.1508254. URL http://doi.acm.org/10.1145/1508244.1508254.

S. Narayanasamy, C. Pereira, and B. Calder. Recording shared memory dependencies using strata. *SIGPLAN Not.*, 41(11):229–240, Oct. 2006. ISSN 0362-1340. doi: 10.1145/1168918.1168886. URL http://doi.acm.org/10.1145/1168918.1168886.

S. Park, Y. Zhou, W. Xiong, Z. Yin, R. Kaushik, K. H. Lee, and S. Lu. Pres: Probabilistic replay with execution sketching on multiprocessors. In *Proceedings of the ACM SIGOPS 22Nd Symposium on Operating Systems Principles*, SOSP '09, pages 177–192, New York, NY, USA, 2009. ACM. ISBN 978-1-60558-752-3. doi: 10.1145/1629575.1629593. URL http://doi.acm.org/10.1145/1629575.1629593.

F. Qin, C. Wang, Z. Li, H.-s. Kim, Y. Zhou, and Y. Wu. Lift: A low-overhead practical information flow tracking system for detecting security attacks. In *Proceedings of the 39th Annual IEEE/ACM International Symposium on Microarchitecture*, MICRO 39, pages 135–148, Washington, DC, USA, 2006. IEEE Computer Society. ISBN 0-7695-2732-9. doi: 10.1109/MICRO.2006.29. URL http://dx.doi.org/10.1109/MICRO.2006.29.

B. Salamat. *Multi-variant Execution: Run-time Defense Against Malicious Code Injection Attacks*. PhD thesis, Irvine, CA, USA, 2009. AAI3359500.

G. Shu, B. Sun, A. Podgurski, and F. Cao. Mfl: Method-level fault localization with causal inference. In *Software Testing, Verification and Validation (ICST), 2013 IEEE Sixth International Conference on*, pages 124–133, March 2013. doi: 10.1109/ICST.2013.31.

D. Song, D. Brumley, H. Yin, J. Caballero, I. Jager, M. G. Kang, Z. Liang, J. Newsome, P. Poosankam, and P. Saxena. Bitblaze: A new approach to computer security via binary analysis. In *Proceedings of the 4th International Conference on Information Systems Security*, ICISS '08, pages 1–25, Berlin, Heidelberg, 2008. Springer-Verlag. ISBN 978-3-540-89861-0. doi: 10.1007/978-3-540-89862-7_1. URL http://dx.doi.org/10.1007/978-3-540-89862-7_1.

F. Sorrentino, A. Farzan, and P. Madhusudan. Penelope: Weaving threads to expose atomicity violations. In *Proceedings of the Eighteenth ACM SIGSOFT International Symposium on Foundations of Software Engineering*, FSE '10, pages 37–46, New York, NY, USA, 2010. ACM. ISBN 978-1-60558-791-2. doi: 10.1145/1882291.1882300. URL http://doi.acm.org/10.1145/1882291.1882300.

M. Tiwari, X. Li, H. Wassel, F. Chong, and T. Sherwood. Execution leases: A hardware-supported mechanism for enforcing strong non-interference. In *Microarchitecture, 2009. MICRO-42. 42nd Annual IEEE/ACM International Symposium on*, pages 493–504, Dec 2009a.

M. Tiwari, H. M. Wassel, B. Mazloom, S. Mysore, F. T. Chong, and T. Sherwood. Complete information flow tracking from the gates up. In *Proceedings of the 14th International Conference on Architectural Support for Programming Languages and Operating Systems*, ASPLOS XIV, pages 109–120, New York, NY, USA, 2009b. ACM. ISBN 978-1-60558-406-5. doi: 10.1145/1508244.1508258. URL http://doi.acm.org/10.1145/1508244.1508258.

M. Tiwari, J. K. Oberg, X. Li, J. Valamehr, T. Levin, B. Hardekopf, R. Kastner, F. T. Chong, and T. Sherwood. Crafting a usable microkernel, processor, and i/o system with strict and provable information flow security. In *Proceedings of the 38th Annual International Symposium on Computer Architecture*, ISCA '11, pages 189–200, New York, NY, USA, 2011. ACM. ISBN 978-1-4503-0472-6. doi: 10.1145/2000064.2000087. URL http://doi.acm.org/10.1145/2000064.2000087.

A. Tulley and S. Shrivastava. Preventing state divergence in replicated distributed programs. In *Reliable Distributed Systems, 1990. Proceedings., Ninth Symposium on*, pages 104–113, Oct 1990. doi: 10.1109/RELDIS.1990.93956.

B. Vandiver, H. Balakrishnan, B. Liskov, and S. Madden. Tolerating Byzantine Faults in Transaction Processing Systems Using Commit Barrier Scheduling. In *ACM SOSP*, Stevenson, WA, October 2007.

K. Veeraraghavan, D. Lee, B. Wester, J. Ouyang, P. M. Chen, J. Flinn, and S. Narayanasamy. Doubleplay: Parallelizing sequential logging and replay. *ACM Trans. Comput. Syst.*, 30(1):3:1–3:24, Feb. 2012. ISSN 0734-2071. doi: 10.1145/2110356.2110359. URL http://doi.acm.org/10.1145/2110356.2110359.

N. Viennot, S. Nair, and J. Nieh. Transparent mutable replay for multicore debugging and patch validation. In *Proceedings of the Eighteenth International Conference on Architectural Support for Programming Languages and Operating Systems*, ASPLOS '13, pages 127–138, New York, NY, USA, 2013. ACM. ISBN 978-1-4503-1870-9. doi: 10.1145/2451116.2451130. URL http://doi.acm.org/10.1145/2451116.2451130.

B. Xin, W. N. Sumner, and X. Zhang. Efficient program execution indexing. In *Proceedings of the 2008 ACM SIGPLAN Conference on Programming Language Design and Implementation*, PLDI '08, pages 238–248, New York, NY, USA, 2008. ACM. ISBN 978-1-59593-860-2. doi: 10.1145/1375581.1375611. URL http://doi.acm.org/10.1145/1375581.1375611.

A. R. Yumerefendi, B. Mickle, and L. P. Cox. Tightlip: Keeping applications from spilling the beans. In *Proceedings of the 4th USENIX Conference on Networked Systems Design and Implementation*, NSDI'07, pages 12–12, Berkeley, CA, USA, 2007. USENIX Association. URL http://dl.acm.org/citation.cfm?id=1973430.1973442.

TaxDC: A Taxonomy of Non-Deterministic Concurrency Bugs in Datacenter Distributed Systems

Tanakorn Leesatapornwongsa
University of Chicago
tanakorn@cs.uchicago.edu

Jeffrey F. Lukman
Surya University
lukman@cs.uchicago.edu

Shan Lu
University of Chicago
shanlu@uchicago.edu

Haryadi S. Gunawi
University of Chicago
haryadi@cs.uchicago.edu

Abstract

We present TaxDC, the largest and most comprehensive taxonomy of non-deterministic concurrency bugs in distributed systems. We study 104 distributed concurrency (DC) bugs from four widely-deployed cloud-scale datacenter distributed systems, Cassandra, Hadoop MapReduce, HBase and ZooKeeper. We study DC-bug characteristics along several axes of analysis such as the triggering timing condition and input preconditions, error and failure symptoms, and fix strategies, collectively stored as 2,083 classification labels in TaxDC database. We discuss how our study can open up many new research directions in combating DC bugs.

Categories and Subject Descriptors D.2.5 [*Testing and Debugging*]: Diagnostics

Keywords Concurrency bugs, distributed systems, software testing

1. Introduction

> *"Do we have to rethink this entire [HBase] root and meta 'huh hah'? There isn't a week going by without some new bugs about* ***races*** *between splitting and assignment [distributed protocols]."* — *h4397*

Software systems are getting more complex and new intricate bugs continue to appear, causing billions of dollars in economic loss. One notorious type of software bugs is concurrency bugs. These timing-related bugs manifest non-deterministically, and hence are extremely difficult to detect, diagnose, and fix. A huge body of work exists in this space that focuses on "local" concurrency (LC) bugs in single-machine multi-threaded software, caused by incorrect interleaving of memory accesses.

Today, beyond single-machine software, distributed software infrastructures have become a dominant backbone for cloud computing and modern applications. Large-scale distributed systems such as scalable computing frameworks [4, 14], storage systems [3, 6, 11, 15], synchronization [7, 10] and cluster management services [5, 29] have emerged as the datacenter operating system. Increasing numbers of developers write large-scale distributed systems and billions of end users rely on the reliability of these systems.

Unfortunately, the reliability of datacenter distributed systems is severely threatened by non-deterministic concurrency bugs as well, which we refer as *distributed concurrency (DC) bugs*. Distributed systems execute many complicated distributed protocols on hundreds/thousands of machines with no common clocks, and must face a variety of random hardware failures [17, 25]. This combination makes distributed systems prone to DC bugs caused by non-deterministic timing of distributed events such as message arrivals, node crashes, reboots, and timeouts. These DC bugs cannot be directly tackled by LC bug techniques, and they cause fatal implications such as operation failures, downtimes, data loss and inconsistencies.

Fighting DC bugs is challenging, particularly given the preliminary understanding of real-world DC bugs. To make progress, we believe a comprehensive bug study is needed. Past studies have closely examined bugs in various software systems [12, 44, 50], which have motivated and guided many aspects of reliability research. There are few bug studies on large-scale distributed systems [25, 39], but they did not specifically dissect DC bugs. One recent paper ana-

ASPLOS '16, April 02 - 06, 2016, Atlanta, GA, USA.

ACM 978-1-4503-4091-5/16/04... $15.00.
http://dx.doi.org/10.1145/2872362.2872374

lyzed non-determinism in MapReduce programs but only discussed five bugs [64]. Thorough studies have also been conducted for LC bugs [21, 45] with many follow-up work to date. To the best of our knowledge, *there is no comprehensive study on real-world distributed concurrency bugs.*

A comprehensive study on real-world DC bugs relies on three key ingredients: detailed bug descriptions by users and developers, open access to source code and patches, and pervasive documentation of the studied systems. Although DC bugs theoretically have existed for decades, all the key ingredients were never aligned, causing the lack of comprehensive DC bug studies. There were only a few popular open-source distributed systems [1, 37, 60], and they do not document bugs in detail. There were a few bug detection and diagnosis papers that discussed DC bugs in real-world proprietary systems [26, 42, 43, 55, 65], but the number of reported bugs is too few for a comprehensive study and they do not release source code and patches. Fortunately, in the advent of open-source cloud computing, many of today's popular datacenter distributed systems provide all the key ingredients.

1.1 TaxDC

This paper presents our in-depth analysis of 104 DC bugs. We believe our study is the largest and most comprehensive to date for DC bugs. The bugs came from four popular datacenter distributed systems: Cassandra [3], HBase [6], Hadoop MapReduce [4], and ZooKeeper [7]. We introduce TaxDC, a comprehensive taxonomy of real-world DC bugs across several axes of analysis such as the triggering timing condition and input preconditions, error and failure symptoms, and fix strategies, as shown in detail in Table 1. The results of our study are stored in the form of 2,083 classification labels in TaxDC database [2].

As our main contribution, TaxDC will be the first large-scale DC-bug benchmark. In the last five years, bug benchmarks for LC bugs have been released [32, 66], but no large-scale benchmarks exist for DC bugs. Researchers who want to evaluate the effectiveness of existing or new tools in combating DC bugs do not have a benchmark reference. TaxDC provides researchers with more than 100 thoroughly taxonomized DC bugs to choose from. Practitioners can also use TaxDC to check whether their systems have similar bugs. The DC bugs we studied are considerably general, representing bugs in popular types of distributed systems.

As a side contribution, TaxDC can help open up new research directions. In the past, the lack of understanding of real-world DC bugs has hindered researchers to innovate new ways to combat DC bugs. The state of the art focuses on three lines of research: monitoring and postmortem debugging [22, 42, 43, 55], testing and model checking [26, 37, 38, 59, 65], and verifiable language frameworks [16, 63]. We hope our study will not only improve these lines of research, but also inspire new research in bug detection tool design, runtime prevention, and bug fixing, as elaborated more in Section 8.

1.2 Summary of Findings

While we provide detailed findings throughout the paper, we first summarize findings on the intricacies of DC bugs:

• Throughout the development of our target systems, new DC bugs continue to surface. Although these systems are popular, there is a lack of effective testing, verification, and analysis tools to detect DC bugs prior to deployment.

• Real-world DC bugs are hard to find because many of them linger in complex concurrent executions of *multiple* protocols. Complete systems contain many background and operational protocols beyond user-facing foreground protocols. Their concurrent interactions can be deadly.

• 63% of DC bugs surface in the presence of hardware faults such as machine crashes (and reboots), network delay and partition (timeouts), and disk errors. As faults happen, recovery protocols create more non-deterministic events concurrent with ongoing operations.

• 47% of DC bugs lead to silent failures and hence are hard to debug in production and reproduce offline.

Nevertheless, through a careful and detailed study of each bug, our results also bring fresh and positive insights:

• More than 60% of DC bugs are triggered by a *single* untimely message delivery that commits order violation or atomicity violation, with regard to other messages or computation. This finding motivates DC bug detection to focus on timing-specification inference and violation detection; it provides simple program-invariant and failure-predictor templates for DC bug detection, failure diagnosis, and runtime prevention.

• 53% of DC bugs lead to *explicit* local or global errors. This finding motivates inferring timing specifications based on local correctness specifications, in the form of error checking already provided by developers.

• Most DC bugs are fixed through a small set of strategies. 30% are fixed by prohibiting the triggering timing and another 40% by simply delaying or ignoring the untimely message, or accepting it without introducing new handling logic. This finding implies unique research opportunities for automated in-production fixing for DC bugs.

• Many other observations are made that enable us to analyze the gap between state-of-the-art tools and real-world DC bugs as well as between research in LC and DC bugs.

In the following sections, we first present our methodology (§2) and then our DC taxonomy (§3-§7). Note that these sections only present the taxonomy, illustrations, examples, and statistics. Later, Section §8 discusses the lessons learned wherein we will connect our findings with the implications to existing tools and opportunities for new research in combating DC bugs. We do not have an exclusive section for related work as we discuss them throughout the paper.

2. Methodology

2.1 Basic Definitions

A *distributed concurrency (DC) bug* is a concurrency bug in distributed systems caused by distributed events that can occur in non-deterministic order. An *event* can be a message arrival/sending, local computation, fault, and reboot. A *local concurrency (LC) bug* is a concurrency bug that happens locally within a node due to thread interleaving. In our model, a *distributed system* is a collection of shared-nothing nodes. Each node can run multiple protocols in multiple threads.

2.2 Target Systems and Dataset

Our study examined bugs from four widely-deployed open-source datacenter distributed systems that represent a diverse set of system architectures: Hadoop MapReduce (including Yarn) [4] representing distributed computing frameworks, HBase [6] and Cassandra [3] representing distributed key-value stores (also known as NoSQL systems), and ZooKeeper [7] representing synchronization services. They are all fully complete systems containing many complex concurrent protocols. Throughout the paper, we will present short examples of DC bugs in these systems. Some detailed examples are illustrated in Figure 2, 4 and 5.

The development projects of our target systems are all hosted under Apache Software Foundation wherein organized issue repositories (named "JIRA") are maintained. To date, across the four systems, there are over 30,000 issues submitted. One major challenge is that issues pertaining to DC bugs do not always contain plain terms such as "concurrency", "race", "atomicity", etc. Scanning all the issues is a daunting task. Thus, we started our study from an open source cloud bug study (CBS) database [2], which already labels issues related to concurrency bugs. However, beyond simple labeling, the CBS work did not differentiate DC from LC bugs and did not dissect DC bugs further.

From CBS, we first filtered out LC bugs, then exclude DC bugs that do not contain clear description, and finally randomly picked 104 samples from the remaining detailed DC bugs, specifically 19 Cassandra, 30 HBase, 36 Hadoop MapReduce, and 19 ZooKeeper DC bugs, reported in January 2011-2014 (the time range of CBS work). We have seen much fewer clearly explained DC bugs in CBS from Cassandra and ZooKeeper than those from HBase and Hadoop MapReduce, which may be related to the fact that they are different types of distributed systems. For example, ZooKeeper, as a synchronization service, is quite robust as it is built on the assumption of event asynchrony since day one. Cassandra was built on eventual consistency, and thus did not have many complex transactions, until recently when Cassandra adopts Paxos. We still see new DC bugs throughout 2014-2015 (some pointed to us by the developers); they can be included into TaxDC in the future.

Triggering (§3)
What is the triggering timing condition?
Message arrives unexpectedly late/early
Message arrives unexpectedly in the middle
Fault (component failures) at an unexpected state
Reboot at an unexpected state
What are the triggering inputs preconditions?
Fault, reboot, timeout, background protocols, and others
What is the triggering scope?
How many nodes/messages/protocols are involved?
Errors & Failures (§4)
What is the error symptom?
Local memory exceptions
Local semantic error messages & exceptions
Local hang
Local silent errors (inconsistent local states)
Global missing messages
Global unexpected messages
Global silent errors (inconsistent global states)
What is the failure symptom?
Node downtimes, data loss/corruption, operation failures, slowdowns
Fixing (§5)
What is the fix strategy?
Fix Timing: add global synchronization
Fix Timing: add local synchronization
Fix Handling: retry message handling at a later time
Fix Handling: ignore a message
Fix Handling: accepting a message without new computation logics
Fix Handling: others

Table 1. Taxonomy of DC Bugs.

2.3 Taxonomy

We study the characteristics of DC bugs along three key stages: triggering, errors & failures, and fixing (Table 1). *Triggering* is the process where software execution states deviate from correct to incorrect under specific conditions. At the end of this process, the manifestation of DC bugs changes from non-deterministic to deterministic. *Errors and failures* are internal and external software misbehaviors. *Fixing* shows how developers correct the bug. We will discuss in detail these categories in their respective sections.

2.4 Threats to Validity

For every bug, we first ensure that the developers marked it as a real bug (not a false positive). We also check that the bug description is clear. We then *re-enumerate* the full sequence of operations (the "*steps*") to a clearer and more concise description such as the ones in Figure 2. Finally, to improve the quality of the taxonimization process, each bug classification is reviewed by *all* authors in this paper. Our study cannot and does not cover DC bugs not fixed by the developers. Even for fixed bugs, we do not cover those that are not described clearly in the bug repositories, a sacrifice we had to make to maintain the accuracy of our results.

Readers should be cautioned not to generalize the statistics we report as each distributed system has unique purpose, design and implementation. For example, we observe 2:1 overall ratio between order and atomicity violations §3.1, however the individual ratios are different across the four systems (*e.g.* 1:2 in ZooKeeper and 6:1 in MapReduce). Like all empirical studies, our findings have to be interpreted with our methodology in mind.

2.5 TaxDC Database

We name the product of our study TaxDC database. TaxDC contains in total 2,083 classification labels and 4,528 lines of clear and concise re-description of the bugs (our version, that we manually wrote) including the re-enumeration of the steps, triggering conditions, errors and fixes. We will release TaxDC to the public [1]. We believe TaxDC will be a rich "bug benchmark" for researchers who want to tackle distributed concurrency problems. They will have sample bugs to begin with, advance their work, and do not have to repeat our multi-people-year effort.

2.6 Detailed Terminologies

Below are the detailed terminologies we use in this paper. We use the term "state" to interchangeably imply *local state* (both in-memory and on-disk per-node state) or *global state* (a collection of local states and outstanding messages). A *protocol* (*e.g.*, read, write, load balancing) creates a chain of events that modify system state. User-facing protocols are referred as *foreground* protocols while those generated by daemons or operators are referred as *background* protocols.

We consider four types of *events*: message, local computation, fault and reboot. The term *fault* represents component failures such as crashes, timeouts, and disk errors. A *timeout* (system-specific) implies a network disconnection or busy peer node. A *crash* usually implies the node experiences a power failure. A *reboot* means the node comes back up.

Throughout the paper, we present bug examples by abstracting system-specific names. As shown in Figure 1, we use capital letters for nodes (*e.g.*, A, B), two small letters for a message between two nodes (*ab* is from A to B). Occasionally, we attach system-specific information in the subscript (*e.g.*, $\text{A}_{\text{AppMaster}}$ sends ab_{taskKill} message to $\text{B}_{\text{NodeManager}}$). We use "/" to imply concurrency (*ac*/*bc* implies the two messages can arrive at C in different orders, *ac* or *bc* first). A dash, "–", means causal relation of two events (*ab-bc* means *ab* causally precedes *bc*). Finally, we use "N*" to represent crash, "N!" reboot, and "N+" local computation at N.

We cite bug examples with clickable hyperlinks (*e.g.*, m3274). To keep most examples uniform, we use MapReduce examples whenever possible. We use the following abbreviations for system names: "c/CA" for Cassandra, "h/HB" for HBase, "m/MR" for Hadoop MapReduce, and "z/ZK" for ZooKeeper; and for system-specific components: "AM" for application master, "RM" for resource manager, "NM" for node manager, "RS" for region server, and "ZAB" for ZooKeeper atomic broadcast.

[1] Please check our group website at `http://ucare.cs.uchicago.edu`

3. Trigger

"That is one monster of a race!" — m3274

DC bugs often have a long triggering process, with many local and global events involved. To better reason about this complicated process, we study them from two perspectives:

1. *Timing conditions* (§3.1): For every DC bug, we identify the smallest set of concurrent events E, so that a specific ordering of E can guarantee the bug manifestation. This is similar to the interleaving condition for LC bugs.
2. *Input preconditions* (§3.2): In order for those events in E to happen, regardless of the ordering, certain inputs or fault conditions (*e.g.*, node crashes) must occur. This is similar to the input condition for LC bugs.

Understanding the triggering can help the design of testing tools that can proactively trigger DC bugs, bug detection tools that can predict which bugs can be triggered through program analysis, and failure prevention tools that can sabotage the triggering conditions at run time.

3.1 Timing Conditions (TC)

Most DC bugs are triggered either by untimely delivery of messages, referred to as *message timing bugs*, or by untimely faults or reboots, referred to as *fault timing bugs*. Rarely DC bugs are triggered by both untimely messages and untimely faults, referred to as *message-fault bugs*. Table 2 shows the per-system breakdown and Figure 3a (TC) the overall breakdown. Since a few bugs are triggered by more than one type of timing conditions (§3.3), the sum of numbers in Table 2 is slightly larger than the total number of DC bugs.

Message Timing Bugs. The timing conditions can be abstracted to two categories:

a. *Order violation* (44% in Table 2) means a DC bug manifests whenever a message comes earlier (later) than another event, which is another message or a local computation, but not when the message comes later (earlier).

b. *Atomicity violation* (20% in Table 2) means a DC bug manifests whenever a message comes in the middle of a set of events, which is a local computation or global communication, but not when the message comes either before or after the events.

LC and DC bugs are similar in that their timing conditions can both be abstracted into the above two types. However, the subjects in these conditions are different: shared memory accesses in LC and message deliveries in DC. The ratio between order violation and atomicity violation bugs are also different: previous study of LC bugs showed that atomicity violations are much more common than order violations in practice [45]; our study of DC bugs shows that this relationship does not apply or even gets reversed in several representative distributed systems.

	Ordering	Atomicity	Fault	Reboot
CA	4	4	6	5
HB	13	9	8	1
MR	25	4	5	3
ZK	4	8	7	5
All	46	25	26	14

Table 2. #DC bugs triggered by timing conditions (§3.1). *The total is more than 104 because some bugs require more than one triggering condition. More specifically, 46 bugs (44%) are caused* only *by ordering violations, 21 bugs (20%)* only *by atomicity violations, and 4 bugs (4%) by multiple timing conditions (as also shown in Figure 3a).*

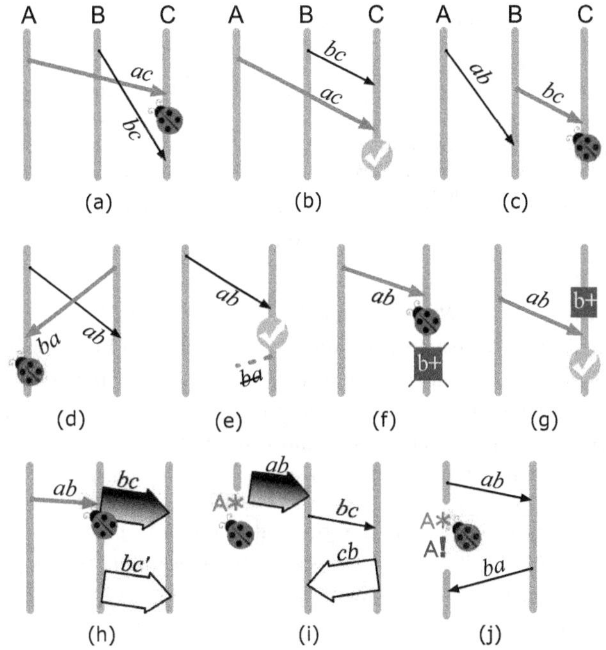

Figure 1. Triggering patterns (§3.1). *The three vertical lines represent the timeline of nodes A, B and C. An arrow with* xy *label implies a message from X to Y. A square box with label* x+ *implies a local state-modifying computation at node X. A thick arrow implies a set of messages performing an atomic operation.* X* *and* X! *implies a crash and reboot at node X respectively (§2.6). All figures are discussed in §3.1*

An order violation can originate from a race between two messages (*message-message race*) at one node. The race can happen between two message arrivals. For example, Figure 1a illustrates *ac*/*bc* race at node C in m3274. Specifically, B_{RM} sends to C_{NM} a task-init message (bc_{init}), and soon afterwards, A_{AM} sends to C_{NM} a task-kill preemption message (ac_{kill}), however ac_{kill} arrives *before* bc_{init} and thus is incorrectly ignored by C. The bug would not manifest if ac_{kill} arrives *after* bc_{init} (Figure 1b). Message-message race can also happen between a message arrival and a message sending. For example, the *ab*/*bc* race in Figure 1c depicts h5780. In this bug, B_{RS} sends to C_{Master} a cluster-join request (bc_{join}) unexpectedly *before* a security-key message (ab_{key}) from A_{ZK} arrives at B, causing the initialization to abort.

Interestingly, message-message race can also occur concurrently across two nodes. For example, Figure 1d illustrates *ab*/*ba* race crisscrossing two nodes A and B in m5358. Specifically, A_{AM} sends ab_{kill} to a backup speculative task at B_{NM} because the job has completed, but concurrently the backup task at B sends $ba_{complete}$ to A, creating a double-complete exception at A. If ab_{kill} arrives early at B, *ba* will not exist and the bug will not manifest (Figure 1e).

An order violation can also originate from a race between a message and a local computation (*message-compute race*). For example, Figure 1f illustrates *ab*/*b*+ race in m4157. First, B_{AM} was informed that a task has finished and B plans to close the job and remove its local temporary files (*b*+). However, just *before b*+, A_{RM} sends to B a kill message (*ab*) and hence the files are never removed, eventually creating space issues. To prevent the failure, the kill message has to arrive after the local cleanup (Figure 1g).

An atomicity violation, as defined above, originates when a message arrives in the middle of a supposedly-atomic local computation or global communication. For example, Figure 1h illustrates m5009. When B_{NM} is in the middle of a commit transaction, transferring task output data (*bc*) to C_{HDFS}, A_{RM} sends a kill preemption message (*ab*) to B, preempting the task without resetting commit states on C. The system is never able to finish the commit — when B later reruns the task and tries to commit to C (*bc*'), C throws a double-commit exception. This failure would not happen if the kill message (*ab*) comes before or after the commit transaction (*bc*).

Fault and Reboot Timing Bugs. Fault and reboot timing bugs (32% in Table 2) manifest when faults and/or reboots occur at specific global states S_i; the bugs do not manifest if the faults and reboots happen at different global states S_j.

Figure 1i illustrates a fault-timing bug in m3858. Here, A_{NM1} is sending a task's output to B_{AM} (*ab*) but A crashes in the middle (A*) leaving the output half-sent. The system is then unable to recover from this untimely crash — B detects the fault and reruns the task at C_{NM2} (via *bc*) and later when C re-sends the output (*cb*), B throws an exception. This bug would not manifest, if the crash (A*) happens before/after the output transfer (*ab*).

Figure 1j depicts a reboot-timing bug in m3186. Here, A_{RM} sends a job (*ab*) to B_{AM} and while B is executing the job, A crashes and reboots (A*, A!) losing all its in-memory job description. Later, B sends a job-commit message (*ba*) but A throws an exception because A does not have the job information. The bug would not manifest if A reboots later: if A is still down when B sends ba_{commit} message, B will realize the crash and cancel the job before A reboots and A will repeat the entire job assignment correctly.

z1264: (1) *Follower F crashed* in the past, (2) *F reboots* and joins the cluster, (3) Leader L sync data with F and send snapshot, (4) *In the middle of step 3-6*, client updates data with Tx-#15; L forwards the update to F, (5) F applies the update in memory only, due to a concurrent sync, (6) L tells F syncing is finished, (7) Client updates data with Tx-#16; F writes update to disk correctly, (8) *F crashes*, (9) *F reboots* and joins the cluster again, (10) L sync data with F, but this time L sends only "diff" starting with Tx-#17 (11) F permanently *loses data* from Tx-#15, inconsistent with L and other followers!

Figure 2. A DC bug in ZooKeeper.

Message-Fault Bugs. Four DC bugs are caused by a combination of messages and faults. For example, in Figure 2, a message (step 4) arrives in the middle of some atomic operation (step 3-6). This message atomicity violation leads to an error that further requires a fault timing (step 8) to become an externally visible failure.

Finding #1: DC bugs are triggered mostly by *untimely messages* (64% in Table 2) and sometimes by *untimely faults/reboots* (32%), and occasionally by a *combination* of both (4%). Among untimely messages, two thirds commit order violations due to message-message or message-computation race on the node they arrive; the others commit atomicity violations.

3.2 Input Preconditions (IP)

The previous section presents simple timing conditions that can be understood in few simple steps. In practice, many of the conditions happen "deep" in system execution. In other words, the triggering path is caused by complex input preconditions (IP) such as faults, reboots, and multiple protocols. Let's use the same example in Figure 2. First, a fault and a reboot (step 1-2) and a client request (step 4) must happen to create a path to the message atomicity violation (step 4 interfering with step 3-6). Second, conflicting messages from two different protocols (ZAB and NodeJoin initiated in step 2 and 4) have to follow specific bug-triggering timing conditions. Even after the atomicity violation (after step 6), the bug is not guaranteed to lead to any error yet (*i.e.*, a benign race). Finally, the follower experiences an untimely fault (step 8), such that after it reboots (step 9), a global replica-inconsistency error will happen (step 11). Put it in a reverse way, before step 8, the global state is S_i and S_i+crash→error, and the only way for the system to reach S_i is from complex preconditions such as a fault, a reboot, and some foreground and background protocols.

Statistically, Figure 3b (IP-FLT) shows that 63% of DC bugs must have at least one fault. In more detail, Figure 3c-e (IP-TO, IP-CR, IP-RB) shows the percentage of issues that require timeouts, crashes and reboots respectively, including how many instances of such faults must be there; the rest is other faults such as disk errors (not shown).

Figure 3f (IP-PR) shows how many "protocol initiations" mentioned in the bug description. For example, if the system needs to perform one execution of background protocol and

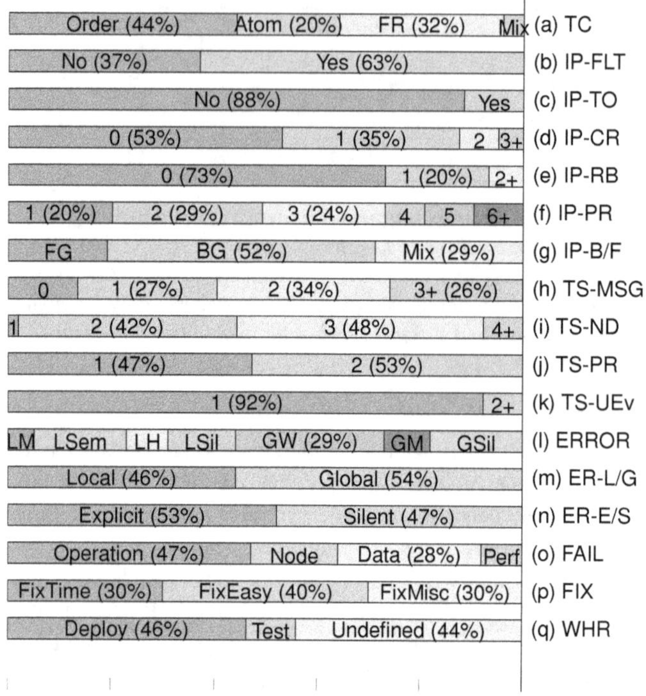

Figure 3. Statistical overview of TaxDC. *Timing Conditions (TC) is discussed in §3.1, Input Preconditions (IP) in §3.2, Triggering Scope (TS) in §3.3, Errors (ER) in §4.1, Failures (FAIL) in §4.2, Fixes (FIX) in §5, and Where Found (WHR) in §7.*

also three concurrent calls to the `write` protocol, then we label it with four protocol initiations. Up to 3 protocol initiations covers three quarters of DC bugs. When we count the number of *unique* protocols involved in all the bugs we study, we record 10 Cassandra, 13 HBase, 10 MapReduce, 6 ZooKeeper unique protocols, or 39 protocols in total. This again highlights the complexity of fully complete systems. Figure 3g (IP-B/F) shows our categorization of protocols that are concurrently running into foreground only, background only, and foreground-background (mix) categories. More than three quarters of the bugs involve some background protocols and about a quarter involves a mix of foreground and background protocols.

Finding #2: Many DC bugs need *complex input preconditions*, such as faults (63% in Figure 3b), multiple protocols (80% in Figure 3f), and background protocols (81% in Figure 3g) .

3.3 Triggering Scope (TS)

We now analyze the triggering scope (TS), which is a complexity measure of DC-bug timing conditions. We use four metrics to measure the scope: message count (TS-MSG), node (TS-ND), protocol (TS-PR), and untimely event (TS-UEv) counts as shown in Figure 3h-k. This statistic is important with respect to the scalability of model checking, bug detection and failure diagnostic tools (§8.2-8.5).

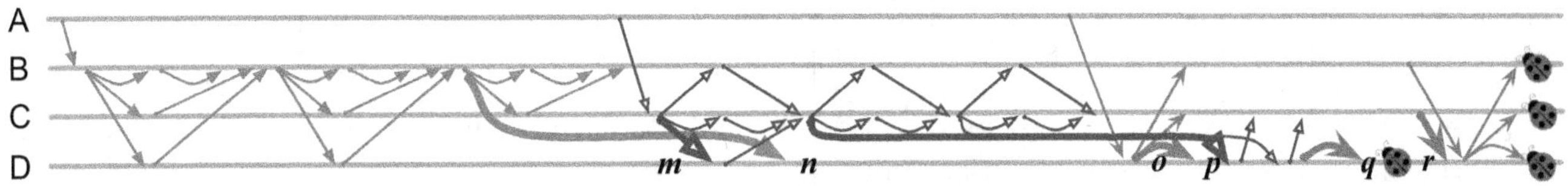

Figure 4. A Cassandra's Paxos bug. *In c6023, three key-value updates (different arrow types) concurrently execute the Paxos protocol on four nodes (we simplify from the actual six nodes). The bug requires three message-message race conditions: (1)* m *arrives before* n*, (2)* o *before* p*, and (3)* q *before* r*, which collectively makes D corrupt the data and propagate the corruption to all replicas after the last broadcast. Note that the bug would not surface if any of the conditions did not happen. It took us one full day to study this bug.*

Message count implies the minimum number of messages involved in E as defined in the beginning of section 3. Figure 3h (TS-MSG) shows that one or two triggering messages are the most common, with 7 messages as the maximum. Informally, zero implies fault timing bugs without any message-related races, one implies message-compute race, two implies message-message as in Figure 1a, and three implies a scenario such as *ac*/(*ab*-*bc*) race where *ab* and *ac* are concurrent or non-blocking message sending operations.

The node and protocol scopes present how many nodes and protocols are involved within the message scope. Figure 3i-j (TS-ND and TS-PR) shows that the scale of node and protocol triggering scope is also small, mostly two or three nodes and one or two protocols.

The untimely events count implies the total number of order violations, atomicity violations, untimely faults and reboots in the triggering timing condition of a bug. Figure 3k (TS-UEv) shows that only eight bugs require more than one untimely events. Four of them are message-fault bugs, each requiring one untimely message and one untimely fault to trigger (*e.g.*, step 4 and 8 in Figure 2). Three are fault-reboot timing bugs, each requiring one untimely fault and one untimely reboot. The last one is c6023, shown in Figure 4, requiring three message-message order violations to happen.

Finding #3: The *timing conditions* of most DC bugs only involve *one to three* messages, nodes, and protocols (>90% in Figure 3h-j). Most DC bugs are mostly triggered by only *one* untimely event (92% in Figure 3k).

4. Errors and Failures

"... we [prefer] debugging crashes instead of hard-to-track hanging jobs." — m3634

4.1 Error Symptoms

From the triggering conditions, we then scrutinize the *first* error that happens immediately after. First errors are the pivotal point that bridges the triggering and error-propagation process. Identifying first errors help failure diagnosis get closer to disclosing bug triggering and root causes and help bug detection get closer to accurately predict failures (§8).

	Local Errors				Global Errors		
	Mem	Sem	Hang	Sil	Wrong	Miss	Sil
CA	2	0	0	4	3	3	7
HB	1	2	1	2	15	3	6
MR	2	13	7	4	14	4	0
ZK	0	6	2	5	1	0	5
All	5	21	10	15	33	10	18

Table 3. First error symptoms of DC bugs (§4.1). *Some bugs cause multiple concurrent first errors.*

We categorize first errors into *local* errors and *global* errors, based on whether they can be observed from the triggering node N_T alone. Here, N_T is the node where triggering ends. It is the receiver node of untimely messages (*e.g.*, node C in Figure 1a) or the node with untimely fault (*e.g.*, node A in Figure 1i). For each error, we also check whether it is an *explicit* or *silent* error. Table 3 and Figure 3l (ERR) show the per-system and overall breakdowns respectively. Some MapReduce bugs caused multiple concurrent first errors of different types.

First, DC bugs can manifest into both local explicit errors and local silent errors. The former includes *memory exceptions* such as null-pointer exceptions (5% in Table 3) and *semantic errors* such as wrong state-machine transition exceptions thrown by the software (19%). Local silent errors include *hangs*, such as forever waiting for certain states to change or certain messages to arrive which are typically observed implicitly by users (9%), and *local silent* state corruption, such as half-cleaned temporary files (13%).

When local error is non-obvious in N_T, we analyze if the error is observable in other nodes communicating with N_T. Many DC bugs manifest into explicit global errors through *wrong messages* (29% in Table 3). Specifically, the communicating node receives an incorrect message from N_T, and throws an exception during the message handling. However, a few DC bugs still lead to silent global errors. These include *missing messages*, where N_T never sends a reply that the communicating node is waiting for in the absence of timeout (9%), and *global silent* state corruption such as replica inconsistencies between N_T and the other nodes (16%).

Finding #4: *Local* and *global* first errors are about equally common; 46% vs. 54% in Figure 3m (ER-L/G). About half of the DC bugs generate *explicit* first errors (53%), including local exceptions and global wrong messages, and the remaining DC bugs lead to *silent* errors (47%), as shown in Figure 3n (ER-E/S). Some of them immediately lead to hangs in the triggering node N_T (9%) or a node communicating with N_T (9%).

4.2 Failure Symptoms

Figure 3o (FAIL) shows that errors from DC bugs will eventually lead to a wide range of fatal failures including node downtimes (17%), data loss/corruption/inconsistencies (28%), operation failures (47%), and performance degradation (8%). A node downtime happens when the node either crashes or hangs (*i.e.*, it may still be heartbeating). It happens to both master/leader nodes and worker/follower nodes in our study. Data-related failures and performance problems are an artifact of incorrect state logic induced from DC bugs. For example, in HBase, concurrent region updates and log splittings can cause data loss. In Cassandra, some dead nodes are incorrectly listed as alive causing unnecessary data movement that degrades performance. Node downtimes and data-related failures could also cause some operations to fail. To avoid double counting, we consider a bug as causing operation failures only when it does not cause node downtimes or data-related failures.

5. Fixes

"We have already found and fix many cases ... however it seems exist many other cases." — *h6147*

We next analyze bug patches to understand developers' fix strategies. In general, we find that DC bugs can be fixed by either disabling the triggering timing or changing the system's handling to that timing (*fix timing* vs. *fix handling*). The former prevents concurrency with extra synchronization and the latter allows concurrency by handling untimely events properly. Since message timing bugs are fixed quite differently from fault timing bugs, we separate them below.

5.1 Message Timing Bug Fixes

The left half of Table 4 shows that only one fifth of message timing bugs are fixed by disabling the triggering timing, through either global or local synchronization. Only a couple of bugs are fixed through extra *global synchronization*, mainly due to its complexity and communication cost. For example, to prevent a triggering pattern $b+/ab$ in Figure 1f, m5465's fix *adds* a monitor on A_{RM} to wait for ba_{done} message from B_{AM} after B finishes with its local computation ($b+$); the result is $b+$-ba-ab global serialization. More often, the buggy timing is disabled through *local synchronization*, such as re-ordering message sending operations within a single node. For example, h5780's fix for ab/bc race in Figure

	Fix Timing		Fix Handling			
	Glob	Loc	Ret	Ign	Acc	Misc
CA	0	0	0	1	3	4
HB	2	7	2	1	7	3
MR	2	8	2	7	8	3
ZK	0	4	0	3	0	1
All	4	19	4	12	18	11

Table 4. Fix strategies for message timing bugs (§5.1). *Some bugs require more than one fix strategy.*

1c forces the sending of *bc* request at B to wait for the receipt of *ab*; the result is *ab-bc* local serialization at B.

The right half of Table 4 shows that fix handling is more popular. Fix handling fortunately can be simple; many fixes do *not* introduce brand-new computation logic into the system, which can be done in three ways. First, the fix can handle the untimely message by simply *retrying* it at a later time (as opposed to ignoring or accepting it incorrectly). For example, to handle bc/ac race in Figure 1a, m3274 retries the unexpectedly-early ac_{kill} message at a later time, right after the to-be-killed task starts. Second, the fix can simply *ignore* the message (as opposed to accepting it incorrectly). For example, to handle ab/ba race in Figure 1d, m5358 simply ignores the unexpectedly-late ba_{finish} message that arrives after A_{AM} sends an ab_{kill} message. Finally, the patch can simply *accept* the untimely message by *re-using* existing handlers (as opposed to ignoring it or throwing an error). For example, m2995's fix changes the node AM to accept an unexpectedly-early expiration message using an existing handler that was originally designed to accept the same message at a later state of AM. m5198's fix handles the atomicity violation by using an existing handler and simply cancels the atomicity violating local operation. The rest of the fix-handling cases require new computation logic to fix bugs.

5.2 Fault/Reboot Timing Bug Fixes

Table 5 summarizes fix strategies for fault/reboot timing bugs. Unlike message timing, only rare bugs can be fixed by controlling the triggering timing either globally or locally (*e.g.*, by controlling the timing of the fault recovery actions). A prime example is an HBase cluster-wide restart scenario (h3596). Here, as A shuts down earlier, B assumes responsibility of A's regions (via a region-takeover recovery protocol), but soon B shuts down as well with the regions still locked in ZooKeeper and the takeover cannot be resumed after restart. The patch simply adds a delay before a node starts region takeover so that it will likely get forced down before the takeover starts.

For the majority of fault timing bugs, their patches conduct two tasks: (1) detect the local/global state inconsistency caused by the fault and (2) repair/recover the inconsistency. The former is accomplished through timeouts, additional message exchanges, or others (omitted from Table 5).

	Fix Timing		Fix Handling			
	G	L	Detect		Recover	
			TO	Msg	Canc	Misc
CA	1	0	3	2	4	6
HB	0	1	3	1	6	1
MR	2	1	1	1	2	1
ZK	0	3	0	1	1	7
All	3	5	7	5	13	15

Table 5. Fix strategies for fault/reboot timing bugs (§5.2). *Some bugs require more than one fix strategy.*

The latter can be achieved by simply canceling operations or adding new computation logic.

Finding #5: A *small number of fix strategies* have fixed most DC bugs. A few DC bugs are fixed by *disabling* the triggering timing (30% in Figure 3p), occasionally through extra messages and mostly through local operation re-orderings. Most DC bugs are fixed by better handling the triggering timing, most of which do not introduce new computation logic — they *ignore* or *delay* messages, *re-use* existing handlers, and *cancel* computation (40%).

6. Root Causes

"This has become quite messy, we didn't foresee some of this during design, sigh." — m4819

It is difficult to know for sure why many DC-bug triggering conditions were not anticipated by the developers (*i.e.*, the root causes). In this section, we postulate some possible and common misbeliefs behind DC bugs.

"One hop is faster than two hop." Some bugs manifest under scenario *bc*/(*ba-ac*), similar to Figure 1a. Developers may assume that *bc* (one hop) should arrive earlier than *ba-ac* (two hops), but *ac* can arrive earlier and hit a DC bug.

"No hop is faster than one hop." Some bugs manifest under scenario *ba*-(*b*+/*ab*), similar to Figure 1f. Developers may incorrectly expect *b*+ (local computation with no hop) to always finish before *ab* arrives (one hop).

"Atomic blocks cannot be broken." Developers might believe that "atomic" blocks (local or global transactions) can only be broken unintentionally by some faults such as crashes. However, we see a few cases where atomic blocks are broken inadvertently by the system itself, specifically via untimely arrival of kill/preemption messages in the middle of an atomic block. More often, the system does not record this interruption and thus unconsciously leaves state changes half way. Contrary, in fault-induced interruption, some fault recovery protocol typically will handle it.

"Interactions between multiple protocols seem to be safe." In common cases, multiple protocols rarely interact, and even when they do, non-deterministic DC bugs might not surface. This can be unwittingly treated as normally safe, but does not mean completely safe.

"Enough states are maintained." Untimely events can unexpectedly corrupt system states and when this happens the system does not have enough information to recollect what had happened in the past, as not all event history is logged. We observe that some fixes add new in-memory/on-disk state variables to handle untimely message and fault timings.

Finding #6: Many DC bugs are related with a few common misconceptions that are unique to distributed systems.

7. Other Statistics

"Great catch, Sid! Apologies for missing the race condition." — m4099

We now present other quantitative findings not included in previous discussions. We attempted to measure the complexity of DC bugs using four metrics: (a) the number of "re-enumerated steps" as informally defined in §2.4, (b) the patch LOC including new test suites for the corresponding bug, (c) the time to resolve (TTR), and (d) the number of discussion comments between the bug submitter and developers. The 25th percentile, median, and 75th percentile for the four metrics are (a) 7, 9, and 11 steps, (b) 44, 172, and 776 LOC, (c) 4, 14, and 48 days to resolve, (d) 12, 18, and 33 comments.

In terms of where the bugs were found, Figure 3r (WHR) highlights that 46% were found in deployment and 10% from failed unit tests. The rest, 44%, are not defined (could be manually found or from deployment). Some DC bugs were reported from large-scale deployments such as executions of thousands of tasks on hundreds of machines.

Due to space constraints, we do not provide cross-cutting analyses (*e.g.*, how many bugs have >2 protocols and >2 crashes with patch >100 LOC and were found in deployment). However, future TaxDC users can easily do so with all the rich statistics stored in TaxDC database.

8. Lessons Learned

"This issue, and the other related issues ... makes me very nervous about all the state combinations distributed between [ZooKeeper and many HBase components]. After this is done, do you think we can come up with a simpler design? I do not have any particular idea, so just spitballing here." — h6060

We now discuss the lessons learned, implications to existing tools and the opportunities for new research in combating DC bugs. Although many high-level directions can be adopted from work on LC bugs, there are many interesting challenges and opportunities unique to DC bugs.

8.1 Fault Paths and Multi-Protocol Interactions

Individual protocols tend to be robust in general. Only 18 DC bugs occur in *individual* protocols *without* any input fault condition; only 8 of them are in foreground protocols. On the other hand, a large majority of DC bugs happen due to concurrent executions of multiple protocols and/or different fault timings (Finding **#2**). This has a tremendous implication to input testing: *all types of verification, testing, and analysis approaches must consider fault injections and multiple protocols as input conditions.* Although recent work has paid attention to this [24, 35, 67], we emphasize that all forms of faults (§2.6) must be exercised.

8.2 Distributed Systems Model Checkers

Assuming the necessary input conditions are exercised, the next question is: can we test different event re-orderings to hit the triggering timing (§3.1)? This is the job of distributed system model checkers (dmck), which are gaining popularity recently [26, 37, 38, 59, 65]. Dmck works by intercepting distributed events and permuting their ordering. The more events included, the more scalability issues will arise due to state-space explosion. To date, *no dmck completely controls the timings of all necessary events* that might contribute to the triggering timing (Finding **#1**). MaceMC [37] only re-orders messages and network disconnections. MoDist [26] exercises timeouts and Demeter [26] intercepts messages and local computation but they do not explore different timing of multiple crashes and reboots. SAMC [38] exercises multiple faults but does not support timeout and thread controls. Also, none of the above include storage faults or timing issues [27]. Therefore, continued research on scalable exploration algorithms is needed, specifically when *all* the necessary events need to be controlled. This could be helped by DC bugs' triggering scope characteristics (Finding **#3**), just like that in LC model checkers [48].

8.3 Domain-Specific Specifications

Now, assuming the necessary events are controlled, the next question is: do we have the specification to judge the manifestation of a bug? This is a plague for many tools. For example, Demeter does not find new bugs [26] and SAMC [38] finds two new bugs. Conversations with the authors suggest that their target systems do not deploy detailed specifications, and thus some bugs are left uncaught. Deploying generic "textbook" specifications (*e.g.*, "only one leader exists") does not help as they could lead to false positives (*e.g.*, ZooKeeper allows two leaders at a single point in time). Many research papers on specifications only deploy few of them [24, 42, 55]. Developers also bemoan the hard-to-debug fail-silent problems m3634 and prefer to see easier-to-debug fail-stop bugs.

On the positive side, 53% of DC bugs lead to explicit first errors (Finding **#4**), implying that sanity checks already in software can be harnessed as specifications (more in §8.4). On the other side, compared to single-machine systems, distributed systems are much more capable of masking errors. Therefore, these error specifications have to be used with caution to avoid false positives. Furthermore, 47% of DC bugs lead to silent first errors (Finding **#4**). Many of them proceed to "silent failures", such as data loss, node hangs, etc. Even if they become explicit errors later, these explicit errors could be far away from the initial triggering conditions (*e.g.*, Figure 4). In short, *no matter how sophisticated the tools are, they are ineffective without accurate specifications.* This motivates the creation or inference of local specifications that can show early errors or symptoms of DC bugs.

8.4 Bug Detection Tools

We now discuss bug detection tools, which are unfortunately rare for DC bugs, although very popular for LC bugs [8, 20, 30, 46, 48, 56]. Bug detection tools look for bugs that match specific patterns. They cannot provide bug-free proof, but can be efficient in discovering bugs when guided by the right patterns. Our study provides guidance and patterns that can be exploited by future DC bug detection.

Generic detection framework. Finding **#1** implies that detecting DC bugs, particularly message-timing DC bugs, should focus on two key tasks: (1) obtaining timing specifications, including order and atomicity specifications among messages and computation; and (2) detecting violations to these specifications through dynamic or static analysis.

Invariant-guided detection. Likely program invariants can be learned from program behaviors, and used as specifications in bug detection [18, 19, 46]. The key challenge is to design simple and suitable invariant templates. For example, "function F_1 should always follow F_2" is a useful template for API-related semantic bugs [18]; "the atomicity of accesses a_1 and a_2 should never be violated" is effective for LC bugs [46]. Finding **#1** about triggering timing and Finding **#4** about error patterns provide empirical evidence that these templates can be effective for DC bugs: "message bc should arrive at C before message ac (ca) arrives (leaves)"; "message ab should never arrive in the middle of event e on node B"; and "message ab should always be replied".

Misconception-guided bug detection. Knowing programmers' misconceptions can help bug detectors focus on specifications likely to be violated. LC bug researchers have leveraged misconceptions such as *"two near-by reads of the same variable should return the same value"* [46] and *"a condition checked to be true should remain true when used"* [53]. Finding **#6** reveals that DC-unique common misconceptions, such as *"a single hop is faster than double hops"*, *"local computation is faster than one-hop message"*, *"atomic blocks cannot be broken"* can help DC bug detection.

Error-guided bug detection. Finding **#4** shows that many DC bugs lead to explicit local/global errors, which implies that timing specifications for many DC bugs can be inferred backward based on explicit errors. For example, program analysis may reveal that a state-machine exception e will arise whenever C receives message ac before bc, which provides a timing specification (ac arrives before bc) whose violation leads to a *local error*; or, the analysis may reveal that exception e arises whenever node B receives a message cb from node C and C only sends cb when ac arrives at C before bc, which provides a timing specification whose violation leads to a *wrong-message global error*; and so on.

Software testing. Testing takes a quarter of all software development resources, and is crucial in exposing bugs before code release. Although many testing techniques have been proposed for LC bugs [9, 51, 57], there have been few for DC bugs [58]. Finding **#2** implies that test input design has to consider faults, concurrent protocols, and background protocols. Finding **#3** implies that *pairwise testing*, which targets every pair of message ordering, every pair of protocol interaction, and so on, will work much more effectively than *all combination testing*, which exercises all possible total orders and interactions of all messages and all protocols. For example, a large number of DC bugs (Figure 3d-f) can be found with inputs of at most two protocols, crashes and reboots.

8.5 Failure Diagnosis

Given failure symptoms, distributed systems developers have to reason about many nodes to figure out the triggering and root cause of a failure. Our study provides guidance to this challenging process of failure diagnosis.

Slicing/dependence analysis. Identifying which instructions can affect the outcome of an instruction i is a widely used debugging technique for deterministic sequential bugs. However, it cannot scale to the whole distributed systems, and hence is rarely used. Finding **#3** indicates that most DC bugs have deterministic error propagation; Finding **#4** shows that many DC bugs have their errors propagate through missing or wrong messages. Therefore, per-node dependence analysis that can quickly identify whether the generation of a local error depends on any incoming messages would help DC bug failure diagnosis to get closer and closer to where the triggering events happen.

Error logging. Error logging is crucial in failure diagnosis. If the first error of a DC bug is an explicit local error, the error log can help developers quickly identify the triggering node and focus their diagnosis on one node. Finding **#4** unfortunately shows that only 23% of DC bugs lead to explicit local errors. This finding motivates future tool to help make more DC bugs lead to explicit local errors.

Statistical debugging. Comparing success-run traces with failure-run traces can help identify failure predictors for semantic bugs [40] and concurrency bugs [33] in single-machine software. The key design question is what type of program properties should be compared between failure and success runs. For example, branch outcomes are compared for diagnosing semantic bugs but not for LC bugs. Finding **#1** and **#3** about triggering timing conditions provide guidance for applying this approach for DC bugs. We can collect all message sending/arrival time at runtime, and then find rare event orderings that lead to failures by contrasting them with common "healthy" orderings (*e.g.*, Figure 1b happens 99.99% of the time while Figure 1a happens 0.01% of the time). Of course, there are challenges. Finding **#2** and **#3** show that many DC bugs come from the interactions of many protocols. Thus, it is not sufficient to only log a chain of messages originated from the same request, a common practice in request logging [13]. Furthermore, some DC bugs are triggered by message-computation ordering. Therefore, logging messages alone is not sufficient.

Record and Replay. Debugging LC concurrency bugs with record and deterministic replay is a popular approach [52, 61]. However, such an approach has not permeated practices in distributed systems debugging. A ZooKeeper developer pointed us to a fresh DC bug that causes a whole-cluster outage but has not been fixed for months because the deployment logs do not record enough information to replay the bug (z2172). There has been 9 back-and-forth log changes and attachments with 72 discussion comments between the bug submitter and the developers. More studies are needed to understand the gap between record-replay challenges in practice and the current state of the art [23, 43].

8.6 Failure Prevention and Fixing

Runtime Prevention. The manifestation of concurrency bugs can sometimes be prevented by injecting delays at runtime. This technique has been successfully deployed to prevent LC bugs based on their timing conditions [36, 47, 68]. Finding **#1** shows that many DC bugs are triggered by untimely messages and hence can potentially be prevented this way. For example, none of the bugs shown in Figure 1a–h would happen if we delay a message arrival/sending or local computation. Of course, different from LC bugs, some of these delays have to rely on a network interposition layer; similar with LC bugs, some delays may lead to hangs, and hence cannot be adopted.

Bug Fixing. Recent work automatically fixes LC bugs by inserting lock/unlock or signal/wait to prohibit buggy timing [34, 41, 62]. Finding **#5** shows that the same philosophy is promising for 30% of studied DC bugs. Our study shows that this approach has to be tweaked to focus on using global messages (*e.g.*, ACKs) or local operation re-ordering, instead of lock or signal, to fix DC bugs. Finding **#5** indicates that 40% of those DC bugs are fixed by shifting message handlers, ignoring messages, and canceling computa-

h9095: (1) RS successfully OPENED region R, (2) RS notifies ZK that region R is OPENED, (3) ZK continues region R state msg to Master, (4) Master starts processing OPENED msg, (5) Meanwhile RS CLOSED region R (asked by Client), (6) RS notifies ZK that region R is CLOSED, (7) Master asks ZK to delete znode for region R, *concurrently racing with step 6!*, (8) ZK deletes region R's znode, (9) Master never assigns region R to any RS. *R becomes an orphan!*

Figure 5. Race of HBase's messages to ZooKeeper.

tion, without adding new computation logic. This presents a unique opportunity for developing new and more aggressive fixing techniques.

8.7 Distributed Transactions

In the middle of our study, we ask ourselves: if DC bugs can be theoretically solved by distributed transactions, why doesn't such technique eliminate DC bugs in practice? Our answers are: first, the *actual implementations of theoretically-proven distributed transactions are not always correct* (as also alluded in other work [10, 49]). For example, new DC bugs continue to surface in complex distributed transactions such as ZooKeeper's ZAB and Cassandra's Paxos as they are continuously modified. Second, *distributed transactions are only a subset of a full complete system.* A prime example is the use of ZooKeeper in HBase for coordinating and sharing states between HBase masters and region servers. Although ZooKeeper provides linearization of updates, HBase must handle its concurrent operations to ZooKeeper, for example, step 6 and 7 in Figure 5; there are many other similar examples.Put simply, there are many protocols that do not use distributed transactions, instead they use domain-specific finite state machines, which should be tested more heavily.

Another approach to eliminate non-deterministic bugs in distributed protocols is by building deterministic distributed systems. However, the technique is still in its infancy, at least in terms of the impact to performance (*e.g.*, an order of magnitude of overhead [31]).

8.8 Verifiable Frameworks

Recently there is a growing work on new programming language frameworks for building verifiable distributed systems [16, 28, 63], but they typically focus on the main protocols and not the full system including the background protocols. One major challenge is that just for the basic read and write protocols, the length of the proofs can reach thousands of lines of code, potentially larger than the protocol implementation. Unfortunately, our study shows that the complex interaction between foreground and background protocols can lead to DC bugs. Therefore, for complete real-world systems, verification of the entire set of the protocols is needed.

8.9 LC bugs vs. DC bugs

There are clearly similarities between LC bugs and DC bugs, as, by definition, they are both timing-related non-deterministic bugs. Many DC bugs contain LC components: untimely messages may lead to unsynchronized accesses from multiple threads or multiple event-handlers [30, 54] in a single machine. It is probably not a surprise that atomicity violations and order violations are two dominant triggering timing conditions for both LC and DC bugs (Finding **#1**). Our observation of the small triggering scope of most DC bugs (Finding **#3**) is similar with that for LC bugs, which may be related to the nature of the bug sets — more complicated bugs may be more difficult to fix, and hence less likely to be included in empirical studies.

There are also many differences between LC bugs and DC bugs, as they originate from different programming paradigms and execution environments. For example, order violations are much more common in DC bugs than those in LC bugs (Finding **#1**); faults and reboots are much more common in DC bugs than those in LC bugs (Finding **#2**); the diagnosis of many DC bugs will have to reason beyond one node, clearly different from that of LC bugs (Finding **#4**); the fix strategies for DC bugs are very different from those of LC bugs, because enforcing global synchronization is difficult (Finding **#5**).

9. Conclude

DC Bugs impact the reliability, availability, and performance of real-world distributed systems. Even with all the redundancy and fault-recovery mechanisms deployed in today's systems, DC bugs make the software as the single point of failure. Combating DC bugs will have a profound impact to future software systems as more organizations are building more distributed system layers on farms of machines and services in this era of cloud computing. The gap between the theory and practice of distributed systems reliability should continue to be narrowed. We hope our work will commence more interdisciplinary actions from diverse researchers and practitioners in the areas of concurrency, fault tolerance and distributed systems to combat DC bugs together.

10. Acknowledgments

We thank the anonymous reviewers for their tremendous feedback and comments. We also would like to thank Chen Tian of Huawei and Yohanes Surya and Nina Sugiarti of Surya University for their continuing supports. This material is based upon work supported by the NSF (grant Nos. CCF-1336580, CNS-1350499, CCF-1439091, CNS-1514256, IIS-1546543) and generous supports from Huawei and Alfred P. Sloan Foundation. Any opinions, findings, and conclusions, or recommendations expressed herein are those of the authors and do not necessarily reflect the views of the NSF or other institutions.

References

[1] `http://www.freepastry.org/`.

[2] `http://ucare.cs.uchicago.edu/projects/cbs/`.

[3] Apache Cassandra. `http://cassandra.apache.org`.

[4] Apache Hadoop. `http://hadoop.apache.org`.

[5] Apache Hadoop NextGen MapReduce (YARN). `https://hadoop.apache.org/docs/current/hadoop-yarn/hadoop-yarn-site/YARN.html`.

[6] Apache HBase. `http://hbase.apache.org`.

[7] Apache ZooKeeper. `http://zookeeper.apache.org`.

[8] Michael D. Bond, Katherine E. Coons, and Kathryn S. McKinley. PACER: Proportional Detection of Data Races. In *PLDI*, 2010.

[9] Sebastian Burckhardt, Pravesh Kothari, Madanlal Musuvathi, and Santosh Nagarakatte. A Randomized Scheduler with Probabilistic Guarantees of Finding Bugs. In *ASPLOS*, 2010.

[10] Mike Burrows. The Chubby lock service for loosely-coupled distributed systems. In *OSDI '06*.

[11] Fay Chang, Jeffrey Dean, Sanjay Ghemawat, Wilson C. Hsieh, Deborah A. Wallach, Michael Burrows, Tushar Chandra, Andrew Fikes, and Robert Gruber. Bigtable: A Distributed Storage System for Structured Data. In *OSDI '06*.

[12] Andy Chou, Junfeng Yang, Benjamin Chelf, Seth Hallem, and Dawson Engler. An Empirical Study of Operating System Errors. In *SOSP '01*.

[13] Michael Chow, David Meisner, Jason Flinn, Daniel Peek, and Thomas F. Wenisch. The Mystery Machine: End-to-end performance analysis of large-scale Internet services. In *OSDI '14*.

[14] Jeffrey Dean and Sanjay Ghemawat. MapReduce: Simplified Data Processing on Large Clusters. In *OSDI '04*.

[15] Giuseppe DeCandia, Deniz Hastorun, Madan Jampani, Gunavardhan Kakulapati, Avinash Lakshman, Alex Pilchin, Swaminathan Sivasubramanian, Peter Vosshall, and Werner Vogels. Dynamo: Amazon's Highly Available Key-value Store. In *SOSP '07*.

[16] Ankush Desai, Vivek Gupta, Ethan Jackson, Shaz Qadeer, Sriram Rajamani, and Damien Zufferey. P: Safe Asynchronous Event-Driven Programming. In *PLDI '13*.

[17] Thanh Do, Mingzhe Hao, Tanakorn Leesatapornwongsa, Tiratat Patana-anake, and Haryadi S. Gunawi. Limplock: Understanding the Impact of Limpware on Scale-Out Cloud Systems. In *SoCC '13*.

[18] Dawson Engler, David Yu Chen, Seth Hallem, Andy Chou, and Benjamin Chelf. Bugs as Deviant Behavior: A General Approach to Inferring Errors in Systems Code. In *SOSP*, 2001.

[19] Michael D. Ernst, Adam Czeisler, William G. Griswold, and David Notkin. Quickly Detecting Relevant Program Invariants. In *ICSE*, 2000.

[20] Cormac Flanagan and Stephen N. Freund. FastTrack: Efficient and Precise Dynamic Race Detection. In *PLDI*, 2009.

[21] Pedro Fonseca, Cheng Li, Vishal Singhal, and Rodrigo Rodrigues. A Study of the Internal and External Effects of Concurrency Bugs. In *DSN*, 2010.

[22] Dennis Geels, Gautam Altekar, Petros Maniatis, Timothy Roscoe, and Ion Stoica. Friday: Global Comprehension for Distributed Replay. In *NSDI '07*.

[23] Dennis Geels, Gautam Altekar, Scott Shenker, and Ion Stoica. Replay Debugging for Distributed Applications. In *USENIX ATC '06*.

[24] Haryadi S. Gunawi, Thanh Do, Pallavi Joshi, Peter Alvaro, Joseph M. Hellerstein, Andrea C. Arpaci-Dusseau, Remzi H. Arpaci-Dusseau, Koushik Sen, and Dhruba Borthakur. FATE and DESTINI: A Framework for Cloud Recovery Testing. In *NSDI '11*.

[25] Haryadi S. Gunawi, Mingzhe Hao, Tanakorn Leesatapornwongsa, Tiratat Patana-anake, Thanh Do, Jeffry Adityatama, Kurnia J. Eliazar, Agung Laksono, Jeffrey F. Lukman, Vincentius Martin, and Anang D. Satria. What Bugs Live in the Cloud? A Study of 3000+ Issues in Cloud Systems. In *SoCC '14*.

[26] Huayang Guo, Ming Wu, Lidong Zhou, Gang Hu, Junfeng Yang, and Lintao Zhang. Practical Software Model Checking via Dynamic Interface Reduction. In *SOSP '11*.

[27] Mingzhe Hao, Gokul Soundararajan, Deepak Kenchammana-Hosekote, Andrew A. Chien, and Haryadi S. Gunawi. The Tail at Store: A Revelation from Millions of Hours of Disk and SSD Deployments. In *FAST '16*.

[28] Chris Hawblitzel, Jon Howell, Manos Kapritsos, Jacob R. Lorch, Bryan Parno, Michael L. Roberts, Srinath Setty, and Brian Zill. IronFleet: Proving Practical Distributed Systems Correct. In *SOSP '15*.

[29] Benjamin Hindman, Andy Konwinski, Matei Zaharia, Ali Ghodsi, Anthony D. Joseph, Randy Katz, Scott Shenker, and Ion Stoica. Mesos: A Platform for Fine-Grained Resource Sharing in the Data Center. In *NSDI '11*.

[30] Chun-Hung Hsiao, Cristiano L. Pereira, Jie Yu, Gilles A. Pokam, Satish Narayanasamy, Peter M. Chen, Ziyun Kong, and Jason Flinn. Race Detection for Event-Driven Mobile Applications. In *PLDI*, 2014.

[31] Nicholas Hunt, Tom Bergan, Luis Ceze, and Steven D. Gribble. DDOS: Taming Nondeterminism in Distributed Systems. In *ASPLOS '13*.

[32] Nicholas Jalbert, Cristiano Pereira, Gilles Pokam, and Koushik Sen. RADBench: A Concurrency Bug Benchmark Suite. In *HotPar*, 2011.

[33] Guoliang Jin, Aditya Thakur, Ben Liblit, and Shan Lu. Instrumentation and Sampling Strategies for Cooperative Concurrency Bug Isolation. In *OOPSLA*, 2010.

[34] Guoliang Jin, Wei Zhang, Dongdong Deng, Ben Liblit, and Shan Lu. Automated Concurrency-Bug Fixing. In *OSDI*, 2012.

[35] Pallavi Joshi, Haryadi S. Gunawi, and Koushik Sen. PREFAIL: A Programmable Tool for Multiple-Failure Injection. In *OOPSLA '11*.

[36] Horatiu Jula, Daniel Tralamazza, Cristian Zamfir, and George Candea. Deadlock Immunity: Enabling Systems To Defend Against Deadlocks. In *OSDI*, 2008.

[37] Charles Killian, James W. Anderson, Ranjit Jhala, and Amin Vahdat. Life, Death, and the Critical Transition: Finding Liveness Bugs in Systems Code. In *NSDI '07*.

[38] Tanakorn Leesatapornwongsa, Mingzhe Hao, Pallavi Joshi, Jeffrey F. Lukman, and Haryadi S. Gunawi. SAMC: Semantic-Aware Model Checking for Fast Discovery of Deep Bugs in Cloud Systems. In *OSDI '14*.

[39] Sihan Li, Hucheng Zhou, Haoxiang Lin, Tian Xiao, Haibo Lin, Wei Lin, and Tao Xie. A Characteristic Study on Failures of Production Distributed Data-Parallel Programs. In *ICSE*, 2013.

[40] Ben Liblit, Alex Aiken, Alice X. Zheng, and Michael I. Jordan. Bug Isolation via Remote Program Sampling. In *PLDI*, 2003.

[41] Peng Liu, Omer Tripp, and Charles Zhang. Grail: Context-Aware Fixing of Concurrency Bugs. In *FSE*, 2014.

[42] Xuezheng Liu, Zhenyu Guo, Xi Wang, Feibo Chen, Xiaochen Lian, Jian Tang, Ming Wu, M. Frans Kaashoek, and Zheng Zhang. D3S: Debugging Deployed Distributed Systems. In *NSDI '08*.

[43] Xuezheng Liu, Wei Lin, Aimin Pan, and Zheng Zhang. WiDS Checker: Combating Bugs in Distributed Systems. In *NSDI '07*.

[44] Lanyue Lu, Andrea C. Arpaci-Dusseau, Remzi H. Arpaci-Dusseau, and Shan Lu. A Study of Linux File System Evolution. In *FAST '13*.

[45] Shan Lu, Soyeon Park, Eunsoo Seo, and Yuanyuan Zhou. Learning from Mistakes — A Comprehensive Study on Real World Concurrency Bug Characteristics. In *ASPLOS '08*.

[46] Shan Lu, Joseph Tucek, Feng Qin, and Yuanyuan Zhou. AVIO: Detecting Atomicity Violations via Access Interleaving Invariants. In *ASPLOS*, 2006.

[47] Brandon Lucia and Luis Ceze. Cooperative Empirical Failure Avoidance for Multithreaded Programs. In *ASPLOS*, 2013.

[48] Madanlal Musuvathi and Shaz Qadeer. Iterative Context Bounding for Systematic Testing of Multithreaded Programs. In *PLDI*, 2007.

[49] Diego Ongaro and John Ousterhout. In Search of an Understandable Consensus Algorithm. In *USENIX ATC '14*.

[50] Nicolas Palix, Gaël Thomas, Suman Saha, Christophe Calvès, Julia Lawall, and Gilles Muller. Faults in Linux: Ten Years Later. In *ASPLOS*, 2011.

[51] Soyeon Park, Shan Lu, and Yuanyuan Zhou. CTrigger: Exposing Atomicity Violation Bugs from Their Finding Places. In *ASPLOS*, 2009.

[52] Gilles Pokam, Klaus Danne, Cristiano Pereira, Rolf Kassa, Tim Kranich, Shiliang Hu, Justin Gottschlich, Nima Honarmand, Nathan Dautenhahn, Samuel T. King, and Josep Torrellas. QuickRec: Prototyping an Intel Architecture Extension for Record and Replay of Multithreaded Programs. In *ISCA*, 2013.

[53] Shanxiang Qi, Abdullah A. Muzahid, Wonsun Ahn, and Josep Torrellas. Dynamically Detecting and Tolerating IF-Condition Data Races. In *HPCA*, 2014.

[54] Veselin Raychev, Martin T. Vechev, and Manu Sridharan. Effective race detection for event-driven programs. In *OOPSLA*, 2013.

[55] Patrick Reynolds, Charles Killian, Janet L. Wiener, Jeffrey C. Mogul, Mehul A. Shah, and Amin Vahdat. Pip: Detecting the Unexpected in Distributed Systems. In *NSDI '06*.

[56] Stefan Savage, Michael Burrows, Greg Nelson, Patrick Sobalvarro, and Thomas Anderson. Eraser: A Dynamic Data Race Detector for Multithreaded Programs. *ACM TOCS*, 1997.

[57] Koushik Sen. Race Directed Random Testing of Concurrent Programs. In *PLDI*, 2008.

[58] Koushik Sen and Gul Agha. Automated Systematic Testing of Open Distributed Programs. In *FSE*, 2006.

[59] Jiri Simsa, Randy Bryant, and Garth Gibson. dBug: Systematic Evaluation of Distributed Systems. In *SSV '10*.

[60] Ion Stoica, Robert Morris, David Karger, M. Frans Kaashoek, and Hari Balakrishnan. Chord: A Scalable Peer-to-peer Lookup Service for Internet Applications. In *SIGCOMM '01*.

[61] Kaushik Veeraraghavan, Dongyoon Lee, Benjamin Wester, Jessica Ouyang, Peter M. Chen, Jason Flinn, and Satish Narayanasamy. DoublePlay: Parallelizing Sequential Logging and Replay. In *ASPLOS*, 2011.

[62] Yin Wang, Terence Kelly, Manjunath Kudlur, Stephane Lafortune, and Scott Mahlke. Gadara: Dynamic Deadlock Avoidance for Multithreaded Programs. In *OSDI*, 2008.

[63] James R. Wilcox, Doug Woos, Pavel Panchekha, Zachary Tatlock, Xi Wang, Michael D. Ernst, and Thomas Anderson. Verdi: A Framework for Implementing and Formally Verifying Distributed System. In *PLDI*, 2015.

[64] Tian Xiao, Jiaxing Zhang, Hucheng Zhou, Zhenyu Guo, Sean McDirmid, Wei Lin, Wenguang Chen, and Lidong Zhou. Nondeterminism in MapReduce Considered Harmful? An Empirical Study on Non-commutative Aggregators in MapReduce Programs. In *ICSE '14*.

[65] Junfeng Yang, Tisheng Chen, Ming Wu, Zhilei Xu, Xuezheng Liu, Haoxiang Lin, Mao Yang, Fan Long, Lintao Zhang, and Lidong Zhou. MODIST: Transparent Model Checking of Unmodified Distributed Systems. In *NSDI '09*.

[66] Jie Yu. A collection of concurrency bugs. `https://github.com/jieyu/concurrency-bugs`.

[67] Ding Yuan, Yu Luo, Xin Zhuang, Guilherme Renna Rodrigues, Xu Zhao, Yongle Zhang, Pranay U. Jain, and Michael Stumm. Simple Testing Can Prevent Most Critical Failures: An Analysis of Production Failures in Distributed Data-Intensive Systems. In *OSDI '14*.

[68] Wei Zhang, Marc de Kruijf, Ang Li, Shan Lu, and Karthikeyan Sankaralingam. ConAir: Featherweight concurrency bug recovery via single-threaded idempotent execution. In *ASPLOS*, 2013.

RID: Finding Reference Count Bugs with Inconsistent Path Pair Checking

Junjie Mao Yu Chen Qixue Xiao Yuanchun Shi

Department of Computer Science and Technology, Tsinghua University

maojj12@mails.tsinghua.edu.cn, yuchen@mail.tsinghua.edu.cn, xqx12@mails.tsinghua.edu.cn, shiyc@tsinghua.edu.cn

Abstract

Reference counts are widely used in OS kernels for resource management. However, reference counts are not trivial to be used correctly in large scale programs because it is left to developers to make sure that an increment to a reference count is always paired with a decrement. This paper proposes inconsistent path pair checking, a novel technique that can statically discover bugs related to reference counts without knowing how reference counts should be changed in a function. A prototype called RID is implemented and evaluations show that RID can discover more than 80 bugs which were confirmed by the developers in the latest Linux kernel. The results also show that RID tends to reveal bugs caused by developers' misunderstanding on API specifications or error conditions that are not handled properly.

Categories and Subject Descriptors F.3.2 [*Logics and Meanings of Programs*]: Semantics of Programming Languages—Program analysis

Keywords reference counting; inconsistency; static analysis

1. Introduction

Reference counts (referred to as refcounts hereinafter) are widely used in operating system kernel subsystems, such as synchronization mechanisms [19], management of dynamically allocated memory blocks [18] and dynamic power management. Misuses of refcounts can thus lead to different phenomena including memory exhaustion, mutual exclusion failures, abnormally high power consumption and security vulnerabilities. For instance, memory leaks due to improper reference count handling in Linux kernel can lead to Denial of Service attacks [29]. Bugs related to wake locks, a refcount-based power management mechanism in Android, have been identified as a significant root cause of abnormal power consumption on smartphones [22]. Several vulnerabilities in Windows kernel have direct relations with refcount usages and can lead to revelation of all system files or execution of arbitrary code with administrative privileges [10].

In OS kernels, refcount mechanisms typically encapsulate an integer as a counter and provide only APIs for incrementing and decrementing the counter. Developers are then required to ensure by themselves that all refcounts are used as intended, which is not trivial in complex programs. A recent survey [27] shows that violations to developers' intention, also known as semantic bugs, have emerged as one of the dominant threats to systems even in relatively mature software including the Linux kernel.

In this paper, we propose *inconsistent path pair checking* to statically detect refcount bugs in OS kernels . An *inconsistent path pair* (abbreviated as IPP) is a pair of two paths that (1) are in the same function, (2) both start from the entry of the function and end at the exit, (3) have different changes to a refcount, and (4) are, at runtime, indistinguishable outside the function by checking arguments and the return value. The definition of IPP does not depend on the context in which the function is called. As a result, IPP checking is also applicable to part of an OS kernel like libraries and drivers. In addition, IPP checking needs no extra assumption on how refcounts should be used in a function. The only information needed is the refcount API specifications which is a common requirement in the existing work [4, 12, 13, 17].

We implement a static checker, called RID, based on inconsistent path pair checking, program abstraction and summary-based inter-procedural analysis. We evaluate RID against the Linux kernel, and the results show that RID is helpful in revealing developers' misunderstanding of kernel API specifications and detecting refcount bugs effectively.

Although we focus on the Linux kernel, we believe the idea of IPP is general and applicable to other programs. We have also applied RID to the Python/C programs in which 100+ bugs are found.

This paper makes the following key contributions:

ASPLOS '16 April 2–6, 2016, Atlanta, Georgia, USA.
Copyright © 2016 ACM 978-1-4503-4091-5/16/04. . . $15.00
DOI: http://dx.doi.org/10.1145/2872362.2872389

1. We propose inconsistent path pair checking, a novel technique for detecting refcount bugs with only the specifications of refcount APIs.
2. We present a summary-based inter-procedural analysis algorithm to detect inconsistent path pairs and implement a prototype which can analyze programs such as Linux kernel and Python/C programs.
3. We analyze the characteristics of bugs and false positives reported from RID by an evaluation against the Linux kernel and three Python/C programs. 83 new bugs are found in Linux kernel and confirmed by kernel developers. We also find an instance which shows an API can still be misused in many places in relatively mature software like Linux.

In the rest of this paper, Section 2 presents related work and discusses the novelty of our work. Section 3 introduces the characteristics of refcounts and describes inconsistent path pairs in more detail. Section 4 proposes our summary-based inter-procedural analysis on inconsistent path pairs, followed by Section 5 which presents the implementation details and limitations. An analysis on evaluation results are presented in Section 6. Section 7 concludes our work.

2. Related Work

2.1 Detecting Refcount Bugs

M. Emmi *et al.*have proposed Referee [4] which uses symbolic model checking to verify the absence of refcount bugs in closed programs where the complete control flow is known. Referee assumes that resources are arranged as an array and are managed independently. An unlimited number of threads have access to the resources. Referee further assumes that any thread manages any resource in exactly the same way (i.e. by the same piece of code). This assumption allows Referee to reduce the verification of all threads and resources to the verification of an arbitrary thread and an arbitrary resource, both of which are identified symbolically. RID, on the other hand, focuses on the analysis of programs in which refcounts are not necessarily independent or changed in the same way.

A. Lal and G. Ramalingam [12] propose a polynomial time algorithm to statically detect refcount bugs in closed programs with only shallow aliasing. They identify the entry function of the program (usually `main()`), initialize all refcounts to 0 at the entry point of the function, insert assertions at the exit claiming that all refcounts must be 0, and verify that the assertions are never violated. Their methodology cannot be applied to open programs either, because it is too strong to assume that all entry functions in open programs like libraries must leave all refcounts unchanged.

Cpychecker, proposed by D. Malcom [17], and Pungi, proposed by S. Li *et al.*[13], analyze refcount bugs in the native implementations of Python/C programs. They rely on the rule that, in any function, the change of a refcount must be equal to the number of references escaped from the function. A reference can escape by the return value of the function or by Python/C APIs that steal references [23]. Pungi adopts the idea of affine abstraction in [12] and analyzes on Static Single Assignment (SSA) form of the program. Note that wrappers to the basic refcount APIs, which is common in subsystems of Linux, are always considered as an error according to the rule above. Thus, to apply the above rule to Linux kernel, a comprehensive list of refcount API wrappers must be given and maintained along with the rapid evolution of the Linux kernel.

Compared to Pungi and Cpychecker, RID checks programs against a weaker property which does not rely on any assumption on how refcounts should be changed in a function. Theoretically any bug found by RID (using a weaker property) should be detectable by the methods of Pungi or Cpychecker (using a stronger property) if the same analysis techniques (e.g. SSA form) are adopted. However, using a weaker property allows RID not to generate false alarms which are raised by Pungi or Cpychecker when the assumption they adopt is too strict for a function, which is common due to the reason presented above. No false alarm suppression techniques is mentioned in Pungi. In Cpychecker, suppressing these false alarms must be done by manually adding GCC attributes to each of these functions. Meanwhile, stronger properties can be easily integrated into RID by introducing corresponding checks on function summaries introduced in Section 4.

2.2 Specification Inference

Specification inference is another category of techniques that can check programs without rules defined by developers. Engler *et al.*use belief analysis to extract API usage patterns [6] and implement checkers based on state machine abstraction [5, 9]. Specification mining [8, 14, 15, 30] is another category of techniques which adopt statistical analysis to infer API usage rules that are commonly followed by a sufficient number of occurrences in the code. Different thresholds are used to filter out less likely rules and the remaining are used for checking. Hector [25], on the other hand, infers the acquisition and release of a specific resource in a function instead of seeking for general usage patterns of resource management APIs.

S. Saha *et al.*have shown that a significant part of API usage rules are under the thresholds used in recent specification mining work and thus cannot be found by these tools [25]. Different from the work above, RID analyzes a program in a bottom-up manner. The behavior of a function is calculated from the function body, rather than from how the function is used. This allows RID to detect bugs involving APIs that are used occasionally or are commonly misused. Examples are presented in Section 6.

2.3 Inconsistency Checking

In literature, various kinds of inconsistencies have been defined and used in static analysis.

D. R. Engler *et al.*define inconsistencies as incompatible beliefs implied by multiple uses of a value [6]. I. Dillig *et al.*[3] further propose a formal description of inconsistent beliefs by considering inconsistency checking as a variance of type inference and show that inconsistency checking is a complement to standard semantic-based approaches such as source-sink analysis. A. Tomb *et al.*[28] detect pieces of program code that have incompatible beliefs but can execute in sequence by solving the reachability problem.

S. Lu *et al.*propose MUVI to infer the access correlations of multiple fields in a data structure [16]. An update to some of these fields is considered inconsistent if the correlated fields are not updated accordingly. The access correlations are inferred by the patterns how multiple data structure fields are accessed in the same function.

M. Gabel *et al.*detect inconsistencies among changes to duplicated code syntactically [7]. Textual similarity of clone code and syntactic filters to change operations are used to extract likely bugs from a large set of similar code fragment pairs.

M. Schäf *et al.*consider a code fragment inconsistent if *it is not part of any normally terminating execution* [26]. Examples include a infeasible path, where the conjunction of branch conditions is not satisfiable, and a branch never taken because the branch condition always evaluates to true at runtime. Instead of detecting new bugs, M. Schäf *et al.*use inconsistency checking for fault localization.

Different from existing work, RID adopts a different notion of consistency, i.e. different refcount changes that are made in two paths in the same function and are indistinguishable outside the function at runtime. With IPP detection, RID can reveal bugs that are challenging to find using inferred beliefs or common usage patterns (illustrated in section 3.4 by example), showing that IPP detection is complementary to existing inconsistency checking techniques.

3. Refcounts and Inconsistent Path Pairs

3.1 Characteristics of Refcounts

A *refcount* is an integer encapsulated in a structure and is used to track the number of references to the structure. Note that a *reference* can be defined in different ways. For example, a refcount of a dynamically allocated object tracks the number of pointers that point to this object in the system. A refcount of a device structure, on the other hand, may track the number of threads that are using the device.

From the analysis and statistics on over 270k functions in Linux kernel, we observe that the following characteristics are commonly followed by the refcount APIs.

1. A refcount is mostly incremented or decremented by 1 at a time.
2. The exact value of a refcount is seldom accessed. Especially, the exact value is hardly used in any branch condition.
3. From any system state, it is possible for the refcount to be decremented to 0.
4. The value of a refcount must always be a non-negative.

The characteristics above applies to over 800 sets of refcount APIs, consisting of more than 1600 functions in Linux kernel. These APIs are found by a syntactical search for functions with similar names except some common antonyms such as 'inc'-'dec' and 'get'-'put'. A similar approach is used to discover paired functions in [15]. 10987 out of 11755 (93.5%) files in Linux kernel release 3.17 have functions calling these APIs directly or indirectly. In this paper, we only consider refcounts used in the common way, i.e. refcounts are changed by 1 at a time and the exact value is not accessed.

We use the Power Management (PM) counts in Linux DPM subsystem to illustrate the characteristics above. The counts are not designed to be accessible outside DPM subsystem. When a thread (typically created or scheduled by a device driver) needs to carry out some operations on a device, it increments the count of the device by calling an API provided by DPM and decrements the count when the operations are completed. When the count reaches 0, the corresponding device is scheduled to be suspended to power-saving mode. Each time the count is incremented, the device is resumed if it is in power-saving mode. A PM count that can never reach 0 under certain system state indicates that the corresponding device will keep active forever, leading to abnormal power drainage. A PM count with a negative value indicates that it is possible for a thread to carry out device operations when the device is in power-saving mode, which can lead to unexpected results.

In this paper, we call any violation to characteristic 3 or 4 above as a *refcount bug*.

3.2 Inconsistent Path Pairs

Our key observation is that inconsistent path pairs often indicates violations to one of the two characteristics of refcounts. We illustrate the point by the example function `foo()` in Figure 1(a). The function `foo()` determines if the device is usable by checking the value of register located at 0x54 (the register is accessible even the device is suspended). The PM count of the device is incremented and more device operations are carried out if the register contains a positive.

Figure 1(b) shows the CFG (control flow graph) of `foo()` with each vertex representing a statement. The two paths in `foo()`, i.e. p_1 and p_2, are shown with different gray scale in the CFG. Note that the PM count of `dev` is incremented in p_1 but not in p_2. Furthermore, the only difference between p_1 and p_2 besides the change to PM count of `dev` is that p_1 carries out some device operations (line 8) while p_2 does not.

```
1  int reg_read(device *d, int reg);
2  void inc_pmcount(device *d);
3
4  int foo(device *dev) {
5    assert(dev != NULL);
6    int v = reg_read(dev, 0x54);
7    if (v <= 0)
8      goto exit;
9    inc_pmcount(dev);
10   // more register reads/writes
11 exit:
12   return 0;
13 }
```
(a)

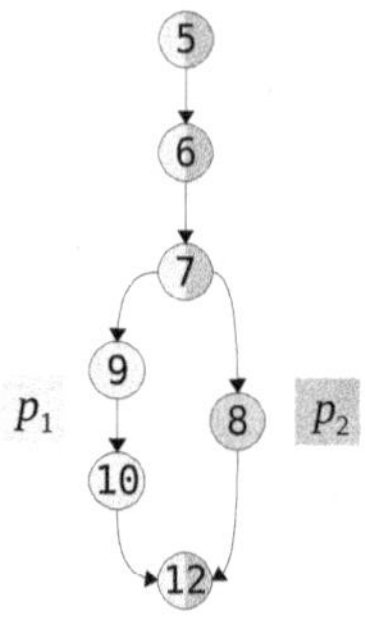

(b)

Figure 1: (a) an example program for illustration, and (b) the control flow graph of the example program with each statement as a vertex. The exception path handling assertion failure is ignored for brevity. The numbers in vertices are the line numbers of the statement the vertices represent. (p_1, p_2) is an inconsistent path pair.

As the exact value of the PM count is not accessible, a caller to foo() can hardly tell which of the two paths is executed at runtime. Especially, given the same structure representing a device, both the paths are feasible and return 0. As a result, it is not possible to determine outside foo() which path is executed by checking the return value at runtime. We call the path pair (p_1, p_2) an *inconsistent path pair.*

The example above leads us to a general definition to *inconsistent path pairs*. An inconsistent path pair, or IPP, is a pair of paths satisfying the following conditions.

1. Both paths are in the same function.
2. Both paths start from the entry of the function and end at the exit.
3. The two paths have different changes to a refcount.
4. It is possible that, given the same arguments, both the paths are feasible and return the same value.

We informally explain why IPPs can reveal refcount bugs with the example function foo(). Assume that, at runtime, the program reaches the entry of foo() with the PM count of dev being n. After p_1 is executed, the PM count is incremented to $n+1$. If the PM count of dev can never be decremented to 0 from the exit of foo(), then characteristic 3 is violated. Otherwise, let p' be a runtime path which starts at the exit of foo() and decrements the PM count of dev to 0. As p_1 and p_2 are indistinguishable outside foo() by checking the arguments passed to foo() or the value returned by foo(), it is possible for the program to follow p' even if p_2 is executed instead of p_1 in foo(). As a result, the PM count of dev is still n at the exit of foo(). After the program executes p', the PM count of dev will be decremented to -1, which violates characteristic 4. In summary, a refcount bug can exist no matter which path in the IPP is taken at runtime.

3.3 Detecting IPP: An Example

To check IPPs in a program, we need to compare any two paths in a function and determine whether the third and fourth condition in the definition of IPP can be satisfied. A precise understanding of refcount changes in a path requires the information of how functions called in the path change refcounts. We use a function summary to record the refcount changes and the return values under different constraints. A summary based inter-procedural analysis is then needed for checking IPPs in programs.

We first introduce how foo() in Figure 1(a) is analyzed. A general introduction to the analysis follows in section 4. Figure 2 shows how we check IPPs in foo(). From a high level of view, the analysis consists of three steps. (I) Enumerate all paths in foo(). (II) Summarize each path independently. (III) Check consistency among summaries of paths, report any inconsistency found and use the union of the consistent summaries as the function summary for foo().

3.3.1 Summaries of the Called Functions

We summarize a function by a set of *summary entries* (referred to as entries hereinafter). Each entry records 1) how refcounts will be changed (by the field *changes*), 2) what can be returned (by the field *return*) and 3) under what constraints can this entry be applied (by the field *cons*). The constraints are on the arguments and the return value of the function.

For example, the summary of reg_read(), shown at the bottom of Figure 2, consists of two entries. The first entry applies when the first argument of reg_read() (written as $[d]$) is not a null pointer and the return value (written as $[0]$) is always nonnegative. The second entry applies when the return value is -1, without any constraints on the arguments. Neither of the entries changes any refcount. The implementation of reg_read() is given in Figure 2 for reference.

The summary of inc_pmcount() has the same form as the summary of reg_read(). The main difference is that inc_pmcount() 1) has no return value, and 2) increments the PM count of its only argument (written as $[d].pm$) when the argument is not null.

3.3.2 STEP I: Enumerating Paths

The first step to summarize foo() is to enumerate all paths in the function and attach a path constraint to each of them. In the example function foo(), there are two paths, i.e. p_1 and p_2 in Figure 1(b). The corresponding path constraints are $v > 0$ and $v \leq 0$, respectively, where v is the local variable in foo(). Both of the paths assert that the first

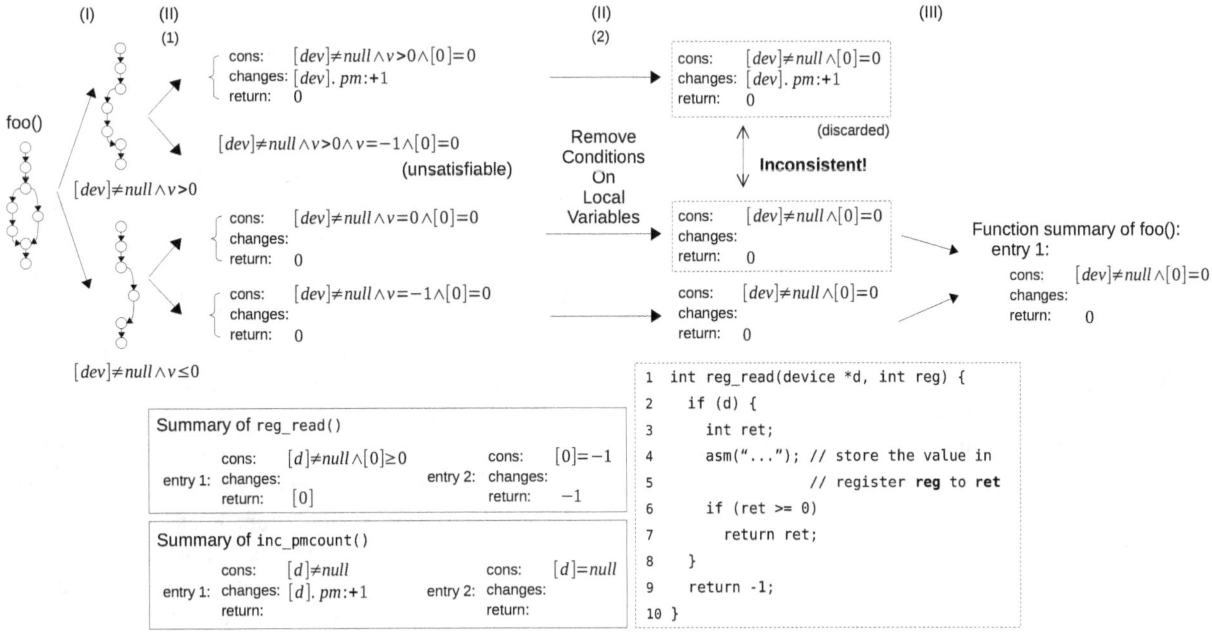

Figure 2: The complete analysis of foo() in figure 1.

formal argument of `foo()` (written as $[dev]$) is not null due to the assertion at line 5.

3.3.3 STEP II: Calculating Summaries for Each Path

Each path enumerated in Step I is summarized independently. The summary of a path is a set of entries, each of which records how refcounts are changed in the path under the constraint in the entry. We ensure that the constraint in an entry can uniquely determine the refcount changes in and the return value of all functions called in the path. As a result, multiple entries may be needed to summarize a path.

We describe as an example how p_2 is analyzed. In p_2, v is non-positive and no refcount is changed. Note that the path constraint of p_2 cannot uniquely determine the return value of `reg_read()`. As a result, two entries are needed to summarize the path, one for each entry in the summary of `reg_read()`. We denote the path constraint of p_2 as c_p and the constraints in the summary of `reg_read()` as c_1 and c_2, respectively. Then one entry summarizing p_2 has the constraint $c_p \wedge c_1$, asserting the local variable v is non-positive and non-negative, i.e. equals to 0, and the other entry has the constraint $c_p \wedge c_2$, asserting v is -1. Both of the entry has no refcount changes recorded since `reg_read()`, the only function called in p_2, does not change any refcounts.

After summaries of paths are calculated, we remove conditions on local variables (v in the example) from the constraints because local variables are discarded when the function returns and thus can not be accessed outside the function.

3.3.4 STEP III: Checking and Merging Summaries of Paths

Any two path summaries calculated in step II are checked for consistency. In Figure 2, the path summaries in dashed boxes are inconsistent because they share the same constraints but have different refcount changes.

The function summary of `foo()` is the union of entries calculated in step II. If two path summaries are inconsistent, we randomly drop one of them.

3.4 Difference Between IPP and other Notions of Inconsistency

The example above also shows that IPP detection is able to reveal bugs that cannot be found by detecting other kinds of inconsistency. Belief analysis can infer that the refcount of `dev` must be non-negative at the entry of `foo` from how the refcount is operated in the function. However, it is still challenging to deduce the bug in `foo` from such beliefs. With only the definition of `foo`, inconsistency detection techniques based on common usage patterns are not able to find the bug, either, as no common usage pattern can be extracted.

4. Inter-procedural Analysis for IPP Checking

As is stated in Section 3.3, how a function changes refcounts depends on the behavior of its callees. Thus an inter-procedural analysis is required. In this section, we describe our inter-procedural analysis in general.

$$
\begin{array}{lcll}
\textit{(Predicate)} & p & := & = \mid \neq \mid > \mid \geq \mid < \mid \leq \\
\textit{(Value)} & v & := & x \mid \textbf{\textit{numeral}} \mid true \mid false \\
\textit{(Instruction)} & inst & := & x = v \\
 & & \mid & x = y.\textbf{\textit{field}} \\
 & & \mid & x = \textbf{\textit{random}} \\
 & & \mid & \textbf{\textit{fn}}\ (v_1, ..., v_n) \\
 & & \mid & x = \textbf{\textit{fn}}\ (v_1, ..., v_n) \\
 & & \mid & \textbf{\textit{return}}\ v \\
 & & \mid & x = v_1\ p\ v_2 \\
 & & \mid & \textbf{\textit{branch}}\ x, l_1, l_2 \\
 & & \mid & \textbf{\textit{branch}}\ l
\end{array}
$$

Figure 3: Syntax of instructions in our abstract programs. x, y are variables, ***numeral*** is a numeral constant, l_i are labels marking positions where the control flow can jump to, ***field*** is a field name, ***random*** is a random number generator, and ***fn*** is a function identifier. Variables in conditional branches must be defined by an (in)equality expression.

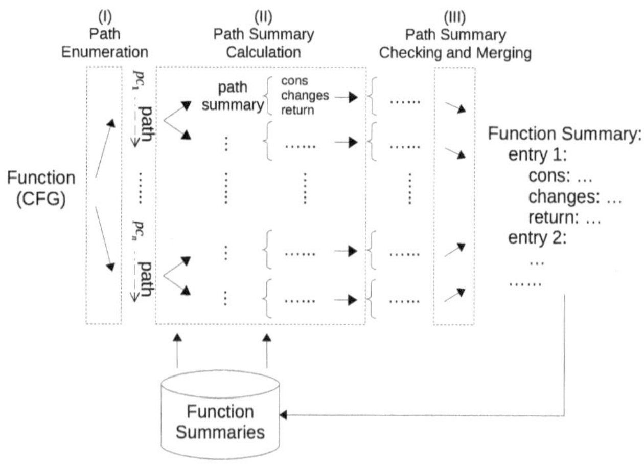

Figure 4: Overview of summary-based IPP analysis on a function

4.1 Program Abstraction

In this paper, we focus on the abstract program defined in Figure 3. The abstraction extends *affine programs* proposed in [12] and [13] by preserving formal arguments, branch conditions and return values, all of which are critical in IPP checking because formal arguments and return values are involved in the definition of IPPs. Another minor difference is that we assume refcounts can only be changed via refcount APIs. As a result, our abstraction ignores arithmetic operations which is mostly used to model changes to refcounts in previous work. A random generator is introduced as an abstraction of operations generating non-deterministic results, such as reading from device registers.

4.2 Summary-based Inter-procedural Analysis

Our summary-based inter-procedural analysis works on the aforementioned program abstraction (see Section 4.1). Functions are traversed and summarized in the reverse topological order of the call graph (recursive calls are randomly broken). A function summary is a set of summary entries, each of which summarizes the refcount changes and the return value of the function under certain constraints (see Section 4.3). Figure 4 shows the process of analyzing a single function. The process consists of the following three steps.

1. **Path Enumeration.** We first enumerate all paths in the given function. Loops are unrolled at most once in a path. Each path has a *constraint* showing when this path will be executed. The constraint is represented by first order formulas with LIA (linear integer arithmetic) theory [2].
2. **Path Summary Calculation.** Each path enumerated is summarized by symbolic execution (defined in section 4.4). After the summaries are calculated, conditions on local variables are removed from the constraints in the summary.
3. **Path Summary Checking and Merging.** After calculating all path summaries, we check whether these summaries are consistent and report any inconsistency found. The function summary is the set of consistent path summaries, and is added to the function summary database for future use.

4.3 Definition of the Summary

Formally, an entry in a summary of function is a triple

$$S = (cons, changes, return)$$

where $cons$ is a constraint on arguments and return values, $changes$ is a map from refcounts to integers, and $return$ is an expression representing the return value. A refcount is represented by an expression in our symbolic execution (see Section 4.4). We denote $cons$ in S by $S.cons$, the map $changes$ in S by $S.changes$, $return$ in S by $S.return$, and the change of refcount rc in S by $S.changes[rc]$.

We restrict that the conjunction of the constraints of any two entries in a function is unsatisfiable. If not, assume there are two entries e_1 and e_2 where $e_1.cons \wedge e_2.cons$ is satisfiable. If the refcount changes in e_1 and e_2 are same for all refcounts, the entries can be merged into a single entry where the constraint is $e_1.cons \vee e_2.cons$. The return expression in the merged entry is $e_1.return$ if $e_1.return = e_2.return$ and $[0]$ otherwise. If the refcount changes in e_1 and e_2 are different, e_1 and e_2 are considered inconsistent and one of them must be dropped (refer to Section 4.5 on how inconsistency are detected).

4.4 Path Summary Calculation

Summary of a path is calculated by executing the paths symbolically. Valuation to variables are expressed by symbolic

(Predicate)	p	$:=$	$= \mid \neq \mid > \mid \geq \mid < \mid \leq$
(Condition)	$cond$	$:=$	$e_1 \; p \; e_2$
(Argument)	arg	$:=$	$[\,\textbf{\textit{ident}}\,]$
(Return Value)	ret	$:=$	$[0]$
(Local Variable)	$local$	$:=$	***ident***
(Field)	$field$	$:=$	$e.$***field***
(Expression)	e	$:=$	***const*** $\mid cond \mid arg \mid ret \mid local \mid field$

Figure 5: Syntax of expressions in the symbolic execution. ***field*** is a field name, ***const*** is a numeral or boolean constant, and ***ident*** is the name of an identifier.

$x = v$	$vmap[x] = vmap[v]$
$x = y.$***field***	$vmap[x] = vmap[y].$***field***
$x =$ ***random*** l	(none)
return v	$return = vmap[v]$
$x = v_1 \; p \; v_2$	$vmap[x] = vmap[v_1] \; p \; vmap[v_2]$
branch x, l_1, l_2	remove any condition previously added by this instruction from $cons$, then $cons = cons \wedge vmap[x]$ if l_1 is taken otherwise $cons = cons \wedge (\neg vmap[x])$
branch l	(none)

Figure 6: How instructions are evaluated in the symbolic execution. ***field*** is a field name.

expressions defined in Figure 5. A *state* in the symbolic execution is a quintuple

$$St = (ip, cons, changes, return, vmap)$$

where ip points to the next instruction to be executed, $cons$ is a path constraint, $changes$ is a map from refcounts to integers, $return$ is the value returned and $vmap$ is a map from variables to values. The initial state is defined as follows.

- ip points to the first instruction in the function.
- $cons$ is $True$.
- $changes$ is an empty map and $changes[x]$ is 0 by default if x is not a key in $changes$.
- $return$ is an empty string.
- For each formal argument arg of the function, the value of $vmap[arg]$ is $[arg]$. Otherwise $vmap[x]$ is x by default, where x can be a numeral constant, a boolean constant or a variable.

Figure 6 shows how instructions (except function calls) are executed in an informal manner. For example, $vmap[x] = vmap[v]$ means the value of key x in $vmap$ is set to the value of key v in $vmap$. Updates to the instruction pointer ip are straightforward and are not shown for brevity.

```
input : The current state s
output: A set of states states
1  inst ← the call instruction pointed to by s.ip
2  summary ← summary of the function called by inst,
   instantiated with s.vmap
3  states ← {}
4  foreach entry in summary do
5      new_constraint ← s.cons ∧ entry.cons
6      if new_constraint is satisfiable then
7          s' ← allocate a new state
8          s'.ip ← pointer to the next instruction of inst
9          s'.cons ← new_constraint
10         s'.changes = s.changes
11         foreach key rc in entry.changes do
12             s'.changes[rc ] ← s'.changes[rc ] +
               entry.changes[rc ]
13         end
14         s'.vmap ← s.vmap
15         ret ← entry.return
16         var ← the variable to which the return value of
           inst is assigned to
17         s'.vmap[var ] ← ret
18         add s' to states
19     end
20 end
21 return states
```

Algorithm 1: Execution of a call instruction. A function summary is instantiated by replacing formal arguments and [0] to actual arguments and the variable holding the return value.

Execution of a call instruction is more complicated as it uses the summary of the called function and can create new states. Algorithm 1 shows how a call instruction is executed in RID. Each entry in the summary of the called function is first *instantiated*, i.e. formal arguments are replaced by the expressions of actual arguments and [0] is replaced by the name of the variable holding the return value of the call. For each entry in the instantiated summary, a new state is created if the conjunction of the constraints in the current state and in the entry is satisfiable (line 6). In the new state s', $s'.cons$ is the conjunction above (line 9), the refcount changes in the entry are added to $s'.changes$ (line 10 to 13), and the expression of the variable holding the return value is updated (line 14 to 17). The execution generates a set of new states each of which will be executed independently.

Each time a return instruction is executed, an entry is created with the constraint, the refcount changes and the expression of the return value in the state. Conditions on local variables are then removed from the constraint.

4.5 Path Summary Checking

With a collection of summary entries $S_1, ..., S_n$, we check if there exist two different entries S_i, S_j satisfying the following conditions:

- $S_i.cons \wedge S_j.cons$ is satisfiable.
- There exists a refcount rc such that $S_i.changes[rc] \neq S_j.changes[rc]$.

Let p_i and p_j be the path represented by S_i and S_j respectively. A pair S_i, S_j satisfying the above conditions indicates that (p_i, p_j) is an IPP defined in section 3.2. This is because the satisfiability of $S_i.cons \wedge S_j.cons$ means we can find an initial state St such that p_i and p_j are both feasible and the same value is returned (recall that $S_i.cons$ and $S_j.cons$ also contains conditions on the return value). Each refcount with different changes in the IPP is reported as a bug. One of the path in each IPP, randomly selected, will be discarded to avoid further reports at the call sites of the function. However, it is possible that RID drops a summary that does not meet the expected behavior of the function, as RID has no idea which summary reflects the *expected* behavior. As a result, RID may give redundant reports or fail to report bugs in callers of the function. A possible solution to this problem is discussed in section 5.4.

The function summary is defined as the set of the path summaries excluding the ones discarded during IPP checking. If the program under analysis respect other rules, a corresponding check on the refcount changes in the function summary can be added.

5. Implementation

We implement the analysis as a pass in the LLVM framework. All constraints are expressed in SMT formulas with linear integer arithmetic theory [1] and solved by Z3 [20].

5.1 Predefined Function Summaries

RID encodes the specifications of refcount APIs by predefined function summaries (referred to as predefined summaries hereinafter). If a predefined summary is given for a function, RID uses the predefined summary without analyzing the body of the function. RID, like existing tools [13, 17], expects that predefined summaries of APIs are given. Usually, predefined summaries are not changed frequently as the specifications of refcount APIs tend to be stable.

Figure 7 lists some examples of predefined summaries RID uses to analyze refcounts in Linux DPM and Python/C programs. The predefined summaries for DPM APIs in Linux is straightforward. API functions beginning with `pm_runtime_get` increment the refcount of the given device and functions beginning with `pm_runtime_put` do the opposite. Wrapper functions based on these APIs have no predefined summaries and are left to be analyzed by RID.

In Python/C, `Py_INCREF()` and `Py_DECREF()` are the basic interfaces to increment or decrement the refcount of a python object. In addition, other APIs may return borrowed reference or steal the caller's reference to an object passed to the function, as is explained in [23]. We briefly introduce some examples in the following paragraphs.

Program	API	summary
Linux	pm_runtime_get pm_runtime_get_sync	cons: $True$ change: $[dev].pm$: +1 return: $[0]$
	pm_runtime_put pm_runtime_put_sync	cons: $True$ change: $[dev].pm$: -1 return: $[0]$
Python/C	Py_INCREF	cons: $True$ change: $[o].rc$: +1 return:
	Py_DECREF	cons: $True$ change: $[o].rc$: -1 return:
	Py_BuildValue PyList_New PyInt_FromLong	cons: $[0] \neq null$ change: $[0].rc$: +1 return: $[0]$ cons: $[0] = null$ change: return: $null$
	PyList_GetItem	cons: $True$ change: return: $[0]$
	PyErr_SetObject	cons: $True$ change: $[type].rc$: +1 $[value].rc$: +1 return:
	PyList_SetItem	cons: $True$ change: return:

Figure 7: Examples of refcount APIs in Linux kernel and Python/C programs, and the predefined summaries of these APIs.

Predefined summaries of APIs returning a new reference usually consist of two entries because these APIs involve memory allocation that can fail. Among the two entries, one returns a new reference successfully when the refcount of the returned object is incremented, and the other returns a null pointer and no refcount is changed. Examples include `Py_BuildValue()`, `PyList_New()` and `PyInt_FromLong()`.

APIs that create new references to the arguments increment the refcount in their summary. In Figure 7, `PyErr_SetObject` is an API of this type and the corresponding predefined summary increment the refcount of $[type]$ and $[value]$, which are the two formal arguments of `PyErr_SetObject()`.

APIs that return a borrowed reference or steal a reference to an object passed to them have simpler summaries as these APIs do not change any refcount. For example, `PyList_GetItem()` returns a borrowed reference and `PyList_SetItem()` steals a reference to the object to be inserted.

The predefined summaries are manually written according to the documentation available in Python source [24]. It is also possible to generate the predefined summaries automatically because the documentation has a well-defined syntax.

5.2 Analysis of Large Scale Programs

Analyzing a complete OS kernel like Linux by symbolic execution with constraint solving is usually unacceptably expensive. To reduce the number of functions we need to analyze, we divide functions in Linux into the following three categories.

1. **Functions with refcount changes.** Functions in this category calls other functions with refcount changes. The basic functions in this category are refcount APIs with predefined summaries.
2. **Functions affecting those with refcount changes.** Functions in this category do not call any functions with refcount changes. However, at some call sites of the functions, return values of the functions can affect how functions in the first category change refcounts.
3. **The others.** This category consists of functions not belonging to the previous two categories.

We classify the functions by a two-phase analysis on the call graph. In the first phase, the set of functions with refcount changes is calculated by traversing all functions in the call graph in reverse-topological order (note that recursive calls are broken in the call graph), with an initial set including the refcount APIs. In the second phase, the functions are traversed in topological order of the call graph. For each function, a static backward slice [21, 31] is calculated. The slice criteria includes the return value and all actual arguments passed to functions with refcount changes. Thus a function called in the slice may affect the behavior of functions with refcount changes and falls into the second category if it is not in the first category.

With the above three categories in mind, we analyze functions from different categories in different ways. Functions with refcount changes are fully analyzed because any two paths in a function may be inconsistent. Functions affecting those with refcount changes are analyzed selectively. This is because these functions have no refcount changes and the only information useful is the conditions on their return values. We avoid analyzing complex functions in this category and assume these functions can return any possible value. In RID, we analyze functions in this category with no more than three conditional branches. Functions in the third category are ignored as no information RID summarizes will be used.

RID also limits the total number of paths to be enumerated in a function and the number of path summaries generated from a path. If a function is not fully analyzed due to the limits, a default summary entry, which has no refcount changes and no conditions on the return value, will be added to the summary of the function. Options are provided to adjust the limitations according to the program to be analyzed.

5.3 Preparation of the Program under Analysis

RID analyzes a single LLVM bitcode file a time. A program containing multiple source files can either be compiled into a single bitcode file, or into multiple bitcode files which can be analyzed separately.

When linking multiple bitcode files in LLVM, we meet an implementation issue that static functions defined in headers have multiple copies. This can significantly increase analysis time in large scale programs because all of the duplicate functions must be analyzed. To avoid the duplication, we mark all function defined in headers as *weak symbols* before linking, so that multiple weak symbols will be merged into a single symbol.

RID can also analyze multiple files separately. In this case, function summaries calculated in one source file will be saved to disk and used when another source file is analyzed. To determine a proper order of the sources, a dependency graph of the sources is built where A depends on B if and only if A uses any symbols defined in B. We then calculate strongly connected components (SCCs) in the dependency graph, link sources in the same SCC into a single file and analyze these SCCs in reverse topological order. Multiple SCCs can be analyzed in parallel as long as the SCCs they depend on have been analyzed. This technique helps reduce the total time needed to analyze a large scale program.

5.4 Limitations

We list the limitations of RID as follows and briefly discuss their influence on the results of the analysis.

First, the abstract program analyzed by RID does not include features such as function pointers, bit operations and stores to data structure fields. When a branch condition is out of the expressive power of linear arithmetic theory used by RID, the branch condition is forgetted. Forgetting some branch conditions or updates other than resources and the return value may make two path indistinguishable to RID though they are actually not. Thus the design decisions above can lead to false positives but no false negatives. In the future, we plan to enhance RID by adopting techniques such as alias analysis [11] and SMT BitVector Theory.

Second, RID unrolls loop at most once. Some bugs cannot be detected if they can only be triggered by executing a loop body multiple times.

Third, RID limits the number of paths analyzed in a function and may not visit all possible paths in a complex function. In the future we plan to investigate whether static slicing is helpful in reducing the number of paths RID need to analyze.

Fourth, randomly dropping one of two inconsistent reference count update summaries in one function, say `bar()`, may hide some of inconsistencies exist in the callers of `bar()`. These inconsistencies in the callers can be revealed by an incremental recheck which uses previously calculated summaries of unaffected functions once the inconsistency in `bar()` is fixed.

6. Evaluation

6.1 Benchmark and Configuration

We evaluate RID against two kinds of sources, i.e. the Linux kernel and a set of native implementaion in Python/C programs.

For the Linux kernel, we use the 3.17 release and concentrate on the DPM (Dynamic Power Management) subsystem which is a necessity for device drivers to support runtime power management. We choose DPM as a representative of refcount APIs because refcount bugs in DPM APIs are known to cause severe errors including system crash, boot hang and abnormally high power consumption. One of the fundamental elements in DPM is a per-device refcount. The count of a device is incremented by 1 whenever the driver is about to execute some device operations and decremented by 1 after the operations are done. The bugs are then double-checked in the upstream kernel and reported to the kernel mail list if they exist in the latest code base.

For the Python/C programs, we focus on the reference count usage of Python objects in the native code, as is done in previous work [13]. Predefined summaries follow the official Python/C API reference manual [23]. We choose three Python/C programs, namely krbV, pyaudio and ldap, and compares the reports of RID with warnings given by cpychecker [17] (the source code of Pungi[13] is not yet available). Cpychecker is a rule-based checker relying on the extra rule discussed in section 2.1, i.e. the change of a reference count of an object must be equal to the number of references escaping from the function. Cpychecker also allows a user to add GCC attributes in the source to indicate that a function steals a reference to an argument or returns borrowed reference.

Examples of predefined summaries used in our evaluation are given in Section 5.1. We omit the full list of predefined summaries due to the large amount of Python/C APIs. The limits of paths enumerated in a function and subcases in a path are set to 100 and 10, respectively. All evaluations are carried out on a Fedora Linux box with eight 2.4GHz x86-64 cores and 8GB memory.

6.2 Bugs Detected and Their Characteristics

RID has found 83 new bugs out of 355 reports in Linux involving DPM. These bugs are reported to kernel mail lists

```
... radeon_crtc_set_config(dev) {
  ...
  ret = pm_runtime_get_sync(dev);
  if (ret < 0)
    return ret;
  ...
  ret = drm_crtc_helper_set_config(set);
  ...
  pm_runtime_put_autosuspend(dev);
  return ret;
}
```

Figure 8: A DPM API misuse detected by RID. pm_runtime_get_sync() increments a refcount regardless of its return value. pm_runtime_put_autosuspend() decrements the refcount.

and confirmed by kernel community developers. Similar bugs fixed in recent Linux development are known to cause system crashes, kernel boot hangs and abnormal power consumption. We show two representative examples to illustrate the characteristics of bugs found by RID.

One typical category of bugs caught by RID reflects the difference between specifications of refcount APIs and programmers' understanding. For example, the function `radeon_crtc_set_config()` in Figure 8, before carrying out further device operations, increments the refcount of the device by calling `pm_runtime_get_sync()` and returns directly if `pm_runtime_get_sync()` returns an error code (which is a negative integer). This reflects that the developer assumes `pm_runtime_get_sync()` should do nothing if it returns an error. This assumption, though widely adopted in Linux, is not true for `pm_runtime_get_sync()` which always increment the refcount, as is shown in the predefined summary in section 5.1. As a result, the increment to the refcount is never balanced by a pairing decrement, which prevents the driver from suspending the device when the device is not in use.

Another category of bugs found reveals the improper error handling when invoking an API that may fail. Figure 9 shows a subsystem specific wrapper to DPM, namely `usb_autopm_get_interface()`, which is commonly used in USB drivers. This wrapper works in a different way from `pm_runtime_get_sync()`, i.e. no refcount is changed if the API returns an error code. With the predefined summary of `pm_runtime_get_sync()`, RID can automatically calculate the precise summary of `usb_autopm_get_interface()` and detect the bug in `idmouse_open()` which does not decrement the refcount when `idmouse_create_image()` fails.

The above examples also show why RID can detect bugs with only the refcount API specifications. The key point is that it is common for a function, which implement a high level functionality, to invoke multiple APIs. A well-written

```
int usb_autopm_get_interface
    (struct usb_interface *intf)
{
  int status;
  status = pm_runtime_get_sync(&intf->dev);
  if (status < 0)
    pm_runtime_put_sync(&intf->dev);
  if (status > 0)
    status = 0;
  return status;
}

int idmouse_open(struct inode *inode,
                 struct file *file)
{
  interface = ...;
  ...
  result =
    usb_autopm_get_interface(interface);
  if (result)
    goto error;
  result = idmouse_create_image (dev);
  if (result)
    goto error;
  usb_autopm_put_interface(interface);
error:
  return result;
}
```

Figure 9: A bug detected by RID. Different from pm_runtime_get_sync(), usb_autopm_get_interface(), a wrapper of DPM in USB subsystem, does not change the PM count when it returns an error code. How this subsystem specific API changes the PM count is automatically summarized in a precise manner.

function then has to deal with all the potential behavior of any API the function calls and to implement a consistent behavior under all these circumstances. In these cases, it is not surprising that the code can reflect the difference between the behavior of APIs and developers' understanding, as the consistent behavior from the developers' point of view is actually inconsistent. RID takes advantage of these different paths and reveals any inconsistency in them to detect refcount bugs without knowing the actual consistent behavior expected by the developers.

6.3 High Percentage of Incorrect API Usage

The example in Figure 8 is a representative of a class of bugs due to the uncommon specification of the `pm_runtime_get()` and `pm_runtime_get_sync()`. After searching the whole kernel for similar call sites using regular expressions, we find 96 calls to the function with error handling (wrapper functions are excluded). Among these call sites, 67 of them (70%) miss the decrement when `pm_runtime_get()` fails (RID has detected 40 of them and the reason why some bugs are missing is discussed in Section 6.4).

Reasons of this unexpectedly high percentage of incorrect uses include the following. (1) The specification of `pm_runtime_get()` is different from most other resource management functions. `pm_runtime_get()` always increments a refcount regardless of its return value, while the common practice for resource management functions is to change nothing if the function returns an error code. (2) Cases are observed where developers of a driver may copy the code from another driver in the same subsystem for common functionality. This allows errors in one driver to be propagated to some others.

By discussing with DPM designers, it is worth noting that the specification of `pm_runtime_get()` has been deliberated and designed in a reasonable way. Balancing the refcount increment on error in the APIs can introduce extra complexity because errors can happen in another thread scheduled by `pm_runtime_get()` after `pm_runtime_get()` has returned.

This clearly shows that, even in relative mature code bases, how an API is commonly used does not necessarily indicates how the API *should* be used. As a result, it is challenging for specification mining techniques to infer the correct pattern in this kind of cases. RID, on the other hand, can reveal these bugs because it checks for IPPs in a function locally, without relying on how APIs are used in other functions.

6.4 False Positives and Missed Bugs

The major source of false positives from RID is operations not covered by RID's program abstraction. For example, a function in a driver may have two paths with different changes to a refcount according to a specific bit in a bitmap which tracks options from the user. As we have not considered bit operations in our abstraction yet, conditions on these bits are dropped. This makes the paths look indistinguishable in RID though they can be distinguished by the value in the bitmap. Another example is the lack of data structure operations in our summary. This prevents us from distinguish two paths by whether they insert(remove) an element to(from) a list passed as an argument.

Figure 10 shows an example missed by RID. This bug is found by the brute force search discussed in Section 6.3. RID cannot detect this bug because no inconsistency exists among the paths in `arizona_irq_thread()`. One path in the function returns `IRQ_NONE` with the PM count of `arizona->dev` incremented and the other paths returns `IRQ_HANDLED` with no PM count changes. To detect this bug, RID needs to look at the callers to this function and determine whether every caller handles these two cases properly. However, `arizona_irq_thread()` is an interrupt handler which is called via function pointers, which is not yet covered by RID. It is possible to extend RID with alias analysis so that the above call relation is included in the call graph,

```
irqreturn_t arizona_irq_thread
  (int irq, void *data)
{
  int ret;
  ret = pm_runtime_get_sync(arizona->dev);
  if (ret < 0) {
    dev_err(...);
    return IRQ_NONE;
  }
  ...... // no return here
  pm_runtime_put(arizona->dev);
  return IRQ_HANDLED;
}
```

Figure 10: A bug missed by RID. One path in the function returns IRQ_NONE with a refcount incremented. The other paths returns IRQ_HANDLED with no refcount changes.

Table 1: Function in different categories and paths analyzed in functions

Category		Count
Functions with refcount changes		2133
Functions affecting those with refcount changes	analyzed	1889
	not analyzed	2803
The others		261391

Table 2: Comparison between RID and Cpychecker.

Test Program	Common	Specific to... RID	Specific to... Cpychecker
krbV-1.0.90	48	86	14
ldap-2.4.20	7	13	1
pyaudio-0.2.8	31	15	1
total	86	114	16

allowing RID to detect bugs of this kind by checking callers of the functions.

6.5 Performance

RID takes 64 minutes to classify the 270k functions in Linux and 67 minutes to analyze the complete Linux kernel with the help of selective analysis presented in Section 5.2. Table 1 shows the number of functions in different categories. The statistics illustrate that we can concentrate on a small portion of the Linux kernel as the other parts have no effects in our analysis. This is because Linux is composed of many functionalities while power management of devices is only one of them. The 2133 functions with refcount changes cover 574 out of 3623 drivers in the Linux kernel we build for evaluation.

6.6 Sanity Check: Refcounts in Python/C Programs

Table 2 lists the number of common bugs found by Cpychecker and RID, along with number of bugs detected by only one of the two tools. We check the reports from these tools manually, as is done in [13]. The result shows RID can detect more bugs than Cpychecker, mainly because of the adoption of SSA form which allows RID handle variables with multiple statical assignment. The same phenomenon is observed in the evaluation of Pungi [13]. Some bugs reported by Cpychecker are missed by RID because of the same reason discussed in section 6.4.

7. Conclusion

In this paper, we propose inconsistent path pair detection, a novel technique to discover refcount bugs. A prototype, called RID, is implemented based on the method. RID looks for a pair of paths in the same function that, given the same argument, have the same return value but different changes to a refcount. At the core of RID is a summary-based inter-procedural analysis that calculates the refcount changes and return value of a function under different constraints on arguments. Our evaluation shows RID detects 83 new bugs in Linux and tends to find bugs caused by developers' misunderstanding on API semantics or improper error handling. RID can also be applied to libraries such as the native implementation of Python/C programs as long as the specifications of refcount APIs are given.

The future work of RID focuses on relaxing the limitations discussed in Section 5.4. Alias analysis can be adopted to complement the call graph. Operations on abstract data structures can be included in summaries to improve the precision of RID on functions with data structure operations. Symbolically executing multiple paths in parallel can be adopted to improve the performance of RID.

Acknowledgments

This research is supported by Natural Science Foundation of China under Grant No. 61170050, National Science and Technology Major Project of China (2012ZX01039-004) and the National High Technology Research and Development Program of China (2015AA011505).

References

[1] Clark Barrett, Pascal Fontaine, and Cesare Tinelli. The smt-lib standard version 2.5. `http://smtlib.cs.uiowa.edu/papers/smt-lib-reference-v2.5-r2015-06-28.pdf`.

[2] Peter Baumgartner, Alexander Fuchs, and Cesare Tinelli. (lia) - model evolution with linear integer arithmetic constraints. In Iliano Cervesato, Helmut Veith, and Andrei Voronkov, editors, *Logic for Programming, Artificial Intelligence, and Reasoning*, volume 5330 of *Lecture Notes in Computer Science*, pages 258–273. Springer Berlin Heidelberg, 2008.

[3] Isil Dillig, Thomas Dillig, and Alex Aiken. Static error detection using semantic inconsistency inference. In *ACM SIGPLAN Notices*, volume 42, pages 435–445, June 2007.

[4] Michael Emmi, Ranjit Jhala, Eddie Kohler, and Rupak Majumdar. Verifying reference counting implementations. In Stefan Kowalewski and Anna Philippou, editors, *Tools and Algorithms for the Construction and Analysis of Systems, 15th International Conference, TACAS 2009, Held as Part of the Joint European Conferences on Theory and Practice of Software, ETAPS 2009, York, UK, March 22-29, 2009. Proceedings*, volume 5505 of *Lecture Notes in Computer Science*, pages 352–367. Springer, 2009.

[5] Dawson R. Engler, Benjamin Chelf, Andy Chou, and Seth Hallem. Checking system rules using system-specific, programmer-written compiler extensions. In Michael B. Jones and M. Frans Kaashoek, editors, *4th Symposium on Operating System Design and Implementation (OSDI 2000), San Diego, California, USA, October 23-25, 2000*, pages 1–16. USENIX Association, 2000.

[6] Dawson R. Engler, David Yu Chen, and Andy Chou. Bugs as inconsistent behavior: A general approach to inferring errors in systems code. In *SOSP*, pages 57–72, 2001.

[7] Mark Gabel, Junfeng Yang, Yuan Yu, Moises Goldszmidt, and Zhendong Su. Scalable and systematic detection of buggy inconsistencies in source code. *ACM SIGPLAN Notices*, 45(10):175–190, October 2010.

[8] Claire Le Goues and Westley Weimer. Specification mining with few false positives. In Stefan Kowalewski and Anna Philippou, editors, *Tools and Algorithms for the Construction and Analysis of Systems, 15th International Conference, TACAS 2009, Held as Part of the Joint European Conferences on Theory and Practice of Software, ETAPS 2009, York, UK, March 22-29, 2009. Proceedings*, volume 5505 of *Lecture Notes in Computer Science*, pages 292–306. Springer, 2009.

[9] Seth Hallem, Benjamin Chelf, Yichen Xie, and Dawson R. Engler. A system and language for building system-specific, static analyses. In Jens Knoop and Laurie J. Hendren, editors, *Proceedings of the 2002 ACM SIGPLAN Conference on Programming Language Design and Implementation (PLDI), Berlin, Germany, June 17-19, 2002*, pages 69–82. ACM, 2002.

[10] Mateus Jurczyk. Windows kernel reference count vulnerabilities - case study. `http://j00ru.vexillium.org/dump/zn_slides.pdf`.

[11] Vineet Kahlon. Bootstrapping: a technique for scalable flow and context-sensitive pointer alias analysis. In Rajiv Gupta and Saman P. Amarasinghe, editors, *Proceedings of the ACM SIGPLAN 2008 Conference on Programming Language Design and Implementation, Tucson, AZ, USA, June 7-13, 2008*, pages 249–259. ACM, 2008.

[12] Akash Lal and Ganesh Ramalingam. Reference count analysis with shallow aliasing. *Information Processing Letters*, 111(2):57–63, 2010.

[13] Siliang Li and Gang Tan. Finding reference-counting errors in python/C programs with affine analysis. In Richard Jones, editor, *ECOOP 2014 - Object-Oriented Programming - 28th European Conference, Uppsala, Sweden, July 28 - August 1, 2014. Proceedings*, volume 8586 of *Lecture Notes in Computer Science*, pages 80–104. Springer, 2014.

[14] Zhenmin Li and Yuanyuan Zhou. PR-miner: automatically extracting implicit programming rules and detecting violations in large software code. In Michel Wermelinger and Harald C. Gall, editors, *Proceedings of the 10th European Software Engineering Conference held jointly with 13th ACM SIGSOFT International Symposium on Foundations of Software Engineering, 2005, Lisbon, Portugal, September 5-9, 2005*, pages 306–315. ACM, 2005.

[15] Huqiu Liu, Yuping Wang, Lingbo Jiang, and Shimin Hu. PF-miner: A new paired functions mining method for android kernel in error paths. In *COMPSAC*, pages 33–42. IEEE, 2014.

[16] Shan Lu, Soyeon Park, Chongfeng Hu, Xiao Ma, Weihang Jiang, Zhenmin Li, Raluca A. Popa, and Yuanyuan Zhou. MUVI: automatically inferring multi-variable access correlations and detecting related semantic and concurrency bugs. In Thomas C. Bressoud and M. Frans Kaashoek, editors, *Proceedings of the 21st ACM Symposium on Operating Systems Principles 2007, SOSP 2007, Stevenson, Washington, USA, October 14-17, 2007*, pages 103–116. ACM, 2007.

[17] D. Malcom. a static analysis tool for cpython extension code. `https://gcc-python-plugin.readthedocs.org/en/latest/cpychecker.html`.

[18] Paul E. McKenney. Overview of linux-kernel reference counting. `http://www.open-std.org/jtc1/sc22/wg21/docs/papers/2007/n2167.pdf`.

[19] Paul E. McKenney and Jack Slingwine. Read-copy update: Using execution history to solve concurrency problems. In *10th IASTED International Conference on Parallel and Distributed Computing and Systems*, October 1998.

[20] Leonardo Mendona De Moura and Nikolaj Bjrner. *Z3: An Efficient SMT Solver*. Springer, 2008.

[21] Robert Oehlmann. Static single-assignment for program slicing on binary intermediate language. Master's thesis, Hamburg University of Technology, 2013.

[22] Abhinav Pathak, Abhilash Jindal, Y. Charlie Hu, and Samuel P. Midkiff. What is keeping my phone awake?: characterizing and detecting no-sleep energy bugs in smartphone apps. In Nigel Davies, Srinivasan Seshan, and Lin Zhong, editors, *The 10th International Conference on Mobile Systems, Applications, and Services, MobiSys'12, Ambleside, United Kingdom - June 25 - 29, 2012*, pages 267–280. ACM, 2012.

[23] Python/c api reference manual. `https://docs.python.org/2/c-api/`.

[24] Refcount behavior of python/c apis. `http://svn.python.org/projects/python/trunk/Doc/data/refcounts.dat`.

[25] Suman Saha, Jean-Pierre Lozi, Gaël Thomas, Julia Lawall, and Gilles Muller. Hector: Detecting resource-release omission faults in error-handling code for systems software. In *Annual IEEE/IFIP International Conference on Dependable Systems and Networks, DSN 2013*, June 2013.

[26] Martin Schäf, Daniel Schwartz-Narbonne, and Thomas Wies. Explaining inconsistent code. In Bertrand Meyer, Luciano

Baresi, and Mira Mezini, editors, *Joint Meeting of the European Software Engineering Conference and the ACM SIGSOFT Symposium on the Foundations of Software Engineering, ESEC/FSE'13, Saint Petersburg, Russian Federation, August 18-26, 2013*, pages 521–531. ACM, 2013.

[27] Lin Tan, Chen Liu, Zhenmin Li, Xuanhui Wang, Yuanyuan Zhou, and ChengXiang Zhai. Bug characteristics in open source software. *Empirical Software Engineering*, 19(6):1665–1705, 2014.

[28] Aaron Tomb and Cormac Flanagan. Detecting inconsistencies via universal reachability analysis. In Mats Per Erik Heimdahl and Zhendong Su, editors, *International Symposium on Software Testing and Analysis, ISSTA 2012, Minneapolis, MN, USA, July 15-20, 2012*, pages 287–297. ACM, 2012.

[29] Security Tracker. Linux kernel memory leak in inotify_init() lets local users deny service. `http://www.securitytracker.com/id/1025321`.

[30] Westley Weimer and George C. Necula. Mining temporal specifications for error detection. In Nicolas Halbwachs and Lenore D. Zuck, editors, *Tools and Algorithms for the Construction and Analysis of Systems, 11th International Conference, TACAS 2005, Held as Part of the Joint European Conferences on Theory and Practice of Software, ETAPS 2005, Edinburgh, UK, April 4-8, 2005, Proceedings*, volume 3440 of *Lecture Notes in Computer Science*, pages 461–476. Springer, 2005.

[31] Mark Weiser. Program slicing. *IEEE Transactions on Software Engineering*, SE-10(4):352–357, July 1984.

Maximizing Performance Under a Power Cap: A Comparison of Hardware, Software, and Hybrid Techniques

Huazhe Zhang
University of Chicago
huazhe@cs.uchicago.edu

Henry Hoffmann
University of Chicago
hankhoffmann@cs.uchicago.edu

Abstract

Power and thermal dissipation constrain multicore performance scaling. Modern processors are built such that they could sustain damaging levels of power dissipation, creating a need for systems that can implement processor *power caps*. A particular challenge is developing systems that can maximize performance within a power cap, and approaches have been proposed in both software and hardware. Software approaches are flexible, allowing multiple hardware resources to be coordinated for maximum performance, but software is slow, requiring a long time to converge to the power target. In contrast, hardware power capping quickly converges to the the power cap, but only manages voltage and frequency, limiting its potential performance.

In this work we propose PUPiL, a hybrid software/hardware power capping system. Unlike previous approaches, PUPiL combines hardware's fast reaction time with software's flexibility. We implement PUPiL on real Linux/x86 platform and compare it to Intel's commercial hardware power capping system for both single and multi-application workloads. We find PUPiL provides the same reaction time as Intel's hardware with significantly higher performance. On average, PUPiL outperforms hardware by from 1.18–2.4× depending on workload and power target. Thus, PUPiL provides a promising way to enforce power caps with greater performance than current state-of-the-art hardware-only approaches.

Categories and Subject Descriptors C.1.3 [*Other Architectural Styles*]: Adaptable architectures; I.2.8 [*Problem Solving, Control Methods, and Search*]: Heuristic methods; D.4.8 [*Performance*]: Measurements

General Terms Performance, Design, Experimentation

ASPLOS '16, April 02-06, 2016, Atlanta, GA, USA

DOI: http://dx.doi.org/10.1145/http://dx.doi.org/10.1145/2872362.2872375

Keywords Adaptive Systems, Power Management, Decision-tree

1. Introduction

Modern processors are constrained by *dark silicon* – their abundance of transistors enables them to draw more power than they can safely sustain [11, 57]. For example, the Exynos 5 processor (in the Samsung Galaxy S4 phone) has a 5.5W peak power – nearly 2× its sustainable heat dissipation, limiting peak speed to less than 1 second [49]. At the other end of the spectrum, future exascale supercomputers have a predicted operating budget of 20 MW [2], making power management a central challenge of supercomputer operating systems [54].

These physical constraints create a need for *power control systems* which guarantee the processor operates within a strict *power cap*. Research power capping systems have been implemented in software [5, 6, 14, 31, 42–44, 62]. The need for power capping has become so great, however, that Intel processors now support power capping in hardware with their Running Average Power Limit (RAPL) interface [7].

Whether implemented in hardware or software, there are two essential properties for a power capping system. The first is **timeliness** – the speed with which a new cap can be enforced. The second is **efficiency** – the performance delivered under the cap. Without timeliness, critical operating bounds can be violated, damaging the hardware. Without efficiency, application performance suffers unnecessarily. It is, of course, trivial to implement a power cap while ignoring performance – simply turn the machine off.

In general, hardware approaches provide superior timeliness – hardware reacts much faster than software – while software approaches have superior efficiency – they find the highest performance set of resources to activate within the power cap. Hardware's timeliness is due to the relatively simple circuits that control key power indicators like processor voltage and frequency. Software's efficiency derives from its ability to consider the complex interactions between multiple resources, allowing it to solve the constrained optimization problem of scheduling the highest performance resource configuration which obeys the power cap.

This paper explores the tradeoffs between timeliness and efficiency in power capping approaches. Specifically, we advocate a *hybrid* approach that includes both software and hardware components, using each to address the challenge to which it is best suited. We instantiate this hybrid approach in PUPiL – for Performance Under Power Limits – a power capping system based on a novel *decision framework.* To ensure a power cap, PUPiL navigates nodes in a decision framework. Each node represents a choice about how to use a particular resource. For example, one node will select how many cores to use in a multicore. After making a decision, PUPiL measures power and performance and uses that feedback to drive the decision at the next node.

We implement PUPiL and test it on a Linux/x86 server with 20 different multithreaded benchmarks under 5 different power caps. We compare PUPiL to both RAPL (Intel's state-of-the-art hardware power capping system [7]) and two software-only approaches. We evaluate the timeliness and efficiency of all approaches for both single and multi-application workloads. Our results show:

- **Efficiency:** For single application workloads, a software-only approach can achieve higher performance than RAPL, but PUPiL achieves the highest performance. Specifically, PUPiL outperforms RAPL by 1.32–1.18× depending on the power cap. (Section 5.2.)
- **Timeliness:** RAPL's speed enforcing the power caps greatly exceeds software-only approaches by orders of magnitude. PUPiL is equivalent to RAPL. (Section 5.3.)
- **Multi-application Efficiency:** We test two types of multi-application workloads: 1) *cooperative* loads where each application requests a subset of available resources and 2) *oblivious* loads where each application requests all resources. For cooperative loads, PUPiL outperforms RAPL by 1.43–1.18× on average depending on the power cap. In the oblivious case, PUPiL outperforms RAPL by 2.56–2.43× depending on the power cap.
- **Energy Efficiency:** While PUPiL is designed to meet power caps, we find that by increasing performance, it also improves energy efficiency compared to RAPL, with 1.05-1.4× average improvements.

These results indicate that PUPiL's hybrid approach provides the timeliness of hardware with significantly greater efficiency. The performance gains are particularly high when enforcing power caps in the oblivious multi-application scenario. The large number of threads and resulting contention in the oblivious multi-application scenario creates a situation where the applications destructively interfere with each other. RAPL's only mechanism for power enforcement is processor voltage and frequency, which does nothing to limit contention. PUPiL, in contrast, manipulates DVFS as well as core allocation, socket usage, memory usage, and hyperthreading. This diversity allows PUPiL to throttle back multiple resources and reduce overall contention, resulting in large performance gains for the same power cap.

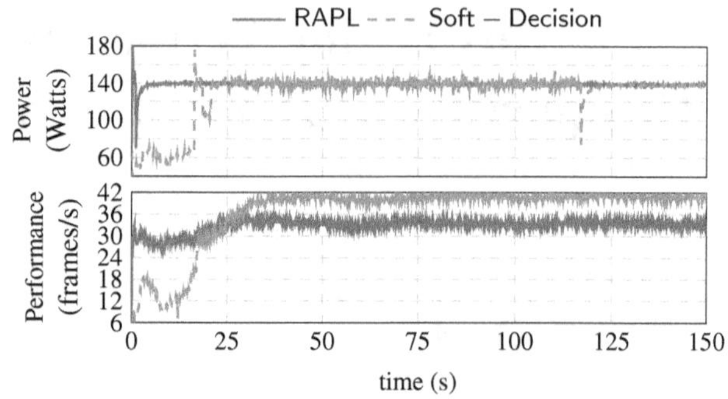

Figure 1. Tradeoff between timeliness and efficiency from hardware and software power capping, running x264.

This paper makes the following contributions:

- Develops a decision framework to maximize performance under a power cap.
- Evaluates this implementation on a real system in multiple usage scenarios.
- Identifies workload properties where Intel's RAPL power capping system fails to deliver best performance.
- Makes all scripts, code, and data collection tools from this evaluation available as open source, so others can test or extend these results[1].

The fundamental contribution of this paper is an empirical demonstration of the need for software and hardware to work together to maximize performance under power caps. The combined software/hardware approach proposed in this paper demonstrates it is possible to achieve significant performance gains over Intel's state-of-the-art, commercial hardware approach – especially for multi-application workloads.

2. Motivational Example

This example highlights the different tradeoffs in hardware and software power capping approaches and motivates the need for a hybrid design. We run the **x264** video encoder on an Intel Linux/x86 system. We compare the timeliness and efficiency of both Intel's RAPL hardware and a software approach that can adjust many settings (presented in Section 3).

Our test system is a dual-socket server with two Intel SandyBridge Xeon E5-2690 processors and 64GB of RAM. These processors support RAPL, but also have a number of configurable resources which affect power and performance tradeoffs, listed in Table 1. Each processor supports 15 frequency settings plus TurboBoost. Each is 8 cores, with hyperthreading, giving a total of 32 virtual cores across both sockets. These processors have a thermal design power (TDP) of 135 Watts, but experimentally we find it extremely rare for any workload to sustain that power consumption.

To illustrate the difference between hardware and software power capping, we set a 140 Watt power cap total for both sockets. RAPL must achieve this power consumption

[1] All source code, scripts, inputs, and patches are available at: https://github.com/PUPiL2015/PUPIL.git.

Table 1. Server resources.

Processor	Cores	Sockets	Speeds (GHz)	TurboBoost	HyperThreads	Memory Controllers	Socket TDP (W)	Configurations
Xeon E5-2690	8	2	1.2–2.9	yes	yes	2	135	1024

by driving each socket to 70 Watts (this is the optimal solution without thread migration, over which RAPL has no control). In contrast, the software approach configures a range of parameters: 1) how many sockets to use, 2) how many cores to use on each socket, 3) whether to use hyperthreads or not, 4) how many memory controllers to use, and 5) the frequency of each socket. For both the hardware and software approaches we measure power and performance (in frames encoded per second) as a function of time.

Fig. 1 illustrates the results, with power shown in the top chart and performance shown on the bottom. Each chart shows time on the x-axis. The hardware approach is represented by the solid line, and the dashed line represents the software approach. Clearly, both approaches meet the power cap – RAPL hits the cap quickly while the software approach operates below the cap for approximately 20 seconds, briefly exceeds it, and finally settles at 140 Watts.

The performance results, however, show that once the software approach converges, it delivers 20% more performance than RAPL. Specifically, after convergence, the software approach averages approximately 41 frames per second while RAPL averages approximately 33.5 frames per second. Software outperforms hardware because it recognizes that hyperthreads do not help this application on this system. Using hyperthreads results in greater power consumption and a small performance loss. The software approach recognizes that it should not make use of hyperthreads and instead it increases the speed of the cores it is using without hyperthreads. Of course, it takes software a long time to recognize and adjust.

These results demonstrate the need for a hybrid approach that enforces power caps with hardware's speed, but has software's flexibility to adapt resource usage to the particular application (or applications) running on the system.

3. Power Capping Methodologies

This section introduces the different power capping approaches we explore in this paper. It first discusses our software approach. It then describes RAPL, a state-of-the-art hardware power capping system. Finally, it introduces PUPiL, a hybrid of software and hardware approaches.

We assume that a computer system is *configurable*; *i.e.,* it has resources or other parameters whose usage can be tuned to navigate performance/power tradeoffs. For each approach, the goal is to configure these resources to meet a power cap in a timely and efficient manner. Timeliness means the cap is quickly enforced. Efficiency means the system delivers maximum performance under the cap.

All three power capping approaches (software, hardware, and PUPiL) operate based on *feedback.* These approaches *observe* their environment, *decide* on a response, and *act* to implement their decisions. This feedback loop is repeated continually, allowing the power capping system to react to application phase changes or other environmental fluctuations. We use this *observe-decide-act* framework as a basis for understanding the methodologies of the three different power capping approaches addressed in this paper.

3.1 Software Power Capping

This section discusses how the software system implements observation, decision, and action.

3.1.1 Observe

In the observation phase, the software collects power and performance feedback.

Power feedback can come from any number of power monitoring mechanisms. For example, external power meters such as a WattsUp device can be used. Other alternatives include on-board power monitoring devices, such as the INA231 [27], or on-chip power monitoring, which is available commercially from Intel [7] and through research prototypes [50].

Performance feedback can also come from a number of sources. High-level performance feedback can come directly from appropriately instrumented applications [21]. It could also come from any number of other sources, including hardware counters that measure floating point computation rate or simply instructions per second [52, 55]. While the methodologies in this paper will work with any metric, the authors personally advocate the use of high-level application-specific feedback, if available as such allows a power capping system to ensure efficiency in terms of real application progress.

One issue with feedback is that real systems are noisy. To meet the efficiency challenge, a power capping system should ensure that it is reacting to persistent phenomena and not some transient effect that momentarily disturbs performance. That is, the system should distinguish between a fundamental change in application workload and a temporary timing fluctuation (*e.g.,* due to a page fault). The power capper should adjust in the first case, but ignore the second case.

To address noise and ensure that the system acts on meaningful feedback, the software approach employs a deviation based filter to remove outliers. Specifically, the software approach measures performance over a window, filters any data that falls more than 3-standard deviations from the mean, and averages the rest. Assuming, X is the list of performance measurements collected, μ is the average of unfiltered X, σ is the standard deviation of unfiltered X, then $X_{feedback}$ is the performance feedback used by the system to make deci-

Algorithm 1 Walking the decision framework.

```
Require: Set of ordered resources R
Require: Power cap P
  Put system in minimal resource configuration
  U ← R                                   ▷ the set of untested resources
  while U ≠ ∅ do                          ▷ While untested resources
    ⟨perf_old, pow_old⟩ ← GetFeedback()
    r ← RemoveNext(U)                     ▷ next resource in order
    set r to highest setting
    wait r.d time units                   ▷ Account for resource delay
    ⟨perf_cur, pow_cur⟩ ← GetFeedback()
    if perf_cur < perf_old then
      return r to lowest setting
    else
      if pow_cur > P then
        s ← BinarySearchResourceSettings(r)
        set r to s
                  ▷ This may return the resource to its lowest setting.
```

sions:

$$\mu = \frac{\sum_i X_i}{N} \tag{1}$$

$$\sigma = \sqrt{\frac{\sum_i (X_i - \mu^2)}{N}} \tag{2}$$

$$X_{feedback} = \frac{\sum_{j \in A} X_j}{size(A)} \tag{3}$$

$$A = \{j \mid |X_j - \mu| < 3\sigma\} \tag{4}$$

3.1.2 Decide

In the decide phase, the software selects a resource configuration. One way to select the best configuration would be to simply walk through all configurations until we find the highest performance configuration that respects the power cap. This approach has the twin drawbacks that it fails to meet the timeliness challenge and it may fail to respect the power cap. In general, the number of possible resource configurations will grow exponentially as we add more resources. Thus exhaustive search is simply not feasible.

Any software approach must find a more intelligent way to explore the configuration space. In this paper, we propose a novel *decision framework*. To begin, the system orders the available resources (the ordering process is described below). It then starts in the lowest resource configuration. Proceeding through resources in order, the approach puts the next resource into its highest setting. Feedback is measured in this new configuration. The software compares the performance feedback of the current configuration to that of last configuration to decide whether 1) performance has improved by using this new resource and 2) the resource usage respects the power cap. Algorithm 1 specifies the decision making process.

Algorithm 1 requires an ordered set of resources. The order is determined by Order() (detailed in Algorithm 2). The algorithm first sets the system to the smallest resource configuration. It then puts the resources into a set of untested resources. While this ordered set of untested resources is non-empty, the algorithm measures power and performance (using the helper function GetFeedback()). It then takes the next resource in order and sets it to its highest configuration setting (using the Set() helper function), waits a resource-specific amount of time, and then measures the feedback again. If this resource provided higher performance, then the algorithm fine tunes the resource setting, otherwise it returns to the lowest setting for this resource. The fine tuning process involves performing a binary search on resource settings to find the highest performance setting that is under the power cap (the BinarySearchResourceSettings() helper function).

We use binary search on a resource-by-resource basis to avoid exhaustive search's overhead. This is an engineering tradeoff. Component-wise binary search is fast, but can get stuck in local extrema and miss the global optimal solution. In exchange, however, it scales well even as the number of configurable resources grows. In practice, this approach works well because resources tend to have a single peak. For example, not all applications can use all cores, but there tends to be a single best core count with no local extrema.

There are four helper functions for this approach. Three are straightforward and their detailed descriptions are omitted for space. We provide a brief overview here. The GetFeedback() function simply measures and returns power and performance data. The $Set()$ function is used to configure the resource. The BinarySearchResourceSettings() function simply does a binary search on the available configurations for a resource. Its goal is to find the highest performance setting that respects the power cap. The ordering function is the fourth helper and it is described below.

The ordering function is essential to Algorithm 1. The software approach establishes the ordering based on the potential impact of each resource. Higher impact resources have precedence over lower impact resources. Algorithm 2 shows the algorithm used for establishing this order. The intuition is to allocate power first to higher impact resources so that we can tune the performance from coarse-grained knobs to fine-grained knobs. We evaluate impact of a resource by the performance improvement that it delivers when activated individually. The one exception is DVFS, which is used at the end to fine-tune power within the cap. To determine impact, we calibrate the system using a well-understood, embarrassingly parallel application. Based on our results, the ordering is insensitive to different applications; *i.e.,* the decision tree finds a near-optimal configuration using the same calibrated ordering for all applications. The detailed process for establishing the order is shown in Algorithm 2.

3.1.3 Act

In the act phase, the software implements the resource allocation proposed by the decision phase. For example, if the decision phase decides to test a resource, the act phase is responsible for actually assigning that resource to the active applications. To implement the act phase, the software requires two pieces of external information. The first is a tim-

Algorithm 2 Ordering Resources in Calibration.

Require: Set of resources R excluding DVFS
Require: a calibration benchmark without inter-thread communication
Put system in minimal resource configuration
$U \leftarrow R$ ▷ the set of disordered resources
while $U \neq \emptyset$ **do** ▷ While disordered resources
  $r \leftarrow$ RemoveNext(U) ▷ next resource in random order
  set r to highest setting
  wait $r.d$ time units ▷ Account for resource delay
  $perf_r \leftarrow$ GetFeedback()
  return r to lowest setting
  add r to O
Sort r in O by $perf_r$
Add DVFS to the last in O **return** O ▷ The set of ordered resources

ing information about how long to expect from when the resource is allocated to when its effects can be observed. This information is required so that the software does not take a new observation before the resources have actually had an effect. The second piece of information is a function that implements the resource allocation. As most resources are allocated in system-specific ways, this function is necessary to maintain the generality of the approach and let it work on multiple systems.

Given this information, the action phase simply consists of setting the resource configuration to that specified by the decision phase and then putting the decision framework to sleep for the time it will take to see the resource effects. To increase efficiency, the software keeps track of the previous resource allocation and only changes those resource settings which changed since the last decision.

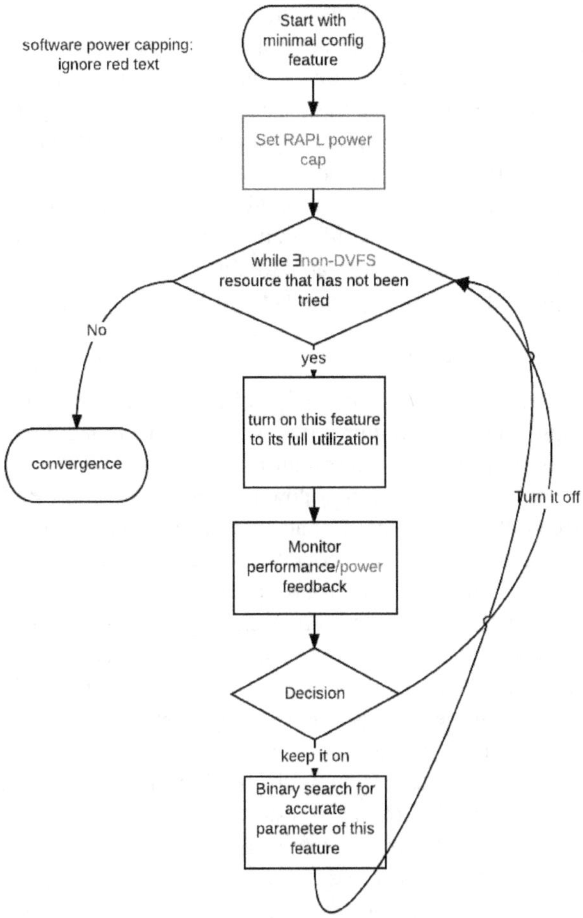

Figure 2. PUPiL's approach to hybrid hardware/software power capping.

3.2 Hardware Power Capping

We briefly outline the approach taken by Intel's RAPL system [7], in terms of observation, decision, and action. RAPL receives a power cap and a time interval through a machine specific register (MSR). RAPL observes various low-level hardware events and estimates power consumption from those event counts. RAPL determines an energy budget that would meet the desired power cap during the specified time interval. For example, if the time interval is 0.5 seconds and the power cap is 100 Watts, the energy budget is 50 Joules.

RAPL sub-divides the user-specified time interval into a set of smaller intervals. For each of these fine-grained intervals, RAPL calculates the remaining energy budget for the remaining time in the user-specified interval and decides the best possible processor speed and voltage. Given this decision, RAPL sets DVFS to the decided state and waits for the next fine-grained interval. More detail on RAPL operation is available in the literature [7].

It is instructive at this point to compare the hardware and software approaches. Software is clearly flexible, the approach in Algorithm 1 will work with any set of available resources – the only requirement is that we must be able to establish an order on these resources. The drawback of software is that configuring the system requires executing Algorithm 1, which can be costly (as shown in Fig. 1). In contrast, RAPL observes only power feedback (not performance), makes decisions by solving a linear equation, and acts by only tuning voltage and frequency only. All three steps can be done within milliseconds and this ensures the timeliness of hardware approach. However, because RAPL lacks performance feedback and considers only DVFS, this hardware approach cannot deliver the highest performance for many applications.

3.3 PUPiL's Hybrid Power Capping

Our goal is to obtain the efficiency of the software approach and the timeliness of hardware approach. Thus, we propose PUPiL, a hybrid power capping system that incorporates software and hardware to achieve the benefits of both.

3.3.1 Timeliness

We need the system to respect the power cap as soon as the cap is set. To achieve this timeliness, hardware power capping approach has to be in charge of capping the power instead of the much slower control loop of software approach. Thus, we set the power cap in hardware first, before exploring other resources. Meanwhile, to avoid interference with the hardware approach, we remove processor speed and voltage from the set of resources controlled by software. Leaving hardware in charge of voltage and speed ensures timeliness and reduces the configuration space software much search.

Fig. 2 illustrates PUPiL's hybrid decision framework. The major difference between the software-only approach and Fig. 2's is that the hybrid approach explicitly sets RAPL before exploring the configuration space determined by the non-DVFS resources. To achieve this in practice, we modify Algorithm 1 so that it first sets the RAPL power cap.

3.3.2 Efficiency

We need to find the optimal configuration for the running application. This requires two modifications to the decision algorithm shown in Algorithm 1.

First, the power cap is now met by hardware so PUPiL need only manage performance. Thus, the hybrid approach excludes all the power condition checks in Algorithm 1 – PUPiL assumes RAPL ensures the power cap.

Second, power distribution among different chips in a multi-socket environment has to be reconsidered. Hardware power capping caps power on a per-socket manner. However, when we consider thread migration as a tunable parameter, the optimal configuration for an application or workload is often asymmetric, so it is necessary to distribute power accordingly instead of using a default even distribution. PUPiL, therefore, uses a core-number based power distribution across different chips. More specifically, PUPiL distributes the dynamic power (power cap minus static power) proportional to the core number being used by each chip. PUPiL achieves this by setting corresponding hardware power cap to each chip. Thus, whenever there is core number configuration adjustment, power distribution adjusts with it.

4. Experimental Setup

This section describes benchmarks, system, metrics, and points of comparison we use to evaluate PUPiL.

4.1 Benchmarks

We use 20 benchmark applications from three different suites including PARSEC (`x264`, `swaptions`, `vips`, `fluidanimate`, `blackscholes`, `bodytrack`) [3], Minebench (`ScalParC`, `kmeans`, `HOP`, `PLSA`, `svmfe`, `btree`, `kmeans_fuzzy`) [40], and Rodinia (`cfd`, `nn`, `lud`, `particlefilter`)[4]. We also use a partial differential equation solver (`jacobi`) and the `swish++` search webserver [24] and `dijkstra` [28]. These benchmarks test a range of important modern applications, both compute-intensive and memory-intensive. All applications run with up to 32 threads (the maximum supported in hardware on our test machine). In addition, all workloads are long running, taking at least 10 seconds to complete. This duration gives us plenty of time to take measurements of system performance and power.

Table 2. System configurations.

Configuration	Settings	Max Speedup	Max Powerup
cores per socket	8	7.9	2.1
sockets	2	2.0	1.7
hyperthreading	2	1.9	1.2
mem controllers	2	1.8	1.1
clock speeds	16	3.2	3.4

4.2 Platform

We use a dual-socket Intel/Linux system with a SuperMICRO X9DRL-iF motherboard and two Xeon E5-2690 processors (see Table 1). This motherboard supports setting RAPL's power capping feature. The system runs Linux 3.2.0. We use the `msr` module, to access the model specific registers that implement RAPL. We use the `cpufrequtils` package to set the processor's clock speed. These processors have eight cores, fifteen DVFS settings (from 1.2 – 2.9 GHz), hyper-threading, and TurboBoost. In addition, each chip has its own memory controller, and we use the `numactl` library to manage memory controller use. In total, the system supports 1024 user-accessible configurations, each with its own power/performance tradeoffs[2]. The thermal design power for these processors is 135 Watts.

Given those specifications, the following resources are configurable: the clock speed of each socket, core use per socket, hyperthreading, the number of sockets in use, and the number of memory controllers in use. Manipulating thread affinities allows us to change the cores per socket, the active sockets and the use of hyperthreading.

As described in Section 3, implementing the software decision system requires ordering the set of resources under consideration. Table 2 lists these resources in the order established by Algorithm 2. For each resource in the table, it lists the speedup and power up (increase in power, analogous to speedup) measured during the ordering process.

4.3 Evaluation Metrics

Our goal is to evaluate the timeliness and efficiency of various power capping approaches. To compare approaches, we must quantify these properties. We evaluate timeliness by measuring settling time. We evaluate efficiency by measuring the performance achieved by a workload under a power cap.

4.3.1 Timeliness

Settling time is a standard metric for a control system [18]. Given a power cap, it may take some amount of time for the controller to stabilize the system at that power. We call the period after which the system stabilizes the *steady state* and we denote the time at which the system enters steady state as

[2] 16 cores, 2 hyperthreads, 2 memory controllers, and 16 speed settings (15 DVFS settings plus TurboBoost)

t_{ss}. If the controller begins work at time t_0, then the settling time is simply:

$$settle = t_{ss} - t_0 \quad (5)$$

4.3.2 Efficiency

Efficiency is the performance delivered under a power cap. We evaluate efficiency using *weighted speedup*. This is a standard metric for multi-application workloads that weights the performance each application achieves in a multi-application scenario by the performance it would achieve in isolation. This metric has been demonstrated to be both consistent and fair [13].

4.4 Points of Comparison

To evaluate PUPiL, we compare it to several other techniques:

- **RAPL:** The primary approach with which we compare.
- **Soft-DVFS:** This is a software approach that sets the DVFS settings using the `cpufrequtils` package. Our implementation is modeled on a prior approach proposing a software-based DVFS control system [31].
- **Soft-Modeling:** This is a software approach that models the power for different configurations in an offline manner. That is, it uses multiple regression to estimate the power and performance of an application as a function of assigned resources (in this case, clockspeed, memory controllers, sockets, cores per socket and hyperthreads). This approach is an extreme case of a predictive model that needs no feedback information at runtime.
- **Soft-Decision:** This is the software-only decision framework described in Section 3.1.
- **Optimal:** This is determined by running each application in every possible system configuration and measuring its performance. The optimal configuration achieves the best speed for a given power cap.

5. Experimental Evaluation

This section evaluates PUPiL's timeliness and efficiency. To enable others to perform similar evaluations, we have made the software and scripts used to perform this evaluation available online. We begin by evaluating single application workloads and then address multi-application workloads.

5.1 Single Application

To evaluate power control methods for single application workloads, we launch each application under a power cap and measure both its performance and settling time. We evaluate 5 different processor power caps: 60, 100, 140, 180, and 220 Watts. When setting the caps for both RAPL and Soft-DVFS, we split the power budget between both sockets evenly as this is the optimal allocation when no other resource is considered. Soft-Decision and PUPiL are free to divide the power cap among the sockets as they see fit when they migrate threads.

Table 3. Comparison of Harmonic Mean Performance.

Power Cap	RAPL	Soft-DVFS	Soft-Modeling	Soft-Decision	PUPiL
60W	.54	-	-	.70	.71
100W	.68	.66	.66	.80	.85
140W	.74	.71	.65	.87	.89
180W	.78	.74	.76	.88	.92
220W	.79	.75	.85	.91	.94

There are no Soft-DVFS or Soft-Modeling data for the 60W cap. For Soft-DVFS, even the lowest p-state exceeds the 60W power cap when using all cores and hyperthreads. For Soft-Modeling, the errors for this cap are extremely large; approximately 70% of the data points for this technique exceed the power cap. This demonstrates a disadvantage of a system that uses no online feedback to correct its models. It has no ability to recover when the models have high error. PUPiL, in contrast, uses a very simple model but the feedback constantly corrects.

5.2 Performance

Fig. 3 shows the performance delivered under each cap for each application. This figure contains one chart for each power cap. The x-axis shows the benchmark, the y-axis shows performance normalized to optimal (1 is the best possible performance). The charts show one bar for each of RAPL, Soft-DVFS, Soft-Modeling, Soft-Decision, and PUPiL.

While results vary per application and power cap, the general trends show that Soft-Decision provides higher performance than RAPL with Soft-DVFS and Soft-Modeling comparable to RAPL. Furthermore, the hybrid approach generally provides the highest performance. The harmonic mean performance for each power cap and power controller is summarized in Table 3. This table shows PUPiL consistently outperforms RAPL and Soft-DVFS across all power caps by at least 18% (at the 180W cap) and at most 32% (at the 60W cap).

Soft-Modeling takes the advantage historical power data and configures the machine based on the predicted power. It, however, has no guarantee of respecting power cap because it has no feedback mechanism. For some applications and power caps (*e.g.,* HOP, swish++ at 100W), it outperforms all other approaches by exceeding the power cap. The average performance of Soft-Modeling is still not good compared to Soft-Decision and PUPiL, despite the fact that it sometimes exceeds the caps. Furthermore, Soft-Decision is very close to PUPiL. These results confirm that multi-resource approaches out perform systems that only manipulate DVFS, whether in software or hardware.

Clearly RAPL performs well on some applications (*e.g.,* `btree` and `svmfe`) and poorly on others (*e.g.,* `dijkstra` and `kmeans`). Fig. 5 shows the computation (in instructions per second) and memory bandwidth (in GB/s) for each benchmark. Blue dots represent applications for which RAPL does well (is within 10% of optimal for the 140 W cap) and red dots show applications for which RAPL achieves poor effi-

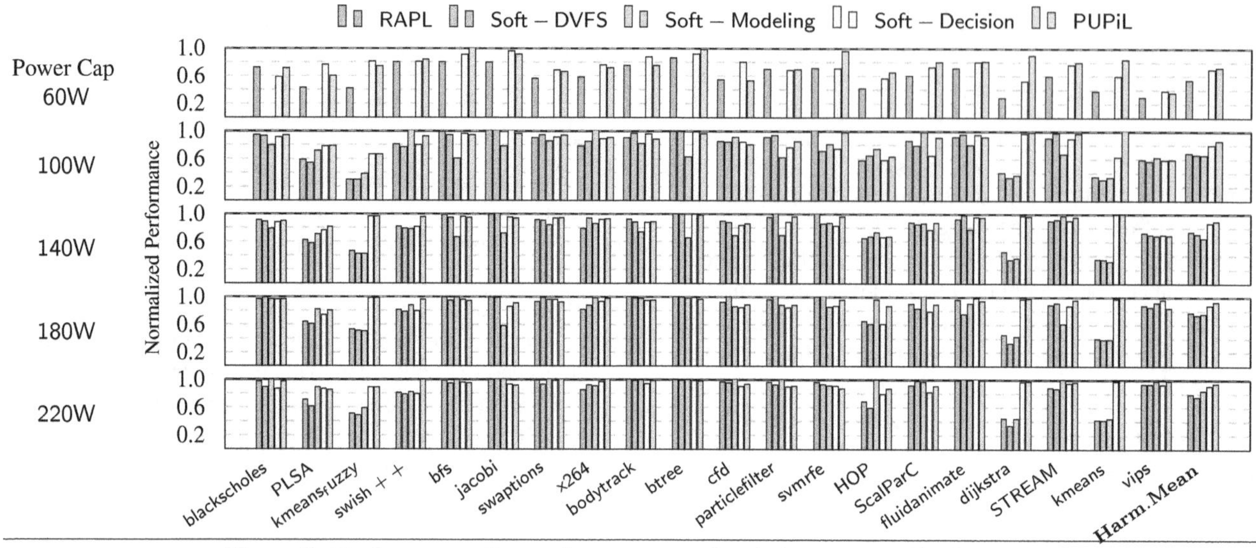

Figure 3. Performance of several power control techniques normalized to optimal.

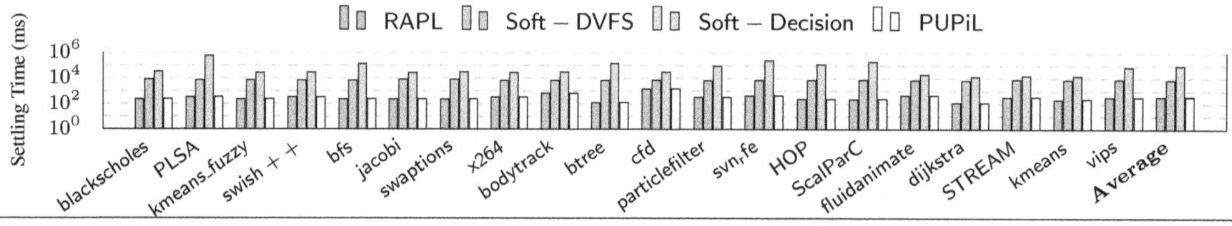

Figure 4. Settling times for several power control techniques.

ciency (greater than 10% from optimal). Clearly simple notions like memory-bound or compute bound are not good predictors of RAPL efficiency. For example, RAPL performs poorly on `STREAM` (which has the highest memory bandwidth), yet does well with `jacobi` (which has the second highest memory bandwidth). RAPL generally performs well for applications that have ample parallelism and scale well to use all 32 virtual cores. RAPL generally performs poorly on applications with scaling issues or limited parallelism. For such applications, it is better to restrict the resources they are using and increase the speed of this small subset.

For example, `kmeans` scales well with more cores on a socket. When `kmeans` is allocated cores on both sockets, however, inter-socket communication becomes a bottleneck, so `kmeans` continues to issue instructions and burn power but without increasing speed. RAPL and Soft-DVFS must reduce clock speed to meet the power cap. In contrast, both Soft-Decision and PUPiL recognize that the second socket decreased performance, and they restrict `kmeans` to a single socket but increase its speed, resulting in higher performance.

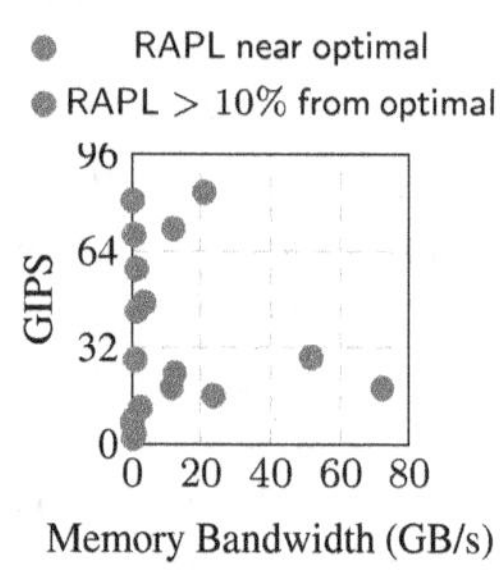

Figure 5. Benchmark characteristics.

5.3 Settling Time

For each application and power cap we measure settling time. Soft-Modeling is omitted as there is no settling time for this offline approach. Fig. 4 shows the settling times for all approaches and applications under the 140 Watt cap. Results for other caps are similar (only 1-2% different) and are omitted for space. Each application is shown on the x-axis and settling time (measured in milliseconds) is shown on the y-axis (in a logarithmic scale).

The data in Fig. 4 demonstrates the tremendous advantages in timeliness that RAPL has over Soft-Decision. On average, across all benchmarks, RAPL's settling time is 356 ms. In contrast, Software-Decision averages 95,000 ms, a difference of approximately 260 × and soft-DVFS averages 7,300ms, a difference of approximately 13 ×. These results demonstrate the claims of timeliness made in the introduction to the paper. RAPL has significant timeliness advantages over software approaches. PUPiL, however, is able to maintain RAPL's timeliness advantages, averaging 365 ms. The small increase in overhead is due to the fact that the power cap is now set through PUPiL's software interface rather than directly setting the register in hardware.

Table 4. Multi-application Workloads.

Name	Benchmarks
mix1	jacobi, swaptions, bfs, particlefilter
mix2	cfd, bfs, fluidanimate, jacobi
mix3	blackscholes, cfd, jacobi, fluidanimate
mix4	particlefilter, blackscholes, swaptions, btree
mix5	x264, dijkstra, vips, HOP
mix6	STREAM, fuzzy-kmeans, HOP, dijkstra
mix7	STREAM, kmeans, vips, HOP
mix8	kmeans, dijkstra, x264, STREAM
mix9	jacobi, swaptions, fussy-kmeans, vips
mix10	cfd, bfs, x264, HOP
mix11	jacobi, blackscholes, dijkstra, fuzzy-kmeans
mix12	btree, particlefilter, kmeans, STREAM

These results demonstrate the main claims in the introduction. Specifically, RAPL's hardware approach addresses the timeliness challenge. The software approach achieves efficiency gains compared to hardware. The mean performance advantage is at least 18%, while for specific applications (*e.g.*, `kmeans`, `dijkstra`) the gains can be over 2×. Finally, PUPiL's hybrid approach meets both the timeliness and efficiency challenges, combining hardware's low settling time with software's high performance.

5.4 Multi-Application Workloads

We evaluate RAPL and PUPiL on multi-application workloads. We begin by dividing our benchmarks into two sets: ones for which RAPL delivers near-optimal performance (blue dots from Fig. 5), and ones for which RAPL is more than 10% from optimal (red dots in Fig. 5). We create multi-application workloads by randomly selecting applications from the two sets. Specifically we create 12 separate mixes, each consisting of four applications. For the first four mixes (1–4), all applications are drawn from the set for which RAPL is near optimal. The mixes 5–8 are all taken from applications for which RAPL performs poorly. The applications in mixes 9–12 include two applications from each set. Table 4 summarizes the workloads: each is given a name – `mixN` – and we list the applications used in that workload. We evaluate the multi-application workload by launching all applications at the same time. We use the weighted speedup for efficiency metrics as described in Section 4.3.2.

We evaluate two separate multi-application scenarios: *cooperative* and *oblivious*. In the cooperative scenario, we assume all applications know that they are running with other applications; each is launched with only 8 threads, so that the total number of active threads is equal to the number of virtual cores. In the oblivious scenario, we assume that each application is launched without regard to the other applications in the system and each requests 32 threads, for a total of 128 alive in the system. We compare the performance achieved by RAPL and PUPiL in these two scenarios.

5.4.1 Cooperative Performance

The performance for the cooperative multi-application scenario is shown in the left column of Fig. 6. There is a chart for each power cap. The y-axes show the ratio of PUPiL to RAPL weighted speedup (higher means PUPiL outperforms RAPL) for each application mix (shown on the x-axes).

Table 5. Ratio of PUPiL to RAPL Performance.

Power Cap	Cooperative	Oblivious
60W	1.43	2.53
100W	1.21	2.56
140W	1.18	2.44
180W	1.18	2.46
220W	1.21	2.43

The performance comparison for the cooperative scenario reveals similar trends to the single-application scenarios. There are several mixes for which PUPiL and RAPL achieve similar performance and others where PUPiL far outperforms RAPL. Table 5 shows the ratios of PUPiL to RAPL performance across all mixes for each power cap. In the cooperative scenario, PUPiL outperforms RAPL by at least 18% across all power budgets.

Single-application performance is not necessarily a good indicator of multi-application performance. For each power cap there are examples where PUPiL far outperforms RAPL. For example, across all power caps PUPiL achieves much higher performance for mix2. This happens despite the fact that all applications in mix2 are drawn from the set for which RAPL provides good individual performance. This result shows that multi-application workloads can have complicated behavior and it justifies the need for an adaptive approach, like PUPiL, that can accommodate the unexpected.

5.4.2 Oblivious Performance

Fig. 6's left column shows the performance for the oblivious multiapp scenario. Recall that in the oblivious scenario, each application requests 32 threads. The performance results show that PUPiL provides significantly better performance than RAPL in the oblivious multi-application case. The summary results across all performance caps are shown in Table 5, which indicates that PUPiL achieves at least 2.4× better aggregate performance than RAPL. Furthermore, this advantage can jump up to as much as 6× for some application mixes.

These results demonstrate that in a system that reflects the oblivious multi-application workload – where every application is trying to claim as many resources as possible – RAPL by itself is simply not sufficient to provide high performance under the power cap. Instead, the flexibility of a system like PUPiL is needed to carefully manage resource usage and deliver high performance. The reason for PUPiL's higher performance is that these oblivious workloads typically bottleneck on some non-computational resource. This bottleneck is usually either intersocket communication bandwidth or memory bandwidth. This bottlenecking in the multi-application scenario is similar to what we have seen in the single application case, but now the consequences are more dire. We explore the reasons for this more in the next section.

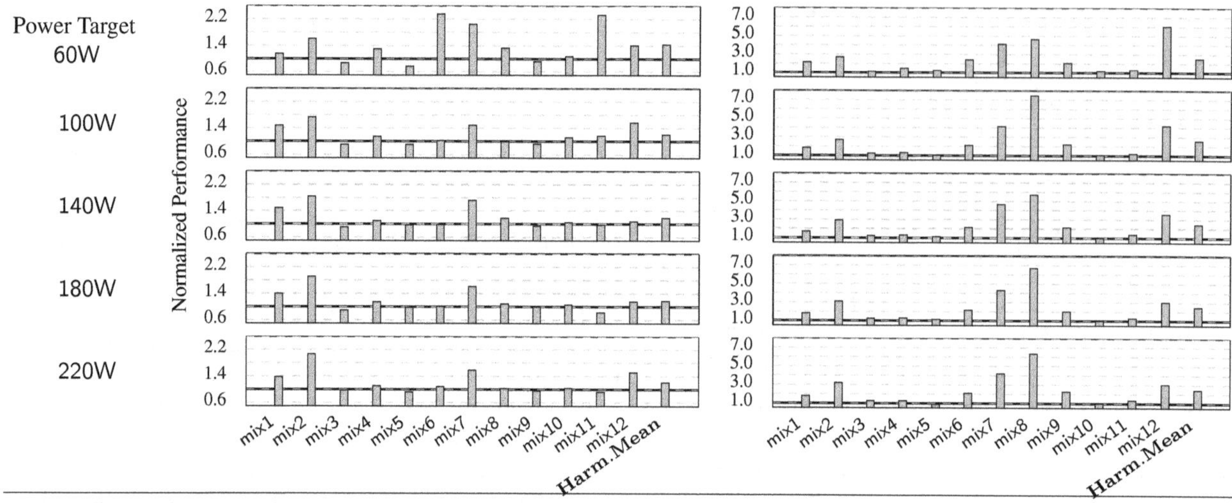

Figure 6. Ratio of PUPiL to RAPL performance in cooperative (left) and oblivious (right) multiapp scenarios.

Table 6. PUPiL and RAPL Multiapp Performance.

Workload	Spin Cycles (%)		Memory Bandwidth (GB/s)	
	RAPL	PUPiL	RAPL	PUPiL
mix7	15	0.23	14.6	23.8
mix8	54	.48	17.5	30.3
mix12	33	.40	14.3	27.0

5.4.3 Detailed Multiapp Data

This section presents some low-level metrics collected to explain the performance difference between PUPiL and RAPL in the oblivious multiapp case. To look for major differences between RAPL and PUPiL we use Intel's VTune tool to collect low-level metrics for the application mixes under both RAPL and PUPiL control.

VTune collects a tremendous amount of data on applications, but when looking at the metrics, two things stood out: *spin cycles* and *memory bandwidth*. This data is shown in Table 6 for the three mixes where PUPiL outperforms RAPL by the greatest amount. For each mix, the table shows the percentage of time spent executing *spin cycles*, cycles for which the processor is retiring instructions, but no forward progress is being made (*e.g.,* test-and-set instructions which fail the test). The table also shows the achieved memory bandwidth in MB/s for these three mixes.

Table 6 shows that under RAPL control these mixes spend significantly larger portions of their time spinning and achieve a significantly smaller memory bandwidth. We believe the problem is that one of the applications in these mixes uses polling synchronization during a fairly long serial portion of operation. The other applications appear to be largely memory limited and are either embarrassingly parallel (no or limited synchronization) or use condition variables to synchronize. Therefore, these other applications need memory bandwidth and yield the CPU when they cannot make progress. The one application that does polling synchronization, however, ruins the behavior of the entire system, as when it gets the CPU it holds it for its entire scheduling quantum while making minimal forward progress. This behavior limits the ability of the other applications to make progress as well. When the mix is scheduled on fewer cores, however, its overall performance increases dramatically. In this case, the polling benchmark (1) has much less contention, (2) finishes its work faster, and (3) yields the cores to other applications more often, boosting the overall performance.

5.5 Energy Efficiency

We compare RAPL's and PUPiL's energy efficiency. We report performance divided by power, which shows how much work can be done per joule. Single application workloads results are shown in Fig. 7. As before, we normalize efficiency of all approaches to the optimal. Soft-decision and PUPiL produce 1.15-1.3× energy efficiency compared to RAPL or Soft-DVFS. Fig. 8 shows the multi-application workload results. PUPiL has a 5–40% improvement of energy efficiency compared to RAPL across different power caps. These results show PUPiL produces good energy efficiency even though saving energy is not PUPiL's primary purpose.

5.6 Sensitivity and Overhead Analysis

Throughout this section we investigate several factors which affect the results. Our results examine sensitivity to various power caps. Performance under very low power caps is difficult for any power management system. In addition, PUPiL provides consistent performance improvements in both single and multiapp scenarios. Further, the use of diverse workloads demonstrates that some applications achieve high performance with RAPL alone, while others need the greater flexibility of PUPiL's hybrid approach.

In a feedback based system, overhead can take two forms: 1) the number of measurements that need to be taken before the system converges and 2) the impact on the converged system. Our results account for both forms of overhead. All

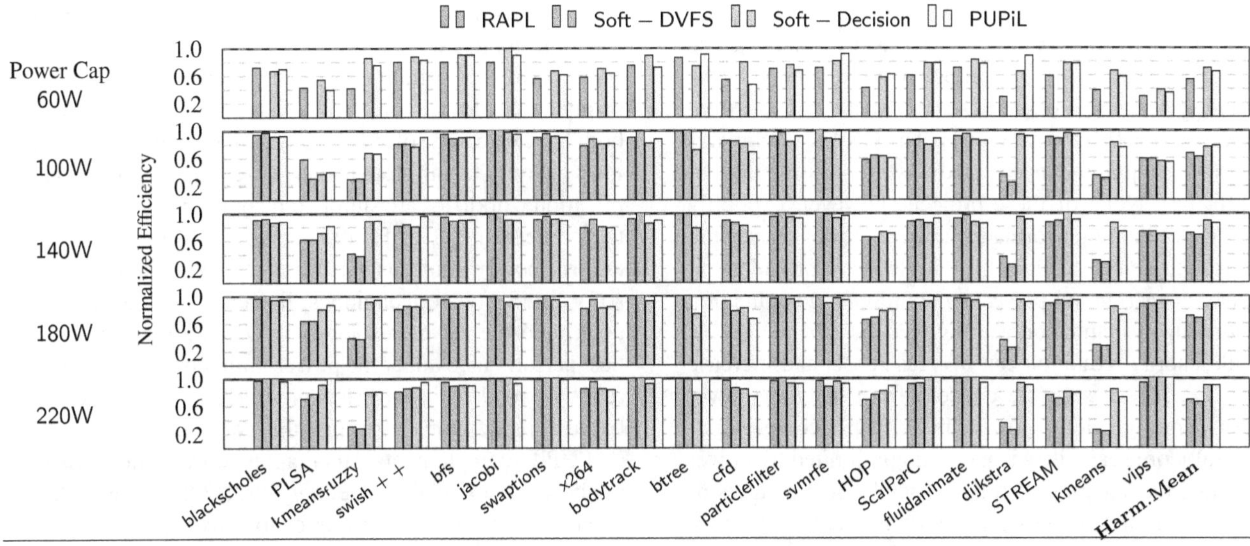

Figure 7. Energy efficiency of several power control techniques normalized to optimal.

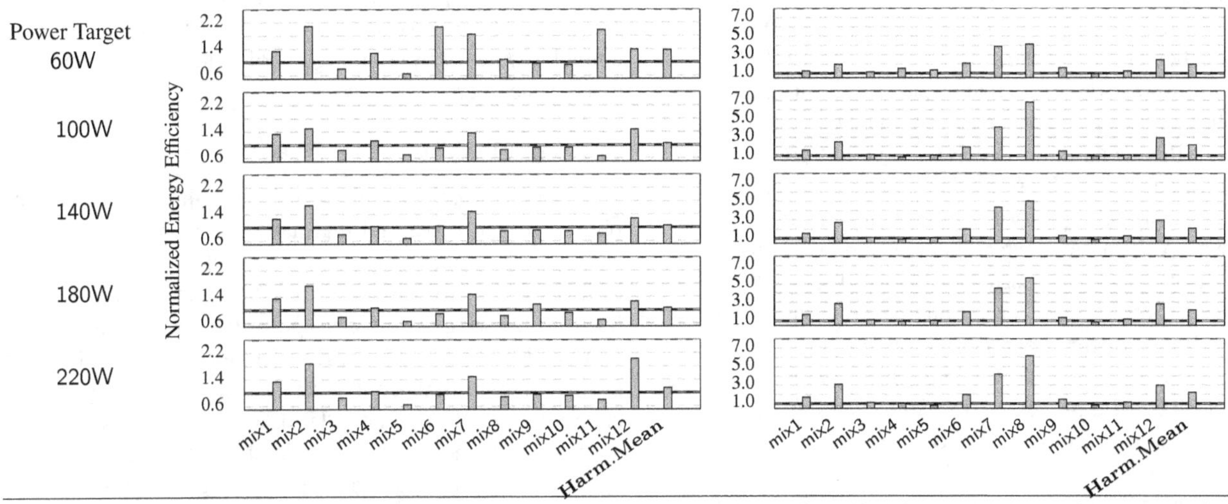

Figure 8. Ratio of PUPiL to RAPL energy efficiency in cooperative (left) and oblivious (right) multiapp scenarios.

reported results include the power and performance impact of the power capping systems themselves. The first type of overhead is measured directly in terms of settling times shown in Fig. 4. Both software approaches have very high, likely unusably high, overhead by this metric. The second type of overhead is accounted for by the comparison to optimal in Fig. 3. This figure shows that the performance impact of the PUPiL runtime system is acceptable in that PUPiL produces the closest to optimal performance.

6. Related Work

As power and energy become first order concerns of computing systems, a number of approaches have been proposed for managing these critical issues. Some approaches focus on minimizing energy, which can reduce costs in data centers and servers [25, 35, 47, 58, 63] or increase battery life in mobile and embedded platforms [15, 20, 26, 30, 39, 46, 56, 64]. These techniques provide performance guarantees (*e.g.,* for meeting quality-of-service or real-time requirements) and minimize power consumption or energy, but they do not provide power guarantees and cannot implement power caps.

To help facilitate energy management, several OS projects have added operating system support for monitoring and allocated energy. The Quanto project facilitates tracking energy usage in networked embedded devices [16]. The Cinder OS allows energy usage to be tracked and allocated across multiple applications in a system [45]. The Koala project also allows energy to be tracked and allocated while supporting several different policies for optimizing energy and performance [51]. Similarly, *power containers* support fine-grain tailoring of heterogeneous resources to varying workloads [48]. LEO is a hierarchical Bayesian learning framework that produces extremely accurate estimates of an application's performance and power consumption [38]. The Coop-I/O project allows applications to coordinate with the operating system to schedule I/O operations in the most energy efficient manner possible [61]. The GRACE OS meets performance requirements for media while minimizing energy [56, 64]. None of these projects, however, explicitly support maximizing performance under a power constraint, which is the subject of this paper. JouleGuard provides energy guarantees (but not power) by coordinating application behavior with system resource usage [20].

While energy reduction can decrease costs and increase battery life, it is a separate concern from meeting power limits. Operating within power limits has become essential as multicore scalability is increasingly limited by power and thermal management [11, 57]. The physical realities of power dissipation in modern processors have led to hardware designs characterized by *dark silicon*. That is, modern processors cannot physically power all transistors at their maximum speed without damage. Thus, some of those transistors are kept dark (meaning they are not powered at all) or dim (meaning they are powered at less than full speed) [53].

These physical realities create a need to limit processor power dissipation. This concern is important enough that Intel's SandyBridge and later processors support power management in hardware [7]. A number software systems have also been proposed to perform power control or *capping*.

Cluster level solutions which guarantee power consumption include those proposed by Wang et al. [59] and Raghavendra et al. [42]. These approaches require some node-level power capper and node-level systems have been developed to manage different individual components including DVFS for a processor (the Soft-DVFS approach in our evaluation) [31], per-core DVFS in a multicore [29], processor idle-time [17, 65], and DRAM [10].

Several researchers have noted that coordinating multiple components provides greater performance under a power cap than management of a single component in isolation [1, 19, 22, 34, 35, 41]. Thus, approaches have been proposed which provide power guarantees while increasing performance through coordinated management of multiple components, including processor and DRAM [5, 8, 9, 14, 32, 46], processors speed and core allocation [6, 44], combining DVFS and scheduling [43, 62], memory and disk speed [33] and combining DVFS and process placement [36]. The VirtualPower project coordinates power management, virtual machine placement, and server consolidation to meet power constraints in a virtualized data center [41]. Despite differences in mechanisms, these techniques all solve a common problem: select the highest performance set of resources that respect a given power limit. All of these projects found higher performance is available through the coordination of multiple resources. With these results, it is not surprising that a hardware solution alone would not achieve high efficiency for some applications.

We take the position that power management should not solely be the domain of hardware, but must be supported by both hardware and software coordinated through the operating system.. The different resources required by different application workloads are simply too complicated for hardware to handle alone [12]. Hardware should be used to quickly enforce power limits, as hardware can simply act faster than software. Software techniques, however, should be used to determine the set of resources to activate that achieve the best performance under the power limit, considering the current workload. This paper has presented a general, decision-based approach for performing this coordination.

PUPiL complements other approaches which schedule applications to minimize energy [23, 37, 60, 66]. PUPiL determines what set of resources to activate, but it does not explicitly assign those resources to applications. Instead, it lets the underlying operating system scheduler perform that work. In this paper, that scheduler was simply the default Linux scheduler. It is likely that further performance gains could be achieved by coupling PUPiL with advanced energy-aware schedulers.

7. Conclusion

This paper investigates hardware and software power capping techniques. We find that hardware techniques provide significantly faster response time – quickly enforcing power limits – while software can provide much greater flexibility – by tailoring resource usage to the current application workload. We have used these observations to formulate and evaluate a hybrid hardware/software power capping system called PUPiL. We evaluate PUPiL and compared it to a pure software approach and to Intel's state-of-the-art hardware approach. Across a number of power targets and workloads, we find that PUPiL achieves nearly the same response time as the hardware approach and the flexibility of the software approach. In both single and cooperative multi-application workloads, PUPiL provides at least 18% greater mean performance than RAPL. In oblivious multi-application workloads, PUPiL provides at least $2.4\times$ the mean performance. We conclude that delivering performance under a power cap cannot be left to hardware alone, but requires the cooperation of both hardware and software. We have developed one such cooperative approach and released the code and test cases so that others can use it, compare against it, or extend it.

Acknowledgments We are grateful to the anonymous reviewers whose suggestions improved the paper. The effort on this project is funded by the U.S. Government under the DARPA BRASS program, by the Dept. of Energy under DOE DE-AC02-06CH11357, by the NSF under CCF 1439156, and by a DOE Early Career Award.

References

[1] V. Anagnostopoulou, S. Biswas, H. Saadeldeen, R. Bianchini, T. Yang, D. Franklin, and F. Chong. "Power-Aware Resource Allocation for CPU- and Memory-Intense Internet Services". In: *E2DC*. 2012.

[2] K. Bergman, S. Borkar, D. Campbell, W. Carlson, W. Dally, M. Denneau, P. Franzon, W. Harrod, J. Hiller, S. Karp, S. Keckler, D. Klein, R. Lucas, M. Richards, A. Scarpelli, S. Scott, A. Snavely, T. Sterling, R. S. Williams, K. Yelick, K. Bergman, S. Borkar, D. Campbell, W. Carlson, W. Dally, M. Denneau, P. Franzon, W. Harrod, J. Hiller, S. Keckler, D. Klein, P. Kogge, R. S. Williams, and K. Yelick. *ExaScale Computing Study: Technology Challenges in Achieving Exascale Systems Peter Kogge, Editor & Study Lead*. 2008.

[3] C. Bienia, S. Kumar, J. P. Singh, and K. Li. "The PARSEC Benchmark Suite: Characterization and Architectural Implications". In: *PACT*. 2008.

[4] S. Che, M. Boyer, J. Meng, D. Tarjan, J. W. Sheaffer, S.-H. Lee, and K. Skadron. "Rodinia: A Benchmark Suite for Heterogeneous Computing". In: *IISWC*. 2009.

[5] J. Chen and L. K. John. "Predictive coordination of multiple on-chip resources for chip multiprocessors". In: *ICS*. 2011.

[6] R. Cochran, C. Hankendi, A. K. Coskun, and S. Reda. "Pack & Cap: adaptive DVFS and thread packing under power caps". In: *MICRO*. 2011.

[7] H. David, E. Gorbatov, U. R. Hanebutte, R. Khanna, and C. Le. "RAPL: Memory Power Estimation and Capping". In: *ISLPED*. 2010.

[8] Q. Deng, D. Meisner, A. Bhattacharjee, T. F. Wenisch, and R. Bianchini. "CoScale: Coordinating CPU and Memory System DVFS in Server Systems". In: *MICRO*. 2012.

[9] Q. Deng, D. Meisner, A. Bhattacharjee, T. F. Wenisch, and R. Bianchini. "MultiScale: memory system DVFS with multiple memory controllers". In: *ISLPED*. 2012.

[10] B. Diniz, D. Guedes, W. Meira Jr., and R. Bianchini. "Limiting the power consumption of main memory". In: *ISCA*. 2007.

[11] H. Esmaeilzadeh, E. Blem, R. St. Amant, K. Sankaralingam, and D. Burger. "Dark silicon and the end of multicore scaling". In: *ISCA*. 2011.

[12] H. Esmaeilzadeh, T. Cao, X. Yang, S. M. Blackburn, and K. S. McKinley. "Looking Back and Looking Forward: Power, Performance, and Upheaval". In: *Commun. ACM* 55.7 (July 2012), pp. 105–114.

[13] S. Eyerman and L. Eeckhout. "Restating the Case for Weighted-IPC Metrics to Evaluate Multiprogram Workload Performance". In: *Computer Architecture Letters* 13.2 (2014), pp. 93–96. ISSN: 1556-6056. DOI: 10.1109/L-CA.2013.9.

[14] W. Felter, K. Rajamani, T. Keller, and C. Rusu. "A performance-conserving approach for reducing peak power consumption in server systems". In: *ICS*. 2005.

[15] J. Flinn and M. Satyanarayanan. "Energy-aware adaptation for mobile applications". In: *SOSP*. 1999.

[16] R. Fonseca, P. Dutta, P. Levis, and I. Stoica. "Quanto: Tracking Energy in Networked Embedded Systems". In: *OSDI*. 2008.

[17] A. Gandhi, M. Harchol-Balter, R. Das, C. Lefurgy, and J. Kephart. "Power capping via forced idleness". In: *Workshop on Energy-Efficient Design*. Austin, TX, 2009.

[18] J. L. Hellerstein, Y. Diao, S. Parekh, and D. M. Tilbury. *Feedback Control of Computing Systems*. John Wiley & Sons, 2004.

[19] U. Hoelzle and L. A. Barroso. *The Datacenter as a Computer: An Introduction to the Design of Warehouse-Scale Machines*. 1st. Morgan and Claypool Publishers, 2009.

[20] H. Hoffmann. "JouleGuard: Energy Guarantees for Approximate Applications". In: *SOSP*. 2015.

[21] H. Hoffmann, J. Eastep, M. D. Santambrogio, J. E. Miller, and A. Agarwal. "Application heartbeats: a generic interface for specifying program performance and goals in autonomous computing environments". In: *ICAC*. 2010.

[22] H. Hoffmann and M. Maggio. "PCP: A Generalized Approach to Optimizing Performance Under Power Constraints through Resource Management". In: *ICAC*. 2014.

[23] H. Hoffmann, M. Maggio, M. D. Santambrogio, A. Leva, and A. Agarwal. "A Generalized Software Framework for Accurate and Efficient Managment of Performance Goals". In: *EMSOFT*. 2013.

[24] H. Hoffmann, S. Sidiroglou, M. Carbin, S. Misailovic, A. Agarwal, and M. Rinard. "Dynamic Knobs for Responsive Power-Aware Computing". In: *ASPLOS*. 2011.

[25] T. Horvath, T. Abdelzaher, K. Skadron, and X. Liu. "Dynamic Voltage Scaling in Multitier Web Servers with End-to-End Delay Control". In: *Computers, IEEE Transactions on* 56.4 (2007).

[26] C. Imes, D. H. K. Kim, M. Maggio, and H. Hoffmann. "POET: A Portable Approach to Minimizing Energy Under Soft Real-time Constraints". In: *RTAS*. 2015.

[27] T. Instruments. http://www.ti.com/product/ina231.

[28] S. Iqbal, Y. Liang, and H. Grahn. "ParMiBench - An Open-Source Benchmark for Embedded Multiprocessor Systems". In: *Computer Architecture Letters* 9.2 (2010). ISSN: 1556-6056. DOI: 10.1109/L-CA.2010.14.

[29] C. Isci, A. Buyuktosunoglu, C.-Y. Cher, P. Bose, and M. Martonosi. "An Analysis of Efficient Multi-Core Global Power Management Policies: Maximizing Performance for a Given Power Budget". In: *MICRO*. 2006.

[30] M. Kim, M.-O. Stehr, C. Talcott, N. Dutt, and N. Venkatasubramanian. "xTune: A Formal Methodology for Cross-layer Tuning of Mobile Embedded Systems". In: *ACM Trans. Embed. Comput. Syst.* 11.4 (Jan. 2013).

[31] C. Lefurgy, X. Wang, and M. Ware. "Power capping: a prelude to power shifting". In: *Cluster Computing* 11.2 (2008).

[32] X. Li, R. Gupta, S. V. Adve, and Y. Zhou. "Cross-component energy management: Joint adaptation of processor and memory". In: *ACM Trans. Archit. Code Optim.* 4.3 (2007).

[33] X. Li, Z. Li, Y. Zhou, and S. Adve. "Performance directed energy management for main memory and disks". In: *Trans. Storage* 1.3 (2005).

[34] M. Maggio, H. Hoffmann, M. D. S. an d Anant Agarwal, and A. Leva. "Power optimization in embedded systems via feedback control of resource allocation". In: *IEEE Transactions on Control Systems Technology (to appear)* ().

[35] D. Meisner, C. M. Sadler, L. A. Barroso, W.-D. Weber, and T. F. Wenisch. "Power management of online data-intensive services". In: *ISCA* (2011).

[36] A. Merkel and F. Bellosa. "Balancing power consumption in multiprocessor systems". In: *EuroSys*. 2006.

[37] A. Merkel, J. Stoess, and F. Bellosa. "Resource-conscious scheduling for energy efficiency on multicore processors". In: *EuroSys*. 2010.

[38] N. Mishra, H. Zhang, J. D. Lafferty, and H. Hoffmann. "A Probabilistic Graphical Model-based Approach for Minimizing Energy Under Performance Constraints". In: *ASPLOS*. 2015.

[39] S. Mohapatra, R. Cornea, H. Oh, K. Lee, M. Kim, N. Dutt, R. Gupta, A. Nicolau, S. Shukla, and N. Venkatasubramanian. "A cross-layer approach for power-performance optimization in distributed mobile systems". In: *IPDPS*. 2005.

[40] R. Narayanan, B. Ozisikyilmaz, J. Zambreno, G. Memik, and A. Choudhary. "MineBench: A Benchmark Suite for Data Mining Workloads". In: *IISWC*. 2006.

[41] R. Nathuji and K. Schwan. "VirtualPower: coordinated power management in virtualized enterprise systems". In: *SOSP*. 2007.

[42] R. Raghavendra, P. Ranganathan, V. Talwar, Z. Wang, and X. Zhu. "No "power" struggles: coordinated multi-level power management for the data center". In: *ASPLOS*. 2008.

[43] K. K. Rangan, G.-Y. Wei, and D. Brooks. "Thread motion: fine-grained power management for multi-core systems". In: *ISCA*. 2009.

[44] S. Reda, R. Cochran, and A. Coskun. "Adaptive Power Capping for Servers with Multithreaded Workloads". In: *Micro, IEEE* 32.5 (2012).

[45] A. Roy, S. M. Rumble, R. Stutsman, P. Levis, D. Mazières, and N. Zeldovich. "Energy Management in Mobile Devices with the Cinder Operating System". In: *EuroSys*. 2011.

[46] R. Sasanka, C. J. Hughes, and S. V. Adve. "Joint Local and Global Hardware Adaptations for Energy". In: *ASPLOS*. 2002.

[47] A. Sharifi, S. Srikantaiah, A. K. Mishra, M. Kandemir, and C. R. Das. "METE: meeting end-to-end QoS in multicores through system-wide resource management". In: *SIGMETRICS*. 2011.

[48] K. Shen, A. Shriraman, S. Dwarkadas, X. Zhang, and Z. Chen. "Power Containers: An OS Facility for Fine-grained Power and Energy Management on Multicore Servers". In: *ASPLOS*. 2013.

[49] Y. Shin, K. Shin, P. Kenkare, R. Kashyap, H.-J. Lee, D. Seo, B. Millar, Y. Kwon, R. Iyengar, M.-S. Kim, A. Chowdhury, S.-I. Bae, I. Hon, W. Jeong, A. Lindner, U. Cho, K. Hawkins, J. Son, and S. Hwang. "28nm High- Metal-Gate Heterogeneous Quad-Core CPUs for High-Performance and Energy-Efficient Mobile Application Processor". In: *ISSCC*. 2013.

[50] Y. Sinangil, S. M. Neuman, M. E. Sinangi, N. Ickes, G. Bezerra, E. Lau, J. E. Miller, H. Hoffmann, S. Devadas, and A. P. Chandraksan. "A Self-Aware Processor SoC using Energy Monitors Integrated into Power Converters for Self-Adaptation". In: *VLSI Symposium*. 2014.

[51] D. C. Snowdon, E. Le Sueur, S. M. Petters, and G. Heiser. "Koala: A Platform for OS-level Power Management". In: *EuroSys*. 2009.

[52] B. Sprunt. "The basics of performance-monitoring hardware". In: *IEEE Micro* 22.4 (2002).

[53] M. B. Taylor. "Is Dark Silicon Useful? Harnessing the Four Horesemen of the Coming Dark Silicon Apocalypse". In: *Design Automation Conference*. 2012.

[54] E. Team. *Key Challenges for Exascale OS/R*. Online document, `https://collab.mcs.anl.gov/display/exaosr/Challenges1`.

[55] P. Team. Online document, `http://icl.cs.utk.edu/papi/`.

[56] V. Vardhan, W. Yuan, A. F. H. III, S. V. Adve, R. Kravets, K. Nahrstedt, D. G. Sachs, and D. L. Jones. "GRACE-2: integrating fine-grained application adaptation with global adaptation for saving energy". In: *IJES* 4.2 (2009).

[57] G. Venkatesh, J. Sampson, N. Goulding, S. Garcia, V. Bryksin, J. Lugo-Martinez, S. Swanson, and M. B. Taylor. "Conservation cores: reducing the energy of mature computations". In: *ASPLOS*. 2010.

[58] A. Verma, G. Dasgupta, T. K. Nayak, P. De, and R. Kothari. "Server workload analysis for power minimization using consolidation". In: *USENIX Annual technical conference*. 2009.

[59] X. Wang, M. Chen, and X. Fu. "MIMO Power Control for High-Density Servers in an Enclosure". In: *IEEE Transactions on Parallel and Distributed Systems* 21.10 (2010).

[60] M. Weiser, B. B. Welch, A. J. Demers, and S. Shenker. "Scheduling for Reduced CPU Energy". In: *OSDI*. 1994.

[61] A. Weissel, B. Beutel, and F. Bellosa. "Cooperative I/O: A Novel I/O Semantics for Energy-Aware Applications". In: *OSDI*. 2002.

[62] J. A. Winter, D. H. Albonesi, and C. A. Shoemaker. "Scalable thread scheduling and global power management for heterogeneous many-core architectures". In: *PACT*. 2010.

[63] Q. Wu, P. Juang, M. Martonosi, and D. W. Clark. "Formal online methods for voltage/frequency control in multiple clock domain microprocessors". In: *ASPLOS*. 2004.

[64] W. Yuan and K. Nahrstedt. "Energy-efficient soft realtime CPU scheduling for mobile multimedia systems". In: *SOSP*. 2003.

[65] X. Zhang, R. Zhong, S. Dwarkadas, and K. Shen. "A Flexible Framework for Throttling-Enabled Multicore Management (TEMM)". In: *ICPP*. 2012.

[66] S. Zhuravlev, J. C. Saez, S. Blagodurov, A. Fedorova, and M. Prieto. "Survey of Energy-Cognizant Scheduling Techniques". In: *IEEE Trans. Parallel Distrib. Syst.* 24.7 (2013), pp. 1447–1464. DOI: 10.1109/TPDS.2012.20. URL: http://doi.ieeecomputersociety.org/10.1109/TPDS.2012.20.

The Computational Sprinting Game

Songchun Fan * Seyed Majid Zahedi * Benjamin C. Lee
Duke University
{songchun.fan, seyedmajid.zahedi, benjamin.c.lee}@duke.edu

Abstract

Computational sprinting is a class of mechanisms that boost performance but dissipate additional power. We describe a sprinting architecture in which many, independent chip multiprocessors share a power supply and sprints are constrained by the chips' thermal limits and the rack's power limits. Moreover, we present the computational sprinting game, a multi-agent perspective on managing sprints. Strategic agents decide whether to sprint based on application phases and system conditions. The game produces an equilibrium that improves task throughput for data analytics workloads by 4-6× over prior greedy heuristics and performs within 90% of an upper bound on throughput from a globally optimized policy.

1. Introduction

Modern datacenters oversubscribe their power supplies to enhance performance and efficiency. A conservative datacenter that deploys servers according to their expected power draw will under-utilize provisioned power, operate power supplies at sub-optimal loads, and forgo opportunities for higher performance. In contrast, efficient datacenters deploy more servers than it can power fully and rely on varying computational load across servers to modulate demand for power [18]. Such a strategy requires responsive mechanisms for delivering power to the computation that needs it most.

Computational sprinting is a class of mechanisms that supply additional power for short durations to enhance performance. In chip multiprocessors, for example, sprints activate additional cores and boost their voltage and frequency. Although originally proposed for mobile systems [36, 37], sprinting has found numerous applications in datacenter systems. It can accelerate computation for complex tasks or accommodate transient activity spikes [41, 49].

The system architecture determines sprint duration and frequency. Sprinting multiprocessors generate extra heat, absorbed by thermal packages and phase change materials [36, 41], and require time to release this heat between sprints. At scale, uncoordinated multiprocessors that sprint simultaneously could overwhelm a rack or cluster's power supply. Uninterruptible power supplies reduce the risk of tripping circuit breakers and triggering power emergencies. But the system requires time to recharge batteries between sprints. Given these physical constraints in chip multiprocessors and the datacenter rack, sprinters require recovery time. Thus, sprinting mechanisms couple performance opportunities with management constraints.

We face fundamental management questions when servers sprint independently but share a power supply – which processors should sprint and when should they sprint? Each processor's workload derives extra performance from sprinting that depends on its computational phase. Ideally, sprinters would be the processors that benefit most from boosted capability at any given time. Moreover, the number of sprinters would be small enough to avoid power emergencies, which constrain future sprints. Policies that achieve these goals are prerequisites for sprinting to full advantage.

We present the computational sprinting game to manage a collection of sprinters. The sprinting architecture, which defines the sprinting mechanism as well as power and cooling constraints, determines rules of the game. A strategic agent, representing a multiprocessor and its workload, independently decides whether to sprint at the beginning of an epoch. The agent anticipates her action's outcomes, knowing that the chip must cool before sprinting again. Moreover, she analyzes system dynamics, accounting for competitors' decisions and risk of power emergencies.

We find the equilibrium in the computational sprinting game, which permits distributed management. In an equilibrium, no agent can benefit by deviating from her optimal strategy. The datacenter relies on agents' incentives to decentralize management as each agent self-enforces her part of the sprinting policy. Decentralized equilibria allow datacenters to avoid high communication costs and unwieldy enforcement mechanisms in centralized management. More-

*These authors contributed equally to this work.

ASPLOS '16 April 2–6, 2016, Atlanta, Georgia, USA.

DOI: http://dx.doi.org/10.1145/2872362.2872383

over, equilibria outperform prior heuristics. In summary, we present the following contributions:

- **Spriting Architecture (§2).** We present a system of independent sprinters that share power – a rack of chip multiprocessors. Sprinting multiprocessors activate additional cores and increase clock rates. Sprints are constrained by chips' thermal limits and rack power limits.
- **Sprinting Game (§3).** We define a repeated game in which strategic agents sprint based on application phases and system conditions. The game divides time into epochs and agents play repeatedly. Actions in the present affect performance and the ability to sprint in the future.
- **Dynamics and Strategies (§4).** We design agents who sprint when the expected utility from doing so exceeds a threshold. We devise an algorithm that optimizes each agent's threshold strategy. The strategies produce an equilibrium in which no agent benefits by deviating from her optimal threshold.
- **Performance (§5–§6).** We evaluate the game for Spark-based datacenter applications, which exhibit diversity in phase behavior and utility from sprinting. The game increases task throughput by 4-6× when compared to prior heuristics in which agents sprint greedily.

2. The Sprinting Architecture

We present a sprinting architecture for chip multiprocessors in datacenters. Multiprocessors sprint by activating additional cores and increasing their voltage and frequency. Datacenter applications, with their abundant task parallelism, scale across additional cores as they become available. We focus on applications built atop the Spark framework, which extends Hadoop for memory caching [46]. In Figure 1, Spark benchmarks perform 2-7× better on a sprinting multiprocessor, but dissipates 1.8× the power. Power produces heat.

Sprinters require infrastructure to manage heat and power. First, the chip multiprocessor's thermal package and heat sink must absorb surplus heat during a sprint [36, 40]. Second, the datacenter rack must employ batteries to guard against power emergencies caused by a surplus of sprinters on a shared power supply. Third, the system must implement management policies that determine which chips sprint.

2.1 Chip Multiprocessor Support

A chip multiprocessor's maximum power level depends on its thermal package and heat sink. Given conventional heat sinks, thermal constraints are the primary determinant of multiprocessor performance, throttling throughput and overriding constraints from power delivery and off-chip bandwidth [31]. More expensive heat sinks employ phase change materials (PCMs), which increase thermal capacitance, to absorb and dissipate excess heat [37, 40]. The quality of the thermal package, as measured by its thermal capacitance and conductance, determines parameters of the sprinting game.

The choice of thermal package dictates the maximum duration of a sprint [40]. Whereas water, air and foam enable sprint durations on the order of seconds [37], PCMs enable durations on the order of minutes if not hours [38, 40, 44]. Our sprint architecture employs paraffin wax, which is attractive for its high thermal capacitance and tunable melting point when blended with polyolefins [35]. We estimate a chip with paraffin wax can sprint with durations on the order of 150 seconds.

After a sprint, the thermal package must release its heat before the chip can sprint again. The average cooling duration, denoted as Δt_{cool}, is the time required before the PCM returns to ambient temperature. The rate at which the PCM dissipates heat depends on its melting point and the thermal resistance between the material and the ambient [35]. Both factors can be engineered and, with paraffin wax, we estimate a cooling duration on the order of 300 seconds, twice the sprint's duration.

Different types of workloads may demand different sprint durations. Sprints for online queries requires tens of milliseconds or less [28]. Sprints for parallel workloads requires seconds or more [37]. And those for warehouse-scale thermal management requires support for hours [41]. In this paper, we study data analytics applications that would prefer to sprint indefinitely. In this setting, the primary determinant of a sprint's duration is the thermal package.

2.2 Datacenter Support

At scale, servers within the same rack share a power supply. Chip multiprocessors draw current from a shared power distribution unit (PDU) that is connected to a branch circuit and protected by a circuit breaker (CB). Datacenter architects deploy servers to oversubscribe branch circuits for efficiency. Oversubscription utilizes a larger fraction of the facility's provisioned power for computation. But it relies on power capping and varied computational load across servers to avoid tripping circuit breakers or violating contracts with utility providers [18, 19]. Although sprints boost computation for complex queries and during peak loads [28, 49], the risk of a power emergency increases with the number of sprinters in a power capped datacenter.

Circuit Breakers and Trip Curves. Figure 2 presents the circuit breaker's trip curve, which specifies how sprint duration and power combine to determine whether the breaker trips. The trip time corresponds to the sprint's duration. Longer sprints increase the probability of tripping the breaker. The current draw corresponds to the number of simultaneous sprints as each sprinter contributes to the load above rated current. Higher currents increase the probability of tripping the breaker. Thus, the tolerance for sprints depends on their duration and power. The breaker dictates the number of sprinters supported by the datacenter rack.

Figure 3 associates the number of sprinters to the tripping probability for a given trip time. Let n_S denote the number

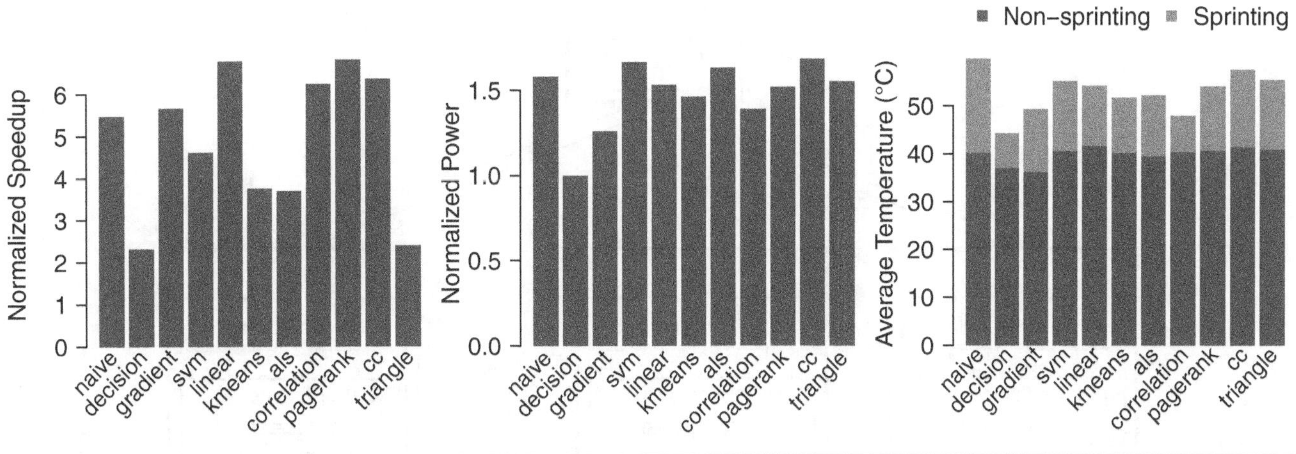

Figure 1. Normalized speedup, power, and temperature for varied Spark benchmarks when sprinting. Nominal operation supplies three cores at 1.2GHz. Sprint supplies twelve cores at 2.7GHz.

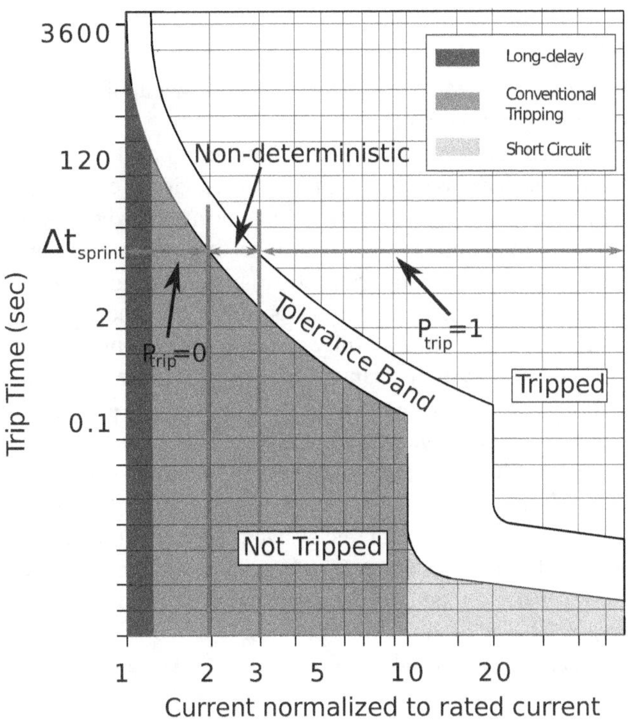

Figure 2. Typical trip curve of a circuit breaker [19].

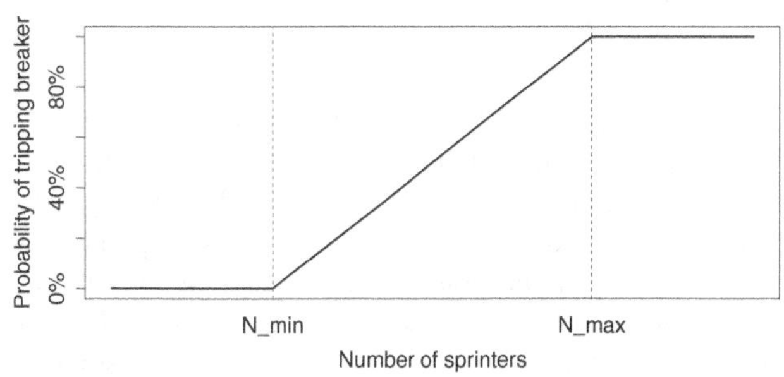

Figure 3. Probability of tripping the rack's circuit breaker.

of sprinters and let P_{trip} denote the probability of tripping the breaker. The breaker occupies one of the following regions:

- **Non-Tripped.** P_{trip} is zero when $n_S < N_{\min}$
- **Non-Deterministic.** P_{trip} is a non-decreasing function of n_S when $N_{\min} \leq n_S < N_{\max}$
- **Tripped.** P_{trip} is one when $n_S \geq N_{\max}$

Note that $N_{\min}$ and $N_{\max}$ depend on the breaker's trip curve and the application's demand for power when sprinting.

Suppose a sprinter dissipates twice as much power as a non-sprinter, as in Spark applications on chip multiprocessors. We find that the breaker does not trip when less than 25% of the chips sprint and definitely trips when more than 75% of the chips sprint. In other words, $N_{\min} = 0.25N$ and $N_{\max} = 0.75N$. We consider UL489 circuit breakers from Rockwell Automation, which can be overloaded to 125-175% of rated current for a 150 second sprint [9, 45, 49].

Uninterruptible Power Supplies. When the breaker trips and resets, power distribution switches from the branch circuit to the uninterruptible power supply (UPS) [22, 23]. The rack augments power delivery with batteries to complete sprints in progress. Lead acid batteries support discharge times of 5-120 minutes, long enough to support the duration of a sprint. After completing sprints and resetting the breaker, servers resume computation on the branch circuit.

However, servers are forbidden from sprinting again until UPS batteries have been recharged. Sprints before recovery would compromise server availability and increase vulnerability to power emergencies. Moreover, frequent discharges without recharges would shorten battery life. The average recovery duration, denoted by $\Delta t_{\text{recover}}$, depends on the UPS discharge depth and recharging time. A battery

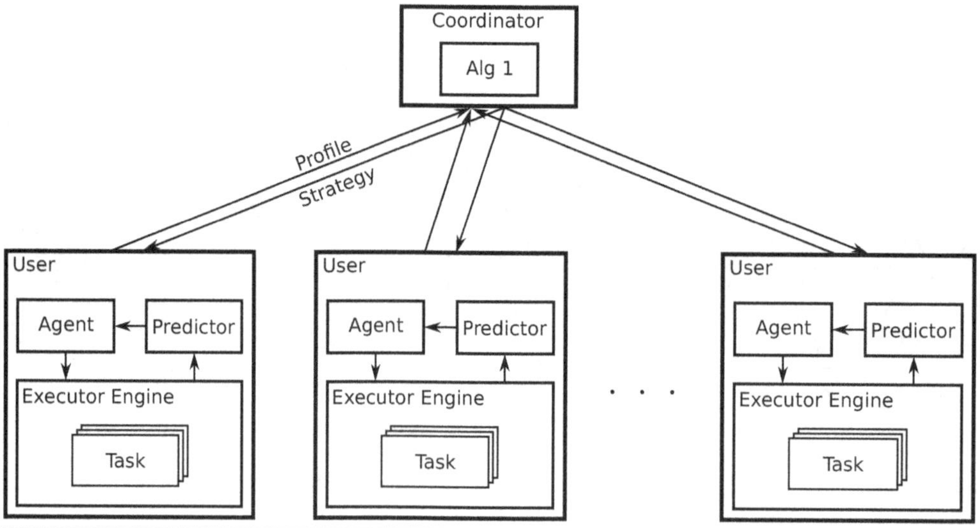

Figure 4. Users deploy task executors and agents that decide when to sprint. Agents send performance profiles to a coordinator and receives optimized sprinting strategies.

can be recharged to 85% capacity in 8-10× the discharge time [10], which corresponds to 8-10× the sprint duration.

Servers are permitted to sprint again after recharge and recovery. However, if every chip multiprocessor in the rack were to sprint simultaneously and immediately after recovery, they would trigger another power emergency. The rack must stagger the distribution of sprinting permissions to avoid dI/dt problems.

2.3 Power Management

Figure 4 illustrates the management framework for a rack of sprinting chip multiprocessors. The framework supports policies that pursue the performance of sprints while avoiding system instability. Unmanaged and excessive sprints may trip breakers, trigger emergencies, and degrade performance at scale. The framework achieves its objectives with strategic agents and coarse-grained coordination.

Users and Agents. Each user deploys three run-time components: executor, agent, and predictor. Executors provide clean abstractions, encapsulating applications that could employ different software frameworks [27]. The executor supports task-parallel computation by dividing an application into tasks, constructing a task dependence graph, and scheduling tasks dynamically based on available resources. Task scheduling is particularly important as it increases parallelism when sprinting powers-on cores and tolerates faults when cooling and recovery powers-off cores.

Agents are strategic and selfish entities that act on users' behalf. They decide whether to sprint by continuously analyzing fine-grained application phases. Because sprints are followed by cooling and recovery, an agent sprints judiciously and targets application phases that benefit most from extra capability. Agents use predictors that estimate utility from sprinting based on software profiles and hardware counters. Each agent represents a user and her application on a chip multiprocessor.

Coordination. The coordinator collects profiles from all agents and assigns tailored sprinting strategies to each agent. The coordinator interfaces with strategic agents who may attempt to manipulate system outcomes by misreporting profiles or deviating from assigned strategies. Fortunately, our game-theoretic mechanism guards against such behavior.

First, agents will truthfully report their performance profiles. In large systems, game theory provides incentive compatibility, which means that agents cannot improve their utility by misreporting their preferences. The coordinator assigned a tailored strategy to each agent based on system conditions. An agent who misreports her profile has little influence on conditions in a large system. Not only does she fail to affect others, an agent who misreports suffers degraded performance as the coordinator assigns her a poorly suited strategy based on inaccurate profiles.

Second, agents will implement their assigned strategies because the coordinator optimizes those strategies to produce an equilibrium. In equilibrium, every agent implements her strategy and no agent benefits when deviating from it. An equilibrium has compelling implications for management overheads. If each agent knows that every other agent is playing her assigned strategy, she will do the same without further communication with the coordinator. Global communication between agents and the coordinator is infrequent and occurs only when system profiles change. Local communication between each user's run-time components (*i.e.*, executor, agent, predictor) is frequent but employs inexpensive, inter-process mechanisms. In effect, an equilibrium permits the distributed enforcement of sprinting policies.

In contrast, the centralized enforcement of coordinated policies poses several challenges. First, it requires frequent and global communication as each agent decides whether to sprint by querying the coordinator at the start of each epoch. The length of an epoch is short and corresponds to sprint duration. Moreover, without equilibria, agents with kernel privileges could ignore prescribed policies, sprint at will, and cause power emergencies that harm all agents. Avoiding such outcomes in a multi-tenant datacenter would require a distributed runtime. The runtime, not the agent, would have kernel privileges for power management, introducing an abstraction layer and overheads.

3. The Sprinting Game

We present a computational sprinting game, which governs demands for power and manages system dynamics. We design a dynamic game that divides time into epochs and asks agents to play repeatedly. Agents represent chip multiprocessors that share a power supply. Each agent chooses to sprint independently, pursuing benefits in the current epoch and estimating repercussions in future epochs. Multiple agents can sprint simultaneously, but they risk tripping the circuit breaker and triggering power emergencies that harm global performance.

3.1 Game Formulation

The game considers N agents who run task-parallel applications on N chip multiprocessors. Each agent computes in either normal or sprinting mode. The normal mode uses a fraction of the cores at low frequency whereas sprints use all cores at high frequency. Sprints rely on the executor to increase task parallelism and exploit extra cores. In this paper, for example, we consider three cores at 1.2GHz in normal mode and twelve cores at 2.7GHz in a sprint.

The repeated game divides time into epochs. The duration of an epoch corresponds to the duration of a safe sprint, which neither overheats the chip nor trips the circuit breaker. An agent's utility from a sprint varies across epochs according to her application's phases. Agents apply a discount factor $\delta < 1$ to future utilities as, all else being equal, they prefer performance sooner rather than later.

3.2 Agent States

At any given time, an agent occupies one of three states—active (A), chip cooling (C), and rack recovery (R)—according to her actions and those of others in the rack. An agent's state describes whether she can sprint, and describes how cooling and recovery impose constraints on her actions.

Active (A) – Agent can safely sprint. By default, an agent in an active state operates her chip in normal mode, with a few processor cores running at low frequency. The agent has an option to sprint, which deploys additional cores and raises the frequency. She decides whether to sprint by comparing a sprint's benefits in the current epoch against benefits from deferring the sprint to a future epoch. If the agent sprints, her state in the next epoch is cooling.

Chip Cooling (C) – Agent cannot sprint. After a sprint, an agent remains in the cooling state until excess heat has been dissipated. Cooling requires a number of epochs Δt_{cool}, which depends on the chip's thermal conductance and resistance, the heat sink and cooling technology, and the ambient temperature. An agent in the cooling state stays in this state with probability p_c and returns to the active state with probability $1 - p_c$. Probability p_c is defined so that $1/(1 - p_c) = \Delta t_{\text{cool}}$.

Rack Recovery (R) – Agent cannot sprint. When multiple chips sprint simultaneously, their total current draw may trip the rack's circuit breaker, trigger a power emergency, and require supplemental current from batteries. After an emergency, all agents remain in the recovery state until batteries recharge. Recovery requires a number of epochs $\Delta t_{\text{recover}}$, which depends on the rack's power supply and its battery capacity. Agents in the recovery state stay in this state with probability p_r and return to the active state with probability $1 - p_r$. Probability p_r is defined so that $1/(1 - p_r) = \Delta t_{\text{recover}}$.

In summary, the states describe and enforce system constraints. A chip that sprints must cool before sprinting again. A rack that supports sprints with batteries must recharge those batteries before doing so again. Agents in cooling or recovery states are constrained, but those in active states will sprint strategically.

3.3 Agent Actions and Strategies

Agents have two possible actions — sprint or do not sprint. Strategic agents decide between these actions to maximize their utilities. Each agent's sprinting strategy depends on various factors, including

- agent's state and her utility from sprinting,
- agent's history of sprinting,
- other agents' states,
- other agents' utilities, strategies, and histories.

Sprinting strategies determine the game's performance. Agents that greedily sprint at every opportunity produce several sub-optimal outcomes. First, chips and racks would spend many epochs in cooling and recovery states, respectively, degrading system throughput. Moreover, agents who sprint at the first opportunity constrain themselves in future epochs, during which sprints may be even more beneficial.

In contrast, sophisticated strategies improve agent utility and system performance. Strategic agents sprint during the epochs that benefit most from additional cores and higher frequencies. Moreover, they consider other agents' strategies because the probability of triggering a power emergency and entering the recovery state increases with the number of sprinters. We analyze the game's governing dynamics to optimize each agent's strategy and maximize her performance.

4. Game Dynamics and Agent Strategies

A comprehensive approach to optimizing strategies considers each agent—her state, utility, and history—to determine whether sprinting maximizes her performance given her competitor's strategies and system state. In practice, however, this optimization does not scale to hundreds or thousands of agents.

For tractability, we analyze the population of agents by defining key probability distributions on population behavior. This approach has several dimensions. First, we reason about population dynamics in expectation and consider an "average" agent. Second, we optimize each agent's strategy in response to the population rather than individual competitors. Third, we find an equilibrium in which no agent can perform better by deviating from her optimal strategy.

4.1 Mean Field Equilibrium

The mean field equilibrium (MFE), a concept drawn from economic game theory, is an approximation method used when analyzing individual agents in a large system is intractable [6–8, 26, 29]. With the MFE, we can characterize expected behavior for a population of agents and then optimize each agent's strategy against that expectation. We can reason about the population and neglect individual agents because any one agent has little impact on overall behavior in a large system.

The mean field analysis for the sprinting game focuses on the sprint distribution, which characterizes the number of agents who sprint when the rack is not in the recovery state. In equilibrium, the sprint distribution is stationary and does not change across epochs. In any given epoch, some agents complete a sprint and enter the cooling state while others leave the cooling state and begin a sprint. Yet the number of agents who sprint is unchanged in expectation.

The stationary distribution for the number of sprinters translates into stationary distributions for the rack's current draw and the probability of tripping the circuit breaker – see Figure 3. Given the rack's tripping probability, which concisely describes population dynamics, an agent can formulate her best response and optimize her sprinting strategy to maximize performance.

We find an equilibrium by characterizing a population's statistical distributions, optimizing agents' responses, and simulating game play to update the population. We specify an initial value for the probability of tripping the breaker and iterate as follows.

- **Optimize Sprint Strategy (§4.2).** Given the probability of tripping the breaker P_{trip}, each agent optimizes her sprinting strategy to maximize her performance. She sprints if performance gains from doing so exceed some threshold. Optimizing her strategy means setting her threshold u_T.
- **Characterize Sprint Distribution (§4.3).** Given that each agent sprints according to her threshold u_T, the game characterizes population behavior. It estimates the expected number of sprinters n_S, calculates their demand for power, and updates the probability of tripping the breaker P'_{trip}.
- **Check for Equilibrium.** The game is in equilibrium if $P'_{\text{trip}} = P_{\text{trip}}$. Otherwise, iterate with the new probability of tripping the breaker.

4.2 Optimizing the Sprint Strategy

An agent considers three factors when optimizing her sprinting strategy: the probability of tripping the circuit breaker P_{trip}, her utility from sprinting u, and her state. An agent occupies either the active (A), cooling (C), or recovery (R) state. To maximize expected value and decide whether to sprint, each agent optimizes the following Bellman equation.

$$V(u,\, A) = \max\{V_S(u,\, A),\;\, V_{\neg S}(u,\, A)\} \qquad (1)$$

The Bellman equation quantifies value when an agent acts optimally in every epoch. V_S and $V_{\neg S}$ are the expected values from sprinting and not sprinting, respectively. If $V_S(u,\, A) > V_{\neg S}(u,\, A)$, then sprinting is optimal. The game solves the Bellman equation and identifies actions that maximize value with dynamic programming.

Value in Active State. Sprinting defines a repeated game in which an agent acts in the current epoch and encounters consequences of that action in future epochs. Accordingly, the Bellman equation is recursive and expresses an action's value in terms of benefits in the current epoch plus the discounted value from future epochs.

Suppose an agent in the active state decides to sprint. Her value from sprinting is her immediate utility u plus her discounted utility from future epochs. When she sprints, her future utility is calculated for the chip cooling state $V(C)$ or calculated for the rack recovery state $V(R)$ when her sprint trips the circuit breaker.

$$V_S(u,\, A) = u + \delta\,[V(C)(1 - P_{\text{trip}}) + V(R)P_{\text{trip}}] \qquad (2)$$

On the other hand, an agent who does not sprint will remain in the active state unless other sprinting agents trip the circuit breaker and trigger a power emergency that requires recovery.

$$V_{\neg S}(u,\, A) = \delta\,[V(A)(1 - P_{\text{trip}}) + V(R)P_{\text{trip}}] \qquad (3)$$

We use $V(A)$ to denote an agent's expected value from being in the active state, which depends on an agent's utility from sprinting. The game profiles an application and its time-varying computational phases to obtain a probability density function $f(u)$, which characterizes how often an agent derives utility u from sprinting. With this density, the game estimates expected value.

$$V(A) = \int V(u,\, A)\, f(u)\, du \qquad (4)$$

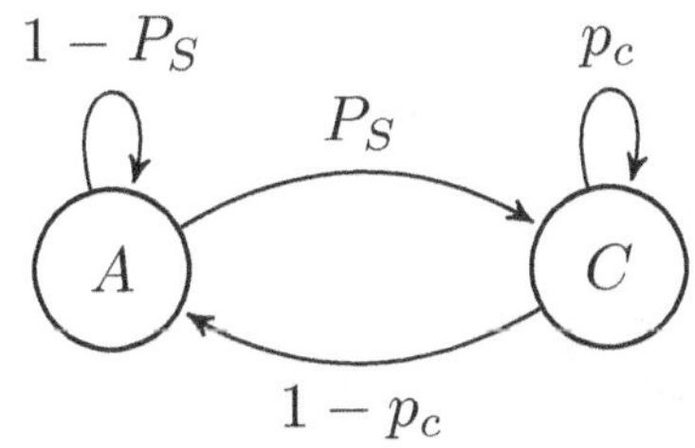

Figure 5. State transitions when agent sprints, chip cools. Assumes an agent is not in recovery.

Value in Cooling and Recovery States. An active agent transitions into cooling and recovery states when she and/or others sprint. Because agents cannot sprint while cooling or recovering, their expected values from these states do not depend on their utility from sprinting.

$$\begin{aligned} V(C) = \;& \delta\;[V(C)p_c + V(A)(1-p_c)]\,(1-P_{\text{trip}}) + \\ & \delta\, V(R) P_{\text{trip}} \qquad (5) \\ V(R) = \;& \delta\;[V(R)p_r + V(A)(1-p_r)] \qquad (6) \end{aligned}$$

Parameters p_c and p_r are technology-specific probabilities of an agent in cooling and recovery states staying in those states. An agent in cooling will remain in this state with probability p_c and become active with probability $1 - p_c$, assuming the rack avoids a power emergency. If the circuit breaker trips, an agent enters recovery. An agent remains in recovery with probability p_r and becomes active with probability $1-p_r$. The game tunes these parameters to reflect the time required for chip cooling after a sprint and for rack recovery after a power emergency – see §2.

Threshold Strategy. An agent should sprint if her utility from doing so is greater than not. But when is this the case? Equation (8), which follows from Equations (2)–(3), states that an agent should sprint if her utility u is greater than her optimal threshold for sprinting u_T.

$$\begin{aligned} V_S(u,\, A) \;&>\; V_{\neg S}(u,\, A) \qquad (7) \\ u \;&>\; \underbrace{\delta\;(V(A) - V(C))\;(1-P_{\text{trip}})}_{u_T} \qquad (8) \end{aligned}$$

Thus, an agent uses threshold u_T to test a sprint's utility. If sprinting improves performance by more than the threshold, an agent should sprint. Applying this strategy in every epoch maximizes expected value across time in the repeated game.

4.3 Characterizing the Sprint Distribution

Given threshold u_T for her strategy, an agent uses her density function on utility to estimate the probability that she sprints, p_s, in a given epoch.

$$p_s = \int_{u_T}^{u_{\max}} f(u)\; du \qquad (9)$$

The probabilities of sprinting (p_s) and cooling (p_c) define a Markov chain that describes each agent's behavior – see Figure 5, which assumes the agent is not in recovery. As agents play their strategies, the Markov chain converges to a stationary distribution in which each agent is active with probability p_A. If N agents play the game, the expected number of sprinters is

$$n_S = p_s \times p_A \times N \qquad (10)$$

As the number of sprinters increases, so does the rack's current draw and the probability of tripping the breaker. Given the expected number of sprinters, the game updates the probability of tripping the breaker according to its trip curve (*e.g.*, Figure 3). Mathematically, the curve is described as follows.

$$P_{\text{trip}} = \begin{cases} 0 & \text{if } n_S < N_{\min} \\ \frac{n_S - N_{\min}}{N_{\max} - N_{\min}} & \text{if } N_{\min} \le n_S \le N_{\max} \\ 1 & \text{if } n_S > N_{\max} \end{cases} \qquad (11)$$

P_{trip} determines n_S, which determines P'_{trip}. If $P_{\text{trip}} = P'_{\text{trip}}$, then agents are playing optimized strategies that produce an equilibrium.

Algorithm 1: Optimizing the Sprint Strategy

```
input : Probability density function for sprinting utilities (f(u))
output: Optimal sprinting threshold (u_T)
j ← 1
P^0_trip ← 1
while P^j_trip not converged do
    u^j_T ← DP solution for Equations (1)–(8) with P^j_trip
    p^j_S ← Equation (9) with f(u), u^j_T
    n^j_S ← Equation (10) with MC solution and P^j_S
    P^{j+1}_trip ← Equation (11)
    j ← j + 1
end
```

4.4 Finding the Equilibrium

When the game begins, agents make initial assumptions about population behavior and the probability of tripping the breaker. Agents optimize their strategies in response to population behavior. Strategies produce sprints that affect the probability of tripping the breaker. Over time, population behavior and agent strategies converge to a stationary distribution, which is consistent across epochs. The game is in equilibrium if the following conditions hold.

- Given tripping probability P_{trip}, the sprinting strategy dictated by threshold u_T is optimal and solves the Bellman equation in Equations (1)–(3).
- Given sprinting strategy u_T, the probability of tripping the circuit breaker is P_{trip} and is calculated by Equations (9)–(11).

In equilibrium, every agent plays her optimal strategy and no agent benefits when deviating from her strategy. In practice,

Table 1. Spark Workloads

Benchmark	Category	Dataset	Data Size
NaiveBayesian	Classification	kdda2010 [43]	2.5G
DecisionTree	Classification	kdda2010	2.5G
GradientBoostedTrees	Classification	kddb2010 [43]	4.8G
SVM	Classification	kdda2010	2.5G
LinearRegression	Classification	kddb2010	4.8G
Kmeans	Clustering	uscensus1990 [1]	327M
ALS	Collaborative Filtering	movielens2015 [2]	325M
Correlation	Statistics	kdda2010	2.5G
PageRank	Graph Processing	wdc2012 [3]	5.3G
ConnectedComponents	Graph Processing	wdc2012	5.3G
TriangleCounting	Graph Processing	wdc2012	5.3G

the coordinator in the management framework finds and maintains an equilibrium with a mix of offline and online analysis.

Offline Analysis. Agents sample epochs and measure utility from sprinting to produce a density function $f(u)$, which characterizes how often an agent sees utility u from sprinting. The coordinator collects agents' density functions, analyzes population dynamics, and tailors sprinting strategies for each agent. Finally, the coordinator assigns optimized strategies to support online sprinting decisions.

Algorithm 1 describes the coordinator's offline analysis. It initializes the probability of tripping the breaker. Then it iteratively analyzes population dynamics to find an equilibrium. Each iteration proceeds in three steps. First, the coordinator optimizes sprinting threshold u_T by solving the dynamic program defined in Equations (1)–(8). Second, it estimates the number of sprinters according to Equation (10). Finally, it updates the probability of tripping the breaker according to Equation (11). The algorithm terminates when thresholds, number of sprinters, and tripping probability are stationary.

The offline algorithm has no performance overhead. The analysis runs periodically to update sprinting strategies and the tripping probability as application mix and system conditions evolve. It does not affect an application's critical path as agents use updated strategies when they become available but need not wait for them.

The algorithm requires little computation. It solves the dynamic program with value-iteration, which has a convergence rate that depends on the discount factor δ. The number of iterations grows polynomially in $(1-\delta)^{-1}$. We implement and run the algorithm on an Intel® Core™ i5 processor with 4GB of memory. The algorithm completes in less than 10s, on average.

Online Strategy. An agent decides whether to sprint at the start of each epoch by estimating a sprint's utility and comparing it against her threshold. Estimation could be implemented in several ways. An agent could use the first few seconds of an epoch to profile her normal and sprinting performance. Alternatively, an agent could use heuristics to estimate utility from additional cores and higher clock rates. For example, task queue occupancy and cache misses are associated with a sprint's impact on task parallelism and instruction throughput, respectively. Comparisons with a threshold are trivial. If an agent decides to sprint, it turns on otherwise disabled cores using CPU-hotplug and increases clock rates using ACPI [39].

5. Experimental Methodology

Servers and Sprints. The agent and its application are pinned to a chip multiprocessor, an Intel® Xeon® E5-2697 v2 that can run at 2.70GHz. Two multiprocessors share 128GB of main memory within a server. An agent runs in normal or sprinting mode. In normal mode, the agent uses three 1.2GHz cores. In sprinting mode, the agent uses twelve 2.7GHz cores. We turn cores on and off with Linux `sysfs`. In principle, sprinting represents any mechanism that performs better but consumes more power.

Workloads. We evaluate Apache Spark workloads [46]. The Spark run-time engine dynamically schedules tasks to use available cores and maximize parallelism, adapting as sprints cause the number of available cores to vary across epochs. Each agent runs a Spark application on representative datasets as shown in Table 1.

Profiling Methods. We collect system profiles that measure power and temperature, using the Intel® Performance Counter Monitor 2.8 to read MSR registers once every second. We collect workload profiles by modifying Spark (v1.3.1) to log the IDs of jobs, stages, and tasks upon their completion.

We measure application performance in terms of the number of tasks completed per second (TPS). Each application defines a number of jobs, and each job is divided into tasks that compute in parallel. Jobs are completed in sequence while tasks can be completed out of order. The total number of tasks in a job is constant and independent

Table 2. Experimental Parameters

Description	Symbol	Value
Min # sprinters	$N_{\min}$	250
Max # sprinters	$N_{\max}$	750
Prob. of staying in cooling	p_c	0.50
Prob. of staying in recovery	p_r	0.88
Discount factor	δ	0.99

of the available hardware resources. Thus, TPS measures performance for a fixed amount of work.

We trace TPS during an application's end-to-end execution in normal and sprinting modes. Since execution times differ in the two modes, comparing traces requires some effort. For every second in normal mode, we measure the number of tasks completed and estimate the number of tasks that would have been completed in the sprinting mode. For our evaluation, we estimate a sprint's speedup by comparing the measured non-sprinting trace and the interpolated sprinting trace. In a practical system, online profiling and heuristics would be required.

Simulation Methods. We simulate 1000 users and evaluate their performance in the sprinting game. The R-based simulator uses traces of Spark computation collected in both normal and sprinting modes. The simulator models system dynamics as agents sprint, cool, and recover.

One set of simulations evaluates homogeneous agents who arrive randomly and launch the same type of Spark application; randomized arrivals cause application phases to overlap in diverse ways. A second set of simulations evaluates heterogeneous agents who launch different types of applications, further increasing the diversity of overlapping phases. Diverse phase behavior exercises the sprinting game as agents and their processors optimize strategies in response to varied competitors'.

Table 2 summarizes technology and system parameters. Parameters $N_{\min}$ and $N_{\max}$ are set by the circuit breaker's tripping curve. Parameters p_c and p_r are set by the chip's cooling mechanism and the rack's UPS batteries. These probabilities decrease as cooling efficiency and recharge speed increase – see §2.

6. Evaluation

We evaluate the sprinting game and its equilibrium threshold against several alternatives. Although there is little prior work in managing sprints, we compare against three heuristics that represent broader perspectives on power management. First, greedy heuristics focus on the present and neglect the future [49]. Second, control-theoretic heuristics are reactive rather than proactive [4, 5]. Third, centralized heuristics focus on the system and neglect individuals. Unlike these approaches, the sprinting game anticipates the future and emphasizes strategic agents who participate in a shared system.

Greedy (G) permits agents to sprint as long as the chip is not cooling and the rack is not recovering. This mechanism may frequently trip the breaker and require rack recovery. After recovery, agent wake-ups and sprints are staggered across two epochs. Greedy produces a poor equilibrium—knowing that everyone is sprinting, an agent's best response is to sprint as well.

Exponential Backoff (E-B) throttles the frequency at which agents sprint. An agent sprints greedily until the breaker trips. After the first trip, agents wait 0 – 1 epoch before sprinting again. After the second trip, agents wait 0 – 3 epochs. After the t-th trip, agents wait for some number of epochs drawn randomly from $[0, 2^t - 1]$. The waiting interval contracts by half if the breaker has not been tripped in the past 100 epochs.

Cooperative Threshold (C-T) assigns each agent the globally optimal threshold for sprinting. The coordinator exhaustively searches for the threshold that maximizes system performance. The coordinator enforces these thresholds although they do not reflect agents' best responses to system dynamics. These thresholds do not produce an equilibrium but do provide an upper bound on performance.

Equilibrium Threshold (E-T) assigns each agent her optimal threshold from the sprinting game. The coordinator collects performance profiles and implements Algorithm 1 to produce thresholds that reflect agents' best responses to system dynamics. These thresholds produce an equilibrium and agents cannot benefit by deviating from their assigned strategy.

6.1 Sprinting Behavior

Figure 6 compares sprinting policies and resulting system dynamics as 1000 instances of *Decision Tree*, a representative application, computes for a sequence of epochs. Sprinting policies determine how often agents sprint and whether sprints trigger emergencies. Ideally, policies would permit agents to sprint up until they trip the circuit breaker. In this example, 250 of the 1000 agents for *Decision Tree* can sprint before triggering a power emergency.

Greedy heuristics are aggressive and inefficient. A sprint in the present precludes a sprint in the near future, harming subsequent tasks that could have benefited more from the sprint. Moreover, frequent sprints risk power emergencies and require rack-level recovery. G produces an unstable system, oscillating between full-system sprints that trigger emergencies and idle recovery that harms performance. G staggers the distribution of sprinting permissions after recovery to avoids dI/dt problems, which reduces but does not eliminate instability.

Control-theoretic approaches are more conservative, throttling sprints in response to power emergencies. E-B adaptively responds to feedback, producing a more stable system with fewer sprints and emergencies. Indeed, E-B may be too

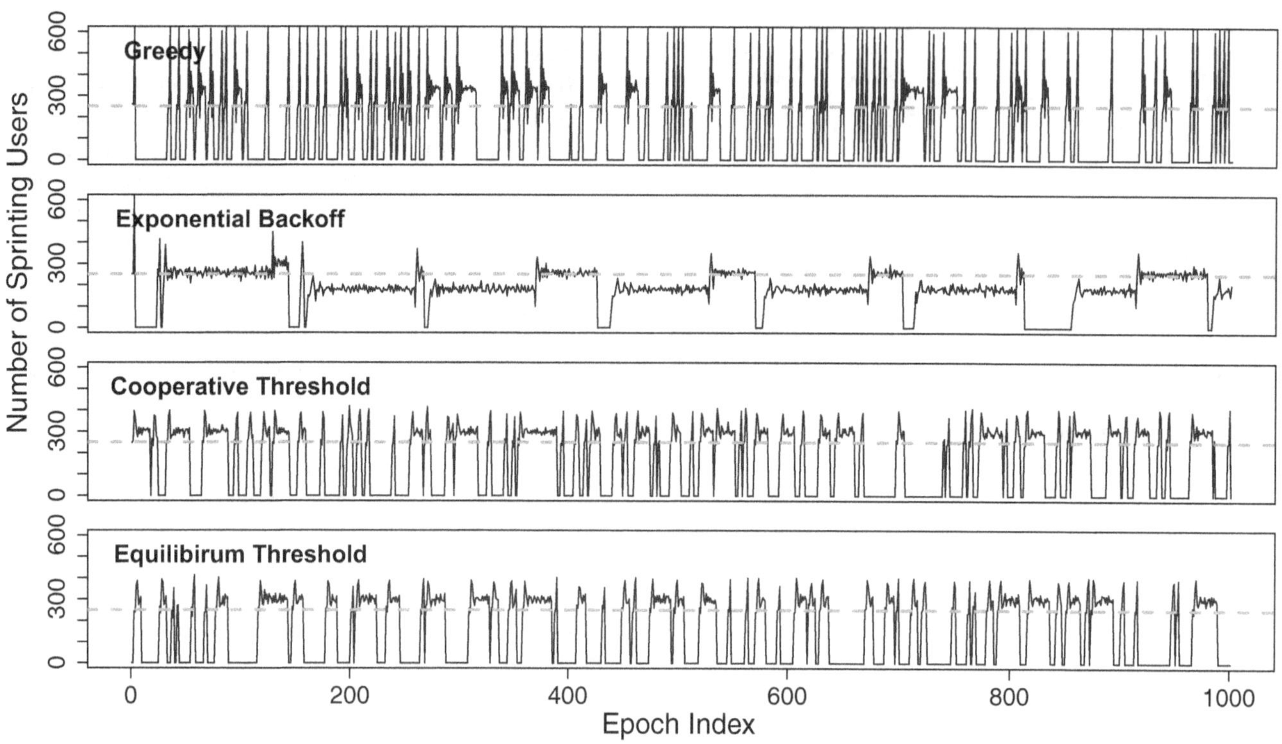

Figure 6. Sprinting behavior for a representative application, Decision Tree. Black line denotes number of sprinters. Grey line denotes the point at which sprinters risk a power emergency, N_{min}.

conservative, throttling sprints beyond what is necessary to avoid tripping the circuit breaker. The number of sprinters is consistently lower than N_{min}, which is safe but leaves sprinting opportunities unexploited. Thus, in neither G nor E-B do agents sprint to full advantage.

In contrast, the computational sprinting game performs well by embracing agents' strategies. E-T produces an equilibrium in which agents play their optimal strategies and converge to a stationary distribution. In equilibrium, the number of sprinters is just slightly above $N_{min} = 250$, the number that causes a breaker to transition from the non-tripped region to the tolerance band. After emergency and recovery, the system quickly returns to equilibrium. Note that E-T's system dynamics are similar to those from the high-performance, cooperative C-T policy.

Figure 7 shows the percentage of time an agent spends in active, cooling, and recovery states. The analysis highlights G and E-B's limitations. With G, an agent spends more than 50% of its time in recovery, waiting for batteries to recharge after an emergency. With E-B, an agent spends nearly 40% of its time in active mode but not sprinting.

Agents spend comparable shares of their time sprinting in each policy. However, this observation understates the sprinting game's advantage. G and E-B sprint at every opportunity and ignore transitions into cooling states, which preclude sprints in future epochs. In contrast, E-T and C-T's sprints are more timely as strategic agents sprint only when estimated benefits exceed an optimized threshold. Thus, a sprint in E-T or C-T contributes more to performance than one in G or E-B.

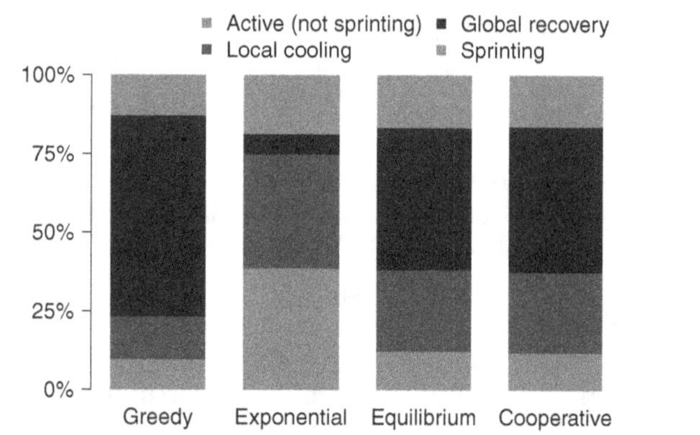

Figure 7. Percentage of time spent in agent states for a representative application, Decision Tree.

6.2 Sprinting Performance

Figure 8 shows task throughput under varied policies. The sprinting game outperforms greedy heuristics and is competitive with globally optimized heuristics. Rather than sprinting greedily, E-T uses equilibrium thresholds to select more profitable epochs for sprinting. E-T outperforms G and E-B by up to 6.8× and 4.8×, respectively. Agents who use their

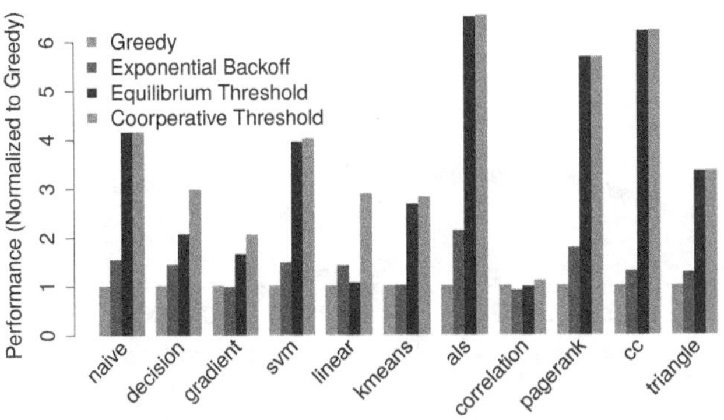

Figure 8. Performance, measured in tasks per second and normalized against greedy, for a single application type.

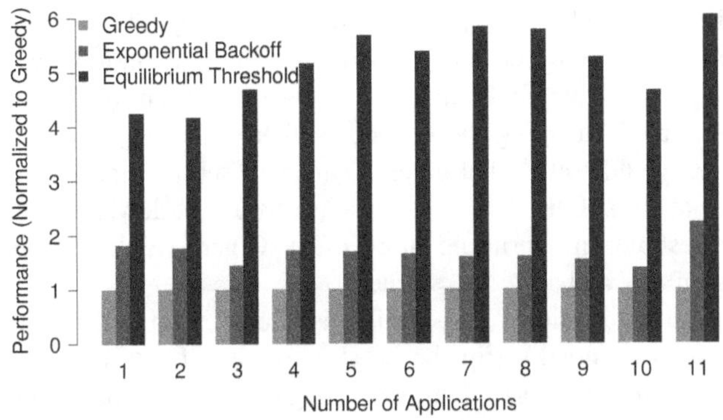

Figure 9. Performance, measured in tasks per second and normalized against greedy, for multiple application types.

own strategies to play the game competitively produce outcomes that rival expensive cooperation. E-T's task throughput is 90% that of C-T's for most applications.

Linear Regression and *Correlation* are outliers, achieving only 36% and 65% of cooperative performance. For these applications, E-T performs as badly as G and E-B because the applications' performance profiles exhibit little variance and all epochs benefit similarly from sprinting. When an agent cannot distinguish between epochs, she sets a low threshold and sprints for every epoch. In effect, for such applications, E-T produces a greedy equilibrium.

Thus far, we have considered agents for applications of the same type that compute together. When agents represent different types of applications, E-T assigns different sprinting thresholds for each type. Figure 9 shows performance as the number of application types increases. We evaluate performance for a system with k types by randomly selecting k applications, finding each agent's strategy under an E-T policy, and repeating ten times to report an average. As before, E-T performs much better than G and E-B. We do not evaluate C-T because searching for optimal thresholds for multiple types of agents is computationally hard.

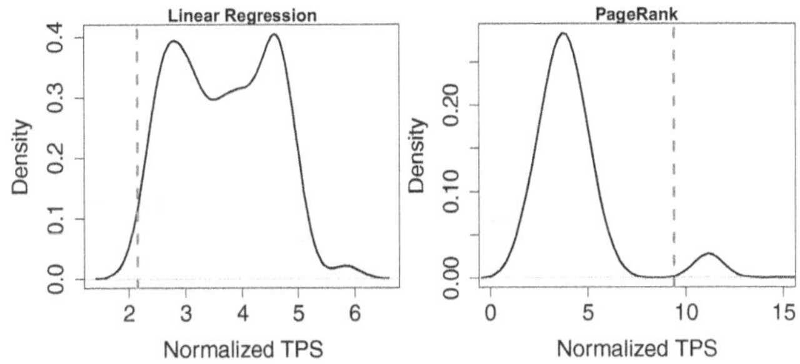

Figure 10. Probability density for sprinting speedups.

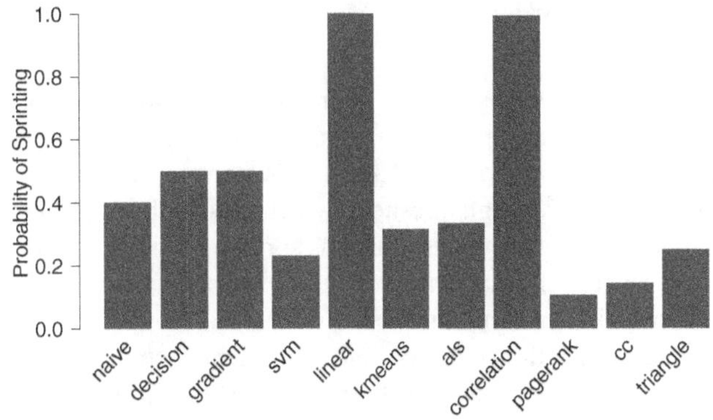

Figure 11. Probability of sprinting.

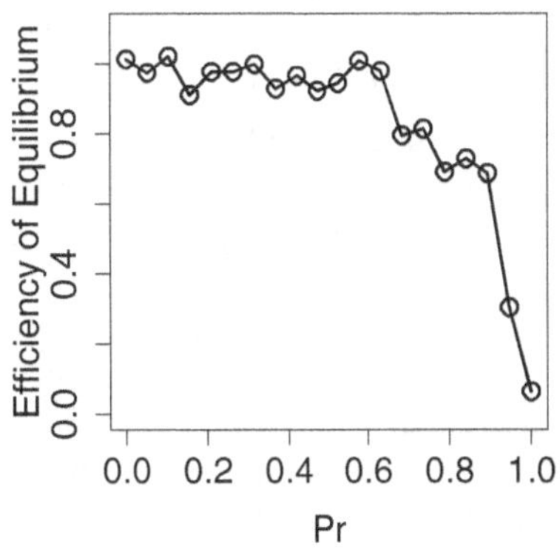

Figure 12. Efficiency of equilibrium thresholds.

6.3 Sprinting Strategies

Figure 10 uses kernel density plots for two representative applications, *Linear Regression* and *PageRank*, to show how often and how much their tasks benefit from sprinting. *Linear Regression* presents a narrower distribution and performance gains from sprinting vary in a band between 3× and 5×. In contrast, *PageRank*'s performance gains can often exceed 10×.

The coordinator uses performance profiles to optimize threshold strategies. *Linear Regression*'s strategy is aggressive and uses a low threshold that often induces sprints. This strategy arises from its relatively low variance in per-

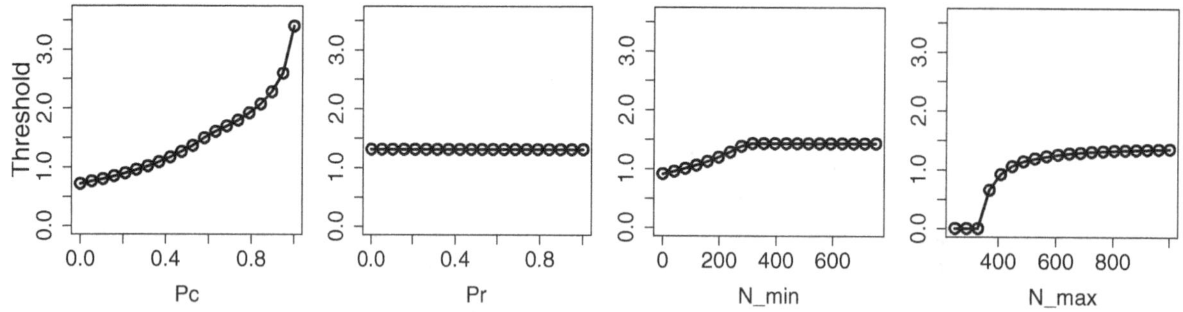

Figure 13. Sensitivity of sprinting threshold to architectural parameters—probability of staying in cooling and recovery p_c, p_r and the tripping curve $N_{\text{min}}, N_{\text{max}}$.

formance gains. If sprinting's benefits are indistinguishable across tasks and epochs, an agent sprints indiscriminately and at every opportunity. *PageRank*'s strategy is more nuanced and uses a high threshold, which cuts her bimodal distribution and implements judicious sprinting. She sprints for tasks and epochs that benefit most (*i.e.*, those that see performance gains greater than $10\times$).

Figure 11 illustrates diversity in agents' strategies by reporting their propensities to sprint. *Linear Regression* and *Correlation*'s narrow density functions and low thresholds cause these applications to sprint at every opportunity. The majority of applications, however, resemble *PageRank* with higher thresholds and judicious sprints.

6.4 Equilibrium versus Cooperation

Sprinting thresholds from equilibria are robust to strategic behavior and perform well. However, cooperative thresholds that optimize system throughput can perform even better. Our evaluation has shown that the sprinting game delivers 90% of the performance from cooperation. But we find that the game performs well only when the penalties from non-cooperative behavior are low. To understand this insight, let us informally define efficiency as the ratio of game performance from equilibrium thresholds (E-T) to optimal performance from cooperative thresholds (C-T).*

The sprinting game produces efficient equilibria because the penalty for non-cooperative behavior is triggering a power emergency. In the sprinting architecture, recovery is relatively inexpensive as batteries recharge and normal system operation resumes in ten epochs or less. However, higher penalties for non-cooperative behavior would degrade the game's performance from equilibrium strategies. Figure 12 shows how efficiency falls as recovery from power emergencies become increasingly expensive. Recall that p_r is the probability an agent in recovery stays in that state.

Prisoner's Dilemma. The sprinting game fails when an emergency requires indefinite recovery and p_r is one. In this extreme scenario, we would like the game to produce an equilibrium in which agents sprint yet avoid tripping the breaker. Unfortunately, the game has no equilibrium that avoids tripping the breaker and triggering indefinite recovery. If a strategic agent were to observe system dynamics that avoid tripping the breaker, which means P_{trip} is zero, she would realize that other agents have set high thresholds to avoid sprints. Her best response would be lowering her threshold and sprinting more often. Others would behave similarly and drive P_{trip} higher.

In equilibrium, P_{trip} would rise above zero and agents would eventually trip the breaker, putting the system into indefinite recovery. Thus, selfish agents would produce inefficient equilibria—the Prisoner's Dilemma in which each agent's best response performs worse than a cooperative one.

Enforcing Non-Equilibrium Strategies. The Folk theorem guides agents to a more efficient equilibrium by punishing agents whose responses harm the system. The coordinator would assign agents the best cooperative thresholds to maximize system performance from sprinting. When an agent deviates, she is punished such that performance lost exceeds performance gained. When applied to our previous example, punishments would allow the system to escape inefficient equilibria as agents are compelled to increase their thresholds and ensure P_{trip} remains zero.

Note that threat of punishment is sufficient to shape the equilibrium. Agents would adapt strategies based on the threat to avoid punishment. The coordinator could monitor sprints, detect deviations from assigned strategies, and forbid agents who deviate from ever sprinting again. Alternatively, agents could impose collective punishment by continuously sprinting, triggering emergencies, and degrading everyone's performance. The threat of collective action deters agents who would deviate from the cooperative strategy.

6.5 Sensitivity Analysis

Figure 13 shows the sprinting threshold's sensitivity to the game's parameters. In practice, server engineering affects cooling and recovery durations (p_c, p_r) as well as the breaker's trip curve $(N_{\text{min}}, N_{\text{max}})$.

*We are informal because the domain of strategies is huge and we consider only the best cooperative threshold. A non-threshold strategy might provide even better performance.

As cooling duration increases, thresholds increase and agents sprint less. Agents are more cautious because sprinting in the current epoch requires many more epochs for cooling. The opportunity cost of sprinting mistakenly rises. As recovery duration increases, the cost of tripping the breaker increases. However, because each agent sprints to pursue her own performance while hoping others do not trip the breaker, thresholds are insensitive to recovery cost. When p_r is one, we have shown how agents encounter the Prisoner's Dilemma – see §6.4.

When $N_{\min}$ and $N_{\max}$ are small, the probability of tripping the breaker is high. Ironically, agents sprint more aggressively and extract performance now because emergencies that forbid future sprints are likely. When $N_{\min}$ and $N_{\max}$ are big, each agent sprints more judiciously as a sprint now affects the ability to sprint in the future.

7. Related Work

The sprinting problem falls into the general category of datacenter power management, but we are the first to identify the problem and propose a game-theoretic approach. The sprinting problem is made interesting by modern approaches to datacenter provisioning.

To minimize total cost of ownership and maximize return on investment, datacenters oversubscribe their servers [12, 17], bandwidth [11], branch circuits [19], cooling and power supplies [18, 23]. In datacenters, dynamic power capping [15] adjusts the power allocation to individual servers, enabling a rich policy space for power and energy management. In servers, managers could pursue performance while minimizing operating costs, which are incurred from energy and cooling [13, 14, 21, 32]. Researchers have sought to allocate server power to performance critical services via DVFS [28, 34].

Economics and game theory have proven effective in datacenter power and resource management [16]. Markets [24, 25] and price theory [42] have been applied to manage heterogeneous server cores. Demand response models have been proposed to handle power emergencies [33]. In addition to performance, fairness in game theory has been studied to incentivize users when sharing hardware in a cloud environment [20, 47, 48].

In this paper, we treat the sprinting management problem as a repeated game and seek an equilibrium that leads sprinting servers to expected behavior. Similar approaches have been applied to power control in wireless communication systems [30]. But we are the first to consider game theory for datacenter management, especially in the context of computational sprinting and power capping.

8. Conclusions

We present a sprinting architecture in which many, independent chip multiprocessors share a power supply. When an individual chip sprints, its excess heat constrains future sprints. When a collection of chips sprint, its additional power demands raise the risk of power emergencies. For such an architecture, we present a management framework that determines when each chip should sprint.

We formalize sprint management as a repeated game. Agents represent chip multiprocessors and their workloads, executing sprints strategically on their behalf. Strategic behaviors produce an equilibrium in the game. We show that, in equilibrium, the computational sprinting game outperforms prior, greedy mechanisms by 4-6× and delivers 90% of the performance achieved from a more expensive, globally enforced mechanism.

Acknowledgments

This work is supported by NSF grants CCF-1149252 (CAREER), CCF-1337215 (XPS-CLCCA), SHF-1527610, and AF-1408784. This work is also supported by STARnet, a Semiconductor Research Corporation program, sponsored by MARCO and DARPA. Any opinions, findings, conclusions, or recommendations expressed in this material are those of the author(s) and do not necessarily reflect the views of these sponsors.

References

[1] US census data (1990) data set. `https://archive.ics.uci.edu/ml/datasets/US+Census+Data+(1990)`.

[2] Movielens dataset. `http://grouplens.org/datasets/movielens/`.

[3] Web data commons: Hyperlink graphs. `http://webdatacommons.org/hyperlinkgraph/index.html`.

[4] Dynamic thermal management for high-performance microprocessors. In *Proceedings of the 7th IEEE International Symposium on High Performance Computer Architecture (HPCA)*, pages 171–182. IEEE Computer Society, 2001.

[5] Control-theoretic techniques and thermal-RC modeling for accurate and localized dynamic thermal management. In *Proceedings of the 8th IEEE International Symposium on High Performance Computer Architecture (HPCA)*, pages 17–28, 2002.

[6] S. Adlakha and R. Johari. Mean field equilibrium in dynamic games with strategic complementarities. *Operations Research*, 61(4):971–989, 2013.

[7] S. Adlakha, R. Johari, G. Y. Weintraub, and A. Goldsmith. On oblivious equilibrium in large population stochastic games. In *Proceedings of the 49th IEEE Conference on Decision and Control (CDC)*, pages 3117–3124. IEEE, 2010.

[8] S. Adlakha, R. Johari, and G. Y. Weintraub. Equilibria of dynamic games with many players: Existence, approximation, and market structure. *Journal of Economic Theory*, 2013.

[9] Allen-Bradley. Bulletin 1489 UL489 circuit breakers. `http://literature.rockwellautomation.com/idc/groups/literature/documents/td/1489-td001_-en-p.pdf`.

[10] Ametek. Selection and sizing of batteries for UPS backup. `http://www.solidstatecontrolsinc.com/download/selection-and-sizing-batteries-tech-paper.pdf`.

[11] H. Ballani, P. Costa, T. Karagiannis, and A. Rowstron. Towards predictable datacenter networks. In *Proceedings of the ACM SIGCOMM Conference (SIGCOMM)*, pages 242–253. ACM, 2011.

[12] L. A. Barroso, J. Clidaras, and U. Hölzle. The datacenter as a computer: An introduction to the design of warehouse-scale machines. *Synthesis Lectures on Computer Architecture*, 8(3): 1–154, 2013.

[13] A. Beloglazov, J. Abawajy, and R. Buyya. Energy-aware resource allocation heuristics for efficient management of data centers for cloud computing. *Future Generation Computer Systems*, 28(5):755–768, 2012.

[14] J. L. Berral, Í. Goiri, R. Nou, F. Julià, J. Guitart, R. Gavaldà, and J. Torres. Towards energy-aware scheduling in data centers using machine learning. In *Proceedings of the 1st International Conference on Energy-Efficient Computing and Networking*, pages 215–224. ACM, 2010.

[15] A. A. Bhattacharya, D. Culler, A. Kansal, S. Govindan, and S. Sankar. The need for speed and stability in data center power capping. *Sustainable Computing: Informatics and Systems*, 3(3):183–193, 2013.

[16] J. S. Chase, D. C. Anderson, P. N. Thakar, A. M. Vahdat, and R. P. Doyle. Managing energy and server resources in hosting centers. In *Proceedings of the 18th Symposium on Operating Systems Principles (SOSP)*, pages 103–116. ACM, 2001.

[17] G. Chen, W. He, J. Liu, S. Nath, L. Rigas, L. Xiao, and F. Zhao. Energy-aware server provisioning and load dispatching for connection-intensive internet services. In *Proceedings of the 5th USENIX Symposium on Networked Systems Design and Implementation (NSDI)*, pages 337–350. USENIX Association, 2008.

[18] X. Fan, W.-D. Weber, and L. A. Barroso. Power provisioning for a warehouse-sized computer. In *Proceedings of the 34th Annual International Symposium on Computer Architecture (ISCA)*, pages 13–23. ACM, 2007.

[19] X. Fu, X. Wang, and C. Lefurgy. How much power oversubscription is safe and allowed in data centers. In *Proceedings of the 8th ACM International Conference on Autonomic Computing (ICAC)*, pages 21–30. ACM, 2011.

[20] A. Ghodsi, M. Zaharia, B. Hindman, A. Konwinski, S. Shenker, and I. Stoica. Dominant resource fairness: Fair allocation of multiple resource types. In *Proceedings of the 8th USENIX Conference on Networked Systems Design and Implementation (NSDI)*.

[21] Í. Goiri, T. D. Nguyen, R. Bianchini, and Í. G. Presa. Coolair: Temperature-and variation-aware management for free-cooled datacenters. In *Proceedings of the 20th International Conference on Architectural Support for Programming Languages and Operating Systems (ASPLOS)*, pages 253–265. ACM, 2015.

[22] S. Govindan, A. Sivasubramaniam, and B. Urgaonkar. Benefits and limitations of tapping into stored energy for datacenters. In *Proceeding of the 38th Annual International Symposium on Computer Architecture (ISCA)*, pages 341–351. IEEE, 2011.

[23] S. Govindan, D. Wang, A. Sivasubramaniam, and B. Urgaonkar. Leveraging stored energy for handling power emergencies in aggressively provisioned datacenters. In *Proceedings of the 7th International Conference on Architectural Support for Programming Languages and Operating Systems (ASPLOS)*, pages 75–86. ACM, 2012.

[24] M. Guevara, B. Lubin, and B. C. Lee. Navigating heterogeneous processors with market mechanisms. In *Proceeding of the 19th IEEE International Symposium on High Performance Computer Architecture (HPCA)*, pages 95–106. IEEE, 2013.

[25] M. Guevara, B. Lubin, and B. C. Lee. Strategies for anticipating risk in heterogeneous system design. In *Proceeding of the 20th IEEE International Symposium on High Performance Computer Architecture (HPCA)*, pages 154–164. IEEE, 2014.

[26] R. Gummadi, R. Johari, and J. Y. Yu. Mean field equilibria of multiarmed bandit games. In *Proceedings of the 13th ACM Conference on Electronic Commerce (EC)*, pages 655–655. ACM, 2012.

[27] B. Hindman, A. Konwinski, M. Zaharia, A. Ghodsi, A. D. Joseph, R. Katz, S. Shenker, and I. Stoica. Mesos: A platform for fine-grained resource sharing in the data center. In *Proceedings of the 8th USENIX Conference on Networked Systems Design and Implementation (NSDI)*, pages 295–308. USENIX Association, 2011.

[28] C.-H. Hsu, Y. Zhang, M. Laurenzano, D. Meisner, T. Wenisch, J. Mars, L. Tang, R. G. Dreslinski, et al. Adrenaline: Pinpointing and reining in tail queries with quick voltage boosting. In *Proceedings of the 21st IEEE International Symposium on High Performance Computer Architecture (HPCA)*, pages 271–282. IEEE, 2015.

[29] K. Iyer, R. Johari, and M. Sundararajan. Mean field equilibria of dynamic auctions with learning. *ACM SIGecom Exchanges*, 10(3):10–14, 2011.

[30] M. Le Treust and S. Lasaulce. A repeated game formulation of energy-efficient decentralized power control. *Wireless Communications, IEEE Transactions on*, 9(9):2860–2869, 2010.

[31] Y. Li, B. Lee, D. Brooks, Z. Hu, and K. Skadron. CMP design space exploration subject to physical constraints. In *Proceedings of the 12th IEEE International Symposium on High Performance Computer Architecture (HPCA)*, pages 17–28. IEEE, 2006.

[32] M. Lin, A. Wierman, L. L. Andrew, and E. Thereska. Dynamic right-sizing for power-proportional data centers. *IEEE/ACM Transactions on Networking (TON)*, 21(5):1378–1391, 2013.

[33] Z. Liu, A. Wierman, Y. Chen, B. Razon, and N. Chen. Data center demand response: Avoiding the coincident peak via workload shifting and local generation. *Performance Evaluation*, 70(10):770–791, 2013.

[34] D. Lo, L. Cheng, R. Govindaraju, L. A. Barroso, and C. Kozyrakis. Towards energy proportionality for large-scale latency-critical workloads. In *Proceeding of the 41st Annual International Symposium on Computer Architecture (ISCA)*, pages 301–312. IEEE, 2014.

[35] A. Raghavan. *Computational sprinting: Exceeding sustainable power in thermally constrained systems*. PhD thesis, University of Pennsylvania, 2013.

[36] A. Raghavan, Y. Luo, A. Chandawalla, M. Papaefthymiou, K. P. Pipe, T. F. Wenisch, and M. M. K. Martin. Computational sprinting. In *Proceedings of the 18th IEEE International Symposium on High Performance Computer Architecture (HPCA)*, pages 1–12. IEEE Computer Society, 2012.

[37] A. Raghavan, L. Emurian, L. Shao, M. Papaefthymiou, K. P. Pipe, T. F. Wenisch, and M. M. Martin. Computational sprinting on a hardware/software testbed. In *Proceedings of the 18th International Conference on Architectural Support for Programming Languages and Operating Systems (ASPLOS)*, pages 155–166. ACM, 2013.

[38] A. Raghavan, L. Emurian, L. Shao, M. Papaefthymiou, K. P. Pipe, T. F. Wenisch, and M. M. Martin. Utilizing dark silicon to save energy with computational sprinting. *IEEE Micro*, 33 (5):20–28, 2013.

[39] A. Raj. CPU hotplug support in Linux(tm) kernel. URL `https://www.kernel.org/doc/Documentation/cpu-hotplug.txt`.

[40] L. Shao, A. Raghavan, L. Emurian, M. C. Papaefthymiou, T. F. Wenisch, M. M. Martin, and K. P. Pipe. On-chip phase change heat sinks designed for computational sprinting. In *Proceedings of the 30th Annual Semiconductor Thermal Measurement and Management Symposium (SEMI-THERM)*, pages 29–34. IEEE, 2014.

[41] M. Skach, M. Arora, C.-H. Hsu, Q. Li, D. Tullsen, L. Tang, and J. Mars. Thermal time shifting: Leveraging phase change materials to reduce cooling costs in warehouse-scale computers. In *Proceedings of the 42nd Annual International Symposium on Computer Architecture (ISCA)*, pages 439–449. IEEE, 2015.

[42] T. Somu Muthukaruppan, A. Pathania, and T. Mitra. Price theory based power management for heterogeneous multi-cores. In *Proceedings of the 19th International Conference on Architectural Support for Programming Languages and Operating Systems*, ASPLOS '14, pages 161–176. ACM, 2014.

[43] J. Stamper, A. Niculescu-Mizil, S. Ritter, G. Gordon, and K. Koedinger. Algebra I 2006-2007. Challenge data set from KDD Cup 2010 educational data mining challenge. `http://pslcdatashop.web.cmu.edu/KDDCup/downloads.jsp`.

[44] F. Volle, S. V. Garimella, M. Juds, et al. Thermal management of a soft starter: Transient thermal impedance model and performance enhancements using phase change materials. *Power Electronics, IEEE Transactions on*, 25(6):1395–1405, 2010.

[45] X. Wang, M. Chen, C. Lefurgy, and T. W. Keller. Ship: A scalable hierarchical power control architecture for large-scale data centers. *Parallel and Distributed Systems, IEEE Transactions on*, 23(1):168–176, 2012.

[46] M. Zaharia, M. Chowdhury, M. J. Franklin, S. Shenker, and I. Stoica. Spark: Cluster computing with working sets. In *Proceedings of the 2nd USENIX Conference on Hot Topics in Cloud Computing*, volume 10, page 10, 2010.

[47] S. Zahedi and B. Lee. Sharing incentives and fair division for multiprocessors. *IEEE Micro*, 35(3):92–100, 2015.

[48] S. M. Zahedi and B. C. Lee. REF: Resource elasticity fairness with sharing incentives for multiprocessors. In *Proceedings of the 19th International Conference on Architectural Support for Programming Languages and Operating Systems (ASPLOS)*, pages 145–160. ACM, 2014.

[49] W. Zheng and X. Wang. Data center sprinting: Enabling computational sprinting at the data center level. In *Proceedings of the 35th International Conference on Distributed Computing Systems (ICDCS)*, pages 175–184. IEEE, 2015.

An Energy-interference-free Hardware-Software Debugger for Intermittent Energy-harvesting Systems

Alexei Colin[1,2], Graham Harvey[1,2], Brandon Lucia[2], and Alanson P. Sample[1]

Disney Research, Pittsburgh[1]
Pittsburgh, USA
graham.n.harvey@disney.com
alanson.sample@disneyresearch.com

Electrical and Computer Engineering[2]
Carnegie Mellon University
Pittsburgh, USA
{acolin, blucia}@andrew.cmu.edu

Abstract

Energy-autonomous computing devices have the potential to extend the reach of computing to a scale beyond either wired or battery-powered systems. However, these devices pose a unique set of challenges to application developers who lack both hardware and software support tools. Energy harvesting devices experience power intermittence which causes the system to reset and power-cycle unpredictably, tens to hundreds of times per second. This can result in code execution errors that are not possible in continuously-powered systems and cannot be diagnosed with conventional debugging tools such as JTAG and/or oscilloscopes.

We propose the *Energy-interference-free Debugger*, a hardware and software platform for monitoring and debugging intermittent systems without adversely effecting their energy state. The Energy-interference-free Debugger re-creates a familiar debugging environment for intermittent software and augments it with debugging primitives for effective diagnosis of intermittence bugs. Our evaluation of the Energy-interference-free Debugger quantifies its energy-interference-freedom and shows its value in a set of debugging tasks in complex test programs and several real applications, including RFID code and a machine-learning-based activity recognition system.

1. Introduction

Energy-harvesting devices are embedded computing systems that eschew tethered power and batteries by *harvesting* energy from the environment [6, 12, 13, 16, 21, 25]. A power system collects energy into a storage element (i.e., a capacitor) until the buffered energy is sufficient to power the computing device. Once powered, the device can operate until energy is depleted and power fails. After the failure, the cycle of charging begins again. These charge-discharge cycles power the system *intermittently* and, consequently, software that runs on an energy-harvesting device also executes intermittently [18, 23]. A power failure may interrupt an execution with a reboot at any point. A reboot clears volatile state (e.g., register file, SRAM), retains non-volatile state (e.g., FRAM), and transfers control to some earlier point in the program (e.g., the start of `main()`). Recent work [18] defined and characterized the *intermittent execution model*, comprising periods of execution interspersed with reboots.

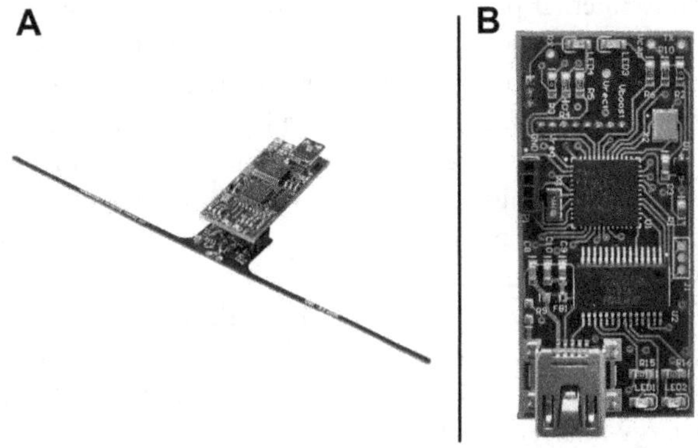

Figure 1: EDB, energy-interference-free system for monitoring and debugging energy-harvesting devices, attached to a WISP [25] (purple PCB) in Panel A and shown in detail in Panel B.

Intermittence makes software difficult to write and understand. A reboot can happen at any point in a program's code, and may occur tens or hundreds of times per second. Reboots complicate a program's possible behavior because reboots are *implicit discontinuities* in the program's control flow that are not expressed anywhere in the code [18, 23]. Even with checkpointing [11, 20, 24] and versioning [18],

ASPLOS '16, April 02-06, 2016, Atlanta, GA, USA

DOI: http://dx.doi.org/10.1145/2872362.2872409

reboots cause control to flow unintuitively back to a previous point in the execution.

Intermittence can cause correct software to misbehave. Intermittence-induced jumps back to a prior point in an execution inhibit forward progress and may repeatedly execute code that should not be repeated. Intermittence can also leave memory in an inconsistent state that is impossible in a continuously powered execution [18, 23]. These failure modes represent a new class of *intermittence bugs.* To avoid intermittence-related malfunction, code must *correctly* leverage non-volatile memory. Writing intermittence-safe code for an energy-harvesting application or runtime system [2, 4, 11, 18, 20, 24] requires the programmer to understand, find, and fix intermittence bugs.

To diagnose intermittence bugs in their code, programmers need to monitor system behavior, observe failures, and examine internal program state. Unfortunately, this simple debugging methodology is unusable for intermittence bugs because existing tools power the target device, masking intermittent behavior. Programmers are left with an unsatisfying dilemma: to use a debugger to monitor the system and never observe a failure; Or to run without a debugger and observe the failure but gain no insight into the system necessary for understanding the bug.

Our work addresses the lack of basic debugging support for intermittent systems with the *Energy-interference-free Debugger* (*EDB*), a complement of hardware and software for *energy-interference-free* monitoring and manipulation of intermittent devices, pictured in Figure 1. EDB can *passively monitor* a target device for its energy level, I/O events (e.g., I^2C, RFID), and program events. Monitoring with EDB, unlike with conventional debuggers, is energy-interference-free, because it is designed to be electrically isolated from the target device. EDB also provides a capability to *actively manipulate* the amount of energy stored on the device. Using this mechanism, EDB can compensate for the energy consumed by arbitrarily expensive tasks, effectively eliminating their impact on the energy state experienced by the program.

Many important intermittence debugging tasks are impossible without energy-interference-free monitoring and manipulation mechanisms. Passive monitoring allows concurrent tracing of energy, program events, and I/O under realistic scenarios. EDB's energy manipulation and compensation mechanism lets a programmer instrument application code with energy-hungry invariant checks (e.g., `asserts`) and trace statements (e.g., `printfs`) without impacting application behavior. The same mechanisms enable *interactive debugging* with breakpoints that can be conditioned on energy level and with access to the state of the target device.

To summarize our main contributions:

- We observe that *energy-interference-freedom* is essential for debugging intermittent, energy-harvesting systems.
- We design and build EDB, a platform for energy-interference-free system monitoring and manipulation.

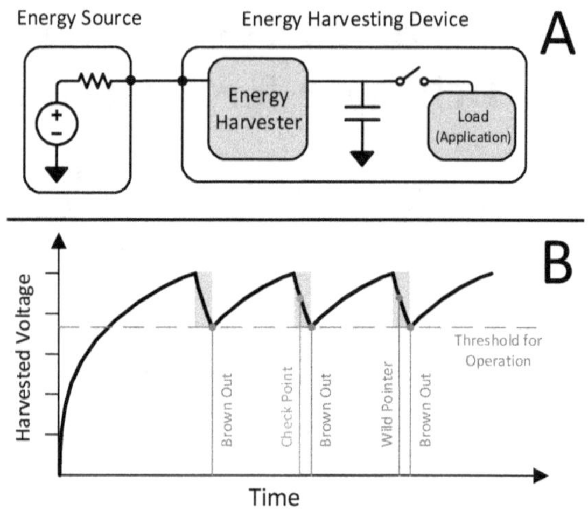

Figure 2: A simplified circuit diagram of an energy harvesting device (Panel A) and characteristic charge and discharge cycles which define its intermittent operation (Panel B).

- We develop debugging primitives for intermittent software, including energy-aware breakpoints, keep-alive assertions, and energy guards.
- We evaluate EDB and show that it is energy-interference-free and is instrumental in intermittence debugging.

2. Intermittence and Energy-interference

This section provides background on the challenges presented by intermittent energy-harvesting devices and illustrates that existing approaches to debugging fail to address these challenges. As a basis for our discussion, we assume an intermittent system that executes a C program that takes longer than a single charge-discharge execution cycle to complete. We assume our device has a mixture of volatile registers and memory, as well as some non-volatile memory. We further assume a checkpointing mechanism that periodically collects a checkpoint of volatile execution context (i.e., register file and stack) like prior work [11, 20, 24]. Note that this checkpointing assumption simplifies the exposition, but our ideas and prototype apply to a system without that support.

2.1 Challenges of Intermittence

Power intermittence complicates understanding and debugging a system, because the behavior of an intermittent system is closely linked to its power supply. This link is illustrated in Figure 2. A simplified energy-harvesting circuit diagram is shown in Figure 2A. An ambient energy transducer (e.g., solar, RF, vibration) connects to an energy storage element (a capacitor), and a load (a microcontroller). Unlike a battery, the ambient energy source has a high source resistance that limits its usable power, resulting in the characteristic "sawtooth" RC charging behavior shown in Figure 2B. The system charges its capacitor until there is enough energy and voltage to operate. Then, active operation begins and the

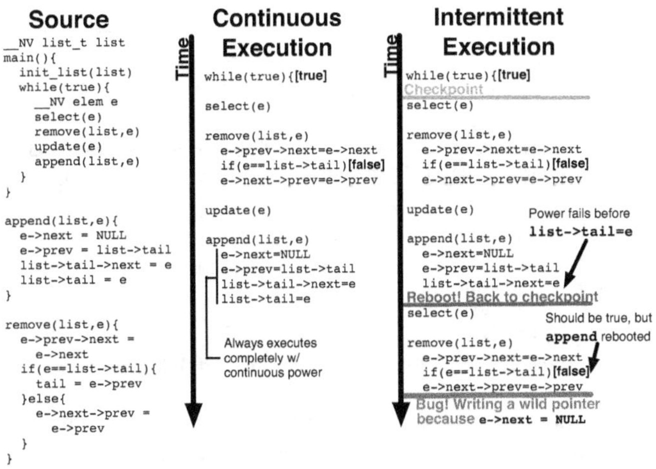

Figure 3: An intermittence bug. The linked-list stays correct with continuous power but is corrupted and leads to a wild pointer write with intermittent power.

capacitor starts to discharge (regions highlighted in green). The device continues actively until the voltage on the storage capacitor drops below a minimum operating threshold (dashed red line), at which point the system loses power and begins another charging cycle. This repeated charging and discharging of the device forces software into an *intermittent execution model* [18] where periods of powered execution are interspersed with reboots.

Figure 3 illustrates how intermittence induces bugs even with runtime support for checkpointing volatile state into non-volatile memory [11, 20, 24]. The code manipulates a linked-list in non-volatile memory using `append` and `remove` functions. A continuous execution completes the code sequentially, as expected. An intermittent execution, however, is not sequential. In the leftmost trace, a checkpoint happens to be collected at the top of the `while` loop and the processing continues until power fails at the indicated point (cf. Figure 2). After the reboot, execution resumes from the checkpoint. This sequence of events later leads to undefined behavior. The execution violates the pre-condition assumed by `remove` that only the `tail`'s `next` should be `NULL`. The reboot interrupts `append` before it can make node `e` the list's new tail but after its `next` pointer is set to `NULL`. When execution resumes at the checkpoint, it attempts to remove node `e` again. The conditional in `remove` confirms that `e` is not the tail, then dereferences its `next` pointer (which is `NULL`). The `NULL next` pointer makes `e->next->prev` a wild pointer that, when written, leads to undefined behavior. This `NULL` pointer dereference cannot happen in a continuous execution and is an example of an *intermittence bug*.

2.2 Energy-interference during Debugging

Debugging intermittence bugs, like the one in Figure 3, using existing tools is virtually impossible. Conventional debuggers supply power to the device-under-test (DUT), which precludes observation of a realistically intermittent execution. Dedicated debugging equipment, like a JTAG [1] debugger, offers visibility into the device's state but is not useful because it provides continuous power and masks intermittence. JTAG power isolator devices [27] exist to decouple debug host power rails from DUT power rails, but these do not help with intermittence debugging, because the JTAG protocol fails if the DUT powers off. The inapplicability of JTAG precludes interactive debugging (e.g., like GDB or LLDB) for intermittent executions. Using a JTAG debugger for the code in Figure 3 would only ever result in the non-failing, continuous execution shown in the middle; the programmer would never see unexpected behavior.

One mostly energy-interference-free tool that can be used for debugging intermittent systems to a limited extent is a mixed-signal oscilloscope. A scope can collect an energy trace by probing DUT's power system and I/O lines. Unfortunately, a scope provides no insight into the internal state of the software running on the DUT. Scope-based debugging is not the interactive process familiar to most programmers. Moreover, oscilloscopes cost thousands of dollars, making them inaccessible to most developers. Using a scope to debug the code in Figure 3 would permit the problematic intermittent execution. However, the scope would not help relate changes in the device's energy state (which it can observe) to the software events that change device state and memory (which it cannot observe). That absent connective information is the key to understanding the failure in this code.

An alternative approach to diagnosing an intermittence bug is to directly write debugging instrumentation code into an application to trace certain program events. In embedded systems, a popular *ad hoc* approach is to toggle an LED at a point of interest. LED-based tracing does not work in energy-harvesting devices, because LEDs are power-hungry and their energy use changes the execution's behavior. As a case in point, it is prohibitively expensive to use an LED to indicate when a WISP energy-harvesting device [25] is executing code, rather than just charging. Powering an LED increases the WISP's current draw by five times, from around 1mA to over 5mA.

Another tracing strategy is to manually instrument code to log program events to non-volatile memory. The resulting trace lacks information about the energy level, unless the developer also spends time, energy, and an ADC channel to log the DUT's energy state. Non-volatile tracing also consumes precious non-volatile storage space. To spare consuming non-volatile storage space, a programmer may write code to stream the event log to a separate, always-on system (e.g., via UART). Powering and clocking an I/O peripheral to transfer the log is expensive in time and energy and adds considerable complexity to code.

All of these instrumentation-based approaches change the point in the program at which energy is exhausted. As a result, the act of debugging alters the intermittent behavior of the application. Furthermore, the value of tracing depends on the events which the programmer decides to trace. To understand the intermittence bug in Figure 3, the programmer needs to log particular events in the `append` and `remove` routines. The bug manifests as a wild pointer write and may appear to crash inexplicably, in code far from the either of those routines, giving little to suggest that `append` and `remove` contain the culpable code.

Energy-interference and lack of visibility into intermittent executions makes prior approaches to debugging inadequate for intermittence debugging.

3. EDB: Energy-interference-free Debugging

EDB is an energy-interference-free platform for intermittence debugging that addresses the shortcomings of existing approaches described in Section 2. This section describes the high-level capabilities and functionality of EDB, while Section 4 describes the co-designed hardware and software implementation that make EDB energy-interference-free.

Figure 4 illustrates EDB functionally. At the top are EDB's *capabilities* that together support the *debugging primitives* at the bottom. The functionality is organized into two parts. The first part is support for *passively monitoring* a device's energy level, program events and I/O, which we call EDB's "passive mode" of operation. The second part is a complementary "active mode" with support for *actively monitoring and manipulating* the target's energy level and internal state (e.g., registers and memory). We combine passive and active mode capabilities, to implement energy-interference-free debugging primitives, including energy and event tracing, intermittence-aware breakpoints, energy guards for instrumentation, and interactive debugging.

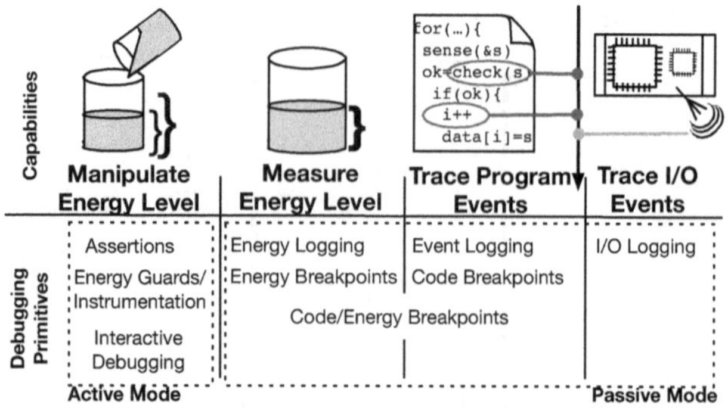

Figure 4: EDB's features and supported debugging tasks.

3.1 Passive Mode Operation

EDB's passive mode operation is built around the three rightmost components at the top of Figure 4. The developer gets the ability to acquire a set of streams and relay them to the host workstation continuously in real-time without active involvement from the target whether it is on or off. Streams instrumental for debugging are the energy level, I/O events on wired buses, messages exchanged over RFID protocol, and program events marked by *watchpoints* in application code. A key advantage of EDB is the ability to gather this data concurrently, letting the developer correlate changes in system behavior with changes in energy state. That correlation is important during development, but, as Section 2 describes, difficult or impossible using existing techniques.

3.2 Active Mode Operation

The capability to manipulate the amount of energy stored on the target device underlies EDB's active mode of operation. Active mode frees debugging tasks from the constraint of the small energy store of the target device. EDB can *compensate* for the energy consumed by a debugging task that involves a costly operation on the target, such as interacting with the programmer, executing arbitrary debug code, or conveying state to the debugger. Before performing an active task the energy on the target device is measured and recorded. While the active task executes, the target is continuously powered. After performing the active task, energy on the target device is restored to the level measured before the active task. Continuously powering active tasks enables them to consume arbitrary amounts of energy. Energy compensation provides the illusion of an unaltered, intermittent execution to the application. Without this support, debugging tasks that require considerable involvement from the target are out of reach.

3.3 Energy-interference-free Debugging Primitives

Using the monitoring and manipulation capabilities described so far, EDB creates a toolbox of energy-interference-free debugging primitives. EDB brings to intermittent platforms familiar debugging techniques that are currently confined to continuously-powered platforms. New intermittence-aware primitives are introduced to handle debugging tasks that arise only on intermittently-powered platforms.

3.3.1 Code and Energy Breakpoints

EDB implements three types of *breakpoints*. A *code breakpoint* is a conventional breakpoint that triggers at a certain code point. An *energy breakpoint* triggers when the target's energy level is at or below a specified threshold. A *combined* breakpoint triggers when a certain code point executes and the target device's energy level is at or below a specified threshold. Breakpoints conditioned on energy level can help catch energy leaks due to unexpected code paths. They initiate an interactive debugging session precisely in problematic iterations when more energy was consumed than expected or when the device is about to brown-out.

3.3.2 Keep-alive Assertions

EDB provides support for using familiar *assertions* on intermittent platforms. When an assertion fails, EDB immediately tethers the target to a continuous power supply to prevent it from losing state by browning out. This *keep-alive* feature turns what would have to be a post-mortem reconstruction of events into an investigation on a live device. A post-mortem analysis is limited to scarce clues in a tiny ad hoc "core dump" that a custom fault handler can manage to save into non-volatile state before the target runs out of energy and resets. The clues available in the interactive session that is automatically opened by EDB for a failing `assert` include the entire live target address space and I/O buses to peripherals.

3.3.3 Energy Guards

EDB can hide the energy cost of an arbitrary region of code if enclosed between a pair of *energy guards*. Code within energy guards executes on tethered power. Code on either side of an energy-guarded region experiences an illusion of continuity in the energy level across the energy-guarded region as if no energy was consumed. EDB implements energy guards using its energy compensation mechanism by recording the target energy level upon entering an energy guard and restoring it upon exiting the guard. Without energy cost, *instrumentation code* becomes non-disruptive and therefore useful on intermittent platforms. Two especially valuable forms of instrumentation impossible without EDB are *complex data structure invariant checks* and *external event tracing*. Extra code added to an application to check invariants on data structures or report when certain events have executed via I/O (e.g. `printf`, LED) can be costly enough to repeatedly deplete the target energy supply and prevent forward progress.

Besides instrumentation, EDB energy guards may also help incorporate non-intermittence-safe third-party code into intermittent applications. As long as third-party library calls are wrapped in energy guards, intermittence failures are guaranteed to not occur within the library. Functionality can now be developed separately from handling intermittence. Similarly, energy guards are useful for gradually porting code from a continuously powered platform. A programmer can start with an energy guard around the entire program and repeatedly exclude a module from the guarded region after verifying its correctness under intermittence, until the entire application is out of the guarded region and intermittence-safe.

3.3.4 Interactive Debugging

EDB supports interactive debugging of a target from a workstation. An interactive session provides full access to view and modify the target's memory, as in a conventional debugger (e.g., GDB, LLDB). A developer can enable code-energy breakpoints and can manually manipulate the target's energy level. An interactive session is entered automatically when a breakpoint is hit or an assertion fails or on demand by a console command. A unique benefit of EDB is its ability to trigger a manipulation of the target's energy state based on the target's program behavior and vice versa.

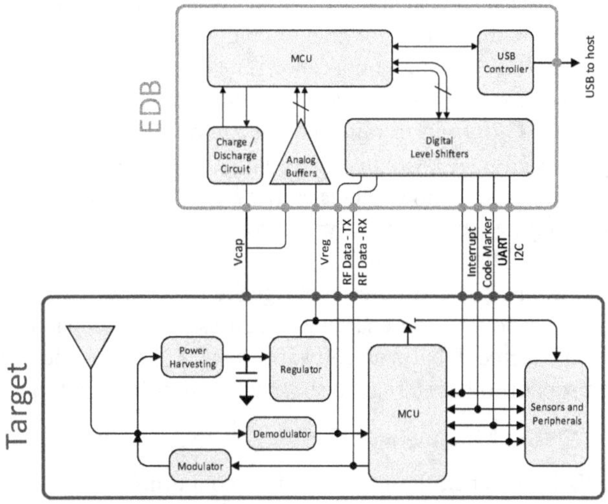

Figure 5: Block diagram of EDB connected to an RF energy-harvesting target. All signal lines are buffered to minimize energy interference. A charge/discharge circuit controls the voltage on the target's energy storage capacitor.

4. Hardware/Software Implementation

EDB's capabilities and debugging primitives are implemented in custom co-designed hardware and software. Figure 5 shows a block diagram of EDB (depicted in green) connected to an RF energy harvesting target (in purple). The labeled wires are physical connections between EDB and the target that carry both analog and digital signals and are exposed through header pins. Our prototype hardware board can connect to any energy-harvesting device with a microcontroller and a capacitor. To support a new device, the applicable physical connections from Figure 5 must be wired and target-side EDB software library of 1200 lines of C code must be ported to the new architecture.

4.1 Energy Level Monitoring

Energy-interference-free measurement of the target's energy level is essential to EDB's passive mode operation (Section 3.1). To measure a device's energy level, EDB uses two physical connections, *Vcap* and *Vreg*, to the target device's energy storage capacitor and its regulated power line, respectively. These signals pass through a dual high impedance, unity gain instrumentation amplifier to minimize leakage current from the target to EDB. These analog voltages are digitized by an analog to digital converter (ADC) and logged or used internally for debugging tasks. While it is *possible* for energy harvesting devices to measure their stored energy levels, doing so uses energy, perturbing the energy state being measured and altering software's intermittent behavior.

4.1.1 Energy Manipulation and Compensation

Energy manipulation and compensation are the basis for EDB's active mode of operation (Section 3.2). EDB has a custom circuit consisting of a low pass filter, keeper diode, and GPIO pins that can charge and discharge the target's energy storage capacitor. This circuit is designed to prevent it from loading down or trickle charging the target while inactive (i.e., in a high impedance state).

To charge the target to a desired voltage level, EDB activates a GPIO pin to raise the voltage on the energy storage capacitor. A basic iterative control loop in EDB's software ensures that the voltage converges to the desired level. Discharging works similarly: the target's energy storage capacitor discharges through a fixed resistive load and a software control loop ensures convergence to the desired level. In our prototype, the charging circuit assumes a capacitive storage element, but with software changes, the same design can support other storage media, such as thin-film batteries.

4.1.2 I/O Monitoring

EDB is designed to enable passive monitoring of arbitrary I/O and attached peripherals, such as sensors, communication buses, and radios. These digital signals (labeled RF Data Tx/Rx, UART, and I2C in Figure 5) connect to a digital buffer and level shifter. We use an extremely low-leakage buffer to prevent leakage current from the target to EDB, and we use the level shifter to match the buffer's voltage level to the target device's voltage level.

Note that while the target device has an on-board regulator, the *Vreg* line may drop below its specified, regulated value during a power failure on the target device. We address the *Vreg* drop with a simple tracking circuit consisting of an analog buffer to keep the level shifter at the target's voltage. This circuit is important because too large a mismatch (i.e., over +/-0.3V [30]) activates the voltage protection diodes in the target's MCU, which perturbs the target's power state.

Our prototype can monitor GPIO, UART, I2C, and RFID RX/TX data lines. A key benefit of EDB is that it monitors data communication lines externally. With external monitoring, messages (e.g., RFID messages) can be decoded even if the target does not correctly decode them due to power failures. EDB's I/O monitoring support aids developers in I/O calibration and debugging I/O related issues in software.

4.1.3 Program Event Monitoring

EDB can track program execution using the *Code Marker* connections in Figure 5. To monitor a code point, the programmer inserts a watchpoint with a unique identifier at that location. EDB's target-side software encodes this identifier onto the Code Marker lines when the program counter passes over the code point. On the debugger-side, transitions on the Code Marker lines are captured and decoded into watchpoint identifiers. EDB can simultaneously monitor $2^n - 1$ distinct watchpoints, where n is the number of GPIO lines allocated to the Code Marker function.

Monitoring program events using EDB is *practically* energy-interference-free. The main energy cost is the target device holding a GPIO pin high for one cycle to encode each traced code point as it executes. We measured the cost of this GPIO-based signaling to be negligible using the methodology described in Section 5. Without EDB, monitoring has a prohibitive cost in code, memory space, and energy. With EDB, events are not only logged without these costs, but also correlated with energy state into a multifaceted profile.

`libEDB` **API**	**Debug Console Commands**
`assert(expr)`	`charge|discharge` *energy_level*
`break|watch_point(id)`	`break|watch en|dis` *id [energy_level]*
`energy_guard(begin|end)`	`trace` *{energy,iobus,rfid,watchpoints}*
`printf(fmt, ...)`	`read|write` *address [value]*

Table 1: Developer's interfaces into EDB.

4.2 Developer's Interfaces into EDB

EDB's debugging primitives are accessible to the end-user through two complimentary interfaces: the `libEDB` API and the host console commands listed in Table 1. The `libEDB` library statically links into the application and exports C macros for inserting assertions, breakpoints, watchpoints, energy guards, and energy-interference-free `printf` calls into the application code. Internally, the library implements the target-side half of the protocol for communicating with the debugger over a dedicated GPIO line and a UART link, which includes routines for reading from and writing to target address space.

The debug console is a command-line interface for interacting directly with EDB and indirectly with the target over a USB connection from a workstation. During interactive debugging in active mode, the console reports assert failures and breakpoints hits and provides commands to inspect target memory. During passive mode debugging, the console delivers traces of energy state, watchpoint hits, monitored I/O events, and the output of `printf` calls. EDB can emulate intermittence at the granularity of individual charge-discharge cycles using the `charge/discharge` commands.

4.3 Implementation Details and Release

We prototyped EDB as a printed circuit board (PCB) that connects to the target device via a board-to-board header. Our core design is also compatible with an implementation as an on-chip component within the target device architecture. EDB software includes 5600 lines of C code for firmware, 1200 lines of C code for `libEDB`, and 1200 lines of Python code for scripting API and host console.

5. Evaluation

The purpose of our evaluation is two-fold. First, we characterize potential sources of energy interference and show that EDB is energy-interference-free with detailed measurements. Second, we use a series of case studies conducted on a real energy-harvesting system to demonstrate that EDB supports monitoring and debugging tasks that are impossible with existing tools.

5.1 Experimental Setup

Our experimental setup consists of the EDB prototype board, a target energy-harvesting device and wireless energy source, and measurement instruments. The EDB board is always connected to a development workstation via USB and to the target device through a dedicated header. EDB is controlled from the workstation programmatically or manually through the console described in Section 4.2.

Our target device is a Wireless Identification and Sensing Platform (WISP) version 5 [25]. The WISP has a 47 μF energy storage capacitor, a turn-on threshold of 2.4 V, a brown-out threshold of 1.8 V, and an active current of approximately 0.5 mA at 4 MHz. The WISP is intermittently powered by RF radiation from an Impinj Speedway Revolution RFID reader. The reader is configured to continuously inventory tags at a transmit power of up to 30 dBm using the SLLURP toolset [3], and its antenna is placed at a distance of 1 m from the WISP. The amount of harvestable energy is inversely proportional to this distance. In our evaluation, we ran a collection of different software applications on the target device. We used a custom test program that manipulates non-volatile linked-list, and another that generates a persistent list of Fibonacci numbers. We also used two real applications, including the official WISP 5 RFID firmware, and a machine-learning-based activity recognition application from prior work [18].

To validate and characterize EDB— especially its energy-interference-freedom — we used some additional measurement equipment that is not normally necessary when using EDB. We collected data in the evaluation using a Tektronix MDO4104 oscilloscope and a Keithley 2450 SourceMeter. The oscilloscope channels were connected to the analog and digital lines between EDB and the WISP in order to record the capacitor voltage, moments when active debug mode starts and ends, and events that trace application progress.

5.2 Energy-interference

EDB's edge over existing debugging tools is its ability to remain isolated from intermittent power in passive mode and to create an illusion of an untouched energy reservoir in active mode. Next, we characterize these two modes of energy-interference and show with measurements that neither compromises EDB's energy-interference-freedom.

5.2.1 Current flow over electrical connections

Any current that flows between the target and the debugger through the connections in Figure 5 may inadvertently charge or discharge the capacitor on the target. As discussed in Section 4, EDB's circuits are designed to minimize the amount of current that can flow across any of these connections to or from the target's power supply. Imperfections in components, such as reverse leakage current in the diodes, inevitably cause some current to flow. We measured the maximum possible current flow over each connection and verified that in the absolute *worst-case*, when all lines are active, the effect it can have on the target power supply is negligible.

We used a source meter to apply a voltage to the driving endpoint of each connection and measure the resulting current. We measured each connection with digital logic endpoints in both *LOW* and *HIGH* states by applying either 0 V or 2.4 V, which is the maximum voltage that can arise on any of the connections. We measured analog endpoints under the worst-case condition of 2.4 V. The sum of the worst-case current flow in either direction across all connections is 0.85 μA or 0.2% of the typical active mode current consumption of the MCU in our target device. Table 2 characterizes the energy interference, showing a breakdown of worst-case current by connection, driving endpoint, and logic state.

Debuger ↔ Target Connection		**DC Current (nA)**		
		Min	Avg	Max
Capacitor sense, manipulate		-2.5100	0.1445	0.8300
Regulator sense, level reference		-0.0300	-0.0029	0.0100
Debugger→Target comm.	high	-0.0200	-0.0004	0.0100
	low	-0.0300	-0.0200	-0.0100
Target→Debugger comm.	high	-0.0200	62.9349	108.2300
	low	-1.9200	-1.7982	-1.7100
Code marker (x2)	high	-0.0200	63.7853	111.5400
	low	-2.1600	-1.9770	-1.8300
UART RX	high	-0.0100	64.8042	111.2600
	low	-2.5500	-1.8909	-1.7200
UART TX	high	-0.0000	66.3433	139.8800
	low	-1.7900	-1.6705	-1.5600
RF RX	high	-0.0400	66.0402	115.0100
	low	-2.3000	-2.1271	-1.9900
RF TX	high	-0.0200	66.5382	117.9600
	low	-2.7300	-2.2726	-2.1600
I2C SCL	high	-0.0400	0.0358	0.0800
	low	-0.3200	-0.1780	-0.1500
I2C SDA	high	-0.0100	0.0367	0.0700
	low	-0.2800	-0.1754	-0.1400
Worst-Case Total Current				836.51 nA

Table 2: Measured worst-case current that can flow over electrical connections between the target device and EDB.

5.2.2 Accuracy of manipulating target energy level

To support debugging tasks presented in Section 3, EDB needs to save, change, and restore the amount of charge in the target's storage capacitor. A large discrepancy between the saved and restored level can undermine the illusion of an unaltered intermittent power supply that EDB presents to the target software. We quantified this energy level discrepancy, ΔE, by measuring the voltage on the capacitor before and after a save-restore operation and applying the expression for the energy stored in a capacitor: $\Delta E = \frac{1}{2}C(V_{\text{restored}}^2 - V_{\text{saved}}^2)$. This quantity was then expressed as a percentage of the maximum energy storable on the target: $\Delta\hat{E} = \Delta E/(\frac{1}{2}CV_{\text{max}}^2)$, where $V_{\text{max}} = 2.4$ V.

We used the charge/discharge commands introduced in Section 4.2 to run 50 trials of a save-restore operation. For each trial, we set an energy-breakpoint at 2.3 V, charged the target capacitor to 2.4 V, waited for the target execution to be interrupted by the breakpoint, and then resumed the target. Table 3 summarizes two independent sets of measurements of $\Delta V = V_{\text{restored}} - V_{\text{saved}}$, ΔE, and $\Delta\hat{E}$: one from our oscilloscope and one from EDB's ADC. The accuracy of EDB's save-restore mechanism, $\Delta\hat{E}$, in our prototype implementa-

	ΔV (mV)		ΔE (μJ)		$\Delta\hat{E}$ (%*)	
	O-scope	ADC	O-scope	ADC	O-scope	ADC
Mean	54	55	1.25	1.25	4.34	4.34
S.D.	16	7.8	0.37	0.18	1.30	0.62

* Energy cost is reported as percentage of 47μF storage capacity.

Table 3: Accuracy with which EDB saves and restores energy level quantified as the difference in capacitor charge before saving and after restoring and measured using either an external oscilloscope or the internal ADC in EDB.

tion of EDB is, on average, 4.34% of the target's $47\mu F$ energy storage capacitor. Our prototype's energy level discrepancy is small enough that it is unlikely to be problematic. We expect that further software optimization will leave a discrepancy closer to the accuracy limit imposed by EDB's ADC. A 12-bit ADC with effective resolution of approximately 1 mV imposes a theoretical lower bound on $\Delta\hat{E}$ of 0.08%.

5.3 Debugging Capabilities

We now illustrate the new capabilities that EDB brings to the development of intermittent software by applying it to debugging tasks that are particularly difficult to resolve using state-of-the-art tools. Energy-harvesting applications in the following case studies execute intermittently and keep state in non-volatile memory to make progress without relying on a runtime checkpointing system. A reboot causes execution to return to the program entry point (i.e., `main`).

5.3.1 Detecting memory corruption early

Memory corruption due to incorrect pointer arithmetic or a buffer overflow is a frequent yet difficult problem to debug. The root cause is obscured behind symptoms that are far from the offending memory write in time and in space. Memory corruption induced by intermittence is harder to diagnose still, because it is not reproducible in a conventional debugger as discussed in Section 2.2. This section studies an application that fails due to an intermittence-induced memory corruption and demonstrates how EDB's support for assertions exposes the root cause.

Application. The code listed in Figure 6 maintains a doubly-linked list data structure in non-volatile memory. On each iteration of the main loop, a node is appended to the linked list if the list is empty or removed from the list otherwise. The node is initialized with a pointer to a buffer in volatile memory. This pointer is retrieved when the node is removed from the list and data is written to the buffer it points to.[1] For illustrative purposes, at the beginning and end of the loop iteration, the code toggles a GPIO pin to indicate that the main loop is running.

Symptoms. After having run on harvested energy for some amount of time, the GPIO pin indicating main loop progress stops toggling. The real oscilloscope trace in the top of Figure 7 shows an early charge-discharge cycle when the main loop is still executing and a later one when it no longer does. After the main loop stops executing, the application never returns to normal, including after reboots on subsequent charge-discharge cycles. The only way to recover is to re-flash the device. Note that the failure problem never occurs when the device runs on continuous power.

Diagnosis. Since the broken final state persists across reboots, one approach is to attach a conventional debugger after the failure and attempt to determine why the main loop stopped running. This approach may help uncover the symptom, but not the root cause, because the information that happens to persist in memory may not be sufficient to follow the chain of events backwards in time. A better approach is to catch the problem at its source by `assert`ing an invariant on the linked-list data structure whenever it is manipulated. However, conventional assertions fall short in this case, because they let the target drain the energy supply, reset, and continue past a failed assertion.

EDB's intermittence-aware `assert` mechanism is designed to tackle this class of bugs. We assert the invariant that the tail pointer points to the last element in the list as shown in Figure 6 and run the program on harvested energy with EDB attached. EDB's console reports the assertion failure, halts the program, starts continuously powering the target, and opens an interactive debug session. This sequence is captured in the bottom oscilloscope trace in Figure 6. The discharge cycle on the right is the one during which the assert fails at instant 1 and the capacitor voltage is seen rising to the level of the tethered power supply.

In the interactive debug session summarized on the right in Figure 6, we check the device's internal state using EDB's commands for inspecting target memory. The tail pointer points to the penultimate element instead of the last one, which is a consequence of an `append` interrupted by intermittence. Because of this inconsistency, the `else`-clause in the `remove` function would dereference a `NULL` pointer, read the buffer pointer from an invalid location, and cause `memset` to write to a wild pointer and corrupt non-volatile state beyond recovery. The `assert` and the interactive session uncovered the precise inconsistency in the data structure before any of these confounding consequences could take place.

5.3.2 Instrumenting code with consistency checks

To aid in debugging, applications often have separate *debug* and *release* build configurations. A debug build includes *instrumentation* code such as checks for consistency of data structures or array bounds. On continuously-powered platforms the convenience of the debug build comes at the cost of slower execution speed, higher memory usage, and higher energy consumption. However, on intermittently-powered platforms, the effect is more dire: the energy overhead of

[1] The role of the memory buffer in this example is to expose undefined behavior during access to the linked list, which takes place with or without the buffer, as an externally observable failure.

Application Code

```
init_list(list)
while (1)
  node = list->head
  while (node->next != NULL)
    node = node->next
  assert(list->tail == node)
  if (node == list->head)
    init_node(new_node)
    append(list, new_node)
  else
    remove(list, node, &bufptr)
    memset(bufptr, 0x42, BUFSZ)
```

Debug Console

```
> run
Interrupted:
ASSERT line: 8
Vcap = 1.9749

*> print node
0xAA10: 0x00BB
*> print list->tail
0xAA20: 0x00AA
*> print list->tail.next
0xAA30: 0x00BB
```

Figure 6: An intermittence bug that corrupts memory, diagnosed using EDB's intermittence-aware `assert` (left) and interactive console (right).

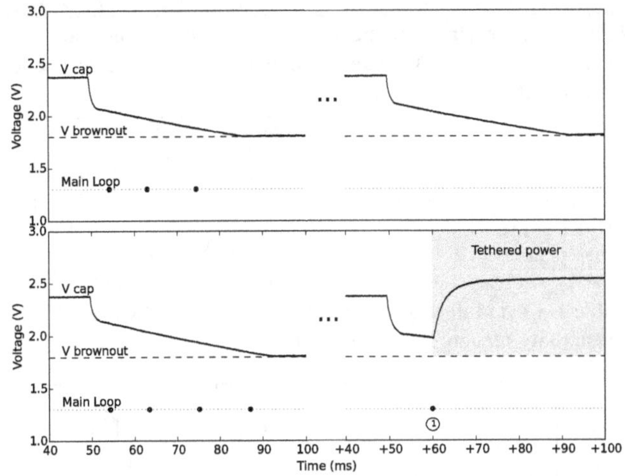

Figure 7: Oscilloscope trace of a memory-corrupting intermittence bug and EDB's intermittence-aware `assert` in action. Without the `assert` (top) the main loop runs at first (left) but mysteriously stops running in later discharge-cycles (right). With the `assert` (bottom), when it fails at instant 1, EDB halts the device and tethers it to a continuous power supply.

instrumentation can render an application non-functional by preventing it from making *any* forward progress. Yet, instrumented energy-harvesting applications must be run on harvested energy to diagnose intermittence-induced bugs, since these bugs are invisible while the device is continuously powered. In this case study we demonstrate how an application can be instrumented with debug code of arbitrary energy cost using EDB's energy guards.

Application. The code in Figure 8 generates the Fibonacci sequence and appends each number to a non-volatile, doubly-linked list. For illustrative purposes, each iteration of the main loop toggles a GPIO pin to track progress. In the debug build, `main` begins with an energy-hungry consistency check that traverses the list and asserts that the previous and next pointers and the Fibonacci value in each node are consistent. This invariant helps detect problems early before they precipitate into mysterious failures akin to the one in Section 5.3.1. With intermittent power, the invariant was violated in several experimental trials.

Symptoms. The application's release build produces an inconsistent list without any indication that there is a problem.

```
main()
  energy_guard_begin()
  for (node in list)
    assert(node->prev->next == node == node->next->prev)
    assert(node->prev->fib + node->fib == node->next->fib)
  assert(list->tail == node)
  energy_guard_end()
  while(1)
    append_fibonacci_node(list)
```

Figure 8: Application code instrumented with a consistency check of arbitrary energy cost using EDB's energy guards.

The debug build stops executing the main loop after having added approximately 555 items to the list. The top trace in Figure 9 shows an early charge cycle when the main loop executes and a later one when it no longer does.

Diagnosis. The energy cost of the consistency check is proportional to the length of the list. Once the list is long enough, the consistency check consumes all the energy available in one charge-discharge cycle and leaves none for the main loop. Once reached, this hung state persists indefinitely because the application cannot make progress in subsequent charge-discharge cycles.

EDB lets the developer keep the consistency check without breaking application functionality by wrapping the check with energy guards as shown in Figure 8. The effect this has on the target energy state is captured in the bottom oscilloscope trace in Figure 9. At instance 1, the target enters the energy guard, and EDB tethers it to a power supply. The capacitor starts charging, while the target continues executing the code within the energy guard. At instance 2, the target exits the energy guard, and EDB cuts the power supply and starts to discharge the capacitor to the level it had at instance 1. After the discharge completes, the target is allowed to continue. This sequence of events later takes place again between instances 3 and 4. With the energy guard around the consistency check, the main loop gets the same amount of energy in both early charge-discharge cycles when the list is short (left) and later ones when it is longer (right).

5.3.3 Tracing events and profiling energy cost

Intermediate results of calculations, frequency of events, and energy cost of operations are valuable clues for quick diagnosis of erroneous code. Directly extracting such information from an energy-harvesting device using existing tools changes the application's behavior. For example, the sample rate of a sensing application may increase by a factor of 100-1000x when powered continuously in the lab relative to when harvesting energy in a realistic deployment. This section demonstrates how EDB's energy-interference-free `printf` and watchpoints can peek under the hood of running code with minimal impact on application behavior.

Application. The activity recognition application outlined in Figure 10 reads an accelerometer sample, classifies the sample as "stationary" or "moving", and records statistics in non-volatile memory.

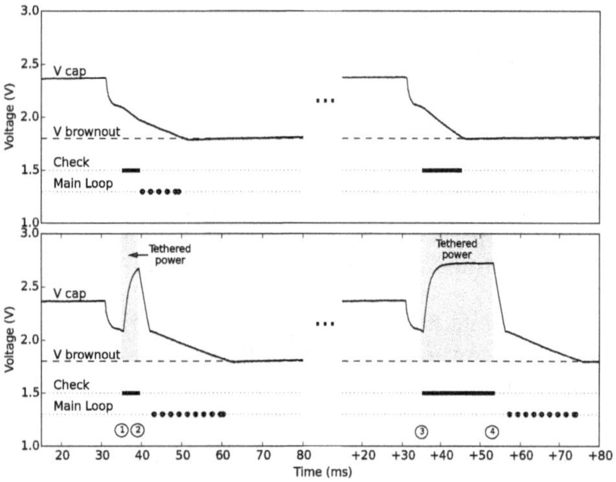

Figure 9: Oscilloscope trace of an application instrumented with a consistency check of high energy cost. Without an energy guard (top), the check and main loop both execute at first (left) but only the check executes in later discharge-cycles (right). With an energy guard (bottom), the check executes on tethered power from instant 1 to 2 and 3 to 4, and the main loop always executes.

Symptoms. There is no evidence that the recorded statistics are based on correct accelerometer readings and classification results. Moreover, the application cannot be tuned to the size of the storage capacitor without the energy profile of one classification operation.

Diagnosis. Information can be extracted from the target device either over traditional debugger interface (e.g. JTAG) or I/O peripherals (e.g. UART or GPIO ports). To relay a data stream via a JTAG debugger, the target device must be on during the entire debugging session. Off-the-shelf USB-to-serial adapters are not electrically isolated from the target UART and permit energy to flow into or out of the device. Encoding information onto GPIO pins and decoding it using an oscilloscope costs pins and significant effort compared to a `printf` call that outputs text to a console on the host.

The measurements in Table 4 demonstrate the impact on application behavior of using UART. The energy cost of the print statement changes the iteration success rate, i.e. the fraction of iterations that successfully complete out of the total attempted. To trace application progress without disrupting its behavior, we instrumented the loop body with an EDB `printf` and three watchpoints as shown in Figure 10. The `printf` produces a stream of intermediate classification results for each iteration. The watchpoints produce a time and energy profile of a loop iteration as well as an independent calculation of the statistics that is useful for manual verification. The energy profile shown in Figure 11 was calculated from the difference between energy level snapshots taken by watchpoints 1 and 2, and watchpoints 1 and 3. Reference classification statistics can be calculated by counting occurrences of watchpoints 2 and 3.

```
main()
  while (1)
    watchpoint(1)
    sample = read_accelerometer()
    class = classify(featurize(sample))
    switch (class)
      case STATIONARY: count[STATIONARY]++
                       watchpoint(2)
      case MOVING:     count[MOVING]++
                       watchpoint(3)
    total++
    printf("t %u s %u m %u\n", total
           count[STATIONARY], count[MOVING])
    stats[STATIONARY] = count[STATIONARY] / total
    stats[MOVING]     = count[MOVING]     / total
```

Figure 10: Tracing and profiling an activity recognition application using EDB's energy-interference-free `printf` and watchpoints.

	Iteration Success Rate	Iteration Cost		Print Cost	
		Energy (%*)	Time (ms)	Energy (%*)	Time (ms)
No print	87%	3.0	1.1	-	-
UART `printf`	74%	5.3	2.1	2.5	1.1
EDB `printf`	82%	3.4	4.7	0.11	3.1

* Energy cost is reported as percentage of 47μF storage capacity.

Table 4: Cost of debug output and its impact on the behavior of the activity recognition application.

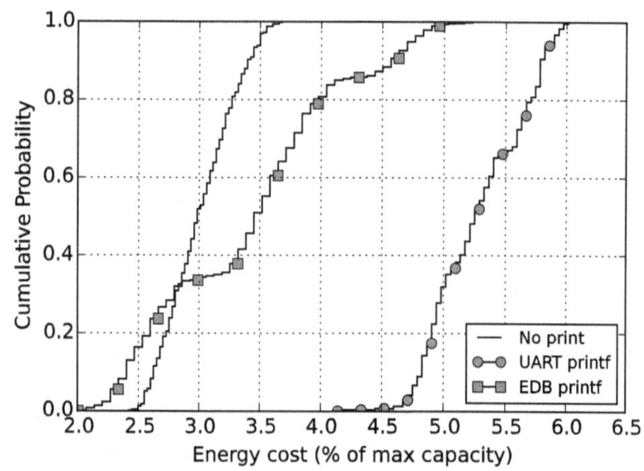

Figure 11: Energy profile of one loop iteration in the activity recognition application when instrumented with different output mechanisms.

5.3.4 Debugging and tuning RFID applications

Energy-harvesting applications that communicate over the RFID protocol are difficult to debug without simultaneous visibility into communication and energy state. This case study demonstrates how EDB can monitor RFID I/O messages and correlate them with available energy.

Application. The WISP RFID firmware [31] decodes RFID query commands from a reader in software and replies with a unique identifier.

Symptoms. The application and reader cannot be characterized and tuned without a measure of the target's performance in different RF environments, e.g. the number of responses per queries received. Correctness cannot be verified without

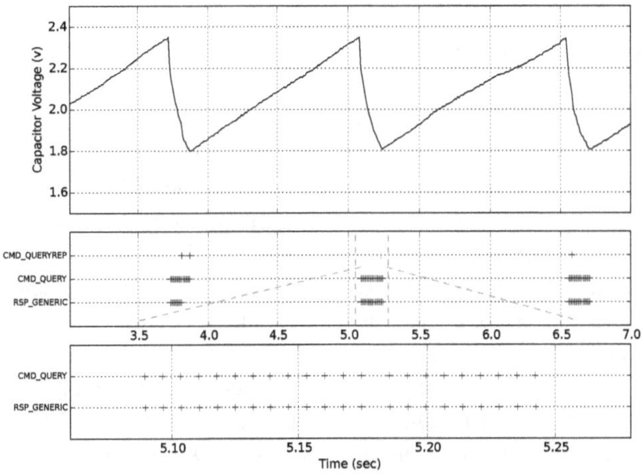

Figure 12: Incoming and outgoing RFID messages correlated with energy level recorded by EDB.

evidence that the application software successfully decodes and acts on each valid incoming query message.

Diagnosis. Both tasks require a trace of incoming messages that reached the target, i.e. bit patterns in the incoming demodulated waveform that *could* have been decoded into valid messages by software. An oscilloscope trace of the raw output from the RF demodulator does not reveal whether the waveform is decodable into a valid message. A decoder is necessary to separate messages that were corrupted in flight from valid messages that the target application failed to parse.

We use EDB to stream RFID message identifiers and target energy readings to the host. From data plotted in Figure 12 we find that in our lab setup the application responded 86% of the time for an average of 13 replies per second. The view focused on one discharge cycle confirms that the application successfully received consecutive incoming query messages and replied. To produce such a mixed trace of I/O and energy using existing equipment, the target would have to be burdened with logging duties that exceed the computational resources left after message decoding and response transmission.

6. Related Work

We discuss several areas of prior work that are especially related to EDB. Some recent work proposes models and emulators for energy-harvesting environments. Much effort is dedicated to improving the reliability of energy-harvesting systems. Earlier work explored debugging in continuously powered sensor nodes.

6.1 Modeling and emulation of energy sources

Ekho [9] is a device that records the amount of energy harvested by a harvesting circuit and reproduces the trace as power input into an application device. Ekho can reproduce problematic program behavior, but it cannot offer insight into this behavior. Complementary to Ekho's features, EDB offers debugging mechanisms for inspecting the program state and correlating program events to the energy level.

Application behavior on an intermittent energy source can be partially inferred from a simulation. Computational RFID Crash Test Simulator (CCTS) [8] can produce a voltage trace representative of a solar harvester with a specified capacitor size and load. CCTS is useful for exploring the design space for a new energy-harvesting application, but not for *in situ* debugging tasks that EDB is designed for.

6.2 Reliability in Intermittent Devices

Prior work pointed out that intermittent execution threatens forward progress [24] and memory consistency [18, 23]. There are three main approaches taken by prior work to combat these threats to reliability. The first approach is to *tolerate intermittent failures* by selectively capturing and restoring program state. The second is to *avoid intermittent failures* through aggressive duty cycling and scheduling. The last is to *eliminate intermittence* with non-volatile hardware.

EDB is related to these approaches because all of them aim to improve correctness of code and reliability of intermittent executions. EDB, however, is largely orthogonal to these approaches as they are mostly changes to the programming or execution model. Instead, the purpose of EDB is to give a programmer visibility into a system to *understand* why intermittence is causing problems, even in emerging programming and execution models.

Tolerating Intermittent Failures. Mementos [24] first equipped energy-harvesting computers to make progress through long-running workloads. Mementos checkpoints volatile state into the device's non-volatile state to preserve execution context and data across power failures. QuickRecall [11] took a similar approach with hardware support and Idetic [20] applied the idea to ASICs.

More recent work [23] observed that even with measures to ensure progress, intermittent execution can leave a system's memory in an inconsistent state. DINO [18] characterized the *intermittent execution model* and addressed these consistency issues with a task-based programming and execution model that selectively preserves both non-volatile and volatile memory across power failures.

Avoiding Intermittent Failures. Other prior work aims to avoid failures due to intermittence by scheduling and duty cycling. Eon [28] is one of the first efforts at avoiding intermittence failures in a solar-powered device. Eon associates computational tasks with their expected energy consumption, and a scarcity of energy causes the system to deschedule expensive tasks. Dewdrop [4] is a scheduler that brings an RF-harvesting device [25] into and out of deep sleep states that consume little energy. Dewdrop schedules tasks based on the likelihood that they will successfully execute, given the available energy. Hibernus [2] assumes hardware with a large capacitor that stores energy during execution. When power fails, Hibernus uses the stored energy to checkpoint volatile state and puts the device to sleep, preserving volatile state and avoiding some failures.

Eliminating Intermittent Failures. Other prior work aims to eliminate intermittence with pervasive non-volatile hardware. Several recent papers [17, 19] discussed different approaches to using microarchitectural non-volatility to prevent power intermittence from leading to intermittent software execution. These efforts require invasive hardware changes and operate more slowly than conventional hardware. However, by making microarchitectural state persistent, these systems prevent progress and consistency issues due to intermittence.

6.3 Debugging in Embedded Wireless Sensor Nodes

Prior to recent interest in energy-harvesting systems [13, 25], there was considerable interest in battery-powered wireless sensor nodes [10, 12]. Sensor nodes necessitated programming [5] and operating system [7, 14] support, which in turn created a need for development and debugging support.

Clairvoyant [32] is the closest work from this era to EDB because, like EDB it provides interactive debugging capabilities. The system tries to minimize its effect on the program being debugged, in terms of memory use, network traffic, and system lifetime. However, because Clairvoyant targets powered nodes, it does not (need to) address energy-interference-freedom. Additionally, Clairvoyant does not discuss features supported by EDB like assertions, energy manipulation, or instrumentation.

Sympathy [22] provides support for debugging *networks* of sensor nodes. The scope of Sympathy is restricted to determining why data collection nodes stop sending data to "sink" nodes in the network. This work uses a series of metrics and an inference step to isolate failures and is largely orthogonal in purpose and mechanism to EDB.

TinyTracer [29] supports lightweight event tracing for sensor node programs written in nesC [5]. Its traces enable execution replay and manual failure analysis. Like TinyTracer, EDB provides lightweight event tracing, although EDB does not trace all events, only marked ones. In contrast, EDB provides fine-grained energy tracing, as well as energy-interference-free active mode tasks. Moreover, EDB's instrumentation support may be able to make TinyTracer energy-interference-free.

T-Check [15] and KleeNet [26] use model checking and symbolic execution (respectively) to *expose* failures in sensor node programs. Both are orthogonal to EDB, as they do not support monitoring or interactive debugging. Additionally, these systems do not address intermittence; however, if we assume they could be re-engineered to work on intermittent systems, they would be complementary to EDB: A developer could use EDB's debugging capabilities to understand and fix failures that they expose.

7. Conclusion

Intermittently executing, energy-harvesting devices present unique system reliability challenges, and our work in EDB presents the first debugging system that is designed to address those challenges. We identified *energy-interference-freedom* as a property that is essential to the utility of a debugging platform for power intermittent systems and built EDB to espouse that property from its circuits to its software. EDB supports passive monitoring of a target device's energy, software events, and I/O. Using its ability to manipulate a target device's energy, EDB also supports active debugging tasks with energy-interference-freedom, including assertions, instrumentation, tracing, and interactive debugging. We evaluated our prototype of EDB, including custom hardware, showing that it is energy-interference-free in both its passive and active tasks, and that it provides invaluable debugging information that is out of reach using existing tools and techniques. We see EDB and its energy-interference-freedom as a key part of future support for reliability in intermittent energy-harvesting devices.

8. Acknowledgements

We thank the anonymous reviewers for their time and valuable feedback. Thanks to Preeti Murthy for beta-testing our EDB prototype. This work was generously supported by Disney Research Pittsburgh and National Science Foundation grant CNS-1526342.

References

[1] IEEE standard for reduced-pin and enhanced-functionality test access port and boundary-scan architecture. *IEEE Std 1149.7-2009*, pages 1–985, Feb 2010.

[2] D. Balsamo, A. Weddell, G. Merrett, B. Al-Hashimi, D. Brunelli, and L. Benini. Hibernus: Sustaining computation during intermittent supply for energy-harvesting systems. *Embedded Systems Letters, IEEE*, PP(99):1–1, 2014.

[3] Ben Ransford. SLLURP - Python Client for LLRP-based RFID Readers. `https://github.com/ransford/sllurp`. Visited August 10, 2015.

[4] M. Buettner, B. Greenstein, and D. Wetherall. Dewdrop: An energy-aware task scheduler for computational RFID. In *USENIX Symposium on Networked Systems Design and Implementation (NSDI)*, Mar. 2011.

[5] D. Gay, P. Levis, R. von Behren, M. Welsh, E. Brewer, and D. Culler. The nesC language: A holistic approach to networked embedded systems. In *Proceedings of the ACM SIGPLAN 2003 Conference on Programming Language Design and Implementation*, PLDI '03, pages 1–11, New York, NY, USA, 2003.

[6] S. Gollakota, M. S. Reynolds, J. R. Smith, and D. J. Wetherall. The emergence of RF-powered computing. *Computer*, 47(1), 2014. doi: http://dx.doi.org/10.1109/MC.2013.404.

[7] L. Gu and J. A. Stankovic. T-kernel: Providing reliable OS support to wireless sensor networks. In *Proceedings of the*

4th International Conference on Embedded Networked Sensor Systems, SenSys '06, pages 1–14, New York, NY, USA, 2006.

[8] J. Gummeson, S. S. Clark, K. Fu, and D. Ganesan. On the limits of effective hybrid micro-energy harvesting on mobile CRFID sensors. In *Proceedings of the 8th International Conference on Mobile Systems, Applications, and Services*, MobiSys '10, pages 195–208, New York, NY, USA, 2010.

[9] J. Hester, T. Scott, and J. Sorber. Ekho: Realistic and repeatable experimentation for tiny energy-harvesting sensors. In *Proceedings of the 12th ACM Conference on Embedded Network Sensor Systems*, SenSys '14, pages 1–15, New York, NY, USA, 2014.

[10] J. Hill, R. Szewczyk, A. Woo, S. Hollar, D. Culler, and K. Pister. System architecture directions for networked sensors. In *Proceedings of the Ninth International Conference on Architectural Support for Programming Languages and Operating Systems*, ASPLOS IX, pages 93–104, New York, NY, USA, 2000.

[11] H. Jayakumar, A. Raha, and V. Raghunathan. QuickRecall: A low overhead HW/SW approach for enabling computations across power cycles in transiently powered computers. In *Int'l Conf. on VLSI Design and Int'l Conf. on Embedded Systems*, Jan. 2014.

[12] J. M. Kahn, R. H. Katz, and K. S. J. Pister. Next century challenges: Mobile networking for "smart dust". In *Proceedings of the 5th Annual ACM/IEEE International Conference on Mobile Computing and Networking*, MobiCom '99, pages 271–278, New York, NY, USA, 1999.

[13] Y. Lee, G. Kim, S. Bang, Y. Kim, I. Lee, P. Dutta, D. Sylvester, and D. Blaauw. A modular 1mm3 die-stacked sensing platform with optical communication and multi-modal energy harvesting. In *Solid-State Circuits Conference Digest of Technical Papers (ISSCC), 2012 IEEE International*, pages 402–404, Feb 2012.

[14] P. Levis, S. Madden, J. Polastre, R. Szewczyk, K. Whitehouse, A. Woo, D. Gay, J. Hill, M. Welsh, E. Brewer, and D. Culler. *Ambient Intelligence*, chapter TinyOS: An Operating System for Sensor Networks. 2004.

[15] P. Li and J. Regehr. T-Check: Bug finding for sensor networks. In *Proceedings of the 9th ACM/IEEE International Conference on Information Processing in Sensor Networks*, IPSN '10, pages 174–185, New York, NY, USA, 2010.

[16] V. Liu, A. Parks, V. Talla, S. Gollakota, D. Wetherall, and J. R. Smith. Ambient backscatter: Wireless communication out of thin air. In *Proceedings of the ACM SIGCOMM 2013 Conference on SIGCOMM*, SIGCOMM '13, pages 39–50, New York, NY, USA, 2013.

[17] Y. Liu, Z. Li, H. Li, Y. Wang, X. Li, K. Ma, S. Li, M.-F. Chang, S. John, Y. Xie, J. Shu, and H. Yang. Ambient energy harvesting nonvolatile processors: From circuit to system. In *Proceedings of the 52Nd Annual Design Automation Conference*, DAC '15, pages 150:1–150:6, New York, NY, USA, 2015.

[18] B. Lucia and B. Ransford. A simpler, safer programming and execution model for intermittent systems. In *Proceedings of the 36th ACM SIGPLAN Conference on Programming Language Design and Implementation*, PLDI 2015, pages 575–585, New York, NY, USA, 2015.

[19] K. Ma, Y. Zheng, S. Li, K. Swaminathan, X. Li, Y. Liu, J. Sampson, Y. Xie, and V. Narayanan. Architecture exploration for ambient energy harvesting nonvolatile processors. In *High Performance Computer Architecture (HPCA), 2015 IEEE 21st International Symposium on*, pages 526–537, Feb 2015.

[20] A. Mirhoseini, E. M. Songhori, and F. Koushanfar. Idetic: A high-level synthesis approach for enabling long computations on transiently-powered ASICs. In *IEEE Pervasive Computing and Communication Conference (PerCom)*, Mar. 2013.

[21] J. A. Paradiso and T. Starner. Energy scavenging for mobile and wireless electronics. *IEEE Pervasive Computing*, 4(1): 18–27, 2005. doi: http://dx.doi.org/10.1109/MPRV.2005.9.

[22] N. Ramanathan, K. Chang, R. Kapur, L. Girod, E. Kohler, and D. Estrin. Sympathy for the sensor network debugger. In *Proceedings of the 3rd International Conference on Embedded Networked Sensor Systems*, SenSys '05, pages 255–267, New York, NY, USA, 2005.

[23] B. Ransford and B. Lucia. Nonvolatile memory is a broken time machine. In *Proceedings of the Workshop on Memory Systems Performance and Correctness*, MSPC '14, pages 5:1–5:3, New York, NY, USA, 2014.

[24] B. Ransford, J. Sorber, and K. Fu. Mementos: System support for long-running computation on RFID-scale devices. In *ASPLOS*, Mar. 2011.

[25] A. P. Sample, D. J. Yeager, P. S. Powledge, A. V. Mamishev, and J. R. Smith. Design of an RFID-based battery-free programmable sensing platform. *IEEE Transactions on Instrumentation and Measurement*, 57(11):2608–2615, Nov. 2008.

[26] R. Sasnauskas, O. Landsiedel, M. H. Alizai, C. Weise, S. Kowalewski, and K. Wehrle. KleeNet: Discovering insidious interaction bugs in wireless sensor networks before deployment. In *Proceedings of the 9th ACM/IEEE International Conference on Information Processing in Sensor Networks*, IPSN '10, pages 186–196, New York, NY, USA, 2010.

[27] SEGGER. J-Link JTAG Isolator . `https://www.segger.com/jtag-isolator.html`, 2015.

[28] J. Sorber, A. Kostadinov, M. Garber, M. Brennan, M. D. Corner, and E. D. Berger. Eon: A language and runtime system for perpetual systems. In *Proceedings of the 5th International Conference on Embedded Networked Sensor Systems*, SenSys '07, pages 161–174, New York, NY, USA, 2007.

[29] V. Sundaram, P. Eugster, X. Zhang, and V. Addanki. Diagnostic tracing for wireless sensor networks. *ACM Trans. Sen. Netw.*, 9(4):38:1–38:41, July 2013. ISSN 1550-4859.

[30] TI Inc. Overview for MSP430FRxx FRAM. `http://ti.com/wolverine`, 2014. Visited July 28, 2014.

[31] WISP. WISP - Firmware Repository for WISP 5.0. `https://github.com/wisp/wisp5`. Visited August 10, 2015.

[32] J. Yang, M. L. Soffa, L. Selavo, and K. Whitehouse. Clairvoyant: A comprehensive source-level debugger for wireless sensor networks. In *Proceedings of the 5th International Conference on Embedded Networked Sensor Systems*, SenSys '07, pages 189–203, New York, NY, USA, 2007.

Programmer Poductivity in a World of Mushy Interfaces: Challenges of the Post-ISA Reality

Moderator: Emmett Witchel
The University of Texas at Austin
witchel@cs.utexas.edu

Abstract

Since 1964, we had the notion that the instruction set architecture (ISA) is a useful and fairly opaque abstraction layer between hardware and software. Software rode hardware's performance wave while remaining gloriously oblivious to hardware's growing complexity. Unfortunately, the jig is up. We still have ISAs, but the abstraction no longer offers seamless portability—parallel software needs to be tuned for different core counts, and heterogeneous processing elements (CPUs, GPUs, accelerators) further complicate programmability. We are better at building large-scale heterogeneous processors than we are at programming them. Maintaining software across multiple current platforms is difficult and porting to future platforms is also difficult. There have been many technical responses: virtual ISAs (e.g., NVIDIA's PTX), higher-level programming interfaces (e.g., CUDA or OpenCL), and late-stage compilation and platform-specific tailoring (e.g., Android ART), etc.

A team of opinionated experts, drawn from the three ASPLOS communities will examine the problem of programmer productivity in the post-ISA world, first from the perspective of their area of expertise and then noting the contributions from the other two communities. What research will save us and how? This wide-ranging debate will frame important research areas for future work while being grounded in frank discussion about what has succeeded in the past. Attendees can expect actionable insight into important research issues as well an entertaining discussion.

Categories and Subject Descriptors C.0 [*Computer Systems Organization*]: General; D.3 [*Software*]: Programming languages; D.4 [*Software*]: Operating systems

Keywords Programmer productivity, portability, instruction set architecture

ASPLOS '16 April 02-06, 2016, Atlanta, GA, USA
ACM 978-1-4503-4091-5/16/04.
DOI: http://dx.doi.org/10.1145/2872362.2876511

RAPID Programming of Pattern-Recognition Processors

Kevin Angstadt Westley Weimer Kevin Skadron

Department of Computer Science
University of Virginia
Charlottesville, VA 22904-4740
{angstadt,weimer,skadron}@cs.virginia.edu

Abstract

We present RAPID, a high-level programming language and combined imperative and declarative model for programming pattern-recognition processors, such as Micron's Automata Processor (AP). The AP is a novel, non-Von Neumann architecture for direct execution of non-deterministic finite automata (NFAs), and has been demonstrated to provide substantial speedup for a variety of data-processing applications. RAPID is clear, maintainable, concise, and efficient both at compile and run time. Language features, such as code abstraction and parallel control structures, map well to pattern-matching problems, providing clarity and maintainability. For generation of efficient runtime code, we present algorithms to convert RAPID programs into finite automata. Further, we introduce a tessellation technique for configuring the AP, which significantly reduces compile time, increases programmer productivity, and improves maintainability. We evaluate five RAPID programs against custom, baseline implementations previously demonstrated to be significantly accelerated by the AP. We find that RAPID programs are much shorter in length, are expressible at a higher level of abstraction than their handcrafted counterparts, and yield generated code that is often more compact. In addition, our tessellation technique for configuring the AP has comparable device utilization to, and results in compilation that is up to four orders of magnitude faster than, current solutions.

Categories and Subject Descriptors C.1.3 [*Processor Architectures*]: Other Architecture Styles—Heterogeneous (hybrid) systems; D.3.3 [*Programming Languages*]: Language Constructs and Features—Concurrent, distributed, and parallel languages; D.3.4 [*Programming Languages*]: Processors—Concurrent programming structures, Patterns

Keywords Automata Processor; Accelerators; MISD

ASPLOS '16, April 2–6, 2016, Atlanta, Georgia, USA..

ACM 978-1-4503-4091-5/16/04...$15.00.
http://dx.doi.org/10.1145/2872362.2872393

1. Introduction

Big-data research is becoming increasingly common in both industry and also academia. In a recent survey of around 1,000 senior decision-makers from nine industries and ten countries, 70% of respondents consider their business's ability to exploit big data critical to their future success [5]. Additionally, the Computer Sciences Corporation reports that the amount of data being generated by individuals and companies will be 44 times greater in 2020 than it was in 2009 [8].

Collected data is often analyzed in a multitude of different ways, and many algorithms in areas such as data-mining, bioinformatics, deep packet analysis, and spam filtering require identification of exact or near-match character patterns. A pattern defines a sequence of data that should be found within another collection of data. For example, a pattern could be all DNA sequences within a Hamming distance of four from "ATCGAC" or all six-letter strings beginning with "se". Conducting such searches through large datasets demands good support from both hardware and software. Current processor technologies are not well-suited for these tasks: single-threaded processing most naturally identifies a single pattern at a time, and therefore requires multiple passes through the data; vector or SIMD processors suffer from inherent branch divergence when analyzing data for multiple patterns; and multi-core processors and clusters often execute far fewer threads than there are patterns to be identified.

Hardware designers are exploring new processing technologies to accelerate pattern identification. One proposed solution is the Automata Processor (AP) [10] by Micron Technology, a non-Von Neumann architecture for direct hardware simulation of non-deterministic finite automata (NFAs). Patterns are encoded as NFAs, which are loaded into a reconfigurable lattice on the processor. Data are then streamed to the processor and the NFAs are executed in lock-step against the data stream. The AP is well-suited for problems that are highly parallel with disjoint or inexact comparisons, such as analyses requiring the identification of multiple patterns against a single data stream. Previous work has demonstrated significant speedups on the AP for several data analysis and pattern-recognition problems, such as biological motif search [18], association rule mining [21], and Brill tagging in natural language processing [23].

The AP, however, is currently challenging to program. Programming consists of specifying NFAs using an XML-based language, which requires both knowledge of automata theory and also the non-standard architecture. This is akin to assembly-level programming on a traditional, Von Neumann architecture. High-level language bindings exist for this XML-based language, but are similarly challenging to use. Regular expressions are a common means for defining NFAs, but their use with the AP also has drawbacks. For problems accelerated by the AP, the regular expression representation is often an exhaustive enumeration of all accepting data sequences. This is difficult to maintain and places an unnecessary burden on the developer, as described further in Section 2.

This paper presents RAPID, a high-level language that maintains the performance benefits of pattern-recognition processors while also providing concise, clear, maintainable, and efficient representations of pattern-identification algorithms. Programs consist of one or more *macros* and a *network*, written in a combination of imperative and declarative styles. A *macro* uses sequential control flow to define an algorithm for matching patterns in an input data stream. Macros in RAPID are similar to C-style macros and macros in low-level Automata Processor programs. The *network* contains a list of macros that are instantiated in parallel, allowing for simultaneous recognition of many patterns in data streams. Macros and networks provide a programming abstraction that maps naturally to pattern-matching problems and the MISD computational model of the Automata Processor, while providing a familiar structure akin to functions or procedures.

We introduce three parallel control structures to facilitate common pattern-matching tasks. These allow the concise specification of multiple, simultaneous comparisons against a single data stream and provide high-level support for variable-offset sliding window comparisons that are integral to many pattern-recognition problems.

We also present algorithms for converting RAPID programs into NFAs for execution with the Automata Processor. While code generation from RAPID for other pattern-recognition processors and CPUs is possible, we choose to focus on the AP because of recent promising results [4, 18, 21, 23] and the overall flexibility of the architecture. These studies have reported speedups ranging from 8x–4000x over single-threaded CPU applications. Acceleration of RAPID programs is achieved via *staged computation*. Imperative statements in the code are executed at compile time to aid in generating finite automata, while declarative statements related to the input data stream are then executed on the Automata Processor.

Producing designs that place and route efficiently on the AP is a challenge. The AP hardware has a finite number of resources, divided into configurable regions. By increasing the utilization of these resources, more NFAs can be loaded, thereby allowing for increased parallel exploration of the data stream. We propose an *auto-tuning tessellation* optimization to increase the density of NFAs loaded into the AP while reducing compile time. Often, the generated finite automata of a RAPID program consist of a repeated NFA design for exploring variations of a pattern. Our optimization determines the maximum quantity of this design that can occupy the smallest programmable portion of the AP and generates a final automaton accordingly. At runtime, this structure can be *tiled* (loaded into multiple, programmable regions) onto the AP by making use of block-level configuration before execution of the search. Automation of this process saves the developer time and reduces the number of possible programming mistakes, while increasing the overall resource utilization and throughput of the AP.

We evaluate the efficiency of compiled RAPID programs against handcrafted equivalents, measuring program size and resource utilization. These programs are based on real-world applications that have previously been shown to have significant speedups when executed on the Automata Processor. This paper makes the following contributions:

- the RAPID programming language, a high-level language for programming pattern identification processors
- a set of algorithms for converting RAPID programs into non-deterministic finite automata
- an auto-tuning tessellation optimization for block-level configuration of the AP, which maintains runtime efficiency and significantly reduces compilation times
- experimental evaluation of the RAPID language against hand-crafted applications demonstrating improved density of loaded NFAs and up to five orders of magnitude faster compilation times when using our tessellation optimization

2. Background and Related Work

Pattern-Recognition Processors. There have been many proposed hardware approaches for accelerating pattern-matching problems [7, 11, 12, 15, 22]. Recently, there has been been a renewed focus on accelerating pattern-recognition problems using devices such as IBM's PowerEN Processor [13], the Titan IC RXP Regular eXpression Processor [20], and the Automata Processor (AP) [10]. The PowerEN processor contains special accelerators alongside traditional cores to allow for improved regular expression performance. The Titan IC processor employs a large lookup table to accelerate regular expression matching. Rather than directly processing a regular expression, the AP executes NFAs using a combination of a modified SDRAM memory array and a reconfigurable routing matrix. The device is a MISD processor according to Flynn's Taxonomy. In this paper we choose to target the AP and leave research into alternate hardware architectures for future work.

Low-Level Automata Programming. The primary programming model for the AP requires developers to design NFAs using an XML-based language called the Automata Network Markup Language (ANML). The ANML definition is passed to placement and routing tools, which generate a binary image of the automaton. This binary image is used to configure AP components to directly execute the NFAs. The language allows for very fine-grained control, but is verbose and not conducive to maintenance. For example, measuring Hamming distance, the number of differences in corresponding characters between two strings, between a five character string and the input data stream requires 62 lines of code [17]. To modify this code for Hamming distance comparisons with a string of length 12 requires 40 lines to be modified or inserted (i.e., 65% of the code in this simple example must be modified to make this change). Modifying the code to support even larger strings requires the modification of an increasing percentage of the code.

Although GUI-based design tools for developing automata exist, there is still an additional level of abstraction the developer must provide. Instead of directly representing the pattern to be matched, the developer must instead provide a finite automaton. The conversion from pattern to automaton is a conceptual burden placed on the developer. Finite automata can be challenging and tedious to design and can feel non-intuitive to developers lacking familiarity with automata theory. In program verification research, for example, generation of finite automata that represent specifications is automated because generating correct designs is difficult [1], and debugging of these automata is also challenging [2]. ANML requires developers to have intimate knowledge of the processor's architecture to design automata that meet hardware constraints. Consequently, changes in newer generations of the hardware could hinder productivity and portability.

Alternatively, developers could program the processor using regular expressions, which abstractly represent their equivalent automata; however, this also has its drawbacks. For many problems, such as motif search or association rule mining, the regular expression representing the search is non-intuitive or may enumerate all possible variations of a given pattern that should be matched. An additional limitation with these programming models is that the patterns to be matched must be known at compile time; i.e., a *specific instance* of a problem must be defined and then compiled.

While other notations exist for defining patterns, such as those used by lexical analyzers [14] and packet filters [16], these representations become cumbersome as pattern complexity increases. For example, motif search does not map well to a list of non-overlapping lexemes. RAPID excels in applications where patterns are best represented as a combination of text and computation.

Languages for Streaming Applications. Streaming applications process a sequence of data that is received in real time. Common examples of these applications include radio receivers and software routers. The AP can be classified as a streaming processor because the hardware detects patterns in real time as data is input.

Languages for streaming applications, such as StreamIt [19], have been studied in great detail. StreamIt provides structures for stream pipelining, splitting and joining, and feedback loops. StreamIt objects may peek and pop from the input stream, store input, and perform computations before outputting a result. The AP architecture, however, does not readily admit to this computational model. Finite automata have no inherent memory, and cannot generally peek at the input stream. Many of the operations allowed by StreamIt are thus not applicable in this domain, and it is not evident how to extend the StreamIt model to describe complex automata nor non-deterministic execution. Additionally, data and control are treated differently in StreamIt and RAPID. A StreamIt program specifies a stream graph: data always enters the program and is transformed and passed downstream until reaching an output. In RAPID, each instruction describes the next step to be taken to identify a pattern: stream data enters the program in the location(s) where the program is currently active, causing control to shift to another statement in the program. Ultimately, StreamIt and RAPID target different architectures and abstractions, and are not directly comparable (e.g., it is not clear how to compile StreamIt programs for the Automata Processor).

Non-Deterministic Languages. Non-determinism is a useful formalism for identifying patterns in parallel within a data stream. In a state machine, non-determinism arises when multiple states are active simultaneously, effectively allowing for parallel exploration of the data stream. Several existing languages contain non-deterministic control structures to facilitate these types of operations.

Dijkstra's Guarded Command Language [9] introduces non-deterministic alternative and repetitive constructs. Each construct is predicated with a boolean "guard" that must be true for the encapsulated statements to execute. The alternative construct chooses one command for which the guard is satisfies and executes it. In the repetitive construct, the program loops, choosing one command with a satisfied guard to execute, until no guards are satisfied. Rather than proposing a concrete language, the Guarded Command Language presents guiding formalisms for supporting non-determinism. RAPID provides similar constructs, but a notion of parallel exploration is incorporated directly into the semantics, allowing RAPID to be more concise than the

Guarded Command Language when processing stream or pattern data.

An additional non-deterministic programming language is Alma-0 [3], a declarative extension of Modula-2. Alma-0 supports the use of boolean expressions as statements, an ORELSE statement allowing for execution of multiple paths through the program, and a SOME statement that is the non-deterministic dual of the FOR statement. While RAPID also treats boolean expressions as statements (see Section 3.1), it differs from Alma-0 in the computational model supported by the language's semantics. In Alma-0, the ORELSE and SOME are defined via backtracking. Execution is single threaded: when an ORELSE statement or a SOME statement is encountered, the program will choose a single option to execute. If an exploration fails, the program backtracks to the last choice point, restoring all program state, and attempts a different option. Rather than choosing a single option to explore and backtracking if computation fails, RAPID programs explore all paths in parallel.

3. The RAPID Language

RAPID allows developers to write concise, clear, and maintainable algorithms for use on pattern-recognition processors, such as the Automata Processor. In particular, RAPID supports searching a stream of data for many patterns in parallel. Programs are written in a combined imperative and declarative style using a C-like syntax. In this section, we present a high-level overview of the control structures and data representations in the RAPID programming language.

3.1 Program Structure

Macros and Networks. Rapid programs consist of one or more *macros* and a *network*. The basic unit of computation in a RAPID program is a *macro*, which define reusable pattern-matching algorithms. Macros in RAPID share similarities with both C-style macros and ANML macros, allowing code to be written once and then used as a "rubber stamp". RAPID macros admit more customized usage than their namesakes in C and ANML; the same macro can generate all designs for a particular problem.

Statements within a macro are executed sequentially and define actions that should be taken to identify a pattern. To facilitate the description of these actions, RAPID provides several control structures, including `if` statements, `while` loops, and `foreach` loops. Unlike some languages, we guarantee in-order traversal when iterating with a `foreach` loop. The language also provides parallel control structures useful for pattern-matching, which we describe later in this section.

Additionally, macros can instantiate other macros. When a macro is called, control shifts to the called macro; all of its statements are executed, and then control returns to the calling macro. While the macro code defines how to identify a pattern in the input stream, the macro parameters can specify the particular characters to match, allowing for comparisons of varying lengths. Consider the macro in Figure 1, which performs a Hamming distance computation between a string parameter, `s`, and the input stream. Changing from comparison against a string of length five to a string of length twelve only requires passing a different string argument to the macro. As noted previously in Section 2, more than half of the code in the ANML model must be modified to make an identical change.

```
1  macro hamming_distance (String s, int d) {
2      Counter cnt;
3      foreach (char c : s)
4          if(c != input()) cnt.count();
5      cnt <= d;
6      report;
7  }
8  network (String[] comparisons) {
9      some(String s : comparisons)
10         hamming_distance(s,5);
11 }
```

Figure 1: A RAPID program for computing Hamming distances

The *network* represents the highest level of pattern-matching within a RAPID program. Statements within a network definition are executed in parallel. The most common use of the network is to define a collection of macros for instantiation, which are executed in parallel at runtime to identify patterns in the input data stream. The network may also have parameters which specify certain values at runtime. For example, Figure 1 contains a RAPID program that computes the Hamming distance for a number of given strings and reports on input within a distance of five. In this example, the network is parameterized on an array of strings, which is used at runtime to specify the comparisons being made.

Reporting. RAPID programs passively observe the input data stream; they cannot modify the stream in any manner. Programs can indicate interesting regions within the stream by using the `report` statement, which generates a *report event*. These events provide the offset in the input data stream at which the report occurred and additional identifying meta data, such as the reporting macro. For the program in Figure 1, reports indicate offsets where the input stream is within a Hamming distance of five from the strings in `comparisons`.

Boolean Expressions as Statements. Inspection of the input data stream is central to the RAPID programming model. Often, pattern identification algorithms only continue if a certain sequence of characters is detected. RAPID provides concise support for this common domain idiom by allowing boolean expressions whenever full statements are allowed. These declarative assertions terminate the thread of computation if the expression returns `false`. Line 5 in Figure 1 illustrates this usage.

```
Counter cnt;
foreach(char c : "rapid") {
    if( c == input() ) cnt.count();
}
if( cnt >= 3 ) report;
```

Figure 2: The above code counts the number of characters matched in "rapid" and reports if the count is at least three

3.2 Types and Data in RAPID

There are five primary data types in RAPID: `char`, `int`, `bool`, `String`, and `Counter`. Both `String` and `Counter` are lightweight objects, while the remaining three are primitive types. Additionally, there is support for nested arrays of these types.

In RAPID, pattern-matching occurs in a stream of a characters. Therefore, the language provides the `char` primitive type for interacting with input data. The input data stream, however, is a stream of bits and does not need to be interpreted as characters. To support this, a `char` may also store escaped hexadecimal values. RAPID also defines two character constants, which represent special symbols in the input stream: `ALL_INPUT` and `START_OF_INPUT`. The former represents any symbol within the input and the latter is a reserved symbol (character `0xFF`) for indicating the start of data. For example, if the input data stream consists of the flattening of an array, the entries would be concatenated into a stream, separated by the `START_OF_INPUT` symbol.

A `Counter` is an abstract representation of a saturating up-counter. Upon instantiation, a counter's value is initialized to zero. Counters provide two functions: `reset()` and `count()`, which set the value to zero and increment by one respectively. Although a program does not have access to the internal value of the counter, it is possible to check its value against integers.

Figure 2 demonstrates the usage of counters and interacting with the input stream. The `foreach` loop iterates over each character in the string "`rapid`" sequentially. If that character matches the next character from the input stream, the counter is incremented. After iterating over the entire string, the program checks if the counter is at least three and reports if so. For example, if the stream contained "`tepid`", the count would be three, and there would be a report, but "`party`" results in a count of one and no report.

The input data stream in RAPID is privileged and is accessed via the `input()` function. A call to this function returns a single character from the head of the data stream. Access to the input data is destructive—no peeking or insertion is allowed during program execution. Calls to `input()` act as synchronization points across active threads in a RAPID program. Similar to how active states in an NFA process the same input symbol, all active threads execute up to an `input()` statement and then receive the same character from the input stream. For example, if the stream contains "`abcd...`", `input()` would return '`a`' to all active threads of computation, and the stream would now contain "`bcd...`". There is no required number of calls to `input()` across threads and also no communication between threads. Threads with fewer calls to input() than another thread will simply terminate earlier. This data model supports the heterogeneity of MISD computations.

RAPID's design represents the input stream as a FIFO only accessible through a special function, `input()`, rather than as a special indexed array. This is for conceptual clarity: arrays afford a notion of random access into the stored data, while pattern-recognition processors support sequential access to an ordered sequential data stream. Global input access is intentionally similar to C's "fgetc" rather than "fread/fseek" or "mmap".

3.3 Parallel Control Structures

In pattern-matching problems, it is often useful to explore multiple possibilities in parallel. For example, a spam filter may wish to check for many black-listed subject lines simultaneously, or a gene aligner may begin matching a sequence at any point in the input stream. To facilitate such operations, RAPID provides both the network environment and also parallel control structures. Networks, as described previously, allow for parallelism at the macro level, which is useful for checking several patterns in tandem. The parallel control structures (`either/orelse`, `some`, and `whenever`) provide finer-grain control over parallel operations.

***Either/Orelse* Statements.** This structure provides basic support for parallel exploration in a pattern-matching algorithm. An `either/orelse` statement consists of two or more blocks, which allows for an arbitrary, static number of parallel computations. Computation splits when an `either/orelse` statement is encountered during execution, and each of the blocks is executed in parallel. When the end of a block is reached, computation continues with the next statement in the program. No blocking or joining occurs, meaning that different paths in the `either/orelse` statement may begin executing the following statement at different times. This behavior is desirable because it allows for the matching of different length patterns containing the same suffix.

As an example usage of the `either/orelse` statement, consider the code fragment in Figure 3, which is adapted from a bioinformatics motif search program [18]. In this problem, candidates in the input stream are separated by the control character '`y`'. The computation should report the candidates within a Hamming distance of `d` from the string stored in variable `s`. We use an `either/orelse` statement to ensure that computation continues to the next candidate when the current candidate does not fall within the threshold. The first block of the `either/orelse` statement performs the Hamming distance comparison, while the second block

```
either {
    hamming_distance(s,d); //hamming distance
    'y' == input();        //next input is 'y'
    report;                //report candidate
} orelse {
    while('y' != input()); //consume until 'y'
}
```

Figure 3: An example usage of an either/orelse statement

consumes input until the control character is reached, always preparing the program to check the next candidate.

***Some* Statements.** In certain cases, for example instantiating macros based on the content of an array, the ability to generate a dynamic number of parallel paths is desirable. The `some` statement provides this functionality.

This statement is the parallel dual of a `foreach` loop. During execution, the program iterates over a provided array or string and instantiates a parallel thread of execution for each item. Similar to an `either/orelse` statement, the execution of each parallel thread continues with the subsequent statement in the program; different threads in the some statement may reach this next statement at disjoint times. The `some` statement in Figure 1 instantiates a Hamming distance macro for each string in the `comparisons` array. The number of parallel threads executed depends on the number of entries in `comparisons`.

***Whenever* Statements.** A common operation in pattern-matching algorithms is a *sliding window* search, in which a pattern could begin on any character within the input stream. The `whenever` statement consists of a boolean guard and an internal statement, which is often a block. The guard specifies a condition on the input stream that must be true or a counter threshold that must be met before the internal statement is executed. At any point in the data stream where this guard is satisfied, the internal statement will be executed in parallel with the rest of the program. A `whenever` statement is the parallel dual of a while statement. Whereas a while statement checks the guard condition before each iteration of the internal statement, a `whenever` statement checks the guard in parallel with all other computations, if any.

The code fragment in Figure 4 will perform a sliding window search for the string "`rapid`". The predicate within the guard will return true on any input, and therefore the block of code will begin execution at every character in the input stream. The `whenever` statement can also perform restricted sliding window searches depending on the predicate in the guard. For example, an application searching through HTTP transaction might use the predicate matching "`GET`" before matching specific URLs.

Sliding window searches are fundamental to stream pattern recognition. All RAPID programs perform a sliding

```
whenever( ALL_INPUT == input() ) {
    foreach(char c : "rapid")
        c == input();
    report;
}
```

Figure 4: Execution of a sliding window search over the entire input stream for the string "`rapid`"

window search on the `START_OF_INPUT` symbol. In the common case, this sliding window search occurs at the topmost level of a RAPID program, i.e. right within the network. To reduce verbosity, RAPID infers this `whenever` statement, only requiring developers to specify a whenever statement when performing a non-default sliding window search.

4. The Automata Processor

Before describing our techniques for transforming RAPID programs into NFAs for acceleration with the AP, we present an overview of the device's architecture and computational model.

The Automata Processor, as described by Dlugosch et al. [10], is a hierarchical, memory-derived architecture for direct execution of homogeneous non-deterministic finite automata. NFAs are a useful model of computation for identifying patterns in a string of symbols. An NFA, formally, is defined as a tuple consisting of: a finite set of states, a finite alphabet, a transition function, the initial state, and the set of accepting states. The finite alphabet defines the allowable symbols within the input string. The transition function takes, as input, a set of currently active states and a symbol, and the function returns a new set of active states.

Traditionally, NFAs are often represented as a directed graph with states as vertices and the transition function encoded as edges. The AP executes an alternate form of NFAs known as *homogeneous* NFAs. These automata restrict the possible transition rules such that all incoming transitions to a state must occur on the same symbol.[1] Because all transitions to a state occur on the same symbol, we can label states with symbols rather than labeling the transitions. We refer to these combined states and labels as *state transition elements* (STEs). An STE *accepts* the symbols in its label, which we we refer to as the *character class* of the STE. Figure 5 depicts an NFA and a behaviorally equivalent homogeneous NFA. Additionally, the AP relaxes the definition of machine acceptance. Instead of accepting if an accepting state is active at the end of input, the AP will report any time an accepting state is active and record the relative offset in the input stream of this activation. This allows for pattern-recognition in streams of data symbols.

[1] NFAs traditionally support ϵ-transitions between a source and target state *without* consuming a symbol. These are not supported in our definition of homogeneous NFAs. An ϵ-transition may be removed by duplicating all incident transitions to the source state on the target state.

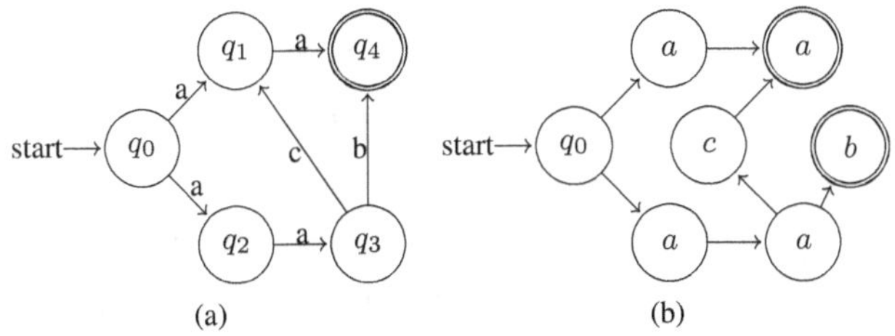

Figure 5: A behaviorally equivalent NFA and homogeneous NFA (both accept exactly aa, aab, and aaca)

The set of languages recognized by both forms of finite automata are equivalent [6]; however, the homogeneous formulation allows for efficient execution directly in hardware. The STEs are stored in a memory array, and transitions between these STEs are embedded in a reconfigurable routing matrix. These two components—the memory array and routing matrix—form the basis of the AP architecture.

An SDRAM memory array serves as a computational medium in the AP, a stark contrast from its traditional role as main memory in a Von Neumann computer system. Arranged as a two dimensional grid, SDRAM data is accessed via row and column addresses. STEs consist of a single column of memory and a detection cell used for storing whether the given STE is active. The design in Figure 5b would require seven columns of SDRAM, one for each of the STEs. The symbol or symbols accepted by an STE are stored in the column of memory, each row representing a different symbol in the alphabet. At runtime, a symbol from the input data stream is decoded and drives one of the rows in the memory array. Simultaneously, all STEs (columns of memory) determine whether they accept that symbol. Accepting STEs (i.e., those currently active as determined via their detection cells) then generate an output signal that is passed through the routing matrix to activate the connected STEs.

In addition to STEs, there may be additional special purpose elements. For example, the current generation AP contains saturating counters and combinatorial logic. These elements connect to the STEs via transition edges and allow for aggregation and thresholding of transitions between STEs. While these elements do not necessarily add any expressive power over traditional NFAs, the use of counters and logic often reduces the overall size of automata. This allows the AP architecture to be flexible. Future implementations might contain additional special purpose elements.

A hierarchical, reconfigurable routing matrix is used to route activation signals between STEs and special elements. Groupings of two STEs form a *GoT*. Several GoTs and a special purpose element (S.E.) are then connected to form a *row* in the routing matrix. Groupings of rows form *blocks*, and groupings of blocks form a *half-core*. Although an AP *chip* consists of two half-cores, there exists no routing between these two units. An AP *board* consists of several AP chips, and this allows for many pattern-recognition searches to occur in parallel. Figure 6 depicts this hierarchy for a half-core. Table 1 provides resource information for the first-generation AP board. We can take advantage of this hierarchical routing to produce efficient automata from RAPID programs.

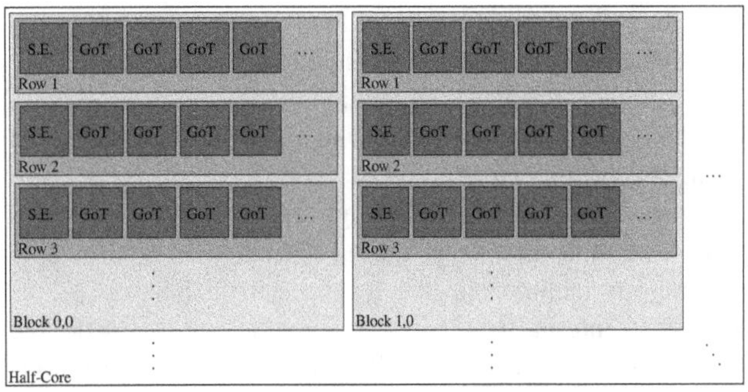

Figure 6: Hierarchical relationships between AP components: *groups of two* (GoT) and a *special purpose element* (S.E.) form a *row*, rows form *blocks*, and blocks form a *half-core*

Table 1: Resources available on the first-generation AP board, containing 32 chips

Total STEs	Total Counters	Total Boolean Logic Elements	Total Blocks	Half-Cores / Chip
1,572,864	24,576	73,728	6,144	2
STEs / Row	**Rows / Block**	**Counters / Block**	**Boolean / Block**	**Blocks / Half-Core**
16	16	4	12	96

5. Code Generation and Staged Computation

In this section, we present techniques for converting RAPID programs into automata for execution on the Automata Processor. The placement and routing tools for the AP accept both regular expressions and an XML-based design language called ANML as input. We choose to generate ANML because this allows for finer-grained control over the resulting automata. Additionally, ANML allows us to explicitly take advantage of future extension to the AP hardware, such as the addition of new special purpose elements.

Our technique takes two files as input: the RAPID program and a file annotating properties of the arguments to the network parameters, such as lengths of arrays and strings. Using this information, our tool converts the RAPID program into two files: an ANML specification and host driver code. The ANML file specifies the configuration of the AP needed to perform the given pattern-matching algorithm given by the RAPID program. The driver code is executed on the CPU at runtime to load the ANML design onto the AP, stream input data to the AP, and collect report events back from the AP. In this section, we focus on the transformation of RAPID into the ANML specification.

We employ a staged computation model to convert RAPID program: comparisons with the input stream and counters occur at runtime, while all other values are resolved at compile time. To aid in partitioning, we annotate all expressions with their return type during type checking. Allowable annotations include the five types listed in Section 3.2 as well as an internal `Automata` type, which we use to denote expressions interacting with the input stream. Expressions annotated with `Automata` or `Counter` are converted into ANML structures (allowing for runtime execution), while the remaining expressions are evaluated during compilation.

At its heart, our conversion algorithm recursively transforms RAPID programs into finite automata in much the same way that regular expressions can be recursively transformed into NFAs. Comparisons with the input stream are transformed into STEs. The particular statement in which the comparison occurs determines how the STEs attach to the rest of the automaton. Rules for transforming automata expressions determine the structure of the STEs within a given statement. We describe the conversion of expressions, statements and counters in turn.

5.1 Converting Expressions

Expression transformation results in the formation of a chain of STEs. No cycles are generated by expressions, but chains may include bifurcations. Figure 7 provides examples of transformations from RAPID expressions to automata structures. The most basic transformation is a comparison between a character and the input stream, which generates a single STE. AND expressions behave as concatenation because reading from the input stream is destructive. The conversion of an OR expression generates a bifurcation in the generated automaton structure. A special case occurs when both sides of the OR expression contain input comparisons of length one. In these instances, we take advantage of STE character classes to specify multiple accepting symbols for a single STE.

Negations of expression generate the most complex structures of all the expression types. Traditionally, an automaton is negated by swapping accepting and non-accepting states. This construction, however, does not work for our use case because RAPID programs consume the same number of symbols for an expression and its negation. The traditional transformation does not maintain this property. Instead, we transform the expression via De Morgan's laws and generate STEs for the resulting statement. After any mismatch in this negation, the remaining symbols do not matter, but still must be consumed. We therefore use *star* states, which match on any character. In practice, complex STE character classes can handle such reserved symbols efficiently.

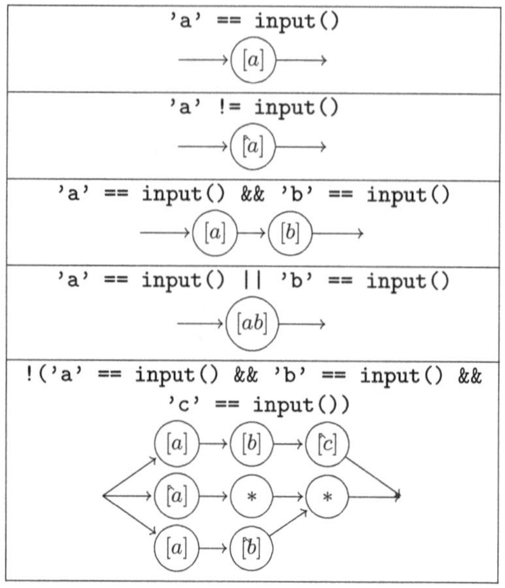

Figure 7: Example transformations of RAPID expressions into automata

5.2 Converting Statements

Statements in RAPID are transformed into the high-level automaton structures, allowing for additional pipelining, feedback loops, and parallel exploration of patterns. We present the overall structures in Figure 8.

A `foreach` loop is unrolled into straight-line pattern-matching. Parallel `either/orelse` and `some` statement are transformed by generating the code for each statement and connecting these structures in parallel into the overall design. This mirrors the language semantics that the `some` statement is the parallel dual of `foreach`. Note that `some` statements typically depend on compile-time parameters (via input annotations on the network) while `either/orelse` statements do not (see Section 3.3).

There is also a similarity between `while` loops and `whenever` statements. `While` loops are transformed to alternately perform predicate checks and execute the body code. This generates a feedback loop structure in the automaton. In a `whenever` statement, predicate checking begins on every character consumed. To support this, we generate a self-activating STE that accepts all symbols (see $*$ node in Figure 8d). This added STE maintains an active transition into the predicate, allowing matching to begin on every symbol consumed. Once the predicate accepts, the body of the `whenever` statement will begin to execute (although the predicate is still checked again in parallel on subsequent input characters).

5.3 Converting Counters

Counters in RAPID are challenging to implement because the state of a hardware counter on the AP cannot be directly accessed. Therefore, counter comparisons in RAPID pro-

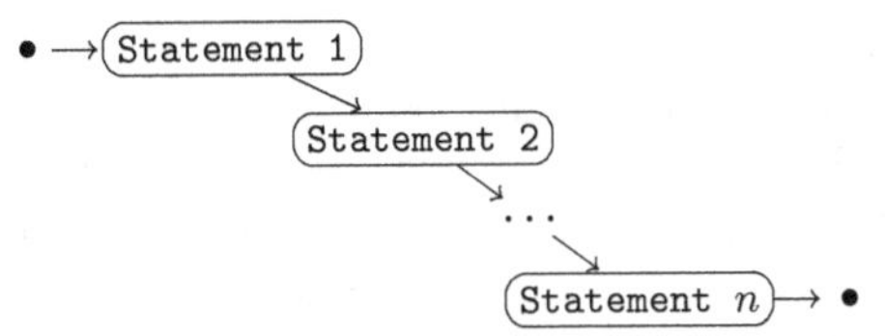

(a) Foreach Loops

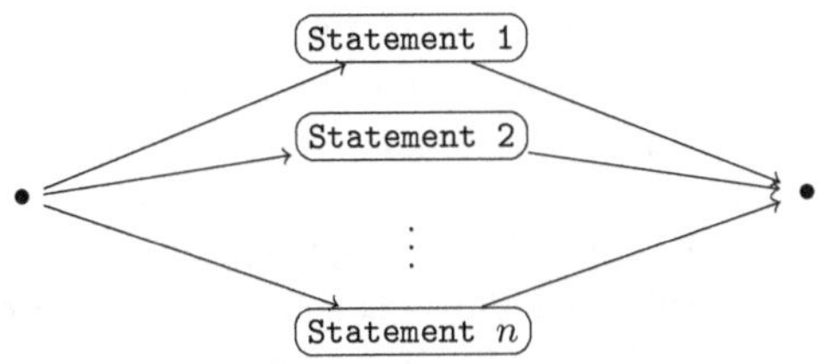

(b) Either/Orelse and Some statements

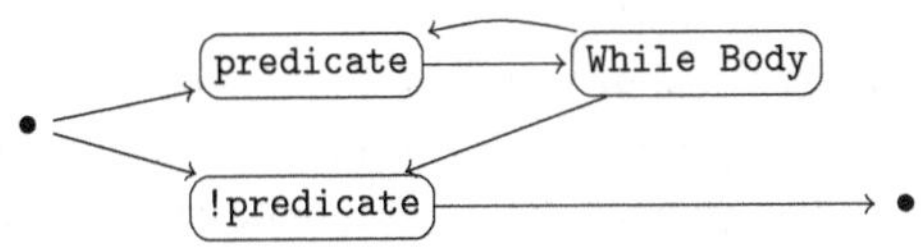

(c) While Loops

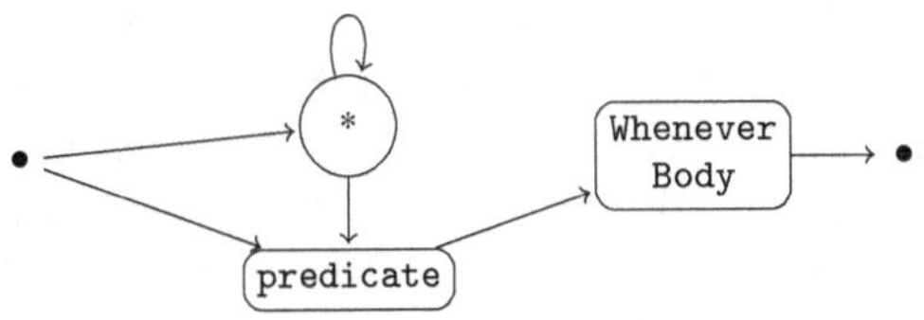

(d) Whenever statement

Figure 8: Automaton designs for RAPID statements

grams are transformed into a pattern-matching operation using a combination of one or more physical saturating counters and boolean logic elements. The basic structure consists of a saturating counter set to latch (once the threshold is reached, the output signal remains active) and an inverter, which allows for detection of the counter target not being reached.

Physical counters on the AP have three connection ports: count enable, reset, and output. `Counter` object function calls to `count()` and `reset()` in RAPID are connected to their respective ports on the counter. Output signals then connect to the next statement in the program.

We follow a set of rules for determining the threshold and outputs of a `Counter` object shown in Table 2. Equality checking with a `Counter` requires the use of two physical counter elements in the AP. While traversing the program, we note which `Counter` objects are used for equality checking. Then during code generation, we emit two counter elements for each.

This technique only allows for one threshold to be checked per counter in the RAPID program. An alternate solution would be to use positional encodings, which duplicate an automaton for each value a counter might have, encoding the count in the position of states within an automaton. While

Table 2: Rules for thresholds and outputs on counters

Comparison	Threshold	True Output
< x	x	inverted
<= x	x+1	inverted
> x	x+1	non-inverted
>= x	x	non-inverted
== x	convert to <= x && >= x	
!= x	convert to < x || > x	

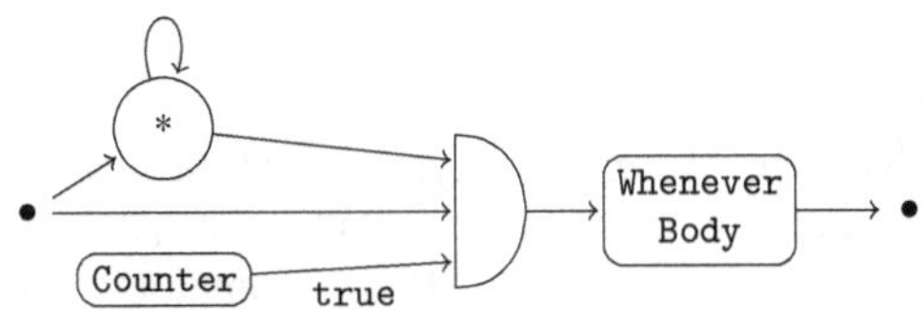

Figure 9: Structure of `whenever` statement with counters

this design allows for easy checking of multiple thresholds, it also significantly increases the number of states in the final automaton and does not support counter resetting. We chose not to implement this technique in our initial compiler because it does not support full, generic functionality.

We must also support the use of `Counter` variables as predicates in a `whenever` statement. For the body of a `whenever` statement to execute, the `Counter` must have reached its appropriate threshold, and the statement itself must have been reached within the control flow of the RAPID program. We use a self-activating STE matching all symbols to track when the statement is reached. We use an AND gate to check both of these conditions before executing the body of the `whenever` statement. This design is demonstrated in Figure 9.

`Counter` threshold checks are also used as assertions or as predicates in `if` statements and `while` loops. Because NFAs do not have dynamic memory (beyond the states themselves), we propose to handle this case by both generating automata and also pre-transforming the input stream. For each such `Counter`, we create a unique reserved input symbol. This new symbol indicates that the threshold for that particular `Counter` has been met. We add an STE matching exactly that symbol linked to the subsequent statement; whenever that symbol is encountered in the input data stream, the appropriate subsequent statement begins execution. This symbol must be injected into the input data stream before the RAPID program begins execution. Actual injection is handled by the runtime code and can occur while data is being streamed to the AP (but before execution of the RAPID program beings).

We attempt to automatically determine the pattern for inserting the count threshold symbol into the input stream. An example pattern is "insert the symbol after every 25 characters in the input stream." Often, the compiler can infer the pattern by counting the number of symbols consumed before the counter check occurs. When certain `while` loops are included in the program, however, it may not be possible to determine where in the input stream to inject the unique symbols. In these cases, we currently output a warning at compile time and rely on the developer to provide the pattern for inserting the control character into the data stream.

6. Auto-tuning Tessellation

The automata designs generated from RAPID programs are often repetitive. Specifically, we found four out of five of our benchmarks reuse the same automaton structure multiple times, only altering the symbol sets of the STEs. RAPID takes advantage of this underlying structural regularity to improve placement and routing times for the AP.

Using current tools for the AP, an automaton can be pre-compiled (i.e., placement and routing can be determined for a small portion of the overall design). State symbols are parameterized, allowing repeated use of pre-compiled designs with different symbols. The developer creates automata that reference this pre-compiled design many times. This design is then placed and routed to be loaded onto the device. Because the individual automata have already been placed, the time needed is significantly reduced compared to processing the entire design at once; however, this process still requires over an hour for designs spanning an entire AP board.

We propose an alternate approach, *auto-tuning tessellation*, that requires seconds to produce final placement and routing data. This optimization approximates filling an entire AP board with a design. Instead of generating a design to fill the entire board, we produce a design on a block-level for the AP (see Section 4). At runtime, we load this design several times onto the AP to fill the entire board. To improve device utilization (the number of automata loaded onto the AP), we attempt to generate dense designs at the block level.

To implement this optimization, we must determine which program elements to generate for tessellation. One option would be to require developers to annotate programs, indicating code sections to tile. This places undue burden upon developers as they would have to analyze programs to determine the best locations to introduce tiling. Instead, we use a heuristic: code iterating over a network parameter within a `some` statement at the top level of the network is tiled. This heuristic captures the intended optimization behavior for all of our benchmarks that support tiling.

Given a portion of the code to tile, we generate an automaton. This design is placed and routed, reporting the block-level device utilization. Then, we iteratively add additional copies of the automaton to the design until just before device utilization increases. This technique improves overall usage by embedding more automata into each block.

7. Evaluation

We evaluate RAPID against hand-crafted designs for five real-world benchmark applications, which were selected based upon previous research demonstrating significant acceleration using the Automata Processor [4, 18, 21, 23].

Table 3 provides descriptions of the benchmarks used. For each benchmark, we chose an instance size representative of a real-world problem. These sizes come either directly from previous work or from conversations with the authors of the previous work. The generation method column indicates the technique used to create the handcrafted code, which ranged from custom Java or Python programs for generating an ANML design to the use of a GUI design tool (Workbench) for crafting automata by hand. The authors of the *ARM* [21] and *Brill* [23] benchmarks provided us with their original code, including a collection of regular expressions for performing the *Brill* benchmark. We recreated the remaining designs, using algorithms and specifications published in previous work.

Table 4 lists design statistics for the benchmarks. We compare the lines of code needed to generate ANML, be it using RAPID or a custom technique in the cases of *ARM* and *Brill*. For *ARM*, the RAPID code requires six times fewer lines to represent, and *Brill* requires about half of the lines of the hand-crafted solution. The regular expression representation for *Brill* is more compact than RAPID. We found developing the regular expressions to be tedious and error-prone and felt that the RAPID program was more intuitive.

We created the *Gappy*, *Exact*, and *MOTOMATA* benchmarks using a GUI design tool. For these, we present the lines of code in ANML, which is roughly equivalent to the number of actions taken within the design tool. ANML file sizes are dependent on the specific instance of a problem. The numbers we present are for a single instance of the problem size listed in Table 3. In all cases, the RAPID program is significantly more compact than the ANML it generates.

As an approximation for the size of the resulting automaton, we measure the number of STEs generated and the number of STEs loaded to the AP after placement and routing. The placement and routing tools modify the original automaton to better match the architectural design of the AP. For most benchmarks, RAPID-generated automata contain fewer device STEs, taking up less space on the device. Only the *Gappy* benchmark requires more device STEs. Although we could optimize the RAPID code to reduce the size of the generated automaton, we found that this more natural design, although larger, has comparable placement and routing efficiency. For *MOTOMATA*, the RAPID version requires approximately half the STEs of the hand-crafted version. The compiled RAPID version makes use of a saturating counter, while the handcrafted version uses positional encoding.

Due to the lock-step execution of automata on the AP, runtime performance of loaded designs is linear in the length of a given input stream. Therefore, we focus on evaluating the space efficiency of RAPID programs. In Table 5, we present the performance of RAPID programs compared to hand-crafted ANML based on placement and routing statis-

Table 3: Description of benchmarks

Benchmark	Description	Generation Method	Sample Instance Size
ARM [21]	Association rule mining	Python + ANML	24 Item-Set
Brill [23]	Rule re-writing for Brill part of speech tagging	Java	219 Rules
Exact [4]	Exact match DNA sequence search	Workbench	25 Base Pairs
Gappy [4]	DNA string search with allowances for gaps between characters	Workbench	25-bp, Gaps $\leqslant 3$
MOTOMATA [18]	Fuzzy matching for planted motif Search in bioinformatics	Workbench	(17,6) Motifs

Table 4: Comparison between RAPID and hand-crafted code with respect to lines of code (LOC) and STE usage

Benchmark		LOC	ANML LOC	STEs	Device STEs
ARM	R	18	214	58	56
	H	118	301	79	58
Brill	R	688	10,594	3,322	1,429
	H	1,292	9,698	3,073	1,514
	Re	218	–‡	4,075	1,501
Exact	R	14	85	29	27
	H	–†	193	28	27
Gappy	R	30	2,337	748	399
	H	–†	2,155	675	123
MOTOMATA	R	34	207	53	72
	H	–†	587	150	149

R – RAPID H – Hand-coded Re – Regular Expression

† The GUI-tool does not have a LOC equivalent metric.

‡ No ANML statistics are provided by the regular expression compiler.

Table 5: Placement and routing statistics

Benchmark		Total Blocks	Clock Divisor	STE Util.	Mean BR Alloc.
ARM	R	1	1	21.9%	20.8%
	H	1	1	23.4%	20.8%
Brill	R	8	1	84.0%	52.6%
	H	12	1	57.9%	65.4%
	Re	10	1	71.4%	60.6%
Exact	R	1	1	10.9%	4.2%
	H	1	1	10.9%	4.2%
Gappy	R	2	1	89.5%	70.8%
	H	2	1	37.5%	77.1%
MOTOMATA	R	1	2	33.6%	75.0%
	H	4	1	17.2%	75.0%

R – RAPID H – Hand-coded Re – Regular Expression

tics for the AP, using version 1.4-11 of the AP SDK to generate the placement and routing information. The total blocks column measures the number of routing matrix blocks (see Section 4) needed to accommodate the design; lower numbers represent a more compact design. STE utilization indicates the percent of used STEs within the routed blocks; high numbers indicate a design with fewer unused STEs. Mean BR allocation is a metric provided by the AP SDK that approximates of the routing complexity of the design. Here, a lower number is better, signifying lower congestion within the routing matrix. The clock divisor indicates whether the clock cycle of the AP must be reduced to accommodate a design. In one instance (the RAPID *MOTOMATA* program), the clock cycle must be halved due to a limitation in signal propagation between counters and combinatorial elements in the current generation AP. However, the RAPID version is four times more compact. Although this is a performance loss for a single instance, it is a net performance gain for a full problem, which will fill the AP board: four times as many instances execute in parallel at half the speed, for a net improvement factor of two. Although RAPID provides a higher level of abstraction than ANML, the final device binaries are more compact, using fewer resources on the AP.

Finally, we evaluate our tessellation optimization by generating designs filling the entire AP Board. The *Brill* benchmark is fixed in size and is not applicable for this optimization. For the remaining benchmarks, we compare generating the "full problem" using non-compiled ANML, pre-compiled designs, and RAPID's tessellation feature (see Section 6 for descriptions). The ANML is generated using a Python script and bindings for the AP tool-chain. We choose problem sizes for each benchmark to ensure that the worst performing technique would still fit on an AP board (6,144 blocks) in each case.

The results of this optimization are given in Table 6. We report the average of ten runs of both the ANML generation and placement and routing steps for each benchmark. We measured each configuration on the same machine using both version 1.4-11 and version 1.6-0 of the AP placement and routing tools, reporting the best result obtained. Neither version of the AP tools could successfully place and route the *ARM* baseline or the *Gappy* benchmark with pre-compiled designs.

To determine the total number of blocks for RAPID tessellation, we multiply the problem size by the number of blocks used by the RAPID program (Table 4) and divide by the number of automata generated in each tile. We use compiler output to determine the total number of blocks for the baseline and pre-compiled techniques.

Our auto-tuning tessellation technique outperforms both the baseline and pre-compiled designs in terms of time and space. We hypothesize that the improved block utilization results from routing complexities within the automata designs. When this complexity is present, the baseline technique cannot provide a more efficient layout than when us-

Table 6: Tessellation optimization

Benchmark		Problem Size (# instances)	Total Blocks	Generate Time (sec)	Place and Route Time (sec)	Total Time (sec)
ARM	B†	8,500	–	5.38	–	–
	P	8,500	6,100	6.53	771.16	770.70
	R	8,500	2,125	3.70	0.41	4.12
Exact	B	46 000	4 730	24.52	22 011.10	22 035.62
	P	46 000	6 075	30.17	1 676.88	1 707.05
	R	46 000	5 750	0.80	0.08	0.88
Gappy	B	2,000	5,354	0.99	9158.00	9158.99
	P†	2,000	–	0.99	–	–
	R	2,000	4,000	9.17	2.20	11.36
MOTOMATA	B	1 500	5 320	1.49	5 874.51	5 875.99
	P	1 500	6 001	1.45	210.62	212.07
	R	1 500	1 500	2.26	0.37	2.63

B – Baseline (No Pre-Compilation)   P – Pre-Compiled Designs   R – RAPID Tessellation

† The current AP software is not able to support placement and routing for this benchmark.

ing our tessellation. The *Exact* benchmark forms chains of STEs, which are simpler to route, and therefore the placement and routing tools are able to overlap some of the automata across blocks in the routing matrix using the baseline technique. Additionally, our technique is up to four orders of magnitude faster during compilation, placement, and routing than the baseline and up to three orders of magnitude faster than using pre-compilation. We do not view the many-hour place-and-route times of the default approach as efficient in practice, especially when our tessellation reduces this time to seconds. Consequently, RAPID tessellation promotes rapid prototyping of designs. By significantly decreasing design testing time, tessellation can increase developer productivity and improve maintainability while maintaining efficient device utilization.

8. Conclusions and Future Directions

This paper presents RAPID, a language for defining pattern-matching algorithms. RAPID is motivated by pattern-recognition processors, such as the Automata Processor, which greatly accelerate pattern detection in streams of data, but lack easy-to-use programming models.

We present techniques for converting RAPID programs to designs that can be executed on the Automata Processor. Although RAPID programs are written at a higher level of abstraction than current hand-crafted code, our evaluation indicates that RAPID programs have similar, if not better, device utilization. We plan to develop additional conversion techniques to support other hardware architectures.

Additionally, we argue that our auto-tuning tessellation technique for generating pattern searches spanning the entire AP board increases developer productivity and program maintainability. Compile times are several orders of magnitude faster than current methods and produce device configurations that maintain high device utilization.

There many options for extending the RAPID language. Generated automata could be optimized to better support the placement and routing tools. The AP has specific constraints for routing between special elements and states. By optimizing RAPID programs for these constraints, we can improve device utilization and also reduce placement and routing times. Further, debugging tools for pattern-matching processor are limited. Tools aiding developers to generate short input sequences to test corner cases of their applications as well as techniques for debugging RAPID would further increase productivity and maintainability.

In conclusion, RAPID raises the level of abstraction for programming pattern-recognition processors, resulting in clear, concise, maintainable, and efficient programs. We develop a notion of macros and networks, which we argue improve program maintainability. The same macro may be called with differing arguments to generate automata for varying instances of a pattern-matching problem. This program structure maps well to pattern-recognition problems and the underlying pattern-recognition hardware. Additionally, RAPID provides parallel control structures to support common tasks in pattern-matching algorithms, such as sliding window searches. Compared to hand-crafted versions of pattern-matching algorithms, the RAPID definition is more concise, needing only a fraction of the lines to implement.

Acknowledgments

We acknowledge the partial support of the NSF (CCF 0954024, CCF 1116289, CDI-1124931); Air Force (FA8750-15-2-0075); Virginia Commonwealth Fellowship; Jefferson Scholars Foundation; and C-FAR, one of six centers of STARnet, a Semiconductor Research Corporation program sponsored by MARCO and DARPA. We would like to thank Micron Technology for their support and expertise as well as the anonymous reviewers for their helpful comments and feedback.

References

[1] R. Alur, P. Černý, P. Madhusudan, and W. Nam. Synthesis of interface specifications for Java classes. In *Proceedings of the 32nd ACM SIGPLAN-SIGACT Symposium on Principles of Programming Languages*, pages 98–109, 2005.

[2] G. Ammons, D. Mandelin, R. Bodík, and J. R. Larus. Debugging temporal specifications with concept analysis. In *Proceedings of the 2003 ACM SIGPLAN Conference on Programming Language Design and Implementation*, pages 182–195, 2003.

[3] K. R. Apt, J. Brunekreef, V. Partington, and A. Schaerf. Alma-0: An imperative language that supports declarative programming. Technical report, 1997.

[4] C. Bo, K. Wang, Y. Qi, and K. Skadron. String kernel testing acceleration using the Micron Automata Processor. In *Workshop on Computer Architecture for Machine Learning*, 2015.

[5] Capgemini. Big & fast data : The rise of insight-driven business. `http://www.capgemini.com/resource-file-access/resource/pdf/big_fast_data_the_rise_of_insight-driven_business-report.pdf`, 2015.

[6] P. Caron and D. Ziadi. Characterization of Glushkov automata. *Theoretical Computer Science*, 233(1):75–90, 2000.

[7] H. D. Cheng and K. S. Fu. VLSI architectures for string matching and pattern matching. *Pattern Recognition*, 20(1):125–144, 1987.

[8] Computer Sciences Corporation. Big data universe beginning to explode. `http://www.csc.com/insights/flxwd/78931-big_data_universe_beginning_to_explode`, 2012.

[9] E. W. Dijkstra. Guarded commands, nondeterminacy and formal derivation of programs. *Communications of the ACM*, 18(8):453–457, 1975.

[10] P. Dlugosch, D. Brown, P. Glendenning, M. Leventhal, and H. Noyes. An efficient and scalable semiconductor architecture for parallel automata processing. *IEEE Transactions on Parallel and Distributed Systems*, 25(12):3088–3098, 2014.

[11] A. Halaas. A systolic VLSI matrix for a family of fundamental searching problems. *Integration VLSI Journal*, 1(4):269–282, 1983.

[12] A. Halaas, B. Svingen, M. Nedland, P. Sætrom, O. Snøve, Jr., and O. R. Birkeland. A recursive MISD architecture for pattern matching. *IEEE Transactions on Very Large Scale Integrated Systems*, 12(7):727–734, 2004.

[13] A. Krishna, T. Heil, N. Lindberg, F. Toussi, and S. VanderWiel. Hardware acceleration in the IBM PowerEN processor: Architecture and performance. In *Proceedings of the 21st International Conference on Parallel Architectures and Compilation Techniques*, pages 389–400, 2012.

[14] M. E. Lesk and E. Schmidt. Lex: A lexical analyzer generator. Technical Report 39, AT&T Bell Laboratories Computing Science, 1975.

[15] H. Lu, K. Zheng, B. Liu, X. Zhang, and Y. Liu. A memory-efficient parallel string matching architecture for high-speed intrusion detection. *IEEE Journal on Selected Areas in Communications*, 24(10):1793–1804, 2006.

[16] S. McCanne and V. Jacobson. The BSD packet filter: A new architecture for user-level packet capture. In *Proceedings of the 1993 USENIX Winter Conference*, USENIX'93, pages 295–270, 1993.

[17] Micron Technoloy. Calculating Hamming distance. `http://www.micronautomata.com/documentation/cookbook/c_hamming_distance.html`.

[18] I. Roy and S. Aluru. Finding motifs in biological sequences using the Micron Automata Processor. In *Proceedings of the 28th IEEE International Parallel and Distributed Processing Symposium*, pages 415–424, 2014.

[19] W. Thies, M. Karczmarek, and S. P. Amarasinghe. StreamIt: A language for streaming applications. In *Proceedings of the 11th International Conference on Compiler Construction*, pages 179–196. Springer-Verlag, 2002.

[20] Titan IC Systems. RXP regular eXpression processor soft IP. `http://titanicsystems.com/Products/Regular-eXpression-Processor-(RXP)`.

[21] K. Wang, M. Stan, and K. Skadron. Association rule mining with the Micron Automata Processor. In *Proceedings of the 29th IEEE International Parallel & Distributed Processing Symposium*, 2015.

[22] H. Yamada, M. Hirata, H. Nagai, and K. Takahashi. A high-speed string-search engine. *IEEE Journal of Solid-State Circuits*, 22(5):829–834, 1987.

[23] K. Zhou, J. J. Fox, K. Wang, D. E. Brown, and K. Skadron. Brill tagging on the Micron Automata Processor. In *Proceedings of the 9th IEEE International Conference on Semantic Computing*, pages 236–239, 2015.

Proactive Control of Approximate Programs *

Xin Sui
Department of Computer Science,
The University of Texas at Austin
xinsui@cs.utexas.edu

Andrew Lenharth
The Institute for Computational Engineering and Science,
The University of Texas at Austin
lenharth@ices.utexas.edu

Donald S. Fussell Keshav Pingali
Department of Computer Science,
The University of Texas at Austin
fussell@cs.utexas.edu,
pingali@cs.utexas.edu

Abstract

Approximate computing trades off accuracy of results for resources such as energy or computing time. There is a large and rapidly growing literature on approximate computing that has focused mostly on showing the benefits of approximate computing. However, we know relatively little about how to control approximation in a disciplined way.

In this paper, we address the problem of controlling approximation for non-streaming programs that have a set of "knobs" that can be dialed up or down to control the level of approximation of different components in the program. We formulate this control problem as a constrained optimization problem, and describe a system called Capri that uses machine learning to learn cost and error models for the program, and uses these models to determine, for a desired level of approximation, knob settings that optimize metrics such as running time or energy usage. Experimental results with complex benchmarks from different problem domains demonstrate the effectiveness of this approach.

1. Introduction

Models should be used, not believed.
Henri Theil

There is growing interest in *approximate computing* as a way of reducing the energy and time required to execute applications [3, 4, 41, 46, 55]. In conventional computing, programs are usually treated as implementations of mathematical functions, so there is a precise output that must computed for a given input. In many problem domains, it is sufficient to produce some approximation of this output; for example, when rendering a scene in graphics, it is acceptable to take computational short-cuts if human beings cannot tell the difference in the rendered scene.

In this paper, we focus on a class of approximate programs that we call *tunable* approximate programs. Intuitively, these programs have one or more *knobs* or parameters that can be changed to vary the fidelity of the produced output. These knobs might control the number of iterations performed by a loop [7, 36], determine the precision with which floating-point computations are performed [38, 43], or switch between precise and approximate hardware [16]; for the purposes of this paper, the source of approximation does not matter so long as the fidelity of the output is changed by adjusting the knobs.

Perhaps the oldest example of a tunable approximate computation is the method used by Archimedes to estimate the value of π by constructing inscribed and circumscribed regular polygons for circles; by increasing the number of sides of the polygons, more accurate estimates for π can be obtained at the cost of additional computation. Iterative algorithms for solving linear or non-linear systems are tunable algorithms since they can produce more accurate solutions if more iterations are executed. Fast multipole methods for solving n-body problems are tunable by design. Not all approximate algorithms are tunable; for example, Kempe's heuristic for graph coloring [13] works for most graphs that arise in register allocation, but if it fails for a particular graph, there is no way to tune it to produce a coloring even if one exists.

Our concern in this paper is the *control problem* for tunable approximate programs: roughly speaking, given a permissible error for the output, we want to set the knobs to minimize computational costs, such as running time or energy, while meeting the error constraint.

For example, consider the GEM algorithm [52] for clustering social networks. Given a social network graph and the number of clusters, GEM produces an assignment of nodes to clusters. The quality of the clustering is estimated using a metric called the normalized cut which is defined in more detail in §4, but roughly speaking, it computes the ra-

* The work presented in this paper has been supported by the National Science Foundation grants CNS 1111766, CCF 1218568, XPS 1337281, CNS 1406355, and DARPA BRASS contract FA8750-16-2-0004.

ASPLOS '16 April 2–6, 2016, Atlanta, Georgia, USA.

DOI: http://dx.doi.org/10.1145/2872362.2872402

tio of inter-cluster edges to intra-cluster edges (lower is better since it means there are fewer edges connecting nodes in different clusters). The GEM program has two components: the first one extracts a representative skeleton of the original graph by picking high degree nodes and clusters this skeleton graph using a weighted kernel k-means algorithm, and the second one projects this clustering to the original graph and uses weighted kernel k-means again to refine this clustering. Weighted kernel k-means is an iterative algorithm, so there are two knobs in GEM, one for each component. For a given input graph, running both components to convergence produces a clustering of some quality; reducing the number of iterations in either component may reduce the computational cost but may impact the quality of the clustering. Given an input graph and some desired output quality, how do we set the knobs for the two components to minimize computational time or energy?

This problem has not been considered in most of the existing literature in this area, which is surveyed in §6. Prior work has focused mostly on the *forward problem* of studying what happens to the output of a tunable approximate program when its knobs are dialed up or down [10, 40, 41, 46], and there is little work on the more difficult *inverse problem* of finding optimal knob settings, given a bound on the output quality. One exception is the Green system [4] but it is targeted for streaming applications in which the system is given a *sequence* of inputs such as a sequence of video frames, and the results from processing an input can be used to adjust knob settings for *succeeding* inputs. This kind of *reactive* control is not useful for applications that are not streaming programs, such as GEM, for which knobs must be set *before* the program is executed; in this paper, we call this *proactive* control.

This paper proposes and evaluates a solution to the proactive control problem for non-streaming programs like GEM that consist of components controlled by one or more knobs and in which the error and cost behaviors are substantially different for different inputs. The rest of the paper is organized as follows.

- We formulate the proactive control problem as a constrained optimization problem, dealing explicitly with the problem of input variability. (§2).
- We describe an error model based on Bayesian networks (§3.1), and a cost model for running time, implemented using the M5 system [34] (§ 3.2).
- We describe the Capri system, which incorporates these models, and discuss two algorithms, implemented in this system, for finding optimal knob settings (§ 3.4).
- We validate the proposed approach using five complex, tunable approximate programs (§ 4 and §5). We also describe the results of a blind test in which we use our system to control a third-party radar application.
- We show that Capri can successfully build models for and tune approximate programs to optimize not just running time but energy as well (§ 5.5).

Related work is described in § 6, and conclusions in § 7.

2. Problem definition

We describe the formulation of the proactive control problem we use in this paper, justifying it by describing other reasonable formulations and explaining why we do not use them. To keep notation simple, we consider a program that can be controlled with two knobs K_1 and K_2 that take values from finite sets κ_1 and κ_2 respectively. We write $K_1 : \kappa_1$ and $K_2 : \kappa_2$ to denote this, and use k_1 and k_2 to denote particular settings of these knobs. The formulation generalizes to programs with an arbitrary number of knobs in an obvious way.

It is convenient to define the following functions.

- Output: In general, the output value of the tunable program is a function of the input value i, and knob settings k_1 and k_2. Let $f(i, k_1, k_2)$ be this function.
- Error/quality degradation: Let $f_e(i, k_1, k_2)$ be the magnitude of the output error or quality degradation for input i and knob settings k_1 and k_2.
- Cost: Let $f_c(i, k_1, k_2)$ be the cost of computing the output for input i with knob settings k_1 and k_2. This can be the running time, energy or other execution metric to be optimized.

In §2.1, we formulate the control problem as an optimization problem in which the error is bounded for the particular input of interest. This optimization problem is difficult to solve, so in § 2.2, we formulate a different problem in which the expected error over all inputs is less than the given error bound. In the final variation of this problem, this error bound is satisfied with some probability, which gives the implementation flexibility in finding low-cost solutions.

2.1 Input-specific error bound

One way to formulate the control problem informally is the following: given an input value and a bound on the output error, find knob settings that (i) meet the error bound and (ii) minimize the cost. This can be formulated as the following constrained optimization problem.

Problem Formulation 1. *Given:*

- *a program with knobs $K_1{:}\kappa_1$ and $K_2{:}\kappa_2$, and*
- *a set of possible inputs I.*

For input $i \in I$ and error bound $\epsilon > 0$, find $k_1 \in \kappa_1, k_2 \in \kappa_2$ such that

- *$f_c(i, k_1, k_2)$ is minimized*
- *$f_e(i, k_1, k_2) \leq \epsilon$*

In the literature, the constraint $f_e(i, k_1, k_2) \leq \epsilon$ is said to define the *feasible region*, and values of (k_1, k_2) that satisfy

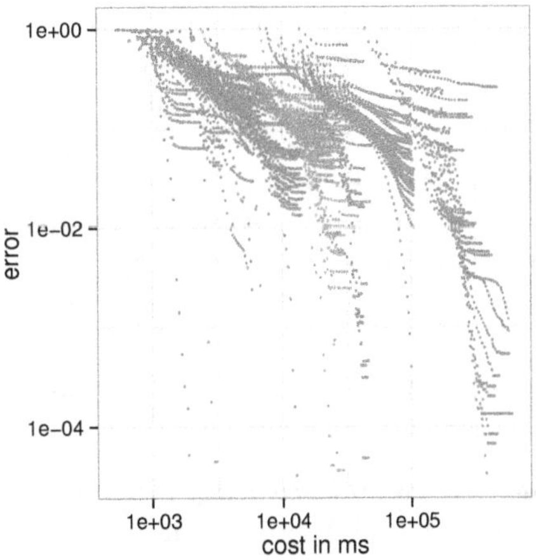

Figure 1. Cost vs. error for GEM benchmark. Each dot represents one knob setting for one input. Different colors represent different inputs.

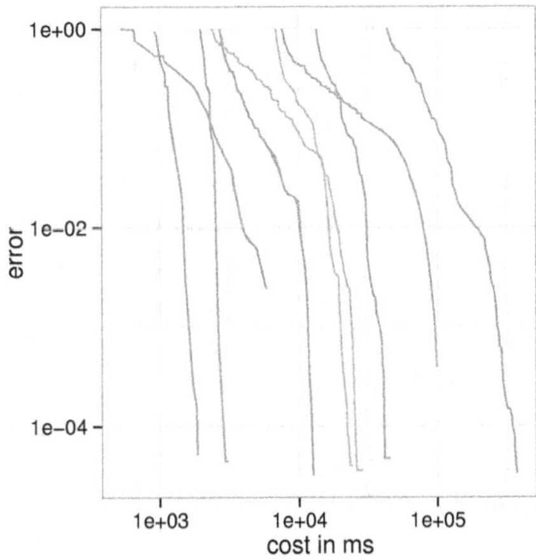

Figure 2. Pareto-optimal curves for GEM benchmark. Different lines represent different inputs.

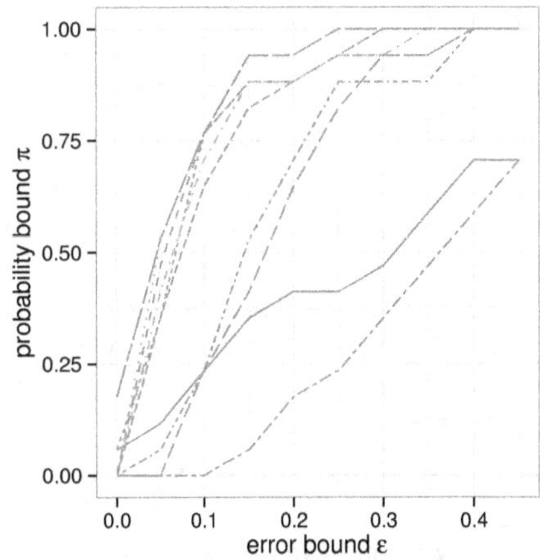

Figure 3. Isoclines for GEM benchmark. Each line represents one knob setting, which is in the feasible region for all (ϵ, π) values below the line.

this constraint for a given input are said to lie within the feasible region for that input. The function $f_c(i, k_1, k_2)$ is the *objective function*, and a solution to the optimization problem is a point that lies within the feasible region and minimizes the objective function.

For most tunable programs, this is a very complex optimization problem. To get a sense of the solution space, we ran the GEM benchmark, discussed in detail in Section 4, with a variety of inputs and different knob settings, and measured both the cost (running time of the program) and the quality degradation of the output of the resulting programs. Figure 1 shows the data. In this graph, each point represents a single input graph and knob settings combination; points that correspond to the same input graph are colored identically. It can be seen that even for a single input graph, there are many knob combinations that produce the same output error, and that these combinations have widely different costs. For a given input graph and output error, we are interested in minimizing cost so only the leftmost point for each such combination is of interest. Figure 2 shows these *Pareto-optimal* points for each input graph.

Since the Pareto-optimal points vary greatly across inputs, it is difficult to predict the knob settings that produce the Pareto-optimal point, for a given input graph and output error, without exploring much of the space of knob settings for a given input. This is intractable for non-trivial systems.

2.2 Controlling expected error

One way to simplify the control problem is to require only that the *expected* output error over all inputs be less than some specified bound ϵ. Since some inputs may be more likely to be presented to the system than others, each input can be associated with a probability that is the likelihood that that input is presented to the system. This lets us give more weight to more likely inputs. Since the cost function is still a function of the actual input, knob settings for a given value of ϵ will be different in general for different inputs, but the output error will be within the given error bounds only in an average sense.

To formulate this as an optimization problem, we assume that the probability of getting input j is $p(j)$.

Problem Formulation 2. *Given:*

- *a program with knobs K_1:κ_1 and K_2:κ_2,*
- *a set of possible inputs I, and*
- *a probability function p such that for any $i \in I$, $p(i)$ is the probability of getting input i.*

For input $i \in I$ and error bound $\epsilon > 0$, find $k_1 \in \kappa_1, k_2 \in \kappa_2$ such that

- *$f_c(i, k_1, k_2)$ is minimized*
- $\sum_{j \in I} p(j) f_e(j, k_1, k_2) \quad \leq \epsilon$

This optimization problem seems more complex than the previous one since it also requires knowing the probability of being asked to solve the control problem for each possible input. However, it is intended to capture the intuition that if we can come up with knob settings that work well for the most common inputs, these knob settings will be acceptable in an average sense. Note that the feasible region for this optimization problem does not depend on the particular input i for which the control problem must be solved, which is a major simplification.

2.3 Controlling probability of error

Formulation 2 has the drawback that even if the *average* error is below ϵ for given knob settings, the error could be large for some likely inputs; if this is unacceptable, there is no way out for the application developer other than to avoid approximation. To solve this problem, we consider a variation of this optimization problem, inspired by Valiant's probably approximately correct (PAC) theory of machine learning [51], in which we are also given a probability π with which the error bound must be met. Intuitively, values of π less than 1 give the control system a degree of slack in meeting the error constraint, permitting the system to find lower cost solutions.

This control problem can be formulated as an optimization problem as follows. For a given error bound ϵ and knob setting (k_1, k_2), consider inputs $j \in I$ that satisfy the error bound (that is, $f_e(j, k_1, k_2) \leq \epsilon$). The sum of the probabilities of these inputs is the probability that the knob setting (k_1, k_2) satisfies the error bound for a random input. This can be written formally as follows:

$$P_e(\epsilon, k_1, k_2) = \sum_{(j \in I) \wedge (f_e(j,k_1,k_2) \leq \epsilon)} p(j)$$

If this value is greater than or equal to π, then (k_1, k_2) is in the feasible region for error bound ϵ. For future reference, we call this value the *fitness* of knob setting (k_1, k_2) for error ϵ; intuitively, the greater the fitness of a knob setting, the more likely it is that it satisfies the error bound for the given ensemble of inputs.

Problem Formulation 3. *Given:*

- *a program with knobs $K_1 : \kappa_1$ and $K_2 : \kappa_2$,*
- *a set of possible inputs I, and*
- *a probability function p such that for any $i \in I$, $p(i)$ is the probability of getting input i.*

For an input $i{\in}I$, error bound $\epsilon{>}0$, and a probability $1{\geq}\pi{>}0$ with which this error bound must be met, find $k_1{\in}\kappa_1$, $k_2{\in}\kappa_2$ such that

- *$f_c(i, k_1, k_2)$ is minimized*
- $\sum_{(j \in I) \wedge (f_e(j,k_1,k_2) \leq \epsilon)} p(j) \geq \pi$

In the rest of this paper, we refer to Problem Formulation 3 as "the control problem".

2.4 Discussion

We conclude this section with a justification of the choices made in the problem formulation, and a presentation of experimental results that demonstrate some of the difficulties in solving the control problem.

Design choices: We have framed the control problem in terms of bounding the expected error but for some problems, it may be preferable to bound the maximum error or some other function of the error distribution. The techniques discussed in this paper apply to such measures but we do not consider them here for lack of space.

In Problem Formulation 3, the feasible region depends on the values of π and ϵ, *but the objective function f_c depends on the actual input.* This is an important design choice. The machine learning techniques used in Section 3 to build models for f_c exploit *features* of the input, and for most problems, these features are the input parameters in the asymptotic complexity of the algorithm (for example, the asymptotic complexity of GEM is $O(N * K + E)$ where N and E is the number of nodes and edges in the graph respectively and K is the number of clusters, so we use N, E, and K as the features for cost estimates). In contrast, our experience is that it is difficult to find input features that are strongly correlated with output error or quality, which is why the feasible region in our formulation depends only on the values of π and ϵ, and not on features of the input. A deeper understanding of how error is related to input features might permit the development of alternative solutions.

Difficulties in solving the control problem: To gain insight into the control problem, it is useful to study the feasible region for given values of the parameters ϵ and π. Notice that this region is independent of the input. It is intuitively reasonable that if a knob setting (k_1, k_2) is in the feasible region for given parameter values (ϵ_1, π_1), then this knob setting is also in the feasible region for points $(\epsilon \geq \epsilon_1, \pi_1)$ (less stringent output error requirement) as well as points $(\epsilon_1, \pi \leq \pi_1)$ (less stringent likelihood of meeting the output error requirement).

Figure 3 illustrates this for the GEM benchmark. Each line in this graph corresponds to one knob setting. This knob setting is in the feasible region for all values of (ϵ, π) on this line or below it. We call this line the *isocline* for the given knob setting. In general, a given point (ϵ, π) will be contained in several isoclines, each of which corresponds to a different setting of knobs, and therefore a different (input-dependent) cost. To solve the optimization problem for a given input, and given ϵ and π values, we must find the lowest cost isocline that contains the point (ϵ, π) (or report that the problem is infeasible if there is no such isocline).

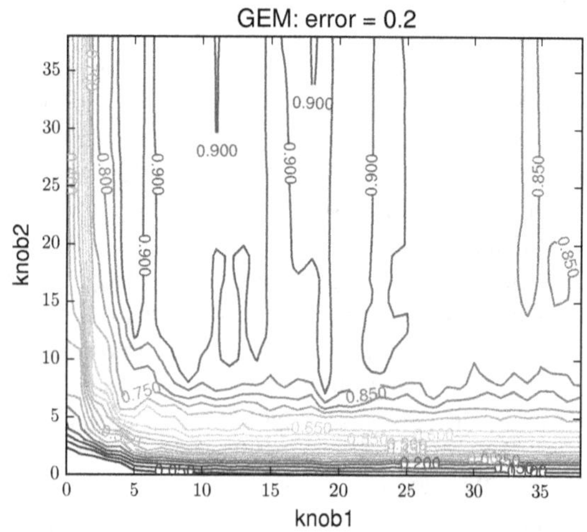

Figure 4. Probability contours for GEM. Lines represent the probability of achieving an error of 0.2.

Figure 4 shows how the probability of meeting a fixed quality bound ϵ changes as knobs are tuned. The x- and y-axes represent knob settings, and each line in the graph is a contour for some probability value. If output quality increases monotonically with knob settings, we would expect the probability contours to be shaped roughly like rectangular hyperbolas, with higher probability contours being closer to the top-right corner of the graph. This can be seen for small values of probability in Figure 4. The more complex contours for higher values of probability arise from the fact that output quality does not increase monotonically with the setting of knob1.

3. A solution to the proactive control problem

To solve the control problem for a given tunable program, we need the following information.

- I and $p(i)$: the set of possible inputs, and the probability of being presented with input $i \in I$.
- $f_e(i, k_1, k_2)$: error function.
- $f_c(i, k_1, k_2)$: cost function.

Figures 1 through 4 show that for the kinds of complex applications considered here, it is difficult if not impossible to derive closed-form analytical expressions for the functions f_e and f_c. Therefore, we use machine learning to learn these functions, given a suitable collection of training inputs.

Figure 5 is a pictorial representation of the Capri system. For a given program, the system must be provided with a set of training inputs, and metrics for the error/quality of the output and the cost (for example for GEM, the quality metric might be the normalized cut and the cost metric might be the running time or total energy, as explained in Section 1). The off-line portion of the Capri system runs the program on these inputs using a variety of knob settings, and learns the functions f_e and f_c. These models are inputs to the controller in the online portion of the system; given an input and values of ϵ and π, the controller solves the control problem to estimate optimal knob settings.

We have implemented Capri in a extensible way to permit easy exploration of different machine learning and optimization strategies. For lack of space, we restrict the discussion to particular choices of these strategies. For f_e, we use a Bayesian network [31]; this is described in §3.1. For f_c, we consider both running time and energy, and use the tree-based model in the M5 system [34]. This cost model uses a classification of the input based on features provided by the application programmer, and is described in §3.2. We explore two solutions to the control problem in §3.4: one uses exhaustive search over the space of knob settings, which is possible when the space of knob settings is small, and the other uses the Precimonious heuristic search strategy [38], which can be used when the space of knob settings is very large. Exhaustive search permits us to evaluate the effects of *model inaccuracy* independently of *algorithmic inaccuracy* introduced by heuristic search methods.

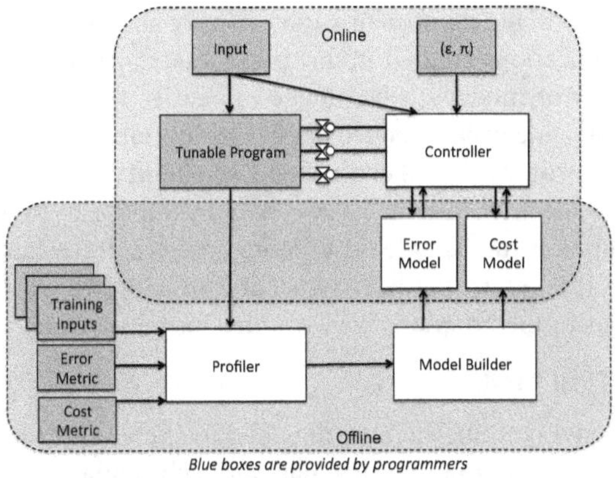

Figure 5. Overview of Capri

3.1 Error Model

An error model can be viewed abstractly as a proxy for the fitness function $P_e(\epsilon, k_1, k_2)$ defined in Section 2.3 (recall that if $P_e(\epsilon, k_1, k_2) \geq \pi$, then (k_1, k_2) is in the feasible region for a given (ϵ, π)).

In Capri , the error model is implemented using a Bayesian network [31]. A Bayesian network is a directed acyclic graph (DAG) in which each node represents a random variable in the model and each edge represents the dependence relationship between the variables corresponding to the nodes of its end points. Each node or variable may take one of many possible states and the probability of a state is directly affected by the states of predecessor nodes, if any, in the graph. To quantify this influence, each node is associated with a conditional probability distribution (CPD). The CPD of a node describes the conditional probability distribution of the node's associated variable, given the states of its dependent variables. When a random variable is continuous (as is the case with errors), Bayesian networks require a closed-form distribution to be specified for that variable. The closed-form distribution is generally not available for real-world applications. Therefore, without making any assumptions about the possible forms of distributions, we discretize the continuous random variables and use a discrete Bayesian network and Bayesian inference to determine the probability that the final error is between 0 and ϵ given a knob setting $(k_1, k_2, ..., k_n)$.

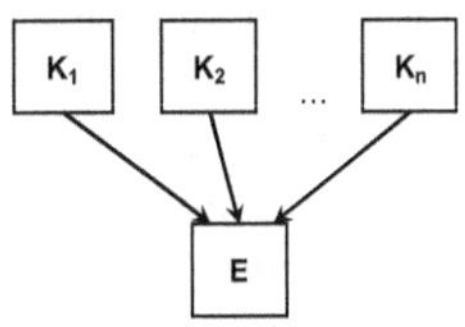

Conditional Probability Distribution(CPD) for E

K_1	K_2	...	K_n	E	Prob
1	1	...	1	0.1	0.1
1	1	...	2	0.2	0.3
...	...	...	...	...	...

Figure 6. Bayesian Network for Error Modeling

There are many ways to model the error probability distribution using a Bayesian network. A simple model for n knobs is shown in Figure 6. In this model, the output error E depends directly on the settings of all of the knobs. Although this is simple, the size of the table for the output error is exponential in the number of knobs. This is not a problem for the applications studied in this paper, but Capri allows different error models to be plugged in easily if desired. For example, one way to reduce the size of this table is to model the errors of individual components and build a network that models the way in which these errors compose to produce the output error. This leads to more complex Bayesian networks that reflect the interconnection structure of the components of the program. We leave this for future work.

3.2 Cost Model

We model both the running time and total energy. For most algorithms, the running time can vary substantially for different inputs; after all, even for simple algorithms like matrix multiplication, the running time is a function of the input size. For complex irregular algorithms like the ones considered in this paper, running time will depend not only the input size but also on other features of the input. For example, the running time of a graph clustering algorithm is affected by the number of vertices and edges in the graph as well as the number of clusters. Therefore, the running time is usually a complex function of input *features* and knob settings.

We use M5 [34], which builds tree-based models, to model the cost function f_c. Input features and knob settings define a multidimensional space; the tree model divides this space into a set of subspaces, and constructs a linear model in each subspace. The division into sub-spaces is done automatically by M5, which is a major advantage of using this system. Intuitively, this model can approximate cost well because the running time does not usually exhibit sharp discontinuities with respect to knob settings. For example, an iterative algorithm to solve the graph clustering problem may have a knob to control the number of iterations. A small change of the knob value corresponds to the small change of the number of iterations, and it is reasonable to assume the iteration space can be divided into areas where the amount of work or energy per iteration does not change dramatically.

3.3 Learning the Models

The error and cost models are built by learning from the data obtained by executing the programs on a set of representative inputs. The program is profiled exhaustively over the knob space. During each execution of the program, the following data is collected for learning the models.

Learning the Bayesian network model Although the topology of the Bayesian network model is fixed, the conditional probability tables are usually not known in advance. We use a standard Bayesian network learning algorithm, Bayesian posterior estimates [31], to learn the CPD's. The user must provide the error metric for evaluating the error in the program output (§4 has several examples).

Learning the cost model The M5 model is constructed automatically from the training data. Each training data point is a vector of input features, knob settings and the running time. The input features are application-specific and need to be specified by the programmer. The details of the learning algorithm are described in the classic M5 paper [34].

Since these models are learnt during the training phase, the time for learning these models is of secondary importance compared to ensuring that the training data sets are representative of the test inputs that will be given to the system when it is deployed.

3.4 Control Algorithms

The control algorithm must search the space of knob settings to find optimal knob settings, using the error and cost models as proxies for f_e and f_c respectively. Our system is implemented so that new search strategies can be incorporated seamlessly. We evaluated two search algorithms: *exhaustive search* and *Precimonious search* [38]. This lets us evaluate model accuracy separately from search accuracy.

- *Exhaustive search:* If the error and cost models are not expensive to evaluate and each knob has a finite number of settings, we can use exhaustive search. We sweep over the entire space of knob settings, and for each knob setting, use the error model to determine if that knob setting is in the feasible region. The cost model is then used to find a minimal cost point in the feasible region.
- *Precimonious search [38]:* In a large search space, heuristics-based search is an effective way to trade-off search cost for quality of the result. Precimonious search, which is based on the delta-debugging algorithm [54], is one such strategy. The algorithm is organized around a data structure called the *change set*; initially, this set consists of all the knobs set to the highest values, and the algorithm attempts to lower these settings iteratively as follows. In each iteration, the settings of all knobs in the change set are lowered by one level. If this new setting satisfies the accuracy constraint, the algorithm continues to the next iteration. Otherwise, the algorithm heuristically tries to find subsets of knobs whose settings can be lowered while still satisfying the accuracy constraint, and then chooses the lowest cost subset from these. Then the algorithm continue to next iteration with this subset as the new change set. Precimonious can quickly prune the search space but the solution it finds may be a local minimum.

3.5 Oracle control

To evaluate the effectiveness of overall control system for given choices of the error model, cost model, and search strategy, it is useful to define an *oracle control*, which solves Problem Formulation 3, for a given input and (ϵ, δ) values, by performing exhaustive search over the knob space and using the actual error and cost at each point in the knob space. In other words, oracle control solves the optimization problem in Problem Formulation 3 by using the actual functions f_e and f_c, instead of using proxies for these functions as Capri does. For most applications and inputs, running the application takes less time than it takes to invoke the oracle control to find optimal knob settings, so the utility of oracle control is only that it permits us to evaluate the effectiveness of the overall system in finding good knob settings.

3.6 Discussion

The approach used in Capri to controlling approximation is called *open-loop control* in classical control theory [24]. Open-loop control uses a model of the system to determine how knobs should be set for a given input, and does not consider whether the control objectives were actually met. Therefore open-loop control has no way to correct for model inaccuracy.

Closed-loop control, also known as *feedback control*, can be used when the input is a function of time; in the classical setting, the input is a continuous function of time, while in many computer applications, the input is a sequence of values, one per time step, such as a stream of video frames. In this setting, the result of controlling the system for one input can be used to adaptively control the system for succeeding inputs, as is done in the Green system [4]. Closed-loop control can be less sensitive than open-loop control to model inaccuracy, which is an advantage. However, in our setting, programs take one input and produce one output (for example, GEM takes one graph as input and produces a partitioning of the graph), so there is no obvious way to use closed-loop feedback control.

Much of the theory of closed-loop control is concerned with stability[1], and powerful techniques based on frequency-domain analysis and Lyapunov's methods have developed for proving the stability of linear and non-linear systems respectively [47]. One advantage of open-loop control is that stability is not an issue since there is no feedback.

4. Applications

We evaluated the Capri system on five complex applications: (i) GEM, the graph partitioner for social networks which was introduced earlier, (ii) Ferret [6], a content-similarity based image search engine, (iii) ApproxBullet (Bullet) [32], a 3D physics game engine, (iv) SGDSVM (SGD) [7], a library for support vector machines and (v) OpenOrd [28], a library for layout graphs. The code for these applications was modified by us to permit control of approximation. In addition, we did a blind test of the system using an unmodified radar processing application [21], written by researchers at the University of Chicago, which was already instrumented for control.

Error/Quality Definition To compute the error/quality of the output, we require the user to provide a distance function that quantifies the difference between an approximate execution and a reference execution for a given input. The reference execution can be the exact execution if such a thing exists or the best execution in the knob space for that input. The error is defined as a normalized version of this distance

$$\text{Error} = (d - d_{min})/(d_{max} - d_{min})$$

where d, d_{max} and d_{min} represent the distance for a execution, the maximum distance and the minimum distance over the knob space for the same input. The distance function is application-specific.

4.1 GEM

As described in §1, GEM [52] is a graph clustering algorithm for social networks.

Knobs: There are two components; both use a weighted kernel k-means algorithm and have a knob controlling the number of iterations. Each knob can be set to one of 40 levels. All input graphs are partitioned into 100 clusters in our experiments.

Error metric: The output of GEM is the cluster assignment of each node in the graph. There is a standard way to measure the quality of graph clustering, using the notion of a *normalized cut*, which is defined as follows:

$$\sum_{k=1}^{N} \sum_{i=1, i \neq k}^{N} \text{edges}(C_k, C_i)/\text{edges}(C_k)$$

where N is the number of clusters, $\text{edges}(C_k, C_i)$ denotes the number of edges between cluster k and cluster i, and $\text{edges}(C_k)$ denotes the edges inside cluster k

The distance function computes the difference of the normalized cut given two clustering assignments. The reference execution is the execution achieving the smallest normalized cut.

Input features for modeling cost: the number of vertices in the graph, the number of edges and the number of clusters.

4.2 Ferret

Ferret [6] performs content-similarity based image search from an image database. Given a query image, Ferret first decomposes it into a set of segments, and for each segment, Ferret finds a set of candidate image matches by indexing its database. After indexing, all of the candidate images are ranked, and the top K images are returned. There are two major computational phases in this process: finding the candidate image set and ranking the candidate images. In the first phase, an algorithm called Multi-probe LSH is used to approximately find $2K$ nearest neighbors of the query image. This algorithm uses multiple hash tables, which map similar images to the same hash bucket with high probability. Besides the mapped hash bucket, Multi-probe LSH probes nearby buckets in each hash table until a specified number of buckets are explored. In the second phase, the Earth Mover's Distance (EMD) between each candidate image and the query image is computed by an iterative optimization algorithm.

[1] Roughly speaking, stability ensures that if the input is bounded, the output is bounded as well (BIBO).

Knobs: There are three knobs in this application. In multi-probe LSH, the number of hash tables per bucket and the number of buckets probed can be changed to trade off error for cost. EMD is computed by an iterative algorithm; executing more iterations trades off error for cost. The first knob can be tuned to change the number of hash tables to up to 4 levels, the second knob can tune the number of probed buckets to up to 10 levels and the third knob can be tuned to change the number of iterations to up to 25 levels.

Error Metric: We adopt a distance function that is widely used in the comparing search engine results [5]. Given two image lists L_1 and L_2 returned by two executions, the distance function is:

$$2\times(k-z)(k+1)+\sum_{i\in Z}|rank_1(i)-rank_2(i)| \\ -\sum_{i\in S} rank_1(i)-\sum_{i\in T} rank_2(i) \quad (1)$$

where Z is the set of images appears in both L_1 and L_2, S and T are the sets of images appearing only in L_1 and L_2 respectively. k, z are the sizes of L_1(or L_2) and Z respectively. $rank_1(i)$ and $rank_2(i)$ are the ranks of the image i in L_1 and L_2.

The reference execution is obtained by setting all knobs to their maximum levels.

Input features for modeling cost: the number of segments in the image.

4.3 ApproxBullet(Bullet)

Bullet is a 3D physics game engine for approximately simulating the rigid body dynamics of objects. The input of Bullet is a set of objects represented by triangular meshes. Bullet simulates the behaviors of the objects in frames. In each frame, Bullet performs two major computations: approximate collision detection and sequential impulse-based constraint solving. The approximate collision algorithm is a simplified version of [32]. It first builds a multi-resolution representation for each object by coarsening its triangular mesh repeatedly [19]. A surface deviation threshold can be specified to control the level of mesh detail used for detecting collisions. The approximate collision detection component outputs a set of collision points to the constraint solver which is based on the iterative Gauss-Seidel method.

The inputs for this benchmark consist of a set of object pairs represented by triangle meshes. We make one object a stationary object and the other one a moving object. The moving object starts from a high position and drops on the stationary object. We only consider the computation in the frame when the two object first collide. Different inputs are created by enumerating object pairs from a set of objects and rotating them randomly.

Knobs: When a coarse mesh is used in the approximate collision detection algorithm, computation will be reduced but the collision detected may be inaccurate. In the constraint solver, the number of iterations can trade-off the accuracy of the solution for cost. The knob for the first component is the surface deviation threshold, and the knob for the second component is the number of iterations for the constraint solver. The first knob can be tuned to 15 levels from the original mesh to the coarsest mesh. The second knob can be tuned up to 20 different levels.

Error metrics: The output of Bullet for one frame is the "delta change vector" of the speed of the moving object. The distance function is the Euclidean distance between the two delta speed vectors of the moving object. The reference execution is obtained by turning both knobs to their maximum levels.

Input features for modeling cost: The number of triangles in each of the triangle meshes representing the objects.

4.4 SGDSVM(SGD)

Support Vector Machines (SVM) are a supervised machine learning method for binary classification. Classifier training is formulated as an optimization problem that can be solved in many ways. SGD [7] is an approximate SVM solver using an iterative stochastic gradient descent algorithm. The input of SGD is a set of training examples and the output is a model to classify new data. In each iteration of SGD, an approximate gradient is computed to update the model parameters. The process stops after a specified number of iterations.

Knobs: The number of training instances and the accuracy of solving the underlying optimization problem can be tuned to trade off higher classification error for faster runtimes. One knob controls the size of the subset, and another knob controls the number of iterations of the stochastic gradient descent algorithm. The first knob can be tuned to randomly sample the training instances at 20 different levels from 5% to 100%. The second knob can be tuned up to 100 levels.

Error metrics: SGD outputs the learned SVM model. The misclassification rate when using the resulting model to classify the test instances is a standard way to measure the quality of the output. The distance function computes the difference of the misclassification rates between the two models resulting from the two executions. The reference execution is the one achieving the minimum misclassification rate for the same input.

Features for modeling cost: The number of training instances, the dimension of a training instance and the number of non-zero entries of the training instances.

4.5 OpenOrd

OpenOrd [28] is a graph layout algorithm for drawing graphs in two dimensions. It specializes the force-directed graph layout algorithm to scale to large graphs. The drawing problem is formulated as an optimization problem where nodes connected by high edge weights attempt to move together but nodes otherwise attempt to push their nearby nodes far away. The optimization problem is solved by initially positioning all the nodes at the origin and iteratively moving the nodes until their relative positions do not change. The iterations are divided into five phases: liquid, expansion, cooldown, crunch and simmer. In each phase, simulated annealing is used to control how far the nodes are allowed to move.

Knobs: In practice, the algorithm is not run until convergence. The number of iterations used in each phase affects how far the resulting solution is from the exact solution as well as the amount of time required to compute it. Since there are 5 phases, the application has 5 knobs. In the experiments, the five knobs can be tuned to 3, 6, 6, 3 and 4 levels respectively.

Error metrics: The objective function minimized by the algorithm is used as the quality metric to measure how well the optimization problem is solved. The reference execution is the one achieving the minimum objective value.

Input features for modeling cost: The number of vertices and the number of edges in the graph.

4.6 Radar processing

We also performed a blind test of the system using a radar processing application [21] developed by Hank Hoffmann at the University of Chicago. Unlike the five applications described above, this code was already instrumented with knobs, so we used it out of the box as a blind test for our system. This code is a pipeline with four stages. The first stage (LPF) is a low-pass filter to eliminate high-frequency noise. The second stage (BF) does beam-forming which allows a phased array radar to concentrate in a particular direction. The third stage (PC) performs pulse compression, which concentrates energy. The final stage is a constant false alarm rate detection (CFAR), which identifies targets.

Knobs: The application supports four knobs. The first two knobs change the decimation ratios in the finite impulse response filters that make up the LPF stage. The third knob changes the number of beams used in the beam former. The fourth knob changes the range resolution. The application can have 512 separate configurations using these four knobs.

Error metrics: The signal-to-noise ratio (SNR) is used to measure the quality of the detection. The reference execution is the one achieving the highest SNR.

Input features for modeling cost: No input features are used in this application.

5. Evaluation

For each benchmark, we collected a set of inputs as shown in Table 1. We would have liked to have more training inputs for GEM, OpenOrd and SGD. To evaluate the error and cost models, inputs were randomly partitioned into training and testing subsets in the proportions shown.

All experiments were run on a machine with two Xeon E5 processors and 32G memory. We used BNLearn [44] for learning Bayesian networks and gRain [23] for performing inference in Bayesian networks. In addition, we used the

Benchmark	#Total	#Train	#Test	Source
Bullet	1783	881	882	[8, 50]
Ferret	3500	1750	1750	[6]
GEM	43	26	17	[25, 53]
OpenOrd	43	26	17	[25, 53]
SGD	30	18	12	[26, 48], synthetic
Radar	128	64	64	synthetic

Table 1. Inputs for benchmarks. Inputs are randomly divided into training set and testing set.

	Bullet	Ferret	GEM	OpenOrd	SGD	Radar
Training time (error)	0.239	0.927	0.109	0.119	0.120	0.072
Training time (cost)	34.44	133.37	7.52	15.00	7.18	3.80
Control (exhaustive)	0.0016	0.004	0.034	0.032	0.020	0.0009
Control (Precimonious)	0.0003	0.0010	0.0008	0.0016	0.0018	0.0006
Max execution time	2.365	2.590	584.951	221.285	388.364	608
Min execution time	0.008	0.038	0.570	2.362	0.594	550
Mean execution time	0.090	0.341	48.348	76.087	92.276	562

Table 2. Training time for error and cost (application execution time) models, running time for Control Algorithm, and Application execution times (all times are seconds)

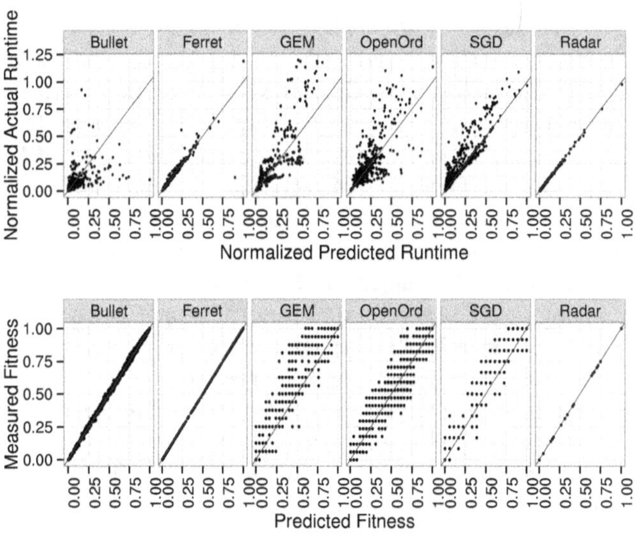

Figure 7. Accuracy of cost and error models

Cubist [1] implementation of the M5 Cost Model. We used Python to implement the Capri system.

We evaluated our system for ϵ ranging from 0.0 to 1.0 and π ranging from 0.1 to 1.0.

5.1 Evaluation of the cost and error models

Training is done offline, so training time is not as important as the accuracy of the cost and error models. Table 2 shows the time for training the error and cost models for the five applications (for these experiments, the cost metric was the running time of the application, and the time for running the applications on the training inputs with different knob settings is excluded). Training time obviously increases with the number of training inputs, but even for Ferret, which has

	Bullet						Ferret						GEM						OpenOrd						SGD					
π || ϵ	0.0	0.1	0.2	0.3	0.4	0.5	0.0	0.1	0.2	0.3	0.4	0.5	0.0	0.1	0.2	0.3	0.4	0.5	0.0	0.1	0.2	0.3	0.4	0.5	0.0	0.1	0.2	0.3	0.4	0.5
1.0	1.0	1.0	1.0	1.0	1.0	1.0	1.0	1.0	1.0	1.0	1.1	1.1	NA	NA	1.3	1.4	1.6	1.9	NA	2.0	2.4	6.3	6.3	5.9	NA	2.5	5.6	14.1	31.3	77.4
0.9	1.0	1.0	1.0	1.0	1.0	1.0	1.1	1.4	1.4	1.6	1.7	1.9	NA	1.1	1.5	1.9	2.2	2.5	NA	2.9	6.5	6.0	5.9	8.4	NA	11.8	30.3	43.0	56.3	94.9
0.8	1.0	1.0	1.0	1.0	1.0	24.3	1.1	1.4	1.6	1.6	1.9	1.9	NA	1.2	1.7	2.1	2.4	2.6	NA	5.2	6.4	8.7	8.7	8.5	NA	39.7	52.5	103.7	165.0	184.0
0.7	1.0	1.0	1.0	1.0	9.0	96.6	1.1	1.4	1.6	1.7	1.9	2.0	NA	1.3	1.7	2.1	2.5	2.7	NA	6.3	6.1	8.5	8.8	8.5	NA	73.3	101.4	139.9	176.1	271.7
0.6	1.0	1.0	1.0	1.7	96.6	141.3	1.2	1.4	1.6	1.7	1.9	2.0	NA	1.4	2.0	2.2	2.6	2.7	NA	6.0	8.5	8.7	8.5	8.5	1.0	97.5	136.7	207.0	302.0	395.3
0.5	1.0	1.0	1.0	39.9	115.4	204.6	1.2	1.4	1.6	1.7	2.0	2.0	NA	1.7	2.3	2.5	2.7	3.0	NA	8.5	8.5	8.6	8.4	8.4	1.0	104.6	161.1	259.1	302.0	418.4

Table 3. Speedups of the tuned programs for a subset of constraint space.

the largest training set, it takes only 0.927 seconds to train the error model and 133.366 seconds (about 2 minutes) to train the cost model.

How accurate are the cost and error models constructed from the training inputs? One way to determine this is to use them to make predictions for the test inputs, and evaluate the accuracy of these predictions against empirical measurements.

Evaluating the accuracy of the cost model for a given application is straightforward: we sweep the space of test inputs and knob settings, and for each point in this space, we compare the running time predicted by the cost model with the actual execution time. The top charts in Figure 7 show the results for the applications in our test suite. In each graph, the x-axis is the predicted running time and the y-axis is the measured running time. If the cost model is perfect, all points should lie on the $y{=}x$ line. Figure 7 shows that this is more or less true for Ferret and Radar. For GEM and SGD, the predicted time is usually less than the actual execution time, and for Bullet and OpenORD, the over-predictions and under-predictions are more or less evenly distributed. Radar implements a regular algorithm in which running time depends on the size of the input. In contrast, GEM and OpenORD implement complex graph algorithms, so they are more irregular in their behavior.

Estimating the accuracy of the error model has to be more indirect since the model does not make error predictions for individual inputs but only for an ensemble of inputs. The error model is a proxy for the fitness function

$$P_e(\epsilon, k_1, k_2) = \sum_{(j \in I) \wedge (f_e(j,k_1,k_2) \leq \epsilon)} p(j)$$

This proxy is constructed during the training phase by letting I be the set of training inputs. One way to evaluate the accuracy of this proxy is to construct another proxy by letting I be the set of test inputs. If the model is accurate, these two proxy functions, which we call the predicted fitness and measured fitness, will be equal.

The bottom charts of Figure 7 show the results of this experiment. The x and y axes in each graph are the predicted and measured fitness respectively. We sweep over the space of (discretized) error values ϵ and knob settings, and for each point in this space, we evaluate the two proxy functions and plot the point in the graph. We see that the error model is very accurate for Bullet, Ferret and Radar, and less so for the other three benchmarks. For GEM and SGD, most of the points lie above the $y{=}x$ line, which means that the predicted fitness is usually less than the actual fitness. Therefore, the feasible region determined by using the model may be smaller than the actual feasible region.

It is important to note that although model accuracy can be improved in many ways, more accurate models do not necessarily enable a system like Capri to produce better solutions to the control problem. For example, the cost model is used only to rank knob settings in the feasible region, so the actual value of the predicted running time for a knob setting is not important; if the predicted running time for every knob setting is a thousand times more than the actual running time, the model is very inaccurate but it will nevertheless rank knob settings perfectly. Similarly, as long as the feasible region returned by an error model contains the optimal knob setting and does not contain spurious knob settings ranked higher by the cost model, that error model is as good as a perfectly accurate model as far as its use in Capri is concerned.

5.2 End-to-end evaluation of the control system

The control algorithm is executed online, so it is important for it to be fast. Table 2 shows that the time for executing the control algorithm is very small; for example, for SGD, it takes 20 milliseconds. This is an acceptable overhead, particularly for large inputs, as can be seen by comparing these times to the max, min, and mean running times for the applications with maximum quality knob settings shown in the table. Using the Precimonious algorithm for control is faster than using exhaustive search, as expected.

Speedup is defined as ratio of the running time at a particular knob setting to the running time with the knobs set for maximum quality.

Table 3 shows speedups for each application for ϵ values between 0 and 0.5 and π values between 0.5 and 1.0 (for lack of space, we show only a portion of the overall constraint space). Each entry gives the average speedup over all test inputs for the knob settings found by the control algorithm based on exhaustive search, given (ϵ, π) constraints in the intervals specified by the row and column indices.

Speedups depend on the application and the (ϵ, π) constraints. For each application, the top-left corner of the constraint space is the "hard" region since the error must be low with high probability. The knob settings must be at or close to maximum, and speedup will be limited. Table entries marked "NA" show where the control system was unable to find any feasible solution for these hard constraints.

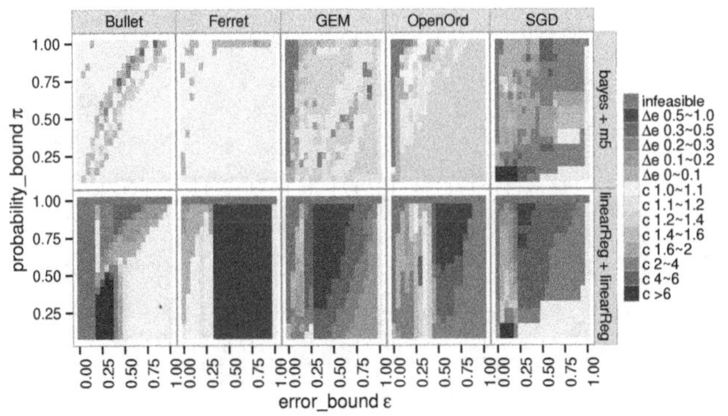

Figure 8. Effectiveness of Capri for constrained optimization of running time. Regions are colored red if error constraint is not met; shade of red encodes difference between achieved and target errors. Regions are colored green to blue if error constraint is met; shade of green-blue encodes ratio of achieved cost to cost of oracle solution, averaged over all test inputs.

In contrast, the bottom-right corner of the constraint space is the "easier" region, so one would expect higher speedups. This is seen in all benchmarks. For SGD, significant speedup can be obtained since the asymptotic complexity of the algorithm is proportional to the product of the number of training instances and the number of iterations; therefore, a ten-fold reduction in both these numbers results in a 100-fold speedup.

Overall, we see that controlling the knobs in these applications can yield significant speedups in running time.

Effectiveness in finding optimal knob settings While Table 3 shows speedups obtained from the knob settings found by the control algorithm in different regions of the constraint space, it does not show how well these constraints were actually met. To provide context, we have evaluated this both for our method and for a similar method using linear regression to model both error and running time (linear regression can be seen as the simplest non-trivial model one can build for these values). The results are shown in Figure 8.

For each (ϵ, π) combination, we evaluated the quality of the achieved control as follows:

- For each test input, use the control algorithm to set the knobs. If no knob settings are returned, the tile is colored grey. Otherwise measure the actual error and the actual running times for this returned knob setting.
- Using the measured actual error for each input, find the probability that the error bound ϵ has actually been met (if all inputs are equally likely, this is just the fraction of inputs for which the actual error is less than or equal to ϵ). If this probability is greater than π, the control algorithm has succeeded in meeting the (ϵ, π) constraint. Give the tile a color between green and blue, depending on how close on average (over all test inputs) the cost is to the cost of the solution found by the oracle described in §3.4. The number associated with the color in each cell represents the average (over all test inputs) of the ratio of the cost of the error and cost method combination to the cost of the oracle.
- If the (ϵ, π) constraint has not actually been met, color the tile red. The shade of red indicates the difference between the achieved error and the error of the solution found by the oracle control.

In short, grey tiles indicate that the control algorithm was unable to find a solution. Red tiles indicate that the algorithm found a feasible solution but failed to satisfy the (ϵ, π) constraint and the shade of red indicates the degree of failure in the average error. Green-blue tiles indicate that the algorithm succeeded, and the color indicates how close the cost is to the optimal cost solution found by the oracle. Ideally, all tiles would be colored light green to light red, indicating that the error bound was met with low cost.

The top set of squares shows the results from using Capri , while the bottom set of squares shows the results from the control system based on linear regression. Overall, the control system using the Bayes model for error and the m5 model for cost performs quite well for all inputs and regions of the constraint space. The only noticeable problem is in SGD, which has a lot of blue squares. A closer study showed that the feasible region found by the Bayes error model is smaller than it should be and did not contain some low-cost points found by the oracle control. This can be attributed to the fact that the predicted fitness function for SGD is somewhat conservative, as seen in Figure 7.

In contrast, the control system based on linear regression performs quite poorly. No solutions are found in most parts of the space, and even when solutions are found, the cost of the solutions is very sub-optimal.

Using the Bayesian network to model error and m5 to model cost is fairly successful across the constraint space: for most points, it finds solutions and the cost difference from the oracle's solution is within 40%.

5.3 Performance of Radar Application

	Radar					
π || ϵ	0.0	0.1	0.2	0.3	0.4	0.5
1.0	1.0	1.0	1.0	1.1	1.1	1.1
0.9	1.0	1.0	1.0	1.1	1.1	1.1
0.8	1.0	1.0	1.0	1.1	1.1	1.1
0.7	1.0	1.0	1.0	1.1	1.1	1.1
0.6	1.0	1.0	1.0	1.3	1.3	1.3
0.5	1.0	1.0	1.0	1.3	1.3	1.3

Figure 9. Speedup of Radar Application

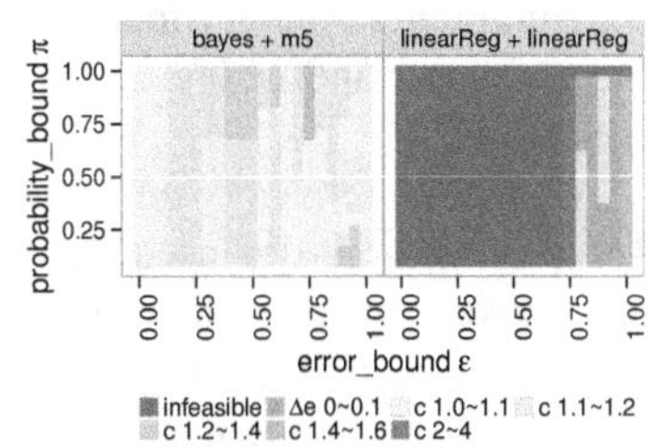

Figure 10. Effectiveness of Capri for Radar application

Table 9 and Figure 10 shows the speedups and the performance of the error and cost models for the radar application for different values of ϵ and π. These results are competitive

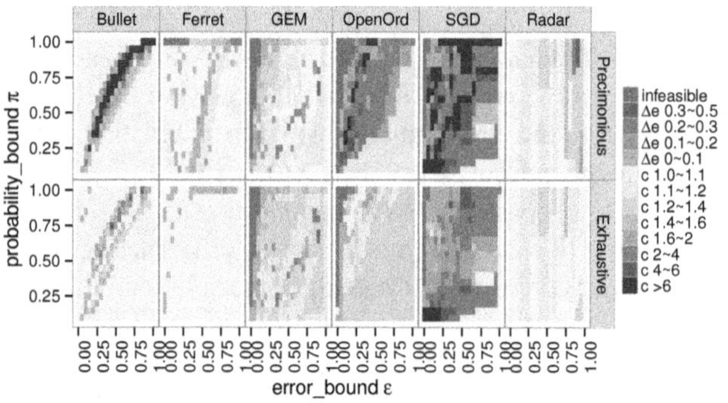

Figure 11. Precimonious search vs. exhaustive search

with the knob settings obtained by manual tuning for this application, which demonstrates the effectiveness of using machine learning to solve the control problem. The models using linear regression were unable to find solutions in most of the constraint space.

5.4 Using Precimonious Search

Table 2 shows that using Precimonious to solve the control problem is significantly faster than using exhaustive search. On the other hand, Figure 11 shows that the knob settings it finds may be worse than the ones found by the exhaustive search, as one might expect. For OpenOrd, we can see that the Precimonious-based system is unable to find knob settings in many more cells, and finds much higher cost knob settings in the top left cells. The main reason for this is that Precimonious uses a greedy search strategy that may get stuck in a local minimum, which in the case of OpenOrd is not the global minimum. This experiment shows that the search strategy in our system is not restricted to exhaustive search, and that other search strategies can be used easily.

5.5 Optimizing Energy Consumption

Finally, we note that a major advantage of our approach is that it can be used to optimize not just running time but any metric for which a reasonable cost model can be constructed. Therefore, in principle, the system can be used to optimize metrics such as energy consumption, bandwidth or memory consumption. In this section, we show the results of applying the system to optimizing energy consumption for the same benchmarks.

We measured energy on a Intel Xeon E5-2630 CPU with 16Gb of memory. We used the Intel RAPL (Running Average Power Limit) interface and PAPI to measure the energy consumption. This machine does not support DRAM counters, so what is being measured is the CPU package energy consumption.

Table 4 shows the power savings obtained for our benchmarks for ϵ values between 0 and 0.5 and π values between 0.5 and 1.0. Each entry gives the average power savings over all test inputs for the knob settings found by our control algorithm given (ϵ, π) constraints in the intervals specified by

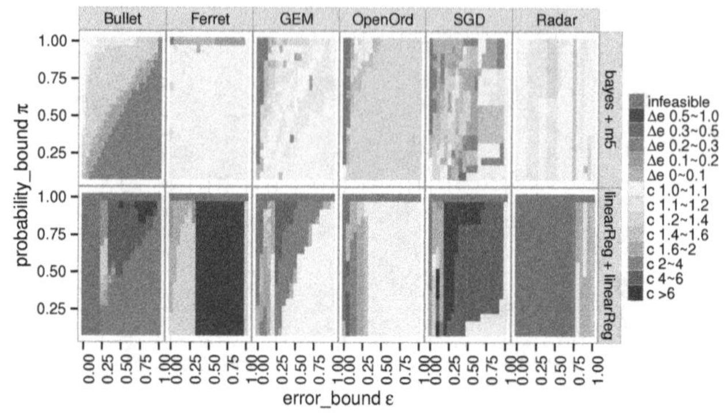

Figure 12. Effectiveness of Capri for constrained optimization of energy usage using exhaustive search

the row and column indices. As expected, savings are greater when the constraints are looser.

Figure 12 shows the performance of our system compared to the linear regression approach on the four applications. We can see that our approach performs very close to the oracle **measuredE + measureP**, while **linearReg + linearReg** does cannot satisfy a great portion of the constraints.

6. Related work

Approximation opportunities in software and hardware Loop perforation [46] explores skipping iterations during loop execution. [35] explores randomly discarding tasks in parallel applications. [36] and [9] explore relaxing synchronization in parallel applications. [49] explores different algorithmic level approximation schemes on a video summarization algorithm. In [39], methods are developed to recognize patterns in programs that provide approximation opportunities. These techniques could be used to provide knobs automatically and thus complement our work.

A distortion model using linear regression was used in [35] to demonstrate the feasibility of their approximation techniques. The results in this paper show that linear regression is not useful for modeling quality and cost.

Researchers have proposed several hardware designs for exploiting approximate computing [15, 16, 29, 33, 42, 45]. Our techniques can be useful in choosing how to most efficiently to map programs onto such hardware and thus increase the effectiveness of such approaches.

Reactive control of streaming applications In this problem, the system is presented with a stream of inputs in which successive inputs are assumed to be correlated with each other, and results from processing one input can be used to tune the computation for succeeding inputs. The Green System [4] periodically monitors QoS values and recalibrates using heuristics whenever the QoS is lower than a specified level. PowerDial [22] leverages feed-back control theory for recalibration. Argo [18] is an autotuning system for adapting application performance to changes in multicore resources. SAGE [40] exploits this approach on GPU platforms. In [17], the authors use simulated annealing to adjust

	Bullet						Ferret						GEM					
π || ϵ	0.0	0.1	0.2	0.3	0.4	0.5	0.0	0.1	0.2	0.3	0.4	0.5	0.0	0.1	0.2	0.3	0.4	0.5
1.0	1.0	1.0	1.0	1.0	1.0	1.0	NA	1.0	1.0	1.0	1.1	1.1	NA	NA	1.3	1.5	1.7	1.9
0.9	1.0	1.0	1.1	1.0	1.0	1.0	1.0	1.5	1.7	1.8	1.8	1.8	NA	NA	1.7	2.0	2.1	2.3
0.8	1.0	1.1	1.0	1.0	1.0	1.0	1.1	1.6	1.8	1.8	1.8	1.8	NA	1.1	1.8	2.1	2.3	2.5
0.7	1.0	1.0	1.0	1.0	1.0	1.0	1.1	1.7	1.8	1.8	1.8	1.8	NA	1.2	1.8	2.3	2.5	2.5
0.6	1.0	1.0	1.0	1.0	1.0	1.2	1.4	1.8	1.8	1.8	1.8	1.8	NA	1.5	2.1	2.3	2.5	2.8
0.5	1.0	1.0	1.0	1.0	1.2	1.3	1.4	1.8	1.8	1.8	1.8	1.8	NA	1.7	2.3	2.5	2.8	2.8

	OpenOrd						SGD						Radar					
π || ϵ	0.0	0.1	0.2	0.3	0.4	0.5	0.0	0.1	0.2	0.3	0.4	0.5	0.0	0.1	0.2	0.3	0.4	0.5
1.0	NA	2.4	6.1	7.2	7.2	8.9	NA	21.6	59.5	83.3	108.3	107.3	1.0	1.0	1.0	1.1	1.1	1.1
0.9	NA	6.0	7.1	7.2	8.9	8.9	NA	51.0	98.0	149.2	168.7	262.7	1.0	1.0	1.0	1.1	1.1	1.1
0.8	NA	6.0	7.2	8.9	8.9	8.9	NA	91.0	192.5	266.0	265.0	319.0	1.0	1.0	1.0	1.1	1.1	1.1
0.7	NA	7.1	7.2	8.9	8.9	8.9	NA	112.7	193.6	265.0	338.2	319.0	1.0	1.0	1.0	1.1	1.1	1.1
0.6	NA	7.2	8.9	8.9	8.9	8.9	1.0	110.2	193.6	345.1	341.8	410.2	1.0	1.0	1.0	1.3	1.3	1.3
0.5	NA	8.9	8.9	8.9	8.9	8.9	1.0	129.9	254.2	345.1	420.2	410.2	1.0	1.0	1.0	1.3	1.3	1.3

Table 4. Energy savings of the tuned programs for a subset of constraint space.

the knob settings. The problem considered in this paper is fundamentally different since it involves proactive control of an application with a single input rather than reactive control for a stream of inputs. However, the techniques described in this paper may be applicable to reactive control as well.

Auto-tuning Auto-tuning explores a space of exact implementations to optimize a cost metric like running time; in contrast, the control problem defined in this paper deals with both error and cost dimensions. [3, 14] have extended the PetaBricks [2] auto-tuning system to include an error bound. In [14], training inputs are grouped into clusters based on user-provided features, and auto-tuning is used to find optimal knob settings for each cluster for given error bounds. For a new input, optimal knob settings for the same error bounds are determined by classifying the input into one of the clusters and using the predetermined knob settings for that cluster. Auto-tuning is used by Precimonious [38] to lower precision of floating point types to improve performance for a particular accuracy constraint.

The main difference between our approach and auto-tuning approaches is that our approach builds error and cost models that can be used to control knobs for any error constraint presented during the online phase, without requiring re-training. Since auto-tuning approaches do not build models, they do not have the ability to generalize their results from the constraints they were trained for to other constraints. Note that the clustering-classification approach can be combined with our approach by clustering the training inputs and building a different model for each cluster.

Programming language support EnerJ [41] proposes a type system to separate exact and approximate data in the program. Rely [10] uses static analysis techniques to quantify the errors in programs on approximate hardware. [37] developed tools for debugging approximate programs. None of these deals with controlling the tradeoff of error versus cost.

Error Guarantees In [55], the author formulated a randomized program transformation which trades off expected error versus performance as an optimization problem.However, their formulation assumes very small variations of errors across inputs, an assumption violated in all of our complex real-world benchmarks applications. They also assume the existence of an *a priori* error bound for each approximation in the program and that the error propagation is bounded by a linear function. These assumptions make it hard to apply this approach to real-world applications. For example, we know of no non-trivial error bounds for our benchmarks. Chisel [30] extends Rely [10] to use integer linear programming(ILP) to optimize the selection of instructions/data executed/stored in approximate hardware. The ILP constraints are generated by static analysis, which propagates errors through the program. While they consider input reliability, i.e. the probability that an input contains errors, they do not deal with input sensitivity of the error function. Moreover, their error propagation method requires that the error function be differentiable and their static analysis technique cannot deal with input-dependent loops, which are common in our benchmarks and many other applications. ApproxHadoop [20] applies statistical sampling theory to Hadoop tasks for controlling input sampling and task dropping. While statistical sampling theory gives nice error guarantees, the application of this technique is restricted. [27] uses neural networks to predict whether to invoke approximate accelerators or executing the precise code for a quality constraint.

Analytic properties of programs Several techniques exist to verify whether a program is Lipschitz-continuous [12]. Smooth interpretation [11] can smooth out irregular features of a program. Given the input variability exhibited in our applications, analytic properties usually provide very loose error bounds and are not helpful for setting knobs.

7. Conclusions

Although there is a large body of work on using approximate computing to reduce computation time as well as power and energy requirements, little is known about how to control approximate programs in a principled way. Previous work on approximate computing has focused either on showing the feasibility of approximate computing or on controlling streaming programs in which error estimates for one input can be used to reactively control error for subsequent inputs.

In this paper, we addressed the problem of controlling tunable approximate programs, which have one or more knobs that can be changed to vary the fidelity of the output of the approximate computation. We showed how the proactive control problem for tunable programs can be formulated as an optimization problem, and then gave an algorithm for solving this control problem by using error and cost models generated using machine learning techniques. Our experimental results show that this approach performs well on controlling tunable approximate programs.

References

[1] Cubist. `https://www.rulequest.com/cubist-info.html`.

[2] Jason Ansel, Cy Chan, Yee Lok Wong, Marek Olszewski, Qin Zhao, Alan Edelman, and Saman Amarasinghe. Petabricks: A language and compiler for algorithmic choice. In *Proceedings of the 2009 ACM SIGPLAN Conference on Programming Language Design and Implementation*, PLDI '09, 2009.

[3] Jason Ansel, Yee Lok Wong, Cy Chan, Marek Olszewski, Alan Edelman, and Saman Amarasinghe. Language and compiler support for auto-tuning variable-accuracy algorithms. *Proceedings of the 2013 IEEE/ACM International Symposium on Code Generation and Optimization (CGO)*, 2011.

[4] Woongki Baek and Trishul M. Chilimbi. Green: A framework for supporting energy-conscious programming using controlled approximation. In *Proceedings of the 2010 ACM SIGPLAN Conference on Programming Language Design and Implementation*, PLDI '10, 2010.

[5] Judit Bar-Ilan, Mazlita Mat-Hassan, and Mark Levene. Methods for comparing rankings of search engine results. *Comput. Netw.*, 2006.

[6] Christian Bienia. *Benchmarking Modern Multiprocessors*. PhD thesis, Princeton University, January 2011.

[7] Léon Bottou. Large-scale machine learning with stochastic gradient descent. In *Proceedings of the 19th International Conference on Computational Statistics (COMPSTAT'2010)*, 2010.

[8] John Burkardt. 3d graphics models. `http://people.sc.fsu.edu/~jburkardt/data/ply/ply.html`.

[9] Simone Campanoni, Glenn Holloway, Gu-Yeon Wei, and David Brooks. Helix-up: Relaxing program semantics to unleash parallelization. In *Proceedings of the 13th Annual IEEE/ACM International Symposium on Code Generation and Optimization*, CGO '15, 2015.

[10] Michael Carbin, Sasa Misailovic, and Martin C. Rinard. Verifying quantitative reliability for programs that execute on unreliable hardware. In *Proceedings of the 2013 ACM SIGPLAN International Conference on Object Oriented Programming Systems Languages and Applications*, OOPSLA '13, 2013.

[11] Swarat Chaudhuri, Sumit Gulwani, and Roberto Lublinerman. Continuity and robustness of programs. *Commun. ACM*, 55(8):107–115, August 2012.

[12] Swarat Chaudhuri and Armando Solar-Lezama. Smooth interpretation. In *Proceedings of the 2010 ACM SIGPLAN Conference on Programming Language Design and Implementation*, PLDI '10, 2010.

[13] Thomas Cormen, Charles Leiserson, Ronald Rivest, and Clifford Stein, editors. *Introduction to Algorithms*. MIT Press, 2001.

[14] Yufei Ding, Jason Ansel, Kalyan Veeramachaneni, Xipeng Shen, Una-May O'Reilly, and Saman Amarasinghe. Autotuning algorithmic choice for input sensitivity. In *ACM SIGPLAN Conference on Programming Language Design and Implementation*, June 2015.

[15] Hadi Esmaeilzadeh, Adrian Sampson, Luis Ceze, and Doug Burger. Architecture support for disciplined approximate programming. In *Proceedings of the Seventeenth International Conference on Architectural Support for Programming Languages and Operating Systems*, ASPLOS XVII, 2012.

[16] Hadi Esmaeilzadeh, Adrian Sampson, Luis Ceze, and Doug Burger. Neural acceleration for general-purpose approximate programs. In *Proceedings of the 2012 45th Annual IEEE/ACM International Symposium on Microarchitecture*, MICRO-45, 2012.

[17] Shuangde Fang, Zidong Du, Yuntan Fang, Yuanjie Huang, Yang Chen, Lieven Eeckhout, Olivier Temam, Huawei Li, Yunji Chen, and Chengyong Wu. Performance portability across heterogeneous socs using a generalized library-based approach. *ACM Trans. Archit. Code Optim.*, 2014.

[18] Davide Gadioli, Gianluca Palermo, and Cristina Silvano. Application autotuning to support runtime adaptivity in multicorearchitectures. In *SAMOS XV*, 2015.

[19] Michael Garland and Paul S. Heckbert. Surface simplification using quadric error metrics. In *Proceedings of the 24th Annual Conference on Computer Graphics and Interactive Techniques*, SIGGRAPH '97, 1997.

[20] Inigo Goiri, Ricardo Bianchini, Santosh Nagarakatte, and Thu D. Nguyen. Approxhadoop: Bringing approximations to mapreduce frameworks. In *Proceedings of the Twentieth International Conference on Architectural Support for Programming Languages and Operating Systems*, ASPLOS '15, 2015.

[21] Henry Hoffmann, Anant Agarwal, and Srinivas Devadas. Selecting spatiotemporal patterns for development of parallel applications. *IEEE Transactions on Parallel and Distributed Systems*, 23(10):1970–1982, 2012.

[22] Henry Hoffmann, Stelios Sidiroglou, Michael Carbin, Sasa Misailovic, Anant Agarwal, and Martin Rinard. Dynamic knobs for responsive power-aware computing. In *Proceedings of the Sixteenth International Conference on Architectural Support for Programming Languages and Operating Systems*, ASPLOS XVI, 2011.

[23] Sren Hjsgaard. Graphical independence networks with the grain package for r. *Journal of Statistical Software*, 46, 2012.

[24] Benjamin Kuo. *Automatic control systems*. Prentice-Hall Publishers, 1991.

[25] Jure Leskovec. Stanford large network dataset collection(snap). `http://snap.stanford.edu/data/`.

[26] Chih-Jen Lin. Libsvm classification dataset. `http://www.csie.ntu.edu.tw/~cjlin/libsvmtools/datasets/`.

[27] Divya Mahajan, Amir Yazdanbakhsh, Jongse Park, Bradley Thwaites, and Hadi Esmaeilzadeh. Prediction-based quality-control for approximate accelerators. In *Second Workshop on Approximate Computing Across the System Stack*, WACAS, 2015.

[28] Shawn Martin, W. Michael Brown, Richard Klavans, and Kevin W. Boyack. Openord: an open-source toolbox for large graph layout. volume 7868, 2011.

[29] Joshua San Miguel, Mario Badr, and Natalie Enright Jerger. Load value approximation. In *Proceedings of the 47th Annual*

IEEE/ACM International Symposium on Microarchitecture, MICRO-47, 2014.

[30] Sasa Misailovic, Michael Carbin, Sara Achour, Zichao Qi, and Martin C. Rinard. Chisel: Reliability- and accuracy-aware optimization of approximate computational kernels. In *Proceedings of the 2014 ACM International Conference on Object Oriented Programming Systems, Languages and Applications*, OOPSLA '14, 2014.

[31] R. E. Neapolitan. *Learning Bayesian Networks*. Prentice Hall, 2003.

[32] Miguel A. Otaduy and Ming C. Lin. Clods: Dual hierarchies for multiresolution collision detection. In *Proceedings of the 2003 Eurographics/ACM SIGGRAPH Symposium on Geometry Processing*, SGP '03, 2003.

[33] Krishna V. Palem. Energy aware computing through probabilistic switching: A study of limits. *IEEE Trans. Comput.*, 2005.

[34] J. R. Quinlan. Learning with continuous classes. In *Proceedings of the Australian Joint Conference on Artificial Intelligence*, pages 343–348. World Scientific, 1992.

[35] Martin Rinard. Probabilistic accuracy bounds for fault-tolerant computations that discard tasks. In *Proceedings of the 20th Annual International Conference on Supercomputing*, ICS '06, 2006.

[36] Martin C. Rinard. Using early phase termination to eliminate load imbalances at barrier synchronization points. In *Proceedings of the 22Nd Annual ACM SIGPLAN Conference on Object-oriented Programming Systems and Applications*, OOPSLA '07, 2007.

[37] Michael Ringenburg, Adrian Sampson, Isaac Ackerman, Luis Ceze, and Dan Grossman. Monitoring and debugging the quality of results in approximate programs. In *Proceedings of the Twentieth International Conference on Architectural Support for Programming Languages and Operating Systems*, ASPLOS '15, 2015.

[38] Cindy Rubio-González, Cuong Nguyen, Hong Diep Nguyen, James Demmel, William Kahan, Koushik Sen, David H. Bailey, Costin Iancu, and David Hough. Precimonious: Tuning assistant for floating-point precision. In *Proceedings of the International Conference on High Performance Computing, Networking, Storage and Analysis*, SC '13, 2013.

[39] Mehrzad Samadi, Davoud Anoushe Jamshidi, Janghaeng Lee, and Scott Mahlke. Paraprox: Pattern-based approximation for data parallel applications. In *Proceedings of the 19th International Conference on Architectural Support for Programming Languages and Operating Systems*, ASPLOS '14, 2014.

[40] Mehrzad Samadi, Janghaeng Lee, D. Anoushe Jamshidi, Amir Hormati, and Scott Mahlke. Sage: Self-tuning approximation for graphics engines. In *Proceedings of the 46th Annual IEEE/ACM International Symposium on Microarchitecture*, MICRO-46, 2013.

[41] Adrian Sampson, Werner Dietl, Emily Fortuna, Danushen Gnanapragasam, Luis Ceze, and Dan Grossman. Enerj: Approximate data types for safe and general low-power computation. In *Proceedings of the 32Nd ACM SIGPLAN Conference on Programming Language Design and Implementation*, PLDI '11, 2011.

[42] Adrian Sampson, Jacob Nelson, Karin Strauss, and Luis Ceze. Approximate storage in solid-state memories. In *Proceedings of the 46th Annual IEEE/ACM International Symposium on Microarchitecture*, MICRO-46, 2013.

[43] Eric Schkufza, Rahul Sharma, and Alex Aiken. Stochastic optimization of floating-point programs with tunable precision. In *Proceedings of the 35th ACM SIGPLAN Conference on Programming Language Design and Implementation*, PLDI '14, 2014.

[44] M. Scutari. Learning Bayesian Networks with the bnlearn R Package. *Journal of Statistical Software*, 35, 2010.

[45] M. Shoushtari, A. BanaiyanMofrad, and N. Dutt. Exploiting partially-forgetful memories for approximate computing. *Embedded Systems Letters, IEEE*, March 2015.

[46] Stelios Sidiroglou-Douskos, Sasa Misailovic, Henry Hoffmann, and Martin Rinard. Managing performance vs. accuracy trade-offs with loop perforation. In *Proceedings of the 19th ACM SIGSOFT Symposium and the 13th European Conference on Foundations of Software Engineering*, ESEC/FSE '11, 2011.

[47] Jean-Jacques Slotine and Weiping Li. *Applied Nonlinear control*. Prenctice-Hall Publishers, 1991.

[48] Soeren Sonnenburg, Vojtech Franc, Elad Yom-Tov, and Michele Sebag. Pascal large scale learning challenge. `http://largescale.ml.tu-berlin.de`.

[49] Karthik Swaminathan, Chung-Ching Lin, Augusto Vega, Alper Buyuktosunoglu, Pradip Bose, and Sharathchandra Pankanti. A case for approximate computing in real-time mobile cognition. In *Second Workshop on Approximate Computing Across the System Stack*, WACAS, 2015.

[50] TF3DM. 3d graphics models. `http://tf3dm.com`.

[51] L. G. Valiant. A theory of the learnable. *CACM*, 27(11), 1984.

[52] Joyce Jiyoung Whang, Xin Sui, and Inderjit S. Dhillon. Scalable and memory-efficient clustering of large-scale social networks. In *ICDM*, 2012.

[53] R. Zafarani and H. Liu. Social computing data repository at ASU, 2009. `http://socialcomputing.asu.edu`.

[54] Andreas Zeller and Ralf Hildebrandt. Simplifying and isolating failure-inducing input. *IEEE Trans. Softw. Eng.*, 28(2):183–200, February 2002.

[55] Zeyuan Allen Zhu, Sasa Misailovic, Jonathan A. Kelner, and Martin Rinard. Randomized accuracy-aware program transformations for efficient approximate computations. In *Proceedings of the 39th Annual ACM SIGPLAN-SIGACT Symposium on Principles of Programming Languages*, POPL '12, 2012.

AxGames: Towards Crowdsourcing Quality Target Determination in Approximate Computing

Jongse Park   Emmanuel Amaro   Divya Mahajan   Bradley Thwaites   Hadi Esmaeilzadeh

Alternative Computing Technologies (ACT) Lab
Georgia Institute of Technology
{jspark, amaro, divya_mahajan, bthwaites}@gatech.edu   hadi@cc.gatech.edu

Abstract

Approximate computing trades quality of application output for higher efficiency and performance. Approximation is useful only if its impact on application output quality is acceptable to the users. However, there is a lack of systematic solutions and studies that explore users' perspective on the effects of approximation. In this paper, we seek to provide one such solution for the developers to probe and discover the boundary of quality loss that most users will deem acceptable. We propose AxGames, a crowdsourced solution that enables developers to readily infer a statistical common ground from the general public through three entertaining games. The users engage in these games by betting on their opinion about the quality loss of the final output while the AxGames framework collects statistics about their perceptions. The framework then statistically analyzes the results to determine the acceptable levels of quality for a pair of (application, approximation technique). The three games are designed such that they effectively capture quality requirements with various tradeoffs and contexts.

To evaluate AxGames, we examine seven diverse applications that produce user perceptible outputs and cover a wide range of domains, including image processing, optical character recognition, speech to text conversion, and audio processing. We recruit 700 participants/users through Amazon's Mechanical Turk to play the games that collect statistics about their perception on different levels of quality. Subsequently, the AxGames framework uses the Clopper-Pearson exact method, which computes a binomial proportion confidence interval, to analyze the collected statistics for each level of quality. Using this analysis, AxGames can statistically project the quality level that satisfies a given percentage of users. The developers can use these statistical projections to tune the level of approximation based on the user experience. We find that the level of acceptable quality loss significantly varies across applications. For instance, to satisfy 90% of users, the level of acceptable quality loss is 2% for one application (image processing) and 26% for another (audio processing). Moreover, the pattern with which the crowd responds to approximation takes significantly different shape and form depending on the class of applications. These results confirm the necessity of solutions that systematically explore the effect of approximation on the end user experience.

ASPLOS '16, April 02 - 06, 2016, Atlanta, GA, USA
Copyright © 2016 ACM 978-1-4503-4091-5/16/04…$15.00
DOI: http://dx.doi.org/10.1145/http://dx.doi.org/10.1145/2872362.2872376

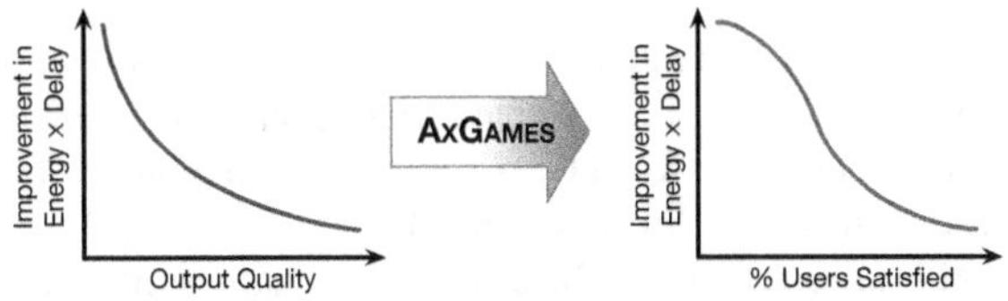

Figure 1: AxGames is a crowdsourcing solution that transforms the tradeoff between quality and energy-performance gains from approximation to the tradeoff between the gains and user satisfaction.

1. Introduction

Power efficiency is a primary concern in modern systems. Battery capacity often limits mobile devices, while power consumption and cooling imposes budgetary constraints on data centers. Moreover, traditional CMOS scaling has slowed to a point that threatens the longstanding cadence of continuously improving performance [1–3]. Meanwhile, emerging workloads must manage ever-growing datasets with high responsiveness and availability to end users. Expert analyses show that in 2011, 1.8 zettabytes (1.8 trillion gigabytes) of information was created and replicated by all sources, with individual consumers responsible for 75% [4]. By 2020, the world's data centers will be responsible for managing 50× this staggering figure [4]. This level of demand for computing raises serious concerns about the capabilities of current computing systems to match emerging trends. Apropos these confluent challenges, a growing body of recent work seeks to exploit a common property of many emerging applications: tolerance to approximate computation. These techniques relax the traditional abstraction of full accuracy in data processing, storage, and retrieval, thus trading losses in output quality for improved performance and efficiency [5–16].

While these techniques provide promising gains, the effects of quality loss on the users are not well understood, leaving approximation techniques in a position of questionable utility. The challenge is determining the level of quality loss that the large majority of users deem acceptable. Discovering this level requires end users, who are not readily available during the development phase. Even after the application is deployed, frameworks that enable users to provide feedback on the quality loss are currently unavailable. To this end, we aim to develop a framework that methodically utilizes crowdsourcing to identify the desirable application output quality without exposing the details of approximation to the users. The objective is to aid the developers in identifying the acceptable level of quality loss and enable the crowd of users to directly help in determining this level. The crowdsourcing process needs to also be engaging and enjoyable enough to retain users. To address these challenges, this paper describes AxGames, a game-based crowdsourcing framework that statistically projects *user-driven* quality targets for approx-

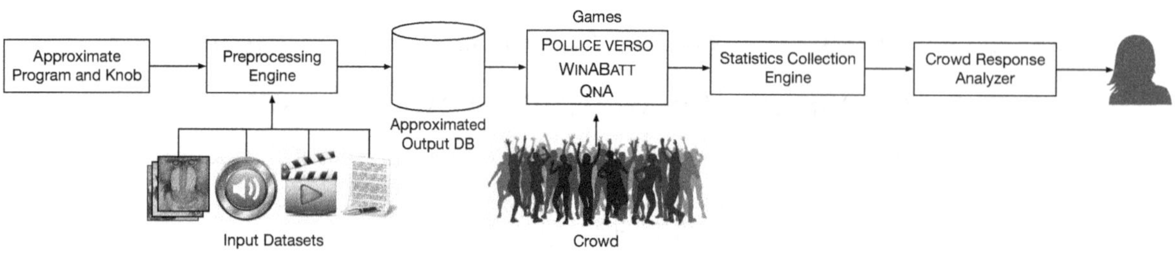

Figure 2: An overview of the AXGAMES crowdsourcing solution which determines the user-driven quality target for a given approximated application.

imate computing. As Figure 1 illustrates, AXGAMES changes the tradeoff between output quality and energy-performance gains to a tradeoff between the gains and the percentage of the users who are satisfied with the output.

AXGAMES comprises three web-based games that enable players to collectively identify the acceptable level of quality for the application in question. The games are designed to find a statistical consensus among the players on which level of quality loss is acceptable. Finding the statistical consensus is imperative in ensuring that the majority of the application users will accept the quality loss caused by the approximation technique. The first game allows the users to express their perception about the quality of the approximated output without regard to the quality-cost tradeoff. The second game enables users to choose a level of quality while considering an abstract cost tradeoff. The third game adds an element of context by asking the players to answer a multiple-choice question about the approximated output. The users are given an incentive to select the lowest output quality that allows them to answer the question. All the three games involve betting, spending, losing, and winning virtual money. The virtual money is an abstract metaphor for compute resources (time, energy, storage) that need to be spent to achieve a higher quality output. The rewarding procedure in the games is designed to place players in competition with previous players. This strategy uses the overall group to act as a check mechanism for the feedback that is provided by the players. While the participants/users play, the games collect statistics about their choices.

We use the Clopper-Pearson exact method [17] to statistically project the acceptable level of accuracy based on the statistics collected by the games. These projections provide a statistical basis for the developers to decide which degree of approximation will provide a satisfactory experience for the users. Our analysis is impartial to the benefits of approximation and independent of the approximation technique that is utilized.

To evaluate our solution, we study seven applications that produce user perceptible outputs and cover a wide range of domains including image processing, optical character recognition, speech recognition, and audio processing. Humans are naturally tolerant to approximation; hence, many approximation techniques target these domains of applications. We recruit 700 participants/users through Amazon's Mechanical Turk to play the games. The study shows that level of acceptable quality changes significantly across applications. For instance, to satisfy 90% of users, the level of acceptable quality loss is 2% for one application and 26% for another. Moreover, the study shows that generally users have higher tolerance to approximation when exposed to the tradeoff between cost and quality. The users' tolerance is even higher when they consider a context. Moreover, the pattern with which the crowd responds to approximation takes significantly different shape and form depending on the class of applications. These results suggest the necessity of solutions that systematically explore the effect of approximation on the end user experience.

By introducing the AXGAMES framework, this paper makes the following contributions:

1. **Crowdsourcing for approximate computing:** We develop a game-based crowdsourcing solution as an effective step towards enabling developers to systematically assess the effect of approximation from the user's perspective.
2. **Statistical inference:** We couple the crowdsourcing with statistical analysis to quantitatively translate raw data from the games to actionable results.
3. **Deployment:** Through deployment on Amazon's Mechanical Turk, we investigate the effectiveness of the proposed solution and show the necessity of the end user feedback by examining a diverse of real applications from different domains.

This study open a new axis, that of user experience, for the growing research in approximate computing. This work also sheds light on previously unexplored effects of approximation on the users. Moreover, it provides a development tool–rather unconventional–for the research community to better assess their innovative approximation techniques. Our tool is open source and is publicly available at http://act-lab.org/artifacts/axgames.

2. Overview

Figure 2 provides an illustration of AXGAMES's overall structure. AXGAMES is comprised of four major components: (1) approximated output database, (2) the three games namely POLLICE VERSO[1], WINABATT, and QNA; (3) the data collection engine; and (4) the crowd response analyzer. This section provides an overview of these components.

Approximated output database. The first step in using the AXGAMES solution is generating outputs of a given approximated application with varying degrees of quality loss. Note that AXGAMES is independent of the approximation technique and does not depend on how approximation is applied in the program. The developer provides a program which: (1) has an approximation knob to vary the degree of quality loss, and (2) can measure the quality loss for an approximated output[2]. For each input in the

[1]Wikipedia: "Pollice verso refers to the hand gesture or thumbs signal used by Ancient Roman crowds to pass judgment on a defeated gladiator."

[2]When developing an approximated program the developer needs to provide both the approximation knob and the quality measurement procedure [8, 10, 12, 13]. Therefore, in this regard, using AXGAMES does not require extra effort.

input dataset, the application is executed with different degrees of quality losses. A database records the approximated outputs, their degree of quality loss, and the setting of the approximation knob. We refer to this database as the approximated output database.

AXGAMES is designed to study a wide range of applications that generate outputs perceivable by humans through output devices such as a monitor or a speaker. Therefore, AXGAMES currently provides a large collection of images, audio, and text. This collection can be used by a wide variety of applications that span different domains to generate their own specific approximated output database. By playing the games, players collectively build a judgment regarding the acceptable quality for the collection of outputs. Additional information may be stored in the approximated output database. For instance, in the QNA game, players will need to answer one simple question for each approximated output. These questions are stored in the database as well. Section 3 discusses these questions and describes the three games in detail. Populating the approximated output database is performed offline to avoid unnecessary involvement of developers with the internals of gaming and crowdsourcing.

The three games. AXGAMES used the approximated output database as an input to its three different games. In all the games, a player is given an initial allowance of virtual money. The player's objective is to earn more money by guessing the statistical common ground among the previous players. In a sense, each player is playing with all of the past players and her guess affects the majority vote for the future players. As the crowd of gamers play the games, the players are *iteratively* converging to a statistical common ground. AXGAMES can then statistically infer the acceptable level of quality from the gamers' choices. Section 3 presents the details of the three games.

Statistics collection engine. As the users play, the games record the player choices and the game state in a database along with the player user IDs. AXGAMES uses this data to perform statistical projections about the percentage of users that deem a certain level of quality acceptable.

User response analyzer. After collecting the statistics from all the players, AXGAMES uses the Clopper-Pearson exact method [17] to calculate the binomial proportion confidence interval [18] for each level of quality loss. These intervals represent the percentage of users that deem a certain level of quality acceptable. Section 4 elaborates on the calculation and use of these intervals to recommend quality targets for the approximated applications.

3. The Three Games

AXGAMES includes three web-based games which aim to enable the crowd to iteratively converge to a statistical common ground. The players register with a unique user ID on the website to play the games without revealing personal information. Each user plays all three games independently and each game is played for 10 rounds. From the player's perspective, all three games revolve around betting, earning, spending, and losing virtual money. The score is the player's balance at the end of the game. We intentionally avoided exposing the direct relationship between virtual money and the computation cost to avoid biasing the gamers in choosing any level of quality. This relationship is a parameter in the games and can be exposed if desired. We also intended to make the games entertaining and enjoyable by using virtual money as the score and as a proxy for compute resources in two of the games. Our surveys show that 84% of the users were entertained when playing the games.

We devised the three games with different intuitions about inferring user-driven acceptable level of quality through crowdsourcing. The first game, POLLICE VERSO, is a betting game. In each round, the player is presented with an approximated output and its corresponding precise version. The player is asked to guess whether or not the majority of other players thought that the approximated output is *good enough*. The player bets money on her guess and wins money back if the guess is correct[3]. This game aims to find a statistical common ground about the acceptability of an approximated output. However, POLLICE VERSO does not have any notion of tradeoff between quality and cost. To include the notion of cost, we designed WINABATT which presents the player with a very low quality output and asks the player "How much would your spend to receive a better output?". The player can spend money to improve the output quality with a slider. The player wins money back depending on how close her choice of quality is to the previous players' selection. The objective of these two games is to find the statistical common ground while players judge the quality of the output in an abstract and context-insensitive manner. To provide some general context to the players, the third game QNA, presents the player with a very low quality output and asks the player a multiple choice question about that specific output. To answer the multiple-choice question, the player can improve the quality of the output by spending money with a slider. The player wins money back based on both the correctness of her answer and the closeness of her choice of quality to the previous players' selection. QNA gives incentive to the players to strike a balance between quality and cost while considering some context. The rest of this section describes these three games in further detail.

3.1 POLLICE VERSO

As Figure 3 illustrates, POLLICE VERSO is a betting game that gives each player an initial allowance of $500 virtual money. By keeping track of players' bets, the game aims to infer the statistical common ground for the acceptable level of quality for a given application. The game randomly selects an approximated output o, and displays o along with its precise counterpart o^*. Internally, we represent each approximated output o with the following tuple:

$$(o,q,s,n,n_{GoodEnough}) \qquad (1)$$

In Equation (1), q is the output quality; s is the setting of the approximation knob that led to this quality; n is the total number of past players that have played this particular output; and $n_{GoodEnough}$ is the number of players who thought the output is good enough. The last two parameters capture the history of the previous players' choices.

After displaying the outputs, a player is asked "How much do you want to *bet* that this approximation is **Good**

[3]POLLICE VERSO shares similarities with A/B testing [19]. However, A/B testing does not incorporate (1) games and betting (provided by all three games) (1) a sense of tradeoff (provided by WINABATT) and (2) a sense of context (provided by QNA) to the users. As the statistical results show, userss tolerance to approximation increases when the tradeoff and/or context is added to the games.

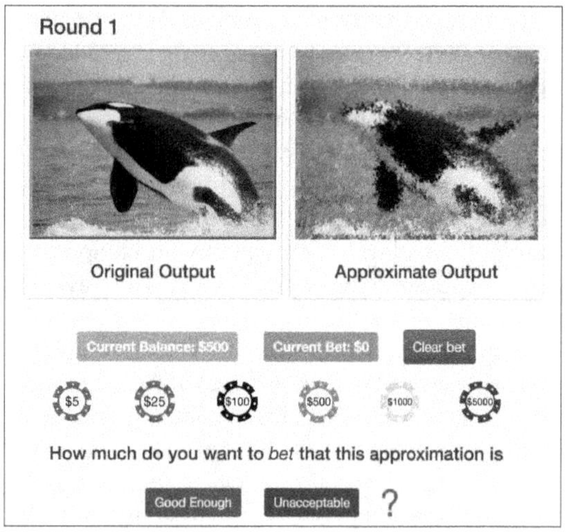

Figure 3: A round of the POLLICE VERSO game when deployed for an approximated implementation of the jpeg application.

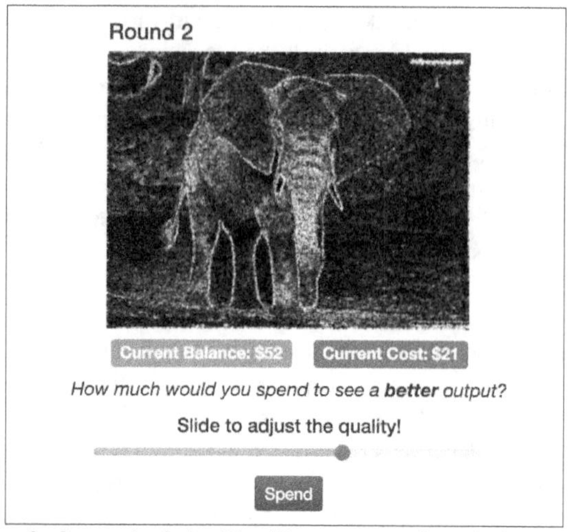

Figure 4: A round of the WINABATT game when deployed for an approximated implementation of the sobel application.

Enough/Unacceptable?" Using the gaming chips shown in Figure 3, the player chooses to bet b amount of money on her answer. The player's choice c, is a binary decision.

Rewarding procedure. The player may win money or lose the bet depending on whether the past players agree with her choice. This rewarding strategy incentivizes the players to gradually come to a statistical common ground without directly interacting with each other. As Equation (2) shows, the winnings w, is a function of the player's choice c, the amount of bet b, and the past player's choices, captured by n and $n_{GoodEnough}$. Note that the values of n and $n_{GoodEnough}$ are updated after the player receives her reward. Therefore, the player's choice affects the winnings of future players.

$$w(c,b,n,n_{GoodEnough}) = b \cdot (reward(c,n,n_{GoodEnough}) - 1) \quad (2)$$

where $reward(c,n,n_{GoodEnough}) =$

$$\begin{cases} 2 \cdot f(c,n,n_{GoodEnough}) & \text{if } 0 \leq f \leq 0.5 \\ -7.8 \cdot f(c,n,n_{GoodEnough}) + 8.9 & \text{if } 0.5 < f \leq 1 \end{cases} \quad (3)$$

As Equation (2) shows, the player wins money proportional to the amount of bet b. The $reward$ function (Equation (3) and Equation (4)) defines this proportion based on whether or not the majority of previous players agree with the player's choice c. In Equation (3), the constants $(2, -7.8, 8.9)$ are picked such that the player loses all her bet in the worst case or quadruples her bet in the best case. Moreover, if the output is controversial, the loss is low and the gain is high. An output is controversial if $n_{GoodEnough}/n \approx 0.5$. That is, almost half of the past players think the output is good enough and the other half thinks otherwise. In Equation (3), f captures the level of agreement between the player's choice with the majority vote of the previous players as presented in Equation (4).

$$f(c,n,n_{GoodEnough}) = agreement(c,n,n_{GoodEnough}) =$$

$$\begin{cases} n_{GoodEnough}/n & \text{if } c = \textit{Good Enough} \\ 1 - n_{GoodEnough}/n & \text{if } c = \textit{Unacceptable} \end{cases} \quad (4)$$

To enable players to make choices primarily based on their own perception, the reward function is hidden. Additionally, they play the game with no knowledge of the majority vote.

3.2 WINABATT

POLLICE VERSO enables users to perceptively judge the quality of an approximated output without regard to the tradeoff between quality and cost. To add this notion of tradeoff, we designed WINABATT as shown in Figure 4. The player starts with $100 of initial allowance and in each round, the game displays an approximated output at its lowest quality and asks the player: "How much would you spend to receive a **better** output?" The player is also given a slider with which she can adjust the output quality. The slider controls the quality and the cost associated with each quality level. Selecting a higher quality translates to spending more virtual money. Unlike POLLICE VERSO, the player's choices in WINABATT are no longer *yay/nay* binary decisions, and the player uses a continuous slider to choose a *level* of quality while considering its cost. If the game was naively designed, the player would always choose the lowest level of quality since it costs the least. However, in WINABATT, the player will be rewarded or penalized depending on how her choice of quality is close to the previous players. Hence, the player is also trying to guess the statistical common ground among the past players in a cost-conscious manner.

Rewarding procedure. To calculate the player's winnings and the statistical common ground, the game internally represents each output with the following tuple:

$$(\mathbb{O}, \mathbb{Q}_c, q_{MA}, n) \quad (5)$$

In Equation (5), $\mathbb{O}$ is the set of different approximated versions of an output; $\mathbb{Q}_c$ is the set of previous players' choice of quality, q_{MA} is the cumulative moving average of the past players' choice of quality; and n is the number of previous players that played the $\mathbb{O}$ set. The q_{MA} captures the statistical common ground among the past n players and is updated based on Equation (6) after the current player is rewarded.

$$q_{MA}^{(n+1)} = \frac{q_{MA}^{(n)} \cdot n + q_c}{n+1} \quad (6)$$

As shown in Equation (7), the player's winnings w, is a function of her choice of quality q_c and q_{MA}. As shown, the player's reward is deducted by her bet money b, which is the cost associated with her choice of quality q_c. This cost function

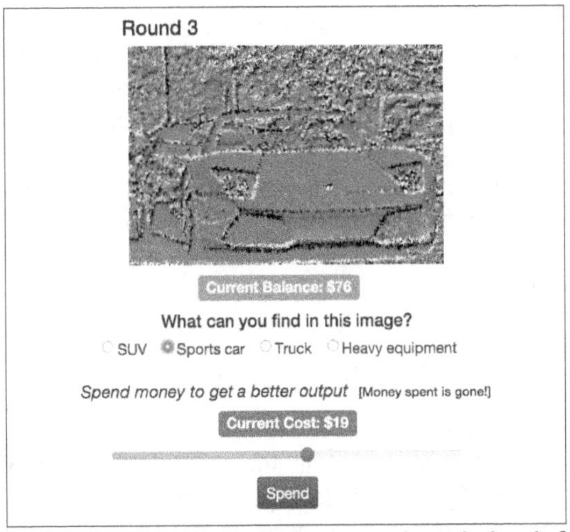

Figure 5: A round of the QnA game when deployed for an approximated implementation of the emboss application.

is linear to avoid bias towards any specific quality with \$5 for the lowest quality version (q_{min}) and \$30 for the highest quality version (q_{max}). The conditional part of Equation (7) is the reward that is determined by $f(q_c,q_{MA})$, which is presented in Equation (8) and captures how the player's choice of quality, q_c, is close to the choice of previous players' moving average, q_{MA}. The constants in Equation (7) is chosen such that the player's winnings, w, is between $-$\$35 and $+$\$35.

$$w(q_c,q_{MA})=-b+\begin{cases}5\cdot f(q_c,q_{MA})-10 & \text{if } f\leq 10\\ 40=5\cdot 10-10 & \text{if } f>10\end{cases} \quad (7)$$

$$f(q_c,q_{MA})=agreement(q_c,q_{MA})=\left(\frac{|q_c-q_{MA}|}{q_{max}-q_{min}}\right)^{-1} \quad (8)$$

This rewarding procedure incentivizes the players to balance the cost and quality *while* guessing the past player's consensus.

3.3 QnA

While WinABatt provides an opportunity to the players to explore the tradeoff between quality and cost, they do so in an abstract and context-insensitive manner. To provide some context to the players, we design the QnA game. As Figure 5 illustrates, in each round, QnA displays an approximated output initially set to its lowest quality level, along with a slider, and a multiple-choice question about the output. The questions are in the form of "What can you find in this image? Sports car / SUV / Truck / Heavy equipment." The player needs to answer the question and can spend money to improve the quality using the slider. Similar to WinABatt, the initial allowance provided is \$100. In contrast to WinABatt, the slider cannot move backwards. This feature is to prevent the players from cheating, increasing the quality to answer the question, and then decrease the quality to minimize the cost. In other words, once the player improves the quality, she cannot recover the cost of seeing the higher quality output.

Rewarding procedure. The winnings are calculated based on the rewarding procedure explained for WinABatt with the exception that the player also pays a \$20 penalty for answering the question incorrectly. There is no extra reward for correct answers. The player wins money back depending on the correctness of her answer and the closeness of her choice of quality to the moving average of the previous players. QnA incentives the players to find a statistical common ground while balancing quality and cost with respect to some context about the output.

4. Statistical Analysis

As mentioned before, the games internally collect the player's choices and decisions for a series of outputs at different levels of quality. To enable the application developer to draw meaningful conclusions from this raw data, we devise a statistical framework that projects the user-driven quality target. Due to the large space of possible inputs and the diversity of users, it is practically infeasible to find a quality target that satisfies the entire population of the users for any arbitrary input. However, coupling the games with statistical analysis provides a pragmatic approach to determine the quality target that, with high confidence, satisfies the large majority of users.

4.1 Binomial Proportion Confidence Interval

We calculate the binomial proportion confidence interval [18] for each level of quality loss. Given the decisions of a *sample population* (players of the games), the binomial proportion confidence interval projects what percentage of the *statistical population* (all the users) are likely to deem a certain level of quality good enough (acceptable). After the players play the games, AxGames calculate this confidence interval for a range of quality losses which resulted from approximating the application-under-study. Based on the confidence interval, we can determine the level of quality loss that is highly likely to satisfy, for example, 90% of the statistical population[4] of the users.

AxGames leverages a commonly used method, the Clopper-Pearson exact method [17] to compute the binomial proportion confidence interval. We chose the Clopper-Pearson method as it has certain advantages over the other available options [20, 21] such as, (1) higher accuracy as the number of samples becomes relatively large, and (2) it can calculate the confidence interval even when the opinion of the sample population is very skewed towards a decision. These features are important in our setup since the games provide a relatively large number of statistical samples, and the large majority of the players are highly likely to think that 1% quality loss is almost always acceptable and similarly a 50% quality loss is almost never good enough. Moreover, the Clopper-Pearson exact method calculates a conservative confidence interval that reduces the risk of being too aggressive when it comes to approximation. The binomial confidence interval is calculated based on a set of binary decisions from the sampled population. For example, in the case of the Pollice verso game, a binary decision comes directly from the player's choice on whether or not an approximated output with the quality of q is good enough. Later in this section we describe how the WinABatt's and QnA's sliders are translated to binary decisions.

[4]Statistical population is the entire pool from which a sample population is drawn. Here, the sample population are the gamers who are drawn from the entire pool of the application users. Thus, statistical population is the entire users.

To calculate the confidence interval, we first need to calculate the sampled binomial proportion for each level of quality. The sampled binomial proportion is calculated for each approximated output by computing the fraction of votes that deem a level of quality good enough to the total number of votes. This sampled binomial proportion is calculated based on the $(n_{Votes}, n_{GoodEnough})^{(q)}$ pair, where n_{Votes} is the total number of decisions on outputs with the quality of q, and $n_{GoodEnough}$ is the number of decisions that deem these outputs good enough. This pair is calculated for each level of quality.

As Equation (9) shows, the Clopper-Pearson exact method computes the one-sided confidence interval of success rate, $\theta^{(q)}$, when the number of sample trials, n_{Votes}, and the number of successes among the trials, $n_{GoodEnough}$, are measured for a sample of the population.

$$\frac{1}{1+\frac{n_{Votes}-n_{GoodEnough}+1}{n_{GoodEnough}\cdot\mathbf{F}[1-\alpha;2\cdot n_{GoodEnough},2\cdot(n_{Votes}-n_{GoodEnough}+1)]}} < \theta^{(q)} \tag{9}$$

In Equation (9), $\mathbf{F}$ is the F-critical value that is calculated based on the F-distribution [22]. The *discontinuous* nature of the binomial distribution precludes any interval with exact coverage for all values of n_{Votes} and $n_{GoodEnough}$ (all possible values of the binomial proportions). However, because of the relationship between the cumulative binomial distribution and the *continuous* F-distribution, we use the common alternative form of the binomial confidence interval that provides exact coverage for all population proportions. $\mathbf{F}[1-\alpha; d_1, d_2]$ is the $(1-\alpha)$ quintile of the F-distribution with d_1 and d_2 degrees of freedom. The $(1-\alpha)\cdot 100\%$ is degree of confidence on the interval. For instance, for 95% confidence interval, α is 0.05 and for 90% confidence interval, α is 0.10. The two degrees of freedom, d_1 and d_2, decide the shape of the F-distribution based on the collected statistics, n_{Votes} and $n_{GoodEnough}$ in our case.

To understand the meaning of $\theta^{(q)}$, we discuss an example deployment of the game that resulted in n_{Votes}=60 and $n_{GoodEnough}$=56 for quality level q=97%. From Equation (9), the lower limit of the 95% confidence interval, $\theta^{(97\%)}$, is 85.4%. That is, with 95% confidence, we can project that at least 85.4% of the users will deem 97% quality level acceptable. This projection is conservative because the Clopper-Pearson exact method calculates a conservative lower bound for the confidence interval. The degree of confidence is the probability of the projection being true. The projection based on 95% confidence interval is true with probability of 0.95.

For each level of quality, AXGAMES projects the fraction of user population (statistical population) that deems that level of quality acceptable. Using this information, the developer can choose the level of quality that satisfies a target majority of users.

Translating a choice of quality to a set of binary decisions. Players in POLLICE VERSO make binary decision on the quality of an approximated output. These yay/nay decisions can be directly used in the Clopper-Pearson statistical analysis. In contrast, the players in WINABATT and QNA, choose a level of quality using a slider. To be able to use the Clopper-Pearson statistical analysis, each chosen level of quality needs to be translated to a series of binary decisions. Intuitively, when a player chooses the quality level of q_c to be good enough, she implies that any level of quality higher than q_c is also good enough. Because of the rewarding procedure, the player has the incentive to choose the lowest acceptable quality. Choosing higher quality translates to a higher cost. The choice of player also implies that lower quality outputs are not good enough, otherwise, she would have chosen a lower quality to pay a lower cost. Based on this intuition, we convert one chosen level of quality, q_c, which is in the range of (q_{min}, q_{max}) to $q_{max} - q_{low} + 1$ binary decisions (Equation (10)).

$$decision(q) = \begin{cases} \text{"}GoodEnough\text{"} & \text{if } q \geq q_c \\ \text{"}Unacceptable\text{"} & \text{if } q < q_c \end{cases} \quad \forall q \in (q_{min}, q_{max}) \tag{10}$$

By using this conversion, the same method of statistical projection can be applied to all three games. Moreover, WINABATT and QNA provide larger number of decisions per round. We did not use this conversion in POLLICE VERSO to enlarge the number of decisions since the players do not have an opportunity to see a range of quality losses for each output. Whereas, WINABATT and QNA allows the players to see the same output at different quality levels using the slider.

5. Evaluation

To evaluate the effectiveness of the AXGAMES crowdsourcing framework, we deploy the three games on the web for seven different applications. We use Amazon's Mechanical Turk to recruit a large number of users to play the games. Using the collected data through the games and our statistical analysis, we measure what level of quality is acceptable for the majority of users. We also study how the acceptable level of quality varies across different applications and how the statistical analysis effectively captures these trends.

5.1 Methodology

Applications. As Table 1 shows, we examine AXGAMES using a wide range of applications from diverse domains that include image processing, audio processing, optical character recognition, and speech to text conversion. AXGAMES is not limited to these applications and can be used with other applications that produce outputs perceptible by humans. As shown in Table 1, our set of programs includes four image processing applications. The emboss application is an image filter that replaces each pixel either by a highlight or a shadow. Applying this filter to an image usually results in an image resembling a paper or metal embossing of the original image. The jpeg application implements the JPEG image compression algorithm. The sobel application is an edge detection algorithm which employs the Sobel operator. The mean is a sliding-window spatial filter that replaces the center pixel with the average (mean) of the pixel values in the window and blurs the image. Additionally, we also evaluate audio-enc, an audio compression engine that compresses WAV files and transforms them into MP3 files [23] . The quality metric for the image processing and audio compression applications is the normalized root mean square error (NRMSE) which is calculated by comparing an approximated output with its precise counter part.

We also use two applications that recognize text and speech. The ocr application is an optical character recognition program that converts raster images of written text to characters. The speech2txt application is a speech recognition engine that con-

Table 1: Applications and their quality metric.

	Description	Domain	Quality Metric
emboss	Embossing filter	Image Processing	Normalized Root Mean Square Error (NRMSE)
jpeg	Lossy compression		
mean	Blurring filter		
sobel	Edge detection		
audio-enc	Audiio encoder	Audio Processing	
ocr	Optial character recognition	Pattern Recognition	Text Similarity Ratio
speech2txt	Speech to text		

verts speech audio files to text [24]. The quality metric for these two applications that produce text output is the text similarity ratio that is computed by comparing the original application output with the approximated application output. We use an open-source implementation of the Gestalt Pattern Matching algorithm [25] to measure the text similarity ratio. This algorithm assigns higher scores to the outputs that *look right* to a human reader. The set of applications have often been used to evaluate the benefits of approximation techniques in the approximate computing literature [5, 6, 8, 13, 26, 27].

Approximation techniques. For the image processing applications, we use a variation of loop perforation [12] as the approximation technique. This technique skips computing some of the pixels and instead, copies the values from neighboring pixels. The rate at which the computation is skipped is the knob for controlling the quality. We refer to this technique as tiling. We chose tiling for image processing applications since it is a simple yet effective coarse-grained approximation technique. For the audio compression and pattern recognition applications, we use the same model used in previous fine-grained approximation works [7, 10, 11, 13, 28] that adds stochastic noise to the computation by leveraging voltage overscaling, bit-width reduction, and reducing the DRAM refresh rate. The rate and the magnitude of noise are the knobs for controlling approximation. We refer to this technique as fine-grained approximation. We use tiling and fine-grained approximation to examine AxGames, since they represent the two main categories of approximation techniques, coarse-grained and fine-grained, respectively. AxGames is general and is not limited to these techniques. This flexibility is inherent in the framework since it only needs a set of approximated outputs with varying degrees of quality loss. Naturally, if the approximation technique changes, the games need to be redeployed in order to understand the user response to the new technique.

Datasets. As part of the AxGames framework, we include the input dataset that contains 200 images, 200 audio files, 200 speech files, and 200 printed text files. We collect this dataset from open-source databases or public data archives such as ImageNet [29], Freesound [30], VoxForge [31], and New York Times TimeMachine [32]. The applications can use this collection to generate the approximated output database which is used in the three games. AxGames also assigns one multiple-choice question to each data element. These questions are used during the QnA game to provide some context to the gamers when they trade quality for cost. The questions are part of the framework and do not need to be regenerated for other applications that produce similar outputs. Additionally, the approximated output database is generated offline by running the application-under-study with different settings of the approximation knob. The AxGames's requirement is to generate each output with varying degrees of quality loss. For our experiments, we generate 51 versions of each output, with quality loss ranging from 0% to 50%, and a step size of 1%.

Game deployment. We separately deploy the three games on the web for each of the seven applications. In each round, each game randomly selects an output from the approximated output database. In the Pollice verso game, the players bet and vote on whether the quality of the approximated output is good enough. Thus, the game randomly picks a quality loss for the displayed output. The following ten quality losses are used for the selected approximated output: 1%, 3%, 5%, 7%, 10%, 15%, 20%, 30%, 40%, and 50%. The other two games use all 51 quality levels which are generated for each approximated output and allow the player to pick any of them. We have made AxGames open source in our artifact portal (http://act-lab.org/artifacts/axgames). The deployed games, which are used for evaluations, are also available through the same portal.

Crowdsourcing through Amazon's Mechanical Turk. To collect a reasonable amount of statistics from a diverse set of users, we leverage a crowdsourcing Internet marketplace, Amazon's Mechanical Turk [33]. The games for each application is played by 100 individual Mechanical Turk workers (turkers)[5]. For the seven applications, 700 turkers contributed to our study. Each turker plays the games once. We do not allow a worker to play the games more than once to avoid bias in statistics from a few heavy gamers. Each game has 10 rounds, our 100 turkers make a total of 1,000 binary decisions in Pollice verso for each individual application. Therefore, each of the 10 discrete levels of quality in Pollice verso receives 100 votes for each application. As discussed in Section 4, in each round of WinABatt and QnA, a player's choice of quality on the slider is translated to 51 binary decisions, which correspond to one of the 51 quality levels of an approximated output. Hence, for each of these two games the turkers make a total of 51,000 (= 100 players $\times$ 10 rounds $\times$ 51 binary decisions per round) binary decisions for each individual application . Thus, each of the 51 levels of quality receive 1000 votes in WinABatt and QnA for each application. This amount of information provides the grounds for making high confidence statistical projections on the acceptable level of quality for each application. We also conduct an optional survey at the end of the games to understand whether or not the games were entertaining. The survey results show that 84% of players were entertained.

Game initialization. The results are reported when the games are deployed with random initial votes for 10 imaginary gamers on each output. These random initial votes are not used in the statistical analysis. To understand the effect of initialization, in a separate experiment, we also asked 10 graduate students to play the games without regard to the rewards. We then extrapolated their choices across all the outputs with the same quality. We observed that both initialization strategies yield similar trends and therefore, we report the results with random initial values. This similarity is the result of recruiting large number of turkers

[5]We received Institutional Review Board (IRB) approval before deploying AxGames. The request was approved in three weeks.

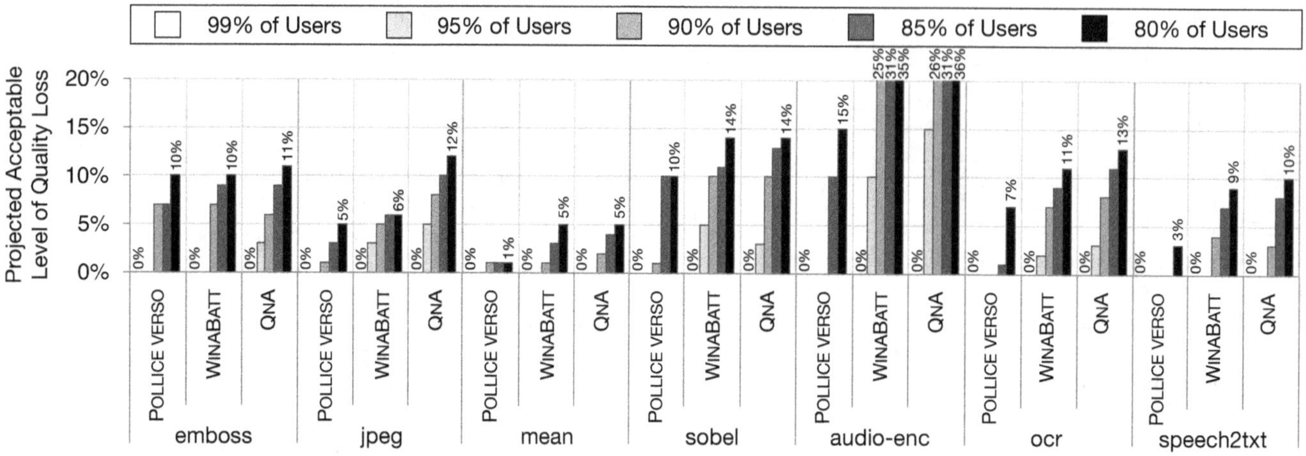

Figure 6: Projected acceptable level of quality loss with 95% confidence. These levels of quality are projected by our statistical analysis based on the game plays of 100 Mechanical Turk workers. Starting from left, each bar corresponds to the level that is projected to satisfy 99%, 95%, 90%, 80%, and 80% of the applications' users. These projections vary significantly across the applications.

and the fact that the human turkers ultimately make decisions based on their own perception of the approximated outputs.

5.2 Statistical Projections

Figure 6 shows the projected acceptable level of quality for each approximated application. The confidence level of these projections is 95%. As shown, each pair of (application, game) yields a set of projections. Starting from left, each bar corresponds to the level that satisfies 99%, 95%, 90%, 85%, and 80% of statistical population of the application users. The details of these projections are provided in Figure 7 and are discussed later in the section. As shown in Figure 6, for all the pairs of (application, game), the projected level of quality loss that satisfies more than 99% of the users is 0%. That is, for developers who aim to satisfy 99% of their users, the specific approximation techniques that are used in our evaluations (tiling and fine-grained approximation) are not a viable option. However, when the target is to satisfy a large majority of the users, starting from 90% of the users, there are opportunities to utilize these approximation techniques across all the image processing applications. Based on the statistics from POLLICE VERSO, if a developer chooses to satisfy 90% of the users, emboss can utilize tiling with 7% quality loss while jpeg, mean, and sobel can utilize tiling with 1% quality loss. Based on POLLICE VERSO, audio-enc and ocr can be only approximated if target is to satisfy 85% or less percentage of the users. For speech2txt, only if the target is to satisfy 80% or less percentage of the users, approximation can be enabled given the statistics from POLLICE VERSO.

As Figure 6 depicts, based on the statistics from QNA, all the applications can be approximated if the target is to satisfy 90% of the users. For this target, the acceptable level of quality loss is 6% for emboss, 8% for jpeg, 2% for mean, 10% for sobel, 26% for audio-enc, 8% for ocr, and 3% for speech2txt. As these results show, there is a clear difference between the three games when they assess the user satisfaction even for one application. This difference emanates from the fact that WINABATT and QNA provide an opportunity for the users to consider tradeoff and context, while POLLICE VERSO does not. We will discuss these differences in more detail later in this section.

User response varies significantly across applications. Another observation from these results is that the user-driven level of acceptable quality varies significantly across applications. Consider the four image processing applications that use the same approximation technique, tiling. Users show relatively higher tolerance to the tiling approximation for two of the applications, emboss and sobel. However, for other applications, especially for mean, the users show significantly lower tolerance. This significant variation in user response to the same approximation technique across different applications shows the necessity of solutions that statistically evaluate the acceptable level of quality. AXGAMES is one such solution, that effectively enables the users to provide statistical feedback to the developers who intend to leverage approximation techniques. With QNA, 90% of the users only accept 2% quality loss for mean while they tolerate 26% for audio-enc. These results shed light on the significant variation of users response to quality loss from approximation for different applications. To this end, AXGAMES provides the grounds for researchers to statistically evaluate their innovations from the users' perspective.

Users show higher tolerance to approximation when they consider cost or context. From the results in Figure 6, it is evident that users show higher level of tolerance to the approximation when playing WINABATT and QNA. Whereas the level of tolerance to approximation is lower in POLLICE VERSO. Intuitively, in these two games the players choose a level of acceptable quality in a cost-conscious manner while also considering the context in the case of QNA. In the case of POLLICE VERSO, the players vote only based on their personal impression of the approximated output without a chance to explore the cost-quality tradeoff. On the other hand, the other two games, WINABATT and QNA, introduce a notion of tradeoff between cost and benefits of approximation. Moreover, the players' choice of quality in QNA is driven by their ability to answer the associated multiple choice question with the output. This analysis shows that these three games collectively provide a deeper understanding of the user' reaction to the approximation technique. The developer may choose to use the results from any of these games on her

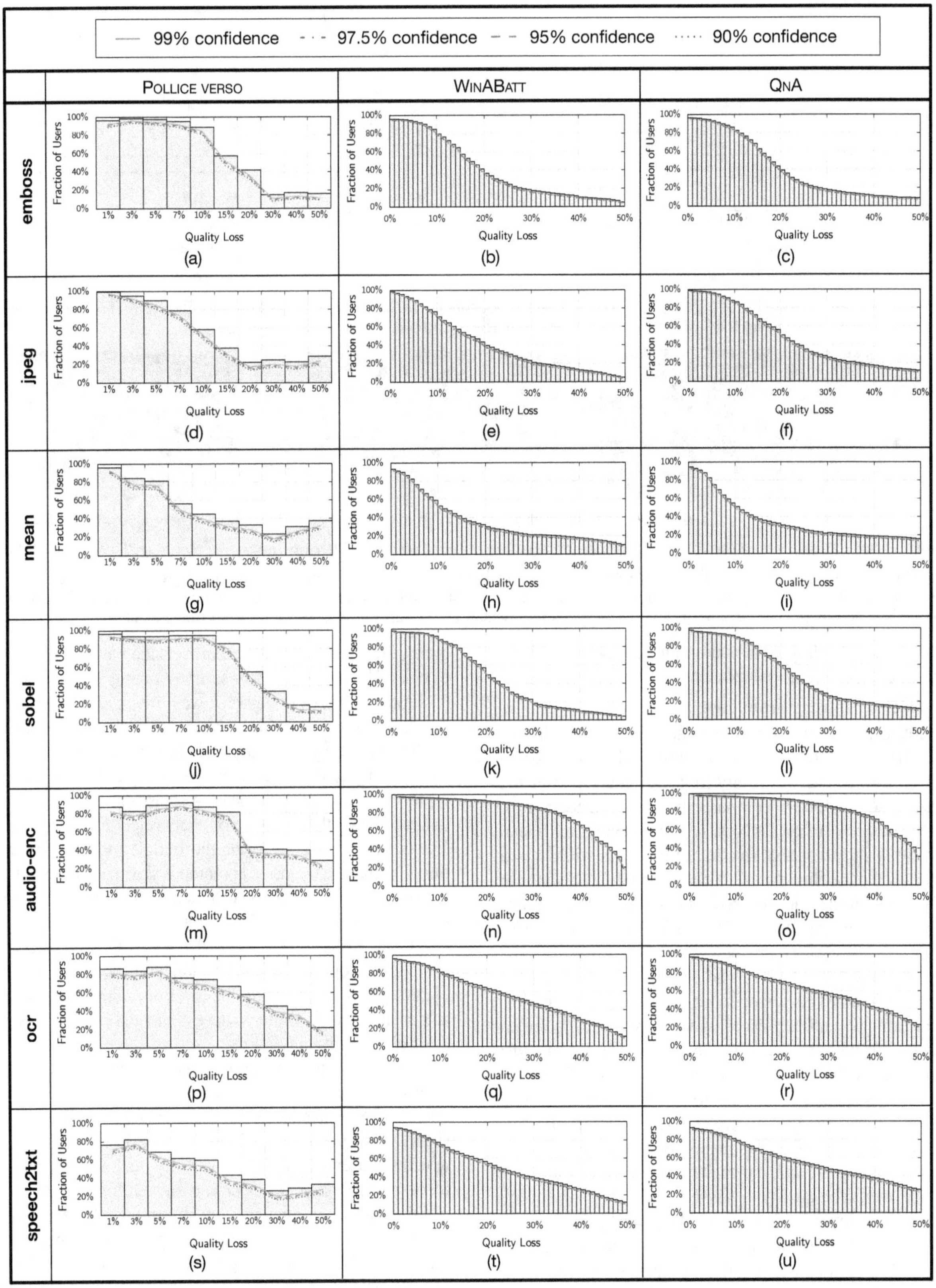

Figure 7: The collected statistics and the statistical projections. The bars show the fraction of players that selected a certain level of quality loss as "Good Enough." The lines represent the lower bound of the binomial confidence interval with different degrees of confidence, including 99%, 97.5%, 95%, and 90%.

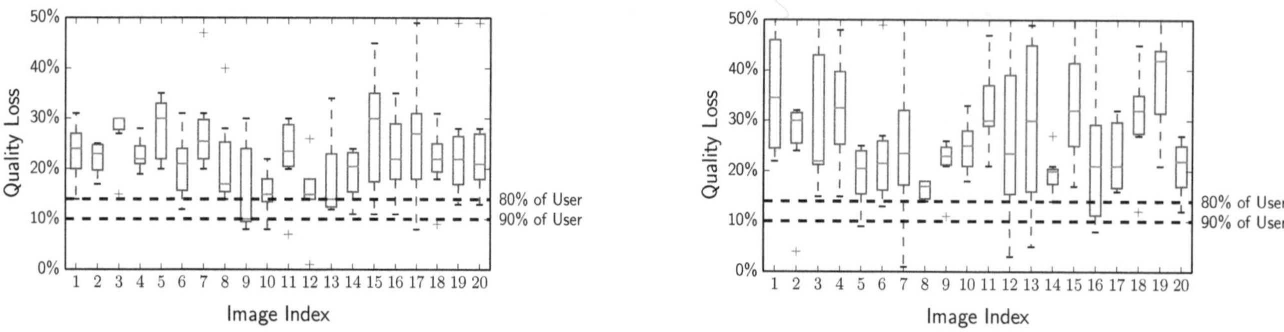

(a) Distribution of the quality choices in WINABATT

(b) Distribution of the quality choices in QNA

Figure 8: The box plot distribution of the players' choices of quality for sobel. The dashed horizontal lines show the projected acceptable level of quality loss that satisfies 80% and 90% of the users with 95% confidence (a) based on WINABATT and (b) QNA.

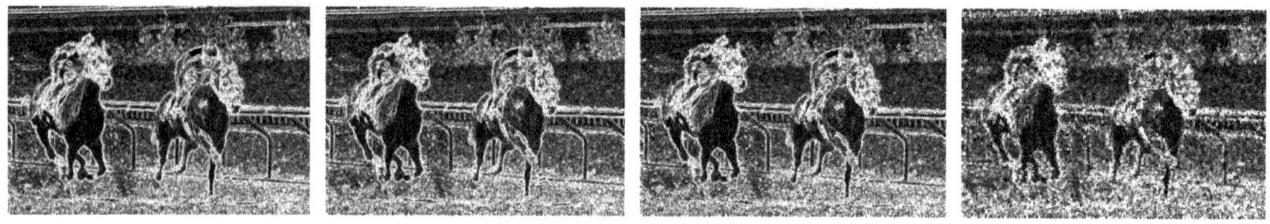

(a) Precise output (b) Output with 10% quality loss. (c) Output with 14% quality loss. (d) Output with 30% quality loss.

Question: *What can you see in the image?* **Correct answer**: *Horse racing* **Wrong answers**: *Bowling, Bridge, Buffalo wings*

Figure 9: Outputs from the edge detection filter, sobel, for image 13 in Figure 8(b). The leftmost output is the precise version and the rest are the approximated outputs. The approximated outputs (b) and (c) have 10% and 14% of quality loss that satisfy 90% and 80% of the users, respectively. The output (d) has 30% of quality loss, which is the median of the votes for the image 13 from the QNA plays.

own discretion depending on her constraints on user experience and her target deployment environment.

5.3 Collected Statistics from the Games

The collected statistics from the games are presented in Figure 7. The bars represent the fraction of players who chose "Good Enough" for each level of quality loss. Our analysis uses the Clopper-Pearson method to computes the one-sided confidence interval for each level of quality loss. This one-sided lower-bound conservatively projects what fraction of the users will deem a particular level of quality loss as "Good Enough." The lines in Figure 7 represent the statistical projections with different levels of confidence, including 99%, 97.5%, 95%, and 90%. As shown, the projection lines fall below the collected statistics from the sampled population (the turkers who played the games). That is because the Clopper-Pearson confidence interval, by definition, covers the sampled statistics in a conservative manner. A point on a projection line with the (x,y) coordinates predicts that *at least* $y\%$ of the users will deem $x\%$ quality loss as "Good Enough." For instance, suppose that we want to use the statistical results from WINABATT to find an acceptable level of quality for emboss. Let's target to find the quality loss level that provides satisfactory experience at least for 90% of the users with 95% confidence level. The quality loss is 7%, which is the x coordinate of the intersection point between the y=90% line and the red dashed projection line in Figure 7(b). The results in Figure 6 are obtained in this manner and also summarizes the statistical data given in Figure 7. As depicted, the results for POLLICE VERSO do not decrease monotonically whereas the results for WINABATT and QNA do. That is because only for these two game, the statistical analysis converts the players' selected level to binary decisions for all the levels of quality loss (see Section 4).

From the results in Figure 7, we observe different patterns for the different classes of applications. For the image processing applications, the graphs have three regions, the top region where the majority of users agree on the low quality loss; the middle region where there is no clear consensus among the users; and the tail where the majority of users reject low quality outputs The quality level from which the middle region starts captures the point that the majority's opinion is shifting. This point of shift in opinion can be found by calculating changes in the derivative of the projection lines. This point of shift may be used by the developers to choose the acceptable level of quality. AXGAMES provides the opportunity to find this point of shift for the developers. Instead of choosing the level of quality loss that certain percentage of users prefer, a developer can optimistically choose this point of shift in opinion.

The audio-enc application, which generates auditory output, shows a different pattern. The gamers show a significantly higher tolerance to the quality loss in the audio outputs. The majority of users tolerate the quality loss up to a significantly high level, after which the user satisfaction drastically declines. For the pattern recognition applications, ocr and speech2txt, the graphs show that the fraction of satisfied users almost linearly decreases as the quality loss increases. These two applications generate textual output. Unlike the other applications, there is not a clear point of shift in the crowd's opinion about the quality loss. These difference are significant and depend on the inherent characteristics of application, its output format, and the applied approximation techniques. Our experimental results show that the AXGAMES

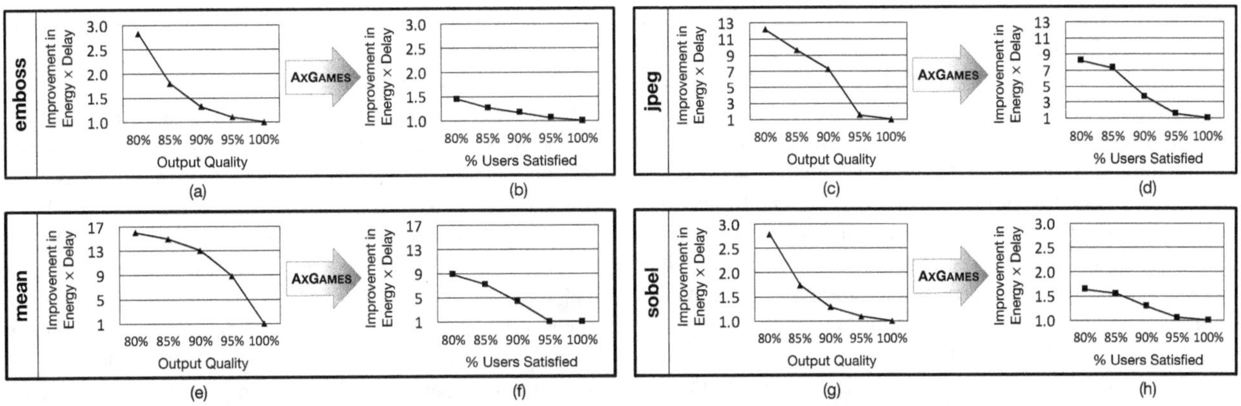

Figure 10: Improvement in energy-delay products vs. output quality (a, c, e, and g), and vs. % users satisfied. (b, d, f, and h). The results in (b), (d), (f), and (h) are based on the statistics collected from the QnA plays.

framework can effectively capture such patterns that need to be taken into account when approximation is employed.

5.4 User Response Variations

We investigate the user response variation across the same approximated images in Figure 8. Figure 8 shows the distribution of the responses from the players for a randomly selected subset of the output images from sobel. The trends are similar for the other applications. This distribution is shown as a box plot. The bottom and top of each box represent the lower and upper quartiles, respectively, and the band near the middle of the box is the 50th percentile (the median). The bottom whisker represents the lowest datum that is still within 1.5 inter quartile range (IQR) of the lower quartile. The top whisker denotes the highest datum that is still within 1.5 IQR of the upper quartile. The dashed horizontal lines show the projected acceptable levels of quality loss that satisfy 80% and 90% of the users with 95% confidence. It is even visually evident that these levels of quality cover their corresponding majority of users.

As expected, there is a large variation in the players choices. That is each player is providing her own personal judgment on the quality of the output, which is one of the main objectives of the games. Interestingly, the variation is higher in the QnA game. We investigate this higher variation in Figure 9 by showing the output image with the highest variation in Figure 8(b), image 13. The associated question with this image is "What can you see in the image: Horse racing/Bowling/Bridge/Buffalo wings?". This question can be answered even with high quality loss (30%) as shown Figure 9. However, it is understandable if a player chooses a lower quality loss to answer the question. Qualitatively, the context provided by the question allows a fraction of the users to choose levels of quality loss that are relatively higher. We speculate that approximation can be applied more aggressively if the output of this image processing is fed to a machine learning algorithm that performs scene detection or object recognition.

5.5 Changing the Tradeoff for Approximate Computing

The AxGames framework enables programmers to *change* the tradeoff between quality and performance-energy gains into the tradeoff between the users' satisfaction and the gains. We demonstrate this ability by measuring the speedup and energy savings for the image processing applications. A full investigating of the benefits of approximation is out of the scope of this work. This study is not to advocate approximation or show how much gains are possible; rather, it is to investigate the users' perspective on the output quality loss. For the performance and energy modeling, we use the same setup as the one used in [9]. We use the MARSSx86 x86-64 cycle-accurate simulator [34] and McPAT [35] for timing and energy modeling, respectively. The processor is modeled after a single-core Intel Nehalem (3.4 GHz with 0.9 V at 45 nm). The use statistics are based on QnA.

Figure 10 shows the improvement in energy-delay product when the output quality and the fraction of satisfied users change from 80% to 100%. The baseline is the application running on the processor without any approximation. Figure 10(a, c, e, and g) represent the tradeoff between quality and the gains from approximation while Figure 10(b, d, f, and h) represent the tradeoff between the user satisfaction and the gains. All applications see a disparity in the energy-delay product improvement for the same level of quality loss and fraction of satisfied users. For instance, in Figure 10(e), mean sees 8.9× energy-delay product improvement with 95% quality. Even though this level of quality seems high, it only satisfies about 80% of users. For mean, as shown in Figure 10(f), to satisfy 95% of users, only 1.3× energy-delay product improvement can be achieved, which is significantly lower than the gains that can be achieved with the 95% quality. Although the results in Figure 10 are specific to the pair of (application, approximation technique), they show a clear change in the tradeoffs when user response is considered.

While many approximate techniques provide significant benefits, their utility cannot be established without understanding the users' perspective. Our framework and our analysis are impartial to approximation techniques and are intended to shed light on how application users react to approximation. The games and the statistical analysis provide an effective mean for developers to understand the user experience before employing approximation. In fact, the developers can explore the tradeoffs and the benefits in a new light that considers users' perspective.

5.6 Discussion

Currently, AxGames is implemented for applications that directly produce human-perceivable outputs, such as image processing, audio processing, and pattern recognition applications. These programs represent a large body of applications that are designed for humans as the end users. These applications can benefit from approximation due to the inherent tolerance of humans to inexact results. In fact, many of the approximate computation research includes such applications [5, 6, 8–10, 12, 13, 27, 28]. Furthermore, these classes of applications, such as Instagram, Microsoft HoloLens, Qualcomm Vuforia, are gaining prominence as the computing services, more and more, aim to provide natural and targeted experiences for the end users. This trend has been amplified by prevalence of mobile devices and will grow in importance as wearable electronics is gaining traction and smart and interactive home/office environments are emerging. Moreover, even complex machine learning algorithms are being deployed in interactive data visualization [36] and analytics tools [37] that allow humans to interact with complex and large amounts of data. Besides the direct use of AxGames in these domains, the results of AxGames can be used as an upper bound for inaccuracy in cases where the approximate output is fed to a machine learning engine. Humans are the ultimate recognition engines.

As an end-to-end attempt toward crowdsourcing the target quality determination, our approach takes an initial and effective step toward enabling the end users to become a helping force in the development and deployment of approximation techniques.

6. Related Work

There has been a substantial amount of effort to leverage crowdsourcing tools and games to solve computationally difficult problems. However, there is a lack of solutions that leverage crowdsourcing or game design for approximate computing which statistically determine the level of quality considered acceptable by the majority of application users. This paper provides one such solution and lies at the intersection of (a) approximate computing, (b) crowdsourcing, and (c) game with a purpose.

Approximate computing. A growing body of recent work explores a variety of approximation techniques. These techniques include (a) approximate storage designs [38, 39] which trade data quality for reduced energy [38] and larger capacity [39], (b) voltage over-scaling [7, 13, 28, 40–43], (c) computation and data sampling [12, 14, 44, 45], (d) loop early termination [46], (e) computation substitution [5, 46–48], (f) memoization [6, 49, 50], (g) limited fault recovery [44, 51–56], (h) precision scaling [10, 57], (i) approximate circuit synthesis [27, 58–63], and (j) neural acceleration [8, 9, 26]. Many of these solutions include applications which produce perceptible outputs for users. Although these techniques report promising benefits from approximate computing, they do not explore the acceptability of the quality loss from the users' perspective.

Crowdsourcing. The reCAPTCHA [64] project is a successful crowdsourcing application in production. This system uses the CAPTCHA, human Turing test, to classify text images from scanned books when other techniques fail. Automan [65] is an automatic crowd programming system which enables the integration of human computation in conventional programming languages and rigorously studies scheduling, budgeting, and statistical quality control in programming with human computational resources. TurKit [66] provides a programming model to integrate human computation in JavaScript using templates which provide close integration with Mechanical Turk. TurKit also supports checkpointing and recovery. Russell et al. [67] developed a web-based tool that leverages crowdsourcing to identify objects and locations in images and annotate them. These research efforts are not concerned with quality loss in approximate computing.

Games with a purpose. Games with a purpose provide an opportunity to engage the crowd in entertaining applications while providing insight to researchers. Several prior works have successfully utilized game-based crowdsourcing to label random images and locate objects [68–70]. Furthermore, Dietl et al. [71] proposed to transform verification tasks into a puzzle games which can be solved by humans. The solution of the puzzle is then translated back and used for proving correctness and verification. Foldit [72] is an online multiplayer game whose players interact with protein structures while they compete and collaborate to optimize the computed energy. They discovered that players of their game are able to search the state space of proteins configurations faster than computational algorithms. We are inspired by these efforts and exclusively developed a solution that uses games with a purpose and crowdsourcing to statistically determine the users' acceptable level of quality for approximate computing.

7. Conclusion

Approximate computing is an emerging area that breaks the long-held fundamental abstraction of near-perfect accuracy in PL [10, 11, 13, 73–75], OS [76], and Architecture [5–9, 26, 38]. While these techniques provide promising gains, they cause quality loss whose effects on the users are not well understood; leaving approximation in a position of questionable utility. Many of these inspiring studies argue that a certain quality loss may be acceptable without systematically considering the users' perspective. It is timely to systematically explore and study users' perspective on the effects of approximation. This paper takes an effective initial step in this direction. This work provided an automated programming tool–rather unconventional–to methodically utilize crowdsourcing in identifying the desirable application output quality from the final users. This readily available tool provides a path for the research community to better assess their innovative approximation techniques. The framework enables developers to conveniently study user responses at scale and gain statistical confidence when deploying approximated applications. Our results from examining a variety of applications show the necessity of solutions such as AxGames since the crowd's response to approximation varies drastically across different applications. Moreover, when the users consider tradeoff and context, they tend of to be more tolerant to approximation. These results suggests that AxGames can add an unexplored, yet important, dimension to the research and development in approximate computing.

8. Acknowledgments

We thank the anonymous reviewers for their insightful comments. We thank Richard Lipton and Faramarz Fekri for discussions that helped refine this work. We also thank Zhijian Li, Nick Liu, Elizabeth Perakis, Akshay Sawant, and Wen Xin for assistance in developing the games. We thank Amir Yazdanbakhsh for his contributions to energy-performance measurements. This work was in part supported by Qualcomm Innovation Fellowship, NSF award CCF#1553192, Semiconductor Research Corporation contract #2014-EP-2577, and a gift from Google.

References

[1] Hadi Esmaeilzadeh, Emily Blem, Renee St. Amant, Karthikeyan Sankaralingam, and Doug Burger. Dark silicon and the end of multicore scaling. In *ISCA*, 2011.

[2] Nikos Hardavellas, Michael Ferdman, Babak Falsafi, and Anastasia Ailamaki. Toward dark silicon in servers. *IEEE Micro*, 31(4):6–15, July–Aug. 2011.

[3] Ganesh Venkatesh, Jack Sampson, Nathan Goulding, Saturnino Garcia, Vladyslav Bryksin, Jose Lugo-Martinez, Steven Swanson, and Michael Bedford Taylor. Conservation cores: Reducing the energy of mature computations. In *ASPLOS*, 2010.

[4] John Gantz and David Reinsel. Extracting value from chaos. http://www.emc.com/collateral/analyst-reports/idc-extracting-value-from-chaos-ar.pdf.

[5] Mehrzad Samadi, Janghaeng Lee, D. Anoushe Jamshidi, Amir Hormati, and Scott Mahlke. Sage: Self-tuning approximation for graphics engines. In *MICRO*, 2013.

[6] Mehrzad Samadi, Davoud Jamshidi, Janghaeng Lee, and Scott Mahlke. Paraprox: Pattern-based approximation for data parallel applications. In *ASPLOS*, 2014.

[7] Hadi Esmaeilzadeh, Adrian Sampson, Luis Ceze, and Doug Burger. Architecture support for disciplined approximate programming. In *ASPLOS*, 2012.

[8] Hadi Esmaeilzadeh, Adrian Sampson, Luis Ceze, and Doug Burger. Neural acceleration for general-purpose approximate programs. In *MICRO*, 2012.

[9] Renée St. Amant, Amir Yazdanbakhsh, Jongse Park, Bradley Thwaites, Hadi Esmaeilzadeh, Arjang Hassibi, Luis Ceze, and Doug Burger. General-purpose code acceleration with limited-precision analog computation. In *ISCA*, 2014.

[10] Adrian Sampson, Werner Dietl, Emily Fortuna, Danushen Gnanapragasam, Luis Ceze, and Dan Grossman. EnerJ: Approximate data types for safe and general low-power computation. In *PLDI*, 2011.

[11] Jongse Park, Hadi Esmaeilzadeh, Xin Zhang, Mayur Naik, and William Harris. Flexjava: Language support for safe and modular approximate programming. In *FSE*, 2015.

[12] Stelios Sidiroglou, Sasa Misailovic, Henry Hoffmann, and Martin Rinard. Managing performance vs. accuracy trade-offs with loop perforation. In *FSE*, 2011.

[13] Michael Carbin, Sasa Misailovic, and Martin Rinard. Verifying quantitative reliability for programs that execute on unreliable hardware. In *OOPSLA*, 2013.

[14] Inigo Goiri, Ricardo Bianchini, Santosh Nagarakatte, and Thu D. Nguyen. Approxhadoop: Bringing approximations to mapreduce frameworks. In *ASPLOS*, 2015.

[15] Joshua San Miguel, Mario Badr, and Natalie Enright Jerger. Load value approximation. In *MICRO*, 2014.

[16] Adrian Sampson, Jacob Nelson, Karin Strauss, and Luis Ceze. Approximate storage in solid-state memories. In *MICRO*, 2013.

[17] C. J. Clopper and E. S. Pearson. The use of confidence or fiducial limits illustrated in the case of the binomial. *Biometrika*, 26(4):404–413, Dec. 1934.

[18] Sean Wallis. Binomial confidence intervals and contingency tests: mathematical fundamentals and the evaluation of alternative methods. *Journal of Quantitative Linguistics*, 20(3):178–208, July. 2013.

[19] A/b testing. https://en.wikipedia.org/wiki/A/B_testing.

[20] Edwin B. Wilson. Probable inference, the law of succession, and statistical inference. *Journal of the American Statistical Association*, 22(158): 209–212, Jun. 1927.

[21] Jeff Sauro and James R. Lewis. Estimating completion rates from small samples using binomial confidence intervals: Comparisons and recommendations. In *HFES*, 2005.

[22] Morris H. DeGroot. *Probability and Statistics*. Chapman & Hall, 1974.

[23] Lame mp3 encoder. http://lame.sourceforge.net.

[24] Speech recognition toolkit. http://cmusphinx.sourceforge.net.

[25] John W Ratcliff and David E Metzener. Pattern matching: The gestalt approach. *Dr. Dobb's Journal*, 13(7):46, 1988.

[26] Amir Yazdanbakhsh, Jongse Park, Hardik Sharma, Pejman Lofti-Kamran, and Hadi Esmaeilzadeh. Neural acceleration for gpu throughput processors. In *MICRO*, 2015.

[27] Amir Yazdanbakhsh, Divya Mahajan, Bradley Thwaites, Jongse Park, Anandhavel Nagendrakumar, Sindhuja Sethuraman, Kartik Ramkrishnan, Nishanthi Ravindran, Rudra Jariwala, Abbas Rahimi, Hadi Esmaeilzadeh, and Kia Bazargan. Axilog: Language support for approximate hardware design. In *DATE*, 2015.

[28] Sasa Misailovic, Michael Carbin, Sara Achour, Zichao Qi, and Martin Rinard. Chisel: Reliability- and accuracy-aware optimization of approximate computational kernels. In *OOPSLA*, 2014.

[29] Jia Deng, Wei Dong, Richard Socher, Li-Jia Li, Kai Li, and Li Fei-Fei. Imagenet: A large-scale hierarchical image database. In *CVPR*, 2009. URL http://image-net.org.

[30] Freesound.org. https://freesound.org.

[31] Voxforge. https://developer.nvidia.com/cuda-llvm-compiler.

[32] The new york times timesmachine. http://timesmachine.nytimes.com.

[33] Amazon's mechanical turk. https://www.mturk.com.

[34] Avadh Patel, Furat Afram, Shunfei Chen, and Kanad Ghose. MARSSx86: A full system simulator for x86 CPUs. In *DAC*, 2011.

[35] Sheng Li, Jung Ho Ahn, Richard D. Strong, Jay B. Brockman, Dean M. Tullsen, and Norman P. Jouppi. McPAT: An integrated power, area, and timing modeling framework for multicore and manycore architectures. In *MICRO*, 2009.

[36] Jaegul Choo, Changhyun Lee, Hannah Kim, Hanseung Lee, Barry L. Drake, and Haesun Park. Apolo: Making sense of large network data by combining rich user interaction and machine learning. In *VAST*, 2014.

[37] Duen Horng (Polo) Chau, Aniket Kittur, Jason I. Hong, and Christos Faloutsos. Apolo: Making sense of large network data by combining rich user interaction and machine learning. In *CHI*, 2011.

[38] Song Liu, Karthik Pattabiraman, Thomas Moscibroda, and Benjamin Zorn. Flikker: Saving refresh-power in mobile devices through critical data partitioning. In *ASPLOS*, 2011.

[39] Adrian Sampson, Jacob Nelson, Karin Strauss, and Luis Ceze. Approximate storage in solid-state memories. In *MICRO*, 2013.

[40] Lakshmi N. Chakrapani, Bilge E. S. Akgul, Suresh Cheemalavagu, Pinar Korkmaz, Krishna V. Palem, and Balasubramanian Seshasayee. Ultra-efficient (embedded) SOC architectures based on probabilistic CMOS (PCMOS) technology. In *DATE*, 2006.

[41] Sriram Narayanan, John Sartori, Rakesh Kumar, and Douglas Jones. Scalable stochastic processors. In *DATE*, 2010.

[42] Rajamohana Hegde and Naresh Shanbhag. Energy-efficient signal processing via algorithmic noise-tolerance. In *ISLPED*, 1999.

[43] Larkhoon Leem, Hyungmin Cho, Jason Bau, Quinn Jacobson, and Subhasish Mitra. ERSA: error resilient system architecture for probabilistic applications. In *DATE*, 2010.

[44] Sasa Misailovic, Stelios Sidiroglou, Hank Hoffman, and Martin Rinard. Quality of service profiling. In *ICSE*, 2010.

[45] Martin Rinard, Henry Hoffmann, Sasa Misailovic, and Stelios Sidiroglou. Patterns and statistical analysis for understanding reduced resource computing. In *Onward!*, 2010.

[46] Woongki Baek and Trishul Chilimbi. Green: a framework for supporting energy-conscious programming using controlled approximation. In *PLDI*, 2010.

[47] Jason Ansel, Cy Chan, Yee Lok Wong, Marek Olszewski, Qin Zhao, Alan Edelman, and Saman Amarasinghe. Petabricks: a language and compiler for algorithmic choice. In *PLDI*, 2009.

[48] John Sartori and Rakesh Kumar. Branch and data herding: Reducing control and memory divergence for error-tolerant gpu applications. *IEEE Transactions on Multimedia*, 15(2), 2013.

[49] Carlos Alvarez, Jesus Corbal, and Mateo Valero. Fuzzy memoization for floating-point multimedia applications. *IEEE Trans. on Computers*, 54 (7), 2005.

[50] Jose-Maria Arnau, Joan-Manuel Parcerisa, and Polychronis Xekalakis. Eliminating redundant fragment shader executions on a mobile gpu via hardware memoization. In *ISCA*, 2014.

[51] Marc de Kruijf, Shuou Nomura, and Karthikeyan Sankaralingam. Relax: an architectural framework for software recovery of hardware faults. In *ISCA*, 2010.

[52] Xuanhua Li and Donald Yeung. Application-level correctness and its impact on fault tolerance. In *HPCA*, 2007.

[53] Xuanhua Li and Donald Yeung. Exploiting application-level correctness for low-cost fault tolerance. *Journal of Instruction-Level Parallelism*, 2008.

[54] Marc de Kruijf and Karthikeyan Sankaralingam. Exploring the synergy of emerging workloads and silicon reliability trends. In *SELSE*, 2009.

[55] Yuntan Fang, Huawei Li, and Xiaowei Li. A fault criticality evaluation framework of digital systems for error tolerant video applications. In *ATS*, 2011.

[56] Vicky Wong and Mark Horowitz. Soft error resilience of probabilistic inference applications. In *SELSE*, 2006.

[57] Swagath Venkataramani, Vinay K. Chippa, Srimat T. Chakradhar, Kaushik Roy, and Anand Raghunathan. Quality programmable vector processors for approximate computing. In *MICRO*, 2013.

[58] Ashish Ranjan, Arnab Raha, Swagath Venkataramani, Kaushik Roy, and Anand Raghunathan. Aslan: Synthesis of approximate sequential circuits. In *DATE*, 2014.

[59] Swagath Venkataramani, Amit Sabne, Vivek Kozhikkottu, Kaushik Roy, and Anand Raghunathan. Salsa: Systematic logic synthesis of approximate circuits. In *DAC*, 2012.

[60] Jin Miao, A. Gerstlauer, and M. Orshansky. Approximate logic synthesis under general error magnitude and frequency constraints. In *ICCAD*, 2013.

[61] Kumud Nepal, Yueting Li, R. Iris Bahar, and Sherief Reda. ABACUS: A technique for automated behavioral synthesis of approximate computing circuits. In *DATE*, 2014.

[62] Avinash Lingamneni, Christian Enz, Krishna Palem, and Christian Piguet. Synthesizing parsimonious inexact circuits through probabilistic design techniques. *ACM Transactions on Embedded Computing Systems*, 12(2s): 93:1–93:26, May 2013.

[63] Avinash Lingamneni, Kirthi Krishna Muntimadugu, Christian Enz, Richard M. Karp, Krishna V. Palem, and Christian Piguet. Algorithmic methodologies for ultra-efficient inexact architectures for sustaining technology scaling. In *CF*, 2012.

[64] Luis Von Ahn, Benjamin Maurer, Colin McMillen, David Abraham, and Manuel Blum. recaptcha: Human-based character recognition via web security measures. *Science*, 321(5895):1465–1468, 2008.

[65] Daniel W Barowy, Charlie Curtsinger, Emery D Berger, and Andrew McGregor. Automan: A platform for integrating human-based and digital computation. In *OOPSLA*, 2012.

[66] Greg Little, Lydia B Chilton, Max Goldman, and Robert C Miller. Turkit: human computation algorithms on mechanical turk. In *UIST*, 2010.

[67] Bryan C Russell, Antonio Torralba, Kevin P Murphy, and William T Freeman. Labelme: a database and web-based tool for image annotation. *International Journal of Computer Vision*, 77(1-3):157–173, 2008.

[68] Luis Von Ahn. Games with a purpose. *Computer*, 39(6):92–94, 2006.

[69] Luis Von Ahn, Ruoran Liu, and Manuel Blum. Peekaboom: a game for locating objects in images. In *CHI*, 2006.

[70] Luis Von Ahn and Laura Dabbish. Labeling images with a computer game. In *CHI*, 2004.

[71] Werner Dietl, Stephanie Dietzel, Michael D Ernst, Nathaniel Mote, Brian Walker, Seth Cooper, Timothy Pavlik, and Zoran Popović. Verification games: Making verification fun. In *FTfJP*, 2012.

[72] Seth Cooper, Firas Khatib, Adrien Treuille, Janos Barbero, Jeehyung Lee, Michael Beenen, Andrew Leaver-Fay, David Baker, Zoran Popovi, and Foldit players. Predicting protein structures with a multiplayer online game. *Nature*, 466(7307):756–760, 2010.

[73] Henry Hoffmann, Stelios Sidiroglou, Michael Carbin, Sasa Misailovic, Anant Agarwal, and Martin Rinard. Dynamic knobs for responsive power-aware computing. In *ASPLOS*, 2011.

[74] J. Bornholt, T. Mytkowicz, and K. McKinley. Uncertain<T>: A first-order type for uncertain data. In *ASPLOS*, 2014.

[75] Michael Ringenburg, Adrian Sampson, Isaac Ackerman, Luis Ceze, and Dan Grossman. Monitoring and debugging the quality of results in approximate programs. In *ASPLOS*, 2015.

[76] Phillip Stanley-Marbell and Martin Rinard. Lax: Driver interfaces for approximate sensor device access. In *HotOS*, 2015.

A DNA-Based Archival Storage System

James Bornholt[†] Randolph Lopez[†] Douglas M. Carmean[‡]
Luis Ceze[†] Georg Seelig[†] Karin Strauss[‡]
† University of Washington ‡ Microsoft Research

Abstract

Demand for data storage is growing exponentially, but the capacity of existing storage media is not keeping up. Using DNA to archive data is an attractive possibility because it is extremely dense, with a raw limit of 1 exabyte/mm^3 (10^9 GB/mm^3), and long-lasting, with observed half-life of over 500 years.

This paper presents an architecture for a DNA-based archival storage system. It is structured as a key-value store, and leverages common biochemical techniques to provide random access. We also propose a new encoding scheme that offers controllable redundancy, trading off reliability for density. We demonstrate feasibility, random access, and robustness of the proposed encoding with wet lab experiments involving 151 kB of synthesized DNA and a 42 kB random-access subset, and simulation experiments of larger sets calibrated to the wet lab experiments. Finally, we highlight trends in biotechnology that indicate the impending practicality of DNA storage for much larger datasets.

Categories and Subject Descriptors B.3.2 [*Memory Structures*]: Design Styles—Mass storage; J.3 [*Life and Medical Sciences*]: Biology and genetics

Keywords Archival storage; molecular computing; DNA

1. Introduction

The "digital universe" (all digital data worldwide) is forecast to grow to over 16 zettabytes in 2017 [14]. Alarmingly, the exponential growth rate easily exceeds our ability to store it, even when accounting for forecast improvements in storage technologies. A significant fraction of this data is in archival form; for example, Facebook recently built an entire data center dedicated to 1 exabyte of cold storage [18].

ASPLOS '16 April 2–6, 2016, Atlanta, GA, USA
Copyright © 2016 ACM 978-1-4503-4091-5/16/04...$15.00
DOI: http://dx.doi.org/10.1145/2872362.2872397

Most of the world's data today is stored on magnetic and optical media [14]. Tape technology has recently seen significant density improvements with tape cartridges as large as 185 TB [25], and is the densest form of storage available commercially today, at about 10 GB/mm^3. Recent research reported feasibility of optical discs capable of storing 1 PB [8], yielding a density of about 100 GB/mm^3. Despite this improvement, storing zettabytes of data would still take millions of units, and use significant physical space. But storage density is only one aspect of archival: durability is also critical. Rotating disks are rated for 3–5 years, and tape is rated for 10–30 years. Current long-term archival storage solutions require refreshes to scrub corrupted data, to replace faulty units, and to refresh technology. If we are to preserve the world's data, we need to seek significant advances in storage density and durability.

Synthetic DNA sequences have long been considered a potential medium for digital data storage [6, 7, 10]. DNA is an attractive possibility because it is extremely dense, with a theoretical limit above 1 EB/mm^3 (eight orders of magnitude denser than tape), and long-lasting, with observed half-life of over 500 years in harsh environments [2]. DNA-based storage also has the benefit of eternal relevance: as long as there is DNA-based life, there will be strong reasons to read and manipulate DNA. The write process for DNA storage maps digital data into DNA nucleotide sequences (a nucleotide is the basic building block of DNA), *synthesizes* (manufactures) the corresponding DNA molecules, and stores them away. Reading the data involves *sequencing* the DNA molecules and decoding the information back to the original digital data. Both synthesis and sequencing are standard practice in biotechnology, from research to diagnostics and therapies.

Progress in DNA storage has been rapid: in 1999, the state-of-the-art in DNA-based storage was encoding and recovering a 23 character message [7]; in 2013, researchers successfully recovered a 739 kB message [6, 10]. This improvement of almost 2×/year has been fueled by exponential reduction in synthesis and sequencing cost and latency; growth in sequencing productivity eclipses even Moore's Law [4]. The volume of data that can be synthesized today is limited mostly by the cost of synthesis and sequencing, but growth in the biotechnology industry portends orders of magnitude cost reductions and efficiency improvements.

We think the time is ripe to consider DNA-based storage seriously and explore system designs and architectural implications. This paper presents an architecture for a DNA-backed archival storage system, modeled as a key-value store. A DNA storage system must overcome several challenges. First, DNA synthesis and sequencing is far from perfect, with error rates on the order of 1% per nucleotide. Sequences can also degrade while stored, further compromising data integrity. A key aspect of DNA storage is to devise appropriate encoding schemes that can tolerate errors by adding redundancy. Existing approaches have focused on redundancy but have ignored density implications. In this work we propose a new encoding scheme that offers controllable redundancy, enabling different types of data (e.g., text and images) to have different levels of reliability and density. The density of our encoding scheme outperforms existing work while providing similar reliability.

Second, randomly accessing data in DNA-based storage is problematic, resulting in overall read latency that is much longer than write latency. Existing work has provided only large-block access: to read even a single byte from storage, the entire DNA pool must be sequenced and decoded. We propose a method for random access that uses a polymerase chain reaction (PCR) to amplify only the desired data, biasing sequencing towards that data. This design both accelerates reads and ensures that an entire DNA pool need not be sequenced.

We demonstrate the feasibility of our system design with a series of wet lab experiments, in which we successfully stored data in DNA and performed random access to read back only selected values. We further evaluate our design using simulations to understand the error-correction characteristics of different encoding schemes, assess their overheads, and make projections about future feasibility based on technology trends. Our results demonstrate the impending practicality of DNA-based archival storage as a solution to exponential growth in demand for data storage.

2. Background on DNA Manipulation

DNA basics. Naturally occurring DNA consists of four types of nucleotides: adenine (A), cytosine (C), guanine (G), and thymine (T). A DNA strand, or *oligonucleotide*, is a linear sequence of these nucleotides. The two ends of a DNA strand, referred to as the $5'$ and $3'$ ends, are chemically different. DNA sequences are conventionally represented starting with the $5'$ nucleotide end. The interactions between different strands are predictable based on sequence. Two single strands can bind to each other and form a double helix if they are complementary: A in one strand aligns with T in the other, and likewise for C and G. The two strands in a double helix have opposite directionality ($5'$ end binds to the other strand's $3'$ end), and thus the two sequences are the "reverse complement" of each other. Two strands do not need to be fully complementary to bind to one another. Such *partial* complementarity is useful for applications in DNA nanotechnology and other fields, but can also result in undesired "crosstalk" between sequences in complex reaction mixtures containing many sequences.

Selective DNA amplification with polymerase chain reaction (PCR). PCR is a method for exponentially amplifying the concentration of selected sequences of DNA within a pool. A PCR reaction requires four main components: the template, sequencing primers, a thermostable polymerase and individual nucleotides that get incorporated into the DNA strand being amplified. The template is a single- or double-stranded molecule containing the (sub)sequence that will be amplified. The DNA sequencing primers are short synthetic strands that define the beginning and end of the region to be amplified. The polymerase is an enzyme that creates double-stranded DNA from a single-stranded template by "filling in" individual complementary nucleotides one by one, starting from a primer bound to that template. PCR happens in "cycles", each of which doubles the number of templates in a solution. The process can be repeated until the desired number of copies is created.

DNA synthesis. Arbitrary single-strand DNA sequences can be synthesized chemically, nucleotide by nucleotide [15, 17]. The *coupling efficiency* of a synthesis process is the probability that a nucleotide binds to an existing partial strand at each step of the process. Although the coupling efficiency for each step can be higher than 99%, this small error still results in an exponential decrease of product yield with increasing length and limits the size of oligonucleotides that can be efficiently synthesized to about 200 nucleotides. In practice, synthesis of a given sequence uses a large number of parallel start sites and results in many truncated byproducts (the dominant error in DNA synthesis), in addition to many copies of the full length target sequence. Thus, despite errors in synthesizing any specific strand, a given synthesis batch will usually produce many perfect strands. Moreover, modern array synthesis techniques [15] can synthesize complex pools of nearly 10^5 different oligonucleotides in parallel.

DNA sequencing. There are several high-throughput sequencing techniques, but the most popular methods (such as that used by Illumina) use DNA polymerase enzymes and are commonly referred to as "sequencing by synthesis". The strand of interest serves as a template for the polymerase, which creates a complement of the strand. Importantly, *fluorescent* nucleotides are used during this synthesis process. Since each type of fluorescent nucleotide emits a different color, it is possible to read out the complement sequence optically. Sequencing is error-prone, but as with synthesis, in aggregate, sequencing typically produces enough precise reads of each strand.

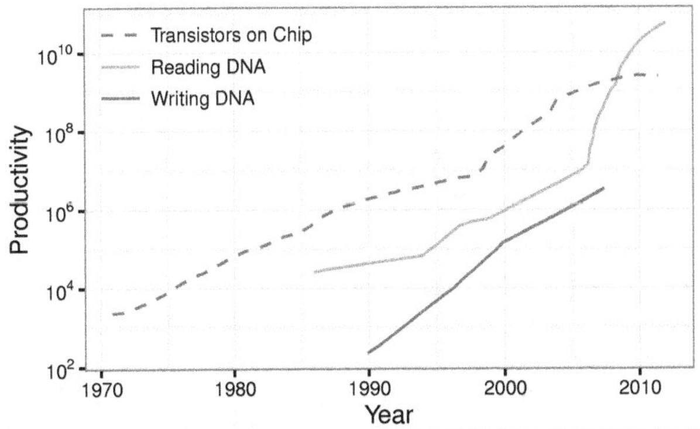

Figure 1. Carlson curves [4]: trends in DNA synthesis and sequencing technology compared to Moore's Law. DNA productivity is measured in nucleotides per person per day. Recent growth in sequencing technology eclipses Moore.

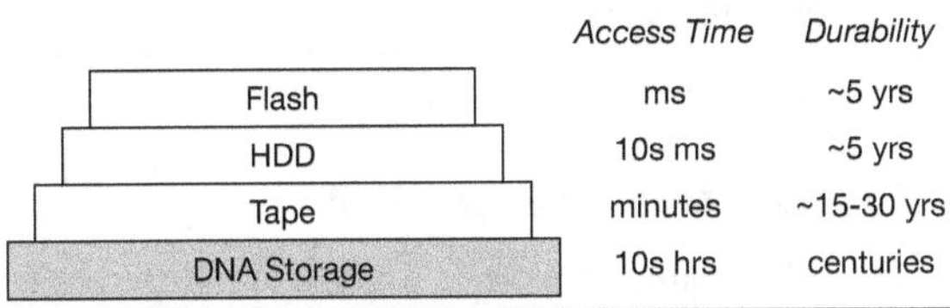

Figure 2. DNA storage as the bottom level of the storage hierarchy

Sequencing and synthesis improvement projections. Today, neither the performance nor the cost of DNA synthesis and sequencing is viable for data storage purposes. However, they have historically seen exponential improvements. Their cost reductions and throughput improvements have been compared to Moore's Law in Carlson's Curves [4], as shown in Figure 1. It shows that sequencing productivity has been growing faster than Moore's Law. Important biotechnology applications such as genomics and the development of smart drugs are expected to continue driving these improvements, eventually making data storage a viable application.

3. A DNA Storage System

We envision DNA storage as the very last level of a deep storage hierarchy, providing very dense and durable archival storage with access times of many hours to days (Figure 2). DNA synthesis and sequencing can be made arbitrarily parallel, making the necessary read and write bandwidths attainable. We now describe our proposal of a system for DNA-based storage with random access support.

3.1 Overview

A DNA storage system consists of a DNA synthesizer that encodes the data to be stored in DNA, a storage container with compartments that store pools of DNA that map to a volume, and a DNA sequencer that reads DNA sequences and converts them back into digital data. Figure 3 shows an overview of the integrated system.

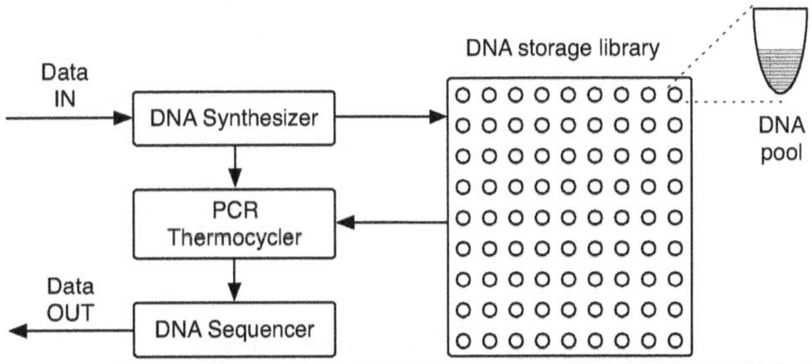

Figure 3. Overview of a DNA storage system.

The basic unit of DNA storage is a DNA strand that is roughly 100-200 nucleotides long, capable of storing 50-100 bits total. Therefore, a typical data object maps to a very large number of DNA strands. The DNA strands will be stored in "pools" that have stochastic spatial organization and do not permit structured addressing, unlike electronic storage media. Therefore, it is necessary to embed the address itself into the data stored in a strand. This way, after sequencing, one can reassemble the original data value. We discuss digital data representation in DNA in Section 4.

3.2 Interface and Addressing

A storage system needs a way to assign identification tags to data objects so they can be retrieved later. We choose a simple key-value architecture, where a `put(key, value)` operation associates `value` with `key`, and a `get(key)` operation retrieves the `value` assigned to `key`. To implement a key-value interface in a DNA storage system, we need: (1) a function that maps a key to the DNA pool (in the library) where the strands that contain data reside; and (2) a mechanism to selectively retrieve only desired portions of a pool (i.e, random access), since the DNA container will likely store significantly more data than the desired object.

We implement random access by mapping a key to a pair of PCR primers. At write time, those primers are added to the strands. At read time, those same primers are used in PCR to amplify only the strands with the desired keys. Because the resulting pool will have a much higher concentration of the desired strands, a sample from that pool is very likely to contain all of those strands.

Separating the DNA strands into a collection of pools (Figure 3) balances a trade-off between storage density, reliability, and performance. The most dense way to store data would be to have all strands in a single pool, but this arrangement sacrifices reliability for two reasons. First, a single pool requires many different primers to distinguish all keys, which increases the chance that two primers react poorly to each other. Second, a single pool reduces the likelihood that a random sample drawn during the read process will contain all the desired data. On the other hand, using a separate pool per key sacrifices density excessively. We therefore use a library of reasonably-sized pools, and use random access within each pool.

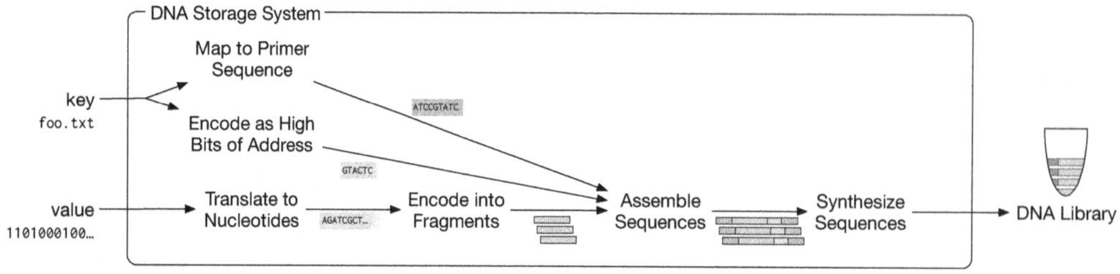

(a) The write process performs `put (key, value)`, generating a DNA library.

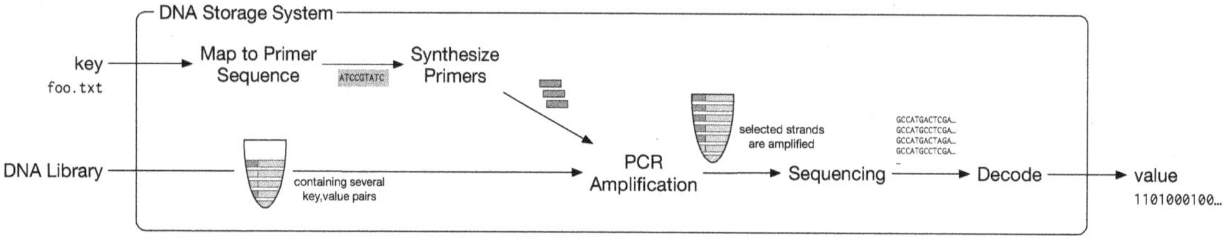

(b) The read process performs `get (key)` on a DNA library, returning the value.

Figure 4. Overview of a DNA storage system operation as a key-value store.

3.3 System Operation

Figure 4 shows flowcharts for the write (`put`) and read (`get`) processes in more detail. The write process (Fig. 4(a)) takes as input the key and value to store. It uses the key to obtain the PCR primer sequences, compute the high part of the address, and to determine the pool in the DNA library where the resulting strands will be stored. The low part of the address indexes the multiple strands generated by chunking the value (see Sec. 4.2). Next, it encodes the data addresses, payloads, and error detection codes, and attaches the primer target sequences, to produce final DNA sequences for the synthesizer to manufacture. The resulting DNA molecules are stored in the storage library for archival.

The read process (Fig. 4(b)) takes as input a key. It uses the key to obtain the PCR primer sequences that identify molecules in the pool associated with that key. Next, the storage system physically extracts a sample from the DNA pool that contains the stored data, but likely also includes large amounts of unrelated data. The sample and the PCR primers are sent to the PCR thermocycler, which amplifies only the desired strands. The resulting pool goes to the DNA sequencer, which ultimately produces the digital data readout. Note that this process might be iterative since it may require multiple samples and sequencing steps to extract all the data associated with the desired keys. The DNA synthesizer is used for both producing the DNA strands that hold data payload as well as synthesizing the PCR primers used to amplify data during the random access read process.

The read process removes a sample of DNA from the pool, and so cumulative reads reduce the quantity of DNA available for future operations. But DNA is easy to replicate, and so the pools can easily be replenished after read operations if necessary. If successive amplification is problematic, a pool can also be completely resynthesized after a read operation.

4. Representing Data in DNA

While DNA has many properties that make it different from existing storage media, there are parallels between traditional storage and DNA storage. At the lowest levels, traditional storage media store raw bits. The storage device abstracts the physical media, which could be magnetic state, or the charge in a capacitor, or the stable state of a flip-flop, and presents to the storage hierarchy raw digital data. In a similar way, the abstraction of DNA storage is the nucleotide: though a nucleotide is an organic molecule consisting of one base (A, C, G, or T) and a sugar-phosphate backbone, the abstraction of DNA storage is as a contiguous string of quaternary (base-4) numerals. This section describes the challenges of representing data in DNA, and presents several encodings that overcome these challenges.

4.1 Representation

The obvious approach to store binary data in DNA is to encode the binary data in base 4, producing a string of $n/2$ quaternary digits from a string of n binary bits. The quaternary digits can then be mapped to DNA nucleotides (e.g., mapping 0, 1, 2, 3 to A, C, G, T, respectively). For example, the binary string 01110001 maps to the base-4 string 1301, and then to the DNA sequence CTAC. However, DNA synthesis and sequencing processes are prone to a wide variety of errors (substitutions, insertions, and deletions of nucleotides), requiring a more careful encoding.

The likelihood of some forms of error can be reduced by encoding binary data in base 3 instead of base 4 [10], as Figure 5(a) illustrates. Each ternary digit maps to a DNA nucleotide based on a rotating code (Figure 5(b)) that avoids repeating the same nucleotide twice. This encoding avoids *homopolymers*—repetitions of the same nucleotide that significantly increase the chance of sequencing errors [20].

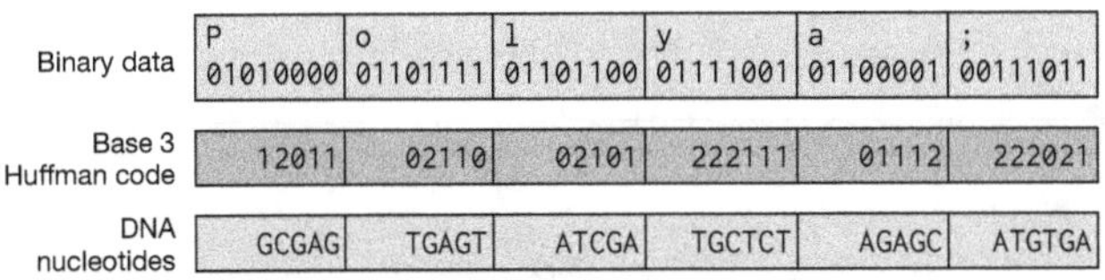

(a) Translating binary data to DNA nucleotides via a Huffman code.

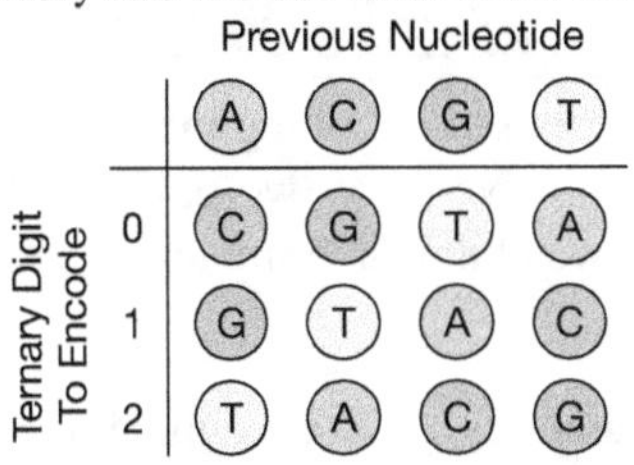

(b) A rotating encoding to nucleotides avoids homopolymers (repetitions of the same nucleotide), which are error-prone.

Figure 5. Encoding a stream of binary data as a stream of nucleotides. A Huffman code translates binary to ternary digits, and a rotating encoding translates ternary digits to nucleotides.

Because base 3 is not a multiple of base 2, mapping directly between the bases would be inefficient: 6 ternary digits ($3^6 = 729$) can store 9 bits of data ($2^9 = 512$), but waste 217 possible states. Instead, we use a Huffman code [13] that maps each binary byte to either 5 or 6 ternary digits. For example, the Huffman code maps the binary string 01100001 to the base-3 string 01112. The rotating nucleotide encoding maps this string to the DNA sequence CTCTG. The code maps more common ASCII characters to 5 digit strings, offering minor compression benefits for textual data, though the effect on overall storage density is insignificant.

4.2 Data Format

Another practical issue with representing data in DNA is that current synthesis technology does not scale beyond sequences of low hundreds of nucleotides. Data beyond the hundreds of bits therefore cannot be synthesized as a single strand of DNA. In addition, DNA pools do not offer spatial isolation, and so a pool contains data for many different keys which are irrelevant to a single read operation. Isolating only the molecules of interest is non-trivial, and so existing DNA storage techniques generally sequence the entire solution, which incurs significant cost and time overheads.

To overcome these two challenges, we organize data in DNA in a similar fashion to Goldman et al. [10], as shown in Figure 6. Segmenting the nucleotide representation into blocks, which we synthesize as separate strands, allows storage of large values. Tagging those strands with identifying primers allows the read process to isolate molecules of interest and so perform random access. Below we describe these designs in detail.

Payload. The string of nucleotides representing the data to be stored is broken into data blocks, whose length depends on the desired strand length and the additional overheads

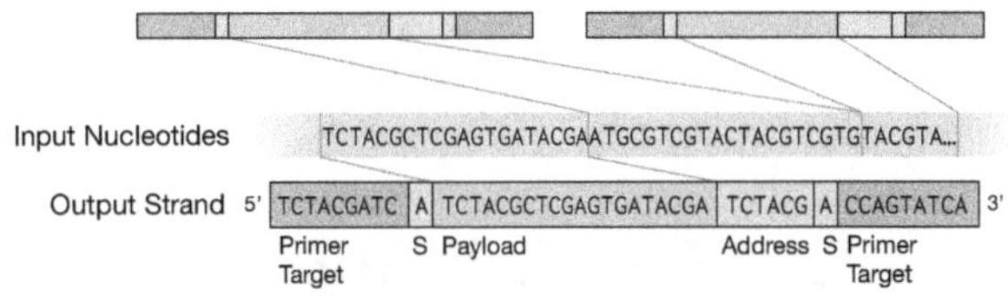

Figure 6. An overview of the DNA data encoding format. After translating to nucleotides, the stream is divided into strands. Each strand contains a payload from the stream, together with addressing information to identify the strand and primer targets necessary for PCR and sequencing.

of the format. To aid decoding, two sense nucleotides ("S" in Figure 6) indicate whether the strand has been reverse complemented (this is done to avoid certain pathological cases).

Address. Each data block is augmented with addressing information to identify its location in the input data string. The address space is in two parts. The high part of the address identifies the key a block is associated with. The low part of the address indexes the block within the value associated with that key. The combined address is padded to a fixed length and converted to nucleotides as described above. A parity nucleotide is added for basic error detection.

Primers. To each end of the strand, we attach primer sequences. These sequences serve as a "foothold" for the PCR process, and allow the PCR to selectively amplify only those strands with a chosen primer sequence.

Random Access. We exploit primer sequences to provide random access: by assigning different primers to different strands, we can perform sequencing on only a selected group of strands. Existing work on DNA storage uses a single primer sequence for all strands. While this design suffices for data recovery, it is inefficient: the entire pool (i.e., the strands for every key) must be sequenced to recover one value.

To provide random access, we instead design a mapping from keys to unique primer sequences. All strands for a particular object share a common primer, and different strands with the same primer are distinguished by their different addresses.

Primers allow random access via a polymerase chain reaction (PCR), which produces many copies of a piece of DNA in a solution. By controlling the sequences used as primers for PCR, we can dictate which strands in the solution are amplified. To read a particular key's value from the solution, we simply perform a PCR process using that key's primer, which amplifies the selected strands. The sequencing process then reads only those strands, rather than the entire pool. The amplification means sequencing can be faster and cheaper, because the probability of recovering the desired object is higher.

Note that not all adapters and primers have the same behavior or effectiveness during PCR. Also, the actual sequences affect the PCR cycle temperatures. Discussing adapter and

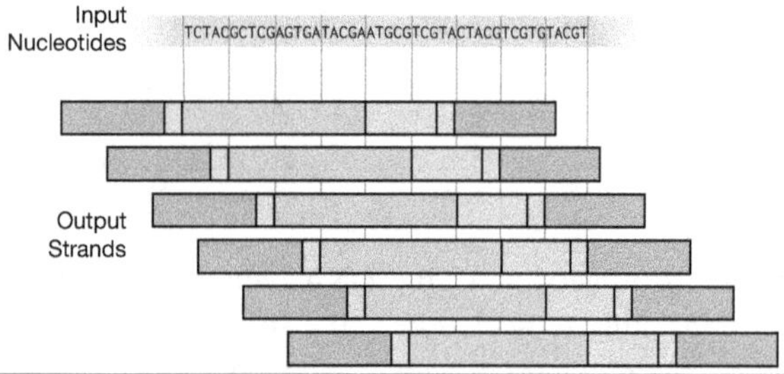

Figure 7. An encoding proposed by Goldman et al. [10]. The payloads of each strand are overlapping segments of the input stream, such that each block in the stream appears in four distinct strands.

primer design is outside the scope of this paper. The hash function that maps addresses to primers can be implemented as a table lookup of primers that are known to work well and have known thermocycling temperatures. For this paper, we used primer designs from prior work [24].

5. Encodings for Reliable Storage

The previous sections described the organization of a DNA-based storage system, and in particular, how data can be broken into strands of DNA. However, the encoding implied by the previous section is naive: each bit of binary data is encoded in exactly one location in the output DNA strands, and so relies on the robustness of DNA for durability. A more robust design would provide redundancy at the data encoding level. This section discusses existing work on encodings for redundancy, highlights the reliability–density trade-off implicit in encoding design, and presents a new encoding with similar reliability to and yet higher density than existing work.

5.1 Existing Encodings

Early work in DNA storage used encodings simpler than the one we describe above. For example, Bancroft et al. [3] translate text to DNA by means of a simple ternary encoding: each of the 26 English characters and a space character maps to a sequence of three nucleotides drawn from A, C, and T (so exactly $3^3 = 27$ characters can be represented). The authors successfully recovered a message of 106 characters, but this encoding suffers substantial overheads and poor reliability for longer messages.

Goldman encoding. We focus on an existing encoding proposed by Goldman et al. [10], shown in Figure 7. This encoding splits the input DNA nucleotides into overlapping segments to provide fourfold redundancy for each segment. Each window of four segments corresponds to a strand in the output encoding. The authors used this encoding to successfully recover a 739 kB message. We use this encoding as a baseline because it is, to our knowledge, the most successful published DNA storage technique. In addition, it offers a tunable level of redundancy, by reducing the width of the segments and therefore repeating them more often in strands of the same length (for example, if the overlapping segments were half as long as in Figure 7, they would be repeated in eight strands instead of four).

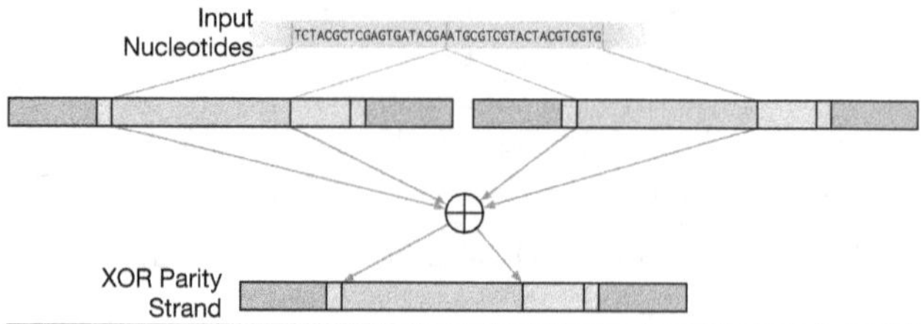

Figure 8. Our proposed encoding incorporates redundancy by taking the exclusive-or of two payloads to form a third. Recovering any two of the three strands is sufficient to recover the third.

5.2 XOR Encoding

While the Goldman encoding provides high reliability, it also incurs significant overhead: each block in the input string is repeated four times. We propose a simple new encoding that provides similar levels of redundancy to prior work, but with reduced overhead.

Our encoding, shown in Figure 8, provides redundancy by a simple exclusive-or operation at the strand level. We take the exclusive-or $A \oplus B$ of the payloads A and B of two strands, which produces a new payload and so a new DNA strand. The address block of the new strand encodes the addresses of the input strands that were the inputs to the exclusive-or; the high bit of the address is used to indicate whether a strand is an original payload or an exclusive-or strand. This encoding provides its redundancy in a similar fashion to RAID 5: any two of the three strands A, B, and $A \oplus B$ are sufficient to recover the third.

The reliability of this encoding is similar to that of Goldman. In Section 6, we show that we successfully recovered objects from both encodings in a wet lab experiment. However, the theoretical density of this encoding is much higher than Goldman—where in their encoding each nucleotide repeats (up to) four times, in ours each nucleotide repeats an average of 1.5 times. In practice, the density difference is lower, due to the overheads of addressing and primers that are constant between the two encodings. Simulation results in Section 7 show our encoding to be twice as dense as that of Goldman, and for all practical DNA synthesis and sequencing technologies, it provides equivalent levels of reliability.

5.3 Tunable Redundancy

Recent work in approximate storage [12, 23] shows that many applications do not need high-precision storage for every data structure. For example, while the header data of a JPEG file is critical to successful decoding, small errors in the payload are tolerable at the cost of some decoding imprecision.

One key advantage of our encoding is that the level of redundancy is tunable at a per-block granularity. For critical data, we can provide high redundancy by pairing critical blocks with many other blocks: if A is critical, produce $A \oplus B$, $A \oplus C$, etc. On the other hand, for blocks that are less critical, we can further reduce their redundancy: instead of including only two blocks in an exclusive-or, we can include n, such that any $n-1$ of the n blocks is sufficient to recover the last, at an average density overhead of $1/n$.

In addition to improving density, tunable redundancy has a significant effect on performance. Both DNA synthesis and sequencing are slower and more error-prone with larger datasets, and this error does not always grow linearly in size. It is often economically viable to synthesize smaller DNA pools with more accurate technology, while larger pools are out of reach. Tunable redundancy allows the storage system to optimize the balance between reliability and efficiency.

5.4 Factors in Encoding Design

As with many encodings in the literature, ours ignores special properties of DNA synthesis and sequencing that make choosing an optimal encoding more complex. In particular, errors in synthesis and sequencing are not uniform: they vary according to location within a strand, and different sequences of nucleotides are more susceptible to undesired reactions.

Synthesis error grows with the length of the strand being synthesized; nucleotides towards the end of the strand are more likely to be incorrect. Some of these errors are easily ignored, because they result in truncations, where the product strand is not of the correct length. Other errors are more insidious, with substitution errors being particularly common.

An improved version of our encoding would tolerate variable substitution errors by not aligning the strands directly. For example, rather than computing $A \oplus B$, we might instead compute $A \oplus B'$, where B' is B in reverse. Since nucleotides at the end of a strand are more error-prone, reversing one strand ensures that the average quality is (roughly) constant along the strand, so that each nucleotide has at least some redundancy information stored in a high-reliability position.

6. Experiments

To demonstrate the feasibility of DNA storage with random access capabilities, we encoded four image files using the two encodings described in Section 5. The files varied in size from 5 kB to 84 kB. We synthesized these files and sequenced the resulting DNA to recover the files. This section describes our experience with the synthesis and sequencing process, and presents results demonstrating that DNA storage is practical and that random access works. We used the results of our experiments to inform the design of a simulator, which we use in Section 7 to perform more experiments exploring the design space of data encoding and durability.

6.1 Materials and Method

This section briefly describes the experimental protocol; see Appendix A for details.

We used as input to the storage system four image files. For each image file `x.jpg`, we generated DNA sequences corresponding to the output of `put(x.jpg, ...)`. We performed these operations using two different encodings – the Goldman encoding and our proposed XOR encoding – described in Section 5. Combined, the eight operations produced 45,652 sequences of length 120 nucleotides, representing 151 kB of data.

(a) `sydney.jpg`, 24301 bytes

(b) `cat.jpg`, 11901 bytes

(c) `smiley.jpg`, 5665 bytes

Figure 9. Three image files we synthesized and sequenced for our experiments.

To demonstrate that DNA storage allows effective random access, we performed four `get` operations: selecting three of the four files encoded with the Goldman encoding, and one of the four encoded with the XOR encoding. The three files retrieved from the Goldman encoding are in Figure 9; we also performed `get(sydney.jpg)` on the XOR-encoded data.

The synthesized sequences were prepared for sequencing by amplification via the polymerase chain reaction (PCR) method. The product was sequenced using an Illumina MiSeq platform. The selected `get` operations total 16,994 sequences and 42 kB. Sequencing produced 20.8 M reads of sequences in the pool. We inspected the results and observed no reads of sequences that were not selected – so random access was effective in amplifying only the target files.

6.2 Results

File Recovery. We successfully recovered all four files from the sequenced DNA. Three of the files were recovered without manual intervention. One file – `cat.jpg` encoded with the Goldman encoder – incurred a one-byte error in the JPEG header, which we fixed by hand. As described, the design of the Goldman encoder provides no redundancy for the first and last bytes of a file, and so this error was due to random substitution in either sequencing or synthesis. We could mitigate this error scenario by trivially extending that algorithm to wrap the redundant strands past the end of the file and back to the beginning.

Sequencing Depth. Figure 10 shows the distribution of sequencing depths over the 16,994 selected sequences. The sequencing depth of a strand is the number of times it was perfectly sequenced. Of the 20.8 M reads from the sequencing

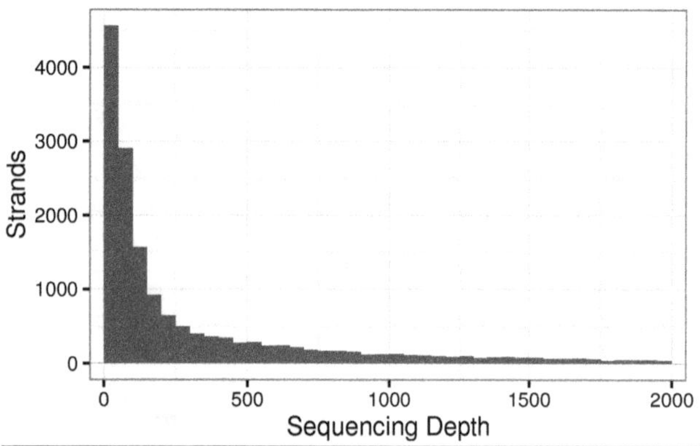

Figure 10. Distribution of sequencing depths over all encoded strands.

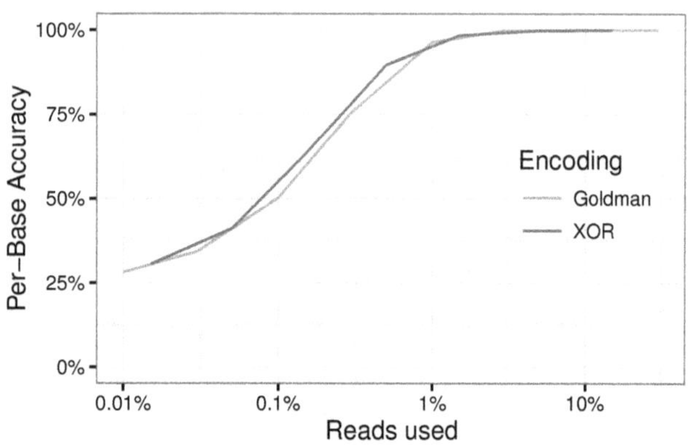

Figure 11. Decoding accuracy as a function of sequencing depth.

run, 8.6 M were error-free reads of a strand in the desired pool. The distribution of reads by sequence is heavily skewed with a mean depth of 506 and median depth of 128. These results suggest that encodings need to be robust not only to missing sequences (which get very few reads), but heavily amplified incorrect sequences.

Reduced Sequencing Depth. The sequencing depth achieved in our experiment is more than sufficient to recover the encoded data. Sequencing technology can reduce sequencing depth in exchange for faster, higher-throughput results. To determine whether our encodings are still effective as sequencing depth reduces, we randomly subsampled the 20.8 M reads we achieved and tried to decode `sydney.jpg` again, using both the Goldman and XOR encodings.

Figure 11 shows that both encodings respond similarly to reduced sequencing depth. The x-axis plots the fraction of the 20.8 M reads used, and the y-axis the accuracy of the decoded file. Both encodings tend to 25% accuracy as the depth reduces, as both decoders randomly guess one of the four nucleotides if no data is available. The accuracy of the two encodings is similar; however, the XOR encoding is higher density than the Goldman encoding.

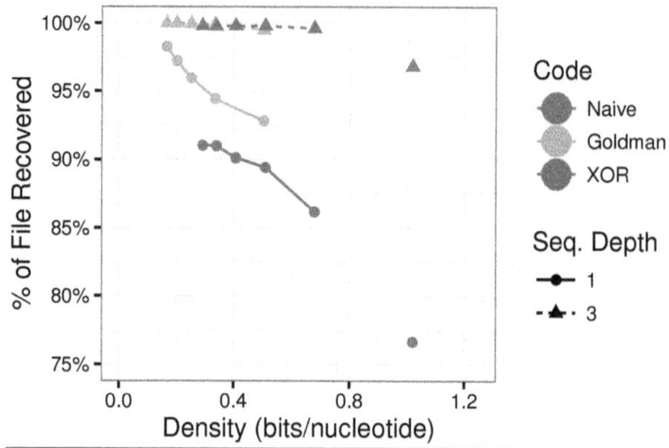

Figure 12. Reliability of encoded data as a function of storage density at different sequencing depths.

Naive Encoding. Figure 8 shows that the XOR encoding is actually a superset of a naive encoding: if we ignore strands which are products $A \oplus B$, we are left with only the naively encoded strands A and B. We attempted to decode `sydney.jpg` while ignoring the XOR products. We found that 11 strands were missing entirely, and even after improving the decoder to arbitrarily guess the values of missing strands, were not able to recover a valid JPEG file. The XOR encoding corrected all these errors at a lower density overhead than the Goldman encoding. These results suggest that even at very high sequencing depths, a naive encoding is not sufficient for DNA storage: encodings must provide their own robustness to errors.

7. Simulation

We used the results of the experiments in Section 6 to inform the design of a simulator for DNA synthesis and sequencing. The simulator allows experimenting with new encodings and new configurations for existing encodings. This section uses the simulator to answer two questions about DNA storage: first, how do different encodings trade storage density for reliability, and second, what is the effect of decay on the reliability of stored data?

Reliability and Density. The encodings we described in Section 5 can be reconfigured to provide either higher density or higher reliability. To examine this trade-off between different encodings, we encoded the `sydney.jpg` file (Fig. 9) with a variety of configurations. These configurations vary the number of strands where a piece of data is included, by changing the overlap between strands for Goldman and increasing the number of XOR copies for XOR.

Figure 12 plots the density achieved by an encoding (x-axis) against decoding reliability (y-axis). The density is calculated as the file size divided by the total number of bases used to encode the file. Figure 12 includes three different encoding mechanisms: a naive encoding with no redundancy, the encoding proposed by Goldman, and our proposed XOR encoding. It presents the results for two

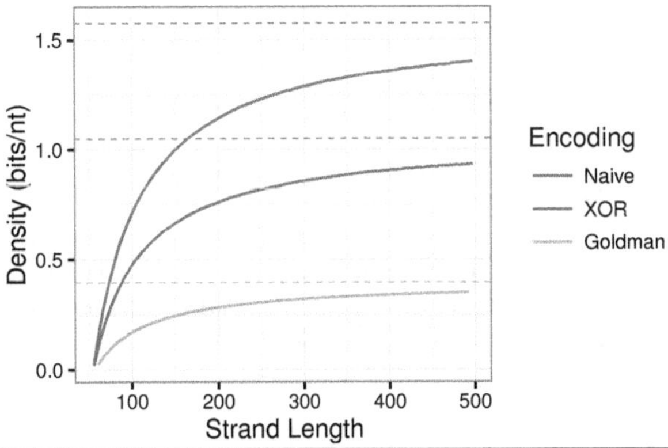

Figure 13. Density of different encodings as a function of the length of each synthesized DNA strand. Dashed lines are asymptotes for infinite-length strands.

sequencing depths, 1 and 3. Naive encoding has the lowest reliability because there is no redundancy. As the sequencing depth increases, the reliability improves, but as observed in the wet lab experiments, even at higher sequencing depths, the Naive encoding is not sufficient to provide full data recovery. For both tunable encodings, additional redundancy increases robustness, but affects density negatively. For sequencing depth of 1, where only a single copy of each strand is available, any error causes information loss if no redundancy is available (red dot). As more redundancy is added (blue and green curves), the encoding becomes more resilient to errors. At sequencing depth 1 and same density, Goldman is more resilient than XOR because it does not combine then replicate bits, it simply replicates them. As sequencing depths increase, XOR becomes as reliable as Goldman because the probability of having no copies at all of the original data lowers significantly.

Density and Strand Length. One limiting factor for DNA storage is strand length: current DNA synthesis technology can only viably produce strands of lengths less than 200, and our wet lab experiments (Sec. 6) used strands of length 120. But future synthesis technology promises to increase this limit, as many fields of biology require longer artificial DNA sequences (for example, the average human gene has on the order of 10^4 nucleotides).

Figure 13 plots the density of different encodings on the y-axis as a function of the strand length on the x-axis. As strand length grows, addressing and other overheads become less significant, and density becomes a function only of the encoding. In the limit, the density of our XOR encoding is 2.6× that of Goldman, and yet our results show similar reliability. The XOR encoding is also two-thirds the density of a naive encoding, which suffers much worse error rates.

Decay. Finally, we used the simulator to evaluate the durability of DNA storage over time. The durability of electronic storage is, in the best case, in the tens of years. In contrast, the half life of single stranded DNA is much longer. To demonstrate the durability of DNA storage, we simulated decay at room temperature, according to rates observed in recent work [11]. Storage at lower temperatures significantly increases the half life of the stored DNA.

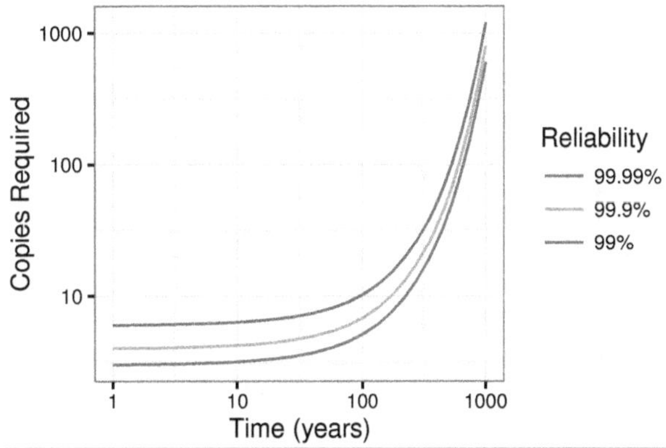

Figure 14. Average number of copies of sequences required to ensure a desired reliability over time.

Figure 14 shows desired timespan on the x-axis and the number of copies of each strand required to achieve a desired reliability after the timespan on the y-axis. Different curves correspond to different desired reliabilities. For example, the 99.99% reliability line says that to have a 99.99% chance of recovering an encoded value after 100 years, we need to store only 10 copies of the strands for that value. The results show that even very few copies are sufficient to provide high reliability long beyond the half lives of existing electronic media. In summary, high reliability for long time intervals does not have much impact on DNA storage density.

8. Discussion and Future Work

The results in Sections 6 and 7 demonstrate a full DNA storage system and its advantages. This section provides a more in-depth examination of experimental data and discusses potential improvements.

The Real Source of Errors. The results in Section 6 showed that error rates in a complete storage pipeline are high enough to require redundant encoding. This section shows where these errors come from, so that we can decide where to focus our attention when attempting to reduce errors.

To answer this question, we synthesized a small subset of strands using a high fidelity on-column synthesis process (Single). In this process, each sequence is synthesized individually resulting in low error rate, but high cost and low throughput incompatible with information storage applications. In contrast, the results in Section 6 were generated using a high-throughput microarray-based synthesis process (Array) that is not high fidelity, but is currently among the lowest cost DNA synthesis alternatives.

Figure 15 compares the overall error distribution for identical strands obtained through Single and Array synthesis as a function of the relative position within the strand. The

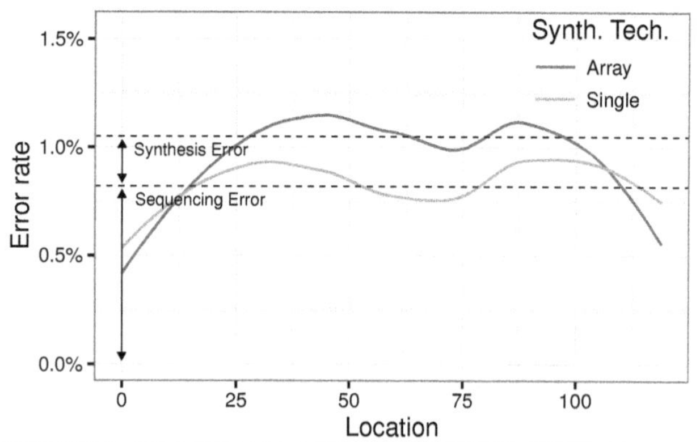

Figure 15. Distribution of DNA errors from two synthesis technologies. Because Single synthesis is effectively error-free, its results reflect sequencing error alone.

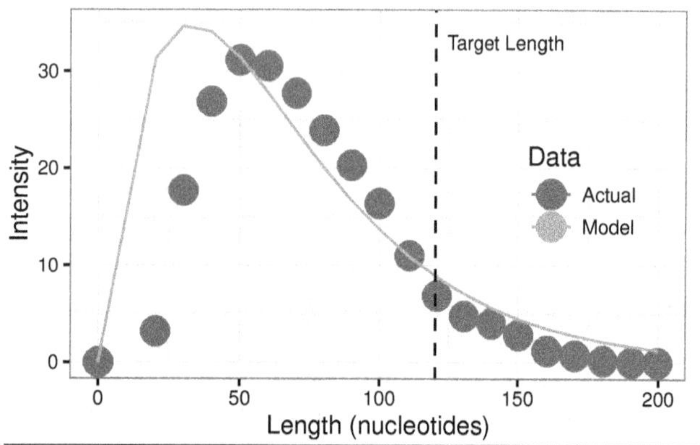

Figure 16. Expected and observed distributions of strand length from DNA synthesis. Sequencing recovers only strands of the target length, but most of the synthesis product is not full length.

overall error rate is due to both sequencing and synthesis errors. However, if we assume that the error rate for Single synthesis is near zero, we can interpret errors measured for those strands as solely due to sequencing. The difference between the error rates for the stands derived from Single and Array can then be interpreted as synthesis errors. We clearly see that sequencing error dominates for all locations: the sequencing error rate is on average an order of magnitude higher. These results show that future technology should focus on improving the accuracy of sequencing.

Synthesis Efficiency. In addition to incorrect strands, micro-array synthesis can produce *truncated* strands. Standard sequencing processes exclude these truncated strands, so they are unused for data recovery and represent waste.

To illustrate the potential losses due to truncation, Figure 16 shows the length distribution of the synthesized strands, as determined by gel electrophoresis (see Appendix A for details). Less than 5% of the pool is of the target length of 120 nucleotides – other strands are either truncated early, or (much more rarely) made longer. This indicates that work in reducing number of fragments could improve synthesis costs by up to about one order of magnitude.

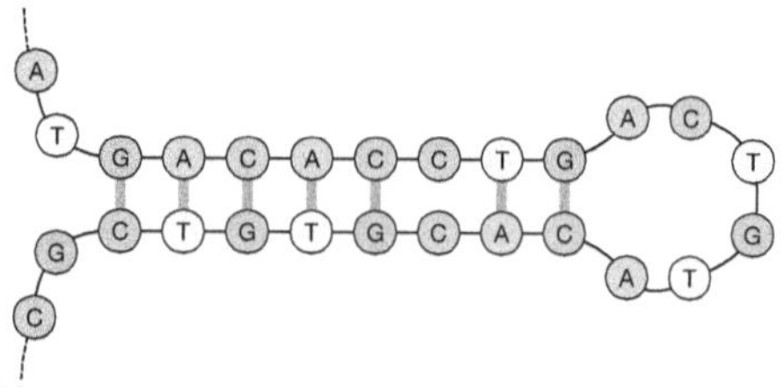

Figure 17. A hairpin, in which a single sequence of DNA binds to itself because nearby regions are self-complementary. Hairpins make DNA amplification and sequencing more error prone.

Avoiding Bad Sequences. The representation we (and others) have used does not avoid more complex sources of error in DNA data representation. For example, Figure 17 shows a *hairpin*, in which a single sequence of DNA binds to itself, folding its two ends together because they are (partially) complementary. The binding of the two ends to each other prevents this strand from being easily amplified and sequenced. A more robust representation would avoid creating sequences that are self-complementary to reduce the chance of this self-hybridization. Of course, restricting self-complementarity also reduces the potential density of the representation, so it presents a trade-off between density and reliability.

Similarly, if different strands are partially complementary, there is a chance they will bind to each other. A more robust encoding would try to mitigate this chance. For example, the mapping in Figure 5(b) from ternary digits to nucleotides need not be static. Instead, it could be selected on a per-strand basis by selecting the encoding that produces the least self-complementary and partially complementary strands.

We intend to explore these directions as future work, but thus far these issues have had little effect on our experiments.

9. Related Work

Encoding data in DNA has a long line of research in the biology community. Early examples encoded and recovered very short messages: Clelland et al. recovered a 23 character message in 1999 [7], and Leier et al. recover three 9-bit numbers in 2000 [16]. The first significant scaling improvements were made by Gibson et al. in 2010, successfully recovering 1280 characters encoded in a bacterial genome as "watermarks" [9] – but note this approach is *in vivo* (inside an organism), whereas ours is *in vitro* (outside), so the technology is very different and inapplicable to large-scale storage. More scaling improvements were made by Church et al. in 2012, who recovered a 643 kB message [6], and Goldman et al. recovered a 739 kB message also in 2012 [10]. However, both these results required manual intervention: Church et al. had to manually correct ten bits of error, and Goldman et al. lost two sequences of 25 nucleotides.

Most recently, Grass et al. recovered an 83 kB message without error [11]. Their design uses a Reed-Solomon code [22], striping the entire dataset across 5000 DNA strands. While this design leads to excellent redundancy, it defeats the desire for random access.

Concurrent with our work, Yazdi et al. [28] developed a method for rewritable random-access DNA-based storage. Its encoding is dictionary-based and focuses on storage of text, while our approach accommodates arbitrary binary data. We do not support rewritability, which adds substantial complexity, because write-once is appropriate for archival items (e.g., photos) that are unlikely to change. If necessary, one can use a log-based approach for rewriting objects, since the density of DNA exceeds the overhead of logging.

The use of DNA as a computing substrate also has a long history: in 1994, Adleman proposed composing Hamiltonian paths with DNA [1]. Researchers have proposed the use of DNA for Boolean circuits [26], neural networks [21], and chemical reaction networks [5]. DNA computing has also begun making inroads in the architecture community: Muscat et al. explore the architectural challenges of DNA strand-displacement circuits [19], and Talawar examines the design of a DNA-based crossbar interconnection network [27].

10. Conclusion

DNA-based storage has the potential to be the ultimate archival storage solution: it is extremely dense and durable. While this is not practical yet due to the current state of DNA synthesis and sequencing, both technologies are improving at an exponential rate with advances in the biotechnology industry. Given the impending limits of silicon technology, we believe that hybrid silicon and biochemical systems are worth serious consideration: time is ripe for computer architects to consider incorporating biomolecules as an integral part of computer design. DNA-based storage is one clear example of this direction. Biotechnology has benefited tremendously from progress in silicon technology developed by the computer industry; perhaps now is the time for the computer industry to borrow back from the biotechnology industry to advance the state of the art in computer systems.

Acknowledgements

We thank Brandon Holt, Emina Torlak, Xi Wang, and the anonymous reviewers for their feedback on earlier versions of this work; Robert Carlson for providing historic information on DNA synthesis and sequencing; and the members of the Sampa, Molecular Information Systems, and Seelig labs at UW, and the Emerging Storage and Computation team at Microsoft Research, for their support of this project. This work was supported in part by NSF grants #1064497 and #1409831, gifts by Microsoft Research, and by the David Notkin Endowed Graduate Fellowship.

A. Appendix: Materials and Method

Primers for the PCR reaction (Fig. 18) were designed to amplify specific files and also to incorporate sequence domains that are necessary for sequencing. Each primer incorporated overhangs that included three sequence domains in addition to the amplification domain necessary for PCR amplification. The first domain included the sequences necessary for binding to the Illumina flow cell during next generation sequencing. The second domain included a custom sequencing-priming region designed for the sequencing primer to bind. This region allows for sequencing of multiple files in the same sequencing run since the sequencing primer region becomes independent of the oligonucleotide pool. These sequences were generated using Nupack [29], software for thermodynamic analysis of interacting nucleic acid strands, in order to avoid the formation of secondary structure that could interfere with the PCR reaction. The third domain consisted of a 12-nucleotide long degenerate region intended to optimize cluster detection in the Illumina sequencing platform.

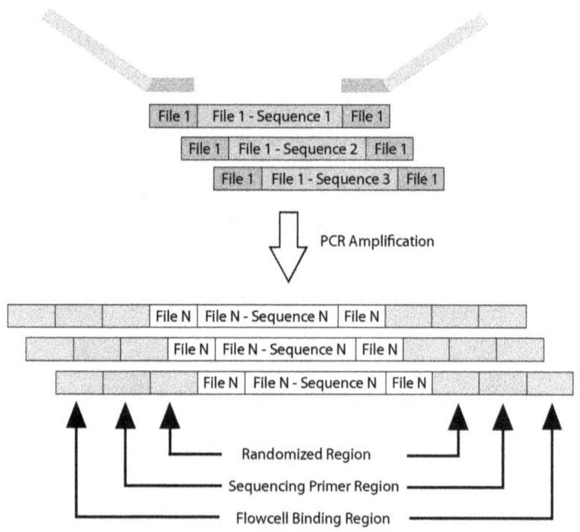

Figure 18. PCR amplifies the strands in the file, and attaches new regions to each end that allow for sequencing.

PCR amplification was performed using Platinum® PCR SuperMix High Fidelity MasterMix from Life Technologies. The cycling conditions were (i) 95°C for 3 min, (ii) 95°C for 20 s, (iii) 55°C for 20 s, (iv) 72°C for 160 s, and (v) looping through (ii)–(iv) 30 times. The PCR amplification output was purified via gel extraction and quantified before next generation sequencing. Finally, the product was sequenced using an Illumina MiSeq sequencing platform.

Synthesis Efficiency. To determine the results in Figure 16, which presents a distribution of strand lengths produced by synthesis, we designed a mathematical model to estimate the nucleotide *coupling efficiency*, which is the probability that a nucleotide will be added to the strand during each of the 120 coupling cycles in the synthesis process. The model says that the likelihood of observing a strand of length n is proportional to

$$\mathit{Intensity} = nN_t p^n (1-p)$$

where N_t is the total number of DNA molecules being synthesized in the array, p is the coupling efficiency, and *Intensity* is the observed flouresence measured from the gel electrophoresis shown in Figure 19. By fitting this model, we estimated the nucleotide coupling efficiency in the synthesis process to be approximately 0.975.

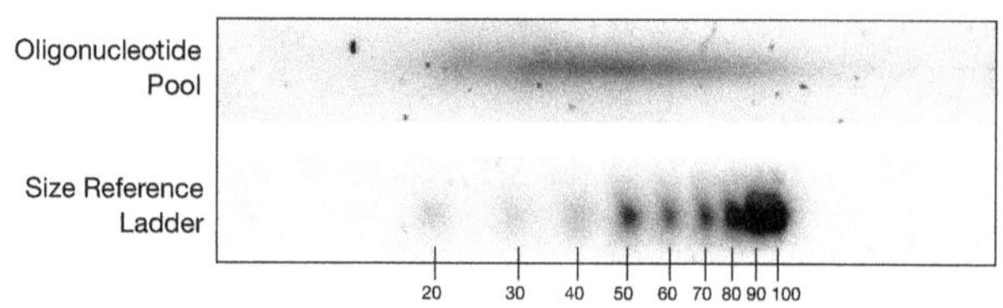

Figure 19. Gel electrophoresis results showing the distribution of strand lengths from the DNA synthesis process.

References

[1] L. Adleman. Molecular computation of solutions to combinatorial problems. *Science*, 266(5187):1021–1024, 1994.

[2] M. E. Allentoft, M. Collins, D. Harker, J. Haile, C. L. Oskam, M. L. Hale, P. F. Campos, J. A. Samaniego, M. T. P. Gilbert, E. Willerslev, G. Zhang, R. P. Scofield, R. N. Holdaway, and M. Bunce. The half-life of DNA in bone: measuring decay kinetics in 158 dated fossils. *Proceedings of the Royal Society of London B: Biological Sciences*, 279(1748):4724–4733, 2012.

[3] C. Bancroft, T. Bowler, B. Bloom, and C. T. Clelland. Long-term storage of information in DNA. *Science*, 293(5536): 1763–1765, 2001.

[4] R. Carlson. Time for new DNA synthesis and sequencing cost curves. http://www.synthesis.cc/2014/02/time-for-new-cost-curves-2014.html, 2014.

[5] Y.-J. Chen, N. Dalchau, N. Srinivas, A. Phillips, L. Cardelli, D. Soloveichik, and G. Seelig. Programmable chemical controllers made from DNA. *Nature Nanotechnology*, 8(10):755–762, 2013.

[6] G. M. Church, Y. Gao, and S. Kosuri. Next-generation digital information storage in DNA. *Science*, 337(6102):1628, 2012.

[7] C. T. Clelland, V. Risca, and C. Bancroft. Hiding messages in DNA microdots. *Nature*, 399:533–534, 1999.

[8] ExtremeTech. New optical laser can increase DVD storage up to one petabyte. http://www.extremetech.com/computing/159245-new-optical-laser-can-increase-dvd-storage-up-to-one-petabyte, 2013.

[9] D. G. Gibson, J. I. Glass, C. Lartigue, V. N. Noskov, R.-Y. Chuang, M. A. Algire, G. A. Benders, M. G. Montague, L. Ma, M. M. Moodie, C. Merryman, S. Vashee, R. Krishnakumar, N. Assad-Garcia, C. Andrews-Pfannkoch, E. A. Denisova, L. Young, Z.-Q. Qi, T. H. Segall-Shapiro, C. H. Calvey, P. P. Parmar, C. A. Hutchison, H. O. Smith, and J. C. Venter. Creation of a bacterial cell controlled by a chemically synthesized genome. *Science*, 329(5987):52–56, 2010.

[10] N. Goldman, P. Bertone, S. Chen, C. Dessimoz, E. M. LeProust, B. Sipos, and E. Birney. Towards practical, high-capacity, low-maintenance information storage in synthesized DNA. *Nature*, 494:77–80, 2013.

[11] R. N. Grass, R. Heckel, M. Puddu, D. Paunescu, and W. J. Stark. Robust chemical preservation of digital information on DNA in silica with error-correcting codes. *Angew. Chem. Int. Ed.*, 54:2552–2555, 2015.

[12] Q. Guo, K. Strauss, L. Ceze, and H. Malvar. High-density image storage using approximate memory cells. In *ASPLOS*, 2016.

[13] D. Huffman. A method for the construction of minimum-redundancy codes. *Proceedings of the IRE*, 40(9):1098–1101, 1952.

[14] IDC. Where in the world is storage. http://www.idc.com/downloads/where_is_storage_infographic_243338.pdf, 2013.

[15] S. Kosuri and G. M. Church. Large-scale de novo DNA synthesis: technologies and applications. *Nature Methods*, 11:499–507, 2014.

[16] A. Leier, C. Richter, W. Banzhaf, and H. Rauhe. Cryptography with DNA binary strands. *Biosystems*, 57(1):13–22, 2000.

[17] M. D. Matteucci and M. H. Caruthers. Synthesis of deoxy-oligonucleotides on a polymer support. *Journal of the American Chemical Society*, 103(11):3185–3191, 1981.

[18] R. Miller. Facebook builds exabyte data centers for cold storage. http://www.datacenterknowledge.com/archives/2013/01/18/facebook-builds-new-data-centers-for-cold-storage/, 2013.

[19] R. A. Muscat, K. Strauss, L. Ceze, and G. Seelig. DNA-based molecular architecture with spatially localized components. In *International Symposium on Computer Architecture*, 2013.

[20] T. P. Niedringhaus, D. Milanova, M. B. Kerby, M. P. Snyder, and A. E. Barron. Landscape of next-generation sequencing technologies. *Anal. Chem.*, 83:4327–4341, 2011.

[21] L. Qian, E. Winfree, and J. Bruck. Neural network computation with DNA strand displacement cascades. *Science*, 475(7356): 368–372, 2011.

[22] I. S. Reed and G. Solomon. Polynomial codes over certain finite fields. *Journal of the Society for Industrial and Applied Mathematics*, 8(2):300–304, 1960.

[23] A. Sampson, J. Nelson, K. Strauss, and L. Ceze. Approximate storage in solid-state memories. In *International Symposium on Microarchitecture*, 2013.

[24] J. J. Schwartz, C. Lee, and J. Shendure. Accurate gene synthesis with tag-directed retrieval of sequence-verified DNA molecules. *Nature Methods*, 9(9):913–915, 2012.

[25] Sony. Sony develops magnetic tape technology with the world's highest recording density. http://www.sony.net/SonyInfo/News/Press/201404/14-044E/, 2014.

[26] K. Takahashi, S. Yaegashi, A. Kameda, and M. Hagiya. Chain reaction systems based on loop dissociation of DNA. In *DNA Computing*, volume 3892 of *Lecture Notes in Computer Science*, pages 347–358. Springer Berlin Heidelberg, 2006.

[27] B. Talawar. A crossbar interconnection network in DNA. In *Workshop on High Performance Computational Biology*, 2015.

[28] S. M. H. T. Yazdi, Y. Yuan, J. Ma, H. Zhao, and O. Milenkovic. A Rewritable, Random-Access DNA-Based Storage System. *Nature Scientific Reports*, 5(14318), 2015.

[29] J. N. Zadeh, B. R. Wolfe, and N. A. Pierce. Nucleic acid sequence design via efficient ensemble defect optimization. *Journal of Computational Chemistry*, 32(3):439–452, 2011.

Generating Configurable Hardware from Parallel Patterns

Raghu Prabhakar
Stanford University
raghup17@stanford.edu

David Koeplinger
Stanford University
dkoeplin@stanford.edu

Kevin J. Brown
Stanford University
kjbrown@stanford.edu

HyoukJoong Lee
Stanford University
Google, USA
hyouklee@stanford.edu

Christopher De Sa
Stanford University
cdesa@stanford.edu

Christos Kozyrakis
Stanford University
EPFL
kozyraki@stanford.edu

Kunle Olukotun
Stanford University
kunle@stanford.edu

Abstract

In recent years the computing landscape has seen an increasing shift towards specialized accelerators. Field programmable gate arrays (FPGAs) are particularly promising for the implementation of these accelerators, as they offer significant performance and energy improvements over CPUs for a wide class of applications and are far more flexible than fixed-function ASICs. However, FPGAs are difficult to program. Traditional programming models for reconfigurable logic use low-level hardware description languages like Verilog and VHDL, which have none of the productivity features of modern software languages but produce very efficient designs, and low-level software languages like C and OpenCL coupled with high-level synthesis (HLS) tools that typically produce designs that are far less efficient.

Functional languages with parallel patterns are a better fit for hardware generation because they provide high-level abstractions to programmers with little experience in hardware design and avoid many of the problems faced when generating hardware from imperative languages. In this paper, we identify two important optimizations for using parallel patterns to generate efficient hardware: tiling and metapipelining. We present a general representation of tiled parallel patterns, and provide rules for automatically tiling patterns and generating metapipelines. We demonstrate experimentally that these optimizations result in speedups up to 39.4× on a set of benchmarks from the data analytics domain.

Keywords Hardware generation; tiling; metapipelining; parallel patterns; reconfigurable hardware; FPGAs

ASPLOS '16 April 2–6, 2016, Atlanta, Georgia, USA.

DOI: http://dx.doi.org/10.1145/http://dx.doi.org/10.1145/2872362.2872415

1. Introduction

The slowdown of Moore's law and the end of Dennard scaling has forced a radical change in the architectural landscape. Computing systems are becoming increasingly parallel and heterogeneous, relying on larger numbers of cores and specialized accelerators. Field programmable gate arrays (FPGAs) are particularly promising as an acceleration technology, as they can offer performance and energy improvements for a wide class of applications while also providing the reprogrammability and flexibility of software. Applications which exhibit large degrees of spatial and temporal locality and which contain relatively small amounts of control flow, such as those in the image processing [22, 7], financial analytics [31, 17, 53], and scientific computing domains [45, 2, 12, 55], can especially benefit from hardware acceleration with FPGAs. FPGAs have also recently been used to accelerate personal assistant systems [24] and machine learning algorithms like deep belief networks [33, 34].

The performance and energy advantages of FPGAs are now motivating the integration of reconfigurable logic into data center computing infrastructures. Both Microsoft [40] and Baidu [33] have recently announced such systems. These systems have initially been in the form of banks of FPGA accelerators which communicate with CPUs through Infiniband or PCIe [30]. Work is also being done on heterogeneous motherboards with shared CPU-FPGA memory [23]. The recent acquisition of Altera by Intel suggests that systems with tighter, high performance on-chip integration of CPUs and FPGAs are now on the horizon.

The chief limiting factor in the general adoption of FPGAs is that their programming model is currently inaccessible to most software developers. Creating custom accelerator architectures on an FPGA is a complex task, requiring the coordination of large numbers of small, local memories, communication with off-chip memory, and the synchronization of many compute stages. Because of this complexity,

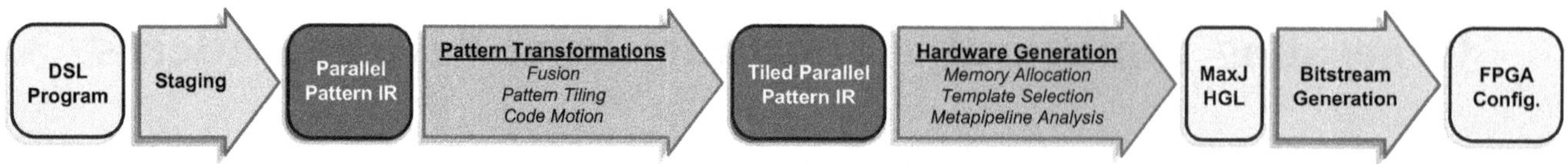

Figure 1. System diagram

attaining the best performance on FPGAs has traditionally required detailed hardware design using hardware description languages (HDL) like Verilog and VHDL. This low-level programming model has largely limited the creation of efficient custom hardware to experts in digital logic and hardware design.

In the past ten years, FPGA vendors and researchers have attempted to make reconfigurable logic more accessible to software programmers with the development of high-level synthesis (HLS) tools, designed to automatically infer register transaction level (RTL) specifications from higher level software programs. To better tailor these tools to software developers, HLS work has typically focused on imperative languages like C/C++, SystemC, and OpenCL [50]. Unfortunately, there are numerous challenges in inferring hardware from imperative programs. Imperative languages are inherently sequential and effectful. C programs in particular offer a number of challenges in alias analysis and detecting false dependencies [19], typically requiring numerous user annotations to help HLS tools discover parallelism and determine when various hardware structures can be used. Achieving efficient hardware with HLS tools often requires an iterative process to determine which user annotations are necessary, especially for software developers less familiar with the intricacies of hardware design [16].

Functional languages are a much more natural fit for high-level hardware generation as they have limited to no side effects and more naturally express a dataflow representation of applications which can be mapped directly to hardware pipelines [6]. Furthermore, the order of operations in functional languages is only defined by data dependencies rather than sequential statement order, exposing significant fine-grained parallelism that can be exploited efficiently in custom hardware.

Parallel patterns like *map* and *reduce* are an increasingly popular extension to functional languages which add semantic information about memory access patterns and inherent data parallelism that is highly exploitable by both software and hardware. Previous work [20, 4] has shown that compilers can utilize parallel patterns to generate C- or OpenCL-based HLS programs and add certain annotations automatically. However, like hand-written HLS, the quality of the generated hardware is still highly variable. Apart from the practical advantage of building on existing tools, generating imperative code from a functional language only to have the HLS tool attempt to re-infer a functional representation of the program is a suboptimal solution because higher-level semantic knowledge in the original program is easily lost. In this paper, we describe a series of compilation steps which automatically generate a low-level, efficient hardware design from an intermediate representation (IR) based on parallel patterns. As seen in Figure 1, these steps fall into two categories: high level parallel pattern transformations (Section 4), and low level analyses and hardware generation optimizations (Section 5).

One of the challenges in generating efficient hardware from high level programs is in handling arbitrarily large data structures. FPGAs have a limited amount of fast local memory and accesses to main memory are expensive in terms of both performance and energy. Loop tiling has been extensively studied as a solution to this problem, as it allows data structures with predictable access patterns to be broken up into fixed size chunks. On FPGAs, these chunks can be stored locally in buffers. Tiling can also increase the reuse of these buffers by reordering computation, thus reducing the number of total accesses to main memory. Previous work on automated tiling transformations has focused almost exclusively on imperative C-like programs with only affine, data-independent memory access patterns. No unified procedure exists for automatically tiling a functional IR with parallel patterns. In this paper, we outline a novel set of simple transformation rules which can be used to automatically tile parallel patterns. Because these rules rely on pattern matching rather than a mathematical model of the entire program, they can be used even on programs which contain random and data-dependent accesses.

Our tiled intermediate representation exposes memory regions with high data locality, making them ideal candidates to be allocated on-chip. Parallel patterns provide rich semantic information on the nature of the parallel computation at multiple levels of nesting as well as memory access patterns at each level. In this work, we preserve certain semantic properties of memory regions and analyze memory access patterns in order to automatically infer hardware structures like FIFOs, double buffers, and caches. We exploit parallelism at multiple levels by automatically inferring and generating *metapipelines*, hierarchical pipelines where each stage can itself be composed of pipelines and other parallel constructs. Our code generation approach involves mapping parallel IR constructs to a set of parameterizable hardware templates, where each template exploits a specific parallel pattern or memory access pattern. These hardware templates are implemented using a low-level Java-based hardware generation language (HGL) called MaxJ.

In this paper we make the following contributions:

- We describe a systematic set of rules for tiling parallel patterns, including a single, general pattern used to tile all patterns with fixed output size. Unlike previous automatic tiling work, these rules are based on pattern matching and therefore do not restrict all memory accesses within the program to be affine.
- We demonstrate a method for automatically inferring complex hardware structures like double buffers, caches, CAMs, and banked BRAMs from a parallel pattern IR. We also show how to automatically generate *metapipelines*, which are a generalization of pipelines that greatly increase design throughput.
- We present experimental results for a set of benchmark applications from the data analytics domain running on an FPGA and show the performance impact of the transformations and hardware templates presented.

2. Related Work

Tiling Previous work on automated loop tiling has largely focused on tiling imperative programs using polyhedral analysis [9, 37]. There are many existing tools—such as Pluto [10], PoCC [38], CHiLL [15], and Polly [21]—that use polyhedral analysis to automatically tile and parallelize programs. These tools restrict memory accesses within loops to affine functions of the loop iterators. As a consequence, while they perform well on affine sections of programs, they fail on commonly occurring data-dependent operations like *filters* and *groupBys* [8]. In order to handle these operations, recent work has proposed using preprocessing steps which segment programs into affine and non-affine sections prior to running polyhedral analysis tools [51].

While the above work focused on the analysis of imperative programs, our work analyzes functional parallel patterns, which offer a strictly higher-level representation than simple imperative *for* loops. In this paper, we show that because of the additional semantic information available in patterns like *groupBy* and *filter*, parallel patterns can be automatically tiled using simple transformation rules, without the restriction that all memory accesses are purely affine. Little previous work has been done on automated tiling of functional programs composed of arbitrarily nested parallel patterns. Hielscher proposes a set of formal rules for tiling parallel operators *map*, *reduce*, and *scan* in the Parakeet JIT compiler, but these rules can be applied only for a small subset of nesting combinations [25]. Spartan [26] is a runtime system with a set of high-level operators (e.g., *map* and *reduce*) on multi-dimensional arrays, which automatically tiles and distributes the arrays in a way that minimizes the communication cost between nodes in cluster environments. In contrast to our work, Spartan operates on a tiled representation for distributed CPU computation and does attempt to optimize performance on individual compute units.

Hardware from high-level languages Generating hardware from high-level languages has been widely studied for decades. CHiMPS [41] generates hardware from ANSI C code by mapping each C language construct in a dataflow graph to an HDL block. Kiwi [44] translates a set of C# parallel constructs (e.g., *event*, *monitor*, and *lock*) to corresponding hardware units. Bluespec [3] generates hardware from purely functional descriptions based on Haskell. Chisel [5] is an embedded language in Scala for hardware generation. AutoPilot [54] is a commercial HLS tool that generates hardware from C/C++/SystemC languages. Despite their success in raising the level of abstraction compared to hardware description languages, programmers are still required to write programs at a low-level and express how computations are pipelined and parallelized. Our work abstracts away the implementation details from programmers by using high-level parallel patterns, and applies compiler transformations to automatically pipeline and parallelize operations and exploit on-chip memory for locality.

Existing hardware synthesis tools are limited in their ability to automatically infer and generate coarse-grained pipelines. A traditional software pipelining approach is typically used on innermost loop bodies consisting only of primitive operations. Optimizations like *unroll-and-jam*, and *unroll-and-squash* [35] also attempt to exploit pipelined parallelism, but target outer parallel loops with inner sequential loops. To pipeline imperfectly nested loops, some commercial high-level synthesis tools like Vivado [1] unroll all inner loops and then employ traditional software pipelining. Not only does this approach generate needlessly large designs for large benchmarks, it also suffers from long compilation times due to the complexity in scheduling a large number of unrolled instructions. More recent works like ElasticFlow [49] and CGPA [29] generate coarse-grained pipelines using FIFOs in between stages for communication. However, they handle only a restricted form of data access patterns and a restricted number of nesting levels. Our metapipelining technique is more general than previous approaches because: (i) metapipeline stages are decoupled using double buffers, therefore not restricting data access patterns, (ii) metapipelines are easily composed and nested to any number of levels, and (iii) metapipelines can handle dynamic rate mismatches as they use asynchronous handshaking for inter-stage synchronization, thereby obviating the need to calculate static initiation interval as well as knowing loop trip counts ahead of time.

Recent work has explored using polyhedral analysis with HLS to optimize for data locality on FPGAs [39]. Using polyhedral analysis, the compiler is able to promote memory references to on-chip memory and parallelize independent loop iterations with more hardware units. However, the compiler is not able to analyze loops that include non-affine accesses, limiting the coverage of applications that can be generated for hardware. Our work can handle parallel pat-

Parallel Pattern Definition		High Level Language Example	PPL Example
Multidimensional			

`Map(d)(m)`	: V_D	`// Size s vector multiplied by 2`
		`x.`**`map`**`{ e => 2*e }`
		`// Addition of two size s vectors`
		`x.`**`zip`**`(y){ (a,b) => a + b }`
			`map``(s){i => 2*x(i) }`
			
			`map``(s){i => x(i) + y(i) }`

`MultiFold(d)(r)(z)(f)(c)`	: V_R	`// Reduction of vector of s elements`
		`x.`**`fold`**`(1){ (a,b) => a * b }`
		
		`// Row summation in s x t matrix`
		`x.`**`map`**`{ row =>`
		`  row.`**`fold`**`(0){ (a,b) => a + b }`
		`}`
			`multiFold``(s)(1)(1){ i =>`
			`  (0, acc => acc + x(i))`
			`}{ (a,b) => a + b }`
			
			`multiFold``(s,t)(r)(zeros(s)){ (i,j) =>`
			`  (i, acc => acc + x(i,j) )`
			`}{ (a,b) =>` **`map`**`(s){ i => a(i) + b(i) } }`

One-dimensional			

`FlatMap(d)(n)`	: V_1	`// Filter positives from s elements`
		`x.`**`flatMap`**`{ e =>`
		`  if (e > 0) [e] else [] }`
			`flatMap``(s){ i =>`
			`  if (x(i) > 0) [x(i)] else [] }`

`GroupByFold(d)(z)(g)(c)`	: $(K,V)_1$	`// Histogram with bin width 10`
		`x.`**`groupByFold`**`(0){ e =>`
		`  (e/10, 1)`
		`}{ (a,b) => a + b }`
			`groupByFold``(s)(0){ i =>`
			`  (x(i)/10, acc => acc + 1)`
			`}{ (a,b) => a + b }`

User-defined Values			
`d :` $Integer_D$	input domain	`m :` $Index_D$ `=> V`	value function
`r :` $Integer_R$	output range	`n : Index =>` V_1	multi-value function
`z :` V_R	init accumulator	`f :` $Index_D$ `=> (`$Index_R$`,` V_R `=>` V_R`)`	(location, value) function
`c : (`V_R`,`V_R`) =>` V_R	combine accumulator	`g : Index => (K, V => V)`$_1$	(key, value) function

Figure 2. Definitions and usage examples of supported parallel patterns.

terns with non-affine accesses by inferring required hardware blocks (e.g., FIFOs and CAMs) for non-affine accesses, while aggressively using on-chip memory for affine parts.

As high-level parallel patterns become increasingly popular to overcome the shortcomings of C based languages, researchers have recently studied generating hardware from functional parallel patterns. Lime [4] embeds high-level computational patterns (e.g., *map*, *reduce*, *split*, and *join*) in Java and automatically targets CPUs, GPUs, and FPGAs without modifying the code. Our compiler manages a broader set of parallel patterns (e.g., *groupBy*) and applies transformations even when patterns are nested, which is common in a large number of real-world applications. Recent work has explored targeting nested parallel patterns to FPGAs [20]. By exploiting the access patterns of nested patterns to store sequential memory accesses to on-chip memory and parallelizing the computation with strip-mining, the compiler can generate hardware that efficiently utilizes memory bandwidth. However, the compiler does not automatically tile patterns for data locality or implement metapipelines for nested parallel patterns, which we show are essential components for generating efficient hardware. Overall, our work is the first to show a complete method for automatically tiling parallel patterns to improve locality for individual compute units and a process for inferring hardware metapipelines from nested parallel patterns.

3. Parallel Patterns

Parallel patterns are becoming a popular programming abstraction for writing high level applications that can still be efficiently mapped to hardware targets such as multicore [32, 36, 46], clusters [18, 52, 26], GPUs [13, 28], and FPGAs [4, 20]. In addition, they have been shown to provide high productivity when implementing applications in a wide variety of domains [48, 42].We refer to the definitions presented in Figure 2 as the parallel pattern language (PPL). The definitions on the left represent the atoms in the intermediate language used in our compiler for analysis, optimization, and code generation. The code snippets on the right show common examples of how users typically interact with these patterns in a functional programming language via collections operations and how those examples are represented in PPL. The syntactic structure is essentially the same except that the input domain is inferred from the shape of the input collection. Using explicit indices in the intermediate language allows us to model more user-facing patterns and more input access patterns with fewer internal primitives.

We separate our parallel patterns into two groups. Multidimensional patterns have an arbitrary arity domain and range, but are restricted to a range which is a fixed function of the domain. One-dimensional patterns can have a dynamic output size. All patterns generate output values by applying a function to every index in the domain. Each pattern then merges these values into the final output in a differ-

```
//data to be clustered, size n x d
val points: Array[Array[Float]] = ...

// current centroids, size k x d
val centroids: Array[Array[Float]] = ...

// Assign each point to the closest centroid by grouping
val groupedPoints = points.groupBy { pt1 =>
  // Assign current point to the closest centroid
  val minDistWithIndex = centroids.map { pt2 =>
    pt1.zip(pt2).map { case (a,b) => square(a - b) }.sum
  }.zipWithIndex.minBy(p => p._1)
  minDistWithIndex._2
}

// Average of points assigned to each centroid
val newCentroids = groupedPoints.map { case (k,v) =>
  v.reduce { (a,b) =>
    a.zip(b).map { case (x,y) => x + y }
  }.map { e => e / v.length }
}.toArray
```

Figure 3. k-means clustering implemented using Scala collections. In Scala, _1 and _2 refer to the first and second value contained within a tuple.

```
points: Array2D[Float](n,d) // data to be clustered
centroids: Array2D[Float](k,d) // current centroids

// Sum and number of points assigned to each centroid
(sums,counts) = multiFold(n)((k,d),k)(zeros((k,d),k)){ i =>
  pt1 = points.slice(i, *)
  // Assign current point to the closest centroid
  minDistWithIndex = fold(k)((max, -1)){ j =>
    pt2 = centroids.slice(j, *)
    dist = fold(d)(0){ p =>
      acc => acc + square(pt1(p) - pt2(p))
    }{ (a,b) => a + b }
    acc => if (acc._1 < dist) acc else (dist, j)
  }{ (a,b) => if (a._1 < b._1) a else b }

  minDistIndex = minDistWithIndex._2
  sumFunc = ((minDistIndex, 0), acc => {
    pt = points.slice(i, *)
    map(d){ j => acc(j) + pt(j) }
  })
  countFunc = (minDistIndex, acc => acc + 1)

  (sumFunc, countFunc)
}{ (a,b) => {
  pt = map(k,d){ (i,j) => a._1(i,j) + b._1(i,j) }
  count = map(k){ i => a._2(i) + b._2(i) }
  (pt, count)
} }

// Average assigned points to compute new centroids
newCentroids = map(k,d){ (i,j) =>
  sums(i,j) / counts(i)
}
```

Figure 4. k-means clustering represented using the parallel patterns in Figure 2 after fusion and code motion.

ent way. The output type V can be a scalar or structure of scalars. We currently do not allow nested arrays, only multidimensional arrays. We denote multidimensional array types as V_R, which denotes a tensor of element type V and arity R. In Figure 2 subscript R always represents the arity of the output range, and D the arity of the input domain.

Map generates a single element per index, aggregating the results into a fixed-size output collection. Note that the value function can close over an arbitrary number of input collections, and therefore this pattern can represent classic parallel operations like *map*, *zip*, and *zipWithIndex*.

MultiFold is a generalization of a *fold* which reduces generated values into a specified region of a (potentially) larger accumulator using an associative combine function. The initial value z is required to be an identity element of this function, and must have the same size and shape as the final output. The main function f generates an index specifying the location within the accumulator at which to reduce the generated value. We currently require the generated values to have the same arity as the full accumulator, but they may be of any size up to the size of the accumulator. Note that a traditional *fold* is the special case of MultiFold where every generated value is the full size of the accumulator. f then converts each index into a function that consumes the specified slice of the current accumulator and returns the new slice. If the pattern's implementation maintains multiple partial accumulators in parallel, the combine function c reduces them into the final result.

FlatMap generates an arbitrary number of values per index. These values are all concatenated into a flattened output. As the output size can only be determined dynamically, we restrict FlatMap to one-dimensional domains so that dynamically growing the output is easily defined. Note that this primitive also easily expresses a *filter*.

GroupByFold reduces generated values into one of many buckets where the bucket is selected by generating a key along with each value, i.e. it is a fused version of a *groupBy* followed by a *fold* over each bucket. The operation is similar to *MultiFold* except that the key-space cannot be determined in advance and so the output size is unknown. Therefore we also restrict this operation to one-dimensional domains.

Example Now that we have defined the operations, we will use them to implement k-means clustering as an example application. For reference, first consider k-means implemented using the standard Scala collections operations, as shown in Figure 3. We will use this application as a running example throughout the remainder of this paper, as it exemplifies many of the advantages of using parallel patterns as an abstraction for generating efficient hardware. k-means consumes a set of n sample points of dimensionality d and attempts to cluster those points by finding the k best cluster centroids for the samples. This is achieved by iteratively refining the centroid values. (We show only one iteration in Figure 3 for simplicity.) First, every sample point is assigned to the closest current centroid by computing the distance between every sample and every centroid. Then new centroid

Pattern		Strip Mined Pattern

`T[ Map(d)(m) ]`	=	`MultiFold(d/b)(d)(zeros(d)){ i =>`
		`  (i, acc => Map(b)(T[m]) )`
		`}(_)`

`T[ MultiFold(d)(r)(z)(g)(c) ]`	=	`MultiFold(d/b)(r)(T[z]){ i =>`
		`  (i, acc => T[c](acc, MultiFold(b)(r)(T[z])(T[g])(T[c])) )`
		`}(T[c])`

`T[ GroupByFold(d)(z)(h)(c) ]`	=	`GroupByFold(d/b)(T[z]){ i =>`
		`  GroupByFold(b)(T[z])(T[h])(T[c])`
		`}(T[c])`

`T[ FlatMap(d)(f) ]`	=	`FlatMap(d/b){i => FlatMap(b)(T[f]) }`

Table 1. Strip mining transformation rules for parallel patterns defined in Figure 2.

values are computed by averaging all the samples assigned to each centroid. This process repeats until the centroid values stop changing. Previous work [43, 11, 14] has shown how to stage a DSL application like k-means, lowering it into a parallel pattern IR similar to ours, as well as how to perform multiple high-level optimizations automatically on the IR. One of the most important of these optimizations is fusing patterns together, both vertically (to decrease the reuse distance between producer-consumer relationships) and horizontally (to eliminate redundant traversals over the same domain). Figure 4 shows the structure of k-means after it has been lowered into PPL and fusion rules have been applied. We have also converted the nested arrays in the Scala example to our multidimensional arrays. This translation requires the insertion of *slice* operations in certain locations, which produce a view of a subset of the underlying data. In our implementation, we use the Delite compiler framework [46] to stage applications. For the remainder of this paper, we will assume a high-level translation from user code to PPL exists and always start from the parallel pattern representation.

4. Pattern Transformations

One of the key challenges of generating efficient custom architectures from high level languages is in coping with arbitrarily large data structures. Since main memory accesses are expensive and area is limited, our goal is to store a working set in the FPGA's local memory for as long as possible. Ideally, we also want to hide memory transfer latencies by overlapping communication with computation using prefetching hardware blocks. To this end, in this section we describe a method for automatically tiling parallel patterns to improve program locality and data reuse. Like classic loop tiling, our pattern tiling method is composed of two transformations: strip mining and interchange. We assume here that our input is a PPL representation of a program and that well known target-agnostic transformations like fusion, code motion, and struct unwrapping have already been run.

Strip mining The strip mining algorithm is defined here using two passes over the IR. The first pass partitions each pattern's iteration domain d into tiles of size b by breaking the pattern into a pair of perfectly nested patterns. The outer pattern operates over the strided index domain, expressed here as d/b, while the inner pattern operates on a tile of size b. For the sake of brevity this notation ignores the case where b does not perfectly divide d. This case is trivially solved with the addition of *min* checks on the domain of the inner loop. Table 1 gives an overview of the rules used by transformer (denoted T) to strip mine parallel patterns. In addition to splitting up the domain, patterns are transformed by recursively strip mining all functions within that pattern. Map is strip mined by reducing its domain and range and nesting it within a MultiFold. Note that the strided MultiFold writes to each memory location only once. In this case we indicate the MultiFold's combination function as unused with an underscore. As defined in Figure 2, the MultiFold, GroupByFold, and FlatMap patterns have the property that a perfectly nested form of a single instance of one of these patterns is equivalent to a single "flattened" form of that same pattern. This property allows these patterns to be strip mined by breaking them up into a set of perfectly nested patterns of the same type as the original pattern.

The second strip mining pass converts array slices and accesses with statically predictable access patterns into slices and accesses of larger, explicitly defined array memory tiles. We define tiles which have a size statically known to fit on the FPGA using array copies. Copies generated during strip mining can then be used to infer buffers during hardware generation. Array tiles which have overlap, such as those generated from sliding windows in convolution, are marked with metadata in the IR as having some reuse factor. Array copies with reuse have generation rules which minimize the number of redundant reads to main memory when possible.

Table 2 demonstrates how our rules can be used to strip mine a set of simple data parallel operations. We use the *copy* infix function on arrays to designate array copies in these examples, using similar syntax as array *slice*. We assume in these examples that common subexpression elimination (CSE) and code motion transformation passes have been run after strip mining to eliminate duplicate copies and to move array tiles out of the innermost patterns. In these examples, strip mining creates tiled copies of input collections that we can later directly use to infer read buffers.

High Level Language	PPL	Strip Mined PPL

// Element-wise Map
val x: Array[Float] // length d
x.map{e => 2*e}
	map(d){i => 2*x(i)}	multiFold(d/b)(d)(zeros(d)){ii =>
		  xTile = x.copy(b + ii)
		  (i, map(b)(b){i => 2*xTile(i) })
		}(_)

// Sums along matrix rows
val x: Array[Array[Float]] // m x n
x.map{ row =>
  row.fold(0){ (a,b) => a + b }
}
	multiFold(m,n)(m)(zeros(m)){ (i,j) =>
	  (i, acc => acc + x(i,j))
	}{(a,b) =>
	  map(n){(j) => a(j) + b(j)}
	}
		multiFold(m/b0,n/b1)(m)(zeros(m)){ (ii,jj) =>
		  xTile = x.copy(b0 + ii, b1 + jj)
		  tile = multiFold(b0,b1)(b0)(zeros(b0)){ (i,j) =>
		    (i, acc => acc + xTile(i,j))
		  }{(a,b) => map(b0){i => a(i) + b(i)} }
		  (ii, acc => map(b0){j => acc(j) + tile(j)})
		}{(a,b) =>
		  multiFold(m/b0)(m)(zeros(m)){ii =>
		    aTile = a.copy(b0 + ii)
		    bTile = a.copy(b0 + ii)
		    (ii, acc => map(b0){i => aTile(i) + bTile(i)})
		  }{(a,b) => map(m){i => a(i) + b(i)}}
		}

// Simple Filter
val x: Array[Float] // length d
x.flatMap{ e =>
  if (e > 0) e else []
}
	flatMap(d){i =>
	  if (x(i) > 0) x(i) else []
	}
		flatMap(d/b)(1){ii =>
		  eTile = x.copy(b + ii)
		  flatMap(b){i =>
		    if (eTile(i) > 0) eTile(i) else []
		}}

// Histogram Calculation
val x: Array[Float] // length d
x.groupByFold(0){ r =>
  (r/10, 1)
}{ (a,b) => a + b }
	groupByFold(d)(0){i =>
	  (x(i)/10, 1)
	}{(a,b) => a + b }
		groupByFold(d/b)(0){ii =>
		  xTile = x.copy(b + ii)
		  groupByFold(b)(0){i =>
		    (xTile(i)/10, 1)
		  }{(a,b) => a + b}
		}{(a,b) => a + b}

Table 2. Examples of the parallel pattern strip mining transformation on Map, MultiFold, FlatMap, and GroupByFold

High Level Language	Strip Mined PPL	Interchanged PPL

// Matrix Multiplication
x: Array[Array[Float]] // m x p
y: Array[Array[Float]] // p x n
z = x.map{row =>
  y.map{col =>
    row.zipWith(col){(a,b) =>
      a * b
    }.sum
  }
}
	multiFold(m/b0,n/b1)(m,n)(zeros(m,n)){(ii,jj) =>
	  ((ii,jj), zTile =>
	    map(b0,b1){(i,j) =>
	      tile = multiFold(p/b2)(1)(0){ kk =>
	        xTile = x.copy(b0 + ii, b2 + kk)
	        yTile = y.copy(b2 + kk, b1 + jj)
	        dprod = fold(b2)(0){ k =>
	          acc => acc + xTile(i,k) * yTile(k,j)
	        }{(a,b) => a + b})
	        (0, elemTile => elemTile + dprod)
	      }{(a,b) => a + b}
	      zTile(i,j) + tile
	  })
	}(_)
		multiFold(m/b0,n/b1)(m,n)(zeros(m,n)){(ii,jj) =>
		  tile = multiFold(p/b2)(b0,b1)(...){kk =>
		    xTile = x.copy(b0 + ii, b2 + kk)
		    yTile = y.copy(b2 + kk, b1 + jj)
		    (0, elemTile =>
		      map(b0,b1){(i,j) =>
		        dprod = fold(b2)(0){ k =>
		          acc => acc + xTile(i,j) * yTile(j,k)
		        }{(a,b) => a + b}
		        elemTile(i,j) + dprod
		    })
		  }{(a,b) =>
		    map(b0,b1){(i,j) => a(i,j) + b(i,j)
		  }
		  ((ii,jj), zTile =>
		    map(b0,b1){(i,j) => zTile(i,j) + tile(i,j)}
		  })
		}(_)

Table 3. Example of the pattern interchange transformation applied to matrix multiplication.

Pattern interchange Given an intermediate representation with strip mined nested parallel patterns, we now need to interchange patterns to increase the reuse of newly created data tiles. This can be achieved by moving strided patterns out of unstrided patterns. However, as with imperative loops, it is not sound to arbitrarily change the order of nested parallel patterns. We use two rules for pattern interchange adapted from a previously established *Collect-Reduce* reordering rule for computation on clusters [11]. These rules both match on the special case of MultiFold where every iteration updates the entire accumulator, which we refer to here as a *fold*. The first interchange rule defines how to move a scalar, strided *fold* out of an unstrided Map, transforming the nested loop into a strided *fold* of a Map. Note that this also changes the combination function of the *fold* into a Map. The second rule is the inverse of the first, allowing us to reorder a strided MultiFold with no reduction function (i.e. the outer pattern of a tiled Map) out of an unstrided *fold*. This creates a strided MultiFold of a scalar *fold*. We apply these two rules whenever possible to increase the reuse of tiled inputs.

Imperfectly nested parallel patterns commonly occur either due to the way the original user program was structured or as a result of aggressive vertical fusion run prior to tiling. Interchange on imperfectly nested patterns requires splitting patterns into perfectly nested sections. However, splitting and reordering trades temporal locality of intermediate values for increased reuse of data tiles. In hardware, this can involve creating more main memory reads or larger on-chip buffers for intermediate results so that less reads need to be done for input and output data. This tradeoff between memory reads and increased buffer usage requires more complex cost modeling. We use a simple heuristic to determine whether to split fused loops: we split and interchange patterns only when the intermediate result created after splitting and interchanging is statically known to fit on the FPGA. This handles the simple case where the FPGA has unused on-chip buffers and allocating more on-chip memory guarantees a decrease in the number of main memory reads. Future work will examine ways to statically model the tradeoff between main memory accesses and local buffers near 100% on-chip memory utilization.

Table 3 shows a simple example of the application of our pattern interchange rules on matrix multiplication. We assume here that code motion has been run again after pattern interchange has completed. In matrix multiplication, we interchange the perfectly nested strided MultiFold and the unstrided Map. This ordering increases the reuse of the copied tile of matrix y and changes the scalar reduction into a tile-wise reduction. Note that the partial result calculation and the inner reduction can now be vertically fused.

Discussion The rules we outline here for automatic tiling of parallel patterns are target-agnostic. However, tile copies should only be made explicit for devices with scratchpad memory. Architectures with hierarchical memory systems effectively maintain views of subsections of memory automatically through caching, making explicit copies on these architectures a waste of both compute cycles and memory.

We currently require the user to explicitly specify tile sizes for all dimensions which require tiling. In future work, tile sizes for all pattern dimensions will instead be determined by the compiler through automated tile size selection using modeling and design space exploration.

Example We conclude this section with a complete example of tiling the k-means clustering algorithm, starting from the fused representation shown in Figure 4. We assume here that we wish to tile the number of input points, n, with tile size b_0 and the number of clusters, k, with tile size b_1 but not the number of dimensions, d. This is representative of machine learning classification problems where the number of input points and number of labels is large, but the number of features for each point is relatively small.

Figure 5 gives a comparison of the k-means clustering algorithm after strip mining and after pattern interchange. During strip mining, we create tiles for both the *points* and *centroids* arrays, which helps us to take advantage of main memory burst reads. However, in the strip mined version, we still fully calculate the closest centroid for each point. This requires the entirety of *centroids* to be read for each point. We increase the reuse of each tile of *centroids* by first splitting the calculation of the closest centroid label from the MultiFold (Figure 5a. line 5). The iteration over the centroids tile is then perfectly nested within the iteration over the points. Interchanging these two iterations allows us to reuse the centroids tile across points, thus decreasing the total number of main memory reads for this array by a factor of b_0. This decrease comes at the expense of changing the intermediate (distance, label) pair for a single point to a set of intermediate pairs for an entire tile of *points*. Since the created intermediate result has size $2b_0$, we statically determine that this is an advantageous tradeoff and use the split and interchanged form of the algorithm.

5. Hardware Generation

In this section, we describe how the tiled intermediate representation is translated into an efficient FPGA design. FPGAs are composed of various logic, register, and memory resources. These resources are typically configured for a specific hardware design using a hardware description language (HDL) that is translated into an FPGA configuration file. Our approach to FPGA hardware generation translates our parallel pattern IR into MaxJ, a Java-based hardware generation language (HGL), which is in turn used to generate an HDL. This is simpler than generating HDL directly because MaxJ performs tasks such as automatic pipelining of innermost loops and other low-level hardware optimizations.

Hardware generation follows a template-based approach. We analyze the structure of the parallel patterns in the IR to determine the correct template to translate the pattern to hardware. Table 4 lists the templates and their corresponding IR constructs in three classes: memories, pipelined execution units, and state machine controllers. *Buffer*, *Double buffer*, and *Cache* are different on-chip memory templates intended to capture both regular and data-dependent access patterns. In particular, the *double buffer* template is used to decouple execution stages and support dynamic rate mismatch between producer and consumer stages. Templates labeled as *Pipelined Execution Units* are used to support different kinds of innermost parallel patterns, as described in Table 4. The *Controller* templates implement a specific form of control flow using asynchronous handshaking signals. The *Sequential*, *Parallel*, and *Metapipeline* controllers all orchestrate execution of a list of templates; *Sequential* enforces linear execution order, *Parallel* enforces parallel execution with a barrier at the end, and *MetaPipeline* enforces pipelined execution. *Tile Memory* controllers correspond to off-chip memory channels that load tiles of data into one of the on-chip memory templates. Each template can be composed with other templates. For example, a *Metapipeline controller* could be composed of multiple *Parallel controller*s, each of which could contain pipelined *Vector* or *Tree reduction* units. We next describe the key features in the IR which we use to infer each of these template classes.

Memory Allocation Generating efficient FPGA hardware requires effective usage of on-chip memories (buffers). Prior to generating MaxJ, we run an analysis pass to allocate buffers for arrays based on data access patterns and size. All arrays with statically known sizes, such as array *copies* generated in the tiling transformation described in Section 4, are assigned to buffers. Dynamically sized arrays are kept in main memory and we generate caches for any non-affine ac-

```
1   (sums,counts) = multiFold(n/b0)((k,d),k)(...){ii =>
2     pt1Tile = points.copy(b0 + ii, *)
3     multiFold(b0)((k,d),k)(zeros(1,d),0){ i =>
4       pt1 = pt1Tile.slice(i, *)
5       minDistWithIndex = multiFold(k/b1)(1)((max, -1)){ jj =>
6         pt2Tile = centroids.copy(b1 + jj, *)
7         minIndTile = fold(b1)((max,-1)){ j =>
8           pt2 = pt2Tile.slice(j, *)
9           dist = distance(pt1, pt2)
10          acc => if (acc._1 < dist) acc else (dist, j+jj)
11        }{ (a,b) => if (a._1 < b._1) a else b }
12
13        (0, acc =>
14          if (acc._1 < minIndTile._1) acc else minIndTile)
15      }{(a,b) =>
16        if (a._1 < b._1) a else b
17      }
18
19
20      minDistIndex = minDistWithIndex._2
21      sumFunc = ... // Fig 4: lines 17-20
22      countFunc = ... // Fig 4: line 21
23      (sumFunc, countFunc)
24    }{(a,b) => ... /* Tiled combination function */ }
25    (0, acc => ... /* Tiled combination function */ )
26  }{(a,b) => ... /* Tiled combination function */ }
27
28  newCentroids = multiFold(k/b1,d)(k,d)(...){ (ii,jj) =>
29    sumsBlk = sums.copy(b1 + ii, *)
30    countsBlk = counts.copy(b1 + ii)
31    (ii, acc => map(k,d){ (i,j) =>
32      sumsBlk(i,j) / countsBlk(i)
33    })
34  }
```

(a) Strip mined k-means in PPL.

```
1   (sums,counts) = multiFold(n/b0)((k,d),k)(...){ ii =>
2     pt1Tile = points.copy(b0 + ii, *)
3     minDistWithInds = multiFold(k/b1)(b1)(map(b1)((max, -1))){ jj =>
4       pt2Tile = centroids.copy(b1 + jj, *)
5       minIndsTile = map(b0){ i =>
6         pt1 = pt1Tile.slice(i, *)
7         minIndTile = fold(b1)((max,-1)){ j =>
8           pt2 = pt2Tile.slice(j, *)
9           dist = distance(pt1, pt2)
10          acc => if (acc._1 < dist) acc else (dist, j+jj)
11        }{ (a,b) => if (a._1 < b._1) a else b }
12      }
13      (0, acc => map(b0){ i =>
14        if (acc(i)._1 < minIndsTile(i)._1) acc else minIndsTile(i) })
15    }{(a,b) =>
16      map(b0){i => if (a(i)._1 < b(i)._1) a(i) else b(i) }
17    }
18    multiFold(b0)(k,d)(zeros(k,d)){ i =>
19      pt1 = pt1Tile.slice(i, *)
20      minDistIndex = minDistWithInds(i)._2
21      sumFunc = ... // Fig 4: lines 17-20
22      countFunc = ... // Fig 4: line 21
23      (sumFunc, countFunc)
24    }{(a,b) => ... /* Tiled combination function */ }
25    (0, acc => ... /* Tiled combination function */ )
26  }{(a,b) => ... /* Tiled combination function */ }
27
28  newCentroids = multiFold(k/b1,d)(k,d)(...){ (ii,jj) =>
29    sumsBlk = sums.copy(b1 + ii, *)
30    countsBlk = counts.copy(b1 + ii)
31    (ii, acc => map(k,d){ (i,j) =>
32      sumsBlk(i,j) / countsBlk(i)
33    })
34  }
```

(b) Pattern Interchanged k-means in PPL.

```
1       For each tile of b0 points:
2         Copy the points tile into local memory
3 - 4     For each point pt1 in the points tile:
5           For each tile of b1 centroids:
6             Copy the centroids tile into local memory
7 - 8         For each centroid pt2 in the centroids tile:
9               Compute distance between pt1 and pt2
10-11           Keep the closest (index,distance) pair
              End
13-16         Keep the closest pair across tiles
            End
20          Extract the index of the closest centroid
21          Add pt1 to row minDistIndex
22          Increment count at minDistIndex
24          Add point and count sums across tiles
          End
25-26     Add point and count sums across tiles
        End

28      For each tile of b1 point sums and counts:
29        Copy the point sums tile into local memory
30        Copy the point counts tile into local memory
31-32     Compute each new centroid as sums(i) / count(i)
        End
```

(c) Pseudocode description of strip mined k-means.

```
1       For each tile of b0 points:
2         Copy the points tile into local memory
3         For each tile of b1 centroids:
4           Copy the centroids tile into local memory
5 - 6       For each point pt1 in the points tile:
7 - 8         For each centroid pt2 in the centroids tile:
9               Compute distance between pt1 and pt2
10-11           Keep the closest (index,distance) pair
              End
            End
13-16       For each point: keep the closest pair across tiles
          End
18-19     For each point pt1 in points tile:
20          Extract the index of the closest centroid
21          Add pt1 to row minDistIndex
22          Increment count at minDistIndex
24          Add point and count sums across tiles
          End
25-26     Add point and count sums across tiles
        End

28      For each tile of b1 point sums and counts:
29        Copy the point sums tile into local memory
30        Copy the point counts tile into local memory
31-32     Compute each new centroid as sum / count
        End
```

(d) Pseudocode description of pattern interchanged k-means.

	Fused		**Strip Mined**		**Interchanged**	
	Main Memory Reads	On-Chip Storage	Main Memory Reads	On-Chip Storage	Main Memory Reads	On-Chip Storage
points	$n \times d$	d	$n \times d$	$b_0 \times d$	$n \times d$	$b_0 \times d$
centroids	$n \times k \times d$	d	$n \times k \times d$	$b_1 \times d$	$(n/b_0) \times k \times d$	$b_1 \times d$
minDistWithIndex	0	2	0	2	0	$2 \times b_0$

(e) Minimum number of words read from main memory and on-chip storage for data structures within k-means clustering after each IR transformation.

Figure 5. Full tiling example for k-means clustering, starting from the fused representation in Figure 4, using tile sizes of b_0 and b_1 for the number of points n and the number of clusters k. The number of features d is not tiled in this example.

	Template	Description	IR Construct
Memories	Buffer	On-chip scratchpad memory	Statically sized array
	Double buffer	Buffer coupling two stages in a metapipeline	Same as metapipeline controller
	Cache	Tagged memory to exploit locality in random memory access patterns	Non-affine accesses
Pipelined Execution Units	Vector	SIMD parallelism	Map over scalars
	Reduction tree	Parallel reduction of associative operations	MultiFold over scalars
	Parallel FIFO	Used to buffer ordered outputs of dynamic size	FlatMap over scalars
	CAM	Fully associative key-value store	GroupByFold over scalars
Controllers	Sequential	Controller which coordinates sequential execution	Sequential IR node
	Parallel	Task parallel controller. Simultaneously starts all member modules when enabled, signals done when all members finish	Independent IR nodes
	Metapipeline	Controller which coordinates execution of nested parallel patterns in a pipelined fashion	Outer parallel pattern with multiple inner patterns
	Tile memory	Memory command generator to fetch tiles of data from off-chip memory	Transformer-inserted array copy

Table 4. Hardware templates used in hardware code generation.

cesses to these arrays. We also track each memory's readers and writers and use this information to instantiate a template with the appropriate word width and number of ports.

Pipeline Execution Units We generate parallelized and pipelined hardware when parallel patterns compute with scalar values, as occurs for the innermost patterns. We implemented templates for each pipelined execution unit in Table 4 using MaxJ language constructs, and instantiate each template with the proper parameters (e.g., data type, vector length) associated with the parallel pattern. The MaxJ compiler applies low-level hardware optimizations such as vectorization, code scheduling, and fine-grained pipelining, and generates efficient hardware. For example, we instantiate a reduction tree for a MultiFold over an array of scalar values, which is automatically pipelined by the MaxJ compiler.

Metapipelining To generate high performance hardware from parallel patterns, it is insufficient to exploit only a single level of parallelism. However, exploiting nested parallelism requires mechanisms to orchestrate the flow of data through multiple pipeline stages while also exploiting parallelism at each stage of execution, creating a hierarchy of pipelines, or *metapipeline*. This is in contrast to traditional HLS tools which require inner patterns to have a static size and be completely unrolled in order to generate a flat pipeline containing both the inner and outer patterns.

We create metapipeline schedules by first performing a topological sort on the IR of the body of the current parallel pattern. The result is a list of stages, where each stage contains a list of patterns which can be run concurrently. Exploiting the pattern's semantic information, we then optimize the metapipeline schedule by removing unnecessary memory transfers and redundant computations. For instance, if the output memory region of the pattern has been assigned to a buffer, we do not generate unnecessary writes to main memory.

As another example, our functional representation of tiled parallel patterns can sometimes create redundant accumulation functions, e.g., in cases where a MultiFold is tiled into a nested MultiFold. During scheduling we identify this redundancy and emit a single copy of the accumulator, removing the unnecessary intermediate buffer. Finally, in cases where the accumulator of a MultiFold cannot completely fit on-chip, we add a special forwarding path between the stages containing the accumulator. This optimization avoids redundant writes to memory and reuses the current tile. Once we have a final schedule for the metapipeline, we promote every output buffer in each stage to a double buffer to avoid write after read (WAR) hazards between metapipeline stages.

Example Figure 6 shows a block diagram of the hardware generated for the k-means application. For simplicity, this diagram shows the case where the *centroids* array completely fits on-chip, meaning we do not tile either the number of clusters k or the number of features d. The generated hardware contains three sequential steps. The first step (Pipe 0) preloads the entire *centroids* array into a buffer. The second step (Metapipeline A) is a metapipeline which consists of three stages with double buffers to manage communication between the stages. These three stages directly correspond to the three main sections of the MultiFold (Figure 4, line 5) used to sum and count the input points as grouped by their closest centroid. The first stage (Pipe 1) loads a tile of the *points* array onto the FPGA. Note that this stage is double buffered to enable hardware prefetching. The second stage (Pipe 2) computes the index of the closest centroid using vector compute blocks and a scalar reduction tree. The third stage (Pipe 3 and Pipe 4) increments the count for this minimum index and adds the current point to the corresponding location in the buffer allocated for the *new centroids*. The third step (Metapipeline B) corresponds with the second outermost parallel pattern in the k-means application. This step streams through the point sums and the centroid counts, dividing each sum by its corresponding count. The resulting new centroids are then written back to main memory using a tile store unit for further use on the CPU.

Our automatically generated hardware design for the core computation of k-means is very similar to the manually op-

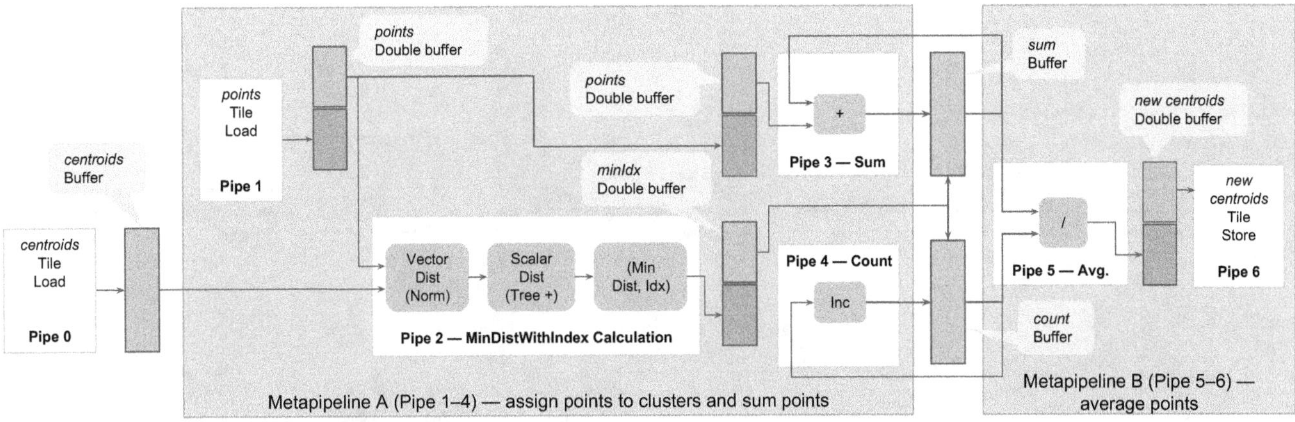

Figure 6. Hardware generated for the k-means application.

Benchmark	Description	Collections Ops
outerprod	Vector outer product	*map*
sumrows	Summation through matrix rows	*map, reduce*
gemm	Matrix multiplication	*map, reduce*
tpchq6	TPC-H Query 6	*filter, reduce*
logreg	Logistic regression	*map, reduce*
gda	Gaussian discriminant analysis	*map, filter, reduce*
blackscholes	Black-Scholes option pricing	*map*
kmeans	k-means clustering	*map, groupBy, reduce*

Table 5. Evaluation benchmarks with major collections operations used by Scala implementation.

timized design described by Hussain et al. [27]. While the manual implementation assumes a fixed number of clusters and a small input dataset which can be preloaded onto the FPGA, we use tiling to automatically generate buffers and tile load units to handle arbitrarily sized data. Like the manual implementation, we automatically parallelize across centroids and vectorize the point distance calculations. As we see from the k-means example, our approach enables us to automatically generate high quality hardware implementations which are comparable to manual designs.

6. Evaluation

We evaluate our approach to hardware generation described in Sections 4 and 5 by comparing the performance and area utilization of the FPGA implementations of a set of data analytic benchmarks. We focus our investigation on the relative improvements that tiling and metapipelining provide over hardware designs that do not have these features.

6.1 Methodology

The benchmarks used in our evaluation are summarized in Table 5. We choose to study vector outer product, matrix row summation, and matrix multiplication as these exemplify many commonly occurring access patterns in the machine learning domain. TPC-H Query 6 is a data querying application which reads a table of purchase records, filtering all records which match a given predicate. It then computes the sum of a product of two columns in the filtered records. Logistic regression is a binary discriminative classification algorithm that uses the sigmoid function in the calculation of predictions. Gaussian discriminant analysis (GDA) is a classification algorithm which models the distribution of each class as a multivariate Gaussian. Black-Scholes is a financial analytics application for option pricing. k-means clustering groups a set of input points by iteratively calculating the k best cluster centroids. In our implementations, all of these benchmarks operate on single precision, floating point data.

We implement our transformation and hardware generation steps in an existing compiler framework called Delite [46]. We write each of our benchmark applications in OptiML [47], a high level, domain specific language embedded in Scala for machine learning. We then compile each of these applications with the modified Delite compiler. During compilation, applications are staged, translating them into PPL representations. The compiler then performs the tiling transformations and hardware optimizations described in Sections 4 and 5 before generating MaxJ hardware designs. We then use the Maxeler MaxCompiler toolchain to generate an FPGA configuration bitstream from our generated MaxJ. We use the Maxeler runtime layer to manage communication with the FPGA from the host CPU. We measure the running times of these designs starting after input data has been copied to the FPGA's DRAM and ending when the hardware design reports completion. Final running times were calculated as an arithmetic mean of five individual run times to account for small runtime variations in main memory accesses and Maxeler's device driver stack.

We run each generated design on an Altera Stratix V FPGA on a Max4 Maia board. The Maia board contains 48 GB of DDR3 DRAM with a maximum bandwidth of 76.8 GB/s. The area numbers given in this section are ob-

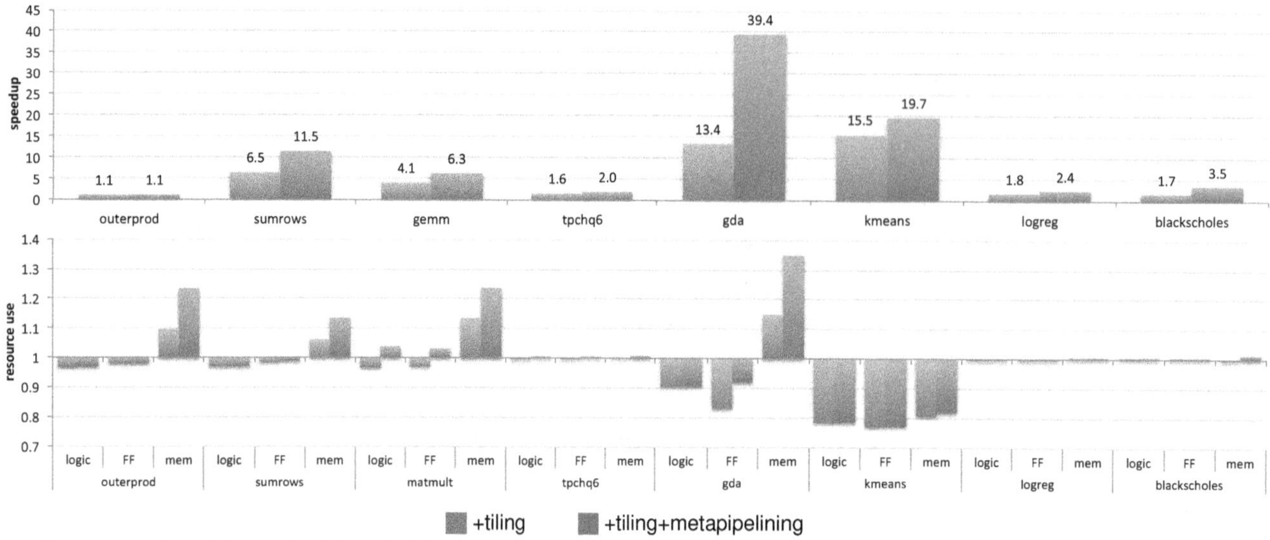

Figure 7. Speedups and resource usages, relative to respective baseline designs, resulting from tiling and metapipelining.

tained from synthesis reports provided by Altera's logic synthesis toolchain. Area utilization is reported under three categories: Logic utilization (denoted "logic"), flip flop usage ("FF"), and on-chip memory usage ("mem").

6.2 Experiments

The baseline for each benchmark is an optimized hardware design implemented using MaxJ. The baseline designs were manually tuned after automatic generation and are representative of optimizations done by state-of-the-art high-level synthesis tools. In particular, each baseline design exploits data and pipelined parallelism within patterns where possible. Pipelined parallelism is exploited for patterns that operate on scalars. Our baseline design exploits locality at the level of a single DRAM burst, which on the MAX4 MAIA board is 384 bytes. To isolate the effects of the amount of parallelism in our comparison, we keep the innermost pattern parallelism factor constant between the baseline design and our optimized versions for each benchmark.

We evaluate our approach against the baseline by generating two hardware configurations per benchmark: a configuration with tiling but no metapipelining, and a configuration with both tiling and metapipelining optimizations enabled.

Impact of tiling alone Figure 7 shows the obtained speedups as well as relative on-chip resource utilizations for each of benchmarks. As can be seen, most benchmarks in our suite show significant speedup when tiling transformations are enabled. Benchmarks like *sumrows* and *gemm* benefit from inherent locality in their memory accesses. For *gemm*, our automatically generated code achieves a speedup of $4\times$ speedup over the baseline for a marginal increase of about 10% on-chip memory usage.

Benchmarks *outerprod* and *tpchq6* do not show a significant difference with our tiling transformations over the baseline. This is because both *outerprod* and *tpchq6* are both memory-bound benchmarks. *Tpchq6* streams through the input once without reuse, and streaming data input is already exploited in our baseline design. *Blackscholes* has a similar data access pattern as *tpchq6*, due to which it achieves a speedup similar to that of *tpchq6*. Hence tiling does not provide any additional benefit. Most of the locality in *logreg* is already captured at burst-level granularity by our baseline. As a result, *logreg* achieves a modest speedup of $1.8x$ over the baseline due to tiling. The core compute pipeline in *outerprod* is memory-bound at the stage writing results to DRAM, which cannot be addressed using tiling. Despite the futility of tiling in terms of performance, tiling *outerprod* has a noticeable increase in memory utilization as the intermediate result varies as the square of the tile size.

In *kmeans* and *gda*, some of the input data structures are small enough that they can be held in on-chip memory. This completely eliminates accesses to off-chip memory, leading to dramatic speedups of $13.4\times$ and $15.5\times$ respectively with our tiling transformations. *gda* uses more on-chip memory to store intermediate data. On the other hand, the tiled version *kmeans* utilizes less on-chip memory resources. This is because the baseline for *kmeans* instantiates multiple load and store units, each of which creates several control structures in order to read and write data from DRAM. Each of these control structures includes address and data streams, which require several on-chip buffers. By tiling, we require a smaller number of load and store units.

Impact of metapipelining The second speedup bar in Figure 7 shows the benefits of metapipelining. Metapipelines increase throughput at the expense of additional on-chip memory used for double buffers. Metapipelining overlaps design compute with data transfer and helps to hide the cost of the slower stage. Benchmarks like *gemm* and *sumrows* naturally benefit from metapipelining because the memory transfer time is completely overlapped with the compute, resulting in speedups of 6.3× and 11.5× respectively. Metapipelining also exploits overlap in streaming benchmarks like *tpchq6* and *blackscholes*, where the input data is fetched and stored simultaneously with the core computation.

The speedup due to metapipelining is largely determined by balancing between stages. Stages with roughly equal number of cycles benefit the most, as this achieves the most overlap. Unbalanced stages are limited by the slowest stage, thus limiting performance. We observe this behavior in *outerprod*, where the metapipeline is bottlenecked by the stage writing results back to DRAM. The metapipeline in *logreg* is bottlenecked at the stage performing dot products of all the points in the input tile with the *theta* vector. As we only parallelize the innermost parallel pattern in this work, only a single dot product is produced at a time, even though the dot product itself is executed in parallel across the point dimensions. On the other hand, applications like *gda*, *kmeans* and *sumrows* greatly benefit from metapipelining. In particular, *gda* naturally maps to nested metapipelines that are well-balanced. The stage loading the input tile overlaps execution with the stage computing the output tile and the stage storing the output tile. The stage computing the output tile is also a metapipeline where the stages perform vector subtraction, vector outer product and accumulation. We parallelize the vector outer product stage as it is the most compute-heavy part of the algorithm; parallelizing the vector outer product enables the metapipeline to achieve greater throughput. This yields an overall speedup of 39.4× over the baseline.

7. Conclusion

In this paper, we introduced a set of compilation steps necessary to produce an efficient FPGA hardware design from an intermediate representation composed of nested parallel patterns. We described a set of simple transformation rules which can be used to automatically tile parallel patterns which exploit semantic information inherent within these patterns and which place fewer restrictions on the program's memory accesses than previous work. We then presented a set of analysis and generation steps which can be used to automatically infer optimized hardware designs with metapipelining. Finally, we presented experimental results for a set of benchmarks in the machine learning and data querying domains which show that these compilation steps provide performance improvements of up to 39.4× with a minimal impact on FPGA resource usage.

Acknowledgments

The authors thank Maxeler Technologies for their assistance with this paper and Jacob Bower for his help running experiments. They also thank the reviewers for their comments and suggestions. This work is supported by DARPA Contract-Air Force FA8750-12-2-0335; Army Contract AHPCRC W911NF-07-2-0027-1; NSF Grants IIS-1247701, CCF-1111943, CCF-1337375, and SHF-1408911; Stanford PPL affiliates program, Pervasive Parallelism Lab: Oracle, AMD, Huawei, Intel, NVIDIA, SAP Labs. Authors acknowledge additional support from Oracle. The views and conclusions contained herein are those of the authors and should not be interpreted as necessarily representing the official policies or endorsements, either expressed or implied, of DARPA or the U.S. Government.

References

[1] Vivado high-level synthesis. `http://www.xilinx.com/products/design-tools/vivado/integration/esl-design.html`, 2016.

[2] Sadaf R Alam, Pratul K Agarwal, Melissa C Smith, Jeffrey S Vetter, and David Caliga. Using fpga devices to accelerate biomolecular simulations. *Computer*, (3):66–73, 2007.

[3] Arvind. Bluespec: A language for hardware design, simulation, synthesis and verification invited talk. In *Proceedings of the First ACM and IEEE International Conference on Formal Methods and Models for Co-Design*, MEMOCODE '03, pages 249–, Washington, DC, USA, 2003. IEEE Computer Society.

[4] Joshua Auerbach, David F. Bacon, Perry Cheng, and Rodric Rabbah. Lime: A java-compatible and synthesizable language for heterogeneous architectures. In *Proceedings of the ACM International Conference on Object Oriented Programming Systems Languages and Applications*, OOPSLA '10, pages 89–108, New York, NY, USA, 2010. ACM.

[5] J. Bachrach, Huy Vo, B. Richards, Yunsup Lee, A. Waterman, R. Avizienis, J. Wawrzynek, and K. Asanovic. Chisel: Constructing hardware in a scala embedded language. In *Design Automation Conference (DAC), 2012 49th ACM/EDAC/IEEE*, pages 1212–1221, June 2012.

[6] David Bacon, Rodric Rabbah, and Sunil Shukla. Fpga programming for the masses. *Queue*, 11(2):40:40–40:52, 2013.

[7] Donald G Bailey. *Design for embedded image processing on FPGAs*. John Wiley & Sons, 2011.

[8] Mohamed-Walid Benabderrahmane, Louis-Noël Pouchet, Albert Cohen, and Cédric Bastoul. The polyhedral model is more widely applicable than you think. In *ETAPS International Conference on Compiler Construction (CC'2010)*, pages 283–303, March 2010. Springer Verlag.

[9] Uday Bondhugula, Albert Hartono, J. Ramanujam, and P. Sadayappan. A practical automatic polyhedral parallelizer and locality optimizer. In *Proceedings of the 29th ACM SIGPLAN Conference on Programming Language Design and Implementation*, PLDI '08, pages 101–113, 2008. ACM.

[10] Uday Bondhugula, Albert Hartono, J. Ramanujam, and P. Sadayappan. A practical automatic polyhedral program optimization system. In *ACM SIGPLAN Conference on Programming Language Design and Implementation (PLDI)*, 2008.

[11] Kevin J. Brown, HyoukJoong Lee, Tiark Rompf, Arvind K. Sujeeth, Christopher De Sa, Christopher Aberger, and Kunle Olukotun. Have abstraction and eat performance, too: Optimized heterogeneous computing with parallel patterns. In *International Symposium on Code Generation and Optimization,*, CGO, 2016.

[12] Samuel Brown et al. Performance comparison of finite-difference modeling on cell, fpga and multi-core computers. In *SEG/San Antonio Annual Meeting*, 2007.

[13] Bryan Catanzaro, Michael Garland, and Kurt Keutzer. Copperhead: compiling an embedded data parallel language. In *Proceedings of the 16th ACM symposium on Principles and practice of parallel programming*, PPoPP, pages 47–56, New York, NY, USA, 2011. ACM.

[14] Craig Chambers, Ashish Raniwala, Frances Perry, Stephen Adams, Robert R. Henry, Robert Bradshaw, and Nathan Weizenbaum. Flumejava: easy, efficient data-parallel pipelines. In *Proceedings of the 2010 ACM SIGPLAN conference on Programming language design and implementation*, PLDI. ACM, 2010.

[15] Chun Chen, Jacqueline Chame, and Mary Hall. Chill: A framework for composing high-level loop transformations. Technical report, Citeseer, 2008.

[16] J. Cong, Bin Liu, S. Neuendorffer, J. Noguera, K. Vissers, and Zhiru Zhang. High-level synthesis for fpgas: From prototyping to deployment. *Computer-Aided Design of Integrated Circuits and Systems, IEEE Transactions on*, 30(4):473–491, April 2011.

[17] Christian de Schryver. *FPGA Based Accelerators for Financial Applications*. Springer, 2015.

[18] Jeffrey Dean and Sanjay Ghemawat. MapReduce: Simplified Data Processing on Large Clusters. In *OSDI*, OSDI, pages 137–150, 2004.

[19] S.A. Edwards. The challenges of synthesizing hardware from c-like languages. *Design Test of Computers, IEEE*, 23(5):375–386, May 2006.

[20] Nithin George, HyoukJoong Lee, David Novo, Tiark Rompf, Kevin J. Brown, Arvind K. Sujeeth, Martin Odersky, Kunle Olukotun, and Paolo Ienne. Hardware system synthesis from domain-specific languages. In *Field Programmable Logic and Applications (FPL), 2014 24th International Conference on*, pages 1–8, Sept 2014.

[21] Tobias Grosser, Armin Groesslinger, and Christian Lengauer. PollyâĂŤperforming polyhedral optimizations on a low-level intermediate representation. *Parallel Processing Letters*, 22(04):1250010, 2012.

[22] Frederik Grull and Udo Kebschull. Biomedical image processing and reconstruction with dataflow computing on fpgas. In *Field Programmable Logic and Applications (FPL), 2014 24th International Conference on*, pages 1–2. IEEE, 2014.

[23] Prabhat K. Gupta. Xeon+fpga platform for the data center. `http://www.ece.cmu.edu/~calcm/carl/lib/exe/fetch.php?media=carl15-gupta.pdf`, 2015.

[24] Johann Hauswald, Michael A. Laurenzano, Yunqi Zhang, Cheng Li, Austin Rovinski, Arjun Khurana, Ronald G. Dreslinski, Trevor Mudge, Vinicius Petrucci, Lingjia Tang, and Jason Mars. Sirius: An open end-to-end voice and vision personal assistant and its implications for future warehouse scale computers. In *Proceedings of the Twentieth International Conference on Architectural Support for Programming Languages and Operating Systems*, ASPLOS '15, pages 223–238, New York, NY, USA, 2015. ACM.

[25] Eric Hielscher. *Locality Optimization For Data Parallel Programs*. PhD thesis, New York University, 2013.

[26] Chien-Chin Huang, Qi Chen, Zhaoguo Wang, Russell Power, Jorge Ortiz, Jinyang Li, and Zhen Xiao. Spartan: A distributed array framework with smart tiling. In *2015 USENIX Annual Technical Conference (USENIX ATC 15)*, pages 1–15, Santa Clara, CA, July 2015. USENIX Association.

[27] H.M. Hussain, K. Benkrid, H. Seker, and A.T. Erdogan. Fpga implementation of k-means algorithm for bioinformatics application: An accelerated approach to clustering microarray data. In *Adaptive Hardware and Systems (AHS), 2011 NASA/ESA Conference on*, pages 248–255, June 2011.

[28] HyoukJoong Lee, Kevin J. Brown, Arvind K. Sujeeth, Tiark Rompf, and Kunle Olukotun. Locality-aware mapping of nested parallel patterns on gpus. In *Proceedings of the 47th Annual IEEE/ACM International Symposium on Microarchitecture*, IEEE Micro, 2014.

[29] Feng Liu, Soumyadeep Ghosh, Nick P. Johnson, and David I. August. Cgpa: Coarse-grained pipelined accelerators. In *Proceedings of the 51st Annual Design Automation Conference*, DAC '14, pages 78:1–78:6, 2014. ACM.

[30] Maxeler Technologies. MaxCompiler white paper, 2011.

[31] Oskar Mencer, Erik Vynckier, James Spooner, Stephen Girdlestone, and Oliver Charlesworth. Finding the right level of abstraction for minimizing operational expenditure. In *Proceedings of the fourth workshop on High performance computational finance*, pages 13–18. ACM, 2011.

[32] M. Odersky. Scala. `http://www.scala-lang.org`, 2011.

[33] Jian Ouyang, Shiding Lin, Wei Qi, Yong Wang, Bo Yu, and Song Jiang. Sda: Software-defined accelerator for largescale dnn systems. Hot Chips 26, 2014.

[34] Kalin Ovtcharov, Olatunji Ruwase, Joo-Young Kim, Jeremy Fowers, Karin Strauss, and Eric S. Chung. Accelerating deep convolutional neural networks using specialized hardware. Technical report, Microsoft Research, February 2015.

[35] D. Petkov, R. Harr, and S. Amarasinghe. Efficient pipelining of nested loops: unroll-and-squash. In *Parallel and Distributed Processing Symposium., Proceedings International, IPDPS 2002, Abstracts and CD-ROM*, April 2002.

[36] Simon Peyton Jones [editor], John Hughes [editor], Lennart Augustsson, Dave Barton, Brian Boutel, Warren Burton, Simon Fraser, Joseph Fasel, Kevin Hammond, Ralf Hinze, Paul Hudak, Thomas Johnsson, Mark Jones, John Launchbury, Erik Meijer, John Peterson, Alastair Reid, Colin Runciman, and Philip Wadler. Haskell 98 — A non-strict, purely functional language. Available from `http://www.haskell.org/definition/`, feb 1999.

[37] Louis-Noël Pouchet. *Interative Optimization in the Polyhedral Model.* PhD thesis, University of Paris-Sud 11, Orsay, France, January 2010.

[38] Louis-Noël Pouchet, Uday Bondhugula, Cédric Bastoul, Albert Cohen, J. Ramanujam, P. Sadayappan, and Nicolas Vasilache. Loop transformations: Convexity, pruning and optimization. In *38th ACM SIGACT-SIGPLAN Symposium on Principles of Programming Languages (POPL'11)*, pages 549–562, Austin, TX, January 2011. ACM Press.

[39] Louis-Noel Pouchet, Peng Zhang, P. Sadayappan, and Jason Cong. Polyhedral-based data reuse optimization for configurable computing. In *Proceedings of the ACM/SIGDA International Symposium on Field Programmable Gate Arrays*, FPGA '13, pages 29–38, New York, NY, USA, 2013. ACM.

[40] Andrew Putnam, Adrian M. Caulfield, Eric S. Chung, Derek Chiou, Kypros Constantinides, John Demme, Hadi Esmaeilzadeh, Jeremy Fowers, Gopi Prashanth Gopal, Jan Gray, Michael Haselman, Scott Hauck, Stephen Heil, Amir Hormati, Joo-Young Kim, Sitaram Lanka, James Larus, Eric Peterson, Simon Pope, Aaron Smith, Jason Thong, Phillip Yi Xiao, and Doug Burger. A reconfigurable fabric for accelerating large-scale datacenter services. In *Proceeding of the 41st Annual International Symposium on Computer Architecuture*, ISCA '14, pages 13–24, Piscataway, NJ, USA, 2014. IEEE Press.

[41] Andrew R. Putnam, Dave Bennett, Eric Dellinger, Jeff Mason, and Prasanna Sundararajan. Chimps: A high-level compilation flow for hybrid cpu-fpga architectures. In *Proceedings of the 16th International ACM/SIGDA Symposium on Field Programmable Gate Arrays*, FPGA '08, pages 261–261, New York, NY, USA, 2008. ACM.

[42] Jonathan Ragan-Kelley, Connelly Barnes, Andrew Adams, Sylvain Paris, Frédo Durand, and Saman Amarasinghe. Halide: A language and compiler for optimizing parallelism, locality, and recomputation in image processing pipelines. In *Proceedings of the 34th ACM SIGPLAN Conference on Programming Language Design and Implementation*, PLDI '13, pages 519–530, New York, NY, USA, 2013. ACM.

[43] Tiark Rompf, Arvind K. Sujeeth, Nada Amin, Kevin Brown, Vojin Jovanovic, HyoukJoong Lee, Manohar Jonnalagedda, Kunle Olukotun, and Martin Odersky. Optimizing data structures in high-level programs. POPL, 2013.

[44] Satnam Singh and David J. Greaves. Kiwi: Synthesis of fpga circuits from parallel programs. In *Proceedings of the 2008 16th International Symposium on Field-Programmable Custom Computing Machines*, FCCM '08, pages 3–12, Washington, DC, USA, 2008. IEEE Computer Society.

[45] M.C. Smith, Jeffrey S Vetter, and Sadaf R. Alam. Scientific computing beyond CPUs: FPGA implementations of common scientific kernels. In *Proceedings of the 8th Annual Military and Aerospace Programmable Logic Devices International Conference*, 2005.

[46] Arvind K. Sujeeth, Kevin J. Brown, HyoukJoong Lee, Tiark Rompf, Hassan Chafi, Martin Odersky, and Kunle Olukotun. Delite: A compiler architecture for performance-oriented embedded domain-specific languages. In *TECS'14: ACM Transactions on Embedded Computing Systems*, July 2014.

[47] Arvind K. Sujeeth, Hyoukjoong Lee, Kevin J. Brown, Hassan Chafi, Michael Wu, Anand R. Atreya, Kunle Olukotun, Tiark Rompf, and Martin Odersky. Optiml: an implicitly parallel domainspecific language for machine learning. In *in Proceedings of the 28th International Conference on Machine Learning, ser. ICML*, 2011.

[48] Arvind K. Sujeeth, Tiark Rompf, Kevin J. Brown, HyoukJoong Lee, Hassan Chafi, Victoria Popic, Michael Wu, Aleksander Prokopec, Vojin Jovanovic, Martin Odersky, and Kunle Olukotun. Composition and reuse with compiled domain-specific languages. In *European Conference on Object Oriented Programming*, ECOOP, 2013.

[49] Mingxing Tan, Gai Liu, Ritchie Zhao, Steve Dai, and Zhiru Zhang. Elasticflow: A complexity-effective approach for pipelining irregular loop nests. In *Proceedings of the IEEE/ACM International Conference on Computer-Aided Design*, ICCAD '15, pages 78–85, 2015. IEEE Press.

[50] The Khronos Group. OpenCL 2.0. `http://www.khronos.org/opencl/`.

[51] Anand Venkat, Mary Hall, and Michelle Strout. Loop and data transformations for sparse matrix code. In *Proceedings of the 36th ACM SIGPLAN Conference on Programming Language Design and Implementation*, PLDI 2015, pages 521–532, New York, NY, USA, 2015. ACM.

[52] Matei Zaharia, Mosharaf Chowdhury, Michael J. Franklin, Scott Shenker, and Ion Stoica. Spark: cluster computing with working sets. In *Proceedings of the 2nd USENIX conference on Hot topics in cloud computing*, HotCloud'10, pages 10–10, Berkeley, CA, USA, 2010. USENIX Association.

[53] GL Zhang, Philip Heng Wai Leong, Chun Hok Ho, Kuen Hung Tsoi, Chris CC Cheung, Dong-U Lee, Ray CC Cheung, and Wayne Luk. Reconfigurable acceleration for monte carlo based financial simulation. In *Field-Programmable Technology, 2005. Proceedings. 2005 IEEE International Conference on*, pages 215–222. IEEE, 2005.

[54] Zhiru Zhang, Yiping Fan, Wei Jiang, Guoling Han, Changqi Yang, and Jason Cong. Autopilot: A platform-based esl synthesis system. In Philippe Coussy and Adam Morawiec, editors, *High-Level Synthesis*, pages 99–112. Springer Netherlands, 2008.

[55] Ling Zhuo and Viktor K Prasanna. High-performance designs for linear algebra operations on reconfigurable hardware. *Computers, IEEE Transactions on*, 57(8):1057–1071, 2008.

DySel: Lightweight Dynamic Selection for Kernel-based Data-parallel Programming Model

Li-Wen Chang Hee-Seok Kim Wen-mei Hwu

University of Illinois

{lchang20, kim868, w-hwu}@illinois.edu

Abstract

The rising pressure for simultaneously improving performance and reducing power is driving more diversity into all aspects of computing devices. An algorithm that is well-matched to the target hardware can run multiple times faster and more energy efficiently than one that is not. The problem is complicated by the fact that a program's input also affects the appropriate choice of algorithm. As a result, software developers have been faced with the challenge of determining the appropriate algorithm for each potential combination of target device and data. This paper presents DySel, a novel runtime system for automating such determination for kernel-based data parallel programming models such as OpenCL, CUDA, OpenACC, and C++AMP. These programming models cover many applications that demand high performance in mobile, cloud and high-performance computing. DySel systematically deploys candidate kernels on a small portion of the actual data to determine which achieves the best performance for the hardware-data combination. The test-deployment, referred to as micro-profiling, contributes to the final execution result and incurs less than 8% of overhead in the worst observed case when compared to an oracle. We show four major use cases where DySel provides significantly more consistent performance without tedious effort from the developer.

Categories and Subject Descriptors D3.4 [*Programming Languages*]: Processors—Code generation, Compilers, Runtime environments

Keywords Graphics Processing Unit, Dynamic Profiling

ASPLOS '16 April 2–6, 2016, Atlanta, Georgia, USA.
Copyright © 2016 ACM 978-1-4503-4091-5/16/04...$15.00
DOI: http://dx.doi.org/10.1145/2872362.2872373

1. Introduction

The demand for computing devices with increased performance at reduced power continues to grow. In the mobile community, such devices enable more functionality and longer battery life. In the high-performance computing community, such devices make exascale computing more feasible. As improvements from the semiconductor fabrication process diminish, architects are compelled to introduce more diversity into all aspects of computing devices: function units, interconnect fabrics, and memory hierarchies. The complicated interactions between these diverse devices and input data present a major challenge in predicting the effect of optimizations performed by the programmers or compilers.

Programmers of these devices must understand and exploit a wider set of architectural entities to achieve high performance, far beyond the traditional instruction set architecture and uniform memory space. CUDA and OpenCL, for instance, are designed for highly parallel execution based on lightweight threads, but high performance often requires carefully crafted work assignment to threads, multi-level tiling, and scheduling of the threads. While achieving high-performance on one device is challenging, preparing code that can achieve high-performance across a diverse set of devices is a daunting and tedious task for even the most skilled programmers.

It is therefore desirable to support performance portability over different device architectures. Popular approaches commonly involve compiler and/or runtime solutions to address this problem. Architecture-specific code transformations must be done by considering detailed facts about the target architecture. Achieving high performance for a particular device and runtime data combination involves finding a good selection and ordering of optimizations along with appropriate values for associated parameters.

Figure 1 demonstrates how different choices of optimizations can result in substantially disparate results of the state-of-the-art Intel OpenCL stack [21] on an Intel i7-3820 CPU. It compares the performance of heuristically selected optimization [13] of `sgemm` and `spmv` (denoted as `spmv-jds`) in Parboil [28] against that of a non-vectorized version and two

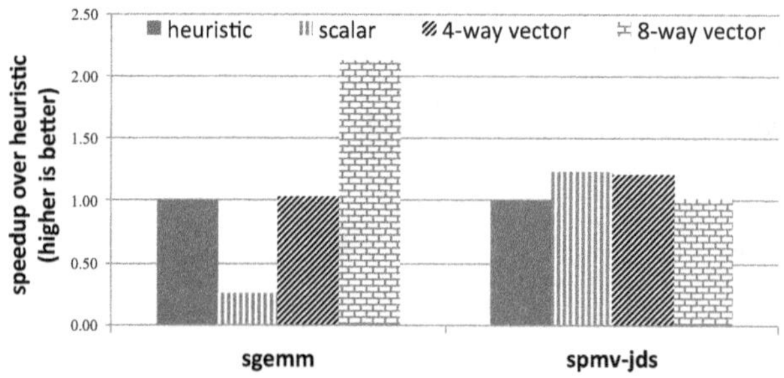

Figure 1. Performance of Intel CPU OpenCL stack with different vectorization strategies.

alternative vectorized versions. The Intel compiler counter-intuitively chooses 4-way vector for regular and control divergence free `sgemm` kernel, while it uses 8-way vector for `spmv` kernel which exercises control divergence. Under control divergence, code generation for work-items using SIMD instructions typically comes with a large overhead due to masking, packing and unpacking, which gets larger with wider SIMD datapath width. In the end, the Intel's heuristic has made suboptimal decisions for both cases, falling short of the best achieved performance by a factor of 2.13x and 1.24x, respectively. One observation is that it clearly demonstrates the importance of choosing the most optimal code. Another observation is any single static heuristic for choosing optimizations will likely fall short due to the complexity of interactions between the device, the computation, and the data.

There is a wealth of prior work [2, 7, 11, 12, 14, 15, 17, 21–23, 27, 35] on estimating the performance of code or determining the effect of a certain type of compile time code transformation. Performance models are widely used to prune the design space for autotuning [11, 22], or to guide optimization strategies [7, 15, 17, 22, 35]. For example, locality-centric scheduling [17] statically analyzes memory access patterns with respect to work-items and kernel loops and employs a heuristic cache model to determine a locality-friendly schedule of OpenCL work-item loops on CPUs. PORPLE [7] relies on GPU memory or cache models to analyze work-item access patterns of regular applications for data placement. However, these approaches address model-specific aspects of the device architecture of interest, while other important factors such as vectorization are not considered or assumed to be decoupled from the aspects being considered. Such assumptions considerably reduces the accuracy of the model-based approach. Moreover, they are limited by ignoring factors that are only known at runtime, such as the actual data shape. As a result, accurately predicting the effect of optimizations is not likely viable at compile time. Optimizations based on inaccurate predictions can lead to disappointing performance outcomes.

Several runtime-based approaches [7, 10, 18, 24, 33] have been proposed to mitigate the problem with static performance prediction approaches. Reactive tiling [24] uses online trained tiling model and chooses likely optimal tiling parameters for the given working set size and system load. PORPLE [7] leverages runtime micro simulation on a CPU to refine the GPU memory or cache models when inputs are irregular and cannot be statically analyzed. Although more information is accessible at runtime, model-driven approaches at runtime can still have limitations and blind spots of unconsidered factors of models like static model-driven approaches, resulting in suboptimal decisions.

In this paper, we propose DySel, a runtime framework that matches the best code arrangement with the actual device and data combination, thereby improving performance and efficiency. With DySel, we remove the burden of determining the most optimal code from an optimizing compiler and allow it to produce several likely candidate variants from the input code. Then the runtime performs *micro-profiling*, a process of deploying the candidates on a small portion of the actual data on the actual device and determines the best version to be used to process the rest of workload. The advantage of this approach is that it can work with virtually any combination of compiler and device architecture as modeling is not required at runtime. When dealing with a large workload, the cost of micro-profiling can be easily amortized and the overall benefit can be much greater than unconditionally executing a single code selected by the compiler. Note DySel is not intended to completely replace whole decision-making procedures for compiler optimizations with run-time profiling. Instead, DySel is designed to relax the conditions for determining the most optimal code from an optimizing compiler. Therefore, with DySel, the optimizing compiler still needs to produce several (typically 2 to 10) likely candidate variants.

We have prototyped our idea on OpenCL and CUDA, two popular kernel-based parallel programming models today. Experimental results demonstrate that our proposed approach correctly chooses the optimal code version with less than 8% overhead in the worst observed case compared to oracle results for both CPU and GPU architectures.

We make the following contributions in this paper:

1. We propose a combined compiler and runtime approach towards optimal code selection.
2. We propose a lightweight runtime micro-profiling technique and discuss the engineering tradeoffs involved in its implementation.
3. We evaluate the DySel idea by implementing a prototype system and performing real-hardware measurements for four important use cases on CPU and GPU.

The rest of this paper is organized as follows. Section 2 introduces the concept of DySel. Section 3 details our implementation. Section 4 and 5 evaluates and discusses the performance of DySel. Section 6 outlines related work and Section 7 concludes.

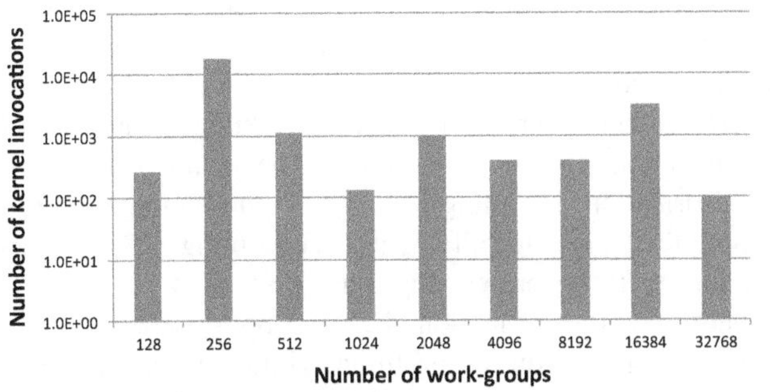

Figure 2. Distribution of number of work-groups among kernel launches in Parboil and Rodinia benchmarks

2. DySel Design

This section provides a background of profiling for kernel-based data-parallel programming, and introduces the idea of *DySel* and the three productive profiling techniques used in DySel.

2.1 Profiling for Kernel-based Data-parallel Programming

DySel evaluates different code variants at runtime in order to determine which variant performs best. It measures performance of each variant on a small portion of the actual data and identifies the best performing one, a process which we call *micro-profiling*. The chosen version will be used to process the rest of workload. The key ingredients of DySel are efficient profiling and accurate performance projection.

Popular kernel-based data-parallel programming models, such as OpenCL, CUDA, OpenACC, and C++AMP, allow over-decomposition of workloads for maximized parallelism. Work-groups in OpenCL, for example, are meant to run **independently** from each other by design and this enables efficient parallel execution on a variety of architectures, such as CPUs and GPUs. With these programming models, workload processing is done via repeatedly executing the kernel code over a small subset of the workload, which often takes place in parallel.

The decomposition makes the number of independent kernel invocations fairly **large** in practice, which helps to amortize the cost of allocating a few of them for evaluation of code variants. The overhead for evaluating code variants can often be amortized over the large number of invocations.

Figure 2 shows accumulated occurrences of kernel invocation in different numbers of work-groups from all OpenCL benchmarks in Parboil [28] and Rodinia [6] benchmark suites. It supports the low-cost profiling hypothesis based on workload decomposition, as significant number of kernel invocations fall into the range of 128 to 32768 work-groups. Kernel invocations with less than 128 work-groups are rarely observed and so dropped from the figure. Kernel launches with small number of work-groups can be sensitive to profiling overhead, but a small number of work-groups also indicates relatively small workloads and performance variation from the level of optimization might not be critical. DySel mainly targets kernels with large work-groups and profiling-based kernel selection is deactivated for small workload.

An individual kernel invocation is assumed to have **similar performance** throughout subsequent invocations. This is due to the nature of data-parallel computing where the same code is used to process large data. Thus, observed performance from a kernel invocation is likely to be indicative for others, which helps keep the required sampling frequency and thus the overhead low. These properties make work-group an ideal granularity for micro-profiling.

Accurate performance projection means that the variant that performs best in micro-profiling is the one that performs best on the whole workload, even in irregular workload or complex variants. Accuracy of DySel can be evaluated by measuring performance difference between the variants on the whole workload, and is further discussed in Section 4.

2.2 Productive Profiling

DySel employs *productive* micro-profiling, where execution from profiling also contributes to workload processing. Each kernel invocation during profiling takes a different part of the workload data. This is a departure from offline profiling, where performance characteristic is extracted while the result is simply ignored. This strategy reduces the overhead of profiling, since workload processed during profiling does not require reprocessing.

Figure 3 shows the three productive profiling techniques used in DySel. In this example, we assume that the compiler produces two implementations as follows. The ratio of workload per work-group between Version A and B is 3 to 2. According to safe point analysis [24] (Section 3.4), DySel launches 2 and 3 work-groups for Version A and B, respectively, in order to make a fair throughput comparison during profiling.

Fully-productive profiling, shown in Figure 3(a), is the most efficient profiling in DySel. Each kernel invocation during profiling takes a different part of the workload data and computes valid contribution to the final output. In Figure 3(a), both versions compute and profile different parts of the workload, and write to the final output. After profiling, Version B is chosen to compute the remaining workload, as Version B turns out to run faster during profiling. Fully-productive profiling can take place as long as the individual invocations do not have overlap in the final output, which is a dominating pattern in data-parallel programming. It is accurate when parts of the workload are roughly equal, which is common in regular applications.

Two variants of productive profiling, called partial-productive profiling, are proposed to overcome the limitations of fully-productive profiling. Hybrid-based partial-productive profiling, shown in Figure 3(b), is designed for irregular workload with a non-overlapping final output. By running a set of ker-

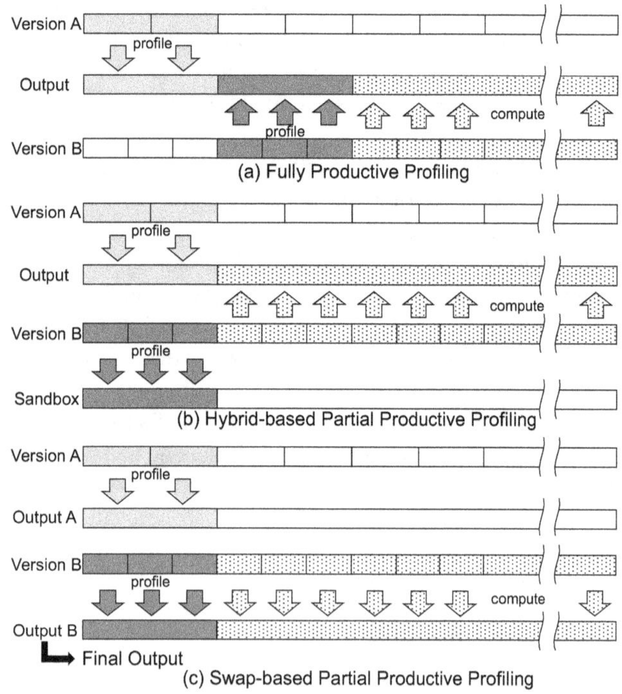

Figure 3. Illustration of proposed productive profiling

nels over the same workload, profiling can be still fair among different kernel innovations. While only the first kernel (Version A in Figure 3(b)) can contribute to the final output, results from others (Version B in Figure 3(b)) are directed into a sandbox and thus unused. After profiling, Version B is chosen to process the remaining workload. Since the final output contains contributions from both Version A and B, we call this profiling hybrid-based.

Swap-based partial-productive profiling, shown in Figure 3(c), is proposed for handling output range variations among work-groups from different kernels by running a set of kernels over the same workload but with their own private output spaces. After profiling, the one selected kernel and output (Version B and Output B in this Figure 3(c)) will remain for the rest of execution while others (Version A and Output A in this Figure 3(c)) are discarded. Since the final output is swapped with Output B, we call this profiling swap-based. It is worth mentioning that swap-based partial-productive profiling can be considered as a speculation approach to version selection.

DySel relies on compilers or programmers to specify which kind of productive profiling a set of kernels. Interaction between DySel and compilers and programmers is discussed with more details in Section 3.

2.3 Applicability

The choice of profiling mode is determined based on programming patterns and optimizations for kernels. First, fully-productive profiling is appropriate for kernels with regular or near-regular workloads. Large workload variations can significantly impact the fairness of comparison among kernels. Therefore, fully-productive profiling is only suitable for applications with regular workload, such as BLAS, or stencil. It can select between kernels with different levels of optimizations such as tiling, thread coarsening, data layout transformation (including padding), input binning [26, 29], loop-interchange, locality-centric scheduling [17], vectorization, software prefetching, data placement [7, 15], and input format transformation [4]. Some optimizations require special treatment during profiling. Tiling and thread coarsening require normalization of throughput using safe point analysis [24] (Section 3.4) to ensure fairness. Data layout transformation, input binning, and input format transformation may require duplication of inputs to meet the assumption of different kernel implementations.

Second, hybrid-based partial-productive profiling supports all patterns and optimizations supported by fully-productive profiling. Additionally, it is applicable to irregular workload. By profiling the same portion of workload across different kernels, unfair throughput comparison can be avoided. The applicable kernels typically have in-kernel loops with varying bounds across work-groups, such as sparse BLAS. Uniform workload analysis [14] (Section 3.4) can be used to detect such in-kernel loops with varying bounds.

Finally, swap-based partial-productive profiling further supports output range variation across kernels, and in theory is applicable to any optimizations, such as privatization, regularization, compaction, output binning, scatter-to-gather [26, 29], kernel fusion, kernel fission, optimizations using atomic operations, and even algorithm change. Although swap-based partial-productive profiling is the most applicable profiling in DySel, it has less output contribution efficiency than fully-productive profiling. It also requires more storage than the hybrid-based profiling due to the need to maintain private output spaces during micro-profiling.

2.4 Orchestration for Profiling and Execution

The way DySel orchestrates micro-profiling and execution at runtime can have significant impact on profiling overhead. We present two orchestration designs in this subsection.

Figure 4(a) shows the overall flow of synchronous DySel. The compiler deposits several code versions to the kernel pool in the executable binary file. Upon execution of the kernel, the runtime dispatches code versions from the pool and executes them (❷) in one of the productive modes described in the previous section, with a few work-groups (❶) assigned using safe point analysis [24] (Section 3.4). The runtime waits until all versions finish execution and compares their execution time to pick the best one. Then the rest of the execution runs with the selected kernel. The implementation is simple. However, it incurs latency penalty if there is large disparity between the best and the worst versions since the latency of the profiling phase is determined by the slowest execution (❸). Furthermore, the total number

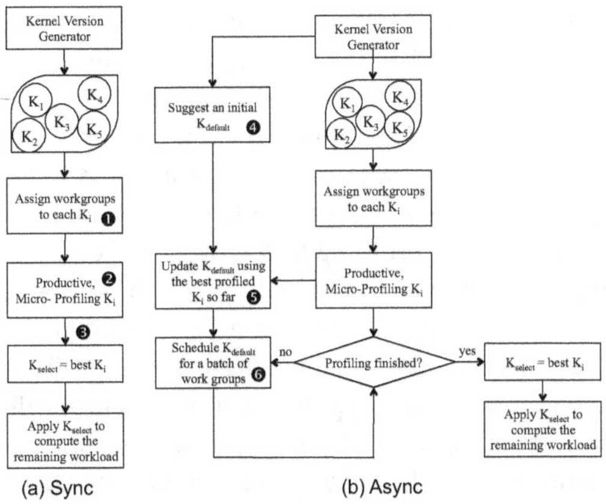

Figure 4. Flows of proposed synchronous and asynchronous DySel

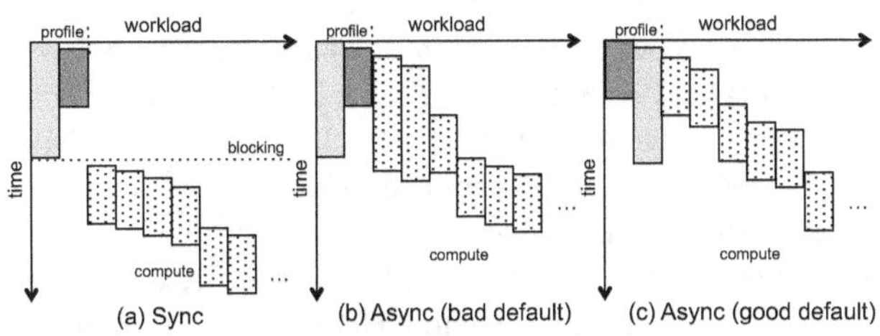

Figure 5. Illustration of timing difference between synchronous and asynchronous DySel

of work-groups used in micro-profiling may not be able to fully utilize the hardware resources.

Figure 4(b) shows the flow for asynchronous DySel. Unlike the synchronous design, the rest of the execution can begin even before profiling is complete, which we denote as eager execution. When the non-profiling execution begins, it runs with the best-performing version so far. To support eager execution, we require that the compiler or programmer suggest an initial version (❹). We will discuss more on the initial selection and its impact on performance later. As profiling progresses, the selection gets updated once a faster version is found (❺). The asynchronous flow must be able to switch to the best kernel found so far, therefore the eager execution is done via launching a series of chunks (❻), instead of a single batch. While it can better tolerate the latency of profiling, the implementation gets more complicated for two reasons. First, it requires careful workload management so that profiling can be done with a higher priority over the eager execution. Second, the eager execution is divided into many chunks, imposing associated kernel launch overhead.

Figure 5 illustrates the execution timing for both synchronous and asynchronous micro-profiling designs. The example assumes that there are four concurrent execution units and two kernels in the kernel pool. The darker gray kernel runs faster than the lighter one. With synchronous flow, the runtime waits for all kernels to finish profiling execution. It

Table 1. Summary of proposed productive profiling

Profiling method	Productive output in profiling	Extra space requirement	Async support
Fully-productive profiling	K	0	Yes
Hybrid-based partial-productive profiling	1	$\leq K-1$	Yes
Swap-based partial-productive profiling	1	$\leq K$	No

underutilizes the execution units while waiting for the slow kernel to complete its profiling execution. The asynchronous flow overcomes this problem by launching useful work on the vacant execution units with the initial version, which is shown Figure 5(b) and (c). However, the quality of the initial selection potentially can impact overall performance, as suboptimal code occupies execution units longer, as shown in Figure 5(b). In either case, the asynchronous flow yields better utilization and throughput compared to synchronous one.

Table 1 summarizes throughput, extra space requirement, and support of asynchronous flows for the three proposed productive micro-profiling modes. Given K kernel variants in the kernel pool, all K profiled portions of the workload contribute to the final workload in fully-productive profiling, while only 1 profiled portion does so in the two partial-productive profiling modes. In terms of extra space requirement, fully-productive profiling directly writes results into the original output space and needs no extra space, while the two partial-productive profiling methods require at most $K-1$ or K copies of space for either sandboxes or private outputs, respectively. It is worth mentioning that extra space requirement can be further reduced if footprint of memory accesses during profiling can be predicted so that a subset of output is allocated for sandboxing. Last, both fully-productive profiling and hybrid-based partial-productive profiling support asynchronous flows, since profiling results are directly written into the distinct, final output space, while swap-based partial-productive profiling cannot support asynchronous flows, because the final output space is not determined until profiling is complete.

3. Implementation

In this section, we first introduce the DySel runtime interface, and then detailed implementations for both CPU and GPU. Lastly, we discuss the analyses to determine the ratios of workload among kernel variants, and the profiling mode.

3.1 Runtime Interface

Unlike traditional runtimes, DySel allows the compilers or programmers to deposit multiple implementations of the same kernel function signature. Figure 6(a) shows the DySel kernel implementation registration API. A DySel-specific

```
DySelAddKernel(
    string kernel_sig,                  // kernel name
    func_ptr implementation,            // kernel implementation
    dim3 wa_factor,                     // work assignment factor
    vector<int> sandbox_index= []       // argument offsets for
                                        // sandboxes/private outputs
);
```

(a) Kernel Implementation Registration API

```
DySelLaunchKernel(
    string kernel_sig,          // kernel name
    bool profiling=true,        // profiling activation flag
    enum mode=fully_async       // profiling mode
);
```

(b) Kernel Launch API

Figure 6. DySel runtime interface

requirement is to provide *work assignment factor*, which is the number of workload units packed into each work-group for accurate profiling. Figure 6(b) shows the DySel kernel launch API. It allows the caller to specify whether profiling is activated or not using a *profiling activation flag* along with *profiling mode*. Compiler analyses required are discussed in Section 3.4.

Work Assignment Factor. An important class of optimizations is designed to utilize resources such as registers or scratchpad memory for improved execution efficiency. Among them, coarsening [19] and tiling change the amount of work assigned to each thread and thus the work assignment per kernel invocation. The runtime needs to know the relative work assignment between variant kernels for fair comparison. Once such workload-changing optimization is done, the compiler needs to inform the runtime about the change. For those kernel variants generated by programmers, DySel requires programmers to specify the relative work assignment ratios.

Profiling Activation Flag. A class of applications, such as stencil operations in partial differential equation (PDE) solvers or sparse matrix-vector multiplication (spmv) in conjugate gradient (CG) iterative solvers, launch a kernel iteratively without changing workload or data shape between iterations. In this scenario, the kernel can be just profiled in the first iteration and the selected variant can be reused for the later iterations. The profiling activation flag allows the user to turn on profiling only for the first iteration.

Profiling Mode. As mentioned previously, different modes of profiling have different applicability, throughput, and cost. Different classes of optimizations require different productive profiling modes for efficient, fair profiling. Asynchronous profiling potentially can reduce overheads of profiling. The DySel interface allows the compilers and programmers to indicate their choices.

3.2 CPU Runtime Implementation

Work distribution and prioritized execution for profiling are two main requirements for the CPU implementation of DySel. We use Intel's TBB [20] that has strong support for both. TBB's work stealing feature provides load balancing over multiple cores while its concurrent task groups allow assigning higher scheduling priority to profiling execution. In the profiling task group, kernel invocation is wrapped by timer calls to measure execution time. Updating the current best variant is done via atomic operation when the execution time of a variant is found to be smaller than the current minimum. Non-profiling task group invokes the current best implementation upon launch. When profiling is activated, it first launches the profiling task group with priority, which is followed by launching the non-profiling task group. Synchronous mode puts a barrier to wait for the profiling task group to finish its execution between the two task group launches, while asynchronous mode schedules both task groups concurrently. When profiling is not activated, it launches the non-profiling task group only.

3.3 GPU Runtime Implementation

Measuring execution time with precision for a kernel with small workload on GPUs requires a high-resolution timer. It is often inaccurate to use wall clock timer or GPU driver event according to our experience. Alternatively, we use in-kernel performance counters to solve this problem. The in-kernel performance counter is CUDA-specific, thus DySel first translates OpenCL code to CUDA code when performing profiling on NVIDIA GPUs. On the other hand, performance comparison takes place on the host. Therefore, the GPU runtime for DySel entails a combined solution where kernel execution timing information is measured on the GPU and used by the DySel runtime code running on the host.

Kernel Code Transformations. Each kernel variant is further replicated into three extended versions: one for profiling, one for non-profiling batch execution, and one for eager execution in the asynchronous profiling mode. First the code for profiling is augmented by inserting performance measurement code, shown in Figure 7(b). It reads the CUDA clock register, as shown in Figure 7(a), at the beginning and the end of the code, and the difference is recorded to a dedicated memory location. The code will be executed over multiple thread blocks because GPU throughput is determined by both latency and parallelism. Atomic operations are used to mark the earliest and the latest cycles among the participating thread blocks. The profiling code is also augmented with a block index offset parameter to shift thread block id so that the kernel will be profiled based on a particular part of the workload. Second, the code for non-profiling batch execution has an additional parameter that indicates the number of thread blocks executed during profiling and a test that suppresses the execution of the thread blocks that have been executed during profiling. This code will also be used when profiling is not activated by supplying a 0 value for the parameter. Finally, the code for eager dispatch in asynchronous profiling mode has the same block id shifting code as the profiling code but does not have measurement code. This code is exclusively used in the asynchronous profiling mode.

```
__device__ unsigned int get_cycle() {
  unsigned int y;
  asm("{\n\t" // use braces for local scope
      " mov.u32 %0, %clock;\n\t"
      "}"
      : "=r"(y) );
  return y;
}
```

(a) CUDA in-kernel clock register

```
unsigned int local_start_stamp;
if((threadIdx.x)==0) {        //only one thread in a  thread block
   local_start_stamp = get_cycle();
   unsigned int old = atomicMin(global_start_stamp + kernel_id, local_start_stamp);
   local_start_stamp= old > local_start_stamp? local_start_stamp: old;
}

//Here is kernel code, between the two measurement codes

__syncthreads();
if((threadIdx.x)==0) {   //only one thread in a  thread block
   unsigned int old = atomicInc(global_count + kernel_id, gridDim.x);
   if(old ==  gridDim.x-1) {  //only last thread block of profiling
      unsigned int local_diff = get_cycle()-local_start_stamp;
      old = atomicMin(global_diff, local_diff );
      if(global_diff <old )
         atomicExch(global_final_selection,kernel_id);
   }
}
```

(b) GPU profiling code

Figure 7. Example of GPU profiling code for a kernel using 1D thread block

Host Code Generation. DySel uses CUDA streams to launch different kernels concurrently on a GPU. By using multiple concurrent streams, profiling of different kernels can be done in parallel, reducing the profiling overhead. In the synchronous mode, `cudaDeviceSynchronize` is called to wait for all streams to finish profiling. The host code then chooses the best one, followed by launching the code for non-profiling batch execution. In the asynchronous mode, DySel calls `cudaStreamQuery` to check the status of each stream for profiling and schedules eager dispatches. After all profiling streams complete, DySel launches the remaining computation in a batch.

3.4 Compiler Analyses

Delivering accurate information on profiling mode and work assignment factor to DySel is critical for both correctness and efficiency. The information can be specified by programmers. However, such an approach is not desirable because inconsistent information can be supplied by the programmer, which may result in unexpected behavior. Compiler-driven approach can supply safe information automatically, though it can be conservative. We outline three important analyses for a compiler to derive such information:

Safe Point Analysis. Relative work assignment among kernel variants can be normalized to the least common multiple (LCM) among all related assignments for a fair comparison. Therefore, the number of work-groups in each variant of a kernel can be defined as the LCM divided by each work assignment factor. For more details, we refer to [24]. In DySel, we further multiply the number returned from safe point analysis by a constant to make the total workload become a multiple of the number of CPU cores or GPU streaming multiprocessors (SMs) in order to fully utilize the hardware.

Uniform Workload Analysis. A large disparity of loop iteration counts among profiling execution may lead to unfair performance comparison. We employ uniform workload analysis to determine whether loop bounds are varying across work-groups. Uniform workload analysis also detects an early break of a loop or an early termination of a kernel. For more details, we refer to [14]. The result of uniform workload analysis determines which profiling mode is applied in DySel. It is worth noting that uniform workload analysis may be conservative for kernels with data-dependent loop bounds. For example, in spmv on a CSR matrix, the given matrix might have an uniform non-zeros per row, but our analysis will flag it as a non-uniform workload since the loop bound is data-dependent. DySel interface provides programmers with an option to select a specific profiling mode by overriding the compiler's decision.

Side Effect Analysis. Whether work-groups have overlapping and variable output ranges is critical for DySel to safely conduct productive profiling. We employ side effect analysis to identify whether output overlapping happens. Here, we either assume no data race in the original OpenCL source code [16] or that the original OpenCL programs are deterministic. Therefore, the current implementation of side effect analysis only detects global atomic operations. Upon detection of global atomic operations, the compiler restricts the micro-profiling to swap-based to ensure correctness. Similar to uniform workload analysis, side effect analysis is used to determine profiling mode, and is also conservative, since atomic operations do not directly imply that memory contention really happen across work-groups. Therefore, DySel also allows the programmers to override the compiler decision.

4. Evaluation

In this section, we evaluate our prototype DySel implementation on several OpenCL/CUDA benchmarks on both CPU and GPU architectures.

4.1 Setup

All experiments are done on a system with an Intel Core i7-3820 CPU with an NVIDIA K20c GPU connected via

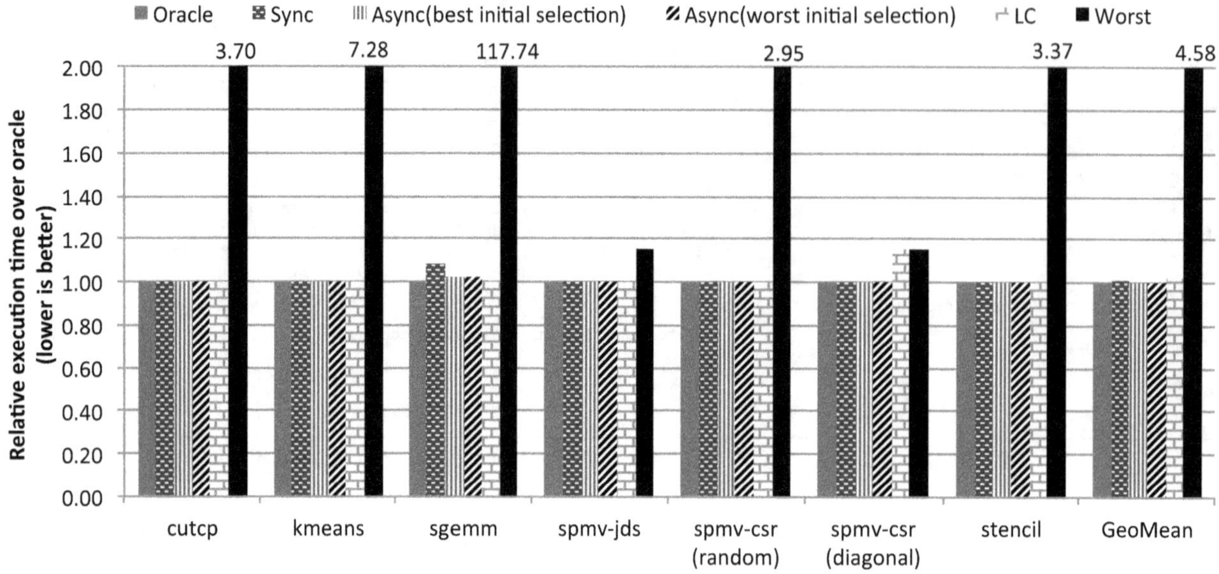

Figure 8. DySel performance results on locality-centric scheduling on CPU for OpenCL

PCI-E interface. For CPU experiments, our DySel starts with OpenCL code, performs all the code transformations described in this paper, produces C source code with calls to the TBB API, and uses the Intel's icc compiler version 15.0.2 with vectorization enabled to generate final executable code. For GPU experiments, DySel starts with OpenCL code, performs the code transformations described in this paper, produces CUDA source code, and uses nvcc version 7.0.27 with -O3 and –arch=sm_35 compile flag to generate executable. The CUDA driver version in use is 346.82. The system runs on 64-bit Ubuntu Server 14.04 LTS.

The experiments are based on benchmarks from Parboil [28], Rodinia [6] and SHOC [9] benchmark suites. Different experiments subscribe to slightly different sets of benchmarks according to their own purposes, which are individually described for each.

The evaluation focuses on the impact of DySel on kernel execution time. To this end, we measure execution time that includes all profiling time, profiling kernel launch overheads, and compute time of the remaining workload for both CPU and GPU architectures. For GPUs, time spent on data transfer among architectures before and after kernel execution is not included since it is the same across variants and profiling modes, but time spent on data transfer required by DySel profiling and variant selection is included.

The oracle results in the following is defined as the single *pure* versions that delivers the shortest runtime for the corresponding benchmarks. Note a *mixed* version that applies different pure versions on different partitions of computation could potentially outperform the "oracle". In this paper, we only compare DySel with the best pure version. For the mixed version, we consider it as the future work.

4.2 Case Study I & II: Single Compile-time Optimization

Performance modeling at compile time can yield the highest accuracy when it is used in isolation from other transformations. We compare DySel's performance to two high-quality compile time optimizations for CPU and GPU in order to compare accuracy and benefit. For CPU, locality-centric scheduling of OpenCL work-items execution [17] is used. For GPU, data placement [7, 15] is chosen.

The purpose of this experiment is to test whether DySel can adaptively and efficiently select the right variant from candidate kernel implementations. When a single standalone optimizer works well, DySel can confirm the version with an ignorable overhead. On the other hand, when the static optimizer makes a wrong decision, DySel can insure that an alternative is chosen to avoid performance loss.

Locality-Centric Scheduling on CPU for OpenCL. We evaluate DySel on the locality-centric scheduling of work-item executions for CPUs using four benchmarks, `sgemm`, `spmv` (denoted as `spmv-jds`), `stencil` and `cutcp`, from Parboil [28], one benchmark, `kmeans`, from Rodinia [6], and one benchmark, `spmv` with scalar dot products on a CSR format matrix without padding (denoted as `spmv-csr`), from SHOC [9]. All of the chosen versions in Parboil are base versions. These benchmarks are selected because their CPU performance is sensitive to the scheduling policy used. The inputs for Parboil and Rodinia benchmarks are all default, while the inputs for `spmv-csr` include a $16k$-by-$16k$ random sparse matrix with 1% probability of non-zeros (the default input in SHOC, denoted as `random`) and a $2M$-by-$2M$ diagonal matrix (denoted as `diagonal`). In `spmv-jds` and `spmv-csr`, DySel applies hybrid-based partial-productive profiling due to irregular workload, while

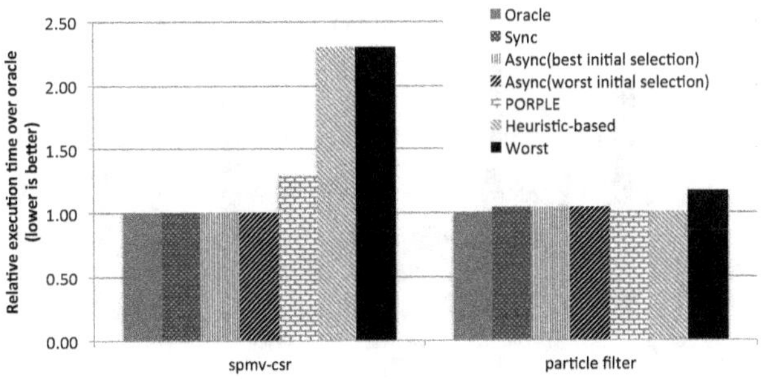

Figure 9. DySel performance results on data placement on GPU

in the rest, DySel applies fully-productive profiling. Since `kmeans`, `spmv-jds`, `spmv-csr` and `stencil` are iterative, DySel profiles only the first iteration.

We use the OpenCL implementation of Kim et al. [17], which is denoted as LC, to generate code from possible combinations in scheduling of work-items execution. LC employs a heuristic that minimizes overall memory access strides in work-items execution in the presence of loops. Possible numbers of different schedules are 60, 3, 6, 2, 2 and 6 for `cutcp`, `kmeans`, `sgemm`, `spmv`, `spmv-csr` and `stencil`, respectively, as schedules are permutation of work-item loops and kernel loops to form loop nesting.

Figure 8 compares performance of DySel and compile-time heuristic over oracle. DySel achieves close to optimal results for all benchmarks with negligible overhead. The results also demonstrate the importance of a data-locality-friendly schedule as the gap between the oracle and the worst is significant. A heuristic-based static selection could have caused a large performance loss with a suboptimal decision. However, DySel correctly selects the optimal schedule for all given benchmarks. In the case of `spmv-csr` with the diagonal input, the LC static heuristic selected incorrectly but DySel avoided the mistake. When no or little performance variation due to input distribution is expected, DySel chooses the optimal from profiling, witnessed by `cutcp`, `kmeans`, `sgemm`, and `stencil`. In a situation where input distribution has a high impact to data locality, such as `spmv-csr`, the static approach works well with a certain input distribution but it cannot cope with all possible cases with equal efficiency. DySel, on the other hand, adaptively chooses between two schedules, yielding close to optimal performance for both cases. Additionally, it also shows that asynchronous mode hides profiling latency better than synchronous mode. The impact of initial version selection in asynchronous mode is marginal in all cases. More discussion about the impact of synchronous mode and the initial version selection in asynchronous mode is shown in Section 5.

Data Placement on GPU. We evaluate DySel on the data placement optimization on GPU using two benchmarks, `spmv-csr` from SHOC [9] and particle filter from Rodinia [6]. For `spmv-csr`, we choose three data placement policies listed in the PORPLE paper [7] for the recent three generations of GPUs, and one data placement policy from a heuristic-based method [15] as the candidates. For particle filter, we choose two data placement policies from the PORPLE paper, one from the heuristic-based method, and one originally from Rodinia as the candidates. The input for `spmv-csr` is the random matrix, which is also used in micro simulation of PORPLE, and the input size for particle filter is 32,000. Both benchmarks use hybrid-based partial-productive profiling due to irregular workload, and `spmv-csr` is profiled for only the first iteration.

Figure 9 demonstrates that DySel can efficiently choose the optimal data placement policies for both benchmarks on a Kepler K20c GPU. On `spmv-csr`, DySel successfully selects the optimal version with a completely negligible overhead, while both PORPLE and the heuristic-based method generate suboptimal versions, falling short of the best achievable performance by a factor of 1.29x and 2.29x, respectively. Interestingly, the heuristic-based method yields the worst performance. Also, the optimal data placement for `spmv-csr` on Kepler is actually generated by PORPLE but with the target on Fermi architectures. On particle filter, DySel successfully selects the optimal version with at most 4% overhead, while both PORPLE and the heuristic-based method generate the optimal version. The original policy from Rodinia delivers the worst performance of a 1.17x slowdown compared to the best performance.

In this evaluation, both benchmarks expose different levels of challenge for static data placement due to irregular workload. PORPLE tends to perform much better than the heuristic-based method, because PORPLE uses more complicated memory and cache models. However, due to lack of runtime information, PORPLE might still make a wrong decision. With DySel, the performance loss from these mistake can be minimized.

4.3 Case Study III: Mixed Compile-time Optimizations

We evaluate multiple mixed and complex optimizations using four Parboil benchmarks: `cutcp`, `sgemm`, `spmv-jds`, and `stencil`. We choose all versions listed in these Parboil benchmarks as the candidates. There are two candidates for `sgemm`, three for `stencil`, four for `spmv-jds` on GPU, two for `spmv-jds` on CPU, and two for `cutcp`. All inputs are the default large datasets in Parboil. The profiling modes are the same as the previous experiment.

The purpose of this experiment is to test DySel's adaptive selection capability when static heuristics cannot easily foresee the impact of combined optimizations for decision making. The relevant optimizations for `cutcp`, `sgemm` and `stencil` are tiling, coarsening, data placement, loop unrolling and prefetching. Particularly, `cutcp` has tiling, coarsening, and data placement using scratchpad; `sgemm` has tiling, coarsening, loop unrolling, and data placement using scratchpad; `stencil` has tiling, coarsening, and data

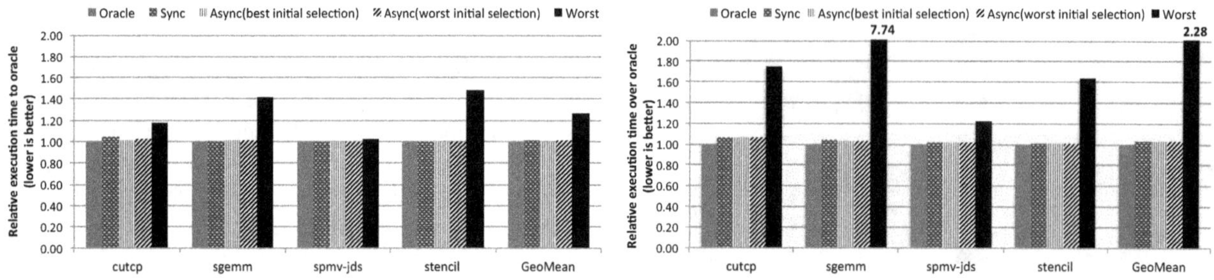

(a) CPU (b) GPU

Figure 10. DySel performance results on mixed compile-time optimizations

placement using scratchpad; `spmv-jds` has tiling, coarsening, loop unrolling, prefetching, and data placement using texture memory, which is only for GPUs. Work assignment factors are 4x and 16x for `cutcp` and `sgemm`, respectively, while `stencil` comes with three versions and work assignment factors relative to the base version are 64x and 128x.

CPU. Figure 10(a) compares the performance of DySel when differently optimized kernels are provided. Again, LC from the OpenCL implementation of Kim et al. [17] is used to compile the kernels. DySel achieves near optimal results for all benchmarks, with only 2% overhead on average compared to oracle. While not shown in Figure 10(a), we note that for all benchmarks, the best variant for CPU execution are naive base versions from the selected benchmark suites, as they allow the greatest flexibility for the compiler in planning how to serialize execution of work-items. GPU-specific optimizations such as data placement and data prefetching using scoreboarding make no difference for CPU. Tiling using scratchpad memory typically leads to negative results on CPUs because there is no latency gain using them after they are lowered to CPU's uniform memory space, resulting in a 1.23x slowdown on average compared to oracle. This result again confirms that the help from runtime can mitigate the stress having to develop complicated models at compile time.

GPU. Figure 10(b) compares the performance of DySel when differently optimized kernels are provided for a Kepler K20c GPU. DySel always selects optimal version among candidates, except `spmv-jds`. In `spmv-jds`, DySel chooses the second best version (which applies loop unrolling, prefetching, and texture memory), which has only 0.8% performance degradation from the best one (texture memory only). We observe that optimizations of loop unrolling and prefetching applied in `spmv-jds` on a Kepler architecture are redundant when texture memory is applied, but they do improve performance when texture memory is not used. The similar situation is also observed in `stencil`, where scratchpad tiling and coarsening along the x-dimension does not improve performance on top of coarsening along the z-dimension on Kepler. These mismatched optimizations may come from a mistake of the experts who write the benchmarks or from non-transferable optimizations across different generations of GPUs. In both cases, it confirms performance prediction for the combined set of optimizations is challenging, and DySel can help resolve the challenge.

4.4 Case Study IV: Input-dependent Optimization

We evaluate an input-dependent version selection scenario using `spmv-csr` from SHOC benchmark suite [9]. We choose two `spmv-csr` versions, one using scalar dot product (denoted as `scalar`) and the other using vector dot product (denoted as `vector`), from SHOC. The optimal version of `spmv` on a CSR-format matrix is highly dependent on sparsity of a matrix [4], which is typically unknown at compile time. We test with two matrices, the random sparse matrix and the diagonal matrix, described in the previous experimental setup. The profiling modes are also the same as the previous experiment.

The purpose of this experiment is to demonstrate DySel's adaptive selection capability when the compiler simply cannot predict the performance, due to lack of critical information, which is sparsity of the actual matrix in this experiment.

CPU. Figure 11(a) shows performance of DySel compared to that of a scalar kernel and a vector kernel for all possible combinations of work-item scheduling for them. DySel correctly selects the optimal one for both inputs, yielding near oracle performance. The selection here is particularly complicated by the dimensions of schedule, kernel version and input data distribution. Here, LC chooses to iterate in-kernel loops first (denoted as `DFO`) for both scalar and vector implementations and uses it unconditionally. However, it does not cope well with unfavorable input distribution from the diagonal matrix, where work-item-loop-first (denoted as `BFO`) schedule is desired. As for version selection among scalar and vector, scalar performs better when `DFO` is chosen mainly because of less overhead having to deal with control divergence. For CPU execution, the vector version is inferior because it uses local memory which incurs the copy cost without any benefit in a CPU. This is a reason why the `BFO` schedule for the vector kernel performs similar to `DFO` in spite of favorable data locality.

GPU. Figure 11(b) demonstrates that DySel can adaptively select the optimal implementations for different matrices on a Kepler GPU. On the random matrix, DySel se-

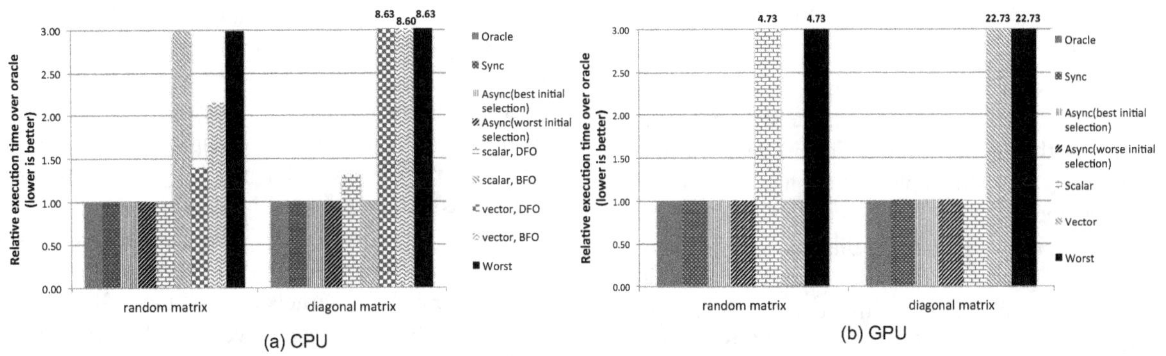

Figure 11. DySel performance results on input-dependent optimization

lects the vector version with at most 0.4% overhead, while the scalar version delivers a 4.73x showdown, due to non-coalescing memory accesses. On the other hand, for the diagonal matrix, DySel selects the scalar version with at most 0.8% overhead, while the vector version delivers a significant 22.73x showdown, due to underutilization of vectors (warps on NVIDIA GPUs).

5. Discussion

5.1 Performance Impact between Sync and Async DySel

Long-running profiling execution that lasts to the end of the profiling phase increases profiling overhead, which is further amplified by the number of vacant execution units waiting for workload. For example, `sgemm` with data locality scheduling shown in Figure 8 is regarded as a pathological case due to its huge variation of 117x between the oracle and the worst. The synchronous profiling overhead is 8%. Nevertheless, asynchronous mode can scatter the overhead, suppressing it down to less than 5%.

The asynchronous DySel GPU implementation is based on CUDA concurrent execution using CUDA streams, in which different kernel invocations are enqueued by the host CPU. It requires the host to query the status of the streams. At the same time, DySel employs micro-profiling, which typically takes extremely small profiling time. Combining these two facts, querying the status often takes a longer latency than profiling time. Therefore, it can only have few or even zero eager dispatches. In the end, synchronous and asynchronous DySel have only marginal difference for GPUs.

One possible solution to further improve asynchronous DySel is to apply CUDA Dynamic Parallelism to avoid the long latency from host queries. However, current CUDA Dynamic Parallelism also suffers from a huge kernel launching overhead on the device [32, 34], which is even larger than the original DySel overhead.

5.2 Profiling Overhead

Among all experimental benchmarks, DySel exposes 8% overhead in the worst case compared to the oracle results. However, since a few of the experimental benchmarks are iterative, their overhead is amortized across iterations and cannot be easily quantized in the above figures.

Here, we further investigate those benchmarks, which are `spmv-jds`, `stencil`, `spmv-csr`, and `kmeans`, by enabling profiling in every iteration. In this experiment, we observe increased overhead.

For CPU, most of the above benchmarks show less than 6% overhead, except `spmv-csr` for the random matrix with observed overhead of 88% to the oracle. Performance profiling using Intel's vtune reveals that the TBB dispatch loop incurs substantial overhead from spin and associated cost, which might have been caused by managing huge number of extremely tiny tasks. A tradeoff is to implement bigger task granularity by serializing several kernel invocations at the expense of load imbalance. Also, profiling accuracy can be a problem when the unit of workload is small, which is the case where system noise can affect the evaluation, particularly for CPUs. In `spmv-csr`, for example, the dynamic selection accuracy is 95%. By increasing the number of executions per kernel during profiling, this can be resolved at the expense of additional profiling overhead. The exact tradeoff and an empirical solution are to be further studied.

Similarly, on GPUs, `spmv-csr` in Case study II has 14.7% overhead; `spmv-jds` in Case study III has 46.5%, while stencil has only 3.7% overhead; `spmv-csr` in Case study IV has 9.9% to 30.5% overhead for different input datasets. We recognize most of the high overhead is from the `spmv` benchmarks (`spmv-csr` and `spmv-jds`). Unlike the other benchmarks, each iteration of `spmv` spends several to several hundred microseconds in non-profiling execution on the GPU, while profiling time takes around a few to 10s of microseconds, which is very close to the GPU kernel launch overhead. In this sense, profiling overheads are completely exposed despite the small portions of the workload DySel profiles. Fortunately, most of these data-parallel kernels with insignificant execution time are either iterative or not performance critical. Also, this overhead should be much less for larger sparse matrices in real applications.

5.3 Performance Advantage over Heuristic Approaches

As mentioned previously, quality and precision of heuristics dictate performance. In this subsection, we highlight performance insurance that DySel provides against decisions made by state-of-the-art heuristic implementations.

From Case study I & II, DySel can provide 1.15x more performance in `spmv-csr` when the diagonal matrix is given to the CPU (in Figure 8). PORPLE [7] and the heuristic-based method [15] making suboptimal data placement policies for GPU, DySel achieves 1.29x and 2.29x improvements over the model-based counterparts (in Figure 9).

In Case study III & IV, it is difficult to judge which version the compiler should generate since the kernels are written by experts [9, 28]. Assuming suboptimal decisions are made, DySel can outperform 1.26x and 2.28x on average for CPU and GPU, respectively (in Figure 10). In Case study IV (in Figure 11), the amount of performance improvement is input-dependent. DySel recovers 2.98x and 8.63x speedups over the worst possible choice for CPU for the random and the diagonal input matrices, respectively. Similarly, it achieves 4.73x and 22.73x speedups on GPU for the same input matrices.

6. Related Work

Various works have covered performance modeling for overall kernel performance or specific optimizations of data-parallel programming.

Dynamic optimization has been studied extensively for performance, which exploits information only available at runtime. Dynamo [3] and Mojo [8] monitor execution traces to capture a sequence of frequently executed basic blocks and replace the trace with a highly optimized instruction sequence. However, their performance suffers in many cases due to high overhead of execution monitoring and runtime compilation. Similarly, modern managed languages typically are supported by runtime optimization [1] for instruction throughput. While aforementioned approaches are focused on finding a better instruction sequence at fine-grained scope such as basic blocks, our work differs as multiple differently implemented kernels are used, which brings a greater impact to performance with low cost profiling overhead. Reactive tiling [24] alters tiling size on-the-fly for working set size optimization, which can also be properly implemented using our approach. ADAPT [31] sharing a similar idea with our work, however, the optimization rules are not performance portable to other architectures. Unlike this work, our approach does not require coupling with a runtime optimizer, making it easier to deploy.

Performance models for GPUs have been studied to provide performance feedbacks for optimization benefits [2, 23]. Several compile-time optimizations for data-parallel programming based on **heuristics** or **modeling** have been done on CPUs [12, 14, 17, 21, 27] and GPUs [7, 11, 15, 22, 35]. DySel relieves the pressure for developing an optimal and costly version as it allows them to generate multiple versions.

Adaptive runtime using **profiling** has been an area of great interest. Charm++ [30] employs a message-passing-driven adaptive runtime for matching an execution unit for a given task at a node level by continuously monitoring the performance over different types of execution units. Unlike Charm++, DySel applies runtime profiling for selecting the optimal versions of kernels on a CPU or GPU. SASSI [25] provided by NVIDIA can deliver flexible **software profiling** for GPU architectures. DySel applies software profiling instructions on CPU and GPU architectures for selecting the optimal versions at runtime.

Model-driven adaptive runtime has been widely studied for both CPUs and GPUs. Reactive tiling [24] switches between kernels of different tile sizes at runtime, from a decision made by subscribing **online** profiling results into a model-based (through curve-fitting) heuristic. Dollinger et al. [10] proposed a model-based adaptive runtime selection for GPUs using offline profiling. Elastic computing [33] dynamically selects the optimal version from multiple implementations of a function based on a cost model built at install time via profiling them. PEPPHER [5] provides offline profiling [18] functionality to help select variants of components and construct a heterogeneous program. In contrast, DySel provides a lightweight **online productive** profiling for multiple variants selection on data-parallel programming without specific models involved.

7. Conclusion

We have discussed and showed the drawback of solely relying on heuristics or performance models to drive transformations on diverse and complicated heterogeneous architectures. We leverage the property of performance similarity across the entire workload processing and introduce micro profiling technique at runtime for a fraction of workload to derive performance characteristics for different kernel implementations. Our proposed approach, DySel, not only overcomes the drawback of model-based approaches but also achieves near-oracle performance with profiling overhead under 8% in the worst observed case from our evaluation of Parboil, Rodinia, and SHOC benchmarks on CPU and GPU. As precise modeling becomes harder to come by for modern architectures, our proposed approach can be a simple yet effective alternative for a wide range of systems and applications.

Acknowledgments

This work is supported by the Starnet Center for Future Architecture Research (C-FAR), the DoE Vancouver Project (DE-FC0210ER26004/DE-SC0005515), and the NVIDIA GCoE at UIUC.

References

[1] M. Arnold, S. Fink, D. Grove, M. Hind, and P. F. Sweeney. Adaptive optimization in the Jalapẽno JVM. In *ACM SIGPLAN Notices*, volume 35, pages 47–65. ACM, 2000.

[2] S. S. Baghsorkhi, M. Delahaye, S. J. Patel, W. D. Gropp, and W.-m. W. Hwu. An adaptive performance modeling tool for GPU architectures. In *ACM SIGPLAN Notices*, volume 45, pages 105–114, 2010.

[3] V. Bala, E. Duesterwald, and S. Banerjia. Dynamo: a transparent dynamic optimization system. In *ACM SIGPLAN Notices*, volume 35, pages 1–12. ACM, 2000.

[4] N. Bell and M. Garland. Implementing sparse matrix-vector multiplication on throughput-oriented processors. In *Proceedings of the Conference on High Performance Computing Networking, Storage and Analysis*, pages 18:1–18:11, 2009. ISBN 978-1-60558-744-8.

[5] S. Benkner, S. Pllana, J. L. Träf, P. Tsigas, U. Dolinsky, C. Augonnet, B. Bachmayer, C. Kessler, D. Moloney, and V. Osipov. PEPPHER: Efficient and productive usage of hybrid computing systems. *IEEE Micro*, 31(5):28–41, 2011.

[6] S. Che, M. Boyer, J. Meng, D. Tarjan, J. W. Sheaffer, S.-H. Lee, and K. Skadron. Rodinia: A benchmark suite for heterogeneous computing. In *Workload Characterization, 2009. IISWC 2009. IEEE International Symposium on*, pages 44–54, 2009.

[7] G. Chen, B. Wu, D. Li, and X. Shen. PORPLE: An extensible optimizer for portable data placement on GPU. In *Proceedings of the 47th Annual IEEE/ACM International Symposium on Microarchitecture*, pages 88–100, 2014.

[8] W.-K. Chen, S. Lerner, R. Chaiken, and D. M. Gillies. Mojo: A dynamic optimization system. In *3rd ACM Workshop on Feedback-Directed and Dynamic Optimization (FDDO-3)*, pages 81–90, 2000.

[9] A. Danalis, G. Marin, C. McCurdy, J. S. Meredith, P. C. Roth, K. Spafford, V. Tipparaju, and J. S. Vetter. The scalable heterogeneous computing (SHOC) benchmark suite. In *Proceedings of the 3rd Workshop on General-Purpose Computation on Graphics Processing Units*, pages 63–74, 2010.

[10] J.-F. Dollinger and V. Loechner. Adaptive runtime selection for GPU. In *Parallel Processing, 2013 42nd International Conference on*, pages 70–79, 2013.

[11] Y. Dotsenko, S. S. Baghsorkhi, B. Lloyd, and N. K. Govindaraju. Auto-tuning of fast Fourier transform on graphics processors. In *ACM SIGPLAN Notices*, volume 46, pages 257–266, 2011.

[12] J. Gummaraju, L. Morichetti, M. Houston, B. Sander, B. R. Gaster, and B. Zheng. Twin Peaks: A Software Platform for Heterogeneous Computing on General-purpose and Graphics Processors. In *Proceedings of the 19th International Conference on Parallel Architectures and Compilation Techniques*, pages 205–216, 2010.

[13] Intel. Vectorizer knobs. `https://software.intel.com/en-us/node/540483`.

[14] P. Jääskeläinen, C. S. de La Lama, E. Schnetter, K. Raiskila, J. Takala, and H. Berg. pocl: A performance-portable OpenCL implementation, 2014.

[15] B. Jang, D. Schaa, P. Mistry, and D. Kaeli. Exploiting memory access patterns to improve memory performance in data-parallel architectures. *IEEE Trans. Parallel Distrib. Syst.*, 22 (1):105–118, 2011.

[16] Khronos OpenCL Working Group and others. The OpenCL Specification. *A. Munshi, Ed*, 2008.

[17] H.-S. Kim, I. El Hajj, J. Stratton, S. Lumetta, and W.-M. Hwu. Locality-centric thread scheduling for bulk-synchronous programming models on CPU architectures. In *Proceedings of the 13th Annual IEEE/ACM International Symposium on Code Generation and Optimization*, pages 257–268, 2015.

[18] L. Li, U. Dastgeer, and C. Kessler. Adaptive off-line tuning for optimized composition of components for heterogeneous many-core systems. In *High Performance Computing for Computational Science-VECPAR 2012*, pages 329–345. 2013.

[19] A. Magni, C. Dubach, and M. F. O'Boyle. A large-scale cross-architecture evaluation of thread-coarsening. In *Proceedings of the International Conference on High Performance Computing, Networking, Storage and Analysis*, page 11, 2013.

[20] J. Reinders. *Intel threading building blocks: outfitting C++ for multi-core processor parallelism.* " O'Reilly Media, Inc.", 2007.

[21] N. Rotem. Intel OpenCL Implicit Vectorization Module, 2011.

[22] S. Ryoo, C. I. Rodrigues, S. S. Stone, S. S. Baghsorkhi, S.-Z. Ueng, J. A. Stratton, and W.-m. W. Hwu. Program optimization space pruning for a multithreaded GPU. In *Proceedings of the 6th annual IEEE/ACM international symposium on Code generation and optimization*, pages 195–204, 2008.

[23] J. Sim, A. Dasgupta, H. Kim, and R. Vuduc. A performance analysis framework for identifying potential benefits in GPGPU applications. In *ACM SIGPLAN Notices*, volume 47, pages 11–22, 2012.

[24] J. Srinivas, W. Ding, and M. Kandemir. Reactive tiling. In *Code Generation and Optimization, 2015 IEEE/ACM International Symposium on*, pages 91–102, 2015.

[25] M. Stephenson, S. K. S. Hari, Y. Lee, E. Ebrahimi, D. R. Johnson, D. Nellans, M. O'Connor, and S. W. Keckler. Flexible software profiling of gpu architectures. In *Proceedings of the 42nd Annual International Symposium on Computer Architecture*, pages 185–197. ACM, 2015.

[26] J. Stratton, N. Anssari, C. Rodrigues, I.-J. Sung, N. Obeid, L.-W. Chang, G. D. Liu, and W.-m. Hwu. Optimization and architecture effects on GPU computing workload performance. In *Innovative Parallel Computing (InPar), 2012*, pages 1–10, 2012.

[27] J. A. Stratton, S. S. Stone, and W. W. Hwu. MCUDA: An efficient implementation of CUDA kernels for multi-core CPUs. In *Languages and Compilers for Parallel Computing*, pages 16–30. 2008.

[28] J. A. Stratton, C. Rodrigues, I. Sung, N. Obeid, L. Chang, N. Anssari, G. D. Liu, and W. W. Hwu. Parboil: A revised benchmark suite for scientific and commercial throughput computing. *IMPACT Technical Report*, 2012.

[29] J. A. Stratton, C. Rodrigues, I.-J. Sung, L.-W. Chang, N. Anssari, G. Liu, W.-m. W. Hwu, and N. Obeid. Algo-

rithm and data optimization techniques for scaling to massively threaded systems. *Computer*, 45(8):0026–32, 2012.

[30] R. Vasudevan, S. S. Vadhiyar, and L. V. Kalé. G-Charm: an adaptive runtime system for message-driven parallel applications on hybrid systems. In *Proceedings of the 27th international ACM conference on International conference on supercomputing*, pages 349–358, 2013.

[31] M. J. Voss and R. Eigemann. High-level adaptive program optimization with ADAPT. In *ACM SIGPLAN Notices*, volume 36, pages 93–102. ACM, 2001.

[32] J. Wang and S. Yalamanchili. Characterization and analysis of dynamic parallelism in unstructured GPU applications. In *Workload Characterization (IISWC), 2014 IEEE International Symposium on*, pages 51–60, 2014.

[33] J. R. Wernsing and G. Stitt. Elastic computing: a framework for transparent, portable, and adaptive multi-core heterogeneous computing. In *ACM SIGPLAN Notices*, volume 45, pages 115–124, 2010.

[34] Y. Yang and H. Zhou. CUDA-NP: Realizing nested thread-level parallelism in GPGPU applications. In *ACM SIGPLAN Notices*, volume 49, pages 93–106, 2014.

[35] Y. Yang, P. Xiang, J. Kong, and H. Zhou. A GPGPU compiler for memory optimization and parallelism management. In *ACM SIGPLAN Notices*, volume 45, pages 86–97, 2010.

Baymax: QoS Awareness and Increased Utilization for Non-Preemptive Accelerators in Warehouse Scale Computers

Quan Chen[*†1] Hailong Yang[*‡1] Jason Mars[*] Lingjia Tang[*]

[*]Clarity Lab, University of Michigan - Ann Arbor, MI, USA
[†]Shanghai Jiao Tong University, Shanghai, China
[‡]Beihang University, Beijing, China
{quanchen, hailong, profmars, lingjia}@umich.edu

Abstract

Modern warehouse-scale computers (WSCs) are being outfitted with accelerators to provide the significant compute required by emerging intelligent personal assistant (IPA) workloads such as voice recognition, image classification, and natural language processing. It is well known that the diurnal user access pattern of user-facing services provides a strong incentive to co-locate applications for better accelerator utilization and efficiency, and prior work has focused on enabling co-location on multicore processors. However, interference when co-locating applications on non-preemptive accelerators is fundamentally different than contention on multi-core CPUs and introduces a new set of challenges to reduce QoS violation.

To address this open problem, we first identify the underlying causes for QoS violation in accelerator-outfitted servers. Our experiments show that queuing delay for the compute resources and PCI-e bandwidth contention for data transfer are the main two factors that contribute to the long tails of user-facing applications. We then present Baymax, a runtime system that orchestrates the execution of compute tasks from different applications and mitigates PCI-e bandwidth contention to deliver the required QoS for user-facing applications and increase the accelerator utilization. Using DjiNN, a deep neural network service, Sirius, an end-to-end IPA workload, and traditional applications on a Nvidia K40 GPU, our evaluation shows that Baymax improves the accelerator utilization by 91.3% while achieving the desired 99%-ile latency target for for user-facing applications. In fact, Baymax reduces the 99%-ile latency of user-facing applications by up to 195x over default execution.

Keywords scheduling; quality of service; warehouse scale computers; non-preemptive accelerators

1. Introduction

Emerging intelligent personal assistant (IPA) workloads including speech recognition [1, 2], image classification [3], face recognition [4] and natural language processing [5, 6] have recently gained tremendous momentum. Several major Internet-service companies including Google [7], Microsoft [8], Apple [9] and Baidu [10] have all released their IPA services providing a wide range of features. Compared to traditional warehouse scale computer (WSC) applications such as web-search, IPA applications are significantly more computationally demanding [11].

Accelerators, such as GPUs, ASICs and FPGAs, have been shown to be particularly suitable for these IPA applications from both performance and total cost of ownership (TCO) perspectives [11]. Therefore, to satisfy the evergrowing user demand at a low cost, datacenters have recently adopted accelerator-outfitted servers for these applications [12, 13]. Meanwhile, since these IPA services generally experience diurnal pattern [14, 15] (leaving the accelerator resources under-utilized for most of the time except peak hours), it is more cost efficient to co-locate user-facing applications and throughput-oriented applications on accelerators. However, accelerator sharing introduces varying amount of performance interference between co-located applications, and thus poses critical challenges for guaranteeing that user-facing applications can meet their quality of service targets.

There has been a significant amount of prior work recognizing the importance, and addressing the problem, of contention due to co-locations to enforce quality of service

ASPLOS '16, April 02-06, 2016, Atlanta, GA, USA

DOI: http://dx.doi.org/10.1145/2872362.2872368

[1] Work was conducted as a postdoc fellow of Clarity Lab at the University of Michigan.

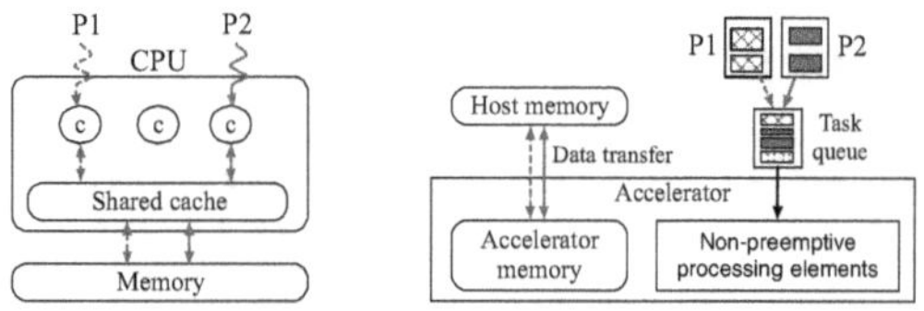

(a) Interference on traditional server (b) Interference on accelerator-outfitted server

Figure 1: Interference between co-located applications on a CMP server and an accelerator-outfitted server. Interference on a traditional server is mainly due to cache and memory bandwidth contention. Interference on an accelerator-outfitted server is caused by both queuing delay for processing elements and PCI-e bandwidth contention.

(QoS) and maximize utilization. However, because traditional datacenter servers use only commodity general purpose processors, these researches have focused exclusively on techniques to predict the QoS interference among co-located applications on multi-core processors [16–22] and simultaneous multi-threading (SMT) processors [23]. These solutions are not adequate for the emerging generation of datacenter architectures that have introduced accelerators as a key element of their design.

Figure 1 compares the performance interference between co-located applications on traditional multicore servers and accelerator-outfitted servers. While performance interference on traditional servers is mainly due to cache and memory bandwidth contention [18, 20, 23], we discover that the performance interference on accelerator-outfitted servers is often caused by queuing delay and PCI-e bandwidth contention. Together they can cause as much as 195x slowdown in terms of the 99%-ile latency for user-facing applications. As shown in Figure 1(b), when a compute task is running on a non-preemptive accelerator, all the following tasks have to wait for its completion before they can get executed. This mechanism introduces severe queuing delay to user-facing services. In addition, the co-located applications contend for the PCI-e bandwidth to transfer data between the host memory and the accelerator memory. The prior techniques based on shared resource contention (e.g., contention on shared cache and memory bandwidth) cannot be applied to this class of non-preemptive hardware that has distinctive data transfer phases.

This paper aims to improve the utilization of accelerator hardware while guaranteeing the required QoS target of user-facing time-sensitive applications in WSCs. We find that four main factors affect the queuing delay and data transfer latency and thus the end-to-end latency of user-facing applications. These factors include the number of tasks in a user-facing query that indicates how many tasks could be delayed, the task execution order that decides which tasks may cause the delay for each user-facing task, the duration and occupancy of throughput-oriented tasks that impact the queuing delay of each task in a user-facing query, as well as the PCI-e bandwidth contention that affects data transfer rate between host memory and accelerator memory.

Because key factors such as the task execution order and PCI-e bandwidth contention may change during runtime, an offline solution is not adequate. A runtime system that can dynamically monitor the accelerator and PCI-e bus, and schedule tasks accordingly is needed to maximize accelerator utilization while satisfying QoS of user-facing applications. To this end, we propose **Baymax**, a runtime system composed of two parts: a *task duration predictor* and a *task re-ordering engine*. The task duration predictor leverages novel models to predict the duration of tasks across different inputs. The task re-ordering engine then intercepts and analyzes task launching function calls before passing control to the accelerator. Based on the precisely predicted task duration, Baymax re-orders compute tasks issued to the accelerator. Meanwhile, Baymax limits the number of concurrent active data transfer tasks to mitigate PCI-e bandwidth contention. By reordering tasks and managing PCI-e bandwidth, Baymax guarantees that QoS of user-facing applications is always satisfied regardless of the order of tasks issued by applications.

To the best of our knowledge, Baymax is the first work that improves the utilization of non-preemptive accelerators while guaranteeing the QoS of user-facing applications on real systems. Specifically, this paper makes the following contributions:

1. **Comprehensive analysis of QoS violation on non-preemptive accelerators -** We identify four key factors that significantly affect the end-to-end latency of user-facing applications when they are co-located with other applications. The analysis motivates the design of a task re-ordering system based on precisely predicted task duration for accelerator co-locations.
2. **Design of online task duration prediction models -** We establish accurate and low-overhead models to estimate the duration of tasks on accelerators.
3. **Design of a task re-ordering mechanism to manage accelerator tasks -** We design a task re-ordering mechanism that intercepts and re-orders task invocations from both user-facing and throughput-oriented applications. The mechanism trades off QoS headroom of user-facing applications for increased accelerator utilization while guaranteeing the satisfactory QoS.
4. **Design of an online mechanism to mitigate PCI-e bandwidth contention -** We design a mechanism that monitors the realtime data transfer pressure on PCI-e bus and mitigates PCI-e bandwidth contention to eliminate QoS violation.

We implement Baymax runtime system combining all the above techniques. Our evaluation using Nvidia K40 GPU demonstrates that Baymax can greatly increase the utilization of accelerators by 91.3% while guaranteeing the 99%-ile latency of user-facing applications within the QoS target.

Compared with the default scheduling, Baymax reduces the tail latency of user-facing applications by up to 195x when co-located with throughput-oriented applications.

2. Understanding Performance Interference on Non-Preemptive Accelerators

We refer to accelerators that do not support context switching during kernel execution (such as ASICs, FPGAs and GPUs) as *non-preemtive*. In this section, we seek to answer the following research questions.

- Is there serious performance interference for user-facing applications when co-located with throughput-oriented applications on non-preemptive accelerators?
- What are the root causes of long tail latency when a user-facing application is co-located with other throughput-oriented applications?
- What can we do to improve the accelerator utilization while guaranteeing that user-facing applications achieve the desired QoS for tail latency?

2.1 Real System Setup

We use the GPU as our non-preemptive accelerator platform throughout this work. Our real system study uses both user-facing applications and throughput-oriented applications. User-facing applications, such as emerging IPA application Sirius [11] and deep neural network service DjiNN [24], run as permanent services on the accelerator, accepting user queries and returning the results with stringent QoS requirement. Throughput-oriented applications on the other hand do not have QoS requirement but only require high throughput. Both user-facing applications and throughput-oriented applications consist of various number of tasks (*kernels* and *memcpy tasks*[1]), and the duration of each task also varies across applications. In this experiment, multiple user-facing applications and throughput-oriented applications submit kernels and memcpy requests to GPU simultaneously. The details on the platform and benchmarks can be found in Section 7.1.

2.2 Long Tail Latency and Low Utilization

Interference between co-located applications often incurs long tail latency for user-facing applications. Figure 2 shows the QoS violation when a user-facing application is co-located with throughput-oriented applications on a Nvidia K40 GPU. In the figure, the x-axis indicates the combination of user-facing application and throughput-oriented application, and the y-axis shows the 99%-ile latency of the user-facing applications normalized to its QoS target (150 milliseconds [15, 25]). The left part of the figure and the right part (shadowed part) of the figure show the results when a user-facing application is co-located with compute intensive throughput-oriented applications and PCI-e intensive throughput-oriented applications, respectively.

[1] A task that runs on processing elements is refer as a *kernel* and a task that transfers data through PCI-e bus is refer as a *memcpy task*.

MPS (Multi-Process Service) scheduling [26] enables concurrent sharing of a GPU among multiple applications. As shown in Figure 2(a), the 99%-ile latency of user-facing queries in 40 out of the 88 co-locations is much larger than the expected QoS target with default MPS scheduling. The 99%-ile latency of user-facing applications is 10.8x of the QoS target on average and up to 195.9x in the worst case.

Priority-based scheduling [27] used in TimeGraph [28] and GPUSync [29] for improving performance of realtime kernels on accelerators executes high priority kernels first if multiple kernels are ready to run. Adopting priority-based scheduling, as shown in Figure 2(b), user-facing applications in 33 out of the 88 co-locations still suffer from QoS violation by 1.6x on average (up to 5.2x in the worst case).

The reason priority-based scheduling polices are not capable to guarantee the QoS of user-facing applications (high priority) is that they are not aware of the duration of tasks. Whenever a user-facing application is not submitting kernels to GPU due to stalls such as CPU synchronization, kernels of throughput-oriented applications may take over the GPU resource with long duration and high occupancy. Because emerging accelerators (e.g., GPU) are non-preemptive, even if a user-facing kernel becomes ready right after the submission of the long throughput-oriented kernel, the user-facing kernel would not be executed until the previous kernel completes. In this case, long queuing delay is added to the user-facing kernel, risking QoS violations.

Meanwhile, as shown in Figure 2(c), the end-to-end latency of user-facing queries in some other co-locations is much smaller than the acceptable QoS target while the GPU utilization is low. Always prioritizing user-facing kernels even if the latency is much smaller than the QoS target wastes the opportunity to improve the utilization. If the kernels are scheduled properly, the QoS headroom can be leveraged for higher utilization.

2.3 Root Causes of Long Tail Latency

In order to show the root causes of long tail latency on non-preemptive accelerators, Figure 3 presents two task execution timelines captured with *nvprof* [30] when co-locating *face* (user-facing) and four compute intensive application *hw*, *stemmer* (user-facing) and four PCI-e intensive application *pf* (details on benchmarks are shown in Table 3). Note that the overlapping of green bars in Figure 3(a) is not kernel preemption, but concurrent kernel execution when using MPS. From the figure we observe that four factors may impact the tail latency of a user-facing application when it is co-located with other applications.

The duration and occupancy of kernels - If the occupancy of a kernel is high, MPS is not able to overlap the kernel with its neighbor kernels to boost concurrent kernel execution. In this case, if the duration of throughput-oriented kernels is long, the execution of user-facing kernels will be delayed significantly.

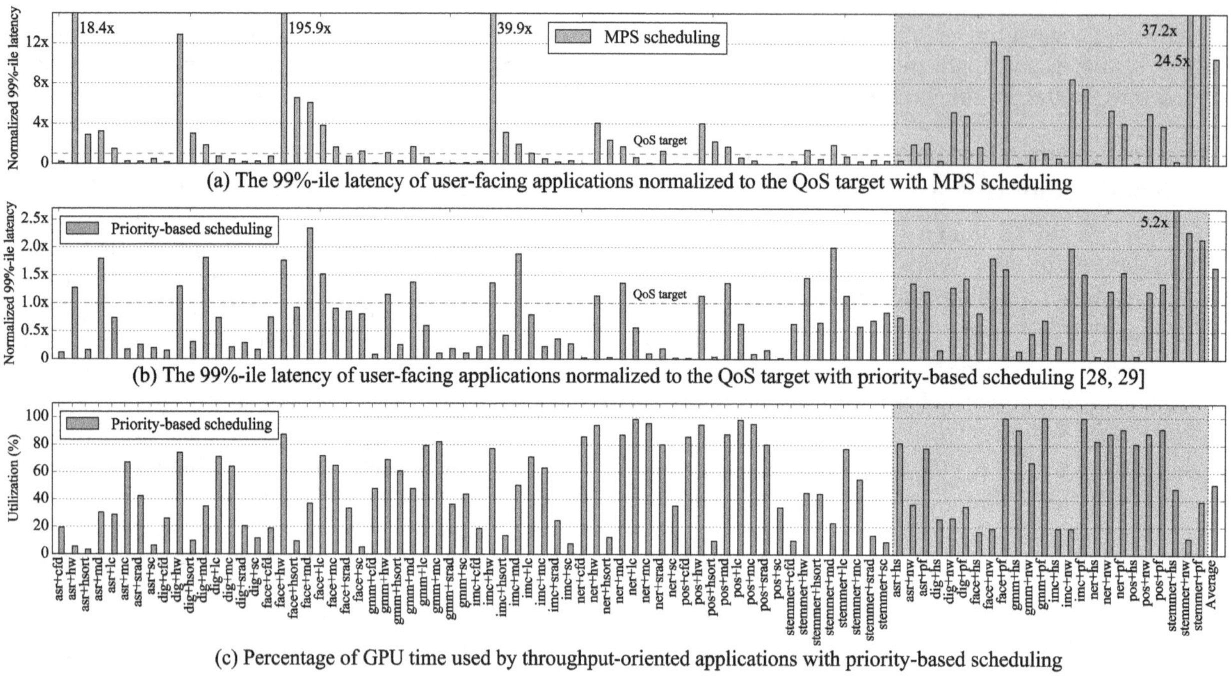

(a) The 99%-ile latency of user-facing applications normalized to the QoS target with MPS scheduling

(b) The 99%-ile latency of user-facing applications normalized to the QoS target with priority-based scheduling [28, 29]

(c) Percentage of GPU time used by throughput-oriented applications with priority-based scheduling

Figure 2: QoS violation of user-facing applications and low GPU utilization at co-locations with default MPS scheduling policy and priority-based scheduling policy.

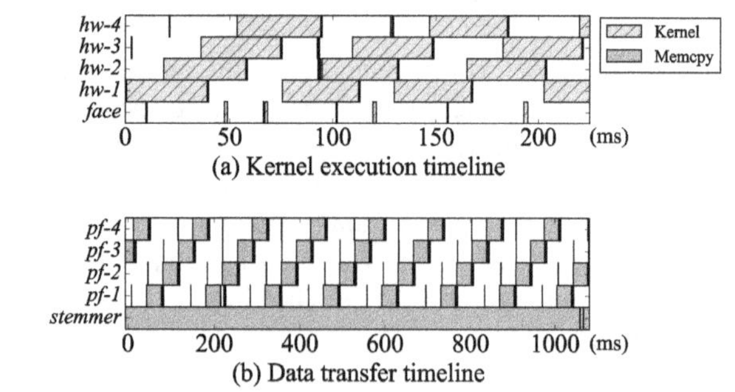

(a) Kernel execution timeline

(b) Data transfer timeline

Figure 3: Kernel execution timeline on GPU and data transfer timeline between host memory and accelerator memory.

The kernel scheduling order - Accelerators, such as GPUs, schedule kernels in the same order as they arrived (even if neighbor kernels can run concurrently when the kernel occupancy is small). If the co-located throughput-oriented applications submit kernels frequently, the user-facing application will be delayed by a large amount of throughput-oriented kernels.

The number of kernels in a user-facing query - The more kernels a user-facing query has, the longer its tail latency could be, because every kernel in the user-facing query can be delayed by throughput-oriented kernels. For example, as shown in Figure 3(a), every kernel of *face* is delayed by at least two kernels of *hw*.

The contention on PCI-e bandwidth - If throughput-oriented applications consume high PCI-e bandwidth, user-facing applications may suffer from slow data transfer due to the contention on PCI-e bandwidth. For example, as shown in Figure 3(b), the memcpy task of *stemmer* is severely slowed down to more than 1000 milliseconds from only 15 milliseconds when it is running alone. This slow down in turn results in long tail latency.

2.4 Design Guidelines of Baymax

Based on the identified root causes of long tail latency, to improve the utilization of non-preemptive accelerator while guaranteeing the QoS of user-facing applications, we design and implement Baymax following four guidelines.

- Baymax should be able to predict the duration of each kernel and memcpy task. In this case, Baymax can quantify the impact of each task on the end-to-end latency of user-facing applications.
- Baymax should be able to re-order all the kernels issued to the same accelerator, no matter how they are submitted by the co-located applications.
- For a user-facing query, Baymax should be able to limit the overall time delayed by the co-located applications regardless of the number of kernels in the query.
- Baymax should be able to monitor realtime data transfer pressure on PCI-e bus and mitigate PCI-e bandwidth contention.

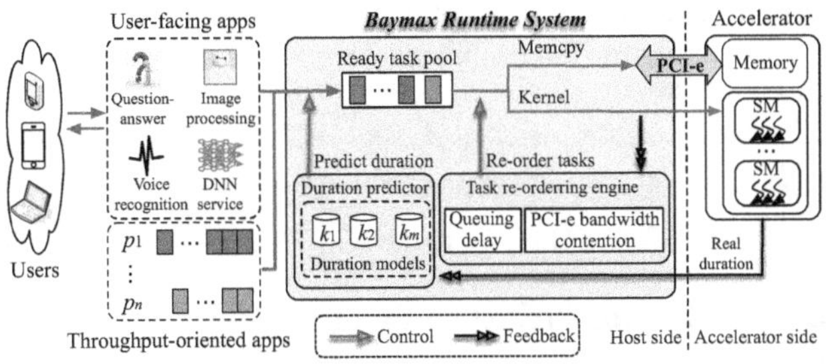

Figure 4: Design of Baymax.

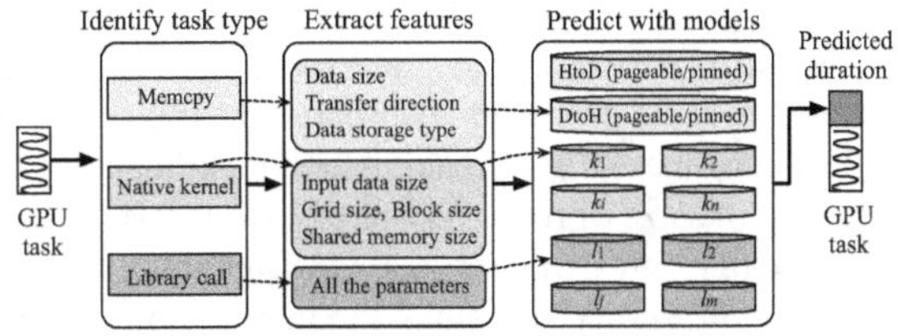

Figure 5: Predict the duration of GPU tasks (memcpy, native kernel, and library call).

3. Baymax Methodology

Figure 4 presents the design overview of Baymax. Limited by the existing GPU design, there is no open interface to schedule tasks that are already launched to the GPU. We therefore design a mechanism to re-order tasks on the CPU side. If such interface is provided in the future, Baymax can be implemented directly on accelerators. The re-ordering decision is based on the QoS target of user-facing applications and the predicted duration of each task.

In Baymax, all the tasks submitted to the accelerator are first pushed into a ready task pool managed by Baymax on the CPU side. This is achieved by simple automatic instrumentation of the original task submission code. The task submission rerouting APIs can be provided to programmers to submit tasks through Baymax. When a task is pushed into the ready task pool, the task duration predictor first predicts its duration leveraging regression models (Section 4).

The *task re-ordering engine* periodically iterates over all the tasks in the ready task pool and decides whether each task can be launched to GPU. If the task is a kernel and its predicted duration is larger than the realtime QoS headroom of any active user-facing query, the kernel will stay in the ready task pool. Otherwise, the kernel is launched to GPU (Section 5). On the other hand, if the task is a memcpy task, the engine decides whether to launch the task based on realtime data transfer pressure on PCI-e bus (Section 6).

Baymax incorporates a feedback mechanism to update the duration models used by the task duration predictor. Once a task completes, the actual duration of the task is fed back to the duration predictor to update its duration model.

4. Task Duration Modeling

In this section, we present the modeling methodology used to predict the duration of GPU tasks.

4.1 Task Duration Predictor

Baymax builds duration models for three types of GPU tasks: *memcpy*, *native kernel*, and *library call*. Native kernels are the kernels defined by programmers. Besides writing their own native kernels, an application can also call APIs defined in highly-optimized GPU libraries (e.g., cuDNN [31] and cuBLAS [32]). For the three types of GPU tasks, Figure 5 shows the methodology to predict their duration.

When a task is submitted to Baymax, the duration predictor identifies the type of the task, extracts the representative features, and selects pre-trained duration model according to the name of the GPU task (function name for native kernels and API name for library calls). Once the duration model is found, Baymax predicts the duration of the task using the extracted features and the model, and attaches the predicted duration to the task. After that, the task is pushed into the ready task pool waiting for launching to GPU.

4.2 Selecting Representative Features

It is challenging to predict the duration of GPU tasks because there is very limited information we can obtain at runtime. Although *nvprof* [30] provides comprehensive performance metrics after measuring the entire task execution, no performance information can be accessed before the task is executed. It is not applicable to rely on these metrics to predict the duration of GPU tasks.

Table 1: Features selected for different types of tasks.

Task Type	Features	Dimension
Memcpy	Data size	1
	Data transfer direction	1
	Data storage (pageable/pinned [33])	1
Native kernel	Input data size	1
	Grid size ($X \times Y \times Z$)	3
	Block size ($X \times Y \times Z$)	3
	Size of required shared memory	1
Library call	All the parameters	/

The only information we can obtain before a GPU task is executed includes its configurations (e.g., grid size, block size etc.) and the parameters passed to the task. We further select the information that strongly impact a task's duration on GPU (e.g., input scale and task configurations) as representative features. Empirically, to capture the correlation between features of a GPU task and its duration, as listed in Table 1, we select different features for different types of GPU tasks.

For a memcpy task, we select data size, data transfer direction and data storage type as its representative features. Data to be transferred from/to GPU can be stored in either *pageable memory* or *pinned memory* [33]. It is much faster (around 4x faster) to transfer data from pinned memory compared with pageable memory while more time is needed to initialize pinned memory when it is allocated.

For a native kernel, we use kernel configuration and input data size as the features. The grid size and the block size determine the scale of thread level parallelism on GPU and the GPU occupancy of the kernel, which significantly affect its duration; the size of required shared memory (both *static shared memory* and *dynamic shared memory*) reflects the efficiency of the kernel leveraging the memory hierarchy on GPU. We train different duration models for native kernels executing different functions, because they often have totally different characteristics.

A library call may consist of multiple kernels, while the actual kernels and their configurations are hidden behind the API. Therefore, we treat all the kernels in a library call as a whole, and use all the parameters of the API as its representative features. For several widely used libraries (i.e., cuBLAS and cuDNN), we only need to train models for them once and use the models in all applications.

Besides fine-grained GPU tasks, the duration predictor also predicts the solo-run duration of each user-facing query when the query is first launched. For a user-facing query, we select its input data size as its representative feature.

4.3 Low Overhead Prediction Models

The QoS target of a user-facing query is in the granularity of hundreds of milliseconds to support smooth user interaction [15, 25]. Therefore, choosing the modeling techniques with low computation complexity and high prediction accuracy for the online duration predictor becomes critical.

We evaluated a spectrum of widely used prediction models (e.g., *Linear Regression* (LR) [34], *Approximate Nearest Neighbor* (ANN) [35], *K-Nearest Neighbor* (KNN) [36] and *Support Vector Machines* (SVM) [37]) to predict task duration and eventually selected LR and KNN for their high accuracy and low overhead. While LR assumes the linear relationship between input and output variables, KNN regression holds no such assumption. Therefore using both LR and KNN allows us to achieve accurate prediction for both linear and non-linear relations. Other evaluated models either require longer calculation time with no accuracy improvement (e.g., SVM), or cannot provide satisfactory accuracy (e.g., ANN). Both KNN and LR achieve low prediction overhead. According to our measurement on real hardware, the duration prediction overhead with KNN model and LR model in Baymax is under 0.05 millisecond.

Suppose a task has p representative features. Let X_i represent an input sample with p features $(x_1, x_2, ..., x_p)$, and n represent the total number of input samples $(i = 1, 2, ..., n)$. The linear regression model is defined as Equation 1, and the Euclidean distance for KNN model between sample X_i and X_l $(l = 1, 2, ..., n)$ is defined as Equation 2. In our case, the input is the task features and the output is the predicted task duration. The primary computation of KNN is to calculate the Euclidean distance between the predicting and training samples, which can be accelerated with different tree searching algorithms such as K-D tree and ball tree. We pick the most efficient KNN searching algorithm when training prediction model according to the number of samples and the number of features in every sample.

$$y_i = \beta_1 x_{i1} + ... + \beta_p x_{ip} + \varepsilon_i, i = 1, ..., n \quad (1)$$

$$d(X_i, X_l) = \sqrt{(x_{i1} - x_{l1})^2 + ... + (x_{ip} - x_{lp})^2} \quad (2)$$

4.4 Minimizing Prediction Error

To achieve high prediction accuracy, we apply both KNN and LR to each task in both user-facing and throughput-oriented applications, and choose the model that fits the data most to predict the task duration at runtime. As shown in Section 7.2, LR model and KNN model achieve different prediction accuracy for user-facing applications and throughput-oriented applications respectively. Since the duration models are trained offline with the profiled performance samples from the workloads, more sample data is usually effective to improve the accuracy of the duration models. Especially, in WSCs, the workloads become stable after certain time scale and the models become more accurate with periodical updates. Moreover, the duration predictor detects the prediction deviation at runtime. If the deviation exceeds a certain threshold, incremental update [38] and parallel update [39] can be applied during runtime with low overhead to refine the duration models, which continuously improves the accuracy of the duration prediction.

5. Task Re-ordering Mechanism

In this section, we describe the mechanism used to re-order native kernels and library calls in Baymax. For ease of description, a kernel can be either a native kernel or a library call in this section.

5.1 Breaking Down the End-to-End Latency

It is important to understand the end-to-end latency breakdown of a user-facing query when it is co-located with other applications before diving into the task re-ordering policy. We first assume the co-located applications do not contend for PCI-e bandwidth (to be mitigated in Section 6).

Figure 6 presents the end-to-end latency breakdown of a user-facing query Q when it is co-located with other applications. The end-to-end latency of a query is the time from the first kernel of the query is issued to the last kernel of the query is returned. As shown in the figure, Q's end-to-end latency is composed of three parts. The first part is the processing time of the queued kernels (black kernels in Figure 6) that are issued before k_1 gets executed (denoted by T_q). The second part is the processing time of Q's own kernels (denoted T_{self}). The last part is the processing time of the kernels (line-filled and white kernels) from the co-located applications between k_1 and k_n (denoted by T_{other}).

5.2 Re-ordering Native Kernels and Library Calls

Let T_{tgt} represent the QoS target of query Q. Only if $T_{self} + T_q + T_{other} \leq T_{tgt}$, Q's QoS is satisfied. In the equation,

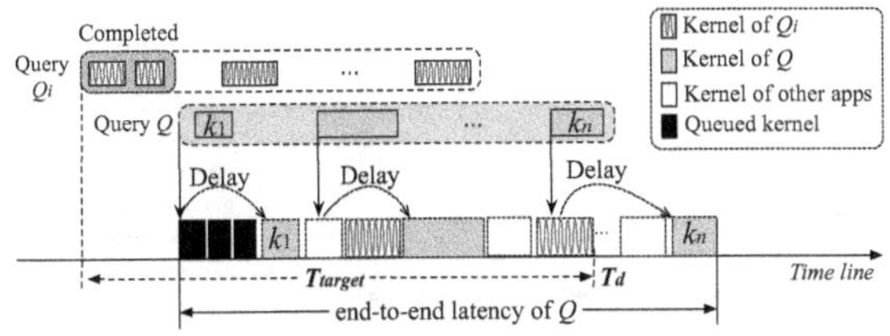

Figure 6: Calculating QoS headroom of Q when its first kernel is launched.

T_{self} is predicted according to the prediction model proposed in Section 4. In this case, to guarantee Q's QoS, the task re-ordering engine in Baymax monitors T_q and reduces T_{other} as follows.

5.2.1 Monitoring Queued Time

To estimate the queuing delay a user-facing query will experience, T_q, Baymax sums up the predicted duration of all the kernels that are already issued to GPU by our re-ordering engine but are not yet executed (still waiting in the GPU queue). Specifically, once a kernel is issued to GPU, we add its predicted duration to T_q, the duration of all the un-executed kernels on GPU. Once a kernel completes, we subtract its predicted duration from T_q.

To eliminate the situation that a user-facing query is significantly delayed by the queued-up kernels on GPU, even if no active user-facing query is running on the GPU, Baymax makes sure that T_q is smaller than the QoS target T_{tgt}. If $T_q > T_{tgt}$, Baymax would not issue any kernel to GPU until some kernels complete. This method would not reduce the GPU utilization because the kernel will be queued up on GPU even if it is issued to GPU.

5.2.2 Calculating QoS Headroom

As discussed above, T_{self} and T_q are known and cannot be reduced when Q is launched. In this case, to guarantee Q's QoS, Baymax makes sure that $T_{other} \leq T_{tgt} - T_{self} - T_q$. We use T_{hr} to represent the free GPU time left for kernels from the co-located applications during the execution of Q (referred as *QoS headroom*). When the first kernel of Q is launched, $T_{hr} = T_{tgt} - T_{self} - T_q$.

Based on T_{hr}, the task re-ordering engine periodically iterates over the ready task pool to check whether each kernel can be safely issued to GPU without causing any QoS violation. Suppose the predicted duration of a kernel is t. If t is larger than T_{hr}, the kernel is delayed until Q completes. On the other hand, if t is smaller than T_{hr}, the kernel is launched to GPU, and at the same time, T_{hr} is reduced by t.

5.2.3 Dealing with Multiple Active User-facing Queries

When multiple user-facing queries are active, more complexity is introduced when calculating the headroom of each user-facing query. Figure 6 describes the method to calculate T_{hr} of query Q when multiple user-facing queries are active. As shown in the figure, if query Q_i is still active when the first kernel of query Q is launched, the un-executed kernels of Q_i have to be completed before T_d so that the QoS of Q_i is satisfied. In this case, when we calculate T_{hr} for Q, the GPU time reserved by the un-executed kernels of Q_i need to be subtracted from T_{tgt} as well. Therefore, we monitor the GPU time each active query still needs to complete the whole query. For Q_i in Figure 6, we estimate Q_i's remaining GPU time by subtracting the time of its completed kernels from its estimated overall GPU time (T_{self} of Q_i).

Suppose there are n active user-facing queries when Q is launched. Let t_1, ..., t_n represent the remaining GPU time required by the n active user-facing queries respectively. Equation 3 calculates Q's QoS headroom when it is issued.

$$T_{hr} = T_{tgt} - T_q - T_{self} - \sum_{i=1}^{n} t_i \tag{3}$$

When multiple queries are active, if the predicted duration of a kernel (denoted by t) is larger than the QoS headroom of any active query, the kernel will be delayed. Otherwise, the kernel is launched and the QoS headroom of each user-facing query is reduced by t.

It is worth noting that Baymax would not result in starvation of any user-facing query even if multiple queries are active concurrently. User-facing kernels are issued in an FIFO order and a throughput-oriented kernel can be issued only when it will not result in QoS violation of any active user-facing query.

5.3 Utilizing Concurrent Kernel Execution

In Section 5.2, we assume that a GPU is not able to concurrently execute multiple kernels. Actually, leveraging emerging MPS technique [26], a GPU is able to execute multiple independent kernels that have low occupancy concurrently.

When concurrent kernel execution happens, T_{hr} calculated in Equation 3 is smaller than the real GPU time available for the co-located applications. In this case, the GPU utilization is not maximized because there is actually more GPU time can be used to process throughput-oriented applications while guaranteeing the QoS of all the active user-facing queries.

To further increase GPU utilization when MPS is enabled, as shown in Figure 7, when kernel k_i of Q is submitted to the ready task pool, Baymax updates the QoS headroom of Q. In this way, the time saved from previous concurrent kernel execution can be refilled to the QoS headroom for executing throughput-oriented applications. Based on Equation 3, the QoS headroom of Q when it submits k_i can be calculated in Equation 4.

$$T_{hr} = (T_{tgt} - T_{used}) - T_q - (T_{self} - \sum_{j=1}^{i} T_j) - \sum_{i=1}^{n} t_i \tag{4}$$

In the equation, T_j is the processing time of kernel k_j, $T_{self} - \sum_{j=1}^{i} T_j$ is the remain GPU time reserved by Q itself, T_{used} is the time from the beginning of Q to k_i is

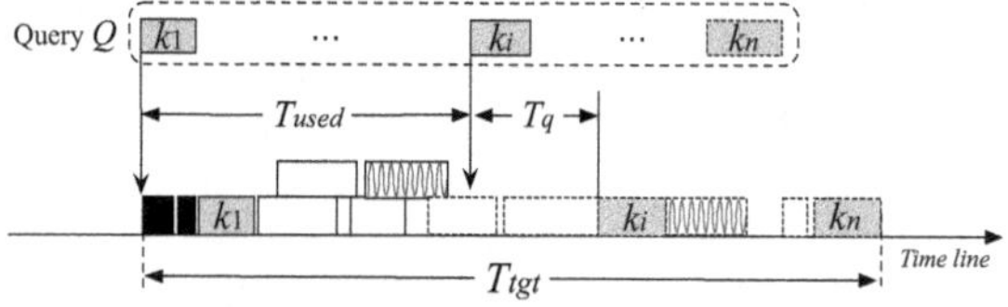

Figure 7: Updating QoS headroom of Q when it submits k_i, if concurrent kernel execution is enabled.

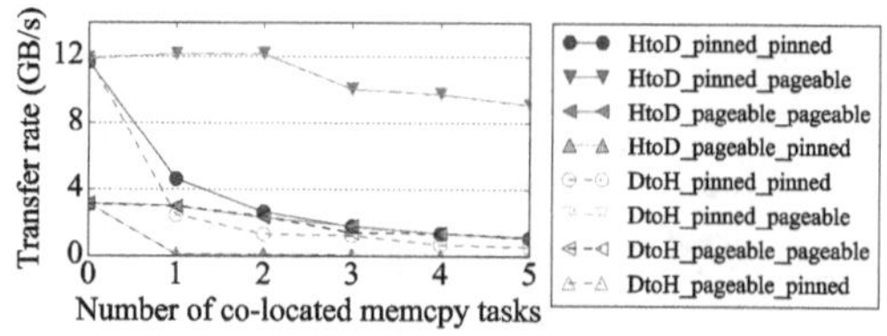

Figure 8: Data transfer rate of *stemmer* when it is co-located with applications that transfer data in the same direction.

submitted, T_q is the realtime queuing time, t_i is the remaining GPU time required by the active user-facing queries launched before Q as calculated and defined in Section 5.2.3.

In summary, the QoS headroom of a user-facing query will be updated when a kernel of the co-located applications is launched to GPU and when a new kernel of the query is submitted to the ready task pool.

6. Mitigating PCI-e Bandwidth Contention

Even if the native kernels/library calls are re-ordered as presented in Section 5, without considering PCI-e bandwidth contention, user-facing applications may still suffer from severe QoS violation. In this section, we analyze the impact of PCI-e bandwidth contention on CPU-accelerator data transfer rate per memcpy task and mitigate the contention for achieving QoS of user-facing applications.

6.1 Characterizing PCI-e Bandwidth Contention

Figure 8 reports the data transfer rate of a user-facing application *stemmer* when it is co-located with several applications that transfer data in the same direction. Data transfers in different directions do not interfere with each other, because PCI-e bus supports full-duplex communication. In the figure, the legends show the data transfer direction. For example, "HtoD_pageable_pinned" means *stemmer* transfers data from pageable memory to GPU, while the co-located applications transfer data from pinned memory to GPU. From the experiment, we have two main observations.

Observation 1: Transferring data from and to pageable memory degrades the performance of its co-located memcpy tasks only when more than three memcpy tasks are running concurrently ("*_*_pageable" in Figure 8). As shown in the figure, when *stemmer* uses pageable memory and transfers data through PCI-e bus alone, the achieved data transfer rate is 3,150MB/s. Because the theoretical peak bandwidth of 16x PCI-e 3.0 bus used in our platform is 15,800MB/s and the effective bandwidth is 12,160MB/s [40], the bus can only support $\lfloor \frac{12160}{3150} \rfloor = 3$ memcpy tasks to transfer data in their full speeds in the same direction. We generalize this observation in Section 6.2.

Observation 2: A single memcpy task that transfers data from/to pinned memory would severely degrade the performance of its co-located memcpy tasks ("*_*_pinned" in Figure 8). As shown in the figure, transferring data from/to pinned memory requires up to 11,883MB/s PCI-e bandwidth, which saturates the whole PCI-e bus. In this case, all the other memcpy tasks will be queued up and have to wait for its completion.

6.2 Managing Memcpy Tasks

Baymax mitigates QoS violations due to PCI-e bandwidth contention by reducing the number of concurrent memcpy tasks and considering data transferring delay when calculating QoS headroom for active user-facing queries.

Let BW_{peak} represent the effective PCI-e bandwidth, BW_{memcpy} represent the peak data transfer rate from/to pageable memory per memcpy task. According to our observation 1, to make sure that memcpy tasks of user-facing applications can always transfer data in full speed, Equation 5 calculates the number of active throughput-oriented memcpy tasks N_{tr} that Baymax should allow in each direction. For our platform N_{tr} is two.

$$N_{tr} = \lfloor BW_{peak}/BW_{memcpy} \rfloor - 1 \tag{5}$$

Baymax periodically iterates over the ready task pool to check whether each memcpy task can safely start to transfer data. If the memcpy task is from a throughput-oriented application and there are already N_{tr} active memcpy tasks, the task is delayed until one memcpy task completes. If the memcpy task is from a user-facing query, it is directly issued to GPU to minimize queuing delay.

According to the second observation, if a memcpy task *mc* uses pinned memory, it may severely delay the data transfer of user-facing queries. Let t represent the predicted duration of *mc*. If t is larger than the QoS headroom of any active user-facing query, *mc* will not be launched. Otherwise, *mc* can start to transfer data, but to avoid QoS violation due to the possible queuing delay caused by *mc*, the QoS headroom of every active user-facing query is reduced by t. This method would not degrade the accelerator utilization. If *mc* does not cause severe queuing delay, the QoS headroom of each active user-facing query will be refilled when a new task is launched as described in Section 5.3.

7. Evaluation

7.1 Experimental Setup

We evaluate Baymax using Nvidia GPU K40. Note that Baymax does not rely on any special hardware features or characteristics of K40 and treats it as a generic non-preemptive accelerator. The detailed setups are summarized in Table 2. MPS [26] is enabled to allow concurrent kernel execution on GPU. As listed in Table 3, We use *Tonic suite* [24] in DjiNN and *Sirius suite* [11] in Sirius as the user-facing applications; use eight most compute intensive and three most PCI-e intensive applications from *Rodinia* [41] as throughput-oriented applications. In order to evaluate the impact of memcpy tasks using both pageable memory and pinned memory, we configure *hs* to use pageable memory, *pf* and *nw* to use pinned memory. To construct the training and testing data sets for our prediction models, we collect a large amount of samples, and randomly choose 90% of the samples to train the model and use the rest to test. For KNN model, we choose the number of nearest neighbors to be 5 ($K = 5$).

Table 2: Hardware and software specifications.

	Specifications
Hardware	CPU Intel Xeon E5-2620 @ 2.10GHz Nvidia GPU Tesla K40
Software	CentOS 6.6 x86_64 with kernel 2.6.32-504 CUDA Driver 340.29, CUDA SDK 6.5, CUDA MPS

Table 3: Benchmarks used in the experiment.

Benchmark Suite	Workloads
Sirius suite in Sirius [11]	asr, gmm, stemmer
Tonic suite in DjiNN [24]	dig, face, imc, ner, pos
Rodinia [41]	heartwall (hw), lavaMD (md), cfd hybridsort (hsort), streamcluster (sc), srad, leukocyte (lc), myocyte (mc), hotspot (hs), nw, pathfinder (pf)

Throughout this section, the QoS is defined as the 99%-ile latency, and the accelerator utilization is measured as the ratio of throughput-oriented application execution time to the whole co-location execution time. The prediction error for the duration of task t (memcpy, native kernel or library call) is calculated in Equation 6.

$$Err_t = \frac{\left|Duration_t^{predicted} - Duration_t^{measured}\right|}{Duration_t^{measured}} \quad (6)$$

7.2 Task Duration Prediction

In this section, we first evaluate the accuracy of the task duration predictor in Baymax. The representative features for different types of tasks are listed in Table 1.

7.2.1 Prediction for Memcpy

In order to build duration models for memcpy tasks, we create a micro kernel to transfer data between main memory and GPU global memory with arbitrary input sizes. The range of data transfer size in our experiment reflects the actual size of memcpy tasks cross all the benchmarks. As shown in Figure 9(a), with the tested data size profiled from all the benchmarks, LR model is able to accurately predict the duration of memcpy across all workloads, which also in accordance with existing literature. The average prediction

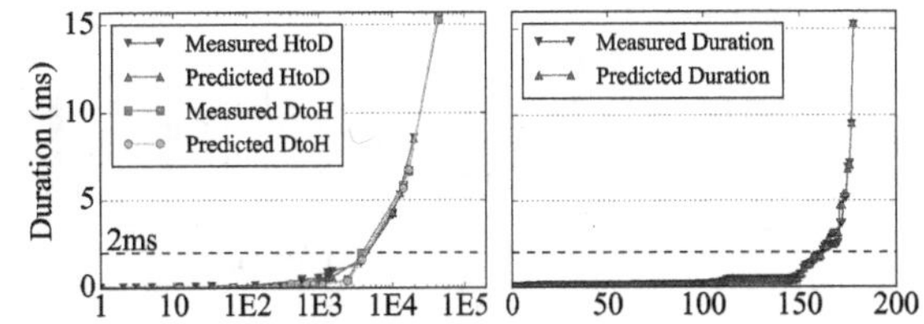

(a) Memcpy (b) Library call

Figure 9: Prediction error for the duration of memcpy tasks and library calls. In (a), the x-axis is the size of data to be transferred (KB); In (b), the x-axis is the library calls. Baymax achieves 3.2% and 6.2% prediction errors on average for memcpy and library call respectively.

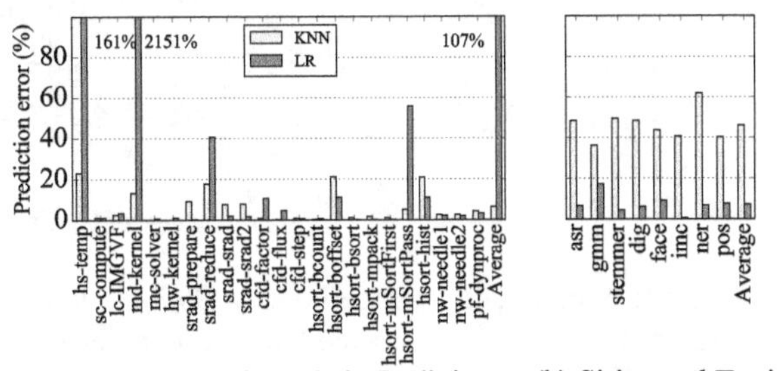

(a) Native kernels in Rodinia (b) Sirius and Tonic

Figure 10: Prediction error for the duration of Sirius, Tonic, and native kernels in Rodinia. KNN model achieves 7.2% prediction error for Rodinia; LR model achieves 5.8% prediction error for Sirius suite and Tonic suite.

error is smaller than 3.2%, when the duration is longer than two milliseconds. Thus, Baymax uses LR to predict the duration of memcpy tasks.

7.2.2 Prediction for Library Call

Library calls take a large portion of GPU execution time across emerging user-facing applications. All the library APIs used in the benchmarks are listed in Table 4. These library calls control which kernel to launch as well as the launch configuration with detailed information hidden behind the APIs.

Table 4: Frequently used library APIs.

Library	API Name
cuBLAS [32]	sgemm/dgemm
cuDNN [31]	convolutionForward, addtensor4d poolingForward, activationForward, softmaxForward

To build duration model for a library call, we analyze every parameter to the library call according to its API definition and extrapolates the size of the input based on the number as well as the data type of the input parameters. Using the input size as the representative feature available at runtime, the prediction fits well into linear regression model

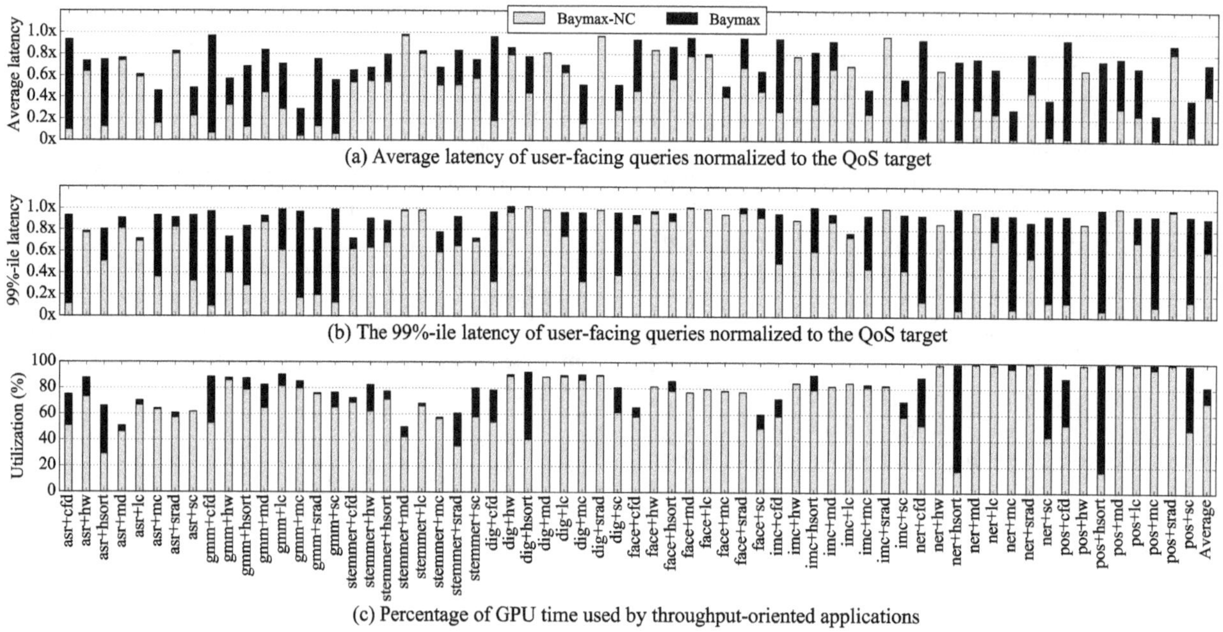

(a) Average latency of user-facing queries normalized to the QoS target

(b) The 99%-ile latency of user-facing queries normalized to the QoS target

(c) Percentage of GPU time used by throughput-oriented applications

Figure 11: Normalized average latency, 99%-ile latency of user-facing queries, and accelerator utilization when user-facing applications are co-located with compute-intensive throughput-oriented applications. Different from Baymax, Baymax-NC does not consider concurrent kernel execution.

as shown in Figure 9(b), which is consistent with the findings in prior work [31, 42]. Across all the 180 calls of the library APIs in all the benchmarks, our models can precisely predict the duration of library calls with the prediction error smaller than 6.2%, when the duration is longer than two milliseconds.

If the duration of a library call or a memcpy task is shorter than two milliseconds, even if its duration is not predicted precisely, it will not affect the latency of the co-located applications seriously.

7.2.3 Prediction for Native Kernel

The behaviors of native kernels are quite diverse across benchmark suites. While Rodinia is composed of classic HPC workloads that exhibit high thread level divergence on GPU, workloads in Sirius and Tonic are speech recognition, nature language processing and DNN computation that rely on large matrix multiplication with almost no divergence. To build duration models for native kernels, we collect performance samples, including features and duration, using *nvprof* [30]. Note that most of the workloads in Rodinia contain iterative kernel invocations in their implementations and we treat each kernel invocation as an individual sample. To provide rigid validation, we use different samples to train model and to evaluate prediction accuracy.

As shown in Figure 10, no single regression model fits both user-facing and throughput-oriented applications perfectly. In general, KNN works better than LR for Rodinia since in some cases (e.g., *hs* and *md*) the prediction of LR goes extremely wrong. This observation reveals that the duration of a kernel and its inputs do not always have a linear relationship. Whereas for Tonic suite and Sirius suite, the computation is more regular and predictable, LR has more advantage over KNN with a constrained sample dataset. The average prediction error of KNN for the kernels in Rodinia is 7.2% on average, and the prediction error of LR for Sirius suite and Tonic suite is 5.8% on average.

7.3 QoS and Throughput

In this section, we evaluate the effectiveness of Baymax in increasing the accelerator utilization while satisfying the QoS requirement of emerging user-facing applications.

Figure 11 presents the average latency, 99%-ile latency of user-facing queries, and the improved accelerator utilization when user-facing applications are co-located with throughput-oriented applications. In the figure, "Baymax" updates the QoS headroom of each user-facing query when a new kernel is issued to squeeze the extra QoS headroom benefited from concurrent kernel execution as presented in Section 5.3. "Baymax-NC", on the contrary, does not squeeze the extra QoS headroom.

Figure 11(a) and Figure 11(b) show that both Baymax-NC and Baymax are able to effectively satisfy the QoS for user-facing applications under different pair-wise co-locations. On the contrary, default MPS scheduling [26] and priority-based scheduling [28, 29] cannot satisfy the QoS for user-facing applications as presented in Figure 2 in Section 2. With MPS scheduling and priority-based scheduling, the 99%-ile latency of user-facing queries is up to 195.9x and 5.2x of the QoS target, respectively.

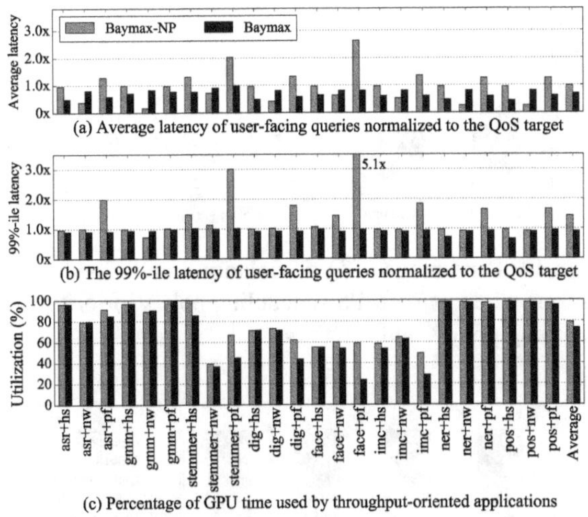

Figure 12: Normalized average latency, 99%-ile latency of user-facing queries, and accelerator utilization when user-facing applications are co-located with PCI-e intensive throughput-oriented applications. Different from Baymax, Baymax-NP does not mitigate PCI-e bandwidth contention.

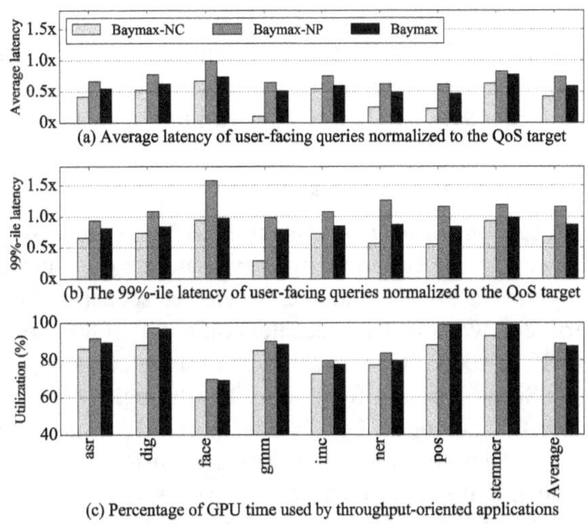

Figure 13: Normalized average latency, 99%-ile latency of user-facing queries, and accelerator utilization when each user-facing application is co-located with all the throughput-oriented applications.

Figure 11(a) and (b) also show that the average latency and 99%-ile latency of user-facing queries in Baymax is higher than in Baymax-NC. This is because Baymax squeezes more QoS headroom to trade off higher GPU utilization. As shown in the Figure 11(c), Baymax-NC increases the accelerator utilization by 70.8% on average, and Baymax further increases the average accelerator utilization by 11.4%. The reason of utilization increasing is that Baymax can utilize the saved GPU time from concurrent kernel execution to execute more throughput-oriented kernels.

Observed from Figure 11, for some co-location pairs (e.g., *dig+hsort* and *ner+hw*), the accelerator utilization is not increased using Baymax compared to Baymax-NC. This is because the kernels of these throughput-oriented applications have large GPU occupancy. In this case, MPS does not have chance to execute multiple kernels concurrently and Baymax cannot squeeze extra GPU time for throughput-oriented applications.

7.4 Mitigating PCI-e Bandwidth Contention

As presented in Section 6, Baymax also mitigates PCI-e bandwidth contention for achieving QoS of user-facing applications. Figure 12 shows the average latency and 99%-ile latency of user-facing queries when they are co-located with PCI-e intensive throughput-oriented applications. As shown in the figure, the QoS requirement of user-facing queries cannot be satisfied if PCI-e bandwidth contention is not mitigated (shown as "Baymax-NP" in Figure 12). As shown in the figure, user-facing queries still suffer from up to 5.1x QoS violation in Baymax-NP.

Even if a user-facing application is not PCI-e intensive, its occasional data transfer can be severely delayed by memcpy tasks from throughput-oriented applications. For example, while less than 10% of GPU time is spent on PCI-e data transfer for *imc* and *face*, they still suffer from severe QoS violation due to the unmanaged and unpredicted PCI-e bandwidth contention in Baymax-NP.

Figure 12(c) shows that the accelerator utilization in Baymax and Baymax-NP are similar for most of the co-locations. This is mainly because existing emerging user-facing applications do not transfer data between CPU and GPU frequently, and the duration of their memcpy tasks is often less than 10 milliseconds (Figure 9). In this case, the memcpy tasks in throughput-oriented applications will not be delayed seriously and the accelerator utilization is not reduced seriously in Baymax compared with in Baymax-NP.

7.5 Beyond Pair-wise Co-locations

To evaluate the robustness of Baymax in dealing with more complex co-location scenarios, we pick all the Rodinia benchmarks in Table 3 to form a mixture of throughput-oriented applications, and co-locate them all with the user-facing applications from both Sirius suite and Tonic suite.

We report the normalized average latency and 99%-ile latency of user-facing queries, and accelerator utilization in this scenario in Figure 13. As shown in the figure, Baymax is robust enough to increase the accelerator utilization while guaranteeing the QoS of user-facing applications. The average latency and 99%-ile latency of user-facing applications with Baymax and Baymax-NC are always within the QoS target as shown in Figure 13(a) and Figure 13(b). On the contrary, Baymax-NP cannot satisfy the QoS of user-facing application (up to 1.6x QoS violation in terms of 99%-ile latency) due to the unawareness of PCI-e bandwidth contention. Compared with Baymax-NP, Baymax can achieve similar utilization improvement while satisfying the QoS of all the user-facing applications. Compared with Baymax-NC, Baymax can further increase the average accelerator utilization from 81.2% to 87.4% as shown in Figure 13(c).

7.6 Applying Baymax in a WSC

In this section, instead of evaluating Baymax on a single GPU, we conduct experiments to evaluate the effectiveness of Baymax in a GPU-outfitted datacenter scenario. In the experiment, we model a datacenter composed of 800 Nvidia K40 GPUs, 100 GPUs for each type of user-facing applications in Sirius suite and Tonic suite. The throughput-oriented workloads are composed of 8000 instances (10 instances assigned to each GPU) evenly selected from Rodinia shown in Table 3. In the experiment, we use pair-wise co-locations, and randomly select throughput-oriented applications to co-locate with each user-facing application.

Figure 14 shows the percentage of co-locations that suffer from QoS violation under different scheduling policies. The first three bars present QoS violation when co-located applications on each GPU are scheduled using the default MPS scheduling policy, priority-based scheduling policy and Baymax, respectively. As shown here, 55% of the user-facing applications suffer from severe QoS violations(>40% degradation) with MPS scheduling, and 37.5% with priority-based scheduling. On the contrary, Baymax is able to maintain the QoS of user-facing applications for most co-locations. Less than 5% of user-facing applications suffer from insignificant QoS violations (less than 2% degradation) with Baymax. In addition to randomly mapping jobs at the cluster level to each GPU (the first three bars), we also present data for Baymax when the cluster-level job mapping is done using *Hungarian algorithm* [43]. When the accelerator utilization for each co-location pair with Baymax is known through profiling, *Hungarian algorithm*, a combinatorial optimization algorithm can be used at the cluster level to select the best mapping of applications to the GPUs that achieve the highest utilization (Denoted by "Baymax+Hungarian"). In other words, this presents the best case utilization Baymax can achieve. As shown here, Baymax+Hungarian also only incur negligible QoS violation.

Figure 15 presents the accelerator utilization of GPUs when the co-located applications are scheduled with MPS scheduling, priority-based scheduling, and Baymax. As shown in the figure, Baymax significantly improves accelerator utilization by selecting appropriate co-locations and scheduling tasks appropriately. On average, Baymax is able to achieve 79.9% accelerator utilization improvement at the WSC level. If Hungarian algorithm is applied to choose co-location pairs at WSC level and Baymax is applied to schedule tasks on the same GPU, the average accelerator utilization is further increased to 91.3%.

Figures 14 and 15 show that Baymax is effective at significantly improving accelerator utilization while guaranteeing the QoS of user-facing applications at the WSC level. On the contrary, default MPS scheduling policy and priority-based scheduling policy result in severe QoS violation and low utilization.

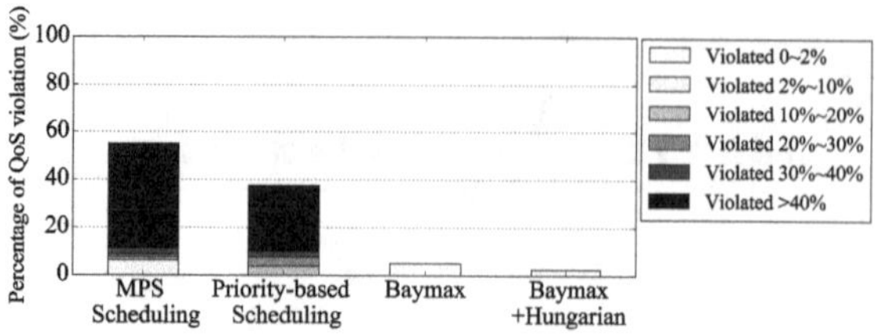

Figure 14: Percentage of QoS violation in all scheduled co-locations when using MPS scheduling policy, priority-based scheduling policy, and Baymax.

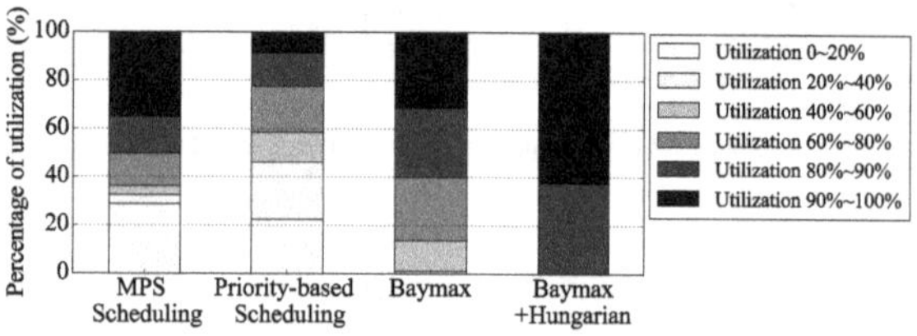

Figure 15: Percentage of accelerator utilization of each GPU at different levels when using MPS scheduling policy, priority-based scheduling policy, and Baymax.

8. Related Work and Limitations

In this section, we discuss the state-of-the-art techniques and their limitations.

8.1 Improving CPU Utilization

There has been a large amount of prior work focusing on improving application QoS and hardware utilization [18, 20, 21, 23, 46]. Recently, techniques have been proposed to improve CPU utilization while guaranteeing the QoS requirement of high priority user-facing applications. Bubble-Up [18] and Bubble-Flux [20] identify "safe" co-locations that bound performance degradation while improving chip multiprocessor utilization. SMiTe [23] further extends Bubble-Up and Bubble-Flux to predict performance interference between applications on simultaneous multithreading (SMT) processors. However, all these interference prediction techniques do not apply to non-preemptive accelerators.

Some other prior scheduling infrastructures, such as Loadleveler [44] and Maui [47], attempt to increase the hardware utilization by allocating jobs to servers using backfilling scheduling algorithm [48]. These infrastructures require users to provide resource requirement of every job. Moreover, as these techniques overlook the interference between co-located jobs, for example, PCI-e bandwidth contention is not considered, they are not able to guarantee the QoS of user-facing applications on accelerators.

Table 5: Comparison between Baymax and prior work

	Loadleveler [44]	GPUSync [29]	Bubble-Flux [20]	GPU-EvR [45]	SMiTe [23]	Quasar [21]	TimeGraph [28]	Baymax
QoS awareness	✓		✓		✓	✓		✓
Improved utilization	✓		✓		✓	✓		✓
Work on accelerator		✓		✓			✓	✓
Commodity HW/driver	✓	✓	✓		✓	✓		✓
Mitigated PCI-e contention								✓
No user-provided info.			✓		✓	✓		✓
Concurrent kernel exec.				✓				✓
Adaptive	✓	✓	✓		✓	✓	✓	✓

In addition to backfilling scheduling policy, rate monotonic scheduling algorithm [49, 50] and its variations [51, 52] are proposed to schedule periodical tasks with different priorities in embedded systems. In rate monotonic scheduling, shorter tasks are given higher priorities to be scheduled earlier. These scheduling algorithms assume that the inter-arrival rate of every task is fixed and the duration of every task is known before scheduling. However, in real world datacenters, the duration of user-facing queries and the inter-arrival rate of queries may vary significantly at runtime, therefore these scheduling algorithms do not apply to those real-world datacenter scenarios.

8.2 Scheduling on Accelerator

Realtime scheduling on accelerator is another research direction related to Baymax. Prior work [28, 29, 53, 54] has proposed techniques to improve the performance of traditional realtime GPU tasks (e.g., frames per second for video processing) when they are co-located with other GPU tasks. TimeGraph [28] and GPUSync [29] use priority-based policies to manage kernel execution on GPUs. High priority kernels are executed first if multiple kernels are launched to the same GPU. GPU-EvR [45] maps concurrent applications to different streaming multiprocessors (SMs) on the same GPU. These techniques assign a fix proportion of GPU time to high priority tasks but cannot guarantee that the realtime tasks do not violate the QoS requirement [45]. In addition, these techniques rely on users to provide task arrival rate, length of time window and the expected GPU time for each type of GPU tasks. Such information is often unavailable in real datacenter environment. In addition, these techniques focus on increasing throughput for high priority tasks, overlooking the long tail latency problem, which is more critical for user-facing applications.

At the hardware level, GPU thread preemption [55, 56] is also proposed to intelligently schedule threads for improved hardware utilization. Tanasic et al. [57] proposed a technique that improves performance of high priority processes by enabling preemptive scheduling on GPUs. The proposed technique requires vendors to add extra hardware extensions and does not work on commodity accelerators. Aguilera et al. [54] proposed a technique to guarantee QoS of high priority tasks by spatially allocating them more SMs on a GPU. This work assumes that programmers can decide how to allocate SMs to the co-located applications. However, commodity GPUs do not support allocating a set of SMs to a specific application.

Other techniques improve application performance on GPUs through addressing the problems of data transfer [58, 59], thread divergence [60], data placement [61], synchronization overhead [62] and configuration tuning [63, 64]. GPU resource sharing has been studied at both system [65, 66] and architecture levels [67, 68] to address the resource contention and performance interference. Table 5 compares our proposed technique, Baymax, with prior utilization improving techniques and GPU scheduling techniques.

9. Conclusion

Baymax improves the hardware utilization in WSCs while guaranteeing the QoS requirement of user-facing applications on the non-preemptive accelerator. To achieve the above purpose, Baymax enables precise kernel duration prediction, QoS aware kernel re-ordering, and PCI-e bandwidth contention aware data transfer management. Through evaluating Baymax with emerging user-facing workloads, we demonstrate the effectiveness of Baymax in eliminating QoS violation due to kernel interference and PCI-e bandwidth contention. We achieve up to 91.3% utilization improvement on average for pair-wise co-locations at the WSC level. Beyond the pair-wise co-locations, Baymax can improve the accelerator utilization by 87.4% without violating the QoS of 99%-ile latency for user-facing applications.

10. Acknowledgements

We thank our anonymous reviewers for their feedback and suggestions. This work was partially sponsored by Google and by the National Science Foundation (NSF) under grant CNS-CSR-1419243. We also would like to acknowledge Xayden, born 5 weeks before the deadline, for being an awesome and easy baby.

References

[1] David Huggins-Daines, Mohit Kumar, Arthur Chan, Alan W Black, Mosur Ravishankar, and Alex I Rudnicky. Pocketsphinx: A Free, Real-time Continuous Speech Recognition System for Hand-Held Devices. In *International Conference on Acoustics, Speech and Signal Processing (ICASSP)*, volume 1, pages 185–188. IEEE, 2006.

[2] Daniel Povey, Arnab Ghoshal, Gilles Boulianne, Lukáš Burget, Ondřej Glembek, Nagendra Goel, Mirko Hannemann,

Petr Motlíček, Yanmin Qian, Petr Schwarz, et al. The Kaldi Speech Recognition Toolkit. 2011.

[3] Herbert Bay, Tinne Tuytelaars, and Luc Van Gool. Surf: Speeded Up Robust Features. In *Computer Vision–ECCV 2006*, pages 404–417. Springer, 2006.

[4] Qualcomm Acquires Kooaba Visual Recognition Company. http://mobilemarketingmagazine.com/qualcomm-acquires-kooaba-visual-recognition-company.

[5] Erik F Tjong Kim Sang and Sabine Buchholz. Introduction to the CoNLL-2000 Shared Task: Chunking. In *the 2nd Workshop on Learning Language in Logic and the 4th Conference on Computational Natural Language Learning-Volume 7*, pages 127–132. Association for Computational Linguistics, 2000.

[6] Marti A Hearst. 'Natural' Search User Interfaces. *Communications of the ACM*, 54(11):60–67, 2011.

[7] Google's Google Now. `http://www.google.com/landing/now/`.

[8] Microsoft's Cortana. `http://www.windowsphone.com/en-us/features-8-1`.

[9] Apple Siri. `https://www.apple.com/ios/siri/`.

[10] Baidu YuYin. `http://yuyin.baidu.com/`.

[11] Johann Hauswald, Michael A. Laurenzano, Yunqi Zhang, Cheng Li, Austin Rovinski, Arjun Khurana, Ron Dreslinski, Trevor Mudge, Vinicius Petrucci, Lingjia Tang, and Jason Mars. Sirius: An Open End-to-End Voice and Vision Personal Assistant and Its Implications for Future Warehouse Scale Computers. In *the 20th International Conference on Architectural Support for Programming Languages and Operating Systems (ASPLOS)*. ACM, 2015.

[12] Andrew Putnam, Adrian M Caulfield, Eric S Chung, Derek Chiou, Kypros Constantinides, John Demme, Hadi Esmaeilzadeh, Jeremy Fowers, Gopi Prashanth Gopal, Jordan Gray, et al. A Reconfigurable Fabric for Accelerating Large-scale Datacenter Services. In *the 41st International Symposium on Computer Architecture (ISCA)*, pages 13–24. ACM/IEEE, 2014.

[13] Nicola Jones. The Learning Machines, 2014.

[14] Luiz André Barroso, Jimmy Clidaras, and Urs Hölzle. The Datacenter as a Computer: An Introduction to the Design of Warehouse-Scale Machines. *Synthesis Lectures on Computer Architecture*, 8(3):1–154, 2013.

[15] Jeffrey Dean and Luiz André Barroso. The Tail at Scale. *Communications of the ACM*, 56(2):74–80, 2013.

[16] Lingjia Tang, Jason Mars, and Mary Lou Soffa. Compiling for niceness: Mitigating contention for qos in warehouse scale computers. In *Proceedings of the Tenth International Symposium on Code Generation and Optimization (CGO)*, CGO '12, pages 1–12, New York, NY, USA, 2012. ACM.

[17] Jason Mars and Lingjia Tang. Whare-map: Heterogeneity in "homogeneous" warehouse-scale computers. In *Proceedings of the 40th Annual International Symposium on Computer Architecture (ISCA)*, ISCA '13, pages 619–630, New York, NY, USA, 2013. ACM.

[18] Jason Mars, Lingjia Tang, Robert Hundt, Kevin Skadron, and Mary Lou Soffa. Bubble-Up: Increasing Utilization in Modern Warehouse Scale Computers via Sensible Co-locations. In *the 44th Annual IEEE/ACM International Symposium on Microarchitecture (MICRO)*, pages 248–259. IEEE/ACM, 2011.

[19] Wei Wang, Tanima Dey, Jason Mars, Lingjia Tang, Jack W. Davidson, and Mary Lou Soffa. Performance analysis of thread mappings with a holistic view of the hardware resources. In *Proceedings of the 2012 IEEE International Symposium on Performance Analysis of Systems & Software (ISPASS)*, ISPASS '12, pages 156–167, Washington, DC, USA, 2012. IEEE Computer Society.

[20] Hailong Yang, Alex Breslow, Jason Mars, and Lingjia Tang. Bubble-flux: Precise Online QoS Management for Increased Utilization in Warehouse Scale Computers. In *the 40th Annual International Symposium on Computer Architecture (ISCA)*, pages 607–618. ACM/IEEE, 2013.

[21] Christina Delimitrou and Christos Kozyrakis. Quasar: Resource-efficient and QoS-aware Cluster Management. In *the 19th International Conference on Architectural Support for Programming Languages and Operating Systems (ASPLOS)*, pages 127–144. ACM, 2014.

[22] David Lo, Liqun Cheng, Rama Govindaraju, Parthasarathy Ranganathan, and Christos Kozyrakis. Heracles: Improving Resource Efficiency at Scale. In *the 42nd International Symposium on Computer Architecture (ISCA)*, pages 450–462. ACM/IEEE, 2015.

[23] Yunqi Zhang, Michael Laurenzano, Jason Mars, and Lingjia Tang. SMiTe: Precise QoS Prediction on Real System SMT Processors to Improve Utilization in Warehouse Scale Computers. In *the 47th Annual IEEE/ACM International Symposium on Microarchitecture (MICRO)*, pages 406–418. IEEE/ACM, 2014.

[24] Johann Hauswald, Yiping Kang, Michael A. Laurenzano, Quan Chen, Cheng Li, Ronald Dreslinski, Trevor Mudge, Jason Mars, and Lingjia Tang. DjiNN and Tonic: DNN as a Service and Its Implications for Future Warehouse Scale Computers. In *the 42nd Annual International Symposium on Computer Architecture (ISCA)*, pages 27–40. ACM/IEEE, 2015.

[25] Vinicius Petrucci, Michael Laurenzano, John Doherty, Yunqi Zhang, Daniel Mosse, Jason Mars, and Lingjia Tang. Octopus-Man: QoS-driven Task Management for Heterogeneous Multicores in Warehouse-Scale Computers. In *the 21st International Symposium on High Performance Computer Architecture (HPCA)*, pages 246–258. IEEE, 2015.

[26] Nvidia Multi-Process Service. `https://docs.nvidia.com/deploy/pdf/CUDA\_Multi\_Process\_Service\_Overview.pdf`.

[27] Carlos Boneti, Francisco J. Cazorla, Roberto Gioiosa, Alper Buyuktosunoglu, Chen-Yong Cher, and Mateo Valero. Software-Controlled Priority Characterization of POWER5 Processor. In *the 35th International Symposium on Computer Architecture (ISCA)*, pages 415–426. ACM/IEEE, 2008.

[28] Shinpei Kato, Karthik Lakshmanan, Raj Rajkumar, and Yutaka Ishikawa. TimeGraph: GPU Scheduling for Real-time Multi-tasking Environments. In *USENIX Annual Technical Conference (ATC)*, pages 17–30. USENIX, 2011.

[29] Glenn Elliott, Bryan C Ward, and James H Anderson. GPUSync: A Framework for Real-time GPU Management. In *the 34th Real-Time Systems Symposium (RTSS)*, pages 33–44. IEEE, 2013.

[30] Profiler User's Guide. `http://docs.nvidia.com/cuda/profiler-users-guide`.

[31] Sharan Chetlur, Cliff Woolley, Philippe Vandermersch, Jonathan Cohen, John Tran, Bryan Catanzaro, and Evan Shelhamer. cuDNN: Efficient Primitives for Deep Learning. *arXiv preprint arXiv:1410.0759*, 2014.

[32] CUDA Nvidia. cuBLAS library. *Nvidia Corporation, Santa Clara, California*, 15, 2008.

[33] David Kirk et al. Nvidia CUDA Software and GPU Parallel Computing Architecture. In *the 6th International Symposium on Memory Management (ISMM)*, volume 7, pages 103–104. ACM, 2007.

[34] George AF Seber and Alan J Lee. *Linear Regression Analysis*, volume 936. John Wiley & Sons, 2012.

[35] Sunil Arya, David M Mount, Nathan S Netanyahu, Ruth Silverman, and Angela Y Wu. An Optimal Algorithm for Approximate Nearest Neighbor Searching Fixed Dimensions. *Journal of the ACM*, 45(6):891–923, 1998.

[36] Gareth James, Daniela Witten, Trevor Hastie, and Robert Tibshirani. *An Introduction to Statistical Learning*. Springer, 2013.

[37] Chih-Chung Chang and Chih-Jen Lin. LIBSVM: A Library for Support Vector Machines. *ACM Transactions on Intelligent Systems and Technology*, 2(3):27, 2011.

[38] Cui Yu, Rui Zhang, Yaochun Huang, and Hui Xiong. High-Dimensional KNN Joins with Incremental Updates. *Geoinformatica*, 14(1):55–82, 2010.

[39] Vincent Garcia, Eric Debreuve, and Michel Barlaud. Fast K Nearest Neighbor Search using GPU. In *Conference on Computer Vision and Pattern Recognition Workshops (CVPRW)*, pages 1–6. IEEE, 2008.

[40] Alex Goldhammer and John Ayer Jr. Understanding Performance of PCI Express Systems. *Xilinx WP350, Sept*, 4, 2008.

[41] Shuai Che, Michael Boyer, Jiayuan Meng, David Tarjan, Jeremy W Sheaffer, Sang-Ha Lee, and Kevin Skadron. Rodinia: A Benchmark Suite for Heterogeneous Computing. In *IEEE International Symposium on Workload Characterization (IISWC)*, pages 44–54. IEEE, 2009.

[42] Sergio Barrachina, Maribel Castillo, Francisco D Igual, Rafael Mayo, and Enrique S Quintana-Orti. Evaluation and Tuning of the Level 3 cuBLAS for Graphics Processors. In *International Parallel and Distributed Processing Symposium (IPDPS)*, pages 1–8. IEEE, 2008.

[43] Harold W Kuhn. The Hungarian Method for the Assignment Problem. *Naval research logistics quarterly*, 2(1-2):83–97, 1955.

[44] Subramanian Kannan, Mark Roberts, Peter Mayes, Dave Brelsford, and Joseph F Skovira. Workload Management with Loadleveler. *IBM Redbooks*, 2:2, 2001.

[45] Haeseung Lee, Al Faruque, and Mohammad Abdullah. GPU-EvR: Run-time Event based Real-time Scheduling Framework on GPGPU Platform. In *Design, Automation and Test in Europe Conference and Exhibition (DATE)*, pages 1–6. IEEE, 2014.

[46] Michael A Laurenzano, Yunqi Zhang, Lingjia Tang, and Jason Mars. Protean code: Achieving Near-Free Online Code Transformations for Warehouse Scale Computers. In *the 47th Annual IEEE/ACM International Symposium on Microarchitecture (MICRO)*, pages 558–570. IEEE/ACM, 2014.

[47] David Jackson, Quinn Snell, and Mark Clement. Core Algorithms of the Maui Scheduler. In *Job Scheduling Strategies for Parallel Processing*, pages 87–102. Springer, 2001.

[48] Ahuva W Mu Alem and Dror G Feitelson. Utilization, Predictability, Workloads, and User Runtime Estimates in Scheduling the IBM SP2 with Backfilling. *IEEE Transactions on Parallel and Distributed Systems*, 12(6):529–543, 2001.

[49] Chung Laung Liu and James W Layland. Scheduling Algorithms for Multiprogramming in a Hard-real-time Environment. *Journal of the ACM*, 20(1):46–61, 1973.

[50] Lui Sha, Ragunathan Rajkumar, and Shirish S Sathaye. Generalized Rate-Monotonic Scheduling Theory: A Framework for Developing Real-time Systems. *Proceedings of the IEEE*, 82(1):68–82, 1994.

[51] Neil C Audsley, Alan Burns, MF Richardson, and AJ Wellings. *Deadline Monotonic Scheduling*. Citeseer, 1990.

[52] Alan Bertossi, Luigi V Mancini, and Federico Rossini. Fault-tolerant Rate-Monotonic First-fit Scheduling in Hard-real-time Systems. *IEEE Transactions on Parallel and Distributed Systems*, 10(9):934–945, 1999.

[53] Glenn A Elliott and James H Anderson. Globally Scheduled Real-time Multiprocessor Systems with GPUs. *Real-Time Systems*, 48(1):34–74, 2012.

[54] Pedro Aguilera, Katherine Morrow, and Nam Sung Kim. QoS-aware Dynamic Resource Allocation for Spatial-multitasking GPUs. In *the 19th Asia and South Pacific Design Automation Conference (ASP-DAC)*, pages 726–731. IEEE, 2014.

[55] Jason Jong Kyu Park, Yongjun Park, and Scott Mahlke. Chimera: Collaborative Preemption for Multitasking on a Shared GPU. In *the 20th International Conference on Architectural Support for Programming Languages and Operating Systems (ASPLOS)*, pages 593–606. ACM, 2015.

[56] Kittisak Sajjapongse, Xiang Wang, and Michela Becchi. A Preemption-based Runtime to Efficiently Schedule Multi-process Applications on Heterogeneous Clusters with GPUs. In *the 22nd International Symposium on High-performance Parallel and Distributed Computing (HPDC)*, pages 179–190. ACM, 2013.

[57] Ivan Tanasic, Isaac Gelado, Javier Cabezas, Alex Ramirez, Nacho Navarro, and Mateo Valero. Enabling Preemptive Multiprogramming on GPUs. In *the 41st International Symposium on Computer Architecuture (ISCA)*, pages 193–204. ACM/IEEE, 2014.

[58] Neha Agarwal, David Nellans, Mike O'Connor, Stephen W Keckler, and Thomas F Wenisch. Unlocking Bandwidth for GPUs in CC-NUMA Systems. In *the 21st International Symposium on High Performance Computer Architecture (HPCA)*, pages 354–365. IEEE, 2015.

[59] Jens Breitbart. Analysis of a Memory Bandwidth Limited Scenario for NUMA and GPU systems. In *the 25th International Symposium on Parallel and Distributed Processing Workshops(IPDPSW)*, pages 693–699. IEEE, 2011.

[60] Ping Xiang, Yi Yang, and Huiyang Zhou. Warp-level Divergence in GPUs: Characterization, Impact, and Mitigation. In

the 20th International Symposium on High Performance Computer Architecture (HPCA)*, pages 284–295. IEEE, 2014.

[61] Guoyang Chen, Bo Wu, Dong Li, and Xipeng Shen. Enabling Portable Optimizations of Data Placement on GPU. *Micro*, 35(4):16–24, July 2015.

[62] Daniel Lustig and Margaret Martonosi. Reducing GPU Offload Latency via Fine-grained CPU-GPU Synchronization. In *the 19th International Symposium on High Performance Computer Architecture (HPCA)*, pages 354–365. IEEE, 2013.

[63] Ankit Sethia and Scott Mahlke. Equalizer: Dynamic Tuning of GPU Resources for Efficient Execution. In *the 47th Annual IEEE/ACM International Symposium on Microarchitecture (MICRO)*, pages 647–658. IEEE/ACM, 2014.

[64] J-F Dollinger and Vincent Loechner. Adaptive Runtime Selection for GPU. In *the 42nd International Conference on Parallel Processing (ICPP)*, pages 70–79. IEEE, 2013.

[65] Vignesh T Ravi, Michela Becchi, Gagan Agrawal, and Srimat Chakradhar. Supporting GPU Sharing in Cloud Environments with a Transparent Runtime Consolidation Framework. In *the 20th International Symposium on High Performance Distributed Computing (HPDC)*, pages 217–228. ACM, 2011.

[66] Khaled M Diab, M Mustafa Rafique, and Mohamed Hefeeda. Dynamic Sharing of GPUs in Cloud Systems. In *the 27th International Parallel and Distributed Processing Symposium Workshops (IPDPSW)*, pages 947–954. IEEE, 2013.

[67] Onur Kayiran, Nachiappan Chidambaram Nachiappan, Adwait Jog, Rachata Ausavarungnirun, Mahmut T Kandemir, Gabriel H Loh, Onur Mutlu, and Chita R Das. Managing GPU Concurrency in Heterogeneous Architectures. In *the 47th Annual IEEE/ACM International Symposium on Microarchitecture (MICRO)*, pages 114–126. IEEE/ACM, 2014.

[68] Rashid Kaleem, Rajkishore Barik, Tatiana Shpeisman, Brian T Lewis, Chunling Hu, and Keshav Pingali. Adaptive Heterogeneous Scheduling for Integrated GPUs. In *the 23rd International Conference on Parallel Architectures and Compilation Techniques (PACT)*, pages 151–162. ACM, 2014.

Analyzing Behavior Specialized Acceleration

Tony Nowatzki Karthikeyan Sankaralingam

University of Wisconsin - Madison

{tjn,karu}@cs.wisc.edu

Abstract

Hardware specialization has become a promising paradigm for overcoming the inefficiencies of general purpose microprocessors. Of significant interest are Behavioral Specialized Accelerators (BSAs), which are designed to efficiently execute code with only certain properties, but remain largely configurable or programmable. The most important strength of BSAs – their ability to target a wide variety of codes – also makes their interactions and analysis complex, raising the following questions: can multiple BSAs be composed synergistically, what are their interactions with the general purpose core, and what combinations favor which workloads? From a methodological standpoint, BSAs are also challenging, as they each require ISA development, compiler and assembler extensions, and either simulator or RTL models.

To study the potential of BSAs, we propose a novel modeling technique called the Transformable Dependence Graph (TDG) - a higher level alternative to the time-consuming traditional compiler+simulator approach, while still enabling detailed microarchitectural models for both general cores and accelerators. We then propose a multi-BSA organization, called ExoCore, which we model and study using the TDG. A design space exploration reveals that an ExoCore organization can push designs beyond the established energy-performance frontiers for general purpose cores. For example, a 2-wide OOO processor with three BSAs matches the performance of a conventional 6-wide OOO core, has 40% lower area, and is 2.6× more energy efficient.

1. Introduction

Hardware specialization has become a promising paradigm for continued efficiency improvements. The insight of this paradigm is that, depending on the type of program or code, relaxing certain capabilities of the general purpose core, while augmenting it with others, can eliminate energy overheads and greatly improve performance.

ASPLOS '16, April 02 - 06, 2016, Atlanta, GA, USA

ACM 978-1-4503-4091-5/16/04…$15.00

DOI: http://dx.doi.org/10.1145/2872362.2872412

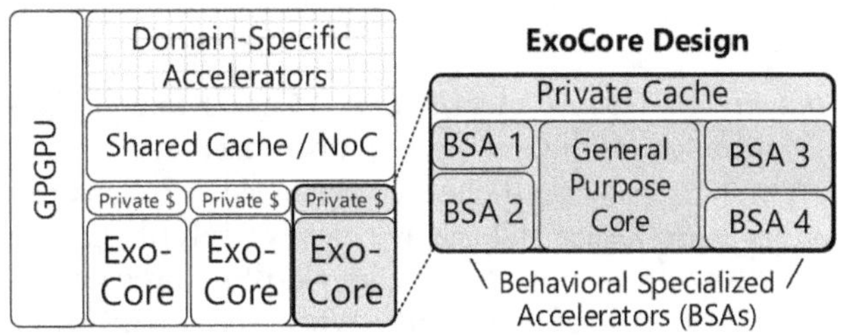

Figure 1: ExoCore-Enabled Heterogeneous System

Within the broad specialization paradigm, approaches can be categorized as either domain specialized or behavior specialized. A domain specialized approach uses hardware customized for a specific domain of computation or even a single algorithm (resembling the SoC paradigm). This allows these accelerators to be extremely efficient for certain domains. Since this approach requires domain-specific information to be conveyed to the architecture, their use is largely non-transparent to the programmer. Examples include accelerators for convolution [42], neural networks [7, 30], approximate computing [3, 13], video encoding [19] and database processing [24, 56].

Behavior specialized accelerators (BSAs), the focus of this work, differ in that they attempt to exploit program behaviors and their inter-relationship to hardware microarchitecture[1]. A well-known example is short-vector SIMD instructions, which exploit local data-parallelism. Research examples include BERET [18], which specializes for hot program-traces, XLOOPS [49], which specializes for loop dependence patterns and DySER [17], which exploits memory/computation separability in data-parallel code. Specializing for program behaviors is advantageous both because fewer accelerators can target a large variety of codes, and because these behaviors are typically analyzable by a compiler, meaning their use can be largely transparent to the programmer. Though non-transparent BSAs have been proposed (eg. LSSD [37]), we focus on transparent BSAs in this work.

Since programs exhibit a variety of behaviors, and BSAs each target different behaviors, it is natural to consider combining them. We propose an organization called ExoCore, as shown in Figure 1. An ExoCore integrates a general purpose core with several BSAs targeted at different program behav-

[1] The line between BSA and DSA can be sometimes blurry. Considering the NPU [13] accelerator, a sophisticated compiler could automatically determine neural-network mappable regions, perhaps making NPU a BSA.

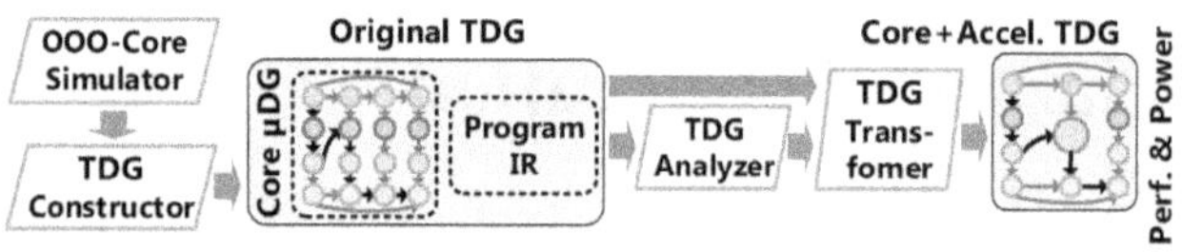

Figure 2: TDG-based Accelerator Modeling Framework

iors. At run-time, depending on the affinity of the code, the execution may migrate to one of the BSAs, a process which is transparent to the programmer. To enable fast switching between cores, without the need for migrating state, BSAs share the virtual memory system and cache hierarchy.

Studying Behavioral Accelerators Considering designs that incorporate multiple synergistic behavior-specialized accelerators, many questions become immediately apparent: can the performance and energy benefits be worth the area costs? Is there opportunity for multiple-BSAs inside applications, and at what granularity? What types of BSAs are synergistic, and is there a minimal useful set? Which type of general purpose core should they integrate with? When accelerators target overlapping regions, how should the decision be made to switch between BSAs?

We argue that thus far, these questions have not been addressed adequately for at least two reasons. First, prior to the advent of "dark silicon", such a design would not have been sensible given that certain portions of the core would go unused at any given time – now the tradeoffs are more plausible. Secondly, we simply lack effective ways to study an organization like ExoCore. Evaluating even one BSA requires extensive effort, including the definition of a new ISA and possibly ISA extensions for the host processor, compiler analysis, transformations and assembler implementation, and finally for evaluation requires either a simulator or RTL model. Exploring ExoCore designs incorporating many BSAs has so far been intractable, and evaluating new BSAs takes considerable effort; a higher-level evaluation methodology, retaining the ability of modeling the effect of *both* the compiler and the detailed interaction of the microarchitecture seems necessary.

Goals and Contributions This paper's goal is to elucidate the potentials of synergistic BSAs. To achieve this, the first thrust of this paper is to propose a novel BSA-modeling methodology, called the transformable dependence graph (TDG). The approach is to combine semantic information about program properties (eg. loop dependence, memory access patterns) and low-level hardware events (eg. cache misses, branch mis-predictions, resource hazards) in a single trace-based dependence graph representation. This dependence graph is transformed, by adding or removing edges, to model how it specializes for certain program behaviors (Figure 2).

Using the TDG as the modeling methodology, we explore a design space of ExoCore organizations that draws accelerators from the literature, evaluating 64 design points across more than 40 benchmarks. Our analysis shows that

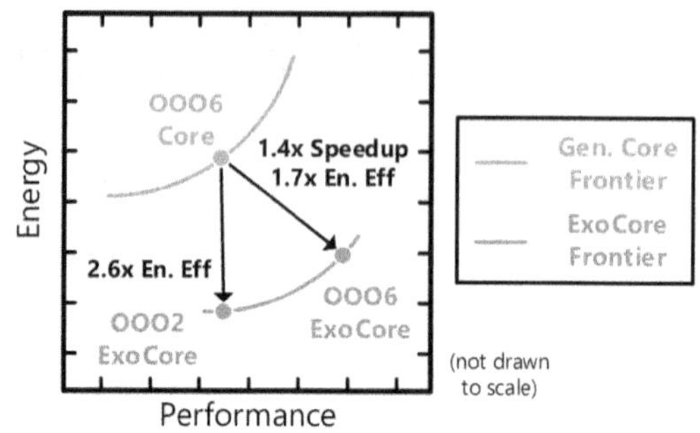

Figure 3: Results of Design-Space Exploration Across 64 ExoCore Configurations

having multiple BSAs can be helpful both within workload domains and within single applications. Understanding this design space would have been intractable without a TDG style approach[2].

To summarize, this paper's contributions are:

- A novel methodology (TDG) for modeling behavior specialized acceleration (see `www.cs.wisc.edu/vertical/tdg` for implementation details), that is practical and accurate (less than 15% error in relative performance and energy efficiency for existing BSAs).
- Defining the ExoCore concept, and developing a synergistic composition of BSAs which significantly pushes the performance and energy frontiers of traditional cores.
- Design-space exploration of ExoCore configurations (Figure 3). Specifically, a 2-wide OOO processor with three BSAs matches the performance of a conventional 6-wide OOO core with SIMD, has 40% lower area and is 2.6× more energy efficient. We also find that BSAs have synergistic opportunities across and *within* workloads.

Paper Organization We first describe the background, intuition, and details of the TDG-based accelerator modeling approach, along with single-accelerator validation (Section 2). We then use the TDG methodology to design and model an ExoCore system with four synergistic BSAs (Section 3). Section 4 has methodology, and Section 5 has results. Section 6 is related work, and Section 7 concludes.

2. Transformable Dependence Graphs

In this section, we describe our approach for modeling behavior specialized accelerators: the Transformable Dependence Graph (TDG). We first describe the requirements for a BSA-modeling framework, then overview our proposed approach, and go into detail with a specific accelerator example. We also discuss implementation, validation, usage and limitations.

[2] We note that TDG is a simulation-modeling technique that does not produce a compiler artifact, or microarchitecture spec, or RTL of the modeled BSA. Its potential usefulness is in research of accelerator ideas and early design-space exploration - it is analogous to a cycle-level trace simulator.

2.1 Insights and Background

Requirements For modeling the workings of behavior specialized accelerators, a useful evaluation approach must capture the following aspects of execution:

1. **General Purpose Core Interaction** Since transparent accelerators selectively target certain code, the general purpose core must be modeled in detail (eg. pipelining, structural hazards, memory-system etc.). In addition, accelerators can interact with different parts of the general purpose core (eg. sharing the LSQ), so this must be modeled as well.
2. **Application/Compiler Interaction** Much of a BSA's success depends on how well the compiler can extract information from the application, both for determining a valid accelerator configuration, and for deciding which accelerator is appropriate for a given region.
3. **Accelerator Behavior** Naturally, the low-level detailed workings of the accelerator must be taken into-account, including the microarchitecture and dynamic aspects of the execution like memory latency.

A traditional compiler+simulator can capture the above aspects very well, but the effort in building multi-BSA compilers and simulators is time consuming, if not intractable. What we require are higher-level abstractions.

Leveraging Microarchitectural Dependence Graphs (μDGs) For a higher-level model of microarchitectural execution, we turn to the μDG, a trace-based representation of a program. It is composed of nodes for microarchitectural events and edges for their dependences. It is constructed using dynamic information from a simulator, and as such, is input-dependent. The μDG has traditionally been used for modeling out-of-order cores [15, 28]. Overall, it offers a detailed-enough abstraction for modeling microarchitecture, yet is still abstract and easy to model modifications/additions of effects.

What is missing from the above is the capability of capturing compiler/application interactions. Our insight is that *graph transformations* on the μDG can capture the effects of behavioral specialization – after all, a BSA simply relaxes certain microarchitectural dependences while adding others. To perform these transformations, we require knowing the correspondence between the program trace and the static program IR. This can be reconstructed from the binary.

2.2 The Transformable Dependence Graph

Approach Overview Putting the above together, the crux of our approach is to build the Transformable Dependence Graph (TDG), which is the combination of the μDG of the OOO core, and a Program IR (typically a standard DFG + CFG) which has a one-to-one mapping with μDG nodes.

As shown in Figure 2, a simulator produces dynamic instruction, dependence, and microarchitectural information, which is used by the constructor to build the TDG. The TDG is analyzed to find acceleratable regions and determine the strategy for acceleration. The TDG-transformer modifies the original TDG, according to a graph re-writing algorithm, to create the combined TDG for the general purpose core and accelerator. As part of the representation, the TDG carries information about overall execution time and energy. The next subsection describes the approach using an example.

Notation To aid exposition, the notation $\text{TDG}_{\text{GPP,ACCEL}}$ refers to a TDG representation of a particular general purpose processor (GPP) and accelerator. $\text{TDG}_{\text{OOO4,SIMD}}$, for example, represents a quad-issue OOO GPP with SIMD. As a special case, the original TDG prior to any transformations (not representing an accelerator) is $\text{TDG}_{\text{GPP},\emptyset}$.

2.3 Transformable Dependence Graph Example

Here we define the components of our approach using a running example in Figure 4, which is for transparently applying a simple fused multiply-accumulate (`fma`) instruction. We intentionally choose an extremely simple example for explanatory purposes, and note how a more complex accelerator would implement that component. Detailed modeling of such accelerators are in Section 3.2.

Constructing the TDG To construct $\text{TDG}_{\text{GPP},\emptyset}$, a conventional OOO GPP simulator (like gem5 [5]) executes an unmodified binary[3], and feeds dynamic information to the TDG constructor (Figure 4(a)). The first responsibility of the tool is to create the original μDG, which embeds dynamic microarchitectural information, including data and memory dependences, energy events, dynamic memory latencies, branch mispredicts and memory addresses. We note that this makes the TDG input dependent, which is similar to other trace-based modeling techniques.

To explain an example, Figure 4(b) shows the μDG for the original OOO core, which in this case was a dual issue OOO. Here, nodes represent pipeline stages, and edges represent dependencies to enforce architectural constraints. For example, edges between alternate dispatch and commit nodes model the width of the processor ($D_{i-2} \xrightarrow{1} D_i$, $C_{i-2} \xrightarrow{1} C_i$). The FU or memory latency is represented by edges from execute to complete ($E_i \rightarrow P_i$), and data dependencies by edges between complete to execute ($P_i \xrightarrow{0} E_j$).

The second responsibility of the constructor is to create a program IR (also in Figure 4(b)) where each node in the μDG has a direct mapping with its corresponding static instruction in the IR. We analyze the stream of instructions from the simulator, using known techniques to reconstruct the CFG, DFG with phi-information, and loop nest structure using straightforward or known techniques [33]. Also, register spill and constant access is identified for later optimization. To account for not-taken control paths in the program,

[3] Our implementation assumes that compiler auto-vectorization is off.

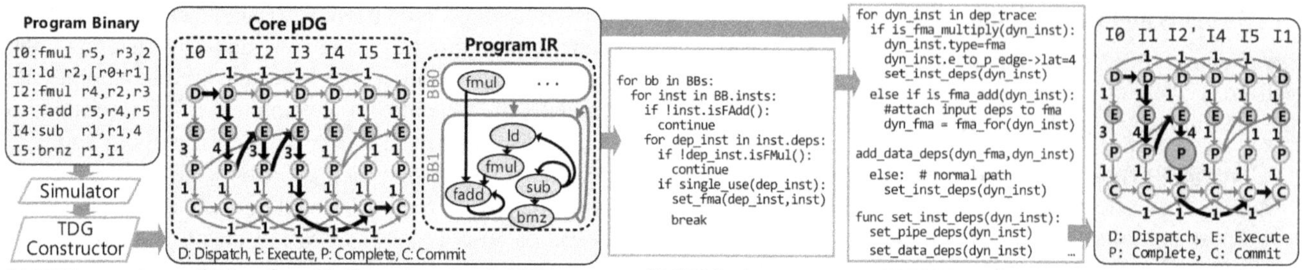

(a) TDG Construction (b) Transformable Dependence Graph (TDG) (c) TDG Analyzer (d) TDG Transformer (e) Core+Accel TDG

Figure 4: Example TDG-Based model for transparent fused multiply-add (`fma`) specialization.

we augment the program IR with the CFG from binary analysis.

TDG Analyzer The next step is to analyze the TDG to determine which program regions can be the legally and profitably accelerated, as well as the "plan" for transformation. This "plan" represents the modifications a compiler would make to the original program. We explain with our example.

Figure 4(c) shows the algorithm (in pseudo-code) required for determining the `fma` instructions. To explain, the routine iterates over instructions inside a basic block, looking for a `fadd` instruction with a dependent `fmul`, where the `fmul` has a single use. The function `set_fma(inst1,inst2)` records which instructions are to be accelerated, and passes this "plan" to the TDG transformer. In concrete terms, a TDG-analysis routine is a C++ module that operates over the TDG's trace or IR, and the "plan" is any resulting information or data-structures that are stored alongside the TDG.

While the above is basic block analysis, more complex accelerators typically operate on the loop or function level. For example, determining vectorizability in SIMD would require analyzing the IR for inter-iteration data dependences.

TDG Transformer This component transforms the original TDG to model the behavior of the core and accelerator according to the plan produced in the previous step. It applies accelerator-specific graph transformations, which are algorithms for rearranging, removing, and reconstructing μDG nodes and dependence edges. In our notation, this is the transformation from $\text{TDG}_{\text{GPP-X},\emptyset}$ to $\text{TDG}_{\text{GPP-Y,ACCEL}}$.

Figure 4(d) outlines the algorithm for applying the `fma` instruction, which iterates over each dynamic instruction in the μDG. If it is an accelerated `fmul`, it changes its type to `fma` and updates its latency. If the original instruction is an accelerated `fadd`, it is elided, and the incoming data dependences are added to the associated `fma`.

This simple example operates at an instruction level, but of course more complex accelerators require modifications at a larger granularity. For instance, when vectorizing a loop, the μDG for multiple iterations of the loop can be collected and used to produce the vectorized μDG for a single new iteration.

Core+Accelerator TDG The core+accelerator TDG represents their combined execution, an example of which is in Figure 4(e), for $\text{TDG}_{\text{OOO2},\texttt{fma}}$. Here, `I2'` represents the specialized instruction, and `I3` has been eliminated from the graph. In practice, more complex accelerators require more substantial graph modifications. One common paradigm is to fully switch between a core and accelerator model of execution at loop entry points or function calls.

Finally, this TDG can be analyzed for performance and power/energy. The length of the critical path, shown in bold in the figure, determines the execution time in cycles. For energy, we associate events with nodes and edges, which can be accumulated and fed to standard energy-modeling tools.

Accel.	Base	P Err.	P Range	E Err.	E Range
OOO8→1	–	3%	0.05→1.0 IPC	4%	0.75→2.75 IPE
OOO1→8	–	2%	0.02→5.5 IPC	3%	0.39→1.7 IPE
C-Cores	IO2	5%	0.84→1.2×	10%	0.5→0.9×
BERET	IO2	8%	0.82→1.17×	7%	0.46→0.99×
SIMD	OOO4	12%	1.0→3.6×	7%	0.30→1.3×
DySER	OOO4	15%	0.8→5.8×	15%	0.25→1.28×

Table 1: Validation Results (P: Perf, E: Energy)

2.4 Implementation: Prism

Our framework's implementation, *Prism*, generates the original TDG using gem5 [5], enabling analysis of arbitrary programs. We implement custom libraries for TDG generation, analysis and transformation (more details on specific modeling edges are in a related paper [38]). Since transforming multi-million instruction traces can be inefficient, Prism uses a windowed approach. Windows are large enough to capture specialization granularity (max ~10000 instructions). The final outputs include cycle count and average power.

Power and Area Estimation Prism accumulates energy event counts for both the GPP and accelerator from the TDG. It then uses McPAT [29] internally for computing power, calling McPAT routines at intervals over the program's execution. We use 22nm technology. The GPP core activity counts are fed to McPAT [29], a state-of-the-art GPP power model. For accelerators, a combination of McPAT (for FUs) and CACTI [34] is used, and for accelerator-specific hardware we use energy estimates from existing publications.

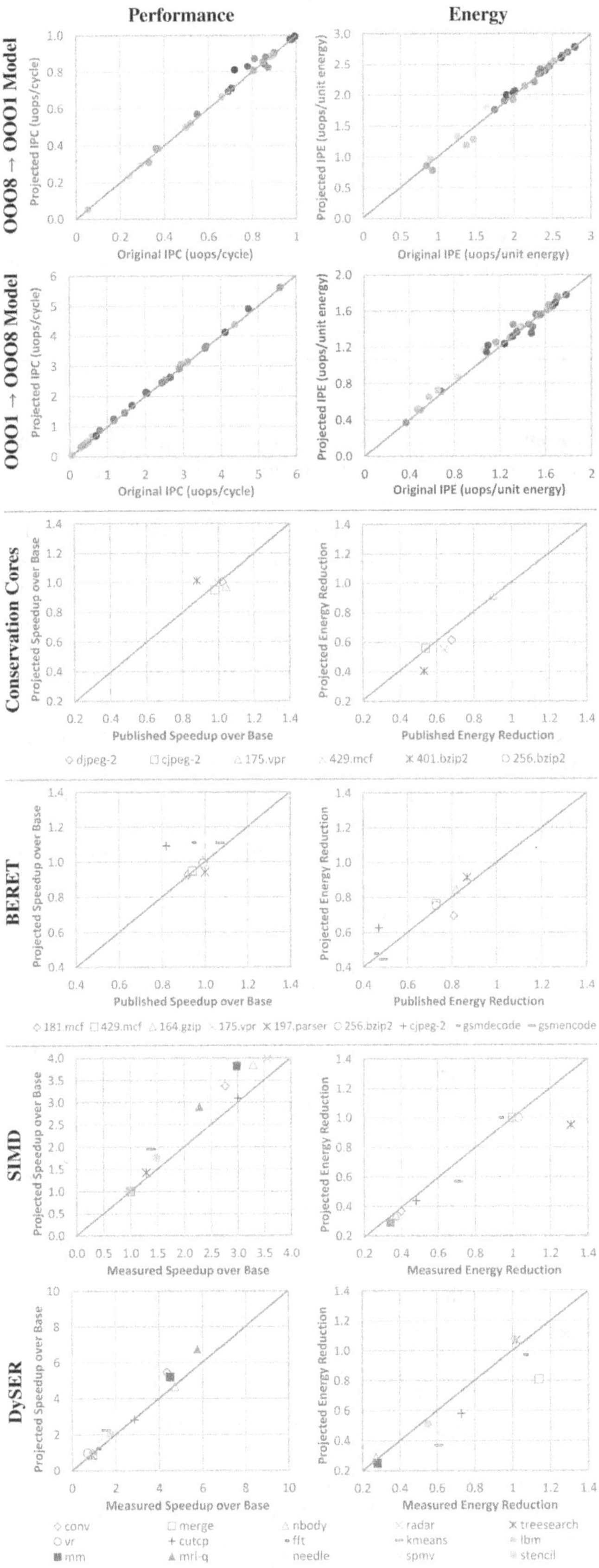

Figure 5: Prism Validation

2.5 Core and Single-Accelerator Validation

We perform validation by comparing the TDG against the published results of four accelerators, each of which use traditional compiler+simulator evaluation. These results used benchmarks from the original publications [17, 18, 53], and Parboil [1] and Intel's microbenchmarks for SIMD. The original μDG is generated by fast-forwarding past initialization, then recording for 200 million instructions. Here, the error is calculated by comparing the relative speedup and energy benefits over a common baseline, where we configured our baseline GPP to be similar to the reported baseline GPP. Note that for SIMD and DySER, we were able to adjust the transformations to match the compiler output, as we had access to these compiler infrastructures.

Table 1 presents a validation summary for the OOO core and accelerators, where column "Base" is the baseline GPP, "Err." is the average error, and "Range" is the range of compared metrics. Figure 5 shows the validation graphs for each architecture, including performance (left) and energy (right). Each point represents the execution of one workload, and the distance to the unit line represents error. The X-Axis is the validation target's estimate (from published results or measured from simulation), and the Y-Axis is the TDG's estimate of that metric. We describe the validation of the core and accelerators below.

OOO-Core To determine if we are over-fitting the OOO core to our simulator, we perform a "cross validation" test: we generate a trace based on the 1-Wide OOO core, and use it to predict the performance/energy of an 8-Wide OOO core, and vice-versa. The first two graphs in Figures 5 show the results. The benchmarks in this study [2] are an extension of those used to validate the Alpha 21264 [9] (we omit names for space). The high accuracy here ($< 4\%$ on average) demonstrates the flexibility of the model in either speeding up or slowing down the execution.

Conservation Cores are automatically generated, simple hardware implementations of application code [53], which are meant as offload engines for in-order cores. We validate the five benchmarks in the above paper, and achieve an average of 5% and 10% average error in terms of performance improvement and energy reduction. The worst case is for 401.bzip2, where we under-predict performance by 15%.

BERET is also an offload engine for hot loop traces, where only the most frequently executed control path is run on the accelerator, and diverging iterations are re-executed on the main processor [18]. Efficiency is attained through serialized execution of compound functional units. We achieve an average error of 8% and 7% in terms of performance improvement and energy reduction. We over-predict performance slightly on cjpeg and gsmdecode, likely because we approximate using size-based compound functional units, rather than more restrictive pattern based (to not over-conform to the workload set).

BSA (**Acronym**)	Exploited App. Behavior	Benefits vs General Core	Drawbacks vs General Core	Granularity	Inspired By
Short-Vector **SIMD**	Data-parallel loops with little control	Fewer instructions and less port contention	Masking/predicated inst penalty	Inner Loops	
Data Parallel CGRA (**DP-CGRA**)	Parallel loops w/ separable compute/memory	Vectorization + fewer insts. on general core	Extra comm. insts, predicated inst penalty	Inner Loops	DySER [17], Morphosys [47]
Non-speculative Dataflow (**NS-DF**)	Regions with non-critical control	Cheap issue width, larger instruction window	Lacks control speculation, requires instr. locality	Nested Loops	SEED [36], Wavescalar [50]
Trace-Speculative Proc. (**Trace-P**)	Loops w/ consistent control (hot traces)	Similar to above, but larger compound insts.	Trace mispeculation requires re-execution	Inner Loop Traces	BERET [18], CCA [8]

Table 2: Tradeoffs of Behavior Specialized Accelerators (BSAs) in this Work

SIMD validation is performed using the Gem5 Simulator's implementation, configured as a 4-Wide OOO processor. Figure 5(e) shows how we attain an average error of 12% and 7% in terms of performance improvement and energy reduction. Our predictions for SIMD are intentionally optimistic, as there is evidence that compilers will continue to see improved SIMD performance as their analysis gets more sophisticated. We remark that our transformations only consider a straight-forward auto-vectorization, and will not be accurate if the compiler performs data-layout transformations or advanced transformations like loop-interchange.

DySER is a coarse grain reconfigurable accelerator (CGRA), operating in an access-execute fashion with the GPP through a vector interface [17]. On the Parboil and Intel microbenchmarks, we attain an average error of 15% for both speedup and energy reduction.

In summary, The TDG achieves an average error of less than 15% for estimating speedup and energy reduction, compared to simulator or published data.

2.6 Using TDG Models in Practice

The TDG can be used to study new BSAs, their compiler interactions and the effect of varying input sets. In practice, running TDG models first requires TDG-generation through a conventional simulator. The generated TDG can be used to explore various core and accelerator configurations. Since the TDG is input-dependent, studying different inputs requires the re-running the original simulation.

Implementing a TDG model is a process of writing IR analysis routines, graph-transformation algorithms and heuristics for scheduling, as outlined in Appendix A.

2.7 Limitations of TDG Modeling

Lack of Compiler Information First, since the TDG starts from a binary-representation, it lacks native compiler information, which sometimes must be approximated in some way. An example is memory aliasing between loop instructions, useful for determining vectorization legality. In such cases, we use dynamic information from the trace to estimate these features, though of course this is optimistic.

Other Sources of Error Another consequence of beginning from a binary representation are ISA artifacts in the TDG. One important example is register spilling. In this case, the TDG includes a best-effort approach to identify loads and stores associated with register spills, which can potentially be bypassed in accelerator transformations.

The graph representation is itself constraining, in particular for modeling resource contention. To get around this, we keep a windowed cycle-indexed data structure to record which TDG node "holds" which resource. The consequence is that resources are preferentially given in instruction order, which may not always reflect the microarchitecture.

Another source of error is unimplemented or abstracted architectural/compiler features. An example from this work is the lack of a DySER spatial scheduler – the latency between FUs is estimated. Of course, TDG models can be made more detailed with more effort.

Flexibility The μDG itself embeds some information about the microarchitectural execution (eg. memory latency, branch prediction results), meaning that its not possible to change parameters that affect this information without also re-running the original simulation. Understanding how those components interact with specialization would require recording multiple TDGs.

Transformation Expressiveness Some transformations are difficult to express in the TDG, limiting what types of architectures/compilation techniques can be modeled. In particular, non-local transforms are challenging, because of the fixed instruction-window that the TDG considers. One example of this would be an arbitrary loop-interchange.

3. Designing ExoCore Systems

Now that we have described an effective modeling technique for studying multiple BSA designs, the TDG, we employ it to study multi-BSA organizations - we call such an architecture an *ExoCore*. As shown earlier in Figure 1, an ExoCore integrates a general purpose core with several other programmable or configurable BSAs targeted at different kinds of program behaviors. At runtime, depending on the

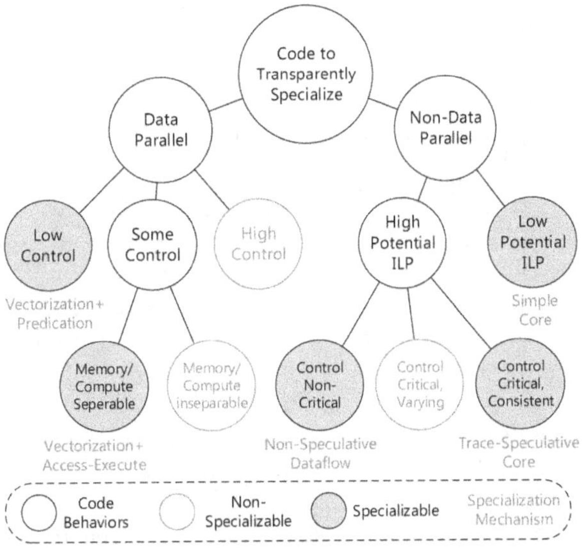

Figure 6: This work's behavior-space.

affinity of the code, the execution may migrate to one of the BSAs, a process which is transparent to the programmer.

In this section, we first discuss how to construct a composition of BSAs to form an ExoCore, then give background on the individual BSAs that comprise it, and finally describe how they are modeled using the TDG.

3.1 Opportunities for Behavioral Specialization

An effective ExoCore design must incorporate accelerators which are *synergistic*, meaning they can effectively work together for added benefits. Intuitively, BSAs that are synergistic will simply specialize different types of behaviors. Figure 6 shows an example taxonomy of program behaviors, where leaf nodes in this tree are program types that can be mapped to specific hardware specialization mechanisms.

With our behavior space outlined, we can now begin to compose a set of BSAs which target those behaviors. Fortunately, we can draw from the existing accelerator literature to fill these niches. Table 2 shows how different accelerators can map onto the specializable behaviors, and gives insights into their benefits and drawbacks versus a general purpose core. We describe these accelerators below; their high-level architecture is in Figure 7.

SIMD Short vector **SIMD** is a well known BSA for targeting data parallel regions, where a limited amount of control and memory irregularity exists.

Data-Parallel Access-Execute Past a certain degree of control, SIMD is no longer effective. An alternate approach is to offload the computation of the loop to a CGRA which natively supports control, and pipeline the CGRA for executing parallel loops (eg. DySER [17], Morphosys [47]). This works well when the memory and computation are separable (fewer communication instructions). Also, these architectures handle some memory irregularity by providing a shuffle network in their flexible input/output interfaces.

We call this design Data-Parallel CGRA (**DP-CGRA**). Its design point has 64 functional units (FUs), and is configured similar to previous proposals [17].

Non-speculative Dataflow In code regions that are not data-parallel, but still have high potential ILP, non-speculative dataflow processors can be highly effective, especially when the control flow does not lie on the critical path.

We model this BSA after the recent SEED [36] architecture, using distributed dataflow units communicating over a bus, and compound FUs (CFUs) for computation. This design targets inlined nested loops with 256 static compound instructions. We refer to this as **NS-DF**, for non-speculative dataflow.

Trace-Speculative Core Often, control is on the critical path, meaning speculation is necessary for good performance, but it is *highly* biased – creating one hot path through a loop. Architectures like BERET [18] exploit this by sequencing through a speculative trace of instructions, using CFUs for energy efficiency. Instructions diverging from the hot loop trace require re-execution on the general core.

We model a trace-speculative BSA similar to BERET, except that we add dataflow execution. This enables the design to be more competitive with an OOO core. We add a loop-iteration versioned store buffer to save speculative iterations. We refer to this design as a **Trace-P** for trace-processor[4]. Compared to NS-DF, Trace-P requires half as much operand storage, and can have larger CFUs, as compound instructions in Trace-P can cross control boundaries.

ExoCore Architecture Organization Putting the above together, Figure 7 shows how an ExoCore combines a general core with the four different BSAs. DP-CGRA and SIMD are integrated with vector datapaths from the general core. All designs besides SIMD are *configurable*, and require a configuration datapath. NS-DF and Trace-P are *offload* architectures, meaning they have their own interfaces to the cache hierarchy, and can power down parts of the core.

We emphasize that the detailed microarchitecture is not the emphasis or contribution of this work. The novel and new ability to model such an architecture using the TDG, and the implications of this design organization are the main contributions.

3.2 TDG-Modeling of BSAs

We now discuss how each BSA is modeled inside the TDG framework. Each accelerator model discusses the analysis plan and transforms, and Figure 8 shows an example code and transform for each BSA.

SIMD (Loop Auto-vectorization) TDG For SIMD we focus on vectorizing independent loop iterations, as this is the most common form of auto-vectorization.

TDG Analysis: First, a pass optimistically analyzes the TDG's memory and data dependences. Memory-dependences

[4] Not to be confused with the Trace Processor from [43]

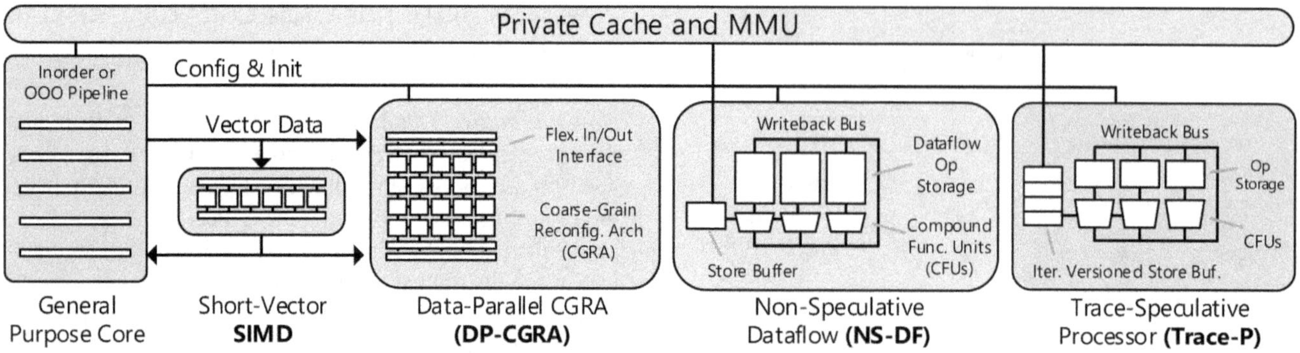

Figure 7: Example ExoCore Architecture Organization

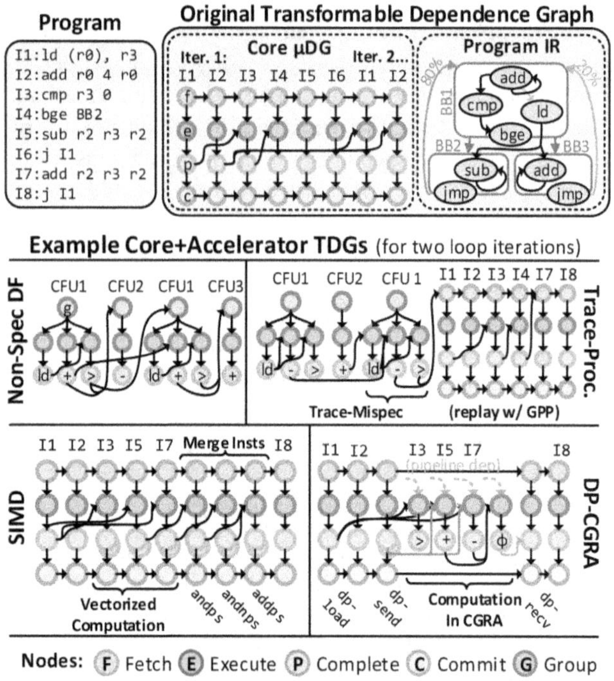

Figure 8: Example TDGs

between loop iterations can be detected by tracking per-iteration memory addresses in consecutive iterations. Loops with non-vectorizable memory dependences are excluded, and considering loop-splitting and loop-reordering to break these dependences is future work. Similarly, loops with inter-iteration data dependences which are not reductions or inductions are excluded.

For vectorizing control flow, the TDG analysis considers an if-conversion transformation, where basic blocks in an inner-loop are arranged in reverse-post order, and conditional branches become predicate-setting instructions. In the case of non-local memory access, packing/unpacking instructions are inserted into the loop body. For alignment, we assume we have the use of unaligned memory operations (like in x86). This analysis also computes where masking instructions would need to be added along merging control paths. The TDG decides whether to vectorize a loop by computing the expected number of dynamic instructions per iteration by considering path profiling information. If it is more than twice the original, the loop is disregarded.

TDG Transform ($TDG_{GPP,\emptyset}$ to $TDG_{GPP,SIMD}$): When a vectorizable loop is encountered, μDG nodes from the loop are buffered until the vector-length number of iterations are accumulated. The first iteration of this group becomes the *vectorized* version, and not-taken control path instructions, as well as mask and predicate instructions, are inserted. Most instructions are converted to their vectorized version, except for non-contiguous loads/stores, for which additional scalar operations are added (as we target non-scatter/gather hardware). At this point, memory latency information is remapped onto the *vectorized* iteration, and the non-vector iterations are elided. If fewer than the minimum vector length iterations remain, the SIMD transform is not used.

Data-Parallel CGRA (DP-CGRA) TDG *TDG Analysis:* The analysis "plan" is a set of legal and profitable loops, potentially vectorized, where for each loop the plan contains the *computation subgraph* (offloaded instructions). Vectorization is borrowed from SIMD, and a slicing algorithm [17] is used to separate instructions between the general core and CGRA. Control instructions without forward memory dependences are offloaded to the CGRA.

Similar to SIMD, a new version of the inner loops is constructed, except here the computation subgraph is removed from the loop, and communication instructions are inserted along the interface edges. If the loop is vectorizable, the computation can be "cloned" until its size fills the available resources, or until the maximum vector length is reached, enabling more parallelism. The analysis algorithm disregards loops with more communication instructions than offloaded computation.

TDG Transform ($TDG_{GPP,\emptyset}$ to $TDG_{GPP,DP\text{-}CGRA}$): The DP-CGRA keeps a small configuration cache, so if a configuration is not found when entering a targeted loop, instructions for configuration are inserted into the TDG. Similar to SIMD, μDG nodes from several loop iterations are buffered until the vectorizable loop length is reached. At this point, if the loop is vectorizable, the first step is to apply the SIMD transformation as described earlier ($TDG_{GPP,\emptyset}$ to $TDG_{GPP,SIMD}$).

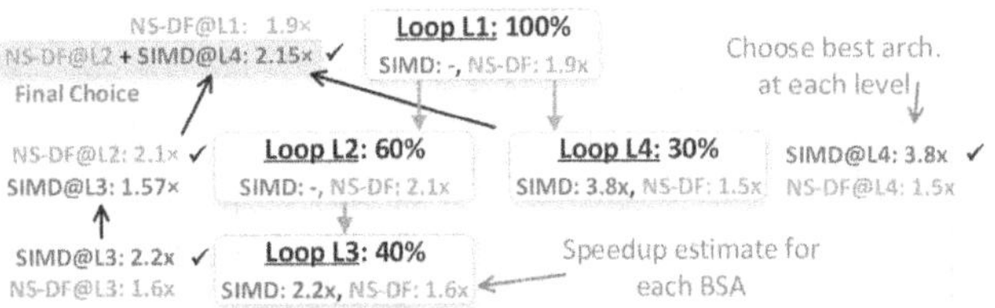

Figure 9: Amdahl Tree – Example of Triple Nested Loop

Offloaded instructions require two additional edges to enforce accelerator pipelining: one for the pipeline depth between computation instances, and one for in-order completion. We model the scheduling and routing latency by adding delay on the data dependence edges.

Non-speculative Dataflow (NS-DF) TDG *TDG Analysis:* The primary analysis here is to find fully inlinable loops or nested loops that fit within the hardware budget. Once a loop nest selected, the control is converted into data-dependences by computing the program dependence graph. This determines where "switch" instructions should be inserted to handle control. Instructions are then scheduled onto CFUs using known mathematical optimization [36] techniques.

TDG Transform ($TDG_{GPP,\emptyset}$ to $TDG_{GPP,NS\text{-}DF}$): This transform operates at basic-block granularity, by inserting edges to enforce control dependences and to force each compound instruction to wait for all operands before beginning execution. It also adds edges to enforce writeback network capacity. Additionally, edges between the general core and NS-DF regions are inserted to model live value transfer time.

Trace-Processor (Trace-P) TDG *TDG Analysis:* The analysis plan is a set of eligible and profitable inner loops and compound instruction schedules. Eligible loops with hot traces are found using path profiling techniques [4]. Loops are considered if their loop back probability is higher than 80%, and their configuration size fits in the hardware limit. A similar CFU scheduling technique is used, but compound instructions are allowed to cross control boundaries.

TDG Transform ($TDG_{GPP\text{-}Orig,\emptyset}$ to $TDG_{OOO,Trace\text{-}P}$): This transform is similar to NS-DF, except that the control dependences are not enforced, and if Trace-P mispeculates the path, instructions are replayed on the host processor by reverting to the $TDG_{GPP\text{-}Orig,\emptyset}$ to $TDG_{GPP\text{-}New,\emptyset}$ transform.

3.3 BSA Selection

A practical consideration is how to choose between BSAs throughout the program execution. This is complicated by the fact that the decision is hierarchical in program scope (eg. target an entire loop nest, or just the inner loop?).

We propose a simple strategy called the Amdahl Tree, as shown in Figure 9. Each node in the tree represents a candidate loop, and is labeled with the speedup of each BSA, and the expected execution time. This speedup can be approximate based on static or profile information. A bottom-up traversal, applying Amdahl's law at each node, can determine the best architecture for a given region. In practice, a profile-based compiler can make BSA selections and embed them in the program binary.

Suite	Benchmarks
TPT	conv, merge, nbody, radar, treesearch, vr
Parboil	cutcp, fft, kmeans, lbm, mm, needle, nnw, spmv, stencil, tpacf
SPECfp	433.milc 444.namd 450.soplex 453.povray 482.sphinx3
Mediabench	cjpeg, djpeg, gsmdecode, gsmencode cjpeg2, djpeg2, h263enc, h264dec, jpg2000dec, jpg2000enc, mpeg2dec, mpeg2enc
TPCH	Queries 1 and 2
SPECint	164.gzip, 181.mcf, 175.vpr, 197.parser, 256.bzip2 429.mcf, 403.gcc, 458.sjeng, 473.astar, 456.hmmer, 445.gobmk

Table 3: Benchmarks

	IO2	OOO2	OOO4	OOO6
Fetch, Dispatch Issue, WB Width	2	2	4	6
ROB Size	-	64	168	192
Instr. Window	-	32	48	52
DCache Ports	1	1	2	3
FUs (ALU,Mul/Div,FP)	2,1,1	2,1,1,	3,2,2	4,2,3

Table 4: General Core Configurations

4. ExoCore Exploration Methodology

The following methodology is used in the design-space exploration in the next section.

Benchmarks Selection Benchmarks were chosen from a wide range of suites (Table 3). These include highly regular codes from Intel TPT [17], scientific workloads from PARBOIL [1], image/video applications from Mediabench [27] and irregular workloads from SPECint. The diversity highlights ExoCore's ability to target a large variety of codes. Also, as much as possible, we picked benchmarks and suites from the respective accelerator publications.

General Core Configurations We considered four different cores of varying complexity, with parameters as outlined in Table 4. The common characteristics are a 2-way 32KiB I$ and 64KiB L1D$, both with 4 cycle latencies, and a 8-way 2MB L2$ with a 22 cycle hit latency. We model 256-bit SIMD.

Area Estimation We use McPAT for estimating area of general cores, and use area estimates from relevant publications [17, 18, 36].

Runtime Accelerator Selection Because we are exploring the potential of ExoCore systems, most of our results use an Oracle scheduler, which chooses the best accelerator for each static region, based on past execution characteristics. The selection metric we use is energy-delay, where no individual region should reduce the performance by more than 10%. One later set of results compares the oracle and Amdahl Tree schedulers.

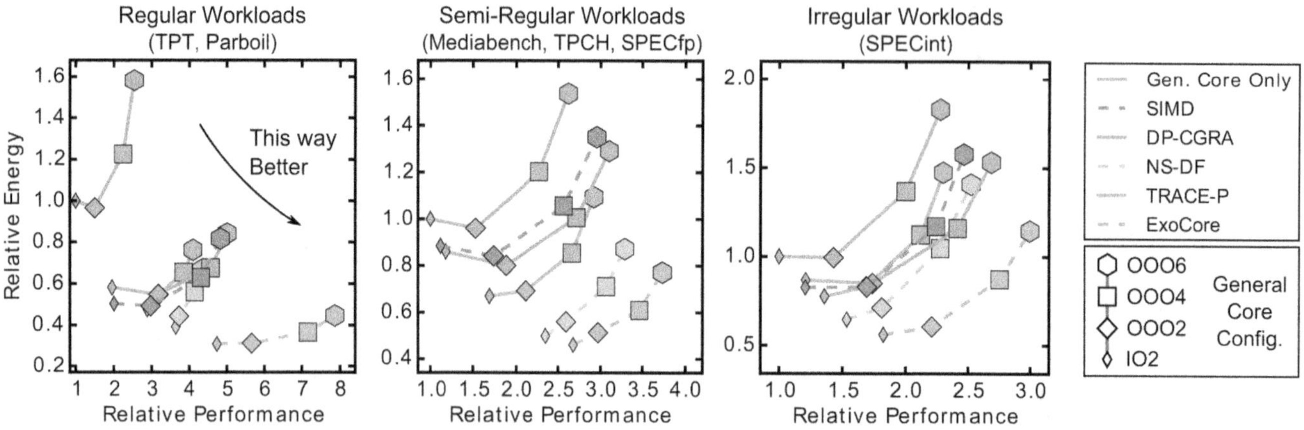

Figure 11: Interaction between Accelerator, General Core, and Workloads

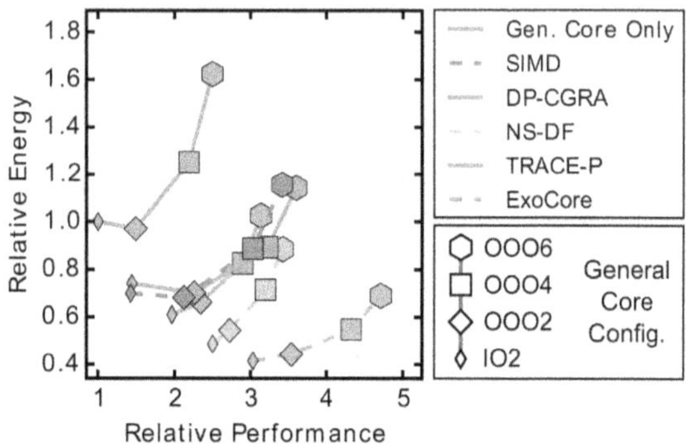

Figure 10: ExoCore Tradeoffs Across All Workloads

5. Design Space Exploration

In this section, we explore a design space comprising the combinations of four general purpose cores and 16 choices for the subset of BSAs (from the set of four BSAs we study). For this section, a "full ExoCore" consists of an ExoCore with all four BSAs. We report three important results first:

- **High Potential of BSAs** Across all workloads, a full OOO2-based ExoCore provides 2.4× performance and energy benefits over an OOO2 core (dual-issue, out-of-order). Compared to an OOO6 core, an OOO6 ExoCore can achieve up to 1.9× performance and 2.4× energy benefits.
- **Design Choice Opportunities** Our analysis suggests that there are several ways to break through current energy, area, and performance tradeoffs. For example, there are four OOO2-based ExoCores and nine OOO4-based ExoCores that achieve higher performance than an OOO6 with SIMD alone. Of these, the $\text{OOO2}_{\text{SIMD+DP-CGRA+NSDF}}$ ExoCore achieves 2.6× better energy efficiency, while requiring 40% less area.
- **Affinity Behavior** ExoCores make use of multiple accelerators, both inside workload domains, and inside applications themselves. Across all benchmarks, considering a full OOO2 ExoCore, an average of only 16% of the original programs' execution cycles went un-accelerated.

We discuss each of these results in the following subsections. We also again emphasize that, in principle, the same analysis could be done by implementing and integrating many compilers and simulators inside the same framework. However it is difficult and impractically time-consuming. See Appendix A for steps in TDG modeling.

5.1 High Potentials of ExoCores

Overall Trends Figure 10 shows geometric mean performance and energy benefits of single-BSA designs as well as full ExoCores across all workloads. Each line in this graph represents the set of designs with the same combination of accelerators (or no accelerators), and each point on the curve represents a different general purpose core. As alluded to, we show that each BSA alone has significant potential, and their combination has even more.

Workload Interaction To observe workload domain specific behavior, Figure 11 divides the previous results into highly regular, semi-regular, and highly irregular workload categories. The major result here is that even on the most challenging irregular SPECint applications, ExoCores have significant potential. A full OOO2 ExoCore can achieve 1.6× performance and energy benefits over OOO2 with SIMD. For OOO6, ExoCore achieves 1.25× performance and 50% energy efficiency improvement. Our findings also confirm the intuitive result that BSAs have a high potential on regular workloads, where ExoCore achieves 3.5× performance and 3× energy improvement for OOO2 core.

5.2 Design Choice Opportunities

An ExoCore organization opens design opportunities which can push traditional energy and performance tradeoffs forward, and this is true for both complex and simple general purpose cores. The TDG enables the exploration of these designs.

To demonstrate this capability, and examine some new opportunities, we perform a design space exploration across

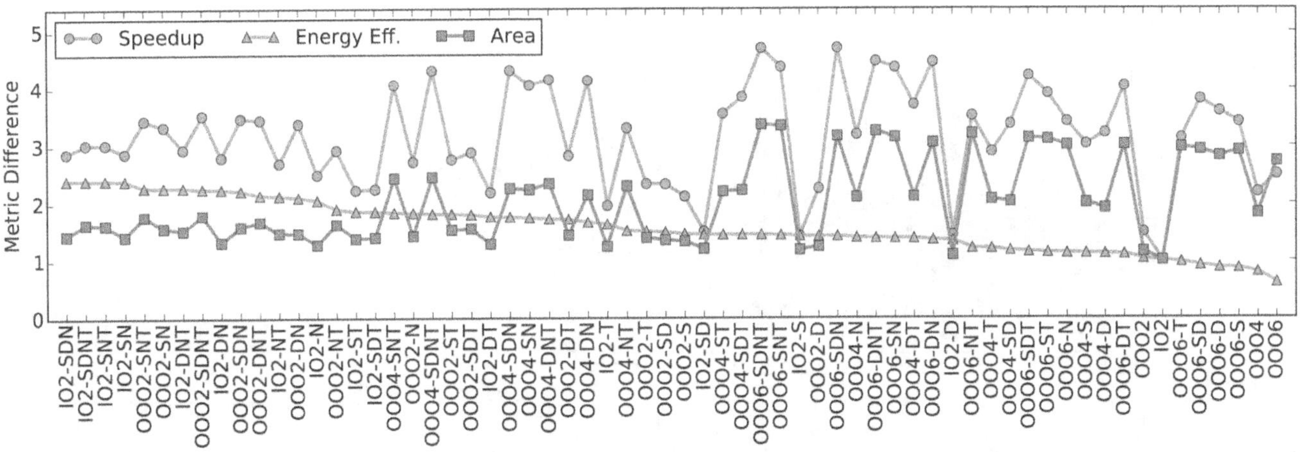

Figure 12: Design-Space Characterization. S: SIMD, D: Data-Parallel CGRA, N: Non-spec Dataflow, T: Trace-Processor

all combinations of general purpose cores and BSAs across all workloads. The resulting performance, energy efficiency and area metrics are shown in Figure 12, where all points are relative to the dual-issue in-order (IO2) design. On the graph, higher is better for performance and energy efficiency, and lower is better for area. There are many valuable quantitative insights.

- **[Performance]** Compared to the OOO6 core with SIMD[5], four OOO2 and nine OOO4 ExoCore configurations match the performance with lower energy and area, by as much as 2×. This gives the designer freedom even if performance is a hard constraint.
- **[Performance]** No in-order ExoCore configuration can match the OOO6 performance. The best achieved is 88% of the OOO6, with almost 1.7× lower area.
- **[Energy]** The OOO2 core with SIMD is the most energy efficient baseline core. Compared to this core, **twelve** in-order and **five** OOO4 ExoCores have higher energy efficiency - by as much as 65% and 25% respectively. In addition to being more energy efficient, these configurations are up to 1.35× (IO2-SDN) and 1.9× (OOO4-SNT) higher performance.
- **[Energy]** A full OOO6 ExoCore achieves the same energy efficiency (within 1%) of the OOO2-SIMD core and has 2.2× higher performance, but is nearly twice the area.
- **[Full ExoCores]** The full IO2 ExoCore is the most energy-efficient among all designs. The full OOO6 ExoCore has the best performance, the next best is the full OOO4 ExoCore, which has 10% lower performance, 1.25× lower energy and 1.36× lower area.

Overall these results suggest two trends. Behavior specialized cores are extremely effective at reducing energy regardless of core type. They provide high performance-improvements for in-order, small and medium-sized OOO cores - but not much for big OOO cores. Therefore, the most high impact opportunity for future BSAs is to improve the performance of OOO cores, while further increasing their energy efficiency. The TDG enables this and other such explorations.

[5] We use OOO6-SIMD as the baseline - since this resembles commercial processors with AVX2 etc. Note that if we had used OOO6 without SIMD as the baseline, the benefits of ExoCores would be even higher.

5.3 Affinity Behavior

We have thus far considered aggregate metrics across workloads, but the TDG also enables application-level analysis, which we perform next.

Inter-application Affinity Figure 13 considers an OOO2-based ExoCore, and shows each benchmark's energy and execution time breakdown. The baseline is the OOO2 alone. Most benchmarks, even irregular workloads, have some potential to effectively use BSAs, ranging from 100% of the program being offloaded, to around 20%. Secondly, some workloads can benefit from multiple BSAs inside a single application. For example, cjpeg-2 makes use of SIMD, NS-DF and Trace-P during its execution.

Considering energy breakdowns in Figure 13, observe that for SIMD and DP-CGRA, the percentage of cycles offloaded is proportional to the energy contribution. For NS-DF, because it can power-gate portions of the general core when in use, the energy reduction is higher than the execution time reduction.

Affinity Granularity To give insight into the dynamic behavior of an ExoCore, Figure 14 shows a trace of execution for two benchmarks. These graphs show the relative performance benefits of a full OOO2 ExoCore over the OOO2 core alone, over time. These graphs demonstrate both that applications can have fine-grain affinity for different accelerators, and that a TDG-based framework can capture and model this behavior.

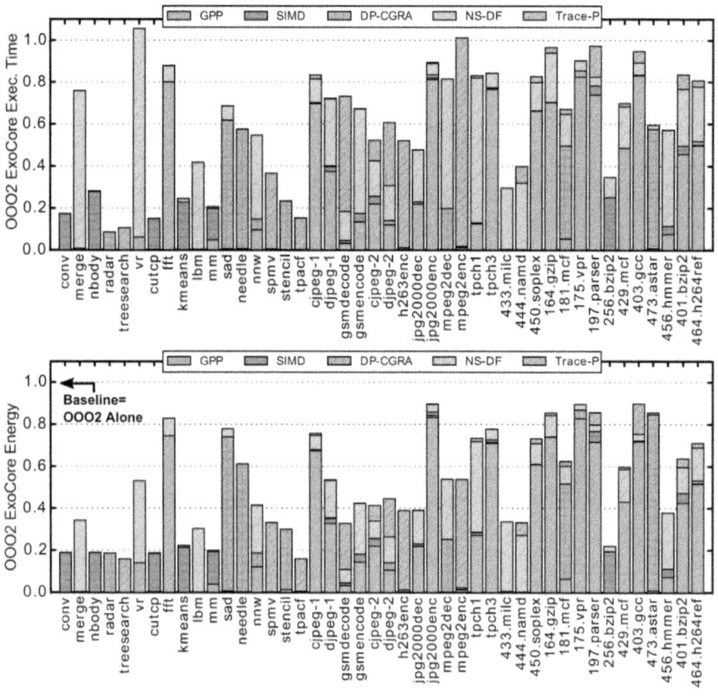

Figure 13: Per-Benchmark Behavior and Region Affinity

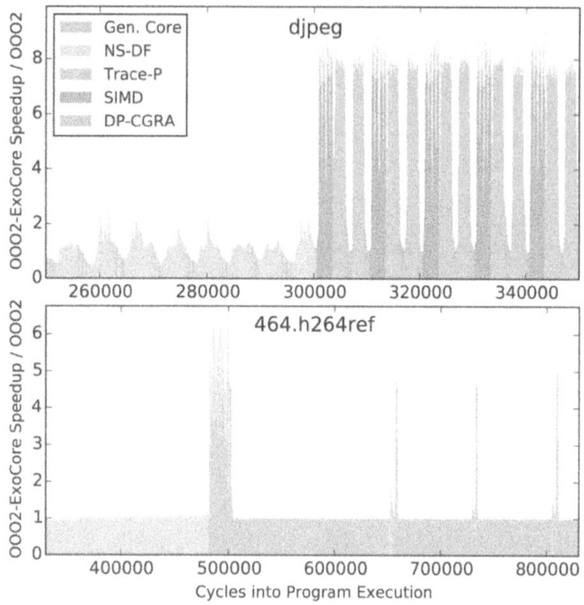

Figure 14: ExoCore's Dynamic Switching Behavior

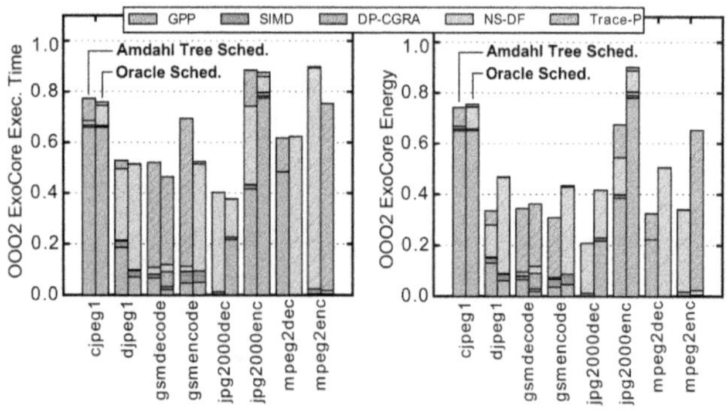

Figure 15: Oracle versus Amdahl Tree Scheduler

5.4 Practicality

Though we have shown that ExoCores have significant potential, an important concern is whether they can practically provide benefits without oracle information. To study this, Figure 15 presents a comparison of the performance and energy of the Amdahl scheduler (left-bar) and the Oracle scheduler (right-bar). Here, the general core is the OOO2, and we are showing challenging benchmarks from Mediabench which require using multiple different accelerators in the same application to be effective.

Compared to the oracle scheduler, our scheduler is slightly over-calibrated towards using the BSAs rather than the general core, meaning it is biased towards energy efficiency – across all benchmarks (including those not shown) the scheduler provides 1.21× geomean energy efficiency improvement, while giving 0.89× performance of the Oracle scheduler. These heuristics can be tuned with more effort to favor different metrics, or to be useful for the OOO4 or OOO6 cores.

5.5 Evaluation Limitations and Extensions

This evaluation has explored *a* design space across cores, accelerators and various metrics. Of course, there is a much larger design space including varying core and accelerator parameters, modifying their frequencies, and including other proposed or novel accelerators. Though we have admittedly just scratched the surface, the TDG can enable insightful modeling of this design space.

The TDG framework and the benefits of combining BSAs suggests that a fruitful area of future work is to see if an ExoCore can be designed to match domain specific accelerators in certain domains.

Also, our TDG transforms are simply written as short functions in C/C++. A DSL to specify these transforms could make the TDG framework even more productive for designers.

6. Related Work

Parallel and Heterogeneous Architecture Modeling An alternative to modeling architectures with the TDG are analytical models. Relevant works include those which reason about the benefits of specialization and heterogeneity [11, 20, 45, 57], high-level technology trend projections [6, 22], or even general purpose processors [10, 12, 14]. There are also several analytical GPU models [21, 32, 39, 40, 46, 54].

The drawback of such models is that they are either specific to the modeling of *one* accelerator or general-purpose core, or they are too generic and do not allow design space explorations which capture detailed phenomenon.

Kismet [16, 23] is a model which uses profiles of serial programs to predict upper-bound speedups for parallelization. It uses a hierarchical critical path analysis to characterize the available and expressible parallelism.

Perhaps the most related technique is the Aladdin framework [44], a trace-based tool that uses a compiler IR interpreter, that enables design space exploration of *domain specific accelerators*. Using such an approach for behavioral specialized accelerators is possible, and should reduce errors from ISA artifacts. The drawback would be that the interaction with the general purpose core in that framework would be more difficult to capture. However, that style of approach may be an avenue for improving accuracy in the future.

Core Heterogeneity Single-ISA heterogeneous architectures have been extensively explored, starting with Kumar et al. [25]. Later work extended this by exploring a large design space of microarchitectural design points [26], and Lee et al. use regression analysis to broaden this design space even further. A related design approach is to use a shared pipeline frontend, but use a heterogeneous backend inside the microarchitecture, like Composite Cores [31].

To a lesser extent, multi-ISA heterogeneity (where all cores are general purpose) have been previously studied, including Venkat et al. [52], who show that heterogeneity in the ISA alone can provide benefits. Our work considers the composition of accelerator-type architectures, which offer tradeoffs beyond those of general purpose architectures.

Relatedly, many past works have explored processor steering methods on heterogeneous architectures [35, 41, 48, 51, 55]. The unique aspect of the scheduling problem in this work is that entry points to different accelerators are restricted by the program's loop structure.

7. Conclusions

In this work, we proposed the ExoCore design which incorporates multiple behavior-specialized accelerators inside a core, and a comprehensive and novel modeling methodology for studying such architectures called the transformable dependence graph (TDG).

The TDG consists of a closely-coupled μDG and Program IR for analysis. This representation allows the study of the combined effects of compiler and hardware microarchitecture as graph transformations. We showed the TDG approach is accurate and allows deep and insightful analysis and design-space exploration.

Broadly, the ExoCore approach could be influential in two ways. First, it simplifies general purpose core design – behavior-specific microarchitecture blocks can be designed and integrated into the core in a modular fashion, without disruptive changes to the core's microarchitecture. Second, it provides a promising approach for exceeding the performance/energy frontier of conventional approaches. Finally, an open question that arises from this paradigm is how powerful must the baseline core be - can one design sufficiently powerful and expressive BSAs, where only a simple in-order core is sufficient, and most of the application time is spent in a BSA.

A. Steps in TDG Model Construction

Here we discuss the practical aspects and steps in constructing a TDG model.

Analysis The first step is identifying the required compiler analysis or profiling information, and implementing a pass to compute it, operating on the IR or trace respectively. Often, the required information (eg. path profiling) already exists because it is common among BSAs. When this information cannot be computed, approximation may be appropriate.

Transformations The next step is to write an algorithm (a "transform") which reads the incoming μDG trace, and modifies dependences to model the behavior of the BSA in question. Depending on the granularity of acceleration, a transform may operate on a single instruction at a time, or it might collect a basic block, loop iteration, or several iterations before it can decide what the final μDG should be. The modified μDG is transient, and is discarded after any analysis (eg. critical path analysis), once it is no longer inside the current instruction window. A transformation should also include a model for how it interacts with the core when it enters and exists a region.

Scheduling Finally, the model must decide *when* to apply the BSA transform (ie. at what point in the code). In a single-BSA system, the BSA's transform can be used at any legal entry point. For multi-BSA systems, the model should provide per-region performance (or other metric) estimates relative to the general purpose core for the BSA based on either the IR or profiling information. This is used with the Amdahl tree to decide which BSA to use in each region.

Validating new BSAs Validating a TDG model of newly-proposed BSAs is similar to validating a cycle-level simulator. Writing microbenchmarks and sanity checking is recommended (eg. examining which edges are on the critical path for some code region).

Acknowledgments

We thank Venkatraman Govindaraju for his help in creating the initial TDG models and validation for DySER and SIMD. We also thank our shepherd, David Wentzlaff, and the anonymous reviewers for their comments and advice.

Support for this research was provided by NSF under the grants CNS-1218432 and CCF-0917238, and by a Google PhD Fellowship.

References

[1] *Parboil Benchmark Suite.* impact.crhc.illinois.edu/parboil/parboil.aspx.

[2] *Vertical Microbenchmarks.* http://cs.wisc.edu/vertical/microbench.

[3] Renée St. Amant, Amir Yazdanbakhsh, Jongse Park, Bradley Thwaites, Hadi Esmaeilzadeh, Arjang Hassibi, Luis Ceze, and Doug Burger. General-purpose code acceleration with limited-precision analog computation. In *ISCA*, 2014.

[4] Thomas Ball and James R. Larus. Efficient path profiling. In *MICRO*, 1996.

[5] Nathan Binkert, Bradford Beckmann, Gabriel Black, Steven K. Reinhardt, Ali Saidi, Arkaprava Basu, Joel Hestness, Derek R. Hower, Tushar Krishna, Somayeh Sardashti, Rathijit Sen, Korey Sewell, Muhammad Shoaib, Nilay Vaish, Mark D. Hill, and David A. Wood. The gem5 simulator. *SIGARCH Comput. Archit. News*, 2011.

[6] Shekhar Borkar and Andrew A. Chien. The future of microprocessors. *Commun. ACM*, 54(5):67–77, 2011.

[7] Tianshi Chen, Zidong Du, Ninghui Sun, Jia Wang, Chengyong Wu, Yunji Chen, and Olivier Temam. DianNao: a small-footprint high-throughput accelerator for ubiquitous machine-learning. In *ASPLOS*, 2014.

[8] Nathan Clark, Manjunath Kudlur, Hyunchul Park, Scott Mahlke, and Krisztian Flautner. Application-specific processing on a general-purpose core via transparent instruction set customization. In *MICRO*, 2004.

[9] Rajagopalan Desikan, Doug Burger, and Stephen W. Keckler. Measuring experimental error in microprocessor simulation. In *ISCA*, 2001.

[10] Lieven Eeckhout. Computer architecture performance evaluation methods. *Synthesis Lectures on Computer Architecture*, 2010.

[11] Peter A. Milder Eric S. Chung, James C. Hoe, and Ken Mai. Single-chip heterogeneous computing: Does the future include custom logic, FPGAs, and GPUs? In *MICRO '10*.

[12] Hadi Esmaeilzadeh, Emily Blem, Renee St. Amant, Karthikeyan Sankaralingam, and Doug Burger. Dark silicon and the end of multicore scaling. *SIGARCH Comput. Archit. News*, 2011.

[13] Hadi Esmaeilzadeh, Adrian Sampson, Luis Ceze, and Doug Burger. Neural acceleration for general-purpose approximate programs. In *MICRO*, 2012.

[14] Stijn Eyerman, Lieven Eeckhout, Tejas Karkhanis, and James E. Smith. A mechanistic performance model for superscalar out-of-order processors. *ACM Trans. Comput. Syst.*, 2009.

[15] Brian Fields, Shai Rubin, and Rastislav Bodik. Focusing processor policies via critical-path prediction. In *ISCA*, 2001.

[16] Saturnino Garcia, Donghwan Jeon, Chris Louie, and Michael Bedford Taylor. Kremlin: Rethinking and rebooting gprof for the multicore age. In *PLDI*, 2011.

[17] Venkatraman Govindaraju, Chen-Han Ho, Tony Nowatzki, Jatin Chhugani, Nadathur Satish, Karthikeyan Sankaralingam, and Changkyu Kim. Dyser: Unifying functionality and parallelism specialization for energy efficient computing. *IEEE Micro*, 2012.

[18] Shantanu Gupta, Shuguang Feng, Amin Ansari, Scott Mahlke, and David August. Bundled execution of recurring traces for energy-efficient general purpose processing. In *MICRO*, 2011.

[19] Rehan Hameed, Wajahat Qadeer, Megan Wachs, Omid Azizi, Alex Solomatnikov, Benjamin C. Lee, Stephen Richardson, Christos Kozyrakis, and Mark Horowitz. Understanding sources of inefficiency in general-purpose chips. In *ISCA '10*.

[20] Mark Hempstead, Gu-Yeon Wei, and David Brooks. Navigo: An early-stage model to study power-contrained architectures and specialization. In *Proceedings of Workshop on Modeling, Benchmarking, and Simulations (MoBS)*, 2009.

[21] Sunpyo Hong and Hyesoon Kim. An integrated GPU power and performance model. In *ISCA '10*.

[22] R. Iyer. Accelerator-rich architectures: Implications, opportunities and challenges. In *Design Automation Conference (ASP-DAC), 2012 17th Asia and South Pacific*, 2012.

[23] Donghwan Jeon, Saturnino Garcia, Chris Louie, and Michael Bedford Taylor. Kismet: Parallel Speedup Estimates for Serial Programs. In *OOPSLA*, 2011.

[24] Onur Kocberber, Boris Grot, Javier Picorel, Babak Falsafi, Kevin Lim, and Parthasarathy Ranganathan. Meet the walkers: Accelerating index traversals for in-memory databases. In *MICRO*, 2013.

[25] Rakesh Kumar, Keith I. Farkas, Norman P. Jouppi, Parthasarathy Ranganathan, and Dean M. Tullsen. Single-isa heterogeneous multi-core architectures: The potential for processor power reduction. In *MICRO*, 2003.

[26] Rakesh Kumar, Dean M. Tullsen, and Norman P. Jouppi. Core architecture optimization for heterogeneous chip multiprocessors. In *PACT*, 2006.

[27] Chunho Lee, M. Potkonjak, and W.H. Mangione-Smith. MediaBench: a tool for evaluating and synthesizing multimedia and communications systems. In *MICRO*, 1997.

[28] Jaewon Lee, Hanhwi Jang, and Jangwoo Kim. Rpstacks: Fast and accurate processor design space exploration using representative stall-event stacks. In *MICRO*, 2014.

[29] Sheng Li, Jung-Ho Ahn, R.D. Strong, J.B. Brockman, D.M. Tullsen, and N.P. Jouppi. McPAT: an integrated power, area, and timing modeling framework for multicore and manycore architectures. In *MICRO*, 2009.

[30] Daofu Liu, Tianshi Chen, Shaoli Liu, Jinhong Zhou, Shengyuan Zhou, Olivier Teman, Xiaobing Feng, Xuehai Zhou, and Yunji Chen. PuDianNao: a polyvalent machine learning accelerator. In *ASPLOS*, 2015.

[31] Andrew Lukefahr, Shruti Padmanabha, Reetuparna Das, Faissal M. Sleiman, Ronald Dreslinski, Thomas F. Wenisch, and Scott Mahlke. Composite Cores: Pushing heterogeneity into a core. In *MICRO*, 2012.

[32] J. Meng, V.A. Morozov, K. Kumaran, V. Vishwanath, and T.D. Uram. GROPHECY: GPU performance projection from CPU code skeletons. In *SC'11*. ACM, 2011.

[33] Tipp Moseley, Dirk Grunwald, Daniel A Connors, Ram Ramanujam, Vasanth Tovinkere, and Ramesh Peri. Loopprof:

Dynamic techniques for loop detection and profiling. In *Proceedings of the 2006 Workshop on Binary Instrumentation and Applications (WBIA)*, 2006.

[34] Naveen Muralimanohar, Rajeev Balasubramonian, and Norman P Jouppi. Cacti 6.0: A tool to model large caches. *HP Laboratories*, 2009.

[35] Sandeep Navada, Niket K. Choudhary, Salil V. Wadhavkar, and Eric Rotenberg. A unified view of non-monotonic core selection and application steering in heterogeneous chip multiprocessors. In *PACT*, 2013.

[36] Tony Nowatzki, Vinay Gangadhar, and Karthikeyan Sankaralingam. Exploring the potential of heterogeneous Von Neumann/Dataflow execution models. In *ISCA*, 2015.

[37] Tony Nowatzki, Vinay Gangadhar, and Karthikeyan Sankaralingam. Pushing the limits of accelerator efficiency while retaining programmability. In *HPCA*, 2016.

[38] Tony Nowatzki, Venkatraman. Govindaraju, and Karthikeyan Sankaralingam. A graph-based program representation for analyzing hardware specialization approaches. *Computer Architecture Letters*, 2015.

[39] Cedric Nugteren and Henk Corporaal. A modular and parameterisable classification of algorithms. Technical Report ESR-2011-02, Eindhoven University of Technology, 2011.

[40] Cedric Nugteren and Henk Corporaal. The boat hull model: adapting the roofline model to enable performance prediction for parallel computing. In *PPOPP*, 2012.

[41] Shruti Padmanabha, Andrew Lukefahr, Reetuparna Das, and Scott Mahlke. Trace based phase prediction for tightly-coupled heterogeneous cores. In *MICRO*, 2013.

[42] Wajahat Qadeer, Rehan Hameed, Ofer Shacham, Preethi Venkatesan, Christos Kozyrakis, and Mark A. Horowitz. Convolution engine: Balancing efficiency and flexibility in specialized computing. In *ISCA*, 2013.

[43] Eric Rotenberg, Quinn Jacobson, Yiannakis Sazeides, and Jim Smith. Trace processors. In *MICRO*, 1997.

[44] Yakun Sophia Shao, Brandon Reagen, Gu-Yeon Wei, and David Brooks. Aladdin: A pre-rtl, power-performance accelerator simulator enabling large design space exploration of customized architectures. In *ISCA*, 2014.

[45] M. Shoaib Bin Altaf and D.A. Wood. LogCA: a performance model for hardware accelerators. *Computer Architecture Letters*, 2015.

[46] Jaewoong Sim, Aniruddha Dasgupta, Hyesoon Kim, and Richard Vuduc. A performance analysis framework for identifying potential benefits in GPGPU applications. In *PPoPP*, 2012.

[47] H. Singh, Ming-Hau Lee, Guangming Lu, F.J. Kurdahi, N. Bagherzadeh, and E.M. Chaves Filho. Morphosys: an integrated reconfigurable system for data-parallel and computation-intensive applications. *Computers, IEEE Transactions on*, 2000.

[48] Tyler Sondag and Hridesh Rajan. Phase-based tuning for better utilization of performance-asymmetric multicore processors. In *CGO*, 2011.

[49] Shreesha Srinath, Berkin Ilbeyi, Mingxing Tan, Gai Liu, Zhiru Zhang, and Christopher Batten. Architectural specialization for inter-iteration loop dependence patterns. In *MICRO*, 2014.

[50] Steven Swanson, Ken Michelson, Andrew Schwerin, and Mark Oskin. Wavescalar. In *MICRO*, pages 291–, 2003.

[51] Kenzo Van Craeynest, Aamer Jaleel, Lieven Eeckhout, Paolo Narvaez, and Joel Emer. Scheduling heterogeneous multi-cores through performance impact estimation (pie). In *ISCA*, 2012.

[52] Ashish Venkat and Dean M. Tullsen. Harnessing isa diversity: Design of a heterogeneous-isa chip multiprocessor. In *ISCA*, 2014.

[53] Ganesh Venkatesh, Jack Sampson, Nathan Goulding, Saturnino Garcia, Vladyslav Bryksin, Jose Lugo-Martinez, Steven Swanson, and Michael Bedford Taylor. Conservation Cores: Reducing the Energy of Mature Computations. In *ASPLOS '10*.

[54] Samuel Williams, Andrew Waterman, and David Patterson. Roofline: an insightful visual performance model for multi-core architectures. *Commun. ACM*, 2009.

[55] Jonathan A. Winter, David H. Albonesi, and Christine A. Shoemaker. Scalable thread scheduling and global power management for heterogeneous many-core architectures. In *PACT*, 2010.

[56] Lisa Wu, Andrea Lottarini, Timothy K. Paine, Martha A. Kim, and Kenneth A. Ross. Q100: The architecture and design of a database processing unit. In *ASPLOS*, 2014.

[57] T. Zidenberg, I. Keslassy, and U. Weiser. Optimal resource allocation with multiamdahl. *Computer*, 2013.

PIFT: Predictive Information-Flow Tracking

Man-Ki Yoon
University of Illinois at Urbana-Champaign
mkyoon@illinois.edu

Negin Salajegheh Yin Chen
Mihai Christodorescu
Qualcomm Research
{msalajeg,yinc,mihai}@qti.qualcomm.com

Abstract

Phones today carry sensitive information and have a great number of ways to communicate that data. As a result, malware that steal money, information, or simply disable functionality have hit the app stores. Current security solutions for preventing undesirable data leaks are mostly high-overhead and have not been practical enough for smartphones. In this paper, we show that simply monitoring just some instructions (only memory loads and stores) it is possible to achieve low overhead, highly accurate information flow tracking. Our method achieves 98% accuracy (0% false positive and 2% false negative) over DroidBench and was able to successfully catch seven real-world malware instances that steal phone number, location, and device ID using SMS messages and HTTP connections.

Categories and Subject Descriptors K.6.5 [*Management of Computing and Information Systems*]: Security and Protection

Keywords Security; information flow tracking

1. Introduction

Information-flow control (IFC) is a fundamental technique in computer security and privacy, allowing fine-grained control over information as it is routed between running programs and processed by them. Information-flow tracking [9, 14, 16] is the underlying mechanism that enables IFC to make decisions. With a robust tracking system, IFC can be used to prevent privacy leaks, ensure the integrity of information by verifying its provenance, and minimize the attack surface of a system by restricting the data accessible to any one program in that system. An information-flow tracking system that supports these goals has to be accurate, scalable, and efficient.

Today there is a large number of information-flow tracking techniques, from static [5] to dynamic [9] and from hardware-based [16] to hybrid [19] to software-only [14]. Static analysis of program code is often constrained to particular languages and particular runtime environments, thus making it inadequate in a real system consisting of programs written in diverse languages. Dynamic information-flow tracking modifies the program, the runtime environment, or the hardware to associate supporting information (called taint state or taint flags) to relevant program data and to propagate this supporting information as the program copies, manipulates, and transforms the data. The dynamic approach is broadly applicable to many programming languages and runtimes, making it attractive in practice, but comes with the implicit overhead of doing additional work per program instruction. Rewriting the program or the runtime to add dynamic information-flow tracking introduces large overheads, which translate to increased power consumption, and is thus impractical for all but strictest security- and privacy-conscious uses. Hardware solutions usually introduce less than 1% overhead, but require re-architecting the system to supplement each storage element (e.g., registers, cache blocks at all levels, main memory) with the storage for the associate taint state. Such re-architecting is undesirable from an engineering perspective.

We approach the challenges of information-flow tracking from the position of simplifying the mechanics of tracking while carefully trading off perfect accuracy for sufficient accuracy. In other words, the question we try to answer is how much performance and simplicity of implementation we can gain by reducing tracking accuracy without endangering the task at hand (qualitative information-flow control). We make the observation that *information flows have distinguishable characteristics in terms of their structure* (e.g., length, duration, instruction distribution). This fact (which we support with empirical evidence and analytical reasoning later in this paper) allows us to discard the requirement that every instruction be analyzed (statically or dynamically). Furthermore, this allows us to design the tracking mechanism in terms of inexpensive syntactic elements of the program, instead of expensive semantic ones.

We discuss the use of statistics over the instruction stream, in particular with respect to *memory loads* and *mem-*

ASPLOS '16 April 2–6, 2016, Atlanta, Georgia, USA.
Copyright © 2016 ACM 978-1-4503-4091-5/16/04…$15.00
DOI: http://dx.doi.org/10.1145/http://dx.doi.org/10.1145/2872362.2872403

ory stores, to determine whether a data value from a source reaches a sink. While in general it might be possible to predict whether a memory operation that reaches a sink (e.g., a memory store to a parameter for a sink function call) operates on data read much earlier from a source, the accuracy of the resulting information-flow would be low if all intermediate execution between source and sink are ignored. We take a more refined view, where an information flow from a source to a sink is divided into segments consisting of a memory-load operation (where sensitive data is loaded into the CPU), a number of manipulations of the data in CPU registers, and one or more memory-store operations (where the derived data, still sensitive, is sent from CPU to memory). The structural characteristics of information flows can predict which memory stores in an instruction stream are related via a CPU-only flow to which memory loads. In other words, we treat the CPU as a black box, where sensitive data goes in via *loads*, and then we can tell which of the outgoing data is also sensitive based on the characteristics of the *stores*. Repeating this prediction process creates a chain of load–store operations that deal with sensitive data, eventually establishing whether an information flow from a source to a sink exists.

The benefits of this approach is to reduce the amount of data to be processed (load–store operations are at least an order of magnitude less frequent than arbitrary CPU operations) and to allow for a non-intrusive design (as monitoring memory loads and stores is easier than monitoring the CPU pipeline). Beyond performance improvements, the reduction in the amount of data means it is possible to move information-flow tracking off the critical path in the architecture, such that the load–store stream is buffered for delayed processing at a more convenient time (while trading prevention for detection, of course).

To evaluate our observation on the structural characteristics of information flows and our design for a predictive tracking mechanism, we consider mobile operating environments such as Google Android on smartphone devices. Mobile devices, though becoming more powerful every year, are significantly constrained in terms of performance and power. Each component either in hardware or software is carefully analyzed for impact on performance and on battery use. In our discussions with engineers from companies in the mobile ecosystem, any overhead over 5% (together with its associated battery impact) is considered unacceptable. Mobile devices commonly suffer from privacy-intruding apps, which collect sensitive data about the user and ship it over the network to a remote service. This combination of factors (strict performance constraints, prevalent well-defined privacy challenges) led us to focus on mobile devices for our evaluation.

In this paper we make the following contributions:

- We observe that information flows in programs have structural characteristics that makes them amenable to analysis and detection using *predictive heuristics* over the instruction stream. We propose the use of such information in a new information-flow tracking mechanism that can be easily deployed in high-performance hardware.
- We design and implement a lightweight and effective heuristic (called PIFT) for information-flow tracking, which relies only on the memory loads and stores issued by the CPU during program execution.
- We present a detailed evaluation on an ARM SoC running Google Android, showing 98% accuracy with limited impact on performance and on added CPU complexity.

2. Overview

The problem of information-flow tracking consists of determining whether sensitive data, once read at program points called *sources*, reaches program points called *sinks*. In the simplest case, a source is a program point where a sensitive data is introduced into the program memory (e.g., a password is read from user input) and a sink is a program point where some data (possibly derived from the sensitive data originated at the source) is sent out of the system.

Threat Model: Since information-flow tracking is useful in security contexts, we define here the type of attacker we consider. Our assumption is that the attacker creates a program to steal sensitive data from a user's device, and convinces the user to run this program on the device. The attacker can design and develop the program in any way they wish, using any programming language, and any supporting runtime libraries they deem suitable. The program is installed on the user's device using standard means for that environment. We make no assumptions about the exact time during execution to access sensitive data or to communicate it. The flow of data from source to sink is of the direct kind, without any indirect, conditional, or control flow-based information flows.

We are interested in mobile environments, and we consider a RISC-style load/store architecture (e.g., ARM), running a software stack designed for interactivity with a single user (e.g., Android OS). It is possible that the techniques in this paper would be applicable to web server, cloud, or scientific workloads, but we have not investigated these options.

Example: Let us consider the following program fragment:

```
String msgX = "type=sms";
...
msgY = msgX + "&imei=" + telMan.getDeviceId();
...
msgZ = msgY + "&dummy";
...
sms.sendTextMessage(phNum, null, msgZ, ...);
```

This code sends out an SMS message that contains the IMEI (International Mobile Equipment Identity) number, a sensitive ID of the mobile device. If we are interested in `getDeviceId()` as a source and `sendTextMessage()` as a sink, the problem is how to determine most efficiently that `msgZ` is sensitive because it was derived from the return value of `getDeviceId()`.

Approach: All information-flow tracking techniques applied to the above example rely on establishing the following relationships:

$$\texttt{getDeviceId()} \longrightarrow \texttt{msgY}$$
$$\texttt{msgY} \longrightarrow \texttt{msgZ}$$

where $a \longrightarrow b$ denotes an information flow from memory location a to memory location b. Together with the information about sources and sinks, these relationships are sufficient to determine that there is an information flow from `getDeviceId()` to `sendTextMessage()`. Typically the problem is solved through expensive statement- or instruction-level tracking, where an additional bit of information (called *taint*) is associated with memory locations and registers to indicate the presence of sensitive data in those locations and where execution of any instruction is supplemented to propagate these bits from the source operands to destination operands.

We explore an alternate design where *not all instructions are tracked for taint propagation.* In particular we are interested in computing taints for memory locations, so we consider the feasibility of *propagating taints from load instructions to store instructions, irrespective of the interceding data manipulation done via registers.* Our intuition behind this goal of avoiding full register-level tracking of previous work [8, 14, 16] is that code for Android-on-ARM platforms exhibits data flows of predictable lengths, not arbitrarily long, and thus the starting and ending memory operations of these data flows likely have *temporal locality.* This temporal locality is induced by the choice of Java as programming language (e.g., prevalence of heap-allocated data), by the Java virtual machine (e.g., register pressure), and by the architectural characteristics of ARM processors (e.g., load–store instruction set architecture).

To test our hypothesis of temporal locality for load–store data flows, we analyzed the native code corresponding to our Java example. During execution, the strings are copied between the character arrays of the `String` instances. For example, suppose the application has just executed `msgX + "&imei="` and `mem[addr`$_1$`,addr`$_2$`]` denotes the corresponding memory address range. The application then executes `telMan.getDeviceId()` which returns the IMEI string located at, say, `mem[addr`$_3$`,addr`$_4$`]`. Now, the concatenation of the two strings is carried out by appending the character array of the second string (i.e., the IMEI string) to the end of the array of the first string (which is now storing `"type=sms&imei="`). The final string is then stored at `mem[addr`$_1$`,addr`$_2$`+L]` where `L=addr`$_4$`-addr`$_3$`+1` is the length of the IMEI string.[1] Assuming that it is sensitive data and its corresponding memory location (`mem[addr`$_3$`,addr`$_4$`]`) has already been tainted, the goal is to propagate the taint to the corresponding part of the new string, i.e., `mem[addr`$_2$`+1, addr`$_2$`+L]`. To achieve this goal, we need to know *when* the characters are stored into the new location.

[1] In fact, L is the twice of the length of the IMEI string because in Java, each character consumes two bytes.

```
0x4004c114: ldrh r6←[r1, r4]  //r6<-mem[addr_s,addr_s+1]
0x4004c116: adds r3, r3, #1
0x4004c118: strh r6→[r0, r4]  //r6->mem[addr_d,addr_d+1]
004004c11a: adds r4, r4, #4
0x4004c11c: cmps r3, r5
0x4004c11e: b
0x4004c114: ldrh r6←[r1, r4]  //r6<-mem[addr_s,addr_s+1]
0x4004c116: adds r3, r3, #1
0x4004c118: strh r6→[r0, r4]  //r6->mem[addr_d,addr_d+1]
004004c11a: adds r4, r4, #4
0x4004c11c: cmps r3, r5
0x4004c11e: b
...
```

Figure 1: The native code for Java string copy. Each character is loaded into a register and then stored to its destination.

Figure 1 shows the stream of ARM instructions that appends a Java string to another one by copying two bytes at a time. Each character of the string is first loaded from the source address into a register (`r6` in this example), and then later it is stored to the destination address. The full-tracking techniques would propagate the taint associated with the source address to register `r6` and then to the destination address. Albeit the taint tracking accuracy is high, this register-level tracking requires a significant modification of the processor hardware architecture, not to mention high performance overhead due to the tracking operation for (almost) every instruction (such as `add`, `mov`, etc.).

Empirical Study of Load–Store Distances: To better understand how loads and stores are distributed in the instruction stream of a program's execution, we instrumented the gem5 simulator system [2, 6] to obtain instruction level execution traces of Android apps running on an ARM processor. While it is possible for loads and stores to appear anywhere in an instruction stream, we are interested in understanding their distribution in regular Android apps, running in the Android environment. Here, we highlight the statistics for a real-world malicious Android app (known as LGRoot), however, we also analyzed a number of app executions (Section 5).

The first metric we consider is the distance between loads and their subsequent stores. In Figure 2a load–store distances from a trace with 2.2 million memory loads and 768 thousand memory stores are plotted as a probability distribution. It is noticeable that the bulk of load–store distance values cluster in the range 0–5, meaning that most stores follow closely after a load. The distribution tapers off past a distance of 10, such that the range 0–10 captures 99% of all loads and stores. This indicates that it is feasible to track loads and related stores with a small window size.

The second metric is the number of stores following a load, i.e., the number of stores that could potentially be

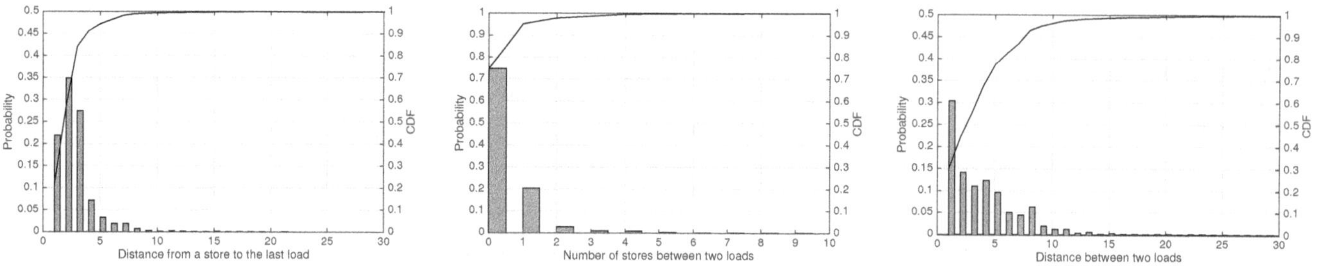

(a) Distance from most recent load to store (b) Number of stores between consecutive loads (c) Distance between consecutive loads

Figure 2: Memory operations exhibit predictable patterns, as shown by the probability and cumulative distributions for various metrics over memory loads and memory stores in an LGRoot malware execution trace. (distance = number of instructions)

tainted from the previous load. If such a number is high, then a heuristic that considers all of these stores as candidates for tainting would result in over-tainting and a large false-positive rate. As Figure 2b shows, the number of stores between consecutive loads is small and thus naturally limits the taint propagation.

The third metric is the distance between consecutive loads. Figure 2c indicates that loads are fairly uniformly spread throughout the program execution, and thus more amenable to tracking over time.

Together Figure 2 show that most computations in an Android program on ARM consists of short-lived, possibly interleaved, *load–process–store* sequences, where the *process* step is strictly local to the CPU and has no memory operations.

Designing a Load–Store Taint Tracker: Given this structural characteristic of information flows, the tracking mechanism would identify stores that are within the correct distance of a load of sensitive data and taint the destination addresses as sensitive. It is important to note that our approach has to handle a certain amount of imprecision due to the fact that it ignores the actual instructions between loads and stores (i.e., process step).

3. PIFT Architecture

In this section, we discuss the system architecture, PIFT algorithm, and hardware design for PIFT. We especially consider a hardware-based approach because of the needs for fast processing of low-level events and for an OS/application-independent solution.

3.1 System Architecture

PIFT architecture (Figure 3) consists of three main components in different levels of Android software hierarchy.

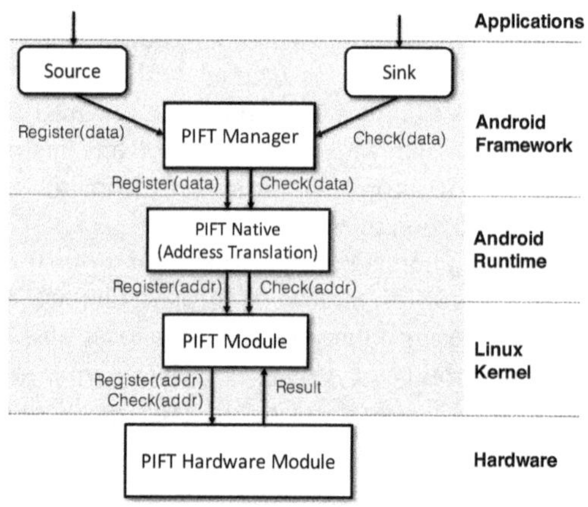

Figure 3: PIFT architecture allows for registering sources and sinks and monitoring data flows.

1. PIFT Manager: We instrument each type of sensitive data source (such as `LocationManager`) so that the data being fetched by an application are registered with our tracking. Similarly, at a sink (such as `SmsManager`) the data being sent out is passed down to the lower level to check if any part of it has been tainted. The registration and check of data are handled by PIFT Manager in the Android Framework level as in [9].
2. PIFT Native: The data is passed down to PIFT Native in the Android runtime layer for address translation. For an object-type data such as IMEI string, it simply obtains the pointer to the data using Java Native Interface (JNI). For a primitive data type such as the GPS location, PIFT Manager passes the object instance that owns the field in addition to the field's name, and then PIFT Native finds the byte offset of the field in the object instance, which is the address of the primitive-type data.
3. PIFT Module: The address is passed down to PIFT Module in the Linux kernel layer. It interacts with the PIFT Hardware Module to register sensitive data's address ranges and make taint queries for check requests. Upon detecting any taint associated with the given address range, it may generate an event to the upper layer to inform of the potential leakage.

3.2 PIFT Taint-Propagation Algorithm

Our taint propagation heuristic works based on memory load and store events. Conceptually speaking, upon loading of a piece of sensitive data from a tainted address range, the

Algorithm 1 TAINT PROPAGATION HEURISTIC

1: $\{r_i = [s_i, e_i]$: address range$\}$
2: $\{R = \{r_i | 1 \le i \le n\}$: tainted address ranges$\}$
3: $\{\mathsf{Inst}_k$: the kth CPU instruction$\}$
4: $\{N_I$: tainting window (TW) size$\}$
5: $\{N_T$: the maximum number of propagation per TW$\}$
6: $\{LTLT$: the last tainted-load time (in CPU inst. seq)$\}$
7: $\{n_t$: the number of taint propagations$\}$

8: $LTLT \leftarrow -\infty, n_t \leftarrow 0$
9: **for each** CPU instruction Inst_k **do**
10:   **if** Inst_k is a memory *load* from r_L **then**
11:     **if** $\exists r_i \in R$ that overlaps r_L **then**
12:       {Starts Tainting Window}
13:       $LTLT \leftarrow k$
14:       $n_t \leftarrow 0$
15:     **end if**
16:   **else if** Inst_k is a memory *store* to r_S **then**
17:     **if** $k \le LTLT + N_I$ **and** $n_t < N_T$ **then**
18:       Taint: Add r_S to R
19:       $n_t \leftarrow n_t + 1$
20:     **else**
21:       Untaint (if enabled): Remove r_S from R
22:     **end if**
23:   **end if**
24: **end for**

algorithm starts a window of instructions called *Tainting Window* (TW). Then, it taints the target addresses of the next few (but upper-bounded) store instructions in that window.

We formalize our taint propagation heuristic algorithm as follows: Let R be the set of memory address ranges that have been tainted, $R = \{r_1, r_2, \ldots, r_n\}$. Each range is defined by $r_i = [s_i, e_i]$ where s_i and e_i are the start and end addresses of the range. Given R, the algorithm works as follows as the CPU executes instructions (see Algorithm 1 and an example in Figure 4):

1. [LINE 10–15] For a memory *load* instruction (e.g., `ldr`, `ldrd`, `ldmia`) that loads a data from $r_L = [s_L, e_L]$, the algorithm queries if there exists any range $r_i \in R$ such that
$$\max(s_i, s_L) \le \min(e_i, e_L).$$
That is, r_i overlaps r_L iff this condition is true. If there exists such an r_i, the algorithm starts (or starts over) the Tainting Window (TW). Its size is measured in the number of instructions from the last tainted-load instruction.

2. [LINE 16–23] For a memory *store* instruction (e.g., `str`, `strh`, `stmdb`) that stores a data to $r_S = [s_S, e_S]$,

   (a) [LINE 17–19] If in the Tainting Window and have not exceeded the maximum number of propagations of the current TW, taint r_S by adding it to R.

   (b) [LINE 20–22] Otherwise, do nothing or, if enabled, untaint r_S by removing it from R.

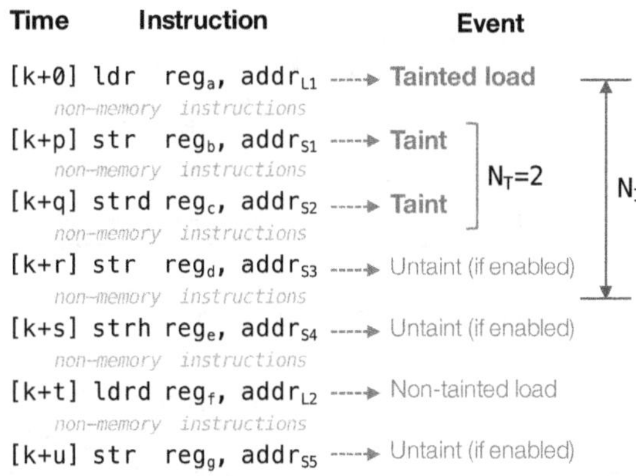

Figure 4: Upon reading of a tainted load (the first line), the Taint Window (TW) of size N_I starts. Within this window, the target address ranges ($1, 2, 4, > 4$ byte-long, depending on the specific store instruction) of the next N_T store instructions become tainted. The store instruction at $[k + r]$ is not tainted because the maximum number of propagations have completed. The store instructions at $[k + s]$ and $[k + u]$ are not tainted because they are outside of the TW. If $N_I > t$ and if the load instruction at $[k + t]$ was a tainted load, then the Tainting Window starts over at $[k + t]$.

This window-based taint propagation tries to achieve both accuracy and efficiency. Since we avoid register-level tracking, we do not know which store instruction(s) write back the processed data to the memory, or even whether this would ever happen or not. For example, in Figure 4, a sensitive data loaded to $\mathtt{reg_a}$ could be written to (after some processing) $\mathtt{addr_{S1}}$ or $\mathtt{addr_{S2}}$ or neither of them. Hence, the propagation algorithm taints multiple ranges (i.e., *overtaints*) and increase the chances of tracking sensitive data flow. However, we limit the number of propagations in a TW in order to prevent the tainted regions in the memory from exploding. We further reduce the tainted regions by *untainting* the target addresses of the store instructions, which have been tainted, that do not fall within a TW because they are likely overwritten by a non-sensitive data. It is, however, possible that they actually contain sensitive data, in which case we might create a false negative. However, our experimental results in Section 5 indicate that untaintings do not degrade the detection accuracy while significantly reducing the tainted regions.

3.3 PIFT Hardware Module

The high-level architecture that illustrates how the on-chip PIFT hardware module (PIFT HW) interacts with the CPU is shown in Figure 5. The PIFT front-end logic, added in the CPU, performs two operations: it 1) tracks the instructions executed by the CPU's instruction unit and 2) generates events to PIFT HW upon observing memory access instructions. It also maintains the instruction counter for each process (indexed by a process-specific ID such as Process

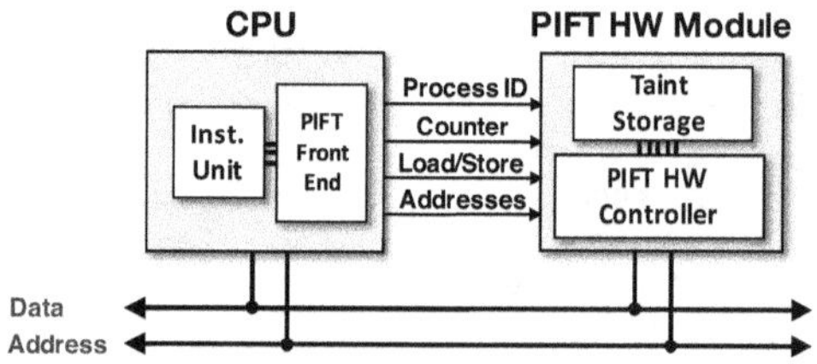

Figure 5: PIFT hardware architecture.

ID (PID) or Translation Table Base Register (TTBR)). For each memory access instruction, PIFT HW receives from the front-end logic 1) the process-specific ID, 2) the process-specific instruction counter, 3) memory access type (load or store), and 4) the read or write address range. Then the PIFT HW controller performs the taint propagation heuristic using the given information and the attached taint storage while the memory sub-system is handling the memory access. For a software-level registration at source (i.e., tainting a new address range), a query at sink (i.e., checking a range's taint), and configuration (parameter setting $\mathtt{N_T}$ and $\mathtt{N_I}$), PIFT software module sends commands and receives responses through an array of memory-mapped ports of PIFT HW. Note that the SW module does not interact with the HW module most of the time; taint lookup and propagation operations are transparent to the software side.

The most frequent operation of the taint tracking is the taint lookup operation, which is carried out on every memory load instruction. Thus, the taint storage is desired to have a very fast lookup-time. One possible option is a cache-like on-chip memory as the taint storage as used in [16, 17, 19]. In our architecture, we use a cache of ranges in which each entry stores arbitrary-length tainted ranges, similar to [17]. Figure 6 shows the structure of our taint storage and illustrates the lookup procedure. Each entry holds the start and end addresses of each tainted range, the associated process-specific ID, and a valid bit. A lookup is a parallel operation; it is hit if any entry 1) has the same process ID, 2) is valid, and 3) contains a range that overlaps (irrespective of being fully/partially) with the one being queried. If hit, the PIFT HW controller starts a new tainting window. The same procedure is carried out for software-level query.

Because of this cache-like taint storage, a query can be very fast and thus take a constant time, provided that the storage is large enough. As will be shown in Section 5.2, the number of ranges created during tracking is sufficiently small so that an on-chip memory with a reasonable size can handle tainted ranges without a secondary storage at, for example, a part of the main memory. To be more specific, each range takes up 12 bytes (excluding the valid bit) - 4 byte for start and end addresses, respectively, and additional 4 bytes for PID value. Accordingly, a small on-chip memory, for example, of 32KB can accommodate approximately 2730 ranges at the same time. If a secondary storage is allocated on the main memory and the entire range entries

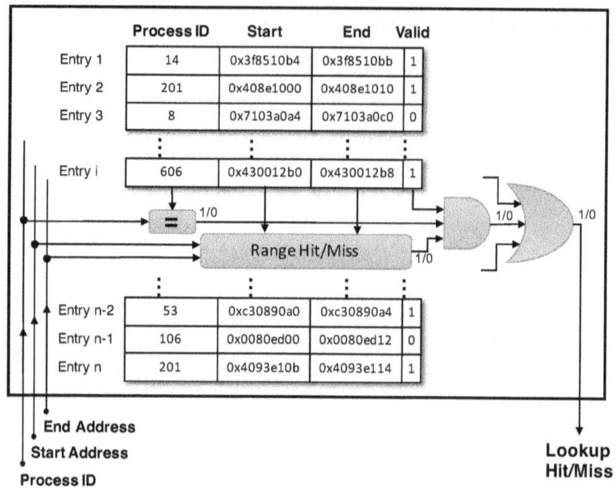

Figure 6: Taint storage and lookup operation.

are written back when a context switch occurs, we can remove the process-specific identification for each entry and thus can store 4096 entries in the 32KB memory. If, however, the storage is not sufficient, one may evict some of the existing entries to the main memory using a replacement algorithm such as LRU (Least Recently Used) as in [17] or may simply drop it. The former case resembles the ordinary data/instruction caches, and hence it may experience delays when there is a 'cache miss'. The latter case does not exhibit a performance overhead, however it may increase the possibility of false negative because it may lose some sensitive data flow.

Another possible option is to taint addresses at a fixed granularity such as a word. That is, instead of keeping track of ranges of arbitrary lengths, we can taint a block as a whole if any part of the block is being tainted. This can be done by storing the $(32 - r)$ most significant bits of the tainted addresses if the granularity is 2^r bytes. This can reduce the size per entry of the taint memory to 4 bytes (or 8 bytes if each entry is tagged with process-specific ID), and also simplify the hardware logic and make queries faster due to the fewer comparisons. However, this may lead to overtaintings. The consequence could be more propagations, hence possibly more entries might be needed than was the case with arbitrary range sizes, and also false positives might be introduced. Witchel *et al.* [20] presents a multi-level address space partitioning method that can associate an arbitrary range with a tag by a series of power-of-two sized ranges.

4. Technical Analysis

The existence of a predictable distance between related loads and stores, empirically measured in Section 2, allowed us to design an end-to-end system as described in Section 3. We have yet to explain analytically why this predictable distance exists for Java applications running on top of the Android-on-ARM platform. This analysis is the purpose of this section.

```
void foo() {                                          Java
    ...
    int key = 123;  //v1
    String msg = "2*key+456=" + bar(key,456);
    ...
}
```

```
...                                                   Bytecode
move v5, v1
const/16 v6, #int 456
invoke-direct {v4, v5, v6}, MainActivity;.bar
move-result v4
invoke-virtual {v3, v4}, StringBuilder;.append
move-result-object v3
invoke-virtual {v3}, StringBuilder;.toString
move-result-object v3
...
```

```
int bar(int x /*v1*/, int y /*v2*/) {                 Java
    return 2*x + y;
}
```

```
const/4 v3, #int 2                                    Bytecode
move v4, v1
mul-int/2addr v3, v4
move v4, v2
add-int/2addr v3, v4
move v0, v3
return v0
```

Figure 7: Java code and corresponding Dalvik bytecode.

```
/* mul-int/2addr vA, vB */

1: mov     r3, rINST, lsr #12     @ r3<- B
2: ubfx    r9, rINST, #8, #4      @ r9<- A
3: GET_VREG(r1, r3)               @ r1<- vB
4: GET_VREG(r0, r9)               @ r0<- vA
5: FETCH_ADVANCE_INST(1)          @ advance rPC, load rINST
6: mul     r0, r1, r0             @ r0 <- op, r0-r3 changed
7: GET_INST_OPCODE(ip)            @ extract opcode from rINST
8: SET_VREG(r0, r9)               @ vAA<- r0
9: GOTO_OPCODE(ip)                @ jump to next instruction
```

Figure 8: Dalvik bytecode `mul-int/2addr` to native code translation.

4.1 Load–Store Distances in Native Code

Android applications are executed by Dalvik virtual machine (VM) that translates each Dalvik bytecode to a sequence of native instructions [3]. Two examples of Java code and their corresponding bytecodes are shown in Figure 7 and the translation rule of bytecode `mul-int/2addr` is shown in Figure 8.

Dalvik is a register-based VM in which the operands of bytecode are *virtual registers*. For example, '`mul-int/2addr v3, v4`' multiplies the value in virtual register v3 by the one in v4 and then writes the result back to v3. Our taint tracking heuristic method takes advantage of the property that *virtual registers reside on the memory*. Hence, each bytecode involves loading operands from the memory and storing the resultant to the memory, if produced. In Figure 8, these correspond to '`GET/SET_VREG(_reg, _vreg)`' which are macros defined as

```
ldr _reg, [rFP, _vreg, lsl #2],
str _reg, [rFP, _vreg, lsl #2],
```

```
0x407c7c40: mov   r3, r7, LSR #12
0x407c7c44: ubfx  r9, r7, #8, #4
0x407c7c48: ldr   r1, [r5, r3 LSL #2]     r1←v4  Tainted Load
0x407c7c4c: ldr   r0, [r5, r9 LSL #2]     r0←v3  Non-tainted Load
0x407c7c50: ldrh  r7, [r4, #2]!
0x407c7c54: mul   r0, r1, r0
0x407c7c58: and   r12, r7, #255
0x407c7c5c: str   r0, [r5, r9 LSL #2]     r0→v3  Tainting
0x407c7c60: add   pc, r8, r12, LSL #6

0x407c5000: mov   r1, r7, LSR #12
0x407c5004: ubfx  r0, r7, #8, #4
0x407c5008: ldrh  r7, [r4, #2]!
0x407c500c: ldr   r2, [r5, r1 LSL #2]     r2←v2  Non-tainted Load
0x407c5010: and   r12, r7, #255
0x407c5014: str   r2, [r5, r0 LSL #2]     r2→v4  Untainting
0x407c5018: add   pc, r8, r12, LSL #6

0x407c7bc0: mov   r3, r7, LSR #12
0x407c7bc4: ubfx  r9, r7, #8, #11
0x407c7bc8: ldr   r1, [r5, r3 LSL #2]     r1←v4  Non-tainted Load
0x407c7bcc: ldr   r0, [r5, r9 LSL #2]     r0←v3  Tainted Load
0x407c7bd0: ldrh  r7, [r4, #2]!
0x407c7bd4: add   r0, r0, r1
0x407c7bd8: and   r12, r7, #255
0x407c7bdc: str   r0, [r5, r9 LSL #2]     r0→v3  Tainting
0x407c7be0: add   pc, r8, r12, LSL #6
```

Figure 9: Native codes translated from `mul-int/2addr`, `move`, and `add-int/2addr` in Figure 7.

respectively. Thus, if there is a data movement (with or without processing) from a virtual register to another within a bytecode, we can find a pair (or more) of load and store instructions associated with them. More importantly, because of the pre-defined translation rules, the distance between the loads and stores *cannot be arbitrary*. For instance, if one of the operands of '`mul-int/2addr v3, v4`', loaded at line 3 and 4 in Figure 8, were tainted, a tainting window of size 5 could propagate the taint correctly to the resultant (line 8).

Accordingly, the data movement over a sequence of bytecodes can be tracked by matching such load and store instructions. Figure 9 shows a gem5 trace of native codes that are translated from the sequence of bytecodes `mul-int/2addr`, `move`, and `add-int/2addr` used in Figure 7. Suppose the sensitive data, `key`, has been tainted. It has been placed in virtual register `v4` (which is copied from `v1`, the first argument of function `bar`, by `move` bytecode). By our heuristic, the taint of `v4` is propagated to `v3` if the TW size was set to at least 5. The next bytecode, `move`, overwrites `v4` with the value in `v2` which in fact is the argument `y`. This store instruction is outside of the TW started by the load of `v4`, and thus becomes untainted. In the last block of native codes (translation of `add-int/2addr`), the load of `v3` starts a new TW which then propagates the taint to itself.

The proper window size varies with bytecode as we can see from the example above; for `add-int/2addr`, the TW size should be at least 5 while `move` needs a size of 2. To examine the adequate sizes for Dalvik bytecodes, we first categorized the total 256 bytecodes into the ones that can move data around in memory and the others (e.g., method invocations, constants, and if-statements). The latter includes 74 bytecodes, of which 10 are unused (based on armv7-a architecture). Then, we examined each of the bytecode in the former group, and measured the longest distance between

Load-Store Distance	Cnt	Example Bytecodes
1	3	`return, return-wide, return-object`
2	26	`move-result, move/16, aget, aput, sput,iput-quick`
3	19	`move-object, sget-object, long-to-int, sget`
4	11	`iput-iput, neg-double, iget-quick, sget-volatile`
5	46	`iget, iget-object, int-to-long, add-int/lit8`
6	21	`int-to-char, sub-long, shl-int/lit8, iget-volatile`
9–12	9	`mul-long/2addr, aput-object, mul-long, shr-long`
Unknown	47	`double-to-int, rem-float, div-int/lit16`

Table 1: Native load & store distances within Dalvik bytecodes.

the loads of actual data and the store instruction. The results summarized in Table 1 show that most of the bytecodes have a short load-store distance. There exist 47 bytecodes of which load-store distances were not measured. Those are the ones for floating-point arithmetic and call ARM's runtime ABI (Application Binary Interface) helper-functions such as `__aeabi_fadd` [1]. Thus, their required window sizes are unknown.

We have also measured how frequently each bytecode is used by analyzing the dex files of the Android system libraries (Core, Framework, and Services) and those of the stock applications (Browser, Contacts, Email, KeyChain, Music, Calculator, Gallery, Phone, Calendar, Dialer, HTMLViewer, Mms, SpeechRecorder). The tables in Figure 10 show the top 30 bytecodes in the number of appearances in applications as well as the system libraries. Most of the frequently appearing bytecodes have a short load-store distance. One exception is `aput-object` bytecode, which puts an object reference into an array of object, that appears more frequently in applications. The relatively long load-store distance is due to type checking. Most of the bytecodes that have long or unknown load-store distances take a very small percentage of the examined lines (less than 0.1% or 0.01%) or even did not appear in the collected dex files. These results indicate the effectiveness of our taint propagation heuristic specifically in Android.

Impact of Dalvik JIT and ART AOT Compilation: While we have run all of our experiments with the default Dalvik optimization settings and the optimization has not impacted our algorithm accuracy, we are interested to investigate the effect of more aggressive optimization on PIFT accuracy. More aggressive optimizations might eliminate or reorder some of the load and store instructions and potentially make it more difficult to predict data tracking. Our initial testing of running apps with and without JIT (Just-In-Time) optimization has shown little impact on the distribution of load and store distances. For example, we profiled the memory operation profile as in Figure 2 without JIT, but the patterns were identical.

Dalvik Bytecode	%	L-S Distance
invoke-virtual	11.06%	
move-result-object	8.98%	2
iget-object	7.10%	5
const/4	5.19%	
const-string	4.85%	
invoke-static	4.45%	
move-result	4.42%	2
invoke-direct	4.31%	
return-void	3.19%	
goto	3.10%	
invoke-interface	3.04%	
const/16	2.82%	
if-eqz	2.82%	
return-object	2.79%	1
aput-object	2.50%	10
new-instance	2.36%	
iput-object	1.97%	5
move-object/from16	1.84%	2
return	1.68%	1
iget	1.46%	5
if-nez	1.40%	
check-cast	1.31%	
sget-object	1.09%	3
add-int/lit8	0.80%	5
iput	0.74%	4
move	0.68%	3
move/from16	0.65%	2
throw	0.64%	
const	0.60%	
move-object	0.53%	3

(a) Applications (1.2M lines)

Dalvik Bytecode	%	L-S Distance
invoke-virtual	12.57%	
iget-object	7.51%	5
move-result-object	7.46%	2
const/4	5.64%	
invoke-direct	4.57%	
move-result	4.16%	2
const-string	3.84%	
invoke-static	3.59%	
goto	3.30%	
if-eqz	3.26%	
move-object/from16	3.22%	2
return-void	2.83%	
iget	2.60%	5
new-instance	2.57%	
iput-object	1.76%	5
if-nez	1.61%	
invoke-interface	1.57%	
const/16	1.50%	
return-object	1.44%	1
throw	1.30%	
iput	1.27%	4
return	1.17%	1
move/from16	1.13%	2
move-exception	1.12%	
add-int/lit8	0.96%	5
check-cast	0.95%	
sget-object	0.91%	3
monitor-exit	0.82%	
invoke-virtual/range	0.74%	
move	0.74%	3

(b) System libraries (1.3M lines)

Figure 10: The distribution of the top 30 Dalvik bytecodes in the number of appearances in Google stock applications and Android libraries dex files. The bytecodes in the highlighted cells are the ones that can move data, irrespective of being a real data or a reference to it. The third column of each table is the load-store distance of such bytecodes.

ART (Android RunTime) is an ahead-of-time compiler for Dalvik bytecode and has become the preferred platform for the most recent Android versions. ART compiles the bytecode of individual Java methods into native versions and provides the linking environment to route calls between the compiled methods. The optimizations applied by ART are a limited subset of Dalvik's JIT optimizations and thus ART does not impact the accuracy of our taint-propagation algorithm.

4.2 Limitations

Native code obfuscation: If an attacker can insert an arbitrarily long, dummy block of native codes between a load of sensitive data and a store using JNI (Java Native Interface), PIFT can be circumvented. For example, one may pass the IMEI `String` instance to the JNI level, obtain the pointer to the character array, load each character onto a register, using `ldr` instruction, do a series of dummy computations, then store the register (i.e., an IMEI character) to the memory. If the extra dummy code is not optimized out by the native code compiler, this could copy the IMEI string to another without any taint propagation.

Implicit flows: A sensitive information flow can be created through control flows [12], which PIFT does not directly address. However, some types of implicit flows are detected by PIFT due to their temporal locality. As an example, a detected case in one of the tested DroidBench applications, `ImplicitFlows_ImplicitFlow1` [4] works by obfuscating the IMEI and then leaking it:

```
for(char c : imei.toCharArray()){
   switch(c){
      case '0' : result += 'a'; break;
      case '1' : result += 'b'; break;
      case '2' : result += 'c'; break;
      ...
```

The `imei` string is already tainted, hence each character load starts a tainting window. Then, since a writing to the `result` string (i.e., each `case` statement) is close enough to the tainted load (in terms of the number of native instructions), the obfuscated string, `result`, gets tainted.

5. Evaluation

The two major goals of a data leak detection algorithm are 1) maximum accuracy and 2) minimum overhead, especially if the system is resource-constrained (e.g., mobile devices). For the evaluation of PIFT, we used DroidBench 1.1 [4] as well as seven real-world malware apps. The test set is representative of real-world apps and their challenges, as it moves data through arrays, lists, callbacks, exceptions, intents, and obfuscates control flow through method overriding, reflection, and object inheritance. In our experience of manually analyzing hundreds of malicious and benign Android apps, the vast majority of information flows are *direct*. Thus we focus on optimizing the common case, and we consciously choose to leave implicit flows and obfuscated apps for future work.

We used the DroidBench apps (a total of 41 leaky and 16 benign apps that ran on gem5 simulator [2]) as-is except for minor modifications for the purposes of automation (so that they can run without user interaction). The sources used in DroidBench are device ID (IMEI), serial number, phone number, and location. The sinks are SMS messages, HTTP queries, and logging functions. We used Android 4.2 Jelly Bean (the highest Android version supported by gem5 simulator), with the Dalvik JIT enabled. In our experiments, the PIFT Native (Figure 3) just prints out the address ranges of source and sink, which then are fed into the PIFT analysis code along with the CPU instruction stream trace obtained by gem5 simulator.

5.1 Accuracy Evaluation

We tested the 57 DroidBench apps and investigated the impact of window size on accuracy. We tried 200 combinations of $N_I = [1, 20]$ and $N_T = [1, 10]$. Figure 11 shows the accuracy heatmap, i.e., (true positive + true negative)/total, of DroidBench apps. When $N_I < 10$, PIFT was not able to detect an app that sends out GPS location, which requires float-

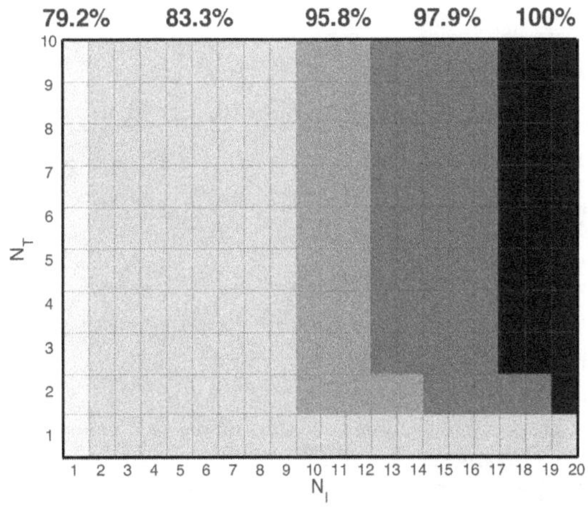

Figure 11: Accuracy of a subset of DroidBench apps for all possible window sizes of $N_I = [1, 20]$ and $N_T = [1, 10]$. For the window size of $N_I = 13$ and $N_T = 3$ the accuracy reaches 97.9%.

ing point-to-string transformation through an ARM runtime ABI. N_I had to be at least 10 for PIFT to detect such a case. Using a window size of $N_I = 13$ and $N_T = 3$, PIFT was able to achieve 98% accuracy, 0% False Positive (0 out of 16) and 2% False Negative (1 out of 41). The one app we did not detect has an implicit data flow which makes it difficult (but not impossible) to detect. To achieve a 100% accuracy, the windows size should be set to $N_I = 18$ and $N_T = 3$. We believe there is a proper upper-bound on the window size for each leakage type, which could be found from a future large-scale experiment.

In all experiments, no false positive occurred. False positive is not likely to occur because the tainting window should be so large that it can span across multiple Java statements. Note that one Java statement is expanded into multiple bytecodes and each bytecode is translated into multiple native instructions, therefore the distance between Java statements will be large in terms of the number of native instructions and with high probability out of the window size. Furthermore, a mis-tainting does not necessarily lead to a false positive because a mis-tainted range should be sent out through a sink to cause a false positive. This, however, is not likely to happen.

We have also tested seven real-life malware samples, which target Android mobile devices and send out various data, such as phone number, location, and device ID, over HTTP connections and SMS messages. The malware samples include four rootkits and three CPU over-clocking apps from a Chinese app store. PIFT successfully detected all the malware given a very small window size of $N_I = 3$ and $N_T = 2$. This result shows our algorithm is very effective for most of current data leaking apps. Here we present the micro-benchmark results for one of the tested rootkits to give insight into the detection rate of PIFT.

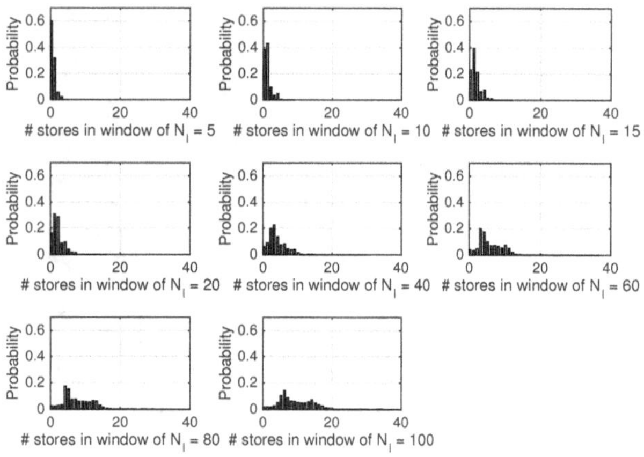

Figure 12: Probability distributions of number of stores in window of size $N_I = 5, 10, 15, 20, 40, 60, 80, 100$ (LGRoot trace).

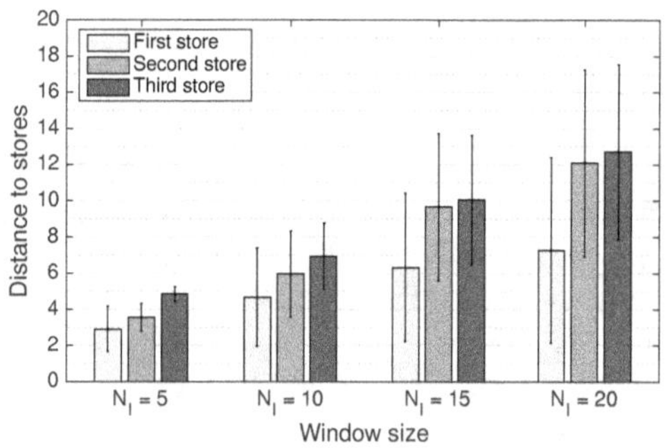

Figure 13: The average distance to the 1st, 2nd, and 3rd stores within an window of size $N_I = 5, 10, 15, 20$ (LGRoot trace).

Load–store distance: For every load instruction, we counted the number of stores in the next N_I instruction, and calculated the probability distribution for different window sizes. As Figure 12 indicates, small window size is acceptable because of the diminishing returns; increasing the window size above 10 or 15 does not capture more stores.

Load–store extended distances: We extended the previous experiment by measuring the distances to the first, the second, and the third stores in the window. Figure 13 shows that the stores are in close proximity of loads, and as a result, we can taint all the three stores after a load without taint explosion.

5.2 Overhead Evaluation

We have analyzed the runtime overhead of a real-world malware—known as LGRoot—with respect to the tainting window parameters and the effects of untainting. Due to the intrinsic limitation of cycle-inaccurate simulation, we performed detailed analyses on factors affecting runtime overhead, e.g., the number of operations, and the size and number of tainted regions.

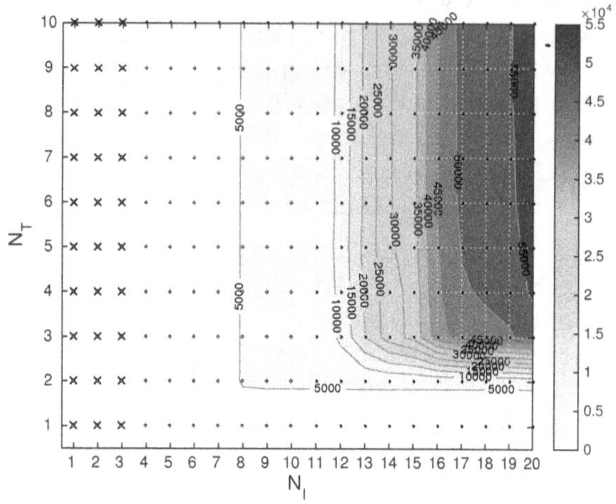

Figure 14: Maximum size of tainted addresses for different tainting window size parameters (N_I and N_T).

Figure 14 shows the maximum size (in bytes) of tainted addresses over time with varying size of tainting window defined by N_I and N_T. The heatmap clearly shows the increasing trend of tainted regions with tainting window parameters. Also, N_T (the maximum number of propagations in a window) outweighs N_I (the tainting window size) in its effect on the tainted region size. This is because a larger N_I increases the chance of a propagation, whereas a larger N_T increases that of overtainting. When the window size is small, N_T does not affect much since we would likely not see the additional store instructions in such a small window. Due to the similar reason, N_T becomes a critical factor for long windows.

Figure 15 shows how the tainted region grows as time progresses, for different window parameters ($N_I = \{5, 10, 15, 20\}$, $N_T = \{1, 2, 3\}$). The sensitive data (i.e., IMEI) is

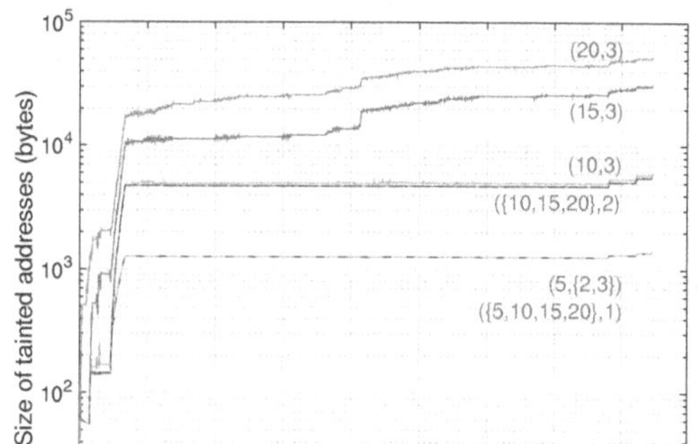

Figure 15: Size of tainted addresses for different tainting window size parameters (N_I and N_T) as time progresses.

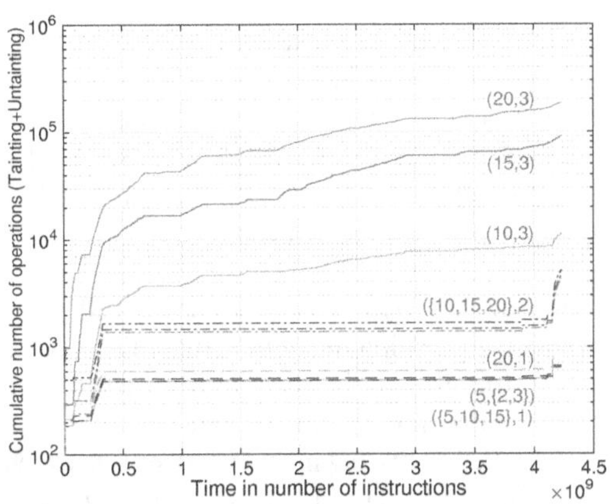

Figure 16: Number of operations (tainting + untainting) for different tainting window size parameters (N_I and N_T) as time progresses.

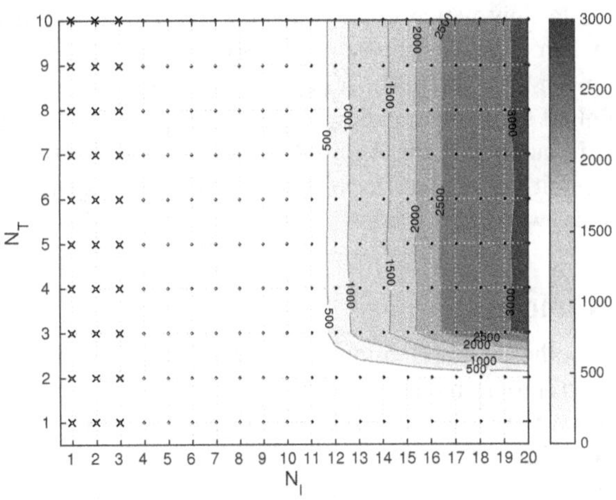

Figure 17: Number of distinct ranges for different tainting window size parameters (N_I and N_T).

fetched at the beginning and then used to compose a message. It is sent out at the end of the trace. Here, notice the flat lines corresponding to $(N_I, N_T) = (\{5, 10, 15, 20\}, \{1, 2\})$ and $(5, 3)$ between them. It is a period when the taints do not propagate because of inactivity on the sensitive data. This can be checked from Figure 16 that shows the number of tainting and untainting operations over time.

The case of $(10, 3)$ is a bit different. The tainted regions do not grow during the period, whereas the tainting/untainting operations keep occurring. This can be explained by situations where some small regions are repeatedly mistainted and then untainted or retainted. If the level of overtaintings exceeds a certain level, those produce a far more overtaintings, which eventually expands the tainted regions exponentially as evidenced by the cases of $(15, 3)$ and $(20, 3)$ in Figure 15. If the parameters are selected properly,

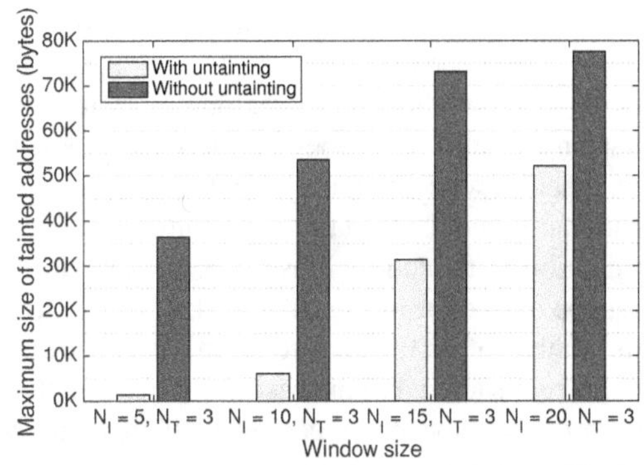

Figure 18: Effect of untainting on the maximum size of tainted addresses.

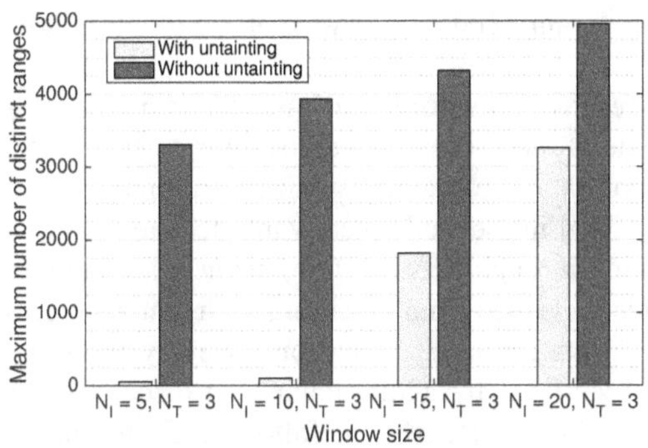

Figure 19: Effect of untainting on the number of distinct ranges.

the tainted regions can be kept reasonably small while not missing sensitive data flows as previously seen.

The number of distinct ranges maintained by PIFT is another important metric to measure the performance overheads since the operations (i.e., query, tainting, untainting) are performed on address ranges. Hence we measured the maximum number of distinct ranges over time for different tainting window size parameters as shown in Figure 17. The trend is similar to that in Figure 14.

For window sizes not larger than $N_I = 10$, there were less than 100 distinct ranges at any time instant over the trace. This result implies that the memory required to store the ranges can be kept very small, which in turn make it possible to make taint queries very fast by removing the need for a secondary storage.

Effects of untainting: The untainting technique can remove possibly-mistainted, non-sensitive data from the tainted ranges and thus can reduce the possibility of tainted region explosion which may introduce significant performance overheads. Hence we evaluate how much untainting can help reduce the performance-related metrics.

Figure 18 compares the maximum sizes of tainted regions when untainting is enabled or disabled. The results show significant reductions in the size of tainted regions due to the untaintings; for the case of $N_I = 5$ and $N_T = 3$, untainting resulted in 26 times smaller tainted regions. Without untainting, the varying window size does not make a considerable difference, whereas with untainting enabled, shorter window could significantly reduce the tainted regions.

The reduction in tainted regions led to fewer number of distinct ranges as shown in Figure 19 which compares the maximum number of distinct address ranges when untainting is enabled or disabled. For the case of $N_I = 5$ and $N_T = 3$, more than 60 times fewer number of distinct ranges were kept when untainting was enabled.

6. Related Work

Information-flow tracking techniques can be *dynamic*, where a program's execution is monitored and analyzed, or *static*, where a program's code is analyzed ahead of execution.

Hardware-based instrumentation: Hardware-based techniques extend the processor architectures to facilitate taint propagation in a fine-grained, software-transparent manner. Suh *et al.* [16] introduced a hardware mechanism in which data coming through network I/O channels are tainted and the CPU is prevented from executing such tainted addresses. The taint propagation is carried out at every register- and memory byte-level by adding taint tags to caches, TLBs, and register blocks. Raksha [8] follows a similar hardware mechanism with additional flexibility by making the propagation and check rules programmable via multi-bit tags that represent different security policies. Flexitaint [19] provides full flexibility in specifying the taint propagation and check rules by allowing software to handle instructions with different rules. Tiwari *et al.* [18] proposed a processor architectural technique that can track complete information flow at the logic gate-level.

Software-based instrumentation: Software-based techniques such as TaintCheck [14] and Panorama [22] use emulation environments or virtualization techniques to enable program instrumentation, where every CPU instruction is checked and therefore incurs a huge overhead. A line of work has focused on *efficient* taint tracking. LIFT [15], built on top of a binary translator, eliminates unnecessary flow tracking when programs executes computations that involve safe data. It also reduces the number of checks by considering spatial and temporal localities of memory references. Ho *et al.* [11] reduces the overhead associated with hardware emulation by dynamically switching between emulated execution (by Qemu) and virtualized execution. TaintEraser [23] performs an application-level taint tracking to reduce overhead due to system-wide instrumentation. It tracks object-level taints at the kernel level and in certain highly utilized functions and turns off tracking to avoid huge overhead. TaintDroid [9] detects data leakage of mobile malware by instrumenting the Dalvik VM interpreter at variable granularity. The Dalvik bytecode translations rules are patched to include taint propagation logic. For native code, TaintDroid does not track taints but apply a heuristic that propagates the taint of input arguments to that of the return value of functions in native code. DroidScope [21] modifies the Android emulator to instrument native and Dalvik instruction traces, API calls, and also to track taints.

Static analysis: AndroidLeaks [10] uses a call graph extracted from an application under test. It applies a reachability analysis to find if there is any path from a sensitive data source to a network sink. Since the analysis is restricted at the Java code-level, flows that involve native code executions cannot be tracked. FlowDroid [5] uses not only the source code but also auxiliary information obtained from application manifest and layout files. Such information are used to identify the application's lifecycle, sensitive data source and sink, which helps reduce both false positives and negatives. FlowDroid does not track native code either. AAPL [13] improves the accuracy by identifying conditional sources and sinks which depend on the input arguments to them, and joint data flow which could potentially be a sensitive data flow when multiple, non-sensitive flows become connected during run-time. EdgeMiner [7] deals with imprecision due to implicit sensitive data flows (especially by callback functions) by analyzing the Android framework and identifying all implicit flows (that is, pairs of callback and registration methods) within the framework.

7. Conclusions

We hypothesized and empirically verified that information flows in programs have stable structural characteristics. Based on these characteristics we introduced in this paper a new lightweight and effective information-flow tracking system called PIFT. PIFT monitors memory accesses (loads and stores) and propagates taint tags across them in a predictive fashion, achieving 98% accuracy on a simulated ARM processor running Google Android, with limited overhead and limited added hardware complexity.

As discussed in Section 4.2, PIFT could be circumvented if the load-store distances are controlled using native-level instructions. A compiler support for PIFT could address such attacks. For example, the compiler could eliminate dummy code inserted between related load/store instructions and could relocate such instructions to be closer to each other (although in general the problem of statically identifying dummy code is undecidable). This necessitates a follow-up study.

Acknowledgments

The authors would like to thank the anonymous reviewers for their valuable comments and suggestions. This work was conducted during Man-Ki Yoon's internship at Qualcomm Research.

References

[1] Run-time ABI for the ARM architecture. http://infocenter.arm.com/help/topic/com.arm.doc.ihi0043d/IHI0043D_rtabi.pdf.

[2] Bbench-gem5. http://www.m5sim.org/BBench-gem5.

[3] Dalvik bytecode. https://source.android.com/devices/tech/dalvik/dalvik-bytecode.html.

[4] DroidBench Version 1.1. http://sseblog.ec-spride.de/tools/droidbench/.

[5] S. Arzt, S. Rasthofer, C. Fritz, E. Bodden, A. Bartel, J. Klein, Y. Le Traon, D. Octeau, and P. McDaniel. Flowdroid: Precise context, flow, field, object-sensitive and lifecycle-aware taint analysis for android apps. In *Proceedings of the 35th ACM SIGPLAN Conference on Programming Language Design and Implementation*, PLDI, 2014.

[6] N. Binkert, B. Beckmann, G. Black, S. K. Reinhardt, A. Saidi, A. Basu, J. Hestness, D. R. Hower, T. Krishna, S. Sardashti, R. Sen, K. Sewell, M. Shoaib, N. Vaish, M. D. Hill, and D. A. Wood. The gem5 simulator. *SIGARCH Comput. Archit. News*, 39(2):1–7, Aug. 2011.

[7] Y. Cao, Y. Fratantonio, A. Bianchi, M. Egele, C. Kruegel, G. Vigna, and Y. Chen. Edgeminer: Automatically detecting implicit control flow transitions through the android framework. In *Proceedings of the 22nd Network and Distributed System Security Symposium*, NDSS, 2015.

[8] M. Dalton, H. Kannan, and C. Kozyrakis. Raksha: A flexible information flow architecture for software security. In *Proceedings of the 34th Annual International Symposium on Computer Architecture*, ISCA, 2007.

[9] W. Enck, P. Gilbert, B.-G. Chun, L. P. Cox, J. Jung, P. McDaniel, and A. N. Sheth. Taintdroid: An information-flow tracking system for realtime privacy monitoring on smartphones. In *Proceedings of the 9th USENIX Conference on Operating Systems Design and Implementation*, OSDI, 2010.

[10] C. Gibler, J. Crussell, J. Erickson, and H. Chen. Androidleaks: Automatically detecting potential privacy leaks in android applications on a large scale. In *Proceedings of the 5th International Conference on Trust and Trustworthy Computing*, TRUST, 2012.

[11] A. Ho, M. Fetterman, C. Clark, A. Warfield, and S. Hand. Practical taint-based protection using demand emulation. In *Proceedings of the 1st ACM SIGOPS/EuroSys European Conference on Computer Systems*, EuroSys, 2006.

[12] M. G. Kang, S. McCamant, P. Poosankam, and D. Song. Dta++: Dynamic taint analysis with targeted control-flow propagation. In *Proceedings of the 18th Network and Distributed System Security Symposium*, NDSS, 2011.

[13] K. Lu, Z. Li, V. Kemerlis, Z. Wu, L. Lu, C. Zheng, Z. Qian, W. Lee, and G. Jiang. Checking more and alerting less: Detecting privacy leakages via enhanced data-flow analysis and peer voting. In *Proceedings of the 22nd Network and Distributed System Security Symposium*, NDSS, 2015.

[14] J. Newsome and D. Song. Dynamic taint analysis for automatic detection, analysis, and signature generation of exploits on commodity software. In *Proceedings of the 12th Network and Distributed System Security Symposium*, NDSS, 2005.

[15] F. Qin, C. Wang, Z. Li, H.-s. Kim, Y. Zhou, and Y. Wu. Lift: A low-overhead practical information flow tracking system for detecting security attacks. In *Proceedings of the 39th Annual IEEE/ACM International Symposium on Microarchitecture*, MICRO, 2006.

[16] G. E. Suh, J. Lee, and S. Devadas. Secure program execution via dynamic information flow tracking. In *Proceedings of the 11th International Conference on Architectural Support for Programming Languages and Operating Systems*, ASPLOS, 2004.

[17] M. Tiwari, B. Agrawal, S. Mysore, J. Valamehr, and T. Sherwood. A small cache of large ranges: Hardware methods for efficiently searching, storing, and updating big dataflow tags. In *Proceedings of the 41st Annual IEEE/ACM International Symposium on Microarchitecture*, MICRO, 2008.

[18] M. Tiwari, H. M. Wassel, B. Mazloom, S. Mysore, F. T. Chong, and T. Sherwood. Complete information flow tracking from the gates up. In *Proceedings of the 14th International Conference on Architectural Support for Programming Languages and Operating Systems*, ASPLOS, 2009.

[19] G. Venkataramani, I. Doudalis, Y. Solihin, and M. Prvulovic. Flexitaint: A programmable accelerator for dynamic taint propagation. In *Proceedings of the 14th IEEE International Symposium on High Performance Computer Architecture*, HPCA, 2008.

[20] E. Witchel, J. Cates, and K. Asanović. Mondrian memory protection. In *Proceedings of the 10th International Conference on Architectural Support for Programming Languages and Operating Systems*, ASPLOS, 2002.

[21] L. K. Yan and H. Yin. Droidscope: Seamlessly reconstructing the os and dalvik semantic views for dynamic android malware analysis. In *Proceedings of the 21st USENIX Conference on Security Symposium*, Security, 2012.

[22] H. Yin, D. Song, M. Egele, C. Kruegel, and E. Kirda. Panorama: Capturing system-wide information flow for malware detection and analysis. In *Proceedings of the 14th ACM Conference on Computer and Communications Security*, CCS, 2007.

[23] D. Y. Zhu, J. Jung, D. Song, T. Kohno, and D. Wetherall. Tainteraser: Protecting sensitive data leaks using application-level taint tracking. *SIGOPS Oper. Syst. Rev.*, 45(1):142–154, 2011.

HIPStR – Heterogeneous-ISA Program State Relocation

Ashish Venkat   Sriskanda Shamasunder   Hovav Shacham   Dean M. Tullsen
University of California, San Diego
{asvenkat | sshamasu | hovav | tullsen}@cs.ucsd.edu

Abstract

Heterogeneous Chip Multiprocessors have been shown to provide significant performance and energy efficiency gains over homogeneous designs. Recent research has expanded the dimensions of heterogeneity to include diverse Instruction Set Architectures, called Heterogeneous-ISA Chip Multiprocessors. This work leverages such an architecture to realize substantial new security benefits, and in particular, to thwart Return-Oriented Programming. This paper proposes a novel security defense called HIPStR – Heterogeneous-ISA Program State Relocation – that performs dynamic randomization of run-time program state, both within and across ISAs. This technique outperforms the state-of-the-art just-in-time code reuse (JIT-ROP) defense by an average of 15.6%, while simultaneously providing greater security guarantees against classic return-into-libc, ROP, JOP, brute force, JIT-ROP, and several evasive variants.

1. Introduction

Heterogeneous chip multiprocessors employ CPU cores of different organization or size that offer varying degrees of micro-architectural complexity [1, 2, 3, 4] and/or core specialization [5, 6, 7, 8]. Owing to their high performance and execution efficiency, these architectures have been showcased, for example, as promising candidates towards achieving energy proportionality in large data-centers [9, 10, 11]. While early work on on-chip heterogeneity [12, 13] restricted cores to implement a single instruction set architecture (ISA), recent findings [14, 15, 16, 17, 18] indicate that a heterogeneous-ISA chip multiprocessor (CMP) is not only a viable option, but has greater potential both in terms of performance and efficiency.

A heterogeneous-ISA CMP synergistically complements architectural heterogeneity with micro-architectural heterogeneity, and allows an application (compiled to each ISA as a fat binary) to dynamically identify the ISA of its preference and migrate execution at any given point of time. In this paper, we leverage this architecture to demonstrate significant new security benefits, and in particular, showcase its ability to defend against an evasive class of buffer overflow exploits called Return-oriented Programming (ROP) [19, 20].

Return-oriented Programming chains together short code snippets in the program (called gadgets) that end with a return or an indirect jump instruction, by overflowing the stack with a carefully constructed sequence of return addresses, and other data required for malicious computation. ROP has been shown to be Turing-complete for multiple ISAs, and over a wide range of applications [19, 21, 22, 23, 24, 25]. Several exploit mitigation techniques have been described in the literature to thwart ROP. These mitigations can be broadly classified as (a) control flow integrity (CFI) techniques [26, 27, 28, 29, 30, 31, 32, 33] that constrain execution to a predefined control flow graph, or (b) randomization techniques [34, 35, 36, 37, 38, 39, 40, 41] that enable a system to exist in one of many random states such that it is hard to predict the exact location or manifestation of a gadget.

The success of randomization techniques is directly proportional to the *entropy* (number of randomizable states) they provide, and the extent to which they are resistant to entropy reduction attacks [42, 43, 44]. In their most powerful form, entropy reduction attacks called just-in-time return-oriented programming (JIT-ROP) [45], completely bypass all randomization, using a single leaked memory disclosure. Therefore, it is critical to design robust and performance-efficient randomization techniques that provide an entropy that is beyond the reach of state-of-the-art exploit generation. In this work, we find that the low overhead of execution migration in a heterogeneous-ISA CMP makes it a natural candidate to repel such attacks, and therefore propose a novel defense mechanism called Heterogeneous-ISA Program State Relocation (HIPStR), that performs dynamic randomization of run-time program state, both within and across ISAs.

First, we leverage a heterogeneous-ISA CMP composed of an ARM core and an x86 core, and non-deterministically migrate execution of a vulnerable process between the two ISAs, in such a way that we render JIT-ROP attacks extremely hard to execute, while still retaining inherent performance gains offered by the architecture. Consequently, we remove one of the last remaining "constants" available

ASPLOS '16, April 02-06, 2016, Atlanta, GA, USA

DOI: http://dx.doi.org/10.1145/http://dx.doi.org/10.1145/2872362.2872408

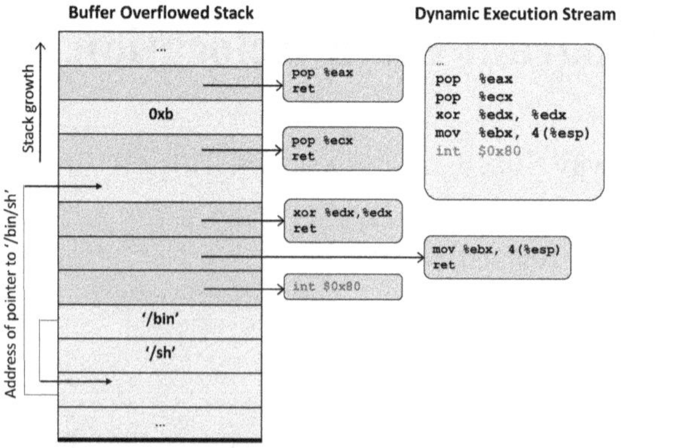

Figure 1. Return-oriented Programming

to the attacker – knowledge of the ISA the program is executing on.

Second, we note that any program, including a return-oriented program, requires a certain amount of program state, in the form of registers and memory, to perform any computation in the target ISA. To this end, we employ a dynamic binary translation engine on both cores that moves the run-time program state of an application to random and attacker-unknown locations, such that legitimate execution that preserves control flow is guaranteed to function as expected, but an attacker-crafted malicious exploit is highly unlikely to function as intended.

To demonstrate the full potential of the proposed security defense, we subject it to a series of malicious ROP-style attacks, including classic return-into-libc, jump-oriented programming, simple brute force, and just-in-time code reuse. Consequently, we make the following major observations:

(1) The sheer amount of entropy provided by our defense renders brute force attacks such as Blind-ROP [46] practically impossible, for current or even distant future microprocessors.

(2) Our ability to perform seamless and instantaneous execution migration across heterogeneous ISAs significantly inhibits just-in-time code reuse attacks, forcing an attacker to construct heterogeneous-ISA exploits that are extremely hard to execute, as shown in Section 7.

(3) Our performance focused migration policy and our optimization techniques help us outperform Isomeron [35], the only other JIT-ROP defense, by an average of 15.6%, while simultaneously providing greater security guarantees against brute force, JIT-ROP, and more tailored attacks geared to break execution path diversification.

(4) We defend against all variants of classic ROP-style attacks [19, 21, 47, 48], and reduce their overall attack surface to such an extent that it is difficult to construct a four-gadget shellcode exploit, let alone achieve Turing-completeness.

2. Background and Related Work

Heterogeneous-ISA CMPs. Architects have established that on-chip heterogeneity is an effective mechanism to improve processor efficiency for both general purpose and embedded computing [2, 3, 8, 12, 13, 49, 50]. In the embedded world, it is not uncommon for architects to exploit both architectural and microarchitectural heterogeneity to realize heterogeneous-ISA MPSoCs that cater to a diverse class of applications such as wireless networks, signal processing, multimedia, packet switching, and cybersecurity [7, 51, 52, 53, 54]. While examples of heterogeneous-ISA chip multiprocessors do exist in the general-purpose market [6, 8], they haven't been targeted for mainstream mixed workloads yet. However, recent research proposals have demonstrated the performance and energy benefits of such architectures [14, 15, 16, 17, 18]. This work showcases the high potential of this architecture from a security standpoint.

Return-Oriented Programming. Buffer overflow vulnerabilities form a major chunk of the security loopholes that plague the Internet today. They rank third amongst the common vulnerability types reported by the National Vulnerability Database, finishing just behind cross site and cryptographic vulnerabilities [55]. These vulnerabilities have been systematically exploited by code reuse attacks such as *return-into-libc* [48], which exploits a buffer overflow on the stack to return into a *libc* function. Despite its ability to subvert control flow without injecting malicious code, return-into-libc is inherently limited to *libc*, and thus incapable of performing arbitrary malicious computation. In recent years, return-into-libc attacks have evolved into a more general and flexible scheme of attacks called Return-oriented Programming (ROP) [19, 20].

Figure 1 shows a ROP attack that spawns a command shell. The attack begins with an attacker injecting an exploit payload on to the stack, exploiting a buffer overflow. The payload is crafted to overwrite the return address with the address of a short code snippet within the program, called a *gadget*, that ends in a return instruction. Once the gadget has executed and the instruction pointer has reached the return instruction, the stack pointer points to the address of the next gadget, and the exploit continues. ROP hinges on the attacker being able to control the stack pointer and use it as the instruction pointer. Several evasive variants of ROP have been described in the literature that use indirect jumps in place of returns (Jump-oriented programming (JOP) [21, 23, 56]), and provide Turing-completeness on different instruction set architectures [22, 25]. The advent of automated exploit compilers has further made ROP a formidable attack technique to defend against [57].

Control Flow Integrity. Abadi, et al. [26] first formalized the idea of CFI. The main idea of that work is to constrain the execution of the program to a predefined control flow graph (CFG) by instrumenting the program to perform ID-checks before every indirect jump. They also observe that it is difficult to implement ideal CFI statically without a runtime mechanism to track function calls and indirect jumps. There has been significant follow-up work on CFI at the hardware, runtime, and compiler levels [27, 28, 58, 59, 60, 61, 62]. More recent work such as CCFIR [32], bin-CFI [31], branch regulation [30], and code pointer integrity [33] have made significant strides in reducing the attack surface, by employing more fine-grained CFI, in the absence of any source or debug information, and at an acceptable degradation in performance. However, several backdoor attacks [63, 64, 65, 66, 67, 68, 69, 70] have been described in the literature to bypass these techniques, thereby exposing the need for a stricter enforcement of CFI. HIPStR is orthogonal to these defenses and could be applied in conjunction. HIPStR also defends against all the above backdoor attacks since we make no assumptions about CFI or memory safety.

Randomization and Obfuscation. Yet another class of ROP defenses randomize the location of gadgets in the process image, making the attack only probabilistic. Several gadget location randomization techniques have been proposed in the literature, at various granularities — module (ASLR [39]), basic block [41], instruction [36], and byte [40] levels. Furthermore, several binary re-writing and gadget obfuscation mechanisms [37, 38, 71, 72, 73, 74] have been proposed to restrict the number of useful gadgets in a program.

In the presence of a memory disclosure vulnerability, these randomization techniques can be bypassed by simple brute-force attacks [43, 46] that exploit a memory disclosure, in just a matter of a few thousand attempts. Moreover, the load-time nature of these techniques makes them highly susceptible to just-in-time code reuse (JIT-ROP) attacks that exploit a single leaked memory disclosure to read code pages in memory, disassemble them, and reconstruct the control flow graph on-the-fly. Snow, et al. [45] show that JIT-ROP can bypass a combination of fine-grained randomization techniques in a matter of 23 seconds. In this work, we demonstrate significant resistance against entropy exhaustion by employing run-time randomization instead of load-time randomization.

As of this writing, Oxymoron [34] and Isomeron [35] are the only two techniques that have claimed full immunity to JIT-ROP. Oxymoron leverages x86 segmentation and page-level randomization to re-encode direct branches as indirect branches in such a way that the target address of a direct branch is hidden from a JIT-ROP attacker, thereby thwarting the reconstruction of a program's control flow graph on-the-fly. However, Davi, et al. [35] describe a backdoor attack to successfully bypass Oxymoron by disclosing a large number of pages using code pointers, such as return addresses or pointers to virtual methods, gleaned off the stack or the heap.

Isomeron, on the other hand, harnesses software diversity and probabilistic execution by randomly switching between two versions of the program, one original and one diversified, at every function call. Our work differs from Isomeron in that we diversify code both within and across the ISA, thus randomizing the architecture itself. Moreover, HIPStR can defend against return-into-libc and JOP attacks owing to its ability to randomize calling conventions and switch between different ISAs at basic block boundaries, unlike Isomeron which is a function-level diversification technique. HIPStR exploits the already existing architectural heterogeneity in modern processors to provide significantly higher entropy and greater reduction in attack surface, at a lower performance overhead than Isomeron.

JIT-hardening. The NVD database shows that JIT environments such as browsers and Adobe Flash are common targets of code reuse attacks. Specifically, JIT-spraying techniques exploit the just-in-time compilation functionality to generate predictable chunks of exploit code in the text section, using carefully crafted JavaScript or ActionScript, called GaJITS [75]. Such environments typically employ JIT-hardening techniques such as page randomization, constant blinding [75], and random NOP insertion on each JIT-compiled page to defend against JIT-spraying. Our technique can be seamlessly integrated into such JIT environments since we already employ dynamic binary translation. Furthermore, unlike Isomeron, we not only defend against JIT-ROP, but also defend against JIT-spraying, because we enforce program state relocation on all JIT-compiled code including JIT-sprayed gadgets.

3. Architectural Overview

In this section, we lay out our security and performance guarantees, briefly recap the multi-ISA compilation and dynamic task migration methodology outlined in prior work [14, 15], and discuss strategies to harness and re-purpose these techniques as a security defense for ROP.

3.1 Security and Performance Guarantees

Security. One of the main goals of HIPStR is to defend against and reduce the attack surface of a wide array of attacks, including but not limited to return-into-libc, ROP, JOP, brute force attacks, JIT-ROP, and JIT-spraying. For any program in execution, HIPStR dynamically randomizes the location of its program state (registers and stack objects) in order to render brute-force attacks infeasible. Furthermore, HIPStR has the ability to detect a potential break-in attempt via JIT-ROP, and when detected, probabilistically migrates execution to a different ISA, thereby imposing serious limitations on JIT-ROP attacks.

Performance. HIPStR makes several careful performance-related decisions in order to provide security guarantees, at an acceptable degradation in performance, and outperform Isomeron, the only other JIT-ROP defense in the literature. First, unlike Isomeron which diversifies execution at every function call and return, HIPStR migrates execution to a different ISA only when a potential security breach is detected, thereby enjoying full security benefits at virtually zero performance overhead due to migration. Second, HIPStR implements several optimizations described in Section 5 in order to speed up the underlying dynamic binary translation framework.

3.2 Multi-ISA compilation

Process migration across heterogeneous ISAs requires expensive program state transformation because the run-time

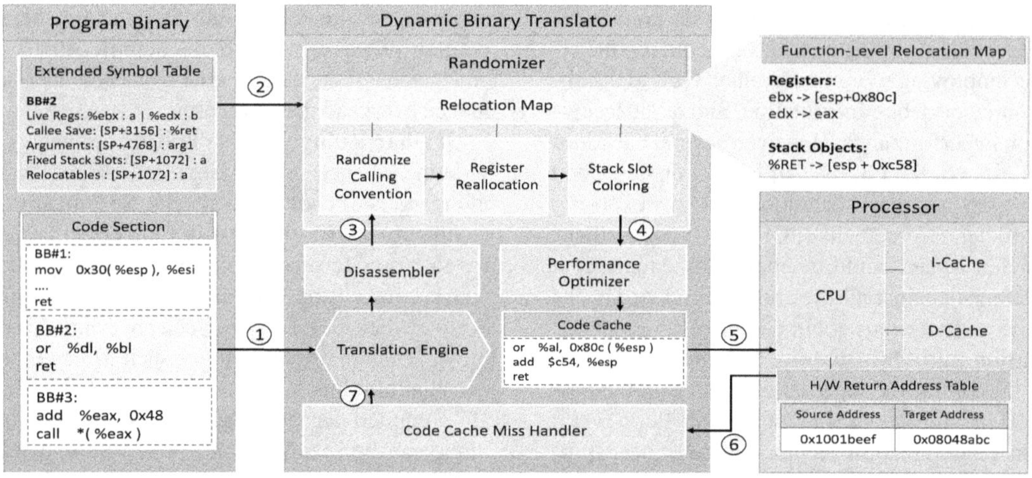

Figure 2. Program State Relocation Architecture

program state (registers and memory) is always present in architecture-specific form. The multi-ISA compilation infrastructure outlined in prior work ensures minimal state transformation by taking advantage of a *symmetrical fat binary* with multiple ISA-specific code sections, a common stack frame organization, and a common ISA-agnostic data section. Furthermore, a multi-ISA runtime transforms the program state (registers and stack) upon migration to a different ISA at specific *equivalence points*, after which point execution can be safely resumed on a different ISA.

3.3 Instruction Set Randomization

From a security standpoint, heterogeneous-ISA CMPs have two major advantages. First, ROP attacks are highly target-ISA dependent. An application that migrates between multiple heterogeneous-ISA cores executes instructions from different instruction sets. If a migration is forced upon execution of every ROP gadget, a successful attack would require chaining gadgets from different ISAs, and yet produce a meaningful result (e.g., spawn a shell). Furthermore, if we make migration probabilistic, we remove the most fundamental assumption of the attacker – knowledge of what ISA the gadget will execute on. The second advantage is that execution migration in a heterogeneous-ISA CMP requires stack transformation. This especially constrains ROP gadgets to save all intermediate state in locations that are immune to run-time stack transformation (e.g., heap memory), thereby significantly reducing the attack surface.

Several fine-grained randomization techniques proposed in prior work have been shown to be broken by JIT-ROP [45] that exploits a single leaked memory disclosure to reconstruct the entire memory image of the process, and thereby bypass all randomization. Instruction Set Randomization in a heterogeneous-ISA CMP, however, severely inhibits JIT-ROP. This is because the decision to migrate execution to a different ISA is made probabilistically at run-time, thereby limiting an attacker's ability to chain gadgets reliably.

While randomization across heterogeneous-ISAs systematically removes the knowledge of what architecture the attacker is executing on, in the next section, we show how randomization within an ISA could further extend the effectiveness of our technique.

3.4 Program State Relocation

Program State Relocation (PSR) comprises a set of dynamic binary code transformations that can be easily deployed in any JIT-based system. The major goal of program state relocation is to shuffle program state (registers and memory) such that it is always found at the expected location during legitimate execution, but it is highly unlikely to be found by a ROP gadget that strays away from the legitimate control flow path.

As shown in Figure 2, the PSR runtime operates in a classic just-in-time dynamic translation mode, processing one basic block at a time. For each basic block in translation, it gathers information about the parent function, which is available from static analysis. Irrespective of the point of entry, the PSR runtime constructs a *relocation map* for every function, if it is being entered for the first time. The relocation map specifies the randomized calling conventions to be followed while calling the function, along with a set of randomized register allocation and stack slot coloring rules to be followed within that function. In Section 5, we describe each transformation in detail. The figure shows an example PSR transformation – BB#2 in the code section is transformed to the basic block shown in the code cache. Note that PSR just requires a simple change in the addressing mode of the instruction *or* in order to relocate its original operands *dl* and *bl* to *al* and *[esp+0x80c]*, as indicated by the relocation map respectively. Note that the return address is also moved to a random location on the stack.

As with classic DBT [76, 77], translation is performed until an indirect or conditional jump is reached, at which point control is transferred to the translated code in the code cache. If a translation for the jump target is not available (a code cache miss), necessary transformations are applied as described above, and control is relinquished to the translated code. To ensure the code cache does not get compromised, we mandate that all return addresses stored on the stack point to original source code instead of the translated version. Furthermore, we make minor changes to the call and return instructions (macro-ops) to perform an extra cycle look-up in a hardware-maintained *Return Address Table* (RAT), in order to translate the source-level address to its corresponding translated version before making the actual control transfer.

The effect of program state relocation is that an object previously found in a register may be relocated to a different register or a random location on the stack, and vice-versa. Due to the sheer number of stack locations available to use for relocating an object, the number of possible dynamic code transformations (entropy) explodes, thereby rendering classic brute force attacks such as Blind-ROP [46] practically impossible on a system implementing PSR. Moreover, since the transformations happen at run-time rather than load-time, a PSR system will always re-randomize upon a crash or reboot, further strengthening its effectiveness.

3.5 Heterogeneous-ISA PSR

Instruction Set Randomization and Program State Relocation each represent strong defenses independently. However, we find that there is significant synergy between the two techniques, and one technique only amplifies the effectiveness of the other. Therefore, we combine them into one solid defense called "Heterogeneous-ISA Program State Relocation"(HIPStR).

The defense leverages, in this particular implementation, a heterogeneous-ISA CMP composed of a low-power ARM core and a high-performance x86 core, that each run a virtual machine capable of performing program state relocation. To continue to reap the full performance/energy benefits of the heterogeneous-ISA CMP, we perform task migration only when an application phase change profits from migration to a different ISA. Additionally, we perform non-deterministic execution migration between the two ISAs only when the PSR runtime detects a possible attempt to compromise security.

In our evaluation, we find that a code cache miss resulting from an indirect control transfer (including returns) is one of the key characteristics of a possible security breach. A code cache miss could result from one of two scenarios. In the legitimate execution scenario, the jump target is valid, but has not been translated yet (compulsory miss), or a translation for it was previously evicted from the code cache (capacity miss). In an attack scenario, the jump target points to a ROP gadget, and therefore a mapping does not exist in the PSR data structures. The PSR virtual machines make no effort to distinguish between the two scenarios. They instead migrate execution to a different ISA (with some probability) on every indirect control transfer that misses the code cache.

Like any JIT system with a sufficiently large code cache, one would expect code cache misses to be infrequent once the application reaches a steady state in execution. Therefore, legitimate execution should experience no meaningful degradation in steady state performance. Furthermore, we perform multiple translations, one for each ISA, when an indirect control transfer results in a compulsory miss, further reducing miss events.

In theory, an attacker could avoid migrating to a different ISA by using gadgets that are already translated indirect jump targets or function call sites, for which the PSR virtual machines already have a mapping in their internal data structures. In our evaluation, we find that the number of such gadgets is insufficient even for the simplest $execve$ exploit.

4. Assumptions and Threat Model

JIT Engine. We model a JIT engine such as a browser environment that performs dynamic binary transformations. Like most browser environments and other code randomization defenses [35, 36] that employ dynamic binary instrumentation, we assume that the JIT engine is checked for vulnerabilities and its address space is protected by memory protection mechanisms such as code signing [78], sandboxing [79], and Intel Software Guard Extensions (SGX) [80].

Fine-grained Randomization. We require no fine-grained randomization techniques (including ASLR) to protect our system, although they would only further strengthen the system since HIPStR is orthogonal to most existing defense mechanisms.

Complete Disclosure. We assume that the attacker has full knowledge of the inner workings of our defense mechanisms. We also assume that the attacker has unfettered access to the binary, source code, and complete control flow graph of the program in execution. Consequently, the attacker has a complete list of all potential ROP/JOP gadgets in the binary, and is capable of mounting attacks ranging from classic ROP [20] to just-in-time code reuse (JIT-ROP) [45] attacks.

Just-in-time Code Reuse. In addition to the ability to snoop into a program's memory, we assume the program in execution exhibits one or more vulnerabilities that allow an attacker to (a) write to memory (by means of a stack/heap based overflow), and (b) read an arbitrary number of bytes from any memory location, using a single leaked memory disclosure.

Brute Force Attacks. We also assume that the system is susceptible to brute force attacks such as Blind-ROP [46]. To this end, we model a system as described by Shacham, et al. [43] that assumes a program executing as a child thread, whose parent re-spawns it upon on a crash. We do not assume any defense mechanism that monitors the frequency of such an event to detect ROP attacks. We instead use it as a metric to demonstrate the effectiveness of PSR against brute force.

5. Design and Implementation

In this section, we present the design and implementation details of Program State Relocation, discuss how our system behaves under different execution scenarios, and finally describe techniques to optimize our system for performance.

5.1 Program State Relocation

As discussed in Section 3, Program State Relocation is a set of transformations that relocate program state (registers and stack objects) within the same ISA. In our implementation, these transformations essentially randomize calling conventions, register allocation, and stack slot coloring. While most of these transformations can be accomplished by a mere change in the addressing mode, some transformations (e.g., procedure call/return) are slightly more involved and might require insertion of a small number of *move* instructions.

Addressing Mode Transformation. Each instruction in a basic block is modified to access its source and destination operands at their new locations, as specified by the function's relocation map. In most cases, this transformation is rather trivial and involves mere changing of addressing modes. If the ISA does not expose a certain addressing mode, the PSR virtual machine emulates it using additional instructions and register temporaries. For example, owing to the variety of addressing modes in x86, we use additional instructions only when more than one operand of an instruction is relocated to memory.

Procedure Call Transformation. The PSR virtual machine instruments all procedure call instructions to perform argument relocation and register spill/restore as specified by the callee's relocation map and the target ABI, respectively. As an optimization, the PSR virtual machine eliminates any redundant caller/callee register save and restore instructions. Furthermore, the virtual machine allocates 2 to 16 pages of randomization space on the stack in addition to the space already used by the callee's locals, temporaries, and spills, effectively providing 13 to 16 bits of entropy for every register or memory access. Note that return addresses are also relocated to random offsets, and therefore even a *nop* gadget that just performs a return incurs an entropy of at least 13 bits.

One of the biggest challenges with procedure call transformation is to preserve the live-ins and live-outs across function call sites, and correctly compute the caller/callee saves upon every function invocation. We take advantage of a single basic block look-ahead liveness analysis to accurately compute this information, and incorporate them into the randomized calling convention. A major source of ROP gadgets include the callee restore sequence that pops a bunch of callee save registers before returning back to the caller. To circumvent this, we perform a randomized scatter of callee saves (spray callee saves to random locations on the stack) at the function call site, and a randomized gather after return.

Indirect Control Transfer. Like any DBT system [76, 77], the PSR virtual machine traps all indirect jumps into the translator. This ensures there exist absolutely no indirect jumps translated into the code cache. As a software fault isolation measure, we terminate the process in case we find an indirect jump target within the code cache's address range. Similarly, we disallow pointers to the code cache to exist as function pointers or return addresses on the stack. We handle function pointers in the same way as indirect jumps.

For function returns however, we always push the source return address on the stack, and take advantage of the return address table (RAT) that contains a mapping from source address (address of the function call site in the native binary) to target address (address of the function call site in the code cache). The call macro-op in the processor is modified to update the RAT with the right mapping, while the return macro-op is modified to perform return address translation as an extra step with a 1-cycle penalty. Upon a RAT miss, we conclude that there was a code cache miss and trap into the translator, for re-translation of that basic block.

5.2 PSR-aware Execution Migration

Our migration policy allows execution migration across heterogeneous ISAs in two specific scenarios. First, we migrate execution whenever an application phase change or the processor's current operating condition demands migration to another core. This is essential because it preserves the performance and energy advantages of a heterogeneous-ISA CMP. On the other hand, we also migrate execution, although probabilistically, when the PSR virtual machine suspects a security breach (specifically, when an indirect control transfer results in a code cache miss).

Prior work on heterogeneous-ISA execution migration suggests that we can be migration-safe at only 45% of the basic blocks [15]. To support instantaneous migration, they employ dynamic binary translation until a point of execution is reached where the stack can be safely transformed. This implies that a ROP exploit that is composed entirely out of the remaining 55% of the basic blocks could completely bypass instruction set randomization.

To circumvent this, we re-purpose the original multi-ISA compilation infrastructure to support an on-demand execution migration. In essence, we transform only those objects on the stack that are absolutely necessary for executing instructions until the next control transfer (jump, call or return), and revert back to the original ISA to execute the next basic block. By doing so, we manage to be migration-safe 78% of the time. Furthermore, we completely avoid jumps to *unintentional* gadgets upon a code cache miss. We do this by taking advantage of an attack detection unit that disassembles from the last seen nearest address (or function boundary) to the program counter, up until the program counter itself. This is a minor change to the PSR virtual machine, which already does sophisticated liveness analysis.

Finally, we ensure that our migration strategy is PSR-aware, which means we not only transform an object from one ISA-form to another, but we fetch the object from its randomized location on one ISA and move it to its new randomized location on the other ISA.

5.3 Execution Scenarios

Legitimate execution. In a legitimate execution scenario, the procedure call transformation ensures that functions are always presented with relocated arguments. Furthermore, basic blocks are also presented with relocated live-ins since execution starts at the intended entry point of the function, thereby preserving the integrity of legitimate program execution.

Stack Unwinding. Libraries such as *libunwind* rely on compiler generated stack frame layout information to unwind the stack in exceptional scenarios such as *setjmp and longjmp*, and C++ exceptions. PSR seamlessly works with *setjmp and longjmp* due to the temporary register spill/restore, performed as a part of the procedure call transformation.

However, C++ exceptions and other debugger routines unwind the stack frame-by-frame, inspecting stack objects at each frame, until the unwind target is reached. Performing PSR on such routines might lead to inconsistent program state. To prevent such inconsistencies, the PSR virtual machine instruments these unwind routines to use the same relocation map as the function that owns the frame being processed. This guarantees that frame objects are always accessed from their appropriate relocated addresses, irrespective of the control flow. Furthermore, we force migration (and thus stack transformation) in the rare event when a *longjmp* is taken, but the corresponding *setjmp* was performed on a different ISA.

ROP attack. In the event of a ROP attack, the buffer overflow itself happens at a relocated stack address. Therefore, there is no guarantee that the return address is overwritten with the gadget address. In case the attacker manages to successfully overwrite the return address, she will find that the gadget at that address fails to work as intended. This is because the PSR virtual machine dynamically transforms every instruction in that gadget to access data from their randomized locations. Note that this is not just true for ROP attacks, but holds for jump-oriented programming, v-table hijack, and other variants. PSR inherently defeats return-into-libc because of the randomized calling conventions.

Crash/Reboot scenarios. To guarantee high quality of service and robustness, most servers re-spawn worker threads upon a crash or a reboot. Several brute force attacks such as Blind-ROP exploit this property of servers to mount repeated attacks until they become compromised. These attacks typically bank on using information leaked in a previous attempt, in order to reduce the overall time-to-attack. This is possible because a process randomized at load-time typically does not get re-randomized every time it spawns a thread. However, a PSR virtual machine performs randomization at run-time, which means we have the ability to re-randomize upon re-spawn. Note that this extends to the PSR virtual machines on both ISAs. Therefore, each time a worker thread re-spawns, the attacker is presented with a re-randomized version of the code cache on both ISAs.

5.4 Performance Optimizations

Machine Block Placement. As with any JIT engine, we take measures to carefully place translated basic blocks in the code cache, so that we incur as few conflict misses in the instruction cache as possible. To further improve the instruction cache performance and fetch bandwidth, we align tight single-entry single-exit loops to cache block boundaries.

Branch Inlining and Superblock Formation. Next, we compose our translated basic blocks into *superblocks* that have a single entry-point, but multiple exit-points. We form superblocks in two steps. First, we fold branches whenever possible. This includes both direct unconditional branches and fall-through cases in conditional branches. Second, we avoid backward branches by inlining a direct branch instruction. Note that this results in code duplication, but it both improves the locality in the instruction cache, and reduces pressure on the branch predictor.

Global Register Cache. While PSR provides extremely high entropy, the sheer number of stack operations could potentially cause severe performance degradation. To optimize for performance, we use a global register cache that holds the most frequently used registers that are relocated to stack objects. We mandate that this cache be only three entries long so that we provide high performance in tight loops, and at the same time provide security guarantees by still spilling frequently to random locations.

PSR with a Register Bias. In this final optimization, we perform PSR with a *register bias*, i.e, at all times, we ensure at least three registers are always relocated to other registers, albeit randomized for each function.

5.5 Prototype Implementation of PSR

Owing to the complex addressing modes in x86 and the possibility of *unintentional* gadgets (unaligned sequence of bytes that end with the byte *c3* indicating a *ret* opcode), x86 not only exhibits greater susceptibility to vulnerabilities, but also presents greater challenges in terms of design and implementation. Specifically, we note that the attack space on ARM is 52X smaller than x86 (measured using Galileo [20] ported to ARM), since ARM enforces strict alignment of instructions. Moreover, the simplicity of the instruction set and lower register pressure on ARM facilitate a smaller engineering effort and better opportunity for performance optimization. Therefore, we choose to implement our more complete PSR prototype, and do most of our PSR measurements, in x86. By doing so, we not only demonstrate high coverage (as the vast majority of the gadgets exist in the x86 code), but also report conservative estimates in both performance and security evaluation.

6. Methodology

Security Evaluation. An important characteristic of a security attack is that it requires the victim program to expose a reasonable *attack surface* to exploit. In the context of ROP, the attack surface is represented by the number of gadgets available in a program that facilitate the construction of a successful exploit. The goal of every randomization defense is to reduce the attack surface (both in terms of availability and functionality), in order to limit the attacker's abil-

Algorithm 1 Brute Force Simulation

$R = \{r_1, r_2 \ldots r_m\}$ /* Set of m registers to load. */
$P = \emptyset$ /* Set of successfully populated registers. */
$X = ()$ /* List of chosen gadgets for the attack. */
$Y = ()$ /* List of return address locations for chosen gadgets. */
$A(g)$ is the randomized return address for gadget g

for all $i = 1$ to m **do**
  r_i is the register to populate
  find g_j in G s.t. g_j populates register r_i, does not clobber any register s in P, and $A(g_j) = \min_{k=1 \ldots n} A(g_k)$
  $P = P + \{r_i\}$
  $X = X + \{j\}$
  $Y = Y + \{A(g_j)\}$
end for

Let B be the number of attempts to populate all registers, then for an average frame size of f
$B = Y[0] + f.X[0] + nf.Y[1] + nf^2.X[1] + \ldots + n^3 f^4.X[3]$

ARM core			
Frequency	2 GHz	I cache	32 KB, 2 way
Fetch width	2	D cache	32 KB, 2 way
Issue width	4	ROB size	20 entries
LQ/SQ size	16/16 entries	Functional Units	Int ALU(2), IntMult/Div(1), FP ALU/Mult/Div(2)
x86 core			
Frequency	3.3 GHz	I cache	32 KB, 2 way
Fetch width	4	D cache	32 KB, 2 way
Issue width	4	ROB size	128 entries
LQ/SQ size	48/96 entries	Functional Units	Int ALU(6), Mult/Div(1), FP ALU/Mult/Div(2), SIMD(2)

Table 1. Architecture detail for ARM and x86 cores

ity to construct meaningful exploits. In our evaluation, we not only subject our defense to state-of-the-art attack mechanisms [19, 21, 45, 47, 48], but also measure its effectiveness against potential attacks that are computationally beyond the reach of today's attacker. For each attack, we report the degree to which the attack surface is reduced by our technique.

We use the 'Galileo' algorithm described by Shacham, et al. [20] to mine a benchmark for every possible instruction sequence that ends with a return instruction. Since every exploit requires some program state in the form of either registers or stack objects, we designate any gadget that successfully populates a register with an attacker supplied value from the stack as *viable*. We evaluate every gadget for its viability on a system, without and with PSR, to measure the attack surface for four major classes of attacks: (a) classic ROP, (b) brute-force, (c) JIT-ROP, and (d) tailored heterogeneous-ISA attacks to defeat HIPStR.

Owing to the sheer number of stack locations available for program state relocation, the number of possible manifestations of a gadget explodes. To evaluate the system against brute force attacks while keeping the experiment tractable, we analyze each gadget to gather data about every perturbation it produces on the state of the program, at a randomly chosen point in its execution. We then simulate a brute force attack by running this data through Algorithm 1. Cheng, et al. [81] showed that the shortest aligned gadget chain generated by gadget compilers such as Q [57] is 17, but to establish the effectiveness of PSR, we consider a much smaller four-gadget shellcode exploit that performs the system call $execve()$, which in theory should be easier to brute force by several orders of magnitude. Although the run-time nature of PSR transformations involve re-randomization upon crash, to keep the experiment tractable, we make the conservative assumption that a failed attempt does not result in re-randomization, and thereby tip the scales in the attacker's favor.

Algorithm 1 simulates a brute force attack to populate the four registers (*eax*, *ebx*, *ecx*, and *edx*) necessary to perform the $execve()$ system call with attacker provided values on the stack. On a system protected by PSR, all program state (registers and stack objects, including the return address) is relocated to a random register or a stack location. Therefore, such an attack should brute force three independent variables in the system: (a) the gadget to execute, (b) relative position(s) of data on the stack, as required by the gadget, and (c) relative position of the return address on the stack, required to chain the next gadget. The attacker should brute force the gadget itself, because it is difficult to determine the potential *viability* of a gadget that will inevitably be subject to PSR. Therefore, we brute force every gadget discovered by the Galileo algorithm. The data for each gadget (the value to load into a register) and the return address both share the same stack frame. In an unsecured system their locations can be easily determined, but with PSR, they can lie anywhere within a stack frame.

To maximize the success of a gadget, our attack *sprays* the data for the gadget on the entire stack frame and brute force the location of the return address within the frame. We model our attack to populate one register at a time, in order to *spray* an entire stack frame with the data for one register, thereby increasing its chances of being read by a gadget. Since we assume the attacker has insight into the inner workings of PSR, we assume a frame size of 8KB, at which PSR provides substantial security benefits at an acceptable degradation in performance. In our algorithm, we also account for register and stack clobbering to ensure that a gadget does not destroy previously established (by an earlier gadget in the exploit) state. The algorithm stops searching for more *viable* gadgets as soon it finds a four-gadget shellcode exploit.

Performance Evaluation. We use the SPEC CPU2006 integer and floating-point C benchmarks to evaluate the proposed defense. We exclude *gcc* and *sjeng* from this set because they perform dynamic memory allocation on the stack either using the *alloca* library function, or by passing variable-length array parameters. While our multi-ISA compilation and runtime infrastructure is capable of working with variable-size stack frames, our PSR implementation does not support this feature yet. All benchmarks are compiled using an LLVM-based multi-ISA compiler at the -O3 optimization level. To model a heterogeneous-ISA CMP, we use the gem5 [82] architectural simulator. The processor model of the ARM core is based on the low-power Cortex A-

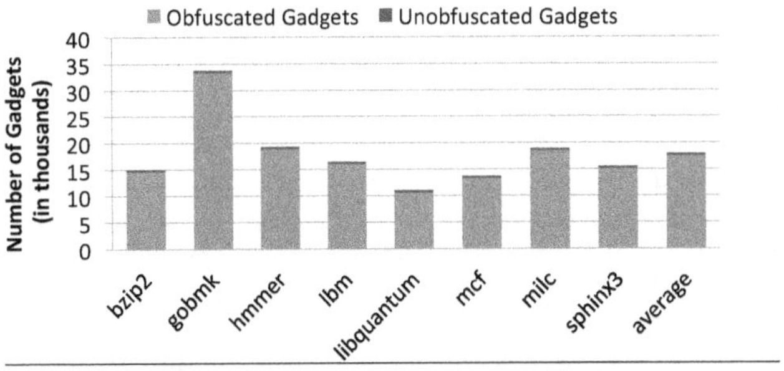

Figure 3. Classic ROP Attack Surface

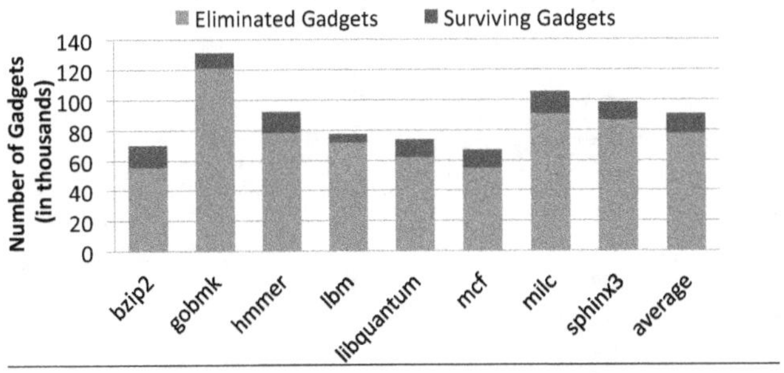

Figure 4. Brute Force Attack Surface

9, while the x86 core is modeled after the high performance Intel Xeon. Table 1 shows the details of each core.

To evaluate the steady state performance and study the effect of various contributing factors, we simulate a portion of the program's execution at different optimization and entropy levels, with different code cache and hardware Return Address Table (RAT) sizes, as follows. We fast forward execution for the first one billion instructions to skip initialization code, and perform cycle accurate simulation for another one billion instructions[83], while running in the context of a PSR virtual machine and with heterogeneous-ISA migrations enabled.

To evaluate the migration overhead at random execution points, we skip the initalization phase and fast forward execution of each benchmark to a random checkpoint and force migration to a different ISA, and report results averaged across ten random checkpoints.

7. Evaluation

7.1 Security Evaluation

Classic ROP-Style Attacks. Figure 3 shows the extent to which PSR reduces the attack surface for classic ROP-style attacks, including return-into-libc, jump-oriented programming, and v-table hijack. We observe that the sheer amount of randomization that each gadget undergoes guarantees that only a very small portion of the attack surface remains unaltered. To be precise, PSR reduces the attack surface of classic ROP by an average of 98.04%. We note that although the remaining 1.96% is unobfuscated by PSR, the attacker has no way of determining which gadgets they are beforehand, since their randomized version is only generated on execution, thereby rendering classic ROP attacks infeasible.

Benchmark	Randomizable Params (avg)	Entropy	Attempts (no reg-bias)	Attempts (reg-bias)
bzip2	6.76	88	9.11×10^{33}	2.34×10^{33}
gobmk	6.53	85	2.34×10^{34}	2.87×10^{34}
hmmer	6.69	87	1.37×10^{34}	1.16×10^{34}
lbm	6.92	90	3.33×10^{34}	3.90×10^{34}
libquantum	6.76	88	1.05×10^{34}	6.45×10^{33}
mcf	6.69	87	3.10×10^{33}	1.71×10^{34}
milc	6.46	84	1.86×10^{34}	2.92×10^{34}
sphinx3	6.92	90	1.14×10^{34}	8.68×10^{33}

Table 2. Inferences from Brute Force Simulation

Brute Force Attacks. As illustrated in Figure 3, PSR modifies a majority of the gadgets that were previously available for ROP. These gadgets, by virtue of PSR's transformations, have either been obfuscated in a way that they no longer perform the attacker intended action, or have been completely eliminated. The former of these are *viable* candidates for a brute force attack since they perform useful computation, just not what an attacker expects them to. Even under the assumption of full memory disclosure, it is impossible to determine the transformations that will be applied on a gadget, without executing it. Also *viable* for a brute force attack are any gadgets introduced by the randomization itself. The attack surface for brute force comprises every gadget available in the program, since there is no way to ascertain which ones will transform to be *viable* gadgets. As shown in Figure 4, we observe that a sizable portion (an average of 15.83%) of all gadgets are *viable* for brute force, and therefore require thorough evaluation.

Table 2 shows the results of our brute force simulation described in Section 6. We observe that PSR successfully renders brute force attacks computationally infeasible, by a considerably large margin. We find that, on an average, a gadget has between six and seven randomizable parameters which could potentially include registers, stack objects, and at least one address on the stack to place the (return) address of the next gadget. In our configuration of 8KB sized stack frames, each parameter has 2^{13} randomizable states, resulting in an average entropy of 87 bits per gadget. Even if a vulnerability allowed an indefinite number of attempts, with each attempt only taking a nanosecond, we find that it is computationally infeasible to perform such a brute force attack with state-of-the-art computing infrastructure. In fact, such an attack would remain computationally infeasible on future processors targeted at exascale computing.

Just-In-Time Code Reuse. Figure 5 shows the reduction in attack surface for each benchmark under both single-ISA and heterogeneous-ISA PSR. Owing to the just-in-time nature of PSR, only the steady state program code that has already been randomized by PSR and is present in the code cache remains vulnerable to JIT-ROP. We find that the number of gadgets already randomized by PSR accounts for only 1.45% of all classic ROP gadgets and 1.92% of those *viable* for brute force, thereby severely constraining the attack surface. Note that a majority of gadgets are now *undiscoverable*, since they lie outside the code cache.

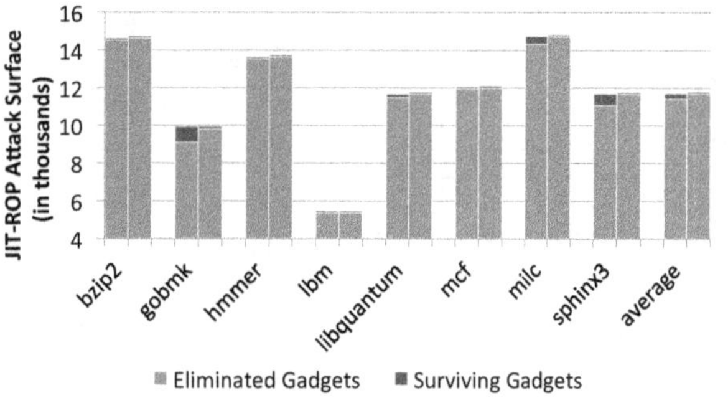

Figure 5. JIT-ROP Attack Surface on (a) PSR, (b) HIPStR

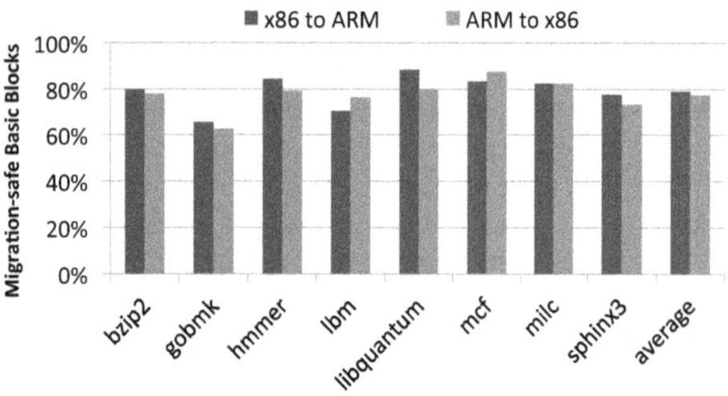

Figure 6. Percentage of Migration-Safe Basic Blocks

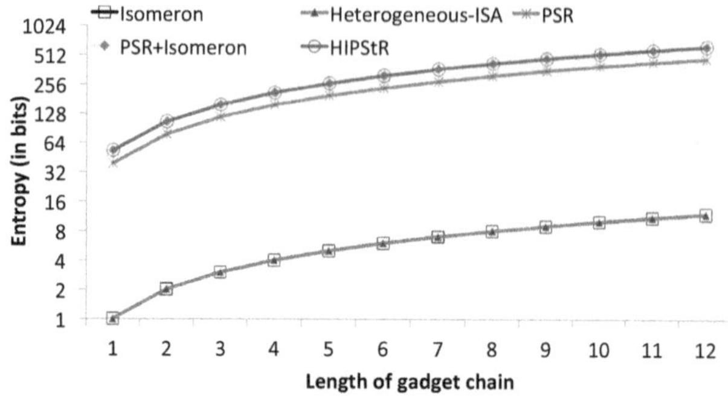

Figure 7. Entropy Comparison

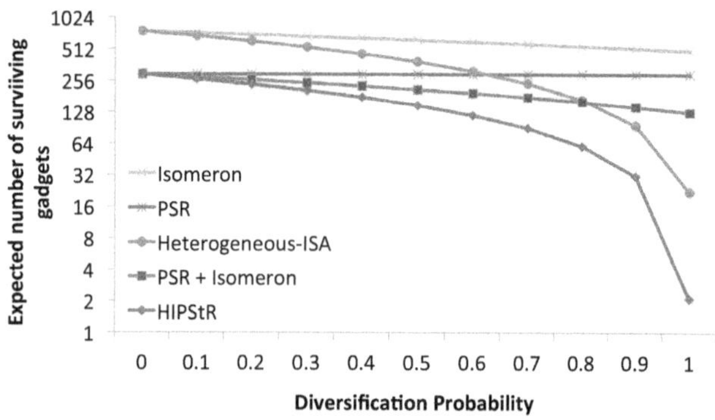

Figure 8. Effect of diversification on attack surface

Although the attack surface has been considerably reduced, the surviving 294 gadgets could potentially be enough to mount a JIT-ROP attack. Recall from Section 3 that the PSR virtual machines suspect a security violation when an indirect control transfer (including returns) misses the code cache, and subsequently migrate execution to a different ISA, albeit probabilistically. Note that the PSR virtual machine can find in its internal structures only those indirect jump targets and function call sites that have been translated so far, and will result in a code cache miss for all others. Any surviving gadget that is *viable* for JIT-ROP must ideally avoid migration to a different ISA, and therefore begin at an already translated indirect jump or function call site. This imposes serious limitations on the JIT-ROP attack surface that has already been weakened by PSR.

We find that out of the 294 surviving gadgets from PSR, 267 gadgets cause a security breach violation in the PSR virtual machine, thereby triggering a probabilistic migration to a different ISA. This leaves the attacker with only 27 gadgets, on average, that do not flag a violation and could potentially bypass migration to a different ISA. Furthermore, as shown in Figure 6, we note that our infrastructure is capable of being migration-safe on an average of 78% of the time, in either direction. This implies that gadgets in the remaining 22% of the basic blocks are still *viable* candidates for JIT-ROP. However, we find that these remaining gadgets are insufficient to even construct a four-gadget shellcode exploit, let alone complex exploits.

Tailored attacks. To further explore the synergy of the HIPStR components, we compare the combined entropy of HIPStR with the two individual components of HIPStR (PSR and heterogeneous-ISA migration) alone, as well as a hybrid of Isomeron and our PSR approach (See Figure 7). We make two important observations. First, any system that implements only Isomeron or only Heterogeneous-ISA migration suffers from extremely low entropy, which cannot be amortized unless the gadget chain is long enough. For example, every one out of as low as 256 attempts will succeed for a gadget chain that is 8 gadgets long. Second, the just-in-time nature of PSR inherently enables re-randomization upon a crash. Therefore, the attacker is always presented with a re-randomized version of the code cache on both ISAs, for every brute force attempt. Although PSR by itself is susceptible to JIT-ROP, this characteristic of PSR makes brute forcing a JIT-ROP attack significantly harder on a system that implements both diversification and PSR.

This might suggest that a system implementing a combination of PSR and Isomeron is as effective as HIPStR. However, we note that entropy as a metric by itself does not completely capture the effect of randomizing the instruction sets. To observe this effect, we turn to tailored attacks that bypass both same-ISA (Isomeron) and heterogeneous-ISA diversification. An attacker who is aware of the diversification could construct exploits that interleave gadgets from both the original and the diversified versions. For example, on HIPStR, one could craft an exploit that alternates gadgets between x86 and ARM, such that the all meaningul computation is performed by x86 gadgets, while the ARM gadgets are all *nops* that switch execution to x86 without clobbering already

Level	Optimizations
-O0	No Optimization.
-O1	Machine Block Placement, Branch Inlining and Superblock Formation.
-O2	-O1 optimizations, Global Register Cache.
-O3	-O2 optimizations, PSR with a register bias.

Table 3. Performance Optimizations for PSR

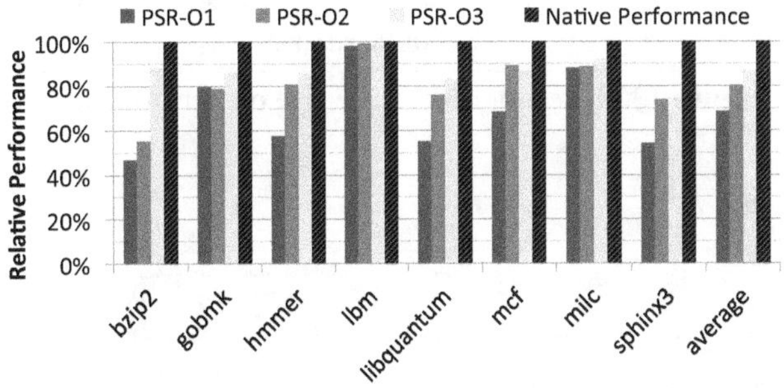

Figure 9. Performance at different optimization levels

established state. Another example of such a tailored attack would be to use those gadgets that are unaffected by diversification, i.e, those gadgets that perform the same intended malicious operation regardless of what ISA/software version they execute.

Figure 8 examines the JIT-ROP attack surface of each technique in the face of such tailored attack mechanisms. When the probability of diversification (the probablility of switching ISAs or program variants between gadgets) is zero, such an attack surface will include all gadgets present in the code cache. As the diversification probability increases, the attacker would find it increasingly harder to brute force a JIT-ROP attack.

We note that the system implementing both PSR and Isomeron is as effective as HIPStR when the diversification probability is zero, but the two systems rapidly diverge in their effectiveness as the probability increases. In fact, at a probability of one, at which we diversify execution for every gadget, HIPStR manages to have an average of just two surviving gadgets in its attack surface, while the attack surface of the system implementing PSR and Isomeron still comprises hundreds of gadgets. It is worth noting here that on HIPStR, we failed to find any surviving gadgets in five out of the eight applications we benchmark, thereby completely thwarting such tailored attacks.

Aside from these eight SPEC applications, we also evaluate the effectiveness of HIPStR on the network facing daemon *httpd*, a classic target of ROP attacks. Our evaluation shows that the attack surface of *httpd* is composed of 169,272 gadgets. PSR successfully obfuscates 99.7% of the gadgets, requiring 1.8×10^{39} attempts to brute-force (still computationally infeasible). Furthermore, while 84 gadgets are available for JIT-ROP, only two survive heterogeneous-ISA migration. These are insufficient to generate even the simplest shellcode exploit.

In our evaluation, we find that it is more likely to find large gadgets that populate multiple registers at a time, and are unaffected by diversification on the same ISA, rather than different ISAs. Note that our experiments only measure the number of surviving gadgets in the face of such tailored attacks. We expect that chaining together these gadgets to craft an exploit payload is a much more daunting task, because not only is brute-forcing such an attack under PSR extremely hard, but heterogeneous-ISA migration involves stack transformation that could potentially clobber the exploit payload on the stack.

The strength of PSR lies in its ability to defeat brute force attacks, while simultaneously reducing the attack surface. It amplifies the entropy of heterogeneous-ISA migration making a brute force attack on the combined defense infeasible. Conversely, heterogeneous-ISA migration has the ability to shield PSR from a JIT-ROP attack attempting to bypass randomization. Together, they form a formidable defense.

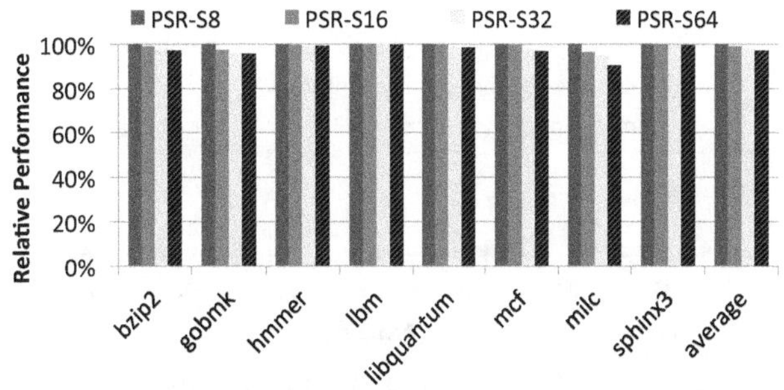

Figure 10. Effect of additional stack memory overhead

7.2 Performance Evaluation

Steady State Performance. Figure 9 shows the steady state performance overhead of PSR and the effect of each performance optimization. We do not gain a significant performance boost from the O1 level of optimizations that we apply to improve the instruction cache performance. However, we observe an average of 13% improvement in performance due to a small global register cache that holds just 3 registers. This, in large part, is due to the fact that short and tight loops operate on a small set of input registers, but dominate most of a program's execution. Finally, we find that operating PSR in a register-bias mode can further improve performance by an average of 5.5%, thereby reducing the overall performance degradation from native execution to just 13.14%.

Since PSR relies on large stack frames to provide higher entropy, it is important to measure the performance effects due to the extra stack memory used. Figure 10 shows the steady state performance overhead at different entropy levels. The performance only drops by an average of 2.96% even after expanding individual stack frame sizes by as much as 64KB. This is because the stack frames become very sparse, and large empty spaces between items (e.g., larger than a cache line) do not place pressure on the cache.

PSR takes advantage of a return address table (Section 3) to protect the code cache from becoming compromised. Figure 11 shows the effect of the RAT size on performance. We

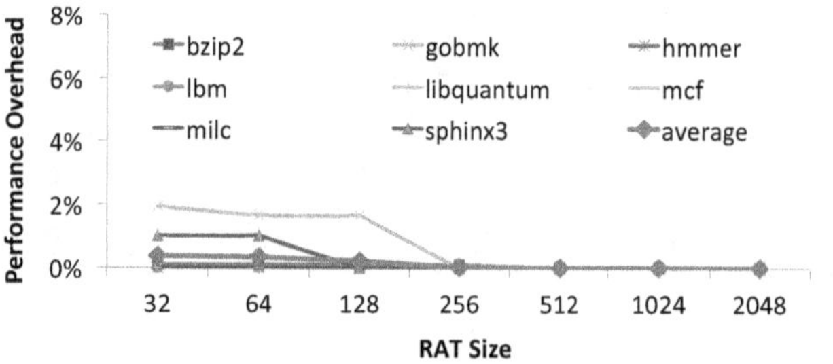

Figure 11. Effect of RAT size on Performance

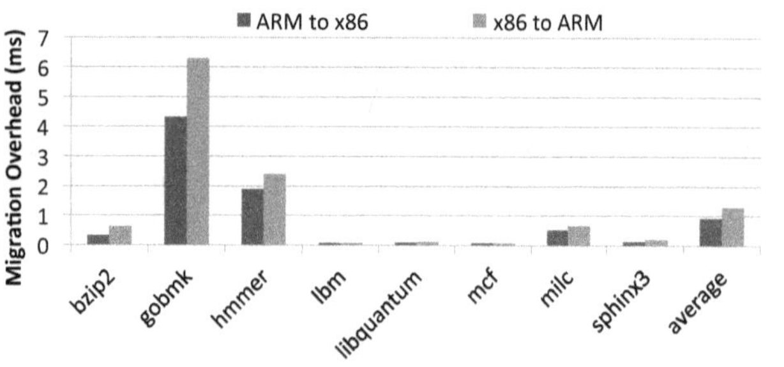

Figure 12. Migration Overhead

incur an average of 0.37% performance overhead even with as small as a 32-entry RAT. In fact, we observe no noticeable degradation in performance with a RAT that can hold just 512 entries. This is because the distance between a *call* and a *return* instruction is generally so short that we seldom incur a RAT miss.

Migration Overhead. Figure 12 shows the state transformation overhead due to heterogeneous-ISA process migration. We report an average migration overhead of 909 microseconds when migrating from ARM to x86, and 1.287 ms in the other direction, resulting in an overall baseline migration overhead of 0.32% resulting from the migrations initiated to improve performance. Our migration policy ensures that we switch ISAs only when a program's ISA preference changes as it enters a new program phase, or when the PSR virtual machine suspects a security breach, i.e, when we encounter an indirect control transfer that results in a code cache miss.

Figure 13 shows the effect of code cache size on migration overhead. We record zero indirect control transfers that miss a code cache as small as 768 KB, resulting in no measurable overhead for security-induced migrations. In steady state execution, it is highly unlikely that we return to a function whose translation has been evicted, or we make an indirect jump or a function pointer call to an evicted region. For example, *gobmk* makes 65,746 function pointer calls within a span of one second, but none miss the code cache.

Finally, Figure 14 compares the performance of HIPStR with Isomeron, the only other technique that defends against JIT-ROP, along with a system that implements both PSR and Isomeron, for the six common applications that we benchmark. Since Isomeron invokes execution path diversification for each function call and return, they report a higher performance overhead. In fact, they mention that this degradation in performance is expected since their program shepherding renders CPU optimizations like branch prediction ineffective [35]. As the diversification probability increases, HIPStR performance only slightly decreases with the smaller code cache, but still manages to provide higher performance than both Isomeron, as well as the combination of PSR and Isomeron. Overall, HIPStR outperforms Isomeron by an average of 15.6% while simultaneously providing signficantly higher entropy, and thereby higher resistance to brute force, JIT-ROP, and tailored attacks that bypass diversification.

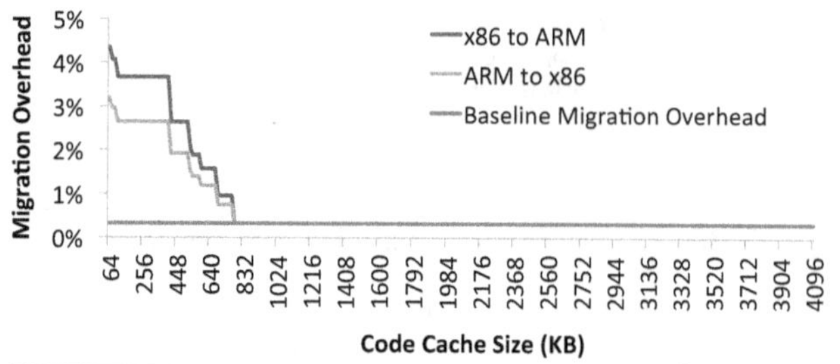

Figure 13. Effect of code cache size on Performance

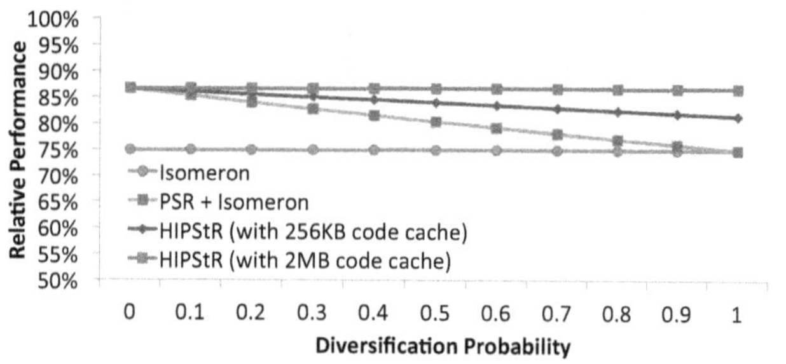

Figure 14. Performance Comparison with Isomeron

8. Conclusion

Heterogeneous-ISA CMPs have been shown to provide significant performance and energy gains. In this work, we showcase their security benefits through a novel defense called HIPStR (Heterogeneous-ISA Program State Relocation) that combines dynamic randomization of program state with non-deterministic process migration between heterogeneous-ISAs. We find that HIPStR outperforms the state-of-the-art JIT-ROP defense by 15.6% while providing greater security guarantees.

Acknowledgements

The authors would like to thank the anonymous reviewers for their helpful insights. The authors are particularly grateful to Arvind Krishnaswamy, Koichi Yamada, and Rajan Palanivel for their numerous suggestions during the early days of PSR's formulation, and for their contributions to the United States Patent US009135435B2 [84]. This research was supported in part by NSF Grant CCF-1302682.

References

[1] R. Kumar, D. M. Tullsen, N. Jouppi, and P. Ranganathan, "Heterogeneous chip multiprocessors," *Computer*, vol. 38, no. 11, 2005.

[2] "Variable SMP - A Multi-Core CPU Architecture for Low Power and High Performance," tech. rep., NVidia, 2011.

[3] P. Greenhalgh, "big.LITTLE Processing with ARM Cortex-A15 & Cortex-A7," tech. rep., ARM, 2011.

[4] M. Hill and M. Marty, "Amdahl's Law in the Multicore Era," *Computer*, July 2008.

[5] "2nd Generation Intel Core vPro Processor Family," tech. rep., Intel, 2008.

[6] "The future is fusion: The Industry-Changing Impact of Accelerated Computing.," tech. rep., AMD, 2008.

[7] "The Benefits of Multiple CPU Cores in Mobile Devices," tech. rep., NVidia, 2010.

[8] J. A. Kahle, M. N. Day, H. P. Hofstee, C. R. Johns, T. R. Maeurer, and D. Shippy, "Introduction to the Cell multiprocessor," *IBM Journal of Research and Development*, July 2005.

[9] L. A. Barroso and U. Hölzle, "The case for energy-proportional computing," *IEEE computer*, 2007.

[10] D. Lo, L. Cheng, R. Govindaraju, L. A. Barroso, and C. Kozyrakis, "Towards energy proportionality for large-scale latency-critical workloads," in *Proceedings of the 41st Annual International Symposium on Computer Architecuture*, 2014.

[11] G. Varsamopoulos, Z. Abbasi, and S. K. Gupta, "Trends and effects of energy proportionality on server provisioning in data centers," in *Proceedings of the 17th Annual International Conference on High Performance Computing*, 2010.

[12] R. Kumar, K. I. Farkas, N. P. Jouppi, P. Ranganathan, and D. M. Tullsen, "Single-ISA Heterogeneous Multi-core Architectures: The Potential for Processor Power Reduction," in *International Symposium on Microarchitecture*, Dec. 2003.

[13] R. Kumar, D. M. Tullsen, P. Ranganathan, N. P. Jouppi, and K. I. Farkas, "Single-ISA Heterogeneous Multi-core Architectures for Multithreaded Workload Performance," in *International Symposium on Computer Architecture*, June 2004.

[14] M. DeVuyst, A. Venkat, and D. M. Tullsen, "Execution migration in a heterogeneous-isa chip multiprocessor," in *Proceedings of the Seventeenth International Conference on Architectural Support for Programming Languages and Operating Systems*, 2012.

[15] A. Venkat and D. M. Tullsen, "Harnessing ISA diversity: Design of a heterogeneous-ISA chip multiprocessor," in *Proceedings of the International Symposium on Computer Architecture*, 2014.

[16] A. Barbalace, M. Sadini, S. Ansary, C. Jelesnianski, A. Ravichandran, C. Kendir, A. Murray, and B. Ravindran, "Popcorn: Bridging the Programmability Gap in heterogeneous-ISA Platforms," in *Proceedings of the 10th European Conference on Computer Systems*, Apr. 2015.

[17] T. Li, P. Brett, R. Knauerhase, D. Koufaty, D. Reddy, and S. Hahn, "Operating system support for overlapping-ISA heterogeneous multi-core architectures," in *Proceedings of the 16th International Symposium on High Performance Computer Architecture*, Jan. 2010.

[18] D. Lustig, C. Trippel, M. Pellauer, and M. Martonosi, "ArMOR: Defending Against Memory Consistency Model Mismatches in Heterogeneous Architectures," in *Proceedings of the 42nd International Symposium on Computer Architecture*, June 2015.

[19] R. Roemer, E. Buchanan, H. Shacham, and S. Savage, "Return-oriented programming: Systems, languages, and applications," *ACM Transactions on Information and System Security*, 2012.

[20] H. Shacham, "The geometry of innocent flesh on the bone: Return-into-libc without function calls (on the x86)," in *Proceedings of the 14th ACM conference on Computer and Communications Security*, 2007.

[21] T. Bletsch, X. Jiang, V. W. Freeh, and Z. Liang, "Jump-oriented programming: a new class of code-reuse attack," in *Proceedings of the 6th ACM Symposium on Information, Computer and Communications Security*, 2011.

[22] E. Buchanan, R. Roemer, H. Shacham, and S. Savage, "When good instructions go bad: generalizing return-oriented programming to RISC," in *Proceedings of the 15th ACM conference on Computer and Communications Security*, 2008.

[23] S. Checkoway, L. Davi, A. Dmitrienko, A.-R. Sadeghi, H. Shacham, and M. Winandy, "Return-oriented programming without returns," in *Proceedings of the 17th ACM conference on Computer and Communications Security*, 2010.

[24] S. Checkoway and E. W. Felten, "Can DREs provide long-lasting security? The case of return-oriented programming and the AVC Advantage," 2009.

[25] T. Kornau, "Return oriented programming for the ARM architecture," *Master's thesis, Ruhr-Universitat Bochum*, 2010.

[26] M. Abadi, M. Budiu, U. Erlingsson, and J. Ligatti, "Control-flow integrity," in *Proceedings of the 12th ACM conference on Computer and Communications Security*, 2005.

[27] C. Cowan, C. Pu, D. Maier, *et al.*, "StackGuard: Automatic adaptive detection and prevention of buffer-overflow attacks," in *Proceedings of the 7th USENIX Security Symposium*, 1998.

[28] L. Davi, A.-R. Sadeghi, and M. Winandy, "ROPdefender: A detection tool to defend against return-oriented programming attacks," in *Proceedings of the 6th ACM Symposium on Information, Computer and Communications Security*, 2011.

[29] H. Etoh, "GCC extension for protecting applications from stack-smashing attacks," 2003.

[30] M. Kayaalp, M. Ozsoy, N. Abu Ghazaleh, and D. Ponomarev, "Branch regulation: low-overhead protection from code reuse attacks," in *Proceedings of the 39th Annual International Symposium on Computer Architecture*, 2012.

[31] M. Zhang and R. Sekar, "Control flow integrity for COTS binaries," in *Proceedings of the 22nd USENIX Security Symposium*, 2013.

[32] C. Zhang, T. Wei, Z. Chen, L. Duan, L. Szekeres, S. McCamant, D. Song, and W. Zou, "Practical control flow integrity and randomization for binary executables," in *Proceedings of the 34th IEEE Symposium on Security and Privacy*, 2013.

[33] V. Kuznetsov, L. Szekeres, M. Payer, G. Candea, R. Sekar, and D. Song, "Code-pointer integrity," in *USENIX Symposium on Operating Systems Design and Implementation (OSDI)*, 2014.

[34] Michael Backes and Stefan Nürnberger, "Oxymoron: Making Fine-Grained Memory Randomization Practical by Allowing Code Sharing," in *Proceedings of the 23rd USENIX Security Symposium*, Aug 2014.

[35] L. Davi, C. Liebchen, A.-R. Sadeghi, K. Z. Snow, and F. Monrose, "Isomeron: Code randomization resilient to (just-in-time) return-oriented programming," July 2015.

[36] J. Hiser, A. Nguyen Tuong, M. Co, M. Hall, and J. W. Davidson, "ILR: Where'd My Gadgets Go?," in *Proceedings of the 33rd IEEE Symposium on Security and Privacy*, 2012.

[37] G. S. Kc, A. D. Keromytis, and V. Prevelakis, "Countering code-injection attacks with instruction-set randomization," in *Proceedings of the 10th ACM conference on Computer and Communications Security*, 2003.

[38] V. Pappas, M. Polychronakis, and A. D. Keromytis, "Smashing the gadgets: Hindering return-oriented programming using in-place code randomization," in *Proceedings of the 33rd IEEE Symposium on Security and Privacy*, 2012.

[39] PaX Team, "PaX address space layout randomization," 2003.

[40] E. Shioji, Y. Kawakoya, M. Iwamura, and T. Hariu, "Code shredding: byte-granular randomization of program layout for detecting code-reuse attacks.," in *Proceedings of the 28th Annual Computer Security Applications Conference*, 2012.

[41] R. Wartell, V. Mohan, K. W. Hamlen, and Z. Lin, "Binary stirring: Self-randomizing instruction addresses of legacy x86 binary code," in *Proceedings of the 2012 ACM conference on Computer and Communications Security*, 2012.

[42] G. F. Roglia, L. Martignoni, R. Paleari, and D. Bruschi, "Surgically returning to randomized lib (c)," in *Proceedings of the 25th Annual Computer Security Applications Conference*, 2009.

[43] H. Shacham, M. Page, B. Pfaff, E.-J. Goh, N. Modadugu, and D. Boneh, "On the effectiveness of address-space randomization," in *Proceedings of the 11th ACM conference on Computer and Communications Security*, 2004.

[44] B.-J. Wever, "Internet Explorer IFRAME src&name parameter BoF remote compromise," 2004.

[45] K. Z. Snow, F. Monrose, L. Davi, A. Dmitrienko, C. Liebchen, and A.-R. Sadeghi, "Just-in-time code reuse: On the effectiveness of fine-grained address space layout randomization," in *Proceedings of the 34th IEEE Symposium on Security and Privacy*, 2013.

[46] A. Bittau, A. Belay, A. Mashtizadeh, D. Mazieres, and D. Boneh, "Hacking Blind," in *Security and Privacy*, July 2014.

[47] H. D. Moore, "Microsoft Internet Explorer data binding memory corruption," 2010.

[48] Solar Designer, "Getting around non-executable stack (and fix)," 1997.

[49] G. Kyriazia, "Heterogeneous Systems Architecture: A Technical Review," tech. rep., 2012.

[50] A. Putnam, A. M. Caulfield, E. S. Chung, D. Chiou, K. Constantinides, J. Demme, H. Esmaeilzadeh, J. Fowers, G. P. Gopal, J. Gray, *et al.*, "A reconfigurable fabric for accelerating large-scale datacenter services," in *Proceedings of the 41st International Symposium on Computer Architecture*, June 2014.

[51] D. Allred and G. Martinez, "Maximizing the Power of ARM with DSP," tech. rep., Texas Instruments, 2010.

[52] S. Dutta, R. Jensen, and A. Rieckmann, "Viper: A multiprocessor SoC for advanced set-top box and digital TV systems," *Design & Test of Computers, IEEE*, vol. 18, no. 5, 2001.

[53] "Intel IXP425 Network Processor," tech. rep., 2006.

[54] Qualcomm, "Snapdragon S4 Processors: System on Chip Solutions for a New Mobile Age," tech. rep., Oct. 2011.

[55] "National Vulnerability Database,"

[56] D. Jang, Z. Tatlock, and S. Lerner, "SAFEDISPATCH: Securing C++ virtual calls from memory corruption attacks," in *Proceedings of the 21st International Symposium on Network and Distributed System Security*, Feb. 2014.

[57] E. J. Schwartz, T. Avgerinos, and D. Brumley, "Q: Exploit Hardening Made Easy.," in *Proceddings of the 20th USENIX Security Symposium*, 2011.

[58] Vasilis Pappas, Michalis Polychronakis, and Angelos D. Keromytis, "Transparent ROP Exploit Mitigation Using Indirect Branch Tracing," in *Proceedings of the 22nd USENIX Security Symposium*, 2013.

[59] C. Cowan, S. Beattie, R. F. Day, C. Pu, P. Wagle, and E. Walthinsen, "Protecting systems from stack smashing attacks with StackGuard," in *Proceedings of the 5th Linux Expo*, 1999.

[60] H. Ozdoganoglu, T. Vijaykumar, C. E. Brodley, B. A. Kuperman, and A. Jalote, "SmashGuard: A hardware solution to prevent security attacks on the function return address," *IEEE Transactions on Computers*, 2006.

[61] G. E. Suh, J. W. Lee, D. Zhang, and S. Devadas, "Secure program execution via dynamic information flow tracking," in *Proceedings of the 11th International Conference on Architectural Support for Programming Languages and Operating Systems*, 2004.

[62] Vendicator, "StackShield: A Stack Smashing Technique Protection Tool for Linux," 2001.

[63] I. Evans, S. Fingeret, J. González, U. Otgonbaatar, T. Tang, H. Shrobe, S. Sidiroglou-Douskos, M. Rinard, and H. Okhravi, "Missing the point (er): On the effectiveness of code pointer integrity1," in *Proceedings of the 36th IEEE Symposium on Security and Privacy*, 2015.

[64] N. Carlini, A. Barresi, M. Payer, D. Wagner, and T. R. Gross, "Control-flow bending: On the effectiveness of control-flow integrity," in *Proceedings of the 24th USENIX Security Symposium*, 2015.

[65] E. Goktas, E. Athanasopoulos, H. Bos, and G. Portokalidis, "Out of control: Overcoming control-flow integrity," in *Proceedings of the 35th IEEE Symposium on Security and Privacy*, May 2014.

[66] E. Goktas, E. Athanasopoulos, M. Polychronakis, H. Bos, and

G. Portokalidis, "Size does matter: Why using gadget-chain length to prevent code-reuse attacks is hard," in *Proceedings of the 23rd USENIX Security Symposium*, Aug. 2014.

[67] N. Carlini and D. Wagner, "Rop is still dangerous: Breaking modern defenses," in *Proceedings of the 23rd USENIX Security Symposium*, Aug. 2014.

[68] Lucas Davi, Daniel Lehmann, and Ahmad-Reza Sadeghi, "The Beast is in Your Memory: Return-Oriented Programming Attacks Against Modern Control-Flow Integrity Protection Te chniques," in *BlackHat USA*, Aug 2014.

[69] L. Davi, D. Lehmann, A.-R. Sadeghi, and F. Monrose, "Stitching the gadgets: On the ineffectiveness of coarse-grained control-flow integrity protection," in *Proceedings of the 23rd USENIX Security Symposium*, Aug. 2014.

[70] F. Schuster, T. Tendyck, C. Liebchen, L. Davi, A.-R. Sadeghi, and T. Holz, "Counterfeit object-oriented programming," May 2015.

[71] S. Bhatkar and R. Sekar, "Data space randomization," in *Detection of Intrusions and Malware, and Vulnerability Assessment*, 2008.

[72] C. Cadar, P. Akritidis, M. Costa, J.-P. Martin, and M. Castro, "Data randomization," tech. rep., Technical Report MSR-TR-2008-120, Microsoft Research, 2008.

[73] K. Onarlioglu, L. Bilge, A. Lanzi, D. Balzarotti, and E. Kirda, "G-Free: defeating return-oriented programming through gadget-less binaries," in *Proceedings of the 26th Annual Computer Security Applications Conference*, 2010.

[74] A. Papadogiannakis, L. Loutsis, V. Papaefstathiou, and S. Ioannidis, "ASIST: architectural support for instruction set randomization," in *Proceedings of the 2013 ACM SIGSAC conference on Computer & Communications Security*, 2013.

[75] C. Rohlf and Y. Ivnitskiy, "Attacking clientside JIT compilers," *Black Hat, USA*, 2011.

[76] J. Smith and R. Nair, *Virtual Machines: Versatile Platforms for Systems and Processes.* Morgan Kaufmann Publishers Inc., June 2005.

[77] F. Bellard, "Qemu, a fast and portable dynamic translator," in *USENIX Technical Conference*, Apr. 2005.

[78] MSDN, "Introduction to code signing,"

[79] J. Ansel, P. Marchenko, Ú. Erlingsson, E. Taylor, B. Chen, D. L. Schuff, D. Sehr, C. L. Biffle, and B. Yee, "Language-independent sandboxing of just-in-time compilation and self-modifying code," *ACM SIGPLAN Notices*, 2011.

[80] Intel, "Software guard extensions programming reference," 2014.

[81] Y. Cheng, Z. Zhou, M. Yu, X. Ding, and R. H. Deng, "ROPecker: A generic and practical approach for defending against ROP attacks," in *Symposium on Network and Distributed System Security (NDSS)*, 2014.

[82] N. L. Binkert, R. G. Dreslinski, L. R. Hsu, K. T. Lim, A. G. Saidi, and S. K. Reinhardt, "The M5 Simulator: Modeling Networked Systems," *Micro, IEEE*, 2006.

[83] T. Sherwood, E. Perelman, G. Hamerly, and B. Calder, "Automatically Characterizing Large Scale Program Behavior," in *Proceedings of the 7th International Conference on Architectural Support for Programming Languages and Operating Systems*, Oct. 2002.

[84] A. Venkat, A. Krishnaswamy, K. Yamada, and R. Palanivel, "Binary Translation driven Program State Relocation," in *United States Patent Grant US009135435B2*, 2015.

ANVIL: Software-Based Protection Against Next-Generation Rowhammer Attacks

Zelalem Birhanu Aweke,[†] Salessawi Ferede Yitbarek,[†] Rui Qiao,[‡] Reetuparna Das,[†]
Matthew Hicks,[†] Yossi Oren,[*] and Todd Austin[†]

[†] University of Michigan   [‡] Stony Brook University   [*] Ben-Gurion University of the Negev

Abstract

Ensuring the integrity and security of the memory system is critical. Recent studies have shown serious security concerns due to "rowhammer" attacks, where repeated accesses to a row of memory cause bit flips in adjacent rows. Recent work by Google's Project Zero has shown how to leverage rowhammer-induced bit-flips as the basis for security exploits that include malicious code injection and memory privilege escalation. Being an important security concern, industry has attempted to defend against rowhammer attacks. Deployed defenses employ two strategies: (1) doubling the system DRAM refresh rate and (2) restricting access to the *CLFLUSH* instruction that attackers use to bypass the cache to increase memory access frequency (i.e., the rate of rowhammering).

We demonstrate that such defenses are inadequte: we implement rowhammer attacks that both avoid using the *CLFLUSH* instruction and cause bit flips with a doubled refresh rate. Our next-generation *CLFLUSH-free* rowhammer attack bypasses the cache by manipulating cache replacement state to allow frequent misses out of the last-level cache to DRAM rows of our choosing.

To protect existing systems from more advanced rowhammer attacks, we develop a *software-based* defense, ANVIL, which thwarts all known rowhammer attacks on existing systems. ANVIL detects rowhammer attacks by tracking the locality of DRAM accesses using existing hardware performance counters. Our detector identifies the rows being frequently accessed (i.e., the aggressors), then selectively refreshes the nearby victim rows to prevent hammering. Experiments running on real hardware with the SPEC2006 benchmarks show that ANVIL has less than a 1% false positive rate and an average slowdown of 1%. ANVIL is low-cost and robust, and our experiments indicate that it is an effective approach for protecting existing and future systems from even advanced rowhammer attacks.

ASPLOS '16, April 02-06, 2016, Atlanta, GA, USA
 ISBN 978-1-4503-4091-5/16/04$15.00
DOI: http://dx.doi.org/10.1145/2872362.2872390

1. Introduction

In recent years, hardware security has grown in importance for all aspects of hardware design. The emergence of viable hardware security vulnerabilities, such as side-channel attacks [2] and malicious circuits [10, 22], ensures that this trend continues today. Perhaps no recent hardware security vulnerability has garnered more concern than the rowhammer attack [24]. The rowhammer attack allows the manipulation of data in a row of a DRAM (referred to as the victim row) by repeatedly accessing (or "hammering") adjacent rows. Serious security concerns arise when, for example, adjacent DRAM rows are **not** within the same memory protection domain [28].

1.1 Rowhammer Attacks

The rowhammer attack exploits the physical architecture of modern DRAMs, which are composed of numerous rows of densely packed capacitive bit cells. The bit cells hold the charge that represent program data values. Natural leakage of charge out of capacitive bit cells requires that the DRAM rows be refreshed (i.e., their charge restored through a refresh operation) regularly. Current DRAM architectures (e.g., DDR3) require a refresh command to be issued every 7.8us [3], refreshing individual rows once every 64ms. The rowhammer attack exploits an electrical cross-talk property within the dense interconnect of modern DRAMs. Repeated accesses to one row (the aggressor) within a single refresh cycle (e.g., 100's of thousands of accesses) speeds up the discharge of bit cells in adjacent rows (victim rows) [11]. This causes bit-flips in the victim rows most sensitive to hammering.

Recent studies have demonstrated the rowhammer attack on a wide variety of commercial system [24, 28]. These attacks used the *CLFLUSH* x86 instruction to flush specific cache lines, thereby allowing high locality rowhammer accesses to reach the DRAM unhindered by on-chip caches. Shortly after viable rowhammmer demonstrations emerged, work began to weaponize the mechanism, i.e., utilize it to breach a secure system. Of note, Google's Project Zero demonstrates two such weaponizations of a *CLFLUSH*-based rowhammer attack [28]. The first attack uses rowhammering to insert malicious code into Google's Native Client sandbox. The second attack is a privilege escalation attack that allows a process to gain write access to its own page tables, and hence gain read-write access to all of physical memory.

1.2 Mitigating Rowhammer Attacks

The response from the hardware industry focuses on protecting both legacy and future systems. For legacy systems, industry employs two mitigation strategies. The first mitigation strategy is to double the refresh rate of DRAM systems, from once every 64ms to once every 32ms. Many hardware manufacturers, for example HP [15] and Lenovo [18], deployed firmware updates that double refresh rates as a rowhammer protection. However, this approach is insufficient, as shown by us in Section 2.1 and by others [24]. The state of the art in rowhammer attacks are effective at causing bit-flips within a 32ms refresh window. The second mitigation strategy involves restricting access to the *CLFLUSH* instruction which attacks use to flush cache lines and gain direct access to DRAM rows. For example, Google recently updated the Chrome Native Client sandbox (which allows local execution of remotely downloaded binaries) to prevent the loading of any code containing the *CLFLUSH* instruction [28]. Again, we show that this protection is insufficient by detailing the first CLFLUSH-free rowhammer attack.

An emerging defense, as suggested by some manufacturers, is that increasing ECC scrub rates could be a rowhammer protection mechanism [14]. But, prior work [24] shows multiple bit-flips per word when executing rowhammer attacks, making this approach of questionable value in protecting existing or future systems.

Protections for future DRAM architectures are beginning to appear in industry announcements and the literature. For example, the upcoming LPDDR4 specification and new DDR4 modules include a targeted row refresh (TRR) capability designed to thwart rowhammer attacks [19, 21]. The mechanism tracks the number of row activations within a fixed time window, and selectively refreshes rows neighboring a too-frequently accessed DRAM row. However, Micron DDR4 documentation [19] suggests that this mechanism is an "optional module", thus there may exist future DDR4 systems still susceptible to rowhammer attacks. In fact, bit flips due to rowhammering in DDR4 system have been reported [7]. Intel has partially disclosed the existence of pseudo-targeted row refresh (pTRR) in Xeon-class Ivybridge architectures to help in the mitigation of rowhammer attacks, but Intel has yet to release the details of this mechanism.

Finally, the architecture literature has seen a few rowhammer protection proposals. For example, one proposal, PARA, utilizes probabilistic adjacent row activation to refresh the neighboring rows of any DRAM row access, with low probability. The idea behind this approach is that the many repeated DRAM row accesses required to hammer a victim DRAM row will result in an early refresh of the victim row with extremely high (cumulative) probability [24]. Such solutions require the introduction of new hardware.

1.3 Contributions of This Work

In this work, we show that current rowhammer mitigation techniques for existing systems (i.e., disallowing cache flush instructions and doubling refresh rates) do *not* work. We demonstrate in this paper two attacks that defeat these protections. Specifically, we demonstrate the first *CLFLUSH-free* rowhammer attack, thereby thwarting efforts to deter rowhammering by restricting access to the *CLFLUSH* instruction. The attack manipulates cache replacement state to ensure high-frequency misses out of the last-level cache to DRAM rows of our choosing. The algorithm is able to efficiently implement a successful rowhammer attack within one 64ms DRAM refresh cycle, creating approximately 220,000 DRAM row accesses [1]. A critical implication of the *CLFLUSH*-free attack is that now any program with access to loads and stores can perform a rowhammer attack. In addition, we demonstrate that is it straightforward to rowhammer DRAM under a double-rate 32ms refresh cycle, underscoring the futility of this popular, but costly, protection mechanism.

As such, existing systems immediately require a more robust means of protection against rowhammer attacks. To this end, we present ANVIL, a software-based rowhammer detector which protects existing and future commodity DRAMs. We implement ANVIL using an existing hardware performance monitoring infrastructure. ANVIL works by monitoring the locality of DRAM row accesses out of the last-level cache. In the event that row access locality becomes too high (i.e., indicating repeated accesses to the same DRAM row), the detector selectively refreshes neighboring potential victim rows with a read operation (for DRAM, a read operation fully refreshes the accessed DRAM row).

We implement ANVIL as a Linux kernel module that utilizes Intel architectures' performance monitoring capabilities to detect DRAM row access locality out of the last-level cache. The performance monitoring capabilities we rely on are also available on AMD-based systems [6]. The detector uses a multi-staged approach to reduce detector overheads, leading to an average slowdown (for non-malicious programs running on real hardware) of about 1%, and worst-case slowdown of 3.2%. In addition, our detector has a latency of only 12ms. This enables the detection of rowhammer attacks that are more than twice as fast as the fastest known technique today. Finally, the detector is accurate, with no false negatives and less than 1% false positives. Beside their small performance impact, false positives are innocuous in that they incur only a small number of extra DRAM

[1]We were the first to disclose the existence of a *CLFLUSH*-free rowhammer attack. The attack was announced on May 10, 2015 on the Google Project Zero rowhammer forum. The details of the attack are being disclosed for the first time in this paper.

read operations. In summary, this paper makes the following contributions:

- We demonstrate attacks that side-step existing measures to protect systems from rowhammer attacks. Our *CLFLUSH*-free attack does not use the *CLFLUSH* instruction, instead, it cleverly manipulates cache replacement state to allow frequent misses out of the last-level cache to hammer DRAM rows of our choosing. Moreover, we demonstrate the ease with which recent rowhammer attacks can work successfully within double-rate 32ms refresh cycles.
- We propose, implement and analyze a *software-based* protection against rowhammer attacks, ANVIL, which successfully thwarts all of the known rowhammer attacks on commodity systems. ANVIL detects rowhammer attacks by tracking the locality of DRAM row accesses using existing hardware performance counters. When a potential attack is detected, it is thwarted by selectively refreshing identified victim DRAM rows with a simple read operation. Running on real hardware, ANVIL has a less than 1% false positive rate, and it uses a multi-stage design to reduce average slowdowns to only 1% across diverse benchmarks.

2. Breaking Current Mitigation Techniques

Multiple techniques have been proposed to protect existing systems from DRAM rowhammering errors. Currently deployed mitigation techniques include doubling the DRAM refresh rate and disallowing cache flush instructions. In this section, we show that these techniques are insufficient to guarantee protection from rowhammer exploits. First, we show that a refresh period of 32ms is sufficient time to implement a rowhammer attack. Second, we show how to implement a rowhammer attack without using the CLFLUSH instruction.

2.1 Rowhammering under a Double Refresh Rate

After DRAM rowhammering errors and their security implications were widely recognized, a number of vendors published BIOS updates that double the rate at which DRAM refreshes its data [15, 18]. By refreshing the DRAM more frequently, it is believed that there is insufficient time to carry out a rowhammering attack. We perform experiments on a commodity platform that show that this belief is indeed false. Even when refresh intervals are reduced to 32ms, it is still possible for a malicious program to cause bit flips by repeatedly accessing two rows adjacent to a victim row using a rowhammering technique dubbed *double-sided rowhammering* [28]. Table 1 lists our experimental results for three rowhammer attacks. The attacks are analyzed on a real system with an Intel core i5-2540M processor (Sandy Bridge) and a 4GB DDR3 DRAM module while running Ubuntu 14.04 LTS. As shown in the results of Table 1, it is possible to employ double-sided rowhammering using the CLFLUSH instruction to flip bits in only 15ms on our DDR3 module—well below the 32ms window of deployed defenses.

Hammer Technique	Minimum Number of DRAM Row Accesses	Time to first bit flip
Single-Sided with CLFLUSH	400K	58 ms
Double-Sided with CLFLUSH	220K	15 ms
Double-Sided without CLFLUSH	220K	45 ms

Table 1: Rowhammer Attack Characteristics: The measured performance of three rowhammer techniques, i.e., single and double-sided rowhammering and with/without CLFLUSH to flush the cache. The experiments are run on a Ubuntu-based Sandy Bridge laptop with a 4GB DDR3 DRAM module. The table gives the minimum number of DRAM row accesses required to induce a bit-flip and the time until the first bit-flip.

Sequence (a) in Figure 1 shows the access sequence used to implement our double-sided rowhammer attack using CLFLUSH instructions. The attack involves three rows: Rows 0 and 2 are the aggressor rows, and Row 1 is the victim row. The aggressor rows are repeatedly activated to increase the discharge rate in the victim row. The attack works by first accessing an address in Row 0 (i.e., $A0_{(row0)}$); Then an address in Row 2 ($A1_{(row2)}$) is accessed. After each access, a CLFLUSH instruction is used to flush all levels of cache at addresses $A0_{(row0)}$ and $A1_{(row2)}$ thereby ensuring the next access goes directly to the DRAM. This sequence is repeated N number of times; for our experiments the minimum value of N was equal to 110k to see a bit flip.

Given the results of our experiment, one might suggest further increases in refresh rate. The problem with this approach, in general, is that increasing the refresh rate comes at the cost of increased power and reduced DRAM throughput—as refresh commands compete with software-requested memory accesses. Going from a 64ms refresh period to the 15ms required to protect our DRAM requires over a 4x increase in refresh power and throughput overhead. Also, as DRAM continues to move to smaller feature sizes, the vendors will likely have to lower the refresh rate more to account for increased density (i.e., future DRAM devices may be more susceptible to rowhammering at the cell level).

2.2 Rowhammering without the CLFLUSH instruction

Modern processors include multiple levels of cache for faster access of frequently used data. It is common to have three levels of cache with the last-level cache capable of

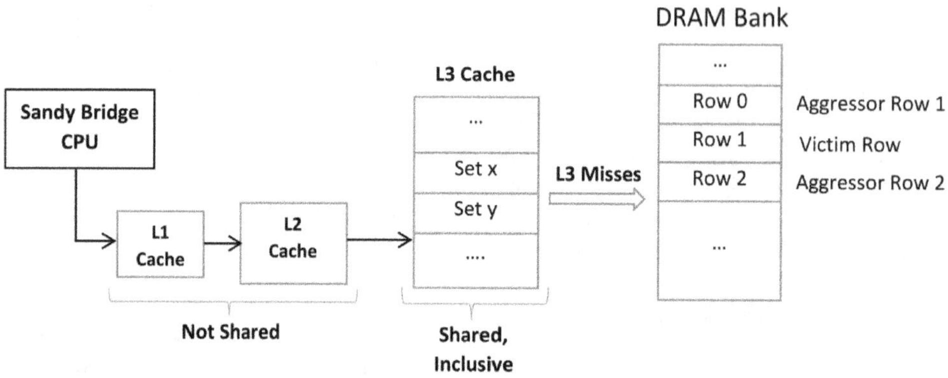

a) CLFLUSH Attack: $(A0_{(row0)}, CLFLUSH(row0), A1_{(row2)}, CLFLUSH(row2))^{N=110K}$

b) CLFLUSH-free Attack: $(A0_{(row0,\ setx)}, X1_{(setx)}, X2_{(setx)}, ..., X9_{(setx)}, X10_{(setx)}, X11_{(setx)}, X1_{(setx)}, X2_{(setx)}, ..., X9_{(setx)}, X12_{(setx)}, A1_{(row2,\ sety)}, Y1_{(sety)}, Y2_{(sety)}, ..., Y9_{(sety)}, Y10_{(sety)}, Y11_{(sety)}, Y1_{(sety)}, Y2_{(sety)}, ..., Y9_{(sety)}, Y12_{(sety)})^{N=110K}$

Figure 1: Memory Access Patterns for CLFLUSH-based & CLFLUSH-free Double-sided Rowhammer Attacks: In (a), a CLFLUSH instruction is used to flush caches after accessing aggressor DRAM rows Row 0 and Row 2. This sequence of operations is repeated N times. In our experiments the minimum value of N observed was 110K. In (b) the CLFLUSH instructions are replaced with sequences of memory accesses that force misses in the L3 cache at addresses that map to aggressor Row 0 and aggressor Row 2. This is done by accessing conflicting data that belong to the same cache set as the aggressor row addresses. *A0:* address in aggressor row 1 and maps to set X; *A1:* address in aggressor row 2 and maps to set Y; *X1, X2, ... X12:* addresses that map to cache set X and evict A0; *Y1, Y2, ... Y12:* addresses that map to cache set Y and evict A1.

storing megabytes of data. In order to repetitively access a DRAM row, memory access to that DRAM row must miss on all cache levels and the DRAM row buffer. One way to achieve this is to use cache flushing instructions like CLFLUSH on the x86 architecture. Previous works on exploiting the rowhammer problem all used the CLFLUSH instruction to bypass caches. One counter measure that has been taken to thwart CLFLUSH-based attacks is to disallow the CLFLUSH instruction [28]. Such measures thwart rowhammmer attacks based on cache flushing, but we show that it is possible to implement a rowhammer attack without using cache flush instructions.

Rowhammering in the presence of caches: Caches are limited in size; given varied enough accesses, eventually a cache will fill and memory accesses will miss in the cache. One way to force a miss from a cache is to evict previously accessed data by accessing conflicting data that belongs to the same cache set. To accomplish this, an *eviction set* that contains addresses that belong to the same cache set is created. Then the addresses in the eviction set are accessed one after the other to force eviction of a particular data element from the cache. If the access sequence is cleverly designed to manipulate the cache eviction policy, it is possible to precisely control which addresses hit in the cache and which addresses miss the cache and make it to main memory. This minimizes the delay between subsequent target misses. By repetitively evicting data from a target address and then re-accessing it, corresponding DRAM rows can be accessed.

Nonetheless, there are significant challenges in devising efficient address reference streams that can implement a rowhammer attack. First, last-level caches in modern processors have high associativity, usually 8-way to 16-way. Because each way can hold the address of the aggressor row, we must generate at least as many conflicting memory accesses that hit the cache as there are ways. Therefore, many memory accesses are required to evict a cache block, which slows down the rowhammering process. In addition, replacement policies used on real hardware are not true LRU, and vendors often do *not* publicly disclose their replacement algorithms. This means that access patterns that assume true LRU replacement policy often do not result in misses on the required target addresses. Missing on the exact target addresses is important as creating extraneous memory acceses dramatically decreases the rate of rowhammering. Finally, creating eviction sets can be a challenge in situations where the mapping of an address to a cache set is via physical address, as the mapping algorithm is not publicly disclosed by manufacturers and user-level application may not have access to the virtual memory mapping.

Demonstration of the attack: In this section we describe how we were able to overcome the challenges mentioned above to do CLFLUSH-free rowhammering. For our demonstration, we use a processor with an Intel Sandy Bridge microarchitecture. The processor has three levels of cache. The last-level cache is an inclusive, shared, physically indexed 12-way cache. It is an inclusive cache, therefore it is enough to evict a word from the last-level cache to bypass the whole cache hierarchy.

One way to create an eviction set is to directly use physical addresses and select memory addresses with the same set-index bits. Previous work in this area has revealed the mapping for an Intel Sandy Bridge microarchitecture with four CPU cores [12]. We discover that our Sandy Bridge microarchitecture based processor with two CPU cores uses a slightly modified version of this mapping. In our eviction set, we have one address that belongs to a row (which we call an aggressor address). Since our cache is a 12-way cache, we need 13 addresses in the eviction set, 12 conflicting address and the aggressor address. We create an eviction set by first picking the aggressor address and then using its physical address to find 12 more addresses with matching cache set mappings. On our Intel Sandy Bridge machine, bits 6 to 16 of the physical addresses are used to map to last-level cache sets. Furthermore, the last-level cache is organized into *slices* [16], with one slice per processor core. Conflicting addresses will have the same cache slice and cache set bits.

The next step is to create an efficient memory access pattern that has a high probability of misses on the aggressor address. Creating such a pattern requires knowing the cache replacement policy of the microarchitecture. We did this by generating a high miss-rate pattern that cyclically accesses the 13 addresses in the eviction set, and using performance counters (particularly the last-level cache miss counter) to determine whether each access was a cache hit or a cache miss. Then we correlate the performance counter results with results from different cache replacement policy simulators that we built. Our results show that one of the replacement algorithms Sandy Bridge favors (it uses more than one) is Bit Pseudo-LRU (Bit-PLRU) which is similar to the Not Recently Used (NRU) replacement policy [20]. In Bit-PLRU, each cache line in a set has a single MRU (Most Recently Used) bit. Every time a cache line is accessed, its MRU bit is set. The least-recently used cache line is the line with the lowest index whose MRU bit is cleared. When the last MRU bit is set, the other MRU bits in the set are cleared.

A time efficient memory access pattern misses the last-level cache only on the aggressor address and one additional conflicting address, and hits on the rest of addresses in the eviction set. This works by always driving the aggressor address to the least recently used position in the replacement state. Sequence (b) in Figure 1 outlines the access pattern we used for our CLFLUSH-free double-sided rowhammer attack. This attack is similar to the CLFLUSH-based attack except here the CLFLUSH instructions are replaced with memory accesses that drive the two aggressor DRAM row addresses to the least recently used (LRU) position in the L3 cache and subsequently evict them, thereby ensuring their next access goes to the aggressor DRAM rows. In Figure 1b, address $A0_{(row0,setx)}$ belongs to Row 0 in the DRAM, and *Set X* in the L3 cache. Address $A1_{(row2,sety)}$ belongs to Row 2 in the DRAM, and *Set Y* in the L3 cache. The two addresses constitute the aggressor addresses. First, data at address $A0_{(row0,setx)}$ is accessed. Then 10 addresses ($X1_{(setx)}$ to $X10_{(setx)}$) that belong to *Set X* are accessed to put $A0_{(row0,setx)}$ to the LRU position of the L3 cache. Then, when data from address $X11_{(setx)}$ is accessed, data at address $A0_{(row0,setx)}$ is evicted from the L3 cache. The next 9 accesses ($X1_{(setx)}$ to $X9_{(setx)}$) hit in the L3. Then, after data at address $X12_{(setx)}$ is accessed, address $X11_{(setx)}$ is put to the LRU position and subsequently replaced by data at address $A0_{(row0,setx)}$. This access sequence is repeated N times, with only two addresses ($A0_{(row0,setx)}$ and $X11_{(setx)}$) missing for each iteration. In *Set Y*, a similar access pattern is used to miss only from addresses $A1_{(row2,sety)}$ and $Y11_{(sety)}$. Using this technique, accesses to Row 0 and Row 2 will always access the DRAM.

Access to the last-level cache on Sandy Bridge takes 26 to 31 cycles [16]. Considering a DRAM access latency of 150 cycles, the access pattern in sequence (b) in Figure 1 takes an estimated (29*20) + (2*150) = 880 cycles. On our test machine, which runs at a nominal frequency of 2.6GHz, this access pattern takes approximately 338 nanoseconds. This allows up to 190K double-sided hammers with-in a 64ms refresh period. This is enough to produce a flip on our test DRAM module—which only requires 110k accesses to produce a bit flip.

In addition to rowhammering, the technique used in the CLFLUSH-free rowhammering attack can be used in other attacks that need to flush the cache at specific addresses. For example the Flush + Reload cache side-channel attack [29] relies on the CLFLUSH instruction. Our CLFLUSH-free cache flushing method can extend this attack to situations where the CLFLUSH instruction is not available (e.g., JavaScript) – a similar approach was explored in [27].

2.3 Attack Implementations

The CLFLUSH-based and CLFLUSH-free attacks were implemented as native C++ applications. The implementations are based on the double-sided rowhammering attack implementation [1]. The CLFLUSH-free rowhammering attack uses the Linux /proc/pagemap utility to convert virtual addresses to physical addresses in order to create conflicting LLC access patterns (eviction set). We demonstrated the attacks on a laptop with an Intel core i5-2540M processor (Sandy Bridge) with a 4GB DDR3 DRAM module.

Table 1 compares the minimum number of DRAM row accesses and the corresponding time required to produce a bit flip for the CLFLUSH-based and CLFLUSH-free attacks for our test DRAM module. Double-sided, CLFLUSH-based rowhammering is the most aggressive of the three.

It is also worth noting that a double-sided CLFLUSH-free rowhammering can produce bit flips faster than single-sided CLFLUSH-based rowhammering.

It is interesting to note that if both of the protection mechanisms detailed in this section are used in tandem (i.e., double refresh plus restricted access to CLFLUSH), such a system would still today have a measure of protection against rowhammer attacks, including those detailed in this paper. As shown in Table 1, we are unable to yet rowhammer memory in less than 32ms without use of the CLFLUSH instruction. While we are unaware of any systems that combine these two protection measures, one that did would likely only acquire a temporary measure of protection against novel rowhammer attacks. We continue to optimize the performance of our CLFLUSH-free attack, and if we are able to reduce its time-to-first bit flip by an additional 13ms, the combined protections will no longer work. Recognizing the tenuous nature of today's rowhammer protections, we feel a better approach to protect systems is to provide in-situ mechanisms that detect and subsequently defeat rowhammer attacks.

In summary, current techniques used to protect systems from rowhammer attacks are insufficient. We show that reducing the DRAM refresh period to 32ms is not sufficient as faster rowhammer attacks are possible using double-sided rowhammering in as little at 15ms. Moreover, by manipulating the LRU chain of the last-level cache, enough DRAM row activations can be performed in a single refresh cycle to flip bits, without using the CLFLUSH instruction.

3. Software-Based Rowhammer Detection and Protection

As Section 2 shows, currently deployed rowhammer defenses are insufficient. What is needed is a more robust solution that can detect rowhammering activity in time to protect any potential victim rows. In this section, we introduce a software technique that uses existing hardware performance counters in commercial processors to detect rowhammering activity and perform selective refresh on potential victim rows.

3.1 Detecting Rowhammer Attacks

Rowhammering relies on repetitively accessing an aggressor DRAM row within a single refresh cycle. We make the observation that this fundamentally requires accesses to the aggressor rows to miss on all cache levels. This reveals two identifying characteristics of rowhammering: *high cache miss rate* and *high spatial locality of DRAM row accesses*. This is in contrast to general memory access patterns where high locality results in high cache hit rates. As such it is straightforward to discriminate between rowhammer attacks and non-malcious programs by looking at DRAM access patterns and rate.

Another property of rowhammer attacks is high *bank locality*. DRAM disturbance errors occur due to repeated opening and closing of a DRAM row. When a row is accessed, it is opened and its data is transfered to a row-buffer. Subsequent accesses to the same row are served by the row-buffer. In order to close the row, a different row located in the same bank must be accessed. Therefore, a rowhammer attack involves repeatedly accessing at least two rows within the same bank—otherwise the row buffer would prevent the rowhammering. This bank locality property can be used to differentiate between "real" rowhammering and false positives that are caused by thrashing access patterns observed in some applications.

To minimize the performance impact of rowhammer detection, we propose a two-stage detection mechanism. In the first stage, we monitor the last-level cache miss rate. If this rate is high enough to successfully implement a rowhammer attack, the second stage samples the physical addresses of the memory accesses that miss from the last-level cache. If the samples reveal DRAM row accesses with high temporal locality, then the detector signals this as a potential rowhammer attack. To reduce the possibility of false positives, the detector also verifies that the samples have high bank locality. If there is enough bank locality among samples, then a protection phase follows.

3.2 Protecting Potential Rowhammer Victims

When the detector identifies potential rowhammering activity, it identifies the potential victim DRAM rows. Victim rows are adjacent to (preceding and following) identified aggressor rows. To protect the victim rows we refresh them by reading a word from them. Reading from a row opens that row which has the effect of refreshing cells in the row [24]. This approach does not incur significant performance penalties even in the case of false positives.

3.3 ANVIL: A Linux-Based Rowhammer Protection Mechanism

To demonstrate the protection mechanism, we built ANVIL, a Linux kernel module that prevents all known forms of rowhammer attacks. The module uses hardware performance counters found in modern processors to get memory access information, such as the addresses of loads and stores and the miss rate of the last-level cache. Specifically, we used performance counters found in Intel microprocessors with Sandy Bridge and later microarchitectures. AMD also provides similar capabilities required for our implementation [6]. In this section we provide details of our implementation. We start by reviewing the performance counter features used in our implementation.

Load Latency Performance Monitoring Facility: The Load Latency performance monitoring facility is part of Intel's Performance Event Base Sampling (PEBS) feature. PEBS uses a debug store mechanism and a performance

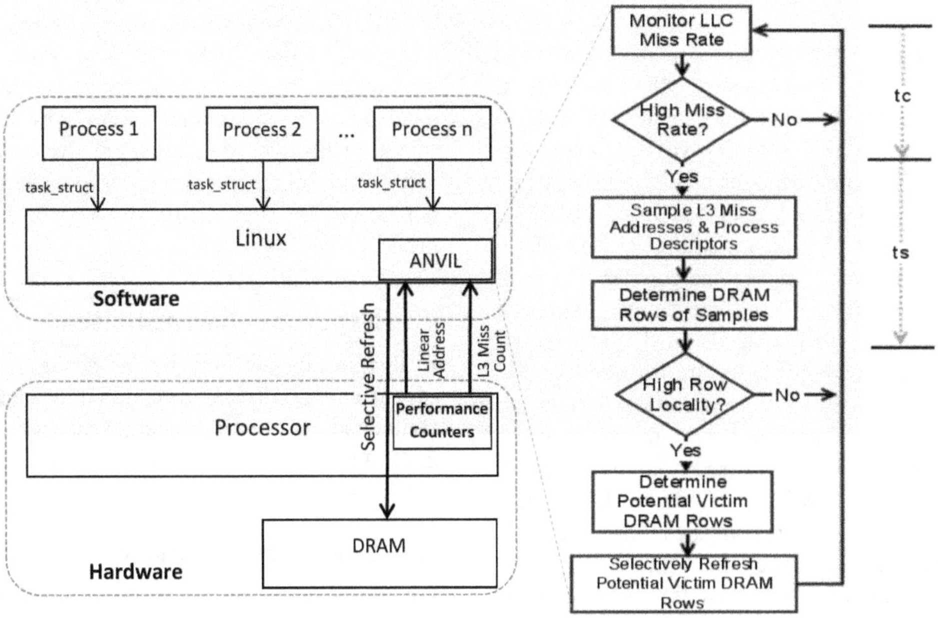

Figure 2: Software-Based Rowhammer Attack Detector: ANVIL is as a kernel module. It gets last-level cache miss count and memory access samples from hardware performance counters. By combining sampled virtual address information and process descriptor structures, samples of DRAM row accesses are obtained. ANVIL then checks the samples for high locality that suggests potential rowhammer activity. Upon detection of potential rowhammer activity, ANVIL performs selective read operations to refresh potential victim DRAM rows.

monitoring interrupt to store a set of architectural states [17]. The load latency facility measures latency of a load operation from the load's first dispatch until final data writeback from the memory subsystem. The load operation is sampled probablistically by hardware. If the latency of the sampled load operation exceeds a latency value specified by a dedicated programmable register, the operation is tagged to carry the following information:

- Load data virtual address
- Data source
- Latency value

When the next event categorized as a precise event (e.g., "load retired", "store retired") occurs, the last update of the load information is written to a PEBS record which then can be read by software. By setting the latency threshold to match last-level cache miss latency, it is possible to sample last-level cache misses. The data source information confirms the source of the load operation.

Precise Store Facility: The Precise Store facility complements the Load Latency facility by providing additional information about sampled store operations. When a precise event occurs, hardware samples the virtual address and data source of the next store that retires. Similar to the Load Latency event, data source information can be used to determine if the store was a miss. The precise store facility is replaced with the Data Address Profiling facility on Intel's Haswell and later microarchitectures [17]. This facility profiles load and store memory events similar to the other facilities, but has support for more events like DRAM access events. While we could implement ANVIL with either performance counter, we use the Precise Store facility for our implementation since it allows our rowhammer detection mechanism to support older micro-architectures.

In addition to the previously mentioned facilities, we utilize the last-level cache miss counter facility that generates an interrupt after N misses. The count is set such that if the miss interrupt arrives before the sample window timer interrupt, we know that the miss threshold has been breached.

Rowhammer Detection: Figure 2 shows the process of detecting a rowhammer activity in ANVIL. In the first stage of the detection phase, the last-level cache miss count event (LONGEST_LAT_CACHE.MISS) is used to measure the last-level cache miss rate. The miss rate is calculated by reading the last-level cache miss count for a time duration of t_c. If this rate is beyond a last-level cache miss threshold, the second stage of the detector is triggered. The last-level cache miss threshold (LLC_MISS_THRESHOLD) is set by considering the minimum cache miss rate that is enough to cause bit-flips within a single refresh period. As will be described in the next section, we set this value based on our empirical observations, but it is adaptable to other systems and attack scenarios.

In the second stage, ANVIL samples virtual addresses for a time duration of t_s using Load Latency (MEM_TRANS_RETIRED.LOAD_LATENCY) and Precise Store (MEM_TRANS_RETIRED.PRECISE_STORE) events. The load latency facility allows sampling of loads that have latency beyond a preset clock cycle value. We set the clock cycle value to match last-level cache miss latency so that we only sample loads that miss in the L3 cache. The counter also provides information about the source of the sample, therefore we can ensure the load is accessing DRAM. The precise store facility is used to sample stores. It also provides information about the source of a store operation. Which facility to use for sampling is selected based on a count of retired memory load operations that missed from the last-level cache (MEM_LOAD_UOPS_MISC_RETIRED_LLC_MISS) for a time duration of t_c. ANVIL compares this value with the total number of last-level cache misses for that duration. If load operations account for more than 90% of all misses then only loads are sampled. On the other hand, if load operations account for less than 10% of all misses, only stores are sampled. For the remaining cases, both stores and loads are sampled. A sampling rate of 5000 samples per second is used which gives an average of 30 samples for a sampling duration of 6ms. The second stage also samples the process descriptor (task_struct) of the process that generated the memory access. This structure is used to determine the physical address and DRAM row of the memory access in combination with the sampled virtual address.

At the end of sampling, sampled DRAM row accesses are sorted and the sample distribution is analyzed to identify high DRAM row locality. DRAM row locality is determined by considering the number of samples, the number of last-level cache misses for the sampling duration and the required last-level cache miss rate for a successful rowhammr attack. For each row that has high DRAM locality, a check is made to see if there are other row access samples from the same DRAM bank. If the cumulative of samples of the other row accesses from the same DRAM bank is high enough, then there is a potential rowhammer attack occurring.

Rowhammer Protection: Once ANVIL detects potential rowhammering activity, it uses the physical addresses of the identified aggressor rows to determine potential victim rows. The kernel module was pre-configured using a reverse engineered physical address to DRAM row and bank mapping scheme. We also make the assumption that sequentially numbered rows are physically adjacent. Two potential victim rows are considered for each potential aggressor row: rows that are directly above and below each potential aggressor row (our approach easily extends to N adjacent rows). ANVIL performs a single read operation per victim row to refresh its value. The number of selective read operations performed on a potential victim row is low enough (once every $t_c + t_s$ in the worst case) that it has little effect on performance of non-rowhammering applications, even if they experience a high incidence of false positive detection. Also, it is not possible for an attacker to use the selective refresh mechanism to rowhammer DRAM rows adjacent to the potential victim row since the selective read rate is well below the minimum access rate for a rowhammer attack. After performing a selective refresh, ANVIL starts the detection process again.

4. Experimental Evaluation

In this section we evaluate the accuracy and performance of our software-based detection mechanism. All tests are conducted on a real physical system with an Intel Core i5-2540M processor and Ubuntu 14.04 LTS with Linux kernel version 4.0.0.

4.1 Benchmark Applications

We use several benchmark programs for our evaluations. To evaluate rowhammer detection accuracy, we use two rowhammer attacks. The first is a CLFLUSH-based double-sided rowhammer attack, *CLFLUSH_hammer*, adapted from the original weaponization [1]. The second application is CLFLUSH-free double-sided rowhammer attack, *CLFLUSH-free_hammer*, used to demonstrate our CLFLUSH-free attack in Section 2[1]. We measure the slowdown incurred on non-malicious programs using SPEC2006 integer benchmarks [9].

4.2 Rowhammer Detection Characteristics

We first evaluate ANVIL's ability to detect rowhammer activity. The evaluation is done for scenarios where the test machine is heavily and lightly loaded. To emulate heavy load, we run the rowhammering applications along with memory-intensive applications (*mcf*, *libquantum* and *omnetpp* running at the same time) from the SPEC2006 integer benchmark suite. The detector parameters used for our evaluations are given on Table 2. The time values are selected to be low enough so that any rowhammering activity can be detected with enough time to deploy protection. With this setting, hammering activity can be detected within 12 milliseconds. The last-level cache miss threshold value was experimentally found by considering the minimum number of memory accesses required to cause a DRAM bit flip. In our experiments the minimum number of memory accesses that caused a flip was 220K for CLFLUSH-based double-sided rowhammering attack. In order to achieve this many activations within a refresh period of 64ms, a minimum of 20.6K activations must occur within 6ms. Therefore, we will use 20K misses in 6ms as a threshold value for the first stage of detection.

[1] Code for the *CLFLUSH-free_hammer* program and ANVIL can be found at `https://github.com/zaweke/rowhammer`

Parameter	Value
LLC_MISS_THRESHOLD	20K
Miss Count Duration (t_c)	6ms
Sampling Duration (t_s)	6ms

Table 2: Rowhammer Detector Parameters to Evaluate Accuracy of Rowhammer Detection

Benchmark	Average Time to Detect	Refreshes per 64ms	Total Bit Flips
CLFLUSH *(Heavy Load)*	12.8 ms	12.35	0
CLFLUSH *(Light Load)*	12.3 ms	10.3	0
CLFLUSH-free *(Heavy Load)*	35.3 ms	4.53	0
CLFLUSH-free *(Light Loaded)*	22.85 ms	5.10	0

Table 3: Rowhammer Detection Result for Rowhammering Programs: The table shows the average time before rowhammer activity is detected and the rate of selective refreshes performed.

Table 3 shows the result of rowhammering detection for applications *CLFLUSH_hammer* and *CLFLUSH-free_hammer* under heavy and light load. For both attacks, the table shows the average time to detect a rowhammer attack within a 64ms refresh cycle in which rowhammering was occurring. This time includes the time to identify and selectively refresh potential victim rows. The table also lists the average selective refresh rate, which are refreshes that occur when the rowhammer detector identifies potential DRAM victim rows. As seen in these results, ANVIL is quite responsive, with response times well within a single refresh cycle, and with only slight increases in response time due to a heavy loaded system. In addition, the selective refresh rates are low, but sufficient for multiple refreshes within a single refresh cycle for any detected victim row. The low selective refresh rate ensures that a clever attacker cannot use the selective refresh to hammer other DRAM rows. Finally, it is good to note that our detector stopped all rowhammering, resulting in zero bit flips for all of the attacks.

4.3 Performance Evaluation

We evaluated the slowdown incurred by ANVIL by analyzing the execution of non-malicious applications from the SPEC2006 integer benchmark suite. We used the parameters listed on Table 2 for the evaluation. In addition to this experiment, we compare the performance overhead of ANVIL with that incurred by doubling DRAM refresh rate. For these evaluations our baseline is an unprotected system with a refresh period of 64ms.

Figure 3 shows relative execution times for ANVIL-protected system relative to our baseline. The ANVIL-protected system has peak and average overheads of 3.18% and 1.17%, respectively. Most of the performance overhead by ANVIL is attributed to the low last-level cache miss rate threshold. *libquantum*, *omnetpp*, *mcf* and *Xalancbmk* crossed the last-level cache miss threshold 95% to 99% of the time. On the other extreme, *h264ref*, *gobmk*, *sjeng* and *hmmer* crossed the threshold less than 10% of the time. This indicates that sampling of addresses in the second stage of the detection phase contributes to almost all of the performance overhead. As can be observed from the results, the overheads of continuously running ANVIL's rowhammer detection are very low. Low enough to protect existing systems from rowhammer attacks, and likely low enough to obviate the need for dedicated hardware-based rowhammer protection mechanisms in future systems.

Benchmark	Refreshes/sec
astar	0.10
bzip2	1.05
gcc	0.71
gobmk	0.19
h264ref	0.00
hmmer	0.00
libquantum	0.06
mcf	0.01
omnetpp	0.02
perlbench	0.00
sjeng	0.00
xalancbmk	0.05

Table 4: Rate of False Positive Refreshes: The table shows rate of superfluous refreshes for SPEC2006 integer benchmarks while running under ANVIL.

Table 4 shows the false positive rate for the SPEC2006 integer benchmarks. The rate is measured as the average number of superfluous selective refreshes per second. The number of false positives is low enough that selective refresh of rows has negligible effect on performance.

4.4 Comparison with Double Refresh Rate

As we have shown in Section 2, doubling DRAM refresh rate is not sufficient to prevent all rowhammering attacks. Equally important is the execution time and power overhead incurred by the increased refresh rate. Previous studies have shown that increasing refresh rate reduces parallelism in the memory subsystem, affecting overall system performance [5, 26]. Figure 3 shows performance overhead of doubling DRAM refresh rate as compared with our software-based protection mechanism. ANVIL's performance overheads are only marginally larger (on average) than doubling the refresh rate, while providing a significantly higher level of protection against rowhammer attacks, as demonstrated in Section 2. As can be observed, memory intensive applications like *mcf* suffer most from doubling DRAM refresh rate thus, their performance benefits greatly from the use of ANVIL's protection.

4.5 Robustness to Potential Future Rowhammer Attacks

As the density of DRAM devices increases, DRAM cells become more susceptible to disturbance errors. It is then expected that for future DRAM devices, rowhammer attacks will be possible with less DRAM row activations. An attacker might take advantage of this to evade detection by our software-based protection mechanism by: 1) Activating DRAM aggressor rows at a high rate such that rowhammer attacks will be faster than they can be detected by the protection mechanism. 2) Spreading out fewer DRAM row activations over a refresh period such that the last-level cache miss rate stays below the last-level cache miss threshold. Our detection mechanism can cope with both situations by adjusting the detector parameters listed on Table 2. To evaluate the effect that more nimble future attacks have on the performance of non-malicious programs, we consider a future scenario where bit flips can occur with 110K DRAM row accesses (i.e., half the number of accesses that produced flips on our experiments).

Figure 4 examines the performance impact on a subset of the SPEC2006 benchmarks for three cases. The benchmarks are selected to be representatives of the memory access characteristics of SPEC2006 benchmark suit. *ANVIL-baseline* is our baseline detector with parameters as given on Table 2. *ANVIL-heavy* considers the case where the 110K DRAM row accesses can occur within 7.5ms (i.e., half the time we observed for our experiments). For this case values of t_c and t_s are set to 2ms while the value of the last-level cache miss threshold remains unchanged at 20K. The third case, *ANVIL-light*, considers a situation where the 110K DRAM row accesses are spread out across a refresh period of 64ms (i.e., half the number of accesses purposely spread out maximally). For this case values of t_s and t_c are set to 6ms, and the last-level cache miss threshold is halved to 10K. As seen in Figure 4, ANVIL has room to grow if future rowhammer attacks become more aggressive. Overheads do grow to detect these more nimble attacks, but only slightly. Decreasing the last-level miss sample period to 2ms has the larger performance impact, which is expected as the sampling overheads are experienced continuously.

Table 5 shows false positive refresh rates due to false positives for *ANVIL-light* and *ANVIL-heavy*. Though both configurations show an increase in false positive rates than *ANVIL-baseline*, they do not incur significant overheads.

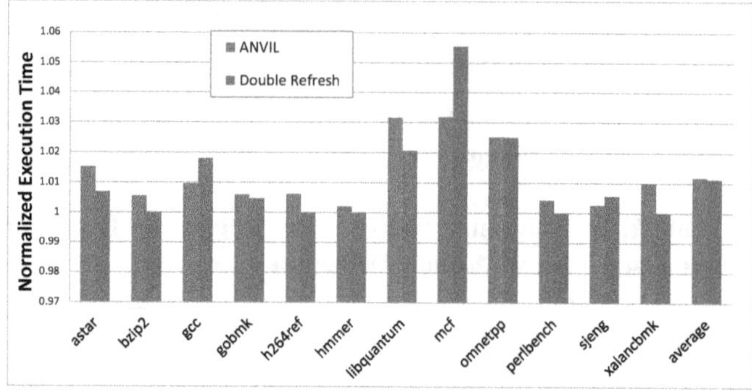

Figure 3: ANVIL's Impact on Non-Malicious Programs: The Figure shows execution times for selected benchmarks on ANVIL-enabled system and a system with doubled DRAM refresh rate. The values shown are normalized to execution time without ANVIL and at a single refresh period.

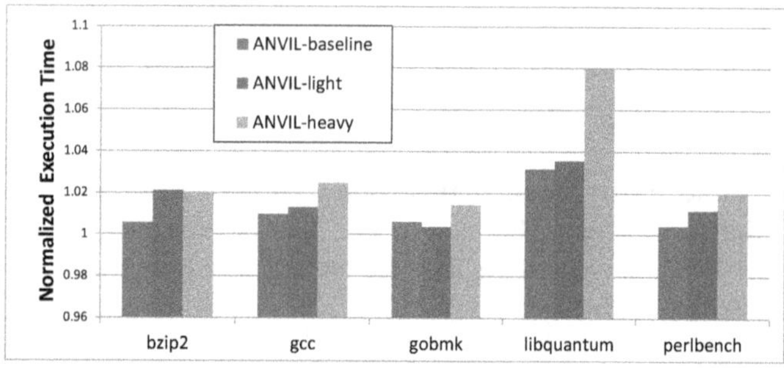

Figure 4: Sensitivity of Execution Overheads to Potential Future Attacks: The figure compares normalized execution times for selected benchmarks running on ANVIL-enabled system with three configurations. *ANVIL-Heavy* is configured to have the highest sampling rate while *ANVIL-Light* has the lowest last-level cache miss threshold.

5. Related Work

Previous works have studied exploitation and prevention of the rowhammer vulnerability. In this section, we detail currently known attacks and proposed mitigations.

5.1 Rowhammer Vulnerability and Its Exploitation

Even if the rowhammer vulnerability on modern DRAMs has been known by manufacturers since at least 2012 [24], the first detailed experimental study was published in 2014 by Yoongu Kim, et. al [24]. Their study shows that bits in a DRAM row (the victim row) can be flipped by repeatedly accessing adjacent rows in the same bank (the aggressor rows). The authors used x86's CLFLUSH instruction to bypass the cache and enable frequent references directly to DRAM.

Leveraging the early attack demonstrations, Seaborn and Dullien [28] demonstrated two security exploits that take advantage of rowhammer-induced bit flips. Their first attack bypasses Google's Native Client (NaCl) sandboxing system. NaCl is a software sandbox, integrated with the Chrome browser, that allows secure execution of untrusted client side applications and plug-ins. NaCl works by carefully scanning code for illegal code operations at load time (e.g., system calls or arbitrary indirect jumps), and by funneling all I/O operations through a security analyzer. The NaCl rowhammer attack works by having a securely loaded NaCl application hammer its own code segment until an illegal arbitrary code jump sequence is formed, then the application jumps to the middle of an instruction where illegal operations can be formed from validated code. Note that the attack is changing code that has been verified and deemed safe. Since the instructions are modified at the hardware level, the sandbox will not be aware of any of these changes. The authors' current proof-of-concept implementation can take advantage of 13% of the possible bit flips within an instruction.

Seaborn and Dullien's second attack takes advantage of the bit flips to bypass the memory page protection mechanism of a Linux system running on x86-64 [28]. The attack works by filling physical memory with page tables for a single process, by repeatedly mmap()'ing a file into its memory. This repeated file mapping sprays the memory with page table entries (PTEs), that are used to translate the newly mmap()'ed virtual addresses. By rowhammering the memory with page tables, there is a non-trivial probability that a PTE will be changed to point to a physical page containing a page table, thereby giving the application access to its own page tables. This will give the attacker full R/W permission to a page table entry, which in effect results in access to all of physical memory.

Even if all of the exploits mentioned above rely on CLFLUSH instruction in x86, the attack we presented in Section 2 demonstrates how rowhammer attacks can be launched without the use of any cache line flush instruction. A concurrent effort similarly demonstrated a CLFLUSH-free rowhammer attack [8]. This attack, which was disclosed two months after our attack, is similar in that it uses cache manipulation to avoid CLFLUSH instruction, but unlike our attack, it is implemented in Javascript. This earlier effort is only an attack and does not detail protections like we describe in this work.

5.2 Rowhammer Mitigation

In this section, we detail both software and hardware techniques that have been proposed and deployed to protect against data corruption and security exploits due to rowhammering.

5.2.1 Protections for Legacy Systems

Software Patches: To date, two open source projects have released patches in response to the security vulnerabilities explained above. Google's NaCl sandbox was patched to disallow the use of CLFLUSH instruction by applications running inside it. The attack mechanism we present in Section 2 defeats this protection and enables malicious applications to effectively hammer rows without using CLFLUSH (or any other explicit cache flush instructions).

Benchmark	Refreshes/sec (ANVIL-light)	Refreshes/sec (ANVIL-heavy)
bzip2	1.61	1.09
gcc	7.12	1.88
gobmk	0.28	0.84
libquantum	0.13	0.08
perlbench	0.06	0.00

Table 5: Rate of False Positive Refreshes for *ANVIL-Heavy* and *ANVIL-Light*: The table shows false positive rates for selected SPEC2006 integer benchmarks while running under two ANVIL configurations. *ANVIL-Heavy* has a relatively small sampling period which reduces the probability of misses with high address locality on non-malicious applications. On the other hand, *ANVIL-light* allows more samples for a longer sampling period thus resulting in a relatively larger false positive rate.

Recently, the Linux kernel was updated to disallow the use of the pagemap interface from the user space, as a measure to make it more difficult to do double-sided rowhammering in Linux-based systems. This change prevents malicious applications from analyzing the physical address space to launch targeted attacks. However, this attack still leaves room for potential attacks that rely on side-channel information to make inferences about the physical memory layout. Furthermore, certain attacks such as the NaCl sandbox escape attack can be implemented by repeatedly picking two random addresses without having any knowledge of the physical address mapping.

Doubling Refresh Rate: Some vendors published BIOS updates that double DRAM refresh rates(i.e. halving the refresh interval from 64ms to 32ms) [13, 15, 18]. Doubling the refresh rate reduces the amount of time an attacker has to mount an attack, since the discharging of a rowhammer'ed bit must be completed within one refresh cycle. However, our empirical studies show that it is still possible to induce bit flips through double-sided hammering even when the refresh period is as low as 16ms. Further increases in refresh rates would have significant effects on system performance and energy consumption [24].

5.2.2 Protections for Future Systems

Currently available hardware-based reliability features are not capable of mitigating DRAM disturbance errors. Error Correcting Codes (ECC) protection, aside from being expensive, is only capable of repairing single-bit flips. Furthermore, ECC will turn the problem of bit-flips into denial of service if the system has to deal with machine check exceptions every time a flip is detected [28].

Due to the inability of current memory controllers and memory modules to deal with rowhammer attacks, multiple hardware enhancements have been proposed. The possibility of having an activation counter for each row in a DRAM module has been considered in literature [23, 24]. However, due to the high overhead of maintaining and updating per-row counters, other alternatives have been recommended.

Probabilistic row refreshing (e.g. PARA) has been proposed as an alternative to per-row counters [23, 24]. In this technique, when an activation command is sent to a row, a random number generator is used to decide if adjacent row has to be refreshed. Since requests to rows that are being hammered will be encountered very frequently, there is a high probability that it will trigger a refresh. Compared to ANVIL, PARA can have lower overhead but requires a modification to the memory controller, therefore it can not be deployed on existing systems.

Project Armor [25] introduces an extra buffer that will cache data from rows with repeated activation commands. By servicing requests to hammered rows from the extra buffer, Armor prevents rows from being accessed repeatedly.

Processor and memory manufacturers are also deploying products with capabilities to perform targeted row refreshes. The current LPDDR4 standard and recent DDR4 modules support targeted refresh of potential victim rows [19, 21]. Intel has published patents on memory controllers that support targeted row refresh [4]. The memory controllers are designed to identify repeated reads to a row. However, the actual physical placement of rows can differ among different manufacturers. Hence, the controller only transmits the row that is being repeatedly accessed, and the memory module is responsible for refreshing the victim rows based on its internal structure.

It is important to note that the mitigation techniques for existing systems (i.e., doubling refresh rate and removing access to CLFLUSH) are shown to be ineffective in this work. We are able to implement the rowhammer attack in a 32ms double-rate refresh cycle, and we can also rowhammer DRAMs without access to the CLFLUSH instruction. While newly proposed hardware enhancements can protect future systems from rowhammer attacks, a software solution is still necessary to protect current hardware. As such, in this paper we detail a low-cost software-based rowhammer detector that thwarts attacks with little performance impact. It is our claim that these protections are appropriate both for existing and future designs.

6. Conclusion

Securing computing systems is a critical design goal. In this paper, we systematically analyze a security vulnerability found in commodity DRAM chips referred to as rowhammer. Rowhammer attacks use the CLFLUSH instruction to accomplish hammering by bypassing processor caches and repeatedly accessing memory.

We demonstrate that existing mitigation techniques such as doubling refresh rates and disallowing CLFLUSH instructions are not sufficient—we show that it possible to rowhammer in as little as 15ms. We also provide the first CLFLUSH-free rowhammer attack that does not require special cache flushing instructions, thereby expanding the rowhammering attack surface.

As an alternative protection mechanism to rowhammering attacks, we design, implement and evaluate ANVIL, the first software-based defense that protects against all known rowhammer attacks. Our defense leverages the insight that rowhammer memory access patterns are fundamentally different from those of normal applications. Compared to prior approaches, ANVIL is more effective, has lower cost, is readily deployable and is adaptable due to its software-based approach. Experiments with a diverse set of benchmarks on a real system show that ANVIL has an average slowdown of 1% and less than 1% false detections, while protecting against all tested rowhammer attacks. We feel that these results show it is viable to protect current and future systems against rowhammer attacks.

Acknowledgments

We extend special thanks to Mark Seaborn of Google for his many valuable inputs to this work. This work was supported in part by C-FAR, one of the six STARnet Centers, sponsored by MARCO and DARPA.

References

[1] Program for Testing for the DRAM "rowhammer" Problem. `https://github.com/mseaborn/rowhammer-test`. Accessed: 2015-08-11.

[2] National Security Agency. TEMPEST: A Signal Problem. `https://www.nsa.gov/public_info/_files/cryptologic_spectrum/tempest.pdf`. Accessed: 2015-08-11.

[3] JEDEC Solid State Technology Association. DDR3 SDRAM Specification, 2010.

[4] K. Bains, J.B. Halbert, C.P. Mozak, T.Z. Schoenborn, and Z. Greenfield. Row Hammer Refresh Command, 2014.

[5] Ishwar Bhati, Mu-Tien Chang, Zeshan Chishti, Shih-Lien Lu, and Bruce Jacob. DRAM Refresh Mechanisms, Penalties, and Trade-Offs. In *IEEE Transactions on Computers, VOL. 64*, 2015.

[6] Paul J. Drongowski. Instruction-Based Sampling: A New Performance Analysis Technique for AMD Family 10h Processors. 2007.

[7] D. Gruss. `https://twitter.com/lavados/status/685618703413698562`. Accessed: 2016-01-21.

[8] D. Gruss, C. Maurice, and S. Mangard. Rowhammer.js: A Remote Software-Induced Fault Attack in JavaScript. *ArXiv e-prints*, July 2015.

[9] John L. Henning. SPEC CPU2006 Benchmark Descriptions. *SIGARCH Comput. Archit. News*, 34(4):1–17, September 2006.

[10] M. Hicks, M. Finnicum, S.T. King, M. Martin, and J.M. Smith. Overcoming an Untrusted Computing Base: Detecting and Removing Malicious Hardware Automatically. In *Security and Privacy (SP), 2010 IEEE Symposium on*, pages 159–172, May 2010.

[11] Rei-Fu Huang, Hao-Yu Yang, M.C. Chao, and Shih-Chin Lin. Alternate Hammering Test for Application-Specific DRAMs and an Industrial Case Study. In *Design Automation Conference (DAC), 2012 49th ACM/EDAC/IEEE*, pages 1012–1017, June 2012.

[12] R. Hund, C. Willems, and T. Holz. Practical Timing Side Channel Attacks against Kernel Space ASLR. In *Security and Privacy (SP), 2013 IEEE Symposium on*, pages 191–205, May 2013.

[13] Apple Inc. About the Security Content of Mac EFI Security Update 2015-001 . `https://support.apple.com/en-us/HT204934`. Accessed: 2015-08-11.

[14] CISCO Inc. Mitigations Available for the DRAM Row Hammer Vulnerability. `http://blogs.cisco.com/security/mitigations-available-for-the-dram-row-hammer-vulnerability`.

[15] HP Inc. HP Moonshot Component Pack Version 2015.05.0. `http://h17007.www1.hp.com/us/en/enterprise/servers/products/moonshot/component-pack/index.aspx`. Accessed: 2015-08-11.

[16] Intel Inc. *Intel 64 and IA-32 Architectures Optimization Reference Manual*. September 2014.

[17] Intel Inc. *Intel 64 and IA-32 Architectures Software Developers Manual, Volume 3 (3A, 3B & 3C): System Programming Guide*. June 2015.

[18] Lenovo Inc. Row Hammer Privilege Escalation Lenovo Security Advisory: LEN-2015-009. `https://support.lenovo.com/us/en/product_security/row_hammer`. Accessed: 2015-08-11.

[19] Micron Inc. *DDR4 SDRAM MT40A2G4, MT40A1G8, MT40A512M16 Data sheet*. 2015.

[20] Aamer Jaleel, Kevin B. Theobald, Simon C. Steely, Jr., and Joel Emer. High Performance Cache Replacement Using Re-reference Interval Prediction (RRIP). In *Proceedings of the 37th Annual International Symposium on Computer Architecture*, ISCA '10, pages 60–71, New York, NY, USA, 2010. ACM.

[21] JEDEC Solid State Technology Association . Low Power Double Data Rate 4 (LPDDR4), 2015.

[22] Yier Jin, Nathan Kupp, and Yiorgos Makris. Experiences in hardware trojan design and implementation. In *Proceedings of the 2009 IEEE International Workshop on Hardware-Oriented Security and Trust*, HST '09, pages 50–57, Washington, DC, USA, 2009. IEEE Computer Society.

[23] Dae-Hyun Kim, P.J. Nair, and M.K. Qureshi. Architectural support for mitigating row hammering in dram memories. *Computer Architecture Letters*, 14(1):9–12, Jan 2015.

[24] Yoongu Kim, R. Daly, J. Kim, C. Fallin, Ji Hye Lee, Donghyuk Lee, C. Wilkerson, K. Lai, and O. Mutlu. Flipping Bits in Memory Without Accessing Them: An Experimental Study of DRAM Disturbance Errors. In *Computer Architecture (ISCA), 2014 ACM/IEEE 41st International Symposium on*, pages 361–372, June 2014.

[25] Mohsen Ghasempour, Mikel Lujan and Jim Garside. Armor: A Run-Time Memory Hot-Row Detector. `http://apt.cs.manchester.ac.uk/projects/ARMOR/RowHammer/index.html`. Accessed: 2015-08-11.

[26] Janani Mukundan, Hillery Hunter, Kyu-hyoun Kim, Jeffrey Stuecheli, and José F. Martínez. Understanding and Mitigating Refresh Overheads in High-density DDR4 DRAM Systems. In *Proceedings of the 40th Annual International Symposium on Computer Architecture*, ISCA '13, pages 48–59, New York, NY, USA, 2013. ACM.

[27] Yossef Oren, Vasileios P. Kemerlis, Simha Sethumadhavan, and Angelos D. Keromytis. The Spy in the Sandbox: Practical Cache Attacks in JavaScript and their Implications. In *Proceedings of the 22nd ACM SIGSAC Conference on Computer and Communications Security, Denver, CO, USA, October 12-6, 2015*, pages 1406–1418. ACM, 2015.

[28] Mark Seaborn and Thomas Dullien. Exploiting the DRAM rowhammer bug to gain kernel privileges. March 2015.

[29] Yuval Yarom and Katrina Falkner. FLUSH+RELOAD: A High Resolution, Low Noise, L3 Cache Side-channel Attack. In *Proceedings of the 23rd USENIX Conference on Security Symposium*, SEC'14, pages 719–732, Berkeley, CA, USA, 2014. USENIX Association.

ProteusTM: Abstraction Meets Performance in Transactional Memory

Diego Didona Nuno Diegues
INESC-ID, Instituto Superior Técnico, Universidade de Lisboa
didona,ndiegues@gsd.inesc-id.pt

Anne-Marie Kermarrec
INRIA
anne-marie.kermarrec@inria.fr

Rachid Guerraoui
EPFL
rachid.guerraoui@epfl.ch

Ricardo Neves Paolo Romano
INESC-ID, Instituto Superior Técnico, Universidade de Lisboa
ricardo.neves,paolo.romano@tecnico.ulisboa.pt

Abstract

The Transactional Memory (TM) paradigm promises to greatly simplify the development of concurrent applications. This led, over the years, to the creation of a plethora of TM implementations delivering wide ranges of performance across workloads. Yet, no universal implementation fits each and every workload. In fact, the best TM in a given workload can reveal to be disastrous for another one. This forces developers to face the complex task of tuning TM implementations, which significantly hampers their wide adoption.

In this paper, we address the challenge of automatically identifying the best TM implementation for a given workload. Our proposed system, ProteusTM, hides behind the TM interface a large library of implementations. Underneath, it leverages a novel multi-dimensional online optimization scheme, combining two popular learning techniques: Collaborative Filtering and Bayesian Optimization.

We integrated ProteusTM in GCC and demonstrate its ability to switch between TMs and adapt several configuration parameters (e.g., number of threads). We extensively evaluated ProteusTM, obtaining average performance $< 3\%$ from optimal, and gains up to $100\times$ over static alternatives.

Categories and Subject Descriptors D.1.3 [*Programming Techniques*]: Concurrent Programming

Keywords Transactional Memory, Recommender Systems, Performance Tuning, Adaptive System

ASPLOS '16, April 02–06, 2016, Atlanta, Georgia, USA.

DOI: http://dx.doi.org/10.1145/http://dx.doi.org/10.1145/2872362.2872385

1. Introduction

The advent of multi-cores has brought parallel computing to the fore-front of software development, fostering research on paradigms to simplify the development of concurrent applications. The Transactional Memory (TM) [35] abstraction is a prominent approach that promotes a simple idiom for synchronizing code: programmers specify only *what* should be done atomically (via serializable transactions), leaving to the TM the responsibility of implementing *how* to achieve it.

Over time, several works have provided evidence [46, 52, 57] on the effectiveness of TM to simplify the development and verification of concurrent programs, enhancing code reliability and productivity. Recently, the relevance of TM was amplified by the standardization of constructs in popular languages (such as C/C++ [49]), and by the integration of hardware support in processors by Intel and IBM [39, 67].

The abstraction vs performance dilemma. Unfortunately, TM performance remains a controversial matter [11]: despite the large body of work in the area, the search for a "universal" TM with optimal performance across all workloads has been unsuccessful. Fig. 1 conveys experimental evidence of the strong sensitivity of TM to the workload characteristics. We report on the energy efficiency (in Fig. 1a) and throughput (in Fig. 1b) of various TMs in different architectures and benchmarks. We normalized the data with respect to the best performing configuration for the considered workload. Fig. 1 shows that, in two different architectures and metrics, the optimal TM configuration differs significantly for each workload. Furthermore, choosing wrong configurations can cripple performance by several orders of magnitude. Interestingly, some TMs used in these experiments were designed to tackle various workloads [27, 29], but configuring them is non-trivial and they still cannot perform well for all workloads.

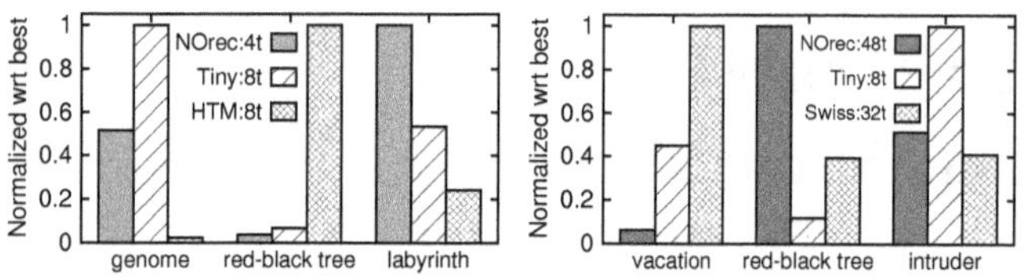

(a) Throughput/Joule on a single-chip 8-core CPU (Machine A in Table 2).

(b) Throughput on a multi-chip 48-core CPU (Machine B in Table 2).

Figure 1: Performance heterogeneity in TM applications.

The problem is that the efficiency of existing TM implementations is strongly dependent on the workloads they face. Performance can be affected by a number of factors, including program inputs [26], phases of program execution [24], tuning of internal parameters [25], as well as architectural aspects of the underlying hardware [12].

Given the vast TM design space, manually identifying optimal configurations, using trial and error on each workload, is a daunting task. Overall, the complexity associated with tuning TM contradicts the motivation at its basis, i.e., to simplify the life of programmers, and represents a roadblock to the adoption of TM as a mainstream paradigm [42].

Contributions. We propose a new system, ProteusTM[1], which allows developers to enjoy the simplicity and ease of usage of the TM abstraction, while sparing them from the burden of tuning TM implementations to specific workloads.

Under the simple and elegant interface of TM, ProteusTM hides a large library of TM implementations. At run-time, ProteusTM relies on an combination of learning techniques to pursue optimal efficiency via multi-dimensional adaptation of the TM implementation and its parameters.

At the heart of ProteusTM lie two key components:

• **PolyTM** is a polymorphic TM library that encapsulates state-of-the-art results from research in TM, and has the unique ability to transparently and dynamically adapt multiple dimensions: (i) switch between different TM algorithms; (ii) reconfigure the internal parameters of a TM; (iii) adapt the number of threads concurrently generating transactions.

• **RecTM** is in charge of determining the optimal TM configuration for an application. Its basic idea is to cast the problem of identifying such best configuration as a recommendation problem [54]. This allows RecTM to inherit two highly desirable properties of state of the art Recommender System (RS) algorithms: the ability to operate with very sparse training data, and to require only the monitoring of the Key Performance Indicator (KPI) to be optimized. This avoids intrusive instrumentation [59] and (possibly inaccurate) static code analysis [65] employed by other machine learning-based solutions.

While building ProteusTM, we solved several challenges:

► *Minimizing the cost of adaptivity.* Supporting reconfigurations across multiple dimensions requires introducing some synchronization, in order to ensure correctness during run-time adaptations. The challenge here is to ensure that the overheads to support adaptivity are kept small enough not to compromise the gains achievable via our self-tuning.

We addressed this challenge by designing lightweight synchronization schemes that exploit compiler-aided, asymmetric code instrumentation. The combination of these techniques allows PolyTM to achieve average and maximum overhead of 1% and 5%, even when considering the most performance sensitive TM implementations.

► *Transparency and portability*: PolyTM encapsulates a wide variety of TM implementations, along with their corresponding tuning procedures. The key challenge here is to conceal these mechanisms without breaking the simple abstraction of TM. Furthermore, one of the key design goals of ProteusTM is to seamlessly integrate with existing TM applications, and to support different machine architectures.

We tackled this issue by integrating PolyTM in GCC, via the standard TM ABI [49], and by exposing to programmers standard C++ TM constructs. Not only this preserves the simplicity of TM, but it also maximizes portability due to the widespread availability of GCC across architectures.

► *Applying Recommender Systems to the TM domain*: Decades of research have established RS as a powerful tool to perform prediction in various domains (e.g., music and news) [16, 19, 45]. The application of RS techniques to performance prediction of TM applications, however, raises unique challenges, which were not addressed by previous RS-based approaches to the optimization of systems' performance [20, 21]. One key issue is that, in conventional RS domains (e.g., recommendations of movies), users express their preferences on a homogeneous scale (e.g., 0 to 5 stars). On the contrary, the KPIs of TM applications can span very heterogeneous scales. As we shall see, this can severely hinder the accuracy of existing RS techniques.

We cope with this issue by introducing a novel normalization technique, called *rating distillation*, which maps heterogeneous KPI values to scale-homogeneous ratings. This allows ProteusTM to leverage state-of-the-art RS algorithms even in the presence of TM applications whose KPIs' scales span across different orders of magnitude.

► *Large search space*: Although RS algorithms are designed to work with very sparse information, their accuracy can be strongly affected by the choice of the configurations [61] that are initially sampled to characterize a TM application. Deciding *which* and *how many* TM configurations to sample is a challenging task, as ProteusTM supports reconfigurations across multiple dimensions, resulting in a vast search space.

RecTM addresses this issue by relying on Bayesian Optimization techniques [8] to steer the selection of the configurations included in the characterization of a TM application. This reduces by up to 4× the duration of the learning process of the RS using Collaborative Filtering (CF) [61].

[1] *Proteus* is a Greek god who can foretell the future and adapt his shape.

We conducted an extensive evaluation of ProteusTM using 15 TM applications, a parameter space of up to 130 configurations, and optimizing 2 metrics: performance and energy efficiency. Our results highlight that ProteusTM obtains quasi-optimal performance (on average $< 3\%$ from optimal) and gains up to 2 orders of magnitude over static alternatives.

While ProteusTM does not solve all challenges of TM (e.g., coping with side-effects of transactions), it drastically improves performance while preserving its simplicity.

The rest of the paper is structured as follows. In §2 we provide background on TM and CF. Then, §3 overviews ProteusTM, which we detail in §4-5. The evaluation follows in §6, with the related work in §7 and conclusions in §8.

2. Background

Next, we provide background on TM and overview Collaborative Filtering techniques for Recommender Systems.

2.1 Transactional Memory

The TM programming model relies on the abstraction of *atomic blocks* to demarcate which portions of code of a concurrent application must execute as atomic transactions. The TM implementation guarantees serializable transactions, by aborting transactions that perform unsafe operations and automatically re-executing them until completion.

Many design and configuration choices have high impact on performance. Next, we discuss their associated trade-offs that are self-tuned by ProteusTM.

TM implementations. The TM abstraction has been implemented in software (STM), hardware (HTM), or combinations thereof (Hybrid TM). A wide variety of STMs have been proposed [34]. STMs pose no restrictions on the number of memory accesses of a transaction, but they require costly code instrumentation to track transactional operations. HTMs do not need instrumentation, but they are best-effort [23, 67]: only transactions whose memory footprint fits in the processor's cache can be executed; otherwise they incur a *capacity abort* and resort to a fall-back synchronization. This is typically a global lock [67], or an STM [14].

Degree of parallelism. The number of concurrently active threads is another parameter with a potentially strong impact on TM performance: a low thread count may lead to subutilizing available processing power; a high one, conversely, may induce excessive contention and lead to thrashing [24].

Contention management. A TM contention manager [30] is in charge of arbitrating conflicts (e.g., by backing off transactions). In HTM, contention management is also responsible for dealing with problematic transactions that might suffer from best-effort caused aborts. Typical approaches allocate a budget of retries to hardware transactions, upon whose exhaustion they resort to the fall-back scheme. Tuning the initial budget, and the retry policy, has significant impact on performance and is strongly workload dependent [25].

2.2 Collaborative Filtering in Recommender Systems

A Recommender System (RS) seeks to predict the rating that a user would give to an item. These ratings can be exploited to recommend items of interest to users [45]. We focus on Collaborative Filtering (CF) [61], a prominent prediction technique used in a RS. To infer the rating of a $\langle$user, item$\rangle$ pair, CF techniques exploit the preferences expressed by other users, and ratings by the user on different items. Ratings are stored in a *Utility Matrix* (UM): rows represent users and columns represent items. Typically, a UM is very sparse, as a user rates a small subset of the items. A CF algorithm reconstructs the full UM, from its sparse representation, by filling empty cells with ratings close to the ones that the users would give.

K-Nearest Neighbors (KNN) and Matrix Factorization (MF) are popular CF techniques [54]. KNN uses a *similarity function* to express the affinity of two rows or columns: a recommendation for a pair $\langle$u,i$\rangle$ is computed with a weighted average of the ratings of the most similar users to u (and/or on the most similar items to i) [54]. MF, instead, maps users and items to a latent factors space of dimensionality d. Each dimension represents a hidden similarity concept: in the movies' domain, a similarity concept may be how much a user likes drama movies, or how much a movie belongs to the drama category. To compute recommendations, MF infers two matrices P and Q, which represent, respectively, users and items in the aforementioned d-dimensional space. The product of P and Q is a matrix R that is similar to a given UM A, i.e., $Q^T P = R \sim A$, containing also predictions for the missing ratings in A [54].

3. ProteusTM in a Nutshell

In essence, ProteusTM applies Collaborative Filtering (CF) to the problem of identifying the best TM configuration that maximizes a user-defined Key Performance Indicator (KPI): e.g., throughput or consumed energy. ProteusTM aims to maximize the efficiency of TM applications by orchestrating various TM algorithms and their dynamic reconfiguration. We now overview the architecture of ProteusTM, depicted in Fig. 2, which enables its self-tuning capabilities. More details shall be provided in the corresponding sections.

- **PolyTM** §4: consists of a Polymorphic TM library comprising various TM implementations. It allows for switching among TMs and reconfigure several of their internal parameters. It exposes transactional operators via an implementation of the standard TM ABI [49] (supported by GCC [38]).
- **RecTM** §5: is responsible for identifying the best configuration for PolyTM depending on the current workload. It is composed, on its turn, by the following sub-modules:

1. Recommender §5.1: a RS that acts as a performance predictor and supports different CF algorithms. It receives the KPIs of explored configurations from the Controller, and returns ratings (i.e., predicted KPIs) for unexplored ones.

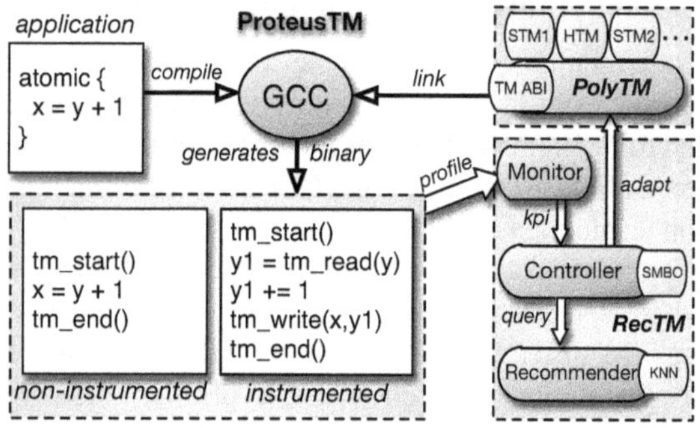

Figure 2: Architecture of the ProteusTM system.

2. Controller §5.2: selects the configurations to be used and triggers their adaptation in PolyTM. It queries the Recommender with the KPI values from the Monitor, obtaining estimates for the ratings of unexplored TM configurations.

3. Monitor §5.3: this module collects the target KPI to (i) give feedback to the Controller about the quality of the current configuration and (ii) detect changes in the workload, so as to trigger a new optimization phase in the Controller.

4. PolyTM: a Polymorphic TM Library

The PolyTM library encompasses a wide variety of TM implementations. It interacts with compilers, like GCC, via the standard TM ABI [38]. Each atomic block, written by the programmer using standard C/C++ constructs [49], is compiled into calls to the various modules of ProteusTM.

For every atomic block, GCC inserts a call to *tm_begin* and *tm_end*, which we direct to PolyTM. Also, two code paths are generated: a non-instrumented path, and a second one in which reads and writes are instrumented with calls to PolyTM. The latter allows our code to arbitrate reads and writes, besides the begin and commit of transactions.

Our system is able to integrate with any new TM backend, as long as this backend maintains its metadata (such as locks, ownership records, etc.) in separate memory regions, i.e., it does not interfere with the original memory layout of the application. This is the case for most TMs we are aware of.

Behind the TM ABI interface, we implemented in PolyTM several TM algorithms[2], and run-time support to switch among them: 4 STMs [15, 22, 27, 29], 2 HybridTMs [14, 47], and 2 HTMs [1, 67]. We take advantage of the dual compilation paths and use the instrumented one for the STMs. In contrast, HTMs — which automatically transactionalize reads and writes — execute the non-instrumented one. As shown in §6.2, the dual path optimization is crucial to minimize overhead.

The compiled code is also instrumented to profile performance metrics in a lightweight and transparent manner. In particular, PolyTM collects the commits and aborts at each thread, and the energy consumed by the system. It also uses a dedicated *adapter thread* to change the TM configuration.

[2] We used open-source TMs by mapping ProteusTM's implementation of the TM ABI to the API of each TM with a thin software layer.

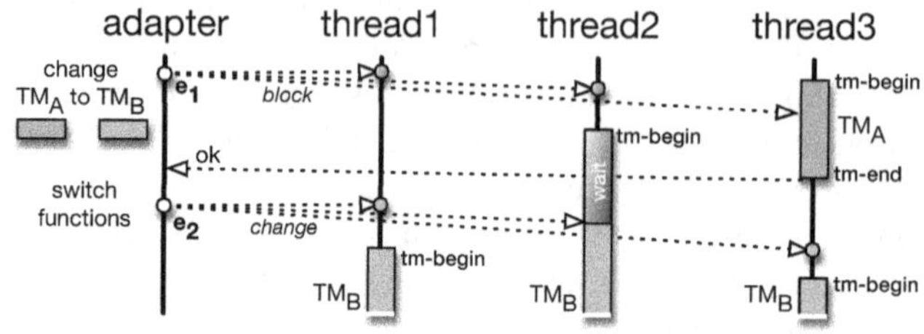

Figure 3: Switching TM algorithm safely in PolyTM.

In the following, we describe the mechanisms used by PolyTM to support run-time configuration changes.

4.1 Switching Between TM Algorithms

Since our library must interact with the compiler via a single ABI, we hide different TM implementations under a common interface defined in PolyTM. Then, each thread uses a set of function pointers to this interface to process transaction operations. To switch between TMs, a thread switches the function pointers to a different implementation.

Running concurrent transactions with different TMs is not safe in general [44, 65]. So, PolyTM enforces an invariant: a thread may run a transaction in mode TM_A only if no other thread is executing a transaction in mode TM_B. We illustrate the problem in Fig. 3: at time e_1 the adapter thread tries to change the TM mode; if thread 2 immediately applied the change, it could run mode TM_B concurrently with thread 1 in TM_A. The above invariant guarantees correctness by forcing thread 2 to wait until e_2 to change to TM_B.

The invariant is enforced via an implementation using the following steps: (i) adapt parallelism degree (i.e., number of threads) from the current value, say P, to 0; (ii) change TM back-end; (iii) adapt parallelism degree back to P.

4.2 Adapting the Parallelism Degree

To adapt the maximum number of active threads we use the synchronization scheme described in Algorithm 1.

Each application thread synchronizes with the adapter thread via a (padded) state variable. When executing a transaction for the first time, a thread is registered in PolyTM. We simplify this in the algorithm by using a maximum number of threads, although PolyTM supports an arbitrary number.

Upon starting a transaction, a thread t sets the lowest bit in its state variable (line 10), whereas the adapter thread sets the highest bit of t's state variable when it wants to disable t (line 4). These writes are performed atomically together with returning the state of t. Then, both adapter thread and t can reason on who wins (a potential race): if t sees only the lowest bit set, it is allowed to proceed and executes the transaction; otherwise, it must wait for the adapter to change

Algorithm 1 Changing the parallelism degree in PolyTM.

```
1: const int RUN ← 1 , BLOCK ← 1 ≪ 32
2: padded var int threadState[MAX_THREADS] ← { 0 }
3: function disable-thread(int t)                  ▷ adapter thread
4:   int val ← fetch-and-add(threadState[t], BLOCK)
5:   while (val & RUN) val ← threadState[t]
6: function enable-thread(int t)                   ▷ adapter thread
7:   threadState[t] ← RUN
8:   signal(t)                ▷ wakes up thread t (locking omitted)
9: function tm-start(int t)                    ▷ application thread
10:  int val ← fetch-and-add(threadState[t], RUN)
11:  if (val & BLOCK)
12:    fetch-and-sub(threadState[t], RUN)
13:    cond-wait(t)         ▷ checks it is still blocked after locking
14:  ▷ ...omitting logic for tm-start...
15: function tm-end(int t)                     ▷ application thread
16:  ▷ ...omitting logic for tm-end...
17:  fetch-and-sub(threadState[t], RUN)
```

the mode (line 13). The adapter inversely checks that only the highest bit is set, or else waits for t to unset the lowest bit (line 5) — because t was already executing a transaction.

We implement these atomic operations with the primitives fetch-and-*op* (e.g., *op* = *add* would be XADD in x86). These primitives always succeed, and are cheaper than the traditional compare-and-swap loop [18, 48]. Furthermore, in the common case of our algorithm — a thread starting a transaction is not concurrently disabled — each thread performs the atomic operation on a variable residing (with high probability) in its cache and without contention. In this case, the latencies (in processor cycles), in our Machine A are 17 cycles for a fetch-and-add and 32 for a compare-and-swap. As such, the cost for managing the number of active threads is quite limited, for instance when compared to the begin and commit of a hardware transaction (>120 cycles [56]).

We also use a conditional variable, associated with each thread t, for t to wait on, in the case it is disabled. We omit the details of its management, for simplicity of presentation.

PolyTM guarantees that a reconfiguration always terminates: a thread eventually commits a pending transaction, or else aborts and checks whether it was disabled — assuming finite atomic blocks. Hence, the duration of a reconfiguration depends on the longest running transaction. This, however, does not impair the efficiency of PolyTM's reconfiguration: in-memory transactions are generally very fast (given that they do not entail I/O) [43, 64].

In addition, the success of a reconfiguration does not rely on threads to eventually call into ProteusTM. This is crucial to cope with applications whose threads may wait for events (e.g., client requests) and do not run atomic blocks often.

We note that, depending on the application, it may not be safe for PolyTM to permanently disable an arbitrary thread: for instance, a web server may have a single thread accepting requests. To account for such cases, in which it is impossible to know the application's semantics, we provide a library call for the programmer to forbid PolyTM from disabling a specific thread (e.g., to tune the parallelism degree). Such a thread may still be disabled temporarily to allow switching the TM algorithm, which is a brief procedure as noted above.

4.3 Adapting the Contention Management

PolyTM's optimization encompasses other configuration parameters related to contention management [31]. Specifically, PolyTM integrates a scheme for HTM [25] that considers two parameters: (i) the budget of retries using HTM for a transaction, (ii) whether, upon a capacity abort, the budget should be decreased by one, halved, or fully consumed.

In fact, different contention management policies can coexist without affecting correctness [31]. Hence, both parameters can be changed at any point without synchronization.

5. RecTM: a Recommender System for TM

RecTM optimizes PolyTM by relying on a novel combination of off-line and on-line learning. In short, it operates according to the work-flow of Algorithm 2:

(i) build a *training set* by profiling the KPI of a base set of applications in the encompassed TM configurations (line 1);
(ii) instantiate a CF-based performance predictor based on the training set obtained off-line in (i) (lines 2 and 3);
(iii) upon deploying a new application or detecting a change of the workload, profile on-line the application over a small set of explored configurations (lines 4 and 5);
$iv)$ recommend a configuration for the workload (line 6).

In the following, we detail the building blocks of RecTM.

5.1 Recommender: Using Collaborative Filtering

RecTM casts the identification of the optimal TM configuration for a workload into a recommendation problem, which it tackles using Collaborative Filtering (CF), an efficient and simple technique for rating prediction [61].

A key challenge to successfully apply CF in predicting the performance of TM applications, is that CF assumes the ratings in a predetermined scale (e.g., a rating of 0 to 10). The absolute KPI values produced by different TM applications, instead, can span orders of magnitude (e.g., from millions [9] to few txs/sec [32]). Further, KPIs of specific configurations provide no indication on the max/min KPI that the application can obtain, impairing their normalization.

Our Recommender tackles this issue with an innovative technique, which we call *rating distillation*. This function maps KPI values of diverse TM applications to a scale that can be fruitfully exploited by CF to identify correlations among trends of heterogeneous applications.

The Rating Heterogeneity Problem. Ratings are stored in a Utility Matrix (UM) A, of which each row u represents a workload and each column i is a TM configuration: $A_{u,i}$ is the rating of configuration i for workload u (i.e., in our domain, it expresses the performance of i in u for a given KPI metric). To illustrate the problem, let us populate the UM directly with sampled KPI values (e.g., throughput):

Algorithm 2 RecTM work-flow

```
Off-line performance profiling of an initial training set of applications.
Rating distillation and construction of the Utility Matrix (§ 5.1).
Selection of CF algorithm and setting of its hyper-parameters (§ 5.1).
Upon the arrival of a new workload (§ 5.3):
    Sample the workload on a small set of initial configurations (§ 5.2).
    Recommend the optimal configuration (§ 5.1).
```

Algorithm 3 Rating Distillation function in ProteusTM.

```
for C_i ∈ C_1 ... C_K do
    Normalize Matrix KPI w.r.t. C_i
    Collect the vector M_w with the max values per row
    Compute mean_i(M_w) and var_i(M_w)
end for
Return C* = argmin_{i∈1...M} var_i(M_w)/mean_i(M_w)
```

$\begin{pmatrix} 1 & 2 & 3 \\ 30 & 20 & 10 \\ 100 & 200 & ? \end{pmatrix}$, which contains information on applications A_1 and A_2 profiled with configurations C_1, C_2 and C_3 and A_3 profiled only at C_1 and C_2. Let us assume that C_i is an application running with a given TM and i threads. From the matrix, we can infer that A_1 can scale, as its performance increases linearly with the number of threads; A_2 does not, since its performance, though higher in absolute value than A_1's, decreases as the number of threads grows. We want to predict the rating for $A_{3,3}$. Note that A_3 exhibits the same linear trends of A_1: for this reason, a likely value for $A_{3,3}$ would be 300. Next, we show why well-known CF techniques can be misled because of the heterogeneity of the ratings' scales in the UM.

The Need for Normalization. The most used similarity functions in KNN CF are the Euclidean, Cosine and Pearson [54]. The first cannot be applied to heterogeneous ratings, because it is based on the scale-sensitive Euclidean distance: in the example above, it would incorrectly regard C_2 as more similar to C_3 than C_1. The other two are scale-insensitive, so they identify C_1 as similar to C_3. However, they would yield an incorrect prediction in absolute value, as it will lie on C_1's scale, which is different from C_3's[3].

A similar shortcoming applies to MF CF. The P and Q matrices — recall §2.2 — are typically obtained via Stochastic Gradient Descent [54]: starting from random matrices, this technique iteratively tries to minimize the fitting error of $P^T Q$ over A. Thus, it is prone to over-fitting around the highest absolute value ratings, yielding poor accuracy.

A solution to these problems is to normalize the entries in the UM. An effective normalization function should: (i) transform entries in the UM so that similarities among heterogeneous applications can be mined and (ii) enable the application of conventional CF techniques.

Note that feature normalization is often performed in Machine Learning (ML): the most notable example is in Artificial Neural Networks, which normalize input features in the range [0,1] [5]. In ML, however, normalization is performed on the input features, whose values are fully known for samples in the training set and for queries. In contrast, in ProteusTM, the normalization has to be performed on the UM, which contains values of the output feature KPI, and whose entries are not all known. Next, we describe how ProteusTM normalizes ratings to meet the two aforementioned requirements and, thus, enables CF to optimize TM applications.

Normalization in the Recommender. If the minimum and maximum KPIs of an application were known *a priori*, they could be mapped to a homogeneous scale with a simple, per workload, normalization. Since KPIs of applications can take arbitrary values, then this *ideal* solution cannot be used.

The rating distillation used by the Recommender approximates the ideal approach with a mapping function that, for any workload w in the UM, ensures: (i) the ratio between the performance of two configurations c_i, c_j is preserved in the rating space, i.e., $\frac{kpi_{w,c_i}}{kpi_{w,c_j}} = \frac{r_{w,c_i}}{r_{w,c_j}}$; and (ii) the ratings of the corresponding configurations, $r_{w,c}$, are distributed (assuming a maximization problem) in the range [0,M_w], so as to minimize the index of dispersion of M_w: $D(M_w) = var(M_w)/mean(M_w)$ (where M_w is defined below).

Property (i) ensures that the information about the relative distances of two configurations is correctly encoded in the rating spaces. Property (ii) aligns the scales that express the ratings of each workload w to use similar upper bounds M_w, which are tightly distributed around their mean value.

We define this function in Algorithm 3. The rating of each row is obtained by normalizing its KPI with respect to a column C*∈ $\{C_1...C_K\}$ (assuming there are K configurations), so to minimize the index of dispersion among the resulting maximum ratings in the normalized domain.

Note that not only does this function reduce the numerical heterogeneity of ratings; it also projects all the elements of the matrix to a semantically common domain: now, a rating k for configuration i can be seen as "configuration i delivers performance that are k times the reference one". While an absolute throughput of 5K txs/sec may correspond to either a good or a bad performance depending on the application, our rating function gives ratings a "more universal" meaning. Also, minimizing the dispersion of the maximum values allows to align the upper extreme of the rating distributions of each application (i.e., matrix row) to a common value: the tighter the distribution around a common value M_w, the closer it approximates an ideal "omniscient" normalization.

Tuning the Recommender. We used Mahout [51], a ML framework containing several CF algorithms. This design choice allows the Recommender to seamlessly leverage a vast library of techniques, rather than binding to a single one.

The Recommender uses the training UM to choose one of the available CF algorithms, to adopt at run-time, and properly tunes its parameters (e.g., similarity function). Deter-

[3] This reasoning applies for user-based KNN. Item-based KNN is not suitable for our domain, as it expresses any unknown rating for a $\langle$u,i$\rangle$ pair as a *weighted average* of the ratings already provided by u itself. Hence, it cannot predict any value outside the range already witnessed by u itself.

mining the best algorithm and its hyper-parameters, given a training set, is a challenge that falls beyond the domain of CF [3]. In our Recommender, we use an approach based on random-search [4] and n-fold cross-validation [6, 37, 62].

5.2 Controller: Bayesian Workload Exploration

The Controller uses Sequential Model-based Bayesian Optimization (SMBO) [37] to drive the profiling of incoming workloads, to quickly identify optimal TM configurations.

SMBO is a strategy for optimizing an unknown function $f : D \rightarrow \mathbb{R}$, whose estimation can only be obtained through (possibly noisy) observation of sampled values. It operates as follows: (i) evaluate the target function f at n initial points $x_1 \dots x_n$ and create a training set S with the resulting $\langle x_i, f(x_i) \rangle$ pairs; (ii) fit a probabilistic model M over S; (iii) use an *acquisition function* $a(M, S) \rightarrow D$ to determine the next point x_m; $iv)$ evaluate the function at x_m and accordingly update M; $v)$ repeat steps (ii) to $iv)$ until a stopping criterion is satisfied.

Acquisition function. Our Controller uses as acquisition function the criterion of *Expected Improvement (EI)* [40], which selects the next point to sample based on the gain that is expected with respect to the currently known optimal configuration. More formally, considering without loss of generality a minimization problem, let D_e be the set of evaluation points collected so far, D_u the set of possible points to evaluate in D and $x_{min} = \arg\min_{x \in D_u} f(x)$. Then the positive improvement function I over $f(x_{min})$ associated with sampling a point x is $I_{x_{min}}(x) = max\{f(x_{min} - f(x), 0\}$. Since f has not been evaluated on x, $I(x)$ is not known *a priori*; however, thanks to the predictive model M fitted over past observations, it is possible to obtain the expected value for the positive improvement:

$EI_{y(x_{min})}(x) = \mathbb{E}[I_{y(x_{min})}(x)] = \int_{-\infty}^{y(x_{min})} (f_{x_{min}} - c) p_M(c|x) dc.$

Here, $p_M(c|x)$ is the probability density function that the model M associates to possible outcomes of the evaluation of f at point x [40]. High EI values are associated either with points that are regarded by the model as likely to be the minimum (high predicted mean), or with points whose corresponding value of the target function the model is uncertain about (high predicted variance). By selecting as next point for evaluation the one that maximizes the EI, SMBO naturally balances exploitation and exploration: on one side it exploits model's confidence to sample the function at points that are supposedly good candidates to be the minimum; on the other, it explores zones of the search space for which the model is uncertain, to increase its predictive power by iteratively narrowing uncertainty zones.

Computing $\mathbf{p}_M(\mathbf{c}|\mathbf{x})$. The Controller computes $p_M(c|x)$ with an ensemble of CF predictors, and obtains predictive mean μ_x and variance σ_x^2 of $p(c|x)$ as frequentist estimates over the output of its individual predictors evaluated at x. It then models $p_M(c|x)$ as a Gaussian distribution $\sim N(\mu_x, \sigma_x^2)$. Assuming a Normal distribution for

Machine ID	Processor / Number of cores / RAM	HTM	RAPL
Machine A	1 Intel Haswell Xeon E3-1275 3.5GHz / 4 (8 hyper-threads) / 32 GB	Yes	Yes
Machine B	4 AMD Opteron 6172 2.1 Ghz / 48 / 32 GB	No	No

Table 2: Machines used in our experimental test-bed.

$p(c|x)$ is frequently done in SMBO [37] and other optimization techniques [50] to ensure tractability. Given a Gaussian distribution for $p_M(c|x)$, $EI_{y(x_{min})}(x)$ can be computed in closed form as $EI_{y(x_{min})}(x) = \sigma_x[u\Phi(u) + \phi(u)]$, where $u = \frac{y(x_{min}) - \mu_x}{\sigma_x}$ and Φ and ϕ represent, respectively, the probability density function and cumulative distribution function of a standard Normal distribution [40].

More in detail, the Controller builds a *bagging* ensemble [7] of k CF learners, each trained on a random subset of the training set. Then, it computes μ_x as the average of the values output by the single predictors, and σ_x^2 as their variance. In ProteusTM, we use 10 bagged models; the cost of employing them instead of a single one is negligible, mainly because they are only queried during profiling phases.

Stopping Criterion. As discussed, SMBO requires the definition of a predicate to stop exploring new configurations.

Our Controller uses a stopping criterion that seeks a balance between exploration and exploitation by relying on the notion of EI: it uses the estimated likelihood that additional explorations may lead to better configurations. More precisely, the exploration is terminated after k steps when: (i) the EI decreased in the last 2 iterations; (ii) the EI for the k-th exploration was marginal, i.e., lower than ϵ with respect to the current best sampled KPI; (iii) the relative performance improvement achieved in the $k-1$-th iteration did not exceed ϵ. In §6.3, we evaluate the effectiveness of this policy.

5.3 Monitor: Lightweight Behavior Change Detection

The Monitor periodically gathers KPIs from PolyTM. These are used for two tasks: (i) while profiling a new workload, they are fed to the Controller, providing feedback about the quality of the current configuration; (ii) at steady-state, they are used to detect a workload change. The Monitor implements the Adaptive CUSUM algorithm to detect, in a lightweight and robust way, deviations of the KPI from the mean value observed in recent time windows [2]. This allows the Monitor to detect both abrupt and smooth changes and to trigger a new profiling phase in our Controller. Note that environmental changes (e.g., inter-process contention or VM migration) are indistinguishable from workload changes from the perspective of our behavior change detection.

6. Evaluation

This section provides an extensive validation of our contributions. We introduce, in §6.1 the test-bed, applications, and accuracy metrics used. In §6.2 we assess the overhead incurred by PolyTM to provide self-tuning capabilities. In

Benchmark	Lines of Code	Atomic Blocks	Description
STAMP [9]	28803	35	Suite of **8** heterogeneous benchmarks with a variety of workloads (genomics, graphs, databases).
Data Structures	3702	12	Concurrent Red-Black Tree, Skip-List, Linked-List and Hash-Map with workloads varying contention and update ratio.
STMBench7 [32]	8623	45	Based on OO7 [10] with many heterogeneous transactions over a large and complex graph of objects.
TPC-C [63]	6690	5	OLTP workload with in-memory storage adapted to use one atomic block encompassing each transaction.
Memcached [58]	12693	120	Caching service with many short transactions that are used to read and update the cache coherently.

Table 1: TM applications used in our evaluation. These 15 benchmarks span a wide variety of workloads and characteristics.

Machine ID	TM Backend	# threads	HTM Abort Budget	HTM Capacity Abort Policy
Machine A	STMs and TSX [67]	1,2,3,4, 5,6,7,8	1,2,4, 8,16,20	Set budget to 0; decrease budget by 1; halve budget
Machine B	STMs	1,2,4,6, 8,16,32,48	N/A	N/A

Table 3: Parameters tuned by ProteusTM. STMs are TinySTM [29], SwissTM [27], NORec [15] and TL2 [22].

#threads	TL2	NOrec	Swiss	Tiny	HTM-opt	HTM-naive
1	3	3	2	3	3	14
4	<1	1	<1	3	3	14
8	<1	<1	<1	4	5	24

Table 4: Overhead (%) incurred by ProteusTM for different TM and # threads. Results are an average across ten runs.

Benchmark (Machine)	# Threads					
	1	2	4	8	16	32
TPC-C (Machine A)	21	91	213	3419	N/A	N/A
Memcached (Machine B)	2	8	28	145	1103	1849

Table 5: Reconfiguration (TM and #threads) latency (μsec).

§6.3, we evaluate the effectiveness of RecTM's components separately. Finally, in §6.4 we evaluate the ability of ProteusTM to perform optimization of dynamic workloads.

6.1 Experimental Test-Bed

We deployed ProteusTM in two machines with different characteristics (described in Table 2) and used a wide variety of TM applications (summarized in Table 1). We considered over 300 workloads, which are representative of heterogeneous applications, from highly to poorly scalable, from HTM to STM friendly [26]. Moreover, we tested three KPIs: execution time, throughput and EDP (Energy Delay Product, a popular energy efficiency metric [36]). We measure energy consumption via RAPL [17] (available on Machine A).

Our system optimizes the KPI by tuning the four dimensions listed in Table 3[4]. Overall, we consider a total of 130 TM configurations for Machine A and 32 for Machine B.

Evaluation metrics. We evaluate the performance of ProteusTM along 2 accuracy metrics: Mean Average Percentage Error (MAPE) and Mean Distance From Optimum (MDFO).

Noting $r_{u,i}$ the real KPI for workload u when running with i as configuration, $\widehat{r}_{u,i}$ the corresponding prediction of the Recommender, and S the set of testing $\langle u,i\rangle$ pairs, **MAPE** is defined as: $\sum_{\langle u,i\rangle \in S} |r_{u,i} - \widehat{r}_{u,i}|/r_{u,i}$.

Noting with i^*_u the optimal configuration for workload u and with $\widehat{i^*_u}$ the best configuration identified by the Recommender, the **MDFO** is: $\sum_{\langle u,\cdot\rangle \in S} |r_{u,i^*_u} - r_{u,\widehat{i^*_u}}|/r_{u,i^*_u}$.

MAPE reflects how well the CF learner predicts performance for an application. MDFO captures the quality of final recommendations output by the Recommender.

6.2 Overhead Analysis and Reconfiguration Latency

We now assess the overhead of PolyTM, i.e., the inherent steady-state cost of supporting adaptation. We compare the performance of a bare TM implementation T with that achieved by PolyTM using T without triggering adaptation.

Table 4 summarizes the results averaged across all benchmarks. The contention management for HTM is set to decrease linearly the retries starting from 5 (a common setting [41, 67]). We also show the overhead of the optimized code path, employed for HTM, and the one resulting from the default GCC instrumentation (fully instrumented path).

These experiments reveal overheads consistently $< 5\%$ across the TM backends. The lower STM overhead is justifiable considering that STMs natively suffer from instrumentation costs that end up amortizing most of the additional overhead introduced by PolyTM.

We also assess the average latency of a typical reconfiguration in PolyTM to switch TM algorithms (which also entails changing the number of threads). The results, shown in Table 5, encompass two heterogeneous workloads: Memcached uses $100\times$ shorter transactions than TPC-C. The results highlight the practicality of our reconfiguration. Even in the worst case of large transactions in TPC-C, the latency is small. In fact, this is only incurred during the exploration phase, which, as we shall see, is very short with ProteusTM.

6.3 Quality of the Prediction and Learning Processes

We now evaluate each of RecTM's components by means of a trace-driven simulation. We collected traces of *real* executions of a subset of the test cases (namely, STAMP and Data Structures), averaging the results over 5 runs.

The data-set was split into a training set (30%) and a test set (70%). The training set is used to choose and tune the CF

[4] ProteusTM also includes HybridTMs: we omit them as HybridTMs never outperformed STMs/HTMs (similarly to recent work [26]).

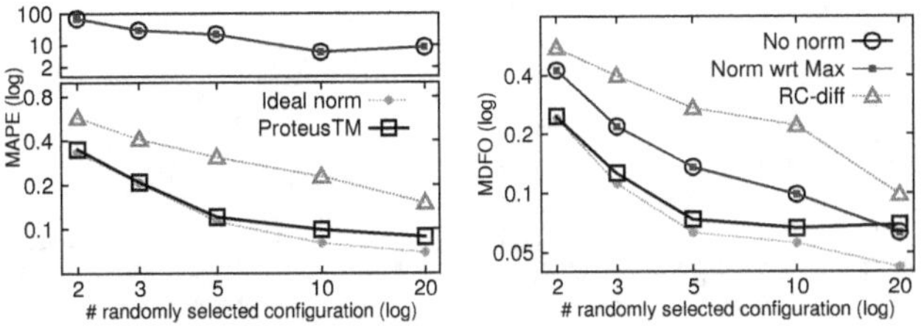

(a) MAPE, KNN Cosine (b) MDFO, KNN Cosine

Figure 4: Rating distillation for Exec. Time on Machine A.

algorithm (§5.1) and to instantiate the predictive model. We used 10 learners for the bagging ensemble, as this is a typical value [37, 62]. To simulate sampling the performance of the application in a given configuration, the corresponding value from the test set is inserted in the UM of the Recommender.

Rating distillation. We assess the effectiveness of the distillation function versus several UM preprocessing techniques: *(i) No normalization:* CF is applied on the UM containing raw KPI samples. This is equivalent to Quasar [21] (see §7); *(ii) Normalization w.r.t. max.:* entries in the UM are relative to the highest value, supposed to be known a priori. It resembles Paragon's approach [20] (see §7), where the machine's peak instructions/sec rate is used as normalizing constant; *(iii) Ideal normalization:* the scheme described in §5.1; *(iv) Row-column subtraction:* noted RC, is typically employed in CF to cope with biases in ratings [54]. It consists in removing from each known rating the average value of the corresponding row; then, the average value per column — computed after the first subtraction — is subtracted; *(v) Rating distillation:* used in ProteusTM (Algorithm 3).

For space constraint we show only a subset of results, focusing on execution time on Machine A with KNN and cosine similarity. We vary the number of *randomly chosen* known ratings per row and compute MAPE and MDFO.

Figure 4 shows that using no normalization, or normalization w.r.t. the maximum performs very poorly, both in terms of MAPE (Figure 4a) and MDFO (Figure 4b). That is because they are both performing a normalization with respect to some constant that has no meaning in the scope of the applications used. RC achieves lower MAPE than the two aforementioned normalizations, yet its accuracy is significantly worse than that of rating distillation, both in terms of MAPE and MDFO. Also, the approach of ProteusTM closely follows the ideal normalization. To ensure a fair comparison, we used the same training set, without forcing the presence of the column used for normalization among the profiled configurations for ProteusTM.

We have obtained other similar results, omitted due to space constraints, with other distance functions in KNN and MF (which is used by other proposals that rely on a RS for performance prediction, see §7) . Our results confirm the key role of rating distillation to enable the use of CF in the domain of performance prediction for TM applications.

Controller. We evaluate the effectiveness of our SMBO approach to the sampling of new workloads. We compare our solution (called EI) with a randomized sampling approach, used in Quasar and Paragon [20, 21] (see §7), and two other SMBO approaches using acquisition functions different from ours: Variance explores configurations with high uncertainty for the underlying model (i.e., high $variance/mean$ ratio); Greedy explores the configuration with highest predictive mean.

Our simulation proceeds in rounds: each one profiles the target workload on the reference configuration chosen by the rating distillation function; then the sampling phase begins. Afterwards, the Recommender produces a recommendation for the optimal configuration, noted $\hat{c^*}$. If such a configuration is explored, then the optimization is concluded; otherwise, a final exploration of $\hat{c^*}$ is performed. The final recommendation c^* is the one which, among those explored, yields the best performance. The MDFO is computed with c^* and the MAPE is an average of MAPEs computed per workload.

Due to space constraints we show only a subset of results. In Fig. 5a, we report the MDFO for EDP (on Machine A). The EI exploration policy is able to identify a high quality solution requiring, on average, less explorations than any competitor. Fig. 5b shows that the 80-th percentile of the DFO obtained by EI — after 5 explorations — is less than 10%. We highlight that the EDP KPI was the most challenging to optimize: hence, the latter result represents a lower bound on our accuracy.

In Fig. 5d, we show the MDFO when optimizing execution time (on Machine B): once again, our EI-based Controller's exploration performs best. Fig. 5c shows the MAPE per explorations. Interestingly, the Variance policy has the best *mean* prediction accuracy. However, as it does not aim at sampling potential optimal solutions, but only at reducing uncertainty, it does not learn the behavior of the target function for potentially good configurations. Thus, the quality of the recommended configurations is significantly worse than EI's (see Fig. 5d).

Finally, we compare our EI policy with random sampling in Figs. 5a and 5d: taking 5% distance as reference, EI achieves a number of explorations vs MDFO trade-off that is up to 4× better than its competitor. This highlights the effectiveness of our SMBO-based approach over simpler sampling techniques used in recent systems [20, 21] (see §7).

Stopping criterion. We now evaluate our stopping heuristic (§5.2), called *Cautious* (C in the plots). We compare it with a *Naive* stopping rule N that blindly trusts the model, by stopping explorations when the expected improvement over the best known configuration falls $< \epsilon$. The results are shown in Fig. 6, portraying the sensitivity of both heuristics to ϵ.

For any fixed ϵ, we observe that the Naive predicate consistently chooses a worse configuration than the one of our

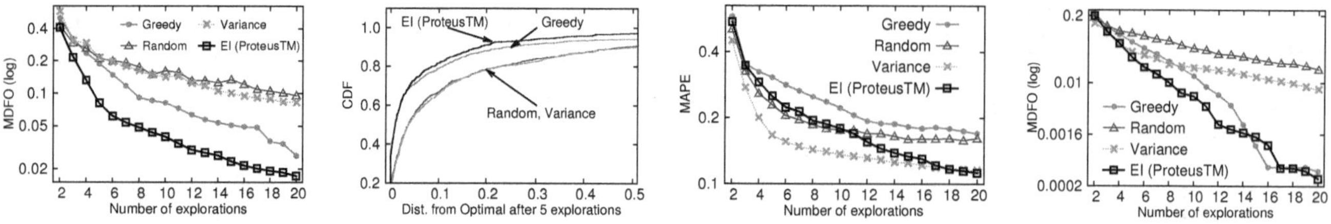

(a) MDFO for EDP (b) CDF of DFO for EDP (c) MAPE for Exec. Time (d) MDFO for Exec. Time

Figure 5: Controller's exploration policies for EDP on Machine A (left figures) and Exec. Time on Machine B (right figures).

Cautious heuristic: blindly trusting the predictive model results in an excessively eager policy, which does not provide the model with enough training data.

As expected, the plots also show that the lower ϵ, the lower the obtained MDFO. Notably, for $\epsilon = 0.01$, the Controller achieves, in 90% of the cases, MDFO of only 5% when considering execution time on and 12% when optimizing EDP. This comes at the price of a higher number of explorations. Although not shown for space constraints, we report that the Controller is able to keep this price very low, by requiring, on average, a similar number of explorations of a policy that performs a fixed amount of explorations and is tuned to deliver the same mean performance. This confirms the effectiveness of the Controller in determining the duration of the profiling, by striking a balanced trade-off between the extent of online exploration and final performance.

Comparison with ML approaches. We now compare ProteusTM with an approach based on the same technique proposed by Wang et. al [65] to automate the choice of the TM algorithm for a given workload. This approach relies on workload characterization data to train a ML-based classifier that is used to predict the best TM configuration for a given workload. The workload characterization uses 17 features: duration of transactions, data access patterns, data contention, etc. Wang et al. also uses static analysis to for other features, e.g., the number of atomic blocks. We did not perform this step but complemented it with contention management features. These are not considered by the authors, but we found them to be highly correlated with performance.

The simulation for ProteusTM evolves as explained above. For the ML competitor, instead, a workload is first profiled over a reference configuration (TinySTM, 4 threads) and then the ML is invoked to predict the best configuration. We then compute the MDFO for this chosen configuration.

We used 300 STAMP and Data Structures workloads, on Machine A, and split them randomly into training and test sets: 30-70 and 70-30 train-test splits. For ProteusTM, the training set is the UM of the selected workloads; for ML approaches, the training set is composed, for each workload, by the aforementioned features and the identifier of the best configuration as target class. The target KPI is throughput.

We consider 3 ML algorithms, implemented in Weka [33]: Decision Trees (CART), Support Vector Machines (SMO), and Artificial Neural Networks (MLP) [5]. Their parameters were chosen via random search optimization [4], which evaluated 100 combinations with cross-validation on the training set.

Fig. 7 reports the CDF of the DFO of each technique over 10 runs. The data shows the superiority of ProteusTM relatively to pure ML approaches. In particular, with 30% training set, ProteusTM already delivers a DFO of 1.6% against the 10% of the ML competitors, and a 90-th percentile of 3.5% against 25% of CART (the best alternative). Also, by increasing the training set to 70%, ProteusTM delivers a DFO of 1.3% and a 90-th percentile of 3%, against 6.8% DFO and 21% 90-th percentile of the best alternative (SMO).

We note that the DFO of ProteusTM is similar (both in mean and 90th percentile) in both cases, whereas ML

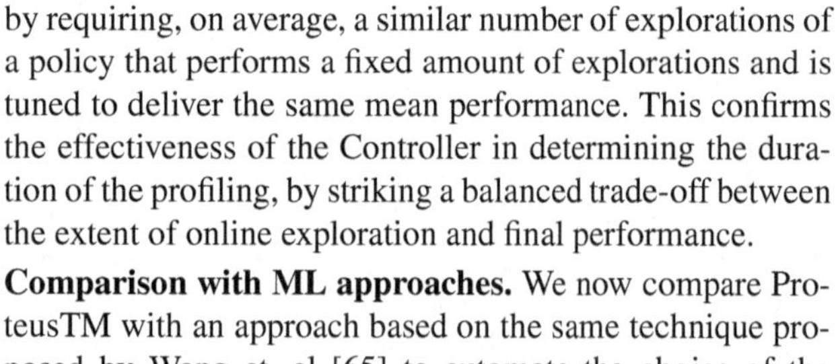

(a) MDFO for EDP, Machine A (b) MDFO for Exec time, Machine B

Figure 6: Comparing early-stop exploration predicates.

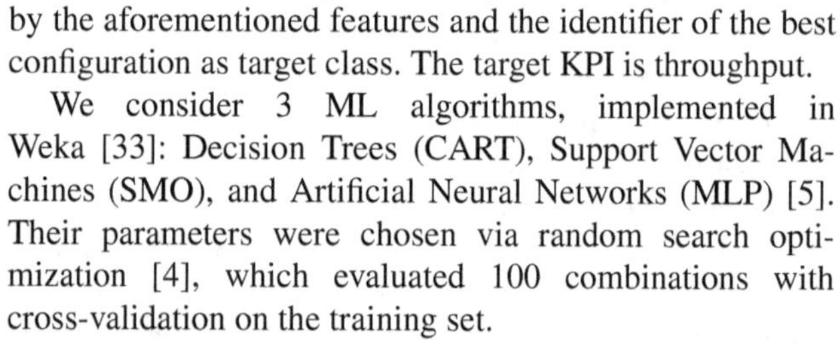

(a) 30% Training data used. (b) 70% Training data used.

Figure 7: Comparison of ProteusTM vs various Machine Learning based techniques.

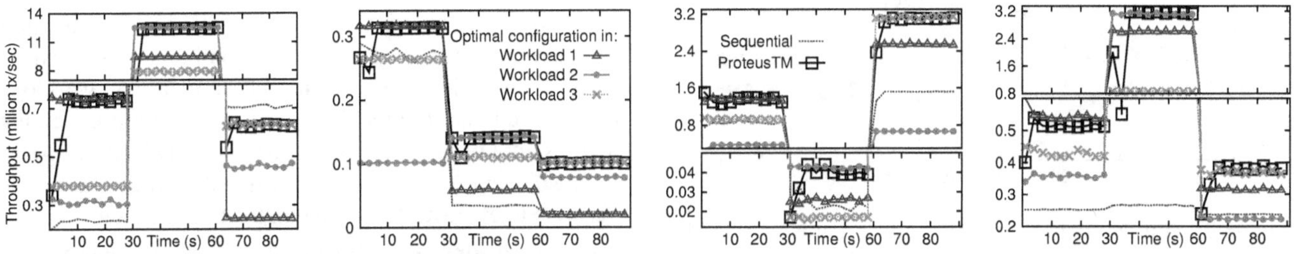

(a) Red-Black Tree (RBT) (b) STMBench7 (c) TPC-C (d) Memcached

Figure 8: Performance of four applications when their workload changes three times. We show the performance obtained with ProteusTM, and three additional fixed configurations, each one corresponding to an optimum in each workload.

greatly benefits from more training data. This difference is explained by the number of explorations used by ProteusTM in its profiling phase (with threshold $\epsilon = 0.01$): at 30% training, the 90th percentile number of explorations is 7, but this lowers to 6 with 70% training set. This means that ProteusTM delivers high accuracy also in presence of scarce training data, by autonomously exploring more.

Our evaluation suggests that detecting similarities on the KPI is more effective than statistically inferring relationships from training data. We argue that this depends on two, tightly intertwined, causes: (i) thanks to our novel normalization, using CF is more robust than ML, as it is based on *direct KPI observations*, rather than on *learning* the mapping of input to output features; (ii) the adaptive profiling phase proved to be more effective than a *one-shot* classification-based solution.

6.4 Online Optimization of Dynamic Workloads

In Fig. 8, we evaluate the ProteusTM system as a whole[5]: 2 TM benchmarks (Red-Black Tree and STMB7 [32]) and 2 TM ports of TPC-C [63] Memcached [58]. For each, we trigger 3 workloads chosen to exemplify contrasting performances. In each case, ProteusTM is totally oblivious of the target application: no workloads of the application are in its training set. This highlights the Recommender's ability to detect similarity patterns between the target workloads and the set of *disjoint* workloads used as training set. We set the Monitor period to 1 sec and the SMBO ϵ to 0.01. In each run, we measure the performance of (i) ProteusTM, (ii) the 3 configurations that perform best in each workload, (iii) the Best Fixed configuration on Average (BFA) across the workloads, and (iv) a Sequential non-instrumented execution.

We draw three conclusions: (i) ProteusTM is able to quickly identify, at runtime, configurations that are optimal or very close. Remarkably, ProteusTM delivers performance that is, on average, only 1% lower than the optimal; (ii) employing *any* of the baseline alternatives yields up to 2 orders of magnitude worse performance; (iii) thanks to our SMBO approach, the performance degradation when exploring is minimal (at most 7 explorations in these use cases). Such cost is usually amortized in long-running services (e.g., databases), in which workload shifts are infrequent [13].

[5] The source materials can be found in `https://github.com/nmldiegues/proteustm`.

Benchmark		Mean Distance from Optimum (MDFO %)			
		Optimal in Workload i			ProteusTM
Name	Workload (Opt Conf)	Opt 1	Opt 2	Opt 3	(explorations)
RBT	1 (NOrec: 7t)	0	137	93	**< 1** (4 expl)
Machine	2 ★ (HTM:8t Half-20)	33	0	71	**2** (4 expl)
A	3 (HTM: 4t GiveUp-4)	154	37	0	**< 1** (7 expl)
STMB7	1 (HTM: 4t Linear-2)	0	20	210	**2** (6 expl)
Machine	2 (Swiss: 4t)	135	0	28	**< 1** (4 expl)
A	3 ★ (TL2: 8t)	390	29	0	**< 1** (3 expl)
TPC-C	1 ★ (Tiny: 4t)	0	273	47	**< 1** (3 expl)
Machine	2(HTM:3t GiveUp-16)	68	0	152	**3** (4 expl)
A	3 (Tiny: 8t)	22	370	0	**< 1** (3 expl)
Memchd	1 ★ (Swiss: 32t)	0	50	26	**4** (3 expl)
Machine	2 (Tiny: 32t)	19	0	258	**< 1** (4 expl)
B	3 (Tiny: 4t)	18	66	0	**< 1** (3 expl)

Table 6: For each benchmark in Fig. 8, we show the MDFO of ProteusTM, each Optimal and BFA (★) configurations. Each workload is labeled with its optimal configuration.

A summary is provided in Table 6 where we list the optimal configurations in each workload. We also show the BFA (with ★) which is always also an optimal configuration in some workload. This data highlights the robustness of ProteusTM to optimize applications with diverse optimal configurations, in terms of TM algorithm (STMB7), parallelism degree (TPC-C) and HTM tuning (RBT and Memchd).

Finally, in Fig. 9, we confirm our claims of §5.3 by using a static TPC-C workload and varying external factors to the application to trigger behavior changes. To simulate these external changes we used the *stress* Unix tool with different configurations over periods of 30 seconds: it either created high CPU, memory or IO usage in each workload. The results are once again positive, in that ProteusTM performs close to the optimal configuration across all workloads.

7. Related work

Our work lies at the intersection of 3 major research fields: optimization of TM systems, performance prediction via RS, and experiment-driven optimization of computer systems.

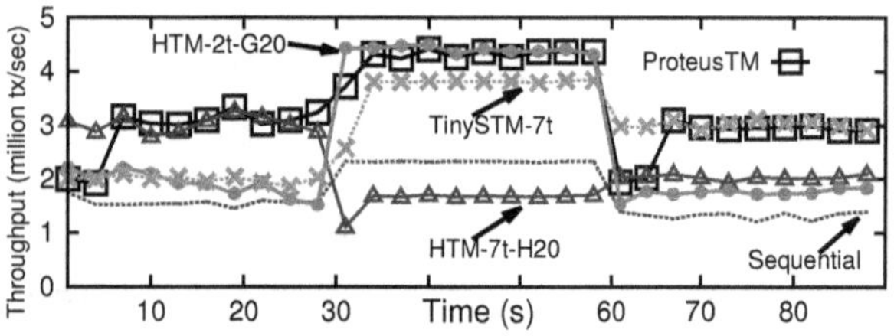

Figure 9: Similar to Fig. 8c, but with a static workload, varying instead the availability of machine resources.

Optimization of TM applications. The most researched problem in TM self-tuning is choosing the number of active threads. Proposed solutions rely on analytical modeling [60], off-line machine learning [59], or exploration-based strategies [24]. Wang et al. [65] use Artificial Neural Networks and programmer heuristics to determine the best TM for an application (excluding HTM). Workload characterization uses static analysis and runtime detailed profiling. Tuner [25] exploits hill climbing and reinforcement learning to adaptively determine the retry-on-abort policy for HTM.

These solutions optimize a single aspect of TM. Moreover, purely exploration-based solutions [24, 25] are impractical in high dimensional spaces, as the number of configurations to explore rapidly grows with the parameters to optimize. ProteusTM, instead, is effective in optimizing in a large space (we considered 130 configurations over 4 parameters). Thanks to the capability of CF techniques to deal with sparse information and to our model to steer online explorations, ProteusTM operates in even higher dimensional problems by simply including more configurations as extra columns of the UM.

In addition, all surveyed solutions need either preliminary code analysis or intrusive instrumentation for workload characterization. These add complexity to the code of TM algorithms and overhead to the application. ProteusTM, conversely, relies solely on profiling high-level KPIs, which incurs minimal overhead and maximizes portability. We stress that ProteusTM's work-flow is fully automated, avoiding the need for programmer heuristics [65]. Finally, ProteusTM avoids off-line training on the target application, unlike other ML approaches [59].

Performance prediction via Recommenders. To the best of our knowledge, Paragon [20], Quasar [21] and U-CHAMPION [53] are the only systems relying on RS for performance prediction, job scheduling and resource provisioning. In common, they characterize an incoming job via *random* sampling of a *fixed* number of configurations and then apply MF-based CF.

ProteusTM differs from these works in three key aspects: (i) it relies on a novel rating distillation function that identifies similarity patterns among the performances of heterogeneous applications (one noteworthy finding of our work is that this pre-processing step, not used in previous works, is of paramount importance to achieve high accuracy in the TM domain); (ii) ProteusTM leverages model-based techniques to determine which and how many configurations to experiment with during the sampling phase of a new workload (we showed that it outperforms random sampling), yielding lower sampling time and higher accuracy; (iii) it integrates both MF- and KNN-based CF, being able to determine the best one to employ, depending on the training data.

Experiment-driven optimization. The classic approach in this field is dynamic sampling: a performance model of the system is initialized, by evaluating its performance corresponding to some randomly chosen configurations; then, the next experiment to run is chosen according to the observations progressively collected [28, 50, 66, 68]. The proposal that is closest to ours is iTuned [28], which optimizes configuration parameters of a database for a target application. It exploits Gaussian processes [55] to build a performance model of the application and uses the EI acquisition function to choose the next experiment to run. However, iTuned does not use knowledge of previous the workloads: by leveraging CF, ProteusTM alleviates the need for the initial static sampling phase, and is able to perform accurate recommendations after a short online adaptive sampling phase.

8. Conclusions

We proposed ProteusTM, the first TM system with multi-dimensional self-tuning capabilities. ProteusTM has been integrated in GCC to expose a standard TM interface, which ensures full transparency, ease of use and portability. Together with this simple abstraction, we provide high performance by relying on a novel technique that leverages Collaborative Filtering and Bayesian Optimization.

Via an extensive evaluation based on a real-word application and well-known benchmarks, we demonstrated the ability ProteusTM to optimize heterogeneous applications in high-dimensional configuration spaces: ProteusTM achieves performance that are, on average, $< 3\%$ from optimum and gains up to $100\times$ relatively to static configurations.

As a final remark, we believe that the methodologies underlying the RecTMdesign could be applicable to optimize the self-tuning of broader and more generic classes of systems than just TM. In particular, its novel ability to normalize the data for the RS, together with the Bayesian-driven exploration of workloads to sample.

As a final remark, we believe that the methodologies underlying RecTM— namely, the techniques of rating distillation and the Bayesian approach to drive the workloads' sampling — can be used to optimize the self-tuning of a broader, more generic class of systems, than just TM.

Acknowledgements

This work was supported by Portuguese funds through Fundação para a Ciência e Tecnologia via projects UID/CEC/50021/2013 and EXPL/EEI-ESS/0361/2013.

References

[1] Allon Adir, Dave Goodman, Daniel Hershcovich, Oz Hershkovitz, Bryan Hickerson, Karen Holtz, Wisam Kadry, Anatoly Koyfman, John Ludden, Charles Meissner, Amir Nahir, Randall R. Pratt, Mike Schiffli, Brett St. Onge, Brian Thompto, Elena Tsanko, and Avi Ziv. Verification of Transactional Memory in POWER8. In *Proceedings of the Annual Design Automation Conference*, DAC, pages 1–6, 2014.

[2] Michèle Basseville and Igor V. Nikiforov. *Detection of Abrupt Changes: Theory and Application*. Prentice-Hall, Inc., Upper Saddle River, NJ, USA, 1993.

[3] James Bergstra, R. Bardenet, Yoshua Bengio, and Balázs Kégl. Algorithms for Hyper-Parameter Optimization. In *Proceedings of the Annual Conference on Neural Information Processing Systems*, NIPS, Granada, Spain, 2011.

[4] James Bergstra and Yoshua Bengio. Random search for hyper-parameter optimization. *J. Mach. Learn. Res.*, 13(1):281–305, February 2012.

[5] Christopher M. Bishop. *Pattern Recognition and Machine Learning*. Springer-Verlag New York, Inc., 2006.

[6] Christopher M. Bishop. *Pattern Recognition and Machine Learning*. 2007.

[7] Leo Breiman. Bagging predictors. *Mach. Learn.*, 24(2):123–140, August 1996.

[8] Eric Brochu, Vlad M Cora, and Nando de Freitas. A Tutorial on Bayesian Optimization of Expensive Cost Functions, with Application to Active User Modeling and Hierarchical Reinforcement Learning. eprint arXiv:1012.2599, arXiv.org, December 2010.

[9] Chi Cao Minh, JaeWoong Chung, Christos Kozyrakis, and Kunle Olukotun. STAMP: Stanford Transactional Applications for Multi-Processing. In *Proceedings of The IEEE International Symposium on Workload Characterization*, IISWC, 2008.

[10] Michael J. Carey, David J. DeWitt, and Jeffrey F. Naughton. The oo7 benchmark. *SIGMOD Rec.*, 22(2):12–21, June 1993.

[11] Calin Cascaval, Colin Blundell, Maged Michael, Harold W Cain, Peng Wu, Stefanie Chiras, and Siddhartha Chatterjee. Software transactional memory: why is it only a research toy? *Communications of the ACM*, 51(11):40–46, 2008.

[12] Mrcio Castro, LusFabrcioWanderley Ges, LuizGustavo Fernandes, and Jean-Franois Mhaut. Dynamic Thread Mapping Based on Machine Learning for Transactional Memory Applications. In *Proceedings of the European Conference on Parallel Processing*, Euro-Par, pages 465–476. 2012.

[13] Carlo Curino, Evan P.C. Jones, Samuel Madden, and Hari Balakrishnan. Workload-aware database monitoring and consolidation. In *Proceedings of the ACM International Conference on Management of Data*, SIGMOD, pages 313–324, 2011.

[14] Luke Dalessandro, François Carouge, Sean White, Yossi Lev, Mark Moir, Michael L. Scott, and Michael F. Spear. Hybrid NOrec: A Case Study in the Effectiveness of Best Effort Hardware Transactional Memory. In *Proceedings of the International Conference on Architectural Support for Programming Languages and Operating Systems*, ASPLOS, pages 39–52, 2011.

[15] Luke Dalessandro, Michael F. Spear, and Michael L. Scott. NOrec: Streamlining STM by Abolishing Ownership Records. In *Proceedings of the ACM SIGPLAN Symposium on Principles and Practice of Parallel Programming*, PPoPP, pages 67–78, 2010.

[16] Abhinandan S. Das, Mayur Datar, Ashutosh Garg, and Shyam Rajaram. Google news personalization: Scalable online collaborative filtering. In *Proceedings of the International Conference on World Wide Web*, WWW, pages 271–280, 2007.

[17] Howard David, Eugene Gorbatov, Ulf R. Hanebutte, Rahul Khanna, and Christian Le. RAPL: Memory Power Estimation and Capping. In *Proceedings of the ACM/IEEE International Symposium on Low Power Electronics and Design*, ISLPED, pages 189–194, 2010.

[18] Tudor David, Rachid Guerraoui, and Vasileios Trigonakis. Everything You Always Wanted to Know About Synchronization but Were Afraid to Ask. In *Proceedings of the ACM Symposium on Operating Systems Principles*, SOSP, pages 33–48, 2013.

[19] James Davidson, Benjamin Liebald, Junning Liu, Palash Nandy, Taylor Van Vleet, Ullas Gargi, Sujoy Gupta, Yu He, Mike Lambert, Blake Livingston, and Dasarathi Sampath. The YouTube Video Recommendation System. In *Proceedings of the ACM Conference on Recommender Systems*, RecSys, pages 293–296, 2010.

[20] Christina Delimitrou and Christos Kozyrakis. Paragon: QoS-aware Scheduling for Heterogeneous Datacenters. In *Proceedings of the Eighteenth International Conference on Architectural Support for Programming Languages and Operating Systems*, ASPLOS, pages 77–88, 2013.

[21] Christina Delimitrou and Christos Kozyrakis. Quasar: resource-efficient and QoS-aware cluster management. In *Proceedings of Architectural Support for Programming Languages and Operating Systems*, ASPLOS, pages 127–144, 2014.

[22] Dave Dice, Ori Shalev, and Nir Shavit. Transactional Locking II. In *Proceedings of the International Conference on Distributed Computing*, DISC, pages 194–208, 2006.

[23] David Dice, Yossi Lev, Mark Moir, and Daniel Nussbaum. Early experience with a commercial hardware transactional memory implementation. In *Proceedings of the International Conference on Architectural Support for Programming Languages and Operating Systems*, ASPLOS, pages 157–168, 2009.

[24] Diego Didona, Pascal Felber, Derin Harmanci, Paolo Romano, and Joerg Schenker. Identifying the Optimal Level of Parallelism in Transactional Memory Applications. *Computing Journal*, pages 1–21, December 2013.

[25] Nuno Diegues and Paolo Romano. Self-Tuning Intel Transactional Synchronization Extensions. In *Proceedings of the USENIX International Conference on Autonomic Computing*, pages 209–219, Philadelphia, PA, 2014.

[26] Nuno Diegues, Paolo Romano, and Luís Rodrigues. Virtues and Limitations of Commodity Hardware Transactional Memory. In *Proceedings of the International Conference on Parallel Architectures and Compilation*, PACT, pages 3–14, 2014.

[27] Aleksandar Dragojević, Rachid Guerraoui, and Michal Kapalka. Stretching Transactional Memory. In *Proceedings of the ACM SIGPLAN Conference on Programming Language Design and Implementation*, PLDI, pages 155–165, 2009.

[28] Songyun Duan, Vamsidhar Thummala, and Shivnath Babu. Tuning Database Configuration Parameters with iTuned. *PVLDB*, 2(1):1246–1257, 2009.

[29] Pascal Felber, Christof Fetzer, and Torvald Riegel. Dynamic Performance Tuning of Word-based Software Transactional Memory. In *Proc. of the ACM SIGPLAN Symposium on Principles and Practice of Parallel Programming*, PPoPP, pages 237–246, 2008.

[30] Rachid Guerraoui, Maurice Herlihy, and Bastian Pochon. Polymorphic Contention Management. In *Proceedings of the International Conference on Distributed Computing*, DISC, pages 303–323, 2005.

[31] Rachid Guerraoui, Maurice Herlihy, and Bastian Pochon. Toward a Theory of Transactional Contention Managers. In *Proceedings of the ACM Symposium on Principles of Distributed Computing*, PODC, pages 258–264, 2005.

[32] Rachid Guerraoui, Michal Kapalka, and Jan Vitek. STM-Bench7: A Benchmark for Software Transactional Memory. In *Proceedings of the ACM SIGOPS European Conference on Computer Systems*, EuroSys, pages 315–324, 2007.

[33] Mark Hall, Eibe Frank, Geoffrey Holmes, Bernhard Pfahringer, Peter Reutemann, and Ian H. Witten. The weka data mining software: An update. *SIGKDD Explor. Newsl.*, 11(1):10–18, November 2009.

[34] Tim Harris, James Larus, and Ravi Rajwar. *Transactional Memory, 2nd Edition.* Morgan and Claypool Publishers, 2nd edition, 2010.

[35] Maurice Herlihy and J. Eliot B. Moss. Transactional memory: Architectural support for lock-free data structures. In *Proceedings of the Annual International Symposium on Computer Architecture*, ISCA, pages 289–300, 1993.

[36] M. Horowitz, T. Indermaur, and R. Gonzalez. Low-power digital design. In *Proceedings of the IEEE Symposium on Low Power Electronics*, pages 8–11, Oct 1994.

[37] Frank Hutter, Holger H. Hoos, and Kevin Leyton-Brown. Sequential Model-based Optimization for General Algorithm Configuration. In *Proceedings of the International Conference on Learning and Intelligent Optimization*, LION, pages 507–523, 2011.

[38] Intel Corporation. Intel Transactional Memory Compiler and Runtime Application Binary Interface. `https://gcc.gnu.org/wiki/TransactionalMemory?action=AttachFile&do=get&target=Intel-TM-ABI-1\_1\_20060506.pdf`, 2009.

[39] Christian Jacobi, Timothy Slegel, and Dan Greiner. Transactional Memory Architecture and Implementation for IBM System Z. In *Proceedings of the Annual nternational Symposium on Microarchitecture*, MICRO, pages 25–36, 2012.

[40] Donald R. Jones, Matthias Schonlau, and William J. Welch. Efficient Global Optimization of Expensive Black-Box Functions. *Journal of Global Optimization*, 13(4):455–492, December 1998.

[41] T. Karnagel, R. Dementiev, R. Rajwar, K. Lai, T. Legler, B. Schlegel, and W. Lehner. Improving in-memory database index performance with Intel Transactional Synchronization Extensions. In *Proceedings of the IEEE International Symposium on High Performance Computer Architecture*, pages 476–487, 2014.

[42] Andi Kleen. Scaling existing lock-based applications with lock elision. *Commun. ACM*, 57(3):52–56, March 2014.

[43] Per-Ake Larson, Spyros Blanas, Cristian Diaconu, Craig Freedman, Jignesh M. Patel, and Mike Zwilling. High-performance Concurrency Control Mechanisms for Main-memory Databases. *Proceedings of the VLDB Endownment*, 5(4):298–309, December 2011.

[44] Yossi Lev, Mark Moir, and Dan Nussbaum. Phtm: Phased transactional memory. In *Workshop on Transactional Computing (Transact)*, 2007.

[45] Greg Linden, Brent Smith, and Jeremy York. Amazon.Com Recommendations: Item-to-Item Collaborative Filtering. *IEEE Internet Computing*, 7(1):76–80, January 2003.

[46] Daniel Lupei, Bogdan Simion, Don Pinto, Matthew Misler, Mihai Burcea, William Krick, and Cristiana Amza. Transactional Memory Support for Scalable and Transparent Parallelization of Multiplayer Games. In *Proceedings of the ACM SIGOPS European Conference on Computer Systems*, EuroSys, pages 41–54, 2010.

[47] Alexander Matveev and Nir Shavit. Reduced Hardware Transactions: A New Approach to Hybrid Transactional Memory. In *Proceedings of the Annual ACM Symposium on Parallelism in Algorithms and Architectures*, SPAA, pages 11–22, 2013.

[48] Adam Morrison and Yehuda Afek. Fast Concurrent Queues for x86 Processors. In *Proceedings of the ACM SIGPLAN Symposium on Principles and Practice of Parallel Programming*, PPoPP, pages 103–112, 2013.

[49] Yang Ni, Adam Welc, Ali-Reza Adl-Tabatabai, Moshe Bach, Sion Berkowits, James Cownie, Robert Geva, Sergey Kozhukow, Ravi Narayanaswamy, Jeffrey Olivier, Serguei Preis, Bratin Saha, Ady Tal, and Xinmin Tian. Design and Implementation of Transactional Constructs for C/C++. In *Proceedings of the ACM SIGPLAN Conference on Object-oriented Programming Systems Languages and Applications*, OOPSLA, pages 195–212, 2008.

[50] Takayuki Osogami and Sei Kato. Optimizing System Configurations Quickly by Guessing at the Performance. In *Proceedings of the ACM SIGMETRICS International Conference on Measurement and Modeling of Computer Systems*, SIGMETRICS, pages 145–156, 2007.

[51] Sean Owen, Robin Anil, Ted Dunning, and Ellen Friedman. *Mahout in Action.* Manning Publications Co., Greenwich, CT, USA, 2011.

[52] Victor Pankratius and Ali-Reza Adl-Tabatabai. Software Engineering with Transactional Memory Versus Locks in Practice. *Theor. Comp. Sys.*, 55(3):555–590, October 2014.

[53] Eric Pettijohn, Yanfei Guo, Palden Lama, and Xiaobo Zhou. User-Centric Heterogeneity-Aware MapReduce Job Provisioning in the Public Cloud. In *Proceedings of the Inter-*

national Conference on Autonomic Computing, ICAC, pages 137–143, 2014.

[54] Anand Rajaraman and Jeffrey David Ullman. *Mining of Massive Datasets*. Cambridge University Press, 2011.

[55] Carl Edward Rasmussen and Christopher K. I. Williams. *Gaussian Processes for Machine Learning*. The MIT Press, 2005.

[56] Carl Ritson and Frederick Barnes. An Evaluation of Intel's Restricted Transactional Memory for CPAs. In *Proceedings of Communicating Process Architectures*, CPA, pages 271–292, 2013.

[57] Christopher J. Rossbach, Owen S. Hofmann, and Emmett Witchel. Is Transactional Programming Actually Easier? *SIGPLAN Not.*, 45(5):47–56, January 2010.

[58] Wenjia Ruan, Trilok Vyas, Yujie Liu, and Michael Spear. Transactionalizing Legacy Code: An Experience Report Using GCC and Memcached. In *Proceedings of the International Conference on Architectural Support for Programming Languages and Operating Systems*, ASPLOS, pages 399–412, New York, NY, USA, 2014. ACM.

[59] Diego Rughetti, Pierangelo Di Sanzo, Bruno Ciciani, and Francesco Quaglia. Machine learning-based self-adjusting concurrency in software transactional memory systems. In *Proceedings of the 2012 IEEE 20th International Symposium on Modeling, Analysis and Simulation of Computer and Telecommunication Systems*, MASCOTS '12, pages 278–285, Washington, DC, USA, 2012. IEEE Computer Society.

[60] Pierangelo Di Sanzo, Francesco Del Re, Diego Rughetti, Bruno Ciciani, and Francesco Quaglia. Regulating Concurrency in Software Transactional Memory: An Effective Model-based Approach. In *Proceedings of the IEEE International Conference on Self-Adaptive and Self-Organizing Systems*, SASO, pages 31–40, 2013.

[61] Xiaoyuan Su and Taghi M. Khoshgoftaar. A survey of collaborative filtering techniques. *Adv. in Artif. Intell.*, 2009:4:2–4:2, January 2009.

[62] Chris Thornton, Frank Hutter, Holger H. Hoos, and Kevin Leyton-Brown. Auto-WEKA: Combined Selection and Hyperparameter Optimization of Classification Algorithms. In *Proceedings of the ACM SIGKDD International Conference on Knowledge Discovery and Data Mining*, KDD, pages 847–855, 2013.

[63] TPC Council. TPC-C Benchmark. `http://www.tpc.org/tpcc`, 2011.

[64] Stephen Tu, Wenting Zheng, Eddie Kohler, Barbara Liskov, and Samuel Madden. Speedy Transactions in Multicore In-memory Databases. In *Proceedings of the ACM Symposium on Operating Systems Principles*, SOSP, pages 18–32, 2013.

[65] Qingping Wang, Sameer Kulkarni, John Cavazos, and Michael Spear. A Transactional Memory with Automatic Performance Tuning. *ACM Trans. Archit. Code Optim.*, 8(4):54:1–54:23, January 2012.

[66] Bowei Xi, Zhen Liu, Mukund Raghavachari, Cathy H. Xia, and Li Zhang. A Smart Hill-climbing Algorithm for Application Server Configuration. In *Proceedings of the International Conference on World Wide Web*, WWW, pages 287–296, 2004.

[67] Richard M. Yoo, Christopher J. Hughes, Konrad Lai, and Ravi Rajwar. Performance evaluation of Intel Transactional Synchronization Extensions for High-performance Computing. In *Proceedings of the International Conference for High Performance Computing, Networking, Storage and Analysis*, pages 1–19. ACM, 2013.

[68] Wei Zheng, Ricardo Bianchini, G. John Janakiraman, Jose Renato Santos, and Yoshio Turner. JustRunIt: Experiment-based Management of Virtualized Data Centers. In *Proceedings of the Conference on USENIX Annual Technical Conference*, ATC, pages 18–18, Berkeley, CA, USA, 2009. USENIX Association.

CSR: Core Surprise Removal in Commodity Operating Systems

Noam Shalev[†] Eran Harpaz[†] Hagar Porat[†] Idit Keidar[†] Yaron Weinsberg[*]

Technion, Israel Institute of Technology[†]
IBM Research, Israel[*]

{noams,seharpaz,hagarp}@campus.technion.ac.il idish@ee.technion.ac.il yaron@il.ibm.com

Abstract

One of the adverse effects of shrinking transistor sizes is that processors have become increasingly prone to hardware faults. At the same time, the number of cores per die rises. Consequently, core failures can no longer be ruled out, and future operating systems for many-core machines will have to incorporate fault tolerance mechanisms.

We present CSR, a strategy for recovery from unexpected permanent processor faults in commodity operating systems. Our approach overcomes surprise removal of faulty cores, and also tolerates cascading core failures. When a core fails in user mode, CSR terminates the process executing on that core and migrates the remaining processes in its run-queue to other cores. We further show how hardware transactional memory may be used to overcome failures in critical kernel code. Our solution is scalable, incurs low overhead, and is designed to integrate into modern operating systems. We have implemented it in the Linux kernel, using Haswell's Transactional Synchronization Extension, and tested it on a real system.

Categories and Subject Descriptors D.4.7 [*Operating Systems*]: Organization and Design

General Terms Design, Reliability

Keywords Operating Systems, Transactional Memory, Reliability, Hotplug, Core Surprise Removal, CSR.

1. Introduction

In today's economies of scale, which rely upon adding more and more servers with cheaper hardware, the observation that failures are the norm rather than the exception [11, 24] has become a guiding light for system designers. Nowadays, constant monitoring, fault tolerance, and automatic recovery are an integral part of any large cloud or data-center system. However, these are mostly focused on machine failures rather than low-level hardware failures such as processor faults.

At the same time, the number of cores per chip constantly increases. Modern consumer machines already contain 32 cores, data center servers include more than 60 cores per machine, while tera-devices with hundreds or even a thousand fault-prone cores are the subject of active research [25, 70]. This was made possible due to constant shrinking in transistor size and voltage supply. However, with hardware shrinking, the probability of physical flaws on the chip significantly rises [8, 16], and chances for processor faults become substantial [66]. With many tens or even hundreds of cores per chip, core failures can no longer be ruled out. Recent studies show that, even on consumer machines, hardware faults are not rare [52], and memory errors are currently dominated by hard errors, rather than soft-errors [63]. We therefore believe that, with technology advances, tolerating failures of individual cores shall become inevitable.

Current operating systems, including Linux and Windows, crash in the face of any permanent core fault and most chip-originated soft errors. As we explain later, the reason for the crash lies in the various kernel mechanisms that require the collaboration of the faulty core. Thus, the failure of a single core, out of hundreds in the foreseeable future, brings down the entire system. Cloud systems, for example, usually consolidate multiple virtual machines on a single server in order to improve its utilization [7, 39, 43, 61, 65]. In such settings, the failure of a single core crashes all the VMs running on the server.

Our goal in this work is to fortify existing operating systems against unexpected core failures, and in particular, allow processes – and VMs – on other cores to operate without interruption. We further elaborate on our goals and design considerations in Section 2.

In Section 3, we present *CSR*, a strategy for overcoming *Core Surprise Removal* in commodity operating systems. CSR is designed for multi-core architectures with reliable shared memory, and incurs virtually no overhead when the

ASPLOS '16, April 2–6, 2016, Atlanta, Georgia, USA.

http://dx.doi.org/10.1145/2872362.2872369

system is correct. Its primary objective is to keep the system alive and running after a core crash, while terminating at most the one user program that had been running on the faulty core. Recovery from that user program's failure can be handled, e.g., using checkpointing mechanisms [20], by application developers, and is out of this work's scope.

CSR's basic fault recovery function overcomes all core failures that happen when the faulty core is either in user-mode or executing non-critical kernel code. In order to cope with failures inside kernel critical sections, we propose in Section 4 a complementary technique based on *lock elision* using *Hardware Transactional Memory (HTM)* [31, 57], which is already incorporated in modern commodity processors [15, 77] and HPC systems [71]. In addition, CSR has a modular design, and it employs deferred execution of the recovery process in order to minimize the vulnerability to cascading failure scenarios, as discussed in Section 5.

In Section 6 we provide a proof-of-concept implementation of CSR in version 3.14.1 of the Linux kernel. We further exemplify the use of Haswell's HTM support[1] for recovery from failures in critical kernel code. HTM prevents critical sections' intermediate values from being written to shared memory, thus avoiding inconsistent states following a crash.

In Section 7, we evaluate CSR via three different experiments. First, we use a virtualized environment to inject thousands of permanent failures at random times. Since our emulated VM does not support HTM, we run CSR in this experiment without using HTM protection for critical kernel sections. We show that, while an unmodified kernel persistently fails, CSR successfully recovers from all failures occurring in user or idle mode, and in roughly 70% of the faults injected during execution of kernel code.

Next, we inject permanent core failures on real systems, during the execution of a hundred different critical and non-critical kernel functions. In these experiments, we use CSR with lock elision, and it successfully recovers from 100% of the faults. Finally, we build a fault-resistant cloud setting by installing CSR on the host OS of a 64-core server over which multiple virtual machines run unmodified Ubuntu. We show that following a core fault, only one VM crashes, while the others resume normal execution.

To conclude, our contributions in this work are:

1. We present CSR, a strategy for overcoming permanent core failures.
2. We propose using HTM for tolerating processor faults that happen during execution of critical kernel code.
3. We implement CSR in Linux, as well as a proof of concept for using HTM for recovery.
4. We evaluate CSR by injecting numerous faults on real and virtualized environments.

[1] The recently found erratum in Intel-TSX instructions did not affect our experiments. Our work comprises a prototype, and the concept of using HTM for our purposes shall remain applicable in future technologies.

2. Design Considerations

We design CSR to overcome core failures, whereby a core stops working without advance notice. Our goal is to take a system from an arbitrary state induced by a failure to a *recovered* state, where the following holds: (1) Interrupts are routed to online cores only. (2) All threads, as well as all types of delayed kernel tasks, are affined to online cores only. (3) All kernel services and subsystems operate using only online cores.

In this section we first argue that core failures merit a different treatment from CPU Hot-Plugging (Section 2.1), and then detail our failure model (Section 2.2) and the extent to which we can overcome failures in kernel code (Section 2.3).

2.1 Why Not CPU Hotplug?

Modern commodity operating systems usually include a *CPU Hotplug* [50, 51] mechanism, which allows one to dynamically plug or unplug a core. Ideally, we would like to simply unplug a faulty core once a failure is detected. However, there is a profound difference between voluntary CPU unplugging and on-line removal of a faulty core: CPU unplugging can use the cooperation of the victim core, thus enabling a completely supervised removal process, including choosing the correct moment to commence the removal, asking the victim core to perform some local tasks, and reading the values stored in its registers. In contrast, a failure can happen any time, depriving the crashed core of the ability to communicate, and leaving its buffers' and registers' contents unknown. The latter suggests that it is impossible to know what the core was doing at the moment of the failure.

2.2 Fault Model

We consider cores prone to *permanent faults* [55] – irreversible physical faults that cause consistent failure. This captures cases such as permanently open or shortcut transistors, slow components that cause timing violations, or a partially burned-out chip [56].

CSR ensures recovery from failures that happen while the faulty core executes in user-mode; other cores can be either in kernel or user mode. Failures in kernel code are partially handled, as we discuss in Section 2.3. CSR is only concerned with the system's survival, whereas application-level recovery is out of scope.

When dealing with core failures, one has to define their scope, namely, which hardware components are affected by the failure. Some designs of future many-core machines [25, 72, 73] assume that the entire internal state of a faulty core (including registers and buffers) may be flushed upon failure. We do not require this in this paper, but rather allow a core's internal state (buffers and registers) to remain unavailable following a crash. We do, however, assume that core malfunction does not destroy its cache. Hence, following a core's failure, it is possible to flush its private cache.

We use such a flush in order to ensure kernel data consistency in the following scenario: a kernel thread updates some OS data structure; next, the core switches to user code, but the changes it had made to kernel data have propagated from its local cache to the shared memory only partially; then the core fails. If one wishes to forgo triggering a cache flush following failure without sacrificing consistency, other solutions are possible. For example, one can configure kernel pages as non-cacheable, or flush the cache in kernel-to-user mode transitions. Note that fault-tolerant cache technologies are currently emerging [33, 42], and it is not unlikely that future caches will provide fault-tolerance features.

For detecting failures and triggering the recovery process, we assume the existence of a reliable *Failure Detection Unit (FDU)*. This can be implemented in hardware, using heartbeats and Machine Check Architecture [2, 32, 37], as suggested in previous works [21, 72, 73]. Upon fault detection, the FDU (1) halts the faulty core, thus preventing it from corrupting shared memory; (2) triggers a flush of its private cache; and (3) reports the error to the OS. Note that a hardware-based FDU implementation can easily provide these requirements. In this work, we simulate the FDU in software using heartbeats (see Section 6.1).

Given such an FDU, we design our core surprise removal strategy to cope with a *fail-stop* [62] model. Namely, a faulty core simply stops executing from some point onward.

CSR is designed for operating systems running on multicore architectures with reliable shared memory. Memory failures are typically addressed using other, complementary, mechanisms, such as error-correcting codes and relocating data [13, 60, 76]. By building upon reliable shared memory, we forgo the need for checkpointing.

2.3 Failures in Kernel Code

Unlike a failure in user-mode, certain failures in kernel-mode might be impossible to recover from by simply terminating the running thread. For example, failure during execution of a critical section might lead to data inconsistency. Failures in kernel code also include *cascading failure* scenarios, whereby the core that executes the recovery procedure crashes before completing the recovery process.

We address kernel-mode failures in two complementary ways: First, we design our algorithm to withstand cascading failures, while striving to minimize the time interval during which a cascading failure may interfere with an ongoing core removal. To this end, we use a strategy of queueing work for later execution. This allows us to migrate the recovery work to other cores in case the core that executes the recovery also fails.

Second, we propose the use of HTM for executing kernel critical sections. This prevents propagation of partial updates resulting from unfinished execution of critical sections to the shared memory. Recall that upon failure detection, the FDU triggers a flush of the faulty core's cache; here, we assume that the system does not flush uncommitted values.

We note that our proposed solution to failures in kernel code is a best-effort one. It guarantees recovery from failures during execution of code that does not access hardware different from RAM, and therefore can be protected with a transaction. Moreover, there are instructions that cannot be executed transactionally, such as a TLB flush, accessing a control register, an IO operation, etc. [36]. We cannot guarantee recovery from failures during execution of code sections containing such instructions.

3. Core Surprise Removal

The current section presents the heart of CSR's recovery approach, and focuses on the common case – failure during execution of user-code or non-critical kernel code. The next section addresses failures during critical kernel code, and in Section 5 we discuss cascading failures.

3.1 Background: OS Mechanisms Used

Our solution utilizes a few common facilities that exist in modern operating systems. We begin with some background and discuss the relevant aspects of these kernel mechanisms.

3.1.1 Deferrable Functions

Operating systems usually support multiple types of delayed tasks for performing work with different urgencies and execution contexts. For readability, we use the Linux terminology for the different delayed tasks types. CSR employs two types of delayed kernel tasks:

Tasklets [47] (Deferred Procedure Calls in Windows), which have three important properties: (1) They always run in interrupt context, and as a consequence, are unable to sleep or block. (2) A tasklet always executes on the core that schedules it. (3) The kernel services all pending tasklets immediately after handling all pending hardware interrupts.

Work-queues [47] (Asynchronous Procedure Calls in Windows), which, in contrast to tasklets, are executed by kernel threads in user context, and therefore are allowed to sleep or block. Furthermore, a work-queue may be bound to a specific processor, or may be unbound, in which case it can be executed by any core.

3.1.2 CPU States and Hotplug

Operating systems manage the state of all cores. For example, Linux uses bitmaps, dubbed *CPU masks*, for each possible state. Each CPU mask represents one state, and contains one bit per core. These masks are accessed globally and used by the kernel in various cases, such as for iterating over per-core data structures.

Linux, for example, defines, among others, an *online* state and an *offline* state. An offline core is not available for scheduling and does not receive or handle interrupts; it is in deep sleep mode, and consumes low power. A core's state can be dynamically changed between online and offline by using the CPU Hotplug mechanism. The CPU Hotplug

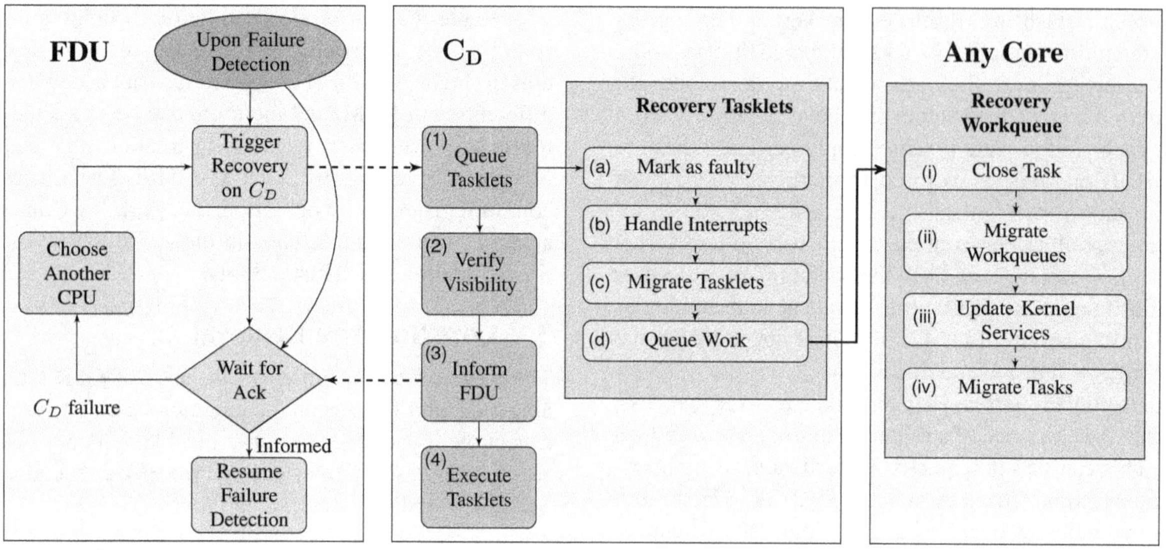

(a) Failure Detection Unit flow. (b) Recovery procedure on recovery core C_D. (c) Delayed tasks, execute on any core.

Figure 1: Recovery flow chart. Dashed lines represent message passing; solid lines represent flow.

feature has various uses [4, 51]. However, as explained in Section 2.1, CPU Hotplug cannot be used for disabling a faulty core, as it does not consider any reliability issues.

3.2 CSR Data Structures

We augment the kernel with two new data structures. First, we define a new processor state, *faulty*, and a corresponding global CPU mask, *faulty_mask*. This mask is the first to be updated upon processor failure, and, as its name suggests, indicates which cores in the system are in a faulty state. The faulty state serves two purposes at two different time intervals:

- While the system is not in a recovered state, namely, following a failure and before CSR's removal procedure has completed, the corresponding bit in the *faulty_mask* indicates to kernel code that hasn't yet adjusted to the failure to treat this core as unavailable for scheduling, migration, updating its data structures, etc.
- After the removal procedure finishes, a core marked as faulty is treated by the kernel as offline, with the exception that it is not permitted to come back online.

Second, we add a new globally accessed work-queue, *recovery-workqueue (RWQ)*. This work-queue is not bound to any processor, namely, different processors can pull its work items and execute them. We use RWQ to defer execution of certain recovery functions to a later time and a different execution context, in order to shorten the time interval during which a cascading failure may require re-execution of the recovery process. Functions queued to this work-queue are less urgent or might need to sleep, and so they are not queued as tasklets.

3.3 Failure Detection Unit

The FDU's operation is shown in Figure 1(a). When a failure is detected, the FDU invokes CSR's *recovery procedure* on a designated non-faulty online core, denoted C_D, which in turn handles the crash. The selection of C_D prefers cores that reside in a different socket in order to reduce the probability for a cascading failure. The ensuing flow in C_D, depicted in Figure 1(b), is described is Section 3.4 below.

After invoking the recovery process on the designated core, the FDU waits for an ack. Meanwhile, if the FDU detects a cascading failure of C_D, it invokes the recovery algorithm again, on another processor, for handling both the first failure and the new one. Once the FDU receives an ack from the designated core, it considers the recovery process done, and resumes normal operation with the faulty core, C_F, removed from the available processors list.

Note that this ack does not function as a keep-alive message. Its purpose is to notify the FDU that the recovery process has reached a point from which its completion is guaranteed; in case of a cascading failure before that point, the FDU cannot know what stages C_D completed before the failure.

3.4 Recovery Procedure

3.4.1 High Level Operation

C_D begins the recovery procedure, as presented in Figure 1(b). C_D's role consists of four primary steps: (1) First, it enqueues four new tasklets for repairing the system's state. These include Hotplug-like operations of modifying CPU masks, resetting interrupt affinities, and migrating tasklets from the removed core, as well as recovery-specific actions that address the surprise nature of the removal. The tasklets are only queued at this point, and are not executed yet. Queuing the tasklets rather than executing them reduces the time interval during which a cascading failure of C_D causes re-execution of the recovery process. (2) Next, C_D takes actions that assure the visibility of the tasklets to the rest of the cores (e.g., flush its write buffer). Once they are visible, other cores can steal them, and so the recovery operation is guaranteed to complete. (3) At this point, C_D sends an ack to the FDU. (4) Subsequently, C_D naturally turns to execute the tasklets found in its tasklets queue in FIFO order, as part of the kernel's normal behavior.

3.4.2 Recovery Work

Recovery Tasklets. The actual core removal process begins with the execution of four tasklets (depicted in the grey box in Figure 1(b)), which we subsequently call *recovery tasklets*. They perform the following:

(a) The first tasklet marks C_F's state as faulty in the corresponding CPU mask. Once a core is marked as faulty, kernel services will treat it as if it is out of the online map. Namely, no tasks will be scheduled or migrated to its run queue, iterations on various CPU masks will skip it, etc. The longer this step's execution gets postponed, the further the system might diverge from a recovered state, e.g., new tasks might get attached to C_F's run-queue.

(b) The next tasklet deals with interrupts. Modern operating systems use SMP IRQ affinity to assign interrupts to specific cores – this means that interrupts that were affined to the faulty core might have been lost. Therefore, to minimize the time interval during which interrupts can be lost, we reset their affinities early in the recovery process.

Next, we deal with interrupts that may have been lost. The loss of an interrupt can cause errors in software components that depend on its arrival. For example, a lost interrupt originating in the NIC may prevent network packets from being delivered to an application. Even worse, a lost Inter-Processor Interrupt (IPI) might prevent imperative kernel procedures from being executed and possibly crash the system. To recover from possible interrupt loss, we send spurious interrupts for all interrupt types that were previously routed to C_F (a technique that was employed in previous Linux versions). In addition, we check if any of the pending functions in C_F's IPI queue need to be migrated, and migrate those that do.

(c) The third tasklet migrates tasklets that are attached to C_F. This has to be performed urgently for two main reasons: first, tasklets embody high priority kernel work that is important to system maintenance and functionality. The second reason lies in our support for cascading failures, as we explain in Section 5 below.

(d) The last tasklet queues additional work that is essential to the recovery process but cannot run in interrupt context, or can endure a short delay in its execution. We divide this work into a number of functions, which we queue to our recovery-workqueue. This work will be executed later by dedicated kernel threads. Most of the work items queued at this step are needed in every operating system, but some of them are OS-dependent.

Queued Work. The following work-items are queued:

(i) Close the running task. We close the task that was running on C_F at the moment of the failure and free its resources. Since we are unable to communicate with C_F, significant data such as the instruction pointer and the register file content is lost. Therefore, we cannot recover the running application's state. It is possible to recover from such failures using a checkpointing mechanism, which could be done at application level.

(ii) Migrate work-queues affined to C_F. As in the tasklets case, we migrate work-items from the work-queues affined to C_F for later execution on other cores.

(iii) Update kernel services. This step is OS-dependent. Here, we update kernel services that might be affected by the sudden departure of C_F from the online map, such as performance events, synchronization services, and memory allocation.

(iv) Migrate C_F's tasks. User processes and kernel threads that were attached to the run-queue of C_F at the moment of the failure will usually still be there (unless the load balancer moved some of them); these must be migrated to other run-queues. The target run-queues for migrated tasks can be chosen in a variety of ways, but this choice is inconsequential as it only has a short-term effect – until the load-balancer kicks in. For the sake of simplicity, CSR moves these threads to the run-queue of the lowest-id correct core, leaving it up to the load-balancing mechanism to correct the overload that might be temporarily formed at the target core.

As in a regular CPU-unplug process, the migration of the run-queue is performed at the end of the removal process, as it does not affect system correctness. Its delay only blocks the execution of the tasks in C_F's run-queue until the end of the recovery process.

It is worth pointing out that CSR's recovery process subsumes the set of recovery actions performed by CPU-Hotplug. Specifically, the following steps are common, at least partially, to both CSR and CPU-Hotplug: (b), (c), (ii), (iii), and (iv). Nevertheless, tasks that perform analogous logical roles in both mechanisms differ in their implementation and order of execution, as CPU Hotplug exploits the cooperation of the unplugged core, and CSR cannot. After the execution of all the above, the system is again in a correct state, as all actions that would have been needed by a hot-unplug operation have been performed.

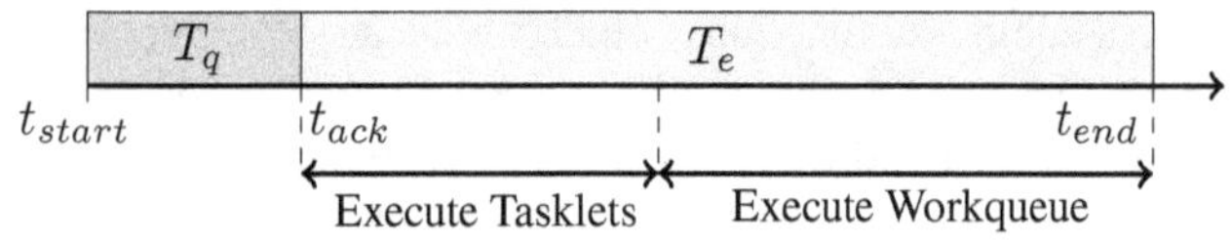

Figure 2: Recovery Periods.

4. Failures in Kernel Code

Kernel code execution usually comprises a small fraction of the total system's runtime. However, a failure in kernel code might have severe consequences. For example, a failure during a migration operation may cause a task to be dequeued from the source queue without being enqueued at the target one. Moreover, a crash of a core holding a kernel lock may leave the system in an inconsistent, or even unrecoverable, state.

In order to prevent the implications such crashes may inflict, we propose to elide the locks [57] protecting kernel critical sections using HTM; HTM mechanisms cause changes to multiple memory locations to appear to be atomic, while providing isolation between parallel executions [31]. We assume that these properties still hold in the presence of failures, namely, the HTM prevents uncommitted changes from propagating, even when a failure occurs during a transaction. Thus, in case of a failure inside a critical section, no changes are written to shared memory, and the system remains in a consistent and recoverable state. Rossbach et al. [59] have proposed TxLinux, an operating system that exploits hardware transactional memory in kernel code for handling concurrency and improving performance. We, on the other hand, exploit HTM abilities in a similar context, but for the purpose of reliability.

Kernel developers devote effort in order to reduce contention among cores. To this end, each core has its own kernel data structures, and accessing another core's data is relatively rare. Therefore, transaction aborts due to data conflicts are likely to be infrequent. Nevertheless, since Intel Transactional Synchronization Extension (TSX) [36] is a *best effort* HTM, (namely, transactions are not guaranteed to commit because of various architectural reasons), and since kernel code executes many sensitive instructions, such as interrupt masking, interrupt sending, TLB and cache operations, which cause aborts, we expect transactions to abort occasionally. Furthermore, due to architectural reasons, some critical sections cannot be executed transactionally, e.g., a context-switch always causes a TLB flush – an operation that leads to abort. In such cases, our solution reverts to using locks. Using HTM in all remaining critical sections keeps the system fault-resistant a majority of the time. Though reliability is not assured while executing uncommon abort-prone sections as discussed above, the simplicity of this solution, and the very low overhead (or even performance gain) it incurs makes it appealing and easily applicable. We prototype this approach in Section 6, for a subset of OS critical sections, to illustrate its feasibility.

Domain	T_q	T_e	
		Tasklets	Workqueue
In-Chip	0.9ms/1.1ms	1.8ms	1.5ms/1ms
Inter-Chip	0.9ms/1.1ms	1.8ms	2.3ms/2.1ms

Table 1: T_q and T_e measurements (Busy/Idle).

An alternative approach to handling failures during critical sections is by using Recovery Domains [44], an organizing principle presented by Lenharth et al., which uses logging and rollback for restoring system state upon failure. Unlike transactional memory systems, the Recovery Domains principle only focuses on recovery from failures and not on isolation between parallel executions. However, this does not constitute a problem, since concurrency in kernel code is already managed by locks. The most prominent advantage of this approach is the ability to cope with critical sections that cannot commit transactionally. However, this approach is likely to incur much higher overhead and complexity, a cost that might not justify the benefits. We do not further explore this path in this paper.

5. Cascading Failures

In this section we elaborate on CSR's tolerance to cascading failures. This relies on the principle that each recovery task is eventually executed by some core exactly once.

We use HTM to avoid inconsistent states resulting from failures during recovery tasks execution. To this end, we have divided the recovery procedure into four tasklets and four work items, each of which is small enough to run as a transaction. We execute each individual tasklet or work item as a separate atomic transaction. Next, we take steps to ensure that recovery items are executed exactly once.

To analyze different cascading failure scenarios, we examine a timeline of the recovery process, as shown in Figure 2. The time at which the failure of C_F is detected is denoted t_{start}, and t_{ack} denotes the time at which the FDU receives the ack from C_D. We denote by T_q the interval between t_{start} and t_{ack}, and by T_e the time between t_{ack} and the end of the recovery process.

Measurements of our implementation on a 64-core machine, presented in Table 1, show that T_q lasts about 1ms, in both busy and idle systems. T_e, can last a bit longer, depending on the system load as well as the chips on which C_D and C_F reside.

In case of a cascading failure, the FDU detects and triggers a recovery procedure on another processor, C'_D. We first discuss the case where C_D fails during T_e. Here, the FDU knows that the recovery tasklets are accessible by the rest of the cores, and if necessary, other cores can read, migrate, and execute those tasklets. T_e itself can be divided into two sub-periods: one that consists of the execution of the recovery tasklets and a second where the work-items queued to RWQ are executed. In the latter case – since RWQ is not bound to any core, failure of C_D during that time does not affect the recovery process. In the former case, as part of step (c) of the recovery procedure, C'_D will take over and execute the recovery tasklets among the rest of C_D's tasklets. Thus, in either case, the recovery tasklets related to C_F's failure are executed, either by C_D before it fails, or by C'_D.

If the failure occurs during T_q, it is impossible to know which stages of CSR C_D has completed. Therefore, in case the FDU detects a failure of C_D without having received an ack from it, the FDU invokes a double recovery procedure on C'_D, to handle the failures of both C_F and C_D.

A failure during T_q can cause the recovery functions to appear more than once on the same queue. We give an example in Figure 3, where C_D completes stage (2) and crashes just before informing the FDU. C'_D then invokes a double recovery procedure (Figure 3(b)), during which it migrates C_D's tasklets. As a result, C'_D has the tasklets for handling C_F's failure twice. To prevent duplicate execution, we give the tasklets unique IDs, and mark completed tasklets in a globally accessed bitmap, as part of the transaction executing them. This bitmap is checked before each tasklet execution to ensure that it has not been executed before.

6. Implementation Issues

As a proof of concept, we implemented CSR in version 3.14.1 of the Linux kernel. Our implementation uses high-priority tasklets to queue the recovery tasklets, and allocates a new unbound workqueue to serve as the recovery-workqueue. We exploit, with some modifications, most of the functions that are used by CPU Hotplug. Eighty-one files of the Linux source were changed, for a total of about 4000 changed and new lines. We next explore some issues that arose during the work.

6.1 FDU and C_D

We implement the FDU using a periodic timer, which times out in predefined constant-length intervals and checks for heartbeats from all online cores (see Figure 4). Online cores send heartbeats to the FDU each timer interrupt. When the FDU detects a core that has stopped sending heartbeats, it considers that core to be faulty, and initiates CSR on another processor, C_D, by sending it an IPI. To simulate the reliability of the FDU, we affine the FDU to core 0 solely and do not crash it during the experiments. This is done only for simplicity, as a reliable FDU can be implemented in hardware, even in a fault-prone environment [21, 72].

Upon receiving the IPI, C_D queues the recovery tasklets and verifies their visibility by using the WBINVD [34] instruction, which flushes its write buffer and private caches by invalidating them and performing a write back.

6.2 Setting a Faulty State

Linux's supervised core-unplug uses the *stop_machine()* mechanism for setting a core offline. The purpose of this mechanism is to prevent a core from going offline during execution of non-preemptible code on another core. This prevents, for example, changes to the online mask while another core iterates on it, and thus avoids inconsistent updates of the removed core's data. The *stop_machine()* function halts the execution of all online cores before the actual removal of the outgoing core from the online mask; thus, it postpones the actual removal of the victim core to a later time, at which no non-preemptible code is executed.

However, in crash failure cases, the use of *stop_machine()* is inadvisable. This is because the update of *faulty_mask* about the failure, as well as interrupt resetting, should happen fast. Deferring or preventing a core from crashing while another core executes non-preemptible code is, of course, impossible. Moreover, since the core will not get back online, consequences of inconsistent updates of its data are limited. We therefore refrain from using *stop_machine()*.

Note that previous works [26, 67] have also proposed to decouple *stop_machine()* from the CPU Hotplug path, for performance and design considerations.

6.3 Handling Lost Interrupts

For handling possible interrupt loss, following resetting the interrupt affinities, we send spurious interrupts for all the interrupt types that were previously routed to the faulty core. However, this does not cover cases of lost Inter-Processor Interrupts: The IPI queue on the faulty core might contain *migratable* callbacks, namely, callbacks that can execute on any core, and their execution is necessary. For example, in order to change the frequency of a chip, an IPI is sent to one

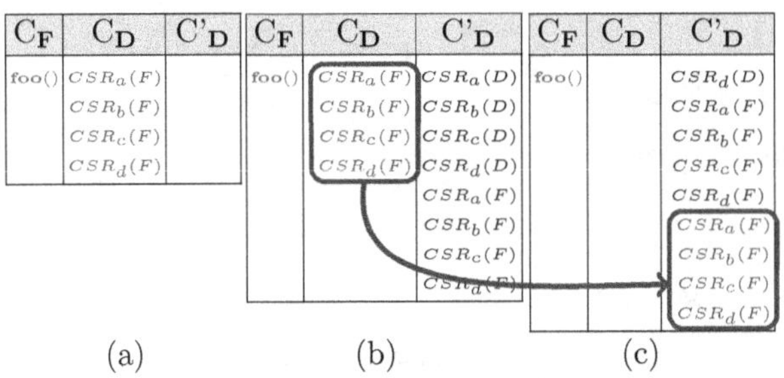

Figure 3: Duplicate queuing of recovery tasklets due to failure during T_q. Columns represent tasklet queues. $CSR_X(Y)$ represents recovery tasklet X for core Y.
(a) C_D queues recovery tasklets for C_F's failure.
(b) C_D fails, C'_D queues recovery tasklets for C_D and C_F.
(c) After executing $CSR_c(D)$, C'_D has duplicates in its queue.

```
for_each_possible_cpu(cpu){
  if (!heartbeats_received(cpu) &&
        !cpu_is_faulty(cpu)){
    mark_cpu_as_faulty(cpu);
    Cd = choose_recovery_cpu();
    send_IPI(Cd,CSR,cpu);
  }
}
```

Figure 4: FDU periodic callback.

of the cores in that chip; if that core fails, the callback needs to be migrated. On the other hand, some functions passed by IPIs should execute exclusively on the core they were sent to (e.g., read MSRs or flush TLB). Only the code that sends the IPI can determine whether the callback should be migrated when its recipient fails.

We therefore provide each callback with a flag indicating whether it is migratable. The flag is set when the IPI is generated and checked during recovery. Linux provides four primitives for broadcasting IPIs, depending on whether the destination is (1) a particular core, (2) a subset of the cores, (3) all of the cores, (4) any of the cores in a subset (*anycast*). By examining the Linux source, we found that only functions that are sent by the anycast primitive are migratable. Thus, we changed the anycast implementation to queue these functions with flag set to true. By default, the other primitives queue functions as not migratable.

6.4 RCU Implications

Read-Copy Update (RCU) [48, 49] is a synchronization mechanism that allows low overhead wait-free reads at the cost of potentially expensive updates – each update must wait for a grace period to elapse before it completes. Specifically, an update thread must wait for a quiescent state to occur on each of the online cores in order to complete its update. As a result, an update operation that begins prior to C_F's crash and does not complete before the crash might wait forever for a quiescent state to occur on the faulty, non-responsive, core. In order to prevent such deadlocks, following a core crash, we explicitly allow all RCU updaters waiting for a quiescent state to occur on C_F to proceed. Likewise, future updates must avoid the waiting for C_F, and stop tracking it, as its future quiescent states will not happen. We therefore iterate over all RCU data-structures and delete all wait list entries corresponding to C_F, thus preventing future RCU updaters from waiting in vain. Figure 5 shows the high level operation of the corresponding code, which is executed as part of stage (iii).

6.5 Using HTM

We gathered statistics about lock usage in kernel code, and found that the run-queue locks are among the most commonly acquired for the workloads we study and the most commonly occur in the kernel source. We therefore chose to elide these locks as a case study for using transactions for recovery. We replaced all kernel critical sections protected by run-queue locks with the lock elision code in Figure 6, using Intel TSX. Here, we assume a convention in the Linux kernel, whereby all accesses to the run-queues are protected by these locks.

Each critical section is executed transactionally, and, as befits a best effort TM, is provided with a fallback path (line 9) [35]. The fallback path retries to execute the transaction, up to a predefined number of times. If the allowed number of retries has been exhausted, the implementation resorts to regular lock acquisition (line 13). To ensure correctness and reciprocity of a transaction with the fallback path, hardware transactions must read the lock as free (line 4), thus inserting the lock value into their read sets. The transactional memory semantics then guarantee that the transaction commits only when there is no ongoing fallback execution.

Though resorting to regular locking compromises our ability to recover from core failures in critical code, it is necessary to prevent livelock. The retries limit value determines a tradeoff – higher values favor reliability, whereas lower ones favor performance, as they shorten the maximum possible time to spend on retrying. Also, too high values may cause abort-prone sections to retry numerous times, thus harming the commit rates of other sections, causing them to resort to locking. We examined different limit values, and found the sweet spot to be at 10000 retries. Our results in the next section show that more than 99% of the transactions commit successfully in a lock-free manner, making failures inside a lock-protected critical section extremely improbable.

Among the 47 kernel critical sections protected by the run-queue locks, only three could not commit transactionally. Not surprisingly, one of them contains the context-

```
rcu_report_crash(cpu){
  // Update all RCU trees
  for_each_rcu_tree{
    struct rcu_node* rnp;
    rnp = rcu_tree_leaf_node(cpu);
    while (rnp != NULL){
      // For future grace periods -
      // Exclude cpu from the initial mask
      remove_from_mask(rnp->qsmaskinit,cpu);
      rnp=rnp->parent;
    }
  }
  // For the current grace period -
  // Artificially report a quiescent state
  rcu_report_qs(cpu);
}
```

Figure 5: RCU recovery.

```
1  RetryTxn:
2  // start the transaction
3  if (_xbegin() == _XBEGIN_STARTED){
4      if (raw_spin_is_locked(&rq->lock)){
5          _xabort(1);
6      }
7      /*** Critical Section Code Here ***/
8      _xend(); // finish the transaction
9  }else{ //Tx failed - fallback:
10     if(retries++ < MAX_RETRIES){
11         goto RetryTxn;
12     }
13     raw_spin_lock(&rq->lock);
14     /*** Critical Section Code Here ***/
15     raw_spin_unlock(&rq->lock);
16 }
```

Figure 6: Lock elision using HTM [35].

Benchmark	Workload Properties			Success Rate	
	user	*system*	*iowait/idle*	*non-system*	*system*
K-means	99%	1%	0%	100%	86%
401.bzip2	99%	1%	0%	100%	72%
410.bwaves	99%	1%	0%	100%	88%
429.mcf	22%	14%	64%	100%	68%
Postmark	5%	21%	74%	100%	70%

Table 2: Recovery rates, without HTM, under random fault injections in user and kernel code.

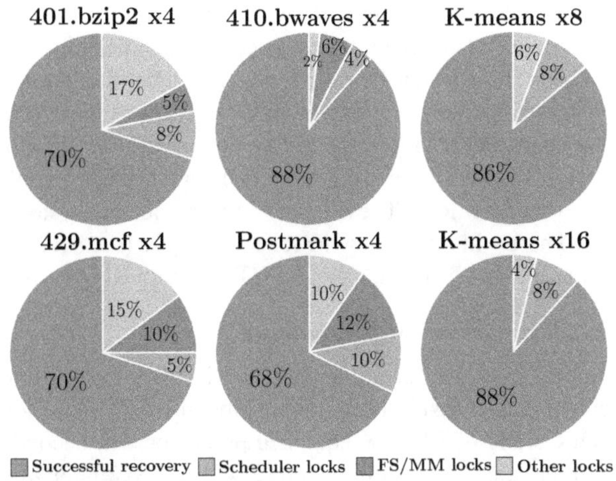

Figure 7: Recovery rates and failure locations under random fault injection in kernel code, no HTM in use.

switch function, which issues a TLB flush – an operation that cannot commit transactionally. The second creates a new kernel thread, and is called only a handful of times during the system's lifetime. We left the first two critical sections with a surrounding lock, compromising our ability to recover from failures in these critical sections. The third critical section has a large data set and could successfully commit after we split it into three smaller sections, after ensuring that such chopping is safe.

Given the above, we conclude that eliding the run-queue locks constitutes a good case study. While the most contended lock in the kernel will be workload-dependent, run-queue locks are commonly used and some of the critical sections they protect have complex behaviors that are challenging for HTM mechanisms. Our work is a proof of concept for using HTM for recovery on a real system. A complete conversion of kernel locking to HTM usage has already been presented on a simulator in TxLinux [59], and in that aspect, TxLinux is complementary to our work.

7. Evaluation

This section presents our evaluation of CSR. We begin in Section 7.1 with a massive random fault injection campaign on a virtualized environment protected by the basic CSR algorithm, without using HTM. Next, in Section 7.2, we evaluate CSR with the lock elision code on real systems. Finally, in Sec. 7.3, we quantify the effects of using HTM on energy and performance using a dedicated scheduler benchmark.

In all experiments, except noted otherwise, the timer interrupt is set to the default period of 4ms and the FDU wakeup period, which can be set to any value higher than the timer interrupt period, is set to 10ms.

7.1 Massive Virtualized Fault Injection Without HTM

We install our CSR-enhanced Linux on a 4-core VM emulated by QEMU [6]. As we employ QEMU without HTM emulation, we run a kernel with only the basic CSR functionality and no lock elision. Hence, kernel critical sections are not protected. We run three sets of experiments, with random fault injections during three different execution modes: (1) user mode, (2) kernel mode, and (3) idle/IO-wait mode.

Emulating Failures. We change the QEMU source, causing it to shutdown a random virtual core at a random time when this core is executing in the desired mode (user, kernel or idle), thus simulating a permanent core fault. This is done by abruptly stopping one of the QEMU threads that simulate the virtual cores. We determine the execution mode by examining the CPL and EIP registers of the victim core. Note that an unmodified kernel crashes following a fault injection during any execution mode.

In each experiment, we start a VM running our kernel, run a given workload, wait for a virtual core to crash during the required execution mode, and allow the system time to recover. In order to verify that the system has indeed recovered, we create a new file, write a timestamp into it, and flush it to disk using **sync**. Thus, a file is created per each successful recovery. We repeat the experiments thousands of times per workload and per execution mode.

The benchmarks we use are K-means of the Metis [46] in-memory MapReduce library; SPEC-CPU™2006 [29] benchmarks, out of which we choose one data-intensive (429.mcf) and two CPU-intensive (401.bzip2, 410.bwaves) applications; and Postmark [40], an IO-intensive filesystem benchmark. Since Postmark and SPEC benchmarks are single threaded, we run four instances of each application, in order to keep all the cores occupied. In order to exercise the scheduling system, we run K-means with 8 and 16 threads on the four cores. We measure the induced workload properties of each benchmark using SYSSTAT [27].

Results. Our results, which appear in Table 2, show that our system recovered in all cases wherein fault injections were performed in user or idle mode, as expected. For fault injections during kernel code execution, the system recovered in about 70% (or more) of the experiments. For each experiment that resulted in a system crash, we extracted the exact code line before which the fault was injected (using the EIP and CPL registers) and analyzed the reason that prevented the system from recovering. We present in Figure 7 a breakdown of the failure reasons into three main categories: (1) holding a *scheduler lock*, such as the run-queue locks; (2) holding a *filesystem or a memory lock*; and (3) holding *other locks*, such as RCU and timer locks. As can be seen, IO-intensive workloads (mcf, Postmark) tend to crash during filesystem and memory operations more often than their computation-intensive counterparts. In addition, all workloads suffer considerably from crashes due to holding a scheduler lock. These failures occur since our system is tested here without eliding the scheduler locks (see Sec. 6.5), which we next evaluate on a real HTM-equipped system.

7.2 Experiments on a Real System

We next evaluate our implementation in two physical environments. The first is a PC running Ubuntu 14.04 on a 1x4x2 Intel Core i7-4770, TSX-equipped processor. The second is a server running Ubuntu Server 12.04 on 4x8x2 Intel Xeon E5-4650 processors.

7.2.1 Crash Simulation

For simulating a crash in a real system, we force a core to hang inside various kernel critical and non-critical sections in an un-interruptible state, thus causing it to stop responding. Figure 8 shows the code snippet we use for crashing an online core. The return value of *fault_injection()* is negative until set to be some core's id by a system call. Once the code is invoked on the victim core, it hangs in an infinite loop, with interrupts disabled, and therefore no possibility to be preempted. Note that this simulates our failure model, where the values in the crashed core's cache is accessible to other cores following a failure.

In order to hang a core on a real system, the code snippet (Figure 8) has to be hard coded into the kernel source. This does not allow us to perform automatic fault injection at random locations as in the virtualized case. Therefore, we manually perform fault injections in one hundred representative kernel functions (a partial list appears in Table 3). For functions that contain critical sections protected by a run-queue lock, we inject a crash in the critical section itself.

7.2.2 Crash and Recovery Timeline

In this set of experiments, we create and affine to each core 10 computation-heavy tasks. These tasks are always hungry for CPU time, and so, at any given moment during the experiment, each correct core should have at least 10 tasks in its run-queue. Next, we crash one of the cores and let CSR recover the system. We repeat the experiment on the PC by placing the code snippet of Figure 8 in the one hundred kernel critical and non-critical sections mentioned above.

Traditional operating systems do not recover from such faults. Linux, for example, uses a watchdog [14] to detect

```
interrupts_disable();
if (fault_injection() == smp_processor_id())
    while(TRUE);
```

Figure 8: Crashing a core.

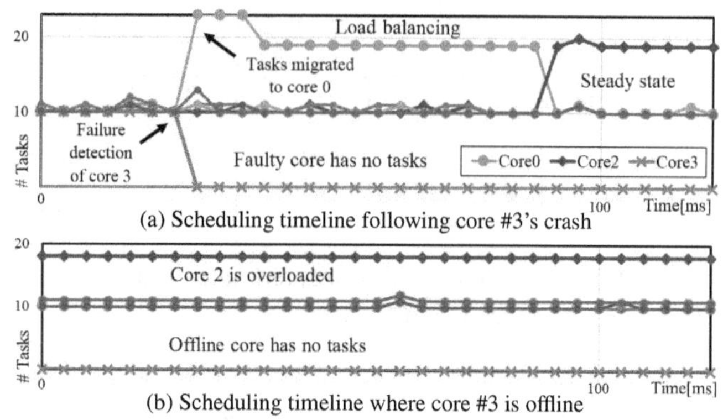

Figure 9: Scheduling timelines for PC system with 8 cores.

lock-ups. Following a fault detection, Linux provides two possible actions (determined at system install time). The first is to reboot the system, and the second is to ignore the fault and resume normally. We configured our unmodified Linux system to the second option and used the method described in Figure 8 to hang a core. We repeated this experiment multiple times, and got a variety of behaviors, all of which led to a system freeze within a few seconds, possibly due to lost interrupts, unanswered IPIs, synchronization problems (held locks, stuck RCU operations), etc.

On the other hand, with CSR, the system successfully recovered in *all* the experiments. Exemplary results of experimenting on the PC and server are shown in Figures 9 and 10, respectively. To improve readability, we increase the FDU timeout to 100ms, show only cores 0-15, and disable hyper-threading on the server, just for the depicted experiments. The number of tasks in each run-queue is sampled every clock interrupt by a tool we implemented, and we plot the resulting scheduling timeline. Figure 9a shows the recovery timeline following a crash of core 3 (out of 8). We see that the system recovers, and the tasks that belong to the faulty core are migrated to the lowest id correct core. After less than 70ms, the load balancing mechanism kicks in and corrects the overload. Perhaps surprisingly, the tasks are migrated to core 2. The reason for this behavior lies in the scheduling-domains approach [41], according to which, in our case, each pair of logical cores constitute a scheduling domain. After the crash of core 3, core 2 constitutes a domain by itself. Therefore, the balancing among the domains causes core 2 to get a double amount of work. To verify this analysis, we examine the system with the same workload and take core 3 offline using CPU-Hotplug in an unmodified Linux kernel. As can be seen in Figure 9b, the load balancing behaves the same in both cases. We conclude that the Linux load balancer is not tuned for considering offline cores, and leave fixing this issue for future work.

Figure 10 shows the scheduling timeline of our server platform, after a crash of core 13 among 32. We see that the system recovers, and the overload formed on core 0 is spread among the rest of the cores.

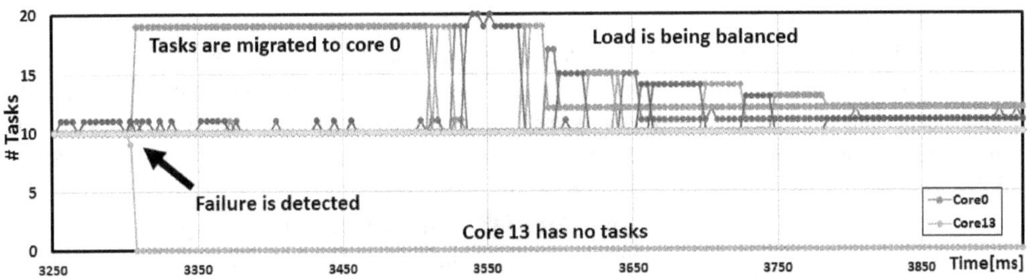

Figure 10: Scheduling timeline, on server with 32 cores (16 shown) following the crash of core 13.

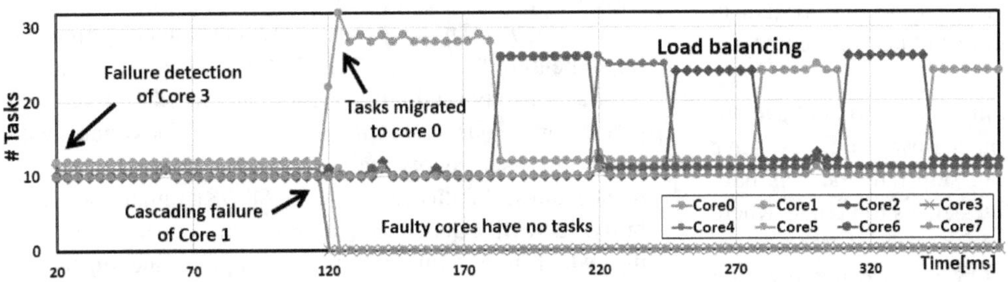

Figure 11: Scheduling timeline, with cascading failures on a PC.

We simulate cascading failures by crashing a core, and immediately afterwards, crashing the core that was nominated by the FDU to execute CSR. Figure 11 presents the resulting scheduling timeline on the PC. Here, the FDU detects core 3 as faulty and nominates core 1 to handle the fault. Core 1 crashes before it sends an ack to the FDU, and 100ms (the FDU wakeup period) later, the FDU considers core 1 to be faulty as well. It then nominates core 2 to perform CSR for both cores 1 and 3, and the system recovers.

7.2.3 Multiple Virtual Machines

Servers nowadays often run multiple VMs. In the absence of support for core surprise removal, a crash of a single core brings down the entire system, along with all running VMs. To demonstrate that CSR eliminates this problem, we conduct the following experiment: We install our CSR-protected Linux on our 64 hardware threads server. Using unmodified QEMU, we create and run four VMs; each is allocated 16 cores and runs an unmodified Ubuntu 14.04. We then set the affinity of VM i to the CPU in socket i and cause a permanent failure to one of the cores in the 4th socket. Thanks to CSR, only the fourth VM, (which has affinity to the fourth chip), suffers from the fault and crashes, while the remaining VMs continue normally. We revert the host OS to an unmodified kernel and repeat the experiment. Not surprisingly, without CSR, all the virtual machines, along with the server itself, crash.

7.3 Lock Elision

We now proceed to quantify the energy and performance implications of using HTM instead of locks in critical kernel code. We use the SysBench [1] benchmark tool, and gather performance, energy consumption (using the RAPL [38] interface), and abort statistics under various workloads on our PC system. Since we apply lock elision on the run-queue lock, we use the *threads* test mode of Sysbench, which is intended for measuring scheduler performance. We set the retries limit to 10000 for all critical sections. By examining the commit rates of each critical section, we found one exceptional critical section (*task_tick*)) that was able to commit, but caused, under some workloads, a significant increase to the total system abort rate. In principle, this code section updates only local data, and should abort rarely. However, the best-effort nature of Intel-TSX causes it to abort under certain workloads due to reasons like cache evictions. To avoid performance penalties, we set the retries limit for this critical section to 10, thus prevent it from contending excessive times with other sections and improve the overall commit rate.

Measurements of our reliable kernel over billions of transactions appear in Table 4. The use of lock elision eliminates expensive atomic instructions. This results in small improvements to the energy consumption and performance.

File	Functions
kernel/sched/core.c	scheduler_tick(), schedule(), ttwu_queue()
kernel/watchdog.c	watchdog_timer_fn()
kernel/timer.c	__run_timers()
kernel/workqueue.c	__queue_work()
kernel/softirq.c	wakeup_softirqd(), __do_softirq()
kernel/events/core.c	update_event_times()
kernel/pid.c	alloc_pid()

Table 3: Functions injected with faults (partial list).

Workload	Commit Rate	Fall-Backs on Locking	Performance Gain	Energy Saving
Idle	61%	0%	-	4%
16-threads	93%	0.1%	0%	1%
32-threads	80%	0.1%	3%	3%
64-threads	42%	0.2%	2%	2%

Table 4: HTM implications on performance and energy.

As can be seen, commit rates are always higher than 40%, meaning that transactions require less than 3 retries on average to commit successfully. The second column shows that the percentage of critical sections that exhaust all retries and resort to locking is negligible, meaning that the vast majority of critical sections execute in a reliable manner.

8. Related Work

To the best of our knowledge, CSR is the first system to address unexpected permanent core failures in commodity architectures and OS.

Reliability Support in OS. A number of works have addressed permanent or intermittent hardware failures: Hive [12], is designed to cope with fail-stop failures. It is built of independent kernels and confines errors to kernels where they occur. However, it is intended for a special architecture, is incompatible with commodity OS, and was not tested on a real system. Dobel and Hartig [18] designed an OS that tolerates soft errors using redundant threads by transferring essential OS code to a dedicated reliable computing base. CSR, on the other hand, does not assume the existence of a reliable core. C^3 [64] provides predictable recovery from intermittent faults in embedded and real-time systems. However, it does not address commodity computers and OSes.

Dolev and Yagel [19] present two self-stabilizing OS principles, which allow an OS to start from any initial state. Unlike CSR, they do not deal with allowing a system to continue to run in case of hardware failures.

Other works have addressed software-induced failures. MINIX3 [30], for example, is a reliable micro-kernel that detects software failures such as deadlocks, and restarts the faulty software component for recovery. Microreboot [10] performs fine-grain rebooting of application components, but is not designed for kernel code. Nooks [68, 69] and SafeDrive [79] provide fault isolation and recovery for device drivers by inspecting their interaction with the kernel, and are thus able to recover from failures in drivers and other kernel extensions without rebooting the OS. Akeso [44] is a system based on the Recovery Domains principle, which uses logging and rollback to tolerate faults in the entire kernel. All efforts mentioned above tolerate software-induced failures only, and except for Akeso [44], none of them tolerates errors in core kernel code.

Transactional Memory. Rossbach et al. have proposed the use of TM in kernel code, and presented TxLinux [59], which exploits TM in order to improve performance. CSR, on the other hand, exploits HTM for reliability. FaulTM [75] utilizes a modified HTM for reducing the overhead of double execution; however, it does not address execution of OS code. Moreover, unlike both of these works, CSR was tested on a real system, taking into account the best-effort nature of real HTM implementations.

CPU-Hotplug. Various works have pointed out CPU Hotplug's shortcomings. Gleixner et al. [26] propose improvements to the CPU-Hotplug path for energy and real-time purposes. Panneerselvam and Swift [54] propose operating system support for dynamic processors, which can dynamically reconfigure the machines' cores at runtime. However, neither of these refers to hardware failures, and both require the cooperation of the victim core.

Many-Core OS. Many-core operating systems is an active area of research. The TeraFlux project [25] encompasses various aspects of teradevice computing, including reliability [21–23, 72]. These works mainly focus on designing and implementing hardware FDUs, but do not consider the OS implications upon failure detection, and are therefore complementary to our work. Other works on OS for systems with large processor counts mainly focus on improving performance and scalability [5, 9, 28, 45, 58, 78], rather than reliability. IBM BlueGene [53] features fault-aware job scheduling, which uses fault prediction to improve the supercomputer's performance, but without considering recovery methods within a faulty node.

9. Conclusions

Existing operating systems cannot recover from unexpected core failures. Thanks to technology scaling, many-core machines are going to be widely deployed in the foreseeable future. However, hardware shrinking introduces new reliability challenges which cannot be addressed by current software.

In this paper we have introduced CSR, a new approach for OS reliability in the face of permanent core faults. We further proposed the use of HTM to cope with faults in kernel critical sections. CSR can be integrated with kernels running on servers with multiple coherence domains [3, 25], preventing entire clusters from crashing following a single core fault. Moreover, a combination of CSR and application-level runtime solutions to re-issue work performed by crashing threads [17, 74] can conceal consequences of failures from user applications.

The CSR principle can be extended to cope with unrecoverable chip-originated soft-errors. Such errors, which are common even today, typically indicate that something is wrong with the chip and therefore it is considered good practice to take the malfunctioning core offline. Since the core is already known to be faulty, expecting it to perform the unplug steps is inadvisable. In addition, Machine Check Exceptions that catch such malfunctions today usually result in a kernel panic. Instead, one can catch the MCE, flush the cache, and revert to CSR upon such errors.

Acknowledgments

This research was funded in part by Hasso-Plattner Institue (HPI), the Intel Collaborative Research Institute for Computational Intelligence (ICRI-CI), and the Technion Funds for Security Research. We thank Chris Rossbach, Emmett Witchel and Mark Silberstein for many insightful suggestions that helped to improve the paper.

References

[1] Alexey Kopytov. SysBench - A Modular, Cross-Platform and Multi-Threaded Benchmark Tool, 2016.

[2] AMD®. Machine Check Architecture. In *AMD64 Architecture Programmer's Manual*, volume 2, chapter 9. May 2013.

[3] E. Argollo, A. Falcón, P. Faraboschi, M. Monchiero, and D. Ortega. COTSon: Infrastructure for Full System Simulation. *SIGOPS Oper. Syst. Rev.*, 43(1):52–61, 2009.

[4] Ashok Raj. CPU Hotplug Support in Linux Kernel. In *Linux Documentation*.

[5] A. Baumann, P. Barham, P.-E. Dagand, T. Harris, R. Isaacs, S. Peter, T. Roscoe, A. Schüpbach, and A. Singhania. The Multikernel: A New OS Architecture for Scalable Multicore Systems. In *22nd Symposium on Operating Systems Principles*. Association for Computing Machinery, Inc., October 2009.

[6] F. Bellard. QEMU, a Fast and Portable Dynamic Translator. In *Proceedings of the Annual Conference on USENIX Annual Technical Conference*, ATEC '05, pages 41–41, Berkeley, CA, USA, 2005. USENIX Association.

[7] N. Bobroff, A. Kochut, and K. Beaty. Dynamic Placement of Virtual Machines for Managing SLA Violations. In *Integrated Network Management, 2007. IM '07. 10th IFIP/IEEE International Symposium on*, pages 119–128, May 2007.

[8] S. Borkar. Designing Reliable Systems from Unreliable Components: The Challenges of Transistor Variability and Degradation. *IEEE Micro*, 25(6):10–16, Nov. 2005.

[9] S. Boyd-Wickizer, A. T. Clements, Y. Mao, A. Pesterev, M. F. Kaashoek, R. Morris, and N. Zeldovich. An Analysis of Linux Scalability to Many Cores. In *Proceedings of the 9th USENIX Conference on Operating Systems Design and Implementation*, OSDI'10, pages 1–8, Berkeley, CA, USA, 2010. USENIX Association.

[10] G. Candea, S. Kawamoto, Y. Fujiki, G. Friedman, and A. Fox. Microreboot: A Technique for Cheap Recovery. In *Proceedings of the 6th Conference on Symposium on Opearting Systems Design & Implementation - Volume 6*, OSDI'04, pages 3–16, Berkeley, CA, USA, 2004. USENIX Association.

[11] F. Chang, J. Dean, S. Ghemawat, W. C. Hsieh, D. A. Wallach, M. Burrows, T. Chandra, A. Fikes, and R. E. Gruber. Bigtable: A Distributed Storage System for Structured Data. *ACM Trans. Comput. Syst.*, 26(2):4:1–4:26, June 2008.

[12] J. Chapin, M. Rosenblum, S. Devine, T. Lahiri, D. Teodosiu, and A. Gupta. Hive: Fault Containment for Shared-memory Multiprocessors. In *Proceedings of the Fifteenth ACM Symposium on Operating Systems Principles*, SOSP '95, pages 12–25, New York, NY, USA, 1995. ACM.

[13] C. Chen and M. Hsiao. Error-Correcting Codes for Semiconductor Memory Applications: A State-of-the-Art Review. *IBM Journal of Research and Development*, 28(2):124–134, March 1984.

[14] Christer Weingel. The Linux Watchdog API. In *Linux Documentation*.

[15] D. Christie, J.-W. Chung, S. Diestelhorst, M. Hohmuth, M. Pohlack, C. Fetzer, M. Nowack, T. Riegel, P. Felber, P. Marlier, and E. Rivière. Evaluation of AMD's Advanced Synchronization Facility Within a Complete Transactional Memory Stack. In *Proceedings of the 5th European Conference on Computer Systems*, EuroSys '10, pages 27–40, New York, NY, USA, 2010. ACM.

[16] C. Constantinescu. Trends and Challenges in VLSI Circuit Reliability. *Micro, IEEE*, 23(4):14–19, July 2003.

[17] J. Dean and S. Ghemawat. MapReduce: Simplified Data Processing on Large Clusters. *Commun. ACM*, 51(1):107–113, Jan. 2008.

[18] B. Döbel and H. Härtig. Who Watches the Watchmen? Protecting Operating System Reliability Mechanisms. In *The Eighth Workshop on Hot Topics in System Dependability*, Berkeley, CA, 2012. USENIX.

[19] S. Dolev and R. Yagel. Towards Self-Stabilizing Operating Systems. *Software Engineering, IEEE Transactions on*, 34(4):564–576, July 2008.

[20] I. Egwutuoha, D. Levy, B. Selic, and S. Chen. A Survey of Fault Tolerance Mechanisms and Checkpoint/Restart Implementations for High Performance Computing Systems. *The Journal of Supercomputing*, 65(3):1302–1326, 2013.

[21] B. Fechner, A. Garbade, S. Weis, and T. Ungerer. Fault Detection and Tolerance Mechanisms for Future 1000 Core Systems. In *High Performance Computing and Simulation (HPCS), 2013 International Conference on*, pages 552–554, July 2013.

[22] A. Garbade, S. Weis, S. Schlingmann, B. Fechner, and T. Ungerer. Fault Localization in NoCs Exploiting Periodic Heartbeat Messages in a Many-Core Environment. In *Parallel and Distributed Processing Symposium Workshops PhD Forum (IPDPSW), 2013 IEEE 27th International*, pages 791–795, May 2013.

[23] A. Garbade, S. Weis, S. Schlingmann, B. Fechner, and T. Ungerer. Impact of Message Based Fault Detectors on Applications Messages in a Network on Chip. *2014 22nd Euromicro International Conference on Parallel, Distributed, and Network-Based Processing*, 0:470–477, 2013.

[24] S. Ghemawat, H. Gobioff, and S.-T. Leung. The Google File System. In *Proceedings of the Nineteenth ACM Symposium on Operating Systems Principles*, SOSP '03, pages 29–43, New York, NY, USA, 2003. ACM.

[25] R. Giorgi, R. M. Badia, F. Bodin, A. Cohen, P. Evripidou, P. Faraboschi, B. Fechner, G. R. Gao, A. Garbade, R. Gayatri, S. Girbal, D. Goodman, B. Khan, S. Koliaï, J. Landwehr, N. M. Lê, F. Li, M. Lujàn, A. Mendelson, L. Morin, N. Navarro, T. Patejko, A. Pop, P. Trancoso, T. Ungerer, I. Watson, S. Weis, S. Zuckerman, and M. Valero. TERAFLUX: Harnessing Dataflow in Next Generation Teradevices. *Microprocessors and Microsystems*, 38(8, Part B):976 – 990, 2014.

[26] T. Gleixner, P. E. McKenney, and V. Guittot. Cleaning Up Linux's CPU Hotplug for Real Time and Energy Management. *SIGBED Rev.*, 9(4):49–52, Nov. 2012.

[27] S. Godard. *SYSSTAT Utilities - System Performance Tools for the Linux Operating System*, 2016. Available at `http://sebastien.godard.pagesperso-orange.fr/`.

[28] G. Heiser. Many-Core Chips — A Case for Virtual Shared Memory. In *Workshop on Managed Many-Core Systems*, Washington DC, USA, Mar 2009.

[29] J. L. Henning. SPEC CPU2006 Benchmark Descriptions. *SIGARCH Comput. Archit. News*, 34(4):1–17, Sept. 2006.

[30] J. N. Herder, H. Bos, B. Gras, P. Homburg, and A. S. Tanenbaum. MINIX 3: A Highly Reliable, Self-Repairing Operating System. In *ACM SIGOPS Operating Systems Review*, 2006.

[31] M. Herlihy and J. E. B. Moss. Transactional Memory: Architectural Support for Lock-Free Data Structures. *SIGARCH Comput. Archit. News*, 21(2):289–300, May 1993.

[32] Intel®. OS Machine Check Recovery on Itanium®-Based Systems. Aug. 2008.

[33] Intel®. Intel® Cache Safe Technology. In *The Intel® Itanium® Processor 9300 Series*. 2014.

[34] Intel®. Instruction Set Reference. In *Intel 64 and IA-32 Architectures Software Developer's Manual*, volume 2, chapter 4. Dec 2015.

[35] Intel®. Intel TSX Recommendations. In *Intel 64 and IA-32 Architectures Optimization Reference Manual*, chapter 12. Sep 2015.

[36] Intel®. Intel® Transactional Synchronization Extensions. In *Intel 64 and IA-32 Architectures Software Developer's Manual*, volume 1, chapter 15. Dec 2015.

[37] Intel®. Machine-Check Architecture. In *Intel 64 and IA-32 Architectures Software Developer's Manual*, volume 3, chapter 15. Dec 2015.

[38] Intel®. RAPL Interface. In *Intel 64 and IA-32 Architectures Software Developer's Manual*, volume 3, chapter 14. Dec 2015.

[39] R. Iyer, R. Illikkal, O. Tickoo, L. Zhao, P. Apparao, and D. Newell. VM3: Measuring, Modeling and Managing VM Shared Resources. *Comput. Netw.*, 53(17):2873–2887, Dec. 2009.

[40] Jeffrey Katcher. Postmark: a New File System Benchmark. Technical report, October 1997. TR3022, Network Appliance.

[41] Jonathan Corbet. *Scheduling Domains*, 2004. Available at `http://lwn.net/Articles/80911/`.

[42] C.-K. Koh, W.-F. Wong, Y. Chen, and H. Li. The Salvage Cache: A Fault-Tolerant Cache Architecture for Next-Generation Memory Technologies. In *Computer Design, 2009. ICCD 2009. IEEE International Conference on*, pages 268–274, Oct 2009.

[43] Y. Koh, R. Knauerhase, P. Brett, M. Bowman, Z. Wen, and C. Pu. An Analysis of Performance Interference Effects in Virtual Environments. In *In Proceedings of the IEEE International Symposium on Performance Analysis of Systems and Software (ISPASS)*, 2007.

[44] A. Lenharth, V. Adve, and S. King. Recovery Domains: An Organizing Principle for Recoverable Operating Systems. In *International Conference on Architectural Support for Programming Languages and Operating Systems - ASPLOS*, pages 49–60, 12 2008.

[45] LSE. *Linux Scalability Effort Homepage*, 2004. Available at `https://lse.sourceforge.net/`.

[46] Y. Mao, R. Morris, and M. F. Kaashoek. Optimizing MapReduce for Multicore Architectures. *Computer Science and Artificial Intelligence Laboratory, Massachusetts Institute of Technology, Tech. Rep*, 2010.

[47] W. Maurer. *Professional Linux Kernel Architecture*. 2008.

[48] P. E. Mckenney, J. Appavoo, A. Kleen, O. Krieger, O. Krieger, R. Russell, D. Sarma, and M. Soni. Read-Copy Update. In *In Ottawa Linux Symposium*, pages 338–367, 2001.

[49] P. E. Mckenney and S. Boyd-wickizer. RCU Usage in the Linux Kernel: One Decade Later. Technical Report, sep 2012.

[50] Microsoft ®. Windows Hot Add CPU.

[51] Z. Mwaikambo, A. Raj, R. Russell, J. Schopp, and S. Vaddagiri. Linux Kernel Hotplug CPU Support. In *Linux Symposium*, 2004.

[52] E. B. Nightingale, J. R. Douceur, and V. Orgovan. Cycles, Cells and Platters: An Empirical Analysis of Hardware Failures on a Million Consumer PCs. In *Proceedings of the Sixth Conference on Computer Systems*, EuroSys '11, pages 343–356, New York, NY, USA, 2011. ACM.

[53] A. J. Oliner, R. K. Sahoo, J. E. Moreira, M. Gupta, and A. Sivasubramaniam. Fault-Aware Job Scheduling for BlueGene/L Systems. In *IPDPS*, 2004.

[54] S. Panneerselvam and M. M. Swift. Chameleon: Operating System Support for Dynamic Processors. In *Proceedings of the Seventeenth International Conference on Architectural Support for Programming Languages and Operating Systems*, ASPLOS XVII, pages 99–110, New York, NY, USA, 2012. ACM.

[55] D. A. Patterson. An Introduction to Dependability. *login*, pages 61–65, 2002.

[56] M. Radetzki, C. Feng, X. Zhao, and A. Jantsch. Methods for Fault Tolerance in Networks-On-Chip. *ACM Comput. Surv.*, 46(1):8:1–8:38, July 2013.

[57] R. Rajwar and J. R. Goodman. Speculative Lock Elision: Enabling Highly Concurrent Multithreaded Execution. In *Proceedings of the 34th Annual ACM/IEEE International Symposium on Microarchitecture*, MICRO 34, pages 294–305, Washington, DC, USA, 2001. IEEE Computer Society.

[58] B. Rhoden, K. Klues, D. Zhu, and E. Brewer. Improving Pernode Efficiency in the Datacenter with New OS Abstractions. In *Proceedings of the 2Nd ACM Symposium on Cloud Computing*, SOCC '11, pages 25:1–25:8, New York, NY, USA, 2011. ACM.

[59] C. J. Rossbach, O. S. Hofmann, D. E. Porter, H. E. Ramadan, A. Bhandari, and E. Witchel. TxLinux: Using and Managing Hardware Transactional Memory in an Operating System. In *SOSP*, 2007.

[60] D. Rossi, N. Timoncini, M. Spica, and C. Metra. Error Correcting Code Analysis for Cache Memory High Reliability and Performance. In *Design, Automation Test in Europe Conference Exhibition (DATE), 2011*, pages 1–6, March 2011.

[61] A. Roytman, S. Govindan, J. Liu, A. Kansal, and S. Nath. Algorithm Design for Performance Aware VM Consolidation. Technical report, 2013.

[62] R. D. Schlichting and F. B. Schneider. Fail-Stop Processors: An Approach to Designing Fault-Tolerant Computing Systems. *ACM Trans. Comput. Syst.*, 1(3):222–238, Aug. 1983.

[63] B. Schroeder, E. Pinheiro, and W.-D. Weber. DRAM Errors in the Wild: A Large-Scale Field Study. In *SIGMETRICS*, 2009.

[64] J. Song, J. Wittrock, and G. Parmer. Predictable, Efficient System-Level Fault Tolerance in C^3. *2013 IEEE 34th Real-Time Systems Symposium*, 0:21–32, 2013.

[65] S. Srikantaiah, A. Kansal, and F. Zhao. Energy Aware Consolidation for Cloud Computing. In *Proceedings of the 2008 Conference on Power Aware Computing and Systems*, HotPower'08, pages 10–10, Berkeley, CA, USA, 2008. USENIX Association.

[66] J. Srinivasan, S. Adve, P. Bose, and J. Rivers. The Impact of Technology Scaling on Lifetime Reliability. In *Dependable Systems and Networks, 2004 International Conference on*, pages 177–186, June 2004.

[67] Srivatsa S. Bhat. *CPU Hotplug: stop_machine()-Free CPU Hotplug.* Available at `http://lwn.net/Articles/533553/`.

[68] M. M. Swift, M. Annamalai, B. N. Bershad, and H. M. Levy. Recovering Device Drivers. *ACM Trans. Comput. Syst.*, 24(4):333–360, Nov. 2006.

[69] M. M. Swift, B. N. Bershad, and H. M. Levy. Improving the Reliability of Commodity Operating Systems. In *Proceedings of the Nineteenth ACM Symposium on Operating Systems Principles*, SOSP '03, pages 207–222, New York, NY, USA, 2003. ACM.

[70] S. Vangal, J. Howard, G. Ruhl, S. Dighe, H. Wilson, J. Tschanz, D. Finan, A. Singh, T. Jacob, S. Jain, V. Erraguntla, C. Roberts, Y. Hoskote, N. Borkar, and S. Borkar. An 80-Tile Sub-100-W TeraFLOPS Processor in 65-nm CMOS. *Solid-State Circuits, IEEE Journal of*, 43(1):29–41, Jan. 2008.

[71] A. Wang, M. Gaudet, P. Wu, J. N. Amaral, M. Ohmacht, C. Barton, R. Silvera, and M. Michael. Evaluation of Blue Gene/Q Hardware Support for Transactional Memories. In *Proceedings of the 21st International Conference on Parallel Architectures and Compilation Techniques*, PACT '12, pages 127–136, New York, NY, USA, 2012. ACM.

[72] S. Weis, A. Garbade, B. Fechner, A. Mendelson, R. Giorgi, and T. Ungerer. Architectural Support for Fault Tolerance in a Teradevice Dataflow System. *International Journal of Parallel Programming*, pages 1–25, 2014.

[73] S. Weis, A. Garbade, and T. Ungerer. Design Exploration of FDUs and Core-Internal Fault-Detection. *Exploiting Dataflow Parallelism in Tera-Device Computing*, 2010.

[74] T. White. *Hadoop: The Definitive Guide.* O'Reilly Media, Inc., 1st edition, 2009.

[75] G. Yalcin, O. Unsal, and A. Cristal. FaulTM: Error Detection and Recovery Using Hardware Transactional Memory. In *Proceedings of the Conference on Design, Automation and Test in Europe*, DATE '13, pages 220–225, San Jose, CA, USA, 2013. EDA Consortium.

[76] G.-C. Yang. Reliability of Semiconductor RAMs with Soft-Error Scrubbing Techniques. *Computers and Digital Techniques, IEE Proceedings*, 142(5):337–344, Sep 1995.

[77] R. M. Yoo, C. J. Hughes, K. Lai, and R. Rajwar. Performance Evaluation of Intel ® Transactional Synchronization Extensions for High-performance Computing. In *Proceedings of the International Conference on High Performance Computing, Networking, Storage and Analysis*, SC '13, pages 19:1–19:11, New York, NY, USA, 2013. ACM.

[78] G. Zellweger, S. Gerber, K. Kourtis, and T. Roscoe. Decoupling Cores, Kernels, and Operating Systems. In *11th USENIX Symposium on Operating Systems Design and Implementation (OSDI 14)*, pages 17–31, Broomfield, CO, Oct. 2014. USENIX Association.

[79] F. Zhou, J. Condit, Z. Anderson, I. Bagrak, R. Ennals, M. Harren, G. Necula, and E. Brewer. SafeDrive: Safe and Recoverable Extensions Using Language-based Techniques. In *Proceedings of the 7th Symposium on Operating Systems Design and Implementation*, OSDI '06, pages 45–60, Berkeley, CA, USA, 2006. USENIX Association.

CASPAR: Breaking Serialization in Lock-Free Multicore Synchronization *

Tanmay Gangwani
University of Illinois at Urbana–Champaign
gangwan2@illinois.edu

Adam Morrison
Technion—Israel Institute of Technology
mad@cs.technion.ac.il

Josep Torrellas
University of Illinois at Urbana–Champaign
torrella@illinois.edu

Abstract

In multicores, performance-critical synchronization is increasingly performed in a *lock-free* manner using atomic instructions such as CAS or LL/SC. However, when many processors synchronize on the same variable, performance can still degrade significantly. Contending writes get serialized, creating a non-scalable condition. Past proposals that build hardware queues of synchronizing processors do not fundamentally solve this problem—at best, they help to *efficiently serialize* the contending writes.

This paper proposes a novel architecture that *breaks* the serialization of hardware queues and enables the queued processors to perform lock-free synchronization *in parallel*. The architecture, called CASPAR, is able to (1) execute the CASes in the queued-up processors in parallel through eager forwarding of expected values, and (2) validate the CASes in parallel and dequeue groups of processors at a time. The result is highly-scalable synchronization. We evaluate CASPAR with simulations of a 64-core chip. Compared to existing proposals with hardware queues, CASPAR improves the throughput of kernels by 32% on average, and reduces the execution time of the sections considered in lock-free versions of applications by 47% on average. This makes these sections 2.5x faster than in the original applications.

Keywords lock-free synchronization; serialization

1. Introduction

The arrival of large multicores such as Intel's Xeon Phi [27] provides renewed impetus to develop highly-threaded applications that share data in a fine-grained manner. Examples of such applications can be found in the traditional domains of numerical and database [15, 63] computing, as well as in the runtimes of emerging programming frameworks, such as Galois [50] for graph analytics, and those of Google's Go [1] and Mozilla's Rust [45] languages.

Fine-grained applications require efficient synchronization to manage shared data structures. For highest performance, they often employ *lock-free* synchronization [25], which avoids the overheads of using locks [13, 15, 19, 35, 47, 59, 61, 63]. Lock-free synchronization forgoes locking by directly manipulating the data structures using atomic instructions such as compare-and-swap (CAS) or load-linked/store-conditional (LL/SC). There are several popular lock-free versions of basic data structures, such as queues [26, 40], stacks [23], LRU caches [9], and priority queues [6]. They provide fast operations on these structures.

Regrettably, while lock-free synchronization provides fast sequential access to shared structures, many-thread synchronization can still lead to substantial contention—e.g., when all the threads attempt to perform a CAS on the head of a queue to update it atomically. For this reason, developers of highly-threaded codes today turn to algorithms that *distribute* synchronization [5, 22, 33, 34, 50, 62].

Unfortunately, these algorithms are difficult to design and debug. Even more importantly, they often provide only *weak* and unintuitive data structure semantics [5, 22, 34, 62]—e.g., items in a distributed queue are removed in an order that is different than their insertion order. Such weak semantics make these distributed algorithms more error-prone and difficult to use, and render them inappropriate for programs that require familiar semantics.

To reduce synchronization bottlenecks, past designs have proposed to queue-up the synchronizing processors in a hardware queue [20, 32, 43, 55, 56, 58, 68]. Other designs have also proposed to forward or prefetch [56, 65] the data accessed in the critical section when a lock is transferred. These proposals attempt to *efficiently serialize* concurrent synchronizations. However, they do not solve the serialization problem itself: serialized writes inherently become slower as the number of synchronizing processors grows. To make synchronization truly scalable, we need to break the serialization of the queue and allow the queued processors to synchronize *in parallel*.

This paper proposes a novel architecture design that *breaks* the serialization of hardware queues and enables the queued processors to perform lock-free synchronization *in*

*This work was supported in part by NSF under grants CCF-1012759, CNS-1116237, and CCF-1536795; by the Israel Science Foundation under grants 1227/10 and 1749/14; and by the Yad HaNadiv foundation.

ASPLOS '16, April 2–6, 2016, Atlanta, Georgia, USA.

ACM 978-1-4503-4091-5/16/04...$15.00.
http://dx.doi.org/10.1145/2872362.2872400

parallel. The scheme, called CASPAR, is applicable to some common lock-free synchronization patterns. The result is low-overhead, highly-scalable synchronization. With CASPAR, it is possible to have non-distributed scalable versions of lock-free data structures.

We present CASPAR in the context of the CAS instruction, although it also applies to other synchronization instructions such as LL/SC. Recall that a CAS takes three operands: a memory address *addr*, an *old* value, and a *new* value. A CAS changes the value in *addr* to *new*, provided the current value in *addr* is *old*. We observe that, in common synchronization patterns, the *new* value that a processor stores on a variable with a CAS does not depend on the *old* value previously read from the variable. Instead, the *new* value is generated locally by the processor. For example, as we will see, this occurs when pushing nodes into a stack.

This observation motivates CASPAR, which exploits it with two new ideas: (i) parallel execution of the CASes in the queued-up processors through eager forwarding of the expected *new* values, and (ii) parallel validation of the CASes and group dequeue of the processors.

The first idea uses the fact that a queued processor may know early-on the *new* value that it will set the shared variable to. Hence, it eagerly forwards it to its immediate successor in the queue, so that the successor processor can use it as its *old* value. As a result, queued processors can perform their CASes early-on and in parallel, and continue execution past the CAS. However, since the value passed is a hint, the successors' execution becomes speculative.

The second idea involves the group validation of CASes and, therefore, the group commit and dequeue of processors. It leverages the fact that the directory knows the values passed between processors and can interrogate a chain of dependent processors in parallel. If all processors validate, a two-phase commit operation dequeues them all in one step.

CASPAR effectiveness. We evaluate CASPAR by augmenting a simulated 64-core multicore with a synchronization hardware queue (representing prior work) and then extending it with the complete CASPAR design. We run five kernels and several applications—including some from the Galois system [50]. The applications are modified to use lock-free data structures. Compared to the design with only the hardware queue, CASPAR: (i) improves the throughput of the kernels by 32% on average, and (ii) reduces the execution time of the sections considered in the lock-free applications by 47% on average. This makes such sections 2.5x faster than in the original, tuned versions. Also, compared to a design with only conventional CAS synchronization, CASPAR improves the kernel throughput by 83% and reduces the execution time of the application sections by 58% on average.

Contributions. This paper makes three contributions:

• The CASPAR architecture, which provides scalable and efficient lock-free synchronization by parallelizing the operation of hardware-queued processors.

• A design for automatically triggering hardware queueing on the unmarked loads of contended CAS variables.

• Simulation-based evaluation of CASPAR using highly-threaded kernels and applications.

2. Motivation

Lock-free synchronization (also referred to as *nonblocking* synchronization [24]) directly manipulates shared data using atomic instructions such as CAS and LL/SC, or transactional memory (TM) instead of using locks (see Section 3 for an example). Performance-critical multi-threaded codes such as operating systems [2, 13, 35], databases [4, 15, 63], language runtimes [19], memory allocators [47, 59, 61], or trading frameworks [3] often utilize lock-free synchronization to avoid the overheads of locking.

Lock-free synchronization has two main performance advantages compared to lock-based solutions. First, it is more efficient, since it has no lock acquire and release operations on the critical path. Indeed, lock-free versions of many basic data structures have fast synchronization operations that write to at most a few variables—queues [26, 36, 48], stacks [66], and priority queues [18, 44]. Second, lock-free algorithms guarantee system-wide progress, and thus eliminate problems such as deadlocks and preemption of the holder of a lock [24].

Performance issues. Lock-free synchronization still has two performance issues when many processors contend to perform a write to the same synchronization variable. First, sometimes CAS or LL/SC atomic instructions fail, and transactions abort. This can place useless work on the critical path. Second, contending writes are *serialized*, as each processor must obtain exclusive access to the contended variable's cache line to update it. This serialization causes the latency of each write to grow with the amount of concurrency, making contending writes non-scalable and slow.

Software approaches. To avoid these issues, developers turn to algorithms that distribute synchronization [5, 22, 33, 34, 50, 62]. However, these algorithms are often complex and provide only weak and unintuitive data structure semantics [5, 22, 34, 62]. For example, consider a FIFO queue algorithm. Instead of synchronizing all operations on a single queue head, we distribute the synchronization. We maintain a queue per producer thread and require a remove operation to iterate over each of these queues until it finds an item to remove [22]. Doing so, however, no longer maintains the cause and effect relation in the program: If thread T_1 adds x_1 to its queue after thread T_0 adds x_0 to its queue, a remove can return x_1 before x_0. We *weakened* the guarantees provided by the queue from global FIFO to per-thread FIFO.

Hardware approaches. Alternatively, there are hardware proposals to make synchronization efficient (Section 8). The most relevant to our work are those that build hardware queues of processors synchronizing on a variable. Specif-

```
1 // Stack consists of linked list of nodes.
2 // The following defines a stack node:
3 struct Node {
4     struct Node* next;
5     void* value;
6 }
7 // Pointer to top of the stack, initially
8 // NULL as the stack is empty:
9 Node* stack = NULL;
```

(a) Definitions

```
10 void push(void* v) {
11     Node *old_top, *new_top = malloc ();
12     new_top->value = v;
13     while (true) {
14         old_top = stack;
15         new_top->next = old_top;
16         if (CAS(&stack, old_top, new_top))
17             return;
18 } }
```

(b) Pushing a value

```
19 void* pop() {
20     Node *old_top, *new_top;
21     while (true) {
22         old_top = stack;
23         if ( old_top == NULL) return NULL;
24         new_top = old_top->next;
25         if (CAS(&stack, old_top, new_top))
26             return old_top->value;
27 } }
```

(c) Popping a value

Figure 1: Treiber's lock-free LIFO stack [66].

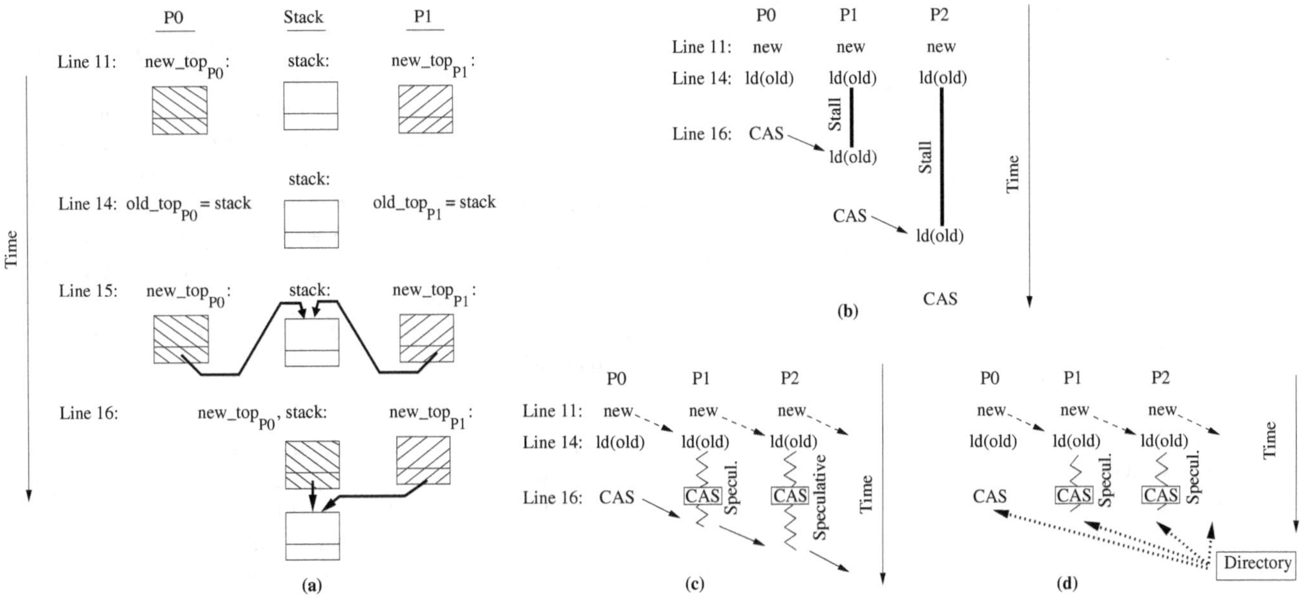

Figure 2: Ideas behind CASPAR.

ically, Goodman et al. [20, 32] proposed QOSB/QOLB, which forms a hardware queue linking the caches of the synchronizing processors. Hardware queues have also been implemented in the directory of DASH [43], and proposed by other researchers [55, 56, 58, 68]. In one of these designs [55], coherence actions are delayed to prevent repeated failure of lock acquire or atomic instructions. Specifically, a processor delays responding to requests on the synchronization variable while the processor is executing the critical section or the code between LL and SC. Finally, other designs proposed to forward or prefetch [56, 65] the data accessed in a critical section while the lock is transferred.

These proposals efficiently serialize concurrent synchronizations. However, they do not solve the serialization problem itself: executing the critical section or performing the lock-free write takes on average proportionally longer as the number of synchronizing processors grows.

Our approach and observation. To make synchronization truly scalable, we need hardware that *breaks* the queue serialization and allows the queued processors to synchronize *in parallel*. To design this hardware, we observe that, in some common synchronization patterns that we describe in the next section, the *new* value that a CAS writes to a variable does not depend on the variable's previous value. We exploit this fact next.

3. Overview of CASPAR

3.1 A LIFO Stack Example

Figure 1 shows the C code of Treiber's lock-free LIFO stack [66]. As shown in Figure 1(a), the stack is a linked list of nodes, each of which holds a value. The top of the stack is the first node in the list. The *push()* (Figure 1(b)) and *pop()* (Figure 1(c)) operations use a CAS.

We focus on the *push()* operation. It allocates a new node, *new_top* (Line 11), whose *next* field is set to point to the current top of the stack, *old_top* (Lines 14–15). It then uses a CAS to set the top of the stack to this *new_top* (Line 16). A CAS failure implies that another thread has modified the top of the stack, and so the *push()* operation retries the CAS using a freshly-read value of *stack*.

Figure 2(a) illustrates the above process. It shows the execution of two processors (P0 and P1) and the state of the stack. The top row corresponds to Line 11, where P0 allocates the new_top_{P0} node and P1 allocates the new_top_{P1} node. The second row is for Line 14, where the processors set their old_top_{P0} and old_top_{P1} to *stack*. The third row is for Line 15, where the processors point $new\_top_{P0}\rightarrow next$ and $new\_top_{P1}\rightarrow next$ to *stack*. Finally, the last row is for Line 16, where both P0 and P1 attempt the CAS but only P0 succeeds. The new_top_{P0} node is inserted at the top of the stack, and P1 has to retry.

The ABA problem. An ABA problem [49] occurs when a thread reads the same value (e.g., *A*) from the *stack* location in Lines 14 and 16 and, in between the two reads, other threads update the location to a different value (e.g., *B*) and then back to *A*. The CAS in Line 16 succeeds, even though the atomicity of the load-to-CAS execution was violated. As in other works, in this paper, we assume implementations that avoid this problem by not recycling a node as long as some thread holds a reference to it [18, 30, 46].

3.2 CASPAR Ideas

In the *push()* operation, the CAS of the successful processor (P0) writes new_top_{P0} to *stack*. Such a value does not depend on the value that P0 did read from *stack* into *old_top*. Instead, it is obtained locally by P0, early-on, with a malloc(). Interestingly, this is the value that the failing processor (P1) will need to read into its own *old_top* when it wants to perform the next successful CAS. To summarize, each processor generates the *new* value for its CAS locally and early-on, and this is the value that its immediate successor will need to read as its *old* value to perform its own CAS. This provides an opportunity for parallelism.

Unfortunately, even the most aggressive proposals for hardware synchronization queues fail to take advantage of this opportunity. Indeed, assume a design based on any of the hardware queues described in Section 2, where requests are queued-up in hardware in the directory. Further, assume that, for highest efficiency, the load-to-CAS execution is designed to be atomic—i.e., a processor reads *stack*, prepares the new value, and then writes the new value with the CAS without any conflicting access allowed to interleave in the middle.

In this design, Figure 2(b) shows the execution timeline of three processors (P0, P1, and P2). Assume that all three generate their *new* values at approximately the same time, and that they attempt to load *old* and queue-up in the P0-P1-P2 order. P0 gets the *old* value, while the others stall (thick lines). Only after P0 completes its CAS can P1's load complete and return the current *old* value—even though it was available as the *new* value that P0 produced long ago. P2 suffers an even longer stall. The operation of the processors is completely serialized.

First idea: parallel CAS execution. CASPAR's first idea is parallel CAS execution, as shown in Figure 2(c). When a processor generates its *new* value locally and early-on, we propose that it *eagerly forwards* the *new* value right away to its immediate successor in the queue (dashed arrows). A processor uses the received value as the response to its load for the *old* value, and has all the information to perform the CAS. Hence, *the CASes are performed early-on and in parallel.* Since the values forwarded may be incorrect under certain conditions, execution past the load becomes speculative (zig-zag lines), and can only commit after a validation step in the background (solid arrows). Such a step would require waiting until the processor reaches the head of the queue, and then verifying that the actual content of the variable matches the value of the earlier hint. In cases when the CAS pattern is not amenable to eager forwarding, CASPAR reverts to the serialization of prior queue designs.

Second idea: parallel CAS validation. CASPAR's second idea is to validate groups of CASes in parallel and, therefore, commit groups of processors at a time. This technique reduces the amount of work done speculatively and, hence, reduces the risk of squashes. It is shown in Figure 2(d). The idea is based on the observation that the directory knows the value that each processor forwarded early-on to its successor. Hence, the directory can later interrogate a chain of queued processors in parallel (dotted lines), to see if the value that a processor's CAS ended-up generating is indeed equal to the value that the processor forwarded early-on to its successor. If this is true for a group of processors that begins with the one at the queue head, the group is committed and dequeued in one shot.

3.3 CASPAR Effectiveness

CASPAR is effective when queued processors can generate their *new* value early-on, independently of the *old* value that they read. This pattern appears in several cases. The most common one is when inserting elements into a shared data structure, as in the *push()* operation of Figure 1(b). This pattern also appears when using atomic swap instructions (like x86's XCHG), setting variables to fixed values, resetting variables (e.g., a counter), and detaching a list by swapping the head pointer with null.

Insertion-heavy scenarios occur in many workloads. For example, they arise in runtimes using a shared work queue for load-balancing task-based parallelism [51], when the task queue is populated, either initially or as part of a bulk-synchronous execution [50, 67]; in update-heavy OS data structures such as the reverse page map or pathname lookup cache [12]; in memory allocators when accessing the main heap [47, 59, 61]; in high-speed networking when enqueuing packets [13]; and in other cases.

We also believe that the CASPAR ideas apply more broadly than lock-free code based on CAS or LL/SC, and can be used to break the serialization in TM (Section 5). We defer exploration of this idea to future work.

CASPAR is not effective when the *new* value created by a queued processor depends on the *old* value that the processor reads. This pattern occurs most commonly when removing elements from a shared data structure. An example is the *pop()* operation of Figure 1(c), where the new value of the stack is obtained by reading the node currently at the top of the stack and accessing its *next* field. It also occurs when inserting elements to a structure using ABA-tagging [49]—i.e., devoting some bits in pointers for a counter that each operation increments, to reduce the chance of an ABA problem. Incrementing such a counter creates a dependency. In all of these cases, CASPAR reverts to the serialization present in prior queue designs.

4. CASPAR Architecture

CASPAR is composed of three modules, which (1) identify contended CASes, (2) efficiently queue-up concurrent CASes operating on a location, and (3) enable parallel operation of the queued-up CASes (i.e., the process that we called *breaking the serialization*). Table 1 lists the modules and where they reside in the architecture. Since module (2) is reminiscent of previously-proposed designs of hardware queues for synchronization (e.g., [20, 32, 43, 56]), we do not consider it a main contribution of this work. Hence, we only outline it briefly.

Module Function	Location
(1): Identify contended CAS locations	Processor core
(2): Efficiently queue-up concurrent CASes	
Enforce load-to-CAS atomicity	Processor core
Queue requests in the directory	Directory module
(3): Parallel operation of queued-up CASes	
Parallel CAS execution with Eager Forwarding	Mostly core + directory
Parallel CAS validation using Group Commits	Mostly directory

Table 1: Components of CASPAR.

For ease of explanation, we divide module (2) into two parts: enforcing load-to-CAS atomicity and enqueuing requests in the directory. Module (3) is also composed of two parts: *Parallel CAS Execution* through eagerly forwarding, and *Parallel CAS Validation* using group commits. The following discussion assumes a generic chip multiprocessor (CMP) with a distributed directory for coherence.

4.1 Identifying Contended CAS Locations

4.1.1 Intuitive Idea

CASPAR dynamically identifies contended CAS locations in hardware, without the need to modify the executable. To understand how it works, consider a CAS such as the one in Line 16 of Figure 1(b). When it has failed a few times in a row, the CASPAR hardware saves the address it contends on (i.e., *stack*) in a table. In addition, every load issued by the processor is dynamically checked against the entries in that table. When a load hits (such as the one in Line 14 of Figure 1(b)), the load becomes a *Triggering Load (TL)*, which exercises the CASPAR hardware. The CASPAR hardware remains active until the corresponding CAS completes, at which point the hardware actions typically complete. In a processor, only a single load at a time can be exercising the CASPAR hardware.

4.1.2 Detailed Design

The two per-processor hardware structures used in this process are shown in Figures 3(a)-(b). One is the Triggering Addresses Table (TAT), which has the addresses identified as "under CAS contention" by this processor. It is a 4-8 entry fully-associative table. Its entries are regularly aged out. The second structure is the Active CAS (AC), which can only contain one of the addresses from the TAT: the one currently exercising the CASPAR hardware.

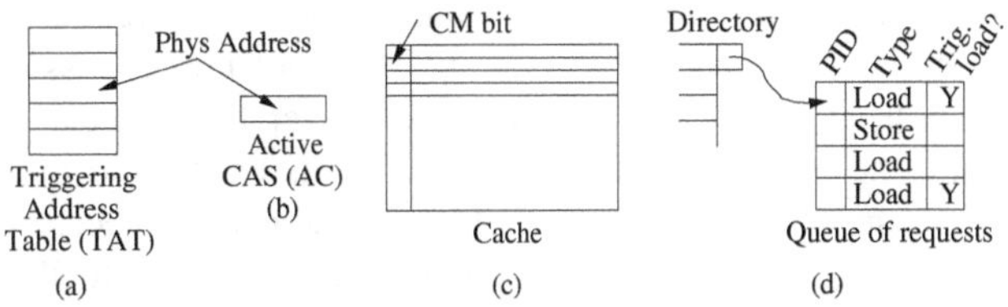

Figure 3: Basic hardware structures in CASPAR.

The address read by each load is compared to the addresses in the TAT. If a load hits and the AC is currently null, then the address read from is stored in the AC and the load becomes a TL. Normally, the AC will retain its value until the corresponding CAS completes. Then, the AC is cleared. If a second load hits in the TAT while the AC is full, that load executes as an plain load (i.e., it is not a TL).

CASPAR does not always need multiple CAS failures to insert an address in the TAT. We will see that a CAS that has encountered a queue in the directory returns a hint that can be used to insert the address accessed in the TAT.

4.2 Efficiently Queueing-up Concurrent CASes

4.2.1 Enforcing Load-to-CAS Atomicity

To support hardware queueing of concurrent CASes directed to the same address, CASPAR enforces Load-to-CAS atomicity. This is shown in Figure 4. A TL requests the memory line in Exclusive state. When the line arrives at the cache, the hardware sets a CAS Mode (CM) bit in the line's cache tag (Figure 3(c)). The cache is now in *CAS Mode*, and rejects any incoming coherence requests for the line. The cache remains in CAS Mode until the corresponding CAS completes. If no CAS to the line executes within a timeout period (e.g., due to a bug), the CAS Mode expires. If an exception occurs, CM is cleared.

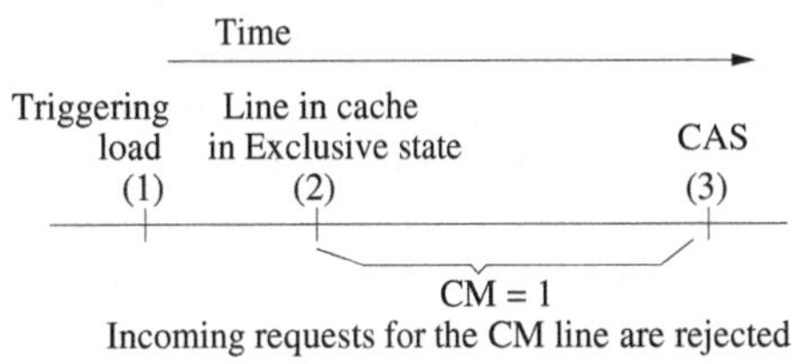

Figure 4: Timeline to enforce Load-to-CAS atomicity.

It is possible that two or more processors end-up waiting on each other—e.g., if two processors execute load-to-CASes to different addresses, but, in between the load and the CAS, they attempt to access the address of the other's CAS location (or false-share it). The timeout mechanism avoids deadlock. A similar timeout mechanism has been proposed for LL/SC [55].

4.2.2 Queueing Requests in the Directory

All the concurrent requesters to a given CAS location are queued-up in hardware by CASPAR in a directory module. As shown in Figure 5, when a TL request from processor P_i arrives at the directory, it is placed at the tail of the hardware queue. The directory continuously issues requests to the current owner of the line on behalf of the processor at the head of the queue. Such requests keep being rejected while the owner has its CM bit set in its cache line tag. When the owner clears the CM bit, the directory succeeds at stealing the line in Exclusive state and sends it to the processor at the head of the queue—as a response to its initial TL. Immediately after that, the directory dequeues the head entry from the directory queue and starts requesting the line from the new owner on behalf of the new entry at the head of the queue.

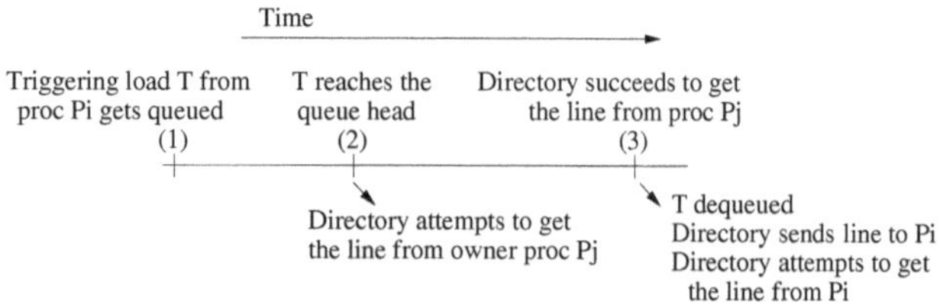

Figure 5: Timeline to queue/dequeue requests.

Figure 3(d) shows the hardware queue. Logically, the directory entry for the contended CAS location has a pointer to the queue. Each queue entry records the requesting processor's ID, the type of request (request to read or to write), and if the read is a TL. A directory module can have multiple queues for different addresses.

A queue entry of Store type is typically due to a CAS from a processor that is unaware that this location suffers contention. Hence, as indicated before, when the directory processes such an entry, it augments its reply to the requesting processor with a hint bit. If the access was indeed a CAS, this bit prompts the requesting processor to save the address in its TAT (if it is not already there).

4.3 Parallel CAS Execution Through Eager Forwards

Prior proposals that build a synchronization queue in hardware process the queue elements sequentially. CASPAR processes them *in parallel* thanks to two ideas: (1) parallel CAS execution through Eager Forwarding and (2) parallel CAS validation using Group Commits. This section describes the first idea; the next one the other.

4.3.1 Intuitive Idea

CASPAR targets codes where the *new* value to store in the CASed location does not depend on the *old* value in that location. With CASPAR, a processor P_i, before obtaining the line with the *old* value from memory, can *forward* its *new* value to the directory; the directory can send it to the successor processor P_{i+1} in the queue. P_{i+1} receives the value as a response to its TL request for its *old* value, and uses this highly-accurate hint of *old* in its CAS. Note that the forwarded value is coupled with its offset in the cache line, so P_{i+1} uses it only if it matches its TL address. With this scheme, both processors can execute the CAS *in parallel.*

Later, when P_{i+1} reaches the head of the queue, the coherence protocol supplies the line to P_{i+1}, as the true response to P_{i+1}'s TL. On reception of the line, the hardware in P_{i+1} compares the value in the line to the *old* value that was received (and used) earlier on. If the validation succeeds, the hardware merges the *new* value produced by P_{i+1} into the line, and allows the protocol to transfer the line to the next processor in the queue.

Typically, the *old* value received from the predecessor will be correct. However, there are events such as branch mispredictions in the predecessor that may cause divergence between the value forwarded and the line received later. In this case, the *old* value used was incorrect and execution needs to be squashed and restarted from the TL issue. To support this, in a TL, the processor performs a checkpoint and enters speculative (i.e., transactional) execution.

CASPAR speeds-up execution because CASes are executed early and in parallel. For now, the validation step that allows processors to exit speculation is serialized. (We relax this property in Section 4.4.) However, processors can continue speculative execution past the CAS, until the *old* value is validated. Then, they commit all the work performed since the TL issue.

A value is forwarded by writing it back to the directory in a fine-grain writeback-like transaction. The directory stores the value in the queue entry of the sender processor and, if there is a successor processor, passes the value to the successor. Note that the successor receives the value as a speculative response to its TL. This means that the successor is expecting a value, which makes our approach different than classical unsolicited forwarding (e.g., [37, 43]).

In practice, the directory does not pass the value to the successor unconditionally. It tries to avoid passing a value to a processor whose *new* value depends on the *old* value. To see why, consider the *pop()* operation in Figure 1(c), where the *new* value depends on the *old* one (Line 24). If a processor executing *pop()* receives a forwarded value, it will dereference it in Line 24, attempting to read data written by the sender of the forward. This will lead to the squashing of the predecessor, if it is still executing speculatively.

Therefore, when the directory receives a forwarded value from P_i, it will only pass it to P_{i+1} if and when P_{i+1} also sends a forwarded value to the directory. The latter forward is a hint that P_{i+1} will not squash the predecessor because its *new* value does not depend on the *old* one. Intuitively, in a queue with push and pop requests, forwarding will only occur between consecutive pushes. Alternatively, we could implement CASPAR on top of a TM design that allows some coherence operations between executing transactions, such as OmniOrder [54]. This would allow a processor to deref-

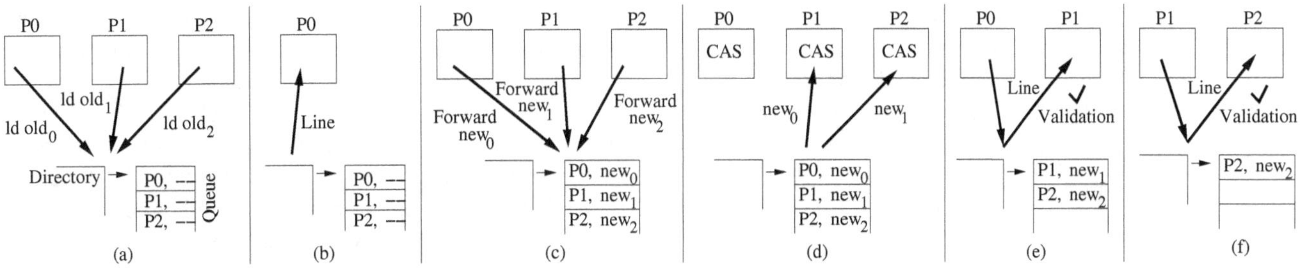

Figure 6: Operation of Eager Forwarding.

erence the received value without squashing the predecessor. We defer this extension to future work.

Figure 6 shows the operation of CASPAR for three processors. In Figure 6(a), all processors issue TLs, and get queued as P_0 first, then P_1, and then P_2. The queue contains no *new* values. In Figure 6(b), the directory provides the line to P_0, which is at the head of the queue. Soon after the TLs reach the directory, the forwarded *new* values also arrive at the directory, and are stored in the queue (Figure 6(c)). The directory immediately sends the *new* values to the successor processors, and all processors now have the data they need to perform the CAS in parallel (Figure 6(d)). As described before, the directory attempts to get the line from P_0. When it succeeds (Figure 6(e)), it pops the first entry from the queue and replies to the next entry's TL by sending the line to P_1. P_1 validates the speculative execution and commits it. The directory repeats the same process for P_2, which is the new head of the queue (Figure 6(f)).

4.3.2 Architectural Components Required

Eager forwarding requires architectural components to: (1) transfer the *new* value to the successor, (2) accept an early *old* value from the predecessor and later validate it, and (3) support speculative execution from the TL until the execution is validated. We describe each one in turn and outline the hardware structures.

A. Transfer the new value. In a conventional pipeline, a CAS instruction performs the read-modify-write of a cache line when it is at the head of the Reorder Buffer (ROB). With CASPAR, a CAS instruction whose address hits in the Active CAS (AC) (Figure 3(b)) has a two-step execution. First, as soon as its *new* value is known, it forwards *new* to the directory. Second, when it reaches the ROB head and we know its *new* value and its *old* value (perhaps speculatively), it performs the read-modify-write as in a conventional system.

Since forwarding the *new* value is on the critical path of the parallel execution, it is performed as soon as *new* is known, bypassing all the other loads and stores by the processor. This is safe because *new* is observed only by the next processor in the directory queue (as it is deposited in the queue rather than in memory), where it is used only as a hint that is validated upon committing (i.e., as a value prediction). As detailed in Section 4.3.4, standard speculative execution conflict checks guarantee that using a forwarded value does not cause memory consistency errors.

B. Old value use and validation. After a processor issues a TL to memory, it may receive a speculative *old* value from the directory. Such a value is stored in the AC structure, and cannot be used until the TL has reached the ROB head and checkpointed. At that point, execution turns speculative, and the thread can use the received *old* value. In particular, the CAS operation may use it, and store the speculative CAS result in the cache.

Eventually, the processor will receive from the directory the line requested by the TL. Then, the hardware compares the value in the incoming line to the speculative *old* value. If the values are different, execution is rolled back to the checkpoint and the value in the line is used rather than the speculative *old* value. Otherwise, the work done so far is useful and correct, and is committed. Note that this value-based validation does not introduce an ABA problem [49]. Since the directory manages the hardware queue, a processor can only see updates from its immediate predecessor; no other processor's updates can interleave between the two.

C. Speculative execution from TL to validation. When a TL reaches the ROB head and the requested line is not in Exclusive (or Dirty) state in the cache, the hardware performs a checkpoint and the processor enters speculative execution. If, instead, the line is already in one of these states, there is no need to become speculative because the CAS will execute with safe data very soon.

As in conventional TM, during speculative execution, data conflicts with incoming coherence transactions cause an abort. If speculative data is about to overflow the cache, the execution can stall rather than abort. There is no danger of deadlock because there is always a non-speculative thread—the one at the head of the queue.

At some point during speculative execution, the requested line is provided by the memory system. If the processor had used a speculative *old* value, then the hardware performs the above validation step, and the transaction commits or aborts. This may occur past the CAS execution.

D. Hardware structures. Figure 7(a) shows the two main hardware structure extensions required for eager forwarding. First, in the processor, the Active CAS (AC) is extended to include the speculative *old* value received (SpecOld) and a set of bits (Trans?, LineArrived?, CASDone? and NewSent?). The speculative *old* value is kept in the AC to compare it to the line's value in the validation step. The bit fields are used by a state machine to track execution states.

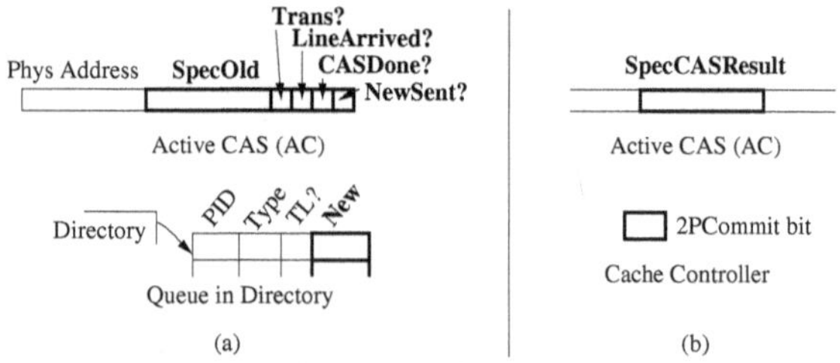

Figure 7: Additional hardware for eager forwarding (a) and parallel CAS validation (b).

In the directory queue, we add one extra field per entry. For the entry of a given processor, the field contains the *new* value forwarded by the processor to the directory.

4.3.3 Timeline

Figure 8 shows a typical timeline of eager forwarding. The events are shown above the horizontal line, while the actions are shown below the line.

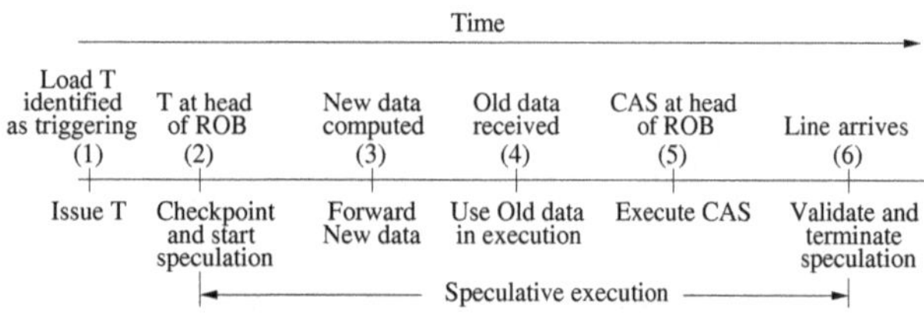

Figure 8: Timeline to perform eager forwarding.

The first event occurs when a load is identified as TL (Section 4.1). Event (2) is when the TL reaches the ROB head. Unless the line is already in Exclusive (or Dirty) state in the cache, the hardware checkpoints and starts speculative execution. Event (3) occurs when a CAS instruction in the pipeline finds that its address matches the one in the AC, and that its register operand with the *new* value to write is already full. In this case, the hardware forwards the *new* value to the directory. Typically, the CAS is not at the ROB head.

When an *old* value is received for a line with the CM bit set, it is saved in the SpecOld field of the AC for later validation. If the processor is in speculative mode, then Event (4) occurs, and the received *old* value is used in the execution.

Event (5) occurs when the CAS instruction reaches the ROB head, the register operands with its *new* value and its *old* (possibly speculative) value are full, and all prior accesses have completed. The CAS then executes, either speculatively (reading from SpecOld) or not (reading from the cache). If the CAS succeeds, the cache is updated. Irrespective of whether the CAS succeeds, execution continues (possibly speculatively).

Finally, Event (6) occurs when the requested line finally arrives for a cache entry marked with the CM bit. The hardware validates the SpecOld field of the AC against the line. If the validation fails, the processor rolls back to the checkpoint; otherwise the speculative execution commits. In all cases, the AC and the CM bit get cleared.

These events may be ordered in slightly different manners. In all cases, it can be shown that the algorithm works.

A processor may forward a *new* value to the directory twice. This may occur in a branch misprediction where *new* is forwarded on both sides of the branch. The directory only takes the first forwarded value. This case may cause the successor processor to fail the validation. However, correctness is guaranteed.

4.3.4 Memory Consistency Issues in Forwarding Data

In CASPAR, the *new* value of a processor (P_i) finds its way to the immediate successor in the queue (P_{i+1}) before P_i performs the CAS. In addition, *new* can bypass all the other outgoing accesses from P_i. This operation causes no memory consistency errors for the following reasons.

First, the forwarded value does not update memory; it is saved in the directory queue and sent to P_{i+1}. Second, if *new*'s value is wrong, the worst that can happen is that P_{i+1} executed past the CAS, gets squashed when its validation fails, and restarts from the TL using the correct value.

Since *new* can bypass earlier accesses in P_i's outgoing buffers, P_{i+1} may observe *new* before it observes other P_i accesses that precede the corresponding CAS in P_i's program order. Figure 9 shows an example, where P_i performs a TL and CAS on location *Stack*. In between the two, the *new* value of *Stack* is forwarded before P_i updates variable *X*. It is possible that P_{i+1} reads the forwarded value of *Stack* and then X. Hence, it observes the new value of *Stack* and the old value of *X*. This will not cause a consistency violation because P_{i+1} turns speculative when it reads *Stack*. Hence, when P_i writes X, it will send an invalidation to P_{i+1} and squash P_{i+1}'s execution.

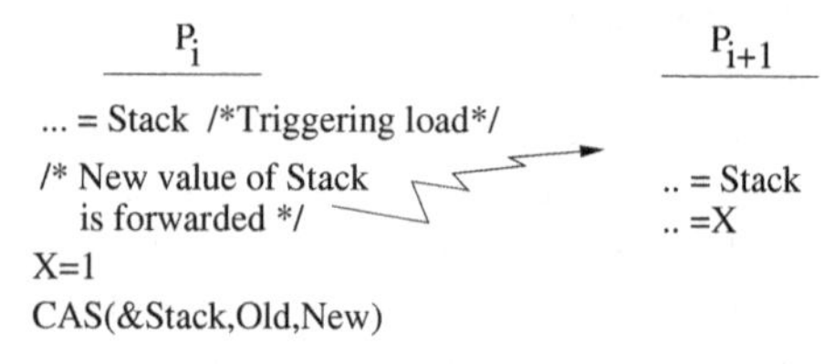

Figure 9: Forwarding causes no consistency violation.

In fact, P_{i+1}'s transaction can commit only if it uses the correct state. The transaction cannot commit until P_i performs the CAS, and P_{i+1} receives the line and validates the *new* value that it used. By this time, all of P_i's accesses that precede the CAS have been completed, including all writes. Such writes would have squashed P_{i+1}'s transaction if it had read an incorrect value. Moreover, P_i cannot read any state generated by P_{i+1} before *new* is validated because P_{i+1}'s execution is speculative.

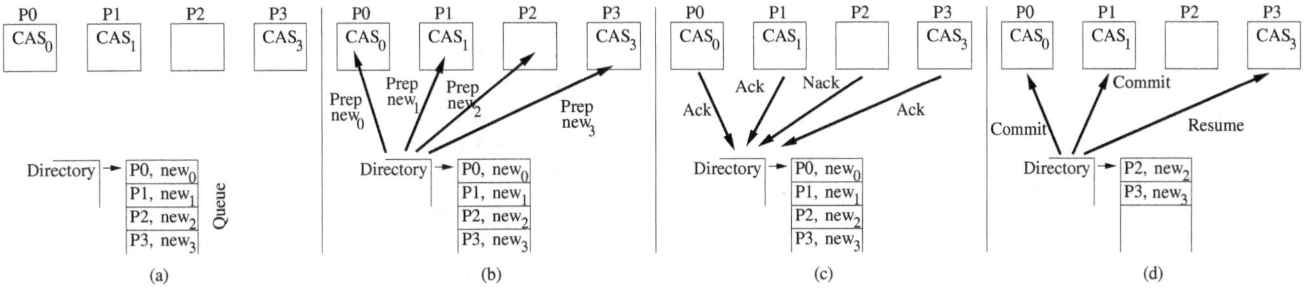

Figure 10: Parallel CAS validation.

4.4 Parallel CAS Validation Using Group Commits

With eager forwarding, the queued processors still perform the CAS validation step sequentially (Figures 6(e)-(f)). In theory, this should not hurt performance because processors do not stall after a CAS waiting for validation: they continue executing speculatively. In practice, however, it is desirable to validate sooner for two reasons. The first one is to reduce the time a processor remains speculative and, hence, exposed to aborts. The second reason is to avoid stalls in codes where a processor repeatedly executes CASes to the same address—a common pattern in codes with fine-grain synchronization.

Indeed, assume that a processor has issued a TL and completed a CAS, but has not received the line yet. It remains speculative. Suppose that it then executes the load for a second load-to-CAS to the same address. Since the AC is still full, the load is not designated a TL but a plain load. The load goes to the cache and stalls, waiting for the line requested by the TL. The pipeline will likely stall soon after. In essence, the processor has overlapped as much speculative execution as it could with the TL, and it now stalls. It will not resume execution until the processor receives the line.

If we have a long queue, it will take on average a long time for the line to reach a processor. As a result, if a processor repeatedly executes CASes to the same address, it will likely stall for long periods.

To solve these two problems, we propose to accelerate the CAS validation by performing it *in parallel*.

4.4.1 Intuitive Idea

We augment the design of Section 4.3 to validate the CASes in groups of queued processors at a time. The idea is to augment the protocol so that the directory orchestrates group-commits in a manner modeled after the *two-phase commit* (2PC) in transactional processing.

Consider a queue of processors, where many have forwarded their *new* values to the directory—which in turn has saved the values and sent them to their successors. When the directory finally obtains the line, rather than sending it to the next processor in the queue for validation, it attempts to *group-validate* a group of processors. To do this, as it dequeues the processor that supplied the line, it checks that the value that the processor forwarded in the past matches the current value in the line. If so, it proceeds to group-validate the next set of contiguous processors in the hardware queue that have provided their *new* values. It does so in three steps.

First, it sends a *Prep* message (for "prepare-to-commit") to all of these processors in parallel. In each message (say to processor P_i), the directory includes the *new* value that the processor had earlier forwarded to the directory (new_i). The goal is for P_i to validate it against the outcome of P_i's CAS. Recall that new_i has already been used by the successor processor P_{i+1}.

Second, when P_i receives the *Prep* message, it compares *Prep*'s value (new_i) to the result of its CAS. If the values match, the validation succeeds. P_i then responds to the directory with an *Ack* message and temporarily sets the pipeline in a quiescent, stalled state to enable a correct 2PC (see Section 4.4.2). If, instead, the values do not match, or P_i has not performed its CAS yet, or P_i has other pending accesses waiting for the same cache line, then P_i responds to the directory with a *Nack* message and does not stop execution.

Third, after the directory gets all the responses, it identifies the set of contiguous processors (starting from the head of the queue) that responded with *Ack*. To these, it sends a *Commit* message and removes them from the queue; they commit their speculative execution and then resume. To the others that sent *Acks*, the directory sends a *Resume* message; they resume executing speculatively. Finally, to the ones that sent *Nacks*, it does not respond.

If the first processor in the queue sent a *Nack*, the group commit fails. We will see that this processor then falls back to the sequential CAS validation of Section 4.3.

Figure 10 shows an example of parallel CAS validation. In Figure 10(a), four processors are queued up and have forwarded their *new* values to the directory (which has passed them to their successors). In addition, P_0, P_1, and P_3 have completed their CAS. Assume also that the directory/memory has attained the line—hence, the line is not in any cache.

In Figure 10(b), the directory initiates a group commit. It sends a *Prep* to the four processors, together with the corresponding *new* values that the processors had forwarded. On reception, processors P_0, P_1, and P_3 compare the *new* value to the outcome of their CAS. Assume that the values match. Hence, as shown in Figure 10(c), they send *Acks* to the directory. P_2 has not completed its CAS yet. Hence it sends a

Nack. In Figure 10(d), the directory finds that, starting from P_0, the set of contiguous processors that responded with *Ack* are P_0 and P_1. So, these two can commit in a group. The directory sends a *Commit* to them and removes their entries from the queue. It sends a *Resume* to P_3.

4.4.2 Architectural Components Required

Parallel CAS validation requires components to: (1) quiesce a processor pipeline in a two-phase commit, (2) commit a load-to-CAS section without the processor ever obtaining the memory line with the CAS data, and (3) seamlessly revert to sequential CAS validation if group validation fails.

A. Quiesce a pipeline in a two-phase commit. We extend the Active CAS (AC) structure to save the result of a speculative CAS execution. Then, if the processor receives a *Prep*, it compares the message's *new* value to the result of the CAS. If they are the same, the processor prepares for a two-phase commit (2PC).

For correctness, the 2PC requires that the processor be able to commit if it is instructed to do so. Thus, its speculative execution must never get squashed after sending an *Ack*. Quiescing the pipeline achieves this: The processor stops issuing new instructions and flushes the pipeline, discarding all the unretired instructions. It also sets a new bit in the cache controller called *2PCommit*. This bit will reject all incoming coherence requests that could cause a squash of the thread—i.e., incoming reads to speculatively written lines, and incoming writes to speculatively accessed lines. Finally, when the write buffer is drained, the processor disables interrupts (like in the x86 CLI instruction), bringing the pipeline to the quiescent state.

Once in quiescent state, the processor sends the *Ack* to the directory. It remains quiescent until the arrival of a *Commit* or *Resume*. Then (after committing the thread if the message was a *Commit*) the *2PCommit* bit is cleared to accept all coherence requests. Interrupts are re-enabled (like in x86's STI instruction) and the processor re-starts issuing instructions.

It is possible that a pipeline cannot get into a quiescent state because the writes in its write buffer end up getting rejected by another processor with its *2PCommit* bit set. This case is detected because the response to the rejected writes indicates that the destination processor does not accept requests. In this case, the processor refuses to participate in the 2PC: it sends a *Nack* to the directory and continues executing. Its CAS will be validated later, either in a group or sequentially with the default algorithm.

B. Commit without ever getting the cache line. A successful parallel CAS validation is fast because the memory line with the CAS data does not need to be transferred between the caches of the processors involved. Instead, these processors commit their load-to-CAS code without ever obtaining the line in their caches.

To see how it works, consider a processor that is executing a load-to-CAS section. The TL caused a cache miss, which triggered the allocation of an MSHR entry and of space for a line in the cache. When the *old* value is received from the predecessor, it is stored in the MSHR and used speculatively. Later, the CAS is performed speculatively and its result is stored in the AC. Suppose that a *Prep* now arrives and its value matches the CAS value in the AC. If and when the *Commit* is eventually received, the hardware simply commits the execution. In addition, it discards the MSHR entry and frees-up the empty cache line.

C. Seamlessly revert to sequential CAS validation. Whenever a group commit fails, our algorithm performs a sequential CAS validation like the algorithm of Section 4.3. Specifically, a failure occurs when the first processor in the queue (P_0) responds to the directory's *Prep* with a *Nack*. This may be because either P_0 has not performed its CAS yet or P_0's CAS fails the validation—i.e., the CAS produces a value different than the one P_0 forwarded to the directory (new_0). In either case, in CASPAR, the directory sends the memory line to P_0, which performs a local CAS validation as described in Section 4.3. The directory also sends *Resumes* to processors that sent *Acks*. As usual, the directory will then try to obtain the cache line from P_0. Once it gets it, it attempts the next parallel CAS validation.

D. Hardware structures. Figure 7(b) shows the two main hardware structure extensions required. First, in the processor, the Active CAS (AC) is extended to include the result of the speculative CAS operation (*SpecCASResult*). Second, in the cache controller, we have the *2PCommit* bit, which rejects incoming coherence requests that could cause a squash of the thread during the two-phase commit.

5. Supporting Other Primitives

CASPAR applies straightforwardly to other atomic instructions, such as LL/SC [29]. LL/SC has an explicit triggering load (i.e., the LL), and so is simple to serialize with hardware queueing. We can then apply parallel execution and validation, which are agnostic to the atomic instruction used.

We believe CASPAR can also be extended to TM, which is increasingly being used for lock-free synchronization [16]. In typical TM designs, programmer-defined transactions that execute read-modify-write (RMW) access sequences to shared variables (e.g., a queue head) will abort on conflict and be serialized. Such transactions can benefit from the CASPAR ideas. Specifically, aborts can be used as the signal to identify the contended variables, similarly to how TLs are identified. Once a RMW sequence of accesses is identified, the written value can be eagerly forwarded to another transaction, allowing the concurrent execution of multiple transactions. Compared to the current CASPAR design, supporting TM presents new challenges, such as the possibility of multiple RMW sequences in a transaction. We defer exploration of this CASPAR extension to future work.

6. Evaluation Environment

We evaluate CASPAR with simulations of a 64-core chip using the Sniper simulator [14]. Table 2 shows the baseline architecture modeled. The core and L1/L2 cache parameters are taken from Nehalem [64]. We implement three designs which incrementally build on top of this baseline (B). They are Queue (Q), EagerForwarding (EF) and CASPAR (C). *Queue* implements basic hardware queueing in each module of the distributed L3 tag directory, similar to past proposals, as per Section 4.2. *EagerForwarding* adds parallel CAS execution with eager forwarding as per Section 4.3. CASPAR further adds support for parallel CAS validation using group commits as per Section 4.4, and is our complete design.

Parameter	Value
Architecture	64 cores on chip
Core	2.66 GHz, 4-wide out-of-order
ROB, Res. Stations	128 entries, 36 entries (unified)
Private L1	32KB WB, 8-way, 4 cycles round trip
Private L2	256KB WB, 8-way, 9 cycles round trip
Shared, NUCA L3	16MB WB, 16-way, 12 cycles (near access)
Cache line size	64B
Coherence	MESI, full-mapped tag directory
Network	2-D torus, 2-cycle hop latency, 64 bits/cycle link
Main memory	120 cycles round trip
Entering quiescence	$\approx$ Time to drain write buffer

Table 2: Architecture simulated.

We use two sets of programs for our evaluation (Table 3): five kernels and four applications. The kernels consist of four computational kernels (*FIFO*, *LPO*, *MBrot*, and *LIFO*) and one standard memory allocation kernel (*Larson*). In the computational kernels, each thread executes a loop where, in each iteration, the thread performs some computation and then synchronizes with a lock-free operation. The memory allocation kernel runs Michael's memory allocator [47], which internally uses lock-free algorithms.

Program	Description
Kernels:	
FIFO	Add/remove from Michael and Scott's lock-free queue [48].
LIFO-push-only (LPO)	Push into a lock-free stack, modeling bulk synchronization [67] or initial population of a work list.
MBrot	Mandelbrot set computation. Computing threads pass results to rendering thread via a multi-producer/single-consumer queue.
Larson	Threads allocate/deallocate objects, while transferring some objects to be freed by other threads [41].
LIFO	Push/Pop into a Treiber's lock-free stack [66].
Applications:	
FFT	1D FFT of a vector of complex values from BOTS.
CC	Connected components computation based on a concurrent union-find algorithm from Galois. Input is USA road network.
IS	Maximal independent set computation from Galois. Input is USA road network.
DT	Delaunay triangulation from a given a set of points from Galois. Input is 5 million 2D points.

Table 3: Programs evaluated.

The applications are FFT from the Barcelona OpenMP Tasks Suite (BOTS) [17] and three graph analytics programs from the Galois system [39, 50]. BOTS includes several task parallel applications from various domains; we evaluate FFT, which uses fine-grained tasks and stresses the task scheduler. We run FFT using the open-source Qthreads parallel runtime [51, 69], which supports multiple scheduling options. We compare schedulers that use lock-free LIFO [66] and FIFO [48] queues to the default lock-based scheduler. Galois [39] provides a domain-specific language and runtime for graph algorithms. The runtime parallelizes graph analytics loops using a work list data structure where threads add/remove work. We evaluate three Galois programs where work list synchronization accounts for a sizable fraction of the execution time. We add lock-free LIFO and FIFO work lists to the Galois 2.2.1 runtime [1], and compare the execution time to the default lock-based work list.

7. Evaluation

7.1 Kernels

Since the threads in the kernels repeatedly perform work and then synchronize using a lock-free algorithm, we use *CAS throughput*—the number of successful CAS operations per unit time—as the performance metric. We measure throughput over 5 ms (13.3 million cycles) of kernel execution time. Figure 11 shows the results, normalized to the throughput of the baseline (B) design. On average, EF and C improve the CAS throughput by 53% and 83%, respectively, over the baseline multicore (B), and by 10% and 32%, respectively, over hardware queues only (Q).

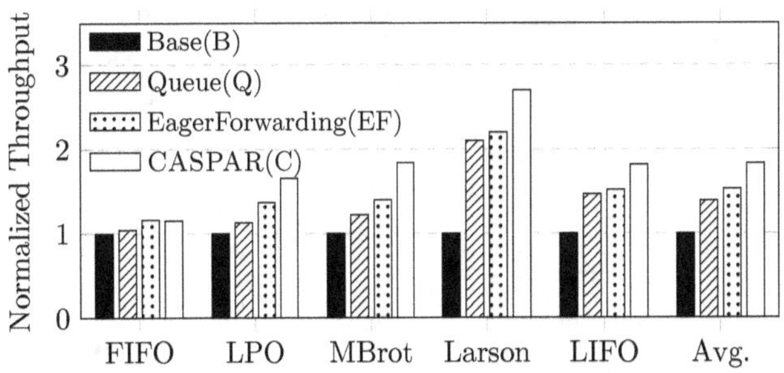

Figure 11: Kernel throughput for the different designs.

The gains vary depending on the kernel characteristics. Hardware queueing (Q) provides benefits in most of the kernels. The benefits are especially large in *Larson* and *LIFO*, where B's CASes frequently fail. Q eliminates CAS failures by enforcing load-to-CAS atomicity.

EF provides additional throughput boost for most kernels. The improvements are largest in the kernels with mostly enqueue operations, namely *LPO* and *MBrot*. The other kernels have both enqueue and dequeue operations; the latter have CAS dependencies as shown in Figure 1(c), which reduce the frequency of eager forwarding.

C improves over EF in all kernels except *FIFO*. To see why, recall that a processor in EF can execute speculatively past a CAS but stalls upon attempting to execute another load to the location that was CASed until the pending cache line arrives (Section 4.4). The wait time for the cache line is proportional to the length of the queue in the directory. On average, the queue size increases by 2.2x from Q to EF, since speculative execution increases the rate at which a

[1]The code is available at `http://git.io/galoisLF`.

core issues TLs. This results in stall cycles for kernels where the work between successive executions of the load-to-CAS section is too small to absorb the wait time for the cache line. This is the case for all kernels under EF except *FIFO*. On the other hand, C uses group commit to dequeue groups of processors at a time. With C, the average queue size is ≈33% of Q's. This reduces the stall and improves the throughput of C over EF in these kernels. In *FIFO*, EF had few stall cycles, and so C and EF perform comparably.

7.1.1 Impact of the Amount of Work

We now measure the change in throughput as we change the amount of work performed between synchronizations. We start with the amount of work in the experiments of Figure 11 and progressively reduce the work. Figures 12(a)-(c) show the throughput of *LPO*, *MBrot* and *LIFO* in each of the architectures. The plots are normalized to the B design for the amount of work in Figure 11.

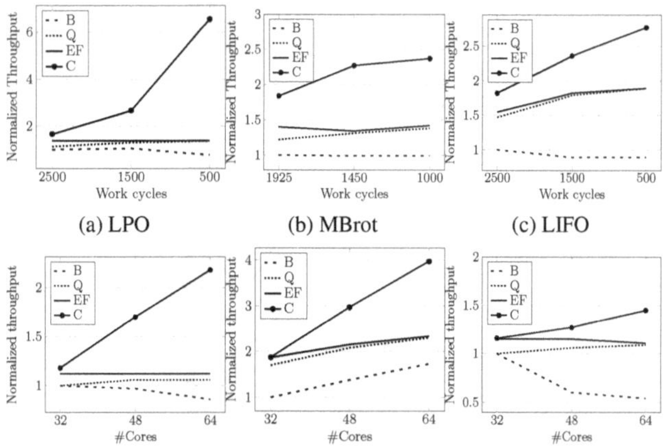

(a) LPO (b) MBrot (c) LIFO

(d) LPO (e) MBrot (f) LIFO

Figure 12: Impact of work size (a-c) & scalability (d-f).

Reducing the work should increase CAS throughput, but it also increases CAS contention. In B, it increases the CAS failure rate. This results in a largely flat or decreasing throughput, which is the number of *successful* CASes per unit time. In Q, hardware queueing improves synchronization efficiency and eliminates CAS failures. Hence, decreasing work increases the CAS throughput in two of the three kernels.

In EF, the throughput is initially higher than in Q because processors perform part of the work speculatively. However, the throughput gap between the two narrows as the available work to speculate on decreases. EF is unable to exploit the reduction in work to improve throughput in two kernels—the processors eventually stall. Finally, C keeps increasing its throughput as the amount of work decreases. This is due to C's parallel validation, which eliminates EF's stalls.

To better compare EF and C, Figure 13 breaks down the normalized execution cycles in EF and C as they run *MBrot* and *FIFO*. We show two variants per kernel: high work and low work between CASes. The cycles are broken down into

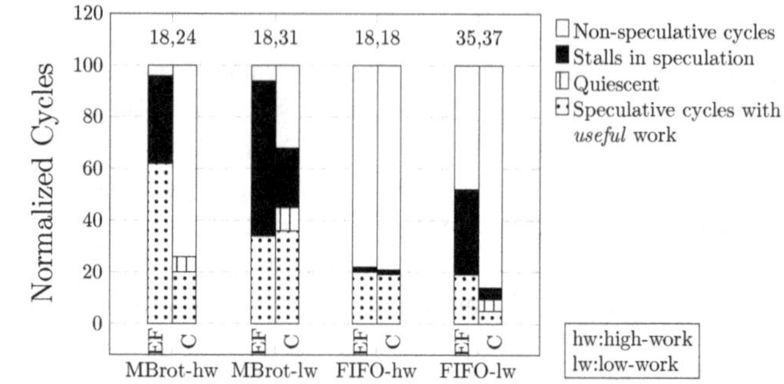

Figure 13: Cycle breakdown for EF and C. The numbers at the top of the bars are the CAS throughput.

non-speculative execution, processor stalls while speculative, quiescent pipeline (C only), and speculative execution of useful work. On top of the bars, we have the CAS throughput in successful CASes per 1,000 cycles.

Consider *MBrot* first. When the work is low, EF stalls frequently. C converts a good fraction of these cycles to non-speculative cycles using group commit. While C suffers from some quiescent pipeline cycles, the result is a large improvement in throughput. When the work is high, EF has fewer stall cycles. In this case, C converts both the remaining stall cycles and a portion of speculative cycles into non-speculative. However, the CAS throughput is not as high because improvements come only from the elimination of the stall cycles.

Consider *FIFO* now. When the work is low, EF has stall cycles and C eliminates most of them, increasing the throughput. When the work is high, however, EF has few stall or speculative cycles. The hardware queue is short and contains both push and pop requests. As a result, C is unable to perform much parallel CAS validation, and does not reduce either type of cycles. As a result, as shown in Figure 11, the EF and C throughputs are similar.

7.1.2 Scalability

We now measure the throughput as we change the number of processors for a fixed amount of work (i.e., the intermediate work amount from Figures 12(a)-(c)). This is shown in Figures 12(d)-(f), which are normalized to B with 32 cores. We note that *LPO* and *LIFO* have high CAS contention. Hence, they scale poorly in B because, with more cores, we have more CAS failures. Q and EF maintain performance for these kernels even at a high core count. C breaks the sequential validation in EF, and scales well. On the other hand, *MBrot* has low CAS contention. Hence, B's throughput improves with additional cores due to parallelization. Q and EF scale better, and C scales linearly.

7.2 Applications

Figure 14 compares the execution time of the applications (both LIFO and FIFO variants) on different architectures. The B bar is now replaced by two bars: L is the *original* lock-based version, and LF is the *lock-free* one. Q, EF, and C use

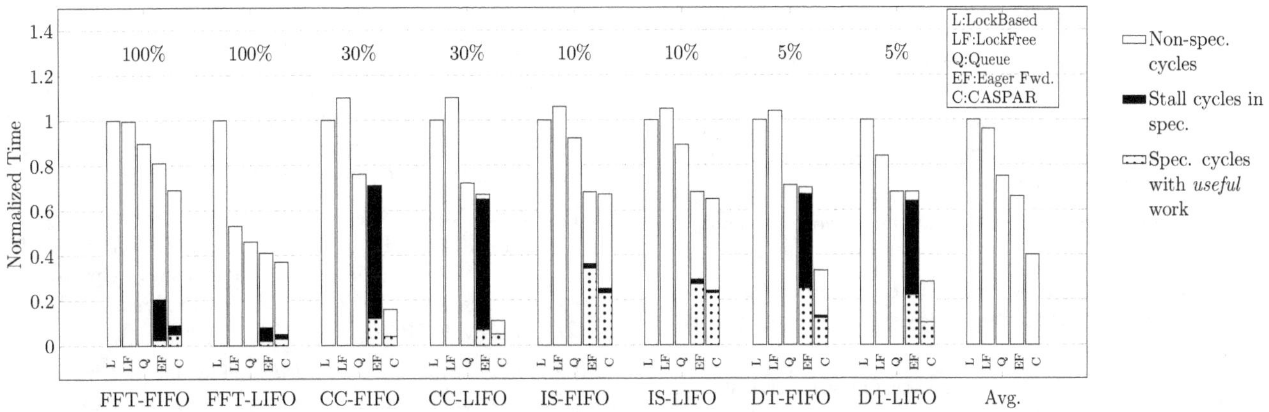

Figure 14: Execution time of the applications.

the latter. The time is normalized to L and broken down into the categories of Figure 13—though the Quiescent cycles are too few to see. The average bars are not broken down. The number above each program is the fraction of the program time that we simulate. In Galois, this is the phase in which the work list is populated.

By taking L and re-writing the synchronizations in a lock-free manner in LF, the execution time decreases by an average of only 4%—in fact, in some programs, the time goes up. As we go from LF to Q, the efficient queue-based synchronization reduces the execution time by 22% on average. Among the applications, *CC* and *DT* have the highest reductions. This is because they have the least work between successive calls to the load-to-CAS region and, as a result, suffered a high CAS failure rate. Going from Q to EF, we see that adding eager forwarding reduces the execution time by 12% on average. The reductions are substantial in *IS*, where there are long queues and data is forwarded effectively. The other programs have smaller gains in EF: in *CC* and *DT*, the processors forward data but soon stall as they re-reference the CAS location; in *FFT*, the hardware queue has as many requests for enqueue as for dequeue operations, hampering data forwarding. Finally, going from EF to C, we see that adding group commits reduces the execution time by 40% on average. The largest reductions occur in *CC* and *DT*, where the processors were stalled, and group commit allows them to make progress. In the other programs, C helps processors commit sooner, transforming speculative cycles into non-speculative ones. However, this does not translate into lower execution time.

Overall, C is a very robust design. On average, it reduces the execution time of these sections of applications by 47% relative to Q, and 58% relative to LF. It makes these lock-free sections 2.5x faster on average than the original, lock-based versions (L).

8. Related Work

TM. Most conflict-serializable TM designs [8, 11, 53, 54, 57] abort when multiple transactions read the same variable and then write to it. In contrast, CASPAR preemptively serializes such regions. Other designs [10, 28] similarly preemptively stall loads to contended locations. These designs place special software routines on the transactions' critical path. DATM [57] and OmniOrder [54] transfer speculative data from one transaction to another. They do so to prevent squashes between transactions that commit serially. In contrast, CASPAR transfers speculative data early so that serialized operations can execute in parallel.

Hardware support for scalable synchronization. The proposals most relevant to our work are those that build hardware synchronization queues [20, 32, 43, 55, 56, 58, 68]. In Section 2, we showed how they relate to our work. Some experimental or commercial machines have implemented other scalable synchronization primitives. They include Full/Empty bits in the HEP [31] and Tera multiprocessors [7]; Fetch&Add with request combining in the NYU Ultracomputer [21]; Fetch&Φ operations in the IBM RP3 [52], the SGI Origin [42], and the Cray T3E [60]; and a versatile Synchronization Processor in Cedar [38].

9. Conclusions and Future Work

This paper proposed CASPAR, an architecture that *breaks* the serialization of hardware queues and enables the queued processors to perform lock-free synchronization *in parallel.* CASPAR executes the CASes in the queued-up processors in parallel through eager forwarding, and validates them in parallel through group commit. Compared to existing proposals with hardware queues, CASPAR improves the throughput of kernels by 32% on average, and reduces the execution time of the sections considered in lock-free versions of applications by 47% on average. This makes such sections 2.5x faster than in the original applications.

CASPAR can be improved in several ways. First, we can dynamically rearrange the placement of processors in the queue so that processors that forward values to the queue are placed next to each other. This would increase eager forwarding effectiveness. Also, CASPAR can leverage TM designs such as OmniOrder [54] that allow passing data between transactions. Finally, we can extend CASPAR to allow breaking serialization in TM.

References

[1] The Go Programming Language. http://golang.org, 2014.

[2] NetBSD producer/consumer queue. ftp://ftp.netbsd.org/pub/NetBSD/NetBSD-current/src/sys/kern/subr_pcq.c, 2014.

[3] fix8: High Performance C++ FIX Framework. http://fix8.org, 2014.

[4] MySQL Concurrent Allocator. https://github.com/twitter/mysql/blob/master/mysys/lf_alloc-pin.c, 2014.

[5] Y. Afek, G. Korland, and E. Yanovsky. Quasi-Linearizability: Relaxed Consistency for Improved Concurrency. In *Proceedings of the 14th International Conference On Principles Of Distributed Systems (OPODIS 2010)*, volume 6490 of *LNCS*, pages 395–410. 2010.

[6] D. Alistarh, J. Kopinsky, J. Li, and N. Shavit. The SprayList: A Scalable Relaxed Priority Queue. In *Proceedings of the 20th ACM SIGPLAN Symposium on Principles and Practice of Parallel Programming*, PPoPP 2015, pages 11–20, 2015.

[7] R. Alverson, D. Callahan, D. Cummings, B. Koblenz, A. Porterfield, and B. Smith. The Tera Computer System. In *Proceedings of the 4th International Conference on Supercomputing*, ICS '90, pages 1–6, 1990.

[8] U. Aydonat and T. S. Abdelrahman. Hardware Support for Relaxed Concurrency Control in Transactional Memory. In *Proceedings of the 43rd Annual IEEE/ACM International Symposium on Microarchitecture*, MICRO '10, pages 15–26, 2010.

[9] S. Bansal and D. S. Modha. CAR: Clock with Adaptive Replacement. In *Proceedings of the 3rd USENIX Conference on File and Storage Technologies*, FAST '04, pages 187–200, 2004.

[10] G. Blake, R. G. Dreslinski, and T. Mudge. Proactive Transaction Scheduling for Contention Management. In *Proceedings of the 42nd Annual IEEE/ACM International Symposium on Microarchitecture*, MICRO '09, pages 156–167, 2009.

[11] C. Blundell, A. Raghavan, and M. M. Martin. RETCON: Transactional Repair Without Replay. In *Proceedings of the 37th Annual International Symposium on Computer Architecture*, ISCA '10, pages 258–269, 2010.

[12] S. Boyd-Wickizer, M. F. Kaashoek, R. Morris, and N. Zeldovich. OpLog: a library for scaling update-heavy data structures. Technical Report MIT-CSAIL-TR-2014-019, MIT Computer Science and Artificial Intelligence Laboratory, September 2014.

[13] J. D. Brouer. Qdisc lockless FIFO. In *Netfilter Workshop*, 2014.

[14] T. E. Carlson, W. Heirman, and L. Eeckhout. Sniper: Exploring the Level of Abstraction for Scalable and Accurate Parallel Multi-core Simulation. In *Proceedings of 2011 International Conference for High Performance Computing, Networking, Storage and Analysis*, SC '11, pages 52:1–52:12, 2011.

[15] C. Diaconu, C. Freedman, E. Ismert, P.-A. Larson, P. Mittal, R. Stonecipher, N. Verma, and M. Zwilling. Hekaton: SQL Server's Memory-optimized OLTP Engine. In *Proceedings of the 2013 ACM SIGMOD International Conference on Management of Data*, SIGMOD '13, pages 1243–1254, 2013.

[16] N. Diegues, P. Romano, and L. Rodrigues. Virtues and Limitations of Commodity Hardware Transactional Memory. In *Proceedings of the 23rd International Conference on Parallel Architectures and Compilation*, PACT '14, pages 3–14, 2014.

[17] A. Duran, X. Teruel, R. Ferrer, X. Martorell, and E. Ayguade. Barcelona OpenMP Tasks Suite: A Set of Benchmarks Targeting the Exploitation of Task Parallelism in OpenMP. In *Proceedings of the 2009 International Conference on Parallel Processing*, ICPP '09, pages 124–131, 2009.

[18] K. Fraser. *Practical lock-freedom*. PhD thesis, University of Cambridge, Computer Laboratory, University of Cambridge, Computer Laboratory, February 2004.

[19] L. Gidra, G. Thomas, J. Sopena, and M. Shapiro. A Study of the Scalability of Stop-the-world Garbage Collectors on Multicores. In *Proceedings of the 18th International Conference on Architectural Support for Programming Languages and Operating Systems*, ASPLOS '13, pages 229–240, 2013.

[20] J. R. Goodman, M. K. Vernon, and P. J. Woest. Efficient Synchronization Primitives for Large-scale Cache-coherent Multiprocessors. In *Proceedings of the 3rd International Conference on Architectural Support for Programming Languages and Operating Systems*, ASPLOS '89, pages 64–75, 1989.

[21] A. Gottlieb, R. Grishman, C. Kruskal, K. McAuliffe, L. Rudolph, and M. Snir. The NYU Ultracomputer – Designing an MIMD, Shared Memory Parallel Machine. In *IEEE Transactions on Computers*, February 1983.

[22] A. Haas, M. Lippautz, T. A. Henzinger, H. Payer, A. Sokolova, C. M. Kirsch, and A. Sezgin. Distributed queues in shared memory: multicore performance and scalability through quantitative relaxation. In *Proceedings of the ACM International Conference on Computing Frontiers*, CF '13, pages 17:1–17:9, 2013.

[23] D. Hendler, N. Shavit, and L. Yerushalmi. A scalable lock-free stack algorithm. In *Proceedings of the 16th Annual ACM Symposium on Parallelism in Algorithms and Architectures*, SPAA 2004, pages 206–215, 2004.

[24] M. Herlihy. Wait-free synchronization. *ACM Transactions on Programming Languages and Systems (TOPLAS)*, 13:124–149, January 1991.

[25] M. Herlihy and N. Shavit. *The Art of Multiprocessor Programming*. Morgan Kaufmann Publishers Inc., San Francisco, CA, USA, 2008.

[26] M. Hoffman, O. Shalev, and N. Shavit. The baskets queue. In *Proceedings of the 11th International Conference on Principles of Distributed Systems*, OPODIS'07, pages 401–414, 2007.

[27] Intel. Intel Xeon Phi Coprocessor. https://software.intel.com/en-us/mic-developer, 2013.

[28] S. A. R. Jafri, G. Voskuilen, and T. N. Vijaykumar. Wait-n-GoTM: Improving HTM Performance by Serializing Cyclic Dependencies. In *Proceedings of the 18th International Conference on Architectural Support for Programming Languages and Operating Systems*, ASPLOS '13, pages 521–534, 2013.

[29] E. H. Jensen, G. W. Hagensen, and J. M. Broughton. A New Approach to Exclusive Data Access in Shared Memory Multiprocessors. Technical Report UCRL-97663, Lawrence Livermore National Laboratory, 1987.

[30] R. Jones, A. Hosking, and E. Moss. *The Garbage Collection Handbook: The Art of Automatic Memory Management*. Chapman & Hall/CRC, 1st edition, 2011.

[31] H. Jordan. Performance Measurements on HEP A Pipelined MIMD Computer. In *International Symposium on Computer Architecture (ISCA)*, June 1983.

[32] A. Kägi, D. Burger, and J. R. Goodman. Efficient Synchronization: Let Them Eat QOLB. In *Proceedings of the 24th Annual International Symposium on Computer Architecture*, ISCA '97, pages 170–180, 1997.

[33] C. Kirsch, H. Payer, H. Röck, and A. Sokolova. Performance, Scalability, and Semantics of Concurrent FIFO Queues. In *Proceedings of the International Conference on Algorithms and Architectures for Parallel Processing (ICA3PP '12)*, volume 7439 of *LNCS*, pages 273–287. 2012.

[34] C. M. Kirsch, M. Lippautz, and H. Payer. Fast and Scalable, Lock-Free k-FIFO Queues. In *Proceedings of the 22nd International Conference on Parallel Architectures and Compilation Techniques*, PACT '13, pages 241–252, 2013.

[35] A. Kivity, D. Laor, G. Costa, P. Enberg, N. Har'El, D. Marti, and V. Zolotarov. OSv—Optimizing the Operating System for Virtual Machines. In *Proceedings of the 2014 USENIX Annual Technical Conference*, ATC '14, pages 61–72, June 2014.

[36] A. Kogan and E. Petrank. Wait-free queues with multiple enqueuers and dequeuers. In *Proceedings of the 16th ACM Symposium on Principles and Practice of Parallel Programming*, PPoPP '11, pages 223–234, 2011.

[37] D. A. Koufaty, X. Chen, D. K. Poulsen, and J. Torrellas. Data Forwarding in Scalable Shared-memory Multiprocessors. In *Proceedings of the 9th International Conference on Supercomputing*, ICS '95, pages 255–264, 1995.

[38] D. Kuck, E. Davidson, D. Lawrie, A. Sameh, C. Q. Zhu, A. Veidenbaum, J. Konicek, P. Yew, K. Gallivan, W. Jalby, H. Wijshoff, R. Bramley, U. M. Yang, P. Emrath, D. Padua, R. Eigenmann, J. Hoeflinger, G. Jaxon, Z. Li, T. Murphy, and J. Andrews. The Cedar System and an Initial Performance Study. In *Proceedings of the 20th Annual International Symposium on Computer Architecture*, ISCA '93, pages 213–223, 1993.

[39] M. Kulkarni, K. Pingali, B. Walter, G. Ramanarayanan, K. Bala, and L. P. Chew. Optimistic parallelism requires abstractions. In *Proceedings of the 2007 ACM SIGPLAN Conference on Programming Language Design and Implementation*, PLDI '07, pages 211–222, 2007.

[40] E. Ladan-Mozes and N. Shavit. An optimistic approach to lock-free FIFO queues. In *Proceedings of the 18th International Symposium on Distributed Computing (DISC 2004)*, volume 3274 of *LNCS*, pages 117–131, 2004.

[41] P.-A. Larson and M. Krishnan. Memory Allocation for Long-running Server Applications. In *Proceedings of the 1st International Symposium on Memory Management*, ISMM '98, pages 176–185, 1998.

[42] J. Laudon and D. Lenoski. The SGI Origin: A ccNUMA Highly Scalable Server. In *Proceedings of the 24th Annual International Symposium on Computer Architecture*, ISCA '97, pages 241–251, 1997.

[43] D. Lenoski, J. Laudon, K. Gharachorloo, W. Weber, A. Gupta, J. Hennessy, M. Horowitz, and M. Lam. The Stanford DASH Multiprocessor. In *IEEE Computer*, March 1992.

[44] I. Lotan and N. Shavit. Skiplist-Based Concurrent Priority Queues. In *Proceedings of the 14th International Parallel and Distributed Processing Symposium*, IPDPS '00, pages 263–268, 2000.

[45] N. D. Matsakis and F. S. Klock, II. The Rust Language. In *Proceedings of the 2014 ACM SIGAda Annual Conference on High Integrity Language Technology*, HILT '14, pages 103–104, 2014.

[46] M. M. Michael. Hazard Pointers: Safe Memory Reclamation for Lock-Free Objects. *IEEE Transactions on Parallel and Distributed System*, 15(6):491–504, June 2004.

[47] M. M. Michael. Scalable lock-free dynamic memory allocation. In *Proceedings of the 2004 ACM SIGPLAN Conference on Programming Language Design and Implementation*, PLDI '04, pages 35–46, 2004.

[48] M. M. Michael and M. L. Scott. Simple, fast, and practical non-blocking and blocking concurrent queue algorithms. In *Proceedings of the 15th Annual ACM Symposium on Principles of Distributed Computing*, PODC '96, pages 267–275, 1996.

[49] M. M. Michael and M. L. Scott. Nonblocking algorithms and preemption-safe locking on multiprogrammed shared memory multiprocessors. *Journal of Parallel and Distributed Computing*, 51:1–26, May 1998.

[50] D. Nguyen, A. Lenharth, and K. Pingali. A Lightweight Infrastructure for Graph Analytics. In *Proceedings of the 24th ACM Symposium on Operating Systems Principles*, SOSP '13, pages 456–471, 2013.

[51] S. L. Olivier, A. K. Porterfield, K. B. Wheeler, M. Spiegel, and J. F. Prins. OpenMP Task Scheduling Strategies for Multicore NUMA Systems. *International Journal of High Performance Computing Applications*, 26(2):110–124, May 2012.

[52] G. Pfister, W. Brantley, D. George, S. Harvey, W. Kleinfelder, K. McAuliffe, E. Melton, V. Norton, and J. Weiss. The IBM Research Parallel Processor Prototype (RP3): Introduction and Architecture. In *Proceedings of the 1985 International Conference on Parallel Processing*, ICPP '85, pages 764–771, 1985.

[53] X. Qian, B. Sahelices, and J. Torrellas. BulkSMT: Designing SMT Processors for Atomic-block Execution. In *Proceedings of the 2012 IEEE 18th International Symposium on High-Performance Computer Architecture*, HPCA '12, pages 1–12, 2012.

[54] X. Qian, B. Sahelices, and J. Torrellas. OmniOrder: Directory-based Conflict Serialization of Transactions. In *Proceeding of the 41st Annual International Symposium on Computer Architecuture*, ISCA '14, pages 421–432, 2014.

[55] R. Rajwar, A. Kägi, and J. R. Goodman. Improving the throughput of synchronization by insertion of delays. In

Proceedings of the 6th International Symposium on High-Performance Computer Architecture, HPCA '00, pages 168–179, January 2000.

[56] R. Rajwar, A. Kägi, and J. R. Goodman. Inferential Queueing and Speculative Push for Reducing Critical Communication Latencies. In *Proceedings of the 17th Annual International Conference on Supercomputing*, ICS '03, pages 273–284, 2003.

[57] H. E. Ramadan, C. J. Rossbach, and E. Witchel. Dependence-aware Transactional Memory for Increased Concurrency. In *Proceedings of the 41st Annual IEEE/ACM International Symposium on Microarchitecture*, MICRO '08, pages 246–257, 2008.

[58] A. Ros and S. Kaxiras. Complexity-effective Multicore Coherence. In *Proceedings of the 21st International Conference on Parallel Architectures and Compilation Techniques*, PACT '12, pages 241–252, 2012.

[59] S. Schneider, C. D. Antonopoulos, and D. S. Nikolopoulos. Scalable Locality-conscious Multithreaded Memory Allocation. In *Proceedings of the 5th International Symposium on Memory Management*, ISMM '06, pages 84–94, 2006.

[60] S. L. Scott. Synchronization and Communication in the T3E Multiprocessor. In *Proceedings of the 7th International Conference on Architectural Support for Programming Languages and Operating Systems*, ASPLOS '96, pages 26–36, 1996.

[61] S. Seo, J. Kim, and J. Lee. SFMalloc: A Lock-Free and Mostly Synchronization-Free Dynamic Memory Allocator for Manycores. In *Proceedings of the 20th International Conference on Parallel Architectures and Compilation Techniques*, PACT '11, pages 253–263, 2011.

[62] N. Shavit. Data Structures in the Multicore Age. *Communications of the ACM*, 54(3):76–84, Mar. 2011.

[63] M. Stonebraker, A. Pavlo, R. Taft, and M. L. Brodie. Enterprise Database Applications and the Cloud: A Difficult Road Ahead. In *Proceedings of the 2014 IEEE International Conference on Cloud Engineering*, IC2E '14, pages 1–6, 2014.

[64] M. E. Thomadakis. The Architecture of the Nehalem Processor and Nehalem-EP SMP Platforms. *Resource*, 3:2, 2011.

[65] P. Trancoso and J. Torrellas. The Impact of Speeding Up Critical Sections with Data Prefetching and Forwarding. In *Proceedings of the 1996 International Conference on Parallel Processing*, ICPP '96, pages 79–86.

[66] R. K. Treiber. Systems Programming: Coping with Parallelism. Technical Report RJ5118, IBM Almaden Research Center, 2006.

[67] L. G. Valiant. A Bridging Model for Parallel Computation. *Communications of the ACM*, 33(8):103–111, Aug. 1990.

[68] E. Vallejo, R. Beivide, A. Cristal, T. Harris, F. Vallejo, O. Unsal, and M. Valero. Architectural Support for Fair Reader-Writer Locking. In *Proceedings of the 43rd Annual IEEE/ACM International Symposium on Microarchitecture*, MICRO '10, pages 275–286, 2010.

[69] K. B. Wheeler, R. C. Murphy, and D. Thain. Qthreads: An API for programming with millions of lightweight threads. In *Proceedings of the 22nd International Parallel and Distributed Processing Symposium*, IPDPS '08, pages 1–8, 2008.

Author Index

Abadal, Sergi 3
Achermann, Reto 353
Alarcón, Eduard 3
Amani, Sidney 175
Amaro, Emmanuel 623
Anderson, Thomas 67
Angstadt, Kevin 593
Asanović, Krste 457
Asmussen, Nils 189
Austin, Todd 743
Awad, Amro 263
Aweke, Zelalem Birhanu 743
Baek, Woongki 385
Balkind, Jonathan 217
Beckmann, Nathan 113
Beeren, Joel 175
Bhattacharjee, Abhishek 233
Bodik, Rastislav 297
Bornholt, James 83, 637
Brown, Fraser 143
Brown, Kevin J.. 651
Cabellos-Aparicio, Albert 3
Carmean, Douglas M. 637
Ceze, Luis 413, 637
Chang, Li-Wen 667
Chen, Peter M. 399
Chen, Quan 681
Chen, Yin 713
Chen, Yu 339, 531
Chen, Zilin 175
Choi, Young-ri 443
Christodorescu, Mihai 713
Chubb, Peter 175
Colin, Alexei 577
Cox, AlanL. 129
Das, Reetuparna 743
de Lara, Eyal 205
De Moraes Garcia, Italo 205
De Sa, Christopher 651
Delimitrou, Christina 473
Dhurjati, Dinakar 297
Didona, Diego 757
Diegues, Nuno 757
Dunn, AlanM. 277
El Hajj, Izzat 353
Elnikety, Sameh 129
Engler, Dawson 143
Erez, Mattan 33
Esmaeilzadeh, Hadi 623
Fan, Songchun 561
Faraboschi, Paolo 353
Fettweis, Gerhard 189
Fu, Yaosheng 217
Fuchs, Adi 217
Fussell, Donald S. 607
Gangwani, Tanmay 789
Garland, Michael 325
Goel, Ashvin 205
Gopinath, K. 99
Gordon, Abel 49
Guerraoui, Rachid 757
Gunawi, Haryadi S. 517
Guo, Qing 413
Haber, Stuart 263
Hall, Mary 325
Han, Jaeung 443
Harpaz, Eran 773
Harris, Tim 457
Härtig, Hermann 189
Harvey, Graham 577
Hasabnis, Niranjan 311
He, Jiaquan 339
He, Yuxiong 129
Heiser, Gernot 175
Hicks, Matthew 743
Hixon, Alex 175
Hoffmann, Henry 545
Hofmann, Owen S. 277
Horne, William 263
Huh, Jaehyuk 443
Hwu, Wen-mei 353, 667
Izraelevitz, Joseph 427
Jeon, Myeongjae 129
Jeon, Seungheun 443
Jiang, Guofei 489
Jin, Guoliang 489
Jingoi, Silviu 205
Joshi, Pallavi 489
Jung, Changhee 159
Kaufmann, Antoine 67, 83
Keidar, Idit 773
Keller, Gabriele 175
Kelly, Terence 427
Kermarrec, Anne-Marie 757
Kim, Dohyeong 503
Kim, Hee-Seok 667
Kim, Hwanju 129
Kim, Jinwoong 385
Kim, Kyungtae 503
Kim, Wook-Hee 385
Klein, Gerwin 175
Koeplinger, David 651
Kolli, Aasheesh 399, 427
Kozyrakis, Christos 473, 651
Krishnamurthy, Arvind 67, 83
Kubiatowicz, John 457
Kuperman, Yossi 49
Kwon, Yonghwi 503
Kwon, Youngjin 277
Ladelsky, Razya 49
Lavrov, Alexey 217
Lee, Benjamin C. 561
Lee, Dongyoon 159
Lee, HyoukJoong 651
Lee, Kevin 205
Lee, MichaelZ. 277
Leesatapornwongsa, Tanakorn 517
Lenharth, Andrew 607
Li, Jialin 83
Li, Xiaodong 339

Liang, Xiaohua........................ 217
Liaqat, Daniyal........................ 205
Lim, Japheth............................ 175
Lin, Felix Xiaozhu.................. 369
Lin, Xiaofeng.......................... 339
Liu, Xu................................... 369
Lopez, Randolph..................... 637
Lu, Shan................................. 517
Lucia, Brandon........................ 577
Lukman, Jeffrey F.................. 517
Lustig, Daniel.......................... 233
Maas, Martin........................... 457
Mahajan, Divya....................... 623
Malvar, Henrique S................. 413
Manadhata, Pratyusa............... 263
Mao, Junjie...................... 339, 531
Markuze, Alex......................... 249
Mars, Jason............................. 681
Martínez, José F....................... 19
Martonosi, Margaret............... 233
Matl, Matthew......................... 217
McKeown, Michael................ 217
McKinley, Kathryn S................. 1
Merritt, Alexander.................. 353
Milojicic, Dejan...................... 353
Morrison, Adam............. 249, 789
Moscovici, Eyal........................ 49
Mukkara, Anurag.................... 113
Muralidharan, Saurav............. 325
Murray, Toby.......................... 175
Nagashima, Yutaka................. 175
Nam, Beomseok...................... 385
Neves, Ricardo....................... 757
Nguyen, Tri............................ 217
Nider, Joel................................ 49
Nöthen, Benedikt.................... 189
Nötzli, Andres......................... 143
Nowatzki, Tony....................... 697
O'Connor, Liam...................... 175
Olukotun, Kunle..................... 651
Oren, Yossi............................ 743
Park, Jongse............................ 623
Payne, Samuel......................... 217
Pelley, Steven.......................... 399
Peter, Simon.............................. 67
Phothilimthana, Phitchaya Mangpo.............................. 297
Pingali, Keshav....................... 607
Porat, Hagar........................... 773
Prabhakar, Raghu................... 651
Prasad, Aravinda....................... 99
Qiao, Rui................................ 743
Rai, Piyush............................. 325
Rixner, Scott........................... 129
Rizkallah, Christine................ 175
Romano, Paolo........................ 757
Roscoe, Timothy.................... 353
Roy, Amit............................... 325
Saidi, Ali................................ 399
Salajegheh, Negin.................. 713
Saldana, Manuel..................... 205
Saltaformaggio, Brendan........ 503
Sample, Alanson P................. 577
Sanchez, Daniel...................... 113
Sankaralingam, Karthikeyan.. 697
Schwan, Karsten.................... 353
Seelig, Georg.......................... 637
Sekar, R.................................. 311
Sethi, Geet.............................. 233
Sewell, Thomas...................... 175
Shacham, Hovav..................... 727
Shahrad, Mohammad............. 217
Shalev, Noam......................... 773
Shamasunder, Sriskanda......... 727
Sharma, Naveen Kr................... 67
Shi, Yuanchun................ 339, 531
Skadron, Kevin....................... 593
Solihin, Yan........................... 263
Strauss, Karin................. 413, 637
Sui, Xin.................................. 607
Sumner, William N.................503
Tang, Lingjia...........................681
Thakur, Aditya........................297
Thwaites, Bradley...................623
To, Wilson..............................205
Torlak, Emina............................83
Torrellas, Josep...................3, 789
Tsafrir, Dan.............. 49, 249, 291
Tullsen, Dean M.....................727
Tuong, Joseph.........................175
Venkat, Ashish........................727
Völp, Marcus..........................189
Wang, Xi...................................83
Wang, Xiaodong.......................19
Weimer, Westley....................593
Weinsberg, Yaron...................773
Wenisch, Thomas F................399
Wentzlaff, David....................217
Williams, R.Stanley................295
Witchel, Emmett............277, 591
Won, Youjip............................385
Xiao, Qixue.............................531
Xu, Dongyan...........................503
Xu, Jianwu..............................489
Xu, Wei...................................339
Xu, Yuanzhong.......................277
Yang, Hailong.........................681
Yitbarek, Salessawi Ferede.....743
Yoon, Man-Ki.........................713
Yu, Xiao..................................489
Zahedi, Seyed Majid...............561
Zellweger, Gerd......................353
Zhang, Huazhe........................545
Zhang, Hui..............................489
Zhang, Tong............................159
Zhang, Xiangyu......................503
Zhou, Yanqi............................217
Zhu, Haishan.............................33

www.ingramcontent.com/pod-product-compliance
Lightning Source LLC
LaVergne TN
LVHW080102011026
849160LV00013B/1017